ENCYCLOPÆDIA IRANICA

EDITED BY

EHSAN YARSHATER

Center for Iranian Studies
Columbia University
New York

Volume VII

DĀRĀ(B)—EBN AL-AṮĪR

Mazda Publishers
Costa Mesa, California
1996

Library of Congress Cataloging-in-Publication Data

Encyclopædia Iranica/ Edited by Ehsan Yarshater.

p. cm.
Includes index
1. Iran—Encyclopedias. I. Yar-Shater, Ehsan.
DS253.E53 1991 91-9733
955′.003—dc20 CIP

 First published in one volume in 1996 by
Mazda Publishers, P.O. Box 2603, Costa Mesa, California 92626 U.S.A.

ISBN: 1-56859-028-8 (bound volume)
ISBN: 1-56859-026-1 (preliminary pages)
ISBN: 1-56859-027-x (binder)

10 9 8 7 6 5 4 3 2 1

ENCYCLOPÆDIA IRANICA

This volume is dedicated to the memory of S. H. Taqizadeh (1878-1970) and Ebrāhīm Pūrdāvūd (1885-1968)

ACKNOWLEDGMENTS

The preparation of this volume was made possible by grants from:

the program for Research Tools and Reference Works of the National Endowment for the Humanities, an independent federal agency;

Keyan Foundation;

Khosrow Eghbal, Richard J. Haas, Khosrow B. Semnani;

Bibliotheca Persica;

and a number of individual donors.

AUTHORS OF ARTICLES IN VOLUME VII

Abbas, Ihsan, University of Jordan, Amman. 664.

Abu El Fadl, Khalid, Princeton University, Princeton, N.J. 360, 362.

Adḳā'ī, Parvīz, Hamadān. 55.

Adle, Chahryar, Centre National de la Recherche Scientifique, Paris. 601, 602.

Aghajanian, Akbar, Fayetteville State University, Fayetteville, N.C. 448.

Ahmad, Shamsuddin, University of Kashmir, Srinagar, India. 203.

Akhtar, M. Saleem, National Institute of Historical and Cultural Research, Islamabad. 32, 358.

Āl-e Dāwūd, ʿAlī, The Greater Islamic Encyclopædia, Tehran. 64, 95, 214, 335, 492, 521.

A'lam, Hūšang, National Library, Tehran (emeritus). 21, 117, 128, 316, 404, 519, 583.

Algar, Hamid, University of California, Berkeley. 20, 73, 452, 570, 575, 653, 656.

Allan, Nigel J. R., University of California, Davis. 26.

Alram, Michael, Kunsthistorisches Museum, Vienna. 36.

Amanat, Abbas, Yale University, New Haven, Conn. 143, 147.

Amiet, Pierre, Musée du Louvre, Paris. 90, 175, 399.

Amir-Mokri, Cyrus, Chicago. 141.

Anderson, Steven C., University of the Pacific, Stockton, Calif. 623.

Ando, Shiro, Institute of Inner Asian Studies, Kyoto. 439.

ʿĀqelī, Bāqer, Našr-e Goftār, Tehran. 32, 133.

Arkun, Aram, Diocese of the Armenian Church of America, New York. 90.

Āryān, Qamar, Tehran. 169.

Asatrian, Garnik S., Institute of Oriental Studies, Academy of Sciences, Yerevan. 405.

Asher, Catherine B., University of Minnesota, Minneapolis. 246

Asmussen, Jes P., University of Copenhagen. 292.

Āšūrī, Dāryūš, Paris. 168.

Atkin, Muriel, The George Washington University, Washington, D.C. 598.

Avery, Peter, University of Cambridge. 492.

Babayan, Kathryn, The University of Michigan, Ann Arbor. 79, 387.

Badian, Ernst, Harvard University, Cambridge, Mass. 51, 421.

Balland, Daniel, Université de Paris-Sorbonne. 61, 62, 140, 146, 150, 160, 204, 268, 273, 485, 510, 513, 522, 626.

Bates, Michael L., The American Numismatic Society, New York. 413, 426.

Bayevsky, Solomon, formerly Institute for Oriental Studies, St. Petersburg. 112.

Bazin, Marcel, Centre National de la Recherche Scientifique, Ivry-sur-Seine, France. 204

Beck, Roger, Erindale College, University of Toronto, Mississauga, Ont., Canada. 421.

Bedrosian, Robert G., New York, N.Y. 167.

Berberian, Manuel, Najarian Associates, Inc., Eatontown, N.J. 635.

Bernard, Paul, Centre National de la Recherche Scientifique, Paris. 234.

Bivar, A. D. H., School of Oriental and African Studies, University of London (emeritus). 257.

Blair, Sheila S., Richmond, N.H. 500.

Blau, Joyce, Institut National des Langues et Civilisations Orientales, Paris. 238.

Blois, François de, The Royal Asiatic Society, London. 432, 438.

Blum, Stephen, York University, North York, Ont., Canada. 451.

Bopearachchi, Osmund, Centre National de la Recherche Scientifique, Paris. 422.

Borjian, Habib, Isfahan. 630.

Bosworth, C. Edmund, University of Manchester (emeritus). 33, 136, 159, 170, 172, 215, 216, 320, 416, 432, 663.

Boucharlat, Rémy, Institut Français de Recherche en Iran, Tehran. 59.

Böwering, Gerhard, Yale University, New Haven, Conn. 229, 338, 341, 572.

Boyce, Mary, School of Oriental and African Studies, University of London (emeritus). 56, 179, 354, 370, 467.

Bozorgmehr, Mehdi, University of California, Los Angeles. 380.

BRESCIANI, EDDA, Università degli Studi, Pisa. 276.
BRUIJN, J. T. P. DE, University of Leiden. 397, 526.

CALMARD, JEAN, École Pratique des Hautes Études, Paris. 398, 566, 569.
CATON, MARGARET, The Institute of Persian Performing Arts, Los Angeles. 77.
CHAUMONT, MARIE LOUISE, Centre National de la Recherche Scientifique, Paris. 55, 420.
CHELKOWSKI, PETER J., New York University, New York. 97.
CHITTICK, WILLIAM C., State University of New York, Stony Brook. 664.
CHOKSY, JAMSHEED, Indiana University, Bloomington. 554.
COLE, JUAN R. I., The University of Michigan, Ann Arbor. 237.
CURTIS, JOHN, The British Museum, London. 64.

DABĪRSĪĀQĪ, MOḤAMMAD, Moʾassasa-ye Loḡatnāma-ye Dehḵodā, Tehran. 216, 569.
DAFTARY, FARHAD, The Institute of Ismaili Studies, London. 151, 354.
DANDAMAYEV, MUHAMMAD A., Institute for Oriental Studies, St. Petersburg. 443, 460, 654.
DIGARD, JEAN-PIERRE, Centre National de la Recherche Scientifique, Ivry-sur-Seine, France. 469, 485.
ḎOKĀʾ, YAḤYĀ, Tehran. 82.
DONNER, FRED M., The University of Chicago. 476.
DUCHESNE-GUILLEMIN, JACQUES, Université de Liège (emeritus). 177, 227.
DURING, JEAN, Centre National de la Recherche Scientifique, Strasbourg. 11, 84, 102, 104, 107, 153, 251, 337, 524, 526, 563, 652.

EDEL'MAN, D. I., Academy of Sciences, Moscow. 27.
EDWARDS, DAVID B., Williams College, Williamstown, Mass. 588.
EHLERS, ECKART, Rheinische Friedrich-Wilhelms-Universität, Bonn. 94, 526.
EIR. 411.
ERNST, CARL W., University of North Carolina, Chapel Hill. 181.
ESLAMI, KAMBIZ, Princeton University, Princeton, N.J. 23.
ESS, JOSEF VAN, Eberhard-Karls-Universität, Tübingen. 31, 417, 418.

FARR, GRANT, Portland State University, Portland, Ore. 383.
FELIX, WOLFGANG, Universität Wien. 342, 419, 423.
FERRIER, R. W., British Petroleum, London. 644.
†FISCHER, KLAUS. 431, 457, 587.
FLOOR, WILLEM, The World Bank, Washington, D.C. 173, 470, 586, 603.
FRANCFORT, HENRI-PAUL, Centre National de la Recherche Scientifique, Paris. 96.
FRYE, RICHARD N., Harvard University (emeritus), Cambridge, Mass. 40.
FUSSMAN, GÉRARD, Collège de France, Paris. 96.

GALL, HUBERTUS VON, Deutsches Archäologisches Institut, Abteilung Teheran, Berlin. 211, 472.
GHANOONPARVAR, MOHAMMAD R., The University of Texas, Austin. 478, 492, 529, 584.
GIGNOUX, PHILIPPE, École Pratique des Hautes Études, Paris. 105, 282, 284, 412, 424.
GNOLI, GHERARDO, Istituto Italiano per il Medio ed Estremo Oriente, Rome. 576.
GREAVES, ROSE L., The University of Kansas, Lawrence. 594.
GRENET, FRANTZ, Centre National de la Recherche Scientifique, Paris. 537.
GREVEMEYER, JAN-HEEREN, Berlin. 65.
GROPP, GERD, Universität Hamburg. 585.
GURNEY, JOHN, The Oriental Institute, The University of Oxford. 251.

HAKIMIAN, HASSAN, School of Oriental and African Studies, University of London. 375.
HAMBLY, GAVIN R. G., University of Texas, Austin. 242.
HANAWAY, WILLIAM L., JR., University of Pennsylvania, Philadelphia. 8, 102, 625.
HASSANPOUR, AMIR, University of Windsor, Windsor, Ont., Canada. 404.
HERMANSEN, MARCIA K., San Diego State University, San Diego, Calif. 220.
HERRMANN, GEORGINA, Institute of Archaeology, University College, London. 7.
HOLE, FRANK, Yale University, New Haven, Conn. 221.
HOONAARD, WILL. C. VAN DEN, University of New Brunswick, Fredericton, N.B., Canada. 643.

†1919-1993

HORTON, MARK, British Institute in Eastern Africa, London. 640.

HOURCADE, BERNARD, Centre National de la Recherche Scientifique, Ivry-sur-Seine, France. 19, 233, 258.

HUFF, DIETRICH, Deutsches Archäologisches Institut, Abteilung Teheran, Berlin. 5.

IVANOV, ANATOL, The State Hermitage Museum, St. Petersburg. 283.

JACOBS, LINDA K., Middle East Technical Assistance, Monterey, Calif. 71.

JAMASPASA, KAIKHUSROO M., K. R. Cama Oriental Institute, Bombay. 7, 355.

KELLENS, JEAN, Collège de France, Paris. 281, 553, 562, 565, 595.

KETTENHOFEN, ERICH, Universität Trier, Germany. 13, 297, 387, 478, 479, 616.

KHALEDOV, A. B., Institute for Oriental Studies, St. Petersburg. 655.

KHALEGHI-MOTLAGH, DJALAL, Universität Hamburg. 135, 315.

KHEIRABADI, MASSOUD, Marylhurst College, Portland, Ore. 5, 60, 351.

KLEISS, WOLFRAM, Deutsches Archäologisches Institut, Abteilung Teheran, Berlin. 66, 331, 347.

KNÖRZER, JUTTA, Toronto. 108.

KOHL, PHILIP, Wellesley College, Wellesley, Mass. 60.

KOHLBERG, ETAN, The Hebrew University, Jerusalem. 35, 339.

KOMAROFF, LINDA, The Metropolitan Museum of Art, New York. 137.

KOTWAL, FIROZE M., H. B. Wadia Atash Bahram, Bombay. 354.

KROELL, ANNE, Centre National de la Recherche Scientifique, Nancy, and École Pratique des Hautes Études, Paris. 127, 647.

KRÖGER, JENS, Museum für Islamische Kunst, Berlin. 401.

KUMAMOTO, HIROSHI, The University of Tokyo. 320, 356, 358, 551.

LAMBDEN, STEPHEN, Newcastle-upon-Tyne, U.K. 661, 670.

LANDAU-TASSERON, ELLA, The Hebrew University, Jerusalem. 574.

LAWSON, TODD, University of Toronto. 662.

LAZARD, GILBERT, École Pratique des Hautes Études, Paris. 34.

LERICHE, PIERRE, Centre National de la Recherche Scientifique, Paris. 589.

LITVINSKY, BORIS, Institute of Near Eastern Studies, Moscow. 619.

LUZHETSKAYA, N. L., Institute for Oriental Studies, St. Petersburg. 511.

MACKENZIE, D. N., Georg-August-Universität (emeritus), Göttingen. 56, 124, 585, 593, 596.

MACKINNON, COLIN, Arlington, Va. 351.

MADELUNG, WILFERD, The Oriental Institute, The University of Oxford. 338, 343.

MAHAMEDI, HAMID, University of California, Berkeley. 129.

MAHDAWĪ DĀMĞĀNĪ, AḤMAD, Harvard University, Cambridge, Mass. 456, 477.

MALANDRA, W. W., University of Minnesota, Minneapoolis. 163.

MANOUTCHEHRIAN, MEHRANGUIZ, Tehran. 142.

MARSHAK, BORIS, The State Hermitage Museum, St. Petersburg. 334.

MELVILLE, CHARLES, University of Cambridge. 255, 256, 475.

METCALF, BARBARA DALY, University of California, Davis. 296.

MODE, MARKUS, Martin-Luther Universität, Halle, Germany. 474.

MOJTABĀʾĪ, FATḤ-ALLĀH, University of Tehran. 85, 161.

MOJTAHED-ZADEH, PIROUZ, School of Oriental and African Studies, University of London. 379.

MOMAYYEZ, MORTAŻĀ, Tehran. 505.

MOMEN, MOOJAN, Biggleswade, Beds., U.K. 10, 233, 450, 477.

MORGAN, DAVID O., School of Oriental and African Studies, University of London. 111, 113.

MURATA, SACHIKO, State University of New York, Stony Brook. 445.

MUSCARELLA, OSCAR WHITE, The Metropolitan Museum of Art, New York. 283.

NAJMABADI, AFSANEH, Barnard College, New York. 520.

NAKHASH, YITZHAK, Princeton University, Princeton, N.J. 377.

NASHAT, GUITY, The University of Illinois, Chicago. 20, 83.

Negahban, Ezat O., University of Pennsylvania, Philadelphia. 254, 337.

Newman, Andrew J., Wellcome Unit for the History of Medicine, The University of Oxford. 9, 100, 132.

†Nūrānī Weṣāl, ʿAbd-al-Wahhāb. 135.

Nurse, Derek, Memorial University, St. John's, Nfld., Canada. 642.

Oberling, Pierre, Hunter College, New York. 63, 209, 250, 423, 492, 522, 573.

O'Kane, Bernard, The American University, Cairo. 479.

Omidsalar, Mahmoud, University of California, Los Angeles. 164, 428, 440, 461, 495, 584.

Omidsalar, Teresa P., University of California, Los Angeles. 164, 461, 495.

Pahlavān, Čangīz, Tehran. 385.

Panaino, Antonio, Università degli Studi "Alma Mater," Bologna. 615.

Parvin, Nassereddin, Geneva. 81, 139, 140, 347, 412, 475, 498, 499, 521, 597, 655.

†Pellat, Charles, Université de Paris. 417.

Perry, John R., The University of Chicago. 308, 390, 568, 646.

Planhol, Xavier de, Université de Paris-Sorbonne. 79, 633.

Poujol, Cathérine, Institut National des Langues et Civilisations Orientales, Paris. 250, 331.

Rajabzadeh, Hashem, Osaka University of Foreign Studies. 113.

Rassekh, Shapour, Geneva. 552, 553.

Rīāḥī, Moḥammad-Amīn, Tehran. 166.

Richard, Francis, Bibliothèque Nationale, Paris. 203, 571.

Richards, D. S., The Oriental Institute, The University of Oxford. 671.

Richter-Bernburg, Lutz, Universität Leipzig. 663.

Rose, Jenny, Mission Viejo, Calif. 449.

Rouhani, Fuad, Geneva. 23.

Rubin, Barnett, Columbia University, New York. 162.

Russell, James R., Harvard University, Cambridge, Mass. 292.

†1923-1995

†1914-1992

Ṣadāqat-Kīš, Jamšīd, University of Shiraz. 103, 106.

Ṣādeqī, ʿAlī-Ašraf, University of Tehran. 387.

Ṣafā, Ḏabīḥ-Allāh, University of Tehran (emeritus). 149.

Safvat, Dariush, University of Tehran. 136.

Šahīdī, Yaḥyā, Tehran. 197.

†Saʿīdī Sīrjānī, ʿAlī-Akbar. 216.

Sajjādī, Ṣādeq, The Greater Islamic Encyclopaedia, Tehran. 292, 555.

Sāmeʿī, Ḥosayn, Tehran. 393, 395.

Šamīsā, Sīrūs, ʿAllāma Ṭabāṭabāʾī University, Tehran. 565.

Sancisi-Weerdenburg, Heleen, University of Utrecht. 50.

Savory, Roger M., University of Toronto (emeritus). 431, 439, 597.

Schimmel, Annemarie, Harvard University (emeritus) and Rheinische Friedrich-Wilhelms-Universität (emeritus), Bonn. 2, 25.

Schmitt, Rüdiger, Universität des Saarlandes, Saarbrücken, Germany. 40, 54, 55, 114, 115, 117, 126, 128, 226, 255, 257, 397, 423, 535, 554, 565, 596.

Shaffer, Jim G., Case Western Reserve University, Cleveland, O. 210.

Shahbazi, A. Shapur, Eastern Oregon State College, La Grande. 41, 114, 297, 312.

Shaki, Mansour, University of Prague (emeritus). 72, 111, 279, 348, 444, 457, 613.

Shokoohy, Mehrdad, London. 83, 170.

Siavoshi, Sussan, Trinity University, San Antonio, Tex. 582.

Sims-Williams, Nicholas, School of Oriental and African Studies, University of London. 336, 649.

Soucek, Priscilla P., Institute of Fine Arts, New York University, New York. 185, 189, 277, 438.

Spooner, Brian, University of Pennsylvania, Philadelphia. 321.

Subtelny, M. E., University of Toronto. 76, 77.

Sundermann, Werner, Akademie der Wissenschaften, Berlin. 418.

Swietochowski, M. L., The Metropolitan Museum of Art, New York. 537.

†1931-1994

TAFAŻŻOLĪ, AḤMAD, University of Tehran. 1, 2, 223, 319, 347, 348, 350, 547, 564.

TARZI, AMIN H., New York University, New York. 523.

THORDARSON, FRIDRIK, University of Oslo. 402.

TISSOT, FRANCINE, Musée Guimet, Paris. 238, 240.

TOPAN, FAROUK, School of Oriental and African Studies, University of London. 643.

VAHMAN, FEREYDUN, University of Copenhagen. 289.

VARJĀVAND, PARVĪZ, Tehran. 11.

VROLIJK, A. J. M., University of Leiden. 174.

WEISKOPF, MICHAEL, Berkeley, Calif. 85.

WILLIAMS, A.V., University of Manchester. 333.

WINDFUHR, GERNOT L., The University of Michigan, Ann Arbor. 362.

WOODS, JOHN E., The University of Chicago. 670.

YAZICI, TAHSİN, İslâm Ansiklopedisi, Istanbul. 202, 598.

YOSHIDA, YUTAKA, Kobe City University of Foreign Studies, Japan. 357, 359, 424.

ZARINEBAF-SHAHR, FARIBA, University of Illinois, Chicago. 373.

ZIAI, HOSSEIN, University of California, Los Angeles. 549.

ADDENDA AND CORRIGENDA*

Volume I

P. 226[a] ABLUTION, ZOROASTRIAN, *for* PADYĀB *read* PĀDYĀB.

P. 641[a] AḤMAD B. KEŻRŪYA, l. 1 *for* **KEŻRŪYA** *read* **ḴEŻRŪYA**; l. 2 *after* ḤĀMED *add* in Supplement.

P. 880[b] ʿALĪ-REŻĀ KHAN QĀJĀR l. 1 *for* AŻOD *read* ʿAŻOD.

P. 973[b] AMĪRḴĪZĪ, signature *for* Ī. *read* IRAJ.

P. 1001[a] AN SHIH-KAO, l. 20 *after Bibliography*: *add* A. Forte, "An Shigao . . . and His Descendants," *The Bukkyō Shigaku Kenkyū* 35/1, 1992, pp. 1-35.

Volume III

P. 1[a] ĀTAŠ, l. 5 *after* unknown *add* (cf. Sogd. fem. *(ʾ)ʾtr*, Scythian *tabītī* "hearth fire").

P. 15[a] ʿATR, l. 42 *after* Egyptians *add* (cf. Sundermann, p. 59 n. 7);

P. 16[a] l. 40 *after* 1914. *add* W. Sundermann, *Mitteliranische manichäische Texte kirchengeschichtlichen Inhalts*, Berlin, 1981.

P. 16[b] ĀΘRAVAN-, l. 5 *after ārmaiti add* ; cf. Wikander, pp. 9 ff.;

P. 17[b] l. 22 *after* books *add* (for continuation in the New Persian tradition of the *Šāh-nāma*, see Tafażżolī, pp. 10-12; for *ʾʾtrwn* in the Manichean tradition, see p. 11); l. 27 *after athornan. add* A. Tafażżolī, "Quelques mots savants d'origine pehlevie dans le *Šāhnāme*," *Stud. Ir.* 22/1, 1993, pp. 7-13. S. Wikander, *Feuerpriester in Kleinasien und Iran*, Lund, 1946.

P. 28[b] AUGUSTINE, l. 21 *after* 1970. *add* E. Feldmann, *Die "Epistula Fundamenti" der nordafrikanischen Manichäer. Versuch einer Rekonstruktion*, Altenberge, Germany, 1987.; l. 22 *after* 1931. *add* L. Koenen, "Augustine and Manichaeism in Light of the Cologne Mani Codex," *Illinois Classical Studies* 3, 1978, pp. 154-95.

P. 49[a] AVESTAN LANGUAGE i, l. 35 *after* A.D. 430 *add* (redated to the 9th or 10th century by de Blois);

P. 51[a] l. 9 *after* 99-106. *add* F. de Blois, "The Middle-Persian Inscription from Constantinople. Sasanian or Post-Sasanian?" *Stud. Ir.* 19, 1990, pp. 209-18.

P. 102[a] AVICENNA xi, l. 57 *after* philologists *add* (see Livshits and Smirnova).

P. 104[a] l. 48 *after* 625-28. add V. A. Livshits and L. P. Smirnova, "Yazyk Danish-nama i rol' Ibn Siny v razvitii persidsko-tadzhikskoĭ nauchnoĭ terminologii" (The language of the *Dāneš-nāma* and the role of Ebn Sīnā in the development of Persian-Tajik scientific terminology), in *Pis'mennye pamyatniki i problemy istorii kul'tury narodov vostoka* (Literary monuments and problems in the historical culture of the Near East) III, Moscow, 1981, pp. 115-63.

P. 107[a] AVICENNA xii, l. 5 *after* 1966. *add* G. Strohmeier, "Avicennas 'Hayy ibn Yaqẓān' und Dantes 'Commedia,'" *AAASH* 29, 1984, pp. 73-80.

P. 123[b] AXTARMĀR, l. 2 *for* AXTARMAR, Man. Mid. Persian *read* ĀXTARMĀR, *ʾxtrmʾr*, Man. Mid. Persian; Sundermann, p. 154;

P. 124[a] l. 13 *after* 1914. *add* W. Sundermann, *Mitteliranische manichäische Texte kirchengeschichtliche Inhalts*, Berlin, 1981.

ĀXWARR, l. 4 *for* It is derived *read* It is perhaps derived.

P. 126[a] ĀY ḴĀNOM, signature *for* O. BERNARD *read* PAUL BERNARD.

P. 128[b] AYĀDGĀR Ī ZARĒRĀN, ll. 58-59 *for* whose name, irregularly, developed into "Zarēr" *read* < Sogd. Zarwar, *z-rwr*; W. Sundermann, "Bruchstücke einer manichäischen Zarathustralegende," in R. Schmitt and P. O. Skjærvø, eds., *Studia Grammatica Iranica. Festschrift für Helmut Humbach*, Munich, 1986, p. 466.

P. 153[a] AYVĀN, l. 12 *after* established *add* (Szemerényi argued for the Akkadian origin of *ayvān* and earlier forms);

P. 155[b] l. 9 *after* 1149. *add* O. Szemerényi, "Semitic Influence on the Iranian Lexicon I," in G. Rendsburg et al., eds., *The Bible World. Essays in Honor of Cyrus H. Gordon*, New York, 1980, pp. 233-37.

P. 157[a] AYVĀN-E KESRĀ. l. 13 *after* Ašūhast *add* (Umēd [Ēmēd] b. Ašawahišt; Justi, *Namenbuch*, p. 333).

P. 169[a] l. 56 *after* 1973. *add* Idem, "Some Remarks on Mithra in the Manichaean Pantheon," *Acta Iranica* 17, 1978, pp. 485-99.

P. 170[b] ĀZĀD, l. 1 *after* **ĀZĀD** *add* (Pers. *sarv-e āzād* "cedar").

---

*Many suggestions by reviewers and other readers have been incorporated. Note especially W. Sundermann's detailed reviews of volumes III and IV in *OLZ* 89, 1994, cols. 309-13, 409-13; and M. Shaki, "An Appraisal of Encyclopaedia Iranica, Vols. IV. and V.," *Archív Orientální* 62, 1994, pp. 326-28.

P. 178[b] ĀZĀDSARV, l. 1 *after* **ĀZĀDSARV** add (lit., "free or noble cypress, cedar").

P. 190[a] ĀZARMĪGDUXT, l. 6 *after* respected one *add* or honorable daughter; *for* refers *read* may refer.

P. 298[b] BĀBAK l. 1 *after* Pābag *add* , Pābak [Justi, *Namenbuch*, p. 242];

P. 299[a] l. 35 *after* table I *add*; M. Alram, *Iranisches Personennamenbuch* IV. *Nomina Propria Iranica in Nummis*, Vienna, 1986, p. 185.

P. 323[b] BABR, l. 1 *after* **BABR** *add* (< Skt. *ryāgbrá*; *Grundriss* II/b, p. 7; Bailey, p. 35);

P. 324[b] l. 19 *after Bibliography*: *add* H. W. Bailey, "Excursus Iranocaucasicus," *Acta Iranica* 4, 1975, pp. 31-35. BABR-E BAYĀN, l. 8 *after* 319 v. 6 *add* ; cf. Sogd. *pwrönk črm nγwδnn* "leopard-skin garment"; N. Sims-Williams, "The Sogdian Fragments of the British Library," *IIJ* 18, 1976, p. 55.

P. 349[a] BĀD, l. 1 *before* wind *add* Mid. Pers. *wād*, etc.;

P. 418[b] BAGŌAS, l. 3 *after* period *add* (for the Iranian form of the name, see Justi, *Namenbuch*, pp. 590-60, 525).

P. 492[b] BAHMAN YAŠT, l. 49 *for* "iron and clay" read "iron ore or ironstone."

P. 500[b] BAHMANŠĪR, l. 34 *after* 770 *add*; it may actually, however, have been derived from the name of the legendary Bahman son of Esfandīār, who was also known as Ardašīr.

P. 516[a] BAHRĀM ii, l. 7 *for* "savior of Bahrām's soul," *read* "*mōbed* of the blessed Wahrām and of Ohrmazd" (F. Grenet, "Observations sur les titres de Kirdīr," *Stud. Ir.* 19/1, 1990, pp. 88, 91).

P. 588[a] BALḴ i, l. 22 *after* occupants. *add paragraph* See also BACTRIA i.

P. 788[b] BARF, l. 5 *after* 144-45 *add* ; cf. Mid. Pers. *snēzag* "snow," Sogd. *šn'yš* "to snow."

PP. 805-06 BARM-E DELAK *for the inscription of Abnūn recently discovered at the site, see* M. Tavoosi and R. N. Frye, "An Inscribed Capital Dating from the Time of Shapur I," *Bulletin of the Asia Institute*, N.S. 3, 1989, pp. 25-38; P. Gignoux, "D'Abnūn à Māhān. Étude de deux inscriptions sassanides," *Stud. Ir.* 20, 1991, pp. 9-22; P. O. Skjærvø, "L'inscription d'Abnūn et l'imparfait en Moyen-Perse," *Stud. Ir.* 21, 1992, pp. 153-60.

P. 825[b] BARSOM, l. 1 *after barəsman) add* "rods, grass, straw" (Boyce, *Zoroastrianism* I, p. 167).

P. 836[b] BĀRŪ, l. 4 *after* Eilers *add* ; but cf. Parth. *bārag* "wall";

P. 837[a] l. 50 *after* 215f. *add* R. N. Frye, "The Sasanian System of Walls for Defense," in M. Rosen-Ayalon, ed., *Studies in Memory of Gaston Wiet*, Jerusalem, 1977, pp. 7-15.

P. 886[a] BAYATĪ, l. 29 *after* Berlin. *add* His papers are to be found in the Staatsbibliothek, Berlin.

Volume IV

P. 60[b] BĀZĪ, l. 10 *after bāzī add*; cf. Middle Pers. *zēn-wāzīg* "play with free use of arms," *gōywāzīg*, *čawgān-wāzīg* "polo"; l. 12 *for* 9th *read* 6th.

P. 172[a] BESMELLĀH i, l. 17 *after* century *add* ; for a proposed Christian origin of the formula, see Paret, p. 11;

P. 172[b] l. 1 *after* no. 1.1.2. *add* R. Paret, *Der Koran. Kommentar und Konkordanz*, Stuttgart, 1993.

P. 193[a] BHAIṢAJYAGURUVAIḌŪRYAPRABHARĀJASŪTRA, l. 5 *for* Two *read* Three; l. 14 *after* ones. *add* A third fragment has recently been published (Kudara and Sundermann); l. 28 *after* p. 20. *add* K. Kudara and W. Sundermann, "Ein weiteres Fragment einiger soghdischen Übersetzung des Bhaiṣajyaguruvaiḍūryaprabhatathāgatasūtra," *AoF* 19, 1992, pp. 350-58.

P. 237[b] BĪD ii, ll. 10-11 *after* willow *add* ," perhaps alluding to Majnūn, the demented lover of Laylā, who is often depicted under a willow), *bīd-e mowalla*, ; l. 12 *for* both an allusion *read* all alluding.

P. 290[a] BĪSOTŪN i, l. 2 *after* god(s)" *add* (cf. Markwart, *Ērānšahr*, p. 71).

P. 381[b] BORZŪYA, l. 13 *after* souvenirs. *add* (F. de Blois, *Burzōy's Voyage to India and the Origin of the Book of Kalīlah wa Dimnah*, London, 1990.; l. 35 *after Ḵodāy-nāma add* (*Xwadāy-nāmag*); l. 36 *after* Barzīn *add* (Šādān-burzēn).

P. 444[b] BREAD, l. 1 *after nān add* (for etymology, see Bailey, *Dictionary*, p. 179, s.v. *nāṃji*);

P. 446[b] l. 16 *after* 593-631. *add* H. W. Bailey, *Dictionary of Khotanese Saka*, Cambridge, 1979).

P. 551[b] l. 3 *after* capital *add* ; for a different interpretation, see DEŽ Ī NEBEŠT.

P. 553[b] BŪRĀN, l. 1 *after* **BŪRĀN** *add* (< Middle. Pers. Bōrān).

P. 562[b] BURIAL iii, l. 10 *for* "beaver" read "badger."

P. 613[a] ČAĞĀNA, l. 3 *for* Sach's *read* Sachs'.

P. 646[a] ČAK, l. 1 *after* **ČAK** *add* (< Middle Pers. *čak* "document"; *Mādayān*, pt. 1, 73.14, 74.3).

P. 648[a] ČAKAR, l. 3 *for Vidēvdād*, 1895, 26 *read Wizīrkard ī dēnīg* 2.6, 17.

P. 658[b] CALENDARS i, l. 16 *after* refs.; *add* Cornillon;

P. 659 table 20, l. 2 *after* Θūravāhara *add* [a]; *below table add* a. Avestan Zaremaya; *Dādistān ī dēnīg*, chap. 16; tr. West, SBE 17, p. xxiv.;

P. 664[b] l. 24 *after* Bīrūnī. *add* According to the Sogdian text M 18400, the year was divided into three seasons of four months each (Kudara and Sundermann, p. 340).; l. 56 *after* 205-23). *add* K. Kudara and W. Sundermann, "Zwei Fragmente einer Sammelhandschrift buddhistischer Sūtras in soghdischer Sprache," *AoF* 14, 1987, pp. 334-49.

P. 675[b] CALENDARS iv, l. 44 *after* "Shenshai" *add* (royalist; Boyce, 1979, p. 190; cf. Sogd. *š'nš'y* "king of kings"; Sundermann; l. 59 *after* 110-15. *add* W. Sundermann, "Soghdisch š'nš'y," *AoF* 10, 1983, pp. 193-95.

P. 720[a] CALLISTHENES, l. 38 *after* 1969. *add Iskandarnameh. A Persian Medieval Alexander Romance*, tr. M. Southgate, New York, 1978.

P. 743[b] CAMPHOR, l. 1 *after kāpūr*, *add* perhaps directly; l. 2 *after kāpūr*; *add* but cf. Sogd. *kpwr* "camphor" < Prakrit *kappūra-*, Sims-Williams, p. 137, suggesting the parallel Middle Pers. derivation *kappūr* > *kāpūr*;

P. 747[b] l. 36 *after* 1984. *add* N. Sims-Williams, "Indian Elements in Parthian and Sogdian," in K. Röhrborn and W. Veenker, *Sprachen des Buddhismus in Zentralasien*, Wiesbaden, 1983, pp. 132-41.

ČAMRŪŠ, l. 1 *after* **CAMRŪŠ** *add* (or Činamrūs; *Mēnōg ī xrad*, chap. 61.11).

P. 758[a] ČANG, l. 1 *after čang add* , mentioned in *Xusrō ī Kawādān ud rēdag*, pars. 62-63.

P. 767[b] ČĀPĀR, l. 32 *after* 1963. *add* B. Geiger, "Zum Postwesen der Perser," *WZKM* 29, 1915, pp. 309-14.

P. 769[b] CAPITAL CITIES i, ll. 52-53 *for* Aspānbūr *read* Aspānvar (Shaki, pp. 94-95);

P. 770[b] l. 13 *before* M. Streck *add* M. Shaki, "Pahlavica," *in A Green Leaf. Papers in Honour of Prof. J. Asmussen*, Acta Iranica 28, 1988, pp. 93-99.

P. 795[a] CARAVAN, l. 3 *after* army," *add* Parth. and Middle Pers. *kārawān* "caravan, military column" [MacKenzie, p. 49], thus equipped with armed troops; pace Dowsett, p. 61;

P. 797[b] l. 41 *after* 1980. *add* C. J. F. Dowsett, "Cause, and Some Linguistically Allied Concepts, in Armenian,"*BSOAS* 33, 1970, pp. 55-71.;

P. 798[a] l. 24 *after* 1983. *add* D. N. MacKenzie, *A Concise Pahlavi Dictionary*, London, 1971.

P. 861[a] CARPETS vi, l. 33 *before* R. Pfister *add* C. Parham, "How Altaic/Nomadic Is the Pazyryk Carpet?" *Oriental Rug Review* 13/5, June-July 1993, pp. 34-39.

Volume V

P. 70[b] CASTRATION, l. 2 *after kardan add* , *ak̲ta kardan.*

P. 84[b] CAUCASUS, l. 3 *after* Caucasus *add* (Qafqāz; Parth. *kpy TWR'*, Kāf-kōf [SKZ 2; A. Maricq, "Classica et Orientalia," *Syria* 35, 1958, p. 336]).

P. 107[b] ČĒČAST, l. 1 *after Čaēčasta- add* ; Ar. and Pers. *Šīz.*

P. 119[b] ČEHR, l. 23 *after* p. 98 *add* ; for a different interpretation, see Shaki, pp. 285, 303-04; l. 38 *after* 83-86 *add* M. Shaki, "Some Basic Tenets of the Metaphysics of the Dēnkart," *Archív Orientální* 38, 1970, pp. 277-312.

P. 123[a] ČELLA i, l. 12 *for* 21 December *read* 22 December; l. 13 *for* 10 Bahman *read* 11 Bahman.

P. 389[a] COX, l. 1 *for* 1970 *read* 1870.

P. 407[b] CHILDREN iii, l. 4 *for nāmaganīh read nāmagānīh.*

P. 419[b] CHILDREN vii, l. 26 *for* Farāḥ *read* Faraḥ.

P. 424[a] CHILIARCH, l. 16 *after* 22.7 *add* ; Middle Pers. *hazārbad*, miswritten *hazār-banda*; Shaki, p. 258 n. 16; l. 45 *after* 174. *add* M. Shaki, "Observations on the Ayādgār ī Zarērān," *Archív Orientální* 54, 1986, pp. 257-74.

P. 486[a] CHIONITES, l. 26 *after* 117; *add* for other citations in Parthian and Middle Persian literature, see *Ayādgār ī Zarērān*, in *Pahlavi Texts*, ed. Jamasp-Asana, pp. 1-18; *Dēnkard*, ed. Madan, p. 643;

P. 525[a] CHRISTIANITY i, l. 20 *for wināhgār read bazaggar*; l. 21 *after* p. 67) *add* or "the Harsh One" (*dabr*; cf. Markwart, *Ērānšahr*, p. 67).

P. 596[b] CIRCUMCISION l. 2 *for ṭaṭhīr read taṭhīr.*

P. 633[b] CITIZENSHIP ii, l. 32 *after* Shaki, *add* 1974,

P. 654[a] CLASS SYSTEM iii, l. 38 *after* sins *delete* of.

P. 655[b] l. 50 *for* scribe *read* chief scribe;

P. 656[a] l. 55 *for dādwa read dādwar*; l. 57 *for sawār read aswār.*

Volume VI

P. 2[b] COFFEEHOUSE, l. 24 *for maʿarakas read maʿrakas.*

P. 47[a] COLOR i, l. 10 *for* Dāyā *read* Dāya.

P. 112[a] COMMUNISM iii, l. 43 *for Żorūrat read Żarūrat.*

P. 121[b] CONCESSIONS ii, l. 39 *for* French Régie *read* Régie.

P. 138[b] CONSPIRACY THEORIES, l. 44 *for* Russia, and Turkey *read* the Russians, and the Ottomans;

P. 139[a] ll. 53-54 *for* Komīta-ye sīāsī-e Īrān (Political committee of Iran) *read* Komīta-ye mellīūn-e īrānī (Committee of Iranian nationalists);

P. 140[a] ll. 50-51 *for* 9 Esfand 1299 Š./28 February 1921 *read* 3 Esfand 1299 Š./22 February 1921;

P. 140[b] l. 53 *for Nowrūz Khan read Shaikh Hādī.*

P. 354[b] COUP D'ETAT OF 1332 Š./1953, ll. 47-48 *for* the spring of 1331 Š. *read* late 1331 and early 1332 Š.; ll. 52-53 *for* Ḥasan Farūst's *read* Ḥosayn Ferdūst's.

P. 457[a] CUNEIFORM SCRIPT, l. 27 *for Persiká read Persikà;*

P. 459 Figure 23 *for xsāyaθiy- read xsāyaθiya-; for būmī read būmī-; for Ahuramazdā-* (genitive noun) *read Auramazdā-* (theonym); *for Ahuramazdāhā* (genitive singular noun) *read Auramazdāha* (theonym, genitive);

P. 460[a] l. 41 *for* mī̆- *read* mī̆-;

P. 462[a] l. 11 *for alt-persischen read altpersischen*

P. 469[b] CURZON, l. 21 *before* B. Busch *add* C. E. Bosworth, "The Hon. George Nathaniel Curzon's Travels in Russian Central Asia and Persia," *Iran* 31, 1993, pp. 127-36.

P. 514[b] CYROPOLIS, l. 3 *for* 559-30? *read* 559-30; ll. 5-6 *for *Kuru(š)-kaġa- read *Kuru(š)-kaθa-*; l. 15 *for* 522?-486 *read* 522-486; l. 43 *for *Kuru(š)-kaġa- read *Kuru(š)-kaθa-*;

P. 515[a] l. 18 *for* though *read* through; l. 54 *after* Tajikistan *add* and northern Central Asia; l. 56 *delete* and northern Central Asia.

P. 515[b] CYRUS i, l. 4 *for Per-sonennamenbuch read Personennamenbuch.*

P. 516[b] CYRUS iii, l. 17 *for* Cabyses *read* Cambyses.

P. 524[b] CYRUS v, l. 24 *for* Achai-menideninschriften *read* Achaimenideninschriften; l. 25 *for* litera-rischer *read* literarischer.

P. 525[a] CYRUS vi, l. 12 *for kṛa- read kāra-*; l. 28 *for* Xenophon, *Anabasis* 1.1.2 *read* Xenophon, *Hellenica* 2.1.11; l. 31 *for* Xenophon, *Hellenica* 2.1.11 *read* Xenophon, *Anabasis* 1.1.2;

P. 525[b] l. 11 *for* Tuyrtaeum *read* Tyrtaeum.

P. 538[b] DABĪR ii, l. 39 *add new paragraph:* A strong hereditary tendency among prominent bureaucratic families continued until quite late. In 14th-century Qazvīn, for example, there were fourteen families of city officials, tax collectors, and bureaucrats (of thirty-three families of notables) who had dominated the region for generations; many had accumulated wealth and landed property. The clan of Ḥamd-Allāh Mostawfī, attested among notables in the city for more than five centuries, is a prime example (*Tārīḵ-e gozīda*, ed. Browne, pp. 798-814).

P. 555[b] DĀDGAR, l. 2 *for* 1348 Š./1959 *read* 1349 Š./1970; l. 12 *for* kešvar *read* ḏākela;

P. 556[a] ll. 3-4 *for* became general director of *read* returned to work in; ll. 4-5 *for* assistant deputy *read* he became deputy minister; ll. 9-10 *for* retained the latter position and became assistant *read* became the acting minister of the interior and deputy; ll. 18-19 *for* on the suspicion that he had been cooperating *read* because of his previous cooperation; l. 24 *for* deputy *read* assistant to the; l. 37 *after* Seventh *add* , Eighth,; l. 41 *after* suspicions *add* (*Eṭṭelāʿāt dar yak robʿ-e qarn*, p. 137); ll. 42-43 *delete* (*Eṭṭelāʿāt dar yak robʿ-e qarn*, p. 137).

P. 565[b] DĀĞ, l. 21 *after* emblems *add* (for references in the *Šāh-nāma*, see Wolff, *Glossar*, p. 360).

P. 577[a] DĀĞESTĀNĪ, l. 18 *for* "head of the royal arsenal" *read* "commander of the *qūrčīs*."

P. 578[b] DAGUERREOTYPE, l. 24 for in the late 1850s *read* by the 1850s.

P. 581[b] DAHAE ii, l. 28 *after* Great *add* at Gaugamela;

P. 582[a] l. 29 *for* S(p)árnoi *read* (S)párnoi.

P. 588[b] DAHRĪ i, l. 6 *after* Zaehner *add Zurvan.*

P. 614[b] DAL'VERZIN TEPE, pl. LVII, legend l. 1 *for* Terracotta *read* Gypsum-coated clay;

P. 615[a] pl. LVIII, legend, l. 1 *for* Terracotta *read* Gypsum-coated clay.

P. 617[b] DĀM-DĀRĪ *for Table 36 substitute*

Table 36

DISTRIBUTION OF PASTURELANDS IN PERSIA, BY GRAZING CAPACITY

(in millions of ha)

Annual Grazing Capacity	Total Area
1 sheep per ha	19
1 sheep per 2 ha	25
1 sheep per 15 ha	56
Total	100

Source: Hourcade, 1977, p. 214.

P. 623[b] DĀM-PEZEŠKĪ ii, signature *add* ḤASAN TĀJBAḴŠ AND (omitted through an oversight).

P. 624[a] DĀMĀD, l. 23 *after* 948/1541). *add* Mīr Dāmād led the Friday prayer service in Isfahan after the enthronement of Shah Ṣafī (1038-52/1629-42; Moḥammad-Maʿṣūm, pp. 82, 96).

P. 626[a] l.11 *after* n.d. *add* Moḥammad-Maʿṣūm Eṣfahānī, *Ḵolāṣat al-sīar*, Tehran, 1368 Š./1989.

P. 640[a] DANCE i, l. 3 *for* Sīālk *read* Sīalk.

P. 646[a] *DĀNEŠ*, l. 25 *for* 35.5 x 21.5 *read* 21.5 x 35.5; ll. 46-49 *for* the wife of Dr. Ḥosayn Khan Kaḥḥāl, himself editor of the newspaper *Esteqlāl-e Īrān* (Iranian independence); in the paper itself she was named as Ḵānom-e Doktor Kaḥḥāl *read* Doktor Kaḥḥāl, Ḵānom-e Doktor [Ḥosayn Khan] Kaḥḥāl; l. 52 *for* executive editor *read* editor in chief; ll. 53-54 *for* and for numbers 4-30 as Dr. Kaḥḥāl himself *read* ; in numbers 4-30 no editor in chief was mentioned; l. 58 *for* 34 x 22 *read* 22 x 34; l. 59 *for* Russian *read* the Rūsī;

P. 646[b] l. 16 *for* 20.5 x 13 *read* 13 x 20.5; l. 20 *after* was *add* reportedly; l. 39 *for* A *read* From 1974 a; ll. 43-44 *for* 22.5 x 13.5 *read* 13 x 21.5; l. 56 *for* 23.5 x 15.5 *read* 15.5 x 23.5; ll. 59-60 *delete* "Negāh-ī be majallāt-e fārsī," *Soḵan* 4/13, Bahman 1331 Š./February 1953,;

P. 647[a] ll. 1-2 *delete* pp. 242-43; 6/2, Farvardīn 1334 Š./April 1955, pp. 183-84; Tīr 1334 Š./July 1955, pp. 468-69. Idem,; l. 4 *after* 1975 *add* , pp. 248-55; ll. 4-6 *delete* Idem, *Fehrest-e majallāt e mawjūd dar Ketāb-ḵāna-ye Āstān-e qods-e rażawī* I, Mašhad, 1364 Š./1985.; l. 12 *after* 1979. *add Fehrest-e majallāt-e mawjūd dar Ketāb-ḵāna-ye Āstān-e Qods-e rażawī* I, Mašhad, 1364 Š./1985.; l. 23 *after* 1989. *add* "Negāh-ī be majallāt-e fārsī," *Soḵan* 4/13, Bahman 1331 Š./February 1953, pp. 242-43; 6/2, Farvardīn 1334 Š./April 1955, pp. 183-84; Tīr 1334 Š./July 1955, pp. 468-69.

P. 654[a] DĀNEŠ-SARĀ-YE ʿALĪ *for* **ʿALI** *read* **ʿĀLĪ**.

P. 654[b] DĀNEŠKĀDA *for* **DĀNEŠKĀDA** *read* **DĀNEŠKADA**; *after* DANEŠKADA *add* DĀNEŠKADA (newspaper). See Supplement; DĀNEŠKĀDA-YE AFSARĪ *for* **DĀNEŠKĀDA** *read* **DĀNEŠKADA**; *after* DANEŠKĀDA-YE AFSARĪ *add* DĀNEŠKADA-YE EṢFAHĀN (newspaper). See Supplement.

P. 655[b] *Delete* **DĀNEŠMAND.** See ʿABD-AL-BĀQĪ TABRĪZĪ.

P. 656[b] DANG *for* **DANG** *read* **DĀNG.**

P. 659 DĀNĪĀL-E NABĪ iii, pl. LXII, legend *after* east. *add* Photograph courtesy Mīrāṯ-e farhangī-e Īrān.

P. 670[b] DĀR AL-ŠŪRA-YE KOBRĀ *for* **ŠŪRA** *read* **ŠŪRĀ**.

Volume VII

P. 14[a] DARBAND, ll. 33-36 *for pahak*) to gates that lay parallel to the Gates of the Alans; they thus equated the name with the fortress of *pahak*) to gatesthat lay parallel to the Gates of the Alans; they thus equated the name with the fortress of *read parhak* the reference in Agathangelos' text (*Patmutʿiwn Hayocʿ* par. 19; cf. *History*, tr. Thomson, p. 36: *Čoray pahak*) to gates that lay parallel to the Gates of the Alans; they thus equated the name with the fortress of.

P. 23[a] D'ARCY, ll. 1-3 *delete* (also known as D'arcy Todd, Major Todd;

P. 23[b] ll. 2-5 *delete* In D'Arcy's later years he served on a military mission to Herat in 1255/1829 in support of Kāmrān against Dōst Moḥammad Khan (Ṭāherī, II, pp. 189-93; see AFGHANISTAN x); l. 11 *for* Clements Markham *read* Maḥbūbī; l. 13 *for* Markham, p. 482 *read* Maḥbūbī, p. 101; ll. 14-17 *delete* B. Ātābāy, *Fehrest-e tārīḵ, safar-nāma, sīāḥat-nāma, rūz-nāma wa joḡrāfīā-ye ḵaṭṭī-e ketāb-ḵāna-ye salṭanatī* , Tehran, 2536=1356 Š./1977.; ll. 23-25 *delete* C. R. Markham, *A General Sketch of the History of Persia*, London, 1874; repr. Liechtenstein, 1977.

P. 46 DARIUS iii, Figure 2 *east of the mountains at the lower right add* 13. Indians.

P. 59[a] DARMESTETER, l. 42 *for* Gilbert Lazard *read* Jean de Menasce

P. 115[a] DĀTA, l. 42 *for* Freiberg *read* Freiburg

P. 116[a] DATAMES, l. l. 46 *for* 21.2.5 *read* 21.1, 21.5

P. 117[a] l. 46 *for* Mineur *read* Mineure

P. 229[a] DEIPNOSOPHISTAÍ, l. 11 *for* Deipno-sophistai *read* Deipnosophistai

SHORT REFERENCES AND ABBREVIATIONS OF BOOKS AND PERIODICALS

AAASH
Acta Antiqua Academiae Scientiarum Hungaricae.

Aarne and Thompson
A. A. Aarne, *Verzeichnis der Märchentypen*, tr. and enl. by Stith Thompson as *The Types of the Folk-Tale: A Classification and Bibliography*, Helsinki, 1928.

ʿAbd-al-Karīm Boḵārī
Afḡān wa Kābol wa Boḵārā wa Ḵīwaq wa Ḵoqand Ḵānlarīnin aḥwāl, ed. and tr. Charles Schefer as *Histoire de l'Asie Centrale par Mir Abdoul Kerim Boukhary: Afghanistan, Boukhara, Khiva, Khoqand depuis les dernières années de règne de Nadir Chah (1153), jusqu'en 1233 de l'Hégire (1740-1818 A.D.)*, Publications de l'École des langues orientales vivantes, 1, I, Būlāq, 1290/1873, II, Paris, 1876; repr. in 1 vol., Amsterdam, 1970.

Abh.
Abhandlungen.

Abu'l-Fedā, *Taqwīm*
Abu'l-Fedā Esmāʿīl b. ʿAlī b. Maḥmūd ʿEmād-al-Dīn Ayyūbī, *Taqwīm al-boldān*, ed. J.-T. Reinaud and W. M. de Slane, Paris, 1840.

Abu'l-Fedā, *Taqwīm*, tr. Reinaud
Abu'l-Fedā Esmāʿīl b. ʿAlī b. Maḥmūd ʿEmād-al-Dīn Ayyūbī, *Taqwīm al-boldān*, tr. as *Géographie d'Aboulfeda, traduite de l'arabe en français*, I and II/1 tr. J.-T. Reinaud, Paris, 1848, II/2 tr. Stanislaus Guyard, Paris, 1883.

Abu'l-Ḡāzī, *Šajara-ye tork*
Abu'l-Ḡāzī, *Šajara-ye tork*, ed. and tr. J. J. P. Desmaisons as *Histoire des Mongols et des Tatares par Aboul-Ghâzi Bèhâdour Khân, souverain de Kharezm et historien Djaghataï, 1603-1664*, 2 vols., St. Petersburg, 1871-74.

ADTD
Ankara Üniversitesi, Dil ve tarih-coğrafya fakültesi dergisi.

***Aḡānī*[1,2,3] (Cairo)**
Abu'l-Faraj ʿAlī b. al-Ḥosayn Qorašī Eṣbahānī, *Ketāb al-aḡānī*, I-XX ed. Naṣr Horīnī, Būlāq, 1285/1868-69, XXI ed. R. E. Brünnow, Leiden, 1888; repr., 21 vols., Cairo, 1323/1905-06; 3rd ed., Cairo, 1345-/1926-.

Agathangelos, *History*, tr. Thomson
Agatʿangelay, *Patmutʿiwn Hayocʿ*, tr. R. W. Thomson as *History of the Armenians*, Albany, N.Y., 1976 (except pars. 259-715).

Agathangelos, *Patmutʿiwn Hayocʿ*
Agatʿangelay, *Patmutʿiwn Hayocʿ*, ed. G. Tēr-Mkrtʿean and S. Kanayeancʿ, Tiflis, 1909; repr. Delmar, N.Y., 1979.

Agathangelos, *The Teaching of St. Gregory*
Agatʿangelay, *Patmutʿiwn Hayocʿ*, tr. R. W. Thomson as *The Teaching of St. Gregory, an Early Armenian Catechism*, Cambridge, Mass., 1970 (pars. 259-715).

***Āʾīn-e akbarī*, ed. Blochmann**
Abu'l-Fażl ʿAllāmī, *Āʾīn-e akbarī*, ed. H. Blochmann, Bib. Ind., 2 vols., Calcutta, 1867-77.

***Āʾīn-e akbarī*, ed. Phillott**
Abu'l-Fażl ʿAllāmī, *Āʾīn-e akbarī*, rev. ed. and tr. D. C. Phillott, 3 vols., Calcutta, 1939-49.

***Āʾīn-e akbarī*, tr. Blochmann**
Abu'l-Fażl ʿAllāmī, *Āʾīn-e akbarī* I, tr. H. Blochmann, II-III, tr. H. S. Jarrett, Bib. Ind., Calcutta, 1868-94.

AirWb.
Christian Bartholomae, *Altiranisches Wörterbuch*, Strassburg, 1904; repr. Berlin, 1961.

AIUON
Annali dell'Istituto universitario orientale di Napoli.

AJA
American Journal of Archaeology.

AJSLL
American Journal of Semitic Languages and Literature.

Akbar-nāma
Abu'l-Fażl ʿAllāmī, *Akbar-nāma*, ed. Āqā Moḥammad ʿAlī and Mawlawī ʿAbd-al-Raḥīm, 3 vols., Bib. Ind., Calcutta, 1877-86.

***Akbar-nāma*, tr. Beveridge**
Abu'l-Fażl ʿAllāmī, *Akbar-nāma*, tr. Henry Beveridge, 3 vols., Bib. Ind., Calcutta, 1897-1939.

AKM
Abhandlungen für die Kunde des Morgenlandes.

Aʿlām-al-šīʿa
Āḡā Bozorg Ṭehrānī, *Ṭabaqāt aʿlām al-šīʿa*, Najaf, 1373/1954.

AMI
Archäologische Mitteilungen aus Iran.

***ANRW* II**
Aufstieg und Niedergang der römischen Welt. Geschichte und Kultur Roms im Spiegel der neueren Forschung II. *Principat*, ed. Hildegard Temporini and Wolfgang Haase, Berlin, 1976-.

Anz.
Anzeiger.
AOASH
Acta Orientalia Academiae Scientiarum Hungaricae.
AoF
Altorientalische Forschungen.
APAW
Abhandlungen der Preussischen Akademie der Wissenschaften.
ARW
Archiv für Religionswissenschaft.
Āryanpūr, *Az Ṣabā tā Nīmā*
Yaḥyā Āryanpūr, *Az Ṣabā tā Nīmā*, 2 vols., Tehran, 1351 Š./1973.
Ašʿarī, *Maqālāt*
Abu'l-Ḥasan ʿAlī b. Esmāʿīl Ašʿarī, *Maqālāt al-eslāmīyīn*, ed. Helmut Ritter, Istanbul, 1929-33.
Ātaškada
Loṭf-ʿAlī Bīg Āḏar, *Ātaškada*, ed. Ḥasan Sādāt-e Nāṣerī, 3 vols., Tehran, 1337-41 Š./1958-62.
Ateş, *Eserler*
Ahmed Ateş, *İstanbul kütüphanelerinde farsça manzum eserler* I. *Üniversite ve nuruosmaniye kütüphaneleri*, Istanbul, 1968.
***Avesta*, ed. Geldner**
K. F. Geldner, ed., *Avesta. Die heiligen Bücher der Parsen*, 3 vols. in 1, Stuttgart, 1886-95.
***Avesta*, tr. Darmesteter**
James Darmesteter, *Le Zend-Avesta: Traduction nouvelle avec commentaire historique et philologique*, 3 vols., Paris, 1892-93; repr. Paris, 1960.
***Avesta*, tr. Wolff**
Fritz Wolff, *Avesta. Die heiligen Bücher der Parsen, übersetzt auf der Grundlage von Chr. Bartholomae's Altiranischem Wörterbuch*, Berlin and Leipzig, 1924.
ʿAwfī, *Lobāb*
Moḥammad ʿAwfī, *Lobāb al-albāb*, ed. E. G. Browne and M. Qazvīnī, Leiden and London, 1906.
ʿAwfī, *Lobāb*, ed. Nafīsī
Moḥammad ʿAwfī, *Lobāb al-albāb*, ed. Saʿīd Nafīsī, Tehran, 1335 Š./1956.
Aʿyān al-šīʿa
Moḥsen Amīn Ḥosaynī ʿĀmelī, *Aʿyān al-šīʿa*, 14 vols. in 15, Damascus, 1935-39.
Bābor-nāma
Ẓahīr-al-Dīn Moḥammad Bābor, *Bābor-nāma*, facs. ed. A. S. Beveridge, GMS 1, Leiden and London, 1905; repr. London, 1971.
***Bābor-nāma*, tr. Beveridge**
Ẓahīr-al-Dīn Moḥammad Bābor, *Bābor-nāma*, tr. A. S. Beveridge as *Bābur-nāma in English (Memoirs of Bābur)*, London, 1922; repr. London, 1969.
Back
Michael Back, *Die sassanidischen Staatsinschriften: Studien zur Orthographie and Phonologie des Mittelpersischen der Inschriften . . .*, Tehran and Leiden, 1978.
Badāʾūnī, *Montaḵab*
ʿAbd-al-Qāder Badāʾūnī, *Montaḵab al-tawārīḵ*, ed. A.-ʿA. Kabīr-al-Dīn Aḥmad and W. N. Lees, 2 vols., Calcutta, 1864-69.
Badāʾūnī, *Montaḵab*, tr. Ranking et al.
ʿAbd-al-Qāder Badāʾūnī, *Montaḵab al-tawārīḵ*, tr. G. S. A. Ranking, W. H. Lowe, and Wolseley Haig, 3 vols., Calcutta, 1884-1925; repr. Patna, 1973.
Baḡdādī, *Farq*, ed. ʿAbd-al-Ḥamīd
Abū Manṣūr ʿAbd-al-Qāher b. Ṭāher b. Moḥammad Baḡdādī, *Ketāb al-farq bayn al-feraq*, ed. M. M. ʿAbd-al-Ḥamīd, Cairo, 1964.
Baḡdādī, *Farq*, ed. Badr
Abū Manṣūr ʿAbd-al-Qāher b. Ṭāher b. Moḥammad Baḡdādī, *al-Farq bayn al-feraq*, ed. Moḥammad Badr, Cairo, 1328/1910.
Bahār, *Sabk-šenāsī*
M.-T. Bahār, *Sabk-šenāsī*, 3 vols., Tehran, 1321 Š./1942.
Bailey, *Dictionary*
H. W. Bailey, *Dictionary of Khotan Saka*, Cambridge, 1979.
Bailey, *Zoroastrian Problems*
H. W. Bailey, *Zoroastrian Problems in the Ninth-Century Books*, Oxford, 1943; repr. with a new introd., London, 1971.
Balāḏorī, *Ansāb*
Abu'l-ʿAbbās Aḥmad b. Yaḥyā b. Jāber Balāḏorī, *Kitāb ansāb al-ašrāf*, IVb ed. Max Schlössinger, Jersualem, 1935, V ed. S. D. F. Goitein, Jerusalem, 1936.
Balāḏorī, *Fotūḥ*
Abu'l-ʿAbbās Aḥmad b. Yaḥyā b. Jāber Balāḏorī, *Kitāb fotūḥ al-boldān*, ed. M. J. de Goeje, Leiden, 1886; 2nd ed., Leiden, 1968.
Balāḏorī, *Fotūḥ*, ed. Monajjed
Abu'l-ʿAbbās Aḥmad b. Yaḥyā b. Jāber Balāḏorī, *Kitāb fotūḥ al-boldān*, ed. Ṣalāḥ-al-Dīn Monajjed, 3 vols., Cairo, 1956-61.
Balʿamī, ed. Bahār
Abū ʿAlī Moḥammad Balʿamī, *Tārīḵ-e Balʿamī*, ed. M.-T. Bahār, Tehran, 1341 Š./1962.
Balʿamī, ed. Rowšan
Abū ʿAlī Moḥammad Balʿamī, *Tārīḵ-nāma-ye Ṭabarī gardānīda-ye mansūb be Balʿamī*, ed. Moḥammad Rowšan, 3 vols., Tehran, 1366 Š./1987.
Balʿamī, tr. Zotenberg.
Abū ʿAlī Moḥammad Balʿamī, *Tārīḵ-nāma-ye Ṭabarī gardānīda-ye mansūb be Balʿamī*, tr. Hermann Zotenberg as *Chronique de . . .Tabari*

traduite sur la version persane d'Abou-ʿAli Moʿhammad Belʿami, 4 vols., Paris, 1867-74.

Bāmdād, *Rejāl*
Mahdī Bāmdād, *Šarḥ-e ḥāl-e rejāl-e Īrān dar qorūn-e davāzdahom wa sīzdahom wa čahārdahom-e hejrī*, 6 vols., Tehran, 1347-57 Š./1966-78.

BAR
British Archeological Reports, International series.

Barthold, *Turkestan* [2,3]
W. W. Barthold, *Turkestan Down to the Mongol Invasion*, 2nd ed., London, 1958; 3rd ed., London, 1969.

Bayānī, *Ḵošnevīsān*
Mahdī Bayānī, *Aḥwāl o āṯār-e ḵošnevīsān: Nastaʿlīqnevīsān*, 3 vols., Tehran, 1345-48 Š./1966-69.

Bayhaqī, ed. Fayyāż
Abu'l-Fażl Bayhaqī, *Tārīḵ-e masʿūdī*, ed. ʿA.-A. Fayyāż, Mašhad, 1350 Š./1971.

Bayhaqī, ed. Nafīsī
Abu'l-Fażl Bayhaqī, *Tārīḵ-e masʿūdī*, ed. Saʿīd Nafīsī, 3 vols., Tehran, 1319-32 Š./1940-53.

Bd.
See *Bundahišn*.

Belgrāmī, *Ḵezāna*
Āzād Belgrāmī, *Ḵezāna-ye ʿāmera*, Cawnpore, 1871.

BGA
Bibliotheca Geographorum Arabicorum, ed. M. J. de Goeje, 8 vols., Leiden, 1870-94.

Bib. Ind.
Bibliotheca Indica, published by the Asiatic Society of Bengal, Calcutta.

Bib. Pers.
Bibliotheca Persica, New York.

Bīrūnī, *Āṯār*
Abū Rayḥān Bīrūnī, *Ketāb al-āṯār al-bāqīa ʿan al-qorūn al-ḵālīa*, ed. Eduard Sachau as *Chronologie orientalischer Völker von Albêrûnî*, Leipzig, 1878; repr. Leipzig, 1923; repr. Baghdad, 1963.

Bīrūnī, *Āṯār*, tr. Sachau
Abū Rayḥān Bīrūnī, *Ketāb al-āṯār al-bāqīa ʿan al-qorūn al-ḵālīa*, tr. Eduard Sachau as *The Chronology of the Ancient Nations*, London, 1879; repr. Frankfurt, 1969.

BNF
Beiträge zur Namenforschung.

***Borhān-e qāṭeʿ*, ed. Moʿīn**
Moḥammad Ḥosayn b. Ḵalaf Tabrīzī, *Borhān-e qāṭeʿ*, ed. Moḥammad Moʿīn, 6 vols., Tehran, 1342-52 Š./1963-73.

Bosworth, *Ghaznavids*
C. E. Bosworth, *The Ghaznavids: Their Empire in Afghanistan and Eastern Iran 944-1040*, Edinburgh, 1963.

Bosworth, *Later Ghaznavids*
C. E. Bosworth, *The Later Ghaznavids, Splendour and Decay: The Dynasty in Afghanistan and Northern India 1040-1186*, Edinburgh, 1977.

Boyce, "Middle Persian Literature"
Mary Boyce, "Middle Persian Literature," in *HO* I/IV, 2/1, Leiden, 1968, pp. 31-66.

Boyce, *Reader*
Mary Boyce, *A Reader in Manichaean Middle Persian and Parthian*, Acta Iranica 9, Tehran and Liège, 1975.

Boyce, *Stronghold*
Mary Boyce, *A Persian Stronghold of Zoroastrianism*, Oxford, 1977.

Boyce, *Zoroastrianism*
Mary Boyce, *A History of Zoroastrianism* I-II, HO I/VIII/1, 2/2A, Leiden, 1975-82.

Boyce and Grenet, *Zoroastrianism*
Mary Boyce and Frantz Grenet, *A History of Zoroastrianism* III, HO I/VIII/1, 2/2, Leiden, 1991.

Brockelmann, *GAL*
Carl Brockelmann, *Geschichte der arabischen Litteratur*, 2nd ed., 2 vols., Leiden, 1943-49; Supplement (S), 3 vols., Leiden, 1937-42.

Browne, *Lit. Hist. Persia*
E. G. Browne, *A Literary History of Persia*, 4 vols., London, 1902-04.

Browne, *Persian Revolution*
E. G. Browne, *The Persian Revolution of 1905-1909*, London, 1910.

Browne, *Press and Poetry*
E. G. Browne, *The Press and Poetry of Modern Persia Partly Based on the Manuscript Work of Mírzá Muḥammad ʿAlí Khán "Tarbiyat" of Tabríz*, Cambridge, 1914.

BSL
Bulletin de la Société de Linguistique de Paris.

BSO(A)S
Bulletin of the School of Oriental (and African) Studies.

***Bundahišn* (DH)**
P. K. Anklesaria, ed., *The Codex DH, Being a Facsimile Edition of Bondahesh, Zand-e Vohuman Yasht, and Parts of the Denkard*, Tehran, n.d. (1350 Š./1971).

***Bundahišn* (TD_1)**
P. K. Anklesaria, ed., *The Bondahesh, Being a Facsimile Edition of the Manuscript TD_1*, Tehran, n.d. (1350 Š./1971).

***Bundahišn* (TD_2)**
T. D. Anklesaria, ed., *The Bûndahishn, Being a Facsimile of the TD Manuscript No. 2 . . .*, Bombay, 1908.

***Bundahišn*, tr. Anklesaria**
B. T. Anklesaria, ed. and tr., *Zand-Ākāsīh: Iranian or Greater Bundahišn*, Bombay, 1956.

Caetani, *Annali*
Leone Caetani, *Annali dell'Islam*, 10 vols. in 12, Milan, 1905-26; repr. 1986.

***CAH*[2,3]**
Cambridge Ancient History, 2nd ed., 12 vols., Cambridge, 1928-39; 3rd ed., vols. 1 and 2 in 4, Cambridge, 1970-75.

***Čahār maqāla*, ed. Qazvīnī**
Aḥmad b. ʿOmar b. ʿAlī Neẓāmī ʿArūżī Samarqandī, *Čahār maqāla*, ed. Moḥammad Qazvīnī, rev. Moḥammad Moʿīn, Tehran, 1331 Š./1952.

Camb. Hist. Iran
The Cambridge History of Iran, Cambridge, 1968-.

Cat. Bankipore
Catalogue of the Arabic and Persian Manuscripts in the Oriental Public Library at Bankipore, 29 vols., Calcutta, 1908-20, Patna, 1918-71.

Cat. Bibliothèque Nationale
Edgar Blochet, *Catalogue des manuscrits persans de la Bibliothèque Nationale*, 4 vols., Paris, 1905-34.

Cat. Bodleian Library
Eduard Sachau, Hermann Ethé, and A. F. L. Beeston, eds., *Catalogue of the Persian, Turkish, Hindustani, and Pushtu Manuscripts in the Bodleian Library*, 3 vols., Oxford, 1889-1954.

Cat. Chester Beatty Library
The Chester Beatty Library: A Catalogue of the Persian Manuscripts and Miniatures, I ed. A. J. Arberry, Mojtaba Minovi, and Edgar Blochet, Dublin, 1959; II-III ed. Mojtaba Minovi, B. W. Robinson, J. W. S. Wilkinson, and Edgar Blochet, Dublin, 1960-62.

CDAFI
Cahiers de la Délégation archéologique française en Iran.

Chardin
Jean Chardin, *Voyages du chevalier Chardin en Perse, et autres lieux de l'Orient . . . Nouvelle édition, soigneusement conférée sur les trois éditions originales, augmentée . . . de notes, etc. . . .*, ed. Louis Langlès, 10 vols., Paris, 1811.

Christensen, *Contributions*
Arthur Christensen, *Contributions à la dialectologie iranienne*, Det Kgl. Danske Videnskabernes Selskab, Hist.-fil. Medd., 2 vols., Copenhagen, 1935.

Christensen, *Iran Sass.*
Arthur Christensen, *L'Iran sous les Sassanides*, 2nd ed., Copenhagen, 1944.

Col. Lect. Series.
Columbia Lectures Series on Iranian Studies.

Corpus Inscr. Iran.
Corpus Inscriptionum Iranicarum, London, 1955-.

CSCO
Corpus Scriptorum Christianorum Orientalium.

Curzon, *Persian Question*
G. N. Curzon, *Persia and the Persian Question*, 2 vols., London, 1892.

***Dādistān ī dēnīg*, pt. 1**
T. D. Anklesaria, ed., *The Dadistan-i Dinik, Part I, Pursishn I-XL*, Bombay, 1913.

DAI
Deutsches Archäologisches Institut.

Dānešgāh-e Tehran
Mortażā Solṭānī, ed., *Fehrest-e rūz-nāmahā-ye fārsī dar majmūʿa-ye Ketāb-ḵāna-ye markazī . . . Dānešgāh-e Tehrān*, Entešārāt-e Ketab-ḵāna-ye markazī o markaz-e esnād 6, Tehran, 1354 Š./1975.

al-Ḏarīʿa
Āqā Bozorg Ṭehrānī, *al-Ḏarīʿa elā taṣānīf al-šīʿa*, 24 vols. in 27, Najaf and Tehran, 1355-98/1936-78.

Dawlatābādī, *Ḥayāt-e Yaḥyā*
Yaḥyā Dawlatābādī, *Tārīḵ-e moʿāṣer yā ḥayāt-e Yaḥyā*, 4 vols., Tehran, n.d.

Dawlatšāh, ed. Browne
Dawlatšāh Samarqandī, *Taḏkerat al-šoʿarāʾ*, ed. E. G. Browne as *The Tadhkiratu 'sh-shuʿará ("Memoirs of the Poets") of Dawlatsháh . . .*, Leiden and London, 1901.

Dehḵodā
ʿAlī-Akbar Dehḵodā, *Loḡat-nāma*, Tehran, 1325-58 Š./1946-79.

***Dēnkard*, ed. Dresden**
M. J. Dresden, ed., *Dēnkart, a Pahlavi Text: Facsimile Edition of the Manuscript B of the K. R. Cama Oriental Institute Bombay*, Wiesbaden, 1966.

***Dēnkard*, ed. Madan**
D. M. Madan, ed., *The Complete Text of the Pahlavi Dinkard*, 2 vols., Bombay, 1911.

***Dēnkard*, ed. Sanjana**
D. P. Sanjana and P. B. Sanjana, *The Dinkard*, 19 vols., Bombay, 1874-1928.

Dīnavarī, ed. Guirgass
Abū Ḥanīfa Dīnavarī, *al-Aḵbār al-ṭewāl*, ed. Vladimir Guirgass, Leiden, 1888.

DMBE
Dāʾerat al-maʿāref-e bozorg-e eslāmī, ed. Kāẓem Mūsawī Bojnūrdī, Tehran, 1367-Š./1988-.

Doerfer, *Elemente*
Gerhard Doerfer, *Türkische und mongolische Elemente im Neupersischen*, 4 vols., Wiesbaden, 1963-76.

Ebn al-Aṯīr
ʿEzz-al-Dīn b. al-Aṯīr, *al-Kāmel fi'l-taʾrīḵ*, ed. C. J. Tornberg, 12 vols., Leiden, 1851-76; repr., 13 vols., Beirut, 1965-67.

Ebn al-Balḵī
Ebn al-Balḵī, *Fārs-nāma*, ed. Guy Le Strange and R. A. Nicholson as *The Fársnáma of Ibnu'l-Balkhí*, GMS, Cambridge, 1921.

Ebn Baṭṭūṭa
Abū ʿAbd-Allāh Moḥammad b. Moḥammad Lawātī Ṭanjī b. Baṭṭūṭa, *Toḥfat al-noẓẓār fī ğarāʾeb al-amṣār wa ʿajāʾeb al-asfār*, ed. and tr. Charles Defrémery and B. R. Sanguinetti as *Voyages d'Ibn Batoutah*, 4 vols., Paris, 1853-58.

Ebn Baṭṭūṭa, tr. Gibb
Abū ʿAbd-Allāh Moḥammad b. Moḥammad Lawātī Ṭanjī b. Baṭṭūṭa, *Toḥfat al-noẓẓār fī ğārāʾeb al-amṣār wa ʿajāʾeb al-asfār*, tr. H. A. R. Gibb as *Travels of Ibn Battuta, A.D. 1325-1354*, 4 vols., Cambridge, 1958-94.

Ebn Esfandīār
Moḥammad b. Ḥasan b. Esfandīār, *Tārīḵ-e Ṭabarestān*, ed. ʿAbbās Eqbāl, 2 vols., Tehran, 1320 Š./1941.

Ebn Esfandīār, tr. Browne
Moḥammad b. Ḥasan b. Esfandīār, *Tārīḵ-e Ṭabarestān*, tr. E. G. Browne as *An Abridged Translation of the History of Ṭabaristān*, Leiden and London, 1905.

Ebn al-Faqīh
Abū Bakr Aḥmad b. Moḥammad Hamaḏānī Ebn al-Faqīh, *Moḵtaṣar Ketāb al-boldān*, ed. M. J. de Goeje, BGA, Leiden, 1886.

Ebn Ḥawqal
Abu'l-Qāsem b. Ḥawqal Naṣībī, *Ketāb ṣūrat al-arż*, ed. J. H. Kramers, BGA, 2nd ed., Leiden, 1938

Ebn Ḥawqal, tr. Kramers
Abu'l-Qāsem b. Ḥawqal Naṣībī, *Ketāb ṣūrat al-arż*, tr. J. H. Kramers and Gaston Wiet as *Configuration de la terre*, 2 vols., Paris and Beirut, 1964.

Ebn al-Jawzī, *Montaẓam*
ʿAbd-al-Raḥmān b. ʿAlī b. al-Jawzī, *al-Montaẓam fī taʾrīḵ al-molūk wa'l-omam*, Hyderabad, 1357-59/1938-40.

Ebn Ḵallekān, ed. ʿAbbās
Abu'l-ʿAbbās Aḥmad b. Moḥammad b. Ebrāhīm b. Ḵallekān, *Wafayāt al-aʿyān wa anbāʾ abnāʾ al-zamān*, ed. Eḥsān ʿAbbās (Ihsan Abbas), 8 vols., Beirut, 1968-72.

Ebn Ḵallekān, ed. Wüstenfeld
Abu'l-ʿAbbās Aḥmad b. Moḥammad b. Ebrāhīm b. Ḵallekān, *Wafayāt al-aʿyan wa anbāʾ abnāʾ al-zamān*, ed. Ferdinand Wüstenfeld, 2 vols., Göttingen, 1835-50.

Ebn Ḵallekān, tr. de Slane
Abu'l-ʿAbbās Aḥmad b. Moḥammad b. Ebrāhīm b. Ḵallekān, *Wafayāt al-aʿyān wa anbāʾ abnāʾ al-zamān*, tr. W. M. de Slane as *Ibn Khallikan's Biographical Dictionary*, 4 vols., Paris, 1842-71.

Ebn Ḵordāḏbeh
Abu'l-Qāsem ʿObayd-Allāh b. ʿAbd-Allāh b. Ḵordāḏbeh, *Kitāb al-masālek wa'l-mamālek*, ed. M. J. de Goeje, BGA, Leiden, 1889; 2nd ed., Leiden, 1967.

Ebn Meskawayh. See Meskawayh.

Ebn al-Mortażā, *Ṭabaqāt*
Aḥmad b. Yaḥyā b. al-Mortażā, *Ṭabaqāt al-moʿtazela*, ed. Susanna Diwald-Wilzer, Beirut and Wiesbaden, 1961.

Ebn al-Nadīm, ed. Flügel
Abu'l-Faraj Moḥammad b. al-Nadīm, *Ketāb al-fehrest*, ed. G. Flügel, 2 vols., Leipzig, 1871-72.

Ebn al-Nadīm, ed. Tajaddod
Abu'l-Faraj Moḥammad b. al-Nadīm, *Ketāb al-fehrest*, ed. M. R. Tajaddod, Tehran, 1350 Š./1971.

Ebn al-Nadīm, tr. Dodge
Abu'l-Faraj Moḥammad b. al-Nadīm, *Ketāb al-fehrest*, tr. Bayard Dodge as *The Fihrist of al-Nadīm*, 2 vols., New York, 1970.

Ebn Rosta
Abū ʿAlī Aḥmad b. ʿOmar b. Rosta, *Ketāb al-aʿlāq al-nafīsa*, ed. M. J. de Goeje, BGA, Leiden, 1892; 2nd ed., Leiden, 1967.

Ebn Rosta, tr. Wiet
Abū ʿAlī Aḥmad b. ʿOmar b. Rosta, *Ketāb al-aʿlāq al-nafīsa*, tr. Gaston Wiet as *Les atours précieux*, Cairo, 1955.

Ebn Saʿd
Moḥammad b. Saʿd, *al-Ṭabaqāt al-kobrā*, ed. Eduard Sachau, 9 vols., Leiden, 1904-40.

Ebn Serapion. See Sohrāb.

Ebn Tağrīberdī
Abu'l-Maḥāsen Jamāl-al-Dīn Yūsof b. Tağrīberdī, *al-Nojūm al-zāhera fī molūk Meṣr wa'l-Qāhera*, 16 vols., Cairo, 1964-72.

Edrīsī
Abū ʿAbd-Allāh Moḥammad Edrīsī, *Nozhat al-moštāq fī eḵterāq al-āfāq*, ed. Enrico Cerulli et al. as *Opus Geographicum*, 6 vols., Naples, 1970-76.

Edrīsī, tr. Jaubert
Abū ʿAbd-Allāh Moḥammad Edrīsī, *Nozhat al-moštāq fī eḵterāq al-āfāq*, tr. P. A. Jaubert as *Géographie d'Edrisi*, 2 vols., Paris, 1836-40.

***EI*[1,2]**
The Encyclopaedia of Islam, 4 vols. and supplement, London and Leiden, 1908-36; 2nd ed., London and Leiden, 1960-.

EIr.
Encyclopædia Iranica, ed. Ehsan Yarshater, London and Costa Mesa, Calif., 1982-.

Ełišē, ed. Tēr-Minasean
Vardapet Ełišē, *Vasn Vardanay ew Hayocʿ paterazmin*, ed. Ervand Tēr-Minasean, Erevan, 1957.

Ełišē, tr. Thomson
Vardapet Ełišē, *Vasn Vardanay ew Hayocʿ paterazmin*, tr. R. W. Thomson as *History of Vardan and the Armenian War*, Cambridge, Mass., 1982.

Elliot, *History of India*
H. M. Elliot and John Dowson, eds., *The History of India as Told by Its Own Historians. The Muhammadan Period*, 8 vols., London, 1867-77.

Eqbāl, *Tārīḵ-e Moḡol*
ʿAbbās Eqbāl, *Tārīḵ-e mofaṣṣal-e Īrān az estīlā-ye Moḡol tā eʿlān-e mašrūṭīyat* I, Tehran, 1320 Š./1941; 2nd ed., Tehran, 1341 Š./1962.

Eskandar Beg
Eskandar Beg Torkamān Monšī, *Tārīḵ-e ʿālamārā-ye ʿabbāsī*, ed. Īraj Afšār, 2 vols., Tehran, 1334-35 Š./1955-56.

Eskandar Beg, tr. Savory
Eskandar Beg Torkamān Monšī, *Tārīḵ-e ʿālamārā-ye ʿabbāsī*, tr. R. M. Savory as *History of Shah ʿAbbas the Great*, 3 vols., PHS 28, Boulder, Colo., and New York, 1979-86.

Eṣṭaḵrī
Abū Esḥāq Eṣṭaḵrī, *Ketāb masālek al-mamālek*, ed. M. J. de Goeje, BGA, Leiden, 1870; 2nd ed., Leiden, 1927; 3rd ed., Leiden, 1967.

Eʿtemād-al-Salṭana, *Maʾāṯer wa'l-āṯār*
Moḥammad-Ḥasan Khan Ṣanīʿ-al-Dawla Eʿtemād-al-Salṭana, *al-Maʾāṯer wa'l-āṯār*, ed. Īraj Afšār as *Čehel sāl tārīḵ-e Īrān dar dawra-ye Pādšāhī-e Nāṣer-al-Dīn Šāh: al-Maʾāṯer wa'l-āṯār*, 3 vols., Tehran, 1363-68 Š./1984-89.

Eʿtemād-al-Salṭana, *Montaẓam-e nāṣerī*
Moḥammad-Ḥasan Khan Ṣanīʿ-al-Dawla Eʿtemād-al-Salṭana, *Tārīḵ-e montaẓam-e nāṣerī*, 3 vols., Tehran, 1298/1881.

Eʿtemād-al-Salṭana, *Montaẓam-e nāṣerī*, ed. Reżwānī
Moḥammad-Ḥasan Khan Ṣanīʿ-al-Dawla Eʿtemād-al-Salṭana, *Tārīḵ-e montaẓam-e nāṣerī*, ed. M.-E. Reżwānī, Tehran, 1363-68 Š./1984-88.

Eʿtemād-al-Salṭana, *Rūz-nāma-ye ḵāṭerāt*
Moḥammad-Ḥasan Khan Ṣanīʿ-al-Dawla Eʿtemād-al-Salṭana, *Rūz-nāma-ye ḵāṭerāt-e Eʿtemād-al-Salṭana*, ed. Īraj Afšār, 3rd ed., Tehran, 2536=1356 Š./1977.

Ethé, *Catalogue*
Hermann Ethé, *Catalogue of Persian Manuscripts in the Library of the India Office*, 2 vols., Oxford, 1903-37.

Eznik, ed. Mariès and Mercier
Eznik Kołbacʿi, *Ełc ałandocʿ*, ed. and tr. Louis Mariès and Charles Mercier as *De Deo*, 2 vols., Paris, 1959.

Fasāʾī
Ḥājj Mīrzā Ḥasan Ḥosaynī Fasāʾī, *Fārs-nāma-ye nāṣerī*, 2 vols., Tehran, 1313-14/1896-97; repr. 2 vols. in 1, Tehran, n.d.

Fasāʾī, ed. Rastgār
Ḥājj Mīrzā Ḥasan Ḥosaynī Fasāʾī, *Fārs-nāma-ye nāṣerī*, ed. Manṣūr Rastgār Fasāʾī, 2 vols., Tehran, 1367 Š./1988.

Fasāʾī, tr. Busse
Ḥājj Mīrzā Ḥasan Ḥosaynī Fasāʾī, *Fārs-nāma-ye nāṣerī*, tr. Heribert Busse as *History of Persia under Qajar Rule*, PHS 15, New York, 1972.

Faustus, ed. Patkanean
Pʿawstos Buzandacʿi, *Patmutʿiwn Hayocʿ*, ed. Kʿ. Patkanean, St. Petersburg, 1883; repr. Delmar, N.Y., 1984.

Faustus, tr. Garsoïan
Pʿawstos Buzandacʿi, *Patmutʿiwn Hayoc*, tr. N. G. Garsoïan as *The Epic Histories Attributed to Pʿawstos Buzand (Buzandaran Patmutʿiwnkʿ)*, Cambridge, Mass., 1989.

Fehrest. See Ebn al-Nadīm.

Fehrest . . . Āṣafīya
Fehrest-e kotob-e ʿarabī wa farsī wa ordū, maḵzūna-ye kotob-ḵāna-ye Āṣafīya-ye Sarkār-e ʿAlī, 3 vols., Hyderabad, 1332-47/1914-28.

Feraq al-šīʿa
Ḥasan B. Mūsā Nawbaḵtī, *Ketāb feraq al-šīʿa*, ed. H. R. Ritter, Leipzig and Istanbul, 1931.

Ferešta
Moḥammad-Qāsem Hendūšāh Estarābādī Ferešta, *Golšan-e ebrāhīmī*, ed. John Briggs, 2 vols., Bombay and Poona, 1831.

Ferešta, tr. Briggs
Moḥammad-Qāsem Hendūšāh Estarābādī Ferešta, *Golšan-e ebrāhīmī*, tr. John Briggs as *History of the Rise of the Mohammedan Power in India . . .*, 4 vols., London, 1829; repr. Calcutta, 1908-10, 1966.

FIZ
Farhang-e Īrān-zamīn.

Gardīzī, ed. Ḥabībī
Abū Saʿīd ʿAbd-al-Ḥayy Gardīzī, *Zayn al-aḵbār*, ed. ʿAbd-al-Ḥayy Ḥabībī, Tehran, 1347 Š./1968.

Gardīzī, ed. Nazim
Abū Saʿīd ʿAbd-al-Ḥayy Gardīzī, *Zayn al-aḵbār*, ed. Muhammad Nazim, Berlin, 1928.

Gazetteer of Afghanistan
L. W. Adamec, ed., *Historical and Political Gazetteer of Afghanistan*, Graz, 1972-.

Gazetteer of Iran
L. W. Adamec, *Historical Gazetteer of Iran*, Graz, 1976-.

GMS
E. J. W. Gibb Memorial Series.

Golčīn-e Maʿānī, *Kārvān-e Hend*
Aḥmad Golčīn-e Maʿānī, *Kārvān-e Hend. Dar aḥwāl wa āṯār-e šāʿerān-e ʿaṣr-e ṣafawī ke be Hend raftand*, 2 vols., Mašhad, 1369 Š./1990.

Golčīn-e Maʿānī, *Taḏkerahā*
Aḥmad Golčīn-e Maʿānī, *Tārīḵ-e taḏkerahā-ye fārsī*, 2 vols., Tehran, 1348-50 Š./1969-71.

Gray, *Foundations*
L. H. Gray, *The Foundations of the Iranian Religions*, K. R. Cama Oriental Institute Publication 5 (repr. from *Journal of the Cama Oriental Institute* 15, 1929), Bombay, 1930.

Grundriss
Wilhelm Geiger and Ernst Kuhn, eds., *Grundriss der iranischen Philologie*, 2 vols., Strassburg, 1895-1904.

***Ḥabīb al-sīar* (Bombay)**
Ḡīāṯ-al-Dīn Moḥammad Ḵᵛāndamīr, *Tārīḵ-e ḥabīb al-sīar*, 3 vols., Bombay, 1272/1955-56.

***Ḥabīb al-sīar* (Tehran)**
Ḡīāṯ-al-Dīn Moḥammad Ḵᵛāndamīr, *Tārīḵ-e ḥabīb al-sīar*, ed. Jalāl-al-Dīn Homāʾī, 4 vols., Tehran, 1333 Š./1954.

Ḥabībābādī, *Makārem*
M.-ʿA. Moʿallem Ḥabībābādī, *Makārem al-āṯār dar aḥwal-e rejāl-e do qarn-e 13 wa 14-e hejrī*, 5 vols., Isfahan, 1337-2535=1355 Š./1958-76.

Haft eqlīm
Amīn Aḥmad Rāzī, *Haft eqlīm*, ed. Jawād Fāżel, 3 vols., Tehran, 1340 Š./1961.

Ḥamza
Abu'l-Ḥasan Ḥamza Eṣfahānī, *Ketāb taʾrīḵ senī molūk al-arż wa'l-anbīāʾ*, ed. and Latin tr. J. M. E. Gottwaldt, 2 vols., St. Petersburg and Leipzig, 1844-48.

Ḥasan Rūmlū, ed. Navāʾī
Ḥasan Rūmlū, *Aḥsan al-tawārīḵ*, ed. ʿAbd-al-Ḥosayn Navāʾī, 2 vols., Tehran, 1349-57 Š./1970-79.

Ḥasan Rūmlū, ed. Seddon
Ḥasan Rūmlū, *Aḥsan al-tawārīḵ*, ed. and tr. C. N. Seddon, 2 vols., Baroda, 1931-34.

Hedāyat, *Rawżat al-ṣafā*
Reżāqolī Khan Hedāyat, *Tārīḵ-e rawżat al-ṣafā-ye nāṣerī*, 2 vols., Tehran, 1270-74/1853-56 (= IX-X of Mīrḵᵛānd, *Tārīḵ-e rawżat al-ṣafā*; XI index by M.-J. Maškūr, 1351 Š./1972).

Henning, "Mitteliranisch"
W. B. Henning, "Mitteliranisch," *HO* I, IV, 1, Leiden and Cologne, 1958, pp. 20-130.

Highlights of Persian Art
R. Ettinghausen and E. Yarshater, eds., *Highlights of Persian Art*, Boulder, Colo., 1979; repr. Bib. Pers., New York, 1982.

HJAS
Harvard Journal of Asiatic Studies.

HO
Bertold Spuler et al., eds., *Handbuch der Orientalistik.*

***Ḥodūd al-ʿālam*, ed. Sotūda**
Ḥodūd al-ʿālam, ed. Manūchehr Sotūda, Tehran, 1340 Š./1961.

***Ḥodūd al-ʿālam*, tr. Minorsky**
Ḥudūd al-ʿālam, tr. Vladimir Minorsky as *The Regions of the World*, 2nd ed., GMS, London, 1970.

Honarfar, *Eṣfahān*
Loṭf-Allāh Honarfar, *Ganjīna-ye āṯār-e tārīḵī-e Eṣfahān*, Tehran, 1344 Š./1965.

Horn, *Etymologie*
Paul Horn, *Grundriss der neupersischen Etymologie*, Strassburg, 1893.

Houtsma, *Recueil*
M. T. Houtsma, *Recueil de textes relatifs à l'histoire des Seljoucides*, 4 vols., Leiden, 1886-1902.

Hübschmann, *Armenische Grammatik*
Heinrich Hübschmann, *Armenische Grammatik*, Leipzig, 1897; repr. Hildesheim and New York, 1972.

Hübschmann, *Persische Studien*
Heinrich Hübschmann, *Persische Studien*, Strassburg, 1895.

İA
İslâm ansiklopedisi, 13 vols. in 15, Istanbul, 1961-88.

Ibn. See Ebn.

IF
Indogermanische Forschungen.

IHQ
Indian Historical Quarterly.

IIJ
Indo-Iranian Journal.

IJMES
International Journal of Middle East Studies.

Iran
Iran. Journal of the British Institute of Persian Studies.

Iranian Studies
Iranian Studies. Journal of the Society for Iranian Studies.

Iranisches Personennamenbuch
Manfred Mayrhofer and Rüdiger Schmitt, eds., *Iranisches Personennamenbuch*, Vienna, 1977-.

Ivanov, *Catalogue*
Wladimir Ivanov, *Concise Descriptive Catalogue of the Persian Manuscripts in the Collection of the Asiatic Society of Bengal*, Calcutta, 1924.

JA
Journal asiatique.

Jacoby, *Fragmente*
Felix Jacoby, *Die Fragmente der griechischen Historiker*, 3 vols., Berlin, 1923-58.

Jāmeʿ al-tawārīḵ. See Rašīd-al-Dīn.

Jāmī, *Nafaḥāt*
ʿAbd-al-Raḥmān Jāmī, *Nafaḥāt al-ons min ḥażarāt al qods*, ed. Mahdī Tawḥīdīpūr, Tehran, 1336 Š./1957.

JAOS
Journal of the American Oriental Society.

JESHO
Journal of the Economic and Social History of the Orient.

JNES
Journal of Near Eastern Studies.

Jovaynī, ed. Qazvīnī
ʿAlāʾ-al-Dīn ʿAṭā Malek Jovaynī, *Tārīḵ-e jahāngošā*, ed. Moḥammad Qazvīnī, GMS, 3 vols., Leiden and London, 1906-37.

Jovaynī, tr. Boyle
ʿAlāʾ-al-Dīn ʿAṭā Malek Jovaynī, *Tārīḵ-e jahāngošā*, tr. J. A. Boyle as *The History of the World-Conqueror*, 2 vols., Manchester, 1958.

JPHS
Journal of the Pakistan Historical Society.

JRAS
Journal of the Royal Asiatic Society.

J(R)ASB
Journal of the (Royal) Asiatic Society of Bengal.

JRGS
Journal of the Royal Geographical Society.

Justi, *Namenbuch*
Ferdinand Justi, *Iranisches Namenbuch*, Marburg, 1895; repr. Hildesheim, 1963.

Jūzjānī, *Ṭabaqāt*
Menhāj-e Serāj Jūzjānī, *Ṭabaqāt-e nāṣerī*, ed. ʿAbd-al-Ḥayy Ḥabībī, 2nd ed., 2 vols., Kabul, 1342-43 Š./1963-64.

Jūzjānī, *Ṭabaqāt*, tr. Raverty
Menhāj-e Serāj Jūzjānī, *Ṭabaqāt-e nāṣerī*, tr. H. G. Raverty, Bib. Ind., 2 vols., London, 1881-99.

Kaḥḥāla
ʿOmar Reżā Kaḥḥāla, *Moʿjam al-moʾallefīn*, 15 vols., Damascus, 1957-61.

Karatay, *Katalog*
F. E. Karatay, *Topkapı Sarayı Müzesi Kütüphanesi farsça yazmalar kataloğu*, Istanbul, 1961.

***Kār-nāmag*, ed. Antia**
E. K. Antia, ed., *Kârnâmak-i Artakhshîr Pâpakân, the Original Pahlavi Text, with Translation in Avesta Characters, Translations into English and Gujarati, and Selections from the Shâhnâmeh*, Bombay, 1900.

***Kār-nāmag*, ed. Sanjana**
D. D. P. Sanjana, ed., *The Kârnâmê î Artakhshîr Pâpakân . . . The Original Pahlavi Text Edited for the First Time . . . Translations into English and Gujarati Languages . . .*, Bombay, 1896.

***Kašf al-ẓonūn*, ed. Flügel**
Ḥājī Ḵalīfa, *Kašf al-ẓonūn*, ed. Gustav Flügel, 7 vols., Leipzig, 1835-58.

***Kašf al-ẓonūn*, ed. Yaltkaya and Bilge**
Ḥājī Ḵalīfa, *Kašf al-ẓonūn*, ed. Şerefeddin Yaltkaya and K. R. Bilge, 2 vols., Istanbul, 1941-43.

Kašf al-ẓonūn: Ḏayl
Esmāʿīl Pasha Baḡdādī, *Ketāb īżāḥ al-maknūn fi'l-ḏayl ʿalā Kašf al-ẓonūn ʿan asāmi'l-kotob wa'l-fonūn*, 2 vols., Istanbul, 1945-47.

Kasrawī, *Āḏarbāyjān*
Aḥmad Kasrawī, *Tārīḵ-e hejda-sāla-ye Āḏarbāyjān*, 2nd ed., Tehran, 1333 Š./1954.

Kasrawī, *Mašrūṭa*
Aḥmad Kasrawī, *Tārīḵ-e mašrūṭa-ye Īrān*, 3rd ed., 3 vols. in 1, Tehran, 1330 Š./1951.

Kayhān, *Joḡrāfīā*
Masʿūd Kayhān, *Joḡrāfīā-ye mofaṣṣal-e Īrān*, 3 vols., 1310-11 Š./1931-32.

Ḵayyāmpūr, *Soḵanvarān*
ʿAbd-al-Rasūl Ḵayyāmpūr, *Farhang-e soḵanvarān*, Tabrīz, 1340 Š./1961.

Kent, *Old Persian*
R. G. Kent, *Old Persian: Grammar, Texts, Lexicon*, 2nd ed., New Haven, Conn., 1953.

Lambton, *Continuity*
A. K. S. Lambton, *Continuity and Change: Aspects of Social and Administrative History in Persia*, Col. Lect. Series, Albany, N.Y., 1988.

Lambton, *Landlord and Peasant*
A. K. S. Lambton, *Landlord and Peasant in Persia: A Study of land Tenure and Land Revenue Administration*, London, 1953.

Langlois, *Historiens*
Victor Langlois, tr., *Collections des historiens anciens et modernes de l'Arménie*, 2 vols., Paris, 1868-69.

Laufer, *Sino-Iranica*
Berthold Laufer, *Sino-Iranica: Chinese Contributions to the History of Civilization in Ancient Iran*, Chicago, 1919.

Lazard, *Premiers poètes*
Gilbert Lazard, *Les premiers poètes persans (IXe-Xe siècle): Fragments rassemblés, édités et traduits*, 2 vols., Tehran and Liège, 1964.

Le Strange, *Lands*
Guy Le Strange, *The Lands of the Eastern Caliphate*, 2nd ed., Cambridge, 1930.

***Loḡat-e fors*, ed. Dabīrsīāqī**
Asadī Ṭūsī, *Loḡat-e fors*, ed. Moḥammad Dabīrsīāqī from the edition of Paul Horn, Tehran, 1336 Š./1957.

Loġat-e fors, ed. Eqbāl
Asadī Ṭūsī, *Loġat-e fors*, ed. ʿAbbās Eqbāl, Tehran, 1319 Š./1940.
Loġat-e fors, ed. Mojtabāʾī and Ṣādeqī
Asadī Ṭūsī, *Loġat-e fors*, ed. Fatḥ-Allāh Mojtabāʾī and ʿA-A. Ṣādeqī, Tehran, 1365 Š./1986.
Lorimer, _Gazetteer_
J. G. Lorimer, *Gazetteer of the Persian Gulf, ʾOmān, and Central Arabia*, compl. and ed. L. Birdwood, 2 vols., Calcutta, 1908-15; repr., Westmead, U.K., 2 vols. in 6, 1970.
Maʾāṯer al-omarāʾ (Calcutta)
ʿAbd-al-Razzāq Šāhnavāz Khan Awrangābādī, *Maʾāṯer al-omarāʾ*, Bib. Ind., 3 vols., Calcutta, 1888-91.
Maʾāṯer al-omarāʾ, tr. Beveridge
ʿAbd-al-Razzāq Šāhnavāz Khan Awrangābādī, *Maʾāṯer al-omarāʾ*, tr. Henry Beveridge, rev. Baini Prashad, Bib. Ind., 3 vols., Calcutta 1911-64; repr. Patna, 1979.
Mādayān, pt. 1
Mâdigân-i-hazâr Dâdistân, ed. J. J. Modi (facs. ed. fols. 1-55), Bombay, 1901.
Mādayān, pt. 2
Mâdigân-i-hazâr Dâdistân, ed. T. D. Anklesaria as *The Social Code of the Parsees in Sassanian Times*, pt. 2, Bombay, 1912.
Maḥbūbī, _Moʾassasāt_
Ḥosayn Maḥbūbī Ardakānī, *Tārīḵ-e moʾassasāt-e tamaddonī-e jadīd dar Īrān* I, Tehran, 1356 Š./1975, II, Tehran, 2537=1357 Š./1978, III, ed. Karīm Eṣfahānīān and Jahāngīr Qājārīya, Tehran, 1368 Š./1989.
Majāles al-nafāʾes
ʿAlī Šīr Navāʾī, *Majāles al-nafāʾes*, tr. Faḵrī Herātī and Ḥakīm Shah Moḥammad Qazvīnī, ed. ʿA.-A. Ḥekmat, Tehran, 1323 Š./1944.
Majmaʿ al-foṣaḥāʾ
Reżāqolī Khan Hedāyat, *Majmaʿ al-foṣaḥāʾ*, ed. Maẓāhir Moṣaffā, 2 vols. in 6, Tehran, 1336-40 Š./1957-61.
Malekzāda
Mahdī Malekzāda, *Tārīḵ-e enqelāb-e mašrūṭīyat-e Īrān*, 7 vols., Tehran, 1327-35 Š./1948-56; 2nd ed., 3 vols., Tehran, 1363 Š./1984.
Mann, _Kurdisch-persische Forschungen_
Oskar Mann, *Kurdisch-persische Forschungen: Ergebnisse einer von 1901 bis 1903 und 1906 bis 1907 in Persien und die asiatischen Türkei ausgeführten Forschungsreise*, pts. 1-2, Berlin, 1909-10; pt. 3, ed. Karl Hadank, 4 vols., Berlin, 1926-1932.
Maqdesī, _Badʾ_
Moṭahhar b. Ṭāher Maqdesī, *Ketāb al-badʾ waʾl-taʾrīḵ*, ed. and tr. Clément Huart as *Le livre de la création et de l'histoire*, 6 vols., Paris, 1899-1919.
Margoliouth and Amedroz, _Eclipse_
D. S. Margoliouth and H. F. Amedroz, eds. and trs., *The Eclipse of the Abbasid Caliphate: Original Chronicles of the Fourth Islamic Century*, 7 vols., Oxford, 1921-22.
Markwart, _Ērānšahr_
Josef Markwart (Marquart), *Ērānšahr nach der Geographie des Ps. Moses Xorenacʿi*, Abh. Akademie der Wissenschaften zu Göttingen, N.S. 3/2, 1901.
Markwart, _Provincial Capitals_
Josef Markwart, *A Catalogue of the Provincial Capitals of Ērānshahr (Pahlavi Text, Version and Commentary)*, ed. Giuseppe Messina, Analecta Orientalia 3, Rome, 1931.
Marshall, _Mughals in India_
D. N. Marshall, *Mughals in India: A Bibliographic Survey* I. *Manuscripts*, Bombay, 1967.
MASI
Memoirs of the Archaeological Survey of India.
Massé, _Croyances_
Henri Massé, *Croyances et coutumes persanes suivies de contes et chansons populaires*, Les littératures populaires de toutes les nations 4, 2 vols., Paris, 1938.
Massignon, _Essai_
Louis Massignon, *Essai sur les origines du lexique technique de la mystique musulmane*, new ed., Paris, 1954.
Masʿūdī, _Morūj_
Abu'l-Ḥasan ʿAlī Masʿūdī, *Morūj al-ḏahab*, ed. and tr. Charles Barbier de Meynard and Abel Pavet de Courteille as *Les prairies d'or*, 9 vols., Paris, 1861-1917.
Masʿūdī, _Morūj_, ed. Pellat
Abu'l-Ḥasan ʿAlī Masʿūdī, *Morūj al-ḏahab*, rev. ed. Charles Pellat, 7 vols., Beirut, 1962-79.
Masʿūdī, _Tanbīh_
Abu'l-Ḥasan ʿAlī Masʿūdī, *Ketāb al-tanbīh wa'l-ešrāf*, ed. M. J. de Goeje, BGA, Leiden, 1894.
Maṭlaʿ-e saʿdayn, ed. Šafīʿ
Kamāl-al-Dīn ʿAbd-al-Razzāq b. Jalāl-al-Dīn Esḥāq Samarqandī, *Maṭlaʿ-e saʿdayn wa majmaʿ-e baḥrayn*, ed. Moḥammad Šafīʿ, 2 vols., Lahore, 1360-68/1941-49.
Maṭlaʿ al-šams
Moḥammad-Ḥasan Khan Ṣanīʿ-āl-Dawla Eʿtemād-al-Salṭana Marāġaʾī, *Maṭlaʿ al-šams*, 3 vols., Tehran, 1300-03/1883-85; repr. Tehran, 2535=1355 Š./1976.
Mayrhofer, _Dictionary_
Manfred Mayrhofer, *A Concise Etymological Sanskrit Dictionary (Kurzgefasstes etymologisches Wörterbuch des Altindischen)*, 3 vols., Heidelberg, 1956-76.

Mayrhofer, *Wörterbuch*
Manfred Mayrhofer, *Etymologisches Wörterbuch des Altindoarischen*, Heidelberg, 1986-.
***MDA* Tabriz**
Majalla-ye Dāneškada-ye adabīyāt (o ʿolūm-e ensānī-) e Dānešgāh-e Tabrīz.
MDAF
Majalla-ye Dāneškada-ye adabīyāt o ʿolūm-e ensānī-e Dānešgāh-e Ferdowsī.
MDAFA
Mémoires de la Délégation archéologique française en Afghanistan.
MDAFI
Mémoires de la Délégation archéologique française en Iran.
MDAM
Majalla-ye Dāneškada-ye adabīyāt (o ʿolūm-e ensānī-e) e Dānešgāh-e Mašhad.
MDAT
Majalla-ye Dāneškada-ye adabīyāt (o ʿolūm-e ensānī-) e Dānešgāh-e Tehrān.
MDOG
Mitteilungen der Deutschen Orient-Gesellschaft.
***Mēnōg ī xrad*, ed. Anklesaria**
Dânâk-u mainyô-i khrad, ed. T. D. Anklesaria, Bombay, 1913.
Meskawayh, *Tajāreb*
Abū ʿAlī Aḥmad b. Meskawayh, *Tajāreb al-omam.* See Margoliouth and Amedroz, *Eclipse*.
***Meyḵāna*, ed. Golčīn-e Maʿānī**
ʿAbd-al-Nabī Qazvīnī, *Tadkera-ye meyḵāna*, ed. Aḥmad Golčīn-e Maʿānī, Tehran, 1340 Š./1961.
***Meyḵāna*, ed. Šafīʿ**
ʿAbd-al-Nabī Qazvīnī, *Tadkera-ye meyḵāna*, ed. Moḥammad Šafīʿ, Lahore, 1926.
MIDEO
Mélanges de l'Institut Dominicain d'Études Orientales du Caire.
Mir. Man
F. C. Andreas and W. B. Henning, *Mitteliranische Manichaica aus Chinesisch-Turkestan*, SPAW I, 1932, 10; II, 1933, 7; III, 1934, 27.
Mīrḵᵛānd (Bombay)
Mīr Moḥammad b. Sayyed Borhān-al-Dīn Ḵᵛāvandšāh Mīrḵᵛānd, *Tārīḵ-e rawżat al-ṣafā*, Bombay, 1266/1849.
Mīrḵᵛānd (Tehran)
Mīr Moḥammad b. Sayyed Borhān-al-Dīn Ḵᵛāvandšāh Mīrḵᵛānd, *Tārīḵ-e rawżat al-ṣafā*, 8 vols., Qom, 1339 Š./1960; IX-X. Hedāyat, *Rawżat al-ṣafā*; XI. Index, M.-J. Maškūr, 1351 Š./1972.
MO
Le monde oriental.
Modarres, *Rayḥānat al-adab*
M.-ʿA. Modarres, *Rayḥānat al-adab fī tarājem al-maʿrūfīn be'l-konya aw al-laqab*, 8 vols., Tabrīz, n.d.
***Mojmal*, ed. Bahār**
M.-T. Bahār, ed., *Mojmal al-tawārīḵ wa'l-qeṣaṣ*, Tehran, 1318 Š./1939.
Monzawī, *Nosḵahā*
Aḥmad Monzawī, *Fehrest-e nosḵahā-ye ḵaṭṭī-e fārsī*, 6 vols., Tehran, 1348-53 Š./1969-74.
Moqaddasī
Abū ʿAbd-Allāh Moḥammad Moqaddasī (Maqdesī), *Aḥsan al-taqāsīm fī maʿrefat al-aqālīm*, ed. M. J. de Goeje, BGA, Leiden, 1877.
Moreley, *Catalogue*
W. H. Moreley, *A Descriptive Catalogue of the . . . Manuscripts in the Arabic and Persian Languages Preserved in the Library of the Royal Asiatic Society*, London, 1854.
Morier, *Journey*
J. J. Morier, *A Journey through Persia, Armenia, and Asia Minor, to Constantinople, in the Years 1808-1809 . . .*, 2 vols., London, 1812.
Morier, *Second Journey*
J. J. Morier, *A Second Journey through Persia, Armenia, and Asia Minor, to Constantinople, between the Years 1810-1816. With a Journal of the Voyage by the Brazils and Bombay to the Persian Gulf . . .*, London, 1818.
Mošār, *Fehrest*
Fehrest-e ketābhā-ye čāpī-e fārsī, based on the 2-volume catalogue of the same title by Ḵānbābā Mošār and the catalogues of the Anjoman-e Ketāb, 3 vols., Tehran, 1352 Š./1973.
Mošār, *Moʾallefīn*
Ḵānbābā Mošār, *Moʾallefīn-e kotob-e čāpī-e fārsī wa ʿarabī*, 6 vols., Tehran, 1340-44 Š./1961-65.
Moses of Khorene
Movsēs Xorenacʿi, *Patmutʿiwn Hayocʿ*, ed. M. Abelean and S. Yarutʿiwnean, Tiflis, 1913; repr. Delmar, N.Y., 1981.
Moses of Khorene, tr. Thomson
Movsēs Xorenacʿi, *Patmutʿiwn Hayocʿ*, tr. R. W. Thomson as *History of the Armenians*, Cambridge, Mass., 1978.
Mostawfī, *Šarḥ-e zendagānī*
ʿAbd-Allāh Mostawfī, *Šarḥ-e zendagānī-e man yā Tārīḵ-e ejtemāʿī o edārī-e dawra-ye qājārīya*, 2nd ed., 3 vols., Tehran, 1343 Š./1964.
Movsēs Xorenacʿi. See Moses of Khorene.
MSL
Mémoires de la Société de linguistique de Paris.
MSS
Münchener Studien zur Sprachwissenschaft.
Müller, *Fragmenta*
Karl and Theodor Müller, eds., *Fragmenta Historicorum Graecorum*, 5 vols., Paris, 1841-85.

Nachr.
Nachrichten.

Nafīsī, *Naẓm o naṯr*
Saʿīd Nafīsī, *Tārīḵ-e naẓm o naṯr dar Īrān*, 2 vols., Tehran, 1344 Š./1965.

Nafīsī, *Rūdakī*
Saʿīd Nafīsī, *Aḥwāl o ašʿār-e Rūdakī*, 3 vols., Tehran, 1309-19 Š./1930-40; 2nd ed., Tehran, 1341 Š./1962.

Naršaḵī
Abū Bakr Jaʿfar Naršaḵī, *Tārīk-e Boḵārā*, ed. M.-T. Modarres Rażawī, Tehran, 1319 Š./1940; 2nd ed. Tehran, 1351 Š./1972.

Naršaḵī, tr. Frye
Abū Bakr Jaʿfar Naršaḵī, *Tārīḵ-e Boḵārā*, tr. R. N. Frye as *The History of Bukhara*, Cambridge, Mass., 1954.

NC
Numismatic Chronicle.

***NDA* Tabrīz**
Našrīya-ye Dāneškada-ye adabīyāt (o ʿolūm-e ensānī)-e Dānešgāh-e Tabrīz.

Nöldeke, *Geschichte der Perser*
Theodor Nöldeke, *Geschichte der Perser und Araber zur Zeit der Sasaniden, aus der arabischen Chronik des Tabari übersetzt*, Leiden, 1879; repr. Leiden, 1973.

***Nozhat al-qolūb*, ed. Le Strange**
Ḥamd-Allāh Mostawfī, *Nozhat al-qolūb*, ed. and tr. Guy Le Strange, GMS, 2 vols., Leiden and London, 1916-19.

NTS
Norsk tidsskrift for sprogvidenskap.

Nyberg, *Manual*
H. S. Nyberg, *A Manual of Pahlavi*, 2 vols., Wiesbaden, 1964-74.

OGI
Wilhelm Dittenberger, ed., *Orientis Graeci Inscriptiones Selectae*, 2 vols., Leipzig, 1903-05.

OLZ
Orientalistische Literaturzeitung.

Osnovy
Osnovy iranskogo yazykoznaniya, Moscow, 1979-.

***Pahlavi Rivayat*, ed. Dhabhar**
B. N. Dhabhar, ed., *The Pahlavi Rivâyat Accompanying the Dâdestân-î Dînîk*, Bombay, 1913.

***Pahlavi Texts*, ed. Jamasp-Asana**
J. M. Jamasp-Asana, ed., *The Pahlavi Texts Contained in the Codex MK*, 2 vols., Bombay, 1897-1913.

Pauly-Wissowa
Georg Wissowa, Wilhelm Kroll, and Karl Mittelhaus, eds., *Paulys Real-Encyclopädie der classischen Altertumswissenschaft*, Stuttgart, ser. 1, 24 vols., 1894-1970; ser. 2, 10 vols. and 15 suppl. vols. and index vol., Munich, 1903-80.

Pʿawstos Buzandacʿi. See Faustus.

Persian Literature
Ehsan Yarshater, ed., *Persian Literature*, Bib. Pers., Albany, N.Y., 1988.

***Persian Rivayats*, ed. Unvala**
M. R. Unvala, ed., *Dârâb Hormazyâr's Rivâyat*, 2 vols., Bombay, 1922.

***Persian Rivayats*, tr. Dhabhar**
B. N. Dhabhar, tr., *The Persian Rivayats of Hormazyar Framarz and Others*, 2 vols., Bombay, 1932.

Phil.-hist. Kl.
Philosophisch-historische Klasse.

PHS
Persian Heritage Series.

Pokorny
Julius Pokorny, *Indogermanisches etymologisches Wörterbuch*, 2 vols., Bern and Munich, 1959-69.

PRGS
Proceedings of the Royal Geographical Society.

Qāżī Aḥmad
Qāżī Aḥmad, *Golestān-e honar*, ed. A. Soheylī Ḵᵛānsārī, Tehran, 1352 Š./1973; 3rd ed., 1366 Š./1987.

Qāżī Aḥmad, tr. Minorsky
Qāżī Aḥmad, *Golestān-e honar*, tr. Vladimir Minorsky and Tatiana Minorsky as *Calligraphers and Painters: A Treatise by Qāḍī Aḥmad, son of Mīr Munshī . . .*, Washington, D.C., 1959.

Qodāma, *Ketāb al-ḵarāj*
Qodāma b. Jaʿfar, *Ketāb al-ḵarāj*, ed. M. J. de Goeje, BGA, Leiden, 1889; repr. Leiden, 1967.

RA
Revue d'assyriologie et d'archéologie orientale.

RAA
Revue des arts asiatiques.

Rādūyānī
Moḥammad b. ʿOmar Rādūyānī, *Tarjomān al-balāḡa*, ed. Ahmed Ateş, İstanbul Üniversitesi Yayınlarından 395, Istanbul, 1949.

Rāmī, *Ḥaqāʾeq*, ed. Emām
Šaraf-al-Dīn Ḥasan b. Moḥammad Rāmī, *Ḥaqāʾeq al-ḥadāʾeq*, ed. M.-K. Emām, Tehran, 1341 Š./1962.

Rašīd-al-Dīn, *Jāmeʿ al-tawārīḵ* (Baku)
Ḵᵛāja Rašīd-al-Dīn Fażl-Allāh b. ʿEmād-al-Dawla, *Jāmeʿ al-tawārīḵ*, I-II ed. A. A. Ali-Zade, III tr. A. K. Arends, Baku, 1957.

Rašīd-al-Dīn, *Jāmeʿ al-tawārīḵ* (Moscow)
Ḵᵛāja Rašīd-al-Dīn Fażl-Allāh b. ʿEmād-al-Dawla, *Jāmeʿ al-tawārīḵ*, ed. A. A. Romaskevicha, A. A. Khetagurova, and A. A. Ali-Zade, Moscow, 1965.

Rašīd-al-Dīn, *Tārīk-e ḡāzānī*
K̲ᵛāja Rašīd-al-Dīn Fażl-Allāh b. ʿEmād-al-Dawla, *Tārīḵ-e mobārak-e ḡāzānī*, ed. Karl Jahn as *Geschichte Ġāzān-Ḫān's*, GMS, London, 1940; as *Geschichte der Ilḫāne Abāġā bis Gaiḫātū (1265-1295)*, the Hague, 1957.

Razmārā, Farhang
Ḥ.-ʿA. Razmārā, ed., *Farhang-e joḡrāfīāʾī-e Īrān. Ābādīhā*, 10 vols., Tehran, 1328-32 Š./1949-53.

REA
Revue des études arméniennes.

REI
Revue des études islamiques.

RHR
Revue de l'histoire des religions.

Rieu, *Persian Manuscripts*
Charles Rieu, *Catalogue of the Persian Manuscripts in the British Museum*, 3 vols. and supplement, London, 1876-95.

RlA
Erich Ebeling et al., eds., *Reallexikon der Assyriologie und vorderasiatischen Archäologie*, Berlin and Leipzig, 1928-.

RMM
Revue du monde musulman.

Rypka, *Hist. Iran. Lit.*
Jan Rypka et al., *History of Iranian Literature*, ed. Karl Jahn, Dordrecht, 1968.

Ṣadr Hāšemī, *Jarāʾed o majallāt*
Moḥammad Ṣadr Hāšemī, *Tārīḵ-e jarāʾed o majallāt-e Īrān*, Isfahan, 1327-32 Š./1948-53; repr. Tehran, 1363 Š./1984.

Ṣafā, *Adabīyāt*
Ḏabīḥ-Allāh Ṣafā (Zabihollah Safa), *Tārīḵ-e adabīyāt dar Īrān*, 1332- Š./1953-; I, rev. ed., Tehran, 1335 Š./1956.

***Šāh-nāma*, Borūḵīm ed.**
Abu'l-Qāsem Ferdowsī, *Šāh-nāma*, ed. ʿAbbās Eqbāl et al., 10 vols. in 5, Tehran, 1313-15 Š./1934-36.

***Šāh-nāma*, ed. Khaleghi**
Abu'l-Qāsem Ferdowsī, *Šāh-nāma*, ed. Djalal Khaleghi-Motlagh, Bib. Pers., Persian Text Series, N.S. 1, New York, 1987-.

***Šāh-nāma*, ed. Mohl**
Abu'l-Qāsem Ferdowsī, *Šāh-nāma*, ed. and tr. Jules Mohl, 7 vols., Paris, 1838-78.

***Šāh-nāma* (Moscow)**
Abu'l-Qāsem Ferdowsī, *Šāh-nāma*, ed. E. E. Bertel's et al., 9 vols., Moscow, 1960-71; new ed., ed. R. M. Aliev and M.-N. O. Osmanov, Tehran, 1350- Š./1971-.

Šahrastānī
Moḥammad b. ʿAbd-al-Karīm Šahrastānī, *Ketāb al-melal wa'l-neḥal*, ed. William Cureton, London, 1846.

Šahrastānī, tr. Gimaret and Monnot
Moḥammad b. ʿAbd-al-Karīm Šahrastānī, *Ketāb al-melal wa'l-neḥal*, tr. Daniel Gimaret and Guy Monnot as *Livre des religions et des sectes*, Paris, 1986.

Samʿānī, ed. Margoliouth
Abū Saʿd ʿAbd-al-Karīm b. Moḥammad Tamīmī Samʿānī, *Ketāb al-ansāb*, facs. ed. D. S. Margoliouth, GMS, Leiden, 1912.

Samʿānī, ed. Yamānī
Abū Saʿd ʿAbd-al-Karīm b. Moḥammad Tamīmī Samʿānī, *Ketāb-al-ansāb*, ed. ʿAbd-al-Raḥmān Yamānī, 7 vols., Hyderabad, 1382-86/1962-76.

Šams-al-Dīn Rāzī, *Moʿjam*
Šams-al-Dīn Moḥammad b. Qays Rāzī, *al-Moʿjam fī maʿāʾīr ašʿār al-ʿajam*, ed. Moḥammad Qazvīnī and M.-T. Modarres Rażawī, Tehran, 1338 Š./1959.

Sartīpzāda
Bīzhan Sartīpzāda, ed., with the collaboration of Kobrā Ḵodāparast, *Fehrest-e rūz-nāmahā-ye mawjūd dar Ketāb-ḵāna-ye mellī-e Īrān*, Tehran, 1336 Š./1957.

Šāyest nē šāyest
J. C. Tavadia, ed. and tr., *Šāyast nē Šāyast, a Pahlavi Text on Religious Customs*, Hamburg, 1930.

***Šāyest nē šāyest*, suppl.**
F. M. Kotwal, ed. and tr., *The Supplementary Texts to the Šāyest nē-šāyest*, Copenhagen, 1969.

Sb.
Sitzungsberichte.

SBE
Sacred Books of the East.

Schlimmer
J. L. Schlimmer, *Terminologie médico-pharmaceutique et anthropologique française-persane*, Tehran, 1874; repr. Tehran, 1970.

Schwarz, *Iran*
Paul Schwarz, *Iran im Mittelalter nach den arabischen Geographen*, Leipzig, 1969.

Sezgin, *GAS*
Fuat Sezgin, *Geschichte des arabischen Schrifttums*, Leiden, 1957-.

Siroux, *Anciennes voies et monuments*
Maxime Siroux, *Anciennes voies et monuments routiers de la région d'Ispahan*, Cairo, 1971.

Sobkī, *Ṭabaqāt* (Cairo¹)
Abū Naṣr ʿAbd-al-Wahhāb b. ʿAlī Tāj-al-Dīn Sobkī, *Ṭabaqat al-šāfeʿīya al-kobrā*, 6 vols., Cairo, 1906.

Sobkī, *Ṭabaqāt* (Cairo²)
Abū Naṣr ʿAbd-al-Wahhāb b. ʿAlī Tāj-al-Dīn Sobkī, *Ṭabaqāt al-šafeʿīya al-kobrā*, ed. M. M. Ṭanāḥī and ʿA. M. Ḥelw, 10 vols., Cairo, 1964-76.

Sofra-ye aṭʿema
Mīrzā ʿAlī-Akbar Āšpazbāšī, *Sofra-ye aṭʿema*, Tehran, 1353 Š./1974.

Sohrāb, tr. Le Strange
Guy Le Strange, "Description of Mesopotamia and Baghdad, Written about 900 A.D. by Ibn Serapion," *JRAS*/1-3, 1895.

Solamī, *Ṭabaqāt*
Moḥammad b. Ḥosayn Solamī, *Ketāb ṭabaqāt al-ṣūfīya*, ed. Johannes Pedersen, Leiden, 1960.

SPAW
Sitzungsberichte der Preussischen Akademie der Wissenschaften.

Spuler, *Iran*
Bertold Spuler, *Iran in früh-islamischer Zeit*, Wiesbaden, 1952.

Spuler, *Mongolen* [2,3,4]
Bertold Spuler, *Die Mongolen in Iran*, 2nd ed., Berlin, 1955; 3rd ed., Berlin, 1968; 4th ed., Leiden, 1985.

Stchoukine, *Îl-khâns*
I. V. Stchoukine, *La peinture iranienne sous les derniers ʿAbbâsides et les Îl-khâns*, Bruges, 1936.

Stchoukine, *Safavis* 1
I. V. Stchoukine *Les peintures des manuscrits safavis de 1502 à 1587*, Paris, 1959.

Stchoukine, *Safavis* 2
I. V. Stchoukine, *Les peintures des manuscrits de Shâh ʿAbbâs ler à la fin des ṣafavîs*, Paris, 1964.

Stchoukine, *Tîmûrides*
I. V. Stchoukine, *Les peintures des manuscrits tîmûrides*, Paris, 1954.

Storey
C. A. Storey, *Persian Literature: A Bio-bibliographical Survey*, Leiden, 1927-.

Storey-Bregel
C. A. Storey, *Persidskaya literatura: Bio-bibliograficheskiĭ obzor*, ed. and tr. Yu. E. Bregel, 3 vols., Moscow, 1972.

Stud. Ir.
Studia Iranica.

Stud. Isl.
Studia Islamica.

Stud. Or.
Studia Orientalia.

Survey of Persian Art
A. U. Pope and P. Ackerman, eds., *A Survey of Persian Art from Prehistoric Times to the Present*, 4 vols., London, 1938-39; 2nd ed., 16 vols., Tehran, 1964, with addenda 1967; 3rd ed. with bibliography and addenda, Tehran, 2535= 1355 Š./1977.

Suter, *Mathematiker*
Heinrich Suter, *Die Mathematiker und Astronomen der Araber und ihre Werke*, Leipzig, 1900.

Sykes, *History of Persia*
Percy Sykes, *A History of Persia*, 3rd ed. with suppl. essays, 2 vols., London, 1930.

Ṯaʿālebī, *Ḡorar*
Abū Manṣūr ʿAbd-al-Malek Ṯaʿālebī, *Ḡorar akbār molūk al-fors*, ed. and tr. Hermann Zotenberg as *Histoire des rois des Perses*, Paris, 1900.

Ṯaʿālebī, *Yatīma* (Damascus)
Abū Manṣūr ʿAbd-al-Malek Ṯaʿālebī, *Yatīmat al-dahr fī maḥāsen ahl al-ʿaṣr*, Damascus, 1304/1886-87.

Ṯaʿālebī, *Yatīma*, ed. ʿAbd-al-Ḥamīd
Abū Manṣūr ʿAbd-al-Malek Ṯaʿālebī, *Yatīmat al-dahr fī maḥāsen ahl al-ʿaṣr*, ed. M. M. ʿAbd-al-Ḥamīd, Cairo, 1377/1957-68.

Ṭabarī
Moḥammad b. Jarīr Ṭabarī, *Ketāb taʾrīḵ al-rosol waʾl-molūk*, ed. M. J. de Goeje et al., 15 vols., Leiden, 1879-1901; repr. Leiden, 1964.

Ṭabarī (Cairo[1])
Moḥammad b. Jarīr Ṭabarī, *Ketāb taʾrīḵ al-rosol waʾl-molūk*, 13 vols., Cairo, 1326/1908; repr. Beirut, 6 vols., 1970.

Ṭabarī (Cairo[2])
Moḥammad b. Jarīr Ṭabarī, *Ketāb taʾrīḵ al-rosol waʾl-molūk*, ed. M. A. Ebrāhīm, 9 vols., Cairo, 1960-68; repr. Beirut, 6 vols., 1970.

Ṭabarī, tr.
Moḥammad b. Jarīr Ṭabarī, *Ketāb taʾrīḵ al-rosol waʾl-molūk*, tr. by various scholars as *The History of al-Ṭabarī*, ed. Ehsan Yar-Shater, Albany, N.Y., 1985-.

***Taḏkerat al-molūk*, ed. Minorsky**
Vladimir Minorsky, facs. ed. and tr., *Tadhkirat al-mulūk: A Manual of Ṣafavid Administration* (circa *1137/1725*), GMS, London, 1943.

Tarbīat, *Dānešmandān-e Āḏarbāyjān*
M.-ʿA. Tarbīat, *Dānešmandān-e Āḏarbāyjān*, Tehran, 1314 Š./1935.

Taʾrīḵ Baḡdād
Ḵaṭīb Baḡdādī, *Taʾrīḵ Baḡdād*, 14 vols., Cairo, 1349/1931.

***Tārīḵ-e bīdārī*, ed. Saʿīdī Sīrjānī**
Nāẓem-al-Eslām Kermānī, *Tārīḵ-e bīdārī-e īrānīān*, ed. ʿA.-A. Saʿīdī Sīrjānī, 2 vols., Tehran, 1346 Š./1967; 2nd ed.,, Tehran, 1362 Š./1983.

***Tārīḵ-e ḡāzānī*.** See Rašīd-al-Dīn.

***Tārīḵ-e gozīda*, ed. Browne**
Ḥamd-Allāh Mostawfī, *Tārīḵ-e gozīda*, facs. ed. E. G. Browne, GMS, Leiden and London, 1910.

***Tārīḵ-e gozīda*, ed. Navāʾī**
Ḥamd-Allāh Mostawfī, *Tārīḵ-e gozīda*, ed. ʿAbd-al-Ḥosayn Navāʾī, 2 vols., Tehran, 1336-39 Š./1957-60.

Tārīḵ-e Sīstān
Tārīḵ-e Sīstān, ed. M.-T. Bahār, Tehran, 1314 Š./1935.

***Tārīḵ-e Sīstān*, tr. Gold**
Tārīḵ-e Sīstān, tr. Milton Gold as *The Tārikh-e Sistān*, PHS, Rome, 1976.

Tārīḵ-e Waṣṣāf
Šehāb-al-Dīn ʿAbd-Allāh Waṣṣāf Ḥażra, *Tajzīat al-amṣār wa tazjīat al-aʿṣār*, ed. M. M. Eṣfahānī, Bombay, 1269/1853.

Tavadia
J. C. Tavadia, *Die mittelpersische Sprache und Literatur der Zarathustrier*, Wiesbaden, 1956.

Tavernier (Paris)
J. B. Tavernier, *Les six voyages de Jean Baptiste Tavernier, ecuyer baron d'Aubonne, en Turquie, en Perse, et aux Indes pendant l'espace de quarante ans . . .*, 2 vols., Paris, 1677-82.

Tavernier (London)
J. B. Tavernier, *The Six Travels of John Baptiste Tavernier . . .*, London, 1684.

TAVO
Tübinger Atlas des Vorderen Orients, Wiesbaden, 1977-.

TDED
Türk dili ve edebiyat dergisi, İstanbul Üniversitesi, Edebiyat fakültesi.

Tedesco, "Dialektologie"
Paul Tedesco, "Dialektologie der westiranischen Turfantexte," *MO* 15, 1921, pp. 184-257.

Thévenot
Jean de Thévenot, *Relation d'un voyage fait au Levant, dans laquelle il est curieusement traité des estats sujets au Grand Seigneur, des moeurs, religions, forces, gouvernemens, politiques, langues et coustumes des habitans de ce grand empire*, 3 vols., Paris, 1665-84.

Thévenot (London)
Jean de Thévenot, *The Travels of Monsieur de Thevenot into the Levant*, 3 vols., London, 1686.

Toḥfa-ye sāmī
Sām Mīrzā Ṣafawī, *Toḥfa-ye sāmī*, ed. Ḥasan Waḥīd Dastgerdī, Tehran, 1314 Š./1935.

Toumanoff, *Généalogie*
Cyrille Toumanoff, *Manuel de généalogie et de chronologie pour l'histoire de la Caucasie chrétienne*, Rome, 1977; supplement, 1978.

TPS
Transactions of the Philological Society.

Ṭūsī, *Fehrest*
Abū Jaʿfar Moḥammad b. Ḥasan Ṭūsī, *Fehrest kotob al-šīʿa wa asmāʾ al-moʾallefīn*, ed. Aloys Sprenger, Calcutta, 1853-55.

Ṭūsī, *Rejāl*
Abū Jaʿfar Moḥammad b. Ḥasan Ṭūsī, *Ketāb al-rejāl*, ed. M. Ṣ. Āl Baḥr-al-ʿOlūm, Najaf, 1381/1961.

Vd.
Vidēvdād, Vendidad, a text of the Avesta.

VDI
Vestnik drevniĭ istorii.

Wolff, *Glossar*
Fritz Wolff, *Glossar zu Ferdosis Schahname*, Berlin, 1935; repr. Hildesheim, 1965.

Wulff, *Crafts*
H. E. Wulff, *The Traditional Crafts of Persia*, Cambridge, Mass., 1966.

WZKM
Wiener Zeitschrift für die Kunde des Morgenlandes.

Y.
Yasna, a group of texts of the Avesta.

Yaʿqūbī, *Boldān*
Aḥmad b. Abī Yaʿqūb Yaʿqūbī, *Ketāb al-boldān*, ed. M. J. de Goeje, BGA, Leiden, 1892; 2nd ed., Leiden, 1967.

Yaʿqūbī, tr. Āyatī
Aḥmad b. Abī Yaʿqūb Yaʿqūbī, *Ketāb al-boldān*, tr. M.-E. Āyatī, Tehran, 1347 Š./1968.

Yaʿqūbī, tr. Wiet
Aḥmad b. Abī Yaʿqūb Yaʿqūbī, *Ketāb al-boldān*, tr. Gaston Wiet as *Les pays*, Cairo, 1937.

Yaʿqūbī, *Taʾrīḵ*
Aḥmad b. Abī Yaʿqūb Yaʿqūbī, *Taʾrīḵ*, ed. M. T. Houtsma as *Historiae*, Leiden, 1883.

Yāqūt, *Boldān*
Šehāb-al-Dīn Abū ʿAbd-Allāh Yāqūt b. ʿAbd-Allāh Ḥamawī, *Moʿjam al-boldān*, ed. Ferdinand Wüstenfeld, 6 vols., Leipzig, 1866-73.

Yāqūt, *Boldān* (Beirut)
Šehāb-al-Dīn Abū ʿAbd-Allāh Yāqūt b. ʿAbd-Allāh Ḥamawī, *Moʿjam al-boldān*, 5 vols., Beirut, 1955-57.

Yāqūt, *Eršād al-arīb*. See Yāqūt, *Odabāʾ*.

Yāqūt, *Odabāʾ*
Šehāb-al-Dīn Abū ʿAbd-Allāh Yāqūt b. ʿAbd-Allāh Ḥamawī, *Moʿjam al-odabāʾ*, ed. D. S. Margoliouth, GMS, 7 vols., Leiden, 1907-31.

Yt.
Yašt, a text of the Avesta.

ZA
Zeitschrift für Assyriologie.

Zādspram
B. T. Anklesaria, ed., *Vichitakiha-i Zatasparam*, pt. 1, Bombay, 1964.

Zambaur
Éduard de Zambaur, *Manuel de généalogie et de chronologie pour l'histoire de l'Islam*, Hannover, 1927.

ZDMG
Zeitschrift der Deutschen Morgenländischen Gesellschaft.

Zereklī, *Aʿlām*[1,2]
K̲ayr-al-Dīn Zereklī, *al-Aʿlām*, 3 vols., Cairo, 1927-28; 2nd ed., 10 vols., Cairo, 1373-78/1954-59.

Zhukovskiĭ, *Materialy*
V. A. Zhukovskiĭ, *Materialy dlya izucheniya persidskikh narechiĭ*, 3 vols., St. Petersburg, 1888-1922; repr. 1 vol., Tehran, 1976.

ZII
Zeitschrift für Indologie und Iranistik.

ZVS
Zeitschrift für vergleichende Sprachforschung.

EDITORIAL NOTES

On the principle that what people looked like is no less informative than their birth or death dates, photographs of the subjects will henceforth accompany biographical articles whenever possible.

The titles chosen for the entries are either in English or in an Iranian language, normally the title that comes earlier in the alphabet. Cross-references ensure that the reader looking under either possible title can find the appropriate article.

DĀRĀ(B) (< *Dārāw < Dāryāw < OPers. Dārayavau-; cf. Pahlavi Dārāy), the name of two kings of the legendary Kayanid dynasty.

i. *Dārā(b) I.*

ii. *Dārā(b) II.*

i. Dārā(b) I

Dārā(b) I was the son of the Kayanid Bahman Ardašīr. According to most of the sources, his mother was Homā Čehrāzād, who married her own father, Bahman (*Šāh-nāma*, Moscow, VI, p. 352; Ṭabarī, I, p. 687; Balʿamī, ed. Bahār, p. 687; Masʿūdī, *Morūj*, ed. Pellat, I, p. 272; Ṯaʿālebī, *Ḡorar*, p. 389; Meskawayh, p. 34; Gardīzī, ed. Ḥabībī, p. 15; Ṭarsūsī, pp. 10-11). In one tradition, however, this marriage was denied, and it was maintained that Homā died a virgin (Ebn al-Balḵī, p. 54). Nevertheless, the former version, which accords with the old Iranian tradition of next-of-kin marriage, is certainly authentic. According to this legend, Bahman died before Dārā was born and appointed Homā his regent. When Dārā was born she did not reveal the news of his birth but had him laid, together with precious jewels, in a casket and exposed on the river Euphrates (*Šāh-nāma*, Moscow, VI, p. 356; Ṭarsūsī, p. 11), the Tigris (Maqdesī, *Badʾ* III, p. 150), the Kor river in Fārs (Ṭabarī, I, p. 689), the Eṣṭaḵr (i.e., Polvār) river in Fārs (Ṯaʿālebī, *Ḡorar*, p. 392), or the Balḵ river (Ṭabarī, I, p. 690). The child was found by a fuller (*Šāh-nāma*, Moscow, VI, p. 356; Ṯaʿālebī, *Ḡorar*, p. 392; *Mojmal*, ed. Bahār, p. 54; Maqdesī, *Badʾ* III, p. 150; Ṭarsūsī, where his name is given as Hormaz) or a miller (Ṭabarī, I, p. 690; Balʿamī, ed. Bahār, p. 690), who called him Dārāb, because he was found in the water (*āb*) among the trees (*dār*; Ṯaʿālebī, *Ḡorar*, p. 394; *Šāh-nāma*, Moscow, VI, p. 358; Ṭarsūsī, pp. 13-14; Balʿamī, ed. Bahār, p. 690: *dār* "hold, take").

This story seems to be based on popular etymology. A similar etiological legend is told about Kawād, the founder of the Kayanid dynasty (*Bundahišn*, TD_2, p. 231; Christensen, 1931, pp. 70-71; idem, 1933-35; Bailey, pp. 69 ff.). It belongs to a type of legend "which is generally associated with the change of dynasties, the end of an era, or a major shift of power" (Yarshater, p. 522; cf. Christensen, 1933-35). In spite of the discontent of his foster-father, who wanted the boy to become a fuller, Dārā, eager to receive an aristocratic education, was first handed over to scholars, who taught him the Avesta and its commentary (*Zand o Estā*); then he was trained in archery, horsemanship, polo, and similar skills. Dārā, who doubted his relationship to the fuller and was curious to find out his true origin, compelled the fuller's wife to reveal his descent. As he was ambitious to reach high positions, Dārā entered the service of Rašnavād, Homā's commander-in-chief (*Šāh-nāma*, Moscow, VI, pp. 358 ff.; Ṯaʿālebī, *Ḡorar*, pp. 394 ff.; Maqdesī, *Badʾ* III, p. 150; Balʿamī, ed. Bahār, pp. 690-91; Ṭarsūsī, pp. 27 ff., with different details). Eventually Dārā was introduced to the queen, who after a reign of thirty years (thirty-two according to *Šāh-nāma*, Moscow, VI, p. 371 v. 312) abdicated in his favor.

Dārā reigned for twelve years (*Bundahišn*, TD_2, p. 240; Ḥamza, p. 13; *Mojmal*, ed. Bahār, p. 55; Ebn al-Balḵī, p. 55; Dīnavarī, ed. Guirgass, p. 31; Masʿūdī, *Morūj*, ed. Pellat, I, p. 272). During his reign he fought with Šoʿayb, the Arab commander from the Qotayb tribe (*Šāh-nāma*, Moscow, VI, pp. 374-75; Ṭarsūsī, pp. 354-72). He also campaigned against Fīlfūs (Philip) of Rūm (i.e., Greece), who was defeated and compelled to pay tribute and agreed to marry his daughter Nāhīd (*Šāh-nāma*, Moscow, VI, p. 377; Ṭarsūsī, p. 380) or Halāy (Ṭabarī, I, p. 697) to Dārā. Although pregnant, she was soon sent back home because of her foul breath. In Rūm she bore Eskandar (Alexander, q.v.; *Šāh-nāma*, Moscow, pp. 375 ff.; Dīnavarī, pp. 31-32; Ṯaʿālebī, *Ḡorar*, pp. 399 ff.; Ṭabarī, I, pp. 696-97; *Mojmal*, ed. Bahār, p. 54; Ṭarsūsī, pp. 390 ff.). This last episode represents an obvious attempt to provide a link between Alexander the Great and the Persian royal house by making him a half-brother of Dārā II (q.v.; Yarshater, pp. 522-23).

The introduction of the Persian postal system was attributed to Dārā I (Ṭabarī, I, p. 692; Ḥamza, p. 39; Ṯaʿālebī, *Ḡorar*, p. 398; Gardīzī, ed. Ḥabībī, p. 16), apparently reflecting a historical fact: the introduction or reorganization of the postal system by Darius I the Great (q.v.). The foundation of the city of Dārābgerd in Fārs was attributed to him in most of the sources (Ḥamza, p. 39; Ṭabarī, I, p. 692; Balʿamī, ed. Bahār, p. 692; Ebn al-Balḵī, p. 55; Ṯaʿālebī, *Ḡorar*, p. 398; Gardīzī, ed. Ḥabībī, p. 16; *Mojmal*, ed. Bahār, p. 55; Ebn al-Balḵī, p. 55; Ṭarsūsī, pp. 353, 452; see DĀRĀB ii), though in some others Dārā II was credited with its foundation (*Pahlavi Texts*, ed. Jamasp-Asana, p. 22; *Tārīḵ-e gozīda*, ed. Browne, p. 99). Babylon was mentioned as his residence (Ṭabarī, I, p. 692; Masʿūdī, *Morūj*, ed. Pellat, I, p. 272), which shows the general tendency in the tradition to link the exploits of the last Kayanid kings with western Iran.

Dārā was supposed, according to the late sources, to have had a son called Fīrūzšāh, whose exploits are related in the popular Persian romance *Fīrūzšāh-nāma*, published under the title *Dārāb-nāma* by Ḥājī Moḥammad Bīḡamī (qq.v.; ed. Ḏ. Ṣafā, Tehran, 1339-41 Š./1960-62).

Bibliography: H. W. Bailey, "Iranian Studies II," *BSOS* 7, 1933-35, pp. 69-86. A. Christensen, *Les Kayanides*, Copenhagen, 1931. Idem, "Notes and Queries," *BSOS* 7, 1933-35, pp. 483-85. Meskawayh, *Tajāreb al-omam*, ed. A. Emāmī, I, Tehran 1366 Š./1987. Abū Ṭāher Moḥammad b. Ḥasan Ṭarsūsī, *Dārāb-nāma*, ed. Ḏ. Ṣafā, I, Tehran, 1344 Š./1365. E. Yarshater, "Were the Sasanians Heirs to the Achaemenids?" in *La Persia nel medioevo*, Rome, 1971, pp. 517-30.

(Aḥmad Tafażżolī)

ii. Dārā(b) II

Dārā II was the son of Dārā I (see i, above) and the last king of the legendary Kayanid dynasty, often identified in sources with Darius III Codomannus (q.v.), the last Achaemenid king (336-31 B.C.E.). His name is recorded as Dārā in the Pahlavi literature and in the majority of the Islamic sources but as Dārāb in Abū Ṭāher Moḥammad Ṭarsūsī's *Dārāb-nāma* (q.v.) and the Persian prose version of the *Eskandar-nāma*. His mother was Māhnāhīd, daughter of Hazārmard (Ṭabarī, I, p. 693); according to a later tradition, however, she was Ṭamrūsīa, daughter of Faṣṭabīqūn and former wife of the king of Oman (Ṭarsūsī, I, pp. 100 ff.). In the legend Dārā II was the half-brother of Alexander (Eskandar) the Great (q.v.). When he came to power he demanded the customary tribute from Alexander, who refused to comply and instead led an army to Iraq on the Euphrates, where he encountered the forces of Dārā coming from Eṣṭaḵr. According to one tradition (Ebn al-Balḵī, p. 55; cf. Ṭabarī, I, pp. 692-30; Meskawayh, pp. 34-35), Dārā II's vizier, whose brother had been killed by *Rašnīn, the vizier of Dārā I, instigated Alexander's attack on Iran. In order to learn the potential of the Iranian army and to become privy to Dārā's plans, Alexander presented himself as an envoy to Dārā II and witnessed the court ceremonial. He was recognized by some courtiers, but he managed to escape before he was arrested. War broke out, and Dārā fled to Kermān, where he asked the emperor of India, Porus (Fūr), to come to his aid but in vain. Dārā was killed by two men, called Māhyār and *Jānūšyār, who were his ministers (*dastūr*), guards, or amirs. Then they led Alexander to the dying king, who asked him to marry his daughter Rowšanak (Roxana), also called Būrān-doḵt, and to avenge his death (*Šāh-nāma*, Moscow, VI, pp. 398 ff.; Ṭabarī, I, pp. 696, 698; Balʿamī, ed. Bahār, p. 698; Ṯaʿālebī, *Ḡorar*, p. 410; Ebn al-Balḵī, p. 56; Masʿūdī, *Morūj*, ed. Pellat, II, pp. 9, 12; Gardīzī, ed. Ḥabībī, p. 16; *Mojmal*, ed. Bahār, pp. 55-56; Maqdesī, *Badʾ* III, p. 150; Meskawayh I, p. 35; Ṭarsūsī, I, pp. 461, 468, II, pp. 85 ff.). Dārā reigned for fourteen (*Bundahišn*, TD_2, p. 240; Ṭabarī, I, p. 694; Ḥamza, p. 13; *Mojmal*, ed. Bahār, p. 55), thirteen (*Ayādgār* 4.4, probably a clerical error), or sixteen years (*Mojmal*, ed. Bahār, p. 55). He was said to have had three sons: Ašk, supposedly the ancestor of the Arsacids, Ardašīr (qq.v.), and a third, whose name has been corrupted (Ṭabarī, I, p. 700; cf. Balʿamī, ed. Bahār, p. 698).

The foundation of the city of Dārā (q.v.; Ṭabarī, I, p. 694), or Dāryā, above Nisibis (Ḥamza, p. 39; *Mojmal*, ed. Bahār, p. 56) has been attributed to Dārā II. In some sources he is reported also to have built the city of Dārābgerd (see DĀRĀB ii). In addition, he is reported to have ordered two copies of the entire Avesta and Zand to be kept respectively in the royal treasury (*ganj ī šāhīgān*) and the fortress of the archives (*diz ī nibišt*; *Dēnkard*, ed. Madan, I, p. 412).

The legend of Dārā and the golden idol, mentioned by Ebn al-Nadīm (ed. Tajaddod, p. 364) among Iranian stories translated into Arabic, may be about Dārā II. A lengthy part of Ṭarsūsī's *Dārāb-nāma* is devoted to his exploits.

Bibliography: *Ayādgār ī jāmāspīg*, ed. G. Messina, Rome, 1939. *Eskandar-nāma*, ed. Ī. Afšār, Tehran, 1343 Š./1964. Meskawayh, *Tajāreb al-omam*, ed. A. Emāmī, I, Tehran 1366 Š./1987. Abū Ṭāher Moḥammad b. Ḥasan Ṭarsūsī, *Dārāb-nāma*, 2 vols., ed. Ḏ. Ṣafā, Tehran, 1344-46 Š./1965-67.

(Aḥmad Tafażżolī)

DĀRĀ, ʿABD-ALLĀH MĪRZĀ. See ʿABDALLĀH MĪRZĀ DĀRĀ.

DĀRĀ B. ROSTAM. See ĀL-E BĀVAND.

DĀRĀ ŠOKŌH (b. near Ajmer, 19 Ṣafar 1024/20 March 1615, d. Delhi, 22 Ḏu'l-ḥejja 1069/12 August 1659), first son of the Mughal emperor Shah Jahān (r. 1037-67/1627-57) and his wife Momtāz Maḥall, religious thinker, mystic, poet, and author of a number of works in Persian. Little is known about his education; one of his teachers was ʿAbd-al-Laṭīf Solṭānpūrī (Raḥmān-ʿAlī, p. 81). Although trained as heir apparent, Dārā Šokōh never showed a serious interest in politics or in military prowess; his father repeatedly promoted him, however, until he finally reached the unprecedented rank of commander of 60,000 *ḏāt*/40,000 *sovār* in 1067/1656. His only major military adventure, the attempt to reconquer the strategic fortress of Qandahār from the Persians in 1062/1652, ended in failure. Instead, Dārā Šokōh's interests were geared to philosophy and mysticism, and it is said that he accepted an appointment as governor of Allāhābād in 1055/1645 only because it was the seat of Moḥebb-Allāh Allāhābādī (d. 1058/1648), the most famous interpreter of the philosophy of Ebn al-ʿArabī (q.v.; d. 638/1240) in that period. Nevertheless, although Dārā Šokōh exchanged numerous letters with Moḥebb-Allāh, he never actually settled in his Allāhābād residence.

Both Jahāngīr (1013-37/1605-27) and Shah Jahān had shown reverence for Sufis and saintly Hindus. Thus when Dārā Šokōh fell seriously ill as a teenager his father took him to Lahore to Mīān Mīr (d. 1045/1635), a shaikh of the Qāderīya order, which was becoming prominent in Sind and the southern Punjab in the late 16th century. The boy was cured and at the same time developed a deep veneration for Mīān Mīr. In his second book, *Sakīnat al-awlīāʾ* (comp. 1052/1642), Dārā Šokōh expressed his devotion to Mīān Mīr, to his saintly sister Bībī Jamāl Ḵātūn, and to Mollā Šāh Badaḵšī (d. 1072/1661), who had continued the spiritual chain after Mīān Mīr's death and under whom Dārā Šokōh and his sister Jahānārā had joined the order in 1030/1640. This book is a useful introduction to mystical life and lore in Lahore and Kashmir, based mainly on firsthand information. Before writing it, Dārā Šokōh had completed, on

Ramażān 27 1049/21 January 1640, *Safīnat al-awlīāʾ*, a set of biographies of saintly people, modeled on ʿAbd-al-Raḥmān Jāmī's *Nafaḥāt-al-ons*. The date was important to Dārā Šokōh, for he had had his first mystical experience of light in the *laylat-al-qadr*, 27 Ramażān 1040/29 April 1630, owing to Mīān Mīr's presence and spiritual power (*Sakīnat al-awlīāʾ*, p. 54). *Safīnat al-awlīāʾ* contains biographies not only of major saints of the different orders, including some women saints, but also of the first four caliphs, the twelve Shiʿite imams, and the founders of the four schools of Islamic law, thus demonstrating the prince's catholic Islamic stance. He always remained bound to the fundamentals of Islam and repeatedly called himself a Hanafite Qāderī; his mystical writings contain nothing that could not be found in the works of other Sufis. An interesting aspect of *Safīnat al-awlīāʾ* is that Dārā Šokōh incorrectly placed Jālāl-al-Dīn Rūmī (d. 672/1273) and his family in the Kobrawī line, or *selsela*. He became familiar with certain Sufi practices, like *ḥabs-e dam*, the retaining of one's breath during the *ḏekr* (q.v.), a practice that he described in detail (*Resāla-ye ḥaqqnomā*, p. 13). He did not, however, believe in exaggerated austerities, which in any case would have been difficult for him as heir apparent to a vast country.

After finishing his first two books Dārā Šokōh may have written *Ṭarīqat al-ḥaqīqa*, which has been attributed to him, though its style is more elaborate than that of his other works; it is in a combination of poetry and prose, and the majority of the poetic quotations are taken from Rūmī. The authenticity of this work is doubtful, however. His next work, *Resāla-ye ḥaqqnomā* (comp. 1056/1646) is one of his most impressive studies of Sufism, in the vein of Ebn al-ʿArabī, by whose philosophy he was deeply influenced; most of the Sufis with whom he corresponded, like Moḥebb-Allāh and Shah Delrobā, were proponents of the theories of *waḥdat al-wojūd* ("unity of being," as developed by Ebn al-ʿArabī, often incorrectly translated "pantheism"). In this small book he tried to explain the four planes of being, rising from *nāsūt* (the world of humanity) to the heights of *lāhūt* (the world of divinity). He considered this booklet to be a compendium of Ebn al-ʿArabī's *Fotūḥāt al-makkīya* and *Foṣūṣ al-ḥekam*, as well as of the *Lamaʿāt* of Faḵr-al-Dīn ʿErāqī (d. 688/1289) and the *Lawāʾeḥ* of Jāmī (d. 898/1492). In his closing verse, which includes the date of completion, he claimed the book to have been divinely inspired. In the *Resāla* Dārā Šokōh called self-knowledge *eksīr-e aʿẓam* (the mightiest elixir), and this phrase was used as the title of his small *dīvān*, in which, under the pen name Qāderī, he expressed his thoughts in traditional images. It is certainly not a great work of poetical art and lacks luster, but some of the verses are interesting because of their bold assertion that "paradise is where there is no *mollā*."

Six years later, in 1062/1652, Dārā Šokōh compiled *Ḥasanāt al-ʿārefīn*, a collection of the *šaṭaḥāt* (theopathic locutions or paradoxes) of 107 saints. Many of the quatrains contained in this book are versified sayings of earlier Sufis. The book is usually regarded as his last contribution to the literature on pure Sufism.

Dārā Šokōh's interest in the esoteric aspects of Islam and his pursuit of genuine *tawḥīd* led him to study other religious traditions as well. An important step on his way to understanding the major religion of his future realm, Hinduism, was a series of conversations with the Hindu sage Baba Lal Das, a member of the reformist Kabirpanthi sect whom he met in the city of Lahore in late 1064/1653 after his return from the disastrous siege of Qandahār. Dārā Šokōh's secretary Chandar Bhan Brahman, a noted poet and master of Persian style, recorded in Persian the text of the discussions, which were conducted in Hindi. These "entretiens de Lahore," as Clément Huart and Louis Massignon have called them, reveal the prince's sound knowledge of Indian mythology and philosophy, which is not amazing at all, as his great-grandfather Akbar (q.v.) had ordered Persian translations of numerous important Sanskrit works. The discussions ranged from purely philosophical concepts to problems of interpretation of the Ramayana.

A book that displays even more clearly Dārā Šokōh's interest in the terms common to Hindu thought and Islamic Sufism is *Majmaʿ al-baḥrayn* (comp. 1065/1655). Its very title, taken from Koran 18:60, underscores his intention to prove that on the level of monistic thought the "two oceans" of Islam and Hinduism become indistinguishable; the book in fact contains a number of Hindu technical terms, which he attempted to explain in Persian.

After finishing this work the prince, by then slightly more than forty years old, embarked upon his major undertaking, a translation of fifty-two Upanishads, for which he had invited the consultation of a good number of Brahmans and pandits. The work, entitled *Serr-e akbar*, was completed in the first half of 1067/1657. Dārā Šokōh was strongly convinced, as he wrote in his introduction, that religious truth is not solely contained in the books explicitly mentioned in the Koran: the Torah, Psalms, and Gospels. In the Koran itself (56:78) a "hidden book," not yet discovered, is mentioned. He argued that this hidden book was the oldest revelation, as contained in the Vedas and in particular the Vedanta. The Upanishads, in his view, embody the same concept of the transcendental unity of the absolute as does the Koran; hence he deemed it necessary to make this wisdom available to his fellow Muslims. To what extent Dārā Šokōh himself was responsible for the translation from Sanskrit is a matter of dispute. Erhard Göbel-Gross has tried to show that his knowledge of Sanskrit was restricted to a certain vocabulary and that he could not read complex texts; the actual work would thus have had to be done by pandits, whose explanations he wrote down in Persian. He could not possibly have foreseen that the Latin translation of this rendering of the Upanishads by A. H. Anquetil Duperron, which appeared in Europe in 1801 under the title *Oupnekʿhat, Id Est Secretum Tegendum*, was to stir immense interest in Indian mystical philosophy among European thinkers and to create an image of India as the home of all mystical wisdom.

Dārā Šokōh was deeply convinced of the reality of mystical experience and apparently believed firmly in miracles, some of which he described in his books. He took Muslim mystics and miracle workers, as well as yogis and sannyasis, with him on his ill-fated expedition to Qandahār. It was quite natural that the more orthodox circles around him should have disapproved of his predilection for mystical thought and practice, as well as of his disinterest in practical political activity. His brother Awrangzēb (q.v., Supp.), frustrated by Shah Jahān's persistent preference for Dārā Šokōh, despite his own greater political and military skills, incited the prince's younger brothers against him. Together they took advantage of Shah Jahān's illness in 1068-69/1657-58 to declare Dārā Šokōh a heretic (*molḥed*), whose possible ascent to the throne would be disastrous for Islam. They began to fight against Dārā Šokōh, who had to flee the capital and was defeated several times. He sought refuge in the southwestern part of the empire but found no support in either Rajastan or the borderlands of Sind. The death of his dearly beloved wife Nādera Begom, mother of his seven children, deprived him of his greatest spiritual support. He sent off some of his few remaining soldiers with her bier so that she might be buried close to Mīān Mīr in Lahore, where a graceful mausoleum had been built for her. The prince himself was shortly afterward treacherously handed over to Awrangzēb's men by his host, Malek Jevān. After a trial for heresy he was executed on 22 Ḏu'l-ḥejja 1069/12 August 1659 and buried in the mausoleum of his ancestor Homāyūn in Delhi.

Dārā Šokōh was a great lover of art and a fine calligrapher. His refined taste is shown by an album (*moraqqaʿ*) that he had prepared for Nādera Begum in 1051/1641, preserved in the India Office Library, London (ms. no. Add. Or. 3129); it contains seventy-eight folios, on which paintings and pieces of calligraphy alternate, as was traditional in Mughal albums. His master in calligraphy was Rašīdā, a nephew of the famous Persian calligrapher Mīr ʿEmād Ḥasanī who, after his uncle's assassination in 1024/1615, found a refuge at the Mughal court. Dārā Šokōh not only mastered *nastaʿlīq* but was also skilled in *nasḵ* and *rayḥānī* (see CALLIGRAPHY). Among surviving manuscripts written by him is a copy of a *maṯnawī* by Jālāl-al-Dīn Rūmī's son Solṭān Walad (d. 712/1312); he sent a Koran in his hand to the shrine of his patron saint, ʿAbd-al-Qāder Jīlānī (d. 562/1166), in Baghdad. In many calligraphic pieces written by him or for him his name was later erased, lest people remember him for his love of art and his skill.

It is difficult to provide a balanced assessment of Dārā Šokōh, the "unfortunate aesthete" with his "uninhibited imagination" (Huart and Massignon, p. 287). European visitors to India in the 17th century, like François Bernier, accused him of having "too exalted an opinion of himself" (p. 6) and of never showing his true religious loyalty, "behaving as a Christian with Christians, as a gentile with gentiles." Niccolò Manucci thought that he had no religion at all (p. 223). Some of the misunderstandings and misgivings about Dārā Šokōh may have originated in his life style and can be explained by the presence of the strange people with whom he surrounded himself, in particular the Persian Jewish merchant Sarmad, who, after studying Christianity, converted to Islam and then, under the shock of his infatuation with a Hindu boy, began to walk around stark naked, reciting daring Persian quatrains. The Muslim nobility understandably did not find the prince's association with such people fitting for a future ruler. Sarmad was executed two years after his master. One may also think of the Hindu secretary Chandar Bhan Brahman and of Moḥsen Fānī (d. 1081/1670), a mediocre Kashmiri poet and disciple of Moḥebb-Allāh Allāhābādī (Schimmel, 1980, pp. 100-01).

Shah Jahān's two sons Dārā Šokōh and Awrangzēb manifested in themselves the two possibilities of Indian Islam: Awrangzēb certainly gained the love of those Muslims more oriented to the Šarīʿa, with their attention centered on Mecca and a distinct Muslim identity; he was equally disliked by mystically minded Muslims and most Hindus. Dārā Šokōh, on the contrary, has been considered truly Indian in spirit. In our century the poet-philosopher Moḥammad Eqbāl (see IQBĀL) spoke of Dārā Šokōh's perpetuation of "the seed of heresy that his ancestor Akbar had sown, while Awrangzēb was sitting in this idol temple like an Abraham [ready to destroy the idols]" (p. 113). The fact that during the days of the emperor Jahāngīr the Naqšbandī reformer Aḥmad Serhendī (d. 1034/1624) had heavily attacked Akbar's attempts to bridge the gap between the two major religious systems of his country and had alerted the Mughal nobility to the necessity of avoiding any rapprochement between Islam and Hinduism may have contributed to the aversion of a good number of Sunni officeholders to the heir apparent; nevertheless, an important faction of the Shiʿite population, among them the influential Bārhā *sayyeds*, sided with him against Awrangzēb (Schimmel, 1980, pp. 92-93, 103). It must not be forgotten, however, that Dārā Šokōh's interest was not so much in the reconciliation of Islam and Hinduism on the political and practical level, on which Akbar had focused; rather, it was focused on the experiential realization that esoteric understanding of both religions provides proof of a single divine principle behind the variety of outward manifestations, just "as the ocean is one and the waves and foam flecks cannot be distinguished from it once they disappear" (*Resāla*, p. 17).

Bibliography: For various editions of Dārā Šokōh's works, see B. J. Hasrat, *Dārā Shikuh. Life and Works*, n.p. (Calcutta), 1953; and A. Schimmel, "Islamic Literatures of India," in J. Gonda, ed., *History of Indian*

Literature, Wiesbaden, 1973, p. 39 n. 178. F. Bernier, *Travels in the Mogul Empire A.D. 1656-1668*, tr. I. Rock, rev. A. Constable, London, 1891; repr. Delhi, 1972. Dārā Šokōh, *Majmaʿ al-Baḥrayn, or the Mingling of the Two Oceans*, ed. and tr. M. Maḥfūẓ-al-Ḥaqq, Calcutta, 1929; ed. M.-R. Jalālī Nāʾīnī, in *Montaḵabāt-e āṯār*, Tehran, 1335 Š./1956. Idem, *Serr-e akbar*, ed. T. Chand and M.-R. Jalālī Nāʾīnī, Tehran, 1344 Š./1965. Idem, *Sakīnat al-awlīāʾ*, ed. M.-R. Jalālī Nāʾīnī, Tehran, 1344 Š./1965. M. Eqbāl, *Romūz-e Bīḵodī*, Lahore, 1917. E. Göbel-Gross, *Sirr-i Akbar. Die Upanishad-Übersetzung Dara Shikohs*, Ph.D. diss. Marburg, 1962. C. Huart and L. Massignon, eds. "Les entretiens de Lahore [entre le prince impérial Dârâ Shikûh et l'ascète hindou Baba La'l Das]," *JA* 209, 1926, pp. 285-334. N. Manucci, *Storia do Mogor or Mogul India 1653-1708 vy Niccolao Manucci Venetian*, tr. W. Irvine, I, London, 1906. Raḥmān-ʿAlī Moḥammad ʿAbd-al-Šakūr, *Toḥfat al-fożalaʾ fī tarājem al-komalāʾ* (*Taḏkera-ye ʿolamā-ye Hend*), Lucknow, 1894; 2nd ed., Lucknow, 1914. A. Schimmel, *Islam in the Indian Subcontinent*, Leiden, 1980, pp. 2, 89, 96-101, 103-04,130, 138, 142-43.

(ANNEMARIE SCHIMMEL)

DĀRĀB.

i. *Modern city and šahrestān.*
ii. *History and archeology.*
iii. *Rock reliefs.*

i. MODERN CITY AND ŠAHRESTĀN

The name Dārāb refers both to a *šahrestān* (subprovince) of Fārs province and to the chief city of that *šahrestān*. The subprovince is bound on the north by the *šahrestān*s of Neyrīz and Eṣṭahbānāt; on the east by Saʿādatābād, a *baḵš* (district) of Bandar-e ʿAbbās(ī) (q.v.); on the south by the *šahrestān* of Lār; and on the west by the *šahrestān*s of Jahrom and Fasā. Its central district (*baḵš-e markazī*) encompasses, beside the capital, several rural subdistricts (*dehestān*s), including Ābšūr, Īzadḵᵛāst, Rūdbāl, Hājīābād, Ḵosūya, Rostāq, Šāhījān, Fasārūd, Fūrk, Kūhestān, Qaryat al-Ḵayr, and Hašīvār (*Farhang-e jofrāfīāʾī*, p. 24).

In the northern region of the *šahrestān* a continuation of the Zagros mountain range runs from northwest to southeast; the land slopes gradually toward the south and southwest. The three highest peaks are, from west to east, Kūh-e Namak (2,863 m), Kūh-e Panjšāh (2,765 m), and Kūh-e Barfdān (3,025 m). Owing to these and other, scattered mountains along its borders, the *šahrestān* enjoys cold winters and hot, dry summers, a more moderate climate than the hot neighboring regions. In 1354 Š./1975 temperatures measured in the city of Dārāb ranged between -0.8° and 45° C respectively (Saʿīdīān, p. 538). The recorded average, however, ranges from -0.4° to 46° C, with annual precipitation of 160 mm (*Farhang-e jogrāfīāʾī*, p. 26).

The region is well watered, owing to abundant seasonal precipitation and a number of permanent springs and rivers, supplemented by *qanāt*s and wells. The largest river is the Rūdbār, which rises in the southern mountains of Neyrīz and in various parts of its course is known as Rūdbāl, Rostam, Āb-e Šūr, and Tang-e Čarḵī. It flows into the Persian Gulf near Bandar-e ʿAbbās. As the soil of Dārāb is also fertile, agriculture is the primary source of livelihood in the *šahrestān*. The leading agricultural products and the main exports from the region include cotton (q.v.), wheat, citrus fruits (q.v.), dates (see DATE PALM), grapes (see ANGŪR), fresh vegetables, and roses. The cotton is usually ginned locally before being exported. In fact, cotton ginning and carpet weaving are the major industrial products of Dārāb. Among other crafts of economic importance is embroidery, characterized by floral designs on white cloth.

According to the census (q.v.) of 1365 Š./1986, the population of Dārāb *šahrestān* was 168,692 (30,755 family units, 84,834 men, and 83,858 women), with 27.4 percent living in urban areas. Of the total population 51.2 percent were below the age of fifteen years, 46.1 percent between fifteen and sixty-four years old, and 2.7 percent sixty-five years old or older (Markaz-e āmār, pp. 1, 10). This population consists mainly of Twelver Shiʿite Muslims whose first language is Persian, though Turkic languages and Arabic are also spoken.

The city of Dārāb, located in the Rūdbār valley 270 km southeast of Shiraz, at 28°45′ N and 54°33′ E and an altitude of 1,120 m (*Farhang-e jogrāfīāʾī*, p. 26), is the capital of the *šahrestān*. Ruins of the ancient city of Dārābgerd, capital of the district of Dārābjerd, the easternmost of five districts of Fārs under the ʿAbbasid caliphate (Le Strange, *Lands*, pp. 288-89; corresponding to the independent province of Šabānkāra in the Mongol period; Bartol'd, tr., pp. 152-53, 161-62), lie 8 km south of the present city (see ii, below).

Bibliography: V. Bartol'd (W. Barthold), "Istoriko-geograficheskiĭ obzor Irana" (A historical-geographical survey of Iran), in V. Bartol'd, *Sochineniya* (Collected works), Moscow, 1971, pp. 31-225; tr. S. Soucek as *A Historical Geography of Iran*, Princeton, N.J., 1984. ʿA. Bayāt, *Kollīyāt-e jografīā-ye ṭabīʿī wa tārīḵī-e Īrān*, Tehran, 1367 Š./1988, pp. 341-43. *Farhang-e jogrāfīāʾī-e Īrān (ābādīhā)* CXIII, Tehran, 1367 Š./1988, pp. 24-27. Moḥammad-Naṣīr Forṣat Šīrāzī, *Āṯār-e ʿajam*, Bombay, 1354/1935, pp. 92-100. Markaz-e āmār-e Īrān, *Natāyej-e sar-šomārī-e nofūs wa maskan. Mehr māh-e 1365. Šahrestān-e Dārāb*, Tehran, 1368 Š./1989. ʿA. Saʿīdīān, *Dāʾerat al-maʿāref-e sarzamīn wa mardom-e Īrān*, Tehran, 1360 Š./1981, pp. 538, 574-76.

(MASSOUD KHEIRABADI)

ii. HISTORY AND ARCHEOLOGY

The modern town of Dārāb, the center of the Ḵamsa tribe of Fārs (Oberling, pp. 123-70), lies on a slightly elevated plateau at the foot of the northern mountains (see i, above) and is separated from the plain to the south by a low mountain ridge (*Gazetteer of Iran* III, pp. 183-84, 372; Gītā Šenāsī).

There is an unusual Friday mosque, possibly of the 17th century; in contrast to the typical Persian courtyard mosque, with porticos, *ayvāns* (q.v.), and domed sanctuary, it is freestanding with four corner towers and a rectangular prayer room surrounded by open porches (Moṣṭafawī, pp. 493-94; tr., pp. 332-34, 354-57; Pohanka, pp. 265-69). About 7 km southwest of the town, in the middle of the plain, are the remains of the ancient city of Dārābgerd/Dārābjerd (Nöldeke, p. 146), now called Qalʿa or Ḵandaq-e Daḥīa after an Islamic shrine outside the fortifications (Forṣat Šīrazī, p. 92). In medieval reports a certain Dārā, perhaps either an Achaemenid king or a local ruler, is named as founder of the city (Ṭabarī, I, p. 692; Ebn al-Balḵī, p. 55; Barbier de Meynard, p. 226; *Nozhat al-qolūb*, pp. 124, 138; Markwart, *Provincial Capitals*, p. 19; see DĀRĀ(B)). According to Ṭabarī (I, p. 815), Ardašīr Bābakān (Ardašīr I, q.v.; 224-40) was educated in Dārāb by the permission of Gōzehr, king of Eṣṭaḵr, whom Ardašīr's father, Bābak (q.v.), later assassinated on his son's orders. From Dārāb Ardašīr is reported to have launched his first territorial conquests. Later, however, he built the town of Ardašīr-Ḵorra (q.v.; Gūr) as his residence.

The importance of Dārāb in early Sasanian history is underscored by the nearby rock reliefs (see iii, below), as well as by a splendid mud-brick building with rich stucco decoration of the time of Šāpūr II (309-79) in the adjacent Ḥājīābād plain (Azarnoush, pp. 159-76). Some authors have suggested that the circular wall of Dārāb was the model for the circular plan of Ardašīr-Ḵorra (Schwarz, *Iran*, p. 94; Stein, p. 193). Ḥamza Eṣfahānī (I, p. 37; cf. Creswell, II, p. 21 n. 3), however, reported that the original layout of Dārāb was triangular and that its circular defensive wall was built in the 8th century by a governor of Fārs under Ḥajjāj b. Yūsof. Although Dārāb was eventually surpassed in size and wealth by Fasā, it remained the capital of a large district throughout most of the Middle Ages. It was particularly known for the manufacture of textiles, jasmine oil, and mineral salts of different colors. Its most famous product was *mūmīā*, a rare bituminous mineral oil used as a medicine; it was collected in a rock cave, whether in the city itself or in the nearby mountains, and formed the most precious part of the tribute to the governor of Fārs (Schwarz, *Iran*, pp. 95-97; Ouseley, pp. 117-21). The reputed unhealthy climate and bad water may have contributed to the total abandonment of Dārāb in about the 12th century or perhaps later (Ebn Ḥawqal, tr. Kramers, II, pp. 268, 273-74, 294; *Nozhat al-qolūb*, ed. Le Strange, p. 139; tr., p. 138).

Unlike the layout of Ardašīr-Ḵorra, that of Dārāb was not geometrically perfect; instead the course of the wall traces an irregular circle about 1,900 m in diameter. The four gates are not located on perpendicular axes, nor do the insignificant ruins within the city reveal a radial or concentric street system. At the north gate are the ruined piers of an aqueduct. The city center is a rocky outcrop with three peaks of different sizes. On the highest, at about 85 m, are the ruins of a citadel, which was enlarged and reinforced at least three times. A rock-cut passage below does not appear to be connected to it (Stein, pp. 191-94). A number of other fortresses are located on the mountains bordering the plain in the north. The most important is Qaṣr-e Šāhnešīn, or Gār-e Sīāh, northwest of Dārāb, where the ceramic finds included prehistoric sherds. Below are the ruins of a *čahār-tāq*, called Golābī, Pesar o Doḵtar, or Oğlan Qiz (> misunderstood Urlangaz), the dome of which was still standing in the 19th century (Ouseley, pl. 36; Forṣat Šīrāzī, pp. 101-02 fig. 10; de Miroschedji, pp. 157-60).

The rock reliefs at Naqš-e Rostam are located on the southern precipices of the mountain ridge between modern Dārāb and the plain. In addition to the reliefs already known (see iii, below), in 1990 another small relief, measuring 65 cm high, was found when the lake was drained; on it is depicted a king facing right and stabbing a lion standing on its hind legs. Farther east is Masjed-e Sangī, also known as Qaṣr-e Doḵtar, a rock-cut mosque of cruciform plan (Fasāʾī, II, pp. 200-01; Stein, pp. 196-99; Ball, pp. 103-07; Bier, pp. 117-30). Donor inscriptions dated 652/1254-55 include a name that has been debated, most recently read as Moḥammad b. Mobārez b. Ḥasan (S. Blair in Bier, p. 117). This building, together with a water-supply system, seems to have been a pious foundation connected with the nearby ruins of Jannat Šahr. A number of other settlements, reaching back to the Neolithic period, were surveyed by Sir Mark Aurel Stein (pp. 183-200), who also dug soundings in several of them.

Bibliography: A. Azarnoush, "Excavations at Hajiabad, 1977. First Preliminary Report," *Iranica Antiqua* 18, 1983, pp. 159-76. W. Ball, "Some Rock-Cut Monuments in Southern Iran," *Iran* 24, 1986, pp. 95-115. C. Barbier de Meynard, tr., *Dictionnaire de la Perse*, Paris, 1861. L. Bier, "The Masjid-i Sang Near Dārāb and the Mosque of Shahr-i Īj. Rock-Cut Architecture of the Il-Khanid Period," *Iran* 24, 1986, pp. 117-30. A. Creswell, *Early Muslim Architecture*, 2 vols., Oxford, 1940. E. Flandin and P. Coste, *Voyage en Perse . . . Perse ancienne* I, Paris, 1843, pp. 31-35, pls. 31-33. Moḥammad-Naṣīr Forṣat Šīrāzī, *Āṯār-e ʿajam*, Bombay, 1354/1935. Gītā Šenāsī, ed., *Map of Islamic Republic of Iran* 169, Tehran, 1363 Š./1984. N. Meshkati, *A List of the Historical Sites and Ancient Monuments of Iran*, Tehran, 1353 Š./1974. P. de Miroschedji, "Un *chahār ṭāq* dans la plaine de Darab," *Iran* 18, 1980, pp. 157-60. M.-T. Moṣṭafawī, *Eqlīm-e Pārs*, Tehran, 1343 Š./1964; tr. R. N. Sharp as *The Land of Pars*, Chippenham, Wilts., U.K., 1978. T. Nöldeke, "Über iranische Ortsnamen auf -kert und anderen Endungen," *ZDMG* 33, 1879, pp. 143-56. P. Oberling, *The Turcic Peoples of Southern Iran*, Ph.D. diss., Columbia University, New York, 1960. W. Ouseley, *Travels in Various Countries of the East, More*

Particularly Persia II, London, 1821, pp. 117-56. R. Pohanka, "Die Masdjed-e Djoume in Darab, Südiran," *Anz. der phil.-hist. Klasse der Österreichischen Akademie der Wissenschaften* 121, 1984, pp. 265-69. A. Stein, "An Archaeological Tour in the Ancient Persis," *Iraq* 3, 1936, pp. 111-230.

(DIETRICH HUFF)

iii. ROCK RELIEFS

Three rock reliefs are now known on the southern precipices of the mountain ridge between modern Dārāb and the plain; they are sited above a recently drained pool.

The best known is the Sasanian relief first recorded by Sir William Ouseley (pp. 145-48) and published by Leo Trümpelmann. It shows in the center the mounted figure of the emperor, wearing the crown of Ardašīr I (q.v.; 224-40). Behind him are rows of Sasanian courtiers; in front are two pleading figures. Under the emperor's horse lies a defeated enemy. Balancing the rows of Sasanians are rows of "Romans" arranged in tiers. There is no universally accepted interpretation of this scene, though the dating suggested by the different hypotheses varies only about thirty years, from the late 230s to the 260s. In these hypotheses what is depicted on the relief is identified either as a little-known victory of Ardašīr in the 230s (e.g., MacDermot, p. 74; Herrmann, 1969, pp. 63-88; idem, 1989, pp. 21-22); as an early relief of Šāpūr I (240-70) before his coronation (e.g., Ghirshman, 1971, pp. 103-06; Calmeyer, pp. 93-94); as the earliest of the victory reliefs of the emperor Šāpūr I (von Gall, pp. 99-104); or as a late relief of Šāpūr I, illustrating his defeat of Valerian (e.g., among others, Hinz, 1969, pp. 148-49, 173-82).

Below this relief is a small bust first noticed by Louis Vanden Berghe, who initially identified it as that of Anāhitā (1978, p. 72; see ANĀHĪD). A. Shapur Shahbazi has suggested that it represents Narseh's queen, Šāpūrduxtak II (1983, p. 265 n. 61).

Finally, the draining of the pool in 1369 Š./1990 revealed a third relief, showing a king stabbing a rampant lion, reported by Dietrich Huff but not yet published (see ii, above).

Bibliography: P. Calmeyer, "Zur Genese altiranischer Motive IV," *AMI*, N.S. 9, 1976, pp. 45-95. E. Flandin and P. Coste, *Voyage en Perse . . . Perse ancienne* I, Paris, 1843, esp. pp. 34-35, pl. 33. H. von Gall, *Das Reiterkampfbild in der iranischen und iranisch beeinflussten Kunst parthischer und sasanidischer Zeit*, Berlin, 1990. R. Ghirshman, *Iran. Parthians and Sassanians*, London, 1962, esp. pp. 160-61 fig. 206. Idem, *Bichâpour* I, Paris, 1971, esp. pp. 91-106. R. Göbl, *Der Triumph des Sāsāniden Shāhpuhr über Gordian, Philippus und Valerian*, Vienna, 1974; review R. Ghirshman, *Artibus Asiae* 37, 1975, pp. 313-18. G. Herrmann, "The Darabgird Relief—Ardashir or Shapur? A Discussion in the Context of Early Sasanian Sculpture," *Iran* 7, 1969, pp. 63-88. Idem, *The Sasanian Rock Reliefs at Naqsh-i Rustam. Naqsh-i Rustam 6. The Triumph of Shapur I*, Iranische Denkmäler 13, Iranische Felsreliefs I, Berlin, 1989, esp. pp. 18-23. E. Herzfeld, *Iran in the Ancient East*, London, 1941, esp. p. 314. W. Hinz, "Das sassanidische Felsrelief von Salmas," *Iranica Antiqua* 5, 1965, pp. 156-58. Idem, *Altiranische Funde und Forschungen*, Berlin, 1969, esp. pp. 145-171, pls. 75-99. B. C. MacDermot, "Roman Emperors in the Sasanian Reliefs," *Journal of Roman Studies* 44, 1954, pp. 76-80. A. Mazaheri, *Der Iran und seine Kunstschätze*, Geneva, 1970, esp. pls. 139-40. W. Ouseley, *Travels in Various Countries of the East, More Particularly Persia*, II, London, 1821, esp. pp. 145-48. E. Schmidt, *Persepolis* III, Chicago, 1970, esp. pp. 127-28. A. Sh. Shahbazi, "Some Remarks on the Sasanian Relief at Darabgird," in Summaries of Papers to be Delivered at the Sixth International Congress of Iranian Art and Archaeology, Oxford, September 1972, p. 76. Idem, "Studies in Sasanian Prosopography," *AMI* 16, 1983, pp. 255-68. D. Shepherd, "Sasanian Art," in *Camb. Hist. Iran* III/2, pp. 1055-1112, esp. p. 1082. J. M. C. Toynbee, *Roman Historical Portraits*, London, 1978. L. Trümpelmann, *Das sasanidische Felsrelief von Darab*, Iranische Denkmäler 6, Iranische Felsreliefs B, Berlin, 1975. L. Vanden Berghe, "La découverte d'une sculpture rupestre à Darabgird," *Iranica Antiqua* 13, 1978, pp. 135-47. Idem, *Archéologie de l'Iran ancien*, Leiden, 1959, esp. p. 46. Idem, *Reliefs rupestres de l'Iran ancien*, Brussels, 1983. E. de Waele, "L'investiture et le triomphe dans la thématique de la sculpture rupestre sassanide," in L. de Meyer and E. Haerinck, eds., *Archaeologia Iranica et Orientalis. Miscellanea in Honorem Louis Vanden Berghe*, Ghent, 1989, pp. 811-30.

(GEORGINA HERRMANN)

DARAB PAHLAN, DASTUR, Zoroastrian priest and author (b. Navsari, Gujarat, 1668, d. Navsari, 1 September 1734), eldest son of Pahlan Fredoon, who was accorded the title "dastur" (high priest) and the privilege of occupying the second chair in the Zoroastrian assembly of the small port of Navsari in 1670 or perhaps earlier; the first chair belonged to the family of Dastur Meherjirana and the third to the family of Dastur JamaspAsa. Darab Pahlan, a brilliant student, learned Avestan, Pahlavi, Pāzand, Sanskrit, and Persian under the tutelage of his father, whom he esteemed highly and to whom he ascribed his own knowledge. He was ordained a priest in Navsari in 1679. He wrote his first book in Persian, *K̲ōlāsa-ye dīn* (Exposition of religion), including his *Rūz-nāma* praising the thirty days of the Zoroastrian calendar month, in 1690, at the age of only twenty-two years; it was inspired by a visit to Surat, where he was the guest of Kaus Bahman and his son Jamshed. Three years later he published his second book, *Farżīyāt-nāma* (Book of duties), composed in Persian couplets, in which he defined the duties of a Zoroastrian from birth to death.

Darab assisted his father in the performance of his priestly duties, including the higher liturgical ceremonies in the Navsari *dar-e mihr* (*dar-e mehr*, q.v.). He also became known as a scribe and in 1694 copied a manuscript of the *Vidēvdād*. After his father's death in 1706 Darab was appointed dastur. He was a capable teacher and had many students in Pahlavi, Persian, and religious studies; foremost among them was Desai Khurshed Tehmulji. Many priests sought his advice, and laymen from various cities wrote to him inquiring about matters of religion, astrology, and prognostication. In particular he defended the rights of the Bhagarias (q.v.), local priests of Navsari, so-called because they distributed among themselves the receipts, or share (*bhāg*), from rituals, in their quarrels with the descendants of the immigrant priests of Sanjan.

Beside the works already mentioned Darab Pahlan wrote *monājāt*s, *Dīvān-e qāmūs*, *Saddar*, *Sroš Hādōxt*, *Enšā-ye Abu'l-Fażl*, all in Persian, and a Persian version of the ninth and tenth chapters of the *Yasna* based on Pahlavi and Sanskrit renderings. He also translated the *Yasna*, the *Vidēvdād*, and the *Ḵorda Avesta* into Gujarati.

He died at the age of sixty-seven years, leaving three sons: Kaus, Barzo, and Bahram.

Bibliography: Darab Pahlan, *The Persian Farziât-nâmeh and Kholâseh-i Dîn*, ed. J. J. Modi, Bombay, 1924.

(KAIKHUSROO M. JAMASP-ASA)

DĀRĀB-NĀMA, prose romance of the 12th century, by Abū Ṭāher Moḥammad b. Ḥasan b. ʿAlī b. Mūsā Ṭārsūsī (or Ṭarṭūsī), in which the adventures of the legendary Kayanid king Dārāb (q.v.), son of Bahman (also called Ardašīr) and Homāy, variously identified as the daughter of king Sām Čāraš of Egypt or of Ardašīr (=Bahman), are recounted. The tale also includes a story of Alexander the Great and his conquest of Persia in one of the Iranian variants of the Romance of Alexander by Pseudo Callisthenes. The text has been edited by Ḏabīḥ-Allāh Ṣafā. (For manuscripts see *Cat. Bodleian Library*, nos. 522, 787; Rieu, *Persian Manuscripts*, Supp., nos. 384 [16th century], 385 [99?/158?]; E. Blochet, *Bibliothèque Nationale, Catalogue des manuscrits persans* III, nos. 1201, 1202, Suppl., nos. 837, 838; Prince of Wales Museum, Bombay, no. 63.19; C. Stewart, *A Descriptive Catalogue of the Oriental Library of the late Tipoo Sultan of Mysore*, Cambridge, 1809, p. 7 no. xiv; Bibliotheca Lindesiana, Aberdeen, 1898, p. 109 no. 132 [1054/1644], now in the John Rylands Library, Manchester, Persian ms. no. 132; Ivanov, *Catalogue*, p. 138 no. 321 [17th century]; Aligarh University Library, no. 10/414 [see Ṭarsūsī, I, p. 25]; Akademiya Nauk, Institut Narodov Azii, *Persidskie i tadzhikskie rukopisi* [Persian and Tajik manuscripts], Moscow, 1964, nos. 1220, 1221; for Turkish versions, see E. Blochet, *Catalogue des manuscrits turques de la Bibliothèque Nationale* 2 vols., Paris, 1932-33, I, A.F. no. 107; II, no. 140; Monzawī, *Nosḵahā* V, pp. 3685-86.)

The story, in brief, is as follows: Homāy, the queen of Persia, is pregnant by her father, Ardašīr/Bahman, and gives birth to a son. She sets him afloat in a box on the Euphrates, where he is found by a launderer and given the name Dārāb. When he reaches the age of thirteen years, after a turbulent youth during which he proves his military prowess, Dārāb meets his mother, and they are reconciled. It is not yet time for him to assume the throne, so he sets off on a long series of adventures on land and sea. In Oman he falls in love with the widowed queen Ṭamrūsīa, of Greek origin. Together they flee by ship for the islands of Greece. The lovers encounter storms at sea, talismans, cannibals, and sea monsters and are saved from trouble by prophetic dreams, magical cures, and divine intervention. Circumstances separate the two, and Dārāb, now thirty years old, reaches an island, where he is crowned king and marries the former king's daughter.

Ṭamrūsīya meets her brother Mehrāsb, and together they undergo adventures among the Greek islands. They separate, and Mehrāsb marries a mermaid (*doḵtar-e ābī*). She returns to the sea after four years, and he sets sail, reaching an island of one-eyed people. He becomes their king and marries Gowharāsā, the former king's widow, whose sister Zankalīsā has married Dārāb. Gowharāsā dies, and Mehrāsb kills all her family. When Dārāb learns of this crime, he conquers the island and imprisons Mehrāsb. Ṭamrūsīa reaches Dārāb's island, and they marry. Dārāb's other wife, Zankalīsā, also arrives and kills her rival, but the newborn son of the latter survives. Dārāb names him Dārāb. Zankalīsā dies of snakebite, and Dārāb *père* sets out with his son to return to Persia.

While passing through Oman Dārāb learns that Homāy has been defeated in a battle with the Caesar of Rūm, who is descended from Salm the son of Ferīdūn and thus distantly related to Dārāb. Dārāb hastens to her aid, but before he can reach her Homāy is captured in battle at Ray. Dārāb rescues her, and she turns the throne over to him. The Caesar is eventually captured and held prisoner at Eṣṭaḵr. More fighting results in the defeat and capture of the Caesar's brother Fīlqūs, whose daughter Nāhīd is demanded by Dārāb as tribute. They are married, but Dārāb sends her back to her father, pregnant, because of her bad breath. She gives birth to Alexander in secret, and to avoid a scandal she leaves him on the mountain where Aristotle lives in a retreat. The infant is eventually found by an old woman, who nourishes him and rears him under the guidance of Aristotle. In the meantime, Dārāb dies, and Dārāb *fils* becomes king.

Alexander conquers the Persian army, and he and Dārāb, half-brothers, finally meet on the battlefield, as Dārāb lies dying. One of his last requests is that Alexander marry his daughter Būrān-doḵt (q.v.), also called Rowšanak. Būrān-doḵt does not agree to this marriage, and, being a spirited and warlike woman, she raises an army and battles with Alexander. The fighting ranges from Aleppo to Eṣṭaḵr in Fārs, where Alexander finally captures Būrān-doḵt. Again she refuses to marry him and escapes, soon proclaiming herself queen of Persia. After more fighting around Eṣṭaḵr, Alexander surprises her as she is bathing, and she finally agrees to marry him.

After they are wed Alexander installs Būrān-doḵt as queen of Persia and sets off to travel around the world with the object of conversing with sages and seeking the Water of Life. He first marches toward India, where he encounters the Indian king Kaydāvar. This king resists Alexander so strongly that he is forced to send to Būrān-doḵt for reinforcements. She herself leads the Persian forces into India and captures the king. Būrān-doḵt continues to aid Alexander in many ways, particularly against wizardry, because she is divinely protected against many natural hazards. In India she and Alexander have several adventures in which she is identified with, or aided by, water.

The campaigns in India end, and Alexander sets sail for the Arabian peninsula, passing through Mecca and pausing in Egypt. There he and Būrān-doḵt part ways, never to meet again. She returns to Persia, and he heads west in search of the Water of Life. The story ends as Alexander dies in Jerusalem and Būrān-doḵt dies shortly afterward in Persia (for a discussion of the relationship between Alexander and Būrān-doḵt and her possible identification with the Iranian goddess Anāhitā, see Hanaway).

This *Dārāb-nāma* should not be confused with another romance of the same name by Shaikh Ḥājī Moḥammad b. Shaikh Aḥmad b. Mawlānā ʿAlī b. Ḥājī Moḥammad, known as Bīḡamī (q.v.), which would be more accurately entitled *Fīrūzšāh-nāma* (q.v.). Ebn al-Nadīm (ed. Tajaddod, 2nd ed., p. 541) listed a *Ketāb Dārā wa'l-ṣanam al-ḏahab*, but its contents are unknown.

Popular romances like the *Dārāb-nama* were most certainly performed, rather than read silently, and therefore their primary existence was in the performance, rather than in a fixed text. The performing, as well as the literary, skills of the storyteller (*naqqāl, qeṣṣaḵᵛān*) must thus have played a large part in the general success of the story. Ṭārsūsī's written text of the *Dārāb-nāma* is simply one version of a long tale, the second part of which (the Alexander Romance) is known to have been recounted by many different storytellers over hundreds of years.

The *Dārāb-nama* is true to its generic nature as a romance. In Persian romances, both popular and courtly, instruction is combined with entertainment. Listeners are instructed in the traditional social and moral values of the Iranian common people, in contrast to those of the courtly elite. Popular romances thus complement courtly romances in preserving and transmitting traditional values. More specifically, the *Dārāb-nama* and other popular romances like the *Fīrūzšāh-nāma*, *Samak-e ʿayyār*, and *Eskandar-nāma* (q.v.) are focused on the moral value of kingship and the social value of relations between men and women.

The model for moral instruction is usually a prince, who matures from a callow youth into a responsible adult, or a hero from among the people (e.g., Samak the *ʿayyār*). In a typical tale the prince or hero leaves home, usually to pursue a woman with whom he has fallen in love. Once separated from his family, he must overcome a series of challenges before being reunited with his beloved and returning home. These challenges serve to test his bravery, instruct him in administrative or military skills, and teach him sexual restraint and a proper attitude toward women. They include a journey to the supernatural world of *parīs* (fairies) or to a culturally different region of the human world. In the *Dārāb-nāma* Dārāb travels about the Greek islands, and Alexander the Great journeys to India and later to the Land of Darkness. In the end the hero returns home, ready to marry and assume the responsibilities of kingship and adult life.

The *Dārāb-nama* links stories from the national legend about the fall of the Achaemenid dynasty with those of the conquest of Persia by Alexander the Great. There are both popular and courtly parallels to the Alexander Romance, which is part of the *Dārāb-nāma*. Regarding the genealogy of Alexander, for example, Ṭārsūsī followed the version of the Pseudo-Callisthenes Romance of Alexander, in which Dārāb and Alexander are half-brothers; the *Eskandar-nāma*, a popular prose romance from the 13th century (ed. Ī. Afšār), and Ferdowsī's account follow this version, whereas the versions of Neẓāmī and Amīr Ḵosrow are different.

Bibliography: ʿA.-Ḥ. Āyatī, "Dārāb-nāma-ye Ṭarsūsī," *Rāhnamā-ye ketāb* 9/4, 1345 Š./1966, pp. 419-25. W. Hanaway, "Anāhitā and Alexander," *JAOS* 102/2, 1982, pp. 285-95. M. Parvīn Gonābādī, "Dārāb-nāma," *Soḵan* 12, 1340 Š./1961, pp. 92-108. Abū Ṭāher Ṭarsūsī, *Dārāb-nāma-ye Ṭarsūsī*, ed. Ḏ. Safā, 2 vols., Tehran, 1344-46 Š./1965-67.

(WILLIAM L. HANAWAY)

DĀRĀBGERD. See DĀRĀB ii.

DĀRĀBĪ. See CITRUS FRUITS.

DĀRĀBĪ, SAYYED **JAʿFAR** b. Abī Esḥāq Mūsawī Borūjerdī Kašfī (b. Eṣṭahbānāt in Fārs, 1189/1775, d. Borūjerd 1267/1851), religious scholar, nephew of the Aḵbārī Yūsuf b. Aḥmad Baḥrānī and father of Sayyed Yaḥyā Waḥīd Dārābī (qq.v.).

His position on the dispute between Aḵbārīs (see AḴBARĪYA) and Oṣūlīs is unclear. Like his contemporaries Mīrzā Moḥammad Aḵbārī (q.v.; d. 1233/1818) and Asad-Allāh Borūjerdī (d. 1271/1854), Dārābī claimed intuitive knowledge (*kašf*) to be an alternative to the rational inquiry propounded by the Oṣūlī school of Twelver Shiʿism. On the other hand, his opposition to the continuation of Friday congregational prayer during the occultation of the twelfth imam, an opposition shared by many Aḵbārī Twelvers, was based on revelations received in a dream (Amanat, pp. 44-47; Ḥabībābādī, *Makārem*, p. 1856).

Dārābī was skilled in koranic exegesis and wrote as well on logic, grammar, Hadith, *oṣūl al-dīn* (fundamental principles of Islam), and theology. He composed both *Ejābat al-możṭarayn* and the abridgment *Kefāyat al-aytām* (completed 1259/1843) for Mīrzā Moḥammad-Taqī Ḥosām-al-Salṭana, governor of Borūjerd (*al-Ḏarīʿa* I, pp. 120-21, XVIII, pp. 88-89; Dānešpažūh, V, pp. 1988-89, VI, p. 2121). At Mīrzā Moḥammad-Taqī's behest, he composed *Toḥfat al-molūk fi'l-sayr wa'l-solūk* (1233/1817-18) in Persian and dedicated it to Fatḥ-ʿAlī Shah (1212-50/1797-1834); in this work he argued for the concurrent authority of the *mojtahed* (jurist) and the political ruler, defining the former as the spiritual deputy of the Imam and the second as the temporal deputy (Amir Arjomand, pp. 225-28; *al-Ḏarīʿa* III, p. 471).

Dārābī performed the *ḥajj* in 1260/1844, the same year as Mīrzā ʿAlī-Moḥammad, the Bāb (q.v.). Neither then nor after his son Sayyed Yaḥyā converted to Babism, a move that he is said to have discussed with his father, did Dārābī himself become a convert (Amanat, pp. 247-48; Balyuzi, pp. 70, 93-94; Browne, 1975, p. 8; idem, 1893, p. 347-48). He witnessed both his son's subsequent involvement and death in the failed Babi uprising in Neyrīz and the execution of the Bāb in 1266/1850.

Bibliography: A. Amanat, *Resurrection and Renewal. The Making of the Babi Movement in Iran, 1844-1850*, Ithaca, N.Y., 1989. S. Amir Arjomand, *The Shadow of God and the Hidden Imam*, Chicago, 1984, pp. 225-29, 232, 235-37. *Aʿyān al-Šīʿa* XV, s.v., pp. 262-63. H. M. Balyuzi, *The Bab. The Herald of the Day of Days*, Oxford, 1973. E. G. Browne, ed. and tr., *The Táríḵ-i-Jadíd, or New History of Mírzá ʿAlí Moḥammad, the Báb*, Cambridge, 1893, pp. 111, 231 n. 2. Idem, ed. and tr., *A Traveller's Narrative Written to Illustrate the Episode of the Bāb*, Amsterdam, 1975, pp. 183, 254. M.-T. Dānešpažūh, ed., *Fehrest-e ketāb-ḵāna-ye ehdāʾī-e Āqā-ye Sayyed Moḥammad Meškāt ba ketāb-ḵāna-ye dānešgāh-e Tehrān*, Tehran, 6 vols., 1332-35 Š./1953-56. *al-Ḏarīʿa* I, pp. 493, 498, 501; III, pp. 144, 471; IX/3, p. 911; XII, p. 232. Fasāʾī, II, pp. 178, 236. M.-T. Lesān-al-Molk Sepehr, *Nāseḵ al-tawārīḵ. Dawra-ye kāmel-e tārīḵ-e qājārīya*, ed. J. Qāʾemmaqāmī, III, Tehran, 1337 Š./1958, p. 121. M.-ʿA. Modarres Tabrīzī, *Rayḥānat al-adab* V, Tabrīz, 1327 Š./1948, pp. 60-62.

(ANDREW J. NEWMAN)

DĀRĀBĪ, SAYYED **YAḤYĀ** (b. Yazd, ca. 1226/1811, d. Neyrīz, 1266/1850), Babi leader usually known as Waḥīd (unique), a title given him by the Bāb (q.v.). The eldest son of Sayyed Jaʿfar Kašfī Eṣṭah-bānātī, he received a Muslim religious education and, like his father, was associated with the Qajar court (see DĀRĀBĪ, JAʿFAR; Sepehr, p. 121; Eʿteżād-al-Salṭana, p. 74).

In 1261/1846 Waḥīd was asked by Moḥammad Shah (1250-64/1834-48) and Ḥājī Mīrzā Āqāsī (q.v.) to investigate the claims being put forth by the Bāb (Nicolas, p. 233; Nabīl, pp. 171-72). He arrived in Shiraz in May, and, after three interviews, during the last of which the Bāb wrote his commentary on the koranic sura 108 (al-Kawṯar), he became a follower (Māzandarānī, pp. 465, 471-72; MacEoin, p. 71; Nabīl, pp. 174-76; Browne, pp. 111-13, 209). Two short essays in which Waḥīd described this encounter have been published (Māzandarānī, pp. 471-77; MacEoin, p. 117). Subsequently Waḥīd traveled extensively to preach Babism (q.v.), visiting Borūjerd to tell his father of the new faith; Isfahan; Ardestān; Tehran, where he stayed with Mīrzā Ḥosayn-ʿAlī Bahāʾ-Allāh (q.v.); Khorasan; Qazvīn, where he remained some months with his sister; Shiraz; and Yazd (Māzandarānī, pp. 465-70). In the winter of 1264/1847-48 he again visited the Bāb, who had been moved to Mākū (Māzandarānī, p. 468).

In 1265/1849, when news of the fighting between followers of the Bāb and government troops at the shrine of Shaikh Ṭabarsī in Māzandarān (see BABISM) reached him in Tehran, Waḥīd was determined to go there, but he learned from Bahāʾ-Allāh that the road was blocked by government troops. Instead he set off to the south, visiting Qom, Kāšān, Isfahan, and Yazd. There is contradictory evidence in the sources about the dates of his final stay in Yazd (Momen, pp. 108-09 and n.), where he succeeded in converting a number of important *ʿolamāʾ* and notables in the town and surrounding area. His activities were opposed, however, by some *ʿolamāʾ*, as well as by the acting governor, Āqā Khan Īravānī (Nabīl, pp. 466-75).

Waḥīd eventually left Yazd and went to Bavānāt and Eṣṭahbānāt, at each place effecting a number of conversions. In late May 1850 he arrived in Neyrīz (Nīrīz), where his father-in-law was imam of the Čenār-sūḵta quarter. Many of the inhabitants of Neyrīz are reported to have come to Eṣṭahbānāt to welcome him to Neyrīz (Nabīl, p. 476). Soon after his arrival in the latter city, however, his preaching of Babism in the Čenār-sūḵta mosque aroused opposition. The governor, Ḥājī Zayn-al-ʿĀbedīn Khan, recruited 1,000 local militia to prevent him and his followers from carrying on their activities. As a result the town became divided, the governor and his forces occupying the *bāzār* quarter and Waḥīd and the Babis the Čenār-sūḵta quarter and later the nearby fort of Ḵᵛāja. A dawn raid by the Babis routed the governor's forces, and further defeats caused him to withdraw to the village of Qoṭra. He then sent to Shiraz for reinforcements. Mīrzā Fażl-Allāh Naṣīr-al-Molk, acting on behalf of Fīrūz Mīrzā Noṣrat-al-Dawla, governor of Fārs, sent three regiments of infantry, together with cavalry and artillery. These forces were also defeated, in a pitched battle that lasted eight hours (Momen, pp. 109-10; Nabīl, pp. 481-88; Fasāʾī, I, pp. 304-05; tr. Busse, pp. 290-94).

In the end Zayn-al-ʿĀbedīn was forced to resort to a

ruse. He sent to Waḥīd a Koran on which he had supposedly sworn to guarantee safe passage for him and his men. When they emerged from the fort, however, they were set upon and killed or captured. Waḥīd himself was captured and put to death on 18 Šaʿbān 1266/6 June 1850 (Eʿteżād-al-Salṭana, pp. 77-78; Nabīl, pp. 488-95; Momen, pp. 110-11; Fasāʾī, I, p. 304; tr. Busse, p. 294). His head and those of some of his followers were sent to Shiraz (Momen, p. 111).

Bibliography: A. Amanat, *Resurrection and Renewal. The Making of the Babi Movement in Iran, 1844-1850*, Ithaca, N.Y., 1989. E. G. Browne, ed. and tr., E. G. Browne, ed. and tr., *The Tārīḵ-i-Jadīd, or New History of Mīrzā ʿAlī Moḥammed, the Bāb*, Cambridge, 1893; repr. as *The New History . . .*, Amsterdam, 1975. Eʿteżād-al-Salṭana, *Fetna-ya Bāb*, 3rd ed., ed. ʿA.-Ḥ. Navāʾī, Tehran, 1362 Š./1983, esp. pp. 74-78. M.-A. Feyżī, *Neyrīz-e moškbīz*, Tehran, 130 Badīʿ=1352 Š./1973, pp. 3-88. Hedāyat, *Rawżat al-ṣafā* X, pp. 456-59. B. Maʿānī, "Neyrīz," in *A Short Encyclopedia of the Bahá'í Faith*, Wilmette, Ill., forthcoming. Idem, "Vaḥīd," in *A Short Encyclopedia of the Bahá'í Faith*, Wilmette, Ill., forthcoming. D. MacEoin, *The Sources for Early Bābī Doctrine and History. A Survey*, Leiden, 1992. F. Māzandarānī, *Ketāb-e ẓohūr al-ḥaqq* III, Tehran, n.d., pp. 461-81. Ḡ. Mawlānā, *Tārīḵ-e Borūjerd* II. *Danešmandān-e Borūjerd*, Tehran, n.d., pp. 307-13. M. Momen, *The Bābī and Bahāʾī Religions, 1844-1944. Some Contemporary Western Accounts*, Oxford, 1981, pp. 106-13. Nabīl Zarandī, *The Dawn-Breakers. Nabīl's Narrative of the Early Days of the Bahāʾī Revelation*, tr. Shoghi Effendi, Wilmette, Ill., 1962, pp. 171-77, 465-99. A. L. M. Nicolas, *Seyyèd Ali Mohammed dit le Bāb*, Paris, 1905, pp. 233-35, 387-409. M. S. Rawḥānī Neyrīzī, *Lamʿāt al-anwār* I, Tehran, 130 Badīʿ=1352 Š./1973, pp. 40-129. M.-T. Lesān-al-Molk Sepehr, *Nāsek al-tawārīḵ. Dawra-ye kāmel-e tārīḵ-e Qājārīya*, ed. J. Qāʾemmaqāmī, 3 vols., Tehran, 1337 Š./1958, pp. 121-24.

(MOOJAN MOMEN)

DARAFŠ-E KĀVĪĀN. See DERĀFŠ-E KĀVĪĀN.

DĀRĀʾĪ, WEZĀRAT-E. See FINANCE MINISTRY.

DARĀMAD (lit., "introduction"), an episode in the course of a musical performance, the nature and length of which vary with the material introduced. The *darāmad* of a modal system (*dastgāh*, q.v.) is thus more developed than that of one of its sections (*gūšas*). Only when the *darāmad* is long enough to constitute a distinct entity is it recognized in the nomenclature of the *gūšas* of a modal system (*āvāz*, q.v., or *dastgāh*), for example, *darāmad-e Šūr* or *darāmad-e Zābol*. In other instances the *darāmad* consists only of the few introductory notes of a melodic type (small *gūša*; Tsuge, p. 225). The general concept of the *darāmad* can also be extended to include the entire group of sections placed at the beginning of a *dastgāh*, expressing the essential character (*māya*) of the mode (Nettl, p. 68) in a relatively restricted register independent of its modulations, so that it can be identified instantly. In both form and function the *darāmad* properly so-called expresses the fundamental character of a *dastgāh* or large *gūša*; in this sense the *darāmad* or *darāmads* of Māhūr represent Māhūr itself, less as a composite modal system (*dastgāh* or *radīf*) than as a fundamental mode (*maqām*). For this reason, though in a free performance *gūša* or *dastgāh* may be omitted, it is impossible to omit the *darāmad*.

The *darāmād* begins in the lower register of the mode, with a fairly limited range and in a slow tempo; it gradually expands to include the essential intervals in a precisely determined order and with typical motifs ("signatures") contributing to its identification (During, pp. 136-39; Nettl, pp. 43-64); in singing it does not normally have a text (for further details, cf. Masʿūdīya, p. 7). Certain *gūšas* that occur (sometimes several in succession) at the beginning of a *dastgāh* and fulfill these same criteria are known either by the generic term *darāmad*; by a proper name, for example, *darāmad-e Ḵārā, darāmad-e Zang-e Šotor* (i.e., "introduction known as Ḵārā," "introduction known as Zang-e Šotor"), and so on; or by its function and position (e.g., second or third *darāmad*). This terminology also varies somewhat in the *radīf* (sequence of *āvāzes* and *dastgāhs*) of each master.

The term *moqaddama* can be considered a synonym for *darāmad* (Nettl, p. 68), though sometimes it has overtones suggesting that it appears first. Measured introductory pieces, in the sense of *moqaddama* or *pīš-darāmad*, like Koroḡlī in Māhūr, have sometimes been called *darāmad*.

The term *darāmad* is not found in other musical traditions, except in the Azerbaijan *radīf*, where it has the meaning of a measured preamble (corresponding to the Persian *pīš-darāmad*); the Azerī equivalent of *darāmad* is called *māya* (mode).

Bibliography: J. During, *La musique iranienne. Tradition et évolution*, Paris, 1984. M. Maʿrūfī, *Radīf-e haft dastgāh-e mūsīqī-e īrānī/Les systèmes de la musique traditonnelle iranienne (radīf)*, Tehran, 1342 Š./1963; 2nd ed., Tehran, 1352 Š./1973. M.-T. Masʿūdīya (Massoudieh), *Radīf-e āvāzī-e mūsīqī-e sonnatī-e Īrān/Radīf vocal de la musique iranienne*, Tehran, 1357 Š./1978. B. Nettl, *The Radif of Persian Music. Studies of Structures and Cultural Context*, Champaign, Ill., 1987. G. Tsuge, "Rhythmic Aspects of the Avaz in Persian Music," *Ethnomusicology* 14, 1970, pp. 205-27.

(JEAN DURING)

DARĀZ-DAST. See DERĀZ-DAST; ARDAŠĪR; BAHMAN.

DARB-E EMĀM, large shrine complex in the old Sonbolestān quarter of Isfahan (number 217 in the official register of Persian national monuments), centered on a burial chamber identified in an 18th-century inscription (see below) as that of Ebrāhīm Baṭḥā (or Ṭabāṭabāʾī?), a descendant of one Ḥasan Moṯannā, and Zayn-al-ʿAbedīn, believed to have been the son of Imam Jaʿfar al-Ṣādeq. The main structure, consisting of entrance portal (*sar-dar*), vestibule, and tomb, was built in 857/1453 and expanded and modified several times during the Safavid period (Figure 1).

The elaborate portal of the main structure, entered on the north side, is faced with tile mosaics, considered among the finest specimens of such work in Persia and comparable to the contemporary mosaics at the Blue Mosque (Masjed-e kabūd) in Tabrīz. The portal opening consists of a pointed arch contained within a rectangular frame in which lozenge- and cross-shaped tiles alternate against a background filled with floral designs; the spandrels are filled with symmetrical compositions of vine stems and flowers. The interior side walls are paneled with geometric designs emanating from central ten-pointed stars, and panels with centralized floral designs flank the doorway.

A Persian inscription in white *ṯolṯ* script (see CALLIGRAPHY) on a dark-blue ground encircles the interior of the portal at the springing of the arch, though the final words have disappeared. The surviving portion reads: "When the ruler of the greatest domain, lord of the mightiest realm, and sovereign protector of the world Abu'l-Moẓaffar Mīrzāda Jahānšāh, may God perpetuate his stewardship, entrusted the government of this province to the care and direction of the prince, the support of the pillars of the religion of Moḥammad Abu'l-Fatḥ Moḥammadī, may God sustain his rule, the great and most just commander and the repository of grandeur and majesty Jalāl-al-Dīn Ṣafaršāh, may God enlarge his fortune. . . ." Partly on the basis of a painted inscription preserved on the walls of the vestibule (Godard, pp. 52-53), Jalāl-al-Dīn Homāʾī suggested completing the portal inscription thus: "undertook the erection of this majestic shrine and mighty edifice, seeking the pleasure of God, in the year 857." Abu'l-Moẓaffar Mīrzāda Jahānšāh, the Qarā Qoyunlu ruler (841-72/1438-67), had captured Isfahan two years earlier. Moḥammadī, called Moḥammad-Solṭān in a Persian poem inscribed under the small dome of the vestibule and dated 857, was Moḥammadī Mīrzā, son of Jahānšāh and at that time ruler of Isfahan as his father's deputy under the tutelage of Lala Ṣafaršāh (Abū Bakr Ṭehrānī, pp. 326-30; pace Godard, pp. 53-54).

Figure 1. Plan of the Darb-e Emām complex, Isfahan. After Golombek and Wilber, II, fig. 126.

In the interior corners of the portal above the tile inscription two *moqarnas* squinches flank a central latticed window framed by three Persian verse couplets in tile work. The semidome (*nīm-kāsa*) rests on a squinch net of tile mosaic.

The tomb chamber itself is covered by an onion-shaped dome on a cylindrical drum. The mosaic facing of the exterior was restored in 1010/1601-02 and again in 1325 Š./1946 by the Department of antiquities (Edāra-ye bāstān-šenāsī; Honarfar, p. 346 n. 1). Fragments of Safavid inscriptions remain on the drum, including the koranic surah LXXVI in Kufic script and the building inscription in white *ṯolṯ* on a turquoise ground.

In the centuries that followed the initial construction of Darb-e Emām a number of additional tombs were constructed in the vestibule and surrounding the shrine. None of the tombstones in the vestibule bears a name or date. Eventually their number forced the closing of the original entrance, during the reign of Shah Solaymān (1077-1105/1666-94). The door was replaced by a long window with a grill of interlaced star patterns, and the shrine had thenceforth to be entered directly from the south. A helmet-shaped dome on a cylindrical drum was raised over the vestibule, thus increasing the space of the shrine itself, without altering the basic plan. The inscription on the exterior of the drum was executed by Moḥammad-Reżā Emāmī in 1081/1671 in *ṯolṯ* on a background of azure tiles with lozenge designs.

In 1127/1715 Shah Solṭān-Ḥosayn constructed a new portal to the east of the original. The date is given in a large inscription band in white on dark-blue tile mosaic, which encircles the three sides of the entrance passage. Below it, immediately above the central doorway, is an Arabic inscription on square tiles in two registers: "The refurbishment of this shrine, dedicated to *mawlānā sayyed-al-sājedīn*, in which are the tombs of the two *sayyed*s Emāmzāda Ebrāhīm Baṭḥā and Emāmzāda Zayn-al-ʿAbedīn, took place on the order of Nawwāb Ḵāqān b. Ḵāqān, the greatest of the Safavid shahs mentioned above [in the upper inscription]. Written by the lowly ʿAbd-al-Raḥīm in 1129 [1717]." The tympanum above the inscriptions on the back wall is faced with tile mosaic in a geometric design. A series of rooms was built leading from this portal to an anteroom south of the shrine (Godard, pp. 55-56).

Today the Darb-e Emām complex encompasses a

number of units arrayed around three square courtyards respectively north, east, and west of the original structure. From the northern courtyard both the original and later portals are visible; from the eastern courtyard a series of blind arches (*tāq-nāmas*), some containing latticed windows and doorways; and from the western courtyard porticos ornamented with *moqarnas* of polychromed stucco and mosaic spandrels (*pošt-e baḡals*). The central portico in this wing once housed a fine 15th-century stained-glass window mounted in plaster; some years ago it was removed and installed in one of the rooms of the Čehel Sotūn (q.v.) in Isfahan.

Bibliography: Abū Bakr Ṭehrānī, *Ketāb-e dīārbakrīya*, ed. N. Lugal and F. Sümer, Ankara, 1964; repr. Tehran, 1356 Š./1977. M.-H. Čahārsūqī, *Mīzān al-ansāb. Šarḥ-e ḥāl-e emām-zādagān-e Eṣfahān*, ed. A. Rawżātī, Qom, 1379/1959. A. Godard, "Iṣfahān," *Āthār-é Īrān* 2/1, 1937, esp. pp. 47-57. L. Golombek and D. Wilber, *The Timurid Architecture of Iran and Turan*, 2 vols., Princeton, N.J., 1988. L. Honarfar, *Ganjīna-ye āṯār-e tārīḵī-e Eṣfahān. Āṯār-e bāstānī wa alwāḥ wa katībahā-ye tārīḵī dar ostān-e Eṣfahān*, Isfahan, 1344 Š./1965, pp. 341-53. A. Rafīʿī Mehrābādī, *Āṯār-e mellī-e Eṣfahān*, Tehran, 1352 Š./1963, pp. 765-72.

(PARVĪZ VARJĀVAND)

DARBAND (Ar. Bāb al-Abwāb), ancient city in Dāḡestān on the western shore of the Caspian Sea (qq.v.), located at 42° 3′ N and 48° 18′ E at the entrance to the narrow pass (3-3.5 km wide) between the Caucasus foothills and the sea.

Name. The ancient city must have been one of the four coastal cities of Caucasian Albania mentioned by Ptolemy in his *Geography* (cf. sketch in Murav'ev, p. 121); nevertheless, specific identification with Gaitara, Albana (Isakov, 1959, p. 147; cf. Hewsen, 1984), Gelda (Kudryavtsev, 1982a, pp. 62, 105), or Telaiba remains hypothetical. In early Armenian sources the city was called Čor/Čoł (*Ełišē*, ed. Tēr-Minasean, pp. 74, 75); in the 11th century Movsēs Dasxurancʿi used both variants, as well as the earlier Armenian genitive Čołay/Čoray as a nominative (pp. 87, 91, 105, 257). This Armenian name is to be connected with Tzour, documented in Byzantine sources as the name of the pass (Procopius, *De Bello Gothico*, 4(8).3-4); Tzon (in some manuscripts Chorytzon; Menander, ed. Blockley, pp. 70 fr. 6.1, 255 n. 48); Zōarou (gen. sing.) in the Greek rendering of Čoray by the Armenian Agathangełos (*Patmutʿiwn Hayocʿ* par. 10: cf. Lafontaine, pp. 178-79); evidently Syriac Ṭūrāyē in the *Chronicle* of Michael the Syrian (Marquart, p. 489; cf. Altheim and Stiehl, p. 110); and Arabic Ṣūl (e.g., Ṭabarī, I/2, pp. 895, 896). According to A. A. Kudryavtsev (1979a, p. 39), the city is still called Churul/Chulli in Dāḡestān languages today (cf. Hübschmann, *Armenische Grammatik*, p. 219). The Middle Persian reading Vīrōi-pahr (*wylwd̠ p'hl*; Nyberg, *Manual* I, p. 114; Utas, p. 118) for the fortress of Darband is unsubstantiated in texts (D. N. MacKenzie, personal communication, 7 July 1990). The name of the pass, documented in many languages and various forms, was also frequently ascribed to the city.

The name Darband is first attested for the city in the 7th-century *Geography* incorrectly attributed to Moses of Khorene ([Pseudo] Moses of Khorene, ed. Soukry, p. 27 ll. 12-13). Although Kudryavtsev (1978, p. 245 and n. 20) reported it from 6th-century Middle Persian inscriptions on the city wall, it has not been possible to corroborate his report. The contemporary Russian name Derbent is derived from modern Persian *darband* (*dar* "gate" + *band* "bar," lit., "barred gate"), referring to the adjacent pass. In Arabic texts the city was known as Bāb wa'l-Abwāb, Bāb al-Abwāb, or simply al-Bāb (Balāḏorī, *Fotūḥ*, index; Masʿūdī, *Morūj*, ed. Pellat, I, pp. 305-06, 312; Yāqūt, *Boldān*, I, p. 439, distinguishing it from Bāb Ṣūl, which has caused considerable confusion). The view of H. S. Nyberg (*Manual* II, p. 56) that Čōl was a city in the vicinity of Darband and the differentiation between Čor and the pass of Čor (Trever, table 42; Hewsen, 1987) are thus incorrect.

Confusion has also arisen from mistaken identification in ancient sources of the pass at Darband with the Dar'yal pass in the central Caucasus (e.g., Procopius; cf. Gagloev; Kretschmer; Gerland). The term Caspian Gates in particular was used inconsistently. Although it originally designated a pass near modern Tehran (Strabo, 11.12.4; see Kolendo, correcting Anderson), it came to be applied also and eventually exclusively to the pass at Darband (Sebeos, p. 173). In some ancient sources the location of the Caspian gates is unclear (Lucan, *Prometheus* 4; Arrian, *Anabasis* 7.10.6; Cassius Dio, *Roman History* 62 [63].8.1). In others (Josephus, *Antiquitates* 18.4.4; John Malalas, *Chronicon* 406, 472) the Dar'yal pass was probably meant; Tacitus (*Annals* 6.33.3) connected the "Caspian route" with the Dar'yal pass and clearly distinguished it from the "passage between the sea and the end of the Albanian mountains" (Aliev, 1986, pp. 113-14; cf. *Histories* 1.6.2: *claustra Caspiarum*, referring to the Darband pass; pace Heubner, p. 34; Koestermann, p. 321). Diodorus Siculus (*Bibliothēkē* 2.2.3) seems to have understood the Caspian Gates as the pass of Darband. Particularly important is Suetonius' remark in his biography of Nero (19.1) that the emperor was preparing for war against the Albanians, with a clear indication that he identified the Caspian Gates with the Darband pass. In the 9th century Theophanes designated both the Dar'yal and Darband passes as the Caspian Gates (*Chronography*, ed. C. de Boor, I, pp. 161, 315-16).

More caution is required in interpreting the terms *porta Caspiaca* (Statius, *Silvae* 4.4.63-64), *Caspiae pylae* (Pomponius Mela, *Chorography* 1.81), *Caspia claustra* (Valerius Flaccus, *Argonautica* 5.124; Lucan, *Pharsalia* 8.22; Claudianus, *In Rufinum* 2.28), and *Alexandri claustra* (Jerome, 77:8; cf. Abel). In other classical texts *Sarmaticae portae* (e.g. Pliny, *Historia*

Naturalis 6.30) or *Sarmatikai pylai* (Ptolemy, *Geography* 5.8.5, 5.8.9) and *portae Caucasiae* (with variants) or *Kaukasiai pylai* are identified with the Dar'yal pass on the Georgian military road (cf. Mittelhaus), *Albaniai pylai* with the Darband pass (Ptolemy, 5.9.15, 5.12.6; cf. Chaumont, 1973; Hewsen, 1987). If, however, the latter were indeed located above the ancient Albanian capital, Cabalaca/Kapałak (Tomas-chek, "Albaniai Pylai"), identification with the Darband pass would be out of the question. The mountain fortress Iouroeipaach, situated at the Caspian Gates (Priscus, fr. 41, *Excerpta* 15; Blockley, pp. 346-47; cf. John Lydus, 3.52: Biraparach; cf. Bandy, pp. 212-13), for which the Romans paid subsidies, is to be identified with the Dar'yal pass (Tomaschek, "Biraparach"; Justi, in *Grundriss* II, p. 535). Peoples advancing from areas north of the Caucasus were able to penetrate into Roman territory through this pass; had they already advanced through the Darband pass to Azerbaijan and into Media, the Romans would hardly have been interested in maintaining a border patrol there (pace Peeters, 1935, pp. 282-83, referring to an inscription from the reign of the emperor Marcianus [450-57] supposedly discovered in Darband in 716; cf. Trever, pp. 273-74). The Greek names Iouroeipaach and Biraparach were derived from the Armenian for "Georgian fortress" (assuming that *Virḳ*=Iberians); *wyrwphrg* is documented in Syriac (Markwart, *Ērānšahr*, p. 103). Confusion arose when Heinrich Hübschmann (*Armenische Grammatik*, p. 36) and Josef Markwart (*Ērānšahr*, pp. 100-02) identified the fortress with that in Darband; Markwart and later Nyberg incorrectly read as *Iwroy pahak*) to gates that lay parallel to the Gates of the Alans; they thus equated the name with the fortress of *pahak*) to gatesthat lay parallel to the Gates of the Alans; they thus equated the name with the fortress of Darband and the derived Greek names Biraparach and Iouroeiparach with the adjacent pass (Asdourian, p. 123; Peeters, p. 285; Dunlop, 1954, p. 19; see ALBANIA, p. 806; for a related but apparently undocumented Virattarak, see Hewsen, 1987; idem, 1984). Other authors who have associated the Greek names with the Caspian Gates have offered only ambiguous documentation (e.g. Ensslin, col. 1953). No Middle Iranian name for the Darband pass appears in the 3rd-century inscriptions on stone; André Maricq has found little support for his identification of *'l'nn TR"* with the Darband pass and his addition of *py[l]ō[n Alban]ōn* to the Greek version (pp. 80-89). Parthian Dar i Alān, from which the name Dar'yal was derived, is to be connected with *Dareine atrapos* (path, ravine), preserved by Menander (fr. 10. 5, *Excerpta* 9; ed. Blockley, pp. 126-27 and n. 149, 266-67; for later Georgian documentation, cf. Tomaschek, "Dareine atrapos"); the Dar'yal pass is also called the Gates of the Alans in the Armenian texts (e.g. Ełišē, ed. Tēr-Minasean, p. 198).

The most frequent and clearest documentation of the name of the pass at Darband is found in the Armenian sources in several variations, here cited uniformly in the nominative (Agathangelos, *Patmutᶜiwn Hayocᶜ* par. 19; tr. Thomson, pp. 36-37: "the sentry of Chor"; Pᶜarpecᶜi, p. 66: "sentry of the wall," probably from a misspelling of *pahak Čoray*; [Pseudo] Moses of Khorene: "city of *pahak Čoray*"; cf. Ełišē, ed. Tēr-Minasean, pp. 12, 94, 198; tr. Thomson, pp. 66, 146, 242; Sebeos, pp. 69, 104, 169, tr. pp. 7, 52, 139; Moses of Khorene, 2.65, 3.12; tr. Thomson, pp. 211, 265; Dasxurancᶜi, p. 13; tr., p. 9). Other documented variants include *kapankᶜ Čoray* "pass/defile of Chor" (Sebeos, p. 173, tr. p. 144), *pahak Honacᶜ* "garrison of the Huns" (Ełišē, ed. Tēr-Minasean, pp. 43, 78, 142; tr. Thomson, pp. 94, 129, 193), *Honacᶜ dur̄n* "gate of the Huns" (Sebeos, p. 173; tr., p. 144), *dur̄n Čoray* (more often written *dur̄n Čołay*) "gate of Chor" (Dasxuranc'i, pp. 70, 82, 110, 148, tr. pp. 55, 155 [with the addition "which is near Darband"], 190), and *drunkᶜ Čołay* (Dasxurancᶜi, p. 110) or simply *drunkᶜ* "gates" (Ełišē, ed. Tēr-Minasean, p. 94; tr. Thomson, p. 146 and n. 8). The "gate of Ṭūrāyē," mentioned in the *Chronicle* of Michael the Syrian (d. 1199), was interpreted by Markwart and Altheim and Stiehl as a translation of Armenian *pahak Čoray*, Ṭūrāyē being recognized as an equivalent of Čor (cf. most recently Dzhafarov, 1985, p. 19). In the 6th century Pseudo Zacharias Rhetor (*Ecclesiastical History* 7.3) wrote of the "gates that guard the way to Persia." The "gate of Chor" corresponds to Arabic Bāb Ṣūl (cf. Ṭabarī, I/2, p. 896) and Sadd Darband, "which is Bāb al-Abwāb" (Ḥamza, I, p. 57). Bāb al-Abwāb/al-Bāb eventually came to designate the city itself (Eṣṭaḵrī, p. 184; Moqaddasī, p. 376; Ebn Rosta, pp. 148-49; Ebn Ḥawqal, p. 342; tr. Kramers, p. 335).

History. Owing to excavations conducted by Soviet archeologists beginning in 1971, the history of Darband can be traced back as far as the late 4th millennium B.C.E.; finds of stone and bronze axes and pottery suggest that the peak of the hill was settled by then. In the 1st millennium B.C.E. the history of Darband was closely linked to events north of the Caucasus and on the Eurasian steppes in general (cf. Kudryavtsev, 1979a, pp. 31-32), and the fortress was important in the defense of areas south of the Caucasus. Similarities between the pottery finds and those from farther north in Dāḡestān strongly suggest an ethnic and cultural unity among the population. In fact, the initial fortification of the hill at the end of the 8th century B.C.E. appears to have been a response by the indigenous population to Scythian invasions from the north (Herodotus, 1.104.2; cf. Kudryavtsev, 1982a, p. 166); it is clear that the strategic location and the natural advantages of the terrain were already appreciated (see sketch in Kudryavtsev, 1982a, p. 30). Archeologists have identified a period of construction subdivided into pre-Scythian (9th-6th centuries B.C.E.: settlement covering 4-5 ha on the protected northeastern side of the hill), Scythian (6th-5th centuries: settlement of the entire hill, ca. 15 ha), and late Scythian (5th-4th centuries) phases. The walls apparently attained a maximum height of 2 m and a maximum thickness of 7 m. The fortress seems to have been destroyed repeatedly during this and the following periods.

The so-called "Albano-Sarmatian period" is dated by the excavators from the 4th century B.C.E. to the Sasanian occupation in the 4th century C.E. At the beginning of this period the hill became the citadel of an expanding city. The varied and often conflicting names in the sources complicate historical interpretation (see above). It appears, however, that, with the political and economic development of Caucasian Albania in the first three centuries C.E., Darband experienced a new prosperity, accompanied by commercial expansion and social differentiation within the population. Neither Albania nor the city of Darband seems to have been conquered by the Romans in their struggle with the Parthians for hegemony in the Caucasus; nor, despite claims in the Armenian sources, is Armenian influence recognizable in the region. Coins and architectural details are evidence of interaction with the Parthians (cf. ALBANIA, p. 807), yet there was probably no direct dependence, and the presence of a Parthian garrison cannot be confirmed.

Both the pass and the citadel first came to the attention of the ancient Mediterranean world through reports of Pompey's campaign in 65 B.C.E. and of Nero's supposed plans for the conquest of Albania. At the time of Pompey's campaign Darband apparently already belonged to the kingdom of Albania and was probably located on its northern border (cartographic representations of the border are based on speculation; cf. Trever, table 42). As attacks by northern peoples became more frequent (Maskʿutʿkʿ and from the end of the 4th century Huns), Darband came to be the most important bastion and the symbolic boundary between nomadic and agrarian ways of life.

Darband was probably drawn into the Sasanian sphere of influence as a result of the victory over the Parthians and the conquest of Caucasian Albania by Šāpūr I (240-70 C.E.; *ŠKZ*, Parth. l. 2, Gk. l. 3; cf. Kudryavtsev, 1979a, p. 35; Akopyan, appendix 2). Šāpūr identified "the gate of the Alans" as the border of his realm but not as the Albanian border (*ŠKZ*, Parth. l. 2; cf. *KKZ*, Parth. l. 12, *KNRm*, Parth. l. 39). Some modern scholars identify "the gate of the Alans" with the pass of Darband (Cereṭeli; Back, pp. 187-88; for another view, see Kasumova, 1979; idem, 1988, p. 88) and would thus interpret Šāpūr's "gate of the Alans" as the Albanian border, but in this author's view that is incorrect. Sasanian rulers must have endeavored to prevent the advance of peoples from the north along the Caspian coast and to protect the northern provinces of their realm. Albania remained Sasanian, though the precise position of its boundaries is obscure; Kudryavtsev (1978, p. 244; idem, 1982a, pp. 67-69), relying on historically worthless information in the so-called *Augustan History*, ascribes renewed Sasanian attempts to dominate Albania to Šāpūr II (309-79), following his defeat of the Romans near Amida in 359 (cf. Akopyan, map presupposing the loss of the entire coastal region before the 5th century). The Sasanians were certainly stronger in the Caucasian kingdoms after the peace treaty of Šāpūr III (383-88) with the Byzantines, concluded in 384 or 387, but a late 4th-century date for the construction of stone fortifications at Darband (Isakov, 1941, p. 156; Gropp, 1975, pp. 317-20, 330-31) can be ruled out. The earlier hypothesis of a gradual Sasanian advance into the northern areas of Caucasian Albania, accompanied by construction of defensive walls, is generally rejected today (Kudryavtsev, 1979a, p. 34). In the 5th century Darband functioned as a border fortress (Ełišē, ed. Tēr-Minasean, p. 198; pace Trever) and the seat of a *marzbān* (Ełišē, ed. Tēr-Minasean, p. 74; Dasxurancʿi, p. 87; on the political role of Darband, see Gignoux). Archeological findings reveal similarities with contemporary Azerbaijan coupled with differences from Dāḡestān (pace Kudryavtsev, 1978, p. 253; idem, 1982a, p. 81, emphasizing contacts with peoples beyond the borders).

During periods when the Sasanians were distracted by war with the Byzantines or protracted battles with the Hephthalites in the eastern provinces, the northern tribes succeeded in advancing into the Caucasus. The first Sasanian attempt to seal off the road along the Caspian seacoast at Darband by means of a mud-brick wall (maximum thickness 8 m, maximum height ca. 16 m) has been dated by Kudryavtsev (1976a, pp. 87-92) to 439-50, in the reign of Yazdegerd II (438-57; cf. Ełišē, ed. Tēr-Minasean, p. 78; cf. Khan-Magomedov, 1966, p. 229: Kavād I; Kudryavtsev, 1978, pp. 250-51: both Yazdegerd and Kavād). It was clearly intended to protect the rich and fertile areas south of the Caucasus from the invading tribes. Little attention has been paid to the possibility that this wall was actually a reconstruction of earlier, damaged defenses. At any rate, in 450 rebellious Armenians and Albanians destroyed the fortifications, and in the regin of Pērōz (459-84) the Huns, led by Ambazuk, temporarily occupied the city.

In about 503 the Sabir Huns advanced on Darband (Dzhafarov, 1979, p. 166; Kasumova, 1988, p. 94). Archeologists date the next reconstruction to the second reign of Kavād I (498-531; cf. Masʿūdī, *Morūj*, ed. Pellat, I, p. 209; Ebn al-Faqīh, p. 343). Probably after 508, though the date is disputed, the long fortification walls at Besh Barmak and Šīrvān/Gil'ginchaĭ were constructed in a combination of mud brick, stone blocks, and baked bricks; as they probably served as models for the massive rebuilding of the fortifications at Darband (Khan-Magomedov, 1979, p. 40), their construction serves as a terminus post quem for the latter. The new city wall at Darband consisted of a core of rough stone blocks set in limestone mortar and faced with limestone slabs. Three building phases have been identified, extending almost to the end of the reign of Ḵosrow I (531-79; Artamonov, 1946, pp. 129, 131; pace Gropp, 1977, pp. 1622-25), who is often credited in the Arabic sources with the entire construction (e.g., Ṭabarī, I/2, p. 896; Balāḏorī, *Fotūḥ*, pp. 195-96);

certainly conditions would have been most favorable after the peace treaty with the Byzantines in 562 (Artamonov, 1962, p. 125). The wall measured 3,650 m on the north side and 3,500 m on the south. These two sides, which were 350-450 m apart (Spasskiĭ), extended on the east to the Caspian shore (cf. Kudryavtsev, 1979, p. 33), enclosing the harbor; the water level was much lower than it is today (Leont'ev and Fedorov; Huff; see CASPIAN). On the southwest the city wall joined the mountain wall (for photographs, see Khan-Magomedov, 1979), which extended west more than 40 km (Arabic sources: 7 farsakhs) into the wooded, virtually impassable mountains. This fortified wall, with its seven gates, apparently connected already existing freestanding fortifications (cf. Khan-Magomedov, 1966, pp. 235-37, 242-43; cf. idem, 1979, p. 208); it was never completed. The stone city wall was 4 m thick and reached a height of 18-20 m. On the north it was reinforced by seventy-three massive rectangular and round towers, spaced ca. 70 m apart, as well as by outworks at strategic points; on the south there were twenty-seven round towers at intervals of 170-200 m.

The northern city wall and the wall of the citadel were constructed first, obviously to protect the inhabitants against imminent invasions from the north. Their foundations are much deeper, and, as a result, the wall is almost entirely preserved today, whereas the southern wall survives only in part. The northern wall follows the winding course of a ravine before straightening out toward the east; the southern wall, on the other hand, presents an almost straight line. Battlements and additional gates were added later; fourteen gates survived as late as 1720.

The impression of antiquity evoked by these fortifications led many Arab historians to connect them with Ḵosrow I and to include them among the seven wonders of the world. In the Middle Ages Alexander the Great (q.v.) was credited with having cordoned off the Darband pass against the tribes of Gog and Magog advancing from the north (Ebn Rosta, p. 149; cf. Ezekiel 38-39; the reference to iron gates in Josephus, *Bellum Judaicum* 7.7.4, cannot be connected with the pass at Darband; cf. Anderson, 1928, pp. 147-48). The Darband fortress was certainly the most prominent Sasanian defensive construction in the Caucasus (Artamonov, 1962, p. 122) and could have been erected only by an extremely powerful central government (Kasumova, 1988, p. 93; for an opposing view, see Gropp, 1977, pp. 1621-22). In construction technique it is similar to other 6th-century fortifications (see Frye, 1977; Cuneo, pp. 60-61), like those at Taḵt-e Solaymān (Huff; for another opinion, see Gropp, 1977). By 1985 twenty-five Middle Persian inscriptions (representing measurements for construction purposes) had been found in the walls of Darband (Kasumova, 1987, p. 102; idem, 1988, p. 93). The paleography belongs to a single period, and the vertical format is clearly late Sasanian, confirming attribution to Ḵosrow I (Gignoux, pp. 304-05). Nevertheless, the readings, particularly of the dated inscription no. 3, remain controversial. Most scholars consider this inscription to belong to the 6th century (e.g., Lukonin, *Camb. Hist. Iran*, p. 683; Kasumova, 1979, p. 117). Kudryavtsev places it in the twenty-seventh year of the reign of Kavād I, that is, 515 (1982a, p. 94), whereas Vladimir Lukonin (1969, p. 45 and n. 23) arrived at the third year of the reign of Ḵosrow I (534, not necessarily the date of completion), and E. A. Pakhomov (1930), M. I. Artamonov (1962, p. 464), and S. Yu. Kasumova (1979) arrived at the thirty-seventh year (567-68). Nyberg and Gerd Gropp differ dramatically, both having read the year as 700 but Nyberg basing his calculations on the Arsacid era, thus arriving at a date in the middle of the 5th century C.E., whereas Gropp used the Seleucid era, which yields the date 389. Neither of these dates has been generally accepted, however.

Movsēs Dasxuranc'i called Darband a city (2.41) and a large city (2.11), even though in the Sasanian period the developed area seems to have extended only as far as the town of Dzhuma-Mechet' (Kudryavtsev 1982a, p. 116 map). The citadel, today the site of Naryn-kala (Artamonov, 1946, p. 123), served as the administrative, political, and military center, where Ḵosrow I stationed sentries (Kramers); the area between the city walls was settled primarily by artisans and merchants. Certain trades, like stonemasonry, were undoubtedly significant, and the city was also a major center of international trade. Driyōš (read by Gignoux, review of Kasumova, 1988) is documented as *āmārgar* (q.v.) of Ādurbādagān (*'twrp'tkn 'm'lkl*) in the Darband inscriptions. The city was for a time also the seat of the catholicos of the Albanian church (Hewsen, 1987), but accounts of the founding of the diocese are legendary (Pseudo Faustus, 3.6); it was moved to Pērōz-Kavād/Partaw in 552. Despite the massive fortifications, in 627 the Khazars, allied with the Byzantine emperor Heraclius (610-41), succeeded in capturing the city, which probably remained under Khazar rule until 22/643, when it was conquered by Sorāqa b. ʿAmr and became part of the Islamic empire (Ṭabarī, I/5, pp. 2663-67).

For Darband in the Islamic period, see DĀḠESTĀN.

Bibliography: Sources. Movsēs Dasxuranc'i, *Patmut'iwn Ałuanic' ašxarhi*, ed. M. Emin, Moscow, 1860; tr. C. J. F. Dowsett as *The History of the Caucasian Albanians by Movsēs Dasxuranċi*, London Oriental Series 8, London, 1961. Ebn al-Faqīh, tr. H. Massé as *Abrégé du livre des pays*, Damascus, 1973. E. Koestermann, ed., *Annalen* II, Heidelberg, 1965. G. Lafontaine, *La version grecque ancienne du livre arménien d'Agathange*, Publications de l'Institut Orientaliste de Louvain 7, Louvain-la-Neuve, 1973. J. Marquart (Markwart), *Osteuropäische und ostasiatische Streifzüge*, Leipzig, 1903. Menander Protector, *The History of Menander the Guardsman*, ed. and tr. R. C. Blockley, ARCA, Classical and Medieval Texts, Papers and Monographs 17, Liverpool, 1985. (Pseudo) Moses of

Khorene, *Géographie de Moïse de Corène d'après Ptolémée*, ed. and tr. A. Soukry, Venice 1881. Łazar P'arpec'i, *History of the Armenians and the Letter to Vahan Mamikonean*, ed. D. Kouymjian, Delmar, N.Y., 1985. Sebeos, *Istoriya Sebeosa* (The History of Sebeos), ed. G. V. Abgaryan, Yerevan, 1979; tr. F. Macler as *Histoire d'Héraclius, par l'évêque Sebèos*, Paris, 1904.

Studies. A. A. Akopyan, *Albaniya-Aluank v greko-latinskikh i drevnearmyanskikh istochnikakh* (Albania-Ałuank' in the Greco-Latin and ancient Armenian sources), Yerevan, 1987. K. G. Aliev, *Kavkazskaya Albaniya (I v. do n. e.—I v. n. e.)* (Caucasian Albania [1st century B.C.E.-1st century C.E.]), Baku, 1974, pp. 56-63, 182-84. Idem, *Antichnye istochniki po istorii Azerbaĭdzhana* (Ancient sources for the history of Azerbaijan), Baku, 1986. F. Altheim and R. Stiehl, "Michael der Syrer über das erste Auftreten der Bulgaren und Chazaren," *Byzantion* 28, 1958, pp. 108, 110, 115. A. R. Anderson, "Alexander at the Caspian Gates," *Transactions of the American Philological Association* 59, 1928, pp. 130-63. Idem, *Alexander's Gate, Gog and Magog and the Inclosed Nations*, Cambridge, Mass., 1932; review F. Abel, *Revue biblique* 42, 1933, pp. 456-57. M. I. Artamonov, "Drevniĭ Derbent" (Ancient Darband), *Sovetskaya arkheologiya* 8, 1946, pp. 121-44. Idem, *Istoriya Khazar* (History of the Khazars), Leningrad, 1962. P. Asdourian, *Die politischen Beziehungen zwischen Armenien und Rom von 190 v. Chr. bis 428 n. Chr.*, Venice, 1911.

M. Back, *Die sassanidischen Staatsinschriften*, Acta Iranica 18, Tehran and Liège, 1978. N. B. Baklanov, *Arkhitekturnye pamyatniki Dagestana* (The architectural monuments of Dāḡestān) I, Leningrad 1935, pp. 20-24. A. C. Bandy, *Ioannes Lydus on Powers. Or the Magistracies of the Roman State*, Philadelphia, 1983. W. Barthold (V. V. Bartol'd), "Derbend," in *EI*[1] I, pp. 940-45. Idem, "K istorii Derbenta" (On the history of Darband), in *Zapiski vostochnogo otdeleniya (Imp.) russkogo arkheo-logicheskogo obshchestva* 19, 1909, pp. xi-xii; repr. in *Sochineniya* (Collected works) II/1, Moscow, 1963, pp. 786-87. Idem, "Novoe izvestie o stenakh Derbenta" (New information on the walls of Darband), *Zapiski vostochnogo otdeleniya (Imp.) russkogo arkheologicheskogo obshchestva* 21, 1913, pp. iv-v; repr. in *Sochineniya* (Collected works) II/1, Moscow, 1963, p. 788. R. C. Blockley, *The Fragmentary Classicising Historians of the Later Empire* II, Liverpool, 1983. A. Ya. Borisov and V. G. Lukonin, *Sasanidskie gemmy* (Sasanian gems), Leningrad, 1963, pp. 60-65. L. S. Bretanitskiĭ and B. V. Veĭmarn, *Isskustvo Azerbaĭdzhana IV-XVIII vekov* (Art of Azerbaijan, 4th-18th centuries), Moscow, 1976; tr. B. Brentjes as *Die Kunst Aserbaidshans vom 4. bis zum 18. Jahrhundert*, Leipzig, 1988, pp. 38-40. G. V. Cereṭeli, "Šapuris carceris 'l'nn TR'

'," in *Yubileĭnyĭ sbornik posvyashchennyĭ Georgiyu Saridanovichu Akhvlediani v svyazi s 80-letiem sodnya rozhdeniya* (Jubilee collection dedicated to Georgi Saridanovich Akhvlediani on the occasion of his eightieth birthday), Tbilisi, 1969, pp. 327-37. M. L. Chaumont, "Conquêtes sassanides et propagande mazdéenne (IIIème Siècle)," *Historia* 22, 1973, pp. 687-90. P. Cuneo, "Le mura di Derbent," *Rivista degli studi orientali* 59, 1985, pp. 57-61. D. M. Dunlop, *The History of the Jewish Khazars*, Princeton Oriental Studies 16, Princeton, N.J., 1954. Idem, "Bāb-al-Abwāb," in *EI*[2] I, pp. 835-36. Yu. R. Dzhafarov, "K voprosu o pervom poyavlenii Sabir v Zakavkaz'e" (On the question of the first appearance of the Sabirs in the Transcaucasus), *VDI*, 1979/3, pp. 163-72. Idem, *Gunny i Azerbaĭdzhan* (The Huns and Azerbaijan), Baku, 1985. Idem, "Sabiry na Kavkaze. Osnovnye etapy istorii (463-558 gg.)" (The Sabirs in the Caucasus. The formative stage of history [463-558]), in *Sovmestnaya nauchnaya sessiya molodykh uchenykh Institutov istorii Akademiĭ nauk Azerbaĭdzhanskoĭ, Gruzinskoĭ i Armyanskoĭ SSR, Tezisy dokladov*, Yerevan, 1980, pp. 39-40. W. Ensslin, "Leo I.," in Pauly-Wissowa XII/1, cols. 1947-62. *Excerpta de Legationibus*. I. *Excerpta de Legationibus Romanorum ad Gentes*, ed. C. de Boor, Berlin, 1903. S. T. Eremyan, "Syuniya i oborona Sasanidami kavkazskikh prokhodov" (Siwnik' and the Sasanians' defense of the Caucasian passes), *Izvestiya Arm. Filiala Akademii Nauk*, 1941/7, pp. 33-40. Idem, *Armeniya po «Ashkharatsuĭts» u (armyanskoĭ geografii VII veka)* (Armenia according to the *Ašxarhac'oyc'* [Armenian geography of the 7th century], Yerevan, 1963, p. 49. R. N. Frye, "The Sasanian System of Walls for Defense," in M. Rosen-Ayalon, ed., *Studies in Memory of Gaston Wiet*, Jerusalem, 1977, pp. 11-12.

V. G. Gadzhiev, ed., *Istoriya Dagestana* (History of Dāḡestān) I, Moscow, 1967, pp. 115-22, 127-31, 146-49, 163-64. Y. S. Gagloev, "O Kaspiĭskikh vorotakh Prokopiya Kesariĭskogo" (On the Caspian Gates of Procopius of Caesaria), *Izvestiya yugo-osetinskogo nauchno-issledovatel'skogo Instituta Akademii Nauk Gruzinskoĭ SSR* 13, 1964, pp. 47-51. E. Gerland, "Die persischen Feldzüge des Kaisers Herakleios," *Byzantinische Zeitschrift* 3, 1894, p. 364. P. Gignoux, "L'organisation administrative sasanide. Le cas du *marzbān*," *Jerusalem Studies in Arabic and Islam* 4, 1984, pp. 1-29. G. Gozalishvili, "Kaspiĭskie vorota" (The Caspian gates), *Trudy instituta istorii i material'noĭ kul'tury im. N. Ya. Marra* 5-6, 1940, p. 470. G. Gropp, "Die Derbent-Inschriften und das Adur Gušnasp," in *Monumentum H. S. Nyberg* I, Acta Iranica 4, Tehran and Liège, 1975, pp. 317-20, 330-31; rev. P. Gignoux, *Stud. Ir.* 5, 1976, p. 304. Idem, "Die Festung Derbent zwischen Hunnen und Sasaniden," *ZDMG*, Suppl. 3/2, 1977, pp. 1619-25. L. N. Gumilev, *Otkrytie Khazarii (Istoriko-geograficheskiĭ etyud)* (Unveiling the Khazars [A historical-geographical study]), Moscow, 1966. I. Gurlev et al., *Dervent. Putevoditel' po gorodu i okrestnostyam* (Darband. Observations on the city and the surrounding area), Makhachkala, 1976. G.-B. Guseĭnov, *Gorod tysyachi legend* (The city of a thousand legends), Makhachkala, 1982. Tʿ. Hakobyn, "Čora pahak," in *Haykakan sovetakan hanragitaran* IV, Yerevan, 1981, pp. 104-05. R. H. Heubner, *Die Historien. Kommentar* I, Heidelberg, 1963. H. Hewsen, "Derbent," in *Dictionary of the Middle Ages* IV, New York, 1984, p. 162. Idem, *Armenia and Georgia. Christianity and Territorial Development from the 4th to the 7th Century*, TAVO, BVI 14, Wiesbaden, 1987. D. Huff, "Zur Datierung des Alexanderwalls," *Iranica Antiqua* 16, 1981, pp. 132-33. M. Isakov, "Ischeznuvshiĭ gorod v Dagestane" (A lost city in Dāḡestān), *Istoricheskiĭ zhurnal*, 1941/6, pp. 156-57. Idem, *Arkheologicheskie pamyatniki Dagestana. Materialy po arkheologii Dagestana* (Archeological monuments of Dāḡestān. Materials for the archeology of Dāḡestān) I, Makhachkala, 1959.

S. Yu. Kasumova, "K tolkovaniyu srednepersidskikh nadpiseĭ iz Derbenta" (On the interpretation of the Middle Persian inscriptions from Darband), *VDI*, 1979/1, pp. 113-26. Idem, "Novye srednepersidskie nadpisi iz Derbenta" (New Middle Persian inscriptions from Darband), in *Etnokul'turnye protsessy v drevnem Dagestane (Sbornik stateĭ)* (Ethnocultural processes in ancient Daghestan [Collected papers]), Makhachkala, 1987, pp. 102-05; review P. Gignoux, *Abstracta Iranica* 11, 1988, p. 27. Idem, "Novye nakhodki srednepersidskikh nadpiseĭ v Derbente" (New discoveries of Middle Persian inscriptions in Darband), *VDI*, 1988/1, pp. 88-95. Idem, "Le sceau du catholicos d'Albanie et du Balāsagān," *St. Ir.* 20/1, 1991, pp. 23-32. S. S. O. Khan-Magomedov, "Arkhitektura drevnego Derbenta (K 150-letiyu sodnya prisoedineniya k Rossii)" (The architecture of ancient Darband [on the 150th anniversary of the annexation to Russia]), *Arkhitektura SSSR* 1957, pp. 53-54. Idem, *Derbent*, Moscow, 1958. Idem, "Steny i bashni Derbentskoĭ kreposti" (Walls and towers of the Darband fortress), *Arkhitekturnoe nasledstvo* 17, 1964, pp. 121-46. Idem, "Rannesrednevekovaya gornaya stena v Dagestane" (The early medieval mountain wall in Dāḡestān), *Sovetskaya arkheologiya*, 1966/1, pp. 227-43. Idem, *Derbent. Gornaya stena. Auly Tabasarana* (Darband. The mountain wall. The villages of Tabasaran), Moscow, 1979. J. Kolendo, "Sur le nom de *Caspiae Portae* appliqué aux cols du Caucase," *Folia Orientalia* 24, 1987, pp. 141-48. A. V. Komarov, "Ob ukrepleniyakh Derbenta i o Kavkazskoĭ stene" (On the fortifications of Darband and the Caucasian wall), *Trudy V arkheologicheskogo s'ezda v Tiflise* (Acts of the fifth archeological congress in Tiflis), Moscow, 1887. S. A. Kovalevskiĭ, "«Karta Ptolemeya» v svete istoricheskoĭ geografii Prikaspiya" (Ptolemy's map in the light of the historical geography of Precaspia), *Izvestiya vsesoyuznogo geograficheskogo obshchestva* 85/1, 1953, pp. 31-48. E. I. Kozubskiĭ, *Istoriya goroda Derbenta* (History of the city of Darband), Temir-Khan-Shura, 1906. J. H. Kramers, "The Military Colonization of the Caucasus and Armenia under the Sasanids," *BSOS* 8, 1935-37, p. 613. K. Kretschmer, "Sarmaticae Portae," in Pauly-Wissowa, IIA/1, cols. 13-14. E. I. Krupnov, *Voprosy skifo-sarmatskoĭ arkheologii* (Questions of Scythian-Sarmatian archeology), Moscow, 1954, p. 193. Idem, *Drevnyaya istoriya severnogo Kavkaza* (The ancient history of the northern Caucasus), Moscow, 1960, pp. 62-63, 66, 75. A. A. Kudryavtsev, "Otchet o rabote Derbentskogo arkheologicheskogo otryada v 1971 g." (Report on the work of the Darband archeological expedition in 1971), in *Rukopisnyĭ fond. Institut istorii, yazyka i literatury im. G. Tsadasy Dagestanskogo Filiala Akademii Nauk SSSR, Makhachkala* 357, Makhachkala, 1972. Idem, *Gorod, ne podvlastnyĭ vekam* (A city unconquered by the centuries), Makhachkala, 1976a. Idem, "Otchet o rabote Derbentskoĭ arkheologicheskoĭ ėkspeditsii v 1976 g." (Report on the work of the Darband archeological expedition in 1976), *Rukopisnyĭ fond. Institut istorii, yazyka i literatury im. G. Tsadasy Dagestanskogo Filiala Akademii Nauk SSSR, Makhachkala* 477, Makhachkala, 1976b. Idem, *Drevnie pamyatniki severo-vostochnogo Kavkaza* (Ancient monuments of the northeastern Caucasus), Makhachkala, 1977a. Idem, *Pervye issledovaniya dosasanidskogo Derbenta. Materialy po arkheologii Dagestana* (Initial investigations of pre-Sasanian Darband. Materials on the archeology of Dāḡestān) VI, Makhachkala, 1977b. Idem, "O datirovke pervykh sasanidskikh ukrepleniĭ v Derbente" (On the dating of the Sasanian fortifications in Darband), *Sovetskaya arkheologiya*, 1978/3, pp. 243-58. Idem, "«Dlinnye steny» na vostochnom Kavkaza" (The "long walls" in the eastern Caucasus), *Voprosy istorii*, 1979a/11, pp. 31-43. Idem, "Otchet o rabote Derbentskoĭ arkheologicheskoĭ ekspeditsii v 1979 g." (Report on the work of the Darband archeological expedition in 1979), *Rukopisnyĭ fond. Institut istorii, yazyka i literatury im. G. Tsadasy Dagestanskogo Filiala Akademii Nauk SSSR, Makhachkala* 632, Makhachkala, 1979b. Idem, *Drevniĭ Derbent* (Ancient Darband), Moscow, 1982a. Idem, "O novoĭ khronologii drevnego Derbenta" (On the new chronology of ancient Darband), *Sovetskaya arkheologiya*, 1982b/4, pp. 165-85. Idem, *Tezisy dokladov nauchnoĭ sessii posvyashchennoĭ itogam ekspeditsionnykh issledovaniĭ Instituta istorii, yazyka i literatury im. G. Tsadasy Dagestanskogo Filiala Akademii Nauk SSSR v 1984-85 gg. (28-29 aprelya 1986 g.)*, Makhachkala, 1986. Idem, "O sinkretizme parfyano-sasanidskikh, greko-rimskikh i mestnykh traditsiĭ v fortifikatsionnoĭ arkhitekture i gradostroitel'stve drevnego i rannesrednevekovogo Derbenta" (On the syncretism of the Parthian-Sasanian, Greco-Roman, and indigenous traditions in fortification architecture and city planning of ancient and early medieval Darband), in *Etnokul'turnye protsessy v drevnem Dagestane (Sbornik stateĭ)* (Ethnocultural processes in ancient Dāḡestān [Collected papers]), Makhachkala, 1987, pp. 52-71. Idem, *Feodal'nyĭ Derbent. Puti i zakonomernosti razvitiya goroda v VI—seredine XIII v.* (Feudal Darband. Directions and regularities in the development of the city in the 6th to mid-13th centuries), Makhachkala, 1991. Yu. Kulakovskiĭ, *Alany po svedeniyam klassicheskikh i vizantiĭskikh pisateleĭ* (The Alans in the light of the classical and Byzantine sources), Kiev, 1899, p. 139.

L. I. Lavrov, *Epigraficheskie pamyatniki severnogo Kavkaza na arabskom, persidskom i turetskom yazykakh. Teksty, perevody, kommentarii, vvedenie i prilozhenie* (Epigraphic monuments of the northern Caucasus in the Arabic, Persian, and Turkish languages. Texts, translations, commentaries, introduction, and supplement) I, Moscow, 1966, p. 156. O. K. Leont'ev and P. V. Fedorov, "K istorii Kaspiĭskogo mor'ya v pozdne i poslekhvalynskoe vremya" (On the history of the Caspian Sea in the late and post Khvalynsk period), *Izvestiya Akademii Nauk SSSR. Seriya geograficheskaya*, 1953/4, pp. 64-74. V. G. Lukonin, "Srednepersidskie nadpisi iz Kara-tepe" (Middle Persian inscriptions from Kara Tepe), in *Buddiĭskie peshchery Kara-tepe v starom Termeze. Osnovnye itogi rabot 1963-1964 gg.* (The Buddhist caves of Kara Tepe in ancient Termez. Basic results of the overall work of 1963-64), Moscow, 1969, pp. 42-46; repr. in *Drevniĭ i ranne-srednevekovyĭ Iran. Ocherki istorii kul'tury* (Ancient and early medieval Iran. Outline history of the culture), Moscow, 1987, pp. 231-34, 271-74. Idem, "Political, Social and Administrative Institutions. Taxes and Trade," in *Camb. Hist. Iran* III/2, pp. 681-746. M. G. Magomedov, *Drevnie i srednevekovye oboronitel'nye sooruzheniya Dagestana* (Ancient and medieval defensive structures of Dāḡestān), Ph.D. diss., University of Makhachkala, 1970. R. M. Magomedov, *Legendy i fakty o Dagestane* (Legends and facts about Dāḡestān), Makhachkala, 1969. F. D. Mamedova, *Politicheskaya istoriya i istoricheskaya geografiya Kavkazskoĭ Albanii (III v. do n. e.-VIII v. n. e.)* (The political history and historical geography of Caucasian Albania [3rd century B.C.E.-8th century C.E.]), Baku, 1986 (to be used with caution). Ya. A. Manandyan, "O mestonakhozhdenii Caspia Via i Caspiae Portae" (The location of the Caspian route and the Caspian gates), *Istoricheskie zapiski* 25, 1948, pp. 59-70. A. Maricq, *Recherches sur les Res Gestae Divi Saporis*, Mémoires de l'Académie Royale de Belgique, Classe des lettres et des sciences morales et politiques, 47/4, Brussels, 1953. K. Mittelhaus, "Kaukasiai Pylai," in Pauly-Wissowa, XI/1, col. 58. S. N. Murav'ev, "Ptolemeeva karta Kavkazskoĭ Albanii i uroven' Kaspiya" (Ptolemy's map of Caucasian Albania and the level of the Caspian), *VDI*, 1983/1, pp. 117-47. H. S. Nyberg, "Materialy po istolkovaniyu pechleviĭskikh nadpiseĭ Derbenda" (Materials for the interpretation of the Pahlavi inscriptions of Darband), *Izvestiya obshchestva obsledovaniya i izucheniya Azerbaĭdzhana* (Baku) 8/5, 1929, pp. 26-32.

E. A. Pakhomov, "O nakhodke sasanidskikh nadpiseĭ v Derbende" (On the discovery of Sasanian inscriptions in Darband), *Kul'tura i pis'mennost' Vostoka* 4, Baku 1929a. Idem, "Pekhleviĭskie nadpisi Derbenda" (The Pahlavi inscriptions of Darband), *Izvestiya obshchestva obsledovaniya i izucheniya Azerbaĭdzhana* 8/5, Baku 1929b, pp. 1-25. Idem, "K istolkovaniyu pechleviĭskich nadpiseĭ Derbenda" (On the interpretation of the Pahlavi inscriptions of Darband), *Izvestiya Azerbaĭdzhanskogo nauchoissledovaniya Institut* 1/2, Baku, 1930, pp. 13-16. Idem, "Krupneĭshie pamyatniki sasanidskogo stroitel'stva v Zakavkaz'e" (Fortified monuments of the Sasanian regime in the Transcaucasus), *Problemy Gosudarstvennoĭ Akademii istorii material'noĭ kul'tury* 9-10, Leningrad 1933, pp. 37-47. P. Peeters, "Sainte Sousanik martyre en Arméno-Géorgie," *Analecta Bollandiana* 53, 1935, pp. 282-85. N. V. Pigulevskaya, "Siriĭskiĭ istochnik VI v. o narodakh Kavkaza" (A Syriac source of the 6th century on the peoples of the Caucasus), *VDI* 1939/1, pp. 109-10. Idem, *Siriĭskie istochniki po istorii narodov SSSR* (Syriac sources for the history of the people of the U.S.S.R.), *Trudy Instituta Vostokovedeniya Akademii Nauk SSSR* 41, Moscow and Leningrad, 1941, pp. 67, 82, 165. P. I. Spasskiĭ, "Derbentskie ukrepleniya" (The Darband fortifications), *Izvestiya Azerbaĭdzhanskogo komiteta okhrany pamyatnikov stariny, iskusstva i prirody* 4/2, Baku, 1929, p. 267-76. W. Tomaschek, "Albaniai Pylai," in Pauly-Wissowa, I/2, col. 1305. Idem, "Biraparach," in Pauly-Wissowa, III/1, col. 489. Idem, "Dareinē atrapos," in Pauly-Wissowa IV/2, cols. 2183-84. K. V. Trever, *Ocherki po istorii i kul'ture kavkazskoĭ Albanii IV v. do n. e.-VII v. n. e.* (Sketches on the history and culture of Caucasian Albania, 4th century B.C.E.-7th century C.E.), Moscow and Leningrad, 1959. B. Utas, "Non-Religious Book Pahlavi Literature as a Source to the History of Central Asia," *AAASH* 24, 1976, 115-24 (esp. pp. 117-18).

(This article has been condensed from a longer study.)

(ERICH KETTENHOFEN)

DARBAND, quarter of Tehran, formerly a village in the summer resort (*yeylāq*) of Šamīrān, situated at an elevation of 1,700 m on the extreme northern edge of the capital, where the Alborz foothills begin. A stream of the same name flows through it, and in July 1987 it flooded, destroying the *bāzār* of Tajrīš. Since the 1950s, when Šamīrān and Tajrīš were gradually incorporated into Tehran, Darband has become the *yeylāq* quarter par excellence, adjacent to the palaces of Saʿdābād; it has a hotel, restaurants, and cafés, which are frequented by members of the more prosperous social classes. Darband has become increasingly popular since the 1970s, especially as the point of departure for hikes and climbs toward the Towčāl (stopping at the Šīrpalā shelter in the Osūn valley). On both winter and summer holidays the square and single main street of this old mountain village, which can be reached easily via urban transportation, are the setting for tens of thousands of strollers, and many boutiques and teahouses (*čāy-ḵāna*s) serve hikers along the whole length of the valley as far as Pas-qalʿa.

Owing to the huge growth in the population of Tehran, as well as the integration of Darband into the city, tourism there remains undiminished, despite the development of other, similar resorts near the capital (e.g., installation of a telpher from Towčāl to Valanjak and construction of a road from Emāmzāda Dāwūd).

(Bernard Hourcade)

DARBANDĪ, Mulla Āqā b. ʿĀbed b. Ramażān, commonly known as Fāżel Darbandī (d. Tehran, 1286/1869-70), Shiʿite scholar and preacher of the Qajar period, renowned for his disputatious and irascible character. His name suggests an origin in the city of Darband or its environs, but the place and year of his birth are not known. He studied in Najaf, where his principal teacher was Mulla Moḥammad Šarīf-al-ʿOlamāʾ Māzandarānī (d. 1245/1829-30), whose patience he frequently tried with his endless objections to the texts being studied and his tendency to brawl with his fellow students. He early formed a high opinion of his own worth and once informed Shaikh Moḥammad-Ḥasan Najafī, author of *Jawāher al-kalām*, a well-known work on the principles of jurisprudence, that it was much inferior to his own writings (Modarres, p. 216). He also argued with the Ottoman civil authorities and with the Hanafite mufti of Baghdad, Shaikh Šehāb-al-Dīn Alūsī, supposedly reducing the latter to shamefaced silence on the question of the permissibility of cursing the Umayyad caliph Moʿāwīa (41-60/661-80; Tonokābonī, p. 111). His verbal attacks on the Babis are said to have brought on an assassination attempt (Algar, p. 166). By his own account Darbandī even quarreled with the dead: He dreamed of the medieval scholar Ebn Abi'l-Ḥadīd (d. 655/1257) and took him to task for alleged misinterpretation of passages in *Nahj al-balāḡa* (Tonokābonī, p. 112).

Darbandī attempted to teach at Karbalāʾ, but the peculiarities of his character made it impossible for him to retain students. He then migrated to Persia, arriving in Tehran soon after the dismissal of the vizier Mīrzā Āqā Khan Nūrī in 1275/1858. In the following Moḥarram he denounced members of the government for alleged immoral conduct in such scurrilous detail that he was temporarily banished to Kermānšāh (Algar, p. 166). Although on another occasion he upbraided Nāṣer-al-Dīn Shah (1264-1313/1747-1896) for failing to trim his opulent mustache, he seems generally to have enjoyed good relations with the monarch, at whose request he wrote *Saʿādat-e nāṣerīya*, a fantastic and highly inaccurate account of the martyrdom of Imam Ḥosayn.

In his way, however, Darbandī was devoted to the cult centered on the martyrdom at Karbalāʾ. When he preached on those tragic events he would weep violently, lacerate his face, throw off his turban, and sometimes even throw himself from the minbar to the ground. A similar emotionalism and lack of restraint pervade his *Eksīr al-ʿebādāt fī asrār al-šehādāt*, a voluminous work in Arabic on the same topic, which was criticized by the early 20th-century scholar of Hadith Ḥosayn Nūrī for the numerous false traditions included in it (Modarres, p. 217). Most of his other writings (listed in Modarres, p. 217) have also been criticized for lack of scholarly precision, but at least in his own time Darbandī enjoyed fame for eloquence in both Persian and Arabic and for erudition in the science of Hadith transmitters.

After his death he was taken to Karbalāʾ for burial.

Bibliography: H. Algar, *Religion and State in Iran, 1785-1906. The Role of the ʿUlamāʾ in the Qajar Period*, Berkeley and Los Angeles, 1969, p. 166. Moḥammad-Ḥasan Khan Eʿtemād-al-Salṭana, *al-Maʾāṯer wa'l-āṯār*, Tehran, 1307/1889, p. 139. A. de Gobineau, *Les religions et les philosophies dans l'Asie centrale*, Paris, 1865, pp. 107-10. M.-M. Kāẓemī, *Aḥsan al-wadīʿa fī tarājem mašāhīr mojtahedīʾl-Šīʿa* I, Najaf, 1968, pp. 47-50. M.-ʿA. Modarres, *Rayḥānat al-adab* II, Tabrīz, n.d. Mīrzā Moḥammad Tonokābonī, *Qeṣaṣ al-ʿolamāʾ*, Tehran, n.d., pp. 107-12.

(Hamid Algar)

DARBĀR. See bār; courts and courtiers.

DARBĀR-e AʿẒAM (lit., "the great court"), a council of ministers established in October 1872 as one of several experiments undertaken in the reign of Nāṣer-al-Dīn Shah (1264-1313/1848-96) to reorganize and rationalize the Persian administration on the model of Western cabinet government. It was composed of the *ṣadr-e aʿẓam* (grand vizier) and nine other ministers—of war, finance, justice, foreign affairs, the interior, education, public works, the court, and commerce and agriculture—who were collectively responsible for the entire government (Ṣanīʿ-al-Dawla [later Eʿtemād-al-Salṭana], pp. 162-66).

The edict establishing the *darbār-e aʿẓam*, drafted by Mīrzā Ḥosayn Khan Mošīr-al-Dawla and approved by Nāṣer-al-Dīn Shah on 20 Šaʿbān 1289/23 October 1872, defined the authority of the individual cabinet ministers, as well as their relation to the central authority (for the text, see Ṣanīʿ-al-Dawla, pp. 162-66). The shah was to appoint and dismiss the *ṣadr-e aʿẓam*, who, as the senior member of the cabinet, wielded extensive authority, appointing and dismissing the other ministers, subject to the shah's approval, and serving as the sole channel of communication with the sovereign. He was empowered to intervene in the internal affairs of each ministry, and no official could be appointed or dismissed without his knowledge. The edict did, however, grant the individual ministers a high degree of autonomy to define and regulate the duties of officials within their ministries. Salaries were determined by the duties of office, rather than by individual rank, as had been the previous practice. Members of the cabinet were to meet in consultation and report to the *ṣadr-e aʿẓam* twice a week.

The establishment of the *darbār-e aʿẓam* represented the culmination of Western-inspired efforts to strengthen and reorganize the central government. Mīrzā Ḥosayn Khan Mošīr-al-Dawla, Persian ambassador to Istanbul, had for some time been urging Nāṣer-al-Dīn Shah to adopt such reforms; in December 1870 the shah recalled him to Tehran to undertake the necessary measures (Bakhash, pp. 77-120; Nashat, pp. 43-94). He was named *ṣadr-e aʿẓam* in November 1871 and immediately took steps to eliminate the overlapping jurisdictions and rationalize the unclear lines of authority that had previously prevailed within the government. He also attempted to end corruption by putting the state finances in order. Although at first he enjoyed the full support of the shah, his efforts, particularly to concentrate power in his own hands, angered many powerful courtiers and officials. The opposition took advantage of the crisis generated by the government's grant to Baron Julius de Reuter of exclusive rights to exploit most Persian natural resources (see CONCESSIONS ii) to bring about Mošīr-al-Dawla's dismissal in September 1873. The shah maintained his interest in reforming the central administration until the end of the decade, but in the remaining years of his rule he grew less enthusiastic. Mostawfī-al-Mamālek and later Amīn-al-Solṭān (q.v.), whom he appointed to the post of *ṣadr-e aʿẓam*, were also not very interested in government by cabinet. As a result, even though the term *darbar-e aʿẓam* survived into the reign of Moẓaffar-al-Dīn Shah (1313-24/1896-1907), the body was actually an independent ministry with nebulous function. In the absence of a *ṣadr-e aʿẓam* the minister of the *darbār-e aʿẓam* was responsible for calling ministerial meetings and seeing that individual ministries prepared reports for the shah (Afżal-al-Molk, pp. 57, 83). During the constitutional period cabinet government came to be called *majles-e wozarāʾ*, or *kābīna* (Amīn-al-Dawla, pp. 235, 273).

Although in the text of Nāṣer-al-Dīn Shah's edict Mošīr-al-Dawla is credited with creation of the *darbār-e aʿẓam*, the principal arguments for ministerial accountability and coordinating the work of the highest state officials had already been set forth in the essay "Ketābča-ye ḡaybī yā daftar-e tanẓīmat" by Mīrzā Malkom Khan in 1276/1859 (Nashat, p. 79).

Bibliography: F. Ādamīyat, *Fekr-e āzādī wa moqaddama-ye nahżat-e mašrūṭīyat*, 1340 Š./1961. Idem, *Andīša-ye taraqqī wa ḥokūmat-e qānūn. ʿAṣr-e sepahsālār*, Tehran, 1351 Š./1972. Ḡolām-Ḥosayn Khan Afżal-al-Molk, *Afżal al-tawārīḵ*, ed. M. Etteḥādīya, Tehran, 1361 Š./1982. Mīrzā ʿAlī Khan Amīn-al-Dawla, *Ḵāṭerāt-e sīāsī-ye Mīrzā ʿAlī Ḵān Amīn-al-Dawla*, ed. H. Farmānfarmāʾīān, Tehran, 1341 Š./1962. S. Bakhash, *Iran. Monarchy, Bureaucracy, and Reform under the Qajars. 1858-1896*, London, 1978. Eʿtemād-al-Salṭana, *Ḵalsa mašhūr be ḵᵛāb-nāma-ye Eʿtemād-al-Salṭana*, ed. M. Katīrāʾī, Tehran, 1348 Š./1969, pp. 97-1911. Idem, *Ṣadr-al-tawārīḵ*, Tehran, 1349 Š./1970. G.-M. Farhād Moʿtamed, *Sepahsālār-e aʿẓam*, Tehran, 1325 Š./1946. Malkom Khan, "Ketābča-ye ḡaybī yā daftar-e tanẓīmāt," in Malkom Khan, *Majmūʿa-ye āṯār-e Mīrzā Malkom Ḵān*, ed. M. Moḥīṭ-Ṭabāṭabāʾī, Tehran, 1327 Š./1948, pp. 2-52. G. Nashat, *The Origins of Modern Reform in Iran, 1870-1880*, Urbana, Ill., 1982. M.-Ḥ. Ṣanīʿ-al-Dawla (Eʿtemād-al-Salṭana), *Merʾāt-al-boldān-e nāṣerī* III, Tehran, 1296/1879.

(GUITY NASHAT)

DĀRČĪNĪ (i.e., *dār-e čīnī*, lit., "Chinese tree/wood," < Mid. Pers. **dār ī čēnīg*; cf. Arm. lw. *daričenik*; Hübschmann, *Armenische Grammatik*, p. 137; Ar. *dārṣīnī*), or commonly *dārčīn*, the dried aromatic (inner) bark of many plants of the genus *Cinnamomum* (fam. Lauraceae) found in eastern, southeastern, and southern Asia (for a description of species, varieties, and their habitats, see Balfour, I, pp. 598-99, 731-32).

History. Some Persian medical authors of the Islamic period have referred to the use of *dārṣīnī* and the related *salīḵa* (see below) in early prescriptions traceable to Galenic pharmacology, which was practiced at the Jondīšāpūr hospital (see BĪMĀRESTĀN) in the Sasanian period, though there is no specific evidence of their use there. These prescriptions included the vaguely characterized *jowārešn* (< Pers. *govārešn*) *al-šahrīārān* "the digestive [compounded] for kings" and *maʿjūn Qobāḏ al-malek* "the electuary of King Qobād" (Ebn Sīnā, III, pp. 314, 350, 333-34; Jorjānī, p. 691).

Cinnamon has been found in Egyptian tombs of the pharaonic period (Meyerhof and Sobhy, in Ḡāfeqī, pp. 471, 475), and cinnamon and cassia bark are mentioned several times in the Old Testament (Heb. *qinnāmōn/kinnamon* and *qēṣīʿāh/keẓi'ah* or *kiddah*; see, e.g., Laufer, *Sino-Iranica*, p. 542 n. 3; *Encyclopaedia Judaica*, s.v. cinnamon) and by such early authors as Herodotus, Theophrastus, Strabo, and Pliny (Laufer, *Sino-Iranica*, p. 541). Although some modern scholars have inferred from the literal sense of *dārčīnī* that the ancients obtained cinnamon by land from China (Renaud and Colin, pp. 129-30 no. 291; Meyerhof in Ebn Maymūn, p. 50 no. 95; Dietrich, p. 197; Dymock et al., p. 204; Mazahéri, p. 441), the sinological evidence does not support their view (Laufer, *Sino-Iranica*, pp. 542-44). It seems more likely that in antiquity cinnamon and related products came mainly from Ceylon and India (cf. Strabo, 1.4.2, 15.1.22, 16.4.19, 16.4.25; Balfour, p. 732).

In the 1st century C.E. Dioscorides described many species or varieties of *kassía* and *kinamómon* (1.12-13) without, however, indicating their origins. The

9th-century Arab translators rendered them as either *dārṣīnī*, traditionally identified with the bark of *Cinnanomum cassia* Bl., or as *salīḵa* (lit., "excoriated (bark)"; Renaud and Colin, pp. 129-30), usually believed to have come from *Cinnamomum iners* Reinw. (or other Indian or Indo-Chinese species; Dymock et al., p. 203). The earliest author of the Islamic period to have provided an independent inventory of *dārṣīnī* species was the Egyptian Esḥāq b. Solaymān Esrāʾīlī (ca. 243-343/858-955; in Ḡāfeqī, Ar. text, p. 107; cf. Ebn al-Bayṭār, I/2, pp. 83-84). A contemporary of Esrāʾīlī, Yūḥannā b. Māsūya (d. 343/955; p. 19), mentioned three kinds of *qerfa* (lit., "rind, skin, bark"): *qerfat al-qaranfol*, the best; *qerfa* that smelled like camphor; and *qerfa* that smelled like *dārṣīnī*. ʿAlī b. Sahl Ṭabarī, author of the earliest surviving medical compendium of the Islamic period (comp. 236/850), named only *qerfa* (p. 398) and *salīḵa* (p. 397).

Abū Manṣūr Mowaffaq Heravī (q.v.; fl. ca. 370-80/980-90), author of the oldest known pharmacological work in Persian, included separate articles on *dārčīnī* and *qerfa* (p. 154) and on *salīḵa* (p. 185). On the other hand, Abū Bakr Rabīʿ Aḵawaynī Boḵārī (d. ca. 373/983), who wrote the earliest medical treatise in Persian, used the terms *dārčīnī*, *dārčīnī-e čīnī* (Chinese *dārčīnī*, pp. 250, 390), *qerfa*, and *salīḵa* (pp. 250, 390 and passim). Ebn Sīnā (d. 428/1037) merely summarized Dioscorides' information. The latest, partly original account of cinnamon in Persian is that by the 18th-century author Moḥammad-Ḥosayn ʿAqīlī Ḵorāsānī, who appears to have known most of the species and varieties and their sources (pp. 410-11: *dārṣīnī*, 688: *qerfat al-dārčīnī* [sic], 513: *salīḵa*). According to him, the best varieties came from Ceylon.

Although William Dymock and his colleagues (p. 203) insisted that cinnamon had not been cultivated in Ceylon before 1770, Alphonse de Candolle (p. 146) claimed that it was native to Ceylonese forests and had always been a principal product of the country. Bozorg b. Šahryār of Rāmhormoz, a Persian ship captain, had mentioned *al-qerfat al-sehīlānīya* "Ceylonese bark" in the 10th century (p. 180).

Medicinal and culinary uses. The numerous uses found for *dārčīn* in post-Galenic and folk medicine were derived principally from its identification as "hot" and "dry" (e.g., Ṭabarī, pp. 397-98; Heravī, p. 154). According to Ebn Sīnā (III, p. 289), when taken internally it would counteract venoms and poisons, relieve catarrh and cough, and cure dim eyesight caused by thick "moisture" in the eyes and liver obstructions. Applied externally, it would cure sores, tetter, freckles, and the like.

Like most other Galenic simples, *dārčīnī* has gradually fallen from use for medical purposes. Nowadays in Persia powdered *dārčīn* is used (in infusions, and usually with *nabāt* "rock candy") only as a "hot" drug against *sardī* ("coldness" of the humoral constitution) and as a stomachic, carminative, or (because of its tannin content) antidiarrheal. A hot infusion of *dārčīn* popularly called *čāyī-dārčīn* (lit., "cinnamon tea") is occasionally drunk, especially in cold weather, as a mild tonic; until not very long ago sidewalk barbers used to serve it to their clients while shaving their heads. Gisho Honda and his colleagues have reported only two kinds of *dārčīn* available in Tehran: *dārčīn-e dorošt* (coarse cinnamon) and *dārčīn-e narm* (soft/delicate cinnamon), identified as from *Cinnamomum cassia* and *Cinnamomum zeylanicum* respectively (p. 3). In 1937 David Hooper and Henry Field reported (p. 100) that "the small, black fruits of the cinnamon tree from China are sold in the bazaars" [of Tehran] under the name *qorfa* (sic) and that "the leaves of cinnamon (taken internally for rheumatism)" were called *barg-e sāḏaj* (*sāḏaj* leaf) in Tehran and *sāḏaj-e hendī* (Indian *sāḏaj*) in Isfahan.

Powdered *dārčīn* is sprinkled on a kind of rice pudding called *šol-e zard* and is included in some pastries, stews, and such regional dishes as the Kermānī pilaw with kohlrabi.

In 1368 Š./1989-90, 27,835 kg (total value: 4,293,195 rials) of "*dārčīn* and *dārčīn*-tree blossoms" were imported from Dubai, which was obviously an intermediary for exports from elsewhere (Gomrok, p. 21).

Bibliography: Abū Bakr Rabīʿ b. Aḥmad Aḵawaynī Boḵārī, *Hedāyat al-motaʿallemīn fi'l-ṭebb*, ed. J. Matīnī, Mašhad, 1344 Š./1965. Moḥammad-Ḥosayn ʿAqīlī Ḵorāsānī, *Maḵzan al-adwīa*, Calcutta, 1844. E. Balfour, *The Cyclopaedia of India and of Eastern and Southern Asia . . .*, 3rd ed., 3 vols., London, 1885. Bozorg b. Šahryār, *Ketāb ʿajāyeb al-Hend . . .*, ed. P. A. van der Lith, Leiden, 1883-86; tr. L. M. Devic as *Les merveilles de l'Inde*, Paris, 1878. A. de Candolle, *Origin of Cultivated Plants*, London, 1886. A. Dietrich, "Dār Ṣīnī," in *EI*², Suppl., pp. 197-98. Dioscorides, *De Materia Medica*, tr. J. Goodyer (1655) as *The Greek Herbal of Dioscorides*, ed. R. T. Gunther, Oxford, 1934. W. Dymock et al., *Pharmacographia Indica . . .*, 3 vols., London, 1890-93. Ebn al-Bayṭār, *al-Jāmeʿ le mofradāt al-adwīa wa'l-aḡḏīa*, 4 pts. in 2 vols., Būlāq, 1291/1874. Ebn Maymūn (Maimonides), *Šarḥ asmāʾ al-ʿoqqār*, ed. and tr. M. Meyerhof as *L'explication des noms de drogues*, Cairo, 1940. Ebn Sīnā, *Ketāb al-qānūn fi'-l-ṭebb*, 3 vols., Būlāq, 1294/1877. Aḥmad Ḡāfeqī, *Ketāb al-adwīa al-mofrada*, partially ed. and tr. M. Meyerhof and G. P. Sobhy as *The Abridged Version of "The Book of Simple Drugs" of Ahmad Ibn Muhammad al-Ghâfiqî by Gregorius Abu'l-Farag (Barhebraeus)* I/1-3, Cairo, 1932-38. Gomrok-e . . . Īrān, *Sāl-nāma-ye āmār-e bāzargānī-e ḵārejī-e . . . Īrān, 1368*, Tehran, 1369 Š./1990. Abū Manṣūr Mowaffaq Heravī, *Ketāb al-abnīa ʿan ḥaqāyeq al-adwīa*, ed. A. Bahmanyār and Ḥ. Maḥbūbī Ardakānī, Tehran, 1346 Š./1967-68. G. Honda et al., *Herb Drugs and Herbalists in the Middle East*, Tokyo, 1979. D. Hooper and H. Field, *Useful Plants and Drugs of Iran and Iraq*, Chicago, 1937. Zayn-al-Dīn Esmāʿīl Jorjānī, *Ḏaḵīra-ye ḵᵛārazmšāhī*, facs. ed. ʿA.-A. Saʿīdī Sīrjānī, Tehran, 2535=1355 Š./1976 A. Mazahéri, *La route de la soie*, Paris, 1983. H. P.

Renaud and G. S. Colin, eds. and trs., *Toḥfat al-aḥbāb fī māhīyat al-nabāt wa'l-aʿšāb*, Paris, 1934. ʿAlī b. Sahl Ṭabarī, *Ferdows al-ḥekma*, ed. M. Z. Siddiqi, Berlin, 1928. Yūḥanna b. Māsūya, "Ketāb jawāher al-ṭīb al-mofrada," ed. P. Sbath, *Bulletin de l'Institut d'Égypte* 19, 1937, pp. 5-27.

(HŪŠANG AʿLAM)

D'ARCY, JOSEPH (also known as D'Arcy Todd, Major Todd, Pers. "Mester Bārūt," "Qūlūnel Khan," "Qonsūl Khan"; b. Portsmouth, England, 14 March 1780, d. Lymington, England, 17 February 1848), major (later lieutenant colonel) in the British Royal Artillery who arrived in Persia in 1226/1811 with the ambassador Sir Gore Ouseley. He was one of a group of British officers and enlisted men who were to reform and equip the Persian army. Before reaching its headquarters in Tabrīz, D'Arcy and his companions were forced to stay in Shiraz for three months, during which D'Arcy was put to work collecting geographical and other information and surveying local sites. His highly accurate and perceptive account of Fīrūzābād pleased Ouseley, who had selected him as commanding officer of the mission partly because of his training in such matters (Ṭāherī, I, pp. 435-36; Ruck, pp. 28, 38). Early in 1227/1812 D'Arcy arrived in Tabrīz, where he commanded more than thirty officers, as well as enlisted men. They accompanied Persian forces led by ʿAbbās Mīrzā (q.v.) against Russian attacks on Ṭāleš and Qarābāḡ. The ensuing victory over the Russians at Solṭānābād, on 29 Moḥarram 1227/13 February 1812, was attributed mainly to D'Arcy's artillery force, which destroyed the Russian magazine (Campbell, p. 226; Wright, 1977, pp. 50-52). In August, however, Britain and Russia made peace, and in October Ouseley ordered an almost total withdrawal of the British forces from the Persian army, though D'Arcy was among those who remained in the country.

By late 1230/1815 the British government had lost interest in the military mission in Persia and had begun to withdraw all British personnel. Before leaving D'Arcy agreed to take five Persian students to Britain to study various sciences and languages. Persian and British sources often disagree on D'Arcy's intentions and the manner in which he supervised the young men after their arrival in London in October 1815. There is evidence to suggest that the idea of an educated and skilled assemblage of Persian experts on both military and nonmilitary matters did seem to both the Persian and British governments, at least at some point, politically prudent. On the other hand, personal financial and professional considerations were often on D'Arcy's mind (Mīnovī, p. 401; Maḥbūbī, pp. 131, 145; Wright, 1985, p. 76; Ruck, p. 29). In any event the whole affair turned into a bitter clash of personalities. The main issue was, of course, money, which came from Persia irregularly and in insufficient amounts. In the end the students left Britain with little regard for the man who, in their opinion, had "neglected" them (Wright, pp. 75-78; for an account by one of the students, see Mīrzā Ṣāleḥ Šīrāzī). In D'Arcy's later years he served on a military mission to Herat in 1255/1839 in support of Kāmrān against Dōst Moḥammad Khan (Ṭāherī, II, pp. 189-93; see AFGHANISTAN x).

Information on D'Arcy's personal life is scant; the only available published source is the work of his great-granddaughter Bertha Ruck, who revealed that he was the father of an illegitimate daughter by a Georgian woman and that, despite the assertion of Clements Markham that he was killed at the battle of Fīrūza, he died peacefully at home in Lymington (Ruck, pp. 106-15, 178; Markham, p. 482).

Bibliography: B. Ātābāy. *Fehrest-e tārīḵ, safar-nāma, sīāḥat-nāma, rūz-nāma wa joḡrāfīā-ye ḵaṭṭī-e ketāb-ḵāna-ye salṭanatī*, Tehran, 2536=1356 Š./1977. M. Atkin, *Russia and Iran, 1780-1828*, Minneapolis, Minn., 1980, pp. 136-37. J. Campbell, "The Russo-Persian Frontier, 1810," *Journal of the Central Asian Society* 18, April 1931, pp. 223-32. ʿAbd-al-Razzāq Donbolī, *Maʾāṯer-e solṭānīya*, Tabrīz, 1241/1826; repr. Tehran, 1351 Š./1972. Maḥbūbī, *Moʾassasāt* I, pp. 101, 106, 131 ff. C. R. Markham, *A General Sketch of the History of Persia*, London, 1874; repr. Liechtenstein, 1977. M. Mīnovī, "Awwalīn kārvān-e maʿrefat," in *Tārīḵ wa farhang*, Tehran, 1352 Š./1973, pp. 380-437. B. Ruck, *Ancestral Voices*, London, 1972. Mīrzā Ṣāleḥ Šīrāzī, *Safar-nāma*, ed. E. Rāʾīn, Tehran, 1347 Š./1968; ed. H. Šahīdī as *Gozāreš-e safar-e Mīrzā Ṣāleḥ Šīrāzī (Kāzerūnī)*, Tehran 1362 Š./1983; ed. Ḡ-Ḥ. Mīrzā Ṣāleḥ as *Majmūʿa-ye safar-nāmahā-ye Mīrzā Ṣāleḥ Šīrāzī*, Tehran, 1364 Š./1985. A. Ṭāherī, *Tārīḵ-e rawābeṭ-e bāzargānī wa sīāsī-e Engelīs wa Īrān*, 2 vols., Tehran, 1354 Š./1975. D. Wright, *The English amongst the Persians during the Qajar Period 1787-1921*, London, 1977. Idem, *The Persians amongst the English. Episodes in Anglo-Persian History*, London, 1985.

(KAMBIZ ESLAMI)

D'ARCY, WILLIAM KNOX (b. Newton Abbot, Devonshire, England, 11 October 1849, d. Stanmore, Middlesex, England, 1 May 1917), petroleum entrepreneur and founder of the oil industry in Persia and the Middle East. The only son of an Irish solicitor, D'Arcy received his early education at Westminster School, London. The family moved to Rockhampton, Queensland, Australia, in 1866, where, after qualifying as a solicitor in 1872, D'Arcy joined his father's practice and later established his own. In 1882 he became involved with mining, forming a syndicate to restore a nearby abandoned gold mine; by 1886 he had become a millionaire. In that year he sold his legal practice and left for England, intending to use his wealth to establish himself in society. He bought a country mansion and a London town house, entertained extravagantly, and emulated the future Edward VI in his fondoness for shooting and frequenting continental spas. In the late 1890s his lavish life style, coupled with banking and stock-market problems in Australia, where he still maintained interests, forced him to undertake new mining investments (Carment, pp. 207-09; Ferrier, 1984).

Antoine Kitabgi (Ketābčī Khan), the Persian commissioner-general at the Paris Exposition of 1900 and close friend of the Persian grand vizier, Atābak-e Aʿẓam Mīrzā ʿAlī-Aṣḡar Khan Amīn-al-Solṭān (q.v.), was a firm believer in the future of a Persian oil industry and had been associated with the negotiations for the concessions (q.v.) granted by the Persian government to Baron Julius de Reuter and others. In October he requested the help of Sir Henry Drumond Wolff, former British minister in Tehran, in locating an English investor for an oil concession (Ferrier, 1982, pp. 28-30; Wolff, II, pp. 328-30). The archeologist Jacques de Morgan (q.v.; 1892, pp. 1-16; idem, 1894-1905, II, p. 87) had documented the presence of oil deposits in western and southwestern Persia. Most London financiers were, however, wary of further investment in the country after cancellation of the tobacco concession, the failure of de Reuter's Persian Bank Mining Rights Corporation, and the scandal over the national lottery swindle (Wright, 1985, pp. 157-60). Nevertheless, Wolff persuaded D'Arcy to apply for the oil concession, describing him in a letter to Ketābčī Khan in November as "a capitalist of the highest order who declares himself disposed to examine the affair" (Wright, 1977, p. 108; Ferrier, 1982, p. 29).

A meeting between Ketābčī Khan and D'Arcy took place in Paris on 8 January 1901. D'Arcy agreed in principle to apply for a concession, and after further negotiations in Paris and London a basic application was drafted; it excluded the northern provinces, in order to avoid antagonizing the Russians (Ferrier, 1982, pp. 32-33). In April Ketābčī Khan and D'Arcy's representative Alfred Marriot called on the British minister in Tehran, Sir Arthur Hardinge. In discussions with Amīn-al-Solṭān and Hardinge on 26 April Marriot assured the vizier that the proposed concession would eventually dwarf the Baku oil industry. Hardinge informed D'Arcy in a letter of 12 May that Ketābčī Khan "had secured in a very thorough manner the support of all the principal ministers and courtiers, not even forgetting the personal servant who brings His Majesty's pipe and morning coffee" (Ferrier, 1982, p. 36). Amīn-al-Solṭān triumphed over court intrigues and Russian opposition, and Moẓaffar-al-Dīn Shah (1313-24/1896-1907) signed the concession on 28 May (Hardinge, pp. 278-79; Ferrier, 1982, pp. 35-40; Kazemzadeh, pp. 356-58, 379-81; Fāteḥ, pp. 250-54). In a letter to the British Foreign Office dated 30 May Hardinge expressed strong support for D'Arcy and the concession. On the other hand, George Curzon (q.v.), then viceroy of India, predicted that D'Arcy's venture would fail, as had the Persian Bank Mining Rights Corporation, with which Curzon himself had been associated, and advised London "not to think the industrial regeneration of Persia is going to make a new start in Mr D'Arcy's hands" (Wright, 1977, p. 108).

In the concession D'Arcy was granted the privilege to "search for and obtain, exploit, develop, render suitable for trade, carry away and sell natural gas, petroleum, asphalt and ozokerite . . . for a term of sixty years"; it was applicable to the entire country except the five northern provinces (for the text, see Hurewitz, pp. 482-84; cf. Ferrier, 1982, pp. 42, 640-43; Lesānī, pp. 65-69). D'Arcy also received the exclusive right to lay pipeline from oil wells to the Persian Gulf and to establish distribution depots, construct and maintain factories, and undertake all other works and services necessary for operation of the concession. These provisions aroused particular opposition from the Russians, who hoped to gain oil concessions in the northern provinces, the value of which would be severely curtailed without access to the Persian Gulf coast.

The concession was to become void if D'Arcy had not established within two years a company or several companies. Within one month from the date at which the first company was established he was to pay the Persian government £20,000 in cash and £20,000 in stocks; he was also to pay an annual sum equal to 16 percent of the net profits of all companies formed. The government was entitled to appoint an imperial commissioner to safeguard Persian interests and to be available for consultation with the concessionaire. Exports and imports would be free from taxes and duties. On the expiration of the concession all assets would become the property of the Persian government, and the concessionaire would have no right of indemnity.

D'Arcy founded the First Exploitation Company in 1903 and made the required initial payments. Drilling had already begun near Qaṣr-e Šīrīn, though no oil had been discovered. D'Arcy had agreed to finance the search himself, and by 1905 he had spent more than £225,000, mortgaged his remaining Australian stock holdings, and exhausted his ability to raise further capital. He began discussions with the French branch of the Rothschild family to sell the concession (Wright, 1977, p. 108; Carment, p. 208).

The intervention of the British government had become crucial. The royal navy, convinced that oil would replace coal as the main source of fuel, wanted a secure source of petroleum supplies, and naval officials thus put D'Arcy in touch with the British Burmah Oil Company with the object of promoting a joint venture. The result was the Concessions Syndicate Ltd., established in 1905 with control of the First Exploitation Company shares and the concession under the trusteeship of D'Arcy. The syndicate provided the necessary capital for Persian operations. Drilling began at a new site, which also proved unsuccessful; two wells were abandoned. In January 1908 a third well was sunk, at Masjed-e Soleymān, 80 miles northeast of Ahvāz, in Ḵūzestān. The syndicate was on the verge of withdrawing from oil exploration entirely, abandoning this well too, when, on 24 Rabīʿ II 1326/26 May 1908, a reservoir of considerable size was struck. A year later the Anglo-Persian Oil Company (q.v.) was founded; it acquired the rights and shares of Concessions Syndicate, Ltd. In 1914 the British government became part owner of the firm, acquiring more than 50 percent of the voting rights, reimbursing D'Arcy for all his previous expenditures, and granting him £900,000 worth of shares. He remained a director until his death.

D'Arcy never visited Persia. His formal relations with the Persian government and the actual drilling operations were entrusted entirely to his representatives.

Bibliography: D. Carment, "D'Arcy, William Knox," in B. Nairn and G. Serle, eds. *Australian Dictionary of Biography* VIII, Melbourne, 1981, pp. 207-09. M. Fāteḥ, *Panjāh sāl naft-e Īrān*, Tehran, 1335 Š./1956. R. Ferrier, *The History of the British Petroleum Company* I. *The Developing Years 1901-1932*, London, 1982. Idem, "D'Arcy, William Knox," in D. Jeremy, ed., *Dictionary of Business Biography*, London, 1984, pp. 12-14. A. Hardinge, *A Diplomatist in the East*, London, 1928. J. Hurewitz, *The Middle East and North Africa in World Politics. A Documentary Record* I, New Haven, Conn., 1975. F. Kazemzadeh, *Russia and Britain in Persia, 1864-1914*, New Haven, Conn., 1968. A. Lesānī, *Ṭelā-ye sīāh yā balā-ye Īrān*, Tehran, 1329 Š./1950. J. de Morgan, "Note sur les gîtes de naphte de Kend-e Chirin," *Annales des mines*, February 1892, pp. 1-16. Idem, *Mission scientifique en Perse*, 5 vols., Paris, 1894-1905. F. Rūḥānī, *Tārīḵ-e mellī šodan-e naft-e Īrān*, Tehran, 1352 Š./1973. J. Šayḵ-al-Eslāmī, "Qażīya-ye tamdīd-e emtīāz-e naft-e janūb," *Āyanda* 14/1-2, 1367 Š./1988, pp. 13-25. C. E. Tugendhat and A. Hamilton, *Oil. The Biggest Business*, London, 1968. H. D. Wolff, *Rambling Recollections* II, London, 1908. D. Wright, *The English amongst the Persians during the Qajar Period 1787-1921*, London, 1977. Idem, *The Persians amongst the English. Episodes in Anglo-Persian History*, London, 1985.

(FUAD ROUHANI)

DARD, ḴᵛĀJA MĪR (b. Delhi, 19 Ḏu'l-Qaʿda 1133/13 September 1721; d. Delhi, 29 Ṣafar 1199/11 January 1785), poet and author of prose works on mystical theology.

Dard's father, Nāṣer-Moḥammad ʿAndalīb (q.v.), was a retired Mughal officer, scion of a family of *sayyeds* (claiming descent from the Prophet Moḥammad) from Bukhara, descended from both Bahāʾ-al-Dīn Naqšband and ʿAbd-al-Qāder Jīlānī (qq.v.). He was a disciple of Pīr Moḥammad Zobayr, great-grandson of Aḥmad Serhendī (q.v.), as well as of Shah Saʿd-Allāh Golšan (d. 1140/1728), a prolific poet in Persian who spent his last years in ʿAndalīb's house. In about 1735 ʿAndalīb had a vision of Imam Ḥasan, and Dard became his father's first disciple; it was he who elaborated the *ṭarīqa moḥammadīya*, the Moḥammadan Path, on the basis of this vision. At the age of fifteen years he wrote his first religious book, *Asrār al-ṣalāt*.

After the death of Pīr Moḥammad Zobayr in 1153/1740 ʿAndalīb consoled his friends by reciting an allegory in Hindi; Dard wrote it down in Persian as *Nāla-ye ʿAndalīb* (lit., "Lament of the nightingale"), a "novel" of some 1,600 printed pages in large folio. In it the adventures of the "nightingale" are recounted, with many digressions on music, yoga, and Islamic theology and practice, reflecting the refined culture of the Mughal aristocracy; in the end the nightingale emerges as the Prophet Moḥammad himself. For Dard the identification of his father with the Prophet remained the central truth (1310/1892b, p. 90).

Dard never left Delhi despite the confused political situation there. He participated in meetings in the Zīnat al-Masājed mosque, where the rhetorical rules of Urdu poetry, based on those of classical Persian, were discussed. Later a number of Urdu poets became his pupils. After 1161/1748 he wrote 111 Persian quatrains, which became the core of his *ʿElm al-ketāb*, composed after his father's death in 1172/1758. In this work he interpreted the verses, demonstrating his erudition by quoting widely from classical Islamic texts, in particular those of Jalāl-al-Dīn Rūmī. He described in detail his own mystical experiences, recounting how God had granted him all the stages of the previous prophets until he had become completely absorbed in Moḥammad, his ancestor, and felt himself to be his true *ḵalīfa* (vicegerent). He expressed the idea that after the stages of *fanāʾ fi'llāh* (annihilation in God) and the *baqāʾ bi'llāh* (remaining in God) there were two loftier stages, "remaining in the Prophet" and "remaining in the spiritual guide," claiming that the last stage had been granted to him alone, as his master and father had been both a *sayyed* and one who had attained "annihilation in the Prophet." This idea was, however, unacceptable to most of his contemporaries.

Dard attacked the doctrine of *waḥdat al-wojūd* (unity of existence) and the popular "shopkeeper shaikhs," refusing to be identified as a Sufi. His creed was not the usual Sufi *hama ūst* "everything is He" but the Naqšbandī *hama az ūst* "everything is from Him." He thus preferred *qorb al-farāʾeż*, proximity reached through observance of religious duties, to *qorb al-nawāfel*, proximity reached by "intoxicated" mystics through supererogations. Nonetheless, his language was permeated with Ebn ʿArabī's "pantheistic" terminology, and his works were efforts to describe the human being as mirror of the divine names, seeking the permanent essence behind shifting manifestations. These ideas are expressed in his *Čahār resāla*, four collections of aphorisms and meditations, each containing 341 pieces, reflecting the numerical value of the letters in Nāṣer, the name of his father and also one of the epithets of God, the Prophet, and ʿAlī. This name permeated all his thought and writings; even the servants of the house had names like Nāṣerqolī. Some aspects of the text reflect the misery in Delhi, for the inhabitants of which he considered the *ṭarīqa moḥammadīya* the only solace.

Although Dard had been raised in the sober Naqšbandī tradition, he was, like his father, extremely fond of music and wrote a booklet, *Ḥormat al-ḡenā* (The dignity of music), which was printed but seems unobtainable. Even the Mughal emperor Shah ʿĀlam II Āftāb (1173-1203/1760-1806, with interruption) attended musical sessions in his home.

There is as yet no thorough study of Dard's theological work. In his Persian poetry he followed the traditional style, whereas in his fragile Urdu verse, for which he is now best known, he developed the language of the heart. His prose works were written in long, rolling sentences with sophisticated imagery.

Dard died at the age of sixty-six years and was buried in a modest graveyard outside the Turkoman Gate in Delhi. His younger brother Aṯar, long his faithful assistant, succeeded him as leader of the *ṭarīqa moḥammadīya*. Dard's veneration of the luminous Prophet, the true guide of his community, reflected a trend also visible in other parts of the Muslim world, one that inspired the political movement of the *ṭarīqa moḥammadīya* a few years after Dard's death.

Bibliography: W. Akhtar, *Ḵ^{v}āja Mīr Dard, taṣawwuf awr šāʿerī*, Aligarh, 1971. Nāṣer-Moḥammad ʿAndalīb, *Nāla-ye ʿAndalīb*, 2 vols., Bhopal, 1308/1890. B. Ansari, "Dard," *EI*^{2} II, p. 137. Ḵ^{v}āja Mīr Dard, *Dīvān-e fārsī*, Delhi, 1309/1891. Idem, *Čahār resāla*, Bhopal, 1310/1892a. Idem, *ʿElm al-ketāb*, Delhi, 1310/1892b. Idem, *Urdu Divan*, ed. Ḵ. Dāʾūdī, Lahore, 1961. Idem, *Asrār al-ṣalāt*, in Aḥmad Serhendī, *al-Mabdaʾ wa'l-maʿād*, Delhi, n.d., pp. 69-92. N. N. Ferāq, *Mayḵāna-ye Dard*, Delhi 1344/1925. Y. Friedmann, *Shaykh Aḥmad Sirhindi*, Montreal, 1971. A. Schimmel, *Pain and Grace*, Leiden, 1976, pp. 31-147.

(ANNEMARIE SCHIMMEL)

DARDESTĀN, the region where Dardic languages are spoken.

i. *Geography.*
ii. *Languages.*

i. GEOGRAPHY

The term Dardestān once described the extreme northwestern region of the Indian subcontinent, extending from Kashmir to Kabul (Emeneau). It is in this region that the Indic languages begin to merge with Southwestern Iranian Darī (q.v.) or Northeastern Iranian Pashto. The alleged eponym of the word Dard is Daradae (Pliny, *Naturalis Historia* 5.9; Ptolemy, *Geography* 4.6.6; see ii, below). The terms Dardic or Dardestān are not, however, in common use in the region; rather, they were adopted by Western scholars after G. W. Leitner used them in his books in the late 19th century (1877, 1887, 1893, 1894, 1895). It has been suggested that *dard* may be a local word for "cave," although other origins have also been given (Dani, pp. 112-15; see ii, below). Another common toponym for the region is Kōhestān, referring to the mountains along the upper Indus in the vale of Kashmir, Indus and Swat Kōhestān, Nūrestān, and Kabul Kōhestān (Jettmar, 1982; idem, 1983).

The geography of the Dardic languages has been described in great detail, with extensive bibliography, by Gérard Fussmann (I), though his treatment of Pashai (Pašaī), the most widely distributed Dardic language, is incomplete for the western reaches. The southern limit of its distribution is the Kabul river, and the extreme western outposts are hamlets in Estālef and villages in Qarābāḡ, on the western slopes of the Kōhdāman valley adjacent to Kabul (Allan, 1974; idem, 1978).

In the time of the Mughal emperor Bābor (932-37/1526-30) Dardic languages were more widespread, but they have retreated as Iranian languages have intruded, Pashto (see AFGHANISTAN vi) from the south, especially in the Pakistan sector of the region, and Afghan Persian (Darī, q.v.) in the west. Pashto speakers, largely concentrated in the foothills, represent a powerful political force, and Darī is the predominant *bāzār* language around Kabul. There are scattered remnants of other languages, like Southeastern Iranian Parachi, found in Kabul Kōhestān, and Burushaski (q.v.; Berger, 1985), found in Hunza and Nagar districts in northern Gilgit (Mueller-Stellrecht). Wakhi (Wāḵī), a mountain (Pamir) Tajik language, is found on the northern margins of Chitral and Gilgit districts (for others, see CHITRAL ii). In southern Indus Kōhestān, Hindki is a buffer between Punjabi/Pashto and the Dardic languages (Gankovskiĭ).

As use of Dardic languages has declined, ethnonyms have shifted. In the west the residents of Kabul Kōhestān became Islamicized in the early 19th century, and Pashto speakers now call them Tajiks, after the Persian speakers across the Hindu Kush mountains in Central Asia, Kōhestānīs or Fārsīwāns (see AFGHANISTAN iv). Many former Pashai speakers have adopted the ethnonym Safi (Allan, 1978; Keiser) and often refer to themselves by the mountain valleys in which they live, for example, Panjšēr, Nejrāw, Tagāw, Laḡmān, Darra-ye Nūr (q.v.), and Peč (Grierson), whereas in Swat and Indus Kōhestān many former Dardic speakers now claim to be Pashtuns, though they speak Urdu. Karl Jettmar (1967) attributed a Central Asian origin to speakers of Dardic languages on the basis of their funerary rites and practices.

The toponym Dardestān is a social and political construct. Its currency toward the end of the 19th century in many ways reflected an attempt by supporters of imperial India to link the Indian northwestern frontier tracts to Kashmir, with which the British had treaties. Once Prime Minister Benjamin Disraeli had been defeated by William Gladstone in 1880, the British abandoned the "forward policy" of maintaining a British presence in the Kabul area. As a consequence the British created the modern entity of Afghanistan. In 1893 adoption of the Durand Line (see BOUNDARIES iii) fixed the limit of Kabul's influence, and the homogeneous linguistic region implicit in the term Dardestān became obsolete.

See also AFGHANISTAN v.

Bibliography: N. J. R. Allan, "The Modernization of Rural Afghanistan. A Case Study," in L. B. Dupree and L. Albert, *Afghanistan in the 1970's*, New York, 1974, pp. 113-25. Idem, "Men and Crops in the Central Hindukush," Ph.D. diss., Syracuse University, Syracuse, N.Y., 1978. H. Berger, "A Survey of Burushaski Studies," *Journal of Central Asia* 8/1, 1985, pp. 33-37. A. H. Dani, *History of the Northern Areas of Pakistan*, Islamabad, 1989. M. Emeneau, "Dialects of Old Indo-Aryan," in H. Birnbaum and J. Puhvel, *Ancient Indo-European Dialects*, Berkeley, Calif., 1966, pp. 123-38. G. Fussman, *Atlas linguistique des parlers dardes et kafirs*, 2 vols., Paris, 1972. Yu. V. Gankovskiĭ, *Istoriya Pakistana*, tr. I. Gavrilov as *The Peoples of Pakistan. An Ethnic History*, Lahore, 1971. G. Grierson, "On Pashai, Laghmani, or Dehgani," in *ZDMG* 54, 1900, pp. 563-98. K. Jettmar, "The Middle Asiatic Heritage of Dardistan (Islamic Collective Tombs in Punyal and Their Background)," *East and West* 17, 1967, pp. 59-82. Idem, "Kafiran, Nuristani, Darden. Zur Klärung des Begriffsystems," *Anthropos* 77, 1982, pp. 254-63. Idem, "Indus Kohistan. Entwurf einer historischen Ethnographie," *Anthropos* 78, 1983, pp. 501-18. R. Keiser, "Social Structure in the Southeastern Hindukush. Some Implications for Pashai Ethno-History," *Anthropos* 69, 1974, pp. 445-56. G. W. Leitner, *Races and Languages of Dardistan*, Lahore, 1877. Idem, *The Results of a Tour in Dardistan*, Lahore, 1887. Idem, "Dardistan," *Imperial and Asiatic Quarterly Review*, n.s. 6, 1893, pp. 422-25. Idem, *Dardistan in 1866, 1886, and 1893*, Woking, Kent, 1894. Idem, *Dardistan in 1895* I. *The Future of Chitral and Neighbouring Countries*, Woking, Kent, England, 1895. I. Mueller-Stellrecht, *Materialien zur Ethnographie Dardistans (Pakistan)* II-III, Bergvölker im Hindukusch und Karakorum 3, Graz, 1980. R. Strand, "Notes on the Nuristani and Dardic Languages," *JAOS* 93, 1973, pp. 297-305.

(NIGEL J. R. ALLAN)

ii. LANGUAGES

The Dardic (< OInd. *darád-* "the people who live next to Kashmir"; cf. *dārada-, darada-*, designating the population of northern India, and modern *dard, dārd*, self-denomination of the speakers of Gurezi, one of the Shina dialects) languages are a group of Indo-European languages spoken in part of Nūrestān and adjacent areas along the Kabul river and its tributaries in the mountain region that encompasses northeastern Afghanistan, northern Pakistan, and northwestern India (see i, above).

In the literature this group is sometimes also called Piśāca (the old term for the population of northwestern India), and Paiśāci (obsolete name of one Middle Indian language of this region).

Classification.

The main languages and dialects of the Dardic group are the following.

Eastern subgroup. The eastern subgroup includes Kashmiri in the Kashmir valley; Shina in the districts of Gilgit and Tangir, north of Kashmir; Phalura (or Palola) and the closely related Sawi; and a number of languages and dialects sometimes referred to generally as Kōhestānī (lit., "of the mountains") in the Indus, Swat, and Panjkora basins: Maiyan (so called by native speakers but Kōhestānī by others) with the Kanywali dialect, Torwali, and Bashkarik (or Diri, known in another dialect variant as Garwi).

Central subgroup. The central subgroup is further subdivided into northern and southern groupings. The northern grouping includes Khowar (or Chitrali, Chitrari, Chatrori, Arniya) and Kalasha in the Chitral (q.v.) region. The southern grouping includes Tirahi, Gawar (or Gawar-bati, lit., "language of the Gawar people"), Katarkalai (or Wotapuri, referring to another dialect), Shumashti, Glangali (closely related Ningalami, reported in the literature but apparently no longer extant), and Pashai, a large group of extremely divergent dialects or closely related languages, in the southern part of Nūrestān and adjacent areas.

Nūrestānī languages. The Nūrestānī languages (also known traditionally as Kafiri languages) are sometimes included as a western subgroup of the Dardic group of languages (see Shaw, 1876, pp. 146-47; Grierson; Morgenstierne, 1945; idem, 1974). They are the languages of Afghan Nūrestān, known as Kafiristan until the people adopted Islam on the eve of the 20th century. This subgroup includes Kati (including the eastern dialect Bashgali), Waigali (or Wai, Wai-alā), and related Tregami (or Gambiri) and Zemiaki; Ashkun and the closely related language or dialect Wamai; and Prasun (or Paruni, Wasin-veri, Veron). These languages have much in common with the Dardic languages and are spoken in close geographical proximity to them, but their origin is not the same (see below). The attribution of the Dameli language, which exhibits both Nūrestānī and Dardic features, is not clear. Some authors also include in the Dardic group the Ḍumaki language, spoken by a people scattered in groups in Hunza and Nagar. Genetically, however, it belongs to the Central Indo-Aryan languages (being close to Gypsy), rather than to the Dardic group.

Linguistic classification.

The Dardic languages are an offshoot of the Indo-Aryan languages of the post-Vedic period. The Nūrestānī languages belong neither to the Iranian nor to the Indo-Aryan group but represent instead an independent branch of the Aryan family of Indo-European languages. This relationship is represented schematically in Table 1.

The main classifying features within this family of

Table 1

ORIGIN OF THE DARDIC LANGUAGES AND THEIR RELATION TO OTHER ARYAN LANGUAGES

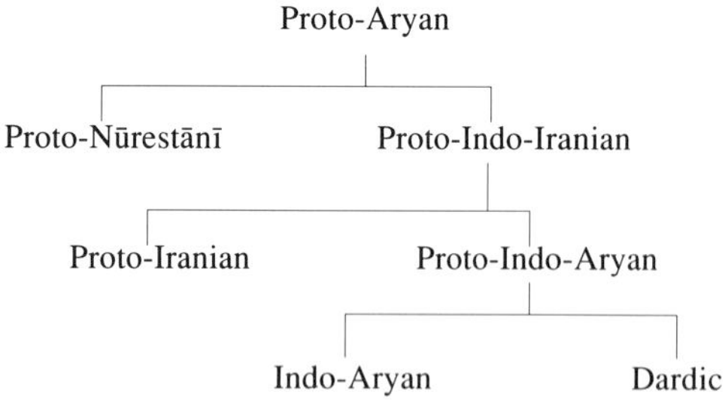

languages is the different phonetic evolution of certain Proto-Aryan consonants.

Development of the Proto-Aryan stops. The Proto-Aryan phonological system included four kinds of stop: voiced and unvoiced, aspirated and unaspirated (**dh, *d, *th, t; *bh, *b*, etc.). In Proto-Indo-Aryan these stops remained separate phonemes, whereas in the Nūrestānī languages the aspiration was lost (**dh* and * *d* > **d*, *th* and **t* > **t*, etc.), leaving a system with two kinds of stop: voiced and unvoiced (*d-t*, etc.). In Proto- Iranian only the voiced aspirate stops lost their aspiration (**dh* and **d* > **d*, etc.), while the unvoiced aspirated stops, with a few exceptions, became fricatives (**th* > **θ*, **ph* > **f*, **kh* > **x*); the system of four stops was thus changed into a system of two stops, voiced and unvoiced, and a fricative (**d* -**t* -**θ*). Examples include Proto-Indo-Aryan (and Old Indian) **khara* "donkey," Dardic (Kalasha) *khār*, Nūrestānī (Kati) *kur*, Proto-Iranian (and Avestan) **xara* (Pers. *k̲ar*).

Development of the Indo-European palatal velars. Indo-European **ǵ(h)*, **ḱ* became Proto-Arian palatal affricates **ǰ́(h)*, **ć* (i.e., *dź(h)*, *tś*). They remained in Proto-Nūrestānī and Proto-Iranian as separate phonemes but merged with the palatalized velars in Proto-Indo-Aryan (see below).

Development of the Proto-Aryan palatalized velars and palatal affricates. In Proto-Aryan the Indo-European velars were palatalized before front vowels: **g(h)*, **k* before *e* and *i* > **ǰ(h)*, **č*. When Proto-Aryan **e* changed into **a*, these palatalized velars became separate phonemes, contrasting with the Proto-Aryan descendants of the Indo-European voiced and unvoiced palatals: **ǰ́(h)*, **ć*. As with the stops, the aspiration remained in Proto-Indo-Aryan but was lost in Nūrestānī and Proto-Iranian, leaving only **ǰ*, **č* and **ǰ́*, ć, which remained as separate phonemes. In Proto-Indo-Aryan **ǰh*, **ǰ́h* and **ǰ*, **ǰ́* then merged into single phonemes *h* and *ǰ*, *č* remained, and **ć* changed to palatal *ś*. In Nūrestānī **ǰ* remained, **ǰ́* changed to *‰(> *z*), and **ć* became the dental affricate *c* (*ts*). In the Iranian languages **ǰ* and **č* remained, while **ǰ́* became *z* or *d* and **ć* became *s* or *θ*. Examples include Indo-European **deḱm̥* "ten" (Latin *decem*, etc.) > (late) Proto-Aryan **daća* > Nūrestānī (Kati) *duc*, Avestan *dasa*, Old Persian **daθa* (Pers. *dah*), Old Indian *daśa*, Dardic (Dameli) *daš*; Indo-European **ǵenu-*/**ǵonu-* "knee" > Proto-Aryan **ǰ́ānu-* "knee" > Nūrestānī (Kati) *jō* (i.e., *dzō*), Old Indian *jānu-*, Avestan *zānu-* (Pers. *zānū*); and Proto-Aryan **aǰ́ham* "I" (cf. Latin *egō*, etc.) > Nūrestānī (Kati) *vúze*, Avestan *azəm*, Old Persian *adam*, Old Indian *aham*, Dardic (Pashai) *ā*.

Development of Indo-European s. Indo-European *s* remained in Proto-Aryan except in a few positions. Proto-Aryan *s* remained in Nūrestānī and Proto-Indo-Aryan but became *h* in Proto-Iranian. Indo-European **s* became **š* after Indo-European **i*, **ə*, **u*, **r*, **k*, **ḱ* in most of Proto-Aryan, but not consistently in Nūrestānī, where in a few words the *s* has remained after *u*, for example, in Kati *músə* "mouse," as opposed to Old Indian *mūṣ-*, Iranian (Persian) *mūš* (for more details, see Morgenstierne, 1945, pp. 225-36; idem, 1973, pp. 227-347; idem, 1974, pp. 6-8; Buddruss).

The Nūrestānī and Dardic languages are therefore genetically quite distinct, and the similarities between them that can be observed today and that have obscured their origins must be ascribed to various causes: their common Proto-Aryan origin, effects of a common substrate, parallel developments resulting from their geographic proximity, converging phonetic developments, and mutual influences and borrowings. As a result of all these trends, Dameli, for instance, now occupies what may be termed an "intermediate" position between the two groups. The separate nature of the Dardic languages is still clear, however, from their close relationship with other Indo-Aryan languages, especially Punjabi, Lahnda, Sindhi, and the dialects of Western Pahari.

The assumption of a connection between the Dardic languages and the Middle Indian Paiśācī language is based partly on their common geographical location and partly on such phonetic features as the devoicing of postvocalic (occasionally also initial) voiced consonants. This feature is not shared by all Dardic languages, however, and may be a regional, rather than a genetic, phenomenon. A genetic relationship between the two groups is therefore doubtful.

The Dardic languages.

The Dardic language group can be further subdivided according to genetic and structural criteria.

1. The four-way opposition among the stops (*dh-d-th-t*, etc.) remains in most of the Kōhestānī languages but is reduced through the merger of the voiced aspirated and unaspirated stops (*dh* and *d* > *d*, etc.) to a three-way opposition elsewhere, except perhaps in Kalasha, Phalura, and some of the dialects of Kashmiri. In some of these languages the loss of the voiced aspirated stops gave rise to a tonal opposition, similar to that found in some neighboring Indo-Aryan languages.

2. In Proto-Khowar-Kalasha intervocalic and final **t* become **δ*, which then became *l* in Northern Kalasha but *r* in Southern Kalasha and Khowar. (There is a similar distribution of the change from **t* in the Gypsy

dialects, to *r* in Syria, to *l* in Europe.)

3. The augment was retained only in Khowar and Kalasha (e.g., *akāren* "they did").

It is possible to distinguish still further subdivisions, for instance, Phalura-Sawi-Shina, and Shumasti-Glangali-Ningalami, but the mutual relationships among the Dardic languages are still unclear at many points, primarily because of insufficient research, so that, for instance, the phonology of several Dardic languages is very scantily known. Furthermore, determination of which similarities should be ascribed to common ancestry and which have been caused by linguistic interaction still remains to be sorted out

History of study of the Dardic languages.

The only Dardic language with a long literary tradition is Kashmiri, which was formerly written in the Śārada and Nagarī alphabets and more recently in the Urdu modification of the Arabic script. Written versions of Khowar, Shina, and Maiyan, also based on the Arabic alphabet, have appeared only recently.

Alhough Dardic languages were occasionally mentioned in travelers' notes and Christian missionaries actually published parts of the Bible in Kashmiri (in the Nagari alphabet) in the 1820s, the study of Dardic languages actually began in the 1830s, when the first professional linguistic data, in the form of compact vocabularies and glossaries, were published by M. P. Edgeworth, R. Leech, G. T. Vigne, and others. Between the 1860s and 1880s more comprehensive information appeared, along with studies of the folklore and ethnography of the region. The most important works of this period were those by J. Campbell, G. W. Leitner, J. H. Knowles, and K. F. Burkhard. At about the same time such scholars as R. B. Shaw and Wilhelm Tomaschek incorporated material on the Dardic and Nūrestānī languages into their studies of comparative Indo-Iranian linguistics.

By the 1890s the study of the Dardic languages had assumed a systematic character. In 1896 G. A. Grierson initiated and supervised the multivolume *Linguistic Survey of India*, an attempt to gather data on all known languages of India and neighboring countries in conformity with general guidelines and a standard questionnaire. The *Survey* included linguistic outlines and lexical and textual material for the Dardic languages and a consolidated dictionary of Dardic vocabulary. Grierson also wrote several works on various Dardic languages, notably a grammar and an extensive dictionary of Kashmiri. A major contribution to the descripton of Shina, Kashmiri, and other languages was made by T. Grahame Bailey, beginning in the first decade of the twentieth century. Georg Morgenstierne devised the accepted genetic classification of the Dardic and Nūrestānī languages. In the 1920s he began to publish descriptions of many Dardic, Nūrestānī, and Iranian languages, as well as texts, vocabularies, and historical essays. In the 1950s Georg Buddruss began publication of texts, vocabularies, and descriptions of languages, supported by profound historical analysis. He drew on a wide range of material to revise the historical-genetic classification of the Nūrestānī languages, thus largely completing the classification of the Aryan language group.

In recent decades research has been focused on the contemporary state of languages (e.g., in the works of B. B. Kachru, B. A. Zakharyin, and A. L. Gryunberg) and on typological and regional analysis of the Dardic languages (e.g., by W. N. Toporov, Gérard Fussman, and others). The material of Dardic languages has also been used for historical analysis of the Indo-Aryan and other languages by R. L. Turner, Manfred Mayrhofer, I. M. Steblin-Kamenskiĭ, and others.

Exchange of loanwords with Iranian languages.

Contact between the Dardic and Iranian languages and the resulting mutual exchange of loanwords varied with several factors. In folklore, particularly poetry, and religious texts there are a large number of Persian words and elements, as well as some from Arabic borrowed through Persian. Such borrowings have often been indirect, through Urdu in the modern Dardic languages of India and Pakistan and through Darī or Pashto (see AFGHANISTAN v, vi) in those of Afghanistan, especially in some of the Pashai dialects. In Kashmiri, the traditional Dardic literary language, they came directly from literary Persian.

Persian and Arab-Persian loanwords fall into large lexical groups. One such group is the concrete nouns (names of animate and inanimate objects and substances): Kashmiri *pādšāh*, Khowar *bāča*, Kalasha *bādša*, Kanyawali *bādšā* "padishah"; Kashmiri *wəz′ɨr* "vizier," *yɨnsān* "human being," *hamdard* "courtier," *k′ɨtāb* "book"; Shina *bădăm* "almond"; Kalasha *biaban* "desert"; Kashmiri *šah(ɨ)r* "city," *kākaz* "paper." Another is names of abstract nouns: Kashmiri *wādɨ*, Khowar *wada* "promise"; Kashmiri *mōǰɨzɨ* "wonders," *yād* "memory," *nūr* "light"; Kalasha *bo* "smell," *khiyal* "thought," *kuwat* "strength"; Khowar *wafā́*, Kashmiri *waphā* "fidelity"; Khowar *itifaq* "unity," *žān* "life, soul." Adjectives constitute another group: Kashmiri *phə̄n′ɨ* "temporal, perishable," *mušk′ul* "difficult," *waphādār* "devoted," *g°ənāgār* "sinful"; Kalasha *bedarkar* "ill, sick"; Khowar *kam* "little, less, few."

Some loanwords occur as the nominal components of compound verbs, as in Persian and other Iranian languages: Khowar *ǰawab d-* "to answer," *wada k-* "to promise"; Kashmiri *taft′īš kar-* "to check," *kar- arz* "to complain," *kar- khošī* "to make merry, to rejoice." Much less often a simple verb has been borrowed, for example, Khowar *neweš-* "to write." Occasionally borrowed conjunctions, particles, and other auxiliaries are found: Kashmiri *agar*, Shina *ăgăr* "if"; Kalasha *albat* "probably"; Kashmiri *hargāh k′ɨ* "if only"; Kashmiri *magar*, Khowar *magam* "however."

In regions of direct contact between various Dardic languages and the adjacent Iranian languages, that is, in the Hindu Kush and part of the Pamirs, there are mutual lexical borrowings between Iranian and Dardic languages, as well as common borrowings from other sources. The Dardic languages have borrowed from live and extinct Iranian languages throughout the entire area of contact. In Khowar several Iranian sources from different periods can be distinguished (Morgenstierne, 1973, pp. 241-55).

In turn, the Iranian languages of this area have borrowed a vast vocabulary from Dardic languages or through Dardic languages from other Indo-Aryan sources. These words are mostly related to local life, traditional household items, plants, and the like, for example, terms for birch bark: Shughni *birūǰ*; Rushani, Bartangi, Roshorvi *birū̌ǰ*; Yazghulami *bəruž*, *bəruǰ*; Ishkashmi *bɨrɨẓ̌*, *bərij*, *bruǰ*; Sanglechi *bᵊrež*, *bᵊrīž*; Zebaki *bruǰ*, *bərež*; Tajik dialect *bəruǰ*, *buruǰ*; Pashto *barǰ*; Khotanese Saka *bruṃja-* "bark." Of special interest is the term for cotton: Shughni *čipōs* (in the collocation *čipōs rūγan* "cotton oil"), Rushani *čipʊs*, Yazghulami *k′əbes*, Wakhi *kəbas*. These terms are all descended from **kap(p)āsa-* (cf. Pali *kappāsa-* < OInd. *karpāsa-*, Khowar *kəbos*, Marathi *kāpūs*, Nepali and Hindi *kapās*, as the word spread eastward following the cultural reality: Burushaski *gupas*, Werchikwar *γupas*, Uighur *käpäz*, *kepäz*, and so on; Turner, no. 2877). Despite the obscure origin of this word in Old Indian (see Mayrhofer, *Dictionary* fasc. 3, pp. 174-75), it certainly came into these Iranian languages from Indo-Aryan, presumably Dardic, languages at a relatively early period, as can be deduced from phonetic transformations: the transition **k* > *č* before **a* in Shughni and Rushani, also typical of indigenous words, and the transition **-p-* > *b* in Yazghulami. Wakhi *kəbas* could havebeen borrowed directly from Khowar or from Indo-Aryan before the change of *p* to *b* in Wakhi. The term for a particular kind of cotton cloth, which continues the same Old Indian prototype *karpāsa-* and has been borrowed by other Iranian languages through other channels, exhibits a more archaic form in Iranian than the one observed in the Dardic languages, for instance, Persian *karbās*, Tajik *karbos*, but Kalasha *kravas*, Khowar *karvas*.

In the Iranian languages of the Pamirs the term for the local style of kerchief is probably a similar borrowing with relatively early phonetic transformations: Shughni-Bajuwi *cēl*, Rushani-Khufi, Roshorvi *cīl*, Yazghulami *cil* (possibly from Rushani), Wakhi *čil*. Among Dardic equivalents are Kalasha *čēl-*, Ḍameli *čel*, Pashai *čilā-* (Turner, no. 4910). Another Iranian borrowing is Shughni *lāq* "old, worn trousers, tatters," *lêq* "old, torn quilt"; Rushani *loq*, Bartangi *löq* "clothes"; Rushani, Khufi, Bartangi *lēq* "old clothes, rags"; Yazghulami *luq* "clothes, fabric, rags" (pl. *laqáθ* "quilts"); Wakhi *luq* "rags." This word is probably related to Indo-Aryan **lakka-* "defective" (Turner, no. 10877) or possibly to Ossetic *lyg*/*lux*, the onomatopoeic origin of which cannot be excluded.

A Dardic source may also be attributed to Shughni *kappur*, Rushani *kapor*, Bartangi *kapör* "gourd, calabash"; Roshorvi *kapir* "gourd snuffbox"; Yazghulami *kapur*, *kapʊr* "elongated calabash"; Tajik dialect *kapar* "calabash," all probably related to Old Indian *karpara* "bowl." Other plant names display similar patterns of borrowing. In the Iranian languages of the Pamirs a large number of terms for useful domestic plants were borrowed from the Dardic languages (and through them from other Indo-Aryan sources): Shughni, Rushani, Khufi, Bartangi, Roshorvi *pīnǰ*, Sarīqoli *penǰ* (and Wanji *punǰev*) "millet"; Wakhi *ṣ̌ax̌*, Shughni (etc.) *x̌āš* "peas, beans"; Wakhi *kroṣ̌*, Ishkashmi *karoṣ̌*, *karå̊š* "cinna"; and so on (for more details, see Steblin-Kamenskiĭ, pp. 24, 30, 33, 42, 46, 49 ff.).

Certain Dardic borrowings in Iranian languages can be linked with traditional taboos on words, which were usually replaced by either descriptive expressions or loanwords. For example, in certain Iranian languages of the area the original terms for the wolf that continue proto-Iranian **u̯ṛka-* (cf. Av. *vəhrka-*, OInd. *vṛka-*, Pers. *gorg*, Yazghulami *warǵ*, etc.) have been replaced by *x̌iθp* in the Barwozi dialect of Shughni and *x̌iθp* in Sariqoli, both borrowed from Wakhi; in Wakhi itself, however, *ṣ̌apt* "wolf" is borrowed from **šapita-* in the precursor of Khowar (continued in modern Khowar as *šapīr*), which was a continuation of Old Indian **śapita-* "cursed," from the verbal stem **śap-* "to curse" (Mayrhofer, *Dictionary*, fasc. 21, p. 396; Turner, no. 12293). The term for wolf is also taboo in other languages of the area, but the substitution is made in a different way; cf. Ormuri *lēwū*, Pashto *lewə* "wolf" < **daiu̯ia-* "of the dēvs" < **daiu̯a-* "dēv, evil spirit." In the non-Indo-European Burushaski language *ūrk* and *urk* in the Werchikwar dialect are borrowed from Iranian Ishkashmi.

The Iranian, Dardic, and other languages of the area also have a common "local vocabulary," which includes words, usually names of local things, household terms, and the like, the source and transmission of which are unknown or in doubt. These words include, for instance, Shughni *tāk* "gown string," Rushani, Khufi *tāk* "collar, lapel," Sariqoli *tok* "button," Yazghulami *tak°* "string at the collar of a woman's gown," Wakhi *tak* "button"; cf. Shina *ṭʌk*, Khowar *ṭʌk* "button, string of a woman's gown," Burushaski *ṭʌk*, Werchikwar *ṭʌk* "collar string, button." Evidently this term initially denoted the common reality in the area: the string fastening the collar of the old local dress (cf. Tajik *yak-tak* "old-fashioned shirt with the string on one side"; on the other hand, Kurdish *tog* "string" is derived from Armenian). When the button appeared in this area the old term for "fastening" was retained in some languages and in others a new word was borrowed from Turkic: Shughni *tukmā́*, Yazghulami *təkmá* "button." Another example of the common regional vocabulary is the term for a large flat cake: Shughni *x̌ipik* "pancake" and Sariqoli *x̌(i)pik* "big flat cake" are borrowed from Wakhi, in which *x̌apik* "kind of cake" is itself derived from Khowar *ṣapik* "cake" (cf. Burushaski *ṣ̌ʌpik*).

In addition, the Dardic and Iranian languages share a number of structural features, also ascribable to a variety of causes, including substrate influence and interaction. In noun morphology the use of nouns like *gal(a)*, originally meaning "flock" (also found throughout Iran; e.g., Pashai *-kuli*, *-ēlā*, Gawar *-gila*, Kashmiri masc. *kyəl*, fem. *kyaǰ*; cf. Shughni *-galā*, *-xēl*, etc.) as plural markers may be noted. In pronominal inflection the remarkable convergence in the forms of the first-person plural pronouns Khowar *ispa* (direct and oblique cases), Wakhi *spo* (genitive) and the influence of the second-person singular pronoun on the second-person plural (e.g., Phalura sing. *tu*, pl. *tus*), is noteworth; it may be compared with the "prefix" *ta-* used in the second-person plural in the Shughni group and Ishkashmi (Schmitt, p. 432). In both the Iranian languages of the area and Dardic (except Kashmiri) the numeral system is vigesimal; for example, fifty-five is expressed as "two score + ten + five" or "two score + fifteen." The numerals from 11 to 19 are expressed as "ten-one" and so on, rather than in the earlier form "one-ten." The syntax is characterized by the word order subject-object-verb in most of the languages, avoidance of indirect speech, and the like (see Edel'man, 1968, pp. 77-98 and maps 2, 5-14).

Bibliography: G. Buddruss, "Nochmals zur Stellung der Nuristan-Sprachen des Afghanischen Hindukush," in *MSS* 36, 1977, pp. 19-38. D. I. Edel'man, *Dardskie yazyki* (The Dardic languages), Moscow, 1965. Idem, *Osnovnye voprosy lingvisticheskoĭ geografii (na materiale indoiranskikh yazykov)* (Fundamental problems of linguistic geography [based on the materials of the Indo-Iranian languages]), Moscow, 1968. Idem, *The Dardic and Nuristani Languages*, Moscow, 1983 (with extensive bibliography). G. Fussman, *Atlas linguistique des parlers dardes et kafirs*, 2 vols., Paris, 1972. G. A. Grierson, *Linguistic Survey of India* I/1-2, Calcutta, 1927-28; VIII/2, Calcutta, 1919. G. Morgenstierne, *Indo-Iranian Frontier Languages*, 4 vols. Oslo, 1929-67. Idem, "Indo-European k' in Kafiri," *NTS* 13, 1945, pp. 225-38. Idem, *Irano-Dardica*, Wiesbaden, 1973. Idem, "Languages of Nuristan and Surrounding Regions" in K. Jettmar, ed., *Cultures of the Hindukush*, Wiesbaden, 1974, pp. 1-10. I. M. Oranskij, "Indo-Iranica IV. Tadjik (Régional) *Buruǰ* 'Bouleau,'" in *Mélanges linguistiques offerts à Émile Benveniste*, Paris, 1975, pp. 435–40. R. Schmitt, ed. *Compendium Linguarum Iranicarum*, Wiesbaden, 1989. R. B. Shaw, "On the Ghalchah Languages (Wakhí and Sari-ḳolí)," *Journal and Proceedings of the Asiatic Society of Bengal* 45, 1876, pp. 139-278. I. M. Steblin-Kamenskiĭ, *Ocherki po istorii leksiki pamirskykh yazykov. Nazvaniya kul'turnykh rasteniĭ* (Outlines for the lexical history of the Pamir languages. Names for cultivated plants), Moscow, 1982. R. L. Turner, *A Comparative Dictionary of the Indo-Aryan Languages*, 2 vols., London, 1963-66.

(D. I. EDEL'MAN)

DĀREMĪ, ABŪ SAʿĪD ʿOṮMĀN b. Saʿīd b. Ḵāled SEJESTĀNĪ, Persian traditionist and jurist (b. ca. 200/816, d. Herat Ḏu'l-ḥejja 280/February 894, sometimes incorrectly reported as 282/896). He belonged to a family of Sejestānī cloth merchants and was educated in a Hanafite environment. Through extensive travel, probably in connection with his business, he became acquainted with Hadith scholarship in Iraq, Syria, and Egypt. In Baghdad he met (Aḥmad) Ebn Ḥanbal (q.v.; 164-241/780-855), but his main teacher seems to have been Yaḥyā b. Maʿīn (d. 233/847), from whom he preserved a collection of notes on earlier traditionists, among them eastern Persian Hanafites like Ebrāhīm b. Rostam Marvazī (cf. Ebn Abi'l-Wafāʾ, I, p. 38). In Egypt he studied with (Abū ʿAbd-Allāh Moḥammad) Šāfeʿī's most important pupil, Yūsof b. Yaḥyā Bowayṭī (d. 231/846). These contacts seem to have led him to a more rigorous reliance on tradition when he settled finally in Herat.

Abū ʿĀṣem Moḥammad ʿAbbādī, who came from the same city, reported (pp. 45 ff.) that Dāremī joined the Shafiʿites, though they had probably not yet succeeded in establishing themselves in the area. As a result, he clashed with the Karrāmīya, adherents of (Abū ʿAbd-Allāh Moḥammad) Ebn Karrām (d. 255/869), who had Hanafite leanings and were less scrupulous in dealing with Hadith, and was forced to leave Herat; a sojourn in Jorjān is attested for the year 273/886-87 (Sahmī, p. 258 no. 505; for additional details, see Ebn Abī Yaʿlā, I, p. 221 no. 298; Sobkī, *Ṭabaqāt* (Cairo²), pp. 302 ff. no. 71; Ḏahabī, XIII, pp. 319 ff. no. 148; Sezgin, *GAS* I, pp. 600-01).

Dāremī's discontent with antitraditionist tendencies persisting among eastern Persian Hanafites is reflected in his two surviving books, both directed at the so-called Jahmīya, a group of theologians, especially influential in Persia, who, because of their transcendentalist and antianthropomorphic outlook, were connected by their opponents with the early Islamic thinker Jahm b. Ṣafwān (executed 128/746); they drew their ideas mainly from the Baghdad Hanafite jurist Bešr Marīsī (d. 218/833). In his *Radd ʿala'l-Jahmīya* (ed. G. Vitestam, Lund and Leiden, 1960) Dāremī followed the line of Ebn Ḥanbal's *Radd ʿala'l-Zanādeqa wa'l-Jahmīya*, attempting to prove that the Jahmīs were heretics and therefore deserved capital punishment. He was criticized for this fanaticism by an unknown individual who had met Bešr personally and maintained that Jahmī theology lay within the radius of normal doctrinal differences. This critic cited Moḥammad b. Šojāʿ Ṯaljī (d. 266/880), whose views were highly influential among Persian jurists and who, like Marīsī, had not completely rejected the traditions adduced against Jahmī theology; both had instead simply interpreted them in metaphorical terms. This attack led Dāremī to write *Radd ʿala'l-Marīsī al-ʿanīd* (ed. M. Ḥ. Feqī, Cairo, 1939; for a more recent reprint of both Dāremī's works, see ʿA. S. Naššār and ʿA. J. Ṭālebī, *ʿAqāʾed al-salaf*, Alexandria, 1971, pp. 254 ff., 359 ff.), in which he in no way softened the aggressiveness of his style.

Bibliography: Abū ʿĀṣem Moḥammad ʿAbbādī, *Ṭabaqāt al-foqahāʾ al-Šāfeʿīya*, ed. G. Vitestam,

Leiden, 1964. Šams-al-Dīn Abū ʿAbd-Allāh Moḥammad Ḏahabī, *Sīar aʿlām al-nobalāʾ*, ed. Š. Arnāʾūt, Beirut, 1401/1981. ʿAbd-al-Qāder Ebn Abi'l-Wafāʾ, *al-Jawāher al-možīʿa fī ṭabaqāt al-Ḥanafīya*, 2 vols., Hyderabad, 1332/1914. Abu'l-Ḥosayn Moḥammad Ebn Abī Yaʿlā, *Ṭabaqāt al-Ḥanābela*, ed. M.-Ḥ. Feqī, 2 vols., Cairo, 1952. J. van Ess, *Theologie und Gesellschaft im 2. und 3. Jahrhundert Hidschra*, Berlin, 1991, II, p. 71; III, pp. 181-82. Ḥamza b. Yūsof Sahmī, *Tārīḵ Jorjān*, Hyderabad, 1369/1950.

(JOSEF VAN ESS)

DARGĀHĪ, MOḤAMMAD (b. Zanjān, 1317/1899, d. Tehran, 1331 Š./1952), first chief of the state police under Reżā Shah (1304-20 Š./1925-41). After receiving his secondary education at ʿElmīya school in Tehran (Hedāyat, p. 386; Modarresī, I, p. 109), Dargāhī attended the gendarmerie officers' college. In 1299 Š./1920 he was appointed chief of police in Qom, with the rank of major. After the coup d'etat of 1299/1921 (q.v.) he was appointed military governor of Qom by the prime minister, Sayyed Żīāʾ-al-Dīn (Afsar, p. 273). In February 1922, after the Cossack Brigade (q.v.) had been merged with the gendarmerie, he was promoted to the rank of colonel and appointed chief of the military police in Tehran. In 1302 Š./1923 Reżā Khan Sardār-e Sepah, the new prime minister, dismissed the Swedish officers who had been in charge of the state police force and appointed Dargāhī as the new chief (Bahār, I, p. 286). He soon became a confidant of Reżā Khan and threw the support of the police behind his effort to put an end to the Qajar dynasty. He remained in charge of the police for six years and in March 1928 was promoted to the rank of brigadier-general.

During his tenure as chief of police there were a number of murders and assassinations in Tehran in which the police were believed to be involved: the murders of American vice-consul Robert Imbrie in 1303 Š./1924 and of Wāʿeẓ Qazvīnī, editor of the newspaper *Naṣīḥat* in 1304 Š./1925; the attempt on the life of Sayyed Ḥasan Modarres in 1305 Š./1926; and the assassination of the poet Moḥammad-Reżā Mīrzāda ʿEšqī (q.v.) in 1303 Š./1924. In 1308 Š./1929 he invited the shah and a number of ministers to open a new prison on the site of the former Qajar palace known as Qaṣr-e Qajar, an occasion that led, for reasons that are still a matter of debate, to his dismissal and arrest on the following day, 13 Āḏar/4 December (*Eṭṭelāʿāt dar robʿ-e qarn*, p. 57). He was detained for some time at the headquarters of the military police but was pardoned, on 14 Ordībehešt 1309/4 May 1930, and appointed chief of military conscription (*Sālnāma-ye Pārs*, 1310 Š./1931, p. 27). He served in this post until 1313 Š./1934, when he was appointed head of the National registry and census office (Edāra-ye koll-e āmār wa ṯabt-e aḥwāl). In 1316 Š/1937 he was dismissed by the shah. Dargāhī never held another government office. He spent the rest of his life as a farmer in Varāmīn.

He was responsible for having expanded the police force, created the state police system under Reżā Shah, and laid the foundations for intelligance gathering and strict police control of society. In the 1930s Moḥammad-Ḥosayn Āyrom (q.v.) and Rokn-al-Dīn Moḵtār perfected this system.

Bibliography: P. Afsar, *Tārīḵ-e žāndārmerī-e Īrān*, Tehran, 1332 Š./1953. Bamdād, *Rejāl*, III, pp. 242-43. M.-T. Bahār, *Tārīḵ-e moḵtaṣar-e aḥzāb-e sīāsī* I, Tehran, 1323 Š./1944. *Eṭṭelāʿāt dar robʿ-e qarn*, Tehran, 1329 Š./1950. M. Hedāyat, *Ḵāṭerāt wa ḵaṭarāt*, 2nd. ed., Tehran, 1344 Š./1965. ʿA. Modarresī, *Ketāb-e Modarres*, I, Tehran, 1366 Š./1987. Mostawfī, *Šarḥ-e zendagānī* III, p. 629.

(BĀQER ʿĀQELĪ)

DARGĀHQOLĪ KHAN ḎU'L-QADR, also known as Moʿtaman-al-Dawla Moʿtaman-al-Molk Sālār-Jang Ḵān-e Dawrān Nawwāb (b. Sangamnēr, Deccan, 1122/1710, d. Awrangābād, 18 Jomādā I 1180/22 October 1766; Malkāpūrī, p. 398; cf. Āzād Belgrāmī, pp. 222-23), Persian official at Hyderabad and Awrangābād, best known for his description of Delhi. He was descended from Ḵāndānqolī Khan Ḏu'l-Qadr, a member of the Būrbūr line of Turkman chiefs in the region of Mašhad, who had emigrated to India in 1048/1638 (Āzād Belgrāmī, pp. 221-22; Kanbō, II, p. 246; cf. Malkāpūrī, pp. 397-98). Ḵāndānqolī Khan's great-grandson, also named Ḵāndānqolī, was Dargāhqolī's father and the first of the family to enter the service of the *neẓām*s (rulers) of Hyderabad. It was he who designed and constructed the township of Neẓāmābād for Neẓām-al-Molk Āṣaf-jāh (d. 1161/1748; Āzād Belgrāmī, p. 222; Malkāpūrī, p. 397-98).

Dargāhqolī Khan became one of the foremost nobles of Persian descent at the Hyderabad court and served with distinction under four *neẓām*s. He was fourteen years old when Neẓām-al-Molk bestowed on him his ancestral rank (*manṣab*) and estate (*jāgīr*); when he was twenty years old he was chosen for Neẓām-al-Molk's suite. He accompanied his master to Delhi and remained with him during the invasion by the Persian Nāder Shah and its aftermath (1151-54/1738-41; Dargāhqolī, pp. 14-20). Neẓām-al-Molk's successor, Neẓām Nāṣer-Jang (1161-64/1748-50), appointed him *kōtvāl* (commandant of the fortress) and *fawjdār* (garrison commander) of Awrangābād, and Ṣalābat-Jang (r. 1164-75/1751-62) elevated him to governor, a position that he held until 1179/1765. During that period he rose to the rank of *haft-hazārī* (commander of 7,000), and under Neẓām ʿAlī Khan (1175-1217/1762-1802) he was granted the extraordinary privilege of *māhī-marāteb* (Dargāhqolī, pp. 43-45, 48, 51; Qureshi, p. 105). He appears to have been an excellent administrator, as well as a generous patron of literature (Malkāpūrī, pp. 400-01, 403). He also built numerous monuments that still survive in Awrangābād (Malkāpurī, p. 401-04; Āzād Belgrāmī, p. 224;

Dargāhqolī, pp. 53, 64-65; Rizvi, p. 258), including his own mausoleum.

Dargāhqolī Khan's *Moraqqaʿ-e Dehlī* (Album of Delhi, a title given it by its first editor, Ḥ.-S. Możaffar Ḥosayn), also known as *Resāla-ye Sālār-Jang* and *Ābādī-e Dehlī*), is a collection of extracts from Dargāhqolī Khan's personal diary of his stay in Delhi, in which he described the city, its monuments, its poets, its *martīya-kᵛāns* (reciters of threnodies), and its musicians on the eve of the conquest by Nāder Shah. Dargāhqolī Khan himself composed *martīyas* (threnodies) in Urdu.

Bibliography: Mīr Ḡolām-ʿAlī Āzād Belgrāmī, *Ḵezāna-ye ʿāmera*, Kanpur, 1288/1871. Dargāhqolī Khan, *Moraqqaʿ-e Dehlī*, ed. Ḥ.-S. Możaffar Ḥosayn, Hyderabad (Deccan), n.d. (1926); ed. with Urdu tr. N. H. Anṣārī, Aligarh, 1981; tr. C. Shekhar and S. M. Chenoy as *Muraqqaʿ-e-Dehli. The Mughal Capital in Muhammad Shah's Time*, Delhi, 1989. Moḥammad-Ṣāleḥ Kanbō, *ʿAmal-e Ṣāleh al mawsūm beh Šāh-jahān-nāmą*, ed. Ḡ. Yazdānī, 2nd ed., rev. W. Qorayšī, 3 vols., Lahore, 1967-72. Abū Torāb Moḥammad ʿAbd-al-Jabbār Khan Malkāpūrī, *Maḥbūb al-zamān men Taḏkera-ye šoʿarāʾ-ye Dakkan*, Hyderabad (Deccan), n.d. I. H. Qureshi, *The Administration of the Mughul Empire*, Karachi, 1966. Rieu, *Persian Manuscripts* II, p. 858. A. A. Rizvi, *A Socio-Intellectual History of the Isnā ʿAsharī Shīʿīs in India*, Canberra, 1986. Storey, I/2, pp. 1118-19.

(M. Saleem Akhtar)

DARGAZĪNĪ, *nesba* (attributive name) for Dargazīn (or Darjazīn, q.v.), borne by several viziers of the Great Saljuqs in the 12th century.

The most distinguished was Abu'l-Qāsem Nāṣer b. ʿAlī, Qewām-al-Dīn Zayn-al-Molk ʿEmād-al-Dawla; he and his relative and successor ʿEmād-al-Dīn Abu'l-Barakāt, at least, also bore the additional *nesba* Anasābādī (after Anasābāḏ, a village in the district of Dargazīn between Hamadān and Zanjān; Yāqūt, *Boldān*, ed. Beirut, I, p. 265, II, pp. 451-52). Of peasant origin, he rose within the Saljuq administration through ambition and intrigue, becoming *ʿāreż al-jayš* (head of the military department), and eventually succeeded Šams-al-Molk ʿOṯmān b. Neẓām-al-Molk as vizier to Sultan Maḥmūd b. Moḥammad b. Malekšāh (511-25/1118-31; for Abu'l-Qāsem's career, see Bondarī, pp. 121-24, 144-50, 160-70; Ebn al-Aṯīr, X, p. 642, 652, 669; Kermānī, pp. 74-77; ʿAqīlī, pp. 255-56; cf. Eqbāl, pp. 265-74; Bosworth, p. 124; Lambton, pp. 251, 263-64; Klausner, pp. 39, 43-44, 54-56, 61, 90, 92-93). He served in the latter office for three years (518-21/1124-27). His rival Anūšervān b. Ḵāled (q.v.) and ʿEmād-al-Dīn Eṣfahānī, who translated and expanded Anūšervān's literary work, preserved in an abridgment by Bondarī, stigmatized Dargazīnī for his plebeian background, hostility to Turkish military commanders, and alleged tenderness toward the Ismaʿilis, supposedly shown at the time when Amir Šīrgīr lifted the siege of Alamūt (q.v.) in 511/1118. Anūšervān secured Abu'l-Qāsem's dismissal, but the latter was restored and served as vizier in 522-25/1128-31. After his second dismissal he persuaded the senior member of the Saljuq dynasty, Sanjar (511-52/1118-57), to appoint him as vizier to Sultan Maḥmūd's brother Ṭoḡrel, who ruled briefly in Azerbaijan in 525/1131 before becoming sultan in 526/1132; in the following years Abu'l-Qāsem served as Sanjar's own vizier, exercising this function, however, through a deputy, Ẓahīr-al-Dīn ʿAbd-al-ʿAzīz Ḥāmedī while himself remaining at Ṭoḡrel's court (Klausner, pp. 54-56). Anūšervān b. Ḵāled denounced Abu'l-Qāsem's financial exactions, tyranny, and general mismanagement of affairs, which aroused much fear and hostility. Opposition to him and his policies mounted, and he was executed by Sultan Ṭoḡrel II (526-29/1132-34) in August 1133.

According to ʿEmād-al-Dīn Eṣfahānī (Bondārī, pp. 181-82; cf. Ebn al-Aṯīr, XI, pp. 45, 64; Kermānī, pp. 79-80; ʿAqīlī, p. 260; Klausner, pp. 52, 77, 87, 93, 108), ʿEmād al-Dīn Abu'l-Barakāt b. Salama Dargazīnī, a maternal kinsman of Abu'l-Qāsem, succeeded Anūšervān b. Ḵāled as vizier to Sultan Masʿūd b. Moḥammad b. Malekšāh (530-32/1136-38). The appointment resulted from the sultan's perception that the state was slipping into disorder under Anūšervān and his hope that Abu'l-Barakāt's kinship to Abu'l-Qāsem would bring with it administrative and financial expertise. These hopes were initially realized: During his two years in office Abu'l-Barakāt curbed the influence of the military and restored some of the prestige of the sultanate. In the process he made powerful enemies, who procured his arrest and dismissal in 532/1138; he was replaced by the *mostawfī* (chief auditor) Kamāl-al-Dīn Ṯābet Qomī, who had already been exercising considerable influence on affairs of the state.

Three other, less distinguished members of the Dargazīnī family served the Saljuq sultans as viziers and officials during the 12th century. Abū Najīb, Šams-al-Dīn (d. 554/1159), son of Abu'l-Qāsem's sister, served in the administrations of various Saljuq atabegs and provincial governors and eventually, in 541/1146, became vizier in Hamadān on behalf of Sultan Masʿūd b. Moḥammad (529-47/1134-52); he remained in that post until the sultan's death.

Abu'l-Fażl Jalāl-al-Dīn, a son of Abu'l-Qāsem, was vizier in 547-49/1152-54, serving Malekšāh III (547-48/1152-53) and Moḥammad II (548-55/1153-60); he died in about 1182.

Finally, a second son of Abu'l-Qāsem, Qewām-al-Dīn, often called Ṭoḡrāʾī, was vizier to Ṭoḡrel III b. Arslān (571-90/1176-94) in the years 578-81/1182-85; he died in about 585/1189.

Bibliography: Sayf al-Dīn ʿAqīlī, *Āṯār al-wozarāʾ*, ed. J. Moḥaddeṯ Ormavī, Tehran, 1337 Š./1958. Qewām-al-Dīn Fatḥ Bondārī, *Zobdat al-noṣra wa nokbat al ʿoṣra*, in Houtsma, *Recueil* II. C. E. Bosworth, "The Political and Dynastic History of the

Iranian World (A.D. 1000-1217)," in *Camb. Hist. Iran* V, pp. 1-202. ʿA. Eqbāl, *Wezārat dar ʿahd-e salāṭīn-e bozorg-e saljūqī*, Tehran, 1338 Š./1959. Nāṣer-al-Dīn Monšī Kermānī, *Nasāʾem al-asḥār*, ed. J. Moḥaddeṯ Ormavī, Tehran 1338 Š./1959. C. L. Klausner, *The Seljuk Vezirate. A Study in Civil Administration 1055-1194*, Cambridge, Mass., 1973. A. K. S. Lambton, "The Internal Structure of the Saljuq Empire," in *Camb. Hist. Iran* V, pp. 203-282.

(C. Edmund Bosworth)

DARĪ, name given to the New Persian literary language at a very early date and widely attested in Arabic (e.g., Eṣṭaḵrī, p. 314; Moqaddasī [Maqdesī], p. 335; Ebn Ḥawqal, p. 490) and Persian texts since the 10th century. The Persian translator of Ṭabarī's *Tafsīr* (between 350/961-62 and 365/975-76; I, p. 5), Abū ʿAlī Moḥammad Balʿamī in his continuation of Ṭabarī's *Tārīḵ* (352/963-64; Gryaznevich and Boldyrev, p. 53), Keykāvūs Rāzī in his *Zarātošt-nāma* (before 368/978, according to Rempis), and Ḥakīm Meysarī in his *Dāneš-nāma* (367-70/978-81; apud Lazard, *Premiers poètes* I, p. 182) all claimed to be writing in *darī*. Ferdowsī (*Šāh-nāma*, ed. Moscow, VIII, p. 254), in his account of the origins of *Kalīla wa Demna*, reported that the Arabic version had been translated by Balʿamī into *darī* on the order of the Samanid Naṣr II (301-31/914-43). The term *darī* also referred to a spoken language as early as the time of Jāḥeẓ (mid-9th century; p. 13); Arabic historians and geographers of the following century also used it in that sense (e.g., Masʿūdī, p. 78; Moqaddasī, p. 335).

Darī was contrasted to Pahlavi, sometimes when the latter term designated literary Middle Persian, as in the *Zarātošt-nāma* (p. 2) and the *Šāh-nāma* (Moscow, VIII, p. 254), and sometimes when it referred to Medo-Parthian dialects, as in Masʿūdī (p. 78) and probably also in the *Šāh-nāma* (I, p. 44, in connection with the word *bīvar* "ten thousand"). It was sometimes also distinguished from *pārsī*. Moqaddesī (p. 259) mentioned *darī* as one of the Iranian dialects "that together are known as *parsī*." A century later Keykāvūs b. Eskandar (in ca. 475/1082-83; p. 208) advised letter writers to avoid the use of "pure *pārsī*" (*pārsī-e moṭlaq*), that is, free of Arabic words, "for it is displeasing, especially *pārsī-e darī*, which is not usual," implying the existence of other kinds of *pārsī*. *Darī* thus seems to have been a variety of *pārsī*, as is confirmed by the expression *pārsī-e darī* (Ar. *al-fārsīya al-dārīya*) frequently found in early text. The variant *pārsī o darī*, which also occurs in Persian manuscripts (e.g., *Šāh-nāma* VIII, p. 254), is a distortion, as Parvīz Ḵānlarī correctly noted (p. 273).

The original meaning of the word *darī* is given in a notice attributed to Ebn al-Moqaffaʿ (Ebn al-Nadīm, ed. Tajaddod, p. 15; Ḵᵛārazmī, *Mafātīḥ al-ʿolūm*, pp. 116-17; Ḥamza Eṣfahānī, pp. 67-68; Yāqūt, *Boldān* IV, p. 846). This notice, which probably reflected the linguistic situation in Persia at the end of the Sasanian period, includes mention of *pahlavī*, literally, "the Parthian language" (or the dialects that grew out of it), *pārsī*, and *darī*. According to Ebn al-Moqaffaʿ, *pārsī* was "the language spoken by the *mowbeds* (priests), scholars, and the like; it is the language of the people of Fārs." It is obvious that this language was none other than Middle Persian, traditionally known as Pahlavi. As for *darī*, "It is the language of the cities of Madāʾen; it is spoken by those who are at the king's court. [Its name] is connected with presence at court. Among the languages of the people of Khorasan and the east, the language of the people of Balḵ is predominant." This notice has given rise to considerable discussion. The etymology given for the name is clear: It is derived from the word for *dar* (court, lit., "gate"). *Darī* was thus the language of the court and of the capital, Ctesiphon (q.v.). On the other hand, it is equally clear from this passage that *darī* was also in use in the eastern part of the empire, in Khorasan, where it is known that in the course of the Sasanian period Persian gradually supplanted Parthian and where no dialect that was not Persian survived. The passage thus suggests that *darī* was actually a form of Persian, the common language of Persia. If that conclusion is correct, what was the relationship between *pārsī* and *darī*, and how did the latter term come to be applied specifically to literary New Persian at the time of its emergence?

On the basis of Moqaddasī's report (p. 335) that *darī* was the chancery language in Bukhara, it has been thought that it was from the beginning a kind of formal Persian. Ḵānlarī (pp. 280-81) put forth the hypothesis that *darī* had been an official and administrative language of the Sasanian court, had become established in the east by officials of the Sasanian kingdom, and had thus became the chancery language of Khorasan. There is no doubt, however, that the official and administrative language of the Sasanians was not *darī* but Middle Persian (so-called Pahlavi). Ebn al-Moqaffaʿ's account clearly indicates that *darī* was a spoken language, and it is obviously as a spoken language that it spread to the east. The founders of Persian literature, who were poets, rather than prose writers, naturally resorted to the language that they spoke. Moqaddasī's statement was made at a time when *darī* had already been in literary use for nearly a century.

New information on the dialectology of Persia at the beginning of the Islamic period now permits a clearer understanding. It is known that ancient Judeo-Persian texts, probably originating in southern Persia (cf. Lazard, 1968), represent local dialects clearly different from those of Khorasan and Transoxania, from which literary Persian originally developed. The recent discovery in Mašhad of a manuscript of the *Qorʾān-e Qods*, a translation of the Koran into a Persian dialect related to early Judeo-Persian, confirms the dialectological significance of details already known from the latter. The work apparently originated in Sīstān in the 11th century. One of the most interesting features common to this *Qorʾān* and early Judeo-Persian is the abundance of words that were well known in literary Middle Persian and unknown in literary New Persian, evidence that there were important differences between the common language spoken in the south and that in use in the north. The former, as represented by literary Middle Persian, retained most its ancient form; the latter evolved from the same Persian language, which had spread throughout the north, but evinced the influence of the dialects that it had supplanted there, particularly Parthian. It thus diverged noticeably from the original form. Both were called *pārsī* (Persian), but it is very likely that the language of the north, that is, the Persian used on former Parthian territory and also in the Sasanian capital, was distinguished from its congener by a new name, *darī* ([language] of the court). It was only natural that several centuries later literary Persian, based on the speech of the northeast, bore the same name.

Bibliography: Dehḵodā, s.v. Darī. P. A. Gryaznevich and A. N. Boldyrev, "O dvukh redaktskiyakh 'Taʾrikh-i Tabarī' Balʿamī" (On two translations of Balʿamī's *Tārīḵ-e Ṭabarī*), *Sovetskoe Vostokovedenie*, 1957/3, pp. 46-59. Jāḥeẓ, *Ketāb al-bayān wa'l-tabyīn*, ed. M. Hārūn, III, Cairo, 1368-69/1949. P. N. Ḵānlarī, *Tārīḵ-e zabān-e fārsī*, new ed., I, Tehran, 1365 Š./1986. Keykāvūs b. Eskandar, *Qābūs-nāma*, ed. Ḡ.-Ḥ. Yūsofī, Tehran, 1346 Š./1967. Keykāvūs Rāzī, *Zarātošt-nāma*, ed. F. Rosenberg, St. Petersburg, 1904; repr. Tehran, 1338 Š./1959. Abū ʿAbd-Allāh Moḥammad Ḵᵛārazmī, *Mafātīḥ al-ʿolūm*, ed. G. van Vloten, Leiden, 1895. G. Lazard, "La dialectologie du judéo-persan," in *Studies in Bibliography and Booklore* 8, 1968, pp. 77-98. Idem, "Pahlavi, parsi, dari. Les langues de l'Iran d'après Ibn al-Muqaffaʿ," in C. E. Bosworth, ed., *Iran and Islam. In Memory of the Late V. Minorsky*, Edinburgh, 1971, pp. 361-91. Idem, "Lumières nouvelles sur la formation de la langue persane. Une traduction du Coran en persan dialectal et ses affinités avec le judéo-persan," in S. Shaked and A. Netzer, eds., *Irano-Judaica* II, Jerusalem, 1990a, pp. 184-98. Idem, "Parsi et dari. Nouvelles remarques," in *Aspects of Iranian Culture. In Honor of R. N. Frye*, Bulletin of the Asia Institute, N.S. 4, 1990b, pp. 239-42. Idem, "Rīšahā-ye zabānī-e fārsī-e adabī," *Īrān-nāma* 11/4, 1371 Š./1993, pp. 569-84. *Qorʾān-e Qods*, ed. A. Rawaqī, Tehran, 1364-65 Š./1985-86. C. Rempis, "Qui est l'auteur du Zartušt-Nâmeh?" in *Mélanges d'orientalisme offerts à Henri Massé . . .*, Tehran, 1963, pp. 337-442. Abū Jaʿfar Moḥammad Ṭabarī, *Tafsīr*, tr. as *Tarjama-ye tafsīr-e Ṭabarī*, ed. Ḥ Yaḡmāʾī, 7 vols., Tehran, 1339-44 Š./1960-65.

(GILBERT LAZARD)

DARĪ IN AFGHANISTAN. See AFGHANISTAN v; PERSIAN LANGUAGE; see also Supplement.

al-ḎARĪʿA elā TAṢĀNĪF al-ŠĪʿA, a comprehensive bibliography of Imami Shiʿite works in twenty-five volumes compiled by Shaikh Moḥammad-Moḥsen Āqā Bozorg Ṭehrānī (q.v.; 1293-1389=1349 Š./1876-1970); it contains about 55,000 entries for works written up to 1370 Š./1950-51. Āqā Bozorg initially conceived the project as a response to the work of Jerjī Zaydān (1278-1332/1861-1914), who was considered to have belittled the Imami contribution to Arabic literature (cf. Zaydān, p. 6). The original title, *al-Ḏarīʿa elā maʿrefat moṣannafāt al-Šīʿa*, was suggested by Āqā Bozorg's teacher Sayyed Ḥasan Ṣadr (Ṣadr-al-Dīn; 1272-1354/1856-1935). Āqā Bozrog began work on 25 Ḏū'l-qaʿda 1329/17 November 1911, shortly after settling in Sāmarrā in Iraq. By 1331/1913 he had produced a one-volume draft of abbreviated titles of works to be cited. He completed a six-volume draft of the entire work three years later and made it available to interested scholars. Technical problems caused repeated delays in publication; some volumes took more than two years to print. Only volumes I-XIX had been published, at Najaf (I-III, XIII-XIV) or Tehran, by the time of Āqā Bozorg's death. The final volume apppeared in Tehran in 1398=1357 Š./1978. A supplement, edited by Aḥmad Ḥosaynī and entitled *Mostadrakāt al-moʾallef*, was published as volume XXVI in Mašhad in 1405=1364 Š./1985.

Most of the volumes were edited by the author's sons, ʿAlī-Naqī (vols. IV-XII, XV, XXIV-XXV) and Aḥmad Monzawī (XVI-XXIII); volumes XIII and XIV were, however, edited by Moḥammad-Ṣādeq Baḥr-al-ʿOlūm (*Ḏarīʿa* XXVI, p. 5). Some volumes include French or English title pages, and from volume XVI on there are author indexes. Beginning with volume XVII titles of Ismaʿili works mentioned in the *Fehrest* of Esmāʿīl Majdūʿ were included; the edition by ʿAlī-Naqī Monzawī was used. The material on poetry, originally planned for volumes IX and X, was published in four separately paginated parts, numbered IX/1 through IX/4.

In preparing his magnum opus Āqā Bozorg read widely in Imami literature and also traveled in Iraq, Persia, Syria, Palestine, Egypt, and the Ḥejāz, in order to visit public and private libraries and to consult their catalogues (*Ḏarīʿa* VI, pp. 400-04, VII, pp. 289-94, VIII, pp. 297-99). He also consulted catalogues of libraries in Turkey, India, Afghanistan, Pakistan, and some European countries (*Ḏarīʿa* XX, p. *hāʾ*) and made use of material that he requested from various scholars. The result is a work of meticulous scholarship and remarkable industry. All branches of Imami literature are fully represented, from koranic exegesis and works of tradition, history, theology, and law to science, poetry, and belles lettres. Major topics are preceded by illuminating introductory remarks, and issues in the history and transmission of problematic texts are treated in a clear and concise manner. Entries vary in length from a few lines to several pages. For many works Āqā Bozorg provided summaries of the contents, as well as lists of manuscripts and printed editions known to him. Where there were doubts about the author's identity he reviewed the available evidence, occasionally offering his own views. Cross-references are provided for works known under more than one title. For those no longer extant Āqā Bozorg noted where he had found references to them.

As Āqā Bozorg noted more than once, ideally a work on the scale of the *Ḏarīʿa* requires the cooperation of a team of scholars, and he was aware that some errors or inaccuracies were inevitable. They are impressively few, however, and the *Ḏarīʿa* is generally a sound and reliable guide. It surpassed by far anything previously available, including the *Kašf al-ẓonūn* by Ḥājī Ḵalīfa (1017-67/1609-57), which contains little on Shiʿite literature, and *Kašf al-ḥojob wa'l-astār* by Sayyed Eʿjāz-Ḥosayn Kantūrī (1240-86/1824-70; see Āqā Bozorg, pp. 149-50). Its importance, which was immediately obvious to Muslim scholars, was soon recognized in the West as well. Carl Brockelmann used it in the second edition of his *Geschichte der arabischen Litteratur* (though he had only the first two volumes at his disposal; cf. *GAL* I, p. 196), and it has since become an indispensable tool for all students of Imami literature.

Bibliography: J. Āl-e Aḥmad, "Moʿarrefī-e jeld-e panjom-e *al-Ḏarīʿa*," *Soḵan* 2/11-12, 1324 Š./1946, pp. 907-09. Āqā Bozorg, *Ṭabaqāt aʿlām al-Šīʿa* II, Najaf, 1374/1954. *Aʿyān al-Šīʿa*, 3rd ed., I/2, Beirut, 1370/1951, p. 468 (with some critical remarks). "Dānešmandān-e moʿāṣer wa āṯār-e ānhā. Šayḵ Āqā Bozorg Ṭehrānī," *Rāhnemā-ye ketāb* 4/5-6, 1340 Š./1961, pp. 525-29. *Ḏekrā al-Šayḵ Āḡā Bozorg al-Ṭehrānī, ṣāḥeb al-Ḏarīʿa*, Najaf, 1391/1971. E. Majdūʿ, *Fehrest al-kotob wa'l-rasāʾel*, ed. ʿA.-N. Monzawī, Tehran, 1344 Š./1965. M.-ʿA. Modarres, *Rayḥānat al-adab* I, Tabrīz, 1346 Š./1965, pp. 52-54. ʿA.-R. Moḥammad-ʿAlī, *Šayḵ al-bāḥeṯīn Āḡā Bozorg al-Ṭehrānī*, Najaf, 1390/1970. S. Nafīsī, "Ketāb-e Ḏarīʿa wa moʾallef-e ān," *Soḵan* 2/11-12, 1324 Š./1946, pp. 887-89. J. Zaydān, *Taʾrīḵ ādāb al-loḡat al-ʿarabīya* III, Cairo, 1931.

(ETAN KOHLBERG)

DARIC (Gk. *dareikós statḗr*), Achaemenid gold coin of ca. 8.4 gr, which was introduced by Darius I (q.v.; 522-486 B.C.E.) toward the end of the 6th century B.C.E. The daric and the similar silver coin, the siglos (Gk. *síglos medikós*), represented the bimetallic monetary standard that the Achaemenids developed from that of the Lydians (Herodotus, 1.94). Although it was the only gold coin of its period that was struck continuously, the daric was eventually displaced from its central economic position first by the biga stater of Philip II of Macedonia (359-36 B.C.E.) and then, conclusively, by the Nike stater of Alexander the Great (336-23 B.C.E.).

The ancient Greeks believed that the term *dareikós* was derived from the name of Darius the Great (Pollux, *Onomastikon* 3.87, 7.98; cf. Caccamo Caltabiano and Radici Colace), who was believed to have introduced these coins. For example, Herodotus reported that Darius had struck coins of pure gold (4.166, 7.28: *chrysíou statḗrōn Dareikôn*). On the other hand, modern scholars have generally supposed that the Greek term *dareikós* can be traced back to Old Persian **dari-* "golden" and that it was first associated with the name of Darius only in later folk etymology (see ACHAEMENID DYNASTY; Herzfeld, p. 146; for the contrary view, see Bivar, p. 621; DARIUS iii). During the 5th century B.C.E. the term *dareikós* was generally and exclusively used to designate Persian coins, which were circulating so widely among the Greeks that in popular speech they were dubbed *toxótai* "archers" after the image of the figure with a bow that appeared on them (Plutarch, *Artoxerxes* 20.4; idem, *Agesilaus* 15.6). The earliest mention of the *dareikós* in an inscription occurs in the reckoning of accounts for the year 429/8 by the priests responsible for administering the temple treasury of Athena Parthenos and other gods at Athens (*Inscriptiones Graecae* I^3, p. 383 ll. 17-18: *dareikó chrysío statêres*; cf. Carradice, pp. 75-76; Melville-Jones, pp. 35-36; for additional references, see Babelon, 1901, pp. 469-72). Eventually, because of the *dareikós*' dominant position as the single regularly issued gold coin of its time, the term became a synonym among the Greeks for any gold coin, for example, the stater issued by Philip (*dareikoì Philíppeioi*; Melville-Jones, pp. 25 ff.).

Introduction of the daric. The discovery in 1312 Š./1933 of a hoard of coins in the famous Apadāna (q.v.) deposit of Darius at Persepolis, which is unfortunately still inadequately published, has been the focus for a long-standing debate over the date when the daric was first minted (Herzfeld, pp. 413-16; Schmidt, p. 110, pl. 84; M. Thompson et al., no. 1789). Altogether eight gold Croesus staters (of the late type known as "light Croeseids") were found, together with four Greek silver staters, under stone coffers containing the foundation tablets for the building, giving rise to the opinion that at the time when the deposit was made (between 519 and 510 B.C.E.) Darius had still not issued darics and sigloi. The date of the first minting of the coins with the image of the archer, that is, of the change from the old, widely circulated Lydian type with the heads of a lion and a bull to a characteristic Achaemenid type, was thus fixed soon after 515 (Herzfeld; Robinson, p. 190; Kraay, p. 32; Bivar, p. 617). In a recent but less persuasive study Michael Vickers (pp. 4 ff.) dated the first issue of the Achaemenid archer after 490. The decisive evidence for a date in the last decade of the 6th century at the latest, has, however, now been discovered by M. C. Root (pp. 8-12), who published a small clay tablet from the Persepolis fortification archive bearing a date in the twenty-second regnal year of Darius (500-499); on the reverse there is a clear impression of two *toxótai* of type II (see below). Darius was thus in fact the first Achaemenid emperor to order the striking of the new gold coin with the image of the royal archer. It has been established with certainty, however, that these coins were not the first to be struck at the Achaemenid imperial mint: As die studies (Naster, 1965, pp. 25 ff., pl. 1), in conjunction with analysis of hoards (Noe, pp. 23ff.; Robinson, pp. 187 ff.; Carradice, pp. 73 ff., pls. 10-11), have shown, some of the earlier Croesus staters (*kroísos statḗr*) of the lion-and-bull type are to be attributed to the Achaemenid emperors, including Darius I, who took over minting of the type from the Lydian king Croesus (after 546 B.C.E.). Toward the end of the 6th century, when Darius undertook the restructuring of the Achaemenid political system, including in particular the financial and tax systems, he ordered the minting of darics and sigloi. The opinion of Laura Breglia (pp. 659 ff.; cf. Price, pp. 211 ff.; Vickers, pp. 4-9) that all the so-called "Croeseids" are to be attributed to the Achaemenids does not, however, seem persuasive (cf. Cahn, pp. 55-57; Root, pp. 1 ff.).

Typology. The fundamental type of the Achaemenid daric and siglos is that bearing the image of the royal archer (*toxótēs*), which remained stereotyped as the obverse, with only a few minor variations. The reverse was without images, and only an irregular oblong incuse can be recognized. It was E. S. G. Robinson who first established, on the basis of the obverse images, the four main types and the relative chronology that are still generally accepted today (cf. Kraay, pp. 32-33; Carradice, pp. 76 ff.; Stronach, pp. 258 ff.).

Type I (Plate Ia). Torso of bearded archer with the crenellated crown (*kídaris*) and sleeved chiton (see CLOTHING ii) facing right, a bow in the left hand and two arrows in the right. It is known so far only on sigloi.

Type II (Plate Ib). Kneeling archer dressed as on Type I, facing right, with drawn bow and a quiver on his back. It is attested on darics, sigloi, and fractional coins in silver.

Type III (Plate Ic). The archer as on Type I but in the *Knielauf* (running with bent knees) position, moving to the right, with a bow in his left hand, a lance in his right, and a quiver on his back. This type is further divided into several subtypes, according to stylistic features. It includes darics, sigloi, and fractional coins in gold and silver.

Type IV (Plate Id). The archer as on Type III, in *Knielauf* position moving to the right, with a bow in his left hand, a dagger in his right, and a quiver on his back. This type is also divided into two subtypes according to stylistic features. It includes darics, sigloi, and fractional coins in silver.

Interpretation of the image on the coin as the Achaemenid emperor has not been entirely accepted; the discussion has been summarized most recently by David Stronach (pp. 266 ff.; the conclusions of Harrisson, pp. 17 ff., are less persuasive). Whether the representation is that of the emperor, of a royal hero, or of a god in special avatar, the image has no convincing parallels in other branches of Achaemenid imperial art, with the exception of isolated occurences on seals, though the individual elements of the composition are firmly anchored in the ancient Persian tradition (Calmeyer, pp. 303 ff.; Stronach). The image of the royal archer is, however, to be found not only on the darics and sigloi issued by the Achaemenid imperial mint but also on satrapal and dynastic coins of Asia Minor, as well as later on the Babylonian double darics issued under Alexander the Great (Göbl, pl. 95 nos. 1895, 1914, 1916-18). At the end of the 5th century, when the Persian satraps in Asia Minor began to strike their own coins, it was deemed necessary to express, through images or inscriptions, that the right of coinage was still a royal prerogative. Darius treated such an encroachment as a crime punishable by death (Herodotus, 4.166; cf. Kraay, pls. 12/206, 55/949-50; Göbl, pl. 95 nos. 1901-02, 1906). In fact, the numismatic evidence does not permit identification of the

PLATE I

a

b

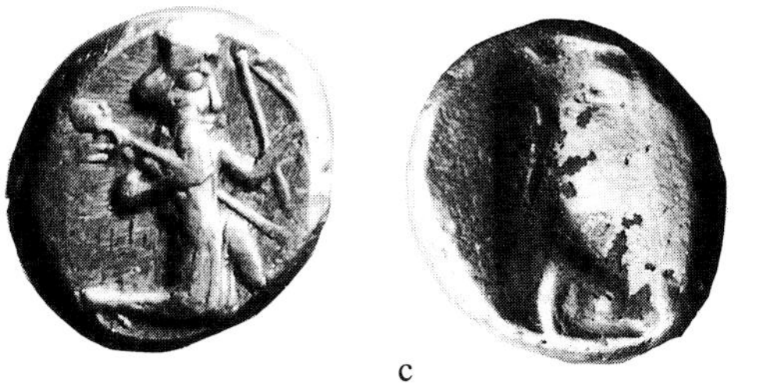

c

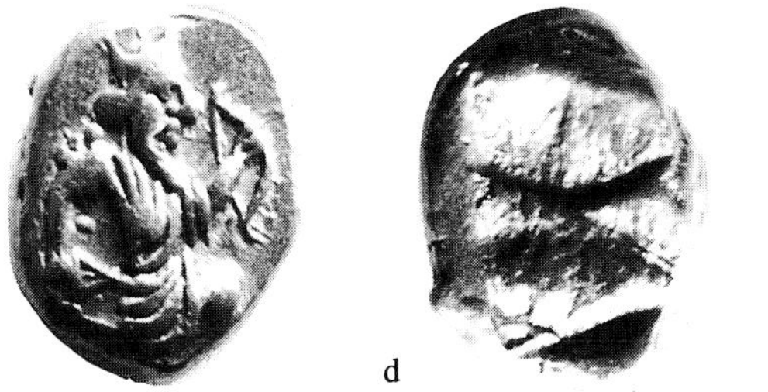

d

a. Siglos, type I, 5.30 gr. b. Daric, type II, 8.24 gr. c. Daric, type III, 8.37 gr. d. Daric, type IV, 8.33 gr. Photographs courtesy of Institut für Numismatik, University of Vienna.

image on the darics and sigloi as anything but that of the emperor; it was adopted by Darius as a dynamic expression of his royal power expressly for his coin issues. These coins were particularly aimed at the Greek west (see below), however, and the choice of image had therefore to be made with reference to its impact on the Greeks among whom the coins would circulate; in addition to their mercantile value, the darics thus had a propaganda function. This type was continued more or less unchanged by Darius' successors; it also served as a model for comparable coin issues by succeeding Persian dynasties, helping to underscore the dynastic principle. As Ian Carradice (pp. 80 ff.) has suggested on the basis of evidence from hoards, types I, II, and III (first version) all seem to have been struck by Darius I. In fact the minting of types I and II appears to have occurred in very close chronological proximity toward the end of the 6th century; perhaps the two types represent parallel issues from two different mint cities. Carradice (pp. 84 ff.) placed the next version of type III around 480 and the introduction of type IV somewhat later, around 450 (cf. Stronach, pp. 261-62). Judging by the quantities of preserved examples of the two latter types, they accounted for the overwhelming bulk of Achaemenid mint production. The peak was clearly reached in the 5th century, though both types were probably still being minted at the beginning of the 4th century; they were thus in circulation for an extremely long time. During the 4th century types III and IV were still minted, but production then declined. One obvious conclusion to be drawn from this pattern is that it was only during the 4th century that the satraps and dynasts of Asia Minor increased their own production of coins and thus partly reduced the amount of imperial currency in use in their own territories.

Minting and mint cities. The central problem of identifying different mint cities can be solved only through comprehensive new finds and detailed die studies. The major mint was certainly Sardis, the seat of the Achaemenid administration for the whole of Asia Minor; it had already been the mint of the former Lydian kings and was kept in operation by the Achaemenids (Kraay, pp. 30 ff.; Bivar, p. 619). As the leading administrative center, Sardis must also have been the collection point for the annual tribute payments from the provinces of Asia Minor, thus ensuring a sufficient supply of precious metals for mint production there. On the basis of evidence from hoards, as well as typological and metrological research, C. M. Kraay (p. 33) has concluded that there were also mint cities in both northwestern and southwestern Asia Minor (cf. Carradice, pp. 84-85). The fact that in the time of Alexander the Great double darics with the image of the great king were being issued in the eastern part of the empire, perhaps in Babylon (Le Rider), suggests that there may already have been a mint there under the Achaemenids. Paul Naster's exemplary die study of the Croeseids (1965, pl. 1), encompassing identical obverse dies and reverse punches on both gold and silver coins, has considerably clarified Lydian minting practice, which must also have been adopted for the later production of darics and sigloi, though few overlapping series of dies and punches have so far been discovered on Achaemenid coins. In fact, identical reverse punches appear on the overwhelming majority of coins within the different typological groups, suggesting that, as the design lacked imagery, it continued in use for a very long time (Noe; Robinson, pp. 191 ff.).

Metrology and denominations At the time of Darius' great tax reform a new weight standard for gold was introduced (Herodotus, 3.89, 3.95). In contrast to the lighter Lydian gold stater of slightly more than 8 gr (8.06-8.19 gr), the new daric weighed ca. 8.4 gr and was thus brought into relation with the old Mesopotamian shekel measure (1 mina: ca. 504 gr, 1/60 mina: 8.40 gr), which had previously been the basic weight standard for Lydian electrum issues (Nau, pp. 6 ff.; cf. Karwiese, pp. 35 ff.). The weight of the silver siglos continued to be based on that of the silver Croesus stater (10.75-92 gr) and was minted as a half-siglos of ca. 5.5. gr. Various other fractions of the daric and the siglos are known, though they generally had no significance in the Achaemenid monetary system and still have not been attested for all types. The hypothesis that the weight of the Achaemenid coinage was raised in two successive stages (Robinson, pp. 189 ff.; Kraay, pp. 32-33; Bivar, pp. 617-18) during Darius' reforms has not been conclusively proved and must await the test of additional material.

The Achaemenids thus at first adopted two different weight standards for gold and silver, with a fixed ratio of value between the denominations; in particular, they attempted to gear the two types of coinage to the needs of the respective groups of recipients and users. Herodotus reported (3.89, 3.95) that the annual tribute payments from the individual satraps were to be made in silver according to the Babylonian weight standard and in gold according to the Euboic weight standard; in fact, the weight of the daric does correspond approximately to that of the Euboic-Attic didrachm (ca. 8.5 gr). The monetary policy that led to the minting of the daric was thus clearly oriented toward the Greek west, where the coin was in direct competition with the Attic tetradrachm, which began during the 5th century to gain acceptance as an international trading currency throughout the entire eastern Mediterranean area and as far away as India.

Under Darius the ratio of value between gold and silver in the new Achaemenid imperial system was corrected from the old Lydian ratio of 1:13.3 to 1.13 (Herodotus, 3.95) and the official exchange rate between the daric and the siglos set at 1:20 (Nau, pp. 14 ff.). The exchange rate with the Attic drachm was 1:25, and the siglos was reckoned equivalent to 7.5 Attic obols (Xenophon, *Anabasis* 1.5.6). The daric also provided the basic standard of value for payments to the Persian army: The pay of a simple soldier, and of a mercenary, was usually calculated at one daric a month (Xenophon, *Anabasis* 1.3.21). From the beginning of the 4th century, however, actual payments must have been made partly in Attic coins, which were apparently preferred by Greek mercenaries; the standard pay was about one Attic drachm a day (Xenophon, *Hellenica* 1.5.4 ff.; cf. W. E. Thompson, pp. 120 ff.).

Circulation. Naturally the main source of evidence on the circulation of coinage comes from hoards. This evidence has most recently been brought together and discussed by Carradice. In general it seems that the circulation patterns of darics and sigloi were fundamentally different; so far there is no single known hoard in which the two types of coins have occurred together. Whereas hoards of sigloi have been found almost exclusively in Asia Minor, and isolated examples have been found only with Greek currency in more distant lands (e.g., Egypt and Afghanistan), darics have been found in closed contexts not only in Asia Minor but also in Greece, Macedonia, and Italy. Nevertheless, the total evidence for the circulation of the daric is extremely meager and does not lend itself to definitive conclusions: No example of type II, III (first version), or IV darics has yet occurred in an archeological context. For the later verions of type III only a few hoards of vastly different sizes (3-2,000 pieces each) have been found, but, as they have not been fully studied, they permit no general conclusions. At any rate, all the finds now known conform without exception to the picture of Achaemenid monetary policy developed by Daniel Schlumberger on the basis of the hoard at Čaman-e Hočūrī near Kabul: The siglos can be identified as a local currency for Asia Minor, whereas it is clear from the importance of the daric in the gold market of antiquity that it was conceived from the beginning as a superregional trading currency. As a continuously minted piece of precious metal with a stable value, it was certainly able to compete with the Attic tetradrachm or the electrum stater from Cyzicus, especially during the 5th century. Its function as a freely circulating means of exchange was nevertheless limited, owing to its relatively high value; it must indeed have been traded primarily as bullion.

See also COINS AND COINAGE.

Bibliography: E. Babelon, *Catalogue des monnaies grecques de la Bibliothèque Nationale. Les Perses achéménides, les satrapes et les dynastes tributaires de leur empire Cypre et Phénicie*, Paris, 1893. Idem, *Traité des monnaies grecques et romaines* I, Paris, 1901; II/1, Paris, 1907; II/2, Paris, 1910. A. D. H. Bivar, "Achaemenid Coins, Weights and Measures," in *Camb. Hist. Iran* II, pp. 610-39. L. Breglia, "Interrogativi sulle 'creseidi,'" *Annali della Scuola Normale Superiore di Pisa*, 1974, pp. 659-85. M. Caccamo Caltabiano and P. Radici Colace, "Argyrion eydokimon (Pollux 3, 87)," *Annali della Scuola Normale Superiore di Pisa*, 1985, pp. 81-101. H. A. Cahn, "Kleinasien," *A Survey of Numismatic Research 1972-1977*, Bern, 1979, pp. 55-57. P. Calmeyer, "Zur Genese altiranischer Motive, VI. TOXOTAI," *AMI* 12, 1979, pp. 303-13. I. Carradice, "The 'Regal' Coinage of the Persian Empire," in I. Carradice, ed., *Coinage and Administration in the Athenian and Persian Empires. The Ninth Oxford Symposium on Coinage and Monetary History*, BAR 343, Oxford, 1987, pp. 73-95. R. Göbl, *Antike Numismatik*, 2 vols., Munich, 1978.

C. M. Harrisson, *Coins of the Persian Satraps*, Ph.D. diss., University of Pennsylvania, Philadelphia, 1982. B. V. Head, *The Coinage of Lydia and Persia from the Earliest Time to the Fall of the Dynasty of the Achaemenids*, London, 1877. E. Herzfeld, "Notes on the Achaemenid Coinage and Some Sasanian Mint-Names," in J. Allan, H. Mattingly, and E. S. G. Robinson, eds., *Transactions of the International Numismatic Congress 1936*, London, 1938, pp. 413-26. G. F. Hill, *Catalogue of the Greek Coins of Arabia, Mesopotamia and Persia in the British Museum*, London, 1922. Idem, "The Coinage of the Ancient Persians," in *Survey of Persian Art* I, pp. 397-405. *Inscriptiones Graecae* I^3, ed. D. Lewis, Berlin, 1981. J. H. Jongkees, "Kroiseios en Dareikos," *Jaarbericht van het Vooraziatisch-Egyptisch Gezelschap Ex Oriente Lux* 9, 1944, pp. 163-68. S. Karwiese, "Aristoteles' Ath. Pol. c. 10. Des Rätsels Lösung?" *Litterae Numismaticae Vindobonenses* 1, 1979, pp. 23-41. C. M. Kraay, *Archaic and Classical Greek Coins*, London, 1976. G. Le Rider, "Tetradrachmes 'au lion' et imitations d'Athènes en Babylonie," *Schweizer Münzblätter* 85, 1972, pp. 1-7. J. R. Melville-Jones, "Darics at Delphi," *Revue belge de numismatique et de sigillographie* 125, 1979, pp. 25-36. P. Naster, "Remarques charactéroscopiques et technologiques au sujet des créséides," *Congresso Internazionale di Numis-matica. Atti* II, Rome, 1965, pp. 25-36. Idem, "Les monnayages satrapaux, provinciaux et régionaux dans l'empire perse face au numéraire officiel des Achéménides," in E. Lipinski, ed., *State and Temple Economy in the Ancient Near East* II, Orientalia Lovaniensia Analecta 6, Louvain, 1979, pp. 597-604. E. Nau, *Epochen der Geldgeschichte*, Stuttgart, 1972. S. P. Noe, *Two Hoards of Persian Sigloi*, Numismatic Notes and Monographs 136, New York, 1956. M. Price, "Croesus or Pseudo-Croesus? Hoard or Hoax? Problems Concerning the Sigloi and Double-Sigloi of the Croeseid Type," in A. Houghton and S. Hurter, eds., *Studies in Honor of Leo Mildenberg*, Wetteren, Belgium, 1984, pp. 211-21. E. S. G. Robinson, "The Beginnings of Achaemenid Coinage," *NC*, 1958, pp. 187-93. M. C. Root, "Evidence from Persepolis for Dating of Persian and Archaic Greek Coinage," *NC*, 1988, pp. 1-12. D. Schlumberger, "L'argent grec dans l'empire achéménide," in R. Curiel and D. Schlumberger, eds., *Trésors monétaires d'Afghanistan*, MDAFI 14, 1953, pp. 3-62. E. F. Schmidt, *Persepolis* II. *Contents of the Treasury and Other Discoveries*, Chicago, 1957. D. Stronach, "Early Achaemenid Coinage. Perspectives from the Homeland," *Iranica Antiqua* 24, 1989, pp. 255-79. M. Thompson, O. Mørkholm, and C. M. Kraay, eds., *An Inventory of Greek Coin Hoards*,

New York, 1973. W. E. Thompson, "Gold and Silver Ratios at Athens during the Fifth Century," *NC*, 1964, pp. 103-23. M. Vickers, "Early Greek Coinage, a Reassessment," *NC*, 1985, pp. 1-44.

(MICHAEL ALRAM)

DARĪGBED (Mid. Pers. **dlykpt'*, *darīgbed* [cf. Arm. *darikʿpet*; see Chaumont, p. 157], variant *dlyk'n srd'r*, *darigān sālār* [Arm. *dranikan-salar*; Chaumont, p. 157] attested in the inscription of Šāpūr I on the Kaʿba of Zoroaster at Naqš-e Rostam, Mid. Pers. l. 33, Parth. l. 27: *drykn s'rr*, Gk. l. 65: *toû epì tôn driganôn*, rather than *drigaiôn*), title of a low-ranking official at the Sasanian court. Although it is rarely attested in Middle Persian, its occurrence as the title of Abursām-Šāpūr, the last name in the list of dignitaries at Šāpūr's court in the inscription at Naqš-e Rostam, is clear evidence that its holder did not have an exalted rank. His actual function is unclear. He was head neither of the courtiers (Sprengling, p. 19) nor of the court servants (Back, p. 363; Hinz, p. 64; Gignoux, p. 22), for those offices were filled by the *paristagbed* Wardbed, whose name appears earlier in the same list (Mid. Pers. l. 33: *plstkpt*; Parth. l. 27: *prštkpt*; Gk. l. 64: *toû epì tês hypēresías*). In the 7th-century Byzantine history of Theophylact Simocatta (3.18.12) the title is given as *darigbedoûm* (Lagarde, p. 188) and is said to have been the equivalent of the Roman (Byzantine) *kouropalátēs*, originally a kind of palace superintendent but by the 6th century simply a commander of the palace guard. In Šāpūr's inscription the *darigān sālār* is named well below the chiliarch (q.v.) and probably was a palace superintendent.

Bibliography: M. Back, *Die sassanidischen Staatsinschriften*, Acta Iranica 18, Leiden, 1978. M. L. Chaumont, "Chiliarque et curopalate à la cour des Sassanides," *Iranica Antiqua* 10, 1973, pp. 139-65. P. Gignoux, *Glossaire des inscriptions pehlevies*, London, 1972. W. Hinz, *Altiranische Funde und Forschungen*, Berlin, 1969. P. de Lagarde, *Gesammelte Abhandlungen*, Leipzig, 1866. M. Sprengling, *Third Century Iran*, Chicago, 1953.

(RICHARD N. FRYE)

DARIUS (NPers. Darīūš, Dārā), name of several Achaemenid and Parthian rulers and princes.

i. *The name.*
ii. *Darius the Mede.*
iii. *Darius I the Great.*
iv. *Darius II.*
v. *Darius III.*
vi. *Achaemenid princes.*
vii. *Parthian princes.*
viii. *Son of Artabanus.*

i. THE NAME

Dārīus (or Dārēus) is the common Latin form of Greek Dareîos, itself a shortened rendering of Old Persian five-syllable Dārayavauš (spelled *d-a-r-y-v-u-š*), the throne name of Darius the Great and two other kings of the Achaemenid dynasty (see iii-v, below), which thus enjoyed considerable popularity among noblemen in later periods (see vi-viii, below). The original Old Persian form was also reflected in Elamite Da-ri-(y)a-ma-u-iš (cf. Hinz and Koch, pp. 289, 291), Babylonian Da-(a-)ri-ia-(a-)muš and so on, Aramaic dryhwš and archaizing drywhwš, and perhaps the longer Greek form Dareiaîos (attested only in Ctesias, Jacoby, *Fragmente* IIIC, pp. 462, 464 frags. 13-14 pars. 24, 33-34; and Xenophon, *Hellenica* 2.1.8-9). On the other hand, the shorter forms Elamite Da-ri-ya-(h)u-(ú-)iš (cf. Hinz and Koch, pp. 290-91), Babylonian Da-(a-)ri-muš and so on, Aramaic drwš, drywš (cf. Schmitt, 1987, pp. 150-51), Egyptian tr(w)š, trjwš, ỉntr(w)š, ỉntrjwš (cf. Posener, pp. 161-63), Lycian Ñtarijeus-, Greek Dareîos (the standard form from Aeschylus onward), and Latin Dārīus, Dārēus are renderings of a haplologically shortened allegro form Old Persian *Dārayauš (replacing normal Dārayavauš), for which further indirect evidence may be found (Schmitt, 1990, pp. 197-98) in *Dariaus, the basis of the toponym Dariaúsa (Ptolemy, *Geography* 6.2.12). The proposal by Chlodwig Werba (p. 148) that Greek Dareîos reflects a two-stem hypocoristic form *Dāraya-v-a- does not take into account the other forms mentioned. Old Persian Dāraya-vauš, which is composed of the present stem *dāraya-* "hold" and the adjective *vau-* "good," must be translated as "holding firm the good" (cf. analogous expressions in Vedic texts) or the like. All attempts to explain it as shortened from a three-part compound name like *Dāraya-vau-manah-, *Dāraya-vau-xšaça-, or *Dāraya-vau-dāta- (cf. Werba, pp. 149-50) are erroneous, however. The ancient etymologies given by both Greek and Persian "authorities" may be passed over in silence.

Bibliography: W. Hinz and H. Koch, *Elamisches Wörterbuch*, 2 parts, Berlin, 1987. M. Mayrhofer, *Iranisches Personennamenbuch* I/2, pp. 18-19 no. 26. G. Posener, *La première domination perse en Égypte. Recueil d'inscriptions hiéroglyphiques*, Cairo, 1936. R. Schmitt, *Die Iranier-Namen bei Aischylos*, Vienna, 1978. Idem, "Review of Segal," *Kratylos* 32, 1987, pp. 145-54. Idem, "The Name of Darius," *Acta Iranica* 30, 1990, pp. 194-99. C. Werba, *Die arischen Personennamen und ihre Träger bei den Alexanderhistorikern*, Ph.D. diss., Vienna, 1982, pp. 141-53.

(RÜDIGER SCHMITT)

ii. DARIUS THE MEDE

In the Old Testament Book of Daniel Darius the Mede is mentioned (5:30-31) as ruler after the slaying of the "Chaldean king" Belshazzar. Daniel is supposed to have flourished during the reigns of Darius and of Cyrus "king of Persia" (Daniel 6.28, 10.1), to be identified with Cyrus the Great (see CYRUS iii; 529-29 B.C.E.). According to the narrative in its present form,

Darius, identified as the son of Ahasuerus (q.v.; Xerxes), a descendant of the Medes, was about sixty-two years old at his succession (Daniel 5:31, 9:1). These references, which do not conform to what is known of the history of the period, have caused problems for scholars trying to unravel the discrepancies in the text, a work of the Hellenistic period, long after the fall of the Achaemenids (see DĀNĪĀL-E NABĪ i).

The Book of Daniel is a collection of moralistic and religious stories, rather than a historical work, and, as such writings were popular among common folk, accuracy was not a prime characteristic. Many explanations of the discrepancies have been proposed by scholars (see listing in Rowley, p. 2), including the suggestion that different authors were involved in the composition of the book at different times. This explanation does not, however, account for the incorrect sequence in which the name of Darius the Mede precedes that of "Cyrus the Persian." Other scholars have proposed that verse 6:28 should be interpreted as referring not to Darius and Cyrus but to Darius as a throne name for Cyrus (Wiseman, p. 15); the age of sixty-two years would certainly fit with the facts known about the life of Cyrus. D. J. Wiseman (pp. 12-14) has suggested further that all the names of the Achaemenid kings were throne names, hence liable to confusion in the minds of subjects living far from the court. As the names of the Achaemenid kings were later lost, even in the Persian tradition, it is not surprising that in an area far from Persia the names and events of the Achaemenid period were reported incorrectly. Failure to recognize the distinction between Mede and Persian is, of course, found in other texts and was not unusual.

The confusion may thus be attributed to the popular nature of the Book of Daniel and its distance in time from the period of the early Achaemenid kings. The same confusion about Darius the Mede persisted in Arabic and Syriac sources (cf. Ṭabarī, I, pp. 647, 652-54, 665-68, 717; Bīrūnī, *Qānūn*, p. 154; idem, *Āṯār*, p. 89; Bar Hebræus, *Chronography*, ed. E. A. W. Budge, p. 31; cf. Yarshater, pp. 54-58).

Bibliography: M. Moʿīn, "Šāhān-e kāyānī wa haḵāmanešī dar *Āṯār al-baqīā*," in M. Moʿīn, ed., *Majmūʿa-ye maqalat-e Doktor Moḥammad Moʿīn* II, Tehran, 1367 Š./1988, pp. 57-87. H. H. Rowley, *Darius the Mede and the Four World Empires in the Book of Daniel*, Cardiff, 1935; repr. 1964 (with extensive bibliography). D. J. Wiseman, "Some Historical Problems in the Book of Daniel," in D. J. Wiseman et al., eds., *Notes on Some Problems in the Book of Daniel*, London, 1965, pp. 9-18. E. Yarshater, "List of the Achaemenid kings in Biruni and Bar Hebraeus," in E. Yarshater, ed., *Biruni Symposium*, New York, 1976, pp. 49-65.

(RICHARD N. FRYE)

iii. DARIUS I THE GREAT

Darius I the Great was the third Achaemenid king of kings (r. 29 September 522-October 486 B.C.E.). He was born in 550 B.C.E. (cf. Herodotus, 1.209), the eldest son of Vištāspa (Hystaspes) and *Vardagauna (Gk. Rhodog(o)únē, NPers. Golgūn; Justi, *Namenbuch*, p. 261; Hinz, 1975a, p. 270). Before his accession to the throne he served Cambyses (529-22 B.C.E.) as a spear bearer in Egypt (Herodotus, 3.139).

Sources.

The primary sources are of four basic kinds. First, there is Darius' record relief (DB) at Bīsotūn (q.v.; for the Old Persian text, see now Schmitt; for the Babylonian text, with some variants, see von Voigtlander); an additional fragment of the relief (Seidl) and one of the Babylonian inscription (von Voigtlander, pp. 63-65) are also known, as are substantial portions of an Aramaic version (Greenfield and Porten). The second category includes texts and monuments from Persepolis (Schmidt; Kent, *Old Persian*; Cameron; Hallock, 1969; cf. evaluations by Lewis, 1977, pp. 4-26; idem, 1990; Bivar, CAH^2, pp. 204-10; Tuplin, pp. 115 ff.), Susa (Schmidt, I, pp. 29-33; ART IN IRAN iii, pp. 574-75), Babylon (Strassmaier; Oppenheim, pp. 559-60; Cardascia, pp. 5-8; Haerinck; van Dijk and Mayer, no. 88; Stolper, 1985, esp. pp. 41-60; Dandamayev, 1992, pp. 3, 5, 10-11 and passim), and Egypt (Posener; Schmidt, I, pp. 26-27; Bresciani, pp. 507-09; Ray, pp. 262-66; Hinz, 1975b; Lloyd). A fragmentary Old Persian inscription from Gherla, Rumania (Harmatta), and a letter from Darius to Gadates, preserved in a Greek text of the Roman period (F. Lochner-Hüttenbach, in Brandenstein and Mayrhofer, pp. 91-98) also belong to this category. The third source is a detailed and colorful narrative by Herodotus (books 3-6; cf. How and Wells). Finally, there are briefer notices by other classical authors (listed and analyzed by Meyer, pp. 3-7; Prášek, II, pp. 10-11; Drews, pp. 20 ff.) and a few references in the Bible (q.v. i.).

Accounts of Darius' accession and rebellions in the provinces. Darius began his "autobiography" in the trilingual (Old Persian, Elamite, Babylonian) inscription on the rock face at Bīsotūn with a genealogy purporting to establish his right to the Achaemenid throne (DB 1.1-11; Table 2), followed by a long account of the Magian usurper Gaumāta (DB 1.26-61). According to this version, after Gaumāta's death at the hands of Darius some provincial magnates rebelled, but Darius slew them all (DB 1.72-3.92). Thereafter his rule was established throughout the empire. He immediately published at Bīsotūn and elsewhere inscriptions providing an exact record of these events, explaining the causes of the rebellions (DB 4.34: "Falsehood [*drauga-*] made them rebellious"; see Schaeder, 1941, pp. 31-32) and his own success (DB 4.61-67; see BĪSOTŪN iii).

In Herodotus' version Cambyses left Patizeithes, a Magian, as "steward of his household" (3.61, 3.63, 3.65) and went to Egypt, whence he sent a trusted Persian, Prexaspes, to murder his full brother Smerdis (i.e., Bardiya, q.v.) in secret (3.31). Only a few

Table 2
FAMILY TREE OF DARIUS THE GREAT

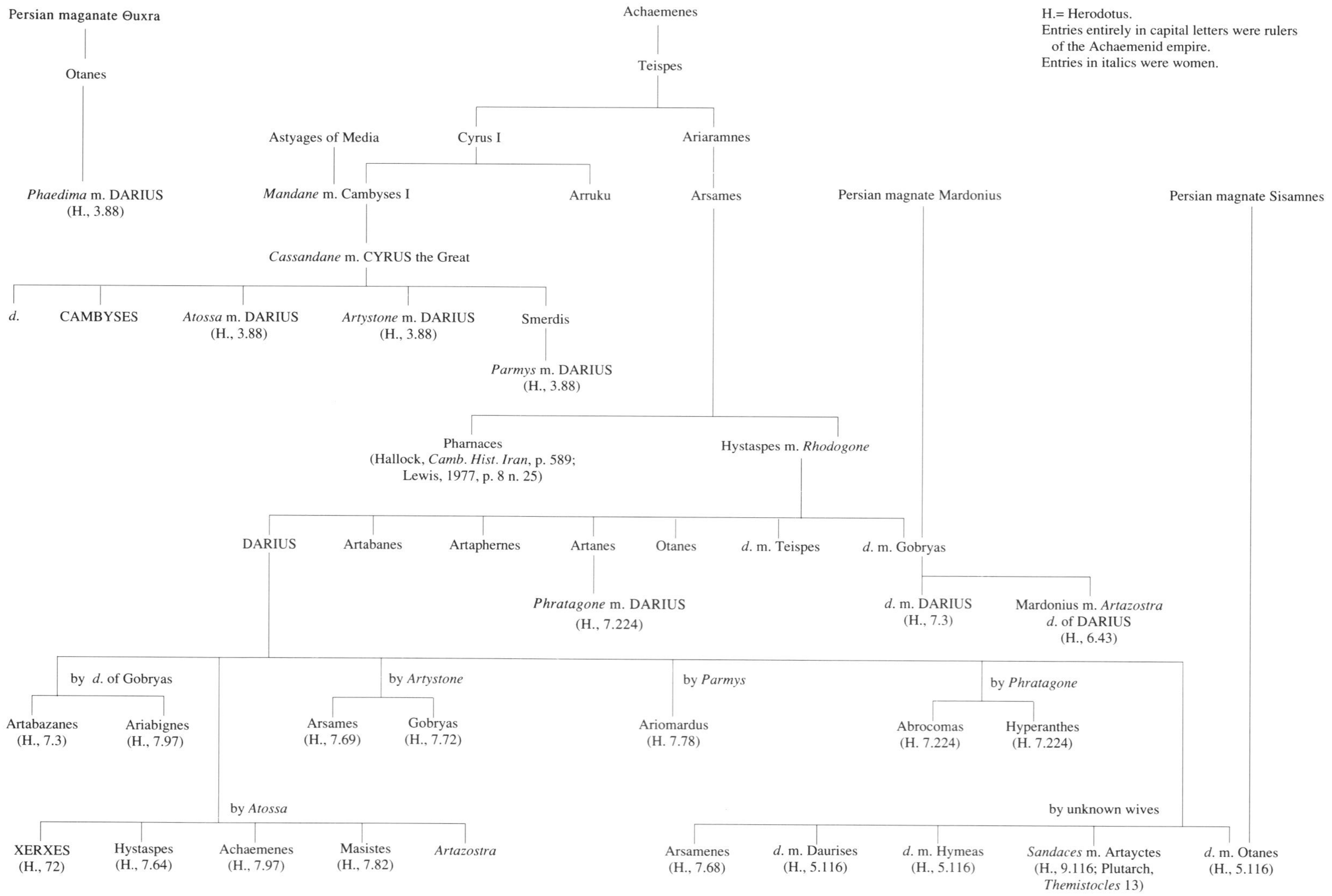

H.= Herodotus.
Entries entirely in capital letters were rulers of the Achaemenid empire.
Entries in italics were women.

Persians, among them Darius, knew of this murder, so that Patizeithes was able to place upon the throne his own brother, also called Smerdis and "greatly resembling the son of Cyrus" (3.61). The imposter was discovered, in the eighth month of his reign, by the Persian noble Otanes (Utāna; 3.68). Five other Persian nobles, Aspathines (see ASPAČANĀ), Gobryas (Gauburuva), Intaphernes (Vindafarnah), Megabyzus (Bagabuxša), and Hydarnes (Vidarna), joined Otanes; Darius had also "hastened to Susa to accomplish the death of the Magian" (3.71). The seven exchanged oaths and at Darius' urging entered the imposter's castle and slew him and his brother (3.71-78); then, joined by other Persians, they slaughtered many Magians (3.71). According to Herodotus, "All peoples of Asia mourned his loss exceedingly, save only the Persians" (3.67), who continued to celebrate the anniversary of this slaughter (3.79). The seven leaders then debated the most suitable mode of government for Persia (for a detailed discussion, see Gschnitzer, 1977; idem, 1988). Otanes urged democracy, but Darius' view that monarchy was "the rule of the very best man in the whole state" prevailed (3.80-88). The seven then resolved to ride out together the next morning and to accept as ruler of the kingdom the one of their number whose horse neighed first after the sun was up (3.84). Darius' groom, Oebares, devised a stratagem that caused his master's horse to neigh first, whereupon Darius was saluted as king (3.84; cf. Widengren, 1959, pp. 244, 255). About the ensuing rebellions Herodotus remarked only that there had been a period of "troubles" after Cambyses' death (3.126), though he did include the story of Oroetes (see below), as well as a legendary account of the revolt of Babylon and its recapture through a stratagem (1.150-58).

Ctesias reported that before leaving for Egypt Cambyses had ordered a Magian named Spendadates to kill and impersonate Tanyoxarkes, the younger son of Cyrus and Amytis and satrap of the Bactrians, Chorasmians, Parthians, and Carmanians. After Cambyses' death Spendadates ascended the throne but was betrayed by one of his own associates. Then seven Persians, Ataphernes, Onaphas, Mardonius, Hydarnes, Norondabates, Barisses, and Darius, plotted and slew him, and Darius won the throne through the "horse trick." Since then the Persians had celebrated the anniversary of the slaughter of the Magians (Ctesias, in Jacoby, *Fragmente*, no. 688 frag. 13.18). Xenophon reported that Tanaoxares, identified as Cyrus' younger son and satrap of Media, Armenia, and Cadusia, had quarreled with Cambyses upon the accession of the latter (*Cyropaedia* 8.8.2), and Plato (*Leges* 3.694-95; *Epistulae* 7.332A) added that in the quarrel one had killed the other. According to Trogus (Justin, 1.9), the trusted friend chosen to kill the "son of Cyrus" was Cometes (i.e., Gaumāta), who did so after Cambyses' death and placed his own brother Oropastes ("who resembled Smerdis very much") on the throne. The rest follows Herodotus' version.

Darius' veracity. Most historians have accepted Darius' testimony as trustworthy and have used it to check and correct classical accounts (cf. Gershevitch), but others have argued for his mendacity (e.g., Balcer; Bickerman and Tadmor; Boyce, *Zoroastrianism* II, pp. 78-89; Cook, pp. 8-9, 46-57; Culican, pp. 64-65; Dandamaev, 1963; Nyberg, pp. 74-75; Olmstead, 1938, pp. 392-416; idem, 1948, pp. 107-18; Rost, 1897a, pp. 107-10, 208-10; idem, 1897b; Wiesehöfer; Winckler; Young, pp. 53-62). The present author subscribes to the former view. In 1889 Hugo Winckler (p. 128) suggested that "perhaps" Darius had lied in claiming to be related to Cyrus (cf. Rost, 1897a, p. 107; idem, 1897b). Subsequently such scholars as A. T. Olmstead, A. R. Burn, and Muhammad A. Dandamayev elaborated on this hypothesis. Their main arguments are of nine basic types. First, Darius' insistence that all his opponents lied arouses suspicion of his own trustworthiness, especially as Herodotus (3.72) had quoted Darius as defending a justifiable untruth (Olmstead, 1938, p. 397; cf. Dandamaev, 1976, p. 121; Balcer, p. 59). This assessment involves a highly biased interpretation of Darius' motives, whereas Herodotus' report is unreliable; not only did he comment elsewhere on the Persians' high regard for truth (1.136), but also it has been suggested that this casuistry "is purely Greek" (How and Wells, I, p. 276 n. 4; similarly Meyer, p. 35 n. 1). Second, it has been argued that Darius was not a royal prince, let alone the rightful heir (Olmstead, 1938, p. 394; Burn, p. 95). As Cambyses and Bardiya had left no sons, however, the nearest to the throne would have been Aršāma (q.v.), Darius' grandfather, who was then too old to take the field. His son Vištāspa (Hystaspes) was in charge of Parthia and Hyrcania (DB 2.92-98) and could not have led an army to Media undetected. The task thus fell to Darius, one of "the Achaemenids" whom Cambyses had besought on his deathbed to restore the Persian monarchy (Herodotus, 3.65, 3.73). Darius' right was supported by other living Achaemenids, including Bardiya's daughter and sisters (Herodotus, 3.88). Third, it has been doubted that a mighty satrap, a son of Cyrus (i.e., Bardiya), could disappear without arousing suspicion (Olmstead, 1938, p. 396; Nyberg, pp. 75-76; Dandamaev, 1976, p. 116; Boyce, II, pp. 80-81). Nevertheless, with the help of court officals the death of Artaxerxes II (q.v.) was kept secret for nearly a year (Polyaenus, *Stratagemata* 7.17) and in the Islamic period that of the Buyid ʿAżod-al-Dawla (q.v.) for three months (Margoliouth and Amedroz, *Eclipse* VI, pp. 78-79).

The fourth argument is based on Herodotus' report that the "true" and "false" Bardiyas were so alike that even the former's mother and sisters were deceived (Olmstead, 1938, p. 396). Yet elsewhere Herodotus reported that Bardiya's mother had died much earlier (2.1) and that his sister, Queen Atossa (q.v), was kept under strict confinement by the false Bardiya precisely to prevent her from communicating with others (3.68; Shahbazi, 1971, p. 43). Fifth, the date Darius claimed for the slaying of Gaumāta was deemed by Olmstead

(1938, pp. 397-98) not to agree with that in Babylonian documents, which give his reign as having lasted "one year and seven months," but Olmstead's chronology was proved incorrect by Arno Poebel (1939). Sixth, in his inscription Darius identified his opponents precisely, except for Gaumāta, whom he styled merely as "the Magian," giving the impression that the latter was fictitious (Dandamaev, 1976, p. 119; cf. Bickerman and Tadmor, pp. 246-61; Boyce, *Zoroastrianism* II, pp. 85-86). But in the Babylonian version of Darius' inscription at Bīsotūn (1.18) it is specified that Gaumāta was "a Mede, a Magian," which, incidentally, is evidence that he was not a priest but a Median nobleman from the tribe of the Magi (as Benveniste adduced in 1938, p. 17, with Herodotus, 1.101; it should be noted that in the Babylonian text, l. 23, Gaumāta's followers are called "nobles").

A seventh argument involves the Babylonian tablets, which, according to Olmstead (1938, p. 403), proved false Darius' repeated claim that he had made the majority of his expeditions "in the same year after I became King." Walther Hinz (1942), Richard Hallock (1960), and Riekele Borger have shown, however, that the period from Darius' first dated victory (13 December 522) to his last (28 December 521) fell within one year, including an intercalated month. Eighth, in Aeschylus' contemporary play *Persae* (773-76) Darius' ghost announces that after a son of Cyrus "ruled Mardos, a disgrace to his country and ancient throne, whom Artaphernes slew by guile." Olmstead argued that Aeschylus thus had no doubt that Mardos was a legitimate ruler (1938, p. 396; similarly Dandamaev, 1976, p. 120). But in fact Aeschylus merely indicated that Cambyses was followed by a disgraceful king officially known as Mardos (Bardiya); no legitimacy is implied (Burn, p. 94 n. 44). Finally, Darius' marriages to Bardiya's daughter and sisters have been interpreted as moves to gain necessary legitimacy (Olmstead, 1938, pp. 396-97). On the contrary, however, they are evidence of Darius' innocence of Bardiya's murder, for otherwise family vengeance would certainly not have permitted him to survive for thirty-six more years (Prášek, I, p. 265).

Other evidence confirms Darius' testimony. First, as J. V. Prášek (I, p. 265) noted, many foreigners, Greeks in particular, served Darius, and some wrote about his affairs unfavorably (e.g., Herodotus, 3.118-19, 3.133, 4.43), yet none suggested that he was a usurper. Second, although a Persian king was expected to conduct his royal duties openly in the capital, the false Bardiya lived secluded in a castle in the mountains (between Ḥolwān and Hamadān; Marquart, 1905, II, p. 159), and, fearing detection, he "never quitted the citadel nor ever gave audience to a Persian nobleman" (Herodotus, 3.68). To claim that this residence was, in fact, the summer capital (Dandamaev, 1976, p. 137) is to ignore the fact that the summer capital was in Ecbatana and that 29 September was too late to be summer in Media. Third, upon his accession the false Bardiya had abolished taxes and military service "for all nations under his rule for a period of three years" (Herodotus, 3.67), the actions of a usurper desperate for popular support and fearful of the warrior nobility, who had the means to raise new armies. No Persian prince would have thus undermined royal authority (Widengren, 1968, p. 521). In addition, under Persian law the king was required to name a successor before leaving on a dangerous expedition. Cyrus had appointed Cambyses, and later Xerxes I (486-65) chose his uncle Artabanus (Herodotus, 1.208, 7.2, 7.52; cf. 7.53, 8.54). That Cambyses left Patizeithes, a Median official, as his viceroy (3.65) is evidence that his brother Bardiya was already dead. Poebel (1938, p. 314) thus concluded that "Darius, in full accord with his earnest claim to personal veracity, had no intention whatever to exaggerate, as has been assumed, nor that he consciously indulged in any inaccuracy, however small it might be" (sic).

Chronology of Darius' reign.

Darius' second and third regnal years were devoted to consolidating his authority. A fresh rebellion in Elam was suppressed by Gobryas (DB 5.3-14), and Oroetes, satrap of Sardis, was executed for the murders of Polycrates, tyrant of Samos; Mithrobates, satrap of Phrygia; and the latter's son (Herodotus, 3.120-29). Darius himself marched against "the rebellious Scythians" of Central Asia, who threatened the northern and eastern flanks of the empire; he crossed the Caspian Sea, defeated the group known as the Pointed-Hat Scythians (*Sakā tigraxaudā*), captured their "king," Skunxa, and installed a loyal leader in his stead (DB 5.20-33; for detailed commentary, see Shahbazi, 1982, pp. 189-96). On his return he added the image of Skunxa and an account of the Elamite and Scythian campaigns to the reliefs at Bīsotūn. In autumn 517 he traveled to Egypt and succeeded in pacifying the rebellious Egyptians by showing respect for their religion and past glory and by ordering the codification of their laws; in turn he received their obeisance and reverence (Polyaenus, *Strategemata* 7.11.7; Diodorus, 1.95.4-5; for details, see Bresciani, pp. 507-09; Ray, pp. 262-64). After he returned to Persia Darius executed Intaphernes for treason (Herodotus, 3.118-19) and sent a naval reconnaissance mission down the Kabul river to the Indus; it explored the eastern borderlands, Sind, the Indian Ocean, and the Red Sea and arrived in Egypt near modern Suez thirty months later (Hinz, 1976, p. 198; Bivar, *CAH*^{2}, pp. 202-04). Following this expedition "Darius conquered the Indians [of Sind], and made use of the sea in those parts" (Herodotus, 4.44).

A major event in Darius' reign was his European expedition. The region from the Ukraine to the Aral Sea was the home of north Iranian tribes (Rostovtzeff; Vasmer) known collectively as Sakā (Gk. Scythians). Some Sakā had invaded Media (Herodotus, 1.103-06), others had slain Cyrus in war (1.201, 1.214; see CYRUS iii), and some groups had revolted against Darius (DB 2.8). As long as they remained hostile his empire was in constant danger, and trade between Central Asia and the shores of the Black Sea was in peril (Meyer, pp. 97-99). The geography of Scythia was only vaguely known (Figure 2), and it seemed feasible to plan a punitive campaign through the Balkans and the Ukraine, returning from the east, perhaps along the west coast of the Caspian Sea (Meyer, pp. 101-04; Schnitzler, pp. 63-71). Having first sent a naval reconnaissance mission to explore shores of the Black Sea (cf. Fol and Hammond, pp. 239-40), in about 513 Darius crossed the Bosporus into Europe (Shahbazi, 1982, pp. 232-35), marching over a pontoon bridge built by his Samian engineer, Mandrocles. He continued north along the Black Sea coast to the mouth of the Danube, above which his fleet, led by Ionians, had bridged the river; from there he crossed into Scythia (Herodotus, 4.87-88, 4.97). The Scythians evaded the Persians, wasting the countryside as they retreated eastward. After following them for a month Darius reached a desert and began to build eight frontier fortresses; owing to Scythian harrassment of his troops and the October weather, which threatened to hinder further campaigning, he left them unfinished and returned via the Danube bridge. He had, however, "advanced far enough into Scythian territory to terrify the Scythians and to force them to respect the Persian forces" (Herodotus, 4.102-55; cf. Meyer, pp. 105-07; Macan, pp. 2-45; Prášek, II, pp. 91-108; Rostovtzeff, pp. 84-85; Junge, 1944, pp. 104-05, 187-88; Schnitzler, pp. 63-71; Fol and Hammond, pp. 235-43; Černenko, with further references). Shortly afterward Megabyzus reduced gold-rich Thrace and several Greek cities of the northern Aegean; Macedonia submitted voluntarily (Herodotus, 4.143, 5.1-30), and Aryandes (q.v.), satrap of Egypt, annexed Cyrene (Libya; 4.167, 4.197-205). Four new "satrapies" were thus added to Darius' empire: *Sakā tyaiy paradraya* "Overseas Scythians," Skudra (Thrace and Macedonia), *Yaunā takabarā* or *Yaunā tyaiy paradraya* (Thessalians and Greek islanders), and Putāyā (Libya).

By 510 B.C.E. the Asiatic Greeks and many islanders had accepted Persian rule and were being governed by tyrants responsible to Darius. There were also pro-Persian parties, the "Medizing Greeks," in Greece itself, especially at Athens (Herodotus, 6.115, 6.124; Gillis, pp. 39-58; on the term "Medism," see Graf). Darius encouraged these tendencies and opened his court and treasuries to those Greeks who wanted to serve him—as soldiers, artisans, mariners, and statesmen (Junge, 1944, pp. 98 ff.). Greek fear of growing Persian might and Persian annoyance at Greek interference in Ionia and Lydia made conflict between them inevitable, however (Meyer, pp. 277-80; Hignett, pp. 83-85). When, in 500 B.C.E., deposed oligarchs of Naxos in the Cyclades appealed to Artaphernes (see ARTAPHRENĒS), Darius' brother and satrap of Lydia, he sent a fleet to Naxos; partly owing to a falling out with Aristagoras (q.v.), tyrant of Miletus, the expedition failed, however. Aristagoras then organized the "Ionian revolt." Eretrians and Athenians supported him by sending ships to Ionia and burning Sardis. Military and naval operations continued for six years, ending with the Persian reoccupation of all Ionian and Greek islands. The prudent statesman Artaphernes then reorganized Ionia politically and financially. As anti-Persian parties gained ascendance in Athens, however, and aristocrats favorable to Persia were exiled from there and from Sparta, Darius retaliated by sending a force, led by his son-in-law Mardonius, across the Hellespont. Owing to a violent storm and harassment by Thracians he was defeated. Darius then sent a second expedition (of about 20,000 men; Hignett, p. 59) under Datis (q.v.) the Mede, who captured Eretria and, guided by Hippias, exiled tyrant of Athens, landed at Marathon in Attica. In the late summer of 490 the Persians were defeated by a heavily armed Athenian infantry (9,000 men, supported by 600 Plataeans and some 10,000 lightly armed "attendants") under Miltiades (Meyer, pp..277-305; Hignett, pp. 55-74).

Meanwhile, Darius was occupied with his building programs in Persepolis, Susa, Egypt, and elsewhere (Hinz, 1976, pp. 177-82, 206-18, 235-42). He had linked the Nile to the Red Sea by means of a canal running from modern Zaqāzīq in the eastern Delta through Wādī Ṭūmelāt and the lakes Boḥayrat al-Temsāḥ and Buḥayrat al-Morra near modern Suez (Hinz, 1975b; Tuplin, 1991). In 497 he again traveled to Egypt, "opened" his "Suez canal" amid great fanfare, executed Aryandes for treason, erected several commemorative monuments, and returned to Persia, where he found that the codification of Egyptian law had been completed (Bresciani, p. 508); a statue of Darius in Egyptian style, found at Susa (*EIr.* II, p. 575 fig. 40), reflects the influence of this journey. Following Datis' defeat at Marathon Darius resolved to lead a punitive expedition in person, but another revolt in Egypt (possibly led by the Persian satrap; Bresciani, p. 509) and failing health prevented him. He died in October 486 and was entombed in the rock-cut sepulcher he had prepared at Naqš-e Rostam (see Schmidt, III, pp. 80-90, pls. 18-39). He had already designated as his successor Xerxes, his eldest son by Queen Atossa (XPf, 27-31; Kent, *Old Persian*, p. 150; Ritter, pp. 20-23, 29-30); the throne thus returned to Cyrus' line.

Darius' empire.

Cyrus and Cambyses had incorporated Elam, Media, Lydia, Babylonia, Egypt, and several eastern Iranian states into a loose federation of autonomous satrapies, subject to irregular taxation (Herodotus, 3.89; 3:120-29; 4.165-67, 200-05; cf. DB 3.14, 3.56; Meyer, pp. 46-47; Lehmann-Haupt, cols. 85-90; Ehtécham, pp. 110-27; Petit, pp. 16-97). They had relied heavily on non-Persian officials and the established institutions of the subject states (Dandamaev, 1975; idem, 1992, pp. 3 ff.; Bivar, *Camb. Hist. Iran*, pp. 610-21), which encouraged particularism among Iranian magnates and nationalism among conquered nations. These tendencies resulted in chaos and rebellion and led to the

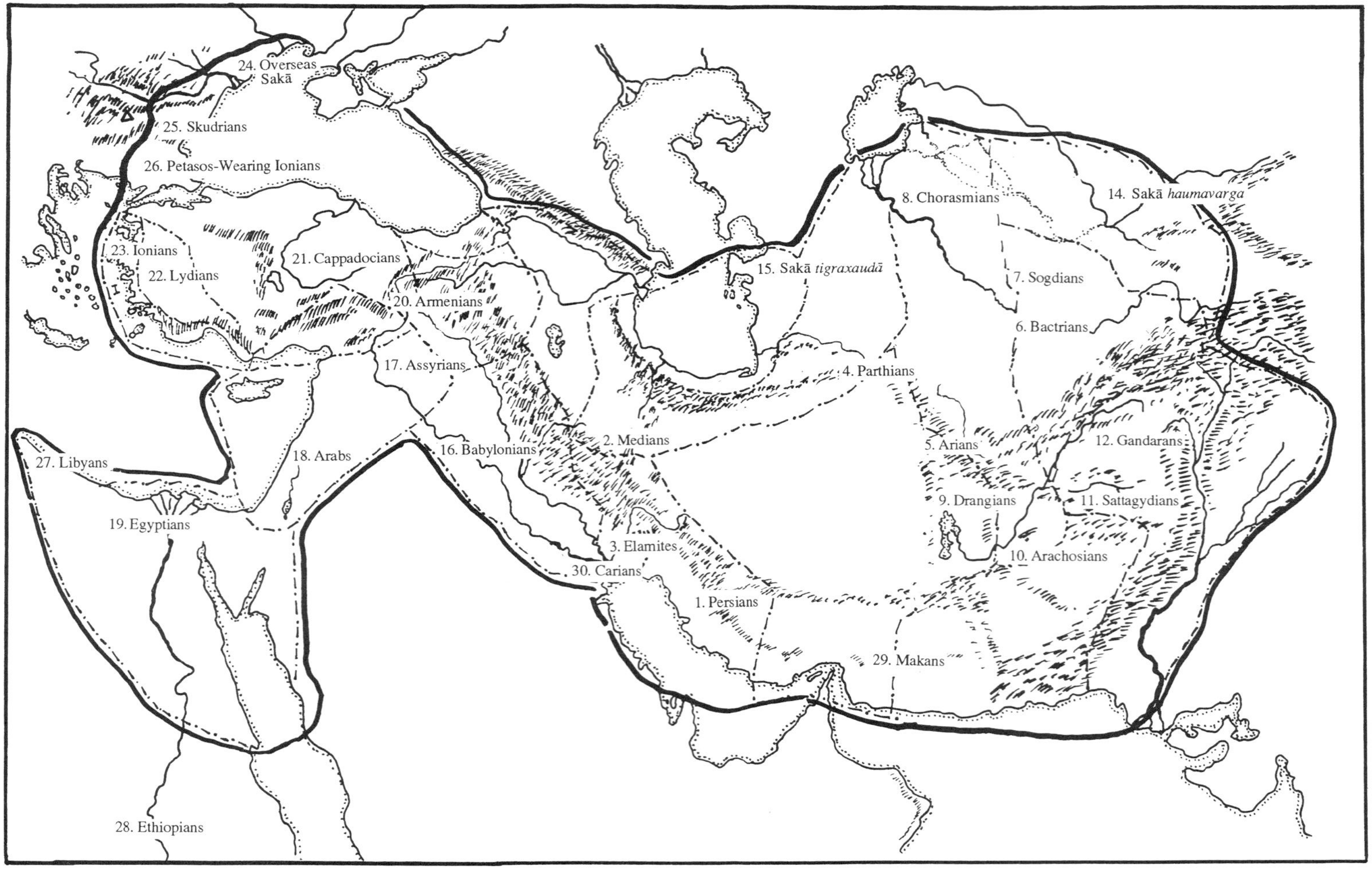

Figure 2. Peoples of the Persian empire, as recorded on the relief on the tomb of Darius I at Naqš-e Rostam (numbered in the order in which the peoples are represented on the relief and named in the accompanying text).

destruction of the Achaemenid federation in 522 B.C.E. (Schaeder, 1941, p. 32; Junge, 1944, pp. 41-43, 51; Stolper, 1985, p. 6). Darius thus faced the task of reconquering the satrapies and integrating them into a strong empire. The accomplishment of his first year was "the actual creation, for the first time, of a real empire: a governmental structure based on the army, on certain classes of the society whose loyalty was to the throne and not to some specific geographical region, and on the charisma, intelligence and moral fortitude of one man, Darius" (Young, p. 63). Darius knew that an empire could flourish only when it possessed sound military, economic, and legal systems, as is clear from his prayer "May Ahuramazda protect this country from a [hostile] army, from famine, from the Lie" (DPd 15-17; Kent, *Old Persian*, p. 135; cf. Tuplin, pp. 144-45). Once he gained power, Darius placed the empire on foundations that lasted for nearly two centuries and influenced the organization of subsequent states, including the Seleucid and Roman empires (Stolper, 1989, pp. 81-91; Kornemann, pp. 398 ff., 424 ff.; Junge, 1944, pp. 150, 198 n. 46). Himself a soldier of the first rank "both afoot and on horseback" (DNb 31-45; Kent, *Old Persian*, p. 140), Darius provided the empire with a truly professional army. Earlier Achaemenids had relied on regional contingents, especially cavalry, apparently recruited as the need arose. Darius put his trust mainly in Iranians, including Medes, Scythians, Bactrians, and other kindred peoples (see ARMY i.3) but above all Persians: "If you thus shall think, 'May I not feel fear of (any) other,' protect this Persian people" (DPe 18-22; Kent, *Old Persian*, p. 136). Thenceforth the mainstay of the imperial army was an infantry force of 10,000 carefully chosen Persian soldiers, the Immortals, who defended the empire to its very last day (Curtius Rufus, 3.3.13).

Darius ruled about 50 million people in the largest empire the world had seen (Meyer, p. 85). His subjects (*kāra*) or their lands (*dahyu*) were several times listed, and also depicted, in varying order at Bīsotūn and Persepolis (Junge, 1944, pp. 132-59; Kent, 1943; Ehtécham, pp. 131-63; Walser; Hinz, 1969, pp. 95-113; Calmeyer), but the definitive account is carved on his tomb (*EIr.* V, p. 722 fig. 46). In the relief on his tomb Darius and his royal fire are depicted upon the imperial "throne" supported by thirty figures of equal status, who symbolize the nations of the empire, as explained in the accompanying inscription (DNa 38-42). The text reflects Darius' status, ideals, and achievements. He introduces himself as "Great King, King of Kings, King of countries containing all kinds of men, King in this great earth far and wide, son of Hystaspes, an Achaemenian, a Persian, son of a Persian, an Aryan [=Iranian], having Aryan lineage" (DNa 8-15; Kent, *Old Persian*, p. 138). Next "the countries other than Persis" are enumerated in what is clearly intended to be a geographical order. According to Herodotus (3.89), Darius "joined together in one province the nations that were neighbors, but sometimes he passed over the nearer tribes and gave their places to more remote ones." Applying this scheme to the lands recorded in the record relief, it is possible to distinguish, beside Persis, six groups of nations, recalling the traditional Iranian division of the world into seven regions (Shahbazi, 1983, pp. 243-46 and fig. 3; cf. Plato, *Leges*, 3.695c, where it is reported that power was divided among seven leading Persians). The sevenfold division of Darius' empire, revealing his geographical conception, is as follows: (1) the central region, Persis (Pārsa), which paid no tribute, though some of its districts sent commodities (Herodotus, 3.97; Koch; cf. Briant, pp. 342-501), possibly to pay for garrisons; (2) the western region encompassing Media (Māda) and Elam (Ūja); (3) the Iranian plateau encompassing Parthia (Parθava), Aria (Haraiva), Bactria (Bāxtri), Sogdiana (Suguda), Chorasmia (Uvārazmī), and Drangiana (Zranka; cf. Herodotus, 3.93, according to whom these lands paid little tribute); the borderlands: Arachosia (Harauvati), Sattagydia (Θatagu), Gandara (Gandāra), Sind (Hindu), and eastern Scythia (Sakā); (5) the western lowlands: Babylonia (Bābiru), Assyria (Aθurā), Arabia (Arabāya), and Egypt (Mudrāya); (6) the northwestern region encompassing Armenia (Armina), Cappadocia (Katpatuka), Lydia (Sparda), Overseas Scythians (Sakā tyaiy paradraya), Skudra, and Petasos-Wearing Greeks (Yaunā takabarā); and (7) the southern coastal regions: Libya (Putāyā), Ethiopia (Kūša), Maka (Maciya), and Caria (Karka, i.e., the Carian colony on the Persian Gulf; Schaeder, 1932, p. 270; Shahbazi, 1983, p. 245 n. 28; Figure 2).

Early in his reign Darius established twenty *archi* (provinces), called "satrapies," assigning to each an *archon* (satrap) and fixing tribute to be paid by neighboring "nations," joined together in each satrapy (Herodotus, 3.89). The list is preserved in the confused but invaluable catalogue of Herodotus (3.90-97; for detailed analysis, see Junge, 1941; Leuze, pp. 25-144; Lehmann-Haupt, cols. 91-109; Ehtécham, pp. 96-102, 127-63; for Babylonian data, see also Dandamayev, 1992, pp. 8-12 and passim). It begins with Ionia and lists the rest in a sequence from west to east, with the exception of "the land of the Persians," which did not pay tax. The nations in each satrapy are enumerated. The fixed annual tributes to Darius' treasury were paid according to the Babylonian talent in silver but to the Euboic talent (25.86 kg) in gold (3.89). The total yearly tribute, according to Herodotus' somewhat contradictory calculations, seems to have been less than 15,000 silver talents (3.95).

Most of the satraps were Persian, members of the royal house or of the six great noble families (Meyer, pp. 47 ff.; Schaeder, 1941, p. 18; cf. Petit, pp. 219-26). They were appointed directly by Darius to administer these tax districts, each of which could be divided into subsatrapies and smaller units with their own governors, usually nominated by the central court but occasionally by the satrap (see ACHAEMENID DYNASTY ii). To ensure fair assessments of tribute, Darius sent a commission of trusted men (cf. OPers. **hamara-kāra-*; Stolper, 1989, p. 86; Dandamayev, 1992, p. 36) to evaluate the revenues and expenditures of each district (cf. Plutarch, *Moralia* 172F; Polyaenus, *Stratagemata* 7.11.3). Similarly, after the Ionian revolt his brother Artaphernes calculated the areas of Ionian cities in parasangs and fixed their tributes (OPers. *bāji-*; see BĀJ) at a rate "very nearly the same as that which had been paid before the revolt," a rate that continued unaltered down to Herodotus' time (Herodotus, 6.42). Contemporary Babylonian documents attest the existence of a detailed land register in which property boundaries, ownership (of cattle and probably other movable goods, as well as of urban and rural real estate), and assessments were recorded (Stolper, 1977, pp. 259-60; Dandamayev, 1992, pp. 11-12). In the Persepolis Elamite texts officials who "write people down" and "make inquiries" are mentioned (see Tuplin, p. 145, with references). To prevent concentration of power in one person, each satrap was normally accompanied by a "secretary," who observed affairs of the state and communicated with the king; a treasurer, who safeguarded provincial revenues; and a garrison commander, who was also responsible to the king. Further checks were provided by royal inspectors with full authority over all satrapal affairs, the so-called "eyes" and "ears" of the king (Meyer, pp. 39-89; Kiessling; Schaeder, 1934; Ehtécham, pp. 56-62; Frye, 1984, pp. 106-26; see also Hirsch, pp. 101-43; Tuplin; Petit, pp. 109-72).

Coordination of the imperial administration was the responsibility of the chancery, with headquarters at Persepolis, Susa, and Babylon (Junge, 1944, pp. 78 ff.; Hinz, 1971; idem, 1976, pp. 226-31; idem, 1979), although such chief cities of the empire as Bactria, Ecbatana (q.v.), Sardis, Dascylium (q.v.), and Memphis also had branches (Ehtécham, pp. 58-62; Tuplin, with full references). Bureaucratic organization was deeply rooted in the Near East (Schaeder, 1941, p. 17), but Darius reformed it in accordance with the needs of a centralized empire. Aramaic was retained as the common language, especially in trade, and "imperial Aramaic" soon spread from India to Ionia, leaving permanent traces of Achaemenid organization (see ART IN IRAN iii, pp. 571-72). Elamite and Babylonian, written in cuneiform, were used in western Asia, and Egyptian, written in hieroglyphics, prevailed in Egypt. Early in his reign, however, Darius appears to have commissioned a group of scholars to create a writing system specifically for Persian (Junge, 1944, p. 63; Hinz, 1973, pp. 15-27; Mayrhofer, pp. 175, 179); the result was the creation of what Darius called "Aryan" script (Old Persian cuneiform, q.v.; cf. DB 4.88-89; Schmitt, p. 73 and n. 89), the simplest cuneiform system, which bears clear traces of having been modeled on the Urartian signs (Mayrhofer, p. 179). Although this script was merely "ceremonial," used for official inscriptions only, it nevertheless contributed to the distinctive identity of the Persian empire.

In keeping with his "very clear creative role" in the patronage of "an Achaemenid canon for imperial art, edicts and administrative mechanisms" (Root, p. 8), Darius introduced (before 500 B.C.E.; Root, pp. 1-12) a new monetary system based on silver coins (Gk. *síglos*) with an average weight of 8 g and gold coins weighing 5.40 g, equaling in value 20 silver coints (see DERHAM i). The gold coin, **dārayaka-*, Gk. *dareikós*, was probably named after Darius (see DARIC), as ancient sources attest (cf. Meyer, p. 75 n. 2; Schwyzer, pp. 8-19; Kent, *Old Persian*, p. 189 [cf. W. B. Henning apud Robinson, p. 189 n. 1]; Brandenstein and Mayrhofer, p. 115; Hinz, 1975a, p. 83; Cook, p. 70; Bivar, *Camb. Hist. Iran*, p. 621; for a different derivation, see ACHAEMENID DYNASTY ii, p. 421).

In order to enhance trade, Darius built canals, underground waterways, and a powerful navy (Hinz, 1976, pp. 206 ff.). He further improved the network of roads and way stations throughout the empire, so that "there was a system of travel authorization by King, satrap, or other high official, which entitled the traveller to draw provisions at daily stopping places" (Tuplin, p. 110; cf. Hallock, 1978, p. 114; Lewis, 1977, pp. 4-5; Bivar, *CAH²*, pp. 204-08). Some standardization of weights and measures was also effected (see Bivar, *Camb. Hist. Iran*, pp. 621-37). Darius appointed loyal subjects, primarily Persians, to senior posts but was eager to listen to and follow the advice of non-Persian counselors as well (Cook, pp. 71-72). He recognized the kinship between the Greeks and Persians and promoted an "open door" policy under which Hellenic aristocrats could enter his service and receive honored positions (Junge, 1944, pp. 95-120, 185-91).

Darius sponsored large construction projects in Susa, Babylon, Egypt, and Persepolis (Hinz, 1976, pp. 235-42). The monuments were often inscribed in the scripts and languages of the empire: Old Persian, Elamite, Babylonian, and Egyptian hieroglyphs. Large numbers of workers and artisans of diverse nationalities, some of them deportees (Dandamaev, 1975; Koch) were employed on these projects, enhancing both the Persian economy and intercultural relations (see DEPORTATIONS). The king was also deeply interested in agriculture. In his letter to Gadates, a governor in Asia Minor, he echoed the Avestan statement (*Vd.* 3.4, 23) "the Earth feels most happy . . . where one of the faithful cultivates corn, grass and fruits" (Lochner-Hüttenbach, in Brandenstein and Mayrhofer, pp. 91-92). Darius' codification of Egyptian law has been mentioned above; he also sanctioned various other local codes (Schaeder, 1941, pp. 25-26; Tuplin, pp. 112-13). Little need be said about Darius' religion (see ACHAEMENID RELIGION). It is clear that he felt himself chosen by Ahura Mazdā: "Ahuramazda, when he saw this earth in commotion, thereafter bestowed it upon me, made me king. I am king, by the favor of Ahuramazda I put it down in its place" (DNa 30 ff.; Kent, *Old Persian*, p. 138); "Ahuramazda is mine; I am Ahuramazda's" (DSk 3-5; Kent, *Old Persian*, p. 145). These sentiments echo Zoroaster's utterances and attest Darius' piety (Hinz, 1976, pp. 242-45). With characteristic Achaemenid tolerance (Schaeder, 1941, pp. 22, 34), however, Darius supported alien faiths and temples "as long as those who held them were submissive and peaceable" (Boyce, *Zoroastrianism* II, p. 127). He funded the restoration of the Jewish temple originally decreed by Cyrus (Ezra 5:1-6:15), showed favor toward Greek cults (attested in his letter to Gadatas), observed Egyptian religious rites related to kingship (Posener, pp. 24-34, 50-63), and supported Elamite priests (Boyce, *Zoroastrianism* II, pp. 132-35). In H. H. Schaeder's opinion (1941, p. 29), "the great politics of the King reveal his clear understanding of what were possible and what necessary . . .; [and] the organizations which he established in the empire earn him the title of the greatest statesman of ancient East."

Bibliography: J. M. Balcer, *Herodotus and Bisitun. Problems in Ancient Persian Historiography*, Stuttgart, 1987. E. Benveniste, *Les Mages dan l'ancien Iran*, Paris, 1938. E. J. Bickerman and H. Tadmor, "Darius I, Pseudo-Bardiya and the Magi," *Athenaeum*, N.S. 56, 1978, pp. 239-61. A. D. H. Bivar, "Achaemenid Coins, Weights and Measures," *Camb. Hist. Iran* II, pp. 610-39. Idem, "The Indus Lands," *CAH*[2] IV, pp. 194-210. R. Borger, *Die Chronologie des Darius-Denkmals am Behistun-Felsen*, Göttingen, 1982. W. Brandenstein and M. Mayrhofer, *Handbuch des Altpersischen*, Wiesbaden, 1964. E. Bresciani, "The Persian Occupation of Egypt," *Camb. Hist. Iran* II, pp. 502-28. P. Briant, *Rois, tributs et paysans. Études sur les formations tributaires du Moyen-Orient ancien*, Paris, 1982. A. R. Burn, *Persia and the Greeks. The Defense of the West, c. 546-478 B.C.*, London, 1962. P. Calmeyer, "Zur Genese altiranischer Motive VIII. Die 'Statistische Landcharte des Perserreiches,'" *AMI*, N.F. 15, 1982, pp. 105-87; 16, 1983, pp. 141-232. G. G. Cameron, "The Persian Satrapies and Related Matters," *JA* 32, 1973, pp. 47-56. G. Cardascia, *Les archives des Murašū*, Paris, 1991. E. V. Černenko, *Skifo-persidskaya voĭna* (The Scytho-Persian war), Kiev, 1984. J. M. Cook, *The Persian Empire*, London, 1983. M. A. Dandamaev (Dandamayev), *Iran pri pervykh Akhemenidakh*, Moscow, 1963; rev. ed. tr. H. D. Pohl as *Persien unter den ersten Achämeniden (6. Jahrhundert v. Chr.)*, Wiesbaden, 1976. Idem, "Forced Labour in the Persian Empire," *AoF* 2, 1975, pp. 71-78. Idem, *A Political History of the Achamaenid Empire*, tr. W. J. Vogelsang, Leiden, 1989. Idem, *Iranians in Achaemenid Babylonia*, Costa Mesa, Calif., 1992. J. J. A. van Dijk and W. R. Mayer, *Texte aus dem Rēš-Heiligtum in Uruk-Warka*, Baghdader Mitteilungen, Beiheft 2, 1980. R. Drews, *The Greek Accounts of Eastern History*, Cambridge, Mass., 1973.

M. Ehtécham, *L'Iran sous les Achéménides*, Fribourg, 1946. A. Fol and N. G. L. Hammond, "Persia in Europe, Apart from Greece," *CAH*[2] IV, pp. 234-53. R. N. Frye, *The History of Ancient Iran*, Munich, 1984. I. Gershevitch, "The False-Bardiya," *AAASH* 27/4, 1979, pp. 337-51. D. Gillis, *Collaboration with the Persians*, Wiesbaden, 1979. D. F. Graf, "Medism. The Origin and Significance of the Term," *Journal of Hellenic Studies* 104, 1984, pp. 15-30. J. C. Greenfield and B. Porten, eds., *The Bisitun Inscription of Darius the Great. Aramaic Version*, Corpus Inscr. Iran., pt. 1, vol. 5, Texts 1, 1982. F. Gschnitzer, *Die sieben Perser und das Königtum des Dareios*, Heidelberg, 1977. Idem, "Zur Stellung des persischen Stammlandes im Achaimenidenreich," in *Ad Bene et Fideliter Seminandum. Festgabe für Karlheinz Deller*, Kevelaer and Neukirchen-Vluyn, Germany, 1988, pp. 87-122. E. Haerinck, "Le palais achéménide de Babylone," *Iranica Antiqua* 10, 1973, pp. 108-32. R. T. Hallock, "The 'One Year' of Darius I," *JNES* 19, 1960, pp. 36-39. Idem, *Persepolis Fortification Tablets*, Chicago, 1969. Idem, "The Use of Seals on the Persepolis Fortification Tablets," in M. Gibson and R. D. Biggs, eds., *Seals and Sealing in the Ancient Near East*, Malibu, Calif., 1978, pp. 127-33. Idem, "The Evidence of the Persepolis Tablets," *Camb. Hist. Iran* II, pp. 588-609. J. Harmatta, "A Recently Discovered Old Persian Inscription," *AAASH* 2, 1954, pp. 1-14. C. Hignett, *Xerxes' Invasion of Greece*, Oxford, 1963. W. Hinz, "Zur Behistun-Inschrift des Dareios," *ZDMG* 96, 1942, pp. 326-49. Idem, *Altiranische Funde und Forschungen*, Berlin, 1969, 63-114. Idem, "Achaemenidische Hofverwaltung," *ZA* 61, 1971, pp. 260-311. Idem, *Neue Wege im Altpersischen*, Wiesbaden, 1973. Idem, *Altiranisches Sprachgut der Nebenüberlieferungen*, Wiesbaden, 1975a. Idem, "Darius und der Suezkanal," *AMI*, N.F. 8, 1975b, pp. 115-21. Idem, *Darius und die Perser. Eine Kulturgeschichte der Achämeniden*, 2 vols., Baden-Baden, 1976-79. S. W. Hirsch, *The Friendship of the Barbarians*, Hanover, N.H., 1985. W. W. How and J. Wells, *A Commentary on Herodotus*, 2 vols., Oxford, 1961.

P. J. Junge, "Satrapie und Nation," *Klio* 34, 1941, pp. 1-55. Idem, *Dareios I. König der Perser*, Leipzig, 1944. R. G. Kent, "Old Persian Texts. The Lists of Provinces," *JNES* 2, 1943, pp. 302-06. M. Kiessling, *Zur Geschichte der ersten Regierungsjahre des Darius Hystaspes*, Leipzig, 1900. H. Koch, *Persien zur Zeit des Dareios. Das Achämenidenreich im Lichte neuer Quellen*. Kleine Schriften aus dem vorgeschichtlichen Seminar der Philipps-Universität Marburg 25, Marburg, 1988. E. Kornemann, *Römische Geschichte* II, Leipzig, 1940. C. F. Lehmann-Haupt, "Satrap," in Pauly-Wissowa IIA/1, cols. 82-188. O. Leuze, *Die Satrapieneinteilung in Syrien und im Zweistromlande von 520 bis 320*, 2 vols., Halle, 1935; repr. in 1 vol., Hildesheim, 1972. D. M. Lewis, *Sparta and Persia*, Leiden, 1977. Idem, "The Persepolis Fortification Texts," in H. Sancisi-Weerdenburg and A. Kuhrt, eds., *Achaemenid History* IV, Leiden, 1990, pp. 1-6. A. B. Lloyd, "The Inscription of Udjaḥorresnet. A Collaborator's Testament," *Journal of Egyptian Archaeology* 68, 1982, pp. 166-80. R. W. Macan, *Herodotus. The Fourth,*

Fifth and Sixth Books II, London, 1895. J. Marquart, *Untersuchungen zur Geschichte von Eran* II, Leipzig, 1905, pp. 158-62. M. Mayrhofer, "Über die Verschriftung des Altpersischen," *Historische Sprachforschung* 102, 1989, pp. 174-84. E. Meyer, *Geschichte des Altertums* IV, Basel, 1954.

H. S. Nyberg, "Das Reich der Achämeniden," in F. Valjavec, ed., *Historia Mundi* III, Munich, 1954, pp. 56-115. A. T. Olmstead, "Darius and His Behistun Inscription," *AJSLL* 55, 1938, pp. 392-416. Idem, *The Persian Empire*, Chicago, 1948, pp. 107-18. A. L. Oppenheim, "The Babylonian Evidence of Achaemenid Rule in Mesopotamia," *Camb. Hist. Iran* II, pp. 529-87. T. Petit, *Satrapes et satrapies dans l'empire achéménide de Cyrus le Grand à Xerxes Ier*, Liège, 1990. A. Poebel, "Chronology of Darius' First Year of Reign," *AJSLL* 55, 1938, pp. 142-65, 285-314. Idem, "The Duration of the Reign of Smerdis, the Magian, and the Reigns of Nebuchadnezzar III and Nebu-chadnezzar IV," *AJSLL* 56, 1939, pp. 121-45. G. Posener, *La première domination perse en Égypte*, Cairo, 1936. J. V. Prášek, *Geschichte der Meder und Perser bis zur makedonischen Eroberung*, 2 vols., Gotha, 1906-10; repr. Darmstadt, 1968; rev. P. R. Rost, *OLZ* 1, 1898, pp. 38-45. J. D. Ray, "Egypt 525-405 B.C.," *CAH*[2] IV, pp. 254-86. H. W. Ritter, *Diadem und Königsherrschaft. Untersuchungen zu Zeremonien und Rechtsgrundlagen des Herr-schaftsantritts bei den Persern, bei Alexander dem Grossen und im Hellenismus*, Wiesbaden, 1965. E. S. G. Robinson, "The Beginnings of Achaemenid Coinage," *NC*, 1958, pp. 187-93. M. C. Root, "Evidence from Persepolis for Dating of Persian and Archaic Greek Coinage," *NC*, 1988, pp. 1-12. P. R. Rost, "Untersuchungen zur altorientalischen Geschichte," *Mitteilungen der Vorderasiatisch-Aegyptischen Gesellschaft* 41/1, Leipzig, 1897, pp. 107-10, 208-10. M. Rostovtzeff, *Iranians and Greeks in South Russia*, 2nd ed., New York, 1969.

H. H. Schaeder, "Die Ionier in der Bauinschrift des Dareios von Susa," *Jahrbuch des Deutschen Archäologischen Instituts*, 1932, pp. 270-74. Idem, "Iranica. I. Das Auge des Königs," in *Abh. der Gesellschaft der Wissenschaften zu Göttingen*, Phil.-hist. Kl., 3rd series 10, 1934, pp. 3-24. Idem, *Das persische Weltreich*, Breslau, 1941. E. F. Schmidt, *Persepolis* I-III, Chicago, 1953-70. R. Schmitt, *The Bisitun Inscriptions of Darius the Great. Old Persian Text.* Corpus Inscr. Iran, pt. 1, vol. I, Texts 1, 1991. H. J. Schnitzler, "Der Sakenfeldzug Dareios' des Grossen," in R. Stiehl and G. A. Lehmann, eds., *Antike und Universalgeschichte. Festschrift für Erich Stier*, Münster, 1972, pp. 52-71. E. Schwyzer, "Awest. *aspərənō* und byzantin. *áspron*. Beiträge zur griechisch-orientalischen Münznamenforschung," *IF* 49, 1931, pp. 11-45. U. Seidl, "Ein Relief Dareios' I in Babylon," *AMI*, N.F. 3, 1976, pp. 125-30. A. Sh. Shahbazi, *Jahān-dārī-e Dāryūš-e Bozorg*, Tehran, 1350 Š./1971. Idem, "Darius in Scythia and Scythians in Persepolis," *AMI*, N.F. 15, 1982, pp. 189-235. Idem, "Darius' *'Haft Kišvar'*," *AMI*, Suppl. 10, Berlin, 1983, pp. 239-46. M. Stolper, "Three Iranian Loan-words in Late Babylonian Texts," in L. Levine, ed., *Mountains and Lowlands*, Malibu, Calif., 1977, pp. 251-66. Idem, *Entrepreneurs and Empire*, Leiden, 1985. Idem, "On Interpreting Tributary Relationships in Achaemenid Babylonia," in P. Briant and C. Herrenschmidt, eds., *Le tribut dans l'empire perse. Actes de la table ronde de Paris, 12-13 décembre 1986*, Paris, 1989, pp. 147-56. J. N. Strassmaier, *Inschriften von Darius*, Leipzig, 1892. C. Tuplin, "The Administration of the Achaemenid Empire," in I. Carradice, ed., *Coinage and Administration in the Athenian and Persian Empires. The Ninth Oxford Symposium on Coinage and Monetary History*, Oxford, 1987, pp. 109-64. Idem, ""Darius' Suez Canal and Persian Imperialism," in H. Sancisi-Weerdenburg and A. Kuhrt, eds., *Achaemenid History* VI. *Asia Minor and Egypt. Old Cultures in a New Empire*, Leiden, 1991, pp. 237-83. M. Vasmer, *Die Iranier in Südrussland*, Leipzig, 1923. E. N. von Voigtlander, *The Bisitun Inscription of Darius the Great. Babylonian Version*, Corpus Inscr. Iran, pt. 1, vol. II, Texts 1, 1978. G. Walser, *Die Völkerschaften auf den Reliefs von Persepolis*, Berlin, 1966. G. Widengren, "The Sacral Kingship of Iran," in *Studies in the History of Religions*, Numen, Suppl., Leiden, 1959, pp. 242-57. Idem, "Über einige Probleme in der altpersischen Geschichte," in J. Meixner and G. Kegel, eds., *Festschrift für L. Brandt zum 60 Geburtstag*, Opladen, Germany, 1968, pp. 517-33. J. Wiesehöfer, *Der Aufstand Gaumāta's und die Anfänge Dareios' I*, Bonn, 1978. H. Winckler, *Untersuchungen zur altorientalischen Geschichte*, Leipzig, 1889. T. Cuyler Young, Jr., "The Persian Empire," *CAH*[2] IV, pp. 1-111.

(A. Shapur Shahbazi)

iv. Darius II

Darius II was the sixth Achaemenid king of kings (r. February 423- March 403 B.C.E.). He had been satrap of Hyrcania. Darius was his throne name; his given name is reported in classical sources as Ochus (Babylonian Ú-ma-kuš or Ú-ma-su; Stolper, p. 115). The Old Persian name may have been either *Vauka (Schmitt, 1977, pp. 422-23; idem, 1982, p. 84) or *Va(h)uš (cf. Stolper, p. 115). His father was Artaxerxes I (q.v.; 465-25 B.C.E.), his mother a Babylonian. Greek authors therefore considered him a bastard (Gk. *nóthos*), though this epithet appeared rather late (Pausanias, 6.5.7). According to Ctesias (Jacoby, *Fragmente* 688 frag. 15.47-51), Darius II ascended the throne after the short reigns of two of his half-brothers, Xerxes II (425-24) and Sogdianus (or Sekyndianus; 424). In the dating formulas of the Babylonian business documents, however, these kings are not mentioned, and Darius II directly succeeds Artaxerxes I. The struggle for the throne probably took place during the first years of Darius' reign, rather than before it, as Greek authors have it (cf. Ctesias, in Jacoby, *Fragmente* 688 frag. 15.47-49; Diodorus, 11.69.6, 12.7.1, 12.64.1). Its effects appear to be reflected in the archive of the Babylonian banking family the Murašūs: In the second year of the reign of Darius II Ochus there was an increase in the number of mortgages, possibly resulting from the fiscal and military demands of his first year (Stolper, pp. 122-23). The names of those who supported Sogdianus and Darius given by Ctesias are confirmed in these cuneiform documents (Stolper, p. 116); these names include that of Parysatis, Darius' wife and half-sister. In discussionss of her presumed pernicious influence at court (e.g., Olmstead, pp. 356, 364; Cook, p. 135) little account is taken of her wealth and landholdings, as they appear in the Murašū tablets.

Iranian evidence for the rule of Darius II is scarce; all his inscriptions refer to building activities. He built at Susa (cf. Kent, *Old Persian*, p. 154, D²Sa, D²Sb, both fragmentary; but cf. Lewis, p. 78, for mention of an unpublished inscription, presumably from Hamadān), and one of the three anepigraphic tombs at Naqš-e Rostam is ascribed to him; he was the last Achaemenid to be buried there.

Darius' reign was conspicuous for frequent revolts, led partly by satraps who had acquired a power base in regions where their families had ruled for generations. Ctesias mentioned a revolt by Darius' full brother Arsites, assisted by Artyphios (qq.v.), son of the satrap Megabyzus, who had mounted a revolt during Artaxerxes' reign. The revolt of the satrap Pissoúthnēs at Sardis was crushed by Tissaphernes (see ČIΘRAFARNAH), probably in 422 (cf. Ctesias, in Jacoby, *Fragmente* 688 frag. 15.53), who bribed Pissoúthnēs' Greek mercenary troops to abandon their commander. Tissaphernes' sojourn in Asia Minor signaled the start of intensified Persian interference in Greek affairs during the Peloponnesian war. The Paphlagonian eunuch Artoxares (q.v.), who had once helped Darius to become king, also attempted a coup at an uncertain date (Ctesias, in Jacoby, *Fragmente* 688 frag. 15.54). In addition, the novelistic tale of the insubordination of Teritouchmes, married to a daughter of Darius II, may well mask a more serious threat to the throne (Ctesias, in Jacoby, *Fragmente* 688 frag. 15.55-56). There is evidence of trouble in Egypt in 410 B.C.E., prelude to a successful revolt in 404 (on its origins, cf. Briant, pp. 138 ff.; Ray, 1987; idem, 1988). Finally, in the heart of the empire the crushing of a Median revolt (Xenophon, *Hellenica* 1.11.19) was followed by a campaign against the Cadusii (q.v.; Gk. *Kadoúsioi*).

Darius II died in 404 in Babylon (Ctesias, in Jacoby, *Fragmente* 688 frag. 16.57). He was survived by Parysatis, who supported her younger son, Cyrus the Younger (see CYRUS vi), in his well-known rebellion against his full brother Artaxerxes II (405-359), reported by Xenophon in the first book of his *Anabasis*. Dependence on Greek sources, notably Ctesias (Sancisi-Weerdenburg, pp. 34 ff.), and the virtual absence of Near Eastern documentation seriously biases current views on the reign of Darius II.

Bibliography: P. Briant, "Ethno-classe dominante et populations soumises dans l'empire achéménide. Le cas d'Égypte," in A. Kuhrt and H. Sancisi-Weerdenburg, eds., *Achaemenid History* III. *Method and Theory*, Leiden, 1988, pp. 137-74. J. M. Cook, *The Persian Empire*, London, 1983. M. A. Dandamaev (Dandamayev), *A Political History of the Achaemenid Empire*, tr. W. J. Vogelsang, Leiden, 1989, pp. 258-73. Idem, *Iranians in Achaemenid Babylonia*, Costa Mesa, Calif., 1992, pp. 115-16. A. Kuhrt, "Survey of Written Sources Available for the History of Babylonia under the Later Achaemenids," in H. Sancisi-Weerdenburg, ed., *Achaemenid History* I. *Sources, Structures and Synthesis*, Leiden, 1987, pp. 147-58. D. M. Lewis, *Sparta and Persia*, Leiden, 1977. A. T. Olmstead, *The History of the Persian Empire*, Chicago, 1948. J. D. Ray, "Egypt. Dependence and Independence (425-343 B.C.)," in H. Sancisi-Weerdenburg, ed., *Achaemenid History* I. *Sources, Structures and Synthesis*, Leiden, 1987, pp. 79-95. Idem, "Egypt 525-404 B.C.," in *CAH²* IV, pp. 254-86. A. Sachs, "Achaemenid Royal Names in Babylonian Astronomical Texts," *American Journal of Ancient History* 2, 1977, pp. 129-47. H. Sancisi-Weerdenburg, "Decadence in the Empire or Decadence in the Sources? From Source to Synthesis: Ctesias," in H. Sancisi-Weerdenburg, ed., *Achaemenid History* I. *Sources, Structures and Synthesis*, Leiden, 1987, pp. 33-45. R. Schmitt, "Thronnamen bei den Achaimeniden," *BNF*, N.F. 12, 1977, pp. 422-25. Idem, "Achaemenid Throne-names," *AION* 42, 1982, pp. 85-95. M. W. Stolper, *Entrepreneurs and Empire. The Murašû Archive, the Murašû Firm and Persian Rule in Babylonia*, Leiden, 1985.

(HELEEN SANCISI-WEERDENBURG)

v. DARIUS III

Darius III (b. ca. 380 B.C.E., d. mid-330; cf. Arrian, *Anabasis* 3.22.6) was the last Achaemenid king.

Sources. The lack of sources for the last century of Achaemenid rule (Frye, p. 135) is especially severe for the life and reign of Darius III. There are no Persian royal texts or monuments, and what is known comes almost solely from Greek historians, who depicted his career mainly as a contrast to the brilliant first few years of Alexander the Great (q.v.). There are a few documents from Babylonia, including the Uruk king list; an astronomical diary that has been interpreted as giving the date of the battle of Gaugamela and of Alexander's entry into Babylon (20 October 331); and some astronomical observations collected by Abraham Sachs, in which Darius' personal name, not mentioned elsewhere, is given in two slightly different transcriptions (cf. Stolper, *CAH²*, with additional references). The main literary sources, all written centuries after Darius' reign, are the Greek accounts of Alexander's career and their derivatives: the universal history of

Diodorus Siculus (q.v.; bk. 17; 1st century B.C.E.); Arrian's *Anabasis* (2nd century C.E., drawing chiefly on two contemporary accounts) and, in Latin, Curtius Rufus (q.v.; probably 1st century C.E.; cf. Rutz), both chiefly based on a romanticized contemporary account by Cleitarchus (q.v.); Plutarch, *Alexander* and some references in the *Moralia* (based on a great variety of sources of variable value; ca. 100 C.E.); and Justin's 3rd-century epitome of Pompeius Trogus' world history (in Latin, based on Greek sources; 1st century B.C.E.). The only useful monumental source is the Alexander mosaic from Pompeii.

Darius' life. Even in antiquity Darius' origin was obscure (see especially Diodorus, 17.5.5-6; Justin, 10.3.3-6; Plutarch, *Moralia* 326F; Strabo, 15.3.24). Furthermore, his life before his accession has received no detailed treatment in modern scholarly literature. He seems to have had some connection with the royal family but probably not a close one. In the Greek tradition he was unanimously depicted as an outsider who had risen to the throne through outstanding bravery, first shown in single combat in an early expedition of Artaxerxes III Ochus (q.v.; 359-38 B.C.E.) against the Cadusii (q.v.). Justin, who gave the fullest account, reported that, although Darius had been an obscure figure (*quidam*) before, he was rewarded for his valor with the satrapy of Armenia and later became king; according to both Diodorus and Strabo, the Achaemenid dynasty had ended with his predecessor, Arses (338-36 B.C.E.). Diodorus also included the Cadusian story but in his introduction called Darius a son of "Arsanes" (i.e., Arsames, OPers. Aršāma (q.v.), the name of the grandfather of Darius I; see iii, above) and grandson of Ostanes, a son of Darius II (424-05; see iv, above). This lineage was clearly the official version, probably adopted, along with the throne name Darius (cf. Dandamaev, p. 112 n. 3), at his accession. In Babylonian documents his personal name appears as Ar-ta-šá-a-ta/u (probably OPers. *Artašiyāta, lit, "happy in Arta"). Of the Greeks only Justin, who was generally well informed about names and must be accepted as reproducing the Greek tradition, mentioned a personal name, Codomannus, which Darius bore before gaining prominence. The name of his mother (by birth or adoption) appears as Sisyngambris (Diodorus) or Sisigambis (Curtius, with numerous manuscript variants). Curtius, in a rhetorical passage (10.5.23), seems to have identified her as a cousin of Ochus, who eliminated a brother of Ostanes with all his sons on his accession. She cannot have been a full cousin, however, for Ochus would not then have spared Darius' life, let alone promoting him. Darius had a brother Oxyathres (whether a full or "official" brother is unknown), who fought loyally for him and was held in honor by Alexander after Darius' death.

At some unspecified time Darius was probably in charge of the royal "postal service," an exalted position, perhaps the same one that is ascribed to the great Parnaka in the Persepolis Fortification tablets. Plutarch (*Moralia* 326F) called him both a "courier" (using the Persian loanword *astándes*) and a slave (as in other sources); he was thus presumably the king's *bandaka* (see BANDA i) in the public service. After the succession ofArses (q.v.) he was one of the king's "friends" at court, and it may be at that time that he was promoted from his satrapy to the postal service; he may in fact already have been elevated by his old patron Ochus, perhaps about 340, when he seems to have married the royal princess Stateira, whom Curtius described as his sister or cousin; his only son by her, Ochus, was six years old when captured by Alexander late in 333. Three daughters by an earlier wife are attested, one married to a Mithridates who died fighting on the Granicus (see below), and two who as adolescents accompanied their father on the campaign that ended in the battle of Issus and were captured along with his mother, wife, and son. One unreliable source reported that he also had another son, Ariobarzanes, whom he had executed for treason.

When the general Bagōas (q.v.) murdered Arses and his sons he installed Darius as king, no doubt because (as reported in the Greek sources) his reputation for valor made him acceptable to the nobles; Darius' probable connection with the royal family and the memory of Artaxerxes Ochus' favor must also have contributed to their acceptance. Bagōas must have thought that the outsider would have to rely on him, but Darius soon eliminated him and assumed full control, at about the time that Alexander the Great succeeded in Macedonia (autumn 336). Darius may have been faced with immediate rebellions in Egypt (see Kienitz, pp. 110, 185 ff., though the chronology and interpretation are unclear) and Babylon; a native king was briefly in occupation of Memphis at about that time, and in the Uruk king list a king with a Babylonian name appears just before Darius. These rebellions cannot have been of major importance, however, as both pretenders quickly disappeared from the record, evidence that their revolts were quickly suppressed; nevertheless, they must have added to Darius' feeling of insecurity.

This insecurity, together with a deceptively easy success against an expedition sent by Philip II into Asia Minor, dissuaded him from strengthening his forces in the west, despite Alexander's preparations for resuming the invasion (cf. Dandamaev, pp. 314-19). He did not establish there a unified command comparable to that of the Rhodian Greek Mentor under Ochus. Mentor's brother Memnon was perhaps the only man who could have handled such a command, but, as a brother-in-law of Artabazus (q.v.), satrap of Phrygia, he had joined in the latter's rebellion against Ochus and long exile in Macedonia. Other commanders, mainly eminent Persians and some even members of the royal family, were unacceptable to a king of doubtful legitimacy who feared their power. Thus, when Alexander invaded Asia Minor early in 334, he was met at the river Granicus by only a small force, divided among several commanders with different strategic ideas. A strike at Alexander himself failed, and after his victory the whole of Asia Minor lay open before him, with the exception of one or two fortified and garrisoned cities, which he at firat bypassed, then conquered.

It was only after receiving Memnon's wife and children as hostages that Darius named him "commander of the seashore and the fleet" (the position once held by Cyrus the Younger; see CYRUS vi). Even then, some troops were actually recalled from the coast, for Darius had decided to meet the invader in person, in a land battle. Memnon was given a free hand only at sea, but Alexander had dismissed his own fleet through fear of Greek disloyalty. Memnon launched a successful counteroffensive, intending to recapture the main island bases and then to carry the war to Greece, where Agis III of Sparta was eager to lead an alliance to overthrow Macedonian domination. But Memnon died, and his successors were less capable. By the time they met Agis off the Greek coast, Darius had been defeated at Issus (in late 333). Agis was given some funds and, after collecting mercenaries, launched his war in Greece, but by then he could receive no further support. Early in 330 he was defeated and killed. Darius himself died soon afterward.

During 334-33 Darius collected an army with unprecedented speed, and by October 333 he was crossing the Taurus mountains; through a failure in Alexander's intelligence, he was able to appear at his rear. But he lacked experience of major command and, persuaded by his advisers that victory was certain, he faced Alexander on the small coastal plain of Issus, where his superior cavalry could not be deployed to envelop the enemy's left. Parmenio, the most experienced Macedonian commander, held it back while Alexander routed the king. For the Persians the battle was a disaster. Darius himself escaped before it was over, and Greek historians were quick to charge him with cowardice—though bravery was his best-attested quality. It is more probable that he had kept his head and had understood that the only chance of saving the kingdom lay in saving himself; had he died, there would have been no plausible successor who could have commanded allegiance and led resistance to the invasion.

His family had fallen into Alexander's hands, however. There is no reason to disbelieve the stories of his anxiety over their treatment and his surprise at Alexander's magnanimity. Nonetheless, that they were hostages dissuaded Darius from attempting a counterattack. While Persia's allies confidently waited for him to do so (the city of Tyre holding out for nearly a year against all Alexander's siegecraft), the king began negotiations for a settlement. The details cannot be recovered, for the documents quoted in Greek sources are as usual fictitious, but it is clear that he faced decisions inconceivable to his predecessors. The minimum terms that offered hope of acceptance were cession of large territories and recognition of Alexander as an equal. In addition, Darius offered a large ransom for his family and a marriage alliance to seal the bargain. It is said that Parmenio advised Alexander to accept, but, quite apart from Alexander's heroic ambition, he could not easily do so. Once peace had been made and the hostages released, he would have to return home, leaving garrisons to guard a long frontier; Darius would then be free to attack at a time of his own choosing. Alexander therefore decided instead to seize his chance of inflicting further humiliation. He rejected all terms and demanded that Darius pay homage to him as his superior. Darius thus had no choice but to fight on.

He had few Greek mercenaries left to form a usable infantry force, but he decided to improve the equipment of his native forces after the Greek model; his cavalry was vastly superior, and he had both elephants (which the enemy had never seen) and the fearsome scythe chariots used by Cyrus the Younger at Cunaxa (q.v.). Furthermore, this time he would be fighting on his own ground. He seems to have awaited Alexander in Mesopotamia and to have offered no opposition when the Greek forces crossed the desert and the Euphrates. But Alexander, probably by chance, traveled farther north to avoid the extreme heat, crossing both the Euphrates and the Tigris. Darius thus had to find suitable ground east of the Tigris; he took a position near the village of Gaugamela north of Arbela (q.v.), with the Maqlūb ridge covering his flank. The plain was large enough for his cavalry, and he had it leveled in order to allow full use of the chariots. But with the decision to await the enemy's attack he had lost the initiative. Alexander moved up slowly, allowing his men to rest while keeping Darius on the alert. He halted overlooking the edge of the plain; the moon was in its last quarter, and in a night attack the disciplined Macedonians would have overwhelmed the motley Iranian forces. Darius thus kept his men under arms all night, while Alexander allowed his troops to rest, then attacked at sunrise, on 1 October 331. As at Cunaxa, the chariots proved useless against disciplined forces, and, despite his improved equipment, Darius had nothing to set against the Greek phalanx. The cavalry, as planned, fought successfully against Alexander's left, commanded by Parmenio, but Alexander, who was on the right, ignored the threat of encirclement, let the Persians pour through a gap in his center, then charged straight at the weary troops in Darius' center, where the king himself commanded. The line was broken, and Darius again had to flee. His army disintegrated, and Alexander never again had to face the grand Persian army in full-scale battle.

Darius fled to Ecbatana (q.v.), hoping either to draw Alexander after him or to gain time while Alexander occupied the other royal capitals. Alexander took the latter course, occupying Babylon (where his army rested for a month) and Susa without opposition and continuing on to Persepolis. En route, at the so-called "Persian Gate," Ariobarzanes (q.v.), commander of Persis, caught Alexander in a trap and inflicted on him the only defeat he is attested to have suffered at Persian hands. Neverthless, Alexander found a way of going around the narrow pass to Ariobarzanes' rear and avenged his defeat; in mid-January 330 he reached

Persepolis and destroyed the lower city. He remained there four months, except for a limited campaign to occupy the rest of Persis, including Pasargadae, while he waited for news of Agis' war in Greece. Having heard nothing by May, he destroyed the terrace and royal buildings at Persepolis, in a symbolic gesture of revenge for Xerxes' destruction in Greece, and set out on the mountain road to Ecbatana. The Greek sources do not provide information on how Darius used the time he had gained at such cost. There is no sign that he assembled another army, either at Ecbatana or farther east, and such a task was probably impossible in winter. When Alexander approached he left him to occupy the city and, with a few remaining nobles and a small force, retreated eastward. Alexander organized Media and slowly followed him, until he heard that Darius had been taken prisoner by his own companions.

The surviving account of Darius' last days is ultimately based on unreliable sources: Darius' Greek mercenaries, who were loyal to the end but had little idea of what was going on, and Persian nobles who later joined Alexander and were unlikely to tell the whole truth. The lead in the plot against Darius was said to have been taken by Bessos (q.v.), satrap of Bactria, who was related to the royal family and may have had as valid a claim to the Persian throne as the king himself. Bessos is contradictorily reported to have been ambitious for the royal dignity and to have hoped to buy his own safety by surrendering Darius. He and several others, including the *hazārapati-* (chiliarch, q.v.) Nabarzanes, bound the king in golden fetters. When Alexander heard of this development from Persian deserters, he hastened to take the king alive, but by the time he arrived, somewhere near Hecatompylus, it was too late. The conspirators, fearing capture, had stabbed Darius and left him to die while they escaped to the east. Bessos then assumed the royal tiara and the throne name Artaxerxes. In later fiction the two rulers met, and Darius uttered a great speech of proud resignation before dying.

It is possible only to guess the realities that lay behind these events, but Alexander's eagerness to reach Darius while he was alive and the conspirators' determination to prevent this meeting and to carry on the war in the east suggest that Darius was ready to do what Alexander had demanded two years earlier: to pay homage to him as a superior and thus to confer some legitimacy on his attempt to assume the Achaemenid succession. Some eminent nobles had joined Alexander after the battle at Gaugamela and had been rewarded with satrapies and honors, but the destruction of Persepolis had largely undone the effect of Alexander's striving for legitimacy. Only recognition by Darius might yet have spared him years of war in the east, which did in fact ensue. Darius' motives are less clear. Several instances in which he put personal honor below his country's interests have been mentioned. Despair for the present and desire to spare Persia further suffering may have been mingled with hope for future recovery. The young "barbarian" might not have been able to hold what he had won, and another chance might have come for Darius. His death was a misfortune for both sides but a disaster for Iran.

Alexander sent Darius' body to be buried "among the royal tombs"; it is not clear where they were, but he cannot have been placed in the unfinished tomb at Persepolis. His monument, if he had one, does not survive, any more than does that of Alexander.

Bibliography: E. Badian, "Alexander in Iran," in *Camb. Hist. Iran* II, 1985, pp. 420-502. A. B. Bosworth, *Conquest and Empire*, Cambridge, 1988. M. A. Dandamaev, *A Political History of the Achamaenid Empire*, tr. W. J. Vogelsang, Leiden, 1989. R. N. Frye, *The History of Ancient Iran*, Munich, 1984. F. K. Kienitz, *Die politische Geschichte Ägyptens vom 7. bis zum 4. Jhdt. vor der Zeitwende*, Berlin, 1953. C. Nylander, "The Standard of the Great King," *Opuscula Romana* 14, 1983, pp. 19-37 (the most important recent work on the Alexander mosaic). W. Rutz, "Das Bild des Dareios bei Curtius Rufus," *Würzburger Jahrbücher für die Altertumswissenschaft* N.F. 10, 1984, pp. 147-59. A. Sachs, "Achaemenid Royal Names in Babylonian Astronomical Texts," *American Journal of Ancient History* 2, 1977, pp. 129-47. J. Seibert, *Alexander der Grosse*, Darmstadt, 1972. M. W. Stolper, "Mesopotamia," in *CAH*[2] VI. H. Swoboda, "Dareios 3," in Pauly-Wissowa, IV/2, cols. 2205-11 (uncritical in treatment but useful in giving all the Greek and Latin references).

(Ernst Badian)

vi. Achaemenid Princes

Darius was the name of two Achaemenid princes in addition to the emperors who bore it.

Eldest son of Xerxes I (486-65 B.C.E.). This Darius was born of Amestris (q.v.) and was thus the brother of Hystaspes, Artaxerxes I (q.v.), Amytis (q.v.), and Rhodogune (Ctesias, in Jacoby, *Fragmente* III.C, p. 462 frag. 13 par. 24; Diodorus, 11.69.2). After the battle of Mycale in 479 B.C.E. Xerxes married Darius to Artaynte, daughter of his brother Masistes and his wife, whom he loved himself (Herodotus 9.108.1-2). In 465-64 Darius was linked to the assassination of Xerxes and also himself fell a victim in the ensuing events, though details of this court revolution are not entirely clear from the sources. According to contemporary opinion, as represented by Ctesias (q.v.; in Jacoby, *Fragmente* III.C, p. 464 frags. 13-14 pars. 33-34), Diodorus Siculus (q.v.; 11.69.1-5), and Justin (3.1.1-5), who differed only slightly in their accounts, Xerxes was murdered by Artabanus (q.v. 2; Ctesias: Artapanus, probably the correct form), the chief of his bodyguards, and some other confidants, whose identities vary in the sources. Artapanus then went to the king's younger son Artaxerxes and accused Darius of the murder; Artaxerxes decided to kill Darius before he could seize the throne. Artapanus' plan to take power for himself failed, however, as the truth came to light at last. A totally different version of these events was given by Aristotle (*Politica* 1311b.36 ff.), who reported that Artapanes (sic) first killed Darius without royal orders, then murdered Xerxes for fear of the king's vengeance.

Bibliography: T. Nöldeke, *Aufsätze zur persischen Geschichte*, Leipzig, 1887, p. 49. [H.] Swoboda, "Dareios 4," in Pauly-Wissowa IV/2, col. 2211.

Son of Artaxerxes II (405-359 B.C.E.). Artaxerxes II (q.v.) designated Darius, his son by Stateira (Plutarch, *Artoxerxes* 26.1) and already fifty years old, as coruler and successor, in order to avoid riot and war between his legitimate sons, comparable to the quarrels at his own accession. Artaxerxes' second wife, Atossa, however, favored Darius' younger brother Ochus, who was of a brutal and impetuous character (Plutarch, *Artoxerxes* 26.2-4; cf. Justin 10.1.2-3). On the occasion of his appointment Darius asked his father for the gift of Aspasia, a beautiful woman of Phocean birth, who had come into the harem of Cyrus the Younger (q.v.) and then of Artaxerxes, who esteemed and loved her greatly (Plutarch, *Artoxerxes* 26.5-27.3; Justin, 10.2.1-6). According to an ancient custom, the king was required to give her to his son, but not much later he appointed her priestess of Anaitis (see ANĀHĪD ii) in Ecbatana, thus effectively taking her away from him (Plutarch, *Artoxerxes* 27.4). In his irritation and fear of a change in the succession and incited by a certain Tiribazus (perhaps the famous satrap of Armenia and then of Lydia), Darius plotted against his father (Plutarch, *Artoxerxes* 27.5-28.5; cf. Justin 10.2.5). The conspiracy was exposed by a eunuch, and Darius was unanimously sentenced to death by the royal judges and executed (Plutarch, *Artoxerxes* 29.1, 29.8-10). The chronology of these events cannot be ascertained precisely; they are commonly dated to 362 or 361 B.C.E. (on the basis of which Darius' birth date is given as ca. 412 B.C.E.), but this date is far from convincing. It is not even certain that the events unfolded in immediate succession. Darius' son Arbupales was one of the Persian leaders killed at the battle of Granicus in 334 B.C.E.

Bibliography: A. T. Olmstead, *History of the Persian Empire*, Chicago, 1948, p. 424. [H.] Swoboda, "Darius 5," in Pauly-Wissowa IV/2, col. 2211.

(RÜDIGER SCHMITT)

vii. PARTHIAN PRINCES

Darius was the name of several petty princes in the Parthian period.

In 64 B.C.E. while his father, Mithridates VI Eupator, king of Pontus (ca. 121/20-63 B.C.E.), was fighting his last, losing campaign against the troops of the Roman general Pompey (106-48 B.C.E.), the child Darius was taken prisoner, along with several brothers and his sister Eupatra, in Phanagoria (Appian, *Mithridatica* 108). He was carried in procession among the defeated kings, princes, and other royal figures at Pompey's triumphal reentry into Rome (Appian, *Mithridatica* 117).

His nephew, son of Pharnaces II (63-47 B.C.E.), was Darius, king of Pontus, appointed by Mark Antony in 39 B.C.E. (Appian, *Bellum Civile* 5.319). He ruled for only about two years before being dethroned by Polemon, son of the rhetor Zeno of Laodicia.

A third Darius, son of Mithridates, was king of Media Atropatene, though almost nothing is known about him. In order to rid himself of his Armenian overlords, he submitted to Pompey in about 65 B.C.E., during the conflict between the Romans and the Armenian king Tigranes. He is said to have ruled later over part of Armenia, under the suzerainty of the Parthians (Appian, *Mithridatica* 106; cf. 117).

(RÜDIGER SCHMITT)

viii. DARIUS SON OF ARTABANUS

A son of the Parthian king Artabanus II (q.v.; r. ca. 10-38 C.E.) named Darius was sent as a hostage to Rome (Josephus, *Antiquitates* 18.4.5) shortly after an interview between Artabanus and the Roman legate for Syria, Vitellius, in 37 C.E. (Suetonius, *Caligula* 14.3; idem, *Vitellius* 2.4; Dion Cassius, 59.27.3).

Darius seems to have led an obscure life in the Roman empire. He is mentioned only once as having ridden before Gaius [Caligula] during one of his repeated crossings of the bridge between Baiae and the bay of Puteoli (Pozzuoli; Suetonius, *Caligula* 19.2). Five fragments of water conduits found at Nemi (ca. 40 km from Rome) bear the inscription "Darii Regis" (Morpurgo, p. 280 no. 109). It has been suggested that the inscription could refer to the hostage Darius (Stein, p. 2), but the could hardly have used the title "king." Alfred von Gutschmid (p. 49 and n. 19) has identified Darius with Vologases I, mentioned as a son of Artabanus II by Josephus (*Antiquitates* 20.3.4), but this identification is untenable (cf. Kahrstedt, p. 18 and n. 9), as it would mean that Darius had been sent back to Artabanus.

Bibliography: A. von Gutschmid, *Kleine Schriften* III, Leipzig, 1893. U. Kahrstedt, *Artabanos III und seine Erben*, Bern, 1950. L. Morpurgo, "Nemi," in *Notizie degli scavi*, Rome, 1931. A. Stein, *in Prosopographia Imperii Romani* III, 2nd ed., Berlin and Leipzig, 1943.

(MARIE LOUISE CHAUMONT)

DARJAZĪN (or Dargazīn), name of two rural subdistricts (*dehestāns*) and a village in the Razan district (*bak̲š*) of Hamadān province. The administrative center for the subdistrict of Upper Darjazīn (Darjazīn-e ʿolyā) is Razan, for Lower Darjazīn (Darjazīn-e soflā) Fāmenīn. The average altitude of the Razan plain is 1,830 m above sea level, and winters are cold. The chief products of the region are grains, fruits (especially grapes), and dairy products. The village of Darjazīn (35° 21′ N, 49° 04′ E) is situated 83 km northeast of Hamadān in Upper Darjazīn subdistrict. The population was 2,825 in 1365 Š./1986 (Meʿmārīān, p. 89).

In the 11th century the Darjazīn area was populated by Mazdakites and the related Ḵorramīs (Anūšervān b. Ḵāled, q.v., apud ʿEmād Kāteb, p. 114 and Yāqūt, *Boldān* II, p. 569); it was also the native city of an important family of viziers (see Dargazīnī). In 1032/1622 Shah ʿAbbās I (996-1038/1588-1629) resettled some of the Sunni population of the Baghdad area around Hamadān (Dehgān, pp. 171-72; Krusinski, p. 70). The Ottoman writer Awlīāʾ Čelebī (IV, pp. 355-57), who passed through the area in 1065/1654, described the layout of the town and the Moḥarram mourning ceremonies of the Shiʿites there and also referred to the garrison and the fort. No trace remains of this fort, which Čelebī associated with the Sasanian king Yazdegerd, possibly referring to Yazdegerd I (399-420). After the Afghan invasion in 1135/1722 Darjazīn became the scene of conflict between Persia and the Ottoman empire, changing hands several times (Ḥazīn, pp. 91-93; Marvī, I, pp. 218, 221, 223). In the mid-19th century Zayn-al-ʿĀbedīn Šīrvānī (p. 311) reported that the population spoke Turkish and belonged to the Shiʿite Qaragozlū clan.

Two noteworthy shrines survive at Darjazīn. The Emāmzāda Aẓhar includes a circular tower with a conical dome 12 m high. A wooden chest in the shrine, part of which has been stolen, bears the date 1056/1646, but the building itself has been dated to the Mongol period. It may be the tomb of Shaikh Salmān ʿĀref Dargazīnī (13th century) or Shaikh Šaraf-al-Dīn Dargazīnī (14th century). The Emāmzāda Hūd, situated 3 km west of the Emāmzāda Aẓhar near the village of Yengī Qalʿa, is probably the *ḵānaqāh* (Sufi monastery) of Shaikh Šayʾ-Allāh Dargazīnī (late 14th century). It is a twelve-sided tower 11 m high (Wilber, p. 189, pls. 213-14; cf. Moṣṭafawī, pp. 204-10; Ḥāfeẓ Ḥosayn, I, pp. 129, 399, 578-79; *Nozhat al-qolūb*, ed. Le Strange, p. 73; cf. Sāzmān, pp. 228, 301; *Dāyerat al-maʿāref*, pp. 415, 481-82).

Bibliography: P. Aḏkāʾī, *Dargazīn tā Kāšān*, Tehran, 1372 Š./1993. Awlīāʾ Čelebī, *Sīāḥat-nāmasī*, ed. A. Jawdat and N. ʿĀṣem, 6 vols., Istanbul, 1314-18/1896-1900. *Dāyerat al-maʿāref-e tašayyoʿ* II, Tehran, 1368 Š./1989. E. Dehgān, "Aqallīyathā-ye Erāq yā Sonnīhā-ye Dargazīn," *Yaḡmā* 7/4, 1333 Š./1954, pp. 171-73. ʿEmād Kāteb Eṣfahānī, *Tārīḵ dawlat Āl Saljūq*, Cairo, 1318/1900. Ḥāfeẓ Ḥosayn b. Karbalāʾī, *Rawżāt al-jenān wa jannāt al-jenān*, ed. J. Solṭan-al-Qorrāʾī, 2 vols, Tehran, 1344-49 Š./1965-70. Ḥazīn Lāhījī, *Tārīḵ-e Ḥazīn*, Isfahan, 1332 Š./1953. J. Krusinski, *Histoire des révolutions de Perse depuis le commencement de ce siècle*, Paris, 1742. Moḥammad-Kāẓem Marvī, *ʿĀlamārā-ye nāderī*, ed. M.-A. Rīāḥī, 3 vols., Tehran, 1364 Š./1985. A. Meʿmārīān, *Farhang-e dehhā-ye Īrān. Ostān-e Hamadān*, Tehran, 1369 Š./1990. M.-T. Moṣṭafawī, *Hegmatāna*, Tehran, 1332 Š./1953. Razmārā, *Farhang* V, p. 174. Sāzmān-e mellī-e ḥefāẓat-e āṯār-e bāstānī-e Īrān, *Fehrest-e banāhā-ye tārīḵī o amāken-e bāstānī-e Īrān*, Tehran, 1345 Š./1966. D. Wilber, *Architecture of Islamic Iran. The Il Khānid Period*, Princeton, N.J., 1955. Ḥājj Zayn-al-ʿĀbedīn Šīrvānī, *Bostān al-sīāḥa*, Tehran, n.d.

(Parviz Aḏkāʾī)

DARMESTETER, JAMES (b. Château-Salins, Alsace, 12 March 1849, d. Paris, 19 October 1894), the great Iranist, was the son of a Jewish bookbinder, who in 1852 moved to Paris to improve his children's educational opportunities. Through the prompting of his elder brother Arsène, himself a distinguished philologist specializing in medieval French, James (who was endowed with a superb intellect in a frail body), after a brilliant school career, enrolled at the École des Hautes Études, where he studied comparative grammar with Michel Bréal and Sanskrit with Abel Bergaigne and made his first contribution to Iranian studies in 1874 with "Notes de philologie iranienne" (*MSL* 4, pp. 300-17). A year later he submitted his prize-winning thesis, *Haurvatāt et Amərətāt. Essai sur la mythologie de l'Avesta*. With these two works he entered on what were to be his lifelong fields of study, Iranian philology and the Zoroastrian religion. Both he approached from a historical point of view, bringing his increasing erudition to bear on tracing connections and developments through attested usages. He read swiftly, mastering languages with ease, and his retentive memory and alert intelligence enabled him to store and use creatively a great mass of knowledge.

In 1877 he received the degree of *docteur ès lettres* for his *Ormazd et Ahriman, leurs origines et leur histoire* (Paris, 1877; repr. Paris, 1971), a study of Iranian dualism. His conclusion, that dualism was the logical development of beliefs evolved in India, was bold and controversial but argued with characteristic lucidity and force. In the same year he was appointed to teach Avestan at the École des Hautes Études and, encouraged by Bréal, set himself the formidable task of making a new translation of the entire Avesta. His publications, which by then included a number of other articles on Iranian subjects, had already earned him an international reputation, and Max Müller invited him to contribute an English translation of Avestan texts to the series Sacred Books of the East. His *The Zend Avesta* Part I. *The Vendīdād* appeared in 1880 as the fourth volume in the series, followed in 1883 by Part II. *The Sīrōzahs, Yasts, and Nyāyis*, the twenty-third volume. In 1883 he also published the two volumes of his *Études iraniennes*, characterized by Karl Geldner as epoch-making. In the first volume, entitled *Grammaire historique du persan*, he established that Old Persian and Avestan were distinct languages, showed that the cradle of modern Persian was Fārs, isolated the Semitic element in Pahlavi, and established that Pārsīk (now more usually termed Pāzand) was only Pahlavi transcribed in Avestan characters.

The second volume, called *Mélanges d'histoire et de littérature iranienne*, is a miscellany of brilliant short studies, for example, his masterly treatment (pp. 301-03) of Hadiš, Iranian divinity of the homestead, until then unrecognized by Western scholars. In the same year Darmesteter published a more general collection of articles, *Essais orientaux*, which included his "La légende d'Alexandre," articles on aspects of Judaism and Buddhism, a comparative study of elements in the *Māhābharata* and the *Šāh-nāma* (which he read extensively, both for its own sake and in connection with the Avestan *Yašt*s), and several articles relating to Afghanistan, the language and history of which greatly interested him.

He had been appointed joint director of the École des Hautes Études in 1880, and in 1882 he became honorary secretary of the Société Asiatique, a post that he held until his death. One of his most arduous duties as honorary secretary was the presentation of detailed annual reports on progress in Oriental studies in France, and his were masterpieces of comprehensiveness and lucidity, in which, it was said (Barbier de Meynard, p. 527), he sometimes surprised authors by bringing out points in their writings the implications of which they themselves had not fully appreciated. Although his own standards of scholarship were rigorous, he was generous in his judgment of others' work.

In 1885 Darmesteter was nominated for the chair of Persian language and literature at the Collège de France. A year earlier Müller had pressed him to complete his contributions to Sacred Books of the East by translating the *Yasna* and *Visperad*, but he had declined on the grounds that it was impossible to render these liturgical works adequately without knowledge of the rituals that they accompanied. In 1886-87 he therefore set out on an eleven-month "philological mission" to India, supported by the French Ministry of education. He spent the first and longest part of this period in the northwest frontier area of the Punjab, April in Peshawar and May to September in Abbottabad. His purpose was to go beyond his few predecessors in the study of Pashto, who had relied mainly on literary texts, and to "provide the philologist and the historian with authentic and immediate specimens of the language and thought of the Afghan people." To this end he engaged two amanuenses, Pīr Moḥammad-ʿAlī at Peshawar and Mawlawī Moḥammad-Esmāʿīl Khan at Abbottabad, to write down the texts of popular songs as dictated by professional singers and to help him with their interpretation. A few other texts of this sort he acquired from collections made by British amateurs of the subject. In a remarkably short time after his return from India he published a representative collection of more than a hundred of these songs in Pashto script, with annotated French translations, under the title *Chants populaires des Afghans* (Paris, 1888). The book contains more than its title suggests, for in the preface he included a thorough analysis of Pashto phonology and morphology, confirming that the language belongs to the Iranian family, as well as a sketch of Afghan literature and history. Almost simultaneously his lively *Lettres sur l'Inde. À la frontière afghane*, appeared; in its historical passages he used the texts of several ballads as illustrations.

Darmesteter also reaped a rich harvest in the still briefer time, a bare three months, that he spent among the Parsis, mostly in Bombay, with short visits to Navsari and other old Parsi centers in Gujarat. His fame as a foreign *dastūr* (q.v.) of their faith had preceded him, and the warmth of his reception contrasted strongly with the sustained hostility that had formerly greeted A. H. Anquetil-Duperron (q.v.). In his work he benefited most from two friendships that he formed, one with the learned Tahmuras Dinshaw Anklesaria (q.v.), the other with E. W. West, the scholarly English engineer who, initially inspired by Martin Haug, had by then spent some twenty years studying Pahlavi texts. Leading Parsi priests, notably Jivanji Jamshedji Modi, and the *dastūr*s of Bombay and Puna—Peshotanji Behramji Sanjana, Jamaspji Minochehr Jamasp-Āsana, and Hoshangji Jamasp-Asana—readily showed him their manuscripts and gave him whatever information he sought; and he was formally welcomed at Navsari by a full assembly of the Bhagaria priests (Darmesteter, I, p. lviii). Accordingly he returned to Paris, in February 1887, with a mass of new information concerning the Avesta itself, the solemnization of Zoroastrian rituals, and the nature of living Zoroastrian beliefs and practices. Side by side with the publication of his Afghan materials he settled to completing his magnum opus, a French translation, richly furnished with notes and commentaries, of the entire Avesta, including thitherto unpublished fragments that he had come to know in Bombay. This masterpiece of learning, the synthesis of some twenty years' labor, was published as *Le Zend-Avesta* in three massive tomes in the Annales du Musée Guimet (1892-93) and received instant acclaim. It did not become generally accessible, however, until 1960, when it was reprinted in three small volumes that could be on every scholar's shelves. The rich store of facts and penetrating and rational observations contained within it did not therefore benefit Zoroastrian studies, lending ballast and sobriety, as fully and speedily as they might have done. Knowledge of the Avestan language has now advanced so greatly that Darmesteter's translations themselves are outdated in many respects, but the notes and commentaries remain invaluable, as do the long introductions to the respective volumes.

The first of these introductions begins with a succinct survey of the knowledge of Zoroaster and his teachings in classical and medieval times, followed by an outline of academic studies of the Avesta down to his own day. Darmesteter then went on to describe the various aids available for an understanding of the sacred texts. He gave due recognition to the usefulness of Vedic but stressed the dangers of relying too much on similarities with Vedic words and on speculative etymologies, rather than on studying the actual usage of Avestan words in context. As an aid to this study he found great value in the Pahlavi *Zand* and in Pahlavi literature generally, looking to Iranian tradition to help illuminate these ancient Iranian texts. Concerning the content of the Avesta, Darmesteter stressed, here and in the introduction to Volume III, the great importance of the *Gatha*s, which, he showed, were cited, imitated, and invoked in every other part of the Avesta (see his detailed references, I, p. xcviii n. 3). He further maintained (I, p. cv) that, once the myths and legends are taken away, "Parsism" (by which he meant the religion of the Pahlavi books and later times) faithfully reproduces the theology and ethics of the *Gatha*s. The difficulties of these most sacred of texts he held to be in their form (I, p. cvii), rather than in their content, to which, he maintained, tradition furnishes a guide. Approaching the texts in this way, he encountered none of the artificial problems created by other Western scholars. That is, he saw the religion as a radical dualism, with Ahura Mazdā (q.v.) directly opposed to Angra Mainyu (see AHRIMAN) and, as creator of good, himself called Spənta Mainyu (III, pp. lxiv, lxvi). Darmesteter was the first to explain the number of the seven great Aməša Spəntas (q.v.) as corresponding to Ahura Mazdā's seven creative acts (III, p. lvi), and he considered the doctrine of the resurrection of the dead as an essential component of the primitive faith, linked with those of an end of time and of rewards and punishments hereafter (III, pp. lxiv, lxvii).

The next section of the introduction to Volume I Darmesteter devoted to the Zoroastrian cult. He gave accounts of the Parsi priests and fire temples and of the ritual offerings and main ceremonies, supplying, as Anquetil had done before him, clear plans and drawings and good photographs. The accounts themselves furnish an admirably clear guide to the various main ceremonies. This first introduction concludes with an analysis of the texts and rituals of the *Yasna*. With the help of Anklesaria, Darmesteter established the existence of two distinct ritual traditions, Irani and Parsi, which vary in a number of mostly small details, whereas, as he pointed out (I, p. cx), there was only one version of the text, with all manuscripts going back to a single original. There follow, in the first volume, the texts of the *Yasna* and *Visperad*, accompanied throughout by ritual instructions. For these Darmesteter relied on two works (I, p. cxi), one (in Gujarati) for the Parsi, the other (in Pahlavi) for the old Irani rites, which he systematically distinguished. On obscure points he also consulted Anklesaria by letter. This was a work of immense and discerning labor and is one of the aspects of his masterpiece that is unlikely to be superseded.

The second, larger volume contains the *Vidēvdād*, *Sīrōza*s, *Yašt*s, and a selection of texts from the *Ḵorda Avesta*. It includes, that is, all the texts that Darmesteter had translated for Sacred Books of the East, but with renderings improved by intervening years of study and notes enriched by an abundance of new materials, especially for the *Vidēvdād*. His introduction to this much-discussed text is judicious and learned, and there are valuable appendices to particular sections, notably one dealing at length with the Zoroastrian funerary customs (derived largely from the work on this subject by J. J. Modi). The *Sīrōza*s and *Yašt*s are also richly annotated, with a wealth of background knowledge.

The third volume is devoted to the Avestan fragments, patiently collected and interpreted largely in the light of the Pahlavi texts in which most are embedded. At the end of them is set the Avestan *Nīrangestān*. The introduction includes one chapter devoted largely to the *Letter of Tansar*, the importance of which Darmesteter was the first to perceive; he subsequently published an edition, with translation and notes (*JA*, 1894). There is other matter in this introduction, however, that some scholars rejected instantly as unsound and that progress in knowledge has shown to be indeed unacceptable. Darmesteter was one of the distinguished Iranists who gave credence to the spurious date for Zoroaster, "258 years before Alexander"; and he was perhaps the only one to make a serious attempt to understand the evolution of the *Avesta* in the light of this false chronology. The task was impossible, and grappling with it led him for once to wholly invalid conclusions. At that time the academic study of oral literature had not begun, and like everyone else Darmesteter thought that he was dealing with a written scripture. From the contents of the *Yašt*s and *Vidēvdād* he reasonably supposed that they were older than the *Gatha*s, and he thus deduced that the latter could not have been the work of Zoroaster himself but must have been composed later to enshrine the teachings of the faith. He held that the unknown author had used a deliberately elevated, archaizing language, knowledge of which he must have obtained from a lost Old Avestan written literature. Furthermore, the parallels that exist between Neoplatonism and Judaism on one hand and Zoroastrianism on the other are striking, and in the 19th century it was natural to suppose that influence had gone from west to east, rather than the other way about. Darmesteter accordingly thought that these similar elements were alien to primitive Zoroastrianism and had been absorbed by the Iranian religion after the time of its prophet. They then came to be interwoven by the putative author of the *Gatha*s with original doctrines. Darmesteter suggested that his date was probably in the 1st century C.E., at the time of the religious revival under "Valakš the Arsacid." The basis of original doctrine was nevertheless suffiiciently strong, he maintained, for the religion to be able to absorb these alien elements without losing its own essential character; and he argued convincingly for its continuity as a living faith through Achaemenid, Seleucid, Parthian, Sasanian, and later times (III, pp. v, xxiii-xxvii, xcvii). This is only one of the points in this introduction where Darmesteter's sound evaluation of historical evidence led him to just conclusions, which, had they gained a hearing at the time, would have saved Zoroastrian studies from much confusion and time-wasting debate. Unfortunately the third introduction has been generally neglected because of the assumption that it represented nothing but a major error, best forgotten, on the part of a great scholar, and so some of his most valuable observations went unregarded.

In 1892, the year in which he published the first two volumes of *Le Zend-Avesta*, Darmesteter became sole director of the École des Hautes Études, with added administrative burdens. He continued to write brilliantly on a whole diversity of subjects, literary and political, contributing to the *Revue critique*, the *Journal des débats*, and the newly launched *Revue de Paris*, the first and last of which he also helped to edit. The range of his interests was remarkable; he was steeped among other things in English literature, on which he wrote perceptively. This interest led to his friendship and then happy marriage with the English poet Mary Robinson, to whom he dedicated *Le Zend-Avesta*.

The accumulation of scholarly, literary, teaching, and administrative activities demanded, however, too much "not of his vast intelligence but of his physical powers" (Barbier de Meynard, p. 532). In July 1894, anxious that the Société Asiatique, which he had served so well, should not think him in any way neglectful because of other calls on his time, he attended the annual general meeting and read a paper on what was to be his last piece of Iranian research, "Les Parthes à Jérusalem" (*JA*, 1894, pp. 43-54). Soon afterward he fell ill and died in October at the age of forty-five years. West, never given to overstatement, wrote of him: "It would be difficult to find a sounder scholar, a more brilliant writer, and a more estimable man, all united in the same individual" (cited by Benveniste), while in another obituary it was said: "In him was realized the perfect ideal of scholarship," a "happy blending of profound learning, daring originality and transparent clearness of expression" (cited by Cordier, p. 221).

Darmesteter's widow eventually married the director of the Pasteur Institute in Paris. When they both died, the Institute inherited Darmesteter's books, which gathered dust there for half a century until, through the efforts of Gilbert Lazard, they were transferred to the library of the Institut d'Études Iraniennes, renamed Bibliothèque James Darmesteter in tribute to him.

Bibliography: R. d'Amat, in *Dictionnaire de Biographie Française*, Paris, 1933, p. 199. C. A. C. Barbier de Meynard, in *JA*, 1884, pp. 519-34. E. Benveniste, "Avant-Propos," in J. Darmesteter, *Le Zend-Avesta* I, repr. ed., Paris, 1960, n.p. H. Cordier, in *JRAS*, 1895, pp. 216-22.

(MARY BOYCE AND D. N. MACKENZIE)

DARRA-YE BARRA (Valley of the lamb), a locality in Fārs province, 2.5 km east-northeast of the Achaemenid royal tombs at Naqš-e Rostam. Several rock-cut monuments are scattered on steep scree and in the cliff on the north side of the valley. They include chambers either hollowed out of the cliff or cut in freestanding blocks; basins and troughs, often called "fire bowls" by archeologists; and platforms of stones and earth. The most outstanding feature, however, is the tallest fire altar so far found in Fārs. It is cut from the living rock in the shape of a cube (4.90 x 2.10 x 3.30 m) without a step (Plate II). A vertical semicircular slab of rock projects above the flat upper surface; on the curved upper surface of this disk and on the top surface of the altar basins have been hollowed out. This monument, which was discovered by ʿAlī Sāmī in the 1950s, has been considered by David Stronach (p. 224, pls. XXI-XXII) among the numerous surviving rock-cut fire altars, though it is very different from the well-known twin altars at Naqš-e Rostam and other monumental examples located in the same region (e.g., at Bāḡ-e Bodra and Kūh-e Šahrak), all of which are provided with steps. As is usual in this part of Fārs, the altar at Darra-ye Barra has been placed in relation to the other monuments (Vanden Berghe, pp. 3-6; Huff), which probably all had funerary functions. Like most of the rock-cut monuments in this area, the altar has been tentatively dated to the Sasanian period.

PLATE II

The fire altar at Darra-ye Barra.

See also ASTŌDĀN; CORPSE.

Bibliography: R. Boucharlat, "Pratiques funéraires à l'époque sassanide dans le sud de l'Iran," in P. Bernard and F. Grenet, eds., *Histoire et cultes de l'Asie centrale préislamique*, Paris, 1991, pp. 71-78. D. Huff, "Zum Problem zoroastrischer Grabanlagen in Fars. I. Gräber," *AMI* 21, 1988, pp. 145-76. ʿA. Sāmī, "Kašf-e čand katība-ye pahlavī. Tang-e bolāḡī,

Tang-e čak čak wa ḡayroh," *Gozārešhā-ye bāstānšenāsī* 4, 1959, pp. 1-172. D. Stronach, "The Kuh-i Shahrak Fire Altar," *JNES* 25/4, 1966, pp. 217-27. L. Vanden Berghe, "Monuments récemment découverts en Iran méridional," *Bibliotheca Orientalis* 10/1-2, 1953, pp. 5-8.

(RÉMY BOUCHARLAT)

DARRAGAZ, DARGAZ (Valley of the tamarisks), a fertile valley about 50-55 km east-west and 30-35 km north-south in the Kopet Dagh range in northern Khorasan, at about 450 m above sea level, in which are located a *šahrestān* (subprovince) and a town of the same name.

i. *Šahrestān and town.*
ii. *Archeological sites.*

i. ŠAHRESTĀN AND TOWN

According to the natives, the area owes its name to the abundance of tamarisk trees (*gaz*) growing in the valley (cf. Curzon, *Persian Question* I, p. 192; Le Strange, *Lands*, p. 394), which is surrounded on all but the northern side by mountains and is accessible through the difficult Allāh Akbar and Hazār Masjed passes. Annual precipitation is 301 mm, and the valley is well watered by seasonal and permanent rivers (i.e., the Darūngar river), *qanāt*s, and wells. The main agricultural products include wheat, barley, cotton, potatoes, sugar beets, fruits and vegetables, and goats and cows are also raised (*Farhang-e joḡrāfīā'ī*, pp. 35-36).

The *šahrestān* of Darragaz is bounded on the north by Turkmenistan, on the west by Qūčān *šahrestān*, and on the east and south by Mašhad *šahrestān*. It contains four districts (*bakš*) and ten rural subdistricts. According to the 1365 Š./1986 census (q.v.), the population was 65,715 (14,124 families), 29,684 living in urban areas, 35,625 classified as rural, and 406 counted as nomads (Markaz-e āmār). They are mainly Shiʿite Muslims speaking Persian, Kurdish, and various Turkish dialects. A cotton gin and several carpet-weaving workshops are located in the valley (*Farhang-e joḡrāfīā'ī*, pp. 35-36)

The main urban center of the *šahrestān* is the town of Darragaz (formerly Moḥammadābād; *Times Index-Gazetteer of the World*, p. 205), situated at 37° 22′ N and 59° 8′ E, about 290 km northwest of Mašhad on the gravel road between Loṭfābād and Qūčān.

Bibliography: ʿA. Bayāt, *Kollīāt-e joḡrāfīā'ī-e ṭabīʿī wa tārīkī-e Īrān*, Tehran, 1988, pp. 184-86. *Farhang-e joḡrāfīā'ī-e Īrān (ābādīhā)* IX, Tehran, 1334 Š./1955. Markaz-e āmār-e Īrān, *Natāyej-e saršomārī-e nofūs wa maskan. Mehr-māh-e 1365. Šahrestān-e Darragaz*, Tehran, 1368 Š./1989.

(MASSOUD KHEIRABADI)

ii. ARCHEOOGICAL SITES

The valley of Darragaz, approximately halfway between the headwaters of the Atrak and Kašafrūd rivers in the south and the fertile foothills (*atak*) of southern Turkmenistan bordering the Kara Kum desert in the north, is relatively fertile and prosperous and contains numerous archeological sites (*tapa*s), some of which date back to at least as early as Chalcolithic times, suggesting that the region was equally prosperous and densely settled during specific prehistoric and historic periods.

Henri Frankfort first published archeological ceramics from Moḥammadābād (see i, above) in 1924, comparing them with those excavated earlier by Raphael Pumpelly at Anau. In 1966 ʿEzzat-Allāh Negahbān visited Darragaz and collected sherds from Yarim (Yarem) Tepe, the largest prehistoric site on the plain, but this work has never been published. The most systematic exploration of the valley was conducted by P. L. Kohl and D. L. Heskel on two short visits in the late summer and early fall of 1978 (1980; 1982). Thirty-two sites in the valley and an additional four on the road north to what was then the Soviet border were identified and their dates and sizes estimated from the distribution of surface remains; Yarim Tepe, which rises ca. 35 m above the contemporary level of the plain and covers an area of ca. 8 ha, was mapped and investigated more intensively.

On the basis of this preliminary work, it appears that Darragaz was densely settled during the Sasanian and early Islamic periods, and a substantial occupation is also suggested for the Achaemenid period. Four sites containing prehistoric materials identical to those excavated by Soviet archeologists in southern Turkmenistan were recorded, and it is believed that the surface materials of many later sites probably cover earlier, prehistoric occupations. It was also determined that the cultural deposit at Yarim Tepe extends ca. 3 m beneath the level of the plain, suggesting that many other early sites may have been buried as a result of alluvial processes.

Although the site of Yarim Tepe is badly eroded, materials collected from the surface suggest occupation throughout the Chalcolithic and Bronze Age; comparable materials are known from the southern Turkmenistan sequence (named after the type site Namazga I-VI, ranging from the early 5th millennium to the middle of the 2nd millennium B.C.E.). Yarim Tepe may also have been occupied on a smaller scale during Achaemenid and Sasanian times. The site, apparently occupied over its full surface, may have covered about 16 ha during the Late Aeneolithic and Early Bronze Age (Namazga III-IV, late 4th-early 3rd millennium B.C.E.), but much of this surface has been lost through erosion and destruction of the site. Diagnostic Early Bronze Age ceramics were collected from the base to the summit of the mound. The possibility of recovering a substantial intact array of Early Bronze architecture thus seems great and would augment considerably understanding of the so-called "urban revolution" in southern Central Asia.

These preliminary investigations in Darragaz clearly link materials recovered in the upper Atrak valley of northeastern Persia with those known from southern Turkmenistan. Archeological materials from Darragaz should thus ultimately play a pivotal role in the reconstruction of the prehistory and early history of Khorasan.

Bibliography: H. Frankfort, *Studies in the Early Pottery of the Near East*, Royal Anthropological Institute, Occasional Papers 6, 8, London, 1925-27. P. L. Kohl and D. L. Heskel, "Archaeological Reconnaissances in the Darreh Gaz Plain. A Short Report," *Iran* 18, 1980, pp. 160-72. Idem, "Arkheologicheskie pamyatniki ravnini Darre Gaz (rasprostranenie sistemi khronologii Namazga na materiali Iranskogo Khorasana)" (Archeological monuments of the Darra Gaz plain [Extension of the Namazga system of chronology to the materials of Persian Khorasan]), *Sovetskaya Arkheologiya* 4, 1982, pp. 33-47. R. Pumpelly, *Explorations in Turkestan. Expedition of 1904* I, Washington, D.C., 1908.

(PHILIP KOHL)

DARRA-YE NŪR (Pašaī Därē-i No: Herrlich et al., pp. 343, 858; lit., "valley of light"; a suggested Pashto etymology, in *Bābor-nāma*, tr. Beveridge, app., pp. xxiii-xxv, is to be rejected), name of a small tributary valley on the right bank of the Konar river in eastern Afghanistan and the corresponding subdistrict of Nangrahār province. The Nūr river rises on the forested Kōṇḍ Ḡar (ca. 4,360 m), a ridge of the Hindu Kush that has been described as a place of pilgrimage (Simpson, p. 803). It flows due south for about 25 km, receiving several tributaries on its right bank, and joins the Konar river near the market town and district seat of Šēwa, at an altitude of 610 m, about 23 km upstream from the confluence of the Konar and the Kābolrūd.

The area seems to have been incorporated into the Afghan state under Amir ʿAbd-al-Raḥmān (1297-1319/1880-1901; Keiser, 1971, p. 11). Owing to abundant forest game (Nāheż, p. 240) and proximity to the winter palace at Jalālābād, the Darra-ye Nūr was a favorite royal hunting ground. As early as 1327/1909 a road was built from Šēwa through the valley to Qalʿa-ye Šāhī(d) (Pašaī Ḵalšaī; Morgenstierne, p. 22) and then to Šokīālī (or Šogīālī), a village halfway to the source of the Nūr river elevated to the status of administrative center of the area (Kohzad, pp. 1-2).

The subdistrict (*ʿalāqadārī*) of Darra-ye Nūr covers 336 km². In 1925 there were about 10,000 inhabitants and in 1358 Š./1979, according to preliminary census (q.v.) returns, 27,606 (Herbordt, p. 208), with a relatively high density of 82 inhabitants per km². The population, concentrated in scattered settlements ranging from compact villages in the upper valley to either dispersed fortified farmsteads (*qalʿa*) surrounded by small tenant houses or tiny hamlets in the lower valley, is supported by intensive irrigated double cropping (Keiser, 1971, pp. 38 ff.; idem, 1984, p. 128; Wutt, 1977; idem, 1981, pp. 73 ff.). In the market-oriented wheat-rice system of the semitropical lower valley rice is the main cash crop, whereas in the temperate upper valley the traditional subsistence wheat-maize farming, with declining goat pastoralism, has recently been giving way to commercial poppy production for the narcotics trade (Keiser, 1971, pp. 31 ff.; idem, 1984, pp. 127 ff.; Ovesen, 1983, p. 174; Wutt, 1981, p. 55).

The inhabitants speak the eastern Pašaī language, the so-called *lağmānī* or *dehgānī* Pašaī, but with dialectal variations strong enough to prevent mutual intelligibility, although some standardization of the language seems to have occurred recently (Buddruss, p. 3; Tanner, p. 282; Keiser, 1984, p. 120). They belong to two geographically distinct endogamous clans, the Sūm in upper Darra-ye Nūr and the Šenganek in the lower valley (sometimes called Tajik and Sāfī respectively; Wutt, 1978, p. 43; Ovesen, 1986, pp. 247-48). A third group, allied with the Sūm, is of mixed origin: Čoğānī (immigrants from the Kōrdar and Arēt [Oyrēt] valleys in the north and east; Tanner, p. 293) and Čelāsī (from Čelās in the neighboring Čawkī valley (Ovesen, 1981, p. 224); they inhabit Kandak and Šemōl, two high villages in a side valley (Wutt, 1978, p. 44 map). Pashtun families from the Sāfī (Sāpī) tribe, some reputedly of *sayyed* (claiming descent from the Prophet Moḥammad) origin, have settled in the lower valley and initiated a strong pashtunization process (Kohzad, p. 5; Wutt, 1981, p. 65).

The Sūm are numerically and socially dominant. They claim descent from a common ancestor (possibly a Tajik Naqšbandī *pīr*), who is said to have come through the Kašmūnd range from the upper Alīngār about ten generations ago and to have converted the valley population to Islam. This tradition suggests a religious, rather than a patrilineal, affiliation and casts doubt on the belief that the Sūm were latecomers to the Darra-ye Nūr (Keiser, 1974, p. 449). The conversion must therefore have taken place later than that of the upper Alīngār in about 990/1582 (Moḥammad Khan). In fact, Islam had already reached the Darra-ye Nūr from a different direction, and the process of islamization lasted for centuries. In 411/1020, when the Ghaznavid Sultan Maḥmūd launched a first successful campaign of conversion from the south, the population of the valley was "*kāfer o botparast*" (infidel and idolatrous), most probably worshiping Hindu gods in this deeply indianized region (Gardīzī, ed. Ḥabībī, p. 185; Wutt, 1981, pp. 107-08). In 1035/1625 *kāfer* communities were still living in the Darra-ye Nūr, notably in the western side valley of Sarōr (Raverty, pp. 109, 141). Several pre-Islamic traditions still survive (e.g., in zoomorphic funerary architecture); others vanished only a few decades ago (Herbordt, p. 207; Wutt, 1981, pp. 92 ff.; Ovesen, 1983, p. 179).

Despite traditional factionalism, in the winter of 1358 Š./1979-80 an alliance of all the clans under Sūm leadership drove all government representatives out of the valley. Since then the Darra-ye Nūr has remained outside government control (Keiser, 1984).

Bibliography: G. Buddruss, *Beiträge zur Kenntnis der Pašai-Dialekte*, Abh. für die Kunde des Morgenlandes 33/2, Wiesbaden, 1959. O. Herbordt,

"Eine Reise nach 'Där-i-Nur' im Nordosten Afganistans" (sic), *Petermanns Mitteilungen* 72, 1926, pp. 206-08. A. Herrlich et al, "Orographische Bemerkungen," in A. Scheibe, ed., *Deutsche im Hindukusch*, Berlin, 1937, pp. 295-351. R. L. Keiser, *Social Structure and Social Control in Two Afghan Mountain Societies*, Ph.D. diss., University of Rochester, New York, 1971. Idem, "Social Structure in the Southeastern Hindu-Kush. Some Implications for Pashai Ethno-History," *Anthropos* 69/3-4, 1974, pp. 445-56. Idem, "The Rebellion in Darra-i Nur," in M. N. Shahrani and R. L. Canfield, eds., *Revolutions and Rebellions in Afghanistan. Anthropological Perspectives*, Institute of International Studies Research Series 57, Berkeley, Calif., 1984, pp. 119-35. A. A. Kohzad, "Dara-e-nour ou la vallée de la lumière," *Afghanistan* (Kabul) 13/1, 1958, pp. 1-6 (not very reliable). C. Masson, *Narrative of Various Journeys in Balochistan, Afghanistan, and the Panjab*, 3 vols., London, 1842; repr. Karachi, 1974; repr. Graz, 1975. Moḥammad Khan Ḡāzī, *Ṣefat-nāma-ye Darvīš Moḥammad Ḵān Ḡāzī*, ed. and tr. G. Scarcia as *Cronaca di una crociata musulmana contro i Kafiri di Laġmān nell'anno 1582*, Serie orientale 32, Rome, 1965. G. Morgenstierne, *Report on a Linguistic Mission to North-Western India*, Oslo, 1932. M.-H. Nāheż, ed., *Qāmūs-e joḡrāfīā'ī-e Afḡānestān* II, Kabul, 1336 Š./1957. J. Ovesen, "Ethnographic Field Research among the Pashai People of Darra-i-Nur," *Afghanistan* (Kabul) 31/2, 1978, pp. 91-99. Idem, "The Continuity of Pashai Society," *Folk* 23, 1981, pp. 221-34. Idem, "A Note on the Relation between Language and Culture. The Pashai Case," in *Monumenta Georg Morgenstierne* II, Acta Iranica, Hommages et Opera Minora 8, Leiden, 1982, pp. 131-40. Idem, "Environment and History in Pashai World-View," *Folk* 25, 1983, pp. 167-84. Idem, "The Construction of Ethnic Identities. The Nūrestānī and the Pašaī (Eastern Afghanistan)," in E. Orywal, ed., *Die ethnischen Gruppen Afghanistans*, Wiesbaden, 1986. H. G. Raverty, *Notes on Afghānistān and Part of Balūchistān* II, London, 1881; repr. Lahore, 1976. W. Simpson, "On the Dara Nur, or Dara Nuh, in Afghanistan," *Proceedings of the Royal Geographical Society* 1, 1879, pp. 802-03. H. C. Tanner, "Notes on the Chugāni and Neighbouring Tribes of Kafiristan," *Proceedings of the Royal Geographical Society* 3, 1881, pp. 278-301. K. Wutt, "Zur Bausubstanz des Darrah-e Nur," *Afghanistan Journal* 4/2, 1977, pp. 54-65. Idem, "Über Herkunft und kulturelle Merkmale einiger Pashai-Gruppen," *Afghanistan Journal* 5/2, 1978, pp. 43-58. Idem, *Pashai. Landschaft, Menschen, Architektur*, Graz, 1981.

(DANIEL BALLAND)

DARRA-YE ṢŪF, name of a valley in northern Afghanistan, drained by a tributary of the right bank of the Balḵāb (q.v.), and of the adjoining mountain district and its administrative center in Samangān province. The direct caravan route from Bāmīān (q.v.) to Mazār-e Šarīf passed through the valley, which has sometimes been erroneously transcribed (e.g., in most Afghan Boundary Commission reports) as Darra Yūsūf/Yūsof.

The Ṣūf river rises on Kōh-e Bandak in the westernmost Hindu Kush, at 3,600 m above sea level, flows 142 km, and joins the Balḵāb at an altitude of 642 m, thus having an average slope of 2.08 m/100 m (Ministry, 1978, p. 16). It alternately flows through uninhabited narrow gorges and widens in small intramontane basins, where its waters are used intensively for irrigation (56 percent of the total flow, according to Garbovskiĭ, p. 100). The river is known under a variety of names along its course: successively Darra-ye Bēd, Darra-ye Dāy Mīrdād (or Walīšān), Darra-ye Ṣūf (properly only the middle tract, between Tang-e Ḥasanī and the Kešenda basin), and Āb-e Kešenda (*Gazetteer of Afghanistan* IV, pp. 184-85). It is fed by both rainfall and snowmelt from the mountains. At Kešenda-ye Pāyān, 7 km above the junction with the Balḵāb, the crest occurs in April and May (2.21 and 2.40 m^3/sec respectively, with a record of 66.8 m^3/sec recorded on 19 April 1976), and low water in July and August (0.15 and 0.40 m^3/sec respectively, being entirely dry an average of fifty-three days a year). The mean annual discharge is 1.49 m^3/sec (record: 1358-67 Š./1969-78).

The district (*woloswālī*) of Darra-ye Ṣūf covers 3,432 km^2, broadly encompassing the drainage area of the river, except for the lower section, which falls within the Kešenda district of Balḵ province. According to preliminary returns of the census (q.v.) of 1368 Š./1979, the sedentary population of Darra-ye Ṣūf was 82,535. The average density of 24 inhabitants/km^2 was the highest in Samangān province. The population is mainly Hazāra (53 percent, concentrated in the southern and central parts of the district), and there are substantial minorities of Uzbeks (9 percent), Aymāq (9 percent), and Persianized Turkmen (25 percent) in the north, as well as smaller communities of Baluch, Arabs, and Pashtun (*Gazetteer of Afghanistan* IV, pp. 181 ff.). The district, with its numerous caves, some of them still inhabited (Griesbach, pp. 204-05; repr. in *Gazetteer of Afghanistan* IV, p. 186), and ruins (e.g., the "ruined city" of Šahr-e Čangīz in lower Walīšān; Amîr Khân, pp. 163-64; *Gazetteer of Afghanistan* IV, p. 552, s.v. Tah-i-Shahr), offers promise of archeological discoveries.

The district center is more precisely known as Qalʿa-ye Sarkārī-e Darra-ye Ṣūf, commonly abridged as Qalʿa on modern topographical maps. In 1886 it consisted of only twenty peasant families clustered around a large mud fort containing the governor's residence and quarters for 100 Hazāra soldiers (Maitland, p. 470; repr. in *Gazetteer of Afghanistan* IV, p. 188; Amîr Khan, p. 161; Sahibdâd Khân, p. 142). The population has not increased much since that time; with only 800 inhabitants in 1352 Š./1973, it still can hardly be considered a town (Centlivres, table facing p. 132). Its economic importance was greatly enhanced, however, with the beginning of exploitation of Jurassic coal deposits in the district, the largest reserves in Afghanistan, amounting to 102 million tons (82 percent of national reserves so far recorded; Chmyrov and Muzyka, p. 107). Mining operations began only in 1339 Š./1960 at Dahān-e Tōr, 25 km south of Qalʿa-ye Sarkārī, though coal had been discovered there in 1886 (Griesbach, p. 207; Dupree, p. 26). The mine is, however, still too isolated to contribute more than 10 percent, usually less, of the small national output (Grötzbach, pp. 124, 309). As a result of the opening of the mine, the Ministry of the interior elevated Qalʿa-ye Sarkārī to the status of a municipality. Its *bāzār* also boomed, expanding to 297 permanent shops in 1352 Š./1973, with at least 40 additional shops on market days, formerly Thursdays but now Mondays and Fridays, the latter having been chosen to coincide with the weekly closing of the mine (Centlivres, pp. 133-37; *Gazetteer of Afghanistan* IV, p. 180; Dupree, pp. 21-22). In the 1970s a new town (Darra-ye Ṣūf-e Naw) was being built 6 km north of Qalʿa-ye Sarkārī (Grötzbach, p. 309).

Bibliography: Amîr Khân, "Journey from Yakatâl by the Dara Yûsûf to Bâmiân and on to Hâjigak and Irâk Kotals," in Afghan Boundary Commission, *Records of Intelligence Party* V. *Miscellaneous Reports*, Simla, 1888, pp. 157-84. P. Centlivres, "Structure et évolution des bazars du Nord afghan," in E. Grötzbach, ed., *Aktuelle Probleme der Regionalentwicklung und Stadtgeographie Afghanistans*, Afghanische Studien 14, Meisenheim am Glan, Germany, 1976, pp. 119-45. V. M. Chmyrov and V. N. Muzyka, "Uglenosnost' Afganistana" (Coalfields of Afghanistan) in S. Abdulla et al., eds., *Geologiya i poleznye iskopaemye Afganistana* (Geology and mineral resources of Afghanistan) II, Moscow, 1980, pp. 106-17. L. Dupree, *The Green and the Black. Social and Economic Aspects of a Coal Mine in Afghanistan*, American Universities Field Staff Reports, South Asia Series 7/5, New York, 1963. E. A. Garbovskiĭ, *Inzhenernaya gidrologiya rek Afganistana* (Engineering hydrology of the rivers of Afghanistan), Leningrad, 1989. C. L. Griesbach, "Report on (a) Journey from Chahârshamba through Maimana, Belchiragh and Hill-Country South of Belchiragh-Sar-i-Pul Road (Gurziwân, Faoghân, &c.), to Sar-i-Pul. Thence through the Sangchârak District, and by Ak Kupruk, Dara Yûsûf, Shisha Walang, and the Kara Kotal, to Kâmard and Bâmiân . . .," in Afghan Boundary Commission, *Records of Intelligence Party* V. *Miscellaneous Reports*, Simla, 1888, pp. 185-215. E. Grötzbach, *Afghanistan. Eine geographische Landeskunde*, Darmstadt, 1990. T. Holdich, *Notes on the Survey of the Dara Isuf and Contiguous Routes by S. A. Ata Muhammad*, 1886, India Office Records, London, L/P & S/7/49/62-63. P. J. Maitland, *Diary of Intelligence Party, with Notes on the Population and Resources of Districts Visited 1884 to 1887*, Afghan Boundary Commission, Records of Intelligence Party II, Simla, 1888. Ministry of Water and Power, *Hydrological Yearbook 1964-1975* Part IV/9-13 *(Murghab, Shirintagb, Sarepul, Balkh and Khulm River Basins)*, Kabul, n.d. (1978?). Idem, *Hydrological Yearbook 1976-1978* Part IV. *North Flowing Rivers (Murghab, Shirin Tagab, Sarepul, Balkh and Khulm)*, Kabul, 1980. Sahibdâd Khân, "Route from Rui to Ak Kupruk, Thence Up the River to Sar-i-Pul (Balkh Ao), and Back to Homakai (or Omakhai), November and December 1885," in Afghan Boundary Commission, *Records of Intelligence Party* V. *Miscellaneous Reports*, Simla, 1888, pp. 139-56.

(DANIEL BALLAND)

DARRAŠŪRĪ, one of the five major tribes of the Qašqāʾī tribal confederation (see CONFEDERATIONS, TRIBAL). According to Zīād Khan Darrašūrī, a former *kalāntar* (chief) of the tribe, whom the author interviewed in spring 1957, the name Darrašūrī comes from that of a valley, the Darra-ye Šūr (Valley of salt), in the area of the tribe's summer quarters (Oberling, p. 226). The tribe is also sometimes called Darrašūlī, however, a name that Vladimir Minorsky connected with that of the Šūl (p. 392).

According to G. F. Magee (p. 20), the Darrašūrī are descendants of a group of Qezelbāš warriors headed by a certain Ḥaydar Mīnbāšī, a subordinate of Robert Sherley, and they were assigned the region that is their present-day summer quarters by Shah ʿAbbās I (r. 996-1038/1588-1629) as a reward for their bravery. The Darrašūrī are said to have joined the Qašqāʾī tribal confederation during the reign of Karīm Khan Zand (r. 1163-93/1750-79; Beck, p. 181). The tribe also contains Lur and Kurdish elements, like the Lek and Vandā *tīra*s (clans), which were absorbed either when the Zand tribal confederation disintegrated in the late 18th century or when the Darrašūrī took over some of the pasturelands of the Mamasanī Lurs in western Fārs province during the 19th century.

According to Zīād Khan, the Darrašūrī tribe comprised about 8,000 families, or 35,000 individuals, in 1336 Š./1957. Lois Beck reported (p. 182) about 45,000 individuals in the 1960s. On the other hand, in 1342 Š./1963 Komīsīūn-e mellī-e Yūnesko (I, p. 144) estimated only about 5,265 families, of which only 782 had become sedentary. According to Persian government statistics, there were about 5,169 Darrašūrī families, or 27,396 individuals, in 1360 Š./1981 (Afšār-Sīstānī, p. 626).

The Darrašūrī summer around Vardašt, southeast of Borūjen, in Isfahan province; this area is the northernmost of all Qašqāʾī summer quarters. Their winter quarters are in the *dehestān* of Māhūr-e Mīlātī, southeast of Behbahān, as well as around Kāzerūn and Lake Fāmūr, in central Fārs; winter headquarters are at Tang-e Čogān, in the Šāpūr valley.

The Darrašūrī were "the greatest horse-breeders and

owners among the Qashqai" (Wilson, p. 60). It has been said that before the Pahlavi period "each family possessed an average of three or four mounts, of which one or two were well bred" (Garrod, 1946, p. 40). The policy of forced sedentarization of the nomadic tribes pursued by Reżā Shah Pahlavī (1304-20 Š./1925-41) resulted in the loss of 80-90 percent of the Darrašūrī horses (Garrod, 1946, p. 40), but, under the leadership of Zīād Khan, the tribe made a speedy recovery after World War II, though William O. Douglas' figure of 20,000 cavalrymen (p. 145) must have been exaggerated.

According to Zīād Khan, the *tīra*s of the Darrašūrī are Narreʾī, Qarreḵlū, Jeyrānlū, Āyeblū, Ḵeyrātlū, Nāderlū, Āhangar, Ṭelābāzlū, Bolvardī, ʿOrojlū, Jānbāzlū, Hemmat-ʿAlī Kīḵāʾī, Šāvāzlū, Īmānlū, Ḵodāverdīlū, ʿAbd-al-Soleymānlū, Ṣādeqlū, Qarā Qoānlū (or Qarā Qoyūnlū), Šāhīn Kīḵāʾī, Nāṣer Kīḵāʾī, Dūndūlū, Qarā Gečlū, Karīmlū, Darzī, ʿAmala-ye Ḥosayn Khan, ʿAmala-ye Naṣr-Allāh Khan, Ṭayyeblū, Asad Kīḵāʾī, Golāblū, Lek, Kezīnlū, Korbīkūš, Vandā, Gowjelū, Čaroḵlū, Mešbī Sīār, Qābezlū, ʿAbu'l-Qārlū, Qarājūllū, ʿOṯmānlū, Rostamī, and Jelāllū (Oberling, pp. 226-27). The name Qarā Qoyūnlū suggests a past association of at least some Darrašūrī with the tribal confederation and nation of that name.

Bibliography: I. Afšār-Sīstānī, *Īlhā, čādornešīnān wa ṭawāyef-e ʿašāyerī-e Īrān*, Tehran, 1336 Š./1987, pp. 625-26. M. Bahman-Beygī, *ʿOrf wa ʿādat dar ʿašāyer-e Fārs*, n.p., 1324 Š./1945, p. 52. L. Beck, *The Qashqa'i of Iran*, New Haven, Conn., 1986, pp. 23, 117, 175-76, 180-82, 182n, 192, 221n, 222n, 231, 311-12, 316-17, 319, 334, 343. G. Demorgny, "Les réformes administratives en Iran. Les tribus du Fars," *RMM* 22, March 1913, pp. 97-98. W. O. Douglas, *Strange Lands and Friendly People*, New York, 1951, pp. 138, 145. H. Field, *Contributions to the Anthropology of Iran*, Chicago, 1939, pp. 88, 123, 219, 221. O. Garrod, "The Nomadic Tribes of Persia To-Day," *Journal of the Royal Central Asian Society* 33, 1946, p. 40. Idem, "The Qashqai Tribe of Fars," *Journal of the Royal Central Asian Society* 33, 1946, pp. 294, 302-303. M. S. Ivanov, *Plemena Farsa* (Tribes of Fārs), Moscow, 1961, pp. 35-37, 39, 44-45, 67, 76, 142-43, 145, 147. Kayhān, *Joḡrāfīā* II, p. 79. Komīsīūn-e mellī-e Yūnesko (UNESCO) dar Īrān, *Īrān-šahr*, Tehran, 1342 Š./1963. G. F. Magee, *The Tribes of Fars*, Simla, 1945. V. Minorsky, "Shūlistān," in *EI*[1] IV, pp. 391-92. P. Oberling, *The Qashqāʾi Nomads of Fārs*, the Hague, 1974, pp. 17-18, 23n, 37n, 79, 106, 140, 156, 163, 165, 180, 203, 204n. M. T. Ullens de Schooten, *Lords of the Mountains. Southern Persia and the Kashkai Tribe*, London, 1956, p. 116. A. T. Wilson, *Report on Fars*, Simla, 1916.

(Pierre Oberling)

DARRŪS, district in northern Tehran east of Qolhak and south of Qayṭarīya, all former suburbs of the city; it is located about 8 km from the center of the modern city.

i. *City quarter*.

ii. *Archaeological artifacts*.

i. City Quarter

Darrūs appears to be an ancient settlement, probably originally known as Garrūs (Kasrawī, p. 12). Until the mid-1940s it was a village of about 500 people located 5 km north of Tehran. Wheat and barley were cultivated there, irrigated by two underground canals (*qanāt*s). Before modern times most of its inhabitants were Armenian peasants who lived in a fortress in the middle of the village (Sotūda, pp. 413-15).

The village, with its walled gardens, was a favored summer resort for the notables of Tehran. Ḥājj Mīrzā Āqāsī (q.v.), grand vizier under Moḥammad Shah (r. 1250-64/1834-48), owned a large summer house there. Mehdīqolī Moḵber-al-Salṭana Hedāyat purchased this house and lived in it, gradually buying up half the village in the first decades of the 20th century. He sequestered this property in a family trust (*waqf*), part of which was devoted to local welfare institutions, including a hospital (Bīmārestān-e Hedāyat), a mosque (Masjed-e Hedāyat), a school, and a public bathhouse (Hedāyat, 1363 Š./1984b, p. 503). He also allocated 12,000 m^2 of land for the establishment of a second hospital, Bīmārestān-e Labbāfī-nežād. The village was incorporated into greater Tehran during the real-estate boom of the 1950s-1970s and is now a residential quarter. By 1335 Š./1956 the population had increased to 4,421, and it has continued to grow steadily.

Bibliography: M. Hedāyat, *Gozāreš-e Īrān*, ed. M.-ʿA. Ṣawtī, Tehran, 1363 Š./1984a, pp. 8-9, 27-28. Idem, *Ḵāṭerāt wa ḵaṭarāt*, Tehran, 1363 Š./1984b, pp. 94, 201, 386-87, 407, 449. Ḥ. Karīmān, *Tehrān dar goḏašta wa ḥāl*, Tehran, 1355 Š./1976, p. 419. Idem, *Qaṣrān* I, Tehran, 1356 Š./1977, pp. 57, 96-100, 511. A. Kasrawī, *Nāmhā-ye šahrhā wa dīhhā-ye Īrān*, Tehran, 1308 Š./1929, pp. 11-12. Dūst-ʿAlī Khan Moʿayyer-al-Mamālek, *Waqāyeʿ al-zamān*, ed. Ḵ. Neẓām Māfī, Tehran, 1361 Š./1982, p. 57. Razmārā, *Farhang* I, p. 88. M. Sotūda, *Joḡrāfīā-ye tārīḵī-e Šemīrān* I, Tehran, 1371 Š./1992, pp. 412-22.

(Sayyed ʿAlī Āl-e Dāwūd)

ii. Archeological Artifacts

In 1322 Š./1943 Iron Age pottery was discovered in Darrūs, on land belonging to Mehdīqolī Moḵber-al-Salṭana Hedāyat, who was prime minister from 1306-12 Š./1927-33 (Ṣamadī, 1334 Š./1955; idem, 1960; there are differences in the French and Persian texts, and both should be consulted). This material was not recovered in a properly controlled archeological excavation, so there is no certainty that it all belongs together or indeed that it is all necessarily authentic. A selection of ten pottery items was presented to the Iran

Bastan Museum in 1331 Š./1952. The group included six vessels in gray ware: a jug with an open, trough-shaped spout and a vertical handle with a projection like a horn at the top; a strainer vessel with a conical base and a vertical handle; three bowls, each with a single horizontal looped handle; and a bulbous jar. This pottery apparently belongs to the Late Western Gray Ware tradition, or Iron II (ca. 1000-800 B.C.E.; Young; see CERAMICS x). There are close parallels with pottery from Necropolis B at Tepe Sīalk. In the cemetery in the adjoining district of Qayṭarīya graves with both Early and Late Western Grey Ware were excavated (Curtis). Also from Darrūs is a curious drinking cup made from yellow clay with a tripod base and an animal's head near the bottom. There is incised geometric decoration on the upper part, and a handle projects from the rim.

Bibliography: J. E. Curtis, "A Grave-Group from Qeytariyeh near Teheran (?)," in L. De Meyer and E. Haerinck, eds., *Archaeologica Iranica et Orientalis. Miscellanea in Honorem Louis Vanden Berghe* I, Ghent, 1989, pp. 323-33. Ḥ. Ṣamadi, "Eṭṭelāʿāt-e ejmālī dar bāra-ye čand ẓarf-e makšūfa dar Darrūs-e Šamīrān," *Gozārešhā-ye bāstān-šenāsī* III, 1334 Š./1955, pp. 137-46. Idem, *Les découvertes fortuites et l'état de la civilisation chez l'homme pre-médique*, Tehran, 1960, pp. 7-12. L. Vanden Berghe, *Archéologie de l'Iran ancien*, Leiden, 1959, pp. 124, 196, pl. 159a. T. C. Young, "A Comparative Ceramic Chronology for Western Iran, 1500-500 B.C.," *Iran* 3, 1965, pp. 53-85.

(JOHN CURTIS)

DĀRŪ, DĀRŪ-ḴĀNA, DĀRŪ-SĀZĪ. See DRUGS.

DĀRŪĠA. See CITIES iii.

DARVĀZ, until partition between czarist Russia and the Afghan kingdom in the last quarter of the 19th century a largely autonomous principality with territory on both sides of the upper course of the Āmū Daryā (q.v.), known as the Panj. Today the portion of the former territory of Darvāz that lies north of the river has been incorporated into Tajikistan, whereas the former southern portion has been designated a district within the Afghan province of Badaḵšān (q.v.).

Before partition Darvāz was bordered on the south by Badaḵšān, on the east by the semiautonomous states of Šeḡnān and Rōšān, which were generally subject to Badaḵšān; and on the north and west by the nearly impassable Darvāz chain, a western extension of the Pamirs (see CENTRAL ASIA i; Figure 3), which separated it from the khanate of Bukhara (q.v.). This area is characterized by steep, narrow gorges and small sheltered hollows where fruit trees are grown. The larger valleys are also narrow, with steeply sloping sides. The amount of land available for cultivation is inadequate, and farmers must struggle in order to subsist (Holzwarth, p. 180). The population consists primarily of Tajiks, who adhere to the Sunnite branch of Islam, though in a few areas (e.g., the Wanj valley) the inhabitants are Ismaʿili Shiʿites. The language spoken is Persian.

The history of the region has been determined by its geographically central but politically peripheral position: On one hand, Darvāz has been the target of repeated incursions by foreign empire builders, but, on the other, its relative isolation, lack of mineral resources, and low agrarian yields have contributed to its continued marginal importance. The combination of these factors has ensured that throughout history foreign conquerors would be able to control the region only for short periods and that power would inevitably revert to native dynasties. This generally unbroken autonomy was apparent very early in the refusal of the local rulers to accept Alexander the Great as their overlord (Moḥammad-Nāder Khan, ed. Kūškekī, pp. 354-68). At the beginning of the 16th century Darvāz was caught up in the fierce struggle between the Uzbeks and the Timurids for control of Central Asia. Sovereignty over the region, as well as over the neighboring region of Badaḵšān, changed hands several times before the final victory of the Uzbeks in 913/1507 (Grevemeyer, pp. 28 ff.; Akhmedov, pp. 61, 73, 108-09). Nevertheless, it seems that such external control was only nominal and that the northern part of Darvāz remained completely independent (Kislyakov, pp. 88-89).

Around the middle of the 17th century the Uzbeks were driven out, and an independent dynasty, with the title *shah-e Darvāz*, was established, at the same time that the indigenous Yarid rulers took control of Badaḵšān, in 1067/1657; thereafter the rulers of Badaḵšān, with their capital in Fayżābād, were the primary rivals of the Darvāz shahs. Several times hostilities broke out between Darvāz and Badaḵšān over the region of Rāḡ, which lay between them (Grevemeyer, pp. 122-23), and Darvāz also laid claim to Šeḡnān (Semenov, pp. 6-7). The main cities of Darvāz were Ḵam and, farther north, the capital, Kalai Khumb (Qalʿa-ye Ḵomb), both on the banks of the Panj. The power of the rulers of Darvāz was based on a kind of patronage system organized within a framework of kinship and client relations. The ruler's privileged followers were entitled to shares in the booty captured in successful raids and in revenues from the land and its population, as well as to exemption from taxes (Holzwarth, pp. 205-06). It was typical of the social milieu during these traditional periods that there was no institutionalized economic structure; nevertheless, the existence of large extended families did lead to an internal division of labor (Holzwarth, pp. 184-85). At the time of the conquest by czarist Russia in 1290/1873 Darvāz was annexed to the Russian vassal state of Bukhara. A number of subsequent boundary agreements among Russia, British India, and Afghanistan delineated zones of influence, which ultimately led to the partition of Darvāz in 1310/1893

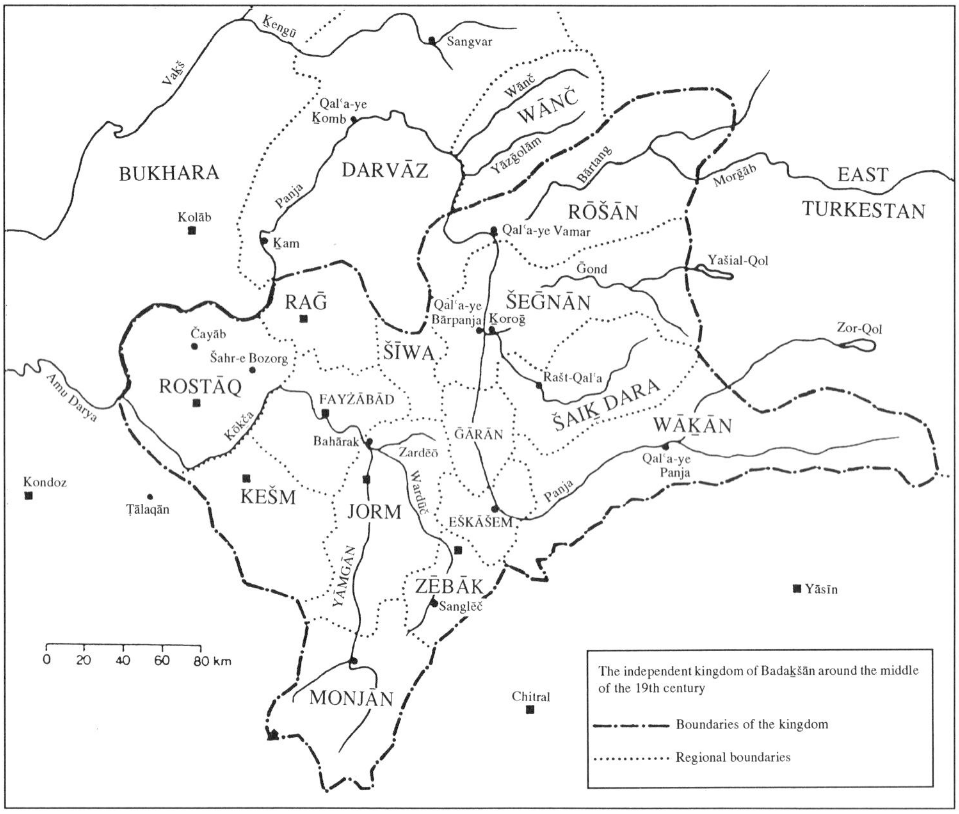

Figure 3. Map of Badakšān in the mid-19th century, showing boundaries of Darvāz. After Grevemeyer, 1982, p. 76.

and again in 1313/1895 (see BOUNDARIES iii). The portion of the region that lay south of the Panj was annexed to Afghanistan in compensation for the loss of Šeḡnān and Rōšān to Russia and its vassal Bukhara.

Bibliography: B. A. Akhmedov, *Istoriya Balkha (XVI-pervaya polovina XVIII v.)* (The history of Balk [16th to the first half of the 18th century]), Tashkent, 1982. *Gazetteer of Afghanistan* I, p. 58. J.-H. Grevemeyer, *Herrschaft, Raub und Gegenseitigkeit. Die politische Geschichte Badakhshans 1500-1883*, Wiesbaden, 1982. W. Holzwarth, "Segmentation and Staatsbildung in Afghanistan. Traditionale sozio-politische Organisation in Badakhshan, Wakhan und Sheghnan," in K. Greussing and J.-H. Grevemeyer, eds., *Revolution in Iran und Afghanistan*, Frankfurt, 1980, pp. 177-235. N. A. Kislyakov, "Istoriya Karategina, Darvaza i Badakhshana" (The history of Qarātekīn, Darvāz, and Badakšān) in *Materialy po istorii Tadzhikov i Tadzhikistana* (Materials on the history of the Tajiks and Tajikistan), Dushanbe, 1945, pp. 71-133. V. Minorsky, "Shughnān," in *EI*[1] IV, pp. 390-91. Moḥammad-Nāder Khan, *Rahnemā-ye Qaṭaḡan wa Badakšān*, ed. Borhān-al-Dīn Kūškekī, Kabul, 1302/1923; ed. M. Sotūda, Tehran, 1367 Š./1988, pp. 228-35; tr. M. Reut as *Qataghan et Badakhshân. Description du pays d'après l'inspection d'un ministre afghan en 1922*, Paris, 1979, pp. 207-17. A. A. Semenov, *Istoriya Shugnana* (The history of Šeḡnān), Tashkent, 1916.

(JAN-HEEREN GREVEMEYER)

DARVĀZA (gateway), generally an entrance opening wide enough to permit passage of vehicles, in contrast to doorways, which are smaller openings to permit passage through a wall or fence (*Wasmuths Lexikon*, pp. 544, 565).

Gateways are found in the walls of every kind of enclosure: castles, fortresses, small or medium-sized settlements, and cities. They are known to have existed from the earliest days of castle and city construction and to have evolved as part of the general development of fortification architecture. From prehistoric times the gateways of castles and fortresses were usually flanked by round or rectangular towers. This combination of entrance with flanking towers was also adopted for *rebāṭs* (fortified monasteries) and caravansaries (q.v.; Kleiss and Kiani, 1983, p. 85: Dayhr). The symbolism of the two-towered plan in palace and other public buildings can be traced to this origin (Diez, p. 193). This type of gate structure could also be adapted to the typical *ayvān* (q.v.) entrance, as in the facade of the Šīr-dār *madrasa* in Samarqand (1019/1610; Diez, p. 81). Gate structures thus also served nondefensive functions, both in fortified cities and in the open countryside.

Only city gates will be treated here. They are sufficient to reveal a continuous development in architectural history, though discussion here will be limited to the Iranian cultural circle. At the beginning of this development, in the 3rd millennium B.C.E., stands the fortified castle settlement of Bolūrābād near Qara Żīāʾ-al-Dīn in western Azerbaijan, a prehistoric site in which a simple, unelaborated opening in the wall marks the gateway (Figure 4a; Kleiss, 1975). At another walled settlement from the 3rd millennium B.C.E., Yak̲valī, east of Mākū, there is evidence that already the line of the fortress walls was laid out in order best to exploit the features of the terrain for defensive purposes. There too, however, the gateway was a simple opening in the walls, without special reinforcement (Figure 4b; Kleiss, 1979).

A more effective defensive layout is represented by the gateway to the strongly fortified settlement of Rāvāz southwest of Mākū, which stands at the junction of the trade routes from Anatolia to Central Asia and from Mesopotamia to the Caucasus and belongs to the 2nd or 3rd millennium B.C.E. (see CASTLES). There an early form of the gateway with flanking projections can be identified (Figure 4c); along with the entire fortifaction wall, which is buttressed by towers or bastions, its placement was dictated by the terrain (Kleiss, 1979, pp. 31-33).

Like Rāvāz, the Urartian remains at Dūčgagī represent a more advanced stage in the evolution of settlements and can be considered those of a full-fledged town (Figure 4d). Located southeast of Mākū on an unfortified clifftop with sheer drops on three sides, it was separated on the fourth side from an outer settlement and protected against assault by a fortified wall in which the simple gateway opening was flanked by a single tower (Kleiss, 1978, pp. 36 ff.). Similarly, the easternmost of the two gates at Qalʿa-ye Esmāʿīl Āqā (Figure 4e), a large fortified Urartian settlement of the 8th-7th centuries B.C.E., was entered through a passage, rather like a dromos, at a point where the topography of the site dictated a step back in the fortification wall (Kleiss, 1977, pp. 64 ff.).

More typical of Urartian fortifications was the 8th-century B.C.E. city wall of Ḥasanlū, with a gateway (Figure 4f) flanked by two massive rectangular towers. In addition, the gate itself was articulated by two flanking projections on the exterior (Dyson and Muscarella, pp. 3-4). At Verak̲ram on the Aras (Araxes) an 8th-century Urartian city wall was elaborated in a later rebuilding by the addition of a small gatehouse (Figure 4g), which was further strengthened by a strongly projecting tower (1974, pp. 82 ff.). On the southern bank of the Aras, east of Jolfā, in the walled 6th-century B.C.E. settlement of Qalʿa-ye Gavūr there is only a simple gate opening (Figure 4h) in one corner of the wall (Kleiss, 1976, pp. 107 ff.). At a 6th- or 5th-century B.C.E. site also known as Qalʿa-ye Gavūr, southwest of K̲ᵛoy, there is a bent-axis gateway (Figure 4i; Kleiss, 1978, pp. 34 ff.). The outer gate of the fortified settlement of Qalʿat southeast of Urmia, also of the 6th century B.C.E., was flanked by two strong rectangular towers (Figure 4k; Kleiss, 1978, pp. 41 ff.). This type of gateway can also be seen on an Assyrian relief representing a "Median" city gate viewed from the front (see, e.g., Kleiss, 1982a). To judge from this relief, the arched gates of the 6th-5th centuries were flanked by towers that rose above the crenellated tops of the adjoining walls and supported enclosed battle platforms encircled by crenellations (Figure 4j). This representation is, however, primarily symbolic, and it is not possible to draw from it conclusions about the proportions of actually existing architecture.

From the 5th and 4th centuries B.C.E. one Achaemenid city gate, the eastern gate of the Ville Royale in Susa (Figure 4l), is known. Its form, a cubical structure projecting from the line of the walls, with a central entrance passage flanked by pairs of deep recesses, can be traced to Hittite models, as at Carchemish (Naumann, p. 301), and to city gates from Palestine and adjacent lands of the 12th-10th centuries B.C.E. (Carter, p. 41 fig. 1; Herzog). The characteristic palace gates of Persepolis are not relevant here.

The ruined gate of Eṣṭak̲r near Persepolis, which, judging from its structure and the technique of working the stone, belongs in the late Achaemenid or Seleucid/Hellenistic period, exhibits an unusual plan (Figure 4m). It stands outside the city of Eṣṭak̲r, which lies to the north of it, between the city and an extensive settlement area that was obviously once surrounded by a fortified wall; the presence of this settlement has been established from the typical relief-carved "Eṣṭak̲r ceramics" found in the area. It is obvious from topographical observations (Kleiss, 1992, pp. 235-36 fig. 2) and investigations (Calmeyer-Seidl, personal communication) that the ruins, which certainly served the function of a gateway on the track of the ancient road from Persepolis (Shiraz) to Pasargadae (Isfahan and Yazd), also served to link the two settlement areas across the caravan route (survey by Kleiss, 1990). Not only the road passed through the gate of Eṣṭak̲r but also a water canal (Figure 4m). Two half-columns and a central column divided the passage into two aisles. The space within the gate structure can thus be viewed as a kind of gatehouse.

Datable to the 4th-1st century B.C.E., in the Seleucid and Parthian periods, is Koi Krylgan Kala, the ruins of the former burial palace of the Chorasmian dynasty, later transformed into a settlement. The plan of the gateway was dominated by two flanking semicircular buttresses (Figure 4n); this arrangement, whether of semicircular or of rectangular towers, was predominant in later gate plans, as well as in city walls (Brentjes, p. 51).

In the Sasanian and early Islamic periods rectangular towers most commonly flanked the gateways in city

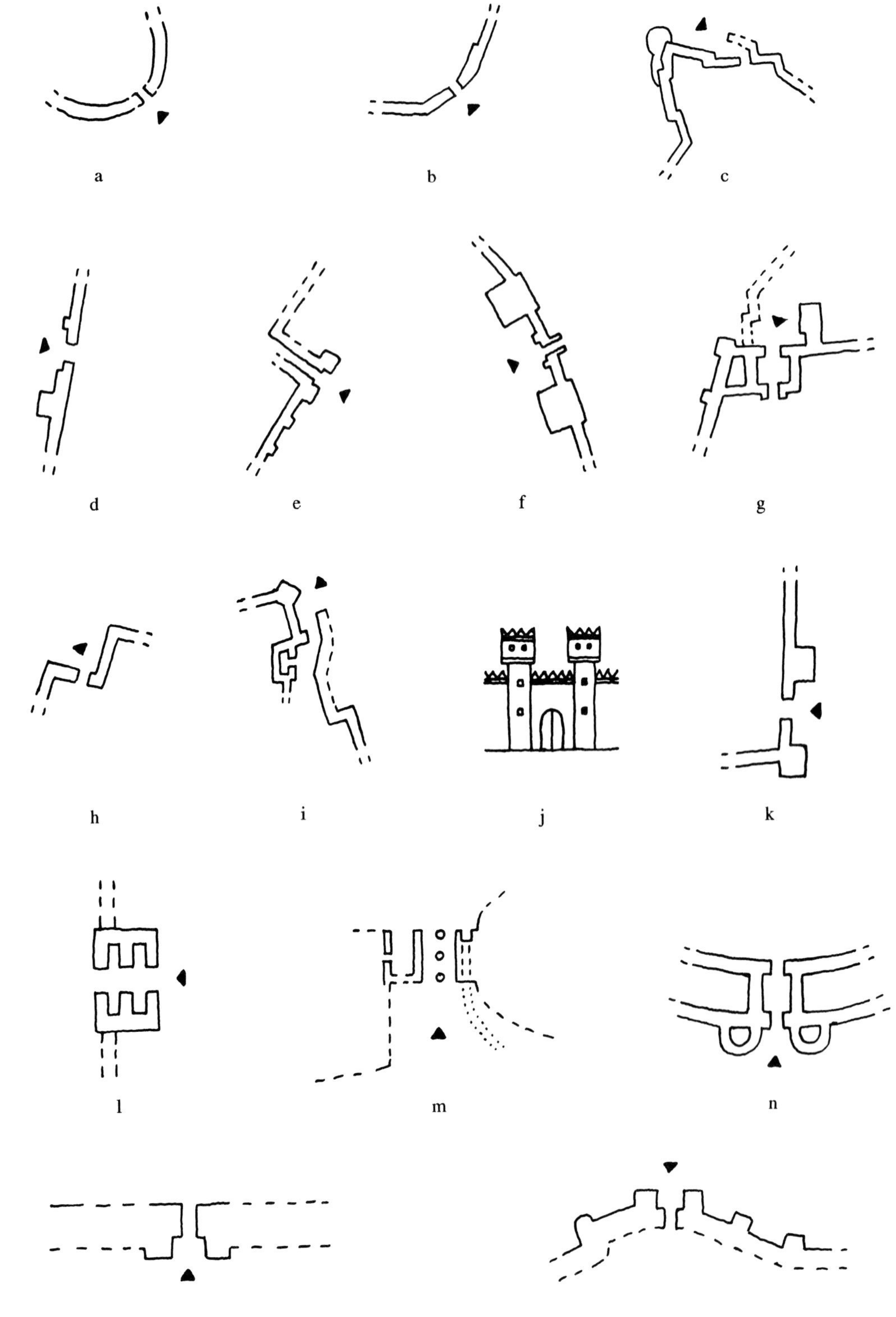

Figure 4. Pre-Islamic city gates: a. Bolūrābād b. Yak̲valī c. Rāvāz d. Dūčgagī e. Qalʿa-ye Esmāʿīl Āqā f. Ḥasanlū g. Verak̲ram h. Qalʿa-ye Gavūr on the Aras i. Qalʿa-ye Gavūr south of K̲^{v}oy j. Assyrian relief of "Median city" k. Qalʿat l. Ville Royale, Susa m. Eṣṭak̲r n. Koi Krylgan Kala o. Dārābgerd p. Qaṣr-e Abū Naṣr.

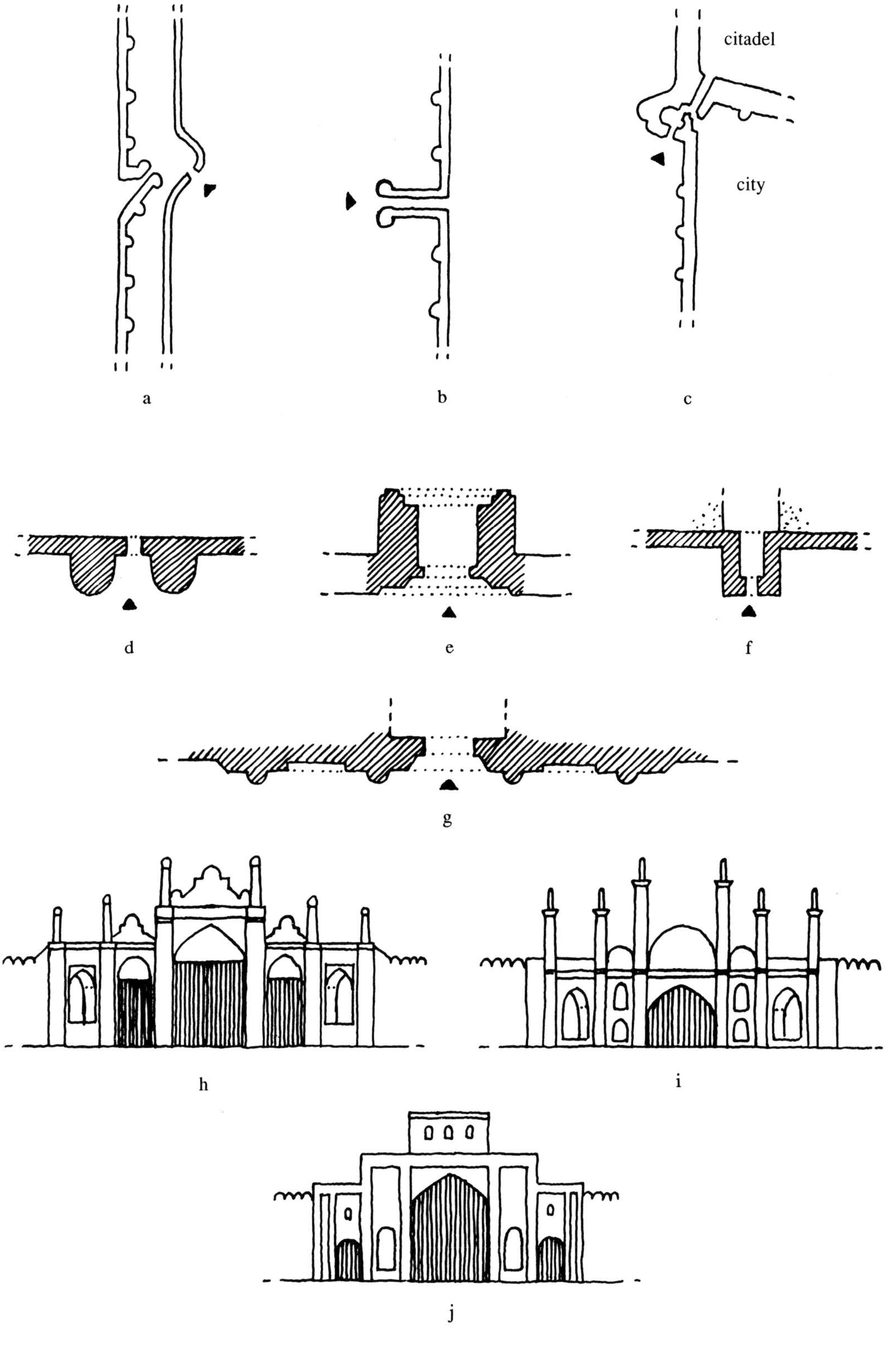

Figure 5. Islamic city gates: a. Herat b. Marūčak, Afghanistan c. Dāmḡān d. Bam e. Ḵᵛoy f. Īzadḵᵛāst g. Tehran h. Qazvīn i. Semnān j. Shiraz.

walls, as is clear from the unexcavated northern gate of the round city of Dārābgerd (Figure 4o; see DĀRĀB ii), here shown with flanking projections, and from the gate of Qaṣr-e Abū Naṣr (Figure 4p), south of Shiraz, with fully developed towers (Whitcomb).

In the later Islamic period in Persia and the areas of its cultural influence heavy semicircular towers flanking gateways in city walls predominated; examples are preserved at Yazd and at Bam (Figure 5d). Unfortunately, a great number of Persian city gates have been completely destroyed in the last 100 years, owing to the increase in modern automobile traffic and breaches in the walls made for thoroughfares. Among the few preserved examples it is nevertheless possible to find solutions other than the two-towered gate facade.

At Marūčak in Afghanistan, for example, a gateway between two circular towers is related to the European type of narrow passage preceding the gate opening (*Zwingertor*; Figure 5b). It is not clear whether there were both exterior and interor gates at Marūčak, but it seems probable. This construction can be dated to the 10th-13th centuries (Ball, I, p. 180; II, pl. 42.1). Another gateway between two exterior round towers has been incorporated into the modern city wall of Herat; the entrance passage is oblique to the fortification wall, which was buttressed by rhythmically placed towers, and there was a simple outer wall without towers and with simple gate openings (Figure 5a; Brandenburg, p. 20 map v).

In the medieval city wall of Dāmḡān (q.v.) a single gateway has been preserved at the point where the city wall meets that of the citadel (Figure 5c); its form is that of a projecting angular buttress of the citadel wall, and the passage makes several turns as it leads into both the citadel and the city area. It is impossible to see into the interior from outside, and thus an attacker could not shoot through the passage (Kleiss, 1982b, p. 376).

In the 18th and early 19th centuries, beside gateways flanked by semicircular towers, as at Bam (Figure 5d), there were also other gateway plans, for example, the passage through a towerlike gatehouse, as at Īzadḵᵛāst near Ābāda (Figures 5f, 6), or an architectonically constructed gate flush with the line of the city wall at Ḵᵛoy in western Azerbaijan, which was reinforced by buttresses betraying European influence (Figure 5e). The remains of the gate at Ḵᵛoy, which is ornamented with stone relief carving and directly connected on the interior to the vaulted street of the *bāzār*, are still well preserved (1977a).

A few examples of 19th-century gateways can still be found in Persia, some of only moderate size (as at Tehran), some well preserved (as at Semnān and Qazvīn), and some reconstructed (as at Shiraz). The southern gateway in the earlier wall of the old city of Tehran, the Moḥammadīya gate (leading to Moḥammadīya and Ray), was built by Moḥammad Shah Qājār (1250-64/1834-48; Figure 5g). Like the gateway at Ḵᵛoy, it is flush with the walls; it is decorated with tiles and flanked by two slightly projecting towers (Kleiss, 1977b). The Qajar gateways at Tehran, Qazvīn, Semnān, and Shiraz had no special defensive function, except that they could be closed at night and for the collection of customs duties. They are nevertheless city portals and are thus lavishly decorated, mainly with tiles. At the Tehran gate in Qazvīn (Figure 5h) and at the Qorʾān gate in Shiraz (Figure 5j) the main vehicle entrances were wide and tall; they were flanked by two pedestrian passageways. The Tehran gate at Semnān and the Moḥammadīya gate in Tehran had only single entrances for vehicles, riders, and pedestrians (Figure 5g, i). The towers that nowadays stand separate from the line of the walls were of course integral parts of the original city walls.

A still well-preserved example of a city gate from the

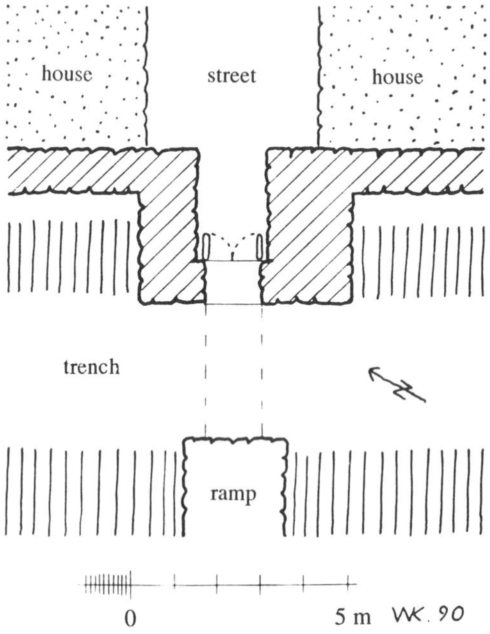

a

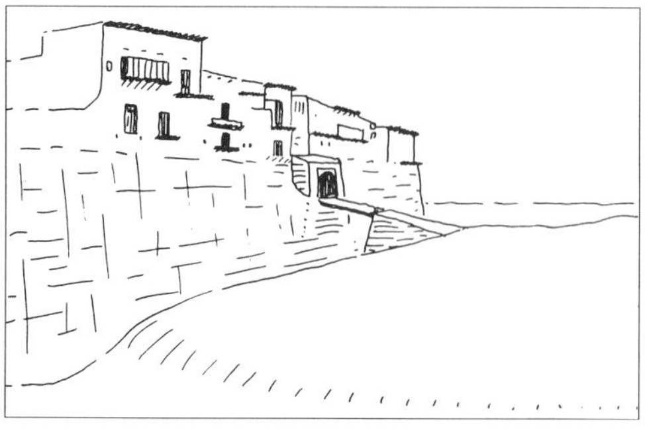

b

Figure 6. Īzadḵᵛāst, city gate: a. Plan b. Elevation. After Amory, p. 42.

18th or 19th century is that at Īzadḵᵛāst (Figure 6). It is the only gate to the city, which is entirely surrounded by steep precipices. On the west side a trench has been dug; it was formerly crossed by means of a wooden bridge. The entrance is through a gatehouse, which stands lower than the houses on both sides of the main street; it juts out from the line of the city wall, which serves at the same time as the foundation for houses built on top of it. The wooden bridge, which is no longer extant, was not a drawbridge. Instead, the outer entrance to the gatehouse was closed by double doors with stone wings, and the closed door could be barricaded on the interior with wooden beams in emergencies. The gate thus provided the inhabitants of the town with sufficient protection from attack.

Bibliography: C. Amory, Jr., *Persian Days*, London, 1928. W. Ball, *Archaeological Gazetteer of Afghanistan*, 2 vols., Paris, 1982. D. Brandenberg, *Herat*, Graz, 1977. B. Brentjes, *Mittelasien*, Vienna, 1977. E. Carter, "Excavations in Ville Royale I at Susa. The Third Millennium B.C. Occupation," *CDAFI* 11, 1980, pp. 7-134. E. Diez, *Die Kunst der islamischen Völker*, Berlin, 1917; repr. Potsdam, n.d. R. H. Dyson and O. W. Muscarella, "Constructing the Chronology and Historical Implications of Hasanlu IV," *Iran* 27, 1989, pp. 1-27. Z. Herzog, *Das Stadttor in Israel und in den Nachbarländern*, Mainz, 1986. W. Kleiss, "Planaufnahmen urartäischer Burgen und Neufunde urartäischer Anlagen in Iranisch-Azerbaidjan im Jahre 1973," *AMI*, N.F. 7, 1974, pp. 79-106. Idem, "Bolurabad I. Die Architektur," *AMI*, N.F. 8, 1975, pp. 15-20. Idem, "Zwei Plätze des 6. Jahrhunderts v. Chr. in Iranisch Azerbaidjan A. Die Bauten," *AMI*, N.F. 9, 1976, pp. 107-16. Idem, "Ergänzung zum Stadttor von Khoy," *AMI*, N.F. 10, 1977a, pp. 323-24. Idem, "Das Muḥammadiyeh-Tor in Alt-Teheran," *AMI*, N.F. 10, 1977b, pp. 341-44. Idem, "Urartäische Plätze in Iran A. Architektur," *AMI*, N.F. 10, 1977c, pp. 53-83. Idem, "Urartäische Plätze und Anlagen des 2.-1. Jahrtausends v. Chr. in Iran A. Architektur," *AMI*, N.F. 11, 1978, pp. 27-59. Idem, "Ravaz und Yakhvali, Zwei befestigte Plätze des 3. Jahrtausends A. Architektur," *AMI*, N.F. 12, 1979, pp. 27-34. Idem, "Darstellungen urartäischer Architektur," *AMI*, N.F. 15, 1982a, pp. 53-77. Idem, "Die islamische Festung am Tepe Hissar bei Damghan," *AMI*, N.F. 15, 1982b, pp. 376-88. Idem, "Brücken aus Zentral- und Südiran," *AMI*, N.F. 25, 1992. Idem and M. Y. Kiani, *Iranian Caravansarais* I, Tehran, 1362 Š./1983. R. Naumann, *Architektur Kleinasiens*, Tübingen, 1971. *Wasmuths Lexikon der Baukunst* IV, Berlin, 1932. D. S. Whitcomb, *Before the Roses and the Nightingales. Excavations at Qasr-i Abu Nasr, Old Shiraz*, New York, 1985.

(WOLFRAM KLEISS)

DARVĀZA TEPE (or Tall-e Darvāza), a village site in the southeastern Kor river basin, in Fārs province, occupied in three stages from 1800 B.C.E. to 800 B.C.E., according to radiocarbon dates of the finds, and characterized by an essential continuity in both architecture and other aspects of material culture. Above virgin soil three levels of occupation have been discovered; in each small irregularly shaped rooms are situated around large, open courtyards. In the most extensively excavated level (phase III) two perpendicular streets divide the settlement into quadrants. Several kilns and what are thought to be "drying racks" are evidence for pottery manufacturing at the site.

Of the ceramic assemblage 93 percent is Shogha (Šoḡā) ware, apparently made at the site (Vanden Berghe, pp. 42-44; Sumner), and a little less than 7 percent Taimuran (Teymūrān) ware. The former is a coarse, handmade ware, probably formed around other pots, as many of the interiors show fabric impressions. The limited corpus of shapes includes bowls and jars with plain or slightly everted rims, handled cups with plain rims, spouted "teapots," and scoops or trays. Freehand designs are painted in black. Major motifs include geometric (cross-hatched diamonds) or naturalistic (birds, fish, goats on mountains) designs painted on an empty field on the body of the vessel; they are enclosed by successive bands of geometric minor motifs, for example, horizontal lines, garlands, and zigzags, which begin at the top of the vessel. Taimuran ware is wheelmade and high-fired; distinctive carinated bowls and jars are coated with a buff slip and carefully painted with horizontal lines, probably applied while the pots were on the wheel. Although Louis Vanden Berghe considered Taimuran ware a late development from Shogha ware, it occurs in all three levels at Darvāza, decreasing slightly in frequency over time.

From the radiocarbon dates Darvāza seems to have been contempory with the Qaleh (Qalʿa) levels at Tal-e Malyan (Malīān) 80 km to the northwest (see CERAMICS viii). A few Qaleh sherds have also been found in the later two occupation levels at Darvāza. No Kaftari (Kaftarī) pottery (found below the Qaleh levels at Tal-e Malyan) has been found at the site. There is, however, a broad resemblance between the Malyan and Darvāza corpuses: Shogha and Kaftari pottery are roughly similar to each other in motifs and shapes, though Kaftari pottery is almost certainly wheelmade; more important, each bears a similar stylistic relations to associated Taimuran and Qaleh wares respectively. The latter two are finer than their Shogha and Kaftari counterparts, with a much more limited range of motifs, among which horizontal lines predominate, and each constitutes a very small percentage of the overall corpus.

Surface surveys in the Kor basin indicate that Shogha sites are located mainly east of the river, whereas Qaleh sites are clustered in the west. Kaftari pottery is found at sites throughout the basin; the Qaleh and Shogha sites are fewer and smaller, indicating a declining population. Imported goods from the Persian lowlands, epigraphic material, and such luxury items as copper and bronze decorations, so common in the preceding Kaftari period, are almost absent from Qaleh and Shogha sites. Whether the provincialism of these sites relative to Kaftari sites is diachronic, representing a "contraction" or adaptation to self-sufficiency; synchronic, representing a shift in population from village to city; or both is unclear. It was breached but not broken by the establishment of a Middle Elamite outpost at Malyan in 1200 B.C.E. Darvāza, however, remained an isolated village until the first influx of Indo-Europeans in the 1st millennium B.C.E.

Bibliography: E. Carter and M. W. Stolper, *Elam. Surveys of Political History and Archaeology*, Los Angeles and Berkeley, 1984. L. K. Jacobs, *Daravazeh Tepe and the Iranian Highlands in the Second Millennium, B.C.*, Ph.D. diss., University of Oregon, Eugene, 1980. M. Nicol, "Darvazeh Tepe," *Iran* 7, 1969, p. 172. Idem, "Excavations at Darvazeh Tepe. A Preliminary Report," *Bāstān-šenāsī wa honar-e Īrān* 5, 1349 Š./1970, pp. 19-22. Idem, "Darvazeh Tepe," *Iran* 9, 1971, pp. 168-69. W. Sumner, *Cultural Development in the Kur River Basin, Iran. An Archaeological Analysis of Settlement Patterns*, Ph.D. diss., University of Pennsylvania, Philadelphia, 1972. L. Vanden Berghe, *Archéologie de l'Īrān ancien*, Documenta et Monumenta Orientis Antiqui 6, Leiden, 1959.

(LINDA K. JACOBS)

DARVĪŠ, a poor, indigent, ascetic, and abstemious person or recluse (Av. *drəgu-*, *driγu-* "the needy one, dependent"; Lommel, pp. 127-28; pace *AirWb.* 777: "poor, needy; Mid. Pers. *driyōš* "worthy poor, needy; one who lives in holy indigence"; Pāzand *daryōš*; NPers. *darγōš* > *daryōš* > *darvīš*). Paul Horn (*Etymologie*, s.v. *dervēš*) connected it with New Persian *derīġ* "regret, sorrow," a connection that Heinrich Hübschmann (*Persische Studien*, p. 62) rightly doubted. (For further discussion of the word, see Lommel, p. 129, with references; *Borhān-e qāṭeʿ*, ed. Moʿīn, II, p. 846.)

i. *In the pre-Islamic period.*
ii. *In the Islamic period.*

i. IN THE PRE-ISLAMIC PERIOD

In Book VI of the *Dēnkard* (q.v.), which deals in some detail with the *driyōš* and his way of life (*driyōšīh*), he is described, on the authority of the ancient fathers of the Mazdean faith (*pōryōtkēšān*), as "he to whom the worldly means of subsistence is merely toward keeping the body hale and healthy (*tuwān xwāstag ī gētīg rāy tan padēxw ud bawandag*), whereupon he is with peace of mind (*axw aziš āsānīg*), of contented disposition (*menišn padiš hunsand*), and free from distress (*widang*); he does not hold the reputable (*čašmag*) and the opulent (*tuwānīg*) in disrespect (*tar-menišn*) but behaves himself in such a way as if to say: 'He with his reputation and wealth, (compared) with my (pious) indigence (*driyōšīh*), he is (just a creature) the same as I am'" (*Dēnkard*, ed. Madan, p. 504). *Driyōšīh* is lavishly praised as the most excellent way of life, and the people are advised to promote its diffusion (*pad mayān kunēd*; *Dēnkard*, ed. Madan, p. 503). He who takes to poverty not out of necessity but because of excellence and the nobility (*wehīh ud burzišn*) of holy indigence (*driyōšīh*) drives away Ahriman (q.v.) and the demons from the world. Only he who takes greater joy from the least means of subsistence than from abundance of wealth can bear the hardships of holy poverty (*Dēnkard*, ed. Madan, p. 503). Men and women living in holy indigence are revered on a par with the righteous men (*ahlawān*), that is, as a group within the priestly estate: "I celebrate the righteous men and women; I celebrate (*yazom*) the *driyōš* men and women" (*Dēnkard*, ed. Madan, p. 621).

In the *Dēnkard* (ed. Madan, p. 588) the requisite features are distinguished from the indispensable features of *driyōšīh* (*čārag ud ačārag ī driyōšīh*). The former are designated as diligence (*tuxšāgīh*) and moderation (*paymānīgīh*), the latter, constituting the quintessence of *driyōšīh*, as contentment (*hunsandīh*) and right-mindedness (*bawandag-menišnīh*). Of these contentment is the most significant epithet of *driyōšīh*, however. The renowned doctor of Zoroastrianism Ādurbād ī Mahrspandān (q.v.) set it out to be the best human quality, which merits the greatest hope of attaining the blessings of the world to come (*hunsandīh . . . wuzurgtom umēd ī mēnōg*; *Pahlavi Texts*, ed. Jamasp-Asana, p. 67), and the high priest Ādurbād ī Zarduštān, in spite of his affluence and high spiritual office, prided himself upon his diligence and moderation in life as a *driyōš* (*Pahlavi Texts*, ed. Jamasp-Asana, p. 81). Contentment was also regarded as the preeminent characteristic of the mystical dervishes in Islam (see ii, below). For example, the poet Ḥāfeẓ wrote: "If there is any merit to be gained in this world, it is that attained by the contented *darvīš*. O Lord, grant me the blessings of holy indigence and contentment" (*Dar īn bāzār agar sūdī'st bā darvīš-e k̲orsand ast/K̲odāyā monʿam am gardān be darvīšī o k̲orsandī*; p. 307).

The word *driyōšīh* thus primarily connotes a pious disposition. In the *Dēnkard* this significant point is stressed in unambiguous terms: "Even a mere pious desire (*kāmag*) for 'intense holy indigence' (*abēr driyōšīh*), with bare necessities of life, may render one righteous, provided (that) he does not look down on those who are not like him" (i.e., the well-to-do; *Dēnkard*, ed. Madan, p. 542). Such sincere longing for *driyōšīh* is regarded as a potent remedy for adverse circumstances and tribulations because it offers bodily comfort (**āsānīh ī tan*), freedom from fear (*abēbīmīh*), and redemption on the day of reckoning (*abēāmāragīh*?; *Dēnkard*, ed. Madan, pp. 579-80). "Many are (those) whose righteousness is owing to their abundance of wealth, and many whose wickedness (*druwandīh*) is because of their 'poverty'" (*driyōšīh*; *Dēnkard* 6.283, ed. Madan, p. 534; Shaked, pp. 110-11).

It is enjoined upon the *driyōš* to instruct the high-ranking (*mehān*) in the matters of the soul (*pad čiš ī ruwān*; *Dēnkard*, ed. Madan, p. 505; Shaked, pp. 58-59) and upon the nobility (*āzād-mardān*) and the opulent to hold the "worthy poor" in reverence (*burzišn*) and redress their grievances (*must wizārdan*; *Dēnkard* 6.146, ed. Madan, p. 505; Shaked, pp. 58-59). In any event they are enjoined to take upon themselves their advocacy (*driyōšān jādaggōwīh*; cf. *Dēnkard*, ed. Madan, p. 504; see DĀDWAR, DĀDWARĪH). The *driyōš* are promised salvation and deliverance from evil in the world to come, provided that they refrain from treating the upper classes and the wealthy with disrespect (*Dēnkard*, ed. Madan, p. 505; Shaked, pp. 58-59). Severe retribution is in store for those who turn a deaf ear to the complaints of the *driyōš* (*Arda-Wīrāz nāmag*; Gignoux, chap. 67), and paradise is promised to those who offer help to the worthy indigent (*arzānīgān*; *Arda-Wīrāz nāmag*; Gignoux, chap. 68).

The term *driyōš* was also used in the sense of "poor" (cf. *pad xrad driyōštar* "poorer in wisdom"; *Mēnōg ī Xrad*, chap. 57.22). In this sense it is applied to needy non-Zoroastrians and heretics, who are equally worthy to receive help and protection because liberality toward the poor drives away the demon of want (*niyāz*) from the world (*Dēnkard* 6.292, ed. Madan, p. 536; Shaked, pp. 112-13).

From all these pronouncements it is clear that the *driyōš* were a group within the learned clergy, a group whose members sought spiritual merit and salvation in self-imposed indigence, contentment, abstemiousness, diligence, and amicability toward high and low, a description that would fit as well the early Sufi dervishes of Islam, were it not for the absence of the components of asceticism and the monastic and hermetic life, which were characteristic of Islamic dervish orders.

The virtues attributed to holy poverty are illustrated by a few anecdotes in the *Dēnkard*. Typical is the story of two learned and pious priests (*hērbads*) who had chosen to live by their own manual labor, as befitting menials. They not only disdainfully refused the magnanimous gifts of the high priest but even admonished him for his merrymaking and life of luxury (*Dēnkard*, ed. Madan, pp. 569-70; Shaked, pp. 178-79; cf. Shaki, pp. 277-79). The mode of life of the hermit Ranj-spōz (he who rejects pain), who lived on wild fruit in a cave, seeking salvation in piety (*Dēnkard*, ed. Madan, pp. 574; Shaked, pp. 186-87), was, on the other hand, "un-Zoroastrian." It is evidently a fabrication based upon the life of Christian hermits who lived in holy dirt and extreme asceticism, a life totally alien to Zoroastrian precepts, in which every disregard of essential bodily wants is a deviation from the sanctified principle of the mean (*paymān*). In the *Dēnkard* (6.282, ed. Madan, pp. 534; Shaked, pp. 108-09) it is explicitly stated: "If the richest person knows how to use and keep (his property), no sin will accrue to him merely on account of his wealth, and if a most indigent person (*driyōštar mardōm*) does not know the proper way of using and keeping (his property), he may become 'worthy of death' (*margarzān*) through misappropriation of one single drahm."

It was in the social interest of the privileged classes to appease the dissatisfaction of the underprivileged, some of whom, like the *škōh* ("the recalcitrant poor"), stood in sharp contrast to *driyōš*, by excessive praise of the *driyōš*, stressing the merits of his meekness, contentment, and resignation to fate. The *škōh*, also unsatisfactorily translated "poor," is described in the *Dēnkard* (6.145, ed. Madan, pp. 505; Shaked, pp. 58-59) as "a person to whom the necessary means of subsistence is not enough and (who) is discontented on that account. He considers himself unfortunate, holds the opulent and reputable people in contempt, whereas he himself ceaselessly strives for high reputation and wealth" (see CLASSES iii).

Bibliography: K. Barr, "Avestan *drəgu-*, *driγu-*," in *Studia Orientalia Ioanni Pedersen . . .*, Copenhagen, 1953, pp. 21-40. P. Gignoux, tr., *Le livre d'Ardā Vīrāz*, Paris, 1984. K̲ᵛāja Šams-al-Dīn Moḥammad Ḥāfeẓ Šīrāzī, *Dīvān*, ed. M. Qazvīnī and Q. Ḡanī, Tehran, n.d. H. Lommel, "Awestisch Drigu. Vāstra und Verwandtes," in J. C. Heesterman, G. H. Schokker, and V. I. Subramoniam, eds., *Pratidānam. Indian, Iranian and Indo-European Studies Presented to F. B. J. Kuiper*, the Hague, 1968, pp. 127-30. J. de Menasce, "Le protecteur des pauvres dans l'Iran sassanide," in *Mélanges d'orientalisme offerts à H. Massé*, Tehran, 1342 Š./1963, pp. 284-85. S. Shaked, *The Wisdom of the Sasanian Sages (Denkard VI)*, Boulder, Colo., 1979, esp. pp. xxxviii-xxxix. M. Shaki, "The Fillet of Nobility," in C. A. Bromberg et al., eds., *Aspects of Iranian Culture in Honor of Richard Nelson Frye*, Bulletin of the Asia Institute, N.S. 4, 1990, pp. 277-79.

(MANSOUR SHAKI)

ii. IN THE ISLAMIC PERIOD

In the Islamic period the term *darvīš*, or dervish, has been variously applied to claimants to the virtue of spiritual poverty, that is, nonattachment, often in conjunction with deliberately chosen or passively accepted material poverty; adherents or practitioners of Sufism, especially its undisciplined or antinomian forms; and mendicants with pretensions to sanctity.

Proposed derivations of the term *darvīš* in folk etymology (e.g., < *dar-pīš* "in front of the door") and the notion that it is cognate with *daryūza* (mendicancy) were no doubt inspired by the practice among many dervishes of begging from door to door (*Borhān-e qāṭeʿ*, ed. Moʿīn, II, p. 846). There is, however, no essential connection between dervishhood and mendicancy; in fact, it is sometimes held that abstention from begging is the mark of a true dervish (see BEGGING ii). The Persian word *darvīš* originally meant simply an indigent person and carried no overtones of ascetic disdain for the world (Dehk̲odā, s.v.). It acquired specialized Sufi overtones through use as a translation for Arabic *faqīr* (poor), a word with connotations of ascetic detachment (see, e.g., Anṣārī, 1954, p. 68; Meybodī, VIII, p. 180; Ḡazālī, pp. 421-25; Hojvīrī, pp. 21-34), which, ironically, came to be reserved in Persian usage for the materially poor. All disquisitions on the virtues of spiritual poverty in early Persian Sufi literature may therefore safely be taken as referring to the dervish and his qualities, even if the words used are *faqīr* and *faqr*.

From the 11th century onward the word *darvīš* was used independently of *faqīr*. Abu'l-Ḥasan Ḵaraqānī (q.v.; d. 425/1034) characterized dervishhood as "an ocean fed from three sources: abstention (*parhīz*), generosity (*saḵāwat*), and freedom from need (*bī-nīāz būdan*)." Correcting the definition of a dervish simply as one who has no worldly goods, he observed that, instead, the dervish is "he whose heart is empty of cares; who speaks without awareness of speech; who hears without awareness of hearing; who eats without awareness of tasting; for whom motion and stillness are as one; and for whom grief and joy do not exist" (p. 110). For Ḵᵛāja ʿAbd-Allāh Anṣārī (q.v.; d. 481/1089) the dervish was one "who does not possess the slightest particle of being." On a certain level this description applies to all creatures, but it is only the one who is conscious of its truth who counts as a dervish. Furthermore, "the dervish is one who abandons both this world and the hereafter and does not even have any religion" (in the sense that the dervish has no selfhood, whereas religion presupposes the selfhood of its practitioner). "The dervish must reside nowhere and recognize nothing. . . . He annihilates his own existence in the existence of God; neither mankind nor self remains for him, neither the seeker nor the sought. Such is the attribute of the dervish" (1368 Š./1989, p. 137). Abū Esḥāq Hojvīrī (d. 465/1073) also tended to identify dervishhood with *fanāʾ* (effacement of separate existence in divine reality), describing the dervish as "a way, not a wayfarer; a place over which something is passing, not a wayfarer following his own will" (tr. pp. 28-29). Abū Saʿīd b. Abi'l-Ḵayr (q.v.; d. 440/1049) echoed this view in a pun suggesting at the same time that dervishes are mediators between man and God: "The dervishes are not they, for if they existed, they would not be dervishes. In their name is their attribute; whoever seeks a path to God must pass by the dervishes, for they are the gate to Him (*dar-e vey īšān-and*; Moḥammad b. Monawwar, I, p. 295).

At the same time that these rarefied descriptions were proliferating, the dervish was becoming increasingly recognizable by his accouterments, above all his cloak; already in the time of Anṣārī it was thought necessary to warn against reliance on externals: "The cloak of the dervish is indeed most precious, but who is truly worthy of it?" (1982, p. 70). Moreover, although the term *darvīš* continued to designate the spiritual ideal to be attained by an individual, dervishes tended to become a category distinct from adherents of the Sufi orders in general and recognizable by their ceaseless traveling, frequent indulgence in mendicancy, and avoidance of social intercourse. In addition to the cloak as outward sign of his state, the *darvīš* therefore gradually added items connected with the needs of the journey, some of them specific to individual orders (Wāʾeẓ Kāšefī). Most typical and significant was the *kaškūl* (q.v.), a begging bowl fashioned of such materials as mother-of-pearl, a gourd, a coconut shell, or carved wood, with an attached chain permitting the *darvīš* to carry it suspended from his wrist. Later examples were often elliptical in shape (Melikian-Chirvani). A further part of the *darvīš*'s equipment was the *nafīr*, or *būq*, a trumpet made from the horn of a ram or deer. Also typical was a hat (q.v.), usually of felt (sometimes called *kōlah-e faqr* "hat of poverty"). On the brim verses in praise of ʿAlī or other inscriptions were sometimes embroidered; one common incription was the Persian verse "There are three denunciations in the hat of poverty: denunciation of this world, denunciation of the hereafter, and denunciation of denunciation." Other characteristic accouterments included the *tabarzīn* (q.v.), a short ax or hatchet carried in the right hand and intended to fend off wild animals or highway robbers; the *čanta*, a patched bag in which essential items were carried slung over the left shoulder; a gnarled staff (*mantešā* or *ʿaṣā*); an animal skin known as *taḵt-e pūst* (Ereshefsky, pp. 49-50); and sometimes a long rosary made of *bang* (q.v.) or other material. The *darvīš* might also carry his own tent (*čādor-e qalantarī*) consisting of simple patches of cloth stitched together; it was used not only while traveling but also when holding a vigil at the tomb of a Sufi.

All these items gradually took on ritual significance and in later centuries were affected even by urban or settled dervishes. As a result of such developments, there came to be some similarity between the *darvīš* and the more radically antinomian *qalandar*; though the *darvīš* might engage in regular Islamic devotions and would, at least in principle, beg only from need, the *qalandar* begged as a matter of course. The gradual approximation between the two cannot be dated with any precision, but it seems to have been well underway by the time of the Mongol invasion in the 13th century. The vast social and demographic dislocations resulting from this invasion favored the further dissemination of antinomian forms of religion (Köprülü, p. 160).

Despite this apparent devaluation of the term *darvīš*, perhaps akin to that of the term *malāmatī* (blameworthy), dervishes were lavishly praised by the great literary figures of the 13th and 14th centuries. Noteworthy, for example, is a *qaṣīda* of Saʿdī, in which he described the face of the dervish as "a mirror in which the light of truth is to be seen" and declared that dervishes "see truth, speak truth, and seek truth;/ Whatever enters their omniscient hearts is truth" (pp. 112-13; cf. Rūmī, III, p. 279, VIII, p. 126). Ḥāfez also found dervishes admirable, in sharp contrast to the Sufis, whom he appears to have regarded as hypocrites and formalists (Ḵorramšāhī, pp. 138-39). In one *ḡazal* he echoed Saʿdī's encomium, describing the intimate company of dervishes as "the loftiest garden of immortality . . . the alchemy that turns blackened hearts to gold" and the dust at the doors of their cells as the source of the water of life (pp. 35-36).

In Sufi hagiography, historical tradition, and literature in general dervishhood and kingship were contrasted as opposite poles of the human condition and parallels between them frequently drawn. The theme perhaps originated with the story of the semilegendary Ebrāhīm b. Adham (d. 160/776 or 173/790), supposedly the scion of a royal family in Balḵ who relinquished power and wealth to become a dervish. It recurred with particular frequency in the Mongol and Timurid periods, when political vicissitudes revealed the hollowness of worldly power and suggested that a dervish might enjoy higher status than a king. Saʿdī said "Were they to desire kingship, /they could plunder the realm of all kings" (pp. 112-13), and Ḥāfeẓ remarked "The good fortune (*dawlat*) that is immune to harm and eclipse—hear it plainly from me!—is that of the dervishes" (p. 35).

By means of this inversion, the dervish became not only the possessor of true kingship and thus the superior of the king but even his patron and protector. Thus Tīmūr was said to have owed his early conquests in Khorasan to the benedictions of a dervish, Bābā Sankū (q.v.), and in legend he was connected with a whole series of other dervishes (Paul, pp. 296-319). Sufis of the Naqšbandī order were able to establish a measure of influence over descendants of Tīmūr; for example, Ḵᵛāja ʿObayd-Allāh Aḥrār (q.v.; d. 896/1490) played a decisive role in the reigns of Sultan Abū Saʿīd (855-73/1451-69) and Sultan Aḥmad (873-99/1469-94). There were also close links between dervishes and kings in post-Timurid Central Asia; a particularly striking example is that of Maʿṣūm Shah Morād (1200-15/1785-1800), the "dervish king" of Bukhara, and his son Amīr Ḥaydar (1215-42/1800-26; Sāmī, pp. 50-52).

It was, however, the Neʿmat-Allāhī order that led the way in making explicit the kingly nature of the dervish calling. The earliest designation of the dervish headgear as *tāj* (crown) was probably owed to Shah Neʿmat-Allāh Walī himself (pp. 160-66), perhaps echoing a Hadith to the effect that the turban is the crown of the Arabs (see ʿAMĀMA). It subsequently became universal, both in Persia and in Ottoman Turkey (see Menzel, pp. 174-99). Neʿmat-Allāh Walī and Sufis of his line were also the first to deal imperiously with monarchs (Farzām, passim) and consistently to include "shah" in their Sufi names (often combined, it is true, with ʿAlī, who was in popular tradition called *šāh-e mardān* "the king of true men").

In view of these various connections between dervishhood and kingship, it is not surprising that the Safavids accomplished the full transition from Sufism to monarchy and then proceeded to eliminate almost all the Sufi orders in Persia, first those of Sunni affiliation and then those with Shiʿite loyalties. As individual or loosely organized practitioners of popular or antinomian religion, dervishes remained fixtures of the religious scene, however. In the 17th century Jean Chardin estimated that there were roughly 20,000 dervishes. He reported, too, that the term *darvīš*, though a generic designation for anyone who chose poverty and detachment from the world, embraced many types of individual wearing a variety of unconventional garbs. Certain distinctions were still made between the *darvīš* and the *qalandar*; the former, it was held, might be genuinely devout and dressed mostly in faded and filthy rags, whereas the latter was universally considered an impostor, recognizable by his brightly colored and outlandish costume and fondness for feathers and animal skins. Despite the essentially solitary nature of dervishhood, there were places in Isfahan where dervishes congregated, notably an ancient plane tree in the cemetery at Emāmzāda Esmāʿīl (q.v.) and a hospice near Masjed-e Masʿūd Beg (Maqṣūd Beg?), where they could rest from their wanderings (pp. 37-38, 209-10).

Organized Sufism reemerged in Persia toward the close of the 18th century, when the Neʿmat-Allāhī order was reintroduced from its base in the Deccan. The earliest leaders, Maʿṣūm-ʿAlīšāh (d. 1212/1797; see DAKANĪ, ʿABD-AL-ḤAMĪD) and his disciple Nūr-ʿAlīšāh (d. 1212/1797), were men of ecstatic and antinomian temperament, and it may be for this reason that they and their initiatic descendants were called dervishes. This designation persisted even after the Neʿmat-Allāhīs had adopted soberer forms and become well integrated into Persian society; it applied to the adherents of such other orders as the Ḏahabīya (q.v.) as well, eventually coming to mean virtually every practitioner of Sufism. The outward appurtenances of traditional dervishhood were nonetheless retained for purely ceremonial and ritual purposes, as is evident from photographs showing the ladies of the Qajar court, initiates of the Ṣafī-ʿAlīšāh branch of the Neʿmat-Allāhīya, wearing the Neʿmat-Allāhī *tāj* and brandishing the *kaškūl* and *tabarzīn* (Modarresī Čahārdehī, pl. 13). The traditional type of unaffiliated wandering dervish continued to exist side by side with the members of the orders, as is plain from Edward Browne's account of his meeting with one of them (pp. 56-61), but even those unorganized dervishes gradually coalesced into something approaching an order, the Ḵāksārīya, which has continued to exist on the fringes of Persian society down to the present, albeit in steadily dwindling numbers.

It may be noted, too, that the members of various heterodox groups in Persia having little or no connection with any form of Sufism have also been designated *darvīš*, for example, the Ḥorūfīs, their successors the Noqṭawīs, and the Ahl-e Ḥaqq of Kurdistan. Another specialized use of the word *darvīš*, encountered in Kurdistan, is in reference to members of the Qāderī order, whereas Naqšbandīs are known as Sufis (Tawakkolī, pp. 169, 225).

The place held by the dervish in Persian culture and folklore can be gauged from the numerous proverbs and idioms in which he is mentioned; the same is true, to a somewhat lesser degree, of Turkish proverbs and popular sayings (Dehkodā, p. 800; Kadri, pp. 730-31; Gölpınarlı, pp. 89-90). In fact the word *darvīš* has entered an extraordinarily wide variety of languages. In Arabic there are also a broken plural *darāwīš* and the form *darwaša*, "to become a dervish or don the garb of a dervish" (Dozy, I, p. 438). In Ottoman Turkish it always designated the adherent of a Sufi order (Pakalın, p. 428; Uludağ, pp. 136-07). In Malay-Indonesian the loanword *darwis* (also sometimes *darwisy*) refers not only to Sufis but also to Buddhist bhikkus, presumably reflecting an Indian usage (Bausani, p. 357). In Chinese there are two forms, *dieli weishi* and *dieleweishi*, the latter used especially by Qāderīs (Gladney, p. 399). The English "dervish," as well as corresponding terms in other European languages, was clearly taken from Turkish, as it is spelled with an "e" rather than an "a" in the first syllable. Western travelers to Turkey also coined the mocking designations "whirling dervishes" and "howling dervishes," referring to adherents of the Mawlawī and Refāʾī orders respectively.

Bibliography: K̲ᵛāja ʿAbd-Allāh Anṣārī, *Ketāb-e ṣad meydān*, ed. S. de Beaurecueil, Cairo, 1954. Idem, *Sok̲anān-e Pīr-e Herāt*, ed. M. J. Šarīʿat, Tehran, 1361 Š./1982. Idem, *Rasāʾel-e K̲ᵛāja ʿAbd-Allāh Anṣārī*, 5th ed., ed. Ḥ. Waḥīd Dastgerdī, Tehran, 1368 Š./1989. H. W. Bailey, "To the Zamasp-Namak," in *Opera Minora*, ed. M. Nawabi, 2 vols., Shiraz, 1981. A. Bausani, "Notes sur les mots persans en malayo-indonésien," *Acta Iranica* 2, Leiden, 1974, pp. 347-79. J. P. Brown, *The Darvishes, or Oriental Spiritualism*, 2nd ed., ed. H. A. Rose, London, 1927; repr. London, 1968. E. G. Browne, *A Year amongst the Persians*, London, 1893. D. Ćehajić, *Derviški redovi u jugoslovenskim zemljama*, Sarajevo, 1986. J. Chardin, *Voyages de Monsieur le Chevalier Chardin en Perse et autres lieux de l'orient* III, Amsterdam, 1711. ʿA.-A. Dehk̲odā, *Amt̲āl o ḥekam*, 6th ed., II, Tehran, 1343 Š./1964. R. Dozy, *Supplément aux dictionnaires arabes*, repr. Beirut, 1968. M. Ereshefsky, "Animal Skin Prayer Rugs," in J. L. Bacharach and I. A. Bierman, eds., *The Warp and Weft of Islam. Oriental Carpets and Weavings from Pacific Northwest Collections*, n.p. (Seattle, Wash.), 1978, pp. 47-52. Ḥ. Farzām, *Rawābeṭ-e maʿnawī-e Šāh Neʿmat-Allāh Walī bā salāṭīn-e Īrān wa Hend*, Isfahan, 1351 Š./1972. Abū Ḥāmed Ḡazālī, *Kīmīā-ye saʿādat* II, ed. Ḥ. K̲adīv Jam, Tehran, 1361 Š./1982. D. C. Gladney, *Muslim Chinese. Ethnic Nationalism in the People's Republic*, Cambridge, Mass., 1991. A. Gölpınarlı, *Tasavvuf'tan dilimize geçen deyimler ve atasözleri*, Istanbul, 1977. R. Gramlich, *Die schiitischen Derwischorden Persiens*, AKM 36/1-4, 1965; 45/2, 1981. K̲ᵛāja Šams-al-Dīn Moḥammad Ḥāfeẓ Šīrāzī, *Dīvān*, ed. M. Qazvīnī and Q. Ḡanī, Tehran, n.d. Abu'l-Ḥasan ʿAlī Hojvīrī, *Kašf al-maḥjūb*, ed. V. Zhukovskii, Leningrad, 1926; tr. R. A. Nicholson as *The Kashf al-Maḥjūb*, London, 1911. G. Jarring, *Dervish and Qalandar. Texts from Kashghar*, Scripta Minora 2, Lund, 1985-86. H. K. Kadri, *Türk Lugatı* II, Istanbul, 1928. Abu'l-Ḥasan K̲araqānī, *Aḥwāl wa aqwāl-e Šayk̲ Abu'l-Ḥasan K̲araqānī*, ed. M. Mīnovī, Tehran, 1354 Š./1975. F. Köprülü, *Türk edebiyatında ilk mutasavvıflar*, Ankara, 1966. B. K̲orramšāhī, *Ḥāfeẓ-nāma* I, Tehran, 1366 Š./1987. R. Lifchez, ed., *The Dervish Lodge*, Berkeley and Los Angeles, 1992. D. B. Macdonald, "Darwīs̲h̲," in *EI²* II, pp. 164-65. A. S. Melikian Chirvani, "From the Royal Boat to the Beggar's Bowl," *Islamic Art* 4, 1990-91, pp. 3-111. T. Menzel, "Beiträge zur Kenntnis des Derwisch-Tāğ," in T. Menzel, ed., *Festschrift für Georg Jacob zum siebzigsten Geburtstag*, Leipzig, 1932, pp. 174-99. Abu'l-Fażl Rašīd-al-Dīn Meybodī, *Kašf al-asrār*, 3rd ed., 10 vols, ed. ʿA.-A. Ḥekmat, Tehran, 1361 Š./1982. M. Modarresī Čahārdehī, *Sayr-ī dar taṣawwof*, Tehran, 1361 Š./1982. Moḥammad b. Monawwar, *Asrār al-tawḥīd*, ed. M.-R. Šafīʿī Kadkanī, 2 vols., Tehran, 1366 Š./1987. Z. Muzaffari, *İşannar-Därvişlär*, Kazan, 1931. Shah Neʿmat-Allāh Walī, *Rasāʾel-e Hażrat-e Sayyed Nūr-al-Dīn Šāh Neʿmat-Allāh Walī* I, ed. J. Nūrbak̲š, Tehran, 2535=1355 Š./ 1976. M. Z. Pakalın, *Osmanlı tarih deyimleri ve terimleri sözlüğü* I, Istanbul, 1971. J. Paul, "Scheiche und Herrscher im Khanat Čağatay," *Der Islam* 67/2, 1990, pp. 278-321. M. Qandīl Baqlī, *Adab al-darāwīš*, Cairo, 1970. Jalāl-al-Dīn Rūmī, *Mat̲nawī*, ed. and tr. R. A. Nicholson as *The Mathnawí of Jalálu'ddín Rúmí*, 8 vols., Leiden, 1925-40. Saʿdī, *Qaṣāʾed wa ḡazalīyāt-e ʿerfānī*, ed. M.-ʿA. Forūḡī, Tehran, 1342 Š./1963. Mīrzā ʿAbd-al-ʿAẓīm Sāmī, *Tārīk̲-e salāṭīn-e Manḡītīya*, ed. L. M. Epifanova, Moscow, 1962. M.-R. Tawakkolī, *Tārīk̲-e taṣawwof dar Kordestān*, Tehran, n.d. S. Uludağ, *Tasavvuf terimleri sözlüğü*, Istanbul, 1991. Ḥosayn Wāʿeẓ Kāšefī Sabzavārī, *Fotowwat-nāma-ye solṭānī*, ed. M.-J. Maḥjūb, Tehran, 1350 Š./1971.

(HAMID ALGAR)

DARVĪŠ, ʿABD-AL-MAJĪD ṬĀLAQĀNĪ. See ʿABD-AL-MAJĪD ṬĀLAQĀNĪ.

DARVĪŠ AḤMAD QĀBEŻ (d. 912/1507), Timurid vizier. From the position of a lowly functionary charged with the task of writing out receipts (*qabż*; hence his nickname Qābeż) in the *dīvān* of the Timurid Solṭān-Ḥosayn Bāyqarā (q.v. Supplement; 873-911/1469-1506) he rose to the rank of *amīr tūmān* (commander of 10,000). In 911/1505-06 he was arrested after accusing Ṣāyen-al-Dīn ʿAlī, keeper of the seal (*mohrdār*) in the *dīvān*, of embezzlement. He was soon released, however, owing to the intervention of the chief amir, Moḥammad-e Walī Beg, who had Ṣāyen-al-Dīn arrested and replaced by Darvīš Aḥmad. After Solṭān-Ḥosayn's death in 911/1506 Darvīš Aḥmad became vizier for his son Moẓaffar Ḥosayn Mīrzā, who ruled jointly with his elder brother, Badīʿ-al-Zamān Mīrzā, in Herat. Darvīš Aḥmad's short term as vizier came to an end in April 1507, when he was killed as the result of a dispute during a drinking party at the home of Amir Yūsof ʿAlī Kükältāš, governor of Herat. Darvīš Aḥmad, a thoroughly corrupt official, was said to have brought many families to ruin by his shameless oppression and exploitation of the population. His death caused rejoicing in the streets. Fearing that the people of Herat might attack the bier if he were accorded a public burial, the governor ordered his body buried secretly in an unmarked grave outside the city.

Bibliography: Ḡīāṯ-al-Dīn Ḵᵛāndamīr, *Dastūr al-wozarāʾ*, ed. S. Nafīsī, Tehran, 1317 Š./1938, pp. 453-56. Idem, *Ḥabīb al-sīar* IV, p. 365 (read Qābeż for Fāyeż).

(M. E. SUBTELNY)

DARVĪŠ ʿALĪ BŪZJĀNĪ. See BŪZJĀNĪ.

DARVĪŠ ʿALĪ, AMĪR NEẒĀM-AL-DĪN **KÜKÄLTĀŠ** KETĀBDĀR, Timurid amir under Solṭān-Ḥosayn Bāyqarā (q.v., Supplement; 873-911/1469-1506) and younger brother of ʿAlī-Šīr Navāʾī (*Bābor-nāma*, fol. 173a). The brothers belonged to an Uighur family that had been affiliated for generations with Solṭān-Ḥosayn's family by ties of foster brotherhood; hence his title Kükältāš (foster brother; Bartol'd, p. 212; Ando, p. 248). During his career Darvīš ʿAlī served as governor of Qom under Abu'l-Qāsem Bābor (853-91/1449-57); after Solṭān-Ḥosayn's conquest of Khorasan in 873/1469 he became state treasurer (*parvānačī*) and later governor of Balḵ in the domain of Solṭān-Ḥosayn's son Mīrzā Ebrāhīm Ḥosayn, as well as royal librarian (*ketābdār*; *Ḥabīb al-sīar* IV, pp. 46, 189; Ando, p. 198). According to the Mughal emperor Bābor (932-37/1526-30), who did not entertain a very high opinion of him, he held these positions largely as a result of ʿAlī-Šīr's influence (*Bābor-nāma*, fol. 173a). Darvīš ʿAlī was married to Āfāq Bīke, a poet and sister of Ḥasan-ʿAlī Jalāyer, one of Solṭān-Ḥosayn's chief amirs (Faḵrī Heravī, p. 129).

Darvīš ʿAlī became involved in his brother's opposition to attempts by the Persian official Majd-al-Dīn Moḥammad to institute centralizing reforms in the Timurid state, especially during the period 892-95/1487-90 (Subtelny, pp. 131 ff.). Fearing for his own position in Balḵ, he mobilized the amirs in a revolt against the sultan, and, making common cause with Solṭān-Ḥosayn's Timurid rival, Solṭān-Maḥmūd Mīrzā, he attempted to oust Mīrzā Ebrāhīm Ḥosayn from Balḵ. Although he was pardoned after the intercession of one of ʿAlī-Šīr's friends, the sultan no longer trusted him, and, when he set out on campaign against Solṭān-Maḥmūd Mīrzā, he imprisoned Darvīš ʿAlī in the fortress of Balḵ. In 899/1494 Darvīš ʿAlī made the pilgrimage to Mecca, and after he returned four years later he was again reinstated, in 904/1498, as amir of the *dīvān-e aʿlā* (*Ḥabīb al-sīar* IV, pp. 188-90, 198, 238; Ando, p. 209).

After ʿAlī-Šīr's death in 906/1501 Darvīš ʿAlī was dismissed from Timurid service and retired to the village of Fayżābād outside Balḵ, which he held free of tax (*Ḥabīb al-sīar* IV, p. 298; ʿAbd-Allāh Morvārīd, pp. 79-80). The Uzbek Moḥammad Šaybānī Khan used him as an envoy in his unsuccessful attempt to negotiate the surrender of Balḵ in 909/1503-04 (*Ḥabīb al-sīar* IV, pp. 298-99). After the death of Moḥammad Šaybānī Khan in 916/1510 Darvīš ʿAlī entered the service of Bābor, himself a member of the Timurid family, in Qondūz; he appears to have been still in Bābor's service when the latter captured Samarkand in the following year (*Bābor-nāma*, fol. 174b). It is not known when he died.

Bibliography: ʿAbd-Allāh Morvārīd, *Šaraf-nāma*, facs. ed. and tr. H. R. Roemer as *Staatsschreiben der Timuridenzeit*, Wiesbaden, 1952. S. Ando, *Timuridische Emire nach dem Muʿizz al-ansāb*, Berlin, 1992. V. V. Bartol'd, "Mir Ali-Shir i politicheskaya zhizn'" (Mīr ʿAlī Šīr and political life), *Sochineniya* (Collected works) II/2, Moscow, 1964, esp. pp. 237-46. Solṭān-Moḥammad Faḵrī Heravī, *Taḏkera-ye jawāher al-ʿajāyeb*, ed. Ḥ. Rāšedī, Hyderabad, 1968. M. E. Subtelny, "Centralizing Reform and Its Opponents in the Late Timurid Period," *Iranian Studies* 21/1-2, 1988, esp. pp. 123-51.

(M. E. SUBTELNY)

DARVĪŠ KHAN, ḠOLĀM-ḤOSAYN (b. Tehran, 1289/1872, d. Tehran, 2 Āḏar 1305 Š./23 November 1926), master musician, renowned teacher, and innovative composer of Persian classical music. He was a transitional figure, both a guardian of tradition and an innovator, introducing changes in style of performance, composition, and construction of instruments.

Ḡolām-Ḥosayn's father, Ḥājī Bašīr Ṭālaqānī, was a postal official and an amateur musician; it was he who first called his son Darvīš, apparently a habit of his. The boy was enrolled in the band at Dār al-Fonūn (q.v.), directed by the Frenchman Alfred Lemaire (Mallāḥ, 1333 Š./1954, p. 68). There he learned to play trumpet and drum; he also played the drum in a children's band formed for the young ʿAzīz-al-Solṭān (q.v.), a favorite of Nāṣer-al-Dīn Shah (1264-1313/1848-96). He became interested in the *setār* and received his first lessons from his father, later studying the *tār* with the master Āqā Ḥosaynqolī, whose best student he is considered to have been (Ḵāleqī, pp. 300-03).

Darvīš Khan was introduced to Prince Šoʿāʿ-al-Salṭana, a son of Moẓaffar-al-Dīn Shah (1313-24/1896-1907), by Kamāl-al-Salṭana, father of his own later student Abu'l-Ḥasan Ṣabā (q.v.). One night Āqā Ḥosaynqolī was playing for the prince and, after starting a particular *dastgāh* (q.v.), asked permission for his pupil Darvīš Khan to finish it. The prince was so impressed with the performance that he invited Darvīš Khan to join his retinue of musicians, which also included Nāyeb Asad-Allāh and Āqā Jān (Mallāḥ, 1333 Š./1954, p. 70). After several months the prince was sent to Shiraz, taking his musicians with him. There Darvīš Khan married Nowrasīda, daughter of Badr-al-Salṭana, a military adviser, and eventually they had a daughter named Qamar (Mallāḥ, 1333 Š./1954, p. 71; Ḵāleqī, p. 303). After his marriage Darvīš Khan began to supplement his income by playing at the parties of local princes. Šoʿāʿ-al-Salṭana became angry and ordered his fingers severed, but Kamāl-al-Salṭana interceded to prevent this misfortune.

After returning to Tehran Darvīš Khan started a small music class. He also asked other princes to help free him from his commitment to Šoʿāʿ-al-Salṭana (Mallāḥ, 1333 Š./1954, p. 71). The infuriated prince sent a servant to summon Darvīš Khan to his presence. The latter asked the servant to wait while he changed his clothes, then escaped through the back entrance and sought refuge with ʿAbbāsqolī Khan, chief custodian of the British embassy. After Darvīš Khan had explained his predicament and played a European piece on the *tār* for the ambassador's wife, the ambassador wrote to the prince, asking him to free Darvīš Khan from his commitment, which the prince agreed to do (Ḵāleqī, pp. 303-05)

Darvīš Khan expanded his music classes and continued to play at private gatherings, one of which was described by the poet ʿĀref Qazvīnī in his *Dīvān* (pp. 128-32). He joined the Sufi order Anjoman-e oḵowwat (q.v.), led by Mīrzā ʿAlī Khan Ẓahīr-al-Dawla, and became director of its orchestra. Ẓahīr-al-Dawla encouraged musical performances, and in 1324/1906 the society sponsored what is considered to have been the first public concert in Persia. It was held in a garden on the outskirts of Tehran and reportedly lasted twenty-four hours (Zonis, p. 144). Darvīš Khan also gave concerts in the hall of the Grand Hotel (Gerānd Hotel).

Traditional performance of a *dastgāh* usually began with a nonmetric *āvāz* or a *čahārmeżrāb* (qq.v.), an improvised instrumental solo. Musical ensembles were small, and solo instrumentalists took turns playing alone or accompanying a singer; in the *taṣnīf* (rhythmic song) and *reng* (a classical dance form) they might also play as an ensemble at the end of the *dastgāh*. The classical *radīf* (repertoire) itself included only a few metric pieces, most of them short. The influence of Western music, with its large orchestras and concert format, was growing in Persia, however. Musicians like Darvīš Khan organized larger orchestras, which encouraged the composition of more ensemble pieces. At one concert rehearsal of the Anjoman orchestra the composer Rokn-al-Dīn Khan Moḵtār introduced a new, metric opening piece. As it came before the *darāmad* (q.v.), it was called *pīšdarāmad* (prelude). Both Moḵtār and Darvīš Khan composed many *pīšdarāmad*s, and Darvīš Khan is credited with having popularized them both through perfomance and through teaching them to his students. Although at first the *pīšdarāmad* was a short piece based on the *darāmad*, Darvīš Khan expanded it to include sections in the major *gūša*s of the *dastgāh*. His *pīšdarāmad*s are known for their variety of rhythm and melody (Mallāḥ, 1337-38 Š./1958-59, 16, p. 22; Khāleqī, pp. 309-13).

At some unknown time Āqā Ḥosaynqolī was invited by His Master's Voice to bring an orchestra to London to record traditional Persian music. Apparently because of the growing popularity of the *pīšdarāmad*, however, these more old-fashioned recordings sold badly in the Persian market (Mallāḥ, 1333 Š./1954, pp. 74-75). Later Darvīš Khan himself made two recording trips with another group of musicians, one to London and one to Tiflis in 1332/1914.

Darvīš Khan was an open and generous teacher. He addressed everyone by a single phrase, "Yā Pīr Jān," which became one of his own nicknames. Both Darvīš and Pīr Jān were appropriate to his association with the Sufis; he used to present his graduating students with the emblem of the Anjoman, two crossed hatchets (*tabarzīn*) and a begging bowl (*kaškūl*), in copper, silver, or gold, depending on the level reached (Maḥmūdī, p. 12). His classes were organized according to three levels of the *radīf*; completion of all three took approximately ten years. Students came twice a week to classes organized according to difficulty. Each had an individual lesson while the others waited and listened in the next room (Nettl, 1974, p. 168). Only about twenty students ever completed the full course and received the gold medal (Maḥmūdī, p. 12). The most talented included Abu'l-Ḥasan Ṣabā, Mūsā Maʿrūfī, Mortażā Ney Dāwūd, Ḥosaynqolī Ġaffārī, Šokr-Allāh (Šokrī), ʿAlī-Moḥammad Ṣafāʾī, ʿAbd-Allāh Dādvar, Ḥosayn Sanjarī, and Arsalān Dargāhī (Khāleqī, pp. 430-42).

Darvīš Khan's own playing on *tār* and *setār* was considered both technically masterly and artistically warm and melodious. The variety he introduced in his performance style is attributed to the European tunes he played on the *tār* (Mallāḥ, 1337-38 Š./1958-59, 22, p. 22), to which he added a sixth string, just before the lowest, doubling the low C string. In this innovation he followed Moštāq-ʿAlīšāh, who had added a resonating string to the *setār*. Both strings are thus known as *sīm-e moštāq* (Caron and Safvate, pp. 166-68).

Darvīš Khan's twenty-four compositions, particularly his *reng*s, are considered among the finest works of his time (Khāleqī, p. 322). They are characterized by variety in both melody and rhythm. He particularly popularized the 2/4 meter in Persian music (Mallāḥ, 1337-38 Š./1958-59, 23, p. 22; for a list of his compositions, see Khāleqī, pp. 312-17).

Darvīš Khan died in 1305 Š./1926 as the result of a collision between a carriage and an automobile. He was a quiet and sensitive person, a great lover of flowers, known not only for hospitality to his friends but also for generosity to the needy, though he himself never had a substantial income. He organized benefit concerts for the poor, orphaned, and victims of fire or famine. His influence on the development of Persian music in the 20th century can be seen in the number, variety, and length of rhythmic pieces, as well as in larger orchestras and the expansion of the audience to include many levels of society. Contrary to the custom of his time, he functioned as an independent musician and paved the way for other musicians to perform with freedom and respect.

Bibliography: A. ʿĀref Qazvīnī, *Kollīāt-e Dīvān-e ʿĀref Qazvīnī*, Tehran, 1347 Š./1968, pp. 128-32, 611-15. Š. Behrūzī, *Čehrahā-ye mūsīqī-e Īrān* I, 2nd ed., Tehran, 1372 Š./1993, pp. 62-64. N. Caron and D. Safvate, *Les traditions musicales. Iran*, Berlin, 1966, pp. 146-49, 166-68. R. Ḵāleqī, *Sargoḏašt-e mūsīqī-e Īrān* I, Tehran, 1333 Š./1954. M. Maḥmūdī, "'Darvīš Ḵān,' ḵāleq-e pīšdarāmad," *Rastāḵīz*, 23 Mordād 2536=1356 Š./14 August 1977, p. 12. Ḥ.-ʿA. Mallāḥ, "Ḡolām-Ḥosayn Darvīš," *Payām-e now* 7/1, 1333 Š./1954, pp. 68-77. Idem, "Ḡolām-Ḥosayn Darvīš," *Majalla-ye mūsīqī* 3/10-11, 1336 Š./1957. Idem, "Sargoḏašt-e Darvīš," *Majalla-ye mūsīqī-e Rādīō Īrān* 15-23, Farvardīn 1337-Āḏar 1338 Š./April 1958-December 1959. B. Nettl, "Nour-Ali Boroumand, a Twentieth Century Master of Persian Music," *Studia Instrumentorum Musicae Popularis* 3, 1974, pp. 167-71. Idem, "Persian Classical Music in Tehran. The Processes of Change," in B. Nettl, ed., *Eight Urban Musical Cultures*, Urbana, Ill., 1978, pp. 146-85. D. Ṣafwat, *Ostādān-e mūsīqī-e Īrān wa alḥān-e mūsīqī-e Īrān*, Tehran, 1350 Š./1971, p. 57. S. Sepantā, *Čašmandāz-e mūsīqī-e Īrān*, Tehran, 1369 Š./1990, pp. 109-21. E. Zonis, *Classical Persian Music. An Introduction*, Cambridge, Mass., 1973, pp. 144, 157, 192.

(MARGARET CATON)

DARVĪŠ REŻĀ (d. 1040/1631), a *qezelbāš* functionary who claimed to be the awaited Mahdī. It is reported in the Safavid chronicles that, in order to gain credibility, he falsely claimed to be an Afšār (Eṣfahānī, p. 118; Wāleh, fols. 43b-44a). At the siege of Yerevan (November 1603-June 1604) he deserted the army, embarked upon a spiritual journey into the Ottoman empire, and spent some time at Anṭākīya, where he was said to have "learned about the occult sciences and magic" (Wāleh, fol. 44a). Darvīš Reżā's official post as *rekābdār* (lit., "stirrup bearer") to the governor of Hamadān required him to participate on the battlefield, an arena in which the *qezelbāš* traditionally had complete control before the incorporation of the *ḡolām*s in to the military under ʿAbbās I (q.v.; 1038/1629). The army at the siege of Yerevan incorporated *ḡolām* troops, and Darvīš ʿAlī's desertion may have been a protest against what he saw as the intrusion of *ḡolām*s into an arena that was the source of much of *qezelbāš* honor, political power, and financial well-being (Chardin, V, p. 228). It is not certain for how long he traveled, but eventually he settled in Kāfūrābād, a village near Qazvīn, probably before the death of Shah ʿAbbās I. There he attracted followers and amassed great wealth through gifts that he received from all parts of the empire (Eṣfahānī, p. 119; Wāleh, fol. 44a). According to Eskandar Beg (1317 Š./1938, p. 84), the governor (*dārūḡa*) and other functionaries of Qazvīn considered Darvīš Reżā a man of God, though, once he had revealed his mahdist ambitions, Eskandar Beg himself characterized him as a heretic.

On 16 Ḏu'l-ḥejja 1040/16 July 1631 Darvīš Reżā rose in rebellion and, surrounded by armed followers, marched from Kāfūrābād to the house of the governor of Qazvīn, Šāhverdī Beg Torkamān, who was ordered to submit to the authority of the Mahdī; Darvīš Reżā thus made public his claim to this role. When the governor refused, the rebels took sanctuary around the tomb of Mīr Faḡfūr (14th century) in the shrine of Šāhzāda Ḥosayn. His disciples declared that their *pīšvā* (example) would bring Faḡfūr back to life (Wāleh, fol. 45a).

The refugees in the shrine were eventually defeated by force; Darvīš Reżā was killed, and his head, along with those of several others, was sent to the shah in Isfahan; it was exhibited in Naqš-e Jahān square there. Eight years later (1049/1639), however, a man claimed to be Darvīš Reżā, who had supposedly never died (Eskandar Beg, pp. 83-85, 240; Eṣfahānī, pp. 119-21; Wāleh, fol. 45a-b; Qazvīnī, p. 59).

Bibliography: Bījan, *Tārīḵ-e jolūs-e Šāh Ṣafī*, British Museum ms. Add. 7655, fol. 30a-b. Moḥammad Maʿṣūm b. Ḵᵛājagī Eṣfahānī, *Ḵolāṣat al-sīar*, Tehran, 1368 Š./1989, pp. 117-22. Sayyed Ḥosayn b. Mortażā Ḥosaynī Astarābādī (Estarābādī), *Tārīḵ-e solṭānī*, ed. E. Ešrāqī, Tehran, 1364 Š./1985. Eskandar Beg Torkamān, *Ḏayl-e tārīḵ-e ʿālam ārā-ye ʿabbāsī*, ed. A. Sohaylī Ḵᵛānsārī, Tehran, 1317 Š./1938. Abu'l-Ḥasan Qazvīnī, *Fawāyed al-ṣafawīya*, ed. M. Mīr-Aḥmadī, Tehran, 1367 Š./1988, pp. 52, 59. Moḥammad-Yūsof Wāleh Eṣfahānī, *Ḵold-e barīn*, British Museum ms. Or. 4132.

(KATHRYN BABAYAN)

DARYĀ (OPers. *drayah-*, Mid. Pers. *drayā*, Av. *zrayah-*; sea, river) in Iranian culture. The role of the sea in Iranian culture evolved through a clearly discernible series of historical phases. In this article an attempt has been made to extrapolate those phases from basic information published in articles on the Black Sea, the Caspian (qq.v.), and the Persian Gulf.

Phase 1. Iranian culture emerged in a continental region, where the only knowledge of the sea was a vague notion (probably pre-Aryan and certainly pre-Iranian) of an external ocean (rather than of an intercontinental sea) encircling the earth, the *zrayah vourukaša* (*Vd*. 19.3 et passim; cf. Herzfeld, 1947, pp. 630-31). Direct acquaintance with the sea doubtless evolved only with the expansion of the Achaemenid empire, which permitted the transformation of old mythic notions into scientific themes. It is perhaps thus that the legend of Fraŋrasyan and Haosravah (*Yt*. 19.56-64, 19.82) came to contain allusions to three great gulfs (*vari*) of the external ocean, possibly the Caspian, the Black Sea, and the Persian Gulf (Herzfeld,

1947, p. 633). A little later precise knowledge of tidal areas, including, it seems, those of the Persian Gulf, began to develop (*Yt.* 8.46; cf. Herzfeld, 1947, pp. 636-37; *Bundahišn*, TD_2, 82 ff.; cf. Herzfeld, 1947, pp. 639-42).

Phase 2. From the moment that direct acquaintance with the sea was achieved a genuine Iranian maritime policy began to develop. This development was nevertheless quite uneven, reflecting the axes of imperial expansion. The Caspian remained practically unknown; knowledge of the Black Sea was very limited, and sources are also almost totally absent. On the other hand, Persian activity in the Mediterranean, the Red Sea, the Persian Gulf, and even the Indian Ocean, along with the conquest of Egypt and attempts to cut through the isthmus of Suez, reinforced the orientation to those areas.

The initiators and principal instruments of Achaemenid maritime policy were at first foreigners, especially Phoenicians and Carians (OPers. *karkā*; DNa 30; Herzfeld, 1947, II, p. 658; idem, 1968, p. 281); the most celebrated were Scylax of Caryanda, admiral under Cambyses and Darius I (qq.v.), who left a periplus in which primarily the Mediterranean and the Black Sea but also the southern coast of Persia as far as the Indus and the Indian Ocean are described (Herodotus, 4.44). But in those southern seas and the Persian Gulf, which was to remain almost exclusively under Persian domination for more than a millennium until the Islamic conquest (as is clear from the name Persian Gulf, in use from the 1st century B.C.E.; Strabo, 2.5.18), it is possible to recognize the emergence of a genuine and original Persian maritime culture. One obvious concrete indication is the very large number of Persian words that passed into the Arabic maritime vocabulary during that long period (Ferrand, 1924) and came to constitute an essential component of it. Already in the pre-Islamic period there was a great sea trade that originated in the Persian Gulf and extended as far as China (Hourani, pp. 38, 46-50). Persians played a considerable role in maritime relations with the Far East (see CHINESE-IRANIAN RELATIONS i-ii, vii), a role that evolved still further in the ʿAbbasid period; the main shipping ports along the Persian coast were successively Sīrāf in the 9th-10th centuries and the island of Qays/Kīš after the Mongol invasion in the 13th century. Even the legendary adventures of Sinbad the Sailor, whose name, if not originally Persian, was certainly Persianized, reflect the preponderance of the Persian element in those distant eastern waters. It still predominated in the eastern trade at the beginning of the 16th century, when the first European navigators arrived in the thalassocracy of Hormoz (Aubin, 1973, p. 140). If it is accepted that there had been no interruption of maritime commerce between the Persian Gulf and India from the 11th to the 14th century, then it is very probable that it was Persian maritime traditions that underlay the Arab pilots' knowledge of the southern seas in that period (Aubin, 1964).

Phase 3. A new phase had already begun, however. From soon after the Mongol invasion in the early 13th century Persian rulers turned progressively away from the sea and abdicated all interest in maritime activity, with sporadic exceptions. Beginning in the 14th century there were frequent references in the texts to the unsuitability of Persians for the sea (Curzon, *Persian Question* II, pp. 389-90). At the same time Persian activity on the Caspian, which had been important in the 8th-13th centuries, gradually gave way to Genoese enterprise; with the arrival of the first Russian traders in the 16th century it approached total extinction. In later centuries Persian rulers increasingly lost interest in the Persian Gulf and the southern seas. The last Persian efforts in the area involved little more than timely attempts to establish shipping ports to serve the interior of the country: at Bandar-e ʿAbbās (q.v) in the 17th-18th centuries, then at Būšehr (q.v.) in the 18th-19th centuries. The shahs also occasionally sought to establish political contacts by sea (e.g., the Persian embassy to Siam in 1685; *Safīna-ye solaymānī*, apud Lescot), though they remained more or less ephemeral. The sea itself, however, was almost totally abandoned to European navigators and Arab pirates. The last manifestations of an expiring power were apparent in the efforts, at once grandiose and absurd, of Nāder Shah (1148-60/1736-47) to revive a Persian fleet, on the Caspian in 1155/1742 and at Būšehr after 1147/1734; in the latter instance he went so far as to have wood for shipbuilding brought, at great expense, from Māzandarān. In the 19th century Persian maritime fortunes reached their lowest point, after the sultan of Muscat established control over part of the Persian coast, including Bandar-e ʿAbbās, in 1207/1793; his hold was broken only in 1285/1868. Persian pilgrims to the Muslim holy places at that period traveled only with the greatest reluctance on seas that seemed to harbor every danger. Many made long detours in order to avoid the perilous passage; those who resigned themselves to it, like the Bāb (q.v.) in 1260-61/1844-45, reported severe sufferings (Nicolas, pp. 206-07).

This decline in Persian maritime interest poses an immense problem in cultural history, one that is still insufficiently explored and for which the reasons remain largely enigmatic. It is obvious that the expansion of the much more powerfully equipped European navies, Portuguese, Dutch, then British in the Persian Gulf and Russian on the Caspian, was an essential element. It was certainly not the only one, however. The period of modern European naval power has also witnessed the flourishing of indigenous maritime cultures, for example, those of the Turkmen on the Caspian and the Arabs in the Persian Gulf. It is thus necessary to seek reasons intrinsic to Persian civilization itself. From the medieval invasions through the reign of the Qajars the domination, except for brief intervals, of dynasties of Turkish and Mongol origin and the massive irruption onto the Persian plateau of populations from the Central Asian land mass no doubt played an equally significant role. Other aspects remaining to be explored include the progressive onset, after the advent of Safavid Shiʿism, of a rigid religious outlook, in which maritime enterprises, judged incompatible with a life of piety, were viewed with scorn and suspicion.

Whatever the explanation, at the end of the 19th century the Persian navy comprised only three ships. One of them was stationed on the Anzalī (q.v.) lagoon of the Caspian, "a small dilapidated paddle-wheel steamer bearing the proud title of 'Shahinshah Nasr-ed-Din,'" a yacht especially constructed for the shah's first voyage to Europe; despite this splendor, upon its arrival in Baku the captain hastily lowered the flag in response to the firing of a warning salvo, which led George Curzon to remark with irony "Such is the majesty of the King of Kings on the Caspian" (*Persian Question* II, p. 394). On the Persian Gulf there was the *Persepolis*, "a screw steamship of 600 tons, of 450 horse-power," armed with four Krupp 7.5 cm cannons and launched from the shipyards of Bremerhaven in 1885. It was commanded by German officers. On the upper Kārūn river, between Ahvāz and Šūštar, there was a small steamboat of 36 tons and slightly less than 30 horsepower, the *Susa* (Curzon, *Persian Question* II, pp. 394-96).

Phase 4. Progress continued to be very slow for the next half-century. On the eve of World War II the Persian navy still did not comprise more than two sloops of 1,050 tons each (both destroyed by the British on 2 Šahrīvar 1320 Š./24 August 1941), five patrol boats, seven hovercraft, and several harbor and auxiliary craft, most constructed in Italy, where the first Persian naval cadets had been sent for training in 1305 Š./1926 and from where the first crews had been recruited in 1932 (*Persia*, pp. 398-99). Only after the war did the building of a genuine Persian naval force (*nīrū-ye daryāʾī*) begin (Gehrke and Mehner, pp. 266-70). Great Britain offered to Persia two frigates (of 2,000 and 1,050 tons respectively) to replace the two units destroyed during the war. In 1343 Š./1964 and 1348 Š./1969 four sloops of 1,000 tons each were delivered to Persia under the American aid program. At the same time Persia was systematically purchasing warships; the first order, placed in 1345 Š./1966, was for four frigates of 1,200 tons each, built in Great Britain and delivered in 1350-51 Š./1971-72. In 1349 Š./1970 a destroyer of 2,300 tons was purchased, also from Great Britain, and in 1351 Š./1972 two 2,200-ton destroyers from the United States. Beginning in 1349-50 Š./1970-71 a substantial fleet of hovercraft was developed (reaching a total of fourteen in the late 1970s). The shah expressly declared his intentions in a speech delivered on 14 Ābān 1351 Š./5 November 1972: not only to ensure the defense of Persian coasts but also to provide a "circle of security" for the country (*ḥarīm-e amnīyat-e Īrān*), of indeterminate radius but extending as far as the Indian Ocean. In 1352 Š./1973 there was a new flurry of orders for ships (eight destroyers, four frigates, twelve gunboats, and fourteen hovercraft). At the same time the number of naval bases was increased. To the already-existing base at Ḵorramšahr were added Bandar-e ʿAbbās (in 1344 Š./1965; from 1352 Š./1973 the general naval headquarters), Ḵārg island (base for hovercraft since 1352 Š./1973), Būšehr, the island of Kīš, Jāsk, and especially Čāh Bahār (q.v.) on the coast of Baluchistan, which permitted Persian control of navigation on the sea of Oman and the Indian Ocean. It is noteworthy that almost nothing was done on the Caspian, where Persia operated only a few patrol boats based at Anzalī and Behšahr (q.v.), without actual combat units. The rebirth of the Persian navy, exclusively an expression of political will, was deliberately oriented toward the region where the government perceived some necessity for it, while at the same time recognizing an arena of potential expansion of influence, which was totally excluded in the Caspian. This strategic vision was confirmed by the war with Iraq in the 1980s. It is still too soon to know, however, whether this cultural graft will take root.

Bibliography: J. Aubin, "Y a-t-il eu interruption du commerce par mer entre le Golfe Persique et l'Inde du XIe au XIVe siècle?" *Studia* (Lisbon) 11, 1963, pp. 165-71. Idem, "Le royaume d'Ormuz au début du XVIe siècle," *Mare Luso-Indicum* 2, 1973, pp. 77-179. G. Ferrand, "L'élément persan dans les textes nautiques arabes," *JA* 204, 1924, pp. 193-257. U. Gehrke and H. Mehner, *Iran. Natur—Bevölkerung—Geschichte—Kultur—Staat—Wirtschaft*, Tübingen and Basel, 1975. *Persia*, Geographical Handbook Series, Oxford, 1945. H. Hasan, *A History of Persian Navigation*, London, 1928. E. Herzfeld, *Zoroaster and His World*, 2 vols., Princeton, N.J., 1947. Idem, *The Persian Empire. Studies in Geography and Ethnography of the Ancient Near East*, Wiesbaden, 1968. G. Hourani, *Arab Seafaring*, Princeton, N.J., 1951. R. Lescot, "Les relations entre l'Iran et le Siam," in D. Bogdanovic and J. L. Bacqué-Grammont, eds., *Iran*, Paris, 1972, pp. 45-49. A. L. M. Nicolas, *Seyyed Ali Mohammed dit Le Bâb*, Paris, 1905. E. Rāʾīn, *Daryā-navardī-e Īrānīān*, 2 vols., Tehran, 1350 Š./1971. A. T. Wilson, *The Persian Gulf*, Oxford, 1928.

(XAVIER DE PLANHOL)

DĀRYĀ, a Tehran morning daily of news and politics, published with a number of interruptions from Ordībehešt 1323 Š./May 1944 to Farvardīn 1330 Š./March 1951. The publisher and managing director was Ḥasan Arsanjānī (q.v.), a radical lawyer and politician (1301-48 Š./1922-69), who had first used the pen name Dāryā for his articles in the paper *Īrān-e mā*. The name Dāryā has no real meaning; in the author's opinion it was formed from the letters of the word *īrād* (objection) spelled backward. Ebrāhīm Faḵrāʾī, publisher of the newspaper *Forūḡ*, was appointed editor-in-chief (*sar-dabīr*).

Dāryā was an independent newspaper, which dealt openly and freely with political and social questions.

Arsānjānī's own powerful pen and irrefutable logic contributed measurably to its frank tone. The paper was thus closed by the government ten times. During these intervals it was replaced by *Nedā-ye ḥaqīqat, Ārmān-e mellī, ʿAlī Bābā,* and *Parvareš,* in the late winter of 1323 Š./1945; *Możaffar, Aḵtar, Zan-e emrūz, Tehrān-e emrūz,* and *Forūḡ* in the autumn of the same year; and *Denā* in Āḏar 1324 Š./December 1948. In Esfand 1324 Š./March 1946 *Dāryā* appeared as the organ of the Āzādī party, which supported Aḥmad Qawām (Qawām-al-Salṭana). Publication ceased permanently in 1330 Š./1951, and Arsanjānī became Qawām's political undersecretary.

Dāryā was published in four to eight pages of six columns each, measuring 36 x 50 cm; the price was 2 rials. It was illustrated and carried advertising. Scattered issues are found in major Persian libraries, the Princeton University library, and the Library of Congress.

Bibliography: Ḥ. Abūtorābīān, *Maṭbūʿāt-e Īrān az Šahrīvar 1320 tā 1326*, Tehran, 1366 Š./1987, p. 81. Ī. Afšār, *Sawād wa bayāż* II, Tehran, 1349 Š./1970, pp. 574-77. Bāmdād, *Rejāl* VI, p. 77. L. P. Elwell-Sutton, "The Iranian Press, 1941-47," *Iran* 6, 1968, pp. 65-104, esp. p. 86. E. Faḵrāʾī, *Sardār-e jangāl, Mīrzā Kūček Ḵān*, 9th ed., Tehran, 1357 Š./1978, p. 448. N. Jāmī, *Goḏašta čerāḡ-e rāh-e āyanda ast*, 2nd ed., Tehran, 1362 Š./1983, p. 559. R. Mach and R. D. McChesney, *A List of Persian Serials in the Princeton University Library*, Princeton, N.J., 1971. J. Mahdī-nīā, *Zendagī-e sīāsī-e Qawām-al-Salṭana*, 2nd ed., Tehran, 1366 Š./1987, pp. 251-54. I. V. Pourhadi, *Persian and Afghan Newspapers in the Library of Congress, 1871-1971*, Washington, D.C., 1979, pp. 15-16. E. Pūr-wālī, "Qeṣṣa-ye por-ḡoṣṣa-ye man o Īrān-e man," *Rūzgār-e-now* 1/7, 1361 Š./1982, pp. 98-100. W.-M. Ṣādeqī-nasab, *Fehrest-e rūz-nāmahā-ye fārsī*, Tehran, 1360 Š./1981, p. 486. B. Sartīpzāda and K. Ḵodāparast, *Fehrest-e rūz-nāmahā-ye mawjūd dar Ketāb-ḵāna-ye mellī-e Īrān*, Tehran, 1356 Š./1977, p. 98. G. Šokrī, "Fehrest-e rūz-nāmahā wa majallahā-ye fārsī dar Moʾassasa-ye āsīāʾī-e Šīrāz," *FIZ* 27, p. 367. M. Zonis, The *Political Elite of Iran*, Princeton, N.J., 1971, pp. 53-61.

(NASSEREDDIN PARVIN)

DARYĀ-YE ḴAZAR. See CASPIAN SEA.

DARYĀ-YE MĀZANDARĀN. See CASPIAN SEA.

DARYĀ-YE NŪR (lit., "sea of light"), one of the largest diamonds in the world, kept and exhibited in the Jewel museum of the Central bank of Persia (Bānk-e markazī-e Īrān). It was mined in the famous Golconda diamond fields in southern India and, with the Kūh-e nūr (lit., "mountain of light," now part of the British crown jewels), was brought to Persia in 1151/1739 as part of the booty from Nāder Shah's Indian campaign. During the unstable period following the assassination of Nāder Shah in 1160/1747 it was held in turn by his grandson Šāhroḵ, ʿAlam Khan Arab Ḵozayma (q.v.), and Moḥammad-Ḥasan Khan Qājār (Jamālzāda, p. 6; Ḏokāʾ, p. 60) and finally came into the possession of Karīm Khan Zand (1163-93/1750-79).

In 1209/1794 the Daryā-ye nūr was removed from the armband of Loṭf-ʿAlī Khan, the last Zand ruler (1203-09/1789-94), by Āḡā Moḥammad Khan Qājār (q.v.; 1209-11/1794-97) in Kermān; it was then inserted in the armband worn by successive Qajar kings. It was the favorite gem of Nāṣer-al-Dīn Shah (1264-1313/1848-96); when wearing armbands became outmoded in the latter part of his reign he wore it variously on his watchband, chest, and hat (Jamālzāda, p. 7). Finally, it was incorporated into one of the royal aigrettes (*jeqqa*), placed within a golden frame decorated with images of the Kayānī crown and two lions and suns ornamented with 475 small brilliants and four rubies (see Ḏokāʾ, p. 60). Możaffar-al-Dīn Shah (1313-24/1896-1907) wore it on his karakul cap during his European tour in 1321/1902 (Meen and Tushingham, 1968, p. 53). When Moḥammad-ʿAlī Shah (1324-27/1907-09) was forced to abdicate and took refuge in the Russian legation in Tehran, he took the crown jewels, including the Daryā-ye nūr, with him; he returned it to the Golestān palace museum only under pressure from the constitutionalists (Taqīzāda, pp. 146-48; Jamālzāda, p. 7). Reżā Shah (1304-20 Š./1925-41) and Moḥammad-Reżā Shah wore it on their military caps en route to their coronations, in 1305 Š./1926 and 1346 Š./1967 respectively (Meen and Tushingham, 1968, p. 53).

The Daryā-ye nūr is a flawless pink diamond, the sixth largest known in the world; it is a rectangular, step-cut tablet, 41.4 x 29.5 x 12.15 mm. Reports of its weight vary between 182 and 186 carats. One of the facets is incised with the words "al-Solṭān ṣāḥeb-qerān Fatḥ-ʿAlī Šāh Qājār 1250." At present the Daryā-ye nūr is set in a frame 2.8 x 2.1 in (Meen and Tushingham, 1968, p. 53; Ḏokāʾ, pp. 60-61).

See CROWN JEWELS.

Bibliography: Bank Markazi Iran, *Les joyaux de la couronne*, Tehran, 1975, pp. 42-43. H. J. Brydges, *The Dynasty of the Kajars*, London, 1833, pp. cxxvi ff. Y. Ḏokāʾ, *Gowharhā*, Tehran, 1346 Š./1968, pp. 58-61. M.-ʿA. Jamālzāda, "Kūh-e nūr, Daryā-ye nūr," *Kāva* 2/2, 1921, pp. 5-8. V. B. Meen and A. D. Tushingham, "The *Darya-i Nur* Diamond and the Tavernier 'Great Table,'" *Lapidary Journal* 21/8, 1967, pp. 1000 ff. Idem, *Crown Jewels of Iran*, Toronto, 1968. S.-Ḥ. Taqīzāda, *Zendagī-e ṭūfānī*, ed. Ī. Afšār, Tehran, 1368 Š./1989.

(YAḤYĀ ḎOKĀʾ)

DARYĀ-YE ʿOMĀN. See ʿOMĀN, SEA OF.

DARYĀ-YE SĪĀH. See BLACK SEA.

DARYĀBEYGĪ (sea lord), originally an Ottoman naval title dating from the 15th century (Lewis, p. 165). In Persia it was first adopted in the 18th century, when Nāder Shah Afšār (1148-60/1736-47) built his fleet. The naval commander in chief bore the title *daryābeygī* or occasionally *sardār* or *sardār-e banāder* (Estarābādī, p. 580; Eskandar Beg, II, p. 665; Lockhart, 1936, p. 11; Floor, 1987, pp. 40-49). Nāder Shah's choice, in 1146/1733, of Būšehr (q.v.) for his shipyards and the residence of the *daryābeygī* led to the eclipse of Bandar-e ʿAbbās (q.v.) as the major Persian Gulf port (Floor, 1979, p. 169; Lockhart, 1938, pp. 92-93; idem, 1936, p. 12). Nevertheless, the commanders of the fleet at Bandar-e ʿAbbās and of a group of two frigates and four smaller vessels on the Caspian Sea (Lockhart, 1936, pp. 7-17) also bore the rank of *daryābegī*. Nāder Shah's naval project did not survive his assassination in 1160/1747, but the title *daryābeygī* was also used to designate the commander of the small fleet assembled under the Zands (Lockhart, 1936, p. 15; Perry, pp. 150-66).

In the early Qajar period *daryābeygī* was simply an honorific, as the state had no navy. Most often it was awarded by the governor of Fārs to the municipal governor of Būšehr and occasionally to other local dignitaries. For example, in 1238/1823 Ḥosayn-ʿAlī Mīrzā Farmānfarmā, bestowed it on the shaikh of Šārja and Raʾs al-Ḵayma, Solṭān b. Ṣaqr, in order to enlist his help in capturing Bahrain (q.v.). When the British navy threatened the Persian Gulf coast in 1256/1840, in response to the Persian siege of Herat, Moḥammad Shah (1250-64/1834-48) himself appointed as *daryābeygī* and governor of Būšehr Shaikh Nāṣer, whose family, of the Mataresh Arabs of Oman (Perry, p. 154), had ruled the city since the mid-18th century (Kelly, pp. 42-43, 220, 347). In 1266/1850 Fīrūz Mīrzā Noṣrat-al-Dawla, governor of Fārs, appointed Mīrzā Ḥasan-ʿAlī Khan, son of Mīrzā ʿAlī-Akbar Qawām-al-Molk of Shiraz, governor of Būšehr and *daryābeygī* (Fasāʾī, I, p. 305). When he was captured by invading British forces during the Anglo-Persian War (q.v.) of 1273/1857 and sent to Bombay Aḥmad Khan Navāʾī ʿAmīd-al-Molk was appointed governor of Būšehr with the title *daryābeygī* (Fasāʾī, I, p. 318).

Despite repeated efforts, the state remained without a fleet until the commissioning of two small vessels from German shipyards, *Persepolis* and *Susa*, in 1300/1883 (Curzon, *Persian Question*, II, pp. 393-96; Rāʾīn, II, pp. 744-61; Ṣafāʾī, pp. 81-82; Lorimer, *Gazetteer* I/1, p. 294), which transformed the position of the *daryābeygī* and permitted the extension of the central authority over Arab tribes on the Persian Gulf coast, for example, the Jawāsem of Lenga (Sadīd-al-Salṭana, pp. 606-12; Šaybānī, pp. 345-52).

By the beginning of the 20th century the entire Persian coastal region was administered by the *daryābeygī* (Busch, pp. 41-47). The title was abandoned when Reżā Shah Pahlavī (1304-20/1925-41) expanded the Persian navy; it subsequently became a surname.

Bibliography: B. C. Busch, *Britain and the Persian Gulf, 1894-1914*, Berkeley, Calif., 1967. Mīrzā Mahdī Khan Estarābādī (Astarābādī), *Dorra-ye nādera*, ed. J. Šahīdī, Tehran, 1341 Š./1962. W. Floor, "A Description of the Persian Gulf and Its Inhabitants in 1756," *Persica* 7, 1979, pp. 165-86. Idem, "The Iranian Navy in the Gulf during the Eighteenth Century," *Iranian Studies* 20/1, 1987, pp. 31-53. J. B. Kelly, *Britain and the Persian Gulf 1795-1880*, Oxford, 1968. B. Lewis, "Daryā-Begi," in *EI*² II, p. 165. L. Lockhart, "The Navy of Nadir Shah," *Proceedings of the Iran Society* 1/1, 1936, pp. 3-18. Idem, *Nadir Shah*, London, 1938. J. Perry, *Karim Khan Zand. A History of Iran 1747-1779*, Chicago, 1979. J. Qāʾem-maqāmī, *Baḥrayn wa masāʾel-e Ḵalīj-e Fārs*, Tehran, 1341 Š./1962. Idem, *Nahżat-e āzādī-ḵᵛāhī-e mardom-e Fārs dar enqelāb-e mašrūṭīat-e Īrān*, Tehran, 1350 Š./1971. E. Rāʾīn, *Daryā-navardī-e Īrānīān*, 2 vols., Tehran, 1350 Š./1971. M.-ʿA. Sadīd-al-Salṭana Kabābī, *Bandar(-e) ʿAbbās wa Ḵalīj-e Fārs*, ed. A. Eqtedārī, Tehran 1363 Š./1984. E. Ṣafāʾī, *Āʾīna-ye tārīḵ*, Tehran, 1353 Š./1974. Ṣadīq-al-Mamālek Šaybānī, *Montaḵab al-tawārīḵ*, Tehran, 1366 Š./1987.

(Guity Nashat)

DARYĀČA. For individual lakes, see entries under the names.

DĀRZĪN, a village (29° 11′ N, 58° 09′ E) on the road between Kermān and Bam on the site of a large early medieval town recorded as Dayr-e Wazīn (or Dīrūzīn), Dārjīn, Dāržīn, and Dārčīn and described as having a fine congregational mosque and many orchards (e.g., Ebn Ḵordāḏbeh, pp. 49, 196; *Ḥodūd al-ʿālam*, tr. Minorsky, pp. 125, 375; Eṣṭaḵrī, pp. 161, 169; Moqaddasī, pp. 461, 465-66; Ebn Ḥawqal, pp. 308, 314; tr. Kramers, II, pp. 302, 309). The town was the center of the region of the same name, which is known to have remained prosperous at least until the end of the 12th century (Afżal-al-Dīn, p. 66). Little is known about it in later periods, except that in 811/1408 a battle between Solṭān Oways, son of the amir Īdkū Barlās, who became independent ruler of Kermān in that year, and the Timurid prince Mīrzā Abā Bakr b. Mīrānšāh was fought in the area (Wazīrī, 1340 Š./1961, p. 243; *Ḥabīb al-sīar* III, p. 57). According to Aḥmad-ʿAlī Khan Wazīrī (1353 Š./1974, p. 96), the site was abandoned, and only in the 19th century was the present village established there.

The ruins of old Dārzīn cover an area 1.5 x 3 km east of the present village. There are abundant surface sherds, mainly underglaze-painted pottery, but earlier wares are also present, including slip-painted and yellow sgraffiato wares. So far the site has not been scientifically excavated, but the ruins of a number of buildings of different periods still stand. The earliest are probably three small forts of similar form (Plate III), built of straw-tempered rectangular mud bricks 27

PLATE III

View of fortress 2 at Dārzīn, from the east.

x 27 x 7 cm. The forts have square plans with round towers at the corners and a semicircular tower in the middle of each of three walls; in the middle of the north wall there is an entrance flanked by two semicircular towers. The walls are about 14 m high, and inside each enclosure there is a series of chambers around a central courtyard at ground level; traces of upper levels are evidence that the buildings probably had three stories. The parabolic profile of the vaults over the chambers and arrow-shaped openings in the curtain walls suggest that these forts may date from the 8th or 9th century; the general layout, too, closely resembles the early palace at Kherbat Menyā, the *rebāṭ* (fortress) of Jabal (ʿO)says, and other Omayyad monuments in Syria.

Only the foundations of the large 10th-12th century mosque (or *madrasa*) survive; the building was constructed of mud brick faced with red-fired brick. It had a central courtyard plan with four *ayvān*s (q.v.). In the vicinity there are also a number of later tombs and ruins.

Bibliography: Afżal-al-Dīn Aḥmad b. Ḥāmed Kermānī, *ʿEqd al-ʿolā le'l-mawqef al-aʿlā*, ed. ʿA.-M. ʿĀmerī, Tehran, 1311 Š./1932. Schwarz, *Iran*, pp. 238-39. M. Shokoohy, "Monuments of the Early Caliphate at Dārzīn in the Kirmān Region (Iran)," *JRAS*, 1980, pp. 3-20. Aḥmad-ʿAlī Khan Wazīrī Kermānī, *Tārīḵ-e Kermān*, ed. M.-E. Bāstānī Pārīzī, Tehran, 1340 Š./1961. Idem, *Jog̲rāfīā-ye Kermān*, Tehran, ed. M.-E. Bāstānī Pārīzī, Tehran, 1353 Š./1974.

(MEHRDAD SHOKOOHY)

DASĀTĪN (Ar. pl. of Pers. *dastān*, q.v.), the term for modes in early musical theory, translated into Arabic as *aṣābeʿ* (fingers) and sometimes also as *mawājeb* "obligations, laws." It originally referred to the eight fundamental octave scales attributed to the Sasanian musician Bārbad (q.v.); as each note is played on a specific lute string by a specific finger, the notes are thus designated, for example, "the free string in the range of the middle finger," "the touch of the index finger on the annular," and so on (Marāg̲ī, 1356 Š./1977, p. 96-99; cf. d'Erlanger, p. 598). These modes are mentioned in general terms in the *Ketāb al-ag̲ānī* (10th century) of Abu'l-Faraj Eṣfahānī, but there is not enough precision to permit individual identification. According to Ṣafī-al-Dīn Ormavī, they consisted of the six *maqām*s (ʿOššāq, Navā, Rāst, Būsalīk, ʿErāq, Nowrūz, and Eṣfahān; d'Erlanger, pp. 466-68). The term *dasātīn* was supplanted by terms like *bardawāt* (Ar. plural of Pers. *parda* "fret"), *maqām*, *šodūd*, *āvāz* (q.v.), and *adwār* and continued to occur in the scholastic treatises only as a memory of the system of the ancients. In Marāg̲ī's writing *dasātīn* meant only a note, implicitly a note on the "neck" (*dasta*) of an instrument, that is, the fret (1366 Š./1987, pp. 29-30).

The image of fingering is also preserved in the use of the term *bardawāt* to refer to the mode or *maqām*.

Bibliography: R. d'Erlanger, *La musique arabe* II, Paris, 1935. ʿAbd-al-Qader b. Ḡaybī Ḥāfeẓ Marāḡī, *Maqāṣed al-alḥān*, ed. T. Bīneš, Tehran, 1356 Š./1977. Idem, *Jāmeʿ al-alḥān*, ed. T. Bīneš, Tehran, 1366 Š./1987. M.-T. Masʿūdīya, *Mūsīqī-e Torbat-e Jām*, Tehran, 1359 Š./1980. ʿAbd-al-Moʾmen Ṣafī-al-Dīn Ormavī, *Resāla al-šarafīya fi'l-nesab al-taʾlīfīya*, tr. R. d'Erlanger as *La musique arabe* III, Paris, 1938.

(JEAN DURING)

DASĀTĪR, the most important tract of the Āḏar Kayvānī sect, almost certainly the work of its founder, Āḏar Kayvān (see ĀẒAR KAYVĀN). The book, written in an invented language, is about supposedly ancient Iranian prophets and includes accounts of events that have no historical basis. It is divided into two parts, the first of which comprises sixteen chapters, or *nāma*s (books), each attributed to a so-called "ancient" prophet, from Mahābād and Jī-Afrām, who supposedly pre-dated Kayūmarṯ, to Sāsān V, whom the author designated as a contemporary of the Sasanian ruler Ḵosrow II Parvēz (r. 590-628). Also included in the list of prophets are certain mythical and historical figures, including Jamšīd, Ferēdūn, Kay Ḵosrow, Zoroaster, and Alexander (q.v.). The second part is a Persian "translation" of the first with commentary, containing many fabricated words; it is ascribed to the sixteenth prophet, Sāsān V.

The author of *Dabestān-e maḏāheb* (q.v.; Malek, I, p. 10) called the language of the *nāma*s "heavenly language" *(āsmānī zabān)*; it has no fundamental connection or resemblance to any living or dead language. The vocabulary is for the most part fabricated. Some words were, however, taken from Persian, Hindi, Avestan, Sanskrit, and Arabic and used in corrupt and distorted forms, sometimes with Persian prefixes or suffixes. The following terms were based on Persian: *jahāḵ* (< *jahān* "world"), *časār* (< *čahār* "four"), *farāsīm* (<*farāzīn* "high"), *forūsīm* (<*forūdīn* "low"), *tanānī* (corporeal), *ravānestān* (the realm of the spirits), *pāsong* (< *pāsoḵ* "reply"), and so on. Words derived from Hindi include *tīm* (< *tīn* "three") and *čahīdan* (< *čāhnā* "to wish"). Among borrowings from Sanskrit are *aham* (I), *sarvah* (all), and *tapas* (mortification). Some terms simulate the structure of Persian, for example, *āhangīdan* (to intend), *pākeš* (sanctification), *čašmīda* (object in view). Others are completely contrived and have no linguistic basis: *samrād* (imagination), *safrang* (interpretation, elucidation), *farnūd* (reason, justification).

Knowledge of the subject matter of *Dasātīr* is possible only through the "translation" and commentary, supposedly by Sāsān V but almost certainly the work of the author of the text. The identity of Sāsān V must itself be the creation of the author, as no one other than he understood the language of the text; supporting this conclusion is the fact that the Persian of the translation and commentary belongs to the 16th-17th centuries. The inclusion of Hindi and Sanskrit words suggests India as the place of composition, even though Mollā Kāvūs Pārsī (father of Mollā Fīrūz; see below), bought the copy of the book in Isfahan in 1192/1778.

On the basis of a description of *Dasātīr* that he noticed in *Dabestān-e maḏāheb*, the 18th-century English orientalist Sir William Jones praised the book and called it a sacred text, equal in importance to the *Avesta* (q.v.) and *Zand*. Jonathan Duncan, at that time governor of Bombay, intended to translate the work into English but died before he could launch the undertaking. His successor as governor, John Malcolm, encouraged Mollā Fīrūz to publish the book and appointed William Erskine to assist him in the English translation. The text and translation were published in two volumes in Bombay in 1818-19 under the title *The Desātir, or the Sacred Writings of the Ancient Persian Prophets, Together with the Commentary of the Fifth Sāsān*. The text was reprinted in 1888, and in the same year Dhunjeebhoy Jamshetjee Medhora published a reprint of the translation and commentary in Bombay.

Some of the fabricated words of the *Dasātīr* found acceptance as genuine Persian vocabulary. From 1062/1652, when *Borhān-e qāṭeʿ* was compiled, until very recently they were included in Persian dictionaries published in both Persia and India. Only after critical reassessment was the language, as well as the contents, of the *Dasātīr* recognized as a forgery (Mojtabāʾī).

Bibliography: For editions of *Dasātīr*, see bibliography of ĀẒAR KAYVĀN. W. Erskine, "On the Authority of the *Desātīr*, with Remarks on the Account of the Mahabadi Religion Contained in the Dabistan," *Transactions of the Literary Society of Bengal* 2, 1818, pp. 395-98. J. J. Modi, "A Parsee High Priest (Dastur Azar Kaiwan, 1529-1614 A.D) with His Zoroastrian Disciples in Patna, in th 16th and 17th Century A.C.," in *Journal of the K. R. Cama Oriental Institute* 20, 1932, pp. 1-85. F. Mojtabāʾī, "Āḏar Kayvān," in *Dāʾerat al-maʿāref-e bozorg-e Eslāmī* I, Tehran, 1368 Š./1989, pp. 247-59. E. Pūr-e Dāwūd, "Dasātīr," *Farhang-e Īrān-e bāstān*, Tehran, 1326 Š./1947, pp. 17-51. Idem, ed., *Hormozd-nāma*, Tehran, 1331 Š./1952. R. Reżāzāda Malek, ed., *Dabestān-e maḏāheb*, 2 vols., Tehran, 1362 Š./1983.

(FATḤ-ALLĀH MOJTABAʾĪ)

DASCYLIUM, Achaemenid satrapy in northwestern Anatolia (Herodotus, 3.120.2; cf. Thucydides 1.129.1: *tēn Daskulitìn satrapeían*; OPers. *tayaiy drayahyā*; DB 1.15; Kent, *Old Persian*, p. 117), part of the Persian empire until the 330s B.C.E. The borders varied, extending as far south as the Mysian plain and the southern Troad and east into the land of the Bithynian peoples; some satraps controlled both sides of the Hellespont. The territory of Dascylium encompassed estates, garrisoned fortresses, and cities and villages in which Persians and other groups were mingled. The name Dascylium was also applied to a number of sites within the satrapy, the most important being the satrapal estate located at modern Hisartepe on the southwestern shore of Lake Manyas, near the village of Ergili.

The relations of Dascylium with the Greeks and Persians are better documented than those of inner Anatolia, though most written sources are accounts by hostile outsiders. Archeological evidence consists principally of administrative documents and monumental remains. The former are bullae with impressions of stamp and cylinder seals (q.v.) from the Dascylium estate (Balkan), the latter carved funerary stelae and traces of platform tombs (Akurgal; Bakır; Mellink, 1990-92; see Sekunda, p. 196 map). On the stelae funerary processions, banquets, and horsemanship are depicted in relief (see, e.g., *EIr.* V, p. 734 fig. 58); they are paralleled elsewhere in Achaemenid Anatolia (see CAPPADOCIA; CILICIA). The inscriptions on some of these monumental remains suggest a local administration composed of several ethnic groups.

Administrative structure. The highest dignitary was the satrap, usually a member of the extended Achaemenid family, who resided on the Dascylium estate. The structure of his court duplicated that of the Achaemenid great king at Susa. The subordinate officials were a mixed group: those who lived on estates of their own, both Persians and Greeks tied to the satrapal court, and such indigenous political authorities as tribal leaders and city governors. All these categories overlapped. Individual officers are mentioned only sporadically in the sources, and it is difficult to reconstruct the hierarchy among them. The satrap was expected to maintain order and thus to ensure a favorable climate for economic activities that would generate tribute (cf. Thucydides, 8.5-6). Dascylium was rich in natural resources, particularly timber, which appears to have been under satrapal control (cf. Xenophon, *Hellenica* 1.1.25; Theophrastus, *Historia Plantarum* 4.5.5; Strabo, 12.572, 12.574-75). There was also gold, but no regular coinage was issued (Pliny, *Naturalis Historia* 37.193; Strabo, 13.591, 14.680; Herodotus, 3.90). In local areas the satrap's responsibilities were delegated to lesser officials (e.g., the Greeks Zenis and Manis; Xenophon, *Hellenica* 3.1).

The fulcrum of Achaemenid control and expansion was the estate system. The satrapal estate itself yielded sufficient revenue to support a luxurious style of life (Xenophon, *Anabasis* 4.4.21, 7.8.8 ff.; idem, *Hellenica* 4.1.15-17, 4.1.24, 4.1.33; cf. 3.4.13; *Hellenica Oxyrhynchia* 21). There were a manor house, some fortifications, barracks and stables (implied by Xenophon, *Hellenica* 3.4.13, 4.1.25), and some sort of construction for use by visiting royalty from Susa (Plutarch, *Agesilaus* 11.3; Arrian, *Anabasis* 1.17.2; *Hellenica Oxyrhynchia* 21; cf. Xenophon, *Anabasis* 1.2.7-9). Judging from the style of surviving funerary monuments, the manor house would have reflected a reworking of Persian and indigenous styles.

History of the satrapy. Before the Achaemenid conquest, in the 540s B.C.E., Dascylium was part of the Lydian kingdom; Greek authors reported traditions associating the name Daskylos or Daskyleion with Lydian royalty (Herodotus, 1.8.1; Nicolaus of Damascus, in Jacoby, *Fragmente* 90, frag. 63; cf. frags. 26, 46, 47). Cyrus II (q.v.; 559-29 B.C.E.) incorporated the province into the Achaemenid empire in 546. The earliest administrative data on Achaemenid Dascylium are from the time of Cambyses II (q.v.; 529-22 B.C.E.): According to Herodotus (3.120-28), Mitrobates governed the satrapy (*nomos*) in Dascylium but was killed by Oroetes, satrap of Sparda (Sardis), probably in the 520s. Under Darius I (q.v.; 522-486 B.C.E.) and

Table 3

THE HOUSE OF MEGABAZUS, THE FIRST SATRAPAL FAMILY AT DASCYLIUM

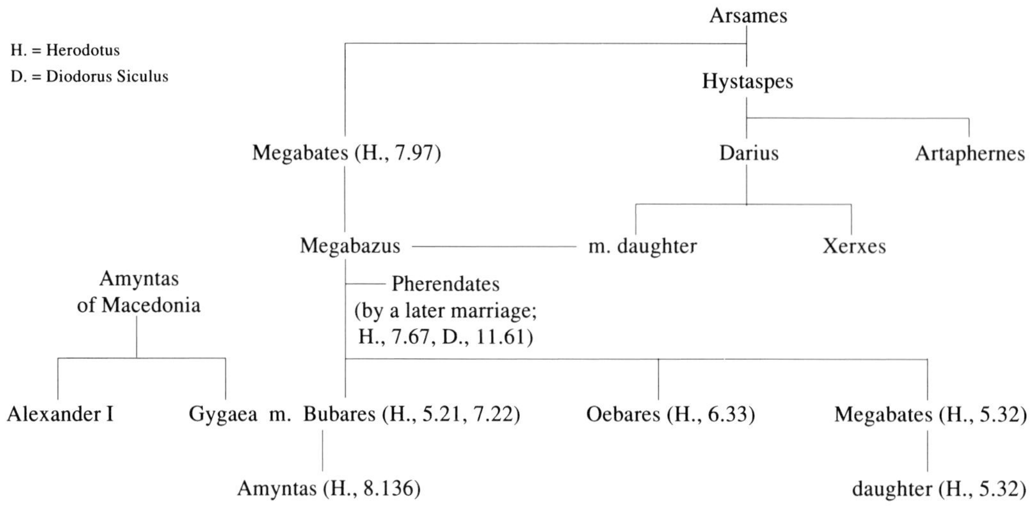

Xerxes I (486-65 B.C.E.) the house of Megabazus seems to have controlled the satrapy (Table 3) and to have furnished personnel for posts in Europe and Asia. Members of the family participated in the war with the European Scythians (ca. 514), and after the victory Darius seems to have left his military forces in the command of Megabazus, who subdued Thrace and Macedonia and subsequently became a senior commander in Xerxes' fleet (Herodotus, 4.143-44, 5.1 ff., 7.97; Justin, 7.3). Megabazus was accompanied on his Balkan campaign by one son, Bubares, who married into Macedonian royalty and supervised the construction of Xerxes' canal south of Macedonia (ca. 483); part of his family remained in Macedonia until the Greek defeat of the Persians in the 470s (Herodotus, 8.136, 5.21, 7.22). A second son, Oebares, was satrap of Dascylium in the 490s (Herodotus, 6.33). Megabates, a younger son of Megabazus, was Achaemenid commander of the fleet that sailed against Naxos in 500/499 and satrap at Dascylium in the early 470s (Thucydides, 1.129; Herodotus, 5.32-35, 6.32). With the Persian withdrawal from Europe, however, the house of Megabazus passed into obscurity, at least for the Greeks; information about Dascylium also becomes scantier once Herodotus' narrative breaks off.

In the later 470s Artabazus (q.v.), son of Pharnaces (Par-na-ka; Hallock, p. 741) and a cousin of Darius I, succeeded Megabazus as satrap of Dascylium (Thucydides, 1.129). The first fifty years of his family's rule is shrouded in obscurity (Table 4). Artabazus commanded the Parthians and Chorasmians in Xerxes' eastern border war (480-79) and was in the Hellespont region in 470 (Herodotus, 7.66, 8.126-29). His social status and military competence account for his appointment to the frontier province of Dascylium at a time when Achaemenid Europe was in collapse. The length and events of his tenure are unknown, but he must have had to devote himself to policing the borders. In the late 460s he commanded troops in Achaemenid campaigns against Egyptian and Cypriote rebels (Diodorus, 11.74.6, 11.77.1-4, 12.3-4), and he probably left the affairs of Dascylium in the hands

Table 4
THE EARLY PHARNACIDS

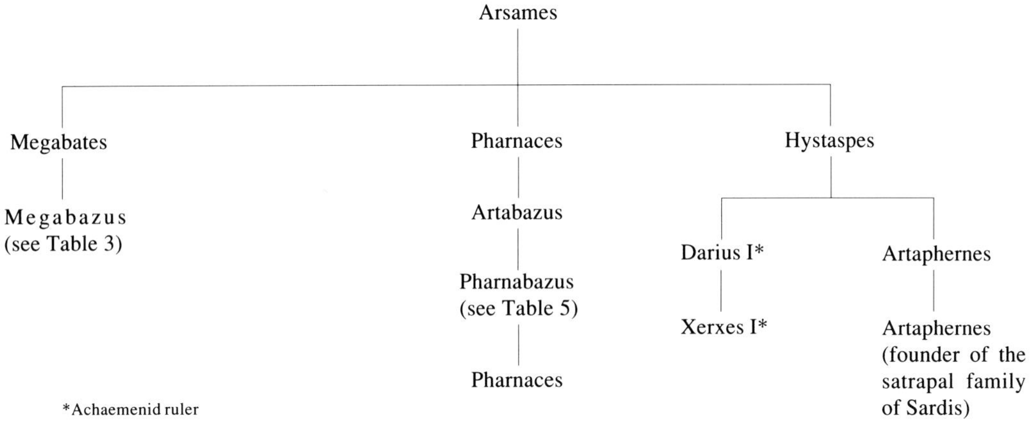

Table 5
FAMILY OF PHARNABAZUS

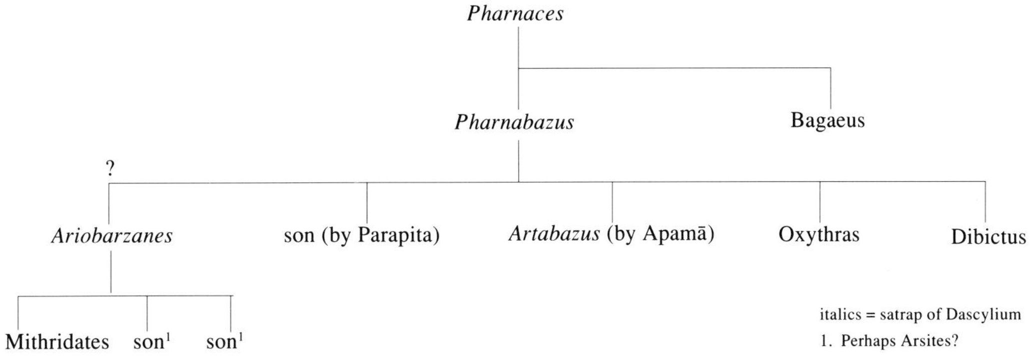

of his son Pharnabazus, for in the 430s Pharnaces, son of Pharnabazus, was satrap; Pharnaces remained active through the 420s (Thucydides, 2.67, 5.1).

Pharnaces' son Pharnabazus ruled Dascylium from at least as early as 413 until 388/7 B.C.E. (Thucydides, 8.108; Table 5). His activities are relatively well documented, as most of them touched on Greek affairs in the Aegean. In fact, he was one of the few Achaemenid nobles to find a place in Greek popular imagination (Athenaeus, 13.570c). From this more abundant documentation it is possible to see how deeply rooted in the political landscape of Dascylium (known to the Greeks as Hellespontine Phrygia) the descendants of the first Pharnaces had become (Thucydides, 8.58.1). Pharnabazus was occupied in warding off external and internal threats to his domain. With royal permission he assembled a fleet under his own command and defeated the Spartans, thus setting the stage for imposition of the "king's peace" upon the Greeks in 387 B.C.E.). Within the satrapy a short-lived rebellion was led by the lesser officer Spithridates (*Hellenica Oxyrhynchia* 21-22; Xenophon, *Hellenica* 3.4.10, 4.1; cf. Weiskopf, 1989). After 388/7 Pharnabazus seems to have divided his time among Susa, Dascylium, and other parts of the Near East, where he twice commanded forces sent to pacify Egyptian rebels (Isocrates, 4.140; Diodorus, 15.29 ff.; Nepos, *Datames* 3; Plutarch, *Artoxerxes* 24). He married several times; Ariobarzanes, probably his son by an unknown wife, was satrap of Dascylium from about 388 to 363 (Xenophon, *Hellenica* 1.4.7, 5.1.28). A younger son, by his wife Parapita, accompanied Pharnabazus on campaign in 395 B.C.E. (Xenophon, *Hellenica* 4.1.39-40; Plutarch, *Agesilaus* 13). In about 388/7 Pharnabazus married Apamā (q.v.), daughter of Artaxerxes II (q.v.; 405-359 B.C.E.), and their son Artabazus (q.v. 2) was satrap of Dascylium in the 360s and 350s (Plutarch, *Artoxerxes* 27; Xenophon, *Agesilaus* 3.3; idem, *Hellenica* 5.1.28; Plutarch, *Alexander* 21). Two other sons, Oxythras and Dibictus, were also resident in the satrapy in the 350s (Polyaenus, 7.33). Pharnabazus' uncle Susamithras and his brother Bagaeus were mentioned in connection with military campaigns (Plutarch, *Alcibiades* 39; Xenophon, *Hellenica* 3.4.13).

Ariobarzanes carried on his predecessor's work and built upon his successes. He extended the territory under his control and intervened in Greek affairs (368; Xenophon, *Hellenica* 7.1.27 ff.; Demosthenes, 23.141, 142, 203), which eventually brought him into conflict with Autophradates (q.v.), satrap of Sparda. There was also civil war within his own family (e.g., Xenophon, *Cyropaedia* 8.8.4); Artaxerxes II installed his grandson, Ariobarzanes' younger half-brother

Table 6
FAMILY OF ARTABAZUS

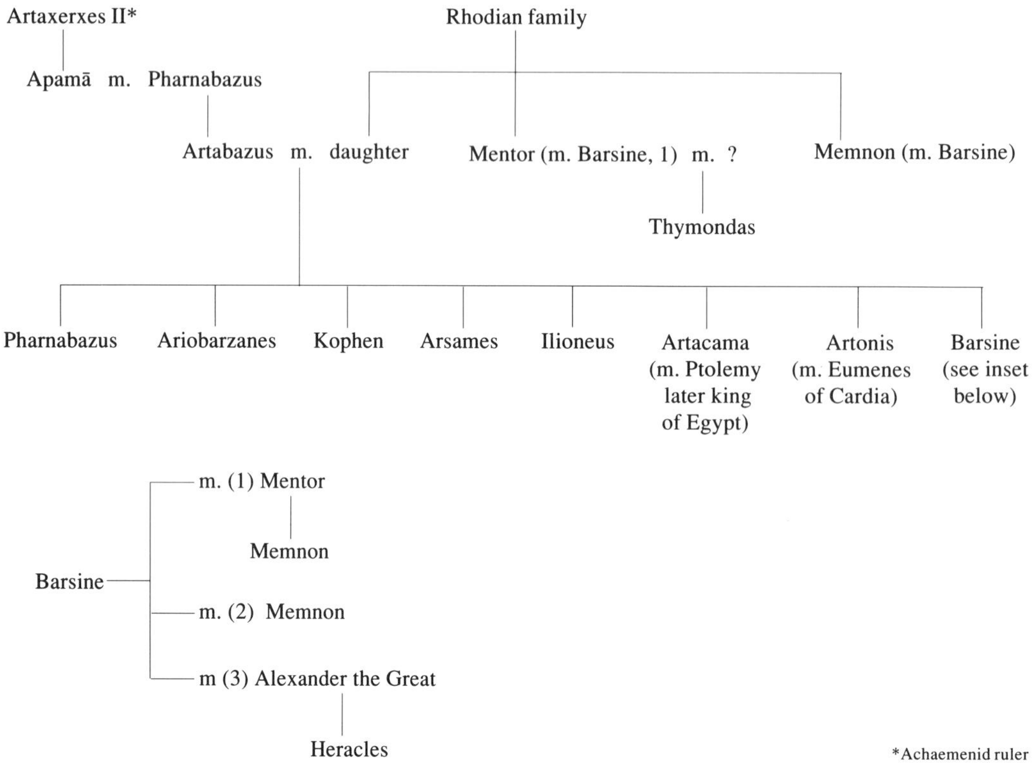

*Achaemenid ruler

Artabazus, in Dascylium; Ariobarzanes himself was sent to Susa and executed (Weiskopf, 1989).

Artabazus was satrap from about 363 into the 350s (Table 6). Although poorly documented, the events of his reign reveal a pattern of continued instability (Demosthenes, 23.154 ff., scholia to 4.19, 3.31; Diodorus, 16.22, 34; Jacoby, *Fragmente* 105, frag. 4). He had married a Rhodian woman in the 360s, and her brothers Mentor and Memnon became important allies (Demosthenes, 23.154 ff.; Diodorus, 16.52). At some time in the 350s Artabazus, Memnon, and their families had to flee to Macedonia (Diodorus, 16.52.3-4; Athenaeus, 6.256c-e; Curtius Rufus, 5.9.1, 6.5.2). The degree of their influence there is uncertain.

Arsites, who may have been one of Ariobarzanes' three sons, succeeded Artabazus as satrap of Dascylium in the 350s and reigned until 334 B.C.E. He was the last Achaemenid satrap of Dascylium (Demosthenes, 23.202). As early as 338 he had assisted Thracian Perinthus against the forces of Philip of Macedon (Pausanias, 1.29; cf. Diodorus, 16.75; Arrian, *Anabasis* 2.12). During his reign Artabazus' family was rehabilitated, in 343/2 B.C.E. (Diodorus, 16.42 ff.). Artabazus himself seems to have settled in the eastern part of the empire, remaining loyal to Darius III (336-31 B.C.E.), eventually surrendering with his sons to the forces of Alexander the Great (q.v.) at Hyrcania in 330 (Arrian, *Anabasis* 3.21.4, 3.23.7; Curtius Rufus, 5.8 ff., 6.5.1-5); he fought for Alexander until 329 and was named satrap of Bactria (q.v.; Arrian, *Anabasis* 3.28.2; Curtius Rufus, 7.3.2, 7.4.33-40). Mentor regained his property in Dascylium and took up a command policing trouble spots in western Anatolia; both estates and command later passed to his brother Memnon (Arrian, *Anabasis* 1.17; Polyaenus, 4.3.15, 5.44.5; Diodorus, 16.50, 16.52, 17.7). Arsites and Memnon fought at Granicus in 334, and Arsites committed suicide after the Persian defeat (Arrian, *Anabasis* 1.16-17). Memnon then led the Achaemenid counterattack but died suddenly in 333, and his nephews Pharnabazus and Thymondas took over his command. Thymondas died in Egypt in the same year (Arrian, *Anabasis* 1.20.2-3, 2.1-2, 2.13, 3.2). Pharnabazus was captured at Cos but escaped; he was still serving near Dascylium in 322, as a cavalry commander in the army of the Greek Eumenes, his brother-in-law (Plutarch, *Eumenes* 7; cf. Briant, 1985, p. 184).

Macedonians then ruled Dascylium. The first was Calas, who later carried out traditional policing actions against the Bithynians (Arrian, *Anabasis* 1.17; Memnon, in Jacoby, *Fragmente* 434, frag. 12.4). The financial structure of the satrapy remained the same, but taxes were paid to the Macedonians. Some time before 323 Calas was succeeded by Demarchus (Arrian, *Events after Alexander* 6), and thereafter the satraps were appointed and deposed by Macedonian dynasties. The fates of Achaemenid officials and the overall survival of Persians in Hellenistic Dascylium are more difficult topics to investigate. One group of lesser officers from a cadet branch of the house of Pharnaces produced the dynasty that ruled Pontic Cappadocia (q.v.) after 302 (Diodorus, 16.90.2, 19.40.2, 20.111.4).

Bibliography: E. Akurgal, "Recherches faites à Cyzique et à Ergili," *Anatolia* 1, 1956, pp. 15-24. T. Bakır, *Höyük* 1, 1988, pp. 75-84. K. Balkan, "Inscribed Bullae from Daskyleion-Ergili," *Anatolia* 4, 1959, pp. 123-28 (cf. D. Kaptan-Bayburtluoğlu, in *Epigraphica Anatolica* 16, 1990, pp. 15-27). H. Berve, *Das Alexanderreich auf prosopographischer Grundlage*, Munich, 1926. R. A. Billows, *Antigonos the One-Eyed and the Creation of the Hellenistic State*, Berkeley, Calif., 1990. K. Bittel, "Zur Lage von Daskyleion," *Archä-ologischer Anz.*, 1953, cols. 1-15. A. B. Bosworth, *A Historical Commentary on Arrian's History of Alexander* I, Oxford, 1980. P. Briant, *Rois, tributs et paysans*, Annales Litteraires de l'Université de Besançon 269, Paris, 1982. Idem, "Les iraniens d'Asie Mineure après la chute de l'empire achéménide," *Dialogues d'histoire ancienne* II, 1985, pp. 167-95 (esp. pp. 181-85). I. A. F. Bruce, *An Historical Commentary on the "Hellenica Oxyrhynchia,"* Cambridge, 1967. A. R. Burn, "Persia and the Greeks," *Camb. Hist. Iran* II, pp. 292-391. J. M. Cook, *The Persian Empire*, New York, 1983. Idem, "The Rise of the Achaemenids and the Establishment of Their Empire," *Camb. Hist. Iran* II, pp. 200-91. M. A. Dandamayev, *Iranians in Achaemenid Babylonia*, Costa Mesa, Calif., 1992. A. W. Gomme, A. Andrewes, and K. J. Dover, *A Historical Commentary on Thucydides* V. *Book VIII*, Oxford, 1981. R. T. Hallock, *Persepolis Fortification Tablets*, Chicago, 1969. W. Heckel, *The Marshals of Alexander's Empire*, London, 1992. S. W. Hirsch, *The Friendship of the Barbarians*, Hanover, N.H., 1985. G. M. A. Hoffmann, *From Croesus to Constantine*, Ann Arbor, Mich., 1975. J. Hofstetter, *Die Griechen in Persien. Prosopographie der Griechen im persischen Reich vor Alexander*, AMI, Ergänzungsband 5, Berlin, 1978. S. Hornblower, *Mausolus*, Oxford, 1982. W. Judeich, *Kleinasiatische Studien*, Marburg, 1892. D. M. Lewis, *Sparta and Persia*, Cincinnati Classical Studies, N.S. 1, Leiden, 1977. M. Mellink, "Anatolia," in *CAH*² IV, pp. 211-33. Idem, "Archaeology in Anatolia," *AJA* 94, 1990, p. 150; 95, 1991, p. 151; 96, 1992, p. 148. R. Schmitt, "Die achämenidische Satrapie *tayaiy drayahyā*," *Historia* 21, 1972, pp. 522-27. Idem, "Achae-menidisches bei Thucydides," in H. Koch and D. N. MacKenzie, eds., *Kunst, Kultur und Geschichte der Achämenidenzeit und ihr Fortleben*, AMI, Ergänzungsband 10, Berlin, 1983, pp. 69-86. R. Sealey, *Demosthenes and His Time. A Study in Defeat*, Oxford, 1993. N. Sekunda, "Persian Settlement in Hellespontine Phrygia," in A. Kuhrt and H. Sancisi-Weerdenburg, eds., *Achaemenid History* III. *Method and Theory*, Leiden, 1988, pp. 175-96. C. G. Starr, "Greeks and Persians in the Fourth Century B.C.," *Iranica Antiqua* 11, 1975, pp. 39-99; 12, 1977, pp. 49-115. C. Tuplin, "The Administration of the Achaemenid Empire," in I. Carradice, ed., *Coinage and Administration in the*

Athenian and Persian Empires, BAR 343, Oxford, 1987, pp. 109-66. G. Walser, *Hellas und Iran*, Erträge der Forschung 209, Darmstadt, 1984. M. Weiskopf, "Achaemenid Systems of Governing in Anatolia," Ph.D. diss., University of California, Berkeley, 1982. Idem, *The So-Called "Great Satraps' Revolt," 366-360 B.C.*, Historia Einzelschriften 63, Stuttgart, 1989.

(MICHAEL WEISKOPF)

DASKARA, DASKARAT AL-**MALEK**. See DASTGERD.

DAŠLĪ (Dashly), oasis situated south of the Āmū Daryā (q.v.), on the desert plain of northern Afghanistan, ancient Bactria (q.v.), now in the province of Jūzjān ca 35 km northeast of Āqča (q.v.; Ball, I, p. 84-85 nos. 256-59). Forty-one archeological sites, representing occupations from the Bronze Age to the Kushan period, have been found distributed over an area 100 km^2; they were explored in the 1970s by a Soviet mission under the direction of Viktor Sarianidi. The two principal Bronze Age sites are Dashly 1 and Dashly 3.

Dashly 1 consists of the remains of a square citadel overlooking a "lower town." After destruction of the citadel the ruins were used as a cemetery, also of the Bronze Age.

Dashly 3 comprises two large architectural complexes. The older complex has been identified as a palace. It is a fortified rectangular compound measuring 88 x 84 m; the outer defenses consisted of a double wall and in the middle of each wall a salient composed of a T-shaped corridor flanked by two L-shaped corridors. On the interior were several houses of simple plan and a large storehouse with long, parallel corridors for jars and other supplies. After its destruction this complex was replaced by a fortress, which was reconstructed several times. The second complex has been incorrectly labeled a temple. It comprises a fairly modest residence and a storehouse, surrounded by a double wall on a circular plan buttressed by square towers, which identify it as a citadel. The complex is approximately 45 m in diameter and is surrounded by closely packed houses and a rectangular outer wall measuring 130 x 150 m. Like the older complex, it must have been the official residence of a dignitary charged with administering a merchant community on the borders of Central Asia.

The tombs dug in the vicinity have been pillaged and their furnishings dispersed through the *bāzār* at Kabul (Amiet). These objects reveal a distinct cultural group with settlements located both north of the Āmū Daryā (Sapalli Tepe), to the west in Turkmenia (Togolok, south of the Morḡāb delta), and south of the Hindu Kush, along the perimeter of the Indus valley (Quetta and Sibri). Aside from connections with India in the 3rd millennium B.C.E., they show affinities with material from Elam at the beginning of the 2nd millennium.

See also AFGHANISTAN viii.

Bibliography: P. Amiet, "Bactriane protohistorique," *Syria* 54, 1977, pp. 89-121. Idem, *L'âge des échanges inter-iraniens. 3500-1700 avant J.-C.*, Paris, 1986, pp. 190-204. W. Ball, *Catalogue des sites archéologiques d'Afghanistan*, 2 vols., Paris, 1982. G. Ligabue and S. Salvatori, eds., *Bactria. An Ancient Oasis Civilization from the Sands of Afghanistan*, Venice, 1988. V. I. Sarianidi, "Afghanistan in the Bronze Period," *Afghanistan* 24/2-3, 1971, pp. 26-38. Idem, "Baktriya v epokhu bronzy" (Bactria in the Bronze Age), *Sovetskaya Arkheologiya* 4, 1974, pp. 49-71. Idem, "Issledovaniye pamyatnikov dashlinskogo oazisa" (Investigations of the monuments of the Dašlī oasis), in G. I. Kruglikova, *Drevnayaya Baktriya* (Ancient Bactria) I, Moscow, 1976, pp. 21-86. Idem, *Drevnie zemledeltsy Afganistana* (Ancient farmers of Afghanistan), Moscow, 1977. Idem, "Le complexe cultuel de Togolok 21 en Margiane," *Arts Asiatiques* 41, 1986, pp. 5-21.

(PIERRE AMIET)

DAŠNAK (Pers. Dāšnāk), short name for Hay Yełapʿoxakan Dašnakcʿutʿiwn (Armenian revolutionary federation [A.R.F.]) or its members. The A.R.F. was founded in Tiflis in 1890 by Russian Armenian intellectuals, including Kʿristapʿor Mikʿayēlean (1859-1905) and Simon Zawarean (1866-1913), soon joined by Stepʿan Zōrean (Ṙostom; 1867-1919). By 1905 it had become the most powerful of all Armenian political parties, with branches in Persia, the Russian and Ottoman empires, Europe, and America. The early focus of its activities was the struggle for the political and economic freedom of Ottoman Armenia, but in 1907 it also officially declared itself in favor of an independent, socialist Russian Armenia. It dominated the short-lived Armenian Republic (1918-20), and after the fall of the latter to the Soviets it became the leading anti-Soviet force among Armenians. Throughout this century it has led the struggle for an independent Armenian state comprised of Armenian territory from the former Soviet Union and Turkey, but it has never asserted claims to the small portion of historical Armenia that is under Persian rule.

Although the party is decentralized geographically, its organization is hierarchical. The lowest level consists of groups of five to fifteen members, which are organized into subcommittees. Each regional chapter is governed by a central committee elected by the two lower levels (Hay Yełapʿoxakan Dašnakcʿutʿiwn, Amerikayi Kedronakan Kōmitē [H.Y.D., A.K.K.], II, p. 248; Tasnapetean, 1989, pp. 162-63). The regional central committee is responsible to the central committee, or bureau, of the party, though until 1919 there were often two or three bureaus, each responsible for a different global region. Members of the bureau are appointed by the general assembly, or world congress, which is composed of delegates from the central committees and other important party bodies (Tasnapetean, 1989, pp. 58, 141, 163). At periodic meetings the general assembly defines overall party principles and strategy; it also has the power to amend the A.R.F. charter and bylaws. In 1898 a "body representing the will of the Dašnakcʿutʿiwn" was established to conduct the external relations of the party and to act in place of the general assembly between meetings. In 1904 it was renamed the A.R.F. council, and in 1907 it was assigned the role of supreme judiciary for internal party matters. In 1919 the council was abolished; a supreme judicial body was established, and the remaining responsibilities of the council were exercised by conferences of members of various high-level party units until 1947, when they were reassigned to the bureau (Tasnapetean, 1989, pp. 58, 72, 141; idem, 1985a, pp. 111, 153).

Shortly after its foundation the A.R.F. began sending representatives to recruit Armenian members in Persia. Among the earliest A.R.F. leaders in Persia were Yonan Dawtʿean, Ishkhan Yovsēpʿ Arłutʿean, Nikol Duman (Nikołayos Tēr Yovhannisean), Ṙostom, Vardan (Sargis Mehrabean), Farhat (Sargis Ōhanǰanean), Karō (Aristakēs Zōrean), Stepʿan Stepʿanean (Balajan), Zakʿkʿi (Bagrat Vardapet Ṫʿawakʿalean), Tsaghik (Satʿenik Matinean), Yovsēpʿ Mirzayean, Vrtʿanēs Pʿapʿazean, Yarutʿiwn Martirosean, Arsēn Mikʿayēlean, and Yovhannēs Khan Masehean. The main A.R.F. center in Persia was in Azerbaijan, and it was the Tabrīz A.R.F. bureau that first published, in 1309/1892, the call for a world congress to define more clearly the objectives, methods, and structure of the party (H.Y.D., A.K.K., I, p. 95). In 1313/1895 the Tabrīz bureau was replaced by the central committee of the Tabrīz branch, responsible for most of Persia. As the Armenian community in Tehran grew in size and importance, a second central committee was established there, in 1329/1911 (Tasnapetean, 1989, p. 34; idem, 1982, p. 226; *Alikʿ* [Tehran], 20 December 1990, p. 51). For similar reasons, at some time between 1312 Š./1933 and 1317 Š./1938 two *mekusi* committees (independent local committees) were established for Persia, in Nor Juła (New Jolfā) at Isfahan and at Ābādān in Ḵūzestān (Tasnapetean, 1985a, p. 149), but, owing to declining membership, the Nor Juła branch was annexed to the Ḵūzestān commettee in 1326 Š./1947 (*Alikʿ*, 20 December 1990, p. 40). After World War II, owing to Soviet occupation and emigration to Soviet Armenia, the Tabrīz central committee was downgraded to a committee (personal interview with a member of the Persian A.R.F.). The central and *mekusi* committees in Persia coordinate the management of their internal affairs, as well as maintaining contact with the bureau, which makes all important general political and ideological decisions.

In the early years the Tabrīz A.R.F. remained particularly important, owing to the strategic location of Azerbaijan and its native Armenian population, which provided a base for activities across the Ottoman and Russian borders. Arms were assembled or repaired in the Xarisx (Anchor) arms workshop in Tabrīz, which was opened in 1308/1891. The monasteries of St. Astuacacin (Derik) in the Salmās district and then St. Tʿadēos in Mākū and St. Stepʿanos Naxavkay in Jolfā were convenient stations for the smuggling of weapons, fighters, and literature into Turkish Armenia; a secondary route passed through Ḵᵛoy to Van. Anzalī, Rašt, and Āstārā were important centers for communication with Baku (Malxas, pp. 145-47, 254-55, 314; Vracʿean; Hangoycʿ, August 1923, p. 82, March 1924, p. 142, May 1924, p. 143; H.Y.D, 1982, p. 231, 1985, pp. 141, 143; idem, A.K.K., I, p. 104; Varantean, II, p. 130; Amurean, 1950, pp. 12-13, 16-17, 19, 30, 32; Stepʿanean, February 1930, p. 88; *Alikʿ*, 20 December 1990, pp. 47, 49-51).

Guerrilla groups crossed the Ottoman border from Azerbaijan to fight Turkish military units and Kurdish tribes encouraged by the Ottoman government to massacre Armenians settled there. In general the Persian monarchy permitted such guerrilla operations in order to weaken Ottoman authority over these tribes, which occasionally also caused trouble on the Persian side of the border. It interfered only under pressure from the Russian or Ottoman governments; for example, after the Xanasor expedition to the province of Van in 1314/1897 many A.R.F. fighters were arrested and nine executed. Party operations were hampered by continued foreign pressure, and during the economic crisis of 1319/1901 the attention of the Armenian community was turned elsewhere. But from 1322/1904 to 1324/1906, during the ferment of the Persian Constitutional Revolution (q.v.), the A.R.F. regained much of its strength (Amurean, 1950, pp. 29-30; Tasnapetean, 1982, pp. 228-30, 235; H.Y.D., A.K.K., II, pp. 97-109). For example, as a result of clashes between Armenians and Tatars in the Caucasus in 1905-06 it was the party that prepared to defend the Persian Armenian population should the conflict spread across the border, which fortunately did not happen (Amurean, 1950, pp. 104-06; Tasnapetean, 1982, pp. 233, 310).

For the A.R.F. the most important period in Persian history was that of the Constitutional Revolution. Individual party members were active among the constitutionalists as early as 1324/1906, and by the time of the anticonstitutional coup by Moḥammad-ʿAlī Shah (1324-27/1907-09) in 1326/1908 (see CONSTITUTIONAL REVOLUTION ii) the party was providing weapons and ammunition, in addition to advice, to the revolutionary leaders in Tabrīz. Monarchist pillaging of Armenian villages, Ottoman incursions into Azerbaijan, and concurrent Kurdish attacks led the party to full involvement by the autumn of that year, an involvement that was further fueled by the success of the Ottoman constitutional revolution and the perceived benefits of democracy for Armenians. The party's commitment can be gauged from the participation of one of the most important A.R.F. leaders, Ṙostom, in such revolutionary activity (Tasnapetean, 1979, pp. 164-69; idem, 1982, pp. 235, 282, 310; Ēlmar, pp. 104-35; Chaqueri, p. 10; Varantean, II, pp. 61-62). In Tabrīz during several episodes in the autumn of 1326/1908 and early

1327/1909 Armenian fighters formed crucial portions of the revolutionary forces led by Sattār Khan and Bāqer Khan (q.v.; Kasrawī, *Mašrūṭa*, p. 713; Browne, *Persian Revolution*, pp. 269-70; Varantean, II, pp. 73-76; "Martiros Č'aruxč'ian), and they helped the constitutionalists to gain control of various parts of Azerbaijan (Ēlmar, pp. 135-63, 170-81; Kasrawī, *Mašrūṭa*, pp. 873-76). Russian occupation of Tabrīz on 9 Rabīʿ II 1327/30 April 1909 halted these activities, but by then the rebellion had spread to other parts of Persia.

Yeprem Khan (Epʿrem Dawtʿean), a member of the Persian A.R.F. since 1896, helped to organize the revolutionaries, including many Armenians, in Rašt and Anzalī. They captured those cities on 27 Moḥarram/8 February and Qazvīn on 14 Rabīʿ II/5 May 1909. Yeprem also organized troops to participate in the march to Tehran, which he entered with Moḥammad-Walī Sepahdār-e Aʿẓam and Baḵtīārī troops on 24 Jomādā II/13 July (Yeprem, pp. 23-34, 40-59; Kasrawī, *Āḏarbāyjān*, pp. 23, 52-59; Shuster, pp. xlii, xlvi; Varantean, II, pp. 82-85; Farrō, November 1924, pp. 67, 71-72). In November the Second Majles appointed him chief of the Tehran police and then of the gendarmerie; during his tenure he instituted a number of reforms (Ēlmar, 290-93). In the winter of 1327-28/1909-10 his forces (including A.R.F. recruits) and the Baḵtīārīs suppressed the counterrevolutionary uprisings of Raḥīm Khan Čalabīānlū (q.v.) in the region of Ardabīl and Mollā Qorbān-ʿĀlī in Zanjān. In April they brought Šāhsevan tribesmen under control (Amurean, 1976, pp. 86-112; Ēlmar, pp. 296-343; Shuster, p. lii; Alka, p. 13; Farrō, December 1924, pp. 68-77, January 1925, pp. 131-37, February 1925, pp. 90-94). After the exiled Moḥammad-ʿAlī landed on Persian soil in July 1911, Yeprem Khan organized three armies and in September successfuly halted the former shah's forces (Ēlmar, pp. 457-93; Shuster, pp. 117-35; Farrō, March 1925, pp. 112-16).

Meanwhile, Duman led the constitutionalist forces defending Tabrīz until December, when Russian troops crushed all opposition and arrested and executed many constitutionalists, including some A.R.F. members (Ēlmar, pp. 184-93; Varantean, II, p. 88; "Parskastan"; Kasrawī, *Āḏarbāyjān*, pp. 356-58; Dēoyeancʿ, pp. 77-90). Yeprem Khan died on 2 Jomādā II 1330/19 May 1912, during a second campaign against the forces of the former shah and his brother Sālār-al-Dawla; another A.R.F. leader, Kʿeṙi (Aršak Gafawean) brought the campaign to a successful close (Ēlmar, pp. 480-93, 522-35; Kasrawī, *Āḏarbāyjān*, pp. 510-27; Farrō, April 1925, pp. 88-93; "Parskastan").

By December 1912, however, the A.R.F. had withdrawn support from what it viewed as a "capitulationist" Persian government, though it helped to ensure that elections were held for the Third Majles before World War I (Abrahamian, 1982, pp. 109-11; Amurean, 1976, pp. 120-22; Ēlmar, pp. 123-24; H.Y.D. Šahstani Kedronakan Kōmitē [Š.K.K.], p. 190; see CONSTITUTIONAL REVOLUTION iii). Party forces continued to defend Armenians in Azerbaijan during three Ottoman occupations, Kurdish attacks, and the chaotic period of World War I and its aftermath. When A.R.F. revolts against the sovietization of Russian Armenia were crushed in mid-1921, approximately 10,000 party leaders, intellectuals, fighters, and their families crossed the Aras and found refuge in Persia (Afanasyan, p. 175; Gēorgean; Minaxorean, pp. 89-97). Their presence ensured A.R.F. predominance over other traditional Armenian parties of Persia and indeed the entire Armenian community, which was centered around the Armenian church.

Despite the party's commitment to socialism in principle, unfavorable conditions in Persia had led to the downplaying of attempts to introduce it there. In the early period village conditions were not conducive to socialist activities (see, e.g., Hangoycʿ, July 1924, pp. 139-40), and in the 20th century Persian governments usually persecuted leftists. Furthermore, following its expulsion from Soviet Armenia after 1921, the A.R.F. became fiercely anti-Soviet throughout the world, though it did not completely abandon its socialist principles.

In Persia the A.R.F. published a series of newspapers to disseminate party views, beginning with *Aṙawōt* (Tabrīz, 1327-29/1909-11); *Alikʿ*, established in Tehran in 1310 Š./1931, is the only Armenian-language newspaper still published in Persia (*Alikʿ*, 20 December 1990, pp. 22-23, 31, 62-63).

Azerbaijan remained the main center of the party in the early 1920s, when its leaders at Tabrīz maintained contact with exiled leaders of the short-lived Republic of Azerbaijan (q.v. iv) and encouraged Kurdish rebellions in Turkey. As a result Turkish and Soviet pressure led the Persian government to arrest some party members (Amurean, 1987, p. 10; Kendal, pp. 64-5; Šahan).

The A.R.F. usually supported the Pahlavi regime (1304-57 Š./1925-79), which in turn generally regarded the party's anti-Soviet stance and lack of claim to Persian territory with favor. The party was generally influential in the Majles, as the two representatives allotted to the Armenian community beginning with the Fifth Majles (1304-06 Š./1925-27) were generally members or willing to coöperate. Only during periods of strong anti-Pahlavi sentiment and the first few years of the Islamic Revolution were leftist Armenians able to elect a representative (Pʿahlevanyan, pp. 106-08; Abrahamian, 1982, pp. 100-01; Połosean, p. 656; Balean Tēr-Yakobean, pp. 74-75, 252-54). The party's only real opposition to the Persian government was focused on the assimilationist policies of Reżā Shah (1304-20 Š./1925-41). From 1315 Š./1936 to 1321 Š./1942 most Armenian and other minority schools were closed; all segments of the Armenian community then united to ensure the perpetuation of the Armenian language and culture. Because of its generally close association with the government, the A.R.F. lost some support during this period (Abrahamian, 1982, p. 163; Amurean, 1987, p. 11; Balean Tēr-Yakobean, pp. 159-61, 230; Pʿahlevanyan, pp. 110-11, 143-44, 191), and in the constitutional crisis at the beginning of World War II a leftist opposition developed among Persian Armenians (*Alikʿ*, 20 December 1990, pp. 39, 41-43). During the Soviet occupation of northern Persia in 1320-25 Š./1941-46 (see AZERBAIJAN v) Persian Armenians elected parliamentary representatives hostile to the A.R.F. (Abrahamian, 1982, pp. 198, 292; Minasean; Demirǰean, pp. 105-13), and the Soviets imprisoned and exiled some A.R.F. leaders.

At the end of 1945 the A.R.F. did not officially oppose a movement to repatriate Armenians to Soviet Armenia, and some individual party members supported it, but the onset of the Cold War, the withdrawal of Soviet territorial claims against Turkey on behalf of Soviet Armenia, and anti-A.R.F. measures during the repatriation process caused the party to shift gradually over the next two years to outright opposition to repatriation (Mandalian, pp. 90-91; Pʿahlevanyan, pp. 181-87; Mouradian; *Alikʿ*, 20 December 1990, p. 46; Atamian, pp. 407-11). The A.R.F. seems to have remained neutral during the period of Moḥammad Moṣaddeq (Cottam, p. 81; see COUP D'ÉTAT OF 1332 Š./1953).

In 1958 the three dioceses of the Armenian church in Persia shifted allegiance from the see of Echmiadzin in Soviet Armenia to that of Cilicia, in Antelias, a village northeast of Beirut. The A.R.F. throughout the world had supported the see of Cilicia since 1956, whereas other Armenian political parties had remained loyal to that of Echmiadzin. The shift in Persia was a result of pressure from the government (and probably from Western powers as well), which, like the A.R.F., feared Soviet influence; it probably also reflected the desire of the A.R.F. to maintain its predominance among Persian Armenians (Ternon, pp. 136-37; Ełiayean, pp. 724-28; Indoyean).

During the Persian Revolution of 1357 Š./1978-79 the Armenian left again regained prominence; the A.R.F. was initially mistrusted by the new government, in which the leftists had some influence, and a number of party members were arrested and interrogated. Members of the Persian left, including the Armenian left, were themselves soon subjected to persecution, however. The leaders of the Islamic Republic became convinced that the A.R.F. was not working against them, and relations returned to normal. Nevertheless, the status of Armenian schools, the religious and cultural rights of the Armenian church, and, in the early 1990s, reverberations of the conflict between Armenians and Azerbaijanis in Karabagh all required negotiation between the Armenian community and the Persian government (*Alikʿ*, 12 March 1990, p. 1, 7 March 1993, p. 2; Balean Tēr-Yakobean, pp. 240-45; Pʿahlevanyan, p. 264; Zenian, pp. 8-9; Abrahamian, 1993, pp. 48, 51; interview with an A.R.F. leader from Persia). Today the A.R.F. is one of the most important political parties among the Armenian diaspora, the only Armenian party permitted to exist (semiofficially) in Persia, and a leading force in the parliamentary opposition in the newly established Republic of Armenia.

See also ARMENIA AND IRAN vi.

Bibliography: E. Abrahamian, *Iran between Two Revolutions*, Princeton, N.J., 1982. Idem, *Khomeinism. Essays on the Islamic Republic*, Berkeley and Los Angeles, 1993. S. Afanasyan, *L'Arménie, l'Azerbaidjan et la Géorgie, de l'indépendance à l'instauration du pouvoir soviétique, 1917-1923*, Paris, 1981. G. Agabekov, *G.G.P.U. (Zapiski chekista)*, tr. H. Bunn as *O.G.P.U. The Russian Secret Terror*, New York, 1931. Alka, "Parskastan. Mi ēǰ parskakan yełapʿ. patmutʿiwnicʿ," *Drōšak* 21, January 1911, p. 13. A. Amurean [Tēr Ōhanean], *H. Y. Dašnakcʿutʿiwnə Parskastanum 1890-1918*, Tehran, 1950. Idem, *H. Y. Dašnakcʿutʿiwn, Epʿrem, parskakan sahmanadrutʿiwn*, 2 vols., Tehran, 1976-79. Idem, "Parskakan hołhi vray. Azat, baycʿ taragir," *Drōšak* 17, 30 September 1987, pp. 9-11. S. Atamian, *The Armenian Community. The Historical Development of a Social and Ideological Conflict*, New York, 1955. B. and S. Bałean Tēr-Yakobean, *Patmutʿiwn iranahayeri*, Glendale, Calif., 1985. C. Chaqueri, "The Role and Impact of Armenian Intellectuals in Iranian Politics, 1905-1911," *Armenian Review* 41, 1988, pp. 1-51. R. W. Cottam, *Nationalism in Iran*, 2nd ed., Pittsburgh, Pa., 1979. V. Demirǰean, "Ancʿkerə Darašambi S. Stepʿanos Naxavkayi Vankʿum 1905-1965 Tʿ. Tʿ.," in V. Demirǰean, ed., *Diwan Atrpatakani hayocʿ patmutʿean* I, Tehran, 1345 Š./1966, pp. 99-130. T. Dēoyeancʿ, "Keankʿis druagnericʿ," *Hayrenikʿ amsagir* 22, January-February 1944, pp. 77-90.

B. Ełiayean, *Žamanakakicʿ patmutʿiwn katʿołikosutʿean hayocʿ Kilikioy 1914-1972*, Antelias, Lebanon, 1975. Ēlmar [Y. Yovhannisean], *Epʿrem*, Tehran, 1964. Farrō, comp., "Epʿremi gorcunēutʿiwn Parskastanum (Grišayi yušerə)," *Hayrenikʿ amsagir* 3, November 1924, pp. 64-72; December 1924, pp. 68-77; January 1925, pp. 131-37; February 1925, pp. 89-96; March 1925, pp. 108-16; April 1925, pp. 86-96. V. Gēorgean, *Lernahayastani herosamartə (1919-1921)*, Bucharest, 1923, pp. 67, 74-75, 111, 141-43, 161, 168-69. *Ḥamāsa-ye Yeprem*, Tehran, 2535-1355 Š./1976. N. Hangoycʿ, comp., "Samsoni yušerə," in *Hayrenikʿ amsagir* 1, August 1923, pp. 78-97; 2, February 1924, pp. 130-44; March 1924, pp. 140-44; April 1924, pp. 130-44; May 1924, pp. 138-44; June 1924, pp. 136-44; July 1924, pp. 138-44; August 1924, pp. 105-09. Hay Yełapʿoxakan Dašnakcʿutʿiwn, Amerikayi Kedronakan Kōmitē, *Diwan H. Y. Dašnakcʿutʿean*, 2 vols., Boston, 1934-38. Hay Yełapʿoxakan Dašnakcʿutʿiwn, Šahstani Kedronakan Kōmitē, "Azdararutʿiwn," *Drōšak* 23, November-December 1913, p. 190. Hayrik, comp., "Yełapʿoxakan aršawə Tʿehrani vray ew Epʿremi gndi derə," *Hayrenikʿ amsagir* 3, May 1925, pp. 26-38. H. Indoyean, *Hayrapetakan patuirakutʿiwn 1956 i Tʿehran*, Beirut, 1959. Kendal, "Kurdistan in Turkey," in *People Without a Country*, ed. G. Chaliand, tr. M. Pallis, London, 1980, pp. 47-106. Malxas [A. Yovsēpʿean], *Aprumner* I, Boston, 1931. J. G.

Mandalian. "The 151 Repatriates from Armenia," *Armenian Review* 4, 1951, pp. 89-100. "Martiros Č'aruxč'ian," in *Drōšak* 20, May-June 1910, p. 51. B. Minasean, "Yušer. Tasə tari, tasn amis ew tasneōt' ōr xorhrdayin banterum ew ašxatank'ayin čambarnerum. T'awrizə, naxk'an karmir banaki grawumə ew grawumic' yetoy," *Drōšak* 21, 20 June 1990, pp. 12-14; 18 July 1990, pp. 10-14; 1 August 1990, pp. 15-18; 15 August 1990, pp. 16-18; 29 August 1990, pp. 15-17; 12 September 1990, pp. 20-24; 26 September 1990, pp. 13-14. V. Minaxorean, "April 2-i gaght'ə (Erewan-T'awriz)," *Hayrenik' amsagir* 2, December 1923, pp. 89-97. C. Mouradian, "Immigration des Arméniens en ASSR," *Cahiers du monde russe et soviétique* 20, 1979, pp. 79-110. L. Nalbandian, *The Armenian Revolutionary Movement*, Berkeley, Calif., 1963. N. Ōdabašean, "Im keank'i patmut'iwnə," *Hayrenik' amsagir* 19, July 1941, pp. 159-68; August 1941, pp. 72-81; September-October 1941, pp. 100-20. H. L. P'ahlevanyan, *Iranahay hamaynk'ə (1941-1979)*, Yerevan, 1989. "Parskastan. Verǰin tarway čakatamartnerə ew 'Dašnakc'ut'ean' masnakc'ut'iwnə (Namak Parskastanic')," *Drōšak* 22, February 1912, pp. 25-28; April 1912, pp. 85-87. T. Połosean, *Raffi taregirk'*, Tehran, 1349 Š./1970. E. Rā'īn, *Yeprem Ḵān-e Sardār*, Tehran, 1350 Š./1971. Šahan [H. Tēr Yakobean], *Alek'sandrapōli dašnagrēn 1930 i kovkasean apstambut'iwnnerə (vergnahatumner). Hator B. P'etruar 18i apstambut'enēn prōmet'ēi hraparakumə*, Marseilles, 1935. W. M. Shuster, *The Strangling of Persia*, New York, 1912. Y. Step'anean, "Nikol Duman (Mahuan 15-ameaki art'iw)," *Hayrenik' amsagir* 8, February 1930, pp. 79-91; August 1930, pp. 133-41; October 1930, pp. 148-60. H. Tasnapetean, ed., *Ṙostom*, Beirut, 1979. Idem, ed., *H.Y. Dasnakc'ut'ean kazmakerpakan kar'oyc'i holovoyt'*, 2nd ed., Beirut, 1985a. Idem, ed., *Niwt'er H.Y. Dašnakc'ut'ean patmut'ean hamar*, 2nd ed., II, Beirut, 1985b; IV, Beirut, 1982. Idem, *H.Y. Dašnakc'ut'iwnĕ ir kazmut'enēn minč'ew Z. Ĕnt'. Žołov (1890-1924)*, tr. B. Fleming and V. Habeshian as H. Dasnabedian, *History of the Armenian Revolutionary Federation Dashnaktsutiwn (1890-1924)*, Milan, 1989. A. Ter Minassian, *La question arménienne*, Paris, 1983. Y. Ternon, *La cause arménienne*, tr. A. A. Mangouni as *The Armenian Cause*, New York, 1985. M. Varandean, *H.Y. Dašnakc'ut'ean patmut'iwn* I, Paris, 1932; II, Cairo, 1950. S. Vrac'ean, "Bagrat vrd. T'awak'aleani namaknerə," *Hayrenik' amsagir* 12, November 1933, pp. 103-10. Yeprem Kān [Ep'rem Dawt'ean], tr. Nerūs as *Az Anzalī tā Tehrān*, Tehran, 1356 Š./1977. D. Zenian, "The Islamic Revolution. A Blessing in Disguise for Iranian-Armenians," in *AGBU* [Armenian General Benevolent Union] *News* 1, September 1991, pp. 8-9.

(ARAM ARKUN)

DAŠT (plain, open ground), Persian term for a very specific type of landscape. In scientific geographical

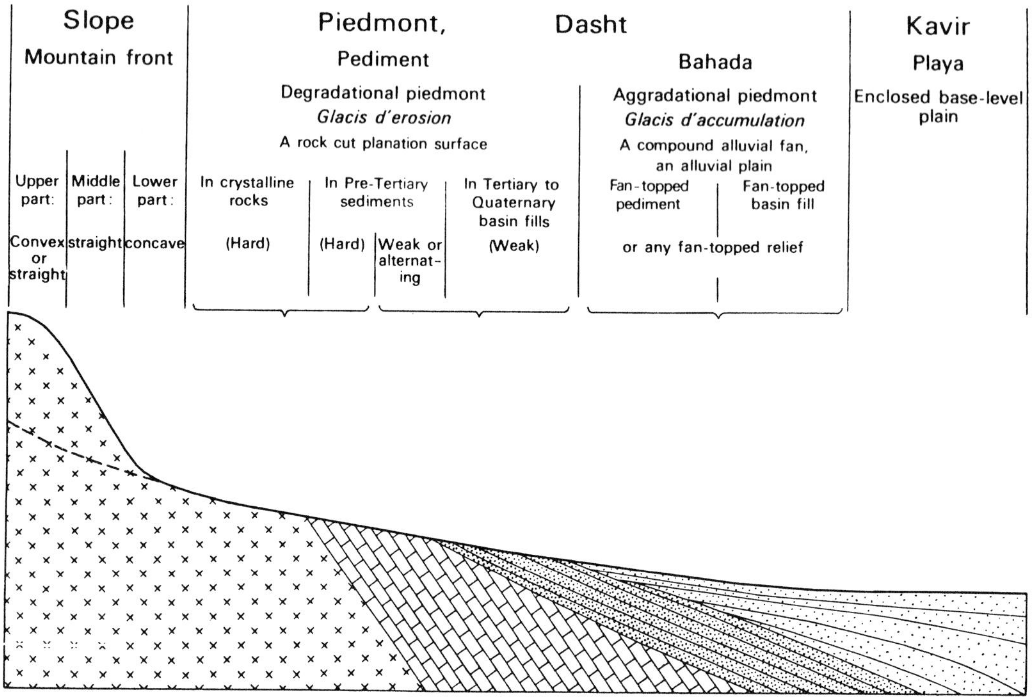

Figure 7. Section showing the composition of *dašt* and adjacent *kavīr*. After Weise.

literature it is applied to the extended gravel piedmonts and plains that are almost ubiquitous in arid central Persia. Sloping down from the upper reaches of the mountains and highlands, *dašt* areas are built up by more or less coarse material like gravels of different sizes and composition (e.g., rocky hammada, pebbled serir). They cover broad expanses of surface and pile up in the interior of mountain ranges, seeming to drown them in their own debris. Geomorphological studies have shown, however, that degradation of the higher parts of the relief coincides with aggradation of its lower parts. *Dašt* slopes are therefore both erosional and depositional features (Figure 7). Such phenomena are called "pediments" and are differentiated into degradational and aggradational piedmonts (Weise, p. 451). The gravel deposits of the *dašt* generally form very thin covers of erosional material; one of the main features of *dašt* areas is their gentle slopes, no more than a few meters per thousand in their lower reaches, though as much as 50 m or more per thousand close to the mountain front. As a precise descriptive term, *dašt* must not be confused with *kavīr* (playa), which refers to surface coverings composed exclusively of very fine materials like clay, silt, and salts of various kinds. The much higher salinity of the *kavīr* leads to the formation of salt crusts, whereas the plains surrounding the *dašt* may develop gypsum crusts or none at all. Furthermore, although the almost total absence of flora and fauna in the *kavīr* convey the impression of an entirely sterile natural environment, *dašt* areas, even under extreme climatic conditions, are characterized by more or less regularly distributed forms of desert or semidesert vegetation and fauna (Bobek; de Misonne; Anderson; Read).

For details of Persian *dašt*s and *kavīr*s, see DESERT.

Bibliography: S. C. Anderson, "Zoogeographic Analysis of the Lizard Fauna of Iran," in *Camb. Hist. Iran* I, pp. 305-71. H. Bobek, "Vegetation," in *Camb. Hist. Iran* I, pp. 280-93. A. Gabriel, "Die Lut und ihre Wege," *Zeitschrift für Erdkunde* 10, 1942, pp. 423-42. S. Jervis Read, "Ornithology," in *Camb. Hist. Iran* I, pp. 372-92. X. de Misonne, "Mammals," in *Camb. Hist. Iran*, I, pp. 294-304. O. Weise, "Morphodynamics and Morphogenesis of Pediments in the Deserts of Iran," *Geographical Journal* 144, 1978, pp. 450-62.

(ECKART EHLERS)

DAŠT-E ARŽAN (also Arjan, Arzan, lit., "plain of the mountain or bitter almond"; Forṣat Šīrāzī, p. 275), a mountain basin ca. 14 x 5-6 km (Manouchehr Kasheff, personal communication) situated 1,500 m above sea level on the road from Shiraz to Kāzerūn. Located on the elevated plain is a small catchment area, fed largely by northern springs. It is surrounded by limestone escarpments, crossed from the south by the Pīra-zan pass (*kotal*). Centuries ago Dašt-e Aržan was covered with forests and was famous for its lush foliage and ample pasturelands; almond trees flourished there. At present the pastures serve as grazing lands. On the eastern flank of the plain are marshes fed by the abundant streams that flow beneath the limestone hills (Mostawfī, p. 4).

According to early Muslim geographers, the lake was 10 farsangs long at high water; the width of 8 farsangs given in *Ḥodūd al-ʿālam* (tr. Minorsky, p. 55) was apparently exaggerated (Eṣṭaḵrī, p. 122; Ebn Ḥawqal, p. 277; Ebn al-Balḵī, p. 153). Lions used to roam the fertile plain (Ebn al-Balḵī, p. 154; *Nozhat al-qolūb*, ed. Le Strange, p. 135). Later travelers confirmed that after a steady rainfall a large lake appeared; lions and wild boars could be found in the meadows (Mohandes et al., pp. 56-57; Forṣat Šīrāzī, p. 275).

The subdistrict of Dašt-e Aržan now belongs to the *šahrestān* (district) of Kāzerūn. Until recently about 720 ha of land were under cultivation, 500 of them dry-farmed in wheat. Some experts have argued that the arable land could be expanded to approximately 2,500 ha through irrigation (Mobaššerī and Qodratnamā, p. 117). According to legend, the village of Dašt-e Aržan, now the administrative center of the subdistrict, was the birthplace of Salmān the Persian, a companion of the Prophet Moḥammad. Ḥājj Mīrzā Ḥasan Ḥosaynī Fasāʾī (ed. Rastgār, I, p. 742; II, pp. 1437-38) reported that certain local families claimed to be related to Salmān and were thus known as Salmānī. A small shrine (*qadamgāh*) shelters a pool fed by a spring; it is popularly believed that Salmān once bathed there (Sadīd-al-Salṭana, p. 39).

Bibliography: R. Badīʿī, *Joḡrāfīā-ye mofaṣṣal-e Īrān*, Tehran, 1361 Š./1982, pp. 36, 162. Edāra-ye joḡrāfīāʾī-e arteš, *Farhang-e joḡrāfīāʾī-e ābādīhā-ye Īrān* CII. *Kāzerūn*, Tehran, 1362 Š./1983, pp. 105-06. Moḥammad-Naṣīr Forṣat Šīrāzī (Forsat-al-Dawla), *Āṯār-e ʿajam*, ed. ʿA. Dehbāšī, Tehran, 1362 Š./1983. Jehād-e Sāzandagī, *Farhang-e ejtemāʿī-e dehāt wa mazāreʿ-e ostān-e Fārs*, Tehran, 1363 Š./1984a, p. 142. Idem, *Farhang-e eqteṣādī-e dehāt wa mazāreʿ-e ostān-e Fārs*, Tehran, 1363 Š./1984b, p. 142. Markaz-e āmār-e Īrān, *Farhang-e ābādīhā-ye kešvar* XXIII, Tehran, 1361 Š./1982, p. 90. Idem, *Farhang-e ābādīhā-ye kešvar* II, Tehran, 1368 Š./1989, pp. 20-21. F. Mobaššerī and Q. Qodratnamā, *Arzyābī-e važʿ-e mawjūd wa emkānāt-e tawseʿa-ye manābeʿ-e āb* IV, Tehran, pp. 117-18. Moḥammad-Ḥasan Mīrzā Mohandes et al., *Do safar-nāma az janūb-e Īrān*, ed. S. ʿA. Āl-e Dāwūd, Tehran, 1368 Š./1989. A. Mostawfī, *Gozārešhā-ye joḡrāfīāʾī-e Lūt Zangī Aḥmad*, Tehran, 1348 Š./1969, pp. 4-6. *Nozhat al-qolūb*, ed. Le Strange, pp. 187, 240. N. Nūḥ, "Dašt-e Aržan," *Majalla-ye talāš* 49, Ḵordād 1354 Š./May-June 1975, pp. 18-19. M.-Ḥ. Pāpolī Yazdī, *Farhang-e ābādīhā wa makānhā-ye maḏhabī-e kešvar*, Mašhad, n.d., p. 247. Razmārā, *Farhang* VII, p. 101. Sadīd-al-Salṭana Kabābī, *Safar-nāma*, ed. A. Eqtedārī, Tehran, 1362 Š./1983. Yāqūt, *Boldān* II, p. 576.

(SAYYED ʿALĪ ĀL-E DĀWŪD)

DAŠT-E NĀWOR (lit. "plain of the lake"), a depression (average elev. 3,100 m) 60 x 15 km with a brackish lake (*nāwor*, *nāvor*, Mong. *nor*) in the center, located at 33° 41′ N and 67° 46′ E, about 60 km west of Ḡaznī. It is now permanently inhabited by Persian-speaking Hazaras and is also the summer grazing ground for Pashto-speaking nomads; formerly the Afghan cavalry also summered there.

Middle and Lower Paleolithic and Mesolithic artifacts have been found in a survey conducted along the lake shores by Louis Dupree (pp. 40, 69-70; Ball, p. 86). The lake may have been mistaken for the source of the Arachōtos river by Ptolemy (6.20.2; cf. Bernard, pp. 182-85), and there is a possible 10th-century reference to it in *Ḥodūd al-ʿālam* (tr. Minorsky, pp. 64, 199).

In 1346 Š./1967 André Boutière, a French geologist, found five badly defaced Kushan inscriptions on a ridge (elev. 4,320 m) overhanging the western edge of Dašt-e Nāwor; they have since been destroyed. DN I and DN II were written in Greek script, probably in the Bactrian language, though there is some doubt on the latter point (Lazard et al., pp. 217-18); DN III and DN V were in a script that has not yet been deciphered; DN IV was in Middle Indian written in Kharoṣṭhī script. DN I, III, and IV together clearly constituted a single trilingual inscription from the reign of the Kushan king Vima Kadphises, in the month of Gorpiaios 279. As all the inscriptions were badly engraved and defaced, readings can be only tentative (Fussman, 1974, for the most part repeated by Mukherjee with occasional acknowledgments; for an attempt at reconstruction from Fussman's photographs, see Davary and Humbach; cf. Lazard). The name of the goddess Šao Nana can be read in DN I, line 2, which suggests that the content of the trilingual inscription was primarily religious. From the evidence published by Robert Göbl (pls. I-III) it is now clear that the titles accompanying Vima's name in DN I and IV are not evidence for a date early in his reign, as originally suggested (Fussman, 1974, p. 38). Nor do the Dašt-e Nāwor inscriptions provide evidence for the dating of Kanishka's reign. Scholars are still debating the correct way of reconciling the date of 279 in Vima's inscription with other chronological schemes (e.g., Fussman, 1974, pp. 38-50; Bivar, 1976).

The script of DN III and V seems to be derived from Aramaic or from Kharoṣṭhī, which was itself derived from Aramaic. In 1353 Š./1974 very few instances of this script were known, one of them from Surkh Kotal (Sork̲ Kōtal). Gérard Fussman (1974, pp. 32-34) suggested that it was meant to express Kambojī, an early language still unattested in surviving examples, which was spoken by a tribe settled in this very region and which may have been Iranian, perhaps even akin to proto-Ormuri. On the basis of evidence surviving from Central Asia, Soviet scholars (Livshits; Rtveladze and Livshits) have, however, proposed that the unknown script from Dašt-e Nāwor was used to transcribe the language of the Yüe-chih invaders of Bactria (q.v.) in the late Hellenistic period. Whether or not this view is accepted, there are now sufficient surviving examples of this script from Central Asia and Afghanistan, particularly from Surkh Kotal, Āy K̲ānom (q.v.), Qara Tepe (old Terme̲d), Issyk, and other sites, to ensure that the language is not Kambojī. It should be emphasized, however, that the scripts from Issyk and some other sites are not exactly like that of DN III; the category of "unknown scripts" still contains several different types (Fussman, 1978, pp. 435-36; idem, 1987, p. 356).

Bibliography: F. R. Allchin and N. Hammond, *The Archaeology of Afghanistan from Earliest Times to the Timurid Period*, London, 1978. W. Ball, *Archaeological Gazetteer of Afghanistan. Catalogue des sites archéologiques d'Afghanistan* I, Paris, 1982. P. Bernard, "Un problème de toponymie antique dans l'Asie Centrale. Les noms anciens de Qandahar," *Stud. Ir.* 3/2, 1974, pp. 171-85. A. D. H. Bivar, "The Kuṣāṇa Trilingual," *BSOAS* 39/2, 1976, pp. 333-40. G. D. Davary and H. Humbach, "Die baktrische Inschrift IDN I von Dasht-e Nāwūr (Afghanistan)," *Abh. der geistes- und sozialwissen-schaftlichen Klasse der Akademie der Wissenschaften und der Literatur im Mainz* 1, 1976, pp. 4-21. R. S. Davies, "The Palaeolithic," in F. R. Allchin and N. Hammond, *The Archaeology of Afghanistan from Earliest Times to the Timurid Period*, London, 1978. G. Fussman, "Documents épigraphiques kouchans," *Bulletin de l'Ecole Française d'Extrême Orient* 61, 1974, pp. 1-66. Idem, "Chronique des études kouchanes (1975-1977)," *JA* 266, 1978, pp. 419-36. Idem, "Chronique des études kouchanes (1978-1987)," *JA* 275, 1987, pp. 333-400. R. Göbl, *System und Chronologie der Münzprägung des Kušān-reiches*, Vienna, 1984. G. Lazard, review of G. D. Davary and H. Humbach, "Die baktrische Inschrift IDN I von Dasht-e Nāwūr (Afghanistan)," *Kratylos* 22, 1977, pp. 171-72. Idem, F. Grenet, and C. de Lamberterie, "Notes bactriennes," *Stud. Ir.* 13/2, 1984, pp. 199-232. V. Livshits, "Nadpisi iz Dil'berdzhina" (Inscriptions from Delbarjīn), in I. T. Kruglikova, ed., *Drevnyaya Baktriya. Materialy Sovetskogo-Afganskoĭ ekspeditsii 1969-1973 gg.* (Ancient Bactria. Materials of the Soviet-Afghan expedition in the years 1969-73), Moscow, 1976, pp. 165-66. B. N. Mukherjee, "Observations on an Unknown Script," *Journal of the Epigraphical Society of India* 4, 1977, pp. 14-21. E. Rtveladze and V. Livshits, *Pamyatniki drevneĭ pis'mennosti* (Monuments of ancient writing), Tashkent, 1985.

(GÉRARD FUSSMAN)

DAŠT-E QALʿA (lit., "plain of the fortress"), small *bāzār* village on an irrigation canal near the junction of the Kōkča and Āmū Darya (q.v.; Panj) rivers in the province of Badak̲šān, northeastern Afghanistan, the site of several earlier settlements. It is the major village on the plain of Torḡay Tīppa (Moḥammad-Nāder Khan, pp. 402-03; tr., 236-37; ed. Sotūda, pp.

251-52), which extends over approximately 220 km^2 and forms part of K̲ᵛāja-ye Ḡār *woloswalī* in Tak̲ār *welāyat*. It was founded in about 1335/1916-1917, and in 1344-54 Š./1965-75 its population was estimated at 400-750, the population of the plain at 1,760-6,472 (Gentelle, p. 53).

The plain around Dašt-e Qalʿa, which has been irrigated and inhabited since the remote past, was thoroughly explored by a French archeological team between 1343 Š./1964 and 1358 Š./1979 (*MDAFA* XXI, XXVI-XXXI).

The first known settlement was a Bronze Age colony from the Mature Indus and post-Harappan periods (Francfort). Although the site was almost abandoned in the early Iron Age (early 1st millennium B.C.E.), it was reoccupied during the Achaemenid period (6th-4th centuries B.C.E.), when a circular fortress and several villages were constructed (Gardin and Lyonnet, pp. 132-36). In the Hellenistic period (3rd-1st century B.C.E.) the large city of Āy K̲ānom (q.v.) was founded, possibly as Alexandria Oxeiana, known in the 2nd century C.E. as Eukratideia. There was no break in occupation during the Kushan period (1st-3rd centuries C.E.). A small Islamic city of the pre-Mongol period, Zūlm, has been discovered (Bernard and Francfort, pp. 27-38), as well as a Timurid fortification on the old Bālā Ḥesār of Āy K̲ānom.

Bibliography: P. Bernard and H.-P. Francfort, *Études de géographie historique sur la plaine d'Aï Khanoum (Afghanistan)*, Paris, 1978. H.-P. Francfort et al., *Fouilles de Shortughaï. Recherches sur l'Asie centrale protohistorique*, Mission Archéologique Français en Asie Centrale, Mémoires 2, Paris, 1989. J.-C. Gardin and B. Lyonnet, "La prospection archéologique de la Bactriane orientale (1974-1978). Premiers résultats," *Mesopotamia* 13-14, 1978-79, p. 99-154. *Gazetteer of Afghanistan* I, s.v. P. Gentelle, *Étude géographique de la plaine d'Aï Khanoum et de son irrigation depuis les temps antiques*, Paris, 1978. Idem et al., *Prospections archéologiques en Bactriane orientale (1971-1978) I. Données paléogéographiques et fondements de l'irrigation*, Mission Archéologique Français en Asie Centrale, Mémoires 3, Paris, 1989. Moḥammad-Nāder Khan, *Rahnemā-ye Qaṭaḡan wa Badak̲šān*, ed. B. Koškakī, Kabul, 1302 Š./1923; repr. and tr. M. Reut as *Qataghan et Badakhshân*, 3 vols., Paris, 1979; ed. M. Sotūda, Tehran, 1367 Š./1988. J. Wood, *A Personal Narrative of a Journey to the Source of the River Oxus . . .*, London, 1841; repr. London, 1976.

(HENRI-PAUL FRANCFORT)

DASTA, the most common term for a ritual procession held in the Islamic lunar month of Moḥarram (q.v.) and the following month of Ṣafar, both periods of mourning for Imami Shiʿites. The procession commemorates the tragic death of Ḥosayn (q.v.), grandson of the prophet Moḥammad and the third imam of the Shiʿites, on the plain of Karbalāʾ on 10 Moḥarram 61/10 October 680. The most spectacular *dasta*s take place on the actual day of the passion, known as ʿĀšūrāʾ (q.v.; Plate IV), and on 20 Ṣafar, known as ʿArbaʿīn (q.v.) or Čella, the fortieth day after Ḥosayn's death.

In all parts of Asia ritual parades lamenting the unjust and sudden deaths of heroes have been performed almost from time immemorial. The mourning processions for Adonis/Tammuz in Mesopotamia and Sīāvoš in Transoxania, as well as the parade commemorating the slaughter of the Magi in Persia, known as Magophonia, are only a few examples. The *dasta* in Moḥarram and Ṣafar developed from simple parades into complex ambulatory rituals occurring annually among the Shiʿites of Persia, Iraq, Bahrain, the Turks of the Caucasus, and the peoples of the Indo-Pakistani subcontinent.

The most salient feature of the *dasta* is the self-mortifiers. These men, aged twelve years and up, are arranged according to height, the smallest in front. Some who strip to the waist (for greater exposure) and strike their chests with their palms are called *sīnazan* (chest beaters); others wear black shirts cut away in the back and beat themselves with chains directly on their flesh; they are known as *zanjīrzan* (beaters with chains). The *šamšīrzan* or *qamazan* (beaters [with] swords) wear white burial shrouds, symbolizing their readiness to sacrifice their lives; they strike their foreheads with long daggers and swords, letting the blood drip down onto the shrouds (Plate V). All these acts of self-mortification are performed in time with the accompanying cymbals and drums. The leader of each subgroup chants dirges in the same rhythm. The entire *dasta* pauses from time to time in front of a religious edifice or the tomb of a local saint or in a large open space, where one group beats itself rhythmically while the others join in the chanting. The tempo quickens until the excitement reaches an uncontrollable pitch, and then the march continues. The cries of the participants, who curse the villains of Karbalāʾ while proclaiming sympathy for Ḥosayn and his companions in martyrdom, are mingled with these mournful songs. Elias Canetti, the Nobel Prize winner in literature, described these processions as "an orchestra of grief, and their effect is that of a crowd crystal. The pain they inflict on themselves is the pain of Ḥosayn, which by being exhibited, becomes the pain of the whole community. Their beating on their chests, which is taken up by the spectators, gives rise to a rhythmic crowd sustained by the emotion of the lament. Ḥosayn has been torn away from all of them and belongs to all of them together" (pp. 150-51)

The commemoration of the martyrdom of Ḥosayn is charged with extreme emotion, not only in Persia, but also throughout the Shiʿite communities of the world. The belief that participation in the annual observances will be an aid to salvation on the Day of Judgment is at least a partial motivation for many mourning rituals. The suffering of Ḥosayn and its commemoration thus

PLATE IV

ʿĀšūrāʾ procession, with onlookers striking themselves on the head as the *dasta* passes, Mehrīz, 1977. Photograph K. Bāyegān.

PLATE V

Dasta on ʿĀšūrāʾ, with *šamšīrzan* or *qamazan* in white shrouds striking their heads with swords or long daggers. After Zereschaguine.

became the very core of the Shiʿite faith. The *dasta* is the most common Shiʿite ritual. The first recorded public mourning ceremonies for Ḥosayn in this form took place in Baghdad in the 10th century. Amir Moʿezz-al-Dawla (334-56/945-67) of the Shiʿite Buyid dynasty ordered the markets closed on the day of ʿĀšūrāʾ in the year 352/963. Processions of Shiʿites then circled the city, weeping, wailing, and striking their heads in grief. The women were disheveled, and everyone wore torn, black clothing. Ḥosayn's murderers were soundly cursed (Ebn Kaṯīr, p. 243)

In the early 16th century the Safavid shah Esmāʿīl I (907-30/1501-24) declared Shiʿite Islam the state religion of Persia, which provided not only legal sanction but also royal backing and encouragement for Moḥarram observances. In turn it was the popular form of Shiʿite Islam, including the *dasta* and other Moḥarram rituals, that helped to spread Shiʿite doctrine across the Persian plateau. Foreign residents, ambassadors, merchants, missionaries, and travelers who spent varying lengths of time in Persia in the 17th and 18th centuries have left very rich accounts of what they saw. These accounts provide nearly a year-by-year record of the development of the pageantry of the *dasta*, chronicling increases in the number of participants costumed to represent various episodes in the battle of Karbalāʾ. Riders on camels and horses were followed by floats with living tableaux on wheels. Various attributes symbolizing the battle were incorporated: standards, banners, flags, guidons, ensigns, turbans, helmets, musical instruments, and a variety of weapons, including swords, axes, bows and arrows, lances, shields, and even firearms. Some of these weapons (e.g., the firearms) may seem anachronistic to westerners, but the Shiʿites are attempting by this means to erase the time that has elapsed since Karbalāʾ and to equate the present with the past. Decorative devotional items were also added to the *dasta*: rugs, mirrors, plumes, lamps, brocades and silks, all of which increased the spectacle. Some of these items were attached to biers and coffins or hung from standards (Plate VI). Each *dasta*, organized by special committees representing various divisions of the town or the guilds, follows a prescribed order and precedence.

In the 1930s Reżā Shah (1304-20 Š./1925-41) restricted Moḥarram rituals, particularly the *dasta* and the *taʿzīya* (passion) plays, on the pretext of their incompatibility with the program of modernization that he was trying to effect in Persia. In fact, however, the shah's move seems to have been at least partially motivated by fear that these powerful public displays could easily be converted into massive political demonstrations. The restrictions were continued under his son, but they failed to eliminate popular attachment to the Moḥarram rituals, as evidenced by their enthusiastic revival during the Revolution of 1357 Š./1978-79 and the advent of the Islamic Republic. In fact, they were among the instruments of mass mobilization for revolution and later for the war with Iraq (1359-67 Š./1980-88). The *dasta* organizations were strategically employed to bring hundreds of thousands of

PLATE VI

Dasta with *naḵl*.

people into the streets of Persian cities to show support for both the Revolution and the fight until final victory in the war.

Bibliography: B. Bayżāʾī, *Nemāyeš dar Īrān*, Tehran, 1344 Š./1965. J. Calmard, "Le mécénat des représentations de Taʿziye," in *Le monde iranien et l'Islam* 2, 1974, pp. 73-126; 4, 1977, pp. 133-62. E. Canetti, *Crowds and Power*, New York, 1978, pp. 143-54. P. Chelkowski, ed., *Taʿziyeh. Ritual and Drama in Iran,* New York, 1979. Idem, "Iran. Mourning Becomes Revolution," *Asia*, May/June 1980, pp. 30-45. Idem, "Shia Muslim Processional Performances," *The Drama Review* 29/3, 1985, pp. 18-30. Idem, "Popular Shiʿi Mourning Rituals," *Alserat* 12/1, 1986, pp. 209-26. Ebn Kaṯīr, *al-Bedāya wa'l-nehāya* II, Cairo, 1358/1939. B. D. Eerdmans, "Der Ursprung der Ceremonien des Hosein Festes," *Zeitschrift für Assyriologie* 9, 1894, pp. 280-307. F. Ḡaffārī, ed., *Vīža-ye nemayešhā-ye sonnatī dar Īrān*, Irān-nāma 9/2, Spring 1991. A. de Gobineau, *Les religions et les philosophies dans l'Asie centrale*, Paris, 1865; repr. Paris, 1957. G. E. von Grunebaum, *Muhammadan Festivals*, London, 1958, pp. 85-94. Ṣ. Homāyūnī, *Taʿzīya dar Īrān*, Shiraz, 1368 Š./1989. A. Kryniski, *Perskiĭ Teatr* (Persian theater), Kiev, 1925. I. J. Lassy, *The Muharram Mysteries among the Azerbaijani Turks of Caucasia*, Helsinki, 1916. P. Mamnoun, *Ta'zija, schi'itisch-persisches Passionsspiel*, Vienna, 1967. H. Müller, *Studien zum persischen Passionspiel*, Freibourg im Breisgau, 1966. M. Rezvani, *Le théâtre et la danse en Iran*, Paris, 1962. B. Zereschaguine, *Voyages dans les provinces du Caucase*, Paris, 1869.

(PETER J. CHELKOWSKI)

DAŠTAKĪ, SAYYED AMĪR JAMĀL-AL-DĪN **ʿAṬĀ-ALLĀH** b. Fażl-Allāh b. ʿAbd-al-Raḥmān Ḥosaynī Heravī (d. 912/1506, 917/1511, or 926/1520; Dānešpažūh and Monzawī, pp. 582-83; Baḡdādī, p. 664, citing the anonymous 16th-century chronicle *Ḵolāṣat al-afkār*, by Mīr Moḥammad-Taqī Kāšānī), a scholar of Hadith in Khorasan in the late Timurid and early Safavid periods. He was from a Sunni family that originally hailed from the Daštak quarter in Shiraz. In the late 15th century he taught at the Madrasa-ye ṣolṭānīya in Herat and preached at Friday services in the main mosque of the city.

The patronage of his three major works reflects the shifting patterns of political dominance in Khorasan. Daštakī completed *Rawżat al-aḥbāb fī sīrat al-nabī wa'l-aṣḥāb* in 888/1483 on commission from the Sunni Mīr ʿAlī-Šīr Navāʾī (q.v.; d. 906/1501), minister to Sultan Ḥosayn Bāyqarā (q.v. Supp.), ruler of Khorasan (874-911/14691506). Probably at about the time of the Safavid conquest of Herat in 916/1510 Daštakī dedicated his *Ketāb toḥfat al-aḥebbāʾ* to Ḵᵛāja Moẓaffar-al-Dīn Betekčī Astarābādī, minister to Shah Esmāʿīl I (907-30/1501-24), and *al-Arbaʿūn ḥadīṯ men aḥādīṯ Sayyed al-Morsalīn fī manāqeb Amīr-al-Moʾmenīn* to Shah ʿAbd-al-Bāqī, who served Amir Najm-e Ṯānī until his death in 918/1512 and succeeded him in command of the Safavid forces in Herat.

Later Twelver biographers disagreed about his religious loyalties and those of his family. Nūr-Allāh Šūštarī (d. 1019/1610-11) and later Daštakīs claimed that the family had practiced *taqīya* (disguise of one's religious beliefs) before the advent of the Safavids. According to Šūštarī, the first of the family to declare open allegiance to Twelver Shiʿism was Sayyed Ṣadr-al-Dīn Moḥammad b. Ebrāhīm Daštakī (d. 903/1498), ʿAṭāʾ-Allāh's uncle and father of Ḡīāṯ-al-Dīn Manṣūr Daštakī (q.v.; Modarres, *Rayḥānat al-adab* III, pp. 367-69; for various views on the Daštakīs' acceptance of Shiʿism, see Šūštarī; Ḵᵛānsārī; *Ḥabīb al-sīar* [Tehran]; Dānešpažūh and Monzawī). After the fall of Herat in 916/1510 Daštakī preached a sermon praising the imams and the shah (Afandī, p. 316; *Ḥabīb al-sīar* IV, p. 515). Daštakī's sermon and later Shiʿite treatises probably reflect realistic assessment of political and religious changes in Persia, rather than a genuine commitment.

Bibliography: Mīrzā ʿAbd-Allāh Eṣbahānī Afandī, *Rīāż al-ʿolamāʾ* III, Qom, 1401/1981, pp. 315-17, 318. *Aʿyān al-Šīʿa* XLI, Beirut, 1400/1980, p. 6. Esmāʿīl Pasha Baḡdādī, *Hadīyat al-ʿārefīn* I, Istanbul, 1951. H. Beveridge and J. T. P. de Bruijn, "Ḵhᵂāndamīr," in *EI*² IV, pp. 1020-22. M.-T. Dānešpažūh and ʿA.-N. Monzawī, eds., *Fehrest-e ketāb-ḵāna-ye ehdāʾī-e Āqā-ye Sayyed Moḥammad Meškāt be ketāb-ḵāna-ye Dānešgāh-e Tehrān* II, Tehran, 1332 Š./1953, pp. 581-84, 760. *al-Ḏarīʿa* I, pp. 421-22; II, p. 480; III, p. 409; IV, pp. 30, 31; VII, pp. 212, 214; XI, pp. 285-86. Fasāʾī, II, p. 91. T. Gandjeï, "Ṣultān Ḥusayn Mīrzā b. Manṣūr b. Bayḳara," in *EI*² III, p. 603. Ghulām Sarwar, *History of Shah Ismāʿīl Safawi*, Aligarh, 1939; repr. New York, 1975, pp. 5, 6, 60, 64-66, 86, 91-92. *Ḥabīb al-sīar* (Tehran) IV, pp. 358-59. Ḥorr ʿĀmelī, *Amal al-āmel fī ʿolamāʾ Jabal ʿĀmel*, ed. A. Ḥosaynī, II, Najaf, 1385/1965-66, p. 170. Moḥammad-Bāqer Ḵᵛānsārī, *Rawżāt al-jannāt fī aḥwāl al-ʿolamāʾ wa'l-sādāt*, ed. A. Esmāʿīlīān, Qom, 1390-92/1970-72, V, pp. 189-94; VII, pp. 177-78, 194-95 n. 1; VIII, p. 71. *Kašf al-Ẓonūn*, ed. Yaltkaya and Bilge, I, pp. 922-23. Qāżī Nūr-Allāh b. ʿAbd-Allāh Šūštarī, *Majāles al-moʾmenīn*, Bodleian Library, ms no. Ouseley 366, fols. 131a-132b (ad. fifth *majles*), 208a (ad. seventh *majles*). Z. V. Togan, "Sur l'origine des Safavides," in *Mélanges Louis Massignon* III, Damascus, 1957, pp. 345-57.

(ANDREW J. NEWMAN)

DAŠTAKĪ, AMĪR SAYYED **ḠĪĀṮ-AL-DĪN** MANṢŪR b. Ṣadr-al-Dīn Moḥammad Šīrāzī Ḥosaynī (866-948/1462-1541), scholar, philosopher, and *motakallem* (theologian) of the late Timurid and early Safavid period, and, for a brief interval under Shah Ṭahmāsb (930-84/1524-76), one of two *ṣadr*s (chief clerical overseers).

His family was originally from Shiraz. In the late 16th century Ḥasan Rūmlū (pp. 303-04) and Aḥmad Ḥosaynī Qomī (I, p. 296) reported that the Safavid shah Esmāʿīl I (905-30/1499-1524) had initially summoned Ḡīāṯ-al-Dīn, who was a student of mathematics and astronomy, from Shiraz to repair the observatory of Naṣīr-al-Dīn Ṭūsī (d. 672/1274) in Marāḡa, but Ḡīāṯ-al-Dīn's contemporary K̲ᵛāndamīr mentioned no such commission, nor did Nūr-Allāh Šūštarī (d. 1019/1610-11).

Although Ḡīāṯ-al-Dīn's father and teacher, Ṣadr-al-Dīn (d. 903/1498), is often accounted the first of the family to have openly professed Twelver Shiʿism, K̲ᵛānsārī (II, pp. 193-94) was skeptical of the family's commitment to the faith in this early period. Like his cousin ʿAṭāʾ-Allāh Daštakī (q.v.), Ḡīāṯ-al-Dīn's branch of the family was probably much influenced in its religious affiliation by the changing political climate in Persia. Ḡīāṯ-al-Dīn himself dedicated an essay to the Ottoman sultan Bāyazīd II (886-918/1481-1512), and K̲ᵛānsārī noted reports that he served Solṭān-Ḥosayn Bāyqarā (q.v., Supp.), Timurid ruler of Khorasan (874-911/1469-1506), as vizier.

Like his father, Ḡīāṯ-al-Dīn criticized the Persian Sunni Jalāl-al-Dīn Davānī (q.v.; d. 908/1502), who initially rejected claims of Shah Esmāʿīl to be "imam of the age." Ḡīāṯ-al-Dīn debated Davānī openly and in such essays as *Ešrāq hayākel al-nūr ʿan ẓolmāt šawākel al-ḡorūr* (*al-Ḏarīʿa* II, pp. 103-04; Brockelmann, *GAL* I, p. 565, SI, p. 782), a treatise in which he attacked Davānī's commentary on *Hayākel al-nūr* by Šehāb-al-Dīn Sohravardī (d. 578/1191), and *al-Moḥākamāt*, in which he evaluated disagreements between his father and Davānī over the Shiʿite-oriented treatise *Tajrīd al-kalām* by Naṣīr al-Dīn Ṭūsī. Ḡīāṯ-al-Dīn's *Ḥojjat al-kalām* was a critique of the thought of Abū Ḥāmed Moḥammad Ḡazālī (d. 505/1111). Moḥammad-Taqī Dānešpažūh (Dānešpažūh and Monzawī, III, pp. 353-54) thought that Mollā Ṣadrā (d. 1050/1640) had been influenced by Ḡīāṯ-al-Dīn's *ešrāqī* (illuminationist; see CORBIN) essay *Merʾāt al-ḥaqāʾeq*.

In 936/1529 Ḡīāṯ-al-Dīn was appointed *ṣadr* at the Safavid court, sharing the post with Sayyed Neʿmat-Allāh Ḥellī (d. 940/1533), who had been appointed a year earlier. Ḥellī, a student of Moḥaqqeq-e Ṯānī ʿAlī Karakī (d. 940/1534), was dismissed after challenging Karakī's ruling permitting Friday prayer during the occultation of the Twelfth Imam. Shortly thereafter Ḡīāṯ-al-Dīn himself challenged Karakī's calculation of the *qebla*. A council was convened in the presence of Shah Ṭahmāsb to settle the disagreement. Karakī triumphed: In 938/1531-1532 Ḡīāṯ-al-Dīn was dismissed and replaced by another student of Karakī. He returned to Shiraz, where he was said to have founded and taught at the Madrasa-ye Manṣūrīya (K̲ᵛānsārī, VII, pp. 176, 194; cf. Forṣat Šīrāzī, pp. 497-98, who reported that the *madrasa* had been founded by Ḡīāṯ-al-Dīn's father). He died there and was buried in the school.

The two failed challenges to Karakī, though based on religious grounds, were certainly fueled by Persian clerics, court officials, and several princes allied to the Tekkelū tribes, whose domination of both the Qezelbāš confederation and the young shah was declining, while the fortunes of the opposing Šāmlū tribe were on the rise. In 939/1532, at the height of the Šāmlū domination of the Safavid confederation, a *farmān* declaring Karakī *nāʾeb al-emām* (deputy of the imam) was issued (for a detailed discussion of these events, see Newman, pp. 96-104).

Qomī (I, p. 297), whose father had studied with Ḡīāṯ-al-Dīn, reported an agreement between Karakī and Ḡīāṯ-al-Dīn to exchange instruction in philosophy and Twelver Shiʿism, an account accepted by Roger Savory (p. 82). In other notices, however, no such exchange is mentioned, and Twelver biographers ascribed such an agreement to Karakī and Jamāl-al-Dīn Estarābādī (d. 931/1524-25), sixth *ṣadr* of the Safavids and a student of Davānī (Rūmlū, pp. 253-56; Šūštarī, fols. 208a-209a, ad. 7th *majles*; K̲ᵛānsārī, II, p. 212, IV, p. 369; *Aʿyān al-Šīʿa* XLI, pp. 176-77).

Šūštarī reported that Ḡīāṯ-al-Dīn replied to questions submitted to the court by the Ottoman sultan, according to K̲ᵛānsārī (VII, p. 192) in the reign of Ṭahmāsb, presumably while he was *ṣadr*. Rūmlū and Qomī mentioned no such reply, however.

The Shiʿite scholar Ṣadr-al-Dīn ʿAlī b. Aḥmad b. Maʿṣūm, known both as Ebn Moḥammad Maʿṣūm and as Sayyed ʿAlī Khan (d. 1118/1706 or 1120/1708), author of *Solāfat al-ʿaṣr*, was a descendant of Ḡīāṯ-al-Dīn.

Bibliography: S. Amir Arjomand, *The Shadow of God and the Hidden Imām. Religion, Political Order, and Societal Change in Shʿite Iran from the Beginning to 1890*, Chicago, 1984, pp. 134-35, 145. *Aʿyān al-Šīʿa* XLVIII, Beirut, 1960, p. 116. M.-T. Dānešpažūh and ʿA-N. Monzawī, eds., *Fehrest-e ketāb-k̲āna-ye ehdāʾī-e Āqā-ye Sayyed Moḥammad Meškāt be ketāb-k̲āna-ye Dāneshgāh-e Tehrān*, Tehran, 1332-35 Š./1953-56, II, pp. 581-84, 760; III, pp. 144-45, 353-54; VI, pp. 2191-92. *al-Ḏarīʿa* I, pp. 108, 378-79; II, pp. 103-04; V, pp. 24-25; VI, pp. 67, 117, 132, 135, 262; XIII, pp. 138-39; XIV, pp. 176-78, 240-41; XVIII, p. 94; XX, pp. 131-32; XXI, p. 352; XXV, p. 253. Mīrzā ʿAbd-Allāh Eṣbahānī, *Rīāż al-ʿolamāʾ* V, Qom, 1401/1981, pp. 250-52. Eskandar Beg, I, pp. 144-45, 148; tr. Savory, I, pp. 231, 236. Moḥammad-Naṣīr Forṣat Šīrāzī (Forṣat-al-Dawla), *Āṯār-e ʿajam*, Bombay, 1354/1935. Fasāʾī, II, p. 139. Moḥammad-Bāqer K̲ᵛānsārī, *Rawżāt al-jannāt fī aḥwāl al-ʿolamāʾ wa'l-sādāt*, ed. A. Esmāʿīlīān, Qom, 1390-92/1970-72, IV, pp. 372-73; VII, pp. 176-99. W. Madelung, "al-Karakī," *EI²* IV, p. 610. A. J. Newman, "The Myth of the Clerical Migration to Safawid Iran. Arab Shīʿite Opposition to ʿAlī al-Karakī and Safawid Shīʿism," *Die Welt des Islams* 33/1, 1993, pp. 66-112. Aḥmad b. Šaraf-al-Dīn Ḥosayn Ḥosaynī Qomī, *K̲olāṣat al-tawārīk̲* I, Tehran, 1359 Š/1980, pp. 149, 160, 195, 218, 296-98. Ḥasan Rūmlū, ed. Seddon, pp. 189-91, 224, 253-56, 303-

04. R. M. Savory, "The Principle Offices of the Safawid State during the Reign of Shah Ṭahmāsp I (930-984/1524-1576)," *BSO(A)S* 24/1, 1961, pp. 81-82. Qāżī Nūr-Allāh b. ʿAbd-Allāh Šūštarī, *Majāles al-moʾmenīn*, Bodleian Library, ms. no. Ousley 366. Modarres, *Rayḥānat al-adab* IV, pp. 258-60. Shah Ṭahmāsb Ṣafawī, *Taḏkera-ye Šāh Ṭahmāsb*, 2nd ed., ed. A. Ṣafarī, Tehran, 1363 Š./1984, pp. 13-14.

(ANDREW J. NEWMAN)

DASTĀN, a term used in three different contexts in Persian music.

Melody. Bārbad (q.v.), the minstrel of the Sasanian king Ḵosrow II Parvēz (591-628), was said to have composed 360 *dastān*s in order to be able to play a new melody each day of the year (Christensen, *Iran Sass.*, p. 485). In contrast to the thirty *laḥn*s (pieces) also composed by Bārbad, the names of these *dastān*s have not been preserved, but among the approximately 170 names of pre-Islamic melodies that have been gathered from various sources (Ṣafwat, pp. 116-18) there are probably several names of *dastān*s. A note by Abū ʿAbd-Allāh Ḵᵛārazmī (p. 238) suggests that the *dastān*s of Bārbad were still fashionable in the 10th century, and some modern scholars believe that they were the sources of the *dastgāh*s (q.v.) that constitute the present modal system (e.g., Joneydī, p. 137). Although there is no doubt some relationship between *dastān*s and *dastgāh*s, the two terms do not share the same meaning: *dastān* came to mean a fingering and, by extension, a scale (see below), whereas *dastgāh* refers to a collection of pieces grouped in relation to a dominant mode. Furthermore, considering their number, it is probable that Bārbad's *dastān*s corresponded to melodies (*gūša*s), rather than to specific modes.

Narrative composition. Dastān is also the name of a narrative genre among Turkish, Azerī (Öztuna, p. 161), and Pashtun minstrels. Among the Uighurs of Turkestan *dastān*s are long compositions that play an important role in classical suites (*moqām*s). *Āvāz-e dastān-e ʿArab* is a *gūša* by which the *āvāz* (song) of Abū ʿAṭā (q.v.) used to be known.

Fingering system. In early Arabic and Persian musical theory *dastān* designated either the fingering of the lute or the ligatures and thus also the modal scale corresponding to the positions of the fingers on the frets (see DASĀTĪN).

Bibliography: J. Baily, *Music of Afghanistan. Professional Musicians in the City of Herat*, Cambridge, 1988. F. Joneydī, *Zamīna-ye šenāḵt-e mūsīqī-e īrānī*, Tehran, 1361 Š./1982. Abū ʿAbd-Allāh Ḵᵛārazmī, *Mafātīḥ al-ʿolūm*, ed., G. van Vloten, Leiden, 1895. M. Maʿrūfī, *Radīf-e haft dastgāh-e mūsīqī-e īrānī/Les systèmes de la musique traditionnelle de l'Iran (radif)*, Tehran, 1352 Š./1973. Y. Öztuna, *Türk musikisi ansiklopedisi*, Istanbul, 1969. D. Ṣafwat, *Ostādān-e mūsīqī-e Īrān wa alḥān-e mūsīqī-e īrānī*, Tehran, 1350 Š./1971.

(JEAN DURING)

DASTĀN. See ZĀL.

DĀSTĀN, story, tale, parable. See FICTION.

DĀSTĀN-SARĀʾĪ (storytelling), term used for written and oral genres of fictional narrative. Other terms used for the same genres include *dāstān-gūʾī*, *dāstān-pardāzī*, *qeṣṣa-gūʾī*, *afsāna-sarāʾī*, and *naqqālī*. In this article primarily the oral forms of storytelling will be discussed. Oral storytelling is generally considered a part of popular culture, but it also touches on literary culture at many points. It is performed in a number of different genres and contexts, of which a general overview will be given here. Storytelling may be classified according to the status of the storyteller, whether amateur or professional; the settings in which it takes place, either private or public; and the subject matter or literary genres of the stories.

In private gatherings traditional folktales are recited by older family members, male or female, as a form of family entertainment. Children may be put to sleep with recitations of such stories as "Sang-e ṣabūr" (Lorimer, pp. 153-56; idem and Lorimer, pp. 19-24). If the gathering includes listeners who are not members of the family, males and females may not both be present together: Female storytellers will address all-female gatherings, and males will perform for male groups (for an extensive discussion of this sort of storytelling, see Mills).

Storytelling in public contexts has been more widely studied. It encompasses a greater variety of performance genres. In pre-Islamic times minstrels performed at royal courts, providing entertainment, as well as news for their audiences. What is known of this practice has been described in detail by Mary Boyce. There are only scattered references to storytellers in Persian texts before the Safavid period. Bayhaqī (ed. Fayyāż, pp. 154, 905) described an incident involving an amateur storyteller (*moḥaddeṯ*) at the court of the Ghaznavid sultan Masʿūd (421-32/1030-41); he also condemned popular storytellers because they related tales of absurdities to please only the ignorant. Professional storytellers were often classed with such other public entertainers as jugglers, wrestlers, tight-rope walkers, and weight lifters (Sīstānī, p. 254; Wāʿeż Kāšefī, 1350 Š./1971, pp. 275-343), all of whom used to perform in squares and open areas of towns and cities.

In the Safavid period, when coffeehouses (q.v.) appeared in Isfahan and became centers of popular entertainment, the nature of professional storytelling began to change. The coffeehouse provided a place where storytellers could appear regularly and entertain a more or less stable audience, which in turn permitted them to tell longer and more complex stories that could be continued from one day to the next and did not have to be concluded in one session (for a broad discussion of such professional storytellers, see Maḥjūb). They also became more free to specialize. The most prominent form of public storytelling was *naqqālī*, still practiced to a limited extent in large cities. In the Safavid and Qajar periods *naqqāl* was most often a generic term for a narrator of stories from the *Šāh-nāma* and such great popular romances as *Abū Moslem-nāma* (see ABŪ MOSLEM ḴORĀSĀNĪ), *Ḥamza-nāma*, *Eskandar-nāma* (q.v.), *Dārāb-nāma* (q.v.), *Samak-e ʿAyyār*, *Ḥosayn-e Kord*, and in late Qajar times *Amīr Arsalān* (q.v.).

Many *naqqāl*s in the Safavid period specialized in single, though extensive stories; they were accordingly known as *Šāh-nāmaḵᵛān*, *Amīr Ḥamzaḵᵛān*, and the like. The names of some famous contemporary *Šāh-nāmaḵᵛān*s were recorded by Mīrzā Moḥammad-Ṭāher Naṣrābādī (pp. 145, 307, 357, 379, 401). In the 20th century, as competition from other forms of entertainment began to restrict the audiences for popular recitations, the *naqqāl*s gradually limited their repertoire to stories from the *Šāh-nāma*.

Already prominent in the Middle Ages were various types of *maddāḥ* (lit., "panegyrists") including the *manāqebḵᵛān*s, who told stories glorifying the Shiʿite imams, and the competing *fażāʾelḵᵛān*s, with stories in praise of the first three caliphs (Qazvīnī, p. 67).

Two specialized genres of oral storytelling were *rawża-ḵᵛānī* and *parda-dārī*. The *rawżaḵᵛān* told stories of the imams Ḥasan and Ḥosayn and the events at Karbalāʾ. They performed at private gatherings in people's homes, as well as in public spaces like shrines and cemeteries, and their function had a religious significance beyond that of simple entertainment. The term *rawża-ḵᵛānī* itself is said to have come from the work *Rawżat-al-šohadā* of Ḥosayn Wāʿeẓ Kāšefī (d. 910/1504). *Parda-dārī* is a form of illustrated storytelling in which the narrator or two narrators working as a team recite stories, usually about important early Shiʿite figures, using a large painting, or *parda*, as a prop. These individuals, who were still functioning in Persia in the 1970s, were usually itinerant, moving from village to village on market days and setting up the *parda* on a wall in a village square (for a discussion of "picture storytelling" in its larger Asian context, see Mair, pp. 119-20).

Popular storytelling has been acknowledged in a number of literary works. The ethical dimensions of popular storytelling were discussed by Wāʿeẓ Kāšefī in a chapter on singers of tales and narrators of stories (1350 Š./1971, pp. 302-05). The poem "Pahlavān-e nāmawjūd" by Abu'l-Qāsem Lāhūtī (1304-77=1336 Š./1887-1957) is about people's reactions to the performance of a storyteller on a summer evening in Kermānšāh (Monīb-al-Raḥmān, I, pp. 194-96). Mahdī Aḵawān-e Ṯālet̲ (pp. 66-68), in his poem "Ādamak," gave the thoughts of an old *naqqāl* as he sees his audience seduced by the attractions of a radio in the coffeehouses of large cities. As *naqqālī* gradually disappears from these coffeehouses, more attention is being paid to it by litterateurs and scholars. For example, ʿAlī-Akbar Saʿīdī Sīrjānī has published a narration of the story of Esfandīār from the *Šāh-nāma* as a *naqqāl* would recite it, and Jalīl Dūstḵᵛāh has published the story of Rostam and Sohrāb from the *ṭūmār*, or notebook, of the famous *naqqāl* of Isfahan, Moršed ʿAbbās Zarīrī.

Bibliography: M. Aḵawān-e Ṯālet̲, *Pāʾīz dar zendān*, Tehran, 1348 Š./1969. M. Boyce, "The Parthian *gosān* and the Iranian Minstrel Tradition," *JRAS*, 1957, pp. 10-45. J. Dūstḵᵛāh, "Naqqālī honar-e dāstān-sarāʾī-e mellī," *Jong-e Eṣfahān* 3, 1345 Š./1966, pp. 73-88. Idem, *Dāstān-e Rostam o Sohrāb*, Tehran, 1369 Š./1990. M. Ḥasanbegī, *Tehrān-e qadīm*, Tehran, 1366 Š./1987. F. Isma'ilbegi Shirazi, *A Study of the Evolutionary Trend and the Current Atmosphere and Condition of Shāhnāmihkhānī in Iran*, Ph.D. diss., Wayne State University, Detroit, Mich., 1973. Ḥ. Lesān, "Šāh-nāma-ḵᵛānī," *Honar o mardom*, N.S. 159-60, 1345 Š./1967, pp. 2-16. D. L. R. Lorimer, *Farhang-e mardom-e Kermān*, ed. F. Vahman, Tehran, 1353 Š./1974. Idem and E. O. Lorimer, trs., *Persian Tales*, London, 1919. M.-J. Maḥjūb, "Taḥawwol-e naqqālī wa qeṣṣa-ḵᵛānī. Tarbīat-e qeṣṣaḵᵛān wa ṭūmārhā-ye naqqālī," *Īrān-nāma* 9/2, 1370 Š./1991, pp. 186-211. V. Mair, *Painting and Performance*, Honolulu, 1988. M. Mills, *Rhetorics and Politics in Afghan Traditional Storytelling*, Philadelphia, 1991. Monīb-al-Raḥmān, *Bargozīda-ye šeʿr-e fārsī-e moʿāṣer*, 2 vols., Aligarh, 1958-63. Mīrzā Moḥammad-Ṭāher Naṣrābādī, *Taḏkera-ye Naṣrābādī*, ed. Ḥ. Waḥīd Dastgerdī, Tehran, 1317 Š./1938. M. E. Page, "Naqqali and Ferdowsi," Ph.D. diss., University of Pennsylvania, Philadelphia, 1977. ʿAbd-al-Jalīl Rāzī Qazvīnī, *Ketāb al-naqż*, ed. J. Moḥaddet̲ Ormavī, Tehran, 1358 Š./1979. K. Sādāt Eškevarī, "Naqqālī wa šāh-nāma-ḵᵛānī," *Honar o mardom* 153-54, 1354 Š./1975, pp. 142-48. Ḏ. Ṣafā, "Mājarā-ye taḥrīm-e Abū Moslem-nāma," *Īrān-nāma* 5/2, 1365 Š./1986, pp. 233-49. Idem, "Ešāra-ī kūtāh be dāstān-gozārī wa dāstāngozārān tā dawrān-e ṣafawī," *Īrān-šenāsī* 1/3, 1368 Š./1989, pp. 463-71. J. Šahrī, *Tārīḵ-e ejtemāʿī-e Tehrān dar qarn-e sīzdahom* V, Tehran, 1368 Š./1989, pp. 506-20. ʿA.-A. Saʿīdī Sīrjānī, *Bīčāra Esfandīār*, Washington, D.C., 1992. Malekšāh Ḥosayn Sīstānī, *Eḥyāʾ al-molūk*, ed. M. Sotūda, Tehran, 1344 Š./1965. Hosayn Wāʿeẓ Kāšefī, *Rawżat al-šohadāʾ*, ed. M. Ramażānī, Tehran, 1334 Š./1955. Idem, *Fotowwat-nāma-ye solṭānī*, ed. M.-J. Maḥjūb, Tehran, 1350 Š./1971.

(WILLIAM HANAWAY)

DAŠTESTĀN, *šahrestān* (subprovince) on the Persian Gulf coast in Būšehr province, bounded on the north and east by Fārs province, on the south by the *šahrestān* of Daštī (q.v.), and on the west by the *šahrestān*s of Būšehr, Tangestān, and Ganāva. The adminstrative capital is Borāzjān (q.v.). According to the census (q.v.) of 1365 Š./1986, the population of Daštestān was 175,406, 42 percent of which lived in urban, the remainder in rural areas (*Natāyej*, p. 2). The *šahrestān* of Daštestān is 6,150 km² and comprises three districts, including a total of two towns, eight rural districts (*dehestān*s), and 197 villages. The districts are, first, Saʿdābād (ca 1,401 km^2, population 6,654) in the northwestern part of the *šahrestān*, in which the town of Saʿdābād and the *dehestān*s of Zīrāh and Mazāreʿī are located; second, Šabānkāra (ca 1,042 km^2) in the northwestern part of the *šahrestān* comprising only one *dehestān*; and the central district (ca 1,707 km^2) in the south, comprising the rural units of Būškān, Ḥūma, Dālakī, Zīārat, and Gīsakān. Borāzjān is in this district.

The climate of Daštestān is warm and dry. The land rises toward the north, with a corresponding drop in temperature and increase in agricultural productivity. The Šabānkāra dam on the Šāpūr river in Šabānkāra *dehestān*, near the village of Dorāhī, irrigates the villages and fields of the southern region, where the major products are tobacco, dates (see DATE PALM), cereals, vegetables, cotton (q.v.), sesame, and limes. Of the 3 million date palms in the province of Būšehr, 2.5 million are in Daštestān. People are also engaged in trade, manufacture of rugs, and weaving of *ʿabā'*s (q.v.). In the Qajar period Daštestān was a center for breeding Arabian horses (Afšār Sīstānī, pp. 829-38).

Archeological sites include two Achaemenid palaces, one in the town of Borāzjān, the other ca 12 km farther north in an area called Sang-e Sīāh (Sarfarāz). The town of Tawwaj, near the coast, was renowned for production of linen fabrics and linen garments known as Tawwazī; it was one of the *ṭerāz* cities of the Buyid ʿAżod-al-Dawla (q.v.; Eṣṭaḵrī, p. 153; Ebn Ḥawqal, p. 293; Moqaddasī, p. 435; Ebn al-Balḵī, pp. 145-46; Yāqūt, *Boldān* I, p. 890; cf. Serjeant, pp. 80-84). Tawwaj was destroyed in the 12th century. A covered *bāzār* and the Mošīr-al-Molk caravansary date from the Qajar period (Sarfarāz); the latter was converted in the 1950s to a prison for political dissidents.

Bibliography: Ī. Afšār Sīstānī, *Negāh-ī be Būšehr*, Tehran, 1369 Š./1990, pp. 15, 35, 139, 295; II, pp. 611, 619, 633, 652, 665, 723, 726, 736, 773. A. Eqtedārī, *Āṯār-e šahrhā-ye bāstānī-e sawāḥel wa jazāyer-e kalīj-e Fārs wa daryā-ye ʿOmān*, Tehran, 1338 Š./1959. ʿA. Farrāšbandī, *Tārīḵ o jografīā-ye Borāzjān*, Shiraz, n.d. Idem, *Gūša-ī az tārīḵ-e enqelāb-e mosallaḥāna-ye mardom-e mobārez-e Tangestān, Daštī wa Daštestān bar ʿalayh-e esteʿmār*, Tehran, 1362 Š./1983. Fasā'ī, ed. Rastgār, II, Tehran, 1367 Š./1988, pp. 1334-39. *Natāyej-e sar-šomarī-e ʿomūmī-e nofūs wa maskan. Mehr-māh-e 1365. šahrestān-e Būšehr*, Tehran, 1365 Š./1986 (?). ʿA.-A. Sarfarāz, "Kašf-e kāḵī az ʿahd-e Kūroš-e kabīr dar sawāḥel-e ḵalīj-e Fārs," *Bāstān-šenāsī wa honar-e Īrān* 7-8, 1971, pp. 19-32. R. B. Serjeant, "Material for a History of Islamic Textiles up to the Mongol Conquest," *Ars Islamica* 10, 1943, pp. 71-104.

(JAMŠĪD ṢADĀQAT-KĪŠ)

DASTGĀH, modal system in Persian music, representing a level of organization at which a certain number of melodic types (*gūšas*) are regrouped and ordered in relation to a dominant mode (*māya*). Each *dastgāh* takes its name from this dominant mode, which is always played in the introductory parts. For example, *dastgāh-e Čahārgāh* comprises not only several *gūšas* belonging to the mode Čahārgāh but also *gūšas* in modes that are both closely (Zābol, Ḥeṣār) and distantly (Moḵālef) related, which are played before the conclusion (*forūd*) in the initial mode. The term *dastgāh* is thus somewhat ambiguous: "The expression *dastgâh-e chahârgâh* . . . means either the major unitary modal complex *chahârgâh* or a whole set of *gushes* traditionally performed with *chahârgâh* at their head as the principal modal nucleus" (Powers, p. 426). Theoretically Čahārgāh can be correctly labeled a *dastgāh* only to the extent that it is composite, that is, comprises a minimal number of varying modal elements; without these elements it must be considered either a *maqām* (as Ḵāleqī suggested, pp. 127-28) or a simple mode (*māya*).

According to some practicing musicians (personal communication), the etymology of the term *dastgāh* can be associated with the idea of "the position (*gāh*) of the hand (*dast*) [on the neck of the instrument]," that is, the scale, for a similar idea of position appears in the names of modes like Dogāh and Segāh. It is more appropriate to translate it as "system," however, for the *dastgāh* is first and foremost a collection of discrete and heterogeneous elements organized into a hierarchy that is entirely coherent though nevertheless flexible

The defining features of the *dastgāh* are thus a certain modal variety subjected to a course of development (*sayr*) that is determined by the preestablished order of sequences, or *gūšas*. This order can, however, vary within certain limits, depending on the repertoire or the taste of the interpreter. This definition is equally applicable to the *āvāz* (q.v.), which is, however, less developed and can itself be included in a *dastgāh* (e.g., Bayāt-e Kord, which can be played separately or as part of *dastgāh-e Šūr*). The extended version of a *dastgāh* like Šūr may encompass as many as fifty *gūšas* (During, 1991), a dozen of which are the most important; an *āvāz* like Bayāt-e Kord, on the other hand, may include only about seven *gūšas*, of which three are essential. Other *āvāz*es, like Bayāt-e Eṣfahān in its extended versions (Maʿrūfī, s.v.), could theoretically also be labeled *dastgāh*.

The overall structure of a *dastgāh* consists of three main parts corresponding to blocs of *gūšas*: the introductory sequence (*darāmad*, q.v.) or sequences, which are developed in the fundamental mode (*māya, maqām*); the sections comprising modulations or transpositions; and the rapid return (*forūd*) to the initial mode. In general there is a gradual progression up the scale, while the return is more rapid, and the ambitus of the melodies is progressively expanded within each section (Nettl, pp. 21-22). In principle the interpreter is always free to determine the content of each *dastgāh* and to modify, up to a point, the order of the *gūšas*, but in practice certain *dastgāh*s (or *āvāz*es), like Šūr and Homāyūn, seem to permit greater liberty than do others, like Čahārgāh and Rāst-Panjgāh, which are more standardized (Nettl, pp. 105-06).

Although there are twelve *dastgāh*s and *āvāz*es, they represent only six or seven scales (During, 1984, p. 105; idem, 1991, passim), in Rūḥ-Allāh Ḵāleqī's view only five (p. 127). In certain instances the features distinguishing *dastgāh*s are purely structural (pauses, *īst*; variable notes; concluding notes; etc.) and connected with motifs (conclusion, or *forūd*; introduction; etc.). *Dastgāh*s can also be distinguished by such other characteristics as the sequence of modulations, the diapason, or the dominant chord (e.g., in the lower register for the *dastgāh*s, in the upper register for the *āvāz*es). All these elements are involved in the definition of "mode" in the broad sense, particularly in eastern music (Powers, pp. 434, 437). Despite their differentiating features, the *dastgāh*s are by no means closed systems but share certain *gūša*s among them: For example, the *gūša* Jāmadarān is played with different adaptations in Bayāt-e Eṣfahān, Afšārī, Homāyūn, and Bayāt-e Tork (During, 1984, p. 142). In principle each *dastgāh* has an expressive coloration, an individual ethos (Joneydī, pp. 218-22), but it cannot always be characterized in a consistent manner. The definition thus remains more fluid and general because the ethos depends in large part on the interpretation. It is nevertheless agreed that Navā is rather serene and meditative, Čahārgāh martial, Māhūr cheerful or majestic, Šūr melancholy, and Homāyūn pathetic; the characters of the other *dastgāh*s are less settled.

Both the term *dastgāh* and the musical form itself are indigenous to Persian (and Azerī) music and were no doubt elaborated during the revival of traditional music in the 19th century. The term is found in an Azerī work of 1301/1884 (Safarova) and, in about 1287/1870, in an unpublished list of terms compiled by Malek-Manṣūrzāda in Baku. The older term that comes closest to it is *āvāz* (Ṣafī-al-Dīn Ormavī, 13th century), and, according to Ḵāleqī (p. 125), when these *āvāz*es were expanded they were called *dastgāh*s. The twelve were thus assembled: seven *dastgāh*s (Šūr, Segāh, Čahārgāh, Māhūr, Homāyūn, Navā, and Rāst-Panjgāh) and five *āvāz*es (Abū ʿAṭā, Bayāt-e Tork, Afšārī, Daštī, Bayāt-e Eṣfahān). The first four of these *āvāz*es (to which Bayāt-e Kord is sometimes added) are considered to have been derived from Šūr and the last from Homāyūn. Among all the *dastgāh*s and *āvāz*es Šūr is the most significant, both because of its scope and because it is the most familiar (Ḵāleqī, p. 129).

In the Azerbaijan tradition, which is very close to the Persian tradition in this respect, twelve *dastgāh*s (or principal *maqām*s) were recognized, seven of them essential (Rāst, Šūr, Segāh, Čahārgāh, Māhūr, Bayāt-e Šīrāz, Homāyūn), the rest less important (Šūštar, Bayāt-e Kord, Bayāt-e Qājār, Navā-Nīšāpūr, Rahāb). To these should be added about ten modes (*moqām*s) and fifteen subsidiary modes (*šoʿba*s; During, 1988, pp. 38-39; cf. pp. 193-98 for information from earlier periods).

Despite all the changes that Persian music has undergone (and despite internal modifications in the *dastgāh*s), the system of twelve *dastgāh*s and *āvāz*es has remained generally the same as when it was codified by the masters of the last century, in particular Mīrzā ʿAbd-Allāh (d. 1337/1918, q.v.). No new *dastgāh* or large *gūša* has been devised since that codification. When an *āvāz* or *dastgāh* has been further developed, it has almost always been through borrowing materials from other *dastgāh*s, rather than through invention, and the rare *gūša*s that have since been added to the traditional corpus (*radīf*) are only melodies or variations that present no novelty from a modal point of view. From this remarkable stability it can be deduced that the system has achieved "canonical" status in Persia (though perhaps less so in Azerbaijan), comparable to that of the twelve *maqām*s and twenty-four *šoʿba*s that prevailed between the 14th and 17th centuries; the breaking down and reassembling of that material produced the present system of *dastgāh*s.

Bibliography: N. Caron and D. Safvate, *Iran*, Paris, 1966. J. During, *La musique iranienne. Tradition et évolution*, Paris, 1984. Idem, *La musique traditionelle de l'Azerbâyjân et la science des muqâms*, Baden-Baden, 1988. Idem, *Le répertoire-modèle de la musique persane. Radif de târ et de setâr de Mirzâ ʿAbdollâh*, Tehran, 1370 Š./1991. Idem, Z. Mirabdolbaghi, and D. Safvat, *The Art of Persian Music*, Wahington, D.C., 1991. Moḥammad-Naṣīr Forṣat Šīrāzī (Forṣat-al-Dawla), *Boḥūr al-alḥān dar ʿelm-e mūsīqī wa nesbat-e ān bā ʿarūż*, ed. M.-Q. Ṣāleḥ Rāmsarī, 2nd ed., Tehran, 1354 Š./1975. F. Joneydī, *Zamīna-ye šenāḵt-e musīqī-e īrānī*, Tehran, 1361 Š./1982. R. Ḵāleqī, *Naẓar-ī be mūsīqī*, 2nd ed., Tehran, 1362 Š./1983. K. Khatschi, *Der Radif*, Regensburg, Germany, 1962. M. Maʿrūfī, *Radīf-e haft dastgāh-e mūsīqī-e īrānī/Les systèmes de la musique traditionnelle iranienne (radif)*, Tehran, 1352 Š./1973. M.-T. Masʿūdīya, *Āvāz-e Šūr*, Regensburg, Germany, 1968. Idem, *Radīf-e āvāzī-e mūsīqī-e īrānī/Radif vocal de la musique iranienne*, Tehran, 1357 Š./1978. Nettl, *The Radif of Persian Music. Studies of Structures and Cultural Context*, Champaign, Ill., 1987. H. Powers, "Mode," in S. Sadie, ed., *The New Grove Dictionary of Music and Musicians*, London, 1980. Z. Safarova, "Traktat Mir Mohsen Navvaba 'Vizuhul agram'" (The treatise of Mīr Moḥsen Nawwāb "Vizuhul agram"), in *Traditsii muzykalnykh kultur. Narodov Blizhnego Vostoka i Sovremennosti* (Traditions of musical culture. The peoples of the Near East and the present), Moscow, 1987, pp. 124-28.

(JEAN DURING)

DASTGERD (< **dasta-kṛta* "made by hand, handiwork"), a term originally designating a royal or seigneurial estate. It is doubtful that it was used in the Achaemenid period, as it is attested only once, in the restored form [*dasta*]*kṛtam* (cf. DSe, ll. 42-43; Kent, *Old Persian*, p. 142). It is widely attested in Middle Iranian inscriptions (ŠKZ Mid.Pers. l. 30, Parth. ll. 16-17, 25, 19-30; NPi Mid.Pers. l. 4, Parth. l. 3, a passage too full of lacunae to permit interpretation of the term; Humbach and Skjærvø, III/1, p. 30, III/2, pp. 31-32) and in Book Pahlavi (cf. *Kār-nāmag* 5.13, ed. Antia, p. 35: *was deh ud dastgird ābādānīh kard*). It was also borrowed in other languages of the Sasanian period (e.g., Arm. *dastakert*, Garsoïan, p. 520; Syr. *dstgrd* (?), Payne Smith, col. 930, and *dsqrtʾ*; Bedjan, p. 439).

Although the etymology seems clear and was well understood by the translator of the Pahlavi psalter (cf. Psalm 134:15, where Syr. *ʿbd ʾydyʾ* "the work of the hands" was rendered *dstklty*; Gignoux, 1969, pp. 241-42 and n. 22), the word has been translated in various ways. It is clear from inscriptions, notably that from Maqṣūdābād in Fārs (de Menasce, p. 424), in which the domain is clearly distinguished from the village, that in the later Sasanian period the word no longer necessarily referred to a "royal" domain, as it had in ŠKZ. The same change is attested in Armenian sources, where the term could refer to the holding of a *naxarar* (a military officer; Garsoïan, p. 520), and from the late Pahlavi sources, where it might simply designate a piece of land (Macuch, p. 243). Such a domain, royal or not, must have included a residence, various other buildings, canals, and the like (Pigulevskaja, pp. 150-53).

The term was also applied to individuals, in phrases like "*dastgerd* of the king" or "of the gods" in ŠKZ (cf. "of God" in Armenian Christian sources; Maricq, repr., p. 56; Perikhanian, p. 460). The rendering *ktisma* in the Greek version of ŠKZ is evidence that the term is correctly translated as "possession" or "creation, creature." It also became a proper noun and was used both as an honorific and as a toponym. An example of the former is *dastgerd-Šābuhr*, referring to Dēnag (q.v.), queen of Mesene (ŠKZ Mid. Pers., l. 30), erroneously associated by W. B. Henning (p. 355) with Hamazasp, king of Georgia, whose name follows hers in the list of dignitaries. As a toponym it was associated by Arabic authors with Daskara or Daskarat al-Malek, a palace or fortified castle surrounded by walls on the road from Ctesiphon (q.v.) to Hamadān, built before the time of Ḵosrow II (590-628 C.E.) and destroyed by the Byzantine emperor Heraclius in 628 (Duri, p. 168; cf. Christensen, *Iran Sass.*, pp. 454-55; Pigulevskaja, pp. 151-52). In a Syriac source of the 5th century a village called Dastgard is mentioned (Bedjan, p. 439), and, according to the acts of the Nestorian councils of 420 and 424, a place called Daskarta in Malka was subject to the catholicos (Pigulevskaja, p. 152). A number of places in Iraq also bore this name (Duri).

Bibliography: M. Back, *Die sassanidischen Staatsinschriften*, Tehran and Liège, 1978. P. Bedjan, *Histoire de Mar-Jabalaha, de trois autres patriarches, d'un prêtre et de deux laïques, nestoriens*, Paris, 1895. A. A. Duri, "Daskara," in *EI²* II, pp. 165-66. N. G. Garsoïan, *The Epic Histories (Buzandaran Patmutʿiwnkʿ)*, Cambridge, Mass., 1989. B. Geiger, "Mittelpersische Wörter und Sachen," *WZKM* 42, 1935, pp. 114-28. P. Gignoux, "L'auteur de la version pehlevie du Psautier serait-il nestorien?" in *Mémorial Mgr. Gabriel Khouri-Sarkis, 1898-1968*, Louvain, 1969, pp. 233-44. Idem, *Glossaire des inscriptions pehlevies et parthes*, London, 1972. W. B. Henning, "A Sassanian Silver Bowl from Georgia," *BSOAS* 24, 1961, pp. 353-56. Hübschmann, *Armenische Grammatik*, p. 135. H. Humbach and P. O. Skjærvø, *The Sasanian Inscription of Paikuli*, 3 pts., Wiesbaden, 1983. M. Macuch, *Das sasanidische Rechtsbuch "Mātakdān i hazār dātistān"* II, Wiesbaden, 1981. A. Maricq, "Res Gestae Divi Saporis," *Syria* 35, 1958, pp. 295-360; repr. in *Classica et Orientalia*, Paris, 1965, pp. 37-101. J. de Menasce, "Inscriptions pehlevies en écriture cursive," *JA*, 1956, pp. 423-31. R. Payne Smith, *Thesaurus Syriacus . . .*, 2 vols., Oxford, 1879. A. Perikhanian, *Sasanidskiĭ sudebnik* (The Sasanian law code), Yerevan, 1973. N. Pigulevskaja, *Les villes de l'état iranien aux époques parthe et sassanide*, Paris and the Hague, 1963.

(PHILIPPE GIGNOUX)

DAŠTĪ, *šahrestān* (subprovince) on the Persian Gulf in Būšehr province, corresponding approximately to the area referred to as Māndestān and Sīf Āl Moẓaffar in early sources (Ebn al-Balḵī, p. 152; Yāqūt, *Boldān* III, p. 217). It is bounded on the north and west by the *šahrestāns* of Daštestān (q.v.) and Tangestān, on the east by the *šahrestān* of Fīrūzābād, and on the south by the *šahrestāns* of Dayyer and Kangān. The administrative center is Ḵormūj, located at 60 m above sea level 82 km from Būšehr. According to the census (q.v.) of 1365 Š./1986, the population of Daštī was 51,409, 36 percent of which lived in urban, the remainder in rural areas; the average population density was thus 8.47 people per km² (*Natāyej*, p. 8). The *šahrestān* of Daštī is 6,065 km² and comprises two districts. The central Ḵormūj district, 3,903 km², comprises the administrative center and two rural subdistricts (*dehestāns*), Ḵormūj and Šanba, with 105 villages. Kākī district, 1,151 km², encompasses the *dehestāns* of Čāġāpūr and Kākī, with a total of forty-four villages.

The climate is hot and humid near the coast, hot and dry inland, and more temperate in the highlands. Water for irrigation comes from springs, wells, *qanāts* (underground aqueducts), and the river Mond. Dry farming (*deym*) is practiced in Kākī; the main products are cereals, dates (see DATE PALM), tobacco, and small quantities of rice (see BERENJ). Persian limes (see CITRUS FRUITS) are produced in Šanba. Most of the population of the *šahrestān* is engaged in agriculture or retail trade; handicrafts include rug weaving.

There are a number of fortresses, rock-cut tombs, and ruined settlements in the *šahrestān* (Eqtedārī, pp. 213 ff., 265-323). In ancient times there were a number of ports in Daštī, reflecting its strategic location near the coast and on the main roads to Fārs and Ḵūzestān. According to *Nozhat al-qolūb* (ed. Le Strange, p. 119), in the 14th century the area was a desert 180 km^2 beside the sea, with no rivers or *qanāt*s. It produced only cereals and cotton (q.v.).

It is not clear from the written sources when the name Daštī was first adopted, but it can be surmised that the *šahrestān*s of Daštī and Daštestān were once part of a single geographical unit. Only from the period of Nāder Shah (1148-60/1736-47) and later is there specific mention of people from Daštī; they were employed as musketeers by the shahs and fought against the British in 1273/1856, 1333/1914, and 1336/1917. They enjoy a reputation as courageous and patriotic people.

In the Qajar period Ḵormūj was a center of learning and the home of several writers and poets, foremost among them Mīrzā Jaʿfar Ḥaqāyeqnegār Ḵormūjī (1225-1301/1810-83), author of *Ḥaqāyeq al-aḵbār-e nāṣerī* (a history of the reign of Nāṣer-al-Dīn Shah, 1264-1313/1848-96) and *Āṯār-e jaʿfarī* (a geography of the world, with special attention to Fārs). The fortress of the hereditary chief Moḥammad Khan Daštī (d. 1299/1881-82), now a ruin, is located in the town of Ḵormūj (Afšār Sīstānī, II, p. 882; Eqtedārī, pp. 213-27).

Bibliography: Ī. Afšār Sīstānī, *Negāh-ī be Būšehr*, Tehran, 1369 Š./1990, pp. 15, 35, 139, 295; II, pp. 611, 619, 643, 652, 665, 723, 726, 746, 773, 881, 886. A. Eqtedārī, *Āṯār-e šahrhā-ye bāstānī-e sawāḥel wa jazāyer-e ḵalīj-e Fārs wa daryā-ye ʿOmān*, Tehran, 1338 Š./1959. M.-Ḥ. Eʿtemād-al-Salṭana, *Merʾat al-boldān*, ed. ʿA.-Ḥ Navāʾī, II-IV, Tehran, 1367 Š./1988. ʿA.-A. Farrāšbandī, *Gūša-ī az tārīḵ-e enqelāb-e mosallaḥāna-ye mardom-e mobārez-e Tangestān, Daštī, wa Daštestān bar ʿalayh-e esteʿmār*, Tehran, 1362 Š./1983. Fasāʾī, ed. Rastgār, II, pp. 1334-43. *Natāyej-e sar-šomarī-e ʿomūmī-e nofūs wa maskan, Mehr-māh-e 1365, šahrestān-e Būšehr*, Tehran, 1365 Š./1986 (?). Razmārā, *Farhang* VII, p. 102. *Safar-nāma-ye banāder-e ḵalīj-e Fārs az mohandesī nāšanāḵta az sālhā-ye 1250-64*, ed. M. Sotūda, Tehran, 1367 Š./1988.

(JAMŠĪD ṢADĀQAT-KĪŠ)

DAŠTĪ, one of the twelve modal systems in the repertoire of traditional music (*radīf*); it is an *āvāz* (q.v.), or auxiliary modal system, derived from or attached to the *dastgāh* (q.v.) Šūr. Its defining feature is the combination of two descending pentachords (G, F, E♭, *D*, C, B♭ and Dp, C B♭, Ap *G*) in such a way that D, the fundamental note of the first pentachord, is lowered a quarter-tone, or *koron* (p), in the second pentachord. This sudden shift from D to Dp confers a very particular character on Daštī, distinguishing it clearly from such related modes as Ḥejāz, Bayāt-e Kord (q.v.), and Bayāt-e rāja. Like all *āvāz*es it begins in the upper register of the scale (D) and finishes in the lower register (G), which is the opening register of Šūr. The principal internal modulation, aside from the shift from the first to the second pentachord, occurs in the ascending sequence D, Ep, F, G, (A♭), in which G is emphasized, before the descent beginning on D. This modulation (*awj*) is sometimes transformed into ʿOššāq: D, Ep, F, G, Ap, B♭ (C) (Caron and Safvate, p. 67).

Daštī is one of those probably ancient modes that have only recently been codified and canonized. It is not mentioned in the classical texts or in related learned traditions in which the features of early Persian music have been preserved. According to Yūsof Forūtan (personal communication), Daštī was borrowed in the 19th century from the vocal repertoire of the Būšehr (q.v.) region, which is celebrated for religious songs. The *taʿzīa* (Shiʿite passion play) may have been one of the means by which it spread. Some of the attached *gūša*s (melodies), like Ḥājīānī and Bīdekānī, came from the same region (Kukertz and Masʿūdīya, pp. 16-17), and the melodies that can be collected there nowadays still show obvious similarities, despite the refinement that this mode has undergone while being integrated into the classical *radīf*. Daštī is also found in the songs of northern Persia. Its popular origins are attested by the *gūša*s of which it is composed (e.g., Gīlakī, Bīdekānī, Čūpānī, Deylamān, Daštestānī). It is because of its coloration and the familiarity with Daštī among the Lors that Daštī is recommended for singing the poems of Bābā Ṭāher (q.v.). For some people this characteristic coloration seems to express rather sprightly and positive feelings (Nettl, p. 10); nevertheless, its dual structure lends another aspect, considered particularly melancholy (Caron and Safvate, p. 67).

The fact that Daštī is also among the *māqām*s (modes) of Iraq must be interpreted as the result of a borrowing either from Persian art music or from the southern Persian popular tradition. It was equally known to musicians from Herat, who played Persian *dastgāh*s. Although it is still found in the art music of Azerbaijan, it is a secondary *māqām* and seldom played; nor does it include the characteristic lowering of the fundamental note by a quarter-tone. In the repertoire of Mīrzā Faraj Rezaiev (Reżāʾīev; 1263-1342/1847-1924) the sequence of *gūša*s Bayāt-e Kord, Ḥājīānī, Gīlakī, Daštī formed part of the development of the Azeri *dastgāh* Bayāt-e Šīrāz. Although the assimilation of Bayāt-e Šīrāz to Daštī has gone out of fashion, it was still mentioned by Mīrzā Moḥammad-Naṣīr Forṣat Šīrāzī (p. 26).

Daštī is unknown in other traditions, and, although some very closely related modes are current in Turkey, Kurdistan, Bukhara, Tajikistan, and Afghanistan, none includes the modulation that is its most defining feature.

One of the most complete versions of Daštī is that of Maḥmūd Karīmī (Masʿūdīya), with the *gūša*s Darāmad (q.v.), Awj, Gīlakī, Bīdekānī, Čūpānī, Daštestānī, Ḡamangīz, Deylamān, and Maṯnawī. In Mūsā Maʿrūfī's version other *gūša*s have been added: Ḥājīānī (highly developed but redundant), Kūča-bāḡī, and Samalī. Gawrī can also be added. The version of Mīrzā ʿAbd-Allāh (q.v.), on the other hand, is very restricted, lasting no more than six minutes and including only the *gūšas* Awj, Bīdekānī, and Ḥājīānī (During, 1991, pp. 151-52). Two very rare *gūšas*, Mamasanī and Sāranj, belong properly to the *radīf* for the *ney* (school of Isfahan; During, 1981). These differences, to which should be added notable variations in performance, are evidence that *āvāz-e Daštī* was codified late and is thus more open to addition of *gūšas* drawn principally from a background of popular songs consisting of *do-baytīs* (Kukertz and Masʿūdīya, pp. 16-17) or folk poetry (Joneydī, pp. 220-21).

Bibliography: N. Caron and D. Safvate, *Iran*, Paris, 1966. J. During, *Anthologie de la musique traditonnelle. Ney par Mohammad Musavi* (recording), Paris, 1981. Idem, *La musique iranienne. Tradition et évolution*, Paris, 1984. Idem, *La musique traditionelle de l'Azerbâyjân et la science des muqāms*, Baden-Baden, 1988. Idem, *Le répertoire-modèle de la musique persane. Radif de târ et de setâr de Mirzâ ʿAbdollâh*, Tehran, 1370 Š./1991. Moḥammad-Naṣīr Forṣat Šīrāzī (Forṣat-al-Dawla), *Boḥūr al-alḥān dar ʿelm-e mūsīqī wa nesbat-e ān bā ʿarūż*, ed. M.-Q. Ṣāleḥ Rāmsarī, Tehran, 1367 Š./1988. F. Joneydī, *Zamīna-ye šenāḵt-e mūsīqī-e īrānī*, Tehran, 1361 Š./1982. J. Kukertz and M.-T. Masʿūdīya, *Musik in Bushehr (Süd Iran)*, Munich and Salzburg, 1975; tr. as *Mūsīqī-e Būšehr*, Tehran, 2536=1356 Š./1977. M. Maʿrūfī, *Radīf-e haft dastgāh-e mūsīqī-e īrānī/Les systèmes de la musique traditionalle de l'Iran (radif)*, Tehran, 1352 Š./1973. M.-T. Masʿūdīya, *Radīf āvāzī-e mūsīqī-e sonnatī-e Īrān/Radīf vocal de la musique iranienne*, Tehran, 1357 Š./1978. B. Nettl, "Attitudes towards Persian Music in Tehran, 1969," *The Musical Quarterly* 56/2, 1969, pp. 73-96. R. Rezayeva-Bakiyava, *Tārzan Mīrzā Faraj*, Baku, 1986. D. Safvate, *Ostādān-e mūsīqī-e Īrān wa alḥān-e mūsīqī-e īrānī*, Tehran, 1350 Š./1971.

(JEAN DURING)

DAŠTĪ, ʿALĪ (b. Karbalāʾ, ca. 1312/1894, d. Tehran, 26 Dey 1360 Š./16 January 1982), man of letters, journalist, and politician.

Life. Daštī, the son of the Shiʿite cleric Shaikh ʿAbd-al-Ḥosayn Daštī, of a family originally from Daštestān (q.v.), received a traditional education in Arabic literature and Islamic sciences and philosophy. In about 1918 he left Iraq for Persia, and, despite his family background and education, turned to journalism and politics, becoming the very antithesis of a religious fundamentalist. Throughout his long life his ideals were "freedom," "reason," and "order." He worked first as a journalist in Shiraz and Isfahan but within two years moved to Tehran as an editor of the weekly *Setāra-ye Īrān*. He received his first major political exposure as an opponent of the Anglo-Persian Agreement of 1919 (q.v.). In 1300 Š./1922 he founded the daily newspaper *Šafaq-e sorḵ*, which he published, with interruptions imposed by the censors, for more than thirteen years (Ṣadr Hāšemī, *Jarāʾed o majallāt* III, pp. 75-79). He was a versatile writer, contributing articles on politics, social issues, and literature throughout most of this period. These articles and the contributions of such colleagues as Rašīd Yāsemī, Saʿīd Nafīsī, ʿAbbās Eqbāl (q.v.), and Mīrzāda ʿEšqī (q.v.) ensured the unique importance of the journal in Persian intellectual life (*Bīst o seh sāl*, tr. Bagley, p. x; Machalski, pp. 133, 139). Many of Daštī's own contributions to this and other periodicals were later reworked in book form (see below).

Daštī's criticism of the 1919 agreement earned him a short spell in prison, the first of four over the next twenty-eight years; he was then exiled to Iraq and received other marks of official displeasure. There are discrepancies in the record of all these events, particularly of the dates. His second arrest, along with seventy or eighty others in public life, following the coup d'etat of 1299/1921 (q.v.) lasted more than three months. During this period he recorded the reflections that eventually formed the first part of his *Ayyām-e maḥbas* and bore the same title (see below).

In the early 1920s Daštī began the serious study of French, a step that opened for him the culture of the West, particularly of the classical world, as well as England and Russia. French and Arabic remained his main languages other than Persian, and he translated such popular sociopolitical writings as Samuel Smiles' *Self-Help* (*Eʿtemād be nafs*, Tehran, 1305 Š/1926; 13th repr., Tehran, 1363 Š./1984), Edmond Demolins's *À quoi tient la supériorité des Anglo-Saxons?* (*Tafawwoq-e Anglo-sākson marbūṭ be čīst?* Tehran, 1302 Š./1923), and Gustave Le Bon's *Lois psychologiques de l'évolution des peuples* (*Nawāmīs-e rūḥīya-ye taṭawwor-e melal*, Tehran, 1302 Š./1923), the latter two from Arabic translations. Although such works were often superficial and naïve, even racist, they had wide influence in Europe, North America, and parts of the Arab world for several decades, and through them Daštī believed that he sensed much of what had made the West so "successful." His attitude to the West was in fact ambivalent. As is clear throughout his writings, he considered himself a patriotic Persian and was deeply resentful of Western colonialism and imperialism. At the same time, however, he saw Western scientific, technological, commercial, and military capabilities and the individualism and sociopolitical attitudes that had supposedly generated them as inescapable facts, to be faced and understood. For him they represented the dark side of forces that in themselves were positive and progressive, forces that Persians had to emulate if they were to be free and self-respecting. Japan and India symbolized classic polarities in their responses to the challenge of the West, whereas Africa was merely an example of the "savage" (*Ayyām-e maḥbas*, pp. 21, 61, 380-81). Yet Daštī (*Ayyām-e maḥbas*, pp. 20-26, 169-70) repeatedly expressed romantic disillusionment with civilization, which he contrasted unfavorably with primitive innocence.

Daštī was among those Persians invited to the Soviet Union in 1927 to celebrate the tenth anniversary of the Bolshevik Revolution. Despite vague allegations to the contrary (Banani, p. 49), there is no real evidence that he ever took more than an optimistic liberal interest in the Soviet regime. He prolonged this trip to tour western Europe. In 1307 Š./1928 he was elected to the sixth session of the Majles as deputy for Būšehr, the beginning of a seven-year career as a bold and skillful parliamentary speaker, though perhaps stronger in his ideas than in carrying them to practical conclusions. At the close of the ninth session (1314 Š./1935) Daštī was again arrested for his writings and his newspaper shut down. After three months, a sick man, he was released to a friend's private clinic, still under strict police supervision. Five months later he was allowed to go home, but comprehensive restrictions on his communication with the outside world continued for a further seven months; this period of ten months was the subject of "Taḥt-e naẓar," the third part of *Ayyām-e maḥbas*. Eventually he resumed his parliamentary career and was elected for Damāvānd in 1318 Š./1939 and 1320 Š./1941 and for a Tehran constituency in 1322 Š./1943. He also cofounded the ʿAdālat (Justice) party in December 1941; unlike its earlier namesake the party was centrist, particularly concerned with reducing military spending and with social, educational, and administrative reforms (*Dam-ī bā Ḵayyām*, tr., p. 25).

In the spring of 1325 Š./1946 Daštī was imprisoned for six months because of his opposition to Prime Minister Qawām-al-Salṭana's apparently pro-Soviet policies and wooing of the Tudeh party (see COMMUNISM ii). After his release in October he paid a prolonged visit to France, which had become a second spiritual home. When he returned to Persia in June 1948 he was appointed ambassador to Egypt, where he served from late 1948 to early 1951. He served as minister without portfolio (*wazīr-e mošāwer*) in the short-lived caretaker cabinet of Ḥosayn ʿAlāʾ, which preceded that of Moḥammad Moṣaddeq. After the coup d'etat of 1332 Š./1953 (q.v.) Daštī was appointed to the Senate, where he remained active for twenty-six years, until the Revolution of 1357 Š./1978-79. He continued to speak with fire and brilliance undiminished, if somewhat tempered by age and wisdom, and without subservience to the court (see Saʿīdī Sīrjānī, p. 345, for reference to a critical letter addressed to the shah). During this period, in 1963, he also spent a year as ambassador to Lebanon. The final three years of his life are particularly obscure, though by all accounts they were sad. He was virtually predestined by his career and his work, as well as by his temperament, for confrontation with the new Islamic regime. There are reports of imprisonments, beatings, injuries, restraints of various kinds, and even half-hearted attempts at suicide (Saʿīdī Sīrjānī, pp. 347 ff.); in his earlier writings he had often discussed suicide as a theoretical concept and a courageous act (e.g., *Ayyām-e maḥbas*, pp. 71-73). The hopes he had nourished for Persia on the world stage had collapsed with the Revolution. His funeral, three years later, seems to have been attended by only a handful of loyal associates.

Daštī's own writings, as well as his translations and adaptations of foreign works that most deeply impressed him, were the main means by which he propagated his ideas, oratory and negotiation being of secondary importance. He came increasingly under the spell of the writings of Anatole France (1844-1924), whom he resembled in many ways, but his empathies remained at once philosophical and romantic, even religious in an ethical sense. To many he was best known for a series of stories set in the fashionable Tehran of the 1930s and 1940s; they were regarded as anything from frivolous to daring to outright immoral (see below). They seem mild enough now but still deserve serious study as social documents of the period.

Perhaps Daštī's innovative and "personal" studies of the principal Persian classical poets will prove the most enduring of his writings; they broke sharply with traditional Persian literary criticism focused on anecdotes, prosody, and *explication de textes*. Like virtually everything he wrote, they were received with great excitement, coming as a complete revelation to many commentators (Saʿīdī Sīrjānī, p. 337). The poet he ultimately seemed to prefer, on various counts, was Saʿdī (see especially his article "Ferdowsī yā Ḥāfeẓ?" in *Sāya* and the study of it by Wickens). His *Bīst o seh sāl*, on the Prophet Moḥammad, is a unique work, respectful, intended even to be reverent, but limited to early "facts" and orthodoxies, stripped of perceived later accretions of miracles and mystification. Despite constant efforts by both the Pahlavi regime and the religious establishment to prevent its publication, it achieved wide circulation (see below) and may have been the greatest single factor in the troubles Daštī suffered in his last decade.

Daštī's character was both colorful and riddled with paradoxes. His quick temper, frankness, and often reckless courage are mentioned in all accounts; he seems also to have been a kind and loyal friend, though some of his friends were less than loyal to him, especially toward the end. By his own lights he was fair and consistent in all his views. Although not without vanity, he was able to accept criticism of his work, for example, of his overfondness at one period for neologisms and Western terminology (Saʿīdī Sīrjānī, p. 346; Kamshad, p. 73). ʿAlī-Akbar Saʿīdī Sīrjānī (pp. 345-46) has stressed his scrupulous care never to use another writer's ideas without acknowledgment. At one period Daštī was something of a dandy, a bon vivant, even a ladies' man; he never married but seems to have adopted a son (Eḥtešāmī, pp. 75-77; Saʿīdī Sīrjānī, pp. 339-40, 347). A few vague allusions to his libertine proclivities resulted, according to Saʿīdī Sīrjānī (pp. 338-40), from his passion for beauty in all things (nature, art, craftsmanship, humanity, etc.) and a propensity to treat women as social equals. He wrote in support of female emancipation, but his position on these matters was often inconsistent.

Whatever personal fortitude and balance Daštī may have achieved in his later life, in his earlier years he seems to have shared some of the outlook of the typical self-indulgent middle-class intellectual. *Ayyām-e maḥbas* contains two major passages perfectly illustrating these attitudes. In part 2 he repeatedly complained of the hardships attending his journey into exile (see above), part of which he was forced to undertake on foot in hot weather and over bad roads; he marveled at the way the lower classes robustly accepted such hardships as a matter of course (e.g., pp. 143-44). In part 3 he described an incident that took place in the hospital where he was convalescing from his prison experiences in 1314 Š/1935: His rest was so disturbed by the cries of a woman in labor and later by the wailing of her child that he devoted a whole essay to the penchant of the human race for procreation, even citing the new Nazi policy of compulsory sterilization of the "unfit" as the perfect solution to such problems (pp. 217-20, 230-31). Even at his most liberal and democratic, he thought primarily of the literate, the intellectual, the comfortably off, the decision makers. His admiration for the doctrine of the survival of the fittest (*nāmūs-e baqāʾ-e ansab*), as he understood it (pp. 50-52, 231), reinforced his preference for "enlightened" capitalism and a strong but just central government; what he could not tolerate was blatant corruption, the arbitrary and oppressive use of power, and entrenched ignorance and superstition.

Works. It is next to impossible at this time to produce a definitive bibliography of Daštī's works that would include every article and editorial that he wrote. The preliminary selective list presented here is derived from a variety of sources, as well as from the works themselves whenever possible. The dates of original publication for some items are uncertain, and some items overlap more than one category.

Daštī published several collections of short stories and novellas. *Fetna* (Tehran, 1323 Š./1944; repr. several times) is a collection of short stories depicting the flaws of Persian social life from several points of view, particularly among women. *Jādū* (Tehran, 1330 Š./1951; repr. several times) and *Hendū* (Tehran, 1333 Š./1954; repr. four times) each includes four short stories.

His works of literary criticism are abundant. *Naqš-ī az Ḥāfeẓ* (Tehran, 1336 Š./1957; rev. and enl. ed., 1349 Š./1970; 7th ed., 1364 Š./1985) is an appreciation of Ḥāfeẓ that broke new ground in Persian literary criticism. Daštī offered little in the way of textual commentary or biographical detail but focused instead on the poet's skillful use of language and his significance in reference to "freedom of thought." He also examined the influence of Saʿdī, ʿOmar Ḵayyām, and Jalāl-al-Dīn Rūmī on Ḥāfeẓ's poetry. He dealt with the *ḡazals* of Rūmī in *Sayr-ī dar Dīvān-e šams* (Tehran, 1337 Š./1958; enl. 3rd ed., 1349 Š./1970; perhaps a 7th ed., 1362 Š./1983), stressing both the poet's distinctive style and his ecstatic outpouring of mystical ideas. As in his other studies, Daštī's technique is impressionistic, albeit here particularly suited to his subject. In *Qalamrow-e Saʿdī* (Tehran, 1338 Š./1959; 3rd ed. with addenda, 1344 Š./1965; reported 6th printing, 1364 Š./1985; tr. Ṣ. Našʾat as *Āfāq adab Saʿdī*) he compared Saʿdī's work with that of earlier poets, underscoring his masterly use (*fasāḥat*) of Persian and offering a critical analysis of his religious beliefs. His *Šāʿer-ī dīr-āšnā* (Tehran, 1340 Š./1961; 2nd ed. with addenda and revisions, 2535=1355 Š./1976; perhaps a 4th ed., 1364 Š./1985.) is a study of the poet Ḵāqānī Šervānī intended to make his work more accessible, despite the difficulties of his language. About 1,000 lines are included as evidence of his true poetic worth. Particularly important in Daštī's literary criticism is *Dam-ī bā Ḵayyām* (Tehran, 1344 Š./1965; 2nd ed. with addenda, Tehran, 1348 Š./1969; 3rd ed. with minor corrections, Tehran, 1355 Š./1976; possibly a fifth printing, 1364 Š./1985; tr. L. P. Elwell-Sutton as *In Search of Omar Khayyam*, London, 1971), a fresh look at Ḵayyām's poetry, including an anthology of all those *robāʿī*s that Daštī thought could plausibly be attributed to him; hundreds of well-known verses were rejected, however. In the second part of the book Daštī presented his personal assessment of the author, his thought, and his weltanschauung. Subsequent works in this genre include *Kāḵ-e ebdāʿ* (originally published in *Yaḡmā*, 1351 Š/1972, and issued separately in Tehran in the same year; 5th ed., 1362 Š./1983), a collection of twelve brief articles in which the ideas of Ḥāfeẓ are analyzed; *Negāh-ī be Ṣāʾeb* (Tehran, 1353 Š./1974; 3rd ed., 1364 Š./1985), a study of the poetry of Ṣāʾeb, with a discussion of the Indian style (*sabk-e hendī*) and some observations on Bīdel (q.v.); and *Taṣwīr-ī az Nāṣer-e Ḵosrow* (Tehran, 1362 Š./1983), similar in approach to Daštī's studies of other poets with inclusion of substantial material from Nāṣer-e Ḵosrow's *Dīvān*, with interpretations.

Daštī was also the author of a number of works of religious criticism. *Taḵt-e pūlād*, published anonymously, is an imagined debate between a *mojtahed* (theologian) and his students (Tehran, 1354 Š./1975). *Bīst o seh sāl* (probably Beirut, n.d. [before 1353 Š./1974]; tr. F. R. C. Bagley as *Twenty Three Years. A Study of the Prophetic Career of Mohammad*, London, 1985; all attributions of this work to other authors are without foundation), published anonymously, was the most controversial of all his publications (see above). *Jabr yā eḵtīār* (*Waḥīd*, 1350 S./1971) is a short treatise on free will versus predestination; appended to the reissue was *Eblīs dar keswat-e ʿerfān*, which he expanded in the final essay of *Parda-ye pendār* (*Eṭṭelāʿāt*, 18-31 Ordībehešt 1353 Š./8-21 May 1974; 4th ed., Tehran, 1363 Š./1984), a collection of essays on Sufism, particularly focused on its antirational, superstitious, and obscurantist manifestations. In *Dar dīār-e ṣūfīān*, a sort of pendant to *Parda-ye pendār*, Daštī gave greater weight to the positive aspects of Sufism (4th ed., 1363 Š./1984). *ʿOqalāʾ bar kelāf-e ʿaql* is a collection of essays on notable instances in which members of the Muslim intelligentsia had adopted "obscurantist" positions (Tehran, 1354 Š./1975; 3rd ed., 1362 Š./1983).

Among Daštī's political memoirs and essays *Ayyām-e maḥbas*, first published in book form in 1303 Š./1924, met with immediate acclaim and was subsequently expanded to include two further sections, "Dar rāh" and "Taḥt-e naẓar." It has been reprinted frequently. *Panjāh o panj*, a collection of political reflections on the first fifty-five years of the Pahlavi regime (1300-55 Š./1921-76), first appeared as a series of thirteen articles in *Kayhān* (1355 Š./1976) and then in book form twice in the same year. *ʿAwāmel-e soqūṭ*, which can apparently be read either as a general analysis of the decline of Persia or as a particularized study of the downfall of the Pahlavi dynasty, appears not to have been published. Three other works, a collection of Daštī's editorials from *Šafaq-e sork* entitled *Sar-maqālahā-ye rūz-nāma-ye Šafaq-e sork*, *Yāddāšthā-ye sīāsī-e Meṣr o Lobnān*, and *Yāddāšthā-ye sīāsī-e zamān-e Reżā Šāh*, have no known printing history but are also said to be "in press."

Other important works by Daštī include *Sāya*, a collection of what he considered some of his best nonpolitical essays (1325 Š./1946; repr. several times in expanded form and with minor alterations; perhaps a 9th printing, 1364 Š./1985); in the latest edition it is divided among literary criticism, social opinions, impressions, and translations. *Maqālāt-e parākanda* has no printing history but is allegedly "in press."

Bibliography: M. ʿĀṣemī, "Daštī," in *Kāve (Kaweh). Deutsch-Iranische Kulturzeitschrift* 75, spring 1982, pp. ii-iii. A. Banani, *The Modernization of Iran. 1921-1941*, Stanford, Calif., 1961 (esp. pp. 48-49, 119). A. Eḥtešāmī, "Āqā-ye Daštī," in A. Eḥtešāmī, *Bāzīgarān-e sīāsat*, Tehran, 1328 Š./1949, pp. 71-83. L. P. Elwell-Sutton, "Political Parties in Iran, 1941-1948," *Middle East Journal* 3/1, 1949, pp. 45-62. R. Gelpke, *Die iranische Prosaliteratur im 20. Jahrhundert* I, Wiesbaden, 1962, esp. pp. 44-69. E. Kᵛāja-Nūrī, "Daštī," in E. Kᵛāja-Nūrī, *Bāzīgarān-e ʿaṣr-e ṭelāʾī*, Tehran, 1357 Š./1978, pp. 154-98. H. Kamshad, *Modern Persian Prose Literature*, Cambridge, 1966. J. E. Knörzer, *ʿAlī Daštī's Prison Days. Life under Reżā Šāh*, Costa Mesa, Calif., and New York, 1994. F. Machalski, *La littérature de l'Iran contemporain* II. *La poésie de l'époque de Reḍā Šāh Pahlavi (1921-1941)*, Wroclaw, 1967. *Raʾy-e ṣāḥeb-naẓarān*, Tehran, 1346 Š./1967 (a valuable collection of reviews of Daštī's studies on Saʿdī, Kāqānī, and Kayyām). ʿA.-A. Saʿīdī Sīrjānī, "Pīr-e mā," in ʿA.-A. Saʿīdī Sīrjānī, *Dar āstīn-e moraqqaʿ*, Tehran, 1363 Š./1984, pp. 329-50. Š. Ṯaqafī, "Mawāred-e tasāhol dar Šīʿa," *Majalla-ye par* 93, Mehr 1372 Š./September-October 1993, pp. 10-13. G. M. Wickens, "Relative Excellence among Classical Poets. A Judgment by Ali Dashti," in D. Amin and M. Kasheff, eds., *Iranica Varia. Papers in Honor of Professor Ehsan Yarshater*, Leiden, 1990, pp. 276-91.

(J. E. KNÖRZER)

DASTJERDĀNĪ, JAMĀL-AL-DĪN, Il-khanid bureaucrat. He first came to prominence as inspector of *awqāf* (pious endowments) in Iraq in 683/1284. Later, during the reign of Arḡūn (q.v.; 683-90/1284-91), he acted as *kāteb* (scribe) to the Jewish administrator Saʿd-al-Dawla, who was attempting to repair the financial ravages of Būqā (q.v.), who is notable for having been the only Mongol to have headed the Il-khanid Persian bureaucracy. During the brief reign of Bāydū (q.v.; 694/1295) Jamāl-al-Dīn served as chief vizier (*ṣāḥeb-dīvān*; Jomādā I 694-Ṣafar 695/March-November 1295). He was restored to that office a few months later by the new ruler, Ḡāzān Khan (694-703/1295-1304), succeeding Šaraf-al-Dīn Semnānī. But his good fortune lasted a very short time: He was brought to trial on charges instigated by one of his predecessors, Ṣadr-al-Dīn Zanjānī, who then succeeded him. During his trial the alleged facts of treasonable correspondence between the influential Amir Nowrūz and the Mamlūks during the reign of Bāydū came to light. Dastjerdānī was said to have prepared, on the orders of Nowrūz, a substitute version of the "genuine" correspondence, in order to present it to Ḡāzān Khan. The version produced at the trial was, however, according to J. A. Boyle (pp. 382-83), a forgery concocted by Nowrūz's enemy Ṣadr al-Dīn. This incident precipitated a crisis leading to Nowrūz's fall and death. Jamāl-al-Dīn was himself executed on 28 Ḏu'l-ḥejja 695/27 October 1296.

Bibliography: J. A. Boyle, "Dynastic and Political History of the Īl-Khāns," in *Camb. Hist. Iran* V, pp. 303-421, esp. pp. 376-83. Rašīd-al-Dīn, *Jāmeʿ al-tawārīk* (Baku), pp. 219, 298, 306, 311-16. Spuler, *Mongolen*[3], pp. 90, 286, 350.

(DAVID O. MORGAN)

DASTŪR (Pahl. *dstwbl*, Man. Mid. Pers. *dstwr*, Man. Parth. *dstbr*, Pāzand and NPers. *dastūr*, all < OIr. **dasta-bara-*(?), the first element of which seems to be cognate with Av. *dąstvā-* "dogma, doctrine" < *dąh-*, *OIr. *dans-* "to teach"; cf. Man. Pers. *dastan* "powerful," Man. Parth. *dast* "capable, able," NPers. *dast* "power, ability," and Dastān, the name of Zāl, father of Rostam, in all likelihood also signifying "powerful"; for the etymology of *dastwar*, see Bailey, *Zoroastrian Problems*, p. 160 n. 5; idem, 1945, p. 8; Bartholomae, p. 26; Darmesteter, I, p. 115; Horn, *Etymologie*, p. 126; Hübschmann, *Persische Studien*, p. 63; Nyberg, *Manual*, II, p. 59; Perikhanian, pp. 445-48).

In Middle Persian. In the Sasanian period *dastwar* had a wide range of meanings, primarily denoting "one in authority, having power." It was most often a generic term referring to Zoroastrian spiritual authorities. It was qualified as *dēn āgāh* "well versed in religious matters" (cf. *dādwar* "judge," q.v., described as *dād āgāh* "well versed in the law"), and *dastwar ī dēn āgāh* was thus an appellation for high-ranking theologians and jurists (in conformity with the concept of *dēn* "religion," q.v.), to whom members of the community turned for authoritative advice or decisions. For example, Wehšābuhr, *mōbedān mōbed* "high priest" in the reign of Ḵosrow I Anōšīravān (531-79), was styled *dastwar ī Ādurbāygān* when summoned to the inquisitorial tribunal convened to try Mazdak (*Zand ī Wahman Yašt*, chap. 2). The famous sage, seer, vizier, and counselor of Guštāsp bore the title *dastwar* Jāmāsp̄ (Gathic Av. *dəjāmāspa-*; *Pahlavi Yasna and Visperad*, p. 205); it also occurs in *Mardbūd ī mōbedān mōbed . . . ud abārīg dastwarān ī mad ēstād hēnd* "Mardbūd, the high priest . . . and the other religious leaders who were present there" (*Mādayān*, pt. 2, p. 39). In the common phrase *pēšēnīgān dastwarān* the term refers to "the ancient fathers of the faith, that is, *pōryōtkēšān*," and the contemporary *dastwarān ēdōn guft* is to be translated "the eminent jurists/theologians have so maintained."

The term *dastwar* is also applied to leaders of evil, that is, non-Zoroastrian, religions: *awēšān dēw dastwar hēnd kēšān druwandīh dēn* "those whose religion is unrighteousness are religious dignitaries representing the demon" (*Pahlavi Yasna and Visperad*, pp. 214-15).

Dastwar occurs in legal texts in the sense of "authorized, legal representative; legal adviser or expert" (see *Dar ī dastwar* "Chapter on the legal representative," in *Mādayān*, pt. 1, p. 5; Perikhanian, p. 14). It is only in this specialized sense that the term designates a distinct juridical office and *dastwarīh* "authorization" a specific function. According to the *Madayān* (pt. 1, p. 6), the *dastwar* is invested with legal power (*dastwarīh*), appears in the law court in the capacity of legal representative (*pad dastwarīh andar ēstēd*), and accordingly pleads one's cause as a lawyer (*dastwarīh ud rāyēnišn ī dādestān kardan*; *Mādayān*, pt. 1, p. 6).

By extension *dastwar* has the sense of "authentic canon, doctrine, dogma," as in the expressions *har čē az wizand ud āšuftagīh ī Aleksandar . . . pad dastwar mānd ēstēd* "Whatever (of the Avesta and Zand) had survived the havoc and disruption of Alexander . . . and remained authoritative" and *Tansar abar mad ān ī *ēwar frāz padīrift ud abārīg az dastwar hišt* "Tansar assumed command; he selected those that were trustworthy and left the rest out of the canon" (*Dēnkard*, ed. Madan, pt. 1, p. 412; Shaki, p. 118). The term also signifies "authority," as in *dēn pad dastwar dār* "regard the religion as your authority" (*Pahlavi Yasna and Visperad*, p. 202) and *axw ī xwēš pad dastwar kunēd* "hold your conscience as your authority" (*Dēnkard*, ed. Madan, pt. 2, p. 528). Through development of this sense the word *dastwarīh* came to mean "judgment; authoritative decision; permission," as attested in *pad rāst dastwarīh ī Tansar* "on the just judgment of Tansar" (*Dēnkard*, ed. Madan, pt. 1, p. 413) and *pad dastwarīh ī pid* "by the father's permission."

In New Persian. In the Islamic period *dastūr* occurs in the Pāzand text of *Škand-gumānīg wizār* (tr. J. de Menasce, chap. 15.91): *Pāwlōs yašą dastūr* "Paul, their religious leader." Although some of the original meanings of the word were retained in this period, the semantic range was increasingly widened to convey different meanings at different times. The Zoroastrian Parsis have employed *dastūr* as the title of a high priest superior to the *mōbed* (Sorūšiān, p. 77), and *dastūrān dastūr* or its New Persian form *dastūr-e dastūrān* "high priest" has replaced the earlier *pēšōbāy* "pontiff," itself adopted in the first centuries of Islam for the Sasanian *mōbedān mōbed* "high priest" (Boyce, *Zoroastrianism* I, p. 164).

The term *dastūr* has been used in profane senses in secular Persian literature. It signifies "prime minister; minister; governmental counselor," the temporal equivalent of Sasanian spiritual dignitaries, and is commonly used in the sense of "command; instruction; obligation; (moral) precept; draft" or "program; model; formulary or recipe, hence prescription." At present it means "rule, regulation, code of law; grammar (*dastūr-e zabān*, lit., "rules of language"); order of the day; procedure of a committee meeting (*dastūr-e jalsa*)." In classical and literary style *dastūrī*, continuing Mid. Pers. *dastwarīh*, and also usually *dastūr* mean "permission." Obsolete meanings include "keeping one's word, promise"; "something given by the vendor free of charge in addition to what is sold"; "customs, tax"; "foundation, pillar"; "master copy, copy"; "bolt of the door."

Dastūr was borrowed in classical Arabic as *dostūr* (pl. *dasātīr*, q.v.), with a variety of meanings, mainly "army pay list; leave; formulary." In modern Arabic *dostūr* refers to a "constitution, statute, regulation." In colloquial Arabic *dastūr* denotes "permission."

Bibliography: H. W. Bailey, "Asica," *TPS*, 1945, pp. 1-38. C. Bartholomae, *Zum sasanidischen Recht* I, Sb. der Heidelberger Akademie der Wissenschaften 9, Abh. 5, Heidelberg, 1918. J. Darmesteter, *Études iraniennes* I, Paris, 1883. *Pahlavi Yasna and Visperad*, Pahlavi Text Series 8, ed. B. N. Dhabhar, Bombay, 1949. A. Perikhanian, *Sasanidskiĭ Sudebnik (Mātakdān ī Hazār Dātastān)* (The Sasanian legal code [*Mādayān i hazār dādestān*]), Yerevan, 1973, pp. 445-48. M. Shaki, "The Dēnkard Account of the History of the Zoroastrian Scriptures," *Archív Orientální* 49/2, 1981, p. 114-25. *Škand-gumanīg wizār*, tr. J. de Menasce as *Škand-Gumanīk Vičār*, Fribourg, 1945. J. S. Sorūšiān, *Farhang-e Behdīnān*, Tehran, 1335 Š/1956. *Zand ī Wahman Yašt*, ed. and tr. B. T. Anklesaria as *Zand i Vohuman Yašt*, Bombay, 1957.

(MANSOUR SHAKI)

***DASTŪR** AL-**AFĀŻEL** FĪ LOĞĀT AL-FAŻĀʾEL* (Manual of the learned for learned words), an early Persian-to-Persian dictionary (*farhang-nāma*), compiled in

India in 743/1342, during the reign of Moḥammad b. Tog̲loq Shah (725-52/1325-52) by Ḥājeb Ḵayrāt Rafīʿ, a poet from Delhi, for his patron Šams-al-Dīn Moḥammad Aḥmad b. ʿAlī Jajnīrī.

Comparisons show that Ḥājeb Ḵayrāt's sources included the early dictionaries *Log̲at-e fors* of Asadī Ṭūsī (11th century) and *Farhang-e Faḵr-e Qawwās* (ca. 700/1300). Although the dictionary includes no corroborative citations, the compiler listed the authors whose prose or poetry he used: Ferdowsī (q.v.; d. ca. 416/1025-26), Abu'l-Qāsem Ḥasan ʿOnṣorī (d. 431/1039), Abu'l-Majd Majdūd b. Ādam Sanāʾī (d. after 528/1134), Ẓahīr-al-Dīn Fāryābī (d. after 598/1201-02), Mojīr-al-Dīn Baylaqānī (d. 597/1197-98), Jamāl-al-Dīn Moḥammad b. ʿAbd-al-Razzāq Eṣfahānī (d. 588/1192), Kamāl-al-Dīn Esmāʿīl (d. 635/1237), Neẓāmī Ganjavī (d. 605/1209), Šaraf-al-Dīn Šafarva (fl. 12th century), Saʿdī, Homām Tabrīzī (d. 714/1314), Nāṣer-e Ḵosrow (b. 304/1004), Sayf Aʿraj, Awḥad-al-Dīn Moḥammad Anwarī (q.v.), Moḥammad b. ʿAlī Sūzanī Samarqandī (d. 569/1173-74), Afżal-al-Din Ḵāqānī Šīrvānī (d. 595/1199), Emām Nāṣerī (fl. 13th century), and other poets of India and Khorasan.

Dastūr al-afāżel contains 2,111 definitions, mostly of nouns and proper names, with only a few infinitives, adjectives, and adverbs. There are many Arabic and a few Turkish words. It is the first Persian dictionary known to have been arranged alphabetically by initial letters, though words beginning with the same letter occur in no particular order. Entries are very short, consisting only of the word and an equivalent (sometimes in Urdu), usually without further explanation or indication of pronunciation. There is occasional evidence of dialectal or local lexical peculiarities, for example Transoxanian *dādar* "brother" and Deylamite *kīā* "hero" (pp. 127, 208).

The work includes words not found in other early dictionaries and was a source for later dictionaries, including *Adāt al-fożalāʾ* (822/1419), *Farhang-e zafāngūyā* (before 837/1433), *Baḥr al-fażāʾel* (837/1433), *Šaraf-nāma-ye Monyarī* (878/1473), *Toḥfat al-saʿādat* (916/1510), *Moʾayyed al-fożalāʾ* (925/1519), *Madār al-afāżel* (1001/1592), and *Farhang-e jahāngīrī* (1017/1608).

Only one manuscript of *Dastūr al-afāżel* is known to have suvived; it was copied ca. 900/1600 and is now kept in the library of The Asiatic Society in Calcutta (Ivanow, no. 517). It was published for the first time in Persia in an edition by Nad̲īr Aḥmad (Tehran, 1352 Š./1973).

Bibliography: W. Ivanow, *Concise Descriptive Catalogue of the Persian Manuscripts in the Curzon Collection, Asiatic Society of Bengal*, Calcutta, 1926. S. I. Baevskii, *Rannyaya persidskaya leksikografiya, 11th-15th vv*. (Early Persian lexicography, 11th-15th centuries), Moscow, 1989, pp. 55-60.

(SOLOMON BAEVSKY)

DASTŪR-E DABĪRĪ, comprehensive manual of letter writing by Moḥammad Meyhanī, consisting of an introduction (*dībāča*) and two chapters (*qeṣm*; comp. D̲u'l-qaʿda 585/December 1189-January 1190). It is known from a single manuscript in the library of the Fatih mosque, Istanbul (ms. no. 4074; Dānešpažūh, p. 27; cf. Monzawī, p. 625).

As stated in the introduction (p. 1), one chapter deals with the prerequisites, style, and manner of *dabīrī*, the secretarial art, and the other with the aims and techniques of correspondence (q.v.). The latter chapter actually comprises samples of a variety of types of correspondence: private letters (*eḵwānīyāt*), social letters (*reqāʿ*), decrees (*solṭānīyāt*), reports (*maḥāżer*), a collective letter (*jamāʿat-nāma*), and a proclamation (*ettefāq-nāma*). In the introduction the author also mentioned samples of securities and legal documents (*sokūk*), but they are missing from the printed text.

The book provides a good example of the plain style of Persian prose of the 10th-12th centuries. The author prescribed eleven rules (*nokta*) for such writing in the opening chapter. The book also contains valuable information on social, administrative, and political conditions in 12th-century Persia.

Dastūr-e dabīrī apparently served as a model for subsequent authors, including Moḥammad Naḵjavānī, author of the 14th-century administrative manual *Dastūr al-kāteb fī taʿyīn al-marāteb* (q.v.).

Bibliography: M.-T. Dānešpažūh, "Dabīrī o Nevīsandegī 5," *Honar o mardom* 106, 1350 Š./1971, pp. 27-38. Moḥammad b. ʿAbd-al-Kārīm Meyhanī, *Dastūr-e dabīrī*, ed. A. Erzi, Ankara, 1962. A. Monzawī, *Fehrest-e moštarak-e nosḵahā-ye ḵaṭṭī-e fārsī-e Pākestān/Comprehensive Catalogue of Persian Manuscripts in Pakistan* V, Islamabad, 1986. D̲. Ṣafā, *Ganjīna-ye soḵan* II, Tehran, 1348 Š./1969.

(HASHEM RAJABZADEH)

DASTŪR AL-KĀTEB FĪ TAʿYĪN AL-MARĀTEB, administrative manual written by Moḥammad Naḵjavānī (ca. 679/1280-after 768/1366), son of Faḵr-al-Dīn Hendūšāh b. Sanjar Naḵjavānī, author of *Tajāreb al-salaf*. The work was commissioned during the reign of the Il-khan Abū Saʿīd (q.v.; 716-36/1316-35) by the vizier G̲īāṯ-al-Dīn Moḥammad, son of the great vizier Rašīd-al-Dīn Fażl-Allāh. It provides a detailed and immensely valuable description of the machinery of government as it existed toward the end of the period of Mongol rule in Persia. It was not, however, completed during the lifetimes of Abū Saʿīd and G̲īāṯ-al-Dīn. It took nearly thirty more years to reach its definitive form and was ultimately dedicated to the Jalayerid sultan Shaikh Oways (757-76/1356-74). According to what is apparently the best manuscript (Köprülü Library, Istanbul, ms. no. 1241), dated 798/1396, Naḵjavānī finished the work in 761/1360, but revision and polishing (in Tabrīz) took until 767/1365-66. The work contains a great deal of information not found elsewhere, for example, information on legal procedures under the late Il-khanids (see Morgan, esp. pp. 174-76). It has been edited by A. A. Alizade (2 vols. in 3 pts., Moscow, 1964-76); the second volume (pt. 2, pp. 40-69) contains an introduction and a discussion of the whole work in English.

Bibliography: D. O. Morgan, "The 'Great *Yāsā* of Chingiz Khān' and Mongol Law in the Īlkhānate," *BSOAS* 49, 1986, pp. 163-76, esp. 174-76.

(DAVID O. MORGAN)

D̲ĀT-AL-SALĀSEL (lit., "provided with chains"), place near Obolla in southern Iraq where in 633 C.E., according to Sayf b. ʿOmar, one of Ṭabarī's informants, K̲āled b. Walīd and an Arab force of about 18,000 men defeated a small Sasanian garrison led by a frontier commander named Hormoz (Ṭabarī, I, pp. 2021, 2023-25; cf. Ebn al-Aṯīr, II, p. 294; Donner, p. 179; for questions about the veracity of Sayf in general and the suggestion that his unique report of this battle is fictional, see Wellhausen, pp. 3-7; Ṭabarī, tr., XI, pp. xiii-xxx, 13 n. 86; Sebeos [d. 66], whose account of the Muslim conquest is the earliest to have survived, did not mention K̲āled in this connection). This engagement was supposedly one of several along the western bank of the Euphrates in that year, during the first phase of K̲āled's invasion of Mesopotamia. At that time the Sasanians were in disarray, owing, first, to a revolt of the imperial army and, second, to the murder of K̲osrow II (590-628, with interruption), followed by the massacre of the royal princes by Šērūye (Kavād II, r. 628). The defense of the borderlands had thus been left to local commanders like Hormoz and magnates (*dehqān*, q.v.) of Sasanian descent like Anūšajān and Qobād (Kavād), who commanded the two wings of the army. Hormoz was allegedly killed by K̲āled (for the legendary character of such reports, cf. Müller, p. 227), but the other two fled with the survivors to Maḏār, where they were subsequently defeated (Ṭabarī, I, pp. 2026-28).

Ṭabarī's assertion that the site was called D̲āt-al-Salāsel because the Persian commanders had chained their troops together (presumably in order to prevent their fleeing from battle) is probably a fabrication (Ṭabarī, I, pp. 2025-26; cf. D̲āt-al-Salāsel in the Ḥejāz in Arabia; Donner, pp. 65, 101-04). Equally the view that the name reflected "the resemblance of the ranks of the armoured Iranian cavalrymen to an iron chain" (Zarrīnkūb, p. 7) is unsubstantiated. A chain fence would, however, have been a useful device for a force fearing a surprise attack by night. Indeed, Sasanian military experts had prescribed related devices: "iron traps [to] be placed in localities, where a night attack is feared" (cf. similar advice in a Byzantine military manual; Inostrancev, pp. 14, 31).

After K̲āled's victories in southern Mesopotamia the Persian frontier defenses near the tip of the Persian Gulf lay open, and he proceeded toward Meysān unhindered, having dispatched Maʿqel b. Moqarren to sack Obolla.

See ʿARAB ii.

Bibliography: F. M. Donner, *The Early Islamic Conquests*, Princeton, N.J., 1981. C. A. Inostrancev, "Sasanian Military Theory," tr. L. Bogdanov, *Journal of the Cama Oriental Institute* 7, 1926, pp. 7-52. A. Müller, *Der Islam im Morgen- und Abendland* I, Berlin, 1885. J. Wellhausen, *Skizzen und Vorarbeiten*. VI/1. *Prolegomena zur ältesten Geschichte des Islams*, Berlin, 1899. ʿA. Zarrīnkūb, "The Arab Conquest of Iran," in *Camb. Hist. Iran* IV, pp. 1-56.

(A. SHAPUR SHAHBAZI)

DĀTA, Old Iranian term for "law" (originally the neuter verbal adjective *dāta-m* from the root *dā-* "to put, place," thus "(the law) set/laid down"; cf. Ger. *Gesetz* and Eng. *law* respectively), attested both in Avestan texts (Old and Younger Av. *dāta-*) and in Achaemenid royal inscriptions (Old Pers. *dāta-*; Kent, *Old Persian*, p. 189). The Old Persian term was incorporated into the languages of several neighboring peoples during the Achaemenid and subsequent periods (e.g., El. *da-ad-da-um*, *da-at-tam*$_6$, *da-tam*$_5$, *da-ad-da-(-ma)* [cf. Hinz and Koch, pp. 246-47, 256, 298], Late Babylonian *da-a-ta/ti/tu*, Hebrew *dt-*, biblical Aram. *dʾt*, *dāt*, inscriptional Aram. [Xanthos] *dt-h*, Syr. *dt-ʾ*, Arm. *dat* (cf. Mid. Pers., NPers. *dād*, etc.).

In the Achaemenid royal inscriptions Old Persian *dāta-* is used in a dual sense. In texts of Darius I (q.v. iii; 522-486 B.C.E.) all the references are to the king's law, by which order was established and guaranteed in his empire (DB I.23: "these countries obeyed my law"; DNa 21-22=DSe 20-21=XPh 18-19: "my law—that held them (firm)"; DSe 37-39 "my law—of that they are afraid"). In two instances in Xerxes' so-called "*daiva* inscription," however, the law of Ahura Mazdā (q.v.) is mentioned ("obey that law which Auramazdā has established"; the man who obeys "both becomes happy while living and blessed when dead"; XPh 49-56; Kent, *Old Persian*, pp. 151-52). Divine law thus apparently applied not only to order on earth but also to welfare in the life to come.

Both these meanings, "king's law" and "divine law," recurred elsewhere. In the royal decree of Artaxerxes I (465-25 B.C.E.) quoted in chapter 7 of the Book of Ezra "the law (*dāṯā*) of your God (i.e., Yahweh)" and "the law of the king" (*dāṯā dī malkā*) are mentioned side by side. Other evidence in the Old Testament confirms this dual meaning; it suffices to mention only the famous immutable "law of the Medes and the Persians" (Daniel 6:9, 6:13, 6:16; Esther 1:19).

It is not surprising that the expression "the king's law/decree (*dātu ša šarri*)" is also attested from Babylonia, but only from the reign of Darius I and later. The phrase occurs in several texts but in obviously different senses (*Assyrian Dictionary*, pp. 122-23). On one hand, the delivery of barley and other produce and the payment due are the subject, whereas in other instances (e.g., a deed recording a slave sale) there are references to trials before a judge whose behavior and decision were to be guided by a law. It is thus evident that this law had been newly imposed in Babylonia by the Achaemenids, most probably by Darius.

It was owing to Darius' legal reforms or, stated more prudently, to his introduction of a special Persian form of law that so many peoples of the empire borrowed the Old Persian term *dāta-*, in semantic contexts obviously extending beyond the native Jewish, Mesopotamian, and other conceptions of "law." Furthermore, there is no doubt that these new developments in the legal and juridical systems were based on royal decrees, which had the force of law. T. Cuyler Young, Jr., correctly noted (p. 95) the passage from DB 1.23-24 in which Darius seems to have equated his law with his command: "By the favor of Auramazdā these countries obeyed my law; as has been said to them by me, thus they used to act." In one document from his twelfth year there is mention of a high official *ša muḫḫi dātu* "in charge of the law," and the title *dātabara* (q.v.) is also attested.

The only independent (untranslated) attestation of Old Persian *dātam* in the Elamite texts is in a Persepolis tablet (PF 1980.31; Hallock, pp. 583-84) in which the term "a former law" occurs, probably referring to a kind of decreed tariff and surely not to a law.

The use of the Avestan term *dāta-* (*AirWb.*, col. 726) corresponds to some extent to the Achaemenid dual usage. On one hand, there are the divine "laws of Ahura Mazdā" (e.g., *Y.* 46.15, 21.1); the religious "law of Zoroaster" (*dāta- zaraθuštri-*), which is more often than not combined with the "law code abjuring the *daēuuas*" (*dāta- vīdaēuua-*, i.e., the *Vidēvdād*); and apparently a deified "law" (*dāta-*; *Yt.* 10.139). On the other hand, profane and trivial occurrences of *dāta-* are not infrequent, including that in *Yašt* 10.84, where there is reference to the pauper who "is deprived of his rights (*dātāiš*)."

See also DĀD, JUDICIAL SYSTEM.

Bibliography: *The Assyrian Dictionary* III. *D*, Chicago, 1959. P. Frei and K. Koch, *Reichsidee und Reichsorganisation im Perserreich*, Freiberg and Göttingen, 1984, pp. 63-64. R. T. Hallock, *Persepolis Fortification Tablets*, Chicago, 1969. W. Hinz and H. Koch, *Elamisches Wörterbuch*, 2 vols., Berlin, 1987. A. T. Olmstead, *History of the Persian Empire*, Chicago, 1948, pp. 119-20, 128 ff., 304-05. T. C. Young, Jr., "The Consolidation of the Empire and Its Limits of Growth under Darius and Xerxes," *CAH*[2] IV, pp. 53-111, esp. pp. 94-95.

(RÜDIGER SCHMITT)

DĀTABARA, title of a high official in the Achaemenid legal and juridical system. It is not attested in Old Persian but only in collateral traditions (El. *da-ud-da-bar-ra*; Late Babylonian *da-(a-)ta-ba-ra/ri*, *-bar-ri*; biblical Aram. *dtbr*, *dəṯāḇar*; talmudic Aram. *dwʾr*, *dwwr*) and in younger Iranian languages (Pahl. *dʾtwbl*, *dādwar*; Inscr. Pahl. *dʾtbry*, *dʾtwbr*; Man. Mid. Pers. *dʾywr*, *dāywar*; Inscr. Parth. *dʾtbr*; Man. Mid. Parth. *dʾdbʾr*, *dādβār*; Pāzand, NPers. *dā(d)war* "judge"; cf. the loan translation Arm. *datawor*). In the sources available Old Iranian **dāta-bara-*, lit., "bearer of the law (DĀTA, q.v.)," designates a high judicial officer, that is, a lawyer but not necessarily a judge. The only Aramaic instance occurs in the Book of Daniel (3:2-3), in an enumeration of higher officials; in the Babylonian documents of the Murašû archives it refers to the same person throughout, a man who had some relation to the satrap of Babylonia but in this context was acting only as witness to the transactions in question (Dandamayev, pp. 41-42).

The title also became a personal name *Dātabara-, which seems to be attested in Aramaic Dtbr on a mortar from Persepolis (Bowman, p. 117, giving the incorrect reading Rtbr).

See also DĀDWAR, DĀDWARĪH.

Bibliography: R. A. Bowman, *Aramaic Ritual Texts from Persepolis*, Chicago, 1970. M. A. Dandamayev, *Iranians in Achaemenid Babylonia*, Costa Mesa, Calif., 1992. W. Hinz, *Altiranisches Sprachgut der Nebenüberlieferungen*, Wiesbaden, 1975, p. 85.

(RÜDIGER SCHMITT)

DATAMES (Gk. Datámēs), Iranian personal name, reflecting Old Iranian *Dātama- or *Dātāma-, either a two-stem shortened form *Dāta-m-a- from a compound name like *Dātamiθra- (q.v.) or an unabridged compound *Dātāma- from *Dāta-ama- "to whom force is given."

The best known bearer of this name (ca. 407 [or earlier]-ca. 362 B.C.E.) was the son of the "Carian" Camisares (whose name was, however, apparently of Iranian origin), who governed part of Cilicia (q.v.) at the beginning of the reign of Artaxerxes II (405-359 B.C.E.), and the Paphlagonian Scythissa, probably a princess (Nepos, *Datames* 1.1). Most available information about Datames is to be found in Cornelius Nepos' *Life of Datames* (bk. 14), but, apart from the notorious shortcomings of this work, it is not easy to reconcile this information with that from other sources.

According to Nepos, at the beginning of his career Datames served in Artaxerxes' palace guard and showed his military talents and bravery in the Cadusian campaign of ca. 385/4 B.C.E. (Nepos, *Datames* 1.1-2; for the date, cf. Sekunda, p. 38). Camisares was killed on this expedition, and his office of governor of "Cilicia next to Cappadocia" was conferred upon his son. In about 384 Datames was commanded by the king to join the campaign of the Lydian satrap Autophradates against "those who had revolted," among them perhaps the Pisidians. He once more distinguished himself by saving the royal army, which was in bitter distress, and was then charged with "more important matters" (Nepos, *Datames* 2.1).

Presumably at about the same time Datames was involved in the quarrel between Artaxerxes and the

Paphlagonian dynast Thuys, his maternal cousin, who had refused obedience to the king. Datames first tried to persuade Thuys to submit (Nepos, *Datames* 2.3), but after having escaped death only through his mother's warning he declared war against Thuys, who was at last captured alive (2.3-5) and brought to the royal court by Datames in person (3.1-4). Datames was generously rewarded and given joint command with Pharnabazus (satrap of Dascylium, q.v.) and Tithraustes over an expeditionary force to Egypt in the later 380s. When Pharnabazus was recalled to the court (perhaps in 373 B.C.E.), the supreme command was bestowed on Datames (3.5).

Before completion of military preparations for a new invasion of Egypt Artaxerxes ordered Datames to subdue a certain Aspis, who at that time held Cataonia (apparently as the official Persian governor) and had begun to disregard the king's authority (Nepos, *Datames* 4.1-2). The choice of Datames for this assignment can be explained only by his positions as satrap of Cappadocia (see Diodorus, 15.91.2, though under the year 362/1 B.C.E.) and supreme commander of the army assembled for the Egyptian expedition. Although there is no sure evidence of the date when Datames received the satrapy, it had probably been earlier than 368/7 B.C.E., perhaps already in the 380s. As for the rebellious Aspis, Datames set out for Cilicia at once, marching day and night with only a small strategic force, and soon succeeded in capturing him (Nepos, *Datames* 4.3-5).

Meanwhile the number of Datames' enemies at court had been growing continuously (Sekunda, p. 51). Datames was warned of developments by his friend Pandantes, the royal treasurer (Nepos, *Datames* 5.3); he then decided to leave the army assembled at Phoenician Akē in command of Mandrocles of Magnesia and to return "with his own men" (*cum suis*) to Cappadocia (5.6). This desertion probably took place in 368 B.C.E. In order to consolidate and extend his domain, Datames occupied part of Paphlagonia (5.6; cf. Polyaenus, *Strategemata* 21.1, apud Sekunda, pp. 45-46). He also attacked Sinope on the Black Sea coast and must have captured it, for he issued coins there. Despite the absence of historical details, some anecdotes from this period of his life are preserved in the account of Polyaenus (*Strategemata* 21.2.5; cf. Sekunda, pp. 46-47).

Datames, already accused by enemies at court of intending to revolt against the king, then decided actually to do so. Although during the Paphlagonian campaign he tried to conceal his plans (Nepos, *Datames* 5.6), he was the first to rise in the great satrapal revolt of the 360s, forming a secret alliance with Ariobarzanes (q.v. 1), satrap of Dascylium. Datames sent his son Arsidaeus against the Pisidians (6.1), but he was killed in battle, so that Datames himself had to take to the field. He achieved a rapid victory with a small force (6.1-8) but failed to subjugate Pisidia. During this campaign his father-in-law, Mithrobarzanes, who commanded part of the cavalry, deserted to the enemy (6.3; but cf. Diodorus, 15.91.2-6, who provided more detail and dated this event to 362/1 B.C.E.).

Of much more consequence was the desertion of his own son Sysinas (or the like), who went over to Artaxerxes and denounced his father as a rebel (Nepos, *Datames* 7.1). At once the king sent a huge army of 171,000 men under Autophradates (q.v.), satrap of Lydia, to Cappadocia to suppress the rebellion (8.2; cf. Sekunda, p. 49). Autophradates, perhaps marching from Akē (Sekunda, p. 49), was able to pass through the Cilician Gates before Datames could take them and to enter Cappadocia itself. Datames, whose force, including Greek mercenaries, was less than a twentieth the size of his adversary's army (cf. Nepos, *Datames* 8.3), chose a defensive position suitable for delaying tactics and thus gained a first victory. Autophradates decided to make peace with Datames and to concentrate his forces against Ariobarzanes, the more dangerous opponent, thus effecting a reconciliation, that is, submission of Datames to Artaxerxes (8.6). Nepos did not provide much detail on ensuing events, recounting only Artaxerxes' repeated attempts to assassinate Datames (9.1; cf. Diodorus, 15.91.7).

Datames' activities during the following years are thus not clear; he seems to have launched several attacks himself, as there is sporadic information in the sources about actions in Pamphylia and even Mesopotamia (Polyaenus, *Strategemata* 7.21.3). For some time during the great satrapal revolt there was actually a danger that the entire western part of the Achaemenid empire, under the leadership of Datames with the support of the Egyptian pharaoh Tachos, might succeed in breaking away from the center and disintegrating into a number of separate autonomous states. As each satrap sought to obtain the greatest gain for himself, however, none could trust the others, and in the end Artaxerxes himself was the winner.

In 362/1 B.C.E. Datames fought another battle, this time with Artabazus, the king's general, who had entered Cappadocia with a great army (Diodorus, 15.91.2) but was unable to gain the victory. At some unknown date, however, Artaxerxes finally succeeded in eliminating Datames by assassination: Mithridates, Ariobarzanes' son, who had already betrayed and captured his own aged father, persuaded Datames to agree to a personal meeting and stabbed him with a hidden sword (Diodorus, 15.91.7; cf. Nepos, *Datames* 9-11; Polyaenus, *Strategemata* 7.29.1), which brought a virtual end to the great satrapal revolt.

Datames was apparently a bold and warlike man, a distinguished strategist. His memory seems to have remained alive in Cappadocia, for he was included in the genealogy of the provincial dynasty (cf. Diodorus, 31.19) in later times (see below). A number of Cilician and other silver coins (mostly from Tarsus) bearing the names Pharnabazus and Datames (in Aramaic or Greek forms) and apparent likenesses survive; they were minted for payment of mercenaries and crews (cf. Sekunda, pp. 41-42; Alram, pp. 109-10; Moysey, with further references). It must be stressed, however, that the difficulty of the Aramaic form *tdnmw* (read as *trkmw* by Lemaire, pp. 302-05), which is not easy to reconcile with the Greek form, remains unresolved.

There were several other known bearers of the name *Dātama. Datámās, leader of the Cadusians during the march to the fortress of Gadatas under Cyrus the Great (559-29 B.C.E.; Xenophon, *Cyropaedia* 5.3.38), was killed near Babylon (5.4.15-16). Another Datámās, a myriarch (i.e., "leader of 10,000" Persian horsemen), participated in Cyrus' triumphal parade (Xenophon, *Cyropaedia* 8.3.17). One *Dātama (El. *Da-(ad/ud-)da-ma*), an official of unknown function in the reign of Darius I (522-486 B.C.E.), is mentioned several times in the Persepolis Fortification tablets (Hinz and Koch, pp. 246, 261, 300), and possibly another was owner of the Persepolitan seal no. 20 (probably from the reign of Xerxes I or Artaxerxes I), which bears a fragmentary Aramaic inscription "seal of *dtm*[" (Schmidt, esp. p. 26). Datames, one of the Cappadocian kings listed in a ficticious genealogy linking the dynasty with Cyrus the Great (Diodorus, 31.19), was said to be the son of Anaphas (q.v.), one of the "seven Persians," and to have succeeded him on the throne; he was also designated as the father of Aria(ra)mnes (see ARIYĀRAMNA 5). This Datames was praised as a brilliant warrior and supposedly died in battle (31.19.2). Finally, there was the Persian Datames who commanded a fleet of ten ships sent to the Cyclades in 334/33 B.C.E., in the reign of Darius III (336-30 B.C.E.; Arrian, *Anabasis* 2.2.2). While anchored near Siphnus he was attacked by the Macedonian Proteas, who captured eight of his ships; Datames himself escaped to the main body of the Persian fleet (2.2.4-5).

Bibliography: M. Alram, *Iranisches Personennamenbuch* IV. *Nomina Propria Iranica in Nummis*, Vienna, 1986. M. A. Dandamaev, *A Political History of the Achaemenid Empire*, tr. W. J. Vogelsang, Leiden, 1989, pp. 301-03. C. M. Harrison, *Coins of the Persian Satraps*, Ph.D. diss., University of Pennsylvania, Philadelphia, 1982, esp. pp. 172-75, 256-65, 321-36, 478-84. W. Hinz and H. Koch, *Elamisches Wörterbuch*, 2 vols., Berlin, 1987. W. Judeich, *Kleinasiatische Studien*, Marburg, 1892, esp. pp. 191-93, 194-97, 204-06. Idem, "Datames," in Pauly-Wissowa IV/2, cols. 2224-25. A. Lemaire, "Recherches d'épigraphie araméenne en Asie Mineur et en Égypte et le problème de l'acculturation," in H. Sancisi-Weerdenburg and A. Kuhrt, eds., *Achaemenid History* VI. *Asia Minor and Egypt. Old Cultures in a New Empire*, Leiden, 1991, pp. 199-206. R. A. Moysey, "The Silver Stater Issues of Pharnabazos and Datames from the Mint of Tarsus in Cilicia," *The American Numismatic Society Museum Notes* 31, 1986, pp. 7-61. A. T. Olmstead, *History of the Persian Empire*, Chicago, 1948, pp. 401, 409-13, 419-22. E. F. Schmidt, *Persepolis* II, Chicago, 1957. N. V. Sekunda, "Some Notes on the Life of Datames," *Iran* 26, 1988, pp. 35-53.

(RÜDIGER SCHMITT)

***DĀTAMIΘRA** (El. Da-da/tam$_5$-mi-ut-ra, Aram. *dtmtr*), Iranian personal name resulting from an inversion of *Miθra-dāta-* "given by Mithra" and continued in the New Persian Dādmehr. It is also attested in the variant *Dāta-miça- (El. Da-da-mi-iš-šá), with persianized second element (Hinz and Koch, pp. 261, 298). Such a name may also form the basis of the shortened Old Iranian *Dātama-, reflected in Greek Datámēs (see DATAMES).

One bearer of this name was a treasurer, who is attested sixteen times in Aramaic documents from Persepolis of the period between the seventh and nineteenth years of Xerxes I (486-65 B.C.E.), that is, 479/8-67/6 B.C.E. (Bowman, pp. 73, 193a). In 467/6 he was replaced by one Bagapāta; in two instances Dātamiθra is explicitly designated "the treasurer, who is in Arachosia" and "the treasurer, who is in *ghštk*," apparently references to his later post (Bowman, pp. 28-29), though its geographical location is unclear.

Bibliography: R. A. Bowman, *Aramaic Ritual Texts from Persepolis*, Chicago, 1970. W. Hinz and H. Koch, *Elamisches Wörterbuch*, 2 vols., Berlin, 1987.

(RÜDIGER SCHMITT)

DATAPHERNES (Gk. Dataphérnēs < Ir. *Dāta-farnah- "to whom *farnah-* [i.e. grace and glory] is given," also reflected in Babylonian Da-da-pir-na-ʾ, Da-da-a-pa-ar-na-ʾ and El. Da-tap-par-na, Da-ud-da-pa-ir-na and variants), name of an Iranian (perhaps Bactrian) officer in the entourage of Bessos (q.v.), murderer of Darius III (q.v.; 336-30 B.C.E.). Although he was one of Bessos' confidants, in the spring of 329 B.C.E. he volunteered, together with Spitamenes, to arrest his master and turn him over to Alexander the Great (q.v.), though in the end he did not do so (Arrian, *Anabasis* 3.29.6-30.1, following Ptolemaeus; for another version, following Aristobulus, cf. Arrian, *Anabasis* 3.30.5; for more details, see Curtius Rufus, 7.5.21-26). Having joined in this treachery and an uprising led by Spitamenes, after the assassination of the latter he was delivered to Alexander by the Dahae (q.v.; Curtius Rufus, 8.3.16).

Bibliography: J. Kaerst, "Dataphernes," in Pauly-Wissowa IV/2, col. 2226. C. Werba, *Die arischen Personennamen und ihre Träger bei den Alexanderhistorikern*, Ph.D. diss., Vienna, 1982, pp. 156-57.

(RÜDIGER SCHMITT)

DATE PALM (*derakt-e kormā, nakl*; *Phoenix dactylifera* L., fam. Palmaceae), dioecious tree of great economic and cultural importance in Persia and the Middle East. It is indigenous to the geobotanical "Sahara-Sind region," a desert or semidesert belt extending from the Indus valley to North Africa (Gauba, 1951, p. 15; for distribution of the date palm in this region, see Dowson and Aten, p. 2; Dowson, tr., pp. 20-37). It is believed by some authorities to be native to the Persian Gulf area (Erbe) and by others to have been derived from the the wild or date-sugar palm of western India (Hindi *ḵarjūra*, *Phoenix sylvestris* Roxb.; Zargarī, IV, p. 525; for a possible linguistic relation between Skt. *kharjura* and *ḵormā* "date" [Mid. Pers. *xurmā*], see Laufer, *Sino-Iranica*, p. 391).

The date palm in historical sources.

Date-palm cultivation is attested in ancient texts and representations from Mesopotamia (e.g., Gauba, 1951, p. 15; cf. Hussain, tr., pp. 1-4; Dowson, tr., p. 25). In the Fertile Crescent the goddess Mylitta (Mesopotamia) or Astarte (Phoenicia) was represented by a female date palm. The attributes of the god Mithra may have included the male palm and the pyramidal cypress (q.v.; Lajard, pp. 7-8, 273), as depicted on a marble relief of Roman provenience kept at the Villa Altieri, Rome (Vermaseren, pp. 152-53 no. 334, fig. 91; cf. Cumont, p. 195).

In the Achaemenid period, according to Strabo (15.2.7, 16.1.14), there was a Persian song on the 360 uses of a date palm. On a contemporary seal Darius is depicted on a chariot between two (female) palms and beneath the winged Ahura Mazdā (q.v.; Plate VII; cf. *Survey of Persian Art*, pls. 123A, G-H, 124D). Zoroastrians regarded the date palm as the most valuable of all trees except the mythical Gōkirin (*Bundahišn*, tr. Anklesaria, p. 157). There is a report of agricultural taxes in the time of Ḵosrow I (531-79 C.E.), including 1 dirham for every four "Persian" date palms and 1 dirham for every six palms yielding dates of inferior quality (*daqal*); isolated palms were exempt from taxation (Ṭabarī, II, p. 962). In particular, dates from the province of Ḥīra in Mesopotamia (*armāv ī hēratīk*), when stuffed with walnuts (cf. the modern *rangīnak*, below), were considered a royal delicacy (*Xusrō i Kavātān*, par. 52; cf. Ṯaʿālebī, *Ḡorar*, p. 708; cf. the Pahlavi commentary on *Vd.* 2.28 in *Avesta*, tr. Darmesteter, II, p. 27). In the Parthian poem *Draxt ī āsūrīg* (q.v.; ll. 1-27), a debate between a she-goat and a female date palm, the latter enumerates the benefits to humankind from her fruits, leaves, fibers, and so on.

A wealth of ancient lore on the date palm is included in the *Ketāb al-felāḥat al-nabaṭīya*, allegedly translated from Syriac by Ebn Waḥšīya in 291/903-04 (VII, pp. 51-271). The Kasdānī (Chaldean?) Yanbūšād is cited (VII, pp. 86-98) on similarities between the date palm and humankind: the existence of males, females, and hermaphrodites (*ḵonṭā*); similarity in the odors of date pollen and semen; the supposed susceptibility of the female palm to falling in love with a nearby male palm; comparable longevity; and erect stature (cf. Dīnavarī, p. 303 no. 26; Qazvīnī, pp. 177-78). Māsī Sūrānī (?) is cited (Ebn Waḥšīya, VII, pp. 55 ff.) as source for the claim that date palms were native to an island named Ḥārakān (the modern Ḵārg?) near the Persian coast; there were four kinds: two that grew at a distance from the sea, the ancestors of the *šahrīz* and

PLATE VII

Impression of cylinder seal, showing Darius I between two palm trees, the British Museum, London, no. 89132. Photograph courtesy of the Trustees of the British Museum.

barenī varieties of date, the ripe fruits of which were black and yellow respectively, and coastal varieties, the *ṣarafān* and *ṭabarzad* (see below).

Abū Ḥanīfa Dīnavarī (q.v; d. ca. 282/895) explored the rich Arabic terminology for the date palm (*nak̲l*; II, pp. 293-324 no. 1061). Persian geographers from the 10th century onward have mentioned many date-growing localities in Persia (e.g., Eṣṭak̲rī, pp. 35, 90, 93-95, 127-28, 153-54, 166, 168, 200, 231, 233-34, 237, 274; *Ḥodūd al-ʿālam*, ed. Sotūda, pp. 91, 103, 127, 132, 141). In the 12th century Ebn al-Balk̲ī (p. 140) reported that in the coastal districts of Korān and Īrāhestān in Fārs date palms were grown in deep pits, in order to make maximum use of the limited winter rain; only the crowns of full-grown trees showed above ground.

Early European travelers also counted dates among the best Persian fruits. Marco Polo (ca. 1272) mentioned the extensive plantations of Yazd, Kermān, and Hormoz, remarking that the inhabitants of Hormoz lived "chiefly upon dates and salted fish" and made from dates and other ingredients "a good kind of wine," which caused "an immediate flux" to those unaccustomed to it (pp. 41, 43, 46, 48). Don García de Silva y Figueroa, the Spanish envoy to Shah ʿAbbās I (996-1038/1588-1629), frequently mentioned date palms in southern Persia, particularly in Mog̲/gestān, a coastal district near Jāsk. On the island of Hormoz he noticed that most local houses were made of canes covered with palm fronds; better houses had flat masonry roofs, where on hot nights wooden "beds" were partitioned off with palm wattles. In Lārestān and Jahrom dates were the staple food and the main article of trade; Figueroa believed those from Lārestān superior in size, color, and taste even to those of Baṣra and Iraq, which had from Xenophon's time always passed for the best in Asia. In Jahrom he reported a "dense forest of palms . . . a good league long and half a league wide," divided by mud walls into about a thousand plots, each containing between twenty and seventy trees belonging to a family or individual and "most of which were higher than the highest church tower in Europe." Some palms bore "up to fifty date clusters," weighing 30 pounds each; the inhabitants claimed that some clusters weighed more than 60 pounds. Figueroa believed that the quality of Jahrom dates was owing to the soil and to careful irrigation with well water (pp. 32, 34, 37, 39, 50-51, 77, 352-54). Later in the 17th century Jean Chardin (p. 157) asserted that Persian dates were tastier than those of Arabia and that the best were from Kahūrestān in Bandar-e ʿAbbās province, Sīstān, Persepolis, and the Persian Gulf littoral, particularly Jahrom. They were exported "dry in bunches, or loose," but mostly "preserved in their own juice . . . in great gourds from 15 to 20 pound weight." He recommended moderation to those unaccustomed to eating dates, for otherwise "they heat the blood," a symptom called *garmī* "heat" in popular Persian medicine, even causing skin eruptions and weakening the sight.

Engelbert Kaempfer, a German physician who accompanied the Swedish ambassador to the court of Shah Solaymān in 1085/1684, discussed all aspects of the "*palma dactylifera*" (pp. 659-754). He recorded many vernacular terms (probably from Bandar-e ʿAbbās and the Hormoz area) related to palms and dates, some of them still used. He also distinguished two kinds of palm in southern Persia: cultivated and wild. The latter, called *Palma sylvestris persica* by Kaempfer and locally nicknamed Abū Jahl, was popularly believed to grow from date pits scattered on sterile soil. It must be the indigenous dwarf palm, *Nannor(r)hops ritchiana* (Griff.) Aitch., with tiny, almost inedible fruit, which grows wild in parts of southern Afghanistan, western Pakistan, and southeastern Persia, reaching a height of 2.5-3 m (Zargarī, IV, p. 528). Among its vernacular names are *marez* in Afghanistan (T̲ābetī, 1355 Š./1976, p. 480), *mazrī* and *kīlū* in Pakistan (Bamber, p. 129), *phiš* in Baluchistan (Mayer, p. 138), and *dāz* (Īrānšahr, Nīkšahr; T̲abetī, 1327 Š./1948, p. 119), *pīš*, *po/ūrk* (Bašākerd), *mazārī*, *k̲ū*, and *kākol-zard* "yellow-crowned" in Persia (Parsa, V, pp. 57-59, VIII, p. 125). The fruit may be eaten during famine (see BALUCHISTAN i, p. 606), and its sturdy fronds (2-3 feet long; Bamber, p. 129) are used to make baskets, mats, cordage, hats, and the characteristic Baluchi sandals; in Afghanistan beads are sometimes made from the date pits (Hamadānī, p. 37; T̲ābetī, 1355 Š./1976, p. 480).

Contemporary production.

As the earlier geographical sources suggest, date palms grow in Persia as far north as the oases along the northern border of the Dašt-e Kavīr (for details, see Dowson, tr., pp. 21, 29-32). Reliable data are available only for the period 1326-59 Š./1947-80. In 1347 Š./1968 about 2 percent of Persian arable land (1,367 km^2) was planted with 20-26 million palms, yielding approximately 325,000 metric tons of dates annually (ʿEnāyat, p. 1; cf. Rūḥānī, pp. 273, 278, 283: 20-21 million, yielding 170,000-310,000 metric tons). Annual domestic consumption, concentrated in the southern coastal provinces, was estimated at 90,000-190,000 metric tons (Rūḥānī, p. 278). In 1369 Š./1990-91, 42,840,453 kg of dates were exported, a total value of Rls. 1,483,785,186 (ca $1,059,847); 39,596,024 kg went to Dubai (Gomrok, 1370 Š./1991, p. 574).

Although Persian dates are among the world's best, adverse factors have impeded their production and export. Aside from inherent factors (e.g., the interval of five to ten years or more before female palms bear fruit, the skill required for hand pollinating trees and harvesting the fruit) that do not permit quick profits, environmental, social, and administrative conditions also play a role. There is a shortage of sweet water for irrigation, and in districts irrigated by saline fluvial or marine waters, especially along the Arvandrūd (q.v.; Šaṭṭ-al-ʿArab) and Bahmanšīr rivers (Ābādān, K̲orramšahr, Mīnū islet), date plantations gradually die (Komīsīūn, II, p. 1650; on similar conditions at

Mīnāb, cf. ʿEnāyat, pp. 57, 68). Another problem is inadequate rural roads connecting the plantations, many of them in remote desert areas, with distribution and packing centers (ʿEnāyat, pp. 49, 70).

The prevailing methods of harvesting, sorting, storing, and packing the crop remain primitive and unsanitary (ʿEnāyat, pp. 55, 56). In the date groves pests and diseases often rage unchecked, with resulting spoilage of about 50 percent of the annual crop; to this percentage must be added the approximately 100,000 tons of dates lost annually through fermentation and spoilage owing to improper handling and storage (ʿEnāyat, pp. 50, 66, 76). The low standard of living among most date cultivators and their inability to invest in better irrigation and drainage systems, sanitary storage and handling facilities, and the like force them to sell their expected crops before the harvest (*salaf-forūšī*), at about 20 percent below market prices. These problems are aggravated by lack of coordination among growers, packers, domestic merchants, and exporters through efficient local cooperatives (q.v.) and trade unions (ʿEnāyat, pp. 50, 57, 66, 72, 76; Edāra, p. 21). Regulation of standards, prices, sales, and exports is nonexistent or inadequate, with the result that goods vary in quality. In these conditions both growers and dealers, fearful of spoilage, often sell at very low prices to unscrupulous middlemen and traders, both Persian and foreign (cf. Sāzmān, pp. 82-84, on the emigration of date-farm laborers from Tangestān province to urban employment and the shift of land especially to cultivation of tobacco, which brings a quicker income).

Government and private processing and packing installations seem inadequate, though no current information is available. In 1347 Š./1968 there were sixteen small private packing houses in Ḵorramšahr (ʿEnāyat, p. 70) and a large state-owned plant equipped with machinery supplied by Hayʾat-e ʿamalīyāt-e eqteṣādī-e Āmrīkā dar Īrān (the American AID mission in Persia), with an annual processing capacity of 3,000-5,000 tons (Faršī, 1339 Š/1960a, p. 86). Before the war between Persia and Iraq in the 1980s there was also a plant producing 5,000 tons of date syrup (*šīra-ye ḵormā*) and about 2,500 tons of residue for cattle feed annually. Nearly 4.2 tons of syrup were obtained from every 6 tons of dates (Edāra, p. 16); it was used in chocolate, biscuits, canned food, and the like.

During the eight years of the war between Persia and Iraq, which involved the most important date-growing areas of both countries, there was severe damage to the plantations of Ḵūzestān and Kermānšāhān (Qaṣr-e Šīrīn and Ḵosravī; Sāzmān, p. 12; Edāra, pp. 29-38). The destruction of dams and irrigation installations flooded the groves, rotting the roots and contributing to a proliferation of weeds and pests, and spraying was prevented by the war. Some statistics, if reliable, suggest the sad state of date cultivation in Ḵūzestān (Edāra, p. 1). In the years 1362-63 Š./1983-84 and 1363-64 Š./1984-85 respective yields were 141,052 and 30,577 metric tons, a drop of more than 78 percent (Edāra, p. 11). War damage in Ḵūzestān may be further estimated from official statistics of date trees and production for the whole country in 1367 Š./1988-89: 12,981,000 palms (of which only 7,844 were fruiting trees), with a yield of 173,940 tons (Markaz-e āmār, p. 54).

Cultivation.

Terminology. The long-standing cultivation of dates in Persia has engendered a rich vocabulary of vernacular terms, which have been generally neglected by Persian philologists. There are only two partial lists of classical Persian equivalents or definitions for terms from the vast Arabic vocabulary related to the *naḵl* or *naḵīl* and *tamr* (generic term for dates). The first is a short list in the earliest extant Arabic-Persian dictionary, by Zamaḵšarī (467-538/1075-1144; I, pp. 106-08; see DICTIONARIES i). The second is a longer list compiled by Maydānī (d. 518/1124; pp. 513-18). Modern studies or lists at this writer's disposal include those by Georges Redard for the hamlet of Ḵūr (partly supplemented by Farahvašī, pp. 21-22; Ḥekmat Yaḡmāʾī, pp. 240-42 and passim), Īraj Afšār and M.-R. Moḥammadī for Bāfq (pp. 193-94), Aḥmad Sāyabānī for the *dehestān* of Fīn (in the *šahrestān* of Bandar-e ʿAbbās); Koji Kamioka and Minoru Yamada for Lārestān (pp. 21-22), Īraj Rūḥānī for Jahrom and adjacent localities (pp. 254-63, 269-72), and Sāzmān-e barnāma wa būdja-ye ostān-e Būšehr for the *šahrestān* of Tangestān (pp. 1-9 and passim). Ahmad Parsa (VIII, pp. 139-41) has included a list of eighty-four names (without a gloss) for date varieties in Makrān. Isolated dialectal terms also occur in some articles and vernacular glossaries (e.g., Sotūda).

Vernacular names for the date palm include *mōlog*, Ḵūr (cf. Mid. Pers. *muγ*); *mok*, Kermān; *moḡ*, Fīn; *moḵ/h*, Tangestān; *moḵ*, *tarak*, Jahrom; *mūg/ḡ* (?) Bandar-e ʿAbbās, Jīroft, and so on (Rūḥānī, p. 272); Baluchi *mòk*, Dezak; *mač*, Zābol; *māč*, Čāhbahār (all recorded by Redard, p. 215 n. 2); and *faṣīl*, Lārestān (cf. *faṣīl* "small young palm" and *naḵīl* "tall old palm" in Tangestān). A young palm grown haphazardly from a date pit is called *pešk* (originally "date pit") and *ḵorost* (< *ḵod-rost*, lit., "grown by itself") in Fīn and *m/harvās* in Tangestān. A date-palm grove or orchard is generally called *naḵlestān*, *bāḡ* (garden), *šahr* (Bašāgerd; Redard, p. 215 n. 1), *mog/ḡestān* (Ḥekmat Yaḡmāʾī, p. 240), or *naḵīlāt* (an Arabic word found in some modern sources).

The date palm is propagated only by planting shoots (*pājūš*; vernacular names: Ar. *faṣīla*; *damīd*, Ḵūr; *dīmīt*, Tangestān, properly a shoot having developed roots while still attached to the mother palm; cf. *mokoš* < *mohkoš* "palm killer," *baḵtakan*, without independent roots and thus a parasite on the mother palm, Jahrom) of male or female palms eight to ten years old. Artificial pollination (*nar māyo*, Ḵūr; *gošn dādan*, Bāfq; *sāḵtan*, Jahrom; *bū dādan*, Tangestān, Ḵūzestān) is performed in two ways: Either the pollen (*garda*) is sprinkled on pistillate flowers (as at Ḵūr; Redard, p. 215), or some staminate spikelets (*toreng*, Bāfq) are placed among the pistillate spikelets, which are then loosely tied together with a string (as at Jahrom, Tangestān, etc.; Sāzmān, p. 93; Rūḥānī, pp. 17-19 with illustrations). This task is performed by skilled workers (*māher*, Jahrom; *zaʿīm*, Bandar-e ʿAbbās, Jīroft, etc.), who usually share the crop with the owner (Rūḥānī, pp. 17, 271). They tie a strong rope belt (*parvanda*, K̲ūr; *parven[d]*, Fīn; *parvand/g*, Tangestān; *parvand,* Jahrom; *parand,* Bandar-e ʿAbbās, etc.; *farvand*, K̲ūzestān, Iraq) 2-3 m long, made from palm leaflets, around the trunk as an aid in climbing (for a more elaborate version with a wooden prop, used in Tangestān, see Sāzmān, p. 6). Depending on the female variety, regional conditions, and so on, two to five male palms are required to pollinate one hundred females. Not all male palms produce suitable pollen for this process (Redard, p. 215; Sāzmān, p. 93; Rūḥānī, pp. 17, 76). In Tangestān newly planted palm shoots are watered from a *kantal*, consisting of two large tin vessels suspended from the ends of a wooden bar that is carried on the shoulders (Rūḥānī, p. 73). Shoots of desirable varieties used to be obtained gratis, but after severe war damage to the palm groves of K̲ūzestān they were selling for Rls. 800-1,000 apiece (Sāzmān, p. 51). Stunted shoots (*kačakī*, Fīn) are discarded, but the edible white medulla (*koj*, *panīr*, lit., "cheese," Jahrom) is enjoyed for its crisp sweetness in Fīn (Sāyabānī, 1362 Š./1983, p. 873).

Felling healthy date palms is considered unlucky, the death of each tree being tantamount to that of a person (Sāzmān, p. 10), but sterile male palms and terminally diseased or infested palms are cut down; the trunks are used in construction (cf. Pliny, *Naturalis Historia* 13.9). According to the traveler Sven Hedin (apud Redard, p. 218 n. 4), the felling of a doomed palm tree is usually postponed until the mourning days of Moḥarram (cf. K̲ūr, where *panīr kardan* "making cheese," i.e., cutting down a palm for its medulla, is usually carried out on a holiday; Ḥekmat Yaḡmāʾī, p. 256 n.).

Crown and terminal bud. Usually the trunk of the date palm is topped by a single crown (*tāj*; *bašn* "top," *Draxt-ī āsūrīg*, l. 25; *kalle mog*, K̲ūr) comprising the fronds (*pīž*), the terminal bud, and the date clusters, though the *tabarzal* palm of Iraq may branch into two, three, or even four crowns (Hussain, tr., p. 41). All these elements are tightly interlaced at the base of the crown, which is protected by layers of tough, intertwined brown fibers (*pīž/j*, K̲ūr). These fibers are separated by soaking, then twisted and braided into cords (*sāzū*, K̲ūr), ropes, mats, and the like (Redard, p. 219; Ḥekmat Yaḡmāʾī, pp. 249-50). When a date palm is to be cut down, the fronds and date stalks are first cut off with a toothed sickle (*dās-e pangbor*, Tangestān) about 30 cm long and curved at the tip; then the top of the trunk is peeled to lay bare "the crisp delicious tissues of the terminal bud" (Milne, p. 276; *dallak*, K̲ūr; *del-e mok̲*, Tangestān) and the underlying pith, which is sawed off at its base. The pith, weighing 3-7 kg, is a crisp white marrow called "palm cheese" (*panīr-e mōg*, K̲ūr; *kūd*, Fīn), bland but highly nutritious (Redard, p. 219). At Fīn (Sāyabānī, 1362 Š./1983, p. 873), Jahrom (Rūḥānī, p. 270), and probably elsewhere the expression *panīr(-e nak̲l)* also refers to the edible marrow (*koj*, Jahrom) of the basal part of the date stalk (20-30 cm long) discarded during pollination. This marrow is sweet in some varieties but somewhat bitter in others (for medicinal uses, cf. Dioscorides, 1.150). Cutting off the terminal bud will kill the palm (pace Pliny, *Naturalis Historia* 13.9), even if the whole tree is not cut down.

Each frond (*šāk̲a*; *be/arašk*, *galga*, K̲ūr; *šāk̲-e boḡ*, *kod-e k̲ormā*, Bāfq; *pīš*, Kermān; *taḡ*, Fīn; *peš*, Lārestān; *gorz*, Tangestān), measuring up to 4-5 m in length, has three parts: the spatulate base (*kava/ešk*, *sāḡarī*, K̲ūr; *kondelū*, Bāfq; *taftūk*, *tagot*, Fīn; *aspakū*, Lārestān; *tūk̲atak*, Jahrom; *tāpūl*, Tangestān), attached to the trunk; the strong, spiny stalk (*bāskīn*, *lows*, K̲ūr; *lot*, Fīn; *tātūk*, Bandar-e ʿAbbās, Jīroft, etc.) and midrib (*gorz*, Tangestān; *taḡ*, Bandar-e ʿAbbās, etc.), 1-2 m long; and the pinnate section, or leaflets (*be/arašk*, K̲ūr; *boḡ*, Bāfq; *balg-e pīs*, Kermān; *pīš*, Fīn; *pīš*, *pūš*, Jahrom), about 40 cm long. The bases of cut fronds are left on the tree to serve as footholds, and each year the dried old bases (*tāpūl*s, etc.; *kaženg*, K̲ūr) are pruned for use as fuel and sometimes as floats for fishing nets; in Tangestān a wooden mallet (*dokū*) and a kind of chisel (*eškena*) are used for this purpose. The copious tough fiber (*sīs*, Bāfq, Fīn; *perī*, Lārestān; *parīče*, Jahrom) from the juncture with the trunk is used in the manufacture of ropes, doormats, and, in Fīn, primitive footwear for laborers (on processing and braiding *parīče* in Jahrom, see Rūḥānī, pp. 251-53). The stalks are also used as fuel and, with the spines removed, for threshing; at K̲ūr women use them for beating laundry. The leaflets are woven or braided into a variety of baskets (mostly for packing or carrying dates), mats, lids, bags, caps, brimmed hats, fans, and so on. They are also bundled into brooms (for braiding and weaving at K̲ūr, see Redard, pp. 217-18; Ḥekmat Yaḡmāʾī, pp. 247-48; for Fīn, Sāyabānī, 1363 Š./1984, pp. 150-54).

Dates and pits. The spadix (*abare* "male spadix," Jahrom) of the palm, whether male or female, develops within a spathe (*kavīle*, K̲ūr; *kāškīlū*, Kermān; *kārček* "dried spathe," Fīn; *tārūne*, Jahrom, Shiraz; *tāre*, Tangestān). At Shiraz a distillate (*ʿaraq-e ṭ/tārūne*) is obtained from the fresh, fragrant male spathes; it is advertised as a "hot" tranquilizer and soporific, an "unequaled nervine," and "very useful for rheumatism, articular pains" (from a brochure published by Iran Targol Co., Tehran; cf. Tonokābonī, p. 730). The fertilized female spadix gradually develops into a cluster of dates (*hūž*, K̲ūr; *pang*, Kermān, Fīn, Lārestān, Jahrom, Tangestān), consisting of a main stalk (*tambar*, K̲ūr; *k̲ošmalg*, Bāfq; *bokom*, *kowsala*, Lārestān; *narī*, Tangestān) branching into many peduncles (*terend/t*, K̲ūr; *teleng*, Fīn; *šen*, Tangestān), to each of which several dates are attached by hard perianths (*kolāhak*, *kūna*; *kolā[h]ū*, K̲ūr; *kālū*, Bāfq; *kofār*, Lārestān; *kalāfa*,

Jahrom, etc.; see Dowson and Aten, p. 70).

Traditionally between five and seven stages of maturation were recognized. Ḥakīm Moʾmen Tonokābonī (comp. 1080/1669-70; p. 215, s.v. *tamr*) reported seven: *ṭalʿ* or *walīʿ*, inflorescence (male or female), when the spadix is still encased in the spathe; *balaḥ* (Pers. *ḡūra-ye k̲ormā*), with tiny green dates; *k̲alāl*, in which the dates are becoming yellow and sweet; *bosr*, when they have become yellow and sweet; *qasb* (in the Ḥejāz; Pers. *k̲ormā-ye sang-šekan*; *qasbak* in Fārs; Jazāyerī, p. 156), in which the dates are still dry; *roṭab*, in which the dates are ripe and juicy; and *tamr*, in which ripe dates have withered slightly on the tree. In modern terminology the equivalents to the *ṭalʿ* and *qasb* stages are not usually distinguished (for names at Fīn, see Sāyabānī, 1362 Š./1983, pp. 873-75). Fresh dates in the *k̲alāl* (*k̲ā/arak*; *hārak*, K̲ūr; *k̲ārak*, Jahrom, Tangestān; *k̲ara/ūk*, Kermān; *harak/g*, Makrān) stage are seldom served or sold other than locally. They are usually boiled, dried until they are very hard and wrinkled, then pitted and threaded on strings; in this form they will keep a long time. Certain varieties are preferred for this purpose: in Makrān (Pakistan) the *mozātī*; in Mīnāb and elsewhere the *hallo*, *mordār-sang*, *šāhānī*, *šakar-pāra*, and *zarag*; in K̲ūzestān and Iraq the *ke/abkāb* (in Iraq *čebčāb*) and *bore/aym* (Dowson and Aten, pp. 84-85, 89, 89-90). Commercial *k̲ārak*s are generally brittle and pleasantly sweet.

Usually each date has a pit (*hasta*; *pešk*, K̲ūr; *kolpī*, Bāfq; *dendel[ū]*, Kermān; *eštak*, Fīn; *astok*, Lārestān), though at Šahdād there is a small (26 x 18 mm) seedless variety, of fine quality, called *bī-dandalū* or *hasekū* (Dowson and Aten, p. 6; Komīsīūn, II, p. 1651). For both genetic and practical reasons date pits are not used for propagation of valued palms. Owing to their nutritious content, however, they are sometimes ground domestically into a meal that is fed, by itself or mixed with herbage, to cattle (ʿEnāyat, pp. 9-10; Rūḥānī, p. 248). According to Ḥekmat Yaḡmāʾī (p. 253), people of K̲ūr used to save them to grind into flour during famine. As there are no mills for date pits in Persia, quantities are exported to other countries in the Persian Gulf area, where they are milled commercially for cattle feed (Edāra, p. 16). In Persia date-pit charcoal is used by smiths to polish gold and silver articles (Rūḥānī, p. 248).

Varieties. Although the generic term for dates in Persia is *k̲ormā* (Mid. Pers. *xurmā*, *armāv*; Parth. *amrāw*; Arm. loanword *armav*; Pashto *k̲orma*; Baluchi *k̲orma*, *hòrmag*, *ormāg*; K̲ūrī *hòrma*; Lārī *ormā*; Redard, p. 216 n. 1; Elfenbein, p. 89), there are approximately 400 varieties of dates (Dowson, tr., p. 82) known by a plethora of vernacular names, many of them synonyms, variants, or corrupted forms. In K̲ūzestān and Kermānšāhān the names are generally those used in Iraq (for descriptions of the most common or important varieties in various parts of Persia, see ʿEnāyat, pp. 23, 28-37; Rūḥānī, pp. 254-63; Sāyabānī, 1362 Š./1983, pp. 875-78; Sāzmān, pp. 106-07; Redard, p. 216; Faršī, 1339 Š./1960b, p. 77; Komīsīūn, II, p. 1651; Dowson, tr., pp. 82 ff.). The most productive variety is the *barḥī*; depending on conditions, each tree may yield up to 250 kg of dates a year. It does not normally live longer than twenty years, however (Wezārat, p. 10). The *sāyer* date palm, which accounts for more than 90 percent of the date crop in K̲ūzestān and ranks first in Persian date exports, produces an average of 18-20 kg of dates a year and remains productive for 100 years, with a peak between the ages of twenty and sixty years (Wezārat, p. 10; Rūḥānī, p. 254; Dowson, tr., p. 64). The best dates in Persia, however, ranked with the famous *daqalat-al-nūr* of Algeria, are the *šāhānī* of Jahrom and the *možāfatī* of Bam. The latter, a dainty, dark-red variety and the most expensive in Persia, is not readily exportable because it is at its best when ripe and juicy and thus subject to spoilage. The *šāhānī*, constituting the greater part of the crop from Jahrom, is the most esteemed variety in Persia. The honey-colored *ašrasī* of Qaṣr-e Šīrīn, rated second quality; the commercially unimportant dates of K̲ūr and Bāfq, harvested and consumed at the *k̲ārak* stage; the seedless *porkū* of Šahdād; and the dark-yellow *batābe* (?; 6-8 cm long) of K̲āš are mainly consumed locally. The inferior *k̲ā/arūk* of Bam is fed to cattle (Faršī, I/7, p. 77; Rūḥānī, p. 255; Dowson, tr., p. 32; ʿEnāyat, pp. 30-31, 37, 60, 71).

Domestic and commercial uses.

Culinary uses. Pitted dates, whole or mashed, are the main ingredient in several Persian confections and a principal component in a few cooked dishes. Hard dates (picked at the *k̲alāl* stage) are cooked and added to *rešta-polow* (a traditional rice dish made on the eve of Nowrūz) and *ʿadas-polow* (lentil pilaf; Montaẓemī, pp. 567, 571; Hekmat, pp. 70-71). Several sweets are made with mashed ripe dates or date syrup, for example, *k̲ormā-berīzū* (Kermān; *k̲ormā-berīz*, Fīn), in which date paste is kneaded with wheat flour fried in ghee (Sotūda, p. 67; Sāyabānī, 1362 Š./1983, p. 879); *čangāl* (Fīn), a paste of soft dates kneaded with roasted and ground wheat grains (Sāyabānī, 1362 Š./1983, p. 879); *ḥalwā-ye k̲ormā*, mashed fresh dates mixed with fried flower, spread on a platter, and cut into lozenges, served at funeral ceremonies and on the holy days of Ramażān and Moḥarram almost everywhere in Persia (for a Šīrāzī variant, see Hekmat, p. 140); *arda-k̲ormā*, date paste kneaded with *arda* (ground sesame) and spices like cardamom and ginger, then flattened and cut into lozenges (Shiraz); and *ḥalwā kanafī*, thick date syrup mixed with hemp seeds (Kermān; Sotūda, p. 64). More complex pastries include *kolomb/pe*, fried mashed dates combined with chopped walnuts, cinnamon, and cloves, then shaped into small balls, wrapped in thin pieces of leavened dough, and baked, usually at Nowrūz (Kermān; Sotūda, p. 137); *komāč/j-e se(he)n*, two layers of dough made from ground wheat and *sehen* (malt) holding a layer of mashed dates, sprinkled with ground walnuts, cumin, and nigella seeds and baked (Kermān; Sotūda, p. 139); *rangīnak*, pitted *roṭab*s, stuffed with walnuts and coated generously with fried flour, then sprinkled with cinnamon, powdered sugar, and sometimes chopped pistachios and then cut into lozenges (originally a Šīrāzī sweet but now popular all over the country; Hekmat, p. 142; Sāyabānī, 1362 Š./1983, p. 880).

Manufacture and uses of date syrup and sap. Date syrup (*šīra-/šahd-e ḵormā; robb, seylān*, Ḵūzestān; *dūšow*, Ḵūr) is obtained either by pressing fresh dates (producing an average of only 2 kg of juice per 100 kg, and thus expensive) or by boiling dates of poor quality to a syrupy consistency and straining them. The residue (*hal*, Ḵūr) of the latter process is fed to cattle (Rūḥānī, pp. 243-44; Sāyabānī, 1362 Š./1983, p. 880; Dowson and Aten, pp. 114, 354). Date syrup is used in various sweets, to preserve or pack choice dates in earthenware jars, and on bread as a main dish. In Ḵūzestān syrup from the surplus date crop is consumed locally and also exported to the islands and emirates of the Persian Gulf; a factory for vacuum-packing the syrup in metal boxes was recently established in Ḵūzestān (ʿEnāyat, p. 28; Rūḥānī, p. 245).

Whereas in Pakistan the sap of *Phoenix sylvestris* is systematically collected to make date sugar (*gūr*; Balfour, I, p. 896), in Persia sterile male date palms and female trees that produce low-quality dates are sometimes tapped for *šīra*: After the young male or female date clusters have been cut off, a container is fixed under the tip of each severed stalk to collect the sap, which continues to rise for weeks or, in female palms, even months. It contains up to 14 percent sucrose, which crystallizes as sugar when the sap is boiled down; the residual molasses is fermented for wine or vinegar (Milne, p. 275). Another alcoholic drink made from dates, *ʿaraq-e ḵormā*, was popular in southern Persia in the 19th century (Schlimmer, p. 179).

The date palm in literature and folklore.

Many casual references to the bountiful, shade-giving date palm are found in classical Persian poetry (see Dehḵodā, s.vv. *naḵl, ḵormā-bon*, etc.). A long, nostalgic poem devoted to praise of the date palm by Ḥabīb Yaḡmāʾī (d. 1363 Š./1984; quoted by Ḥekmat Yaḡmāʾī, pp. 268-70), a native of Ḵūr, is, however, unique in Persian literature.

Information about contemporary folklore concerning the date palm is scanty. The ill fortune associated with cutting down a healthy tree has already been mentioned. At Ḵūr two palm-wood sticks (*jarīdatayn*) inscribed with the Throne verse (Koran 2:256) are placed under the arms of a dead person, to serve him or her as a staff on Resurrection Day (Ḥekmat Yaḡmāʾī, pp. 254-55). In addition, the funeral procession is headed by a man who carries two green palm fronds on his shoulders, to be buried with the corpse; it is believed that, as long as these fronds remain fresh, the dead individual will be free from "the torment and pressure of the tomb" (Ḥekmat Yaḡmāʾī, p. 377). During the mourning ceremonies on ʿĀšūrāʾ (q.v.; 10 Moḥarram) a large wooden structure called a *naḵl*, which somewhat resembles a date palm, is paraded in some parts of Persia as the symbolic bier of Imam Ḥosayn.

In the past there seem to have been craftsmen, called *naḵlband* (lit., "date-palm tier/assembler"), who made ornamental wax replicas of date palms and artificial plants, flowers, and fruits (*Borhān-e qāṭeʿ*, ed. Moʿīn, s.v.; *Ānand Rāj*, s.v.).

Bibliography: Ī. Afšār and M.-R. Moḥammadī, *Vāža-nāma-ye yazdī*, Tehran, 1369 Š./1990. E. Balfour, *The Cyclopaedia of India and of Eastern and Southern Asia . . .*, 3rd ed., 3 vols., London, 1885; repr. Graz, 1967-68. C. J. Bamber, *Plants of the Punjab*, Lahore, 1916. J. Chardin, *Travels in Persia*, London, 1927. F. Cumont, "The Dura Mithraeum," ed. and tr. E. D. Francis, in J. R. Hinnells, ed., *Mithraic Studies* I, Manchester, U.K., 1975, pp. 151-214. Abū Ḥanīfa Dīnavarī, *Ketāb al-nabāt. Le dictionnaire botanique*, ed. M. Ḥamīd-Allāh, II, Cairo, 1973. Dioscorides, *De Materia Medica*, tr. J. Goodyer (1655), ed. R. T. Gunther as *The Greek Herbal of Dioscorides*, Oxford, 1934. V. H. W. Dowson, *Date Production and Protection, with Special Reference to North Africa and the Near East*, Rome, 1982; tr. R. Sanadgol as *Tawlīd o morāqabat-e ḵormā . . .*, Tehran, 1370 Š./1991. Idem and A. Aten, *Dates. Handling, Processing and Packing*, Rome, 1962. *Draxt-ī āsūrīg*, ed. and tr. Y. Māhyār Nawwābī, Tehran, 1346 Š./1967.

Ebn Waḥšīya, *Ketāb al-felāḥat al-nabaṭīya*, facs. ed., 7 vols. in 5, Frankfurt, 1984. Edāra-ye koll-e kešāvarzī-e Ḵūzestān, *Āmār-nāma-ye naḵīlāt-e ostān-e Ḵūzestān*, n.p., 1365 Š./1986 (mimeograph). J. Elfenbein, *A Vocabulary of Marw Baluchi*, Naples, 1963. R. ʿEnāyat, *Ḵormā-ye Īrān*, Tehran, 1347 Š./1969 (mimeograph). L. Erbe, "Date," in *Encyclopedia Americana* VIII, 1984, p. 519. B. Farahvašī, *Vāža-nāma-ye ḵūrī*, Tehran, 2535=1355 Š./1976. M.-H. Faršī, "ʿElal-e rokūd-e ṣāderāt-e ḵormā-ye Īrān," *Īrān-e ābād* 1/8, 1339 Š./1960a, pp. 83-86. Idem, "Ḵormā-ye Īrān," *Īrān-e ābād* 1/7, 1339 Š./1960b, pp. 76-78. García de Silva y Figueroa, *L'ambassade de Don Garcia de Silva Figueroa en Perse*, tr. A. de Wicquefort, Paris, 1667. E. Gauba, "Botanische Reisen in der persischen Dattelregion," *Annalen des Naturhistorischen Museums in Wien* 57, 1949-50, pp. 42-52; 58, 1951, pp. 13-32; 59, 1952-53, pp. 119-34. Gomrok-e Īrān, *Sāl-nāma-ye āmār-e bāzargānī-e ḵārejī-e . . . sāl-e 1369*, Tehran, 1370 Š./1991. N. Hamadānī, "Balūčestān," *Īrān-e ābād* 1/11, 1339 Š./1960, pp. 35-39. ʿA. Ḥekmat Yaḡmāʾī, *Bar sāḥel-e Kavīr-e namak*, Tehran, 1368 Š./1989. F. Hekmat, *The Art of Persian Cooking*, New York, 1961; repr. Tehran, 1349 Š./1970. W. B. Henning, "A Pahlavi Poem," in *Selected Papers*, Acta Iranica 15, Leiden, 1977, pp. 349-56. M. Honari, "Importance de palmier-dattier dans la vie des habitants de Xor," *Objets et mondes* 11, 1971, pp. 49-58. A. A. Hussain (ʿA.-A. Ḥosayn), *Date Palms and Dates with Their Pests in Iraq*, Baghdad, 1974; tr. ʿA. Ṭabīb-nežād as *Deraḵt-e ḵormā wa āfāt o bīmārīhā-*

ye ān dar ʿErāq, Ahvāz, 1368 Š./1989. M.-M. Jaʿfarī, "K̲ormā-bon wa vāžahā-ye vābasta be ān dar fārsī-e Dāstestān," *Pažūheš-nāma-ye Farhangestān-e zabān-e Īrān* II, 1356 Š./1977, pp. 63-94. Ḡ. Jazāyerī, *Zabān-e k̲ᵛorākīhā*, 3rd ed., Tehran, 1354 Š./1975. E. Kaempfer, *Amoenitatum Exoticarum Politico-Physico-Medicarum . . .*, Lemgoviae (Lemgo), 1712. K. Kamioka and M. Yamada, *Lārestāni Studies* I. *Lāri Basic Vocabulary*, Tokyo, 1979. Ṣ Kīā, "K̲orma-bon wa vāžahā-ye vābasta be ān dar fārsī-e Jahrom," *Pažūheš-nāma-ye Farhangestān-e zabān-e Īrān* I, 1354 Š./1976, pp. 85-102. Komīsīūn-e mellī-e Yūneskū dar Īrān, *Īrānšahr*, 2 vols., Tehran, 1342-43 Š./1963-64. F. Lajard, *Recherches sur le culte du cyprès pyramidal chez les peuples civilisés de l'antiquité*, Paris, 1854. Markaz-e āmār-e Īrān, *Sar-šomārī-e ʿomūmī-e kešāvarzī-e 1367*, Tehran, 1371 Š./1992.

Abu'l-Fatḥ Aḥmad b. Moḥammad Maydānī Nīšābūrī, *al-Sāmī fi'l-asāmī*, facs. ed., Tehran, 1345 Š./1966. J. L. Mayer, *English-Baluchi Dictionary*, Lahore, 1909; repr. Lahore, 1975. L. and M. Milne, *Living Plants of the World*, New York, n.d. R. Montaẓemī, *Honar-e āšpazī . . .*, 9th ed., Tehran, 1361 Š./1982. H. J. Moore, Jr., "*Palmae*," in K. H. Rechinger, ed., *Flora Iranica* 146, Graz, 1980. G. Pāk, "'Māhīā,' 'mok̲' dar janūb," *Honar-e mardom* 128, 1352 Š./1973, pp. 58-73. A. Parsa, *Flore de l'Iran* V, Tehran, 1950; VIII, Tehran, 1960. Marco Polo, *The Travels of Marco Polo*, tr. W. Marsden, ed. M. Komaroff, New York, 1953. Zakarīyāʾ Qazvīnī, *ʿAjāʾeb al-mak̲lūqāt wa ḡarāʾeb al-mawjūdāt*, 4th ed., Cairo, 1970. G. Redard, "Le palmier à Khur," in W. B. Henning and E. Yarshater, eds., *A Locust's Leg. Studies in Honour of S. H. Taqizadeh*, London, 1962, pp. 213-19. Ī. Rūḥānī, *K̲ormā*, Tehran, 1367 Š./1988. A. Sāyabānī, "K̲ormā-ye Fīn (moḡ)," *Āyanda* 9/12, 1362 Š./1983, pp. 871-83. Idem, "Ṣanāyeʿ-e dastī az derak̲t-e k̲ormā," *Āyanda* 10/2-3, 1363 Š./1984, pp. 150-59. Sāzmān-e barnāma wa būdja-ye ostān-e Būšehr, *Barrasī-e k̲ormā wa masāʾel-e ān dar šahrestān-e Tangestān* I, n.p., 1364 Š./1985 (mimeograph). M. Sotūda, *Farhang-e kermānī*, Tehran, 1335 Š./1956.

Ḥ. T̲ābetī, *Derak̲tān-e jangalī-e Īrān*, Tehran, 1326 Š./1947. Idem, *Jangalhā, derak̲tān o derak̲tčahā-ye Īrān*, Tehran, 1355 Š./1976. Moḥammad-Moʾmen Ḥosaynī Tonokābonī (Ḥakīm Moʾmen), *Toḥfat al-moʾmenīn* (*Toḥfa-ye Ḥakīm Moʾmen*), Tehran, 1360 Š./1981. M. J. Vermaseren, *Corpus Inscriptionum et Monumentorum Religionis Mithriacae* I, the Hague, 1956. F. Viré, "Nak̲l̲," in *EI²* VII, pp. 923-24. Wezārat-e āb o barq, *K̲ormā*, Tehran, 1349 Š./1970. *Xusrō i Kavātān ut rētak*, ed. and tr. D. Monchi-zadeh, in *Monumentum Georg Morgenstierne* II, Acta Iranica 22, Leiden, 1982, pp. 47-91. Abu'l-Qāsem Maḥmūd b. ʿOmar Zamak̲šarī, *Pīšrov-e adab/Moqaddemat al-adab*, ed. M.-K. Emām, 2 vols., Tehran, 1342 Š./1963. R. Zamānī, "Deh-e Salm," *Honar o mardom* 119-20, 1351 Š./1972, pp. 30-38. ʿA. Zargarī, *Gīāhān-e dārūʾī*, 4th ed., IV, Tehran, 1369 Š./1990.

(HŪŠANG AʿLAM)

DATES AND DATING in Old and Middle Iranian. The only dating formulas preserved in an Old Iranian language are those found in Old Persian in the Bīsotūn inscriptions of Darius I (qq.v.). They have a ponderous air, suggesting a chronicle addressed to posterity, rather than a system meant for everyday use. No year is mentioned in them, and, though the months are named (see *EIr.* IV, p. 659 table 20), the days are generally indicated only by numerals. For example, "on the ninth of Garmapada" is written *garmapadahyā māhyā IX raučabiš θakatā āha avaθā . . .*, that is, "in the month (locative) of Garmapada (genitive) 9 days (instrumental plural as general, here nominative plural) were gone past (nominative plural feminine), then. . . ." Only the thirtieth and last day of a month is referred to as such, for example, *θūravāharahyā māhyā jiyamnam patiy* "in the month of Thuravahara, at the end" (see Kent, *Old Persian*, pp. 203, s.v. *māha-*, 205, s.v. *raucah-*, for references only). By contrast, the formulas used in the translation of the inscriptions into Aramaic, the language of administrative correspondence in the Achaemenid empire, are simple, as in *b 27 lṭbt* "on the 27(th) in Tebeth" (Greenfield and Porten, pp. 24 ff.).

By the time of the earliest dated Middle Iranian documents, the Parthian ostraca from Nisa of the 1st century B.C.E., the Zoroastrian (so-called Avestan) calendar was in use (see *EIr.* IV, pp. 660-61 tables 21-23). On most of these ostraca no more than a year (of the Arsacid era) is indicated, for example, *ŠNT IC XX XX X III III III* = **sard 159* "year 159" (i.e., 89 B.C.E.). On the other hand, some have month and day but no year, and a very few are dated in full, for example, *ŠNT IC XX XX XX X III III YRḤʾ prwrtyn YWMʾ srwš* = **sard 176, māh Frawartīn, rōč Srōš* "year 176 (i.e., 72 B.C.E.), (first) month Frawardīn, (seventeenth) day Srōš" (see D'yakonov and Livshits, p. 147, Nov. 100 + Nov. 91). The same form is found in a Parthian parchment sale contract from Avroman (q.v.): *ŠNT IIIC YRḤʾ ʾrwtt* = **sard 300 māh arwatāt* "year 300, (third) month (H)arwatāt" (i.e., January-February 53 C.E.; Henning, "Mitteliranisch," p. 29). In the only surviving dated Parthian inscription, actually of the Sasanian period, the month appears before the year, as in the accompanying Middle Persian version: *YRḤʾ* (Pers. *BYRḤ*) *prwrtyn ŠNT XX XX X IIIIIIII* "(first) month Frawardīn, year 58" (i.e., 266 C.E.; see Back, p. 378, ŠVŠ 1). The same is true of the later Middle Persian inscriptions at Persepolis, for example, *BYRḤ tyr QDM ŠNT X IIIIIIII YWM ʾwhrmzdy* "(fourth) month Tīr in year 18 (of Šāpūr II, i.e., 327 C.E.), (first) day Ohrmazd" (Back, p. 495, ŠPs II), and of several inscriptions from the walls of the synagogue at Dura-Europos, like *BYRḤ prwrtyn QDM ŠNT 15 WYWM lšnw* "(first) month Frawardīn in year 15, and (eighteenth) day Rašn" (see Geiger, pp. 300 ff.). Similar formulas are found in late Middle Persian documents, particularly ostraca of the 6th century from Persia and papyri from Egypt, the latter datable to the short Sasanian occupation from 618 to 629 C.E. On most only a day is mentioned, as in *YWM tyl*, *YWM gwš* "(thirteenth) day Tīr," "(fourteenth) day Gōš," and the like, or month and day, as in *BYRḤ spndrmt YWM ʾltʾ* "(twelfth) month Spandarmad, (twenty-fifth) day Ard" (Papyrus Heidelberg Pahl., unpublished). The same pattern was followed in Book Pahlavi texts of the Islamic period, the colophons of manuscripts being dated according to the Yazdegerdī era, as in *BYN YWM Y ʾwhrmzd MN BYRḤ spndrmt ŠNT Y IIII IIII C XX XX XX pnc ʾḤL MN ŠNT Y XX (Y) ʿL(H) bg yzdkrt MLKʾʾn MLKʾ Y štrʾydʾlʾn* "on the (first) day Ohrmazd of the (twelfth) month Spandarmad, year 865 after the year 20 of his late majesty Yazdegerd, king of kings, son of Šahrīār" (*Dēnkard* 949.10-11).

In literary texts of Manichean origin, in both Parthian and Middle Persian, a more elaborate expression of dates is found; it is reminiscent of the Old Persian style, owing to the use of the word *saxt* "passed" (corresponding to Old Pers. *θakata-*). Various forms occur. For example, the date of the crucifixion of Jesus, with the name of the month "translated" from the Syriac Nisan, is given in Parthian as *pd myhr mʾh pd sxt cfʾrds* "in the (seventh) month Mihr, on the fourteen(th day) passed" (*Mir. Man.* III, p. 882 p 20-21). The time of Mani's death appears as *pd sxt cwhrm mʾh šhryywr pd dwšmbt ʾwd jmʾn ʿywnds* "on the fourth (day) passed, (sixth) month Šahrewar, on Monday and (at) the hour eleven" (*Mir. Man.* III, p. 864 d 57-58) and as *pd cfʾr sxt šhryywr mʾh šhrywr rwc dwšmbt ʾwd ʿywnds jmʾn* "on the four(th day) passed, month Šahrewar, day Šahrewar, Monday and the hour eleven" (*Mir. Man.* III, p. 861c 23 ff.). In one Middle Persian text the festival of Greater Tīragān is referred to both as *pd hʾn rwc ʿy chʾrdh sxt* "on that day fourteen passed" and as *pd chʾrdh rwc ʿy tyrmʾ* "on day fourteen of Tīr month" (M 16; Boyce, *Reader*, pp. 183-84 dn 2).

Documents from Topraq-qalʿa in Ḵᵛārazm from the 2nd or 3rd century C.E. (the era is still uncertain) and later ossuary inscriptions from Toq-qalʿa, probably of the 8th century, are dated similarly to the earliest Parthian examples. Only the Aramaic ideograms differ slightly, for example, *BŠNT VII C VI YRḤʾ βrwrtn BYWM βrwrtn* "year 706, (first) month Frawardīn, (nineteenth) day Frawardīn" (Toq-qalʿa, no. 25; Henning, 1965; Livshits, 1968).

From the earliest records in Sogdian (beginning of the 4th century C.E.) to the latest (10th century C.E.) a form of the word **saγt* appears in dating formulas. In the Ancient Letters *krt ZNH δykh kδ X-myk mʾxw kδ X IIIII sxth* "made this letter when (it was) the 10th month, when the 15(th day) passed" (AL IV) and *npʾxšt ZNH δykh pr ʾtδrtyk YRḤʾ pr X sγth* "written this letter in the third month, on the 10(th day) passed" (AL III) occur (see Reichelt, "Glossar," p. 53, s.v. *sγt-*). One Buddhist text is dated according to the Central Asian twelve-year animal cycle (*EIr.* IV, p. 667 table 33) *pr myw srδ wxwšw-my mʾxy pncδs sγtyh* "in the tiger year, in the sixth month, on the fifteen(th day) passed" (Benveniste, p. 113 P8.166). This locative form of the word is spelled phonetically in a Manichean text (S 40), *1 sγtyʾ . . . 15 sγtyʾ* "on the 1(st day) passed . . . on the 15(th)" and so on (Henning, 1937, p. 134, s.v. *sγtyʾ*), as in a Christian text (C 2) **xwšmyq sγtyʾ knwn ʾḥry mʾxy* "on the sixth (day) passed in the month Latter Kanon," but also *xwšmyqy sγdyʾ cn mʾx nwʾ nysn mʾxy* "on the sixth (day) passed from the new moon in the month Nisan." It also occurs as accusative singular feminine *qw knwn ʾḥry mʾx *pwn, nwmyq sγtʾ* "until the month Latter Kanon, the ninth (day) passed" (Sims-Williams, p. 225, s.v. *sγt-*). The latest form of the word occurs as *mʾkr srδ wxšmyk mʾxy XX sγδʾ* "year of the monkey, the sixth month, the 20(th day) passed" (Pelliot Chinois 2782; Sims-Williams and Hamilton, p. 39). When dating by the regnal years of local rulers the Sogdians used another style, however. For example, one Buddhist text is dated *ʾwyn βγy βγpʾwr xʾy ʾnkwyn X III III-myk srδy ʾʾz pr nʾk srδy ʾprtmy mʾxyh* "it was in the 16th year of the lord the Son of Heaven Kʿai-ngywan (=728 C.E.), in the year of the dragon, in the first month" (MacKenzie, I, p. 10, Intox. 34-35). Similar formulations are found in several of the documents from Mount Mug, in which the Sogdian names of the months and days are also used (*EIr.* IV, p. 665 tables 27-28), as in *trxwn MLKʾ X srδ ʾʾz mʾxy msβwγycy myδ ʾsmʾn rwc* "it was the year 10 of King Tarkhun, in the (tenth) month Masvoghich, (twenty-seventh) day Asman-roch" (i.e., 25 March 710 C.E.; Livshits, 1962, pp. 21-22 Nov. 3- 4, R 1). The word *ʾʾz*, understood as "was," may originally have been part of an expression **sarδ-āz* for "year" (Gershevitch, pp. 200 ff.).

In Khotanese Saka dates are generally expressed in numerals, though the months are often named (*EIr.* IV, p. 667 table 32). With cardinal numbers, as in *salī (?) māśt[ä] 8 haḍā 27* "year ?, month 8, day 27" (Or. 9268, 1 b 1; Bailey, II, p. 13) or *salī 21 māśta rarūya haḍā-t-ū jsa 18* "year 21, month Raruya (second summer month), day 18 from them" (Hedin 4.1; Bailey, IV, pp. 23, 74-75). A day expressed by an ordinal appears in the genitive-dative singular, as in *skarihveri māśti didye haḍai* "in the month Skarhvāra on the third day" (Hedin 6.18; Bailey, IV, pp. 25, 80). The word *haḍāa-* "day" originally meant, in all likelihood, "passed" (see Bailey, *Dictionary*, p. 447), a striking parallel to the idiom found in the other languages mentioned above.

Bibliography: M. Back, *Die sassanidischen Staatsinschriften*, Acta Iranica 18, Tehran and Liège, 1978. H. W. Bailey, *Khotanese Texts* I-III, Cambridge, 1945-56, repr. in 1 vol., Cambridge, 1969; IV, Cambridge, 1961, repr. Cambridge, 1979; V, Cambridge, 1963, repr. Cambridge, 1980; VI, Cambridge, 1967. E. Benveniste, *Textes sogdiens*, Paris, 1940. I. M. D'yakonov and V. A. Livshits, "Novye nakhodki dokumentov v staroĭ Nise" (New discoveries of documents at ancient Nisa), *Peredneaziatskiĭ sbornik* (Inner Asian collection) II, Moscow, 1966, pp. 133-57, 169-73. B. Geiger, "The Middle Iranian Texts," in *The Excavations at Doura-Europos*, Final Report 8/1, New Haven, Conn., 1956. I. Gershevitch, "Sogdians on a Frogplain," *Mélanges linguistiques offerts à Émile Benveniste*, Paris, 1975, pp. 195-211. J. C. Greenfield and B. Porten, *The Bisitun inscription of Darius the Great. Aramaic Version*, London, 1982. W. B. Henning, *Ein manichäisches Bet- und Beichtbuch*, Berlin, 1937. Idem, "The Choresmian Documents," *Asia Minor*, N.S. 11, 1965, pp. 166-79. V. A. Livshits, *Sogdiĭskie dokumenty s gory Mug* (Sogdian documents from Mount Mug) II, Moscow, 1962, pls. II-XVIa. Idem, "The Khwarezmian Calendar and the Eras of Ancient Chorasmia," *AAASH* 16, 1968, pp. 433-46. D. N. MacKenzie, ed., *The Buddhist Sogdian Texts of the British Library*, Acta Iranica 10, Tehran and Liège, 1976. H. Reichelt, *Die soghdischen Handschriftenreste des Britischen Museums* II, Heidelberg, 1931. N. Sims-Williams, *The Christian Sogdian Manuscript C 2*, Berliner Turfantexte 12, Berlin, 1985. Idem and J. Hamilton, *Documents turco-sogdiens du IXe-Xe siècle de Touenhouang*, London, 1990.

(D. N. MacKenzie)

DATIS (Gk. Dâtis), Iranian personal name, reflecting Old Iranian *Dātiya- (cf. El. Da-ti-ya; see below), rather than *Dāti-, as previously assumed (cf. Old Pers. final *-iya-*, reflected in Gk. *-is*, as in Bṛdiya-/Smérdis). The name is formed with the hypocoristic suffix *-iya-* attached to the well-attested but ambiguous stem **dāta-* (Schmitt, p. 468 n. 38a).

One famous bearer of this name is known, Datis the Mede, though little information on him is available (Herodotus, 6.94.2; Diodorus, 10.27.1); he seems to have been a kind of specialist on Greek affairs under Darius I (522-486 B.C.E.). Together with Artaphernes, son of Artaphernes (see ARTAPHRENĒS) and nephew of Darius, he led the large Persian amphibious expedition against Greece in 490 B.C.E., with the goal of subduing Eretria and Athens. He succeeded the unfortunate Mardonius (Herodotus, 6.94.2; Nepos, *Miltiades* 4.1), who in 492 had suffered military and naval defeats in Thrace and off Mount Athos. Although he is mentioned together with Artaphernes several times (Herodotus, 6.119.1, 7.8b.3, 7.10b.1, 7.74.2), Datis seems to have been the actual commander, for he alone is named in the narrative of the campaign (cf. Diodorus, 11.2.2). About his life and career before 490 B.C.E. nothing is known from the classical sources (but see below).

In the spring of 490 B.C.E. a great Persian army gathered in the Cilician plain, whence it embarked on 600 triremes, sailing along the coast to Samos, passing through the Cyclades, and burning Naxos, which had not previously been captured (Herodotus, 6.95-96). The next stations were Delos and Carystos (6.97-99), where the Persians enslaved their captives. The first main objective of the expedition, Eretria, was taken through betrayal on the seventh day; it was sacked and burned, and its inhabitants were deported (6.100-01) and settled in Arderikka (q.v. 2; see also DEPORTATIONS i), about 40 km from Susa (6.119.1-4).

Up to that point the expedition had been totally successful, and a few days later the Persians set sail for Attica. On the advice of the exiled former tyrant Hippias, who was with Datis, they landed at Marathon (Herodotus, 6.102, 107.1); Diodorus' story (10.27.1-3) about a defiant message sent by Datis to the Athenians and Miltiades' reply is certainly pure fabrication (cf. also the remarks in Plato, *Leges* 3.698e). Details on the battle of Marathon (q.v.) are missing or rather vague in Herodotus' account (6.111-16); the purpose and execution of several military operations are not patent, and it is unclear whether or not Datis made the first decisive move (cf. Nepos, *Miltiades* 5.4). After long and heavy fighting the Athenians, led by Miltiades, gained the victory at Marathon, even before the arrival of the Spartans, to whom they had appealed for help (Herodotus, 6.120). They pursued the fleeing Persians to the shore and tried to set fire to their ships (6.113.2, 6.115.1) but were able to capture only seven. The remainder of the fleet hastened to reach Athens, rounding Cape Sounion before the people of the city and its harbor, Phaleron, heard news of the battle and could prepare for defense (6.115-16). According to Pliny (*Naturalis Historia* 35.57), the leaders of both Greeks and Persians, including Datis, were portrayed in a painting of the battle at Marathon (by Phidias' brother or nephew Panaenus?) in the so-called "painted hall" at Athens.

Datis and his forces, having achieved nothing on the Greek mainland and having taken only the Cyclades, returned to Asia (Herodotus, 6.116, 6.118.1-3). Ctesias reported (cf. Jacoby, *Fragmente* IIIC, p. 462 frag. 13 par. 22), contrary to Herodotus' account, that Datis fell at Marathon and that his corpse was not handed over to the Persians, but this story is not supported by other evidence.

Details of Datis' subsequent life are unknown, though his sons Harmamithres and Tithaeus (Títhaios) were cavalry leaders under Xerxes I (486-65 B.C.E.) ten years later (Herodotus, 7.88.1). The authenticity of reports of Datis' dedications in 490 B.C.E. to the temple of Athena at Lindos, chief city of Rhodes, included in a temple chronicle of the Hellenistic period (Jacoby, *Fragmente* IIIB, p. 512), has been questioned repeatedly (see most recently Baslez). On the basis of an ostracon found in the Athenian agora, on which the Athenian nobleman and leader Aristeides is characterized as the "fellow of Datis" (Raubitschek, pp. 240-41), it has been argued that Datis had fairly close contacts with Greek officials. Evidence from Herodotus and other sources that Datis showed respect for Greek deities, especially the Delian Apollo, may point in the same direction. It is certainly in harmony with Datis' apparent efforts to speak Greek, though rather haltingly, so that Greek *datismós* became a kind of synonym for "barbarism." A similar allusion is found in the proverbial expression "Datis' song" (*tò Dátidos mélos*; Aristophanes, *Pax* 289; cf. Raubitschek, pp. 234-37).

D. M. Lewis (pp. 194-95) recognized that this Datis was also mentioned once, in the Elamite form Da-ti-ya, on one of the Persepolis Fortress tablets, Q-1809. Da-ti-ya was a person of high rank who was returning "from Sardis to the king at Persepolis" in the eleventh month of the twenty-seventh year of Darius (i.e., January-February 494 B.C.E.), carrying "a sealed document of the king." He is recorded as having been recipient of a rather large ration of beer. Lewis interpreted this text as evidence that before the famous expedition of 490 B.C.E. Datis had gained experience in the Ionian revolt, perhaps on a tour of inspection to coordinate the final campaigns to end the revolt early in 494 B.C.E.

Bibliography: M.-F. Baslez, "Présence et traditions iraniennes dans les cités de l'Égée," *Revue des Études Anciennes* 87, 1985, pp. 137-55, esp. pp. 138-41. A. R. Burn, "Persia and the Greeks," in *Camb. Hist. Iran* II, pp. 292-391, esp. pp. 313-18. N. G. L. Hammond, "The Expedition of Datis and Artaphernes," in *CAH*[2] IV, pp. 491-517. D. M. Lewis, "Datis the Mede," *Journal of Hellenic Studies* 100, 1980, pp. 194-95. A. E. Raubitschek, "Das Datislied," in K. Schauenburg, ed., *Charites. Studien zur Altertumswissenschaft*, Bonn, 1957, pp. 234-42. R. Schmitt, "Perser und Persisches in der alten attischen Komödie," in *Orientalia J. Duchesne-Guillemin Emerito Oblata*, Acta Iranica 23, Leiden and Tehran, 1984, pp. 459-73, esp. pp. 467-68. [H.] Swoboda, "Datis 1," in Pauly-Wissowa, IV/2, cols. 2227-29.

(RÜDIGER SCHMITT)

DAULIER DESLANDES, ANDRÉ (b. Montoire-sur-le-Loir, 1621, d. Paris, 23 October 1715), author of *Les Beautez de la Perse . . .*, a brief but valuable description of Safavid Persia in the years 1075-76/1664-65.

No information on his early years has yet come to light, but in 1663 he joined the French jeweler Jean Baptiste Tavernier (1605-89) on his sixth voyage to the Orient, apparently entrusted with the interests of other merchants who had invested in Tavernier's commercial venture. He was the only Catholic in the party, which included seven other young men with different skills, including a physician, all Huguenots (Joret, pp. 164-65; Kroell, pp. 9-10). They reached Isfahan on 25 Jomādā I 1075/14 December 1664, and Daulier took up residence in the Augustinian convent there, while Tavernier stayed at the home of another French jeweler and the rest of the party in the suburb of Jolfā. Daulier learned to his dismay that Tavernier had negotiated the sale of a large part of the valuable merchandise privately, with Raphaël du Mans (q.v.) acting as his interpreter; his dismay was all the greater becaus eht purchaser had been Shah ʿAbbās II (q.v.; 1052-77/1642-66). In a letter to his brother Pierre, a secretary in the Compagnie Française des Indes Occidentaux, Daulier described his sense of helplessness at these events. He said little of his travel from Tabrīz to Isfahan, however, choosing rather to refer to the description of Pietro della Valle (q.v.), but he emphasized the elegance and comfort of Persian houses, which he contrasted with their unassuming facades. Daulier also described a party held by the shah at the royal palace; he had attended and been called upon to play a spinet that an Armenian had brought from the Netherlands (letter published with annotations in Kroell, pp. 9-19; cf. Tavernier, II, pp. 188-89).

On 8 Šaʿbān 1075/24 February 1665 the travelers, including Jean de Thévenot, a scholar of oriental studies with whom Daulier had become friendly, left Isfahan for India. A month later, while still in Bandar-e ʿAbbās (q.v.), Daulier decided to return to France instead (Kroell, p. 10). He and de Thévenot went back to Shiraz and visited Persepolis (Thévenot, London, II, p. 139); then de Thévenot left for India via Baṣra, and Daulier proceeded to France.

After a two-year assignment as director of the Compagnie Française des Indes Orientaux (see EAST INDIA COMPANIES iii) at Bordeaux Daulier settled in Paris, where in 1673 he published *Les Beautez . . .*, with a map and seven engravings drawn from his own sketches by the well-known artists Israël Silvestre and Antoine Paillet, both official artists by royal appointment (Faucheux, pp. 87-89). His account is noted for its recording of precise distances in Persia and its clear descriptions of the principal cities, enhanced by the engravings. With Daulier's consent the unconnected narrative of the adventures of a pilot on the king's galleys was added to the edition (pp. 83-135). During his years in Paris Daulier often encountered Tavernier and other travelers who had visited the east (Galland, p. 503). His private papers are now kept in the manuscript division of the Bibliothèque Nationale, Paris; they include a manuscript of the narrative of an adventurous Armenian merchant, Philippe de Zagly (Gulbenkian).

Bibliography: A. Daulier Deslandes, *Les Beautez de la Perse ou la description de ce qu'il y a des plus curieux dans ce royaume*, Paris, 1673. L. E. Faucheux, *Catalogue raisonné de toutes les estampes d'Israël Silvestre*, Paris, 1857. A. Galland, *Journal parisien d'Antoine Galland, 1708-1715*, Paris, 1919. R. Gulbenkian, "Philippe de Zagly, marchand arménien de Julfa, et l'établissement du commerce persan en Courlande en 1696," *REA*, N.S. 7, 1970, pp. 361-99. C. Joret, *Jean Baptiste Tavernier, écuyer, baron d'Aubonne, chambellan du Gran Électeur, d'après des documents nouveaux et inédits*, Paris, 1886. A. Kroell, *Nouvelles d'Ispahan, 1665-1695*, Paris, 1979. R. du Mans, *Estat de la Perse en 1660*, ed. C. Schefer, Paris, 1890. J. B. Tavernier, *Les six voyages . . .*, 6 vols., Paris, 1713. U. Thieme and F. Becker, *Allgemeines Lexikon der bildenden Künstler von der Antike bis zur Gegenwart* XXVI, Leipzig, 1932, pp. 146-47. P. della Valle, *I viaggi di Pietro della Valle*.

Lettere dalla Persia, ed. F. Gaeta and L. Lockhart, Il nuovo Ramusio 6, Rome, 1972.

(ANNE KROELL)

DAURISES (Gk. Daurísēs, apparently reflecting the same Old Persian original as El. Da-a-ú/hu-ri-sa/ša, connected with Younger Av. *daiŋ́hāuruuaēsa-* "wandering up and down the country"; cf. Hinz, p. 80), name of a Persian general during the Ionian revolt, a son-in-law of Darius I (522-486 B.C.E.). In 497 B.C.E., together with other Persian commanders, he pursued the Ionians who had attacked Sardis. After the victory they divided the rebellious Ionian cities among themselves and destroyed them; Daurises sacked those on the Hellespont, including Dardanus, Abydus, Percote, Lampsacus, and Paesus (Herodotus, 5.116-17). He then heard of the revolt in Caria and hastened to that province (5.117); he defeated the rebels twice, at the River Marsyas and near Labraunda (5.119.1-5.120). Then, while marching toward Pedasus, Daurises was lured into an ambush and killed, together with other officers (5.121).

Bibliography: W. Hinz, *Altiranisches Sprachgut der Nebenüberlieferungen*, Wiesbaden, 1975. [F.] Stähelin, "Daurises," in Pauly-Wissowa, Suppl. III, col. 327.

(RÜDIGER SCHMITT)

DAVĀL-PĀ(Y), or *doval-pā* (colloq. *dūāl-pā*; Kurdish *dolpā*; Kermānī *dohol-pā*), an imaginary evil anthropoid creature characterized by flexible legs (*pā*) resembling leather straps (*da/ovāl* < Pahl. *dawāl* "hide, leather"), which he uses as tentacles to grip and enslave human beings, who then have to carry him on their shoulders or backs and labor for him until they die of fatigue.

The earliest references to such creatures in Persian sources seem to be in the *Šāh-nāma*. In the story of the expedition of the Kayanid king Kaykāvūs to Māzandarān they are called *sost-pāyān* (limp-legged) and are identified as a race of strong horsemen (*savārān-e pūlādḵāy* "steel-chewing riders") with legs of *davāl*, among whom the king of Māzandarān lived (Moscow, II, p. 111). Elsewhere the *narm-pāyān* (soft-legged) are said to have fought the army of Alexander the Great (q.v.) after he left Ethiopia (*zamīn-e Ḥabaš*); they are described as tall, naked creatures without horses or armaments, who fought by hurling stones (Moscow, VII, p. 71).

The tradition of a fabulous limp-legged being, found only in mysterious or out-of-the-way places, seems to have been elaborated by imaginative or credulous seafarers and other travelers in the Islamic period. Moḥammad Ṭūsī (d. ca. 589/1193; pp. 499-500) quoted a certain seafarer, Walīd b. Moslem, who recounted the adventures of a man with scars on his face and neck, who, after escaping from the island of the dog-faced people, found a group of good-looking anthropoid creatures with short, limp legs and long tails in a district called Fāṭūr. When he approached, one of them sprang up, twined its tail around him, clutched his neck with its claws, and made him carry it about all day long while it picked fruit from trees and ate it. This nightmare went on until the traveler managed to get the creature drunk, so that it relaxed and fell off. The man then killed some of its fellows and fled.

Later versions of the myth are mainly elaborations of Ṭūsī's account, with one significant change: the substitution of strap-like legs for the prehensile tail. About a century later Zakarīyāʾ Qazvīnī (tr., pp. 173-74) reported it on the authority of a seafarer named Yaʿqūb b. Eṣḥāq Sarrāj, who had supposedly met the scarred narrator. According to this version, both the limp-legged and the dog-faced peoples dwelt on the same island, Jazīra Sagsār (lit., "island of the dog-headed"), in the Baḥr al-Zanj (i.e., the western Indian Ocean). One of the limp-legged creatures twined its legs around the narrator, but eventually a tree branch blinded it; then the narrator fed the creature grape juice, causing its legs to relax, and cast it off.

Qazvīnī's version was included, with further elaborations, among the adventures of Sinbad the Sailor in the later versions of *Alf layla wa layla* (q.v.; nights 557-58; tr., III, pp. 360-63). The evil creature, known to previous visitors to the island as Šayk al-Baḥr (Old man of the sea), is a handsome old fellow with legs like straps of buffalo hide. Sinbad uses a large dried pumpkin shell to produce the wine that frees him; eventually he is rescued by seafarers who land on the island. Šayḵ-al-Baḥr reappears in the story of the king Sayf-al-Molūk (night 765; tr., IV, pp. 495-96), who is cast away with some of his retinue (*mamālīk*) on an unknown island abounding in fruit trees, from which they hasten to eat. One of his companions comes across an odd-looking, long-faced fellow sitting among the trees; the old man calls him by name and offers to give him ripe fruit. When he approaches, Šayḵ-al-Baḥr climbs on his shoulders, twines one leg round his neck with the other dangling, and commands, "Get going! You cannot free yourself from me!" The victim cries out to his companions "Get off this island, because one of its inhabitants is riding on my shoulders and the others are looking for you!" Alarmed, the king and his men hurry back to their boat and sail away.

The tale of Sinbad and Šayḵ-al-Baḥr was adapted in the popular Persian story *Sargoḏašt-e Salīm-e jawāherī* (The story of Salīm the jeweler), where, for the first time, the creature is expressly referrred to as *davāl-pā*. In the story Salīm flees from a land inhabited by a tribe of apes to an island where grapevines and pomegranate and apple trees grow in abundance and the houses are built of mud and wood. He meets the chief *davāl-pā*, a white-bearded man, who tricks him into carrying him home by promising him bread and meat. The *davāl-pā* jumps onto Salīm's back and twines his legs around his waist; he nibbles at Salīm's ears or pokes a *javāldūz* (large packing needle) into his neck in order to steer him.

The modern version of the *davāl-pā* (see, e.g., Ṣādeq

Hedāyat (p. 176; Massé, *Croyances* II, p. 353; tr., p. 345) includes a few new features. The old man now usually sits by the roadside, imploring passersby to carry him across a nearby stream. Once he is on a victim's back, a long leg comes out of his belly and twists around the carrier's waist; then, firmly grasping the latter with his hands, he orders *Kār bokon, bede (be) man* (Work, [and] give [your earnings] to me). In order to be rid of him, the carrier has to make him drunk. Similar descriptions of the *davāl-pā*, with varying details, are found in local superstitions in many parts of Persia. For instance, in Lorestān and Īlām the *davāl-pā* clings to his victim even when the latter is in mortal agony; the only way to be rid of him is to stick a *javāldūz* into his body (Asadīān et al., p. 166; cf. the myth of the imaginary *merdezmā* [i.e., *mardāzmā*, lit., "man tester"] in Baḵtīārī folklore; Ḵosravī, p. 434). In contemporary Persian the expression *meṯl-e dūālpā* (like the *davāl-pā*) refers to someone who clings tenaciously to other people and importunes them with wearisome requests or commands.

Bibliography: *Alf layla wa layla*, tr. ʿAbd-al-Laṭīf Ṭasūjī Tabrīzī as *Hazār o yak šab*, 5 vols., Tehran, 1316 Š./1937. M. Asadīān Ḵorramābādī et al., *Bāvarhā wa dānestahā dar Lorestān o Īlām*, Tehran, 1358 Š./1979. Ṣ. Hedāyat, *Neyrangestān*, 2nd ed., Tehran, 1334 Š./1955. ʿA. Ḵosravī, *Farhang-e Baḵtīārī*, Tehran, 1368 Š./1989. Massé, *Croyances*; tr. C. A. Messner as *Persian Beliefs and Customs*, New Haven, Conn., 1954. Zakarīyāʾ Qazvīnī, *ʿAjāʾeb al-maḵlūqāt wa ğarāʾeb al-mawjūdāt*, ed. F. Saʿd, 3rd ed., Beirut, 1978; tr. (possibly by Qazvīnī himself), ed. N. Sabūḥī, 2nd ed., Tehran, 1361 Š./1982. ʿA. Šarafkandī (Hažār), *Farhang-e kordī-fārsī*, 2 vols., Tehran, 1368-69 Š./1989-90. *Sargoḏašt-e Salīm-e jawāherī*, Tehran, n.d. Moḥammad b. Maḥmūd Ṭūsī, *ʿAjāyeb al-maḵlūqāt*, ed. M. Sotūda, Tehran, 1345 Š./1966. M.-T. Wāʿeẓ Taqawī, *Farhang-e eṣṭelāḥāt-e Kermān*, 2nd ed., Kermān, 1363 Š./1984, p. 219.

(HŪŠANG AʿLAM)

DAVALLŪ. See QAJAR TRIBES.

DAVĀN (local pronunciation *do:ʾu:*), village located 12 km northeast of Kāzerūn in Fārs; a distinctive dialect is spoken there.

i. *The village.*
ii. *The Davānī dialect.*

i. THE VILLAGE

Davān is located at 29° 23′ N, 51° 55′ E, in a narrow valley at the foot of Mount Davān in the greater Zagros range. It is divided into upper (*maʿale[maḥalla]-ye bār*) and lower (*maʿale[maḥalla]-ye duman*) quarters. The climate is hot and dry. In the 1970s the only source of water was a group of nine springs located at the southeastern end of the village. Arable land is very limited and located mostly in the foothills; dry farming is the prevailing form of agriculture. Products include barley, wheat, and fruits—grapes, figs, pomegranates, and pears (locally called *xormor*). In 1354 Š./1975 there were thirty-three orchards.

Some ruins dating from the Parthian and Sasanian periods are located approximately 4 km to the south of the village. Davān was mentioned by some medieval Islamic historians and geographers (e.g., Eṣṭaḵrī, p. 112; Ebn al-Balḵī, p. 137; *Nozhat al-qolūb*, ed. Le Strange, p. 117). It was the birthplace of the theologian and philosopher Jalāl-al-Dīn Davānī (q.v.; 830-908/1426-1502/03), whose tomb, known as Maqbara-ye Šayḵ-e ʿĀlī, is venerated locally.

In the last forty years there has been a sharp decrease in population, from 2,747 people in 1330 Š./1951 to 966 in 1365 Š./1986 (Razmārā, *Farhang* VII, p. 103; Markaz-e āmār, p. 26). The Davānīs, who are divided among twelve clans (*ṭāyefa*), belong to the Shaikhi branch of Shiʿite Islam and maintain close contact with the Shaikhis of Kermān. They speak both Persian and a local dialect (see ii, below).

Bibliography: ʿA. Laḥsāʾīzāda and ʿA. Salāmī, *Tārīḵ o farhang-e mardom-e Davān*, Tehran, 1370 Š./1991. Markaz-e āmār-e Īran, *Sar-šomarī-e ʿomūmī-e nofūs wa maskan. Mehr-māh-e 1365. Farhang-e ābādīhā-ye kešvar. Šahrestān-e Kāzerūn*, 4-92, Tehran, 1368 Š./1989. Ṣandūq-e taʿāwon-e Davānīhā (Markaz-e Tehran), *Taqwīm-e sāl-e 1354*, Tehran, 1354 Š./1975.

(HAMID MAHAMEDI)

ii. THE DAVĀNĪ DIALECT

Davānī (local pronunciation: *devani*) is spoken in the village of Davān and belongs to the Fārs group of Iranian dialects spoken in the western and northwestern regions of the province of Fārs (see Lecoq; for published material on Davāni, see Ḥosāmzāda Ḥaqīqī; Mahamedi, 1979; idem, 1982; Morgenstierne; Ṣādeqī; Salāmī), an area of Lorī speakers. It thus shares the general characteristics of such other Fārs dialects as Somğūnī, Būrengūnī, and Māsarmī, but it also presents some unique features.

Phonology.

Consonants. Davānī has dental affricates *ts* and *dz*, unknown in the neighboring dialects, as in *tse* "what" and *berendz* "rice" and *andzi* "fig," which contrast with *č* and *ǰ*, as in *čiš* "eye" and *tāǰ* "throne." The fricative *δ* is a variant of *d* after vowels, as in *baδ* "bad." There is a tendency for *k* and *g* to be palatalized before front vowels: *koḵa* "brother," *beg̱a* "say." Beside the regular *r* (single flap), there is also a trilled *r̄*, as in *mor* (NPers. *morğ*) "hen," contrasting with *mor̄* "round." Old Iranian *rθ* and *fr* have both become *hl*, as in *pohl* (Av. *pərəθu*, Mid. Pers. *puhl*, NPers. *pol*) "bridge" and *ba:hl* (Av. *vafra*, Mid. Pers. *wafr*, NPers. *barf*) "snow." Old Iranian *nd* has been assimilated and simplified to *n*, as in *ganom* (NPers. *gandom*) "wheat" and *ben-* (NPers. *band-*) "to tie." There is also the peculiar change of *n* to *r* in *kur-* (NPers. *kon-*) "to do," *kor-* (NPers. *kan-*) "to dig," and *zar-* (NPers. *zan-*) "to hit." Middle Persian intervocalic *b* and *w* have both become *v*, as in *lav* (Mid. and NPers. *lab*) "shore, side" and *meivene* (Mid. Pers. *band-* and *wēn-*) "I tie, I see." Initial *b*, when followed by a closed vowel, is pronounced *v* by some speakers, as in *bi/vi* "was."

Vowels. The vowel system of Davānī is essentially the same as that of Persian. The long vowels *a:*, *e:*, *o:* of various origins contrast with short *a*, *e*, *o*, as in *bar* "shore," *ba:r* (NPers. *bahr*) "share," *ser* "head," *se:r* (NPers. *sīr*) "full," *mor* (NPers. *morḡ*) "hen," *mo:r* (NPers. *mohr*) "seal." The long variants of *ā* (back *a*), *i*, *u* (*ā:*, *i:*, *u:*) are not separate phonemes. Both *o* and *e* have a reduced variant *ə*, as in *dərəs* beside *doros*, *dorost* "right" and the enclitic pronouns *-əm*, *-ət*, *-əš*, *-ən*. In the final position *o* is sometimes found for original *ā*: *injo* (NPers. *īnjā*; cf. colloq. Shirazi *īnjo*) "here." There are two diphthongs, *ou* (*o*[u]) and *ei* (*e*[i]), for example, *tou* "you," *peiš* "before, front"; *ei* has the variant *e:*, as in *meikore* and *me:kore* "I do."

Morphology.

Nouns. The plural marker is usually *-gal*, as in *beččekgal* "children," *sālgal* "years," *gapgal* "conversations," but occasionally *-ā* (*-hā*), as in *šāhā* "kings," *unā* "those," *kehā* "who."

Personal pronouns. The personal pronouns are singular *ma*, *tou*, *u*; plural *mu*, *šumu*, *unā*; and enclitic *-m*, *-t*, *-š*, *-mu*, *-tu*, *-šu* (or with the joining vowels *e*, *ə*, *o*; unattached in ergative constructions: *om*, *ot*, etc.). The enclitic pronouns are used as possessive pronouns (*ser-eš* "his head," *dass-om* "my hand") and in several verbal constructions: as direct or indirect object and as agent in the ergative construction and with impersonal verbs (for examples, see below).

Demonstrative pronouns. The demonstratives are *i* "this," *un* "that," *iyā* (*inā*) "these," and *unā* "those."

Prepositions. The most common prepositions are *a* (corresponding to Pers. *az* and *be*) "from, to, in" and *an* (Pers. *andar*) "in," as in *a Kāziri še* "he went to Kāzerun," *tou a Širāz amesse?* "have you come from Shiraz?" *ma a xuna kār meikore* "I work at home," *Sardār an ma:jjed-e* "Sardār is in the mosque." The preposition *ve* (Pers. *be*) is used in such phrases as *ve ī zelli* "so soon."

The verb. The verbal system of Davānī is based on the present stem (for the present indicative, imperative, and subjunctive) and the past stem (for the preterit, imperfect, past subjunctive, perfect, and pluperfect). The verbal endings are set out in Table 7. The *-ā* in *-t-ā* and *-en-ā* is probably the attention-drawing particle *(h)ā* found in many dialects in Persia. The modal prefixes are *mei* in the present indicative and imperfect; *be* (also *bo*) in the subjunctive, imperative, and sometimes the intransitive preterit (*bošel/beše* "he went"); and *hā* (or *hu*) in the present subjunctive and imperative of a small group of verbs. There are two negations, as in classical Persian: *na-*, negation of statement, and *ma-*, prohibition. The negation *na* is prefixed to the stem and *mei* but replaces *be* and *hā*; *ma* is used with the imperative and replaces any modal prefix. The lexical preverbs *vā* and *var/ver* are common; they may precede or replace the modal prefixes and provide new meanings, for example, *xor-* "to eat," *vā xor-* "to drink," *vā meixore* "I am drinking"; *avār-* "to bring," *var/ver avār-* "to pick, to separate," *ver avār* "pick!"

The enclitic copula and the negative copula are shown in Table 7. A special form of the third person singular, *he*, meaning "there is (for)," is used in possessive constructions, for example, *tse tou he?* "what do you have?" *panss-um boč he* "I have five goats," *tou-t sad sāl de omr he* "you will live for another hundred years."

Present stems can be divided into two groups. The first consists of stems in *-e-* that add *-t* in the third person singular, for example: *meixat-e-t* "he sleeps, he is sleeping" < *-xat-e-* "to sleep." The *-e-* is elided before vocalic endings, as in *(ma) meiters-e* "I am afraid" < *-ters-e-* "to fear." The second group includes stems ending in *-r* or *-n*, which are dropped in the third-person singular present indicative and subjunctive and second-person singular imperative, with accompanying change of the vowel quality. The ending is nil or *-t-ā*, for example, *meivit(-ā)* "he sees" < *-ven-* "to see," *boxut(-ā)* "he may eat" and *buxu* "eat!" < *-xor-* "to eat." The verb *-še-* "to go" is inflected according to this class, as in *bošut-ā* "he may go."

The present indicative is formed by prefixing *mei-* and suffixing a personal ending to the present stem, as in present stem *kor-/kur-* (short form *ku-*) "to do": singular *(ma) meikore*, *(tou) meikore*, *(u) meiku* or

Table 7
PERSONAL PRONOUNS AND VERB CONJUGATIONS

		Personal Pronouns		Conjugation		
		Stressed	Enclitic	Endings	"to be"	"not to be"
Singular	1st	ma	-m	-e	-e	nise
	2nd	tou	-t	-e; nil	-e	nise
	3rd	u	-š	-t, -tā	-ā; he	ni, nissā
Plural	1st	mu	-mu	-u	-i	nisən
	2nd	šumu	-tu	-i	-i	nissi
	3rd	unā	-šu	-en, -enā	-enā, -anā	nissanā

meikutā; plural *(mu) meikoru*, *(šumu) meikori*, *(unā) meikoren(-ā)*.

The present subjunctive is formed by adding a modal prefix (*hā* or *be*) to the present stem and suffixing the personal endings, for example, *hāδe* "I/you may give," *huvene* "I/you may tie," *beire* "I may come," *bokutā* "he may do." The imperative is formed in the same way as the subjunctive, except in the second-person singular, which takes the ending *-a* with stems of the first group but none with stems of the second group, for example, singular *beδa*, *heδa* "give," *bega* "say," *beška* "break," *boku* "do," *vazu* "return," *huči* "sit," *heδe dass-e hasan huvene-š bā injā* "go (and) chain Ḥasan's hand (and) bring him here"; plural *begai* "say."

Past stems are formed differently from intransitive and transitive verbs. The past stems of intransitive verbs are formed in *-eδ-*, corresponding to present stems in *-e-*, as in *xateδ* "slept," *šeδ* "went," *beδ* "was," or to different present stems, for example, *ameδ* "came" (present stem *-r-* "to come"), *so:teδ* "burned," *mordeδ* "died." Some verbs have the past stem formative *-esseδ*, instead of *-eδ-*, for example, *dovesseδ* "ran," *nalesseδ* "groaned."

Past stems of transitive verbs end in either consonants or vowels. Those ending in consonants include *košt* "to kill" and *xond* "to read." Stems ending in vowels are either monosyllabic or bisyllabic, for example, *di:-* "saw," *ze-* "hit," *go-* "said," *ge-* "took," *ersā-* "sent," *xeri-* "bought," *buri-* "cut," *duši-* "milked."

Causative verbs are formed by adding *-n-* to the present stem, to which *-i-* is added to form the past stem, for example: *čar-* "to graze," *čarn-*, *čarni-* "to cause to graze"; *čiy-* "to sit," *čeyn-*, *čeyni-* "to cause to sit down"; *xat-* "to sleep," *xatn-*, *xatni-* "to cause to sleep."

The perfect stem is formed from the past stem plus *-s(s)e-*, for example: *hāise-* "have sat down," *amesse-* "have come," *šesse-* "have gone," *bise-* "have been," *dise-* "have seen."

The simple past tense of intransitive verbs is formed by attaching the personal ending to the past stem. The third-person singular has no ending and may lose the final consonant of the stem. Examples are *ameδe* "I/you came," *ama* or *amaδ* "he came," *še* "he went," *ameδen-ā* "they came." Expressions like *še-š* "he went" and *Hasan-əš ama* "Ḥasan came" are probably borrowed from Persian.

The continuous past is formed by prefixing *mei* to the simple past, as in *mei-šeδ* "he was going," *mei-ama* "he was coming," *mei-δovesseδen* "they were running."

The past subjunctive is formed from the perfect stem plus the inflected present subjunctive of the auxiliary verb "to be," as in *bāyas dovesse but/vut* "he must have run," *bāyas amesse but/vut* "he must have come," *šesse be/ve* "I/you might have gone," *dovesse ben/ven* "they might have run."

The perfect is formed by suffixing the personal endings to the perfect stem, which loses its final *-e* before vocalic endings. The third-person singular has no ending: *(ma) amesse* "I have come," *(u) šesse* "he has gone," *šessu* "we have gone," *(unā) hāyisən* "they have sat down."

The pluperfect is based on the perfect stem plus the simple past form of the auxiliary verb "to be," for example, *(ma) šesse beδe/veδe* "I had gone," *(u) amesse bi/vi* "he had come."

Transitive verbs take the ergative construction in the past tenses. The verb appears in its stem form, and the agent indicating the logical subject is expressed as an enclitic pronoun attached to any word near the verb or to the verb itself. When the agent is a noun or an independent pronoun the corresponding enclitic pronoun must still appear. In the past subjunctive and the pluperfect the auxiliary verb "to be" remains unchanged in all forms, as *but* or *vut* and *bi* or *vi* respectively. Examples of the simple past include *o-š ze* "he struck," *go-t* "you said," *ame injā-š ejāza dā* "he came here and gave permission," *bonā-š ke nasiyat-mu kardan* "he began to advise us," *unā-šu Hasan ersā* "they sent Ḥasan"; of the continuous past *Hasan-əm meidi* "I was seeing Ḥasan"; of the perfect *tou-t xarse* "you have eaten," *gosse-mu* "we have said," *pos-eš-ešu i juri ver sar-eš avarse* "they have done this to his son"; of the past subjunctive (*bāyas*) *tou-t gosse but/vut* "you must have said it"; of the pluperfect *ma-m dise bi/vi* "I had seen," *oš gosse bi/vi* "he had said."

The impersonal verbs *mā* "to want, to wish" and *šā* "can, to be able" are also combined with enclitic pronouns to express what would be the subject in English, for example, *tou-t ne meiša ma hu-zere* "you cannot hit me," *agarət pil mā* "if you want money."

The passive is formed from *še-* "to go" plus an infinitive construction: *nu a xardan še*, literally, "bread went to eat." The passive is used only when the agent is not expressed. When the agent is expressed the ergative construction is used.

Lexicon.

To illustrate the lexical characteristics of Davānī as a Fārs dialect, some words denoting family relationships are listed here: *bāva* "father," *dey* "mother," *koka* "older brother," *borāk* "younger brother," *xāk* "sister," *pos*, *bečček* "son," *dot* "daughter," *zan* "wife," *ši*, *mira* "husband," *bā-gutu* "grandfather," *nena* "grandmother," *āmu* "uncle" (father's brother), *ālu*, *xālu* "uncle" (mother's brother), *āma* "aunt" (father's sister), *xāla* "aunt" (mother's sister), *xasi* "wife's mother," *dey ši* "husband's mother," *nā bavei* "stepfather," *zey bāvei* "stepmother," *dot-e pos* "grandchild" (son's daughter), *pos-e dot* "grandchild" (daughter's son), *āris* "bride," *damā* "bridegroom," *hamāris* (cf. Šīrāzī *hamrūs*) "sister-in-law" (wife of husband's brother), *hamriš* (cf. Šīrāzī *hamrīš*) "brother-in-law" (husband of wife's sister), *peyza* (cf. Šīrāzī *pīzāda*) "stepchild."

Local place names include those of the nine springs from which the village obtained its water in the 1970s: *bal-e passe*, *bal-e ḡeni*, *baryā-ye duman*, *baryā-ye bār*, *ouw-e mašīrī*, *dere-ye x^vāja rajob*, *bal-e maʿd-e x^vāja*, *ouw-e lordeḵ*, and *ouw-e nayeḵ*. Among orchards are *zer-e deh*, *lehraḵ*, *zer-e monāra*, *bar-e* *sovaδu, garr-e māhar, gaft-e monseri, pasbardeḵ, barḵo, tel-e kateḵ,* and *derey-e dāsbanu.*

Bibliography: Č. Ḥosāmzāda Ḥaqīqī, "Gūyeš-e Davān," in *Proceedings of the First Congress of Iranian Studies*, Tehran, 1349 Š./1970, pp. 77-98. P. Lecoq, "Les dialectes du sud-ouest de l'Iran," in R. Schmitt, ed., *Compendium Linguarum Iranicarum*, Wiesbaden, 1989, pp. 341-49. H. Mahamedi, "On the Verbal System in Three Iranian Dialects of Fars," *Stud. Ir.* 8, 1979, pp. 277-97. Idem, "The Story of Rostam and Esfandīyār in an Iranian Dialect," *JAOS* 102, 1982, pp. 451-59. G. Morgenstierne, "Stray Notes on Persian Dialects," *NTS* 19, 1960, pp. 123-29. ʿA.-A. Ṣādeqī, "Yāddāšt-ī dar bāra-ye sāḵtemān-e vājī-e lahja-ye Davānī," *Majalla-ye zabān-šenāsī* 5, 1367 Š./1988, pp. 2-8. A. Salāmī (Davānī), "Sāḵt-e feʿl dar gūyeš-e Davānī," *Majalla-ye zabān-šenāsī* 5, 1367 Š./1988, pp. 9-28 (mentioninng two unpublished theses unavailable to the present author: M. Ḡolāmī, "Gūyeš-e Davānī," B.A. thesis, Jondīšāpūr University, 1354 Š./1975; Q. Forqānī, "Barrasī-e gūyeš-e Davānī az naẓar-e vāžegān wa sāḵtmān-e dastgāhhā-ye feʿlī," M.A. thesis, Shiraz University, 1355 Š./1976). This article is based mainly on data collected by the author during several trips to Davān in 1351-54 Š./1972-75 and 1359-60 Š./1980-81.

(HAMID MAHAMEDI)

DAVĀNĪ, JALĀL-AL-DĪN MOḤAMMAD b. Asʿad Kāzerūnī Ṣeddīqī (b. Davān, q.v., near Kāzerūn in Fārs, 830/1426-27, d. 908/1502), often referred to as ʿAllāma Davānī, leading theologian, philosopher, jurist, and poet of late 15th-century Persia. He began his studies with his father, who had been a student of Mīr Sayyed Šarīf-ʿAlī b. Moḥammad Gorgānī (d. 816/1413), but while still young he moved to Shiraz, where he studied theology, philosophy, logic, principles of Islamic jurisprudence (*oṣūl-e feqh*), and Hadith under such scholars as Homām-al-Dīn Golbārī; Ṣafī-al-Dīn Ījī (d. 864/1450); Moḥyi'l-Dīn Moḥammad Kūškenārī Anṣārī, who had in turn been taught by Ebn Ḥajar ʿAsqalānī (d. 852/1449); and Moḥammad Kāzerūnī. The latter two were also students of Šarīf-ʿAlī Gorgānī.

Davānī was closely associated with contemporary courts throughout his career. In Shiraz, while still young, he was appointed *ṣadr* (religious supervisor) by Yūsof, son of the Qara Qoyunlu Jahānšāh (ca. 841-73/1438-68). He soon resigned the post, however, and took up teaching at the Madrasa-ye Begom, known as Dār al-Aytām. He wrote his *Aḵlāq-e jalālī* (q.v.), also known as *Lawāmeʿal-ešrāq fī makārem al-aḵlāq* (for discussion, see Rosenthal, pp. 210-23; Lambton; Woods, pp. 37, 101, 115-18), in Persian for the Āq Qoyunlu Ozun Ḥasan (857-82/1453-78) at the request of the latter's son Ḵalīl. His *ʿArż-nāma* was written for Ḵalīl himself during his brief reign as sultan (882-83/1478). Davānī later accepted the post of chief judge of Fārs from Sultan Yaʿqūb (883-96/1478-90). His discussion on the commentary of ʿAlī b. Moḥammad Qūščī (d. 879/1474) on *Tajrīd al-kalām* by Naṣīr-al-Dīn Ṭūsī (d. 672/1274) was dedicated to both these sons of Ozun Ḥasan. Davānī did oppose the centralization policies of Sultan Yaʿqūb during the last years of his reign (Woods, p. 157), but he was later on good terms with Sultan Rostam (898-902/1493-97). In addition to his association with the Turkmen rulers of Shiraz, he also enjoyed the respect of the Timurid sultan Abū Saʿīd (855-73/1451-69). He dedicated his well-known illuminationist commentary on *Hayākel al-nūr* by Sohravardī (d. 578/1191), entitled *Šawākel al-ḥūr fī šarḥ Hayākel al-nūr* (872/1468), and his *Anmūḏaj al-ʿolūm* (1411/1990-91, pp. 263-333) and *Resāla dar bayān-e māhīyat-e ʿadālat wa aḥkām-e ān* to Sultan Maḥmūd I of Gujarat (862-917/1458-1511). His *Eṯbāt al-wājeb al-qadīm* (apparently unpublished) was written for the Ottoman sultan Bāyazīd II (886-918/1481-1512; *al-Ḏarīʿa* I, pp. 106-07).

Davānī's work was criticized by Ṣadr-al-Dīn Moḥammad Daštakī (q.v.; d. 903/1498), another student of Golbārī. In 903/1497 a local coup against the Āq Qoyunlu ruler in Shiraz, Qāsem Beg Pornāk, whom both Davānī and Daštakī had supported, resulted in great material loss to both men (Ḵᵛānsārī, II, pp. 243-44; Ḥasan Rūmlū, I, p. 7). After their deaths Daštakī's son Ḡīāṯ-al-Dīn Manṣūr Daštakī (q.v.) continued his father's critique of Davānī's work. The arguments between Davānī and the Daštakīs generated glosses on Qūščī's commentary on *Tajrīd al-kalām*, on the commentary of Moḥammad b. Moḥammad Rāzī Bowayhī (d. 766/1365; *al-Ḏarīʿa* V, p. 132) on *Maṭāleʿ al-anwār* by Maḥmūd b. Abī Bakr Ormavī (d. 689/1290), and on Sohravardī's *Hayākel al-nūr*. Ḡīāṯ-al-Dīn also criticized Davānī's *Anmūḏaj al-ʿolūm.*

Davānī's religious proclivities in this period, like those of the Daštakī family, were the source of later dispute. Before Shah Esmāʿīl's capture of Tabrīz in 907/1501 and his establishment of Twelver Shiʿism as the state religion of Persia, Davānī referred in his *ʿArż-nāma* to Ozun Ḥasan as the "envoy of the 9th century" and "*ḡāzī* in the path of God." In his *Aḵlāq-e jalālī*, completed about 880/1475, he described the sultan as "the shadow of God, the caliph of God, and the deputy of the Prophet" (Woods, pp. 37, 101, 115-18). At another point, when questioned on the identity of "the imam of the age," he replied that the Sunnis believed it was Sultan Yaʿqūb and the Shiʿites the twelfth imam, Moḥammad b. Ḥasan (Šūštarī, fols. 206b-208a, ad. 7th *majles*; ʿA. Davānī, p. 185; Woods, pp. 151, 283 n. 56). Just two years earlier, in 905/1499, he had composed his *Šarḥ al-aqāʾed al-ʿażodīya*, an openly anti-Imamī Shiʿite commentary in a rationalist Ašʿarī vein.

In later sources, however, it was asserted that Davānī had been practicing *taqīya* (disguise of one's religion) during an especially chaotic period in Persian history. The authors of these sources cited his *Resālat al-zawrāʾ*, completed after he experienced a vision of Imam ʿAlī al-Reżā (q.v.) in Najaf in 872/1467, as evidence of his attachment to the Prophet's family; it includes poems in praise of the Imam and disavowing the first three caliphs. It was also criticized by Ḡīāṯ-al-Dīn Daštakī. Davānī's short *Nūr al-hedāya*, though undated, is avowedly Imami (Šūštarī, fol. 207a; Ḵᵛānsārī, II, p. 240; ʿA. Davānī, pp. 75-78, 173-87) and was almost certainly written as the Safavid shah Esmāʿīl I (907-30/1501-24) was advancing on Fārs. Nevertheless, Davānī is said to have rejected the shah's messianic claims (Ḵᵛānsārī, VII, pp. 194-95 n. 1, VIII, p. 71). In the event, Davānī died in November 1502 before the capture of Shiraz in 909/1504, when Sunni clerics who refused to convert to the new faith were put to death (Ḵᵛānsārī, VII, pp. 194-95 n. 1; ʿA. Davānī, pp. 182-84, 187-92). He is buried in Davān in a mausoleum known as Boqʿa-ye Šayḵ-e ʿĀlī.

Among Davānī's students were Kamāl-al-Dīn Ḥosayn Ardabīlī (d. 950/1543), also a pupil of Ḡīāṯ-al-Dīn Daštakī; Mīr Ḥosayn Yazdī (d. 910/1504), appointed chief judge of Yazd by Sultan Yaʿqūb; and Jamāl-al-Dīn Ḥosayn Moḥammad Estarābādī (d. 931/1525), who served jointly with Qewām-al-Dīn Eṣfahānī as *ṣadr* under Shah Ṭahmāsb (930-84/1524-76).

See also AḴLĀQ-E JALĀLĪ.

Bibliography: *Aʿyān al-šīʿa* XLIII, pp. 287-89; XVI, pp. 286-88; XLVIII, p. 116. Brockelman, *GAL* II, pp. 217-18; S II, pp. 306-09. Idem, "al-Dawwānī," in *EI*[1] I, p. 933. *al-Ḏarīʿa* I, pp. 106-07; IV, pp. 227-28; VI, pp. 67, 116, 132, 134; XII, pp. 63-64; XIII, pp. 138-39, 352; XIV, pp. 240-41; XVIII, pp. 359-60; XXIV, p. 385. ʿA. Davānī, *Šarḥ-e zendagānī-e Mollā Jalāl-al-Dīn Davānī* (with *Nūr al-hedāya*), Qom, 1334 Š./1956. Jalāl-al-Dīn Davānī, *Šarḥ al-aqāʾed al-ʿażodīya*, Delhi, 1898. Idem, *Aḵlāq-e jalālī*, Lahore, 1923; partial tr. W. F. Thompson as *Practical Philosophy of the Muhammadan People*, London, 1839; repr. Karachi, 1977. Idem, *Resālat al-zawrāʾ*, Tehran, 1364 Š./1943. Idem, *Resāla dar-bayān-e māhīyat-e ʿadālat wa aḥkām-e ān*, Tehran, 1324 Š./1945. Idem, *Šawākel al-ḥūr fī šarḥ Hayākel al-nūr*, ed. M. A. Haq and M. Y. Kokan, Madras, 1953. Idem, *ʿArż-nāma*, ed. Ī. Afšār as "ʿArż-e sepāh-e Ūzūn Ḥasan," *MDAT* 3/3, 1335 Š./1956, pp. 26-66; partial tr. V. Minorsky as "A Civil and Military Review in Fars in 881/1476," *BSOAS* 10/1, 1940, pp. 147-62. Idem, *Nūr al-hedāya*, Qom, 1375/1955. Idem, *Dīvān*, ed. Ḥ. ʿAlī, Baghdad, 1973. Idem, *Ḵalq al-afʿāl*, in *Kalemāt al-moḥaqqeqīn*, Tehran, 1402/1981, pp. 492-96. Idem, *Ṯalāṯ rasāʾel*, ed. S. A. Tūyserkānī, Qom, 1411/1990-91 (contains a list of Davānī's works). Moḥammad-ʿAlī b. Moḥammad-Nabī Davānī, "Resāla-ī dar šarḥ-e ḥāl-e Jalāl-al-Dīn Davānī," ed. M. Baḵtīār, *MDAT* 17, 1349 Š./1970, pp. 447-56. Fasāʾī, II, p. 250. *Fehrest-e ketāb-ḵāna-ye ehdāʾī-e Āqā Sayyed Moḥammad Meškāt ba ketāb-ḵāna-ye Dānešgāh-e Tehrān*, ed. ʿA.-N. Monzawī and M.-T. Dānešpažūh, Tehran, 1332/1952, I, pp. 47-48, 56-57; II, p. 581; III, pp. 10-11, 122-23, 232-34, 258-59, 271-72, 279-80, 290-91, 452-53, 464-65, 472-73, 523, 662, 667-72; V, pp. 37-38, 571-72, 705-06; VI, pp. 2219-20, 2240-51. *Ḥabīb al-sīar* IV, pp. 604-05, 607 n. Ḥasan Rūmlū, ed. Seddon, I, pp. 9, 71-72. Reżāqolī Hedāyat, *Rīāż al-ʿārefīn*, ed. M. Hedāyat, Tehran, 1316 /1898, pp. 328-30. Moḥammad-Bāqer Ḵᵛānsārī, *Rawżat al-jannāt*, ed. A. Esmāʿīlīān, II, Qom, 1390-92/1970-72, pp. 239-47. A. K. S. Lambton, "al-Dawānī," in *EI*[2] II, p. 174. Modarres, *Rayḥānat al-adab* II, pp. 232-36. Mošār, *Moʾallefīn* V, pp. 314-17. Nafīsī, *Naẓm o naṯr* I pp. 265-67. Aḥmad b. Šaraf-al-Dīn Ḥosayn Ḥosaynī Qomī, *Ḵolāṣat al-tawārīḵ*, ed. E. Ešrāqī, 2 vols., Tehran, 1359-63 Š./1980-84, I, pp. 78-79, 128, 160, 297, 422; II, p. 756. F. Rosenthal, *Political Thought in Medieval Islam*, Cambridge, 1958. Qāżī Nūr-Allāh b. ʿAbd-Allāh Šūštarī, *Majāles al-moʾmenīn*, Bodleian Library, ms. no. Ouseley 366. E. Wāʿez Jawādīpūr, "Davān kojā'st wa Davānī kī'st?" *Taḥqīq dar mabdaʾ-e āfarīneš* 1/3, 1341 Š./1962, pp. 26-34, 4, 99. 16-20. J. E. Woods, *The Aqquyunlu Clan, Confederation, Empire. A Study in 15th/9th Century Turko-Iranian Politics*, Minneapolis, Minn., 1976.

(ANDREW J. NEWMAN)

DĀVAR. See DĀTABARA.

DĀVAR, ʿALĪ-AKBAR (b. Tehran, 1302/1885, d. Tehran, 21 Bahman 1315 Š./10 February 1937), journalist, politician, statesman, and founder of the modern Persian judicial system, as well as of several state enterprises in the time of Reżā Shah (1304-20 Š/1925-41). He was the son of Kalb-ʿAlī Khan Ḵāzen Ḵalwat, a government employee, and was educated at the Dār al-fonūn (q.v.), from which he received his diploma in humanities in 1327/1909 (ʿĀqelī, pp. 12-13). With the help of the Persian Democratic party (Ferqā-ye demokrāt-e Īrān), he began his career at the Ministry of justice (Wezārat-e ʿadlīya), where he was appointed to the district court (Ṣadīq, p. 265). In 1328/1910, at the age of twenty-five years, he became district attorney for Tehran. In this period he also wrote political articles for the radical newspaper *Šarq*, which was edited by Sayyed Żīāʾ-al-Dīn Ṭabāṭabāʾī (ʿĀqelī, p. 16). In 1329/1911 Ḥājj Ebrāhīm Panāhī, a merchant in Tabrīz, provided financing for him to study in Switzerland while serving as guardian for Panāhī's minor child. In 1920 Dāvar received a law degree from the Université de Genève and became a doctoral candidate. After the announcement of the Anglo-Persian Agreement of 1919 (q.v.) he joined with other Persian intellectuals abroad in opposing it and wrote several newspaper articles (Afšār, pp. 454-74). Nevertheless, when the news of Żīāʾ-al-Dīn's coup d'etat of 1299 Š./1921 (q.v.) reached him in Switzerland Dāvar abandoned work on his doctoral thesis in law and returned to Persia to enter politics. He first became director of public education and then director-general of the Ministry of education (Wezārat-e maʿāref; Ṣadīq, p. 268).

In the elections of 1301 Š./1922 Dāvar became representative for Varāmīn to the Fourth Majles. During this period he briefly published the newspaper *Mard-e āzād*, for which he wrote radical editorials read mostly by the Persian intelligentsia (K̲ᵛāja Nūrī, p. 10); organized 330 young intellectuals in the Radical party (Ḥezb-e rādīkāl; ʿĀqelī, p. 33); and formed a group in the Majles to support the minister of war, Reżā Khan (Bahār, II, p. 91). In the elections for the Fifth Majles in 1303 Š./1924 he became deputy from Lār. Five other members of the Radical party were also elected. Dāvar rose to prominence in the Majles and joined with ʿAbd-al-Ḥosayn Teymūrtāš, and Fīrūz Mīrzā Fīrūz (Noṣrat-al-Dawla) to lead support for Reżā Khan. On 25 Bahman 1303 Š./14 February 1925 Dāvar presented a bill to appoint Reżā Khan commander-in-chief of the army. On 9 Ābān 1304 Š./31 October 1925 he also introduced legislation to depose the Qajar dynasty and entrust the state to Reżā Khan, pending the convening of a constituent assembly (Majles-e moʾassesān) to amend certain articles in the Addendum to the Constitution (q.v.). Eighty of eighty-five deputies in the Majles had cosigned the bill. In this historic session of the Majles it was Dāvar who gave detailed replies to questions raised by Sayyed Ḥasan Modarres and Dr. Moḥammad Moṣaddeq (Amīr Ṭahmāsbī, pp. 248-67; ʿĀqelī, pp. 71-85; Makkī, p. 337). He was then put in charge of organizing the constituent assembly and became spokesman for the Committee to amend the constitutional law (Komīsīūn-e moṭāleʿa), which paved the way for transfer of kingship to Reżā Khan and his descendants (Ṣadīq, 1352 Š./1973b, pp. 303-05; Amīr Ṭahmāsbī, pp. 427, 507, 615-17).

Under Reżā Shah Dāvar became head of the Ministry of public utilities and trade (Wezārat-e fawāʾed-e ʿāmma wa tejārat) in the cabinet of Moḥammad-ʿAlī Forūḡī (28 Āḏar 1304 Š./19 December 1925). In this position he oversaw preparations for constructing the Persian railroad. He founded a school of business, the Madrasa-ye tejārat, in Tehran and laid the foundations for a Persian chamber of commerce (q.v.). In 1305 Š./1926 he was again elected representative from Lār to the Sixth Majles (ʿĀqelī, p. 91), and in February 1927 he was appointed minister of justice in the cabinet of Ḥasan Mostawfī.

The judicial system established in 1324/1906-07 by Mīrzā Ḥasan Khan Mošīr-al-Dawla had evolved gradually, but it still suffered from organizational deficiencies, particularly the proliferation of religious and secular jurisdictions and absence of a uniform legal code, most notably in civil and criminal areas. In 1306 Š./1927 the government decided to revoke capitulations (q.v.) to foreign powers, which had permitted their citizens to be tried in special courts, and to bring the entire judiciary under Persian control; in exchange the foreign powers insisted that the government take measures to centralize and modernize the Persian judicial system (Komīsīūn-e mellī, p. 993). Dāvar seized this opportunity, and on 27 Bahman 1305 Š./17 February 1927 he was granted discretion by the Majles to compile a new legal code on the basis of reformed principles and to select a body of qualified judges. Dāvar appointed committees of experts to formulate new legislation; in a very short period 120 separate legal bills were ratified by the judiciary committee of the Majles. The most important was the civil code (q.v.), and in addition there were the basic judicial law, the criminal code, the commercial code, and the code for religious courts (Ṣadīq, 1352 Š./1973a, p. 126). On 5 Ordībehešt 1306 Š./25 April 1927 the new legal system was inaugurated in the presence of Reżā Shah, who at the same time officially terminated the capitulations (Šafā, I, p. 56).

In the seven years that he served as minister of justice Dāvar founded new courts throughout Persia and selected suitable judges, both from among those already serving and from among qualified religious jurists (*mojtaheds*) and government employees. It was also he who organized the recording of documents and properties in appropriate registries (see DAFTAR-E ASNĀD-E RASMĪ). Other achievements included combining the ministerial schools of law and political science into the Higher school of law and political science (Madrasa-ye ʿālī-e ḥoqūq wa ʿolūm-e sīāsī) under the supervision of the Ministry of education, in 1306 Š./1927, and organizing courses in jurisprudence in the Ministry of justice. Dāvar also formulated rules and regulations for the office of defense attorney (ʿĀqelī, pp. 188-89).

The most important criticism of Dāvar's performance as minister of justice was that he retained for himself power to intervene in the judgments of the courts and to remove disobedient judges; this power was embodied in an amendment weakening Article 82 of the Constitutional law, which had established an independent judiciary. The amendment was ratified by the Majles judiciary committee on 26 Mordād 1310 Š./17 August 1931 (Afšār, pp. 363-71; for some cases under the amendment, see Kasrawī, pp. 256-57, 272, 288-90, 305-40).

In 1311 Š./1932 the Persian government unilaterally abrogated the oil treaty with the British (see ANGLO-PERSIAN OIL COMPANY), who filed a complaint with the Permanent Court of International Justice. The Persian government denied the jurisdiction of the court over its internal affairs, and the British appealed to the Council of the League of Nations. In February Dāvar headed a delegation to Geneva to respond to the complaint; the defense was successful, and the court found in favor of Persia, denying the court jurisdiction (Fāteḥ, p. 292; ʿĀqelī, pp. 207-41).

In September Dāvar was appointed minister of finance in the cabinet of Moḥammad-ʿAlī Forūḡī. During the next five years he strove to strengthen the Persian economy, founding or enlarging numerous state enterprises and monopolies. He instituted barter transactions with Germany and the Soviet Union, exporting agricultural products in exchange for industrial goods. In order to promote and standardize exports and to streamline the distribution system, he also centralized the management of state companies (Wakīlī, pp. 32-98). Forūḡī's government resigned in 1314 Š./1935, and Dāvar expected to be named prime minister; instead the shah appointed Maḥmūd Jam, reappointing Dāvar as minister of finance. Dāvar considered this choice a sign of the shah's disfavor and feared for his life. Fear and the increasing pressures of work, especially the problem of ensuring sufficient grain for Tehran in the drought year 1315 Š./1936, contributed to his suicide from an overdose of opium in February 1937 (Taqīzāda, pp. 220-22).

Dāvar was a capable, ambitious, and courageous statesman, devoted to his work. As a politician, he was machiavellian, believing that the end justifies the means (Afšār, pp. 457-59; Golšāʾīān, pp. 611-22). Aside from his judicial and economic reforms, his legacy included his influence on a group of capable administrators of the next generation, including ʿAlī Amīnī, ʿAbbāsqolī Golšāʾīān, Aḥmad Matīn Daftarī, and Allāhyār Ṣāleḥ.

Bibliography: M. Afšār Yazdī, *Sīāsat-e Orūpā dar Īrān*, tr. Żīāʾ-al-Dīn Dehšīrī, Tehran, 1357 Š./1978, pp. 454-74. ʿA. Amīr Ṭahmāsbī, *Tārīḵ-e šāhanšāhī-e aʿlāḥażrat Reżā Šāh Pahlavī*, Tehran, 1305 Š./1926. B. ʿĀqelī, *Dāvar wa ʿadlīya*, Tehran, 1369 Š./1990. M.-T. Bahār, *Tārīḵ-e moḵtaṣar-e aḥzāb-e sīāsī-e Īrān* II, Tehran, 1363 Š./1984. Bāmdād, *Rejal*, II, pp. 427-29. "Faʿʿālīyathā-ye sīāsī-e ʿAlī-Akbar Dāvar dar Orūpā," *Āyanda* 5, 1358 Š./1979, pp. 305-13. M. Fāteḥ, *Panjāh sāl naft-e Īrān*, Tehran, 1335 Š./1956. Fīrūz Mīrzā Fīrūz, *Majmūʿa-ye mokātabāt, asnād, ḵāṭerāt wa āṯār-e Fīrūz Mīrzā Fīrūz (Noṣrat-al-Dawla)*, ed. M. Etteḥādīya (Neẓām Māfī) and S. Saʿdvandīān, 2 vols., Tehran, 1369-70 Š./1990-91, index, s.v. Dāvar. ʿA. Golšāʾīān, "Yāddāšthā-ī čand rājeʿ be marḥūm-e Dāvar," in Q. Ḡanī, *Yāddāšthā-ye Doktor Qāsem Ḡanī*, ed. S. Ḡanī, XI, London, 1984, pp. 607-52. M. Hedāyat, *Ḵāṭerāt wa ḵaṭarāt*, Tehran, 1329 Š./1950. E. Ḵᵛāja Nūrī, *Bāzīgarān-e ʿaṣr-e ṭelāʾī. Dāvar*, Tehran, 1357 Š/1978. A. Kasrawī, *Zendagānī-e man, dah sāl dar ʿadlīya, čerā az ʿadlīya bīrūn āmadam*, Piedmont, Calif., 1990. Komīsīūn-e mellī-e Yūnesko (UNESCO), *Īrānšahr* II, Tehran, 1347 Š./1968, p. 997. Ḥ. Makkī, *Tārīḵ-e bīst sāla-ye Īrān* III, Tehran, 1357 Š/1978. R. Pahlavī, *Safar-nāma-ye Ḵūzestān*, Tehran, 2535=1355 Š./1976. ʿĪ. Ṣadīq, "ʿAlī-Akbar Dāvar," in ʿĪ. Ṣadīq, *Čehel goftār*, Tehran, 1352 Š./1973a, pp. 119-29; repr. *Rāhnemā-ye ketāb* 16, 1352 Š./1973, pp. 745-53. Idem, *Yādgār-e ʿomr* I, Tehran, 1352 Š./1973b. [Š. Šafā, ed.], *Gāh-nāma-ye panjāh sāl šāhanšāhī-e Pahlavī*, 5 vols., Paris, n.d. (1364 Š./1985?). Ṣ.-Ḥ. Taqīzāda, *Zendagī-e ṭūfānī. Ḵāṭerāt-e Sayyed Ḥasan Taqīzāda*, ed. Ī. Afšār, Tehran, 1367 Š./1988, pp. 216-49. ʿA. Wakīlī, *Dāvar wa šerkat-e markazī*, Tehran, 1343 Š/1964.

(BĀQER ʿĀQELĪ)

DĀVARĪ ŠĪRĀZĪ, MĪRZĀ MOḤAMMAD (b. Shiraz 1238/1822-23, d. Shiraz, 1283/1866), poet, calligrapher, and painter of some renown in Qajar Persia and a contemporary of Moḥammad Shah (1250-64/1834-48) and Nāṣer-al-Dīn Shah (1264-1313/1848-96). He was the third son of the famous poet and calligrapher Mīrzā Moḥammad-Ṣafī Weṣāl, with whom he studied Arabic grammar and theology; he also studied with his older brother Aḥmad Weqār. Dāvarī tried his hand at various kinds of poetry, but he excelled at *qaṣīda*s (odes). Some of his *qaṣīda*s rank among the best known in Persian; they also attest to his mastery of Arabic language and literature. In addition, he was well versed in Turkish and composed several *qeṭʿa*s (fragments) in that language. In fact, his *molammaʿāt*—verses with *meṣrāʿ*s (hemistichs) or *bayt*s (distichs) in alternating languages—in Persian, Arabic, and Turkish are among the finest in that genre. His other works include a *dīvān* of about 15,000 verses, *Resāla dar ʿelm-e ʿarūż*, *Resāla dar maʿānī wa bayān*, and an unpublished Turkish-Persian dictionary, the whereabouts of which do not appear to be known (Dāvarī Šīrāzī, introd., pp. 15, 29).

Dāvarī was also a master of *nastaʿlīq* calligraphy (q.v.) and a painter. The best specimen of his calligraphy is a copy of the *Šāh-nāma* now preserved in the Reżā ʿAbbāsī Museum in Tehran. It took him five years to finish and includes drawings by himself and the painter Loṭf-ʿAlī, as well as one drawing by Dāvarī's brother Farhang. At the end of the manuscript there is a beautiful *maṯnawī* by Dāvarī in which he described his five-year labor. Individual portraits by him are preserved in several public and private collections. After the death of his brother Ḥakīm (1239-74/1824-58) he traveled to Tehran to be received at the court of Nāṣer-al-Dīn Shah; the shah granted him a generous lifetime annuity (Dāvarī Šīrāzī, introd., p. 21).

According to several anecdotes, Dāvarī had a short temper and was quick to take offense. He was pious and devoted to the Shiʿite imams, whom he eulogized in several *qaṣīda*s and *maṯnawī*s. He is buried in the shrine of Sayyed Mīr Aḥmad at Shiraz.

Bibliography: Browne, *Lit. Hist. Persia* IV, pp. 319-22. Dāvarī Šīrāzī, *Dīvān-e Dāvarī*, ed. ʿA. Nūrānī Weṣāl, Tehran, 1370 Š./ 1991, pp. 9-30. Aḥmad b. Abu'l-Ḥasan Dīvānbegī, *Ḥadīqat-al-šoʿarāʾ*, ed. ʿA-Ḥ. Navāʾī, Tehran, 1366 Š./1987, pp. 604-13. N. Ḵosravānī, "Dāvarī Šīrāzī," *Armaḡān* 11, 1309 Š./1930, pp. 201-06. Y. Māhyār Nawwābī, *Ḵāndan-e Weṣāl Šīrāzī*, Tabrīz, 1335 Š./1956. ʿA. Rūḥānī Weṣāl, *Golšān-e Weṣāl*, Tehran, 1319 Š./1940, pp. 294-300.

(ʿABD-AL-WAHHĀB NŪRĀNĪ WEṢĀL)

DAVĀZDAH EMĀMĪ. See SHIʿISM.

DAVĀZDAH HŌMĀST. See Supplement.

DAVĀZDAH ROḴ (Twelve combats), designation of a relatively long episode in the *Šāh-nāma* (2,500 verses; Moscow, V, pp. 86-234), in which a battle takes place on the borders of Tūrān between Iranians under the command of Gūdarz and Turanians under the command of Pīrān. The battle begins when Hūmān, a brother of Pīrān, challenges the Iranians and is killed by Bīžan, Gūdarz's grandson, in single combat. Then the two armies join in an inconclusive battle. Finally the two sides agree that the battle should be decided by single combat between eleven pairs of heroes from the two armies. In each encounter the Iranian warrior kills his adversary, and in the eleventh Pīrān is slain by Gūdarz. Then Gostaham, an Iranian hero who had not been chosen by Gūdarz for single combat, sets off in pursuit of Pīrān's two brothers and kills them in a fight. He himself is seriously wounded, however, and is taken by Bīžan to Kay Ḵosrow, who saves his life by tying his own armlet, which has healing powers, around Gostaham's arm and appointing physicians to tend him.

The story is one of the finest in the *Šāh-nāma*, in terms of plot, dramatic description, and insight into human nature. In some manuscripts it is entitled "Yāzdah roḵ," referring to the eleven single combats; in others "Davāzdah Roḵ," including the battle between Gostaham and Pīrān's brothers as the twelfth combat; and in still others "Razm-e Gūdarz o Pīrān" (Battle of Gūdarz and Pīrān).

Bibliography: J. Ḵāleqī-Moṭlaq, "Dar bāra-ye ʿonwān-e Davāzdah roḵ," in Ḥ Yaḡmāʾī, ed., *Moḥīṭ-e adab. Bozorgdāšt-nāma-ye Sayyed Moḥammad Moḥīṭ Ṭabāṭabāʾī*, Tehran, 1358 Š./1978, pp. 156-63.

(DJALAL KHALEGHI-MOTLAGH)

DAWĀ. See DRUGS.

DAWĀ(T)DĀR (lit., "keeper, bearer of [the royal] inkwell or inkstand"), title of various officials in medieval Islamic states.

At an early stage in the development of the vizierate under the ʿAbbasid caliphs the vizier bore an inkstand (*dawāt*) as emblem of his office; it was usually suspended from the wrist on a chain and carried in a sleeve or, in a slimmer version (*dawāt laṭīfa*), in his boot (Helāl Ṣābeʾ, pp. 66-68; tr. pp. 55-56; cf. Mez, pp. 91-92). The *dawāt-e wezārat* was still one of the insignia of the viziers of the Saljuq sultan of Anatolia (Ebn Bībī, apud Uzunçarşılı, pp. 96, 98-99).

From the ʿAbbasids the emblem and associated functions must have passed to the provincial successor dynasties of the Iranian world, though the process is barely documented. Sīmjūr, the prominent Turkish slave commander of the Samanid Esmāʿīl b. Aḥmad (279-95/892-907), is designated in the sources *dawātī* (Gardīzī, ed. Ḥabībī, p. 149: *davītdār/divītdār*), probably because of some civil function that he exercised as a tax collector in the Herat region (Merçil, p. 73). In the Ghaznavid administration one of the responsibilities of the *dawātdār*, an official of the Dīvān-e wezārat, seems to have been keeping records of important official documents (Nāẓim, p. 131).

Under the Great Saljuqs the *dawātdār* was at first a civilian official, but, as with many household and some nominally administrative posts (e.g., custodianship of the royal wardrobe, the washing bowls, etc.), it tended to fall into the hands of the Turkish military. Hence Żīāʾ-al-Dīn Qara Arslān is mentioned as *amīr-e dawāt* for the Saljuq sultan ʿEzz-al-Dīn Keykāvūs I (607-16/1210-19; Ebn Bībī, apud Uzunçarşılı, p. 91). When the office was developed to its full extent under the Mamluks of Egypt and Syria, the *dawādār* was invariably a Turkish and later a Circassian *mamlūk* and one of the principal commanders of the state, functioning, inter alia, as master of ceremonies at court (Maqrīzī, I/1, p. 118; Ebn Ḵaldūn, II, pp. 12, 24; tr., II, pp. 15-16, 28).

The title was continued under the Ottomans; in Safavid Persia, however, the *dawātdār*s were officials of only moderate rank and emoluments. According to *Taḏkerat al-molūk* (tr. Minorsky, pp. 63, 89, 133), there were both a *dawātdār-e mohr-e angoštar* (or *dawātdār-e aḥkām*) and a *dawātdār-e arqām*, whose duties included affixing seals to official documents.

Bibliography: Ḥ. Anwārī, *Eṣṭelāḥāt-e dīvānī-e dawra-ye ḡaznavī wa saljūqī*, Tehran, 2535=1355 Š./1976, pp. 37-38. D. Ayalon, "Dawādār," in *EI*[2] II, p. 172. W. Björkman, *Beiträge zur Geschichte der Staatskanzlei im islamischen Ägypten*, Hamburg, 1928, index, s.v. *dawādār*. Ebn Ḵaldūn, *Moqaddema*, ed. E. Quatremère, Paris, 1858; tr. F. Rosenthal as *The Muqaddimah. An Introduction to History*, 3 vols., New York, 1958. Helāl Ṣābeʾ, *Rosūm dār al-ḵelāfa*, ed. M. ʿAwwād, Baghdad, 1383/1964; tr. E. A. Salem as *The Rules and Regulations of the ʿAbbāsid Court*, Beirut, 1977. Maqrīzī, *al-Solūk le-maʿrefat al-molūk*, ed. E. Quatremère as *Histoire des Sultans Mamlouks de l'Egypte*, 2 vols., Paris, 1837-45. E. Merçil, "Sîmcûrîler. I. Sîmcûr ed-Devâtî," *Tarih Dergisi* 32, 1979, pp. 71-88. A. Mez, *The Renaissance of Islam*, tr. S. Khuda Bukhsh, Patna, 1937. M. Nāẓim, *The Life and Times of Sulṭan Maḥmūd of Ghazna*, Cambridge, 1931. İ. H. Uzunçarşılı, *Osmanlı devleti teşkilâtına medhal*, Istanbul, 1941, p. 49 and index, s.v. *Devâdar*.

(C. EDMUND BOSWORTH)

DAWĀMĪ, ʿABD-ALLĀH (b. Ṭā near Tafreš, 1309/1891; d. Tehran, 20 Dey 1359 Š./10 January 1981), a master of classical Persian vocal music with a perfect command of the *radīf* (repertoire), as well as a gifted player of the Persian drum (*tonbak*) and a virtuoso of rhythmic (*żarbī*) pieces and songs (*taṣnīf*). His father, Abu'l-Qāsem, was a performer in *taʿzīa* (the Shiʿite passion play) and a singer. Dawāmī received his early education from the village mullas. At the age of nine years he went to Tehran, where he studied at the Tarbīat school. After his graduation in 1325/1907 he was hired by the Ministry of post and telegraphs (Wezārat-e post o telegrāf) but was dismissed seven years later, in 1332/1914, because he had taken unauthorized leave to accompany Darvīš Khan (q.v.) to Europe in order to produce musical recordings. After his return to Persia he went to work in the Ministry of finance (Wezārat-e dārāʾī), where he remained until his retirement in 1323 Š./1944 (ʿAskarī; Loṭfī, p. 10; Wayszāda, 1356 Š./1977a; Mašḥūn, p. 47).

Dawāmī did not receive a systematic musical education; rather he learned melodies at first hearing and continued practicing until he could sing them perfectly (Ḵāleqī, p. 409). He was introduced to the social circles of Tehran by Rokn-al-Dīn Moḵtār, a fellow student at the Tarbīat school and a skilled musician, who admired his singing. In this new milieu Dawāmī met the prominent singer ʿAlī Khan Nāyeb-al-Salṭana, with whom he studied for three years (ʿAskarī; Loṭfī, pp. 10-11; Wayszāda, 1356 Š./1977a). It was also through his association with Moḵtār that he met all the great musicians of the period, including Darvīš Khan, who, impressed by Dawāmī's skill in singing and playing the Persian drum, invited him to join his orchestra, which included the master vocalist Sayyed Ḥosayn Ṭāherzāda, as well as Mošīr Homāyūn Ḥabīb-Allāh Šahrdār (Wayszāda, 1356 Š./1977a).

In 1332/1914, in response to an offer from the Baidaphon company in Germany, Darvīš Khan, Dawāmī, and several other musicians left for Berlin, planning to travel via Russia. Owing to the outbreak of World War I, however, they were forced to stop in Tiflis, where they produced a few recordings, which they sent to Berlin. One of these recordings, of which a copy is kept in the archives of Radio Iran, is a song by ʿĀref (q.v.; Wayszāda, 1356 Š./1977a).

Dawāmī remained actively involved in music, collaborating with Darvīš Khan and Ṭāherzāda, until the coup d'état of 1299/1921 (q.v.), when he decided to withdraw from the musical scene. The reason he gave for such an early retirement was his fear that, because musicians were at that time not appreciated as artists in Persia, his public involvement in music could jeopardize his career at the ministry. He later refused an offer to join Radio Tehran (Wayszāda, 1356 Š./1977a). The real reason, however, may have been his voice, which was not much appreciated by the public and had already earned him the nickname ʿAbd-Allāh Do-dāng (ʿAbd-Allāh Two Notes; Šahrdār, p. 39) because of its narrow range.

In the 1950s-70s Dawāmī once again returned to the musical mainstream and made an important contribution by training outstanding students and recording the *radīf*s and *gūšas* of traditional Persian music. In 1330 Š./1951 the Department of fine arts (Edāra-ye koll-e honarhā-ye zībā) initiated evening music classes under the direction of Moḵtār, who invited Dawāmī to teach singing. In 1350 Š./1971 Dawāmī recorded his repertoire of *radīf*s on six tapes, running a total of three hours, for the Ministry of culture and fine arts (Wezārat-e farhang o honar). In 1354 Š./1975 he accepted an offer from the Center for preservation and dissemination of Persian music (Markaz-e ḥefẓ o ešāʿa-ye mūsīqī-e īrānī) to teach singing, which he continued to do until his death. He was also asked by the Center to record any early song that he could remember. His former student the renowned vocalist Moḥammad-Reżā Šajarīān was assigned to supervise the recording sessions, which took place during 1356-57 Š./1977-78, but the tapes were never delivered to the Center. Furthermore, Šajarīān recorded, and now has in his possession, close to 140 *taṣnīf*s sung by Dawāmī (Šajarīān, pp. 161-64).

Among the other notable students trained by Dawāmī are Maḥmūd Karīmī, Marżīya, Ḵāṭera Parvāna, Parīsā, Ḥosayn ʿAlīzāda, Parvīz Meškātīān, and Nūr-al-Dīn Rażawī Sarvestānī (Loṭfī, p. 13; Wayszāda, 1356a; Šajarīān, pp. 156-57).

Bibliography: Ḥ. ʿAskarī, personal interview, 1370 Š./1991. Š. Behrūzī, *Čehrahā-ye mūsīqī-e Īrān* I, Tehran, 1367 Š./1988, pp. 360-68. J. During and Z. Abdolbaghi, *The Art of Persian Music*, Washington, D.C., 1991, pp. 38, 175, 219-21. R. Ḵāleqī, *Sargoḏašt-e mūsīqī-e Īrān* I, Tehran, 1333 Š./1954. M.-R. Loṭfī, *Mūsīqī-e āvāzī-e Īrān (Dastgāh-e šūr). Radīf-e Ostād ʿAbd-Allāh Dawāmī*, Tehran, 1354 Š./1975. Ḥ. Mašḥūn, "Naẓar-ī be mūsīqī-e żarbī-e Īrān" in Sāzmān-e jašn-e honar, *Do maqāla dar bāra-ye mūsīqī-e Īrān*, Shiraz, 1348 Š./1969, pp. 3-54. Ḥ. Naṣīrīfar, *Mardān-e mūsīqī-e sonnatī wa novīn-e Īrān* I, Tehran, 1369 Š./1370. ʿA. Šaʿbānī, *Šenāsāʾī-e mūsīqī-e Īrān*, Tehran, 1351 Š./1972, pp. 187-88. Ḥ. Mošīr Homāyūn Šahrdār, "Pīānū dar mūsīqī-e Īrān," in A. Jāhed, ed., *Dīvān-e Amīr Jāhed* I, Tehran, 1333 Š./1954, p. 33. M.-R. Šajarīān, "Dar kenār-e Ostād Dawāmī," *Kelk* 22, 1370 Š./1991, pp. 156-64. S. Sepantā, *Čašmandāz-e mūsīqī-e Īrān*, Tehran, 1356 Š./1977. Idem, *Tārīḵ-e taḥawwol-e żabṭ-e mūsīqī dar Īrān*, Isfahan, 1366 Š./1987. S. Wayszāda, "Mūsīqī-e īrānī be kojā mīravad? Goftogū bā Ostād ʿAbd-Allāh Dawāmī pedar-e āvāz-e Īrān," *Eṭṭelāʿāt*, 6 Dey 1356 Š./27 December 1977a, p. 21. Idem, "Emkān-e talfīq-e šeʿr-e now wa mūsīqī-e īrānī. Goftogū bā Ostād ʿAbd-Allāh Dawāmī," *Eṭṭelāʿāt*, 8 Dey 1356 Š./29 December 1977b, pp. 21, 25.

(DARIUSH SAFVAT)

DAWĀT (inkwell), a utilitarian receptacle that also served as a symbol or metaphor for the instrument of state, with a long history in Islamic Persia (see DAWĀ(T)DĀR). As a container for ink the *dawāt* could be attached to, or set within, a pencase (*qalamdān*); free standing; or carried suspended from a belt. Practical considerations dictated that the container be cylindrical, in order to prevent the accumulation of dried ink and other matter in the corners. Inkwells from early Islamic Persia have been preserved in glass, pottery, and bronze or brass (Allan, 1982b, p. 44). The metal versions, of which the earliest extant examples are dated to the 10th or 11th century, are by far the most numerous (Allan, 1982a, p. 32; idem, 1982b, pp. 44-45; Melikian-Chirvani, 1986, pp. 73-74); the vast majority of those surviving belong to the 12th-16th centuries. Because the cylindrical boxes usually have domical lids they resemble miniature architectural monuments.

The cylindrical containers from 12th- and early 13th-century Persia, which perhaps most closely resemble contemporary tomb towers, have flat shoulders on which the "drums" of the lobed domical lids rest; the latter are surmounted by knobbed finials (Plate VIII). Some well-preserved inkwells of this type have three trilobed loops attached about halfway up the wall of the container and three corresponding horizontal loops on the vertical rim of the lid; cords strung vertically through these loops made it possible for the inkwell to be suspended. This arrangement differed from that prevailing in the earlier 10th- or 11th-century versions, which were equipped with internal vertical channels, from base to lid, for suspension (Allan, 1982a, p. 32; Melikian-Chirvani, 1986, fig. 2).

The 12th- and early 13th-century inkwells are generally inlaid with figural, abstract, and epigraphic ornament in silver and copper. Most of them have been attributed to Khorasan or Transoxania, on the basis of

PLATE VIII

Bronze inkwell inlaid with silver and copper, Khorasan, late 12th or early 13th century, signed Moḥammad al-Bayyāʿ. The Metropolitan Museum of Art, New York, Rogers Fund, 1935, no. 35.128 a, b.

both the ornament and the content and style of the inscriptions (see, e.g., Allan, 1982a, pp. 32 ff.; Melikian-Chirvani, 1986, pp. 75-78). Characteristic decorative features include friezes of figures or medallions enclosing astrological symbols, with pacing animals (real or fantastic) or rows of birds as subsidiary motifs. The abstract ornament includes knots and arabesques. The heads of dragons, hares, or even bovines are frequently inserted among figures and within abstract ornament. Animated inscriptions in Arabic are also characteristic of metalwork from this region; they are usually invocations with a standardized vocabulary and word order (Melikian-Chirvani, 1982, p. 117).

Inkwells were characterized in Persian poetry and historical works from the 10th century on as symbols of royal and by extension ministerial office, a notion perhaps dating back to Sasanian Persia. For example, the early 12th-century Persian poet from Khorasan Adīb Ṣāber Termeḏī referred to the inkwell as an instrument of government (*dawāt . . . ālat-e dawlat ast*), punning on the dual meaning of the word *dawlat* as "good fortune" and "government" (Melikian-Chirvani, 1986, pp. 70-71). It has been proposed that certain extant inkwells of the 12th and 13th centuries, expressing celestial and royal symbolism through both their decoration and Arabic inscriptions, may in fact represent the so-called "state inkwell" (*dawāt-e dawlat*). Such identifications should be regarded as tentative, however, as very similar inscriptions are found on a variety of contemporary and later objects without clear royal contexts (e.g., Komaroff, 1992, pp. 63, 76 n. 108, 147, 166-67). Furthermore, the depiction of such scenes of "royal" entertainment as wine drinking and musicians are also found on other kinds of contemporary objects, most notably the so-called "Bobrinsky bucket" of 559/1163, now in the Hermitage, St. Petersburg; it was probably made for a religious dignitary (for the latest reading of the inscriptons, see Melikian-Chirvani, 1982, pp. 71, 82-83 nn. 61-62). Not all such objects were produced for patrons of royal or ministerial rank, as is clear from one late 12th- or early 13th-century example decorated with three figural cartouches, in one of which a seated figure is shown writing; it is accompanied by the Persian inscription "for the teacher" (*moʿallem-rā*; Melikian-Chirvani, 1982, p. 124).

This general type of inkwell, with some variations, seems to have been produced into the 14th century. Some of the later versions are not clearly of Persian provenience, however, and may represent Mesopotamian, Syrian, or Egyptian workmanship (see, e.g., Melikian-Chirvani, 1986, figs. 14-16).

Several smaller cylindrical inkwells with bulbous, dome-shaped covers (Plate IX) survive from the 16th and 17th centuries (Komaroff, 1992, pp. 255-56, 260-61, figs. 35, 51, 54-56); two of them, one of brass inlaid with silver and gold and the other of silver inlaid with semiprecious stones, are still attached to tubular pencases (*Survey of Persian Art*, pl. 1387A; Rogers, no. 110). This type of combined inkwell and pencase was also known in the 15th century and is depicted in

PLATE IX

Brass inkwell inlaid with silver, Persia, early 16th century, signed Mīrak Ḥosayn Yazdī. Victoria & Albert Museum, London, no. 454-1888. Photograph L. Komaroff.

Timurid manuscript illustrations (Komaroff, pp. 124, 131 n. 29). The identical Persian poetic inscriptions on three extant inkwells of this type (see, e.g., Plate IX), all signed by the same craftsman, Mīrak Ḥosayn Yazdī, suggest that they may well have been intended as "state inkwells." One poem includes the phrase *dawāt-e dawlat* and an indication that it is through the inkwell that the affairs of the world may be resolved. According to a second, the inkwell is used for the sultan's signature, suggesting that these three inkwells were perhaps commissioned by, or for, the first Safavid ruler, Shah Esmāʿīl I (907-30/1501-24; Melikian-Chirvani, 1986, pp. 81-83).

Bibliography: J. W. Allan, *Islamic Metalwork. The Nuhad Es-Said Collection*, London, 1982a. Idem, *Nishapur. Metalwork of the Early Islamic Period*, New York, 1982b. E. Baer, "An Islamic Inkwell in the Metropolitan Museum of Art," in R. Ettinghausen, ed., *Islamic Art in the Metropolitan Museum of Art*, New York, 1972, pp. 199-211. Idem, *Metalwork in Medieval Islamic Art*, Albany, N.Y., 1983. L. Komaroff, *The Golden Disk of Heaven. Metalwork of Timurid Iran*, Costa Mesa, Calif., 1992. A. S. Melikian-Chirvani, *Islamic Metalwork from the Iranian World, 8-18th Centuries*, London, 1982. Idem, "State Inkwells in Islamic Iran," *The Journal of the Walters Art Gallery* 44, 1986, pp. 74-94. J. M. Rogers, ed. and tr., *The Topkapı Saray Museum. The Treasury*, Boston, 1987.

(LINDA KOMAROFF)

DAʿWAT AL-ESLĀM, a biweekly Persian journal published in Bombay by Ḥājj Sayyed Moḥammad Dāʿī-al-Eslām (q.v.) from 1 Ramażān 1324/19 October 1906 until the end of 1326/1909; it was the organ of an association of the same name, which had its center in Bombay. The journal was religious, and its contributors engaged in polemics against faiths other than Islam and against other, more nationalist Persian publications in India. It also included world news and news about Indian Muslims. It was frequently endorsed by ranking religious leaders and received financial assistance from wealthy believers.

All the articles in the first issue were published in both Persian and Urdu. Beginning with the second issue, the articles were published in Persian with a supplement in Urdu, consisting mainly of translations of the Persian articles. The first fourteen issues were lithographed on sixteen double-column pages, measuring 12.5 by 28 cm; the remainder were set in type and measured 16.5 by 19.5 cm. There were no illustrations. The title page contained the name and address of the paper, subscription price, and date of publication. The annual subscription rate for India was 3 rupees with the Urdu supplement and 2 rupees without it (3 annas for a single issue), for Persia 1 toman, for the Ottoman empire 1 *majīdī*, for the Caucasus and Turkestan 2 rubles, and for other regions 4.5 French francs.

Serial collections are kept in the central library of Tehran University, the library of Āstān-e qods-e rażawī in Mašhad, the Asia Institute at Shiraz, the library of the University of Cambridge, and the Bibliothèque Nationale at Versailles.

Daʿwat al-Eslām was also the name of an underground newspaper published in Tehran during the month of Rabīʿ I 1327/March 1909.

Bibliography: Browne, *Press and Poetry*, pp. 85-86. N. Dānešvar ʿAlawī, *Tārīḵ-e mašrūṭa-ye Īrān o jonbeš-e waṭanparastān-e Eṣfahān o Baḵtīārī*, Tehran, 1335 Š./1956. I. Hamed, "Un journal persan de l'Inde," *RMM* 2, 1908, p. 146. H. Mawlānā, *Sayr-e ertebāṭāt-e ejtemāʿī dar Īrān*, Tehran, 1358 Š./1969, p. 114. Bāmdād, *Rejāl* VI, pp. 255-56. H. L. Rabino, *Ṣūrat-e jarāyed-e Īrān wa jarāyed-ī ke dar ḵārej az Īrān be zabān-e fārsī ṭabʿ šoda ast*, Rašt, 1329/1911. Ṣadr Hāšemī, *Jarāʾed o majallāt* II, pp. 290-92. U. Sims-Williams, *Union Catalogue of Persian Serials and Newspapers in British Libraries*, London, 1985, p. 119. G. Šokrī, "Fehrest-e rūznāmahā wa majallahā-ye fārsī dar moʾassesa-ye Āsīaʾī-e Dānešgāh-e Šīrāz," *FIZ* 27, 1366 Š./1987, p. 367. M. Solṭānī, *Fehrest-e majallahā-ye fārsī az ebtedā tā sāl-e 1320-e šamsī*, Tehran, 1356 Š./1967, pp. 56-57. Idem, *Fehrest-e majallāt-e mawjūd dar ketāb-ḵāna-ye Āstān-e qods-e rażawī* I, Mašhad, 1361 Š./1982, p. 148.

(NASSEREDDIN PARVIN)

DAʿWAT-E ESLĀMĪ (The Islamic call), a monthly religious journal published in Kermānšāh from Jomādā II 1346/November-December 1927 to Tīr 1315 Š./June 1936. Beginning in the fourth year only ten issues were published a year, with a religious treatise substituted for the other two. The first issue was identified as number 3, apparently because the publisher and director of the magazine, Sayyed Moḥammad-Taqī Wāḥedī Bodalā, had previously edited two issues of another religious journal, *Kowkab-e daraḵšān*, published by Mīrzā Aḥmad Jawāherī Borūjerdī. Wāḥedī was a preacher and director of the Moʾassasa-ye dīnīya-ye daʿwat-e eslāmí (Religious institute for the Islamic call).

Daʿwat-e eslāmī was identified on its title page as a journal of religion, Koran commentary, ethics, and criticism, and its editors were interested in refuting the arguments of Christian and Bahai missionaries. Poetry was also included. The title page occupied the entire front cover and included a list of the contents of the issue, as well as a verse from the Koran related to *amr be maʿrūf* (q.v.). During the first two years most issues contained twenty-four pages, but later they consisted of forty-eight single-column pages measuring 16.5 x 21 cm. The journal carried no illustrations or advertising. An annual subscription initially cost 12 *qerān*s, but when the format was changed the price rose to 25 rials. Runs of this journal can be found in the Central Library of Tehran University, the library of Āstān-e qods-e rażawī in Mašhad, and the library of Princeton University in Princeton, New Jersey.

Bibliography: R. Ralph and R. D. MacChesney, *A List of Persian Serials in the Princeton University Library*, Princeton, N.J., 1971. Ṣadr Hāšemī, *Jarāʾed o majallāt* II, pp. 287-88. M. Solṭānī, *Fehrest-e majallahā-ye fārsī az ebtedā tā sāl-e 1325-e šamsī*, Tehran, 1356 Š./1977, pp. 55-56. Idem, *Fehrest-e majallāt-e mawjūd dar Ketāb-ḵāna-ye Āstān-e qods-e rażawī*, Mašhad, 1361 Š./1982, p. 147.

(NASSEREDDIN PARVIN)

DAWLATĀBĀD, name of several localities in Afghanistan that have grown up around civil or military government buildings. Some have never developed into large settlements. For example, a former Nūrzay encampment 72 km northeast of Farāh, formerly a fording place across the Farāhrūd and a toll station on the caravan road between Qandahār and Herat, remains only a village, with a population of about 400 adult males (Central Statistics Office [C.S.O.], p. 1171; Imām Sharīf, p. 220; repr. in *Gazetteer of Afghanistan* II, p. 62). Another village 25 km southeast of Tāšqorḡān (Ḵolm) contained 200 Arab families in the 1880s and a population of some 300 adult men in the 1970s (C.S.O., p. 882; Maitland, II, pp. 46, 465; repr. in *Gazetteer of Afghanistan* IV, pp. 195, 564). Two other settlements, however, expanded into small towns, both now famous for carpet production.

Dawlatābād(-e Balḵ). This Dawlatābād, a former stage on the great caravan route between Afghanistan and Bukhara via Keleft (Maitland, II, p. 199), is now a district seat in Balḵ province and the only town in the northern part of the large Balḵāb (q.v.) oasis. The population (6,111 inhabitants in 1358 Š./1979) includes a mixture of Turkmen, Uzbeks, and Hazāra (Nāheż, p. 271). Owing to its close proximity to Mazār-e Šarīf (26 km) and its distance from the modern road network, the town has recently entered a period of decay: The cotton gin built in 1316 Š./1937 has closed down, and the once prosperous biweekly *bāzār* (397 shops, mostly specializing in cloth or food and open on Mondays and Thursdays) was reported to be partly inactive in 1357 Š./1978 (Jebens, p. 223), though it remains an important center of trade in embroidered cotton caps of various styles, including a cheap local type (Jebens, pp. 225-26, 409).

Dawlatābād is the center of a densely populated and highly productive district (*woloswālī*) of 864 km^2, with 65,397 inhabitants in 1358 Š./1979 (for further statistical information, see BALḴ v). Since the settlement there of Teke Turkmen refugees from the U.S.S.R. in the 1930s (see list of villages in Franz, p. 207), the district has become the most prominent carpet-weaving center in the whole region of Mazār-e Šarīf (Parsons, pp. 78-79); merchants from Mazār-e Šarīf entirely control production.

The district is rich in protohistoric, Achaemenid, Kushan, and Kushano-Sasanian mounds, for example, the unexcavated Dawlatābād Tepe (Ball, p. 87) and the more important mounds near Delbarjīn (q.v.), 28 km west of Dawlatābād, which were excavated in 1969-77 by a joint Soviet-Afghan team (Kruglikova, 1974-77; idem, 1986; idem and Sarianidi, p. 16 map; erroneously located in Jawzjān province by Ball, p. 91). The so-called "Dawlatābād minaret" of the 12th century is actually located in the village of Zādīān, 14 km northeast of Dawlatābād, where it is known by the name *zīārat-e* Kᵛāja (or Ḥażrat-e) Ṣāleḥ (Sourdel-Thomine, pp. 122 ff.; Nāheż, p. 272).

Dawlatābād(-e Maymana). This Dawlatābād is a district seat in Fāryāb province. It evolved from the Turkmen village of Qōzī Bāy Qalʿa, founded soon after 1293/1876 on the right bank of the Šīrīn Tagāw (Tagāb) river by Ersārī immigrants from Panjdeh (Maitland, II, p. 159, partly repr. in *Gazetteer of Afghanistan* IV, p. 68; cf. Peacocke, pp. 289, 293). As the village was exposed to raids by the Sāreq Turkmen, a fort was built there in 1301/1884 and garrisoned with 100 Afghan soldiers (Maitland, II, pp. 156, 159; Peacocke, p. 91, with two plates). This small military post has burgeoned into a thriving new town, owing to three main factors. First was the general rural recolonization of this once depopulated area. Second was the situation of the village at the junction of the main road linking Maymana to Andk̲ūy (q.v.; asphalted only between Andkūy and Dawlatābād) with the direct road to Šeberḡān through the Dašt-e Laylī. Third was elevation to the rank of an administrative center first of a subdistrict (*ʿalāqadārī*), then, in 1343 Š./1964, of a district (*woloswālī*). It has a large biweekly *bāzār* of perhaps 400 shops (Grötzbach, p. 121: only 180 shops and 14 *sarāy*), most open only on Sundays and Wednesdays; there are also four mosques, a military camp, a secondary school for boys and one for girls, and various other administrative facilities (Radojicic, p. 15). Residential quarters (*šahr-e now*) were under construction in 1355 Š./1976, in order to house the growing population of civil servants. According to the preliminary returns of the census (q.v.) of 1358 Š./1979, however, the municipal population amounted to only 2,434 inhabitants; most of the shopkeepers and their employees lived in the surrounding villages.

The district of Dawlatābād has an area of 2,599 km^2. In incorporates two former subdistricts, Dawlatābād proper in the north (originally attached to Āqča, q.v.) and K̲ayrābād in the south (administered from Maymana). Their combined populations were put at 650-850 families in 1886, including Turkmen newcomers in Dawlatābād and long-established Uzbek peasants in K̲ayrābād (Yate, p. 234; Maitland, II, pp. 531, 544; repr. in *Gazetteer of Afghanistan* IV, pp. 69, 392). By 1358 Š./1979 the total population had grown to 26,812 sedentary inhabitants, nearly all concentrated in the Šīrīn Tagāw valley. This tremendous increase can be accounted for by both natural growth and immigration of Pashtun settlers from southern Afghanistan and Turkmen refugees from the neighboring U.S.S.R. (Radojicic, p. 15).

Carpet weaving, originally a specialty of the Turkmen settlements of the district (see Franz, p. 211), has recently been introduced in the more numerous Uzbek villages, where work of lesser quality is produced. It does not seem to have penetrated the remaining Pashtun and Arab villages. Production is now controlled by dealers from Kabul and Andk̲ūy, and the Dawlatābād *bāzār* plays no significant part in the trade (Parsons, pp. 123-24; cf. Klieber, p. 149). That it was once more important is clear from the fact that the typical modern red Turkmen carpet with large blue or black octagonal designs (*fīl-pāy*) is still usually called Dawlatābād (O'Bannon, p. 115). Cotton weaving (*alāča, karbās*) was also formerly widespread in the area (Nāheż, p. 274).

For further statistical information on the district, see FARYĀB.

Bibliography: W. Ball, *Archaeological Gazetteer of Afghanistan*, 2 vols., Paris, 1982. Central Statistics Office, *Aṭlas-e qarīahā-ye Afḡānestān*, Demographic Research Report Series 1, 3 vols., Kabul, 1353 Š./1975. E. Franz, "Zur gegenwärtigen Verbreitung und Gruppierung der Turkmenen in Afghanistan," *Baessler-Archiv*, N.F. 20/1, 1972, pp. 191-238. E. Grötzbach, *Städte und Basare in Afghanistan*, TAVO B16, Wiesbaden, 1979. Imām Sharīf, "Second Journey in the Taimanī Country, September and October 1885," in P. J. Maitland, *Reports on Tribes, Namely, Sārik Turkomans, Chahār Aimāk Tribes, and Hazāras*, Afghan Boundary Commission, Records of Intelligence Party IV, Simla, 1891, pp. 212-20. A. Jebens, *Wirtschafts- und sozialgeographische Untersuchung über das Heimgewerbe in Nordafghanistan*, Tübinger Geographische Studien 87, Tübingen, 1983. H. Klieber, *Afghanistan. Geschichte, Kultur, Volkskunst, Teppiche*, Landsberg am Lech, Germany, 1989. I. T. Kruglikova, *Dil'berdzhin* (Delbarjīn), 2 vols., Moscow, 1974-77. Idem, *Dil'berdzhin. Khram dioskurov* (Delbarjīn. Temple of the Dioscuri), Moscow, 1986. Idem and V. I. Sarianidi, "Pyat' let raboty sovetsko-afghanskoi arkheologicheskoi ekspeditsii" (Five years of work of the Soviet-Afghan archeological expedition), in *Drevnyaya Baktriya* (Ancient Bactria), Moscow, 1976, pp. 3-20. P. J. Maitland, *Diary of Intelligence Party*, Afghan Boundary Commission, Records of Intelligence Party I-II, Simla, 1888. M.-Ḥ. Nāheż, ed., *Q̈āmūs-e joḡrāfīāʾī-e Afḡānestān* II, Kabul, 1336 Š./1957. G. W. O'Bannon, *The Turkoman Carpet*, London, 1974. R. D. Parsons, *The Carpets of Afghanistan*, 3rd rev. ed., Woodbridge (Suffolk), U.K., 1990. W. Peacocke, *Diary between September 1884 and October 1886*, Afghan Boundary Commission, Records of Intelligence Party III, Simla, 1887. S. Radojicic, *Report on Hydrogeological Survey of Certain Settlements along the Afghanistan Ring Road*, UNICEF Assisted Rural Water Supply Project, Kabul, 1976 (roneo). J. Sourdel-Thomine, "Deux minarets d'époque seldjoukide en Afghanistan," *Syria* 30/1-2, 1953, pp. 108-36. C. E. Yate, *Northern Afghanistan, or Letters from the Afghan Boundary Commission*, Edinburgh and London, 1888; repr. Lahore, 1976.

(DANIEL BALLAND)

DAWLATĀBĀDĪ, SAYYED **ʿALĪ-MOḤAMMAD** (b. Dawlatābād, 1341/1868, d. Tehran, Šawwāl 1341/May-June 1923), prominent politician and deputy of the Persian parliament. He was the third son of Ḥājj Sayyed Mīrzā Hādī Dawlatābādī, reputed to have been leader of the Azalī Babis (*Tārīk̲-e bīdārī*, ed. Saʿīdī Sīrjānī, 2nd ed., I, p. 649), and a younger brother of Yaḥyā Dawlatābādī (q.v.). ʿAlī-Moḥammad received his first formal schooling in Najaf, where his father had gone to continue his own religious studies, in 1292-94/1875-77. His family then returned to Isfahan, where he studied with Mollā Moḥammad Kāšī and Jahāngīr Khan Qašqāʾī and then with Hājj Mīrzā Badīʿ and ʿAlam-al-Hodā Kalbāsī. It is unclear from the sources what intellectual currents these men represented and therefore the kinds of ideas to which ʿAlī-Moḥammad was exposed under their tutelage. Later, in Tehran, both ʿAlī-Moḥammad and his brother Yaḥyā seem to have been students of the philosopher Āqā Mīrzā Abu'l-Ḥasan Jelwa, suggesting the heterodox tendencies with which both have been identified (Dawlatābādī, p. 17; Dawlatābādī, *Ḥayāt-e Yaḥyā* I, p. 112).

The oppression of the prince Ẓell-al-Solṭān's government in Isfahan and his animosity toward the Dawlatābādī family (Dawlatābādī, pp. 13-15; Dawlatābādī, *Ḥayāt-e Yaḥyā* I, pp. 39-44, 111-17) did much to shape ʿAlī-Moḥammad's political outlook. He became active in the constitutional movement and a key figure in several important episodes. He seems to have played a role, through his friend the Ottoman ambassador Šams-al-Dīn Beg, in obtaining from the Qajar court accession to the demands of the clerics who had taken sanctuary (*bast*, q.v.) in the shrine of Shah ʿAbd-al-ʿAẓīm (q.v.) in December 1905 (*Tārīḵ-e bīdārī*, ed. Saʿīdī Sīrjānī, I, pp. 357-59; Dawlatābādī, *Ḥayāt-e Yaḥyā* II, pp. 19-21; Šarīf Kāšānī, I, p. 33; see CONSTITUTIONAL REVOLUTION ii); he may also have participated in the exodus to Qom in July 1906 (Dawlatābādī, *Ḥayāt-e Yaḥyā* II, p. 71).

After going underground in the wake of the coup by Moḥammad-ʿAlī Shah (1324-27/1907-09) in 1326/1908 (Šarīf Kāšānī, I, p. 194), ʿAlī-Moḥammad emerged as one of the leaders of the Moderate party Ḥezb-e eʿtedāl during the Second Majles. Though bitter rivals of the Democrats (Ḥezb-e demokrāt), ʿAlī-Moḥammad and his colleagues joined them in forming the National defense committee (Komīta-ye defāʿ-e mellī) in the wake of Russian and British occupation of Persia during World War I (Dawlatābādī, *Ḥayāt-e Yaḥyā* III, pp. 120, 332). The committee, which became a provisional government, with ʿAlī-Moḥammad as an integral member, was based in Kermānšāh. From the small number of references to him in the memoirs of his brother Yaḥyā and Yaḥyā's own detachment from political parties in this period, it appears that the brothers were not closely associated in their public lives; indeed, there may have been some coolness between them (see, e.g., *Ḥayāt-e Yaḥyā* III, pp. 120-21).

ʿAlī-Moḥammad was elected to represent consituency of Lorestān in the Fourth Majles, which convened in 1299/1921; he served as deputy until his death two years later.

Bibliography: Sayyed ʿAlī-Moḥammad Dawlatābādī, *Ḵāṭerāt-e Sayyed ʿAlī-Moḥammad Dawlatābādī*, ed. Ḥ. Dawlatābādī, Tehran, 1362 Š./1983. M. Etteḥādīya, *Peydāyeš wa taḥawwol-e aḥzāb-e sīāsī-e mašrūṭīyat*, Tehran, 1361 Š./1982. M. Malekzāda, *Tārīḵ-e enqelāb-e mašrūṭīyat-e Īrān*, 2nd ed., Tehran, 1363 Š./1984. Moḥammad-Mahdī Šarīf Kāšānī, *Wāqeʿāt-e ettefāqīya dar rūzgār*, Tehran, 1362 Š./1983.

(CYRUS AMIR-MOKRI)

DAWLATĀBĀDĪ, ṢEDDĪQA (b. Isfahan, 1300/1883, d. Tehran, 6 Mordād 1340 Š./28 July 1961), journalist, educator, and pioneer in the movement to emancipate women in Persia. Her mother, Ḵātema, was descended from a family of local *ʿolamāʾ*, and her father, Mīrzā Hādī Dawlatābādī, was a prominent *mojtahed* (theologian) of Isfahan. Ṣeddīqa spent her childhood in Tehran, where she was privately tutored in Persian, Arabic, and French. At the age of twenty years she was married to an elderly physician, but the marriage ended in divorce in 1339/1921.

In 1336/1917 she founded Maktab-ḵāna-ye šarʿīāt, the first school for girls in Isfahan, the beginning of her lifelong commitment to social service. A year later she established Šerkat-e ḵawātīn-e Eṣfahān (Association of women of Isfahan; Bāmdād, pp. 78-79) and in 1337/1919 *Zabān-e zanān* (Voice of women), the third Persian newspaper founded and managed by a woman. The newspaper aroused the hostility of fanatics, who repeatedly attacked its office and finally forced Dawlatābādī to close it after only three years of publication. She then moved to Tehran, where a year later she resumed publication of *Zabān-e zanān* in magazine format (Ṣadr Hāšemī, *Jarāʾed o majallāt* III, pp. 6-11).

In 1301 Š./1922 Dawlatābādī went to Paris to pursue her education. She studied family hygiene, then attended the Sorbonne, where she received a bachelor's degree in psychology and education. During this period she published in French journals articles on the control of Persian women over personal property and the superiority of the rights of Islamic women to those of European women. In 1926, as the representative of Persian women, she presented a paper at the International Congress of Women in Paris (Winsor). In 1306 Š./1927 she returned to Persia and was hired by the Ministry of education (Wezārat-e farhang) as an inspector for girls' schools.

Dawlatābādī never wore the veil, and in 1315 Š./1936 she became director of the Women's center (Kānūn-e bānovān), sponsored by the Ministry of education as the first step in a program to eliminate veiling of Persian women. In this post, where she remained for the rest of her working life, she organized literacy classes for women, as well as classes on homemaking, family hygiene, and raising children. She also lectured and wrote on social issues, including women's rights (e.g., *Majalla-ye zabān-e zanān*, Ḵordād 1323 Š./June 1944, pp. 3-4; Tīr/July, p. 16; Šahrīvar/September, pp. 7-10; Farvardīn 1324/April 1945, pp. 4-6; Ḵordād/June, p. 12).

She died in August 1961 and was buried in Zarganda, Tehran, next to her older brother Yaḥya Dawlatābādī (q.v.).

Bibliography: B. Bāmdād, *Zan-e īrānī az enqelāb-e mašrūṭīyat tā enqelāb-e safīd*, ed. and tr. F. R. Bagley as *From Darkness into Light. Women's Emancipation in Iran*, Hicksville, N.Y., 1977. *Majalla-ye nūr-e ʿālam* 10, Šahrīvar 1340 Š./September 1961, pp. 6-9. *Majalla-ye sapīda-ye fardā* 11-12, Tīr 1334 Š./July 1955, pp. 27-31. F. Qavīmī, *Kar-nāma-ye zanān-e mašhūr-e Īrān . . .*, Tehran, 1352 Š./1973, pp. 109-11. P. Šayḵ-al-Eslāmī, *Zanān-e Rūznāmanegār*, n.p., 1351 Š./1992, pp. 88-99. M. Winsor, "The Blossoming of a Persian Feminist," *Equal Rights* 13/23, 1926.

(Mehranguiz Manoutchehrian)

DAWLATĀBĀDĪ, sayyed **YAḤYĀ** (b. Dawlatābād near Isfahan, 17 Rajab 1279/8 January 1863, d. Tehran, 4 Ābān 1318 Š./26 October 1939), celebrated educator, political activist, and memoirist of the constitutional and postconstitutional periods. Yaḥyā was the second of the five sons of an affluent family of landowning *ʿolamāʾ*. His father, Ḥājj Sayyed Mīrzā Hādī Dawlatābādī, was an influential local *mojtahed* and leader of the clandestine Azalī branch of Babism (q.v. i) in Persia. A haphazard education at traditional koranic schools (*maktab*) left a negative impression on young Yaḥyā, an impression further reinforced at the Ṣadr *madrasa* in Isfahan and later the Moʿtamad-al-Dawla *madrasa* in Najaf in Iraq, where he joined his father in 1290/1873. Residing in Najaf added to his distaste for the conservative clerical milieu and its suffocating conformity (Dawlatābādī, *Ḥayāt-e Yaḥyā* I, pp. 11-18, 28-34).

After the family returned to Isfahan in 1294/1877 Yaḥyā witnessed his father's involvement in an extremely complex struggle for control of the city, with some of the influential *ʿolamāʾ*, most notably Moḥammad-Bāqer Najafī Eṣfahānī and his son Moḥammad-Taqī, better known as Āqā Najafī (q.v.), on one side and the powerful prince-governor of Isfahan, Masʿūd Mīrzā Ẓell-al-Solṭān, on the other (Dawlatābādī, *Ḥayāt-e Yaḥyā* I, pp. 37-44). The ambitious Mīrzā Hādī, whose Babi affiliation was a stigma impossible to disguise by any measure of dissimulation (*taqīya*), was able to build a popular base in Isfahan, at first with the tacit backing of Ẓell-al-Solṭān, who hoped thus to weaken Najafī's domination of the city. Soon, however, Hādī was denounced by Najafī as a heretic, which encouraged Ẓell-al-Solṭān to put into action his own covetous land-grabbing schemes at the expense of Yaḥyā's father. Having become a pariah, Yaḥyā found his stay in Isfahan becoming increasingly hazardous, in spite of his attempts to distance himself from the rival Bahai faction among the Babis, whose exiled leadership he bedeviled consistently.

Yaḥyā, after a year and a half of self-imposed exile in Tehran and Mašhad, as a result of his denunciation (*takfīr*) by the *ʿolamāʾ*, returned to Isfahan in 1299/1882; there he frequented the local literati. An encounter with the ascetic Babi preacher Shaikh Moḥammad Manšādī Yazdī influenced him, as well as two other, later proponents of the Constitutional Revolution (q.v.), Naṣr-Allāh Beheštī (later Malek-al-Motakallemīn) and Jamāl-al-Dīn Wāʿeẓ Eṣfahānī. Yaḥyā was also impressed by Mīrzā Āqā Khan Kermānī (q.v.), then a refugee from his native province. Āqā Khan's intellectual disposition and rhetoric, blending modernism and esoteric thought, served as a model for the receptive Yaḥyā (*Ḥayāt-e Yaḥyā* I, pp. 62-68).

After fresh denunciations, partly elicited by his repeated defiance of the *ʿolamāʾ* and Ẓell-al-Solṭān, Mīrzā Yaḥyā was banished from Isfahan a second time, between 1303/1886 and 1306/1888. He paid a short visit to Aleppo, then returned to the ʿAtabāt (q.v.), where for a year he occasionally audited Mīrzā Ḥasan Šīrāzī's lectures on jurisprudence before embarking on the Ḥajj (pilgrimage) via Alexandria and Cairo. He returned as far as Būšehr in 1304/1887, but news of fresh Babi persecutions in Isfahan forced him to retreat to the relative safety of the ʿAtabāt. He did finally return to Isfahan in 1306/1888 but was unable to stay there. By decree of Nāṣer-al-Dīn Shah (1264-1313/1848-96) Yaḥyā and his father settled in the capital, where they found a protector in the person of the vizier Mīrzā ʿAlī-Aṣgar Khan Amīn-al-Solṭān (q.v.; *Ḥayāt-e Yaḥyā* I, pp. 69-90, 111-12, 118-19).

In Tehran Yaḥyā instructed members of the nobility in calligraphy. While attending the lectures of the celebrated jurist Mīrzā Ḥasan Āštīānī, presumably in order to stave off suspicion of Babi heresy, he also had an opportunity to observe at close quarters the growing power of the *ʿolamāʾ* in a time of political turmoil. He was present when an angry crowd briefly stormed the royal citadel during the protest against the monopolistic Tobacco Régie (q.v.) of 1309-11/1891-92. In the meantime interest in speculative thought brought him to Mīrzā Abu'l-Ḥasan Jelwa, the leading philosopher of his time. None of these activities was able to assuage the moral crisis that he was experiencing at that time, however, a crisis exacerbated by increasing harassment, confiscation of family property, and diminishing income (*Ḥayāt-e Yaḥyā* I, pp. 108-22).

The social quarantine imposed upon Yaḥyā because of his Babi associations finally came to an end only during the reign of Moẓaffar-al-Dīn Shah (1313-24/1896-1906). The reformist Mīrzā ʿAlī Khan Amīn-al-Dawla (q.v.) was appointed vizier in 1314/1897, which encouraged Yaḥyā to try to change his father's course "according to the needs of the time and move in the direction of fundamental actions that could bring progress, development, and freedom of the country" (*Ḥayāt-e Yaḥyā* I, pp. 176-77). Although he remained a member of the *ʿolamāʾ*, establishing secular schools and furthering modern education became the focus of his attention for the next ten years, perhaps the most fruitful period of his career. As a founding member of the Council of education (Anjoman-e maʿāref, q.v.), to which he was appointed by Amīn-al-Dawla in 1315/1898 (*Ḥayāt-e Yaḥyā* I, p. 188; Eḥtešām-al-Salṭana, pp. 322 ff.), he brought his considerable imagination and discretion to bear in working with the daring but abrasive aristocrat Maḥmūd Khan Eḥtešām-al-Salṭana, the determined and intransigent Mīrzā Ḥasan Rošdīya, and others. In his memoirs Dawlatābādī may have overstated his own achievements and criticized his rivals too harshly, yet he should be credited with his persistence in establishing new schools and preparing the earliest elementary textbooks and school curricula. Eḥtešām-al-Salṭana (p. 529) characterized him as an honest and dedicated colleague, who nevertheless suffered from "extreme selfishness and self-centeredness" (*ḵod-ḵᵛāhī-e mofraṭ wa ḵod-pasandī-e bīandāza*). In 1316/1899 Yaḥyā founded the Madrasa-ye motabarreka-ye sādāt, which was dedicated to teaching the children of the poor among the descendants of the Prophet Moḥammad (*sādāt*). By promoting modern schooling for this group he not only challenged arcane scholasticism but also attempted to shaped the students into a constituency that could compete with seminarians (*ṭalaba*) educated in traditional *madrasa*s. He was also partly responsible for establishing at least three other schools, the Adab, Kamālīya, and Dāneš, but his involvement led to personal quarrels and drained his finances (Dawlatābādī, *Ḥayāt-e Yaḥyā* I, pp. 178-204, 237-67).

The events leading up to the Constitutional Revolution (1924-29/1906-11) opened a new chapter in the lives of Yaḥyā Dawlatābādī and his younger brother ʿAlī-Moḥammad (q.v.). They were among the early members of a small but influential revolutionary circle of Azalī persuasion, which also included Jamāl-al-Dīn Eṣfahānī and Malek-al-Motakallemīn, among others. At the same time Yaḥyā established amicable ties with the proreform Ottoman ambassador Šams-al-Dīn Beg, whose sympathy he hoped to evoke for the cause of constitutionalism in Persia. During the crucial protest of the *ʿolamāʾ* in the shrine of Shah ʿAbd-al-ʿAẓīm, which ultimately led to the "constitutional decree," in 1324/1906 (see CONSTITUTIONAL REVOLUTION ii), Yaḥyā acted as a political broker between the reformist faction led by Sayyed ʿAbd-Allāh Behbahānī and the government of ʿAyn-al-Dawla (qq.v.). According to his version of those events, he was the first to include in the list of otherwise mundane requests submitted by the *ʿolamāʾ* a general demand for "reform in all affairs," which was soon articulated by himself and his collaborators as a demand for creation of a "justice bureau" (*dīvān-e ʿadālat*) and a "national house of consultation" (*mašwarat-ḵāna-ye mellī*) to execute the "law of equity" (*qānūn-e mosāwāt*) in all parts of Persia (*Ḥayāt-e Yaḥyā* II, pp. 22-24). Neither of these ideas was by any means novel in the dissident milieu of the time.

In spite of his ardent support for constitutionalism, Dawlatābādī's public role was compromised by his Bābī background, for which he was almost ostracized from the circles around the leading proconstitutionalist *ʿolamāʾ*, Behbahānī and Sayyed Moḥammad Ṭabāṭabāʾī. Furthermore, his hopes of close collaboration with such members of the reformist nobility as Eḥtešām-al-Salṭana and Mahdīqolī Khan Mokber-al-Salṭana, in order to combat opposition from the royalists, achieved limited results His stigma as a Babi may also have barred him and his cohorts from election as deputies to the first constitutional Majles. In an attempt to strengthen his political stand, Dawlatābādī even tried, with little success, to patch up old differences with Shaikh Fażl-Allāh Nūrī, Behbahānī's bitter opponent and later the leader of the anticonstitutional *ʿolamāʾ*. These setbacks did little to diminish Dawlatābādī's revolutionary zeal, however.

In 1325/1907, when the revolutionary activities of the *anjomans* (q.v.) were at a peak, Dawlatābādī helped to form the influential Anjoman-e markazī-e aṣnāf (Central association of guilds) in the Tehran *bāzār*, drawing on members who were loyal to his father. As the mentor and spokesman for this *anjoman*, he had by mid-1326/1908 become sufficiently committed to the radical (*tondrow*) constitutionalist wing to be singled out by Moḥammad-ʿAlī Shah (1324-27/1907-09) as one of eight antimonarchist activists within the Majles and the *anjomans*. Dawlatābādī's guilt was further confirmed in the eyes of the shah when he emerged as a prominent member of the Defense committee (Komīsīyūn-e modāfaʿa) responsible for recruiting the militia forces of the *anjomans* to defend the Majles. It was only his personal circumspection that saved him on the night preceding the coup of 23 Jomādā I 1326/23 June 1908, when the Majles was bombarded. He sought refuge in a safe house while some of his revolutionary friends were arrested and executed. Having received verbal assurance of his safety from the British embassy, he then moved to the British-protected village of Qolhak north of Tehran, where his father had a family retreat adjacent to the British summer residence. After some negotiation with the court he welcomed an offer of voluntary exile and left Persia shortly afterward.

He arrived in Istanbul during the period of ferment preceding the revolution of the Young Turks but was received unenthusiastically by the Anjoman-e saʿādat (q.v.), which was dominated by exiled Azerbaijani constitutionalists suspicious of his background and motives. His acquaintance with political leaders of the Committee for union and progress (Etteḥād o taraqqī komītasī), including Prince Ṣalāḥ-al-Dīn, leader of the federalist Aḥrār party; Ṭalʿat Pasha, later a member of the Young Turk triumvirate; and Shaikh Jamāl-al-Dīn, *šayḵ-al-Eslām* (the highest religious official) of Istanbul, helped to boost Dawlatābādī's morale, though these men offered little practical help in furthering the Persian cause.

Dawlatābādī returned to Tehran in October 1909, three months after the city had been retaken by constitutionalist forces in July. His hesitation proved well founded. Despite his personal acquaintance with most of the revolutionary leaders, his efforts to steer a middle course between the newly organized Eʿtedalīyūn (moderates) and the radicals of the Democratic party drove him farther into isolation. His condescending disposition to "advise" people in power marginalized him still further. Although he eventually tilted toward the Democrats, he never abandoned his self-appointed role as an "interparty mediator" (*moṣleḥ-e ḏāt-al-bayn*; *Ḥayāt-e Yaḥyā* III, p. 121). His political views on the need for the separation of religious and secular authorities, expressed in his treatises *Armaḡān-e Yaḥyā* and *Rāhnemā-ye entekābāt-e Majles-e šūrā-ye mellī*, in which he called for election of nonclerical figures, did not enhance his stature among the *ʿolamāʾ*. His frustration at the outcome of the revolutionary process reached a new height when, after the parliamentary election in June 1911, his credentials as deputy from Kermān to the Second Majles were heatedly challenged by his clerical opponents. Accused of having "corrupt beliefs," he was forced to present his resignation and to refrain temporarily from all political activity. Seeking a pretext to leave Persia, in July 1911 he went to Europe at the invitation of the organizers of the International Congress of the Races, a philanthropic gathering in London (*Ḥayāt-e Yaḥyā* III, pp. 144-52).

On the eve of World War I the domestic situation in Persia and fear of partition loomed large in the minds of patriots like Dawlatābādī. Soon after his return to Tehran he joined the nationalist "emigrants" (*mohājerīn*), who left the capital for Qom in November 1915, as a protest against the threat of Russian aggression. Subsequently he became a prominent member of the newly formed National defense committee (Komīta-ye defāʿ-e mellī) in Hamadān and then in Kermānšāh (*Ḥayāt-e Yaḥyā* III, pp. 300 ff.). The committee, set up with German backing, became a provisional government in charge of conducting the national resistance against the Anglo-Russian occupation. After several military defeats during 1334/1915 and 1335/1916 the nationalists retreated to Qaṣr-e Šīrīn, under the temporary protection of Sanjābī tribal chiefs, and soon after to Baghdad and then to Istanbul. Dawlatābādī arrived in Istanbul in early 1916 to find an atmosphere of gloom among the exiles, whose ranks were riddled with factionalism and personal animosities. The resourceful Dawlatābādī was able to renew his ties with the Young Turks, and it was perhaps at Ṭalʿat Pasha's suggestion that he first traveled to Berlin and then to Stockholm (*Ḥayāt-e Yaḥyā* IV, pp. 32-40), at that time the center of intelligence gathering and espionage. On the pretext of participating in the International Socialist Congress, he appears to have engaged in some intelligence activities (*Ḥayāt-e Yaḥyā* IV, p. 53). Soon after the Bolshevik Revolution of October 1917 and the ensuing Russian withdrawal from the Caucasian and Antolian fronts, including Persian Azerbaijan, Dawlatābādī hastened back to Persia. Benefiting from generous German assistance, he apparently was entrusted with the task of organizing a pro-German nationalist resistance against imminent British advances in the north of Persia (*Ḥayāt-e Yaḥyā* IV, pp. 160-66), a resistance already apparent in Shaikh Moḥammad Ḵīābānī's uprising in Tabrīz and the Jangalī movement in Gīlān (see COMMUNISM i).

The general armistice of October 1918, combined with the demise of the Young Turks and imperial Germany, put an end to this resistance. The formidable task of political reorientation prompted Dawlatābādī to turn for support to the victorious British. In Isfahan he managed to penetrate the clandestine Āhan committee (Komīta-ye āhan), which was apparently set up to create a unified pro-British front in chaotic postwar Persia (*Ḥayāt-e Yaḥyā* IV, pp. 114-15, 167 ff.). He was soon deprived of any meaningful role in this perfunctory organization, however, possibly because he was not trusted by other pro-British participants. The growing unpopularity of the 1919 Anglo-Persian agreement (q.v.) in Persia, moreover, dictated that Dawlatābādī should accentuate his differences with the prime minister Mīrzā Ḥasan Khan Woṯūq-al-Dawla and his allies. The Āhan committee was later transformed in Tehran into the Zarganda committee and became one of the groups supporting the coup d'etat of 1299 Š./1921 (q.v.). In the treacherous political climate of postwar Tehran Dawlatābādī's advocacy of political harmony and austere patriotism, as expressed in his criticism of the 1919 Anglo-Persian Agreement (q.v.) and of the rigged election of the Fourth Majles only prolonged his political quarantine.

The rise of Reżā Khan Sardār-e Sepah (later Reżā Shah), especially after the collapse of the government of Sayyed Żīāʾ-al-Dīn Ṭabāṭabāʾī in June 1921, opened new prospects for Dawlatābādī. He soon managed to develop a close, though ephemeral, rapport with Reżā Khan, who was admired as a champion of security and national renewal by many frustrated constitutionalists like Dawlatābādī. Reżā Khan, on the other hand, detected in Dawlatābādī a clerical advocate of modernity willing to promote his cause in return for long-sought admission to the main political arena. As the opposition *ʿolamāʾ* were intimidated by the new military regime, in January-February 1923 Dawlatābādī was able to win election as deputy from Isfahan to the Fifth Majles, where he came to play a notable role as an early promoter of Reżā Khan. He was an influential member of a committee of eight liberal politicians (including Moḥammad Moṣaddeq and Ḥasan Taqīzāda) who for a while advised Reżā Khan on domestic and foreign affairs (*Ḥayāt-e Yaḥyā* IV, p. 325).

In 1303 Š./1924 Dawlatābādī initially supported Reżā Khan's call for republicanism, yet he later also entertained conspiratorial suspicions about the degree of British involvement in the affair. After the collapse of the republican trend Dawlatābādī and his liberal cohorts in the Majles were faced with the disagreeable choice of supporting the moribund Qajar dynasty or Reżā Khan's demand for change in the monarchy. Despite understandable trepidation, Yaḥyā was one of four deputies who, on 9 Ābān 1304 Š./31 October 1925, spoke out and voted against abolition of the Qajar dynasty and investiture of Reżā Shah Pahlavī. This gesture of resistance, fortified by references to the Constitution of 1324/1906, sealed Dawlatābādī's political fate, and he, along with other veteran politicians, was relegated to a political oblivion from which he never reemerged. After a three-year residence in Brussels, where he served as an informal cultural attaché, he retired to Tehran and completed his famous memoirs, *Tārīḵ-e moʿāṣer yā ḥayat-e Yaḥyā*. He died in 1318/1939 and was buried at his own summer home at Zarganda in Qolhak, which was later expanded to include a public library. His tomb was destroyed after the Revolution of 1357 Š./1979.

Yaḥyā Dawlatābādī best epitomized the spirit of modernism in the quarter-century between the assassination of Nāṣer-al-Dīn Shah in 1313/1896 and the accession of Reżā Shah Pahlavī in 1324 Š./1925, the crucial era in the shaping of modern Persia. Not only did he witness the major developments of his own time and record them for posterity, bu talso he himself helped to influence the emergence of modern education, the growth of constitutionalism, revolutionary and postrevolutionary events, and the rise of the Pahlavi dynasty. His primary themes were separation of clerical and political authority, the importance of education and later of economic planning, devotion to the Constitution, condemnation of political factionalism, and above all morality and patriotism, all rooted in the Western-inspired modernism of his generation, though his attraction to many of them also reflected his religious inclinations. Indeed, it was his persistence in preserving a private Babi identity while trying to assimilate to the liberal polity of his time that proved the greatest obstacle to his political success. Although he never referred to his Babi affiliation in the four volumes of his memoirs, his career demonstrated the formidable barriers the majority political culture placed in the way of reformers of nonorthodox background. In the eyes of the *ʿolamāʾ* no one better symbolized the heretical nature of modernism than Dawlatābādī, even though he attempted to preserve his Islamic garb all his life.

Dawlatābādī's self-censorship and his self-righteous tone undermined the quality of the otherwise remarkable record of his life contained in his memoirs, among the best produced by men of his generation. He should be recognized for his successful blend of insight, thoroughness, organization, and relative impartiality in his account of the history of modern Persia. His literary style, though slightly marred by a constant use of the present tense in an effort to convey contemporaneity, combined the erudition of a seasoned writer with the flexibility of a politician and the analysis of a historian. It was based on diaries and notes that he had kept over the years. He completed the first edition of the memoirs in 1314 Š./1935 and revised it in 1316 Š./1937, an exercise in which he at times sacrificed immediate impressions to hindsight.

Bibliography: Sayyed ʿAlī-Moḥammad Dawlatābādī, *Ḵāṭerāt-e Sayyed ʿAlī-Moḥammad Dawlatābādī*, ed. Ḥ. Dawlatābādī, Tehran, 1362 Š./1983. Mīrzā Maḥmūd Khan Eḥtešām-al-Salṭana, *Ḵāṭerāt-e Eḥtešām-al-Salṭana*, ed. M.-M. Mūsawī, 2nd ed., Tehran, 1366 Š./1987, index. M. Hedāyat, *Ḵāṭerāt wa ḵaṭarāt*, Tehran, 1344 Š./1965, index. M. Moṣaddeq, *Ḵāṭerāt wa taʾallomāt-e Moṣaddeq*, ed. Ī. Afšār, Tehran, 1365/1986, p. 83. A.-ʿA. Mowarreḵ-al-Dawla Sepehr, *Īrān dar jang-e bozorg*, Tehran, 1336 Š./1957, pp. 237-76. A. Nīkū-hemat, "Ḥājj Mīrzā Yaḥyā Dawlatābādī," *Waḥīd* 12, 1353 Š./1974, pp. 927-31. Ḥ. Saʿādat Nūrī, "Ḥājj Mīrzā Yaḥyā Dawlatābādī," *Armaḡān* 36, 1345 Š./1966, pp. 336-45. S. Ḥ. Taqīzāda, *Zendaḡānī-e ṭūfānī. Ḵāṭerāt-e Sayyed Ḥasan Taqīzada*, ed. Ī. Afšār, Tehran, 1367 Š./1988, pp. 36, 59, 124, 198-203. *Tārīḵ-e bīdārī*, ed. ʿA.-A. Saʿīdī Sīrjānī, index.

(ABBAS AMANAT)

DAWLATḴĒL, tribal name common among the eastern Pashtun at various levels of tribal segmentation, not to be confused with Dawlatzī (q.v.). There are minor sections of Dawlatḵēl within the Sadōzī Otmānzī (ʿOṯmānzī) Mandaṛ in the northeastern extremity of the Peshawar basin, the Otmānḵēl (ʿOṯmānḵēl) in the lower Swat valley, the pashtunized Mollāgorī on the northern side of the Khyber Pass, their Malekdīnḵēl and Zakkāḵēl Afrīdī neighbors, the Laškarzī Ōrakzī of the upper Ḵānkī valley, and the Aḥmadzī (q.v.) and Otmānzī (ʿOṯmānzī) Wazīr and the ʿAlīzī Masʿūd of Waziristan. Within the tribes of the Lōdī confederacy a Dawlatḵēl section is recorded among the Nīāzī, the Sūrī, and two subdivisions of the Lōḥāṇī: the Yasīnḵēl Mamāḵēl and the Sālār Marwat of Lakkī (*Dictionary*, pp. 53-54; Hart, p. 45; Ḥayāt Khan, pp. 91, 184-86, 189, 223; King, p. 220; Merk, p. 85; Neʿmat-Allāh, II, p. 50; Šēr Moḥammad Khan, pp. 191, 223-26, 229-30, 248). In fact, the name is so common as to be almost meaningless.

The Dawlatḵēl Mamāḵēl Lōḥāṇī appear to be the only tribal unit of importance that bears the name. Having outnumbered and eventually absorbed all other Mamāḵēl clans, it became the leading tribe among the Lōḥāṇī, a genealogically and economically related group of nomadic tribes. Centuries ago the Dawlatḵēl used to migrate and trade between the highlands of eastern Afghanistan (Kaṭawāz) and the Indus lowlands (Dērajāt). Having lost Kaṭawāz to the Solaymānḵēl in the Timurid period, they found new summer quarters in the Solaymān mountains (Ḥayāt Khan, p. 189). The tribe gradually shifted from a pastoral life to cultivation in their winter quarters, where they replaced the Lōdī tribes that had moved into Hindustan in the 15th-16th centuries (*Gazetteer*, p. 26; Tucker, p. 42). Bitter intertribal conflicts over cultivable land ensued, in the course of which the Dawlatḵēl won control of the upper Dērajāt around Ṭānk by the beginning of the 17th century. Until the late 18th century they seem to have remained mainly nomadic, carrying on trading expeditions as far as Kabul and Qandahār (Raverty, V, p. 488).

At that time massive sedentarization reportedly occurred as part of an agricultural-development scheme undertaken by the chief of the Dawlatḵel around Ṭānk. It included construction of "an enormous dam" across the Gōmal river, so that early in the 19th century the area was described as well cultivated and irrigated (Edwardes, I, pp. 350, 358; Elphinstone, p. 368). By the mid-19th century the Dawlatḵēl were completely sedentarized, the first of the Lōḥānī tribes to give up nomadism and long-distance trading (Lumsden, pp.

91-92). During the same period internal feuds and a long-standing guerrilla war against the Sikhs greatly weakened the tribe (Edwardes, I, pp. 359 ff.; Šēr Moḥammad Khan, p. 226), which dropped in size from 8,000-9,000 families in the late 18th century, a figure including several vassal tribes and many allogenous tenants (*hamsāya*) of various origins, to only 1,387 individuals according to the Indian census of 1881. At that time it was the weakest of all Lōḥāṇī tribes (Elphinstone, p. 375; Ḥayāt Khan, p. 190; Ibbetson, p. 72; Raverty, IV p. 325, V, p. 487). This decline is clearly reflected in the numerous encroachments by the Bēṭanī (q.v.) on Dawlatkēl lands in the second half of the 19th century. In 1910 R. T. I. Ridgeway (p. 106) described the Dawlatkēl as "a very small and feeble tribe," and they have apparently remained so until today.

Genealogical details of Dawlatkēl tribal organization have been provided by Moḥammad Ḥayāt Khan (p. 185) and Šēr Moḥammad Khan (p. 223). The most important section is the Kaṭīkēl, from which originated the headman of both the tribe and all the formerly united Lōḥāṇī tribes (Ḥayāt Khan, p. 189).

Bibliography: *A Dictionary of the Pathan Tribes on the North-West Frontier of India*, Calcutta, 1899. H. B. Edwardes, *A Year on the Punjab Frontier in 1848-49*, London, 1851; repaginated repr. Gurgaon, India, 1989. M. Elphinstone, *An Account of the Kingdom of Caubul*, London, 1815; repr. Graz, 1969. *Gazetteer of the Dera Ismail Khan District 1883-84*, Lahore, 1884. D. M. Hart, *Guardians of the Khaibar Pass*, Lahore, 1985. M. Ḥayāt Khan, *Ḥayāt-e Afḡān*, Lahore, 1867; tr. H. Priestley as *Afghanistan and Its Inhabitants*, Lahore, 1874; repr. Lahore, 1981. D. Ibbetson, *Panjab Castes*, Lahore, 1916; repr. New Delhi, 1981; repr. Lahore, 1982. L. W. King, *The Orakzai Country and Clans*, Lahore, 1900; 2nd ed., Lahore, 1984. H. B. Lumsden, *The Mission to Kandahar*, Calcutta, 1860. W. R. H. Merk, *Report on the Mohmands*, Lahore, 1898; repr. as *The Mohmands*, Lahore, 1984. Kᵛāja Neʿmat-Allāh, *Makzan-e afḡānī*, tr. B. Dorn as *History of the Afghans*, 2 vols., London, 1829-36; repr. London, 1965; repr. Karachi, 1976. H. G. Raverty, *Notes on Afghānistān and Part of Balūchistan*, London, 1881-88; repr. Lahore, 1976. R. T. I. Ridgway, *Pathans*, Calcutta, 1910; repr. Peshawar, 1983. Šēr Moḥammad Khan, *Tawārīk-e koršīd-e jahān*, Lahore, 1311/1894. H. S. Tucker, *Report of the Land Revenue Settlement of the Dera Ismail Khan District of the Punjab 1872-79*, Lahore, 1879.

(DANIEL BALLAND)

DAWLATŠĀH, MOḤAMMAD-ʿALĪ MĪRZĀ

DAWLATŠĀH, MOḤAMMAD-ʿALĪ MĪRZĀ (1203-37/1789-1821), eldest son of Fatḥ-ʿAlī Shah (1212-50/1797-1834) and powerful prince-governor of western provinces of Persia. He was born in the resort village of Navā in Māzandarān to Zībā-čehr Kānom, a Georgian (Čūš) slave girl of the Tzicara Chwili family owned by Fatḥ-ʿAlī Shah, and was senior by seven months to ʿAbbās Mīrzā (q.v.). Proximity in age between these and other princes later contributed to a prolonged succession crisis in the Qajar house.

Upon his father's accession in 1212/1797 Moḥammad-ʿAlī was appointed nominal governor of Fārs and soon after, at the age of twelve years, governor of Qazvīn, Kamsa, and Gīlān. His military gifts soon surfaced in confrontations with ʿAlī Pasha, the *mamlūk wālī* of Ottoman Iraq, whose appointment in 1220/1805 was made without Persian consent, which had customarily been sought by the Ottoman court (Bāb-e ʿālī). The new *wālī*'s hostile attitude encouraged the shah to give refuge to ʿAbd-al-Raḥmān Khan Bābān of Šahrazūr, the most powerful Kurdish frontier chief, and his numerous tribesmen. ʿAlī Pasha viewed this move as a breach of frontier protocol and caused a rift in relations between the two powers. When, in 1221/1806, ʿAlī Pasha attacked ʿAbd-al-Raḥmān Khan inside Persian territory Moḥammad-ʿAlī Mīrzā responded by crossing into Iraqi Kurdistan, accompanied by other military chiefs, and capturing Solaymānīya, taking prisoner the Ottoman governor and a large body of troops (Hedāyat, *Rawżat al-ṣafā* I, pp. 426-30; Eʿtemād-al-Salṭana, *Montaẓam-e nāṣerī* III, pp. 1478-79, 1482-83; Kormūjī, p. 13-14). In this campaign the young prince revealed valor and political skill, but his success was also facilitated by the *wālī*'s retreat, in compliance with the Ottoman sultan's desire to maintain peace with Persia in hopes of forging an alliance against the common Russian threat. ʿAlī Pasha dispatched the celebrated Arab Shiʿite jurist Shaikh Jaʿfar Najafī, author of *Kašf al-ḡeṭāʾ*, to negotiate with Moḥammad-ʿAlī Mīrzā in Kermānšāh; he persuaded the deeply religious prince to advise his father to cease hostilities and release the captured prisoners in exchange for reinstatement of ʿAbd-al-Raḥmān in Šahrazūr.

Following the age-old tradition of assigning frontier provinces to senior sons, in 1224/1809 the shah formally appointed Moḥammad-ʿAlī Mīrzā governor-general (*wālī*) of the entire frontier region from Kermānšāh, Zohāb, and Sonqor to Hamadān, Lorestān, Baktīārī, and Kūzestān; he served in this post unchallenged for the rest of his life. He was also given the title *dawlatšāh*, which emboded a subtle reference to regal prospects. Assignment of so large a territory to Moḥammad-ʿAlī Mīrzā, who governed with a miniature version of the Tehran court, represented Fatḥ-ʿAlī Shah's policy of creating semiautonomous princely governorships in hopes of lessening rivalry among his sons; he supplemented the appointments with numerous gifts of concubines and jewelry. Governing a strategically important region on the Ottoman frontier posed fresh challenges to the ambitious Moḥammad-ʿAlī Mīrzā. The disputed sovereignty over the Kurdish frontier tribes was further complicated by the shifting loyalties of the Bābān chiefs, who tried to play the neighboring states off against each other. Moreover, the security of Persian pilgrims to the holy cities of Iraq, which was frequently violated, and obstacles to the flow of overland trade between Baghdad and Kermānšāh were thorny issues that prevented conclusion of a defensive treaty between the Persian and Ottoman empires against Russia, a treaty that Great Britain strongly favored. In 1227/1812 ʿAbd-al-Raḥmān was defeated in skirmishes with Ottoman troops of a new *wālī* in Iraq, ʿAbd-Allāh Pasha, and again took refuge with Moḥammad-ʿAlī Mīrzā, who then attacked Ottoman territory at the head of a large force, advancing to the vicinity of Baghdad. Mediation by Shaikh Jaʿfar Najafī put an end to Persian looting and destruction in exchange for reinstatement of the Bābān chief as governor of Šahrazūr. Despite the appointment in 1231/1816 of Dāwūd Pasha, a more forceful *wālī* of Baghdad, the Persians retained this advantage for nearly a decade (Hedāyat, *Rawżat al-ṣafā* I, pp. 481-82; Eʿtemād-al-Salṭana, *Montaẓam-e nāṣerī* III, pp. 1504-05).

The policy of backing Kurdish warlords against Baghdad as a guarantee for security of the Persian frontiers reached a climax in 1236/1821, when Dawlatšāh again attacked Baghdad on the pretext of protecting ʿAbd-al-Raḥmān's son and successor, Maḥmūd Pasha Bābān, whom the Ottomans accused of disloyalty. Dawlatšāh's operation was coordinated with a campaign by ʿAbbās Mīrzā, who, after being defeated in the first round of the Russo-Persian war (1220-28/1805-13), was seeking victory over the Ottomans on the Erzurum (Arz-e Rūm) front in Anatolia. Moḥammad-ʿAlī advanced deep into Iraq but was stopped by the formidable walls of Baghdad and dissuaded from taking the city by the intervention of Shaikh Mūsā Najafī, son of Shaikh Jaʿfar. This campaign ended abruptly, however, with the prince's death from cholera at Ṭāq-e Garrā during his withdrawal. Dawlatšāh's death led to a temporary lull in the troubled relations between Persia and the Ottoman empire; shortly afterward some of the disputed issues were partially settled in the treaty of Erzurum in 1238/1823 (Ḥedāyat, *Rawżat al-ṣafā* I, pp. 597-604).

Dawlatšāh's military ventures were partly motivated by intense competition with ʿAbbās Mīrzā. The principles of Qajar succession had not yet been fully established, and the two brothers' valor and military leadership seemed crucial to their nomination to the throne. Despite his seniority, Dawlatšāh's descent from a slave was a fundamental obstacle. ʿAbbās Mīrzā was descended from the Qajar family on both sides, which favored his claim. Āqā Moḥammad Khan (q.v.) had supposedly named pure Qajar lineage as the prime prerequisite for succession, but it was resisted by royal princes who preferred either primogeniture or an open contest to determine the ablest candidate. Moḥammad-ʿAlī Mīrzā viewed the succession as his legitimate right and resented his exclusion, particularly as he possessed superior martial qualities, a record of repeated military victories, and a robust physique, in contrast to ʿAbbās Mīrzā, who had a weak constitution and had been defeated in the war with Russia. The shah's efforts to preserve a balance of power among his sons were further complicated by the growing involvement of European powers and their support of rival candidates. Article 4 of the treaty of Golestān (1228/1813) left the door open for Moḥammad-ʿAlī Mīrzā's succession. It required the tsar "to recognize the Prince who shall be nominated heir-apparent, and to afford him assistance in case he should require it to suppress any opposing party" (Hurewitz, p. 198). Not surprisingly, in 1233/1818 Prince Alexei Petrovich Ermolov, the Russian emissary to Persia, who was frustrated by ʿAbbās Mīrzā's resistance to his territorial demands, began to court Moḥammad-ʿAlī Mīrzā and promised support for his claim to the succession (Atkin, p. 153; Algar, p. 83). Although this rapprochement brought no concrete results, it may have influenced Moḥammad-ʿAlī Mīrzā's aggressive policy toward Ottoman Iraq. His death removed the most formidable challenge to ʿAbbās Mīrzā's succession and reduced the intensity of the civil war fought in 1249-50/1834-35 between ʿAbbās Mīrzā's son Moḥammad Shah (1250-64/1834-48) and the surviving senior sons of Fatḥ-ʿAlī Shah.

Moḥammad-ʿAlī Mīrzā's impressive military record was not incongruent with a certain degree of cultural refinement and political competence. Under his rule Kermānšāh and the western provinces enjoyed an exceptional period of prosperity and social calm, enhanced by trade and pilgrim traffic, as well as by the expansion of the rich agricultural base. He also tolerated ethnic and religious diversity in the province. Large communities of the Kurdish Ahl-e Ḥaqq (q.v.) residing in the Kermānšāh region served in his army, and their chiefs benefited from the prince's patronage. Although he showed respect for jurists like Shaikh Jaʿfar Najafī, the prince preferred the celebrated Arab theologian and philosopher Shaikh Aḥmad Aḥsāʾī (q.v.), founder of Shaikhism; at the prince's invitation and with his financial support the saintly Aḥsāʾī lived in Kermānšāh for eight years (1229-37/1814-21), providing a counterbalance to the stern legalism of the *mojtahed*s. At Moḥammad-ʿAlī Mīrzā's request he wrote a number of treatises on theological subjects, including *al-ʿEṣma wa'l-rajaʿa* on corporeal resurrection. The prince's interest in the hereafter went beyond eschatological conjecture, and he sought to guarantee his own salvation by convincing Aḥsāʾī to produce a testament, comparable to an indulgence, to his good conduct in this world. On his deathbed Dawlatšāh made sure that this testament would be placed in his coffin (Algar, pp. 68, 70).

Dawlatšāh's religious outlook did not diminish his curiosity about the West. Āqā Sayyed Aḥmad Behbahānī, a relatively enlightened son of Āqā Moḥammad-ʿAlī and a resident of India, dedicated to the prince a voluminous tome on family history and an account of modern Europe and the New World entitled *Merʾāt al-aḥwāl-e jahānnemā*. One of the earliest such works in Persian, it seems to have been a source of Dawlatšāh's knowledge of European history and contemporary affairs, which impressed the British envoy Sir Gore Ouseley when he met him in 1224/1809. Dawlatšāh's erroneous insistence that the Portuguese, rather than the Spaniards, had been the first explorers of the New World incensed Ouseley, however. In keeping with the fashion in the time of Fatḥ-ʿAlī Shah, Dawlatšāh also composed poetry under the pen name (*ta*k*alloṣ*) Dawlat (Ḵayyāmpūr, *So*k*anvarān*, p. 213). In addition to his *Dīvān*, he also compiled a biographical dictionary of his own contemporaries, *Maʿāṣer-e Dawlatšāh*, which is unpublished. His interest in astronomy and occult sciences, history, and literary theory exemplifies the Qajar princes' attachment to Persian high culture. He patronized buildings in Qazvīn, Šūštar, Dezfūl, and Kermānšāh, including the Gargar dam in Šūštar. In competition with ʿAbbās Mīrzā he also tried to modernize his army along European lines, first by employing French officers from the mission of General Alfred de Gardane to Persia in 1223/1808 and soon after by commissioning British instructors.

European observers judged Dawlatšāh differently. Some admired his robustness, articulacy, and assertiveness, whereas his critics judged him volatile and imperious. In 1226/1811 he allegedly threatened to stab himself if his father denied him permission to attack Baghdad (Atkin, p. 115). His bitterness at being denied the succession is clear from some anecdotes from his childhood (e.g., ʿAżod-al-Dawla, pp. 122, 124).

Given the intense rivalry between ʿAbbās Mīrzā and Dawlatšāh, Fatḥ-ʿAlī Shah's anxiety over their simultaneous presence in the annual military review at Solṭānīya in 1223/1808 is comprehensible, as is his careful manipulation of protocol involving the two at the court in Tehran. The seat on his right during public audiences and on other occasions was awarded alternately to Moḥammad-ʿAlī Mīrzā and ʿAbbās Mīrzā, symbolizing the shah's deliberate ambiguity over the final choice of his successor. His intense grief at Moḥammad-ʿAlī Mīrzā's death may have reflected his loss not only of a capable son but also of a counterbalance in the complex princely politics of his kingdom.

Dawlatšāh was survived by twenty-four children, including seven adult sons, of whom the eldest, Moḥammad-Ḥosayn Mīrzā, succeeded him as governor of Kermānšāh and was himself succeeded by his brother Ṭahmāsb Mīrzā Moʾayyad-al-Dawla, known for both literary and technological pursuits. The governorship of Kermānšāh remained in Dawlatšāh's house until the death of still another son, Emāmqolī Mīrzā ʿEmād-al-Dawla, in 1292/1875.

Bibliography: ʿAbd-Allāh Aḥsāʾī, *Resāla-ye šarḥ-e aḥwāl-e Šay*k* Aḥmad b. Zayn al-ʿĀbedīn Aḥsāʾī*, tr. M.-Ṭ. Kermānī, 2nd ed., Kermān, n.d., pp. 27-28, 34-35. H. Algar, *Religion and State in Iran. The Role of the Ulama in the Qajar Period*, Berkeley, Calif., 1969, pp. 54, 76. A. Amanat, *Resurrection and Renewal. The Making of the Babi Movement in Iran, 1844-50*, Ithaca, N.Y., 1989, pp. 56, 63-64. M. Atkin, *Russia and Iran, 1780-1828*, Minneapolis, Minn., 1980, pp. 113, 115-17, 153, 156. Solṭān-Aḥmad Mīrzā ʿAżod-al-Dawla, *Tārī*k*-e ʿażodī*, ed. ʿA.-Ḥ. Navāʾī, 3rd ed., Tehran, 1355 Š./1976. Bāmdād, *Rejāl* III, pp. 430-31. ʿAbd-al-Razzāq Donbolī, *Maʾāṯer-e solṭānīya*, Tabrīz, 1241/1825-26, pp. 184-85, 219-25, 242-62, 367. ʿAlīqolī Mīrzā Eʿteżād-al-Salṭana, *Eksīr al-tawārī*k, ed. J. Kayānfar, Tehran, 1370/1991, pp. 125, 183-85. R. Hedāyat, *Rawżat al-ṣafā* IX, pp. 348, 575. J. C. Hurewitz, *The Middle East and North Africa in World Politics* I, New Haven, Conn., 1975. P. A. Jaubert, *Voyage en Arménie et en Perse, fait dans les années 1805 et 1806*, Paris, 1821, chaps. 23, 31. Idem, "Histoire persane de la dynastie des Kadjars," *JA* 13, 1834, pp. 211-13. H. Jones (Brydges), *Account of the Transaction of His Majesty's Mission to the Court of Persia in the Years 1807-1811*, London, 1834, pp. 248-49. Moḥammad-Jaʿfar Ḵormūjī, *Ḥaqāyeq al-a*k*bār-e nāṣerī*, ed. Ḥ. Ḵadīv Jam, 2nd ed., Tehran, 1363 Š./1984. J. Morier, *A Second Journey through Persia, Armenia and Asia Minor to Constatinople*, London, 1818, pp. 195-97. Mošār, *Moʾallefīn* IV, p. 239. S. Nafīsī, *Tārī*k*-e ejtemāʿī wa sīāsī-e Īrān dar dawra-ye moʿāṣer* I, Tehran, 1335 Š./1956, pp. 327-28. M.-R. Naṣīrī, *Asnād wa mokātabāt-e tārī*k*ī-e Īrān (Qājārīya)* I, Tehran, 1366 Š./1987, pp. 164-65, 208-09, 233-39, 253-57. W. Ouseley, *Travels in Various Countries of the East* III, London, 1821, pp. 347-49. E. Pakravan, *Abbas-Mirza*, Paris, 1973, index. Moḥammad-Taqī Lesān-al-Molk Sepehr, *Nāse*k* al-tawārī*k I, Tehran, 1344 Š./1965, pp. 209, 225-28, 329.

(ABBAS AMANAT)

AMĪR **DAWLATŠĀH** b. Amīr ʿAlāʾ-al-Dawla Boḵtīšāh Ḡāzī **SAMARQANDĪ** (b. ca. 842/1438, d. 900/1494 or 913/1507), author of *Taḏkerat al-šoʿarāʾ* (Memorial of poets), a book containing biographies of about 150 poets with specimens of their poetry, as well as historical information. Dawlatšāh was one of the few authors before the 16th century to have devoted a work entirely to poets, arranged more or less chronologically. His is the second such full-length Persian *taḏkera* of poets to have survived, the first being *Lobāb al albāb* by ʿAwfī (q.v.). The only other earlier work known to have been of the same type, Abū Ṭāher Ḵāṭūnī's *Manāqeb al-šoʿarāʾ*, has apparently been lost. Dawlatšāh was unaware of these earlier works, however (Nafīsī, *Naẓm o naṯr* I, pp. 13, 87-88).

The title "amir" in his name and information given by ʿAlī-Šīr Navāʾī (*Majāles al-nafāʾes*, p. 108), to whom the *Taḏkerat al-šoʿarāʾ* was dedicated, indicate that Dawlatšāh belonged to the the ruling elite. His father, ʿAlāʾ-al-Dawla Boḵtīšāh, was a confidant of the Timurid Šāhroḵ (807-50/1405-47), and his brother Amir Rażī-al-Dīn ʿAlī, who wrote poetry in Persian and Turkish, served Abu'l-Qāsem Bābor in Khorasan (853-61/1459-

57). Dawlatšāh himself wrote poetry and was for a time a companion of Sultan Ḥosayn Bāyqarā (875-912/1470-1506), but he eventually withdrew from court and government service (Dawlatšāh, ed. Browne, pp. 11, 337-38, 455-56; Ḵayyāmpūr, *Soḵanvarān*, p. 399). As Dawlatšāh completed *Taḏkerat al-šoʿarāʾ* in 892/1486, when he was about fifty years old, he was probably born in 842/1438 (Dawlatšāh, ed. Browne, pp. 11, 403). His death was reported by Ḥājī Ḵalīfa (*Kašf al-ẓonūn*, ed. Yaltkaya and Bilge, I, cols. 387-88) and by Esmāʿīl Pāšā Baḡdādī (col. 364) as having occurred in 913/1507, though Charles Rieu, on the authority of *Merʾāt al-ṣafāʾ* by Moḥammad-ʿAlī Borhānpūrī (comp. 1148/1735), proposed the year 900/1494 (*Persian Manuscripts* I, p. 364).

Taḏkerat al-šoʿarāʾ is divided into a lengthy preface with a biographical notice about the author; a preamble on ten poets who composed in Arabic; seven chapters on poets who composed in Persian, from Rūdakī to Dawlatšāh's contemporaries; and an epilogue on six great men of letters who lived in the author's time (e.g., ʿAbd-al-Raḥmān Jāmī, ʿAlī-Šīr Navāʾī) with a biographical sketch of Sultan Ḥosayn Bāyqarā. It is written in flowing prose, in a style between the epistolary and the ornate. Its chief merit is the information that it provides on the lives and works of poets who lived after the composition of *Lobāb al-albāb*. It should not, however, be overlooked that the author paid little heed to the veracity of the information that he collected, some of which belongs to the realm of fairy tales. Furthermore, the earlier the poet, the more frequent are the errors and flaws. Nevertheless, a critical reader can find much reliable and useful information, especially about periods closer to the author's own time.

Editions of *Taḏkerat al-šoʿarāʾ* have been published by an anonymous editor (Bombay, 1887); E. G. Browne (Leiden and London, 1901); and Moḥammad Ramażānī (Tehran, 1338 Š./1959). It was translated into Turkish in the mid-16th century (*Kašf al-ẓonūn*, ed. Yaltkaya and Bilge, cols. 387-88). According to Browne (*Lit. Hist. Persia* III, p. 436), a second, abridged Turkish translation, by Solaymān Fahmī, appeared under the title *Safīnat al-šoʿarāʾ* in 1259/1843. In modern Turkish there is a translation in four volumes by Necâti Lugal (Istanbul, 1977). A German translation was published by Josef von Hammer (*Geschichte der schönen Redekünste Persiens* . . ., Vienna, 1818).

Bibliography: Bahār, *Sabk-šenāsī* III, pp. 184 ff. Esmāʿīl Pāšā Baḡdādī, *Hedayāt al-ʿārefīn* I, Istanbul, 1951. Browne, "The Sources of Dawlat-shah," *JRAS*, 1899, pp. 37-60. Idem, *Lit. Hist. Persia* III, index, s.v. Dawlatshāh. Golčīn-e Maʿānī, *Taḏkerahā* I, pp. 264-66. C. Huart and [H. Massé], "Dawlat-shāh," in *EI*[2] II, p. 179. M. F. Köprülü, "Devlet-şah," in *İA* III, pp. 560-62. Ṣafā, *Adabīyāt* IV, 4th ed, Tehran, 1366 Š./1977, pp. 531-34.

(ḎABĪḤ-ALLĀH ṢAFĀ)

DAWLATZĪ (singular Dawlatzay), ethnic name common among the eastern Pashtun on both sides of the Durand Line (see BOUNDARIES iii). The different tribal units bearing the name do not seem to be connected with one another. They are found in four different geographical locations, three on the Pakistani side of the boundary and one in Afghanistan.

In Pakistan. One of the seven subtribes of the Ōrakzī is called Dawlatzī. Its strength was estimated at 1,550 fighting men in 1900 and 2,100 in 1908, that is 6-7 percent of the tribe's total population (King, p. 16; *Frontier*, p. 193). These Dawlatzī are Sunnites, though in one source it is erroneously reported that some of them are Shiʿite (*Dictionary*, p. 54). Their winter settlements are located in the lower Mastura valley, and they thus control several passes on the border between independent tribal territory and the settled district of Kōhāt (in the North-West Frontier Province, Pakistan). Early contacts with the British were alternately peaceful, during which they received annual allowances for guarding the passes (Aitchison, pp. 513 ff.), and hostile, when there were innumerable raids and counterattacks (Paget and Mason, pp. 395 ff.; King, pp. 162 ff.; *Frontier*, pp. 210 ff.; Wylly, pp. 367 ff.; Aitchison, pp. 498 ff.). The former ruling family of Bhopal (Madhya Pradesh, India) is said to have been descended from the Fīrōzḵēl, one of three branches of these Dawlatzī (King, p. 38).

Two minor fractions of the great Kākaṛ tribe also bear the name Dawlatzī, one belonging to the ʿAlīḵēl (also ʿAlīzī) section of the Sanjarḵēl subtribe, the other to the Domaṛ, an adopted subtribe, both living in the Zob district of Baluchistan. They counted 700 and 50 fighting men respectively in 1899 (*Dictionary*, pp. 54-55).

Finally, there are three Dawlatzī fractions among the northeastern Pashtun, the first among the Malīzī Yūsofzī in the central Barandū valley in Būnēr (*Dictionary*, p. 55: 1,500 fighting men in 1899; for a list of their villages, see Ridgway, p. 200; cf. Bellew, p. 175; Ḥayāt Khan, tr., p. 112); a second among their southern neighbors, the Amāzī (also Anāzī) ʿOṯmānzī Mandaṛ of the Sadūm valley (Mardān district; see Ridgway, pp. 185-86); and the third among the pashtunized Manṣūr Gadūn (also Jadūn) of the Hazāra district, east of the Indus (Ridgway, p. 239). In the latter instance, however, the Dawlatzī of the English authors are consistently called Dawlazī in indigenous sources (Ḥayāt Khan, pp. 154-55; Šēr Moḥammad, p. 204); the former is possibly a hypercorrective form of the latter. Similarly, Dawlatzī Yūsofzī is the form given in all Persian sources, but in 1184/1770 Raḥmat Khan, in his *Ḵolāṣat al-ansāb*, spelled it Dawlazī Yūsofzī (Neʿmat-Allāh, tr., p. 125 n. 50).

In Afghanistan. The best-known group of Dawlatzī belongs to the confederation of Ḡelzay tribes, though its status is somewhat controversial. According to Afghan genealogists the Dawlatzay constitute merely a section of the Ṣāleḥḵēl subtribe of the Solaymānḵēl tribe (Ḥayāt Khan, p. 164; Šēr Moḥammad, p. 214).

Although most Dawlatzī acknowledge the connection, it has been reported that the Solaymānk̲ēl do not (Robinson, p. 159), considering the Dawlatzī an independent, non-Ḡelzay tribe. Similar situations are frequent among the Pashtun and usually reflect the genealogical transposition by adoption of a loose political alliance between a larger tribe and a smaller, vassal tribe.

The number of sedentary Dawlatzay families is unknown, but two villages named Dawlatzay are listed in the province of Kabul, two others in Paktīā, and one each in Nangrahār and Samangān (Nāheż, pp. 274-75). In the unpublished survey of Afghan nomads conducted in 1357 Š./1978 560 nomadic Dawlatzay families and 553 seminomadic ones were enumerated. In 1357 Š./1978 most of the former owned flocks and wintered in the K̲ōst basin of Paktīā, spending the summer on the northwestern slopes of the Solaymān mountains (Saydābād district). Most of the seminomads were landless peasants having a permanent winter settlement in Nangrahār and summer quarters in the vicinity of Kabul, where they performed any kind of unskilled work available, from harvesting in the countryside to casual labor in town. In addition, sixty-five nomad families, fifteen of harvesters, the rest pastoral, were migrating from southern Afghanistan to the upper Tarnak valley; 150 agricultural-pastoral semi-nomadic families from Čārbōlak, west of Balk̲, summered in northern Hazārajāt.

From its original home in southeastern Afghanistan the tribe separated geographically in two stages. In the late 19th century several hundred families were transplanted to Afghan Turkestan under the northern Afghanistan pashtunization scheme then in progress; in the 1880s 300 Dawlatzay families were reportedly living (perhaps only in winter) in the Balk̲ oasis, and 30 others near Aybak (Samangān; Maitland, pp. 176, 461, 488; partly repr. in *Gazetteer of Afghanistan* IV, pp. 196, 254). Since the 1930s such impoverished lineages as the Māṇīwāl of Čārbōlak have also left southeastern Afghanistan (Robinson, p. 159), following the decline of trading nomadism across the border. The development of service nomadism among some other sections of the Dawlatzī is another aspect of the same process of proletarization.

In the 1930s some 200 nomadic Dawlatzay families from ten different sections were migrating between the basins of northwestern British India, where they camped in winter (in the Kurram Agency of the North-West Frontier Province and the Lōralāy district of Baluchistan), and the highlands of central Afghanistan, where they summered (Behsūd district of Hazārajāt; Robinson, p. 159). All were purely trading nomads, without land or flocks. Like other Ḡelzay nomads, the Dawlatzī penetrated into the heart of Hazārajāt during their participation in the military conquest of the area in 1310/1892-93 (Fayż Moḥammad, p. 715). In subsequent decades they took an active part in the flourishing summer nomad *bāzārs* of central Afghanistan (Ferdinand, pp. 144, 148; see BĀZĀR v). But in 1357 Š./1978 only one section, the Qalandark̲ēl, comprising forty families, was still migrating across the Durand Line, though no longer carrying on trade or traveling via the Hazārajāt highlands (Balland, 1988, p. 185; idem, 1991, pp. 226-27).

Bibliography: C. U. Aitchison, ed., *A Collection of Treaties, Engagements and Sanads Relating to India and Neighbouring Countries* XI, Delhi, 1933; repr. Delhi, 1983. D. Balland, "Le déclin contemporain du nomadisme pastoral en Afghanistan," in E. Grötzbach, ed., *Neue Beiträge zur Afghanistanforschung*, Schriftenreihe der Stiftung Bibliotheca Afghanica 6, Liestal, Switzerland, 1988, pp. 175-98. Idem, "Nomadism and Politics. The Case of Afghan Nomads in the Indian Subcontinent," *Studies in History* (New Delhi) 7/2, 1991, pp. 205-29. H. W. Bellew, *A General Report on the Yusufzais*, Lahore, 1864; repr. Lahore, 1977. *A Dictionary of the Pathan Tribes on the North-West Frontier of India*, Calcutta, 1899. Fayż Moḥammad, *Serāj-al-tawārīk̲*, 3 vols., Kabul, 1131-33/1913-15. K. Ferdinand, "Nomadic Expansion and Commerce in Central Afghanistan. A Sketch of Some Modern Trends," *Folk* 4, 1962, pp. 123-59. *Frontier and Overseas Expeditions from India* II, Calcutta, 1908; repr. Quetta, 1979; repr. Delhi, 1983. M. Ḥayāt Khan, *Ḥayāt-e-Afḡān* I, Lahore, 1867; tr. H. Priestley as *Afghanistan and Its Inhabitants*, Lahore, 1874; repr. Lahore, 1981. L. W. King, *The Orakzai Country and Clans*, 2nd ed., Lahore, 1984. P. J. Maitland, *Diary, with Notes on the Population and Resources of Districts Visited 1884 to 1887*, Afghan Boundary Commission, Records of Intelligence Party II, Simla, 1888. M. Ḥ. Nāheż, ed. *Qāmūs-e jоḡrāfīāʾī-e Afḡānestān* II, Kabul, 1336 Š./1957. Neʿmat-Allāh Heravī, *Tārīk̲-e afḡānān*, tr. B. Dorn as *History of the Afghans*, 2 pts., London, 1829-36; repr. London, 1965; repr. Karachi, 1976. W. H. Paget and A. H. Mason, *Record of Expeditions against the North-West Frontier Tribes since the Annexation of the Punjab*, London, 1884; repr. as *Tribes of the North-West Frontier*, Delhi, 1980. R. T. I. Ridgway, *Pathans*, Calcutta, 1910; repr. Peshawar, 1983. J. A. Robinson, *Notes on Nomad Tribes of Eastern Afghanistan*, New Delhi, 1935; repr. Quetta, 1978; repr. Quetta, 1980. Šēr Moḥammad Khan, *Tawārīk̲-e k̲oršīd-e jahān*, Lahore, 1311/1894. H. C. Wylly, *From the Black Mountain to Waziristan*, London, 1912.

(DANIEL BALLAND)

DAWR (Ar. and Pers.), period, era, or cycle of history, a term used by Ismaʿilis in connection with their conceptions of time and the religious history of mankind. The early Ismaʿilis conceived of time (*zamān*) as a progression of cycles or eras, *dawr*s (Ar. pl. *adwār*), with a beginning and an end. On the basis of their eclectic temporal vision, which reflected Greek, Judeo-Christian, and Gnostic influences, as well as the eschatological ideas of earlier Shiʿites, they worked out a view of history, or rather hierohistory, in terms of the eras (*dawr*s) of different prophets recognized in the

Koran. This prophetic interpretation of history was, moreover, combined with the Isma'ili doctrine of the imamate, which had been inherited from the Imami Shi'ites.

The Isma'ilis thus believed from early on that the hierohistory of mankind comprised seven prophetic eras (*dawr*s) of various durations, each inaugurated by the speaker-prophet or enunciator (*nāṭeq*) of a revealed message that in its exoteric (*ẓāher*) aspect contained a religious law, or *šarī'a*. The *nāṭeq*s of the first six eras were Adam, Noah, Abraham, Moses, Jesus, and Moḥammad respectively. Each was succeeded by a legatee (*waṣī*), also called "foundation" (*asās*) or "silent one" (*ṣāmet*), who revealed to the elite the inner (*bāṭen*) meanings of the message for his *dawr*. These inner meanings represented the unchangeable truths (*ḥaqā'eq*) of Isma'ili gnosis. Each *waṣī* was, in turn, succeeded by seven imams, who guarded the true meaning of the message in both *ẓāher* and *bāṭen* aspects. The seventh imam of each *dawr* became the *nāṭeq* of the following *dawr*, abrogating the *šarī'a* of the previous *nāṭeq* and promulgating a new one (*Feraq al-šī'a*, pp. 61-63; Qomī, pp. 83-85, apud Stern, pp. 49-55; Madelung, pp. 48 ff.; Daftary, pp. 104-05, 136-40). This pattern would change only in the seventh, final *dawr* of hierohistory.

In the sixth *dawr*, the era of the Prophet Moḥammad and Islam, the seventh imam was Moḥammad b. Esmā'īl b. Ja'far al-Ṣādeq, who had gone into concealment. On his reappearance as the *qā'em* (restorer of justice on earth and true Islam), or *mahdī*, he would become the seventh *nāṭeq*, ruling over the final, eschatological *dawr*. Moḥammad b. Esmā'īl would abrogate the law of Islam; his own divine message would not entail a new law, however, but would consist of the full revelation of the esoteric truths (*ḥaqā'eq*) concealed in all the previous messages, the immutable truths of all religions, which had previously been accessible only to the elite of mankind. In this final, messianic age there would be no need for religious law. Moḥammad b. Esmā'īl, the last of the *nāṭeq*s and imams, would rule in justice as the eschatological *qā'em* and would then bring to an end the physical world. His *dawr* would thus mark the end of time and human history (Ebn Ḥawšab, pp. 189, 191-92, 197 ff.; Ja'far b. Manṣūr Yaman, 1952, pp. 14 ff., 50, 97, 104, 109, 113-14, 132-33, 138, 150, 170; Abū Ya'qūb, 1966, pp. 181-93; idem, 1980, pp. 47-56; Corbin, pp. 30 ff.; Halm, pp. 18-37; Walker, pp. 355-66).

The whole cycle from Adam to the advent of the *qā'em* as the seventh *nāṭeq* was also called the "era of concealment" (*dawr al-satr*), because the truths were concealed in the laws. By contrast, the seventh *dawr*, when the truths would be fully revealed to mankind, was designated the "era of revelation, or manifestation" (*dawr al-kašf*), an era of pure spiritual knowledge with no need for religious laws. The Isma'ilis also used the expression *dawr al-satr* in reference to a period when the imams were hidden (*mastūr*) from the eyes of their followers, in contradistinction to *dawr al-kašf*, when the imams were manifest and accessible.

This Isma'ili view of history was evidently first committed to writing in Persia and Transoxania by prominent early *dā'ī*s (missionaries) and authors there, notably Moḥammad b. Aḥmad Nasafī (d. 332/943-44), whose major treatise *Ketāb al-maḥṣūl* has not survived, and Abū Ḥātem Rāzī (d. 322/934), whose ideas on the subject were primarily expounded in his *Ketāb al-eṣlāḥ*, which is still unpublished. Both these early Isma'ili theologians envisaged hierohistory in terms of the scheme of seven prophetic eras, though they disagreed on some details. In fact, they became the protagonists in a scholarly debate over religious obligations and certain metaphysical issues, later joined by Nasafī's disciple Abū Ya'qūb Sejestānī. Subsequently the *dā'ī* Ḥamīd-al-Dīn Kermānī acted as arbiter in this controversy (Kermānī, pp. 176-212). Nasafī and Abū Ḥātem devoted much energy and imagination to accommodating other religions, notably those of the Zoroastrians and the Sabaeans, within their scheme of seven prophetic eras, assigning these religions to specific *dawr*s and *nāṭeq*s. Abū Ḥātem also introduced the concept of an interim period (*dawr al-fatra*), marked by the absence of imams and occurring at the end of each prophetic *dawr*, between the disappearance of the seventh imam of that era and the advent of the *nāṭeq* of the following era. According to him, the Zoroastrians belonged to the fourth era, the *dawr* of Moses, and Zoroaster himself had appeared during the interim period at the end of that *dawr* (pp. 52 ff., 59, 69 ff., 160 ff., 171-77; Abū Ya'qūb, 1966, pp. 82-83; Corbin, pp. 187-93; Madelung, pp. 101-14; Stern, pp. 30-46; Daftary, pp. 234-39).

The cyclical prophetic view of hierohistory elaborated by the early Isma'ilis was retained by the Fatimid Isma'ilis, who refined or modified certain aspects of it, especially in connection with the duration of the sixth *dawr*, the era of Islam; the number of imams during that era; and the *qā'em* and his functions (see, e.g., Ja'far b. Manṣūr Yaman, 1984, pp. 21 ff., 57 ff., 67 ff., 101, 105, 109, 112, 164 ff., 201 ff., 217, 219, 229 ff.; Qāżī No'mān, pp. 40-368; Daftary, pp. 176-79, 218-20, 234). Some authors of the Fatimid period introduced new concepts into the cyclical scheme. The Persian Nāṣer-e Ḵosrow (394-ca. 471/1004-ca. 1078), for instance, distinguished between a grand cycle (*dawr-e mehīn*), encompassing the entire sequence of the seven *nāṭeq*s, and a small cycle (*dawr-e kehīn*), coinciding with the latter part of the grand cycle and including the era of Islam and thereafter (pp. 62-64, 126-27, 157, 169-70, 245, 256, 331).

Later Isma'ilis introduced further innovations into the earlier interpretation of hierohistory expressed in terms of the seven prophetic *dawr*s. On the basis of astronomical calculations the Yamanī Ṭayyebīs conceived of a grand eon (*kawr a'ẓam*) comprised of countless cycles, each divided into seven *dawr*s, which would be consummated in the *qā'em* of the "great resurrection" (*qīāmat al-qīāmāt*). Furthermore, the grand eon was held to progress through successive cycles of concealment (*satr*) and revelation (*kašf* or *ẓohūr*), each composed of seven *dawr*s (see e.g. Ḥāmedī, pp. 149 ff., 205-27, 232 ff., 258-72; Walīd, pp. 100 ff., 121-28; Corbin, pp. 37-58; Daftary, pp. 140-41, 291 ff., 295).

The Nezārī Ismaʿilis of the Alamūt period (487-654/1094-1256) in Persia followed a religious and political path of their own and, unlike the Ṭayyebī Ismaʿilis, were not particularly concerned with the earlier cyclical view of history, though they generally adhered to the scheme of seven prophetic eras. However, in connection with elaborating their own doctrines, they allowed for transitory eras of resurrection (*qīāmat*) during the *dawr* of the Prophet Moḥammad, who, like the five enunciating prophets before him, had initiated an era of concealment (*dawr-e satr*). In the era of Islam, and in special honor of Moḥammad's greatness, there could be occasional anticipatory eras of resurrection, each offering a foretaste of the *qīāmat* that was to occur at the end of Moḥammad's era, ushering in the seventh and final millennium in the religious history of mankind. The condition of *qīāmat* could in principle be granted at any time, to mankind as a whole or to the elite, by the current Nezārī imam, for every imam was potentially also a *qāʾem*. As a result, in the era of Moḥammad human life could alternate, at the will of the imam, between *dawr*s of *qīāmat* and *satr*, the normal condition of human life. The Nezārīs, however, interpreted the *qīāmat* symbolically and spiritually as the manifestation of the unveiled truth in the person of the Nezārī imam, whereas *satr* meant concealment of the true spiritual reality of the imam, when truth was again hidden in the *bāṭen* of the laws, requiring the strictest observance of the *šarīʿa* and *taqīya*, or dissimulation (Ṭūsī, pp. 61-63, 83-84, 101-02, 110, 117-19, 128-49; Corbin, pp. 117 ff.; Hodgson, pp. 148 ff., 225-38; Daftary, pp. 386 ff., 404 ff., 410-11).

Bibliography: Abū Ḥātem Rāzī, *Aʿlām al-nobūwa*, ed. Ṣ. Ṣāwī and Ḡ.-R. Aʿwānī, Tehran, 1356 Š./1977. Abū Yaʿqūb Sejestānī, *Eṯbāt al-nobūwāt*, ed. ʿĀ. Tāmer, Beirut, 1966. Idem, *Ketāb al-efteḵār*, ed. M. Ḡāleb, Beirut, 1980. H. Corbin, *Cyclical Time and Ismaili Gnosis*, London, 1983. F. Daftary, *The Ismāʿīlīs. Their History and Doctrines*, Cambridge, 1990. Ebn Ḥawšab Manṣūr Yaman, *Ketāb al-rošd wa'l-hedāya*, ed. M. Kāmel Ḥosayn, in W. Ivanow, ed., *Collectanea* I, Leiden, 1948. H. Halm, *Kosmologie und Heilslehre der frühen Ismāʿīlīya*, Wiesbaden, 1978. Ebrāhīm b. Ḥosayn Ḥāmedī, *Ketāb kanz al-walad*, ed. M. Ḡāleb, Wiesbaden, 1971. M. G. S. Hodgson, *The Order of Assassins*, the Hague, 1955. Jaʿfar b. Manṣūr Yaman, *Ketāb al-kašf*, ed. R. Strothmann, London, 1952. Idem, *Sarāʾer wa asrār al-noṭaqāʾ*, ed. M. Ḡāleb, Beirut, 1984. Ḥamīd-al-Dīn Kermānī, *Ketāb al-rīāż*, ed. ʿĀ. Tāmer, Beirut, 1960. W. Madelung, "Das Imamat in der frühen ismailitischen Lehre," *Der Islam* 37, 1961, pp. 43-135. Nāṣer-e Ḵosrow Qobādīānī, *Wajh-e dīn*, ed. Ḡ.-R. Aʿwānī, Tehran, 1356 Š./1977. Qāżī Abū Ḥanīfa Noʿmān b. Moḥammad, *Asās al-taʾwīl*, ed. ʿĀ. Tāmer, Beirut, 1960. Saʿd b. ʿAbd-Allāh Qomī, *Ketāb al-maqālat wa'l-feraq*, ed. M.-J. Maškūr, Tehran, 1342 Š./1963. S. M. Stern, *Studies in Early Ismāʿīlism*, Jerusalem and Leiden, 1983. Naṣīr-al-Dīn Moḥammad Ṭūsī, *Rawżat al-taslīm*, ed. and tr. W. Ivanow, Leiden, 1950. Ḥosayn b. Aḥmad Walīd, *Resālat al-mabdaʾ wa'l-maʿād*, ed. H. Corbin in *Trilogie Ismaélienne*, Tehran and Paris, 1340 Š./1961, pp. 99-130. P. E. Walker, "Eternal Cosmos and the Womb of History. Time in Early Ismaili Thought," *IJMES* 9, 1978, pp. 355-66.

(FARHAD DAFTARY)

DAWR (Ar. and Pers. "circle"), a term applied to scales and also to rhythmic cycles, both commonly diagramed as circles (*dāʾera*, *dawr*) in the classical musicology of Persian, Arab, and Turkish groups. Such diagrams are particularly appropriate for representing both the cyclical nature of the scales, which characteristically return to their points of departure an octave higher, and the periodic nature of rhythmic formulas, defined by the return of identical patterns at specific intervals.

The scales of *maqām*s, or cycles (*adwār*, *šodūd*), were often represented by circles with eight notes indicated by letters of the alphabet distributed around the circumference, for example, the ninety-one cycles described by ʿAbd-al-Qāder Marāḡī in 818/1415. In some scales notes separated by a perfect fifth were linked by lines, so that it was possible to evaluate easily the degree of harmony (Marāḡī, 1366 Š./1987, pp. 82-85, 87-94; Ḥosaynī, pp. 52-57). Rhythmic cycles (*adwār-e īqāʿ*) were also represented by circles, with dots and letters or syllables distributed around the circumference. By tracing the circumference of the circle with the finger and pronouncing the syllables in turn, it was possible to produce a complete rhythmic formula, ending at the point of departure (Marāḡī, 1366 Š./1987, pp. 217-22). This type of representation is still in use in certain musical traditions. According to Ṣafī-al-Dīn Ormavī (d. 693/1294) and Marāḡī, the syllables were disposed in this fashion in order to symbolize the cyclical nature of the rhythmic paradigm, usually called "cycle" (*dawr*) or "rhythmic cycle" (*dawr-e īqāʿ*) but sometimes "principles" (*oṣūl*) or "metric principles" (*baḥr-e oṣūl*; cf. *Maʿrefat*, p. 195).

The scale.

The term *dawr* seems to have been applied to the scale for the first time in a musicological context in the work of Ṣafī-al-Dīn. In his *Ketāb al-adwār* (650/1252) and *Resālat al-šarafīya* (665/1267) he elaborated on the works of Abū Yūsof Yaʿqūb Kendī (ca. 185-252/802-66), Fārābī (q.v.; d. 339/950), and Avicenna (q.v.; d. 428/1037), notably in listing and systematically analyzing the scales and modes then in use and arranging them according to a new system. The information and description of method provided in these works, particularly in connection with the modal scales, were simply repeated by the majority of later authors, particularly Qoṭb-al-Dīn Maḥmūd Šīrāzī (634-710/1236-1311) in his Persian encyclopedia *Dorrat al-tāj le-ġorrat al-dobbāj*; the unknown author of *Šarḥ-e Mawlānā Mobārakšāh bar adwār* (777/1375); Marāġī in *Jāmeʿ al-alḥān* and the abridgment *Maqāṣed al-alḥān* (817/1414); and Zayn-al-ʿĀbedīn Moḥammad Ḥosaynī in *Qānūn-e ʿelmī wa ʿamalī-e mūsīqī* (ca. 905/1500).

After having established a basic scale of seventeen intervals Ṣafī-al-Dīn derived every possible tetrachord (*jens*) according to rigid and restrictive rules, then combined them in order to construct a number of theoretical scales. He thus obtained and named seven "types" (or divisions) of the fourth and twenty-eight of the fifth, among which were several that were actually played (*Šarḥ*, pp. 288-89, 300), the others being purely theoretical. He reduced the divisions of the fifth to twelve by suppressing defective examples and repetitions, presenting a table in which each of the seven divisions of the fourth was linked to each of the twelve divisions of the fifth. He thus obtained a total of eighty-four octave scales, called *adwār* (cycles) or *šodūd* (from *šadd* "tuning"), forty-three of which were consonant according to his criteria, seventeen semidissonant, and twenty-four dissonant. Qoṭb-al-Dīn added seven consonant cycles to this basic repertoire. Later the commentator on Ṣafī-al-Dīn's *Ketāb al-adwār* added forty-nine theoretical cycles (*Šarḥ*, pp. 344-50), four of which he designated as playable (Māhūrī, Bayḏa, Hadra, Farah; he thus established forty-eight consonant cycles, including those already mentioned, but this time with their full octave spans.

The forty-eight cycles described in the *Šarḥ-e Mawlānā* can be divided into three categories, reflecting different conceptual approaches. The first consisted of twelve *šodūd*, later known as *maqāmāt* (p. 376): ʿOššāq, Navā, Būsalīk (Abū Sālīk), Rāst, ʿErāq, Eṣfahān, Zīrafkand, Bozorg, Zangūla, Rahāvī, Ḥosaynī, and Ḥejāzī. The second category included the six *āvāzes* (*āvāzāt*): Gavešt (Ar. Kowašt), Gardānīya, Nowrūz, Salmak, Māya, Šahnāz, the last three of which were not mentioned by Ṣafī-al-Dīn in his *Resāla-ye šarafīya* but are included in the *Šarḥ* (pp. 390-91). By adding the first three, along with a second form of Ḥejāz, Nahoft, and Moḥayyer-Ḥosaynī, to the twelve *maqāms*, the author of the *Šarḥ* brought the total to eighteen important modal scales (actually seventeen, as Ḥejāz was included twice), all of which had been cited by Ṣafī-al-Dīn (1938, pp. 127-36). The third category consisted of five branch modes, or *šoʿbas* (pl. *šoʿab*), generally similar to the *āvāzes* (cf. p. 131): Gardānīya, Panjgāh, Salmak, Moḥayyer, and Māhūrī. The author of the *Šarḥ* also mentioned "composite" modes (*morakkabāt*), though he gave only one example. Six of the *maqāms* were identified as *mawājeb* (*mawājeb/aṣābeʿ-e setta*), or fingered (pp. 466-68). Finally, the term *baḥr* (pl. *boḥūr*) was applied to modes resulting from displacement of the tonic in the scale of Rāst: Dogāh (tonic on the second note), Segāh (tonic on the third note), Čahārgāh, Panjgāh, and so on (p. 109).

Qoṭb-al-Dīn Šīrāzī, a disciple of Ṣafī-al-Dīn and the first compiler of his work, also provided an explanation of the cycles in *Dorrat al-tāj*, but he differed from his teacher on certain points. It is clear that not all the cycles named by Ṣafī-al-Dīn were in use, for Qoṭb-al-Dīn mentioned only twenty-nine.

In the *Šarḥ*, on the other hand, each of the forty-eight cycles or modal scales (*adwār*) was named. Furthermore, with two exceptions (the *āvāzes* Salmak and Māya), they were also cited by type, or genre (*ajnās*, *boʿd*): *āvāz*, *mawājeb*, and so on. The individual names were assigned by the author, who nevertheless recognized that masters of the art also "could very well have given them names" (p. 392). Among the forty-eight cycles in the theoretical repertoire the names of thirty-two were of Persian, sometimes of pre-Islamic origin. In the *Šarḥ* the cycles themselves were explained in detail, but the explanations must be interpreted with care because of distortions owing to the constraints of the method used. Furthermore, no information was given on the internal structure of the modes; they were treated simply as scales, and even the tonics were not specified, though their links and degrees of relationship were often mentioned.

In elaborating Ṣafī-al-Dīn's method Marāġī, like Qoṭb-al-Dīn, arrived at ninety-one cycles, which he classified as *maqāms*, *āvāzes*, and *šoʿab*. The twelve *maqāms* were designated *adwār* or *šodūd* by the Arabs and *maqams* or *parda* (frets) by the Persians, "some of them counting eight notes, others nine" (1356 Š./1977, p. 57). Marāġī warned against errors in naming the scales (pp. 57, 61) and claimed to have reestablished the truth, especially in relation to Qoṭb-al-Dīn, whom he considered a dilettante (p. 65). The six *āvāzes* were identical with those of Ṣafī-al-Dīn, and he also mentioned twenty-four *šoʿab*. This new classification, in which the *maqām* and *šoʿba* (sometimes called *ʿoṣūl* and *forūʿ* respectively) were distinguished, marked a turning pont in modal organization. It was repeated by the majority of later authors (cf. Shiloah), notably the 15th-century author of a treatise dedicated to the Ottoman sultan Moḥammad II (848-86/1444-81, with interruption), often identified as Fatḥ-Allāh Moʾmen Šīrvānī, and ʿAbd-al-Ḥamīd Lāḏeqī (ca. 1500), to whom *Ketāb al-fatḥīya* is attributed, as well as in two nonscientific Persian works, *Resāla-ye mūsīqī-e bahjat al-rūḥ* (ca. 1600; apocryphally attributed to Ṣafī-al-Dīn) and the anonymous *Maʿrefat-e ʿelm-e mūsīqī*. In the Safavid period the science of intervals and even the concepts of cycle, genre, scale, and transposition thus disappeared as major preoccupations of Persian musicians; even Moḥammad-Naṣīr Mīrzā Forṣat Šīrāzī (d. 1338/1920), in his *Boḥūr al-alḥān*, did not venture the slightest explanation.

Rhythmic cycles.

Notation of rhythmic cycles. Conjoint or fundamental rhythm (*żarb al-aṣl*) consists of simple beats at regular intervals without any accent. According to

Avicenna, "certain people condemn conjoint rhythm, whereas others do not reject it but do not recognize it as a kind of rhythm. All the old melodies of Khorasan and Persia are based on conjoint rhythm, because this rhythm is equal and because it regularizes the soul . . . all the disjoint rhythms are variatons of this fundamental rhythm" (cited by Šīrvānī, p. 166). Fārābī considered the basic definition of rhythm to be a series of regularly spaced beats, the last of which was followed by a *disjunction*, a silence, for example, *ta ta ta/ ta ta ta*. He developed and introduced about twenty variations, encompassing all the known rhythmic patterns of his time and taking actual musical practice into account (Sawa, p. 4).

The measure of time, indispensable to the expression of rhythm, is based on the science of metrics. The metric units could be represented in three basic ways. In the first, "time A" (*zamān-e alef*), the simple number of beats (*naqra*) was noted, eventually by means of the syllable *ta*, equivalent to one beat. The second consisted of alphabetical letters (Marāḡī, 1366 Š./1987, p. 214). The third method involved various syllabic systems: *sabab*, or "time B" (*zamān-e be*), conventionally represented by the syllable *tan* (–, two beats); *watad*, or "time J" (*zamān-e jīm*), represented by *tanan* (⏑–, three beats); the lesser *fāṣela*, or "time D" (*zamān-e dāl*), represented by *tananan* (⏑⏑–, four beats); the greater *fāṣela*, or "time Ḥ" (*zamān-e ḥe*), represented by *tanananan* (⏑⏑⏑–, five beats). The *t* of each syllable corresponded to an accented beat, the other letters indicating only the length of the interval separating one beat from the next. The transcription *tananan tan* (pronounced *ta a ta*) was used instead of *tan tan tan* (pronounced *ta ta ta*) when the second beat was not accented. Rhythmic markers (*afāʿīl*) like *fāʿelon*, *fāʿelaton*, and the like were also used, but this method of representation disappeared after the lifetime of Marāḡī.

Ṣafī-al-Dīn described the rhythmic cycle known as "the first Ṯaqīl" as "a series of beats separated by rests, some of them longer than others. The whole series can be encompassed in a cycle of sixteen beats separated by equal intervals of the value 'a.' . . . You can drop six beats and include only five. Between the first and the second there will thus be a rest J (= three beats), then another between the second and third; an interval D (= 4 beats) separates the third accented beat from the fourth; an interval B (= two beats) will separate the fourth from the fifth and another interval D (= four beats) the fifth from the first, in those instances in which the cycle is repeated" (Šīrvānī, pp. 165-66).

Ḥosaynī (p. 67) described the same cycle: "In the quantity of beats in the cycles of the first Ṯaqīl, one can pronounce eight heavy *sabab*s (two units), which are equivalent to sixteen beats (*naqra*). Of these eleven are silent, and five are played. In order to explain better, in place of these eight *sabab*s, two *watad*s (*tanan* = three beats), two *fāṣela*s (*tananan* = four beats), and one *sabab-e ḵafīf* (*tan* = two beats) have been substituted in this way: *tanan tanan tananan tan tananan*.

The old rhythmic cycles, and sometimes new ones as well, were characterized by three (sometimes four) variations, based on tempo, each form containing double the number of beats in the preceding: Ṯaqīl (modern *kabīr*), slow; Wasaṭ, twice as fast; Ḵafīf (modern *ṣaḡīr*), four times as fast; and eventually Sarīʿ, eight times as fast. These different cycles are represented appropriately by concentric circles, the inner circle representing the shortest. In late treatises they are related to a typology of listeners: the old, the young, and infants or people with white, swarthy, and dark skin (Ṣafī-al-Dīn, 1346 Š./1967; Rajabov, pp. 64, 91).

According to the *Šarḥ* (pp. 517-18), several cycles were played sequentially during a composition, but care was taken to ensure that within each cycle each note in the melody was of identical duration. In order to avoid mistakes in these combinations, the author established a table of proportions among the eight basic rhythms. As fractional relations had thus been developed, the science of rhythm, of metric intervals, converged with that of musical intervals.

Evolution (Table 8). In the course of the ages the notation of rhythm has passed through several stages and has been perfected to the point at which theories and analyses of meter have been entirely dropped, while the descriptions have become more pragmatic. In the later writings (e.g., *Bahjat al-rūḥ*) the distinction between low-pitched (*bam*) and high-pitched (*zīr*) strokes was taken into account; they are essential elements in the physiognomy of a rhythmic cycle. Fārābī had already distinguished three types of accents, that is loud, medium, and soft (*qawī*, *motawaṣṣeṭ*, *layyena*, respectively; Sawa, pp. 4-10), corresponding in a general way to the different timbres. Similarly Marāḡī described the mnemonic gestures that in modern times are linked with playing the *naqqāra* (small drum) with flats and sharps. No author, however, explained the rhythmic cycles themselves according to their characteristic timbres and dynamics. According to Rodolphe d'Erlanger (*Šarḥ*, p. 609), a preliminary effort at such a dynamic articulation may be reflected in what authors, beginning in the late 14th century, designated the "fundamental cadence of the cycle" (*żarb al-aṣl*, but in a different sense from the conjoint rhythm or series of beats mentioned above). This cadence consisted in accentuation of the first beat of the cycle and of one other beat, generally located in the last third of the cycle.

It is significant that the methods of analysis and technical terms used to describe rhythm in early sources are no longer in use in Persia, though they remain current in neighboring cultures. The concept of rhythm in the true sense has been borrowed directly from French, although the more general notion of *wazn* (measure) is also in use. This "decadence" was already noticeable in the late work *Bahjat al-rūḥ*, where the older term *naqra* had been replaced by the more ambiguous *żarb*, which sometimes means beat in the sense of striking and at other times a rhythmic cycle.

Table 8

RHYTHMIC CYCLES IN TRADITIONAL PERSIAN MUSIC

Marāḡī[a]	Šīrvānī	Lāḏeqī	*Bahjat al-rūḥ*	*Maʿrefat*	Amīr Ḵān	20th century[c]
Ṯaqīl 16[b]	Ṯaqīl 24	Ṯaqīl 24	Ṯaqīl	Ṯaqīl	Ṯaqīl 12	Tu, Ar, Ta-Uz
Ṯaqīl-e Awwal 16	Ṯaqīl-e Awwal					Tu (or Hazaj)
Ṯaqīl-e Ṯānī 16	Ṯaqīl-e Ṯānī					
		Nīm-Ṯaqīl 24	Nīm-Ṯaqīl	Nīm-Ṯaqīl	Nīm-Ṯaqīl 7	Tu, Ar, K 24
Ṯaqīl-e Ramal 24	Ṯaqīl-e Ramal					
Ramal 12	Ramal		Ramal	Ramal	Ramal 10	Tu, Ar
	Ramal (long)	Ramal (long)				
	Ramal-e Ḵafīf 6	Ramal (short)				
Hazaj a 10	*Hazaj*		Hazaj	Hazaj-e Kabīr	Ḥejāz-e Kabīr 1	Tu 22
Hazaj b 6						
	Hazaj-e Ḵafīf 8	Hazaj (rapid)		Hazaj-e Ṣaḡīr		
	Hazaj-e Ṯaqīl 16					
	Ḵafīf	Ḵafīf	Ḵafīf	Ḵafīf	Ḵafīf 24	Tu, K, Uz, Ar
Ḵafīf-Ṯaqīl 20	Ḵafīf-Ṯaqīl 8					
		Čār Ḵafīf				
Fāḵtī (old) 28	Fāḵtī 4	Fāḵtī	Fāḵtī	Fāḵtī	Fāḵtī Żarb 4	Tu, Ar, K
Fāḵtī (new) 20						
		Fāḵtī-e Ṣaḡīr 18	Fāḵtī-e Ṣaḡīr			
	=Ṯaqīl-e Awwal 18	Barafšān 17	Barafšān	Barafšān	Barafšān 5	Tu 16
Moḵammas 16	Moḵammas	Moḵammas	Moḵammas	Moḵammas	Moḵammas 13	Tu, Ar, K, Ta-Uz 16
Čanbar 16			Čanbar	Čanbar	Čanbar 14	Tu 12, K 22
			Dawr a, b 14?	Dawr (Dawr-e Aṣl)	Dawr-e Tamām 14	Tu, Ar
			Nīm-Dawr	Nīm-Dawr	Nīm-Dawr 7	Tu 9, Ar 14, K 24
		Se Żarb				
Čahār Żarb 12	Čahār Żarb	Čahār Żarb	Čahār Żarb	Čahār Żarb		
			Panj Żarb			
			Do-yak		Do-yak 3	Pers, Tu, Ar, Ka 16
		Tork Żarb (ʿAmal)	Tork Żarb	Tork Żarb	Tork Żarb 10	Tu 18, Ar, K
Torkī Aṣl 20	Torkī Aṣl	Torkī Aṣl				
Torkī Aṣl (old) 24		Torkī Aṣl (old)				
Torkī-e Ḵafīf 12		Torkī-e Ḵafīf				
Torkī-e Sarīʿ 6		Torkī-e Sarīʿ				
		Torkī (small) 10				
			Awfar	Awfar	Awfar 5	Tu, Ta-Uz
	Awsaṭ 10	Awsaṭ	Awsaṭ		Awsaṭ 5	Ar, Tu
		Ravān	Dawr-e Ravān	Ravān-e Awfar		Tu, Ar

			Farʿ 9?		Farʿ 5	Ar, Tu 32
			Šāh-nāma		Šāh-nāma 17	
			Moqaddam			
			Akol			
	Żarb-e Pīšrow					
			Żarb-al-Molūk	Żarb-e Molūk	Żarb-e Molūk 5	
				5 cycles of Mohammad Tanbūrī		
				Żarb al-Aṣl		Pers
			Żarb-al-Qadīm	Dawr-e Qadīm	Żarb-e Qadīm 20	
	Samāʿī	Samāʿī	Dawr-e Amāʿ	Dawr-e Samāʿ		Tu, Ta-Uz 4
				Dawr-e Hendī		Tu 7
				Tarjomānī		
		Rekāb				
		Mohajjal				
		Rāh-Kord				
	Żarb-e Rabīʿ					
5 cycles of Marāḡī						
Żarb-al-Fatḥ 50, 49	Żarb-al-Fatḥ	Żarb-al-Fatḥ 88		Żarb-al-Fatḥ	Żarb-al-Fatḥ 24	Tu
Żarb-e Šāhī 30	Šāh Żarb	Żarb-e Šāhī				
Qamarīya 5		Żarb-e Qamarīya				
Żarb-e Jadīd 14		Żarb-e Jadīd				
Meʾatayn 200	Meʾatayn	Meʾatayn	Meʾatayn	Meʾatayn	Meʾatayn 200	
			5 cycles of Saljūqī			
			Qalandarī			
			Šīrāzī			
			Aḵlāṭī			
			Żarbī			Tu
			Ḥarbī			Tu, Pers 2
				Żarb-al-ʿEšq		
				Motarraj		
				Čahārgāh?		
				Barbaṭ		

a. Cycles in italics were mentioned by Ṣafi-al-Dīn.

b. The number following the name of the cycle indicates the number of beats in that cycle.

c. This column shows that many of these rhythms are still in use, sometimes in various forms. Per: Persia, Tu: Turkey, Ar: Arab traditions in the east, Ka: Kashmir, Ta-Uz: Tajik-Uzbek tradition.

For the extremely analytical and relatively simple perception of the early writers, a doubtless richer but less precise global vision has been substituted. After the revival of Persian music at the beginning of the 19th century Persian rhythmic structure was thoroughly revised, with the loss of certain features that have been preserved in the Turkish and Arabic traditions: long periods (of twelve, sixteen, twenty-eight, or more intervals), asymmetrical or halting rhythms (*aqsaq*, *lang*, with five, seven, nine, ten, thirteen, or more beats), the playing of several different formulas in a single composition (e.g., *zanjīr*, *żarbayn*), and the identification of each formula by name.

Fundamental rhythms. Fārābī, following Kendī (d. 256/870), described the "fundamental Arab rhythms" (*Ketāb al-mūsīqī al-kabīr*, in d'Erlanger, 1935-40, p. 40), applying analytical principles from classical metrics. The result was seven formulas and several derivations that could be expanded into cycles of three, four, and five beats and their multiples. Their names (e.g., Hazaj, Ramal, Ḵafīf, Ṯaqīl) were drawn from prosody. These names, multiplied and varied according to the needs of the music, recur in the headings to all chapters on rhythm in later theoretical works.

Fārābī emphasized that these seven formulas did not encompass the entire diversity of rhythms in use in his time. Later authors did indeed mention other formulas, a number of which were typically Persian. According to Marāḡī (1366 Š./1987, pp. 221-22), Fāḵtī was known only to Persians (though it was no longer very common); a form of Ṯaqīl, or Čahār Żarb, was attributed to an Azeri musician (*Šarḥ*, p. 503): "The original name (of Ṯaqīl) in Persian was Hargapūter" (sic; *Šarḥ*, p. 472); "it is called Barafšān among the Persians" (Šīrvānī, p. 165). According to Lāḏeqī (p. 473), "some musicians of this period" had given it the name *parafšān* "beating of wings" and had added one beat to it. Among the people of Tabrīz Čanbar was the same as light Hazaj, that is, in 6/8; "the majority of the melodies of the people of Tabrīz are in this rhythm" (Marāḡī, 1366 Š./1987, p. 221; Lāḏeqī, p. 477).

The most important works written after the time of Ṣafī-al-Dīn and including new information on rhythmics were those of Marāḡī, Šīrvānī, and Lāḏeqī and finally *Bahjat al-rūḥ* and *Resāla-ye mūsīqī* by the last great master at the Safavid court, Amīr Khan Kawkabī Gorjī (ca. 1700; Dānešpažūh, pp. 170-75). Marāḡī added to the old cycles (which he simply incorporated from the work of Ṣafī-al-Dīn without adding anything original) a Čahār Żarb and two Torkī Aṣl and mentioned that there were at least twenty other cycles, "the explanation of which would be too long" (1356 Š./1977, p. 46; 1366 Š./1987, p. 223). Nevertheless, he then presented five that he had "composed" (*eḵterāʿ*), including a Żarb-al-Fatḥ of fifty beats, composed in celebration of the Jalāyerid "conquest" of Tabrīz by Ḡīāṯ-al-Dīn Shaikh ʿAlī, and Meʾatayn, a cycle of 200 beats (1366 Š./1987, pp. 227-28). These cycles were repeated by Šīrvānī, whose inventory hardly differed from that of Marāḡī. Lāḏeqī also cited them, but, except for Żarb-al-Fatḥ, he described them as no longer in use, without mentioning their author.

Lāḏeqī, who doubtless represented the Ottoman, rather than the Persian, tradition, first described eighteen cycles "widely current in our days," then three new and less common rhythmic cycles and nine obsolete cycles, among them four that had been the creations of Marāḡī. Fourteen of these cycles were later cited in *Bahjat al-rūḥ*. This small treatise is distinguished from earlier writings by its unscientific approach. It includes mention of about thirty rhythmic cycles, of which two new ones (Farʿ and Do-yak) would remain in use for a long time, whereas the others would disappear (Table 8). Finally, the number of rhythmic cycles was limited to twenty-four, probably to achieve symmetry with the twenty-four *šoʿba*s (secondary modes) of the system propagated by Marāḡī: "[T]he twenty-four rhythms are played in the presence of kings. . . . Seven cycles were created by the slave of the Sultan Mālekšāh Saljūqī for the players of *naqqāra*s." The author named five of them (see Table 8) but said no more about them, for "they are not played in the presence of kings. . . . They are theoretical (*qāl*) and produce no mood (*ḥāl*). Seven other cycles were invented by Ḡolām Šādī . . . : Żarb-al-Qadīm, Żarb-al-Molūk, large and small Hazaj, large and small Fāḵtī, Šāh-nāma" (*Bahjat al-rūḥ*, pp. 39-40).

As far as rhythm was concerned, the author of *Bahjat al-rūḥ* exhibited considerable originality in relation to earlier works. He enumerated all the rhythmic cycles in use, with their names and some of their characteristics. His transcription was the most original and the most complete that can be found in the older treatises, but it is also the most incoherent and hermetic. He used a great number of onomatopoeic designations, which apparently reproduce the sonorities of the percussion instruments (probably the *daf*, q.v., or the *naqqāra*), for example, *tan, tana, tanī, tanā, tanana, dīm, der, dernā, dertan*, and so on. The interpretation of these paradigms presents several difficulties and often varies from one manuscript to another. Furthermore, he described the rhythms not as a series of beats (*naqra*) but as a total number of low-pitched (*bam*) and higher-pitched (*zīr*) sounds (*żarb*). The positions of the beats were not represented on the axis of beats as in earlier works. The author was content simply to note that a particular rhythmic cycle was composed, for example, of seven *żarb*s, five of them *bam* and two *zīr*. It is thus often difficult or impossible to determine the relations among the beats and the syllabic paradigms. The same problem arises from the transcriptions of Amīr Khan: In chapter 9 of his *Resāla* he gave the name of twenty-one *oṣūl* with the number of beats for each and six detailed examples of "the manner of playing the *oṣūl*," chosen from among the oldest *oṣūl*. Čanbar thus is said to have fourteen beats and to be played *dek dak dakā dek/dakā dakā dek/dek dakā dek/dek dak/dakā dek dak dak/dakā dek dak dak/dakā dek dak dak*.

One minor anonymous source, *Maʿrefat-e ʿelm-e*

mūsīqī, probably dating from the 17th century, provides a simple list of the rhythmic cycles then in use but without any description. The rhythms were derived from different pulses, and the experts were supposed to have established five fundamental patterns (*ʿoṣūl*): Motarraj, Awfar, Čahārgāh (actually the name of a mode), Żarb, and Mok̲ammas. This work marks a new stage in the Persian rhythmic tradition. The six basic rhythmic patterns of Ṣafī-al-Dīn and the other early writers had been assimilated to the seventeen fundamental cycles "that were established by K̲ᵛāja Saʿīd b. ʿAbd-al-Moʾmen, Ostād ʿAlī, Ostād Rūḥparvār, Mawlānā Ḥosaynī and ʿOwaybī, and K̲ᵛāja ʿAbd-al-Qāder (Marāḡī)" (*Maʿrefat*, p. 195); except for the last, none of the cited musicians is otherwise known.

The inventory given in *Maʿrefat-e ʿelm-e mūsīqī* is distinguished by the addition of several new rhythmic patterns and by a recasting of the old classification. The basic rhythms are no longer those inherited from the classics, nor are those of Marāḡī mentioned separately. Some names appear for the first time, notably Dawr-e hendī, which is still played in Turkey. The author cited active musicians who had apparently not left works of their own, which had not been done in the past. From these specific features, which are to some extent characteristic also of *Bahjat al-rūḥ*, it can be deduced that a page had been turned in Persian musicology.

Table 8 encompasses the different rhythmic cycles in use in Persia, arranged according to several representative features. The modern Persian tradition has preserved only three names of rhythmic patterns, through the intermediary of the *gūšas* and *rengs* that bear their names: Żarb-e ʿoṣūl in 6/8 and Ḥarbī and Dotā-yakī (Do-yak?) in 2/4.

Bibliography: M.-T. Dānešpažūh, *Modāwamat dar oṣūl-e mūsīqī-e Īrān. Nemūna-ī az fehrest-e āṯār-e dānešmandān-e īrānī wa eslāmī dar ḡenāʾ wa mūsīqī*, Tehran, 2535=1355 Š./1976. J. During, *La musique traditionnelle de l'Azerbāyjān et la science des muqāms*, Baden-Baden, 1988. R. d'Erlanger, *La musique arabe* VI, Paris, 1959. Zayn-al-ʿĀbedīn Moḥammad Ḥosaynī, *Qānūn-e ʿelmī wa ʿamalī-e mūsīqī*, Dushanbe, 1987. ʿAbd-al-Ḥamīd Lāḏeqī, *al-Resāla al-fatḥīya*, tr. R. d'Erlanger in *La musique arabe* IV, Paris, 1939, pp. 259-498. ʿAbd-al-Qāder b. Ḡaybī Ḥāfeẓ Marāḡī, *Maqāṣed al-alḥān*, ed. T. Bīneš, Tehran, 2nd ed., 1356 Š./1977. Idem, *Jāmeʿ al-alḥān*, ed. T. Bīneš, Tehran, 1366 Š./1987. *Maʿrefat-e ʿelm-e mūsīqī*, ed. Y. Ḏokāʾ, Tehran, 1350 Š./1971, pp. 190-98. A. Rajabov, *Naḡma-ye neyāgān*, Dushanbe, 1988. *Resāla-ye mūsīqī-e bahjat al-rūḥ*, ed. H. L. Rabino di Borgomale, Tehran, 1346 Š./1967. Ṣafī-al-Dīn ʿAbd-al-Moʾmen Ormavī, *al-Resāla al-šarafīya fi'l-nesab al-taʾlīfīya*, tr. R. d'Erlanger in *La musique arabe* III, Paris, 1938, pp. 5-182. *Šarḥ-e Mawlānā Mobārakšāh bar adwār*, tr. R. d'Erlanger in *La musique arabe* III, Paris, 1938, pp. 185-565. G. Sawa, "Al-Fârâbî's Theory of the Iqâʿ. An Empirically Derived Medieval Model of Rhythmic Analysis," *Progress Reports in Ethnomusicology* 4, 1983, pp. 2-32. A. Shiloah, "The Arabic Concept of Mode," *Ethnomusicology* 34/1, 1981, pp. 19-42. Fatḥ-Allāh Moʾmen Šīrvānī (attributed), tr. R. d'Erlanger as "Traité anonyme dédíeé au Sultan Osmânli Muhammad II (XVe s.)," in *La musique arabe* IV, Paris, 1939, pp. 3-252. M. H. Ungay, *Türk mûsikîsinde usuller*, Üsküdar, Turkey, 1981.

(Jean During)

DAWRA. See Supplement.

DAWRAQ (or Dawraq al-Fors), name of a district (*kūra*; Moqaddasī, pp. 406-07), also known as Sorraq, and of a town that was sometimes its *chef-lieu* in medieval Islamic times. The town lay 78 km southeast of Ahvāz (q.v.); its modern successor is Šādagān, situated 30° 40′ N, 48° 40′ E.

According to early geographers, Dawraq was a fine and prosperous town, through which pilgrims from Fārs and Kermān passed en route to Mecca (see Le Strange, *Lands*, p. 247; Schwarz, *Iran*, pp. 370-74; *Ḥodūd al-ʿālam*, tr. Minorsky, p. 130). Abū Dolaf's mention (sec. 67, comm. pp. 111-12) in the 10th century of Sasanian ruins, which he attributed to Qobāḏ b. Dārā (i.e., Kawād I, 488-531), points to a pre-Islamic history for the place. It lay on the banks of a river of the same name, which flowed into the head of the Persian Gulf and was connected by a canal with the lower Kārūn river. The marshy area between Dawraq and the Persian Gulf was, and still is, known as Dawraqestān, and on the coast there was an anchorage for ships arriving from India.

In 999/1590-91 the district of Dawraq fell temporarily into the hands of the Mošaʿšaʿa *wālī* (governor) of Ḥowayza, Sayyed Mobārak b. Moṭṭaleb; in 1029/1620 Emāmqolī Khan, *beglerbeg* of Fārs, regained it for Shah ʿAbbās I (q.v.; Eskandar Beg, pp. 951-52). In the 18th century the Kaʿb Arabs took over from the Afšār tribe, and Shaikh Salmān built a new settlement called Fallāḥīya south of Dawraq, which subsequently fell into ruins; in the late 19th century the descendants of Salmān were still in possession of Fallāḥīya (Curzon, *Persian Question* II, pp. 322-25; Lockhart).

In 1302 Š./1933 the name of Fallāḥīya was changed to Šādagān, which is now the administrative center of a *bak̲š* (district) of the same name in the *šahrestān* (subprovince) of K̲orramšahr in the province of K̲ūzestān; in 1339 Š./1960 the *bak̲š* had a population of ca. 55,000 people (Razmārā, *Farhang* VI, p. 228).

Bibliography: Abū Dolaf Mesʿar b. Mohalhel Yanbūʿī, *al-Resāla al-ṯānīya*, ed. and tr. V. Minorsky as *Abū-Dulaf's Travels in Iran (circa 950 A.D)*, Cairo, 1955. L. Lockhart, "*Dawrak̲*," *EI²* II, p. 181. J. Perry, *Karim Khan Zand*, Chicago, 1979, pp. 32-33, 161-63.

(C. Edmund Bosworth)

DAWTĀNĪ (or Daftānī, sg. Dawtānay/Daftānay), Pashtun tribe of the Lōdī confederation, still mainly nomadic. The Dawtānī have sometimes been included among the Lōḥāṇī tribes because of common migratory patterns (*Gazetteer of Afghanistan* VI, pp. 162-64). All indigenous accounts point to a wholly independent status, however (Ḥayāt Khan, p. 183; Šēr Moḥammad Khan, p. 222). J. A. Robinson (p. 160) has provided the best discussion of internal subdivisions of the tribe, and most of the segments he described were recorded in the Afghan nomad survey of 1357 Š./1978 (unpublished).

In the survey 1,215 Dawtānī nomadic families (about 6,800 individuals) were enumerated. The majority were herders (*māldār*), who gathered in summer on the high pastures of northern Dašt-e Nāwor in Hazārajāt (Balland and Kieffer, p. 78). The remainder were mainly impoverished nomads scattered in summer camps throughout the Ḡaznī basin and the upper Tarnak valley around Moqor (eastern Afghanistan), where they looked for daily labor, usually as harvesters (*darawgar*). Most Dawtānī nomads wintered in the North-West Frontier Province of Pakistan, in either southern Waziristan or Dērajāt. A minority wintered in southern Afghanistan, mainly in the Qandahār oasis (17 percent), where some owned houses, or in the middle Helmand valley (6 percent). From a social geographical point of view, four different subgroups can thus be distinguished (see Table 9). A fifth group consisted of sedentary Dawtānī settled in southern Waziristan or in eastern Afghanistan.

Such social geographical fragmentation is typical of Pashtun tribes in eastern Afghanistan. It is the result partly of a general crisis that has impoverished and depastoralized many nomads in the area in the second half of the 20th century (Balland, 1988a, pp. 182 ff.) and partly of earlier developments specific to the tribe, which can only roughly be reconstructed.

In the earliest sources on the Dawtānī tribe they are described as sedentary rice and wheat growers living around Wāna in southern Waziristan (Broadfoot, p. 394; Elphinstone, p. 387; Neʿmat-Allāh, II, p. 128 n.

Table 9
SUBGROUPS OF THE DAWTĀNĪ,
1357 Š./1978

	Winter Location	Number of Families	Percentage
māldār	North-West Frontier Province	782	64
	southern Afghanistan	196	16
darawgar	North-West Frontier Province	151	13
	southern Afghanistan	86	7

72). In the mid-19th century territorial pressure from the Aḥmadzī (q.v.) Wazīr gradually ousted the Dawtānī from that region; villages were destroyed, and a growing proportion of the inhabitants was forced to adopt a nomadic life. H. B. Lumsden (p. 97) was the first to mention nomadic Dawtānī. This remarkably late process of nomadization apparently took place rapidly, the number of Dawtānī nomadic families reportedly increasing from about 200 in the 1860s (Foujdar Khan, p. LXXXVI) to 1,000 in the 1890s (King), that is, from about one third of the tribe (Broadfoot, p. 394: estimated at 600 families in 1839) to more than half (*Gazetteer of Afghanistan* VI, pp. 162-64). The need for new seasonal grazing lands increased correspondingly. After the Hazārajāt war of 1309-10/1892, in which they did not participate, the Dawtānī secured access to the large summer pasturelands that they presently hold in Nāwor (Balland, 1988b, p. 272). Competition from the Wazīr limited the availability of winter grazing in the middle Gōmal area, however, and, though pasturelands were available downstream in the Dērajāt and neighboring Žōb district of Baluchistan, they soon became overcrowded (Robinson, p. 160).

The scarcity of winter grazing, coupled with permanent insecurity during the biannual migration through Wazīr territory (King; *Gazetteer of Afghanistan* VI, pp. 162-64; *Military Report*, pp. 147-48), induced several Dawtānī lineages to give up all grazing in India and to take up new winter quarters in less populated southern Afghanistan, thus creating a major geographical division within the tribe (Balland and Kieffer, p. 85). This shift, already in full swing in the 1930s (Robinson, pp. 161, 164), was intensified during the following decades: The entire main nomadic section of the tribe, the Bāzārḵēl, wintered in southern Waziristan in 1311-13 Š./1932-34, but in 1357 Š./1978 two of every three Bāzārḵēl families were spending the winter in southern Afghanistan. The number of Dawtānī nomads whose migratory route crossed the Durand Line (see BOUNDARIES iii) had thus remained more or less constant since the 1890s, despite demographic growth (according to Robinson, pp. 161 ff., 976 families in 1311-13 Š./1932-34, 933 families in 1357 Š./1978).

Nomadic Dawtānī also increasingly engaged in trading activities. Although they were not yet considered a major trading (*powindah*) tribe in 1860, they gained that status within two decades (Lumsden, p. 91; Raverty, IV, pp. 491, 499; *Gazetteer of Afghanistan* VI, pp. 162-64; for later periods, see Ferdinand, pp. 144, 148). Some even took part in the external trade of Bukhara (Tucker, p. 188). In 1357 Š./1978, however, according to an unpublished survey, only twelve families of the Bāzārḵēl section still reported trade as a significant activity.

In 1357 Š./1978 Dawtānī nomads migrating along the Gōmal route made up the largest single nomadic group crossing the border between Afghanistan and Pakistan, a position held by the Nāṣer in the 19th century and the Solaymānk̲ēl in the first half of the 20th century (Balland, 1991, p. 227). Since then, however, land conflicts between the Dawtānī and the Wazīr have come to an end, especially as the latter are now more dependent upon remittances from the Persian Gulf than on local resources and have consequently abandoned their previous claims to the Zarmelān plain and the adjacent Gōmal valley (Ahmad, p. 5).

Bibliography: A. S. Ahmad, "Nomadism as Ideological Expression. The Case of the Gomal Nomads," *Nomadic Peoples* 9, 1981, pp. 3-15; repr. in A. S. Ahmad, *Pakistan Society*, Karachi, 1986, pp. 211-27. D. Balland, "Le déclin contemporain du nomadisme pastoral en Afghanistan," in E. Grötzbach, ed., *Neue Beiträge zur Afghanistanforschung*, Liestal, Switzerland, 1988a, pp. 175-98. Idem, "Nomadic Pastoralists and Sedentary Hosts in the Central and Western Hindukush Mountains, Afghanistan," in N. J. R. Allan, G. W. Knapp, and C. Stadel, eds., *Human Impact on Mountains*, Totowa, N.J., 1988b, pp. 265-76. Idem, "Nomadism and Politics. The Case of Afghan Nomads in the Indian Subcontinent," *Studies in History* (New Delhi) 7/2, 1991, pp. 205-29. Idem and C. M. Kieffer, "Nomadisme et sécheresse en Afghanistan. L'exemple des nomades Paštun du Dašt-e Nāwor," in Equipe écologie et anthropologie des sociétés pastorales, ed., *Pastoral Production and Society*, Cambridge and Paris, 1979, pp. 75-90. J. S. Broadfoot, "Reports on Parts of the Ghilzi Country, and on Some of the Tribes in the Neighbourhood of Ghazni; and on the Route from Ghazni to Dera Ismail Khan by the Ghwalari Pass," *Royal Geographical Society Supplementary Papers* 1, 1886, pp. 341-400. M. Elphinstone, *An Account of the Kingdom of Caubul*, London, 1815; repr. Graz, 1969. K. Ferdinand, "Nomad Expansion and Commerce in Central Afghanistan," *Folk* 4, 1962, pp. 123-59.

Nawab Foujdar Khan, "Statements Regarding Trade Carried on by the Povindah Merchants," in R. H. Davies, *Report on the Trade and Resources of the Countries on the North-Western Boundary of British India*, Lahore, 1862, pp. LXXXV-XCV. M. Ḥayāt Khan, *Ḥayāt-e Afḡān*, Lahore, 1867; tr. H. Priestley as *Afghanistan and Its Inhabitants*, Lahore, 1874; repr. Lahore, 1981. L. W. King, letter dated 30 November 1894, National Archives of India, Foreign Department, Secret F, February 1895, No. 575. H. B. Lumsden, *The Mission to Kandahar*, Calcutta, 1860. *Military Report on Waziristan 1935*, Calcutta, 1936. K̲ᵛāja Neʿmat-Allāh, *Mak̲zan-e afḡānī*, tr. B. Dorn as *History of the Afghans*, 2 vols., London, 1829-36; repr. London, 1965; repr. Karachi, 1976. H. G. Raverty, *Notes on Afghānistān and Part of Balūchistan*, London, 1881-88; repr. Lahore, 1976. J. A. Robinson, *Notes on Nomad Tribes of Eastern Afghanistan*, New Delhi, 1935; repr. Quetta, 1978; repr. Quetta, 1980. Šēr Moḥammad Khan, *Tawārīk̲-e k̲oršīd-e jahān*, Lahore, 1311/1894. H. S. Tucker, *Report of the Land Revenue Settlement of the Dera Ismail Khan District of the Punjab 1872-79*, Lahore, 1879.

(Daniel Balland)

DĀWŪD, DĀʾŪD, the biblical David (for linguistic discussion of the name, see Jeffery, pp. 127-28), mentioned in a number of passages in the Koran as the hero who fought with and killed Jālūt (Goliath; 2:251), the prophet who received the Book of Psalms (Zabūr) from God (4:163, 17:55), and the king who was given the power to rule, enforce justice, and distinguish between truth and falsehood (*faṣl al-k̲eṭāb*, 38:20, 2:251). Dāwūd is said to have been God's vicegerent (*k̲alīfa*) on earth (38:26) and, with his son and successor, Solaymān (Solomon), represented as a man endowed with knowledge (27:15) whose judgment was sought in matters of dispute (21:78, 38:20-25). The birds and the mountains joined with Dāwūd in praise of God (21:79, 34:10, 38:18-19; cf. *Psalms* 98:8, 148:9-11), and God gave him the ability to soften iron (34:10) and taught him to make coats of mail (21:81).

These brief and fragmentary references were expanded in postkoranic literature, and much relevant information, mainly derived from Jewish sources, was added to them. In the Hadith literature the foci are Dāwūd's willingness to do penance, his pious acts, and his performance of religious duties, but other events and circumstances of his life are mentioned as well. His adventures with Ṭālūt (Saul), his fight with Jālūt and the miraculous nature of his slingstones, his infatuation with Bathsheba, Satan's plot against him, the episode of Uriah the Hittite (cf. 2 Samuel 11-12), the revolt of his son Absalom and the latter's death, the numbering of Banū Esrāʾīl, and their unhappy fate are fully developed in histories, commentaries on the Koran, and biographies of the prophets.

Among Persian Sufis Dāwūd has figured as a supreme example of devotion. Shaikh Farīd-al-Dīn ʿAṭṭār (q.v.; d. 618/1221), relating Dāwūd's name to the Arabic root *w-d-d* (to love), attributed all Dāwūd's achievements to his love for God and described Psalms as *zabūr-e ʿešq* (psalms of love; 1356 Š./1977, pp. 294-96; 1342 Š./1963, pp. 2, 42; 1338 Š./1959, pp. 17, 34). Dāwūd's divine gifts, particularly the charm of his voice and its supernatural effect on men, birds, wild beasts, and even inanimate objects; the ecstatic participation of mountains in his songs of praise to God; and the waxy ductility of iron in his hands have been favorite themes of Sufi poetry and have been treated and interpreted variously in Persian mystical writings. Among sayings attributed to the Prophet Moḥammad that are frequently quoted and elaborated in Sufi literature are God's words addressed to Dāwūd (e.g., Meybodī, VI, p. 477; ʿAṭṭār, 1338 Š./1959, p. 100; Rūmī, bk. 1, p. 177; see Forūzanfar, pp. 28-29).

Bibliography: Abū Esḥāq Ebrāhīm b. Manṣūr b. K̲alaf Nīsābūrī, *Qeṣaṣ al-anbīāʾ*, ed. Ḥ. Yaḡmāʾī, Tehran, 1340 Š./1961, pp. 264-81. Shaikh Farīd-al-Dīn ʿAṭṭār, *Asrār-nāma*, ed. S.-Ṣ. Gowharīn, Tehran,

1338 Š./1959. Idem, *Manṭeq al-ṭayr*, ed. S.-Ṣ. Gowharīn, Tehran, 1342 Š./1963. Idem, *Moṣībat-nāma*, ed. ʿA. Nūrānī Weṣāl, 1356 Š./1977. Balʿamī, ed. Bahār, pp. 539-60. B. Forūzanfar, *Aḥādīṯ-e maṯnawī*, Tehran, 1334 Š./1955. Abu'l-Ḥasan ʿAlī b. ʿOṯmān Hojvīrī, *Kašf al-maḥjūb*, ed. V. Zhukovskiĭ, Leningrad, 1926; repr. Tehran, 1358 Š./1979, pp. 413, 524-25. A. Jeffery, *The Foreign Vocabulary of the Qurʾān*, Baroda, 1938; repr. Lahore, 1977. Masʿūdī, *Morūj*, ed. Pellat, I, pp. 60-64. Abu'l-Fażl Rašīd-al-Dīn Meybodī, *Kašf al-asrār wa ʿoddat al-abrār*, ed. ʿA.-A. Ḥekmat, 10 vols., Tehran, 1338-39 S./1959-60. Jalāl-al-Dīn Moḥammad Balḵī Rūmī, *Maṯnawī*, ed. R. A. Nicholson, Leiden, 1925. Moḥammad b. Jarīr Ṭabarī, *Jāmʿ al-bayān fī tafsīr al-Qorʾān* II, Cairo, 1321/1903, pp. 375-81. Abū Esḥāq Aḥmad b. Moḥammad Ṯaʿlebī Nīšābūrī, *Ketāb ʿarāʾes al-majāles fī qeṣaṣ al-anbīāʾ*, ed. Beirut, 1981, pp. 270-92.

(FATḤ-ALLĀH MOJTABĀʾĪ)

DĀWŪD B. MOʾMEN. See JEWISH PERSIAN LITERATURE.

DĀWŪD KHAN, MOḤAMMAD (b. Kabul, 1288/1909, d. Kabul, 7 Ṯawr 1357 Š./27 April 1978), prime minister (1332-42 Š./1953-63) and first president of Afghanistan (1352-57 Š./1973-78). His father, Moḥammad ʿAzīz Khān, was a brother of Moḥammad Nāder Shah (1308-12 Š./1929-33). The family belonged to the Yaḥyāḵēl lineage of the royal Moḥammadzay clan of the Bārakzay tribe of the Dorrānī (q.v.) Pashtuns.

Dāwūd lived and studied in Europe from 1300 Š./1921 to 1309 Š./1930 while his father and for part of that time his uncle remained in exile during the reign of Amān-Allāh Khan (q.v.), representing a rival branch of the clan. After Aman-Allāh's abdication in 1307/1929 Nāder Khan led the opposition to a usurper and succeeded in claiming the throne (See AFGHANISTAN x); Dāwūd Khan returned to Afghanistan and spent the year 1310 Š./1931 studying at the infantry officers' school. In 1312 Š./1933 both Nāder Shah and Dāwūd Khan's father, who was serving as ambassador to Germany, were assassinated by supporters of Amān-Allāh Khan. Nāder Shah's son Moḥammad Ẓāher became king, and his uncle Moḥammad Hāšem Khan effectively ruled Afghanistan as prime minister. Dāwūd Khan joined Moḥammad Hāšem's household. He married Nāder Shah's daughter Zaynab in 1313 Š./1934.

Dāwūd Khan's adolescent sojourn in Europe had left him acutely conscious of the backwardness of Afghanistan. Throughout his career he thus combined a strong desire to modernize the country with a close identification with the military. Nāder Shah had made him a major general in 1321 Š./1932; he subsequently served as military commander of several provinces and in 1318-26 Š/1939-1947 of the central forces at Kabul. In 1325 Š./1946 the prime minister, another uncle, Shah Maḥmūd Ḡāzī, named him minister of defense (Adamec, p. 114).

By that time this branch of the royal family had become divided into two factions. Dāwūd and his uncle Moḥammad Hāšem led the faction favoring tough, activist Pashtun nationalist rule, while Shah Maḥmūd and the king were associated with liberalizing experiments and greater inclusiveness. After a disagreement with Shah Maḥmūd, Dāwūd was sent to Paris as ambassador in 1347 Š./1948. He returned a year later to serve as minister of the interior (*wazīr-e dāḵela*) and head of tribal affairs (*raʾīs-e qabāʾel*; Adamec, p. 114). In the latter position Dāwūd exacerbated the dispute between Afghanistan and the new state of Pakistan, vigorously promoting demands for self-determination in the Pashtun tribal territories of Pakistan (Dupree, pp. 477-98).

In 1332 Š./1953 Dāwūd seized power from his uncle in a bloodless coup. During his tenure as minister (known as "Dāwūd's decade") he transformed the Afghan state. He immediately sought foreign aid to build the national army. When the United States, then embarking on an alliance with Pakistan, refused him, he turned to the Soviet Union, which, beginning with an agreement in 1333 Š./1955, provided the bulk of both military equipment and training for the Afghan army. Moscow also provided development aid, as did Washington, D.C., after 1335 Š./1956 (Dupree, pp. 522-23).

Although Dāwūd's links to Moscow earned him the nickname "the Red Prince," he was an autocratic modernizer, rather than a communist. He maintained a policy of nonalignment (*bīṭarafī*), playing off the United States and the Soviet Union against each other. The aid that he obtained enabled him to carry out the major elements of his state-building policy: centralizing control of weapons in a modern army and gendarmerie; strengthening commercial agriculture and exports by investing in economic infrastructure, particularly dams and roads; relying on state enterprises, rather than private joint-stock companies, as the main source of capital accumulation; expanding modern education in order to train personnel for the new state institutions; and creating a national transportation and communication network.

The increasing strength of the central government enabled Dāwūd to institute some modernizing reforms as well. In 1338 Š./1959 he decided that the army was strong enough to challenge both tribal leaders and the religious establishment. He placed several influential tribal khans under house arrest and announced that he would thenceforth collect land tax in Qandahār, home province of his Dorrānī cotribesmen, who had long been exempted from taxation; the army suppressed the resulting protests. On independence day in 1338 Š./1959 he and his chief military commanders appeared on the reviewing stand with their wives unveiled. He let it be known that any women who wished could follow their example. He arrested those *ʿolamāʾ* who protested these measures, as well as others who had spoken out against his ties to the Soviet Union (Dupree, pp. 530-38).

Dāwūd remained a Pashtun nationalist. In 1342 Š./1963 confrontation with Pakistan, which controlled the principal land route from Afghanistan to the sea, led to an economic crisis that forced him to resign (Dupree, pp. 530-38). For the next decade Moḥammad-Ẓāher Shah ruled directly, inaugurating a system called Demokrāsī-e now (New democracy), with an elected consultative parliament (Wolesi jerga). Dāwūd was the main target of a provision of the constitution adopted in 1343 Š./1964 (see CONSTITUTIONAL HISTORY OF AFGHANISTAN), in which members of the royal family were forbidden to stand for election or to serve as ministers.

He maintained his ties with members of the new intelligentsia and the Soviet-trained officer corps, groups largely created by his policies and with which he therefore enjoyed special relations. Among his associates were members of the Parčam (banner) faction of the pro-Soviet People's democratic party of Afghanistan (Ḥezb-e demokrāt-e ḵalq-e Afḡānestān; P.D.P.A.), led by Babrak Kārmal. In the early 1970s a series of bad harvests, a decline in foreign aid, and Ẓāher Shah's passive style of rule created a crisis for the regime. With the help of Soviet-trained army officers, including members of Parčam, Dāwūd again seized power, in July 1973. Instead of taking the throne, however, he proclaimed Afghanistan a republic and himself president. Although Parčamīs served him in important posts, he soon became wary of excessive dependence on them and the Soviets (Bradsher, pp. 57-59). By 1354 Š./1975 most had been dismissed, and Dāwūd, ever alert for new opportunities, was courting the newly rich monarchs of the Persian Gulf, especially the shah of Persia. The still tiny band of Islamic revolutionaries in Afghanistan staged an abortive uprising against him in 1354 Š./1975 and established bases in Peshawar, Pakistan.

In Moscow in 1356 Š./1977, when Soviet leader Leonid Brezhnev warned Dāwūd about his growing ties with the shah, he replied that Afghanistan would have relations with whomever it pleased. The Soviets then increased their support for the P.D.P.A. By the time that Dāwūd moved against the party in April 1978 it was too late (Bradsher, pp. 63-66). P.D.P.A. cells in the army launched a coup, during which Dāwūd was killed.

See also AFGHANISTAN x, xi.

Bibliography: L. W. Adamec, *A Biographical Dictionary of Contemporary Afghanistan*, Graz, 1987. R. T. Akhramovich, *Afganistan posle vtoroĭ mirovoĭ voĭny. Ocherk istorii*. Moscow, 1961; tr. C. J. Lambkin as *Outline History of Afghanistan after the Second World War*, Moscow, 1966. H. S. Bradsher, *Afghanistan and the Soviet Union*, Durham, N.C., 1983. L. Dupree, *Afghanistan*, Princeton, N.J., 1973; repr. Princeton, N.J., 1980. M. J. Fry, *The Afghan Economy. Money, Finance, and the Critical Constraints to Economic Development*, Leiden, 1974. Yu. V. Gankovskiĭ et al., *Istoriya Afganistana*, Moscow, 1982; tr. V. Baskakov as *A History of Afghanistan*, Moscow, 1985. H. Kakar, "The Fall of the Afghan Monarchy in 1973," *IJMES* 5/9, 1978, pp. 195-214. L. B. Poullada, "Afghanistan and the United States. The Crucial Years," *Middle East Journal* 5/35, spring 1981, pp. 178-90. M. N. Shahrani, "State Building and Social Fragmentation in Afghanistan. An Historical Perspective," in A. Banuazizi and M. Weiner, eds., *The State, Religion and Ethnic Politics. Afghanistan, Iran and Pakistan*, Syracuse, N.Y., 1986, pp. 23-74.

(BARNETT RUBIN)

DAY (Av. *daδuuah-*, Pahl. *day* "creator"), an epithet of Ahura Mazdā (q.v.) that became the name of the tenth month, as well as of the eighth, fifteenth, and twenty-third days in each month of the Zoroastrian calendar (q.v. i). Younger Avestan *daδuuah-/daθuš-* is a perfect active participle of the verb *dā-* (IE. *$*dheh_1$-*, OInd. *dhā-*, NPers. *dādan*) "to place, put, create." In the last sense it was commonly used for the creative acts of Ahura Mazdā, for example, in the words of Darius I (DNa 1-3; Kent, *Old Persian*, pp. 137-38) ". . . Ahuramazdā who created (*adā*) this earth, who created yonder heaven" and in Zarathustra's rhetorical question (*Y.* 44.3) "Who created (*dāt*) the path(s) of the sun and the stars?" A noun of agent *dātr̥-* (OInd. *dhātr̥-*) "creator" is another common epithet of Ahura Mazdā in both Old and Younger Avestan, as in *Yasna* 44.7, where Mazdā is invoked as the "creator of everything" (*vīspanąm dātārəm*), and in the invocation formula "O Ahura Mazdā . . . creator (*dātarə*) of the material world . . ." (*Yt.* 1.1, etc.; cf. Kellens). *Daδuuah-* could mean either "who has created" or, more likely, "who creates" (with present sense comparable to that of *vīδuuah-* "knowing, wise"; cf. Wackernagel and Debrunner, p. 914), that is, "creator." Although *dātr̥-* can be construed with either the accusative or genitive, *daδuuah-* has ceased to function as a participle and never takes an object. In the formula "We worship the Creator (*daδuuaŋ- həm*), Ahura Mazdā" the object of creation is thus unspecified. In Pahlavi translations of Avestan texts *daδuuah-* is always glossed with *dādār*. In the Sogdian calendar the Old Iranian genitive of *daθušō* has been preserved as *δšcyh, δšcyy/δyšcyy/δəšci,/* and *δtš/δatš/*, whereas Pahlavi *day* is derived from the nominative singular *daδuuā*.

In the calendar reform in the 5th century B.C.E. (cf. Hartner, pp. 756 ff.) the names of Zoroastrian *yazata*s (benign divinities) were given to the twelve months and the thirty days of each month. The tenth month was named *daθušō* (*māh-*) "(month) of the creator"; the first day of each month was called *ahurahe mazda* (*aiiarə*) "(day) of Ahura Mazdā," and the eighth, fifteenth, and twenty-third days also bore the epithet *daθušō* (*aiiarə*) "(day) of the Creator." The thirty-day month was thus divided into two segments of seven days, followed by two segments of eight days (see Nyberg, pp. 128-34).

In Pahlavi, in which *daθušō* appears as *day*, the eighth, fifteenth, and twenty-third days are further specified by the days following, for example, *day pad ādur*, *day pad mihr*, *day pad dēn*. According to the *Bundahišn* (30.10-31.8, 33.15-34.2), the establishment of the names of the deities (thirty *amahraspands*; see AMƏŠA SPƏNTA) for the thirty days of the month was an essential part of the material creation, especially the creation of finite time, which places a limit on the life span of Ahriman (q.v.). As participants in the battle against Ahriman the three Days function not only as mere day names but also as Ohrmazd's coworkers, designated as "space" (*gāh*), "religion" (*dēn*), and "time" (*zamān*). In the same text (119.9-13) the "flower" that belongs to each of the thirty *amahraspands* is listed: for the Days they are respectively the citron (*wādrang*), the *kʾltk* (?), and the fenugreek (*šambalī dag*).

Bibliography: W. Hartner, "Old Iranian Calendars," in I. Gershevitch, ed., *Camb. Hist. Iran* II, pp. 714-92. W. B. Henning, "Zum soghdischen Kalender," *Orientalia* 8, 1939, pp. 87-95. J. Kellens, "Ahura Mazdā n'est pas un dieu créateur," in C.-H. de Fouchécour and P. Gignoux, *Études irano-aryennes offertes à Gilbert Lazard*, Paris, 1989, pp. 217-28. H. S. Nyberg, "Questions de cosmogonie et de cosmologie mazdéennes II," *JA* 219, 1931, pp. 1-134, 193-244. J. Wackernagel and A. Debrunner, *Altindische Grammatik* II/2, Göttingen, 1954.

(W. W. MALANDRA)

DĀYA, wet nurse (Mid. Pers. *dāyag*, Av. *daēnu-*, "female animal," Kurdish *dā*, *dī*, *dīa* "mother," Sanglechi *dāya* "nurse"; cf. Oss. *dääin*, *däyun* "to suck," Pashai *dōy* "to milk"). Despite the mammalian instinct to suckle the young, in some societies or social groups women other than the mothers are employed to nurse infants. In some cultures it is even forbidden for women to nurse immediately after giving birth, perhaps a vestige of the ancient belief that colostrum is indigestible and thus harmful to the infant (Deruisseau, p. 548). Early Muslim physicians expressed this concern in the claim that the humors in the new mother's body are such that her milk may be harmful. In the 11th century Ebn Sīnā (p. 305) and in the 12th century Esmāʿīl Jorjānī (p. 209) recommended that new mothers wait a few days before breast feeding. In addition to this concern, the social activity of upper-class mothers must have contributed to perpetuation of wet nursing (Deruisseau, p. 550). Even in the 11th-century text *Vīs o Rāmīn* the wet nurse complains that Vīs's mother surrendered her daughter immediately after birth and took no interest in her upbringing until she reached her teens (Gorgānī, p. 46).

Wet nurses can be either human females or other mammals; in the latter instance the infant may be placed directly under the animal's udders (Radbill, p. 21; Brunning, p. 7; Schlieben, p. 25; Tran, pl. I). In legend heroic infants are often suckled by animal nurses (Thompson, I, motif no. B535), for example, Midas by ants, Cyrus by a bitch, and Croesus, Xerxes, and Lysimachus by mares (Radbill, p. 23; Herodotus, 1.122; cf. Binder, pp. 18-22). In the *Šāh-nāma* of Ferdowsī Zāl is nursed by the legendary bird Sīmorḡ, who feeds him on blood, and Ferēdūn by the cow Barmāya (ed. Khaleghi, I, pp. 61, 167, 169). The reverse practice, in which human females nurse animals, is also attested since antiquity and persists in some cultures (Tran, pl. 58/144; Jelliffe and Jelliffe, p. 170 fig. 9.7; Radbill, p. 26). In 19th-century Persia lactating women suckled puppies, in order to relieve the discomfort of swollen breasts (Katīrāʾī, p. 36).

In Zoroastrian sources (Māhyār Nawwābī, p. 480; Dhabhar, p. 154) there is evidence that children were often suckled by wet nurses in pre-Islamic Persia. In Gorgānī's *Vīs o Rāmīn*, based on a Parthian original, the *dāya* plays a prominent role. In the *Šāh-nāma* Sām's own former wet nurse is the only one who dares tell him of the birth of his albino son, Zāl; Rostam is breast-fed by ten wet nurses (ed. Khaleghi, I, pp. 164, 270). The Sasanian Yazdegerd I sends many wet nurses with his son Bahrām, whom he has put in the care of the Arab king Monḏer, but Monḏer chooses four noblewomen, two Persians and two Arabs, to nurse Bahrām. After four years the prince is weaned, with great difficulty (*Šāh-nāma*, ed. Mohl, VII, p. 269). According to Ebn al-Balḵī (p. 111), the Sasanian Yazdegerd III (632-51) owed his life to the sagacity of his wet nurse, who, when he was an infant, anticipated the threats to his life and rushed him away to Eṣṭaḵr, where the nobles raised him in safety.

The Koran (65:6, 2:233) left the choice of suckling or hiring a wet nurse to the mother. In Persia both pre-Islamic custom and Islamic scriptural sanction thus ensured that the practice of wet nursing continued, especially among the upper classes. The 11th-century author Keykāvūs b. Eskandar (pp. 147, 153; cf. Naṣīr-al-Dīn Ṭūsī, p. 222) considered employment of intelligent, chaste, and kind wet nurses one of the duties of a father toward his children. The special kinship between the male infant and his wet nurse carried with it a sexual taboo (Koran 4:27) against marriage with the wet nurse or with individuals suckled by her; this taboo required a clear definition of the concept of suckling in Islamic law. There was disagreement among early authorities over the extent of breast feeding that defined this specific type of foster parentage (*reżāʿa*). Some companions of the Prophet Moḥammad thought at least five feedings, others three, others only one (Ebn al-Naqqāš, pp. 560-62; cf. Šāfeʿī, pp. 159-62; Ḥāfeẓ, pp. 192-93; Hojawī, pp. 321-23; Māzerī, II, pp. 161-68). In Shiʿite law it is stipulated that a child must be suckled at least fifteen times in sequence by one woman before this condition of foster parentage is established (Abū Jaʿfar Ṭūsī, IV, p. 204; Qomī, I, p. 524).

In pre-Islamic Persia, as in many other cultures, it

was believed that bad characteristics could be transferred through the nurse's milk to the child (Māhyār Nawwābī, p. 480; cf. Radbill, p. 22; Tansillo, pp. 25-27, 37, 39; Jelliffe and Jelliffe, pp. 167-69). Imam ʿAlī b. Abī Ṭāleb is reported to have said that the same care should be taken in choosing a wet nurse as in selecting a wife, because breast feeding can influence the character of the child (Qomī, I, p. 523; cf. Ḡazālī, II, p. 27; Katīrāʾī, p. 37; Massé, *Croyances et coutumes*, p. 49; Šahrī, p. 46; Hedāyat, p. 116). By extension the word *dāya* thus also assumed the meaning "tutor," even a male tutor. In the *Šāh-nāma*, for instance, Rostam is called the *dāya* of Sīavoš (for other examples from the *Šāh-nāma*, see Dehkodā, s.v.). According to folk belief in Persia, not only the character but also the mood of the nursing woman may influence the baby's constitution. For example, if the wet nurse is upset, her *šīr-e jūš* (milk of anxiety) may produce a speech impediment in the child (Šahrī, VI, p. 47; Hedāyat, p. 40).

Before bottle feeding with baby formula was introduced in Persia wealthy and middle-class families hired wet nurses for their children (Mostawfī, *Šarḥ-e zendagānī* I, p. 154; Katīrāʾī, p. 36; Massé, *Croyances et coutumes*, p. 49; Sheil, p. 149). Nomadic women were especially sought (Polak, I, p. 195). There is a remarkable similarity in descriptions of the ideal wet nurse in Indian, Greek, Roman, Arabic, and Persian sources. She should be between twenty-five and thirty-five years old, of good complexion, of medium build with a broad chest, wise, and good-natured. She should have given birth between twenty days and slightly more than two months before wet nursing begins, and she must not have miscarried. Her nipples must be firm and moderately large and her milk white, sweet, and neither too watery nor too thick; it can be tested by allowing a drop to fall on a level fingernail, where it should bead and adhere and should run when the fingernail is inclined (Jorjānī, p. 209; Ebn Sīnā, pp. 366-67; Rabban Ṭabarī, pp. 97-98; *English Translation* II, pp. 225-28; Deruisseau, pp. 552-53; Katīrāʾī, p. 36; Šahrī, VI, pp. 46-47). Sometimes wet nurses were hired for infants suffering from diarrhea, vomiting, and bellyache after being nursed by their own mothers (Šahrī, VI, p. 45).

The wet nurse was prohibited from having sexual intercourse while nursing (Jorjānī, p. 209; Ebn Sīnā, p. 369) and was expected to maintain personal hygiene and always to smell good. In winter she was to warm her breast before suckling and in summer to cool her nipples in water. She was to feed the infant at regular intervals and to test her milk every few days to ensure that it had a pleasant taste. If the taste was unpleasant, she was to improve it by eating apples, persimmons, melons, and other efficacious foods. The infant's natural parents would make sure that such foods were available to her (Šahrī, VI, p. 48; Katīrāʾī, p. 36; Jorjānī, p. 209; Ebn Sīnā, pp. 367-68; Rabban Ṭabarī, p. 98). Once the foster child was grown and independent the wet nurse often assumed an important position in his household (Gorgānī, pp. 46, 99-100, 110-11; cf. Livy, 3.44.7; Apuleius, *Metamorphoses* 8.10; Virgil, *Aeneid* 4.632-33 apud Rosen, p. 558).

In Persia Muslim women believe that nursing a Christian child might bring them harm, whereas a woman who has nursed a *sayyed* (claiming descent from the Prophet) is assured that her breasts will not burn in the fires of hell. If a wet nurse should stop lactating, she should sit facing Mecca while *āš-e rešta* (see ĀŠ) and two sous (*šāhī*) worth of milk are pounded in a mortar and served to her (Massé, *Croyances et coutumes*, p. 49; Hedāyat, p. 194).

Bibliography: G. Binder, *Die Aussetzung des Königskindes Kyros und Romulus*, Meisenheim am Glan, Germany, 1964. H. Brunning, *Geschichte der Methodik der künstlichen Säuglingsernährung*, Stuttgart, 1908. L. G. Deruisseau, "Infant Feeding," in *Ciba Symposia* II/5, 1940, pp. 548-56. E. B. N. Dhabhar, *Saddar Nasr and Saddar Bundehesh*, Bombay, 1909. Ebn al-Naqqāš, *Eḥkām al-aḥkām al-ṣādera men bayn šafatay Sayyed al-Anām*, ed. R.-F. ʿAbd-al-Moṭalleb, Cairo, 1409/1989. Ebn Sīnā, *al-Qanūn fi'l-ṭebb*, bk. 1, tr. O. C. Gruner as *A Treatise on The Canon of Medicine of Avicenna, Incorporating a Translation of The First Book*, London, 1930. *An English Translation of the Sushruta Samhita, Based on Original Sanskrit Text*, 2nd ed., tr. and ed. K. K. Bhishagratna, 3 vols., Varanasi (Benares), 1963. Abū Ḥāmed Ḡazālī, *Kīmīā-ye saʿādat*, 2 vols., ed. Ḥ. Ḵadīv Jam, Tehran, 1361 Š./1982. Faḵr-al-Dīn Asʿad Gorgānī, *Vīs o Rāmīn*, ed. M. Todova and A. Gowakavira, Tehran, 1349 Š./1970.

ʿAbd-al-Raḥmān b. Moḥammad Ḥāfeẓ, *Ketāb ḵolāṣat al-feqh ʿalā maḏhab al-Emām al-Šāfeʿī*, Cairo, 1284/1964. Ṣ. Hedāyat, *Neyrangestān*, Tehran, 1342 Š./1963. Šaraf-al-Dīn Mūsā b. Aḥmad Hojawī, *al-Rawż al-morbeʿ be-šarḥ zād al-mostaḡneʿ*, ed. M. Bahūtī, n.p. (Cairo?), 1370/1960. D. B. Jelliffe and E. F. P. Jelliffe, *Human Milk in the Modern World*, Oxford, 1978. Esmāʿīl Jorjānī, *Ḏaḵīra-ye ḵᵛārazmšāhī*, ed. ʿA.-A. Saʿīdī Sīrjānī, Tehran, 2535=1355 Š./1976. M. Katīrāʾī, *Az ḵešt tā ḵešt*, Tehran, 1348 Š./1969. ʿOnṣor-al-Maʿālī Keykāvūs b. Eskandar, *Gozīda-ye Qābūs-nāma*, ed. Ḡ.-Ḥ. Yūsofī, Tehran, 1362 Š./1983. Y. Māhyār Nawwābī, "Andarz-e Āzarbād Mār-spandān," in M. Ṭāwūsī, ed., *Majmūʿa-ye maqālāt-e Māhyār Nawwābī*, Shiraz, 2535=1355 Š./1976, pp. 456-84. M. Māzarī, *al-Moʿlem be-fawāʾed Moslem*, 2 vols., Tunis, 1987-88. J. E. Polak, *Persien. Das Land und seine Bewohner*, 2 vols., Leipzig, 1865. ʿAbbās Qomī, *Safīnat al-beḥār*, litho. ed., 2 vols., Beirut, n.d. ʿAlī b. Rabban Ṭabarī, *Ferdaws al-ḥekma*, ed. M. Z. Ṣeddīqī, Berlin, 1928. S. X. Radbill, "The Role of Animals in Infant Feeding," in W. D. Hand, ed., *American Folk Medicine. A Symposium*, Berkeley, Calif., 1980, pp. 21-31. G. Rosen, "The Roman Nurse," *Ciba Symposia* II/5, 1940, pp. 558-59. A. M. Šāfeʿī, *al-Ṭalāq wa ḥoqūq al-awlād wa'l-aqāreb*, Beirut, 1986. J. Šahrī, *Tārīḵ-e ejtemāʿī-e Tehrān dar qarn-e sīzdahom*, 6 vols., Tehran, 1369 Š./1990. E. Schlieben, *Mutterschaft und Gesellschaft. Beiträge zur Geschichte des Mutter- und Säug-lingsschutzes*, Osterwieck, Germany, 1927. H. P. Schmidt, "The Senmurw," *Persica* 9, 1980, pp. 1-85. Lady [M. L.] Sheil, *Glimpses of Life and Manners in Persia*, London, 1856. S. Thompson, *Motif-Index of Folk-Literature*, rev. ed., 6 vols., Bloomington, Ind., 1955. L. Tansillo, *The Nurse. A Poem*, tr. W. Roscoe, London, 1798. V. T. T. Tran, *Isis Lactans. Corpus des Monuments Greco-Romains d'Isis allaitant Harpocrate*, Leiden, 1973. Abū Jaʿfar Moḥammad b. Ḥasan Ṭūsī, *al-Mabsūṭ fī feqh al-emāmīya*, 8 vols, ed. M.-B. Behbūdī, Tehran, 1388/1968. Naṣīr-al-Dīn Ṭūsī, *Aḵlāq-e nāṣerī*, ed. M. Mīnovī and ʿA.-R. Ḥaydarī, Tehran, 2536=1357 Š./1978.

(MAHMOUD OMIDSALAR AND THERESA OMIDSALAR)

DĀYA, NAJM-AL-DĪN ABŪ BAKR ʿABD-ALLĀH b. Moḥammad b. Šāhāvar b. Anūšervān Rāzī (573–654/1177–1256), mystic and author. The epithet *dāya* (wet nurse) was apparently bestowed upon him after he wrote *Merṣād al-ʿebād* (for editions of Dāya's works cited here, see below), in which he frequently used breast feeding as a metaphor, and because he had nurtured so many disciples. He referred to himself by this epithet only in the introduction to his late work *Manārāt al-sāʾerīn* (Rīāḥī, introd., *Merṣād*, pp. 15-17). The patronymic Ebn Dāya (Nāyeb-al-Ṣadr, p. 153) is spurious.

Dāya was born in Ray (Ṣafadī, pt. 15; Faṣīḥ, II, p. 262) but left there in 599/1202-03 (*Baḥr al-ḥaqāyeq*, apud *Merṣād*, tr., p. 8). He visited, Ḵ^{v}ārazm, Khorasan, Azerbaijan, Arān, the Ḥejāz, Egypt, Syria, and Anatolia. In Ḵ^{v}ārazm he studied Hadith with Shaikh Najm-al-Dīn Kobrā (Ṣafadī, pt. 15) and Majd-al-Dīn Baḡdādī. Although ʿAbd-al-Raḥmān Jāmī (*Nafaḥāt*, p. 435) and later biographers listed him among the disciples of Najm-al-Dīn Kobrā, Dāya referred to Majd-al-Dīn as "my own shaikh" (*Merṣād*, pp. 205, 233, 398, 530). From a comparison of his work with Baḡdādī's *Resāla-ye toḥfat al-barara* the influence of the latter is obvious.

After fleeing the Mongol invasion of Ḵ^{v}ārazm Dāya spent a year in Ray waiting for the situation to improve (*Merṣād*, pp. 18-19; *Resāla-ye marmūzāt*, p. 4) before leaving for Hamadān. Escaping from the second Mongol attack on Hamadān, which ended in a general massacre (April 1221), he and his disciples sought safety with the Saljuq rulers of Anatolia, who were well known for their patronage of learning. They went first to Erbel in northern Iraq, then to Dīārbakr (q.v.), and finally arrived in Qayṣarīya (modern Kayseri) in October 1221. En route to Qayṣarīya, in Malaṭya, Dāya met Šehāb-al-Dīn ʿOmar Sohravardī, who sent him with a letter of introduction to the Saljuq sultan ʿAlāʾ-al-Dīn Keyqobād I in Sīvās (*Merṣād*, pp. 21-26; Ebn Bībī, fol. 234). Despite Ebn Bībī's reference to gifts granted by the sultan, Dāya failed to win the sultan's patronage and soon left for Arzenjān (q.v.; *Marmūzāt*, p. 5). Jāmī's account (*Nafaḥāt*, p. 435) of a meeting with Jalāl-al-Dīn Rūmī and Ṣadr-al-Dīn Qūnawī is certainly apocryphal. In Arzenjān in 622/1225 Dāya composed the treatise *Resāla-ye marmūzāt-e asadī*, dedicated to Dāwūd b. Bahrāmšāh, the Menguchekid ruler of the town. In the same year he went to Baghdad (Algar, introd., in *Merṣād*, tr., p. 13) and then, as ambassador from the ʿAbbasid caliph al-Nāṣer le-Dīn Allāh (575-622/1180-1225), visited Jalāl-al-Dīn Ḵ^{v}ārazmšāh in Tabrīz (Nasavī, p. 280). He spent the rest of his life in Baghdad, where he was a leader in a Sufi *ḵānaqāh* (Forūzānfar, pp. 38–39) and composed books in Arabic. He died in 654/1256 (Ṣafadī, pt. 15; Jāmī, *Nafaḥāt*, p. 435; Ebn al-ʿEmād, V, p. 265; Faṣīḥ, II, p. 313). Until recently his tomb still stood in the Šūnīzīya cemetery in Baghdad, where many Sufis are buried.

In Dāya's teaching mystical love is combined with obedience to the laws of Islam. He considered it possible to attain mystical knowledge in three ways: through divine grace alone, the method followed by the *majḏūb*, the mystic drawn spontaneously to God; through performance of the five pillars of Islam, the method followed by ascetics; and through Sufi practice, especially *ḏekr* (q.v.) and retreats. His writings, often polemical, prejudiced, and spiteful, reflect the religious and intellectual disputes of his age. He was a Hanafite, adhering to rationalist Ashʿarite theology, and an enemy of the philosophers because of their claim that the intellect (*ʿaql*) could reach gnosis (*maʿrefa*; *Merṣād*, pp. 31, 115, 140, 182, 200, 371). He has thus been criticized by some modern writers (e.g., Kasrawī; Daštī).

Dāya's magnum opus is *Merṣād al-ʿebād men al-mabdaʾ ela'l-maʿād*. It is divided into five parts (*bāb*), each in several chapters (*faṣl*). In the first part, the introduction, he described how and why the book came to be written. The second part, "Concerning the origin of existent beings," deals with the nature of man, God, and the universe. In the third, "Concerning the life of man," he discussed various stages of the mystical path, prophethood, the role of the shaikh, *ḏekr* rituals, and mystical intuition. In the fourth part, "Concerning the return of the souls of the felicitous and the wicked," he discussed mystical psychology. The last part, "Concerning the wayfaring of different classes of men," has considerable value as a description of society in the 13th century. Beside the historical and social information contained in the *Merṣād*, 455 verses of early Persian poetry, including the earliest attestations of two quatrains of ʿOmar Ḵayyām, are preserved in it (*Merṣād*, pp. 31, 200; *Čahār maqāla*, ed. Qazvīnī, comm. pp. 314-15; Forūḡī and Ḡanī, p. 32; Mīnovī, 1335 Š./1956, p. 70). A rare example of a quatrain (*dobaytī*, q.v.) in the old dialect of Azerbaijan provides evidence that the dialect was identical with, or very closely related to, that of Ray (*Merṣād*, pp. 95, 590).

While he was still in Persia Dāya had decided to write the book, at the request of his disciples. He completed the first recension after his escape to Anatolia and made a clean copy in Ramażān 618/November 1221 in Qayṣarīya. Two years later, with Sohravardī's encouragement, he dedicated a revised version to Sultan Keyqobād, presenting it to him on 1 Rajab 620/31 July 1223 in Sīvās (*Merṣād*, pp. 15-26, 545). Many manuscripts of both recensions survive. Apart from minor stylistic changes, the second is distinguished by its account of Dāya's meeting with Sohravardī, references to the sultan, a Fahlavi *do-baytī*, and the dedication added to the title. The only critical edition, based on both recensions, was prepared by Moḥammad-Amīn Rīāḥī (Tehran, 1352 Š./1973, cited here; repr. with different pagination, Tehran, 1365 Š./1986, 1366 Š./1987). Rīāḥī has also edited a volume of selections from the text under the title *Bargozīda-ye Merṣād* (Tehran, 1361 Š./1972, 1366 Š./1987, 1368 Š./1989). An earlier selection, *Talḵīṣ merṣād al-ʿebād fī kašf serr al-īјād* (Tehran, 1301/1884), was mistakenly attributed to Najm-al-Dīn Kobrā. A 15th-century Turkish translation by Qāsem b. Maḥmūd Qarā-Ḥeṣārī, entitled *Eršād al-morīd ela'l-morād fī tarjoma Merṣād al-ʿebād toḥfatan le-Ṣolṭān Morād* and dedicated to Morād II (823-48/1421-44; Ateş, 1945, p. 111), remains unpublished. Hamid Algar has published an English translation (*The Path of God's Bondsmen from Origin to Return*, Delmar, N.Y., 1982).

The style of the *Merṣād* is characteristic of that of the preachers of the time. The author began each chapter in relatively simple scholarly prose, but, when he arrived at the subject of love, his language became elegant and passionate. The book was one of the most widely disseminated mystical works of its time and had major influence on the later mystical literature of Persia (see Rīāḥī, introd., *Merṣād*, pp. 71-74; idem, 1368 Š./1989). Although Dāya did not himself found a Sufi order, he stated the principles of 13th-century Sufism in simple language and a logical order.

Other works by Dāya include *Resāla-ye ṭoyūr* (together with Y. Hamadānī, *Rotbat al-ḥayāt*, ed. M.-A. Rīāḥī, Tehran, 1362 Š./1983, pp. 83-110), an allegory addressed to a vizier named Jamāl-al-Dīn Šaraf Solḡūr Bu'l-Fatḥ, perhaps a specimen of the kind of panegyric known as *faṣṣālī* and incorporating features of the Persian dialect spoken in Ray; *Resāla-ye ʿešq o ʿaql* (ed. T. Tafażżolī, Tehran, 1345 Š./1966), also known as *Meʿyār al-ṣedq wa meṣdāq al-ʿešq*, written in Persian, apparently before the *Merṣād* and encompassing some of the same themes; *Resāla-ye marmūzāt-e asadī dar mazmūrāt-e dāwūdī* (ed. M.-R. Šafīʿī Kadkanī, Tehran, 1352 Š./1973), in Persian, dedicated in 621/1224 to Dāwūd b. Bahrāmšāh and covering much the same subject matter as the *Merṣād*, though the last four chapters contain new material on kingship; an Arabic commentary on the Koran entitled *Baḥr-al-ḥaqāʾeq wa'l-maʿānī fī tafsīr al-sabʿ al-maṯānī*, also known as *ʿAyn al-ḥayāt* and *al-Taʾwīlāt al-najmīya* (Algar), which survives in many manuscripts but no published edition (see especially a copy under the second title in four volumes in the Dār-al-Kotob, Cairo, completed in a fifth volume by ʿAlāʾ-al-Dawla Semnānī; Minovī, 1345 Š./1966, pp. 30-32); *Manārāt al-sāʾerīn ela'llāh wa maqāmāt al-ṭāʾerīn be'llāh*, an Arabic adaptation of the *Merṣād* written about thirty years after the original, preserved in several manuscripts (Mīnovī, 1345 Š./1966, pp. 27-28); *Resālat al-ʿāšeq ela'l-maʿšūq* in Arabic, on the sayings of Abu'l-Ḥasan Ḵaraqānī (Minovī, 1345 Š./1966, p. 29); and three treatises in Persian entitled respectively *Serāj al-qolūb*, *Ḥasrat al-molūk*, and *Toḥfat al-ḥabīb* (Flügel, III, p. 253). Dāya also wrote about 300 verses in Persian, which can be found scattered throughout his own works and biographies of him and have been collected by Maḥmūd Modabberī.

Bibliography: H. Algar, "Bahrü'l-Hakâik ve'l-Meâni," in *Türkiye Diyanet Vakfı İslam Ansiklopedisi* IV, pp. 515-16. A. Ateş, "Hicrî VI-VIII (XII-XIV) asırlarında Anadolu'da farsça eserler," *Türkiyat mecmuası* 7-8/2, 1945, pp. 94-135. S. Ateş, *İşari tefsir okulu*, Ankara, 1974, pp. 139-60. H. Corbin, *L'homme de lumière dans le soufisme iranien*, Paris, 1971, pp. 154-61. ʿA. Daštī, "Ṣūfī-e kūček," in *Dar dīār-e Ṣūfīān*, Tehran, 1354 Š./1975, pp. 207-38. Ebn Bībī, *al-Awāmer al-ʿalānīya fi'l-omūr al-ʿalāʾīya*, Aya Sofya library, Istanbul, ms. no. 2985; partially ed. N. Lugal and A. Sadik Erzi, Ankara, 1957. Ebn al-ʿEmād, *Šaḏarāt al-ḏahab fī aḵbār man ḏahab*, 8 vols., Beirut, n.d. Faṣīḥ Aḥmad b. Jalāl-al-Dīn Moḥammad Ḵᵛāfī, *Mojmal-e faṣīḥī*, ed. M. Farroḵ, 2 vols., Mašhad, 1339 Š./1960. G. Flügel, *Die arabischen, persischen und türkischen Handschrifter der Kaiserlich-königlichen Hof-bibliothek zu Wien* III, Vienna, 1867. M.-ʿA. Forūḡī and Q. Ḡanī, eds., *Robāʿīyāt-e Ḥakīm Ḵayyām-e Nīšābūrī*, Tehran, 1321 Š./1942. B. Forūzānfar, *Manāqeb-e Awḥad-al-Dīn*, Tehran, 1347 Š./1968. A. Kasrawī, *Ṣūfīgarī*, 4th ed., Tehran, 1337 Š./1958. H. Landolt, "Stufen der Gotteserkenntnis und das Lob der Torheit bei Najm-e Razi," *Eranos-Jahrbuch* 46, 1977, pp. 175-204. Majd-al-Dīn Baḡdādī, *Toḥfat al-barara*, Majles Library, Tehran, ms. no. 598. M. Mīnovī, "Az Ḵazāʾen-e Torkīya," *MDAT* 4/2, 1335 Š./1956, pp. 42-75. Idem, introd., in Najm-al Dīn Dāya, *Resāla-ye ʿešq o ʿaql*, ed. T. Tafażżolī, Tehran, 1345 Š./1966. M. Modabberī, ed., *Ašʿār-e Šayḵ Najm-al-Dīn Rāzī Dāya*, Tehran, 1363 Š./1984. Šehāb al-Dīn Moḥammad Ḵorandazī Nasavī, *Sīrat Jalāl-al-Dīn*, Cairo, n.d. Nāyeb-al-Ṣadr Moḥammad-Maʿṣūm Šīrāzī, *Ṭarāyeq al-ḥaqāyeq* I, Tehran, 1318/1900. M.-A. Rīāḥī, "Ḥāfeẓ bā yakī az pīrān-e ḵānaqāhhā," in *Golgašt dar šeʿr o andīša-ye Ḥāfeẓ*, Tehran, 1368 Š./1989, pp. 235-321. Ṣafā, *Adabīyāt* III/2, pp. 1189-96. Ṣalāḥ Ḵalīl Ṣafadī, *al-Wāfī be'l-wafayāt*, Malek Library, Tehran, ms. no. 788, pt. 15.

(MOḤAMMAD-AMĪN RĪĀḤĪ)

DAYEAKUTʿIWN (< *dayeak*, Arm. lw. < Mid. Pers. *dāyag*; cf. NPers. *dāya*, q.v., "wet nurse"; cf. Vedic *dhāpáyatē* "suckles"; Skt. *dhātrī*, Prakrit *dhattī* "wet nurse"), a form of child rearing practiced in Armenia and other parts of the Caucasus. In modern Armenian *dayeak* means only "wet nurse," but in its earliest attestations (4th-5th centuries) it referred to one entrusted with educating and nurturing a child for an extended period. At that time the young sons of Armenian lords (*naxarar*s) were sent to be raised and educated by other lords, sometimes in distant districts. Probably at age fifteen years a youth (*san*) would return home, perhaps with a bride from his "adopted" family. Between him and the host lord (*dayeak*) there was a lifelong bond, and marriage between the two houses might advance the interests of both.

When *dayeakutʿiwn* originated among the Armenians cannot be determined accurately. References to *dayeak*s abound in historical sources from the 4th and 5th centuries (e.g., Agathangelos, q.v.; Faustus, q.v.; Łazar Pʿarpetsʿi), evidence that the institution was already pervasive. Moses of Khorene, a later author whose dates are a matter of debate, projected *dayeakutʿiwn* into Armenian prehistory. It perhaps arose as a response to almost continuous warfare among dynastic lords and the centralizing, or "feudalizing," crown. In 4th- and 5th-century Armenia the Arsacid dynasty tried on more than one occasion to exterminate recalcitrant lordly families and to confiscate their lands. As such a family might include thousands of individuals, this effort meant that every male member had to be killed. Should even one male infant survive, he could (on reaching majority) reclaim all the lands of his clan and, under the prevailing customary law of Armenia, could be restored to his full prerogatives. Under such uncertain circumstances the clans took such precautions as *dayeakutʿiwn* in order to prevent total annihilation. Custody of surviving noble children was of paramount importance among the *naxarar*s, who stood to gain from merging their houses with those of their wards. Beyond ensuring a clan's survival in dangerous times, *dayeakutʿiwn* thus also served as a means of drawing lordly families together.

Łazar Pʿarpetsʿi, author of a history of the Armenians, also referred (2.60, p. 204) to Persian *dayeak*s, apparently confirming the existence of this institution in Persia in the late 5th century. Among Armenians *dayeakutʿiwn* remained part of customary law and is thus not mentioned in extant formal codes and church canons; in Persia, however, "guardianship" became the focus of precise legal formulation in the later Sasanian Law Book.

After the 5th century *dayeakutʿiwn* is more difficult to trace in Armenia, perhaps because of the nature of the sources. Although the term was used occasionally between the 6th and 15th centuries, it was not as frequent as before. In one form or another the institution did endure into the 19th century, though information on more recent survivals comes from Georgia and other parts of the Caucasus, rather than from Armenia.

Bibliography: H. Acharyan, *Hayeren armatakan barharan* I, Yerevan, 1971, pp. 618-19. R. Bedrosian, "Dayeakut'iwn in Ancient Armenia," *Armenian Review* 37, 1984, pp. 23-47. A. Grigolia, "Milkrelationship in the Caucasus," *Bedi Karthlisa* 41-42, 1962, pp. 148-67. Łazar Pʿarpetsʿi, *History of the Armenians*, tr. R. Bedrosian, New York, 1985.

(ROBERT G. BEDROSIAN)

DĀYERAT AL-MAʿĀREF-E FĀRSĪ, the first general encyclopedia in Persian compiled along modern lines. It includes about 30,000 entries translated from the *Concise Columbia Viking Desk Encyclopedia*, supplemented by approximately 10,000 original articles on Persia. Although originally planned for two volumes (*Dāyerat al-maʿāref* I, p. 2), it is now scheduled for three, each measuring 31 x 21 cm, in a triple-column format based on that of its American model. The first two volumes (*alef-sīn* and *sīn-lām*) were published in 1345 Š./1966 and 1356 Š./1977 respectively; the third volume was still in preparation in early 1373 Š./1994.

In 1335 Š./1956 the Franklin Book Programs, Inc. (q.v.), of New York undertook production of the encyclopedia at its Tehran office; the first editor was Ḡolām-Ḥosayn Moṣāḥab (1289-1358 Š./1910-1979), who oversaw publication of the first volume and preparation of the work up to the letter *ḡayn* in the second. Moṣāḥeb held a doctorate in mathematics from the University of Cambridge and was interested in both modern and traditional sciences, including the Islamic sciences (Aqṣā, p. 2). Among the innovations that he introduced into Persian typesetting in *Dāyerat al-maʿāref* were special attention to word spacing, the use of numerals and scientific symbols, and a comprehensive system of abbreviations that helped to limit the size of the volumes considerably. He also adopted strict rules for linking Persian characters, precise use of punctuation, and the International Phonetic Alphabet, albeit with some arbitrary variations (e.g., *ă* and *ŏ* for the diphthongs *aw* and *ow* and of *ŝ* for *šīn*), in order to show the precise pronunciation of words; every article was carefully edited for overall accuracy and consistency. Particularly significant was the systematization of entries, in which Persian and Arabic names were given in a strict order (given name, patronymic, title, family name), with extensive cross-referencing. Under Moṣāḥab's direction a special committee, which included Aḥmad Ārām, Moṣṭafā Moqarrabī, Ṣafī Aṣfīaʾ, and several other literary and scientific figures, introduced a considerable number of neologisms and scientific terms into the Persian language, particularly in the fields of geography, physics, and mathematics (Aqṣā, p. 2). Some of these neologisms were adapted from scientific terms in English (e.g., *yūnīdan*, *yūneš* "to ionize, ionization") or based on Persian nouns (e.g., *qoṭbīdan* "to polarize" from *qoṭb* "pole").

Moṣāḥab's extensive introduction to the first volume includes an explanation of the methodological principles and innovations embodied in *Dāyerat al-maʿāref* and provided useful guidelines for subsequent encyclopedic undertakings. After Moṣaḥab resigned in 1355 Š./1976 Reżā Aqṣā became editor (Aqṣā, p. 6).

Dāyerat al-maʿāref may be criticized for the preponderance of foreign entries, especially biographies, that are of little use to the average Persian reader. The quality of the Persian articles in the compilation is uneven. The abundance of abbreviations relative to the size of the encyclopedia complicates the reader's task. Nonetheless, *Dāyerat al-maʿāref* can be considered the forerunner of modern encyclopedic compilations in Persian and is quite useful as a desk reference.

Bibliography: R. Aqṣā, "Marḥūm-e Doktor Ḡolām-Ḥosayn Moṣāḥab. Tadāwom-e talāš-ī bozorg barāye enteqāl-e ʿelm," *Keyhān-e farhangī* 7/6, Mehr 1368 Š./September-October 1989, pp. 1-6.

(DĀRYŪŠ ĀŠŪRĪ)

DAYLAMITES. See BUYIDS, DEYLAMITES.

DAYR (monastery), in early Islamic Arabic and Persian literature usually a building in which Christian monks (*rāheb*) lived and worshiped. The term eventually took on a number of metaphorical and symbolic meanings as well.

Most *dayr*s were located in rural regions, in deserts or on mountaintops (Yāqūt, *Boldān*, Beirut, II, p. 495), and provision had to be made for defense, as well as for safe travel of visitors and supplies. Some monasteries thus consisted of strongly fortified buildings, surrounded by large estates comprising farms, orchards, water sources, and irrigation channels. In some contexts, however, *dayr* means the isolated and austere abode of a single hermit or a small group of hermits. In the larger monasteries numbers of monks lived a communal life and spent their time in worship and performing work for community needs: farming, sheepherding, manufacturing, even buying and selling. Usually the monastery was dedicated to an angel or saint of the Christian religion or to the memory of the founder.

Christian monasteries had been established throughout the Sasanian empire; in the eastern domains of the caliphate they persisted until some time after the fall of the ʿAbbasids, or even longer. At the time of the Arab conquest in the mid-7th century there were numerous monasteries in the northwestern and western provinces of the Sasanian empire, from the vicinity of Madāʾen (Ctesiphon, q.v.) to that of Naṣībīn on the present border between Syria and Turkey; some maintained schools in which mainly Christian theology was taught, in Syriac. As some visitors and students chose to settle permanently nearby, monasteries often evolved into large villages or small towns, some with commercial or strategic importance.

Many early place names included the word *dayr*, suggesting that they had originally been the sites of monasteries, even though often no trace of such structures survived by the time they were first mentioned in chronicles: Dayr Aʿwar on the outskirts of Kūfa, where the Persian general Rostam-e Farroḵzād camped for a short time on his march from Madāʾen to Qādesīya (Ṭabarī, I, p. 2255); Dayr Kaʿb between Madāʾen and Kūfa, near which the Arabs defeated a Persian force under the command of Naḵīrajān (Balāḏorī, *Fotūḥ*, p. 262); Dayr-e Gačīn (q.v.) near Qom, reputedly built on the order of Ḵosrow I Anōšīravān (531-79; Qomī, p. 26; cf. Dayr Kardašīr, mentioned in Yāqūt, *Boldan*, Beirut II, p. 529) or, according to another source, dating from the time of the Kayanids (*Mojmal*, ed. Bahār, pp. 54, 463); Dayr al-ʿĀqūl (q.v.) southeast of Baghdad, near the site of which caliphal troops defeated the army of the Saffarid Yaʿqūb b. Layṯ in 262/876 (Masʿūdī, *Morūj*, ed. Pellat, V, p. 109); Dayr Meḵrān (Meḵnār?) in the Bagratid territory in Armenia, mentioned by the poet Ḵāqānī as "my final refuge" (p. 45; for its location, see Minorsky, p. 144); and Dayr-e Aflāṭūn near Konya, where Jalāl al-Dīn Rūmī and his followers visited (Aflākī, I, pp. 284, 551). According to Ebn Ḥawqal, there was a Christian monastery at Vazkarda near Samarkand in the 10th century (p. 498; cf. Le Strange, *Lands*, p. 465). Among villages in modern Persia are Dayr-e Mawlā near Sanandaj, Dayr-e ʿAlī near Salmās, and Dayr-e Mīr in the Mamasanī district (Pāpolī Yazdī, p. 270).

At the larger monasteries celebrations of Christian festivals were often attended by citydwellers, including Muslims, who took the opportunity to drink wine and to talk to Christian boys and girls without fear of being questioned by the *moḥtaseb* (guardian of public morals; see CITIES iii). Not a few such pleasure seekers were poets and men of letters. For this reason, in the minds of many Muslims the word *dayr* acquired the connotation of a convivial meeting place or a tavern. It was also applied to the temples of Zoroastrians and Hindus in expressions like *dayr-e Moḡān* (monastery of the Magians) and *dayr-e Barahmanān* (monastery of the Brahmans). Ḥāfeẓ and other poets frequently used the expression *dayr-e Moḡān* symbolically, with mystical overtones. Like the Christians, the Zoroastrians had protected (*ḏemmī*) status in the realm of Islam and were permitted to make and consume wine; Muslims often went to Zoroastrian quarters to find what they euphemistically called *dayr-e Moḡān* (or *sarā-ye Moḡān* "palace of the Magians"), meaning a tavern. Wine and goblets were also called *mey-e moḡāna*. On the other hand, *dayr-e Barahmanān* was used by only a few poets, notably Ḵāqānī (Dehḵodā, s.v. *dayr*), generally referring to the cells of Hindu ascetics who lived in forests (Geden, p. 803). In fact, of course, a Hindu ascetic's cell did not resemble a Christian monastery, but Ḵāqānī's mental picture of a "Brahman monastery" must have been derived from stories that he had heard.

In Sufi literature *dayr* metaphorically represents the universe and the unity of existence (Bāḵarzī, pp. 244-45) or occasionally the material world (*nāsūt*; *Merʾāt al-ʿoššāq*, p. 150; cf. ʿErāqī, p. 414). In Sufi parlance *dayr-e Moḡān* referred to an assembly of mystics and saints (Hedāyat, p. 39). The fact that Christian monasteries served as hostelries, providing temporary lodging for pilgrims and travelers, gave rise to literary uses of the word *dayr*, by itself or in constructs, as a metaphor for the transitory life of this world, comparable to *falak* (revolving firmament) and *čarḵ* (the wheel of fortune). Such examples as *dayr-e ḵākī* (earthly), *dayr-e sepanjī* (transient), *dayr-e šešjehatī* (six-sided), *dayr-e kohan* (decrepit), and *dayr-e mīnā* (enamel) are listed and explained in dictionaries (e.g., Dehḵodā, s.v. *dayr*).

Bibliography: Šams-al-Dīn Aḥmad Aflākī, *Manāqeb al-ʿārefīn*, ed. T. Yazıcı, 2 vols., Ankara, 1959-61. Abu'l-Mafāḵer Yaḥyā Bāḵarzī, *Awrād al-aḥbāb wa foṣūṣ al-ādāb*, ed. Ī. Afšār, Tehran, 1345 Š./1966. Faḵr-al-Dīn ʿErāqī, *Kollīyāt*, ed. S. Nafīsī, Tehran, 1336 Š./1957. A. S. Geden, "Monasticism (Hindu)" in J. Hastings, ed., *Encyclopaedia of Religion and Ethics* VIII, New York, 1915, pp. 802-05. Reżāqolī Hedāyat, *Rīāż al-ʿārefīn*, ed. M. Hedāyat, Tehran, 1316 Š./1937. Ḵāqānī Šervānī, *Dīvān*, ed. A. ʿAbd-al-Rasūlī, Tehran, 1316 Š./1937. *Merʾāt al-ʿoššāq*, ed. E. E. Bertel's, in E. E. Bertel's, *Sufizm i Sufiĭskaya literatura* (Sufism and Sufi literature), Moscow, 1965. V. Minorsky, *Iranica. Twenty Articles*, Tehran, 1343 Š./1964. M.-Ḥ Pāpolī Yazdī, *Farhang-e ābādīhā wa makānhā-ye maḏhabī-e kešvar*, Mašhad, 1368 Š./1989. Ḥasan b. Moḥammad Qomī, *Ketāb-e tārīḵ-e Qom*, tr. Ḥasan b. ʿAlī Qomī, ed. S. J. Ṭehrānī, Tehran, 1313 Š./1934. D. Sourdel, "Dayr," in *EI*[2] II, pp. 194-95.

(QAMAR ĀRYĀN)

DAYR AL-ʿ**ĀQŪL** (lit., "the monastery at the bend in the river"; cf. Syriac *ʿaqûlâ* "bend"; Payne Smith, II, cols. 2963-65), a medieval town in Iraq situated on the Tigris 15 farsangs (= 80 km) southeast of Baghdad. It presumably grew up around a Christian monastery, but the latter had apparently disappeared by the time of Šābeštī (10th century), who did not mention its existence in his *Ketāb al-dīārāt*. The medieval geographers described Dayr al-ʿĀqūl as the primary town of the fertile district (*ṭassūj*) in central Nahravān, with busy markets, prosperous agriculture and palm groves, and a Friday mosque; Maqdesī (Moqaddesī, p. 122) considered it the most important town on the Tigris between Baghdad and Wāseṭ, comparable in prosperity to the towns of his native Palestine. Because of its position on the river, it was a station for levying customs dues, with barriers (*maʾāṣer*) laid across the river to halt traffic (Ebn Rosta, p. 186; tr. Wiet, p. 215). By the time of Yāqūt, in the 13th century, the town had declined somewhat; the course of the river had changed, and Dayr al-ʿĀqūl was a mile from its banks, in the midst of a desert (*Boldān*, ed. Beirut, II, pp. 520-21); Ḥamd-Allāh Mostawfī described it a century later as only a small town (*Nozhat al-qolūb*, ed. Le Strange, p. 41; tr. p. 48). It was subsequently completely deserted; its site is marked today by ruins known locally as al-Dayr situated to the north of modern ʿAzīzīya (Hāšemī, p. 529; cf. Le Strange, *Lands*, pp. 35-36).

The district of Dayr al-ʿĀqūl was the site of the decisive battle between the Saffarid Yaʿqūb b. Layṯ's invading forces and the defending caliphal army of al-Moʿtamed (256-79/870-92) and his brother al-Mowaffaq, which took place on Sunday, 9 Rajab 262/Palm Sunday, 8 April 876, at a village called Estarband (?) between Dayr al-ʿĀqūl and Sīb Banī Kūmā (Ṭabarī, III, pp. 1892-94; Masʿūdī, *Morūj* VIII, pp. 42-45; ed. Pellat, pars. 3159-61; Ebn al-Aṯīr, VII, pp. 290-92; Ebn Ḵallekān, ed. ʿAbbās, VI, pp. 413-19; tr. de Slane, IV, pp. 312-19; cf. Nöldeke, pp. 190-91; Bāstānī Pārīzī; Bosworth, p. 113; Duri; *Tārīḵ-e Sīstān*, pp. 231-33.). The caliphal forces had numerical superiority, and al-Mowaffaq was able to impede deployment of the Saffarid troops by flooding the low-lying surrounding land.

Bibliography: M.-E. Bāstānī Pārīzī, *Yaʿqūb-e Layṯ*, Tehran, 1344 Š./1965, pp. 244-61. C. E. Bosworth, "The Ṭāhirids and Ṣaffārids," in *Camb. Hist. Iran* IV, pp. 90-135. A. A. Duri, "Dayr al-ʿĀḳūl," in *EI*[2] II, p. 196. T. Hāšemī, *Mofaṣṣal jogrāfīat al-ʿErāq*, Baghdad, 1930. T. Nöldeke, "Yakub the Coppersmith and His Dynasty," in T. Nöldeke, *Sketches from Eastern History*, Edinburgh, 1892, pp. 176-206. R. Payne Smith, *Thesaurus Syriacus*, 4 vols., Oxford, 1879-1901.

(C. EDMUND BOSWORTH)

DAYR-E **GAČĪN** (lit., "gypsum hospice"), Sasanian caravansary (q.v.) situated in the desert halfway between Ray and Qom, on the ancient route from Ray to Isfahan (Plate X). It is recorded in most early Muslim geographies (see, e.g. Ebn Rosta, p. 191), with the name sometimes given in Arabic as Dayr al-jeṣṣ. According to Moḥammad b. Qays Rāzī (ed. Modarres Rażawī, p. 192), the name referred to a dome built with gypsum that once stood there. Eṣṭaḵrī (pp. 230-31) and Ebn Ḥawqal (pp. 403-04) noted that the caravansary, "a fortified construction," was built of baked bricks and gypsum, with a well of salt water inside and two circular cisterns outside to collect rain water for drinking. It housed a garrison of state guards, apparently to maintain control of the route through the nearby Sīāhkūh and Karkaskūh, well known for the gangs of robbers alluded to in a tale recorded by Neẓām-al-Molk (p. 80). The caravansary was ascribed to the Sasanian period by Abū Dolaf (p. 19), Yāqūt (*Boldān* II, p. 690), Zakarīyāʾ Qazvīnī (p. 371), and Ḥasan b. Moḥammad Qomī (p. 26); although writers like Yāqūt attributed it to Ardašīr I (224-40) and gave the Sasanian name Kerd-Ardašīr, others, like Qomī, recorded it as a work of Ḵosrow I Anōšīravān (531-79). It is not unlikely that the building dates from early Sasanian times and was restored at the time of Anōšīravān.

During the Islamic period the caravansary underwent major reconstruction at least twice. The first occasion was in the reign of the Saljuq sultan Sanjar (511-52/1118-57), whose vizier Abū Naṣr Aḥmad

PLATE X

View of Dayr-e Gačīn from the southwest.

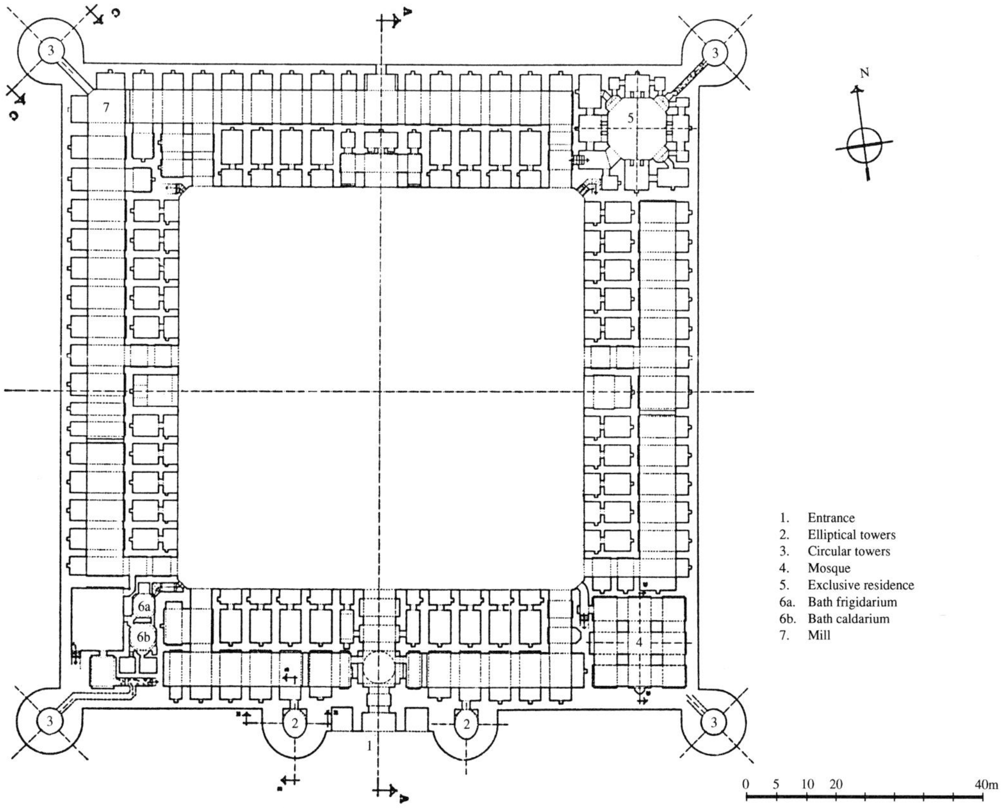

Figure 8. Plan of Dayr-e Gačīn. After Shokoohy, p. 450.

Kāšī repaired the road between Ray and Qom, restored Dayr-e Gačīn, and made the nearby village of Kāj into an endowment for it (Nāṣer al-Dīn Monšī, p. 68). The second was apparently during the Safavid period, when most of the old vaults, built with large Sasanian bricks measuring 36 x 36 x 8 cm, were dismantled and new vaults were built with smaller bricks 25 x 25 x 5 cm on top of the old walls. A large number of the Sasanian bricks were left around the site and were reused later in surrounding buildings.

The caravansary is a fortified square enclosure, with round towers at the corners and two towers, semielliptical in plan, flanking the main entrance in the middle of the southern wall (Figure 8). The corridors to the towers retain their original vaults with parabolic profiles and the towers themselves their Sasanian domes, also parabolic in profile. The domes of the entrance towers are elliptical in plan, an unusual feature in Persian architecture. Inside the enclosure there is a large central courtyard surrounded by four *ayvān*s (q.v.) and forty rooms, each with a vaulted anteroom and, behind, a row of stables with sixty-six raised niches in the walls for use as sleeping platforms. The plan is similar to that of other Islamic caravansaries in Persia, and it is not clear how much of it is of the Sasanian period and how much of the Saljuq reconstruction. Outside the enclosure the cisterns, domed with Sasanian bricks, are also preserved; one of them still holds water.

Dayr-e Gačīn is one of the largest caravansaries in Persia, and, apart from the usual accommodations, includes some uncommon features. Inside the enclosure each corner was built on a different plan for a specific function. In the northwest corner there is a mill, in the southwest a small courtyard with a bathhouse and kitchen. The northeast corner was built as a private apartment around a small courtyard and must have been intended for the use of royalty or high-ranking officials. Among such personages was the Safavid shah Esmāʿīl I (907-30/1501-24), who took this route on his campaign from Fārs to Fīrūzkūh and Māzandarān (Qāżī Aḥmād, p. 268). A mosque was constructed in the southeast corner of the enclosure; it is square in plan, and in the center of the sanctuary there are four massive piers of Sasanian brick, arranged as in a *čahārṭāq* (q.v.). As with the rest of the structure, the original roof has been replaced by later Islamic vaults, but it is likely that the mosque is on the site of a Sasanian fire temple that had a domed *čahārṭāq* in the center.

Bibliography: Abū Dolaf b. Mohalhel, *al-Resālat al-ṯānīya*, ed. V. Minorsky, Cairo, 1955. M. Y. Kiani, *Iranian Caravansarais*, Tokyo, 1978, pp. 27-28. *Mojmal*, ed. Bahār, pp. 54, 463. Nāṣer al-Dīn Monšī Kermānī, *Nasāʾem al-asḥār*, ed. J. Moḥaddeṯ, Tehran, 1338 Š./1959. Neẓām al-Molk, *Sīar al-molūk (Sīāsat-nāma)*, ed. H. Darke, Tehran, 1341 Š./ 1962. Qāżī Aḥmad Ḡaffārī Qazvīnī, *Tārīḵ-e jahānārā*, Tehran, 1343 Š./1964. Abū Yaḥyā Zakarīyāʾ Qazvīnī, *Āṯār al-belād*, Beirut, 1960. Ḥasan b. Moḥammad Qomī, *Ketāb-e tārīḵ-e Qom*, Pers. tr. Ḥasan b. ʿAlī Qomī, ed. S. J. Ṭehrānī, Tehran, 1313 Š./1934. Šams-al-Dīn Moḥammad b. Qays Rāzī, *al-Moʿjam fī maʿayīr ašʿār al-ʿajam*, ed. M. Qazvīnī, Leiden and London, 1909; 2nd ed., ed. M.-T. Modarres Rażawī, Tehran, 1336 Š./1957. M. Shokoohy, "The Sasanian Caravanserai of Dayr-i Gachīn, South of Ray, Iran," *BSOAS* 46, 1983, pp. 445-61. M. Ṭabāṭabāʾī, *Rāhnemā-ye jog̠rāfīā-ye tārīḵī-e Qom* I, Qom, 1355 Š./1976, pp. 66, 208-09.

(MEHRDAD SHOKOOHY)

DAYSAM b. Ebrāhīm KORDĪ, ABŪ SĀLEM, Kurdish commander who ruled sporadically in Azerbaijan (q.v.) between 326/938 and 344/955 after the period of Sajid domination there.

Daysam is described as the son of a Kurdish mother and an Arab father who had been a partisan of the Kharijite Hārūn Wāzeqī at Mosul during the caliphate of al-Moʿtażed (279-89/892-902). A Kharijite like his father, Daysam rose to prominence in the service of Yūsof b. Abi'l-Sāj. Owing largely to Kurdish backing, he had taken control of Azerbaijan by 326/938, but his position there was soon threatened by the northward expansion of the Deylamites (q.v.), particularly Moḥammad b. Mosāfer of Ṭārom and his sons Marzbān and Vahsūdān. The Gīlanī general Laškarī b. Mardī expelled Daysam, who then sought help from the Ziyarid Vošmgīr in Ray; he recovered his principality, only to lose it again to Marzbān b. Moḥammad in 330/941-42. He was invited back from exile in Armenia by pro-Kurdish, anti-Deylamite elements in Azerbaijan but was nevertheless forced to surrender to Marzbān, who then extended his dominion as far as Dvin and Arrān (333/944-45). Daysam was back in Azerbaijan in 341/952, but two years later he had been expelled thence yet again and was seeking help from the Hamdanids. With aid from Sayf-al-Dawla, ruler of Aleppo (333-56/945-67), he took advantage of Vahsūdān b. Moḥammad's preoccupation with quelling a revolt in Darband, reappeared in Azerbaijan, and took Salmās (344/955-56), but he was again obliged to retreat into Armenia when Marzbān appeared. The Artsrunid prince Deranikʿ, son of Gagik, then handed him over to Marzbān, who blinded and imprisoned him; when Marzbān died in 346/957 his supporters killed Daysam.

Bibliography: A. A. Bykov, "Daisam ibn Ibrāhkhīm al-Kurdī i ego monetui (Iz istorii Azerbaidzhana i Armenii X v.)" (Daysam b. Ebrāhīm Kordī and his coins [from the history of Azerbaijan and Armenia in the 10th century]), *Epigrafika Vostoka* 10, 1955, pp. 14-37. Ebn al-Aṯīr, VIII, pp. 349-50, 480, 500. Ebn Ḥawqal, pp. 334, 354; tr. Kramers, pp. 326-27, 347. W. Madelung, "The Minor Dynasties of Northern Iran," in *Camb. Hist. Iran* IV, pp. 232-35. Margoliouth and Amedroz, *Eclipse* I, pp. 398-404; II, pp. 148-51. Aḥmad Monajjem-bāšī, *Bāb fi'l-Šaddādīya men ketāb Jāmeʿ al-dowal*, tr. V. Minorsky as *Studies in Caucasian History*, London, 1953, pp. 11, 161-62, cf. pp. 113-14.

(C. EDMUND BOSWORTH)

DE BODE. See Supplement.

DE BRUIN (or de Bruyn), CORNELIS, also known as Corneille Le Brun or Le Bruyn (b. the Hague 1652, d. Utrecht 1726 or 1727), Dutch painter and author of two accounts of his travels in Persia and other eastern lands. From early childhood he showed a keen interest in foreign countries and travel, and his love for drawing and painting was partly motivated by their usefulness in representing accurately what travelers had seen during their visits to foreign lands. In the Hague, de Bruin studied painting with the master Theodoor van der Schuur. Nicolaas Witsen, a wealthy travel enthusiast and burgomaster of Amsterdam, who had visited "North and East Tartary" in 1666, was so impressed with de Bruijn's enthusiasm for both travel and art that he decided to finance his first trip abroad.

De Bruin left for Italy on 1 November 1674; he remained there for four years before departing for Smyrna, whence he visited Asia Minor, and Egypt. In 1684 he returned to Venice, where he lived for eight years and studied painting with Carl Loth. On 19 March 1693 he arrived in the Hague; he spent the next five years writing his first travelogue (*Reizen van Corn. de Bruyn door de vermaardste deelen van Klein Asia, de eylanden Scio, Rhodus, Cyprus enz. mitsg. de voornaamste steden van Aegypten, Syrien en Palestina*, Delft, 1698) and preparing the 215 engravings that illustrate it. A French version (*Voyage au Levant . . . dans les principaux endroits de l'Asie Mineure*) was published by H. de Krooneveld in Delft in 1700 and reprinted in Amsterdam in 1714 (though Paris is given as the publisher's address); it was the basis for an English translation (*A Voyage to the Levant. Or Travels in the Principal Parts of Asia Minor, etc.*, London, 1702).

On 28 July 1701 de Bruin again left the Hegue, this time for Russia, Persia, and the East Indies; he did not return until 24 October 1708. Witsen had interests in the Russia trade and close contacts with the Vereenigde Oostindische Compagnie (V.O.C., Dutch East Indies company); he also financed this trip and facilitated de Bruin's access to important people and support from Dutch circles in the countries where he traveled. De Bruin arrived in Persia, at Darband, on 7 Rabīᶜ I 1115/21 July 1703, and from there he generally followed the standard route of European travelers: Šamāḵī, Ardabīl, Qom, Kāšān, Isfahan, Shiraz, Bandar ᶜAbbās. He arrived in Isfahan on 4 Šaᶜbān 1115/13 December 1703 and remained for almost a year, during which he was frequently entertained by Frans Kastelein, the local V.O.C. director, and his staff, who also provided him with information and contacts. Through these contacts he was introduced to all levels of Persian society and introduced at court, where he made a drawing of Shah Solṭān Ḥosayn (1105-35/1694-1722).

De Bruin's travel account does not provide major new insights into Persian society, life, and customs, but it is a straightforward, thorough, and balanced account, without the elements of fantasy that mar most other works by contemporary travelers to Persia, particularly in their discussions of Persepolis. It is thus both a reliable and a richly illustrated work that throws light on changes and adjustments in the country since the visits of the 17th-century travelers. As de Bruin drew most of the illustrations from life, they are much more accurate and reliable than those of his predecessors. In particular he devoted much of his time to making drawings of Persepolis and to correcting the errors of Engelbert Kaempfer, Jean Chardin, and other earlier visitors. He also carved his name on Xerxes' portal in 1116/1704.

After returning from Asia de Bruin spent most of his time writing his second book and preparing 320 engravings; the work was published in Amsterdam in 1711 (*Corn. de Bruins Reizen over Moskovie door Persie en Indie, verrykt met 300 konstplaten, vertoonende . . . voor al derz. oudheden, en wel voornamentlyk heel uitvoerig die van het . . .hof van Persepolis*); it was reprinted in Amsterdam in 1714. According to de Bruin's own testimony, 1,000 copies of the first Dutch edition were printed. In the same year he published critical remarks on Kaempfer and Chardin (*Aanmerkingen over de Printverbeeldingen van de overblijfselen van het oude Persepolis uitgegeven door de Heeren Chardin and Kaempfer*, Amsterdam, 1714). In 1718 a French translation (*Voyage de Corneille Le Brun par la Moscovie, en Persia, et aux Indes Orientales*, 6 parts. in 2 vols., Amsterdam) of the second travel account appeared, combined with the criticisms of Kaempfer and Chardin (pt. 5), and the Dane Eberhard Isbrand Ides' account of his own three-year voyage as Russian ambassador to China (pt. 6); this work was reissued in eight parts and five volumes under the title *Voyage au Levant etc.* in Paris in 1725 (reissued in 1732). A similar five-volume edition, edited and "considerably augmented" by Antoine Banier, was published in Rouen in the same year, with the plates reduced in size. An English translation of the account of de Bruin's journey to Russia (*The Present State of Russia . . . Being an Account of the Government of That Country etc.*) appeared in London in 1723 and a Russian translation (*Puteshestvie cherez Moskoviyu*, from the 1718 French edition) in 1872-73. In 1737 an English translation of de Bruin's entire second travel account (*Travels into Muscovy, Persia, and Part of the East-Indies . . . Embellished with above 300 Copper Plates . . . with Remarks on the Travels of Sir John Chardin and Mr. Kaempfer . . .*, 2 vols., London, also based on the 1718 French edition) was published with irregular pagination; another (*A New . . . Translation . . . of Mr. Cornelius Le Brun's Travels into Muscovy, Persia and Divers Parts of the East-Indies, etc.*, London) appeared in one volume in 1759.

De Bruin spent the remainder of his life pursuing his interest in art and visiting friends in various towns in the Netherlands. On one of those lengthy visits, to the home of David van Mollem in Utrecht, he died. Although all editions of de Bruin's books carry the information that the illustrations were drawn from life by de Bruin himself, it is not clear who made the engravings from his drawings (see, e.g., his observations in the preface to the 1700 French translation of his first book*). The 1711 Dutch edition of the second travel account includes the name "M. Pool sc." on some of the engravings. Only a few of de Bruin's paintings are known to have survived. Among them is a portrait of "a kneeling naked woman and a negro," sold at Christie's auction house in London, 12 July 1963 (catalogue of De Witt Institute in London). Another, "David and Abigail," is in the Galleria Colonna in Rome (Benezit, p. 369). A full-page engraving (by G. Valck) of a portrait of de Bruin by G. Kneller appears in the first Dutch edition of each of his travel accounts.

Bibliography. A. J. van der Aa, *Biographisch Woordenboek der Nederlanden* II, Haarlem, 1854, pp. 1489-91. E. Benezit, *Dictionnaire critique et documentée des peintres*, 8 vols., Paris, 1948-53; repr. 10 vols., Paris, 1976. Johan van Gool, *De Nieuwe Schouburg der Nederlantsche Kunstschilders and Schilderessen*, the Hague, 1750; repr., Soest, the Netherdlands, 1971, II, pp. 112-16. C. Krimm, *Geschiedenis van de Beeldende Kunsten in de Nederlanden* II, Amsterdam, 1864, p. 177. P. A. U. Thieme, *Allgemeines Lexicon der Bildende Kuenstler* V, Leipzig, 1911, p. 159. P. A. Tiele, *Nederlandsche Bibliographie van Land- en Volkenkunde*, Amsterdam, 1854, pp. 51-52.

(WILLEM FLOOR)

DE GOEJE, MICHAËL JAN (b. Dronrijp, Friesland, 18 August 1836, d. Leiden, 17 May 1909), Dutch orientalist and chief editor of Ṭabarī's world history, *Taʾrīḵ al-rosol wa'l-molūk* (*Annales*, 15 vols., Leiden, 1879-1901; repr. Leiden, 1964). He was the second son of a Protestant minister. In 1854 he went to Leiden University to study theology and also took courses in Hebrew, Arabic, Syriac, and Aramaic under T. W. J. Juynboll (1802–61). In 1856 he switched to the faculty of literature and studied Arabic and classics under R. P. A. Dozy (q.v.; 1820–83). He received his doctorate in 1860 with a thesis on North Africa as described in Yaʿqūbī's *Ketāb al-boldān* (*Specimen Literarium Inaugurale Exhibens Descriptionem al-Magribi Sumtam e Libro Regionum al-Jaqubii* . . ., Leiden, 1860). In the previous year he had been appointed assistant curator of the collection of oriental manuscripts in the university library. In 1869 he was promoted to curator, a position he held until his death; in this capacity he was the main contributor to the catalogue of the collection (see below). Three years earlier, in 1866, he had succeeded to Juynboll's chair, at first as a kind of adjunct professor of Arabic; from 1869 to 1906 he had regular professorial status.

De Goeje received an honorary doctorate from the University of Cambridge in 1896 and was an associate member of the British Academy and the Institut de France. He was also active in public life, serving for several decades as a Liberal member of the municipal council of Leiden and as a member and later president of the municipal board of education.

De Goeje's main interest lay in Islamic geography and historiography, particularly of the ʿAbbasid period; few of the relevant Arabic textual sources were available in his time. From 1860 to his death in 1909 he therefore devoted himself to the edition, alone or in collaboration, of twenty Arabic texts, all with extensive indexes and Arabic-Latin glossaries. The introductions on the authors and the works themselves were, however, usually limited to two or three pages. After publishing a partial edition and translation of Edrīsī's *Ketāb nozhat al-moštāq* (*Description de l'Afrique et de l'Espagne par Edrîsî*, Leiden, 1866) jointly with Dozy, de Goeje embarked upon the Bibliotheca Geographorum Arabicorum, which eventually included seven volumes of texts by the most prominent geographers of the 9th and 10th centuries (Eṣṭaḵrī, Ebn Ḥawqal, Maqdesī [Moqaddasī], Ebn Faqīh, Qodāma b. Jaʿfar, Ebn Ḵordāḏbeh, Ebn Rosta, Yaʿqūbī, Masʿūdī) and one volume of glossary, indexes, and addenda. No less important are his editions of such historical texts as Balāḏorī's *Ketāb fotūḥ al-boldān* (Leiden, 1866), the third part of the anonymous *Ketāb al-ʿoyūn wa'l-ḥadāʾeq fī aḵbār'l-ḥaqāʾeq* (with P. de Jong), and the sixth part of Ebn Meskawayh's *Tajāreb al-omam* (the latter two in Fragmenta Historicorum Arabicorum, 2 vols., Leiden, 1869–71).

De Goeje's main fame, however, rests on his edition of Ṭabarī's history of the world until the year 302/915. In 1858, when he took up the idea of preparing a printed edition, no complete copy of the text was known to exist, though manuscripts of single volumes were dispersed in libraries throughout Europe and the Near East; some had already been published. It was not, however, until 1871, when eight volumes were discovered in the Kōprülü library in Istanbul, that a reconstruction of the original text began to seem possible. De Goeje invited a number of European orientalists to participate in the project, among them his most intimate friend, Theodor Nöldeke (1836–1930). De Goeje not only coordinated the project but also edited a large part of the text himself, prepared the indexes and glossaries, and concluded the work with an introductory volume in Latin. The publication of this edition, consisting of almost 10,000 pages, extended over twenty-two years and was one of the largest undertakings of 19th-century orientalism. De Goeje's extensive correspondence about the project is preserved with the collection of oriental manuscripts in the library of Leiden University.

De Goeje left no large works of research or synthesis, his main contributions of this kind being the modest volumes of his Mémoires d'Histoire et de Géographie Orientales: I. *Mémoire sur les Carmathes du Bahraïn* (Leiden, 1862; 2nd ed., Leiden, 1886); II. *Mémoire sur le Fotouho's-Scham attribué à Abou Ismaïl al-Baçri* (Leiden, 1864); III. *Mémoire sur la conquête de la Syrie* (Leiden, 1864; 2nd ed., Leiden, 1900); IV. *Mémoire sur les migrations des Tsiganes à travers l'Asie* (Leiden, 1903). He wrote more than a hundred articles, many for popular Dutch magazines like *De Gids* and *De Nederlandsche Spectator*, and numerous book reviews. He also contributed to the work of other orientalists by careful proofreading and by revising books like William Wright's *Grammar of the Arabic Language* and his edition of the *Reḥla* of Ibn Jobayr (*The Travels of Ibn-Jubayr*). At the age of seventy-one years de Goeje accepted the editorship of the first edition of *The Encyclopaedia of Islam* but was soon forced to resign owing to ill health; he did not live to see the first volume in print.

Other works written or edited by de Goeje include *Catalogus Codicum Orientalium Bibliothecae Academiae Lugduno-Batavae* III-V (III-IV with de Jong; Leiden 1865–73); *Catalogus Codicum Arabicorum Bibliothecae Academiae Lugduno-Batavae* (I with M. T. Houtsma, II, pt. 1, with Juynboll), Leiden, 1888–1907; *Historia Khalifatus Omari II, Jazidi II et Hischámi* (Leiden, 1866); *Das alte Bett des Oxus Amû-Darja* (Leiden, 1875); *Diwân Poëtae Abu'l-Walîd Moslim ibno'l–Walîd al-Ançârî* (Leiden, 1876); *The Kâmil of el-Mubarrad* XII (critical notes to Wright's edition of the text; Leipzig, 1892); ʿArīb Qortobī, *Tabari Continuatus* (Leiden, 1897); *Selections from the Annals of Tabari* (Semitic Studies Series 1, Leiden, 1902); Ebn Qotayba, *Liber Poësis et Poëtarum* (Leiden, 1904); and *Selections from Arabic Geographical Literature* (Semitic Studies Series 8, Leiden, 1907).

Bibliography: A. A. Bevan, "Michaël Jan de Goeje," *JRAS*, 1909, pp. 849–50. H. Cordier, "M. J. De Goeje, associé étranger de l'Académie des Inscriptions et Belles-Lettres," *Journal des savants*, N.S. 7, 1909, pp. 326–31. M. T. Houtsma, "Levensbericht van M. J. de Goeje," in *Levensberichten der afgestorven medeleden van de Maatschappij der Nederlandsche Letterkunde. Bijlagen tot de Handelingen 1909-1910*, Leiden, 1910, pp. 34–59 (detailed information on de Goeje's life). Idem et al., eds., *Feestbundel aan Prof. M. J. de Goeje*, Leiden, 1891. C. Huart, "Michael Jan de Goeje," *JA*, 10th ser., 14, 1909, pp. 191–96. A. Kluyver, "Michael-Jan de Goeje," *Journal of the Gypsy Lore Society*, N.S. 3, September 1909, pp. 1–4. P. K. Kokowtsow, "Michail Jan de Gue," *Izvestiya Imperatorskoĭ Akademii Nauk*, 6th ser., 3, 1909, pp. 713–18. C. Snouck Hurgronje, "Michaël Jan de Goeje," *Internationales Archiv für Ethnographie* 19, Leiden, 1910a, pp. 49–54. Idem, "Michaël Jan de Goeje" in *Jaarboek der Koninklijke Akademie van Wetenschappen*, Amsterdam, 1910b, pp. 107–66 (with complete bibliography); tr. M. Chauvin as *Michaël Jan de Goeje, par C. Snouck Hurgronje*, Leiden, 1911; rev. C. J. Lyall, "Michael Jan de Goeje, par C. Snouck Hurgronje . . .," *JRAS*, 1911, pp. 843–48. H. Untersweg, *Michael Jan de Goeje, 1836–1909*, Graz, 1909. C. van Vollenhoven, "Professor De Goeje (1836–1909)," *Leidsch Jaarboekje*, Leiden, 1910. A. J. Wensinck, "Goeje, Michaël Jan de-," in P. C. Molhuysen and P. J. Blok, eds., *Nieuw Nederlandsch Biografisch Woordenboek* I, Amsterdam, 1911, cols. 946–47.

(A. J. M. VROLIJK)

DE MECQUENEM. See Supplement.

DE MORGAN, Jacques (b. Huisseau-sur-Cosson, near Blois, 3 June 1857, d. Marseilles, 14 June 1924), French archeologist and prehistorian. He came from an exceptionally gifted family, in which cultivation of humane learning was combined with scientific rigor. His father, Eugène, sometimes called "Baron" de Morgan, an engineer specializing in mineral prospecting, was interested in entomology and prehistory. He initiated his two sons, Henry, the elder, and Jacques, into fieldwork, excavating with them the Campigny fault near Rouen, which had lent its name to the first phase of the European neolithic. Through his father Jacques became acquainted with Gabriel de Mortillet, who was connected with the museum of national antiquities in Saint-Germain and who, during investigations of Merovingian cemeteries, taught him how to catalogue excavated objects. De Morgan wanted to be a professional geologist like his father, and his personal fortune had permitted him to travel and study abroad since his early youth. In 1879 he began to publish the results of his research, illustrated with drawings that were remarkable for their finesse and documentary precision. He received his final training at the École des Mines, from which he was graduated in 1882. He was then appointed to head a survey expedition to Scandinavia and subsequently conducted surveys in Germany, Austria, Turkey, India, and as far away as the kingdom of Perak in what is now West Malaysia. In this last area he took up geography and ethnology, mastering the physical anthropology and language of the Sakai blacks (de Morgan, 1886).

He went next to Russian Armenia, as manager of a copper mine at Akhtala. At that time he believed that "the Caucasus is of special interest in the study of the origins of metals; it is the easternmost point from which prehistoric remains are known; older than Europe and Greece, it still retains the traces of those civilizations that were the cradle of our own" (Vachon-France) His interest in the eastern origins of civilization eventually led to neighboring Persia. The scientific reports that he wrote upon his return from the Caucasus were published in Paris in 1889-90 (*Mission scientifique au Caucase* I. *Études archéologiques et historiques. Les premiers âges des métaux dans l'Arménie russe*; II. *Recherches sur les origines des peuples du Caucase*). Immediately thereafter the

French ministry of public education entrusted him with his first official mission to Persia. En route he paused to explore the necropolis at Telovan near Tbilisi, then went on to Tehran, whence he paid visits to Māzandarān, to Gīlān, and farther west to Ṭāleš, in order to study dialects. From Ṭāleš he traveled south across Kurdistan and Luristan, combining both geological and archeological investigations. He was the first to recognize, at Qaṣr-e Šīrīn, the presence of oil in the vast fold system of the Zagros. Although he had undertaken his mission on behalf of the French government, he conducted this survey out of friendship for the Persian government. At first, however, neither France nor Persia was interested, and it was only in 1320/1902 that exploitation began, under the leadership of the Englishman William Knox D'Arcy (q.v.).

De Morgan's journey ended in Susiana, where he attempted to retrace the routes of the Assyrian campaigns in Elam. He remained for a long time at Susa (Šūš), from which the expedition led by Marcel Dieulafoy (q.v.) had departed six years earlier. In the vast field of ruins his curiosity was aroused particularly by the high mound known as the "citadel," at the foot of which he recovered some flints and some very early potsherds. This discovery must have been decisive in leading him to reopen excavations at the site. Upon his return to Tehran he confided in the French minister, René de Balloy, who was eager to obtain for France a monopoly of archeological research in Persia. It took a little time, however, before these efforts, under de Morgan's guidance, were successful. In the meantime he published his *Mission scientifique en Perse* (5 parts comprising 10 vols., Paris, 1894-1905), including four volumes of geological studies; two volumes of archeological studies on tombs and other monuments that were still visible; one volume devoted to Kurdish dialects and the languages of northern Persia; one volume of Mandaean texts; and two volumes of geographical studies.

After his return to France, in November 1891, he planned, once he had put his notes in order, to go back to Persia and to pursue his studies in the southern and eastern provinces. Before he could do so, however, he was invited to take over as acting director of the Egyptian antiquities service; he remained in this interim appointment until 1897. De Morgan's talents as an administrator and diplomat ensured his favorable reception by foreign, especially English, Egyptologists. He took up his post in 1892, and during the next five years he founded, with Giuseppe Botti, the museum of Greco-Roman antiquities at Alexandria; saved the temple of Kom Ombo (Kawm Ombū) from destruction; undertook publication of a general catalogue of the monuments and inscriptions of ancient Egypt; and, just before his departure, laid the cornerstone for the Cairo museum of ancient Egyptian antiquities (de Morgan, 1895; idem, 1896). His exploration of the pyramids of Dashur (Dahšūr) brought to light the royal treasures of the Middle Kingdom. But, as always, his primary personal interest was in prehistory, and he can be considered the father of prehistoric archeology in Egypt. He began excavation of the extremely important Proto-Dynastic site of Nagada (Naqqāda); unfortunately, however, he entrusted the continuation of the work to Émile Amélineau, who proceeded with disastrous clumsiness (for details of de Morgan's career in Egypt, see Vachon-France).

In the meantime, in 1312/1895 Nāṣer-al-Dīn Shah (1264-1313/1848-96) had signed a treaty granting to France a monopoly of archeological exploration in Persia. The Délégation en Perse (see DÉLÉGATIONS ARCHÉOLOGIQUES FRANÇAISES i) was then established under the French ministry of public education and fine arts, and its direction was entrusted to de Morgan; he was chosen over Dieulafoy, who never forgave him. De Morgan left Egypt in 1897 with the intention of creating a "French archeological service" in Persia, in order "to investigate these little-known regions from every scientific vantage point." He decided, however, to concentrate most of his own efforts at the site of Susa, in order to further knowledge of Elamite civilization, as opposed to that of the Achaemenid Persians, whom he considered lacking in originality—a debatable judgment, to say the least—and to that of the Medes, who had "never written their history," a conclusion that still stands.

In fact, from de Morgan's own writings it seems clear that he was less interested in Elamite history than in the overall prehistory of the East. In 1902 he declared: "In the Nile valley I developed the conviction that the first civilizations, from which the Egyptian empire arose, came from Chaldea and that the Mesopotamian plains had therefore been the cradle of human progress. Susa, because of its very early date, provided the possibility of solving the greatest and most important problem, that of our origins. This city, in my view, belonged to that primordial world that had witnessed the discovery of writing, the use of metals, the beginnings of art. If the great problem of origins was to be solved one day, it was in Chaldea, and especially at Susa, that it was necessary to seek the basic elements" (1902, p. 16).

It was probably this primary interest in "origins," rather than in historical periods, that led de Morgan to decide, before he had even begun to excavate, that he did not "have to deal with well-preserved monuments that require careful delineation; the ruins were amorphous, and the remains of superimposed walls showed traces of a series of total destructions of the city. . . . It was thus necessary to undertake a general exploration of the site, without taking into account the natural strata, which cannot be recovered" (1900, pp. 50-51). He thus divided the enormous mound of the acropolis, which was at that time 30-35 m high, into sections, each 5 m wide and 5 m deep, which constituted the first "level"; below them similar trenches were excavated, constituting the earliest "levels." From the beginning of his work, then, de Morgan, despite his exceptional cultivation and dedication, condemned the architectural remains at Susa to total destruction for all time; the excavation consisted simply of removing an estimated 2,450,000 m^3 of dirt, as in any public-works project. De Morgan imposed his method, backed by considerable means, on a small team, the most competent members of which were two former colleagues from Egypt, Gustave Jéquier, in particular, and J. E. Gautier. For work on texts he had called upon the Dominican father Vincent Scheil, a renowned Assyriologist.

The team began work in December 1897, but it had to contend with attacks by plunderers, who carried out their depredations without restraint in a province that was mostly out of the control of the central government. To ensure the safety of the expedition and its finds, de Morgan built an enormous castle of medieval aspect on the northernmost point of the acropolis. Wanting to obtain as soon as possible an idea of the sequence of periods, he had dug at the southern tip a series of five successive soundings, which revealed at the bottom traces of an archaic civilization with fine ceramics and above it an apparently derivative civilization with "crude" painted ceramics, both from before the historical periods of Elam. His far too brief summary report on this sounding was to be repeated almost without change in the final excavation report published ten years later (1912).

Meanwhile work in the trenches was yielding impressive results, as masterpieces of Babylonian civilization, captured by the Elamites as spoils of war, began to appear. The victory stele of Naram-Sin and a series of Kassite *kudurru*s ("boundary stones") were intermingled with masterpieces of Elamite metalwork and sculpture. In 1318/1900 Moẓaffar-al-Dīn Shah (1313-24/1896-1907) signed a supplementary treaty granting to France all the antiquities discovered at Susa. And the discoveries continued, crowned by the appearance of the stele bearing the law code of Hammurabi. They were published, starting in 1900, in Mémoires de la Délégation en Perse (M.D.P.).

As work at Susa was carried on in the winter, Henry and Jacques de Morgan used the summers to resume excavation of the late Bronze and Iron Age cemeteries in Ṭāleš. The publication ("Recherches au Talyche persan," in *M.D.P.* VIII, 1905, pp. 251-341) shows that, in the field of prehistory, de Morgan was a good archeologist. At Susa, on the other hand, the "investigations" had become tedious, and he often abandoned direction of the work to his colleagues. In 1322/1903-04 the temples of Inshushinak and Ninhursag of Susa were badly excavated; then, in 1324/1906, virgin soil was reached in the necropolis, revealing clearly both the beauty of the archaic ceramics and the presence of copper, which indicated a date later than had been expected. Disappointed, de Morgan had, in addition, to face the hostility of certain colleagues and in France the very unjust accusation of laxity in the financial management of the mission. He thus decided not to return to Susa after 1325/1907. His health shattered, he resigned from the mission in 1912.

He had previously entrusted to the Hellenist Edmond Pottier the task of publishing the pottery from Susa, though the information on periodization that he provided for Pottier was as false as it was sketchy, basically limited to the succession of two "styles" of pottery ("Étude historique et chronologiqe sur les vases peints de l'acropole de Suse," in *M.D.P.* XIII, Paris, 1912, pp. 27-103). On the other hand, he devoted himself to synthetic publications, primarily on prehistory but also on oriental numismatics. His major works remain *L'humanité préhistorique* (Paris, 1921) and especially the three-volume *La préhistoire orientale* (Paris, 1925-27), which appeared posthumously. Salomon Reinach was charged with providing, in *Revue archéologique* (1924), a detailed assessment of the career and personality of Jacques de Morgan, who was a great archeologist but made the mistake, characteristic of his time, of undertaking as a prehistorian work on a historical site like Susa. The world owes to him exceptional collections of artifacts irreparably deprived of their archeological contexts.

(For a complete bibliography of De Morgan's publications, comprising more than 130 works, see Vachon-France.)

Bibliography: J. de Morgan, "Note sur les terrains crétacés de la vallée de la Bresle," *Bulletin de la Société des Géologues de France*, 3e sér., 7, 1879. Idem, "Exploration dans la presqu'île malaise. Moeurs, coutumes et langages des Negritos Sakayes et Seumangs," *Bulletin de la Société normande de Géographie*, 1886. Idem, "Compte-rendu des travaux archéologiques exécutés par le Service des Antiquités de l'Égypte et par les savants étrangers pendant les années 1894 et 1895," *Bulletin de l'Institut d'Égypte* 3e sér. 6, 1895. Idem, "Note sur les travaux du Service des Antiquités de l'Égypte et de l'Institut égyptien pendant les années 1892-1893-1894," *Xeme Congrès des Orientalistes*, Geneva, 1896. Idem, "Ruines de Sus," in *M.D.P.* I, Paris, 1900, pp. 50-54. Idem, *La Délégation en Perse du Ministère de l'instruction publique 1897 à 1902*, Paris, 1902. Idem, "Observations sur les couches profondes de l'Acropole de Suse," in *M.D.P.* XIII, Paris, 1912, pp. 1-25. S. Reinach, "Nouvelles archéologiques et correspondance. Jacques de Morgan (1856-1924)," *Revue archéologique* 34, 1924, pp. 204-22. C. Vachon-France, "Jacques de Morgan, Directeur général des Antiquités de l'Égypte, *La revue de Marseille* 79, September-October 1968, pp. 13-26.

(PIERRE AMIET)

DEAD SEA SCROLLS, parchment and papyrus scrolls written in Hebrew, mainly of the 1st centuries B.C.E. and C.E., found in caves around Qomrān on the northwest coast of the Dead Sea and considered to represent a sect of Judaism. A number of Iranian elements can be discerned in these documents, particularly pertaining to dualism, a characteristic of Iranian religions. Until the discovery of the Qomrān manuscripts the doctrine of two spirits was only sporadically attested in Jewish literature, but it is clear that the spirits under God's command were not always good and benevolent; for example, God is said to have sent an evil spirit between Abimelech and the citizens of Shechem (Judges 9:23) and Saul to have been troubled by an "evil spirit" after the "spirit of God" departed from him (I Samuel 16:14). In apocryphal, Christian, and rabbinical literature the good and the evil spirits are opposed to each other. For example, in the apocryphal Gospel of Judas (2nd century C.E.) the spirits of truth and error that serve men are mentioned, as well as a third spirit personifying the ability to choose: "and in the midst is the Spirit of intelligence, who is able to turn wherever he chooses." In most texts, however, only good and evil spirits are named, as in the Gospel of St. John; in the Gnostic treatise *Hermas* there is reference to the holy spirit and the evil spirit who dwell together in man.

In contrast to these laconic references, the manual of discipline (or community rule) found among the Qomrān documents includes a small treatise on the two spirits as propounded by the Qomrān sect, founded in the mid-2nd century B.C.E. The fact that God created all things is stressed, followed by the specification "He created man to have dominion over the world and made for him two spirits, that he might walk by them until the appointed time of his visitation; they are the spirits of truth and error. In the abode of light are the origins of truth, and from the source of darkness are the origins of error. In the hand of the prince of lights is dominion over all sons of righteousness; in the ways of light they walk. And in the hand of the angel of darkness is all dominion over the sons of error; and in the ways of darkness they walk. And by the angel of darkness is the straying of all the sons of righteousness, and all their sin and their iniquities and their guilt, and the transgressions of their works in his dominion. . . . But God in the mysteries of his understanding and in his glorious wisdom has ordained a period for the rule of error, and in the appointed time of punishment he will destroy it forever. And then shall come out forever the truth of the world" (Burrows, pp. 374-76).

As André Dupont-Sommer and K. G. Kuhn independently observed, these words are immediately reminiscent of the Zoroastrian doctrine of the two spirits, as embodied in the ethical and eschatological dualism of the Gathas. Kuhn also noted that the Jewish document differs from Iranian doctrine on one important point: specifiying predestination, rather than the free choice of Zoroastrian theology. He did not, however, look beyond the Gathas and orthodox Zoroastrianism. Henri Michaud, on the other hand, sought a connection to Zurvanism but unfortunately based his argument on Plutarch's dubious testimony; the question must now be reexamined in the light of R. C. Zaehner's *Zurvan, a Zoroastrian Dilemma.*

It is possible to explain the contrast between the free choice offered by Zoroaster and the predestination espoused at Qomrān without resorting to Zurvanism; for example, it could have resulted from an adaptation of gathic doctrine to the context of Jewish religion. But there is at least one feature of the Qomrān manual that betrays a nongathic source: identification of the good and evil spirits with light and darkness respectively. In addition, the essential gathic emphasis on the role of the two spirits in the drama of choice was so alien to the Jewish milieu that it could be accommodated only through conception of a third spirit (see above).

The opposition between predestination and free choice, the identification of the spirits with light and darkness, and the claim that the two spirits were created by God are all features of the Zurvanite myth of a god of time or destiny, father of Ohrmazd (light) and Ahriman (q.v.; dark). As this kind of theology prevailed in Iranian religions in the period of the New Covenant Jewish community at Damascus (1st century B.C.E.), it is more likely than the ancient gathic theology to have been known to the Qomrān sect. This conclusion is borne out by Flavius Josephus' report that "The sect of the Essenes holds that Destiny is master of all things and that nothing happens to men but what has been decreed by it" (*Antiquitates* 13.5.9). In the Dead Sea scrolls several references to casting lots provide further corroborative evidence: "According to each man's inheritance in truth he does right, and so he hates error; but according to his possession in the lot of error he does wickedly in it, and so he abhors truth" (from the manual of discipline; Burrows, p. 376); "Thou has cast for man an eternal lot" (from the Thanksgiving psalms; Burrows, p. 404).

The Middle Persian term *mēnōg* has a complex of meanings that are strikingly similar to those of the Hebrew term *rūah*, used in at least three senses at Qomrān: the two spiritual entities, the two opposing qualities in man, and the numerous qualities and faculties in man (Shaked, 1972, p. 436). Nevertheless, "The complex of notions associated with the idea of *mēnōg* forms part of a coherent system in Iran, and stands in complementary opposition to the term *gētīg*, while in Judaism the development, though not actually contradicting anything found originally in Judaism, never comes to form anything like a coherent system" (Shaked, 1972, p. 437). Ohrmazd is said to be all-knowing, Ahriman ignorant; perhaps the most distinctive epithet of God in the scrolls is *El de'oth* "the God of knowledge" (Shaked, 1972, p. 440).

In the creation myth recorded by the Armenian Eznik of Kołb in the 5th century Zurvan says to Ahriman "I have made Ohrmazd reign above thee," which implies that Ohrmazd reigns in the *mēnōg* but Ahriman in this world. Similarly, at Qomrān the present age is said to be dominated by the evil spirit: "So shall they do year by year all the days of the dominion of Belial. . . . And [the world] has wallowed in the ways of wickedness in the dominion of error until the appointed time of judgment which has been decreed" (Burrows, pp. 373, 376).

There is also a single allusion to belief in physical resurrection, a Zoroastrian doctrine, in the Qomrān scrolls, in hymn 17 (Vermès, p. 186): "For the sake of Thy glory Thou hast purified man of sin . . . that . . . he may partake of the lot of Thy Holy Ones; bodies gnawed by worms may be raised from the dust to the counsel [of Thy truth] . . . that he may stand before Thee with the everlasting host."

Bibliography: Boyce, *Zoroastrianism* III, pp. 417-18, 421-27. M. Burrows, *The Dead Sea Scrolls*, New York, 1955. J. J. Collins, "The Mythology of Holy War in Daniel and the Qumran War Scroll," *Vetus Testamentum* 25, 1975, pp. 604-05. J. Duchesne-Guillemin, "Le zervanisme et les mss. de la Mer Morte," *IIJ* 1, 1957, pp. 96-99. A. Dupont-Sommer, "L'instruction sur les deux esprits dans le Manuel de discipline," *RHR* 142, 1952, pp. 5-35. H. W. Huppenheimer, "Belial in the Qumran texts," *Theologische Zeitung* 15, 1959, pp. 81-89. K. G. Kuhn, "Die Sektenschrift und die iranische Religion," *Zeitschrift für Theologie und Kirche* 42, 1952, pp. 211-310. H. Michaud, "Un mythe zervaniste dans un des manuscrits de Qumran," *Vetus Testamentum* 5, 1955, pp. 137-47. S. Shaked, "Qumran and Iran. Further Considerations," *Israel Oriental Studies* 11, 1972, pp. 433-46. Idem, "Iranian Influence on Judaism. First Century B.C.E. to Second Century C.E.," in W. D. Davies and L. Finkelstein, eds., *The Cambridge History of Judaism* I, Cambridge, 1984, pp. 308-25. G. Vermès, *Les manuscrits du désert de Juda*, Paris, 1953. D. Winston, "The Iranian Component in the Bible, Apokrypha and Qumran," *History of Religions* 5, 1966, pp. 188-89. R. Zaehner, *Zurvan, a Zoroastrian Dilemma*, Oxford, 1955.

(JACQUES DUCHESNE-GUILLEMIN)

DEATH among Zoroastrians. At death among Zoroastrians the body is swiftly disposed of (see CORPSE), but rites for the soul are prolonged. They are also complex, partly because, although Zoroastrianism is a salvation faith, offering hope of heaven and threat of hell, it maintains rites that, as Brahmanic parallels show, are an inheritance from very ancient, pre-Zoroastrian, times and belong with quite different beliefs. These beliefs were that the soul, after lingering on earth for three days (a belief retained in Zoroastrianism), needed before its departure consecrated offerings to provide for it in the underworld kingdom of the dead; and that it required such offerings again on the thirtieth day after death, the first anniversary day, and then annually for thirty years, or roughly a generation. Thereafter it was held to have been fully accepted into the ranks of departed souls, who received such offerings collectively only once a year, at the festival of Hamaspathmaēdaya.

Presumably in the early days of the faith converts clung so strongly to these age-old observances that the religious authorities were forced to allow them to be continued, "zoroastrianizing" them as far as possible and blending them with new ones that had the wholly different intention of helping the soul to attain heaven above, after which it should have no further need of anything. Indeed, according to Zoroaster's teaching, the soul's fate depends solely on the sum of the individual's thoughts, words, and acts, the good being weighed against the bad, so that no observances should avail it in any way. But human weakness (including the force of natural affections) and human illogicality enabled his followers to maintain this doctrine while at the same time performing many rites for the departed soul's benefit.

The oldest attestation of the rites of Hamaspathmaēdaya is in *Yašt* 13.49-52. Those for the individual soul during the three days after death, termed comprehensively in Pahlavi *sedōš* (*stwš*), were apparently referred to in the lost *Huspārām Nask*, or more probably in its Pahlavi commentary, according to a citation in the *Nērangestān*. They are known in more detail from texts set down in post-Sasanian times (notably the supplement to the *Šāyest nē šāyest*, the *Pahlavi Rivāyat*, the *Saddar*s, and the *Persian Rivāyats*) and from living usage. They are a mixture of "inner" and "outer" rituals and (unlike the necessarily more public funerary rites) attracted little attention in the past from foreign observers. There are some imprecise allusions by Greek writers in Achaemenid times, but the first detailed account by a non-Zoroastrian was given by A. H. Anquetil du Perron (II, pp. 585-87). This was amplified by Delphine Menant (pp. 195-204), whose description was further expanded by J. J. Modi (pp. 72-82). Details in which Irani usages differed from those of the Parsis were later recorded by Ardašīr Ādargošasp and Ardeshir Khodadadian.

The *sedōš* rite which was regarded as the most important (Anquetil du Perron, II, p. 587), having apparently the most ancient component, is that solemnized in the last watch (*ušahin gāh*) of the third night. This, called by the Iranis the *yašt-e šavgīre*, approximately the "dawn service," consists of a set of *yašt-e keh*, the "lesser service" (to the Iranis a *drōn* service, to the Parsis *bāj-e panj-tāy*; see Boyce and Kotwal, pp. 63-65). The last of these has the dedication (*ḵšnūman*) for the "*fravašis* of the just," *ašaonąm fravašayo* (Pahlavi *ardā frawaš* or *fraward*), and during it food and clothing are consecrated so that their essence may sustain and clothe the newly departed soul in the hereafter. The clothing is called by the Iranis *sedra* (because it includes the sacred shirt) or *šavgīre* after the service (Boyce, *Stronghold*, p. 154), by the Parsis *šiav* or simply *jāme* (*Persian Rivayats*, tr. Dhabhar, p. 422 n. 3; Modi, p. 81). "New clothes, newly washed" are required (*Persian Rivayats*, ed. Unvala, I, p. 152.19; tr. Dhabhar, p. 168; Boyce, *Stronghold*, p. 154), and these belong thereafter to the celebrant priest; hence they were also called *jāme-ye ašōdād* (*Persian Rivayats*, ed. Unvala, II, p. 41.7; tr. Dhabhar, p. 422). He may keep them, share them with the family, or give them to the poor. All kinds of food may be consecrated except meat, from which the bereaved family abstains for the three days. The *gōšodā*, or sacrificial offering, is therefore represented by eggs (*Persian Rivayats*, ed. Unvala, I, p. 153.1; tr. Dhabhar, p. 168). The special Avestan text for the consecration is the *Staomi*, that is, *Yasna* 26 (so called from its first word, "I praise"). This consists of praise and worship of the *fravašis*, among them those "of all near relatives who have died in this house" (*Y*. 26.7). In the Yazdi region among the objects consecrated is a coin or piece of silver, a custom going back conceivably to Seleucid times and reflecting the Greek one of placing Charon's obol with the dead (Boyce, *Stronghold*, p. 155; Boyce and Grenet, *Zoroastrianism*, pp. 66, 191).

Two other *yašt-e keh* are solemnized before that to Ardā Fravaš. The first is dedicated jointly to Rašnu, who holds the scales of justice, and Aštād (q.v.), *yazata* of justice itself. This part of the service is thus linked with the specifically Zoroastrian belief that the departing soul is about to face judgment. The second *yašt-e keh* is dedicated to the "good Vayu," of whom it is said "When the soul of a just person passes over the Činwad way, the good Vayu takes (its) hand and bears it to its own place" (*ruwān ī ašawān ka pad *činwad widarag widērēd, Wāy ī weh dast abar gīrēd ud ō ān ī xwēš gāh barēd*; *Bundahišn*, tr. Anklesaria, chap. 26.29). These three short acts of worship made up the *yašt-e šavgīre* according to the oldest sources (*Šāyest nē šāyest*, suppl. 17.4; *Dādestān ī dēnīg* 21.2; *Pahlavi Rivāyat of Āturfarnbag* 128.2; *Saddar Naṯr* 87.2; see Kreyenbroek, p. 152 n. 51). The earliest authority for the current practice of solemnizing a fourth *yašt-e keh* dedicated to Sraoša after that to Vayu is the *Persian Rivāyat of Kāma Bohra*, dated A.Y. 896 (=1525-26; *Persian Rivayats*, ed. Unvala, II, p. 41.6; tr. Dhabhar, p. 422). It is noteworthy that still in this late development the *yašt-e keh* dedicated to Ardā Fravaš is kept as the last, that is, the one nearest to dawn and the soul's departure.

The addition of this fourth service was remarkable, for three is the dominant number in Zoroastrian observances, but it was in the spirit of the declaration that "during three days all worship should be performed for Srōš, because for three days Srōš can save his (the dead man's) soul from the grasp of demons" (*andar 3 rōz hamāg yazišn ī srōš abāyēd kardan ēd rāy čē ruwān az dast ī dēwān 3 rōz srōš be tuwān buxtan*; *Šāyest nē šāyest*, suppl. 17.3). The oldest source, the *Nērangestān*, refers only to "a *Yasna* (being performed) three times during the *sedōš*" (*pad sedōš se bār yašt-ē*; ms. HJ, ed. Sanjana, fol. 70r l. 5; tr., p. 155). In known usage these *Yasna*s all have the *ḵšnūman* of Srōš, as do the five *yašt-e keh* performed daily, one in each of the five watches (*gāh*s). The last "inner" ritual to be added to the *sedōš* was a *Vīdēvdād* with the *ḵšnūman* of Srōš, solemnized in the *ušahin gāh* (midnight to dawn). This observance is mentioned in the 9th-century *Pahlavi Rivāyat of Āturfarnbag* (chap. 144), where it is said that for the *sedōš* the *Vīdēvdād* is "very proper" (**šāyēndadar*; ed. Anklesaria, 1969, I, pp. 80/146; II, p. 122). In the Persian *rivāyat* of Kāma Bohra three *Vīdēvdād*s are enjoined (*Persian Rivayats*, ed. Unvala, I, p. 155.5; tr. Dhabhar, p. 169 and glossary, p. 656, s.v. "Vendidad of Sarosh"). For modern times Menant (p. 198, followed by Modi, p. 76) says only that the three *Vīdēvdād*s were "sometimes" solemnized, and latterly this usage has been abandoned (*Šāyest nē šāyest*, suppl., p. 109 n. 3).

The "outer" observances of the *sedōš* are performed usually at the home of the deceased. On each of the three days in the *ēvsrūsrim gāh*, just after sunset, priests recite the *Srōš Yašt sar-e šab* (*Y*. 57), solemnize an *Āfrīnagān* of Srōš, and say the *Patēt ī Vidardagān,* the formal confession of sins on behalf of the dead. In the *ušahin gāh*, the *Māh Niyāyeš* is recited, with *Srōš Yašt Hadōxt* (*Yt*. 11), and again the *Patēt*. A number of other prayers are said daily by priests and members of the family (*Šāyest nē šāyest*, suppl., p. 109 n. 3), with all the obligatory prayers uttered twice, the repetition being on behalf of the departed soul. Throughout the three days food used to be given regularly for the soul's sake to a dog (q.v. ii). In the third *gāh* of the third day priests, relatives, and friends gather for what the Iranis call the Yašt-i sevvom "service of the third (day)," the Parsis *ūthamnā* "Last (of the outer observances)." They recite the *gāh* prayers, *Srōš Yašt Hadōxt*, and *Patēt*. A Pāzand prayer is said imploring Sraoša's protection for the departed soul, and either now or at the *čahārom* "(service of the) fourth (day)" those present undertake to perform meritorious acts on behalf of the soul. Among the Iranis these take the form of saying specific numbers of Avestan prayers (Khudayar Dastur Sheriyar, p. 433), among the Parsis of gifts to charities or pious foundations (Modi, p. 76). In the small hours of the third night an animal was sacrificed (in latter-day usage a sheep or goat), and fat from it was offered at dawn on the soul's behalf to a sacred fire. This act is referred to in the *Nērangestān* and later works as the Hōm *drōn*, the sacrifice being consecrated by a *drōn* service with the *ḵšnūman* of Haoma (Boyce, pp. 77-78 with n. 107). So much importance was given to this offering that Dastur Nōshervān Kermānī, writing to the Parsis in A.Y. 967 (=1596-97) declared that, if it were not made, all previous ceremonies performed for the soul were useless (*Persian Rivayats*, ed. Unvala, I, p. 75.14-15; tr. Dhabhar, p. 70).

The *čahārom* service was held just after sunrise on the fourth day, its distinctive element being an *Āfrīnagān ī Dahmān* (see DAHM YAZAD), solemnized as a blessing for the soul at its moment of judgment. Afterward those attending shared the meat of the sacrifice, thus marking the end of the period of abstinence. In Persia blood sacrifices came to be offered again for the departed soul on the thirtieth and anniversary days, *sīrōza* and *sālrōz* (Boyce, *Stronghold*, p. 157), the *šavgīre* and food offerings being consecrated then also. But only the *čahārom* sacrifice is enjoined in the *Persian Rivayats*. On the two latter occasions, and on the tenth day after death, the Iranis solemnize an *Āfrīnagān ī Dahmān* just after sunset in the *ēvsrūsrim gāh*, whereas the Parsis celebrate an *Āfrīnagan* of Ardā

Fravaš then. The rites of the *sālrōz* are then maintained for thirty years as fully as family means allow or piety suggests, and are sometimes continued long beyond this obligatory term.

There are references in the *Persian Rivayats* to reciting the *Staomi* on commemorative days for the dead, presumably that is, to what Parsis call the Satum rite. This is a domestic one, and consists of consecrating, by recital of *Yasna* 26, ritually pure food for the soul's sake, a share being set aside for the dog (Modi, pp. 402-04). In pious Parsi families this rite was performed thrice daily (at mealtimes) during the first month, and monthly thereafter, and was then continued in conjunction with the anniversary ceremonies. The observance appears to have been alluded to by Theopompus in the 4th century B.C.E. (cf. Athenaeus, *Deipnosophistae* 6.60.252; Clemen, 1920a, p. 25; idem, 1920b, p. 131). The Farokši ceremony was also regularly performed for the departed. With the accumulation of family rites, pious individuals could thus devote an immense amount of time to the service of the dead, but in duty and affection, not grief, which, unduly indulged in, is a sin for Zoroastrians.

Pahlavi and Persian texts give yet other observances that it is good to perform for the soul's benefit: founding a *gahāmbār*, paying for the *barašnom-e nō šabe* (the purification of nine nights) to be undergone vicariously, or the performance of the *getī-karīd* (lit., "world purchased"). The first two are still frequently carried out by traditionalists, the former chiefly among Iranis, but the soul ceremonies generally are greatly curtailed by reformers in both communities.

Bibliography: B. T. Anklesaria, ed., *The Pahlavi Rivāyat of Āturfarnbag and Farnbag-Srōš*, 2 vols., Bombay, 1969. H. A. Anquetil du Perron, *Zend-Avesta*, 3 pts, 2 vols., Paris, 1771. A. Ādargošasp, *Āʾīn-e kafn o dafn-e Zartōštīān*, Tehran, 1348 Š./1969. M. Boyce, "Haoma, Priest of the Sacrifice," in M. Boyce and I. Gershevitch, eds., *W. B. Henning Memorial Volume*, London, 1970, pp. 62-80. Idem and F. Kotwal, "Zoroastrian *bāj* and *drōn* I," *BSOAS* 34/1, 1971, pp. 56-73. C. Clemen, *Fontes Historiae Religionis Persicae*, Bonn, 1920a. Idem, *Die griechischen und lateinischen Nachrichten über die persische Religion*, Giessen, 1920b. A. Khodadadian, *Die Bestattungssitten und Bestattungsriten bei den heutigen Parsen*, Ph.D. diss., Berlin, 1974. Khudayar Dastur Sheriyar, "Chaharum Ceremony (in Persia)," in J. J. Modi, ed., *Sir Jamsetjee Jejeebhoy Madressa Jubilee Volume*, Bombay, 1914, pp. 432-34. G. Kreyenbroek, *Sraoša in the Zoroastrian Tradition*, Leiden, 1985. D. Menant, *Les Parsis*, Paris, 1898; repr. Osnabrück, 1975. J. J. Modi, *The Religious Ceremonies and Customs of the Parsees*, 2nd ed., Bombay, 1937; repr. Bombay, 1986. *Nērangestān*, ed. D. P. Sanjana, Bombay, 1894; tr. S. J. Bulsara as *Aērpatastān and Nīrangastān*, Bombay, 1915.

(MARY BOYCE)

DEATH. For death in other religions, see FUNERARY RITES.

DECCAN (or Dakhan, Pers. Dakan < Sk. *dakshiṇa*, "right [hand]," i.e., south), the south-central plateau of India, bounded on the north by the Narbada river, on the west by the Sea of Oman, on the east by the Bay of Bengal, and on the south by the Tungabhadra river. The main plateau is divided into three regions: Maharashtra, Karnataka, and Telang-Andhra.

i. Political and literary history.

ii. Architecture and art.

I. POLITICAL AND LITERARY HISTORY

Outline of political history.

Although the Deccan was in commercial contact with Persia and Arabia from ancient times, it first became a part of the Islamic world in 695/1296, when the Delhi sultan ʿAlāʾ-al-Dīn Kaljī (695-715/1296-1316) invaded the Hindu kingdom of the Yadavas, with its capital at Deogiri (now Daulatabad), and made it a vassal state. The succeeding Kaljī and Tughluqid sultans undertook further expeditions against the Hindu kingdoms of the Hoysalas (at Dwarasamudra), the Kakatiyas (at Warangal), and the Pandyans (at Madura). Although at first these expeditions were essentially raids that left the Hindu dynasties intact, gradually a series of local revolts and reconquests from Delhi led to the incorporation of these realms into the empire.

Sultan Moḥammad b. Toḡloq (725-52/1325-51) made Deogiri the secondary capital of his realm in 728/1328, transferring most of the Muslim population of Delhi there the following year; he briefly controlled the entire Deccan, as well as the Tamil and Malabar country in the extreme south. In 736/1336 a former Hoysala officer of the Tughluqids rebelled and founded the Hindu kingdom of Vijayanagar in the far south.

Meanwhile the centurions (*amīrān-e ṣada*) in the Deccan also revolted against the Tughluqids in 746/1345, and in 748/1347 ʿAlāʾ-al-Dīn Ḥasan took the title *bahmanšāh*. The Bahmanid dynasty (q.v.), recognized by the ʿAbbasid pretender in Cairo, ruled the Deccan (first from Golbarga, then from Bīdar, q.v.) as an independent kingdom until the early 16th century, when increasingly restive governors effectively divided the realm into five minor kingdoms, ruled respectively by the Neẓāmšāhīs in Ahmadnagar (q.v.), the ʿĀdelšāhīs in Bījāpūr (qq.v.), the ʿEmādšāhīs in Berar, the Barīdšāhīs (q.v.) in Bīdar, and the Qoṭbšāhīs in Golconda. To these may be added the minor state of Khandesh, with its capital at Borhānpūr (q.v.) in the northern Deccan, ruled by the Fārūqīs (q.v.) from the late 14th century. Struggles among these small Deccani sultanates led to the conquest of Vijayanagar by a confederation of the princes of Ahmadnagar, Bījāpūr, and Golconda in 973/1565; the absorption of Berar by Ahmadnagar in 982/1574; and the conquest of Bīdar by Bījāpūr in 1028/1619.

The Mughals represented a more serious threat, however. Akbar I (q.v.; 963-1014/1556-1605) enrolled the Fārūqīs as tributaries and after 999/1590 as military allies against Ahmadnagar. In their quest for allies the rulers of Ahmadnagar, Bījāpūr, and Golconda, who had adopted Twelver Shiᶜism at various times, consistently cultivated relations with the Safavids of Persia, sometimes addressing them in the manner of vassals to an overlord (Islam, II, pp. 107-99). Akbar conquered Khandesh in 1009/1601, and Jahāngīr (1014-37/1605-27) took Ahmadnagar in 1043/1633. Awrangzēb (1068-1118/1658-1707) spent the last years of his reign campaigning against the two surviving sultanates, defeating Bījāpūr in 1097/1686 and Golconda the following year. The Mughals had already begun to lose their hold on the Deccan, however, owing to resistance from the Marathas, who had founded their own kingdom under Shivaji in 1085/1674. Although the Marathas founded an explicitly Hindu state and assumed rights of taxation, they acknowledged theoretical Mughal supremacy and, from their capital in the western hills, functioned as an efficient war machine throughout the Deccan and northern India until they came under British domination in the early 19th century. In 1137/1724 the Mughal viceroy in the Deccan, Neẓām-al-Molk Āṣaf-jāh, declared himself an independent ruler. The Āṣafjāhī dynasty of *neẓāms* (q.v.) ruled (at first from Awrangabad and then from Hyderabad) throughout the period of French and British imperialism up to 1948, when their domain was incorporated into the Indian Union. Presently the region is divided among the Indian states of Madhya Pradesh, Andhra Pradesh, Karnataka, and Maharashtra.

Persian literature and culture in the Deccan.

With the transfer of the Muslim population to Deogiri in 729/1329 the Persian culture that flourished in the Delhi sultanate was transplanted to the Deccan. The leading court poet Amīr Najm-al-Dīn Ḥasan Dehlavī (655-737/1275-1336) was one of those forced to move (Ṣafā, *Adabīyāt* III, pp. 817-31). Tughluqid officials in Deogiri and elsewhere sponsored works in Persian on such subjects as lexicography and Islamic law, and at nearby Rawża (now Khuldabad) the Sufi circle around the Češtī Shaikh Borhān-al-Dīn Ḡarīb (d. 738/1337; see ČEŠTĪYA) produced an extensive mystical literature, including recorded oral teachings (*malfūẓāt*), hagiographies, and speculative treatises (Ernst, p. 116 and passim). Legends about Sufis in the Deccan before the Ḵaljī conquest are late hagiographical inventions unsubstantiated by contemporary documents. After the brief period of Tughluqid rule the Deccan sultans contributed to a remarkable flourishing of Persian literature. Persian culture always existed in tension with local Indic cultural traditions, however, as it was totally dependent upon court patronage and elite Sufi circles. The different types of Persian literature produced in the Deccan may be categorized as follows.

Court poetry and belles-lettres. The sultans of the Deccan were great patrons of Persian poetry, and some were known as poets themselves. Of the many poets who came from Persia and Central Asia to India seeking their fortunes (according to Golčīn-e Maᶜānī, more than 700 in the Safavid period alone; I, pp. [5-18]), a large portion came to the Deccan courts (see Sherwani and Joshi, II, pp. 77-103). Moḥammad-Qāsem Ferešta (I, p. 302; tr. Briggs, II, pp. 215-16) reported that the Bahmanid Moḥammad Shah (780-99/1378-97) even tried unsuccessfully to lure Ḥāfeẓ from Shiraz, but the reliability of this story has been questioned (e.g., Ḡanī, p. 136 n. 1; cf. Ḥāfeẓ, comm., II, pp. 1193-95). His successor Aḥmad Shah Walī (825-39/1422-36) made Golbarga a center of Persian culture. After the establishment of the minor Deccan sultanates Moḥammadqolī Qoṭbšāh (d. 1020/1611) and his descendants eagerly welcomed talented Persian poets at Golconda. At Bījāpūr Ebrāhīm ᶜĀdelšāh (d. 1035/1627) employed Ẓohūrī Toršīzī (d. 1026/1617; Ṣafā, *Adabīyāt* V, pp. 977-88, 1717-14), who wrote his *Seh naṯr* as an introduction in rhyming prose to his patron's Dakhanī Urdu treatise on poetry and music, *Ketāb-e nowras*. Many critics regard Ẓohūrī as a chief exponent of the luxuriant "Indian style" (*sabk-e hendī*). Even the Mughal court poet Abu'l-Fayż Fayżī (q.v.; Ṣafā, *Adabīyāt* V, pp. 838-57) was impressed with his "extremely flowery" style (Golčīn-e Maᶜānī, II, p. 827).

Stylistically the Persian poetry produced in the Deccan did not differ notably from that produced in northern India or Persia; many poets circulated among all three areas. For example, Moḥammad Amīn (d. 1047/1637-38), who produced at Golconda an admired epic quintet (*ḵamsa*) in imitation of Neẓāmī's works, went on to Bījāpūr and then back to Persia before finally obtaining a satisfactory position from the Mughals (Sherwani and Joshi, II, pp. 98-99). Borhānpūr also became an important center of literary patronage under the Mughal viceroy ᶜAbd-al-Raḥīm Ḵān-e Ḵānān (q.v.; d. 1036/1627), who surrounded himself with a large circle of Persian poets, mentioned in ᶜAbd-al-Bāqī Nehāvandī's *Maʾāṯer-e raḥīmī* (comp. 1025/1616), which is dedicated to him. They included Nawᶜī Ḵabūšānī (d. 1019/1610), author of *Sūz o godāz*, a *maṯnawī* on the Indian theme of a widow (*satī*) who immolates herself on her husband's funeral pyre (Ṣafā, *Adabīyāt* V, pp. 881-92). In the late 18th century, while Delhi court taste was turning toward Urdu poetry, Persian anthologies continued to appear in the Deccan; the prolific Ḡolām-ᶜAlī Āzād Belgrāmī (q.v.; d. 1200/1786) composed three (*Yad-e bayżā*, *Sarv-e āzād*, and *Ḵezāna-ye ᶜāmera*), his Hindu student Lačmī Narāyan Šafīq (d. after 1214/1799) composed two (*Gol-e raᶜnā* and *Šām-e ḡarībān*), and several other scholars compiled their own *taḏkeras* at Awrangabad (Naqawī, pp. 255, 275, 378, 383, 393, 415, 425, 445, 489). Although in the 19th century Persian literary activity waned in favor of Urdu, Hyderabad continued as a center for Persian studies, and the former court libraries there (the Āṣafīya, now the Andhra Pradesh Oriental Manuscript Research Library, and the Salar

Jang) still have the finest Persian collections in the region.

Historical works. Historiography in the Deccan was modeled on the epics and chronicles of the Ghaznavids and Ghurids, which had formed the basis for the court culture of the Delhi sultanate (q.v.). The first great historical work produced in the Deccan was ʿAbd-al-Malek ʿEṣāmī's *Fotūḥ al-salāṭīn* (comp. 751/1351), which celebrated the triumph of the Bahmanids over the Tughluqids in epic *maṯnawī*s modeled on those of Ferdowsī's *Šāh-nāma*. Āḏarī Ṭūsī (q.v.; d. 866/1461-62) wrote *Bahman-nāma* (British Library, London, ms. no. Or. 2780/3; Bodleian Library, Oxford, ms. no. 2544/3) for Aḥmad I Walī (825-39/1422-36), modeling it on the prose history *Toḥfat al-salāṭīn* by Mollā Dāwūd Bīdarī (d. 817/1414-15). In fact, the close literary relationship between Persia and the Deccan is particularly exemplified by Āḏarī's career; he was initially a poet at the courts of the Timurid Šāhroḵ (807-50/1405-47) and Olоḡ Beg (850-53/1447-49), then a disciple of the Sufi Shah Neʿmat-Allāh Walī before going to India; after he completed his service with Aḥmad Shah Bahmanī he returned to Khorasan (Ṣafā, *Adabīyāt* IV, pp. 323-32). The Sufi shaikh ʿAyn-al-Dīn Bījāpūrī (d. 795/1393) wrote a continuation of the 13th-century chronicle *Ṭabaqāt-e nāṣerī* of Menhāj-e Serāj Jūzjānī. The latter and the *Toḥfat al-salāṭīn* of Bīdarī are lost, but they were used as sources by historians of the Bahmanid successor states, like Ferešta and Sayyed ʿAlī Ṭabāṭabā; some excerpts can also be found in the modern Urdu history of the Deccan by M. A. Molkapūrī, whose library of unique manuscripts of Bahmanid texts was unfortunately destroyed in the Hyderabad flood of 1908. Ṭabāṭabā's *Borhān-e maʾāṯer*, written in 1004/1596 for Borhān Neẓāmšāh II, is a history of the Bahmanid and Neẓāmšāhī dynasties. The most famous Deccan history, however, is Ferešta's *Golšan-e ebrāhīmī*, written for Ebrāhīm ʿĀdelšāh between 1015/1606-67 and 1033/1623-24; it is a general history of Indian dynasties focused on Bījāpūr, with an important appendix on Sufi shaikhs. The work attracted the attention of the British in the late 18th century, and most of it was translated into English. Important Bījāpūr chronicles include the *Taḏkerat al-molūk* of Rafīʿ-al-Dīn Ebrāhīm Šīrāzī (q.v.; comp. 1020/1611-12) and the *Tārīḵ-e ʿādelšāhī* of Nūr-Allāh (b. Sayyed Moḥammad ʿAlī; d. 1077/1666-67). The transition from the Mughals to the Āṣafjāhī *neẓām*s in the Deccan can best be measured from the voluminous biographical dictionary *Maʾāṯer al-omarāʾ*, compiled by Ṣamṣām-al-Dawla Šahnavāz Khan (vizier to the first *neẓām*) and completed by Āzād Belgrāmī; almost every important political figure of the 17th and 18th centuries is included. Numerous other significant monographic histories in Persian, most unpublished, were devoted to the reigns of individual sultans of the different Deccan kingdoms (including the Marathas) down to the end of the 19th century (Sherwani and Joshi, II, pp. 102-07, 575-88; Storey, I, pp. 738-65, 1330-33). The able Bahmanid minister ʿEmād-al-Dīn Maḥmūd Gāvān (813-86/1411-81) wrote a memorable collection of state letters, *Rīāż al-enšāʾ*, which includes correspondence with eminent Sufis and authors like ʿAbd-al-Raḥmān Jāmī, Ḵᵛāja Aḥrār (q.v.), and Šaraf-al-Dīn Yazdī. The Persian Shiʿite scholar Shah Ṭāher (d. 956/1549), adviser to Borhān Neẓāmšāh of Ahmadnagar, also left a collection of official letters (*Monšaʾāt-e Šāh Ṭāher*) that is of some historical importance. In addition, a treatise on political theory, written in 984/1576 by ʿAbd-al-Laṭīf Monšī and entitled *Nafāʾes al-kalām wa ʿarāʾes al-aqlām*, was dedicated to Raja ʿAlī Khan Fārūqī (985-1005/1577-96), the last independent ruler of Khandesh; the unique manuscript is in the Khuda-Bakhsh collection in the Oriental Public Library at Patna (ms. no. 948, H.L. no 946).

Sufi literature. Sufi literature was initiated under the Bahmanids, when the Češtī Sufis at Rawża, led by Borhān-al-Dīn Ḡarīb's successor, Zayn-al-Dīn Šīrāzī (d. 771/1370), began to compile *malfūẓāt* (Ernst, pp. 80, 134-38, 321 n. 226). Zayn-al-Dīn had no successors in Rawża, but later Sufis of Borhānpūr, like Bahāʾ-al-Dīn Bājan (d. 912/1507), claimed to have inherited the authority of Borhān-al-Dīn. In the meantime leadership of the Češtīs passed to Moḥammad Ḥosaynī Gīsūderāz (d. 825/1422), who had left Delhi for Golbarga in 800/1398 and become attached to the Bahmanid court. A prolific author, he was a major force in transmitting the heritage of Persian Sufism in the Deccan. He wrote many mystical treatises in Persian, including *Ḥaẓāʾer al-qods*, *Asmār al-asrār* (q.v.); commentaries on classical works on Islamic law, theology, and Sufism; letters; and poetry. His descendants also made literary contributions to Sufism (Siddiqi, pp. 199-206; Hussaini, passim). The writings by members of other Sufi orders (*selsela*) prominent in the early Bahmanid period, particularly the Jonaydīs, are now known only through later references (Siddiqi, pp. 95-107, 207-09). The Bahmanid rulers encouraged the immigration of Sufi masters from Persia and Iraq as part of a policy of favoring foreigners (*āfāqī*) over Indians. The Neʿmat-Allāhī order became established at Bīdar when its founder, Shah Neʿmat-Allāh Walī (731-834/1330-1431), sent one of his grandsons to act as a guide for the prince who later became Aḥmad II Bahmanī (839-62/1436-58); the order thrived in the Deccan until its leaders decided to return to Persia in the late 17th century. The Qāderī order arrived at Bīdar from Baghdad, also in the 15th century, and later spread to Bījāpūr and Golconda (Eaton, pp. 56-58; Siddiqi, pp. 69-95).

At Golconda the Qoṭbšāhīs, who continued to favor Shiʿism, concentrated their patronage on Dakhani Urdu and Telegu poetry in honor of the imams and on scholarship and poetry in Arabic. There is little evidence of Sufi activity at Ahmadnagar, and in Bījāpūr the ʿĀdelšāhīs seem not to have become patrons of Sufism until the late 16th century, when Sunni Islam replaced Shiʿism there under Ebrāhīm ʿĀdelšāh (Eaton, pp. 70-79). At that time many Češtī and Qāderī Sufis settled in the city, and the Šaṭṭārī order from northern India also established centers at Bījāpūr and Borhānpūr. An exceptionally strong literary tradition was initiated by Češtī authors like Šams-al-Dīn Mīranjī (d. 905/1499), Borhān-al-Dīn Jānam (d. after 1006/1597), and Amīn-al-Dīn ʿAlāʾ (d. 1086/1675), who wrote poetry in Dakhani Urdu addressed to a wide readership. Their Persian works (often translations or commentaries on the Dakhani texts), on the other hand, were aimed at a more specialized Sufi audience (Eaton, pp. 135-74, 243-81).

As the Mughals expanded into the Deccan, so did Sufi orders that were well established in their domain. Disciples of Aḥmad Serhendī (q.v.; d. 1034/1624), leader of the Mojaddedī Naqšbandīs, settled in Borhānpūr, and separate Naqšbandī lineages were established at the convents (*ḵānaqāhs*) of Shah Mosāfer Ḡojdovānī at Awrangabad and Shah ʿEnāyat-Allāh (d. 1117/1705) at Balapur in Berar. The Šaṭṭārī master Moḥammad Ḡawṯ (d. 971/1563) had flourished under the Mughals, and his disciples from Gujarat developed a major center in Borhānpūr, a city to which many Sufis from Sind were also attracted. The successive leaders of this Šaṭṭārī lineage were Laškar Moḥammad ʿĀref (d. 993/1585), ʿĪsā Jond-Allāh (d. 1031/1622), and Borhān-al-Dīn Rāz-e Elāhī (d. 1083/1672); ʿĪsā in particular was a prolific writer on mystical topics (e.g., *ʿAyn al-maʿānī*) and a commentator on Islamic law and theology. Among other significant works produced by this school were Ebrāhīm Šaṭṭārī Jannatābādī's *Āʾīna-ye ḥaqāʾeqnomā*, a commentary on Moḥammad-Šīrīn Maḡrebī's *Jām-e jahānnomā* based on the metaphysics of Ebn al-ʿArabī. At the end of the Mughal period there was also a renaissance of the Češtī order in the Deccan under the leadership of Neẓām-al-Dīn Awrangābādī (q.v.; d. 1142/1728), who followed the instructions of his teacher in Delhi, Shah Kalīm-Allāh Jahānābādī (d. 1142/1729). Neẓām-al-Dīn's relationship with Neẓām-al-Molk Āṣaf-jāh was so close that the latter wrote a biography of him (Nizami, 1980-85, I, pp. 290 ff., V, pp. 81-181). A good survey of Sufism under the later *neẓāms* has yet to be written.

As many important Persian Sufi writings from the Deccan remain in manuscript or have not survived, biographical works that include excerpts from them are extremely valuable. Among the most important is the pan-Indian hagiography *Aḵbār al-aḵyār* by ʿAbd-al-Ḥaqq Dehlavī (qq.v.). Also of great value for the Deccan is Moḥammad Ḡawṯī's *Golzār-e abrār* (comp. 1022/1613), which is devoted especially to the saints of Gujarat and western India. Other significant Persian hagiographies for the Deccan are the anonymous *Fatḥ al-awlīāʾ* (1020/1610) on the saints of Rawża and Borhānpūr, composed for ʿAbd-al-Raḥīm Ḵān-e Ḵānān; *Rawżat al-awlīāʾ* (comp. 1161/1748) by Āzād Belgrāmī on the saints of Khuldabad and Awrangabad; *Meškāt-e nobūwat* (1220/1804-05) by ʿAlī Mūsawī on saints of the Deccan, including Hyderabad; and *Rawżat al-awlīāʾ. Taḏkera-ye awlīāʾ-e Bījāpūr* (comp. 1241/1825-26) by Moḥammad-Ebrāhīm Zobayrī (Storey, I, pp. 979, 984, 1024; Ernst, pp. 91-92, 209-12; Eaton, pp. 334-35). Most of these collections were either produced under royal patronage or include traditions of political origin, so that their accounts must often be measured against the traditions found in *malfūẓāt* texts and other Sufi writings. As use of the Persian language declined during the 19th century, the history of Sufism in Hyderabad and the rest of the Deccan must be supplemented with works written in Dakhani Urdu and other local languages for the benefit of devotees.

Other kinds of literature. Various minor Persian works were written on the subjects of music, Islamic law, astronomy, and the like, and some translations from Arabic (generally on religious topics) and Sanskrit (on veterinary science and music) were produced. Perhaps the most noteworthy of these works is the well-known Persian dictionary *Borhān-e qāṭeʿ* (q.v.), composed by Moḥammad-Ḥosayn Borhān Tabrīzī for ʿAbd-Allāh Qoṭbšāh in 1062/1652. It was the target of caustic criticism by the 19th-century poet Mīrzā Asad-Allāh Ḡāleb in his *Qāṭeʿ-e borhān*.

Bibliography: T. N. Devare, *A Short History of Persian Literature at the Bahmani, the Adilshahi, and the Qutbshahi Courts, Deccan*, Poona, 1961. R. M. Eaton, *Sufis of Bijapur 1300-1700. Social Roles of Sufis in Medieval India*, Princeton, N.J., 1978. C. W. Ernst, *Eternal Garden. Mysticism, History, and Politics at a South Asian Sufi Center*, Albany, N.Y., 1992. ʿAbd-al-Malek ʿEṣāmī, *Fotūḥ al-salāṭīn yā Šāh-nāma-ye Hend*, ed. M. Ḥosayn, Agra, 1938; tr. M. Husain as *Futūḥu's Salāṭīn or Shah Nāma-i Hend of ʿIṣāmī*, New York, 1977. Q. Ḡanī, *Baḥṯ dar āṯār o afkār o aḥwāl-e Ḥāfeẓ* I, Tehran, n.d. A. Golčīn-e Maʿānī, *Kārvān-e Hend*, 2 vols., Mašhad, 1369 Š./1990. Ḥāfeẓ, *Dīvān-e Ḥāfeẓ*, ed. P. Nātel Ḵānlarī, 2nd ed., 2 vols., Tehran, 1362 Š./1983. M. Husain, *Tughluq Dynasty*, Calcutta, 1963. K. Hussaini, *Sayyid Muḥammad al-Ḥusaynī Gīsū Darāz. On Sufism*, Delhi, 1985. R. Islam, *A Calendar of Documents on Indo-Persian Relations (1500-1750)*, 2 vols., Karachi, 1982. O. Khalidi, *Hyderabad State under the Nizams, 1724-1948*, Wichita, Kans., 1985. Idem, *Dakan under the Sultans, 1296-1724*, Wichita, Kans., 1987. M. A. Molkapūrī, *Maḥbūb al-waṭan. Taḏkera-ye salāṭīn-e Dakan* I. *Dar bayān-e salāṭīn-e Bahmanīya*, Hyderabad, n.d. (in Urdu). ʿA. Naqawī, *Taḏkera-nevīsī-e fārsī dar Hend o Pākestān*, Tehran, 1343 Š./1964. ʿAbd-al-Bāqī Nehāvandī, *Maʾāṯer-e raḥīmī*, ed. S. Hidayat Husain, 4 vols., Calcutta, 1924. K. A. Nizami (Neẓāmī), "Gīsū Darāz," in *EI*² II, pp. 1114-16. Idem, "Ṣūfī Movement in the Deccan," in H. K. Sherwani and P. M. Joshi, *History of Medieval Deccan (1295-1724)* II, Hyderabad, 1973, pp. 173-99. Idem, *Tārīḵ-e mašāyeḵ-e Češt* II, V, Delhi, 1980-85 (in Urdu). Nūr-Allāh, *Tārīḵ-e ʿādelšāhī*, ed. A. M. Ḵāledī, Hyderabad, 1384/1964. Rafīʿ-al-Dīn Ebrāhīm Šīrāzī, *Taḏkerat al-molūk*, ed. A. M. Ḵāledī, rev. C. W. Ernst, Costa Mesa, Calif., in press. P. S. M. Rao, *Eighteenth Century Deccan*, Bombay, 1963. Ṣamṣām-al-Dawla Šahnavāz Khan and ʿAbd-al-Ḥayy,

Ma'āṯer al-omarā', tr. H. Beveridge, rev. B. Prashad, 2 vols., Calcutta, 1941-52; repr. Patna, 1979. H. K. Sherwani and P. M. Joshi, *History of Medieval Deccan (1295-1724)*, 2 vols., Hyderabad, 1973-74 (a valuable survey of political and cultural history). M. S. Siddiqi, *The Bahmani Ṣūfīs*, Delhi, 1989. Sayyed ʿAlī Ṭabāṭabā, *Borhān-e ma'āṯer*, Delhi, 1355/1936; partial tr. J. S. King as *The History of the Bahmanī Dynasty, Founded on the Burhān-i Ma'āsir*, London, 1900. A. Wink, *Land and Sovereignty in India. Agrarian Society and Politics under the Eighteenth-Century Maratha Svarājya*, Cambridge, 1986.

(Carl W. Ernst)

ii. Art and Architecture

The development of centers of Islamic culture and learning in the Deccan under the Bahmanid sultans (see BAHMANID DYNASTY) and their successors introduced new architectural forms and artistic traditions to the region. Deccani monuments generally reflect the taste current in such other Indian Islamic centers as Delhi (q.v. ii), Mandu, Gujarat, and Multan, but certain buildings and manuscripts reveal direct connections with Persian artistic traditions. They were probably produced by, or even for, recent arrivals from Persia. Often the most strikingly Persian features are calligraphy and decoration (qq.v.), suggesting that several of the Persian émigrés were scribes also trained in the art of illumination. The architectural and artistic evidence suggests that both religious bonds and the long-standing commercial links between Persia and the Deccan provided important conduits for cultural traditions. Initially enthusiasm for Persian architecture, calligraphy, illumination, and painting was probably restricted to court circles in the Deccan, but eventually some imported features were fused with local traditions in a distinctive regional style.

Architecture.

The first Islamic monuments in the Deccan followed precedents set in Delhi. For example, the congregational mosque of Dawlatābād (718/1318 and later) was constructed with pillars gathered from Hindu monuments, and 14th-century Bahmanid tombs at Golbarga have the heavy sloping walls and low domes characteristic of Tughluqid mausolea (Davies, pp. 451-52, 471-72; Merklinger, 1981, pp. 11-16). During the 15th century, however, Deccani culture became more cosmopolitan, especially at the new capital, Bīdar (q.v.), or Moḥammadābād, established by Aḥmad Shah Bahmanī (825-39/1422-36) in 827/1424. Bīdar remained the capital of both his descendants and their successors the Barīdšāhīs (q.v.; 897-1028/1491-1619).

Bahmanids. Persian connections are evident in both palatial architecture and mausolea at Bīdar. Aḥmad Shah was a member of the Sufi order of Shah Neʿmat-Allāh Walī Kērmānī (730-834/1329-1431), and this personal tie, cemented by marital alliances between the two families, led to the transfer of Persian artistic traditions to the new capital. That Aḥmad Shah sent lavish gifts to Kermān and financed construction of a mausoleum over Neʿmat-Allāh's grave there may have encouraged Persian craftsmen to migrate to the Deccan (Golombek and Wilber, I, pp. 394-95, II, pls. 401-02; cf. Farzām; Bāstānī-Pārīzī, pp. 578-82). The cosmopolitan artistic climate of Bīdar is manifest in Aḥmad Shah's own tomb. The manner in which its hemispherical dome rests on an octagonal drum has been compared to Timurid examples, but the basic type of square tomb was so widely diffused in the Indian subcontinent that any connection to Persia was probably indirect (Merklinger, 1981, pp. 10-16, 113-14). The proportions and such embellishment as wall niches and corner finials resemble those of earlier tombs in Multan, for example, that of Šams-al-Dīn Sabzavārī (729/1329 and later; Khan, pp. 204-14), and numerous 15th-century tombs in the Delhi region (Nath, pp. 76-83; Brown, pp. 27-28, 66). It is, rather, the polychrome interior wall paintings that demonstrate a direct religious and artistic connection with Persia. Numerous inscriptions are combined with ornamental medallions and interstitial designs of floral sprays. In the inscriptions prayers appropriate to a tomb are juxtaposed with texts more characteristic of a *ḵānaqāh*, or Sufi monastery, reflecting Aḥmad Shah's ties to Shah Neʿmat-Allāh. Those just above the prayer niche (*meḥrāb*), giving Aḥmad Shah's titles and death date, bear the signature of a certain Šokr-Allāh Qazvīnī Naqqāš, who may have been responsible for the interior decoration of the entire tomb (Yazdani, pp. 114-28); if so, he must have combined the skills of both calligrapher and decorator. Verses composed by Neʿmat-Allāh are inscribed above the entrances, and the text of one of his mystical treatises encircles the walls just above the dado. Concentric inscription bands in the dome include two versions of Neʿmat-Allāh's spiritual lineage, one through the Qāderīya order and the other to Ḥasan Baṣrī. Above and below these texts are panels containing the *dorūd*, a benedictory prayer that concludes at the apex of the dome with blessings on the twelve Shiʿite imams (Yazdani, pp. 115-21, pls. LXXIII-LXXIV; Merklinger, 1981, p. 113 no. 40, fig. 8, plan 9; Sherwani, p. 131 illus. 10). The variously shaped medallions and floral sprays in Aḥmad Shah's tomb are executed in black, white, gray, and gold against a deep-red ground, a color scheme that may reflect the range of pigments available in Bīdar (Yazdani, pls. LXXIII-LXXIV). On the other hand, the medallion shapes, the arabesque schemes framed by them, and the lush blossoms between them have numerous parallels in the decorative repertoire of the *naqqāš*, or "painter-decorator," in 15th-century Persia (Lentz and Lowry, pp. 204-11; Grube, pp. 178-80, figs. 27-30). Disturbed conditions in Persia in the middle decades of the century seem to have encouraged skilled craftsmen to emigrate to both India and Turkey, so that particularly close parallels to the paintings in Aḥmad Shah's tomb are found in illuminations, bookbindings, and preparatory sketches from the court of the Ottoman sultan Moḥammad II (855-86/1451-81; Necipoğlu, p. 138 fig. 1; Raby and Tanındı, pp. 53, 59-60, figs. 55-59).

A new phase in artistic links between Persia and the Deccan was apparent during the third quarter of the 15th century, when Persian features appeared in both funerary and palatial architecture. Examples include the tombs of ʿAlāʾ-al-Dīn Aḥmad Shah II Bahmanī (d. 862/1458) and that of Neʿmat-Allāh's son and successor, Ḵalīl-Allāh (d. 864/1460; Merklinger, 1981, p. 16 no. 52, figs. 9, 162, 175, pl. 10), as well as several sections of the Bīdar citadel. Persian features include the framing of arches with twisted-rope moldings and revetments in both mosaic faience and polychrome-painted tiles. The plan of Ḵalīl-Allāh's tomb, with a two-story octagonal screen around an open center and vaulted recesses in each side wall, is based on the design of garden pavilions like the *namakdān* at the shrine of ʿAbd-Allāh Anṣārī (q.v.) near Herat. A carved stone inscription over the main doorway was signed by a certain Moḡīṯ Qārī Šīrāzī (Golombek, pp. 70-71, figs. 142-43; Yazdani, pp. 141-44; Merklinger, 1981, no. 55, pp. 16, 104, 114, fig. 13, pl. 11). Traces of ceramic tiles on the exterior resemble better-preserved revetments on the square domed tomb of ʿAlāʾ-al-Dīn, where a large inscription in white *ṯolṯ* (see CALLIGRAPHY) against a blue ground encircles the structure and panels of repeating floral ornament are arranged in vertical strips and horizontal panels (Yazdani, pp. 130-32, pls. LXXVI-LXXVII; Merklinger, 1981, no. 52, pp. 5, 95, figs. 9, 175, plan 10; Crowe, 1986a, pp. 86, 91; idem, 1986b, p. 44, figs. 6, 9-10).

The citadel at Bīdar contains structures with tile decorations founded by various Bahmanid and Barīdšāhī rulers. Those tile decorations closest in style and technique to the revetments at ʿAlāʾ-al-Dīn's tomb are panels set into the walls of a columned audience hall and adjacent chambers, probably erected in the 1460s (Yazdani, pp. 62-65, pls. XXIII, XXVII-XXIX). Like the earlier paintings at Aḥmad Shah's tomb these designs belong to a widely disseminated artistic vocabulary of Persian origin (Necipoğlu, pp. 137-38, figs. 1, 8; Raby and Tanındı, pp. 53-60, figs. 56, 62-63; Beattie, p. 23, fig. 67). Technical features of the Bīdar tiles suggest that they were produced from locally available materials by craftsman trained in Persia but assisted by local workers; unfortunately, perhaps because local materials were not suitable for glazing, many tiles have lost their glazing, so that the original designs are also largely lost (Crowe, 1986b, pp. 44-45).

The continued attraction of the Deccan for Persians was also demonstrated by the career of Maḥmūd Gāvān, a native of Gīlān, who came as a merchant to Dabol in 856/1453, entered the service of ʿAlāʾ-al-Dīn Aḥmad II, rose to become *wakīl* (chief minister) and *malek-al-tojjār* (chief of the merchants' guild) under Homāyūn (862-65/1458-61), and continued to serve the Bahmanids until his death in 886/1481. During his years in India Maḥmūd maintained an active correspondence with leading figures of Timurid Persia. Sultan Ḥosayn Bāyqarā (q.v., Suppl.) is even said to have invited him to join his court (Sherwani, p. 229). The Russian merchant Athanasius Nikitin, who spent several months in Bīdar in about 876/1471, described Maḥmūd as "a Khorassanian boyar" and commented "Khorassanians rule the country and serve in war" (p. 14). It is thus appropriate that it was Maḥmūd who sponsored the most strikingly Timurid of all Bīdar buildings, a *madrasa* (religious school) completed in 877/1472. This structure, now partially destroyed, once had an entrance facade marked by a central vaulted portal, corner minarets, and a courtyard surrounded by three stories of chambers, with a central *ayvān* (q.v.) on each side. The height and pierced-stone window screens reflect local taste, but the basic plan and the scheme of the tile revetments have numerous close parallels in Timurid architecture (Yazdani, pp. 91-100, pls. L-LVI; Merklinger, 1976-77). The plan has particularly close analogies to that of the Timurid *madrasa* at Ḵargerd in Khorasan (846/1442; O'Kane, pp. 211-15 no. 22, figs. 22.1-2). The exterior tile revetments include a well-executed inscription signed by ʿAlī Ṣūfī. Details of the vaults, which include *moqarnas* (oversailing courses of niche sections set at angles to one another) in the transition zone, also suggest the presence of a Persian craftsman (Merklinger, 1981, no. 61, pp. 78, 102, 104-05, 115, figs. 129, 179, 182).

Successor dynasties. Only a few years after Maḥmūd Gāvān's death the Bahmanid state dissolved into five smaller kingdoms, but some aspects of his cultural legacy continued. Later Deccani architecture includes no exact replicas of the plan of his *madrasa*, but simplified versions of the entrance facade did appear as a kind of grand portal. The most striking instances are at burial complexes, or *dargāh*s, near Golbarga, associated with important Sufis, in particular the Češtī saint Moḥammad Bandanavāz Gīsūderāz (d. 825/1422) and Serāj-al-Dīn Jonaydī (d. 781/1380), spiritual guide of the first Bahmanid rulers (Sherwani, pp. 33, 82; Merklinger, 1981, pp. 108, 110 no. 19, plan 13). The entrance to Jonaydī's tomb, known as Šayḵ Rawża, is a two-story version of the facade at the Bīdar *madrasa*, complete with central *ayvān* and corner minarets; it stands like a stage set in front of a much smaller nine-domed building (Merklinger, 1981, plan 13, fig. 43). In the Gīsūderāz complex a three-story version of the *madrasa* facade was placed in front of an earlier, lower house (Merklinger, 1981, fig. 44 top). Both these facades were probably erected in the early 16th century under the patronage of another native of Persia, Yūsof ʿĀdelšāh, a close associate of Maḥmūd Gāvān and progenitor of the ʿĀdelšāhī dynasty (q.v.; Merklinger, 1981, p. 41).

The main innovations in Deccani architecture of the 16th and 17th centuries were either permutations of local traditions or reflections of Mughal practice. Decorative or structural elements of Persian origin, which had first appeared in mid-15th-century Bahmanid monuments at Bīdar, were integrated into the vocabulary of local craftsmen and continued in sporadic use until the Mughal conquest. That portals derived from the facade of the Bīdar *madrasa* continued to be associated with Sufi *dargāhs* is evident from the 17th-century Rawża at Afżalpūr (Merklinger, 1981, p. 91, fig. 159). In the Bīdar citadel tile revetements appeared on the facades of a gateway known as the Šarza Darvāza, dated to 909/1503, and a pavilion in the Takt Maḥall, probably of similar date (Yazdani, pp. 32-34, 66-74, pls. XXXI-XXXVII).

Persian craftsmen seem also to have been employed by the most powerful Barīdšāhī ruler, ʿAlī (949-87/1542-80). His tomb, completed in 984/1576, is notable for its garden setting; the inscriptions, executed in ceramic tile, were signed by Kᵛājagī Šīrvānī and ʿAbd-al-Fattāḥ. ʿAlī's name is also linked with the Rangīn Maḥall, an apartment in the Bīdar citadel faced with ceramic-tile revetments in a Persian style (Yazdani, pp. 44-49, 151-59, pls. VIII-XIV, XCV).

Tombs built by the Qoṭbšāhī rulers at Golconda also retain traces of ceramic-tile revetments, but it is the royal ʿĀšūr-kāna at Hyderabad, used both for Moḥarram ceremonies and for storing such ritual paraphernalia as the standards (*ʿalams*; see ʿALAM VA ʿALĀMAT) carried in processions, that provides the clearest evidence of an artistic link with Persia. Three walls of this structure are faced with mosaic faience, with floral decoration in a Safavid style. Other features of the tiles show accommodation to local traditions, however, notably renditions of ritual *ʿalams* bearing religious texts and embellished with finials. There are also calligraphic cartouches in the "*ṭoḡrā* style" containing prayers and the names and titles of two Qoṭbšāhī rulers, Moḥammadqolī (988-1021/1580-1612) and ʿAbd-Allāh (1035-83/1626-72). Dates on the tiles range from 1001/1593 to 1005/1596, though there were probably subsequent additions (Bilgrami, pp. 21-25; Safrani; Crowe, 1986a, p. 31, fig. 6). Although these tiles contain no calligrapher's signature, an inscription dated 1007/1597 in the Hyderabad congregational mosque is signed by Ḥosayn b. Moḥammad Fakkār Šīrāzī, who may have been both a potter and a calligrapher (James, 1987, pp. 345-46).

Illustrated and illuminated manuscripts.

In India the production of books was closely associated with the spread of Islam, and, according to the sources, there were substantial libraries in the Deccan during the 15th and 16th centuries, probably containing both imported and locally produced volumes (Sherwani, pp. 203-04; Skelton, pp. 98-99; Zebrowski, 1983, pp. 61, 68). Recently two illustrated manuscripts have been attributed to Bahmanid Bīdar, a copy of Ferdowsī's *Šāh-nāma* dated 841/1438 (British Library, London, ms. no. Or. 1403; Rieu, *Persian Manuscripts* II, pp. 534-35) and a two-volume anthology of the *Kamsa*s of Neẓāmī and Amīr Kosrow Dehlavī dated 840/1436, now in The Chester Beatty Library, Dublin (Persian ms. no. 124; Wilkinson, I, pp. 45-53). The *Šāh-nāma*, which once belonged to Charles Mohl and was used in his edition of the text, has been linked to India through unusual features of both text and illustrations; it may have been produced for a member of the Češtīya order, though no specific connection with Bīdar has been established. A note in the anthology documents its purchase by ʿĀdelšāh in 920/1514; the ascription to Bahmanid patronage rests on similarities between its paintings and tile decoration at Bīdar (Brend).

After the fall of the Bahmanids the Nēẓāmšāhīs of Ahmadnagar, the ʿĀdelšāhīs of Bījāpūr, and the Qoṭbšāhīs of Golconda sponsored the production of paintings and illuminated manuscripts. Their patronage was sporadic, however, and appears to have reflected the divergent interests of individual rulers. Most Deccani paintings of the period show a mixture of Persian and Indian features, but there is considerable variation among them. Artistic activity in these media reached its highest level during the late 16th and early 17th centuries, shortly before these states were absorbed into the Mughal empire.

Neẓāmšāhīs. At Ahmadnagar, which fell to the Mughal army in 1008/1600, the best-documented illustrated manuscript is a copy of Āftābī's *Taʿrīf-e ḥosaynšāhī*, composed and illustrated at the court of Ḥosayn Neẓāmšāh I (961-73/1553-65), now in the Bhrata Iltihasa Samshodaka Mandala, Poona. Both the Persian text and the illustrations commemorate the splendors of Ḥosayn's court and his role in the victory of the Deccani Muslim rulers over the Hindu ruler of Vijayanagra in 973/1565. In the twelve illustrations landscape and architectural settings of Persian derivation are combined with a figure style borrowed from earlier Sultanate painting, like that produced at Mandu in Malwa ((Losty, pp. 53-54; Barrett, 1958, pp. 8-9, pl. 12; Zebrowski, 1983, pp. 17-19).

ʿĀdelšāhīs. A different blend of Persian and Indian elements appears in the compendium *Nojūm al-ʿolūm*, an anonymous text on cosmology, astronomy, astrology, and animal lore dated to 978/1570-71 and said to have belonged to the library of Ebrāhīm ʿĀdelšāh II (988-1037/1580-1627) in Bījāpūr; most of it is now in The Chester Beatty Library (Indian ms. no. 2; Arnold, pp. 2-4; Binney, no. 117, pp. 141-47). Some compositions exhibit Persian conventions in both setting and figure style, while others contain figures clearly Indian in dress and posture. There are also depictions of local royal customs. In one scene a figure in Persian dress is carried on a litter by both Muslim and Hindu attendants, a form of royal travel described in detail by Nikitin (pp. 9, 12, 14; Losty, no. 50, pp. 53, 71-72). In another painting a ruler of Vijayanagra is enthroned on a multileveled structure known as the "throne of prosperity" (Barrett and Gray, pp. 117, 120-21). The specific mixture of Hindu and Muslim customs depicted in this text suggests that it too commemorates the victory of 973/1565.

Three of the ʿĀdelšāhī rulers at Bījāpūr are remembered for their interest in both painting and Persian culture. Esmāʿīl (916-41/1510-34) was himself a skilled painter, musician, and poet. His enthusiasm for Persian culture and language was combined with a disdain for local customs and Dakhani Urdu. His relations with the Safavid ruler Shah Esmāʿīl I (907-30/1501-24) were particularly cordial, and his courtiers even adopted the Safavid *tāj* (turban). Esmāʿīl's preference for both Shiʿism and Persian culture was emulated by his grandson ʿAlī I (965-88/1558-80), who is said to have had an extensive library, as well as a workshop of nearly sixty people producing books (Zebrowski, 1983, pp. 60-61). The cumulative effects of this patronage of manuscripts are also evident in the reign of ʿAlī's successor, Ebrāhīm II, who in 1009/1601 was obliged to send to the Mughal emperor Akbar (q.v.; 963-1014/1556-1605) a gift of 2,000 books from the royal collection, many of which were illustrated (Zebrowski, 1983, p. 67-68).

Ebrāhīm, the most celebrated Deccani patron of the arts, is said to have been himself a painter and skilled calligrapher, who appreciated the work of artists of various origins. One painter, Farrok̲ Ḥosayn, is listed among his intimates (Zebrowski, 1981, pp. 171-73, 179; idem, 1983, pp. 68-70). Ebrāhīm is also said to have given refuge to the Dutch painter Cornelius Heda, who was shipwrecked in India on his way to the court of Shah ʿAbbās I (q.v.; 996-1038/1588-1629) at Isfahan (Zebrowski, 1983, pp. 95-96). The paintings that have been securely linked with Ebrāhīm ʿĀdelšāh are idealized single-page portraits of him now scattered among various public and private collections; they show him in opulent court dress silhouetted against a lush landscape, riding an elephant, or playing music, themes consonant with the tone of his own musical treatise, *Ketāb-e nowras* (Skelton; Knižkova; Zebrowski, 1983, pp. 69-76). The style of these paintings is an amalgam of Persian, Indian, and European features. The fundamental scheme, with faces shown in three-quarter view and landscapes with high horizons, is Persian, but in the volumetric treatment of human figures the soft, rounded contours used in portraits from Ahmadnagar were combined with a precision of shading derived from European art. Vibrant colors and a sense of rhythm add to the sensuous effect (Zebrowski, 1983, pp. 76-103). Under Ebrāhīm's successors portraits were affected by the more austere canon in vogue at the Mughal court (Zebrowski, 1981, pp. 174-82; idem, 1983, pp. 139-52).

Qoṭbšāhīs. Although the most accomplished Deccani paintings were produced at the ʿĀdelšāhī court in Bījāpūr, it was the Qoṭbšāhīs of Golconda and Hyderabad who manifested the greatest enthusiasm for Persian calligraphy, illumination, and painting. Their dedicatory inscriptions or seals are found on manuscripts that would otherwise have been assumed to be of Persian provenience. Several can be linked with Ebrāhīm Qoṭbšāh (957-88/1550-80) or his successor Moḥammadqolī Qoṭbšāh. One Shirazī scribe and illuminator, ʿAbd-al-Qāder Ḥosaynī, evidently emigrated to Golconda, where he copied and illuminated several manuscripts of the Koran for the Qoṭbšāhīs. The earliest, which bears a *waqf* (endowment) dedication of 970/1562-63 in the name of Ebrāhīm, is now in the library of Āstān-e Qods-e Rażawī, Mašhad. All these manuscripts contain illuminations in the gold-and-blue style typical of 16th-century Shiraz, but the inclusion of unusual colors and the use of an Indian system of verse counts reveal their Deccani origin (James, 1992, pp. 196-98 no. 47; Sotheby's, pp. 20-24 lot 17). Another scribe, Bābā Mīrak Herātī, copied Esmāʿīl b. Ḥosayn Jorjānī's *D̲ak̲īra-ye k̲ᵛārazmšāhī* at Golconda in 980/1572; this manuscript, now in The Chester Beatty Library (uncatalogued Indian ms. no. 30), contains illuminations in a purely Persian style (Losty, p. 70 no. 47; Zebrowski, 1983, pp. 156-57, fig. 120).

Even more striking is the Safavid style of illumination and illustration in the Urdu and Persian *Kollīyat* of Moḥammadqolī Qoṭbšāh, now in the Salar Jang Museum, Hyderabad. The illuminations resemble those of the *D̲ak̲īra* of 980/1572, and the paintings appear to be the work of two different Persian painters, one of whom included figures wearing turbans in the Safavid style. Again details of execution like the color scheme and the use of marbled paper affirm the Deccani origin of the paintings (Zebrowski, 1983, pp. 158-69, figs. 121-22; idem, 1986, figs. 13 and facing p. 1). The scribe of the Hyderabad *Kollīyat*, Zayn-al-Dīn ʿAlī Šīrāzī, also prepared other manuscripts for Moḥammadqolī, including an album now in The Chester Beatty Library (Persian ms. no. 225; Wilkinson, III, p. 5, pl. 6; James, 1987), in which examples of calligraphy and painting from Persia are combined with those produced in the Deccan; the calligraphy includes pieces signed by Moḥammad-Reżā and Moḥammad Šīrāzī and cut-paper work by Morād D̲u'l-Qadr.

During the reign of ʿAbd-Allāh Qoṭbšāh a new, hybrid style of painting, in which Indian and Persian elements were mingled, was developed. The ruler and his court are depicted in several paintings, five inserted in an earlier Persian copy of the *Dīvān* of Ḥāfeẓ (ms. no. 1974.6-17[1-5], formerly part of Add. 16762), and another single-page painting, all now in the British Museum, London. In the Ḥāfeẓ paintings courtiers rendered in the Persian fashion are juxtaposed with servants and entertainers in a style reminiscent of earlier Sultanate painting (Barrett, 1960; Zebrowski, 1983, pp. 178-80). In the single sheet (no. 1937.4-1001) the ruler and his officials are portrayed in the profile view characteristic of Mughal portraits, whereas attendants or servants are depicted in three-quarter view, a combination that demonstrates the growing importance of Mughal contacts and the waning prestige of the Safavid style; these trends were intensified in subsequent reigns (Zebrowski, 1983, pp. 178-88).

Bibliography: T. W. Arnold, *The Library of A. Chester Beatty. A Catalogue of the Indian Miniatures* I, London, 1936. D. Barrett, *Painting of the Deccan. XVI-XVII Century*, London, 1958. Idem, "Some Unpublished Deccan Miniatures," *Lalit Kala* 7, April 1960, pp. 8-13. Idem and Gray, *Indian Painting*, Geneva, 1963. M.-E. Bāstānī-Pārīzī, *Tārīḵ-e Kermān*, Tehran, 1364 Š./1985. M. Beattie, *Carpets of Central Persia*, Westerham, Kent, 1976. S. ʿA. A. Bilgrami, *Landmarks of the Deccan*, Hyderabad, 1927. E. Binney, *Indian Miniature Painting . . . I. The Mughal and Deccani Schools*, Portland, Ore., 1973. B. Brend, "The British Library's *Shahnama* of 1438 as a Sultanate Manuscript," in R. Skelton et al., eds., *Facets of Indian Art*, London, 1986, pp. 87-93. P. Brown, *Indian Architecture (Islamic Period)*, Delhi, 1956. Y. Crowe, "Coloured Tilework," in G. Michell, ed., *Islamic Heritage of the Deccan*, Bombay, 1986a, pp. 86-91. Idem, "Some Glazed Tiles in 15th-Century Bidar," in R. Skelton et al., eds., *Facets of Indian Art*, London, 1986b, pp. 41-46. P. Davies, *The Penguin Guide to the Monuments of India* II, London, 1989. Ḥ. Farzām, "Solṭān Aḥmad Bahmanī wa Šāh Neʿmat-Allāh Walī," in M.-R. Daryāgašt, ed., *Kermān dar qalamrow-e taḥqīqāt-e īrānī*, Kermān, 1370 Š./1991, pp. 264-72. L. Golombek, *The Timurid Shrine at Gazur Gah*, Art and Archaeology Occasional Paper 15, Toronto, 1969. Idem and D. Wilber, *The Timurid Architecture of Iran and Turan*, 2 vols., Princeton, N.J., 1988. E. Grube, "Notes on the Decorative Arts of the Timurid Period, II" *Islamic Art* 3, 1989, pp. 175-208.

D. James, "The 'Millennial' Album of Muhammad-Quli Qutb Shah," *Islamic Art* 2, 1987, pp. 243-54. Idem, *After Timur. Qurʾans of the 15th and 16th Centuries*, London, 1992. A. N. Khan, *Multan. History and Architecture*, Islamabad, 1403/1983. H. Knižkova, "Notes on the Portrait of Ibrahim ʿAdil Shah II of Bijapur in the Náprstek Museum, Prague," in R. Skelton et al., eds., *Facets of Indian Art*, London, 1986, pp. 116-23. T. W. Lentz and G. D. Lowry, *Timur and the Princely Vision. Persian Art and Culture in the Fifteenth Century*, Los Angeles and Washington, D.C., 1989. J. P. Losty, *The Art of the Book in India*, London, 1982. E. S. Merklinger, "The *Madrasa* of Maḥmūd Gāwān in Bīdar," *Kunst des Orients* 11, 1976-77, pp. 144-57. Idem, *Indian Islamic Architecture. The Deccan 1347-1686*, Warminster, England, 1981. R. Nath, *History of Sultanate Architecture*, New Delhi, 1978. G. Necipoğlu, "From International Timurid to Ottoman. A Change of Taste in Sixteenth-Century Ceramic Tiles," *Muqarnas* 7, 1990, pp. 136-70. A. Nikitin, "Travels," in R. H. Major, ed., *India in the Fifteenth Century*, London, 1857, pp. 3-32. B. O'Kane, *Timurid Architecture in Khurasan*, Costa Mesa, Calif., 1987. J. Raby and Z. Tanindi, *Turkish Bookbindings in the 15th Century*, London, 1993. S. H. Safrani, "Golconda Alums," in S. H. Safrani, ed., *Golconda and Hyderabad*, Bombay, 1992, pp. 73-80. H. K. Sherwani, *The Bahmanis of the Deccan. An Objective Study*, Hyderabad, n.d. R. Skelton, "Documents for the Study of Painting at Bijapur in the Late Sixteenth and Early Seventeenth Centuries," *Arts Asiatiques* 5/2, 1958, pp. 97-125. Sotheby's, *Oriental Manuscripts and Miniatures*, London, 27 April 1994. J. V. S. Wilkinson, ed., *The Chester Beatty Library. A Catalogue of the Persian Manuscripts and Miniatures*, 3 vols., Dublin, 1959-62. G. Yazdani, *Bidar. Its History and Monuments*, Hyderabad, 1947. M. Zebrowski, "Transformations in Seventeenth Century Deccani Painting at Bijapur," *Chhavi* 2, 1981, pp. 170-82. Idem, *Deccani Painting*, Berkeley and Los Angeles, 1983. Idem, "Painting," in G. Michell, ed., *Islamic Heritage of the Deccan*, Bombay, 1986, pp. 92-109.

(PRISCILLA P. SOUCEK)

DECORATION, the use of consciously designed patterns to embellish building surfaces and objects for aesthetic effect, one of the most characteristic features of art and architecture in Islamic Persia. Both the quantity and quality of surface patterns attest the esteem they enjoyed among artists and patrons alike.

Despite the obvious importance of decorative or ornamental schemes in Persian Islamic art, few attempts have been made to deal with this phenomenon in a comprehensive way. During the 19th century such authors as Alois Riegl, Owen Jones, and Oscar Wilde used examples from Persian and other Islamic art in their attempts to explain the appeal of decorative or ornamental patterns in aesthetic, psychological, and even physiological terms (Gombrich, pp. 51-59). Riegl sought, through studying the internal formal evolution of decorative forms, to integrate patterns from Persian carpets with their ancient, and particularly classical, antecedents; his work provided a model for later studies by Ernst Kühnel and Maurice Dimand (Gombrich, pp. 180-90; Grabar, p. 39). Despite progress in identifying or classifying the features of Persian decorative patterns, however, few scholars have attempted to explain why particular designs were used in specific periods, regions, or circumstances, even though it can be observed that in a given area or epoch the form and character of ornament are often consistent within a particular craft and sometimes even among different media, despite the varied techniques in which they are executed. Such consistency raises the questions how these clearly differentiated vocabularies of ornament arose, why they were consciously perpetuated, and whether or not certain types of ornament conveyed specific meanings or general moods to an observer.

The introduction of new decorative modes or techniques often followed such major historical shifts as the Islamic conquest in the mid-7th century, the Mongol invasion in the first half of the 13th century, and the establishment of European trading companies in the 17th century. Nevertheless, in a broad sense the ornamental tradition of Islamic Persia was pluralistic and cumulative. A newly introduced feature might acquire its own distinctive niche within the existing repertoire and be used in conjunction with previously established types of decoration, each of which retained its visual identity, thus contributing to a distinctive historical rhythm of episodic innovation against a stable background. Individual decorative elements can often be traced over several centuries during which time their appearance shows only minor variations. In such a tradition ornament became both a vehicle of continuity and the source of subtle variations on familiar themes. The persistence of distinct visual categories over long periods may have been related to a broader cultural appreciation of normative structures also apparent in Persian literature, in which poetic forms or vocabularies of imagery were repeated, with minor variations, sometimes for centuries (Yarshater, pp. 18-20).

Despite this conservatism, patterns and designs may be classified not only typologically but also geographically and chronologically. Consequently, specific designs can be diagnostic of historical epochs and regional divisions, as well as indicating transfer of decorative themes from one medium or region to another. A systematic investigation of the history and use of decoration in Persia should thus provide insight into a variety of economic and social factors for which written documentation is often scanty, including the training, organization, and migration of craftsmen and the relative economic importance or social status of various crafts.

In this article, the historical development of the Persian ornamental repertoire will be surveyed, with the purpose of providing a foundation for addressing these more general questions. Treatment of this development will be divided into two basic epochs, from the Islamic conquest to the Mongol invasion and from the latter to the mid-19th century. Although there was considerable continuity between these two epochs, Mongol rule brought to a close a period of gradual internal artistic evolution and opened an era in which change was increasingly stimulated by the importation of foreign decorative themes and techniques, often at the instigation of the ruling dynasty.

From the advent of Islam to the Mongol conquest, ca. 750-1250.

This period can be subdivided into two phases. In the first, approximately from 750 to 1050, a distinctive artistic culture, in which pre-Islamic and Islamic elements were fused, developed in Persia. This process was centered in the east, especially Khorasan and Transoxania. In the second phase, from 1050 to about 1250, the cultural center of gravity shifted westward, first to central and then to northwestern Persia, even though the east retained considerable artistic vigor until the Mongol invasion.

Phase 1. The political fusion of former Sasanian territories with those of the city-states of Khorasan and Transoxania under Islamic rule created a new cultural region with a mixed legacy of artistic traditions from both areas, as well as from more distant Asian regions like India and China. Moreover, as this region was tied administratively to Iraq, it was also affected by trends that developed there, particularly in Baṣra and Baghdad.

For the first Islamic centuries the organization and content of decoration can be established through examination of metalwork, ceramics, and architecture. The Sasanian practice of putting royal portraiture on coinage and metalwork almost ceased, but such other royal emblems as the mythical bird Sīmorḡ and birds and animals bearing ribbons or garlands became major decorative themes, appearing, often in roundels, on metalwork, ceramics, textiles, and even architecture of Islamic date (Harper, pp. 16-19). A small gold ewer bearing the titles of the Buyid Abū Manṣūr (ʿEzz-al-Dawla) Amīr Baḵtīār (356-67/967-78) and decorated with roundels suggests that the synthesis of Sasanian themes, Sogdian techniques, and Arabic inscriptions characteristic of eastern Persian metalwork was also popular in western Persia and Iraq (Lowry; Plate XI). An amalgamation of pre-Islamic and Islamic decorative features is also evident in a group of slip-painted ceramics from 10th- and 11th-century Khorasan, especially those painted in black with touches of red on a pure white ground. On the most impressive examples designs echoing the vegetal ornament of Sogdian metalwork are combined with Arabic inscriptions (Raby, pp. 187-99, figs. 12, 18, 20; Plate XII). Those inscriptions range from wishes of good fortune or good health for an anonymous owner to edifying aphorisms and proverbs and even Hadith (Shishkina and Pavchinskaya, pp. 53-56). The practice of using inscriptions as the principal embellishment on ceramics appears to have originated at Baṣra in Iraq during the 9th century, possibly with the support of the ʿAbbasid caliphs; one

PLATE XI

Gold ewer of the Buyid Abū Manṣūr Amīr Baḵtīār, western Persia, 356-67/967-78; 13.7 x 16 cm. Courtesy of the Freer Gallery of Art, Smithsonian Institution, Washington, D.C., no. 43.1.

PLATE XII

Interior of ceramic bowl, Khorasan, 10th-11th centuries; 39.2 x 11.2 cm. Courtesy of the Freer Gallery of Art, Smithsonian Institution, Washington, D.C., no. 57.24.

potter signed as the caliph's craftsman: *ṣāneʿ amīr-al-moʾmenīn*). It was, however, more fully refined in the wares of Khorasan and Transoxania (Qūčānī, pp. 94-95; Keall and Mason).

Architectural decoration in early Islamic Persia also exhibited features drawn from both Sasanian and Sogdian practice. Two types characteristic of the Islamic period had pre-Islamic antecedents: creation of decorative patterns through the use of specially cut or molded bricks, documented in pre-Islamic wall paintings at the Sogdian city of Panjīkant, and the use of carved or molded stucco to highlight certain parts of a building, a well-established tradition in Persia and Iraq under the Sasanians (Belenizki, pp. 101, 116-18; Kröger, pp. 63-65, 144-60). In the mid-10th-century Samanid mausoleum at Bukhara the earlier approach of accenting parts of the building through use of patterned brickwork was expanded to enhance both interior and exterior walls, and other decorative forms derived from the local wood-carving tradition were applied to the transition zone (Voronina, pp. 6-7, 25, pls. 1-2; Ainy, pls. 33, 50, 51). In later Islamic buildings brick or terracotta decoration was used to highlight key areas of exterior facades, but the flexibility of carved or painted stucco was preferred for interior decoration. The earliest carved-stucco wall decoration in Khorasan and Transoxania, for example, in the nine-bay mosque near Balḵ, where all interior surfaces once had stucco revetments, reflected the taste of ʿAbbasid Iraq. On the arch spandrels, intrados, and impost blocks at Balḵ the stucco decoration included patterns based on the grape leaf and grapevine, whereas the pier capitals were ornamented with abstract vegetal ornament (Melikian Chirvani, 1969, pp. 3-9). Analogous ornament is known from 9th-century residential structures at Sāmarrā, north of Baghdad. Those discovered in "House III" are particularly close in the details of their patterns to the decorations at Balḵ (Creswell, pl. 78/a, d-f.)

Phase 2. Persian art and architecture from the mid-11th to the mid-13th century are notable for the intricacy and elaboration of geometric, calligraphic, and vegetal ornament. Although the same categories of decoration were used throughout Persia, there were regional differences in their application, particularly on buildings. In Khorasan, Transoxania, and Sīstān attention was focused on the exteriors of buildings. Portals, minarets, and entire facades were framed or articulated with contrasting areas of geometric and calligraphic ornament (Hutt and Harrow, pls. 10, 14, 64-66, 76-78, 80-82; Pope, pp. 96-98). In northeastern Persia the outer walls of tombs were articulated with niches and often covered with a decorative veneer of intricate geometric patterning executed in brickwork or unglazed and glazed terracotta strips (Hutt and Harrow, pls. 12, 60-61, 126-27; Seherr-Thoss, pp. 74-85).

In central Persia mosques were often left virturally unadorned, except for inscription bands around the bases of domes or carved stucco ornament, often of great intricacy, on prayer niches (*meḥrāb*; Pope, pp. 106-29, 146-62). This tradition of stucco ornament was probably ultimately derived from the undulating grapevines used in ʿAbbasid Iraq, but in 12th-century examples the organic unity of the individual leaf was nearly lost in the lacy network of geometric units that covered the surface, creating patterns within patterns (Plate XIII). Paradoxically, as individual elements of vegetation became more abstract, the vines to which they were attached were endowed with ever greater energy, being woven together to create a dense network on several levels (Shani, pp. 67-74). This interweaving of two or more distinct strands of vegetation in a composition on multiple levels, in which individual forms and structures are complementary, was widely used in later centuries, especially on carpets and polychrome ceramic revetments.

A taste for intricate decoration is also evident in 12th- and 13th-century metalwork from Khorasan, where bronze or brass was inlaid with silver and copper in figural, vegetal, calligraphic, and geometric patterns. The inclusion of symbols for heavenly bodies, the sun, moon, planets, and constellations of the zodiac, underscores the link between metal vessels and cosmological themes (Melikian Chirvani, 1982, pp. 55-135). Some of the finest pieces bear inscriptions stating that they were made in Herat, and some are signed by more than one craftsman. The most important craftsman was probably the *naqqāš*, or designer, who evidently planned and executed the inlaid decoration (Ettinghausen, 1943, pp. 193-99).

The city of Kāšān achieved preeminence in ceramic production during the 12th and 13th centuries; both tableware and architectural revetments were produced

PLATE XIII

Stucco decoration from the congregational mosque, Zavāra, 529/1135. Photograph P. Soucek.

there in several decorative techniques, including molding and underglaze and overglaze painting (Ettinghausen, 1936). Luster-painted tiles and tablewares from Kāšān exhibit a wide decorative repertoire and were highly prized and widely exported. Some are ornamented with intertwined arabesques, vine patterns in which stems and leaves grow one from the other, resembling those in stucco carving; others resemble inlaid metalwork in prominence of inscription bands and geometric schemes. Most striking, however, are the depictions of courtly life: enthroned figures with attendants, retinues of horsemen, or couples conversing (Watson, pp. 45-109 and passim). The inscriptions that are such a prominent feature of both tiles and vessels are also varied. Although koranic quotations occur only on architectural revetments, poetry, some of it composed by the potters themselves, appears on both tiles and tableware. Modern commentators have often pointed out the lack of correspondence between the themes of the poetry and the scenes depicted (e.g., a tile with wrestlers inscribed with verses about a hunt from the *Šāh-nāma*; Watson, pp. 122-31, 146-56; Bahrami, pp. 75-81, 90-95, 114-22, 126-30). Several of the craftsmen responsible for the decoration of these objects signed with the epithet *naqqāš* (Watson, pp. 180-81). The most elaborate compositions on polychrome wares, for example, the scene of the siege of a fortification on a platter or a continuous narrative drawn from the Persian national epic on a beaker, both in the Freer Gallery of Art, Washington, D.C., suggest a link between the designers of ceramic vessels and the artists who executed wall paintings or manuscript illustrations (Simpson, pp. 15-24).

From the Mongol invasion to ca. 1850.

This period can also be divided into two phases. The first, approximately from 1250 to 1650, was characterized by successive links to the artistic traditions of China. The second, approximately from 1650 to 1850, was marked by a fascination with things European, known initially via India, then directly through European contacts. An intrinsic conservatism in the artistic process slowed the pace of change, and the degree of change varied from medium to medium. Nevertheless, after ca. 1250 innovation was primarily stimulated by foreign taste and imported techniques. Furthermore, one addition to the decorative repertoire was often followed by others from the same source, so that both the sinicization and europeanization of Persian taste were incremental processes. At the same time, however, the new elements were as much assimilated as imitated, creating hybrid Sino-Persian and Euro-Persian decorative idioms.

Phase 1. In the 13th and early 14th centuries the formulation of a new decorative vocabulary was accompanied by a change in the structure of patronage fostered by the Mongol conquest. During the first Islamic centuries Persian art appears to have rested largely in the hands of individual urban craftsmen who learned and transmitted their skills within an established artisan tradition. Beginning in the Il-khanid period (654-754/1256-1353), the initiative seems to have shifted gradually to various courts. Members of these courts began to participate in the design and production of art and architecture, though the degree and character of court-sponsored artistic production appears to have varied from one dynasty or ruler to another and certain crafts were more affected than others. In general, however, the transfer of design or production of crafts to a court appears to have fostered a harmonization of designs among various media, a development probably dependent on the primary role of the *naqqāš*, or painter-decorator, in creating patterns to be executed in various media. Over time a court atelier could build up an archive of patterns and designs, thus providing for continuity between generations of artists or even, in periods of political turmoil, from one court or dynasty to another. These court repositories may also have included objects of foreign origin. When court-based design and the importation of foreign taste and techniques coincided, the impact of a given innovation was thereby multiplied.

The initial Mongol invasion brought a virtual cessation of artistic production and architectural patronage from the 1220s to the 1260s, but after the consolidation of Il-khanid control the less devastated areas in central and western Persia began to revive. Structures were repaired and new building projects begun, particularly after the conversion of Ḡāzān Khan (694-703/1295-1304) to Islam in 694/1295. Extensive use of glazed-ceramic revetments was an innovation of the period, and carved or molded plaster ornament reached a new level of elaboration, though in both media the patterns continued pre-Mongol traditions (Wilber, pp. 79-87; Plate XIV). The Kāšān ceramic workshops also resumed production, initially returning to their familiar decorative repertoire; in the 1270s new themes of Chinese origin were introduced on luster-painted tiles manufactured for the palace of Abaqa Khan (q.v.; 663-80/1265-82) at Taḵt-e Solaymān in Azerbaijan: the dragon, the phoenix, the crane, the deer, the lotus, and distinctive cloud forms and floral motifs (Naumann, pp. 80-98; Watson, pp. 131-49, 190-91; cf. *EIr*. V, p. 320 pl. XXIX).

Absorption of these themes into the Persian decorative repertoire was selective and gradual. Most immediately popular was the lotus, which appears in several distinct configurations: as an isolated blossom, a floral spray set within a polylobed frame, or alternating with a six-petaled flower or trilobed buds attached to a vine. Typically the lotus appears in a distinct, often inconspicuous zone in an ensemble that otherwise continues local pre-Mongol traditions (Baer, pp. 15-16 figs. 9, 11a-11b, 13). The longevity of pre-Mongol decorative schemes is illustrated by a silk textile, now in the Erzbischöflichen Dom- und Diozesanmuseum, Vienna, with the name and titles of Abū Saʿīd (q.v.; 717-36/1317-35), on which the field decoration bears a strong resemblance to pre-Mongol metalwork of Khorasan (Wardwell, pp. 108-11 figs. 45-46).

PLATE XIV

Vault with ceramic-tile revetment, Madrasa-ye Emāmī, Isfahan, ca. 755/1354. Photograph P. Soucek.

The advent of the Timurids (771-912/1370-1506) marked a new stage both in the development of court-based artistic production and in the assimilation of Chinese decorative themes to Persian taste. Many 15th-century designs were also widely used in the Safavid period (907-1145/1501-1732). Although initially Tīmūr had hoped to add China to his empire, his successors were content to cultivate commercial links and diplomatic exchanges, in order to procure coveted goods from China. Fortunately, the formative stages of Timurid taste coincided with the reign of the second Ming emperor, Yung-lo (1398-1424), who actively promoted contacts with the Near East, a policy blocked by his immediate successor but revived on a limited scale by the fourth emperor, Hsuan-te (1425-35), before it was definitively abandoned by his successors (Hok-Lam, pp. 232-36, 301-03). By 840/1435, however, a sufficient quantity of Chinese goods had already reached Persia to permit the unimpeded progress of a second, broader phase of sinicization. Chinese silks, porcelain, paper, and other goods had a profound impact on the decorative traditions of Persia, but once again the adoption of new designs was gradual and highly selective (Crowe, pp. 168-78).

In 15th-century manuscripts Chinese blue-and-white ceramics are often depicted in use, and imitations were made in 15th-century Mašhad and during the Safavid era in several regions of the country. From the 15th to the 17th century Persian blue-and-white ceramic vessels emulated the forms and decoration of late 14th- and early 15th-century Ming wares (Bailey, pp. 179-90; Mason and Golombek, pp. 465-74; Rogers, pp. 122-23, 127-29).

Adaptation and absorption of Chinese designs continued on several fronts. The lotus scroll became a vine, thus emulating the arabesque, with which it was often contrasted or intertwined; the two elements in such combinations were called by 15th-century authors *ḵatāʾī* and *eslīmī* respectively (O'Kane, 1992, pp. 76-78, pl. 14) and emerged as major features of tile revetments in the Timurid and Safavid periods. In the 15th century they were often executed in cut-tile mosaic as focal points in larger ensembles, in which large areas of wall surface were covered with revetments simulating ornamental brickwork, known as *bannāʾī* decoration. Simple geometric designs and pious phrases in square Kufic script (cf. *EIr*. IV, pp. 686-88 figs. 43-46) were widely used on Timurid *bannāʾī* panels (O'Kane, 1987, pp. 59-78; Golombek and Wilber, I, pp. 117-36). In Safavid architecture, however, Sino-Persian vegetal ornament is clearly dominant. Large areas on the surfaces of major religious monuments, including the exteriors of domes, were covered with painted tiles decorated with intricate networks of vegetation on several levels (Scarce, pp. 282-86; Hutt and Harrow, pls. 40, 51, 64-65, 69, 91). Decorative schemes incorporating three or even four systems of interwoven *eslīmī* and *ḵatāʾī* fill the main fields in some 16th- or

17th-century carpets (Ettinghausen, 1979, pp. 18-19 figs. 19-24).

In another decorative scheme of Chinese inspiration elaborate versions of lotus or peony blossoms were combined with plume-like leaves with serrated edges, in order to create a clump or scroll often inhabited by birds, dragons, or other creatures of Chinese derivation. This decorative theme was widely used in Ottoman court design, where it was known as *sāz qalamī* (reed-pen style), beginning in the 1520s; it was associated there with a painter from Tabrīz known as Šāhqolī (Denny, pp. 103-06; Necipoglu, pp. 148-54). In Safavid Persia this decorative vocabulary was most often used in *ḥall-kārī* (lit., "pulverized work"), a type of manuscript illumination in which finely ground gold or silver particles suspended in a solution of glue and water were used as a painting medium (Ṣādeqī Beg, pp. 40, 74 ll. 95-96; Dickson and Welch, I, p. 264; Rogers, pp. 31-32, 123-24; Plate XV, central panel). Patterns in this style were probably also used in other contexts at the Safavid court; in a manuscript of the *Šāh-nāma* copied for Shah Ṭahmāsb (930-84/1524-76) they are depicted in both wall paintings and throne decoration, and they can be found on a ruby-and-turquoise-encrusted gold vessel, apparently of Persian manufacture, now in the Art Museum of Georgia at Tiflis (Dickson and Welch, II, pls. 14, 16, 52; Javakhishvili and Abramishvili, pl. 216). During the 17th century the elaborate blossoms and feathery leaves of the *ḥall-kārī* repertoire were transformed into a continuous vine and used for panels of wall decoration, as well as field designs for carpets (Scarce, pp. 286-90; Beattie, pp. 27, 50-56).

Yet another decorative repertoire with a Chinese pedigree that became prominent in the 15th century was an idealized landscape, in which features of the garden and the royal hunting preserve were combined; it is inhabited by both mythological creatures like the dragon and phoenix and more familiar birds and animals (Plate XV, margin). Frequently they are locked in combat with each other or with human figures (Aslanapa, pp. 59-91). In these settings creatures of Chinese origin are integrated into an indigenous scheme centered on the clash of predator and prey, a combination that in the late 16th century Ṣādeqī Beg Afšār (pp. 45, 76 ll. 120-21; Dickson and Welch, I, p. 265) identified as *gereft o gīr* (lit., "caught and catch"). Despite the theme of conflict, this Chinese hunting preserve was very popular on various media from the 15th to the 17th century and sometimes appears to have acquired paradisiac connotations (Soucek, pp. 7-13). It appears frequently in wall paintings depicted in 15th-century manuscripts, as well as in decorative ensembles of the Safavid period (Lentz and Lowry, pp. 182-83, 191-99; Luschey-Schmeisser).

Just as the Sino-Persian repertoire reached a peak of popularity during the early 17th century a new design vocabulary connected with plants and gardens appeared. It, too, consisted of several distinct yet interdependent modes: the individual flowering plant, the flower-filled trellis, a flowering plant with a bird or butterfly or both, and a miniature garden with flowers and birds. The European source of all these motifs is apparent in the use of modeling and shading to suggest a third dimension, but each was also adapted to Persian taste in a hybrid decorative idiom.

Phase 2. The historical coincidence of the reign of Shah ʿAbbās I (q.v.; 996-1038/1588-1629) with a period of European economic expansion was catalytic for the development of Euro-Persian decoration. Eager to expand the markets for Persian silk, over which he had a monopoly, the shah sought the cooperation of Armenian merchants, traditionally active in the silk trade, and concluded agreements with various European groups. In order to finance their purchases of silk, both Armenians and Europeans sold imported goods in Persia, particularly European and Indian textiles. This trade was particularly intense during the middle decades of the 17th century, when the effective demise of the Persian state monopoly allowed Armenian and European merchants greater freedom in procuring and

PLATE XV

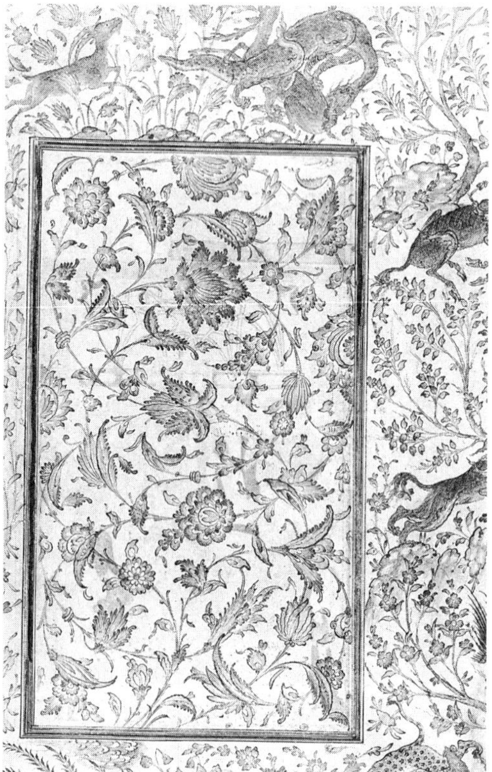

Illuminated page, opaque watercolor, ink, and gold on paper, probably from a manuscript of K͟ᵛāndamīr's *Ḥabīb al-sīar*, Persia, ca. 1590-1600; 38.7 x 23.8 cm. Courtesy of the Arthur M. Sackler Gallery, Smithsonian Institution, Washington, D.C., no. S.1986.201, fol. 211b.

selling goods. In time this large-scale importation of foreign goods would undermine the position of traditional Persian artisans, who found it increasingly difficult to compete against them. Initially, however, the new goods stimulated Persian craftsmen to new accomplishments.

The new decorative vocabulary appeared in different contexts. Luxury textiles and lacquer-painted bookbindings and objects can be connected with the taste of Persian rulers and their close associates, but the inclusion of these new floral designs on carpets and ceramics probably reflects a broader popularity, stimulated by familiarity with both European and Indian goods. European modes of drawing clumps of plants entered the repertoire of artists at the Mughal court and appear in many different materials. The flower-filled lattice was also widely used in Mughal art and architecture (Skelton, pp. 42-45, 67-69, 75-76, 78-81, 83-90).

In Persia some ceramic and carpet decoration blends elements from both the Sino-Persian and Euro-Persian modes. For example, luster-painted vessels with miniature landscapes, often attributed to mid-17th-century Isfahan, incorporate not only the traditional repertoire of animals, birds, trees, rocks, and pools from the Chinese landscape but also oversized clumps of iris from the new vocabulary of Euro-Persian ornament (Lane, pp. 102-04; Watson, pp. 163-69). A similar insertion of oversized europeanizing flowers into the traditional theme of a Sino-Persian garden is found on some blue-and-white ceramic vessels and in wall paintings at the Čehel Sotūn (q.v.) at Isfahan, where a traditional Chinese hunting park was painted over with large bird-and-flower paintings in a modeled style (Allen, pp. 58-59; Gray, pp. 324-26 fig. 220).

A full gamut of designs ranging from purely Sino-Persian to completely Euro-Persian appears on carpets attributed to Kermān in the 16th to 18th centuries (see CARPETS ix-x). In the most conservative schemes only two Sino-Persian designs, *ḵaṭāʾī* and *sāz* scrolls and a stylized garden with animal combats, appear (Housego, pp. 118-23; Beattie, pp. 33-39). In others horizontal rows of flowering plants are set within a network of intertwined *ḵaṭāʾī* on several levels (Beattie, p. 73 no. 47). More common, however, are carpets with designs characteristic of 17th-century Mughal taste, with staggered horizontal rows of plants or a plant-filled lattice (Beattie, pp. 48-49, 80-81 nos. 12-14, 55-57).

Despite this wide diffusion of Euro-Persian decoration, specific types were linked to court circles. For example, even though the practice of arranging flowers in a lattice frame was probably known in 17th-century Persia, its subsequent popularity is often linked to Nāder Shah Afšār (1148-60/1736-47), not only because he brought back considerable booty from his Indian campaign but also because the scheme was used in the decoration of his palace. In Shiraz under the Zand dynasty (1163-1209/1750-94) the theme remained popular for carved stone revetments, tilework, and textiles (Housego, pp. 130-34).

Similarly, an enthusiasm for "bird and flower" decoration is often associated with the court painter Šafīʿ ʿAbbāsī, who was active during the middle decades of the 17th century and who designed both textiles and album paintings. Works attributed to him often show a single plant around which a bird or butterfly hovers (Welch, pp. 90-91, 99-100 nos. 58, 64; Bier, pp. 174-75 nos. 18-20). The most influential variant of this theme, used in lacquer painting, was one in which flowers of different species, often with one or more birds, are grouped in a dense cluster. By the 1670s painters at the Safavid court were decorating objects with such designs, which continued to be common during the 18th and 19th centuries (Plate XVI). Sometimes there is only a single clump of flowers, but in other examples blossoming plants are linked in a vine spray or grouped in a miniature garden, the latter often with a singing nightingale silhouetted against a full-blown rose, hence the appelation *gol o bolbol* (rose and nightingale; Diba, pp. 244-45, 252 figs. 2, 11; Robinson, pp. 177-79 figs. 157, 160, 167-69).

Even as the new hybrid forms of Euro-Persian design grew more prominent in court circles, the older traditions of vegetal, geometric, and calligraphic ornament

PLATE XVI

Panel from mid-19th-century Persian lacquer-painted bookbinding, from a 16th-century manuscript of Neẓāmī's *Ḵamsa*. Courtesy of the Arthur M. Sackler Galllery, Smithsonian Institution, Washington, D.C., no. S.1986.59.

remained in use. The latter two types predominated in the decoration of Qajar religious architecture, and the arabesque was frequently engraved on metalwork during the 17th-19th centuries (Melikian Chirvani, 1982, pp. 260-355; idem, 1983, pp. 311-32; Scarce, pp. 290-94). As late as the 19th century the Persian decorative repertoire retained its characteristic diversity, with new elements added and many earlier ones continuing. This accumulated heritage furnished inspiration for various revivals of Persian artistic and handicraft traditions in the later 19th and 20th centuries.

Bibliography: L. Ainy, *Central Asian Art of Avicenna Epoch*, Dushanbe, 1980. J. Allen, *Islamic Ceramics*, Oxford, 1991. O. Aslanapa, "The Art of Bookbinding," in B. Gray, ed., *The Arts of the Book in Central Asia*, Paris, 1979, pp. 59-91. E. Baer, "The Nisan Tasi. A Study in Persian-Mongol Metal Ware," *Kunst des Orients* 9, 1973-74, pp. 1-46. M. Bahrami, *Gurgan Faïences*, Cairo, 1949. G. A. Bailey, "The Dynamics of Chinoiserie in Timurid and Early Safavid Ceramics," in L. Golombek and M. Subtelny, eds., *Timurid Art and Culture. Iran and Central Asia in the Fifteenth Century*, Leiden, 1992, pp. 179-90. M. H. Beattie, *Carpets of Central Persia*, Westerham, Kent, 1976, pp. 27, 50-56. A. M. Belenizki, *Mittelasien. Kunst der Sogden*, Leipzig, 1980. C. Bier, ed., *Woven from the Soul, Spun from the Heart*, Washington, D.C., 1987. K. A. C. Creswell, *Early Muslim Architecture* II, Oxford, 1940. Y. Crowe, "Some Timurid Designs and Their Far Eastern Connections," in L. Golombek and M. Subtelny, eds., *Timurid Art and Culture. Iran and Central Asia in the Fifteenth Century*, Leiden, 1992, pp. 168-78.

W. Denny, "Dating Ottoman Turkish Works in the Saz Style," *Muqarnas* 1, 1983, pp. 103-21. L. Diba, "Lacquerwork," in R. W. Ferrier, ed., *The Arts of Persia*, New Haven, Conn., 1989, pp. 243-53. M. B. Dickson and S. C. Welch, *The Houghton Shahnameh*, Cambridge, 1981. R. Ettinghausen, "Evidence for the Identification of Kāshān Pottery," *Ars Islamica* 3, 1936, pp. 44-76. Idem, "The Bobrinsky 'Kettle.' Patron and Style of an Islamic Bronze," *Gazette des Beaux-Arts* 24, 1943, pp. 193-208. Idem, "The Taming of the Horror Vaccui in Islamic Art," *Proceedings of the American Philosophical Society* 123, 1979, pp. 15-28. L. Golombek and D. Wilber, *The Timurid Architecture of Iran and Turan*, 2 vols., Princeton, N.J., 1988. E. H. Gombrich, *The Sense of Order*, Oxford, 1979. O. Grabar, *The Mediation of Ornament*, Washington, D.C., 1992. B. Gray, "The Tradition of Wall Painting in Iran," in R. Ettinghausen, and E. Yarshater, eds., *Highlights of Persian Art*, Boulder, Colo., 1979, pp. 313-29. P. O. Harper, *The Royal Hunter*, New York, 1978. Hok-Lam Chan, "The Chien-wen, Yung-lo, Hung-hsi, and Hsuan-te Reigns," *The Cambridge History of China* VII. *The Ming Dynasty, 1368-1644*, pt. 1, ed. F. W. Mote and D. Twitchett, Cambridge, 1988, pp. 128-204. J. Housego, "Carpets," in R. W. Ferrier, ed., *The Arts of Persia*, New Haven, Conn., 1989, pp. 118-49. A. Hutt and L. Harrow, *Islamic Architecture. Iran* I, London, 1977. A. Javakhishvili and G. Abramishvili, *Jewellery and Metalwork in the Museums of Georgia*, Leningrad, 1986. E. J. Keall and R. B. Mason, "The ʿAbbasid Glazed Wares of Siraf and the Basra Connection. Petrographic Analysis," *Iran* 29, 1991, pp. 51-66. J. Kröger, "Décor en stuc," in L. Vanden Berghe and B. Overlaet, eds., *Splendeur des Sassanides*, Brussels, 1993, pp. 63-65. A. Lane, *Later Islamic Pottery*, 2nd ed., London, 1971. T. W. Lentz and G. D. Lowry, *Timur and the Princely Vision. Persian Art and Culture in the Fifteenth Century*, Los Angeles and Washington, D.C., 1989. G. D. Lowry, "On the Gold Jug Inscribed to Abu Mansur al-Amir Bakhtiyar ibn Muʿizz al-Dawla in the Freer Gallery," *Ars Orientalis* 19, 1989, pp. 103-15. I. Luschey-Schmeisser, "Ein neuer Raum in Nayin," *AMI*, N.S. 5, 1972, pp. 309-14.

R. B. Mason and L. B. Golombek, "Differentiating Early Chinese-Influence Blue and White Ceramics of Egypt, Syria, and Iran," in E. Pernicka and G. A. Wagner, eds., *Proceedings of the XXVIIth International Symposium on Archaeometry*, Heidelberg, 1990, pp. 465-74. A. S. Melikian Chirvani, "La plus ancienne mosquée de Balkh," *Arts Asiatiques* 20, 1969, pp. 3-20. Idem, *Islamic Metalwork from the Iranian World*, London, 1982. Idem, "Qajar Metalwork. A Study in Cultural Trends," in E. Bosworth and C. Hillenbrand, eds., *Qajar Iran*, Edinburgh, 1983, pp. 311-28. R. Naumann, *Takht-i Suleiman*, Munich, 1976. G. Necipoğlu, "From International Timurid to Ottoman. A Change of Taste in Sixteenth-Century Ceramic Tiles," *Muqarnas* 7, 1990, pp. 136-70. B. O'Kane, *Timurid Architecture in Khurasan*, Costa Mesa, Calif., 1987. Idem, "Poetry, Geometry and the Arabesque. Notes on Timurid Aesthetics," *Annales Islamologiques* 26, 1992, pp. 63-78. A. U. Pope, *Persian Architecture*, New York, 1965. ʿA. Qūčānī, *Katībahā-ye sofāl-e Neyšābūr*, Tehran, 1364 Š./1985. J. Raby, "Looking for Silver in Clay. A New Perspective on Samanid Ceramics," in M. Vickers, ed., *Pots and Pans*, Oxford, 1986, pp. 179-203. B. W. Robinson, "Lacquer, Oil-Paintings and Later Arts of the Book," in *Treasures of Islam*, Geneva, 1985, pp. 176-205. J. M. Rogers, *Islamic Art and Design. 1500-1700*, London, 1983.

Ṣādeqī Beg Afšār Tabrīzī, *Qānūn al-ṣowar*, ed. A. Yu. Kaziev as *Ganun ös-söuvär (Traktat o zhivopisi)* (*Qānūn al-ṣowar* [Text and illustrations]), Baku, 1963. J. Scarce, "Tilework," in R. W. Ferrier, ed., *The Arts of Persia*, New Haven, Conn., 1989, pp. 271-94. S. P. Seherr-Thoss, *Design and Color in Islamic Architecture*, Washington, D.C., 1968. R. Shani, "On the Stylistic Idiosyncrasies of a Saljuq Stucco Workshop from the Region of Kashan," *Iran* 27, 1989. [G. V. Shishkina and L. V. Pavchinskaya,] *Terres secrètes de Samarcande*, Paris, 1992. M. S. Simpson, "The Narrative Structure of a Medieval Iranian Beaker," *Ars Orientalis* 12, 1981, pp. 15-24. R. Skelton, *The Indian Heritage. Court Life and Arts* under Mughal Rule, London, 1982. P. Soucek, "The New York Public Library Makhzan al-asrār and Its Importance," in Ars Orientalis 18, 1988, pp. 1-37. V. Voronina, Architectural Monuments of Middle Asia, Leningrad, 1969. A. Wardwell, "Panni Tartarici. Eastern Islamic Silks Woven with Gold and Silver," Islamic Art 3, 1988-89, pp. 95-173. O. Watson, Persian Lustre Ware, London, 1985. A. Welch, Shah Abbas and the Arts of Isfahan, New York, 1973. D. Wilber, The Architecture of Islamic Iran. The Ilkhanid Period, Princeton, N.J., 1955. E. Yarshater, "The Development of Iranian Literatures," in E. Yarshater, ed., Persian Literature, New York, 1988, pp. 3-37.

(PRISCILLA P. SOUCEK)

DECORATIONS, honors granted by the Persian government. Although in general Western usage orders are badges reflecting the distinction of belonging to select societies, whereas decorations and medals are awarded in recognition of various types and levels of civil or military achievement or service, in Persia there are no orders in the Western sense, but only decorations and medals. Nonetheless, decorations (nešān), elaborate combinations of badges and accessories, are frequently referred to, especially in Western writings, as "orders." The recipient of such an honor has the right to wear a collar or chain from which the decoration itself is suspended by a badge, a sash in a specified color, and a large pendant star adorned with the relevant insignia. Medals (medāl) are awarded either collectively or individually in recognition of services performed for the nation and are usually reserved for junior and noncommissioned officers or for lower-echelon civil servants.

These honors are to be distinguished from commemorative medallions (for illustrations of such medallions, see Mošīrī, 1354 Š./1975; idem, 1355 Š./1976; Rabino di Borgomale; Šahīdī).

Qajar period (1193-1342/1779-1924).

The practice of awarding such honors was initiated by Fatḥ-ʿAlī Shah (1212-50/1797-1834), who introduced the Lion and sun (nešān-e šīr o ḵoršīd) in 1223/1808, apparently inspired by the Red Crescent adopted by the Ottoman sultan Salīm III (1203-22/1789-1807). It was bestowed on military men and civilians, native and foreign.

Nāṣer-al-Dīn Shah (1264-1313/1848-96) increased the repertoire of honors to include the Temtāl-e Amīr-al-Moʾmenīn (referring to Imam ʿAlī and bearing his image; Plate XVII.a), which was reserved for the shah; the Sun (Āftāb) for royal women; and the Royal portrait (Temtāl-e homāyūn). At first he reserved diamonds for the highest decorations, especially that with the royal portrait (Šahīdī, p. 208). The Amīr-al-Moʾmenīn was introduced after the Qajars recaptured Herat in 1273/1856; it was worn by the shahs at public ceremonies and national festivals (Hedāyat, Rawżat

al-ṣafā II, pp. 702-04; Sepehr, I, p. 295; Eʿtemād-al-Salṭana, 1988, p. 1275). The Āftāb was introduced in 1290/1873 specifically for presentation to queens and princesses, including the empress Augusta of Germany and Queen Victoria, during the shah's European tour in that year (Reuters despatch; The Freemason, June 28, 1873, p. 421). The shah's wife Anīs-al-Dawla received it on his birthday in 1306/1888 (for text and illustrations, see Šahīdī, pp. 224-25, 235-36; Eʿtemād-al-Salṭana, Rūz-nāma-ye ḵāṭerāt, p. 596; idem, 1988, p. 1722). In 1314/1896 Moẓaffar-al-Dīn Shah (1313-24/1896-1907) awarded it to the wife of the Ottoman ambassador Šams-al-Dīn Beg (Sepehr, I, p. 296). During his reign decorations were made of silver (Sepehr, p. 297).

Under Fatḥ-ʿAlī Shah the central medallion with eight radiating points framed a lion against a rising sun; it was ornamented with jewels (see Mošīrī, 1354 Š./1975, p. 13). The crown prince ʿAbbās Mīrzā (q.v.) issued a similar decoration for military valor; it bore a legend on the obverse and a distich composed for the occasion on the reverse (Rabino di Borgomale, 1945, pp. 68-69). Under Moḥammad Shah (1250-64/1834-48) there were eight classes of the lion and sun, corresponding to military rank, from four-star general to noncommissioned officer, each with three grades (for text and illustrations, see Šahīdī, pp. 187-207); under Nāṣer-al-Dīn Shah the number was raised to nine with the creation of the rank of mīr panj (comparable to lieutenant general). The lion was shown holding a raised sword in one paw, and the decoration was set with diamonds. For civilians rubies and sapphires replaced the diamonds, and the lion was depicted reclining without the sword (Šahīdī, pp. 205-07). In 1278/1861 Nāṣer-al-Dīn Shah created three new categories of the lion and sun, which became the highest decorations during his reign; they were the Aqdas (Plate XVII.b), the Qods, and the Moqaddas (for the text of his edict, see Eʿtemād-al-Salṭana, 1988, pp. 1399-1405; Sepehr, p. 291). Each consisted of a central medallion set within a twelve-pointed star and bearing the image of the lion and sun with a crown above; it was set with diamonds and rubies. The highest was the Aqdas (Eʿtemād-al-Salṭana, 1988, p. 1449), reserved for kings and prime ministers; among those who received it was the Ottoman sultan ʿAbd-al-ʿAzīz, in 1280/1863. Ambassadors and dignitaries of comparable status received the Qods (e.g., Mīrzā Yūsof Khan Mostawfī-al-Mamālek; Eʿtemād-al-Salṭana, 1988, p. 1821). The Moqaddas was intended for ministers, governors, and the like (Mostawfī, Šarḥ-e zendagānī I, pp. 118-19; for illustrations, see Šahīdī, pp. 17, 219-20; cf. Mošīrī, 1354 Š./1975, pls. 10-11). In 1289/1872 the vizier Mīrzā Ḥosayn Khan Mošīr-al-Dawla Sepahsālār established five classes of the lion and sun for foreigners and Persian civil servants (nešān-e šīr o ḵoršīd-e ḵāreja), on the pattern of the French Légion d'honneur (Mostawfī, Šarḥ-e zendagānī I, pp. 118-19; Sepehr, p. 297). Thenceforth civilians and foreigners no longer received the Moqaddas; those who would previously have been eligible for it received instead the Lion and sun, first class (Plate XVII.c). The different classes were represented by the number of points in the framing star: from eight for the first class to four for the fifth class. The Lion and sun, first class, was parallel to the military Lion and sun given to three-star generals and was awarded with a green sash (Sepehr, p. 297; cf. Afżal-al-Molk, pp. 43, 194, 200, 421, 429).

The Royal portrait was intended for high-ranking officials and foreign dignitaries. It consisted of an oval medallion 12-14 cm long with the portrait of the shah; it was framed in diamonds, rubies, and sapphires and had a crown at the top (Šahīdī, pp. 200, 213; Mošīrī, 1354 Š./1975, ills. 3, 9, 38). There were three classes of this decoration (Sepehr, I, p. 295).

Except for the lower classes of the Lion and sun, all these honors were awarded with the sash (*ḥamāyel*). The shah's sash was light blue. The grand vizier and four-star generals wore plain green; when the vizier was wearing the Royal portrait his sash was bordered with dark-blue stripes. Ambassadors generally wore dark blue with the Royal portrait, a darker blue with the first class of the Lion and sun. The commander-in-chief of the armed forces wore a blue sash bordered with green stripes, three-star generals red with green border stripes and two-star generals red with white border stripes, brigadier generals plain red, and colonels plain white. These sashes could also be awarded separately (Šahīdī, pp. 214-15; Eʿtemād-al-Salṭana, 1988, pp. 1240, 1300, 1316, 1318, 1617).

The eighth and ninth classes of the Lion and sun for military personnel were considered medals. In 1269/1852 Dār al-fonūn (q.v.) began awarding gold, silver, and copper medals bearing the image of the lion and sun to outstanding students. The Madrasa-ye nāṣerī and Madrasa-ye neẓām-e dawlatī also granted medals (Šahīdī, pp. 226-29; Rabino di Borgomale, 1974, pl. 44/51; many examples are in the collection of the Sepah bank museum in Tehran). Later this system was replaced by the ʿElmī medal, with three classes, for the dissemination and advancement of knowledge; it was bestowed upon students, teachers, university professors, writers, and scientists, both Persian and foreign (Šahīdī, pp. 226-35; cf. Sepehr, p. 297).

From the latter half of Naṣer-al-Dīn Shah's reign to the end of the Qajar period the Lion and sun and the Royal portrait underwent a kind of "inflation," being awarded with increasing frequency (Amīn-al-Dawla, pp. 17-18; Mostawfī, *Šarḥ-e zendagānī* I, p. 105). The Lion and sun for foreigners became particularly known in Russia, to the point that in the last decade of the 19th century Anton Chekhov satirized the eagerness of his countrymen to possess it (pp. 130-33; tr., pp. 219-25; cf. Spasskii, p. 99).

Pahlavi period (1304-20 Š./1925-41).

A new system of official honors was instituted by the Pahlavi dynasty, though two decorations were continued, with major modifications, from the Qajar period. The five classes of the Lion and sun for civilians persisted under the name Homāyūn, and the Amīr-al-Moʾmenīn became the military Ḏu'l-faqār (the name of ʿAlī's sword). The complete Pahlavi *nešān* included the badge, the star, and the sash (Plate XVIII.a).

Among the new decorations introduced there were

PLATE XVII

a

b

c

Decorations of the Qajar period. a. The Temṯāl-e Amīr-al-Moʾmenīn. b. The Aqdas. c. The star of the Lion and sun, first class.

three royal honors (*nešānhā-ye salṭanatī*). The Pahlavī, with two classes, was introduced in 1304 Š./1925, as the highest Persian honor. The first class was limited to reigning monarchs and foreign heads of state; the second class was for male members of the royal family and heirs apparent of foreign monarchies. The badge consisted of a central medallion framed by four Pahlavi crowns forming a cross, each set off from the central medallion by two gold loops joined by a blue enameled ring; on the medallion was an enameled image of Mount Damāvand with the rising sun above it. The star of the order was similar to the badge, except that, instead of rings and loops, the medallion was surrounded by five rays. The sash was cornflower blue with yellow borders. There was also a Pahlavī badge of honor, the frame of which retained the crowns, separated by paired gold loops connected by blue-enameled rings (Werlich, p. 243).

The other new decorations were intended for women and were introduced under Moḥammad-Reżā Shah (1320-57 Š./1941-79). The Haft peykar (Pleiades, referring to Ṯorayyā, the shah's second wife), with three classes, was adopted in 1336 Š./1957. The first class was reserved for Ṯorayyā and foreign queens and first ladies. The badge consisted of a royal-blue enameled medallion with the seven stars of the constellation Pleiades set in diamonds within a white-enameled frame set with twenty-four gold stars within a gold rim, the whole topped by the royal crown in red enamel; it was set within a star frame. The star was identical but larger than the badge and was worn with a sash of light yellow bordered with blue stripes. The second class was for princesses and the third for other distinguished women (see Werlich, pp. 243-44; Mofakkam, pp. 1-2; Mošīrī, 1355 Š./1978, p. 48). The Āryāmehr, with two classes, was introduced on 4 Mehr 1346 Š./26 September 1967, expressly for Queen Faraḥ to wear during the coronation ceremony. Only she was entitled to wear the first class; the second class was reserved for the shah's sisters Šams and Ašraf. The badge consisted of a gold star with sixteen radiating swallowtails, each covered with diamonds, and in the center a gold Pahlavi crown on a blue-enameled disk framed in diamonds. The star was identical but larger than the badge, and the sash was royal blue (Werlich, p. 243).

Civil honors. The two main Pahlavi civil decorations (*nešānhā-ye rasmī-e kešvarī*), the Tāj-e Īrān and the Homāyūn, each with five classes, were instituted on 26 Bahman 1317 Š./15 February 1939 for high-ranking Persian civil servants and foreigners who had performed outstanding service for Persia (Mofakkam, p. 4). The Tāj-e Īrān, first class, was intended for the prime minister and former prime ministers, and there could be no more than ten poeple at one time entitled to wear it; the recipient received the title *janāb* (excellency) and was entitled to a state funeral. One exception was made for Jamšīd Āmūzgār, minister of finance, who received the decoration in 1350 Š./1971 for his role in oil negotiations and his arrangement of a meeting of the Organization of Petroleum Exporting Countries (OPEC) in Tehran (Alam, p. 201). The second class (Plate XVIII.a) could be held by only fifty people at one time and the third class by 150. The badge consisted of a blue-enameled medallion, bearing the Persian crown and rimmed in gold overlaid with a green-enameled laurel wreath, set within a green-bordered white-enameled star, each point tipped with a gold globe. The star consisted of a second, larger badge superimposed upon a gold sunburst. The sash was of yellow moiré silk, with light-blue borders (Werlich, p. 244).

The Homāyūn (Plate XVIII.b) was a simplified and modernized version of the original Qajar Lion and sun. The badge consisted of a central medallion bearing an enameled disk of the lion with upraised sword and the rising sun, framed within a six-pointed star; the star was a similar badge superimposed upon a sunburst with eight points (Plate XVIII.b); the third class consisted only of the star, with no badge (Plate XVIII.c). The first class was worn with a green sash bordered in red, the second class suspended from a red-bordered green ribbon by means of a rosette. There was also a Homāyūn medal, with three grades, of gold, silver, and bronze, intended for lower-ranking civil servants. In the last decades of the Pahlavi dynasty it ceased to be awarded (Werlich, pp. 244-45; Mofakkam, p. 4).

Various badges of honor and medals were issued by ministries and government agencies during the Pahlavi period. For example, the Ministry of education (Wezārat-e farhang, later Wezarat-e āmūzeš o parvareš) awarded four badges of honor for scholars and scientists and one medal for administrative staff and students. The Nešān-e dāneš for science, with two grades, both of gold, was awarded to high-ranking scholars and scientists. The Farhang, with three grades, was awarded to prominent educators, teachers, and administrative staff of the ministry; the first grade was of gold, the second and third of silver. There was also a Farhang medal, with two classes, each with two grades, for teachers, lower administrative staff, and honor students; the first grade was of silver, the second of bronze. The Honar, with three classes, was awarded to prominent people in the fine arts; the first class was of gold, the second and third of silver. The Sepās, with three classes, was awarded to civil servants and to people who had made financial contributions to educational institutions; the first class was of gold, the second of silver, and the third of bronze (*Āʾīn-nāma*).

Military honors. By the order of Reżā Khan Sardār-e Sepah (Ḥokm 86, 20 Asad 1301 Š./11 August 1922) the Ḏu'l-faqār (Plate XVIII.d) became the highest Persian military honor. It was awarded in two categories, to officers and to lower ranks, for demonstrating exceptional courage or sustaining injury or death in the line of duty (Farmān 271, 21 Farvardīn 1304 Š./10 April 1925). After the Sepah decoration was introduced, on 30 Farvardīn 1303 Š./19 April 1924, the Ḏu'l-faqār was reserved exclusively for those who had fought in foreign wars (Farmān 271). Only Reżā Shah

PLATE XVIII

a

b

c

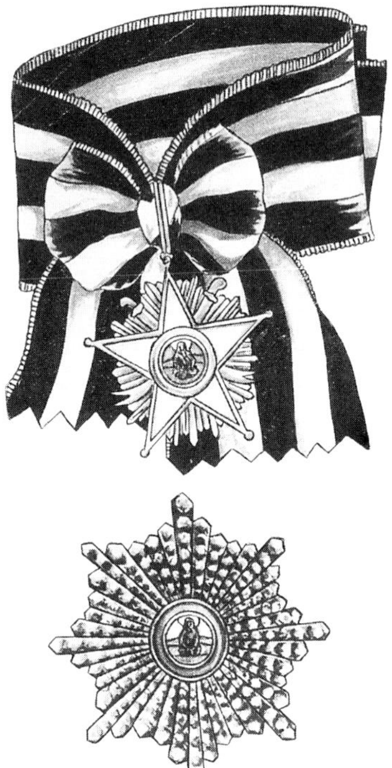

d

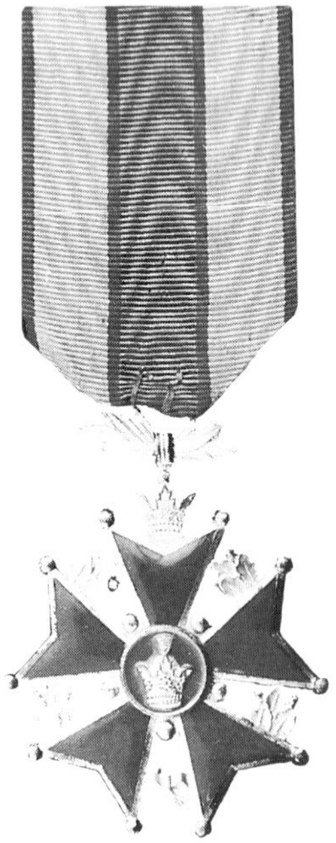

e

Decorations of the Pahlavi period. a. The Tāj-e Īrān, second class, including ribbon with rosette, badge, and star; photograph courtesy of Hooshang Batmanglidj. b. Star worn as part of the Homāyūn, first and second class; photograph courtesy of Hooshang Batmanglidj. c. The complete Homāyūn, third class; photograph courtesy of Hooshang Batmanglidj. d. The Ḏu'l-faqār, first class. e. The Ḵedmat, with ribbon and star.

himself and a handful of army officers received it during his reign. After the unsuccessful attempt to assassinate Moḥammad-Reżā Shah on 15 Bahman 1327 Š./4 January 1948 the armed forces "requested" that the shah grant himself the order of D̲u'l-faqār. The Sepah, with three gold and silver grades, was intended for military men who fought courageously in internal wars (Farmān 206). There was also a Sepah bronze medal for ranks below officer (*Āʾīn-nāma-ye Esfand-e 1319*, art. 5).

Many other, lesser honors were introduced for military personnel in war and peace. Reżā Shah created two service decorations that survived to the end of Pahlavi rule, the Līāqat and the Eftek̲ār. The Līāqat was the higher, a badge of honor awarded to military officers for distinguished service in peace or war (*Āʾīn-nāma-ye Esfand-e 1319*, art. 5). In 1316 Š./1937 the Eftek̲ār was also established in recognition of distinguished service. Medals corresponding to the Eftek̲ār (1333 Š./1954) and the Līāqat (1338 Š./1959) were introduced for the upper ranks of enlisted men. Moḥammad-Reżā Shah introduced five new war honors: the K̲edmat decoration (Plate XVIII.e) and medal in 1328 Š./1949, the Sepāhī medal in 1332 Š./1953, both examples of honors given collectively for outstanding service (*Aʾīn-nāma-ye 1350 Š.*, p. 39); the Farr medal in 1332 Š./1953 for continuing military education (*Aʾīn-nāma-ye 1338 Š.*, p. 46); the Čatr badge in 1338 Š./1959 for successful parachute jumps in difficult circumstances (Farmān 9150); and the Pādāš medal in 1332 Š./1953 for perseverence in the performance of duty (*Āʾīn-nāma-ye 1350 Š.*, p. 40).

The military awarded a number of other honors, including the Bāznešastagī badge for retirement, with four classes (1959 Š./1970; *Āʾīn-nāma-ye 1350 Š.*, p. 82); the Jāvīd badge and medal (1322 Š./1943) and Sarbolandī badge (1350 Š./1971) were awarded respectively to the families of military personnel who died or had been killed (*Āʾīn-nāma-ye 1338 Š.*; *Āʾīn-nāma-ye1350 Š.*, p. 61). Two military honors were designed for civilians who assisted the military, the Hamkārī badge (Esfand 1335 Š./1957; Farmān 5828, *Āʾīn-nāma-ye 1338 Š.*, p. 81) and the Šajāʿat medal (*Āʾīn-nāma-ye 1338 Š.*).

Commemorative medals included one commemorating the coup d'etat of 1299/1921 (q.v.); medals for active participants in the operations against the Soviet-backed autonomous government of Azerbaijan in 1325/1946 (*Dastūr-e ʿamalīyātī* 717; see AZERBAIJAN v); the Rastāk̲īz and Bīst o hašt-e Mordād (28 Mordād/18 August) for active participants in the coup d'etat of 1332 Š./1953 (q.v.; Farmān 7973; *Āʾīn-nāma-ye 1350 Š.*, pp. 67, 69).

Islamic Republic (1357 Š./1979-present).

After a lapse of twelve years civil honors were revived. New regulations governing their award were approved by the cabinet of President ʿAlī-Akbar Hāšemī Rafsanjānī on 27 Ābān 1369 Š./18 November 1990. There are three categories of such decorations: high (*ʿālī*), specialized (*tak̲aṣṣoṣī*), and general (*ʿomūmī*).

There are four high decorations. The highest, the Enqelāb-e eslāmī, is awarded to the president of the republic after his inauguration. The other three are awarded by the president at the suggestion of ministers and with the approval of the cabinet. The Esteqlāl and Āzādī are intended for those who are deemed to have contributed to the goals of the regime; during each presidential term the former can be awarded only four times, the latter eight. The Jomhūrī-e eslāmī, with three grades, is awarded to foreign heads of state, heads of international organizations, and other foreign dignitaries who have contributed to the stated goals of the regime, including expansion of the Islamic revolution; defense of the world's poor; struggle against political, economic, and cultural colonialism; support for Persian international policies; and cooperation in the expansion of relations between the Islamic Republic and their own countries.

Specialized decorations include the Dāneš (erudition), Pažūheš (research), Līāqat wa modīrīyat (merit and management), and ʿAdālat (justice).

General decorations include the Sāzandagī (constructiveness), K̲edmat (service), Kār o tawlīd (work and producton), Šajāʿat (bravary), Īt̲ār (sacrifice), Taʿlīm o tarbīat (education), Farhang o honar (culture and art), and Adab-e fārsī (Persian literature).

Bibliography: G̲.-Ḥ. Afżal-al-Molk, *Afżal al-tawārīk̲*, ed. M. Etteḥādīya and S. Saʿdvandīān, Tehran, 1361 Š./1982. *Āʾīn-nāma-ye nešānhā wa medāl-hā-ye wezārat-e farhang*, 15 Farvardīn 1324 Š./4 April 1945. A. Alam, *The Shah and I*, ed. A. Alikhani, London, 1991. A. P. Chekhov, "Lev i solntse" (Lion and sun), in *Povesti i rasskazy, 1887-1889* (Stories and tales, 1887-1889), Moscow, 1931; tr. C. Garnett as "The Lion and the Sun," in *Love and Other Stories*, London, 1922. Moḥammad-Ḥasan Khan Eʿtemād-al-Salṭana, *Merʾāt al-boldān*, eds. ʿA.-Ḥ. Navāʾī and M.-H. Moḥaddet̲, 3 vols., Tehran, 1367 Š./1988. Jomhorī-e eslāmī-e Īrān, *Āʾīn-nāma-ye eʿṭā-ye nešānhā-ye dawlatī*, 1369 Š./1990. P. V. A. McLoughlin, *The Orders of Knighthood, Decorations, and Awards of Honour of All Nations*, London, 1963. Idem, "Decorations and Orders," in *Encyclopedia Americana* VIII, 1966, pp. 565-66. M. Mofak̲k̲am, *Ketāb-e nešānhā-ye salṭanatī wa rasmī-e kešvar-e Īrān*, Tehran, 1347 Š./1968. M. Mošīrī, *Nešānhā wa medālhā-ye Īrān*, Tehran, 1354 Š./1975. Idem, *Ketāb-e sekka wa nešān dar dawrān-e šāhanšāhī-e Pahlavī*, Tehran, 1355 Š./1976. H. L. Rabino di Borgomale, *Coins, Medals, and Seals of the Shahs of Iran (1500-1941)*, n.p., 1945. Idem, *Album of Coins, Medals, and Seals of the Shâhs of Iran (1500-1948)*, ed. M. Moshiri, Tehran, 1353 Š./1974. Y. Šahīdī, "Nešānha-ye dawra-ye qājār," *Barrasīhā-ye tārīk̲ī* 6/3, 1350 Š./1971, pp. 185-240. ʿA.-Ḥ. Sepehr, *Merʾāt al-waqāyeʿ-e moẓaffarī*, ed. ʿA.-Ḥ. Navāʾī, I, Tehran, 1368 Š./1989, pp. 291-300. I. G. Spasskii, *Inostrannye i russkie ordena do 1917 goda* (Foreign and Russian orders until the year

1917), Leningrad, 1963. R. Werlich, *Orders and Decorations of All Nations,* 2nd ed., Washington, D.C., 1974. Wezārat-e jang, *Taqwīm-e neẓāmī, 1304,* Tehran, 1304 Š./1925. Wezārat-e maʿāref wa awqāf, *Qānūn-e šūrā-ye ʿālī-e maʿāref, 20 Ḥūt 1300,* Tehran, 1301 Š./1922.

(YAḤYĀ ŠAHĪDĪ)

DEDE BEG ḎU'L-QADAR. See ABDĀL BEG.

DEDE ʿOMAR RŪŠANĪ (b. Güzel Ḥeṣār, Aydın province, in western Anatolia, at an indeterminate date; d. Tabrīz, 892/1487), Turkish Sufi who wrote poetry in both Persian and Turkish. His mother belonged to the powerful Aydınoğlu family of western Anatolia, and his *nesba* (attributive name) is a deliberate play on the name of his birthplace, *rūšanī* (< *rowšan* "bright") being a direct Persian translation of Turkish *aydınlı* (< *aydın* "bright").

Dede ʿOmar studied at Bursa with Jandārlı Ebrāhīm Pasha (d. 832/1429) and later in Šamāḵī under Sayyed Yaḥyā Servānī (d. 867/1463), the second saint (*pīr*) of the Ḵalwatīya Sufi order. He served the latter as deputy (*qāʾem-maqām*) and after Sayyed Yaḥyā's death remained in Azerbaijan as leader of the Rūšanīya branch of the Ḵalwatī order. While actively propagating the order in the regions of Qarabāğ, Bardaʿa, Ganja, and Tabrīz, he met and initiated into the order Edrīs, brother of the Āq Qoyunlu Ozun Ḥasan (857-82/1453-78). The ruler invited Dede ʿOmar to Tabrīz, and his wife Saljūq Ḵātūn built a retreat (*zāwīa*) for him there near Bāğ-e Šemāl. Dede ʿOmar spent the final years of his life in Tabrīz and was buried in the *zāwīa* (*Mazārāt-e Tabrīz,* fol. 3a). He raised from seven to twelve the number of the names of God recited in the *ḏekr* (q.v.), a type of change that was customary for a recently founded order. His successor, Ebrāhīm Golšanī, founded the Golšanīya order.

Dede ʿOmar was the author of a *dīvān* of poetry containing his three Persian *maṯnawī*s, *Meskīn-nāma, Nāy-nāma,* and *Selsela-ye mašāyeḵ-e Ḵalwatīān,* as well as *ğazals* and a number of works in Turkish genres (for manuscripts, see *Türkçe yazma,* pp. 34 ff.). In the *Nāy-nāma* the influence of Jalāl-al-Dīn Rūmī's *Maṯnawī* is particularly clear. One volume of the *dīvān* was published under the title *Āṯār-e ešq* in Istanbul in 1315/1897.

Bibliography: Moḥyī Golšanī, *Manāqeb-e Ebrāhīm Golšanī,* ed. T. Yazıcı, Ankara, 1982. Ḥāfeẓ Ḥosayn Karbalāʾī Tabrīzī, *Rawżāt al-jenān wa jannāt al-janān,* ed. J. Solṭān-al-Qorrāʾī, I, Tehran, 1344 Š./1965, pp. 472-76, comm. pp. 601-02. Kamāl-al-Dīn Moḥammad Ḥarīrī, *Ṭebyān wasāʾel al-ḥaqāʾeq fī bayān salāsel al-ṭarāʾeq,* Süleymaniye Kütüphanesi, Istanbul, Ibrahim Efendi kısmı, ms. no. 431, fols. 67b-69a. Jalāl-al-Dīn Maḥmūd Ḥolwī, *Lomẓāt,* Dil ve Tarih-Coğrafya Fakültesi Kütüphanesi, Ankara, İsmail Saib Kitapları ms. no. 1/722, fols. 299b-300a. Moḥammad-Mortażā Ḥosaynī Wāseṭī Zabīdī, *ʿEqd al-jawhar al-ṯamīn fi'l-ḏekr wa ṭoroq al-elbās wa'l-talqīn,* Türk Tarih Kurumu Kütüphanesi, Ankara, Muhammed Tancı ms. (uncatalogued), p. 60. F. de Jong "Ḵhalwatiyya," in *EI*[2] IV, pp. 991-93. B. G. Martin, "A Short History of the Khalwati Order of Derwishes," in N. R. Keddie, *Scholars, Saints and Sufis. Muslim Religious Institutions since 1500,* Berkeley, Calif., 1972, pp. 275-305. *Mazārāt-i awlīā-ye Tabrīz,* Dil ve Tarih-Coğrafya Fakültesi, Ankara, İsmail Saib Kitapları ms. no. I/835. B. M. Tahir, *Osmanlı Müellifleri* I, Istanbul, 1915, p. 69. Tarbīat, *Danešmandān-e Āḏarbāyjān,* pp. 319-20. Abu'l-Ḵayr Aḥmad b. Moṣleḥ-al-Dīn Moṣṭafā Ṭāškūprīzāda, *Šaqāyeq al-noʿmānīya fī ʿolamāʾ al-dawlat al-ʿoṯmānīya,* ed. A. S. Fırat, Istanbul, 1985, p. 264; tr. M. M. Efendi as *Hadaik üş-şakayik,* Istanbul, 1989, pp. 281-82. Ministry of education, Ankara, *Türkce yazma divanlar kataloğu,* Istanbul, 1947.

(TAHSİN YAZICI)

DEDE YŪSOF SĪNAČĀK (b. Yenice on the Vardar in Ottoman Māqadūnīā [modern Macedonia] at an indeterminate date, d. Istanbul, 861/1546), Mawlawī Sufi shaikh, poet, and author. He was born to a family of scholars originally from Edirne and educated by his father. He became shaikh of the Mawlawī convent (*mawlawī-ḵāna*) at Yenice, but he moved to Istanbul when the governor expropriated the endowments of the convent (Ṯāqeb Dede, II, pp. 20-22). According to Qenālīzāda (p. 1085) and Āšeq Čelebī (fol. 98a), Dede Yūsof then gave up studying the religious sciences and went to Egypt, where he became a disciple of the mystic Ebrāhīm Golšanī (d. 940/1533), founder of the Golšanīya order. He seems to have continued his association with Golšanī for only a short time before making the pilgrimage to Mecca and traveling on to Jerusalem, where he remained for several years in the Mawlawī convent; he then went on to Iraq to visit the tombs of the Shiʿite imams, and thence to Konya, where he became shaikh of the Mawlawī order. He finally settled in Istanbul, where he died in the retreat of Sütlüce in 953/1546.

Dede Yūsof is best known for his *Jazīra-ye maṯnawī,* a selection of 366 verses from Rūmī's *Maṯnawī.* It enjoyed great popularity among the Mawlawīs and became the subject of commentaries by ʿElmī Dede (d. 1020/1611), ʿAbd-al-Majīd Sīvāsī, Ğāleb Dede (d. 1213/1799) in his *Lamaḥāt al-lamaʿāt baḥr al-Maṯnawī be šarḥ Jazīrat al-maṯnawī,* the Turkish poet and calligrapher Ebrāhīm Jevrī (d. 1065/1654-55), and ʿAbd-Allāh Bosnavī (d. 1054/1644; Süleymaniye Kütüphanesi, Istanbul, Nafiz Paşa ms. no. 528). A similar selection from Solṭān Walad's *Rabāb-nāma* is lost. Dede Yūsof's own poetry, written in Persian, though considered to be of high quality, reveals Ḥorūfī (cf. ʿAšeq Čelebī, fol. 98b) and Shiʿite tendencies; it remains unpublished.

Bibliography: Pīr Moḥammad ʿĀšeq Čelebī, *Mašāʿer al-šoʿarāʾ,* ed. G. M. Meredith-Owens, London, 1971. ʿA Gölpinarli, *Mevlânâʾdan sonra Mevlevîlîk*, 2nd ed., Istanbul, 1983, pp. 124-27. Qenālīzāda Ḥasan Čelebī, *Taḏkerat al-šoʿarāʾ*, ed. Ī. Kutluk, II, Ankara, 1981, pp. 1085-86. B. M. Tahir, *Osmanlı Müellifleri*, Istanbul, 1915, I, pp. 117, 120; II, p. 351. Šayḵī Moḥammad Efendī, *Waqāyeʿ al-fożalāʾ*, ed. A. Özcan, Istanbul, 1989, p. 663. Ṯāqeb Dede, *Safīna-ye nafīsa-ye Mawlawīān* II, Cairo, 1283/1866-67, pp. 20-23.

(TAHSİN YAZICI)

DĒDMARĪ, ḴᵛĀJA MOḤAMMAD-AʿẒAM b. Ḵayr-al-Zamān Kašmīrī (1103-79/1691-1765), historian, poet, and Sufi of Kashmir. He was born in the Dēdmar quarter of Srinagar, hence his *nesba* (attributive name) Dēdmarī. From his early years he studied traditional Islamic sciences with renowned scholars at the *madrasas* of Mollā ʿAbīd and ʿAbd-al-Razzāq in Srinagar. As a young poet he benefited from the guidance of the poet Nūr-al-Dīn Šāreq (d. 1127/1714) and later studied with Moḥammad-Reżā Moštāq Kašmīrī (d. 1143/1730) and Mollā ʿAbd-al-Ḥakīm Sāṭeʿ (1143/1730). Moḥammad-Aʿẓam joined the Naqšbandī order of Sufis in 1119/1706 and remained under the spiritual guidance of Mollā Moḥammad-Morād Naqšbandī (d. 1131/1718), leader of the order in Kashmir, for twelve years.

Ḵᵛāja Moḥammad-Aʿẓam, a prolific writer, used the pen name Aʿẓam for his poetry. Although no collection of his poems has survived, several chronograms and poems scattered throughout his *Wāqeʿāt-e Kašmīr* show that he was accomplished in the art. *Wāqeʿāt-e Kašmīr* is a compendium of political, social, literary, and intellectual information about Kashmir from ancient times to the year 1148/1735 (Rieu, *Persian Manuscripts* I, pp. 300-01). Ḵᵛāja Moḥammad-Aʿẓam also wrote on mysticism and the Sufi orders of Kashmir. His works include *Fayż-e Morād*, *Resāla-ye fawāʾed al-Reżā*, *Resāla-ye ferāq-nāma*, *Qawāʿed al-mašāyeḵ*, *Resāla-ye eṯbāt al-jabr*, *Tajrabat al-ṭālebīn*, *Ašjār al-ḵold*, and *Ṯamarāt al-ašjār*.

He was buried in Dēdmar.

Bibliography: Moḥammad-Aʿẓam Dēdmarī, *Wāqeʿāt-e Kašmīr*, Srinagar, 1936, pp. 291-93. Pīr Ḡolām-Ḥasan Kūyhāmī, *Tārīḵ-e Ḥasan* I, ed. Ḥasanšāh, Srinagar, 1954, pp. 372-73.

(SHAMSUDDIN AHMAD)

DEER. See ĀHŪ, GAVAZN.

DEFRÉMERY, Charles-François (b. Cambray, France, 18 December 1822, d. St.-Valéry-en Caux, France, 18 August 1883), French orientalist and scholar. His father was a notary. After finishing at the Lycée Louis-le-Grand he studied Arabic with J. T. Reinaud and Caussin de Perceval at the Collège de France and the École des Langues Orientales; at the latter he also studied Persian with the historian Étienne de Quatremère, whose disciple he became. In 1848 it had been intended to entrust him with the first courses in the history of the Islamic world at the École des Langues Orientales, but other matters took priority, and the courses were not introduced. After Quatremère's death in 1857 he hoped to succeed to the chair at the École des Langues Orientales, but Charles Schefer received the appointment instead. Nevertheless, Defrémery taught Arabic beginning in 1859 and was named to Caussin's chair at the Collège de France after the death of the latter in 1871. From 1869 Defrémery was a member of the Académie des Inscriptions et Belles-Lettres, where he and MacGuckin de Slane were entrusted with overseeing the publication of *Historiens arabes des Croisades*.

Defrémery was a scrupulous and careful historian, the author of numerous scholarly notes and reviews in *Journal Asiatique* and the *Mémoires* of the Institut de France. Aside from his publications on the history of Arabic-speaking lands and early French literature, he left a number of works on Persian history and literature.

His editions of Persian texts included two sections from Mīrḵᵛānd's *Rawżat al-ṣafāʾ fī sīrat al-anbīāʾ wa'l-molūk wa'l-ḵolafāʾ* (*L'histoire des sultans du Kharezm*, Paris, 1842; *Histoire des Samanides*, Paris, 1845, with translation); Ḵᵛāndamīr's *Ḥabīb al-sīār* (with translation, "L'histoire des Khans mongols du Turkistan et de la Transoxiane," *JA*, 4e sér. 19, 1852, pp. 58-94, 216-88; 20, 1852, pp. 370-406); and Ebn Baṭṭūṭa's *Reḥla* (with B. R. Sanguinetti; 4 vols., Paris, 1853-59, with translation). In 1858 he published in Paris a translation of Saʿdī's *Golestān* (*Gulistan ou parterre des roses*) and, in *Journal Asiatique*, "Coup d'oeil sur la vie et les écrits de Hafiz"; the next year his translation of several extracts from Saʿdī's *Būstān* appeared in the same journal. In 1873 his translation from Chaghatay Turkish of the memoirs of the Mughal emperor Bābor appeared in *Journal des Savants*; two years earlier he had published a notice about the dictionary of eastern Turkish by Pavet de Courteille.

In 1844 Defrémery's notice on ʿAbd-al-Razzāq Samarqandī's *Maṭlaʿ-e saʿdayn wa majmaʿ-e baḥrayn* appeared in *Journal Asiatique*. In 1854 the firm of Firmin-Didot in Paris brought out his *Mélanges d'histoire orientale*, followed by *Mélanges de critique, de philologie et de géographie*, both containing considerable important material on history as well. A long study devoted to the "Ismaéliens ou Batiniens" of Persia and Syria appeared in *Journal Asiatique* in 1854 and 1856.

Defrémery was first and foremost a historian, particularly concerned with establishing solid factual foundations for and applying the most scrupulous rigor to Islamic history. Much of his work remains useful to this day.

He died at the age of sixty years, after a long illness.

Bibliography: Barbier de Meynard, *Catalogue de la bibliothèque de M. Defrémery*, Paris, 1884. J. Darmesteter, "Rapport sur les travaux . . ., "*JA*, 8e sér., 4, 1884, pp. 27-29. J. Richardot, "Defrémery," in *Dictionnaire de biographie française* X, Paris, 1963, cols. 536-37.

(FRANCIS RICHARD)

DEH (village) in Persia and Afghanistan. The Persian word *deh* (Paštō *kəlay*, Ar. *qarya*) has a more precise meaning than Persian *ābādī* (q.v.) "inhabited place," which can refer to cities and towns, on one hand, and isolated farms (*mazraʿa*), on the other. A *deh* is a rural settlement perceived as an autonomous social and spatial unit.

The village as a spatial entity.

Villages in Persia and Afghanistan can be classified in four main types, according to formal features linked with ecological and cultural determinants (de Planhol, *Camb. Hist. Iran*, pp. 418 ff.).

Ancient clustered villages. The most common type is a dense clustered village, varying in size from around a hundred to several thousand inhabitants. It was characteristic of early settlements that have withstood successive stages of "beduinization" (de Planhol, 1968, pp. 209-13) and are now inhabited by different ethnic groups, like Persian or Tajik, on one hand, and Azeri or Uzbek, on the other. It is clear from toponymic analysis that linguistic turkicization of the latter did not disrupt the continuity of settlement. In Azerbaijan, for example, the great majority of village names in the Sahand area are of Iranian origin (de Planhol, 1966, pp. 304-05); in the Ḵalḵāl district most of the village names mentioned by Yāqūt in the early 13th century or by Ḥamd-Allāh Mostawfī in ca. 741/1340 can still be found (Bazin, 1980, II, p. 81); and in the small district of Ḵalajestān a number of old Iranian toponyms with the suffixes *-gerd/jerd* or *-gān/jān* are still in use (e.g., Dastjerd, Fowjerd, Vasfūnjerd, Tīzagān, Mowjān, Kardījān), though Ḵalaj invaders either settled or converted the local population to their eastern Turkish language at a very early date (Bazin, 1974, p. 26).

These old villages are located mainly in two particular kinds of setting. In the mountains they are usually built on the lower slopes overlooking irrigated valley bottoms or, when the slopes are steep, on cliffs, as in the Hindu Kush (Hallett and Samizay, 1975). On the alluvial fans of arid piedmonts, on the other hand, they are built at the outlets of *qanāt*s or along canals, with their main street(s) usually paralleling the main water channel(s) (Roaf), though the latter may also pass through several domestic compounds (English, pp. 50-51). Access to water produces a social gradient within each village: The cleaner and more abundant the water, the wealthier and more powerful are the inhabitants. Close to the village is a cluster of intensively cultivated gardens and orchards, surrounded by mud walls. Extensive open fields of annual crops encircle the village or are concentrated downstream. In irrigated areas new settlements are frequently dispersed among older ones, but they are completely lacking in the dry-farmed lands.

The clustered village may be generally described as a "huddled and haphazard agglomeration" of square individual habitations (*ḵāna*; de Planhol, *Camb. Hist. Iran*, p. 420), but several house types may be distinguished, largely depending on altitude (Kartsev, pp. 42-43). Their main variant features are the number of stories, the type of roof, and the building materials. Single-story houses organized around inner courtyards typify the low-lying areas, whereas in high mountain valleys houses may have up to three stories, with the ground floor, often partly dug out of the cliff, used to shelter animals. There are also various intermediate forms (for examples, see Desmet-Grégoire and Fontaine, pp. 49 ff.). The shape of the roof depends upon the availability of timber. Wherever poplars are grown flat terraced roofs predominate, whereas in dry low-lying areas domes or vaults of sun-dried or fired bricks are more common, though locally they may be replaced by tamarisks or reeds plastered with mud, as in Sīstān (for Afghan examples, see Jentsch, 1980a, pp. 72 ff.; Szabo and Barfield, pp. 118 ff.; for Persian examples, see Bazin, 1974, pp. 82-83 and map 37; Behforūz, pp. 13 ff.; Desmet-Grégoire and Fontaine, pp. 54 ff. and map 14). In Afghanistan, however, the flat roof is more traditional in the east, the dome and vault in the west, the two regions divided approximately by a line running from Qaṭaḡan through the central Harīrūd valley to the Qandahār oasis (Szabo and Barfield, maps pp. 118, 134). Mud brick is by far the most common building material in villages (Beazley and Harverson, pp. 12 ff.; Engler). Because of its cost baked brick is used infrequently, especially in Afghanistan. In mountainous areas combinations of mud and stone are used, with the proportion of stone increasing at higher elevations. Some mountain villages are built almost entirely of stone, as in the central Hindu Kush. Timber is used for walls only in wooded regions like Nūrestān (Szabo and Barfield, p. 112 et passim).

Fortified settlements. In Persia and Afghanistan, where perched villages are uncommon (de Planhol, 1983, pp. 97 ff.), purely architectural forms have evolved to meet the settlers' defensive needs. For example, watch towers dot many villages in Nūrestān, the Solaymān mountains, and other mountainous areas in central Afghanistan (Edelberg, pp. 145 ff.; Jentsch, 1980a, pp. 66 ff.), and ladder systems are also in use for circulation within villages of Nūrestān, reflecting a tradition in the high mountain ranges of Central Asia. The most common defensive adaptation by far, however, is the fortified village or farmstead (*qalʿa*), sometimes inaccurately called "castle" or "fort" (Klinkott, p. 116). Fortified villages, or fortress villages, appear to be the dominant type of defensive settlement in Persia, whereas fortified farmsteads housing extended families predominate in Afghanistan (Bruno; Hallett and Samizay, 1972; de Planhol, 1958; Rozenfel'd; Turri). The typical *qalʿa* is a square or rectangle enclosed by a mud-brick wall, with a projecting round tower (*borj*) at each corner. In larger examples there may be additional towers along the walls, sometimes flanking the entrance. A maximum of twelve towers has been recorded near Kabul. A few towerless *qalʿa*s are also known in eastern Afghanistan (Jentsch, 1980a, p. 85). Dwellings are built against the inner face of the wall, their doors and windows all facing onto a central courtyard; hence the designation of such settlements as "settlements with habitable walls" (Tolstov).

Similar fortified settlements have been known in Central Asia since the Bronze Age, and fortified rectangular villages were common there in the time of Alexander the Great (q.v.). Quadrangular buildings with central courtyards and corner towers dating from the 2nd millennium B.C.E. have also been excavated in northern Afghanistan (Sarianidi, pp. 30 ff.). According to A. Z. Rozenfel'd, the *qalʿa* has little defensive value and thus cannot be explained as a technical solution; instead, he considers that it probably belongs to the Iranian cultural complex. This assessment appears to be contradicted, however, by the fact that at present *qalʿa*s are concentrated mainly in the most insecure areas; when the threat is from external enemies, *qalʿa* villages predominate, whereas family *qalʿa*s are intended to protect against local marauding.

In Persia all *qalʿa* villages are located in easily invaded plains and broad valleys (Lambton, *Landlord and Peasant*, 3rd ed., pp. 8-9), for example, the Varāmīn plain south of Tehran (de Planhol, 1964, pp. 9 ff.) and the valleys and basins of central Persia between Isfahan and Qom (Bazin, 1974, pp. 81-82), Fārs, and Khorasan on both sides of the Afghan-Persian boundary, that is, wherever villagers have been threatened by nomads or invaders of whatever origins. The fluctuating security of territory along major travel routes is illustrated by the conversion of abandoned caravansaries into settlements resembling *qalʿa*s, as near Qom (Bazin, 1974, p. 82).

Extended-family *qalʿa*s (Paštō *kalā*), on the contrary, are concentrated primarily in southeastern Afghanistan. They may be combined with less monumental but more crowded *qalʿa* villages in loose agglomerations of fortified settlements, as at Deh Afḡānān in the Meydān valley (Szabo and Barfield, pp. 160 ff.), or dispersed among traditional clustered villages (Wald, p. 80). There is a close connection between the prevalence of this type of settlement and several structural characteristics of Ḡilzay society, in which internal insecurity is emphasized to a degree unmatched elsewhere. Outside this area diffusion of the family *qalʿa* has been restricted to the upper social classes, symbolizing nothing more than the owner's status (Schurmann, p. 360).

Changes reflecting demographic pressure are part of the normal evolution of the *qalʿa*, especially during periods of greater security. The inner courtyard first becomes crowded with new buildings; then new houses are constructed outside the wall. Scattered *qalʿa*s with fewer defensive features appear: The corner towers may completely disappear or shrink to no more than symbolic decorative appendages, as in most of the *qalʿa*s built recently in Afghanistan, including Hazārajāt (Bero). Moreover, rooms with large windows opening to the outside may be added to older traditional *qalʿa*s, either just above the monumental entrance gates or high in corner towers.

Loose settlements. Loosely structured settlements, including the agglomerations of Ḡilzay *qalʿa*s mentioned above, are generally of nomadic origin (for those north of Qom, see Bazin, 1974, pp. 82-83; for the Ḡaznī basin, see Balland). The layout is often more or less regular, especially in villages built under official sedentarization schemes (see village plans in Kraus, pp. 16 ff.); the houses, flat-roofed or vaulted, according to local traditions, are not clustered but rather stand side by side, with open space between them, like tents in a nomadic camp. No tree or garden can be seen nearby, and tents or huts may be intermingled with the houses for summer comfort. Settled nomads are actually often seminomads, and a main village is thus usually associated with one or several temporary camps on pasturelands and sometimes with a second village or a few hamlets built on complementary agricultural land, as in northern Khorasan (Pāpolī Yazdī, 1991, pp. 214 ff.). Many such villages are named for their founding clans or lineages, like those of Šāhsevan clans southeast of Ardabīl and Kurdish clans north of Ḵalḵāl (Bazin, 1980, II, pp. 81 ff.). An exception is found in northern Badaḵšān, where a similar loose but less regular layout typifies old Tajik villages (Kussmaul, p. 499; Patzelt and Senarclens de Grancy).

Scattered hamlets of the Caspian lowlands. A completely different rural landscape has evolved in the humid conditions of the Caspian provinces of Gīlān and Māzandarān. True villages are lacking; the basic settlement unit is the *maḥalla*, a loose agglomeration of a few dozen to several hundred scattered farmsteads (Bromberger, 1989, pp. 34 ff.). Each farmstead is itself composed of several separate buildings scattered amid trees and a vegetable garden within a fenced enclosure: a house, a cow shed, a storage shed for rice, a silkworm nursery, and so on, each with a wooden framework and a peaked roof of thatch or tile. The *maḥalla*s are interspersed with orchards and fields of tobacco or tea along alluvial rims and ancient shorelines, quite distant from the extensive treeless rice fields.

The village as a socioeconomic microcosm.

Villages, including the Caspian *maḥalla*s, are the basic units of social and territorial affiliation in rural areas. Related lineages form the human nuclei, to which newcomers may have been added by spontaneous or state-controlled immigration. In such instances the later arrivals live in distinct quarters (Centlivres and Centlivres-Demont, p. 14).

The basic statistical unit. Much of the available information about rural areas in Persia and, to a lesser degree, in Afghanistan has been collected at the village level. As delimitation of villages varies according to different government sources, however, that is not a guarantee of accuracy. Uncertainty is greatest in the Caspian lowlands and Ḡilzay country, where the so-called "villages" are generally artificial groupings of *maḥalla*s (see, e.g., Bazin, 1980, I, pp. 100-01) and *qalʿa*s respectively. In other areas, too, it is often difficult to ascertain whether a small settlement is an independent village or a *mazraʿa* attached to a larger village nearby (see, e.g., Patzelt and Senarclens de Grancy, p. 225). Gazetteers of inhabited places in Persia thus include from 14,721 (Mofakkam Pāyān) to 80,717 names (Pāpolī Yazdī, 1989), and estimates of the total number of villages range from 42,000 to 58,000. A figure of 48,592 was used by the Persian government for purposes of land reform (McLachlan, p. 686). In Afghanistan conflicting figures have been published: In 1339 Š./1960 the Ministry of agriculture and irrigation enumerated 14,205 villages (*Survey*), a figure that was increased to 15,270 after the agricultural census of 1346 Š./1967 (*Natāyej*); the Ministry of interior, on the other hand, listed 20,753 villages, of which 15,599 were classified as "independent villages" and 5,154 as "associated subvillages" (*Aṭlas*). Although the Ministry of agriculture's figures for villages and the Ministry of interior's enumeration of "independent villages" are similar, they only partly coincide. Combining both lists would produce a total of 22,425 inhabited places (computed from *Aṭlas*). It is thus necessary to use the data from gazetteers with caution.

For Persia the following village gazetteers have been published: *Farhang-e joḡrāfīāʾī-e Īrān* in 1328-36 Š./1949-57 (Razmārā, *Farhang*), which remains the only source providing data on languages and religious affiliations, together with population, economic activities, and products; *Farhang-e ābādīhā-ye kešvar* (Markaz-e āmār; Schweizer), providing demographic data from the census of 1345 Š./1966 and the most detailed figures on land use, crafts, and equipment in each enumerated village; a subsequent edition of the same gazetteer, providing population data for 1355 Š./1976 but with less detail than its predecessor; and the *Farhang-e joḡrāfīāʾī-e rūstāhā-ye Īrān* (Sāzmān), which is still being published and which includes useful sketches of locations.

Aside from the somewhat outdated gazetteer produced by the British during the late 19th and early 20th centuries (in four successive editions, the fourth, which is not the best, reissued with only minor editorial updating by L. W. Adamec as *Gazetteer of Afghanistan*), the following village gazetteers are available for Afghanistan: the Persian and Pašto editions of *Qāmūs-e joḡrāfīāʾī-e Afḡānestān*, edited by M.-H. Nāheż, totally different in content but both concerned mainly with purely locational information, and the more recent *Aṭlas-e qaryahā-ye Afḡānestān*, in which no attempt has been made to arrange names in alphabetical order, including only crude demographic data and unsystematic references to location on maps (see CENSUS ii). Neither includes data on economic activities and products. Although such data were collected at the village level during the agricultural census of 1346 Š./1967, they have been released only as aggregates for whole districts. The same procedure was followed after the census of 1358 Š./1979. The preparatory work for the latter included collection of data on the infrastructure of all Afghan villages (mosques, mills, shops, etc.), which have also never been published.

The village and land ownership. Some decades ago Persia was primarily characterized by a system of large property holdings, so that the village was the usual unit for measuring land ownership (Lambton, *Landlord and Peasant*, passim). Every village, large or small, was in turn divided into six *dāng* and every *dāng* into sixteen *šaʿīr*, so that the village consisted of ninety-six *šaʿīr*. The main distinction was between *šeš-dāng* villages, each owned by a single person, and *ḵorda-mālek*, a rather ambiguous expression embracing both peasant property (rather rare) and small properties under absentee ownership. Some landlords owned dozens of villages. The village headman (*kadḵodā*) was generally an agent of the landlord or of one of the main landlords in *ḵorda-mālek* villages. If the landlord managed his own estate, he also had an overseer (*mobāšer*) in the village.

All efforts to change this agrarian structure had therefore to be implemented at the village level. The first stage in the land reform of Moḥammad-Reżā Shah Pahlavī (1320-57 Š./1941-59) was limitation of land ownership to one village per person (Lambton, 1969). The numerous measures adopted in the second stage, including organized partition or sale of estates and fixing of better conditions for tenancy, were also focused on the village level, as was the third stage, intended to complete the processes by producing a full-fledged system of direct exploitation (see LAND REFORM). The "reintegration phase" of the 1970s (Planck) reflected a more ambivalent attitude toward the village, however. On one hand, most of the agricultural cooperatives (q.v.; *šerkat-e sehāmī-e zerāʿī*) were organized at the village level, but, on the other hand, foreign or national agribusinesses encompassed groups of villages and favored concentration of the rural population in the *šahrak*, a kind of company town, as in the area of the Dezfūl irrigation project area (Ehlers, 1975, pp. 198-204). Unrealistic policies aimed at generalizing this pattern throughout the country certainly contributed to dissatisfaction with the shah's regime among the rural population. After the Revolution of 1357 Š./1978-79 attempts by former landlords to recover their estates and by local communities to achieve further partition of land were undertaken at the village level, but no decisive policy was adopted at the national level.

In Afghanistan, where large landed estates had not developed to the same degree as in Persia, the village has never been the unit of measure for land ownership. Moreover, implementation of the land reforms of 1354 Š./1975 and 1357 Š./1978, incomplete though it was, suffered from inadequate or nonexistent cadastral surveys at the village level.

Organization of agricultural production. The village is also a technical and economic unit for agriculture and animal husbandry, reflecting varying degrees of cooperation and collective organization among its inhabitants. Wherever irrigated cultivation predominates, the tilled area of the village normally coincides with one irrigation unit (called *dašt* in central Persia), drawing water from a single source, though in larger villages the land may be divided into two or more autonomous *dašt*s (for examples, see Bazin, 1974, p. 38). In every *dašt* irrigation is supervised by an elected *mīrāb*, who controls the distribution of water from field to field on a strictly organized cycle. He is a leading personality in village life (Amat). Concern for rational distribution of water may lead to collective crop rotation in systems of common fields (Grötzbach). At a lower level of organization small collective units (called *bona* in the Tehran region, *tāq* in Isfahan, *ṣaḥrā* in Khorasan, *bonkūh* in Dezfūl) played an important technical and social role in the villages of central and southern Persia before land reform by implementing cooperation in agricultural work (Ehlers and Safi-Nejad). A "field watcher" (*daštbān*) may also be appointed to keep flocks and wild animals off the fields.

In dry-farming areas various patterns of collective organization can be observed, depending on the age of the villages and the relation between agriculture and animal husbandry. In villages of recently sedentarized nomads individual crop rotation usually predominates, resulting in a mosaic of fields. In older villages common fields are alternately cultivated and left fallow; during fallow periods they serve as pastures for common flocks and herds tended by shepherds (called *nak̲īrjī* for cattle and *čūpān*, q.v., for flocks in Azerbaijan). A further step in collective organization can be observed in Kalārdašt, where fields owned by several adjoining villages and planted with the same crop stretch for miles (de Planhol, 1964). Additional features of collective organization may include the concentration in one place outside the village of the inhabitants' threshing floors (as in Azerbaijan and eastern Afghanistan), common reserves of animal dung to be used for fuel (as in Azerbaijan), and common animal pens (as in eastern Afghanistan).

Infrastructure and local institutions. A few decades ago Persian and Afghan villages were generally poorly provided with communal institutions. Some did not even have mosques, though larger settlements might have several, even sometimes both Shiʿite and Sunni mosques, as at Hešajīn (in the Kāḡad̲konān *dehestān* of K̲alk̲āl). Local shrines (*emāmzāda*, q.v.; *zīārat*), whether located within or outside the built-up areas, could draw pilgrims from large distances (Einzmann). Almost everywhere trading activity was limited to one or a few unspecialized shops; the entire countryside was heavily dominated economically by city *bāzār*s, according to a "primacy model of settlement" (Bonine). Weekly markets, which are known only in some parts of the Perso-Afghan area, were more often located in cities than in villages (see BĀZĀR ii). Finally, although elementary schools gradually became more standard in villages, the only administrative structure present in all of them was embodied in the headman (*kadk̲odā* in Persia, *mālek*, *qaryadār*, or *arbāb* in Afghanistan), who acted as liaison between the villagers and district or provincial administrators (Centlivres and Centlivres-Demont, pp. 242 ff.).

In Persia these traditional structures were severely altered in the course of the White Revolution that accompanied land reform. Several new village institutions were instituted: for example, village councils (*anjoman-e deh*), "houses of equity" (*k̲āna-ye enṣāf*, i.e., boards of mediation), and cooperatives (q.v.), in all of which former tenants who had become small landowners participated. The school network was expanded and complemented by an educational corps (*sepāh-e dāneš*), small welfare centers were established with the help of a health corps (*sepāh-e behdāšt*), and technical aid was made available through a rural-development corps (*sepāh-e tarwīj o ābādānī*). There were efforts to bring safe drinking water and electricity to villages and to connect villages to towns by means of roads or tracks suitable for buses and jeeps. All these improvements were, however, distributed very unequally, both among villages and among the inhabitants of a single village. Rural society actually changed dramatically, owing to the ascent of a group of new landowners constituting a "petite bourgeoisie," which succeeded in monopolizing all the new functions within the village (Vieille; Khosrovi, 1969). The landless *k̲ošnešīn*, who saw no change in his miserable condition, often had no choice but to leave the village for the city (Khosrovi, 1973). This trend was more pronounced in larger or more centrally located villages, in which more improvements had accumulated, than in smaller or more remote ones, which remained largely outside the modernization process. After the Revolution of 1357 Š./1978-79, which was fundamentally an urban movement, the institutions of the Pahlavi regime were replaced by new ones, including local committees and units of the *pāsdārān* (revolutionary guards) or "reconstruction crusade" (*jehād-e sāzandagī*). The most important change, however, has been the opening of more rural areas through a dense network of roads, on one hand, and electricity (and television), on the other; the consequences of this change cannot yet be properly assessed (Bazin, 1989).

In Afghanistan the pace of modernization has been much slower. Many villages, for example, in Hazārajāt and Badak̲šān, are still days distant from the nearest motorable road (Centlivres and Centlivres-Demont, p. 68 map). Furthermore, after 1358 Š./1979 the war has reversed the modernizing trend, thus intensifying the contrast with Persia. Most of the village schools and basic health centers that were opened during the 1970s have now been closed, with resulting drastic reductions in the educational and sanitary levels of villagers. According to official statistics, only 583 primary schools were operating in the entire country in 1369 Š./1990, compared to 4,136 in 1358 Š./1979, a decline of 86 percent. The road network has suffered severely from the hostilities and lack of maintenance. Rural electrification is nonexistent, though a few notables own diesel generators from which they may operate Japanese televisions sets equipped with video cassette recorders, thus considerably adding to their social prestige among villagers. On the institutional side, the regime claims to have created numerous agricultural cooperatives (*kōparātīf-e zerāʿatī*), but whether or not all of them are really operative remains questionable (679 claimed cooperatives, with a total membership of 99,202, in 1369 Š./1990, compared to 126, with 14,340 members in 478 villages, in 1356 Š./1977).

Bibliography: Āmārgīrī-e rūstāʾī jehād-e sāzandagī, *Farhang-e ejtamāʿī-e dehāt wa mazāreʿ*, 24 vols., Tehran, 1358 Š./1979. Idem, *Farhang-e eqteṣādī-e dehāt wa mazareʿ 1318*, 24 vols., Tehran, 1360-61 Š./1981-82. B. Amat, "L'organisation paysanne pour la distribution de l'eau pour l'irrigation dans les villages de la steppe. L'institution du mirab," *Afghanistan Journal* 3/3, 1976, pp. 86-90. *Aṭlas-e qaryahā-ye Afḡānestān*, 3 vols., Demographic Research Report Series 1, Kabul, 1353 Š./1974. D. Balland, "Vieux sédentaires tadjik et immigrants pachtoun dans le sillon de Ghazni (Afghanistan oriental)," *Bulletin de l'Association de Géographes Français* 417-18, 1974, pp. 171-80. M. Bazin, *La vie rurale dans la région de Qom (Iran central)*, Paris, 1974. Idem, *Le Tâlech, une région ethnique au nord de l'Iran*, 2 vols., Paris, 1980; tr. M.-A. Farščīān as *Ṭāleš, manṭaqa-ī qawmī dar šemāl-e Īrān*, 2 vols., Mašhad, 1367 Š./1988. Idem, "L'adaptation des techniques modernes de transport dans les campagnes iraniennes," in Y. Richard, ed., *Entre l'Iran et l'Occident*, Paris, 1989, pp. 91-103. E. Beazley and M. Harverson, *Living with the Desert. Working Buildings of the Iranian Plateau*, Warminster, U.K., 1982. F. Behforūz, *Bīābān. Pažūheš-ī dar masāken-e rūstāʾī-e manṭaqa-ye bīābānī-e šarq-e Kāšān. Abūzaydābād wa rūstāhā-ye manẕūma-ye ān*, Tehran, 2536=1356 Š./1977. M. Bero, "Zur traditionellen ländlichen Bauweise im Hasaradschat, östliches Zentralafghanistan," *Archiv für Völkerkunde* 35, 1981, pp. 31-46. M. E. Bonine, *Yazd and Its Hinterland*, Marburg, 1980. C. Bromberger, *Habitat, architecture et société rurale dans la plaine de Gilân (Iran septentrional)*, Paris, n.d. (1986); tr. as *Habitat, Architecture and Rural Society in the Gilân Plain (Northern Iran)*, Bonn, 1989. A. Bruno, "Case-forti in Afghanistan," *Castellum* (Rome) 12, 1970, pp. 69-90.

P. Centlivres and M. Centlivres-Demont, *Et si on parlait de l'Afghanistan?* Neuchâtel and Paris, 1988. N. N. Cheboksarov, ed., *Tipy traditsionnogo sel'skogo zhilishcha narodov yugo-zapadnoĭ i yuzhnoĭ Azii* (Types of traditional rural dwellings of the peoples of southwestern and southern Asia), Moscow, 1981, chaps. 4-5. *Də Afḡānestān joḡrāfiāʾī qāmūs*, 6 vols., Kabul, 1340-50 Š./1962-721. H. Desmet-Grégoire and P. Fontaine, *La région d'Arāk et de Hamadān. Cartes et documents ethnographiques*, Paris, 1988; tr. A. Karīmī as *Arāk wa Hamadān. Naqšahā wa asnād-e mardom-negārī*, Mašhad, 1370 Š./1991. L. Edelberg, *Nuristani Buildings*, Århus, 1984; review M. Klimburg, "Notes on the Architecture of Nuristan," *Archiv für Völkerkunde* 41, 1987, pp. 41-52. E. Ehlers, *Traditionelle und moderne Formen der Landwirtschaft in Iran. Siedlung, Wirtschaft und Agrarsozialstruktur im nördlichen Khuzistan seit dem Ende des 19. Jahrhunderts*, Marburg, 1975. Idem, "The Iranian Village. A Socio-Economic Microcosm," in P. Beaumont and K. McLachlan, eds., *Agricultural Development in the Middle East*, New York, 1985, pp. 151-70. Idem and J. Safi-Nejad, "Formen kollektiver Landwirtschaft in Iran. Boneh," in E. Ehlers, ed., *Beiträge zur Kulturgeographie des islamischen Orients*, Marburg, 1979, pp. 55-82. H. Einzmann, *Religiöses Volksbrauchtum in Afghanistan. Islamische Heiligenverherung und Wallfahrtswesen im Raum Kabul*, Wiesbaden, 1977. A. E. Engler, "Aus Erde vom Ackerboden," in P. Bucherer-Dietschi, ed., *Bauen und Wohnen am Hindukusch*, Liestal, Switzerland, 1988, pp. 27-39. P. W. English, *City and Village in Iran. Settlement and Economy in the Kirman Basin*, Madison, Wis., 1966.

E. Grötzbach, "Formen des zelgengebundenen Feldbaus und dessen Auflösungserscheinungen im Hindukusch (Nordost-Afghanistan)," *Die Erde* 101, 1970, pp. 23-40. S. Hallett and R. Samizay, "Fortress Housing. The Afghan Qala," *Research* 4/1, 1972, pp. 22-32. Idem, "Nuristan's Cliff-Hangers," *Afghanistan Journal* 2/2, 1975, pp. 65-72. Idem, *Traditional Architecture of Afghanistan*, New York, 1980. C. Jentsch, "Die ländlichen Siedlungen in Afghanistan. Eine erste Bestandsaufnahme und ein Überblick," in C. Jentsch and R. Loose, *Zur Geographie der ländlichen Siedlungen in Afghanistan. Zwei Beiträge*, Mannheim, 1980a, pp. 9-93. Idem, "Zur Höhengrenze der Siedlung in afghanischen Hochgebirgen," in C. Jentsch and H. Liedtke, eds., *Höhengrenzen in Hochgebirgen*, Saarbrücken, 1980b, pp. 353-65. V. N. Kartsev, *Zodchestvo Afganistana* (The architecture of Afghanistan), Moscow, 1986. K. Khosrovi, "La réforme agraire et l'apparition d'une nouvelle classe en Iran," *Études Rurales* 34, 1969, pp. 122-26. Idem, "Les paysans sans terre en Iran. Les Khochnechin," *Sociologia Ruralis* 13/3-6, 1973, pp. 289-93. M. Klinkott, *Islamische Baukunst in Afganisch-Sīstān*, Berlin, 1982. R. Kraus, *Siedlungspolitik und Erfolg, dargestellt an Siedlungen in den Provinzen Hilmend und Baghlan, Afghanistan*, Meisenheim am Glan, Germany, 1975. F. Kussmaul, "Siedlung und Gehöft bei den Taḡiken in den Bergländern Afḡanistans," *Anthropos* 60, 1965, pp. 487-532. A. K. S. Lambton, *The Persian Land Reform 1962-1966*, Oxford, 1969. K. S. McLachlan, "Land Reform," in *Camb. Hist.*

Iran I, pp. 685-713. Markaz-e āmār-e Īrān, *Farhang-e ābādīhā-ye kešvar/Village Gazetteer Based on National Census of November 1966*, 27 vols., Tehran 1347-50 Š./1968-71, Idem, *Farhang-e ābādīhā-ye kešvar bar asās-e saršomarī-e aban 1355*, 23 vols., Tehran, 1361 Š./1982. L. Mofakkam Pāyān, *Farhang-e ābādīhā-ye Īrān*, Tehran, 1339 Š./1960. M.-H. Nāheż, ed., *Qāmūs-e joḡrāfīā'ī-e Afḡānestān*, 4 vols., Kabul, 1335-39 Š./1956-60. *Natāyej-e eḥṣā'īyagīrī-e sarwē-ye moqaddamātī-e zerā'atī-e 1346* II. *Eḥṣā'īya-ye nofūs-e zerā'atī, ta'dād-e zamīndār wa māldār, sāḥa-ye zamīn-dārī*, Kabul, n.d. (roneo).

M.-Ḥ. Pāpolī Yazdī, *Farhang-e ābādīhā wa makānhā-ye maḏhabī-e kešvar*, Mašhad, 1368 Š./1989. Idem, *Le nomadisme dans le nord du Khorassan*, Paris, 1991. G. Patzelt and R. Senarclens de Grancy, "Die Ortschaft Ptukh im östlichen Wakhan," in R. Senarclens de Grancy and R. Kostka, eds., *Grosser Pamir*, Graz, 1978, pp. 215-47. U. Planck, "Die Reintegrationsphase der iranischen Agrar-reform," *Erdkunde* 29/1, 1975, pp. 1-9. X. de Planhol, "Les villages fortifiés en Iran et en Asie centrale," *Annales de Géographie* 67, 1958, pp. 256-58. Idem, "Un village de montagne de l'Azerbaidjan iranien, Lighwan (versant Nord du Sahend)," *Revue de Géographie de Lyon* 35/4, 1959, pp. 395-418. Idem, "Recherches sur la géographie humaine de l'Iran septentrional," *Mémoires et Documents du Centre de Documentation Cartographique et Géographique* 9/4, 1964, pp. 3-79. Idem, "Aspects of Mountain Life in Anatolia and Iran," in S. R. Eyre and G. R. J. Jones, eds., *Geography as Human Ecology*, London, 1966, pp. 291-308. Idem, *Les fondements géographiques de l'histoire de l'Islam*, Paris, 1968. Idem, "Geography of Settlement," in *Camb. Hist. Iran* I, pp. 409-67. Idem, "Les limites orientales de l'habitat perché méditerranéen," in P. Flatrès and X. de Planhol, eds., *Études sur l'habitat perché*, Paris, 1983, pp. 95-111. R. Rainer, *Traditional Building in Iran*, Graz, 1977. S. Roaf, "Settlement Form and Qanat Routes in the Yazd Province," in P. Beaumont, M. Bonine, and K. McLachlan, eds., *Qanat, Kariz, and Khattara. Traditional Water Systems in the Middle East and North Africa*, London, 1989, pp. 58-60. A. Z. Rozenfel'd, "Qal'a (Kala)—tip ukreplennogo iranskogo poseleniya" (The *qal'a*—a type of fortified Iranian settlement), *Sovetskaya Etnografiya* 1, 1951, pp. 22-38.

V. I. Sarianidi, *Drevnie zemledel'tsy Afganistana* (Ancient farmers of Afghanistan), Moscow, 1977. Sāzmān-e naqša-bardārī-e kešvar, *Farhang-e joḡrāfīā'ī-e rūstāhā-ye Īrān*, Tehran, 1370 Š./1991-. H. F. Schurmann, *The Mongols of Afghanistan*, the Hague, 1962. G. Schweizer, "Dorfinventur in Iran," *Orient* 12, 1971, pp. 178-81. *Survey of Population and Agricultural Characteristics of a Sample of 413 Villages in Afghanistan, 1339*, Kabul, 1964. A. Szabo and T. J. Barfield, *Afghanistan. An Atlas of Indigenous Domestic Architecture*, Austin, Tex., 1991 (including monographs on four villages). S. P. Tolstov, "Gorodishcha s 'jilymi stenami'" (Villages with habitable walls), *Kratkie Soobshcheniya Instituta Istorii Material'noi Kultury* (Moscow) 17, 1947, pp. 4-5. E. Turri, "Villaggi fortificati in Iran e Afghanistan," *Rivista Geografica Italiana* 71, 1964, pp. 20-34. P. Vieille, "Les paysans, la petite bourgeoisie rurale et l'état après la réforme agraire en Iran," *Annales. Economies, Sociétés, Civilisations* 27/2, 1972, pp. 347-72. H.-J. Wald, *Landnutzung und Siedlung der Pashtunen im Becken von Khost*, Opladen, Germany, 1969.

(DANIEL BALLAND AND MARCEL BAZIN)

DEH-BOKRĪ, Kurdish tribe of Kurdistan. Henry Rawlinson (p. 34 n.), who visited northwestern Persia in 1838, referred to the Deh-bokrīs as a clan (*tīra*) of the Mokrī tribe. According to Basile Nikitine, the Deh-bokrīs were probably local inhabitants who were absorbed by the Mokrī tribe; he also suggested that the name Deh-bokrī was derived from Deh Mokrī (p. 165). According to a tribal legend, the Deh-bokrī chiefs had originated in Dīārbakr (q.v.) and their name reflects that origin, but, as Vladimir Minorsky pointed out (p. 191), it is much more likely that the name Deh-bokrī is derived from that of the village of Deh-e Bokr, situated 12 km southwest of Mahābād.

William Eagleton reported (p. 22) that the Deh-bokrīs "intermittently fought the Bilbas [see BELBĀS] during the eighteenth and nineteenth centuries but have since been fragmented." At the beginning of World War I, when Turkish forces penetrated into Kurdistan and Azerbaijan, they were joined by horsemen from the Bāna, Mangūr, Māmaš, and Deh-bokrī tribes. In December 1914 the Turks and their Kurdish allies defeated Persian forces at Mīāndoāb, then seized Tabrīz. In September 1921 the Deh-bokrīs and other Kurdish tribes of the Mahābād region participated in an uprising led by the Šaqāqī bandit and Kurdish nationalist Esmā'īl Āqā Sīmko/Semītqū (Arfa, pp. 27, 59).

The Deh-bokrīs played an important role in events in northwestern Persia during and immediately after World War II. When the Soviets occupied Kurdistan in August 1941, they at once started to replace Persian government officials with Kurds. By an agreement with Soviet authorities, the Persian government appointed the aged chief of the Deh-bokrīs, 'Alī Āqā Khan Amīr Asad, governor of Mahābād, but this appointment was strenuously opposed by the leaders of the other tribes in the region, like the Mangūr, Māmaš, Pīrān, Gowrīk, and Zarzā tribes. It was even rejected by several Deh-bokrī clan leaders. As a result, Amīr Asad was gradually rendered powerless (Arfa, p. 72).

When the autonomous Kurdish Republic was declared at Mahābād in February 1946 two Deh-bokrī leaders received cabinet portfolios: 'Abd-al-Raḥmān Īlkānīzāda became foreign minister and Esmā'īl Āqā

Īlḵānīzāda minister of roads. Major Jaʿfar Karīmī was appointed army chief of staff (Eagleton, pp. 69, 79).

The Deh-bokrīs have become sedentary, except for a few shepherds who summer the tribal flocks on neighboring high pastures. In 1342 Š./1963-64 the tribe was estimated at 4,700 households (Komīsīūn-e mellī, I, p. 123). The Īlḵānīzāda, ʿAlīyār, Qahramān, and ʿAbbāsī clans live in the *baḵš* of Būkān, southeast of Mahābād; the Karīmī clan lives along the Sāwj Bolāḡ river, north of Mahābād; and the ʿAzīzī, Pīrotī, Maʿrūfī, and Fatḥānī clans live in and around the town of Mahābād (Komīsīūn-e mellī, I, p. 123; Eagleton, p. 22). According to Minorsky (p. 191), the chief center of the tribe is the village of Deryās, 11 km north of Mahābād. There is also a group of Deh-bokrīs in the Saqqez region, comprising about 1,330 households (Komīsīūn-e mellī, p. 128), but very little is known about it.

Bibliography: Ī. Afšār Sīstānī, *Īlhā, čādornešīnān wa ṭawāyef-e ʿašāyerī-e Īrān* I, Tehran, 1366 Š./1987, pp. 199, 200, 256. H. Arfa, *The Kurds. An Historical and Political Study*, London, 1966. W. Eagleton, Jr., *The Kurdish Republic of 1946*, London, 1963. Komīsīūn-e mellī-e Yūnesko dar Īrān, *Īrān-šahr*, 2 vols., Tehran, 1342-43 Š./1963-64. M.-J. Maškūr, *Naẓar-ī be tārīḵ-e Āḏarbāyjān*, 1349 Š./1971, p. 194. V. Minorsky, "Sāwdj-Bulāḳ," in *EI*[1] IV, pp. 186-92. B. Nikitine, *Les Kurdes*, Paris, 1956. H. C. Rawlinson, "Notes on a Journey from Tabriz through Persian Kurdistan . . . in October and November 1838," *JRGS* 10, 1841, pp. 1-64. Razmārā, *Farhang* IV, pp. 98, 226.

(PIERRE OBERLING)

DEH MORĀSĪ ḠONDAY, a Bronze Age archeological site located at 34° 90′ N, 65° 30′ E, adjacent to the village of Deh Morāsī, approximately 27 km southwest of Qandahār and 6.5 km east-southeast of Pahjwāʾī in southeastern Afghanistan (Ball and Gardin, I, p. 90 no. 287). It is situated on a plain bounded by the Arḡandāb, Tarnak, and Dūrī rivers on the west, east, and south respectively. The mound (Pašto *ḡonday*) rises approximately 5.3 m above the surrounding plain and covers an area of 1.12 ha. The excavations at Deh Morāsī Ḡonday and at the nearby sites of Saʿīd Qaʿla Ḡonday (or Tepe; Shaffer, 1978a, pp. 149-65), 13 km to the northeast; Šamšīr Ḡār cave (Dupree, 1958), 9.5 km to the northwest; and Mondīgak (Casal), 60 km due north, account for most of what is known about Afghanistan in the Bronze and Early Iron Ages (Shaffer, 1978a; idem, 1992, I, pp. 459-64).

Deh Morāsī Ḡonday was discovered in 1951 by the Second Afghan Expedition of the American Museum of Natural History, New York; it was excavated by Louis Dupree (q.v.; 1963). Four trenches were opened, but only the largest (2 x 6 m) was excavated to sterile soil, at a depth of 6.6 m. The total exposed surface was small, so that it was impossible to define structures or patterns of settlement within the site. As a result, knowledge is limited to a narrowly defined cultural sequence derived from the stratigraphy and artifacts recovered.

Four sequential occupations were identified and designated Morāsī I-IV, but analysis indicates no significant differences among I-III, and they should therefore be considered a single analytical unit. Radiocarbon dates from this and sites with comparable material suggest that Morāsī I-III was occupied between 2500-2200/2000 B.C.E. The Morāsī IV deposits were disturbed and contained pottery from the South Asian early historic (after 500 B.C.E.) and Islamic periods; combined with intrusive Kushan burials in upper levels of occupation III, they thus suggest a long period of abandonment following Morāsī III.

Present data indicate that Deh Morāsī Ḡonday was a small Bronze Age agricultural village, dependent on cultivation of barley and raising of sheep, goats, and cattle. Although complete buildings or rooms were not defined, fragmentary mud-brick walls suggest that this ancient village may have resembled those found in the same region today. The only complete architectural feature was a small trapezoidal mud-brick stucture found in Morāsī II. Associated with it were goat remains, a copper tube, a terra-cotta female figurine, a steatite stamp seal, a fragment from an alabaster bowl, and a magnetite nodule that showed signs of use; Dupree interpreted the structure as a small household shrine (1963, p. 81). More important, the painted pottery associated with Morāsī I-III bears strong stylistic similarities to that from Saʿīd Qaʿla Ḡonday, Mondīgak late Period III-IV, Damb Sakaat (in the Quetta valley of Pakistan), and Šahr-e Sūḵta (in Persian Sīstān) Period III. These similarities, as well as parallels with terra-cotta figurines, stone tools, beads, metal artifacts, stamp seals, and other artifacts suggest that Bronze Age social groups throughout this region were closely linked in cultural networks encompassing urban centers like Mondīgak and Šahr-e Sūḵta, as well as small villages like Deh Morāsī Ḡonday. All these sites were abandoned after 2000 B.C.E., but the causes of the abandonment and the fate of the populations have yet to be determined in the archeological record.

Bibliography: W. Ball and J.-C. Gardin, *Archaeological Gazetteer of Afghanistan. Catalogue des sites archéologiques d'Afghanistan*, 2 vols., Paris, 1982. J.-M. Casal, *Fouilles de Mundigak*, 2 vols., Paris, 1961. L. Dupree, "Shamshir Ghar. Historic Cave Site in Kandahar Province, Afghanistan," *Anthropological Papers of the American Museum of Natural History* 46/2, 1958, pp. 141-311. Idem, "Deh Morasi Ghundai. A Chalcolithic Site in South-Central Afghanistan," *Anthropological Papers of the American Museum of Natural History* 50/2, 1963, pp. 59-135. J. G. Shaffer, "The Later Prehistoric Periods," in F. R. Allchin and N. Hammond, eds., *The Archaeology of Afghanistan*, London, 1978a, pp. 71-186. Idem, *Prehistoric Baluchistan*, Delhi, 1978b. Idem, "The Indus Valley, Baluchistan, and Helmand Traditions. Neolithic through Bronze Age," in R. W. Ehrich, ed.,

Chronologies in Old World Archaeology, 2nd ed., 2 vols., Chicago, 1992, I, pp. 441-64; II, pp. 425-46.

(JIM G. SHAFFER)

DEH-E NOW, site of a group of four rock-cut tombs of the 4th-3rd centuries B.C.E., located about 25 km south of Bīsotūn (q.v.) in Kermānšāhān, three of them in the mountains between the villages of Deh-e Now (Kurd. Di Nū) and Esḥāqvand (in Western sources often incorrectly rendered Sakavand; Kurd. Issaqavand), the fourth near the village of Sorḵa-deh (Kurd. Sūrḵa-deh). They provide important evidence for the development of *astōdān* (q.v.; ossuary) burial in Persia (Plate XIX). The group of three tombs has been hewn out of the sloping face of an isolated rock outcropping known locally as Farhād-taš (de Morgan, p. 300: Ferhatach) "the stone of Farhād," which is most easily accessible from Deh-e Now. The fourth, discovered by Oskar Mann (p. 328), is on the left bank of the Gāmāsāb river between Šamsābād and Sorḵa-deh, hewn into the cliff about 50 m above the river; it is known locally as Oṭāq-e Farhād (the chamber of Farhād).

The three tombs near Deh-e Now together extend across a surface a little more than 10 m wide, though at different heights above the ground. The facades are generally similar, each with a panel carved as a door bordered on three sides by a stepped frame (Plate XIX.a-c); the actual opening to the burial space is in the upper half of the panel. Above the entrance to the central tomb is a group of figural sculptures, important for the dating and understanding of this group of monuments. The tomb near Sorḵa-deh (Plate XIX.d) is of similar design, except that, like the remaining two tombs near Deh-e Now, it has no figural sculptures.

The dimensions of the chambers at Farhād-taš vary (Figure 9). Whereas the tomb on the left is a niche, rather than an actual chamber (width, including frame, ca. 3 m; width of opening 2.10 m; depth 0.84 m), the central tomb consists of a larger cavity 1.63 m wide and 1.75 m deep. The tomb on the right, the highest above the ground, consists of a chamber 2.10 m^2 (Figure 10.b). It is likely that this tomb is the oldest of the three, its highly placed entrance and its relatively spacious chamber linking it to the earlier monumental tombs of Media (von Gall, 1966; Huff, 1971; von Gall, 1988). As for the small tomb near Sorḵa-deh, its chamber is unfinished (maximum width 2.33 m, maximum depth 1.50 m), so that no conclusions can be drawn (Figure 10.a).

There remains the question whether or not the three tombs near Deh-e Now can be connected with Zoroastrian burial practices. It is not possible to identify all of them as *astōdāns*. Although the right-hand tomb may well have served as a repository for one or several corpses in outstretched position, the central chamber seems too small for such a burial, though it would be more than spacious enough for ossuaries. Even the left-hand tomb would permit the laying out of a corpse diagonally, though from the evidence of other rock-cut tombs in Media a trough in the floor would be expected for this purpose (von Gall, 1966, figs. 7, 8; idem, 1988, pl. 29c). It is thus possible that at least the two smaller tombs were *astōdāns*.

Of the sculptures above the opening to the central tomb the largest is a figure standing in relief against a ground that still shows the marks of the pick with which the surface of the panel was roughly prepared. Ernst Herzfeld (p. 206) interpreted this figure as the Magian usurper Gaumāta (March-September 522 B.C.E.); indeed it is striking to find represented in the center of Media a personage in the long Persian dress, unarmed, and with lifted hands, undoubtedly in an act of prayer (see CLOTHING ii). Gaumāta is depicted in similar dress on the rock relief at Bīsotūn (ca. 521 B.C.E; Luschey, p. 74). The hairdo covering the ears is clear evidence, however, that the figure near Deh-e Now cannot have been carved earlier than the mature Persepolis friezes. Furthermore, some of the evidence cited by Herzfeld in support of his interpretation (pp. 205-06) is no longer considered valid. For example, Fort Sikayauvatiš, where Gaumāta was slain, is not to be identified with Sakavand, which he considered a simplified spelling of the original Kurdish Issaqavand, composed from the proper name Issaq (Esḥāq). Sikayauvatiš must in fact be sought in the vicinity of Mount Bīsotūn (Kent, *Old Persian*, pp. 118, 209, 220; Luschey, p. 67).

To the right of the large figure there is a smaller panel reaching only as high as his waist but cut more deeply into the rock face than the large panel and breaking through the boundary of the latter on the right. On this panel three elements can be distinguished: to the left, immediately before the large figure and probably connected with it, a tall, unfinished object, evidently intended to be an incense burner, a royal and divine attribute (Gropp, p. 175; von Gall, 1972, p. 279); in the middle a low fire altar; and beside it a man wearing trousers and a tiara with a projection in front (von Gall, 1972, pp. 279-80) stoking the fire with a hook. The working of this panel, with a toothed chisel, represents a technical stage beyond that of the rough pick work on the surface of the large panel (Nylander, pp. 53 ff.). It therefore appears likely that there were two phases, the first in the Achaemenid period, when the larger figure was begun and left unfinished, the second probably in the early Hellenistic period, when the smaller panel and the actual chamber and its frame were carved. The smaller figure, apparently an *ātravaxš* (q.v.; Koch, pp. 159 ff.), was probably the later owner of the tomb, shown venerating the much larger figure. The latter's Elamite-Persian dress, in an area where the Median costume with trousers would be expected, suggests that a high Achaemenid state official is depicted. It would thus seem impossible to date this figure later than the breakdown of the Achaemenid empire (pace Huff, 1990, pp. 93-94; Boyce and Grenet, *Zoroastrianism*, pp. 98-99, favoring a Parthian date on the grounds of the figure's uncovered head and gesture). It

PLATE XIX

a

b

c

d

The rock-cut tombs near Deh-e Now. a. General view of the tombs at Farhād-taš. b. Left-hand tomb at Farhād-taš. c. Reliefs above the entrance to the central tomb at Farhād-taš. d. Rock-cut tomb near Sorḵa-deh.

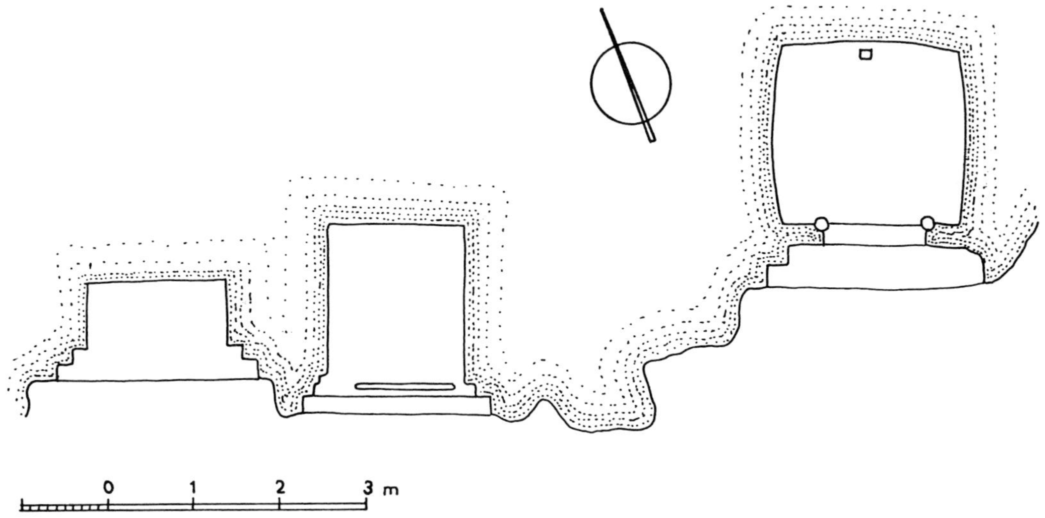

Figure 9. Plan of the rock-cut tombs at Farhād-taš near Deh-e Now.

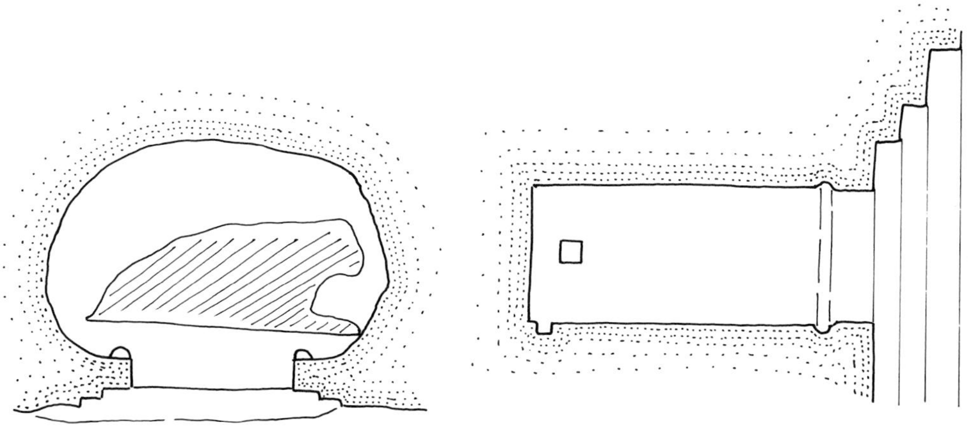

a b

Figure 10. a. Plan of the rock-cut tomb near Sork̲a-deh. b. Section of the right hand tomb at Farhād-taš.
Scale 1:50.

is not impossible that, at least in the later re-interpretation, the larger figure was understood as Gaumāta, but it must be emphasized that in Achaemenid art, particularly seals, the two priests flanking the fire altar, normally the magus and the *ātrevaxš*, are usually equal in height (von Gall, 1988, pp. 565-66).

Together with the evidence that two of the four tombs could have been *astōdān*s, this interpretation supports the view that the three tombs near Deh-e Now were those of Magians (von Gall, 1974, p. 143). According to Herodotus (1.140), the Magians were the first to practice open exposure of the dead. Undoubtedly the tombs near Deh-e Now and Sorḵa-deh represent an important stage in the development from the monumental Median rock-cut tombs with columned antechambers (von Gall, 1966; idem, 1974; idem, 1988; Huff, 1971) to the smaller rock-cut *astōdān*s found in Fārs (Gropp, pp. 205 ff.; von Gall, 1974, pp. 142 ff.; Huff, 1988).

Bibliography: H. von Gall, "Zu den 'medischen' Felsgräbern in Nordwestiran und Iraqi Kurdistan," *Archäologischer Anz.* 1966, pp. 19-43. Idem, "Persische und medische Stämme" *AMI*, N.F. 5, 1972, pp. 261-83. Idem, "Neue Beobachtungen zu den sog. medischen Felsgräbern," in *Proceedings of the IInd Annual Symposium on Archaeological Research in Iran 1973*, Tehran, 1974, pp. 139-54. Idem, "Das Felsgrab von Qizqapan. Ein Denkmal aus dem Umfeld der achämenidischen Königsstrasse," *Bagdader Mitteilungen* 19, 1988, pp. 557-82. M. Golzārī, *Kermānašāhān-e bāstān*, Tehran, n.d. (ca. 1974). G. Gropp, "Bericht über eine Reise in West- und Südiran," *AMI*, N.F. 3, 1970, pp. 173-230. E. Herzfeld, *Iran in the Ancient Near East*, London and New York, 1941. D. Huff, "Das Felsengrab von Fakhrikah," *Istanbuler Mitteilungen* 21, 1971, pp. 161-71. Idem, "Zum Problem zoroastrischer Grabanlagen in Fars I. Gräber," *AMI*, N.F. 21, 1988, pp. 145-76. Idem, "Das Grab von Doğubayazıt. Seine Stellung unter den urartäischen und iranischen Felsgräbern," in *X. Türk Tarih Kongresi 1986* I, Ankara, 1990, pp. 87-95. H. Koch, *Die religiösen Verhältnisse der Dariuszeit*, Göttinger Orientforschungen 4, Wiesbaden, 1977. H. Luschey, "Studien zu dem Darius-Relief von Bisutun," *AMI*, N.F. 1, 1968, pp. 63-94. O. Mann, "Archäologisches aus Persien," *Globus* 83, 1903, pp. 327-31. J. de Morgan, *Mission scientifique en Perse* IV/1, Paris, 1896. C. Nylander, *Ionians in Pasargadae*, Uppsala, 1970. F. Sarre and E. Herzfeld, *Iranische Felsreliefs*, Berlin, 1910. A. S. Shahbazi, *The Irano-Lycian Monuments*, Tehran, 1975. L. Vanden Berghe, *Archéologie de l'Iran ancien*, Leiden, 1959.

(Hubertus von Gall)

DEHBĪD, town in the *šahrestān* of Ābāda (q.v.), Fārs (30° 37′ N, 53° 12′ E), situated on the Shiraz-Isfahan road in a plain (elev. 2,300 m) 191 km northeast of Shiraz. The climate is dry and temperate. The Dehbīd river, which rises in the Gerdāb and Bīdestān mountains, flows south of the town, where it joins the Sīvand river. In the 10th century Dehbīd was mentioned by Maqdesī (Moqaddasī, p. 457) and Eṣṭaḵrī (p. 129) as a village and stage on the road from Eṣṭaḵr to Yazd and Khorasan. The construction of an octagonal caravansary (for a plan, see *EIr.* IV, p. 801 fig. 63[1]) in the late 16th century enhanced its importance and prosperity, which continued into the Qajar period. The caravansary stood near the hill known as Qaṣr-e Bahrām-e Gūr (Bahrām Gūr's palace), near which, according to local legend, the Sasanian king Bahrām V (420-38) was trapped in quicksand and vanished (Āl-e Dāwūd, pp. 35, 200-01, 254, 273); the upper portion of the mound probably dates from the Sasanian period (Moṣṭafawī, p. 364). Near the end of the reign of Nāṣer-al-Dīn Shah (1264-1313/1848-96) the caravansary was in ruins (Āl-e Dāwūd).

Today Dehbīd is a small town, with a population that has grown from 2,711 (856 households) in 1355 Š./1976 to 7,574 (1,505 households) in 1365 Š./1986 (Markaz-e āmār, 1361 Š./1982, p. 15; idem, 1368 Š./1989, pp. 20-21). The cause of this expansion may have been migration from surrounding villages. The town has a power station, a piped water supply, and a telephone network. There are a public library, a rural cooperative, and offices of several government agencies. The people are Shiʿite and are primarily occupied in agriculture, animal husbandry, and the service sector. Cottage industries include weaving of pile carpets, as well as *jājīm*s and *zīlū*s; weaving of vegetal fibers; and making soap. The chief agricultural products of the region are wheat, barley, pulses, grapes, apricots, and peaches. Sheep and goats are reared in abundance; in 1360 Š./1981 there were approximately 4,000 head of sheep in Dehbīd (Jehād-e sāzandagī, 1363 Š./1984b, p. 25).

A white-stone shrine, known as Boqʿa-ye šohadāʾ or Boqʿa-ye Solṭān Ebrāhīm, is situated 14 km southwest of Dehbīd. It consists of a courtyard 7.20 m^2, surrounded by four *ayvān*s (q.v.), the largest of which contains a prayer hall (*šabestān*), with its back wall oriented toward Mecca. It is elaborately decorated with glazed tiles (*moʿarraq*). Particularly fine is the tile-mosaic facing of the *moqarnas* (oversailing courses of niches set at angles to one another) over the entrance to the prayer chamber. The architecture of the shrine suggests either the Āq Qoyunlū or the Timurid period. Located about 3 km from Boqʿa-ye šohadāʾ is a cluster of several mounds known collectively as Qaṣr-e Yaʿqūb (Moṣṭafawī, pp. 6-7).

Bibliography: S. ʿA. Āl-e Dāwūd, ed., *Do safarnāma az janūb-e Īrān*, Tehran, 1368 Š./1989. Edāra-ye joḡrāfīāʾī-e arteš, *Farhang-e joḡrāfīāʾī-e ābādīhā-ye Īrān* XCIII, 1361 Š./1982, p. 75. Fasāʾī, ed. Rastgār, II, p. 873. *Gazetteer of Iran* III, pp. 205-06. Jehād-e sāzandagī, *Farhang-e ejtemāʿī-e dehāt o mazāreʿ-e ostān-e Fārs*, Tehran, 1363 Š./1984a, p. 25. Idem, *Farhang-e eqteṣādī-e dehāt o mazāreʿ-e ostān-e Fārs*, Tehran, 1363 Š./1984b, p. 25. Markaz-e āmār-e Īrān, *Āmār-nāma-ye ostān-e Fārs*, 1364 Š./1985. Idem, *Farhang-e ābādīhā-ye kešvar* (based on the census of 1355 Š./1976) XXIII, Tehran, 1361 Š./1982. Idem, *Sar-šomārī-e ʿomūmī-e nofūs o maskan-e šahrestān-e Ābāda* (based on the census of 1365 Š./1986), Tehran, 1368 Š./1989. M.-T. Moṣṭafawī, *Eqlīm-e Pārs*, Tehran, 1343 Š./1964. Razmārā, *Farhang* VII, p. 106.

(SAYYED ʿALĪ ĀL-E DĀWŪD)

DEHESTĀN (in modern Persian administrative usage a rural district consisting of a number of villages), the name of a region in medieval Gorgān and a town in Bādḡīs (qq.v.) and another in Kermān (Yāqūt, *Boldān*, II, p. 492).

Dehestān in Gorgān. The region of Dehestān (or perhaps Dahestān) lay southeast of the Caspian Sea, north of the Atrak river and the present-day province of Gorgān (qq.v.); it is now in the Turkmenistan Republic. Its name was probably derived from that of the Iranian steppe people the Dáai or Dahae (q.v.), a component tribe of which, the Aparna (q.v.), were progenitors of the Parthian ruling family (Bivar, p. 27; Lukonin, p. 686). Dehestān was somewhat vaguely defined by the classical Arabic and Persian geographers, and it is not unlikely that the physical configuration of the region, involving the Caspian shorelands and those along the course of the lower Atrak, has changed over the centuries. Maqdesī (Moqaddasī, pp. 358-59) described it as a rural area (*rostāq*) with twenty-four villages; its administrative center (*madīna*) was at Āḵor, but in this frontier region facing the Turkish steppes the most flourishing settlement was clearly the *rebāṭ* (stronghold), which was furnished with gates, markets, and a mosque. Ebn Ḥawqal (pp. 383, 388-89, 398; tr. Kramers, pp. 373, 378-79, 388) located it 50 farsangs from Abaskūn (q.v.) and mentioned another Dehestān situated on a peninsula jutting out from the eastern shore of the Caspian. In *Ḥodūd al-ʿālam* (p. 60, comm. p. 193) the latter was called Dehestān-e Sor (Sar?) and described as a resort only of fishermen and hunters of falcons and aquatic birds.

The town/*rebāṭ* of Dehestān was a pre-Islamic foundation attributed to the Arsacid Narsēh (Markwart, *Provincial Capitals*, pp. 12, 53-54) or to the Sasanian Qobād b. Fīrūz (*Nozhat al-qolūb*, p. 160; tr. p. 157). Its importance reflected above all its strategic position at a historic point of entry for steppe barbarians into civilized Iranian lands. At the time of the early Arab expansion north from Khorasan (late 7th century) Dehestān was held by a Turkish tribal group, the Ṣūl (Čöl?), ancestors of the celebrated Ṣūlī family of scholars in Arabic in the early ʿAbbasid period; in 98/715, in the time of the Arab governor Yazīd b. Mohallab, this group expelled the Persian *marzbān* of Gorgān, Fīrūz b. Qūl(?), and overran Gorgān (Ṭabarī, II, p. 1323; tr. XXIV, p. 48).

In late Samanid times Dehestān, along with Abīvard and Farāva (qq.v.), two other frontier towns on the northern rim of Khorasan facing the Kara Kum desert, came within the orbit of the Ḵʷārazmšāhs (see CHORASMIA ii) and then, after the fall of the last indigenous Persian line in 408/1017, passed to the Ghaznavids. In 426/1035 the Ghaznavid sultan Masʿūd I (421-32/1030-41) was forced to assign Dehestān, Farāva, and Nasā to the Saljuq chiefs Ṭoḡrel Beg, Čaḡrī Beg, and Yabḡū, who promised to act as frontier guards against further incursions from the steppes (Bayhaqī, ed. Fayyāż, p. 641; cf. Barthold, *Turkestan*³, p. 308; idem, 1962, pp. 105, 107). Thenceforth Dehestān remained in the hands of the Saljuqs until the decay of their power in the east, after which it was ruled by one Eḵtīār-al-Dīn Aytaq, who was forced, however, to flee to the Ḵʷārazmšāh Il-Arslan in 556/1161, abandoning Dehestān to be sacked by the Oghuz Turks (Barthold, 1962, p. 123). The region played some role in the campaigns of the Ḵʷārazmšāhs in eastern Persia during the subsequent decades (Barthold, *Turkestan*³, p. 338). Although it was mentioned several times in the 13th century (Jovaynī, ed. Qazvīnī, II, pp. 244, 274, III, p. 105; tr. Boyle, II, pp. 507, 538, 616), there is no record of its fate during the Mongol invasion.

In the 17th century the region was held by Turkmen tribesmen as vassals of the khans of Ḵīva (Barthold, 1962, p. 136), but gradually it ceased to be mentioned in the sources. From inscriptions on the mosque in the extensive ruins of what is now Mašhad-e Meṣrīān, built in the reign of the Ḵʷārazmšāh ʿAlāʾ-al-Dīn Moḥammad (596-617/1200-20), it seems clear thatthey were the site of the *rebāṭ* of Dehestān (Minorsky).

Bibliography: V. V. Barthold, *K istorii orosheniya Turkestana* (On the history of the irrigation of Turkestan), St. Petersburg, 1914; repr. in *Sochineniya* (Collected works) III, Moscow, 1962, pp. 96-231. Idem, *An Historical Geography of Iran*, tr. S. Soucek, Princeton, 1984, pp. 117-19. A. D. H. Bivar, "The Political History of Iran under the Arsacids," in *Camb. Hist. Iran* III/1, pp. 21-99. Eṣṭaḵrī, pp. 207, 214, 219, 226, 246. *Ḥodūd al-ʿālam*, tr. Minorsky, p. 133, comm. pp. 385-86. Le Strange, *Lands*, pp. 379-80. V. G. Lukonin, "Political, Social and Administrative Institutions. Taxes and Trade," in *Camb. Hist. Iran* III/2, pp. 680-746. Markwart, *Ērānšahr*, pp. 51, 73, 310. V. Minorsky, "Mas̲h̲had-i Miṣriyān," *EI*² VI, pp. 716-17. Moqaddasī, pp. 24, 312. Schwarz, *Iran* VI, p. 816. B. Spuler, "Dihistān 2," *EI*² II, p. 253.

Dehestān in Bādḡīs. The town of Dehestān lay northeast of Herat in the Paropamisus mountains, where the modern shrine of Ḵʷāja Dehestān is located; it was described by 10th-century geographers as half the size of Pūšang and seems to have been the center of the southern part of the district of Bādḡīs, though the governor (*solṭān*) lived at the smaller Kūḡanābād (Eṣṭaḵrī, pp. 268-69; Ebn Ḥawqal, pp. 440-41; tr. Kramers, p. 426; Moqaddasī, p. 308; cf. *Nozhat al-qolūb*, p. 153; tr. p. 151). By the early 13th century

Bavan (or Babna) had replaced Dehestān as the administrative center in the southern part of Bādḡīs (Yāqūt, *Boldān* I, p. 512). The houses of Dehestān were built of mud brick, but the indifferent water supply, brought largely through underground channels (*asrāb*), limited agriculture there (Moqaddasī, p. 308).

Dehestān played no significant role in history, nor does it seem to have had much cultural significance. Samʿānī did not record any scholar from there, and Yāqūt (*Boldān* II, p. 492) mentioned only Moḥammad b. Aḥmad b. Abi'l-Ḥajjāj Dehestānī Heravī, probably a traditionist.

Bibliography: Markwart, *Ērānšahr*, p. 150. Idem, *Wehrot und Arang*, Leiden, 1936, p. 40. B. Spuler, "Dihistān 1," *EI*², p. 253 (where the historical information is related to the Transcaspian Dehestān and not the one in Bādḡīs).

(C. EDMUND BOSWORTH)

DEHESTĀNĪ, AʿAZZ-AL-MOLK NEẒĀM-AL-DĪN ABU'L-MAḤĀSEN **ʿABD-AL-JALĪL** b. ʿAlī, twice vizier to the Saljuq sultan Barkīāroq (q.v.; 487-98/1094-1105).

In Rabīʿ I 493/January-February 1100, after Barkīāroq succeeded in taking control of Baghdad, he appointed Dehestānī vizier with the honorific Neẓām-al-Dīn. Slightly later, however, Barkīāroq was defeated at Espīdrūḏ near Hamadān by his brother Moḥammad b. Malekšāh, and Dehestānī was captured; he was well treated by Moḥammad's vizier, Moʾayyad-al-Molk b. Neẓām al-Molk, and was appointed civil governor of Baghdad. In the second battle between Barkīāroq and Moḥammad, in 494/1101, Barkīāroq was victorious, and Dehestānī again became vizier (Ṣafar 494/December 1101). Barkīāroq's extreme indigence and inability to pay his troops led Dehestānī to impose stringent financial mulcts and demands for taxation. Early in 495/1101, as he accompanied Barkīāroq at the siege of Isfahan, where Moḥammad was installed, he was murdered, either as an act of private vengeance or by an assassin of the Ismaʿilis, whose adherents in the region had recently been slaughtered by Barkīāroq's troops. Dehestānī was succeeded as vizier by Ḵaṭīr-al-Molk Abū Manṣūr Moḥammad b. Ḥosayn Maybodī.

The hostile picture of Dehestānī provided by Anūšervān b. Ḵāled (q.v.; Bondārī, p. 89) is that of a rapacious tyrant, but in Ebn al-Aṯīr's more balanced view (ed. Beirut, X, p. 336) he was generous and noble-minded, driven to his exactions only by the parlous state of his master's finances; he especially enjoyed the confidence of the merchant community, and the contemporary poet Abū Bakr Aḥmad Arrajānī included in his *dīvān* two Arabic *qaṣīdas* (odes) dedicated to Dehestānī.

Bibliography: Fatḥ b. ʿAlī Bondārī, *Zobdat al-noṣra wa noḵbat al-ʿoṣra*, in Houtsma, Recueil II. C. Defrémery, "Recherches sur le règne du sultan seldjoukide Barkiarok (485-498 de l'hégire 1092-1104 de l'ère chrétienne)," *JA*, ser. 5/2, 1853, pp. 254-61, 265-66, 287. Ebn al-Jawzī, *al-Montaẓam*, IX, pp. 112, 120. Ebn al-Aṯīr, ed. Beirut, X, pp. 294, 298-99, 304-05, 307-08, 311-12, 335-36. ʿA. Eqbāl, *Wezārat dar ʿahd-e salāṭīn-e bozorg-e saljūqī*, Tehran, 1338 Š./1959, p. 115-16, 151. C. L. Klausner, *The Seljuk Vezirate. A Study of Civil Administration 1055-1194*, Cambridge, Mass., 1973, pp. 39, 50, 53. Moḥammad b. ʿAlī Rāvandī, *Rāḥat al-ṣodūr wa āyat al-sorūr*, ed. M. Eqbāl, London, 1921, p. 139. M. F. Sanaullah, *The Decline of the Saljūqid Empire*, Calcutta, 1938, pp. 44-45.

(C. EDMUND BOSWORTH)

DEHESTĀNĪ, ḤOSAYN b. Asʿad b. Ḥosayn Moʾayyadī, Persian translator of the Arabic work *al-Faraj baʿd al-šedda* by Abū ʿAlī Moḥassen b. ʿAlī b. Dāwūd Tanūḵī (327-84/939-94), a collection of poems, anecdotes, sayings, and didactic remarks arranged in thirteen chapters on the general theme of joy following hardship; the translation, *Faraj-e baʿd az šeddat*, was dedicated to Dehestānī's patron ʿEzz-al-Dīn Ṭāher b. Zangī Faryūmadī, governor or vizier of Khorasan under the Il-khanid Abaqa Khan (663-80/1265-82; Spuler, *Mongolen*³, pp. 342-43). Nothing is known about Dehestānī except for what is contained in his own brief introductory remarks about how he prepared his translation (I, pp. 11-13).

Tanūḵī's work had already been translated a few decades earlier by Sadīd-al-Dīn Moḥammad ʿAwfī (q.v.); although that translation was lost, ʿAwfī had incorporated most of it into his *Jawāmeʿ al-ḥekāyāt* (ʿAwfī, 1352 Š./1973, introd., pp. 27-53; idem, *Lobāb*, I, introd., pp. *kj-kd*; Ṣafā, *Adabīyāt* II, p. 1030). As it is not yet possible to distinguish independently which portions of ʿAwfī's text were taken from Tanūḵī's original, Dehestānī's translation can be said to be the earliest available Persian translation.

Bibliography: Sadīd-al-Dīn Moḥammad ʿAwfī, *Jawāmeʿ al-ḥekāyāt wa lawāmeʿ al-rewāyāt* I, pt. 3, ed. B. Moṣaffā (Karīmī), Tehran, 1352 Š./1973. Ḥosayn b. Asʿad Dehestānī, *Faraj-e baʿd az šeddat*, ed. E. Ḥākemī, 3 vols., Tehran, 1363-64 Š./1984-85. H. Ethé, "Neupersische Literatur," in *Grundriss* II, pp. 329-30. Rieu, *Persian Manuscripts* II, p. 751. Ṣafā, *Adabīyāt* III/2, pp. 1234-36.

(MOḤAMMAD DABĪRSĪĀQĪ)

DEHḴᵛĀRAQĀN. See ĀẔARŠAHR.

DEHḴODĀ, MĪRZĀ ʿALĪ-AKBAR QAZVĪNĪ (also known as Daḵow; b. Tehran, ca. 1297/1879, d. Tehran, 7 Esfand 1334 Š./26 February 1956), scholar, poet, and social critic. His father, Ḵānbābā b. Āqā Khan b. Mehr-ʿAlī Qazvīnī, a landowner in Qazvīn before moving to Tehran, died when ʿAlī-Akbar was only nine years old. ʿAlī-Akbar studied Arabic, jurisprudence (*feqh*), theology, and philosophy with Shaikh Ḡolām-Ḥosayn Borūjerdī for ten years; he also came under the influence of the liberal cleric Ḥājj Shaikh Hādī Najmābādī (Dehḵodā, 1334 Š/1955, p. 4). He was a member of the first class at the School of political sciences (Madrasa-ye ʿolūm-e sīāsī), which was opened in 1317/1899; he left without taking his first-year examinations but returned two years later (Mostawfī, Šarḥ-e zendagānī II, pp. 71, 79). After graduation he was employed as secretary to Moʿāwen-al-Dawla Ḡaffārī Kāšānī, Persian ambassador to the Balkans, and went to Europe with him in 1321/1903; he remained there for two years, mainly in Austria, and returned to Persia in 1323/1905 (Dehḵodā, 1334 Š./1955, p. 4). In 1324/1906 he was engaged by Ḥājj Moḥammad-Ḥosayn Amīn-al-Żarb (q.v.) as interpreter for the French engineers who were building the high-way between Khorasan and Tehran ("Do yādgār," p. 178). After the promulgation of the constitutional decree in 1324/1906 Mīrzā Jahāngīr Khan Šīrāzī and Mīrzā Qāsem Khan Tabrīzī conceived the idea of publishing the newspaper Ṣūr-e Esrāfīl and hired Dehḵodā as editorial secretary and contributor, at a monthly salary of forty tomans (Taqīzāda, in Loḡat-nāma, p. 395; see CONSTITUTIONAL REVOLUTION ii, vi).

The constitutional period was an era of journalistic efflorescence. Most journalists, however, had no real writing skill, were ill acquainted with the world outside Persia, and lacked understanding of such concepts as freedom, equality, and constitutional government. The journals for which they worked often disappeared after the first few issues. Ṣūr-e Esrāfīl, however, reflected its founders' passionate devotion to liberal ideas. Dehḵodā, a gifted writer, was trained in political theory, and, thanks to his knowledge of French and his European travel, he also had a sophisticated under-standing of world affairs. He was thus able, through his well-reasoned and clearly written political articles in Ṣūr-e Esrāfīl, to attract a wide audience, particularly for his satirical series Čarand parand (q.v.), which was the main reason for the the rise in the number of printed copies of the newspaper to a high of 24,000 (Mostawfī, Šarḥ-e zendagānī II, pp. 249-50), far higher than those of even the best contemporary publications.

After the coup d'etat of Moḥammad-ʿAlī Shah (1324-27/1907-09) in 1326/1908 Dehḵodā, fearing retalia-tion from the court and the reactionary clergy, joined several other notable constitutionalists in taking ref-uge at the British legation in Tehran (Dawlatābādī, Ḥayāt-e Yaḥyā II, p. 342; Taqīzāda, 1358 Š./1979, p. 76; Mostawfī, Šarḥ-e zendagānī II, p. 262). Owing to the intervention of British officials, he received a safe-conduct and left for Baku and eventually Paris, where he remained for about a year and a half, until 11 Moḥarram 1328/23 January 1910. This exile was one of the most stressful periods of his life. Not only did the agents of the Persian government persecute his relatives and associates, but he himself was also suf-fering from depression and poverty (Dehḵodā, 1368 Š./1989, p. 803; Afšār, 1358 Š./1979c, p. 520; idem, 1359 Š./1980, p. 423), yet he never slackened in his literary and journalistic activity. From Paris he went

to Switzerland, where in Yverdon he published a new series of Ṣūr-e Esrāfīl, which appeared 1 Moḥarram-15 Ṣafar 1327/23 January-8 March 1909; it was printed in Paris (Dehḵodā, 1358 Š./1979a, p. 114). The cost of publication and smuggling copies to Persia, where distribution was not permitted, were high, but eager readers passed each copy from hand to hand (Mostawfī, Šarḥ-e zendagānī II, p. 263). Nevertheless, Dehḵodā's desperation reached such a point that he began to think of suicide. Instead, he went to Germany and resumed publication there, but again there were difficulties, and he moved on to Istanbul, hoping for assistance or employment from the Persian community there (Dehḵodā, 1368 Š./1989, p. 803; Dawlatābādī, Ḥayāt-e Yaḥya III, p. 101). With the help of Mīrzā Abu'l-Ḥasan Khan Moʿāżed-al-Salṭana, the head of Anjoman-e saʿādat (q.v.), he, Ḥājj Mīrzā Yaḥyā Dawlatābādī (q.v.), and Ḥosayn Dāneš undertook publication of a newspaper called Sorūš. It seems that Persian mer-chants living in Istanbul assumed the cost of the early numbers of this journal. Again, however, the difficul-ties of ensuring that copies reached Persian subscrib-ers caused the cessation of publication after fourteen or fifteen issues (Raʿdī Āḏarakšī, p. 428; Moʿīn, p. 5; Reżwānī, pp. 504-05; Ṣadr Hāšemī, Jarāʾed o majallāt III, pp. 34-35).

After the overthrow of Moḥammad-ʿAlī Shah Dehḵodā returned to Persia, on 11 Moḥarram 1328/23 January 1910 (Ṣadr Hāšemī, Jarāʾed o majallāt III, p. 25). In the same year he was elected by the people of both Kermān and Tehran to represent them in the Second Majles. His popularity in Kermān was owing to his criticisms in Čarand parand of the heavy-handed government of Fīrūz Mīrzā Noṣrat-al-Dawla (Mostawfī, Šarḥ-e zendagānī II, p. 291; Ṣūr-e Esrāfīl nos 3, p. 4; 6, p. 5; 13, p. 4; 16, p. 5; 19, p. 4; 21, p. 4). In 1332/1914, with Persia in the grip of British and Russian occupation, Dehḵodā took refuge with the Baḵtīārī tribes in Čahār Maḥāl. After his return he served for a short period in the Ministry of education (Wezārat-e maʿāref) with the title "head of the secre-tariat" (raʾīs-e kābīna) and in the Ministry of justice (Wezārat-e ʿadalīya) with the title "head of the office of investigation" (raʾīs-e edāra-ye taftīš). In 1303 Š./1924 he was appointed director of the Madrasa-ye ʿolūm-e sīāsī, where he served until 1320 Š./1941 ("Sālšomār," p. 429; Dehḵodā, 1358 Š./1979a, pp. xv-xvi, xix).

During his stay among the Baḵtīārī Dehḵodā con-ceived the idea of compiling an encyclopedic dictio-nary of the Persian language, and on his return to Tehran he applied himself to assembling the prelimi-nary materials. He also continued his literary and scholarly activities, publishing articles in such jour-nals as Īrān-e konūnī, Āftāb, and Dāneš (Dehḵodā, 1358 Š./1979a, pp. xii-xvi; Ṭabāṭabāʾī, p. 238).

In the atmosphere of strict censorship under Reżā Shah (1304-20 Š./1925-41) Dehḵodā put aside his political activities and devoted himself entirely to scholarly and literary work. The fruit of this period of his life includes the four-volume collection of aphorisms *Amṯāl o ḥekam* (4 vols., Tehran, 1304-11 Š./1925-32) and the first volume of his *Loḡat-nāma*, which appeared in 1318 Š./1939, as well as a number of scholarly articles on Persian literature and language. He continued to concentrate on the *Loḡat-nāma* through the first decade of Moḥammad-Reżā Shah's reign (1320-57 Š./1941-79). In 1330 Š./1951 Moḥammad Moṣaddeq came to power, and the movement to nationalize the oil industry was gaining momentum; in the prevailing atmosphere of political excitement Dehḵodā once more turned to politics, joining the Anjoman-e havādārān-e ṣolḥ (Society of the supporters of peace), a group with socialist tendencies. Although the leaders of the Tudeh party (see COMMUNISM ii) sought to attract the support of well-known Persian cultural figures, Dehḵodā instead declared his support for Moṣaddeq (*Bāḵtar-e emrūz*, 23 Tīr 1332 Š./15 July 1953). After the coup d'etat of 1332 Š./1953 (q.v.) and the restoration of the shah to power, Dehḵodā withdrew entirely from political activity and devoted the rest of his life to the *Loḡat-nāma*. He was, however, interrogated several times on the allegation that he had been chosen president of the ruling council (Šūrā-ye salṭanatī) that was supposed to have been formed after the shah's flight to Rome on 25 Mordād 1332/16 August 1953 (Dehḵodā, 1360 Š./1981b; idem, 1358 Š./1979a, p. xxi; Moḥīṭ Ṭabāṭabāʾī, p. 467). He is buried in the Ebn Bābūya cemetery in southern Tehran.

Although Dehḵodā never enjoyed wealth or affluence, he was always open-handed. He devoted the royalties from *Amṯāl o ḥekam* to subsidies for printing new books and for the care of the sick (Dehḵodā, 1358 Š./1979a, pp. xxiii-xxiv; Dabīrsīāqī, 1358 Š./1979, p. 455).

Social thought. Dehḵodā's youth coincided with the last decade of Nāṣer-al-Dīn Shah's rule, when, owing to the major role of the clerics in the successful campaign aginst the tobacco concession, new populist forces were unleashed in Persian politics (see CONSTITUTIONAL REVOLUTION i). Religious leaders wielded considerable influence in everyday life, and many of them became prominent landowners (see CLASS SYSTEM iv). In the new liberalizing atmosphere after promulgation of the Constitution Dehḵodā, who had seen the effects of modernization in Europe and was well informed about the reformist ideas of Western thinkers and statesmen, strongly criticized the undue influence of the mullas, their intellectual rigidity, their corruption, and the blind obedience of the Persian people. His fierce attacks on the royalist Shaikh Fażl-Allāh Nūrī, who vehemently opposed reform movements and considered modern educational institutions "contrary to religious law" (*ḵelāf-e šarīʿat*), brought about the temporary suspension of publication of *Ṣūr-e Esrāfīl* (nos. 4, p. 6; 5, p. 2; 6, pp. 6-7; Dehḵodā, 1364 S./1985, p. 17-23, 314; Taqīzāda, in *Loḡat-nāma*, p. 395; Torkamān, pp. 262-63).

Dehḵodā was a firm believer in equality before the law, regardless of religious belief (*Ṣūr-e Esrāfīl*, no. 22, p. 3), and he fervently supported emancipation of women, particularly abolition of the veil (*Ṣūr-e Esrāfīl*, no. 11, p. 6). Owing to his early exposure to the ideas of Najmābādī, he was convinced that, over the course of centuries, Islam itself had been unduly manipulated by religious jurists (*šarīʿatsāzān*). He himself, as one who had to earn his living, was aware of the difficulties faced by ordinary folk and the widespread injustices of the landlord-peasant system. Aside from his campaign against what he considered religious superstition, the greater part of his articles were written in support of the peasants and laborors. One of his most important proposals was for establishment of an agricultural bank, to which large landowners would turn over one-tenth of their holdings at a reasonable price, to be converted into small shares and transferred to the peasants, who would pay for them in installments (see, e.g., *Ṣūr-e Esrāfīl*, nos. 18, p. 22, 19, pp. 1-2, 21, p. 2).

Dehḵodā also wrote and translated a series of articles on the Russian Revolution, striving to familiarize his readers with social and political topics through explanation and criticism of the various political parties and factions involved. He was personally convinced that, in the conditions prevailing in Persia, the program of the Social democrats (Ejtemāʿīyūn-e ʿāmmīyūn) was most appropriate (*Ṣūr-e Esrāfīl*, no. 28, pp. 1-4). After he was elected to the Majles he joined the Eʿtedālīyūn (Moderate) faction ("Sālšomār," p. 428; Bāmdād, *Rejāl* II, p. 429; Mostawfī, *Šarḥ-e zendagānī* II p. 320).

Prose and poetry. Dehḵodā's prose enjoys a special distinction in the Persian literature of this century. His profound familiarity with Persian classical literature, both prose and verse; his prodigious store of current proverbs, partly derived from his work on *Amṯāl o ḥekam*; and his early involvement in journalism, with the concomitant need to attract large numbers of readers, all helped to develop a clearly understandable style far removed from the ornate artificiality that characterizes the prose of the Qajar period. His knowledge of French, though it brought him awareness of Western literature, never led him to adopt a "Western" coloration or to incorporate French borrowings into his own work. Even *Čarand parand*, which was filled with puns, ambiguities, allusions, and intimations (*īhāmāt, kenāyāt, talmīḥāt*), owed its success to the fact that it was intelligible to ordinary folk and at the same time entertaining to the intellectual elite and sophisticated men of letters. In Dehḵodā's serious political articles convoluted and artificial expression is also lacking, though his editorials in *Sorūš* and his satirical pieces for *Īrān-e konūnī* do not have the same bite as the original *Čarand parand* series in *Ṣūr-e Esrāfīl*. The difference is so great in fact that some have suspected that the latter was actually written by Mīrzā Jahāngīr Khan (Moḥīṭ Ṭabāṭabāʾ). The pieces in the numbers of *Ṣūr-e Esrāfīl* printed in Switzerland were, however, written months after the execution of Mīrzā Jahāngīr Khan, and it therefore seems certain that Dehḵodā himself wrote them after what he called five months of silence (*Ṣūr-e Esrāfīl* [Yverdon], no. 1,

p. 7). The disparity in tone may instead be attributed to the change in Dehkodā's own circumstances. He wrote for *Ṣūr-e Esrāfīl* as a member of the disenfranchised elements in Persian society, but six years later he had become a deputy to the Majles and himself a member of the ruling elite.

Although Dehkodā was not primarily a poet and his poems are mainly exercises in versification, he has nevertheless earned a place in the history of contemporary poetry. His modest output includes *ḡazal*s and other pieces in the classical style, each written exclusively in the language of the time of the poet being emulated. For example, in "Līsak" (Dehkodā, 1334 Š/1955, p. 113), which was composed in imitation of Rūdakī, there is not a single word or expression that was not to be found in the Persian lexicon of the 10th century. Similarly, at the request of Ḥabīb Yaḡmāʾī he composed a poem in the style of Bahrāmī Saraksī (*Yaḡmā* 3, 1329 Š./1950, p. 81; Dehkodā, 1334 Š./1955, p. 86). Some of these "imitations" are actually superior in lucidity, expository power, and elegance of expression to the originals, including even some from Saʿdī's *Būstān* (e.g., Dehkodā, 1334 Š/1955, pp. 119, 120, 31).

Dehkodā also wrote a *mosammaṭ* and two *maṯnawī*s (in both Turkish and Persian; Dehkodā, 1334 Š./1955, pp. 124-32), also in the popular (*ʿawāmāna*) manner. Because of his ingenious use of slang expressions his poetry includes the best examples of popular Persian verse ever written. A third group of poems consists of *maṯnawī*s in which he used allegory and narrative to expound his social ideas; as these pieces were aimed at the educated class, he did not hesitate to use all manner of allusions to the Koran and works of *feqh* and belles lettres, as well as archaic expressions. In *Enšāʾ Allāh gorba ast* (God willing it's a cat!) his powerful portrayal of the mien and behavior of a hypocritical *ākūnd* (q.v.) is almost without equal in Persian literature (Dehkodā, 1334 Š/1955, p. 5). Among other literary works were annotations to the *Dīvān* of Nāṣer-e Kosrow (ed. S. N. Taqawī, Tehran, 1307 Š./1928, pp. 619 ff.), the *Dīvān* of Sayyed Ḥasan Ḡaznavī (ed. M.-T. Modarres Rażawī, Tehran, 1328 Š./1949, pp. 361-76), *Loḡat-e fors* (unpubl.), and the *Dīvān* of Ḥāfeẓ, which appeared in the journals *Yaḡmā* and *Dāneš*. He also wrote a biography of Abū Rayḥān Bīrūnī (q.v.), edited the *Ṣeḥāḥ al-fors* (*Yaḡmā* 3, 1329 Š./1950, pp. 321-26, 366-70, 416-20, 480-85; *Dāneš* 3, pp. 197-202, 269-72, 371-78, 491-98, 549-54, 637-42) by Moḥammad b. Hendūšāh Nakjavānī and the *dīvān*s of Manūčehrī Dāmḡānī, Farrokī Sīstānī, Sūzanī Samarqandī, and (parts of) Masʿūd-e Saʿd-e Salmān (Moʿīn, 1335 Š./1956, pp. 295-301). Editing and publication of his monumental *Loḡat-nāma* (q.v.) were completed after his death under the supervision of the late Moḥammad Moʿīn.

In all his writing Dehkodā was a perfectionist and a meticulous craftsman. He was a nationalist, outspoken in his convictions, indifferent to the wrath of powerful men, and a firm believer in Persian culture (Dehkodā, 1358 Š./1979c, pp. 912-14; Afšār, 1358 Š./1979c, p. 522).

Bibliography: Ī. Afšār, "ʿAlī-Akbar Dehkodā," *FIZ* 3, 1334 Š./1975, pp. 408-10. Idem, "Mobārezāt-e Dehkodā wa yārān-aš ʿalayh-e Moḥammad-ʿAlī Šāh dar Orūpā," *Negīn*, 1358 Š/1979a, 167, pp. 23-34; 168, pp. 28-34; 169, pp. 26-33. Idem, "Nokta-ī maktūm-mānda az Dehkodā. Kīāl-e tābeʿīyat-e ʿoṯmānī," *Negīn*, 172, 1358 Š./1979b, pp. 23-26. Idem, "Ṣūr-e Esrāfīl," *Āyanda* 5, 1358 Š./1979c, pp. 509-47. Idem, ed., *Awrāq-e tāzayāb-e mašrūṭīyat wa naqš-e Taqīzāda*, Tehran, 1359 Š./1980, p. 241. Bāmdād, *Rejāl* II, pp. 429-30. M. Dabīrsīāqī, "*Amṯāl o ḥekam*-e Dehkodā," *Āyanda* 5, 1358 Š./1979, pp. 451-60. Idem, "Kāṭerāt-ī az Dehkodā wa az zabān-e Dehkodā," *Nāma-ye nūr* 10/11, 1359 Š./1981, pp. 13-48. ʿA.-A. Dehkodā, *Abū Rayḥān Bīrūnī*, Tehran, 1324 Š./1945. Idem, *Dīvān-e Dehkodā*, ed. M. Moʿīn, Tehran, 1334 Š./1955; ed. M. Dabīrsīāqī, Tehran, 1360 Š./1981a (review Ḥ. Aṣīl, *Āyanda* 8, 1361 Š./1982, pp. 271-79). Idem, *Maqālāt-e Dehkodā*, ed. M. Dabīrsīāqī, 2 vols., 1358-64 Š./1979a-85. Idem, *Nāmahā-ye sīāsī-e Dehkodā*, ed. Ī. Afšār, Tehran, 1358 Š./1979b. Idem, "Nāma-ye Dehkodā be Edāra-ye eṭṭelāʿāt-e Emrīkā," *Āyanda* 5, 1358 Š./1979c, pp. 912-14. Idem, "Nāma-ī az Dehkodā be Yaḡmāʾī," *Āyanda* 7, 1360 Š./1981b, pp. 78-79. Idem, "Nāma-ye tāzayāb-ī az Dehkodā," *Āyanda* 15, 1368 Š./1989, pp. 803-06. "Do yādgār az ʿAlī-Akbar Dehkodā," *Āyanda* 8, 1361 Š./1982, pp. 178-83. W. Dorūdīān, *Dehkodā-ye šāʿer*, Tehran, 1355 Š./1976; 2nd ed., Tehran, 1358 Š./1979.

M. Golbon, "Rūz-nāma-negārī-e Dehkodā wa rūz-nāma-ye *Rūḥ al-qodos*," *Āyanda* 5, 1358 Š./1979, pp. 490-99. *Moḏākarāt-e Majles. Dawra-ye awwal-e taqnīnīya*, Tehran, 1325 Š./1946, pp. 331-60. M. Moḥīṭ Ṭabāṭabāʾī, "Doktor Moṣaddeq o Dehkodā," *Āyanda* 5, 1358 Š./1979, pp. 462-67. M. Moʿīn, "Dehkodā," in Dehkodā, *Loḡat-nāma*, pp. 379-94. Idem, "Čerāḡ-ī ke kāmūš šod," *Yaḡmā* 9/6, 1335 Š./1956, pp. 294-301. B. Moʾmenī, *Ṣūr-e Esrāfīl*, Tehran, 1357 Š./1978. M. Moṣaddeq, *Kāṭerāt wa taʾallomāt-e Moṣaddeq*, ed. Ī. Afšār, Tehran, 1358 Š./1979, pp. 85-86. ʿA. Qanbarzāda, *Aḥwāl o afkār-e Ostād ʿAlī-Akbar Dehkodā*, Tehran, 1355 Š./1976. Ḡ. Raʿdī Āḏarakšī, "Šeʿr-e Dehkodā," *Āyanda* 5, 1358 Š./1979, pp. 432-49. M.-E. Reżwānī, "Sorūš-e Rūm o Sorūš-e Ray," *Āyanda* 5, 1358 Š./1979, pp. 501-08. "Sālšomār-e zendagānī-e Dehkodā," *Āyanda* 5, 1358 Š./1979, pp. 428-30. ʿA.-A. Sīāsī, *Gozāreš-e yak zendagī*, London, 1366 Š./1987, pp. 89-90, 393-95. M.-A. Ṭabāṭabāʾī, "Yād-ī az Dehkodā," *Āyanda* 7, 1360 Š./1981, pp. 237-39. S. Ḥ. Taqīzāda, "Dehkodā," in Dehkodā, *Loḡat-nāma*, pp. 394-96; repr. in *Āyanda* 5, pp. 565-69. Idem, *Zendagānī-e ṭūfānī. Kāṭerāt-e Sayyed Ḥasan Taqīzāda*, Tehran, 1358 Š./1979, pp. 73, 92, 95, 106, 124, 342. M. Torkamān, *Rasāʾel, eʿlāmīyahā, mokātabāt wa rūz-nāmahā-ye Šayk-e Šahīd Fażl-Allāh Nūrī* I, Tehran, 1362 Š./1983. Ḡ.-Ḥ. Yūsofī, "Dakow," in Ḡ.-Ḥ.

Yūsofī, *Dīdār-ī bā ahl-e qalam* II, Mašhad, 1358 Š./1979, pp. 149-84.

(ʿALĪ-AKBAR SAʿĪDĪ SĪRJĀNĪ)

DEHLAVĪ, SHAH WALĪ-ALLĀH QOṬB-AL-DĪN AḤMAD ABU'L-FAYYĀŻ (1114-76/1703-62), leading Muslim intellectual of India and writer on a wide range of Islamic topics in Arabic and Persian; more than thirty-five of his works are extant (for an annotated list, see Baljon, pp. 8-14). He was educated by his father, the well-known scholar Shah ʿAbd-al-Raḥīm ʿOmarī (1131/1719), founder and principal of the Raḥīmīya Madrasa in Delhi. At the age of fifteen years Shah Walī-Allāh was initiated into the Naqšbandī Sufi order by his father and assigned to teach at the Raḥīmīya, of which he became principal in 1131/1719. In 1143/1731 he made the pilgrimage to Mecca. He remained fourteen months in Medina studying Hadith, Islamic law (*feqh*), and mysticism with such eminent scholars as Shaikh Abū Ṭāher Kordī Madanī; he was much influenced by the emerging cosmopolitan tendency in Hadith scholarship, a blend of North African, Ḥejāzī, and Indian traditions of study and verification (Voll, p. 266). He also developed a particular respect for the *Mowaṭṭaʾ* of Mālek b. Anas (d. 179/796) and later wrote two commentaries on it, in Arabic and Persian (respectively entitled *Mosawwā* and *Moṣaffā*; facs. ed., 2 vols., Karachi, 1980).

Shah Walī-Allāh returned to India in 1145/1732 and devoted himself to teaching, writing, and leadership of his Sufi order. During the next decade he wrote his major work, *Ḥojjat-Allāh al-bāleḡa* in Arabic (ed. S. Sābeq, 2 vols., Cairo, 1952-53); in it he called for restoration of the Islamic sciences through the revival of Hadith studies within a proper framework. Other works range over the entire gamut of the Islamic religious sciences, from koranic and Hadith studies to law and mysticism. Many of his works are characterized by a systematic historical approach coupled with concern for explaining and reconciling divisive tendencies; in these writings his mystical outlook was kept in the background. He also formulated a unique set of terms and concepts (e.g., *ertefāqāt*) to explain the mystical theophanies underlying historical development (*eqterābāt*). One group of Shah Walī-Allāh's successors, best exemplified by his closest disciple and cousin, Moḥammad ʿĀšeq (1187/1773), seems to have been influenced by his mystical inclinations; in fact, there is some evidence that he had envisioned establishing his own eclectic Sufi order (*Tafhīmāt* II, pp. 5-98).

Shah Walī-Allāh's works in Persian include *Alṭāf al-qods fī maʿrefa laṭāʾef al-nafs* (ed. ʿA. Sorātī, Gujranwala, India, 1964; tr. G. H. Jalbani, ed. D. Pendlebury as *The Sacred Knowledge of the Higher Functions of the Mind*, London, 1982), in which the psychospiritual journey of the Sufi is detailed (Hermansen, 1988b, pp. 12 ff.); *Entebāh fī salāsel awlīāʾ Allāh*, on Sufi rituals, chains of authority (*esnād*), and hagiography (Baljon, p. 11; the sections on transmission of Hadith and *feqh*, ed. M. ʿA. Ḥanīf as *Ettehāf al-nabīh fī mā yoḥtaj elayh al-moḥaddeṯ wa'l-faqīh*, Lahore, 1969); *Faṭh al-raḥmān fī tarjamat al-Qorʾān*, an annotated Persian translation of the Koran (compl. 1151/1738; Karachi, n.d.), in which he tried to strike a balance between literal rendering and fidelity to the sense of the text; *al-Fawz al-kabīr fī-oṣūl al-tafsīr*, a study of the principles of koranic commentary in which he elaborated on stylistic and exegetical elements of five major themes (Karachi, 1964; tr. G. H. Jalbani as *The Principles of Quran Commentary*, Islamabad, 1985); *Hamaʿāt*, an early work focusing on the historical development of Sufism and the practices and relative orientations of major Sufi orders (Lahore, 1964; sections tr. Mir Valiuddin as *Contemplative Disciplines in Sufism*, ed. G. Khakee, London, 1980); *al-Moqaddama fī qawānīn al-tarjama*, a still-unpublished short treatise on the proper translation of the Koran; *Saṭaʿāt* (ed. Ḡ. M. Qāsemī, Hyderabad, Sind, 1964; tr. G. H. Jalbani as *Sufism and the Islamic Tradition. The Lamahat and Sataʿat of Shah Waliullah*, ed. D. B. Fry, London, 1980), a treatise on mystical philosophy reflecting the emanationist outlook of the school of Ebn al-ʿArabī (q.v.); *Qorrat al-ʿaynayn fī tafżīl al-šayḵayn* (facs. ed., Lahore, 1976) and *Ezālat al-ḵafā ʿan ḵelāfat al-ḵolafāʾ* (facs. ed., Lahore, 1976), two works supporting the Sunni position on the succession of the early caliphate (Rizvi, pp. 249-56); and *al-Tafhīmāt al-elāhīya* (ed. Ḡ. M. Qāsemī, 2 vols., Hyderabad, Sind, 1969-70), which is partly in Arabic, a summation of Shah Walī-Allāh's thoughts on various topics at a mature age.

Shah Walī-Allāh also wrote a number of small literary and didactic treatises, including *Hawāmī* (Delhi, 1308/1890), a Persian commentary on the Šāḏelī Sufi litany *Ḥezb al-baḥr*. His Persian letters are preserved in several Indian libraries (Rizvi, pp. 224-28). Ḵāleq Aḥmad Neẓāmī edited and translated into Urdu selections from one set under the title *Šāh Walī-Allāh Dehlavī ke sīāsī maktūbāt* (Aligarh, 1950; repr. Delhi, 1969); this collection stimulated considerable debate over whether Shah Walī-Allāh's role in history was primarily that of a scholar with mystical inclinations or that of a Muslim nationalist.

Dehlavī was married twice and had five sons and one daughter (Baljon, p. 4). His shrine is in a cemetery at Delhi. His teachings were carried on by his descendants, particularly his sons Shah ʿAbd-al-ʿAzīz (d. 1239/1823) and Shah Rafīʿ-al-Dīn (d. 1234/1818) and his grandson Shah Esmāʿīl Šahīd (d. 1246/1831). The reforming and Muslim nationalist tendencies of this notable family have sometimes been designated the "Walī-Allāhī movement" (Sindhī; Ahmad, pp. 201-17). Today Shah Walī-Allāh is invoked as an intellectual pregenitor of all major religious movements in Muslim South Asia. Groups with a more puritanical outlook hostile to Sufism find support for their own ideas in his emphasis on the fundamentals of the Islamic sciences and his rejection of certain local customs. Islamic modernists like Muhammad Iqbal (q.v.; d. 1938) and Fazlur Rahman (d. 1988) have seen in him a thinker who responded to the intellectual crisis of his time by accommodating divergent legal and ideological factions, calling for a renewed *ejtehād* (Peters; Baqā), and searching for the spirit behind the literal injunctions of tradition.

Bibliography: M. Āšeq, *al-Qawl al-jalī fī ḥayāt al-Walī*, facs. ed., Delhi, 1989. F. M. Asiri, "Shah Wali Allah as a Mystic," *IC* 26, 1952, pp. 1-15. A. Ahmad, "The Waliullahi Movement," in *Studies in Islamic Culture in the Indian Environment*, Oxford, 1964, pp. 201-17. J. M. S. Baljon, *Religion and Thought of Shāh Walī Allāh*, Leiden, 1986. M. Baqā, *Oṣūl al-feqh aur Šāh Walī-Allāh*, Islamabad, 1973. A. S. Bazmee Ansari, "Al-Dehlawī, Shāh Walī Allāh," in *EI²* II, pp. 254-55. Shah Walī-Allāh Dehlavī, *Anfās al-ʿārefīn*, ed. Ẓ Aḥmad, Delhi, 1897; tr. M. Farūqī Qāderī, Lahore, 1974. Idem, *Foyūż al-ḥaramayn*, ed. and tr. M. Saʿīd, Karachi, n.d. Idem, *al-Joz' al-laṭīf fi-tarjamat al-ʿAbd al-Żaʿīf*, ed. and tr. M. Hedāyat Ḥosayn, *JASB* 14, 1912, pp. 161-75. A. J. Halepota, *Philosophy of Shah Wali Allāh of Delhi*, Lahore, 1970. M. S. Hasan Maʿsumi, "An Appreciation of Shah Waliyullah al-Muhaddith al-Dihlawi," *IC* 21, 1947, pp. 340-53. M. K. Hermansen, "The Current State of Shāh Walī Allāh Studies," *Hamdard Islamicus* 11/3, 1988a, pp. 17-30. Idem, "Shāh Walī Allāh's Theory of the Subtle Spiritual Centers (*Laṭā'if*). A Sufi Theory of Personhood and Self-Transformation," *JNES* 47/1, 1988b, pp. 1-25. R. Peters, "Idjtihād and Taqlīd in 18th and 19th Century Islam," *Die Welt des Islams* 20/3-4, 1980, pp. 131-45. F. Rahman, "The Thinker of Crisis—Shāh Waliy-Ullah," *The Pakistan Quarterly*, summer 1956, pp. 44-48. A. A. Rizvi, *Shāh Walī Allāh and His Times*, Canberra, 1980. ʿU. Sindhī, *Šāh Walī-Allāh aur unkī sīāsī taḥrīk*, Lahore, 1970. Storey, pp. 20-22, 179, 1020-21, 1137, 1201, 1353, 1262. J. O. Voll, "Hadith Scholars and Tarīqahs. An ʿUlema' Group," *Journal of Asian and African Studies* 15, July-October 1980, pp. 264-73.

(MARCIA K. HERMANSEN)

DEHLĪ. See DELHI.

DEHLORĀN (Deh Lorān), the name of a *šahrestān* (subprovince) in Īlām province in southwestern Persia, and of the main town. The *šahrestān*, which is located on the Iraqi border, comprises four districts (Ḥūma, Ābdānān, Zarrīnābād, and Mūsīān) inhabited mainly by the Lor tribes of Jā'īrvand, Maḥmūdvand, Bāpīrvand, and Dūst-ʿAlīvand. The Dehlorān plain is bounded on the east and west by the Mayma and Doveyrej rivers respectively and on the north and south respectively by the Sīāhkūh and Ḥamrīn mountains. It is approximately 600 km², including areas on both sides of the flanking rivers, and lies at the base of the Zagros mountains in a semiarid steppe where rain-fed agriculture is possible but unpredictable and transhumant herders camp over the winter. Rain falls only in the winter, averaging about 350 mm annually. There is seldom frost in the winter, but temperatures can reach 50° C. in the summer. The plain is relatively isolated, being surrounded by arid, dissected, and uninhabited lands. Nevertheless, the plain itself is relatively fertile; its situation between the forested mountains of the Zagros and the well-watered Mesopotamian lowlands is attractive for settlement and seasonal grazing. In the census (q.v.) of 1355 Š./1976 the population of the *šahrestān* was recorded at 52,295 (9,207 family units, 27,612 men, 24,683 women; Markaz-e āmār; *Farhang*, pp. 23-26; Razmārā, *Farhang* V, pp. 194-95).

The Dehlorān plain is best known for the excavations conducted at several prehistoric sites, which elucidated the origins and development of sedentary agricultural villages and towns in the region, and for surveys documenting the history of settlement into the modern era. As a relatively small and remote rural area, it has always been affected by political, economic, and technological developments in the adjacent regions of Ḵūzestān, the Zagros mountains, and Mesopotamia. Beginning as early as the 3rd millennium B.C.E. and throughout its subsequent history it was under the political control of kingdoms in one or another of these regions. Although no cuneiform texts have been found at any of the Dehlorān sites, the most prominent mound, Tepe Musiyan (Mūsīān), is possibly to be identified as ancient Urua, an Elamite city known from Mesopotamian texts (Carter and Stolper, p. 212 n. 275). As early as the 3rd millennium Dehlorān may have been on a trade route linking the Zagros mountains with Mesopotamia; in the 1st millennium the route linking the Achaemenid capitals of Susa and Ecbatana passed through the region (Gautier and Lampre, p. 59; Carter and Stolper, p. 150, including earlier references; for the Persian period, see Olmstead, passim).

The plain had a different character when people first established villages there in the 8th millennium B.C.E. Flash floods deposited silt over the entire plain, constantly regenerating its fertility and creating seasonal marshes, which abounded with fish, attracted game and migratory fowl, and provided moist, easily tilled soil for the first agriculturalists. By 4000 B.C.E., however, the marsh had deteriorated to about half its original size (Kirkby), a change reflected in the botanical remains from ʿAlīkoš (q.v.) and Tepe Sabz, both situated on the edge of the original marsh and abandoned as it retreated (Helbaek; Woosley and Hole). The pattern of settlement implies that villages were moved in response to changing environmental conditions; as long as possible they were situated to take advantage of high water tables, and the villagers did not resort to irrigation for watering crops (Helbaek).

Deposition of silt across the plain continued into the 2nd millennium, at which time it had accumulated to a depth of ca. 4 m. Then rivers began to cut the channels that are apparent today, leaving much of the plain difficult to farm without irrigation (Kirkby). The local inhabitants adapted by moving their relatively small villages and towns as need arose and by practicing transhumant herding. Despite notable fluctuations the population remained relatively low until the Sasanian and early Islamic periods, when every available land surface was farmed, long canals were constructed across the plain, and water-driven mills were strategically located (Neely, 1974). At that time the population may have reached 20,000-25,000 (a density of 75/km²). Following this enormous investment in agriculture, which was probably carried out by imperial edict, residents largely abandoned the plain around 1250 C.E., perhaps as a result of environmental degradation and political instability, leaving it in the hands of nomadic pastoralists down to the present (Neely, 1974, p. 36).

In the early 20th century the plain was occupied by two distinct tribal and ethnic groups. Nomadic Lors, speakers of an Indo-European language closely related to Persian, occupied the plain in winter and migrated to mountain pastures in the summer; tribal Arabs migrated between the poor summer pastures in the Tigris river basin and Dehlorān, replacing the Lors there during the summer months (personal observation). From the 18th century Dehlorān was the winter headquarters of the "*wālī* of Pošt-e Kūh," a tribal leader descended from a Ḵoršīdī *atābeg* originally appointed by the Safavid shah ʿAbbās I (996-1038/1588-1629) in 1004/1596 to govern Lorestān (Amanolahi; Lorimer; Mortensen). The ruins of the fort of the last *wālī*, Ḡolām-Reżā (r. until 1304 Š./1925), lie atop Čogā Safīd (q.v.). In the 20th century a customs post was installed close to the site, near the border crossing at Bayāt. During the 1920s the British exploited a tar seep lying about 6.5 km east of the town and constructed a narrow-gauge railway to move the bitumen to market (local informants; cf. Lorimer, p. 62). At that time petroleum geologists carried out a series of seismic soundings and established the presence of a major oil deposit straddling the international border, but, partly because the neighboring Ḵūzestān oilfields are larger, producing wells were never bored. After World War II the tribal inhabitants were settled in villages. The village of Dehlorān, which had a military post, grew into a small town of Kurdish and Lor families. Dehlorān was invaded and taken by Iraqi forces on the first day of the war between Persia and Iraq in 1980.

The first archeological exploration in Dehlorān was conducted by a French archeological mission in 1903 (see DÉLÉGATIONS ARCHÉOLOGIQUES FRANÇAISES), under the direction of J.-E. Gautier and Georges Lampre, who dug trenches at Tepe Mūsīān, Tepe Ḵazīna, and Tepe ʿAlīkoš. The French encountered difficulties with the local tribes, however, and abandoned further work there.

Exploration was resumed in 1961, when Frank Hole and Kent Flannery did a cursory survey of the plain and dug a sounding at ʿAlīkoš. They followed up in 1963 with more extensive excavations at ʿAlīkoš and Tepe Sabz, a village of the 5th millennium B.C.E.; they also briefly reexamined one of the old French trenches at Mūsīān. In 1968 Henry Wright excavated at Tepe Farroḵābād, a site occupied in the 5th-2nd millennia. During the winter of 1969-70 Hole excavated 6th-millenium layers at Čogā Safīd while James Neely conducted an intensive survey of sites in the plain and Michael Kirkby studied its geomorphological history. Collectively these projects have elucidated the archeological sequence from the first settlements in the 8th millennium B.C.E. into the modern era. The construction of this sequence, based on limited stratified soundings at several sites and on intensive surveys of the plain, incorporated changes in artifacts, architecture, faunal and floral remains, settlement patterns, irrigation works, and population sizes. As a result Dehlorān is one of the best-known archeological regions of Persia.

Bibliography: S. Amanolahi, *The Tribes of Iran* I. *The Tribes of Luristan. Bakhtiari, Kuh Gilu and Mamasani*, Human Relations Area Files, New Haven, Conn., 1988. ʿA. Bayāt, *Kollīyāt-e joḡrāfīā-ye ṭabīʿī wa tārīḵī-e Īrān*, Tehran, 1367 Š./1988, pp. 449-53. E. Carter, *Elam in the Second Millennium B.C. The Archaeological Evidence*, Ph.D. diss., The University of Chicago, 1971. Idem and M. W. Stolper, *Elam. Surveys of Political History and Archaeology*, Near Eastern Studies 25, Berkeley, Calif., 1984. *Farhang-e joḡrāfīāʾī-e Īrān (ābādīhā)*, Tehran, 1367 Š./1988. J.-E. Gautier and G. Lampre, "Fouilles de Moussian," *Mémoires de la Délégation en Perse* 8, 1905, pp. 59-149. H. Helbaek, "Plant Collecting, Dry-Farming, and Irrigation Agriculture in Prehistoric Deh Luran," in F. Hole, K. V. Flannery, and J. A. Neely, eds., *Prehistory and Human Ecology of the Deh Luran Plain*, Memoirs of the Museum of Anthropology 1, Ann Arbor, Mich., 1969. pp. 383-426. F. Hole, ed., *Studies in the Archaeological History of the Deh Luran Plain*, Memoirs of the Museum of Anthropology 9, Ann Arbor, Mich., 1977. Idem, ed., *Archaeological Perspectives on Western Iran*, Washington, D.C., 1987. Idem, K. V. Flannery, and J. A. Neely, eds., *Prehistory and Human Ecology of the Deh Luran Plain*, Memoirs of the Museum of Anthropology 1, Ann Arbor, Mich., 1969. F. Hole and M. Shaw, *Computer Analysis of Chronological Seriation*, Rice University Studies 53, Houston, Tex., 1967. M. Kirkby, "Land and Water Resources of the Deh Luran and Khuzistan Plains," in F. Hole, ed., *Studies in the Archaeological History of the Deh Luran Plain*, Memoirs of the Museum of Anthropology 9, Ann Arbor, Mich., 1977, pp. 251-88. D. L. R. Lorimer, A *Report on Pusht-i-Kuh*, 1908, unpublished. Markaz-e āmār-e Īrān, *Sar-šomārī-e ʿomūmī-e nofūs o maskan. Ābān-māh-e 1355. Šahrestān-e Dehlorān*, Tehran, 1358 Š./1979. I. D. Mortensen, Nomads of Luristan, New York, 1993. J. A. Neely, "The Deh Luran Region," *Iran* 8, 1970, pp. 202-03. Idem, "Sassanian and Early Islamic Water-Control and Irrigation Systems on the Deh Luran Plain, Iran," in T. E. Downing and

M. Gibson, eds., *Irrigation's Impact on Society*, Anthropological Papers 25, Tucson, Ariz., 1974, pp. 21-42. Idem and H. T. Wright, *Early Settlement Patterns on the Deh Luran Plain*, Technical Reports of the Museum of Anthropology 26, Ann Arbor, Mich., 1994. A. T. Olmstead, *History of the Persian Empire*, Chicago, 1948. C. Renfrew, "Sources and Supply of the Deh Luran Obsidian," in F. Hole, K. V. Flannery, and J. A. Neely, eds., *Prehistory and Human Ecology of the Deh Luran Plain*, Memoirs of the Museum of Anthropology 1, Ann Arbor, Mich., 1969, pp. 429-33. Idem, "The Later Obsidian of Deh Luran—The Evidence of Chogha Sefid," in F. Hole, ed., *Studies in the Archaeological History of the Deh Luran Plain*, Memoirs of the Museum of Anthropology 9, Ann Arbor, Mich., 1977, pp. 289-311. A. Woosley and F. Hole, "Pollen Evidence of Subsistence and Environment in Ancient Iran," *Paléorient* 4, 1978, pp. 59-70. H. T. Wright, "A Consideration of Interregional Exchange in Greater Mesopotamia, 4000-3000 B.C.," in E. Wilmsen, ed., *Social Exchange and Interaction*, Anthropological Paper 46, Ann Arbor, Mich, 1972, pp. 95-105. Idem, ed., *An Early Town of the Deh Luran Plain. Excavations at Tepe Farukhabad*, Memoirs of the Museum of Anthropology 13, Ann Arbor, Mich., 1981. Idem and G. A. Johnson, "Population, Exchange and Early State Formation in Southwestern Iran," *American Anthropologist* 77, 1975, pp. 267-87. H. T. Wright et al., "Early Fourth Millennium Developments in Southwestern Iran," *Iran* 13, 1975, pp. 129-48.

(FRANK HOLE)

DEHQĀN, arabicized form of Syriac *dhgn*ʾ (Margoliouth, p. 84a), borrowed from Pahlavi *dehgān* (older form *dahīgān*). The original meaning was "pertaining to *deh*" (< OPers. *dahyu*), the latter term not in the later sense of "village," but in the original sense of "land."

i. *In the Sasanian period.*
ii. *In the Islamic period.*

i. IN THE SASANIAN PERIOD

The term *dehqān* was used in the late Sasanian period to designate a class of landed magnates (*Mojmal*, ed. Bahār, p. 420) considered inferior in rank to *āzādān*, *bozorgān* (qq.v.; *Zand ī Wahman Yasn* 4.7, 4.54), and *kadag-xwadāyān* "householders" (*Ardā Wīrāz-nāmag* 15.10, where *dahīgān* should be read for *dādagān*). According to some early Islamic sources, the rank of the *dehqān* in the Sasanian period was also inferior to that of the *šahrīgān* "chief of the small cantons" (Yaʿqūbī, *Taʾrīḵ* I, p. 203; Masʿūdī, ed. Pellat, I, sec. 662; Christensen, *Iran Sass.*, p. 140).

The origin of the *dehqān* class is usually attributed in both Zoroastrian Pahlavi books of the 9th century and early Islamic sources to Wēkard/t, brother of Hōšang, the legendary Iranian king (*Dēnkard*, ed. Madan, pp. 438, 594, 688; Bīrūnī, *Āṯār*, pp. 220-21; Masʿūdī, ed. Pellat, I, sec. 662; Christensen, pp. 68, 134, 151, 156). In some sources the innovation is credited to Manūčehr (Ṯaʿālebī, p. 6; Ṭabarī, I, p. 434; Balʿamī, ed. Bahār, p. 345; Ebn al-Balḵī, p. 37). Nevertheless, as the term *dehgān* is not attested in early Sasanian documents but is sometimes mentioned in the Pahlavi books and frequently occurs in descriptions of late Sasanian administration in early Islamic sources, it is admissible to suppose that *dehqān*s emerged as a social class as a result of land reforms in the time of Ḵosrow I (531-79). He is reported to have admonished future kings that they should protect the *dehqān*s, just as they would protect kingship, because they were like brothers (Ṯaʿālebī, *Ḡorar*, p. 6). According to one source (*Mojmal*, ed. Bahār, p. 73), his own mother had been the daughter of a *dehqān* descended from Frēdon. In the late Sasanian period *dehqān*s and princes (*wāspuhragān*; Ar. *ahl al-boyūtāt*) used to have audience with the king on the second day of the Nowrūz and Ḵorram-rūz (also Ḵorrah-rūz, Navad-rūz) festivals; the latter, celebrated on the first day of the tenth month (Day, q.v.), was their special feast day, on which the king ate and drank with the *dehqān*s and cultivators (Bīrūnī, *Āṯār*, pp. 218, 225; for this feast, see idem, I, 1954, p. 264; Gardīzī, ed. Ḥabībī, pp. 239, 254; Qazvīnī, p. 83).

Management of local affairs was the *dehqān*s' hereditary responsibility, and peasants were obliged to obey them (cf. Ṭabarī, I, p. 434; Balʿamī, ed. Bahār, p. 345; Ebn al-Balḵī, p. 37), but their landed estates must have been smaller than those of noble landowners. They probably represented the government among the peasants, and their main duty was to collect taxes (Christensen, *Iran Sass.*, pp. 112-13). They were divided into five subgroups according to social status, each distinguished by dress (Masʿūdī, ed. Pellat, I, par. 662).

The Arab conquest (q.v.) of the Sasanian empire began with sporadic attacks on the lands of the *dehqān*s of the Sawād, the cultivated areas of southern Iraq. After the defeat of the Persian army and the gradual disappearance of the nobles who administered the country, the local gentry, that is, the *dehqān*s, assumed a more important political and social role in their districts, towns, and villages. Some were able to protect their settlements from the conquering armies by surrendering and agreeing to pay the poll tax (*jezya*). For example, the *dehqān* of Zawābī in Iraq made a treaty with the Arab commander ʿOrwa b. Zayd, in which he agreed to pay a tax of 4 dirhams for each inhabitant of his district. Besṭām, *dehqān* of Bors, also in Iraq, agreed with Zahra to construct a bridge for his army. When the Arab forces arrived at Mahrūḏ near Baghdad the local *dehqān* agreed to pay a sum of money to Hāšem b. ʿOtba, in order to deter him from killing any of the district's inhabitants. Šīrzād, the *dehqān* of Sābāṭ, a village near Madāʾen (see CTESIPHON), was able to save 100,000 peasants from the Arabs. There are similar reports for other parts of the Sasanian empire, for example, Sīstān, Herat, and

Balḵ (Balāḏorī, *Fotūḥ*, ed. Monajjed, pp. 307, 318, 324, 484, 516; Ṭabarī, I, pp. 2421, 2426, 2461; Gardīzī, ed. Ḥabībī, p. 102). *Dehqāns* who refused to collaborate with the Arabs either fled or lost their lives (e.g., Balāḏorī, ed. Monajjed, pp. 324, 420, 422, 464, 466, 514; Ṭabarī, I, pp. 2421-23). The fact that the last Sasanian king, Yazdegerd III (632-51), sought support from the *dehqāns* of Isfahan and Kermān is evidence of the rising power of this class at the end of the Sasanian empire (Ṭabarī, I, pp. 2875-77).

In the early Islamic period, as in late Sasanian times, the *dehqāns* had the task of collecting taxes. They were also responsible for cultivation of the land, maintaining bridges and roads, and providing hospitality to certain travelers (Ṭabarī, I, p. 2470). The lands of *dehqāns* in regions of the Sawād where the population had accepted Islam were left to them, and they were exempt from the poll tax (Balāḏorī, p. 325).

It may be inferred from various reports that in early Islamic times some *dehqāns* functioned almost as local rulers, especially in eastern Persia, and that any man of wealth or social prestige might thus be called *dehqān*. Sometimes the same person was called *dehqān* in one source and *marzbān* (governor) in another. For example, in one report Ṭabarī referred to men with the title *marzbān* of Kermān and Marv and in another called the same men *dehqān* (I, pp. 2872-77; cf. Dīnavarī, p. 148: *ʿāmel* of Marv; Gardīzī, 102: *sālār* and *dehqān* of Marv). Balāḏorī (p. 466) mentioned the revolt of the *dehqān* of Šūš, whereas Dīnavarī (p. 140) called the same person *marzbān*. Dēwāštīč (q.v.), the last ruler of Panjīkant, had the title of "lord" or "king" in the Sogdian documents excavated at Mount Mugh but was designated *dehqān* by Ṭabarī (II, p. 1446; *Dokumenty* II, pp. 132 ff.). In Persian poetry before the 12th century the title *dehqān* meant "ruler, amir, lord," especially in eastern Persia (e.g., Masʿūd-e Saʿd, p. 374; Nāṣer-e Ḵosrow, p. 107; Sūzanī, pp. 200, 224, 311, 326, 436, 485). *Dehqāns* were sometimes mentioned together with princes, grandees, local rulers, learned men (*aḥbār*), knights, and army commanders (Ṭabarī, I, p. 3249, II, 1237; Naršaḵī, pp. 9-13, 54, 84-85; *Mojmal*, p. 328; cf. Balāḏorī, ed. Monajjed, p. 505).

The Arabs often consulted *dehqāns* on political and social affairs, and in some instances the latter were able to intervene on behalf of one of the parties to a conflict (e.g., Ṭabarī, II, pp. 1420, 1569). In the first half of the 9th century Sahl b. Sonbāṭ, who first sheltered Bābak Ḵorramdīn (q.v.) in his castle but later betrayed him to Afšīn (q.v.), was a *dehqān*. Another *dehqān*, Ebn Šarvīn Ṭabarī, was appointed to bring Bābak's brother ʿAbd-Allāh to Baghdad as a captive; on the way ʿAbd-Allāh asked to be treated in the manner of the *dehqāns*, and Ebn Šarvīn gave him wine (*Mojmal*, ed. Bahār, p. 357; Ṭabarī, III, p. 1231). *Dehqāns* enjoyed great respect and prestige at the court of the Samanids (204-395/819-1005). The poet Rūdakī, in an ode (*qaṣīda*) describing a banquet at the court of Naṣr b. Aḥmad (301-31/913-43), mentioned a *dehqān* called Pīr Ṣāleḥ, who sat with the nobles (*ḥorrān*) facing the ranks of the amirs and the grand vizier, Moḥammad Balʿamī (*Tārīḵ-e Sīstān*, p. 319). In the early Islamic centuries many important political figures of eastern Persia were *dehqāns* (e.g., the Samanid amir Aḥmad b. Sahl b. Hāšem, q.v.) or descendants of *dehqān* families (e.g., the Saljuq grand vizier Neẓām-al-Molk, q.v.; Gardīzī, p. 151; Ebn Fondoq, pp. 73, 78).

In the first centuries of Islam many *dehqāns*, as the heirs of Sasanian gentry, led comfortable, even luxurious lives similar to those of their forebears. Jāḥeẓ (*Boḵalāʾ*, p. 71; tr. p. 98) mentioned the table etiquette observed by the *dehqāns*. According to Balāḏorī (ed. Monajjed, p. 524; cf. Ṭabarī, II, pp. 1417-18), Saʿīd b. ʿAbd-al-ʿAzīz, governor of Khorasan under the Omayyad caliph Yazīd II (101-05/720-24), was called *ḵodīna* (lady, wife of a *dehqān*; cf. Sogdian *γwt(ʾy)ynk*) because of his elegant garments and his flowing hair style. *Dehqāns* used to offer presents to the caliphs and local rulers at the Nowrūz and Mehragān festivals, just as their ancestors had done in Sasanian times. Ṭabarī (II, pp. 1635-38) described in detail those offered to Asad b. ʿAbd-Allāh Qasrī, governor of Khorasan, at the Mehragān feast at Balḵ in 120/738. Hārūn al-Rašīd (170-93/786-809), on his way from Baghdad to Ṭūs, fell ill in a village in Bayhaq and had to stay there four months as the guest of a *dehqān*, who served him with magnificence and offered him precious gifts when he departed (Ebn Fondoq, pp. 47-48).

Aside from their political and social significance, the *dehqāns* played an important cultural role. Many participated in the courts of caliphs or governors, and after the establishment of the Persian dynasties in the east they served kings, princes, and amirs as learned men who were well informed on the history and culture of ancient Iran. Bayhaqī (p. 299) reported that Zīād b. Abīhi (d. 56/675), while still governor of Baṣra, had in his service three *dehqāns*, who told him stories of Sasanian grandeur and pomp, causing him to think Arab rule much inferior. In the *Tārīḵ-e Sīstān* (p. 106) a number of wise sayings, similar to the Pahlavi *andarz* (q.v.), are attributed to a certain Zoroastrian *dehqān* named Rostam b. Hormazd, who reportedly uttered them at the request of ʿAbd-al-ʿAzīz b. ʿAbd-Allāh, an Omayyad governor of Sīstān (cf. *Šāh-nāma*, ed. Moscow, IX, p. 211 vv. 3380-83). The 9th-century author Jāḥeẓ (1385/1965, I, p. 115, II, p. 125) also quoted some pieces of folklore from *dehqāns*. In both Arabic and Persian sources the names of many learned persons and men of letters, including theologians, who were *dehqāns* or decendants of *dehqān* families are mentioned (Ebn Fondoq, pp. 116, 149). Some were patrons of Islamic religious scholars; for example, Ebn Fondoq (p. 185) mentioned a wealthy *dehqān* from Sabzavār who, in 418/1027, founded a religious school for a Koran commentator named Ebn Ṭayyeb. The majority of *dehqāns* favored Persian culture, however, and some were patrons of renowned Persian poets. Rūdakī (p. 458) related that the *dehqāns* gave him money and riding animals. Farroḵī in his youth served a *dehqān* in Sīstān and received an annual pension from him. According to one tradition, Ferdowsī himself was a *dehqān* (*Čahār maqāla*, ed. Qazvīnī, text, pp. 58, 75).

Most of the credit for preservation of the stories in the national epic, the *Šāh-nāma*; pre-Islamic historical traditions; and the romances of ancient Iran belongs to the *dehqān*s. Abū Manṣūr Maʿmarī (q.v.), who compiled the prose *Šāh-nāma-ye abū-manṣūrī* (346/957), now lost, wrote in his preface, which does survive, that in gathering his material he summoned a number of *dehqān*s from various cities of Khorasan (pp. 34-35). Ferdowsī often cited *dehqān*s as sources, apparently oral ones, for his narratives (e.g., *Šāh-nāma*, ed. Moscow, I, p. 28 v. 1, II, p. 170 v. 15, III, pp. 6-7 vv. 8, 19, IV, p. 302 vv. 19-20, VI, p. 167 v. 25). Other poets, too, referred to traditions from the *dehqān*s (e.g., Asadī, p. 21 v. 1; Īrānšāh, p. 17; Neẓāmī, pp. 436, 508). The term *dehqān* thus also came to be defined as "historian, versed in history" (*Borhān-e qāṭeʿ*, ed. Moʿīn, II, p. 905). The profound attachment of the *dehqān*s to the culture of ancient Iran also lent to the word the sense of "Persian," especially "Persian of noble blood," in contrast to Arabs, Turks, and Romans in particular (e.g., *Šāh-nāma*, ed. Moscow, I, p. 21 v. 128, IX, pp. 307 v. 7, 319 vv. 105-06; Nāṣer-e Ḵosrow, pp. 83, 156, 288; Farroḵī, pp. 274, 282, 314; Abū Ḥanīfa Eskāfī apud Bayhaqī, ed. Fayyāż, p. 856; ʿOnṣorī, pp. 137, 239). According to Ṭabarī (I, p. 1040), Marvazān, governor of Yemen in the time of Ḵosrow I, had two sons, one Ḵorrah-Ḵosrow, who liked to recite Arabic poetry, and another, unnamed, a knight (*aswār*) who spoke Persian and lived in the manner of the *dehqān*s. Sometimes the word *dehqān* meant a Zoroastrian (*Šāh-nāma*, ed. Moscow, IX, pp. 97 v. 1483, 134 v. 2106; Farroḵī, p. 294; Neẓāmī, p. 238; Ḵāqānī, p. 411; Moʿezzī, pp. 604, 612; Qaṭrān, p. 254).

With the development of the *eqṭāʿ* (q.v.) system of land grants from the 11th century and the decline of the landowning class, the *dehqān*s gradually lost their importance, and the word came to mean simply a farmer (e.g., Nāṣer-e Ḵosrow, p. 118; Ebn Fondoq, pp. 28, 266), though in the 12th and 13th centuries it was still occasionally used in its original sense (e.g., Jovaynī, pp. 53, 55; Najm-al-Dīn Rāzī, p. 514).

Bibliography: (For cited works not found in this bibliography and for abbreviations found here, see "Short References.") M. Ābādī, "Pīšīna-ye dehqān dar adab-e fārsī," *Honar o mardom* 179, 1356 Š./1977, pp. 64-70. Abū Manṣūr Maʿmarī, "Moqaddama-ye Šāh-nāma-ye abū-manṣūrī," in M. Qazvīnī, *Bīst maqāla-ye Qazvīnī* II, Tehran, 1332 Š./1953, pp. 5-90. *Ardā Wirāz-Nāmag*, ed. M. Haug, Bombay and London, 1872. Barthold, *Turkestan*[3], pp. 180-81. Asadī Ṭūsī, *Garšāsp-nāma*, ed. Ḥ. Yaḡmāʾī, Tehran, 1317 Š./1938. Abu'l-Ḥasan ʿAlī b. Zayd Bayhaqī, *Tārīḵ-e Bayhaq*, ed. A. Bahmanyār, Tehran, 1317 Š./1938. Ebrāhīm

b. Moḥammad Bayhaqī, *al-Maḥāsen wa'l-masāwī*, ed. F. Schwally, Giessen, 1902. Abū Rayḥān Bīrūnī, *al-Qānūn al-masʿūdī fi'l-hayʾa wa'l-nojūm*, ed. S. H. Baranī, 3 vols., Hyderabad, 1954-56. A. Christensen, *Les types du premier homme et du premier roi dans l'histoire légendaire des Iraniens* I, Stockholm, 1917. C. Dennett, *Conversion and Poll Tax in Early Islam*, Cambridge, Mass., 1950, pp. 22-23, 29-30, 32-33. Najm-al-Dīn Dāya, *Merṣād al-ʿebād*, ed. M.-A. Rīāḥī, Tehran, 1352 Š./1973. Dehḵodā, s.v. Ebn Fondoq. *Dokumenty s gory Mug* (Documents from Mount Mugh) II, Moscow, 1962. Farroḵī Sīstānī, *Dīvān*, ed. M. Dabīrsīāqī, Tehran, 1342 Š./1963. E. Ḥākemī, "Maʿānī-e dehqān dar zabān o adab-e fārsī," *Soḵan* 26/11-12, 1357 Š./1978, pp. 1231-37. Īrānšāh b. Abi'l-Ḵayr, *Bahman-nāma*, ed. R. ʿAfīfī, Tehran, 1370 Š./1991. Abū ʿOṯmān ʿAmr b. Baḥr Jāḥeẓ, *al-Ḥayawān*, ed. ʿA. Hārūn, I-II, Cairo, 1385/1965. Idem, *Ketāb al-boḵalāʾ*, ed. G. van Vloten, Leiden, 1900; tr. C. Pellat as *Le livre des avares*, Paris, 1951. Montajab-al-Dīn ʿAlī b. Aḥmad Jovaynī, *ʿAtabat al-kataba*, ed. M. Qazvīnī and ʿA. Eqbāl, Tehran, 1329 Š./1940. Ḵāqānī Šervānī, *Dīvān*, ed. Ż. Sajjādī, Tehran, 1338 Š./1959. A. K. S. Lambton, *Landlord and Peasant*. Idem, "Dihḵān," in *EI*[2] II, pp. 253-54. J. P. Margoliouth, *Supplement to the Thesaurus Syriacus of R. Payne Smith, S.T.P.*, Oxford, 1927. Masʿūd-e Saʿd-e Salmān, *Dīvān*, ed. Ḡ.-R. Rašīd Yāsamī, Tehran, 1318 Š./1939. M. Mīnovī, "Dehqānān," *Sīmorḡ* 1, 1351 Š./1973, pp. 8-13. Abū ʿAbd-Allāh Moḥammad Moʿezzī Nīšāpūrī, *Dīvān*, ed. ʿA. Eqbāl, Tehran, 1318 Š./1939. Nāṣer-e Ḵosrow, *Dīvān*, ed. M. Mīnovī and M. Moḥaqqeq, Tehran, 1353 Š./1974. Neẓāmī Ganjavī, *Šaraf-nāma*, ed. Ḥ. Waḥīd Dastgerdī, Tehran, 1316 Š./1937. Nöldeke, *Geschichte der Perser*, p. 440. ʿOnṣorī Balḵī, *Dīvān*, ed. M. Dabīrsīāqī, Tehran, 1342 Š./1963. M. I. Osmanov, "O znachenii termina 'dixkan' v 'Shax-name' Firdousi" (The meaning of the term *dehqān* in the *Šāh-nāma* of Ferdowsī), *Kratkie Soobshcheniya Insitituta Narodov Azii* 39, 1963, pp. 6-9. Qaṭrān Tabrīzī, *Dīvān*, ed. M. Naḵjavānī, Tabrīz, 1333 Š./1954. Zakarīyāʾ Qazvīnī, *ʿAjāʾeb al-maḵlūqāt wa ḡarāʾeb al-mawjūdāt*, ed. F. Wüstenfeld, Leipzig, 1848. E. Quatremère, "Sur l'ouvrage intitulé Kitab-alagānī," *JA*, 2nd sér. 15, 1835, p. 532. Abū ʿAbd-Allāh Jaʿfar b. Moḥammad Rūdakī, *Āṯār-e manẓūm*, ed. A. Mirzayev, Dushanbe, 1958. Ḏ. Ṣafā, "Dehqānān," *Amūzeš o parvareš* 22/1, 1326 Š./1947, p. 43. Idem, *Ḥamāsa-sarāyī dar Īrān*, Tehran, 1333 Š./1954, pp. 62-64. Šams-al-Dīn Moḥammad Sūzanī Samarqandī, *Dīvān*, ed. N. Šāh-Ḥosaynī, Tehran, 1338 Š./1959. J. Wellhausen, *Das arabische Reich und sein Sturz*, Berlin, 1902. *Zand ī Wahman Yasn*, ed. D. T. Anklesaria, Bombay, 1957.

(Aḥmad Tafażżolī)

ii. IN THE ISLAMIC PERIOD. SEE AGRICULTURE; EQTĀʿ; FARMING; LAND TENURE.

DEHQĀN, AḤMAD. See Supplement.

DEIOCES (Gk. Dēïókēs), name of a Median king; this Greek form, like Assyrian Da-a-a-uk-ku (i.e., Daiukku) and Elamite Da-a-(hi-)(ú-)uk-ka, Da-a-ya-u(k)-ka, and so on, reflects Iranian *Dahyu-ka-, a hypocoristic based on *dahyu-* "land" (cf. Schmitt).

According to the detailed account of Herodotus (1.96-101), Deioces, son of Phraortes (Ir. *Fravartiš; 1.96.1), father of Phraortes, and grandfather of Cyaxares (q.v.; 1.73.3, 103.1, etc.), plotted cleverly to establish autocratic rule over the Medes, who at that time lived in separate, autonomous villages, or rather townships. In a period of great lawlessness all over Media he made every effort to enforce justice in his own village; his reputation as an impartial judge thus gradually spread, until finally he claimed that this role was too troublesome and refused to continue administering justice (1.96.2-97.1). Lawlessness then reigned anew, worse than before, so that the Medes assembled and at last resolved to elect a king to rule over them (1.97.2-3); they elected Deioces, who is said to have ruled for fifty-three years (1.98.1, 102.1).

He ordered a strong fortress city to be built, with walls arranged in seven concentric rings; all government authority was centralized in this capital, which in Old Persian was called Hagmatāna (Gk. Agbátana or Ekbátana; modern Hamadān; see ECBATANA). He retired to his palace, within the innermost of the seven rings, and surrounded himself with a kind of bodyguard; he enforced law and order by introducing "watchers and listeners" throughout his realm (1.100.2), the forerunners of the Achaemenid "king's eyes" or "ears" (see ACHAEMENID DYNASTY ii). He also initiated a regulated court ceremonial, so that people should regard him as "of a different kind" (*heteroîos*; 1.99.2). In other Greek sources (Diodorus, 8.16.1; Themistius, *Orationes*, ed. Schenkl, 2.131.15; Polyaenus, 7.1; Dio Chrysostomus, 2.77, 56.4, 64.22) where Deioces is mentioned almost nothing has been added to the information provided by Herodotus.

Herodotus' account seems to have been based on an oral tradition; from it scholars have deduced that Deioces was the founder of the Median royal dynasty and the first Median king to gain independence from Assyria. But it must be stressed that Herodotus' report is a mixture of Greek and eastern legends and is not historically reliable. It has also been supposed (cf. Diakonoff, p. 109) that the Median king on whom Herodotus' account is centered was actually Deioces' son Phraortes, and it is therefore impossible to give the exact dates of Deioces' reign, which probably spanned most of the first half of the 7th century B.C.E. I. M. Diakonoff and others have suggested ca. 727-675 B.C.E., counting back from the date when Cyrus (q.v.) seized power.

It is thus useful to look for some corroboration from the cuneiform sources, and indeed George Smith (p. 98) noticed already in 1869 that in Neo-Assyrian texts one Daiukku is mentioned several times in the reign of Sargon II (721-05 B.C.E.). In the annals for this king's eighth year (i.e., 715 B.C.E.; Luckenbill, pp. 6 ff. ll. 75-100; Lie, pp. 18 ff. ll. 101-26) and in the so-called Display Inscription (*Prunkinschrift*) from Khorsabad (l. 49) Deioces is named as a Mannean provincial governor (*šaknu*) ruling, somewhat independently, a district bordering both the Mannean and the Assyrian kingdoms. The exact location of his estate is not known with certainty; it was perhaps in the valley of the Zarrīnrūd. Deioces, whose son was held hostage by the Urartians, supported the Urartian king Rusā I (730-14 B.C.E.) against the Mannean ruler Ullusunu, ultimately without success, for Sargon intervened and eventually captured Deioces and exiled him and his family to Hamath (modern Ḥamāt) in Syria. Deioces may already have taken part in a rebellion against the Mannean king Iranzu the year before; one of the governors listed in the Assyrian annals for that year, the governor of Messi, is not named and may have been Deioces, but the identification cannot be made with certainty.

The so-called House of Deioces (Bît-Da-a-a-uk-ku, i.e., "place or province of Deioces"), on which scholars used to base their historical reconstructions, never existed, however; the notion arose from a misreading of [KUR *bît*]-Da-a-a-uk-ki for [KUR Ma]-da-a-a "the land of the Medes" in Sargon's annals for the year 713 (Luckenbill, p. 28 l. 140; Lie, pp. 28-29 l. 166). The House of Deioces cannot therefore have been one of the objectives of that year's Assyrian campaign, which was directed eastward into Ellipi and Media.

Any connection between the governor mentioned by Sargon and the Median dynasty of later periods is thus only hypothetical; there is not a single authentic cuneiform source to confirm that Sargon's Daiukku and Herodotus' Deioces were the same person. Stuart Brown (p. 76) is correct in stressing that "it is improbable in the extreme that a Mede who was the governor of a Mannean province for less than a year . . . could have become associated . . . with the founding of the Median state." Nevertheless, the onomastic evidence suggests that the relevant Neo-Assyrian sources and the classical tradition can be brought together. The Old Iranian name *Dahyuka- was not uncommon even in later periods; in the Achaemenid period the Old Persian form *Dahyuka- occurred in a variety of Elamite renderings on the Persepolis Fortification Tablets (cf. Schmitt, p. 145; for additional references to unpublished texts, see Hinz and Koch, pp. 247, 258-59, 303). These references were apparently to different officials in various administrative districts, among them one subordinate who was to apportion fodder rations for horses.

Bibliography: (For abbreviations found in this

bibliography, see "Short References.") S. C. Brown, "The Mêdikos Logos of Herodotus and the Evolution of the Median State," in A. Kuhrt and H. Sancisi-Weerdenburg, eds., *Achaemenid History* III. *Method and Theory*, Leiden, 1988, pp. 71-86. G. G. Cameron, *History of Early Iran*, Chicago, 1936, esp. pp. 150 ff., 175 ff. I. M. Diakonoff, "Media," in *Camb. Hist. Iran* II, pp. 36-148, esp. pp. 80 ff., 89 ff., 109, 112-13. E. A. Grantovskiĭ, *Rannyaya istoriya iranskikh plemen Peredneĭ Azii* (The early history of the Iranian peoples of Nearer Asia), Moscow, 1970, esp. pp. 249-52. W. Hinz and H. Koch, *Elamisches Wörterbuch*, 2 vols., Berlin, 1987. [F. W.] König, "Bît-Daiukku/i," in *RlA* I, p. 38. A. G. Lie, *The Inscriptions of Sargon II, King of Assyria* I. *The Annals*, Paris, 1929. D. D. Luckenbill, *Ancient Records of Assyria and Babylonia* II, Chicago, 1927. J. Miller, "Deiokes," in Pauly-Wissowa IV/2, col. 2399. R. Schmitt, "Deiokes," *Anz. der Österreichischen Akademie der Wissenschaften* 110, 1973, pp. 137-47. G. Smith, "Assyrian History. Additions to the History of Tiglath-Pileser II," *Zeitschrift für Ägyptische Sprache* 7, 1869, pp. 92-100, 106-12.

(RÜDIGER SCHMITT)

DEIPNOSOPHISTAÍ (Banquet of the Sophists), a miscellany in the form of dialogues ostensibly conducted at table, including approximately one hundred passages pertaining to Persia; it is the only extant work of Athenaeus (see ATHENAIOS OF NAUCRATIS), an Egyptian-born author who lived in Rome in the early 3rd century C.E. Charles Gulick (I, p. viii) suggested that one of the participants in the dinner conversation, a man named Ulpian, may have been modeled on the jurist Ulpian of Tyre, who was murdered in the presence of the emperor Alexander Severus in 228; if this identification is correct, then *Deipnosophistaí* was probably completed shortly after that date.

The information on Persia is generally mediocre and unreliable, with emphasis on titillating anecdotes of the luxury and moral laxity at the Persian court, almost entirely compiled from earlier sources, including *Cyropaedia* (q.v.) of Xenophon (ca. 429-375 B.C.E.); *Perì Kyzíkou* by Agathocles (fl. 5th-early 4th century B.C.E.); *Persiká* of Ctesias (q.v.; fl. late 5th-early 4th century B.C.E.); *Physikē' Akróasis*, incorrectly attributed to Aristotle (Rose, p. 236); *Perì hēdonês* by Heracleides of Pontus (fl. 4th century B.C.E.); *En stathmoîs Persikoîs* by Amyntas (fl. late 4th century B.C.E.); the lost *Bíos Arch ta* by Aristoxenus of Tarentum (fl. late 4th century B.C.E.); *Perì Aléxandron historíai* by Chares of Mitylene (q.v.; fl. late 4th century B.C.E.); *Bíoi* by Clearchus of Soloi (fl. late 4th century B.C.E.); *Persiká* by Dino (fl. late 4th century B.C.E.); *Persiká* by Heracleides of Cumae (fl. late 4th century B.C.E.); *Perì phyt(ik)ôn historía* by Theophrastus (ca. 372-ca. 287 B.C.E.); *Historíai* of Duris (q.v.; fl. late 4th-early 3rd century B.C.E.), a notoriously unreliable author; an unnamed work by Timaeus (fl. early 3rd century B.C.E.); *Epistolaí* by Hieronymus of Rhodes (fl. 3rd century B.C.E.); *Historikà hypomnḗmata* of Carystius of Pergamum (fl. late 2nd century B.C.E.); *Geographiká* by Strabo (ca. 63 B.C.E.-ca. 21 C.E.); and *Tà metà Polybion* by Poseidonius (fl. 2nd century C.E.). Athenaeus' work, though thus preserving valuable fragments of earlier writings, must be used with utmost care.

Reports about the Achaemenids. According to Athenaeus (912.513-14), the Persians were the first men in history to become notorious for luxurious living. He quoted from an address by the sensualist Polyarchus, preserved in Aristoxenus' *Bíos Arch ta*, in which he claimed that the Persians rewarded anyone who invented a new pleasure. Polyarchus then described the luxuries with which the king of Persia surrounded himself: his servants, his sexual pleasures, his perfume, his elegance and conversation, and his entertainments (Athenaeus, 12.545-46; cf. 12.512a-b).

The Persian kings wintered in Susa and summered in Ecbatana, spending the autumn in Persepolis and the rest of the year in Babylon (Athenaeus, 12.513-14; cf. Xenophon, *Cyropaedia* 8.6.22, where it is said that Cyrus customarily spent the winter in Babylon and the spring at Susa). Athenaeus drew from Heracleides (12.514b; cf. Müller, *Fragmenta* II, p. 95) his description of the arrangements in one of these palaces. The king's official throne was of gold with four short posts studded with jewels, over which an embroidered purple cloth was draped. Adjacent to his private chamber there was a court named for his Persian bodyguard, one thousand chosen men known as the "apple bearers" because of the "golden apples" that adorned the butts of their spears. A report by Clearchus (Athenaeus, 12.514d; cf. Müller, *Fragmenta* II, p. 304) suggests that the Greek authors at least associated this emblem with eunuchs (q.v.), for, after describing the supposed excesses of the Medes, who castrated many men from neighboring tribes, he claimed that "apple bearing" was continued by the Persians, who avenged themselves on the Medes in this way. The king was accustomed to pass through the court of the apple bearers, walking on Sardis carpets reserved for his exclusive use; when he reached the outer court, he would mount his chariot or his horse, for he never went on foot outside the palace. Supposedly 300 women customarily watched over him at night, entering through the court of the apple bearers to sing and play the harp by lamp light while he took his pleasure of them. Concubines even attended him while he was hunting. Heracleides' description was supplemented by an excerpt from Chares, who reported that at the head of the king's bed there was a chamber, called the "royal cushion," large enough to contain five couches and filled with 5,000 talents of gold coins, while at the foot of the bed there was a chamber called the "royal footstool," large enough for three couches and containing 3,000 talents in silver money. Above the bed itself a golden vine, studded with jewels, formed a kind of canopy (Athenaeus, 12.514b-f; cf. Jacoby, *Fragmente* II B, p. 658), .

Dino (Athenaeus, 12.514a-b; cf. Muller, *Fragmenta* II, p. 92) is cited as the source for a description of the king's fragrant headdress of myrrh and an aromatic known as *lábyzos*; a special attendant carried a golden stool by which the king descended from his chariot, so that no one need touch him in support. Such a stool is represented in the procession on the reliefs at Persepolis (see, e.g., *Survey of Persian Art* VII, pl. 94B). Athenaeus also reported (10.434d), without naming his source, that Darius I (q.v.; r. 521-486 B.C.E.) had inscribed on his tomb "I could drink much wine and yet carry it well" (cf. Schmitt, pp. 26, 30); the trilingual inscription carved on his tomb at Naqš-e Rostam includes no such reference, however (Kent, *Old Persian*, pp. 138-40). Much of Athenaeus' other information on drinking at the Achaemenid court was taken from Ctesias, who had reported that the Persian king was allowed to get drunk only on the day of the sacrifice to Mithra, and from Duris, who added that on that day the king alone could dance "the Persian"; such dancing was unique to the Persians, who, according to Duris, learned to dance as routinely as they learned to ride (10.434d-e; cf. Müller, *Fragmenta* I, p. 55, II, p. 472; see DANCE i).

Dino provided information on the royal meals in the time of Xerxes I. Only the choicest foodstuffs from all over the empire were served, for Xerxes disapproved of foreign food or drink, and his successors actually forbade them; he forbade purchasing Attic figs until he could seize them without buying them, apparently a reference to a proposed expedition to Athens. The most complete report on meals, however, came from Heracleides. The king normally breakfasted and dined entirely alone, though sometimes his wife and some of his sons joined him. All those who were to serve him had first to bathe and don white clothes. The guests were divided into two categories, those who dined outdoors in full view and those who dined indoors, in a separate room, where the king could see them through a curtain while remaining invisible himself. On great public holidays, however, all the guests might dine in the great hall with the king. Furthermore, he frequently sent a eunuch to invite a dozen or so companions to drink with him in his private room after dinner; at these sessions the guests, who were not served the same wine as the king, sat on the floor, while he reclined on a couch with golden feet. They left only when thoroughly drunk. Throughout the dinner the royal concubines played the lyre and sang, one of them as soloist, the rest as chorus. Despite all this supposed splendor, however, Heracleides emphasized the small portions and general parsimony of the meals served both at court and in the homes of Persian notables (see COOKING i) and commented that it was customary for guests to carry away any morsels of their food that they did not finish (Athenaeus, 14.652b-c, 4.145b-e; cf. Müller, *Fragmenta* II, pp. 91, 96).

Clearchus (Athenaeus, 12.514-d-e; cf. Müller, *Fragmenta* II, p. 304) claimed that the king took steps to prevent his bodyguards from becoming soft with luxury: "To those, at any rate, who supplied him with any delicacy he gave prizes for the invention, yet when he served these dainties he did not sweeten them by bestowing special honors, but preferred to enjoy them all alone, showing his sense!" From Timaeus Athenaeus drew the story of Democedes (q.v.; 12.522b-c; cf. Müller, *Fragmenta* I, p. 212), a Greek physician from Croton who was captured by the Persians after the death in battle of Polycrates of Samos in 522 B.C.E. and served at the court of Darius I. Greek notables like Pausanius, king of the Spartans, and Dionysius, tyrant of Sicily, deliberately adopted Persian dress (Athenaeus, 12.535e, citing Duris), and Greek exiles who submitted to Persia, like Themistocles of Athens and Demaratus of Sparta, were required to wear it; among the cities given to Themistocles was Gambreium in Asia Minor, which was to provide his clothing (Athenaeus, 1.29f-30a; cf. Thucydides, 1.138.5).

Reports about Alexander and his successors. Carystius reported that the Persian kings' habit of getting drunk was emulated by Alexander, who used to carouse in an ass-drawn chariot (10.43-44; cf. 10.434f-435a). He also adopted Persian dress, and Demetrius Poliorcetes, son of his general Antigonus, was noted for wearing expensive Persian shoes (Athenaeus, 12.535f, citing Duris). The Parthian kings, according to Athenaeus (12.513f-14a), continued the Achaemenid practice of shifting the capital according to the season, spending the spring in Rhagae, the winter in Babylon, and the rest of the year in Hecatompylos (cf. Strabo, 16.1.16). Citing Poseidonius, Athenaeus reported that at banquets the Parthian king reclined alone on a separate, more elevated couch; his table, with native dishes, was set somewhat apart, "as to a departed spirit." The "king's friend" sat on the ground, while the king tossed him morsels of food as if to a dog; often, on some slight pretext, he would order this favorite to be taken away and flogged with staves or knouts, after which, covered in blood, he would prostrate himself before the king and do obeisance (4.152f-153b; cf. Müller, *Fragmenta* III, pp. 254, 258).

Greek imports from Persia. Among the products that Athenaeus reported as having originated in Persia were peaches ("Persian apples," *mêla persiká*), oranges ("Median apples," *mēdiká*), plums ("Persian sour apples," *oxýmala persiká*; 3.82e-83a), and walnuts ("Persian nuts," *persiká*, 2.53e, 54b), though he did not mention the cock and the rose, which had also originated in Persia. Two supposed Persian drinking vessels, *sannákra* (a cup; 11.497e-f) and *batiákē* ("a Persian saucer"; 11.784a-b) are not attested elsewhere. Among Persian words used in Greek Athenaeus cited *parasángēs* "parasang," *astándēs* "courier," *ággaros* "mounted courier," and *schoînon* "rush, reed," a measure of land (3.122a).

Bibliography: (For cited works not found in this bibliography, see "Short References.") C. B. Gulick, ed. and tr., *Athenaeus. The Deipnosophists*, 7 vols., London, 1927-41; repr. Cambridge, Mass., 1961. P. Huyse, "Persisches Wortgut in Athenaios' Deipno-sophistai," *Glotta* 68, 1990, pp. 93-104. G. Kaibel, *Athenaei Naucraticae Deipnosophistarum Libri XV*, 3 vols., Leipzig, 1887-90; repr. Stuttgart, 1965 (the standard edition). V. Rose, *Aristotle's Pseudepigraphies*, Leipzig, 1863. R. Schmitt, "Achaemenideninschriften in griechischer literarischer Überlieferung," in *Barg-e sabz/A Green Leaf. Papers in Honor of Professor Jes P. Asmussen*, Acta Iranica 28, Leiden, 1988, pp. 17-38.

(JACQUES DUCHESNE-GUILLEMIN)

DEITY. See Supplement. See also ACHAEMENID RELIGION; AHRIMAN; AHURA MAZDĀ; MANICHEISM; ZOROASTRIANISM.

DEJLA. See ARVANDRŪD; ŠAṬṬ AL-ʿARAB; TIGRIS.

D̲EKR (lit., "remembrance"), the act of reminding oneself of God.

i. *In Sufism*.
ii. *In the Babi and Bahai religions*.

i. IN SUFISM

Among Sufis *d̲ekr* is the most common prayer practice. The term and its derivatives occur in about 250 koranic verses. The Koran itself (e.g., 7:63, 38:1) and other scriptures (e.g., 21:7) are referred to as *d̲ekr* or as *d̲ekrā* and *tad̲kera* (reminder; e.g., 6:90, 74:49), and the Prophet Moḥammad is called *mod̲akker* (admonisher; 88:21). In most instances *d̲ekr* has the basic meaning of "mentioning" God's name or "remembering" God, as in "Remember Me and I will remember you" (2:152); "O believers, remember God incessantly" (33:41); and the frequently cited verses 5:91, 7:205, 13:28, 18:24, and 33:35. This meaning recurs in numerous canonical Hadith (Wensinck, II, pp. 178-82) and often also in the noncanonical Hadith frequently cited by Sufis. One example of the latter is the *ḥadīṯ qodsī*, "I am the Companion of one who remembers Me" (*anā jalīso man d̲akaranī*; Tostarī, p. 26; Šeblī in Qošayrī, p. 467; ʿAyn-al-Qożāt, p. 24; Meybodī, V, p. 393, VII, p. 541, VIII, pp. 218-19, 388 [uttered by Bāyazīd], X, p. 260; for Daylamī's attribution to ʿĀʾeša, see Sak̲āwī [d. 902/1467], pp. 95-96), another the *ḥadīṯ nabawī*, "The best *d̲ekr* is the secret one" (Aḥmad b. Ḥanbal, nos. 1477, 1559, 1623; Sarrāj, ed. Nicholson, p. 42). The Prophet is also reported to have compared *d̲ekr* assemblies (*majāles al-d̲ekr*) to the meadows of paradise (Moḥāsebī, 1940, p. 331; Qošayrī, p. 466) and to have likened *d̲ekr* to the angels' glorification of God: "No company sits remembering God, without the angels surrounding them and divine Presence (*sakīna*) covering them" (Wensinck, II, p. 494; Moḥasebī, apud van Ess, p. 201). *D̲ekr* formulas were also adopted in Muslim everyday life, for example, *al-ḥamdo le'llāh* (Praise belongs to God) and *sobḥān Allāh* (Glory be to God). The most beautiful names of God (*al-asmāʾ al-ḥosnā*) were recited to the rhythm of prayer beads (*tasbīḥ*) or as litanies (*awrād, aḥzāb*).

While theologians (*motakallemūn*) explored the variety of meanings in the word *d̲ekr* (Tahānawī, pp. 512-13), scholars of religious law (*foqahāʾ*) concentrated upon minute regulation of ritual prayer (*ṣalāt*). Nevertheless, the term *majāles al-d̲ekr* was used by such scholars of law as Anas b. Mālek (d. 91-93/709-11) for prayer and other religious assemblies said to have existed since the time of the Prophet (Makkī, II, p. 23; cf. Meier, 1976, p. 236).

From the basic meaning of *d̲ekr* in the Koran and Hadith Sufis derived the notion of "recollection" of God (*d̲ekr*) as a principal prayer practice and central doctrinal concept. Although patterns of historical influence have not been conclusively demonstrated, the Sufi *d̲ekr* includes aspects resembling the repetition of the name of God and hesychastic prayer of eastern Christianity, as well as features similar to the meditation techniques of Yoga (Anawati and Gardet, pp. 235-58). Possible affinities between Sufi forms of *d̲ekr* and the shamanistic practices of Central Asia have been doubted (Meier, 1954, p. 131). As a devotional practice *d̲ekr* is clearly distinct from Muslim ritual prayer (*ṣalāt*) and personal supplication (*doʿāʾ*, q.v.). It is, however, closely associated with intimate colloquy with God (*monājāt*) and with ecstatic prayer accompanied by music and dance (*samāʿ*).

In practice the Sufi *d̲ekr* reflects the mystic's concentration upon God's presence within the human soul, to the exclusion of all else. The Sufi repeats a short *d̲ekr* formula either aloud or "in the heart," seeking to turn away from all distractions and to erase all barriers to awareness of God's presence. The struggle against forgetting God (*ḡafla, nesyān*), the antithesis of *d̲ekr*, reaches a point at which the Sufi is so much with God that he is unaware of even the act of *d̲ekr* itself. *D̲ekr* is understood to be both an act of speaking and an act of hearing: The uninterrupted repetition of God's name is experienced as hearing God speak. For Sufis it thus fends off the insinuations of Satan, counteracts the egocentric drives of the lower soul, and cleanses the mirror of the heart from the tarnish of worldly concerns. They can then be free for God alone. Unlike the ritually obligatory *ṣalāt*, *d̲ekr* is voluntary, and performance is not bound to any particular time (Qošayrī, p. 467), though eventually Sufis came to prefer

Thursday nights for their collective *ḏekr*. They do not understand *ḏekr* as an exercise in self-mortification (despite the term *sayf al-morīdīn* "novices' sword"; Qošayrī, p. 465); rather, it is a mystical way of reaching ecstasy (*wajd*), union with and immersion (*esteḡrāq*) in God.

The Sufi *ḏekr* developed from an individual method of prayer among the classical Sufis of the 9th century into a prayer ceremony of the Sufi confraternities (*ṭarīqas*) beginning in the 12th century. Sahl b. ʿAbd-Allāh Tostarī (d. 283/896) was one of the earliest Sufis who adhered to a regular *ḏekr* practice and offered a rudimentary yet coherent *ḏekr* theory. Throughout his life Tostarī observed the method of recollecting God by repeating the mental prayer "God is my witness" (*Allāh šāhedī*; Qošayrī, pp. 83-84; Böwering, pp. 45-49, or in the words of Ebn al-ʿArabī [d. 638/1240], p. 174: "God is with me, God looks at me, God sees me"), in order to actualize God's presence in the silence of his heart. In the conviction that God takes care of the mystic at every moment of his existence, he understood the practice of *ḏekr* as man's daily spiritual sustenance (*qūt*) and interpreted it experientially as the breakthrough to God, Who Himself effects His own recollection within the mystic's heart (*al-ḏekr be'l maḏkūr*, *ḏekr Allāh be'llāh*; Böwering, pp. 201-07). According to Tostarī, God reveals Himself in the inmost recesses of the human soul (*serr al-nafs*) as the Lord of the primordial covenant alluded to in the koranic phrase *alasto be rabbekom* (Am I not your Lord? 7:172). In this covenant the preexisting souls of all humanity had acceded to the lordship of God before the beginning of time. Through anamnesis the mystic rediscovers this moment in preexistence in pharaoh's blasphemous proclamation of his own lordship, *anā rabbokom al-aʿlā* (I am your Lord Most High; 79:24). By listening to God, the true speaker of the koranic word, the mystic ironically perceives the actual essence of belief flowing from pharaoh's tongue of unbelief and remembers in his experience the moment when God, in preexistence, affirmed His oneness and lordship for human consciousness. That there is only One Who can truly say "I" is the ultimate truth of Islamic mysticism captured in the act of *ḏekr* (Böwering, pp. 185-201). Rowaym b. Aḥmad (d. 303/915-16) corroborated Tostarī's theory of *ḏekr*: "The people heard their first *ḏekr* when God addressed them saying, 'Am I not your Lord?' This *ḏekr* was secreted in their hearts even as its occurrence was secreted in their intellects. So when they heard the *ḏekr*, the secret things of their heart appeared, and they were ravished, even as the secret things of their intellects appeared when God informed them of this, and they believed" (Kalābāḏī, pp. 126-27; tr. pp. 166-67).

The ecstatic quality of this "I" was first given consistent expression in the paradoxical utterances (*šaṭḥ*) of Bāyazīd Besṭāmī (q.v.). His statements "Glory be to Me!" (*sobḥānī*), "I am He" (*anā Howa*), "I am I and thus am 'I,'" and "I am I; there is no God but me" gave vivid expression to a human consciousness merging with the divine. In these expressions there was room neither for the human self nor for God but only for the ultimate and absolute "I," called "God" as the object of faith but "I" as the subject of mystical experience. Whereas it was Bāyazīd who laid the ecstatic foundations for Sufi prayer, Ḥallāj (d. 309/922) became famous for bringing the *ḏekr* experience into the open with his public proclamation *ana'l-Ḥaqq* ("I am the Real," i.e., God). There were, however, Sufis, who favored a more sober approach to *ḏekr*. Abū Bakr Wāseṭī (d. after 320/932), for example, held that the first Sufi word was "Allāh" uttered by the first caliph, Abū Bakr (d. 13/634) and that it was the task of the believer to find peace in the *ḏekr* (Sarrāj, ed. Nicholson, pp. 91, 122-23). He voiced reservations about the unmitigated practice of *ḏekr* (*man ḏakara eftarā* "One who performs recollection fabricates lies"; Sarrāj, ed. Arberry, p. 12) and saw its legitimate goal as mystical vision (*mošāhada*): "*Ḏekr* is leaving the field of forgetfulness as one enters the space of vision dominated by fear and intense love" (Qošayrī, p. 467). Many other classical Sufis contributed aphorisms to the chapters on *ḏekr* included in the widely disseminated Sufi manuals of the 10th and 11th centuries.

There is sufficient evidence that the classical Sufis performed *ḏekr*, originally a predominantly solitary exercise, also in groups and employed shouting and dancing as the body language of ecstasy. At Qayrawān in the 9th century these collective perfomances were known as *mašhad al-ḏekr* (Meier, 1976, p. 243); they came to be associated with *samāʿ*, the practice of listening to music and poetry recitation, especially in the Sufi circles of Baghdad. Jonayd (d. 298/910), one of the leading shaikhs of Baghdad and a sober mystic disinclined to show signs of rapture (Qošayrī, p. 202), defined the basic prerequisites of *samāʿ* as a fixed time and place and the presence of brethren (Sarrāj, ed. Nicholson, pp. 186, 272). Abū Naṣr Sarrāj (ed. Nicholson, pp. 285-88) recorded some of the features of those sessions, like emotional gesticulation and shouted ejaculations, and compared the dancing Sufis to a flock of sheep stirred by the wolf. In sessions of *samāʿ* preference was given to the spontaneous show of emotion resulting from overwhelming experience. Although Ḥakīm Termeḏī (d. between 295/907 and 310/922) and others criticized dancing, clapping hands, jerking the head, and swaying during *ḏekr* (Radtke, p. 129), still others approved throwing off the turban and tearing the clothes. Dancing, whirling, and leaping up were understood as the expression and result of trance, rather than as means for achieving ecstasy. There were provisions, however, that made it permissible to provoke the emotion artificially (*tawājod*) or to conform to the movement of another dancer (*mowāfaqa*), especially that of a respected person (Qošayrī, pp. 201-06).

With time, *ḏekr* and *samāʿ*, which had originally been independent forms of religious expression, became intermingled. Although it appears impossible to define with precision the various stages of transition, the process had been completed by the time of Aḥmad Ḡazālī (d. 520/1126), thus well before the emergence of Sufi confraternities. Aḥmad Ḡazālī understood *ḏekr* as the merging of the practitioner with the cosmic consciousness of creation, which spontaneously proclaims God the one and only Lord (Gramlich, 1983, pp. 18-19). As an exercise, it served Aḥmad Ḡazālī as the prelude to *samāʿ*. The group assembled after either the morning or evening prayer and, following litanies and the recital of *ḏekr* formulas, listened to koranic verses recited by a beautiful voice and interpreted by the shaikh. Then the singer (*qawwāl*) stepped forward to chant songs apt to induce dance and ecstasy (Robson, text p. 167; tr., p. 105).

In their attempt to explain Sufi teachings to a larger public the authors of the Sufi handbooks, from Sarrāj's *Lomaʿ* (ed. Nicholson, p. 219) through Qošayrī's *Resāla* (p. 465) to Moḥammad Ḡazālī's *Eḥyāʾ* (Anawati and Gardet, pp. 214-234), established a ranking of three degrees of *ḏekr*, an ordering already formulated in substance by Tostarī's disciple Ebn Sālem (Sarrāj, ed. Nicholson, p. 219). The *ḏekr* of the tongue (*ḏekr al-lesān*) is the mere recital of the *ḏekr* formula; that of the heart (*ḏekr al-qalb*) is total inner concentration on God's name without moving the tongue; and that of the innermost being (*ḏekr al-serr*) is the experience of total absorption by the reality of the One Who is recollected (*al-maḏkūr*). In each of these modes recollection has initially to be established with effort, but then it begins to flow spontaneously. As the mystic advances through these three ranks of *ḏekr*, a process of interiorization takes place. In the *ḏekr al-lesān* the Sufi is aware of three entities: the subject, the object, and the act of recollection. In the *ḏekr al-qalb* he is conscious only of the division between the subject and the object of recollection. Finally, in the *ḏekr al-serr* no duality remains, and total *fanāʾ* (passing from existence) is achieved (see BAQĀʾ WA FANĀʾ). In later Sufi theory the latter two stages were collapsed into a single second stage, and recollection of the organs and limbs (*ḏekr al-jawāreḥ*) was added as the third, in an attempt to describe the permeation of and sovereignty over the whole body by *ḏekr* (*solṭān al-ḏekr*; see e.g., Maʿṣūm-ʿAlīšāh, I, p. 236).

The Sufi confraternities further transformed the *ḏekr*, which had begun as a free method of prayer, into an elaborate liturgical ceremony. They developed a dual tradition, including the solitary *ḏekr*, whether uttered aloud (*jalī*) or imperceptibly (*ḵafī*), and the collective *ḏekr*, performed by the group aloud in unison. They also distinguished between *ḏekr moqayyad*, performed at a fixed time and place, and *ḏekr moṭlaq*, which was free of such constraints (Ebn ʿAṭāʾ-Allāh, p. 5). This same distinction determines whether or not a *ḏekr* is bound to a fixed ritual (Qoššāšī, pp. 146-47; Meier, 1957, p. 202). Ideally *ḏekr*, as an act of reminding oneself of God, should become the mystic's permanent state and an activity performed uninterruptedly. It is of prime importance that the *ḏekr* formula be implanted in the practitioner's heart by the Sufi shaikh through *talqīn* (infusion), an act derived from Muslim funeral custom (Qošayrī, p. 737; Gramlich, p. 389). The most common *ḏekr* formula in the *ṭarīqa* tradition is the Muslim declaration in which the negation *lā elāha* (there is no god) is combined with the affirmation *ellā Allāh* (but God). Other preferred forms are "Allāh" and the pronoun *howa* "He." The principal requirements for the solitary *ḏekr* are a state of ritual purity while reciting the formula; solitude in a small, dark, and empty room; a position facing the *qebla* with eyes closed, legs crossed, and hands on the knees; elimination of all distracting thoughts (*nafy al-ḵawāṭer*) and breathing controlled with minute regularity (*ḥabs al-nafas*); the presence of the *pīr* before one's heart (a practice of visual representation, sometimes aided by contemplation of the ephebe, or *šāhed*; Gramlich, p. 393; cf. Ritter, 1978, pp. 434-503); and the presence of God before one's eyes (*morāqaba*) through and beyond the image of the *pīr*.

Three basic forms of the Sufi *ḏekr* can be distinguished, according to the beats (*żarb*) of the rhythmic movements and regular breathing performed by the seated individual practitioner. The common historical roots of the three basic forms can be traced in the Kobrawī *ḏekr*, for the essential elements were already set forth in the *Merṣād al-ʿebād* (pp. 271-88; tr. pp. 271-85) of Najm-al-Dīn Dāya (q.v.; d. 654/1256), who followed the practice of Najm-al-Dīn Kobrā (d. 618/1221). The Neʿmat-Allāhīs practice a two-beat *ḏekr*, called *ḏekr-e haykalī* or *ḥamāyelī*, accompanied by bodily movements when the practitioner is alone or performed mentally when others are present. As *lā elāha* is pronounced the head is drawn up in a half-circle from the navel to the throat around the right side of the chest, the seat of the carnal soul (*nafs*); while *ellā Allāh* is pronounced it is returned in another half-circle to the navel around the left side of the chest, the seat of the higher soul or spirit (*rūḥ*; Gramlich, pp. 396-98).

The Naqšbandīs perform a three-beat *ḏekr* without visible motion or perceptible sound. Sitting quite still, the practitioner presses the tongue to the palate and holds his breath beneath the navel. Without moving, he draws the *lā* from beneath the navel to the top of the head (first beat), then directs the *elāha* from the vertex to the right shoulder (second beat), and finally drives the *ellā Allāh* from the shoulder into the heart (third beat). The breath should be held as long as possible and released only after an uneven number of completed repetitions, ideally twenty-one; then the exercise is repeated on a new breath (Gramlich, pp. 398-401). The principles regulating the Naqšbandī *dekr*, as ascribed to ʿAbd-al-Ḵāleq Ḡojdovānī (d. after 617/1220) and developed by Bahāʾ-al-Dīn Naqšband (d. 791/1389), have become standard in the confraternity (summarized in Trimingham, pp. 202-04).

The Kobrawī Sufi ʿAlāʾ-al-Dawla Semnānī (d. 736/1336), following Nūr-al-Dīn Esfarāyenī (d. 717/1317), developed a four-beat *dekr* (Qoššāšī, pp. 155-58) that was adopted by the Hamadānīya (see ʿALĪ HAMADĀNĪ). Holding his breath, the Sufi inclines his head to the level of the navel and inaudibly pronounces the formula in four beats: *lā*, while jerking the head back into the upright position, *elāha* while tracing a half-circle with the head around the right side of the chest and returning it to the position of the navel, *ellā* while jerking the head back up again, and *Allāh* while describing a half-circle with the head around the left side back to the navel. The principal shaikhs of the Neʿmat-Allāhīya, Ḏahabīya (q.v.), and Ḵāksārīya developed further variations of these basic forms of *dekr*, which are generally kept secret from the uninitiated (Gramlich, p. 404-07). These variations, often employed as means of shaping a practitioner's character, rest on the assumption that through recollection one assumes the traits of the divine names (*takalloq be asmāʾ Allāh*, a phrase of Abu'l-Ḥosayn Nūrī, d. 295/907-08) and actualizes the perfections latent within man as created in God's image (ʿAṭṭār, II, pp. 54-55).

The collective *dekr* ceremonies of the *ṭarīqa* tradition, based on a number of *dekr* formulas, most commonly *lā elāha ellā Allāh*, included minute regulation of respiratory rhythm and precisely prescribed postures, according to the traditional practice within a particular confraternity. Such traditions frequently included the use of musical instruments like drums and pipes and the recital of poetry and eulogies to saints. The shaikh, or *pīr*, occupied the most important place in a Sufi session (*ḥażra*) or circle (*ḥalqa*). He also directed the exercise of a person practicing *dekr* in seclusion (*ḵalwa*), especially the forty-day retreat (*arbaʿūn*; see ČELLA ii).

An especially well-known form of communal *dekr* is that of the Mawlawī *ṭarīqa*. Although it is also performed individually, the Mawlawī *dekr*, usually called *samāʿ*, is best known in its collective form. A group of adepts assembles in a circular room (*samāʿ-ḵāna*) around the shaikh, who sits on his sheepskin facing the *qebla*. Participation presupposes initiation; musicians must be present, and a particular style of dress (conical cap and sleeveless gown) is imposed. The group first sits in a circle, then stands together and dances in an ordered circle, each person turning on his own axis, with head and arms in precisely prescribed positions. All begin and end with the music as they perform their studied ritual of whirling. Unlike earlier forms of *samāʿ*, in the Mawlawī *dekr* ecstasy has become the goal of the dance, rather than its result (Ritter, 1933).

Bibliography: (For abbreviations found in this bibliography, see "Short References.") Aḥmad b. Ḥanbal, *al-Mosnad*, Beirut, 1398/1978. G. C. Anawati and L. Gardet, *Mystique musulmane. Aspects et tendances, expériences et techniques*, 2nd ed., Paris, 1968. Farīd-al-Dīn ʿAṭṭār, *Taḏkerat al-awlīāʾ*, ed. R. A. Nicholson, 2 vols., London and Leiden, 1905-07. ʿAyn-al-Qożāt Hamadānī, *Tamhīdāt*, ed. ʿA. ʿOsayrān, Tehran, 1382/1962. G. Böwering, *The Mystical Vision of Existence in Classical Islam*, New York, 1980. Ebn al-ʿArabī, *Mawāqeʿ al-nojūm*, Cairo, 1325/1907. Ebn ʿAṭāʾ-Allāh Eskandarī, *Ketāb meftāḥ al-falāḥ wa-meṣbāḥ al-arwāḥ*, Cairo, n.d. J. van Ess, *Die Gedankenwelt des Ḥāriṯ al-Muḥāsibī*, Bonn, 1961. R. Gramlich, *Die schiitischen Derwischorden Persiens* II. *Glaube und Lehre*, Wiesbaden, 1976. Idem, *Der reine Gottesglaube*, Wiesbaden, 1983. ʿAlī b. ʿOṯmān Hojvīrī Jollābī as*Kašf al-maḥjūb*, ed. V. A. Žokofskī, Tehran, 1336 Š./1957; tr. R. A. Nicholson as *The Kashf al-Maḥjūb. The Oldest Persian Treatise on Sufism*, new ed., 1936; repr. London, 1959.

Abū Bakr Kalābāḏī, *Ketāb al-taʿarrof le maḏhab ahl al-taṣawwof*, ed. A. J. Arberry, Cairo, 1352/1933; tr. A. J. Arberry as *The Doctrine of the Ṣūfīs*, Cambridge, 1935. D. B. Macdonald, "Emotional Religion in Islam as Affected by Music and Singing, Being a Translation of a Book of the *Iḥyāʾ ʿulūm ad-dīn* of al-Ghazzālī," *JRAS*, 1901, pp. 195-252, 705-48; 1902, pp. 1-28. Idem, *Religious Attitude and Life in Islam*, Chicago, 1909. Abū Ṭāleb Makkī, *Qūt al-qolūb*, 4 vols. in 2, Cairo, 1932. Maʿṣūm-ʿAlīšāh, *Ṭarāʾeq al-ḥaqāʾeq*, ed. M.-J. Maḥjūb, 3 vols., Tehran, 1339-1345 Š./1960-66. F. Meier, "Der Derwischtanz. Versuch eines Überblicks," *Asiatische Studien* 8, 1954, pp. 107-36. Idem, *Die Fawāʾiḥ al-ǧamāl wa-fawātiḥ al-ǧalāl des Naǧm ad-Dīn al-Kubrā*, Wiesbaden, 1957. Idem, *Abū Saʿīd-i Abū l-Ḫayr*, Leiden, 1976. Abu'l-Fażl Meybodī, *Kašf al-asrār wa ʿoddat al-abrār*, ed. ʿA.-A. Ḥekmat, 10 vols., Tehran, 1331-39 Š./1962-70. Ḥāreṯ b. Asad Moḥāsebī, *Ketāb al-reʿāya le ḥoqūq Allāh*, ed. M. Smith, GMS, N.S. 1, London, 1940. M. Molé, "La danse extatique en Islam," in *Sources orientales* VI. *Les danses sacrées*, Paris, 1963, pp. 145-280. ʿAbd-al-Karīm Qošayrī, *al-Resāla al-qošayrīya*, 2 vols., ed. M. Maḥmūd, Cairo, 1966. Ṣafī-al-Dīn Aḥmad Qoššāšī, *al-Semṭ al-majīd*, Hyderabad, 1328/1910. B. Radkte, *al-Ḥakīm at-Tirmiḏī*, Freiburg, 1980. Najm-al-Dīn Dāya Rāzī, *Merṣād al-ʿebād*, ed. M.-A. Rīāḥī, Tehran, 1352 Š./1973; tr. H. Algar as *The Path of God's Bondsmen from Origin to Return*, Delmar, N.Y., 1982. H. Ritter, "Der Reigen der 'Tanzenden Derwische,'" *Zeitschrift für Vergleichende Musikwissenschaft* 1, 1933, pp. 28-40. Idem, *Das Meer der Seele*, Leiden, 1978. J. Robson, *Tracts on Listening to Music*, London, 1938. Moḥammad b. ʿAbd-al-Raḥmān Saḵāwī, *al-Maqāṣed al-ḥasana fī bayān kaṯīr men al-aḥādīṯ al-moštahera ʿala'l-alsena*, ed. ʿA. Ṣeddīq Ḡemārī and ʿA. ʿAbd al-Laṭīf, Beirut, 1979. Abū Naṣr Sarrāj, *al-Lomaʿ fi'l-taṣawwof*, ed. R. A. Nicholson, London and Leiden, 1914; ed. A. J. Arberry as *Pages from the Kitāb al-Lumaʿ of Abū Naṣr al-Sarrāj*, London, 1947. Moḥammad-ʿAlā b. ʿAlī Tahānawī, *Kaššāf eṣṭelāḥāt al-fonūn*, 2 vols., Calcutta, 1862. Sahl b. ʿAbd-Allāh Tostarī, *Tafsīr al-Qorʾān al-ʿaẓīm*, Cairo 1329/1911. J. S. Trimingham, *The Sufi Orders in Islam*, Oxford, 1971. A. J. Wensinck, *Concordance et indices de la tradition musulmane*, 8 vols., Leiden, 1936-88.

(GERHARD BÖWERING)

ii. IN THE BABI AND BAHAI RELIGIONS

In Babi and Bahai usage *ḏekr* refers to both a person (see Lawson) and an activity (see Scholl). In such phrases as *ḏekr Allāh al-aʿẓam* (the mightiest remembrance of God or the remembrance of God the Mightiest) it refers to the manifestation, or prophet, of God (*maẓhar-e elāhī*). In the writings of the Bāb (q.v.) it is a reference to himself (Lawson). In the writings of Bahāʾ-Allāh (q.v.) it may refer either to himself or to the Bāb (1984, pp. 190, 194; 1967, p. 7). This usage reflects the Shiʿite interpretation of certain koranic passages (e.g., 3:58 and 20:124) as references to the imams. *Ḏekr*, the "mention" or "remembrance" of God, also denotes prayer and the recital and reading of the scripture, as well as sharing the Sufi meaning of repetitive, ritual chanting (see i, above).

In the histories of the Babi period several practices resembling the Sufi *ḏekr* are recorded. For example, in the *Tārīḵ-e jadīd* of Mīrzā Ḥosayn (p. 157; cf. Mīrzā Jānī, p. 231) it is recorded on the authority of Ḥaydar Beg that the Babis of Zanjān used to chant "Allāh abhā" (God is Most Glorious) ninety-two times (equal to the numerical value of the name Moḥammad) from their barricades during the upheaval in 1266-67/1850-51 (see BABISM ii); Moḥammad-Nabīl Zarandī (p. 552-53) listed the invocations used. Babi prisoners in Tehran in 1268-69/1852 are reported to have chanted invocations (Moḥammad-Nabīl, p. 632). Other instances are also recorded.

Bahāʾ-Allāh provided formulas to be chanted and also set aside a special day for this activity (ʿAbd-al-Bahāʾ, tr., p. 38), but, apart from the ritual invocation of the words "Allāh abhā" as part of personal daily devotions, there is not at present much in Bahai practice that corresponds to the Sufi practice of *ḏekr*. The phrase *mašreq al-aḏkār* refers both to the practice of reciting prayers and scripture at dawn and to the place in which such recitations are carried out (see BAHAI FAITH ix).

Bibliography: ʿAbd-al-Bahāʾ, *Taḏkerat al-wafāʾ*, Haifa, 1924; tr. M. Gail as *Memorials of the Faithful*, Wilmette, Ill., 1971. Bahāʾ-Allāh, *Alwāḥ-e nāzela ḵeṭāb be molūk wa roʾasā-ye arż*, Tehran, 1347 Š./1968; partial tr. Shoghi Effendi as *Proclamation of Bahá'u'lláh to the Kings and Leaders of the World*, Haifa, 1967. Idem, *Montaḵabātī az āṯār-e Ḥażrat Bahāʾ-Allāh*, ed. Shoghi Effendi, Hofheim-Langenhain, Germany, 1984. B. T. Lawson, "The Terms 'Remembrance' (*dhikr*) and 'Gate' (*báb*) in the Báb's Commentary on the Súra of Joseph," in M. Momen, ed., *Studies in Honor of the Late Hasan M. Balyuzi*, Los Angeles, 1988. Mīrzā Ḥosayn Hamadānī, *Tārīḵ-e jadīd*, tr. E. G. Browne as *Táríkh-i-Jadíd, or New History of Mírzá 'Alí Muḥammad the Báb*, Cambridge, 1893. Ḥājī Mīrzā Jānī Kāšānī, *Ketāb al-noqṭat al-kāf*, ed. E. G. Browne, Leiden and London, 1910. Moḥammad-Nabīl Zarandī, tr. Shoghi Effendi as *The Dawn-Breakers. Nabíl's Narrative*, Wilmette, Ill., 1962. S. Scholl, "The Remembrance of God. An Invocation Technique in Sufism and the Writings of the Báb and Bahá'u'lláh," *Bahá'í Studies Bulletin* 2/3, 1983, pp. 73-98.

(MOOJAN MOMEN)

ḎEKRĪS. See BALUCHISTAN i.

DELĀRESTĀQ (also Delārostāq, Dīlārostāq), *dehestān* (administrative district) in the *šahrestān* of Āmol (Lārījān *baḵš*), on the northeastern slope of Mount Damāvand (q.v.) in Māzandarān (Razmārā, *Farhang* III, p. 122). It is a small, isolated region, located between Lārījān and Nūr and thus forming part of the conglomeration of mountain valleys in the central Alborz. For a long time it was difficult of access owing to the altitude and especially to the steepness of the slopes in the lower part of the valley bordering the Harāz river (Sotūda, pp. 463 ff.).

The population consists of only 1,300 inhabitants of eleven small villages and hamlets (Census, 1365 Š./1986). As is general in Lārījān, most of the villagers winter in the neighborhood of Āmol, and only agricultural families and herdsmen remain all year in the mountains. Although a few families from the village of Razān (or Razon) call themselves Mongols (Sotūda, pp. 463 ff.), the basic population of Delārestāq has been settled there since time immemorial, and all speak the Gīlakī dialect of Āmol. Until the beginning of the 20th century they were governed by local princes who resisted the successive political authorities (de Planhol, p. 20).

The heart of this pastoral district is a vast plateau, only a small part of which is cultivated (in wheat, barley, and potatoes); it is overlooked by the steep, snowy slopes of Mount Damāvand. The main village, Nāndal (or Lāndāl), is located on this plateau and is often damaged by earthquakes; it serves as the point of departure for ascents of the north face of Damāvand. In the summer herds of cattle and especially flocks of *zeli* sheep (without fat tails) from the Āmol region graze on the high pastures. Summer visitors from Māzandarān and Tehran have become numerous, especially since the construction of the road from Panjāb along the main Harāz route and passing through the neighboring valley of Namārostāq.

According to tradition, Delārestāq was part of the region in which legends linked with Mount Demāvand were set, and many shrines (*takīyas* and *emāmzādas*) attest the symbolic and mythical richness of this small plateau (Sotūda, passim). According to Ebn Esfandīār (p. 57), Ferēdūn was born in Var, a village in Delārestāq the location of which is at present unknown, though H. L. Rabino (p. 115) seems to have recorded its existence in the 19th century; Ferēdūn was supposed to have grown up among cattle herders at Šalāb in the vicinity of Āmol, which seems to fit the present pattern of seasonal migrations between the two districts. Near the village of Kahrūd in the lower part of Delārestāq, where the climate is relatively mild, there are ruins of a castle known only as Robāṭ, which overlooks the entrance to the Harāz valley and Lārījān beyond. Rabino identified them as the celebrated fortress of Prince Manōčehr of Lārījān, who was supposed to have rebuilt it as a palace; it was destroyed by Sayyed Fak̲r-al-Dīn Marʿašī in 783/1381 (Rabino, p. 115; cf. Sotūda, p. 478).

Bibliography: (For cited works not found in this bibliography, see "Short References.") X. de Planhol, "Un haut pays du versant aride de l'Alborz. Le Larid̲jan (haute vallée du Harâz)," in X. de Planhol, *Recherches sur la géographie humaine de l'Iran septentrional*, Paris, 1964, pp. 17-36. H. L. Rabino, *Mázandarán and Astarábád*, GMS, N.S. 7, London, 1928. M. Sotūda, *Az Āstārā tā Estārbād* III. *Māzandarān-e ḡarbī*, Tehran, 1335 Š./1956.

(BERNARD HOURCADE)

DELBARJĪN, urban site 40 km northwest of Balk̲ (q.v.), on the northern limit of an oasis irrigated by the Balk̲āb (q.v.), near a defensive wall built during the Greek period (ca 329-130 B.C.E.) to protect the oasis. It was probably founded in the 5th century B.C.E. and flourished up to about the 6th century C.E. Study of the fortifications excavated by a Soviet-Afghan mission in 1348-56 Š./1969-77 suggests that the earliest stage of the citadel may date from the Achaemenid period, as the closest parallels to the construction methods and ceramic finds are of that period (Dolgorukov, pp. 75-77, 85). It was, however, only in the final phase of Greek hegemony (ca. 150 B.C.E.), when the city may have been known as Eucratideia (Strabo, 11.11.2; Ptolemy, 6.11.8), or at the beginning of the Kushan period (ca. the beginning of the common era) that the site assumed its final configuration: a city protected by a quadrangular rampart (383-93 m^2), with a circular citadel in the center. The northeast corner of the walled enclosure was occupied by a temple precinct (Figure 11/I, II), and suburbs of considerable size lay south and east of the city (Dolgorukov; Pugachenkova, 1984). The earliest city wall consisted of a rather thin curtain of *pak̲sa* (tamped earth mixed with water) and unbaked brick, built on a glacis of *pak̲sa* and pierced with arrow slits, with hollow quadrangular towers at intervals. At the beginning of the Kushan period a second wall, also with towers, was constructed outside the original rampart, forming an interior gallery typical of Central Asian fortifications. The main gate was originally located between two bastions several stories high in the middle of the southern wall in the direction of Balk̲ (Figure 11/VIII); when subsequently the entrance was shifted farther to the east these bastions were enlarged and joined in a single flanking tower (Pugachenkova, 1984). It was also during the Kushan period that the citadel was surrounded by a rampart, circular in plan and again with an internal gallery. This rampart was eventually destroyed and replaced by a solid wall, which was further strengthened with round towers during the last phase (Figure 11/CVII, CVIII). The fortifications ultimately lost their military function and were adapted for dwellings. The date of final abandonment of the rampart can be determined from a tomb situated on the ruins of the southern wall, in which a Hephthalite coin of the 5th century C.E. was found (Vaĭnberg and Kruglikova, 1984, p. 126 no. 124)

Excavations at the main temple in the northeast corner of the wall (Figure 11/I) revealed six construction phases, evidence for the complex architectural and religious history of this sanctuary over the centuries of its existence (Kruglikova, 1986; Bernard, 1990). It may have been established at the end of the Greek period, though, like the temples at nearby Āy-K̲ānom (q.v.) and Tak̲t-e Sangīn, it had few Greek features. In plan it was originally wider than deep, 22 x 16 m, with a cella surrounded by narrow chambers. The entrance consisted of a deep recess between two projecting rooms. In the Kushan period the temple was lengthened toward the back (22 x 44 m), but the facade and entrance reproduced the original disposition, with new rows of columns and pilasters on stone bases of Attic type (Pugachenkova, 1976, pp. 134-37). From decorative wall paintings it is clear that the temple was dedicated first to the Greek Dioscuroi (or their father, Zeus) and in the 2nd century C.E. to the Indian god Shiva, who was depicted seated with his wife Parvati on the bull Nandi (Kruglikova, 1976-84, I, pp. 87-96; Bernard, 1987). Other paintings were found in a series of humbler sanctuaries built against the northern rampart during the Kushan period (Figure 11/II; Kruglikova, 1976-84, I, pp. 96-110, II, pp. 120-45). In addition to representations of worshipers in local dress (full trousers tucked into boots, tunics of rich materials, coats with single lapels, daggers suspended in horizontal position), there are a dancing Shiva, a god mounted on a giant bird, and a helmeted Athena holding a mirror, the last a hellenized synthesis of the two Iranian goddesses Arštāt (see AŠTĀD), god-

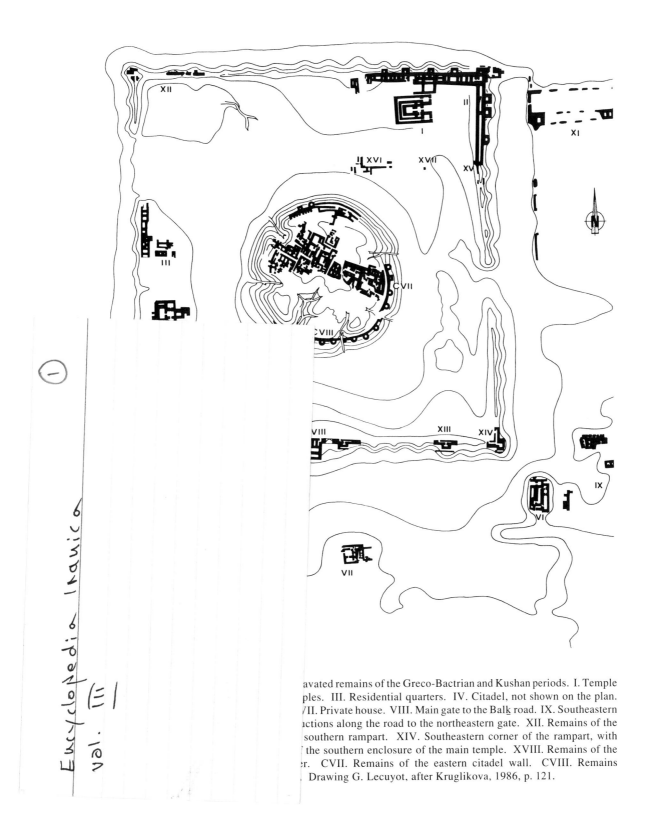

avated remains of the Greco-Bactrian and Kushan periods. I. Temple
ples. III. Residential quarters. IV. Citadel, not shown on the plan.
/II. Private house. VIII. Main gate to the Balḵ road. IX. Southeastern
ıctions along the road to the northeastern gate. XII. Remains of the
southern rampart. XIV. Southeastern corner of the rampart, with
' the southern enclosure of the main temple. XVIII. Remains of the
ːr. CVII. Remains of the eastern citadel wall. CVIII. Remains
. Drawing G. Lecuyot, after Kruglikova, 1986, p. 121.

(1)

Encyclopedia Iranica
vol. III

dess of justice, and Ardoxšo/Aši (q.v.), protectress of women (Grenet). The unbaked clay head of a goddess wearing a diadem was discovered in the earliest, perhaps Greco-Bactrian phase of a sanctuary in the western part of the city (Figure 11/X; Sokolovskiĭ). During the last period a small chapel was built in honor of Hercules/Vahrām in one of the bastions flanking the southern gate (Figure 11/VIII); it contained an unbaked clay statue of the god represented in the nude in the Greek style (Pugachenkova, 1977; idem, 1984, pp. 106-07). Toward the end of the city's existence a Buddhist sanctuary was built in the southeastern suburb of the town (Figure 11/VI; Kruglikova and Pugachenkova, pp. 61-69).

Two houses were excavated in the southern suburbs of the town (Figure 11/V, VII; Pugachenkova, 1976; Kruglikova and Pugachenkova, pp. 5-47, 91-103). One of them (Figure 11/V), built around 100 B.C.E., recalls, in its orthogonal plan, imposing dimensions (84 x 57.5 m), and axial reception hall preceded by a garden court surrounded on three sides by a corridor, the type of patrician house of the Greco-Bactrian period found at Āy Ḵānom. The subdivision of the west wing into separate apartments suggests a patriarchal residence housing several branches of the same family. A large water tank, built against the northwest corner and formerly fed from a shallow aquifer, is the oldest known example of a vaulted ceiling of the "Balḵī" type developed from four squinches on a square plan (Besenval, pp. 65, 131).

The inscriptions are all in the Bactrian language (Livshits, 1976, pp. 163-69; idem, 1979, pp. 95-97), except for one in Brahmi (Vorob'eva-Desyatovskaya); they were painted on the walls and on ostraca or engraved on vases and on a stone stele (Livshits and Kruglikova, pp. 98-112; Lazard et al.). They are too damaged to yield any significant historical information, however.

The chronology of the site cannot be determined with certainty. It is not clear whether the foundation of the walled city and the first quadrangular rampart around the ancient citadel, as well as the first phases of the great temple, dates from the end of the Greco-Bactrian period (ca. 150 B.C.E.) or the beginning of the Kushan period. Furthermore, the style of the later paintings, which are comparable to those of Balalyk Tepe and to the oldest frescoes at Panjīkant, both in Sogdia, indicates a date in the 5th-6th centuries C.E., according to some authorities (Belenitskiĭ and Marshak), whereas others argue from the numismatic finds that the final phase cannot have been later than the end of the 4th or the early 5th century C.E. (Vaĭnberg and Kruglikova, 1976; idem, 1984; Pugachenkova, 1984, p. 105). Despite these uncertainties, however, the mural paintings at Delbarjīn, which were applied directly to the earthen walls, with or without a preliminary undercoat of whitewash, provide valuable information on local cults and on the origins and development of Bactrian painting, in which an increasingly rich palette and shading were used to suggest depth and volume (Buryĭ, 1976, pp. 11-124; idem, 1979, pp. 146-62).

Bibliography: A. M. Belenitskiĭ and B. I. Marshak, "The Paintings of Sogdiana," in G. Azarpay, *Sogdian Painting. The Pictorial Epic in Oriental Art*, Berkeley and Los Angeles, 1981, pp. 11-77. P. Bernard, "Nouvelles découvertes dans la Bactriane afghane," *AIUON* 39, (N.S. 29), 1979, p. 119-39. Idem, in *Abstracta Iranica* 10, 1987, pp. 60-62. Idem, "L'architecture religieuse de l'Asie Centrale à l'époque hellénistique," in *Akten des XIII. Internationalen Kongresses für klassische Archäologie, Berlin 1988*, Mainz, 1990, pp. 51-59. P. Besenval, *Technique de la voûte dans l'Orient ancien* I, Paris, 1984. V. P. Buryĭ, "Tekhnika zhivopisi" (The painting technique), in I. T. Kruglikova, ed., *Drevnyaya Baktriya* I, Moscow, 1976, pp. 111-24. Idem, "Tekhnika rospiseĭ pomishcheniya 16" (The wall-painting technique in Building 16), in I. T. Kruglikova, ed., *Drevnyaya Baktriya* II, Moscow, 1979, pp. 146-62.

V. S. Dolgorukov, "Oboronitel'nye sooruzheniya Dil'berdzhina" (The fortifications of Delbarjīn), in I. T. Kruglikova, ed., *Drevnyaya Baktriya* III, Moscow, 1984, pp. 58-92. F. Grenet, "L'Athéna de Dil'berdžin," in F. Grenet, ed., *Cultes et monuments religieux dans l'Asie Centrale préislamique*, Paris, 1987, pp. 41-45. Idem and N. Sims-Williams, "The Historical Context of the Sogdian Ancient Letters," in *Transition Periods in Iranian History. Actes du symposium de Fribourg-en-Brisgau, 22-24 mai 1985*, Louvain, 1987, p. 118. I. T. Kruglikova, ed., *Dil'berdzhin (Raskopki 1970-1972 gg)* (Delbarjīn [Excavations 1970-1973]) I, Moscow, 1974. Idem, ed., *Drevnyaya Baktriya. Materialy sovetsko-afganskoĭ ekspeditsii 1969-1973 gg.* (Ancient Bactria. Materials from the Soviet-Afghan expedition, 1969-73), 3 vols., Moscow, 1976-84. Idem, "Les fouilles de la mission archéologique soviéto-afghane sur le site gréco-kushan de Dilberdjin en Bactriane (Afghanistan)," *Comptes rendus de l'Académie des Inscriptions et Belles-Lettres*, 1977, pp. 407-28. Idem, *Dil'berdzhin. Khram Dioskurov. Materialy sovetsko-afganskoĭ arkheologicheskoĭ ekspeditsii* (Delbarjīn. Temple of the Dioscuroi. Materials from the Soviet-Afghan archeological expedition), Moscow, 1986. Idem and G. A. Pugachenkova, eds., *Dil'berdzhin (Raskopki 1970-1973)* (Delbarjīn [Excavations 1970-73]) II, Moscow, 1977. G. Lazard, F. Grenet, and C. de Lamberterie, "Notes bactriennes," *Stud. Ir.* 13, 1984, pp. 199-239. V. D. Livshits, "Nadpisi iz Dil'berdzhina" (Inscriptions from Delbarjīn), in I. T. Kruglikova, ed., *Drevnyaya Baktriya* I, Moscow, 1976, pp. 163-69. Idem, "Dva ostraka iz Dil'berdzhina" (Two ostraca from Delbarjīn), in I. T. Kruglikova, ed., *Drevnyaya Baktriya* II, Moscow, 1979, pp. 95-97. Idem and I. T. Kruglikova, "Fragmentu baktriĭskoĭ monumental'noĭ nadpisi iz Dil'berdzhina" (Fragments of a Bactrian monumental inscription from Delbarjīn), in I. T. Kruglikova, ed., *Drevnyaya Baktriya* II, Moscow, 1979, pp. 98-112. G. A. Pugachenkova, "Antichnoĭ i rannesrednevekovoĭ arkhitektury severnogo Afganistana" (The ancient and early medieval architecture of northern Afghanistan), in I. T. Kruglikova, ed., *Drevnyaya Baktriya* I, Moscow, 1976, pp. 125-62. Idem, "Gerakl v Baktrii" (Hercules in Bactria), *VDI*, 1977/2, pp. 77-92. Idem, "Raskopki yuzhnykh gorodskikh vorot Dil'berdzhina" (Excavations of the southern city gate at Delbarjīn), in I. T. Kruglikova, ed., *Drevnyaya Baktriya* III, Moscow, 1984, pp. 93-111. V. M. Sokolovskiĭ, "Rekonstruktsiya dvukh skul'pturnykh izobrazheniĭ iz Dil'berdzhina (Raskop X)" (Reconstruction of two sculptural representations from Delbarjīn [Excavated area X]), in I. T. Kruglikova, ed., *Drevnyaya Baktriya* II, Moscow, 1979, pp. 113-19. B. I. Vaĭnberg and I. T. Kruglikova, "Monetye nakhodki iz raskopok Dil'berdzhina" (Coins from the excavations at Delbarjīn), in I. T. Kruglikova, ed., *Drevnyaya Baktriya* I, Moscow, 1976, pp. 172-82. Idem, "Monetye nakhodki iz raskopok Dil'berdzhina (II)" (Coins from the excavations at Delbarjīn. II), in I. T. Kruglikova, ed., *Drevnyaya Baktriya* III, 1984, pp. 125-40. I. M. Vorob'eva-Desyatovskaya, "Nadpis' brakhmi iz Dil'berdzhina" (The Brahmi inscription from Delbarjīn), in I. T. Kruglikova, ed., *Drevnyaya Baktriya* I, Moscow, 1976, pp. 170-71.

(PAUL BERNARD)

DELDĀR-ʿALĪ b. Moḥammad-Moʿīn NAṢĪRĀBĀDĪ, Sayyed Ḡofrān-maʾāb (b. Naṣīrābād near Lucknow, 1166/1753, d. Lucknow ca. 1235/1820), Shiʿite cleric of northern India who helped to establish the Shiʿite form of Friday prayers and propagated the rationalist Oṣūlī school of jurisprudence in the Avadh (q.v.) region.

In Deldār-ʿAlī's native village, Naṣīrābād in the district of Rai Bareli, influential *sayyeds* (claiming descent from the Prophet Moḥammad) perhaps first began to embrace Shiʿism in the 18th century, encouraged by grants of land from the Shiʿite *nawwābs* of Avadh (Sayyed Moḥammad, p. 47). Nevertheless, Deldār-ʿAlī pursued his early Islamic studies primarily with Sunni teachers in the small intellectual centers of northern India; one of them was the renowned Mollā ʿAbd-al-ʿAlī Ferangī-Maḥallī. When, in 1189/1775, Nawwāb Āṣaf-al-Dawla established his capital at Lucknow, Deldār-ʿAlī made his way there and soon entered the circle of the chief minister, Ḥasan Reżā Khan. The leading state functionaries were looking for young Shiʿite talent, and Deldār-ʿAlī struck them as promising. A notable offered to pay for his studies in Iraq, where he spent the years 1193-95/1779-81 at Najaf and Karbalāʾ, forsaking the conservative Aḵbārī legal teachings then popular in northern India for the rationalist Oṣūlī school (*Āʾīna*, fols. 44-55; Kentūrī, I, pp. 1315-36; Ardestānī, I, 92-91 [pages of Persian text numbered in Western sequence]).

On his return to Lucknow Deldār-ʿAlī accepted the patronage of the notables; beginning in 1200/1786 he was pressed into performing Friday prayers, despite initial reservations about whether such prayers were permissible during the occultation of the twelfth imam. His teaching and writing helped to spread Oṣūlī rationalism among young clerics in Avadh. He opposed the influence of both Sufis and Aḵbārīs and succeeded in gaining perquisites for Shiʿite clerics that had earlier been monopolized by less professional groups; for instance, earlier in the 18th century such Islamic charitable and other taxes as *zakāt* and *ḵoms* had been collected and distributed informally by Shiʿite physicians. The *nawwāb* granted him nine tax-free villages, as well as an annual stipend of Rs. 5,000 (*Āʾīna*, fols. 65-67; Cole, pp. 179-80).

Deldār-ʿAlī also promoted the establishment of Friday prayers throughout the realm and set up an informal network of Shiʿite higher education in the homes of clerics whom he himself helped to train. He and his students issued informal legal rulings for Shiʿites and discouraged them from appealing to the courts, which were still manned largely by Sunni judges. He refused, however, to establish a formal Shiʿite court system for Avadh, fearing that such an institution would bring him into conflict with the authoritarian *nawwābs*, who were not always attentive to the rule of Islamic law. He also refused to challenge their intervention in religious matters, as when one *nawwāb* insisted on celebrating *ʿīd al-ażḥā* (the main Muslim feast day) a day too early. Deldar-ʿAlī argued that Shiʿite clerics should acquiesce, as Avadh was still part of the Sunni Mughal empire and clerics were obliged to practice pious dissimulation (*taqīya*) of their true opinions even from Shiʿite *nawwābs*. As a result of such attitudes Persian clerics like Aḥmad Behbahānī (q.v.) criticized Deldār-ʿAlī for what they regarded as excessive subservience to the state (*Āʾīna*, fols. 142b-46a; Behbahānī, fols. 166b-68b).

Deldār-ʿAlī had five sons; the eldest, Sayyed Moḥammad Naṣīrābādī, succeeded him as leader of the Friday prayers at Lucknow.

Deldār-ʿAlī was a prolific writer. His works include *Fawāʾed-e āṣafīya wa mawāʿeẓ-e ḥasanīya* (Nāṣerīya Library, Lucknow, Hadith Shiʿa, ms. no. 152), a collection of Friday sermons in Persian made in 1200/1786); *Asās al-oṣūl* (Lucknow, 1320/1902) and the more mature *Montaha'l-afkār* (Lucknow, 1330/1912), on Oṣūlī principles of jurisprudence, both in Arabic; *Merʾāt al-ʿoqūl* (3 vols., Lucknow, 1320/1902), on *oṣūl al-dīn*, in Arabic; *Resāla fī aḥkām al-arażīn* (Raza [Reżā] Library, Rampur, ms. no. 2182), his most important work on land tenure, in

Arabic; *Ṣawārem al-elāhīyāt* and *Ḥosām al-Eslām* (both in Persian; Calcutta, 1218/1803), *Ḏu'l-feqār* (in Persian; Ludhiana, 1281/1848-49), *al-Šehāb al-ṯāqeb* (in Arabic; India Office Library, London, ms. no. 2182), and *Resāla dar radd-e maḏhab-e ṣūfīya* (in Persian; Nāṣerīya Library, Kalām Shiʿa, ms. no. 111), all anti-Sufi polemics; and *Najāt al-sāʾelīn* (Nāṣerīya Library, Feqh Shīʿa, ms. no. 256) and *Ajwebat al-sāʾelīn* (Asiatic Society of Bengal Library, Calcutta, Curzon ms. no. 1016), which are collections of his legal rulings.

Bibliography: Sayyed ʿAbbās Ardestānī, *al-Ḥeṣn al-matīn fī aḥwāl al-wozarāʾ wa'l-salāṭīn*, National Archives of India, New Delhi, ms. no. 235a-b. *Āʾīna-ye ḥaqqnemā*, Nāṣerīya Library, Lucknow, Rejāl Shīʿa, ms. no. 1 (the major source for Deldār-ʿAlī's life, written in Lucknow around 1816 by an anonymous disciple). Āqā Aḥmad Behbahānī, *Merʾāt al-aḥwāl-e jahānnemā*, British Library, London, Add. ms. no. 24052. J. R. I. Cole, *Roots of North Indian Shiʿism in Iran and Iraq. Religion and State in Awadh, 1722-1859*, Berkeley, Calif., 1988. Sayyed Eʿjāz Ḥosayn Kentūrī, *Šoḏūr al-ʿeqyān fī tarājem al-aʿyān*, National Library, Calcutta, mss. nos. Buhar 278-79. Āḡā Mahdī Lakhnavī, *Sawāneḥ-e ḥayāt-e ḥażrat-e Ḡofrān-maʾāb*, Karachi, 1982 (a somewhat hagiographical treatment). S. A. A. Rizvi, *A Socio-Cultural History of the Isna ʿAshari Shiʿis in India*, 2 vols., Delhi, 1986. Sayyed Moḥammad, *Maḵzan-e aḥmadī*, Agra, 1299/1882.

(JUAN R. I. COLE)

DELDĀR, YŪNES MELA RAʾŪF (b. in the *sanjaq* of Ḵoy in the Ottoman empire, 20 February 1918; d. Erbīl, Iraq, 12 October 1948), Kurdish poet and humanist. While a student of law in Baghdad he joined the Hiwā (Hope) party, the first legally recognized Kurdish organization to work for the unification of Kurdistan.

Many of his poems in the classical Kurdish style, characterized by quantitative rhythm and monorhyme, were first published in the influential Kurdish literary journals *Ronākī* (Erbīl, 1935-36) and *Galawēz* (Baghdad, 1939-49), which played major roles in the development of Kurdish language and literature in Iraq and Persia. He also introduced new romantic and realistic elements into Kurdish poetry, which up to then had followed purely classical patterns. Most of his poems have been set to music, and one of them, *Ay raqīb* (O enemy), is regarded by most Kurds as their national anthem.

Bibliography: Y. M. R. Deldār, *Dīvān*, 2nd ed., Erbīl, 1971. K.-M. Maʿrūf, "Deldār, šāʿer-ī šorešgar o pēškawtenḵuwāz," *Hēvī* (Paris) 4, 1985, pp. 32-27. ʿA.-M. Rasūl, *al-Wāqeʿīya fi'l-adab al-kordī*, Sidon, Lebanon, 1966.

(JOYCE BLAU)

DÉLÉGATIONS ARCHÉOLOGIQUES FRANÇAISES, bodies established by the French government to conduct archeological investigations in Persia and Afghanistan respectively.

i. *Délégation Archéologique Française en Iran.*
ii. *Délégation Archéologique Française en Afghanistan.*

i. DÉLÉGATION ARCHÉOLOGIQUE FRANÇAISE EN IRAN

Archeological research in Persia began with the explorations of the British geologist W. K. Loftus in 1847 and was continued by Marcel and Jane Dieulafoy (qq.v.) in 1884-86. The main site to catch the interest of these investigators was Susa in Ḵūzestān, one of the capitals of the Achaemenid empire and mentioned in the Bible as the palace where Esther was chosen queen by Ahasuerus (Esther 2; M. Dieulafoy, 1888). C. Babin mapped the three major areas of the site (the acropolis; the Apadāna, q.v. ii; and the "Ville royale") while the Dieulafoys excavated the Achaemenid palace in the Apadāna. Since their early efforts Susa has remained the largest excavation site in Persia, under the direction of the Délégation en Perse (D.P.), which underwent many changes of name and became Délégation Archéologique Française en Iran (DAFI) after World War II. In 1982 the DAFI and the Institut Français d'Iranologie merged under the name Institut Français de Recherches en Iran (IFRI).

In 1312/1895 René de Balloy, the French minister in Tehran, obtained from Nāṣer-al-Dīn Shah (1264-1313/1848-96) a French monopoly of archeological exploration in Persia. Two years later Jacques de Morgan (q.v.), a mining engineer who had already visited Persia in 1889-91 and had advised on the terms of this agreement, was appointed delegate general to Persia from the French Ministère de l'Instruction Publique (ministerial decree, 19 April 1897), and the French parliament allocated 100,000 gold francs for the establishment of the D.P., with an annual budget of F. 130,000.

De Morgan assumed direction of the D.P., which he retained until 1912. His own archeological investigations were focused on the prehistory of Susa and achieving a first appreciation of the stratigraphy of the site (de Morgan et al.). The major discoveries included a prehistoric necropolis with painted ceramics of Susa style A (4th millennium B.C.E.); clay tablets with a proto-Elamite pictographic script that is still undeciphered; Elamite temples from the second half of the 2nd millennium B.C.E.; the stele of Hammurabi, with his law code; the stele of Naram Sin; the Manishtusu obelisk; and a bronze statue of Queen Napirasu. These and other finds, for example, the famed archers' frieze excavated by the Dieulafoys, which Moẓaffar-al-Dīn Shah (1313-24/1896-1907) had seen in the Musée du Louvre in Paris, led, in 1900, to a convention in which France was granted the exclusive right to excavate in the

Persian empire and to keep all the antiquities discovered; the Persian government was to be compensated for gold and silver objects only (Bagherzadeh, p. xv).

An increasing number of investigators were also working at other sites under the sponsorship of the D.P.: Tepe Mūsīān on the plain of Dehlorān (q.v.; Gautier and Lampre, pp. 92-148), "dolmen" fields in Gīlān province, ancient Sasanian irrigation systems in K̲ūzestān (Graadt van Roggen), fossil fish at Marāḡa in Azerbaijan (de Mecquenem). These investigators included the botanist L.-C. Watelin, J.-E. Gautier, Roland de Mecquenem, Paul Toscanne, G. Pézard, and the hydrologist D. L. Graadt van Roggen. The results of this work were published in the *Mémoires* of the successive avatars of the Délégation (for a complete catalogue of those related to Elamite sites in K̲ūzestān, see Amiet, pp. 602-06).

Following de Morgan's resignation no successor was chosen immediately; the funds of the renamed Mission Archéologique de Perse (M.A.P.) were allotted to several scholars working in different parts of Persia: de Mecquenem and the architect Maurice Pillet at Susa; Charles Fossey at Hamadān, Ray, and Sar-e Pol; G. and Maurice Pézard at Līān near Būšehr (Pézard). J. V. Scheil and Pillet edited the various volumes of the *Mémoires*.

Field work was halted during World War I. In 1920 de Mecquenem was named director of the M.A.P., and he and Scheil resumed the work at Susa and in the adjacent region, with funds provided by the French Ministère d'Instruction Publique and the Académie des Inscriptions et Belles-Lettres. Between 1920 and 1938 de Mecquenem excavated Elamite levels, the 4th-millenium B.C.E. necropolis, and the post-Achaemenid *donjon*. In 1939 he initiated work at the large site of Čoḡā Zanbīl (q.v.), where he explored the ziggurat (de Mecquenem and Michalon). His assistant Louis Le Breton surveyed small sites of the 6th-4th millennia in Susiana. Meanwhile, outside the Susiana plain more modern methods of research and more controlled exploration of stratigraphy were adopted at Tepe Gīān near Nehāvand (Contenau and Ghirshman) and Tepe Sīalk near Kāšān (Ghirshman, 1938).

In 1308 Š./1929 the Persian government renounced the terms of its treaty on antiquities with the French; thenceforth all finds, with the exception of clay tablets, elements of architectural decoration, and valuable objects considered components of the Persian patrimony, were to be divided equally between the Iran Bastan Museum in Tehran and the Louvre (Bagherzadeh, p. xvi).

After a further suspension of activity during World War II Roman Ghirshman became director of the Mission Archéologique en Iran (M.A.I.) in 1946. Until 1951 he focused his own efforts on the "Ville royale" at Susa, dating from the 2nd millenium B.C.E.; he was assisted by the architect Hermann Gasche and the epigrapher M.-J. Steve. Then he turned his own attention to Čoḡā Zanbīl, where he continued to work until 1961 (*M.D.A.I.* 39-42); in the meantime other members of the renamed Délégation Archéologique en Iran (D.A.I.) continued the work at Susa, at the acropolis (4th-3rd millennium B.C.E.), the Apadāna, and the "Ville des artisans" (Achaemenid, Parthian, and Sasanian periods; Ghirshman, 1954), and also investigated the Sasanian city of Ayvān-e Kark̲a (Ghirshman, 1952, pp. 10-12), Masjed-e Solaymān, and Bard-e Nešānda (q.v.; Ghirshman, 1976).

In 1968 Jean Perrot became the fourth director of the DAFI and under his guidance close ties of cooperation were forged with the department of archeology at the University of Tehran, the Persian department of antiquities (Edāra-ye koll-e bāstān-šenāsī), the Persian Center for archeological research (Markaz-e pažūheshā wa kāveshā-ye bāstān-šenāsī), and the National organization for the preservation of historic monuments of Persia (Sāzmān-e mellī-e ḥefāẓat-e āṯār-e bāstānī-e Īrān). In 1348 Š./1969 the system of dividing excavated antiquities between the two countries was terminated. All finds, recorded on cards in both Persian and French, are kept in the regional museum at Susa, except for those of greatest importance, which are sent to the Iran Bastan Museum in Tehran (Bagherzadeh, p. xviii).

Beginning in the late 1960s the new staff gathered by Perrot, including archeologists, epigraphers, geophysicists, natural scientists, geologists, and engineers, tended to be more interdisciplinary and more international in composition; for example, it included Persian archeologists and American anthropologists. The goal remained a comprehensive reassessment of the societies of Susa and the Susiana plain from the 6th millennum B.C.E. onward. The excavations at Susa and such nearby sites as Jaʿfarābād (Dollfus), Jovī, and Band-e Bāl have been focused on establishing a solid stratigraphical basis for the chronology of the region (Vallat, pp. 16-17), the indispensable framework for the study of the natural environment, population trends, shifts in settlement, strategies of subsistence, international trade (see COMMERCE i), and successive stages of political integration; comprehensive reports of this effort are published in CDAFI, of which fifteen volumes had appeared by 1987. French excavations in Persia were suspended after the Revolution of 1357 Š./1978-79.

Bibliography: (For abbreviations found in this bibliography, see "Short References.") P. Amiet, *Elam*, Auvers-sur-Oise, France, 1966. F. Bagherzadeh, "Jean Perrot, un ami de l'Iran," in F. Vallat, ed., *Contribution à l'histoire de l'Iran. Mélanges offerts à Jean Perrot*, Paris, 1990, pp. xv-xxi. T. Berthoud and J. Françaix, *Contribution à l'étude de la métallurgie de Suse aux IVème et IIIème millénaires*, Gif-sur-Yvette, France, 1980. R. Boucharlat and O. Lecomte, *Fouilles de Tureng Tepe sous la direction de J. Deshayes* I. *Les périodes sassanides et islamiques*, Paris, 1987. G. Contenau et R. Ghirshman, *Fouilles de Tepe Giyan près de Nehavend*, Paris, 1935. J. Dieulafoy, *À Suse. Journal de fouilles 1884-1886*, Paris, 1888. M. Dieulafoy, *Le livre d'Esther et le Palais d'Assuerus*, Paris, 1888. Idem, *L'acropole de Suse d'après les fouilles exécutées en 1884-1886*, Paris, 1893. *L'évolution des sociétés complexes du sud-ouest de l'Iran. Actes du séminaire CNRS/NSF de Bellevaux (24-29 juin 1985)*, Paléorient 11/2, Paris, 1985. G. Dollfus, "Les recherches à Djaffarabad de 1969 à 1971," *CDAFI* 1, 1971, pp. 17-86. J.-E. Gautier and G. Lampre, "Fouilles de Moussian," in *Recherches archéo-logiques*, M.D.P. 8, Paris, 1905, pp. 59-148. R. Ghirshman, *Fouilles de Sialk près de Kashan*, Paris, 1938. Idem, *Rapport préliminaire* I. *Cinq campagnes de fouilles à Suse (1946-1951)* I, M.M.A.I. 33, Paris, 1952. Idem, *Suse. Village perse-achéménide*, M.M.A.I. 36, Paris, 1954. Idem, *Tchoga Zanbil (Dur-Untash)* I. *La ziggurat*, M.D.A.I. 39, Paris, 1966. Idem, *Tchoga Zanbil (Dur-Untash)* II. *Temenos, temples, palais, tombes*, M.D.A.I. 40, Paris, 1968. Idem, *Terrasses sacrées de Bard-è Néchandeh et de Masjid-i Solaiman. L'Iran du sud-ouest du VIIIe s. av. notre ère au Ve s. de notre ère*, M.D.A.I. 45, 2 vols., Paris, 1976. D. L. Graadt van Roggen, "Notice sur les anciens travaux hydrauliques en Susiane," in *Recherches archéologiques*, M.D.P. 7, 1905, pp. 167-207.

L. Le Breton, "The Early Periods at Susa. Mesopotamian Relations," *Iraq* 19, 1957, pp. 79-124. W. K. Loftus, *Travels and Researches in Chaldaea and Susiana in 1849-52*, London, 1857. R. de Mecquenem, "Contribution à l'étude des fossiles de Maragheh," *Annales de paléontologie* 13, 1924, pp. 133-60. Idem and J. Michalon, *Recherches à Tchogha Zembil*, M.M.A.I. 33, Paris, 1953. J. de Morgan, *Mission scientifique en Perse. Études géographiques*, 5 vols. in 8 parts, Paris, 1894-1905. Idem, *La Délégation en Perse du Ministère de l'Instruction Publique de 1897 à 1902*, Paris, 1902. Idem, G. Jéquier, and G. Lampre, *Recherches archéologiques. Fouilles à Suse en 1897-98 et 1898-99*, M.D.P. 1, Paris, 1900. J. de Morgan and R. de Mecquenem, "Les fouilleurs de Suse," *Iranica Antiqua* 16, 1980, pp. 1-48. J. Perrot, "Un siècle de fouilles à Suse," in *Suse. Dernières découvertes*, Dossiers Histoire et Archéologie 138, Dijon, 1989, pp. 12-15. Idem, "La séquence archéologique de Suse et du sud-ouest de l'Iran antérieurement à la période achéménide," in *L'évolution des sociétés complexes du sud-ouest de l'Iran. Actes du séminaire CNRS/NSF de Bellevaux (24-29 juin 1985)*, Paléorient 11/2, Paris, 1985, pp. 133-40. M. Pézard, "Mission à Bender-Bouchir," *M.A.P.* 15, 1914. M. Pillet, *Le palais de Darius I à Suse*, Paris, 1914. M.-J. Steve and H. Gasche, *L'acropole de Suse*, M.M.A.I. 46, 1971. F. Vallat, "L'inscription trilingue," *JA* 260, 1972, pp. 247-52. Idem, "Une histoire cinq fois millénaire," in *Suse. Dernières découvertes*, Dossiers Histoire et Archéologie 138, Dijon, 1989, pp. 16-17. J. Yoyotte, "Les inscriptions hiéroglyphiques. Darius et l'Égypte," *JA* 260, 1972, pp. 253-66.

(Francine Tissot)

ii. Délégation Archéologique Française en Afghanistan

The Délégation Archéologique Française en Afghanistan (DAFA) was established after the independence of Afghanistan was recognized in 1921. Amir Amān-Allāh Khan (q.v.), later king, in his efforts to modernize the country, rejected the help of his near neighbors and turned to France. Among the projects that he promoted was the DAFA, first proposed by Sardār ʿAbd-al-ʿAzīz Khan and Philippe Bonin, respectively Afghan and French ambassadors to Persia, who were probably inspired by the example of the Mission Archéologique de Perse. Alfred Foucher, a well-known authority on the ancient history of Afghanistan, was entrusted with the difficult task of negotiating an agreement. After a hard journey through Persia and the Hindu Kush he reached Kabul in the spring of 1922 (Foucher, I, p. 10). On 9 September a convention was signed by Amān-Allāh Khan, his minister Fayż-Moḥammed Khan, and Foucher. The newly appointed ambassador to France, Maḥmūd Beg Ṭarzī, carried it to Paris, where it was ratified by the French minister for Foreign Affairs, Philippe Berthellot. Foucher became the first director of the DAFA (Courtois).

By the terms of the agreement the French government had the exclusive privilege to conduct surveys and excavations in Afghanistan for a period of thirty years; at the expiration of that period the convention was renewed, with amendments, until 1357 Š./1978. The initial program of the DAFA included research on the art of Gandhara, Buddhist and Hellenistic sites, and the Silk Road (Courtois, p. 18). It was stipulated that the finds, with the exception of gold and jewelry, were to be divided equally between Afghanistan and France (Hackin, 1933, p. 1). In 1344 Š./1965 the system of sharing finds was terminated, and Afghanistan assumed the right to all of them. Archeological material collected by the DAFA is kept at the Kabul museum and the Musée des Arts Asiatiques-Guimet in Paris. Research results and excavation reports were published in *MDAFA* (1-32, 1942-89).

The activity of the DAFA can be divided into three periods. From 1923 to 1925 the work was limited to surveys, based on the model of the Archaeological Survey of India. Foucher's colleagues included the architect André Godard, who had previously worked in Persia; Joseph Hackin, director of the Musée Guimet; and Jules Barthoux. They followed the ancient trails of Buddhist monks, Chinese pilgrims, and the various invaders of the land. Stupas, monasteries, and columns were recorded in the Kabul area, in Kāpīsā, and around Jalālābād, where the major site was Hadda (Foucher, I, pp. 138-48, 150-53). In November 1923 the team visited Bāmīān (q.v. ii; Godard et al.) on the way to Balḵ, where Foucher and his wife remained for eighteen months, seeking remains of the Greek period, with disappointing results (Foucher, I, pp. 55-121).

In the second phase (1926-40) the first full-scale excavations were undertaken. Although Foucher had returned to France in 1925, he remained director of the DAFA (Dollot, pp. 276-79) up to 1946. Meanwhile Barthoux began excavations at Hadda (1926-28), where eight monasteries and 500 stupas were recorded, as well as approximately 15,000 sculptures and fragments; only 3,000 of the latter reached Kabul, owing to opposition of the inhabitants led by the mullas (Barthoux, 1933; idem, 1930). About half those finds were sent to France, and the other half were placed in the Kabul museum (Bāḡ-e bālā), where they suffered some damage during the revolt of Bačca(-ye) Saqqā (q.v.) in 1308 Š./1929.

The other major figure in the DAFA in the early days was Hackin. He returned to Bāmīān in 1930 with his wife, Ria, and the architect Jean Carl. They worked rapidly but carefully, with the help of the local inhabitants, making surveys, plans, and photographs of the grottoes and their decoration. The painted cupola from nearby Kakrak was restored and sent to Kabul (Hackin and Carl). Hackin joined the Croisière Jaune, a motor expedition to Central Asia and China sponsored by André Citroën in 1931 (Le Fèvre) but returned to Bāmīān three years later (Brühl) and undertook excavations on several monuments in the Kabul area: Ḵayr-Ḵāna (Hackin and Meunié) in 1935, Sāka, and Goldarra (Hackin, 1959, pp. 13-18; Fussman, 1976). In 1936 he turned to the desert of Afghan Sīstān (Hackin, 1959, pp. 19-21) but soon returned to the Hindu Kush, where he worked for a while at Qondūz (Hackin, 1937; Curiel and Fussman), before moving on to Šotorak in Kāpīsā (Meunié) and Fondoqestān in Parvān province (Hackin, 1959, pp. 49-58).

In April 1937 the Hackins and Carl began excavations at Begram. On 17 May the first of the famous "Begram glasses" was unearthed. A total of 216 items was eventually found in a single room (no. 10); beside the glasses, they included bronzes, coins, and ivories, among them the well-known "casket IX" and figurines of river goddesses (Hackin, 1939). Two years later the excavations were resumed, and in room 13 ivories, bronzes, plaster casts, and Chinese lacquers were found (Hackin, 1954). Considerable restoration work was conducted, first at the site by Ria Hackin and Carl and later in Paris by P. Hamelin and P. André (Hamelin). During World War II the Begram discoveries were stored in various embassies in Kabul and Peshawar, after a sharing agreement had been reached between Hackin and the king himself. The Afghan share was sent to the new Kabul museum in Dār al-Amān and the French share to the Musée Guimet. Hackin and his wife died at sea in February 1941 while trying to return to Afghanistan. Roman Ghirshman continued the excavations at Begram, but no further hoards were found (1948). He also resumed the exploration of Nād-e ʿAlī in Sīstān (Hackin, 1959, pp. 23-25).

During the third phase (1946-82) there was a major shift in the orientation of the DAFA. After World War II Daniel Schlumberger, a specialist in the late Hellenistic period in the Near East, became director, serving from 1946 to 1963. The French monopoly of archeological research in Afghanistan was gradually eroded, as missions from other countries were granted permission to work in the country, under the control of a newly developed cultural administration in Kabul. The Afghan Institute of archeology, distinct from the Kabul museum, was established; its last director was Zemaryalai Ṭarzī. In this phase the French program took on new dimensions. Prehistoric sites related to the Indus civilization were excavated: Mondegak (Qandahār province) in the late 1950s (Casal) and twenty years later Šortoḡay (Taḵār province; Francfort). The Islamic monuments at Jam (Maricq and Wiet), Bost (q.v.), and Laškarī Bāzār were also investigated (Schlumberger).

Schlumberger discovered two other major sites, the large mound at Sorḵ-kotal and Āy Ḵānom (q.v.). At the former coins and inscriptions, as well as a wealth of architectural and sculptural fragments, yielded new data on the religious monuments of Bactria during the early Kushan period. Following Schlumberger's untimely death in 1973, the final publication of the architecture at Sorḵ-kotal was entrusted to Gérard Fussman (Schlumberger et al.; Fussman and Guillaume). The excavations at Āy Ḵānom were led by Schlumberger's successor as director of the DAFA, Paul Bernard. The publications that have appeared so far reveal the scope and quality of the work at this important site (Bernard).

The last fieldwork carried out by the DAFA in Afghanistan was a survey of northeastern Bactria, under the direction of Jean-Claude Gardin. It led to the discovery of a large number of sites and the remains of irrigation systems, all dated by surface pottery, which provided a basis for a broad history of the area over the last 5,000 years (Gardin and Lyonnet; Gentelle). Political events in Afghanistan in 1358 Š./1979 halted this work; Gardin, the last director, was entrusted with the transfer to the Kabul museum of the material collected by the DAFA over the years, after it had been recorded and studied by his associates in Kabul for later publication in France. When this work was completed in 1361 Š./1982 the headquarters of the DAFA were closed.

Bibliography: (For abbreviations found in this bibliography, see "Short References") J. Barthoux, *Les fouilles de Haḍḍa* III. *Figures et figurines, album photographique*, MDAFA 6, Paris, 1930. Idem, *Les fouilles de Haḍḍa. Stûpas et sites, texte et dessins*, MDAFA 4, Paris, 1933. P. Bernard, ed.,

Fouilles d'Aï Khanoum I (*Campagnes 1965, 1966, 1967. 1968*). *Rapport préliminaire*, 2 vols., Paris, 1973. O. Brühl, "Derniers travaux de la DAFA en Afghanistan," *RAA* 8, 1934, pp. 116-19. J.-M. Casal, *Fouilles de Mundigak*, MDAFA 17, 2 vols., Paris, 1961. J. C. Courtois, "Summary of the History of Archaeological Research in Afghanistan," *Afghanistan* (Kabul) 16/2, 1961, pp. 18-29. R. Curiel and G. Fussman, *Le trésor monétaire de Qunduz*, MDAFA 20, Paris, 1965. R. Dollot, *L'Afghanistan. Histoire, descriptions, moeurs et coutumes, folklore, fouilles*, Paris, 1937. A. Foucher, *La vieille route de l'Inde, de Bactres à Taxila*, MDAFA 1, 2 vols., Paris, 1942-47. H.-P. Francfort, *Les palettes du Gandhāra*, MDAFA 23, Paris, 1979. G. Fussman and O. Guillaume, *Surkh-kotal en Bactriane* II. *Les monnaies, les petits objets*, MDAFA 32, Paris, 1989. G. Fussman and M. Le Berre, *Monuments bouddhiques de la région de Caboul* I. *Le monastère de Gul Dara*, MDAFA 22, Paris, 1976.

J.-C. Gardin and B. Lyonnet, "La prospection archéo-logique de la Bactriane orientale 1974-1978. Premiers résultats," *Mesopotamia* 13-14, 1978-79, pp. 99-154. P. Gentelle, "Données paléo-géographiques et fondement de l'irrigation," in J.-C. Gardin, ed., *Prospections archéologiques en Bactriane orientale* I, Paris, 1989. R. Ghirshman, *Bégram. Recherches archéologiques et historiques sur les Kouchans*, MDAFA 12, Cairo, 1946. A. Godard, Y. Godard, and J. Hackin, *Les antiquités bouddhiques de Bāmiyān*, MDAFA 2, Paris and Brussels, 1928. J. Hackin, *L'oeuvre de la Délégation Archéologique Française en Afghanistan, 1922-1932*, Tokyo, 1933. Idem, *Recherches archéologiques à Bégram (chantier no. 2, 1937)*, MDAFA 9, 2 vols., Paris, 1939. Idem, *Nouvelles recherches archéologiques à Bégram (1939-1940)*, MDAFA 11, 2 vols., Paris, 1954. Idem, *Diverses recherches archéologiques en Afghanistan (1933-1940)*, MDAFA 8, Paris, 1959. Idem and J. Carl, *Nouvelles recherches archéologiques à Bāmiyān* MDAFA 3, Paris, 1933. Idem and J. Meunié, *Recherches archéologiques au col de Khair Khaneh près de Kâbul*, MDAFA 7, Paris, 1936. P. Hamelin, *Matériaux pour servir à l'étude des verreries de Begram*, Cahiers de Byrsa (Tunis) 3-4, 1953-54. G. Le Fèvre, *La croisière jaune*, Paris, 1933. A. Maricq and G. Wiet, *Le minaret de Djam. La découverte de la capitale des sultans ghorides (XIIe-XIIIe siècles)*, MDAFA 16, Paris, 1959. J. Meunié, *Shotorak*, MDAFA 20, Paris, 1942. D. Schlumberger, *Lashkari Bazar, une résidence royale ghaznévide et ghoride* IA. *L'architecture*, MDAFA 18, Paris, 1978. Idem, M. Le Berre, and G. Fussman, *Surkh Kotal en Bactriane* I. *Les temples*, MDAFA 25, Paris, 1983.

(FRANCINE TISSOT)

DELHI SULTANATE, Muslim kingdom established in northern India by Central Asian Turkish warlords at the turn of the 13th century and continuing in an increasingly persianized milieu until its conquest by Bābor (q.v.) in 932/1526.

i. *Political and cultural history.*
ii. *Architecture.*

i. POLITICAL AND CULTURAL HISTORY

Although the influence of Persian civilization upon that of northern India under the sultans of Delhi has long been treated as a foregone conclusion, attempts to identify the extent of the processes by which that influence was transmitted involve the historian in a web of hypotheses and generalizations (for the historiography of the sultanate, see Hardy, 1960; Rashid; Hasan; Sarkar; Nizami, 1983). As Carl W. Ernst (p. 6) has expressed it, "'influence' is nothing but a rather physical metaphor suggesting a flowing in of a substance into an empty vessel. This is hardly a satisfactory model for the complicated process by which people of one culture interpret and put to new uses themes and symbols from another culture." Because of its origins and subsequent history the sultanate provided for three and a quarter centuries a unique opportunity for the continual transmission to India of a broad range of cultural manifestations emanating from the Persian plateau: language and literature, customs and manners, concepts of kingship and government, religious organization, music, and architecture.

Persian influence in northern India before the sultanate. Islam had already entered India via Sind and up the Indus; by the late 10th century Ismaʿili communities had been established in and around Multan, but they were Carmatians from Bahrain (qq.v.) and probably constituted a wholly Arab element. The seepage of Persian influences into northwestern India resulted, in the first instance, from the transfer of political power on the Persian plateau from ʿAbbasid governors to local dynasts. The early Saffarids Yaʿqūb b. Layṯ (d. 265/879) and ʿAmr b. Layṯ (d. 289/902) exercised a loose sway over what are today the Indo-Afghan borderlands, in which dissidents from the Persian plateau had probably established themselves free from ʿAbbasid surveillance (Bosworth). The Samanids (204-395/819-1005) later extended their hegemony over the same area, including the Kabul valley, Gardīz, Ḡazna, and Zābolestān, leading to penetration of these lands by Persian or persianized officials, traders, and adventurers. Under their aegis rebellious slave commanders like Alptigin (q.v.), Sebüktigin, and the latter's son Maḥmūd used Ḡazna as a base for raids across the Indus and into Hindustan. A century later the Saljuq vizier Neẓām-al-Molk, in his *Sīāsat-nāma* (p. 147), described these raids, emphasizing that plunder and adventure, as much as piety, had motivated them. The Ghaznavid Maḥmūd himself (388-

421/998-1030) may well have viewed these raids as providing the means to play an active role on the Persian plateau, but after the defeat of his son Masʿūd (421-32/1031-41) by the Saljuqs at Dandānqān in 431/1040 the fulcrum of Ghaznavid power shifted east into the Punjab, and Lahore became the capital of the rump empire. The later Ghaznavids, though ethnic Turks, were wholly assimilated to Persian culture; Persian was the language of the court, and Ghaznavid Lahore must have been a typical Persian city. The first flowering of Persian poetry on Indian soil took place there, led by Abu'l-Faraj b. Masʿūd Rūnī (q.v.), the panegyrist of Sultan Ebrāhīm b. Masʿūd (451-92/1059-99) and his son Masʿūd III (492-508/1099-1115), and Masʿūd-e Saʿd-e Salmān (Marek, pp. 714-15). It was also in Lahore that ʿAlī b. ʿOṯmān Hojvīrī, whose *Kašf al-maḥjūb* was one of the earliest accounts in Persian of Sufi theory and practice, finally settled and died (ca. 465-69/1072-77; Hojvīrī, pp. x-xi).

Although the ethnic origins of the Ghurid, or Shansabanid, dynasty (ca. 390-612/1000-1215) remain uncertain, there can be no doubt that the conquest of Ḡazna by the Ghurids' Turkish *ḡolāms* in 545/1150 marked the end of Ghaznavid rule west of the Indus. The last two Ghaznavids, Ḵosrow Shah (547-55/1152-60) and Ḵosrow Malek (555-82/1160-86), controlled only the Punjab, and under their rule the cities there must have experienced further persianization. In 582/1186 the Ghurid ruler Ḡīāṯ-al-Dīn Moḥammad (558-99/1163-1203) occupied Lahore, where he established a condominium with his younger brother Moʿezz-al-Dīn Moḥammad, to whom he delegated the eastern and southern possessions of the dynasty. Thenceforth Moʿezz-al-Dīn was responsible for the extensive conquests in Hindustan. Delhi was captured in 588-89/1192, Ajmer in 589/1193, and Qannauj in 595/1198; Ghurid suzerainty thus extended in a great arc from Mount Abū in Rajasthan through Gwalior to Bundelkhand. Farther east Baḵtīār Ḵaljī proceeded into Bihar and Bengal in 599-601/1202-04, capturing the cities of Nadia and Lakhnawti (Jūzjānī, *Ṭabaqāt* I, pp. 422-32). Following the assassination of Moʿezz-al-Dīn in 599/1206 his territories were partitioned among his principal amirs: Tāj-al-Dīn Yildiz in Ḡazna; Nāṣer-al-Dīn Qobāča in Multan, Uch, and Bhakkar; and Qoṭb-al-Dīn Aybak (q.v.) in Lahore, Ajmer, and Delhi, the last city being held by his lieutenant Šams-al-Dīn Iltutmiš. In Bihar and Bengal the situation remained fluid: Baḵtiār had either died or been assassinated, and successive commanders endeavored to hold those distant provinces and to determine the basis of their legitimacy by dealing with various power brokers in the northwest (Eaton, 1993, pp. 38-39). Eventually Aybak emerged more or less supreme, though he had had to come to terms with Qobāča and probably, contrary to tradition, never assumed the title "sultan." Nor was his son Ārām Shah able to succeed him after his premature death. His successor was his favorite *ḡolām*, the far-sighted and resolute Iltutmiš (607-33/1211-36), who is counted the first and among the greatest of the sultans of Delhi.

The Turkish *ḡolāms* of the Ghurids who laid the foundations of Muslim rule in India were no barbarian conquerors; rather, despite their origins in Central Asia, they were effective agents and purveyors of Persian civilization on the subcontinent. Aybak himself had, as a young slave, been educated by a *qāżī* (religious judge) in Nīšāpūr, where he had acquired a reputation as a reciter of the Koran (Jūzjānī, I, p. 416). Iltutmiš had belonged to a learned man of Bukhara, who educated him thoroughly before selling him to a merchant, who took him to Baghdad and thence to Ḡazna (Jūzjānī, I, p. 442). Qobāča, too, seems to have been a man of considerable polish; it was in his time that the *Čāč-nāma* (q.v.) was rendered from Arabic into Persian, and he provided temporary refuge from the Mongols for both Šadīd-al-Dīn ʿAwfī (q.v.) and Abū ʿAmr Jūzjānī. He appointed the latter to a position at the Fīrūzīya *madrasa* at Uch, which may have been his own foundation (Jūzjānī, I, p. 420). The biographical notices on prominent amirs of the early Delhi sultanate incorporated into Jūzjānī's *Ṭabaqāt-e nāṣerī* confirm the impression of a cultivated persianized ruling elite. The earliest surviving buildings erected by the sultans of Delhi also reflect Persian antecedents (see ii, below).

The Ghaznavid and Ghurid invaders constituted a well-defined ruling elite, reinforced by adventurers of all kinds from the Muslim lands farther west. Neẓām al-Molk reported that, after news of the booty that Alptigin had acquired in the Indus frontier region became known, men flocked from Khorasan, Transoxania, and Sīstān to serve under him (Neẓām-al-Molk, p. 146). Few of these early invaders would have brought wives with them, relying principally upon Indian slave women to provide for their domestic needs and bear them sons. Apart from soldiers, little is recorded about early migrants from Persia and the borderlands into what later became the Delhi sultanate. There must have been writers from the Ghaznavid court at Lahore and in the late Ghurid period *ʿolamāʾ* like Jūzjānī. It can be assumed, too, that among immigrants to northern India there were armorers, metalworkers, tentmakers and furnishers, manufacturers of cavalry gear, and other craftsmen, though none is mentioned in the sources. Merchants must have followed the armies to convert the plunder (often unwieldy and practically useless in the hands of common soldiers) into cash; the vast majority of Indian captives must thus have become objects of commerce. Traders and craftsmen alike most probably came from urban centers in the eastern Persian world and, with bureaucrats and *ʿolamāʾ*, provided the nucleus of the free, nonmilitary Persian-speaking population of such centers as Multan, Uch, Bhakkar, Lahore, Dipalpur, and Bhatinda in the

Punjab, as well as Delhi.

The dynastic history of the sultanate. Iltutmiš was succeeded by five descendants, the last of whom died in 664/1266, but usurpation and murder more often determined the succession at Delhi. In that year his former *ḡolām* Ḡīāṯ-al-Dīn Balban seized the throne, ruling for two decades (664-86/1266-87) in grim splendor amid the trappings of "Sasanian" kingship (Nizami, 1961, pp. 95-105); after his death his grandson and great-grandson were soon ousted, and the throne was then seized by the Turkish or turkicized Ḵaljīs (689-720/1290-1320; on this dynasty, see Haig; Nigam; Lal, 1967). After the murder of the last of the line, Qotḇ-al-Dīn Mobārak Shah (716-20/1316-20), by his favorite the sultanate was restored by Ḡāzī Malek, governor of Dipalpur (Punjab), who mounted the throne as Ḡīāṯ-al-Dīn Toḡloq and founded the Tughluqid dynasty (720-817/1320-1414), under which the sultanate of Delhi reached its greatest extent but also experienced the beginning of fragmentation into smaller states. Ebn Baṭṭūṭa described Ḡāzī Malek as a Qarāʾūnā Turk from southern Afghanistan, though in India the term Qarāʾūnā may have meant descendants of Turks by Indian mothers (Ebn Baṭṭūṭa, III, p. 649). Under the Tughluqids, especially Moḥammad b. Toḡloq (725-52/1325-51) and Fīrūz Shah (752-90/1351-88), the Delhi sultanate reached the zenith of its splendor (on the Tughluqids, see Haig; Husain, 1938; idem, 1963). Even before Tīmūr's devastating raid on Punjab and Delhi in 800/1398-99, however, the Tughluqid state had contracted to a mere shadow of its former self, and the adventurers who ruled after Tīmūr's withdrawal, Mallū Khan, Dawlat Khan Lōdī, and Ḵeżr Khan, had no claims to legitimacy and controlled little more than the countryside immediately surrounding Delhi. Keżr Khan's successors came to be known as the Sayyed dynasty (817-55/1414-51), probably because of spurious claims to descent from the Prophet Moḥammad; they were eventually swept away by the Lōdīs (855-932/1451-1526), themselves part of a larger infiltration of Afghan tribes into the Punjab and the Ganges plain, from which local dynasties also eventually emerged in Bengal and Malwa. The most significant legacy of the Sayyeds and Lōdīs was architectural. The last Lōdī sultan was killed at Panipat fighting the invading forces of Bābor.

Although the extent of Persian immigration into India before the 1220s is a matter of guesswork, events during the 13th century undoubtedly contributed to an increase. The garrison towns and administrative centers in the upper Jumna-Ganges plain (e.g., Baran, Etawah, Badaon, Qannauj) must have become even more persianized after the arrival of successive waves of refugees from the west. The first such wave was the result of campaigns by Čengīz Khan (q.v.) in Transoxania and Khorasan in 616-19/1219-22; he actually reached the Indus in 618/1221 and briefly threatened the Punjab (Jovaynī, ed. Qazvīnī, II, pp. 139-42). Many fugitives sought sanctuary in Delhi during the reign of Iltutmiš and undoubtedly stimulated a greater diffusion of Persian customs and values in lands that had previously been unstable marches on the frontiers of the Islamic world. Jūzjānī is an example, having fled from Tūlak south of Herat, arrived by boat in Uch, where he was warmly received by Qobāča, and then passed on to Delhi, where he enjoyed a moderately successful career in the service of the sultanate (Jūzjānī, I, pp. 420, 447).

The Mongol invasion of Persia continued into the 1250s, and it must be assumed that the exodus also continued, though presumably limited to persons of means or possessing marketable skills. A further stage in the spread of Persian influence must have followed Hülegü's invasion of Persia in 653-56/1255-58; many refugees crossed the Indus during the reign of Sultan Nāṣer-al-Dīn Maḥmūd Shah (644-64/1246-66), and the impetus may have continued during the late 1270s and 1280s after the Negüderis or Qarāʾūnās had occupied Zābolestān in what is now southern Afghanistan, a region that became a bone of contention between Il-khanids and Chaghatayids (see CHAGHATAYID DYNASTY). The latter successfully asserted their hegemony in the borderlands northwest of the Indus and engaged in protracted internal dynastic struggles between Mongol traditionalists and those newly converted to Islam (e.g., ʿAlāʾ-al-Dīn Tarmašīrīn, 726-34/1326-34). Among the refugees who came to Delhi was the party with which Ebn Baṭṭūṭa traveled in 734/1333. The most prominent member was the *qāżī* of Termeḏ, who was accompanied by his women and children, three brothers and a nephew, and two notables from Bukhara and Samarqand respectively, each with an entourage of servants and hangers-on (Ebn Baṭṭūṭa, pp. 606-07). This group was probably typical of such refugees, representing high Persian culture. Sultan Moḥammad b. Toḡloq was especially renowned for his hospitality to foreigners (see Jackson), among whom the "Ḵorāsānīs" (a term used indiscriminately in Delhi to include refugees from Persia proper, the borderlands across the Indus, and Turkestan) were especially numerous. Ebn Baṭṭūṭa mentioned the sultan's practice "of honouring strangers and showing affection to them and singling them out for governorships or high dignities of state" (p. 595). ". . . Well known is his generosity to foreigners, for he prefers them to the people of India, singles them out for favour, showers his benefits upon them . . . and confers upon them magnificent gifts" (p. 671). When the Il-khanate in Persia collapsed in 736/1336 Tughluqid Delhi provided a *carrière ouverte aux talents*, thus ensuring that Muslim India would become a cultural extension of Persia.

Perhaps more than elsewhere in the Muslim east, the political style of the rulers of Delhi reflected traditional concepts of Persian kingship, for Iltutmiš and his successors lacked any other obvious tradition to draw upon (Hardy, 1978a). Indigenous Rajput polities offered no meaningful exemplars, and it is unlikely that the Turks in northern India retained memories of the steppe *imperium* of the Oḡuz or Qarakhanids. The ʿAbbasid caliphate had provided a legitimizing mechanism, but its demise in 658/1258 left a mere fictive device. On the other hand, the culture of the courts of eastern Persia, that is, Samanid Bukhara, in whose service Alptigin had grown gray (Neẓām-al-Molk, p. 139), and the persianized milieux of the Ghaznavids and Ghurids offered a dynamic, ultimately Sasanian concept of *šāhānšāhī* to set against contemporary Hindu notions of kingship or the threatening universalism of the Chinghizids. This concept could be harnessed to the idea, prevalent from the time of the first Mongol incursions across the Indus, that the central functions of the rulers of Delhi were chastisement of the idolaters of Hindustan and defense of the sultanate against the Mongol infidels (Ahmad, p. 12). In his determination to enhance his authority Ḡīāṯ-al-Dīn Balban, who claimed descent from Afrāsīāb (q.v.), sought to overawe his turbulent followers with the splendid ceremonial of pre-Islamic Persia (Nizami, 1985, pp. 148-52). It is surely no coincidence that his grandsons were named Kay Ḵosrow, Kay Qobād, Kay Kāvūs, and Fīrūz. The greatest poet of the Delhi sultanate, Amīr Ḵosrow Dehlavī (q.v.; 651-725/1253-1325; see Rypka, *Hist. Iran. Lit.*, pp. 257-59), in his *Qerān al-saʿdayn*, an account of the reconciliation of Balban's son Boḡrā Khan, ruler of Bengal, with his own son Moʿezz-al-Dīn Kay Qobād in 686/1287, glorified the external symbols of kingship and authority. ʿEsāmī (q.v.), with his *Fotūḥ al-salāṭīn*, composed in the Deccan (q.v.) in 750-51/1349-50, aspired to write the *Šāh-nāma* of India.

By the time of Amīr Ḵosrow's death Persian was firmly established as the language of polite learning, diplomacy, and higher administration among the Muslims of the subcontinent. This success owed as much to the diffusion of the Sufi orders throughout northern India, especially during the 14th century, as to elite patronage of panegyric and belles lettres. The process had begun a century earlier, with the establishment of Moʿin-al-Dīn Češtī (q.v.; d. 633/1236) in Ajmer, Ḥamīd-al-Dīn Nāgawrī (d. 675/1276) in Rajasthan, and Qoṭb-al-Dīn Baḵtīār (d. 633/1235) in Delhi (Lawrence, pp. 20-44). From them flowed the great Češtī tradition in India, embodied in Qoṭb-al-Dīn's disciple Farīd-al-Dīn Masʿūd "Ganj-e Šekar" (664/1265); the latter's spiritual heir, Neẓām-al-Dīn Awlīāʾ (d. 725/1325), who counted the poets Amīr Ḵosrow Dehlavī and Amīr Ḥasan Sejzī (d. 729/1328) as his friends; and Awlīāʾ's successor, Nāṣer-al-Dīn Maḥmūd "Čerāḡ-e Dehlī" (d. 757/1356). Other orders, notably the Sohravardīya and the Ferdowsīya, had established themselves after the Turkish invasions, the former chiefly in the Punjab, the latter in Bihar and Bengal (Lawrence, pp. 60-71, 72-79). At the time of Tīmūr's invasion of Hindustan (800/1398-99) the leading disciple of Čerāḡ-e Dehlī, Moḥammad Ḥosaynī "Gīsū Derāz" (d. 825/1422), abandoned Delhi for the Deccan, where he established himself at Golbarga (Eaton, 1978, pp. 50-52). By that time, however, Sufis had spread far and wide through Muslim territory in India. Their propensity to preserve their conversations (*malfūẓāt*), letters (*maktūbāt*), and hagiology (*taḏkera*) in Persian did much to encourage dissemination of that language. Little survives from before the time of Awlīāʾ, but Sejzī's *Fawāʾed al-foʾād*, in which Awlīāʾ's table talk over about fifteen years is recorded, is perhaps the most important example of the *malfūẓāt* genre. Ḥamīd Qalandar, in his *Ḵayr al-majles*, attempted to do the same for Čerāḡ-e Dehlī but lacked his predecessor's talents as a mystic and as a poet.

Sīar al-Awlīāʾ by Amīr Ḵord (q.v.), though not properly a *taḏkera*, is in the *taḏkera* tradition, containing biographical notices on the early Češtīs, especially Awlīāʾ. Although Amīr Ḵord wrote during the reign of Fīrūz Shah Toḡloq, he had access to much older oral and probably written material that is now lost. Moḥammad-Akbar Ḥosaynī, the son of Gīsū Derāz, also composed a *malfūẓāt* of his father's conversations, *Jawāmeʿ al-kālem*, which includes important material on earlier Češtī shaikhs. Other orders developed their own literary traditions, among which the *Maktūbat-e ṣadī* of the Ferdowsī shaikh Šaraf-al-Dīn b. Yaḥyā Manerī "Maḵdūm-al-Molk" (d. 782/1381) was particularly celebrated. Without such works and the spiritual dynamism of the Sufi orders that inspired them, it may be doubted that the Persian language and the Persian cultural ethos would have pervaded Hindustan so deeply during the sultanate period.

Bibliography: (For cited works not found in this bibliography and for abbreviations found here, see "Short References.") A. Ahmad, *Studies in Islamic Culture in the Indian Environment*, Oxford, 1964. Idem, *An Intellectual History of Islam in India*, Edinburgh, 1969. C. E. Bosworth, "Notes on the Pre-Ghaznavid History of Eastern Afghanistan," *Islamic Quarterly* 9, 1965, pp. 12-24. S. Digby, *War-Horse and Elephant in the Delhi Sultanate. A Study of Military Supplies*, Oxford, 1971. R. M. Eaton, *Sufis of Bijapur, 1300-1700*, Princeton, N.J., 1978. Idem, *The Rise of Islam and the Bengal Frontier, 1204-1760*, Berkeley, Calif., 1993. Ebn Baṭṭūṭa, *Reḥla*, tr. H. A. R. Gibb as *Travels in Asia and Africa, 1325-1354*, Cambridge, 1971. C. W. Ernst, *Eternal Garden. Mysticism, History, and Politics at a South Asian Sufi Center*, Albany, N.Y., 1992. W. Haig, ed., *Cambridge History of India* III, Cambridge, 1928. P. Hardy, *Historians of Medieval India*, London, 1960. Idem, "The Growth of Authority over a Conquered Political Elite. The Early Delhi Sultanate as a Possible Case Study," in J. F. Richards, ed., *Kingship and Authority in South Asia*, Madison, Wis., 1978a, pp.

192-214. Idem, "Unity and Variety in Indo-Islamic and Perso-Islamic Civilization," *Iran* 16, 1978b, pp. 127-35. M. Hasan, ed., *Historians of Medieval India*, Meerut, India, 1968. R. Hillenbrand, "Political Symbolism in Early Indo-Islamic Mosque Architecture. The Case of Ajmir," *Iran* 26, 1988, pp. 105-17. ʿAlī b. ʿOṯmān Hojvīrī, *Kašf al-maḥjūb*, tr. R. A. Nicholson as *The Kashf al-Mahjūb. The Oldest Persian Treatise on Sūfism*, new ed., London, 1936; repr. London, 1976. M. Husain, *The Rise and Fall of Muhammad bin Tughluq*, London, 1938. Idem, *Tughluq Dynasty*, Calcutta, 1963. P. Jackson, "The Mongols and the Delhi Sultanate in the Reign of Muhammad Tughluq (1324-1351)," *Central Asiatic Journal* 19, 1975, pp. 118-57. K. S. Lal, *Twilight of the Sultanate*, Bombay, 1963. Idem, *History of the Khaljis, A.D. 1290-1320*, London, 1967. B. B. Lawrence, *Notes from a Distant Flute. Sufi Literature in Pre-Mughal India*, Tehran, 1968. J. Marek, "Persian Literature in India," in Rypka, *Hist. Iran. Lit.*, pp. 713-34. M. Mujeeb, *The Indian Muslims*, London, 1967. R. Nath, *A History of Sultanate Architecture*, New Delhi, 1978. Neẓām-al-Molk, *Sīāsat-nāma*, ed. H. Darke, Tehran, 1340 Š./1962. S. B. P. Nigam, *Nobility under the Sultans of Delhi, A.D. 1206-1398*, Delhi, 1968. K. A. Nizami, *Some Aspects of Religion and Politics in India during the Thirteenth Century*, Aligarh, 1961. Idem, *On History and Historians of Medieval India*, Delhi, 1983. Idem, "Impact of Iranian Traditions on the Administrative Institutions, Concepts and Practices of the Early Delhi Sultanate," in K. A. Nizami, ed., *State and Culture in Medieval India*, Delhi, 1985, pp. 142-57. A. Rashid, "The Treatment of History by Muslim Historians in Sufi Writings," in C. H. Phillips, ed., *Historians of India, Pakistan, and Ceylon*, London, 1961, pp. 128-38. S. A. Rizvi, *A History of Sufism in India*, 2 vols., Delhi, 1978-82. J. N. Sarkar, *History of History-Writing in Medieval India. Contemporary Historians*, Calcutta, 1977. A. Schimmel, *Islam in the Indian Subcontinent*, Leiden, 1980. Idem, "Persian Poetry in the Indo-Pakistani Subcontinent," in E. Yarshater, ed., *Persian Literature*, Albany, N.Y., 1988, pp. 405-21. Amīr Ḥasan Sejzī, *Fawāʾid al-fuʾād*, tr. B. B. Lawrence as *Nizam ad-Din Awliya. Morals for the Heart*, New York, 1992. E. Thomas, *The Chronicles of the Pathan Kings of Delhi*, London, 1871; repr. Delhi, 1967. A. Welch and H. Crane, "The Tughluqs. Master Builders of the Delhi Sultanate," *Muqarnas* 1, 1983, pp. 123-66. A. Wink, *Al-Hind. The Making of the Indo-Islamic World* I, Delhi, 1990. H. N. Wright, *The Coinage and Metrology of the Sultans of Delhi*, Oxford, 1936. T. Yamamoto, M. Ara, and T. Tsukinowa, *Delhi. Architectural Remains of the Sultanate Period*, 3 vols., Tokyo, 1968-70.

(GAVIN R. G. HAMBLY)

ii. ARCHITECTURE

Although parts of the Indian subcontinent had experienced the impact of Persian culture since the invasion by the Ghaznavid sultan Maḥmūd (388-421/998-1030) in the 10th century, Delhi was little affected before 588/1192, when the Ghurid general Qoṭb-al-Dīn Aybak (q.v.) defeated Prithvi Raj Chauhan, the last Hindu ruler of the city. By 589/1193 Aybak had taken Delhi itself and had established Islam as the new state religion; the Friday sermon (*ḵoṭba*) was read in the name of the Ghurid ruler Moʿezz-al-Dīn Moḥammad (569-602/1173/1206). Medieval Persian institutions, already established in Ghurid Afghanistan, were also implanted in Delhi (see i, above).

The Ghurids. Among the first acts of the new conqueror was the construction of a mosque, known today as the Qowwat-al-Eslām, on a temple plinth in the citadel of the former Chauhan rulers. In its initial phase it consisted of a prayer chamber, an open courtyard, and galleries on the south, north, and east sides; according to a Persian inscription dated 587/1191, the supports of the galleries were taken from twenty-seven dismantled temples (Page, p. 29), but it is possible that this inscription was added later (Horovitz, p. 13). A second inscription suggests that much of this phase had been completed by 592/1196 (Page, p. 29). The mosque was probably modeled loosely on the Saljuq mosques of Persia, with an arcaded screen that was visually related to them (Tsukinowa, p. 37); nevertheless, owing to the predominant use of spolia that were trabeated, not arcuated, the mosque had the aspect of a rearranged Hindu temple. Aybak was evidently dissatisfied with this appearance, for in front of the trabeated prayer chamber he inserted an enormous screen pierced by five corbeled arches, the central one larger than the others, dated 20 Ḏu'l-qaʿda 594/23 September 1198; as a result the courtyard facade of the sanctuary approximated those of the great Saljuq mosques in Persia, for example, the congregational mosque at Isfahan (Tsukinowa, pp. 45, 57; Plate XX). The decorative motifs and calligraphy on this screen are closely related to those on other Ghurid structures in Afghanistan (e.g., the Šāh-e Mašhad *madrasa*, or religious school, in Ḡarjestān, dated 561/1165-66; Casimir and Glatzer). At the same time that he inserted the screen Aybak also began construction of an enormous minaret, known today as Qoṭb Menār, south of the mosque. It has been proposed that this structure may originally have been intended to serve as his tomb, in the tradition of the Persian tomb towers like the Gonbad-e Qābūs in Gorgān (Trousdale, p. 104).

Aybak's successor, Šams-al-Dīn Iltutmiš (607-33/1211-36), greatly enlarged the mosque and completed the Qoṭb Menār, about 626/1229. The extensions of the Qowwat-al-Eslām generally followed the same scheme as the original; the first courtyard was surrounded on the north, east, and south by a larger porticoed courtyard, which also enclosed the minaret, and the sanctuary was extended on either side, with new mihrabs and extensions of the arcaded screen.

The completed minaret reached an estimated height of 79 m. (Cunningham, pp. 196-97). Its tapering form and height recall the "minaret" at Jām (65 m high), erected in 526/1132 by the Ghurid Ḡīāṯ-al-Dīn Moḥammad b. Sām (558-99/1163-202; Maricq and Wiet, p. 27; Plate XXI), and the alternating curved and angular projecting forms of its base are clearly related to those of the minaret of Ḵᵛāja Sīāhpūš in Afghan Sīstān (Nath, 1978, p. 25). Unlike the brick minarets of Afghanistan and Persia, however, the Qoṭb Menār was constructed of red and pink local stone. This monument may be interpreted as an expression of the victory of Islam in infidel India, as well as a declaration of the newly established supremacy of Moʿezz-al-Dīn Moḥammad and later of Iltutmiš himself. The historical inscriptions on the minaret indicate that first the Ghurid overlords and later the independent Iltutmiš considered themselves part of the greater Persian and Islamic world and adopted Persian royal titulary. For example, in four separate places the ruler is proclaimed as master of Arabs and non-Arabs (*ʿarab o ʿajam*; Page, pp. 30-33).

Persian influence on the architecture of the newly established Ghurid splinter state in Delhi was manifest in the very types of buildings constructed, particularly mausolea. Iltutmiš built tombs for himself and his son Nāṣer-al-Dīn Maḥmūd but in quite different styles. That for Nāṣer-al-Dīn at Malikpur, dated 629/1231 and known locally as Solṭān Ḡārī, consists of an underground crypt and heavy enclosure walls that give the appearance of being fortified; it is difficult to trace these features to any specific tradition, but there may have been links with contemporary tombs, probably built originally as *rebāṭ*s (fortified outposts) in the Multan region, which had been under Ghurid domination since 571/1175-76 (Edwards, p. 192; Bosworth, *Later Ghaznavids*, p. 29). In any event, according to the later chronicle of the Tughluqid Fīrūz Shah (*Fotūḥat-e fīrūzšāhī*, apud Navqi, p. 6), the tomb was established as a *madrasa*, an institution that had originated in Persia. Iltutmiš's own tomb, a square stone structure originally surmounted by a corbeled dome, recalls in plan and elevation tombs in persianized Central Asia, for example, the mausoleum of the Samanids at Bukhara (Pope, *Survey of Persian Art*, pl. 264; Plate XXII).

The Ḵaljīs. Although the buildings discussed above were clearly modeled on Persian prototypes, indigenous Indian building techniques were still in use, often in modified form (e.g., the corbeled dome of Iltutmiš's tomb). By the turn of the 14th century true vaulting techniques, including the use of keystones, had been mastered, as attested by the southern gate-

PLATE XX

Screen on the courtyard of the Qowwat al-Eslām mosque, Delhi, added by the Ghurid Qoṭb-al-Dīn Aybak, 594/1198. Photograph C. B. Asher.

way known as ʿAlāʾī Darvāza (710/1311), part of the final extension to the Qowwat al-Eslām by ʿAlāʾ-al-Dīn Ḵaljī (695-715/1296-1316). The facade of the gateway is embellished with carved red and white stone, reflecting the tradition of contrasting bands of colored stone in Syria and Anatolia, probably familiar through artisans or patrons fleeing the Mongols. ʿAlāʾ-al-Dīn's uncompleted enlargement of the mosque, like that of Iltutmiš before him, did not change the original character of the building, however. Persian inscriptions on the facade, in which he is referred to as a "king of Darius-like splendor," underscore his strong attachment to the Persian cultural realm (Page, p. 34).

Aside from royally endowed buildings little is known about architecture in Delhi during the early Sultanate and Ḵaljī periods. Knowledge of painting and the applied arts is also minimal. From coins it appears that indigenous motifs sometimes appeared on standard Islamic coin types like those minted under the Ghaznavids and Ghurids (Wright, esp. pp. 68-69).

The Tughluqids. Although the Tughluqids were dynamic patrons of architecture, the increasing austerity of their imperial buildings evoked few Persian

PLATE XXI

Remains of the Qoṭb Menār, Qowwat al-Eslām mosque, Delhi, begun by Qoṭb-al-Dīn Aybak, ca. 1200, completed by Šams-al-Dīn Iltutmiš ca. 626/1229. Photograph C. B. Asher.

forms other than those already current in Delhi. For example, the mosque of Moḥammad Shah II (725-52/1325-51) in Begumpur, in a southern suburb of the city, is only an elaboration of the Saljuq-inspired mosque type developed earlier in the sultanate period (Welch and Crane, p. 130). The leading architectural patron of the dynasty, Fīrūz Shah (752-90/1351-88), did, however, develop an elaborate building program of explicitly Persian inspiration. In keeping with the image of an ideal ruler portrayed in such Persian texts as Neẓām-al-Molk's *Sīar al-molūk*, he concerned himself with building canals, wells, sluices, forts, *madrasa*s, mosques, and other public amenities, though in reality much of this activity was designed to divert attention from his shrinking domain and political impotence (Asher, 1992, p. 7).

One building type that probably reflected actual Persian prototypes was the octagonal tomb, which became increasingly popular in pre-Mughal Delhi. It consisted of a central chamber surrounded by a veranda. Important examples are the tombs of the general Ẓafar Khan (built 723-25/1323-25) and Ḵān-e Jahān Telangānī (d. 770/1368), prime minister under Fīrūz Shah. The type appears to have been ultimately derived from such Persian tombs as that at Naṭanz (dated 389/999), now incorporated into a later mosque (Blair, p. 47). The mode of transmission is unclear, though it is notable that a type once favored for saints in Persia was used for royalty and high-ranking secular figures in India.

The later sultanate. After the invasion of Tīmūr in 801/1398 the prestige of Delhi suffered considerably. Some octagonal tombs were built in the persianate tradition established by Fīrūz Shah, notably those of Mobārak Shah (824-38/1421-35), Sekandar Shah Lōdī (894-923/1489-1517; Plate XXIII), and the high-ranking ʿĪsā Khan Nīāzī (954/1547-48). Particularly under Sekandar Shah there was an attempt to revive the city's fortunes. The Afghan Šīr Shah Sūr, who temporarily ousted the Mughals from India, ruled Delhi in the years 947-52/1540-45; he built the Qalʿa-ye kohna mosque in the Dīn-panāh section of the city. The sanctuary consists of a single-aisled sanctuary of three bays; it is unique to India, but at that time the building type was favored specifically by Afghan families like the Sūrīs. The ornamentation may also reveal Persian influence (Asher, 1989, pp. 74-75). The exterior and interior are richly faced with red and white stones, some of which are inlaid in intricate geometric patterns reminiscent of tile patterns on Timurid buildings.

Bibliography: (For cited works not found in this bibliography and abbreviations found here, see "Short References.") Aḥmad Khan, *Āṯār al-ṣanādīd*, Delhi, 1847; repr. Delhi, 1965. M. Ara, *Dargāhs in Medieval India*, Tokyo, 1977. C. B. Asher, "From Anomaly to Homogeneity. The Mosque in 14th- through 16th-Century Bihar," in

PLATE XXII

Facade, tomb of Iltutmiš, in the Qowwat al-Eslām mosque, Delhi, ca. 1225. Photograph C. B. Asher.

PLATE XXIII

Tomb of Sekandar Shah Lōdī, in the Bāḡ-e Jor, known today as the Lodi Gardens, Delhi, ca. 1517. Photograph C. B. Asher.

G. Bhattacharya and D. Mitra, eds., *Studies in Art and Archaeology of Bihar and Bengal. Nalinikikanta Satavatsiki. Dr. N. K. Bhattasali Centenary Volume*, Delhi, 1989, pp. 67-84. Idem, *The Architecture of Mughal India*, Cambridge, 1992. S. Blair, "The Octagonal Shrine at Natanz. A Reexamination of Early Islamic Architecture in Iran," *Muqarnas* 1, 1983, pp. 69-94. P. Brown, *Indian Architecture. Islamic Period*, 5th ed., Bombay, 1968. M. J. Casimir and B. Glatzer, "Šāh-i Mašhad, a Recently Discovered Madrasah of the Ghurid Period in Ġarğistān (Afghanistan)," *East and West* 21/1-2, 1971, pp. 53-68. A. Cunningham, ed., *Archaeological Survey of India Reports* I, Calcutta, 1871. H. Edwards, *The Genesis of Islamic Architecture in the Indus Valley*, Ph.D. diss., Institute of Fine Arts, New York University, 1990. Idem, "The Ribat of Ali b. Karmkah," *Iran* 29, 1991, pp. 85-94. J. Hoag, *Islamic Architecture*, New York, 1977. J. Horovitz, "The Inscriptions of Muhammad ibn Sam, Qutbuddin Aibeg, and Iltutmish," *Epigraphia Indo-Moslemica*, 1911-12, pp. 12-34. A. M. Husain, *Tughluq Dynasty*, New Delhi, 1976. Jūzjānī, *Ṭabaqāt. List of Muhammadan and Hindu Monuments. Delhi Province*, 4 vols., Calcutta, 1916-22. A. Maricq and G. Wiet, *Le minaret de Djam*, Paris, 1959. R. Nath, *History of Sultanate Architecture*, New Delhi, 1978. S. A. A. Naqvi, "Sultan Ghari, Delhi," *Ancient India* 3, Calcutta, 1947, pp. 4-10. Idem, *Monuments of Delhi*, New Delhi, 1979. Neẓām-al-Molk, *Sīar al-molūk (Sīāsat-nāma)*, tr. H. Darke as *The Book of Government or Rules for Kings*, New Haven, Conn., 1960. J. A. Page, *A Historical Memoir on the Qutb, Delhi*, Calcutta, 1926. W. Trousdale, "The Minaret of Jam, a Ghorid Monument In Afghanistan," *Archaeology* 18/2, 1965, pp. 102-08. T. Tsukinowa, "The Influence of Seljuq Architecture on the Earliest Mosques of the Delhi Sultanate Period in India," *Acta Asiatica* 43, 1982, pp. 37-60. A. Welch, "Architectural Patronage and the Past. The Tughluq Sultans of India," *Muqarnas* 10, 1993, pp. 311-22. Idem and H. Crane, "The Tughluqs. Master Builders of the Delhi Sultanate," *Muqarnas* 1, 1983, pp. 123-66. H. N. Wright, *The Coinage and Metrology of the Sulṭāns of Delhi*, Delhi, 1936; repr. New Delhi, 1974. T. Yamamoto, M. Ara, and T. Tsukinowa, *Delhi. Architectural Remains of the Delhi Sultanate Period*, 3 vols., Tokyo, 1967-70.

(CATHERINE B. ASHER)

DELĪKĀNLŪ, tribe of the Ḵalḵāl region in eastern Persian Azerbaijan. In spite of its Turkish name (*deli* "young, wild, frolicsome"; Doerfer, *Elemente* II, pp. 660-62), the tribe is apparently of Kurdish origin, like its neighbors the Šaṭrānlū and Qolūqjānlū tribes; Moḥammad Mardūḵ includes it in his list of Kurdish tribes (I, p. 190). Although most of the Delīkānlū are now Turkophone, as recently as 1330 Š./1951 Kurdish was still spoken at Āqbāš (Razmarā, *Farhang* IV, p. 26, s.v.), one of the Delīkānlū villages (Oberling, p. 54).

The Delīkānlūs occupy about twenty villages in the *dehestāns* of Garm, Ganjgāh, Kīvī, and Ḵoreš Rostam (Oberling, p. 54). In 1311 Š./1932 Maḥmūd Kayhān (*Joḡrāfīā* II, p. 108) estimated their number at 400 households, in 1339 Š./1960 the Persian high command at 480 households (Oberling, p. 53) and M. J. Maškūr (p. 184) at 400 households, and in 1352 Š./1973 Mardūḵ (I, p. 90) at 200 households.

Bibliography: (For cited works not found in this bibliography, see "Short References.") M. Mardūḵ Kordestānī, *Tārīḵ-e Kord o Kordestān o tawābeʿ yā Tārīḵ-e Mardūḵ*, Tehran, 1351 Š./1973. M.-J. Maškūr, *Naẓar-ī be tārīḵ-e Āḏarbāyjān*, Tehran, 1349 Š./1970. P. Oberling, *The Turkic Peoples of Iranian Azerbaijan*, New York, 1961. Persian army files at Tabriz.

(PIERRE OBERLING)

DELKAŠ, QĀRĪ MOLLĀ KARĀMAT-ALLĀH TANBŪRĪ BOḴĀRĀʾĪ (b. Bukhara at an indeterminate date, d. Bukhara, 1320/1902), Tajik poet and musician known and revered for melodies performed on the *tanbūr* (a long-necked lute), the instrument from which his nickname was derived (ʿAynī, p. 312). He was a student and friend of Aḥmad Dāneš (q.v.), a leader of the Tajik progressive movement in Bukhara in the late 19th century. Like other disciples of Dāneš, including Tāš-Ḵvāja ʿAṣīrī, Moḥammad-Ṣeddīq Ḥayrat, Možṭareb, Šams-al-Dīn Maḵdūm (Šāhīn), and Raḥmat-Allāh Wāżeḥ, Delkaš was trained in both music and literature (*Istoriya*, 1966, p. 310). Although little is known about his life and thought, there is no doubt that he was influenced by Dāneš. That relationship did not prevent his appointment as court secretary to Amir ʿAbd al-Aḥad (1303-30/1885-1910) in 1319/1901; in fact, the amir was seeking to attract poets and musicians to his court, in order to preserve them from the "pernicious influences" of the progressives ("Dilkaš," 1980). A year later, however, Delkaš died of tuberculosis, paralleling in this way ʿAbd-al-Qāder Ḵᵛāja Savdo (Sawdāʾ), who had been named official poet in 1306/1889 and had also died of tuberculosis (Bečka, p. 526).

Delkaš left no *dīvān* of his poetry; his works must be collected from various contemporary anthologies and notes (*bayāż*) by poets. His name is mentioned in *Toḥfat al-aḥbāb* by Wāżeḥ (p. 47), evidence that he was already a respected artist before his brief stay at court. He was also mentioned in *Taḏkerat al-šoʿarāʾ* by Moḥtaram, compiled after 1323/1905 to glorify the power of the amir (Akademiya Nauk, Tashkent, ms. no. 2252), and in *Afżal al-taḏkār*, compiled in 1322/1904 at the request of the amir, in order to discredit Dāneš and his followers (Hodizade, 1968, p. 282). ʿAynī (pp. 311-12) published a *ḡazal* and a *robāʿī* by Delkaš, drawn from Afżal's compendium. From the accessible samples of his poetry it seems that Delkaš's style is simpler than that prevailing in his time and in that sense closer to the style of oral literature.

Bibliography: (For abbreviations found in this bibliography, see "Short References.") *Afżal al-tadkār*, Tashkent, 1336/1918. S. ʿAynī, *Namūna-ye adabīyāt-e tājīk,* Moscow, 1926. J. Bečka, "Tajik Literature from the 16th Century to the Present," in J. Rypka, *Hist. Iran. Lit.*, pp. 485-545. "Dilkaš," in *Uzbek Sovet Ensiklopediyasi*, Tashkent, 1978, p. 38. "Dilkaš," in *Ensiklopediya-i tojiki soveti*, Dushanbe, 1980, p. 290. R. Hodizade, *Istochniki k izucheniyu tadzhikskoĭ literatury vtoroĭ poloviny XIX v.* (Sources for the study of Tajik literature of the second half of the 19th century), Stalinabad, 1956. Idem, *Tanbury Dilkaš*, Dushanbe, 1964. Idem, *Adabīāt-e tojik dar nimai duvvumi asri XIX*, Dushanbe, 1968. *Istoriya tadzhikskogo naroda* (History of the Tajik people) II, Dushanbe, 1964. Raḥmat-Allāh Wāżeḥ, *Toḥfat al-aḥbāb fī tadkerat al-aṣḥāb*, Tashkent, 1288/1871.

(CATHÉRINE POUJOL)

DELKAŠ, an important modal unit (*šāh gūša*) linked to the *dastgāh* (q.v.) Māhūr, constituting one of its four main modulations, perhaps the most important in expressive function, which contrasts strongly with that of Māhūr itself. Delkaš differs from the initial mode of Māhūr by a displacement on the fifth, with a modulation in Šūr on G and a pause on F: (C, D, E,) F, *G*, A B♭, C, (D). Playing centers around *G*; the melody begins in the higher notes and then, after the sounding of an A, descends toward C in Māhūr. These developments can be fairly long and may consist of three or four distinct phases, including the melody (*gūša*) Ḥājī Ḥasanī (Maʿrūfī, p. 15). Although compositions entirely in Delkaš are very rare, the majority of compositions in Māhūr include passages in this mode. Delkaš is a well-codified *gūša*, and all its classical variants are quite homogeneous, though they lend themselves to improvisation nonetheless.

In Azeri classical music (During, pp. 115-17) the *maqām* (*moqām*) Delkaš occupies the same position in Māhūr and also in Rāst. Its modal structure is identical to that of its Persian counterpart, but the intervals and the melodic line are slightly different. Furthermore, it is often played as an independent *moqām*, free of any reference to Māhūr and associated with Šahnāz (on the same scale), with developments in Bayāt-e Kord on the fifth in the descending scale (transposed to C, with F as dominant): C, B♭, A♭, G, F, E♭, D, *C*, (B♭). The diagnostic motif is the initial jump C-F-C.

There is also a composite *maqām* known as Delkašīda, invented in the 19th century by Ottoman musicians but unrelated to those under the Persian and Azeri homonyms. Nevertheless, an Arabic form of this mode sometimes exhibits some affinities (d'Erlanger, pp. 124-25).

Bibliography: J. During, *La musique traditionnelle de l'Azerbayjan et la science des muqams*, Baden-Baden, 1988. Idem, *La répertoire-modèle de la musique iranienne*, Tehran, 1991. R. d'Erlanger, *La musique arabe* V, Paris, 1949. M. Maʿrūfī, *Les systèmes de la musique traditionnelle iranienne (radif)*, Tehran, 1352 Š./1973. M. T. Massoudieh (Masʿūdīya), *Radif vocal de la musique iranienne*, Tehran, 1357 Š./1978.

(JEAN DURING)

DELLA VALLE, PIETRO (b. Rome, 11 April 1586, d. Rome, 21 April 1652), one of the most remarkable travelers of the Renaissance, whose *Viaggi* is the best contemporary account of the lands between Istanbul and Goa in the early 17th century. He was born into a distinguished aristocratic Roman family, received a thorough education in the classics, had a knowledge of music and letters and an interest in medicine and the sciences, and, as a member of the Accademia degli Umoristi, played a prominent part in Roman and Neapolitan intellectual and cultural circles (Maylender, pp. 369-81). Through this select group he was in touch with the outstanding orientalists of the period, including Diego de Urrea Conca and the Vecchietti brothers (Gabrieli, 1926-27, pp. 105-14; idem, 1938, pp. 504-09, 529-30; Fischel, pp. 7-17). In 1611 he participated in an expedition of the Spanish fleet against pirates on the Barbary coast. Whether it was this experience, rejection in love, or, as he put it, simply the quest for glory, he decided to undertake a pilgrimage to the Holy Land, sailing for Istanbul from Venice in June 1614. He stayed at Istanbul from August 1614 to September 1615, then went by sea to Alexandria before traveling overland to Cairo, Mount Sinai, and Gaza, eventually reaching Jerusalem in time for Easter 1616 (Della Valle, 1843, I, pp. 51-52, 134-35, 164-65, 264-307, 344, 346, 481-82; II, pp. 95, 165).

On his return journey, while at Aleppo, he totally changed the direction and scope of his travels, deciding to join a caravan destined for Baghdad. The motive behind this apparently impulsive decision was to offer his services to Shah ʿAbbās I (q.v.; 996-1038/1588-1629) in a "crusade" against the Ottomans; two years of traveling through the Ottoman empire had only strengthened his antipathy for them (Della Valle, 1843, I, pp. 259, 267, 283, 291, 348, 511-13). At Baghdad he equally impulsively fell in love with Maʿanī Jowayrī, daughter of a Nestorian Catholic father and an Armenian mother. After a short, passionate courtship they married in December 1616, and the progress and ultimate tragedy of their love is an engaging leitmotiv throughout the rest of their travels together (I, pp. 397-405; II, pp. 291, 303-15). This alliance provided Della Valle with another reason to meet Shah ʿAbbās I, whose reputation for religious tolerance encouraged his own vision of establishing a colony of Chaldean and Nestorian Christians at Isfahan under the shah's benevolent protection.

Della Valle left Baghdad in January 1617, surmounted the difficulties of the snowbound passes of Kurdistan, and reached Isfahan in February. Shah ʿAbbās was in the north, and Della Valle had to wait almost a year in the capital before deciding to find the shah for himself, traveling through Kāšān, Fīrūzkūh, and the Alborz mountain range, finally reaching the court at Faraḥābād in February 1618 (Della Valle, 1843, I, p. 596). After eventually being granted an audience, he followed Shah ʿAbbās and part of the Safavid army to Ardabīl (q.v.), which was threatened by an Ottoman attack. Tabrīz was lost briefly, but after a Safavid victory over a branch of the Turkish forces the campaign was abandoned for that season. By November 1618, after victory celebrations in Qazvīn, Shah ʿAbbās was ready to return to his usual winter quarters at Faraḥābād and Ašraf (now Behšahr, q.v.), but Della Valle, who was unwell, went back to Isfahan, where he hoped the Augustinians and Carmelites (q.v.) would restore him to health (I, pp. 818-20, 836-37).

He stayed in Isfahan from December 1618 to October 1621, a time of gradual convalescence, absorption in the problems of his wife's relatives, pursuit of plans for an alliance with the Cossacks in a renewed war against the Ottomans, and efforts to establish a Chaldean colony (Della Valle, 1843, II, pp. 107-09). With the frustration of these hopes he decided to return to Europe via India. As soon as he recovered his health, he set off for the Persian Gulf through Shiraz, but the Persian and English blockade of the Portuguese on Hormuz prevented his sailing (II, pp. 289-90). While waiting at Mīnāb, near Bandar(-e) ʿAbbās (q.v.) Maʿanī, who was several months pregnant, caught fever; the child was stillborn, and Maʿanī died shortly afterward. Della Valle had her body embalmed in camphor, so that it could be buried in his family sepulcher at Rome, a decision that involved him in innumerable difficulties throughout the rest of his journeys. A more immediate problem was his own health, as he too succumbed to the same fever; in a state of semiconsciousness he was taken to Lār, where he slowly recovered his spirits and health between January and June 1622 (II, pp. 325-53). By that time Hormuz had fallen, and after another short stay in Shiraz it was possible to leave for Surat on an English East India Company (q.v.) ship in January 1623, with Maʿanī's coffin covered with clothes at the bottom of a large leather chest; their adopted daughter, a young Georgian called Mariuccia, dressed as a man to escape the attention of port officials.

It was more than another three years before Della Valle returned to Europe. He progressed slowly down the western coast of India as far as Calicut, staying from April 1623 to November 1624 at Goa (Della Valle, 1843, II, pp. 592-789), whence he sailed for Muscat and Baṣra; then, traveling overland to the Mediterranean via Aleppo, he finally reached Naples in February and Rome in late March 1626, nearly twelve years after he had left Italy. The rest of his life was spent in Rome in the pursuit of his literary and scholarly, especially musical, interests, except for a brief banishment for his part in a brawl in the Vatican (Bianconi, pp. xxxiv-ix; Blunt, pp. 304-07). He died in April 1652 and was buried by Maʿanī's side in the church of Ara Coeli in Rome. Some time after his return he had married Mariuccia, who bore him fourteen sons, a turbulent but mostly undistinguished progeny.

From the beginning of his travels Della Valle wrote regularly to a learned friend at Naples, Mario Schipano, who, he hoped, would edit his unsystematic, verbose outpourings, written at great speed and inordinate length, into digestible form (Della Valle, 1843, I, pp. 473-74). In all there were thirty-six letters (only one of which was mislaid by Schipano), containing more than a million words. It was only two years before his death that the first volume of letters was published, slightly edited with the excision of a few personal details; the second and third volumes, edited by four of his sons, followed in 1658. Aside from the immediacy and vivacity of these letters, Della Valle displayed excellent narrative and descriptive skills, powers of acute observation, and a genuinely scholarly breadth of learning. He refused to comment on what he had not witnessed himself or checked against the best authorities (I, pp. 130-31, 141, 254, 860-61). He had attempted to learn some oriental languages, particularly Turkish and later Persian but also Arabic and Hebrew (I, pp. 131-33, 141-42, 522-24, 860-62; II, p. 51). With Maʿanī's knowledge of Armenian, Arabic, Persian, and Georgian, between them there were few levels of Safavid society with which they could not converse.

Given these opportunities and his own qualities of mind and spirit, together with prodigious industry and curiosity, it is no surprise that Della Valle's eighteen letters from Persia provide one of the most detailed sources of information for most aspects of Persian life in the second half of Shah ʿAbbās' reign. Like most 17th-century travelers, he offered a catalogue of information on festivals (Della Valle, 1843, I, pp. 504-06, 536-41, 550-54, 829-30; II, pp. 31-32, 70, 73-75, 96-97, 129), architecture (I, pp. 443, 453-61, 502-03, 602, 673-76, 705-07, 742-44, 779-84, 840-41; II, pp. 104, 116-20, 247-68, 376-79, 415-16), and customs and pastimes (I, pp. 443, 627-28, 677, 691-93, 709-10, 713-14; II, pp. 7-26, 37-38, 401-03, 475) of the main towns through which he passed, as well as food and drink (I, pp. 443-47, 503-04, 653-54, 669, 689, 752, 836; II, pp. 105-07, 283-85), dress (I, pp. 568-72, 591, 639-40; II, pp. 288-89), flora, crops, drugs, and spices (I, pp. 413-18, 472, 634, 668-69, 823; II, pp. 105, 206-10) of rural and urban society. Much precise economic detail is found on prices, weights, and currency (I, pp. 471, 586, 631-33); industries and workshops (I, pp. 562, 566-72, 584, 706); and the cultivation and marketing of silk (I, pp. 566-67, 590, 847-48; II, pp. 57-59, 171). More unusual are his descriptions of the Safavid legal and administrative system, derived from his own personal experience or based on close observation. Several incidents reveal the system at work, for example, a brawl in the *bāzār* at Kāšān (I, pp. 564-66), a case of his own brought before the provincial court at Shiraz (II, pp. 387-89), and two others involving the *dīvānbegī* (q.v.) at Isfahan (II, pp. 78-83, 166-67, 175-76). His first-hand observations on military affairs are also of value; they include information on the composition, preparation, tactics, arms, and pay of the Persian forces in battle against the Ottomans (I, pp. 686-87, 759-69, 803-09, 865-67), as well as a description of the war against the Portuguese in the south (II, pp. 178-80, 322-26). Scattered throughout the letters are Della Valle's disparaging comments on the Qezelbāš military elite, whose pretensions to nobility he ridiculed and whose domination over Persians from older backgrounds he thought insufferable (I, pp. 644, 679, 762, 788). The group in Safavid society that attracted his deepest concern and affection was the Georgians, whether crypto-Christians or apostates. He was impressed by their personal qualities, their courage and civilized courtesy; he obtained a great deal of information about their plight, especially that of the Georgian royal family (I, pp. 469-71, 597-99, 745-47, 844-45; II, pp. 146-57, 393-99). Other minorities, especially the Chaldean relatives of Maʿanī (I, pp. 854-59; II, pp. 107-08), Armenians (I, pp. 598-600, 846-52; II, pp. 84-94, 214-17), Jews (II, p. 72), Zoroastrians (I, pp. 497-500), and Indians (I, pp. 489-97, 534-36; II, pp. 426-29, 447-52) are also frequently mentioned.

The thread that runs through all his Persian letters, however, giving them a certain cohesion, is the account of Shah ʿAbbās and his court: the magnificent feasts at Solṭānīya and Ašraf, ambassadorial receptions, the closing (*qoroq*) of the Isfahan *bāzār* to the general public, Armenian epiphany celebrations, polo and wolf baiting, Āšūrāʾ (q.v.), and the festival of *ābrīzān* (I, pp. 636-73, 707-11, 752-58; II, pp. 7-32). Della Valle's description of ʿAbbās is a masterly, exact portrait of the shah, aged forty-seven years when Della Valle first saw him at Ašraf. He left a verbatim account of their discussion, the topics involved, ʿAbbās' mannerisms, his sense of fun, his skill in drawing information out of visitors, and his curiosity about their customs and forms of government. Characteristically Della Valle tried to see beyond ʿAbbās' public persona and to understand his quixotic changes of temperament, the moods of impenetrable melancholy, the inconsistencies in his religious views, and particularly his attitude toward his sons (I, pp. 636-73, 729-31, 737-40, 755-56, 867-69; II, pp. 197-98, 210-11). It was in these letters, rather than the account he published after his return to Europe (Della Valle, 1628), that Della Valle provided a vivid insight into the complex, tormented personality of the greatest of Safavid rulers.

Different from almost all other 17th-century travelers to Persia in his motivation, education, and cultural sophistication, Della Valle reacted to the intellectual and cultural life of Persia in a particularly interesting way. His gradual appreciation of these aspects of Persian society, culminating in the few months at Lār, reveals a world that few foreigners ever reached (II, pp. 326-53). Although few of his own literary or scholarly projects were completed, he left in his incomparable letters a fitting memorial to Persian life as he understood it in the early 17th century, as well as to his own extraordinary personality, at times arrogant and pretentious but always intelligent, high-spirited, and full of panache.

The most recent complete edition of Della Valle's letters is that of G. Gancia, *Viaggi di Pietro Della Valle, il Pellegrino*, 2 vols., Brighton, England, 1843, but Luigi Bianconi, ed., *Viaggio in Levante di Pietro Della Valle*, Florence, 1942, is useful for the earlier letters; some of those from Persia have been edited with valuable introduction, notes, and comments by Franco Gaeta and Laurence Lockhart, *I viaggi di Pietro Della Valle. Lettere dalla Persia* I, Rome, 1972. Complete French, German, and Dutch translations are available, but only the letters from India and the return journey have been translated into English, by G. Havers, as *The Travels of Sig. Pietro Della Valle into East India and Arabia Deserta . . .*, London, 1665, and *The Travels of Pietro Della Valle in India*, ed. E. Grey, 2 vols., London, 1892. G. Bull has translated and abridged selections from all the travels, *The Pilgrim. The Travels of Pietro Della Valle*, London, 1989. A Persian translation of the Persian letters has been published by Šoʿāʿ-al-Dīn Šafā, *Safar-nāma-ye Petro Delā Vāla*, Tehran, 1348 Š./1969.

Della Valle's other published works include *Delle conditioni di Abbas re di Persia*, Venice, 1628; "Informatione della Georgia," printed in J. Thévenot, *Relations de divers voyages curieux qui n'ont point este' publiees . . .*, I, Paris, 1663; "Della musica dell'eta nostra," written in 1640 but first published in the collection of G.-B. Doni, Florence, 1763; "De Recentiori Imperio Persarum Subiectis Regionibus," in *17 saggi di iranisti italiani*, Rome, 1977, pp. 287-303.

Bibliography: M. Alemi, "I 'teatri' di Shah Abbas nella Persia del XVII secola dai inediti del diario di Pietro Della Valle," *Storia della Città* 46, 1989, pp. 19-26. R. Amalgia, "Per una conoscenza piu completa della figura e del'opera di Pietro Della Valle," *Rendiconti dell'Accademia Nazionale dei Lincei*, Classe di scienzi morali, storiche e filologiche, ser. 8/6, 1951, pp. 375-81. C. Bertacchi,

"C. E. Biddulph e Pietro Della Valle a proposito di un'escursione nel deserto salato persiano," *Bollettino della Società Geografica Italiana* 29, 1892, pp. 427-34. F. Bertotti, "Un viaggiatore romano e un poeta persiano. Pietro Della Valle estimatore e divulgatore di Hafiz," *Islam. Storia e civiltà* 31, 1990, pp. 121-27; tr. as "Petro Delā Vāla mosāfer-e rūmī wa Ḥāfeẓ Šīrāzī," *Ḥāfeẓ-šenāsī* 11, 1368 Š./1989, pp. 137-44. L. Bianconi, *Viaggio in Levante di Pietro Della Valle*, Florence, 1942. P. G. Bientenholz, *Pietro Della Valle 1586-1652. Studien zur Geschichte der Orientkenntnis und des Orientbildes in Abendlande*, Basel and Stuttgart, 1962. W. Blunt, *Pietro's Pilgrimage. A Journey to India and Back at the Beginning of the Seventeenth Century*, London, 1953. I. Ciampi, *Della vita e delle opere di Pietro Della Valle, il pellegrino*, Rome, 1880. W. J. Fischel, "The Bible in Persian Translation," *Harvard Theological Review* 45, 1952, pp. 3-45. G. Furlani, "Pietro Della Valle sui Yezidi," *Oriente moderno* 24, 1944, pp. 17-26. G. Gabrieli, "I primi accademici Lincei e gli studi orientali," *Bibliofilia* 28, 1926-27, pp. 99-115. Idem, "Il 'Linceo' di Napoli," *Rendiconti dell' Accademia Nazionale dei Lincei*, ser. 6/14, 1938, pp. 499-565. J. D. Gurney, "Pietro Della Valle. The Limits of Perception," *BSO(A)S* 49, 1986, pp. 103-16. G. de Lorenzo, "Pietro Della Valle's Letters on India," *East and West* 2, 1952, pp. 205-17. M. Maylender, *Storia della Accademie d'Italia* V, Bologna, 1930. A. M. Piemontese, "Pietro Della Valle," *Bibliografia italiana dell'Iran (1462-1982)* I, Naples, 1982, pp. 153-60. G. Rocchi, *Funerale della Signora Sitti Maani Gioerida Della Valle celebrato in Roma l'anno 1627 . . .*, Rome, 1627. E. Rossi, "Importanza dell'inedita grammatica turca di Pietro Della Valle," in *Atti del XIX Congresso Internazionale degli Orientalisti*, Rome, 1938, pp. 202-09. Idem, "Versi turchi e altri scritti inediti di Pietro Della Valle," *Rivista degli studi orientali* 22, 1947, pp. 92-98. Idem, "Pietro Della Valle orientalista romano (1586-1652)," *Oriente moderno* 32, 1953a, pp. 49-64. Idem, "Poesie inedite in persiano di Pietro Della Valle," *Rivista degli studi orientali* 28, 1953b, pp. 108-17.

(John Gurney)

DELOUGAZ, PINHAS PIERRE (b. Ukraine, 16 July 1901, d. Čoḡā Mīš, Persia, 29 March 1975), archeologist and excavator of the ancient site of Čoḡā Mīš (q.v.) in Persia. The son of Simon and Zipporah Silverman Delougaz, he was raised in a rural setting and received his earliest education in Russian and Hebrew literature and thought from tutors at home. In 1913 he was sent to the Gymnasium Herzlia in Tel Aviv, where he remained throughout World War I. The Bolshevik Revolution in 1917 cut off the flow of funds from home, and he was thus forced to become self-reliant at an early age. At school he had concentrated on mathematics and science, while acquiring a knowledge of Arabic and a familiarity with Near Eastern life from Arab friends. From 1922 to 1926 he studied mathematics and physics at the Sorbonne in Paris, where he developed an interest in architecture, art, and eventually archeology.

Delougaz began his career in field archeology as assistant architect with the Harvard University-Baghdad School expedition to Nuzi in northern Iraq in 1928-29. From 1929 to 1931 he was with Edmund Chiera at the excavation at Khorsabad in Iraq, beginning his long association with the Oriental Institute of The University of Chicago. Beginning in 1931 he directed the Oriental Institute excavation at Ḵafāja in the Dīāla valley of central Iraq, and in 1938, after the final season, he moved to the United States, where he studied at The University of Chicago from 1939 to 1942. He became a member of the faculty there in 1949 and served as professor of archeology from 1960 to 1967. In the 1950s and 1960s he conducted excavations at Beth Yerah (Ḵerbat al-Kerak) in Israel and a survey expedition in Turkey and western Persia. In 1961 he began excavating at Čoḡā Mīš, a large prehistoric and protohistoric site in north-central Ḵūzestān, to which he devoted the remainder of his archeological career. He moved to the University of California at Los Angeles (U.C.L.A.) as professor of Near Eastern archeology in 1967, and the excavation at Čoḡā Mīš was sponsored jointly for several seasons by that university and the Oriental Institute. In 1970 he also assumed the directorship of the Museum of Cultural History at U.C.L.A. He died of a heart attack while working in the field and is buried in Tel Aviv.

Delougaz was known for his ability to interpret sites and the finds from them and for his methodological rigor, particularly a new type of pottery classification. He was also able to convey the technical aspects of field work to students with clarity. He was particularly gifted at identifying the functions of artifacts the use of which was not obvious to modern eyes.

His many publications include *Plano-Convex Bricks and the Method of Their Employment and the Treatment of Clay Tablets in the Field* (Chicago, 1933); *The Temple Oval of Khafajah*, (Oriental Institute Publication 53, Chicago, 1940); *Pre-Sargonid Temples in the Diyala Region* (with Seton Lloyd; Chicago, 1942); *Pottery from the Diyala Region* (Oriental Institute Publication 63, Chicago, 1952); "Chogha Mish Excavation Report" (with Helene Kantor; *Iran* 13, 1975, pp. 176-77); "The 1973-74 Excavation at Chogha Mish" (with Kantor; IIIrd Annual Symposium on Archaeological Research in Iran, Tehran, 1975, pp. 93-102); "Some New Evidence Pertaining to Sites in Southwestern Iran and Southern Mesopotamia in the Protoliterate Period" (in *The Memorial Volume of the Vth International Congress of Iranian Art and Archaeology*, Tehran, 1972, pp. 26-33); "The Prehistoric Architecture at

Chogha Mish"(in *The Memorial Volume of the VIth International Congress of Iranian Art and Archaeology*, Tehran, 1976, pp. 31-48); and *Chogha Mish* I. *The First Five Seasons, 1961-1971* (with Kantor; Oriental Institute Publications 101, Chicago, 1991).

Bibliography: *Who's Who in America*, 38th ed., I, Chicago, 1974-75, p. 771. *Who Was Who in America* VI, Chicago, 1976.

(EZAT O. NEGAHBAN)

DELŠĀD ḴĀTŪN, eldest daughter of the Chobanid Demašq Ḵᵛāja (q.v.) and Tūrsīn Ḵātūn, granddaughter of the Il-khanid sultan Aḥmad Takūdār (q.v.; Aharī, p. 184; tr., p. 83). After the fall of the Chobanids (q.v.) in 727/1327 Delšād Ḵātūn was brought under the protection of her aunt Baḡdād Ḵātūn, who had become wife of the il-khan Abū Saʿīd (q.v.) after having first been married to Ḥasan-e Bozorg Jalāyer. When Delšād attained maturity she was presented to Abū Saʿīd, who married her in 733/1333 and became so devoted to her that Baḡdād Ḵātūn regretted her action (Šabānkāraʾī, p. 295; Ḥāfeẓ-e Abrū, ms., fol. 527b). Abū Saʿīd died without an heir in 736/1335, and a remote cousin, Arpā Khan, was chosen as his successor by the vizier, Ḡīāṯ-al-Dīn Moḥammad (q.v.). Delšād Ḵātūn, who was pregnant, fled with her cousin ʿAli Jaʿfar, grandson of Īrenjīn (Īrenčīn), to ʿAlī Pādšāh, the Oirat amir of Dīārbakr (q.v.) and uncle of Abū Saʿīd; seven months later, on 6 Šawwāl 736/18 May 1336, she gave birth to a daughter (Mostawfī, pp. 91, 94, 98). Shortly afterward ʿAlī Pādšāh was defeated and killed by Ḥasan-e Bozorg, a rival claimant to the throne, who then married Delšād Ḵātūn; in her new position she brought about the death of Meṣr Ḵᵛāja, who had killed her father (Aharī, p. 162; tr., p. 63).

Although married to Ḥasan-e Bozorg, she remained to some extent a partisan of her Chobanid kinsmen, some of whom found temporary asylum in Baghdad (Mostawfī, 1371 Š./1993, p. 27; Ḥāfeẓ-e Abrū, 1350 Š./1971, p. 219). When, in the summer of 748/1347, her cousin Malek Ašraf led an expedition against the capital, she reportedly persuaded Ḥasan-e Bozorg, who wanted to flee to the fortress of Komāḵ on the Euphrates, to stay and defend the city (for a different version, see Faṣīḥ, p. 74). When the Chobanid army withdrew Delšād prevented the Jalāyerids from pursuit and even welcomed some of Malek Ašraf's associates (Mostawfī, 1371 Š./1993, pp. 42-44; Ḥāfeẓ-e Abrū, pp. 226-67). According to Ṣalāḥ-al-Dīn Ḵalīl Ṣafadī (p. 24), she was poisoned by her husband, who suspected her sympathies with Malek Ašraf. Ṣafadī also reported that she enjoyed undisputed power over Jalāyerid Iraq, as well as considerable influence in Syria, and that after her death, on 8 Ḏu'l-qaʿda 752/27 December 1351, Ḥasan-e Bozorg seized her agents and associates. Delšād Ḵātūn was said to have been charitable to the poor. She was buried at Najaf (Ṣafadī, p. 24).

Delšād Ḵātūn bore three sons to Ḥasan-e Bozorg: Oways, who succeeded his father in 757/1356; Qāsem, who died in 769/1367-68 and was buried in Najaf; and Zāhed, who was born on 9 Jomādā II 752/3 August 1351, shortly before his mother's death, and died in 773/1371-72. Various daughters are mentioned only fleetingly in the sources (Naṭanzī, pp. 163, 165; Ḥāfeẓ-e Abrū, pp. 242, 244; Samarqandī, pp. 251-52).

Bibliography: Abū Bakr Qoṭbī Aharī, *Tārīḵ-e Šayḵ Oways*, ed. and tr. J. B. van Loon, the Hague, 1954. Faṣīḥ Aḥmad Ḵᵛāfī, *Mojmal-e faṣīḥī*, ed. M. Farroḵ, III, Mašhad, 1340 Š./1961. Ḥāfeẓ-e Abrū, *Ḏayl-e Jāmeʿ al-tawārīḵ*, Bibliothèque Nationale, Paris, ms. no. Suppl. persan 209; ed. Ḵ. Bayānī, 2nd ed., Tehran, 1350 Š./1971. Moʿīn-al-Dīn Naṭanzī, *Montaḵab al-tawārīḵ-e moʿīnī*, ed. J. Aubin, Tehran, 1336 Š./1957. Ḥamd-Allāh Mostawfī, *Ḏayl-e Ẓafar-nāma*, tr. M. D. Kyazimova and V. Z. Pirieva, Baku, 1986. Idem, *Ḏayl-e Tārīḵ-e gozīda*, ed. Ī. Afšār, Tehran, 1372 Š./1993. Moḥammad Šabānkāraʾī, *Majmaʿ al-ansāb*, ed. M.-H. Moḥaddeṯ, Tehran, 1363 Š./1984. Ṣalāḥ-al-Dīn Ḵalīl Ṣafadī, *al-Wāfī be'l-wafāyāt*, ed. S. Dedering, XIV, Wiesbaden, 1982. ʿAbd-al-Razzāq Samarqandī, *Maṭlaʿ al-saʿdayn wa majmaʿ al-baḥrayn*, ed. ʿA. Navāʾī, Tehran, 1353 Š./1974.

(CHARLES MELVILLE)

DEMARATUS (Attic Dēmárātos, Ionic Dēmárētos, Laconian Dāmárātos, lit., "wished by the people"), king of Sparta (from at least as early as 510 B.C.E.) who took refuge with Darius I (q.v.). He was a son of King Ariston, of the ancient lineage of the Eurypontidae. Demaratus' name is said to have reflected the Spartans' desire that Ariston have a son. Demaratus married Percalum (Pérkalon, not Pérkalos), whom he had abducted from her intended bridegroom, Leotychidas (Herodotus, 5.75.1, 6.63.3, 6.65.2, 6.70.3).

As relevant hints in several sources (e.g., Plutarch, *Mulierum Virtutes* 245d-e; Polyaenus, *Strategicon* 8.33) seem unreliable, there is little point in enumerating supposed events of his long reign, though in 510 B.C.E. he and his coruler, the other Spartan king, Cleomenes, were actively committed to freeing Athens from the Peisistratids (Pausanias, 3.7.8). Eventually Demaratus and Cleomenes became bitter enemies, though Herodotus' legendary reports probably simply reflect topoi. For example, Cleomenes and his followers, including Leotychidas, supposedly claimed that Demaratus was not Ariston's legitimate son and therefore not the legitimate king; through trickery they brought about his abdication before the battle of Marathon, in about 491 B.C.E. (Herodotus, 6.65-67, 6.74.1, 6.75.3; cf. Pausanias, 3.4.3-5, 3.7.7-9). The real reason for Demaratus' abdication, however, was doubtless his friendly attitude toward the Persians (*mēdismós*) and his opposition to Cleomenes, who had attacked Aeginetan allies of the Persians (Herodotus, 6.50-51, 6.64).

Demaratus remained for a while in Sparta and even held office (Herodotus, 6.67.1), but after an affront by his successor, Leotychidas, he took refuge with Darius, who "received him generously and gave him land and cities" (Herodotus, 6.70.1-3). Demaratus appears to have occupied an important position at the Persian court, but it is doubtful that the relevant reports reflect historical truth. For example, in the dispute among Darius' sons over the succession, Demaratus is said to have argued in favor of Xerxes, the first son born after Darius' own accession (Herodotus, 7.3.1-4; cf. Plutarch, *Artoxerxes* 2.4). Xerxes, during his invasion of Greece (Herodotus, 7.101.1) in 480 B.C.E., supposedly consulted Demaratus repeatedly; nevertheless, his warning about the fearless resistance of the Spartan army and his advice favoring a naval attack on Sparta and occupation of the island of Cythera went unheeded (Herodotus, 7.101-04, 7.209, 7.234-35; cf. Diogenes Laertius, 1.72; Diodorus, 11.6.1-2; cf., however, Ctesias, in Jacoby, *Fragmente* IIIC, p. 463, fr. 13 par. 27).

According to Xenophon (*Hellenica* 3.1.6), in 401-399 B.C.E. Pergamum, Teuthrania, and Halisarna (Athenaeus, 1.29-30: also Gambreium) were ruled by two descendants of Demaratus, Eurysthenes and Procles (cf. Xenophon, *Anabasis* 2.1.3, 7.8.17), which suggests that Demaratus himself had been in feudal service to the great king and had held the hereditary rank of a vassal until his death. Xenophon (*Hellenica* 3.1.6) also remarked that Demaratus had received those cities as a reward for his participation in the campaign against Greece, presumably Xerxes' expedition. Members of Demaratus' family obviously were among the oral sources from which Herodotus drew much of his information and some specific stories. It has been supposed, too, that in the Hellenistic period some Demaratids returned to Sparta, perhaps while Lysimachus ruled Asia Minor (305-281 B.C.E.; Homolle; for anecdotal, sometimes fictitious accounts, see Plutarch, *Lycurgus* 20.5, *De Herodoti Malignitate*, pp. 864-65, *Themistocles* 29.7-8; Herodotus, 7.239.2-4; cf. Polyaenus, *Strategicon* 2.20; Justin, 2.10.13-14, 8.65; Seneca, *De Beneficiis* 6.31.4-12).

Bibliography: (For cited works not found in this bibliography and abbreviations found here, see "Short References.") W. Aly, *Volksmärchen. Sage und Novelle bei Herodot und seinen Zeitgenossen*, Göttingen, 1921, esp. pp. 156 ff. W. Burkert, "Demaratos, Astrabakos und Herakles. Königsmythos und Politik zur Zeit der Perserkriege," *Museum Helveticum* 22, 1965, pp. 166-77. J. M. Cook, *The Persian Empire*, London, 1983, esp. pp. 17, 74. D. Hereward, "The Flight of Damaratos," *Rheinisches Museum*, N.F. 101, 1958, pp. 238-49. J. Hofstetter, *Die Griechen in Persien. Prosopographie der Griechen im persischen Reich vor Alexander*, Berlin, 1978, pp. 45-46 no. 77. T. Homolle, "Inscriptions de Délos," *Bulletin de Correspondance Hellénique* 20, 1896, pp. 502-22. [B.] Niese, "Damaratos," in Pauly-Wissowa IV/2, cols. 2029-30. G. Walser, "Griechen am Hofe des Grosskönigs," in E. Walder, ed., *Festgabe Hans von Greyerz* . . ., Bern, 1967, pp. 189-202, esp. pp. 193-94.

(RÜDIGER SCHMITT)

DEMAŠQ K̲ᵛĀJA, third son of the amir Čobān (q.v.), possibly born in 699/1300, when his father was on campaign in Damascus. He was married and remained devoted to Tūrsīn (or Tursān) K̲ātūn, despite the opposition of her father, Īrenjīn (Īrenčīn; Waṣṣāf, pp. 639-40; Ḥāfeẓ-e Abrū, ms., fol. 506b). She bore him four daughters, of whom the eldest was Delšād K̲ātūn (q.v.).

After the death of Čobān's rival Sevīnč (Sevenj) in 718/1318 Demašq K̲ᵛāja seized control of the Šabānkāra district in Fārs, which he divided up among his supporters (Šabānkāraʾī, p. 180; cf. Naṭanzī, p. 9). In the revolt of the amirs against Čobān in the following year Shaikh ʿAlī, son of Īrenjīn, seized Demašq K̲ᵛājā, plundered his possessions, and almost killed him, believing himself to be acting with Abū Saʿīd's support (Waṣṣāf, p. 641; Ḥāfeẓ-e Abrū, 1350 Š./1971, pp. 146-47; Samarqandī, p. 41; Melville). The amirs were defeated, however, and, as a result, Čobān's position became unassailable; Demašq K̲ᵛāja, who was noted for his prudence and clear thinking, became his vicegerent (*nāʾeb-e koll*; Šabānkāraʾī, p. 278).

As Demašq K̲ᵛāja's power grew, so did his arrogance and the consequent resentment of the amirs at court. Abū Saʿīd, who was only a nominal ruler, complained of his behavior to Čobān and requested that one of Demašq K̲ᵛāja's brothers, either Jelāʾū Khan or Shaikh Maḥmūd, replace him. Demašq K̲ᵛāja blamed the sultan's disfavor on slanders by the vizier, Rokn-al-Dīn Ṣāyen (Ḥāfeẓ-e Abrū, pp. 168-69) and succeeded in having Ṣāyen removed from court. Demašq K̲ᵛāja then acquired full control of affairs (*Tārīk̲-e gozīda*, ed. Browne, p. 607), but his rudeness to the sultan and his tyrannical behavior increased. The situation came to a head with the supposed discovery that Demašq K̲ᵛāja was trespassing in the sultan's harem (Ebn Baṭṭūṭa, tr. Gibb, II, pp. 337-38; Abu'l-Fedāʾ, p. 87; Ḥāfeẓ-e Abrū, pp. 168-69). On this pretext Abū Saʿīd moved decisively against him, and Demašq K̲ᵛāja, while trying to escape from Solṭānīya, was captured by the amir Meṣr K̲ᵛāja and executed on 5 Šawwāl 727/24 August 1327. This harem intrigue was not mentioned by the contemporary authors, who reported instead that Abū Saʿīd was goaded into action by the hostility of the amirs (*Tārīk̲-e gozīda*, ed. Browne, p. 608; Šabānkāraʾī, pp. 280-81). Among the latter was Nūrīn Tağāy, who had previously been banished from court by Demašq K̲ᵛāja until Čobān intervened in his favor (Ḥāfeẓ-e Abrū, ms., fols. 523b-24a; Samarqandī, p. 86). According to Aharī (p. 55; tr., p. 154), Abū Saʿīd was distressed at Demašq K̲ᵛāja's death, but this report was probably simply a gesture of respect to Delšād K̲ātūn; in fact, Abū Saʿīd then ordered the arrest of Čobān and his other sons in different parts of the empire.

Demašq K̲ᵛāja was buried in a mosque at Tabrīz that was built in his memory by his sister Bag̲dād K̲ātūn (Ḥāfeẓ Ḥosayn, p. 523).

Bibliography: (For cited works not found in this bibliography and abbreviations found here, see "Short References.") Abu'l-Fedāʾ, *al-Mok̲taṣar fī ak̲bār al-bašar*, ed. and tr. P. M. Holt as *The Memoirs of a Syrian Prince*, Wiesbaden, 1983. Abū Bakr Qoṭbī Aharī, *Tārīk̲-e Šayk̲ Oways*, ed. and tr. J. B. van Loon, the Hague, 1954. ʿA. Eqbāl, *Tārīk̲-e mofaṣṣal-e Īrān az estīlā-ye Mog̲ol tā eʿlān-e mašrūṭīyat* I. *Az ḥamla-ye Čengīz tā taškīl-e dawlat-e tīmūrī*, Tehran, 1341 Š./1962, pp. 333, 335-37, 341. Faṣīḥ Aḥmad K̲ᵛāfī, *Mojmal-e faṣīḥī*, ed. M. Farrok̲, 3 vols., Mašhad, 1340 Š./1961. *Ḥabīb al-sīar* III, pp. 210-12, 214, 216. Ḥāfeẓ-e Abrū, *D̲ayl-e Jāmeʿ al-tawārīk̲-e rašīdī*, Bibliothèque Nationale, Paris, ms. no. Suppl. persan 209; ed. K̲. Bayānī, 2nd ed., Tehran, 1350 Š./1971. Ḥāfez Ḥosayn Karbalāʾī Tabrīzī, *Rawżat al-jenān wa jannāt al-janān*, ed. J. Solṭān-al-Qorrāʾī, I, Tehran, 1344 Š./1965. C. Melville, "Abū Saʿīd and the Revolt of the Amirs in 1319," in D. Aigle and J. Aubin, eds., *L'Iran face à la domination mongole*, forthcoming. Moʿīn-al-Dīn Naṭanzī, *Montak̲ab al-tawārīk̲-e moʿīnī*, ed. J. Aubin, Tehran, 1336 Š./1957. Moḥammad Šabānkāraʾī, *Majmaʿ al-ansāb*, ed. M.-H. Moḥaddet̲, Tehran, 1363 Š./1984.

(CHARLES MELVILLE)

DEMETRIUS, name of two Greco-Bactrian kings.

Demetrius I, son of Euthydemus I. While still crown prince of Bactria Demetrius conducted, on behalf of his father, negotiations with the Seleucid Antiochus III in 206-05 B.C.E.; Antiochus considered Demetrius "worthy of kingship because of his distinction, conversational rapport, and capacity for leadership" and promised him one of his own daughters in marriage. Having succeeded to the throne of Bactria, Demetrius campaigned in India, making apparently extensive conquests (Polybius, 11.39). On the obverse of his silver coins he is portrayed wearing the elephant-scalp headdress of Alexander the Great (q.v.), with the reverse type of a youthful Hercules crowning himself with a garland. On a commemorative "pedigree coin" of the later Euthydemid king Agathocles, presumably a son of Demetrius (Allan), Demetrius is portrayed with the title Aníkētos (invincible), which had been borne by Alexander himself. Subsequently, after the appearance in Bactria of the rival prince Eucratides around 175 B.C.E., he returned from India (Justin, 41.6, where he is described as king of India) and besieged Eucratides' small escort with an army said to have numbered 60,000; he was nevertheless outmaneuvered, defeated, and apparently slain. The curious allusion to "the grete Emetrius, the King of Ynde" in Geoffrey Chaucer's *Knight's Tale* (ll. 2155-57) is thought by some to echo Demetrius' story, as found in medieval sources was derived from the lost histories of Trogus (Bivar).

Demetrius II. Demetrius II was presumably another son of Demetrius I; he is known only from Greco-Bactrian coins with the reverse type of a standing Athena.

Bilingual Indo-Bactrian coins in the name of Demetrius Aníkētos, in particular a remarkable tetradrachm with the royal portrait wearing the *kausía* (sun hat), though usually attributed to Demetrius II, or III, are similar in monogram and arrangement of the legend to late issues of Menander (ca. 155-46 B.C.E.) and were probably commemorative issues of an unnamed ruler.

Bibliography: (For abbreviations found in this bibliography, see "Short References.") J. Allan, "Indian Coins Acquired by the British Museum," *NC*, 1934, pp. 229-31. A. D. H. Bivar, "The Death of Eucratides in Medieval Tradition," *JRAS*, 1950, pp. 7-13. O. Bopearachchi, *Monnaies gréco-bactriennes et indo-grecques. Catalogue raisonné*, Paris, 1991, pp. 49-59, 65-66, 99, 164-67, 195. R. Curiel and G. Fussman, *Le trésor monétaire de Qunduz*, Paris, 1965, pls. II-VII. A. K. Narain, *The Indo-Greeks*, Oxford, 1957, pp. 23-28 and passim. W. W. Tarn, *The Greeks in Bactria and India*, Cambridge, 1951, chap. 4. R. B. Whitehead, "Notes on Indo-Greek Numismatics," *NC*, 1923, pp. 294-343.

(A. D. H. BIVAR)

D̲EMMĪ. See PEOPLE OF THE BOOK.

DEMOCEDES (Gk. Dēmokḗdēs), Greek physician attached to the court of Darius I (q.v.) and praised as "the most skillful physician of his time" by Herodotus (3.125.1). He was born in Croton in southern Italy, the son of Calliphon, a priest of Asclepius in Cnidus. Democedes seems to have worked first as a physician in the civil service of Aegina and Athens before entering the service of Polycrates, the famous tyrant of Samos (Herodotus, 3.131.1-2). Around 522 B.C.E. he, together with Polycrates and his entourage (3.125.2-3), fell into the hands of the Lydian satrap Oroites and was sent as a captive to Susa (3.129.1).

Herodotus described the career of Democedes in great detail, obviously from reliable sources (perhaps oral reports that he heard in Magna Grecia). He once healed, without further trauma, a sprained ankle that Darius had received while hunting and that his Egyptian physicians were unable to treat (3.129.1-130.5). As a result, Democedes received immense rewards; he was held in high esteem at court and, despite his foreign origin, ate in the presence of the king. Democedes was thus the first of a series of Greek physicians at the Persian court; although he lived in luxury, he nevertheless wanted to return to Greece, but his requests were denied (3.132). He apparently remained in Persia for several years and at some point cured Darius' wife Atossa, daughter of Cyrus the Great (qq.v.), of a breast ulcer (3.133). As a reward he was permitted to go to Greece, with fifteen Persian noblemen and three Phoenician ships, to conduct a preliminary reconnaissance of the coastal regions for a planned military campaign (3.133.2-136). After completing most of the assignment the party stopped at Tarentum, and Democedes escaped, with the help of Aristophilides, the Tarentinian king. He returned to his native Croton, where he was protected from Persian recapture (3.136-137.4), and soon married the daughter of the famous wrestler Milon (3.137.5); the other Persian agents returned to Persia with their reports and maps (3.138.1).

Almost no useful additional information is to be found in other sources (Himerius *apud* Photius, *Bibliotheca* 243, ed. Bekker, p. 376a34; Timaeus *apud* Athenaeus, 12.522b-c; Aelian, *Varia Historia* 8.17; Dio Cassius, 38.18.5; Dio Chrysostom, 77/78.10-11; Suda, s.v. Dēmokḗdēs; Tzetzes, *Chiliades* 3.544-60). Only Iamblichus (*De Vita Pythagorica* 257, 261) touched upon another aspect of Democedes' biography.

It seems probable that, like Ctesias (q.v.) a century later, Democedes was the ultimate source for a number of Greek narratives about internal matters at the Persian court and especially the harem, though it is not certain that he left even any medical writings.

Bibliography: (For abbreviations found in this bibliography, see "Short References.") A. R. Burn, "Persia and the Greeks," in *Camb. Hist. Iran* II, pp. 292-391, esp. p. 299. J. M. Cook, *The Persian Empire*, London, 1983, esp. pp. 17, 141. A. Griffith, "Democedes of Croton. A Greek Doctor at the Court of Darius," in H. Sancisi-Weerdenburg and A. Kuhrt, eds., *Achaemenid History* II. *The Greek Sources*, Leiden, 1987, pp. 37-51. J. Hofstetter, *Die Griechen in Persien. Prosopographie der Griechen im persischen Reich vor Alexander*, Berlin, 1978, pp. 46-47 no. 79. P. Huyse, "Die persische Medizin auf der Grundlage von Herodots Historien," *Ancient Society* 21, 1990, pp. 141-48. G. Walser, "Griechen am Hofe des Grosskönigs," in E. Walder, ed., *Festgabe Hans von Greyerz . . .*, Bern, 1967, pp. 189-202, esp. pp. 196-97. E. Wellman, "Demokedes," in Pauly-Wissowa V/1, col. 132.

(RÜDIGER SCHMITT)

DEMOCRACY. See ANJOMAN; CONSTITUTIONAL REVOLUTION i-v; ELECTIONS.

DEMOCRAT PARTY. See CONSTITUTIONAL REVOLUTION v.

DEMOGRAPHY, the statistical study of characteristics of human populations.

i. *In Persia since 1319 Š./1940.*
ii. *In Afghanistan.*
iii. *In Tajikistan.*

i. IN PERSIA SINCE 1319 Š./1940

Since World War II Persia, formerly a rural and tribal country dominated by elderly notables and with low population growth, has come to have a majority of young urban dwellers, mostly literate and multiplying rapidly. In 1358 Š./1979, for the first time in history, the proportions of urban dwellers and individuals classified as literate both passed the threshold of 50 percent. Such social changes have, however, been accompanied by great stability in natural demographic components, particularly fertility, which has changed very little, thus raising questions about the depth of the changes themselves. Unless otherwise noted, the statistics presented here have been drawn directly from the censuses of the general population conducted by Markaz-e āmār-e Īrān (Statistical center of Persia) in November 1956, 1966, 1976, and 1986 (see CENSUS); a demographic survey was conducted in 1991.

In 1995 Persia had about 63 million inhabitants, increasing at a rate of about 1.8 million a year. Population density (38.5 per km^2) differs sharply from that prevailing at the beginning of the century, when the total population of this large country was fewer than 10 million, increasing by only 100,000 a year, with a density of 6.0 per km^2. Since World War II the Persian population has nearly doubled every twenty years (2.9 percent a year), and migration to the cities has increased enormously (Table 10). Like most comparable countries Persia experienced a demographic "boom" beginning in the 1950s (with a 2.5 percent annual increase), entering a phase of "demographic transition," characterized by a continued high birth rate and a rapid decline in the death rate. Despite the impression gathered from examining the raw data, however, the rate of population growth has not accelerated but has remained stable. For extraneous reasons (including factors like registration for military service and food coupons) the census of 1365 Š./1986 was more nearly complete, whereas those of 1335 Š./1956, 1345 Š./1966, and 1355 Š./1976 were underreported by 7.5, 5.0, and 2.5 percent respectively (Bharier, 1968); if only natural growth had been taken into account, the Persian population in 1365 Š./1986 would have been recorded at between 45 and 47 million, rather than the nearly 50 million reported in the census (Amani,

1988).

Distribution. The geographical distribution of the Persian population is very uneven. The heaviest concentration is in the western part of the country, northwest of an imaginary line drawn from Ābādān to Gorgān, where 64 percent of Persians live on 27 percent of the territory (72.4/km^2). This high density reflects stability among the large rural population, rather than growth of the cities, with the exception of the region around Tehran (308/km^2). In the province of Hamadān population density is 77/km^2, in that of Māzandarān 73/km^2, and in that of Gīlān 140/km^2. The rest of the country, comprising 73 percent of the territory, is largely desert (q.v.; 14.9/km^2), with a population concentrated around cities and on several irrigated plains. The southern regions (Fārs, Baluchistan, Kermān) have experienced higher population growth than those of the north and west (the central plateau, the Caspian provinces, Azerbaijan, and even Kurdistan), however. The census of 1365 Š./1986 provides evidence of the effects of regional wars, with heavy increases in Khorasan and Baluchistan, where Afghan refugees have settled, and, on the other hand, abandonment of the *šahrestāns* (subprovincial units) on the Iraqi frontier, especially those of Ābādān and Ḵorramšahr (Figure 12).

The continuous high rate of population increase since the 1950s has had the direct effect of lowering the age of the population, 50 percent of which is now under seventeen years old. The proportion below fifteen years old will drop below 40 percent before the end of the century, however, as the "postwar" generations age; a very gradual increase in life expectancy will not lead to a significant increase in the number of older people (Table 11; Figure 13).

Early census findings that men outnumbered women did not reflect genuine demographic facts; rather, they resulted from cultural features linked to the traditional status of women (underreporting of girls) and the higher value placed on boys (Table 12). The ratio was reversed in the age group between fifteen and thirty years, on the other hand, for men seek to avoid military service, and women, once married, are normally counted (Behnam and Amani, p. 17). In the census of 1365 Š./1986 the sex ratio corresponded more closely to biological reality.

Fertility and mortality. The birth rate is about 43 percent, that is, between six and seven children born alive per woman, among the highest in the world, comparable to rates in several neighboring countries (e.g., Syria 7.5, Turkey 4.3, Jordan 6.5 infants per woman). It has not changed noticeably from that observed in the rural zone in 1344 Š./1965 (Chasteland et al.). In the absence of reliable government figures, the fertility of Persian women can only be estimated, but it is certain that for three decades the level remained stableuntil 1365 Š./1986, while the economic and social development of the country was supposed to have led to a lowering of the number of infants born per woman (Bauer). It is is also certain that the government's family policies, both before and after the Revolution of 1357 Š./1978-79, have had very little direct impact and that, in this respect, the deeply rooted cultural and social characteristics of Persian women and families have, despite a few innovations, evolved little in forty years (Table 13). Since 1986 the fertility rate has been declining rapidly, the average number of children born to women was only 4.4 in 1991 (compared to 6.2 in 1986). The fertility rate varies noticeably with place of residence (urban or rural) and especially with educational level. Regional differences are equally noteworthy, distinguishing the central plateau and the Caspian provinces from peripheral regions, especially those in the south (Figure 14).

The government first adopted a policy of promoting birth control in maternal- and child-health centers in 1332 Š./1953, but consciousness raising began only in 1339 Š./1960, when importation of birth-control pills was authorized (Sardari and Keyhan, p. 780). In fact, it was not until 1345 Š./1966 that the government began to devote serious attention to this issue, establishing the High council of family planning (Wāḥed-e jamʿīyat wa tanẓīm-e ḵānavāda), creating a special ministerial post (*moʿāwen-e vazīr*; Sardari and Keyhan), and, on 15 Ḵordād 1346 Š./5

Table 10
EVOLUTION OF THE POPULATION OF PERSIA, 1900-91

Year	Total Population (in millions)	Growth Rate (in percentages)	Urban Population (in percentages)	Literacy (in percentages)	Population Density per km^2
1317-18/1900	9.86	1.1	21.0	n.a.	6.0
1319 Š./1940	14.55	1.5	22.0	n.a.	8.8
1335 Š./1956	18.95	2.2	31.4	14.9	11.5
1345 Š./1966	25.78	3.1	39.0	29.4	15.7
1355 Š./1976	33.71	2.7	46.9	47.5	20.5
1365 Š./1986	49.86 (47.50[a])	3.9 (3.0[a])	54.2	61.7	30.3
1370 Š./1991	55.83	2.5	57.0	71.4	38.5

a. Estimated total excluding the migratory component (Amani, 1988).
Sources: Bharier, 1972; Markaz-e āmār, 1335-71 Š./1956-92.

June 1967, adopting the Law for the protection of the family (Qānūn-e ḥemāyat-e ḵānavāda). The new policy received massive support from international organizations, but this support produced a greater impact in the media (e.g., the Isfahan communication program in 1349 Š./1970; Lieberman, p. 149) than on actual behavior. In the private sector 4.2 million sets of birth-control pills were sold in 1350 Š./1971, compared to 900,000 in the public centers (Moore et al., p. 403). In 1355 Š./1976 abortion, already widely practiced (11-17 percent of births in the years 1339-46 Š./1960-67; Jalali et al., p. 218), was legalized, but by 1357 Š./1978 only 11 percent of Persian women had accepted the principle of family planning (Aghajanian, 1992). In 1358 Š./1979 the government of the Islamic Republic abolished the laws for protection of the family and legal abortion; although contraception was not forbidden, the administration ceased all significant activity in this area until 1359 Š./1980, when a *fatwā* (legal opinion) from Ayatollah Rūḥ-Allāh Ḵomeynī (Khomeini) confirmed the lawfulness of contraception, permitting the Ministry of health (Wezārat-e behdārī) to resume its contraception programs. Between 1362 Š./1983 and 1366 Š./1987, 6-7 million people, 31 percent of the relevant population, received contraceptive devices each year, aside from sales in the private sector (according to data published in Markaz-e āmār, 1367 Š./1988). The new family-planning policy thus reached populations that had previously been hesitant or poorly informed, which naturally helped to lower the birth rate more rapidly than before, though it remained very high. After the war between Persia and Iraq the demographic policy of

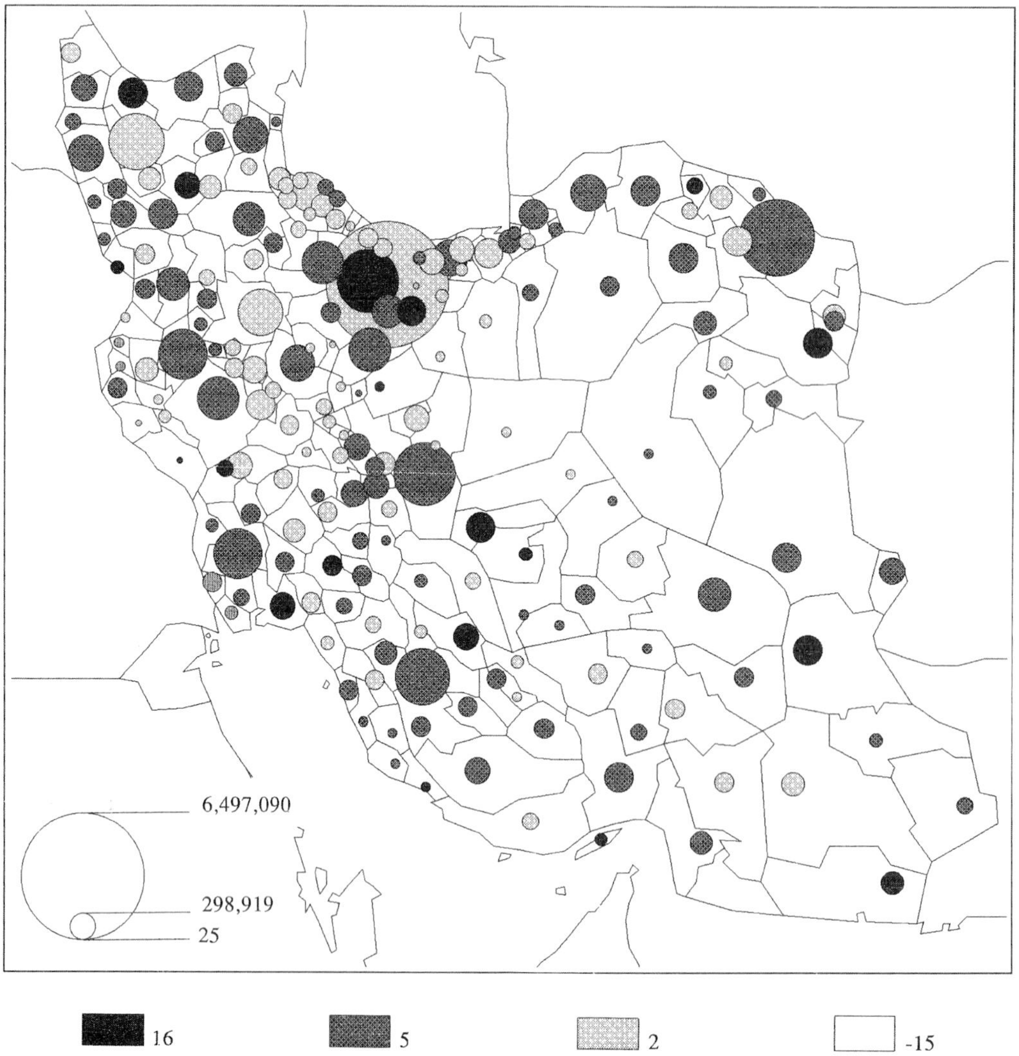

Figure 12. Distribution of population and growth in Persia, by *šahrestān*, 1365-70 Š./1986-91.

Table 11
EVOLUTION OF THE PERSIAN POPULATION BY AGE GROUP, 1335-1379 Š./1956-2000

Year	0-14 Years	15-64 Years	Over 65 Years	Median Age
1335 Š./1956	42.2	53.8	4.0	20.2
1345 Š./1966	46.1	50.0	3.9	16.9
1355 Š./1976	44.4	52.1	3.5	17.4
1365 Š./1986	45.5	51.5	3.0	17.0
Urban	*42.8*	*54.3*	*2.9*	
Rural	*48.6*	*48.2*	*3.2*	
1379 Š./2000 (projected)	36.4	59.5	3.6	

Sources: Markaz-e āmār, 1335-65 Š./1956-86.

Table 12
PERCENTAGES OF MALES IN THE TOTAL PERSIAN POPULATION, 1335-65 Š./1956-86

	1335 Š./1956	1345 Š./1966	1355 Š./1976	1365 Š./1986
Total	103.6	107.3	106.2	104.6
20-24 years	87.7	88.9	92.3	102.5
25-29 years	94.8	94.4	91.7	100.6
Over 65 years	108.2	114.3	111.1	102.0

Sources: Amani, 1988; Markaz-e āmār, 1335-65 Š./1956-86.

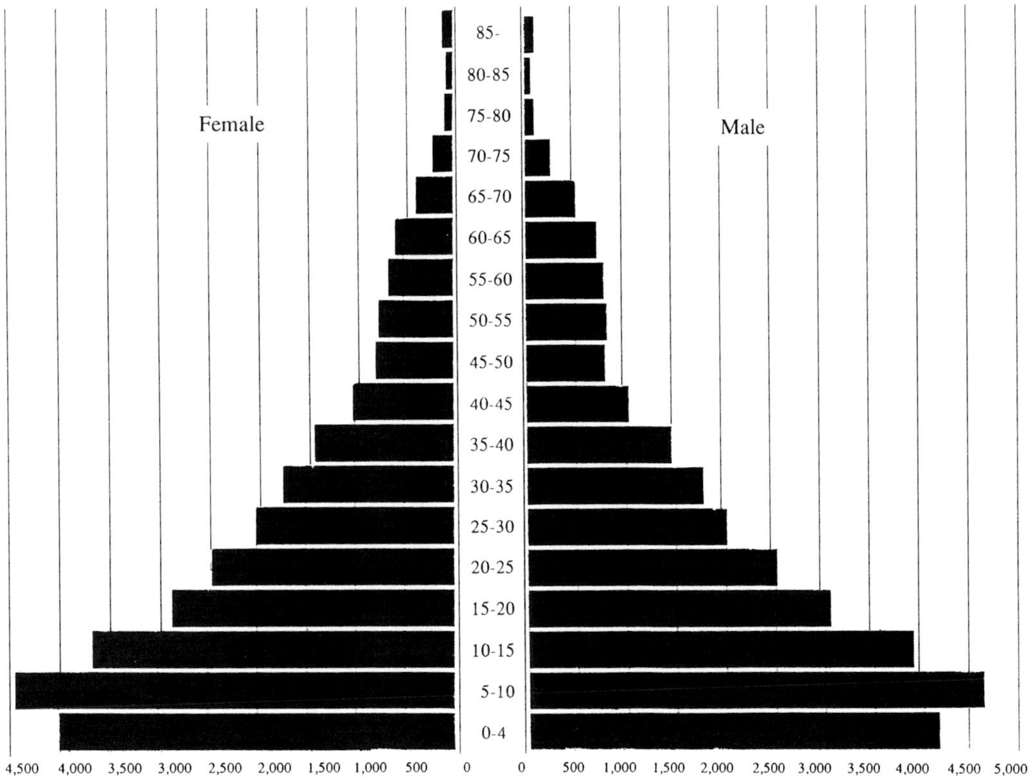

Figure 13. Population tree, Persia, 1370 Š./1991. After Markaz-e āmār, 1371 Š./1992.

the Islamic government changed radically. Following a conference on population and development, held at Mašhad on 18 Mehr 1367 Š./10 September 1988, all propaganda encouraging large families was abandoned, and a new Malthusian policy has been very actively pursued, in order to bring about a reduction in the rate of population increase to 2.3 percent by 1377 Š./1998.

The general mortality rate (9 per thousand), and especially the mortality rate among children (88 per thousand), dropped markedly after 1329 Š./1950, but it, too, remained high (Table 14). The differences between city and country were particularly great because of the lack of medical equipment in rural areas: According to the *Population Growth Survey* (Markaz-e āmār, 1357 Š./1978), the infant mortality rate was 130 per thousand in the country for the years 1351-55 Š./1973-76, compared to 76 per thousand in the city (general mortality: 13.9 and 8.3 per thousand respectively). Life expectancy at birth rose from forty-six years in 1338 Š./1959 to sixty-two years in 1369 Š./1990; in contrast to the situation in most countries, in Persia men seem to live longer than women, but the hypothesis of a higher mortality rate among women has not been confirmed. The war between Persia and Iraq, in which almost 50,000 people died each year, did not alter the overall demography of Persia but did result in changes in numbers of female heads of household (7.1 percent of households) and the rates of remarriage.

The main consequence of longer life expectancy has been the spread of permanent cohabitation of two and even three generations. This situation has consequences for behavior, both demographic (fertility, marriage) and social (aggravation of generational conflict), the effects of which are just beginning to appear. Average family size (five people) has remained stable or increased slightly, further evidence of both the decline in mortality and the stable fertility rate. The differences between city and country reflect both greater fertility in rural areas and increasing cohabitation of generations, which is easier and more traditional than in the urban zones.

Marriage. The average age for first marriage (nineteen years for women, twenty-three years for men) and the proportion of married women between ten and forty-nine years old (58 percent in 1355 Š./1976, 57 percent in 1365 Š./1986) remain generally quite stable, and celibates are still rare (1.1 percent in the age group fifty to fifty-four years; Table 15). These figures reveal a conservatism in behavior that is in sharp contrast to the upheavals that the country has experienced in other areas since World War II. The difference in ages of men and women at first marriage dropped from 5.9 years in 1335 Š./1956 to 3.5 years in 1370 Š./1991. In 1358 Š./1979 the legal marriage age was lowered from eighteen to thirteen years for girls and from twenty to fifteen years for boys. In 1344 Š./1965 an investigation of rural areas revealed that 19.7 percent of girls were married before the age of fourteen years (33.3 percent in the Kāzerūn region; Chasteland et al., p. 180), reflecting a deeply rooted social practice independent of the law.

The sociology of marriage was upset by the revolution in Persia in 1357 Š./1978-1979. There was an immediate boom in marriages, which increased from 1.8 million in 1357 Š./1978 to 3.0 million in 1358 Š./1979, reaching 4.1 million in 1362 Š./1983 before stabilizing at 3.4 million. This phenomenon was provoked not by Islamic legislation but by the arrival at marriageable age of larger generations and by the "revolutionary spirit," which had caused ruptures in the traditional family structure and permitted meetings (e.g., at demonstrations and in political action)

Table 13
FERTILITY IN PERSIA, 1900-91

Year	Birth rate (in percentages[a])	Number of children per woman (in numbers per thousand): Persia	Urban[a]	Rural[a]	Female Literacy (in percentages)	Female Employment (in percentages)
1317-18/1900		8-9.0				
1335 Š./1956					7.3	9.2
1335-45 Š./1956-66	48.0	7.3				
1345 Š./1966					17.4	12.6
1345-55 Š./1966-76	43.0	6.7				
1355 Š./1976		6.3	4.4	7.8	35.5	12.9
1355-65 Š./1976-86	43.0	6.3	5.4	7.8		
1345 Š./1986		6.2	5.3	7.6	51.0	8.2
1370 Š./1991		4.4			67.1	

a. Estimated.
Sources: Ladier; Markaz-e āmār, 1335-71 Š./1956-92.

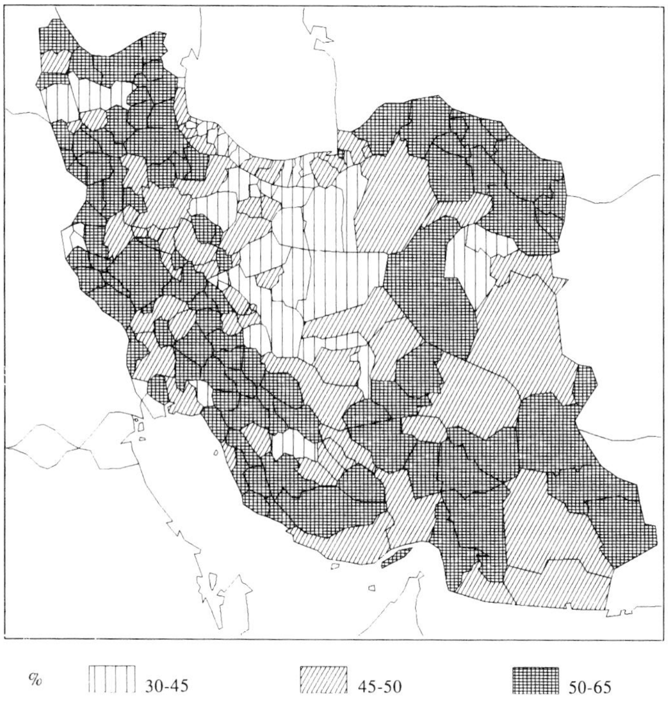

Figure 14. Birth rate in Persia per 1,000, by *šahrestān*, 1365 Š./1986.

Table 14
MORTALITY IN PERSIA, 1329-69 Š./1950-90

Year	General Mortality (per thousand)	Infant Mortality (per thousand)	Life Expectancy (in years)
1329-34 Š./1950-55	22	189	46
1339-44 Š./1960-65	18	156	51
1344-49 Š./1965-70	16	143	53
1349-54 Š./1970-75	14	129	56
1354-59 Š./1975-80	12	115	58
1359-64 Š./1980-85	10	101	60
1364-69 Š./1985-90	9	88	62

Sources: Markaz-e āmār, 1335-71 Š./1956-92.

Table 15
THE PERSIAN FAMILY, 1335-70 Š./1956-91

	Number of Family Members			Average Age at First Marriage		Polygamous Marriages
Year	Total	Urban	Rural	Men	Women	(in percentages)
1335 Š./1956	4.76	4.72	4.77	24.9	19.0	1.1
1345 Š./1966	4.98	5.00	4.98	25.0	18.4	1.0
1355 Š./1976	5.01	4.86	5.17	24.1	19.7	1.3
1365 Š./1986	5.10	4.84	5.45	23.6	19.8	2.2
1370 Š./1991	5.18	4.86	5.61	24.5	21.0	

Sources: Amani, 1988; Markaz-e āmār, 1335-71 Š./1956-92.

that led to marriage alliances contrary to familial traditions. The divorce rate remained stable (10 percent of marriages).

Polygamy accounts for 2-3 percent of all marriages and thus remains marginal demographically, except in certain rural regions of Fārs (Chasteland et al., p. 195) and Ḵūzestān, as well as in traditional lower-income social groups; the rate reached as high as 3.5-13.8 percent, depending upon age, among the skilled laborers of the Iranian Oil Refinery Company in 1335 Š./1956 (Miller and Windle, p. 309). Long-lasting "temporary" marriages (*ṣīḡa*) have never been counted but do not seem to have a notable effect on demography.

Migration. Migrations involve only a small, though growing part of the population; the proportion of people counted in the *šahrestāns* of their birth dropped from 89 percent in 1335 Š./1956 to 77.6 percent in 1365 Š./1986 (Table 16). International migrations were of little importance until the end of the 1970s, but, owing to the Revolution of 1357 Š./1978-79 and then to the war between Persia and Iraq, about 3 million people went into exile in the United States and Europe (Bozorgmehr and Sabbagh, p. 33), as well as in India and Turkey. Emigration on this scale is a new phenomenon but one with ancient roots; it has involved particularly the middle classes and the most highly educated and skilled groups. Large-scale foreign immigration is also new in Persia. In the 1970s more than 1 million Afghan and southeast Asian (Philippine) workers, as well as workers from industrialized nations, lived in Persia on a temporary basis and were rarely counted. In the census of 1365 Š./1986 the nationalities of the 865,307 foreigners counted were specified for the first time: 87.3 percent Afghans, 9.7 percent Iraqis, 1.5 percent Pakistanis, and so on. Refugees from Iraq, mainly Kurds and Iraqis of Persian origin, were not counted because they had been assimilated or lived provisionally in camps. These census data are underestimates, but they reflect a new situation; according to some estimates (Amani, 1988, p. 547), there were actually about 3.5 million foreigners (7 percent of the total population) in Persia in 1365 Š./1986.

Since 1335 Š./1956, 90 percent of internal migrations have been from the country to the cities, the population of which has multiplied 4.5 times (Clark, p. 105), whereas, in the period 1279-35 Š./1900-56, 61 percent of such migrations were between cities, especially toward Tehran, where 48 percent of the inhabitants were migrants; the proportion of migrants was 52 percent in Ābādān, 45 percent in Arāk, and only 25 percent in Mašhad (Bharier, 1972). This very rapid development of the cities reflects the departure of about 50 percent of the natural demographic surplus of the villages, the population of which has grown 71 percent in four decades (Table 17). This migration does not, however, fit the definition of a "rural exodus." On the contrary, Persia is confronted simultaneously with the growth of new districts surrounding already heavily populated cities (Zandjani, 1992) and the persistence of a very large rural population.

The proportion of migrants in Tehran is declining, even though the absolute numbers are growing. Julian Bharier (1972, p. 58) has calculated that, between 1279 Š./1900 and 1335 Š./1956, 42 percent of migrants settled in Tehran and 22 percent in the oil cities; from 1335 Š./1956 to 1345 Š./1966 this proportion rose to 50 percent for Tehran (with only 5 percent for Isfahan and Mašhad), but in 1355-65 Š./1976-86 only 33.3 percent of the 3,277,794 migrants from their native *šahrestāns* moved to the capital, 7 percent to the province of Isfahan, 6.7 percent to Khorasan, and 5.8 percent to Fārs. The position of Tehran as an urban center remained stable over four decades (26.2 percent of city dwellers in 1355 Š./1956, compared to 25.7 percent in 1365 Š./1986, including the suburbs), but in the same period the population living in cities of more than 100,000 inhabitants grew from 15.7 to 36.4 percent, of which 21 percent were concentrated in the five largest cities, each larger than 1 million inhabitants. The concentration of migrants in cities was accelerated by the war between Persia and Iraq and particularly affected the large provincial cities, which

Table 16
MIGRATORY POPULATIONS IN PERSIA, 1335-70 Š./1956-91

	Population Born Elsewhere than in Residence (in percentages)			Population Born Outside Persia	
Year	Total	Urban	Rural	Numbers	Percentages
1335 Š./1956	11.0	?	?	44,796	0.23
1345 Š./1966	13.1	26.4	4.6	57,115	0.22
1355 Š./1976	15.5	27.2	5.3	178,911	0.53
1365 Š./1986	22.4	30.8	12.4	891,798	1.78
1370 Š./1991	25.9	32.5	17.1	906,988	1.60

Sources: Markaz-e āmār, 1335-71 Š./1956-92.

evolved from regional centers into urban metropolises (Zanjānī and Raḥmānī). With the arrival of the Afghans and the peasants of southern Khorasan Mašhad became the second city of Persia (1,463,000). Shiraz (850,000 in 1365 Š./1986) was disrupted by the influx of refugees coming from Ābādān, and Tabrīz (971,000) received a large number of Kurds. Tehran received populations from all over the country, mainly Azerbaijan and Kurdistan; like all the large metropolises of Persia, the capital has become surrounded by immense suburbs with a population of 900,000 people, swallowing up rural areas from Varāmīn to Haštjerd (Rahnema'i).

The nomadic population (see ʿAŠĀYER) was counted for the first time in the summer of 1987 (Tīr 1366 Š.) by the Statistical center of Persia (Markaz-e āmār, 1367 Š./1988). The total was 1,152,099 people, grouped in 96 tribes (*īl*) and 547 independent clans (*ṭāyefa-ye mostaqell*); the figures are not comparable with the estimates in the previous general censuses (337,176 nomads counted in 1355 Š./1976; Amirahmadi). Because of economic development and an authoritarian settlement policy, particularly under Reżā Shah (1304-20 Š./1925-41), the number of people practicing pastoral nomadism has been sharply declining since the beginning of the 20th century, when it was estimated at 2.5 million, 32 percent of the rural population, compared to 5 percent today (Bharier, 1972, p. 59). From the cultural and economic point of view this population is little favored; 83 percent are illiterate, and only 32 percent of children between six and eleven years old are in school, compared to 81.7 percent for Persia as a whole.

Social and economic characteristics (Tables 18-20, Figure 15). The literacy rate of the population (54.2 percent) has risen rapidly since 1335 Š./1956, especially in rural areas, which nevertheless remain far behind the cities (Table 18). These signs of progress go hand in hand with attendance at primary school (91.5 percent in the cities, 72.6 percent in the villages). Young adults are thus largely literate (75.2 percent of those between fifteen and twenty-four years old), especially in the cities, but 58.1 percent of the generation between twenty-five and sixty-four years old were still illiterate in 1365 Š./1986 (Markaz-e āmār, 1365 Š./1986).

The census of 1365 Š./1986 for the first time furnished information on the knowledge of Persian among the population (Figure 15; 82.7 percent of

Table 17
URBANIZATION IN PERSIA, 1335-70 Š./1956-91

Year	Urban Population (in thousands)	Rate of Annual Increase (in percentages)		Number of Cities[a]	Number of Cities with Population over 100,000	Population of Tehran (in thousands)
		Urban	Rural			
1335 Š./1956	5,953			199	9	1,512
1345 Š./1966	9,794	5.41	2.1	272	14	3,015
1355 Š./1976	15,854	4.59	1.9	373	23	4,549
1365 Š./1986	26,844	5.49	2.0	496	41	6,042
1370 Š./1991	31,836	3.50	1.2	514	47	6,475

a. Agglomerations of more than 5,000 inhabitants and important administrative centers are classified as cities.
Sources: Zanjānī and Raḥmānī, 1368 Š./1989; Markaz-e āmār, 1335-71 Š./1956-92.

Table 18
LITERACY RATES IN PERSIA, 1335-70 Š./1956-91[a]

Year	Men			Women		
	Total	Urban	Rural	Total	Urban	Rural
1335 Š./1956	22.2	45.2	10.8	7.3	20.6	1.0
1345 Š./1966	40.1	61.5	25.4	17.9	38.3	4.3
1355 Š./1976	58.8	74.4	43.6	35.6	55.7	17.4
1365 Š./1986	71.0	80.5	60.1	51.0	65.2	36.0
1370 Š./1991	80.1	86.7	72.6	67.1	76.8	54.2

a. Among the population more than ten years old in 1335 Š./1956, more than seven years old in 1345 Š./1966, more than six years old in 1355 Š./1976, 1365 Š./1986, and 1370 Š./1991.
Sources: Markaz-e āmār, 1335-1371 Š./1956-92.

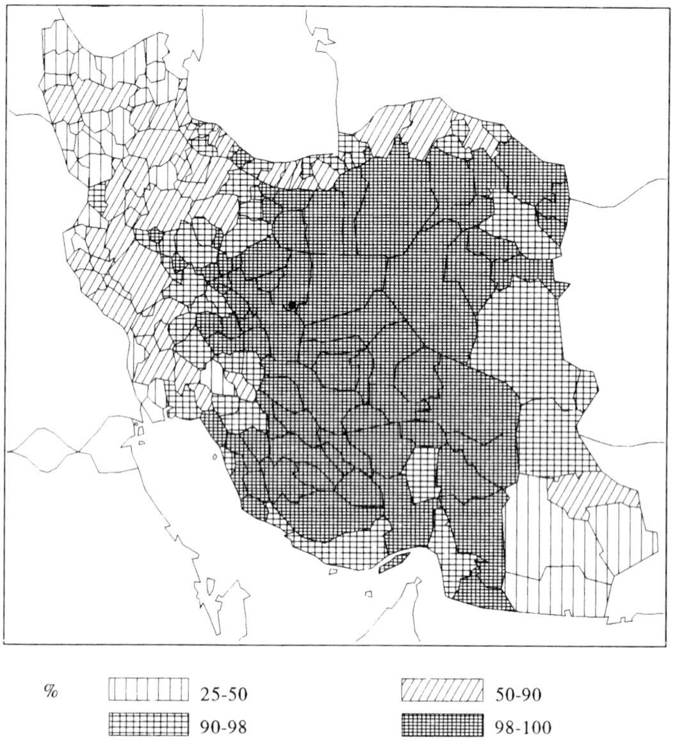

Figure 15. Knowledge of Persian, as represented by percentages of those claiming to understand it, by *šahrestān*, 1365 Š./1986.

Table 19
RELIGIOUS MINORITIES IN PERSIA, 1335-65 Š./1956-86

Year	Christians	Zoroastrians	Jews
1335 Š./1956	114,528	15,723	65,232
1345 Š./1966	149,427	19,816	60,683
1355 Š./1976	168,593	21,400	62,258
1365 Š./1986	97,557	32,589	26,354

Sources: Markaz-e āmār, 1335-65 Š./1956-86.

Table 20
EMPLOYMENT TRENDS IN PERSIA, 1335-65 Š./1956-86

	Working Population			Rate of Employment		Salaried Workers	
Year	Agriculture	Industry	Service	Men	Women	Private	Public
1335 Š./1956	56.7	19.5	23.8	81.5	9.2	48.1	7.6
1345 Š./1966	47.5	26.5	24.0	77.4	12.6	38.4	9.7
1355 Š./1976	34.0	34.2	31.8	70.8	12.9	34.9	19.0
1365 Š./1986[a]	30.0	26.1	43.9	69.5	8.2	17.0	31.4

a. In 1365 Š./1986 the population six years old or older is included, in other years ten years old and older.

Sources: Markaz-e āmār, 1335-65 Š./1956-86.

Persians claimed to speak Persian (73.1 percent in rural areas), but the differences were very great between the central plateau, where nearly all inhabitants spoke it, and the peripheral regions, where people claiming inability to speak Persian were sometimes in the majority (Kurdistan 60 percent, Azerbaijan 59 percent, Īlām 47 percent, Zanjān 34 percent). It is not surprising that the level of literacy is lower where there are fewer Persian speakers (Hourcade and Taleghani, 1988, p. 225).

From the religious point of view the Persian population is quite homogeneous, as 99.3 percent are Muslims, either Shiʿite or Sunni (Table 19). Religious minorities, more and more concentrated in the cities (52.3 percent in Tabrīz in Tehran in 1365 Š./1986; cf. de Mauroy, 1973), are less numerous because of accelerating emigration (Jews, Armenians); only the Zoroastrians have increased. Many Assyro-Chaldean refugees from Iraq have passed through Persia but have not settled there.

Economic activity among the population has profoundly altered in four decades, reflecting the decline of agriculture, the increase in the service sector, and the decline of industrial employment (Table 20). The political and economic crisis revealed by the census of 1365 Š./1986 is clear evidence that modernization of the economy and of Persian society has often been only superficial and easily reversed (e.g., female employment). The decline in private white-collar employment and the equivalent rise in the number of government bureaucrats (almost one third of the employed population) do not reflect the reality of the labor market, which is actually dominated by an informal economy. Reported unemployment remains low (5.5 percent), but it involves mainly the young (10.4 percent of the generation between twenty and twenty-four years old).

Despite urban development and its direct consequences, the population of Persia has preserved for more than forty years a large part of its basic cultural and economic character. This stability is particularly clear in the status of women and the demographic evolution of the country, reinforced by crisis conditions and the recent decrease in the rate of population growth.

Bibliography: C. Adle and B. Hourcade, eds., *Téhéran. Capitale bicentenaire*, Bibliothèque iranienne 37, Paris, 1992. A. Aghajanian, "Status of Women in Iran," in *Women and Population Dynamics. Perspectives from Asian Countries*, New Delhi and London, 1989, pp. 167-76. Idem, "Status of Women and Fertility in Iran," *Journal of Comparative Family Studies* 23/3, 1992, pp. 361-74. I. Ajami, "Differential Fertility in Peasant Communities. A Study of Six Iranian Villages," in C. A. O. van Nieuwenhuijze, ed., *Commoners, Climbers and Notables. A Sampler of Studies on Social Ranking in the Middle East*, Leiden, 1977, pp. 391-408. M. Amani, "La population de l'Iran," *Population* 27/3, 1972, pp. 411-18. Idem, "Vue d'ensemble sur la situation démographique de l'Iran," *Revue de géographie de Lyon* 48/2, 1973, pp. 141-63. Idem, "Accroissement et évolution de la population en Iran," in *Les disparités démographiques régionales. Ve colloque national de démographie du CNRS*, Paris, 1978, pp. 577-82. Idem, "Naissances et taux de natalité et de mortalité de l'Iran de 1877 à 1950," *Population* 37/1, 1982, pp. 175-77. Idem, "La population de l'Iran au recensement de 1986," *Population* 43/3, 1988, pp. 537-54. B. Amirahmadi, "The Socio-Econonomic Census of Nomadic Tribes in Iran in July 1987," *Journal of Official Statistics* 9/3, 1993, pp. 691-703. J. Bauer, "Demographic Change, Women and the Family in a Migrant Neighborhood of Tehran," in A. Fathi, ed., *Women and the Family in Iran*, Leiden, 1985, pp. 158-86. M. Bazin, "La population de l'Iran in 1976," *Monde iranien et l'Islam* 4, 1976-77, pp. 237-42. D. Behnam and M. Amani, *La population de l'Iran*, Paris, 1974. Idem, "A Note on the Population of Iran 1900-1966," *Population Studies* 22, 1968, pp. 273-79. J. Bharier, "The Growth of the Towns and Villages in Iran, 1900-1966," *Middle Eastern Studies* 8/1, 1972, pp. 51-61; repr. in J. A. Momeni, ed., *The Population of Iran. A Selection of Readings*, Honolulu and Shiraz, 1977, pp. 331-41. M. Bozorgmehr and G. Sabbagh, "High Status Immigrants. A Statistical Profile of Iranians in the United States," *Iranian Studies* 21/3-4, 1988, pp. 5-36.

J.-C. Chasteland et al., *Étude sur la fécondité et quelques carac-téristiques démographiques des femmes mariées dans quatre zones rurales d'Iran*, Tehran, 1968. B. D. Clark, "Iran. Changing Population Patterns," in J. L. Clarke and W. B. Fisher, eds., *Populations of the Middle East and North Africa. A Geographical Approach*, London, 1972, pp. 68-96. E. Farahani, "Abridged Life Tables of Iran, 1965-1966," *Genus* 34/1-2, 1978, pp. 215-25. F. Firoozi, "Iranian Censuses 1956 and 1966. A Comparative Analysis," *The Middle East Journal* 24, 1970, pp. 220-28. Idem, "Tehran. A Demographic and Economic Analysis," *Middle East Studies* 10/1, 1974, pp. 60-76. H. Firouzbakhch, "A Structural-Demographic Approach to Revolution. The Case of the Iranian Revolution of 1979," *Civilisations* 38/2, 1988, pp. 85-164. L. Henri, "Aspects démographiques d'une région rurale de l'Iran," *Population* 3, 1953, pp. 590-92. B. Hourcade, "La population iranienne d'après le recensement de 1976," *Population* 4, 1981, pp. 1171-76. Idem, "Migrations intérieures et changement social en Iran (1966-1976)," *Méditerranée* 4, 1983, pp. 63-69. Idem and M. Taleghani, "La population de l'Iran en 1986, entre les conflits irakien et afghan," *Mappemonde* 1, 1988, pp. 18-22. Idem, "La population iranienne d'après le recensement de 1986," *Stud. Ir.* 18/2, 1989, pp. 247-54. G. H. Jalali, H. Peyman, and A. Majd, "Study of Abortion at Farah Maternity Hospital,

Tehran," *Iranian Journal of Public Health* 2/4, 1974, pp. 212-18. F. Kazemi, *Poverty and Revolution in Iran*, New York, 1980. M. Ladier, "La fécondité des ethnies principales d'Iran," *Cahiers d'Études sur la Méditerranée Orientale et le Monde Turco-Iranien* 16, 1993, pp. 314-34. S. S. Lieberman, "Family Planning in Iran. Results of a Survey and a Mass Media Campaign," *Iranian Studies* 5/4, 1972, pp. 149-79. Markaz-e āmār-e Īrān, *Sar-šomārī-e ʿomūmī-e nofūs o maskan*, Tehran, 1335 Š./1956; 1345 Š./1966; 1355 Š./1976; 1365 Š./1986. Idem, *Population Growth Survey of Iran. Final Report 1973-1976*, Tehran, 1357 Š./1978. Idem, *Sar-šomārī-e ejtemāʿī-eqteṣādī-e ʿašāyer-e kūčanda 1366*, Tehran, 1367 Š./1988. Idem, *Sāl-nāma-ye āmārī-e kešvar 1370*, Tehran, 1371 Š./1992. H. de Mauroy, "Mouvements de population dans la communauté assyro-chaldéennes en Iran," *Revue de géographie de Lyon* 43/3, 1968, pp. 333-65. Idem, "Les minorités non musulmanes dans la population iranienne," *Revue de géographie de Lyon* 48/2, 1973, pp. 165-206. M. K. Miller and C. Windle, "Polygyny and Social Status in Iran," *Journal of Social Psychology* 51, 1960, pp. 307-11. ʿA.-A. Mohājerānī, "Tawzīʿ-e makānī-e jamʿīyat-e Īrān," *Taḥqīqāt-e joḡrāfīāʾī* 4/2, 1368 Š./1989, pp. 35-59. J. A. Momeni, "The Difficulties of Changing the Age at Marriage in Iran," *Journal of Marriage and Family* 37, 1975a, pp. 545-51. Idem, "Polygyny in Iran," *Journal of Marriage and the Family* 37, 1975b, pp. 453-56. Idem, ed., *The Population of Iran. A Selection of Readings*, Honolulu and Shiraz, 1977. R. Moore, K. Asayesh, and J. Montague. "Population and Family Planning in Iran," *Middle East Journal* 28/4, 1974, pp. 396-408. H. Moṭīʿī Langarūdī, "Tarākom-e jamʿī-e Īrān," *Taḥqīqāt-e joḡrāfīāʾī* 2/1, 1366 Š./1987, pp. 95-112.

A. A. Nazari, *Population Geography of Iran*, Tehran, 1989. A. Nizard, "La population de l'Iran au recensement de 1956," *Population* 23/1, 1968, pp. 145-50. N. Pakdaman, "Étude critique du recensement général de l'Iran," *Tiers-Monde* 6/21, 1965, pp. 231-46. A. A. Paydarfar, "Marital Fertility and Family Structure among the Urban Population of Iran," *Journal of Comparative Family Studies* 18/3, 1987, pp. 389-402. M. T. Rahnemaʾi, "L'extension de Téhéran et les mutations de l'environnement rural," in C. Adle and B. Hourcade, eds., *Téhéran. Capitale bicentenaire*, Paris, 1992, pp. 321-48. A. M. Sardari and R. Keyhan, "The Prospect of Family Planning in Iran," *Demography* 5/2, 1968, pp. 780-84. *Sāl-nāma-ye āmārī-e kešvar 1370*, Tehran, 1371 Š./1992, p. 48. G. P. Smith, "A Note on Babi and Bahaʾi Numbers in Iran," *Iranian Studies* 17/2-3, 1984, pp. 295-301. United Nations, *Population and Family Planning in Iran*, New York, 1971. H. Zandjani (Ḥ Zanjānī), "Évolution de la population iranienne d'après les recensements," *Population* 6, 1977, pp. 1277-83. Idem, "Téhéran et sa population. Deux siècles d'histoire," in C. Adle and B. Hourcade, eds., *Téhéran. Capitale bicentenaire*, Paris, 1992, pp. 251-66. Idem and F. Raḥmānī, *Rāhnemā-ye jamʿīyat-e šahrhā-ye Īrān 1335-1370*, Tehran, 1368 Š./1989.

(BERNARD HOURCADE)

ii. IN AFGHANISTAN

The demography of Afghanistan is one of the least known in the world, owing to the lack of a complete census (q.v. ii) combined with important but poorly documented structural changes since 1359 Š./1980. It is thus difficult to ascertain the current situation. As recently as thirty years ago the total population of the country could be estimated no more precisely than at 8-15 million inhabitants (Office suisse [OSEC], p. 11; cf. Pulyarkin, p. 34). Even more problematic than the scarcity of statistical material is the reliability of what is available. Most data are mere estimates, subject to government manipulation, with the result that conflicting figures have often been released (N. H. Dupree, 1987, p. 367; Table 21). The best-known example, and the most important factor contributing to demographic uncertainty about Afghanistan, is the successive estimates

Table 21
ESTIMATES OF THE POPULATION OF AFGHANISTAN AT VARIOUS DATES

Date	Source	Estimate (in millions) Sedentary	Nomadic
1870	MacGregor, p. 32	4.90	
1890	Kakar, 1979, pp. 181-82	4.50	
1925	Furon, p. 22	7.00	
1948	Shah, p. 18	9.60	2.00
1961	*Survey of Progress, 1961-62*, Kabul, pp. 46-47	11.40	2.40
1970	*Statistical Pocket-Book of Afghanistan*, Kabul, 1350 Š./1971, pp. 3-4	14.28	2.80
1973	*SYA 1355*,[a] p. 16	13.62	2.30
1978	*SYA 1357*,[a] p. 38	13.66	1.45
1979a	Census[b]	13.05	0.77
1979b	*SYA 1358*,[a] p. 31	13.05	2.50
1982	*SYA 1361*,[a] p. 6	14.11	2.50
1983	*SYA 1362*,[a] p. 5	14.08	1.50
1990	*SYA 1369*,[a] p. 6	16.12	1.50

a. *Statistical Yearbook of Afghanistan*, published annually under different titles from 1354 Š./1975.
b. Central Statistics Office.

of the nomadic population, which have been constantly and capriciously inflated (Khalidi, 1991, p. 104). Moreover, official figures became more and more unrealistic in the 1980s, as the government deliberately ignored the flight of millions of refugees (see below) and the resulting decline in the resident population; instead an increase was officially proclaimed. In such a context any attempt to reconstruct the demographic evolution of the country involves insuperable difficulties and can be only very approximate; it is nevertheless certain that there has been a considerable increase in the population during the last century.

Vital statistics. Whatever the actual growth in population has been, the basic determinant is clear: Afghanistan has entered a period of "demographic transition," characterized by a decline in the crude death rate and stability or even growth of the crude birth rate, hence a boom in natural growth. This transitional phase began comparatively late: An antimalaria program was launched in 1327 Š./1948, and it was only in the late 1950s that the first steps were taken to control other endemic lethal diseases like typhus and smallpox, measures that eventually reduced the general mortality rate. Progress remained slow, however. In 1358 Š./1979, according to the results of the partial census conducted in that year, mortality, and especially infant mortality, was still very high (28.7 per thousand and 190 per thousand respectively), and life expectancy at birth (thirty-nine years) was one of the lowest in the world (Khalidi, 1989, pp. 18 ff.). Lack of safe water supplies (accessible to only about 10 percent of the rural population and 30 percent of urban dwellers; Ministry of Public Health, p. 7), poor health-care facilities (1 physician per 9,840 settled inhabitants in 1358 Š./1979, 1 hospital bed per 2,400 settled inhabitants), and low literacy rates, especially among women (8.8 percent), contributed to a high, though declining morbidity.

In the same census the unadjusted birth rate was 47.9 per thousand, but it has been suggested that it could actually have been near 52 per thousand (Trussell and Brown, pp. 142, 146; Spitler and Frank, pp. 2-3). The natural growth rate was therefore close to 2.6 percent a year, higher in villages (2.7 percent) than in towns (2.2 percent). High natality was supported by four factors. First, marriage was nearly universal, only 1.9 percent of the population remaining single at sixty-five years of age or older (Chu et al., p. 64). Second, women were exposed to long periods of childbearing, owing to the prevalence of early marriages: About 31 percent of the population married before the age of twenty years; in a survey conducted in 1351-52 Š./1972-73 on a sample of 20,257 households scattered throughout the country it was found, in addition, that 6.3 percent of females aged ten to fourteen years and 49.7 percent of those aged fifteen to nineteen were married, compared to only 0.6 and 7.6 percent of men in the respective age groups (Chu et al., pp. 65 ff.). The individual mean age of marriage has been estimated at 17.8 years for rural females, 19.5 for urban females, 26.2 for rural males, and 26.7 for urban males (Trussell and Brown, p. 138). Third, the divorce rate was very low (less than 0.1 percent). Finally, there was no official family-planning policy. The only body concerned with family planning, the privately sponsored Afghan Family Guidance Association, founded in 1347 Š./1968, had a negligible impact: In 1351-52 Š./1972-73 only 3 percent of all married women aged fifteen years or older reported having knowledge of contraception, and only one third of that total claimed actually to have used contraceptive methods; moreover, few among those who had never used contraceptives expressed a desire to use them if available (Chu et al., pp. 117 ff.). As could be expected, knowledge and practice of family planning were more widespread in the better-educated middle and upper urban classes, hence the large differential in fertility observed between towns and villages (respectively 5.3 and 8.8 children per woman of childbearing age in 1358 Š./1979, corresponding to respective crude birth rates of 29 and 51.3 respectively; Khalidi, 1989, p. 13). The average household was, however, larger among city dwellers (6.31 persons) than among villagers (6.16) or nomads (5.6; de Benoist, p. 87), owing to lower infant mortality in towns (130 per thousand) and to the fact that many migrants to towns shared living quarters with friends or relatives.

The age structure of the Afghan population exactly reflected these vital statistics. In 1358 Š./1979, 45.4 percent of the population was less than fifteen years old, and only 3.9 percent was sixty-five years old or older (Khalidi, 1989, p. 7). Such an age structure supports a prediction of continuous high and perhaps increasing population growth.

There was an excess of men over women (51.4 and 48.6 percent of the population respectively, 106 men per 100 women) in 1358 Š./1979. This disparity seems mainly to reflect underreporting of young, marriageable women, possibly combined with high maternal mortality.

The results of the 1358 Š./1979 census (Central Statistics Office [C.S.O.]; Khalidi, 1989) are on the whole consistent with those of the demographic survey in 1351-52 Š./1972-73 (Kerr, pp. 62 ff.; Chu et al.). The only significant exception is life expectancy at birth, put at 34.6 years in the survey, though it has been suggested that this figure is an underestimate (Trussell and Brown, p. 146; Spitler and Frank, p. 7). It can therefore be assumed that the demographic situation in the late 1970s was fairly well established. The same cannot be said about the 1990s.

The civil war, which began in 1357 Š./1978, brought considerable change, especially in mortality, which has not only ceased to decline but has actually increased. The immediate causes have been both situational and structural. First, it has been convincingly suggested that approximately 875,000 people, that is, about 7 percent of the total prewar population, lost their lives in the fighting and bombing between 1357 Š./1978 and 1366 Š./1987 (Khalidi, 1991, p. 106); as the victims were mainly men, there are indications that the traditional deficit of females has been succeeded by a deficit of males (Khalidi, 1991, pp. 110-11, estimating that the sex ratio had dropped to 86 men to 100 women in 1987). Similarly, greater losses in adult age groups have increased the dependency index, especially the proportion of those under twenty years of age (about 60 percent, up from 55 percent). Structural changes include significant deterioration of health facilities, reduced access to health care, and resurgence of malaria as a major epidemic disease, owing to the disruption of the control mechanism (420,000 reported cases in 1364 Š./1985-86, compared to only 36,000 in 1358 Š./1979). Life expectancy at birth must thus have dropped to thirty-eight years, the lowest in the world, while infant mortality has increased to 220 per thousand and maternal mortality to 690 per 100,000 deliveries; in the mid-1980s 21 percent of all pregnancies were unsuccessful because of malnutrition and poor health (U.N. Coordinator, 1988, pp. 80 ff.; idem, 1991, p. 23).

Owing to these factors and provided that natality has kept to its prewar level, natural growth should have slowed, but that cannot be stated with certainty.

Migration patterns (Table 22, Figures 16-17). Geographic mobility, both internal and external, has always been significant in Afghanistan, even without reference to nomadic migrations among its population. During the war, however, it took on unprecedented dimensions. Data on migration patterns gathered in the 1358 Š./1979 census have never been processed, and it is thus difficult to determine the prewar figures. According to the sample survey of 1351-52 Š./1972-73, about 75 percent of the settled population was living in the localities of birth, 16 percent elsewhere in the same provinces, and 8 percent in different provinces; 0.6 percent had been born outside Afghanistan. Mobility was much higher in towns; 50 percent of urban dwellers were not living in their birthplaces, but the proportion was only 20 percent in the rural population (Kerr, p. 71), an indication of strong currents of migration from rural to urban settings. These currents are deeply rooted: Hazāra villagers, for example, were already migrating to Kabul in the 19th century (Burnes, p. 231). Such migrations accelerated rather slowly after the mid-20th century, following the extension and modernization of the road network (Jung, p. 5): In 1358 Š./1979 only 15 percent of the total sedentary population lived in cities, a proportion that is reported to have increased to more than 18 percent during the decade of the civil war. Kabul has been the main destination of rural emigration, the only urban center to draw migrants from the entire nation (Barrat, pp. 125 ff.; Jung, pp. 4-5); all other towns have continued to draw migrants only from their own regions. Migrations from one rural region to another, mainly the permanent transfers of nomadic groups, were also important in the past, especially from southern to northern Afghanistan (Tapper; Barfield; Kakar, 1979, pp. 131 ff.), but data that would permit determination of their present importance and permanence are lacking (but see examples in Gille, pp. 14-15).

Permanent or temporary emigration of labor to foreign countries, especially India, is another long-established tradition (Balland, 1991). Longer-distance emigration, for example, to Australia (Schinasi; Cigler; Stevens), was always marginal. In recent decades emigration has taken two successive forms. After the first oil "shock" (1352 Š./1973) temporary emigration of Afghan workers to Persia and the Persian Gulf states was paramount; the numbers in the late 1970s have been estimated at 400,000 and 300,000 respectively (Wiebe, p. 98). Such economic emigration was followed by political emigration of "refugees" (*mohājerīn*), not at all a novelty in Afghan history; in the past several refugee colonies had been established in neighboring countries, for example, by Sadōzī in Multan in the second half of the 17th century (Khan, pp. 3-4) and Hazāra in Quetta and Persian Khorasan (where they became known as Barbarī) in the 1890s and again in 1903-04 (Banbury, pp. 9-10; Kakar, 1971, p. 174). But the events of 1357-58 Š./1978-79 (the communist coup, civil war, Soviet intervention) provided unprecedented impetus to political emigration, which took on the dimensions of a hemorrhage (Table 22). In a few years more than one Afghan of every three became a refugee, constituting the largest community of refu-

Table 22

OFFICIALLY REGISTERED REFUGEES IN PAKISTAN AND PERSIA

Date	Pakistan	Persia[a]
December 1978	18,000	540,000
April 1979	80,000	
August 1979	185,000	670,000
January 1980	400,000	
December 1980	1,400,000	810,000
December 1981	2,400,000	940,000
December 1982	2,700,000	1,500,000
December 1983	2,900,000	1,600,000
Decmeber 1984	3,050,000	1,700,000
December 1985	3,150,000	1,800,000
December 1986	3,250,000	1,900,000
December 1987	3,330,000	2,200,000
December 1988	3,450,000	2,350,000

a. The figures include Afghan workers, in addition to true refugees.

Sources: For Pakistan, 1979-80, Lieberman, p. 293 n. 2; for 1980-87, Gille, p. 4; for 1988 and Persia, Sliwinski, p. 69.

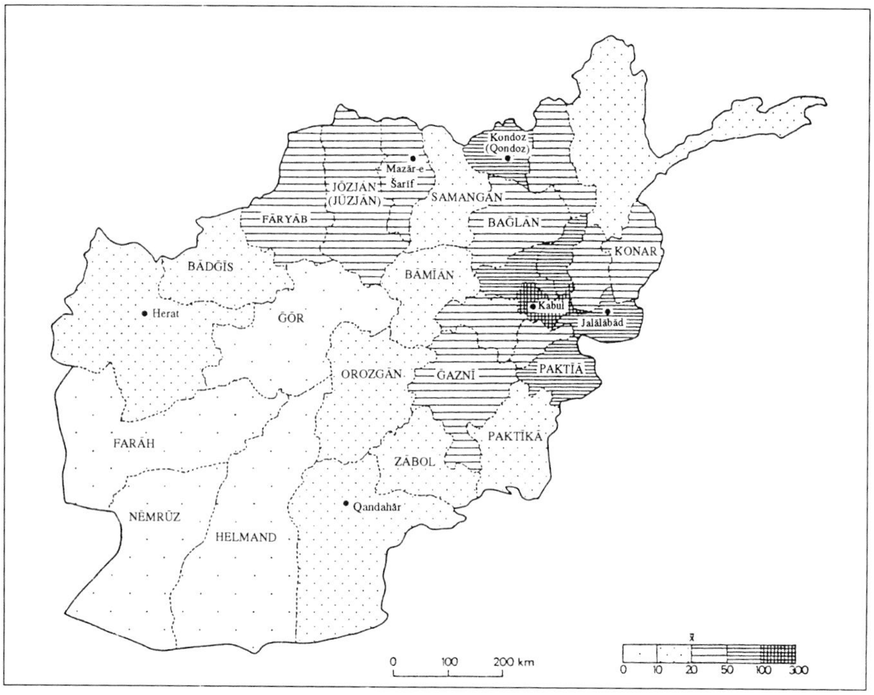

Figure 16. Population density in Afghanistan, by province, according to the censut of 1358 Š./1979; figures represent inhabitants per km². After Central Statistics Office.

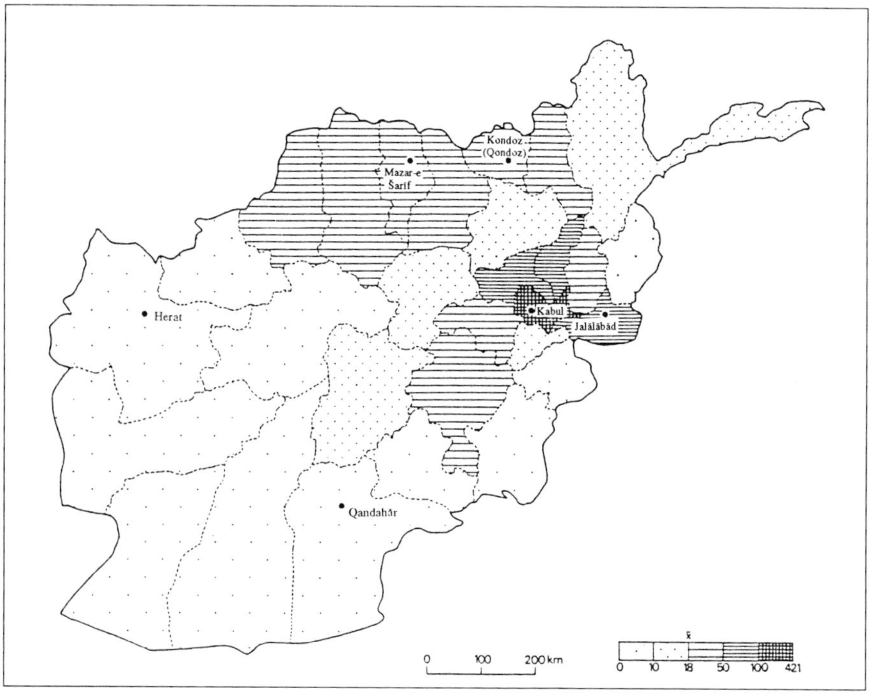

Figure 17. Population density in Afghanistan, by province, at the end of the 1980s; figures represent inhabitants per km². After Eighmy.

gees in the world (see DIASPORA ix-x). In 1366 Š./1987, 3.3 million were enumerated in Pakistan, 2.2 million in Persia, 40,000 in India, 20,000 in Europe, 15,000 in the United States, and 10,000 in other countries, including Canada, Australia, and the Gulf states (Gille, p. 4). Most of these refugees were crowded into hundreds of camps and spontaneous suburban settlements scattered along the Persian and Pakistani borders, where they found a cultural environment close to their own. Refugees came from all regions of Afghanistan, in proportions broadly inverse to their proximity to the relevant boundaries. Consequently the geographical distribution (Figures 16, 17), as well as the ethnic composition, of the resident population of Afghanistan underwent dramatic change. How durable these changes will prove remains to be seen, however. As soon as the communist regime collapsed in April 1992 a massive movement of voluntary repatriation began. In 1992, 1.275 million refugees from Pakistan and 250,000 from Persia reportedly returned to Afghanistan, assisted by the United Nations High Commissioner for Refugees (U.N.H.C.R.) and the World Food Programme. It seems, however, that some of them returned only temporarily (U.N. Office, pp. 6-7). It was anticipated that up to 2 million more refugees would return in 1993, but actual repatriation lagged far behind those expectations; an estimated half-million returned during the first nine months of 1993, 350,000 of them from Persia. The U.N.H.C.R. anticipated only 235,000 returns during the following six months (U.N.O.C.H.A., p. 5). Whatever the pace of repatriation, it seems obvious that a certain proportion of refugees will never return, for example, those Khirghiz and other Turkic-speaking peoples who were resettled in Anatolia in 1361 Š./1982, a total of about 4,500 individuals (N. H. Dupree, 1987, p. 388; Franz), but also many of those who have been successfully integrated into the labor market in Persia and Pakistan.

Foreign immigration also played a role in the historical demography of Afghanistan. Aside from the successive waves of conquest that have produced the present-day ethnic kaleidoscope of the country, mention should be made at least of the 300,000-400,000 refugees from Soviet Central Asia who arrived in the 1920s and 1930s (Balland, 1975-77, p. 33; Centlivres and Centlivres-Demont) and of 100,000 refugees from war-torn Tajikistan in 1371 Š./1992.

Bibliography: D. Balland, "La diaspora des Turcs de Basse-Asie centrale soviétique au XXe siècle," *Bulletin de la Section de Géographie du Comité des Travaux historiques et scientifiques* 82, 1975-77, pp. 23-28. Idem, "Une tradition migratoire. Les mercenaires afghans en Inde," in R. Blanadet, ed., *Aspects du monde tropical et asiatique. Hommage à Jean Delvert*, Paris, 1991, pp. 17-28. T. J. Barfield, "The Impact of Pashtun Immigration on Nomadic Pastoralism in Northeastern Afghanistan," in J. W. Anderson and R. F. Strand, eds., *Ethnic Processes and Intergroup Relations in Contemporary Afghanistan*, Asia Society, Occasional Paper of the Afghanistan Council 15, New York, 1978, pp. 26-34 (mimeograph). J. Barrat, *Kabul, capitale de l'Afghanistan/Kabul, Capital of Afghanistan*, Paris, n.d. (1970). A. de Benoist, *La composition des ménages nomades d'Afghanistan d'après les données du recensement de 1979*, Thèse de 3e cycle, Université de Paris V, 1984. N. L. Bunbury, *A Brief History of the Hazara Pioneers (Indian Army) 1904 to 1933*, unpublished typescript, India Office Library, London, T 14019. A. Burnes, *Cabool*, London, 1842; repr. Graz, 1973.

P. Centlivres and M. Centlivres-Demont, "Frontières et phénomènes migratoires en Asie centrale. Le cas de l'Afghanistan de 1880 à nos jours," in M. Centlivres-Demont, ed., *Migrations en Asie/Migrationen in Asien*, Ethnologica Helvetica 7, Bern, 1983, pp. 83-114; repr. in P. Centlivres and M. Centlivres-Demont, eds., *Et si on parlait de l'Afghanistan?* Neuchâtel-Paris, 1988, pp. 247-74. Central Statistics Office, Afghanistan, *Natāyej-e moqaddamātī-e nok̲ostīn sar-šomārī-e nofūs be asās-e parāses-e nomūnawī*, Kabul, 1360 Š./1981 (mimeograph). S. Chu, R. N. Hill, and S. Graham, *National Demographic and Family Guidance Survey of the Settled Populations of Afghanistan* I. *Demography*, n.p. (Washington, D.C.), 1975. M. Cigler, *The Afghans in Australia*, Melbourne, 1986. L. Dupree, *Population Review 1970. Afghanistan*, American Universities Field Staff Reports 15/1, Hanover, N.H., 1970; repr. in H. Brown and A. Sweezy, eds., *Population. Perspective, 1971*, San Francisco, 1972, pp. 29-53. N. H. Dupree, "The Demography of Afghan Refugees in Pakistan," in H. Malik, ed., *Soviet-American Relations with Pakistan, Iran and Afghanistan*, London, 1987, pp. 366-94. Idem, "Demographic Reporting on Afghan Refugees in Pakistan," *Modern Asian Studies* 22/4, 1988, pp. 845-65.

G. Eger, "Einfluss- und Hinderungsfaktoren einer Geburtenregelung und -beschränkung in Kabul/Afghanistan," *SSIP (Sozialwissenschaftlicher Studienkreis für Inter-nationale Probleme) Bulletin* (Basel) 43, 1976, pp. 12-34. T. H. Eighmy, *Afghanistan's Population Inside and Out. Demographic Data for Reconstruction and Planning*, USAID, n.p., 1990. E. Franz, "Turkstämmige Afghanistanflüchtlinge in der Türkei," in E. Grötzbach, ed., *Neue Beiträge zur Afghanistanforschung*, Schriftenreihe der Stiftung Bibliotheca Afghanica 6, Liestal, Switzerland, 1988, pp. 67-69. R. Furon, *L'Afghanistan*, Paris, 1926. E. Gille, ed., *Les réfugiés afghans*, supp. to *Les Nouvelles d'Afghanistan* 35-36, 1987. C. L. Jung, *Some Observations on the Patterns and Processes of Rural-Urban Migrations to Kabul*, Asia Society, Occasional Paper of the Afghanistan Council 2, n.p. (New York) n.d. (mimeograph). H. K. Kakar, *Afghanistan. A Study in Internal Political*

Developments, 1880-1896, Kabul, 1971. Idem, *Government and Society in Afghanistan. The Reign of Amir ʿAbd al-Rahman Khan*, Austin, Tex., 1979. G. B. Kerr, *Demographic Research in Afghanistan. A National Survey of the Settled Population*, Asia Society, Occasional Paper of the Afghanistan Council 13, New York, 1977 (mimeograph). N. A. Khalidi, *Demographic Profile of Afghanistan*, National Australian University, Research Note of the International Population Dynamics Programme 106, Canberra, 1989 (mimeograph). Idem, "Afghanistan. Demographic Consequences of War, 1978-1987," *Central Asian Survey* 10/3, 1991, pp. 101-26. A. N. Khan, *A History of the Saddozai Afghāns of Multān*, Lahore, 1977. S. S. Lieberman, "Afghanistan. Population and Development in the 'Land of Insolence,'" *Population and Development Review* 6/2, 1980, pp. 271-98. C. M. MacGregor, *Central Asia* II. *A Contribution towards the Better Knowledge of the Topography, Ethnology, Resources, and History of Afghanistan*, Calcutta, 1871. P. A. Martino and S. F. Schutz, eds., *National Demographic and Family Guidance Survey of the Settled Population of Afghanistan* III. *Tables*, n.p. (Washington, D.C.), 1975. Ministry of Public Health, Afghanistan, *Country Profile*, Kabul, 1985 (mimeograph).

Office suisse d'expansion commerciale, *Afghanistan. Structure économique et sociale. Commerce extérieur*, ser. A, Rapport spécial 58, Lausanne, 1950 (mimeograph). V. A. Pulyarkin, *Afganistan*, Moscow, 1964. M. Schinasi, *The Afghans in Australia*, Asia Society, Occasional Paper of the Afghanistan Council 22, New York, 1980 (mimeograph). S. M. Shah, *Afghan General and Commercial Directory 1327 (1948-49)*, Karachi, n.d. (1948). M. K. Sliwinski, "Afghanistan. The Decimation of a People," *Orbis* 33/1, 1989, pp. 39-56 (cf. criticisms in Khalidi, 1991). Idem, "On the Routes of 'Hijrat,'" *Central Asian Survey* 8/4, 1989, pp. 63-93 (to be used with caution; cf. review in *Abstracta Iranica* 13, 1990, pp. 117-18). J. F. Spitler and N. B. Frank, *Afghanistan. A Demographic Uncertainty*, Bureau of the Census, International Research Document 6, Washington, D.C., 1978. C. Stevens, *Tin Mosques and Ghantowns. A History of Afghan Cameldrivers in Australia*, Melbourne, 1989. N. Tapper, "The Advent of Pashtūn *Māldārs* in North-Western Afghanistan," *BSOAS* 36/1, 1973, pp. 55-79; repr. slightly revised as "Abd al-Rahman's North-West Frontier. The Pashtun Colonization of Afghan Turkistan," in R. Tapper, ed., *The Conflict of Tribe and State in Iran and Afghanistan*, London, 1983, pp. 233-61. J. Trussell and E. Brown, "A Close Look at the Demography of Afghanistan," *Demography* 16/1, 1979, pp. 137-55. United Nations, *Consolidated Appeal by the Secretary-General of the United Nations for Emergency Humanitarian Assistance for Afghanistan (January to September 1993)*, Geneva, 1993. United Nations Coordinator for Humanitarian and Economic Assistance Programmes Relating to Afghanistan, *First Consolidated Report*, Geneva, 1988. Idem, *Afghanistan. Operation Salam Programme for 1992*, Geneva, 1991. United Nations Office for the Coordination of Humanitarian Assistance, *United Nations Consolidated Inter-Agency Appeal for Humanitarian Assistance for Afghanistan 1 October 1993-31 March 1994*, Geneva, 1993. D. Wiebe, "Die afghanischen Arbeitskräftewanderung in die islamischen Staaten," *Orient* 20/2, 1979, pp. 96-100.

(DANIEL BALLAND)

iii. IN TAJIKISTAN

The population of Tajikistan grew at an unprecedented rate during the 20th century. From an estimated 1,034,400 people in 1913 within the present boundaries of the republic (143,100 km^2), it rose to 5,092,603 in 1989, the year of the last Soviet census, and to an estimated 5,600,000 in 1993, an increase of 440 percent over eighty years. The increase was not a steady one, however. Two phases can be distinguished. Between 1913 and 1922 the population dropped to 956,300 (-7.6 percent) as a consequence of civil war and famine (for a general review, see Buttino). Recovery was slow; during the period 1929-59 the population grew only 64 percent (from 1,207,000 inhabitants in 1929 to 1,484,900 in 1939 and 1,980,547 in 1959), but in the next thirty years it grew more than 157 percent (to 2,899,602 inhabitants in 1970 and 3,806,220 in 1979), as the region continued in the phase of demographic transition (see below). There has thus been an almost fivefold overall increase in less than sixty-five years. The average population density, which barely exceeded 7 inhabitants per km^2 in 1913 and 10 in 1939, is now approaching 40.

Causes of demographic evolution. Two main factors account for this evolution. The primary factor is high natural growth. The Soviet regime emphasized modernization of health services through such measures as vaccination campaigns, construction of hospitals and dispensaries, and provision of safe drinking water. In Tajikistan the ratio of hospital beds per 10,000 inhabitants rose from 0.4 in 1913 to 28.6 in 1940, 98.8 in 1980, and 105.8 in 1990; the ratio of physicians per 10,000 inhabitants from 0.2 in 1913 to 4.1 in 1940, 23.5 in 1980, and 27.1 in 1990 (*Narodnoe khozyaistvo TSSR* [The national economy of the Tajik S.S.R.], various editions). The mortality rate consequently declined from 14.1 per thousand in 1940 to 8.2 per thousand in 1950 and 5.1 per thousand in 1960; for reasons that are unclear, perhaps more efficient registration of deaths, it then increased to 6.3 per thousand in 1970 and 8 per thousand in 1980 before declining again through the 1980s (7 per thousand in 1985, 6.2 in 1990). Life expectancy at birth reached 69.4 years in 1990, the highest figure in former Soviet Central Asia, with a comparatively slight difference between that for males (66.8 years) and that for females (71.9 years). Infant mortality remained high, however (58.1 per thousand in 1980, 40.7 in 1990, the second highest rate in the U.S.S.R., after Turkmenistan); even in the capital, Dushanbe, where the medical infrastructure is comparatively advanced, infant mortality was 32.9 per thousand in 1990, though it had declined significantly from 59 per thousand in 1980. In the provincial town of Kurgan Tyube, in the Vakhsh (Vak̲š) valley south of Dushanbe, it dropped from 80.5 to 40 per thousand in the same period. A comparative analysis of selected causes of death in the republics of the former U.S.S.R. shows that Tajikistan had the highest rate of death from infectious disease (12.8 percent of all deaths) but the lowest rate of deaths from neoplasms (8.4 percent) and afflictions of the circulatory system (31 percent); the epidemiology of the region thus clearly reflects the low level of socioeconomic development in Tajikistan (Cole and Cole, pp. 6 ff.).

On the other hand, the birthrate remained very high, owing to lack of sex education, prevalence of Muslim conservative attitudes, and early marriage (see below). It has steadily increased from 30.6 per thousand in 1940 to 33.5 in 1960, 37 in 1980, and 38.8 in 1990, by far the highest in Soviet Central Asia. The corresponding fecundity index was 174 births per 1,000 women aged fifteen to forty-nine years in 1990, compared to 150 in 1960. This increase may be explained by a general improvement in female health and by the fact that the steadily increasing number of women of childbearing age counterbalances the effects of a real decrease in individual fertility (from a maximum average of 6.3 children per woman in 1975 to 5.5 in 1984 and 5.1 in 1989; Blum, p. 357; Gosudarstvennii Komitet [G.K.S.], p. 314).

The natural growth rate consequently soared from 16.5 per thousand in 1940 to 28.4 in 1960, 29 in 1980, and 32.6 in 1990, with an absolute maximum so far of 35.2 in 1986, a typical example of "high" demographic transition.

Tajikistan was unique in Soviet Central Asia in the age and sex structure of its population. It had the highest proportion of youngsters fourteen years old and under (43.2 percent in 1990), the lowest proportion of elders aged sixty-five years or more (3.8 percent), and the highest dependency index (i.e., population in these two age groups as a percentage of population aged fifteen to sixty-four years: 88.6 in 1990, compared to 92.3 in 1979). Tajikistan also had the highest ratio of males to females: 98.7 in 1990, compared to 97.7 in 1979. The excess of females reflected higher mortality among adult males.

Marriage statistics reflected the impact of traditional Muslim standards. The marriage rate was very high and concentrated among young people. In 1970, 40.4 percent of women aged eighteen and nineteen years were married (49.6 percent among rural women in this age group), a proportion that had declined only slightly since 1959 (43.8 percent and 52.3 percent, respectively) and was the highest in Central Asia (Blum, p. 346). It was undoubtedly an important factor in the high fertility rate and generally large family size.

The momentum of natural growth was further enhanced by the second determining factor, massive immigration of European populations, mainly Russians. In the first decades of the Soviet regime the number soared from a mere few thousand to several hundred thousand; a parallel though perhaps less massive influx of Ukrainians, Belorussians, and Germans also took place (Table 23). Half this immigrant population, mainly technicians, professionals, and skilled workers, was established in Dushanbe (195,000 Russians out of a total population of 388,000 in 1989). Until the 1960s continuing immigration of Europeans considerably lowered the ratio of Tajiks (Table 23). Since the mid-1970s, however, the number of Russians leaving Tajikistan has surpassed immigration; the trend approached a hemorrhage after the proclamation of Tajik independence in 1991. It is reported that more than 75 per cent of the Russian population (300,000 out of 388,000) left Tajikistan between 1989 and 1993 (Rotar'). Russian Jews and Tatars have also left in massive numbers.

The population of Tajikistan is characterized by high mobility; in 1989, 22.8 per cent of the inhabitants were not living in their birthplaces. Mobility was significantly higher among Russians (56.7 percent) than among Tajiks (18.4 per cent) or Uzbeks (17 per cent).

Ethnic and geographical factors. All these general trends and characteristics conceal considerable demographic variation among national groups. In general the European minorities have accepted family planning and birth control (Watters, p. 80), for example, whereas local Muslims have not. This difference has contributed to the continuous decline of the European proportion of the total population from a peak of more than 16 percent in 1959 to 12 percent in 1979 and 9 percent in 1989 (Table 23). The Muslims themselves are not demographically homogeneous. The Uzbeks, who account for almost a quarter of the total population, are less fertile than the Tajiks, whose birth rate was as high as 42.9 per thousand in 1989, 4 index points above the general birth rate for the republic (Watters, p. 76; G.K.S., p. 185).

The proportion of the population in cities, thus more secularized, better educated, and more receptive to such Western (Russian) cultural ideas as family planning, sharply increased, from about 9 percent in 1913 and 7 percent in 1922, when the region was the least urbanized in Central Asia, to 17 percent in 1939, 33 percent in 1959, and 38 percent in 1975. Since 1975, however, it has been steadily declining (35 percent in 1979, 32 percent in 1990)

Table 23

ETHNIC COMPOSITION OF THE TAJIK A.S.S.R./S.S.R.

Nationality	1926	(%)	1939	(%)	1959	(%)	1970	(%)	1979	(%)	1989	(%)
Tajiks	617,125	74.6	883,996	59.5	1,051,173	53.1	1,629,920	56.2	2,237,048	58.8	3,172,420	62.3
Uzbeks	175,627	21.2	353,478	23.8	455,038	23.0	665,662	23.0	873,199	22.9	1,197,841	23.5
Tatars	950	0.1	18,296	1.2	56,893	2.9	70,803	2.4	79,529	2.1	79,442	1.6
Kirghiz	11,410	1.4	27,968	1.9	25,665	1.3	35,485	1.2	48,376	1.3	63,832	1.3
Kazakhs	1,636	0.2	12,712	0.9	12,555	0.6	8,306	0.3	9,606	0.2	11,376	0.2
Turkmen	4,148	0.5	?		7,115	0.4	11,043	0.4	13,991	0.4	20,487	0.4
Russians	5,638	0.7	134,916	9.1	262,611	13.2	344,109	11.9	395,089	10.4	388,481	7.6
Ukrainians	1,090	0.1	17,360	1.2	26,921	1.3	31,671	1.1	35,826	0.9	41,375	0.8
Germans					32,588	1.6	37,712	1.3	38,853	1.0	32,671	0.6
Jews	9,459	1.2	35,744	2.4	12,415	0.6	14,615	0.5	14,667	0.4	14,766	0.3
Others					37,573	2.0	50,276	1.7	60,063	1.6	69,912	1.4
Total Population	827,083[a]	100.0	1,484,440	100.0	1,980,547	100.0	2,899,602	100.0	3,806,220	100.0	5,092,603	100.0

a. When Tajikistan was elevated from an autonomou S.S.R. to a full-fledged S.S.R. in 1929 the Khodzhent (Kojand) district in the Fergānā valley was attached to it from Uzbekistan, in order to provide an economic base for the new republic. This area had 205,000 inhabitants in 1926. Tajikistan as defined by its present boundaries thus had 1,032,000 inhabitants in 1926 (Krader, p. 182).

Sources: Successive U.S.S.R. censuses. The data for 1939 were collected with the assistance of A. Blum.

because of the increasing differential in fertility between cities and villages: Respective birthrates were 28.5 and 43.6 per thousand in 1990, with respective extremes of 22.4 in Dushanbe and 48.8 in rural Kurgan Tyube oblast; in 1989 the fertility index was 3.4 children per woman in towns, 6.1 in the countryside. Urban and rural death rates were, however, very similar: 6.4 and 6.2 per thousand respectively, with respective extremes of 4.8 in Khorog city and 6.9 in rural Gorno-Badakhshan. The similarity reflects differences in age structure, rather than medical facilities. The gap in natural growth between urban and rural dwellers thus reached 15.3 per thousand, to the advantage of the latter, an unprecedented figure (cf. 13 per thousand in 1980, 14 per thousand in 1985). It should be emphasized that ethnic Tajiks remain predominantly village dwellers (74.5 percent in 1970).

It is not yet possible to assess all the demographic consequences of the civil war that broke out in 1991. Current press estimates are 40,000 dead and another 40,000 refugees in northern Afghanistan at the end of 1993 (compared to 60,000-70,000 in 1992).

See also CENTRAL ASIA ii.

Bibliography: A. Blum, "La transition démographique dans les républiques orientales d'URSS," *Population* 42/2, 1987, pp. 337-58. M. Buttino, "Study of the Economic Crisis and Depopulation of Turkestan, 1917-1920," *Central Asian Survey* 9/4, 1990, pp. 59-74. J. P. Cole and R. P. Cole, *Causes of Death in the USSR in 1989*, University of Nottingham, Department of Geography Working Paper 15, Nottingham, 1992. Gosudarstvennii Komitet SSSR po Statistike, *Demograficheskii ezhegodnik SSSR 1990* (Demographic yearbook, U.S.S.R., 1990), Moscow, 1990. S. I. Islomov, *Demografiya Tadzhikistana* (Demography of Tajikistan), Dushanbe, 1985. L. Krader, *Peoples of Central Asia*, Bloomington, Ind., 1966. I. Rotar', "Slavyane v Srednei Azii. Adaptatsiya ili begstvo?" (Slavs in Central Asia. Adaptation or flight?), *Nezavisimaya Gazeta*, 29 April 1993. Kh. S. Salimov, *Naselenie Srednei Azii* (The population of Central Asia), Tashkent, 1975. *Sovetskii Tadzhikistan za 50 let. Sbornik statisticheskikh materialov* (Soviet Tajikistan after 50 years. Collection of statistical material), Dushanbe, 1975. Statkomitet Soobshchestvo nezavisimykh gosudarst, *Demograficheskii ezhegodnik 1991* (Demographic yearbook, 1991), Moscow, 1991. K. Watters, "The Current Family Planning Debate in Soviet Central Asia," *Central Asian Survey* 9/1, 1990, pp. 75-86.

(DANIEL BALLAND)

DEMOTIC CHRONICLE, Egyptian papyrus document of the early 2nd century B.C.E. (Bibliothèque Nationale, Paris, Pap. dem. no. 215 v), in which anti-Persian themes, especially focused on Cambyses (q.v.), Xerxes, and Artaxerxes III (q.v.), were elaborated in Ptolemaic Egyptian sacerdotal and intellectual surroundings (Bresciani, 1985, pp. 506, 525-26). The Persian conquerors of Egypt are called "Medes" (hieroglyphic *Mdj*, Demotic *Mtj* probably < Aram. *mdy*).

The document consists of a series of oracular sayings divided into "tablets," followed by exegetical and prophetic paraphrases that are political in tone. The beginning, including the first columns of the text and the pseudepigraphic narrative foreword, is lost but, on the basis of comparable documents, may be reconstructed as follows: A court prophet interprets for the king, probably Nectanebus I (r. 378-60 B.C.E.), founder of the Thirtieth Dynasty, the sayings of obscure oracles written on "tablets." In these sayings there are allusions to historical and dynastic events before the reign of Nectanebus I, to those of his own reign (see Bresciani, 1986, pp. 44-45), and to the future destiny of Egypt, including the disastrous arrival of the "Medes" (second Persian domination, 343-32 B.C.E.), then that of the Greeks, and finally the advent of an indigenous ruler who would revolt against the Greeks (almost surely Horunnofri-Harmachi, king of Upper Egypt from 205-04 to 186 B.C.E.).

In the surviving portion of the text the "Medes" are first mentioned (col. 3.18-20) as a point "post quem" for the indigenous dynasties (XXVIII-XXX) that ruled after the first Persian domination in Egypt (524-404 B.C.E.), which began with the conquest by Cambyses. It is therefore probable (Bresciani, 1981, pp. 219-20) that in the lost beginning of the papyrus there were sayings and exegetical comments on the history of Egypt preceding the Twenty-Eighth Dynasty; in particular such tragedies as the Assyrian and Persian invasions may have been described, as well as the Achaemenid kings of the Twenty-Seventh Dynasty, judged in terms of punishment and rewards, just as the rulers from the Twenty-Eighth Dynasty to the Ptolemaic period are judged. A comparable passage in the "Law of the Temples" (Bibliothèque Nationale, Pap. dem. no. 215 r, col. c ll. 7-8; Bresciani 1981, pp. 217-18), in which the reigns of Cambyses and Darius I (q.v.) are judged in a similar way, suggests the nature of the text: ". . . Cambyses conquered Egypt. He was the cause of his own death, for punishment, and he was not able to return to his country. Darius succeeded him in the entire world, thanks to his charity (=goodness)."

Another series of sayings in the Demotic Chronicle (cols. 4.18-23, 5.1-4, 14-16) is connected with the second Persian domination, which followed the defeat of Nectanebus II by Artaxerxes III; the "Medes" are said to have thrown Egypt and its inhabitants into misfortune, but God liberated the country and forced the "Medes" to return to their own. This description recalls that of the conquest by the "Medes" and the subsequent liberation given in the "Prophecy of the Lamb," a political text similar to the Chronicle

(Staatsbibliothek, Vienna, Pap. Vindob. D.10.000): "I will rule Egypt after the Persian (Darius III, q.v.) who had turned his face to Egypt will be gone (from Egypt), returning to the foreign lands and to his places. Iniquity will have an end, and right and order will exist again in Egypt" (Bresciani, 1990, pp. 815, 818).

Bibliography: (For abbreviations found in this bibliography, see "Short References.") E. Bresciani, "La morte di Cambise ovvero dell' empietà punita," *Egitto e Vicino Oriente* 4, 1981, pp. 217-22. Idem, "The Persian Occupation of Egypt," in *Camb. Hist. Iran* II, pp. 502-28. Idem, "Oracles d'Égypte et prophéties bibliques," *Le Monde de la Bible* 45, 1986, pp. 44-45. Idem, ed., *Letteratura e poesia dell'antico Egitto*, 2nd ed., Turin, 1990. J. Johnson, "The Demotic Chronicle as an Historical Source," *Enchoria* 4, 1974, pp. 1-17. F. K. Kienitz, *Die politische Geschichte Ägyptens vom 7. bis zum 4. Jarhundert vor der. Zeitwende*, Berlin, 1953, pp. 136 ff. W. Spiegelberg, *Die sogenannte demotische Chronik des Pap. 215 der Bibliothèque Nationale zu Paris*, Leipzig, 1914.

(EDDA BRESCIANI)

"DEMOTTE" *ŠĀH-NĀMA*, illustrated manuscript, now dispersed, of Ferdowsī's epic poem, often identified by the name of a former owner, the Paris dealer Georges Demotte (active ca. 1900-23). A more accurate designation is "the great Mongol *Šāh-nāma*," for it is generally believed to have been produced for a patron associated with the Il-khanid court (Grabar and Blair, pp. xi-xiv, 46-55) and is particularly renowned for the intrinsic quality of its paintings. The large format of the manuscript and the incorporation of Chinese motifs into the paintings are characteristic of other Il-khanid examples, like Rašīd-al-Dīn's *Jāmeʿ al-tawārīḵ* (Rice and Gray; Gray, pp. 15, 17-19). The paintings in the *Šāh-nāma* are exceptional, however, for their depiction of emotion, particularly grief, which is achieved through the figures' gestures and postures, often echoed and amplified by the expressive use of settings. Some features of the compositions continued in use in later 14th-century and 15th-century paintings, but the expressive quality of the illustrations in the Mongol *Šāh-nāma* was rarely matched in later works.

The Mongol *Šāh-nāma* has also acquired notoriety from the circumstances surrounding its appearance on the art market and the subsequent dispersal of its pages in various public and private collections.

Demotte is said to have acquired the manuscript in Paris in about 1910; he bought it from Shemavan Malayan, brother-in-law of the well-known dealer Hagop Kevorkian, who had brought it from Tehran. The manuscript is thought to have belonged to the Qajar royal library, for it was photographed while still bound (Plate XXIV) by Antoin Sevrugin, court photographer to the rulers Nāṣer-al-Dīn Shah (1264-1313/1848-96) and Moẓaffar-al-Dīn Shah (1313-24/1896-1907; Lowry, 1988a, p. 68; idem, 1988b, pp. 32-33). Moḥammad-ʿAlī Shah (1324-27/1907-09) and members of his household are said to have been selling manuscripts from the dynastic collection as early as 1908, in order to meet personal expenses. Some of these manuscripts were transmitted to Paris, where collectors were learning to appreciate Persian painting (Robinson, p. 1).

It is reported that when the manuscript of the Mongol *Šāh-nāma* came into Demotte's hands it was still bound but that, after he had failed to find a purchaser at the desired price, he removed the binding in order to sell the pages separately, an approach that was well received by collectors (Robinson, p. 1). In 1913 Demotte sold several pages to the collector Charles Vever, and by 1914 ten illustrations from the manuscript had been published by W. P. Schulz (II, pls. 20-29; Lowry, 1988b, pp. 32-34). Over the next sixty years illustrations from this manuscript were gradually dispersed by Demotte and other dealers.

Dispersed paintings from the *Šāh-nāma* have been repeatedly exhibited and published by scholars. There have been two particularly noteworthy attempts to record and analyze the scattered miniatures. In 1939 Doris Brian prepared an inventory of all fifty-eight known miniatures, and in 1980 Oleg Grabar and Sheila Blair published a more thoroughly documented list, along with a series of hypotheses about the original state of the manuscript and a historical interpretation of the paintings. They argue that the manuscript originally contained about 280 folios and as many as 180 illustrations, of which, beside the fifty-eight identified illustrations, only a few unillustrated text pages are known to have survived (pp. 10-12).

Their study also revealed that changes to the *Šāh-nāma* after it reached Paris went far beyond removal of the binding (Grabar and Blair, pp. 2-10), a conclusion that is confirmed by more recent information about the pages purchased by Vever, which are now in the Arthur M. Sackler Gallery, The Smithsonian Institution, Washington, D.C. A close examination of Vever's pages, which include some bifolios, reveals that they had been subjected to a complex process of alteration and restoration, which has been documented for other pages as well. The apparent purpose of these changes was to increase the number of salable pages by splitting leaves originally illustrated on both sides into two separate sheets, each with a painting on one side; the remaining side of each new "page" was thus blank. Various kinds of damage resulting from this process were repaired in various ways; blank pages were covered with new text, either an existing text page or newly written, and miniatures were often partly repainted. Sometimes miniatures were glued to pages from different sections of the text (Lowry, 1988a pp. 58, 65, 68, nos. 66-73; Grabar and Blair, pp. 2-12, 177-82). Contiguous unillustrated pages from the story of

PLATE XXIV

Photograph by Antoin Sevrugin of the "Demotte *Šāh-nāma*" in its binding, taken while it was still in the Qajar royal library in the late 19th century; the illustration of Bahram Gūr hunting is now in the Fogg Museum, Harvard University. Courtesy of the Myron Bement Smith Collection, Freer Gallery of Art and Arthur M. Sackler Gallery Archives, Smithsonian Institution, Washington, D.C., neg. no. 40.7.

Sīāvūš are thus now paired with illustrations about Ferēdūn, Rostam, Eskandar, and Ardašīr; one illustration of Ferēdūn and another of Eskandar are now backed by identical verses from the Sīāvūš story (Lowry, 1988a, pp. 58, 65, nos. 66, 67, 71, 73; Grabar and Blair, p. 177, nos. 3, 7, 8, 37, 43, 44). The creation of these new "pages" must have been accomplished by persons literate in Persian, including a trained calligrapher, but the forgeries (q.v. ii) were clearly aimed at buyers ignorant of the language.

Although the surviving portions of this *Šāh-nāma* manuscript carry no direct information about its original owner or the circumstances surrounding its manufacture, since its first appearance in Paris it has been associated with 14th-century Persia. Various opinions have been expressed about its illustrations, which reflect tensions between the Il-khanid dynasty and Persian subjects; it was probably commissioned by Rašīd-al-Dīn's son Ḡīāṯ-al-Dīn Moḥammad in about 1335 (Grabar and Blair, pp. xi-xiii, 46-55).

Bibliography: S. S. Blair, "On the Track of the 'Demotte' *Shāhnāma* Manuscript," in F. Déroche, ed., *Les manuscrits du Moyen-Orient. Essais de codicologie et de paléographie*, Varia Turcica 8, Istanbul and Paris, 1989, pp. 125-31. D. Brian, "A Reconstruction of the Miniature Cycles in the Demotte Shāh Nāmah," *Ars Islamica* 6, 1939, pp. 97-102. O. Grabar and S. Blair, *Epic Images and Contemporary History. Illustrations of the Great Mongol Shahnama*, Chicago, 1980. B. Gray, *The World History of Rashid al-Din*, London, 1978. G. Lowry, *An Annotated and Illustrated Checklist of the Vever Collection*, Washington, D.C., 1988a. Idem, *A Jeweler's Eye. Islamic Arts of the Book from the Vever Collection*, Washington, D.C., 1988b. D. T. Rice and B. Gray, *The Illustrations to the "World History" of Rashid al-Din*, Edinburgh, 1976. W. P. Schulz, *Die persisch-islamische Miniaturmalerei*, 2 vols., Leipzig, 1914. B. W. Robinson, "Ismāʿīl II's Copy of the *Shāhnāma*," *Iran* 14, 1976, pp. 1-8.

(PRISCILLA P. SOUCEK)

DĒN (Av. *daēnā*, trisyllabic in Old Av., disyllabic in Young Av.; Mid. Pers. *dēn*; NPers. *dīn*), theological and metaphysical term with a variety of meanings: "the sum of man's spiritual attributes and individuality, vision, inner self, conscience, religion."

In the Gathas *daēnā* (which is only "ahuric") denotes "vision, conscience, individuality." Stanley Insler (p. 69) suggests "conception," which is, however, irrelevant to the theological or metaphysical connotations of *daēnā*; for instance, "their own soul and their own inner self (hardly to be read "conception"; Insler, p. 271) did vex them" (*Y*. 46.11). In Middle Persian *dēn* is defined as *xēm* "character, conscience" and *xēm* as *xōg* "nature, habit" (*Dēnkard*, ed. Madan, II, p. 511; Shaked, p. 70). It is maintained that Ohrmazd first and foremost created *xēm* and *dēn* (*Dēnkard*, ed. Madan, II, p. 499; Shaked, p. 50), *dēn* clearly standing for "conscience, inner self."

In the sense of religion *dēn* (*weh-dēn* "the good religion," *māzdēsn dēn* "the religion of Mazdā worship") is a brilliance from the nature of Ohrmazd; its principle is the mind/thought of Axw, Ahū (q.v.; "the supreme lord"), and its manifestation is the recitation and practice of the holy words (*mānsr*), which itself is the mean (*paymān*; *Dēnkard*, ed. Madan, I, p. 326; de Menasce, 1973, pp. 309-10). The essence of the Mazdean religion is the wisdom of Ohrmazd, with knowledge and action (*kunišn*) as its essential elements; its purpose or function is to purify (ms.: heal) the mixed (i.e., Ahriman-ridden; see AHRIMAN) creation (*Dēnkard*, ed. Madan, I, p. 329; de Menasce, 1973, p. 313) by conquering and destroying the adversary (*Dēnkard*, ed. Madan, I, p. 351; de Menasce, 1973, p. 331). The religion is God's wisdom, His word (logos), the substratum par excellence of the principle of creation, the holy words of the religion, the divine Ahunwar (q.v.), who gives the world its being and maintains its existence. In the fashioning of Wahman "the good mind" the religion dwelt with him (*Bundahišn*, tr. Anklesaria, p. 19, chap. 1.53). Ahura Mazdā (q.v.) created man with his vision (*daēnā*; *Y*. 46.6). The bond of religion (*paywand ī dēn*), which denotes "adopting a righteous religious authority in time and not deviating from his authority," is one of three bonds (the others being *paywand ī gēhān* "the bond of the world" and *paywand ī frašegird* "the bond of the renovation") that men should observe (*Dēnkard*, ed. Madan, II, p. 492; Shaked, p. 36). In the domain of government the Mazdean religion, the supreme spiritual power, and royalty, the temporal power, are twins, for sovereignty is essentially religion and religion sovereignty: Royalty (*xwadāyīh*) is founded on the religion and the religion on royalty, and the exaltation of Iranian royalty (*ērīh xwadāyīh*) cannot be separated from submission to the Mazdean religion (*Dēnkard*, ed. Madan, I, p. 47; de Menasce, 1973, p. 65). The omniscient Mazdean religion is likened to a mighty tree with one trunk (the mean), two main boughs (action and abstention), three branches (good thoughts, good words, and good deeds), four small branches (the estates of the priests, warriors, husbandmen, and artisans), five roots (the lord of the house, the village headman, the tribal chieftain, the ruler, and the highest religious authority, the representative of Zoroaster on earth, Zarathuštrōtom), and above them all the head of all heads (*sarānsar*), the king of kings, the ruler of the whole world (*Škand Gumānīg Wizār* 1.11; de Menasce, 1945, p. 24; Zaehner, 1956, p. 86).

In the Avesta (q.v.) *daēnā* in the sense of "conscience" is one of the five spiritual faculties, together with *axw* "vital strength," *baoδah* "perception," *urvan* "soul," and *fravaši* "the everlasting and heavenly tutelary of material beings" (*Y*. 26.4).

Dēn is not only divine wisdom but also its emanation as innate human wisdom (*āsn-xrad*), a principle with far-reaching implications, for all beneficial knowledge thus of necessity falls within the compass of *dēn*. This important feature is apparent not only from the contents of the Avesta, which is a miscellaneous accumulation encompassing both the words of the Prophet and the authoritative pronouncements of the ancient fathers of the faith, but also from various explicit interpretations in Middle Persian literature. According to the *Dēnkard* (q.v.; ed. Madan, I, p. 335; de Menasce, 1973, p. 318), "all wise words uttered in virtue of the innate wisdom (*āsn-xrad*), whether by the people who were before the advent of the Mazdean religion or by those who had come afterward and were ignorant of the good religion, are in conformity with the revelations of the *dēn*." *Dēn* is thus the totality of all sagacious knowledge of mankind because this knowledge encompasses the diffusions of the innate wisdom, the essence of Ohrmazd. In the account of the history of the Mazdean scriptures given in the *Dēnkard* (ed. Madan, I, p. 415) it is said that "all wise words spoken by the religious authorities, throwing light on religious precepts, [are] an exposition of the Avesta, even though they had not derived them from any revelation of the Avesta" (for a full account of this passage, see Shaki, 1981, p. 121). On this point it is declared in *Dādestān ī dēnīg* (q.v.; chap. 89; West, p. 258) that the customs and laws of the holy rulers who lived before Zarathustra in Xwanirah, for example, Yawišt ī Fryān, Gōbadšāh, and Pešōtan, contributed to the advancement of the *dēn*, that is, Mazdean wisdom. In a significant sentence in the *Dēnkard* (ed. Madan, I, p. 411) "the incorporation of every knowledge in the Mazdean religion and its safekeeping (ms.: endurance)" are mentioned.

Apart from these considerations, the miscellaneous contents of the encyclopedic *Dēnkard* attest to the omnifarious nature of the *dēn*. It is to be noted that the term *dēnkard* itself resolves into *dēn-kardag*, in which *kardag* (from the root *kun-* "establish, prescribe, enact") means "orthodox traditional law, teaching; *sunna*" pronounced by the ancient teachers of the religion (*pōryōtkēšān*; see Shaki, 1978, pp. 291-92). Hence *Dēnkard* denotes "traditional teachings and expositions of the Mazdean wisdom (*dēn*)," that is, everything that has been incorporated in the *dēn* by virtue of its merit, including such foreign teachings as Greek and Indian philosophy and sciences. Ādurbād ī Ēmēdān (q.v.), the last redactor of the *Dēnkard*, described the book aptly as *dēnkard nibēg kardag ast ī az wisp-pēsīd dēn paydāgīh*: "The scripture of the *Dēnkard* is a book of orthodox expositions revealed from the omniscient Mazdean *dēn* (wisdom)" (*Dēnkard*, ed. Madan, I, p. 405; de Menasce, 1973, p. 379). The generally accepted description of the book as "acts of the religion" therefore reflects a misapprehension; it should, rather, be described as the "compendium of Mazdean wisdom."

Dēn, the deification of the religion, and the deities of space (Gāh) and time (Zamān) are the three divine instruments of creation, as assistants of Ohrmazd (*Bundahišn*, tr. Anklesaria, p. 40, chap 3.12). The *yazatā* Daēnā is a daughter of Ahura Mazdā and Ārmaiti (q.v.; *Y*. 17.16), but, according to an inscription found at Arebsun in Anatolia, she is the sister and wife of Ahura Mazdā (Boyce, *Zoroastrianism* II, p. 275). In the *Dēn yašt* (q.v.; *Yt*. 16) Daēnā praises the deity (Razišta) Čistā (q.v.), embodiment of "the most true wisdom," which impregnates the Mazdean religion.

The *daēnā*/*dēn* represents a person's deeds (*kunišn*), his inner self. In the Pahlavi commentary on *Yasna* 26.6 *daēnā* is glossed by *kunišn* "deed" (*Y*. 45.2, 48.4, 51.21). The fathers of the faith considered *dēn* to be "that which one always does" (*Dēnkard*, ed. Madan, II, p. 473; Shaked, p. 14); because "of thoughts (*menišn*), words (*gowišn*) and deeds (*kunišn*) it is the deed that counts (on the day of reckoning), for words are unreliable, thought unascertainable, but deeds are palpable, and (it is) by deeds that men are judged" (*Čīdag handarz ī pōryōtkēšān* 24-26; Kanga, p. 24). On the day of judgment the soul of a dead man, at the dawn after the third day, goes along the path created by time for both the just and the wicked to the Činwad bridge (see ČINWAD PUHL; *Vd*. 19.29), created by Ahura Mazdā, where he is met, according to his deserts, either by a beautiful maiden or by a hag, the personification of his deeds, his inner self (Daēnā/Dēn), a name used by the Prophet for this eschatological figure (*Y*. 31.20).

A full account of the personification of the *daēnā* "inner self" as a woman is first given in *Haδōxt nask* (2.11): When a just man dies after the third night "his own *daēnā* appears in the form of a maiden, beautiful, queenly, white-armed . . . as beautiful as the most beautiful of creatures . . . (proclaiming) . . . 'Youth of good thought, good words, good deeds, good inner self (*daēnā*) I am your very own inner self (*daēnā*; *azəm tē . . . ahmi . . . yā hava daēna x^vaepaiθe.tanvō*).'" The concept of this female figure is a relic of the pagan past, a myth recounted in the *Vīdēvdād* (19.30), according to which when the soul of a just man reaches the Činwad bridge "there comes that beautiful one, strong, fair of form, accompanied by two dogs at her sides. She comes over the high Hara and takes the souls of the just over the Činvad bridge . . . to the ramparts of the invisible *yazatas*" (Boyce, 1984, p. 80).

The *daēnā* of the bridge appeared in early Sasanian times in the inscription of Kerdīr at Sar Mašhad (KSM) as Kerdīr's own *dēn*, leading his "ideal body" (*hangirb* "likeness") over the Činwad bridge. The high priest, in his vision of the hereafter, related "and now comes a maiden, appearing from the east, and I have not seen a nobler woman than she" (KSM 35; Back, p. 452); "he who is righteous his own *dēn* leads him to paradise, and he who is wicked his own *dēn* leads him to hell" (KSM 29; Back, p. 445; Gignoux, 1968, ll. 42-43). The story is repeated in the *Ardā Wīrāz* (q.v.) *nāmag* (4.11; Gignoux, 1984, pp. 48, 157; Vahman, 1986, pp. 194-95), where the woman is said to be the personification of one's own *dēn* and deeds (*ān ī xwēš dēn ud ān ī xwēs kunišn*), and in the *Mēnōg ī Xrad* (2.125; Nyberg, *Manual*, pt. 1, p. 73), where she introduces herself as the just man's "good deeds." According to the *Wizīdagīhā ī Zādspram* (31.5) the *dēn*, personified as a beautiful woman, takes care of the soul of the righteous person in paradise, teaching it the speech of the spirits.

The two distinct referents of Daēnā, that is, the maiden of the bridge and the *yazatā* of religion, have led the majority of Iranists to posit two distinct nouns from the same root *di-* "see" (against which, see Nyberg, pp. 114 ff.). It is argued that the *daēnā* of religion represents "that which is seen or recognized (as the truth)," as against the *daēnā* as the maiden of the bridge, "who sees or recognizes (the truth)" (Lommel, pp. 150-51; Boyce, *Zoroastrianism* I, p. 238). It is thus suggested that there may be two pairs of Avestan words, *daēnā*/Daēnā "conscience/the maiden of the bridge" and *daēnā*/Daēnā "religion/the *yazatā* of religion" (Boyce, *Zoroastrianism* I, pp. 239-40). In Manichean Middle Persian *dēn* denotes "religion; the Manichaean community" (Boyce, 1977, p. 38).

Bibliography: (For cited works not found in this bibliography and abbreviations found here, see "Short References.") M. Back, *Die sassanidischen Staatsinschriften*, Acta Iranica 18, Leiden, 1978. M. Boyce, *A Word-List of Manichaean Middle Persian and Parthian*, Acta Iranica 9a, 1977. Idem, *Zoroastrians, Their Beliefs and Practices*, London, 1979. Idem, *Textual Sources for the Study of Zoroastrianism*, Manchester, 1984. P. Gignoux, "L'inscription de Kartīr à Sar Mašhad," *JA* 256, 1968, pp. 387-418. Idem, "Der Grossmagier Kirdīr und seine Reise in das Jenseits," in *Orientalia J. Duchesne-Guillemin Emerito Oblata*, Acta Iranica 23, Leiden, 1984, pp. 191-206, esp. 198, 200. Idem, *Le livre d'Ardā Virāz . . .*, Paris, 1984. S. Insler, *The Gathas of Zarathustra*, Acta Iranica 8, Leiden, 1975. M. F. Kanga, ed. and tr., *Čītak handarz ī pōryōtkēšān*, Bombay, 1960. H. Lommel, *Die Religion Zarathustras nach dem Awesta dargestellt*, Tübingen, 1930; repr. Hildesheim, 1971. J. de Menasce, *Škand-Gumānīk Vičār* . . ., Fribourg, 1945. Idem, tr., *Le troisième livre du Dēnkart*, Travaux de l'Institut d'Études Iraniennes 5, Paris, 1973. M. Molé, "Daēnā, le pont Činvat et l'initiation dans le Mazdéisme," *RHR* 157, 1960, pp. 155-85. H. S. Nyberg, *Die Religionen des alten Iran*, tr. H. H. Schaeder, Leipzig, 1938. J. C. Pavry, *The Zoroastrian Doctrine of a Future Life*, New York, 1929, pp. 28-48 (on the maiden of the bridge). H. P. Schmidt, "Is Vedic *dhénā-* related to Avestan *daēnā-*?" in *Monumentum H.S. Nyberg* II, Acta Iranica 5, Leiden and Tehran, 1975, pp. 163-79 (for diverse unconvincing etymologies of *daēnā* proposed by various authors, see pp. 163-67). S. Shaked, *The Wisdom of the Sasanian Sages (Dēnkard VI) by Aturpāt-i Ēmētān*, Persian Heritage Series 34, Boulder, Colo., 1979. M. Shaki, "The Social Doctrine of Mazdak in the Light of Middle Persian Evidence," *Archív Orientální* 46/4, 1978, pp. 289-306. Idem, "The Dēnkard Account of the History of the Zoroastrian Scriptures," *Archív Orientální* 49/2, 1981, pp. 114-25. F. Vahman, "A Beautiful Girl," in *Papers in Honour of Professor Mary Boyce* II, Acta Iranica 25, Leiden, 1985, pp. 665-73. Idem, *Ardā Wirāz Nāmag. The Iranian "Divina Commedia"*, London, 1986. E. W. West, *Dādistān-ī Dīnīk*, Pahlavi Texts 2, SBE 17, Oxford, 1882, pp. 2-276. R. C. Zaehner, *Zurvan. A Zoroastrian Dilemma*, Oxford, 1955 (see index p. 481 on various aspects of the *dēn*). Idem, *The Teachings of the Magi*, London, 1956.

(MANSOUR SHAKI)

DĒN-DIBĪRĪH. See DABĪRE, DABĪRĪ.

DĒN YAŠT (*Yašt* 16 of the Avesta), a relatively short text, consisting for the most part of repetitive or formulaic sentences (Lommel, pp. 154-56; *Avesta*, tr. Darmesteter, II, pp. 593-97). Although the title implies a hymn to Daēnā, the text is devoted exclusively to the invocation of a female divinity named Čistā (q.v.), whose name is related etymologically to *čisti-* (intuition, idea) but in no other way. Except for several formulaic repetitions, she is mentioned only in this text and in *Yašt* 10.126 and thus appears to have been only a minor goddess, worshiped sporadically. The text consists of three distinct parts: strophes 1-4, containing the only original formulary material, with the archetypal sacrifice by Zarathustra introduced in strophe 2; strophes 5-13, with the continuation of Zarathustra's invocation, requesting from Čistā the visual power that characterizes the fish *kara*, the virile stallion, and the vulture, which, according to *Yašt* 14, Vərəθraγna (see BAHRĀM) had granted to him (*Yt*. 16.7, 16.10, 16.12, corresponding to *Yt*. 14.29, 14.31, 14.33); and strophes 14-20, with enumeration of three other archetypal worshipers: the woman Huuōuuī (strophe 15, invocation in the past tense *yazata*), the priest, and the leader of the nation (strophes 17 and 19 respectively, invocation in the present tense *yazamaide*).

The fundamental study of the *Dēn Yašt* was published in 1934 by Émile Benveniste (q.v.; Benveniste and Renou, pp. 56-64). It remains useful, except for some metrical corrections and the rather loose treatment of the chronology of some parts of the text. The prerogatives of Čistā clearly suggest that she was a goddess of travel. The epithets accorded to her in the first part of the text leave no doubt on this point; the principal epithet, *razišta-*, which belonged to the good path, was hers by simple hypallage. The benefits requested in the second part, especially sharpness of vision and swift legs, are the most useful qualities for the traveler. It is this identification that explains the connection between Čistā and Daēnā: Both guide travelers on the road, the path of religion, in acccordance with the later sense of *daēnā-* (Benveniste and Renou, p. 63), as well as the ritual path and the road to the hereafter, reflecting older ideas. In this connection there are curious correspondences with the last Gatha (*Y*. 53). The only two worshipers named explicitly, Zarathustra and Huuōuuī, belonged to the circle in which the Gathas were worshiped. Furthermore, *čistā-* was a component of the name of Zarathustra's daughter Pouručistā, who plays a central role in *Yasna* 53. These details cannot be solely owing to chance, for the word *daēnā-* is attested in each of the five first strophes of the Gatha. Nevertheless, the precise relation between the two divine personalities remains unclear. According to *Yašt* 16.1, Čistā- and Daēnā- were two names for a single divinity (*cistąm . . . yąm vaŋ^{v}hīm daēnąm māzdaiiasnīm*). Although this evidence was dismissed by Benveniste (Benveniste and Renou, p. 63), Ilya Gershevitch (p. 167) has accepted it. In addition, in *Yašt* 126 Čistā is described as the *upamana* of Daēnā (*cistąm . . . daēnaiiå māzdaiiasnōiš upamanəm*). The meaning of *upamana-* is unfortunately far from clear in such expressions as *dāmōiš upamana-* (see DĀMI-), but it approximates "alter ego." It seems likely, then, that *čistā-* is a metonymic designation for Daēnā, personifying her capacity for seeing the road and for herself being seen (cf. Lankarany, pp. 146-47).

The fact that the noun is more frequently qualified by a passive verbal adjective "she who is noticed" than by an abstract suffix denoting "the capacity for noticing" does not compromise this interpretation. Although Daēnā does distinguish the road, she is herself also distinguished, as clearly as the dawn is distinguished, by the *uruuan* "soul" of the dead at the end of the third night. She reveals herself as beautiful or ugly to the gods who watch over the hereafter, depending upon whether the departed was good or bad.

Bibliography: (For cited works not found in this bibliography, see "Short References.") E. Benveniste and L. Renou, *Vṛtra- et Vṛθragna*.

Étude de mythologie indo-iranienne, Cahiers de la Société Asiatique 3, Paris, 1934. A. Christensen, *Études sur le Zoroastrisme de la Perse antique*, Copenhagen, 1928. I. Gershevitch, *The Avestan Hymn to Mithra*, University of Cambridge Oriental Publications 4, Cambridge, 1959. F.-T. Lankarany, *Daēnā im Avesta. Eine semantische Untersuchung*, Reinbeck, Germany, 1985. H. Lommel, *Die Yäšt's des Awesta*, Göttingen and Leipzig, 1927. H. S. Nyberg, *Religionen des alten Iran*, Leipzig, 1938.

(JEAN KELLENS)

DĒNAG (< Mid. Pers. *dēn*, q.v.), name of several Sasanian queens; it was not feminine by derivation but was clearly reserved for feminine prosopography (Schmitt, p. 269). In the Middle Persian inscription ŠKZ (l. 25; Back, p. 339) the name designated the mother of King Bābak (Mid. Pers. Pābag) and grandmother of the founder of the Sasanian dynasty, Ardašīr I (q.v.; 224-40 C.E.).

Dēnag was also the name of one of Bābak's daughters (ŠKZ, l. 29; Back, p. 350), born about 140 (Lukonin, 1969, p. 32); she was both Ardašīr's sister and his wife, in conformity with the Zoroastrian law of consanguineous marriage so favored by the Sasanians. She was granted the title "queen of queens" (*bānbišnān bānbišn*; see BĀNBIŠN) and is believed to be represented on the far right of the investiture relief of Ardašīr at Naqš-e Rajab (Hinz, p. 126). This queen must also have been the mother of Šāpūr I (240-70) and would have lost her title "queen of queens" after the death of her husband (Henning, p. 44). The inscription on an oft-published amethyst seal in the Hermitage in St. Petersburg (Borisov and Lukonin, no. 979) could refer to her (Henning, p. 44 n. 3), rather than to the wife of Yazdegerd II (438-57), as has often been claimed (Justi, *Namenbuch*, p. 84; Christensen, *Iran. Sass.*, p. 289). It reads *dynky ZY MLKTʾn MLKTʾ mḥysty PWN tny šʾpstn* "Dēnag queen of queens, the principal (or oldest?) in the harem" (lit., "the body of eunuchs"; for a different reading, see de Blois, p. 36). Following W. B. Henning ("Mitteliranisch," p. 45), most scholars (with the exception of Lukonin, 1960) have accepted attribution of this seal to the queen's personal eunuch (cf. Shaked, p. 223; Khurshudyan, p. 98), but, as the representation on it is that of a woman (cf. Gignoux and Gyselen, 1989, p. 882) and as Dēnag is nowhere attested as a masculine name, this attribution seems unacceptable.

A third woman with the name Dēnag was queen of Mesene (ŠKZ, l. 30; Back, p. 355), probably the wife of Šāpūr, king of Mesene and a son of Šāpūr I. She was granted the title Dastgerd-Šābuhr (Gignoux, no. 309; see DASTGERD), doubtless by her husband, rather than by the Sasanian king of kings. She may have ruled Mesene after her husband's death in about 260 (Lukonin, 1969, p. 42). She is believed to have had many children, of whom seven are known (Lukonin, 1969, p. 197 table), if in fact they were all born to her.

According to the 10th-century author Ṭabarī (II, p. 872; cf. Justi, *Namenbuch*, p. 84), the wife of Yazdagerd II was also called Dēnag; she reigned at Ctesiphon (q.v.) during the war between her two sons, Ohrmazd III (457-59) and Pērōz (459-84; cf. Christensen, *Iran Sass.*, p. 289).

The name is also attested in Coptic Manichean in the form Dinak, the name of a probably female catechumen (Polotsky, p. 59).

Bibliography: (For cited works not found in this bibliography and abbreviations found here, see "Short References.") M. Back, *Die sassanidischen Staatsinschriften*, Acta Iranica 18, Tehran and Liège, 1978. F. de Blois, "Middle-Persian Funerary Inscriptions from South-Western Iran," in *Medioiranica*, Orientalia Lovaniensia Analecta 48, Louvain, 1993, pp. 29-43. A. Ya. Borisov and V. G. Lukonin, *Sasanidskie gemmy* (Sasanian gems), Leningrad, 1963. M.-L. Chaumont, "À propos de quelques personnages féminins figurant dans l'inscription trilingue de Šāpuhr Ier à la Kaʿba de Zoroastre," *JNES* 22, 1963, pp. 194-99. R. N. Frye, *The History of Ancient Iran*, Munich, 1984. Ph. Gignoux, *Noms propres sassanides en moyen-perse épigraphique*, Iranisches Personennamenbuch II/2, 1986. Idem and R. Gyselen, *Bulles et sceaux sassanides de diverses collections*, Paris, 1987. Idem, "Sceaux de femmes à l'époque sassanide," *Archaeologia Iranica et Orientalis* 2, 1989, pp. 877-96. W. B. Henning, "Notes on the Great Inscription of Šāpūr I," in *Prof. Jackson Memorial Volume. Papers on Iranian Subjects*, Bombay, 1954, pp. 40-54. W. Hinz, *Altiranische Funde und Forschungen*, Berlin, 1969. E. S. Khurshudyan, "O dvukh sasanidskikh gemmakh" (On a pair of Sasanian gems), in *Pis'mennye pamyatniki i problemy istorii kul'tury narodov vostoka* (Essays on monuments and problems in the cultural history of the peoples of the east), Moscow, 1990, pp. 92-102. V. G. Lukonin, "Reznoĭ ametist s izobrazheniem tsaritsy tsarits Denak" (The engraved amethyst with the representation of the queen of queens Dēnag), in *Issledovaniya po istorii kul'tury narodov vostoka* (Inquiries on the cultural history of the peoples of the east), 1960, pp. 379-85. Idem, *Kul'tura sasanidskogo Irana* (The culture of Sasanian Iran), Moscow, 1969. H. J. Polotsky, *Manichäische Handschriften der Sammlung A. Chester Beatty* I. *Manichäische Homilien*, Stuttgart, 1934. R. Schmitt, Review of P. Gignoux and R. Gyselen, *Bulles et sceaux sassanides de diverses collections*, *Stud. Ir.* 17, 1988, pp. 266-71. S. Shaked, "Some Legal and Administrative Terms of the Sasanian Period," *Monumentum H. S. Nyberg* II, Acta Iranica 2/5, Tehran and Liège, 1975, pp. 213-25.

(PHILIPPE GIGNOUX)

DENIKE, BORIS PETROVICH (b. Kazan, 15 January 1885, d. Moscow, 13 October 1941), the first Russian historian of the medieval art of the Near and Far East. He first studied Russian art at Kazan University, from which he was graduated in 1911. In 1913 in Berlin he became acquainted with the work of A. von Le Coq's expedition to eastern Turkestan. As a result he published "O pamyatnikakh kultury i iskusstva Turfana (Rezul'taty ekspeditsii A. Lekoka v Kitaĭskii Turkestan)" (On the monuments of the culture and art of Turfan [Results of the expedition of A. Le Coq in Chinese Turkestan]), which appeared in *Izvestiya obshchestva arkheologii, istorii i etnografii* (Kazan, 30, 1915, pp. 1-11) and in which he reviewed the literature on the problem of Greco-Buddhist art.

After the Bolshevik Revolution in 1917 he turned his attention to study of the architectural monuments of Bulgaria and the Golden Horde, as well as to the medieval art of Persia and China, study that culminated in *Iskusstvo Vostoka* (The art of the East, Kazan, 1923), the first publication on the art of Islamic peoples to appear in Russia. In the early 1920s he moved to Moscow, where he was appointed lecturer on Oriental art at Moscow University; in 1925 he became professor of Oriental art, a position he held until his death. In the same year he was appointed director of the Museum of Oriental Cultures in Moscow (now the Museum of Art of the Peoples of the Orient). Two years later he published *Iskusstvo Sredneĭ Azii* (The art of Central Asia; Moscow, 1927), the first study on this subject published in the Soviet period.

In 1926-28 Denike headed an archeological expedition to Termez (Termeḏ); the final report was never published, but several members of the expedition published articles on aspects of the finds. Denike himself wrote several on the stucco decorations of the palace and also published several studies of architectural decoration in wood (see the selected list of his publications, below). Eventually he produced a synthesis of these studies in *Arkhitekturnyĭ ornament Sredneĭ Aziĭ* (Architectural ornament of Central Asia; Moscow, 1939).

In 1938 he published *Zhivopis Irana* (Painting of Iran; Moscow, 1938), still the best work in Russian on Persian and Central Asian miniature painting, even though much new material has emerged in the fifty years since his death.

Among his many other works on Iranian subjects are "Zadachi izucheniya iskusstva Afganistana" (Problems in the study of the art of Afghanistan), *Afganistan* (Moscow) 1, 1923, pp. 118-30; "Ekspeditsiya Muzeya vostochnikh kultur v Termez. Predvaritelnyĭ otchet" (The expedition of the Museum of eastern culture in Termez. Preliminary report), *Kultura Vostoka* 1, 1927, pp. 9-18; "Ob odnom do-mongolskom pamyatnike Sredneĭ Azii" (On one pre-Mongol monument of Central Asia), *Trudy Etnografo-arkheologicheskogo muzeya* 1, 1927, pp. 41-42; "Ekspeditsiya Muzeya vostochnikh kultur v Sredniyu Aziyu 1927 goda" (Expedition of the Museum of eastern culture to Central Asia in 1927), *Kultura Vostoka* 2, 1928, pp. 3-16; "Reznaya shtukovaya stennaya dekoraziya v Termeze" (Carved stucco wall decoration in Termez), *Trudy sektsiĭ Instituta iskusstvoznaniya, Rossiĭskaya assotsiatsiya nauchno-issledovatel'skikh institutov obshchestvennykh nayk* 3, 1928, pp. 61-65; "O reznikh dereviyannikh dveriyakh v Sredneĭ Azii" (On carved wooden doorways in Central Asia), *Trudy sektsii arkheologii i iskusstvoznaniya, Rossiĭskaya assotsiatsiya nauchno-issledovatel'skikh institutov obshchestvennykh nayk* 4, 1928, pp. 178-79; "Termez (Raboty ekspeditsiĭ Muzeya vostochnikh kultur v 1927 godu)" (Termez [Work of the expedition of the Museum of eastern culture in 1927]), *Novy Vostok* 22, 1928, pp. 208-23; "La décoration en stuc sculptée de Termez," *Cahiers d'art* 1, 1930, pp. 41-44; "Prikladnoye iskusstvo Sredneĭ Azii" (Additions to the art of Central Asia), in *Khudozhestvennaya kultura sovetskogo Vostoka* (The artistic culture of the Soviet East), Moscow and Leningrad, 1931, pp. 53-75; "Izobrazheniye fantasticheskikh zvereĭ v termezskoĭ reznoĭ dekoratsii" (Representations of fantastic animals in Termez stucco decoration), *Iskusstvo Sredneĭ Aziĭ. Trudy sektsii istorii iskusstva Instituta arkheologii i iskusstvoznaniya, Rossiĭskaya assotsiatsiya nauchno-issledovatel'skikh institutov obshchestvennykh nayk* 5, 1930, pp. 81-85; "Novoye v izuchenii arkhitektury i arkhitekturnoĭ dekorazii v srednevekovoĭ Persii" (Innovations in the study of architecture and architectural decoration in medieval Persia), *Akademiya arkhitektury* 1-2, 1935, pp. 93-106; "Quelques monuments de bois sculpté au Turkestān occidental," *Ars Islamica* 2/1, 1935, pp. 69-83; "Reznaya dekorovka zdaniya, raskopannogo v Termeze" (The carved decoration of a building excavated in Termez), in *III. International Congress of Persian Art*, Leningrad, 1939, pp. 39-43; "Syuzhety Nizami Gandzhavi v iskusstve Azerbaidzhana i Vostoka v XV-XVII vv." (Subjects from Neẓāmī Ganjavī in the art of Azerbaijan and the East in the 15th-17th centuries), *Nizami* (Baku) 4, 1947, pp. 71-102.

Bibliography: B. V. Veĭmarn, "B. P. Denike—istorik iskusstva" (B. P. Denike—art historian), *Narody Azii i Afriki* 1, 1976, pp. 218-26.

(ANATOL IVANOV)

DENKĀ (DINKHA) **TEPE**, a Bronze and Iron Age site situated in the Ošnū valley of Azerbaijan (q.v.), southwest of Lake Urmia, and 15 miles west of the major Iron Age site of Hasanlu (Ḥasanlū) in the Soldūz valley. The mound is 20 m high and 400 m in diameter, but much of the northern side has been washed away by the Gadār river. In 1315 Š./1936 Sir Mark Aurel Stein (1940, pp. 367-76) excavated on the northern slopes for six days, recording only

Bronze Age material. A team from The University of Pennsylvania and The Metropolitan Museum of Art, New York, excavated there in 1345 Š./1966 and 1347 Š./1968 as part of regional research connected with the Hasanlu project. These excavations revealed Islamic remains (Dinkha I), below which a cemetery (missed by Stein) was found on the north side; the burials (Dinkha II and III) contained cultural material paralleling that of Hasanlu periods IV and V respectively (Muscarella, 1968; idem, 1974; idem, 1988, pp. 15-19, 80). This material belongs to what is known as the Late Western Gray Ware (Iron II) and Early Western Gray Ware (Iron I) periods (see CERAMICS vi) in northwestern Persia, dating from the 14th century to ca. 800 B.C.E. All the evidence suggests that both periods represent the same culture, which continued to occupy the area for centuries. The Iron Age remains from Dinkha have been fully published (Muscarella, 1974).

Directly below the Iron Age cemetery and at the center of the mound Bronze Age (q.v.) architecture and burials (Dinkha IV) parallel to those of the Bronze Age culture of Hasanlu VI were recovered; this period began about the 18th century B.C.E. and terminated in the 16th or 15th century. Except for the pottery most of the finds from this period have not been published (Muscarella, 1968; Kramer, 1974). At the center of the mound the Bronze Age remains consisted of a massive fortification wall over which a later settlement had been built. The Bronze Age architectural remains below the Iron Age cemetery included two stone tombs containing multiple burials. The pottery associated with the architecture and tombs includes painted and buff ware, including Khabur (Ḵābūr) wares similar to those encountered in Hasanlu VI and at many sites in Anatolia, northern Syria, and northern Mesopotamia. These finds indicate that in the Old Babylonian and Old Assyrian periods Hasanlu and Dinkha together constituted the easternmost extension of a large cultural zone that was more prominently represented in the west. The presence at Dinkha but not at Hasanlu of polychrome pottery related to that from northern Persia (Haftavan [Haftavān] Tepe), Anatolia, and the Caucasus remains to be investigated (Edwards, 1986). It seems to postdate the Khabur-ware level at Dinkha and may indicate a new cultural presence there. Its occurrence also suggests that the social orientation of the occupants of the site had shifted from the west to the north.

The succeeding Iron Age at Dinkha and Hasanlu reflects a major cultural break with the Bronze Age, attested by completely new pottery forms, mainly monochrome gray and gray-orange wares, which continued in use throughout the Iron I and II periods; extramural burials in a separate cemetery area; and different architectural plans. These features most probably indicate the entry of a new population, whose ethnic background and language remain unknown, though various suggestions have been put forward: Iranian, Hurrian, Mannean. One hundred five Iron Age burials were excavated, thirty-three from period III, the rest from later period II. Dinkha III burials consisted of ten brick-lined tombs and twenty-three inhumations; all contained the characteristic monochrome wares. Four burials included weapons, thirty jewelry; only one yielded a cylinder seal, of Mitannian style, and only one burial included gold, in the form of earrings. There appears to have been no special relation between the type of tomb and the quantity or type of grave goods. No iron artifacts were found, and thus technologically Dinkha III belonged to the late Bronze Age. The Dinkha II burials consisted of nineteen infant burials in urns, twelve inhumations, thirty-one brick-lined tombs, and six stone-built tombs. The burials were richer in pottery and other goods than those of the preceding period, and both bronze and iron artifacts were common: 171 pieces of bronze and eighty-one pieces of iron jewelry, as well as sixteen iron and three bronze weapons. As in Dinkha III, there was no correlation between burial goods and type of tomb. One burial contained horse bits, and the fragmentary skeleton of a horse was found just outside. Very little Dinkha II and no Dinkha III architecture was encountered in the limited excavations. Although Hasanlu remains the northern type site for Iron Age architecture and a vast array of different artifacts, the pottery from Dinkha is the largest corpus of Iron Age wares published to date.

Bibliography: R. H. Dyson, Jr., "The Archaeological Evidence of the Second Millennium B.C. on the Persian Plateau," in *CAH*, 3rd ed., II/1, pp. 686-715. M. Edwards, "'Urmia Ware' and Its Distribution in North-Western Iran in the Second Millennium B.C. A Review of the Results of Excavations and Surveys," *Iran* 24, 1986, pp. 57-77. A. Gilbert et al., "Faunal Remains from Dinkha Tepe, Northwestern Iran," *Journal of Field Archaeology* 4, 1977, pp. 329-51. C. Hamlin, "The Early Second Millennium Ceramic Assemblage of Dinkha Tepe," *Iran* 12, 1974, pp. 125-53. O. W. Muscarella, "Excavations at Dinkha Tepe, 1966," *Bulletin of The Metropolitan Museum*, November 1968, pp. 187-96. Idem, "The Iron Age at Dinkha Tepe, Iran," *The Metropolitan Museum Journal* 9, 1974, pp. 35-90. Idem, *Bronze and Iron. Ancient Near Eastern Artifacts in The Metropolitan Museum of Art*, New York, 1988, pp. 18, 80.

(OSCAR WHITE MUSCARELLA)

DĒNKARD (lit., "Acts of the religion"), written in Pahlavi, is a summary of 10th-century knowledge of the Mazdean religion; the editor, Ādurbād Ēmēdān (q.v.), entitled the final version "The Dēnkard of one thousand chapters." This version, described by Jean de Menasce on the title page of his translation (1958) as a "Mazdean encyclopedia," consisted of about 169,000 words, according to E. W. West (*Grundriss*

II, p. 91). It was divided into nine books of unequal importance, but the first two and the beginning of the third are lost.

Ādurbād Ēmēdān, who is known to have left a *rivāyat* (ed. B. T. Anklesaria, Bombay, 1962), reconstructed a partially destroyed work compiled at the beginning of the 9th century by Ādurfarnbag ī Farroxzādān (q.v.), who transmitted it to his son Zardošt. The only nearly complete manuscript, known as "manuscript B" (Bombay ms. no. 55; Dhabhar, 1923), is now in the K. R. Cama Oriental Institute (q.v.) in Bombay; it is dated 1659. It was brought from Persia to Surat in India in 1783 and lent by its owner to Dastur K. Rustamji, who returned it with a good number of folios missing. For the most part these folios have been restored from other copies (cf. Dresden, 1966, pp. 13-18). According to the colophons of B and other copies, the original manuscript must have been made in Baghdad and dated 1020. Manuscript B consists at present of 322 folios; the total number of the original must have been 392. The other manuscript that is important for the transmission of the text is K 43 in Copenhagen, which consists of two parts, on fols. 177-261 and 262-303 respectively (see CODICES HAFNIENSES). Among modern copies of manuscript B are DE (in the collection of Dastur Edalji Darabji Sanjana) and M 58 (Haug ms. no. 13; Unvala p. 66), the latter dated 1866. Other manuscripts contain parts or extracts of the *Dēnkard*: DH, known for its text of the *Bundahišn* (q.v.; in the collection of Dastur Hoshang Jamasp, fols. 250 ff.), and University of Cambridge mss. Add. nos. 328-29 (containing only the conclusion of the *Dēnkard*). For the reconstruction of the lost folios ms. no. 24 II in the Dastur Meherji Rana Library in Navsari and mss. nos. 10-13 (dated 1866-69) in the Mulla Feroze Library in Bombay are useful, as they contain copies of different books of the *Dēnkard* and the six missing folios (Dhabhar, pp. 10-11).

The text has been edited twice. The first edition was by Dastur Peshotan Bahramji Sanjana, who published eight volumes during his lifetime, between 1869 and 1897; publication of volumes IX-XIX was completed by his son Darab in 1928. D. M. Madan also published a complete text in two volumes (Bombay, 1911). In 1966 M. J. Dresden published a facsimile of manuscript B, with the addition of the missing folios.

The first translations were those of L.-C. Casartelli (some chapters of Book III, in 1881 and 1886) and West (the beginning of Book V and Books VII-IX, in SBE 18, 37, 47). More recently, Marijan Molé published a French translation of Book VII and part of Book V (1967), de Menasce a complete French translation of Book III (1973), and Shaul Shaked an English translation of Book VI (1979). Numerous fragments have also been translated and commented on, notably by H. W. Bailey and R. C. Zaehner. Nevertheless, it would be worth having more modern translations of certain books. Recently Aḥmad Tafażżolī and Žāla Āmūzgār have translated into Persian some parts of Books V, VII, and IX.

The *Dēnkard* is primarily an apology for Mazdaism. More specifically, Books III-V are devoted to rational apologetics, Book VI to moral wisdom, and Books VII-IX to exegetical theology. The work was the product of a Persian milieu already largely islamicized and was thus intended both as a reply to Muslim attacks upon dualism and as a compendium of what could be saved of the scriptures. The main task at such a late date was to produce an encyclopedia of the religious sciences as known in the 9th-10th centuries. The *Dēnkard* is not, however, a systematic treatment; it is, rather, a compilation of preserved materials, no doubt carried out under the direction of an official master. The compiler, who is named in the last chapter (420) of Book III, is said to have had information from the "ancient sages," the *pōryōtkēšān*, clearly of the Sasanian period. According to de Menasce, Ādurfarnbag ī Farroxzādān may have been a contemporary of the caliph al-Maʾmūn (198-218/813-33), but the final redaction dates from the 10th century.

The original *Dēnkard* must have consisted of basic texts specifically related to the Avesta (q.v.), along with glosses or commentaries on them (e.g., the Zand), the whole constituting what was called the *dēn* (q.v.) "the religion."

Book III, which comprises almost half the work, consists of more than 400 chapters, some of them very short, of varied content and without any overall plan (cf. the chapter titles in Pahlavi transcription in de Menasce, 1958, pp. 82-116). What lends it at least some semblance of unity is the polemic against the "bad religions," the practitioners (*kēšdārān*) of which are explicitly identified when they are Manicheans or Jews but not when they are Muslims, an understandable precaution. Almost every chapter begins with the words "From the exposition of the good religion" (*az nigēz ī weh dēn*). This expression probably refers, not to a literary source, but only to a method of interpreting the revelation or Mazdean wisdom. De Menasce (1958, pp. 12 ff.) has recognized several distinct literary forms in this work, including numerous short chapters of two or three pages and rare long chapters on important subjects (e.g., chap. 80 on marriage to blood relatives, chap. 157 on medicine, chap. 123 on cosmogony, q.v.). In accordance with the apologetic perspective that characterizes Book III, another series of chapters deals with good precepts (*andarz*, q.v.), the counsels of Zoroaster or other leaders of the good religion, in contrast to evil precepts (*drāyišn*). De Menasce has argued that, although the presentation does not appear to conform to an overall plan, when all areas of faith, which are linked to myth, and of ethics, which are often dependent upon the laws of purity, are taken into account, they can be seen to be grouped, not haphazardly, but according to key words that serve as links. On the intellectual level, although Book III does not contain a systematic description of the revelation, it is arranged in order to develop the theme of cosmic dualism in a rational and philosophical manner and to explain the situation of mankind in the world of "mixture" (*gumēzišn*). On the social level it shows the complementarity of religion and kingship, and on the level of the individual it includes an analysis of the virtues and vices and the final destiny of the soul. Here and also in his discussion of Book VI (see below) de Menasce has clearly delineated the correspondences between the latter two categories, the play of which seems infinitely varied.

From the fifty chapters dealing with the refutation of false doctrines (a theme to which *Škand gumānīg wizār* of Mardānfarrox Ohrmazddādān, the book of polemics against Manicheism and Judeo-Christianity, is entirely devoted) those Islamic principles that were most disputed can be singled out: the notion of the "seal of prophecy" claimed by Moḥammad, the debate over idolatry (veneration of the stars as sacred entities being no more idolatrous in the eyes of a Mazdean than the koranic claim that God had ordered the angels to adore Adam), and belief in an eternal hell, which contradicts the Mazdean belief in divine mercy and the separation of the principles of good and evil. The *kēšdārān* who professed these evil doctrines are described throughout Book III. The metaphysical and philosophical point of view is always predominant. In the chapter on medicine (cf. Casartelli, 1886, pp. 530-58; de Menasce, 1958, pp. 158-68), for example, different types of medicine; the qualities of a good physician, who must treat the soul, as well as the body; and definitions of illness and health, always from the perspective of man's destiny in this world and in the hereafter, are set forth, but there is no treatise on anatomy and the vital functions of the kind provided, for example, in chapters 29 and 30 of the *Wizīdagīhā ī Zādspram*, so valuable for the reconstruction of a history of the sciences in this period. The compiler of the *Dēnkard* assumed that these principles were known.

Book IV is the shortest, presented as a selection of sentences from the *Āʾīn-nāma* (q.v.), a text dealing with customs, arts, and sciences. One chapter of Book III (142; de Menasce, 1958, p. 147) is of this same genre. Book IV seems particularly incoherent in its organization. It consists of a philosophical explanation of the "issuing" of the Aməša Spəntas (q.v.) from the first principle. The author also explained the role of the Persian sovereigns in the defense of Mazdaism, beginning with Darius III (q.v.; 336-31 B.C.E.), always the ancient starting point in later Pahlavi literature, and ending with K̲osrow I (590-628 C.E.). Then the function of created beings is defined, which provides an occasion for speculations on time, fate, and action, that is, on determination and free will, on music, and on the more abstract concepts of metaphysics. De Menasce thinks that this mixture of metaphysics and history resulted from dislocations occasioned by condensation of a more detailed work, such that the original can no longer be reconstructed. The compiler then turned, without transition, to meteorological questions, then to observations of astronomers and data contained in the "Book of the measurement of the earth" (*Nibēg ī zamīg paymānīh*) and physicians' observations. Then he returned to the relationship between religion and royalty, to a digression on penal law, and to the four qualities of the elements: hot, cold, dry, and moist. Finally, he insisted on the essential role of Persia in the moral education of humanity, owing to Persian sovereignty over foreign peoples. An enumeration of scientific works from Greece and India (the *Almagest* of Ptolemy and works of logic, rhetoric, astrology, and astronomy) reveals foreign influence from the 3rd century onward, and Book IV ends with considerations on the afterlife and the necessity for practicing the golden rule of Mazdaism, that is, the ethical triad of good thoughts (*humat*), good words (*hūxt*), and good actions (*huwaršt*; Gignoux, 1989).

Book V contains the replies of Ādurfarnbag (in a work entitled the "Book of the Daylamite") to a certain Yaʿqūb son of K̲āled, who sought to inform himself about Mazdaism. The instruction that the first editor of the *Dēnkard* provided for a possible convert is not characterized by doctrinal rigor but is, rather, an abridged account of human history up to the time of Zoroaster and of his message, which is subsumed in the obligation to struggle against demons and to perform the worship due to the gods. This exposition is followed by a statement of the principal tenets of the Mazdean faith: belief in paradise and hell, rewards and punishments in the afterlife, the rites of confession of sins, purification, dietary laws, alms, endogamous marriage, feasts, and the protection of the four elements. All this material is clearly nationalist and Persian in orientation, expressing the hope of a Mazdean restoration in the face of Islam and its Arab supporters, and it is thus not of direct value to the historian of religions. It was also a necessary response to Manichean and other detractors, who, emphasizing the universalism of their own religion, reproached the Mazdeans for the parochial character of their own. The second part of Book V consists of thirty-three questions addressed to the Christian Bōxt-Mārā: eleven related to the metaphysics of existence and the operation of the evil principle; three treating the conditions of revelation, especially the oral teaching of the Avesta, evidence suggesting that the text was written down quite late (and that only a few copies existed in the Sasanian period); four dealing with worship; and thirteen devoted to ritual purity in response to objections raised by Bōxt-Mārā.

Book VI is a collection of *andarz*, a literary genre with antecedents in late Avestan literature, known through extracts from the *Bariš nask*. It is a book of practical wisdom said to have been inherited from the ancient sages. Shaked distinguishes two groups of aphorisms, respectively religious and profane in character (see ANDARZ i, p. 13). Those of *Dēnkard* VI are clearly of a more intellectual type than those in smaller, more popular collections, like the *andarz* attributed to Ādurbād ī Mahrspandān (q.v.) or the more clearly narrative texts that belong to the same literary genre (e.g., *Xusrō ī Kawādān ud rēdag-ē* and *Draxt (ī) āsūrīg*, q.v.). Book VI is in fact a compilation, grouped into large sections distinguished from one another by their initial formulas. A certain number of passages are repeated in the book, further evidence that it is not a homogeneous composition. Some collections have been extracted in later Persian and Arabic works (e.g., *Jāwīdān kerad*). Shaked has divided the book into six parts. The first, from the beginning to A6d, is devoted to religious subjects, with emphasis on personal piety and devotion to the gods. In the second, from B1 to B47, the creations of Ohrmazd and Ahriman (q.v.), the two wisdoms, and proportion (*paymān*) and excess (*frēhbūdīh*) are contrasted; the probable source was the ethical principles of Aristotle. The third, from B48 to C47, is related to the second, in that it is devoted to the array of human qualities treated in a more practical manner. The fourth part, C48 to C83, deals with clusters of different qualities or activities, and the fifth, D1 to D12, includes the names of authors and morally edifying anecdotes. The last part, E1 to E45, is a conglomeration of aphorisms on various religious themes.

These *andarz* are seldom referred to doctrine but rather are devoted to human behavior, ranging from personal ethics to the interior vision of the soul. The necessity for self-knowledge is set forth; it requires questioning oneself about one's own origins, religious identification, and ultimate end. Education, the basis of knowledge, leads to wisdom. One thus arrives at correct conduct, fulfilling the duty of mankind, which is to repel demons from this world. The regulation of family relations is also dealt with, and education by means of writing is recommended. The views of good people must be solicited, and their company, like that of the sages, is praised, for they correspond in the material world to the gods in the spiritual world; what separates them is only a matter of degree, rather than of substance, for the soul of the just man is divine. Faith is indispensable to attaining the status of the just (*ahlawīh*), and religious observance is through the triad "thought, word, action." Religion assures man of happiness. Knowledge and recitation of the scriptures are said to be the means of realizing the *dēn*, but advice not to teach the Avesta, and still less the Zand, to everyone is doubtless evidence of the importance still accorded to oral instruction.

Shaked believes (1969, pp. 214 ff.) that he has found traces of esoteric belief in these texts, not of asceticism in general, for there is no deprecation of the things of this world but only encouragement to cultivate them with moderation in order not to encroach on the spiritual domain. It is necessary to preserve a balance between the two poles of human existence. Possession of material goods is a good thing, as are reputation and social status, but they should be put to good use and not enjoyed only for themselves. Nevertheless, poverty, though not misery, is also praised, for it is possible to draw benefit from it. The poor must not, however, scorn the rich or complain of their own lot. The value accorded to poverty, conferring a certain spiritual sanctity, resembles that in the Judeo-Christian tradition. The problem of human liberty is also treated: The notion of fate (*baxt*, *brēh*) is ambiguous in Mazdaism, but, according to Shaked (1979, pp. xli ff.), it does not refer to Zurvanism, as some have tried to demonstrate (Zaehner, pp. 254 ff.). Finally, the conditions of human life are clearly summarized (D1a) as twenty-five functions, organized under five headings: destiny (*brēh*), action (*kunišn*), custom (*hōg*), substance (*gōhr*), and inheritance (*abarmānd*).

Book VII has for a long time been recognized as that of the "legend of Zoroaster," the content of which can be viewed as parallel to that of the beginning of book V and chapters 5-26 of the *Wizīdagīhā ī Zādspram* and chapter 47 of the *Pahlavi Rivāyat*. The Persian *Zardošt-nāma* echoes the same traditions. Book VII was first translated by West and more recently by Molé (who brought together the texts, including the *Wizīrkard ī dēnīg* but not the *Zādspram*; 1967, pp. 26-49); its chapters have been analyzed in broad outline by de Menasce (1958, p. 64): 1. on the prophet as repository of *xwarrah* since the reign of Gayōmard, through the line of the Kayanids; 2. on the genealogy of Zoroaster; 3. on his miraculous infancy until the first interview (*hampursagīh*) with Ohrmazd and on the sorcerers' vain attempts to kill him by fire, then by throwing him under the hooves of bulls and horses and into the lair of a wolf, and finally by means of a sorcerer's evil eye, as well as on the meeting with Wahman (the Aməša Spənta); 4. on revelations received during his seven encounters with Ohrmazd and miracles against the demons, the conversion of Wištāsp after the visit of the Aməša Spəntas, and a visionary experience, apparently shamanistic in nature (rather than an illumination of the sort that Paul received on the road to Damascus); 5. on Zoroaster's actions from the time of Wištāsp's acceptance of the religion until his own death, including the institution of ordeals, revelations on medicine (*biziškīh*), physics (*čihr-šnāsīh*) and other sciences, miraculous curing rituals, and so on; 6. on miracles after Zoroaster's death, including the appearance of Wištāsp on earth riding a celestial chariot; 7. on the history of Iran until the Arab conquest, highlighting several kings and celebrated religious figures; 8. on miracles up to the end of the millennium of Zoroaster and the advent of the first savior, his son Ušētar; 9. on miracles during the thousand years of Ušētar until the advent of Ušētarmāh; 10. on miracles during the thousand years of Ušētarmāh until the advent of Sōšyans; 11. on miracles during the fifty-seven years of Sōšyans until the renewal (*frašgird*) of creation. The *Spand nask* and perhaps even the *Zand ī Wahman Yašt* have been suggested as sources for this book, though, owing to the late character of the latter and uncertainty over the existence of an antecedent Avestan *yašt* (cf. Gignoux, 1986), this connection is problematic.

Book VIII is particularly precious because it provides a summary of the contents of the Sasanian Avesta, which is partly lost, and the commentary on it. It probably consisted of three parts, each of seven chapters; the parts were entitled respectively "Gāhānīg" (seven *nasks* from the gathic texts), "Hadag-mānsarīg" (a collection of sacred formulas related to ritual), and "Dādīg" (devoted to juridical texts; for a table of contents of the Avesta, after Dēnkard VIII, see AVESTA, p. 37). This organization, which is believed to correspond to the twenty-one words of the prayer Ahunwar (q.v.) and may have had astrological connotations, perhaps represents the Sasanian archetype of the Avesta; it reflects the incomplete Pahlavi translation of the Avestan texts, though it may include Avestan texts that are only late compilations. Even so, it accounts for only about a quarter of the original Avesta. Besides, as Jean Kellens has argued (see AVESTA), what the priests of the Sasanian period knew about the old Avestan texts and the ancient *yašts* has survived almost in its entirety. This book also provides information concerning penal and agrarian law, which is complementary to the laws of obligation presented in the *Mādayān ī hazār dādestān*.

Book IX is a book of *zand*, making explicit the content of the gathic *nasks* analyzed in book VIII: the *Sūtkar*, *Varštmānsar*, and *Bag nasks*, which are commentaries on the three great Mazdean prayers: Ahunwar, Ašem vohū (q.v.), and Yeŋhē hātąm. It concludes with a commentary on *Yasna* 54. Although the first two *nasks* are mythical or historical evocations in the midrashic style, the *Bag nask* is more a kind of meditation, serving as a gloss on the text. The teaching emphasizes the necessity for union between Zoroaster and the believer, between the master and the disciple, and with the Aməša Spəntas.

Although the *Dēnkard* as a whole contains a good number of historical allusions, they are most often shrouded in myth and thus of dubious reliability. For example, the report, in the last chapter of Book III, according to which Alexander (q.v.) burned a copy of the Avesta and another example fell into the hands of the Greeks, who translated it into their own language, has often been accepted as historical (e.g., Hansen, pp. 64 ff.), though it is now recognized that there was no written Avesta before the Hellenistic period and that the first edition took place in the Sasanian period, at the earliest (AVESTA).

The style of this monumental work has often been considered difficult and full of pitfalls because of its conciseness and the fact that it often seems to consist of summaries. There is thus still much work to be done before the full richness of this impressive work can be understood in detail.

Bibliography: (For cited works not found in this bibliography and abbreviations found here, see "Short References"). H. W. Bailey, *Zoroastrian Problems in the Ninth-Century Books*, Oxford, 1943; 2nd ed., Oxford, 1971. M. Boyce, "Middle Persian Literature," pp. 43-45, 52-53. L.-C. Casartelli, *La philosophie religieuse du Mazdéisme sous les Sassanides*, Paris, 1881. Idem, "Un traité pehlevi sur la médecine," *Le Muséon* 5, 1886, pp. 530-58. B. N. Dhabhar, *Descriptive Catalogue of Some Manuscripts Bearing on Zoroastrianism and Pertaining to the Different Collections in the Mulla Feroze Library*, Bombay, 1923. M. J. Dresden, "Note on the 'B' Manuscript of the Dēnkart," in *Dr. J. M. Unvala Memorial Volume*, Bombay, 1964, pp. 198-268. Idem, *Dēnkart. A Pahlavi Text*, facsimile ed., Wiesbaden, 1966. Ph. Gignoux, "Sur l'inexistence d'un Bahman Yasht avestique," *Journal of Asian and Aftican Studies* 32, 1986, pp. 53-64. Idem, "Thought, Word and Deed. A Topic of Comparative Religion," *International Congress Proceedings*, Bombay, 1991, pp. 41-51. O. Hansen, "Die Berliner Hephthaliten-Fragmente," *La Nouvelle Clio* 3, 1951, pp. 41-69. M. J. Maškūr, *Goftār-ī dar bāra-ye Dēnkard*, Tehran, 1325 Š./1946. J. P. de Menasce, *Une encyclopédie mazdéenne, le Dēnkart*, Paris, 1958. Idem, "Un chapitre cosmogonique du Dēnkart," *Pratidānam. Indian, Iranian, and Indo-European Studies Presented to F. B. J. Kuiper*, the Hague, 1968, pp. 193-200. Idem, *Le troisième livre du Dēnkart*, Travaux de l'Institut d'Études Iraniennes 5, Paris, 1973. Idem, "Zoroastrian Pahlavī Writings," in *Camb. Hist. Iran* III/2, pp. 1166-95. M. Molé, *Culte, mythe et cosmologie dans l'Iran ancien*, Paris, 1963. Idem, *La légende de Zoroastre*, Travaux de l'Institut d'Études Iraniennes 3, Paris, 1967. S. Shaked, "Esoteric Trends in Zoroastrianism," *The Israel Academy of Sciences and Humanities Proceedings* 3/7, 1969, pp. 175-221. Idem, *The Wisdom of the Sasanian Sages (Dēnkard VI) by Aturpāt-i Ēmētān*, Persian Heritage Series 34, Boulder, Colo., 1979. M. Shaki, "Some Basic Tenets of the Eclectic Metaphysics of the Dēnkart," *Archív Orientální* 41, 1973, pp. 133-64. Idem, "The Social Doctrine of Mazdak in the Light of Middle Persian Evidence," *Archív Orientální* 46, 1978, pp. 289-306. Idem, "The Dēnkard Account of the History of the Zoroastrian Scriptures," *Archív Orientální* 49, 1981, pp. 114-25. A. Tafażżolī and Ž. Āmūzgār, *Osṭūra-ye zendagī-e Zardošt*, Tehran, 1372 Š./1993. J. C. Tavadia, *Die mittelpersische Sprache und Literatur der Zarathustrier*, Leipzig,

1956, pp. 45-73. J. M. Unvala, *Collection of Colophons of Manuscripts Bearing on Zoroastrianism in Some Libraries of Europe*, Bombay, 1940. E. W. West, *Pahlavi Texts* IV. *Contents of the Nasks*, SBE 37, Oxford, 1892; repr. Delhi, 1965. Idem, *Pahlavi Texts* V. *Marvels of Zoroastrianism*, SBE 47, Oxford, 1897. R. C. Zaehner, *Zurvan. A Zoroastrian Dilemma*, Oxford, 1955.

(PHILIPPE GIGNOUX)

DENMARK, relations with Persia.

i. *Political, economic, and cultural relations.*
ii. *Danish-Iranian Society.*

i. POLITICAL, ECONOMIC, AND CULTURAL RELATIONS

Danish-Persian relations have been concentrated in three main areas: politics and diplomacy; trade and other economic relations; and Iranian studies in Denmark, including collections of Persian art in Danish museums.

Political and diplomatic relations. In 1937 archeological excavation on a farm in Jutland led to the discovery of two Sasanian coins, one of Pērōz (459-84) and the other of Ḵosrow I (531-79), part of a hoard found in a vase. The circumstances in which these coins reached Denmark are not yet certain (see Welin; COMMERCE iv; a fragment found more recently is in the Royal coin and medallion collection; Anne Kromann, personal communication).

In 1687 a ship belonging to the Danish East Asian Company (Det Østasiatisk Kompagni) seized a Bengali ship and brought it into the port of Trankebar, a Danish colony on the southeastern coast of India. The merchandise belonged to Armenians from Jolfā at Isfahan in Persia. The Danes sent the ship with its cargo to Copenhagen, where four years later a Persian ambassador arrived to negotiate compensation for the merchandise. On 11 December 1691 he presented to King Christian V (1670-99) his credentials and a letter from the Safavid shah Solaymān (1077-1105/1666-94) addressed to a former king, Christian III (1534-59); it included a comprehensive inventory of the disputed merchandise and the names of the Armenian merchants (partially published in Boisen, 1965, p. 66). Although the ambassador returned empty-handed, the exquisitely embroidered envelope in which he had carried his credentials and the letter is kept in the Danish Museum of Decorative Art (von Falsach and Bernsted, p. 39).

From the end of the 19th century the Danish ambassador to St. Petersburg was also accredited to Persia and other countries in the region. There is little evidence of significant diplomatic contact between the two countries, however, until 1312 Š./1933, when the first Danish consulate was established in Tehran (*Udenrigsminisetriet Kalender*, Copenhagen, 1934), following negotiations between the Danish construction firm Kampsax and the Persian government (see below). It was elevated to an embassy and a Persian embassy was established in Copenhagen after the state visit of Moḥammad-Reżā Shah (1320-57 Š./1941-79) in 1958 (*Corps Diplomatique*, Copenhagen, 1959; *Udenrigsministeriet Kalender*, Copenhagen, 1963). The Danish royal family paid an official visit to Persia in 1341 Š./1962 (Boisen, 1965, pp. 6-9).

Since the Persian revolution of 1357 Š./1978-79 Denmark and Persia have enjoyed generally good relations, though, because of the considerable market for Danish exports in Persia (see below) and consequent fear of economic retaliation, the Danish government has adopted a somewhat cautious position on human rights in Persia. Danish diplomats have usually voted for resolutions condemning violations of human rights, but in the instance of Salman Rushdie the Danish government, despite strong criticism in the national press, has never issued a condemnation of Persia.

The number of Persians living in Denmark probably never exceeded 150 until after the Persian revolution. Beginning in the 1980s thousands of Persians took advantage of a liberal Danish refugee policy to immigrate. In the late 1980s, however, increasing ethnic tensions and a flourishing criminal trade in transporting illegal immigrants led the Danish authorities to adopt greater restrictions on refugees. The Persian community in Denmark numbered 8,800 people in 1993 (*Statistisk Årbog*, Copenhagen, 1993, p. 59), mainly students in universities and other institutions of higher learning but also writers, poets, film producers, artists, and musicians. According to Danish statistics, Persians constitute the largest single refugee group obtaining higher education in Denmark (unpublished report, University of Copenhagen, 1993). Nevertheless, the difficulty of learning Danish and the high standard of the Danish educational system, as well as "culture shock" because of previous unfamiliarity with Danish culture, have somewhat hampered assimilation. Among Persian organizations and clubs the most active is the Anjoman-e Īrānīān (Persian society), which until December 1992 published the monthly journal *Mohājer* (Immigrant). There is a good collection of Persian books in the "refugees' library" administered by the Danish Ministry of social affairs, as well as large numbers of Persian books in municipal libraries in the major cities of Denmark.

Trade and other economic relations. Danish-Persian economic relations essentially began with the construction of the Trans-Persian Railway by the Danish firm Kampsax. After the failure of an American firm to complete the railroad over a number of years the Persian government signed a contract with Kampsax in 1312 Š./1933 for the construction of more than 1,000 kilometers of track between Bandar-e Šāhpūr in the south and Bandar-e-Šāh (qq.v.) on the Caspian coast. The projected cost was about 600 million tomans ($100 million), and the railroad was to be completed in six years. Because of the difficult mountainous terrain to be crossed the work crew of 55,000 men also had to construct 250 tunnels and 550 bridges. Despite limited available resources, this project was completed in five and a half years, one of the most successful ever carried out in Persia (Boisen, 1946; idem, 1965, pp. 93-105; Maḥbūbī, *Moʾassasāt* II, pp. 351-52).

As an oil-exporting country, Persia maintained a favorable balance of trade with Denmark for many years. From the early 1960s Danish exports to Persia also increased, as Persian oil revenues permitted significant increases in imports from Western countries. The discovery of oil and gas in the North Sea in the mid-1970s permitted Denmark to attain self-sufficiency, and oil imports have dropped to a very low level. Table 24 shows the volume of trade between the two countries in 1977 and 1978 and in 1990 and 1991.

Danish exports to Persia consist primarily of agricultural products, cheese, butter, grains, cooking oil, powdered milk, and the like. Feta cheese, deliberately developed to resemble the Persian goat cheese, is particularly important. In recent years industrial goods, including cold-storage units, slaughterhouses, agricultural machinery, and the like have accounted for a substantial share of exports. According to trade statistics for 1990, Danish agricultural exports amounted to 446 million kroner, industrial exports to 419 million, and other commodities to 17 million. Persian exports to Denmark include mainly carpets (q.v.), dried fruits, and raw and semiprocessed materials.

Iranian Studies. The first chair in Iranian philology was established at the University of Copenhagen in 1919, but Danish interest in Iranian studies in Denmark began in the 17th century, when Frederik III, duke of Gottorp, sent a delegation to Persia; the secretary was the German Adam Olearius (1603-71), who left a valuable description of the journey. Olearius arrived in Isfahan in August 1637; while there he learned Persian. When he returned, in April 1639, he was accompanied by a Persian named Ḥaqverdī, who remained with him in Schleswig until his death. It was with Ḥaqverdī's assistance that Olearius was able to publish, in 1654, an edition with a free German translation of part of Saʿdī's *Golestān*. The Persian type fonts were made in Holland, and Olearius himself undertook the setting of the Persian text. This work and a subsequent Danish translation by N. L. N. Boisen (1803-75), *Fra det Persiske* (1853), were used as texts at the University of Copenhagen.

Table 24
VOLUME OF TRADE BETWEEN DENMARK AND PERSIA
(in 1,000 Danish kroner[a])

Year	Persian Imports to Denmark	Danish Exports to Persia
1977	1,795,782	542,656
1978	1,043,936	509,623
1990	57,813	866,207
1991	63,344	1,158,272
1992	69,849	1,063,162

a. 1 kroner=ca. $0.14.
Source: *Statistik Årbog 1992*, Copenhagen, 1993.

Almost a century after Olearius' expedition the Danish king Frederik V (1746-66), encouraged by J. D. Michaelis of Göttingen, sent another expedition to the east to collect materials about the the Old Testament and the Orient that produced it. This ill-fated expedition departed in 1761; the only member to survive fatal illness on the long and dangerous journey was Carsten Niebuhr (1733-1815), who managed to visit Persepolis, where he copied the Achaemenid inscriptions for the first time. His description of the journey, together with a map and drawings, was published in Copenhagen and Hamburg in several volumes: *Beschreibung von Arabien* (Copenhagen, 1772) and *Reisebeschreibung nach Arabien und andern umliegenden Ländern* (I-II, Copenhagen, 1774-78; III, Hamburg, 1837). Thanks to Niebuhr's work the study of the cuneiform inscriptions at Persepolis was placed on a scientific basis. Although the German G. F. Grotefend is generally acknowledged to have deciphered the Old Persian inscriptions at Persepolis, it was the Danish cleric F. C. C. H. Münter (1761-1830) who, in his *Undersøgelse om de Persepolitianske Inscriptioner* (1800), identified the vertical wedge and correctly argued that it was used to separate words. He also recognized the repeated word groups that constitute the title "king of kings."

The Dane Rasmus Rask (1787-1832) first recognized the genitive plural form in Old Persian *n(a)* and *m(a)* and published other linguistic discoveries in his valuable short publication *Om Zendsprogets og Zendavestas Ælde og Ægthed*, written in 1821 and published in Copenhagen in 1826. Rask had begun to study Icelandic while still at school, and his quest for the origins of this ancient Scandinavian language led him across Finland and Russia to Persia and India. While in Persia in 1819-20 he learned Persian, and in Bombay he learned Avestan and Pahlavi (Middle Persian); with some difficulty he collected old manuscripts in these two languages, which are now in the Royal Library in Copenhagen. Some of the Avestan manuscripts that Rask collected are believed to be the oldest in existence, dating from about 1324. Rask returned to Denmark in 1823 and worked on linguistic papers until his death in 1832, but he never produced a major work on his eastern discoveries. It was N. L. Westergaard (1815-78), the first professor of Indo-Asiatic philology at the University of Copenhagen, who continued Rask's work of collecting manuscripts. On a journey to Persia and India in 1841-44 he was able to buy and copy some old Zoroastrian manuscripts and learned much about this religion. His irritation with the refusal of the Zoroastrians of Yazd and Kermān to sell him their manuscripts is clear from his diary (Royal Library, Copenhagen, Ny Kgl. Samling ms. no. 1320). Nevertheless, he brought some interesting examples back to Denmark, including a copy of *Mēnog ī xrad* (K 23). One of his greatest achievements was publication of the collection of texts in the Avestan language, *Zandavesta or the Religious Books of the Zoroastrians* I. *The Zend Texts* (Copenhagen, 1854). All the Avestan type fonts were made in Copenhagen under his supervision. Westergaard was also the first European to publish a Pahlavi text, the *Bundahišn* (q.v.; 1851), based on a manuscript collected by Rask. Westergaard included in this work two Middle Persian texts from the Sasanian inscription of Ḥājīābād of the time of Šāpūr I (241-72). Between 1931 and 1944 Arthur Christensen and Kaj Barr (qq.v.) published the entire collection of manuscripts assembled by Rask and Westergaard in twelve volumes (see CODICES HAFNIENSES).

The printed lecture lists of the University of Copenhagen reveal that classical Persian literature, for example, Saʿdī's *Golestān* (see above), was taught at intervals by A. M. F. van Mehren from 1875 to 1895, sometimes as part of "Arabic and Persian for beginners." Van Mehren also included Ḥāfeẓ (in 1872, 1878, 1882, and 1883) and Wāʿeẓ Kāšefī's *Anwār-e sohaylī* (q.v.; 1883) in the curriculum. Jens Lassen Rasmussen, who had studied Persian in Paris with Silvestre de Sacy, published an article about the odes of Ḥāfez in 1816 ("Nogle Oder af Hafiz," *Theologisk Bibliothek* 9, 1916, pp. 37-70), and in 1892 Harald Rasmussen (1853-1904) received a university prize for his dissertation *Studier over Hafiz med Sideblik til andre persiske Lyrikere*. After van Mehren's retirement in 1898 his pupil Edvard Lehmann (1862-1930), lecturer in the history of religion, taught Persian, introducing Ferdowsī's *Šāh-nāma*; he also taught Avestan and Middle Persian, as well as the history of the Zoroastrian religion.

The first professor of Iranian studies at the University of Copenhagen was Christensen (1875-1945), who was appointed in 1919. His unique range included Sasanian history, Iranian languages and dialects, Persian language and literature, and Iranian religions, ancient and modern. He wrote more than 300 books and articles on such subjects. He visited Persia on three occasions. In 1961 the Institute of Iranian Philology was established at the university, with Christensen's library as a nucleus. Christensen was succeeded by his student and later collaborator Kaj Barr (1896-1970), who taught until 1966; although widely acknowledged as one of the best scholars in the field, he published relatively little. In 1966 Jes P. Asmussen succeeded Barr; he has published a variety of books and articles on Iranian subjects, especially Manicheism and Persian Jewish dialects. In 1968 Fereydun Vahman became lecturer in Iranian philology; he has published works on Pahlavi and Western Iranian dialects, as well as a two-volume Danish-Persian and Persian-Danish dictionary. In recent years the curriculum of the Institute has been expanded with the introduction of subjects related to modern Persian cultural history.

The systematic translation of Persian literary works into Danish began with Christensen. In his *Muhammedanske Digter og Tænker* (Islamic poets and philosophers; Copenhagen, 1906) he included specimen texts in classical Persian drawn from the works of Ferdowsī, Farīd-al-Dīn ʿAṭṭār, Nāṣer-e Ḵosrow, and Saʿdī. He also translated parts of Ferdowsī's *Šāh-nāma* into Danish verse (*Firdausis Kongebog*; Copenhagen, 1931) and later the *Robāʿīāt* of ʿOmar Ḵayyām (Copenhagen, 1943). Christensen also wrote five short stories revealing the influence of the style of the modern Persian writer Moḥammad-ʿAlī Jamālzāda, which were serialized in Danish newspapers. They were based on his observations in Persia or included motivs from Persian folktales. These and several other stories were published together under the title *Experimentierne på Crackwell Hill og andre Fortællinger* (Copenhagen, 1938). In the 1980s several Persian literary works were translated into Danish: In 1984 Bent Hunø published an anthology of works by Saʿdī, Ḥāfeẓ, Rūdakī, Ferdowsī, and Ḵayyām; Verner Jul Andersen published a translation of Hedāyat's *Būf-e kūr* (q.v.) in 1989; Sigrid Hansen and Issa Ghaffari published Forūḡ Farroḵzād's *Tawallod-ī dīgar* in 1990 and translated his *Īmān bī-āvarīm be āḡāz-e faṣl-e sard* in 1992; Søren Theisen and Ḡolām-Reżā Ḵ^{v}ājaʾīān translated Ṣamad Behrangī's *Māhī-e sīāh-e kūčūlū* in the same year. Ḥosayn Ṣafā and a group of Persian teachers publish a quarterly journal for younger readers, *Javāna*; it has a wide readership in Scandinavia. Manīža Āhanī publishes a biannual literary journal, *Vāža*.

Danish museums contain important collections of Persian art; most notable is the David Samling, which houses rich collections of Sasanian glass and silver, as well as miniatures and other works from the Islamic period (von Falsach). The Danish National Museum, the Ny Glyptotek, and the Rosenborg Palace collection also contain important Persian works.

Bibliography: J. P. Asmussen, "Iransk filologi," in *Københavns Universitets 1479-1979* VIII, Copenhagen, 1979, pp. 576-694. K. Barr and A. Christensen, *Codices Avestici et Pahlavici Bibliothecae Universitatis Hafniensis*, 12 vols., Copenhagen, 1931-44. I. Boisen, *Banen skal bygges paa seks aar*, Copenhagen, 1946. Idem, *Danmark og Iran gennem tiderne*; tr. D. Hohnen as *Iran and Denmark through the Ages*, Copenhagen, 1965. K. von Falsach, *Islamisk Kunst*, Copenhagen, 1990. Idem and A. M. K. Bernsted, *Woven Treasures. Textiles from the World of Islam*, Copenhagen, 1993. A. Geijer, *Statistical Yearbook of Denmark*, Copenhagen, 1993. U. S. L. Welin, "Arabisk mynt," in *Kulturhistorisk Leksikon for nordisk middelalder* I, Copenhagen, 1956, pp. 182-91.

(FEREYDUN VAHMAN)

ii. DANISH-IRANIAN SOCIETY

The Danish Iranian Society (Dansk Iransk Selskab, Anjoman-e Īrān o Dānmārk) was founded in Copenhagen on 14 October 1976 to further ties between Denmark and Persia in cultural, social, and economic matters and to further personal contacts between Danes and Persians through meetings, exhibitions, publications, exchange of scholars and artists, and similar activities. The leading figures in launching the society were Mehrangīz Dawlatšāhī, at that time Persian ambassor to Denmark, and Birte Saxild, whose husband, Jørgen, was director of the Kampsax firm, which had built the Trans-Persian Railway (see i, above). A few weeks after its establishment the society already had about 200 members, and the number increased in subsequent years. Birte Saxild served as president until 1984 and was succeeded by Jes P. Asmussen. After the Revolution of 1357 Š./1978 in Persia, however, the membership declined sharply; although in 1994 it seemed to be stable, the possibility that the society will come to an end in the next few years cannot be excluded.

Among the society's most important activities is sponsoring lectures on the culture, defined as broadly as possible, of ancient and modern Persia and on cultural relations between Persia and Denmark, the latter including reports of diplomats since the time of Shah ʿAbbās I (996-1038/1588-1629), of Danish archeological expeditions to Persia, and of language studies. Danish, Persian, and other foreign lecturers have addressed the society on such topics as "Persian Poetry and Mysticism," "*Šāh-nāma*, the National Epic of the Iranians," "Rūmī and Sufism," "Treasures from Ancient Iran in the National Museum of Denmark" (in connection with an exhibition of the collection), "The Architecture of Isfahan," and "Ṣādeq Hedāyat and Modern Persian Literature." They have included Annemarie Schimmel, Bozorg Alavī, Arild Hvidtfeldt, Hans Munk Hansen, and Fereydun Vahman.

The society is not sponsored by the Danish government but itself sponsors performances of traditional Persian music and exhibitions of modern Persian art and Persian minatures, bookbindings, lacquer penboxes, and carpets. Whenever possible these arrangements are made in collaboration with the Danish Royal Library, the David Samling (containing Persian miniatures, ceramics, and other decorative arts; von Falsach), the Danish National Museum, and the museum of Rosenborg Castle (where a collection of rare Safavid carpets, including the famous "Coronation carpet," is housed; see CARPETS ix, Plate CXI; cf. Martin).

Bibliography: K. von Falsach, *Islamisk Kunst*, Copenhagen, 1990. F. R. Martin, *Die persischen Prachstoffe im Schloss Rosenborg in Kopenhagen*, Stockholm, 1901. *Vedtægter for Dansk Iransk Selskab/Asās-nāma-ye Anjoman-e Īrān o Dānmārk*, Copenhagen, n.d.

(JES P. ASMUSSEN)

DENŠAPUH, short form of Vehdenšapuh (Mid. Pers. *Wehdēnšābuhr), Sasanian *hambārakapet* (quartermaster; Faustus, tr. Garsoian, p. 530) involved in the campaign of Yazdagerd II (438-57) to force Christian Armenians to abjure their faith and return to Zoroastrianism (Łazar Pʿarpecʿi, pp. 293, 309-10, 314, 317, 319; Ełišē, ed. Tēr-Minasean, pp. 19-139; cf. Hübschmann, *Armenische Grammatik*, p. 37 no. 56); a gem bearing his name is preserved in the British Museum in London (Thomas, no. 117; cf. Nöldeke, *Geschichte der Perser*, p. 444). Stepʿanos Tarawnacʿi (p. 83) claimed that Denšapuh "increased adultery and lit an Ohrmazd fire in Rštunikʿ," a district south of Lake Van. These claims are references to the Sasanian suppression of sacerdotal celibacy and encouragement of marriage between next of kin, as well as to the conversion of churches into fire temples, as at Echmiadzin (Ējmiacin).

Bibliography: (For cited works not found in this bibliography, see "Short References.") Łazar Pʿarpecʿi, *Patmagirkʿ hayocʿ*, ed. G. Tēr-Mkrtčʿean and S. Malxasean, Tiflis, 1904; repr. Delmar, N.Y., 1985; tr. R. W. Thomson as *The History of Lazar Pʿarpecʿi*, Atlanta, 1991. Stepʿanos Tarawnacʿi, *Tiezerakanpatmutʿiwn*, St. Petersburg, 1885. E. Thomas, *Early Sassanian Inscriptions, Seals and Coins*, London, 1868.

(JAMES RUSSELL)

DENTISTRY (*dandān-pezeškī*) in Persia. No specific information about dentistry in pre-Islamic Persia has survived, but a reference in the Avesta (*Vd.* 2.29) indicates that oral and dental diseases were not uncommon among Iranians. Significant advances in medicine were achieved, particularly at the college hospital at Gondēšāpūr (q.v.; in the Islamic period Jondīšāpūr), which was founded under the Sasanians and continued to function in the early Islamic period. As Abū Bakr Moḥammad Rāzī (d. 313/925) based his discussion of dental therapy (1955) on the methods of Bok̠tīšūʿ b. Jewarjīs (d. 185/801), the latter's son Jebrāʾīl (for both these men, see BOK̠TĪŠŪʿ), and other physicians trained at Gondēšāpūr, it can be inferred that dentistry was part of the program of study at the hospital, inherited from pre-Islamic times.

Dental medicine before the Mongol invasion. The ancient tradition endured into the Islamic period. There is reason to suppose that such physicians as Māsarjawayh (Māsarjūya), a Persian employed at the Omayyad court in Damascus and probably trained at Gondēšāpūr, also did dental work (Sāmarrāʾī, I, pp. 291-92, 305). Ebn al-Nadīm (ed. Flügel, p. 59) ascribed a book entitled *Ketāb al-asnān* (Book of teeth) to Abū ʿObayda Maʿmar b. Moṯannā, nicknamed Saḵt (110-207/728-822), an author of Persian descent; if the title is correct, it must have been one of the first monographs on the subject written by a Persian in the Islamic period, but Ebn Ḵallekān (ed. ʿAbbās, V, p. 239) gave the title as *Resālat al-ensān* (Treatise on mankind), which seems more in keeping with Abū ʿObayda's other writings.

More is known about dentistry under the ʿAbbasids and the autonomous dynasties that arose on Persian soil. The fact that Rāzī, when writing on drugs for dental ailments (1955, III, pp. 130, 136), frequently cited prescriptions of the Boḵtīšūʿ family and other physicians from Gondēšāpūr (e.g., Ḥonayn b. Esḥāq [192-260/808-73], Esḥāq b. Ḥonayn [d. 289/911], and Yūḥannā b. Māsawayh [Māsūya; d. 243/857]) is evidence that this branch of medicine was practiced in Persia. According to Ebn Abī Oṣaybeʿa (p. 99), Ḥonayn b. Esḥāq wrote *Resāla fī ḥefẓ al-asnān* (Treatise on the preservation of the teeth), a source for Rāzī (1955, III, p. 145-50), who noted that it was about hygiene of the gums and teeth. Ebn Abī Oṣaybeʿa also mentioned (I, p. 83) *Resāla fi'l-sewāk wa'l-sonūnāt* (Treatise on toothpicks and tooth powders) by Yūḥannā b. Māsawayh; this and another work by the same writer, *al-Masāʾel*, were also cited by Rāzī (1955, III, pp. 117, 141, 142, 150). If Yūḥannā b. Māsawayh is to be identified with Māsawayh the Younger, as Cyril Elgood has supposed, he deserves credit for being the first to use gold to fill dental cavities and to diagnose sympathetic toothache (Elgood, 1951, pp. 93-95, 287). The renowned physician ʿAlī b. Rabban Ṭabarī (d. 247/861), a contemporary of Yūḥanna, discussed dental ailments in several passages of his medical compendium *Ferdows al-ḥekma* (pp. 47, 188, 189); he described the loss of milk teeth and the growth of molars and prescribed medications to toughen the gums, stop hemorrhages, whiten the teeth, and hasten the growth of teeth in children.

Rāzī himself made much more detailed observations of the teeth and dental diseases (1955, III, pp. 93-155). It is clear that he had personally tested the properties of many of the drugs that he prescribed. He believed that most dental diseases are related to nerves in the roots (1955, III, p. 106). In accordance with the prevalent theory of hot and cold diseases, he divided his prescriptions for toothache and other dental ailments into corresponding categories (1955, III, p. 147 and passim). For tooth extraction without recourse to forceps, he recommended that a thick ointment of wild tarragon root (*ʿāqerqarḥā*) mixed with vinegar or wine be rubbed on the gums, in order to soften them and loosen the tooth, but he advised care in application, so that other teeth would not fall out (Rāzī, 1908, pp. 11, 12; idem, 1955, III, pp. 98, 152). His prescriptions for toothache included drops, poultices, and cauterization, then widely used for many diseases (1945, p. 42); for some kinds of toothache he prescribed eardrops (1955, III, pp. 93, 95) or letting blood from the gums, but he found that gum inflammation could often be healed by rinsing the mouth with damask-rose oil (1955, III, p. 121). For prevention of tooth decay and disease he advised rinsing twice monthly with milkweed (*yattūʿ*) root stewed in wine (1945, p. 99). A section on the teeth and jaws in an early work, *Ketāb al-ṭebb al-manṣūrī*, now lost, was almost certainly the first work ever written on the structure of the tooth and the functioning of the jaw (Malvin, p. 66).

ʿAlī b. ʿĪsā Ahvāzī (d. 384/994) included in his general medical work *al-Kāmel le'l-ṣenāʿa* (or *al-Ṭebb al-malekī*) a section on dental and gingival diseases and injuries (pp. 302-04); his prescriptions are mostly mixtures of substances like tarragon root with vinegar or other liquors, opium, and camphor. Abū'l-Faraj Ebn Hendū (d. 410/1019 or 420/1029), a native of Ray, in his categorized lists of body parts, diseases, and remedies, placed teeth in the category of organs (pp. 112-13). The botanist Mowaffaq-al-Dīn ʿAlī Heravī (10th century; pp. 85, 115, 125, 151) noted the value of several plant products for relief of toothache, and Abū Rayḥān Bīrūnī (q.v.; d. 442/1050) also drew attention to the effects of certain herbs in relieving toothache (I, nos. 284, 623) and advised against the use of the poison hellebore.

Abu'l-Ḥasan Aḥmad b. Moḥammad Ṭabarī, physician to the Buyid prince Rokn-al-Dawla, devoted several chapters to treatment of dental ailments in the sixth discourse of his *Ketāb al-moʿālajāt al-boqrāṭīya* (Tehran University, Central library, ms. no. 6331; cf. Sāmarrāʾī, I, pp. 534-35). In the late 10th century Abū Bakr Aḵawaynī Boḵārī (q.v.) not only made interesting observations about causes of tooth decay, for example, food particles wedged between the teeth and malnutrition, but also described apparently tested methods for relieving and curing the problem and preventing further decay. He rejected the opinion of the ancients who had classified teeth as either bone or nerve, though he recognized toothache as resulting from irritation of the nerves. If the ache could not be relieved by drugs, he recommended lancing the root and removing the nerve (pp. 296-97, 299, 302-03).

Avicenna (q.v.) included some noteworthy clinical observations on toothaches and other diseases of the teeth and gums in his encyclopedic *Qānūn* (pp. 97-98) and recommended cold water for quick relief of toothache. He regarded teeth as bone, which he considered capable of growth at all times, and thus claimed that teeth next to the site of an extracted tooth would grow larger (p. 95). Like earlier physicians, he advised use of medication, as well as forceps, for extracting rotten teeth but emphasized that extraction of a tooth that was not loose is dangerous because it can injure the jawbone, cause eye trouble, and lead to fever through infection (pp. 99-100). He classified possible treatments by method of administration: drugs to be chewed, poultices, mouthwashes, compresses, cauterization, fumigation, and bloodletting; he also identified eight factors that help to keep teeth sound (p. 96). For severe toothache he prescribed a compress of salt, millet, heated olive oil, and melted candle wax, to be applied repeatedly to the site of the inflammation. The proper way to cauterize was to insert a red-hot needle smeared with olive oil into a cavity or a hole made with a very thin metal rod, in order to kill the nerve (pp. 97-98).

A century later the renowned physician Esmāʿīl Jorjānī (d. 531/1136-37) also wrote extensively on dental anatomy and diseases. Among the subjects discussed in his *Ḏaḵīra-ye ḵᵛārazmšāhī* (q.v.) are different types of teeth and roots, the baby teeth and why they are lost and replaced, and medications for hastening the growth of children's teeth (1976. pp. 18-19, 112, 209). He reported his observations of pyorrhea and receding gums and gave details on remedial drugs (p. 379). Emphasizing the importance of oral and dental hygiene, he advised on the use of toothpicks and explained how teeth become discolored (pp. 387, 390). He appears sometimes to have used local anesthetics (p. 388). His prescriptions for toothache include poultices, fumigation, nosedrops, and injections into tooth cavities (p. 389). Like some earlier physicians he believed that rot was caused by worms hatched in the teeth (p. 363).

In the Mongol period and later. In the Mongol period Najm-al-Dīn Maḥmūd Šīrāzī (d. 720/1320) devoted chapters 50-51 of the first discourse and chapter 101 of the third discourse of his medical compendium *Ḥāwī* to dental and gingival diseases and treatments. The outstanding physician of the Timurid period was Borhān Nafīs (q.v.); in his lengthy *Šarḥ al-asbāb wa'l-ʿalāmāt*, a commentary on an earlier *Ketāb al-asbāb wa'l-ʿalāmāt* by Najm-al-Dīn Samarqandī, he discussed in detail the anatomy of teeth and associated nerves and the causes of loosening and loss of teeth, discoloration, and abscesses at the roots. He recommended bloodletting and cupping for toothache and mentioned a "popular antidote" composed of castor (*jond-e bīdastar*; see BEAVER), asafetida (*ḥaltīt*), pepper, ginger, opium, honey, and *felūnīā* (*Philanium romanum*; henbane?; see Schlimmer, pp. 227, 456-57), which people rubbed on sore teeth or pressed into cavities (fols. 157-64).

From that time until the beginning of the Qajar period detailed information on dentistry in Persia is not available, probably owing to a general stagnation of scientific activity and reluctance to innovate in the Safavid and ensuing periods. Particularly in medicine Persians were content to rely on earlier authorities. Unlike ophthalmology dentistry never became a separate specialty before the modern period and was practiced mainly by physicians. There is no evidence before the Safavid period that barbers and masseurs performed dental work and minor surgery; professional physicians and surgeons had apparently been the only providers of dental treatment. Under the Safavids and long afterward, however, barbers and masseurs did perform dental work, especially extractions (Elgood, 1951, pp. 143, 249). Nevertheless, some contemporary medical writings did touch on dental matters. Moḥammad Heravī, in his medical dictionary, written in both Arabic and Persian, described the properties of a number of drugs used in dental treatment (s.vv. *sandarūs*, *ʿāqerqarḥā*). Yūsof Heravī, who was apparently his son and wrote on medical subjects in prose and verse, advised on treatments for various diseases of the teeth and gums in his best known work, *Ṭebb-e yūsofī* (comp. Herāt, 917/1511; pp. 46-50). Ḡīāṯ-al-Dīn Eṣfahānī discussed these diseases in his *Merʾāt al-ṣeḥḥa fi'l-ṭebb* (Tehran University, Central library, ms. no. 293) and recommended treatment of tooth decay by removal of the decayed matter with a sharp instrument and filling of the cavity with a special substance (Elgood, 1970, p. 143). The outstanding physician of the Safavid period was Moḥammad Ḥosaynī Nūrbaḵš, whose *Ḵolāṣat al-tajāreb* was used as a medical textbook for many years in Persia, India, and the Ottoman empire. It embodies some of his own research and clinical experience. He described in detail such ailments as receding, loosening, and bleeding of the gums; caries (*kerm-ḵordagī*); and loosening and loss of teeth, discussing causes and prescribing treatments. For various kinds of toothache he recommended narcotics, fumigation, and cauterization and for certain severe cases injection of a few drops of nitric acid (*tīzāb*) mixed with opium into the cavity; he cautioned, however, that no acid should touch the gums (fols. 189-92).

The medical writings of the Zand period have hardly been studied, but there are passages on dentistry in the manuscripts of ʿEmād-al-Dīn Maḥmūd Šīrāzī's *Manāfeʿ al-tašrīḥ* and Ḥakīm Moḥammad-Hāšem ʿAlawī Khan's *Šarḥ-e mūjaz bar al-Qānūn* (cf. marginal notes to his *Šarḥ al-asbāb wa'l-ʿalāmāt*), Mīrzā Ḥakīm Naṣr's *Asās al-ṣeḥḥa* and *Šefāʾ al-asqām*, and Ḥakīm Sayyed Moḥammad-Ḥosayn Šīrāzī's *Majmaʿ al-jawāmeʿ* (Mīr, pp. 72, 73, 85-86, 192, 197).

In the Qajar period dentists at first held fast to the old methods but later, as more and more Persians acquired knowledge of European medicine, they began to change. Although such well-known medical writers of the early years as Mīrzā Aḥmad Tonokābonī, physician to Fatḥ-ʿAlī Shah (1212-50/1797-1834) and author of *Moṭleb al-soʾāl* and *Borʾal-sāʿa* (pp. 77-78, 206-07), and Fīlsūf-al-Dawla Kāẓem Raštī, author of *Ḥefẓ al-ṣeḥḥa*, did occasionally deviate from traditional practice, Persian acquaintance with European medicine seems to have begun after *Kīmīā'l-šefāʾ* had been translated from Turkish into Persian by Moḥammad-ʿAlī Khan Šīrāzī in 1246/1830 (Dānešpažūh, in Ebn Hendū, p. 202).

It is, however, difficult to give a date for the actual introduction of modern dental practice in Persia. The first European surgeons posted to Persia by the British East India Company (q.v.), for example, Andrew Jukes and John McNeill, probably performed dental, as well as general, surgery. The first mention of false teeth occurs in a letter dated 24 Ḏu'l-ḥejja 1273/15 August 1856, addressed by the grand vizier, Mīrzā Āqā Khan Nūrī, to the special Persian envoy to Europe Farroḵ Khan Amīn-al-Dawla (q.v.), in which he instructed the latter to engage and bring to Persia a "reliable doctor for making substitute teeth" (Amīn-al-Dawla, II, p. 178). No mention of such a doctor has yet been found in the sources, but only four years later, in 1277/1860, the shah's personal physician Dr. Joseph Tolozan brought from Paris a dental technician, "Sāpīvafor"), who remained in Persia for many years and received the honorific Mosannen-al-Salṭana. He not only made dentures but also taught the technique in Tehran (Eʿtemād al-Salṭana, *Rūz-nāma-ye ḵāṭerāt*, p. 881; Hedāyat, p. 69; Maḥbūbī Ardakānī, p. 376). According to Eʿtemād-al-Salṭana, the first "tooth-making workshop" was opened in the reign of Nāṣer-al-Dīn Shah (p. 126). During this period Mīrzā ʿAlī Doktor, French-trained and a teacher of medicine and anatomy at Dār al-fonūn (q.v.), incorporated material on oral and dental diseases and European methods of treatment in his textbook (pp. 224-25); Mīrzā Abu'l-Ḥasan Khan Doktor, also a teacher at Dār al-fonūn and head of the government hospital, translated a book on anatomy that included the structure and physiology of the teeth (*Tašrīḥ*, Tehran, 1308/1891, pp. 45-48). These books represent the first efforts to propagate modern dentistry in Persia. Sufferers of toothache from all classes, however, continued to have recourse to barbers, goldsmiths, and druggists for extractions, fillings, and medication (Najmī, pp. 201-02; Sīmjūr, p. 12) until the enactment of the Medical practice law of 1339/1921, which provided that only those holding licenses from the Ministry of education could practice dentistry (Komīsīūn, II, p. 1406).

At about the same time two foreign dentists, Drs. Melczarski, a Pole, and Stump, an Austrian, arrived in Persia to treat patients and to train Persian dentists. In 1300 Š./1921 Dr. Moḥsen Sayyāḥ, apparently the first fully qualified Persian dentist, returned to the country and, together with a Dr. Stepanian, trained in the United States, was licensed by the Ministry of education to initiate classes to train dental technicians. Together these men laid the foundations of scientific dental education in Persia (Maḥbūbī Ardakānī, p. 376; Sīmjūr, p. 14; Golparvar, p. 47).

After the accession of Reżā Shah (1304-20 Š./1925-41) plans for training dentists were outlined in a report by the Health department (*Dovvomīn rāport-e šeš-māha-yeṣeḥḥīya-ye koll*, 1305 Š./1926, pp. 4-5), and under regulations approved by the High council of education (Šūrā-ye ʿālī-e maʿāref) in the summer of 1307 Š./1928 the government medical college (Madrasa-ye ʿālī-e ṭebb) in Tehran was required to include courses on oral and dental diseases in its curriculum (Maḥbūbī Ardakānī, p. 262). In 1309 Š./1930 a college of dentistry (Madrasa-ye ʿālī-e dandān-pezeškī), was attached to the medical college, offering a five-year diploma course; the first class included fifteen candidates. Melczarski was the first director and Sayyāḥ his deputy. The staff was strengthened by the addition of Dr. Ašot Haratūnīān and Dr. Šahrīār Salāmat, who had studied under Melczarski. Haratūnīān also found time to complete the diploma course and afterward served for many years as a professor and associate dean in the Faculty of dentistry at Tehran University (Golparvar, p. 49).

During those early years such equipment as pedal drills and vulcanizers for hardening rubber compounds came into common use in Persia, replacing pincers, files, forceps, and cauterizing rods (Sīmjūr, pp. 16-18).

Under Sayyāḥ, who succeeded Melczarski as director in 1313 Š./1934, the school was incorporated as a department in the Faculty of medicine when Tehran University was established in the same year. The first professors in the department were Sayyāḥ, oral diseases and dental anatomy; Dr. Maḥmūd Sīāsī, oral and dental therapy and hygiene; Dr. Ḥasan Rīāżī, periodontics and orthodontics; Haratūnīān, dental technology; Dr. Ḥaydar Sarḵoš, denture fitting; and Dr. Aḥmad Farhād, radiology (Sīmjūr, p. 19). Beginning in the summer of 1316 Š./1937 applicants for admission were required to hold secondary-school diplomas. University statutes enacted in autumn of the same year provided that a number of dental students should be selected annually for training in the denture laboratory. In 1317 Š./1938 the department set up a clinic for oral and dental diseases (*Rāhnemā-ye dānešgāh* 1, 1317-18 Š./1938-39, pp. 16, 32, 54).

In the academic year 1355 Š./1956 the department of dentistry was detached from the Faculty of medicine and established as a separate faculty with Sayyāḥ as its first dean (Maḥbūbī Ardakānī, pp. 377, 379; Golparvar, p. 49; Komīsiūn, II, p. 1441); it comprised departments of orthodontics, prosthodontics, dental surgery, practical dentistry, and oral diseases. In 1338 Š./1959 a school of dental nursing, offering a two-year course, was added. New chairs of dental anatomy, dental injuries, prosthodontics, periodontics, and surgery of the jaw and face were established in September 1961 (Bīnā, p. 74). In 1344 Š./1965 a two-year diploma course in oral hygiene was instituted (Maḥbūbī Ardakānī, pp. 377-78). A new building was opened on the Tehran University campus the next year, and subsequently the faculty established dental wards, with trained specialists and modern equipment, in most of the hospitals affiliated with Tehran University.

Several other universities also established faculties of dentistry: the National University (Dānešgāh-e mellī) in Tehran in 1344 Š./1965, Pahlavī University in Shiraz in 1348 Š./1969, and Isfahan University in 1354 Š./1975. Dental departments in private hospitals and clinics and individual dentists also contributed to improving standards of oral and dental health in the larger cities and provincial capitals. In remote towns and villages, however, dental surgery and extractions are still performed by general practitioners.

Traditional methods, handed down from father to son, remain in use among isolated communities, where modern doctors rarely if ever visit. In Lorestān, for example, the following treatments for toothache have been recorded in modern times: rubbing ground cloves, animal fat, or bark of the wild plum on the base of a sore tooth; cauterizing cavities with a red-hot packing needle; putting soot from an oil lamp on the tooth; and burning paper in an enameled bowl and smearing the resulting soot on the tooth with a piece of cotton cloth (Asadīān Ḵorramābādī et al., p. 262).

As already mentioned, manufacture of false teeth was introduced in Persia in the time of Nāṣer-al-Dīn Shah. After World War I the industry expanded under the tutelage of Melczarski. Most Persian dental technicians and denture fitters in Persia today were trained by him and his successors, and they continue to train apprentices who then set up independently after passing licensing tests administered by the Ministry of health (Wezārat-e behdāšt). Some of them also illegally extract and fill teeth and fit crowns.

Bibliography: (For cited works not found in this bibliography, see "Short References.") ʿAlī b. ʿĪsā Ahvāzī, *al-Kāmel le'l-ṣenāʿa/al-Ṭebb al-malekī*, Būlāq, 1294/1877. Moʿtamad-al-Aṭebbāʾ Farroḵ Khan Amīn-al-Dawla, *Majmūʿa-ye asnād wa madārek-e Farroḵ Ḵān Amīn-al-Dawla (Ḡaffārī)*, ed. K. Eṣfahānīān and Q. Rowšanī, 2 vols., Tehran, 1347 Š./1968. M. Asadīān Ḵorramābādī et al., *Bāvarhā wa dānestahā dar Lorestān wa Īlām*, Tehran, 1358 Š./1979. Avicenna (Ebn Sīnā), *al-Qānūn fi'l-ṭebb* III, Tehran, 1343/1925. Š. Bīnā, "Gozāreš," *Majalla-ye Dāneškada-ye dandān-pezeškī-e Dānešgāh-e Tehrān* 11, 1355 Š./1976, pp. 73-74. Abū Rayḥān Bīrūnī, *Ketāb al-ṣaydana*, tr. Abū Bakr b. ʿAlī Kāšānī, ed. M. Sotūda and Ī. Afšār, Tehran, 1358 Š./1979. Abū Bakr Aḵawaynī Boḵārī, *Hedāyat al-motaʿallemīn*, ed. J. Matīnī, Mašhad, 1344 Š./1965. Ebn Abī Oṣaybeʿa, *ʿOyūn al-anbāʾ fī ṭabaqāt al-aṭebbāʾ* I, Cairo 1299/1881. Abu'l-Faraj Ebn Hendū, *Meftāḥ al-ṭebb wa menhāj al-ṭollāb*, ed. M.-T. Dānešpažūh, Tehran, 1368 Š./1989. C. Elgood, *A Medical History of Persia and the Eastern Caliphate*, Cambridge, 1951. Idem, *Safavid Medical Practice*, London, 1970. Gīāt-al-Dīn Eṣfahānī, *Merʾāt al-ṣeḥḥa fi'l-ṭebb*, Tehran University, Central library, ms. no. 293. M.-Ḥ Eʿtemād-al-Salṭana, *al-Maʾāter wa'l-āṯār*, Tehran, 1307/1889. Fīlsūf-al-Dawla Kāẓem b. Moḥammad Raštī, *Ḥefẓ al-ṣeḥḥa*, Tehran, 1304/1887. M.-T. Golparvar, *Tārīḵ-e ʿelm jehat-e dānešjūyān-e dandān-pezeškī*, Tehran, 1366 Š./1987. M. Hedāyat, *Ḵāṭerāt wa ḵaṭarāt*, Tehran, 1363 Š./1984. Moḥammad b. Yūsof Heravī, *Baḥr al-jawāher*, Tehran, 1288/1871. Yūsof b. Moḥammad Heravī, *Ṭebb-e yūsofī*, Lucknow, 1294/1877. Bahāʾ-al-Dawla Moḥammad Ḥosaynī Nūrbaḵš, *Ḵolāṣat al-tajāreb*, Tehran University, Central library, ms. no. 1400. Esmāʿīl Jorjānī, *al-Aḡrāż al-ṭebbīya wa'l-mabāḥeṯ al-ʿalāʾīya*, facs. ed., Tehran, 1345 Š./1966. Idem, *Ḏaḵīra-ye ḵvārazmšāhī*, facs. ed. ʿA.-A. Saʿīdī Sīrjānī, Tehran, 1355 Š./1976. Komīsīūn-e mellī-e Yūnesko (UNESCO) dar Īrān, *Īrānšahr*, 2 vols., Tehran, 1343 Š./1964. Ḥ. Maḥbūbī Ardakānī, *Tārīḵ-e taḥawwol-e Dānešgāh-e Tehrān*, Tehran, 1350 Š./1971. E. K. Malvin, *Dentistry. An Illustrated History*, New York, 1985. M.-T. Mīr, *Pezeškān-e nāmī-e Pārs*, Shiraz, 1348 Š./1969. Mīrzā ʿAlī Doktor, *Jawāher al-ḥekma*, Tehran, 1304/1887. Abū Manṣūr Mowaffaq-al-Dīn ʿAlī Heravī, *Ketāb al-abnīa ʿan ḥaqāʾeq al-adwīa*, ed. A. Bahmanyār and Ḥ. Maḥbūbī Ardakānī, Tehran, 1347 Š./1968. Borhān-al-Dīn Nafīs Kermānī (Borhān Nafīs), *Šarḥ al-asbāb wa'l-ʿalāmāt*, Tehran University, Central library, ms. no. 6354. M. Najmābādī, *Tārīḵ-e ṭebb dar Īrān pas az Eslām*, Tehran, 1353 Š./1974. N. Najmī, *Dār al-ḵelāfa-ye Tehrān*, Tehran, 1356 Š./1977. Abū Bakr Moḥammad b. Zakarīā Rāzī, *Borʾ al-sāʿa*, tr. A. Ṭabīb Tonokābonī, Tehran, 1326/1908. Idem, *Man lā yaḥẓoroho'l-ṭabīb*, Tehran, 1334 Š./1945. Idem, *al-Ḥāwī fi'l-ṭebb*, 22 vols., Hyderabad, 1955. K. Sāmarrāʾī, *Moḵtaṣar taʾrīḵ al-ṭebb al-ʿarabī*, Baghdad, 1984. K. Sīmjūr, "Tārīḵča-ye dandān-pezeškī," *Majalla-ye dandān-pezeškī-e Dānešgāh-e Tehrān* 11, 1355 Š./1976, pp. 73-74. Najm-al-Dīn Maḥmūd b. Elyās Šīrāzī, *al-Ḥāwī fī ʿolūm al-tadāwī*, Tehran University, Central library, ms. no. 6356. ʿAlī b. Rabban Ṭabarī, *Ferdows al-ḥekma*, ed. M.-Z. Ṣeddīqī, Berlin, 1928. Mīrzā Aḥmad Tonokābonī, *Moṭleb al-soʾāl* and *Borʾ al-sāʿa*, Tehran, 1297/1880.

(ṢĀDEQ SAJJĀDĪ)

DEOBAND, country town northeast of Delhi (q.v.) in what is now the Saharanpur district of Uttar Pradesh, India, where an influential Dār al-ʿolūm was founded by a group of religious scholars in 1867 as an expression of a major religious reform movement partly inspired by British educational models. The goal was to train a class of religious scholars dedicated to a version of Islam stripped of many customary practices deemed deviant. The curriculum was based on the *dars-e neẓāmī* developed at the Farangī Maḥall in Lucknow in the 18th century, though with less emphasis on "rational" studies in favor of a thorough grounding in the Koran and Hadith. Although the Deobandis were originally apolitical, by the 1920s many of them supported the Indian nationalist movement and later opposed the creation of Pakistan.

As part of a 19th-century trend away from Persian in favor of modern vernaculars, Urdu, with its heavy admixture of Persian vocabulary and forms, was the language of instruction. In this respect the Deoband school led in establishing Urdu as the language of Indian Muslims. Many Arabic and Persian religious texts were translated into Urdu. Nevertheless, as Sufis, many of the teachers continued to cherish the great tradition of Persian mystical poetry. For example, Moḥammad Yaʿqūb Nanawtawī, the first principal (*sadr modarres*; 1867-88) and a revered spiritual guide (*mūršīd*), was said to recite Rūmī's *maṯnawī*s silently, lest the whole forest burn from his passion (Metcalf, 1982, p. 166).

Bibliography: Z. Faruqi, *The Deoband School and the Demand for Pakistan*, Bombay, 1963. Y. Friedmann, "The Attitude of the Jamʿiyyat-i ʿulamaʾ-i Hind to the Indian National Movement and the Establishment of Pakistan," in G. Baer, ed., *The ʿUlamaʾ in Modern History. Studies in Memory of Professor Uriel Heyd*, Israeli Oriental Society, Asian and African Studies 7, Jerusalem, 1971, pp. 157-83. B. D. Metcalf, *Islamic Revival in British India. Deoband, 1860-1900*, Princeton, N.J., 1982.

(BARBARA DALY METCALF)

DEPORTATIONS, forced transfers of population from one region to another. Deportations should be distinguished from other, somewhat similar sanctions that may occur together with them, for example, expropriation and massacre, exile of individuals and their immediate families or adherents, enslavement or military conscription of conquered peoples, and forced sedentarization of nomads.

i. *In the Achaemenid period.*
ii. *In the Parthian and Sasanian periods.*
iii. *In the Islamic period.*

i. IN THE ACHAEMENID PERIOD

The practice of uprooting whole communities and transplanting them in distant lands is well attested in ancient times, particularly in Mesopotamia (Oded, pp. 33 ff.). The Achaemenids adopted the same practice whenever a particular people was too troublesome or revolted after subjugation (Grosso) and occasionally even when craftsmen of an industrious nation fell into their hands. Cambyses (q.v.) deported to Susa 6,000 Egyptians together with their king, Amyrtaius, and many artisans (Ctesias, *Persica* 13.30; Diodorus, 1.46, 4). Darius I (q.v.) established Barcaean captives from northwestern Africa in a village in Bactria, which was still flourishing in Herodotus' time (Herodotus, 4.204). He also settled Peonians of Thrace in Asia Minor, though most of them returned during the Ionian revolt (Herodotus, 5.14-15, 5.17, 5.98). Other instances include the deportation of Milesians to Ampé at the mouth of the Tigris (Herodotus, 6.20), of Carians and Sitacemians to Babylonia (Arrian, *Anabasis* 3.8, 5, 11.5; cf. Shahbazi, p. 245), of Eretrians to Ardericca in Elam (Herodotus, 6.119; Philostratus, *Vita Apollonii* 1.24), of Beotians to the Tigris region (Diodorus, 17.110), and of Sidonian prisoners sent by Artaxerxes III (q.v.) to his palaces at Susa and Babylon (Grayson, p. 114).

Mass deportations were in fact an effective means of procuring craftsmen and unskilled labor. Darius I mentioned (DSf 45-55; Kent, *Old Persian*, pp. 143) the use of Median, Egyptian, Babylonian, and Sardian artisans in the construction of his palace at Susa. There is no record that these deportees were ill treated. They were given land and allowed to preserve their languages and cultures, but they could not travel freely and were subject to taxation and the corvée (Herodotus, 2.204, 6.119; Diodorus, 17.110; cf. Narain, pp. 2-5). Their precise legal status and degree of dependence in this early period are not always clear, however.

Bibliography. (For cited works not found in this bibliography, see "Short References.") A. K. Grayson, *Assyrian and Babylonian Chronicles*, Locust Valley, N.Y., 1975. F. Grosso, "Gli deportati in Persia," *Rivista di filologia e di istruzione classica* 86, 1958, pp. 350-75. A. K. Narain, *The Indo-Greeks*, Oxford, 1957. B. Oded, *Mass Deportations and Deportees in the Neo-Babylonian Empire*, Wiesbaden, 1979. R. G. Penella, "Scoplianus and the Eretrians in Cissia," *Athenaeum* 52, 1974, pp. 295-300. A. S. Shahbazi, "Darius' *Haft-Kišvar*," in H. M. Koch and D. N. MacKenzie, eds., *Kunst, Kultur und Geschichte der Achämenidenzeit und ihr Fortleben*, Berlin, 1983, pp. 239-46.

(A. SHAPUR SHAHBAZI)

ii. IN THE PARTHIAN AND SASANIAN PERIODS

The Parthian period.

Although there were several mass deportations under the Achaemenids (see i, above), reports of such events from the Parthian period are rare. According to Isidore of Charax (Jacoby, *Fragmente*, no. 781, fr. 2.7), Phraates I (ca. 176-71 B.C.E.; incorrectly identified as Phraates II by Chaumont, 1988, p. 61 n. 28; cf. Justin, 41.5.9) settled the Mards in Charax, which had been founded near Rhages/Ray by the Seleucids. They may have been transported again, for Pliny (*Naturalis Historia* 6.47) located them on the northeastern borders of the Parthian empire.

After the defeat of Crassus at Carrhae (q.v.) in May 53 B.C.E. 10,000 troops were supposed to have been taken prisoner (Plutarch, *Crassus* 31.7) and settled in Alexandria Margiana (later Marv; Pliny, *Naturalis Historia* 6.47; incorrectly identified as Seleucia by Solinus, 48.3; cf. Justin, 42.4.4; Cassius Dio, 40.27.4). Horace (3.5.5-8) reported that the deportees married native women and entered the service of the Parthians (cf. de Plinval); whether or not they were forced into service is uncertain (pace Wolski, citing Velleius Paterculus, 2.82.5, and Florus, 2.20.4). N. V. Pigulevskaja assumed that they must have helped to guard the Parthian borders in the east, and G. A. Pugachenkova considered that they had participated in fortifying the city (Frumkin, p. 146). The hypothesis that some of these legionnaires fled to China, became soldiers for the Hsiung-nu, and founded the city of Li-Jien (Li-jun; Dubs; Ferguson, pp. 599-601; Dauge) should be viewed with caution.

It is not known how many of the Roman prisoners taken in the war between Antony (q.v.) and the Parthians in 36 B.C.E. suffered deportation (Plutarch, *Antony* 50.1: 24,000 casualties). The peace treaty concluded in 20 B.C.E. included a provision that the legion standard and the prisoners be returned (Cassius Dio 53.33.2; cf. 49.24.5), though most of them must have died in the interim. In Roman propaganda the return was celebrated as a major victory (e.g., Augustus' claim of spoils in the so-called *Res Gestae* 29; Brunt and Moore; cf. Pompeius Trogus' exaggerated report in the Epitome of Justin, 42.5.11, from which it would be possible to conclude incorrectly that the captives had been settled throughout the Parthian empire). Cassius Dio (q.v.; 54.8.1) described prisoners who had committed suicide from shame or who did not wish to return.

Strabo (11.14.15) mentioned that the Armenian king Tigranes the Great (r. from ca. 95 B.C.E.), in order to populate his newly established capital, Tigranocerta (Tigranakert), deported the inhabitants of twelve Greek cities that he had destroyed (11.14.15, 12.2.9; Pauly-Wissowa VIA/1, col. 982; for the site of Tigranocerta, see Whitby, p. 217). Appian (*Mithridatica* 67) reckoned the total number of these deportees at 300,000. Plutarch (*Lucullus* 21.4, 26.1) mentioned masses of people transported from Cilicia and Cappadocia and of Arabs (Skēnitai) resettled in northern Mesopotamia for reasons of commercial policy (cf. Pliny, *Naturalis Historia* 6.142; Manandian, 1963, p. 43); they included inhabitants of Adiabene, Assyria, and Gordyene, whom Tigranes forcibly settled in Tigranocerta. After the invasion of the city by L. Licinius Lucullus in 69 B.C.E., apparently with the help of the Cilicians settled there (Cassius Dio, 36.2.3; but cf. Manandian, 1963, pp. 119-20), the deported Greeks were permitted to return to their homes (Strabo, 12.2.9). The reports of this episode transmitted by Moses of Khorene (2.56; tr. Thomson, p. 199) from Artašês are not useful.

Great skepticism should also be adopted toward the reports by Faustus that Tigranes had deported the entire Jewish population of Palestine to Armenia (ed. Patkanean, pp. 145-46; tr. Garsoian, p. 175; cf. Widengren). Moses' version, which was based on that of Faustus, is still more fantastic (2.19; tr. Thomson, pp. 155-58 and n. 8, on the supposed deportation of the residents of Marisa; cf. Widengren, p. 138), as is the passage in which he claimed the presence of large numbers of inhabitants of Ptolemais in Palestine among the captives (2.14; tr. Thomson, pp. 152-53; pace Manandian, 1965, pp. 62-66).

The Sasanian period.

Reports of deportations in the Sasanian period are scattered among sources of varying reliability and in a number of different languages. It is therefore preferable to begin by establishing the facts that can be gleaned from the sources.

Šāpūr I (240-70). In his inscription on the Kaʿba-ye Zardošt at Naqš-e Rostam Šāpūr I declared that he had defeated the Roman emperor Valerian and deported him with the pretorian guards and the officers of the Roman army to Persis (260; Back, ŠKZ, Mid. Pers. l. 15, Parth. l. 11, Gk. l. 25; cf. Kettenhofen, pp. 97-99). Ṭabarī (I, p. 827) claimed that Valerian worked on construction of the dam at Tostar, the ruins of which can still be seen today (cf. Dīnavarī, ed. Guirgass, p. 49; Ṯaʿālebī, *Ḡorar*, p. 527, erroneously attributing foundation of the city to Šāpūr II). Šāpūr also mentioned people from the Roman empire (Anērān) whom he had carried off as booty and "settled in the empire of Ērān, in Persis, in Parthia, Ḵūzestān, in Āsōristān (q.v.; Iraq) and in all the other provinces where we and our forefathers and ancestors had royal estates" (Back, ŠKZ, Mid. Pers. ll. 20-21; Parth. ll. 15-16; Gk. ll. 34-35). The Arabic *Chronicle of Seert* (pp. 220-23) includes mention of the provinces of Iraq, Ḵūzestān, and Fārs, as well as cities founded by Šāpūr's father, Ardašīr I (q.v.; 224-40), which he rebuilt and populated with Roman captives: Šāḏ-Šāpūr, identical with Dayr Meḵrāq in the province of Mēšān; Bīšāpūr (q.v.) in Fārs (cf. Ebn Qotayba, p. 654; Ṯaʿālebī, *Ḡorar*, p. 494; Maqdesī, *Badʾ* III, p. 157; *Acta Martyrum* II, p. 208); and Wuzurg-Šāpūr, later known as ʿOkbarā (Ar. Marw-Ḥābūr; cf. Seybold, p. 745). Šāpūr was also said to have rebuilt the ruined city of Gondēšāpūr, near the modern village of Šāhābād, and settled Roman prisoners there (cf. Ṭabarī, I, pp. 826-27; Yaʿqūbī, *Taʾrīḵ*, p. 180; Dīnavarī, ed. Guirgass, p. 48; Ebn Qotayba, p. 654; Ḥamza, I, p. 49; Maqdesī, *Badʾ* III, p. 157; Ṯaʿālebī, *Ḡorar*, p. 494; Yāqūt, *Boldān* II, p. 130), but no archeological traces of an earlier settlement have been found (Adams and Hansen, pp. 53-54). He called it Wēh Antiōk Šāpūr (Ṭabarī, I, p. 831: Beh-az-andīw-Sābūr; *Chronicle of Seert*, p. 221: Anṭīšābūr, with the gloss *ant badal Sābūr*; cf. Delehaye and Peeters, p. 387 n. 6; Honigmann and Maricq, pp. 21 n. 1, 46 n. 3; see BĒṮ LAPAT).

In the *Chronicle of Seert* it is reported that Šāpūr allocated agricultural land and living quarters to the deportees, among whom were many Christians; indeed, the spread of Christianity in the Sasanian empire was correctly attributed to his deportations (p. 221). In Rēw-Ardašīr (Rīšahr; Ar. text, p. 222:

Yarānšahr) in Fārs Christians were supposed to have built two churches in the time of Šāpūr I, one for the Romans and one for the Carmanians (al-Karmānūn; emended by Seybold, p. 745, to al-Šoryānūn, but cf. Delehaye and Peeters, p. 388 n. 2).

According to Zosimus (1.27.2), after the conquest of Antioch (q.v.) during Šāpūr's first campaign (probably in 253; Balty: 252) a portion of the inhabitants was carried off, along with vast quantities of booty; for captured clerics, cf. Baldus, pp. 257-59; Peeters, 1924, p. 292). The inhabitants of Hatra had already been carried off by the Sasanians when the 4th-century author Ammianus Marcellinus described the place as "an old city, long deserted" (*Res Gestae* 25.8.5); the same must have been true of Dura-Europos (q.v. i) on the Euphrates, which Ammianus also referred to as deserted (23.5.8; on the controversial dating of the conquest, see MacDonald, pp. 45-68). After the conquest of Nisibis Šāpūr is supposed to have killed the soldiers and taken prisoners (Ṭabarī, I, p. 826; cf. Kettenhofen, 1982, pp. 44-46). Eutychius (Saʿīd b. Baṭrīq) described this event in greater detail without inspiring greater credence (CSCO L, pp. 108 l. 15-110 l. 4); he also specifically referred to the deportation of the inhabitants, though alluding only briefly to deportations from other cities of the Roman east. It is difficult to place in historical context the error-ridden report in the *Chronicle of Seert* that Šāpūr founded a city in Kaškar, which he called Ḥasar-Šābūr (emended to Ḵosrow-Šābūr by Seybold, p. 745; cf. Chaumont, 1988, p. 72 n. 82), and settled it with people from the east.

Šāpūr II (309-79). Only a few scattered fragmentary accounts of Šāpūr II's deportations survive. There is in fact a surprising report that the king, disregarding economic considerations and political advantage, ordered the execution of many inhabitants of the cities and fortresses that he captured during his decades of conflict with Rome, perhaps out of retaliation for stubborn resistance (e.g., Ammianus, *Res Gestae* 20.7.15). Ammianus mentioned deportations after the conquests of Bezabde/Bēṯ Zaḇdai (20.7.15; cf. *Acta Martyrum* II, pp. 316-24), the fortress of Reman/Busan (18.10.2; for identification, see Dillemann, p. 157), Ziata/Eğil (19.6.2), Amida (19.9.2; cf. Masʿūdī, *Morūj*, ed. Pellat, I, pp. 300-01; Ṯaʿālebī, *Ḡorar*, p. 530), and Singara/Senjār (Syr. Šīgār; 20.6.7-8; Ṯaʿālebī, *Ḡorar*, p. 530; *Acta Martyrum*, II, p. 154). About Ziata he said that many thousands were led away in slavery, but he alluded only briefly to their destinations; about the captives from Singara he noted only that they were transported to the farthest reaches of the empire. In the writings of Zonaras (13.8.3), Jacob of Edessa (Brooks, text, p. 269, tr., p. 310), and Eutychius (p. 121) there are only general references to these deportations. From Bezabde 9,000 men and women (exaggerated to 50,000 in the Gk. translation of *Acta Martyrum*; Wiessner, 1967, p. 116) are supposed to have been transported, with their bishop, priests, and deacons, to Ḵūzestān (*Acta Martyrum* II, pp. 316-24). Šāpūr allowed those who were prepared to worship the sun and moon and forswear their gods to settle at Dūrsak (in Bēṯ Darayē, q.v.), a site praised for its virtues; twenty-five were thus settled, and their offspring were supposedly still living there at the time that the *Acta Martyrum* were composed. Of the others 275 people were said to have been executed (cf. Fiey, 1970, pp. 372-73).

According to the Arab sources, captives were taken to Ḵūzestān: Ērān-Xwarrah-Šāpūr/Šūš; Ērānšahr-Šāpūr, the royal residence founded by Šāpūr II (Syr. Karkā də Lādān, to be identified with Ḥadīṯa, mentioned by Ḥamza, I, p. 53, the ruined site of Ayvān-e Karḵa); and Tostar/Šūštar (Ṭabarī, I/2, pp. 840, 845; Ṯaʿālebī, *Ḡorar*, p. 530; Masʿūdī, *Morūj*, ed. Pellat, I, p. 301; Delehaye and Peeters, p. 288). According to Ṯaʿālebī, residents of Boṣrā and Ṭowāna (location unknown) were settled with residents of Singara and Amida at Tostar and Šūš, but he seems to have fallen into some confusion (Fiey, 1970, p. 140, erroneously attributing the deportation to Šāpūr I; cf. Ebn Qotayba, p. 654). Captives from different regions, for example, ʿArab, Šīgār, Bēṯ Zaḇdai, Arzōn, Qardū, and Armen (Armenia; *Acta Martyrum* II, p. 154), were supposed to have been settled in the city of Ērānšahr-Šāpūr and thirty families from each city of the empire mingled with them, in order to make it more difficult for them to flee to their homelands (*Acta Martyrum* II, p. 209).

Arab authors also knew about deportations within the Sasanian empire. According to Ṭabarī (I, p. 843; cf. Lieu, p. 498), 12,000 people of "good family" were transferred from Eṣṭaḵr, Isfahan, and other places to populate Nisibis, which had been ceded to Šāpūr II under the terms of the peace treaty with the Roman emperor Jovian in 363 (cf. Julian, 1.27A; Lieu, p. 498). According to the *History of Karḵā də Bēṯ Slōḵ*, the village of Tešʿīn (Syr. "ninety") was named for ninety families from Mēšān settled there by Šāpūr (II?; Hoffmann, p. 48; on the reliability of the sources, cf. Fiey, 1964). He deported Arab tribes without altering their tribal structure (Ṭabarī, I, pp. 839-40); the Taḡleb were settled in Dārīn and Ḵaṭṭ, ʿAbd-al-Qays and a few groups of Tamīm in Hajar, people from Bakr b. Wāʾel in Kermān, and Ḥanẓala in Ramalīya (Ḵūzestān; Ṭabarī I, p. 839) or Tawwaj in Fārs (Ṯaʿālebī, *Ḡorar*, p. 529, mentioning that their chiefs were settled in Pērōz-Šāpūr; Caskel, p. 962).

Faustus furnished a wealth of dubious "information" on deportations from Armenia (though accepted without question by Grousset, pp. 144-45). The numbers given arouse suspicion, as do grotesque exaggerations, for instance, the claim that "men without number were carried off by elephants, and tender young boys too numerous to count were led away into captivity" (ed. Patkanean, 4.24; cf. 4.25). Forty thousand families from the completely demolished city of Tigranakert were supposed to have been carried off into captivity (4.24). Although the Persians were unsuccessful in their siege of Artagerkʿ, they carried off men and cattle from the surrounding countryside (4.55). From Artašat the entire population, 9,000 Jewish and 40,000 Armenian families, was deported (4.55; for archeological findings, see Koshelenko, p. 69), from Vałaršapat 19,000 families, though the following passage (4.55) contains the contradictory report that the Persians killed all the adult males in the land and led only the women and children into captivity. From Ervandašat 20,000 Armenian and 3,000 Jewish families were deported, from Zarehawan in Bagrevand 5,000 Armenian and 8,000 Jewish families, from Zarišat 14,000 Jewish and 18,000 Armenian families, from Van 15,000 Armenian and 18,000 Jewish families, from Naxčavan/Naḵjavān (where all the captives were initially assembled) 2,000 Armenian and 16,000 Jewish families. These captives were resettled in Āsōristān and Ḵūzestān; of those left behind all the adults were supposedly killed in Šāpūr's camp at Zarehawan and the boys castrated and then deported to Persia (4.55; cf. Hewsen; cf. Moses of Khorene's reports, tr. Thomson, pp. 292-94, based on Faustus; see ARMENIA AND IRAN ii).

From Bahrām IV to Kavād I (388-531). According to the *Liber Calipharum* (CSCO IV, text, pp. 136-37, tr., pp. 106-07), the Roman populations of Sophene, Armenia, Mesopotamia, Syria, and Cappadocia, 18,000 in all, were captured and led into exile by the "Huns" in 395. When the prisoners reached the Sasanian empire the Persians freed them, settled them in Slōk (Wēh Ardašīr) and Kōkbā (Kōḵē), and provided them with food. Although their release is mentioned in the text, neither the reason for it nor the number involved is given (there is a lacuna in the text at this point). Yazdegerd I (399-420) allowed 1,330 to return home, but around 800 remained in Persia. The author of the text praised the king for his goodness and gentle treatment of the deportees.

Ṭabarī (I, p. 871) provided an entirely legendary account of the advance of Bahram V (q.v.; 420-38) into southern Arabia, a great bloodbath there, and the carrying away of many of the inhabitants as slaves.

In the time of Yazdegerd II (438-57) there were a number of deportations during the reprisals after the Armenian uprising. The treacherous Vasak of Siwnikʿ was said to have carried off children of the Mamikonians, Kamsarakans, and other families that had been involved in the revolt; they were later entrusted to those who would care for their interests (Pʿarpecʿi, text, pp. 75-76, tr., p. 300). The priests and leaders of the rebellious Armenians, whom Łazar Pʿarpecʿi named individually, were deported to the province of Gorgān; later, when Yazdegerd was at war with the Hephthalites in the eastern empire, these captives were moved to the citadel at Nīšāpūr (Pʿarpecʿi, text, pp. 75, 86, 87, tr., pp. 300, 306, 307), where they were subsequently tortured and executed (Pʿarpecʿi, text, pp. 86-104, tr., pp. 306-16).

In the first year of his reign Pērōz (459-84) is supposed to have freed the Armenian nobles from their imprisonment and settled them in Areia; in his sixth year they were sent back to their homeland (Pʿarpecʿi, text, pp. 108-10, tr., pp. 319-20). It is not clear from where Ełišē, who was writing in the late 6th century, took his reports on the deportation of the populations of Artašat, Gaṙni, Ani, Artagerkʿ, Erkaynordkʿ, Arxni, Barjraboł, Xoranist, Caxanist, Ołakan, Arpʿaneal, Van, Gṙeal, Kapoyt, Orotn, and Vašakašat before the battle of Awarayr in 451 (tr. Thomson, p. 119; many of these place names are attested only in this text). The deportation, supposedly by Vasak, of priestly families from Gaṙni, Eramunkʿ, Drasxanakert, Vardanašat, the fortresses of Awšakan, Pʿaṙaxot, Sardeankʿ, the city of Jołakert, the fortress of Armavir, and the towns of Kuaš, Aruč, and Ašnak, as well as from Aragacotn and the city and province of Artašat is also known only from Ełišē's history. His report resembles in many respects that of Pʿarpecʿi, but his claim to be an eyewitness of the events is untrue; his history reflects much more clearly the prevailing point of view in the late 6th century, a clue to determining the period in which his text was written (tr. Thomson, pp. 18-19).

During the war with the Byzantine empire in the time of the emperor Anastasius Sasanian troops under Kavād I (488-531, with interruption) succeeded in capturing Theodosioupolis (modern Erzurum) and Amida (Christensen, p. 7). Constantinus, the military governor of Theodosioupolis, was deported to Persia (Zacharias Rhetor, 7.3; Michael the Syrian, 9.7) along with many others (cf. Malalas, 16.9; Theophanes, I, p. 144; Wright, p. 37). The conquest of Amida and the deportation of the population were mentioned frequently by both Byzantine and Arab authors (though there is no mention of deportations in the works of Evagrius, 3.37, and Georgius Cedrenus, p. 628; for confusion with Hamadān, see Eutychius, CSCO L, p. 191; Yāqūt, *Boldān* I, p. 194; cf. Nöldeke, *Geschichte der Perser*, p. 138 n. 3). Only Joshua the Stylite mentioned the number of deportees, more than 80,000; others were stoned outside the city walls, and still others suffered a miserable death. The old, the maimed, and those who had hidden themselves were not deported (pp. 42-43). According to Zacharias (7.4), the "nobles, all the high officials, and the craftsmen were transported into the Sasanian empire, accompanied by a Sasanian commander." The captives were taken to Rām-Kavād (later Arrajān, q.v.; Mid. Pers. *wyḥcʾmtʾ kwʾtʾ*, attested on a seal; Gignoux, p. 15 no. 1.3; cf. Sundermann, pp. 98-99; Ḥamza, I, p. 55: Beh az-Āmid Kavād; Dīnavarī, ed. Guirgass, p. 68: Abar-Qubāḏ; Yāqūt, *Boldān*, I, p. 194: Abaz-Qubāḏ) on the border between Ḵūzestān and Fārs (Ṭabarī, I, pp. 887-88; cf. Metzler, p. 198). According to Procopius (*De Aedificiis* 3.2.7), Mayyāfāreqīn had been spared by Kavād; the deportation of its inhabitants is mentioned only in Arabic sources (Dīnavarī, ed. Guirgass,

p. 68; Ṯaʿālebī, *Ḡorar*, pp. 594-95; Yāqūt, *Boldān* I, p. 194). Zacharias' report that Kavād's prisoners of war were returned to their homes was based on texts (or documents?) sympathetic to the Sasanians (7.5; cf. Procopius, *De Bello Persico* 1.7.34-35; Pauly-Wissowa, XXIII/1, col. 363). In 501-02 Kavād ordered the Lakhmid Noʿmān to enter Byzantine territory; he laid waste the area around Ḥarrān and Edessa (modern Urfa) and carried off 18,500 people (Joshua the Stylite, chap. 52; Wright, pp. 40-41). In the last year of Kavād's reign, and at his behest, the Lakhmid Monḏer III invaded Byzantine territory (Rothstein, pp. 79-81); Zacharias (8.5) described the advance to Hemesa/Ḥemṣ, Apamea, and the region of Antioch and the deportation of many prisoners. Theophanes (I, p. 178) and Jacob of Edessa (Brooks, pp. 298-99, 319) reported that the Saracens and Persians carried off booty and prisoners, whereas Malalas (18.32) mentioned only the associated destruction.

Ḵosrow I Anōšīravān (531-79). Ḵosrow I captured Antioch in 540; the city was completely destroyed, and royal treasures were carried away (John Lydus, 3.54; John of Ephesus, 6.4-5; Michael the Syrian, 9.4; cf. Procopius, *De Bello Persico* 2.9.16; Masʿūdī, *Morūj*, ed. Pellat, I, p. 307; *Chronicon Anonymum ad Annum 1234*, tr. CSCO CIX, p. 152; Sebeos confused Syrian Antioch with the city of the same name in Pisidia, p. 69, tr., p. 7; cf. ANTIOCH, p. 123). According to a single source, the inhabitants suffered little, however (*Chronicum Anonymum ad Annum 846*, CSCO III, p. 229; tr, CSCO IV, p. 174). Jacob of Edessa, on the other hand, knew of the deportation of prisoners of war from the cities of Sura, Beroea, Antioch, Apamea, Callinicum, and Batnai in Osrhoene (Brooks, text, pp. 300-01, tr., pp. 320-21) to Wēh Antīōk Ḵosrow/Rūmagān (Ar. Rūmīya), a city that Ḵosrow had founded in the vicinity of Ctesiphon (q.v.; Procopius, *De Bello Persico* 2.14.1: Antiocheia Chosroou; Ḥamza, I, p. 57: Beh-az-Andīv-e Ḵosrow); it is not clear whether it was identical with Māhōzē Ḥədattā, mentioned in the Syriac conciliar acts (see, e.g., Pauly-Wissowa, Supp. IV, col. 1116; Honigmann and Maricq, p. 46; cf. Chabot, p. 676; Fiey, 1967b, p. 37; see ARCHEOLOGY iv, p. 304). The most detailed information on the building of this city was provided by Procopius (*De Bello Persico* 2.14.1-4), who drew on a source friendly to the Sasanians, so that the reliability of certain details may well be debatable. Ṭabarī (I, pp. 898, 959-60) and Ṯaʿālebī (*Ḡorar*, pp. 612-14) elaborated this tradition, according to which the city was built on the plan of the Syrian metropolis and Ḵosrow did everything in his power to make the residents want to stay. Barāz, a Christian from Gondēšāpūr, is said to have been entrusted with the governorship. According to Procopius, the inhabitants were fed at the expense of the royal treasury. Baths, racetracks, and musical performances were also provided. The inhabitants were "the king's people," subject only to him; supposedly even an escaped slave who reached the city and was claimed as a relation by one of the residents could not then be repossessed (cf. Masʿūdī, *Morūj*, ed. Pellat, I, pp. 232-33; Dīnavarī, ed. Guirgass, p. 70; Eutychius, pp. 207-08; *Chronicle of Seert* 7.2).

On the other hand, John of Ephesus reflected the Roman point of view (6.4) in his reports of the deportation of an enormous number of prisoners under Ḵosrow I: In the year 573 the cities of Apamea and Daras (present-day Dara) were taken and their residents carried off in captivity (CSCO III, p. 230, tr., IV, p. 174: 98,000; Michael the Syrian, 10.9, Budge, I, p. 78: 90,000); the Sasanian general Āḏarmahān is supposed to have deported 292,000 people from Apamea and the surrounding area (6.6; cf. similar reports in CSCO CIX, pp. 161-62; Michael the Syrian, 10.9, Budge, I, p. 78, all based on John's report, though the numbers vary from 92,000 to 292,000). Elsewhere John (6.19) reckoned the total number of deportees from Daras, Apamea, and other, unnamed cities at 275,000. He gave no details on the destination of these captives, other than "the land of the Persians" (6.6, 6.19; cf. 6.14). In this connection Bar Hebraeus, whose reports are often unreliable, mentioned the conquest of Aleppo and the "bitter captivity" of the cities of Antioch, Aleppo, and Apamea (Budge, I, p. 74). Theophylact Simocatta (3.5.2-4) referred to the fortress of Giligerdōn, in which the residents of the conquered city of Daras were sheltered (for the location, see Kettenhofen, 1988, pp. 96-101). They were, however, rescued and brought back to the Byzantine empire (Photius, I, no. 65). Certainly belonging to the genre of hagiography is the story of 2,000 (300 in CSCO CIX, p. 162; Michael the Syrian, 10.10, Budge, I, p. 78; *Chronicle of Seert*, pp. 224-25, where the story is set in the time of Šāpūr I) beautiful virgins whom Ḵosrow selected as gifts for the heathen barbarians; in their Christian zeal they threw themselves into the river and drowned, in order to avoid being forced to betray their religion (John of Ephesus, 6.7; cf. Fiey, 1970, pp. 359-60).

Resettlement of tribes and peoples within the Sasanian empire during the reign of Ḵosrow I was frequently mentioned. He settled the people of the Bārez in different parts of the empire (Ṭabarī, I, p. 894; for the name, see Nöldeke, *Geschichte der Perser*, p. 157). He is supposed to have left only eighty of the people of Ṣūl alive and to have settled them in Šah-Rām-Pērōz, the seat of a Nestorian bishop (Ṭabarī, I, pp. 894-95; Guidi, 1889, p. 414; Markwart, *Ērānšahr*, p. 73). Ṭabarī (I, p. 895) also mentioned the resettlement of 10,000 people (Abḵāz, Banjar, Balanjar, Alān) in Azerbaijan and neighboring regions (cf. Nöldeke, *Geschichte der Perser*, p. 157; Altheim and Stiehl, 1954, pp. 138-39 and nn. 1-2). The people identified by Balāḏorī (*Fotūḥ*, pp. 194-95) as Sīāsījūn/Sīāsījīya (but cf. Kramers: *nešāstagān* "warrior"?) were resettled in Ḵosrow's newly built cities Šāberān, Masqaṭ, Bāb al-Abwāb

(Darband, q.v.), Dabīl (Arm. Dvin, q.v.), and Našawā/Naxčavan/Nakjavān and the castles of Wayṣ, Kelāb, and Sāhyūnis. Sogdians and Persians were resettled in the city of Soḡdabīl in Jorzān (Georgia; for location, see Minorsky, 1930, map 2; Christensen, *Iran Sass.*, p. 369). Ebn Ḵordāḏbeh's report (p. 30; cf. Altheim and Stiehl, 1954, p. 44) of Ḵosrow's deportation of members from every family (*az har ḵāna*) to Farḡāna is probably based on popular etymology.

Ḵosrow II Parvēz (590-628, with interruption). A few reports have survived from the time of Ḵosrow II, who conquered Jerusalem in May 614 and deported its population, along with the patriarch and the holy cross, to Ctesiphon (Peeters, 1924, p. 307). According to Sebeos (p. 116, tr., p. 69), 57,000 people were taken prisoner and 35,000 of them deported; later the king is supposed to have mercifully ordered the rebuilding of the city and the return of the prisoners, as well as expulsion of the Jews, but there is no factual basis for these reports (for anti-Jewish polemics, differing in detail, see, Theophanes, I, pp. 300-01; CSCO CIX, p. 178; Michael the Syrian, 11.1; for a report that 90,000 perished at the hands of the Jews, see *Georgius Cedrenus*, p. 715). An account of this deportation is preserved in Georgian and Arabic, though embellished with hagiographical details, including many for which historical evidence has still not been adduced (Graf; Peeters, 1923; CSCO CCII-CCIII). Eutychius' version (p. 216) is largely legendary.

Deportations from Mesopotamia occurred earlier than those from Jerusalem. According to the *Chronography* of Theophanes (I, pp. 293, 295), Daras was taken in the year 606, and an unspecified number of people were taken prisoner and carried off from Mesopotamia, Syria, Palestine, and Phoenicia. In 609 the Sasanians conquered Edessa and transplanted the residents to Sīstān and Khorasan (Bar Hebraeus, ed. and tr. J. B. Abbeloos and T. J. Lamy, II, Louvain, 1874, p. 125, apud Fiey, 1970, p. 63 n. 94); Jacob of Edessa barely mentioned the deportation but reported that the exiles returned after the murder of Ḵosrow (Brooks, text, pp. 306-07, tr., p. 323). In the *Chronicon Paschale* (I, p. 699) and Sebeos' history (Macler, pp. 61-62) only Edessa is mentioned as having fallen into the hands of the Persians. Theophanes (I, p. 299) reported the deportation of many thousands from Caesarea in Cappadocia (cf. Michael the Syrian, 11.1); Georgius Cedrenus (pp. 714-15) those from the cities of Asia, from Damascus (Theophanes, p. 300), and from "the whole of Egypt, Alexandria, and Libya to Ethiopia"; Jacob of Edessa (Brooks, pp. 306, 323) those from the "entire Roman empire to Bithynia, Asia, and the Black Sea"; Michael the Syrian (11.1) that of "prisoners without number." Many of these reports are unconfirmed, and some are very much exaggerated (e.g., Theophanes, I, p. 300).

After the conquest of Karin/Erzurum in 610 Bishop John led the deportees to Hamadān, which the king had granted to them (Macler, p. 63; cf. p. 36). Ṭabarī (I, p. 1003) referred only generally to this incident, noting that Sasanian troops conquered the Roman lands, killed the soldiers, and carried off the children into captivity.

Outstanding problems.

Many questions remain unanswered. In sources like the *Syriac Chronicle* the conquest of a city (see Guidi, 1891, p. 19) may be mentioned but not the deportation of its inhabitants; even when such deportations are reported the numbers given are unreliable (e.g., Faustus, ed. Patkanean, pp. 145-46; tr. Garsoian, p. 175). Many texts leave the impression that entire populations of towns and villages were carried off in captivity, but these reports are generally exaggerations, as is clear from the brief intervals separating the repeated deportations from Antioch in the mid-3rd century C.E. (see above). Only a few clues are available, however, to the criteria for selection (age, skills, etc.). Joshua the Stylite, for example, reported (chap. 53; Wright, pp. 42-43) that older and disabled people were exempted from the deportation from Amida in 503. According to the church history of Zacharias Rhetor (7.4), "the notables, all high officials, and the craftsmen were gathered and led away by a Sasanian governor" (cf. Rubin, 1960, n. 1038). According to one report, in 614, after the prisoners were questioned about their occupations, the skilled craftsmen were taken away; the remainder were forced to live under such harsh conditions that many perished (CSCO CCIII, pp. 16-17), which Paul Peeters (1924, p. 307) considered common practice among the Sasanians.

Although no generalizations are possible about the Parthian period, deportation of populations seems not to have been a common feature of royal policy. On the other hand, the Sasanians, who were engaged in great military struggles with Rome and Byzantium, seized upon such measures and continued to rely on them into the 7th century (pace Altheim and Stiehl, 1954, p. 24). Some scholars (e.g., Pigulevskaja, p. 125) even consider the prospect of capturing prisoners to have been the motivating force behind the military campaigns. Especially the peoples of the provinces along the eastern frontiers of the Roman empire must have endured several deportations. Among the places to which the prisoners were taken several provinces stand out: Under Šāpūr I the home province of Fārs and the region along the lower Tigris; under Šāpūr II, as under the Achaemenids (cf. Herodotus, 6.119), especially Ḵūzestān (for the only contrary report, see Ammianus, *Res Gestae* 20.6.7; cf. Ḥamza, I, p. 53: "in the country"); under Kavād I the border territory between Fārs and Ḵūzestān; under the two Ḵosrows Āsōristān. Settlement of new groups in these provinces was mentioned several times, and the purpose may have been to increase the population. It is even more difficult to learn from limited sources about the deportation of peoples within the Sasanian empire. Why, for example, were the Kadisēnoi deported to Giligerdōn (Theophylact, 3.5.5.) or herdsmen from Kermān to the district of Māsabaḏān (*Acta Martyrum* II, p. 322; cf. Fiey, 1969, p. 182; Procopius, *De Bello Persico* 2.28.17, 2.28.30). According to the *Acta Martyrum* (II, pp. 209-10), Šāpūr I gathered craftsmen from among his subjects, settled them, and erected for them a workshop beside his palace. The report that, after the conquest of Nisibis in 363 and the forced exile of the Roman population (Ammianus, *Res Gestae* 25.9.5-13), the city was settled by Persians is plausible; the same thing must have happened in neighboring cities.

It seems certain from many indications not only that families were kept together but also that larger groups (like residents of a single village or even a city) were resettled together. In Gondēšāpūr the clergymen from Antioch who had been deported there elected a successor to their late bishop (*Chronicle of Seert*, pp. 221-22; cf. Baldus, pp. 257-59). Also, although the picture painted by Procopius (*De Bello Persico* 2.14) is biased, the settlement of at least a large proportion of the deported Antiochenes in Rūmagān seems established, as Ḵosrow entrusted control of their affairs to Barāz, a Christian (Ṭabarī, I, pp. 959-60); the creation of a special quarter with five wards (see ANTIOCH, p. 124) calls to mind several later comparisons. John of Ephesus mentioned an address to more than 30,000 prisoners (6.19). That captives from different locations were settled in a single city is also clear from the report in the *Acta Martyrum* according to which thirty families from every city in the empire were settled at Karḵā ḏə Lāḏān, though the numbers are certainly exaggerated. Such measures were probably influenced by a desire to avoid a ghetto situation.

On practical arrangements for the transport of prisoners of war information is very poor. The *Dēnkard* (8.26, apud Christensen, *Iran Sass.*, p. 215) contains reports on the conduct of wars, but it does not provide any information on deportations. Ammianus Marcellinus (*Res Gestae* 19.9.2, 20.6.8) mentioned that the prisoners taken from Amida and Singara had their hands fastened behind their backs (cf. Eḷišē, tr. Thomson, p. 93), a practice that was already attested in the Near East in the 3rd century B.C.E. According to Eḷišē (tr. Thomson, p. 238), the princes deported after the battle of Awarayr (451) were chained hand and foot, but his text contains many exaggerated reports. In the *Chronicle* of Michael the Syrian (10.9) the fettering of men and women before their deportation following the conquest of Apamea in the 6th century was reported; according to the *Chronicon Anonymum ad Annum 1234*, the men were killed and the women and children put in chains. It was also reported that the Sasanian general Šahrvarāz sent the prisoners that he had taken in Syria to Ḵosrow II in chains (tr. CSCO CIX, pp. 162, 176; for reports of

individual clerics carried off in chains, see Bedjan, pp. 257-58, 264; cf. Peeters, 1946, pp. 154-59; CSCO CCIII, p. 22). Nevertheless, it is improbable that all prisoners of war were chained. Nor is there any information on the branding of deportees. That the expulsion of great masses of human beings from the conquered cities was accompanied by great privation is clear from Ammianus' compassionate description of the many infirm and elderly women who were among them; many faltered and seemed unlikely to survive, so that they were left behind with their calf muscles or hamstrings cut (*Res Gestae* 19.6.2.). A glimpse of the deportees' fate can be gained from the *Annals* of Zonaras: Prisoners received only scant daily rations, just enough for survival, and once a day they were led to water "like cattle" (12.23; cf. Lieu, p. 478). A report that Šāpūr I put prisoners to death on the return march in order to block a narrow valley that had previously been opened by draft animals (Zonaras, 12.23) is less believable and represents a literary convention. Cattle were taken along with the prisoners (Joshua the Stylite, chap. 52; Wright, pp. 40-41).

The sources provide no details on how deportees were transported, whether or not they were arrayed in a specific order, and what measures were taken to prevent escape; nor is it clear that they were allowed to carry cooking utensils or how provisions were obtained. Prisoners could not have been left to die in large numbers on the way, for the specific purpose of the deportation was to resettle them, in order to take advantage of their technical skills. The Sasanians were always quick to recognize the superior accomplishments of their enemies and to make use of them for their own purposes (Lieu, p. 478). Especially hydraulic engineers, metalworkers, irrigation specialists, construction workers, stonemasons, textile workers, physicians, teachers, and other skilled people were sought (cf. Faustus, ed. Patkanean, 5.4; Trever, p. 272). For example, Afsā (ʾpsʾy; Back, ŠVŠ 1. 9) the scribe, who had been born in Carrhae, must have been among the deportees who participated in construction of Šāpūr I's monument in Bīšāpūr; Greek letters found on it are further evidence of foreign participation (Ghirshman, 1938, p. 13; idem, 1962, figs. 180-86; Back, p. 381; pace Christensen apud Ghirshman, 1936, p. 128). The rectangular plan of this city (Ghirshman, 1962, fig. 176) confirms the influence of Roman prisoners; Gondēšāpūr and Ērānšahr-Šāpūr, founded by Šāpūr II in the 4th century (Vanden Berghe, pp. 66-67; Ghirshman, 1962, p. 180), were both, to judge from their plans, also laid out by Romans. Roman specialists laid out irrigation canals and were thus responsible for the economic development of Ḵūzestān, as has been confirmed by archeological evidence (Adams, 1962, fig. 5): The partially preserved dam at Šūštar, known today as Band-e Qaysar (Ṭabarī, I, p. 827; Nöldeke, *Geschichte der Perser*, p. 33 n. 2), as well as the bridges over the Āb-e Dez at Dezfūl (qq.v.) and over the Karḵa at Ērānšahr-Šāpūr, betray the use of Roman prisoners of war (Altheim and Stiehl, 1954, p. 22). Furthermore, elements of Roman iconography have been recognized in the Sasanian rock reliefs (Peeters, 1924, p. 299; Ghirshman, 1962, p. 159; for a contrary view, see BĪŠĀPŪR, p. 287) and traces of Roman building techniques even at Ṭāq-e Kesrā and in the monuments of Ṭāq-e Bostān (Fiey, 1967a, p. 400; ARCHEOLOGY iv, p. 304). Particularly when the technique was not of Persian origin, for example, in the floor mosaics at Bīšāpūr, the participation of foreigners is certain (cf. von Gall; Lieu, p. 479; Göbl, pp. 290-91). The story that olive trees were planted in Iraq by Roman prisoners (Ṭabarī, I, p. 845; Masʿūdī, *Morūj*, ed. Pellat, I, p. 299; Ṯaʿālebī, *Ḡorar*, p. 528) is entirely legendary, however (Nöldeke, *Geschichte der Perser*, pp. 56 n. 2, 66 n. 2). Unfortunately, the author of the *Chronicle of Seert* did not specify the origins of the people that Kavād I settled in new villages in Arbāyestān and employed in agricultural production; as they received permission to construct a church, they must have been Roman prisoners (p. 125).

In the time of Šāpūr II deported craftsmen included especially silk weavers and embroiderers (cf. Ṯaʿālebī, *Ḡorar*, p. 530; *Acta Martyrum* II, p. 209). He settled them almost exclusively in the fertile lands of Ḵūzestān, which were a center of the textile industry. Their numbers were augmented under Ḵosrow I, in whose reign the silk industry became so important that the empire was no longer limited to transit trade in silk, which it monopolized, but itself manufactured textiles for export (Pigulevskaja, pp. 159-69). Masʿūdī reported that, after the resettling of the deported Roman prisoners in Ḵūzestān, the manufacture of silk brocade (*al-dībāj al-tostarī*) and other kinds of silk surpassed that of linen and carpets (*Morūj*, ed. Pellat, I, p. 301; Ebn Ḥawqal, p. 256; Christensen, *Iran Sass.*, p. 127; Huart and Delaporte, p. 378; see BYZANTINE-IRANIAN RELATIONS, p. 594). Maqdesī (*Badʾ* III, p. 157) remarked on the flourishing of medicine at Gondēšāpūr and Tostar/Šūštar after the settlement of captives there (cf. Procopius, *De Bello Gothico* 8.10.11-14; Ṭabarī I, p. 845; *Chronicle of Seert* 7.2).

Urbanization and social conditions within the Persian empire were generally advanced by the captives' skills. Nevertheless, the state might agree to release them in exchange for ransom, which represented a considerable source of funds (see, e.g., ŠKZ, Parth. text l. 4, Gk. text l. 9; Back, p. 501 n. 163; Procopius, *De Bello Persico* 2.5.29-30, 2.13.2-6; cf. Altheim and Stiehl, 1954, p. 47).

The Sasanian kings did not consider the use of Roman captives as footsoldiers in the army; rather, because of these captives' skills, they could ease the task of Sasanian troops (Lieu, p. 478). The military purposes behind the resettlements within the empire are clear, as modern authors have correctly emphasized (Christensen, *Iran Sass.*, pp. 369-70; Altheim and Stiehl, 1954, pp. 138-39). It was Clément Huart's opinion that the Parthian king's resettlement of the Mards was intended to provide guards for the Caspian Gates (Huart and Delaporte, p. 322, though Isidore of Charax provided no basis for this conclusion). The creation of a professional army and the organization of border defenses similar to the Roman limes required the formation of numerous contingent forces. Ṭabarī mentioned (I, p. 894) the settlement of the Bārez in various places where they were to support the military; the Ṣūl were supposed to do the same at Šahrām-Pērōz, and other peoples were settled in the borderlands of the Caucasus in order to protect the Sasanian empire from invasion from the north (see, e.g., Procopius, *De Bello Persico* 2.28.17, 2.28.30). The settlement of Arab tribes in distant Bahrain (q.v.) and Kermān under Šāpūr II seems, on the other hand, to have been intended to populate regions with unattractive climates, while at the same time bringing them under control (cf. Ammianus, *Res Gestae* 20.6.7; Altheim and Stiehl, 1965, p. 361).

Legal and social status of prisoners.

The preserved texts provide very little information on the legal status of deported Roman prisoners. Ammianus (*Res Gestae* 19.6.2) and more often Procopius (*De Bello Persico* 1.7.32, 2.5.26, 2.9.14), as well as the author of the *Chronicle of Seert* (4.3) and Ṭabarī (I, p. 894), referred to the institution of slavery (*ʿobūdīya*; Christensen, *Iran Sass.*, p. 213; Downey, p. 544; Altheim and Stiehl, 1954, p. 48; Rubin, p. 330; for an opposing view, see Lieu, p. 481). According to Zacharias Rhetor, deportees were more correctly designated as "the king's prisoners of war" (7.4; Procopius, *De Bello Persico* 2.14.3: "the king's subjects"; cf. 2.26.4 for the Roman point of view). Ḵosrow I insisted on this designation and declared the prisoners subject to his authority alone. This arrangement seems already to have been the practice under Šāpūr I, for, according to his inscription (Back, ŠKZ), deportees were generally settled on fallow crown lands and in royal cities, which they helped to build. From one report by Procopius (*De Bello Persico* 2.14.4) it can be concluded that noble Persians also had the right to enslave prisoners but that, if the latter then escaped to Rūmagān and were claimed as relatives by residents there, they could not be repossessed by their owners. It cannot be determined from the sources whether the legal status of deportees was the same in all periods and in all places or in what form they paid taxes. They seem, however, not to have lived in oppressive conditions. When a prisoner returned to his homeland, his former legal status was restored according to the Roman doctrine of postliminium (cf. Ammianus, *Res Gestae* 19.9.6). On the numbers of those born in captivity in Persia there is no information (Lieu, p. 478).

In the *Chronicle of Seert* it is reported that Šāpūr I provided prisoners with land for cultivation and the use of living quarters (pp. 221, 223; cf. Mārī b. Solaymān, in Peeters, 1924, p. 292; Pigulevskaja, p. 127), but it cannot be determined whether they could own the land. From all appearances prisoners of war and their descendants did not play an active political role in the Sasanian state administration. During Šāpūr's reign they are supposed even to have enjoyed freedom of religion and to have had the right to build monasteries and churches (though the report is anachronistic as far as monasteries are concerned; *Chronicle of Seert*, p. 221). Accounts of the martyrdom of Pusai, descendant of a Roman prisoner of war, provide valuable clues: As a gifted craftsman, he was admitted to membership in a cooperative (Syr. *knūšyā)* that erected a workshop next to the governor's palace in Ērānšahr-Šāpūr. He was greatly honored and rewarded because of his skill and was named overseer of the workshop (Syr. *rēš ummānē*) and eventually of the workshops in all provinces of the empire (*Acta Martyrum* II, p. 210; cf. Wiessner, 1967, p. 168). Sozomenus called him overseer of all the royal workshops (2.11.1). In the longer account of the martyrdom of Simeon (Wiessner, 1967, p. 176) this official was called master of the royal workshops (Syr. *kārōgbeḏ*, explained in the text as *ʾahīḏ ummānē ḏə malkā*; *Patrologia Syriaca* I/2, cols. 773-76). In this capacity Pusai was ordered to visit the craftsmen in the city of Šāḏ-Šāpūr (*Acta Martyrum* II, p. 210). Whether or not these reports are reliable, they do suggest the heights to which one of "the king's subjects," the descendant of a deported Christian, might rise (cf. Wiessner, 1968; Pigulevskaja, pp. 159-61; Lieu, pp. 484-85). On the other hand, Procopius' description of the "Roman city" (Procopius, *De Bello Persico* 2.14.1-2) where a bath and a racetrack were erected and an especially refined life style provided must be treated with reserve, though it must also be assumed that captives received adequate provisions. Procopius' report (*De Bello Persico* 1.7.32-34) that Kavād I had humanely allowed the prisoners from Amida to return to their homes after a short time (cf. Zacharias Rhetor, 7.5.) also inspires a certain reserve. In the shorter account of the martyrdom of Simeon the mercy of Šāpūr II toward deportees is stressed (*Patrologia Syriaca* 1/2, col. 959). John of Ephesus, who wrote from the Roman point of view, emphasized the close watch kept on captives (p. 239; Fiey, 1967b, p. 27, characterizing the city as no less than a "labor concentration camp"). It is uncertain whether, under the terms of an agreement between Ḵosrow II and the Byzantine emperor Maurice in 591, all Roman deportees and their descendants were repatriated (Fiey, 1967a, p. 416). In the account of Mebodes, repeated by Theophylact (5.7.1-2), the rescue of prisoners who had grown old in captivity was the pretext for Maurice's military campaign to Ctesiphon, but this report must be viewed with caution.

How the deportation of Roman prisoners affected the indigenous populations is also unknown; very probably the latter bore resettlement on their own land with considerable resentment. There is no indication in the sources of much internal unrest or of many attempts to escape. Procopius' report (*De Bello Persico* 1.7.34) that Kavād I's prisoners only pretended to escape is unfounded. Certainly the description of a failed attempt to rescue more than 30,000 captives after the defeat of the emperor Tiberius II, who was held responsible for the failure, is tendentious (John of Ephesus, 6.19; but see Lieu, p. 499). Theophylact reported (3.5.6-7) on the escape and flight of the deportees from Daras imprisoned at Giligerdōn and mentioned the common fate of the people of different origins (Roman prisoners of war and Kadisēnoi) imprisoned there.

The impact of deportations.

It is difficult to assess the impact of increased numbers of skilled workers and their technical knowledge on the functioning of the overall Persian economy. One of the most significant consequences of the deportations carried out under the two Šāpūrs was the spread of Christianity in the Sasanian empire (*Chronicle of Seert*, pp. 221-22; Christensen, *Iran Sass.*, p. 266; Downey, p. 261; Gagé, p. 359; Fiey, 1974; Chaumont, 1988, p. 158). The claim in the *Chronicle of Arbela* that, when that city was conquered, there were more than twenty bishoprics in the Sasanian empire seems improbable (pace Chaumont, 1988, pp. 32-35). Already in the 3rd century the high priest Kirdēr included *krestyānē* (Christians from the Roman empire resettled by the Sasanians, according to Brock, 1975, pp. 91-95; cf. idem, 1982, pp. 3-4; Lieu, p. 482) among the followers of suppressed religions. Owing to the deportations of Christian prisoners under the two Šāpūrs and despite a decade of persecutions under Šāpūr II, three of the five bishops of Ḵūzestān who attended the first synod in Seleucia in 410 came from cities in which Roman prisoners had been settled (Fiey, 1969, p. 238). At the council of 424 Rēw-Ardašīr, to which prisoners had been deported under Šāpūr I, was designated as the metropolitan see of the ecclesiastical province of Fārs (Chabot, p. 681). In the acts of the synod of that year a bishopric by the name of Šḇīṯā ḏə Bəlašparr (captivity of Bəlašparr; Guidi, 1889, p. 414; for the location, see Fiey, 1968, III, pl. I) is attested; if Šḇīṯā was identical with Šwīta (Fiey, 1970, p. 382; cf. Chabot, p. 82), then there is also a reference to the captivity of Gorgān. It is clear from their names that these bishoprics had been established as the result of deportations. Nothing shows the role of Roman prisoners in the establishment of Christian worship in the Sasanian empire better than the insistence of many authors that some of the Sasanian kings were converted to Christianity, though there is no historical evidence to support this claim (Eutychius, p. 214; cf. Garsoïan, p. 568). Reports on the deportation of Christian prisoners form the basis for many legends, like that of the conversion of Marv to Christianity (*Chronicle of Seert*, pp. 253-58; cf. Sachau, 1918; Messina; Lieu, pp. 486-87) or of Mār Aḥḥa (cf. Fiey, 1965, pp. 621-25); it has been suggested, however, that earlier and more reliable reports were incorporated into the account of the martyrdom of Qandīda (Ar. Qandīra; *Chronicle of Seert*, p. 238), who was killed in the time of Bahrām II (cf. Brock, 1978; Lieu, pp. 483-84).

Theodor Nöldeke commented that the "old barbaric custom of transplanting the residents of entire cities and countrysides remained common among the Sasanians" (p. 116), but he did not attempt a more differentiated picture; it is often overlooked, for example, that the Sasanians' enemies shared in this "barbaric custom." Without attempting to provide complete coverage or to assess motivation, the following sources can be cited: Herodian (6.4.6), Ammianus (*Res Gestae* 24.1.9), *Panegyrici Latini* (4(8).21.1), Libanius (59.83-85), Joshua the Stylite (chap. 79); Jacob of Edessa (Brooks, text, p. 300, tr., p. 320; cf. Michael the Syrian, 10.13; Zacharias Rhetor, 8.5), *Chronicum Pseudo-Dionysianum Vulgo Dictum* (CSCO XCI, pp. 179-80, tr., CXXI, pp. 133-34), Theophylact Simocatta (2.5.3), and John of Ephesus (6.34). Even after the two great empires had achieved a certain balance of power and the Sasanians had come to be recognized as equal in diplomatic negotiations (cf. Garsoïan, p. 577), deportation of human beings remained a tool of policy until the 7th century. The technological benefits gained through the exploitation of their skills must have been highly prized by Sasanian rulers, who transported them over long distances, often more than several hundred kilometers, to Persia.

Bibliography: (For cited works not found in this bibliography and abbreviations found here, see "Short References.") N. Abbott, "Jundī Shāhpūr. A Preliminary Historical Sketch (Appendix)," *Ars Orientalis* 7, 1968, pp. 71-73. *Acta Martyrum et Sanctorum*, ed. P. Bedjan, 7 vols., Paris and Leipzig, 1890-97. R. M. Adams, "Agriculture and Urban Life in Early Southwestern Iran," *Science* 136, 1962, pp. 116-19. Idem, *Land behind Baghdad. A History of Settlement on the Diyala Plain*, Chicago, 1965. Idem and D. P. Hansen, "Archaeological Reconnaissance and Soundings in Jundī Shāhpūr," *Ars Orientalis* 7, 1968, pp. 53-70. F. Altheim and R. Stiehl, *Asien und Rom. Neue Urkunden aus sasanidischer Frühzeit*, Tübingen, 1952. Idem, "Staatshaushalt der Sasaniden," *La Nouvelle Clio* 5, 1953, pp. 267-321; repr. in F. Altheim and R. Stiehl, *Ein asiatischer Staat. Feudalismus unter den Sasaniden und ihren Nachbarn*, Wiesbaden, 1954, pp. 3-46. Idem, "Šāpūr II. und die Araber," in F. Altheim and R. Stiehl, *Die Araber in der alten Welt* II, Berlin, 1965, pp. 344-56. J. P. Asmussen, "Christians in Iran," in *Camb. Hist. Iran* III/2, pp. 924-48. M. Back, *Die sasanidischen Staatsinschriften*, Acta Iranica 18, Tehran and Liège, 1978. H. R. Baldus, *Uranius Antoninus. Münzprägung und Geschichte*, Antiquitas 3/11, Bonn, 1971. J.-C. Balty, "Apamée (1986). Nouvelles données sur l'armée romaine d'orient et les raids sassanides du milieu du IIIe siècle," *Comptes Rendus de l'Académie des Inscriptions et Belles-Lettres*, 1987, pp. 213-41. G. Bardy, *Paul de Samosate. Étude historique*, Louvain and Paris, 1923. P. Bedjan, ed., *Histoire de Mar-Jabalaha, de trois autres patriarches, d'un prêtre et de deux laïques nestoriens*, Paris and Leipzig, 1895. A. G. Bokshchanin, *Parfiya i Rim. Vozniknovenie sistemy politicheskogo dualizma v Peredneĭ Azii* (Parthia and Rom. The rise of the system of political dualism in western Asia) II, Moscow, 1966. R. Boucharlat, "Suse à l'époque sasanide," *Mesopotamia* 22, 1987, pp. 357-66. S. P. Brock, "Some Aspects of Greek Words in Syriac," in A. Dietrich, *Synkretismus im syrisch-persischen Kulturgebiet*, Abh. der Akademie der Wissenschaften zu Göttingen, Phil.-hist. Kl. 3/96, 1975, pp. 91-95. Idem, "A Martyr at the Sasanid Court under Vahran II. Candida," *Analecta Bollandiana* 96, 1978, pp. 167-81; repr. in S. P. Brock, *Syriac Perspectives on Late Antiquity* IX, London, 1984, pp. 169-81. Idem, "Christians in the Sasanian Empire. A Case of Divided Loyalties," *Studies in Church History* 18, 1982, pp. 1-19. E. W. Brooks, "The Chronological Canon of James of Edessa," *ZDMG* 53, 1899, pp. 261-327. P. A. Brunt and J. M. Moore, eds., *Res Gestae Divi Augusti. The Achievement of the Divine Augustus*, 2nd ed., Oxford, 1970. E. A. Budge, tr., *The Chronography of Abū'l Faraj . . . Bar Hebraeus*, 2 vols., London, 1932. A. Cameron, "Agathias on the Sasanians," *Dumbarton Oaks Papers* 23, 1969-70, pp. 69-183. W. Caskel, "Bakr b. Wā'il" in *EI²* I, pp. 962-64. J.-B. Chabot, *Synodicon orientale ou Recueil de synodes nestoriens . . .* , Paris, 1902. M. L. Chaumont, "Les Sassanides et la christianisation de l'empire iranien au IIIe siècle de notre ère," *RHR* 165, 1964, pp. 165-202. Idem, *La christianisation de l'empire iranien des origines aux grandes persécutions du IVe siècle*, CSCO 499, Louvain, 1988. A. Christensen, *Le règne du roi Kawādh I et le communisme mazdakite*, Det Kgl. Danske Videnskabernes Selskab, Historisk-filologiske Meddelelser 9/6, Copenhagen, 1925. *Chronicle of Seert*, ed. A. Scher, tr. J. Périer, Patrologia Orientalia 5/2, Paris, 1908. *Chronicon Paschale*, ed. L. Dindorf, 2 vols., Bonn, 1832.

Y. A. Dauge, *Le barbare. Recherches sur la conception romaine de la barbarie et de la civilisation*, Brussels, 1981. N. C. Debevoise, *A Political History of Parthia*, Chicago, 1938. F. Decret, "Les conséquences sur le christianisme en Perse de l'affrontement des empires romain et sassanide. De Shâpûr Ier à Yazdgard Ier," *Recherches Augustiniennes* 14, 1979, pp. 91-152.

H. Delehaye and P. Peeters, *Acta Sanctorum Novembris Collecta Digesta Illustrata* IV, Brussels, 1925. G. Downey, *A History of Antioch in Syria from Seleucus to the Arab Conquest*, Princeton, N.J., 1961. H. H. Dubs, "A Roman City in Ancient China," *Greece and Rome*, 2nd ser., 4, 1975, pp. 139-48.

Ebn Qotayba, *Ketāb al-maʿāref*, ed. Ṯ. ʿAkkāša, Cairo, 1960. J. Ferguson, *China and Rome*, ANRW, ser. 2, 9/2, 1978. J. M. Fiey, "Vers la réhabilitation de l'*Histoire de Karka d'Bēṯ Slōḥ*," *Analecta Bollandiana* 82, 1964, pp. 189-222. Idem, *Assyrie chrétienne* III, Beirut, 1965. Idem, "Topographie chrétienne de Mahozé," *L'Orient Syrien* 12, 1967a, pp. 397-420. Idem, "Topography of al-Madaʾin," *Sumer* 23, 1967b, pp. 3-38. Idem, "Diocèses syriens orientaux du Golfe persique," in *Mémorial Mgr. Gabriel Khouri-Sarkis (1898-1968)*, Louvain, 1969, pp. 177-219. Idem, "L'Élam, la première des métropoles ecclésiastiques syriennes orientales," *Melto* 5, 1969, pp. 221-67; repr. *La parole de l'Orient* 1, 1970, pp. 123-53. Idem, *Jalons pour une histoire de l'église en Iraq*, CSCO 310, Louvain, 1970. Idem, "Les commu-nautés syriaques en Iran des premiers siècles à 1552," in *Commémoration Cyrus. Hommage universel* III, Acta Iranica 3, Tehran and Liège, 1974, pp. 279-97. Idem, "Martyropolis syriaque," *Le Muséon* 89, 1976, pp. 5-38. G. Frumkin, *Archaeology in Soviet Central Asia*, HO VII/3/1, Leiden and Cologne, 1970.

J. Gagé, "Comment Sapor a-t-il 'triomphé' de Valérien?" *Syria* 42, 1965, pp. 343-88. H. von Gall, "Die Mosaiken von Bishapur," *AMI*, N.S. 4, 1971, pp. 193-205. N. Garsoïan, "Byzantium and the Sasanians," *Camb. Hist. Iran* III/1, pp. 568-92. *Georgius Cedrenus . . .*, ed. I. Bekker, I, Corpus Scriptorum Historiae Byzantinae 33, Bonn, 1838. R. Ghirshman, "Inscription du monument de Châpour 1er à Châpour," *RAA* 10, 1936, pp. 123-29. Idem, "Les fouilles de Châpour (Iran)," *RAA* 12, 1938, pp. 12-19. Idem, *Bîchâpour* II. *Les mosaïques sassanides*, Paris, 1956. Idem, *Iran. Parther und Sasaniden*, Munich, 1962. P. Gignoux, *Catalogue des sceaux, camées et bulles sassanides . . .*, Paris, 1978. R. Göbl, review of R. Ghirshman, *Bîchâpour*, *WZKM* 53, 1957, pp. 290-91. P. Goubert, *Byzance avant l'Islam* I, Paris, 1951. G. Graf, "Die Einnahme Jerusalems durch die Perser 614 nach dem Bericht eines Augenzeugen," *Das Heilige Land* 67, 1923, pp. 19-29. R. Grousset, *Histoire de l'Arménie des origines à 1071*, Paris, 1947. I. Guidi, "Ostsyrische Bischöfe und Bischofssitze im V., VI. und VII. Jahrhundert," *ZDMG* 43, 1889, pp. 388-414. Idem, *Un nuovo testo siriaco sulla storia degli ultimi Sasanidi*, Leiden, 1891. A. Günther, *Beiträge zur Geschichte der Kriege zwischen Römern und Parthern*, Berlin, 1922. W. B. Henning, "The Great Inscripton of Šāpūr I," *BSOS* 9, 1937-39, pp. 823-49; repr. *Acta Iranica* 14, pp. 601-27. H. Hewsen, "The Successors of Tiridates the Great. A Contribution to the History of Armenia in the Fourth Century," *Revue des Études Arméniennes* 13, 1978-79, pp. 99-123. W. Hinz, *Altiranische Funde und Forschungen*, Berlin, 1969. G. Hoffmann, *Auszüge aus syrischen Akten persischer Märtyrer*, Leipzig, 1880. E. Honigmann and A. Maricq, *Recherches sur les* Res Gestae Divi Saporis, Brussels, 1953. C. Huart and L. Delaporte, *L'Iran antique. Élam et Perse et la civilisation iranienne*, 2nd ed., Paris, 1943. Julian, *Panegyric in Honour of the Emperor Constantius*, tr. W. C. Wright, I, London and Cambridge, 1913. E. Kettenhofen, *Die römisch-persischen Kriege des 3. Jahrhunderts n. Chr. . . .*, Wiesbaden, 1982. Idem, "Das Staatsgefängnis der Sāsāniden," *Die Welt des Orients* 19, 1988, pp. 96-101. G. A. Koshelenko, *Drevneĭshie gosudarstva Kavkaza i Sredneĭ Azii* (The ancient states of the Caucasus and Central Asia), Moscow, 1985. J. H. Kramers, "The Military Colonization of the Caucasus and Armenia under the Sassanids," *BSOS* 8, 1935-37, pp. 613-18.

J. Labourt, *Le christianisme dans l'empire perse sous la dynastie sassanide (224-632)*, Paris, 1904. S. N. C. Lieu, "Captives, Refugees and Exiles. A Study of Cross-Frontier Civilian Movements and Contacts between Rome and Persia from Valerian to Jovian," in P. Freeman and D. Kennedy, eds., The *Defence of the Roman and Byzantine East. Proceedings of a Colloquium Held at the University of Sheffield in April 1986*, BAR 297/2, Oxford, 1986, pp. 475-505. D. MacDonald, "Dating the Fall of Dura-Europos," *Historia* 35, 1986, pp. 45-68. H. A. Manandian, *Tigrane II et Rome. Nouveaux éclaircissements à la lumière des sources originales*, tr. H. Thorossian, Lisbon, 1963. Idem, *The Trade and Cities of Armenia in Relation to Ancient World Trade*, tr. N. G. Garsoïan, Lisbon, 1965. G. Messina, "Al-Biruni sugli inizi del christianesimo a Merv," in *Al-Biruni Commemoration Volume*, Calcutta, 1951, pp. 221-31. D. Metzler, *Ziele und Formen königlicher Innenpolitik im vorislamischen Iran*, Münster, 1977. V. Minorsky, "Transcaucasica," *JA* 217, 1930, pp. 41-112. Idem, *A History of Sharvān and Darband in the 10th-11th Centuries*, Cambridge, 1958. T. Nöldeke, *Aufsätze zur persischen Geschichte*, Leipzig, 1887.

Łazar Pʿarpecʿi, *History of the Armenians and the Letter to Vahan Mamikonean*, ed. and tr. D. Kouymjian, Delmar, N.Y., 1985. *Patrologia Syriaca* I/2, ed. I. Parisot et al., Paris, 1907. P. Peeters, "Un nouveau manuscrit arabe du récit de la prise de Jérusalem par les Perses, en 614," *Analecta Bollandiana* 38, 1920, pp. 137-47. Idem, "La prise de Jérusalem par les Perses," *Mélanges de l'Université de Saint-Joseph* 9, 1923, pp. 3-42; repr. in P. Peeters, *Recherches d'histoire et de philologie orientales* I, Brussels, 1951, pp. 78-116. Idem, "S. Démétrianus évêque d'Antioche?"

Analecta Bollandiana 42, 1924, pp. 288-314. Idem, "Observations sur la vie syriaque de Mar Aba, catholicos de l'église perse (540-552)," *Miscellanea Giovanni Mercati* 5, Vatican, 1946, pp. 104-08; repr. in P. Peeters, *Recherches d'histoire et de philologie orientales* II, Brussels, 1951, pp. 154-59. N. V. Pigulevskaja, *Les villes de l'état iranien aux époques parthe et sassanide. Contribution à l'histoire sociale de la Basse Antiquité*, Paris and the Hague, 1963. G. de Plinval, "Horace et le sort des prisonniers d'Orient," in *Mélanges de philologie, de littérature et d'histoire anciennes offerts à J. Marouzeau . . .*, Paris, 1948, pp. 491-95. K. Regling, "Crassus' Partherkrieg," *Klio* 7, 1907, pp. 357-94. G. Rothstein, *Die Dynastie der Laḫmiden in al-Ḥîra*, Berlin, 1899. B. Rubin, *Das Zeitalter Iustinians* I, Berlin, 1960. J. R. Russell, "Šābuhr I," in *Dictionary of the Middle Ages* X, 1988, pp. 599-600.

E. Sachau, "Vom Christentum in der Persis," *SPAW*, Phil.-hist. Kl., 39, 1916, pp. 958-60. Idem, "Die Christianisierungs-Legende von Merw," in *Zeitschrift für die Alttestamentliche Wissenschaft*, Beiheft 33, Giessen, 1918, pp. 399-409. M. Schottky, *Media Atropatene und Gross-Armenien in hellenistischer Zeit*, Bonn, 1989. Sebeos, *Patmutʿiwn i Herakln*, ed. G. V. Abgaryan, Yerevan, 1979; tr. F. Macler as *Histoire d'Héraclius par l'évêque Sebèos . . .*, Paris, 1904. C. F. Seybold, review [of *The History of the Governors of Egypt . . .*,] *ZDMG* 66, 1912, pp. 742-46. H. Sonnabend, *Fremdenbild und Politik. Vorstellungen der Römer von Ägypten und dem Partherreich in der späten Republik und frühen Kaiserzeit*, Frankfurt, 1986. W. Sundermann, "Ein Bruchstück einer soghdischen Kirchengeschichte aus Zentralasien?" *AAASH* 24, 1976, pp. 95-101. J. Szidat, *Historischer Kommentar zu Ammianus Marcellinus Buch XX-XXI* II, Wiesbaden, 1981.

Theophanes, *Chronography*, ed. C. de Boor, 2 vols., Leipzig, 1883-85. R. W. Thomson, *History of Vardan and the Armenian War*, Cambridge, Mass., 1982. K. V. Trever, *Ocherki po istorii i kul'ture kavkazskoĭ Albanii IV, do n.è-VII v. n.è* (Sketches for the history and culture of Caucasian Albania, 4th century B.C.E.-7th century C.E.), Moscow and Leningrad, 1959. L. Vanden Berghe, *Archéologie de l'Irān ancien*, Leiden, 1959. H. Volkmann, *Die Massenversklavungen der Einwohner eroberter Städte in der hellenistisch-römischen Zeit*, 2nd ed., Stuttgart, 1990. M. Whitby, "Arzanene in the Late Sixth Century," in S. Mitchell, ed., *Armies and Frontiers in Roman and Byzantine Anatolia*, BAR 156, Oxford, 1983, pp. 205-18. G. Widengren, "The Status of the Jews in the Sassanian Empire," *Iranica Antiqua* 1, 1961, pp. 117-62. G. Wiessner, *Zur Märtyrerüberlieferung aus der Christenverfolgung Schapurs II.*, Abh. der Akademie der Wissenschaften zu Göttingen, Phil.-hist. Kl. 3/67, Göttingen, 1967. Idem, "Zum Problem der zeitlichen und örtlichen Festlegung der erhaltenen syro-persischen Märtyrerakten. Das Pusai-Martyrium," in *Paul de Lagarde und die syrische Kirchengeschichte*, Göttingen, 1968, pp. 231-51. M. Wissemann, *Die Parther in der augusteischen Dichtung*, Frankfurt, 1982. J. Wolski, "Le rôle et l'importance des mercenaires dans l'état parthe," *Iranica Antiqua* 5, 1965, pp. 103-15. W. C. Wright, ed. and tr., *The Chronicle of Joshua the Stylite, Composed in Syriac A.D. 507*, Cambridge, 1882.

(ERICH KETTENHOFEN)

iii. IN THE ISLAMIC PERIOD

There is no standard Persian term for deportation. In the histories the verbs *kūčānīdan* and *kūč dādan* "to force to migrate" and *soknā dādan* "to resettle" are often used. From ancient to modern times centralizing monarchs of sprawling, ethnically diverse Eurasian empires have moved nomads, peasants, and townspeople across "their" chessboards in the hundreds of thousands. The ultimate motive has probably always been the demonstration of imperial power and symbolic demarcation of territory (cf. Oded, pp. 11, 31), but more pragmatic reasons for removal and relocation respectively can also be identified (see Table 25). Removal is designed either to punish rebellion and to guard against a repetition by fragmenting and exiling the troublemakers or to depopulate a frontier region to hamper an invader ("scorched earth"). The corresponding reasons for relocating people are either to promote the economic development of a particular city or region or to provide for defense of an underpopulated frontier. Removal and relocation exhibit a schematic complementarity, either A:A/B:B or A:B/B:A (cf. Perry, 1975, pp. 203-04). Often the main motive is the capture of a useful population, as in the systematic removal of merchants and artisans from conquered cities like Tabrīz for resettlement in Ottoman Istanbul under Mehmet II (848-86/1454-81, with interruption) and Selim I (918-26/1512-20; İnalcık, pp. 519-20), but sometimes a mixture of motives is apparent.

Deportation is the sanction of choice in a large, newly established empire under a strong, centralizing ruler. Not surprisingly, it is barely known from the considerable periods of fragmentation under petty

Table 25
SCHEMATIC DISTRIBUTION OF MOTIVES FOR DEPORTATION

	Removal	Relocation
A	punishment/ intimidation	economic development
B	scorched earth	defense of frontiers

rulers, as after the ʿAbbasid, Saljuq, Il-khanid, and Timurid dispensations. On the other hand, it appears not to have been employed at the height of the Saljuq or Il-khanid empires; it is not among the policies advocated in such classic manuals of administration as the *Sīāsat-nāma* of Neẓām-al-Molk, though from Ghaznavid times on the formation of an army from varied ethnic groups remained one motive for uprooting populations. Systematic deportation seems to have been initiated under Tīmūr (771-807/1370-1405) and most widely practiced by the Safavid shah ʿAbbās I (996-1038/1588-1629) and by Nāder Shah Afšār (1149-60/1736-47). Before the 14th century it was overshadowed as a stratagem for demographic engineering by massive incursions and voluntary migrations of Turkish and Mongol nomads, with consequent flight of refugees from conquered and threatened cities. These population movements were generally from east to west, and the thrust of the imperial constructs that arose with them was also westward. Only after the turkicization of Azerbaijan and Anatolia and the establishment of other nomadic invaders in new Persian territories was there a demographic withdrawal eastward, most dramatically apparent in Safavid expansion but reflected in detail in the upsurge of deportations from west to east that began in the late 14th century and peaked during the 17th and 18th centuries.

Tīmūr's deportations. In Persia Tīmūr came closest to the primarily acquisitive deportation (*sürgün*) policy of the Ottoman sultans. As he methodically expanded his territory from the province of Transoxania in 784-808/1382-1405, he treated both settled and nomadic populations as part of the booty, deporting selected groups of the former to serve in Samarqand and of the latter to defend the frontiers of Turkestan. In 785/1383 he transplanted the Jāvūn-e Qorbānī Mongols from Ṭūs and Kalāt to Samarqand (Manz, p. 102; Roemer, VIb, p. 49), and when he recaptured Tabrīz in 788/1386 he sent scholars, artisans, and craftsmen in large numbers to Samarqand (Roemer, VIb, p. 58). After his defeat of the Ottoman Bāyazīd in 806/1403 he resettled captives from Amasya and Qayṣarīya (30,000-40,000, according to some accounts), chiefly Qara Tatar nomads, in Transoxania; they rebelled at Dāmḡān en route and were slaughtered in large numbers (Barthold, p. 701; Manz, pp. 80, 102). This particular incident apparently contributed to the myth of Safavid origins, for during the journey Tīmūr was said to have visited K̲ᵛāja ʿAlī, then head of the Ṣafawī order, at Ardabīl (q.v.) and to have been so impressed by his miracles that he granted his request for 30,000 "Turkmen" prisoners from Anatolia, the forebears of the seven Turkmen tribes that helped to found the Safavid dynasty a century later (Roemer, VIa, pp. 205-06). Deportees to Transoxania on such occasions included nomads from the Jalayerid confederation of Iraq (Manz, p. 193 n. 67).

The forced transfer of these and other groups from India, the Qepčāq steppe, Iraq, Syria, and the Persian plateau to Samarqand or the ranges of Khorasan and Transoxania left the home territories open to the Čaḡatāy nomads of Tīmūr's invading armies. During the struggles over succession some of his garrisons were expelled from Persia, and many of his Transoxanian transplants, including Kurds and Qara Tatars, deserted to their ancestral homes or elsewhere (Manz, p. 102); in at least one instance, one of Tīmūr's successors reversed his policy: Oloḡ Beg issued a decree in 814/1411 permitting Muslim captives forcibly resettled in Samarqand by Tīmūr to return to their homes (Woods, p. 88). Nevertheless, such massive exchanges of population have left marks throughout southwestern Asia.

Deportations by Shah ʿAbbās I. Shah ʿAbbās inherited a state threatened by the Ottomans in the west and the Uzbeks in the northeast. He bought off the former, in order to gain time to defeat the latter, after which he selectively depopulated the Zagros and Caucasus approaches, deporting Kurds, Armenians, and others who might, willingly or not, supply or support an Ottoman campaign. The Kurds and other warrior nomads were transplanted chiefly to northern Khorasan, in order to help repel Uzbek and Turkmen incursions; urban and rural Armenians and Georgians were resettled in selected Persian cities, in order to promote commerce, crafts, and agriculture. On one occasion ʿAbbās is said to have intended to transplant 40,000 Kurds to northern Khorasan but to have succeeded in deporting only 15,000 before his troops were defeated. His efforts resulted in the rise of five distinct Kurdish "states" northwest of Mašhad: Čenārān, Bām or Mīānābād, K̲abūšān (later Qūčān, the most important), Darragaz, and Bojnūrd (qq.v.); the last three survived well into the 19th century (Fraser, app. B, pp. 42-43). ʿAbbās is also credited in local tradition with having transplanted to Baluchistan the Kurds who are still there (Jane Fair Bestor, private communication). According to legend, he also deported the Qajar tribe from Qarabāḡ and Ganja to Marv (30,000 families), Khorasan, and Estarābād (Hedāyat, *Rawżat al-ṣafā* IX, p. 5; cf. Bākīk̲ānof, p. 173), though it appears to have been established in most of these regions earlier (Eskandar Beg, II, p. 643). If the legend is true these transfers would be classic instances of deportation for the definition and defense of the fragile northern frontiers against the Uzbeks, Turkmen, and Lazgīs; the Zīādoḡlū Qajars of Ganja ultimately succumbed to the Russians in 1804 (Bakīk̲ānof, p. 173).

Shah ʿAbbās' most renowned deportation was on the pattern B:A, involving both scorched-earth tactics and the capture of a useful population. This transfer had been anticipated by Shah Ṭahmāsb (930-84/1524-76), who in 941/1534-35 retreated before the invading Ottomans, destroying crops and settlements and driving refugees, including Armenians, before him. During his campaign in northern Azerbaijan in 1013-14/1603-05 ʿAbbās destroyed all crops and immovable property and herded the population, sometimes of complete towns like Aqčaqalʿa and Jolfā, "out of harm's way," onto the plain of Ararat (Eskandar Beg, II, p. 667 ff.). The prisoners, who included Turks, Georgians, and perhaps as many as 75,000 Armenians, were then marched southeast. Of the Armenians who survived about 6,000 families (according to some accounts, only 3,000) were settled in New Jolfā, across the river from Isfahan. Others were established on lands around the capital and in the Baḵtīārī foothills; 500 families were sent to Shiraz at the governor's request, chiefly to engage in viticulture (Eskandar Beg, II, pp. 667 ff.; Tournebize; Gregorian, p. 661 ff.). From the shah's point of view the operation was a success: The Ottoman army was obliged by famine and consequent disaffection to retreat from the Aras and winter at Van, and the transplanted communities (particularly that at Isfahan) eventually flourished and contributed greatly to the commercial and economic efflorescence of the later Safavid period.

In 1024/1615 ʿAbbās deported peasants from wartorn Qarabāḡ and Šīrvān, refugees who had fled thence to Georgia, and 2,000-3,000 Georgian and Ganjaʾī "rebels" to Faraḥābād, his favorite Caspian resort, "both to develop that province and to requite their ingratitude" (Eskandar Beg, II, pp. 881, 903). In the same year he transferred the Qazāqlū (Qazāqlar, Qaramānlū) from Qarabāḡ to lands at Dārābjerd in Fārs, probably to ensure their loyalty (Eskandar Beg, II, pp. 882-23, 1086; Bākīḵānof, p. 173). In a rare example of "fragmentation and exile" counter to this geographical pattern, the Borjalu tribe was removed from Arāk to Šīrvān (Bākīḵānof, p. 173).

The cited examples constitute a small part even of the documented instances of mass deportation carried out during the Safavid period, which may have affected as many as 100,000 families. With accompanying massacres, induction of male captives into the army, and sale of women and children into slavery, it is clear that Shah ʿAbbās saw himself as physically molding his realm, defining its frontiers, culling or stocking selected pastures and cities, and determining the centers of economic growth by shunting his subjects from one point to another. So far as can be ascertained, most of his transplants remained: The Armenian communities weathered subsequent calamities and maintained their identity (though the descendants of the Faraḥābād colony migrated to Tabrīz), whereas the Georgians (often pressed into the army) tended to become assimilated into the variegated population of Isfahan and other Safavid cities and provinces (Roemer, VIa, pp. 271-72; *Persia*, p. 363).

Deportations by Nāder Shah. For Nāder Shah there is a score of documented episodes, involving perhaps 150,000 families, the greatest volume and consistency of deportations in Persia. Like Tīmūr, whom he also emulated in other ways, he aimed to transplant populations, chiefly nomadic, from the interior of Persia to Khorasan and the frontiers of Turkestan. Following the policy of Shah ʿAbbās, he settled some in the Atrek valley to absorb Turkmen raids and others on agricultural land around Mašhad, Nīšāpūr, Ḵabūšān and Torbat-e Jām to increase production. His principal use for deracinated tribesmen (Baḵtīārī, Kurds, Baluch, Afghans, Turkmen, etc.) was in his army, which was in almost perpetual movement from Dāḡestān to Delhi, from Bukhara to Baghdad; many of them were thus never permanently relocated.

In 1141/1728, even before his coronation, Nāder Shah deported a group of Abdālī tribesmen from Herat to Jām, Langar, and Mašhad; a few years later he dispatched 60,000 more to settle at Mašhad, Nīšāpūr, and Dāmḡān (Marvī, I, p. 198; Estarābādī, p. 95; Lockhart, p. 54). In 1151/1738 he transported some Ḡelzāy Afghans to Nīšāpūr and Gorgān, then moved some Abdālī from there to Qandahār in order to weaken the Ḡelzāy further (Estarābādī, p. 303). In 1143/1730, after recapturing Tabrīz from the Ottomans, Nāder Shah deported and dispersed in the vicinity of Mašhad 56,000 families from assorted tribes from the whole length of the Zagros, Afšār, Moqddam, Kurds, and Baḵtīārī (Estarābādī, pp. 134-35; Lockhart, pp. 51-52). At least 25,000 more families captured in his northwestern campaigns in 1148-54/1735-41 followed: Zīādōglū Qājārs, Šaqāqī Kurds, Georgians, and Turks (Marvī, I, p. 254; Lambton, *Landlord and Peasant*, p. 133; Perry, 1975, p. 209). A total of at least 13,000 families of the turbulent Baḵtīārī were sent to northern Khorasan on at least two occasions (Estarābādī, pp. 189, 283; Marvī, II, p. 247). Nāder Shah continued this policy into his last years, when his primary motivation was undoubtedly exile and fragmentation, rather than redistribution of useful populations: Lor and Baḵtīārī tribesmen who rebelled against excessive taxes in about 1159/1746 were savagely put down and deported to Jām and Langar (Marvī, III, p. 1093).

There appear to be no extant accounts sympathetic to Nāder Šhah's deportees, but it can be guessed that the conditions under which they were escorted over distances ranging from 200 to 1,000 miles were no better than those under Tīmūr or ʿAbbās. One of Nāder Shah's bureaucrats, who was twice put in charge of deporting families of the ʿAlīvand and Ḵalīlvand sections of Moqdam to Kalāt (1,000 miles away), reported only that he spent some time in Marāḡa, the assembly point, organizing the move and that, on the second occasion, they were given six months to complete the journey, perhaps because it was winter and an immediate start impracticable (Marvī, I, pp. 313-14; II, p. 666). Allowing for a few weeks' initial delay, the party would thus have averaged about 7 miles a day.

Karīm Khan Zand and his successors. After Nāder Shah's assassination most of the deportees serving in his army in Khorasan and an indeterminate number of the resettled tribesmen deserted and made their way home (Perry, 1979, pp. 3-4). The leader of one such Zagros clan, Karīm Khan Zand, eventually came to rule an ostensibly neo-Safavid state in western Persia (1165-93/1751-79). He sought, with considerable success, to reverse the voluntary and forcible depopulation of his realms, chiefly by establishing secure communications and inviting refugees and deportees, including tribal groups, to return (Lambton, *Landlord and Peasant*, p. 141). His only deportations of the classic type were of rebellious Bak̲tīārī, who in 1178/1764 were rounded up without bloodshed and resettled, the Haft Lang near Qom and Varāmīn, the Čahār Lang around Fasā and Kangān in Fārs (Perry, 1979, p. 111). Karīm Khan did, however, settle tribal hostages from his northern territories in his capital at Shiraz and built up a standing army from contingents of Lor, Lak, Kurd, and other Zagros tribes, a modified form of resettlement (Perry, 1979, p. 225).

The collapse of Karīm Khan's successors in Fārs before the rising power of the Qajars brought a brief recrudescence of forcible demographic engineering under Āḡā Moḥammad Khan Qājār (fl. 1784-97; shah from 1211/1796). He moved groups of ʿAbd-al-Malekī and K̲ᵛājavand from Fārs to Māzandarān, where they were to help defend Estarābād against the Turkmen of the Gorgān steppe; they were later used by the Qajars in the Russian wars and remained in Māzandarān into this century (*Persia*, p. 363; Lambton, p. 1104). For the rest of the Qajar period there is little sign of a consistent policy of mass deportation. The new capital, Tehran, was situated midway between the source and target areas of most deportations of the previous three centuries; it commanded the populous province of Māzandarān and continually attracted voluntary migrants from Azerbaijan. Artificial measures to populate it were thus unnecessary.

"Exile and fragmentation" were again used as sanctions during the reign of Reżā Shah Pahlavī (1304-20 Š./1925-41) as part of a concerted policy of disarmament and resettlement of the nomadic tribes. Of the three principal targets, the Turkmen, the Qašqāʾī, and the Lors of Pīš-e Kūh, only the last were deported in large numbers. In the late 1920s families of the Sagāvand, whose chief had been killed at military headquarters, were moved under escort to settle near Qazvīn; their flocks suffered severe losses on the way (Wilber, p. 133). Others were sent to Varāmīn. The Beyrānvand, who had ambushed a government detachment, were "decimated and exiled in their thousands to the distant province of Khorassan" (Black-Michaud, p. 218; *Persia*, pp. 343, 387).

It is worth emphasizing the salient differences between forced sedentarization, practiced only in this century, and deportation. Certain tactics, like the killing of leaders and destruction of strongholds, are common to both. Sedentarized nomads were, however, generally disarmed, stripped of their flocks, and settled on agricultural land; they were thus rendered completely dependent upon the government for protection and provisions and often in unequal competition with an existing sedentary population. Most of them subsequently perished. Deportees in former centuries, if they survived the journey, were encouraged to resume their former transhumant life with their own livestock on ranges somewhat similar to those from which they had come and to keep their weapons, ostensibly for use in the service of the state. Ideally, they were relocated to places where they would be less troublesome and more profitable to the state. Although in practice there were much suffering and waste and deportees often returned home when coercion was relaxed, for six centuries the policy was evidently perceived as cost effective in Persia.

Although no regular and reliable figures have been preserved, estimates from the periods of Shah ʿAbbās and Nāder Shah can be combined and compared with figures from Neo-Assyrian deportations under Tiglath-Pileser III, Sargon II, and Sennacherib (cf. Perry, 1975, p. 203; Oded, pp. 20-21). Shah ʿAbbās and Nāder Shah were active for a total period of sixty-two years, during which they deported approximately 1.5 million people in thirty-five separate instances. The three Neo-Assyrian monarchs ruled for a total of fifty-nine years, during which they deported approximately 1.1 million people in ninety-five recorded instances. It thus appears that, though the overall scale of deportations is generally comparable, the Persian rulers deported people less frequently but in greater numbers.

Bibliography: (For cited works not found in this bibliography and abbreviations found here, see "Short References.") ʿAbbāsqolī Āqā Bākīk̲ānof, *Golestān-e eram*, ed. A. A. ʿAlīzāda, Baku, 1970. W. Barthold, "Tatar," in *EI*[1] IV, 1934, pp. 700-02. J. Black-Michaud, "An Ethnographical and Ecological Survey of Luristan, Western Persia. Modernization in a Nomadic Pastoral Society," *Middle Eastern Studies* 10/2, 1974, pp. 210-28. Mahdī Khan Estarābādī, *Jahāngošā-ye nāderī*, ed. S.-J. Šahīdī, Tehran, 1341/1962. J. Fraser, *Narrative of a Journey into Khorasan, in the Years 1821 and 1822*, Edinburgh, 1834. V. Gregorian, "Minorities of Isfahan. The Armenian Community of Isfahan 1587-1722," *Iranian Studies* 7, 1974, pp. 652-80. H. İnalcık, "Mehmet II," *İA* VII, pp. 506-35. A. K. S. Lambton, "Īlāt," in *EI*[2] III, 1971, pp. 1093-1110. L. Lockhart, *Nadir Shah*, London, 1938. B. Manz, *The Rise and Rule of Tamerlane*, Cambridge, 1987. Moḥammad-Kāẓem Marvī, *ʿĀlamārā-ye nāderī*, ed. M.-ʿA. Rīāḥī, 3 vols., Tehran, 1364 Š./1985. B. Oded, *Mass Deportations and Deportees in the Neo-Assyrian Empire*, Wiesbaden, 1979. J. Perry, "Forced Migration in Iran during the Seventeenth and Eighteenth Centuries," *Iranian Studies* 8, 1975, pp. 199-215. Idem, *Karim Khan Zand. A History of Iran, 1747-1779*, Chicago, 1979. *Persia*, Geographical Handbook Series, Oxford, 1945. H. R. Roemer, "The Safavid Period," in *Camb. Hist. Iran* VIa, pp. 189-350. Idem, "Tīmūr in Iran," in *Camb. Hist. Iran* VIb, pp. 42-97. F. Tournebize, "Schah Abbas I, roi de Perse et l'émigration forcée des Arméniens de l'Ararat," *Huschardjan. Festschrift aus Anlass des 100 jahrigen Bestandes des Mechitaristen-Kongregation in Wien (1811-1911)*, Vienna, 1911, pp. 247-52. D. N. Wilber, *Riza Shah Pahlavi*, Hicksville, N.Y., 1975. J. Woods, "The Rise of Timurid Historiography," *JNES* 46/2, 1987, pp. 81-108.

(JOHN R. PERRY)

DERAFŠ ("banner, standard, flag, emblem"; Av. *drafša-*, Mid. Pers. *drafš*, equivalent to OInd. *drapsá-*; see Horn, *Etymologie*, no. 553; *AirWb.*, col. 771) in ancient Iran. The use of the banner as a religious, royal, or military symbol was common among Indo-Iranians (Wikander, pp. 60-62, 96-97; Kramrisch; Kuiper) and Near Eastern peoples (Sarre, pp. 233-44; Nylander, pp. 22-23; for bronze "standards" with animal heads in western Iran, see Moorey). In the Avesta Bactria "with tall banners" (*ərəδβō.drafša-*; *Vd.* 1.7), a fluttering "bull banner" (*gaoš drafša-*; *Y.* 10.14), and banners of enemies of Iran (*Y.* 57.25; *Yt.* 1.11, 4.3, 8.56) are mentioned.

In the Achaemenid period each Persian army divisios had its own standard (Herodotus, 9.59), and "all officers had banners over their tents," by which they were recognized in the camp (Xenophon, *Cyropaedia* 8.5.13; cf. 6.3.4; for evidence of a similar tradition among the Parthians, see below). One such banner is held by a Persian warrior depicted on a Greek vase (the "Duris cup" in the Louvre; Pottier, p. 105 fig. 20). It is a square plaque in saltire, the upper and lower quarters painted black and the side ones white (Plate XXV/b). The origin of this form is Urartian, as is shown by a similar banner (Plate XXV/a) held by a worshiper facing a lion-mounted god on an Urartian bronze disk from Altıntepe (Taşyürek, p. 942 fig. 7; pl. CCXVIII/4-5). The standard of Cyrus (q.v. iii) the Great, "a golden eagle mounted upon a lofty shaft," remained the royal banner of the Achaemenids (Xenophon, *Cyropaedia* 7.1.4) and at Cunaxa marked the position of Artaxerxes II (qq.v.; Xenophon, *Anabasis* 1.10.12; cf. a similar eagle on the chariot of Darius III, q.v.; Curtius Rufus, 3.3.16). At Persepolis six "audience scenes" (in the Throne Hall and among the "Treasury reliefs"; Schmidt, p. 166, pls. 98, 99, 123; Tilia, pp. 175-208, figs. 3, 5, 7, 9, 18, 32) include depictions of Persian soldiers carrying square plaques on poles (Plate XXV/c), which Kurt Erdmann (pp. 62-63) first recognized as banners (the ensigns could have been added in color; Nylander, p. 26). The royal standard is also shown on the "Alexander mosaic" from Pompeii (a Roman copy of a Hellenistic painting of about 320 B.C.E.; Hölscher, pp. 122-69, 270-88), in which Alexander the Great (q.v.) is represented fighting Darius III at Issus (against the view of Rumpf, pp. 233-35, that it depicts a Macedonian attack signal, see Nylander, pp. 26-34). The banner, which is affixed atop a long lance, is a rectangular plaque of dark red (probably representing a purple original; Ackerman, p. 2767), separated by a clear red line from a border of dark red with yellow dots; there is a dark-red fringe along the lower edge. Within the field a golden bird, its head crowned with what appears to be a cockscomb, is partially preserved (Plate XXV/d). Some scholars have thus identified the bird as a cock (q.v.), called the "Persian bird" by the Greeks and "the holy bird" in the Avesta (Sarre, p. 348; Nylander, p. 29 n. 44). Others (Ackerman, p. 2767 n. 4, with references) have considered it an eagle, the usual Achaemenid royal emblem. As the eagle or the related royal falcon (*varəγna*; Stricker; Shahbazi, 1984) symbolized *farr* (q.v.), or God-given glory, and, as the eagle was associated with the Achaemenid family (Achaemenes was said to have been raised by an eagle; Aelian, *De Natura Animalium* 12.21; in Ezra 18:13 "Eagle of the East" refers to Cyrus; and in Aeschylus, *Persae* 205-10, the Persian king is personified by an eagle), an eagle or a foyal falcon seems more appropriate for the banner of Darius III. Indeed, a miniature banner in the form of a square tile (12.3 cm^2) of Egyptian blue frit showing a falcon with outstretched wings and the sun-disk crown on its head, the whole framed by a border of triangles (Plate XXV/e), was discovered at Persepolis by ʿAlī Samī in 1327 Š./1948 (Īrān-Bāstān Museum, Tehran, no. 2436; Sāmī, fig. facing p. 100; Luschey). Although the origins of this motif can be traced to the Egyptian Horus falcon, its appearance at Persepolis is related to Iranian traditions concerning the "glory-bringing *varəγna* bird" of the Avesta (Luschey, p. 260 and n. 20). It also clearly recalls the royal Achaemenid emblem, "a golden eagle with outstreched wings," described by Xenophon (see above). Similar birds were embossed on two Achaemenid gold roundels from the "Oxus treasure" (Dalton, pp. 13-15, pls. XII/33, XXI/34). What appears to be a cockscomb on the banner in the Alexander mosaic is thus to be explained as the vestige of a misunderstood, or misrepresented, sun disk.

Under the Seleucids and Parthians the local rulers of Persis claimed a royal heritage and continued to use traditional Persian dynastic symbols (Shahbazi, 1977, p. 199; Wiesehöfer, pp. 103-08). Early Persid coins (3rd-2nd centuries B.C.E.) are adorned with a banner shaped as a square plaque in saltire, each quarter enclosing a roundel, with tassels along the lower edge (Hill, pp. clx-clxxii; Wiesehöfer, pp. 103-36, figs. 3-7; Plate XXV/f). Sometimes an eagle was added as a finial above the banner (Plate XXV/g), suggesting an even closer association with the Achaemenid royal banner. Ferdinand Justi (*Grundriss* II, pp. 486-87), followed by Friedrich

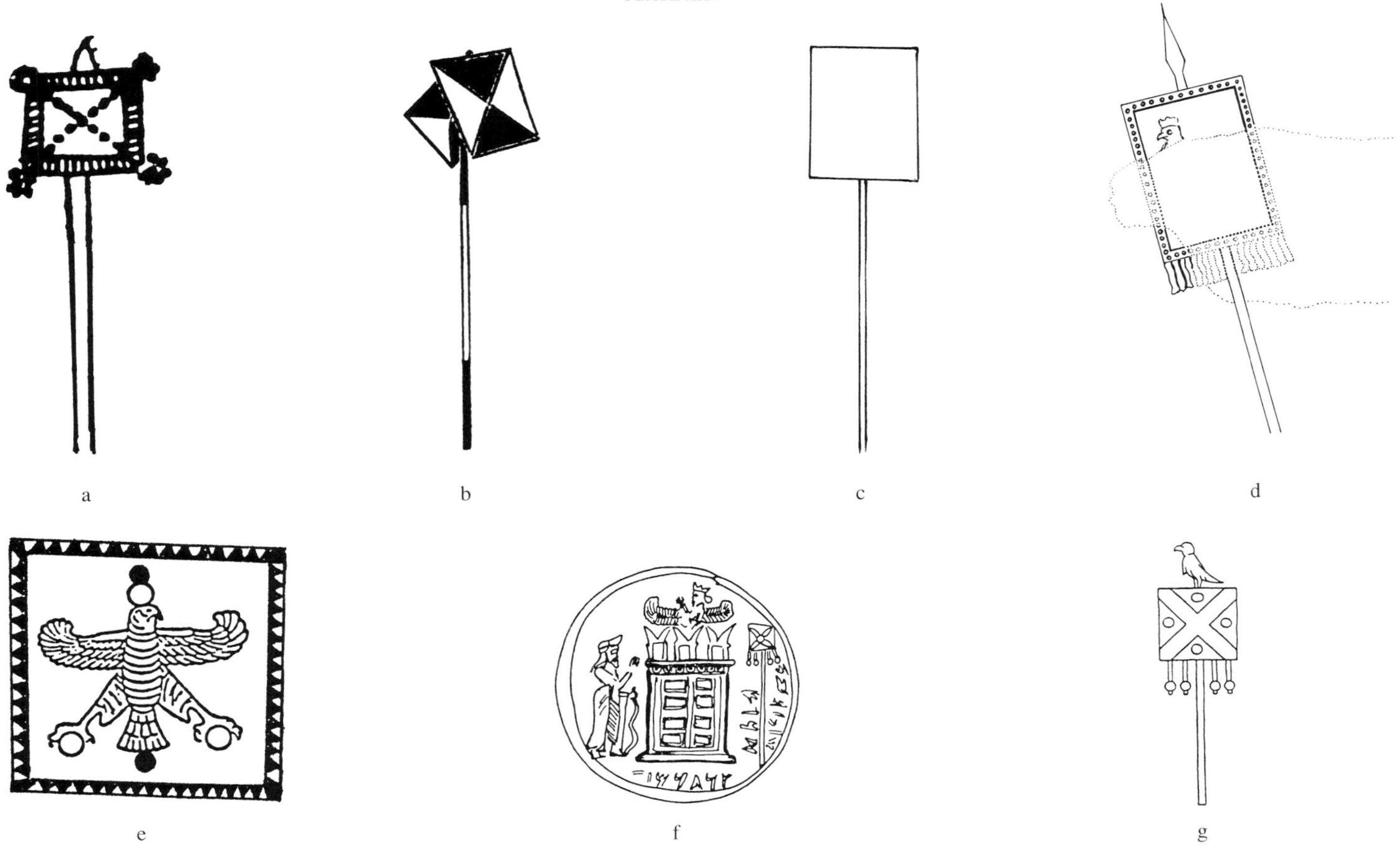

Drawings of ancient banners and standards. a. Urartian banner on a bronze disk from Altıntepe; after Taşyürek, p. 942 fig. 7. b. Persian banner from the "Duris cup"; after Ackermann, p. 2767 fig. 958. c. Achaemenid banner; after a photograph by the author of the Persepolis Treasury relief. d. Reconstruction of the banner of Darius III on the "Alexander mosaic" from a drawing by W. Zahn, 1832; after Nylander, p. 31 fig. 11. e. Miniature banner from Persepolis; after Sāmī, p. 100 fig. f. Persid banner; after a Persid coin. g. Persid banner from a coin; after Ackermann, p. 2786 fig. 959.

Sarre (p. 350) and Oskar Mann, identified this banner with that on the "Alexander mosaic" and took both as representations of the Derafš-e Kāvīān (q.v.). Eagle banners were also used by the Parthians and Armenians (F. C. Andreas apud Sarre, pp. 354-55). The Arsacids additionally used a flag adorned with the image of the sun (Tertullian, *Apologeticum* 16; cf. Ackerman, p. 2769 n. 3) and, as standards distinguishing units of 1,000 soldiers, silken banners bearing the image of a dragon (Lucian, *Hist. Conscr.* 20; cf. Christensen, tr., pp. 37-38; Ackerman, p. 2769 n. 1).

Four Sasanian banners are represented in sculptured scenes. One is an unfurled cloth flag (Plate XXVI/d) carried by a dignitary depicted on the rock relief at Bīšāpūr (q.v.) attributed to Šāpūr II (309-79; Sarre and Herzfeld, pp. 213-14, fig. 101; Ghirshman, figs. 225-26; Schmidt, III, p. 137). The remaining three are from Naqš-e Rostam in Fārs. On one, attributed to Bahrām II (q.v.; 274-93), a lance terminates in a ring with two lateral downcurving appendages; below is a crossbar with a large tassel dependent from each end (Plate XXVI/a; Sarre, pp. 357-58; Schmidt, III, p. 130). On the second (Plate XXVI/b), carried by a heavily armed attendant in the equestrian combat of Hormozd II (302-09; Sarre, pp. 256-57; Schmidt, III, p. 135, pls. 91, 93A), there is a crossbar with tassels at the ends and two (originally three) plain ribbons dependent from it. Finally (Plate XXVI/c), a mounted armed attendant in a relief attributed to Šāpūr II (Schmidt, III, pp. 136-37, pl. 95) carries a standard with a crossbar and end tassels, topped by three fluted globes similar to those surmounting Sasanian crowns.

As in feudal Europe, Sasanian magnates and nobles had their own coats of arms and banners (Faustus, 3.7; 4.2, 3, 20; 5.1, 43, tr. Garsoïan, pp. 73, 108, 150, 185, 226; *Šāh-nāma*, Moscow, II, pp. 212 ff., IV, pp. 41 ff., V, pp. 188-206). The *Šāh-nāma*, reflecting Parthian and Sasanian social practices, includes the following examples (note the consistency of forms in references to individual banners): Kāvūs, a golden sun crowned with a moon encased in purple (II, p. 212 l. 547); his son Farīborz, a sun banner (IV, pp. 26 l. 294, 41 l. 513); Tōs-e Nowda, an elephant banner (II, p. 213 l. 554; IV, pp. 33 l. 399, 41 l. 508); Gōdarz, a golden lion banner (II, p. 213 ll. 556-57; IV, pp. 27 l. 300, 43 l. 527); Gēv, a black banner with a wolf as

PLATE XXVI

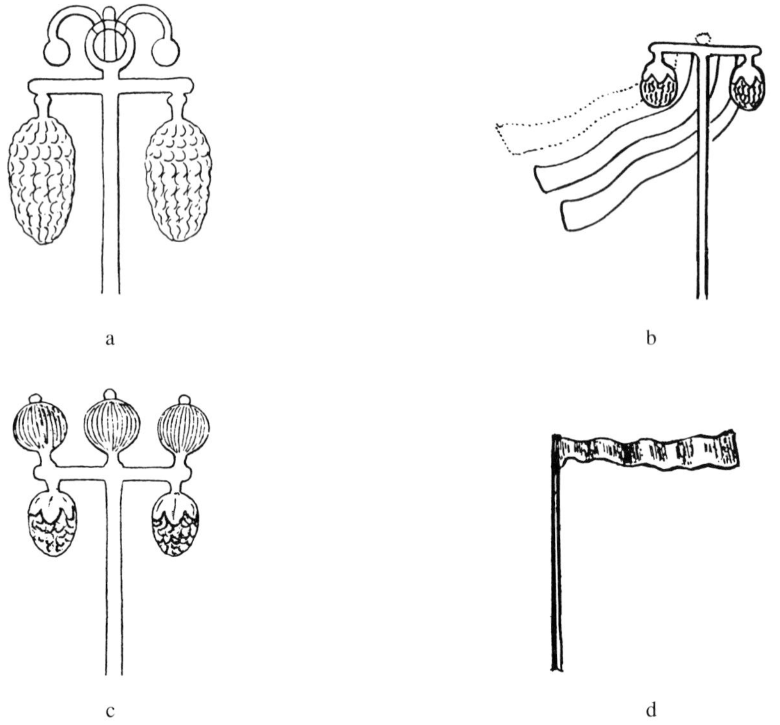

Drawings of Persian standards and banners of the Sasanian period. a. Standard of Bahrām II from a relief at Naqš-e Rostam; after Sarre, p. 357 fig. 20. b. Standard from the relief of Bahrām II at Naqš-e Rostam; after Sarre, p. 357 fig. 19. c. Standard of Šāpūr II (?) at Naqš-e Rostam; after Schmidt, III, pl. 95. d. Banner of Šāpūr II (?) at Bīšāpūr, from a drawing byEugène Flandin of the rock relief at Bīšāpūr; after Sarre and Herzfeld, p. 213 fig. 101.

its emblem (II, p. 214 ll. 577-78; IV, pp. 27 l. 304, 43 l. 526); Gorāza, a wild-boar banner crowned with a golden moon (II, p. 215 l. 588; IV, pp. 29 l. 324, 42 l. 524); Rostam (and his son Frāmarz), a dragon banner atop a lance crowned with a golden lion (II, p. 214 l. 566; IV, pp. 29-30 ll. 345-46, 185 l. 1112, 189 l. 177); Gostahm, a moon banner (IV, pp. 28 l. 318, 42 l. 515); Aškaš, a leopard banner (IV, p. 28 l. 322); and Zanga-ye Šāvorān, a Homāy (the royal falcon) banner (IV, p. 29 l. 328). When Bahrām-e Čōbīn (q.v.) received the supreme command, Hormozd IV (579-90) gave him the dragon banner of Rostam, saying, "You are indeed a second Rostam" (VIII, p. 345 ll. 508-14). The true reason, however, was Bahrām's Arsacid descent, through which he was heir to the traditional Arsacid dragon banner (Shahbazi, 1994, p. 159).

See also ʿALAM VA ʿALĀMAT; BANNERS.

Bibliography: (For cited works not found in this bibliography and abbreviations found here, see "Short References.") P. Ackerman, "Standards, Banners, and Badges," *Survey of Persian Art* VI, pp. 2766-82. A. Christensen, *Smeden Kāväh og det gamle persiske rigsbanner*, Det Kgl. Danske Videnskabernes Selskab, Historisk-Filologiske Meddelelser 2/7, 1919; tr. J. M. Unvala as "The Smith Kāveh and the Ancient Persian Imperial Banner," *Journal of the Cama Oriental Institute* 5, 1925, pp. 22-39. O. M. Dalton, *The Treasure of the Oxus*, 3rd ed., London, 1964. K. Erdmann, review of E. F. Schmidt, *Persepolis* I, *Bibliotheca Orientalia* 13, 1956, pp. 62-63. R. Ghirshman, *Persian Art. 249 B.C.-A.D. 651. The Parthian and Sassanian Dynasties*, New York, 1962. G. F. Hill, *British Museum Catalogue of the Greek Coins of Arabia, Mesopotamia and Persia . . .*, London, 1922. T. Hölscher, *Griechische Historienbilder des 5. und 4. Jahrhunderts v. Chr.*, Würzburg, 1973. S. Kramrisch, "The Banner of Indra," in K. B. Iyar, ed., *Art and Thought. Issued in Honour of Dr. Ananda K. Coomaraswamy . . .*, London, 1947, pp. 197-201. F. B. J. Kuiper, review of J. Duchesne-Guillemin, *Symbols and Values in Zoroastrianism*, *IIJ* 11, 1958-59, pp. 125-33. H. Luschey, "Ein königliches Emblem," *AMI* 5, 1972, pp. 257-60. O. Mann, "Kāveh o derafš-e kāvīānī," *Kāveh* 1, 24 January 1916, pp. 3-5. P. R. S. Moorey, "A Note on Pre-Achaemenid Bronze Standard Tops from Western Iran," *Iran* 15, 1977, pp. 141-46. C. Nylander, "The Standard of the Great King—A Problem in the Alexander Mosaic," *Opuscula Romana* 14/2, 1983, pp. 19-37. E. Pottier, *Douris*, London, 1909. A. Rumpf, "Zum Alexander-Mosaik," *Mitteilungen des Deutschen Archäo-logischen Instituts. Athenische Abteilung* 77, 1962, pp. 229-41. ʿA. Sāmī, *Persepolis*, tr. R. Sharp, Shiraz, 1970. F. Sarre, "Die altorientalischen Feldzeichen, mit besonderer Berücksichtigung eines unveröffentlichten Stücks," *Klio* 3, 1903, pp. 331-71. Idem and E. Herzfeld, *Iranische Felsreliefs*, Berlin, 1920. E. F. Schmidt, *Persepolis* I, III, Chicago, 1953, 1970. A. S. Shahbazi, "From *Pārsa* to *Taxt-e Jamšīd*," *AMI* 10, 1977, pp. 197-207. Idem, "On Vāreγna, the Royal Falcon," *ZDMG* 134/2, 1984, pp. 314-17. Idem, "The Parthian Origins of the House of Rustam," in C. A. Bromberg, ed., *Iranian Studies in Honor of A. D. H. Bivar*, Bulletin of the Asia Institute, n.s. no. 7, Bloomfield Hills, Mich., 1994, pp. 155-65. B. H. Stricker, "Varəγna, the Falcon," *IIJ* 7, 1963-64, pp. 310-17. O. A. Taşyürek, "Darstellungen des urartischen Gottes Haldi," in S. Şahin, E. Schwertheim, and J. Wagner, eds., *Studien zur Religion und Kultur Kleinasiens. Festschrift für Friedrich Karl Dörner . . .* II, Leiden, 1978, pp. 940-55. A. B. Tilia, *Studies and Restorations at Persepolis and Other Sites of Fārs* II, Rome, 1978. J. Wiesehöfer, *Die "dunklen Jahrhunderte" der Persis*, Munich, 1994. S. Wikander, *Der arische Männerbund*, Lund, 1938.

(A. SHAPUR SHAHBAZI)

DERAFŠ-E KĀVĪĀN, the legendary royal standard of the Sasanian kings.

In the *Šāh-nāma* (ed. Khaleghi-Motlagh, pp. 66-70, vv. 184 ff.) it is recorded that, when the blacksmith Kāva revolted against the tyrant Żaḥḥāk, he draped his leather apron from a wooden spear as a standard. As a result of the revolt, the throne passed to a prince of the ancient royal house, Ferēdūn, who adorned the apron with gold and brocade, gems, and tassels of red, yellow (or blue), and violet and called it *derafš-e kāvīān*, "the standard of the *kay*(s)" (i.e., *kāvīs* "kings") or "of Kāva." Each succeeding king added jewels until even at night it shone like the sun. In early Islamic sources this story was elaborated in various ways. According to the 10th-century historians Ṭabarī (I, pp. 2174–75) and Masʿūdī (*Morūj*, ed. Pellat, III, p. 51), the banner was made of panther skin and was 8 x 12 cubits, about 5 x 7.5 m; Ḵᵛārazmī cited sources to the effect that it was of bear or lion skin (p. 115; cf. Maqdesī, *Badʾ* III, p. 142: goat or lion skin). In the 14th century Ebn Ḵaldūn (q.v.; III, pp. 168-69) reported that it "had a magic square of a hundred fields woven into it in gold," reflecting the belief that an army carrying a banner with such a square would never be defeated in war. It was also sometimes called the "standard of Jamšēd," the "standard of Ferēdūn" (*Šāh-nāma*, Moscow, I, p. 202 v. 1007; VI, p. 113 v.704), and the "royal standard" (*derafš-e kayī*; *Šāh-nāma*, ed. Khaleghi, I, p. 147 v. 939; cf. Ṯaʿālebī, *Ḡorar*, pp. 38-30).

According to the *Šāh-nāma*, when the army was mustered five *mowbed*s (priests) would bring the standard forth from its storehouse, and it would be carried with the king or army commander on campaign; it was often mentioned with the adjectives "auspicious" or "blessed" (*homāyūn*, *ḵojasta*; I, p. 118 v. 656; V, p. 102 v. 294). In battle the standard served as a rallying point for the troops (*Šāh-nāma*, ed. Moscow, III, p. 42 v. 621; cf. III, p. 173 v. 2654; IV, pp. 97-98 vv. 1384 ff. and 1389, 140 v. 386, 147 vv. 498 ff.; V, pp. 207 v. 2094, 331 v. 1615, 398 v. 2758; VI, p. 100 vv. 517 ff.; Ṭabarī, I, p. 609; cf. Procopius, *Persian Wars* 1.15).

There is no direct mention of the Derafš-e Kāvīān in the Avesta or in Achaemenid or Parthian sources, but several scholars have argued that it is depicted in a damaged portion of the Alexander mosaic from Pompeii, the subject of which is the victory of Alexander the Great over Darius III (qq.v.) at the battle of Issus (Levy, pp. 439-40; *Grundriss* II, pp. 486-87; Justi, *Namenbuch*, p. 160; Sarre, p. 348; Mann, pp. 3 ff.). Xenophon (*Anabasis* 1.10.12) mentioned, however, that the standard of the Achaemenid king was a golden eagle on a shield carried on a spear. Arthur Christensen (pp. 19-20; idem, *Iran Sass.*, p. 502–04) accepted the Derafš-e Kāvīān as the royal standard of the Sasanians and argued that the myth of Kāva had its genesis in the Sasanian period, reflecting the fame of the house of Kārēn, which traced its lineage to Qārēn, son of Kāva. Stig Wikander (1942, pp. 170, 203; idem, 1946, pp. 97 ff.) agreed but argued that the standard was adopted not by the Kavis of the Gathas but by the eight Kavis of the *Yašt*s, the *mairyō* (Mid.Ir. *mērag*, Ved. *marya*). He argued further that Derafš-e Kāvīān became the national banner of Iran in the Parthian period.

In the battle of Qādesīya (ca. 16/637), in which the invading Arabs defeated the Sasanian army, the standard fell into the hands of Żerār b. Ḵaṭṭāb. He received 30,000 dinars for it, though its real value was said to be 1.2 or even 2 million dinars (Ṭabarī, I, p. 2337; Ebn al-Aṯīr, II, p. 482). After the jewels were removed the caliph ʿOmar is said to have burned the Kāvīān standard (Balʿamī, ed. Bahār, p. 148).

Bibliography: (For cited works not found in this bibliography and abbreviations found here, see "Short References.") A. Christensen, *Smeden Kåväh og det gamle persiske rigsbanner*, Det Kgl. Danske Videnskabernes Selskab, Historisk-filologiske Meddelelser 2/7, Copenhagen, 1919. Ebn Ḵaldūn, *al-Moqaddema*, tr. F. Rosenthal as *The Muqaddimah*, 3 vols, Princeton, N.J., 1967. Ebn Meskawayh, *Tajāreb*, facs. ed., ed. L. Caetani, I, London, 1909, p. 13; ed. A. Emāī, I, Tehran, 1366 Š./1987, p. 8. Ebn Rosta, p. 196. J. Ḵāleqī-Moṭlaq (Dj. Khaleghi-Motlagh), "Taqaddos-e parčam," *Īrān-šenāsī* 4, 1371 Š./1992, pp. 700-02. Ḵᵛārazmī, *Mafātīḥ al-ʿolūm*, ed. G. van Vloten, Leiden, 1895. Lazard, *Premiers poètes* II, p. 154 v. 110. M. A. Levy, "Beiträge zur aramäischen Münzkunde Erans und zur Kunde der älteren Pehlevi-Schrift," *ZDMG* 21, 1867, pp. 421-65. O. Mann, "Kāva wa Derafš-e Kāvīānī," *Kāva* 1/1 (Berlin), 1334/1916; repr., Tehran, 1356 Š./1977. Masʿūdī, *Morūj*, ed. Pellat, III, p. 63. Idem, *Tanbīh*, pp. 85-88. Ḏ. Ṣafā, "Derafš-e Kāvīān," *Sāl-nāma-ye kešvar-e Īrān* II, Tehran, 1326 Š./1947, pp. 18-22. R. Šahmardān, "Derafš-e kāvīānī," *Barrasīhā-ye tārīḵī* 10/1, 1354 Š./1975, pp. 253-72. F. Sarre, "Die altorientalischen Feldzeichen," *Klio* 3, 1903, pp. 333-71. *Tarjama-ye Tafsīr-e Ṭabarī*, 2nd ed., ed. Ḥ. Yaḡmāʾī, V. Tehran 1353 Š./1974, pp. 1154 ff. S. Wikander *Vayu* I, Lund, 1942. Idem, *Der arische Männerbund*, Lund, 1946.

(Djalal Khaleghi-Motlagh)

DERAḴT (Mid. Pers. *draxt*), tree, shrub. Two other words for "tree" occur in Pahlavi literature: *wan* (Av. *vanā-*, Pashto *wana*, Pers. *bon*) and *dār*, also meaning "wood" (Av. *dārav-/drav-* "tree stem, wood," Caspian dialects, Kurd., etc., *dār* "tree"; *AirWb.*, cols. 738-39, 1353; Morgenstierne, p. 87 no. 260); both *bon* and *dār* are obsolete in modern Persian usage, except in compounds like *sarv-bon* "cypress tree," probably *nār-van* "elm tree," *dār-bast* "trellis, scaffolding,"and Šīrāzī *bon(-e)gāh* "grove," and *dār* in the sense of "gibbet" and "wooden frame." In the *Bundahišn* a distinction is made between *dār* and *draxt*: Perennial plants that yield no food, like the cypress (q.v.), plane, and box trees and the tamarisk are called *dār o draxt*, but *draxt* is also said to designate any perennial plant, whether it produces food or not. Curiously, perennial fruit trees like the date palm (q.v.), the myrtle, the lote, and the grapevine are called simply *mēwag* "fruit" (NPers. *mīva*; tr. Anklesaria, 16.8-10; tr. Bahār, p. 87).

The *Bundahišn* (q.v.; tr. Anklesaria, 4.12-18), along with other legendary or historical sources, reveals the basically animistic Mazdean conception of the vegetable kingdom, which is reflected in tree symbolism (cf. the animistic, representative, and symbolic stages distinguished in the general development of tree worship; Barns, pp. 448-51). In the Mazdean tradition plants, like other natural phenomena, were believed to have souls (Pahl. *mēnōg*; see, e.g., *Bundahišn* 4.12, 4.14, 4.16, 4.18); all "Ahura Mazdā-given, clean plants," instinct with divine spirit, were venerable (*Yasna* 16.89, 17.12, 17.16; tr., pp. 194-95, 198, 199; for the few, despicable plants created by Ahriman, see GĪĀH), and this principle underlay all Mazdean plant lore, as well as what may have been a kind of tree cult. Mazdeans believed that Ahura Mazdā (q.v.; *Bundahišn*, tr. Anklesaria, 6D.1-4, 6E.1, 16.3) created fifty-five kinds (*sardag*) of grains and twelve of medicinal plants, which grew from the semen of the "uniquely created bull" at its death, as well as 130,000 *sardag*s (species? 100,000 in *Indian Bundahišn* 9.2-4, 27.2, tr. West, p. 110; cf. *Zādspram* 3.38, tr., p. 12) derived from 10,000 *sardag*s (genera? 1,000 in *Zādspram* 23, tr. pp. 57, 110; cf. 3.38, tr., p. 12) in turn derived from a single *mādagwar sardag* (archetype?). From the combined seeds of all these plants a cosmic or archetypal tree, *wan-ī was-tōhmag* (multiseeded tree) or *wan-ī harwisp-tōhmag* (allseed tree; *Zādspram* 3.39, tr., p. 12), grew in the middle of the mythical sea Frāxwkard (Av. *vourukaša-*; *Bundahišn*, tr. Anklesaria, 6D.3, 16.3-4; *Zādspram* 3.38-39; tr., p. 12). This fabulous tree was also known as *frārōn/tuxšāg bizešk* "righteous/diligent physician," *hamāg-bizešk* "all-healer" (*Bundahišn*, tr. Anklesaria, 24C.8; Av. *vīspō-biš*, lit., "all-remedy [tree]"; *AirWb.*, cols. 1468-69), and *wan-ī jud-bēš* "antipain tree" (*Mēnōg ī xrad*, ed. Anklesaria, 61.37-39; tr., p. 82). These allusions to the healing virtues of this fantastic tree probably reflect the belief that it embodied the twelve kinds of medicinal plants mentioned above, as well as the belief that the 10,000 *sardag*s were intended by Ohrmazd to counter the 10,000 diseases devised by Ahriman (q.v.; *Bundahišn*, tr. Anklesaria, 6D.3).

A number of features of the multiseeded tree are described in the *Bundahišn*. For example, within (under?) its trunk (*ēwan*) there are nine mountains with holes (*sūrāgōmand*) from which spring 9,999 streams. The mythical bird Sīmorḡ (Mid. Pers. Sēn murw) is said to perch on it every year to mix its seeds with water, which Tištar (Sirius) then rains down on all the regions of the world, thus propagating all kinds of plants. The immaculate sacred plant, the "white Hōm" (Av. *haoma*), also called *gōkirin* (Av. *gaokərənə-*) *draxt*, was planted by Ohrmazd near the multiseeded tree, in order to keep away decrepitude (*zarmān*) by imparting immortality to anyone who partakes of it (tr. Anklesaria, 14C.9, 16.4-5, 6D.6; Boyce, *Zoroastrianism* I, pp. 88-89, 137-38). Although the multiseeded tree seems to have been invulnerable, the *gōkirin* was not; Ahriman produced a huge frog (*wazaγ*), his largest animal, to spoil or destroy the *gōkirin*. Ohrmazd, in order to restrain the frog, created his largest animals, two *kar* fish, which constantly circled the *gōkirin* (*Bundahišn*, tr. Anklesaria, 24A.1-4). Whereas on a spiritual level the "white Hōm" was the *rad* (chief, lord, patron) of plants (16.5), among actual trees the date palm (q.v.) "is worth all the plants in the sky and on the earth" (16.1; cf. 17A.2).

Most forms of tree worship include belief in tree oracles (Barns, p. 455); in the *Šāh-nāma* (Moscow, VII, pp. 88-91) Alexander the Great (q.v.), after crossing a desert, came to an inhabited and woody country (probably western India), where he learned of a wonderful tree with one male and one female trunk; the foliage of the former provided oracles in the daytime, that of the other at night. The male prophesied that Alexander's reign would last only fourteen years, the female that he would die soon, in a foreign land.

According to a Zoroastrian tradition recorded by Daqīqī, the Kayanid king Goštāsp commemorated his conversion to Zoroastrianism by planting at Balḵ a wonderful cypress sapling, later known as Sarv-e Kāšmar, which in a few years attained a height of 40 cubits and a comparable diameter (*Šāh-nāma*, Moscow, VI, pp. 68-71). Belief in a sacred, divine, or "cosmic" tree may lead to reverence for, even worship of, individual trees believed to harbor the divine spirit or to embody the souls of personages who might serve as intercessors with the deity. Trees with particular remarkable features lend themselves to such beliefs: Evergreens and very old trees may symbolize immortality; size may suggest the greatness of the associated holy person; and an isolated position may underscore the uniqueness of God or the holy person. Although supposedly "fruitless" cypresses and plane trees have been particularly favored in Persia for these purposes, any other noticeable species may become foci of devotion: date palms in central and southern regions, oaks in western Persia, Siberian elms (*deraḵt-e āzād*, *Zelkova crenata* Desf.) in the Caspian provinces, pistachio trees in Khorasan, various fruit trees in Lorestān and Īlām (Asadīān et al., pp. 234-35).

Aside from the much later identification of the cypress of Kāšmar (or Bost) as the sacred tree of the Persians, the only "historical" reference to such an act of devotion and votive offering by a Persian notable is that of Herodotus (7.31), who reported that at Callatebus in Asia Minor the Achaemenid Xerxes (486-65 B.C.E.) found a plane tree so beautiful that he decorated it with golden ornaments and put it under the care of one of his Immortals. The animistic attitude toward venerable trees has continued in Persia to the present day, but with the transfer of devotion to Muslim saints, particularly Twelver Shiʿites. Distinguished trees have often generated belief in their sacred origin and association with saints, who work miracles or grant wishes through the intermediary of "their" trees. Hence the multitude of holy trees (*deraḵt-e fāżel* "eminent tree"; Ouseley, I, p. 313; Moḥammad-Pādšāh, III, s.v.; *deraḵt-e fażl* "tree of dis-tinction/grace"; Yule in Polo, pp. 134-35), now usually designated *deraḵt-e naẓar-karda* (blessed tree; *āqā-dār* in Gīlān and Māzandarān). There can be little doubt that the two historically attested magnificent cypresses at Kāšmar and Faryūmad inspired the legends that they were planted by Zoroaster or Goštāsp, and many an *emāmzāda* (q.v.) owes its existence to the proximity of an outstanding tree. Manučehr Sotūda (pp. vi-vii) noted that ten remarkable trees recorded in 1906-12 by H. L. Rabino di Borgomale, then British consul at Rašt, "are now each flanked by a building named Emāmzāda Ḥasan, Emāmzāda Ebrāhīm, and the like." The sanctity of a given tree is usually revealed by a Shiʿite saint in a dream to a person who then usually lays claim to the potentially lucrative custodianship (*tawlīat*) of the tree and the shrine eventually constructed there. Dūst-ʿAlī Moʿayyer-al-Mamālek (pp. 16, 28, and photograph p. 173), an intimate and son-in-law of the Qajar Nāṣer-al-Dīn Shah (1264-1313 Š./1848-96), reported such a story, deliberately circulated, which led to construction of an *emāmzāda* beside a plane tree in the private quarters of the shah's palace. Sometimes two or more prominent trees of the same species together constitute a sacred spot; the once prosperous Haft Tan (seven persons) in a suburb of Sārī included seven majestic Siberian elms, of which only a few have been spared by the ravages of time. In Māzandarān such a spot is called a *godargāh* (passage, implying that a saint has passed by), according to Jawād Nūšīn, who reports eighteen *emāmzādas* and several *godargāhs* in Kalārostāq (pp. 79-81). In Lorestān and Īlām lote trees, considered "paradisiacal," grow on plains or mountain passes trodden by holy persons (Asadīān et al., pp. 234-35).

Many remarkable "sacred" trees have been described by European travelers in Persia and by some native authors (see Massé, *Croyances et coutumes* I, pp. 221-23). To those trees may be added the controversial solitary plane tree described confusingly by Marco Polo (I, p. 127) as "the Arbre Sol . . . in Tonocain/Timocain" (i.e., the districts of Tūn and Qāyen in Khorasan); Guy Le Strange's guess (*Lands*, p. 356 n. 1) that it was the fabled "cypress of Zoroaster" is certainly wrong. Other additions to the list include the majestic old cypress in the courtyard of Emāmzāda Sayyed Ḥamza in Kāšmar; the still verdant wild pistachio tree, about 6.5 m tall and 860 years old, shading the tomb of Shaikh Aḥmad Jāmī (q.v.; d. 536/141) in Torbat-e Jām; and another wild pistachio tree, 400-500 years old, at the tomb of Zayn-al-Dīn Abū Bakr Tāybādī (d. 791/1389) in Tāybād (Abrīšamī, p. 39). Shaikh Abū Saʿīd b. Abi'l-Ḵayr (q.v.; d. 440/1048-49), forty years before his death, designated the site of his tomb at the foot of a large mulberry tree at Meyhana (Moḥammad b. Monawwar, pp. 37, 304, 371). The tombs of many Sufis and other saintly men buried in Herat province are shaded by old wild pistachio trees (Saljūqī, notes, pp. 52, 75, 103, 106, 120, 121, 130). Even dead "sacred" trees usually retain their status (see, e.g., *Nozhat al-qolūb*, ed. Le Strange, pp. 279-80; Saljūqī, p. 55 and notes, p. 24).

There are many legendary or semihistorical allusions to the symbolism of trees in pre-Islamic Persia, sometimes with apocalyptic import. Herodotus (1.107-08) reported the legend of Astyages (q.v.), king of Media, who saw in a dream a vine growing from the private parts of his pregnant daughter Mandane, who was married to Cambyses I (q.v.); he also reported (7.27) that the wealthy Lydian Pythius had offered a miniature golden plane tree and vine to Darius I when the latter passed through en route to Greece. These gifts may have been meant as charms, fetishes, or symbols of potential victory. Xenophon described, on the authority of Antiochus of Arcadia, a golden plane tree that was revered at the Achaemenid court; it was adorned with jewels from all over the empire, and royal audiences were held beneath it. The Macedonians who looted Persepolis had seen both that tree and a golden vine that were sometimes kept in the royal bedchamber (*Hellenica* 7.1.38). This golden tree was last mentioned when the Seleucid Antigonus Monophthalmos seized it at Susa in 316 B.C.E. (cf. Eddy; cf. Rawlinson, IV, p. 170).

Herodotus also reported (7.19) that Xerxes, contemplating an invasion of Greece, saw himself in a dream crowned with an olive branch from which other branches spread over the earth, a vision that the Magi interpreted as portending not only victory over Greece but also conquest of the world. Another prophetic dream of a tree is related in the *Bahman Yašt* (q.v.; ed. and tr. Rāšed Moḥaṣṣel, 1.3, 1.6-11, pp. 49-50, cf. 3.19-28, pp. 53-54; tr. West, 1.1-5, pp. 192-93, cf. 2.14-22, pp. 198-201), where Zoroaster is reported to have dreamed of a tree with four branches, of gold, silver, steel, and "mixed-up" iron, which Ohrmazd interpreted as symbolizing four future periods in Iranian history after Zoroaster's own millennium: the reigns of Goštāsb, Kay Ardašīr, Ḵosrow I, and finally a calamitous age of invasion by demons. In the *Šāh-nāma* (Moscow, V, pp. 54-55 vv. 787-92) there is an account of a jeweled artificial tree shading the throne of Kay Ḵosrow. Reminiscent of this tree is the one that the ʿAbbasid caliph al-Moqtader (296-320/908-32) had in Baghdad (Ḵaṭīb, p. 103; Qazvīnī, pp. 210-11).

Sacralization of trees presupposes legal sanctions against profaning or destroying them, or at least an ethical attitude condemning such acts; but the only protection for trees in Persia seems to have been the awe inspired by them, expressed in this hemistich by the poet Neẓāmī Ganjavī (d. 605/1209): "Anybody felling a tree will be short-lived" (p. 427 v. 5). A dramatic instance is the early belief that the caliph al-Motawakkel (232-47/847-61), who ordered the sacred cypress of Kāšmar felled despite warnings of his entourage and the supplication of local Mazdeans, was murdered before the pieces of the tree reached Baghdad. In general, however, Persia has suffered from continuous deforestation over the centuries. In addition to the traditional indiscriminate and wasteful felling of trees for fuel and other uses, during the last few decades much wooded land has been cleared for cultivation, particularly in the Caspian provinces. Reżā Shah (1304-20 Š./1925-41) established an anuual tree-planting day (15 Esfand/6 March), which was nominally observed during the reign of Moḥammad-Reżā Shah (1320-57 Š./1941-79), but it had little impact. In the charter of Moḥammad-Reżā Shah's "White Revolution" (promulgated on 6 Bahman 1341 Š./26 January 1963) many forests and pastures were nationalized, which provided some measure of protection, as destructive exploitation of these resources was forbidden. In addition, a long-term program of reforestation and preservation resulted in establishment of such agencies as Sāzmān-e jangalbānī o marāteʿ-e kešvar (Organization of conservation of forests and rangelands), Sāzmān-e ḥefāẓat-e moḥīṭ-e zīst (Department of environmental protection), and Anjoman-e mellī-e ḥefāẓat-e manābeʿ-e ṭabīʿī o moḥīṭ-e ensānī (National society for the conservation of natural resources and the human environment), the last under royal patronage. A seminar on the natural vegetation of Persia was convened in Tehran 8-11 Tīr 1354 Š./29 June-2 July 1975 (Dānešgāh). The application of protective measures was greatly facilitated by adequate provision of kerosene fuel to villagers and the expansion of the electric-power network. Since the Revolution of 1357 Š./1979 acute shortages of kerosene and electricity, as well as indifference to the natural environment, have resulted in the increased use of firewood and charcoal by villagers and city dwellers (see FORESTS).

Bibliography: (For cited works not included in this bibliography and abbreviations found here, see "Short References.") M.-Ḥ. Abrīšamī, "Īrān-šenāsān-e ḵārejī wa noḵostīn gāmhā dar bāb-e tārīḵ-e kešāvarzī-e Īrān," in 'A. Mūsawī Garmārūdī, ed., *Majmūʿa-ye maqālāt-e Anjomanvāra-ye barrasī-e masāʾel-e īrān-šenāsī*, Tehran, 1369 Š./1990, pp. 33-60. *Alf layla wa layla*, tr. E. W. Lane as *The Thousand and One Nights . . .*, 3 vols., London, 1839-41. M. Asadīān Ḵorramābādī et al., *Bāvarhā wa dānestahā dar Lorestān o Īlām*, Tehran, 1358 Š./1979. M. Bahār, "Deraḵt-e moqaddas," *Alefbā* 1, 1352 Š./1973, pp. 93-96. *Bahman Yašt*, ed. and tr. M.-T. Rāšed Moḥaṣṣel as *Zand-e Bahman Yasn*, Tehran, 1370 Š./1991; tr. E. W. West as *Bahman Yast or Zand-i Vohûman Yasno*, SBE 5, Oxford, 1880; repr. Delhi, 1965, pp. 189-235. T. Barns, "Trees and Plants," in J. Hastings, ed., *Encyclopaedia of Religions and Ethics* XII, Edinburgh, 1921; repr. Edinburgh, 1980, pp. 448-57. *Bundahišn*, tr. M. Bahār as *Bondaheš*, Tehran, 1369 Š./1990. Dānešgāh-e Tehrān, Markaz-e hamāhangī-e moṭālaʿāt-e moḥīṭ-e zīst, *Noḵostīn semīnār-e barrasī-e masāʾel-e pūšeš-e gīāhī-e Īrān/Proceedings of the First Seminar on Problems of the Natural Vegetation of Persia, June 29-July 2, 1975*, Tehran, 1975. S. K. Eddy, *The King Is Dead. Studies in the Near Eastern Resistance to Hellenism, 334-31 B.C.*, Lincoln, Neb., 1961. N. Emāmī, "Deraḵt wa gīāh dar afsāna wa osṭūra," *Pažūheš-nāma-ye Dāneškada-ye Jondī Šāpūr* I/1, 1356 Š./1977, pp. 28-38. *Indian Bundahišn*, ed. and tr. R. Behzādī as *Bondaheš-e hendī . . .*, Tehran, 1368 Š./1989; tr. E. W. West as *Bundahiš*, SBE 5, Oxford , 1880; repr. Delhi, 1965, pp. 1-151. Ḵaṭīb Baḡdādī, *Taʾrīḵ Baḡdād* I, Cairo, 1349/1931. *Mēnōg ī xrad*, tr. A. Tafażżolī as *Mīnū-ye ḵerad*, Tehran, 1354 Š./1975. Moḥammad b. Monawwar, *Asrār al-tawḥīd fī maqāmāt al-Šayḵ Abī Saʿīd*, ed. Ḏ. Ṣafā, Tehran, 1354 Š./1975. Dūst-ʿAlī Moʿayyer-al-Mamālek, *Yāddāšthā-ī az zendagānī-e ḵoṣūṣī-e Nāṣer-al-Dīn Šāh*, 3rd ed., Tehran, 1361 Š./1982. Moḥammad-Pādšāh, *Farhang-e Ānand Rāj*, ed. M. Dabīrsīāqī, 2nd ed., 7 vols., Tehran, 1363 Š./1984. G. Morgenstierne, *An Etymological Vocabulary of Pashto*, Oslo, 1927. Neẓāmī Ganjavī, *Ḵosrow o Šīrīn*, ed. Ḥ. Waḥīd Dastgerdī, Tehran, 1313 Š./1934. J. Nūšīn, *Owżāʿ-e tārīḵī, sīāsī, eqteṣādī wa joḡrāfīāʾī-e šahrestān-e Čālūs*, 2nd ed., Tehran, 1355 Š./1976. W. Ouseley, *Travels in Various Countries of the East (1810-12)*, 4 vols., London, 1819-23. Marco Polo, *The Book of Ser Marco Polo the Venetian . . .*, tr. and ed. H. Yule, 3rd ed., ed. H. Cordier, 2 vols., London, 1929. Zakarīyāʾ Qazvīnī, *Āṯār al-belād wa aḵbār al-ʿebād*, ed. F. Wüstenfeld, Göttingen, 1848. G. Rawlinson, *The Five Great Monarchies of the Ancient Eastern World . . .*, 4 vols., London, 1862-67. "Rūz-e deraḵt-kārī," *Īrān-e novīn*, 14 Esfand 1353 Š./5 March 1975, p. 3. F. Saljūqī, ed., *Resāla-ye mazārāt-e Herāt*, Kabul, 1346 Š./1967. M. Sotūda, *Az Āstārā tā Estārbād* I/1, Tehran, 1349 Š./1970. *Zādspram*, tr. M.-T. Rāšed Moḥaṣṣel as *Gozīdahā-ye Zādesparam*, Tehran, 1366 Š./1987.

(HŪŠANG AʿLAM)

DERĀZ-DAST (having long hands; OPers. **darga-dasta-*; cf. Younger Av. *darəγō.gava-* "with long hands," *AirWb.* col. 694), epithet of King Bahman-Ardašīr (q.v.) mentioned in the Persian sources (*Mojmal*, ed. Bahār, p. 30; Ebn al-Balḵī, p. 52; *Tārīḵ-e gozīda*, ed. Browne, p. 98), probably translating a Pahlavi form like *dērang/d-dast*. It is also recorded in the Arabic forms *ṭawīl-al-yadayn* (Bīrūnī, *Āṯār*, pp. 37, 111; Ebn al-ʿEbrī, pp. 87, 113) or *ṭawīl-al-yad* (Ebn al-Nadīm, ed. Tajaddod, p. 307). Another variant of this epithet is Arabic *ṭawīl-al-bāʿ* (Ṭabarī, I, p. 686; Ḥamza, 1961, p. 37; Bīrūnī, *Āṯār*, p. 105; Ḵᵛārazmī, p. 100), Persian *derāz-bāzūg*, literally "having long arms" (Gardīzī, ed. Ḥabībī, p. 15), derived from Pahlavi **drāz-bāzūg*, Avestan *darəgō.bāzav-* (*AirWb.* col. 695). It is also recorded as *derāz-angol*, literally "having long fingers," rendering Pahlavi *dērand/g-angust* (*Ardā Wīrāz Nāmag*, ed. Haug and West, chap. 4.19; ed. Vahman, p. 91. 3), Avestan *darəγō.angušta-* (*AirWb.* col. 694). The classical authors recorded the title of Artaxerxes I (q.v.) as Makrócheir in Greek (Plutarch, *Artoxerxes* 1.1) and Longimanus in Latin (Nöldeke, 1887, pp. 49-50; idem, 1920, p. 13 and n. 4).

Both the Greek and the Islamic authors had two explanations for this epithet. The old Greek authors like Dino (q.v.) took the word "hand" in its figurative sense of "power" (Nöldeke, 1887; idem, 1920). The same explanation is found in some Islamic sources (Ebn al-Balḵī, p. 52; *Mojmal*, ed. Bahār, p. 30, Bīrūnī, *Āṯār*, p. 37; *Tārīḵ-e gozīda*, ed. Browne, p. 98; Ṭabarī, I, p. 686; Ḥamza, 1961, p. 37; Meskawayh, pp. 33 ff.). But the later Greek authors, like Plutarch (*Artoxerxes* 1.1) and Strabo (15.3.21), as well as some Islamic authors, interpreted it in a literal sense (e.g., Bīrunī, *Āṯār*, p. 111; *Mojmal*, ed. Bahār, p. 30; *Šāh-nāma*, ed. Moscow, VI, p. 320 v. 1668).

The first explanation seems preferable, for the word *dast* is used in a number of Iranian languages with the meaning "power, authority" (e.g., Man. Mid. Parth. *dast* "capable, able"; Pahl. *dastwar* "authority"; NPers. *dast* "power"). Furthermore, another, similar epithet of Bahman-Ardašīr, *rēwand-dast* "having prosperous hands" (Bīrūnī, 1355/1936, p. 25), derived from **raēvas.dasta-/zasta-* (cf. Av. *raēvas.čiθra-* "of rich descent," *AirWb.* 1485; cf. Hinz, p. 196) may confirm such a supposition.

Bibliography: (For cited works not found in this bibliography, see "Short References.") *Ardā Wīrāz Nāmag. The Book of Arda Viraf*, ed. M. Haug and E. W. West, Bombay and London, 1872; ed. F. Vahman, London and Malmö, 1986. Bīrūnī, *Ketāb al-jamāher fī maʿrefat al-jawāher*, Hyderabad, 1355/1936. Ebn al-ʿEbrī, *Taʾrīḵ*, ed. A. Ṣāleḥānī, Beirut, 1890. Abu'l-Ḥasan Ḥamza Eṣfahānī, *Ketāb taʾrīḵ senī molūk al-arż waʾl-anbīāʾ*, Beirut, 1961. W. Hinz, *Altiranisches Sprachgut*, Wiesbaden, 1975. Ḵᵛārazmī, *Mafātīḥ al-ʿolūm*, ed. G. van Vloten, Leiden, 1895. Ṣ. Kīā, *Aryāmehr*, Tehran, 1346 Š./1967, pp. 142-46. Meskawayh, *Tajāreb*, ed. A. Emāmī, I, Tehran, 1366 Š./1987. M. Moʿīn, "Derāz-dast, derāz-angol, rīvand-dast," *Indo-Iranica* 4/2-3, 1949-50, pp. 25-29; repr. in M. Moʿīn, *Majmūʿa-ye maqālāt*, ed. M. Moʿīn, II, 1367 Š./1988, pp. 331-35. T. Nöldeke, *Aufsätze zur persischen Geschichte*, Leipzig, 1887. Idem, *Das iranische Nationalepos*, 2nd ed., Berlin and Leipzig, 1920.

(AḤMAD TAFAŻŻOLĪ)

DERBEND. See DARBAND.

DERHAM. See DIRHAM.

DERHAM B. NAŻR (or Naṣr or Ḥosayn), commander of *ʿayyārs* (q.v.) or *moṭawweʿa*, orthodox Sunni vigilantes against the Kharijites in Sīstān during the period immediately preceding the rise of the Saffarid brothers to supreme power there. Derham was chosen by the Sunni forces in the field to succeed the *ʿayyār* leader Ṣāleḥ b. Nażr Kenānī (nowhere mentioned as a brother of Derham) in Jomādā II 244/October 858; he seems to have remained in command until ousted three years later by his own subordinate the Saffarid Yaʿqūb b. Layṯ (Moḥarram 247/April 861). His later years are obscure, but he may have been reconciled with Yaʿqūb and employed as an envoy to the ʿAbbāsid caliph, probably al-Moʿtamed (256-79/870-92; Eṣṭaḵrī, pp. 246-47; Ebn Ḥawqal, pp. 419-20; tr. Kramers, pp. 407-08) or imprisoned at Sāmarrā (Ṭabarī, III, p. 1892).

Bibliography: (For cited works not found in this bibliography and abbreviations found here, see "Short References.") W. Barthold, "Zur Geschichte der Ṣaffāriden," in *Orientalistische Studien Theodor Nöldeke* . . ., ed. C. Bezold, I, Giessen, 1906, pp. 171-91. C. E. Bosworth, *Sistan under the Arabs, from the Islamic Conquest to the Rise of the Saffarids (30-250/651-864)*, Rome, 1968, pp. 109, 114, 117-19. Ebn al-Aṯīr, VII, pp. 64, 185, 390. Ebn Ḵallekān, ed. ʿAbbās, VI, pp. 402-03; tr. de Slane, IV, pp. 301-02. *Tārīḵ-e Sīstān*, pp. 194, 199-200, 202; tr. Gold, pp. 154, 158-59, 160.

(C. EDMUND BOSWORTH)

DERUSIANS. See TRIBES, PERSIAN.

DEŚANĀ, Khotanese term with two meanings: "showing" (< Skt. *deśayati* "shows"), that is, "preaching" the law, and "profession" of faith or "confession" of sins (Bailey, 1962, p. 18; cf. Edgerton, s.v.). In the second meaning *deśanā* also refers to a particular genre of Khotanese religious text (Emmerick, 1992, p. 37).

Two texts from this group are known to have been translated from Sanskrit originals: the *Bhadracaryādeśanā* (q.v.) and the *Deśanā-parivarta* (chapter of confession), which Johannes Nobel (p. xlvii) considered the nucleus of the *Suvarṇabhāsottamasūtra* (Sutra of golden light), to which other chapters were gradually added. Together the Khotanese versions of these two texts form the main part of manuscript P 3513 (fols. 43-58, 59-75, respectively) in the Pelliot collection of the Bibliothèque Nationale, Paris, preceding another *deśanā* text (fols. 76-84; see below). According to P. O. Skjærvø (forthcoming), the text of the *Deśanā-parivarta* in P 3513, one of the earliest published Late Khotanese Buddhist texts (Pelliot), has occasionally been badly distorted to suit the meter. Other *deśanā* texts appear to have been composed in Khotan, including two attributed to the prince Tcūṃ-ttehi: (Hamilton, p. 48; Kumamoto, p. 231; Takata, in Emmerick and Skjærvø, p. 49). One of them, on fols. 76–84, was published and translated by H. W. Bailey (1951, pp. 62-66; 1962); a variant of the beginning is in P 3510, fols. 9-10, from the same collection (Bailey, 1951, p. 53). The other text by Tcūṃ-ttehi: is found on fols. 1-8 of P 3510 (Bailey, 1951, pp. 47-52) and has been translated by Ronald Emmerick (1980). Both these texts are written in verse in the first-person singular. There is a similar text in the first-person singular, stressing the speaker's faith in the Amitābha Buddha (Khot. Armyāya baʾysä) and Sukhāvatī (*suhāva*; Ethnographic Museum, Stockholm, Hedin ms. 23; Bailey, 1945-63, IV, pp. 36-37, 129-35); the beginning is lost, but the end is preserved.

The *Karmāṃ Deśanā* (Emmerick, 1977; idem, 1992, p. 38), of which three variants exist (Bailey, 1951, pp. 66-71), differs from those already mentioned in that only the first few verses are in the first person; the remainder is a series of doctrinal discussions about *karma* "act." In this text the word *deśanā* is used in the first meaning given above. Mark Dresden has catalogued the "Invocation of Prince Tcū-syau" (Bailey, 1951, pp. 146-48; cf. Kumamoto, p. 232) as *deśanā*, though it, along with two other texts (Bailey, 1945-63, V, pp. 249-55) identified as *deśanā* by Shūyo Takubo, should be classified as *namo* texts (Emmerick, 1992, p. 37), usually long lists of the Buddhas and other deities to whom homage is paid (see, e.g., Bailey, 1951, pp. 91-93, 100-04; idem, 1945-63, III, pp. 30-31, 50-52, 53-54, 55-57, 97-98, 98-99, 112-16, 117). They belong to the same genre of *Buddhanāmasūtras* as the *Bhadrakalpikasūtra* (q.v.) but were probably composed in Khotan, rather than translated.

Bibliography: J. P. Asmussen, *The Khotanese Bhadracaryādeśanā*, Copenhagen, 1961. H. W. Bailey, *Khotanese Texts*, 5 vols., Cambridge, 1945-63. Idem, *Khotanese Buddhist Texts*, London, 1951. Idem, "The Profession of Prince Tcūṃ-ttehi:," in E. Bender, ed., *Indological Studies in Honor of W. Norman Brown*, New Haven, Conn., 1962, pp. 18-22. M. J. Dresden, "Khotanese (Saka) Manuscripts. A Provisional Handlist," *Varia 1976*, Acta Iranica 12, Tehran and Liège, 1977, pp. 27-85. F. Edgerton, *Buddhist Hybrid Sanskrit Grammar and Dictionary*, 2 vols., New Haven, Conn., 1953. R. E. Emmerick, "The Confession of Acts," *Varia 1976*, Acta Iranica 12, Tehran and Liège, 1977, pp. 87-115. Idem, "The Verses of Prince Tcūṃ-ttehi:," *Stud. Ir.* 9/2, 1980, pp. 185-93. Idem, *A Guide to the Literature of Khotan*, 2nd ed., Tokyo, 1992. Idem and P. O. Skjærvø, *Studies in the Vocabulary of Khotanese* II, Vienna, 1987. J. Hamilton, "Sur la chronologie khotanaise au IXe-Xe siècle," in M. Soymié, ed., *Contributions aux études de Touen-houang* III, Paris, 1984, pp. 47-53. H. Kumamoto, "Some Problems of the Khotanese Documents," in R. Schmitt and P. O. Skjærvø, eds., *Studia Grammatica Iranica. Festschrift für Helmut Humbach*, Munich, 1986, pp. 227-44. J. Nobel, *Suvarṇabhāsottamasūtra. Das Goldglanz-sūtra. Ein Sanskrittext des Mahāyāna-Buddhismus*, Leipzig, 1937. P. Pelliot, "Un fragment du *Suvarṇabhāsasūtra* en iranien oriental," *MSL* 18, 1913, pp. 89-125. P. O. Skjærvø, *The Khotanese Suvarṇabhāsottamasūtra*, Habil. thesis, Mainz 1983.. T. Takata, "Tcūm-ttehi:," in R. E. Emmerick and P. O. Skjærvø, *Studies in the Vocabulary of Khotanese* II, Vienna, 1987, pp. 49-50. S. Takubo, *Tonkō-Shutsudo Utengo Himitsu Kyōten-shū-no Kenkyū* (Studies on esoteric sutras in Khotanese found in Dunhuang), Tokyo, 1975.

(Hiroshi Kumamoto)

DESERT (Pers. *bīābān*; *kavīr*; *lūt*; see below), area of low precipitation that supports little vegetation and lacks surface water. Secondary characteristics typically include poor soils, salinity, high winds, and extreme temperatures, accompanied by high rates of erosion and sand accumulation. Global wind patterns maintain these conditions in zones that encircle the earth in the subtropical latitudes, both north and south of the equator.

In the northern hemisphere the arid zone extends from the Atlantic through North Africa and southwestern Asia into northern India. East of Persia the high mountain barrier separating Central Asia from the subcontinent produces an extension of the arid zone through more temperate latitudes from the Caspian (q.v.) as far as Mongolia and China. This aridity dates from the Quaternary or, in some parts, the Tertiary (Fisher, p. 92; Kohl, p. 25). Despite great variation in altitude, from below sea level at the Caspian shore and in the Turfan depression to more than 2,000 m above sea level on parts of the Iranian plateau, the zone evinces a remarkable degree of continuity, in soils and landforms, plant communities, and fauna, as well as in human technological adaptation and cultural response. This continuity has been reinforced over thousands of years by coadaptation between natural processes and various technologies that have been developed to accommodate the problems of aridity.

Paradoxically this Asian arid zone appears to have served as a conduit for population movements and cultural influences since the earliest evidence of human occupation. Where it passes through southwestern and central Asia it comprises the theater of Iranian history. The Iranian plateau lies athwart the zone, forming a bridge between its subtropical extension into the subcontinent and its temperate extension through Central Asia. Consequently, although deserts make up no more than 20 percent of the total land surface of the world, they have been a dominant feature in Iranian geography.

In this article the information currently available on Iranian desert regions is summarized from the general perspective of their historical significance.

Desert Types.

The general Persian word for desert is *bīābān*. As throughout most of the arid zone agriculture and settlement depend upon sustained investment, Persians generally expect to find *bīābān* where *ābādī* (settled, irrigated agriculture, q.v.) ends. The term *bīābān* covers a broad range of different types of desert, from completely barren expanses at one extreme to plains with significant percentages of vegetation cover at the other. There are no scientific criteria for defining the limits at which the more productive types of *bīābān* merge into Western categories of semidesert and steppe. The most common terms for different types of barren *bīābān* are *lūt* (cf. *lok̲t* "bare"), which is generally the default term for barren surfaces; *kavīr* (according to Tomaschek, 1885, p. 582, < *gaver* < *gav*, cognate with *cavitas*, though Barthold, 1984, p. 134 preferred < Ar. *qafr*, pl. *qefār* "barren desert"; cf. Curzon, *Persian Question* II, pp. 246-47) for playas; and *rīg* or *rīgzār* for areas of shifting sand. *Kavīr* is generally equivalent to *solonchak* in the Russian literature on Central Asia. Various vernacular terms are also in use, sometimes associated with special conditions. For example, *daqq* is used for relatively small areas of *kavīr* in Khorasan, *kaffa* similarly in Kermān. In Central Asia the Turkic term *takyr* is used, and farther east the Mongolian term *nor* is found. West of the plateau the most common term is Arabic *sabḵa*.

Iranian *kavīr*s have attracted special interest (see especially the works of Bobek; Gabriel; Stratil-Sauer; and Krinsley, but the most accessible description and explanation is in Jackson et al., pp. 7-14; see also Cooke and Warren, pp. 215-28 for comparative discussion) and may be unique in the variety of their composition and surface types. They offer a prospect of desolate waste that extends almost continuously from within 50 km of Tehran to Afghanistan and the Persian Gulf. To H. B. Vaughan, the first European to provide a firsthand description, the *kavīr* looked like "a vast frozen sea stretching away . . . as far as the eye could reach in one vast glittering expanse" (1893, p. 105). As similar landscapes lie close to many of the major cities of Iranian history *kavīr* is often considered to be the characteristically Iranian desert type. It is composed of fine-grained sediments, saline to varying degrees, accumulated at the lowest part of a closed drainage basin in conditions where evaporation far exceeds precipitation and runoff. The texture varies according to the nature of the sediments, which may be silts or clays. The surface is often level, smooth, and hard, dry except after rain and ideal for all forms of transport. Similar surfaces are used for racing in the western United States and Australia. They may be treacherous, however; in some parts heavy traffic may break through the crust into deep, viscous mud. In other parts the crust may be divided into polygonal plates, which can grow and buckle as the salt crystallizes. Folding makes such areas impassable, comparable to and reminiscent of polar snowfields. In size *kavīr*s vary from a few score square meters to thousands of square kilometers.

The climate in such basins is extreme. In the driest, like the central deserts of the Iranian plateau, average annual precipitation (some of which may fall as snow in the north) is typically less than 100 mm and is restricted to the cooler months. Actual precipitation events are infrequent and may not occur for years at a time. Although records are inadequate and unreliable, annual mean temperatures appear to vary typically from 16° to more than 20° C. Summer maximums in some parts exceed 50° C. and may be among the highest in the world.

The second most prevalent type of desert is sand (Pers. *rīg*, Darī and Tajik *rēg*, less commonly *šen*; often referred to in the scientific literature by the term "erg," drawn from research in North Africa). Areas of dunes, partly shifting, partly vegetated and stable, partly regular (e.g., in crescent-shaped barchans), partly tangled and irregular, occur in various sizes on the leeward (southeastern) side of most basins (see Cooke and Warren, pp. 255-327, for comparative discussion). The deserts of Central Asia and the subcontinent are mostly sand-covered, but the largest impassable area lies on the Iranian plateau in southeastern Persia.

Other types of barren surface are typically called *lūt*. The best known are the undulating gray gravel plains characteristic of southeastern Persia, especially between Kermān and Bīrjand, and of southwestern Afghanistan (see the works of Gabriel, a physical geographer who traveled in the area in the 1920s and 1930s). But similar surfaces recur throughout the arid zone.

The typical *bīābān*, however, is not barren but supports some vegetation. Apart from the Caspian littoral, most of the arid zone may be considered *bīābān*, often including the mountainous areas (which are also largely barren except in sheltered valleys). The term *bīābān* may even be applied to the few upland areas with reliable average precipitation over about 350 mm per year, sufficient to support rainfed agriculture (except during the short growing season), as in parts of Azerbaijan, Kurdistan, Persian Khorasan, northeastern Baluchistan (Pakistan), and the central and eastern highlands of Afghanistan. Typical *bīābān* conditions, therefore, are broad plains with inland drainage, broken irregularly by minor ranges and rock outcrops. Average annual precipitation ranges between 100 and 400 mm, generally restricted to the cooler months, with highest probability in autumn and spring (although the monsoon often brings summer humidity in the south and occasionally even rain). There is great variation from year to year, and the low precipitation is complemented by low humidity and high insolation, with high rates of evaporation (especially during the summer) and diurnal temperature ranges not uncommonly exceeding 30° C. Strong winds blow constantly for weeks at a time throughout the warmer part of the year, especially in the north and east of the plateau; they are known as *bād-e sad o bīst rūz* (120-day wind) in Sīstān. Dust devils are ubiquitous, and dust storms are not uncommon. The wind deflates large quantities of material, producing here and there (beside sand) such fantastic topographical features as yardangs, known locally as *kalūt*, east of Ḵabīṣ. Vegetation cover varies from less than 5 percent to as much as 30 percent, even more in favored locations, and consists mostly of low perennial shrubs, dominated by communities of *Salsola* and *Zygophyllum* (*qīč*) up to about 1,300 m and communities of *Artemisia* (*dermāna*), *Ephedra*, and *Amygdalus* at higher altitudes, with such psammophytes as saxaul (*Haloxylon spp.*) in sandy areas and halophytes like tamarisk (*Tamaryx spp.*; *gāz*) in drainage channels or saline depressions with high water tables. In the south wild date palms (q.v.; *Phoenix dactylifera*) and dwarf palms (*Chamaerops spp.*) replace tamarisks. The barren, gravelly surface between perennial shrubs is filled for a few weeks in spring with a flush of annuals, which are particularly important in the regime of pastoralists, whether nomadic or based in villages.

Much of this typical *bīābān* is endowed with groundwater supplies that may be good and even plentiful, though varying in depth from as much as 100 m or more on the upper slopes of alluvial fans to very shallow levels close to the centers of plains. Soil conditions are often adequate to justify investment in irrigated agriculture.

Unfortunately the current state of research does not allow even a preliminary assessment of how much territory falls within each of these categories. The map in Figure 18 is based on data from a number of sources. It is designed to provide a generalized representation of the sizes and locations of large desert areas relative to other major features. An exact map is not possible because the available sources are derived from incompatible attempts by individual investigators, each of whom has generalized from limited firsthand knowledge. The problem is especially noticeable with regard to the boundaries of *kavīr* and sand. The 2,000-m contour was chosen, and generalized, in order to bring out the saucer-like form of the Iranian plateau and the continuation of the arid zone eastward through Central Asia and Chinese Turkestan, as well as to show the approximate boundaries of mountainous areas (most of them arid and barren except in river valleys). At elevations below the contour line only large areas of sand and playa are marked. There are also many smaller areas of playa, sand, and hamada and serir surfaces, often gypsiferous, sometimes rolling or hilly. Determination of the exact limits and sizes of desert areas awaits definitive interpretation of satellite imagery.

Major desert areas.

For most parts of the arid zone data from field research are not yet sufficiently detailed to support more than brief general descriptions of particular deserts (see above; Figure 18). The following brief general description will serve as a guide to the literature, which lacks a modern synthesis.

The Iranian plateau. The central part of the Iranian plateau resembles a saucer. Alluvial fans sloping down from the ranges of the Alborz, Zagros, and Paropamisus ranges into the arid interior represent the rim. They enclose a system of endorheic basins. A few of these basins in the northwest and southwest contain permanent lakes (e.g., Urmia, Neyrīz, and Bak̲tagān, q.v.). Sīstān, Jāz Mūrīān, Māškel, and Lora in the south and southeast, on the borders of Afghanistan and Pakistan, contain unreliable or intermittent lakes, depending upon river flow from the mountains to the east. Most of the remainder, the vast majority of the basins, contain playas of varying sizes (Persia, pp. 86-97). The largest basins, which lie in the geosyncline that forms the center of the saucer, constituting almost half of Persia, have the severest desert conditions. The barren wastes that occupy the greater part of them are commonly labeled Dašt-e Kavīr (also Kavīr-e Namak) and Dašt-e Lūt. These names are not in local use, however (cf. Gabriel, 1952, pp. 301-02 n. 49), do not appear in historical sources, and are probably derived from the mapping inquiries of foreign explorers in the 19th century. With few exceptions (always smaller areas) local communities tend to refer to all playas and other barren expanses as *kavīr*, *lūt*, or *bīābān*, without naming them. The most common local terms for the largest barren area are Great Kavīr (Kavīr-e bozorg) for the largest northern basin and simply *lūt* for its elongated continuation to the south.

The Great Kavīr is completely barren for more than 350 km from west to east and up to about 150 km from north to south. With the southern *lūt* and its continuation through minor watersheds to the south, past Narmāšīr into Jāz Mūrīān and through Sīstān into Kharan (Pakistan), it forms a continuous stretch of absolute barrenness from the alluvial fans of the Alborz mountains in the north to the edge of the plateau in Baluchistan, more than 1,200 km to the southeast. In altitude these central deserts slope from about 1,000 m in the north to about 250 m on the lowest *kavīr* just east of Šahdād (K̲abīṣ) in the southwest. Average annual rainfall throughout these deserts is well under 100 mm. Near the center of the Lūt, which is in the driest part of the plateau, between the *kavīr* on the west and the erg on the east, the wind has carved out deep furrows, leaving broken ridges that increase in height and density toward the south. These fantastically eroded forms, called *kalūt* and yardangs by physical geographers, resemble passageways between ruined buildings and have sometimes been mistaken by foreign travelers for ruins of ancient cities (hence *šahr-e lūt* in the travel literature; see Gabriel, 1935, p. 185; Dresch).

The erg on the eastern side of the southern Lūt is the largest area of sand on the Iranian plateau, measuring approximately 160 km from north to south and as much as 65 km from east to west. Much of it is not only deep but also tangled without clear differentiation in waves and troughs or other types of dune formation, especially in the south. Within the central basins smaller *rīg*s are widely distributed, especially along the southern shore of the Great Kavīr (for a firsthand description, see Gabriel, 1935, pp. 225-34). Similar conditions continue eastward into Afghanistan (q.v. i), broken by the uplands of Kūhestān (Qāʾenāt) in southern Khorasan and farther south by the low ridge that checks the westward flow of the Helmand to form the large oasis of Sīstān. This eastern desert basin (in southwestern Afghanistan) is about 400 km from west to east and 250 km from north to south and is broken only by the courses of the Helmand itself and some seasonal rivers, of which the K̲āšrūd (Afghanistan) and the Māškel (Persia and Pakistan) are the most significant. The largest continuous erg in Afghanistan is the Rīgestān (24,000 km^2), southwest of Qandahār (Balsan). The Gowd-e Zereh (lake basin), which

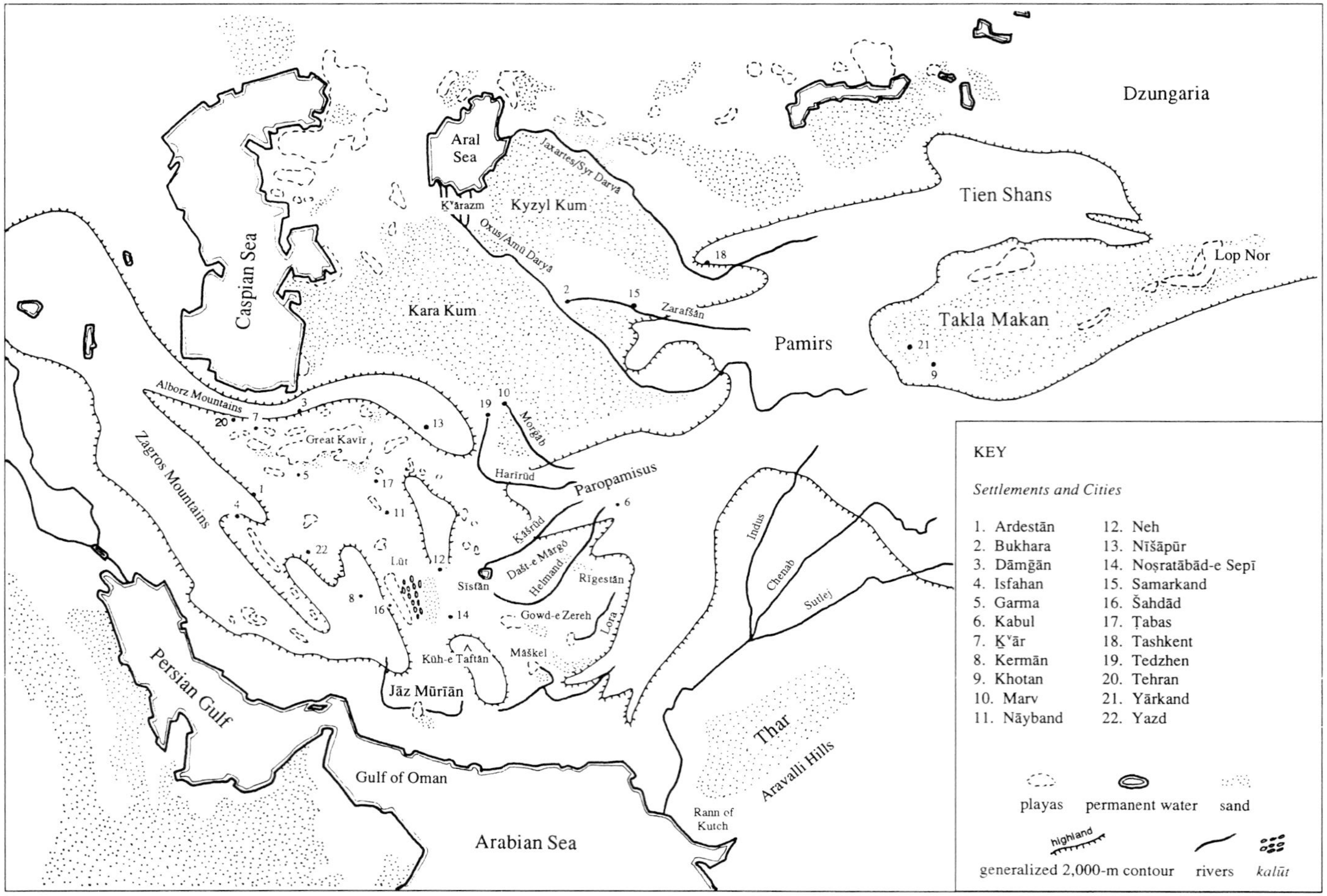

Figure 18. Location of major desert areas in relation to other features. *Sources*: Anders; Dresch; works by Gabriel; Hedin; Kohl; *Persia*; the author's field notes.

occasionally receives excess drainage from Sīstān, is separated from Kharan (in Pakistan) only by the low Chaghai hills, which, with the highlands around the extinct volcano Kūh-e Taftān, cause the Māškel river to form a lake (*hāmūn*) comparable to though much smaller than the lake of Sīstān. The desert north of the Helmand is known as Dašt-e Mārgō (11,500 km^2).

East of the Iranian plateau the desert conditions continue: southeast into India and around the northern side of the Paropamisus, through a succession of large desert areas, broken by occasional rivers and skirted by the former Silk Route.

The extension into India. The Thar, or Great Indian Desert, in Sind (Pakistan) and Rajasthan (India), together with such adjoining areas as the Thal (between the Indus and Chenab rivers) and Cholestan, south and east of Bhawalpur, both in Punjab (Pakistan), stretches ca. 650 km from southwest to northeast and is up to 350 km wide, covering more than 200,000 km^2. Colonization of the Thar has resulted exclusively from the westward extension of Indian influence, as political forces have sought to control the arterial routes across it, whereas the pastoral economy of the desert, though culturally mixed, has been more closely related to that of the predominantly Muslim populations to the west.

The extension into Central Asia (q.v. i). Northeast of the Iranian plateau is the Kara Kum (lit., "black sand," because dark with vegetation). The sands cover about 250,000 km^2, sloping from east to west between the Oxus river (Āmū Daryā, q.v.) and the Caspian, comprising about 60 percent of Turkmenistan. About 5 percent of the area consists of active barchans. Mean annual precipitation ranges between 70 and 150 mm. The vegetation is more plentiful and supports a richer array of fauna than in the deserts of the plateau (where, however, it may have been greater in the past); animals include antelope, wolves, and wildcats, as well as the flocks of Turkmen pastoralists. Beside the Oxus other, smaller rivers enter the desert from the south and supply irrigation systems before disappearing into the sand. The Oxus now feeds a canal that irrigates large areas along the southern edge of the Kara Kum and another in the direction of Bukhara (q.v.), which also receives water from the Zarafšān. Recent archeological research shows evidence of earlier courses of the Oxus and other rivers that supported ancient settlement patterns; they demonstrate the basic instability of the local hydrology (Kohl). The Oxus appears to have flowed into the Caspian, at least for a brief period, as late as the 14th century.

On the other side of the Oxus lies the area known as Transoxania, or Mā warā' al-Nahr, where a series of important towns border the Kyzyl Kum (lit., "red sand"). This desert covers more than 300,000 km^2, with mean annual precipitation of 100-200 mm, and extends up to the Jaxartes (Syr Daryā). It slopes gently from about 600 m in the southeast to about 50 m at the Aral Sea in the northwest. There is sufficient vegetation to support seminomadic herding not only of karakul sheep and camels (q.v.) but also of horses.

Both these deserts contain occasional playas (called *takyr*) among the dunes. Similar conditions continue eastward into Dzungharia and the Tarim Basin (China), where the Takla Makan, one of the world's largest accumulations of sand, with mean annual precipitation of only 10-40 mm, covers more than 270,000 km^2 (see CHINESE TURKESTAN i).

The Iranian experience of deserts.

The arid zone appears to have functioned as a conduit for both populations and cultural influences as early as the Paleolithic (Barthold, 1984, pp. 5, 87; Smith, p. 37; Kohl, pp. 35-44). The evolving synthesis of research on later prehistoric and protohistoric periods suggests that it continued in this function (Dyson; Voigt). The swift progress of Arab armies in the 7th century is a later example. Similarly, in subsequent centuries conversion to Islam was consolidated more quickly throughout this zone, from North Africa to Central Asia, than outside it. Since the 1st millenium B.C.E. Persian cultural influence has moved through this conduit in both directions. For example, religious influences spread early to the west, affecting both Greek and Roman paganism and the Judeo-Christian tradition (on the impact of Mithraism and Manicheism in the west, see, e.g., COSMOGONY AND COSMOLOGY ii-iii; DUALISM; for Iranian elements in the udeo-Christian tradition, see BIBLE iii; DEAD SEA SCROLLS). Later Persian literary and bureaucratic practices spread mainly to the east and predominated in Central and South Asia into the 20th century.

Interdependence of bīābān and ābādī. The distribution of settlements further illustrates the importance of the arid zone as a conduit. Most towns with Iranian names, from Baghdad (Iraq) to Yārkand (China) lie within this zone. Others nestle to one side in fertile valleys surrounded by barren mountains. The oldest were founded on rivers that drain into the deserts. Some of these rivers (e.g., the Jaxartes, Zarafšān, and Zāyandarūd) have supported major agricultural and urban development close to the mountains, whereas others (e.g., the Oxus, Morḡāb, and Helmand) have produced major oases in the desert. But most cities, a good example being Nīšāpūr, were founded on rivers that probably never provided a reliable perennial water supply. Instead, their seasonal rivers supported development through exploitation of groundwater by means of *qanāt*s. Some later foundations on arid plains (e.g., Yazd and Kermān) depended entirely on the development of *qanāt*s in arid plains. Whether or not they were founded on rivers, most Iranian cities look out over arid plains, which merge into sand and salt desert. Larger areas of desert generally provide the transition from predominantly Iranian to non-Iranian cultural areas, especially Russia in the north, Mongolia and the interior of China in the east, and India in the southeast.

Between these irreducible areas of barren playa and shifting sand, the legacy of earlier geological periods, most of the arid zone consists of *bīābān*, endowed with soil and groundwater resources that have permitted conversion into *ābādī* by means of investment in irrigation engineering and agricultural development. Until recently political stability has always encouraged this type of investment, which has pushed back the margins of the *bīābān*. New areas were continually being colonized; some settlements have been sustained, while others have reverted to *bīābān*. There is abundant textual, ecological, and archeological evidence (including visible ruins) of this type of fluctuation, reflected in these lines by Rūdakī (10th century): "Many a desert waste was once a pleasant garden / And pleasant gardens have appeared where once was desert" (Ṣafā, *Adabīyāt* I, p. 384). To a significant extent, therefore, the limits of the *bīābān* have always been determined not by natural factors alone but also by historical factors that have led at particular times to decisions to develop certain areas, rather than others. The distinction between desert and sown is as much the result of the socioeconomic dynamic and cultural choice as of natural endowment.

Whatever lay beyond the city and its agricultural hinterland at any particular time has been considered *bīābān*, land that the urban government did not control. (Land that contained no investment was not worth controlling.) But these vast areas of social exclusion were not empty. When the surrounding urban economies were disrupted or in recession the *bīābān* offered the only refuge and alternative source of livelihood. When the urban economies were expanding they reabsorbed population from the *bīābān* (Spooner, 1972). The ecological carrying capacity of the *bīābān* has always been limited by low natural productivity, but it could be enhanced to some extent by exploitation of the surrounding urban economies even in bad times. Its products have included xerophytic plants with medicinal and other properties, charcoal (q.v.) processed from woody shrubs, and salt. Charcoal has always been in demand both as a preferred fuel in neighboring cities and for use in smelting locally mined ores (especially iron and copper, q.v.). For many, life in the *bīābān* has depended on supplementing local food production by development of these markets, but the dominant livelihood in the *bīābān* has always been nomadic pastoralism.

Nomads have usually migrated in regular seasonal patterns, designed to satisfy their animals' need for water and palatable forage (however sparse) throughout the year. But, as they have the flexibility to adapt their movements to shifting circumstances, pastoralism has often constituted the economic base from which other possibilities have been opportunistically exploited. Where possible nomads have used the deserts seasonally, migrating to cool mountain pastures for the late spring and summer. The most successful pastoral operation in the central deserts is managed by the Sangsarī, who are transhumant pastoralists based on the village of Sangsar in the Alborz mountains north of Semnān. They migrate in the autumn and spring between their high mountain pastures and the northeastern margins of the Great Kavīr, on either side of the provincial boundary between Khorasan and Semnān, and produce meat for sale in Tehran. Through the Sangsarī the *bīābān* along the shore of the Great Kavīr, most of which has a vegetation cover of 15 percent or less (apart from the carpet of spring annuals that define a good year), makes a significant contribution to the national economy.

Just as city dwellers regard the *bīābān* as the frontier, so residents of the *bīābān* have always been ready to encroach on settled society. The settled population along the desert margins has lived in fear of raiders, who appear suddenly out of the desert and disappear back into it. The desert has also served the purposes of small armies. In the 19th century Baluch raided north through the central deserts, at one point threatening settlements close to Tehran (see BALUCHISTAN i). As late as the 1950s the main road to Mašhad from southern Khorasan was the scene of regular ambushes by Turkmen at the point where it crosses shifting sand north of Gonābād (for earlier evidence, see travelers' accounts, e.g., Truilhier). In the late 1950s Bāṣerī (q.v) outlaws from the Ḵamsa confederation in Fārs who had moved north through the deserts routinely molested travelers between settlements along the northern shore of the Great Kavīr. For settled communities the *bīābān* has thus been synonymous not only with anarchy and insecurity but also with tribalism (see ʿAŠĀYER; CONFEDERATIONS; TRIBES).

The desert zone has served as a deterrent to invaders from outside. In the 19th century the British regarded it as the ultimate buffer between India and Russia, a view that led, directly or indirectly, to much of the exploration and travel from which current information about deserts in that zone is derived.

Travel and trade in the desert. Apart from the need to protect the *ābādī* from eruptions of raiders out of the *bīābān*, cities have had to ensure the security of arterial routes through it. The prosperity of each city has depended as much upon trade as upon local production. The overwhelming proportion of all long-distance travel has involved crossing or skirting major deserts, within and between the plateau and Transoxania, between Transoxania and China, and between the plateau and India and the Mediterranean. Long-distance travel was always daunting if not dangerous. The city dweller was not prepared to deal with dust storms, salt bogs, extreme temperatures, and lack of water, fodder, and provisions, much less brigands and robbers. Although the deserts are crisscrossed by arterial and lesser routes (Spooner 1969; idem, 1972), where possible traffic skirts the severer regions, zigzagging along the margins from one city and its agricultural hinterland to the next; most travelers have preferred the difficulties of mountain routes to the dangers of the deserts. On major routes oases formerly provided important staging posts for trade between cities. The prosperity of those oases rose and fell with the economies of the cities. On the plateau the most celebrated oases, each described by travelers from the 10th century to very recently, were Garma (Jarmaq), Nāyband (Nāband), and Noṣratābād Sepī (Sanīj), each benefiting from the opportunity to provide a resting place for caravans crossing the central deserts between west and east (or southwest and northeast). There were also minor routes, especially across the Lūt from Šahdād to Deh-e Salm and Neh, and many lesser oases along the margins, which provided similar but inferior services, with less security. Nāṣer-e Ḵosrow, who passed through Garma to Ṭabas in 444/1052, mentioned (p. 129) water tanks beside small domes at every 2 farsangs; the domes served to mark the route; they must have been intended to service travelers. The 10th-century traveler Maqdesī (Moqaddasī, p. 491) also mentioned the route north from Jarmaq across the Great Kavīr to Dāmḡān (q.v.). These early sources lack detailed information about natural and social conditions. Eṣṭaḵrī (pp. 227-37; cf. Ebn Ḥawqal, pp. 287-88) provided more detail about the oases themselves (for a summary of some medieval reports, see Le Strange, *Lands*, pp. 322-33). The actual routes were rarely engineered or equipped with bridges, but in the 16th century Shah ʿAbbās I (q.v.; 996-1037/1588-1629) had a stone causeway (*sangfarš*) 3 m wide and nearly 30 km long built across a narrow *kavīr* south of Garmsār (Ḵᵛār), in order to shorten the route from Isfahan to Mašhad. It is unclear when it fell into disrepair, but it still survives (Gabriel, 1952, p. 85).

Some oases have provided niches in a settled economy for individuals and communities that have chosen to avoid cities, especially those, like the Zoroastrians outside Yazd and the Ismaʿilis and Bahais in isolated parts of the Qāʾenāt and Baluchistan, that are out of favor with orthodox religious authorities.

Perceptions of the desert. Areas of *bīābān* that were not colonized or close to major oases remained the domain of nomadic pastoralists. From the dichotomy of interests between nomads and villagers in and around the *bīābān* arose the characteristic social distinction between the life of settled agriculture (*ābādī*) and the nomadic life of the *bīābān*; the governing factor was the ability of the cities to colonize the *bīābān* by investing in development of *qanāt*s. The cultural elaboration of this distinction is deeply rooted in Persian traditions and differs in interesting ways from comparable traditions. For example, in Persian literature there is no role for the nomad equivalent to the role of the Bedouin in Arabic literature.

Although the *bīābān* had to be crossed, it was never a place to tarry. But it not only represented the antithesis of civilized life; its importance in the historical record has also been distorted by the urban monopoly of literacy. Moreover, urban prejudices against the *bīābān* and the tribal and nomadic forms of life that characterized it, though at first mildly contested by Western interest in the primitive life of the wilderness, have more recently been reinforcd by Western stereotypes of the ecological impact of traditional pastoralism. Nonetheless, many of the intangibles of Iranian urban life and culture are derived from the surrounding *bīābān*. City dwellers benefit from low humidity and abundant sunlight, enjoying not only the clear horizons of the *bīābān* but also its unique range of light and color. It also ensures pleasantly cool summer nights and warm winter sunshine. The *bīābān* is the backdrop for the "good life," from picnic sites beside springs or streams on the threshold of the desert within easy reach of the *ābādī*; they are popular sites for open-air activity on the last day of the Nowrūz holiday (*sīzdah-bedar*). The Sasanians displayed a similar orientation when they constructed large enclosures (OPers. *paradayadām*, Av. *pairi-daēza-* > Gk. *paradeisos* > Eng. "paradise"; NPers. *pālīz*, Pers. and Ar. *ferdows*) to minimize the dangers and enhance the pleasures of the *bīābān*. This taste for experiencing the *bīābān*, but with the comforts and security of the *ābādī*, epitomizes the Iranian perception of the natural environment, which has persisted to the present day.

Environmental change and conservation. Another significant dimension of the relationship between *bīābān* and *ābādī* can be observed in the effects of human exploitation of the natural resources of the *bīābān*. The sparse vegetation has been systematically grazed to varying degrees, depending upon accessibility. It has also provided construction materials for winter shelters (*āḡol*) for shepherds and their animals; been consumed as fuel for heating, cooking, and processing pastoralists' milk products; and plundered over wide areas for charcoal production. Whether or not the extent of barren desert and of sand movement and the incidence of dust storms have increased as a result of persistence of these traditional technologies as the population has risen in the modern period remains an open question. Equally unclear is whether the *bīābān* has undergone desertification recently or steadily since the original spread of nomadic pastoralism and later*qanāt*-based settlement. Nor has it been determined whether urban environments have suffered as a consequence of desertification.

Historical references, as well as modern experience and experimentation, suggest that natural vegetation cover, which is removed when land is prepared for crop production, is also reduced by any increase in human activity. It has been shown as well that vegetation cover can, with careful management, be restored. Reconstruction of the history of vegetation cover in particular areas of *bīābān* has been attempted by means of palynological (Moore and Stevenson) and even dendrochronological (Bhadresa and Moore) studies, but the results so far are inconclusive. In the first half of the 19th century travelers from India (e.g., Forster, p. 190) reported difficulty in finding firewood in places where it is available today, which suggests that conditions may have improved. But travelers' reports are inconsistent, and, as no quantitative data are offered, it is possible that expectations simply varied (for discussion, see Edāra).

In the 1950s increasing awareness of diminishing wildlife populations, especially game species, and increasing severity of sand and dust storms led to a series of government initiatives. In Persia two agencies developed long-term programs for reversing desertification by improving the productivity of the 125 million ha classified as rangeland (the area likely to be used by pastoralists out of the 165 million ha that constitute the total territory of Persia; see ECOLOGY AND ENVIRONMENTAL PROTECTION). The Forest and range organization (Sāzmān-e jangalhā wa marāteʿ-e kešvar) focused on stabilizing sand dunes and enhancing forage in the more heavily grazed areas. The Department of the environment (Sāzmān-e ḥefāẓat-e moḥīṭ-e zīst) concentrated on the conservation of vegetation and wildlife in areas that were of less economic importance. The department of geography at Tehran University also developed a special program of research on the central deserts; the university established a desert-research center in the late 1970s. In the mid-1970s a "national spatial strategy plan," which involved the first systematic study of the whole of Persia, including the desert areas, was formulated in the Sāzmān-e barnāma (Plan organization).

The long drought of the late 1960s and early 1970s made desertification an issue in all the countries of the arid zone. China, India, Persia, Pakistan, and the Soviet Union all contributed case studies to the United Nations Conference on Desertification in Nairobi in 1977. Afghanistan submitted a country report. Persia led an effort to involve Afghanistan, India, and Pakistan in designing a project to deal with "transnational" problems of desertification in the region. In recent years the Research institute of forests and rangelands (Moʾassa-ye taḥqīqāt-e jangalhā wa marāteʿ) in the Persian Ministry of agriculture (Kowsar), the Central Arid Zone Research Institute in Jodhpur (India), the Arid Zone Research Institute in Quetta, the Agricultural Research Council and the Irrigation Research Council (Pakistan), and the desert-research institutes in Repetek (Turkmenistan) and Lan-chou (China) continue to be involved in these international efforts.

As a result of these activities specific conservation technologies have advanced considerably, but there has been little improvement in overall land-use policies or in ability to prevent further desertification. Areas close to arterial routes and concentrations of population attract investment relatively easily but also tend more readily to become "desertified" from overexploitation. Desertification occurs around all settlements as a consequence of the activities described above, an ecological price not infrequently paid for increased production. The *bīābān* today often bears the scars of past (discontinued) investment. Although it was initially assumed by international experts that for optimum resource management it was necessary simply to reduce the level of human exploitation and to modernize traditional practices, some research findings indicate that the problem is more complex. Attempts to redevelop may require greater investment than was originally necessary. For example, where investment has been discontinued in recent times, whether because of insecurity or other economic disruption, agricultural land has reverted not only to *bīābān* as expected but also to severer desert conditions than before, as a result of the loss of seed reserves and of soil erosion. In one documented instance in Kar (a small *dehestān*, q.v., in southeastern Semnān province), reduction in agricultural investment has led to encroachment of sand, unknown earlier. It appears, therefore, that much of the present *bīābān* is not simply pristine wilderness but rather a product of long coadaptation of human populations, domesticated species, and natural processes over centuries, even millennia. The effects of traditional technologies, unchanged over long periods, have been cumulative, with the result that radical removal of the human factor now, even where it has become excessive, may not be the best road to conservation.

The balance of the historical relationship between *ābādī* and *bīābān* has undergone significant shifts in recent decades. Motorization of long-distance traffic in the 1960s for the first time made it more practical to travel around the deserts than through them. The oases on the routes through the deserts consequently sank into isolation and decline. Ignored by the government, the deserts soon became the domain of smugglers. But, with the beginning of national spatial planning in the mid-1970s, the deserts began to be reincorporated into the larger society. For the first time the Persian government sees the *bīābān* not simply as the area between cities and the antithesis of urban life but also as so many square kilometers of national territory with economic, political, and strategic assets. It is not possible to predict how these changes will in the long term affect the significance of the *bīābān* in Persian culture.

Bibliography: (For cited works not included in this bibliography and for abbreviations found here, see "Short References.") The deserts are neglected in most standard sources on the Iranian cultural area; in the following selection the emphasis is on firsthand accounts and investigations and guides to further work.

K. E. Abbott, "Geographical Notes Taken during a Journey in Persia in 1849 and 1850," *JRGS* 25, 1855, pp. 1-78. B. Allchin and A. Goudie, "Climatic Change in the Indian Desert and North-West India during the Late Pleistocene and Early Holocene," in W. C. Brice, ed., *The Environmental History of the Near and Middle East since the Last Ice Age*, London, 1978, pp. 307-18. S. A. Anders, *Central Asia Atlas*, Stockholm, 1966. O. Aurenche et al., eds., *Chronologies in the Near East. Relative Chronologies and Absolute Chronology 16,000-4,000 B.P.*, BAR 379, 2 vols., Oxford, 1987.

F. Balsan, *Au Registan inexploré (sud-afghan)*, Paris, 1973. Barthold, *Turkestan*[3] (esp. pp. 64-179 for the historical geography of Transoxania). Idem, *An Historical Geography of Iran*, tr. S. Soucek, ed. C. E. Bosworth, Princeton, N.J., 1984 (the most carefully researched and argued work of its type, drawing particularly on Russian sources, but selective rather than exhaustive and with scant attention to deserts). P. Beaumont, "Salt Weathering on the Margin of the Great Kavir, Iran," *Geological Society of American Bulletin* 79, 1968, pp. 1683-84. R. Bhadresa and P. D. Moore, "Desert Shrubs. The Implications of Population and Pattern Studies for Conservation and Management," in B. Spooner and H. S. Mann, eds., *Desertification and Development. Dryland Ecology in Social Perspective*, London, 1982, pp. 269-76. C. E. Biddulph, "A Journey across the Western Portion of the Great Persian Desert," *Proceedings of the Royal Geographical Society*, N.S. 13, 1891, pp. 645-57. H. Bobek, *Features and Formation of the Great Kavir and Masileh*, Tehran, 1959. Idem, "Zur Kenntniss der südlichen Lut. Ergebnisse einer Luftbildanalyse," *Mitteilungen der Österreichische Geographische Gesellschaft* III, Heft 2/3, Vienna, 1969, pp. 155-92. C. E. Bosworth, *Sistan under the Arabs, from the Islamic Conquest to the Rise of the Saffarids (30-250/651-864)*, Rome, 1968 (with information on Kharijite activities in Sīstān). S.-W. Breckle, "The Significance of Salinity," in B. Spooner and H. S. Mann, eds., *Desertification and Development. Dryland Ecology in Social Perspective*, London, 1982, pp. 277-92. W. C. Brice, ed., *The Environmental History of the Near and Middle East since the Last Ice Age*, London, 1978. F. A. Buhse, "Die grosse persische Salzwüste und ihre Umgebung," *Deutsche Rundschau für Geographie und Statistik* 15, 1892, pp. 49-59 (on botany and geology between Dāmḡān and Yazd).

C. Clerk, "Notes in Persia, Khurasan, and Afghanistan," *JRGS* 31, 1861, pp. 47-54. R. U. Cooke and A. Warren, *Geomorphology in Deserts*, London, 1973. L. Costantini and M. Tosi, "The Environment of Southern Sistan in the Third Millennium B.C. and Its Exploitation by the Proto-Urban Hilmand Civilization," in W. C. Brice, ed., *The Environmental History of the Near and Middle East since the Last Ice Age*, London, 1978, pp. 165-83. D. M. Currie, *Report to the Government of Pakistan on Desert Areas of West Pakistan*, Food and Agricultural Organization Report 564, Rome, 1956. Curzon, *Persian Question*, esp. II, pp. 246-67 (for a list of foreign desert travelers and their routes). *Dar rahgoḏar-e kavīr*, Tehran, 1353 Š./1974 (with excellent illustrations, including plans of desert towns superimposed on satellite images). M. J. Dresch, "Reconnaissance dans le Lut (Iran)," *Bulletin de l'Association de Géographes Français* 362-63, 1968, pp. 143-53. R. H. Dyson, "The Relative and Absolute Chronology of Hissar II and the Proto-Elamite Horizon of Northern Iran," in O. Aurenche et al., eds., *Chronologies in the Near East. Relative Chronologies and Absolute Chronology 16,000-4,000 B.P.*, BAR 379, II, Oxford, 1987, pp. 647-73. J. P. Ferrier, *Caravan Journeys and Wanderings in Persia, Afghanistan, Turkistan, and Baluchistan*, London, 1857. W. B. Fisher, "Physical Geography," in *Camb. Hist. Iran* I, pp. 3-110. G. Forster, *A Journey from Bengal to England*, 2 vols., London, 1798. H. Freitag, "Notes on the Distribution, Climate and Flora of the Sand Deserts of Iran and Afghanistan," *Proceedings of the Royal Society of Edinburgh* 89B, 1986, pp. 135-46.

A. Gabriel, *Im weltfernen Orient*, Munich and Berlin, 1929. Idem, *Durch Persiens Wüsten*, Stuttgart, 1935. Idem, *Aus den Einsamkeiten Irans*, Stuttgart, 1939. Idem, *Weites, wildes Iran*, Stuttgart, 1942. Idem, *Die Erforschung Persiens*, Vienna, 1952 (detailed illustrated review of explorer-travelers in Persia, esp. pp. 56-60, 93-99, 174-99, 243-52, 301-17). M. Ganji, "Post-Glacial Climatic Changes on the Iranian Plateau," in W. C. Brice, ed., *The Environmental History of the Near and Middle East since the Last Ice Age*, London, 1978, pp. 149-63 (focused on desert areas). I. P. Gerasimov, "Ancient Rivers in the Deserts of Soviet Central Asia," in W. C. Brice, ed., *The Environmental History of the Near and Middle East since the Last Ice Age*, London, 1978, pp. 319-34. F. J. Goldsmid, ed., *Eastern Persia. An Account of the Persian Boundary Commission 1870-71-72*, 2 vols., London, 1876. S. Hedin, *Overland to India*, 2 vols., London, 1910 (with detailed illustrated description of two routes across the Great Kavīr). L. Horne, "The Demand for Fuel. Ecological Implications of Socio-economic Change," in B. Spooner and H. S. Mann, eds., *Desertification and Development. Dryland Ecology in Social Perspective*, London, 1982, pp. 201-15. A. Houtum-Schindler, *Eastern Persian Irak*, London, 1896. J. Humlum, *La géographie de l'Afghanistan*, Copenhagen, 1959. E. Huntington, "The Basin of Eastern Persia and Sistan," in *Explorations in Turkestan 1904*, Washington, D.C., 1905, pp. 219-324. Isidore of Charax, *Parthian Stations by Isidore of Charax. An Account of the Overland Trade*

Route between the Levant and India in the First Century B.C., ed. and tr. W. H. Schoff, Chicago, 1976. W. Ivanow, "Notes on the Ethnology of Khurasan," *Geographical Journal* 67, 1926, pp. 143-58. M. P. A. Jackson et al., *Salt Diapirs of the Great Kavir, Central Iran*, Geographical Society of America Memoir 177, Boulder, Colo., 1990. A. Kar, "Aeolian Processes and Bedforms in the Thar Desert," *Journal of Arid Environments* 25, 1993, pp. 83-89. P. Kardavānī, *Šahdād tā Deh-e Salm*, Tehran, 1354 Š./1975. N. de Khanikoff, "Mémoire sur la partie méridionale de l'Asie centrale," in *Recueil de voyages et de mémoires* VIII, Paris, n.d. (1861), pp. 239-451 (critical review of earlier work, with firsthand description and useful notes on routes, especially vegetation, around central deserts and between Neh and Kermān). P. L. Kohl, *Central Asia. Palaeolithic Beginnings to the Iron Age*, Paris, 1984 (synthesis of Soviet and other work on the archeology of Central Asia, including information on the physical geography of the desert areas and arguments for the origin of arid conditions and the changes in river courses; see esp. pp. 17-34). A. Kowsar, "Floodwater Spreading for Desertification Control . . .," *Desertification Control Bulletin* 19, 1991, pp. 3-18. D. B. Krinsley, *A Geomorphological and Paleoclimatological Study of the Playas of Iran*, Washington, D.C., 1970. G. S. Kust, "Desertification Assessment and Mapping in the Pre-Aral Region," *Desertification Control Bulletin* 21, 1992, pp. 38-43.

C. MacGregor, *Narrative of a Journey through the Province of Khorasan and on the North-West Frontier of Afghanistan in 1875*, 2 vols., London, 1879 (esp. I, pp. 75 ff.). M. A. Martin, "Conservation at the Local Level. Individual Perceptions and Group Mechanisms," in B. Spooner and H. S. Mann, eds., *Desertification and Development. Dryland Ecology in Social Perspective*, London, 1982, pp. 145-69. S. F. Minchin, *Kharan*, Baluchistan District Gazetteer Series VIIA, Bombay, 1907. ʿA.-A Mohājer, *Zīr-e āsmān-e kavīr*, Tehran, 1940 Š./1961. P. D. Moore and A. C. Stevenson, "Pollen Studies in Dry Environments," in B. Spooner and H. S. Mann, eds., *Desertification and Development. Dryland Ecology in Social Perspective*, London, 1982, pp. 249-67. A. Mostawfī, *Lūt-e Zangī Aḥmad*, Tehran, 1348 Š./1969. Idem, *Ḥawza-ye masīla*, Tehran, 1350 Š./1971. Idem, *Šahdād wa joḡrāfīā-ye tārīḵī-e Dašt-e Lūt*, Tehran, 1351 Š./1972. Nāṣer-e Ḵosrow Qobādīānī, *Safar-nāma-ye Nāṣer-e Ḵosrow*, ed. N. Wazīnpūr, Tehran, 1350 Š./1971. A. E. Nyerges, "Pastoralists, Flocks and Vegetation. Processes of Co-adaptation," in B. Spooner and H. S. Mann, eds., *Desertification and Development. Dryland Ecology in Social Perspective*, London, 1982, pp. 217-47. *Persia*, Geographical Handbook Series, n.p., 1945. M. P. Petrov, *Pustyny zemnogo shara*, Leningrad, 1973; tr. R. Lavoott as *Deserts of the World*, New York, 1976 (esp. chap. 2, based on primary research in the deserts of Central Asia). M. Polo, *The Book of Ser Marco Polo, the Venetian . . .*, ed. and tr. H. Yule, 3rd ed., 2 vols., ed. H. Cordier, 1903 (the first European description of the route from Kērmān to Ṭabas and Khorasan but with little detail). K.-H. Rechinger, *Flora Iranica*, Graz, 1963-. W. R. Rickmers, *The Duab of Turkestan*, Cambridge, 1913. Sāzmān-e barnāma, *National Spatial Strategy Plan, 1976*, Tehran, unpublished.

Sāzmān-e ḥefāẓat-e moḥīt-e zīst, *Case Study on Desertification, Iran. Turan*, submitted to U.N. Conference on Desertification, Nairobi, 1977; repr. in A. and M. Biswas, eds., *Desertification*, Oxford, 1980, pp. 181-251. E. F. Schmidt, *Flights over Ancient Cities of Iran*, Chicago, 1940. S. K. Seth, "The Desiccation of the Thar Desert and Its Environs during the Protohistorical and Historical Periods," in W. C. Brice, ed., *The Environmental History of the Near and Middle East since the Last Ice Age*, London, 1978, pp. 279-305. P. E. L. Smith, *Palaeolithic Archaeology in Iran*, Philadelphia, 1986. B. Spooner, "Mosawwada-ī jehat-e barrasī-e jāmeʿ az kavīrhā wa bīābānhā-ye wasaṭ-e falāt-e Īrān," in Ī. Afšār and M. Mīnovī, eds., *Yād-nāma-ye īrānī-e Mīnorskī*, Tehran, 1348 Š./1969, pp. 36-48. Idem, "The Iranian Deserts," in B. Spooner, ed., *Population Growth. Anthropological Implications*, Cambridge, 1972, pp. 245-68. Idem, "Insiders and Outsiders in Baluchistan. Western and Indigenous Perspectives on Ecology and Development," in P. Little et al., eds., *Lands at Risk in the Third World. Local-Level Perspectives*, Boulder, Colo., 1987, pp. 58-68 (on relations between nomad and settled communities). Idem, "Desertification. The Historical Significance," in R. Huss-Ashmore and S. H. Katz, *Stress and Coping in African Food Systems* I. *Microperspectives*, London, 1989, pp. 111-62. Idem and L. Horne, eds., *Cultural and Ecological Perspectives fom the Turan Program, Iran*, Expedition 22, Philadelphia, 1980. B. Spooner and H. S. Mann, eds., *Desertification and Development. Dryland Ecology in Social Perspective*, London, 1982. G. Stratil-Sauer, *Geographische Forschungen in Ostpersien*, Abh. der Geographischen Gesellschaft Wien 17/2-3, Vienna, 1953-56. Idem and O. R. Weise, *Zur Geomorphologie der südlichen Lut und zur Klimageschichte Irans*, Würzburger Geographische Arbeiten, Mitteilungen der Geographischen Gesellschaft Würzburg, 41, Würzburg, 1974. P. M. Sykes, *Ten Thousand Miles in Persia*, London, 1902.

C. E. Tate, *The Frontiers of Baluchistan*, London, 1909 (esp. pp. 49-70 on winds and cold in southwestern Afghanistan). W. Tomaschek, "Zur historischen Topographie von Persien," in *Kaiserliche Akademie der Wissenschaften* (Vienna) Phil.-hist. Classe, Sb. 102, 1883, pp. 145-231; 108, 1885, pp. 561-652 (critical discussion, with map, of available information on the boundaries of the central deserts; their geography, geology, climate; and the eastern and southern desert routes). W. M. Truilhier, "Mémoire descriptif de la route de Tehran à Meched et de Meched à Jezd, reconnue en 1807," *Bulletin de la Société de Géographie* 9, 1838. pp. 109-45, 249-82, 313-29. H. B. Vaughan, "A Journey through Persia (1887-1888)," *Royal Geographical Society Supplementary Papers* 3, 1893, pp. 89-115. Idem, "Journeys in Persia (1890-1891)," *Geographical Journal* 4, 1896, pp. 24-41, 163-75. M. Voigt, "Relative and Absolute Chronologies for Iran between 6,500 and 3,500," in O. Aurenche et al., eds., *Chronologies in the Near East. Relative Chronologies and Absolute Chronology 16,000-4,000 B.P.*, BAR 379, II, Oxford, 1987, pp. 615-46. Aḥmad-ʿAlī Wazīrī Kermānī, *Joḡrāfīā-ye mamlakat-e Kermān*, ed. M. Bāstānī Pārīzī, in *FIZ* 14, 1345-46 Š./1966-67, pp. 20-286. C. E. Yate, *Khurasan and Sistan*, Edinburgh, 1900. M. Zohary, *On the Geobotanical Structure of Iran*, Bulletin of the Research Council of Israel 2, Section D (Botany), Supplement, Tel Aviv, 1963.

(BRIAN SPOONER)

DESMAISONS, JEAN-JACQUES-PIERRE (Petr Ivanovich Demezon; b. Chambéry, in the kingdom of Sardinia, 1807, d. Paris, 1873), diplomat and compiler of an important Persian-French dictionary. Desmaisons was the son of a physician; he attended the Collège Royal in Chambéry, then went to St. Petersburg to study oriental languages with Henry Wlangali (Vesselovskiĭ, pp. 23-26; *Zapiski*, p. 8). In 1829 he entered the university at Kazan, where he received a doctorate in oriental literature the next year. In February 1831 he was appointed senior master of oriental languages (Persian and Arabic) at the Neplyuev institute in Orenburg and in September translator for the frontier commission of that city (Desmaisons, I, p. 2). In 1834 he was sent to Bukhara disguised as a Muslim merchant; he submitted several reports on the political and economic situation in the khanate, which the Russians were planning to annex. For his success he was awarded the order of St. Anne, 3rd degree, and 3,000 rubles (Savel'ev, p. 26; Chabrov, pp. 109-15; *Zapiski*, pp. 130-31; cf. pp. 17-81, for copies of Desmaisons's reports, drawn from the state archives of Orenburg and the archives of the Russian Ministry of foreign affairs).

In 1836 Desmaisons was named professor in the Asiatic department of the Russian Ministry of foreign affairs. He was a member of the Russian diplomatic mission to Tehran in 1840-41 (Vesselovskiĭ, p. 25). Two years later he was named director of training in oriental languages in the Asiatic department, responsible to the imperial chancellery for translation of Tatar documents and works on Muslim jurisprudence (Desmaisons, I, p. 2). He became a Russian national and traveled to Persia and the Ottoman empire. In 1846 he received from King Charles Albert of Sardinia (1831-49) the title of baron and authorization to continue in the service of Russia (Desmaisons, I, p. 2). In 1850 he reached the highest diplomatic rank in the Asiatic department, dragoman, 5th class.

In 1857 Desmaisons retired to Paris, where he undertook his edition and translation of the *Ketāb-e šajara-ye torkī* by Abu'l-Ḡāzī Bahādūr Khan, based on a manuscript discovered by V. I. Dahl in Orenburg (Kononov, pp. 68-69, 241); it was published by the Imperial academy of sciences of St. Petersburg in two volumes under the title *Histoire des Mogols et des Tartares* (1871-74). Desmaisons' *Dictionnaire persan-français*, compiled during repeated visits to Persia in the years 1858-69, was published posthumously, in Rome in 1908. For each entry he customarily mentioned his sources, which included the Persian works *Bahār-e ʿAjam* and *Borhān-e qaṭeʿ* (q.v.; see DICTIONARIES i), as well as the Turkish-Arabic dictionary *al-Oqīānūs al-basīṭ fī tarjoma al-Qāmūs al-moḥīṭ* and the Persian-Turkish lexicon *Lesān-e ʿAjam yā Farhang-e šoʿūrī*. In addition, he relied on earlier European dictionaries like Jacobus Golius' *Lexicon Arabico-Latinum* . . . (Leiden, 1653); Franciszek Meniński's *Thesaurus Linguarum Orientalium Turcicae, Arabicae, Persicae* . . . (3 vols., Vienna, 1680); G. W. Freytag's *Lexicon Arabico-Latinum* (4 vols., Halle, 1830-37), J. A. Vullers' *Lexicon Persico-Latinum Etymologicum* (2 vols., Bonn, 1855-64), and Albert de Biberstein-Kazimirski, *Dictionnaire arabe-français* (2 vols., Paris, 1860).

Bibliography: G. N. Chabrov, "Poezdka v Bukharu perevodchika P. I. Demezon (1833-1834)" (The journey to Bukhara of Baron P. I. Desmaisons [1833-34]), *Trudy Sredneaziatskogo gosudarstvennogo universiteta im. V. I. Lenina* 94, 1957, pp. 117-48. J.-J.-P. Desmaisons, *Dictionnaire persan-français, publié par ses neveux*, 4 vols., Rome, 1908. A. N. Kononov, *Istoriya izucheniya turkskikh yazukov v Rossii dooktyabrskiĭ period* (History of the study of Turkish languages in Russia of the prerevolutionary period), Leningrad, 1972. P. S. Savel'ev, *Bukhara v 1835* (Bukhara in 1835), St. Petersburg, 1836. N. I. Vesselovskiĭ, *Istoriya Imperatorskogo Russkogo Arkheologicheskogo obshchestva za pervoe pyatidesyatiletie ego sushestvovaniya 1846-1896* (History of the Imperial Russian society of archeology during the first fifty years of its existence, 1846-96), St. Petersburg, 1900. *Zapiski o bukharskom khanstve* (Notes on the khanate of Bukhara), Moscow, 1983, esp. pp. 5-83.

(CATHÉRINE POUJOL)

DEUTSCHES ARCHÄOLOGISCHES INSTITUT (D.A.I.), research institution administered by the German foreign ministry, with a number of branches, including the Abteilung Teheran in Persia. The central headquarters and presidential office are located in Berlin, where normally a general meeting of the board of directors of the entire institute is held once a year.

The D.A.I. originated as a royal Prussian institute in Rome in 1829 and was converted to a national institution in 1874. Its foreign branches include those of Rome, Athens (since 1874), Istanbul and Cairo (since 1929), Madrid (since 1943), Baghdad (since 1956), and Tehran (since 1961), and there are also three scholarly commissions in Germany itself. Some foreign branches also administer smaller stations, for example, the Ankara station of the Istanbul branch; other stations, like those in Damascus and Ṣanʿāʾ, are administered directly by the president of the D.A.I.

Like all branches of the Institute, the Abteilung Teheran has a director (with the title Erster Direktor and Professor at the D.A.I.) and a deputy (with the title Wissenschaftlicher Direktor). The director is a voting member of the board of the D.A.I. The Abteilung Teheran has two scientific advisers, at present Hubertus von Gall (classical archeology) and Dietrich Huff (architectural studies).

In the 1930s the D.A.I. supported a forerunner of the Abteilung Teheran, a station in Isfahan directed by Wilhelm Eilers; its work was brought to a halt in 1941 after the outbreak of World War II. Between 1929 and 1938 Ernst Herzfeld published nine volumes of *Archäologische Mitteilungen aus Iran* under the sponsorship of the Isfahan station; a new annual series under the same title began publication in 1968 under the sponsorship of the Abteilung Teheran. Herzfeld also issued four fascicles of the large-format *Iranischen Denkmäler*, with illustrations of architectural, archeological, and epigraphic monuments; this series was reinstated by the Abteilung Teheran in 1975, with publication of fascicle 5, and a total of thirteen fascicles had appeared by 1994. Herzfeld, Friedrich Sarre, Karl Bergner, Ernst Kühnel, Walther Hinz, Eilers, Kurt Erdmann (q.v.), and their colleagues laid the scholarly foundation for German participation in archeological research in Persia before and between the two world wars, especially the German excavations at Persepolis before 1317 Š./1938.

As a continuation of this tradition, the Abteilung Teheran was established in 1961 after the initiation of excavations at Taḵt-e Solaymān by Hans Henning von der Osten and Rudolf Naumann in 1959. Von der Osten, a Near Eastern archeologist, was named the first director, and after his premature death in the same year Heinz Luschey, a classical archeologist by training, succeeded him, serving until 1971, with Wolfram Kleiss as deputy director from 1967. In 1971 Kleiss became director and Peter Calmeyer deputy director.

The activity of the Abteilung Teheran encompasses the entire territory of the Islamic Republic of Persia from prehistory to the 19th century, including the medieval Christians of Azerbaijan. In addition to *Archäologische Mitteilungen aus Iran* and *Iranische Denkmäler*, the branch publishes the *Teheraner Forschungen*, the Ergänzungsbände of the *Archäologische Mitteilungen*, and *Führer zu Archäologischen Plätzen in Iran*, all issued at irregular intervals.

Although the excavations of the Sasanian and Mongol periods at Taḵt-e Solaymān were directed from the Abteilung Istanbul (under Naumann, its first director) until 1354 Š./1975, in 1355 Š./1976 they were transferred to the Abteilung Teheran, with Huff as field director. In 1342-46 Š./1963-67 Luschey conducted archeological explorations at Bīsotūn (q.v.), which yielded remains ranging from the prehistoric era to the reign of the Mongols. Excavations were also conducted, from 1347 Š./1968 to 1357 Š./1978, in the Urartian fortress and settlement of Bastām/Rusa-i-URU.TUR (q.v.), discovered by Kleiss in 1346 Š./1967. At Fīrūzābād Huff was able to combine excavation and architectural research with restoration projects at various Sasanian monuments before 1357 Š./1978.

Owing to political developments in the Near East, particularly the Islamic Revolution in Persia in 1357 Š./1978, archeological activities at all these sites were interrupted, and so far it has not been possible to resume work. In addition, before 1357 Š./1978 members of the Abteilung Teheran had no problem obtaining access to work on excavated objects in the Iran Bastan Museum, the archeological museum in Tehran, but since then it has become increasingly difficult.

The general surveys conducted between 1346 Š./1967 and 1357 Š./1978, which had provided a partial topographic map of Azerbaijan, especially the surveys of remains from the Urartian period, came to a virtual end in 1358 Š./1979, for they could not be continued in insecure regions of the country.

In 1362 Š./1983 the members of the Abteilung Teheran were transferred from Tehran to Berlin, followed in 1364 Š./1985 by the director, a temporary abandonment of a German archeological presence in Persia. At headquarters in Berlin the members of the Baghdad and Teheran branches, both closed in the Near East but still independent, are housed together with a single library, into which the former library of the Isfahan station has now been incorporated. In the D.A.I. quarters in Tehran there is a larger reference library, which is at the disposal of foreign scholars for consultation. The photographic archive is now located in Berlin.

Since 1358 Š./1979 work in Persia has continued in month-long excursions into the country from the base at the D.A.I. quarters in Tehran. It includes exploration of old caravan routes and systematic photographing of caravansaries (q.v.), road stations, and old bridges and dams (qq.v.); photographing of Zoroastrian cult buildings; and recording of rock reliefs of all periods and of Qajar frescos. Of course, such investigations have been limited to those parts of the country that were not inaccessible to foreigners because of war or similar conditions. During these surveys of the old travel routes numerous prehistoric and historic sites have been observed, and topographic knowledge of the country has thus been considerably enhanced.

The members of the Abteilung Teheran also continue to study the art of relief carving in Persia, with emphasis on Persepolis and on Sasanian and Qajar rock reliefs. They are also revising the topographic map of prehistoric Persia. One focus of research is constructions for controlling the flow of water, from the Achaemenid to the Safavid period, as well as Islamic secular architecture in general. The corpus of finds from the survey, especially the ceramics, represents another essential problem for study.

As at present no excavation is possible in Persia, intensive work on the preparation and publication of the finds from excavations before the Islamic Revolution of 1357-58 Š./1979 is going forward. In recent years the members have also been able to travel to countries bordering on Persia, particularly the Caucasus and the southern states of the former U.S.S.R., in order to visit archeological sites and museums that offer comparative objects of interest in the study of Persian archeology and associated disciplines.

The members of the Abteilung Teheran supplement their publication activity by giving university courses and lectures, conducting tours, and participating in regional and superregional congresses and special scientific meetings. In the D.A.I. buildings in Tehran the guestrooms are available to traveling foreign scholars.

(WOLFRAM KLEISS)

DĒV. See *DAIVA, DĒW, DĪV.

DEVIL. See AHRIMAN; DĪV; EBLĪS.

DĒW (demon) in the Pahlavi books. The concept of the *dēw* (invariably written with the Aram. ideogram *ŠDYA*, more often in the pl. ŠDYA'n', often to be translated "demons" even in the sg.) was central to the theology and ritual of Zoroastrianism; as Émile Benveniste (q.v.; p. 41) first observed, the term *vi.daēva-* ("rejecting the *daēva*s") qualified the faithful Zoroastrian with the same force as *mazdayasna-* ("Mazdā worshiper") and *zaraθuštri-* (Zoroastrian). Rejection of the *dēw*s is linked to Zoroaster's reform, and, as personifications of every imaginable evil, they are mentioned throughout Zoroastrian religious books.

*Dēw*s play an important role in the cosmogonic drama (see COSMOGONY AND COSMOLOGY i). In the *Bundahišn*, for example, just after Ohrmazd's creation of the *amahraspand*s (see AMƎŠA SPƎNTA) the evil spirit Ahreman (see AHRIMAN), also known in Pahlavī as Gannāg Mēnōg, is said to have "miscreated" his *dēw*s, the antitheses of the *amahraspand*s, from the demonic essence (Pahl. *dēwān xwadīh*), by which Ahreman is said to "make himself worse." For Zoroastrians there is a salutary irony in the very conception of demons, for Ahreman produced his creation in that form, and from that creation he became "useless" (Pahl. *akār*), owing to the ignorant and ultimately self-destructive nature of demons. The will of Ahreman and the demons is to smite, and they will ultimately turn their destructiveness upon themselves (see, e.g., de Menasce, chaps. 162, 203; Williams, 1990, chap. 48). In the simplest and most graphic representations, in the *Bundahišn* and similar mythological texts, the *dēw*s are devils of varying powers, ranging from the six archdemons (*kamālīgān dēwān*) who oppose the *amahraspand*s to myriad minor and nameless demons who, when the sun sets, rush out from hell to destroy the world (Williams, 1990, chap. 9). They are responsible for all corruption and destructiveness, cosmic, climatic, corporeal, moral, and social. The present world is a mixture just because the *dēw*s have entered it at every level; in the bodies of men they are present in the form of disease, pain, grief, and so on. They are sometimes objectified as having claws, faces, hair, and feet and as producing semen (e.g., Gignoux, chap. 70.2). There are even stories of *dēw*s' having had sexual intercourse with humans, as in the tale of J̌am and his sister J̌amag, who mated with a female and a male demon respectively, thus bringing noxious creatures into being (*Bundahišn*, tr. Anklesaria, 14B.1; Williams, 1990, chap. 8e). *Dēw*s can also take the form of abstract notions (e.g., heresy, denial) or climatic disorders (e.g., whirlwinds, lightning, drought).

There is some question about how the ontological status of Ahreman and the *dēw*s was understood, for, as all were said to be devoid of truth, even their existence was sometimes denied (Shaked, 1967). This line of thought is several times apparent in the philosophical third book of the *Dēnkard* (q.v.) but also in more "popular" texts like *Čīdag handarz ī pōryōtkēšān* (par. 3) and *Ardā Wīrāz* (q.v.) *nāmag* (5.7). Shaul Shaked (1967, pp. 228 ff.) suggests that reference to the nonexistence of demons reflects the doctrine that Ahreman and the demons have no physical (*gētīg*) form of their own; the presence of demons in physical form is thus entirely parasitic upon the forms created by Ohrmazd, and their reality in this world is a lie. Although they have no being (*astīh*, *stī*), they are nevertheless a force of evil will in the physical world, from which Shaked deduces that their presence in the world is not regarded as an ontological fact but "merely" as an anthropological or psychological phenomenon (1967, p 264). Like many other "anthropological and psychological" (religious?) phenomena, however, the *dēw* has many levels of meaning and function. For example, in the statement "Every day you should worship the sun three times and commit yourselves to the *yazad*s (deities) and pronounce the existence and eternity of the *yazad*s and the nonexistence and destruction of Ahreman and the *dēw*s, (saying) that in the end they shall come to nonexistence and being smitten" (*abdom be ō anastīh ud zadagīh rasēnd*; Shaked, 1979, chap. E31c), the affirmation that the *yazad*s exist and Ahreman and the *dēw*s do not exist is not contradicted by the last phrase, in which the expectation of annihilation of the demons is proclaimed. Both affirmations express faith and determination, but the religious function, as well as the philosophical logic, of such expressions must be considered. Indeed, in texts like the *Vīdēvdād*, *Šāyest nē šāyest*, and *Ardā Wīrāz-nāmag* the evil of Ahreman and the *dēw*s was taken as utterly real and producing catastrophic effects on the world if unrestrained.

Except in the *Ardā Wīrāz-nāmag* and similar texts consisting of admonitions and warnings of dire punishments to be meted out by *dēw*s in hell, Zoroastrian writers did not refer to *dēw*s simply to strike fear in the faithful. Their concern was more practical: *Dēw*s are not simply a psychological or eschatological threat but rather a present reality in an embattled world. They can be smitten by the righteous kindling fire in the night, but it is easier for men to expel them from their bodies than for the *yazad*s themselves to do so; cursing the demons (*nifrin kunišn*) is a religious act (de Menasce, chaps. 123, 225, 236). Man's daily duty and eschatological role are to smite demons through good action and prayer (Williams, 1990, chap. 48.79 ff.). Demons shrink from fire, which should therefore be kept burning in a house where there is a pregnant woman; it protected Zoroaster's own mother from the onslaught of 150 *dēw*s trying to destroy the unborn prophet (Tavadia, chap. 10.4). *Dēw*s are particularly attracted by the organic productions of human beings, from excretion, reproduction, sex, and death (Williams, 1989). Two of the most powerful *dēw*s are the whore J̌eh, who attacks men and women, and the *druj ī nasuš*, the demon of pollution; much of the *Vīdēvdād* is devoted to measures to be taken against the attacks of physical pollution. In the philosophical texts, where there are attempts at rationalization and analysis of religious values, it is, however, the *dēw* Āz (q.v.) who is said to be most dangerously opposed to true human nature, for it is capable of destroying the *asnxrad* "innate wisdom" of man (de Menasce, chap. 316). Āz is responsible for evil religion, heresy, and misunderstanding of Zoroastrian doctrines; it prevents men from knowing the Creator and, in their deviation, they see God as a demon and the demons as gods, the lie as true and the true as a lie (de Menasce, chap. 77). Death itself is demonized as Astwihād (q.v.), who casts a noose of mortality around men's necks from birth. Although the *dēw*s may win a temporary victory for Ahreman, at the end of time they will be utterly vanquished (see, e.g. Williams, 1990, chap. 48).

Despite all the strategies for counterattacking the *dēw*s, the religion of the Pahlavi books is basically optimistic. In Zoroastrianism evil is not a creative force and is secondary in the cosmic order, implying the priority and ontological superiority of good (Shaked, 1967, p. 234). Man as a species thus stands between the *yazad*s and the *dēw*s; the former are immortal in essence and inseparable from their bodies (*mēnōg*), men are immortal in essence but separable from their bodies (moving from *gētīg* to *mēnōg* condition), but *dēw*s are mortal in essence and inseparable from their bodies, which may be destroyed (de Menasce, chap. 51).

See also *DAIVA.

Bibliography: (For cited works not found in this bibliography and for abbreviations found here, see "Short References.") E. Benveniste, "Que signifie *Vidēvdāt*?" in *Henning Memorial Volume*, London, 1970, pp. 37-42. Boyce, *Zoroastrianism* I, pp. 85-108. P. Gignoux, *Le livre d'Ardā Vīrāz*, Paris, 1984. J. de Menasce, *Le troisième livre du Dēnkart*, Paris, 1973. *Šāyest nē šāyest*. S. Shaked, "Notes on Ahreman, the Evil Spirit and His Creation," *Studies in Mysticism and Religion Presented to G. G. Scholem*, Jerusalem, 1967, pp. 227-34. Idem, *The Wisdom of the Sasanian Sages (Dēnkard VI) by Aturpāt-i Ēmētān*, Boulder, Colo., 1979. A. V. Williams, "The Body and the Boundaries of Zoroastrian Spirituality," *Religion* 19, 1989, pp. 227-39. Idem, *The Pahlavi Rivāyat Accompanying the Dādestān ī Dēnīg*, Copenhagen, 1990.

(A. V. WILLIAMS)

DĒWĀŠTĪČ (Ar. Dēwāšanj, Dēwāšenī), ruler of Sogdia (87?-104/706?-22), referred to as "prince of Panč" (Panjīkant) and as "king of Sogdia, ruler of Samarkand" in the portion of his archives discovered at the castle on Mount Mug (Moḡ), east of Samarkand, on the upper course of the Zarafšān river. The latest dates given in the archives are in legal and economic texts in which his "fourteenth year of rule at Panč" and his "second (year of rule) at Samarkand" are mentioned. Before the accession of Dēwāštīč, whose father was Yodḵsetak, Panjīkant was ruled by the Turk Čukin Čur Bilgä, and Dēwāštīč's descendants actually considered Čur to have been his father (Livshits, 1979 pp. 56-68). This anomaly could be explained if Dēwāštīč had married Čur's daughter and immediate successor, a possibility suggested by Sogdian coins from the time of Dēwāštīč, which are inscribed with the phrase "Nana, mistress of Panč," ostensibly referring to the goddess "Nana the mistress." The reference is unusual, however, as Sogdian coins of the 7th and 8th centuries always bore the names and titles of the rulers, rather than those of deities. The Parḡar region east of Panjīkant was under Dēwāštīč's rule, though lands closer to Panjīkant are not mentioned in the documents as his possessions, which suggests that Parḡar may have been his personal estate. It was included in the region of Bottam (Ebn Ḵordāḏbeh, p. 40).

While at Panjīkant Dēwāštīč shared power with the notables who presided over the urban community. The fragmentary nature of the sources does not permit acceptance of any of the ingenious hypotheses proposed for the date of his assumption of the Sogdian throne at Samarkand (variously given as 711-13, 718, and 721). King Ṭarḵūn perished in a coup in 91/709-10, and the usurper Ḡūrak became king of Samarkand (Ṭabarī, II, pp. 1229-30). Ṭarḵūn's two minor sons were taken under the protection of Dēwāštīč at Panjīkant; he thus attained grounds for his own pretensions and claim to the throne (Arabic letter from Mount Mugh, *Documents* 1:1; *Sogdiĭskii sbornik*, p. 56). After Samarkand, was occupied by the Arabs under Qotayba b. Moslem in 93/712 Ḡūrak was temporarily driven out (Ṭabarī, II, pp. 1250, 1508). Although both men had partisans among the Sogdians of Samarkand, Ḡūrak was incomparably the stronger. Both alternately submitted to the Arabs and sought help against them from the Turks and Chinese. Ḡūrak appealed to China in 100/719 (Chavannes, p. 204), while Dēwāštīč remained loyal to the Arabs in 99-101/718-20. He was considered a Muslim and enjoyed the protection of Jarrāḥ b. ʿAbd-Allāḥ, governor of Khorasan, to whom he was obliged to send Ṭarḵūn's two sons at the beginning of 719 (*Sogdiĭskii sbornik*, p. 55). Nevertheless, local cults also flourished in Panjīkant (Grenet, 1984, pp. 17-26). When Sogdia rebelled in 103/722 Ḡūrak, in a reversal, called upon its people to submit to Arab rule. Dēwāštīč, whose active participation against the Arabs has not been documented, feared an alliance with Ḡūrak, and before the new Arab governor, Saʿīd b. ʿAmr Ḥarašī, marched against the rebels in 104/722-23 he left for the citadel at Abḡar (modern Mount Mug) in Parḡar. After a number of episodes the Arabs sent a detachment against the Sogdians, who were defeated near the village of Kūm and retreated to the castle of Dēwaštīč. Dēwāštīč and others in his party surrendered to the Arabs (Ṭabarī, II, pp. 1439-49).

Excavations at Panjīkant have revealed that the Arabs burned one of the temples, the palace of Dēwāštīč, and houses, conceivably only of those citizens who had departed with Dēwāštīč. After his capture Dēwāštīč was treated as an honored prisoner, and, though Ḥarašī's superior in Baghdad seems to have wished to set him free, he was subsequently killed and his head sent to Iraq, one of reasons for the removal of Ḥarašī as governor of Khorasan (Ṭabarī, II, pp. 1148, 1453). In Ṭabarī's account of the events of 104/722 (II, p. 1446) Dēwāštīč is identified as a "noble" (*dehqān*, q.v.) of Samarkand; together with one document from Mount Mug (*Documents*, no. 1:1), this evidence confirms that Dēwāštīč's claim to the Sogdian throne was considered legitimate by the Arabs until the events of 104/722. The wall paintings of his burnt palace in the Panjīkant citadel include depictions of the coronation of a Sogdian king and the reception of an Arab by the king of Sogdia, probably Dēwāštīč himself (Azarpay et al., pp. 64-67, figs. 30-31, pl. 24).

Bibliography: (For cited works not found in this bibliography and for abbreviations found here, see "Short References.") G. Azarpay et al., *Sogdian Painting. The Pictorial Epic in Oriental Art*, Berkeley and Los Angeles, 1981. Barthold, *Turkestan*[3], pp. 188-90. M. Bogolyubov and O. Smirnova, *Khozyaĭstvennye dokumenty* (Economic documents), Sogdiĭskie dokumenty s gory Mug (Sogdian documents from Mount Mugh) 3, Moscow, 1963. E. Chavannes, *Documents sur les Tou-Kiue (Turcs) occidentaux*, St. Petersburg, 1903. *Documents from Mt. Mugh*, Corpus Inscr. Iran. II/3, Moscow, 1963. A. Freĭman, *Opisanie, publikatsii i issledovanie dokumentov s gory Mug* (Descriptions, publications, and studies of documents from Mount Mugh), Sogdiĭskie dokumenty s gory Mug (Sogdian documents from Mount Mugh) 1, Moscow, 1962. I. Gershevitch, "The Soghdian Word for 'Advice' and Some Muγ Documents," *Central Asiastic Journal* 7/1, 1962, pp. 83-94; repr. in I. Gershevitch, *Philologia Iranica*, ed. N. Sims-Williams, Wiesbaden, 1985, pp. 33-51. F. Grenet, *Les pratiques funéraires dans l'Asie Centrale sédentaire*, Paris, 1984. Idem, "Les 'Huns' dans les documents sogdiens du Mont Mugh," *Études irano-aryennes offertes à Gilbert Lazard*, Stud. Ir. 7, Paris, 1989, pp. 165-84. A. Isakov, *Tsitadel' drevnego Pendzhikenta* (The citadel of ancient Panjīkant), Dushanbe, 1977. V. Livshits, *Yuridicheskie dokumenty i pis'ma* (Legal documents and letters), Sogdiĭskie dokumenty s gory Mug (Sogdian documents from Mount Mugh) 2, Moscow, 1962. Idem, "Praviteli Pancha (Sogdiĭtsy i tyurki)" (Rulers of Panč [Soghdians and Turks]), *Narody Azii i Afriki* 4, Moscow 1979, pp. 56-68. O. Smirnova, *Ocherki iz istorii Sogda* (Sketches from the history of Sogdia), Moscow, 1970. *Sogdiĭskii sbornik. Sbornik stateĭ o pamyatnikakh sogdiĭskogo yazyka i kul'tury, naĭdennykh na gore Mug v Tadzhikskoĭ SSR* (Sogdian miscellany. Articles on monuments of the Sogdian language and culture found on Mount Mugh in the Tajik S.S.R.), Leningrad, 1934. Yu. Yakubov, *Rannesredne-vekovye sel'skie poseleniya gornogo Sogda (K probleme stanovleniya feodalizma)* (Early medieval agricultural settlements of upper Sogdia [On the problem of the establishment of feudalism]), Dushanbe, 1988.

(BORIS MARSHAK)

DEYHĪM. See CROWN.

DEYLAM, BANDAR-E, a port on the Persian Gulf (30° 3′ N, 50° 9′ E) in the province of Būšehr at an elevation a little above 1 m. The town is situated in a coastal plain, 10 km north of the cape of Tonūb, 72 km south of Behbahān (q.v.) and 217 km northwest of Būšehr (q.v.). The climate is warm and humid. The shallow harbor is now unsafe, and larger ships cannot dock there at all.

There are few historical references to Bandar-e Deylam, which is located near the ruined medieval towns of Sīnīz and Mahrūbān (sometimes called Mahrūyān; *Hodūd al-ʿālam*, tr. Minorsky, pp. 127, 377-78); a Persian traveler during the reign of Moḥammad Shah Qājār (r. 1250-64/1834-48) provided the following description: "The population of Bandar-e Deylam is one hundred households. All the houses are made of stone and brick. The fortress is built in the shape of a square, each side of which measures a hundred *d̲arʿ*s in length [1 *d̲arʿ*=1.04 m]. Bandar-e Deylam is the place at which the borders of Fārs, K̲ūzestān, and Bak̲tīārī meet. It provides a thoroughfare for Arabs and Lors" (Āl-e Dāwūd, pp. 85-86).

The ancient ruins of Mahrūbān are located 10 km from the port. They occupy an area 4.3 by 1 km and include remains of the corners and foundations of the fortifications, of three large caravansaries, and of the congregational mosque (Eqtedārī, 1348 Š./1969, pp. 3-4). Traces of the old Dutch fortress at Tonūb, with workshops and other installations, are also still visible (Eqtedārī, 1359 Š./1980, p. 751).

In 1365 Š./1986 the population of Bandar-e Deylam was 12,947 (2,247 households); the literacy rate among the 10,117 people six years old and older was 66 percent (Markaz-e āmār, p. 18). They speak Persian, and most are Twelver Shiʿites. Most of the inhabitants are engaged in dry farming, animal husbandry, hunting, forestry, and fishing. A few are employed in industry and construction or on a seasonal basis in the countries of the Persian Gulf littoral. The chief products of the region are grain and dates (see DATE PALM). Bandar-e Deylam has electricity, piped water, a telephone network, and most government services.

Bibliography: (For cited works not found in this bibliography and abbreviations found here, see "Short References.") S. ʿA. Āl-e Dāwūd, ed., *Do safar-nāma az jonūb-e Īrān*, Tehran, 1368 Š./1989. Curzon, *Persian Question*; tr. Ḡ. Waḥīd Māzandarānī as *Īrān wa qażīya-ye Īrān*, 2nd ed., 2 vols., Tehran, 1350 Š./1971, II, p. 482. A. Eqtedārī, *Āt̲ār-e šahrhā-ye bāstānī-e sawāḥel o jazāyer-e k̲alīj-e Fārs o daryā-ye ʿOmān*, Tehran, 1348 Š./1969, pp. 3-5. Idem, *K̲ūzestān o Kohgīlūya o Mamasanī* III, Tehran, 1359 Š./1980, pp. 750-51. ʿA. Farajī et al., *Joḡrāfīā-ye kāmel-e Īrān* I, Tehran, 1366 Š./1987, p. 439. Fasāʾī, ed. Rastgār. Jehād-e sāzandagī, *Farhang-e ejtemāʿī-e dehāt o mazāreʿ-e ostān-e Būšehr*, Tehran, 1363 Š./1984, p. 34. Markaz-e āmār-e Īrān, *Sar-šomārī-e ʿomūmī-e nofūs o maskan, 1365. Šahrestān-e Ganāva*, Tehran, 1365 Š./1986. M.-Ḥ. Pāpolī Yazdī, *Farhang-e ābādīhā wa makānhā-ye mad̲habī-e kešvar*, Mašhad, 1367 Š./1989, p. 106.

(SAYYED ʿALĪ ĀL-E DĀWŪD)

DEYLAM, JOHN OF (Yoḥannān Daylomāyā, d. 120/738), Eastern Syrian saint and founder of monasteries in Fārs. In addition to the brief details of his life given by the 9th-century Syriac writers Thomas of Margā and Īšōʿdnaḥ of Baṣra, there are two complete biographies in Syriac, one in prose (edited and translated by Brock), of which an Arabic version is also known, and one in the form of an extended verse panegyric. The account of John of Deylam in the Ethiopian synaxary (Budge, pp. 168-70) is related to the latter; although abbreviated, it contains a few additional details (Brock, p. 179 n. 84; for summaries of later Arabic traditions, see Fiey). On a Sogdian version, see below.

According to the Syriac sources, John was born in Ḥdattā on the Tigris and entered the monastery of Bēt̲ ʿĀbē while still a child. After living for a time as an anchorite he was captured by raiders from Deylam, who took him to their own land. There he spent many years performing numerous miracles and converting many of the Deylamites. Subsequently, under the protection of the caliph ʿAbd-al-Malek b. Marwān (65-86/685-705) and his governor of Iraq, Ḥajjāj, John traveled to Arrajān in Fārs, where he founded several monasteries; two of them were assigned to Persian- and Syriac-speaking monks respectively, so that neither community should be forced to celebrate services in a foreign language. Despite some chronological confusion and the legendary accretions typical of Syriac hagiographical literature, there is no reason to doubt the essential historicity of this biography (cf. Brock, pp. 131-33, 178-81).

Numerous fragments of a Sogdian version of the life of John are preserved in the Staatsbibliothek, Berlin (Preussischer Kulturbesitz, Orientabteilung); they belong to manuscript C3, found at Bulayïq (q.v.), which also contains the life of Serapion. Two of these fragments have been described by Olaf Hansen (pp. 97 bottom, 98-99) and by Werner Sundermann, who corrects Hansen's erroneous identifications of one of them as the conclusion of a work by (rather than about) John of Deylam and of the other as part of a history of the church in Central Asia. Until the Sogdian text is published it is difficult to comment on its affinities, but it is clearly derived from a Syriac life much more detailed than the text published by S. P. Brock.

Bibliography: (For abbreviations cited here, see "Short References.") S. P. Brock, "A Syriac Life of John of Dailam," *Parole de l'Orient* 10, 1981-82, pp. 123-89. E. A. W. Budge, *The Book of the Saints of the Ethiopian Church* I, Cambridge, 1928. J. M. Fiey, "Jean de Dailam et l'imbroglio de ses fondations," *Proche Orient Chrétien* 10, 1960, pp.

195-211. O. Hansen, "Die christliche Literatur der Sogdier," in *HO* I/IV/2/1, 1968, pp. 91-99. W. Sundermann, "Ein Bruchstück einer soghdischen Kirchengeschichte aus Zentralasien?" *AAASH* 24/1, 1976, pp. 95-101.

(NICHOLAS SIMS-WILLIAMS)

DEYLAMĀN (Daylamān), district and town in Gīlān. The district is about 37 km north-south by 23 km and is located at an elevation of about 2,000 m on the northern slope of the western Alborz (q.v.) east of the Safīdrūd. It is bordered on the north by Lāhījān, on the east by the Jawāherdeh highlands, on the south by ʿAmmārlū, and on the west by the region of Raḥmatābād. It is relatively cool in summer, and the winters are harsh and cold (Fukai, p. 1; Sotūda, pp. 14-15).

The district includes the headwaters of the Polāmrūd and the valleys of various tributary streams (Fukai, pp. 1-5). Many ancient sites are found there, particularly including cemeteries: Morād Tappa and Moḥammad Sālār near Sīākārbon, the cemeteries at Pīla Šāh and Arūškī, Āqā Sayyed Moḥammad northeast of Langol, Zarkūl northwest of Āsīābar, the cemetery north of Īšakūh, Lūr-e Taḵt and Lūr near Lūr, Sū Gol northeast of Qešlāq, the cemetery at Sīāhkūh, Bābā Molḥed at Sīāhkal and another Bābā Molḥed south of the tomb of Bābā Walī, the cemetery at Yahūdī Maḥalla, and Ḵarsāḵānī near the town of Deylamān (Sotūda, pp. 49-50).

Clandestine excavations at these sites have produced material from the 2nd millennium B.C.E., indicating the archeological importance of the area, but much more valuable information has been provided by the scientific excavations conducted from 1960 to 1964 by the Institute of Oriental Culture of the University of Tokyo at several sites, including Ghalekuti (Qalʿa-ye Kūtī) I and II and Ḥasanī Maḥalla. The excavated tombs yielded grayish brown, burnished red-brown, and dark brown pottery vessels; bronze and iron weapons; bronze mirrors; glass vessels; bone implements; and personal ornaments.

The material from Ghalekuti I and nearby Lāsūlkān is of the early Iron Age, spanning the late 2nd and early 1st millennia B.C.E. (Fukai and Ikeda, p. 3). This period encompassed the transition from the Bronze to the Iron Age and the period when native states were first established in the Alborz highlands. The tombs at Ghalekuti I include pit graves, stone chambers, and a few that do not fit either category. Grave goods included the kinds of objects already mentioned. Dwellings were also uncovered (Egami et al., pp. 10-21; Fukai and Ikeda, 1971, p. 3). The material from Lāsūlkān is of a later phase of the Iron Age; four circular stone tombs and two pit burials were excavated there. A study of the skeletons uncovered at both sites revealed both dolichocephalic and brachycephalic types as well as some with characteristics of both (Egami et al., p. 28). At Ghalekuti II stone chambers, pit burials, and shaft graves yielded an assemblage of material of the Early Iron Age and a second of the Parthian or Sassanian period, ca. 200 B.C.E.-600 C.E. (Fukai and Ikeda, pp. 3-4; Toshihiko and Fukai, 1968, p. 51), identified by comparative analysis of pottery and tool finds. At Ḥasanī Maḥalla, east of the village of Deylamān, eight grave shafts yielded iron and bronze implements (Toshihiko and Fukai, 1968, p. 27) of the same periods. At Nowrūz Maḥalla the Japanese excavated nine pit graves and six shaft graves, and at Ḵorramrūd seventeen horizontal underground tombs and one original type were discovered, all contemporary with those at Hasanī Maḥalla (Fukai and Ikeda, 1971, pp. 3-4).

All the tombs so far excavated in the Deylamān region have been tentatively assigned to two general periods: from the end of the Bronze Age to the early Iron Age (late 2nd millennium B.C.E.) and from the late Achaemenid through the Sasanian period.

See also DEYLAMITES.

Bibliography: N. Egami, *Dailaman* II. Tokyo University Iraq-Iran Archaeological Expedition, Report 7, Tokyo, 1966. Idem, S. Fukai, and S. Masuda, *Dailaman* I. *The Excavation at Ghalekuti and Lasulkan, 1960*, Tokyo University Iraq-Iran Archaeological Expedition, Report 6, Tokyo, 1965. S. Fukai, *Study of Iranian Art and Archaeology. Glassware and Metalwork*, Tokyo, 1968. Idem and J. Ikeda, *Dailaman* IV. *The Excavation at Ghalekuti II and I, 1964*, Tokyo University Iraq-Iran Archaeological Expedition, Report 12, Tokyo, 1971. J. Ikeda, *Human Remains from the Tombs in Dailaman 2*, Anthropological Studies of West Asia 2, Tokyo, 1968. H. L. Rabino, *Mázandarán and Astarábád*, GMS, N.S. 7, London, 1925. M. Sotūda, *Az Āstārā tā Estārbād* II, Tehran, 1351 Š./1972. S. Toshihiko and S. Fukai, *Dailaman* III. *The Excavations at Hasani-Mahalleh and Ghalekuti, 1964*, Tokyo University Iraq-Iran Archaelogical Expedition, Report 8, Tokyo, 1968.

(EZAT O. NEGAHBAN)

DEYLAMĀN, melody (*gūša*) incorporated into the *radīf* of Āvāz-e Daštī by Abu'l-Ḥasan Ṣabā (d. 1336 Š./1957), who borrowed it from the regional repertoire of northern Persia. It thus does not occur in the early *radīfs* of Mīrzā ʿAbd-Allāh, Mūsā Maʿrūfī, and Āqā Ḥosaynqolī but is included in that of ʿAbd-Allāh Dawāmī (q.v.) in the version of Maḥmūd Karīmī (Massoudieh, pp. 99-100), where it serves as the conclusion to Daštī (q.v.), lasting 2 minutes and 20 seconds, before the *gūša* Maṯnawī. From the modal point of view, this *gūša* is characterized by an initial motif that begins in the upper register, on the upper seventh (C) of the concluding note (D) of Daštī, and is followed by a slow descent centered around the focal note A. This mode is particularly sweet and melancholy, especially in the version established and popularized by Ḡolām-Ḥosayn Banān (q.v.).

Bibliography: M. T. Massoudieh (Masʿūdīya), *Radif vocal de la musique iranienne*, Tehran, 1357 Š./1978.

(JEAN DURING)

DEYLAMĪ, ʿABD-AL-RAŠĪD. See ʿABD-AL-RAŠĪD DAYLAMĪ.

DEYLAMĪ, ABU'L-FATḤ NĀṢER b. Ḥosayn b. Moḥammad b. ʿĪsā b. Moḥammad b. ʿAbd-Allāh b. Aḥmad b. ʿAbd-Allāh b. ʿAlī b. Ḥasan b. Zayd b. Ḥasan b. ʿAlī b. Abī Ṭāleb, Zaydī imam with the title Nāṣer le-Dīn Allāh (d. 444/1052-53). According to Yemenite sources, he first sought support for his imamate in Deylamān (q.v.), where he was born and raised, or in Gīlān. He is not mentioned in local Caspian sources, however. His ancestors had lived in Abhar (q.v.; Ebn Ṭabāṭabā, pp. 8-9).

Between 430/1039 and 437/1046 he arrived in the Yemen and, in the latter year, gained allegiance among the tribe of Hamdān in the region of Bawn. In April he seized and pillaged Ṣaʿda, killing many tribesmen of Ḵawlān. A month later he entered Ṣanʿāʾ, where he was welcomed by Yaḥyā b. Abī Ḥāšed, chief of the Ḥāšed of Hamdān, who was in control of the town. Abu'l-Fatḥ was recognized as imam and was able to appoint officials and gather the land tax and *zakāt*. He then returned to his permanent base at Ḏībīn, near which he fortified a mountain and built his residence; in 600/1204 it was restored, enlarged, and renamed Ẓafār by Imam Manṣūr ʿAbd-Allāh b. Ḥamza. In 438/1046-47 Abu'l-Fatḥ returned to the region of Ṣanʿāʾ and received the allegiance of Manṣūr b. Abi'l-Fotūḥ, chief of Ḵawlān ʿĀlīa, who built a palace for him at ʿAlab, southwest of Ṣanʿāʾ. Ebn Abi'l-Fotūḥ also mediated the allegiance of some chiefs of the tribe of ʿAns and of Jaʿfar, son of the imam Manṣūr Qāsem ʿĪānī and leader of the Ḥosaynīya Zaydī sect, to Abu'l-Fatḥ, who appointed Jaʿfar *amīr-al-omarāʾ* and conceded one fourth of the revenues to him. Ebn Abī Ḥāšed and Jaʿfar soon fell out with the imam, however, and, when he also offended Ebn Abi'l-Fotūḥ by his conduct in Ṣanʿāʾ, he was forced to abandon ʿAlab. Jaʿfar brought Ṣanʿāʾ under his own control.

The imam returned to Ḏībīn and fought battles with Jaʿfar around Aṯāfet and ʿAjīb. The rapid expansion of the power of the Ismaʿili leader ʿAlī b. Moḥammad Ṣolayḥī from 439/1047 further reduced tribal support for the imam, and he was forced to move from place to place. Ṣolayḥī defeated and killed him and seventy of his followers at Najd-al-Jāḥ in Balad ʿAns in 444/1052-53, according to the best sources, though 446/1054-55 and other dates are also given. According to one Ismaʿili source (see Hamdānī, p. 82), he had appealed to Najāḥ, ruler of Zabīd, for help against Ṣolayḥī. He was buried in Ofayq near Radmān. His descendants continued to live in Ḏamār until modern times.

Abu'l-Fatḥ was the author of a large commentary on the Koran, which is extant in manuscript in Yemen: *al-Borhān fī tafsīr ḡarīb al-Qorʾān*, in which he is said to have put forward many eccentric views. The manuscripts of a shorter koranic commentary, *al-ʿAhd al-akīd fī tafsīr al-Qorʾān al-majīd*, and a collection of his answers to legal and theological questions of several of his disciples also survive. Abu'l-Fatḥ's views clearly reflected his education among the Caspian Zaydīs but seem to have been rather independent of any particular doctrinal school. To some extent his teaching may have prepared the ground for the systematic introduction of Caspian Zaydī doctrine and literature in the Yemen under the imams Motawakkel Aḥmad b. Solaymān (d. 566/1170) and Manṣūr ʿAbd-Allāh b. Ḥamza (d. 614/1217).

Bibliography: Ḥosayn b. Aḥmad ʿArašī, *Bolūḡ al-marām fī šarḥ mesk al-ḵetām* . . ., ed. A. Karmalī, Cairo, 1939, pp. 36-37. ʿAbd-al-Raḥmān Ebn al-Daybaʿ, *Qorrat al-ʿoyūn be-aḵbār al-Yaman al-maymūn*, ed. M. Akwaʿ, I, Cairo 1391/1971, pp. 239-41. Ebrāhīm Ebn Ṭabāṭabā, *Montaqelat al-ṭālebīya*, ed. M. M. Ḵarsān, Najaf, 1388/1968. ʿAbd-Allāh Moḥammad Ḥabšī (Ḥebšī), *Moʾallafāt ḥokkām al-Yaman*, ed. E. Niewöhner-Eberhard, Wiesbaden, 1979, pp. 28-29. Ḥ. F. Hamdānī, *al-Ṣolayḥīyūn*, Cairo, 1955, pp. 82-83. W. Madelung, *Der Imam al-Qāsim ibn Ibrāhīm*, Berlin, 1965, pp. 205-06. Ḥomayd al-Moḥallī, *al-Ḥadāʾeq al-wardīya*, British Library, London, ms. no. 3786, fols. 109b-114a. ʿAbd-al-Bāqī Yamanī, *Taʾrīḵ al-Yaman*, ed. M. Ḥejāzī, Cairo 1384/1965, pp. 48-49. Yaḥyā b. Ḥosayn b. Qāsem, *Ḡāyat al-amānī*, ed. S. ʿA. ʿĀšūr, Cairo, 1968, pp. 246-50.

(WILFERD MADELUNG)

DEYLAMĪ, ABU'L-ḤASAN ʿALĪ b. Moḥammad (fl. 10th century), an obscure yet important author on the early Persian Sufism prevalent in Fārs. A contemporary of Abū ʿAbd-al-Raḥmān Moḥammad b. Ḥosayn Solamī (325-412/936-1021), he was a disciple and transmitter (*rāwī*) of Abū ʿAbd-Allāh Moḥammad Ebn Ḵafīf Šīrāzī (d. 371/982). Later he may have become attracted to the philosophical orientation of Abū Ḥayyān ʿAlī b. Moḥammad Tawḥīdī (320-414/932-1023; see below). Little else is known about his life, and references to him in the Sufi sources are only incidental.

Deylamī's fame rests on his works. His *ʿAṭf al-alef al-maʾlūf ʿala'l-lām al-maʿṭūf* (ed. J. C. Vadet, Cairo, 1962; tr. J. C. Vadet as *Le traité d'amour mystique d'al-Daylamī*, Geneva, 1980; for analysis of the Greek sources of the text fragment on pp. 29-30, see Walzer) is a treatise on mystical love (*maḥabba*; *ʿešq*) in which Sufi and philosophical reflections are blended. In it Bāyazīd Besṭāmī, Abu'l-Qāṣem Jonayd, Ḥosayn b. Manṣūr Ḥallāj (cf. Massignon, 1963, pp. 230-39), and Ebn Ḵafīf are cited as Sufi proponents of *ʿešq*, though initially the last opposed the notion (*ʿAṭf al-alef*, p. 5). Deylamī's Arabic biography of Ebn Ḵafīf is extant in a 14th-century Persian translation by Rokn-al-Dīn Yaḥyā b. Jonayd Šīrāzī (*Sīrat-e Ebn-e Ḵafīf*, ed. A. Schimmel Tarı, Ankara, 1955; Ar. retr. E. Dasūqī Šatā, *Sīrat al-šayḵ al-kabīr*, Cairo 1397/1977). Deylamī also compiled a *mašyaḵa*, a biography of Sufi masters of Fārs, apparently partly identical with a manuscript in Istanbul (Köprülü Library, ms. no. 1589; cf. Massignon, 1963, p. 229), which is the principal source for the early Sufi tradition of Shiraz. Extracts from it were included in the *mašyaḵa* of Abū Šojāʿ Moḥammad b. Saʿdān Maqārīżī (d. 509/1115) and *Tārīḵ mašāyeḵ-e Fārs* by Ṣāʾen-al-Dīn Ḥosayn b. Moḥammad b. Salmān (d. 664/1266). These two works in turn were among the sources for the guidebook to the tombs of Shiraz by Jonayd Šīrāzī (d. 791/1388) and its Persian paraphrase by his son ʿĪsā b. Jonayd Šīrāzī, in which some circumstantial details of Deylamī's life can be traced (see below).

Beginning in about the middle of the 10th century Deylamī appears to have lived twenty-five years in Shiraz, for that is the time span over which he claimed to have known Abū Aḥmad Fażl b. Moḥammad Kabīr (d. 377/987-88), Ebn Ḵafīf's attendant, who lived for fifty years in a room on the roof of Ebn Ḵafīf's *rebāṭ* (Jonayd, p. 46; ʿĪsā b. Jonayd, p. 88). Deylamī recalled an encounter with Abū Aḥmad Ḥasan b. ʿAlī Šīrāzī (d. 385/995; Jonayd, p. 47; ʿĪsā b. Jonayd, p. 89) and reported on the inheritence and Sufi ways of Abū ʿAmr ʿAbd-al-Raḥīm Eṣṭaḵrī (Jonayd, pp. 51-52; ʿĪsā b. Jonayd, pp. 93, 95; cf. Böwering, pp. 81-82). He is known to have visited Arrajān, Mecca (*ʿAṭf al-alef*, pp. 107, 114), and Antioch, where he met a clairvoyant black mystic coming down Mount Lokām (Qošayrī, pp. 114-15; cf. Gramlich, p. 327). A passage in Qefṭī's *Taʾrīḵ al-ḥokamāʾ* (p. 211) places Deylamī with a group of others in the presence of the Buyid vizier Moʿayyad-al-Molk Abū ʿAlī Aḥmad b. Ḥosayn Rokḵajī, who took office in 392/1002.

In Shiraz Deylamī met Abū Naṣr Sarrāj (d. 378/988-89) and Abū ʿAbd-Allāh Ḥosayn b. Aḥmad Šīrāzī, known as Bayṭār (d. 363/974 in Ahvāz; Jonayd, pp. 47, 104-05; ʿĪsā b. Jonayd, pp. 88, 145). He also reported hearing Tawḥīdī's account of a discourse by Bayṭār in the mosque of Ahvāz (Jonayd, p. 104) and an impassioned controversy in Shiraz between Tawḥīdī and the local shaikhs, led by Abuʿl-Ḥosayn Aḥmad b. Moḥammad b. Jaʿfar Bayżāwī, known as Ebn Sāleba (d. 415/1024; Jonayd, pp. 54, 105; ʿĪsā b. Jonayd, p. 97, 145). These fragments from Deylamī's *mašyaḵa*, a gloss in Tawḥīdī's *Moqābasāt* (p. 163 no. 19), and Qefṭī's note (p. 211) about Deylamī's reception by Abu'l-Qāsem Wattār Modlejī, in 382-83/992-993 vizier in Shiraz for Ṣamṣām-al-Dawla (for whom Tawḥīdī wrote one of his works; cf. Stern, p. 127) offer but a tenuous basis for a historical link between Tawḥīdī and Deylamī. Such a link, postulated by Louis Massignon (1963, p. 229) and J. C. Vadet (*ʿAṭf al-alef*, tr., pp. 2, 8, 26), could, however, explain the strong mixture of Sufi reflections on mystical love with philosophical ones evinced in *ʿAṭf al-alef*.

Bibliography: (For cited works not given in detail, see "Short References.") G. Böwering, *The Mystical Vision of Existence in Classical Islam*, Berlin and New York, 1980. C. Brockelmann, *GAL*, S I, p. 359. R. Gramlich, *Das Sendschreiben Al-Qušayrī's über das Sufitum*, Wiesbaden, 1989. L. Massignon, *Recueil de textes inédits concernant l'histoire de la mystique en pays d'Islam*, Paris, 1929, pp. 81-82. Idem, "La notion de l'essentiel désir," in *Mélanges Joseph Maréchal* II, Brussels and Paris, 1950, pp. 263-96; repr. in L. Massignon, *Opera Minora* II, Beirut, 1963, pp. 226-53. Jamāl-al-Dīn Abu'l-Ḥasan ʿAlī b. Yūsof Qefṭī, *Taʾrīḵ al-ḥokamāʾ*, ed. J. Lippert, Leipzig, 1903. Abu'l-Qāsem Qošayrī, *al-Resāla al-qošayrīya fī ʿelm al-taṣawwof*, ed. ʿA Maḥmūd and M. b. Šarīf, Cairo, 1359/1940. ʿĪsā b. Jonayd Šīrāzī, *Taḏkera-ye hazār mazār*, ed. ʿA. Nūrānī Weṣāl, Shiraz, 1364 Š./1985. Abu'l-Qāsem Moʿīn-al-Dīn Jonayd Šīrāzī, *Šadd al-ezār fī ḥaṭṭ al-awzār ʿan zowwār al-mazār*, ed. M. Qazvīnī and ʿA. Eqbāl, Tehran, 1328 Š./1959. H. Ritter, "Philo-logika VII. Arabische und persische Schriften über die profane und die mystische Liebe," *Der Islam* 21, 1933, pp. 84-109. Sezgin, *GAS* I, p. 664. S. M. Stern, "Abū Ḥayyān al-Tawḥīdī," in EI^2 I, pp. 126-27. Storey, I/2, p. 1053. Abū Ḥayyān ʿAlī b. Moḥammad Tawḥīdī, *Moqābasāt*, ed. Ḥ. Sandūbī, Cairo, 1347/1929, p. 163 no. 19. R. Walzer, "Fragmenta Graeca in Litteris Arabicis," *JRAS*, 1939, pp. 407-22. M. Weisweiler, *Verzeichnis der arabischen Handschriften*, Leipzig, 1930, pp. 33-35. Abu'l-ʿAbbās Aḥmad Zarkūb Šīrāzī, *Šīrāz-nāma*, ed. B. Karīmī, Tehran, 1310 Š./1931, p. 99.

(GERHARD BÖWERING)

DEYLAMĪ, ABŪ MOḤAMMAD ḤASAN b. Abi'l-Ḥasan (b.) Moḥammad b. ʿAlī b. ʿAbd-Allāh (or Moḥammad), Shiʿite author and traditionist. He is described in the biographical sources as a contemporary of ʿAllāma Ḥellī (d. 726/1325), of ʿAllāma's son Faḵr al-Moḥaqqeqīn (d. 771/1369-70), and of Šahīd-e Awwal Šams-al-Dīn Moḥammad (d. 786/1384), yet all that can be gleaned from his own writings is that he composed his *Ḡorar al-aḵbār* (see below) about a century after the fall of Baghdad in 656/1258 (cf. *al-Ḏarīʿa*, XVI, p. 36). The earliest author known to have cited him is Ebn Fahd Ḥellī, in *ʿOddat al-dāʿī* (completed 16 Jomādā I 801/24 January 1399). ʿAbd-Allāh Efendī (d. 1130/1718), who was perhaps the first to attempt an assessment of Deylamī's dates, found (pp. 338-40) an apparent inconsistency in the sources: Deylamī cited in his *Eršād al-qolūb* (pp. 182 ff.) the *ketāb* of Warrām b. Abī Ferās (d. 605/1208), known as *Majmūʿat Warrām*, but *Kanz al-fawāʾed* by Abu'l-Fatḥ Moḥammad b. ʿAlī Karājakī (d. 449/1057) contains citations supposedly from Deylamī's *Ketāb al-tafsīr*; furthermore, a work by Deylamī was also cited by Ebn Šahrāšūb (q.v.; d. 588/1192) in *Manāqeb āl Abī Ṭāleb*. Āqā Bozorg Ṭehrānī (*al-Ḏarīʿa* IV, p. 271 no. 1257; 1390/1970, p. 84) attempted to resolve this problem by arguing that the author cited by Karājakī and Ebn Šahrāšūb was distinct from the author of *Eršād al-qolūb*. In fact, the Deylamī mentioned by Ebn Šahrāšūb was Šīrawayh b. Šahradār (d. 509/1115), and in the available versions of Karājakī's work there is no reference to any Deylamī. ʿAbd-Allāh Efendī must have taken the abbreviation *Kanz* in Majlesī's *Beḥār al-anwār* as referring to Karājakī's work, rather than to *Kanz jāmeʿ al-fawāʾed* by ʿAlam b. Sayf b. Manṣūr Najafī Ḥellī (fl. 937/1530-31; cf. editor's introduction to Deylamī's *Aʿlām al-dīn*, pp. 15-16). Nothing is known about Deylamī's life, except that he appears to have led a solitary existence (cf. *Aʿlām al-dīn*, pp. 33, 326).

Deylamī wrote at least five works (the first three cited as sources by Majlesī, pp. 16, 33). *Eršād al-qolūb elā'l-ṣawāb al-monjī man ʿamela behe men alīm al-ʿeqāb* (ed. Bombay, 1315; ed. Beirut, 1398/1978; Pers. tr. H. Mostarḥemī, Tehran, 1338 Š./1959; ʿA. Reżāʾī, Tehran, 1396-97/1976-77) as known today comprises two volumes, the first dealing with ethics, the second with the virtues (*fażāʾel*) of ʿAlī. The earliest known manuscript containing both volumes predates 1024/1615 (cf. *al-Ḏarīʿa* I, pp. 517-18 no. 2527). There are strong indications, however, that the second volume did not originally belong to the *Eršād* and may not even have been written by Deylamī. First, in his introduction to the first volume he described the work as consisting of fifty-five (in some versions fifty-four) chapters; the number of chapters in that volume is in fact fifty-four, the last of which is called in some versions *ḵātema* (conclusion). Second, there is a marked difference in the way the sources are treated in the two volumes: In the first Deylamī identified hardly any of his sources, one of the few exceptions being Warrām's book (see above), whereas the author of the second was careful to identify his. Third, Deylamī's name does not appear in the second volume. Finally, it makes little sense for a work on ethics to be combined with a work of *fażāʾel* (cf. ʿAbd-Allāh, p. 340; Ḵᵛānsārī, p. 291). There was an abridgment (*talḵīṣ*) by Šaraf al-Dīn Yaḥyā b. Ḥosayn Baḥrānī, a student of ʿAlī Karakī (d. 940/1534; *al-Ḏarīʿa* IV, p. 419 no. 1849), but it is not clear whether it was of one or both volumes.

Aʿlām al-dīn fī ṣefāt al-moʾmenīn (ed. Qom 1408/1987, based on Imam Reżā library, Mašhad, ms. 381) is a work of *adab* (belles lettres) and *mawāʿeẓ* (exhortations) dealing with such subjects as God's unity, the importance of knowledge (*ʿelm*), the characteristics of the believer, and the need to lead a life of renunciation (*zohd*); it is interspersed with speeches and supplications of ʿAlī and other imams, as well as poetry and hortatory traditions. All the sources cited and identified by the author were Imami Shiʿite. One of the cited works was *Ketāb al-borhān ʿalā ṯobūt al-īmān* by Abu'l-Ṣālāḥ Ḥalabī (d. 447/1055-56), which is quoted in its entirety (pp. 44-58); it is not known to have survived independently (cf. Qomī, I, p. 97).

Ḡorar al-aḵbār wa dorar al-āṯār fī manāqeb al-aṭhār consists of fifty chapters on the virtues of ʿAlī and the defects of his opponents. It is fully preserved in manuscript form in the Tehran University library (*Fehrest-e . . . Meškāt*, pp. 1437-39 no. 1273; for another, incomplete manuscript, see *al-Ḏarīʿa* XVI, p. 36 no. 156). According to Rudolf Mach and Eric L. Ormsby (p. 60 no. 258), there is also a manuscript in the Princeton University library, but the text in question is a much later work.

The only evidence that Deylamī composed *al-Arbaʿūna ḥadīṯan* appears to be Āqā Bozorg's statement (*al-Ḏarīʿa*, I, p. 414 no. 2144) that a manuscript of such a work was in the possession of ʿAlī Akbar Bojnūrdī and was later damaged. As *Ḡorar* opens with a version of the tradition about the *arbaʿūna ḥadīṯan*, it is not inconceivable that the text in question was in fact the *Ḡorar*.The fifth work, *Ketāb al-tafsīr*, is not known to be extant. A passage from it is cited in Najafī Ḥellī's *Kanz jāmeʿ al-fawāʾed* (pp. 798-99); other fragments, cited in the same work either as simply from Deylamī (pp. 77, 93, 144, 197, 256-57, 261, 422, 511-12, 552, 563, 595, 609, 689-90, 710-11) or as from his *Ketāb* (p. 116), were probably also taken from his work on koranic exegesis.

Bibliography: (For cited works not given in detail, see "Short References.") ʿAbd-Allāh Efendī, *Rīāż al-ʿolamāʾ* I, ed. A. Ḥosaynī, Qom, 1401/1980-81. Āqā Bozorg Ṭehrānī, *Nawābeḡ al-rowāt fī rābeʿ al-meʾāt*, Beirut, 1390/1970. Idem, *al-Ḥaqāʾeq al-rāhena fi'l-meʾa al-ṯāmena*, Beirut, 1395/1975, p. 38. *Aʿyān al-šīʿa* XX, p. 443; XXIII, pp. 120-26. Hāšem b. Solaymān Baḥrānī, *Ketāb al-borhān fī tafsīr al-Qorʾān*, Qom, 1394/1974, I, pp. 294, 499-500; II, pp. 460-63; III, pp. 159, 234; IV, pp. 84, 135, 222, 330, 368. C. E. Bosworth, *Bahāʾ al-Dīn al-ʿĀmilī and His Literary Anthologies*, Manchester, 1989, p. 47. Brockelmann, *GAL* S II, p. 261. *al-Ḏarīʿa* II, pp. 238-39 no. 949. Esmāʿīl Bāšā Baḡdādī, *Hadīyat al-ʿārefīn* I, Istanbul, 1951, p. 287. *Fehrest-e . . . Meškāt* III/3, Tehran, 1335 Š./1956. Ḥorr ʿĀmelī (Moḥammad b. Ḥasan Mašḡarī), *Amal al-āmel* II, Najaf, 1385/1965, p. 77. E. Ḥ. Kantūrī, *Kašf al-ḥojob wa'l-astār ʿan aḥwāl al-kotob wa'l-asfār*, Calcutta, 1330/1912, pp. 39 no. 171, 53 no. 250, 392 no. 2169. Moḥammad-Bāqer Ḵᵛānsārī, *Rawżāt al-jannāt*, ed.

ʿA. Esmāʿīlīān, II, Qom, 1392/1972. R. Mach and E. L. Ormsby, *Handlist of Arabic Manuscripts (New Series) in the Princeton University Library*, Princeton, N.J., 1987. Moḥammad-Bāqer Majlesī, *Beḥār al-anwār* I, Tehran, 1335 Š./1956. M.-ʿA. Modarres, *Rayḥānat al-adab* II, Tehran, 1367/1948, pp. 36-37. ʿAlam b. Sayf Najafī Ḥellī, *Kanz jāmeʿ al-fawāʾed*, Qom, 1407/1987. ʿAbbās Qomī, *al-Konā wa'l-alqāb* II, Najaf, 1376/1956, pp. 216-17.

(ETAN KOHLBERG)

DEYLAMĪ, ŠAMS-AL-DĪN ABŪ ṮĀBET MOḤAMMAD b. ʿAbd-al-Malek ṬŪSĪ (d. ca. 593/1197), original though obscure Sufi author of the 12th century. Jāmī (*Nafaḥāt*, p. 355) cited him as a teacher of the 13th-century Sufi Maḥmūd Ošnohī (Landolt, p. 210) and "a great master and scholar whose teachings on the true reality of time, as set forth in his writings, are rarely found in the works of others." Deylamī was the author of about two dozen works on a variety of philosophical, theological, and mystical topics. Except for one minor treatise that has appeared in print (*Ḡāyat al-emkān fī derāyat al-makān*, wrongly attributed by Raḥīm Farmaneš to ʿAyn-al-Qożāt Hamadānī, app. pp. 1-54), Deylamī's works are extant in manuscript only; most important among them are two collections of his writings (Süleimaniye library, Istanbul, Şehid Ali Paşa ms. no. 1346; Dil ve Tarih-Coğrafya Fakültesi library, Ankara, İsmail Saib ms. no. 4120/2). Despite confusion in the sources (reflected in Brockelmann, *GAL* II, p. 207; cf. Arberry, p. 49; Böwering, p. 231), it is certain that Deylamī flourished in the second half of the 12th century and probably died in 593/1197.

Most of Deylamī's works were written in Arabic, but a few were also written in Persian. It is difficult to establish an exact chronology of these writings because he appears to have systematically reworked many of them, including in his revisions frequent cross-references to his other treatises. It is therefore best to arrange them according to content, divided between major works and minor treatises. The minor works are listed in *Kašf al-ẓonūn* and *Kašf al-ẓonūn*.

Deylamī's major works, all written in Arabic, include a commentary on the Koran, a summary of glosses on Sufi sayings, a collection of Hadith, an epitome of Sufi ethics, a compendium of Sufi cosmology, and an abstract of Sufi theology. His Koran commentary, the longest of his writings, is extant in at least eight manuscripts. One of the oldest, copied in 794/1392, bears the title *Fotūḥ al-Raḥmān fī ešārāt al-Qorʾān* (Beyazıt Umumi Kütüphanesi, Istanbul, Veliyeddin Efendi ms. no. 430). On the other copies the title is given as *Taṣdīq al-maʿāref*, the title by which the author himself referred to the work in his other writings. In his introduction to the commentary Deylamī stressed the radical change in his intellectual outlook from a critical stance toward Sufism in his early writings to a favorable appreciation of Islamic mysticism at later stages of his life. The body of the work is a continuous yet eclectic commentary on selected koranic verses from all suras presented in sequence. It consists of two parallel levels of interpretive glosses on koranic phrases, specimens of Sufi sayings, and items of the author's own explanation.

Šarḥ ketāb al-anfās, a summary of glosses on Sufi sayings, has erroneously been identified as a commentary on the teachings of Abu'l-Qāsem Jonayd (d. 298/910) and Ebn ʿAṭāʾ (d. 309 or 311/921-22 or 923-24) or as a gloss on the so-called *Ketāb al-serr fī anfās al-ṣūfīya*, wrongly attributed to Jonayd (cf. Sezgin, *GAS*, I, p. 648). In *Šarḥ ketāb al-anfās*; *ʿOyūn al-maʿāref*, his collection of Hadith; and *Eṣlāḥ al-aḵlāq*, his epitome of Sufi ethics, Deylamī employed a similar method of quoting Sufi statements and lengthy expressions of his own views.

His compendium on Sufi cosmology, entitled *Merʾāt al-arwāḥ wa ṣūrat al-wejāh*, is extant in two manuscripts that offer a glimpse of the scope of the revisions undertaken by the author, for one manuscript appears to represent the first and the other a revised version. The work is divided into two sections, each subdivided into chapters. It is preceded by a chart providing a sketch of Deylamī's cosmology, depicting the universe from the highest heaven to its lowest point. The author explained this chart as the reflection of a mystical vision in which he perceived the form and image of the invisible world as mirrors within mirrors, reflecting the nature and qualities of the spirits as if in a magnificent kaleidoscope. He defined the basic design and composition of the invisible world, explained its component parts, enumerated seven layers (*badan* "body," *nafs* "soul," *qalb* "heart," *īmān* "faith," *ʿaql* "intellect," *rūḥ* "spirit," and *serr* "inmost being"), and described the two conduits through which spiritual energy passes from the highest spirit (*al-rūḥ al-aʿlā*) and the most hidden reality to the lower world.

In his abstract of Sufi theology entitled *Jawāher al-asrār* Deylamī tried to define the theological foundations on which he anchored the world of his visions. He declared that he changed the original title of the work, *Kašf al-ḥaqāʾeq be-konh al-daqāʾeq* upon divine inspiration. The work, which was completed at the beginning of September 1193, is divided into fourteen chapters composed in the scholastic style of Islamic dialectical theology, frequently proceeding by answers to rhetorical questions. Its main thrust is on the nature of the human intellect, the vision of God, the compatibility of time and space with the idea of God, and the interpretation of Islamic monotheism in mystical experience (cf. Böwering, pp. 233-35). The frequent cross-references to most of Deylamī's other writings in Arabic and Persian seem to indicate that the work was revised by the author toward the end of his life. In his theological argumentation he relied on the *Maqālāt feraq ahl al-qebla*, a work of the Baghdad Muʿtazilite

Abu'l-Qāsem Kaʿbī Balḵī, which, as Deylamī observed, the author had begun to compile in 279/892. Deylamī also included exegetical disquisitions on Koran 42:11, 2:30, and 24:35, supported by quotations from the Old Testament in arabicized Hebrew.

Deylamī's writings encompass much unpublished and original material. Although he did not equal the philosophical prominence of Yaḥyā Sohravardī (d. 587/1191), he bridged the gap in 12th-century Sufism between ʿAyn-al-Qożāt Hamadānī (q.v.) and Najm-al-Dīn Kobrā, foreshadowing ideas that emerged in the Kobrawī school and the Ḥorūfī sect. Deylamī's arguments are frequently directed ad hominem and not free of inconsistencies. His thought is firmly based in theological reasoning and strongly permeated by visionary elements. In fact, the central purpose of his work may best be understood as providing a framework of thought for mystical vision. His writings mark a stage of transition in Sufi thought, breaking away from *karāmāt* (Sufi miracles) and legend and turning toward *wāqeʿāt* (Sufi visions) and dreams. The visionary world of the mystic is treated as totally real and fully identical with the spiritual world of the invisible realm. The twinship and correspondence of the inner world of man and the upper world of the unseen provide the platform for Deylamī's thought on the bipolarity of divine nature, his notions of three-dimensional time and eternal space, and his stress on intuitive knowledge and direct vision of the divine.

Bibliography: (For cited works not given in detail, see "Short References.") A. J. Arberry, "The Works of Shams al-Dīn al-Dailamī," *BSOAS* 29, 1966, pp. 49-56. G. Böwering, "The Writings of Shams al-Dīn al-Daylamī," *Islamic Studies* 26, 1987, pp. 231-36. R. Farmaneš, *Aḥwāl o āṯār-e ʿAyn-al-Qożāt*, Tehran 1339 Š./1960. Kaḥḥāla, X, p. 257. H. Landolt, *Le révélateur des mystères*, Paris, 1986.

(Gerhard Böwering)

DEYLAMITES, people inhabiting a shifting region in northern Persia and adjacent territories, including the Deylamān uplands.

i. *In the Pre-Islamic period.*
ii. *In the Islamic period.*

i. In the Pre-Islamic Period

In antiquity the Deylamites (Gk. Dolomîtai and variants) were mountain tribes, usually identified by 10th-century Arab geographers with the inhabitants of Deylam, the highlands of Gīlān. A considerably broader distribution extending as far as southern Armenia and the Caucasus can be deduced, however (Minorsky, p. 193).

The earliest mention of the Deylamites occurs in Polybius' universal history, of the late 2nd century B.C.E. (5.44.9), in which, in the description of Media, Greek *Delymaîoi is to be read in place of geographically impossible Elymaîoi (i.e., Susiana), as the tribes named immediate after them (Anariákai, Kadoúsioi, Matíanoi) were all in the north. It is also possible that the "Elymaioi" mentioned by Plutarch (*Pompey* 36.2; 1st century B.C.E.) with the Medes were actually Deylamites. In the later 2nd century C.E. Ptolemy (6.2) listed *Delymaís as a place in northern Choromithrene, which was located southeast of Ray and west of the Tapuroi (i.e., Ṭabarestān). There, too, the toponym was corrupted to Elymaís (Markwart, *Ērānšahr*, p. 126 n. 1).

In the Pahlavi *Kār-nāmag* (tr., p. 47) it is recorded that in the final years of the crumbling Parthian empire Artabanus (q.v.) V (or IV) mobilized all the troops from Ray, Damāvand (q.v.), Deylamān, and Pateška͏ᵛārgar, evidence that the region south of the Alborz (q.v.) was inhabited by Deylamites. More precisely in the *Nāma-ye Tansar* (tr., p. 30) it is stated that Deylamān, Gīlān, and Rūyān (later part of Ṭabarestān) all belonged to the kingdom of Gošnasp of Ṭabarestān and Parešvār, the latter apparently the Alborz region. Gošnasp made his submission to Ardašīr I (224-70) only after thorough consideration and kept his realm by the guarantee of Ardašīr himself. The dynasty was still ruling there in the time of Pērōz I (459-84; cf. Masʿūdī, *Tanbīh*, p. 99-100). Kavād I (488-531) appointed his eldest son, Qābūs (Kāōs), king of Ṭabarestān (*Nāma-ye Tansar*, tr., p. 70; Ebn Esfandīār, tr. Browne, pp. 92-94). Toward the end of his reign (while the Roman emperor Justin I [d. 527] was still alive), Kavād dispatched Būya (Gk. Bóēs), "bearing the title *wahriz*" (Gk. *ouarízēs*), against King Gurgēn of Iberia (Procopius, *De Bello Persico* 1.12.10). That Būya had come from Deylam can be deduced from a tradition according to which the *wahriz* (i.e., Ḵorrazād b. Narsē b. Jāmāsp) who conquered Yemen during the reign of Ḵosrow I (531-79), in about 570, had formerly been governor of Deylam (Masʿūdī, *Tanbīh*, p. 260; Ḥamza, p. 138). The troops of the *wahriz* also included Deylamites (Nöldeke, *Geschichte der Perser*, p. 167). Procopius (*De Bello Gothico* 4.14.5-7, 4.14.9) reported, from a western point of view, on the Dolomîtai at the siege of Archeopolis in the disputed territory of Lazica during the reign of Ḵosrow I (about 552): They were independent allies of the Persians, living in inaccessible mountains in the heart of Persia (i.e., Media) and fighting as infantrymen, each armed with sword, shield, and three javelins and accustomed to warfare on mountainous terrain. Some time later, according to Agathias (3.17.6-9, 3.17.18-22), the Dilimnîtai, "the largest tribe of those dwelling on this side of the river Tigris in the region of Persis" (i.e., in central Persia, or Media), undertook a fruitless attack against the Hunnic Sabirs, who were in the service of the Romans, and vainly charged the fortress of Phasis in Colchis (q.v.). Agathias characterized them as very warlike and independent allies of the Persians, skillful warriors in close combat or at a distance, using sword, pike, and sling. In a fragment from Theophanes (preserved in Photius, *Bibliotheca* 64) it is related that in the battles between Persians and Romans during the reign of Justin II (565-78), which broke out in 572, the Deylamites (Gk. *tò Dilmainòn éthnos*) joined forces with the Persians and the Sabirs. When power passed from Ohrmazd IV (579-90), to whom the Deylamites had submitted, to Ḵosrow II in 590 a certain Zoarab, leader of the Deylamites, rose up against the latter and joined the party of Bahrām VI Čōbīn (q.v.; 590-91; Theophylact Simocatta, 4.4.17, 4.3.1). When Bahrām Čōbīn's rising failed the Deylamites joined the rebellion of Besṭām (see BESṬĀM O BENDOY), a maternal uncle of Ḵosrow II (probably 592-95; cf. Nöldeke, *Geschichte der Perser*, p. 486). After the fall of Besṭām the *šahr-wahriz* (i.e., governor of Deylam) fought against the remnants of his army, consisting of Deylamites and Armenians, in alliance with Smbat Bagratuni, *marzbān* (margrave) of Gorgān (Sebeos, tr., pp. 43-46). Incidentally it was reported (Balāḏorī, *Fotūḥ*, p. 282) that Ḵosrow II had a personal guard of 4,000 Deylamites. When the Arabs conquered Persia the Deylamites remained virtually unsubdued, ruled by their own dynasty until the 9th century (cf. Minorsky, p. 190; Markwart, *Ērānšahr*, p. 127; see ii, below).

Christianity entered Deylam fairly early; in 554 there was a diocese of Āmol and Gīlān (Chabot, pp. 109, 366). The religion obviously survived for a long time in these iunaccessible regions: The Nestorian patriarch Timothy I (780-823) elevated both Gīlān and Deylam to the status of metropolis (Thomas of Marga, I, pp. 252-53; II, pp. 467-68), though evidence from a letter of the patriarch suggests this separate status was limited to the years 795-98 (cf. Braun). These arrangements were, in fact, not stable; in about 893 Elias, metropolitan of Damascus, mentioned only Media (=Ray) as a metropolis, and the lists compiled by Ebn al-Ṭayyeb (d. 1043) and ʿAbdīšōʿ, metropolitan of Nisibis (d. 1318), are silent about them (Sachau, pp. 21 ff.). The metropolis of Deylam does, however, reappear in the lists given by the early 14th-century historians of the Nestorian patriarchs, ʿAmr b. Maṭṭā and slightly earlier Salibhā b. Yūḥannā (*Maris Amri et Slibae*, pp. 126, 132). It seems that remnants of Christianity must have survived up to that time.

Bibliography: (For cited works not given in detail, see "Short References.") O. Braun, "Ein Brief des Katholikos Timotheos I über biblische Studien des 9. Jahrhunderts," *Oriens Christianus* 1, 1901, p. 299-313. J.-B. Chabot, *Synodicon Orientale ou Recueil de synodes nestoriens . . .*, Paris, 1902. *Kār-nāmag ī Ardašīr*, tr. T. Nöldeke as "Geschichte des Artachšīr i Pāpakān," *Bezzenbergers Beiträge* 4, 1878, pp. 22-69. *Maris Amri et Slibae De Patriarchis Nestorianorum Commentaria*, ed. E. Gismondi, Rome, 1896. V. Minorsky, "Daylam," in EI^2 II, pp. 189-94. *Nāma-ye Tansar*, tr. M. Boyce as *The Letter of Tansar*, Rome, 1968. E. Sachau, "Zur Ausbreitung des Christentums in Asien," *APAW*, Phil.-hist. Kl. 1, 1919, pp. 1-80. Sebêos, *Patmutʿiwn i Herakln*, tr. F. Macler as *Histoire d'Héraclius par l'évêque Sebèos*, Paris, 1904. Thomas of Marga, *Historia Monastica*, ed. and tr. E. H. W. Budge as *The Book of Governors*, 2 vols., London, 1893.

(WOLFGANG FELIX)

ii. IN THE ISLAMIC PERIOD

In the early Islamic centuries the Deylamites lived in the Alborz mountains and along the shore of the Caspian (qq.v.) north of Qazvīn, between Gīlān in the west and Ṭabarestān (Māzandarān) in the east. Whatever their actual origins, at that time they and their Gilite neighbors were commonly considered closely related and frequently mentioned together. It was claimed that the two peoples were descended from two brothers, Deylam and Gīl, of the Arab tribe Banū Ḍabba; this legend of the Arab origins of the Deylamites seems to have been known already at the time of the early expansion of Islam (see Ṭabarī, I, pp. 1992, 2352; III, p. 2367). Deylamites were certainly known among Arabs from the time of the Persian conquest of Yemen in about 570, and during the early days of Islam the Deylamites Fīrūz and Gošnasp (Jošnas) played a leading role among the Persian Abnāʾ (q.v.), backing the new religion in Yemen. Fīrūz Deylamī's family emigrated to Palestine and Syria, where several of his descendants became well-known Muslim traditionists. Deylamites may also have participated in raids in northern Arabia. Abū Dolaf b. Mohalhel (sec. 25; Yāqūt, *Boldān*, s.v. Deylamestān) mentioned a place called Deylamestān, located 7 farsangs from Šahrazūr, where in pre-Islamic times Deylamites used to camp while they carried out their raids into the lowlands of Mesopotamia.

Whatever the original language of the Deylamites may have been, in the Islamic period they spoke a northwestern Iranian dialect very similar to the language of the Gilites. Apart from other characteristics of northwestern Iranian, the guttural pronunciation of *h* as *ḵ*, noted as Gilite by Maqdesī (Moqaddasī, p. 368; e.g., both Ḵošam and Hawsam, Ḵašūya and Hašūya), and an *ī* sound added between consonants and *ā* (Lāhījān=Līāhījān, Došmanzār=Došmanzīār, Amīrkā=Amīrkīā, presumably pronounced Lyāhījān, Došmanzyār, and Amīrkyā respectively) were probably characteristic of Deylamite, as well as of Gilite. The question whether or not the report by Eṣṭaḵrī (p. 205) about a tribe in the Deylamite highlands that spoke a language different from Deylamite and Gilite and a similar report by Abū Esḥāq Ṣābī about a tribe in the region of Rašt (Madelung, 1987, pp. 14-15) attest the survival of a non-Iranian language among them must be left open.

In the first Islamic centuries. During the early centuries of Islam the Deylamites successfully resisted frequent Arab efforts to conquer their land. Some Deylamite mercenaries seem, however, to have joined the Arabs even before the battle of Qādesīya (16/637) and afterward accepted Islam (Ṭabarī, I, pp. 2340-41). Sayf b. ʿOmar reported a battle at Vājrūḏ in the year 18/639 in which the Arabs under Noʿaym b. Moqarren defeated the Deylamites and killed their leader Mūtā (Ṭabarī, I, pp. 2650-53). Qazvīn surrendered to Barāʾ b. ʿĀzeb, governor of Ray, in 24/645 and continued to function as a fortified border town against the Deylamites, as it had in the Sasanian period. Its garrison converted to Islam, and a group settled in Kūfa, where it was known as the Ḥamrāʾ of Deylam, presumably because its members were largely of Deylamite extraction. In Hadiths ascribed to the Prophet Moḥammad Qazvīn was praised as a border fortress, its martyrs equal in merit to the martyrs of the battle of Badr (Ebn al-Faqīh, p. 283). The Deylamites were commonly described, together with the Turks, as the most barbarous and odious enemies of the Muslims (Ṭabarī, II, pp. 285, 320, 722, 748, 1391), against whom religious war (*jehād*) was most meritorious.

In the historical sources numerous Muslim raids on Deylamān are mentioned summarily, but little detailed information is offered. Ḥajjāj b. Yūsof, the Omayyad governor in Iraq (73-95/694-714), seems to have been particularly eager to subdue the stubborn enemy and is reported to have had a detailed map of their country prepared for himself. Eventually he sent his son Moḥammad to invade the land. The campaign ended in failure, however, and instead Moḥammad built a mosque in Qazvīn (Ebn al-Faqīh, p. 283). The Dabuyid *espahbad*s of Ṭabarestān (see DABUYIDS) continued to claim suzerainty over the Deylamites and Gilites until the Muslim conquest of Ṭabarestān in 144/761. They maintained the border fortifications along the Čālūs river to guard against Deylamite incursions. Both Deylamites and Gilites, however, repeatedly aided the *espahbad*s against Muslim invaders of Ṭabarestān, especially during the campaign of Yazīd b. Mohallab in 98/716-17, during which Yazīd sent his *mawlā* Ḥayyān Nabaṭī, of Deylamite origin and leader of the non-Arab client troops in Khorasan, as envoy to deceive the *espahbad*, in order to extricate himself from a dangerous situation (Balāḏorī, *Fotūḥ*, p. 339; Ebn Esfandīār, I, p. 163; Ṭabarī, II, pp. 1291, 1329).

In 144/761 ʿOmar b. ʿAlāʾ conquered the territory as far as Rūyān, which was not considered part of Ṭabarestān and had in earlier times been Deylamite. The border town and district from which the Muslims raided Deylamān was Mozn, where a group of Deylamites seeking Muslim protection (*mostaʾmena*) were settled (Ebn al-Faqīh, pp. 304-07). In 201/816-17 ʿAbd-Allāh b. Ḵordāḏbeh conquered the Deylamite regions of Lārez and Šerrez for Islam (Ṭabarī, III, pp. 1014-15). This conquest does not, however, seem to have been permanent.

It was most likely after the Muslim conquest of Ṭabarestān that the dynasty of Deylamite kings known as Jostanids rose to power. They are first mentioned in the sources around 176/792, when the ʿAlid rebel Yaḥyā b. ʿAbd-Allāh found refuge with one of them, perhaps the presumed founder of the dynasty, Jostān. In 189/805 the caliph Hārūn-al-Rašīd (170-93/786-809) received the visit of Marzobān b. Jostān in Ray. The history of the dynasty can be traced until the first half of the 11th century, but the extent of its authority outside its own tribe is uncertain. The Jostanid seat of power was in Rūḏbār, a side valley of the Šāhrūd basin (not the Rūdbār of the Safīdrūd near Manjīl), where one dynast is reported to have built the fortress of Alamūt (q.v.) in 346/860-01.

Little is known about the religion of the Deylamites in this period. There may have been a few Christians and Zoroastrians among them, but the bulk were pagans. According to Bīrūnī (*Āṯār al-bāqīa*, p. 224), the Deylamites and Gilites lived by the rule laid down by the mythical Afrīdūn, according to which men were the absolute masters in their families. The Zaydī imam Nāṣer le'l-Ḥaqq broke up this order, evidently when he imposed the laws of Islam on his converts (see below). Bīrūnī added caustically that this change rather led to a return of the devils and demons (*marada*) to dominate their houses, suggesting that the Zaydī converts of Nāṣer remained pagan at heart. Zaydī Islam began to spread from Rūyān into Deylamān during the lifetime of the Zaydī imam Qāsem b. Ebrāhīm Rassī (d. 246/860). When the ʿAlid Ḥasan b. Zayd established Zaydī rule in Ṭabarestān in 250/864, Zaydī Deylamites became his most effective, if not always reliable, warrior supporters. The Zaydī doctrine spreading among the Deylamites at that stage was that of Qāsem, whose followers were later known as the Qāsemīya. After the overthrow of Ḥasan b. Zayd's brother Moḥammad in Ṭabarestān in 287/900 the ʿAlid Ḥasan b. ʿAlī Otrūš Nāṣer le'l-Ḥaqq became active in summoning the population to Islam in the village of Kaylākejān (Gīlākjān) among the more western Deylamites and in Hawsam (modern Rūdsar) among the Gilites. All Deylamites and Gilites east of the Safīdrūd were converted. His doctrine differed from that of Qāsem, and its adherents became known as the Nāṣerīya.

The Deylamite expansion. As Nāṣer le'l-Ḥaqq gradually widened his support among the Deylamites and Gilites, he compelled an oath of allegiance from the Jostanid king Jostān b. Vahsūdān. In 301/914 his followers inflicted a crushing defeat on a Samanid army on the river Būrrūd west of Čālūs (q.v.), and he was able to restore the Zaydī ʿAlid reign in Ṭabarestān with solid backing from the Deylamites and Gilites, who now, under their tribal leaders, erupted en masse from confinement in their homeland. After Nāṣer's death in 304/917 Nāṣerī Deylamites and Gilites for centuries made pilgrimage to his tomb in Āmol and remained deeply attached to his descendants, preferring them as candidates for the Zaydī imamate.

Nāṣer's successor, Ḥasan b. Qāsem Dāʿī, quickly

came into conflict with the Deylamites, partly because of their loyalty to the house of Nāṣer and partly because he sided with the civil population of Ṭabarestān against the often unruly and overbearing Deylamite warriors. In 309/921, after an abortive attempt to conquer Khorasan and a conspiracy of Deylamite and Gilite leaders to kill Dāʿī, the latter murdered seven of them in Gorgān, provoking widespread disaffection. Many rebels joined the Samanids, and one of them, the Gilite Mardāvīj b. Zīār, eventually killed Dāʿī in battle, in 316/928, in revenge for his uncle, king of the Gilites.

As the Zaydī ʿAlid reign in Ṭabarestān collapsed, various Deylamite and Gilite leaders, with their personal followers, sought their fortunes either as mercenaries or by trying to establish independent principalities wherever conditions were propitious. At first the Deylamites Mākān b. Kākī and Asfār b. Šīrūya were the chief rivals. The latter began by serving the Samanids, then established himself as ruler over Ray, Qazvīn, Zanjān, Abhar, Qom, and Karaj. In 319/931 he was seized and killed by his former follower Mardāvīj, founder of the Ziyarid dynasty. Mardāvīj quickly captured Hamadān, Dīnavar, and Isfahan from the caliph's governors and wrested Ṭabarestān and Gorgān from Mākān. Threatened by the revolt of his vassal ʿAlī b. Būya, founder of the Buyid dynasty (see BUYIDS), in Karaj, he moved south in 322/932, seized Ḵūzestān, and extracted recognition of his suzerainty from ʿAlī, who was in control of Shiraz and Fārs. Mardāvīj made plans for the conquest of Iraq, hoping to overthrow the ʿAbbasid caliphate and to restore Persian kingship, crowning himself with a crown shaped like that of Ḵosrow Anūšīrvān (531-79). He was murdered by his Turkish troops in Isfahan, however. His plans reflected the strong attachment to Persian royal traditions among the Deylamites and Gilites in that period. Asfār had also intended for a time to crown himself Persian king and had set up a golden throne for himself in Ray. It fell to the Buyids, however, to realize some of these ambitions.

As a result of the murder of Mardāvīj all the southern territories were lost to his brother and successor, Vošmgīr. Ziyarid rule was thenceforth based in Gorgān and usually included Ṭabarestān. It lasted until the last quarter of the 11th century but was under Saljuq suzerainty after 433/1041.

The most successful actors in the Deylamite expansion were the Buyids. The ancestor of the house, Abū Šojāʿ Būya, was a fisherman from Līāhej, the later region of Lāhījān, who, together with his five sons, joined the army of Nāṣer le'l-Ḥaqq. Three of his sons rose to royal power. ʿAlī ʿEmād-al-Dawla established his reign in Fārs in 322/934. With his backing, Ḥasan Rokn-al-Dawla first seized Isfahan in 323/935 and later, from 335/946, ruled Ray, while Aḥmad Moʿezz-al-Dawla, after invading Kermān in 324/936, seized southern Iraq and entered Baghdad, the seat of the ʿAbbasid caliphate, in 334/945. The long-term presence of three Buyid principalities led to a massive migration of Deylamites to each of them, where they were provided with military fiefs, especially around Shiraz in Fārs, in Mesopotamia south of Baghdad, and in the region of Ray. ʿAlī ʿEmād-al-Dawla retained the supreme leadership among the Buyid amirs. In 325/937 he ascended a throne in Shiraz and adopted the title *šāhanšāh*, partly as a claim to legitimacy independent of the caliphate, partly as an appeal to Persian national sentiments among the population in Fārs and among the Deylamites and Gilites, and partly as an assertion of supremacy over his brothers, who ruled in their own domains. While thus adopting the traditional title of Persian royalty, the Buyids also promoted the ideology of a reign of the Deylamites (*dawlat al-Deylam*) to replace the Arab reign of the ʿAbbasids and Qorayš. This ideology was reflected already in Ḥamza Eṣfahānī's *Taʾrīḵ*, written in 350/961, and was fully developed by ʿEmad-al-Dawla's nephew and successor, ʿAżod-al-Dawla (q.v.), the greatest of the Buyid rulers. ʿAżod-al-Dawla forced the ʿAbbasid caliph to recognize Buyid sovereignty unequivocally and to renounce all rights to interfere in intra-Buyid relations. He compelled Abū Esḥāq Ṣābī to write *Ketāb al-tājī fī aḵbār al-dawla al-deylamīya* (now largely lost), glorifying the Deylamites and their reign. In it Abū Esḥāq set forth, apparently for the first time, the Buyid claim to descent from the Sasanian king Bahrām Gūr (Bīrūnī, *Āṯār al-bāqīa*, p. 38). The weakness and continuous internal rivalries of the later Buyid rulers, however, gave the ʿAbbasid caliphs the opportunity to reassert their traditional role as sovereign arbitrators. A major weakness of Buyid rule was the fact that the Deylamites remained footsoldiers, so that from the beginning the Buyids were forced to employ Turkish horsemen in large numbers to balance their armies. Fighting between the two ethnic elements became endemic under the later Buyids. The Turkish element also quickly intruded into the ruling house. ʿAżod-al-Dawla himself was half Turkish, the son of a Turkish concubine, and some of the later Buyids had more Turkish than Deylamite blood. By 453/1062 Buyid rule had been overthrown by the Saljuq Turks.

The Deylamite expansion also reached northwest to Azerbaijan and beyond. There it was led by the Sallarid, Mosaferid, or Langarid (not Kangarid) dynasty, founded by Sal(l)ār b. Asvār, whose name was islamized and arabicized as Moḥammad b. Mosāfer. He was a son-in-law of Jostān b. Vahsūdān, and the Sallarid dynasty always remained closely connected with the Jostanid house through marriage ties and in rivalry for power over the Deylamites. Probably in the later 9th century Moḥammad b. Mosāfer took possession of the mountain stronghold of Šamīrān and from there gained control over Ṭārom (Ṭarm), the region extending along the middle course of the Safīdrūd before its confluence with the Šāhrūd. After Jostān b. Vahsūdān was murdered by his brother

ʿAlī, who then entered ʿAbbasid service and was eventually appointed governor of Ray, Ebn Mosāfer avenged his death by killing ʿAlī in 307/919. He also killed ʿAlī's brother Kosrow Fīrūz, who had seized power in Rūdbār of Alamūt, but could not prevent the succession of the latter's son Mahdī Sīāhčašm, in Alamūt. While the Mosaferids gradually succeeded in gaining control of a large portion of the highlands of Deylamān, the Jostanids seem to have held on to Alamūt most of the time. Because of his extreme tyranny, in 330/942 Ebn Mosāfer was seized by his sons Vahsūdān and Marzobān, with the connivance of their mother, and imprisoned. Vahsūdān remained to rule Ṭārom, and in the same year Marzobān invaded Azerbaijan and expelled the Kurd Deysam, whose Deylamite troops mostly went over to their countrymen. Sallarid reign in Azerbaijan lasted until 373/973 and at times extended to parts of Armenia and the Muslim principalities in Transcaucasia. In Ṭārom the dynasty continued to survive for some decades after accepting Saljuq overlordship in 434/1043-44.

Beside establishing their own principalities Deylamites came to serve as mercenaries in various established states. In the east the Samanids welcomed Deylamite adventurers as allies. In Egypt the Fatimid caliph al-ʿAzīz (365-86/975-96) was particularly fond of the Deylamite and Turkish elements in his army. The first such group arrived there in 368/978-79, led by the Turk Alptegin Šarābī, who had deserted from the army of the Buyid Moʿezz-al-Dawla. The Deylamites were settled by al-ʿAzīz in a special quarter of Cairo, west of the mosque of al-Azhar (Maqrīzī, I, pp. 74, 263, II, pp. 8, 10).

In that period Deylamān was a battleground of indigenous and foreign powers, each seeking to dominate it. After the fall of the Zaydī state in Ṭabarestān, various Zaydī ʿAlids (q.v.) succeeded in establishing petty jurisdictions in towns in the Caspian coastal regions of Deylamān and eastern Gīlān. Most important was Hawsam in Gīlān, on the border of Deylamān, where Nāṣer le'l-Ḥaqq had been active and where the center of Nāṣerīya scholarship was located. In the highlands the Jostanids and Mosaferids were rivals for domination. The Jostanids tended to favor the Zaydīs and at times encouraged ʿAlid claimants to the imamate. The Mosaferids came under Ismaʿili influence. Both Ziyarids and Buyids tried to exert influence in their former homelands by backing or opposing Zaydī ʿAlid pretenders.

Ismaʿili Shiʿism spread among the initially Zaydī Deylamites from an early date, partly because of disenchantment with the conduct and quarrels among some of the ʿAlid leaders after the death of Nāṣer le'l-Ḥaqq. The Ismaʿili *dāʿī* Abū Ḥātem Rāzī (d. 322/934) in particular gained many converts, among them Asfār, Mardāvīj, and the Jostanid Sīāhčašm, though their allegiance to the Ismaʿili movement may have been superficial. Among the Sallarids both sons of Moḥammad b. Mosāfer, Vahsūdān and Marzobān, as well as their vizier, Jaʿfar b. ʿAlī (formerly in the service of Yūsof b. Abi'l-Sāj and Daysam, q.v.), are known to have been active Ismaʿilis. Ebn Ḥawqal (p. 349) noted the presence of numerous Ismaʿilis in Azerbaijan under Marzobān in 344/955.

The Ismaʿilism of all these early converts was of the Qarmaṭī branch, recognizing Moḥammad b. Esmāʿīl as the expected *mahdī* and rejecting the Fatimid imamate. Later Fatimid Ismaʿilism also spread among the Deylamites. The prominent Ismaʿili *dāʿī* Moʾayyad fi'l-Dīn Šīrāzī, whose father had been *dāʿī* in Fārs, succeeded in converting the Buyid ruler of Fārs Abū Kālījār (q.v.) and numerous Deylamites in his army before 438/1046. While still a *dāʿī* for the Fatimid caliph al-Mostanṣer (427-87/1036-94) Ḥasan b. Ṣabbāḥ became active among the mountain Deylamites. In 483/1090 he seized the fortress of Alamūt from a Zaydī ʿAlid and made it his residence. After the death of al-Mostanṣer Alamūt became the center of the Nezārī Ismaʿili movement and later the residence of the Nezārī imams. Other mountain fortresses in Deylamān, like Maymūndez, Lamasar, and Šamīrān, were seized and fortified later. While the Deylamite highlands came solidly under Nezārī Ismaʿili control Zaydī activity persisted, on a reduced scale, in the Deylamite and Gilite littoral, including Lāhījān.

The fall of Alamūt in 654/1256 and the destruction of the Nezārī castles by the Mongols did not put an end to Nezārī activity in the mountains of Deylamān. Alamūt was repeatedly recaptured and restored by them. In the second half of the 14th century Kodāvand Moḥammad, imam of the Moḥammadšāhī line, found wide support among the Ismaʿilis in Deylamān and eventually established himself in Alamūt. In the coastal regions Zaydī ʿAlids, both of the Qāsemīya and Nāṣerīya schools, remained active in competition with petty local lords. Few details are known about their history until the rise of the Amīr (Kār) Kīāʾī dynasty. Sayyed ʿAlī Kīā b. Amīr Kīā Malāṭī became lord of eastern Gīlān in 769/1367-68, with the help of the Imami Shiʿite Marʿašī *sayyeds* (claiming descent from the Prophet Moḥammad) ruling Māzandarān, and gained formal recognition as imam by the Zaydī scholars of Lāhījān and Rānekūh. Kodāvand Moḥammad was expelled from Alamūt by ʿAlī Kīā. Although he was able to return once more after the latter's death, ʿAlī Kīā's son Rāżī Kīā (798-829/1395-1426) took definitive control over the highlands. The later rulers of the Amīr Kīāʾī dynasty were nominally Zaydī but reigned in Lāhījān on the basis of dynastic succession without claiming the imamate.

After the rise of the Safavids the Amīr Kīāʾī sultan Aḥmad Khan embraced Imami Shiʿism in 933/1526-27, and the Zaydī community disintegrated over the course of the century. Nezārī Shiʿites were last mentioned in the highlands in the 16th century. As the former Deylamite territories were fully integrated into a Persian state for the first time in history, the inhabitants were mostly converted to Twelver Shiʿism, to which in former centuries a few Deylamites had been attracted. Administratively the former Deylamite territories became part of the province of Gīlān, and the population is considered Gilite. Only a small district south of Lāhījān is still called Deylamān.

Bibliography: (For cited works not given in detai, see "Short References.") Abū Dolaf b. Mohalhel, *Resāla*, ed. V. Minorsky as *Abu Dulaf's Travels in Iran*, Cairo, 1954. F. Daftary, *The Ismaʿilis*, Cambridge, 1990, index s.v. Daylam, Daylamān. K. Inostransev, *Sasanidskie etyudy (Etudes Sassanides)*, St. Petersburg, 1909, pp. 111 ff.; tr. K. Kāẓemzāda as *Taḥqīqāt-ī dar bāra-ye Sāsānīān*, Tehran, 1351 Š./1972, pp. 115 ff. M. S. Khan, "The Contents of the Kitāb al-Tājī Manuscript of Abū Isḥāq al-Ṣābī," *Islamic Studies* 8, 1969, pp. 247-52. W. Madelung, "Abū Isḥāq al-Ṣābī on the ʿAlids of Ṭabaristān and Gīlān," *JNES* 26, 1967, pp. 17-57. Idem, "The Assumption of the Title Shāhānshāh by the Būyids and the 'Reign of the Daylam (*Dawlat al-Daylam*),'" *JNES* 28, 1969, pp. 84-108, 168-83. Idem, "Further Notes on al-Ṣābī's *Kitāb al-Tājī*," *Islamic Studies* 9, 1970, pp. 81-88. Idem, "The Minor Dynasties of Northern Iran," in *Camb. Hist. Iran* IV, pp. 198-249 (p. 225 l. 24: for Vushmgīr read Vahsūdān). Idem, *Arabic Texts Concerning the History of the Zaydī Imāms of Ṭabaristān, Daylamān and Gīlān*, Beirut, 1987 (edition of the extant fragment of Abū Esḥāq Ṣābī's *Ketāb al-Tājī* on the Deylamites, together with other relevant source material). Maqrīzī, *Keṭaṭ*, 2 vols., Būlāq, 1270. V. Minorsky, *La domination des Dailamites*, Paris, 1932. Idem, "Daylam," in *EI*², pp. 189-94 (excellent and comprehensive, with references to earlier literature). M. Sotūda, *Az Āstārā tā Estārbād*, 6 vols., Tehran, 1349-56 Š./1970-77, esp. II (for archeological remains and historical geography).

(WILFERD MADELUNG)

DEYM. See ĀBYĀRĪ; AGRICULTURE; BĀRĀN; FARMING.

DEŽ, DEZ (fortress, castle; Mid. Pers. *diz*; OPers. *didā*- "wall, fortress"; Av. *daēz*-; Yidgha *lizo* "fort"). See BĀRU; CASTLES.

Bibliography: *AirWb*, cols. 673-74. Kent, *Old Persian*, p. 191. G. Morgenstierne, *Indo-Iranian Frontier Languages*, 3 vols., Oslo, 1929-56, II, p. 225.

(WOLFRAM KLEISS)

DEŽ, a weekly of news and politics associated with the Tudeh Party (see COMMUNISM ii) that began publication on 6 Ḵordād 1322 Š./27 May 1943 in Tehran and continued with some interruptions until June 1953. Its publisher and director was Nowḏar Āšūrī. From 1950 until the summer of 1953 it was published with interruptions in place of *Be sūy-e āyanda* (q.v.), the unoficial organ of the then underground Tudeh Party. Issues of *Dež* are found in the Central Library of Tehran University, the Asian Institute in Shiraz, and the Library of Congress.

Bibliography: Ḥ. Abū-Torābīān, *Maṭbūʿāt-e Īrān az Šahrīvar-e 1320 tā 1326*, Tehran, 1366 Š./1987, p. 83. G. Šokrī, "Fehrest-e rūz-nāmahā wa majallahā-ye fārsī dar Moʾassasa-ye Āsīāʾī," *FIZ* 27, 1365 Š./1986, p. 365. W. Ṣādeqī-nasab, *Fehrest-e rūz-nāmahā-ye fārsī-e 1320 tā 1332*, Tehran, 1360 Š./1981, p. 150. I. V. Pourhadi, *Persian and Afghan Newspapers in the Library of Congress, 1871-1978*, Washington, D.C., 1979, p. 16.

(NASSERADDIN PARVIN)

DEZ, River. See ĀB-E DEZ.

DEŽ-E BAHMAN (Fortress of Bahman, Pahl. Wahmandiz), according to legend a fortress in Azerbaijan conquered by the Kayānian king Kay Ḵosrow, son of Sīāvaš and grandson of Kāvūs, king of Iran. According to the *Šāh-nāma* (ed. Khaleghi, II, pp. 460-67), after Kay Ḵosrow returned from Tūrān to Iran two prominent courtiers, Ṭūs and Gūdarz, consulted about the royal succession. Ṭūs proposed Farīborz, Kāvūs' son, while Gūdarz put forward the name of Kay Ḵosrow. Finally, Kāvūs declared that both candidates should be sent to Ardabīl, where the fortress of Bahman was located, and that the one who succeeded in taking it would be his heir. Farīborz and Ṭūs made the first attempt, but the grounds of the fortress, the abode of demons (*dīv*s) and sorcerers (*jādūs*), heated up, forcing their army to withdraw. Then Kay Ḵosrow, accompanied by Gīv, son of Gūdarz, advanced. Kay Ḵosrow wrote a letter pleading with God for assistance. He tied the letter to a long spear, which he gave to Gīv to hurl at the fortress wall. When the letter hit the wall it raised an uproar, and the world became cloudy. At Kay Ḵosrow's command the army then shot arrows at the fortress, killing many demons. Afterward the air cleared, and Kay Ḵosrow, accompanied by Gūdarz, entered the fortress, where he beheld an extensive city with numerous gardens and palaces. He ordered construction of a high dome, where he installed Ādur Gušnasp (q.v.), one of the three great Zoroastrian fire temples (*Šāh-nāma*, ed. Khaleghi, II, pp. 463-67), the fire from which is said to have then appeared on the ears (*gūš*; *Tārīḵ-e Sīstān*, pp. 35-36) or on the mane (*buš*; *Bundahišn*, TD_2, p. 125) of his horse.

The fortress was probably originally located in eastern Iran. Later, when eastern Iranian traditions about Kay Ḵosrow, Ādur Gušnasp, and Čēčast (q.v.) were transferred to the west, the fortress, too, came to be located in Azerbaijan. In the Zoroastrian tradition it has been located on Mount Asnwand (Av. Asnuuant), and it is related that it was the assistance of Ādur Gušnasp that enabled Kay K̲osrow to conquer "Bahmandez" (*Ātaš Nyāyišn* no. 5, in Dhalla, pp. 146-47; *Zand-i Khurtak Avistāk*, p. 38). As Asnwand was sometimes identified with Sabalān, the fortress has also been located there (*Nozhat al-qolūb*, ed. Le Strange, p. 81). The story of events involved in the overthrow of the image shrine on Lake Čēčast and the installation of Ādur Gušnasp in Pahlavi (e.g., *Bundahišn*, TD_2, p. 125) and Persian (e.g., *Tārik̲-e Sīstān*, pp. 35-36) texts is obviously connected with the conquest of this fortress. According to one account (*Nozhat al-qolūb*, ed. Le Strange, p. 81), it was also called Rūyīndez (Dež-e Rūīn, q.v.).

Bibliography: (For citated works not given in detail, see "Short References.") Qewām-al-Dīn Fatḥ Bondārī, tr., *Šāh-nāma*, ed. ʿA. ʿAzzām, 2 vols. in 1, I, Tehran, 1349 Š./1970, pp. 197-98. M. N. Dhalla, ed., *The Nyaishes*, New York, 1908. *Mojmal*, ed. Bahār, pp. 47, 50. Šahmardān b. Abi'l-K̲ayr, *Nozhat-nāma-ye ʿalāʾī*, ed. F. Jahānpūr, Tehran, 1362 Š./1983, pp. 328-29. *Tārīk̲-e gozīda*, ed. Browne, p. 93. *Zand-i Khurtak Avistāk*, ed. B. N. Dhabhar, Bombay, 1927.

(AḤMAD TAFAŻŻOLĪ)

DEŽ-E GONBADĀN (Fortress of Gonbadān), a fortress where the Iranian hero Esfandīār (q.v.), son of the Kayānian king Goštāsb, was imprisoned. At the instigation of Gorazm (Ṭabarī, I, p. 677: Qorazm) Goštāsb began to mistrust Esfandīār and finally accused him of laying claim to the throne of Iran; he ordered Esfandīār put in chains and sent to Dež-e Gonbadān, while he himself left Balk̲ for Sīstān. When Arjāsb, king of Tūrān and Goštāsb's adversary, learned of Goštāsb's absence and Esfandīār's captivity he attacked Balk̲, capturing Goštāsb's two daughters and killing his father, Lohrāsb. Goštāsb returned to Balk̲, but Arjāsb repelled his attacks. Finally, Goštāsb's vizier, Jāmāsb, released Esfandīār, who defeated Arjāsb and sent him fleeing to Tūrān (*Šāh-nāma*, ed. Moscow, VI, pp. 124-32, 141-52, 157-63; Ṭabarī, I, pp. 678-79; T̲aʿālebī, *Ḡorar*, pp. 282-98).

Because Ṭabarī (I, p. 680) and Meskawayh (*Tajāreb*, p. 55) both translated the name of this fortress as "Women's fortress" and T̲aʿālebī (*Ḡorar*, p. 280) recorded it as *kamīd̲ān* (a misspelling of *kamand̲ān*), Reinhold von Stackelberg (pp. 103-04) concluded that Gonbadān is a misspelling of *kanbadān*, an abbreviation of **kanbandān* (< **kanibandān* < *kanī*, Av. *kainī-* "woman" + *band-* "to fasten"). This view was accepted by Josef Markwart (p. 156 n. 3). In geographical sources of the Islamic period Dež-e Gonbadān was identified with Gerdkūh, which is approximately 3 farsangs west of Dāmḡān (*Mojmal*, ed. Bahār, p. 52; *Nozhat al-qolūb*, ed. Le Strange, p. 161; *Tārīk̲-e gozīda*, ed. Browne, p. 97; Bondārī, I, p. 335). On the other hand, Qewām-al-Dīn Fatḥ Bondārī recorded the name of the fortress as Šabdez, according to Dāwūd Monchi-Zadeh a misrepresentation of **sepaddez* < **spand-dez*, which he equates with Sepadkōh (*Šāh-nāma*, ed. Moscow, IV, pp. 72 v. 1002, 88 v. 1235, etc.) in the region of Kalāt(-e nāderī) or Kabūd Gonbad; he compares the latter with Pahlavi Spandādkōh (*Bundahišn*, TD_2, p. 79 ll. 9-10; Monchi-Zadeh, pp. 191-92). This identification requires further evidence, however.

Bibliography: (For citated works not given in detail, see "Short References.") Balʿamī, ed. Bahār, pp. 661-62. Qewām-al-Dīn Fatḥ Bondārī, tr., *Šāh-nāma*, ed. ʿA. ʿAzzām, 2 vols. in 1, Tehran, 1349 Š./1970. Ebn al-Balk̲ī, p. 51 (with mistaken identification of the fortress as Eṣṭak̲r). Gardīzī, ed. Ḥabībī, p. 14. J. Markwart, *Wehrot und Arang*, Leiden, 1938. D. Monchi-Zadeh, *Topograpisch-historische Studien zum iranischen Nationalepos*, Wiesbaden, 1975. R. von Stackelberg, "Persica," *ZDMG* 54, 1900, pp. 103-04.

(AḤMAD TAFAŻŻOLĪ)

DEŽ Ī NEBEŠT (Mid. Pers. *diz ī nibišt* "fortress of archives," lit. "writing"), supposedly one of two repositories (the other being *ganj ī šāhīgān*, ms.: *špykʾn* "royal treasury") in which copies of the Avesta (q.v.) and its exegesis (*zand*) were deposited for safekeeping. Five somewhat different versions of this legend are recounted in Pahlavi literature. In the *Dēnkard* (ed. Madan, I, p. 412; Nyberg, *Manual* I, p. 108) the vicissitudes of the Zoroastrian scriptures are reported this way: "Dārāy, son of Dārāy, commanded that two written copies of all the Avesta and Zand, even as Zoroaster had received them from Ohrmazd, be preserved, one in the royal treasury and one in the fortress of archives" (Zaehner, pp. 7-8; Shaki, 1981, p. 118; Bailey, *Zoroastrian Problems*, p. 230). In another passage (ed. Madan, I, p. 405; Nyberg, *Manual* I, p. 111), however, it is the original Dēnkard, an exposition of the Mazdean religion written down by command of Kay Wištāsp, that was deposited in the royal treasury; suitable copies were made and distributed, and one of them was sent to be preserved in the fortress of archives. "During the ruin that was brought upon the country of Iran . . . by the sinister Alexander (q.v.) that which was in the fortress of archives was burnt" (de Menasce, 1973, p. 379; West, pp. xxx-xxxi). In yet another passage of the *Dēnkard* (ed. Madan, I, p. 437; Nyberg, *Manual* I, p. 110) it is reported that "whatever Zoroaster taught and partly wrote together with the Avesta and Zand Jāmāsp wrote in gold on cowhides and kept in the royal treasury" (ms.: *ganj ī xwadāyān*). In the *Šahrestānīhā ī Ērān* (Markwart, *Provincial Capitals*, p. 9) another depository is mentioned in the east: After Zoroaster announced the religion, King Wištāsp ordered 1,200 chapters (*fragard*) engraved in scriptural (i.e., Avestan) characters (*dēn dibīrīh*, q.v.) on gold tablets and deposited in the treasury of the Warahrān fire at Samarkand. On the destruction of the Zoroastrian scriptures it is reported in the *Ardā Wīrāz-nāmag*: "The accursed Alexander the Roman (i.e., Greek) . . . came to Iran with heavy tyranny . . . slew the sovereign of Iran and burnt . . . the whole of the Avesta and the Zand as written in liquid gold on prepared cowhides . . . and deposited in the *KLYTʾ npst* in Staxr Pābagān" (Gignoux, 1984, pp. 37, 145; Vahman, pp. 76, 191; Bailey, *Zoroastrian Problems*, p. 152; Henning, 1944, p. 136; Nyberg, *Manual* I, p. 107). Both the reading and the interpretation of *KLYTʾ npst*, the locality of the *diz ī nibišt*, have given rise to controversy. Contextual comparison reveals that *KLYTʾ npst* in the *Ardā Wīrāz-nāmag* (see ARDĀ WĪRĀZ) cannot be any place other than the *diz ī nibišt* of the parallel accounts; the heterogram *KLYTʾ* stands for *diz* and the slightly miswritten *npst* for *npšt*, *nibišt*. H. W. Bailey, having identified *KLYTʾ* with *diz*, nevertheless unconvincingly interpreted it as Aramaic *QRYTʾ* "village" (*Zoroastrian Problems*, p. 151). H. S. Nyberg correctly rejected the reading *QRYTʾ* and proposed *qellaitā* "cell," a plausible reading for depository. Although he cited *diz ī nibišt* three times (Nyberg, *Manual* I, pp. 108, 111), he nevertheless construed *npst*, *nipast* as depository, taken it as a gloss for *KLYTʾ* (Nyberg, *Manual* II, p. 141). Walter Belardi (pp. 27-28), having accepted Nyberg's reading, considered *kellaitā* a technical term in Middle Persian and *nipast* a verbal adjunct; he thus read *pad kellaitā nipast nihāt estāt* "had been placed in a depository." The term *diz ī nibišt* is preserved in Ṭabarī (I, p. 676), where the manuscripts have the corrupt forms *dr bšt*, *dr bbšt*, and *dr byšt*.

Another area of disagreement has been the location of the *diz ī nibišt*. W. B. Henning, in the introduction to his edition of inscription KNRm, identified *diz ī nibišt* with the Kaʿba-ye Zardošt, which he believed was referred to as *bwn BYTʾ* (interpreted as *bunxānag*, q.v., "foundation house") in the same inscription (KNRm 7 = KKZ 3; Back, p. 391). In discussing the relevant passage of the inscription KKZ, the present author questioned this proposition, linking *bwn BYTʾ* instead to the *ādurān* and *kardagān* "fires and religious rites," and interpreted the phrase as "principal property, capital" (Shaki, 1974, pp. 334-35). To demonstrate the significance of the phrase and assess the purpose of the Kaʿba-ye Zardošt, we will recall the relevant passage where Kirdīr declares: "... and all of these fires and rites (*ādurān ud kardagān*), which have been mentioned in this inscription, were in a most profitable manner (*KN gwnktly*, *ōh gōnagtar*, cf. Av. *gaona*—"profit," *AirWb.*, col. 412) entrusted to me as benefice (*wāspuhragān* "private property") by Šāpūr the king of kings, ordering "Yours shall be these as principal property (resources; *ʾYKt bwny BYTʾ ZHN ʾyw YHWWN*), "do as you deem it best for the gods and us," (KKZ 2-3; Back, pp. 390-91). From the tenor of the sentence it is evident that the royal grant concerns the resources (*BYTʾ*) derived from the revenues of the fires and rites conferred on Kirdīr as a most profitable benefice for the administration of these religious foundations.

Architecturally the Kaʿba-ye Zardošt, like its prototype, the Zendān-e Solaymān, is a tower with a hardly accessible narrow chamber under the roof, situated in a funerary region beyond the compass of social and cultural life; it would thus be quite impractical as a depository, whether for regalia or for ritual objects, as suggested by R. N. Frye (p. 177 n. 14), or for documents, as proposed by Henning. There is therefore no point in looking for the *diz ī nibišt* in a tower like the Kaʿba, which was in all likelihood the mausoleum of Queen Atossa (q.v.; Boyce, *Zoroastrianism* II, p. 117).

That repositories for documents did exist in Iran is attested in the Bible. In ancient Persia there were three houses of treasures (*bēṯ ginzayyā*) where books (*sēp̄ar*) and records (*dukranayyā*) were kept, analogous to the *diz ī nibišt* for royal archives: at Susa (Esther 6:1), at Babylon, and at Ecbatana (Ezra 5:17-6:2). From the Sasanian period only one such repository is known, the *ganj ī šāhīgān* "royal treasury." It was not only a treasury but also a depository for documents, as is clear from the declaration by Bozorgmehr-e Boḵtagān (q.v.), the grand vizier of Ḵosrow Anūšīravān (531-79), that he had deposited his *Ayādgār* (see AYĀDGAR Ī WUZURGMIHR) there for safekeeping (*Pahlavi Texts*, ed. Jamasp-Asana, p. 85).

Bibliography: M. Back, *Die sassanidischen Staatsinschriften*, Acta Iranica 18, Tehran and Liège, 1978; reviewed by D. N. MacKenzie in *IF* 87, 1982, pp. 281-97. W. Belardi, *The Pahlavi Book of the Righteous Viraz* I, Rome, 1979. M. Boyce, "A Tomb for Cassandane," in *Orientalia J. Duchesne-Guillemin Emerito Oblata*, Acta Iranica 23, Tehran and Liège, 1984, p. 71 (on the purpose of the Kaʿba-ye Zardošt). G. R. Driver, *Aramaic Documents of the Fifth Century B.C.*, Oxford, 1957. R. N. Frye, "Religion in Fars under the Achaemenids," in *Orientalia J. Duchesne-Guillemin Emerito Ooblata*, Acta Iranica 23, Tehran and Liège, 1984 pp. 171-78. P. Gignoux, *Glossaire des inscriptions pehlevies et parthes*, London, 1972a. Idem, "L'inscription de Kirdīr à Naqš-i Rustam," *Stud. Ir.* 1, 1972b, pp. 177-205. Idem, *Le livre d'Ardā Vīrāz*, Paris, 1984. W. B. Henning, "The Murder of the Magi," *JRAS*, 1944, pp. 133-44. Idem, *The Inscription of Naqš-i Rustam*, Corpus Inscr. Iran. 3/2/2, London, 1957. W. Hinz, *Zarathustra*, Stuttgart, 1961. H. Humbach, "Bunxanag et Kaʿba-ye Zardušt," in *Acta Iranica* 3, 1974. pp. 203-08. D. N. MacKenzie, in *Indogermanische Forschungen* 87, 1982. Idem,

"Kirdēr's Inscription," in *The Sassanian Rock Reliefs at Naqsh-i Rustam*, Iranische Denkmäler, Lieferung 13, ser. 2, *Iranische Felsreliefs* I, Berlin, 1989. J. de Menasce, tr., *Le troisième livre du Dēnkart*, Paris, 1973. M. Shaki, "Two Legal Terms for Private Property," in P. Gignoux and A. Tafazzoli, eds., *Mémorial J. de Menasce*, Louvain, 1974, pp. 327-36. Idem, "The Dēnkart Account of the History of the Zoroastrian Scriptures," *Archív Orientální* 49, 1981, pp. 114-25. F. Vahman, *Ardā Wirāz Nāmag. The Iranian "Divina Commedia"*, London, 1986, esp. pp. 225-27. E. W. West, tr., *Contents of the Nasks*, Pahlavi Texts 4, SBE 37, Oxford, 1892. R. C. Zaehner, *Zurvān. A Zoroastrian Dilemma*, Oxford, 1955.

(MANSOUR SHAKI)

DEŽ-E **RŪYĪN** (or Rūyīn-dež, Brazen fortress), castle belonging to the Turanian king Arjāsb (see ARJĀSP) and conquered by Esfandīār (q.v.), son of the Kayanid king Goštāsb. It has also been called "brazen city" (*al-madīna al-ṣofrīya*; Ṯaʿālebī, *Ḡorar*, p. 522). In Goštāsb's absence Arjāsb attacked Balḵ, killing Lohrāsb, Goštāsb's father, and taking captive the king's two daughters, Homāy and Behāfarīd (*Šāh-nāma*, Moscow, VI, pp. 142 vv. 102 ff., 202 vv. 641 ff.; Ṭabarī, I, p. 678: Ḵomānī and Bāḏāfara), whom he imprisoned in Dež-e Rūyīn. Goštāsb returned to Balḵ, but it was only when Esfandīār was released from Dež-e Gonbadān (q.v.) that Arjāsb was defeated and fled to Tūrān (*Šāh-nāma*, Moscow, pp. 141-52, 157-63; Ṭabarī, I, pp. 678-79; Ṯaʿālebī, *Ḡorar*, pp. 282-98). Then Esfandīār set out, accompanied by the captive Turanian Gorgsār, to whom he had promised command of Dež-e Rūyīn, in order to exact vengeance for Lohrāsb's blood and to free his two sisters. After completing *haft ḵᵛān* "the seven labours," Esfandīār arrived at the fortress, to which he gained entrance by disguising himself as a merchant. He killed Arjāsb, freed his two sisters, and set fire to the fortress (*Šāh-nāma*, Moscow, pp. 166-90, 192-204, 212; Ṭabarī, I, pp. 679-80; Ṯaʿālebī, *Ḡorar*, pp. 300-38), which was described as a single, fortified castle reaching to the heavens, in which there were fountains and all kinds of plants and trees, so that the inhabitants had no need for the outside world (*Šāh-nāma*, Moscow, pp. 169 vv. 54-59, 184 vv. 305-11; Ṯaʿālebī, *Ḡorar*, p. 304). This feat of Esfandīār was often alluded to by classical Persian poets (e.g., Ḵāqānī, pp. 243, 257, 412, 719, 787; Qaṭrān, p. 312).

Because the city of Bukhara was also designated as *madīnat al-ṣofrīya* (Ṯaʿālebī, *Ḡorar*, p. 522) and *šārestān-e rūīn* (Naršaḵī, pp. 26, 30, 61), Josef Markwart concluded that *dež-e rūyīn* was an epithet for Paykand, a city 5 farsangs west of Bukhara (1938, pp. 160-61; idem, *Provincial Capitals*, p. 35). According to one account (*Nozhat al-qolūb*, ed. Le Strange, p. 81), Dež-e Bahman (q.v.) has also been called the "Brazen castle."

Bibliography: (For citated works not given in detail, see "Short References.") Balʿamī, ed. Bahār, pp. 662-66. Qewām-al-Dīn Fatḥ Bondārī, tr., *Šāh-nāma*, ed. ʿA. ʿAzzām, 2 vols. in 1, I, Tehran, 1349 Š./1970, pp. 336-51. Ebn al-Balḵī, p. 52. Gardīzī, ed. Ḥabībī, p. 14. Afżal-al-Dīn Ebrāhīm Ḵāqānī Šervānī, *Dīvān*, ed. Ż. Sajjādī, Tehran, n.d. J. Markwart, *Wehrot und Arang. Untersuchungen zur mythischen und geschichtlichen Landeskunde von Ostiran*, Leiden, 1938. Meskawayh, *Tajāreb al-omam*, ed. L. Caetani, VII/1, Leiden, 1909, pp. 56-58; tr. A. Emāmī, I, Tehran, 1369 Š./1980, pp. 84-85. *Mojmal*, ed. Bahār, p. 52. Ḥakīm Šaraf-al-Zamān Qaṭrān Tabrīzī, *Dīvān*, ed. M. Naḵjavānī, Tabrīz, 1333 Š./1954.

(AḤMAD TAFAŻŻOLĪ)

DEŽ-E **SAFĪD** (White fortress), Iranian fortress located near the border with Tūrān and conquered by Sohrāb, son of the Iranian hero Rostam by the Turanian princess Tahmīna. Sohrāb, searching for his father, advanced into Iran and arrived at this fortress, which was guarded by another Iranian hero, Hojīr. Hojīr came out alone to fight Sohrāb but was defeated and taken prisoner. Then Gordāfarīd, Goždaham's daughter (see below), put on armor and advanced on Sohrāb, but she was defeated and captured. Sohrāb, however, realized that she was a woman and released her. He then took possession of the fortress and plundered it (*Šāh-nāma*, ed. Khaleghi, II, pp. 130-37).

The guardianship of Dež-e Safīd seems to have been in the hands of the Goždaham family. According to some manuscripts of the *Šāh-nāma*, Goždaham was the castellan (*kūtvāl*) of this fortress during the above-mentioned episode (ed. Khaleghi, I, p. 130 n. 1). He seems to have held the same post (*deždār*) from as early as the reign of the Kayanian king Nōḏar (*Šāh-nāma*, ed. Mohl, I, p. 408 vv. 331-32; cf. ed. Khaleghi, I, p. 305 v. 306). After the murder of the Iranian prince Sīāvaš, on the order of Afrāsīāb, the Iranian hero Gīv, son of Gūdarz, was sent on a secret mission to Tūrān to find Kay Ḵosrow, son of Sīāvaš, and bring him to Iran. Gīv succeeded in locating the young prince and his mother, Farangīs. On the journey to Iran they crossed the river Oxus (*Šāh-nāma*, ed. Khaleghi, II, pp. 419-50) and, according to one tradition, arrived at Dež-e Safīd, where Gostaham, son of Goždaham, lived, apparently also as castellan (Šahmardān, p. 325; cf. *Šāh-nāma*, ed. Moscow, II, p. 182 vv. 175-76; ed. Khaleghi, p. 130 n. 12).

Bibliography: Šahmardān b. Abi'l-Ḵayr, *Nozhat-nāma-ye ʿalāʾī*, ed. F. Jahān-pūr, Tehran, 1362 Š./1983.

(AḤMAD TAFAŻŻOLĪ)

DEZFŪL (< Dez-pol "Fortress bridge"), *šahrestān*

(subprovincial administrative unit) and city in northern Ḵūzestān province.

i. *Geography.*

ii. *Dezfūlī and Šūštarī dialects.*

i. Geography

The *šahrestān* is bounded on the north by Lorestān province, on the west by Īlām province, and on the east and south by Īza, Šūštar, and Ahvāz *šahrestān*s. It covers an area of 7,884 km^2 and consists of three districts (*baḵš*): Markazī (including the rural districts Šamsābād, Šarqī, Šamʿūn, and Nāẓer), Šūš (including the rural districts Ḥosaynābād, Farāzīn, Čanāna, and Sorḵa), and Sardašt (including the rural districts Mīānkūh, Līvūs, Šāhī, and Sardašt), with 526 settlements. The climate is characterized by hot summers and moderate winters, with average annual rainfall of 250 mm; temperatures range between 3° C in winter and 49° C in summer. The humidity varies between 22 and 73 percent (Saʿīdīān, p. 498).

According to the census of 1365 Š./1986, the population of the *šahrestān* was 365,695 (64,225 family units, 189,343 men, and 176,352 women), 191,136 (52.3 percent) living in urban (151,420 in Dezfūl, 39,716 in Šūš) areas, 161,151 (44.1 percent) living in rural areas, and 13,408 commuting between the two. Population density was recorded as 46.4 per km^2. According to the census, 48.4 percent of the population of Dezfūl *šahrestān* was below the age of fifteen years, 48.8 percent between the ages of fifteen and sixty-four years, and 2.7 percent were sixty-five years and older. The literacy rate among those six years old and older was 60.15 percent. The population consisted of Persians, Kurds, Lors, and Arabs, mainly Persian-speaking Shiʿite Muslims. A small Zoroastrian minority (0.13 percent) was also recorded.

Sugarcane, which has been cultivated in the Dezfūl region for more than a thousand years (see, e.g., Moqaddasī, p. 405), is still an important economic factor; a modern sugar refinery with a capacity of more than 300 tons has been built in Haft Tappa near the town of Dezfūl. Other major agricultural products of the *šahrestān* include wheat, barley, clover, alfalfa, sesame, maize, and grass peas; sheep are the most important livestock. Agriculture and local supplies of electricity have been greatly increased since the completion, in 1350 Š./1971, of a modern reservoir dam across the Dez river northeast of the city of Dezfūl (see BARQ i).

The center of the *šahrestān* is the city of Dezfūl, situated at 32° 23′ N, 48° 24′ E (*Gazetteer of Iran* I, p. 458), on the left bank of the Āb-e Dez (q.v.). The population is more than 150,000 (see above), compared to more than 16,000 at the end of the 19th century (Curzon, *Persian Question* II, p. 304). The name Dezfūl appears to refer to a Sasanian bridge built over the Āb-e Dez by Šāpūr II (309-79; Le Strange, *Lands,* p. 238). The Sasanians also built a fortress nearby to defend it (Matheson, p. 155). The area surrounding the bridge and the fortress became the site of a settlement that developed into the city of Dež-Pol or Dezfūl (Bayāt, p. 275), though this name apparently did not come into use until the 12th century (Lockhart, p. 350). The 10th-century writer Eṣṭaḵrī called it Qanṭarat-al-Andāmeš (p. 197; cf. Yāqūt, I, p. 372). It was also known as Qaṣr al-Rūnāš (Yāqūt, IV, p. 111; for the names, Qanṭarat al-Rūm, Qanṭarat al-Rūd, and Qanṭarat al-Zāb, see Le Strange, *Lands*, p. 238 and references; Lockhart, p. 350). The stone foundation of the bridge is still visible; the upper part was repeatedly reconstructed in brick, during the early Islamic, Saljuq, and Qajar periods (Matheson, p. 155). In the 14th century Ḥamd-Allāh Mostawfī (*Nozhat al-qolūb*, p. 111) described it as 520 paces long and 15 paces wide, with forty-two arches; Šaraf-al-Dīn Yazdī, who visited the area in 795/1393, also provided a detailed description (Barthold, p. 187).

The chief local manufacture of Dezfūl, according to George Curzon, who visited the area in the late 19th century, was indigo (with 120 factories in town), the cultivation of which had been introduced there in the early 19th century (*Persian Question* II, p. 304); Dezfūl was also noted for fine reed pens (Lockhart, p. 350).

Bibliography: (For cited works not given in detail, see "Short References.") W. Barthold, *Istoriko-geograficheskiĭ obzor Irana*, tr. S. Soucek, ed. C. E. Bosworth as *An Historical Geography of Iran*, Princeton, N.J., 1984. ʿA. Bayāt, *Kollīyāt-e jografīā-ye ṭabīʿī wa tārīḵī-e Īrān*, 1367 Š./1988, pp. 275-78. L. Lockhart, "Dezfūl," in *EI*^{2}, pp. 350-51. Markaz-e āmār-e Īrān, *Natāyej-e sar-šomārī-e nofūs wa maskan-e mehr-e māh-e1365. Šahrestān-e Dezfūl*, Tehran, 1368 Š./1989. S. A. Matheson, *Persia. An Archaeological Guide*, London, 1972.

(Massoud Kheirabadi)

ii. Dezfūlī and Šūštarī Dialects

Dezfūlī and Šūštarī are two closely related Persian dialects spoken by the indigenous inhabitants of Dezfūl and Šūštar in Ḵūzestān province. The sedentary Iranian communities of Ḵūzestān, the inhabitants of which speak Lor dialects for the most part, seem to be located in a band along the foothills of the Zagros. The plain to the south and west is largely populated by Arabs. Dezfūl (population 151,420 in 1368 Š./1989; Markaz-e āmār, 1368 Š./1989; see i, above) and Šūštar (population 26,173 in 1355 Š./1976; Markaz-e āmār, 1355 Š./1976), 55 km apart, are two non-Lor islands within this larger ensemble.

Accurate statistics on speakers of Dezfūlī and Šūštarī are not available. Furthermore, population figures are misleading, as Dezfūl has experienced considerable immigration in this century, and many speakers of the two dialects have migrated to such nearby cities as Ahvāz and Masjed-e Solaymān.

Dezfūlī and Šūštarī are clearly of the Southwest Iranian type (cf. Schmitt, ed., pp. 295, 341-49) but diverge sharply from standard Persian in phonology, morphology, and vocabulary. The differences are particularly striking in verbal morphology. Dezfūlī and Šūštarī share features with surrounding Lor dialects but are distinct from them. The differences between Dezfūlī and Šūštarī result primarily from variation in low-level phonological processes.

Phonology. Dezfūlī has an underlying seven-vowel system /ī, ē, e, a, ā, o, ū/ and Šūštarī a six-vowel system /ī, e, a, ā, o, ū/. Dezfūlī *ū* is pronounced with considerable fronting, except before *n* and *m*. Three additional phones, Dezfūlī [*ȫ*] and Šūštarī [*ē*, ō], are probably best considered surface realizations of other underlying phonemes. Dezfūlī *ȫ* is a tense, front-rounded midlevel vowel. Šūštarī has]no front-rounded vowels.

The vocalic systems of Dezfūlī and Šūštarī can be derived from an early New Persian type of system but have been rearranged by historic processes of raising, merger, fronting, and laxing. In both dialects early New Persian *ō* has merged with *ū*, as in *pūs* "skin" (Persian *pūst*). In Šūštarī, but not in Dezfūlī, early New Persian *ē* has merged with *ī*, as in Dezfūlī *dēr*, Šūštarī *dīr* "late" (Persian *dīr*). All tense vowels were laxed before *h*, as in Dezfūlī and Šūštarī *pe:* "fat," *ka:* "straw," *ko:* "mountain" (Persian *pīh*, *kāh*, *kūh*).

Under certain conditions early New Persian *ō* and *ū* were fronted to Dezfūlī-Šūštarī *ī*, as in *bīd* "he was," *k̠ī* "blood," *rī* "face" (early N.Pers. *būd*, *k̠ūn*, *rō*(*y*)). Such fronting is common in western Iranian dialects and appears to have occurred before dentals and historic *y* (which later disappeared). Fronting did not occur before labials, palatals, or velars, which suggests an assimilation process in which Dezfūlī and Šūštarī *ū*, presumably after early New Persian *ō* had merged with it, was fronted in anticipation of the fronted articulation of the dentals.

Early New Persian *ā* merged with *ū* before nasals, as in *dūna* "seed," *dūm* "snare" (early New Persian *dāna*, *dām*), a process that could have occurred only after the fronting of *ū* to *ī*, as this secondary *ū* did not become *ī*.

The Dezfūlī and Šūštarī consonantal system is close to that of Persian, but the Arabic pharyngeals *ʿ* and *ḥ* have been borrowed in Arabic loanwords. These phones occasionally also occur in words not of Arabic origin, for example *ʿas* "bone." In both dialects the distinction between *q*, a voiceless velar stop, and *ḡ*, a voiced palatal fricative, is maintained, whereas in standard Persian the two have merged in a single phone, primarily realized as a voiced velar stop. Dezfūlī and Šūštarī *y* and *v* occur only in prevocalic position.

Postvocalic *b* was spirantized after *a*, *ā* in words of Iranian origin, for example, Dezfūlī and Šūštarī *var* "on" (early NPers. *abar*). Between vowels *d* and *g* have been dropped sporadically, as in *mār* "mother," *kuak* "boy" (Pers. *mādar*, *kūdak* "child").

The chief synchronic phonological processes in Dezfūlī and Šūštarī are the raising and fronting of low vowels by a following high vowel or glide and the reduction of syllable-final *y*, *w*, *n*, and *h*, as in *bēn* "between" (Ar. *bayn*); Dezfūlī *dȫr*, Šūštarī *dōr* "around" (Ar. *dawr*); Dezfūlī *lȫ* and Šūštarī *lō* "lip," Dezfūlī *ȫ*, Šūštarī *ō* "water" (Persian *lab*, *āb*) but Dezfūlī *lȫva* and Šūštarī *lōwa* "lips"; Dezfūlī *ȫva*, Šūštarī *ōwa* "waters"; and Šūštarī *ūmē* "you came" (< *ūma* + *ī*) but *ūmēya* "you have come" (< *ūma* + *i* + *a*). A following *ī* raises *ā* to Dezfūlī *ȫ*, Šūštarī *ō*, as in Dezfūlī *dȫrī* "you (sg.) have" (Pers. *dārī*), Šūštarī *ōhī* "you come" (subj.). These processes work under different conditions in the two dialects.

In both Dezfūlī and Šūštarī the syllable-final *n* is deleted and the preceding vowel nasalized, as in *dẽ:dũ* "tooth." Syllable-final *h* becomes vowel length, as in *ka:* "straw."

Morphology. The morphology of nouns in Dezfūlī and Šūštarī exhibits more or less the same categories as colloquial Persian, though some of the devices differ. The plural suffixes are *-ū* and *-(h)ā*. The former is restricted to animate nouns; the latter may occur with either animate or inanimate nouns. The latter is realized as *-hā* after low vowels in Šūštarī and after the low tense vowel in Dezfūlī, for example, Šūštarī *k̠ūnahā* "houses," Dezfūlī and Šūštarī *piāhā* "men." Otherwise it is realized as *-ā*, as in Dezfūlī and Šūštarī *asbā* "horses." Dezfūlī *-ā* replaces the low, lax final vowel, as in *k̠ūna* "house," *k̠ūnā* "houses." Inanimate plural subjects take the plural verb, as in Šūštarī *ī ārdā bīzehes:en a* "this flour (pl.) has been sifted."

The Dezfūlī and Šūštarī *eżāfa*, *-e*, functions as in Persian.

The antecedent of a restrictive relative clause is marked by the enclitics Dezfūlī *-ē*, Šūštarī *-ī*. An indefinite noun singled out from another indefinite noun or nouns is also marked with the enclitics, as in Dezfūlī *dasmāl-e sēa-ē bebā:dom* "I'll tie on a black kerchief."

In both dialects definite objects are marked with an enclitic suffix realized as *-na* after low vowels, *-a* otherwise, as in *k̠ūnana* "the house," *piāna* "the man," *asba* "the horse."

In both dialects there is also a contrastive suffix, stressed *-ka*, which, like colloquial Persian *-é*, singles out a definite noun and contrasts it with another noun or nouns, as in *dok̠tarka mord* "the girl (as opposed to some other person understood in the discourse) died." Both also have a deictive suffix, stressed *-(h)a*, which may occur with the demonstrative adjective. The suffix is realized as *-ha* after low vowels, otherwise as *-a*, as in *ū dūnaha* "that seed," *ū aspa* "that horse."

When the contrastive or deictive suffixes are used no *eżāfa* is permitted between noun and adjective, as in Šūštarī *kuak-e kūčīk* "small boy," *kuak kūčīk:a* "the small boy" and Šūštarī *kīf-e gap* "large sack," *ū kīf gapa* "that large sack."

The personal pronouns are Dezfūlī *mo*, *to*, *ū*, *omū̃*, *šomū̃*, *ūšū̃* and Šūštarī *mo*, *to*, *ū*, *amā*, *šamā*, *ūšū̃* The objective and possessive pronouns are the enclitics *-(o)m*, *-(e)t*, *-(e)š*, *-(o)mū̃*, *-(e)tū̃*, *-(e)šū̃*. In both dialects the demonstrative adjectives are *ī* "this, these" and *ū* "that, those." Both also have a separate category of demonstrative pronouns, that is, Dezfūlī *ha*, *īā̃* (this), *hanū̃* (these), *hū̃*, *ūā̃* (that), *hūnū̃* (those); Šūštarī *(i)he*, *īā̃* (this), *(ū)hū̃*, *ūā̃*, (that), *(ū)hūnū̃* (those). The adjectives *ī* and *ū* may also be used pronominally.

Dezfūlī and Šūštarī verbal morphology diverges from that of Persian in important ways. Alone among reported Persian dialects they have an unstressed modal prefix *be-* to mark the present indicative and past continuous, as in *bebīnom* "I see," *bedīdom* "I used to see." The present subjunctive is signaled by the absence of a prefix, as in *bīnom* "(that) I see." Verbs based on the present stem are stressed on the personal endings; verbs based on the past stem are stressed on the last syllable of the stem, as in *begoróm*, "I take," *goróftom* "I took," *begoróftom* "I was taking."

In compound verbs the incorporated nominal constituent is stressed. If the incorporated constituent ends in a consonant, the verbal prefix is realized as *-e* and is closely attached to the nominal, as in *sēl-e konom* "I watch" (< *sēl* "watch"). If the incorporated constituent ends in a vowel, the verbal prefix is realized as *-b* and is closely attached to the nominal, as in *doʿā-b konom* "I pray" (< *doʿā* "prayer"). The same rules hold true when a direct object precedes a simple verb, as in *ketāb-e ḵūnom* "I read books" and Šūštarī *jūma-b pūšom* "I'm putting on a shirt." When preceded by the negative prefix, stressed *na-*, the *-b* is nasalized, as in Dezfūlī and Šūštarī *namḵerom* "I don't buy."

A handful of verbs take unstressed forms of *me-* as prefix, for example, Dezfūlī *maḵom*, Šūštarī *moḵom* "I want," Šūštarī *merom* "I go." In Dezfūlī both prefixes must occur with a few verbs, like *bemīām* "I come,"*bemīārom* "I bring." Dezfūlī and Šūštarī *darom*, *dunom*, *tarom* "I have, know, am able" do not take the prefix.

The personal endings for the present stem in Dezfūlī are *-(o)m*, *-ī*, *-a*, *-ēm*, *-ē*, *-(e)n*, in Šūštarī *-(o)m*, *-ī*, *-a*, *-īm*, *-īt*, *-(e)n*. The endings for the past stem are identical phonetically, except for the third-person singular, which is unmarked. The past endings are enclitic and are identical with present-tense forms of "to be."

A past continuous is formed by prefixing *be-* to the past tense, as in *beḵeridom* "I used to buy," *ḵerīdom* "I bought."

In preverbal formations the preverb occurs just before the verbal stem and is preceded by the negative and *be-*, as in Dezfūlī *bedervōrdeneš* "they would take it out" and Šūštarī *namvārsaden* "they would not get up" (< *na-* + *be-* + *varsād-* + *-en*).

Present and past perfects are formed from past-tense verbs plus present or past third-person singular of "be," as in Dezfūlī and Šūštarī *raftom a* "I have gone," *raftī a* "you have gone," *raftom bid* "I had gone." A formation corresponding to the Persian perfect construction (past participle + "to be") is used with certain intransitive verbs, like "sit," "stand," and "sleep," to show state of being, as in Šūštarī *varsādám*, *varsādḗ* "I am standing, you are standing" (< *varsada* + *-m*, *-i*).

Inchoative forms expressing change of state or process are built on the simple present stem plus *-(e)h-es:a* (Mid. Pers. *-īhist*). The form is often attached to intransitives and can express futurity. The vowel before *h* is completely assimilated to the following vowel, as in Dezfūlī and Šūštarī *berasohom* "I arrive," *berasīhī* "you arrive" Šūštarī *šā lerhes be vazīr* "the king turned to the minister," and Dezfūlī *ō̃ rēzehes zemī̃* "water spilled on the ground."

There is a corresponding transitivizing morpheme *-(e)nīd* (Mid. Pers. *-ēnīd*), as in Dezfūlī and Šūštarī *časbenīdā* "to stick (something to something)." Inchoative and transitivized verbs often occur in pairs, for example, Šūštarī *tapehes mī̃ botrī* "it got stuffed in the bottle" and *mo tabnīdomeš mī̃ botrī* "I stuffed it in the bottle."

The distinction between "be" and "become" is expressed with the inchoative. Dezfūlī *bies:ā* and Šūštarī *bues:ā* "become" are simply inchoativized forms of Dezfūlī and Šūštarī *bīdā* "be" (present stem *-bū-*), as in Šūštarī *garm a* "it is warm," *garm-e bua*, "it's getting warm," *garm bues* "it got warm." "Be" and "become" are identical in the subjunctive, as in Šūštarī *buwom*, *buwi*, "I be, you be" and so on. Persian *šodan*, *gaštan* "become" and the subjunctive stem *bāš-* do not occur in Dezfūlī or Šūštarī.

The imperative is the simple stem in the singular and the stem plus personal ending in the plural, as in Dezfūlī and Šūštarī *ī ketāba ḵū̃* "read (you sg.) this book," Dezfūlī *ī ketāba ḵūnē* (Šūštarī *ḵūnīt*) "read (you pl.) this book." The imperative is negated by the stressed prefix *má-*.

Wishes may be expressed by a precative consisting of present stem + *-ā-*, as in Šūštarī *vanhām* "may I be placed." The Dezfūlī and Šūštarī precative of "be" is based on the stem *bā-*, as in Dezfūlī and Šūštarī *bām* "I be," Šūštarī *bō*, Dezfūlī *bō̃ī* you (sg.) be." Unreal conditions and wishes about the past are expressed with a verb in the past continuous that may have unstressed *-ē* as a suffix, as in Dezfūlī *aga ī ketāba beḵo:dom-ē* "if I had read this book."

Vocabulary. The Dezfūlī and Šūštarī vocabulary is distinctively western Iranian, for example, *bes:-/beh-*"throw" (Pahl. *wistan*, *wih-*), Dezfūlī *bō̃ī*, Šūštarī *bōhī* "arm" (Pahl. Psalter *bʾdwky* = *bāhūg*), *bua* "father," *es:a-/os:ūn-* "take," *gap* "large," *īsū̃*, *ūsū̃* "now, then," *kot-ī* "a little," *mēra* "husband" (Pahl. *mērag*), *mī̃* "in," Dezfūlī and Šūštarī *nāhā* "in front of," *piā* "man," *pē* "with," *pet* "nose," *sī* "for" (Pers. *sū* "direction"), Dezfūlī *šū̃:d*, *šūn-* "throw" (Pers. *šānd* "winnow"), *tares:-/tar-* "able to," *vā:d-/van* "put, place" (vs. Pers. *afkandan*), *zūna* "wife."

Bibliography: C. MacKinnon, *The Phonology and Morphology of Dezfuli-Shushtari. A Study in West Persian Dialectology*, Ph.D. diss., University of California, Los Angeles, 1974. Markaz-e āmār-e Īrān, *Sar-šomārī-e ʿomūmī-e nofūs wa maskan. Šahrestān-e Šūštar*, Tehran, 1355 Š./1976. Idem, *Sāl-nāma-ye āmārī*, 1358 Š./1989. B. V. Miller, "O dialekte g. Shushtera" (On the dialect of the city of Šūštar), *Iran* III, Leningrad, 1929, pp. 71-93. M.-B. Nīrūmand, *Neṣāb-e Šūštar*, Tehran, 1349 Š./1970. R. Schmitt, ed., *Compendium Linguarum Iranicarum*, Wiesbaden, 1989.

(COLIN MACKINNON)

DEZKŪH (or Šāhdez), a medieval mountain fortress situated in central Persia on the summit of Mount Ṣoffa, about 8 km south of Isfahan. No information is available on the construction date of this strategically situated fortress, which guarded the routes to Isfahan, but, like some other ruins in the same region, it may have been built as early as the Sasanian period (Minasian, pp. 17-18, 20, 61-62, pls. 1-45). Ebn al-Aṯīr attributed (X, pp. 109-10) the construction of this fortress, which he called the "fortress (*qalʿa*) of Isfahan," to the Saljuq sultan Malekšāh (465-85/1072-92), but this attribution does not seem reliable. It is more likely that Malekšāh merely rebuilt the fortress as a major military outpost of Isfahan, the chief Saljuq capital; it was from his time that the fortress became more generally designated as Šāhdez, reflecting his reconstruction of the existing Dezkūh (Ẓahīr-al-Dīn, p. 40; Rāvandī, p. 156).

The historical importance of Dezkūh is particularly related to the activities of the Nezārī Ismaʿilis in Persia during the early Alamūt period (487-654/1094-1256). Ismaʿili *dāʿī*s (q.v.; missionaries) had been active in the region of Isfahan during the11th century, and by the 460s/1170s ʿAbd-al-Malek b. ʿAṭṭāš, the chief *dāʿī* of Persia and Iraq at the time, had established his headquarters at Isfahan. Ḥasan Ṣabbāḥ's seizure of Alamūt in 483/1090, which marked the effective foundation of the Nezārī state in Persia, further encouraged the *daʿwa*, or missionary activities, of Aḥmad b. ʿAbd-al-Malek b. ʿAṭṭāš (q.v.), who had succeeded his father as *dāʿī* of Isfahan. Aḥmad, posing as a schoolmaster, gradually succeeded in converting the garrison of Dezkūh, comprised mostly of Deylamī soldiers with Shiʿite tendencies. By 494/1100, or possibly a few years earlier, Aḥmad had gained possession of Dezkūh, which he fortified like other Nezārī mountain castles in Persia (Ẓahīr-al-Dīn, pp. 40-41; Rāvandī, pp. 155 ff.; Rašīd-al-Dīn, 1338 Š./1959, p. 120; idem, 1960, pp. 69-74; Kāšānī, p. 156; Mīrkᵛānd, Tehran, IV, pp. 306 ff.; Hodgson, pp. 85-86; Daftary, pp. 354-55).

The Nezārī capture of Dezkūh was a serious blow to the Saljuqs, especially as soon afterward Aḥmad b. ʿAbd-al-Malek began to collect taxes in the districts around the fortress. Accordingly, the chief focus of the anti-Nezārī campaign conducted by Sultan Moḥammad b. Malekšāh (498-511/1105-18) was Dezkūh. The sultan with a large force besieged the fortress in 500/1107, but the tactics of Aḥmad, who involved the Sunnite *ʿolamāʾ* of Isfahan in a long religious disputation, in which he argued that the Ismaʿilis were also true Muslims, delayed the conquest for almost a year, until the *ʿolamāʾ* had rendered their judgment. Eventually battle was joined; Aḥmad and his small band of Nezārīs fought the Saljuqs gallantly from tower to tower. In the final assault most of the Nezārī defenders of Dezkūh were killed; Aḥmad was captured and later executed in Isfahan (Ẓahīr-al-Dīn, pp. 41-42; Rāvandī, pp. 158-161; Bondārī, pp. 90-91; Ebn al-Aṯīr, X, pp. 151-52; Ebn al-Qalānesī, pp. 151-56, containing the text of the victory statement issued on the occasion; Rašīd-al-Dīn, 1338 Š./1959, pp. 121-22; Kāšānī, pp. 156-57; Hodgson, pp. 95-96; Lewis, pp. 53-55; Daftary, pp. 361-62). The conquest of Dezkūh is celebrated in one of the versions of the introduction to the *Bahman-nāma* (Storey-de Blois, V, 564-65).

Dezkūh was demolished soon after on the sultan's orders, as he feared its recapture by the Nezārīs. The extensive ruins have been investigated and described by Caro O. Minasian (1897-1972), who was evidently the first person to identify and study the site in modern times (pp. 21-39, 52-54).

Bibliography: (For cited works not given in detail, see "Short References.") Fatḥ b. ʿAlī Bondārī, *Zobdat al-noṣra wa nok̲bat al-ʿeṣra*, in Houtsma, *Recueil* II. F. Daftary, *The Ismāʿīlīs. Their History and Doctrines*, Cambridge, 1990. Ebn al-Aṯīr, *al-Kāmel fi'l-tārīk̲* X, Cairo, 1303/1885. Ebn al-Qalānesī, *D̲ayl tʾarīk̲ Demašq*, ed. H. F. Amedroz, Leiden, 1908. M. G. S. Hodgson, *The Order of Assassins*, the Hague, 1955. Honarfar, *Eṣfahān*, pp. 63 ff. Abu'l-Qāsem ʿAbd-Allāh Kāšānī, *Zobdat al-tawārīk̲. Bak̲š-e Fāṭemīān wa Nezārīān*, ed. M.-T. Dānešpažūh, 2nd ed., Tehran, 1366 Š./1987. B. Lewis, *The Assassins. A Radical Sect in Islam*, London, 1967. M. Mehryār, "Šāhdez kojā'st?" *Našrīya-ye Dāneškada-ye Adabīyāt-e Eṣfahān* 1, 1343 Š./1964, pp. 87-157. C. O. Minasian, *Shah Diz of Ismaʿili Fame. Its Siege and Destruction*, London, 1971. Rašīd-al-Dīn Fażl-Allāh, *Jāmeʿ al-tawārīk̲. Qesmat-e Esmāʿīlīān*, ed. M.-T. Dānešpažūh and M. Modarresī Zanjānī, Tehran, 1338 Š./1959. Idem, *Jāmeʿ al-tawārīk̲. Tārīk̲-e Āl-e Saljūq*, ed. A. Ateş, Ankara, 1960. Moḥammad b. ʿAlī Rāvandī, *Rāḥat al-ṣodūr wa āyat al-sorūr*, ed. M. Eqbāl, London, 1921. Ẓahīr-al-Dīn Nīšāpūrī, *Saljūq-nāma*, Tehran, 1332 Š/1953.

(FARHAD DAFTARY)

DHABHAR, BAHMANJI NUSSERWANJI (b. 1869 in Navsari, d. 1952 in Bombay 1952), eminent Parsi scholar of Bhagaria (q.v.) stock. He received his schooling at the Sir Cowasjee Jehangir Madressa and trained at the same time as a Zoroastrian priest. He was initiated *ervad* (the 1st priestly qualification) and *marāteb* (the 2nd and final priestly qualification) at the Wadi Dar-e Mihr in Navsari, and matriculated in 1890. He then enrolled at Elphinstone College, Bombay, and in 1893 received the B.A. with distinction in mathematics, his optional subjects being English and Persian. He gained the M.A. from Mulla Firoze Madressa in 1898, having studied Avestan and Pahlavi, and was at once invited to conduct classes in these languages at the Madressa, which he continued to do until almost the end of his long life. At the same time he held full-time teaching posts in French, English, and mathematics, first at the Fort High School and then at the Sir Jamshetjee Jeejeebhai Parsi Benevolent Institution. He was deeply respected for his clear and sound methods and his care for his students. He studied Sanskrit and German privately, but his chief devotion was to Iranian languages, literature, and history. Not long after obtaining his M.A. he began to teach Zoroastrian studies at the Sir Jamshetjee Jeejeebhai Parsi Benevolent Institution, and from 1914 to 1940 he was superintendent of Zoroastrian studies for the various schools in Gujarat administered by the Bombay Parsi Panchayat. He visited each of them annually, advising and examining their pupils. He was a member of the governing board of his own old school in Navsari, its honorary secretary for nearly twenty-five years, and an active member of the managing committees of the two Bombay schools for priests' sons—the Athornan Madressa in Dadar and the M. F. Cama Athornan Institute in Andheri. Everywhere he won regard for his abilities, quiet devotion to his duties, and total lack of ostentation. He was generally active in the affairs of his community and a member of its various learned societies. He seldom took part in any of the current religious controversies, but when he did, he argued with courtesy and great soundness of judgment.

Dhabhar's lasting fame rests on his numerous fine scholarly publications. His editions of Pahlavi texts, all published in Bombay, have earned him the reputation of the best of all Parsi editors. They include the *Saddar Naṣr and Saddar Bundehesh* (1909), *The Epistles of Mānūshchīhar* (1912), *The Pahlavi Rivāyat accompanying the Dādistān ī Dīnīk* (1913), *Zand-i Khūrtak Avistāk* (1927), *Andarj-i Aōshnar-i Dānāk* (1930), and his last work, the *Pahlavi Yasna and Visperad*, with an invaluable glossary (1949). He was also a meticulous and lucid translator into English. In 1932 he published his masterly *The Persian Rivayats of Hormazyar Framarz and others*, including in it a rendering of the *Saddar Bundehesh*, and in 1943 he completed *Translation of the Zand-i Khūrtak Avistāk* (publ. posthumously in 1963). The former work was provided with an admirable index, and both were elucidated by learned notes, in which he drew not only on his deep knowledge of Pahlavi and Avestan texts, but also on his priestly familiarity with rituals and observances. His patient scholarship is also shown in his *Descriptive Catalogue of some manuscripts bearing on Zoroastrianism ... in the Mulla Feroze Library*, and his *Descriptive catalogue of all manuscripts in the First Dastur Meherji Rana Library, Navsari* (both published in 1923). He also edited or indexed works of other Parsi scholars. He wrote some studies in Gujarati, and a number of his learned articles in English and Gujarati were reprinted as a tribute in a single volume as *Essays on Iranian Subjects*.

Dhabhar married Shirinbai Rājā, who bore him a son and daughter. He lived in Parsi Colony, Dadar, Bombay, but kept his ancestral home in Sāngā Wād, Navsari, where he took his family during the Christmas and summer holidays. He then indulged temperately, like many another good Bhagaria, in his favorite drink, palm-wine toddy. He lived a life of quiet simplicity, dressing regularly in white trousers, long black coat, and white priestly turban. His width of learning in no way shook his orthopraxy, and the octogenarian Ervad Eruch D. Daboo of Navsari recalls him officiating at *navjote*s (initiations) and marriages with scrupulous recitation of all the traditional prayers. Failing sight led him to pass his last few years in seclusion, and he died, as he was born, on the day Bahman of the Zoroastrian calendar.

Bibliography: Anonymous life-sketch in B.N. Dhabhar, *Essays on Iranian Subjects*, Bombay, 1955.

(MARY BOYCE AND FIROZE M. KOTWAL)

DHALLA, DASTUR MANECKJI NUSSERWANJI (b. 22 September 1875, Surat; d. 25 May 1956, Karachi), Parsi priest and scholar. In 1878 Dhalla came to Karachi with his father, married at the age of nine, and was ordained a priest (*navar*) in 1890. For a while he abandoned his studies and worked to augment the family's meagre income, but his scholarly interest never waned. At the age of nineteen he became the editor of a monthly magazine called *Golšan-e dāneš* (1st issue published September 1894). In its second year Dhalla took over the ownership of the magazine, but shortage of funds forced him to close it down in December 1896. On 21 March 1895 he delivered his first sermon on *ātaš* (q.v., fire). In the same year he published for free circulation a booklet in Gujarati, followed by five others during the next three years. On 21 September 1900 he delivered his first lecture in Bombay at the Framji Cawasji Institute. Later on the lectures he gave in Bombay and elsewhere in India made him famous in the Zoroastrian community. In August 1901 Dhalla went to Bombay to pursue his studies, and in 1904 he completed in three years the five-year course of the M. A. program in Avestan and Pahlavi studies at Sir Jamsetjee Jejeebhoy Madressa. On 15

May 1905 he was sent by the Parsi community to the United States to study with A. V. W. Jackson at Columbia University, where he received his Master's degree in 1906 and Ph.D. in May 1908. His doctoral thesis entitled *The Nyaishes or Zoroastrian Litanies* (New York, 1908). Experiences at Columbia University changed Dhalla's outlook. His fascination with conventional ritualistic religion faded. He now considered ethics as the highest form of religion and felt attracted to mysticism. His antagonism for western culture turned to amity. He returned to Bombay in December 1908 and on 19 September 1909 was appointed the High Priest of the Parsis in Karachi. In 1910 he initiated the idea of holding a Zoroastrian conference, but the controversy it created involving orthodox Parsis soon aborted the idea. In the same year he started the religious journal *Aša*, which was published for less than a year. In 1914 he again went to the United States to deliver lectures and while there published his *Zoroastrian Theology*. In recognition of his services, the Parsis of Karachi established a fund in 1915, from which he received a monthly honorarium. In 1922 he went to the United States for the third time and published his *Zoroastrian Civilization*.

Dhalla labored relentlessly all his life to make his co-religionists understand their own faith better. His motto in life was "plain living and high thinking." He was well respected by his colleagues and community for his amiable nature and sincerity. For his scholarly achievements, he received the title of Shams-ul-Ulema (Šams-al-ʿOlamāʾ), the first Parsi in Karachi to receive such an honor. As a youth he upheld reformist views and involved himself in religious disputes through speeches and articles. But soon he found that such dispute hampered his studies and desisted from them as far as possible. Nevertheless, for forty-seven years he was considered a reformist Dastur by the majority of orthodox laymen and conservative priests. He was embroiled in the problem of proselytizing (the Juddin Question) that plagued the community; even though he held liberal views in the matter, he always sided with the orthodox majority. Besides the books cited above and a few others in Gujarati, his works include: *The Adornment of Priests* (Karachi, 1899), *Footholds of Purity* (Karachi, 1900), *Our Perfecting World* (New York, 1930), *History of Zoroastrianism* (New York, 1938, repr. 1963, 1977, 1985), *Homage unto Ahura Mazda*, (Karachi, 1941-47), *Ancient Iranian Literature* (Karachi, 1949), *Mankind Whither Bound?* (Karachi, 1950), and *World's Religions in Evolution* (Karachi, 1953).

Bibliography: *Athornan Namu*, Meherwanji C. Behramkamdin Dasturna, Bombay, 1923. Dastur M. N. Dhalla, *An Autobiography*, Karachi, 1975.

(KAIKHUSROO M. JAMASPASA)

DHĀR, QĀŻĪ KHAN BADR. See DHĀRVĀL.

DHĀRAṆĪ, magic spells in the Buddhist Mahayanist and Tantric (esoteric) traditions.

i. *In Khotanese*.
ii. *In Sogdian*.

i. IN KHOTANESE

Introduction. *Dhāraṇīs* are, explained traditionally as "(capacity) to hold (Skt. *dhṛ-*) in memory"; shorter spells are called mantras. In the Buddhist Sanskrit texts *dhāraṇīs* can be recognized readily because they are often introduced by *tad yathā* (*syād yathā*) "thus" and end in *svāhā* "Hail!" Elements constituting *dhāraṇīs* are invocational formulae of the type "homage (*namo*) to so-and-so," vocatives of various Buddhas' names, and imperative verb forms or meaningless onomatopoetic syllables. *Dhāraṇīs* were incorporated into Mahāyāna sutras from early times, e.g., chap. 21 (*dhāraṇī-parivarta*) of the *Saddharmapuṇḍarīka* (the Lotus Sutra), chap. 9 of the *Laṅkāvatāra*, or chap. 7 (*Sarasvatī-parivarta*) of the *Suvarṇabhāsottama-sūtra* (Sutra of Golden Light). In the later Tantric tradition numerous shorter texts were composed with such *dhāraṇīs* as their main part. Such texts are referred to as *dhāraṇīs* (not to be confused with the *dhāraṇīs* or *mantras* proper, which form the central part of them), as *sūtras*, or as *dhāraṇī-sūtras*.

Since *dhāraṇīs* are more often transcribed than translated, it is not surprising that we have few *dhāraṇīs* in the Khotanese language. What we have are translations from Sanskrit of either known or unknown originals. Some may be local compositions by the Khotanese, but their *dhāraṇī* part is written in Sanskrit in Khotanese spelling as are the translations. The following are examples of such texts.

Texts with known originals. 1. *Anantamukhanirhāradhāraṇī-sūtra* (q.v.; Inagaki). 2. *Aparimitāyuḥ-sūtra* (q.v.). The transliteration given in Bailey (V, pp. 243ff.) omits the repetition of *dhāraṇīs*. Copies of Tibetan and Chinese translations of this sutra were mass-produced in Dunhuang under Tibetan rule. The latest count indicates the existence in various collections of 842 copies in Chinese (288 in London, 29 in Paris, 509 in Beijing, 11 in Kyoto, 5 in Taiwan), and 1899 copies in Tibetan (660 in London, 657 in Paris, 313 in Bejing, 218 in Japan, 51 in St. Petersburg). More copies in the Tibetan version are reported to remain unclassified in the India Office Library (Ueyama, pp. 438f.). 3. *Jñānolka-dhāraṇī*. The manuscripts of the Petrovsky collection have been published in facsimile by R. E. Emmerick and Vorob'ëva-Desjatovskaja (plates 2-6). The whereabouts of the folio in Japan (first published in facsimile in *Seiiki Kōko Zufu* 2, 1915, and transliterated from a reproduced photo in the wrong order in Bailey, V, pp. 313f. as Otani 1-2) is unknown. 4. *Sumukha-(dhāraṇī) sūtra*. Following R. E. Emmerick (1979) two fragments of the Sanskrit text have been published together with corrresponding Khotanese passages (Bongard-Levin and Vorobyova-Desyatovskaya, 1980-81 and 1986a; see also idem, 1986b). Emmerick has published another fragment of the Sanskrit *Sumukhadhāraṇī* from the Crosby collection in the Library of Congress (1986).

Texts without known originals and given provisional titles. 1. *Amṛta-prabha-dhāraṇī*. 2. *Avalokiteśvara-dhāraṇī* (qq.v.).

Texts found with other Khotanese texts but not translated into Khotanese. 1. *Buddhoṣṇīṣa-vijaya-dhāraṇī*. This popular esoteric text is at the beginning of the long scroll Ch. c. 001 (lines 1-11 in Bailey, V, p. 368; a few more syllables can be read on pl. CXLVI in Stein) at the British Library (Ind. Off.). 2. *Kauśika-prajñā-pāramitā* (see Conze, 1973, pp. 157ff.). The Sanskrit text in Khotanese spelling includes the *dhāraṇī* (Bailey, V, pp. 356ff) and two more fragments (probably scribal exercises; Bailey, III, pp. 102, 118). 3. *Sitāta-patra-(dhāraṇī-)sūtra*. The Sanskrit text with many *dhāraṇīs* in Khotanese spelling is found in two manuscripts (Bailey, V, pp. 359ff, 368ff.).

Other texts originally containing *dhāraṇīs* are, e.g., the *Adhyardhaśatikā* (q.v.; Conze, 1973, pp. 184ff.), the *Prajñāpāramitā-hṛdaya-sūtra* (Skjærvø, 1988), and the *Vajracchedikā* (Kumārajīva's Chinese version), although extant Khotanese versions do not extend to the *dhāraṇī* part.

See also BUDDHISM iii.

Bibliography: H. W. Bailey, *Khotanese Texts*, Cambridge, 1945-63. G. M. Bongard-Levin and M. I. Vorobyova-Desyatovskaya, in *Indologica Taurinensia* 8-9, 1980-81, pp. 45ff. Idem, in *Peredneaziatskiĭ Sbornik* 4, Moscow, 1986a, pp. 156ff. Idem, *Indian Texts from Central Asia (Leningrad Manuscript Collection)*, Bibliographia Philologica Buddhica Series Minor 5, Tokyo, 1986. E. Conze, *The Short Prajñāpāramitā Texts*, London, 1973. R. E. Emmerick, *A Guide to the Literature of Khotan*, Tokyo, 1979. Idem, in G. Bhattacharya, ed., *Deyadharma. Studies in the Memory of Dr. D. C. Sircar*, Delhi, 1986, pp. 165-67 (with two plates). Idem and Vorob'ëva-Desjatovskaja, *Saka Documents* VII. *The St. Petersburg Collection*, Corpus Inscrip. Iran., pt. II, vol. 5, Plates VII, London, 1993. H. Inagaki, *The Anantamukhanirhāra-Dhāraṇī Sūtra and Jñānagarbha's Commentaryt*, Kyoto, 1987. P. O. Skjærvø, in *A Green Leaf. Papers in Honour of Professor Jes P. Asmussen*, Acta Iranica 28, Leiden, 1988, pp. 157-71. M. A. Stein, *Serindia. Detailed Report of Explorations in Central Asia and Westernmost China*, Oxford, 1921, repr. Delhi, 1980. D. Ueyama, *Studies of the Buddhists of Dunhuang*, Kyoto, 1990 (in Japanese).

(HIROSHI KUMAMOTO)

ii. IN SOGDIAN

No *dhāraṇī* in Sogdian script has so far been encountered in Turfan MSS; those found among the Tun-huang MSS are:

1. *Nīlakaṇṭha-dhāraṇī* in Brahmi (47 lines) and its interlinear transcription in Sogdian script (60 lines) by the same scribe (Or. 8212 [175]; de la Vallée Poussin and Gauthiot); it is imperfect at the beginning by three phrases. According to Lévi, the *dhāraṇī* is identical with that of Sahasrabhujāryāvalokiteśvara *(T[aishō] T[ripṭaka]* XX, no. 1061), which in turn is almost the same as Nīlakaṇṭhāvalokiteśvara's *dhāraṇī* (*T.T.*, XX, no. 1111; cf. the Sogdian title given in the text *1-LPw δsty ʾʾryʾβṛʾwkδʾyšβr nyṛknt nʾm tʾrny* "*dhāraṇī* named thousand-handed Avalokiteśvara Nīlakaṇṭha"; on the Skt. and Tibetan versions see Wu chi-yu, pp. 67-68; Tsukamoto et al., pp. 129-30). This *dhāraṇī* is followed by a short, unidentified mantra named *wyspw ʾʾγδʾk δβrʾynʾk δrzyʾwr ptsrwm* "*hṛdaya* mantra fulfilling all the wishes."

2. *Dhāraṇī* of the *Amoghapāśahṛdaya-sūtra*, which is imperfect at the end, occupies lines 202-33 of P[elliot Sogdien] 7 (Benveniste, pp. 93-104); it is known from line 229 that the MS belonged to a man named *kryʾn* (Skt. *kalyāṇa*). Among the extant versions of the *Amoghapāśahṛdaya-dhāraṇī* in Sanskrit, Tibetan, and Chinese (cf. Meisezahl, 1962; Meisezahl, 1965; Emmerick; and Tsukamoto et al., pp. 123-26), the shorter ones, i.e., those found in *T.T.* (XX, nos. 1093-94) and in a Sanskrit MS from Tun-huang are close to the Sogdian.

3. *Kṣitigarbha-dhāraṇī*, contained in P 18 (Benveniste, pp. 200-01). This *dhāraṇī* (28 lines) is similar to the *dhāraṇīs* found in *T.T.* (XX, no. 1159B) and a Tun-huang Chinese MS S.4543. An interesting feature of this text is that Skt. *-l-* is sometimes transcribed with *-rr-* in Sogdian script.

4. Sixteen unidentified *dhāraṇīs* found in P 8 (Benveniste, pp. 105-17); P 8 (lines 61-62) names itself *ʾʾryʾβrʾwkδyšβr pwtystβ mxʾstβ 100 ʾštʾ nʾm swtr γwβtyʾkh pwstk* (= *Avalokiteśvarasyanāmāṣṭaśatakastotra-sūtra*). They are short spells against troubles and misfortunes preceded by homage to Avalokiteśvara. The first four are also found in P 8bis, which is another copy of the same text.

Three more mantras in Siddham script are quoted in P 14 and 15 (Benveniste, pp. 137-41). They are *Fo pu san mei yeh chou* (P 14, 30; *T.T.* XX, p. 204a), *Ch'u hu shên chou* (P 15, 14; *T.T.* XX, p. 191a), *Ching shui chên yen* (P15, 15; *T.T.* XVIII, p. 595a). The *prajñāpāramitāhṛdaya-mantra* is translated into Sogdian in P 16, 19-21 (cf. Benveniste, p. 143; Bailey, pp. 936-37).

Bibliography: H. W. Bailey, "Irano-Indica, IV," *BSO(A)S* 13, 1951, pp. 920-38. E. Benveniste, *Textes sogdiens*, Paris, 1940. R. E. Emmerick, "Amoghapāśahṛdaya," *EIr* I, pp. 979-80. S. Lévi, in *JRAS*, 1912, pp. 1063-66. R. O. Meisezahl, in *Monumenta Nipponica* 17, 1962, pp. 265-328. Idem, in *Mikkyogaku mikkyoshi ronbunshu*, Koyasan, 1965, pp. 179-216. *Taishō Tripṭaka*, ed.

J. Takakusu and K. Watanabe, Tokyo, 1924-32. K. Tsukamoto et al., *Bongo butten no kenkyu* IV. *Mikkyo kyoten hen*, Tokyo, 1989. L. de la Vallée Poussin and R. Gauthiot, in *JRAS*, 1912, pp. 629-45. Wu chi-yu, in *Contributions aux études de Touen-houang* III, Paris, 1984, pp. 55-75.

(YUTAKA YOSHIDA)

DHARMAŚARĪRA-SŪTRA, a short Buddhist text belonging to the Mahāyānist tradition. Two different versions of the Sanskrit text, a fragment of the Khotanese version, and a Chinese translation have been published so far.

One folio belonging to the German Turfan collection with the complete Sanskrit text in North Turkestan Brāhmī (formerly called "the slanting type") was published by Stönner. Part of the same text is also found on a fragment published as Nr. 893 in Waldschmidt. A different text in the St. Petersburg (Leningrad) collection, also bearing the title "Dharmaśarīra-sūtra" but twice as long as the Turfan text, was published by G. M. Bongard-Levin and M. I. Vorobyova-Desyatovskaya (1985, pp. 66-76). This is written in South Turkestan Brāhmī (formerly called "the upright type") on five folios. The Khotanese version is found on two folios numbered 6 and 7 in the St. Petersburg collection, also in the upright type of Brāhmī, and was published by G. M. Bongard-Levin and E. N. Tyomkin. The Chinese text (late 10th century C.E.) is in the *Taishō Tripiṭaka* (XVII, no. 766; XII, no. 356 with a similar title translated in the 2nd century C.E. is a different text).

The main part of the sutra is a list of qualities leading to or attained by Enlightenment. These qualities are classified according to number (e.g., eight salvations) and arranged generally in ascending order. Sometimes details of an item are given. The list is preceded by a prologue and followed by an epilogue.

Of the two versions of the Sanskrit text, the shorter one from Turfan seems more primitive. Most of its qualities generally reappear in the same order in the longer Leningrad text. The Chinese version represents the more developed form and is by far the longest. The Khotanese version, on the other hand, is different in that the list in the extant text is extremely short, mentioning only a few items. A passage which praises itself as the essence of the doctrines of other major Mahāyāna sutras, such as the *Prajñāpāramitā* and *Saddharmapuṇḍarīka*, is absent from any other version. The Khotanese version is more like an abbreviated paraphrase of the sutra than the translation of a Sanskrit text not yet discovered.

Bibliography: G. M. Bongard-Levin and E. N. Tyomkin, in *IIJ* 11/4, 1969, pp. 269-80 (repr. with misprints in G. M. Bongard-Levin, *Studies in Ancient India and Central Asia*, Calcutta, 1971, pp. 257-72). G. M. Bongard-Levin and M. I. Vorobyova-Desyatovskaya, eds., P*amyatniki Indiĭskoĭ pis'mennosti iz Tsentral'noĭ Azii* I, Moscow, 1985. Idem, *Indian Texts from Central Asia (Leningrad Manuscript Collection)*, Bibliographia Philologica Buddhica Series Minor 5, Tokyo, 1986. H. Stönner, in *SPAW*, 1904, pp. 1282-87. *The Taisho Shinshu Daizokyo. The Tripitaka in Chinese*, ed. J. Takakusu and K. Watanabe, 85 vols., Tokyo, 1924-32. E. Waldschmidt, ed., *Sanskrithandschriften aus den Turfanfunden*, pt. 3, Wiesbaden, 1971.

(HIROSHI KUMAMOTO)

DHĀRVĀL or **DHĀR**, QĀŻĪ KHAN BADR MOḤAMMAD (or Ḥosayn) DEHLAVĪ, 15th-century Persian lexicographer in India, so named because he settled in Dhār (hence his *nesba* Dhārvāl), capital of the Ghurid principality of Malwa.

A native of Delhi, he studied there with two leading philologists of the time, Qāżī Borhān-al-Dīn of Bodhānāand Šayḵzāda Āšeq, the author of a dictionary used by Enjū Šīrāzī (Dhārvāl, p. 1; Rieu, *Persian Manuscripts*, p. 491; Nafīsī, *Naẓm o naṯr*, p. 194). He specialized in the study of the Persian vocabulary. From Delhi he went to Jaunpur, the capital of the Sharqid kingdom (796-881/1394-1477), which was becoming an important center of patronage for scholars. Under the governorship of Qadr Khan, the scholarly brother of the Ghurid ruler Hūšang Shah, the town of Dhār had become a center of scholarship. Qāżī Khan emigrated there, making use of his *Adāt al-fożalā*ʾ as an introduction (Dhārvāl, p. 2).

Dhārvāl was one of the first Indian scholars to compile a Persian dictionary. His *Adāt al-fożalā*ʾ (822/1419 or 812/1409) is small book divided into two parts, the first an alphabetical list of Persian words and the second a list alphabetized by first and last letter of compounds and poetical phrases. It was compiled on the basis of several earlier dictionaries, with the addition of words and phrases found by the author in a number of classical Persian poets. The book survives in manuscript and was used by Enjū Šīrāzī, the author of *Farhang-e jahāngīrī*. His second work was an Arabic to Persian dictionary entitled *Dastūr al-eḵwān*. A brief introduction in Persian lists a number of authors, mostly classical Persian poets (Anwarī, Saʿdī, Neẓāmī, etc.), from whose works the Arabic words had been chosen. It seems that a major use of the dictionary was to define the Arabic words found in Persian poetry, rather than to assist students of Arabic. It contains 16,000 words, arranged alphabetically by word (not root), with Persian translations. Verbs are given in the form of infinitives or participles, the form in which they would be used in Persian. Several equivalent words or phrases are often given for a single Arabic word, and Arabic idioms are sometimes explained. In the introduction to the latter work Dhārvāl mentions that he had also written a *taḏkera* of poets (*al-Ḏarīʿa* VIII, p. 150).

Bibliography: M. A. ʿAbbāsī, *Tafṣīlī fehrest-e maḵṭūṭāt-e fārsīya-ye Panjāb Public Library*, supp. I, Lahore, 1966. M. Bašīr Ḥosayn, *Fehrest-e-maḵṭūṭat-e Šafīʿ*, Lahore, 1392/1972. Dehḵodā, I, pp. 180, 317-18. Qāżī Khan Badr Moḥammad Dhārvāl, *Adāt al-fożalāʾ*, ms. no. 473 *qāż*, Punjab Public Library, Lahore. Idem, *Dastūr al-eḵwān*, ed. S. Najafī Asad-Allāhī, 2 vols., Tehran, 1349-50 Š./1970-71; review in *Rāhnemā-ye Ketāb* 18, 1354 Š./1975, pp. 83-86 and *Soḵan* 24, 1354 Š./ 1975, pp. 842-44. ʿA.-A. Ḥekmat, *Sarzamīn-e Hend*, Tehran, 1337 Š./1958. ʿA.-Ḥ. Ḥosaynī, *al-Hend fi'l-ʿahd al-eslāmī*, Hyderabad (Deccan), 1392/1972. ʿA.-N. Monzawī, *Farhang-nāmahā-ye ʿarabī be fārsī*, Tehran, 1337 Š/1958. Storey, III, pp. 11-12. Rypka, *Hist. Iran. Lit.*, pp. 430, 721.

(M. Saleem Akhtar)

DHŪTA-SŪTRA, name of a Buddhist Sogdian text discovered at Tun-huang (B. M. Or. 8212 [160]; facs. ed. in MacKenzie, pls. 37-66). The name of the sutra goes back to Hans Reichelt, who first studied it; the word *δʾw-tʾ* (< Skt. *dhūta-*) recurs several times in the text. Reichelt's edition was extensively commented upon by Émile Benveniste and the most recent, revised edition was published by D. N. MacKenzie.

The text, written on a scroll, comprises 297 lines; although it lacks both the beginning and end, the contents suggest that what has survived is close to the end of a sutra. In the text the Buddha explains to the bodhisattvas Maker of Light (*rwxšny-wnʾy*) and Cittarājā (*pʾzn xwtʾw* = Chin. *hsin wang*) that all existence is one and the same without two *saṃjñā*s (conceptions; ll. 64-65), and that what is lying and deceitful in the three worlds is all done from the mind and heart (ll. 142-43), which must, therefore, be trained with a discipline (*dhūta*) so that one may be able to attain true understanding.

That the Sogdian text was translated from Chinese is put beyond doubt by the word *sry* "head" employed in the rationalization of the name *dhū(-ta)* (ll. 270-77), since *t'ou (t'o)*, the Chinese transcription of Skt. *dhū(-ta)*, means "head, leader." Demiéville (apud Benveniste, 1933b, pp. 239-41) proposes to identify it with an apocryphal Chinese sutra *Fu wei hsin wang p'u sa shuo t'ou t'o ching* "Dhūta-sūtra uttered by the Buddha for the Bodhisattva Cittarāja," the beginning of which is known from a few Tun-huang Chinese MSS (S.2474 publ. in the *Taishō Tripiṭaka* LXXXV, no. 2886; Pelliot chinois 2052; for others see *Tun huang i shu tsung mu so yin*, Peking, 1962, p. 409). He also draws attention to the part (ll. 228-31) corresponding to another apocryphon, *Brahmajāla-sūtra* (*Taishō Tripiṭaka* XXIV, no. 1484, p. 1008a).

The Sogdian text may perhaps be dated to the 8th or 9th century because: 1. The Chinese original *Fu wei*... is listed as an apocryphon in the *Wu chou lu* of 695 C.E. and is believed to have been composed in the Wu chou period (684-705; cf. Yabuki, p. 263). 2. The back of the Sogdian text was reused for writing several Chinese texts, one of which contains a title, "Military governor of Ho hsi [entitled] T'ai pao," presumably referring to the ruler of Tun-huang Chang i ch'ao (r. 851-72).

Bibliography: É. Benveniste, "Notes sur les textes sogdiens bouddhiques du British Museum (= Notes I)," *JRAS* 7 1933a, esp. pp. 33-44. Idem, "Notes sur le fragment sogdien du *Buddhadhyānasamādhisāgarasūtra* (= Notes II)," *JA* 223, 1933b, esp. pp. 239-41. Idem, "Notes sogdiennes (= Notes VII)," *JA* 239, 1951, esp. pp. 123-24). D. N. MacKenzie, *The Buddhist Sogdian Texts of the British Library*, Acta Iranica 10, Tehran and Liège, 1976, text, pp. 33-51, notes, pp. 40-48; reviewed by N. Sims-Williams, *IIJ* 20, 1978, pp. 256-60. H. Reichelt, *Die soghdischen Handschriftenreste des Britischen Museums* I, Heidelberg, 1928, pp. 15-32. *Taishō Tripiṭaka*, ed. J. Takakusu and K. Watanabe, Tokyo, 1924-32. K. Yabuki, M*eisha yoin*, Tokyo, 1932, pp. 263-66.

(Yutaka Yoshida)

DHYĀNA TEXT, designation of a Buddhist Sogdian text of 405 lines discovered at Tun-huang (B.M. Or. 8212 [85]; facs. ed. in MacKenzie, pls. 67-108; *Taishō Tripiṭaka* XV, no. 643, pp. 690c6-692c27). The name applied by Hans Reichelt, who first studied the text, is still in common use among Sogdianists, though the original text was later shown by S. Matsunami to have been the *Kuan fo san mei hai ching*. A very badly preserved little fragment in Berlin, perhaps of the same text, is mentioned by Olaf Hansen (p. 86).

Benveniste and Weller commented extensively upon Reichelt's edition, while comparing the text to the Chinese original, of which a French translation was provided by P. Demiéville (apud Benveniste, 1933b, pp. 195-213); the most recent revised edition was published by MacKenzie (text, pp. 53-77, notes, pp. 49-70).

The *Kuan fo san mei hai ching*, elaborating upon the ways and merits of contemplating the Buddhas, was translated into Chinese by Buddhabhadra at the beginning of the 5th century (for discussion of the Skt. title see Nanjio, Demiéville et al., and Weller). When the Chinese text shows variant readings, the Sogdian translation almost always agrees with the old manuscript of the 7th century preserved in Japan (cf. Weller, pp. 350-51; for a similar case see Kudara and Sundermann, pp. 334-40).

Bibliography: E. Benveniste, "Notes sur les textes sogdiens bouddhiques du British Museum (= Notes I)," *JRAS*, 1933, esp. pp. 44-48. Idem, "Notes sur le fragment sogdien du Buddhadhyānasamādhisāgarasūtra (= Notes II)," *JA* 223, 1933, esp. pp. 213-39. P. Demiéville et al., *Répertoire du canon bouddhique sino-japonais. Fascicule annexe du Hōbōgirin*, rev. ed., Paris and Tokyo, 1978. O. Hansen, "Die buddhistische Literatur der Sogdier," *HO* I/IV, 2/1, pp. 83-90. K. Kudara and W. Sundermann, "Zwei Fragmente einer Sammelhandschrift buddhistischer Sūtras in soghdischer Sprache," *AoF* 14, 1987, pp. 334-49. D. N. MacKenzie, *The Buddhist Sogdian Texts of the British Library*, Acta Iranica 10, Tehran and Liège, 1976; reviewed by N. Sims-Williams in *IIJ* 20, 1978, pp. 256-60 and by W. Sundermann in *BSO(A)S* 40, 1977, pp. 634-35. B. Nanjio, *A Catalogue of the Chinese Translation of the Buddhist Tripiṭaka*, Oxford, 1883. H. Reichelt, *Die soghdischen Handschriftenreste des Britischen Museums* I, Heidelberg, 1928, pp. 33-56. *Taishō Tripiṭaka*, ed. J. Takakusu and K. Watanabe, Tokyo, 1924-32. F. Weller, "Bemerkungen zum soghdischen Dhyāna-Texte," *Monumenta Serica* 2, 1936-37, pp. 341-404; 3, 1938, pp. 78-129.

(YUTAKA YOSHIDA)

DĪA (pl. *dīāt*), the prescribed blood money or wergild paid in compensation for a wrongful death or certain other physical injuries. The system of *dīa* is similar to other forms of compensation prevalent in Roman, Germanic, Anglo-Saxon, and other ancient legal systems (A. Diamond, pp. 144-58). Its inception, however, is in the system of private vengeance prevalent in pre-Islamic Arabia. Tribes in pre-Islamic Arabia would at times renounce their right to vengeance in return for compensation often in form of camels or young brides (Edris, p. 230). While maintaining the basic structure of pre-Islamic *dīa*, Islamic law modified the practice in significant respects by setting restrictions on the right to talion, and limiting *dīa* to specific types of goods (Anderson, pp. 811-12; ʿĀmelī, X, p. 308). There is a broad agreement on the basic theory of *dīa* among Islamic schools of law, which is usually discussed together with *qeṣāṣ*; but this field is marred with disagreements over details. The focus of this article is on the Shiʿite law.

i. In Shiʿite law.

ii. The revival of dīa in the Islamic Republic of Iran.

i. IN SHIʿITE LAW

There is broad agreement on the basic theory of *dīa* (often discussed together with *qeṣāṣ*), but disagreements are common over details. The focus here is on the Jaʿfarī school of the Shiʿite law.

All schools agree that the *dīa* of a free male Muslim is 100 camels but disagree over whether *dīa* can be paid in other types of goods or in money. The Shiʿite school maintains that the full fixed *dīa* is of six primary types: 100 camels (of certain ages, depending on the offense), 200 cows, 1000 sheep, 100 two-piece garments, 1000 dinars in gold coinage, or 10,000 dirhams in silver coinage. The offender or the party bearing the financial liability chooses the type of *dīa*, but in case of intentional crimes a settlement has to be reached by both parties. A minority opinion argues that the choice of *dīa* should be determined according to the trade of the offender (e.g., a goldsmith would pay in gold coinage; ʿĀmelī, pp. 176, 184-86; Moḥaqqeq Ḥellī, p. 246; Ebn al-Barrāj, p. 357).

Dīa is an option in the case of deliberate (*ʿamd*) and quasi-deliberate (*šebh ʿamd*) crimes against persons. Unlike some Sunni schools, the Shiʿite school does not place much weight on the tools used in a crime as a means of distinguishing between deliberate and quasi-deliberate offenses. Rather, the emphasis is on whether the offender had a specific or general intent. In contemporary times deliberate homicide would be murder, while quasi-deliberate homicide would be manslaughter.

The Shiʿite school (as well as the Hanafites and Malikites) holds that in case of intentional homicide or injury the remedy is *qeṣāṣ* (punishment or talion); *dīa* is not a co-equal alternative. Consequently, if the heirs of a victim forgive the offender an automatic right to *dīa* does not arise. Nevertheless, *dīa* could be payable through a settlement (*ṣolḥ*) in which the offender agrees to pay an amount that may be more or less than the specified *dīa* (Moṭahhar Ḥellī, p. 678). Schools that consider *dīa* to be a co-equal alternative to *qeṣāṣ* do not require that the offender consent to paying *dīa*; the choice is entirely that of the victim or the heirs (Zoḥaylī, pp. 286-88).

Dīa, however, might become the only legal recourse if certain legal deficiencies preclude the application of talion. For example, if talion cannot be enforced because strict equality is not achievable, the only option other than an outright pardon is the right to full or partial *dīa*. Accordingly, no talion is admitted in the case of fractured bones or if experts testify, in a case not involving murder, that talion is likely to endanger the life of the offender. Furthermore, a right to *dīa* is the only recourse if talion is not possible because of certain evidentiary deficiencies (ʿĀmelī, pp. 77-80; Moṭahhar Ḥelli, pp. 660, 678; Ebn al-Barrāj, pp. 474-75). *Dīa* is also the only legal remedy in the case of accidental injuries. Whether a rule of strict liability or negligence applies to tort liability is a debated issue (ʿĀmelī, pp. 150, 154-55; Goadby, pp. 62-74).

Islamic law divides injuries, whether intentional or accidental, into four groups: 1. *Aṭrāf*, an injury that involves the total loss of an organ (18 specified organs); 2. *manāfeʿ*, an injury that involves the total loss of a physiological or intellectual function (7 functions); 3. *šejāj*, an injury to the face (8 types); and 4. *jorūḥ*, injuries to the body. The full amount of *dīa* is due for a loss of an organ or function (the first two types). Therefore, a loss of both legs, for example, would elicit one full *dīa*. A proportional *dīa* is due for a partial loss. Hence a loss of one arm or leg would elicit half a *dīa*. A crippling of both legs would elicit two thirds of the *dīa*. Whether several full *dīa*s could be compounded for the loss of several organs or functions is a contested issue (Moḥaqqeq Ḥellī, pp. 235, 279; Ebn al-Barrāj, p. 475).

A specified partial *dīa* is prescribed in the case of *šejāj*. Most *jorūḥ* injuries do not have a specified prescribed *dīa*. Rather, an assessment of the actual loss suffered (*ḥokūmat ʿadl*) is applied, determined by reference to the market value of a slave before and after a similar injury. In comparison to their Sunni counterparts, the province of *ḥokūmat ʿadl* is somewhat restricted in Shiʿite law. Shiʿite law specifies the *dīa*s of several *jorūḥ* that would be covered by *ḥokūmat ʿadl* in Sunni law.

Shiʿite sources state that the terms *arš* and *ḥokūmat ʿadl* are synonymous (Moṭahhar Ḥellī, p. 684; ʿĀmelī, p. 285). Both terms refer to injuries that do not have a specified *dīa*. Most Sunni sources state that *arš* refers to money payable for a bodily injury that has a specified partial *dīa*. Nevertheless, Shiʿite sources in actuality often use *ḥokūmat ʿadl* to refer to compensation for surplus or excess injuries. For instance, if a victim's hand is severed above the wrist, he/she is entitled to *dīa* for the hand up to the wrist and to a *ḥokūmat ʿadl* for any loss above the wrist (*ḥokūma fi'l-zāʾed*; Ebn al-Barrāj, p. 373; Moṭahhar Ḥellī, p. 698).

There is much disagreement over the *dīa* of a Christian, Jew, or Zoroastrian (*ḏemmī*s). The majority opinion in the Jaʿfarī school maintains that it is 800 dirhams. The *dīa* of a slave is his market value, but it cannot exceed the *dīa* of a free person. The *dīa* for a partial loss is determined by referring to the proportional value if the loss had afflicted a free Muslim (Moḥaqeq Ḥellī, pp. 205, 247; Moṭahhar Ḥellī, pp. 683-84). There is some disagreement over the *dīa* of a woman. The majority view is that the *dīa* of a woman is half that of a man. The Shiʿites (as well as the Malikites and Hanbalites) maintain that a woman's *dīa* is equal to that of a man until it reaches two-thirds of the value. This leads to peculiar results. For example, if a woman loses three fingers, she is entitled to thirty camels; but if she loses four fingers, she is now entitled to twenty camels (Ebn al-Barrāj, pp. 486-87; ʿĀmelī, p. 41).

A unique aspect of Shiʿite law of *dīa* is the *radd*, by which a part of the *dīa* is remitted if the victim or the heirs wish to exact talion from an offender with a higher *dīa* value. For example, if a man murders a woman her heirs are entitled to exact talion provided they remit half of the *dīa* to the heirs of the offender. This procedure receives wide application to permit the exaction of talion between people of unequal *dīas*. Other schools would permit talion without remitting the discrepancy in value.

The Jaʿfarī school adopted another unique position in prescribing several specific *dīa*s for each stage of fetal development (called *ḡora*). Other schools prescribe a single *dīa* for an unborn child but disagree as to which stage it becomes due. The Jaʿfarī school was also the only school that set specified *dīa*s for the mutilation of a corpse.

In deliberate and quasi-deliberate offenses a particularly heavy *dīa* (*dīa moḡallaẓa*) is prescribed. The ages and sexes of the camels are varied so that the *dīa* will be of higher value. Additionally, the offender is personally liable for the *dīa*, which is payable in one year in the case of a deliberate offense and in two years in the case of a quasi-deliberate offense. Other schools hold that the offender is not personally liable for the *dīa* in a quasi-deliberate offense and prescribe different grace periods for the payment. In an accidental tort the *ʿāqela* of the offender is liable for the *dīa*, which is payable in three years unless the amount payable is one-third of the full *dīa* payable in one year (Moḥaqqeq Ḥellī, pp. 197, 245-46; Moṭahhar Ḥellī, pp. 679-80; ʿĀmelī, pp. 175-81).

Although existing in various forms in several ancient legal systems (Drew, p. 185; Diamond, p. 158), the *ʿāqela* grew out of the tribal organization of pre-Islamic Arabia, where the tribe of the offender was responsible for any blood money incurred by the offender. There is much disagreement in Islamic law on what constitutes the *ʿāqela* of a person and on the extent of its liability. In Shiʿite law the majority view is that the *ʿāqela* of a person are the male relatives from the father's side. This includes brothers, uncles, and cousins but not sons or fathers. The *ʿāqela* cannot be held liable for any deliberate or quasi-deliberate offense or for any amount of money due by settlement or admission. They are only responsible for an amount that exceeds one-twentieth of the *dīa*. There are differences of opinion over how the money is to be apportioned among the members of the *ʿāqela* and as to whether the public treasury (*bayt al-māl*) or the offender becomes liable if the *ʿāqela* cannot pay. The *ʿāqela* of *ḏemmī*s is the public treasury because, according to Shiʿite sources, they pay poll tax (*jezya*; Ebn al-Barrāj, pp. 357, 503-05; Moṭahhar Ḥellī, pp. 732-39; ʿĀmelī, pp. 308-15; Moḥaqeq Ḥellī, pp. 289-91).

The public treasury is also responsible for the *dīa* of a person found killed in a public place such as a public road or mosque. However, if the deceased is found with evidence of wrongdoing in a locality or on private property, resort is made to *qasāma*, which is similar to the ancient legal procedure of compurgation. The residents of the area are asked to take fifty oaths that they neither killed the deceased nor know who the killer is. According to Shiʿite law and the majority of Sunni schools, if there is a *lawaṯ* (independent evidence of wrong doing such as known hostility or any material evidence), then the locality or the *ʿāqela* of the owner of the property is responsible for the *dīa*. If there is no *lawaṯ*, then taking the oaths shields the suspects from liability and the public treasury pays the *dīa* (Ebn al-Barrāj, pp. 500, 513; Moḥaqqeq Ḥellī, pp. 222-25; ʿĀmelī, pp. 72-5).

The laws of *dīa*, to various degrees, are partially in force in several Middle Eastern countries such as Persia, Saudi Arabia, Yemen, the United Arab Emirates, Oman, and Sudan. However, the *dīa* practices of these countries are intermingled with customary practices and modern criminal law concepts. Certain practices such as *ʿāqela* and *qasāma* for the most part have fallen out of use. Furthermore, the tribes of Sinai, Sudan, and Somalia apply *dīa* laws derived from customary practices rather than *šarīʿa* principles.

Bibliography: Šahīd Awwal Šams-al-Dīn ʿĀmelī, *al-Lomʿa al-demašqīya*, ed. M. Kalāntar, Najaf, 1398/1978, X, pp. 105-329. J. N. D. Anderson, "Homicide in Islamic Law," *BSO(A)S* 13/4, 1951. M. Cherif Bassiouni, ed., *The Islamic Criminal Justice System*, London, 1982. A. S. Diamond, *Primitive Law. Past and Present*, London, 1971. K. F. Drew, *The Laws of Salian Franks*, Philadelphia, 1991. ʿAbd-al-ʿAzīz Ebn al-Barrāj Ṭarābolsī, *Mohaḏḏab*, Tehran, 1406/1986, II, pp. 453-516. ʿA. A. Edrīs, *Dīa*, Beirut, 1986. F. M. Goadby, "The Moslem Law of Civil Delict as Illustrated by the Mejelle," *Journal of Comparative Legislation* 21, 3rd Ser., 1959. Abu 'l-Qāsem Moḥaqqeq Ḥellī, *Šarāʾeʿ al-eslām*, ed. M. ʿAlī, Beirut, 1983, IV, pp. 245-92. Faḵr-al-Moḥaqqeqīn Moṭahhar Ḥellī, *Īżāḥ al-fawāʾed*, Qom, 1387/1967, IV, pp. 655-755. M.-Ḥ. Bāqer Najafī, *Jawāher al-kalām*, ed. R. Estādī, Tehran, 1404, XLI-XLII. Abū Jaʿfar Moḥmmad b. Ḥasan Ṭūsī, *Mabsūṭ*, ed. M. Behbūdī, Tehran, n.d., VII, pp. 2-243. E. Tyan, "Diya," *EI*[2] II, pp. 340-43. W. Zoḥaylī, *al-Feqh al-eslāmī wa adellatoho* VI, Damascus, 1985, pp. 297-327.

(KHALID ABU EL FADL)

ii. THE REVIVAL OF *DĪA* IN THE ISLAMIC REPUBLIC OF IRAN

The abolishment of the secular penal code (Qānūn-e jazāʾ), which had been adopted from the French code since the 1906-11 Constitutional revolution (q.v.), and the establishment of *dīāt, ḥodūd, qeṣāṣ*, and *taʿzīrāt*, the four pillars of Islamic penal law, has constituted the main agenda of the Islamic Republic of Iran for reconstruction of the Judicial system since its inception in 1357 Š./1979 (see JUDICIAL SYSTEM). Thus, on 24 Āḏar 1361 Š./15 December 1982, the Islamic penal law of blood money (Qānūn-e mojāzāt-e eslāmī-e dīāt), comprising 210 articles, was ratified by the Majles (for the text see Waṭanī, pp. 236-85). It was a codified and revised version of a chapter on *dīāt* in Ayatollah Khomeini's *Taḥrīr al-wasīla* (3rd ed., Beirut, 1401/1981, II, pp. 553-607). The law of *dīāt* had been enforced until 7 Āḏar 1370 Š./28 November 1991 when the Discretionary Council (Šūrā-ye maṣlaḥat-e neẓām) approved the new Islamic Penal Law (Qānūn-e mojāzāt-e eslāmī), comprising *ḥodūd, qeṣāṣ, dīāt*, and *taʿzīrāt*, that had been ratified in July 1991 by the Majles (for the text see Qorbānī, pp. 406-779). The fourth book of the law (arts. 294-496) is on *dīāt*. Article 294 defines *dīa* as a property to be given to a victim of crime or to his/her guardian (*walī*) or blood warden (*walī-e dam*) in compensation for his/her life or bodily injuries and defects. Article 295 defines three major subjects of *dīa*: non-deliberate crime (*ḵaṭāʾ-e maḥż*); quasi-deliberate crime (*šebh-e ʿamd*); and deliberate crime (*ʿamd*); which is primarily the subject of *qeṣāṣ*. The *dīa* of the life of a male Muslim (art. 297) includes one of the following options: either 100 healthy camel, or 200 healthy cows, or 1,000 healthy sheep, or 200 of new Yemeni cotton garments (*ḥolla*), or 1,000 dinar (q.v.; gold coin), or 10,000 dirham (q.v.; silver coin). The *dīa* of the life of a female Muslim is one-half of that of a male Muslim. In the case of bodily injuries the *dīa* of Muslim male and female is equal up to the ceiling of one-third of the full amount of the *dīa* of a male Muslim; but when it exceeds the one-third ceiling, the *dīa* of female is one-half of that of the male. Articles 302-496 provide detailed rulings on personal responsibilities in various actions that are subject of *dīa* as well as the *dīa* of bodily injuries of various organs.

Bibliography: F. Qorbānī, *Majmūʿa-ye kāmel-e qawānīn-e jazāʾī*, Tehran, 5th ed. 1372 Š./1993. F. Ṣāleḥī, *Dīa yā mojāzāt-e mālī*, Tehran, 1371 Š./1992. M.-Ḥ. Waṭanī, ed. *Majmūʿa-ye kāmel-e qawānīn wa moqarrarāt-e jazāʾī*, Tehran, 1364 Š./1985.

(KHALID ABU EL FADL)

DĪĀLA, RIVER. See ARVANDRŪD; ŠERVĀNRŪD.

DIALECTOLOGY. Introduction. The terms dialect and language overlap. In general, language refers to the more or less unified system of the phonology, grammar, and lexicon that is shared by the speakers of a country, or geographic region, or a socially defined group, whereas dialect (Pers. *lahja, gūyeš*) focuses on varieties of a language. In that sense, any dialect can be considered a language, and vice versa. In popular usage, dialect also refers to a speaker's accent (*lahja*, but not *gūyeš*), i.e., peculiarities in his pronunciation, including stress and pitch (such as a German accent, or the noticeable "melody" of Isfahani Persian vs. that of Tehran).

More commonly, dialect refers to groups that are noticeably different grammatically, phonologically, and lexically. They may be either closely related varieties of the same language (such as Khorasani vs. Tehrani Persian, or the Persian spoken in Persia proper vs. the variety spoken in Afghanistan, Darī, vs. Tajiki Persian) or of more distantly related languages (such as Kurdish vs. Persian, or Pamir dialects vs. Pashto). It is not always possible to distinguish whether a dialect is a variety of one language or of two closely related languages. Mutual intelligibility is one criterion, but intellibility is very much a factor of linguistic and cultural exposure. Social identity often overrides linguistically defined dialectal relationships. Speakers of socially lower status tend to identify themselves with those of higher status.

The recognition of linguistic and dialectal differences by indigenous writers and travellers alike throughout Persian history is well known. Early writers remark on the diversity of languages, including non-Iranian languages preserved among Iranians. *Loḡat-e fors* quotes mainly eastern poets at a time when New Persian had already established itself as a literary language. Regional dialects of Persian were observed, most notably by geographers (e.g., Eṣṭak̲rī, pp. 91, 167, 314; Ebn Ḥawqal, pp. 254, 348, 490; Maqdesī, pp. 334-35, 368, 378, 398, 418), often with evaluative comments as to their elegance, coarseness, etc. Dictionaries of Persian began to record the geographic origin of certain words.

As to the dialects of the New Iranian period, important sources are secular and religious texts in local and regional dialects, written since the early centuries of Islam. Those texts, as well as the dialects of local religious minorities, mainly Zoroastrian and Jewish, preserve the local tongues where Persian or Turkic have eliminated them (see the various bibliographical studies by Afšār and the overview of dialectological studies in Iran by Yarshater, 1970). On the other hand, important especially for the study of the pre-Islamic diversity is the so-called N*ebenüberlieferung*, i.e., Iranian words and loans in non-Iranian languages, most notably Armenian (see Schmitt, 1989).

Dialectology as an academic subfield of the discipline of linguistics developed in the 19th century, together with the comparative-historical study of Indo-European, to which especially the study of Old Iranian contributed considerably. (Note the early distinction of the IE languages into a western centum-group and an eastern satəm-group, epitomized by the reflexes of IE velar palatals, **ḱn̥tom* "100" in Latin and Avestan, respectively.) The second half of that century was also the beginning of the systematic study of pre-Islamic Iranian texts as well as systematic field work and study of the modern spoken Iranian languages and dialects.

Dialectology is essentially comparative. It has the objective of identifying linguistic relationships in geographic, historical, and social space. The comparative objective involves the study of the two main forces of dialectical divergence and convergence; that is, on the one hand, the retention, loss, and innovation of linguistic features, and their diffusion both internally throughout the lexicon, phonology, and grammar and externally, i.e., diffusion by social and geographic contact. On the other hand, it involves the study of groupings, mostly in terms of geography and history, by the identification of bundlings of isoglosses, i.e., overlapping patterns of lines of shared differentiation, either innovative or conservative. These coinciding objectives reflect the two main original approaches of comparative-historical linguistics, namely the genealogic S*tammbaum* theory and the "wave" theory, the former assuming a single origin and subsequent splits, the latter multiple sources.

The latter also leads to the identification of a *Sprachbund*, i.e., the development of similarities shared by areally adjacent or symbiotic dialects and languages, whether genetically related or not. Diachronically, this may involve reflexes of an extinct local languag, of an incoming group, or of a superimposed dominant language. The comparative-historical approach to dialectology has more recently been extented to that of linguistic typology, i.e., the systematic study of isoglosses and more importantly of phonological, morphological, and syntactic (sub-)systems or types, irrespective of genetic relationship.

These approaches are historical in the sense that they imply the reconstruction of the diachrony of change and the temporal sequence of changes. (Note the observations by biochemists that their reconstruction of the tree of diversification of the DNA of all humankind closely resembles the one reconstructed by linguists for all human languages; see Cavalli-Sforza.) The dating of such changes, specifically their major diachronic groupings into Old, Middle, and New and/or Modern, is, however, largely a crutch, based on major political events. Old Persian refers to a period between the 6th and 3rd centuries B.C.E. and Old English to a period from the Germanic invasion of the Isles to about 1,100 C.E. Many so-called Middle Iranian languages continued in one or another form, medium, and function well after the coming of Islam. The terminology here is also in part correlated with the extant text corpuses, not only chronology/history. (Note also discontinuity in available text corpuses.) No Iranian dialect or language can be studied throughout its entire history. The lesser known dialects or languages are as a rule lumped together with the dating of the emergence of a new nationally or regionally dominant language.

Lack of change and diversion in some aspects of modern or middle dialects, even if confined to one or a few items, tended to be considered evidence for their greater "originality" and tended to attract greater attention than change.

Iranian dialectology. Basic bibliographical overview. The most recent comprehensive analysis with major attention to dialectal dynamics is the *Compendium Linguarum Iranicarum* (Schmitt, ed., 1989). Major earlier studies include the monumental and fundamental *Grundriss der iranischen Philologie*

(1896-1904), Hans Reichelt (1927), the *Iranistik* (1958), I. M. Oranskiĭ (1960, 1963, 1975, 1979), and the largely bibliographical surveys in the *Current Trends* (Sebeok, ed., V-VI). Further, we have two comprehensive works edited by Rastorgueva, largely organized by topic (1975) and arranged according to historical stages and dialect groups (1979-82).

i. Important specialized studies. In terms of groupings, the most decisive studies were by Wilhem Geiger (in *Grundriss*), and, based on observations by Mann and ultimately Friedrich Andreas (q.v.), those by Paul Tedesco, with reference to the evidence of the Middle Iranian Turfan texts, and by Wolfgang Lentz with reference to variations in the New Persian of the *Šāh-nāma*. There are also studies by Harold Bailey, David MacKenzie (1961), Gernot Windfuhr (1975), and Pierre Lecoq.

ii. Phonology, morphology, and syntax. On phonology we have studies by V. S. Sokolova (I. Baluchi, Kurdish, Ṭālešī, Tātī-Persian; II. Ossetic, Yaḡnōbī, Pamir languages), and by Don Stilo on the typology of waves of palatalization affecting Iranian and non-Iranian alike in the area stretching from Persia into the Caucasus and beyond. W. L. Heston studies typological-comparative syntax of noun phrases, pronouns, passives, nominalized verb forms, and coordination and subordination in early New Persian, Middle Persian, Sogdian, and Khotanese. C. P. Masica included Iranian evidence, confined to contemporary standard Persian, Kurdish, and Baluchi, as part of his study on a small number of syntactic types across Eurasia. Hans Seiler traced relative clauses and nominal subordination from Old Iranian to Modern Persian as part of a general linguistic-typological study (see also Haider and Zwanziger). M. M. Sakhokiya's work is a typological study of possessives, transitivity, and ergativity in Old Iranian, Old Armenian, and Old Georgian; J. R. Payne (1980) conducts a typological study of the loss of ergative constructions in the Pamir languages, and Bossong's extensive typological study concerns the case systems of some twenty-six modern Iranian languages (see CASES). Iranian in the general context of universal syntactic typology of agency and its morphological representation is discussed in numerous specialized and general linguistic-typological studies by Gilbert Lazard (see bibliography). Gernot Windfuhr (1985) included Persian, as representative of much of Iranian, in his general model of verbal categorizations and their multidimensional interrelationships and shifts (see also Windfuhr, 1987). The category of inference is discussed by Windfuhr (1982; see also Lazard, 1985). Harald Haarmann included Persian as part of his study of this category across Eurasia.

The systematic cartographic analysis of variety and groups has so far been limited. Besides Edel'man (1968), recent less selective areal studies are the lexical maps published by the *Linguistic Atlas of Afghanistan* (Redard, 1974). Confined to the Central dialects, but of general import for the study of Iranian dialectology, especially in terms of its inclusion of socio-linguistic issues, is the study by Krahnke, which includes numerous maps and identifies two intersecting directions of isoglottic waves.

Groupings. Iranian languages belong to the Indo-European language family, specifically to those languages which in their documented texts identify themselves as Aryan (q.v.). There has been much recent debate about the original areas of Indo-European as a whole. In one theory Indo-European is considered one of the language groups, together with Afro-Asiatic and Dravidian, that are suggested to have originated in the Near East (Gamkrelidze and Ivanov).

The staging area of the Aryan branch of Indo-European was most likely the steppes of Central Asia, from the Caspian and Aral Seas and north. Members of one group of Aryans appear to have moved, by the beginning of the 2nd millennium B.C.E., to much of the south. Most important was the move of one group, the so-called Indo-Aryans, to the southeast, first to the area of Afghanistan and then to northwest India. The group now identified as Iranians, or Irano-Aryans, appears to have remained for some time and expanded toward the west and the east. Most decisive was the move of some of them onto the Iranian plateau. There Iranians first established rulerships, and ultimately world empires, encompassing multi-ethnic, multi-linguistic, and multi-cultural hosts. The Iranization of the area proceeded relatively slowly. The earliest staging areas for the Iranian plateau itself appear to have been in the northeast, the southwest, and the northwest. They are also the major geographically definable, even "natural," focal points of linguistic symbiosis and turmoil (see MacKenzie, 1961; Windfuhr, 1975; and below). These appear to be the same staging areas as for Turkic since the end of the first millennium C.E. Today, Turkic and other languages have erased Iranian in the north, as Iranian languages once did to their predecessors.

The dialectological division of early Iranian is essentially based on comparative reconstruction. Iranian names of persons and places are first recorded in Mesopotamian documents of the early first millennium B.C.E. They give evidence for dialectal differentiation even at that stage. Today, Iranian languages and dialects cover an area approximately as large as that of the modern Indo-Aryan languages (see Edel'man, 1968, map 1). Ever since the earliest records, they exhibit great variety and differentiation (Schmitt, pp. 4-31; for variety in Achaemenid times, see Rossi). This variety is addressed in detail in the major recent comprehensive studies (Rastorgueva, 1975, 1979-87; Schmitt).

Iranian languages and dialects are grouped into western and eastern categories, the former again into southwestern and northwestern, in spite of the recognition of numerous intersections at any time and in any directions. It should be noted that except for the sequence Old > Middle > New Persian, and Middle Sogdian >Yaḡnōbī, no direct predecessors or successors of the other dialects are known. This suggests greater linguistic variety at the earlier stages than that found in the documented evidence.

The incipient western division is already evident in the two attested Old Iranian languages, namely Old Persian and Avestan. This distinction is continued in documented Middle Iranian, which also shows the further distinction between West Iranian, i.e., Middle Persian and Parthian versus East Iranian, namely Sogdian, Saka (Khotanese and Tumshuqese), Choarasmian (see CHORAZMIA iii), and Bactrian (q.v.). Both distinctions are continued in the modern dialects, which may be listed as follows (excluding now extinct dialects): Western Iranian: Superimposed on all is Persian, and its regional varieties, most prominently the Persian varieties in Persia, Afghanistan, and Tajikistan, and lesser known ones such as Tātī-Persian in the southeast Caucasus. The two most widely spread western dialect groups are: in the west, Kurdish dialects found in western Persia, northern Iraq and Syria, eastern Turkey, and southern Armenia; and in the east, Baluchi found in West Pakistan, eastern Persia, southern Afghanistan, and Turkmenistan. Less widely spread dialects are: In the west, Zāzā (see DIMILI) in eastern Turkey and Gōrānī near Mosul and in the central Zagros; in the northwest and the center, the broad band of Tātī and Tālešī dialects stretching from Azerbaijan to the center, to which belong Semnānī east of Tehran, and the Central dialects (q.v.) between Tehran, Hamadān, and Isfahan; in the north, Gīlakī on the northwest shores and Māzandarānī (formerly called Ṭabarī) on the northeast shores of the Caspian; in the southwest and south, the Lorī dialects, the dialects in Fārs, Lārestān and Baškard, and those of along the Persian Gulf coast. Pashto is the most widely spread of the eastern Iranian languages. The remaining eastern languages, each confined to small areas, include: Parāčī and Ōrmuṛī, roughly north and south of Kabul respectively; Yidga, Munjī, Wak̲ī, and the so-called Pamir languages with their own multiple subdivisions, roughly north and northeast of Kabul; Yaḡnōbī in southern Tajikistan, and Ossetic in the central Caucasus.

Alternative grouping. The term East Iranian is a misnomer, since it includes Ossetic and its predecessors in the Caucasus. As to the western division, it was recognized early on that the north-south division essentially is a reflex of the old geographic-political division between Media and Persis. This observation was revived by W. B. Henning, and more recently amply documented by Ehsan Yarshater (e.g., 1969), based on his extensive documentation of the contemporary Iranian dialects stretching from northern Azerbaijan to the center around Isfahan. That is, dialectologically, Persian and Perside dialects such as Lorī have to be recognized as representatives of a small sub-group which began to split from the remainder of West Iranian as early as the 5th century B.C.E. One therefore may speak of a division into North Iranian (instead of East Iranian), and South Iranian (instead of West Iranian), of which the southwestern dialects reflect an early regional split.

Divergence. i. Phonology. Early divergences involve prominently 1. the reflex of the old Aryan palatals, 2. fricative clusters, and 3. initial semivowels.

1. The Aryan palatals *ḱ/*ǵ changed over an affricate stage, i.e., *tś/*dź, to s/z in common Iranian, but to *θ/d* > *h/d* in Persian, e.g., *ḱ: common Ir. *das* (10)> Pers. *dah*; *ǵ: common Ir. *zān-* (know) > Pers. *dān-*; also, Aryan *ḱw and *ǵw changed to *sp* and *zb*, but to *s* and *z* in OPers., e.g., *aḱw- (horse)> common Ir. *asp-*, but Pers. *as-* (NPers. *savār* "mounted" rider'< *asa-bār-*).

2. Already in Old Persian, the fricative cluster Ir. *θr had become a strident, which later changed to *s*, also found in Baluchi, Kurdish, and K̲ūrī. It developed to *(h)r* in other dialects, e.g., *puθr-* (son) > Pers. *pes-ar*, but > *puhr* > *pūr* elsewhere. This change is found extended later to other fricative clusters, in various dialects to different extent, and generally not affecting all lexemes. Both *fr and *xr >*(h)r* in much of the lexicon of the Central dialects, e.g., **fra-vaxš* (call forth, sell) > *(h)r-ōš*, but Pers. *for-ūš* from *√*wač-* (to say, call) and preverb **fra-* (forth);*xr-: *(h)rīd* vs. Pers. *k̲arīd* (to buy).

3. Initial semivowels *w and *y tended to remain unchanged, but in Persian and other dialects they changed to voiced stops, first *w > *b* or *(g)w*, then *y >*j* or *ž*; e.g., *w: **wāt-* (wind)> *wād/wāy* but *bād* in Persian, **ward-* (flower, rose) > *vel*, etc., but > *gol* in Persian (with additional late change of *rd >l*); *y: **yav-* (barley) remains *yow* or *yā* in many dialects, but *jow* in Persian. In turn, initial voiced stops developed into fricatives in a number of eastern dialects. Also, postconsonantal semivowels tend to affect the respective consonants. This includes old initial *dw (e.g., **dwar-* "door" > *bar*, vs. Pers. *dar*).

ii. Morphology and lexicon. Early divergence involves prominently: 1. pronominal suffixes and their development, 3rd singular *-*šai* vs. *-*hai* (both conditioned variants of original Indo-Ir. *-*sai*) > -*š* vs. -*ē*/-*ī*, respectively, reflected in modern dialects (e.g., in Pers. *bīnī-aš* vs. K̲ūrī *nāk-e* "nose-his"); and 2. 3rd person demonstratives, 'this/that', Persian and others *īn/ān* vs. reflexes of **im-*/**aw-* elsewhere (OPers. also had **im-*, still fossilized in Persian *em-* as *em-rūz/-šab/-sāl* (today, tonight, this year)).

Early lexical divergence is found already in Old Iranian, e.g., Old Persian *gaub-* vs. Avestan *wāč-* (say; e.g., Pers. *gū(y)-/gof-t*, Sangsarī *vāž-/vā-t*; note the recently introduced Pers. *vāža* "word"). It should be noted that in regard to some of the early differences in phonology, morphology, and lexicon, the imperial Old Persian of the Achaemenid inscriptions already was no longer *echtaltpersisch*. Of course, there never can be a "pure" dialect.

Loss, retention, and innovation. Typologically, Old Iranian as an Indo-European language is synthetic, i.e., it is morphologically marked by a very high degree of nominal and verbal inflection, syntactically by relative free word order. The breakdown of this system is largely the consequence of phonological change, including conditioned variations and contradictions, and, more importantly, of shifts in stress patterns. Thereby inflectional endings become reduced and ultimately lost, as is the case with most of the distinctions of gender, case, and number in the nominal system, and the distinctions of tense, mood, and aspect as well as of active and passive, and the multiple derivative formations in the verb system.

Beginning as early as the 4th century B.C.E., the complex nominal case system was ultimately reduced to a morphologically unmarked system, and the verb system to a binary opposition of so-called present and preterite. This resulted initially in virtually inflection-less languages, except for the distinction of three persons in the singular and plural of the verbs and pronouns. Concomitantly, there was a process of innovations by periphrasis in the verb system, and by prepositions and postpositions in the nominal system, typologically resulting in an analytic language, with remnants of inflection distinctions.

i. Verb system. The distinctions between the categories of person, as well as those of tense and mood, in the sense of traditional grammar, were as follows:

A. Tense. The tense system inherited from Aryan consists of three sub-systems, namely present, aorist, and perfect. 1. The present system was marked by a range of formants (including zero), added to various forms of the root (e.g., present formant *-a* in *bar-a* "to carry, bear," but formant *-nau* in *kṛ-nau* "to make, do"). Actually, this system had temporal distinctions. They were marked by differences in the personal endings, generally speaking by the addition of *-i* in the present tense and its absence in the past tense. In addition, the past forms tended to be marked by a so-called augment, i.e., a prefix-like marker *a-* (for example Old Persian present indicative *baranti* "they carry" vs. imperfect *a-baran(t)* "they carried"; cf. Old Gk. *e-*). 2. An aorist system developed, at least partially, as the distinction between a present and past aorist, on the model of the present system. 3. The perfect system had distinctly different endings from those of the present. It also partially developed a distinction between present, with its own endings quite dissimilar to those of the other two subsystems, and past endings, on the model of the present system.

B. Aspect. The distinctions between the inherited system of present-perfect-aorist is not one of time and tense, but one of aspect. That is, the morpho-syntactical markers express the speaker's view of whether an action or a situation is 1. ongoing or habitual; 2. (just) done; or 3. done. It is the augment and the personal endings that indicat tense, present and past (e.g., 1. pres. *kṛ-nau-ti* "makes"; 2. aorist *čar-t* [<**kert*] "made"; 3. perfect [reduplicated) *ča-k(a)r-a* "has made").

C. Verbal voice. There was a further distinction of what is called "verbal voice." This involves the distinction between active and so-called "middle" verbal voice, the former indicating the active involvement of the agent/subject, the latter indicating that the action or situation affected the agent, often translated as passive. Morphologically, this is marked in personal endings (e.g., imp. 2nd sing. active ending zero vs. middle ending *-swa*/*-hwa* in *dāh* "give!" vs. *dāhwa* "give for yourself, accept"; *bara-ti* "carries" vs. *bara-tai*" is carried"). In addition, there was the so-called passive, generally expressed by a marker *-y-*; there was its "opposite," the "causative" (e.g., act. *kṛ-nau-ti* "makes," pass. *kṛ-ya-ti* "is being made," caus. *kār-aya-ti* "causes to make').

D. Mood. In addition, the speaker could convey possibility (subjunctive forms, generally marked by *-ā*), suggestion (optative, generally marked by *-ī*; e.g., from *kar-*: ind. *kṛ-nau-ti* "he makea," subj. *kṛ-nau-a-t* "he shall make," opt. *kṛ-nu-yā-t* "he may make," imp. *kṛ-nu-di* "he must make!" or from bar-: *bar-a-ti* "he carries," *bar-ā-t* [<*bar-a-a-t*] "he shall carry," *bar-a-i-t* "he may carry," *bar-a-tu* "he must carry!"), and a wealth of other modalities, such as future marked by *-sya* (e.g., *wax-šya* "I will say" and *sau-šya-nt-* "going to save, future savior").

The most crucial loss was that of the inherited threefold distinction of aspects, i.e., of present, aorist, and perfect, each of which had a present and a past tense. In virtually all of the modern languages/dialects, and certainly in Persian, a new ternary system of aspects has re-emerged.

Already in Old Persian and Younger Avestan the perfect had merged with the aorist into a past system. Subsequently, with the loss of the distinction between primary and secondary personal endings and the loss of the so-called augment *a-* marking past, the formal distinction between present and past was lost. New past/perfect forms developed. They are already found in both Old Persian and Avestan: they are based on the old perfect participle in **-ta*, followed by forms of "to be"; the past agent is expressed by the oblique of the noun, pronoun, or corresponding personal suffix, e.g., *imā tayat manā kṛta-m āhā* (this [is] what by me is made, i.e., I had made it, Mid. Pers. *-m kard*, *be-m-ka(rd)* or similar, found in most NW dialects; for origin of this construction see Pirejko, 1979). Most modern Iranian dialects still have this way of expressing past forms of the verb. It used to be called the passive construction, because in Latin or English it only can be conveyed literally in the passive mood. It now tends to be called the ergative (i.e., the "doer case"), indicating that in past tenses, the transative agent (the "doer") is specially marked, usually by an oblique case ending. (The term was first used for a similar phenomenon in Caucasian languages, which tent to indicate the agent by a special marker, sometimes also in non-past tenses; see Boeder, 1979.) It is also widely found in ancient Near Eastern Languages such as Sumerian (see Steiner, 1979).

Typologically, these forms and their derivatives in the modern dialects resulted in the re-establishment of the ternary distinction of aspect, e.g., contemporary Persian (see Windfuhr, 1985; inferential added, see below):

	imperfective	aorist	perfective
Present	mī-rav-ad	raf-t	raf-t-a ast
Past	mī-raf-t	raf-t	raf-t-a būd
Infer.	mī-raf-t-a ast	raf-t-a ast	raf-t-a būd-a ast

Taking Persian as reference for Iranian in general, without assuming that these categories are pan-Iranian today, *raf-t* implies not only the past, "he/she went," but occasionally a sense of the present, as for an example "there she goes," and even the future, such as *šāyad mā ham raf-t-īm* "we will certainly/ perhaps go too."

The loss of the inherited Aryan past imperfective, marked by the prefix *a-*, is not universal. Some dialects, such as Yaḡnōbī (continuing earlier Sogdian), derive their past/preterite from the present stem. In the west, Gōrānī and Ṭālešī base their past imperfective forms on the old present stem, so the ergative construction did not affect them (although it affected the perfective and aorist); Ṭālešī has prefix *a-* plus present stem plus *ī*, Gōrānī has present stem plus *ēn*: Gōrānī imperf. past 3rd sing. masc. *ūs-ēn-e* "he was sleeping" vs. Ṭālešī *-ī* and Gōrānī *-ēn*, both derived from earlier optative endings **-ē/-ēn*, which already in OIr. could express imperfective past (e.g., Av. formal opt. *-ōi-t* in *yavata xšyōit Yimo* "as long as Yima would rule"; Y. 9.5). The Ṭālešī prefix a- may be a retention of the old augment a-.

As to other categories, dialects have developed multiple ways of differentiating their verb systems after the virtual collapse of the old system. Such development appears to be, at least partially, conditioned externally, such as through interference from Turkic. Differentiation is achieved mostly by periphrasis, which in some cases resulted in new synthetic forms. Such is the case with the widespread development of imperfect markers, serving to disambiguate this aspect from the unmarked perfective aspect. The markers were derived variously from the original temporal/locational adverbs, frequently from **hama-*, (a cognate of Eng.) "same," such as **ham-ayawa-*, e.g., early New Persian *hamē* (contemporary NPers. *mī-*), to which functionally corresponds **hadā* "same time/place," reflected in dialectal variants *de-*, *a(d)-* (Kurdish etc.). Similarly widespread is the development of periphrastic constructions expressing *Aktionsarten*, such as the progressive (Eng. "I am doing"), by a great variety of means, such as verbs semantically connotating continuity or incipiency, e.g., Persian of Persia: *dār-am mī-rav-am*; Kabuli Persian *raf-t-a mē-rav-om*; Tajiki Persian *raf-t-a īst-od-a am*, all meaning "I am going, am about to go" (*dār-* "to hold, keep," *rav-* "to go," *īst-* "to stand, be in"), or constructions based on locative markers added to the nominalized verb, e.g., Gīlakī *kara amon dar-a* "he is coming" (*kar* "work, doing," *amo-n* "coming," *dar-* "in (to)," *-a*, 3rd sing. copula). Likewise frequent are modal constructions. These include a future marked by *kām-* (wish) or forms derived from "to want, wish" with various etyma. Particularly noteworthy is the frequent development of the category of inference, expressing hearsay, assumption, conclusion, and in general the distancing of a speaker, i.e., conveying that he/she did not witness an action or situation (example from cotemporary Persian literature: "*Be-ṭowr-e kollī ānče az har kojā dar-yāfta-am in ast ke ostād Mākān mard-e rāzdār-ī būda . . . kamtar šūḵī mīkarda . . . hīč-kas be zendegī-e dāḵelī-e ū wāred našoda būda ast* "In general what I could find out from here and there was that Ostād Mākān was a secretive man. . . He rarely made any jokes . . . Nobody had gotten through to his inner life"; ʿAlawī, pp. 13-14).

Again, there are retentions. Inflectional mood, such as the subjunctive derived from an earlier marker *-ā* (note the relic *b-ā-d* "may he be," as in *zenda b-ā-d* "may he live" in contemporary Persian), was retained in a good number of dialects, as was the inflectional passive/inchoative derived from *-yā*, still preserved in early Judeo-Persian and some Persian dialects (e.g., Sangesarī: *ešt-ende* "he stands up" vs. *ešt-i-nde* "he will stand up"; Zāzā: *araq-y* "to drink liquor").

ii. Nominal system (see CASES). The most serious loss was that of the distinction between nominative and accusative. These were the two morphological cases that distinguish the two most crucial syntactic cases, namely subject and direct object. Most modern dialects innovated by the grammaticalization of preposition and/or postpositions, mostly with inherent directional meaning, e.g., Persian *-rā* to mark the specific object, originally "for the sake of, concerning" to include later directional and indirect object function, or Sangsarī *-de* from **antar->dar* "in(to)." The greatest variety is found in the eastern dialects. In addition, a more rigorous word order developed, typologically resulting in the (unmarked) order of S-O-V (subject-object-verb, compare English S-V-O). Still, many modern dialects did retain reflexes of earlier inflectional distinctions, generally indicated by the opposition of unmarked direct case and marked oblique case: sing. *-i*(<**-ahya*) and plur. *-ān* (< **-ānām*), even in the early stages of the most reduced Middle West dialect, Middle Persian (see CASES). Typologically, the function of the oblique, which derives from an original genitive/dative, was extended, as the morphologically marked form, to also, or exclusively, mark that of specific direct object. In several dialects this was later further disambiguated by adpositions (e.g., Sangsarī dir. obj. 3rd sing. near deictic *nē-de*, where *nē* is the oblique, and *-de* the specific direct object marker; see CASES).

Gender. Most notably, the distinction between masculine and feminine gender is preserved in many eastern as well as western dialects. Most conservative in terms of retention is Pashto, the nominal inflection of which also retains reflexes of the free accentual system of Indo-Iranian.

Iranian dialectology and history. In terms of retention, then, the two extremes are Eastern Iranian Pashto and Western Iranian Persian. And, contrary to an impression still widely advertized, modern Western Iranian dialects on the whole may be more conservative than Eastern Iranian. It may be noted that all evidence for the retention of the nominal oblique in Middle and Modern dialects, East as well as West, follows the merger of the earlier distinctions in Old Persian, rather than that in Avestan.

Some of the problems involved in the study of dialects include the criteria for groupings. They are often based on the selection of a few features. Nevertheless, even on the basis of a few forms, specialists are often able to eeconstruct the full pattern of the paradigm involvred. Another problem is that descriptions are often based on the information of only one or few informants, usually from the older generation, on the assumption that they preserve an older, and thus more original, stage of their dialect. Only more recently have generational differences and those in local subdivisions been addressed (e.g., Yarshater, 1969). In general, the systematic study of the socio-linguistic aspect of dialectology has been largely neglected. One such neglected study is social affiliation, which often involves diglossia, i.e., the use of different varieties or styles of a dialect or language, as well as bilingualism and multilingualism, characterized by a speaker using different languages in different social contexts, or language switch, and language loss, all contributing to linguistic diversity and groupings. Similarly, studies of the effects of linguistic substrates, adstrates, and superstrates is little developed. Interference between Iranian and non-Iranian, however, especially on the margins of the Iranian speaking areas, has attracted the continuous attention of scholars, such as Iranian and Armenian, Turkic, Arabic, Indo-Aryan, and Dravidian Brahui.

Overall, the available data, not only for the earlier stages, result in frustration. Nevertheless, the objective of clearly identifying the synchrony of a linguistic system as a functioning system at any one point in time, so as to establish systemic certainty prior to comparing items or parts thereof, is increasingly being accomplished.

The focus on selective features and feature clusters allows one to trace at least to some degree larger movements where historical evidence is lacking. In his study of the origins of Kurdish, MacKenzie (1961, pp. 68-86) suggests a path and diachrony of the moves of the Kurds and other Iranian groups into and within northwest Persia and the Fertile Crescent. Windfuhr (1975) suggests a symbiotic area of pre-Persians, -Kurds, and -Baluch in the northeast prior to their moving into their present areas, namely southwest, northwest, and southeast Peria, respectively. As another example, the isolated change of **Θr* > *š* found in some lexical items in Sangsarī in the foothills some 300 km east of Tehran should be linked to a similar change found in Middle Eastern Iranian. The distinctive formation of the present indicative based on the old present participle in **-ant* is found in the Māzandarānī dialects; in Sangsarī and neighboring dialects; in Harzandī (where it is reduced to the subjunctive stem), now in northern Azerbaijan, and in Zāzā, now in eastern Turkey (e.g., Sangesarī: *ner-end-ī*, Zāzā: *niš-ann-ān* "I sit down"). This reflects the retention of a feature that may go back to Old Iranian and suggests earlier contingency among these dialects. Both Eastern Iranian Pashto and Western Iranian Kurdish have subjunctive/counterfactual formations with prefix *be-* and affix *-ā-* (e.g., Pashto perfect conditional I and III: *lwedəlay w-āy*, *lwedəlay ba w-āy* "if it had fallen, (then) it would have fallen"; Kurd: *bī-kawt-im-āyā*, *(bi)kawt-(i/ā) bam (āyā)* "if I fell I had fallen").

The continuing dialectical dynamics is shown by the fact that these dialect groups have considerably adjusted to the dialectal features of their hosts on all levels, which provides evidence for the relative ease of change. This includes syntactic features. For example, it was early recognized that in the Southwestern dialects dependent nouns and adjectives follow the head noun, but vice versa in the Northwestern dialects. The seeming Southwestern feature is found in much of Western Iranian, except for Tātī and Ṭālešī and related dialects. The latter also have postpositions as opposed to Perside prepositions. But fossilized personal pronouns derived from **haca-* (from; e.g., *čemen* "mine"< **haca mana* "from me") suggest an earlier stage with prepositions, as opposed to postpositions in Turkic.

There is much evidence for ethnic and linguistic dynamics through the ages. To cite just one indigenous source, the multilingual and erudite medieval Kurd Bitlisi in his *Šaraf-nāma*, a history of the Kurds written in chancery Persian with poetry and poetic verve, suggests that the Kurds' origin may well be multiple. Known and assumed moves, by force or voluntarily, on a large or small scale, most recently as an effect of the wars of Persia, Afghanistan, and Tajikistan, continue to turn the dialectal kaleidoscope and hologram.

See also AFGHANISTAN v. LANGUAGES; AZERBAIJAN vii. THE IRANIAN LANGUAGES OF AZERBAIJAN; BALUCHESTAN iii. BALUCHI LANGUAGE AND LITERATURE; CENTRAL ASIA xiii. IRANIAN LANGUAGES; CENTRAL

DIALECTS; CHORASMIA iii. THE CHORASMIAN LANGUAGE; and entries under individual languages and dialects.

Bibliography: Major overviews: *Grundriss. Iranistik* I. *Linguistik*, HO I/4, Leiden, 1958. I. M. Oranskiĭ, *Vvedenie v iranskuyu filologiyu* (Introduction to Iranian philology), Moscow, 1960. Idem, *Iranskie jazyk*, Moscow, 1963, tr. J. Blau as *Les langues iraniennes*, Paris, 1977; tr. K. Kešāvarz as *Moqaddama-ye feqh al-loğa-ye īrānī*, Tehran, 1358 Š./1979. Idem, *Die neuiranischen Sprachen der Sowjetunion*, 2 vols., Paris and The Hague, 1975. Idem, *Iranskie jazyki v istoricheskom osvescheniĭ* (The Iranian languages in historical view), Moscow, 1979. V. S. Rastorgueva, ed., *Opyt istoriko-tipologicheskogo issledovaniya iranskikh jazykov* (Essays on the historical-typological study of Iranian languages), 2 vols., Moscow, 1975. Idem, ed., *Osnovy iranskogo jazykoznaniya yazyki*, 4 vols., Moscow, 1979-87. H. Reichelt, in *Grundriss der indogermanischen Sprach-und Altertumskunde* II, Berlin and Leipzig, 1927, pp. 1-84. R. Schmitt, ed., *Compendium Linguarum Iranicarum*, Wiesbaden, 1989. Sebeok et al., eds., *Current Trends in Linguistic*, 6 vols., The Hague, 1963-70, V, pp. 450-77; VI, pp. 9-135.

Comprehensive etymologies: *Air Wb.* Horn, *Etymologie*. Hübschmann, *Persische Studien*. *Iranisches Personennamenbuch*.

Dialectology: Ī. Afšār, "Ketāb-šenāsī-e fārsī-e čāp šoda dar Īrān dar bāra-ye gūyeshā-ye Īrānī," in *Études Irano-Aryennes offertes à Gilbert Lazard*, Paris, 1989, pp. 3-27. Idem, "Ketāb-šenāsī-e zabānhā wa lahjahā-ye īrānī," *FIZ* 3, 1334 Š./ 1955, pp. 78-93. B. ʿAlawī, *Čašmhā-yaš*, 3rd ed. 1357 Š./1978. F. C. Andreas, *Iranische Dialektaufzeichnungen aus dem Nachlass von F.C. Andreas*, ed. A. Christensen, Berlin, 1939. Č.-ʿA. Aʿẓamī Sangsarī and G. L. Windfuhr, *Vāža-nāma-ye sangsarī bā moqaddama-ī az dastūr-e ān*, Tehran, 1351 Š./ 1972. H. W. Bailey, "Persia. ii Language and Dialects," in *EI*[1] III, pp. 1050-58. W. Boeder, "Ergative Syntax and Morphology in Language Change. The South Caucasian Languages," in F. Plank, ed., *Ergativity. Towards A Theory of Grammatical Relations*, London and New York, 1979, pp. 435-80. G. Bossong, *Empirische Universalienforschnung. Differentielle Objektmarkierung in den neuiranischen Sprachen*, Tübingen, 1985. L. L. Cavalli-Sforza, "Easiest To Get, e.g., Genes, Peoples and Languages," *Scientific American*, Nov. 1991, pp. 104-10. A. Christensen, *Contributions à la dialectologie iranienne*, 2 vols., Copenhagen, 1930-35. D. I. Edel'man, *Osnovnye voprosy lingvisticheskoĭ geografii. Na materiale indo-iranskikh yazykov* (Fundumental problems of linguistic geography. Based on data of the Indo-Iranian languages), Moscow, 1968. Idem, *Sravitel'naya grammatika vostochnoiranskih yazykov. Fonologiya* (Comparative grammar of the East Iranian languages. Phonology), Moscow, 1986. R. E. Emmerick, "Indo-Iranian languages. The Iranian Languages," in *The New Encyclopedia Britannica, Macropaedia* IX, Chicago, 1976, pp. 450-57. A. Erhart, *Struktura indoíránských yazykov* (The structure of the Indo-Iranian languages), Brno, 1980. B. Farahvašī, *Vāža-nāma-ye ḵūrī*, Tehran, 1355 Š./1976. Th. Gamkrelidze and V. V. Ivanov, "The Ancient Near East and the Indo-European Problem," *Soviet Studies in History* 2/2, 1983, pp. 1-53. W. Geiger, "Allgemeine Übersicht über die Dialekte und ihre Gruppierung," in *Grundriss* I/2, pp. 412-23. G. A. Grierson, *Linguistic Survey of India*. X *Specimens of Languages of the Ēranian Family*, Calcutta, 1921. H. Haarmann, *Die indirekte Erlebnisform als grammatische Kategorie. Eine eurasische Isoglosse*, Wiesbaden, 1970. H. Haider and R. Zwanziger, "Relatively Attributive. The 'ezâfe'- Construction from Old Iranian to Modern Persian," in J. Fisiak, ed., *Historical Syntax*, Paris and The Hague, 1984, pp. 137-72. W. B. Henning, "The Ancient Language of Azerbaijan," *TPS*, 1954, pp. 157-77. W. L. Heston, *Selected Problems in Fifth to Tenth Century Iranian syntax*, Ph.D. Dissertation, University of Pennsylvania, 1976. W. Ivanov, "The Gabri Dialect," *Revista degli Studi Orientali* 15, 1934, pp. 1-58; 16, 1935, pp. 31-97; 17, 1936, pp. 1-39. K. J. Krahnke, *Linguistic Relationships in Central Iran*, Ph.D. Dissertation, University of Michigan, 1976.

G. Lazard, "Dialectologie de la langue persane d'après les textes de Xme et XIme siècles ap. J.-C.," *NDA* Tabrīz 13, 1340 Š./1961, pp. 241-58. Idem, *La langue des plus anciens monuments de la prose persane*, Paris, 1963. Idem, "La dialectologie du judéo-persane," *Studies in Bibliography and Folklore* 8, 1968, pp. 77-98. Idem, "Pahlavi, pârsi, dari: Les langues de l'Iran d'après Ibn al-Muqaffaʿ," in *Iran and Islam*, ed. C. E. Bosworth, 1971, pp. 361-91. Idem, "The Rise of the New Persian language," in *Camb. Hist. Iran* IV, pp. 595-632. Idem, "Le morpheme *râ* en persan et les relations actancielles," *Bulletin de la Société de linguistique* 77/1, 1982, pp. 177-207. Idem, "Actance Variation and Categories of the Object," in F. Plank, ed., *Ergativity. Towards A Theory of Grammatical Relations*, London and New York, 1984, pp. 269-92. Idem, "L'inférentiel ou passé distancié en persan," *St. Ir.* 14, 1985, pp. 27-42. Idem, "Formes et fonctions du passif et de l'antipassif," *Actances* 2, 1986, pp. 7-57. Idem, "Échelles de transitivité," in G. François-Geiger, ed., *La Transitivité et ses correlats*, 1987, pp. 109-19. P. Lecoq, "La classement des languages irano-aryennes occidentales," in C.-H de Fouchécour and Ph. Gignoux, eds., *Études Irano-Aryennes offertes à Gilbert Lazard*, Paris, 1989, pp. 247-64. W. Lentz, "Die nordiranischen Elemente in der neupersischen Literatursprache bei Firdôsī," *ZII* 4, 1926, pp. 251-316. D. N. MacKenzie, "Gender in Kurdish,"

BSO(A)S 16, 1954, pp. 529-41. Idem, *Kurdish Dialect Studies*, 2 vols., London etc., 1961-62. Idem, "The Origins of Kurdish," *TPS*, 1961, pp. 68-86. Y. Māhyār Nawwābī, *Zabān-e konūnī-e Āḏarbāyjān*, Tabrīz, 1333 Š./1954. O. Mann and K. Hadank, *Kurdish-Persische Forschungen*, I, II, III. 1-2, IV. 1-2, Berlin, 1906, 1932. A. Marʿašī, *Vāža-nāma-ye gūyeš-e Gīlakī*, Rašt, 1363 Š./1984. C. P. Masica, *Defining a Linguistic Area. South Asia*, Chicago, 1976. M. Moʿīn, "Zabān o lahjahā dar *Borhān-e qāṭeʿ*," in *Borhān-e qāṭeʿ*, ed. M. Moʿīn, I, pp. XCVII-CX. G. Morgenstierne, *Report on A Linguistic Mission to Afghanistan*, Oslo, 1926. Idem, *Indo-Iranian Frontier Languages*, 2 vols., Oslo, 1929-38. Idem, *Report on a Linguistic Mission to North-Western India*, Oslo, 1932. Idem, "Bemerkungen zum Wort-Akzent in den Gathas und im Pashto," *MSS* 42, 1983, pp. 167-75. M. Mortażawī, *Zabān-e dīrīn-e Āḏarbāyjān*, Tehran, 1365 Š./1986. *Neue Methodologie in der Iranistik*, Wiesbaden, 1974 (Lentz's Festschrift).

J. Payne, "The Decay of Ergativity in the Pamir Languages," *Lingua* 51, 1980, pp. 147-86. Idem, "Iranian languages," in B. Comrie, *The Languages of the Soviet Union*, Cambridge, 1981, pp. 158-79. Idem, "Iranian Languages," in ed. B. Comrie, *The World's Major Languages*, London, 1987, pp. 514-22. L. Pirejko, "On the Genesis of the Ergative Construction in Indo-Iranian," in F. Plank, ed., *Ergativity. Towards A Theory of Grammatical Relations*, London and New York, 1979, pp. 481-88. N. Rāst, "Fehrest-e maʾāḵeḏ-e zabānhā wa lahjahā-ye Īrānī," *FIZ* 1, 1332 Š./1953, pp. 1-40. V. S. Rastorgueva, *Opyt sravitel'nogo izucheniya tadzhiksikh govorov* (Comparative study of the Tajiki dialects), Moscow, 1964. G. Redard, "Panorama linguistique de l'Iran," *Asiatische Studien* 8, 1954, pp. 137-48. Idem, "Projet d'un Atlas linguistique de l'Iran," in *Akten des 24. Internationalen Orientalisten-kongresses*, Wiesbaden, 1959, pp. 440-44. Idem, "État des travaux et publication. Quelques cartes onomasiologiques," in *Atlas linguistique des parlers iraniens. Atlas de l'Afghanistan*, University of Bern Institut für Sprachwissenschaft, Arbeitspapiere 3, Bern, 1974, pp. 7-19. A. V. Rossi, "La varietà linguistica nell'Iran achemenide," *AIOUN* 3, 1981, pp. 141-96. M. M. Sakhokija, *Posessiv'nost', perekhodnost' i ergativ'nost'. Tipologocheskoe sopostavlenie drevnepersidskikh, drevnearmjanskikh i drevnegruzinskikh konstrukciĭ* (Posessivity, transitivity, and ergativity. Typological comparison of the Old Persian, Old Armenian, and Old Georgian constructions), Tbilisi, 1985. R. Schmitt, "Aryans," in *EIr* II, pp. 684-87. H. J. Seiler, *Relativsatz, Apposition und Attribut*, Wiesbaden, 1960. V. S. Sokolova, *Ocherki po fonetike iranskihkh yazykov* (Studies on the phonetics of the Iranian languages), Moscow, 1953. J. S. Sorūšīān, *Farhang-e Behdīnān*, ed. M. Sotūda, Tehran, 1335 Š./1954. M. Sotūda, *Farhang-e Semnānī. Amṯāl o eṣṭelāḥāt o ašʿār*, Tehran, 1356 Š./1977. G. Steiner, "The Intransative-Passival Conception of the Verb in Languages of the Ancient Near East," in F. Plank, ed., *Ergativity. Towards A Theory of Grammatical Relations*, London and New York, 1979, pp. 185-216. D. L. Stilo, "The Tati Language Group in the Sociolinguistic Context of Northwestern Iran and Transcaucasia," *Iranian Studies* 14, 1981, pp. 137-87. P. Tedesco, "Dialektologie." G. L. Windfuhr, "Isoglosses. A Sketch on Persians and Parthians, Kurds and Medes," in *Monumentum H. S. Nyberg* II, Acta Iranica 5, Tehran and Liège, 1975, pp. 457-72. Idem, "The Verbal Category of Inference in Persian," *Monumentum George Morgenstierne* II, Acta Iranica 22, Leiden, 1982, pp. 263-87. Idem, "A Spatial Model for Tense, Aspect, and Mood," *Folia Linguistica* 19, 1985, pp. 415-61. Idem, "Convergence. Iranian Talyshi and Turkic Azari," *Select Papers from SALA-7. South Asian Languages Roundtable Conference*, Bloomington, Ind., 1987, pp. 385-405. E. Yarshater, *A Grammar of Southern Tati Dialects*, The Hague, 1969. Idem, "Iran and Afghanistan," in Th. A. Sebeok, ed., *Current Trends in Linguistics* VI, The Hague, 1970, pp. 669-89. Idem, "Zabānhā wa lahjahā-ye īrānī," in Dehḵodā, I, *Moqaddama*, pp. 9-25. V. A. Zhukovskiy, *Materialy dlya izucheniya persid-skikh' narechiĭ* (Materials for the study of Persian dialects), 3 vols., St. Petersburg, 1888-1922.

(GERNOT L. WINDFUHR)

DĪĀRBAKR. See AMIDA.

DIASPORA, Iranian. See also DEPORTATIONS.

i. *In Pre-Islamic times.*
ii. *Persians in India.*
iii. *Persians in Southeast Asia.*
iv. *Persians in Ottomon Turkey.*
v. *Persians in the Caucasus and Central Asia in the late 19th and early 20th century.*
vi. *Persians in Iraq.*
vii. *Persians in southern ports of the Persian Gulf.*
viii. *In the Post-revolutionary period.*
ix. *Afghan refugees in Pakestan.*
x. *Afghan refugees in Persia.*

i. IN PRE-ISLAMIC TIMES

The Achaemenid empire attained its fullest extent under its first three kings; and for the next two centuries or so Iranians colonized in numbers the most attractive of its non-Iranian territories. Alexander's conquest of the empire in the 4th century B.C.E. led, under his successors, to those colonists being cut off from Persia, but they proved generally able to maintain their ethnic and cultural identity under alien rule for many generations. Those who settled in Babylonia and Armenia (q.v.) are not considered here as part of this diaspora, because Iran in time regained those lands, and Babylonia (q.v.) in particular became an integrated part of the Parthian and Sasanian empires.Information about the original colonists is meager, but at its best for Egypt (largely from Aramaic papyri) and Asia Minor (from notices by Greek writers, a small number of tomb-carvings, Aramaic inscriptions, and significant devices on satrapal coins). There is also the evidence of personal and place names. That of personal names can only be safely used, however, to identify Iranians where there is additional information, or when such names occur in groups, or in significant associations and settings, because during the Achaemenid period Persian names were sometimes adopted quite extensively by their non-Iranian subjects (e.g., in Lydia; Zgusta; Boyce and Grenet, p. 206). Even in post-Achaemenid times some Persian names (notably Miθradāta/Mithradates, and other Mithra-names) were used by non-Iranians in western regions. Conversely, some individuals of Persian descent under Macedonian rule are known to have adopted Greek names. The hereditary high priests (*archimagoi*) of the temple of Anaitis at Hypaipa in Lydia provide a striking instance (Robert, 1976, pp. 31-33; Boyce and Grenet, p. 224). For all regions except Egypt most of the evidence for the Iranian diaspora comes from post-Achaemenid times.

Most satrapies of the empire were governed by Persians, the wealthier and most important ones being generally entrusted to royal princes; but some of the minor non-Iranian satrapies became hereditary fiefs in the families of Persian nobles, who settled permanently there. Damascus may have been one instance, but the certain examples are Dascylium and Eastern Armenia (qq.v). All satrapal courts would have been frequented by the local Iranian nobility, and, reflecting the customs and manners of the imperial court, would have been centers of Persian culture. In foreign parts which were attractive to Iranians many Persian landowners received their estates from the king with the duty of rendering military service when called on. Many of these fiefdoms were probably granted as a result of confiscations after conquest, but the smaller populations of those days would also have allowed for new estates to be created in fertile areas. The Iranians were not an urban people, and the way of life which these expatriates followed appears to have reflected that of Iran itself, with the nobles living for much of the year on their estates. In Cappadocia, with important high-roads and passes that needed guarding, many hilltop fortresses are recorded (Strabo 12.2.9), a number of which were presumably from Achaemenid times the seats of Persian nobles. In Lydia, with its fertile river-valleys, the only dwelling of a Persian landowner to be described (Xenophon, *Anabasis* 7.8.9-23) was a fortified manor house on his own estate. He had armed retainers in his service, as well as slaves to work the land; and when the house was attacked by Greek raiders, a beacon was lit which brought a Persian neighbor to his aid, with his own body of fighting men. Some official forces also responded to the alarm, and the marauders were driven off. The incident suggests a number of Persian estates in this, and doubtless other, fertile regions of western Asia Minor, with mutual support among the landowners and in general effective Persian vigilance and control.

The royal road which led from Sardis, Lydia's capital, east to Susa and Persepolis was said to pass for its whole length "through country that is inhabited and safe" (Herodotus 5.52.3). This great highway made much of central Asia Minor accessible to Iranian colonists, who were attracted by its valleys and wide plains. Noble fiefholders naturally had an interest in developing their estates, and this interest was quickened in them as Zoroastrians, for whom good cultivation of the land is a religious duty. Cyrus the Younger (q.v.), when satrap in Asia Minor, is reported to have given incentives to "anyone that was a skillful manager, ... stocking the land of which he had the direction and securing income from it" (Xenophon, *Anabasis* 9.16) and to have been ready himself to labor on his own estates, planting for instance fruit trees with his own hands (Xenophon, *Oeconomicus* 4.24). It seems that nobles must have brought skilled farmworkers with them from Iran, for in the 4th century C.E. many villages scattered about Cappadocia were entirely inhabited by Iranians, descendants of the original colonists (St. Basil, *Letter* 258). A satrapal coin from Level Cilicia (a rich and favored area for Iranian settlement) shows on the reverse a ploughman in Iranian clothes, driving a team of oxen (Starr, p. 92). Such country people, living in small, culturally unified communities, appear to have been among the most stable and conservative groups in the Iranian diaspora.

Among them were to be found ex-soldiers. Great centers of imperial power, such as Memphis or Sardis, and important frontier posts were garrisoned by imperial troops, Iranians among them, whose Persian officers formed another element in the provincial aristocracy. Sometimes groups of Iranian soldiers were given grants of land with the obligation to serve again if called on. Achaemenid armies were generally accompanied by women, and the long survival of some of these settlements must owe much to their being, like those of the peasant farmers, ethnically and culturally homogeneous, founded by Iranian families. It is thought that the Hyrcanians who gave their name to Hyrcanis in Lydia (Strabo 13.4.13) were such a group of military colonists, as were the Maebozani of Gölmermere (Robert, 1982; Boyce and Grenet, p. 218). A Greek poet of the 4th century B.C.E. spoke of "Bactrian maidens dwelling beside the Halys river," that is, in Cappadocia (Athenaeus, *Deipnosophists* 14.636), and they may well have been among the descendants of Bactrian ex-soldiers.

In nobles' households there were scribes, probably

mostly of Iranian stock and certainly of Iranian cultural heritage, who used Persian chancellery Aramaic as a written language, and whose distant descendants were still to be found in eastern Asia Minor in Roman imperial times, writing letters on their lords' behalf (Diodorus 19.23; Russell, pp. 47-48.), or drawing up the texts of inscriptions (Grégoire, pp. 434-47; Boyce and Grenet, pp. 268, 272-74). Other scribes must have staffed the satrapal chancelleries and judicial courts, where the most distinguished of their order would have sat as judges. There are records of Persians as members of Babylonian judicial panels (Cook, p. 174). In a trilingual inscription at Xanthos, capital of Lycia (where there is abundant evidence from monuments and personal names of an Iranian presence), the Aramaic text has a sprinkling of Persian words. Recording a religious foundation, it sheds light by its choice of terms on the local Zoroastrianism (Dupont-Sommer; Humbach, pp. 30-32; Boyce and Grenet, p. 476). In the first century C.E. an inscription from near Amorion in Phrygia (by then, at that place, in Greek) records the endowment by a local landowner of an annual soul-ceremony (a characteristic Zoroastrian observance) during the festival of Mehragān (Ramsay; Vermaseren, I, pp. 50-51; Boyce and Grenet, pp. 259-60).

Zoroastrian priests themselves were an important element in the Iranian diaspora. Armies would have been accompanied by many priests, some ministering to officers, others to men, and when ex-soldiers were settled on the land, their priests with their families presumably remained with them. Other priests are likely to have come out with the peasant farmers, and more exalted ones with the nobility. Originally they were known collectively in eastern Mediterranean lands as *magousaioi*, a Greco-Semitic plural for Persian *magu* "Mage, priest" (Cumont, 1896-99, I, p. 9, n. 5; Telegdi, p. 229; Boyce and Grenet, p. 256); but in time, locally at least, this term came to be used for Persian colonists generally (Bardesanes, apud Cumont, 1896-99, I, p. 10, n. l.; St. Basil, L*etter* 258), with Greek *magoi* used for the priests themselves. As these usages suggest, to outside observers all Iranians were Zoroastrians, ethnic and religious labels being used interchangeably, and this probably reflects the broad reality.

As in Persia, so in the diaspora, in addition to priests who ministered to lay families in the traditional way, there were temple priests. There is a fair amount of information about Zoroastrian sanctuaries in Asia Minor, the oldest according to tradition being at Zela in Pontic Cappadocia, founded in the 6th century B.C.E. by Cyrus II the Great (q.v.) himself or his generals. According to the Iranian custom of worshipping in high places, the sanctuary was established on a hill, banked up yet higher and encircled by a wall (Strabo 11.8.4; Julius Caesar, *The Alexandrian Wars*, chap. 77; Cumont, 1906, p. 191). Later this hill bore one of the imposing temples to Anāhīd (q.v.), by which the presence of Iranians is strikingly attested in Asia Minor. One other temple has been identified in Cappadocia, from a fragmentary inscription at ancient Nitalis (Harper), but most are known from Lydia and south-west Phrygia. There were two royal foundations, built by Cyrus the Younger and Artaxerxes II (q.v.) at Hiera Kome (Hierocaesarea) and Hypaipa, and others, probably founded by Persian nobles, at Celenae-Apamea, Gölmermere, Kula, Philadelphia and Sariçam (see Boyce and Grenet, index, s.vv.). Achaemenid foundations have been excavated at Hypaipa, but otherwise the meagre remains (including inscriptions) come from imperial Roman times, when peace returned to the region after many vicissitudes. These temples "of the Persian goddess" flourished then and were wealthy. Their priests were culturally Hellenized (the inscriptions are all in Greek), and the high priests took part in the public life of what was then the Roman province of Asia. But it is recorded that at Hierocaesarea and Hypaipa the liturgies were in an unknown language, presumably Avestan, and sacred fires were reverently maintained (Pausanias 5.27.5-6). The continuance of traditional forms of worship down to this time is attested also for Cappadocia, where there were separate sanctuaries for sacred fires and cult statues (Strabo 15.3.15). The existence of fire temples in the 3rd century C.E. in Syria, Cilicia, Cappadocia, and Armenia is attested in the inscription of the Sasanian high priest Kartīr at Kaʿba-ye Zardošt (l. 8). Temples were clearly important in enabling expatriate Iranian communities to maintain their identity by providing them with centers for religious and social life, while the great holy places, by attracting pilgrims for their annual feast-days, would have brought together Iranians from wide areas. In western Asia Minor records of "Persian" temples cease from the 3rd century C.E. when they were suppressed by Christian edict, but still in the 6th century Ḵosrow I Anōšīravān negotiated with a Byzantine emperor to have fire temples rebuilt in his domains, most probably in Cappadocia (Ṭabarī, I, pp. 1000-01; Nöldeke, *Geschichte der Perser*, p. 288; Boyce and Grenet, p. 257).

In the 2nd-3rd centuries C.E. Bardesanes wrote of "the descendants of Persians who lived out of Persia" as being still numerous in Egypt, Phrygia, and Galatia, and maintaining their traditional customs there. Traces of them in Egypt generally amount to little more than proper names, but from the 3rd century B.C.E. there is reference to a *mithraion* - presumably a Zoroastrian sanctuary - in Fayoum (Wilcken, pp. 71-72.), and there is record from the 4th century C.E. of "Basilios the Persian" practicing, presumably as a member of a community, what appears to have been a popular form of Zoroastrianism (Cumont, 1896-99, II, p. 20, n. 7; Boyce and Grenet, p. 359).

The use of Greek by educated Persians of the western diaspora made possible the circulation of

Zoroastrian ideas in the eastern Mediterranean world in Greco-Roman times. Persian poets, may have helped, descendants of the minstrel-poets who undoubtedly found a living among Iranian expatriates of earlier times. The existence has been traced of Persian Sibyllists oracles, probably the first non-Greeks to adopt the genre of Sibylline oracles, through which they conveyed Persian prophecies and expectations (Boyce and Grenet, pp. 370-81). In time such oracles grew generally into longer poems, through which doctrine could be conveyed. It thus appears to have been through Persians of the western diaspora that Zoroastrianism made a powerful contribution to religion and thought in the Hellenistic world.

In the east Iran lost Arachosia and Gandhara under Seleucus I to the Mauryan empire. These were lands of ancient Iranian settlement, which received new colonists in Achaemenid times. Light is shed on the Iranians there chiefly by inscriptions of the 3rd century B.C.E., consisting of translations or paraphrases of the decrees of the emperor Aśoka (q.v.). These were written in good Persian chancellery Aramaic, with some local usages, and show the scribes to have interpreted Aśoka's concepts in the light of Zoroastrian beliefs (for references see Boyce and Grenet, pp. 136-45). They evidently had a good knowledge of Northwestern Prakrit; and these eastern Iranians are the likely agents for the postulated contribution of Zoroastrianism to Mahayana Buddhism. Later, under Muslim rule, Zoroastrians of this eastern diaspora are known to have maintained themselves in some numbers locally, but in ever-increasing poverty, down to at least the 17th century C.E. (Firby, p. 70; Boyce, p. 161 n. 35).

Trade took some Iranians further east in the Sasanian period, and small Zoroastrian communities existed in China down into medieval times (Lieu, index s.v. "Zoroastrians"; see CHINESE-IRANIAN RELATIONS i). Their numbers appear to have been increased by fugitives after the Arab conquest (q.v.) of Persia, but little is known of them.

Bibliography: St. Basil, *Collected Letters*, Loeb Library, 1934, IV, pp. 34-47. M. Boyce, *Zoroastrianism. Its Antiquity and Constant Vigour*, Columbia Lectures on Iranian Studies 7, Costa Mesa, Calif., 1992. M. Boyce and F. Grenet, *A History of Zoroastrianism* III, Leiden, 1991. J. M. Cook, *The Persian Empire*, London, 1983. F. Cumont, *Voyage d'exploration archéologique dans le Pont et la Petite Arménie*, n.p., 1906. Idem, *Textes et monuments figurés relatifs aux mystères de Mithra*, 2 vols., Brussells, 1896-99. A. Dupont-Sommer, in *Comptes rendus des séances de l'Académie des inscriptions et belles-lettres*, 1974, pp. 132-49. N. K. Firby, *European Travellers and Their Perceptions of Zoroastrians in the 17th and 18th Centuries*, Berlin, 1988. H. Grégoire, "Note sur une inscription gréco-araméenne trouvée à Faraša (Ariaramneia-Rhodandos)," *Comptes rendus des séances de l'Académie des inscriptions et belles-lettres*, 1908, pp. 434-47. R. P. Harper, "A Dedication to the Goddess Anaitis at Ortaköy (Nitalis ?)," *Anatolian Studies* 17, 1967, p. 193. H. Humbach, "Die aramäischen Nymphen von Xanthos," *Die Sprache* 27, 1981, pp. 30-32. S. Lieu, *Manichaeism in the Later Roman Empire and Medieval China*, Manchester, 1985, 2nd ed., Tübingen, 1992. L. Raditsa, "Iranians in Asia Minor," *Cambr. Hist. of Iran* III/1, pp. 100-15. W. M. Ramsay, "Inscriptions d'Asie Mineure," *Revue des études grecques* 2, 1889, pp. 17-37. L. Robert, "Types monétaires à Hypaipa de Lydie," *Revue numismatique* 18, 1976, pp. xx-xx. Idem, "Mermere antique et moderne. Les carrières, les iraniens," *Bulletin de correspondance hellénique* 106, 1982, pp. 367-73. J. R. Russell, *Zoroastrianism in Armenia*, Harvard Iranian Series 5, 1987. N. V. Sekunda, "Achaemenid Colonization in Lydia," *Revue des Études Anciennes* 87, 1985, pp. 7-30. Idem, "Persian Settlement in Hellespontine Phrygia," *Achaemenid History* III, ed. A. Kuhrt and H. Sancisi-Weerdenburg, Leiden, 1988, pp. 175-96. Idem, "Achaemenid Settlement in Caria, Lycia, and Greater Phrygia," ibid., VI, Leiden, 1991, pp. 83-143. A. Shahbazi, *Irano-Lycian Monuments*, Tehran, 1975. C. G. Starr, "Greeks and Persians in the Fourth Century B.C., Part 2," *Iranica Antiqua* 12, 1977, pp. 49-115. S. Telegdi, "Essai sur la phonétique des emprunts iraniens en araméen talmudique," *JA*, 1935, pp. 177-256. M. J. Vermaseren, *Corpus Inscriptionum et Monumentorum Religionis Mithriacae*, The Hague, I, 1956. S. Wikander, *Feuerpriester in Kleinasien und Iran*, Lund, 1946. U. Wilcken, "Papyrus-Urkunden," *Archiv für Papyrusforschung* 7, 1924, pp. 71-72. L. Zgusta, "Iranian names in Lydian inscriptions," *Charisteria Orientalia praecipue ad Persiam pertinentia. Festschrift J. Rypka*, ed. F. Tauer et al., Prague, 1956, pp. 397-400.

(MARY BOYCE)

ii. PERSIANS IN INDIA. See INDIA; PARSIS.

iii. PERSIANS IN SOUTHEAST ASIA. See CHINESE-IRANIAN RELATIONS.

iv. IN OTTOMAN TURKEY

The first major migration of Persians to Anatolia in the Islamic era occured in the 13th century when the invading Mongol armies laid waste much of the country. The majority (including Najm-al-Dīn Dāya and the family of the mystic and poet Rūmī, qq.v.) were from Khorasan, which was totally devastated by the Mongols. The next wave of the Persian diaspora to Anatolia started under the Safavids due to the religious persecution of the Sunnis in Persia and the Ottoman occupations of Azerbaijan and the susequent deportation of skilled workers to Anatolia. The third wave took place in the 19th century, this time due to favorable commercial conditions after the opening of the Tabrīz-Trabzon-Istanbul trade route in the 1830s (Zarinebaf-Shahr, 1993, pp. 207-08). In the 19th century the most numerous groups of Persians in Ottomon Turkey were merchants who traveled constantly between the Persian commercial centers and the Ottoman cities. Some of them eventually settled permanently in the Ottoman empire.

The Mongol empire, linking China to Persia and Russia, stimulated trade between the East and the West. The silk route started in China and passed through Central Asia and Persia, ending up in Anatolia. With the rise of the Ottoman state, the trade route shifted farther west to Bursa, the Ottoman capital. In the 15th century, caravan trade between Tabrīz and Bursa increased greatly in volume. Persian merchants, mostly from Tabrīz and Gīlān, dominated the silk trade between these two commercial centers. They had their own caravansary (*ʿajam ḵānī*) in Bursa, which was built by Bayezid II in 1490 (Inalcik, p. 52).

The beginning of Ottoman-Safavid conflict inflicted heavy economic losses on the Persian merchants in Bursa, many of whom chose to settle in Aleppo and Istanbul, where Selim I's ban on the sale of Persian silk was not effective (Masters, pp. 29-30). The third most important Ottoman center for Persian merchants was the city of Izmir, which became an important commercial center in the 17th century and offerred new trading opportunities with the Venetian, French, Dutch, and British merchants who were turning to Izmir in increasing numbers (Goffman, p. 141).

The treaty of Erzurum in 1238/1823 initiated a new era in Persian-Ottoman relations. It reduced and regularized the customs rates on Persian goods. Persian merchants were required to pay only 4 percent customs duties on their goods, a rate equal to that charged to Ottoman Muslim merchants. Besides, they became exempt from all extra dues, tolls, and taxes. A later treaty signed in 1263/1847, entitled the two governments to appoint consuls (*bālyūz*) in each other's major cities and ports to protect the interests of their subjects (*Ecnebi*, pp. 4, 8). The opening of the Istanbul-Trabzon-Tabrīz route in 1830 provided a major boost to trade between the two states. Trabzon became the entrepôt for Tabrīz, which had suffered an economic setback due to a shift in the trade route to the Persian Gulf in the 17th century. Europeans also carried on the bulk of their trade with Tabrīz via this route (Zarinebaf-Shahr, 1993, p. 208). The number of Persian merchants in Istanbul rose greatly in the second half of the 19th century. According to Ḵān-Malek Sāsānī (pp. 94-95, 107-08), the Persian consul in Istanbul , the number of Persian families residing in Istanbul had grown to about 4,000 families by the end of the 19th century, 80 percent of whom were from Azerbaijan. They included prosperous rug merchants, booksellers, factory owners, shopkeepers, coachmen, etc. Merchants were concentrated in the Valide Hani at the commercial heart of the city, where they also held religious processions in the month of Moḥarram. It became an active center for the dissemination of news about Persia during the Constitutional Revolution (1324-27/1906-09; q.v.).

According to Table 26, major concentrations of Persians in Anatolia were in commercial centers located on a trade route stretching from Erzurum to Izmir. The sharp drop in their number within thirty-one years may be explained by the decline in trade between the two countries and a rise in the number of those who took Ottoman citizenship. According to Sāsānī (pp. 95-97), the Young Turk government encouraged the Azeri Persians to become Ottoman citizens and did not enforce on them the regulation preventing Persians from marrying Ottoman sub-

Table 26

THE NUMBER OF PERSIAN SUBJECTS IN THE ASIAN SECTION OF OTTOMON TURKEY IN THE YEARS 1305/1888 AND 1338/1919-20

City	1888	1919-20
Istanbul	16,000	
Adana	2,714	485
Izmir	955	210
Aleppo (Ḥalab)	850	185
Erzurum	721	50
Samsun (Sāmsūn)	664	235
Van	448	-
Ankara	350	112
Damascus	322	47
Urfa	281	49
Trebzon	270	95
Eskişehir	230	28
Balikesir (Bālekesrī)	200	44
Ismir Dependencies	200	95
Atapazar (Āṭabāzār)	194	65
Adaliya (Anṭālīya)	175	-
Mersin	129	22
Konya (Qūnīa)	112	-
Bayezit	96	-
Ayintap (ʿAynṭāb)	66	-
Beirut	55	-
Maraş (Marʿaš)	38	-
Tyr (Ṣūr)	-	110
Akka (ʿAkkā)	-	90
Akhisar (Āq Ḥeṣār)	-	80
Manisa (Mağnīsa)	-	50
Kasaba (Qaṣaba)	-	30
Bursa	-	20
Salihi (Ṣāleḥī)	-	15
Aydin	-	3
Total (excluding Istanbul)	9,069	2,120

Source: Ḵān-Malek Sāsānī, pp. 97-99, with minor adjustment.

jects. This regulation, established in 1286/1869, provided that the children of Persians from an Ottoman mother automatically became Ottoman subjects (*Ecnebi*, I, p. 17).

Persians of Istanbul had their own cemetery in the Asian part of the city. The cemetery is said to have been constructed originally by the daughter of Shah Sultan Ḥosayn, Ḥūrī Solṭān, in 1774 (Zarcone, 1992). It was enlarged in 1290/1873. A study by Thierry Zarcone shows a sharp increase in the number of tombs in the 19th century. Zarcone has estimatd that three-quarters of the deceased were from Azerbaijan (1992, p. 2).

The well-established and prosperous Persian community in Istanbul attracted many Persian intellectuals who feared persecution in Persia on the eve of the Constitutional Revolution. The Persian newspapers *Aḵtar* and *Šams*, which were printed in Istanbul, voiced the discontent and the political demands of the Persian community there. Following Moḥammad-ʿAlī Shah's coup in the summer of 1326/1908 (see *EIr* VI, pp. 176-87), the number of Persian refugees in the Ottoman Turkey increased again. They formed the political association, Anjoman-e saʿādat (q.v.), which was active promoting the Constitutional Revolution.

Bibliography: *Aḵtar* (newspaper), nos. 1-10, 1908-09. *Cevdet dahiliye* 4312. *Ecnebi defteri* I, pp. 1-26. S. Deringil, "The Struggle against Shiʿism in Hamidian Iraq," *Die Welt Des Islam* 30, 1990, pp. 45-62. E. Glassen, "Muharrem Ceremonies (*azādāri*) in Istanbul at the End of the 19th and the Beginning of the 20th Centuries," in Th. Zarcone and F. Zarinebaf-Shahr, eds.,*Les Iraniens D'Istanbul*, Louvain, 1993, pp. 113-40. D. Goffman, *Izmir and the Levantine World, 1550-1650*, Seattle, 1989, p. 141. H. Inalcik, "Bursa I. XV Asir Sanayi ve Ticaret Tarihine Dair Vesikalar," *Belleten* 24, 1960, pp. 45-65. A. Ḵān-Malek Sasānī, *Yādbūdhā-ye sefārat-e Estānbūl*, Tehran, 1354 Š./1975. B. Masters, *The Origins of Western Economic Dominance and the Islamic Economy in Aleppo, 1600-1750*, New York, 1988. M.-A. Rīāḥī, *Zabān o adab-e fārsī dar qalamrow-e ʿOṯmānī*, Tehran, 1369 Š./1990, pp. 150-70. *Šams* (newspaper), nos. 2-7, 1880-81. T. Zarcone, "The Persian Cemetery of Istanbul," paper presented at a conference entitled "Art funeraire et cimetiere dans le monde Islamique," Istanbul, September 1991. Idem and F. Zarinbaf-Shahr, eds., *Les Iraniens d'Istanbul*, Louvain, 1993.F. Zarinebaf-Shahr, *Tabriz under Ottoman Rule, 1725-1730*, Ph.D. Dissertation, The University of Chicago, 1991.

(FARIBA ZARINEBAF-SHAHR)

v. IN CAUCASUS AND CENTRAL ASIA IN THE LATE 19TH AND EARLY 20TH CENTURIES.

The number of Persians in the Russian empire or its territories increased steadily in the second half of the 19th century. They consisted primarily of migrants from Persia's northern provinces (chiefly Azerbaijan), who traveled to Caucasus and, to some extent, to Central Asia in search of employment. Although the bulk of migrants were involved in some form of short-term or circular migration, many stayed in Russia for longer periods or even settled there.

The first traces of migration were recorded as early as 1855. The British consul in Tabrīz, K. E. Abbott, reported more than 3,000 passes issued by the Russian consulate in two months alone (Seyf, pp. 161-62). However, the process gathered pace after the 1880s, and by the turn of the century it had achieved a scale and consistency that was sufficient to win the attention of many scholars, travelers, and commentators of the time (Orsolle, p. 49; Gordon p. 9; Wigham, p. 402; for a study of the phenomenon see Hakimian, 1985 and 1990) .

According to the returns from the first national census of Russia, some 74,000 Persian subjects were enumerated in the various parts of the empire as of 28 January 1897 (see Table 27). Of these roughly 28 percent (21,000) were females. The largest single grouping was in the Caucasus region, which accounted for 82 percent of the total. Within the region the four major towns of Baku, Elisavetpol (Ganja), Erivan, and Tbilisi accounted for as many as 53,000 or about 72 percent of all Persians in the whole empire. Next to Caucasus in numbers of Persian residents was Central Asia, where numbers surpassed 10,000. According to the same source, Per

Table 27
GEOGRAPHICAL DISTRIBUTION OF PERSIANS IN THE RUSSIANEMPIRE, 28 JANUARY 1897

	Persian Subjects		
	Male	Female	Total
All Russia	53,268	20,652	73,920
European Russia	2,455	745	3,200
(Astrakhan)	(564)	(247)	(811)
Poland	1	—	1
Caucasus	42,080	18,325	60,405
(Baku)	(17,266)	(6,702)	(23,968)
(Tbilisi)	(6,108)	(2,034)	(8,142)
(Erivan)	(5,065)	(3,158)	(8,223)
(Elizavetpol/ Ganja)	(8,134)	(4,542)	(12,676)
(Daghestan)	(1,287)	(564)	(1,851)
Central Asia	8,598	1,573	10,171
(Transcaspian)	(7,466)	(1,433)	(8,899)
(Samarkand)	(1,067)	(125)	(1,192)
Siberia	134	9	143

Source: Based on the First National Census of Russia (Hakimian, 1990, p. 47).

sian-speakers (as distinct from Persian subjects) numbered only about 32,000, suggesting the predominence of Azeri-speaking Azerbaijanis among the migrants.

Other records of the migratory movements or of Persians residing in Russia are not as systematic and reliable as those in Table 1. Many travelers' accounts and political memoirs attest to the importance of the numbers involved, yet they are often contradictory or incomparable. Further useful information is, however, available from data on passports and visas issued at the Russian consulates in Tabrīz, Mašhad, Rašt, and Estarābād (Ethner, p. 60). These data reinforce a picture of consistently rising numbers of Persian travelers to Russia, averaging about 13,000 per year for the period 1876-1890 and rising to over 67,000 at the turn of the century. By 1913 over a quarter of a million Persians (274,555) were reported to have entered Russia (Entner, p. 60). However, this excludes illegal migration, which by many accounts was also substantial (Sobotsinskii, apud Entner, p. 60, gives the figure of 200,000 illegal immigrants for 1911; Belova, p. 114). Equally large numbers of Persians were reported to have left Russia each year (e.g., 213,373 in 1913). It has been estimated that net immigration to Russian territories amounted to about 25,000 each year on average between 1900-13. The total number of Persians in Russia before World War I is thus likely to have been about half a million (Hakimian, 1990, pp. 49-50).

Characteristics. An overwhelming majority of these migrants, and particularly those from Azerbaijan, were common laborers in pursuit of work. It is believed that the largest numbers left Persia regularly around April and September, when agricultural work in Transcaucasia was at its peak; movements declined subsequently in summer and winter (Minorsky, p. 206). The rest of the immigrants came from a variety of social background and included merchants, traders, artisans, etc. who traveled to Russian empire in the face of expanding economic relations between the two countries (*Mašrūṭa*, p. 85). Data on the social composition of migrants are rare, but according to Russian consular reports as high as 93 percent of the total 59,121 visas issued in Tabrīz in 1904 were issued to workers. For Rašt the corresponding figure was much lower, about 27 percent of a total of 3,027, suggesting the importance of trade and mercantile activities for travelers from the Caspian littoral (Minorsky, p. 205).

Minorsky's visa data also show Azerbaijan as the principal Persian province from which migrants set off for Russia: 90 percent of all permits issued in 1904 were issued in Azerbaijan (59,121 in Tabrīz and 3,148 in Urmia compared with 5,459 in Mašhad, 3,027 in Rašt, and 652 in Estarābād respectively; Minorsky, p. 205). Parallel to this, many peasants left Khorasan each winter to seek work in Central Asia (Sykes, p. 392). Others departed from as far south as Sīstān, although their number was far more modest (Abdullaev, pp. 51-52).

Most Persians took up simple manual jobs in Russian towns or in the countryside. In some parts such as Elisavetpol, agricultural lands were almost exclusively operated by Persians who took up occupations normally refused by local workers on grounds of inferior pay and conditions of work (Belova, p. 115). Similar accounts are available from the Baku guberniya and Tbilisi, where many Persians worked in the cotton fields on a seasonal basis. Persians were also attracted to a variety of other occupations. In Baku they reportedly worked as shopkeepers, mechanics, masons, carpenters, coachmen, carters, and laborers (Gordon, p. 8).

As a measure of their dexterity, Persians had earned themselves a reputation of being the "best masons" in Transcaucasia (Orsolle, p. 49). Most new buildings in Tbilisi were attributed to Persian construction workers and masons. In Baku much loading and unloading of ships relied on porters from Ḵalḵāl and Ardabīl (q.v.). Many also toiled on the roads and in railway construction (e.g., on the Trans-Caspian railway and the new railway from Tbilisi to Alexandropol and Kars; Gordon, pp. 8-9).

In many branches of production in the Caucasus Persians comprised sizeable proportions of the work force. In the Baku oil industry, for instance, their numbers and share in the work force rose steadily after 1893: from 11 percent in 1893 to 29.1 percent in 1915, constituting the largest single national grouping in the industry, which reached a total of 13,500 by 1915 (Abdullaev, p. 51). Similarly, in the province of Elisavetpol over a quarter of permanent workers in the copper smelting plant of Kedabek were Persians (Belova, p. 116).

The majority of these Persians, however, held low-paying jobs that had little or no security. Average daily earnings of unskilled Persians in 1904 are reported as 60-70 kopeks, or 20 kopeks lower than the general average rate of pay. Persian dock workers in Baku worked fifteen to eighteen hours a day (often at night), ate badly, and many slept under trees and in gardens (Belova, p. 118). According to another source, the fact that most Persians of Tbilisi shared one room among three or four people hampered attempts to contain the periodic incidence of cholera in the town (Dāneš, p. 316). Moreover, under a 1903 law, foreign workers were denied the protection of safety regulations at work. Even the oil workers in Baku were no exception to this. Their economic and political insecurity was highlighted during the 1905 labor unrests, when thousands were forcibly extradited (Belova, p. 121).

Causes. Much of the critical literature around the Constitutional period has identified growing economic hardship and political oppression at home, in particular affecting the peasant, as the principal forces behind the Persians' drive into Russia in the closing decades of the last century (Marāḡaʾī, pp.

24-25; Reżāzāda Malek, p. 13; Chaqueri, IV, pp. 82, 99; Pavlovitch, p. 625; Kazemi and Abrahamian, pp. 294-95; *Mašrūṭa*, p. 85; Ādamīyat and Nāṭeq, pp. 378-96). Although relevant, however, it is doubtful whether economic and political factors alone can provide an adequate explanation of this phenomenon (Hakimian, 1990, pp. 55-57). Other writers have stressed the role of incentives, namely, savings opportunities in the face of better work prospects and differential earnings abroad, which were accentuated by the depreciation of the Persian currency (Gordon, p. 9; Gilbar, p. 153; Wigham, p. 402; Orsolle, p. 49). Russia's powerful economic drive and industrial transformation in the closing decades of the century and the attendant critical labor shortages in the bordering provinces are thought to have reinforced these opportunities for migrants (Hakimian, 1990, pp. 57-62; Belova, pp. 115-16). Limited data on currency remittances by returning migrants seem to reinforce this picture. Minorsky gives a figure of 1.8 million rubles for Azerbaijani migrants alone in 1904 (p. 211); Entner cites 3 million rubles converted by the Russian Bank in 1909 (p. 61). Both figures exclude unofficial transactions.

Social and political significance. Interaction with the Russian society and polity in general helped to widen many migrants' social and political awareness. It also fostered socialist thinking and values among them, leading some observers to attribute the emergence of an industrial working class in Persia to the migratory movements in these years (Abdullaev, p. 50). With the rise of the social democratic movement in the Caucasus Persian migrants, helped by the Hemmat organization in Baku (estab. 1904), founded the group Ejtemāʿīyūn-e ʿāmmīyūn (q.v.) with subsequent branches in Persian towns (Tehran, Mašhad, and Tabrīz; Chaqueri, I, pp. 16, 35-36). Revolutionary assistance to comrades in Persia included, inter alia, the delivery of printed propaganda from Caucasus and the despatch of militant workers from the Caucasus to fight alongside Sattār Khan during the seige of Tabrīz (Tria, pp. 324-33).

According to other accounts too, the politicization of Persian workers in Russia was extensive during a period beset by revolutionary turmoil in both countries. In the 1906 strike in the copper mines and plants of Alaverdi in Armenia about 2,500 Persian Azerbaijanis were believed to constitute the core of strikers (Abdullaev, p. 51). This politicization was also reflected in the forcible extraditions of 1905 referred to above (Belova, p. 121).

Persians also took part in political activities between World War I and the October Revolution. In 1914 workers residing in Baku took part in street demonstrations against the outbreak of war (Chaqueri, IV, p. 48). Soon after the October Revolution, a group of Persian workers in Baku founded the party ʿEdālat, which was to become the Communist Party of Persia in 1920.

Bibliography: Z. Z. Abdullev, "Bourgeoisie and Working Class, 1900s," in Issawi, pp. 42-52; F. Ādamīyat and H. Nāṭeq, *Afkār-e ejtemaʿī wa sīāsī dar āṯār-e montašer našoda-e dawrān-e Qājār*, Tehran, 1356 Š./1977. N. K. Belova, "Ob Otkhodnichestve iz Severozapadnogo Irana, v Kontse XIX- nachale XX Veka," *Voprosy Istoriĭ* 10, 1956, pp. 112-21. C. Chaqueri (Ḵ. Šākerī), ed., *Asnād-e tārīḵī-e jonbeš-e kārgarī, sosīāl-demokrāsī wa komūnīstī-e Īrān* I, Florence, 1969; IV. *Āṯār-e Avetīs Solṭānzāda*, rev. ed. Tehran and Florence, 1986. Mīrzā Reżā Khan Dāneš, *Īrān-e dīrūz*, Tehran, 1345 Š./1966. M. L. Entner, *Russo-Persian Commercial Relations, 1828-1914*, The University of Florida Monographs 28, Gainsville, 1965. G. G. Gilbar, "Persian Agriculture in the Late Qajar Period, 1860-1906. Some Economic and Social Aspects," *Asian and African Studies* 12, pp. 312-65. E. Gordon, *Persia Revisited*, London, 1896. Ḥājj Zayn-al-ʿĀbedīn Marāḡaʾī, *Sīāḥat-nāma-ye Ebrāhīm Beg*, Tehran, 1353 Š./1974. H. Hakimian, "Wage, Labor and Migration. Persian Workers in Southern Russia," *IJMES* 17/4, 1985, pp. 443-62. Idem, *Labour Transfer and Economic Development. Theoretical Perspectives and Case Studies from Iran*, Hemel Hempstead, 1990. Idem, in *IJMES* 17/4, 1985, pp. 443-62. C. Issawi, ed., *The Economic History of Iran 1800-1914*, Chicago, 1971. F. Kazemi and E. Abrahamian, "The Non-revolutionary Peasantry of Modern Iran," *Iranian Studies* 11, 1978, pp. 259-304. V. Minorsky, "Dvizhenie persidskikh rabochikh na promysly v Zakavkaze," *Sbornik Konsulskikh Doneseniy* (Consular Reports) 3, St. Petersburg, 1905. E. Orsolle, *La Caucase et la Perse*, Paris, 1885. M. Pavlovitch, "La situation agraire en Perse à la veille de la révolution," *RMM* 12, December 1910, pp. 616-25. R. Reżāzāda Malek, *Ḥaydar Ḵān-e ʿAmū Oḡlī*, Tehran, 1352 Š./1973. A. Seyf, *Some Aspects of Economic Development in Iran, 1800-1906*, Ph.D. dissertation, Reading University, U.K., 1982. P. Sykes, *A History of Persia*, 2 vols., II, London, 1930. T. Tria, "La caucase et la Révolution Persane," *RMM* 13, 1911, pp. 324-33. N. Troinitsky, ed., *Premier re-censement général de la population de l'Empire de Russie, 1897. Relevée général pour tout l'Empire des resultats du depouillement des données du premier recensement de la population en 1897*, St. Petersburg, 1905, I, pp. 236-37, 244-45; II, pp. 6-7, 24-25, 42-43, 60-61, 78-79. H. J. Wigham, *The Persian Problem*, London, 1903.

(HASSAN HAKIMIAN)

vi. IN IRAQ

Shiʿite Persian merchants first came to Iraq during the two periods of Safavid occupation of the country (914-40/1508-33 and 1032-48/1622-38), procuring a good share of the commerce of Baghdad (Longrigg, pp. 19, 57). Early in the 17th century there were still no Persians in Baṣra, the population of which was composed mainly of Arabs and some Turks (Teixeira, pp. 27-30). At that time there were a few thousand Persians in Karbalā, Najaf, Kāẓemayn, and Baghdad. Many of them, however, escaped to Persia following the second Ottoman occupation of Baghdad in 1048/1638, which had resulted in the killing of some 1,700 Persians (ʿAzzāwī, IV, pp. 229, 234-35). The Persian colony in Iraq until 1638 was composed mostly of merchants and other individuals who came to the country in search of economic opportunities. There were no significant numbers of Persian students and *ʿolamāʾ* in Iraq at that time, since the main Shiʿite academic centers were in Persia.

It was only from the 18th century that Persian *ʿolamāʾ* and students arrived in Iraq on a massive scale. The capture of Isfahan by the Sunni Afghans in 1135/1722 displaced hundreds of families of *ʿolamāʾ*, many of whom fled to Iraq during 1135-77/1722-63. The center of Shiʿite scholarship shifted from Persia to Iraq, first to Karbalā and then to Najaf. At that time the Persian language gained much ground in Karbalā, Najaf, Baghdad, and Baṣra. In Karbalā and Najaf, the Persian religious families managed to overshadow the Arab *ʿolamāʾ* and succeeded in dominating the religious circles (Kerkūklī, pp. 52-63; Amīn, II, pp. 22-25; ʿAzzāwī, IV, pp. 269-70; Perry, pp. 172, 220; Cole, pp. 5, 20, 22, 26). By the 20th century Persians were also to be found in significant numbers in Baghdad, Baṣra, and Tawayrej. The socio-economic and religious position of Persians in Iraq was bolstered by Ottoman-Qajar agreements (e.g., Treaty of Erzurum in 1823, see Hurewitz, I, p. 220) which facilitated the influx of pilgrims, and regulated the corpse traffic, from Persia to the shrine cities. Their privileged status, relative importance, and large proportion among the population of the shrine cities, most notably in Karbalā, gave the Persians an advantage over the Arab Shiʿite population of Iraq, enabling the Persians to retain their vested economic interests and strong socio-religious links with their families and co-religionists in Persia.

The Persian community in Iraq enjoyed the status of Persian subjects, over whom Persian consular offices held extra-territorial jurisdiction. The status of Persians in the country was a major cause of strained Ottoman-Qajar relations even after their privileges were officially confirmed in 1292/1875. An agreement between the two states recognized the status of Persian consuls and consular dragomans in the Ottoman empire as carrying the same privileges enjoyed by their European counterparts. The exclusive authority of the Persian consuls over Persian subjects in matters of civil and criminal law and of succession was affirmed by the 1875 agreement. While Persian subjects were declared amenable to the jurisdiction of Ottoman courts in cases of violation of the law, and in mixed civil and commercial cases, certain powers of assistance and protection in the proceedings were reserved for the Persian consular representatives. The agreement also established the exemption of Persian subjects from taxes to which Ottoman subjects were liable. Although it was declaired that all provisions relating to Persian subjects in the Ottoman empire should equally apply to Ottoman subjects in Persia, Persians were the main beneficiaries of the agreement (Lorimer, *Gazetteer* I, pt. 1B, p. 1425).

The formation of the modern state of Iraq in 1921 changed the privileged status of Persians. Iraq was no longer the frontier to which Persian nationals could emigrate as easily as in the past. The state's advocacy of Pan-Arabism also served to undermine the position of Persians. The blow to their status was reinforced by the policies of the Iraqi government and by Persia's diminishing influence in Iraq. Following the establishment of the monarchy, both British officials and successive Iraqi governments gave much attention to the question of Persians in Iraq. British Officials argued that there was no need to accord Persians the privileges and capitulations enjoyed by European nationals under the Anglo-Iraqi agreement of 1924 (Nakhash, p. 100).

The Iraqi government was anxious to diminish Persian influence in the country. In an effort to abolish the privileges and immunities enjoyed by Persian nationals in Iraq, successive Iraqi governments adopted and implemented a series of laws and regulations. The Iraqi Nationality law of 1924 had an impact on virtually every person of Persian origin residing in Iraq. Under this law, Persians were automatically considered Iraqi nationals unless they themselves renounced such status by a fixed date, which was extended twice until set for January 1928. The Iraqi Nationality law was followed by the introduction in 1927 of a law prohibiting the employment of foreigners in government posts. A law regulating the appointments and promotions of civil as well as religious judges was introduced in 1929. Among other things, it prohibited the appointment of persons who had not acquired Iraqi nationality and did not have a good knowledge of Arabic as religious judges (*qāżīs*) in the religious (*šarʿī*) courts. In December 1935 the Iraqi parliament passed a law which prohibited foreign nationals from practicing certain trades and works. It applied to various crafts and professions traditionally practiced by Persian residents in the shrine cities. Holy shrine regulations 25 of 1948 and 42 of 1950 had a direct impact on Persian functionaries and servants at the shrines. The administration of the shrines was given to the director general of *awqāf* and it was stipulated that all servants of the shrines should be Iraqi nationals subject to the Directory of *awqāf* (Dāʾerat al-awqāf; Nakash, pp. 100-02).

The number of Persians in Iraq on the eve of the formation of the monarchy was put by the British rough census of 1919 at 80,000 (FO 371/4152/175918). It may very well be, however, that the number of Persians in Iraq was higher than 80,000, particularly if one takes into account cases of mixed marriages and families whose members resided in Iraq for several generations. The number of Persians in Iraq decreased markedly under the monarchy. The decrease was most noticeable in Karbalā. Whereas early in the 20th century Persians constituted some 75 percent of the city's population, by 1957 their percentage had decreased sharply to some 12 percent (Iraq census of 1957, I, pt. 3, p. 75). Persians had either accepted Iraqi nationality or left the country.

The position of Persians in Iraq was further undermined under the Baʿṯ regime (1968). It was estimated that some 60,000 Shiʿites of Persian origin were deported from Iraq to Persia in 1974. Further deportations took place in the period leading up to the Iran-Iraq war and in the month that preceded the war in 1980, when some 35,000 Shiʿites of Persian origin were said to have been deported from Iraq to Persia (Gotleib, p. 154; *The Washington Post*, 11 April 1980, p. A18). The deportation of Shiʿites who were accused of being of Persian origin, was facilitated by the introduction of Law no. 666 of May 1980. This law enabled the government to abrogate the Iraqi citizenship of every citizen of a foreign origin who was found disloyal to the state. Implementation of this law resulted in massive deportations of Shiʿites who were accused of being of Persian origin (ʿOḏrī, pp. 281-94).

See also ʿATABĀT; IRAQ.

Bibliography: M. Amīn, *Maʿāden al-jawāher wa nozhat al-ḵawāṭer* II, Beirut, 1981. ʿA. ʿAzzāwī, *Taʾrīḵ al-ʿErāq bayna eḥtelālayn* IV-V, Baghdad, 1949-53. F. Barrak, *al-Madāres al-yahūdīya wa'l-īrānīya fi'l-ʿErāq. Derāsa moqārena*, Baghdad, 1984. J. Cole, "Shiʿi Clerics in Iraq and Iran, 1722-1780. The Akhbari-Usuli Conflict Reconsidered," *Iranian Studies* 18, 1985, pp. 3-33. Gotleib, "Sectarianism and the Iraqi State," in M. Curtis, ed, *Religion and Politics in the Middle East*, Boulder, 1981, pp. 153-56. Iraq Census, *Modīrīyat al-nofūs al-ʿāmma. al-Majmūʿa al-eḥṣāʾīya le-tasjīl ʿāmm 1957*, Baghdad, 196. J. C. Hurewitz, ed., *The Middle East and North Africa. A Documentary Record*, 2 vols., 2nd ed. New York, 1975. R. Kerkūklī, *Dawḥat al-wozarāʾ fī taʾrīḵ waqāʾeʿ Baḡdād al-zawrāʾ*, Beirut and Baghdad, n.d. Y. Nakash, "The Shiʿites of Iraq, Princeton, N.J., 1994. ʿA.-K. ʿOḏrī, *Moškelāt al-ḥokm fi'l-ʿErāq*, London, 199. J. Perry, *Karim Khan Zand: A History of Iran, 1747-1779*, Chicago, 1979. P. Teixeira, *The Travels of Pedro Teixeira*, tr. W. Sinclair, London, 1802. 1919 Census of Iraq by Religion, FO 371/4152/175918.

(YITZHAK NAKASH)

vii. IN THE PERSIAN GULF STATES

The history of Persian settlement on the southern coast of the Persian Gulf dates from as early as the Sasanian period. Early settlers have to some extent been absorbed into the local population, whereas many of the immigrants of modern times are still considered as Persian nationals.

Immigration of Persian nationals to the Arab coasts of the Persian Gulf in more modern times began in the mid-19th century when the Qāsemī family's rule in Sharjah expanded and its influence in the Musandam Peninsula grew wider. Its ties with the Qāsemīs of Bandar Lenga in Persia encouraged many Persian families of the coastal regions of the Persian Gulf, the Strait of Hormuz, and the Gulf of Oman to migrate to the opposite coasts. The early immigrants were of the merchant class who initially settled in Sharjah. As the silting up of Sharjah's creek affected its commercial significance in the early 20th century, the Persian merchants gradually left Sharjah for the growing town of Dubai. Immigration of Persians to Kuwait and Bahrain also increased in the late 19th and early 20th centuries (Hay, p. 120).

Under Karīm Khan Zand (1163-93/1750-79) Persia recaptured the port of Baṣra from the Ottomans in 1190/1776, which caused British merchants and many of Baṣra residents to leave this city for Kuwait (Taylor, pp. 26-27). When Baṣra was reoccupied by the Ottomans at the turn of the 19th century, Kuwait continued its new significance as a commercial center of the Persian Gulf. This commercial significance, together with the interactions between Kuwait and the Persian provinces of Ḵūzestān and Fārs, encouraged a number of Persian merchants to migrate to Kuwait. Bahrain's political predicament vis-à-vis invasions of the Omanis, the Wahhābīs, the Turks and the British in the mid-19th century drew Bahrain closer to Persia in general and the governorates of Būšehr and Lenga in particular. When in the 1860s Bahrain's authorities established close ties with Persia as a dependent state, a sizable number of Persians moved there (Qāʾemmaqāmī, p. 42). The next wave of Persian immigrants moved to Bahrain in the 1920s.

Sweeping reforms under Reżā Shah Pahlavī (1304-20 Š./1925-41), including the banning of women's traditional veil and introduction of compulsory military service, encouraged the more traditionalist families of the southern regions of Persia to move across the sea to Kuwait, Qatar, and the Trucial States (now United Arab Emirates; Hay, p. 120). Traveling between Persia and the ports of the southern coast of the Persian Gulf was, up to the year 1324 Š./1945, free of any restrictions. In fact economic and social ties between the two shores were so close that any attempt to restrict frequentation was doomed to fail. Everyone from the southern coast was entitled to a boundary pass permit and could remain in Persia indefinitely (Hay, p. 148). Persia introduced some regulations in 1324 Š./1945, and in 1338 Š./1959 restriction of movements to and from Persia was implemented (Hay, p. 148).

The success of the first groups of new immigrants in the southern coast resulted in their supremacy over the economy, especially in Dubai, where the state became dependent on its mercantile interaction with the Persian coast, which in turn led to exceptionally friendly relations with Persia. The socioeconomic success of early Persian immigrants of the modern times encouraged new waves of Persian immigrants, which began in the 1950s when Persia was going through a long period of economic and political uncertainty. An economic boom in the Arab Emirates in the 1950s and 1960s provided further incentive for immigration, which continued until the early 1970s when the Persian economy started to prosper. Of the new immigrant families, the Behbahānī and Maʿāref of Kuwait, the Jawaherī and K̲onjī of Bahrain, the Darvīš of Qatar, and the Galahdārī of Dubai have substantial economic and political influence (Mojtahed-Zadeh, 1993, p. 9).

Persian immigrants in Kuwait, the eastern provinces of Saudi Arabia, Qatar, and Bahrain, experienced a great deal of ethnic and religious confrontation, but not in Dubai and other emirates (Mojtahed-zadeh, 1994, p. 173). The 1970 census of the state of Kuwait placed the number of Persian immigrants at 39,129, which comprised 5 percent of a total population of 800,000 (*Population Census, Kuwait, 1970*).

With the influx of immigrants from other countries to Kuwait in the 1950s, about 40-50,000 of older generations of Persian immigrants found it necessary to assume Kuwaiti nationality to keep their economic stronghold (Razavian, p. 150). The number of Persian immigrants in Kuwait was put at 19,919 in 1957; 30,790 in 1965; and 39,129 in 1970 or 9 percent of the total population (*Population Census of Kuwait, 1970*). Iraq's invasion and occupation of Kuwait (August 1990-January 1991) led to the displacement of about half of Kuwait's population of 2 million. Of these, about 5,000 Persian families went to Persia (*Echo of Iran*, p. 3). Restoration of the state of Kuwait in January 1991 was followed by the adoption of a new policy of reducing that emirate's population to about 1 million. Implementation of this policy has made it difficult for most of the displaced Persian families to return to Kuwait (Mojtahed-zadeh, 1994, p. 75).

Of Bahrain's total population of 217,000 in 1972 (*Bahrain's Population Census 1972*), 35,000 were Baharinahs (*Baḥārena*, i.e., Shiʿites of Bahrain). Of this total, only 5,000 were ʿOṭūbī Arabs, to which the ruling K̲alīfa family belongs. The remaining 177,000 were regarded as immigrants, of which 37,000 were classed as non-Bahrainis. Of these, 5,000 were regarded as Persians who were still subjects of the Persian government. The percentage of Persian nationals fell from 8.4 percent in 1941 to 2.3 percent in 1971 (Razavian, p. 308). This was mainly owing to the political difficulties created by Persia's renewal of sovereignty claims to Bahrain.

Dubai's total population was estimated in 1973 at 100,000, of which 80,000 were said to have been foreign immigrants. Of this figure, 50 percent were Persian immigrants of the more recent decades (Dubai Municipality Statistics, 1973).

With Persia's economic boom of the 1970s, immigration to the southern coast of the Persian Gulf diminished. There were even instances of voluntary repatriation among the immigrants of the recent decades. Persia's Revolution of 1357 Š./1978-79 resulted in the introduction of new measures in the Arab states of the Persian Gulf restricting Persian immigration to those countries, whereas Dubai became one of the most popular exit routes for the political refugees from Persia.

Bibliography: *Echo of Iran*, Echo Publications 38135, London, 1990. R. Hay, *The Persian Gulf States*, Washington, D.C., 1959. P. Mojtahedzāda (Mojtahed-Zadeh), tr. Ḥ. R. Malek-Moḥammadī Nūrī as "Kešvarhā wa marzhā dar manṭaqa-ye žeopolītīk-e K̲alīj-e Fārs," The Institute for Political and International Studies, Tehran, 1993, p. 173. Idem, "Negāh-ī be tārīk̲-e K̲alīj-e Fārs," *Eṭṭelāʿāt-e sīāsī wa eqteṣādī* 8/79-80, March-April 1994, pp. 4-9, 75. J. Qāʾemmaqāmī, *Baḥrayn wa masāʾel-e K̲alīj-e Fārs*, Tehran, 1962, p. 42. M. T. Razavian, *Persian Communities of the Persian Gulf*, Ph.D. dissertation, University of London, 1975. Brief Notes of Captain Robert Tylor, Assistant Political Agent in Turkish Arabia," *Records of the Bombay Government*, N. S., 24 .

(Pirouz Mojtahed-Zadeh)

viii. Diaspora in the Postrevolutionary Period

Migration waves. This article presents a statistical profile of the Persian diaspora worldwide. In general, Persian immigration came in two distinctive waves before and after the Revolution of 1978-79. Persians who emigrated before the Revolution were mostly students while those who left after the Revolution were mainly exiles or political refugees (Bozorgmehr and Sabagh, 1991; Jones). The industrialization drives of the Shah in the 1960s created a need for educated and skilled labor in Persia. Despite a rapid growth in the enrollment of college students, Persian universities could not absorb the large number of high school graduates. Thus, Persia became one of world's premier exporters of college and university students, most of whom pursued higher education in the advanced industrial countries of Europe and North America. In comparison to students, there were fewer economically motivated immigrants since employment opportunities were abundant in Persia. Although students initially were temporary migrants, they formed the original links in the subsequent migration chains of Persians. Improved personal incomes enabled the parents and relatives of students to visit them abroad, paving the way for immigration and family reunification. After the Revolution, many students decided to settle abroad. Although Persian emigrants are increasingly visiting Persia, and even returning, there is no evidence to suggest that the majority of exiles will repatriate unless conditions change drastically in their homeland.

The second wave consisted of a more sizable number of Persians than the first. While the earlier exiles fled the Revolution, the later ones included draft-age men escaping the Iran-Iraq war. The exile outflow has continued to this day. For instance, in spite of the difficulty and expense of immigration from Persia to the United States, roughly the same proportion (29%) immigrated during 1985-1990 and 1975-80. As a result, with an estimated 270,100 refugees, Persia ranked tenth among principal sources of the entire world's refugees in the late 1980s (World Refugee Survey, 1988 in *Review*, Table 4).

Worldwide distribution. Since there are no reliable data on the total Persian diaspora population in the world, the estimates of this population are exaggerated. For example, according to one source, "More than a million, and perhaps, as many as two million [Persians], remained in exile." This source further quotes Ayatollah Ḥosayn-ʿAlī Montaẓerī, a high-ranking official, as saying, "we have several million refugees abroad" (World Refugee Survey, 1988 in *Review*, p. 73). In the absence of comprehensive worldwide data, the data presented here are culled from national population censuses of some of the receiving countries. Table 28 shows the distribution of Persians in countries with recent census data on Persians available at the time of this writing. Around 1990 there was a total of half a million Persians in Germany, France, Sweden, Norway, USA, Canada, Australia, and Israel, but if we include Turkey, they could well exceed one million.

With 285,000 Persians in 1990, the USA has by far the largest number of Persian immigrants among the above-mentioned countries, with the exception of Turkey, for which no reliable data are available. According to the World Refugee Survey 1989 (in *Review*, p. 67), "although Persians probably comprise the largest refugee population in Turkey, little is known about them since their refugee status ... is not recognized and they are not provided shelter or other services." The number of Persians in that country is estimated at between several hundred thousand and a million. The next two largest Persian concentrations are in Israel (121,300) and Germany (89,700). France only has 7,000 Persians despite the disproportionate attention it gets as the main center of Persian political opposition. Germany, Sweden, and Norway emerged as important destinations only after the Revolution because their lenient asylum policies have attracted Persians (Table 28; Kamalkhani, pp. 30-31). On the other hand, Israel, the United States, Canada, Great Britain, and France were countries of significant Persian immigration even before the Revolution.

Population trends in destination countries. The Persian population in the United States more than doubled from 121,500 in 1980 to 285,000 in 1990 due to natural increase and immigration. Of the Persians in the United States, half are concentrated in California. The contiguous states of New York/New Jersey and Washington, D.C./Maryland/Virginia contain the next two largest numbers of Persians. Only twelve states have about 84 percent of the Persian population of the United States; the remaining states each contain fewer than 3,000 Persians. California, especially Los Angeles, is the most ethnically diverse Iranian center in the country, including Muslims, Jews, Christians (Armenians and Assyrians), Bahais, and Zoroastrians (Bozorgmehr and Sabagh, 1989; Kelley and Friedlander; Light et al., 1993; Dallalfar; Hannasab; Hoffman; Naficy, pp. 81-88). New York is the only other state which, in addition to Persian Muslims, has a sizable number of Persian Jews. About 80,000 Persians reside in Los Angeles, making it by far the largest concentration of this group in the United States, and one of the largest outside Persia (Sabagh and Bozorgmehr).

Persian immigration to Canada continues unabated; the Iran-born population increased from 13,950 in

Table 28

DISTRIBUTION OF PERSIAN DIASPORA IN SELECTED COUNTRIES CIRCA 1990

Region and Country	Year	Population
North America		
United States	1990	285,000
Canada	1991	38,900
Europe		
West Germany	1990	89,700
Sweden	1990	39,000
Great Britain	1991	32,300
France	1990	7,000
Norway	1990	5,900
Oceania		
Australia	1991	13,900
Asia		
Israel	1991	121,300
Japan	1992	4,500
Total	—	637,500

Sources: Australian of Bureau Investigation Research, Melbourne, 1993. Great Britain Office of Population Censuses and Surveys, *Ethnic Group and Country of Birth*, London, 1991 (1991 Census). Institute National de la Statistique et des Etudes Economiques, *Recensement de la Population 1990. Nationalities*, Paris, 1992. Israel Central Bureau of Statistics, *Statistical Abstract of Israel, 1992*, Jerusalem, 1992. Japan, Ministry of Justice, *Annual Report of Statistics of Legal Residents*, Tokyo, 1993. System d' Observation Permanente de Migation, *Trends in International Migration*, Paris, Organization for Economic Cooperation and Development, 1992. Statistics Canada, 1991 Census, *Ethnic Origin*, Ottawa, 1993. US Department of Commerce, Bureau of the Census, *Census of Population and Housing, 1990*, Public-Use Microdata Sample, A Sample, United States [Machine-readable datafile], Washington, D.C., 1993.

1986 to 30,715 in 1991. According to Canada's single-response classification (i.e., persons only of one ethnic origin), there were 38,920 Persians in Canada in 1991. There were an additional 4,300 persons who gave a multiple response to the ethnic origin question, i.e., Persian and other origins (Statistics Canada). One province (Ontario) contained 22,510 or over half (58%) of all Persians in Canada. Like those in the United States and Canada, Persians in Australia are heavily concentrated in one region; over three-fourths live in the two states of New South Wales and Victoria (Australian Bureau of Statistics).

The Persian population in United Kingdom increased drastically from 8,200 in 1971 to 28,070 in 1981, but only slightly to 32,300 by 1991. Persian immigration to Israel is not a recent phenomenon (Pliskin, pp. 37-44). Almost 41 percent of Persians currently living in Israel immigrated before the establishment of the state in 1948; only 15 percent have done so from 1975 to 1991. The median year of immigration for Persians to Israel is 1958 (i.e., half arrived before and half after this date; Israel Central Bureau of Statistics). Although the influx of Persians to Australia dates back to the 1970s, there were only 3,670 Persians in this country in 1981 and 7,500 in 1986 (Adibi, 1993).

Family reunification. In the absence of surveys, sex ratio (the number of males per 100 females) is used as an indicator of family reunification. The more balanced the sex ratio, the higher the likelihood of family reunification and, in turn, settlement in the receiving country. As a consequence of family migration (reunification) and natural increase since the Revolution, the sex ratio of the Persian diaspora has become more balanced in most countries. Over half of the population of Persian ethnic origin in Israel were born there, resulting in a very balanced sex ratio. According to the 1991 Canadian census, Persians in Canada had a balanced sex ratio (58% male and 42% female). The Australian Persian population also had a balanced sex ratio. In the United States, males made up 57 percent and females 43 percent of the Persian population (Table 29).

Demographic and socioeconomic characteristics. Since the most extensive data on the Persian diaspora in any country are available for the United States, Table 29 presents data on selected demographic, social, and economic characteristics of this population in 1990. The most interesting new demographic development among Persians is the emergence of the generation born in the United States and the one born in Persia but raised in the United States. The age distribution of Persians shows that there are 69,080 Persians under 15 years of age (Table 29), of whom 47, 670 were born in the United States and the rest were born in Persia and raised in the United States.

Many of the Persians residing in the United States are former college students and educated exiles; half of Persians twenty-five years and older have a bachelor's or higher degree. This high level of education accounts for the heavy concentration of Persians in the top two occupations of managers and professionals (i.e., 43% of employed persons 16 years and over). A substantial clustering in sales (20%) reflects Persians' high rate of self-employment (21%). This self-employment proclivity is partially accounted for by the presence of entrepreneurial minorities from Persia, especially Jews and Armenians. As a whole, Persian males have a higher level of education, hold more prestigious jobs, and are more entrepreneurial than Persian females.

Table 29

SELECTED DEMOGRAPHIC AND SOCIOECONOMIC CHARACTERISTICS OF IRANIANS IN THE UNITED STATES OF AMERICA, 1990*

Characteristics	Number	Percent
Age		
0-15	69,080	24
16-24	34,340	12
25-34	69,620	24
35-44	55,540	20
45-54	25,840	9
55-64	16,680	6
65+	13,880	5
Sex		
Male	160,960	56
Female	124,009	44
Total	284,969	100
Immigration		
Born in US	58,850	21
1985 to 1990	69,870	24
1980 to 1984	41,800	15
1975 to 1979	77,305	27
Before 1974	37,150	13
Education**		
Completed 4 years or more of college	88,370	51
Occupation***		
Managerial	22,640	18
Professional Specialty	30,716	25
Sales	24,980	20
Class Workers***		
Wage and Salary	98,860	79
Self-Employed	26,610	21

*These numbers are based on ancestry (Iranian) and place of birth (Iran).

**Persia-born persons 25 years and over.

***Persia-born employed persons 16 and over. The self-employed include 940 (0.7%) unpaid family workers.

Source: Department of Commerce, Bureau of the Census, *Census of Population and Housing, 1990*, Public-Use Microdata Sample, A Sample, United States [Machine-readable data file], Washington, D. C., 1993.

The statistical profile of Iranian immigrants in the United States shows them to be even more educated, skilled, and entrepreneurial than Americans, as well as most other foreign-born groups in the United States. According to the 1990 U.S. census, Iranian-born persons ranked third in educational achievement after Indians and Taiwanese among major immigrant groups in the United States. Reflecting this high level of education, Iranians once again ranked third after Indians and Taiwanese in holding the top occupations of managers and professionals. By comparison, only 20 percent of the native-born population of the United States had a bachelor's degree or higher, and only 27 percent were employed in these two top occupations. The median household income of Iranians ($36,000) ranked fifth in the United States, and was higher than that of the native-born ($30,000).

The data on Iranians in the United States show the extreme socioeconomic selectivity of this population vis à vis Persia's population. There is some evidence that Persians in the United States are of higher status than Persians in Turkey, Germany, and Australia (Bauer, pp. 77-101; Adibi, 1993). Yet Persians in Australia were more educated than the native-born Australians in 1986; 27 percent of Persians were employed in managerial and professional jobs. An equal proportion of Persians were employed as plant and machine operators and as laborers, a slightly higher percentage than that of the total Australian population. The rest held para-professional, trade, clerical, personal services and sales occupations (Adibi, 1993).

The rapid population growth, concentration in a few countries, and high overall socioeconomic characteristics of the Persian diaspora call for more research on the adaptation of this population.

Bibliography: H. Adibi, "A Study of the Iranian Population in Australia," unpub. paper, 1993. A. Ansari, *The Making of the Iranian Community in America*, New York, 1992. Bauer "A Long Way Home. Islam in the Adaptation of Iranian Women Refugees in Turkey and West Germany," in A. Fathi, pp. 77-101. M. Bozorgmehr and G. Sabagh, "High Status Immigrants. A Statistical Profile of Iranians in the United States," *Iranian Studies* 21/3-4, 1988, pp. 5-36. Idem, "Survey Research among Middle Eastern Immigrant Groups in the United States. Iranians in Los Angeles," *MESA Bulletin* 23/1, 1989, pp. 23-34. Idem, "Iranian Exiles and Immigrants in Los Angeles," in A. Fathi, pp. 121-44. A. Dallalfar, "Iranian Women as Immigrant Entrepreneurs," *Gender and Society* 8/4, 1994, pp. 541-6. A. Fathi, ed., *Iranian Refugees and Exiles Since Khomeini*, Costa Mesa, Calif., 1991. F. Gilanshah, "Iranians in the Twin Cities," *Journal Institute of Muslim Minority Affairs* 7/1, 1983, pp. 117-23. S. Hannasab, "Acculturation and Young Iranian Women. Attitudes Toward Sex Roles and Intimate Relationships," *Journal of Multicultural Counseling and Development* 19/1, 1991, pp. 11-21. D. Hoffman, "Cross-Cultural Adaptation and Learning. Iranians and Americans at School," in H. Touba and C. Delgado-Gaitan, eds., *School and Society*, New York, 1988, pp. 163-80. A. Jones, "Iranian Refugees. The Many Faces of Persecution," Issue Paper, U. S. Committee for Refugees, Washington, D.C., 1984. Z. Kamalkhani, *Iranian Immigrants and Refugees in Norway*, Bergen, Norway, 1988. R. Kelley and J. Friedlander, eds., *Irangeles. Iranians in Los Angeles*, Berkeley and Los Angeles, 1993. I. Light et al., "Internal Ethnicity in the Ethnic Economy," *Ethnic and Racial Studies* 16/4, 1993, pp. 581-97. Idem, "Beyond the Ethnic Enclave Economy," *Social Problems* 41/1, 1994, pp. 65-80. J. Lorentz and J. Wertime, "Iranians," in *Harvard Encyclopedia of American Ethnic Groups*, Cambridge, MA, 1980, pp. 521-24. J. Momeni, "Teʿdād o naḥwa-ye tawzīʿ-e Īrānīān dar Ayālāt-e Mottaḥeda-ye Āmrīkā dar sāl-e 1980," *Īrān-nāma* 2/2, 1984, pp. 17-21. H. Naficy, *The Making of Exile Cultures. Iranian Television in Los Angeles*, Minneapolis, 1993. K. Pliskin, *Silent Boundaries. Cultural Constraints on Sickness and Diagnosis of Persians in Israel*, New Haven, 1987. G. Sabagh and M. Bozorgmehr, "Are the Characteristics of Exiles Different from Immigrants? The Case of Iranians in Los Angeles," *Sociology and Social Research* 71/2, 1987, pp. 77-84. Idem, "Secular Immigrants. Religiosity and Ethnicity among Iranian Muslims in Los Angeles," in Y. Haddad and J. Smith, eds., *Muslim Communities in North America*, Albany, NY, 1994, pp. 445-73. World Refugee Survey, 1988 in Review, 1989 in Review, United States Committee for Refugees, New York, 1989, 1990.

(MEHDI BOZORGMEHR)

ix. AFGHAN REFUGEES IN PAKISTAN

Since the coup d'etat of April 1978 and the Soviet occupation of Afghanistan beginning the following year, over 5 million refugees have fled Afghanistan. Of these refugees as many as 3.5 million settled in Pakistan. Before limited repatriation began in 1992, there were 3.2 million registered and perhaps another half million unregistered Afghan refugees in Pakistan (N. Dupree, p. 852). Historically, Afghans have moved back and forth across the Afghan-Pakistani border, and before 1978 there were Afghan communities in most cities of Pakistan.

Refugees arrived in Pakistan in waves. A small number left Afghanistan as early as 1973 after the coup that deposed Moḥammad-Ẓāher Shah (see AFGHANISTAN x). Approximately 80,000 refugees trickled into Pakistan during 1973-78. The flow dramatically increased after the 1978 coup that established the Communist government of Nūr-Moḥammad Tarakī. The heavy-handed efforts of the Tarakī government to effect social change and the resulting anti-government violence was the major impetus for the refugee migration. By the end of 1979 the Afghan refugee population in Pakistan had reached 400,000 (N. Dupree. p. 850).

The Soviet presence in Afghanistan beginning in late 1979 opened the flood gate. By 1984 the refugee population in Pakistan had reached 3 million, and two years later the official count was 3.2. million (N. Dupree, p. 852). Although refugees came from all over Afghanistan, most of them were from the areas of heavy fighting near the Pakistani border. In addition, the people in the Afghan-Pakistan border areas are largely Pushtuns who share a common ethnic heritage with the Pushtuns living in Pakistan. Eighty-five percent of the refugees in Pakistan are ethnic Pushtuns (N. Dupree, pp. 861-62).

Settlement in Pakistan. Most of the Afghans in Pakistan are housed in 320 refugee camps called refugee tentage villages. Two-thirds of these camps are in the Northwest Frontier Province of Pakistan, with some camps also in Baluchistan. A few camps were established in the Punjab, but historical animosity between the Punjabis and the Afghans dissuaded Pakistani officials from settling Afghans there. Each camp was originally planned to house 10,000 refugees, but most of them now hold many more. The refugee camp at Sorḵāb, Baluchistan is reported to contain 150,000 refugees (N. Dupree, p. 863).

Three-quarters of the Afghan refugees in Pakistan are estimated to be women, the elderly, and children under fifteen years of age. Forty-eight percent are children (N. Dupree, p. 863). The high ratio of women and children is partly due to the high mortality rate among men as a result of the war, partly because of high birth rates in the camp, and partly because men migrate to cities looking for jobs. Most of the refugees in the camps are farmers, traders, or pastoralists. Refugees from the small Afghan middle class, primarily from Kabul, stayed only briefly in the camps, settling either in Pakistani cities or resettling in the West (Farr, 1988, p. 142).

The movement of Afghans is not restricted in Pakistan, nor are Afghans confined to the camps. As a result, many refugees have moved to major cities to work and establish businesses. Most cities of Pakistan, particularly Peshawar and Quetta, now have large Afghan settlements. Some Pakistanis find the presence of Afghans in urban areas objectionable, since the Afghans in the cities are largely young men and crowd the already overloaded municipal facilities. Pakistanis blame the Afghan refugees for the increased crime and violence in Pakistan and for the worsening drug problem (Farr, 1990, p. 138).

Camp life. Refugees have found it difficult to maintain much of their traditional lifestyle. Traditional family structure is therefore challenged. It is difficult, for instance, to maintain living arrangements for extended family. The seclusion of women becomes more difficult in the camps, as they play a more active role because men are often absent or have been killed in war. Marriage becomes more difficult since it is harder to find the appropriate spouse. A very limited number of intermarriages with the Pakistani community have taken place.

Traditional age stratification is also threatened in the Afghan refugee community, since the young must take a more active leadership role, threatening the traditional status of the elders. The younger male adults are often better able to operate in the refugee setting, where knowledge of modern ways and the ability to deal with international agencies are important.

Economic life. Despite attempts by Pakistani officials to provide work in the camps, Afghan refugees have consistently penetrated the local Pakistani economy. Although this has occurred primarily in the areas of high refugee concentration, Afghan laborers, shopkeepers, truck drivers, craftsmen, and traders are now found in most parts of Pakistan. Trucking and shipping has been an important means of income to the Afghans. Many refugees brought with them their heavy trucks now used in Pakistan. Afghans have also opened retail shops in major urban centers. Usually small and selling inexpensive items, these shops are nontheless gaining a growing foothold in the *bāzār*s of Peshawar, Quetta, and Islamabad. Many Afghan craftsmen now work in Pakistan; the best tailors of traditional clothes in Pakistan are now Afghans.

Refugee status. The Afghan refugees' status in Pakistan depends in part on how the refugee situation is defined, both by the refugees themselves and by the Pakistanis. The refugees refer to themselves as immigrants (*mohājerīn*), which has a reference to the flight of the Prophet Moḥammad from Mecca to Medina in 622 C.E. This reference obliges the Pakistanis, as good Muslims, to offer them sanctuary (Farr, 1993, p. 119).

While there are differences between the Afghan and Pakistani Pushtuns, many of the refugees see themselves as simply traveling from one area of their ethnic homeland to another. Indeed, the Afghans have never accepted the Pakistan-Afghan border, known as the Durand Line and drawn by the British in 1893, as a legitimate international boundary. In addition, the Afghans have historically controlled much of the area where they are now refugees, especially the area around Peshawar. As a result the refugees feel that they are, to some degree, entitled to be in this area.

Reptriation. Since the summer of 1992 and the fall of the Najīb-Allāh government in Kabul, some repatriation of the Afghan refugees has begun. The United Nations High Commissioner for Refugees (UNHCR) estimated that by the fall of 1993 approximately 1.6 million Afghan refugees had returned to Afghanistan from the camps in Pakistan. Most have returned to the four border provinces of Qandahār, Paktīā, Nangrahār, and Konar, where the majority of them had come from and from which it is easy to continue doing business in Pakistan and even to return there quickly if things become difficult in Afghanistan. These refugees return to a very difficult situation where their chances of survival over the first year are marginal. The UNHCR has used the incentive of rewarding them with cash and wheat if they turn in their refugee cards, but with little success. Refugees from other parts of Afghanistan, especially the area around Kabul, are not returning, and refugee repatriation from Pakistan has ceased temporarily. In fact, additional refugees are now trying to leave Kabul as fighting has intensified between the rival parties. It is not known how many of the remaining 1.6 million Afghans in Pakistan will remain; certainly some will. As time passes and the refugees increasingly penetrate Pakistani society, find jobs, and adapt to Pakistani conditions, fewer will return. Already a generation of Afghans which has never seen Afghanistan has come of age in the camps.

Bibliography: Z. I. Ansari, "Hijra in the Islamic Tradition," in E. W. Anderson and N. Dupree, eds., *The Cultural Basis of Afghan Nationalism*, London, 1990, pp. 3-20. P. Centlivres and M. Centlivres-Demont, "Socio-Political Adjustment among Afghan Refugees in Pakistan," *Migration World* 15/4, 1987. L. Dupree, *Afghanistan*, Princeton, N. J., 1980 (general discussion on conditions in Afghanistan before the 1978 coup). N. Dupree, "Demographic Reporting on Afghan Refugees in Pakistan," *Modern Asian Studies* 22/4, 1988, pp. 845-65 (discussion of the refugee population and demographics). D. Edwards, "Marginality and Migration. Cultural Dimensions of the Afghan Refugee Problem," *International Migration Review* 20/2, 1986, pp. 313-38. G. Farr, "The Afghan Middle Class as Refugees and Insurgents," in G. Farr and J. Merriam, eds, *Afghan Resistance. The Politics of Survival*, Denver, 1988, pp. 127-50. Idem, "Afghan Refugees in Pakistan. Definitions, Repatriation, and Ethnicity," in E. W. Anderson and N. Dupree, eds., *The Cultural Basis of Afghan Nationalism*, London, 1990, pp. 134-43 (general discussion of camp life). Idem, "Refugee Aid and Development in Pakistan. Afghan Aid after Ten Years," in R. Gorman, ed., *Refugee Aid and Development*, Westport, Conn., 1993, pp. 111-26, (discusses Pakestan's reaction to the refugees). R. G. Wiring, "Repatriation of Afghan Refugees," *Journal of South Asian and Middle Eastern Studies*, 12/2, 1988, pp. 22-41.

(GRANT FARR)

X. AFGHAN IMMIGRANTS IN PERSIA

Prior to the Soviet invasion of Afghanistan in 1979, the majority of Afghans living in Persia were migrant workers. Their number in the 1970s was estimated to be around 200,000 to 250,000 individuals. The occupation launched waves of immigrants and refugees to Persia, most of whom moved to Khorasan while the rest settled in Tehran and other cities. In later years large groups moved to other provinces in the east, center, and south of the country.

Statistical Data. There are no precise statistics or demographic patterns for Afghan immigrants in Persia. Gathering reliable data about them is difficult because single men and heads of household constantly move between the two countries as well as inside Persia. The first official head count included in the census of 1986 showed the Afghan presence at 755,257 (56 percent male and 44 percent female), of whom 85 percent were under forty years of age (44 percent below 15 and 41 percent between 15 and 39). Roughly 84 percent had settled in Khorasan (56 percent), Tehran (16 percent), and Sīstān and Baluchistan (11.5 percent). Another 10 percent lived in the provinces of Isfahan, Kermān, Māzandarān, and Fārs; the remaining 6 percent were scattered in other parts of the country. About 50 percent lived in cities (Markaz-e āmār, 1365 Š., pp. 6, 72-73). It is likely that the immigrants' ignorance of census-taking and fear of persecution on the part of those without identification cards resulted in a low count. A year later the United Nations High Commissioner for Refugees (UNHCR) put the number of Afghan immigrants in Persia at between 2 and 2.5 million, 700,000 of whom were living in Khorasan (250,000 in Mašhad), 200,000 to 300,000 in Tehran, 250,000 in Sīstān and Baluchistan, 50,000 in Isfahan, and the remainder in other provinces (*Refugees*, no. 38, February 1987). In January 1988 the High council on Afghans (Šūrā-ye ʿālī-e Afāḡena) of the Ministry of the interior (Wezārat-e kešvar) released a figure of 2.2 million immigrants, of whom 24 percent lived in Sīstān and Baluchistan, 12 percent in Khorasan, 11 percent in Semnān, 9 percent in Isfahan, 8 percent in Kermān, 8 percent in the Central province, 7 percent in Yazd, 6 percent in Hormozgān, 5 percent in Fārs, 5 percent in Būšehr, and the remainder in other provinces. Figures for 1993 from the same agency show the number of refugees at 2.8 million. The majority have been absorbed into the job market and generally work in agriculture, construction, and the service sector, while a small percentage (roughly 3 percent) live in refugee camps. Afghan workers initially earned 20 percent less than their Persian counterparts, but with the greater need for manpower their wages have reached parity.

Education. Immigrant children carrying identification cards can attend public schools without fee, as Persian children do. Children with no identification cards may go to schools established in some cities (e.g., Mašhad, Torbat-e Jām, Tehran, Zāhedān) by immigrants themselves. Teachers of these schools, themselves refugees, often moonlight for extra income. There are also schools set up in the refugee camps. The rate of enrollment of Afghan children in schools and the literacy rate of the immigrant population are considerably higher than before their immigration to Persia.

Health and Hygiene. Immigrants carry into Persia

illnesses such as tuberculosis, malaria, cholera, measles, sexually transmitted diseases, and skin ailments that are common in Afghanistan and often compounded by malnutrition and hunger (*Refugees*, no. 26, Feb. 1986). New arrivals are required to report to checkpoints and undergo medical examination and treatment, but many enter the country without reporting to any of the fourteen quarantine centers at the border. A joint study, conducted in the spring of 1988 by the UNHCR and the Ministry of health (Wezārat-e behdārī) of 2,800 Afghan households in 133 centers in the rural areas of Bīrjand and Qāʾen in Khorasan, found two-thirds of the centers without lavatories and hygienic drinking water supplies. The primary cause of death in early infancy (3-28 days) was tetanus (64 percent in Qāʾen, 37 percent in Bīrjand).

Legal status. Faced with the two fundamental issues of intermarriage between Afghan men and Persian women and Afghan ownership of property, the Ministry of the interior (Wezārat-e kešvar) instructed the Department of recording documents (Edāra-ye koll-e ṯabt-e asnād) that the identification cards issued to immigrants are solely for the purposes of identification, statistics, receipt of food ration coupons, and the purchase of tickets for domestic travel. They do not have the validity of birth certificates and, therefore, cannot be used for the conclusion of transactions (business and marriage/divorce contracts, power of attorney, etc.) that must be registered officially (directive 6847 M.P., 29 Āḏar 1359/20 December 1980). In practice, however, Afghan men have married Persian women in religious ceremonies not registered with the civil authorities and have assumed ownership or tenancy of property and business establishments with letters of agreement (*qawl-nāma*).

Crime. The presence of more than 2 million, mostly tribal, Afghans in Persia and the violent acts committed by some have created a stereotype, often associating them with violence. A broadcast by Radio Iran on 19 Esfand 1372/10 March 1994 put the number of Afghan prisoners in Persian jails at 3,776, about 4 percent of Persia's prison population. A study of 730 Afghan prisoners in Mašhad (based on a random sampling of 10 percent) found that 40 percent were convicted on narcotics charges, 13.5 percent on murder, 12.5 percent on sexual crimes, 5.5 percent on illegal travel, 5.5 percent on weapon possession, 5.5 percent on assault and battery, and 5.5 percent on other charges (Tabrīznīā and Aržang, p. 105). A 1366 Š./1987 study found that out of 789 persons convicted of murder in Persia about 10 percent were Afghans (ʿAbdī, p. 49). While the rate of murder among the Afghan immigrants is higher than that among the host population, in 77 percent of the cases both perpetrator and victim were immigrants. The high rate of murder and outbreaks of violence among the immigrants may be due, on the one hand, to the weakening of the traditional order and patriarchal mechanisms for conflict resolution and, on the other, to the immigrants' lack of faith in the machinery of justice and law enforcement in Persia. These factors holds true especially for the majority of the immigrants who do not have identification cards.

Return and repatriation. The repatriation of Afghan immigrants assumed primary importance after the Soviet evacuation of Afghanistan in 1989. The Persian government turned to the United Nations for assistance in their repatriation, although it had received minimal aid from the world body for refugee relief. Repatriation efforts, however, have been frustrated by the absorption of many into the Persian job market and by the lack of opportunity at home for a comparable lifestyle. On 31October 1992 the governments of Persia and Afghanistan and the UNHCR signed an agreement for the formation of a tripartite commission to oversee repatriation efforts, which met for the first time on 13 May 1993 in the Ministry of the interior. According to Persian officials, since 1992 every day about 1,500 refugees have returned to Afghanistan, while 400 of them reentered Persia (*New York Times*, Aug. 31, 1992).

Social, political, and cultural ramifications. Afghans living in Persia quickly adapted to their new environment and began to enjoy new opportunities which have permanently changed their lives. Considering the rural origins of the majority, urban life has been a major factor for change. Young immigrants now living in cities, for the most part single men far from their families and traditional patriarchal roots, have been quick to alter their social habits (dressing differently, consuming fast foods, attending movies, etc.). In a few areas with large concentrations of Afghans one can still find the traditional elder (*kalān*) presiding over the community affairs and settling disputes by virtue of his patriarchal mediation. The immigrants, even those living in refugee camps, have never clustered into ghettos. Camp residents are free to leave and reenter their temporary homes; children receive education and health care. Industrial workers have learned new skills, which will probably have an impact on the future economy of Afghanistan. A large number of immigrants find the atmosphere in Persia congenial to their religious traditions. With the desire of many parents to send their children to school the need for education among the immigrants is on the rise. Those who earlier had balked at sending their daughters to school are now inclined to do so. Another major change is the greater uniformity of pronunciation between the Persian spoken in Persia and the one used by the immigrants, as the latter gradually pick up the accent of their hosts. Immigrants without family names have been given surnames, based on place of origin, father's name, etc., on their identification cards. Better health care in Persia has resulted in the abatement or disappearance of viral and skin infections and the reduction of infant mortality, particularly in the cities. Women who had never before consulted a physician are more likely to do so now. The presence of law enforcement agencies in Persia has encouraged refugees to go to authorities when they have complaint against anybody. The role of women, too, has been changing. Afghan women have been going beyond their traditional confinement to the home and are organizing and engaging in social and cultural activities in Persia. Whereas they had been opposed to having their pictures taken, even for identification cards, now, with the assent of their husbands, they appear in family photographs taken for official purposes.

Bibliography: ʿA. ʿAbdī, *Masāʾel-e ejtemāʿī-e qatl dar Īrān*, Tehran, 1367 Š./1988. Markaz-e āmār-e Īrān, *Sar-šomārī-e ʿomūmī-e nofūs o maskan. Mehr-māh-e 1365, koll-e kešvar*, Tehran, 1370 Š./ 1991-92. Š. Tabrīznīā and M. Aržang, "Mohājarat. Yak model-e āmārī," *Majalla-ye k̲āvarān*, Ābān-Āḏar 1370 Š./Oct.-Dec. 1991.

(ČANGĪZ PAHLAVĀN)

DĪBĀ. See ABRĪŠAM.

DĪBĀ, MAḤMŪD KHAN. See ʿALĀʾ-al-MOLK.

DIBĪR, DIBĪRĀN MAHIST. See DABĪR.

DICHŌR, city conquered by Šāpūr I (240-70) during his second campaign against Rome in 253 (252, according to Balty), as recorded in his inscription at Kaʿba-ye Zardošt (Parth. l. 7: *dykwl*, Gr. l. 16). The exact location in northern Syria or southeastern Asia Minor has not yet been established. Martin Sprengling's identification (pp. 95-96, pl. 2 l. 13) of the city with Diacira, mentioned by Ammianus Marcellinus (24.2.3.; Talmudic Ihi Dakira), modern Hīt on the Euphrates in Iraq, is untenable; that of Ernest Honigmann with Zevkir, south of Gaziantep in Turkey, is speculative. This uncertainty underscores the fact that the routes followed by the Sasanian army, or parts of it, cannot yet be reconstructed with certainty.

Bibliography: M. Back, *Die sassanidischen Staatsinschriften*, Acta Iranica 18, Tehran and Liège, 1978, p. 302. J.-C. Balty, in *Comptes rendus des séances de l'Académie des inscriptions et belles-lettres*, Paris, 1987, pp. 213-41. W. Ensslin, "Zu den Kriegen des Sassaniden Schapur," *Sb. Bayer. Akad. der Wissenschaften. Phil.-hist. Kl.* 5, 1947, p. 103 and n. 1. P. Gignoux, *Glossaire des inscriptions Pehlevies et Parthes*, p. 51 and n. 58. F. Grenet, in *Notes et monographies techniques* 23, Paris, 1988, pp. 133-58. E. Honigmann, in *Académie Royale de Belgique. Classe des Lettres* 47/4, 1953, pp. 154-55. E. Kettenhofen, *Die römisch-persischen Kriege des 3. Jahrhunderts n. Chr.*, TAVO, Beihefte B 55, 1982, pp. 74-77. A. Maricq, "Res Gestae Divi Saporis," *Syria* 35, 1958, p. 311; repr. in *Classica et Orientalia*, Paris, 1965, p. 53. D. S. Potter, *Prophecy and History in the Crisis of the Roman Empire*, Oxford, 1990, pp. 46-47, 290-308. M. Sprengling, *Third Century Iran. Sapor and Kartir*, Chicago, 1953.

(ERICH KETTENHOFEN)

DICKSON, MARTIN BERNARD (b. Brooklyn, 22 March 1924, d. Princeton, 14 May 1991), Iranist and Central Asianist specialized in Safavid history. It was as a cryptographic technician for the OSS that he began his training in Persian at the University of Michigan (1943). He served in both the Asian and Eastern European theaters of war, adding Russian and Chinese to his repertoire of languages. After the war he left the army to receive his BA at the University of Washington (1948) in Far Eastern Languages and Literature. Unable to pursue his interests in Chinese Turkestan, for China was in the midst of Mao's revolution, Dickson turned first to Turkey, where he studied with Zeki Velidi Togan, and then to Persia. He did his graduate work at the Department of Oriental Languages and Literature at Princeton University, where he received his Ph.D in 1958 and became profesor of Persian studies (1959-91). In his dissertation, *Shah Tahmasb and the Uzbeks (The Duel for Khurasan with ʿUbayd Khan. 930-946/ 1524-1540)*, he defined the Safavid political system, focussing on the civil war (924-42/1524-36) that erupted upon the accession of Shah Ṭahmāsb. Dickson's magnum opus, the edition of *Houghton Shahnameh* (2 vols., Cambridge, Mass. 1981), entailed a two-decade long (1960-80) collaborative project with the Safavid art historian Stuart Cary Welch. Their analytic comments on the 16th-century Safavid painting not only delineate the Turkman and Timurid sources of the Safavid idiom, but also try to recapture the personalities of the artists responding to the actors and themes of the stories they painted.

Bibliography: Other published works: "Uzbek Dynastic Theory in the Sixteenth Century," *Trudy XXV-ogo Mezhdunardnogo Kongressa Vostokovedov*, Moscow, 1963, pp. 208-16; "The Fall of the Safavi Dynasty," *JAOS* 82/4, 1962, pp. 503-17 (review of L. Lockhart's *The Fall of the Safavi Dynasty and the Afghan Occupation of Persia*).

(KATHRYN BABAYAN)

DICTIONARIES

i. *Persian dictionaries.*
ii. *Arabic-Persian dictionaries.*
iii. *Bi/Multiligual dictionaries.*
iv. *Specialized dictionaries.*
v. *Slang dictionaries.*

i. PERSIAN DICTIONARIES

The history of Persian lexicography can be divided roughly into: 1. early lexicography in Persia; 2. lexicography in India; 3. lexicography in the Ottoman empire; and 4. modern lexicography in Persia. Dictionaries treated in separate articles will not be discussed here.

Early lexicography in Persia (4th-9th/10th-15th cent.). The first Persian dictionary about which some information has come to us is the one compiled by the 5th/11th-century poet Qaṭrān Tabrīzī (but see Ebn al-Nadīm, ed. Flügel, p. 143 on Abu'l-Qāsem Jarrāḥ) which, according to *Loḡat-e fors* (Dabīrsīāqī, p. 14), was mostly comprised of popular words. According to Moḥammad Naḵjavānī (intro. p. 8), it had only 300 entries. It is called *Montaḵab* by Qara-Ḥeṣārī (Dabīrsīāqī, p. 14). This dictionary was one of the sources of Sorūrī Kāšānī's *Farhang-e Sorūrī* and of Enjū Šīrāzī's *Farhang-e jahāngīrī*. Nothing is known about the *Resāla* or *Farhang* of Abū Ḥafṣ Soḡdī (not to be confused with his namesake, q.v., reported as one of the early Persian poets) mentioned by Sorūrī and Enjū Šīrāzī, which must have been compiled no earlier than the late 11th century as it is not mentioned by Asadī (d. 465/1072) and Naḵjavānī (d. ca. 768/1366).

The first extant Persian dictionary is *Loḡat-e fors* of the poet Asadī Ṭūsī (q.v.). Entries are arranged according to their final letters and illustrated by examples from poetry. Over ten manuscripts are known to have reached us (see ed., Mojtabāʾī and Ṣādeqī, pp. 4-16), all of which differ in the number of entries and verses as well as the entry definitions. The author's original copy seems to be represented by the abridged manuscript used by ʿAbbās Eqbāl as the basis of his edition (Tehran, 1319 Š./1940). A version compiled by one of Asadī's students was discovered two decades ago in the Punjab library (ed., Mojtabāʾī and Ṣādeqī). According to its introduction, Asadī had distributed parts of the dictionary without giving anyone a complete version. Later this student collected them, arranged the dictionary, and added supporting verses to illustrate the definitions. This seems to suggest that the dictionary was actually a number of word-lists that Asadī gave his students to complete and to provide with examples found in poetry, which may also explain differences in the title, text, and prefaces found in various manuscripts.

Entries are either defined by their synonyms or explained. Some geographical names, as well as some corrupt words, are also listed in the book. It was used by nearly all subsequent Persian lexicographers, and for some of them it served also as a model (see below).

The second dictionary compiled in Persia is Moḥammad Naḵjavānī's *Ṣeḥāḥ al-fors* (2,300 entries, comp. 728/1328), which depends on Asadī's dictionary but is arranged on the model of the Arabic *Ṣeḥāḥ al-loḡa* by Jawharī Fārābī (Dehḵodā, intro., p. 187). Entries are arranged first according to their final letters, in chapters called *bāb*, then their initial letters, in sections named *faṣl*. Proficient in both Arabic and Persian, Naḵjavānī was more cautious than subsequent lexicographers in choosing his entries. Corrupt words (e.g., *rāzījaz*, *kāmvažīž*, *vāzanj* for *razījar*, *kāmvarīž*, *vāzīj*) are rare, and some verses are attributed to the wrong poet (e.g., ʿOnṣorī's distich to Kesāʾī, s.v. *kūdara*). Some proper nouns are also listed (e.g., *Ās*, *Aras*). It was used by Enjū Šīrāzī, Sorūrī, and Wafāʾī.

Next is *Majmūʿat al-fors* by Abu'l-ʿAlāʾ ʿAbd-al-Moʾmen Jārūtī, known as Ṣafī Kaḥḥāl, about whom almost nothing is known. It is mainly based on Asadī's work but also contains words from the *Šāh-nāma* as well as distichs by Sanāʾī, Sūzanī, Anwarī, Ḵāqānī, and Saʿdī. Since the latest poet mentioned is Saʿdī (d. ca. 690/1291), the book was probably compiled in the late 13th or early 14th century (Nafīsī's suggestion of 9th/15th century, *Naẓm o naṯr*, p. 258, is untenable). It contains 1,542 entries including corrupt forms (e.g., *najm*, *karzīān*, *laḡn* for *bečam*, *korozmān*, *naḡn*). Many definitions are without example.

Meʿyār-e jamālī (comp. 744-45/1343-44) by Šams-e Faḵrī Eṣfahānī is a dictionary of 1,580 entries, including corrupt forms, arranged on the model of *Loḡat-e fors*; all supporting verses are composed by the author. It was used by Wafāʾī, Enjū Šīrāzī, Sorūrī, ʿAbd-al-Rašīd Tatavī, and Awbahī.

Persian Lexicography in India. The influence of the Persian language and literature in India and the need for Persian manuals and dictionaries led Indian men of letters to compile dictionaries as early as the end of the 13th century. The first extant dictionary compiled in India is *Farhang-e Qawwās* by Faḵr-al-Dīn Mobārakšāh Qawwās, a poet at the court of ʿAlāʾ-al-Dīn Ḵaljī (695-715/1295-1316), who was still living in the time of the compilation of *Dastūr al-afāżel* (743/1342, q.v.; Dabīrsīāqī, p. 32). This dictionary, arranged thematically, is divided into five chapters (*baḵš*); each chapter is divided into sections (*gūna*) comprised of a number of sub-sections (*bahra*). It set the example for later dictionaries compiled in India and further influenced many of them. Textual evidence (e.g., use of the same examples, repetition of certain errors) shows that Qawwās used *Loḡat-e fors* as a major source, although he also quotes verses by poets, both Persian and Indian, who lived after Asadī's time.

Baḥr al-fażāʾel by Moḥammad b. Qewām Balḵī Keraʾī (comp. 837/1433) is a dictionary divided in two parts which are further divided into twenty-eight and fourteen chapters (*bāb*), respectively. Entries are arranged according to their initial letters in the first part and thematically (names of cities, drugs, nicknames, etc.) in the second part, which is comprised of thirty-six sections (*faṣl*). The author states in his introduction that he used as his source the works of poets (e.g., Rūdakī, ʿOnṣorī, Neẓāmī, Saʿdī) and the earlier dictionaries *Moqaddemat al-adab* of Maḥmūd Zamaḵšarī, *al-Sāmī fi'l-asāmī* of Abu'l-

Fażl Maydānī, *Seḥāḥ al-fors* of Nak̲javānī, etc.

Šaraf-nāma-ye Monyarī/Ebrāhīmī (comp. 878/1473) by Ebrāhīm Qewām Fārūqī is divided into thirty-one chapters (*bāb*) according to the initial letters of the entrees, and then every *bāb* is divided into sections (*faṣl*) according to the final letters; the rest of the arrangement is alphabetical. The book is dedicated to and named after the author's spiritual mentor Šaraf-al-Dīn Aḥmad Monyarī. In his introduction, the author explains a few grammatical points as well as some Turkish suffixes. The work contains about 11,000 entries illustrated by poems from Ferdowsī to Ḥāfeẓ. The author mentions as his sources Asadī's dictionary, *Adāt al-fożalāʾ* of Badr-al-Dīn Dhārvāl, *Farhang-e zafān-e gūyā* of Badr-al-Dīn Ebrāhīm (qq.v.), the annonymous *Lesān al-šoʿarāʾ*, *Mawāʾed al-fawāʾed*, etc. At the end of the 10th/16th century, Mīrzā Ebrāhīm b. Šāh-Ḥosayn Eṣfahānī abridged this dictionary and renamed it *Farhang-e Mīrzā Ebrāhīm*. *Šaraf-nāma* is the source of many later dictionaries (e.g., *Madār al-afāżel*, *Farhang-e jahāngīrī*, *Majmaʿ al-fors*, *Farhang-e rašīdī*; see Dabīrān).

Moʾayyed al-fożalāʾ (comp. 925/1519) by Moḥammad Lād Dehlavī is arranged first according to the initial and then the final letters of the words. Every letter of the alphabet is divided into three chapters devoted to Arabic loanwords, Persian words, and Turkish elements respectively. The author's main sources were *Šaraf-nāma* and the annonymous *Qonyat al-ṭālebīn*, but he also mentions *Ṣorāḥ*, *Tāj*, *Lesān al-šoʿarāʾ*, *Adāt al-fożalāʾ*, *Dastūr al-afāżel* (q.v.), *Zafān-e gūyā*, etc. (Dabīrsīāqī, pp. 72-74).

Madār al-afāżel of Allāhdād Fayżī Serhendī (comp. 1001/1592) is a detailed dictionary comprising 12,000 entries arranged according to the first and then final letters. The author mentions as his sources *Tājayn*, (i.e., *Tāj al-maṣāder* of Bayhaqī and *Tāj al-loḡa* of Jawharī or the annonymous *Tāj al-asmāʾ*), *Ṣorāḥ*, *Mohaḏḏab al-asmāʾ*, *Qonyat al fetyān* for Arabic and on *Zafān-e gūyā*, *Adāt al-fożalāʾ*, *Šaraf-nāma-ye Monyarī*, *Moʾayyed al-fożalāʾ*, etc. for Persian words. Some definitions are provided with supporting verses (Dabīrsīāqī, pp. 101-02).

Farhang-e rašīdī by ʿAbd-al-Rašīd Tatavī (q.v.; comp. 1064/1653), a dictionary of 8-9,000 entries in alphabetical order, is an abridgement of *Farhang-e jahāngīrī* and *Farhang-e Sorūrī*, correcting some of their errors and omitting the corrupt forms as well as Arabic and Turkish words found in them. Mistakes and corrupt forms recorded in *Farhang-e rašīdī* are mentioned by ʿAlī Khan Ārzū (q.v.) in his *Serāj al-loḡāt*.

Bahār-e ʿAjam is a dictionary of about 10,000 entries, including a considerable number of idioms and expressions, in alphabetical order, compiled in 1152/1739 by Tīk Čand Bahār. In his introduction the author mentions as his source about 100 *dīvān*s and correspondence collections of the Persian and Indian poets of the Safavid period.

The anonymous *Šams al-loḡāt*, compiled by the order of Joseph Barretto in 1219/1805, contains simple words, idioms, expressions, and proverbs in alphabetical order. Examples are at times provided for illustration. The author names in his introduction the earlier dictionaries (e.g., *Madār al-afāżel*, *Kašf al-loḡāt*, *Montak̲ab al-loḡāt*, *Farhang-e rašīdī*, *Farhang-e jahāngīrī*) he based his work on; a few more are quoted in the text. It also contains a number of corrupt forms.

Haft qolzom is an extensive dictionary of 27,709 entries compiled by Abu'l-Moẓaffar Ḡāzī-al-Dīn Ḥaydar, the king of Awadh, in 1229-30/1813-14 and arranged and edited by Mawlawī Qabūl Moḥammad in seven volumes (*qolzom*). The first six volumes are devoted to Persian words and idioms, arranged according to their first and final letters respectively. The last volume discusses Persian alphabet, morphology, prosody, rhyme, figures of speech, etc. The Persian material is taken mainly from *Borhān-e qāteʿ* (q.v.). No examples support entry definitions. Like its source, it contains a number of corrupt words.

Ḡīāṯ al-loḡāt by Moḥammad Rāmpūrī (comp. 1242/1826) contains approximately 15,000 Persian, Arabic, and Turkish entries arranged alphabetically according to the two initial letters. Determinative and attributive compounds are also recorded, but without mentioning their figurative or metaphorical application. Sources are mentioned for many entries, but no examples are cited.

Before turning to the Ottoman Empire and its contribution to Persian lexicography, we must mention a few dictionaries written in Persia during the period we considered as the Indian period of Persian lexicography. They depend on the same tradition and use earlier dictionaries produced in both Persia and India:

Farhang-e Wafāʾī or *Resāla-ye Ḥosayn Wafāʾī* (comp. 933/1526) by Ḥosayn Wafāʾī is based mainly on *Ṣeḥāḥ al-fors*. The author has also used *Meʿyār-e jamālī*, the dictionary of Šams-al-Dīn Moḥammad Kašmīrī and some other sources for a limited number of entries. Another dictionary written in the same period is *Toḥfat al-aḥbāb*, compiled in 936/1529 by the calligrapher Solṭān-ʿAlī Awbahī for Saʿd-al-Dīn Mašhadī, the vizier of Khorasan. It comprises 2,483 entries arranged according to their first and last letters respectively. The entries are almost the same as those recorded by Asadī, plus a number of corrupt forms. The examples are also the same as those quoted by Asadī, besides some verses by later poets (Anwarī, Sūzanī, Sanāʾī, Kamāl-al-Dīn Esmāʿīl, Moʿezzī, etc.). No source is cited by the author (Dabīrsīāqī, pp. 74-78).

A more scholarly and better documented dictionary written a few decades later is *Majmaʿ al-fors* by Sorūrī Kāšānī. Two versions of this dictionary exist. The old version (comp. 1008/1599) is shorter and has an introduction in which Shah ʿAbbās I (q.v.) is praised. The new version is more extensive and seems to have been compiled (1028/1618) after the author had access to *Farhang-e jahāngīrī*, *Šāmel al-loḡa* of Qara-Ḥeṣārī, and *Toḥfat al-saʿāda* of Maḥmūd b. Żīāʾ-al-Dīn Moḥammad. In addition to 10,043 Persian entries, it contains a chapter on metaphorical expressions, the size of which is nearly one-sixth of an identical chapter in *Farhang-e jahāngīrī*. In his introduction, the author mentions as his sources nineteen dictionaries, but thirty-four more dictionaries, some Arabic, are quoted in the text. The author's critical assessment of earlier dictionaries and his careful choice of examples from reliable texts make his work very valuable, even more so than *Farhang-e jahāngīrī* (Dabīrsīāqī, pp. 124-32).

Persian lexicography in the Ottoman empire. Persian lexicography in the Ottoman empire apparently began in the 9th/15th century. Unlike those compiled in India, almost all dictionaries produced in the Ottoman empire are bilingual (Persian-Turkish). The earliest extant dictionary is the anonymous *Oqnūm-e ʿAjam*, containing about 5,000 entries arranged alphabetically according to the initial and final letters. It was used by the author of *Farhang-e Neʿmat-Allāh* (d. 969/1561-62). A manuscript preserved in Bodleian was copied in 898/1492 (Dabīrsīāqī, pp. 261-62).

Loṭf-Allāh b.Yūsof Ḥalīmī is the author of three bilingual dictionaries, namely *Baḥr al-ḡarāʾeb*, *Šarḥ Baḥr al-ḡarāʾeb* or *Qāʾema*, and *Neṯār al-malek/ molūk*, compiled in the Ottomon empire in the 9th/ 15th century. *Qāʾema* is an expanded version of *Baḥr al-ḡarāʾeb* and contains about 5,500 Persian entries defined with examples chosen from poetry. *Neṯār al-malek* was compiled after *Qāʾema* in 872/ 1467. It was apparently a source of *Majmaʿ al-fors* (Dabīrsīāqī, pp. 262-66).

Šāmel al-loḡa of Ḥasan Qara-Ḥeṣārī, compiled around 900/1495 and dedicated to Sultan Bāyazīd (r. 887-918/1482-1512), is based on *Ṣeḥāḥ al-fors*, *Meʿyār-e jamālī*, Qaṭrān's dictionary (which he called *Montaḵab*), and *Qāʾema*. It was one of the sources of *Majmaʿ al-fors*. Other noteworthy Persian-Turkish dictionaries are *Wasīlat-al maqāṣed* by Ḵaṭīb Rostam Mawlawī (comp. 903/1497); *Toḥfa-ye Šāhedī*, a short dictionary in verse composed in 920/1514 by Ebrāhīm b. Ḵodāydede Šāhedī Qūnawī (d. 957/1550); and *Ṣeḥāḥ-e ʿajamīya* or *seḥāh al-ʿAjam* by Moḥammad b. Pīr-ʿAlī Bergavī (d. 981/1573). The last dictionary was originally a Persian-Arabic lexicon with interlinear Turkish translation; in some manuscripts the Arabic equivalents are omitted. Two reductions exist in manuscript (Dabīrsīāqī, pp. 268-80).

Loḡat-e Neʿmat-Allāh (comp. before 947/1540) by Neʿmat-Allāh Aḥmad Rowšanīzāda (d. 969/1561) contains 8-10,000 entries with examples in verse. It has the same arrangement as *Oqnūm-e ʿAjam* and is based on *Qāʾema*, *Wasīlat al-maqāṣed*, *Šāmel al-loḡa*, and the two versions of *Ṣeḥāḥ-e ajamīya* (ibid., pp. 280-82). Lastly, we should mention *Lesān al-ʿAjam* (also called *Nawāl al-fożalāʾ*), a dictionary of nearly 18,000 entries compiled by Ḥasan Šoʿūrī Ḥalabī (d. 1105/1693). It is based in the first place on *Farhang-e jahāngīrī* and *Majmaʿ al-fors*, then on *Šaraf-nāma*, *Ṣeḥāḥ al-fors*, *Ṣeḥāḥ-e ʿAjam-e kabīr* and *Ṣeḥāḥ-e ʿAjam-e ṣaḡīr* of Faḵr-al-Dīn Hendūšāh Naḵjavānī, *Meʿyār-e jamālī*, *jāmeʿ al-loḡāt* of Nīāzī Ḥejāzī, anonymous *Šarḥ-e al-sāmī fi'l-asāmī*, and earlier Persian-Turkish dictionaries (Dabīrsīāqī, pp. 284-90).

Persian lexicography after 1300 Š./1921. Persian lexicography in this period is influenced to some degree by western methodology, although traditional methods are still predominant in most of dictionaries. The most important dictionaries written in this period are *Farhang-e Nafīsī* by Alī-Akbar Nafīsī Nāẓam-al-Aṭṭebāʾ (5 vols., Tehran, 1938-55), *Farhang-e Neẓām*, by Moḥammad-ʿAlī Dāʿī-al-Eslām (5 vols., Hyderabad, 1346-58/1926-39, repr. Tehran, 1985), *Loḡat-nāma* by Dehḵodā, *Farhang-e farsī* by Moḥammad Moʿīn (6 vols., Tehran, 1963-73), and *Loḡat-nāma-ye fārsī* by a number of scholars (Tehran, 1961- Š./1982-; qq.v.).

See also ĀNANDRĀJ; ANJOMANĀRĀ; BORHĀN-e QĀṬEʿ; FARHANG-e JAHĀNGĪRĪ.

Bibliography: (For cited works not given in detail, see "Short References.") S. I. Bayevski, *Ranniyaya persidskaya leksikografiya* (XI-XC vv.), Moscow, 1989. *Borhān-e qāteʿ*, ed. M. Moʿīn, I, pp. LIX-CXVI. Ḥ. Dabīrān, "Šaraf-nāma-ye Monyarī," *Pažūheš-nāma-ye Farhangestān-e zabān-e Īrān* 2, 1356 Š./1977, pp. 97-122. M. Dabīrsīāqī, *Farhanghā-ye fārsī*, Tehran, 1368 Š./1989. M.-ʿA. Dāʿī-al-Eslām, *Farhang-nevīsī-e fārsī*, Hyderabad, 1347/ 1928. Dehḵodā, Intro., pp. 178 ff. ʿA. Joveynī, "Negāh-ī ba farhang-nāmahā-ye fārsī," *Zabān o adabīyāt-e fārsī* 1, 1360 Š./1981, pp. 75-84. P. de Lagarde, *Persische Studien*, Göttingen, 1884. D. N. MacKenzie, "Ḳāmūs ii. Persian Lexicography," in *EI²* IV, pp. 525-27. Monzawī, *Nosḵahā* III, pp. 1919-2046. S. Nafīsī, "Farhanghā-ye fārsī," in *Borhān-e qāṭeʿ*, ed. M. Moʿīn, I, Tehran, 1330 Š./1951, pp. LXIV-LXXVII. Moḥammad b. Hendūšāh Naḵjavānī, *Ṣeḥāḥ al-fors*, ed. ʿA.-ʿA. Ṭāʿatī, Tehran, 1341 Š./ 1962. Š. Naqawī, *Farhang-nevīsī dar Hend o Pākestān*, Tehran, 1341 Š./1962. Faḵr-al-Dīn Mobārakšāh Qawwās Ḡaznavī, *Farhang-e qawwās*, ed. Nadīr Aḥmad, Tehran, 1353 Š./1974. Ḡīāṯ-al-Dīn Moḥammad Rāmpūrī, *Ḡīāṯ al-loḡāt*, ed. M. Dabīrsīāqī, 2 vols., Tehran, 1337 Š./1958. Rypka, *Hist. Iran. Lit.*, pp. 429-37. Šams-e Faḵrī Eṣfahānī, *Meʿyār-e jamālī*, ed. Ṣ. Kīā, Tehran, 1337 Š./1958. Moḥammad-Qāsem Sorūrī Kāšānī, *Majmaʿ al-fors*, ed. M. Dabīrsīāqī, 3 vols., Tehran, 1337-41 Š./1958-62. Storey, III/1, pp. 1ff.

(ʿALĪ AŠRAF ṢADEQĪ)

ii. ARABIC-PERSIAN DICTIONARIES

From the outset of the Islamic period Persian scholars played an active role in Arabic lexicography.

Moḥammad Fīrūzābādī's monolingual dictionary, *Qāmūs*, gave its name as the generic term for a dictionary in Arabic. Bilingual lexicography began during the 11th century soon after Arabic-Persian translation literature and, indeed, New Persian literature in general in Khorasan and Transoxiana. At least sixty bilingual prose dictionaries, and some thirty more in verse (including commentaries on these) were produced in Persia, India, and Turkey up to the later 19th century. They may be classified into five broad types: 1. topical vocabularies, limited to and/or arranged in accordance with particular subjects or a defined corpus, including Koranic and professional glossaries; 2. dictionaries of Arabic action nouns (*maṣāder*-type); 3. dictionaries of Arabic nouns, including adjectives and, sometimes, particles (*asāmī*-type); 4. universal dictionaries, not limited to particular topics or parts of speech and arranged in alphabetical or rhyme order; and 5. pedagogical vocabularies in verse (*neṣāb*-type). Most classical dictionaries are internally classified, whether according to topic, morphology, or alphabetical order (by initial then subsequent letters, or by final then other letters, i.e., rhyme order); the hierarchy of categories is generally *qesm/ketāb*, *bāb*, *faṣl*. Titles, which are often fanciful rhyming or punning phrases or chronograms, do not usually bear translation.

1. Topical. The earliest bilingual dictionary attested is *al-Bolḡa al-motarjem fi'l-loḡa* (comp. 438/1046-47) by Adīb Kordī Nīšāpūrī (Monzawī, p. 265; ed. M. Mīnovī and F. Ḥarīrčī, Tehran, 1976). It is divided into forty *bāb*s listing Arabic words and phrases and Persian glosses under headings such as the names of God, parts of the body, animals, plants, etc. The historian Abu'l-Fażl Bayhaqī (d. 470/1077, q.v.) is reputed to have compiled a Persian-Arabic vocabulary (ed. Ḥekmat, pp. 384-98) comprising a secretary's list of 370 useful Arabic words and phrases in no special order (Monzawī, p. 267). *Al-Merqāt*, also known as *al-Ṣaḥā'ef* (ed. J. Sajjādī, Tehran, 1967), is a Persian-Arabic glossary for beginners in twelve chapters, listing body parts, ailments and medicines, foods and drinks, etc. It is attributed to the poet Adīb Naṭanzī (d. 497/1103, q.v.; Monzawī, p. 272; Storey, pp. 6, 81).

Qāżī Abū ʿAbd-Allāh Ḥosayn Zawzanī (d. 486/1093) produced the first Koran glossary, *Tarjomān-e Qor'ān* (Monzawī, pp. 269-70). The following century saw at least two more, the *Tarājem al-aʿlām* of Abu'l-Maʿālī Aḥmad Ḡaznavī, following the suras in reverse order, and an anonymous imitation of this (Monzawī, p. 284). Two more were produced under the Saljuqs of Anatolia (Rūm) in the latter half of the 12th century by the prolific lexicographer Ḥobayš Teflīsī, the alphabetically-ordered *Jawāmeʿ al-bayān* and the *Wojūh al-Qor'ān* (558/1263), which treated only polysemous words. Post-Mongol examples include the anonymous *Mostaḵleṣ* (711/1311-12), arranged in order of suras and with the addition of grammatical notes; the *Tarjomān-e Qor'ān* attributed to Mīr Sayyed Šarīf Jorjānī (d. 816/1413), extending from suras *Mā'eda* to *Nās*; and an alphabetical recension of this by ʿĀdel b. ʿAlī (Monzawī, pp. 318-20).

Teflīsī also compiled the [*bayān/loḡāt/tarjomān al-*] *Qawāfī*, a dictionary of Arabic rhyming words (Monzawī, pp. 290-91; Storey, p. 88). In Khorasan Moḥammad Ṭabīb Heravī compiled in 924/1518 a dictionary of Arabic medical terms (perforce including many Greek, Syriac, and Latin loanwords), the *Jawāher al-loḡa*, which he revised and reissued in 938/1532 as *Baḥr al-jawāher* (Tehran, 1288/1871; Monzawī, p. 325). A traditional technical glossary in semi-modern guise can be seen in the *Ketāb kaššāf eṣṭelāḥāt al-fonūn* of Moḥammad Tahānavī (fl. ca. 1745), edited by ʿAbd-al-Ḥaqq et al with an English title page and appendix at Calcutta in 1862 (2 vols.; offset repr. Tehran, 1967). This dictionary defines, in Persian, Arabic and other terms used in the Islamic sciences.

2. *Maṣāder*-type. The nonsegmental nature of Arabic morphology presents peculiar problems to lexicographers. Early Arabic topical dictionaries appended after their lists of nouns lists of infinitives (*maṣāder*), and this convention evolved into two distinct genres: dictionaries of nouns (*asmā'*) and of verbs (*maṣāder*).This practice was continued into the early centuries of Arabic-Persian lexicography and considerably elaborated. The first of the latter type, *Ketāb al-maṣāder* of Zawzanī (ed. T. Bīneš, 2 vols., Mašhad, 1961-66), presupposes a solid knowledge of Arabic, being arranged in order of morphological complexity of the infinitives and the characteristic vowels of conjugated forms (Monzawī, p. 268; Storey, pp. 80-81). The *Tāj al-maṣāder* of Abū Jaʿfar Bayhaqī (d. 544/1150; ed. ʿA. Jovaynī, Tehran, 1983) follows essentially the same arrangement, but in strict alphabetical order within the morphological sections; it is, in fact, an unacknowledged expansion of Zawzanī's work from 5,000 to 10,000 entries (Monzawī, pp. 279-80; Storey, pp. 84-85). Both works, but especially the latter, gained immediate popularity; since Bū Jaʿfarak never left home except to visit the mosque, scholars flocked to his house to hear and memorize his dictionary. A 15th-century *Ketāb al-maṣāder* composed in Sīstān by Abū Bakr Bostī shows interesting dialect variants in the glosses, e.g., *al-ʿaks*: *bāškūna kardan* (cf. Persian *vāžgūn*). The principal utility of this type of dictionary lay in the fact that the same Arabic verb can have two or more infinitives. From the perspective of modern scholarship, they illustrate the important process of incorporation of Arabic verbal nouns into Persian by means of auxiliary verbs.

3. *Asāmī*-type. The first of this genre, *al-Sāmī fi'l-asāmī*, compiled in 497/1104 by Abu'l-Fażl Aḥmad Maydānī Nīšābūrī (d. 518/1124; facs. ed. Tehran, 1966; ed. M. M. Hendawī, Cairo, 1967; note that vol. 2 of Tehran edition was published in 1975), was topically classified into four parts (*qesm*): religion, animals, the celestial, and the terrestrial, and it was

further subdivided by *bāb* and *faṣl* (Monzawī, pp. 273-74; Storey, pp. 81-82). It was followed by *al-asmā fi'l-asmā'* (Monzawī, p. 275), an expansion of the work by Maydānī's son Abū Saʿd Saʿīd (d. ca. 539/1144); where the father's book had an introduction in Arabic, the son's had one in Persian. Two famous and similarly-titled works were composed in the 13th century. The *Mohaḏḏeb al-asmā'* of Qāżī Maḥmūd b. ʿOmar Zanjī (Rabenjanī?) Sanjarī (Sejzī?; ed. M.-Ḥ Moṣṭafawī, Tehran, 1985), an Arab by descent and resident near Samarqand, includes phrases, adjectives, and particles, ordered alphabetically (*ketāb*) and by initial vowel (*bāb*), and glossed succinctly in Persian without supporting citations. It makes systematic use of abbreviations which later became standard, such as *mīm* (*maʿrūf* "known") to designate a noun so common as not to require definition, and *jīm* (*jamʿ* "plural"). The anonymous *Tahḏīb al-asmā'*, also called *Tāj al-asāmī* (ed. ʿA.-ʿA. Ebrāhīmī, Tehran, 1988), is similarly arranged but confined strictly to nouns (Monzawī, pp. 301-03; Storey, pp. 92, 109). The former inspired the *Moṣarreḥat al-asma'* of Loṭf-Allāh Ḥalīmī (d. 922/1516), a Persian tutor at the Ottoman court who also compiled several Persian dictionaries. His contemporary Ebrāhīm Šabestarī (d. ca. 916/1510) in western Persia compiled *al-Loḡa fī tarjamat al-esm* (Monzawī, p. 327). In the waning of the Safavid period Mahdīqolī Khan Ṣafā was commissioned by Shah Solṭān Ḥosayn (1105-35/1694-1722) to compile the *Samā' al-asmā'*. Arranged alphabetically by final letter, the work has a long introduction acknowledging sources from Zamaḵšarī to the *Borhān-e qāṭeʿ* (q.v.; Monzawī, p. 343).

4. Universal. Adīb Naṭanzī in the late 11th century compiled the elaborate *Dastūr al-loḡa* or [*Ketāb al-*] *ḵalāṣ*, perhaps for the Saljuqid vizier Ḵᵛāja Neẓām-al-Molk. The bulk of the 7,000 entries are alphabetically ordered by initial, with glosses sometimes in Arabic instead of Persian; appended are some topical sections on names of months, days, etc. and a verse grammar of Arabic. This work was the first to distinguish by diacritics the letters representing Persian consonants not found in Arabic (Monzawī, pp. 270-72; Storey, p. 81). Maḥmūd Zamaḵšarī (d. 538/1144), Moʿtazilite polymath of Chorasmia and author of the important Arabic dictionary *Asās al-balāḡa*, also compiled the Arabic-Persian *Moqad-demat al-adab* (ed. J. G. Wetzstein, Leipzig, 1844-45; ed. M.-K. Emām, 2 vols., Tehran, 1963) for the Ḵᵛārazmšāh Atsïz Ḡarča'ī (q.v.). Unlike the *Asās al-balāḡa*, which is ordered alphabetically by initial of the root, the *Moqaddema* is a cumbersome hybrid, organized morphologically under nouns, verbs, particles, inflexion of nouns, inflexion of verbs (*qesm*), then partly semantically (synonyms and antonyms) and partly alphabetically by rhyme. One manuscript includes Chorasmian instead of Persian glosses (Haywood, pp. 118-19; Monzawī, pp. 276-77; Storey, pp. 82-84). Also at the court of Atsïz was Rašīd-al-Dīn Vaṭvāṭ (d. 573/1177-78), to whom is attributed the Arabic-Persian vocabulary known from its opening words as *Ḥamd o ṯanā* (Monzawī, pp. 282-83; Storey, III, pp. 85-87). This, too, arranges the material under parts of speech, but also juxtaposes synonyms and antonyms. The earliest strictly alphabetical bilingual dictionary (albeit by rhyme) is the *Qānūn-e adab* (comp. 545/1150-51; ed. Ḡ.-R. Ṭāher, 3 vols., Tehran, 1971-72) of Ḥobayš Teflīsī (Monzawī, pp. 286-89; Storey, III, p. 87), expressly designed to help Persian poets find rhymes and as a thesaurus for men of letters. Appendixes included the measures of *maṣdars*, plurals, and biographies of Arab poets, poetesses, and notables. Although Teflīsī's lexicographical works still show dialect differences, they mark the coming of age of literary Persian in the northwest of the Persian world, namely Azerbaijan and eastern Anatolia, to which it had spread from Khorasan more than a century before, and the continuing Persianization of the Turkish élite here as formerly in the east (the *Qānūn* inspired a Persian-Turkish glossary of 1190/1776, the *Alsena-ye ṯalāṯa* "trilinguum" of Saʿd-al-Dīn Mostaqīm-zāda).

There seems to have been by this time an increased need for dictionaries of classical Arabic to serve an enlarged body of professionals who generally functioned in vernacular Persian or Turkish. The anonymous *Jawāmeʿ al-loḡāt* (alphabetic by root initial), written for an atabeg dynast in 641/1243, focused on secretarial vocabulary, and Sadīd-al-Dīn Moḥammad Nasafī's *al-Ṣaḥīfa* [*al-ʿaḏrā'*] *al-sadīdīya* of 649/1251 declared in its Arabic preface that it was compiled for the benefit of Turkoman jurists (*faqīhs*; Monzawī, p. 305). Lexicographers could by now rely on an extensive corpus of monolingual and bilingual dictionaries. The famous Arabic rhyme-order dictionary by Jawharī, *al-Ṣaḥāḥ/Ṣeḥāḥ fi'l-loḡa*, completed at Nīšāpūr around 398/1007 (Haywood, pp. 68-76), was abridged with a Persian translation as *al-Ṣorāḥ men al-Ṣaḥāḥ* by Abu'l-Fażl Jamāl-al-Dīn Moḥammad Qaršī at Kāšḡar in 681/1282. Keeping the rhyme arrangement and the Koranic and Hadith citations and proverbs, Qaršī dispensed with the verse citations and glossed each of the 40,000 entries with a single Persian word or expression. It proved a continuing success, inspiring numerous editions and commentaries (Calcutta, 1259/1843; Monzawī, pp. 306-10; Storey, pp. 78-80). In 725/1324 appeared the *Taršīḥ al-fażā'el*, an abridgement of Zamaḵšarī's *Moqaddemat al-adab*. The *Ṣaḥāḥ* and other works are acknowledged as sources for the popular *Kanz al-loḡāt* of Moḥammad b. Maʿrūf, written around 870/1465 for Solṭān-Moḥammad, the ruler of Gīlān. Primarily in rhyme order, the *Kanz* still segregates infinitives from other vocabulary; it concentrates on Koran and Hadith vocabulary and includes citations. Conversely, the *Dastūr al-eḵwān* (ca. 827/1424; ed. S. Najafī Asad-Allāhī, 2 vols., Tehran, 1970-72) by Qāżī Khan Badr

Dhārvāl (q.v.) is arranged alphabetically by word (not root) initials, and devotes itself chiefly to the Arabic vocabulary of poetry and secular literature in Persian, without citations (Monzawī, p. 316; Storey, pp. 97, 99).

Arabic and Persian lexicography was henceforth practiced increasingly in India, where the rich and comparatively peaceful courts of a cultured Muslim elite attracted both native and immigrant scholars. These efforts bore fruit in the *Montaḵab al-loḡāt-e šāh-jahānī* (comp. 1046/1636-37), the first serious and comprehensive prose dictionary for beginners and general readers of Persian. Compiled by ʿAbd-al-Rašīd Tattavī (q.v.), author of the the *Farhang-e rašīdī*, it is arranged in word-initial alphabetical order. Its rejection of rare vocabulary and ease of use made it immensely popular for centuries (lithographs are still available), and marked the establishment of Persian as the language of culture and administration in north India (Monzawī, pp. 339-40; Storey, pp. 101-02). Meanwhile, the celebrated Arabic *Qāmūs* of Fīrūzābādī (d. 817/1414) had become the subject of translations and commentaries: by ʿAbd-al-Raḥmān b. Ḥosayn in 1027/1618, by Mollā Mīrzā Moḥammad b. Ḥosayn Šīrvānī in Isfahan (both called *Tarjamat* [*wa šarḥ*] *al-Qāmūs*), by Moḥammad b. Moḥammad-Šafīʿ Qazvīnī in 1117/1705 under the patronage of Shah Solṭān Ḥosayn (*Tarjomān al-loḡa*), and by Mawlawī Moḥammad Ḥabīb-Allāh Eṣfahānī in Delhi in 1149/1736-37 (*Qābūs*) for the Mughal Moḥammad Shah (Monzawī, pp. 337-38, 344-45; Storey, pp. 96-97). These generally followed the rhyme order of their model. The most complete of them, however, which incorporated the results of other lexicographical classics, used the "modern" alphabetical order by root initial. This was the *Montaha 'l-arab fī loḡāt al-ʿArab* of ʿAbd-al-Raḥīm Ṣafīpūrī. Completed in 1241/1825 with the encouragement of British orientalists at Fort William College, Calcutta, it went through several editions and was soon regarded in both India and Persia as the most important Arabic-Persian dictionary available. Despite its many errors, it became a principal resource of subsequent Persian dictionaries such as *Farhang-e Ānandrāj*, *Farhang-e Nafīsī*, and *Loḡat-nāma-ye Dehḵodā* (Monzawī, p. 347; Storey, p. 104). Arabic dictionaries continued to be translated into the present century, e.g., *al-Monjed* as *Farhang-e Ḵalīlī* in 1951 (Monzawī, p. 367).

5. *Neṣāb*-type. Versified vocabularies, exploiting the mnemonic value of rhyme and rhythm for rote learning, began with the *Neṣāb al-ṣebyān* of Abū Naṣr Farāhī (d. 640/1242). This work encapsulates 1365 Arabic terms and their Persian equivalents, covering the fields of religion, history, science, and literature in 200 *bayt*s, arranged in 38 strophes and using 9 metres. The abundance of manuscripts, printed editions, commentaries, and imitations of the *Neṣāb* attests to its enormous success; it and its congeners were staples of traditional elementary schools throughout the Turco-Persian world. There were at least 24 Arabic-Persian imitations, and the genre was also exploited for learning Turkish, Hindi, English, and French vocabularies well into the 19th century (Monzawī, pp. 292-96, 299-300, 312-15, 321-25, 341, 365; Storey, pp. 88-91, 95, 98, 100, 102, 104-10; Naqawī, pp. 199-204; Dutt). One ingenious example of this genre, attributed implausibly to the poet Jāmī, is the *Neṣāb-e tajnīs-e alfāẓ*, in which the Persian glosses, as homographs of Arabic words, are reglossed in Persian (e.g., *Meṣr šahr o šahr māh o māʾ āb o ḵawf sahm* /*Sahm tīr o ajneḥa če bāl bāšad bāl jān*), and so on (Monzawī, p. 314). Such curiosities have little value now, except perhaps as indices of their educational and cultural milieu.

Bibliography: (For cited works not given in detail, see "Short References.") Manuscripts and editions are listed in Storey, III/1 pp. 78-110 (esp. those produced in Persia and India); and in two works of ʿAlī-Naqī Monzawī: *Farhang-nāmahā-ye ʿarabī ba-fārsī*, Tehran, 1337Š./1958, and an article of the same name and similar content in Dehḵodā, Introd., pp. 265-372 (esp. dictionaries produced in Persia and Turkey); references in the text are to this article. These works miss a number of manuscripts in India and Pakistan (cf. Naqawī, pp. 281-85) and modern editions. Several critical editions have been issued by the Bonyād-e farhang-e Īrān in recent decades. See also M. Dabīrsīāqī, *Farhanghā-ye fārsī*, Tehran, 1989. Ḥājeb Ḵayrāt Dehlavī, *Dastūr al-afāżel*, ed. Naḏīr Aḥmad, Tehran, 1352 Š./1973. C. Dutt, "Persian '*Niṣābs*' or Rhymed Vocabularies," *Indo-Iranica* 14/1, 1961, pp. 14-31. L. P. Elwell-Sutton, *Bibliographical Guide to Iran*, Brighton and New Jersey, 1983. B. Forūzānfar, *Farhang-e tāzī be fārsī* I, Tehran, 1319 Š./1940. J. A. Haywood, *Arabic Lexicography*, Leiden, 1960. Idem and D. N. MacKenzie, "Ḳāmūs," in *EI*[2] IV, pp. 524-27. ʿA.-A. Ḥekmat, *Pārsī-e naḡz*, Tehran, 1323 Š./1944; repr. Tehran, 1330 Š./1951. Ḥasan Ḵaṭīb Kermānī, *Molaḵḵaṣ al-loḡāt*, ed. M. Dabīrsīāqī and Ḡ.-Ḥ. Yūsofī, Tehran, 1362 Š./1983. S̱. Kīā, *Vāžahā-ye moʿarrab dar montaha'l-ʿarab. Vāžahā-ye moʿarrab dar Ṣorāḥ*, 2 vols. in one, Tehran, 1352 Š./1973. A. Ḵorāsgānī, *Qaṭarāt dar šarḥ-e Neṣāb*, Tabrīz, 1387-1967-68. Monzawī, *Nosḵahā* III, pp. 1941-2046. Š. Naqawī, *Farhang-nevīsī-e fārsī dar Hend o Pākestān*, Tehran, 1341 Š./1962. V. S. Rybalkin, *Arabskaiya leksikograficheskaya tradiciya*, Kiev, 1990. Rypka, *Hist. Iran. Lit.*, pp. 429-37.

(JOHN R. PERRY)

iii. BI/MULTILINGUAL DICTIONARIES

Dictionaries dealing with more than one language can be divided into two general categories of Asian and European. In terms of the number of dictionaries compiled, Asian languages other than Arabic include Turkish (more than 40 titles), Urdu (12 titles), Armenian (8 titles), Pashto (5 titles), Hindi (4 titles), Chinese (3 titles), Japanese (2 titles), and Syriac, Hebrew, Gujarati, and Bengali (1 title each). European languages include English (more than 125 titles), French (63 titles), German (35 titles), Russian (34 titles), Latin and Italian (8 titles each), Spanish (3 titles), and Greek, Esperanto, and Swedish (2 titles each).

The most common type of dictionary is bilingual. Persian is the source language in all Syriac, Bengali, Greek, and Latin dictionaries as well as in most Turkish (80 percent), Urdu (75 percent), Armenian (75 percent), Russian (67 percent), French (50 percent), Hindi (50 percent), and Swedish (50 percent) dictionaries. On the other hand, it is the target language in 75 percent of Pashtu dictionaries, about 67 percent of German, Spanish, and English dictionaries, and in all dictionaries of Gujarati and Esperanto.

History. Excluding Arabic, Turkish was the first language for which a bilingual Persian dictionary was compiled. The oldest such dictionary is the *Ṣeḥāḥ al-ʿAjam* by Fak̲r-al-Dīn Hendūšāh b. Sanjar Nak̲javānī (ca. 731/1330; ed. Ḡ.-Ḥ Bīgdelī, Tehran, 1361 Š./1982). By the 17th century about eleven Persian-Turkish dictionaries had been compiled, the most famous of which is *Lesān al-ʿAjam* (1076/1665) by Ḥasan Šoʿūrī. Also in the 17th century three Persian-Latin dictionaries appeared by C. Ravius (*Specimen Lexici Arabico-Persici-Latini*, Leyden, 1645), Angelo de St. Joseph (*Gazophylacium Linguae Persarum, Triplici Linguarum Clavi Ilalicae, Gallicae, nec non specialibus praeceptis ejusdem linguae reseratum*, Amsterdam, 1685) and Edmond Casteli (London, 1686). In the 18th century, the first English, Italian, and German dictionaries were published. John Richardson published the first Persian-English dictionary in Oxford in 1777. By the end of that century three other English dictionaries were compiled, two of which were published in India (R. Jones, 1792; Gladwin, 1788). F. M. Meninski provided in his mutilingual dictionary (Vienna, 1780) equivalents of Persian words in German, Italian, Latin, Turkish, and Arabic. The number of dictionaries and languages covered (especially European languages) began to increase in the 19th century. Fifteen dictionaries were written for Turkish, most of which were compiled in Ottoman Turkey. The most famous of them is *Lahja-ye ʿOt̲mānī* (1889) by Aḥmed Rafīq Pasha. Four other Latin dictionaries (considered to be the last of such dictionaries) were also written in this century, the most significant of which is Ioannis Vullers (Lexicon Persico-Latinum, 2 vols and a suppl., Bonn, 1855-67). Close to twenty English dictionaries were written in this century, including the well-known Persian-English dictionary of F. Steingass (1892) and a versified English-Persian dictionary, called *Neṣāb*, by Farhād Mīrzā Moʿtamed-al-Dawla (Tehran, 1296/1879). The first dictionaries of French (15 titles), Russian (4 titles), Hindi (3 titles), Armenian, Greek, Bengali, and German (each 1 title) were also compiled in this century. The French dictionaries of J. B. Nicolas (*Dictionaire Français-Persan*, 2vols., Paris, 1857-85), Jean Desmaison (*Dictionaire Persan-Français*, St. Petersburg, 1859-68), and A. B. Kazimirski (*Vocabulaire Français*, Paris, 1883) are more significant that the others. A dictionary by Moḥammad-Ḥasan Khan Ṣanīʿ-al-Dawla (*Dictionaire des homonymes*, Tehran, 1883) and another one attributed to Nāṣer-al-Dīn Shah (*Dictionaire manuel Français-Persan*, Tehran, 1878) are also worth mentioning. The only Armenian dictionary of this century was compiled by H. A. Bezjian (Constantinople, 1826). The first Persian-Russian and Hindi-Persian dictionaries were written by Mīrzā ʿAbd-Allāh Ḡaffārof (Moscow, 1814) and Ṣāḥeb Fīrūz (Lahore, 1840) respectively.

The majority of bi/multilingual dictionaries were, however, compiled in the 20th century, as were the first dictionaries of Pushtu (5 titles), Chinese and Spanish (3 titles), Japanese, Esperanto, and Swedish (2 titles), and Hebrew, Syriac, and Gujarati (1 title each). In the first quarter of the century nine dictionaries of French, six Russian, four Urdu, four English, two German, and two Turkish were compiled. The most important Russian dictionary of this period was produced by L. N. Demitriv (Mašhad, 1906), while the most noteworthy English work was compiled by Arthor Wollaston (London, 1904). In the second quarter of the century, ten English, ten Russian, seven French, four Turkish, two German, two Pashtu, one Armenian, one Greek, one Hindi, and one Gujarati dictionaries were compiled. The Persian-English (Tehran, 1934) and English-Persian (Tehran, 1941) dictionaries of Solaymān Haïm are the most important English dictionaries published in this period, still considered dependable and widely used. Other noteworthy dictionaries of this period include B.V. Miller's Persian-Russian dictionary (Moscow, 1950), Garegin Giragosian's Persian-Armenian dictionary (Tehran, 1933), Saʿīd Nafīsī's French-Persian dictionary (Tehran, 1930), and Nūr-Allāh Golestānī's French-Persian dictionary (Tehran, 1943). In the third quarter of this century twenty-three dictionaries of English, seventeen German, twelve French, eleven Russian, seven Turkish, four Urdu, two Pashto, two Italian, and one Hebrew were compiled. Haïm's dictionaries continued to be the most notable English dictionaries followed by those of Anne Lambton (London, 1954), ʿAbbās and Manūčehr Ārīānpūr (Tehran, 1967), and S.A.J. Reporter (Tehran, 1955, 1973). In other languages, the Persian-German, German-Persian dictionary by Bozorg ʿAlawī and H. F. Junker (Leipzig, 1965, Tehran, 1971) and the Persian-French, French-Persian dictionary by Mortażā Moʿallem (Tehran, 1971) should be mentioned. In the last quarter of this century, more than fifty dictionaries of English, five Italian, three Chinese, three Spanish, two Japanese, two Russian, two Armenian, two Esperanto, two Swedish, one Urdu, and one Turkish were compiled, with varying merits. Prior to the 20th century, Persian was more often a source language, while in the 20th century, with the number of dictionaries increasing, Persian has become more and more a target language.

Places of publication. Early Persian-Turkish dictionaries were compiled in Ottomon Turkey. From 731/1330, when *Ṣeḥāḥ al-ʿAjam* was compiled, to 1967, when Ibrahim Olgun and Cemsit Drahsan published their *Farhang-e fārsī-torkī*, about two-thirds of all Persian-Turkish dictionaries were produced in Turkey. Most Persian-English dictionaries were published in England, particularly in London and Oxford, and in the Indian subcontinent. From 1777, when J. Richardson's Persian-Arabic-English dictionary was published, until 1954, when Ann Lambton's *Persian Vocabulary* came out, seventeen Persian dictionaries were produced in England, of which three were English-Persian and the rest Persian-English. E. Castell's 1686 Hebrew-Syriac-Ethiopic-Arabic-Persian-Latin and S. Veston's 1802 Persian-Arabic-English-French-German-Latin-Greek dictionaries were also published in London. In the subcontinent twenty-one dictionaries (mainly Persian-English) were published between 1877 and 1952. Two Turkish dictionaries by Ebrāhīm b. Nūr Moḥammad (1849) and Šāh Jahān Begom (1886); three Hindi dictionaries by Gladwin (1801), Ṣāḥeb Fīrūz (1840), and ʿAdālat Khan (1890); and ten Urdu dictionaries were also published in the subcontinent. In the United States an English-Persian, Persian-English dictionary was published by J. Accardi in 1977. With the growth of the Iranian diaspora there in the 1980s seversl English-Persian and Persian-English dictionaries were published.

By 1976 twenty Russian dictionaries had been published in the former USSR, namely in Moscow, Saint Petersburg (Leningrad), Tbilisi, Baku, Yerevan, and Tashkent. One was published in Tabrīz (1917). Also in Moscow and Saint Petersburg three French dictionaries by Desmaison (Persian-French), A. Handjeri (French-Arabic-Persian-Turkish), and Mīrzā Šafīʿ Goštāsb (Persian-Russian-French) were published. In Baku a Persian-Russian-Azeri dictionary by Mīr Bābāyef was published in 1945, while in Yerevan, Ārām Būdāḡīān published his Persian-Armenian dictionary in 1961. Four years later a Pahlavi-Persian-Armenian-Russian-English by G. M. Naʿlbandīān was published in Yerevan.

Dictionaries published in Germany and Austria include the Persian-Latin dictionary by Vullers (1855-64), two Persian-French dictionaries by J. T. Zenker (1866-76) and A. Bergè (1912), six German dictionaries from R. Hans (1900) to Wilhelm Eilers (1965), and a Turkish-Arabic-Persian dictionary (1866). Five dictionaries have appeared in Paris, namely a Latin-Persian dictionary (1828) and four French dictionaries by Nicolas (1857), Bergé (1867), Kazimirski (1883), and Gilbert Lazard (1989). Three dictionaries have so far appeared in Italy, namely Desmaison's Persian-French dictionary (1908-14) and two Persian-Italian dictionaries by A. Giodiergui and A. Bausani (1978). Other countries where Persian dictionaries have appeared include Japan (two titles in 1976) and China (two titles in 1981 and 1982). All five Pushto-Persian dictionaries produced so far have been published in Afghanistan.

Bi-multilingual dictionaries published in Persia include eighty-four English (mainly English-Persian), fifty-one French (including one by M. Ḥ. Ṣanīʿ-al-Dawla, Tehran, 1863), twenty-seven German, eight Turkish, five Armenian, five Russian, five Italian, three Spanish (1984-85), two Esperanto (1984), two Swedish (Swedish-Persian, 1988; Persian-Swedish, 1989), one Hebrew-Persian (1966), a Chinese-Persian (1981), an Urdu-Persian (1986), and a multi-language (1933) dictionaries.

Bibliography: Ī. Afšār, "*Ketāb-šenāsī-e farhanghā-ye fārsī-orūpāʾī*," in Dehḵodā, introd, pp. 373-78. M. Dabīrsīāqī, *Farhanghā-ye fārsī wa farhang-gūnahā*, Tehran, 1368 Š./1989. M. Raḥmat-Allāhī, *Ketāb-šenāsī-e farhanghā-ye do-zabāna wa čand-zabāna-ye fārsī*, Theran, 1366 Š./1987.

(ḤOSAYN SĀMEʿĪ)

iv. SPECIALIZED DICTIONARIES

Until the turn of the century, the number and coverage of specialized dictionaries were small and limited. But since then many such dictionaries have appeared, particularly within the last few decades. In these bilingual or multilingual dictionaries equivalents are mostly given in a European language, predominantly in English. Even in the case of monolingual dictionaries, English, French, or German equivalents are often added to the definition.

Before the 20th century. The oldest extant Persian texts that may be considered as dictionaries treat medical or pharmacological subjects. They include *Tanwīr* by Abū Manṣūr Ḥasan Nūḥ Qamarī Boḵārī (4th/10th cent.; ed. M.-K. Emām, Tehran, 1973), in which 321 Persian and Arabic medical terms are defined; the *Ketāb al-abnīa ʿan ḥaqāʾeq al-adwīa* by Abū Manṣūr Mowaffaq Heravī (5th/11th cent., q.v.), which describes in alphabetical order various drugs and their virtues (eds. A. Bahmanyār and Ḥ. Maḥbūbī Ardakānī, Tehran, 1967); and a rather free translation of Abū Rayḥān Bīrūnī's *Ṣaydana* by Jalāl-al-Dīn Abū Bakr Kāšānī (7th/13th cent.; ed. M. Sotūda and Ī. Afšār, Tehran, 1979). Then we have *Meftāḥ al-ḵazāʾen* (in MS), or its revised version *Eḵtīārāt-e badīʿī*, by Zayn-al-Dīn ʿAlī b. Ḥosayn Aṭṭār (d. 806/1403) and *Jawāher al-loḡa* (comp. 924/1518), and *Baḥr al-jawāher* (comp. 938/1531; Tehran, 1288/1877) by Moḥammad b. Yūsof Ṭabīb Heravī. Heravī's son, Yūsof b. Moḥammad, wrote the Arabic-Persian *Loḡāt-e yūsofī* as well as a Hendī-Persian dictionary in verse (Dehḵkodā, intro., p.

296). A manuscript of the former exists in Ṣādeq Kīā's collection in the Central Library of Tehran University. Three dictionaries have come down to us from the 11th/17th century, namely *Alfāẓ al-adwīa* by Ḥakīm Nūr-al-Dīn Šīrāzī, compiled in India in 1038/1628 (Lucknow, 1888); *Ṣaḥāḥ al-adwīya* by Ḥosayn b. Zayn-al-ʿĀbedīn in 1062/1652, a manuscript copy of which is in the Library of Madrasa-ye ʿĀlī-e Sepahsālār (now called Šahīd Moṭahharī); and *Toḥfat al-moʾmenīn* or *Toḥfa-ye Ḥakīm Moʾmen* by Moḥammad Moʾmen Ḥosaynī Tonokābonī (several editions). Two important dictionaries were compiled in the 18th century, namely *Makzan al-adwīa* by Mīr Moḥammad-Ḥosayn ʿAlawī Šīrāzī (many editions) and *Mīzān al-adwīa* by Saʿīd Moḥammad Lakhnavī, containing 476 Hindi words with their Persian definitions (Kanpur, 1332/1914). Of dictionaries compiled in the 13th/19th century, mention should be made of *Farhang-e naṣīrīya* by Ḥakīm Moḥammad-Naṣīr and a Persian-French-German-Arabic dictionary of Johann Schlimmer (*Terminologie medico-pharmaceutique*, Tehran, 1291/1874, repr. Tehran, 1970).

There are also two dictionaries of legal and religious terms from the 17th century, namely a versified one called *Abwāb al-ʿolūm* by Darvīš Jāmī and *Entekābīya*, compiled by Mollā Ebrāhīm in India. The Malek Library in Tehran holds a manuscript copy of the latter (Monzawī, *Noskahā* III, pp. 1920, 1961). A French-Russian-Ottoman-Persian dictionary of military terms was reportedly published in Saint Petersburg in 1306/1889 (Raḥmat-Allāhī, no. 627).

The 20th century. In this century specialized dictionaries have appeared at an accelarating pace: 12 dictionaries were published in during1920-49, 51 during 1950-69, and 249 in the next two decades. Of these 68 percent are Persian-English (or vice versa), 14 percent Persian and a second language, 9 percent multilingual, and 9 percent monolingual (Table 30). Of the total number of dictionaries published during this period, 24 percent deal with technology; 15 percent with applied sciences; 11 percent with medicine, pharmaceutics, and health; 10 percent with

Table 30

DISTRIBUTION OF SPECIALIZED DICTIONARIES IN 1920-1980 BASED ON LANGUAGE

Language/Year	1920-40	1950-60	1970-80	TOTAL
Monolingual	4	7	18	29
English-Persian	0	28	184	212
French-Persian	3	3	6	12
Russian-Persian	3	2	6	11
Others-Persian	1	7	12	20
Multilingual	1	4	23	28
Total	12	51	249	312

Table 31

DISTRIBUTION OF SPECIALIZED DICTIONARIES IN 1920-1980 BASED ON GENERAL FIELDS

Fields/Year	1920-40	1950-60	1970-80	TOTAL
Technology	0	10	66	76
Applied sciences	3	9	34	46
Medicine and related fields	0	5	30	35
Economics and administration	2	6	22	30
Social sciences and Western philosophy	0	0	26	26
Mathematics and statistics	0	1	20	21
Islam and other religions	1	8	9	18
Psychology and psychiatry	0	5	4	9
Military sciences	4	2	2	8
Law	1	3	4	8
Library and information sciences	0	0	8	8
Agriculture ans related fields	0	1	5	6
Linguistics and literature	1	0	5	6
Arts	0	0	6	6
Others	0	1	8	9
Total	12	51	249	312

economics, banking, management, and accounting; 8 percent with social sciences, western philosophy, education, political science, and population; 7 percent with modern mathematics and statistics; 6 percent with logic and Islamic philosophy; and the remaining 19 percent with military science, library science, journalism, printing, law, agriculture, linguistics, literature, cinema, music, and sports (Table 31).

Specialized dictionaries continued to appear at a remarkable pace in the 1990s. By the end of 1992, fifty-two such dictionaries had been published, of which thirty are English-Persian, thirteen monolingual, eight multilingual, and one German-Persian. Nine of them deal with technology, seven with social sciences and western philosophy, six with economics and administration, six with applied sciences, five with Islamic culture and religious sciences, and nineteen with other fields.

Bibliography: M. Dabīrsīāqī, *Farhanghā-ye fārsī wa farhang-gūnahā*, Tehran, 1368 Š./1989. L.-M. Raḥmat-Allāhī, *Ketāb-šenāsī-e farhanghā-ye do-zabāna wa čand-zabāna-ye fārsī*, Tehran, 1366 Š./1987. A. Yārmoḥammadī, "Ketāb-nāma-ye farhang-nāmahā-ye mawżūʿī," *Našr-e dāneš* 3/1, 1981, pp. 48-53.

(Ḥosayn Sāmeʿī)

v. Slang Dictionaries. See SLANG.

DIDYMA (Gk. tà Dídyma, probably of Carian origin), district ca. 20 km south of the Ionian Miletus and site of a pre-Greek (Pausanias, 7.2.6) sanctuary of Apollo, to which a famous oracle was attached. Didyma was connected to Miletus by a partially paved sacred way via Panormus on the sea. The 6th-century temple, which incorporated its smaller predecessor, was destroyed by the Persians in 494 B.C.E., after the failure of the Ionian revolt (Herodotus, 6.19.3; according to Strabo, 14.1.5, however, it was Xerxes who destroyed the temple). The hereditary priests, the Branchidae, descended from a shepherd named Branchus said to have been granted the prophetic gift by Apollo himself, were expelled, and the bronze statue of Apollo, by Canachus of Sicyon (Pausanias, 2.10.5), was carried away to Ecbatana; Seleucus I Nicator brought it back in around 300 B.C.E. A huge bronze knucklebone (weighing ca. 100 kg) has been excavated at Susa; it must have been part of the Persian loot from Miletus or Didyma.

A new sanctuary of great dimensions was planned by Alexander the Great (q.v.); construction seems to have begun under Seleucus and to have continued until the 2nd century C.E. (cf. Pausanias, 7.5.4), but it was never finished.

Bibliography: [L.] Bürchner, "Didyma 1," in Pauly-Wissowa, V/1, cols. 437-41. J. Fontenrose, *Didyma. Apollo's Oracle, Cult and Companions*, Berkeley, Calif., 1988. M. Rostovtzeff, *Iranians and Greeks in South Russia*, New York, 1922, p. 236. T. Wiegand, *Didyma*, 2 vols. in 4, Berlin, 1941-58.

(Rüdiger Schmitt)

DIEU, Louis (Ludovicus) de, Dutch Orientalist (b. Vlissingen, Flushing, April 7, 1590; d. Leiden, Dec. 23, 1642). His father Daniel de Dieu (1540-1607) was a Calvinist minister at Brussels, who in 1585 fled from the Spanish army to Flushing in the Protestant province of Zeeland. Louis studied theology and Oriental languages (Hebrew, Syriac, Ethiopic, and Arabic) in Leiden with Thomas Erpenius and Jacob Golius. As a minister of the Dutch Reformed Church, he served first in his native province and then from 1619 onwards in Leiden. In 1636 he was appointed governor of Walloon College, a hostel for theology students from the southern Netherlands (present-day Belgium) associated with the University of Leiden.

As a scholar De Dieu was renowned for his interpretations of biblical texts, which were based on a wide and profound linguistic learning. His studies were mainly concerned with the early and more recent translations of the Bible. He also wrote a comparative grammar of a number of Semitic languages (*Grammatica linguarum Orientalium. Hebraeorum, Chaldaeorum et Syrorum inter se collatarum*, Leiden, 1628).

His first acquaintance with Persian was through the Jewish-Persian translation of the Pentateuch by Rabbi Yaʿqūb b. Ṭāʾūs, which was printed in a polyglot Bible at Constantinople (1546). In 1635 two Persian texts fell into his hands, which further stimulated his interest in the language. They contained lives of Christ and St. Peter, originally written in Portugese by the Jesuit priest Jerome Xavier (1549-1617) and then translated into Persian at the command of the Mughal emperor Akbar (q.v.; Storey, I, pp. 163-66). De Dieu published both texts together with a Latin translation and annotations, intending to correct what he viewed as "misrepresentations" of Christian beliefs on the part of the Catholic missionary (*Historia Christi,* and *Historia S. Petri*, Leiden, 1639). At the request of the printers of these books he also wrote an elementary grammar (*Rudimenta linguae Persicae*, Leiden, 1639), with the first two chapters of the Book of Genesis from the Persian Pentateuch of Rabbi Ṭāʾūs attached as reading material. It is a small book of eighty-two pages which describes the basic morphological rules of Persian in four chapters (the elements of the Persian language, the verb, nouns and pronouns, particles) according to the categories of classical grammar. However, occasionally he also turned his attention to the analytical structure of Persian, in particular in those cases where parallels could be drawn with the Dutch language. His work was the first Persian grammar published in Europe.

Some confusion has arisen as to the actual authorship of *Rudimenta*. Only a few years after its appearance, a German scholar visiting the Netherlands, Christian Rau, made the suggestion that the grammar was not written by De Dieu himself, but by Johannes Elichman (fl. 1600-39), a physician from Silesia living in Leiden, who was renowned for his extensive knowledge of Oriental languages. This remark by Rau was accepted by Joseph von Hammer and misled Gernot Windfuhr (p. 13) to say: "De Dieu is probably the pseudonym for Johann Elichman." In the preface to his edition of the *Historia Christi*, De Dieu fully acknowledged the help he received from the lexicographical collections of his Leiden colleagues Elichman and Golius, but there are no grounds for supposing that the grammar was not his own work.

Bibliography: J. von Hammer, in *JA* 12, 1833, p. 49. W. Juynboll, *Zeventiende eeuwsche beoefenaars van het Arabisch*, Leiden, 1931, pp. 202-03. Th. H. Lunsingh Scheurleer and G. H. M. Posthumus Meyjes, eds., *Leiden University in the Seventeenth Century*, Leiden, 1975. Chr. Rau (Ravius), *Panegyricae orationes duae de linguis orientalibus*, Utrecht, 1643, p. 12. G. Windfuhr, *Persian Grammar. History and State of its Study*, The Hague, 1979.

(J.T.P. DE BRUIJN)

DIEULAFOY, JANE HENRIETTE MAGRE (b. Toulouse, 29 June 1851, d. Château de Langlade, Haute-Garonne, 25 May 1916), French archeologist, explorer, folklorist, novelist, playwright, and journalist. Jane was born into a wealthy and cultivated family of merchants. She studied at Couvent de l'Assomption d'Auteuil (1862-1870) in Paris. In May 1870, she married Marcel Dieulafoy (q.v.) and joined him in the army of the Loire during the Franco-Prussian war of 1870. From that time, she adopted masculine costume and a short haircut in her extensive travels and her mundane Parisian life. They formed a strange couple which later became a favorite target of journalists and cartoonists. She studied drawing and sculpture, knew English and Spanish, could read Italian and Portuguese, and acquired some knowledge of Moroccan Arabic and Persian. During Marcel's appointments at Toulouse (1871-79) as the architect in charge of historical monuments, she accompanied him on his travels in England, Italy, Spain, Upper Egypt, and Morocco. When Marcel obtained an unpaid assignment in Persia, Jane decided to accompany him. From the start, she imposed herself as a "collaborateur" (she used the masculine form purposely). She covered on horseback all the Persian itinerary of the voyage (1881-82) from Marseilles to Athens, Istanbul, Poti, Erevan, Jolfā, Tabrīz, Qazvīn, Tehran, Isfahan, Persepolis, Shiraz, Sarvestān, Fīrūzābād, and to Susa via Būšehr and Mesopotamia. Despite multiple hardships, and notably a serious illness of Marcel and herself, she kept an enthusiastic diary of the expedition. Persia fascinated her. She wrote profusely on history, archeology, arts, architecture, handicrafts, ethnology, folklore, geography, economics, etc. She encountered and depicted, with a sense of humor, all kinds of people ranging from the simple muletteer to high ranking officials and the Shah. She managed to penetrate into the *andarūns* (q.v.) and provided us with vivid descriptions of the lives of secluded women of all ranks. This intrusion was facilitated by the fascination of Persians with the camera obscura she carried along with a cumbersome photographic material. Besides all the main monuments and archeological remains, she photographed and processed on the spot many portraits of men, women, various social groups, etc. All drawings and engravings illustrating her travel accounts and Marcel Dieulafoy's publications were made from these photographs.

Upon the return from this first Persian mission, she published the journal of the expedition in *Le Tour du Monde* (45-49, 51) and wrote extensively on Persia in various periodicals. With the help of Louis de Ronchaud, the general secretary of fine arts, the Dieulafoys obtained an official mission for Susa. The team, including the young engineer C. Babin and the naturalist F. Houssay, left Paris in December 1884. After some diplomatic difficulties, excavations were carried out during the cold season (March-April 1885; December 1885-March 1886) despite serious difficulties due to insecurity and the rivalry between Arab and Lor tribes and the Dezfūlīs who provided the labor force. Periods of stormy weather and floods hampered the work considerably. Transportation of heavy remains, notably two bull protomes, to the ship on the Kārūn river, was made in scorching heat and constant fear of Arab attacks (March-April 1886). Further difficulties arose from pilgrims of the tomb of Daniel, the *ʿolamāʾ* of Dezfūl, the governor Moḥsen Khan Moẓaffar-al-Molk, and the customs officers, mainly the Ottomans at Amara. On the other hand, Jane recognized that half of the collection was due to "the generosity of the king and his son Masʿūd Mīrzā Ẓell-al-Solṭān and partly to the constant backing of Shaikh Mezʿal of Banī Kaʿb (*En mission...*, p. 306).

Upon the mission's return to Paris, Jane published in *Le Tour du Monde* the journal of the expedition and prepared the exhibition of the monuments in the Louvre (two rooms were to bear her name), notably the enamelled-brick archers frieze which she entirely restored and reconstructed. At the inauguration of the Dieulafoy rooms, she was awarded the coss of the Légion d'Honneur by President Sadi Carnot (20 October 1886).

While writing her travel accounts she had developed a taste for a literary career. Her first historical novel, *Parysatis* (Paris, 1890), inspired by the history of Susa, was awarded a prize by the Académie française and was turned into as a lyrical drama by

Camille Saint-Saëns (Béziers, 1902). It was followed by historical novels inspired by the French Revolution (*Volontaire 1791-1793*, Paris, 1892; *Frère Pélage*, Paris, 1894). She turned to the psychological novel with *Déchéance* (Paris, 1897), where she took position against divorce, although she was othewise considered a determined feminist. In 1904, she presided over the jury of "La vie heureuse," forerunner of the literary award "Prix Femina."

Aside from their busy daily life in their Paris literary salon, which also featured private theatrical performances, the Dieulafoys remained interested in historical and archeological research. They pursued it in Spain and Morocco (twenty three travels between 1888 and 1914); the Susa mission was given, to their great disappointment, to Jacques de Morgan from 1897. Jane wrote historical, geographical, and biographical works on Spain. In 1913-14, she militated for the enrollment of women in the military auxiliary services. In 1914-15, while Marcel was assigned to public works in the corps of engineers at Rabat, she directed the excavation works of the 12th-century Yaʿqūb al-Manṣūr Mosque near Rabat. She died at the family domaine of Langlade, Pompertuzat, near Toulouse.

Despite her ardent feminism and desire to have "*une vie d'homme*," her personality remains rather puzzling. She always claimed to form with Marcel an ideal couple. After her death, he claimed as hers half of the honors that had been bestowed on him. She shares Marcel's responsibility for the positive contributions made to Persian archeology as well as the errors made, notably in historical interpretations. Her description of Persia and the Persians is not free from obvious mistakes either (e.g., she mistranslated *kadḵodā* as "l'image de Dieu and " Salmān-e Pāk as "Soleiman le Pur," called Rostam Beg Āq Qoyunlū "une roi mogol," and took a carder for a harpist; *Une amazone*, pp. 92, 176, 317, 334). She was highly prejudiced against the mullas (ibid., p. 63) and shared Marcel's feelings that the conditions then prevalent in Islamic countries was a drawback on the progress of "civilization" (Gran-Aymeric, pp. 305 f.).

Bibliography: Major works: *La Perse, la Chaldée et la Susiane 1881-1882*, Paris, 1887; repr. two vols. (with a choice of illustrations) as *Une amazone en Orient. Du Caucase a' Persépolis 1881-1882* (vol. 1); *L'Orient sous le voile. De Chiraz a' Bagdad 1881-1882* (vol 2) , Paris, 1989; tr. ʿA.-M. Farahvašī (Motarjem Homāyūn) as *Safar-nāma-ye Mādām Dīūlāfūā*, Tehran, 1332 Š./1953. *A Suse 1884-1886. Journal des fouilles*, Paris, 1888; repr. with a choice of illustrations as *En mission chez les Immortels. Journal des fouilles de Suse 1884-1886*, Paris, 1990; tr. F. L. White as *At Susa, the Ancient Capital of the Kings of Persia*, Philadelphia, 1890. *Rose d'Hatra* and *L'Oracle* (short stories), Paris, 1893. *Aragon et Valence*, Paris, 1901. *L'épouse parfaite* (translation from Fray Luis de León), Paris, 1906. *Castille et Andalousie*, Paris, 1908. *Isabelle la Grande*, Paris, 1920.

Sources: J. Darmesteter, "Parysatis et le roman historique," *Revue Bleue*, 1890, p. 2. F. Desplantes, *Une exploratrice, Madame Jane Dieulafoy*, Rouen, 1889. *Dictionnaire de biographie française*, Paris, 1965, LXII, cols. 331-32. E. and J. Gran-Aymeric, "Jane Dieulafoy, les grands archéologues," *Archeologia*, Dijon, no. 189, pp. 77-81. Idem, *Jane Dieulafoy. Une vie d'homme*, Paris, 1991. E. Pottier, "Les antiquités de Suse rapportées par la mission Dieulafoy," *Gazette des Beaux-Arts*, Paris, 1886. Idem, *Madame Dieulafoy (1851-1916)*, Angers, n.d.

(Jean Calmard)

DIEULAFOY, MARCEL-AUGUSTE, French archeologist (b. Toulouse, 3 August 1844, d. Paris, 25 February 1920). He thoroughly represented a generation of learned Frenchmen of the 19th century who were without university education and specialized training. But their familiarity with classical civilization combined with technical education led them to take an interest in wide-ranging aspects of history and archeology.

Marcel Dieulafoy belonged to a cultivated noble family that had also produced an 18th-century playwright. His uncle was a professor of surgery and his older brother, Georges, was a celebrated teacher of internal pathology. In 1863 Marcel Dieulafoy was accepted at École Polytechnique, where he studied civil engineering; he then became an engineer in the French bureau of roads and bridges. In 1868 he took up his first assignment, in the commune of Aumale (now Sour al-Ghozlane) in Algeria; there he discovered the Arabic-speaking orient in association with Roman antiquities, and this combination was decisive for his future interests. In 1870 he was appointed to the navigation service on the Garonne and married Jane Magre (1851-1916; see DIEULAFOY, JANE), a fellow citizen of Toulouse who subsequently played a major role in the shaping of his career. During the Franco-Prussian war (1870-71) Dieulafoy served as an engineering officer at Nevers. After his demobilization he was placed in charge of the supply services for the department of Haute Garonne, then in 1874 of the municipal services of Toulouse. In the latter capacity he particularly distinguished himself during the serious floods of 1875.

Marcel's leisure activities had already led him to an interest in medieval archeology. He became acquainted with Eugène-Emmanuel Viollet-le-Duc, under whom he worked for four years in the commission of historic monuments and who influenced the direction of his own personal research. As his wife was to explain later, "Marcel was deeply persuaded that Sasanian Persia had had an overwhelming influence on the origins of Islamic architecture and that it was through the study of the monuments of Ḵosrow and Šāpūr that it would one day be possible to substitute for ingenious theories reasoning based on solid foundations." With Viollet-le-Duc's encouragement Dieulafoy left his post in 1880 and requested an unpaid assignment in Persia (Cognat, pp. 5-6).

He took the opportunity to visit Athens and Constantinople en route. When he arrived in Tehran he was seriously ill and came under the care of François Tholozan, the perecited by the Magusaean magi in a real liturgical context. Something about the ill fit of the interpretations with the underlying narratives (especially the first), an allegorical dissonna. From there he made an expedition to Susa, where the traces of the palace explored thirty years earlier by W. K. Loftus remained visible, permitting an immediate comparison with the remains at Persepolis.

On this journey Dieulafoy gathered the material for his great work *L'art antique de la Perse* (5 vols. in folio, 1884-89), illustrated with superb photographs, which remains an indispensable work of reference, especially in view of what has since been lost, notably at the Ayvān-e Kesrā (q.v.). In the first volume the monuments of Mašhad-e Morḡāb (i.e., Pasargadae) are described and discussed: "The tombs and the palace . . . were not original conceptions or copies of monuments built in the countries bordering on Fārs, but rather reproduced, with adaptation to Aryan customs, the previously existing structures of the Greeks in Ionia and Lycia." The second volume is devoted to a description of the buildings at Persepolis, the columns of which Dieulafoy considered to be copies of the Ionic orders. In the third volume the Persepolitan sculptures were presented on the assumption that "both Greek statuary and Persian statuary are derived from the schools of Assyria." In the fourth volume Dieulafoy turned his attention to the vaulted monuments of Sarvestān and Fīrūzābād in Fārs, which he attributed to the Achaemenid period. This error led him to conclude that the vault and the dome had originated in a popular building tradition, which he supposed had then developed further in the Parthian and Sasanian periods. He put forward this hypothesis in the final volume, drawing upon comparisons with the Islamic architecture of Syria and the medieval architecture of France, both of which he believed had evolved directly from that of ancient Persia.

A brief visit to Susa greatly impressed Marcel, who returned with a wish to resume explorations there. The director of the French national museums, who had just created the department of oriental antiquities at the Louvre, obtained for him a modest sum, which was augmented by the minister of public instruction; the army and the navy also provided material and supplies. The Dieulafoys returned to Persia in 1884, with a team consisting of a young engineer, Chrles Babin, and the naturalist Marcel Houssaye. The Persian government at first refused to authorize the excavations, but the intervention of Tholozan made the difference. Permission was granted on the condition that the tomb of Daniel must not be touched except for repairs, for which the French government would be responsible at its own expense. The antiquities discovered were to be divided between the two countries, with the exception of those made of precious metals, which were all to be turned over to the Persian government. The Persian government subsequently waived its right to share in the finds, however, apparently because they consisted mainly of bricks and stone fragments (Gran-Aymeric, pp. 96, 135).

The work was carried out during the winters of 1303/1885 and 1304/1886. Unlike most archeologists of his time, Dieulafoy was more interested in architecture than in "museum objects." He wanted to complete the excavation of the great columned hall, which William Kennett Loftus had identified on the basis of an inscription that he had copied there; the hall was identified by the term *apadāna* (q.v.) and said to have been built by Darius (q.v.; r. 521-486 B.C.E.), then burned, and finally restored by Artaxerxes II (q.v.; r. 405-359; Cagnat, p. 9)

Dieulafoy's work was slowed by the discovery of numerous tombs of the Parthian period, which aroused the protests of the workmen, even though they were not the tombs of Muslims. The trenches had been sunk only 2 m before the floor of the building was reached. It was possible to salvage one almost complete capital, consisting of two bull protomes and an element with volutes. Dieulafoy then concentrated his efforts 50 m farther south, where he was seeking the entrance to the *apadāna*, opening a trench 60 m long and 4 m wide. He thus discovered, upside down on the pavement of a court, the enameled-brick wall revetment representing a frieze of lions. In the following year he extended the excavations farther to the west and found there, in a disordered pile, the enameled bricks that permitted him to reconstruct the archer frieze. Limited finances prevented him from expanding the field of operations farther to the south, which would have led to the discovery of Darius's actual residence; it was uncovered more than twenty years later by Roland de Mecquenem.

A few trenches were also dug in other parts of the site but without much result. In addition, a small building in the neighborhood of Susa was investigated. The discovery there of Achaemenid column bases led Dieulafoy to identify it as an Achaemenid fire temple (*āyadana*, q.v.; Dieulafoy, *L'Acropole*, pp. 411 ff.). In fact, the plan that was recovered was very uncertain. Nor was it recognized that the column bases had been brought from Susa and were older than the building, which was probably a residence constructed after the Achaemenid period.

The excavations were conducted under difficult conditions. The archeologists lived in tents, exposed to the heavy storms of early spring and to the attacks by robbers and pilgrims who came to make their devotions at the tomb of Daniel, in a region where the central government had little control. Nevertheless, Dieulafoy managed to send the antiquities discovered to France without loss; everything that remained in situ was doomed to destruction.

Dieulafoy confided to his wife the task of publishing the details of the work in her book *À Suse, journal des fouilles* (Paris, 1888); unfortunately, however, she indulged her preference for anecdote at the expense of archeological precision. Dieulafoy himself undertook an elaborate synthesis entitled *L'Acropole de Suse d'après les fouilles exécutées in 1884, 1885, 1886 sous les auspices du Musée du Louvre* (Paris, 1893). There he provided a good description of the geography and some historical information on the country of Elam, of which Susa had been the capital. But, having discovered representations of both black and white men among the enameled-brick archers, he was led to conclude that the indigenous population of Susiana had been black; he identified them as "négritos." Although Houssaye's examination of the excavated skeletons did not actually confirm this daring hypothesis, Dieulafoy went on to identify the black archers as the Susianan "platoon" of the Immortals, the royal guard mentioned by Herodotus (7.83), and the whites as Aryan immigrants and thus the Persian contingent of the guard (Dieulafoy, *L'Acropole*, p. 43).

Babin had prepared a new plan of Susa, on which the entire enormous site, encompassing a total of 123 ha, was identified as the Persian "acropolis," comprising the palace, or *apadāna*, in the north and the citadel in the west. The city proper was supposed to have extended over an immense area to the west. Although the fortifications of the "acropolis" had not been excavated, they were nevertheless reconstructed on the plan with "a wide, deep moat and a triple surrounding wall, reinforced by towers provided with casemates . . .," all purely imaginary. As for the *apadāna*, its southern wall having escaped attention because it was built of mud brick, Dieulafoy thought that it had never existed and that the enormous room, covering about 1 ha, had been open on that side. He went farther: "The model of the *apadāna* walled on only three sides was preserved through the centuries, and . . . the throne rooms of the Parthian palace at Hatra . . . of the Persian palaces of Shah ʿAbbās and his successors at Isfahan . . . were built on this model." This conclusion is obviously incorrect.

It is curious to observe that after the publication of the results of his mission, which had enriched the Louvre with a splendid collection, Dieulafoy practically ceased to be interested in Persia, though he never forgave Jacques de Morgan (q.v.) for reopening the excavations at Susa in 1315/1897. He took a post in the administration of the railroads and also threw himself into biblical studies, for which his training as an engineer had ill prepared him. In 1895 he was elected to the Académie des Inscriptions et Belles-Lettres, and from that time on he devoted himself with more competence, though not perhaps with greater success, to research on the history of architecture, notably in a study of the Château Gaillard, built by Richard the Lion-Hearted. He also took a particular interest in the civilization of Spain and Portugal, notably in sculpture and the theater of Pedro Calderón de la Barca.

At the beginning of the World War I Dieulafoy was eager to return to service at the age of seventy years; he was assigned the duties (largely theoretical) of a lieutenant colonel in the corps of engineers at Rabat, which provided the opportunity for some final excavations in a mosque. In 1919 he sent a final communication to the Académie, on the subject of Daniel and Balthazar (ref. Reinach, p. 364). He died early the next year after a short illness.

Bibliography: E. and J. Gran-Aymeric, *Jane Dieulafoy. Une vie d'homme*, Paris, 1991. R. Cagnat, *Notice sur la vie et les travaux de M. Marcel Dieulafoy*, Institut de France, Académie des Inscriptions et Belles-Lettres, 1921. S. Reinach, "Notice biographie et bibliographie," *Revue archéologique* 3, 1920, pp. 363-64.

(PIERRE AMIET)

DIEZ, ERNST, Austrian historian of Iranian and Islamic art (b. 27 January 1878, d. 8 July 1961). Diez belonged to the first generation of European art historians, who, starting with studies in European art, soon developed an interest in Asian cultures.

Diez studied with Josef Strzygowski in Graz until 1902 and later became his assistant. Strzygowski maintained that the art of Europe and the Mediterranean countries could not be understood without knowledge of the ancient Near East and Christian, Armenian, Islamic, and Indian art. Under Strzygowski's influence, Diez became interested in European, Byzantine, Islamic, Indian, and Far Eastern art, but he focussed mainly on Islamic art, particularly on questions concerning Persian architecture.

In 1908 he joined the Berlin State Museums and in 1909 was on the staff of the Islamic Department headed by Friedrich Sarre. This post enabled him to join in the preparation of the exhibition of Islamic art in Munich in 1910 and eventually drew his interest to Islamic art. He concentrated on the theoretical principles of art as well as the general outlines of artistic development. He was also interested in the historical study of monuments within well-defined regional boundaries, which led him to publish a number of broad surveys. As a student of the Vienna school, which considered Asia as a single region, Diez was perhaps one of the last scholars to write individual studies as well as general art histories on Islamic (*Die Kunst der islamischen Völker*, Berlin, 1915), Far Eastern (*Einführung in die Kunst des Ostens. China and Japan*, Hellerau, 1922), and Indian (*Die Kunst Indiens*, Potsdam, 1925) art. His comprehensive survey of Islamic art, which focussed on the architecture, was the first study devoted to this field in the German language.

In spring of 1911 Diez returned to Vienna to become an assistant of Strzygowski. Believing, like his teacher, that the knowledge of Islamic art in northeastern Persia was of prime importance for understanding Islamic art in general, he made a research trip with Oskar von Niedermayer to Persia in the years 1912-14. The journey took them as far as Afghanistan, India, and a number of other Islamic countries. During his stay in Khorasan (10 March-10 April 1913), he surveyed architectural monuments but could not reach an agreement with the Persian authorities to excavate the city of Nīšāpūr. He published the results of his studies and observations during the expedition in two volumes (*Churasanische Baudenkmäle*, Berlin, 1918 and *Persien, islamische Baukunst in Churasan*, Hagen, 1923). The first volume gave a survey of a number of important buildings in Khorasan, including tombtowers and part of the sanctuary of Mašhad. The second volume contained a discussion on construction principles of Persian brick buildings. Diez again took up the questions treated in these volumes in his article in the *Survey of Persian Art* (pp. 916-29) and in a more general work on Persian art (*Iranische Kunst*, Vienna, 1944). Among other results of the expedition was a volume published by Niedermayer on Afghanistan (*Afghanistan*, Leipzig, 1924), which included contributions on art history by Diez.

Diez returned to Vienna after serving in World War I and taught Early Christian and Islamic art. This was the beginning of a long teaching career which, from 1926 until his return to the Vienna University in 1939, took him to the Bryn Mawr College, Pennsylvania, U.S.A. During this period he was able to travel to India and the Far East. From 1943 to 1948 Diez taught Islamic art in Istanbul.

In 1925 he and H. Glück published *Die Kunst des Islam* (Berlin, 1925), which went through several editions. Diez was a contributor to the first edition of the *Encyclopaedia of Islam*. Other contributions include "Indian Influence on Persian Art and Culture" (*Eastern Art* 1, 1928, pp. 117-22), "Sino-Mongolian Temple Painting and Its Influence on Persian Illumination" (*Ars Islamica* 1, 1934, pp. 160-73), "A Stylistic Analysis of Islamic Art" (*Ars Islamica* 3, 1936, pp. 201-12 and 5, 1938, pp. 36-45), and "Simultaneity in Islamic Art" (*Ars Islamica* 4, 1937, pp. 185-89). His continued interest in the art of the Islamic countries, India, and the Far East is reflected by the contributions to his memorial volume, which appeared shortly after his death.

Bibliography: O. Aslanapa, ed., *Beiträge zur Kunstgeschichte Asiens. In Memoriam Ernst Diez*, Istanbul, 1963; reviewed by M. Meinecke, *Der Islam* 45, 1969, pp. 180-83. E. Kühnel, "In Memoriam Ernst Diez 1878-196," *Kunst des Orients* 4, 1963, p. 110 (with a bibliography by D. Brehm and D. Duda, pp. 111-12).

(JENS KRÖGER)

DIGOR, Ossetic tribal name. The Digors, who number about 80,000 people or one-sixth of the Ossetic population, live mainly in the western districts of the former North Ossetian Autonomous Soviet Socialist Republic (ASSR), at the upper reaches of the Iräf (Russ. Urukh) river, but also in the Mozdok region of the same ASSR and in the Ozrek region of the former Kabard-Balkar ASSR (Isaev, p. 4).

In the indigenous dialect the name for both the tribe and its territory is *Digor(ä)*; the corresponding adjective with suffix *-on* is *digoron* "Digorian" (*digoron ävzag* "the Digor language"). In Iron, the Ossetic literary language, the forms are *Di̱gur*, *di̱guron*. This name is also used for the Digors by the neighboring peoples of the North Caucasus (Abaev, 1959-89, I, p. 380). The origin and etymology of the word Digor is obscure. A connection with *Adi̱γe*, the indigenous name of the Circassians (see ČARKAS), has been suggested (**di̱γ-* plus the Circassian demonstrative pronoun *a-* "that"?), but hardly proved (Abaev, 1958-89, I, p. 380; Volkova, pp. 110ff.).

In former times the name Digor was apparently applied to a tribal community in the North Caucasus whose territory extended to the west beyond the borders of present-day Digoria. Pseudo-Moses of Khorene mentions Aštigor and Dik'or among the tribes of Sarmatia (the North Caucasus), at the upper reaches of the Kuban' and Terek rivers (p. 26; cf. Marquart, pp. 169-72). Unfortunately the text is ambiguous, and it is not clear whether both of these tribes are reckoned among the Alans or regarded as distinct nationalities (see also Miller, 1887, pp. 104 ff.; Gagloĭti, pp. 152 ff.; Volkova, pp. 110 ff.; *Istoriya* I, pp. 45-46; Markwart, *Ērānšahr*, p. 105). Aštigor can be analysed as *Aš* (cf. *As*, an ancient tribal name used for the Alans; see ASII) and *Digor*, that is, "the Digor branch of the As."

In Georgian, Russian, and West European sources from the 17th century and later Digor is found as a tribal and geographic name in the same sense it is used today; thus in the Georgian geography of Prince Vaxušti Bat'onišvili (1696-1757) the Digors (*digori*, *digorelni*) are frequently mentioned among the Ossetic tribes (index, p. 1006).

Like their Kabardian and Balkar neighbors, the majority of the Digors are traditionally Muslims, unlike their Iron kinsmen, who are mostly Christian. However, tribal pre-Islamic religious ideas and practices have largely held their ground or entered symbiotic relations with the Islamic creed (for a number of Digor religious and folkloric texts, see *Iron adämi̱ sfäldi̱stad* I-II, passim; see also Kaloev, passim).

The Digor dialect differs to a considerable extent from Iron, upon which the standard written language is founded. Digor literary publications are rare, and most Digor writers use Iron in their works. In Digor schools Iron is taught (along with Russian); administrative and political business is carried out in Iron (and Russian). Among the few Digor writers whose works have appeared in print, the lyric poet Baγärati Sozur (Russ. Sozur Bagraev, 1888-1928) may be mentioned; his collection of poems, *Zärdi duar* (The door of the heart), from 1926, is reckoned among the classics of Ossetic literature.

The relationship of Digor and Iron, the two main dialects of modern Ossetic, can be described in terms of a marginal versus a focal dialect. In oral communication each dialect is hardly comprehensible to the speakers of the other dialect. In their grammatical structure, however, they are almost identical, although the morphological materials used differ somewhat. In all essentials Digor represents an older stage of the language, but both dialects share the same general trend of development. Grammatical innovations are largely common, and there is every reason to believe that both are derived from a fairly homogeneous proto-dialect.

In both dialects the prosodic pattern is in principle the same, word accent being subordinate to clause accent. In Digor ancient short (weak) *i* and *u* (< **i*, **u*) have been retained as two distinct phonemes, whereas in Iron they have been levelled under *i̲*. In Digor initial *γ-* (<**g-*) remains as a voiced velar spirant; in Iron it has become a voiceless velar stop *q*. In Digor *q*, originally alien to Ossetic, is found in loanwords only. Both dialects have introduced voiceless glottalized stops (*p'*, *t'*, *k'*, *c'*, *č'*), no doubt through influence from the neighboring North Caucasian languages.

The Digor noun has retained two declensions, one ending in *-ä* in the nominative singular, the other in zero (<**-ā* and **-ah*, respectively); in Iron both declensions have merged. The case systems of both dialects are closely related. In addition to the four cases inherited from Old Iranian (the nominative, the genitive, the locative-inessive, the ablative-instrumental) Iron has developed a series of (historically) secondary cases, namely the superessive, the allative, the dative, the equative, and the comitative; of these only the last mentioned is lacking in Digor. Both dialects make extensive use of postpositions, nouns, or particles that are added to the genitive (occasionally to some of the other cases too) and thus constitute a system of (synchronically) secondary cases.

In both dialects transitive and intransitive verbs are kept distinct in the past tense. In the first and second person singular of the present indicative of the verb "to be" an enigmatic initial *d-* is common to both dialects (*dän*, *dä*). In Iron the present indicative plural of the same verb is apparently derived from a stem **st(ā)*: *stäm*, *stut*, *sti̲*; in the singular **ah-* is used. In Digor **ah-* is used in both the plural and singular. The past tense of the verb "to be" is in Digor derived from the stem **ad-* (<**hāta-*): *ad-tän*, etc. In Iron the past tense is based on **būta-*: *ui̲d-tän*, etc.; *ad-* is found, however, in the Iron optative of the past tense (*fä-c-ad-ain*, beside *fä-ui̲d-ain*). The inherited modal system (the indicative, the subjunctive, the optative, the imperative) has been retained in the present tense in both dialects; in the past tense the formation of an optative mood is a common innovation. In both dialects a future tense has been formed, originating from a periphrasis consisting of the present stem plus **čanah-* "wish" plus the verb "to be": Iron *cär-ži̲n-än*, Digor *cär-žän-än* "I will live" (**čara-čana(h)-ah-*). An innovation common to both dialects is a bidimensional system of aspectual and spatial preverbs, which at the same time express the direction of the action and the position of the observer (e.g., Dig. *ba-cäun* "to enter" from the point of an observer who is outside, *ärba-cäun* "to enter" when the observer is inside). In Digor this feature is less fully developed than in Iron.

As to vocabulary, Digor has been exposed to Kabardan influences to a larger extent than Iron. The Kabardan loanwords are, however, mostly limited to the semantic fields of economic life (agriculture, husbandry, etc.). The basic core vocabulary, lexical items denoting the elementary human experiences, is largely the same in both dialects; this applies to inherited vocabulary as well as to borrowings.

See also ALANS; ASII.

Bibliography: V. I. Abaev, "Ocherk raskhozdeniĭ ironskogo i digorskogo dialektov" (A sketch of the differences between the Iron and the Digor dialects) in *Osetinskiĭ yazyk i fol'klor* (Ossetic language and folklore) I, Moscow and Leningrad, 1949, pp. 357-493. Idem, *Istoriko-etimologicheskiĭ slovar' osetinskogo yazyka* (A historical-etymological dictionary of the Ossetic language), 4 vols., Moscow and Leningrad, 1958-89. Idem, "O dialektakh osetinskogo yazyka," (On the dialects of the Ossetic language) in *Indo-Iranica. Mélanges présentés à Georg Morgenstierne à l'occasion de son soixante-dixième anniversaire*, Wiesbaden, 1964, pp. 1-7. Yu. S. Gagloĭti, *Alany i voprosy etnogeneza Osetin* (The Allans and the problem of the origin of the Ossets), Tbilisi, 1966. *Iron adämi̲ sfäldi̲stad* (The creation of the Ossetic people) I-II, Ordzhonikidze, 1961. M. I. Isaev, *Digorskiĭ dialekt ozetinskogo yazyka* (The Digor dialect of the Ossetic language), Moscow, 1966. *Istoriya Severo-osetinskoĭ ASSR* (The history of the North Ossetic ASSR) I, Moscow, 1959. B. A. Kaloev, *Osetiny* (The Ossetes), Moscow, 1967. J. Marquart, *Osteuropäische und ostasiatische Streifzüge*, Leipzig, 1903. V. Miller, *Osetinskie etyudy* (Ossetic studies) 3, Uchenyya zapiski imperatorskago Moskavskago universiteta, Otdel istoriko-filologicheskiĭ (The learned transactions of the Imperial University of Moscow, Historical-Philological section), vyp. 8, Moscow, 1887. Idem, "Die Sprache der Osseten," in *Grundriss* I, Supplement, Strassburg, 1903. Ps.-Moses of Khorene, *Géographie de Moïse de Corène*, ed. A. Soukry,

Venice, 1881. F. Thordarson, "Ossetic," in R. Schmitt, ed., *Compendium linguarum Iranicarum*, Wiesbaden, 1989. Vaxušti Bat'onišvili, *Aγc'era sameposa sakartvelosa*, in S. Q'auxčišvili, ed., *Kartlis cxovreba* (The Life of Georgia) IV, Tbilisi, 1973. N. G. Volkova, *Etnonimy i plemennye nazvaniya severnogo Kavkaza* (Ethnic and tribal names of the North Caucasus), Moscow, 1973.

(FRIDRIK THORDARSON)

DILL (*ševed, ševīd, šebet*, etc.), *Anethum graveolens* L. (fam. Umbellifera), an herb widely cultivated in Persia. The main use of its feathery leaves is as the sole herb in all dishes in which the main ingredient is fava beans (*bāqelā*, q.v.), for example, *bāqelā polow* (pilau with fava beans), *kūfta-ye ševed-bāqelā* (meatballs with dill and fava beans), *ḵoreš-e bāqelā* (a stew with chunks of meat, as well as dill and fava beans) and its well-known Gīlānī variant *bāqlā qātoq*, but also in *ševed polow* (a plain pilau sometimes served as a dietary dish, e.g., for patients with diarrhea), and in gherkin pickles. It is also one of the herbs in *sabzī polow* (a rice dish with green herbs; for recipes, see Ramazani, pp. 112-13, 121-22, 192, 263-64; Montaẓemī, p. 597; Ḵāvar, pp. 38-40).

Dill seeds, to which properties similar to those of fennel (*rāzīāna*) seeds were ascribed in Galenic medicine, are still sometimes used as a diuretic (cf. Schlimmer, pp. 40-41), stomachic, carminative, etc. (for a full inventory of the medicinal virtues and uses of dill, see ʿAqīlī, s.v. *šebatt*, pp. 541-42).

Bibliography: Sayyed Moḥammad-Ḥosayn ʿAqīlī Ḵorāsānī, *Maḵzan al-adwīa*, Calcutta, 1844. Z. Ḵāvar (Marʿašī), *Honar-e āšpazī-e Gīlān*, Tehran, 1366 Š./1987. R. Montaẓemī, *Honar-e āšpazī* . . ., 9th ed., Tehran, 1361 Š./1982. V. Mozaffarian, *The Family of Umbelliferae in Iran. Keys and Distribution*, Tehran, 1983, p. 126. N. Ramazani, *Persian Cooking*, New York, 1974.

(HŪŠANG AʿLAM)

DIMDIM (Pers. Demdem or Domdom), name of a mountain and a fortress where an important battle between the Kurds and the Safavid army took place in the early 17th century.

Mount Dimdim (elev. ca. 2,000 m) is located between the Bārāndūz river and the tributary Qāsemlū near the shore of Lake Urmia, a few kilometers west of the Urmia-Mahābād road; the nearby village of Bālānīj is about 18 km south of Urmia. According to Kurdish oral tradition (reported by Eskandar Beg, I, p. 792), the fortress on top of the mountain dates from the pre-Islamic period. In about 1609 the ruined structure was rebuilt by Amir Khan Lapzērīn, ruler of Barādūst, who sought to maintain the independence of his expanding principality in the face of both Ottoman and Safavid penetration into the region. In 1609 Eskandar Beg described it as a formidable stronghold consisting of five separate forts with well-protected cisterns and pits for storing ice and snow (pp. 796-97). Today portions of the walls and heaps of building stones and bricks are still visible (Pedrām).

The battle of Dimdim occupies a prominent place in Safavid historiography. Shah ʿAbbās I (q.v.; 996-1038/1588-1626) had recognized Amir Khan's hereditary right to rule over Barādūst and Urmia, but the rebuilding of Dimdim was considered a move toward independence that could threaten Safavid power in the northwest; in fact, neither the Safavids nor the Ottomans had yet gained firm control of Kurdistan, Azarbaijan, and Armenia. Many Kurds, including the rulers of Mokrī (west and south of Lake Urmia), rallied around Amir Khan. After a long and bloody siege led by the Safavid grand vizier Ḥātem Beg, which lasted from November 1609 to the summer of 1610, Dimdim was captured; all the defenders were massacred. Shah ʿAbbās ordered a general massacre in Barādūst and Mokrī (Eskandar Beg, pp. 809-14; Falsafī, pp. 190-94) and resettled the Turkish Afšār tribe in the region (Adīb-al-Šoʿarāʾ, pp. 11-73) while deporting many Kurdish tribes to Khorasan. The two principalities did survive, though much weakened, and the amirs of Barādūst fought two more battles against the Safavids at Dimdim (Eskandar Beg, pp. 889-91; Adīb-al-Šoʿarāʾ, pp. 52-55). In 1142/1729 Ṭahmāsbqolī Sepahsālār (the future Nāder Shah, 1148-60/1736-47) defeated Yūsof Pasha, the Ottoman governor of Urmia, at Dimdim and ordered the fortress destroyed (Adīb-al-Šoʿarāʾ, pp. 76-77).

Although Persian historians (e.g. Eskandar Beg and Adīb-al-Šoʿarāʾ) depicted the first battle of Dimdim as a result of Kurdish mutiny or treason, in Kurdish oral traditions (e.g., *Baytī dimdim*; see BAYT), literary works (Dzhalilov, pp. 67-72), and histories it was treated as a struggle of the Kurdish people against foreign domination; in fact, *Baytī dimdim* is considered a national epic second only to *Mam ū Zīn* by Aḥmadī Ḵānī (q.v.). It is known in both the Kūrmānjī and Sorānī dialects of Kurdish and in Armenian. Most of the collected ballads portray the defenders of Dimdim as martyrs (*šahīd*) in a holy war (*xeza*; see, e.g., Dzhalilov, pp. 81, 97, 98). The earliest literary account is attributed to the poet Faqē Ṭayrān (ca. 1590-1660), and a number of modern writers, poets, playwrights, and historians have devoted works to the revolt.

Bibliography: Mīrzā Rašīd Adīb-al-Šoʿarāʾ, *Tārīḵ-e Afšār*, ed. P. Šahrīār Afšār and M. Rāmīān, Tabrīz, 1346 Š./1967. M.-T. Dānešpažūh, ed., "Seh sanad-e tārīḵī wa joḡrāfīāʾī-e dawrān-e ṣafawī," *Waḥīd* 8/2 1349 Š./1971, pp. 207-20 (includes two letters on Dimdim). "Dimdim," in *Kurdskie epicheskie Pesni-Skazy*, Moscow, 1962, pp. 210-30. O. Dzh. Dzhalilov, *Kurdskiĭ geroicheskiĭ epos "Zlatorukiĭ Khan"* (The Kurdish heroic epic "Gold-hand Khan"), Moscow, 1967, pp. 5-26, 37-39, 206 (including ballads with musical notation, short stories, and a facsimile of the work by Faqē Ṭayrān). N. Falsafī, *Zendagānī-e Šāh ʿAbbās-e Awwal* III, Tehran, 1339 Š./1960, pp. 190-94. M.-M. Ḥamabor, "Ḵānī Lapzēřīn ū qalāy Dimdim," *Rošinbīrī nö* 103-04, 1984, pp. 168-227, 105, 1984, pp. 206-42. ʿA.-H. Ḥosaynī, *Baytī Dimdim*, n.p. (Europe), 1981. J. Jalil, "Dim-dim," in Q. Mrad and J. Jalil, *A'frānd'inēd Nvīsk'ārēd K'ordēd Armanistānēya Sovētīe*, Yerevan, 1961, pp. 55-72. Idem, "Amar-ē jalālī," in J. Jalil, *K'ilāmē č'yā*, Yerevan, 1970, pp. 25-62. Idem, *Amar-ē jalālī*, Baghdad, 1982 (includes a bibliography of Soviet and Iraqi literature on Dimdim). Ḥ. Jindī, "The Armenian Variants of the Kurdish Epic Dimdim," in "Countries and People of the Near and Middle East" (in Armenian), pp. 174-82. M.-Ṣ. Karīm, *Šahīdānī qalāy Dimdim* (story), Solaymānīya, Iraq, 1958; 2nd ed., Baghdad, 1982. O. Mann, *Die Mundart der Mukri-Kurden* I, Berlin, 1906, pp. 12-24; pt. 1 tr. as *Toḥfa-ye moẓaffarīya be zimānī kurdī mukrī*, Baghdad, 1975, pp. 20-69, 201-21. ʿA. Mardūḵ, "Rēpařīnī Dimdim ū qalāčoy Kūrdānī Mokrī," *Hīwā/Hêvî* (Paris) 1, 1983, pp. 27-44. M. Pedrām, "Bar farāz-e Demdem," *Honar o mardom* 151, 1354 Š./1975, pp. 44-48 (with photographs). A. Šāmīlov, *Dimdim. (Roman)*, Yerevan, 1966; in Roman characters, Stockholm, 1983. Idem, *Dimdim*, Baghdad, 1975. M. Tawfīqverdī, *Qalāy Dimdim*, Baghdad, 1961. M.-A. Zakī, "Amīr Ḵānī Brādost ū qalāy Dimdim," *Galāwēž* 1/3, 1940, Baghdad, pp. 23-30; 4, pp. 33-42. J. A. Zīřo, *Šořišā Dimdim*, 1983, Baghdad. Taped recitations of *Baytī dimdim* are preserved in the ethnomusicological archive at the University of Illinois, Urbana; York University, Toronto, Canada; and the Iraqi Academy-Kurdish Corporation, Baghdad.

(AMIR HASSANPOUR)

DIM(I)LĪ (or Zāzā), the indigenous name of an Iranian people living mainly in eastern Anatolia, in the Dersim region (present-day Tunceli) between Erzincan (see ARZENJĀN) in the north and the Muratsu (Morādsū, Arm. Aracani) in the south, the far western part of historical Upper Armenia (Barjr Haykʿ). They are also found in Bingöl, Muş, and the province of Bitlis, as well as around Diyarbekir (Dīārbakr), Siverek, and Sivas (for details, see Lerch, p. xxi; Haykuni, p. 84; Andranik, pp. 111-16; Hadank, pp. 8-9; Erevanian, pp. 1-20; Halajian, 1973, pp. 9-100; Gasparian, p. 195; Bruinessen, 1978, p. 30). About 300,000 Dimlīs live in western Europe, mainly in Germany. Some of them are political refugees. The total population of Dimlīs at present is unknown, but it can be estimated at 3-4 million.

The people call themselves Dimlī or Dīmla, apparently derived from Deylam (Andranik, p. 161 n. 1; Hadank, pp. 2, 11-12; Minorsky, 1932, p. 17; idem, 1965, p. 159 n. 21), as appears from Armenian *delmik*, *dlmik*, and the like (Yuzbashian, pp. 146-51), which must be derived from **dēlmīk* "Deylamite." The Deylamite origin of the Dimlīs is also indicated by the linguistic position of Dimlī (see below).

Among their neighbors the Dimlī are known mainly as Zāzā, literally "stutterer," a pejorative perhaps owing to the relative abundance of sibilants and affricates in their language (Hadank, p. 1; MacKenzie, p. 164; cf. *zāzā* "dumb" in Arm. dialects of the Vaspurakan area). Armenians also call them Delmik, Dlmik, Dmlik (see below), Zaza (Alevi) Kʿrder, Čʿarkʿəčʿikʿ (Halajian, *Dersimi azgagrakan nyutʿer* [*DAN*], passim; Mkrtčʿian, pp. 54-55), and Dužik or Dužik Kʿrder, the last after the name of a mountain in Dersim (Spiegel, II, p. 65). The Armenian term Kʿrder, literally "Kurds," in this context denotes social status or mode of life, rather than nationality. Even those Armenian authors who use the term Kʿrder explicitly distinguish the Dimlī from the ethnic Kurds (Halajian, *DAN*, p. 242; for similar use of the term in the Middle Ages, see Minorsky, 1943, p. 75). In Turkish the Dimlī are known as Dersimli and Qezelbāš (i.e., Shiʿite).

The appearance of the Dimlī in the areas they now inhabit seems to have been connected, as their name suggests, with waves of migration of Deylamites (q.v. ii) from the highlands of Gīlān during the 10th-12th centuries. Unlike the Kurds, the Dimlīs are mainly sedentary cultivators, though animal husbandry occupies a considerable place in their economic activities. They are especially renowned as horticulturists.

Dimlī society is tribal, a sociopolitical, territorial, and economic unit organized according to genuine or putative patrilineage and kinship, with a characteristic internal structure. It encompasses forty-five subtribes, each divided into smaller units. The most prominent are Ābāsān, Āğājān, Ālān, Bāmāsūr(ān), Baḵtīār(lī), Dūžīk, Davrēš-Gulābān, Davrēš-Jamālān, Haydarān(lī), Hasanān(lī), Korēšān, Mamikī, and Yūsufān. The names of some small subtribes consist of patronymics combined with the Turkish word *uşak* (servant), for example, Ā(r)slānušāğī, Ābāsušāğī, Farhādušāğī, Šāmušāğī, Tōpūzušāğī, and Ḵōčušāğī (Spiegel, I, p. 758; Andranik, pp. 156-57; Molyneux-Seel, p. 68; Dersimi, pp. 18-19, 24-28). The chiefs of the most important subtribes, called *seyīd*s (*sayyeds*), are both religious and secular clan leaders and thus exercise considerable influence upon the tribesmen.

Religion

As the names Alevi (ʿAlawī) and Qezelbāš imply, most Dimlīs are Shiʿites, often considered extremist, though some are Sunnis. The religious beliefs of the majority, in common with those of most Shiʿite extremist groups, are characterized by great variety. They venerate ʿAlī b. Abī Ṭāleb (q.v.) as the most important incarnation of God, but they also profess an admixture of indigenous primitive and some Christian beliefs. Within this framework the cult practice of the Dimlī inhabitants of each individual region displays specific features, reflecting the absence of a centralized religious institution, like those in Christianity and Islam, that might standardize cult practice and dogma. God is known as Hŭmāy, Hōmā, and Haq (Adontz, pp. 11-12; Tēr Minasian, p. 22; Asatrian, 1991, p. 10; idem and Gevorgian, p. 502).

The Dimlīs themselves call their religion by the Turkish term *yōl-ušāḡī* "followers of the [true] path" (Molyneux-Seel, p. 64), a designation with mystical overtones. The influence of folk Sufism on Dimlī religious beliefs is so thoroughly blended with indigenous elements as to permit no definite identification. It may be reflected, however, in the hierarchy of the priesthood, the structure of the community, and the cult of Xizir (Ḵāżer, Ḵeżr) Īlyās; in the last, however, elements of the Armenian Surb Sargis (Saint Sergius) are also recognizable. The feast of Ḵizir, considered an incarnation of ʿAlī/God, coincides with ʿAli-bayrami (the feast of ʿAlī), also known as Aḡa-bayrami (God's feast) among the Qezelbāš of the Mākū region, as well as with the Armenian feast of Surb Sargis (Asatrian and Gevorgian, p. 503 n. 25; Müller, pp. 29-30; see also Abeghian, pp. 95-97). It is usually celebrated in February. Christian elements are assimilated to Shiʿite conceptions (as in the example of Xizir) or have been adopted directly from the Armenian population of Dersim, for example, the rites of communion, baptism, and worship at Christian shrines and churches (e.g., the Sūrb Kārāpēt monastery, Hālvōrī vānk in the Dūžīkbābā mountains, and Dēr Ōvā [Arm. Tēr Ohan, Saint John] monastery near Sēlpūs/zdāḡ). There are also perceptible remnants of "nature worship," including worship of mountains (e.g., Mūnzūrdāḡ, Dūzīkbābā, Sēlpūs/z, Sēl), rocks, springs (e.g., Kānīyē Hazratē Xizirī "the spring of Ḵeżr" on the slopes of Dūžīkbābā and Kānīyē ānmāhūtyan "the spring of immortality" at the foot of Sēlpūs), trees (mainly oaks), and animals (snakes, rabbits, etc.). The cult of the snake, considered a holy creature, is most distinctive. It has been symbolized by a stick called *čūē haqī* (God's stick), the top of which is carved in the form of a snake's head. It is preserved in a green cloth bag suspended from a wooden pillar (*ērkyan*) in the sanctuary of the village of Kiştim near Dersim. The stick is believed to be a piece of the rod of Moses and the bag a copy of the one carried by St. John the Baptist (Halajian, *DAN*, pp. 475-80; Molyneux-Seel, p. 67). The *čūē haqī* is used in cult ceremonies on the feast of Xizir Īlyās, which is celebrated after a three-day fast, during which, according to some reports (Mkrtčʿian, p. 51), even cattle and other livestock are not fed. On this day thousands of pilgrims gather in the village to gaze upon the holy staff (*ēvlīyā keštīmī* "the saint of Kiştim"; for details, see Dersimi, pp. 97-98; Halajian, *DAN*, pp. 475-80; Haykuni, p. 133; Erevanian, p. 79; Müller, pp. 27-28; Asatrian and Gevorgian, p. 508).

One noteworthy trait of Dimlī religious rituals is the equal participation of women, which has often served their detractors as an excuse for accusing them of ritual promiscuity and calling them by derogatory names (e.g., *čirāḡ-kušān*, *čirāḡ-sōndurān*, *mūm-sōndurān*, *ḵurōs-kušān* "candle extinguishers") suggesting participation in orgies (e.g., Fontanier, p. 168; Mkrtčʿian, p. 51).

The Dimlīs' profound hatred of the Turks, in contrast to their mild and friendly attitude toward Armenians, may partly reflect the fact that they, like the Ahl-e Ḥaqq (q.v.) and Yazīdīs, rigorously deny that they are Muslims and stress their claim to follow a distinct religion (Bruinessen, 1991, p. 12; Molyneux-Seel, p. 64). Antagonism to the Turks has also acquired a clear nationalistic character, which is currently being expressed in the powerful upsurge of a Dimlī separatist movement in Turkey (Taławarian, p. 79; Asatrian, 1992a, pp. 104-05; idem, 1992b, pp. 8-9; idem, 1993, p. 7).

Beside special public places for performing their religious ceremonies (*tekke*), the Dimlīs, like the Yazīdīs, also worship in private houses, including those of their religious leaders (Taławarian, p. 64; Müller, p. 228; Asatrian, 1992a, p. 105). They are mostly monogamous, though, according to some authors, polygamy, limited to no more than four wives, is also exercised. Divorce is strictly forbidden. Dimlīs do not practice circumcision (Trowbridge, p. 348; Müller, p. 25; Asatrian, 1992a, p. 106; Mkrtčʿian, p. 55).

Four clans (Āḡājān, Bāmāsūrān, Kurēšān, and Davrēš-Jamālān) are the traditional custodians of Dimlī religious doctrine. Religious offices are hereditary. The highest, that of *pīrī-pīrān* (cf. Pers. *pīr-e pīrān*, elder of elders) may also be conferred by ordination within the hereditary line. Successively lower levels are *pīr*, *seyīd*, *dede*, *muršīd*, and *rayvar* (cf. Pers. *rahbar*). Such terms as "mulla" and *ulem* (Ar. and Pers. *ʿālem*) are never used in non-Sunni Dimlī religious affairs. The *pīrī-pīrān* is the theocratic head of the community. His wife (*ana*) enjoys almost equal rights in managing family affairs (Halajian, *DAN*, pp. 464-65). *Dede*s and *seyīd*s, who never shave or have their hair cut, perform wedding and funeral rites (Haykuni, p. 86). *Rayvar*s, the lowest class of clergy, have the social status of ordinary laymen (*ṭālebs*). They are not paid for their services, which include visiting members of the congregation, performing daily religious rites, and ensuring that the religious and ethical norms of the community are observed. They can punish the guilty but are not allowed to show clemency. Only the *pīrī-pīrān*, upon the application of the supreme council (*jamāʿat*), a mixed secular and clerical body, may forgive sins. The nonreligious affairs of the *rayvar*s are attended to by their families or lay volunteers (Halajian, pp. 463 ff.).

A curious social aspect of the Dimlī community is the institution of *moṣāḥeb* (perhaps "holy brotherhood"). Similar institutions, called *birē āxiratē* and *xūškā āxiratē* (brotherhood and sisterhood of the next world), and *šarṭ-e eqrār* exist also among the Yazīdīs and Ahl-e Ḥaqq respectively (Asatrian, 1985; idem and Gevorgian, p. 507).

Language

Dimlī (Zāzā) belongs to the Northwest Iranian language group (Windfuhr; see DIALECTOLOGY). It is known from several dialects, Sīvērēk, Kōsā, Čabāḵčūr, Kiḡī, Bujāq, Ōvāǰiḡ, and others, which, however, do not differ greatly.

Phonology. The Dimlī phonological system is the same in all dialects, with only slight variations. The vowel system consists of eight phonemes and two diphthongs (Cabolov), which are transcribed variously in the recorded texts:

/*a*/	/*i*/	/*u*/
/*ā*	/*ī*/	/*ū*/
/*ē*/	/*ō*/	
/*ai*/	/*au*/	

The long vowel phonemes have no significant allophones, whereas the range of allophones of the short vowels and diphthongs is quite wide: /*a*/: [*a*, *i*, *ĕ*]; /*i*/: [*ĭ*, *a*, *e*]; /*u*/: [*o*, *ü*], etc.; /*au*/: [*au*, *aū*, *ou*, *eu*]; /*ai*/: [*ai*, *ēi*, *aī*], etc.

The Dimlī consonant phonemes are:

/*p*/	(/pʿ/)	/*b*/	/*m*/			
/*t*/	(/*t*ʿ/)	/*d*/	/*n*/			
/*k*/	(/*k*ʿ/)	/*g*/	/*x*/	/*γ*/	/*q*/	
(/*c*/ [*ts*]	/*j*/ [*dz*]	/*c*ʿ/ [*tsh*])				
/*č̣*/ [*tš*]	/*ǰ*/ [*dž*]	/*č*ʿ/ [*tšh*]				
/*v*/	/*w*/	/*y*/	/*r*/	/*r̄*/	/*l*/	/*s*/
/*z*/	/*š*/	/*h*/	(/ʿ/	/*ḥ*/)		

The affricates *c*, *j*, and *c*ʿ and the aspirated series *p*ʿ, *t*ʿ-, *k*ʿ are found mainly in northern dialects (Erzincan, Dersim). Armenian influence is the most likely explanation of the existence of these phonemes, which are not otherwise found in modern West-Iranian languages (Vahman and Asatrian, p. 268). The /*č̣*/ represents a mediopalatal surd affricate (= -*tš*-, Arm. *č*, Kurmānjī *ç̣*), which is apparently common to all Dimlī dialects. Historically Dimili *j* correspons to Middle Iranian *ǰ*, while *č̣*, *c*, and *c*ʿ all continue Middle Iranian *č*; for instance, *jau* "barley" (< *MIr. *ǰau*), *c*/*c*ʿ*im* "eye" (< **čehm* < **čašm*), and *c*ʿ*ilā* "lamp, candle" (< **čirāḡ*); *cīcag* "flower" < **čīčag*, cf. Turk. *çiçek*, etc.).

The opposition between a rolled *r̄* and a simple flap *r* is found also in Kurmānjī. The marginal phonemes /ʿ/ and /*ḥ*/ occur in some dialects under the influence of Kurmānjī Kurdish.

In certain dialects older *š* is commonly represented by *s*, for example, *sit* or *šit* "milk" (cf. Parth. *šift*), *gōs* or *gōš* "ear" (cf. Pers. *gūš*), *hŭsk* "dry" (cf. Pers. *ḵošk*, Kurdish *hišk*), *mask(a)* "churning bag" (cf. OPers. *maškā*-, NPer. *mašk*); *sim*- "drink" (probably from MIr. **šām*- from older **čyāma*-, cf. NPers. *ā-šām*-, Khotanese *tsām*- "to digest"); and *sōn*- or *šōn*- "flow" (possibly from **xšaudna*-). Conversely *š* also replaces original *s*, for example, *šīr* "garlic" (cf. NPers., Kurdish *sīr*). There is also worth mentioning the initial *s*- in *sol*(*a*), "salt," which is probably also from *š*- (cf. Parth. *šwryn* "salt[y]," NPers. *šūr*); one, however, cannot exclude the possibility of its original character (cf. Mid. Pers. *sōr*, Baḵtīārī, *sūr*, Balūčī *sōr*, Brahui *sōr*; see Henning, 1947, p. 55). Of more uncertain interpretation is *ša* "black," whose *š* may be from **sy* (cf. Sogd. *š*ʾ*w* but Parth. *sy*ʾ*w*, NPers *sīāh*), and *r̄āšt* or *r̄āst* "right" (cf. Parth. *r*ʾ*št* but NPers. *rāst*, Kurdish *r̄āst*). A similar situation is seen in the language of those Armenians of Dersim who belong to the so-called Mirakʿian tribe, in which Armenian *š* has become *s*, for instance, *sun* "dog" < *šun* and *us* "late" < *uš*. In this dialect Armenian *ǰ*, *č*, *č*ʿ have become *j*, *c*, *c*ʿ (e.g., *jur* "water" < *ǰur*, *cut* "chicken" < *čut*, and *c*ʿ*or* "dry" < *č*ʿ*or*).

In the dialect of northern Dersim the voiceless and voiced stops *k*-, *g*- are sometimes palatalized in initial position, for instance, *čē* or *kē*, *kaya* "house, home" (cf. NPers. *kada*, Ṭālešī *ka*), *čanā*, *čayna*, *čēnak*ʿ or *k*ʿ*aynak*ʿ "girl, maiden" (cf. Av. *kainiiā*-, Mid. Pers. *kanīg*), and *ǰī* "excrement" (from MIr. **gūh*, cf. Pers. *goh*, Kurdish *gū*).

Morphology. Nouns and pronouns. Two grammatical genders are clearly distinguished in substantives, adjectives, pronouns, and verbal forms. The nominative singular masculine is unmarked; the feminine usually takes the ending short unstressed -*i*. The plural endings are -(*ā*)*n*, -*ī*, and -*ē* for both genders. There are two cases, direct and oblique, which are distinguished in the singular: masculine -*ī*/-*θ*, feminine -*ē*/-*i*/-*θ*, but not in the plural. The *eżāfa* is masculine singular -*ĕ*/, -*ō*/, -*dē*/, -*di*/, -*dō* and feminine singular -(*y*)*ă*, -*dă*(*y*). The plural form for both genders is usually -*ē*, as in *nē p*ʿ*ōstālē min* "these my shoes."

The two cases are distinguished in the personal pronouns, as well. In addition, the third person pronouns

Table 32

PERSONAL PRONOUNS IN DIMLI

		Direct Case	Oblique Case	Possessive
Singular	1	*az*	*mi*(*n*)	
	2	*ti*	*t*ʿ*ū*, *t*ʿ*ō*	
	3 masc.	*ō*, *āy*(*ō*)	*ăy*, *ādi*	*ǰay*
	fem.	*ā*, *yā*	*ā*, (*ā*)*yā*, *ādă*(*y*)	*ǰāy*
Plural	1	*mā*	*mā*	
	2	*šimā*	*šimā*	
	3	(*y*)*ē*	(*y*)*ĭni*	*ǰē*

have a possessive form derived from Old Iranian **haca* "from" plus the oblique form of the pronoun (Table 32).

To be compared with the possessive forms are Kurdish *žē*, Aftarī *ǰūn*, Tākistānī *ǰā*, *ǰanā*, Ṭālešī *čay*, *čavōn*, Semnāni masc. *žo*, fem. *žin*, and the like.

Verbs. The verbal system is based on two stems, present and past, which correspond to the older present stem and past (passive) participle. The present tense is formed from the present stem plus the formant *-an-*/*-(i)n-* derived from the Old Iranian present participle in **ant(a)-* (cf. Pers. *-anda*) for instance, *barm-an-* "weep, cry" (Parth. *bram-*). If the stem ends in *r* this is assimilated to the following *n*: *kar-* but *kan-an-* "do," **yar-* but *yan-n-* "come." The present stem without *-an-* occurs in the subjunctive (aorist) and imperative, for instance, *karō* "may he be." Some verbs take the preverb *bi-* in the subjunctive and imperative, for instance, *bērī* "come!" The imperfect is made from the present stem plus the suffix *-ǟnī* or *-inī* without personal endings, for example, *ti āgayrā-ynī* "you were walking."

The endings of the present tense (gender marked only in the singular) are:

	Singular	Plural
1	*-ān, -ōn, -in*	*-ī̌ma, -ēma*
2 masc.	*-ē*	*-ē*
fem.	*-āy*	
3 masc.	*-ō*	*-ē*
fem.	*-ā*	

The endings of the past tense are regular. Occasionally the feminine third-person singular of intransitive verbs takes the feminine ending *-i* (masc. *-Ø*). The past tense of the transitive verbs takes the so-called "(split) ergative" construction, in which the (logical) direct object is in the direct case and the agent in the oblique case, for example, *tʿō az ašt-ā(n)* "you have left me," literally, "by-you I left-am" (cf. Kurmānjī *ta az kuštim* "you have killed me").

A secondary (regular) conjugation is formed by affixing *-ā-* to the present stem, past stem *-āy-*, for example, *r̄āmā* "he ran away."

The passive of transitive verbs is expressed either by periphrastic constructions or by a secondary conjugation (as in Gūrānī and Mokrī Kurdish) formed with the passive morpheme *-ya-*: present stem in *-(y)ēn-*, past stem in *-(i)yā-*. This passive is conjugated as an intransitive verb and is used only when the agent is not expressed or is unknown.

Both the infinitive and the active (present!) participle are formed from the past stem. The infinitive ends in *-ǐš* from Middle Iranian *-išn* (only exceptionally used with past stems) and the participle in *-ōγ*, *-ōx*, probably borrowed from the Armenian suffix for the noun of agent *-oł*/*-oγ*, as intervocalic *k* does not become *x* or *γ* in Dimlī (cf. Asatrian, 1987, p. 160). Examples or the infinitive: *āmāyīš* "to come" (cf. Mid. Pers. *āmadišn*), *kardǐš* "to do," *r̄āmāyīš* "to run away," *r̄ōtiš* "to sell," *wandǐš* "to read," *wātiš* "to say." Examples of the present participle: *r̄āmāyōx* "runner," *r̄ōtōx* "seller, vendor," *kardōγ* "doer, maker," *wandōγ* "reader."

A characteristic feature of Dimlī is the use of postposition *-rī*, *-rā* to form the ablative, as in *harzanī-ri* "from Harzand" (cf. Kurdish where *-rā* expresses the instrumental).

Linguistic position of Dimlī. After their migration in the Middle Ages, for almost a millennium the Dimlīs had no direct contact with their closest linguistic relatives. Nevertheless, their language has preserved numerous isoglosses with the dialects of the southern Caspian region, and its place in the Caspian dialect group of Northwest Iranian is clear. The Caspian dialects comprise Ṭālešī, Harzan(d)ī, Gūrānī, Gīlakī, Māzandarānī, and some dialects in Tātī-speaking areas and in the area around Semnān. Historically the Caspian dialects belong to the "Northwest Iranian group of languages" and are related to Parthian (see Windfuhr). The isoglosses are of historical phonetic, morphological, and lexical order.

The typically North Iranian and Northwest Iranian phonetic features found in Dimlī include the developments of Indo-European **ḱ* and (Indo-Iranian) **ts* to **s*, **ḱw* to **sp*, **ǵ(h)* to **z*, **dw-* to *b-* and the preservation of **θr* from Indo-European **tr*. Examples of **s* from Indo-European **ḱ* and Indo-Iranian **ts* include *sar̄a* "year" (cf. Parth. *srd*, Pers. *sāl*), *pas* (cf. Av. *pasu-*), *dis* or *dus* "kind, form" (cf. Mid. Pers. *dēs*), *māsī* "fish" (cf. Skt. *matsya-*, Av. *masiia-*, Pers. *māhī*). Examples of **-sp-* from Indo-European **ḱw* include *aspār* "horseman" (OIr. **aspa-bāra-*, cf. OPers. *asabāra*, Pers. *savār*, Kurdish *siyār*), *āspiǰ/ža* "louse" (cf. Av. **spiš-*, Pers. *šepeš*). Examples of **z* from Indo-European **ǵ(h)* include *zāmā* "son-in-law" (cf. Ṭālešī *zāmā*, Kurdish *zawā*, Pers. *dāmād*), *zān-* "know" (cf. Av. *zanā-*, Pers. *dān-*), *zar̄n* "gold" (cf. Av. *zaraniia-*, Pers. *zarr*); *az* "I" (cf. Av. *azəm*), *dēs* and *dēz* "wall" (cf. Av. *daēza-*), *barz* "high" (cf. Av. *bərəzaṇt-*, Pers. *boland*). Examples of *b-* from Old Iranian **dw-* include *bar* "door" (Parth. *br*, but Pers. *dar*), *bīn* "other, this" (cf. Parth. *byd*, but Mid. Pers. *did*, Pers. *dīgar*). Old Iranian **θr* further became **hr*, which in initial position acquired a supporting vowel in the modern languages, as in *hǐra/ē/i* "three" (cf. Parth. *hry*, Av. *θrāiiō*, versus Pers. *se* < **çaiiah*), but between vowels became *r*, for instance, *mār(i)* "mother" (cf. Av. *māθrō*, gen. of *mātar-*), *āwrǟ* (cf. Av. *apuθrā-* < **ā-puθra-*, but Kurdish *āvis*, Pers. *ābestan* < **āpuçā-*).

Other typical early Northwest Iranian phonetic features include: Preservation in initial position of Old Iranian **č* and **ǰ* (as *ǰ* or *j* [*dz*]), which in other positions became *ǰ* and *ž* or *z*, respectively, for example, **č*: *či* "what" (cf. Pers. *če*), *čarx* "wheel"; *pōnj* or *pōnǰ* "five" (cf. Pers. *panj*), *r̄ōǰ* "day" (cf. Av. *raocah-*, Pers. *rūz*), *vāǰ-* "say" (cf. Parth. *wāž-*), *(a)ǰēr* "downward, below" (cf. Kurdish *žēr*, Pers. *zīr*); *(a)ǰōr* "upward, above" (cf. Kurdish *žōr*, Mid. Pers. *azabar*); *lōǰina* "flue, aperture" (cf. Mid. Pers. *rōzan*); *ǰana* or *ǰiina* "woman, wife" (cf. Av. *jaini-*, Kurdish *žin*, Pers. *zan*), *dažlz* "ache, pain" (from OIr. **daǰi-*?).

Dimlī *gōn(i)* "blood" corresponds exactly to Parthian *gwxn*, the relation of which to Old Iranian **wahuni-* (Gūrānī *winī*, *wun*, Pers. *ḵūn* = Kurdish, all from **xwaun-*, a transformation of OIr. **wahuni-*) is uncertain.

The phonetic isoglosses of Dimlī in modern times overlap to varying degree with those of the Caspian dialects, Kurdish, Persian, the Central dialects (q.v.), and the like (see Henning, 1954, pp. 174-76; Windfuhr). The most characteristic are the following. Initial **x-* became *h-* or was lost, as in Gūrānī, for example Old Iranian initial **x-* became *h-* or was lost, as in *har* "donkey" (Av. *xara-*, Gūrānī, Lorī *har*, versus Kurdish *kʿar*, Pers. *ḵar*, etc.), *yānī* "spring, well" for **hānī* (Mid. Pers. and Parth. *xānīg*, Gūrānī *hāna*, versus Kurdish *kānī*). Initial **xw-* became *w-*, as in the Kandūlāyī dialect of Gūrānī, for example, *wala* "ash" (versus Kurdish *xwalī* "soil"), *wă(y)* "sister" (versus Pers. *ḵᵛāhar*), *war-* "eat" (versus Pers. *ḵordan*). Initial **fr-* became **hr-*, which either received a supporting vowel, as in *harā* "wide, far" (versus Pers. *farāḵ*), or became *r̄-*, as in *r̄ōtiš* "sell" (also in the Central dialects, versus Pers. *forūḵt*).

Survey of typical phonetic developments. Dimlī has preserved the Middle Iranian *maǰhūl* vowels *ō*, *ē* (cf. *gōslš* "ear," *bō(y)* "smell," *gēs* "hair," etc.). The corresponding diphthongs are secondary, however; *au* is from older **-aw-*, **-ap-*, **-ab-*, **-ag-*, or **-af-*, whereas *ai* is the result of phonetic combinatory changes.

The Old Iranian voiceless stops **p*, **t*, **k* remained in initial position or became the apirates *pʿ*, *tʿ*, *kʿ*; **t* and **k* also remained after *s* and *š*, but became *d* and *g* after *r*. Examples of **p* include *pas* "lamb, ram" (see above) and *pʿīza* "belly" (cf. Av. **pāzah-* "chest," Parth. *pʾzʾh* "in front"). Examples of **t* include *tʿau* "fever" (cf. Pers. *tab*), *tʿars* "fear" (Cf. Pers. *tars*), *kʿārd(i)* "knife" (cf. Pers. *kārd*), *pʿōrd* "bridge" (also *pʿird* influenced by Kurdish; cf. Kormānjī *pʿir*, Southern Kurdish *pird*; Pers. *pol*); *ăstik*, *ăsta* "bone" (cf. Av. *ast-*); *ăstāra* "star" (cf. Pers. *setāra*). Examples of **k* include *kʿār* "work" (cf. Pers. *kār*); *čē*, *kaya* "home"(see above); *kŭtik* "dog" (cf. Sogd. *ʾkwty* /*əkuti*/, Oss. *kuj*, Kurdish *kūčlčik*, etc.), *hŭslšk* "dry" (see above), *varg* "wolf" (cf. Av. *vəhrka-*, Pers. *gorg*); exceptionally *k* remained in *hāk* "egg" (Fārs dialects *hāg*, *Ḵ*ūrī *xeik*).

Between vowels **p* became *-u-*/*-w-*, and **t* became *y* or was lost. Examples of **p* include *āu* "water" (cf. Pers. *āb*); *āwră* "pregnant" (see above); *šau* "night" (cf. Pers. *šab*); *ārya*, *āyra* "mill" (from OIr. **ār-θry-*? cf. Kurdish *āš*, NPers. *ās-yāb*< **āç-*); *kawtiš* "fall down" (cf. Mid. Pers. *kaft*). Examples of **t* include *čē*, *kaya* "house" (from **kata-*, see above) and *wā(y)* "wind" (cf. NPers. *bād*). Exceptionally we find *d*, as in *ǰidā* "separated, different" (cf. Kurdish *ǰihē*, Pers. *jodā*). Note the secondary *-t-* in the group *sr* > *str* in *astiri*, *ĭštrī* "horn," as in Kurdish *strī*, from Old Iranian **srū-*.

The Old Iranian voiced stops **b* and **d* are preserved only in initial position, **g* in initial position and in the group **rg*. The group **rd* became *r̄*. Between vowels the voiced stops were mostly lost. On the palatalization of *g* to *ǰ*, see above. Examples of **b-* include *bō(y)* "smell" (cf. Pers. *bū*), *bizlža* "goat" (cf. Pers. *boz*), *b(i)raw(i)* "eyelash" (< **bruwa-*; cf. Pers. *abrū*), *aspār* "horseman" (OIr. **aspa-bāra-*). Examples of **d* include *darg* "long" (cf. Av. *darəγa-*, Pers. *dīr*), *pāī* "foot" (cf. Av. *pāδ-*, Pers. *pā*), *sar̄a* (see above), *var(a)* or *val(a)* "neck" (but NPers. *galū*, Baḵtīārī *gyēl*, Māzandarāni and Gīlakī *gĕl*); *zar̄a* "heart" (cf. Av. *zərəδaiia-*, but Gūrānī *zil*, Pers. *del*), *gara* or *gar̄a* "complaint" (but Pers. *gela*, Kurdish *gilī*), *kʿōl(i)* "hornless (goat)" (from OIr. **kr̥du-*?). It should be noted that Dimlī words with *-i-* before *rll*, as in *ādir* "fire," *mil* "neck," *vil* "flower," are likely to be loanwords from other Iranian dialects (cf. *mol* and *vel* in Fārs dialects). Examples of **g-* include *gōslš* "ear" (cf. Pers. *gūš*), *gā(w)* "cow" (cf. Pers. *gāv*), but *ǰī* or *gī* "excrement" (see above); *darg* "long" (see above); *r̄au* "swift" (cf. Av. **raγu-*).

The Old Iranian spirants, **f*, **θ*, **x*, developed variously. The **f* was lost in the cluster **-ft-* in *slšit* "milk" (cf. Parth. *šyft*). On **fr*, see above. The group **-θn-* became *-sn-* in *ārāsna*, *ārisna* "elbow" (cf. Avestan *araθni-*, but OPers. *arašni-*, Pers. *araš*). Similarly **x* was lost in the cluster **xš-*, as in *šau* "night" (see above), but remained in words such as *čarx* (from Persian?). On initial **x-* and **xw-* , ee above.

On Old Iranian **s* and **z*, as well as the interchange of *s-* and *š*, see above. The Old Iranian groups **-st-*, * *-sn-*, and **-sr-* are preserved (on **sp*, see above), as in *ăsnāwi* "swimming" (versus Pers. *šenā*); *hars(i)* "tear" (cf. Av. *asru-*, Pers. *ašk* from **asruka-*), *askaft* "cave" (from **skăfta-*, versus Pers. *šekāft*). Old Iranian **š* remained in Dimlī, as opposed to Kurdish, where intervocalic *š* regularly became *h*. Example include *goš* or *gōs* "ear" (Kurdish *guh*), *šaš* "six" (= Pers.), *pāšna* "heel" (= Pers., but Kurdish *pa(h)nī*), *pānušna*, *r̄ōšls(a)yā* "light, illumination" (cf. Pers. *rowšanāʾī*, but Kurdish *r̄ō(h)nāyī*), *tayšan* "thirsty" (cf. Pers. *tešna*, but Kurdish *tʿī(h)n*).

Old Iranian **y-* became *ǰ-*, as in Persian, but **w* became *v* (rather than *b-* or *g-*, as in Kurdish, Persian, etc.). Examples of **y* include *ǰau* or *jau* "barley" (cf. Av. *yauua-*, Pers. *ǰou*, Kurdish *ǰa*, but Gūrānī *yaw*, *yaya*), *ǰidā* (see above). Examples of **w* include *vazd* (cf. Av. *vazdah-*, but Kurdish *baz*), *vayšān* or *vaysān* "hungry" (but Kurdish *birčī*, Pers. *gošna* for *gorosna*), *vāris* "rain" (but Pers. *bāreš*), *vā(y)* (see above), *vayva* "bride" (cf. Kurdish *būk*, Judeo-Pers. *bayōg*), *varg* "wolf" (see above), *vinī* "lose, waste" (cf. Mid. Pers. *wanī*), *vāz-* "run" (cf. Pers. *vazīdan* "to blow" of the wind), *văšls* "grass" (cf. Parth. *wʾš*, Av. *vāstra-*? "fodder"). Where *b-* occurs instead of *v-* it may be assumed to be a borrowing from Kurdish or Persian, for instance, *bar* "stone" (cf. Kurdish, Lorī *bard*) and *gumān* "doubt, surmise" and *guna* "sin" from New Persian via Kurdish.

Old Iranian **m* was preserved in all positions in Dimlī but not in Kurdish, where it became *v* between vowels;

examples include *maḡwă* "fruit" (cf. Pers. *mīva*), *dām(i)* "trap" (Pers. *dām*, but Kurdish *dāw*), *āmōr* "counting" (cf. Pers. *āmār*), *ām(i)nān* "summer" (cf. Mid. Pers. *hāmīn*, but Kurdish *hāvīn*), *(h)arma(y)* "shoulder, forearm" (cf. Av. *arəma-*), *mīr* "dough" (cf. Pers./Ar. *ḵamīr*, but Kurdish *havīr*).

Morphological isoglosses. The most important morphological isoglosses which link Dimlī with the Caspian dialects are the pronominal possessive forms from **hača* plus the pronoun and the formation of the present indicative from the old present participle in **-ant(a)-*. The past stem of the secondary conjugation ends in *-ā* from **-ād*, as in Parthian. Exclusive to Dimlī are the infinitive ending *-īš* from **-išn* and the ablative use of postposition *-rī/ā* (Asatrian, 1990, p. 162; idem, 1992c, p. 26).

Lexical isoglosses. These isoglosses include Old Iranian **arma-* "forearm" (Dimlī *(h)arma(y)*, Ṭālešī *ām*, cf. Oss. *ărm*, versus **bāzu-* in Pers. *bāzū*, etc.); Middle Persian *āyišm* "moon" (Dimlī *ăš/smă*, *āsmi*, Tatī *ušmā*, Ṭālesī *ovšim*, Harzanī *öšma*); Dimlī *baurān* "dove" (Oss. *bälon* "domestic dove"; cf. Lithuanian *balañdis* "dove"); Old Iranian **bram-* "weep, cry" (Parth. *bram-*, Dimlī *barm-*, Māzandarānī *barm-*, Harzanī *beram* "weeping," Ṭālešī *bāme*, Tātī *berām*, Gīlakī *barmā*, Aftarī *burme*; cf. in the Central dialects Nāʾīnī *biremba*; versus Pers. *gerya*, etc.). Old Iranian **kanya-* "woman, girl" (Dimlī *kʿaynakʿ*, *čanā*, Harzanī *kīna*, Ṭālešī *kīna*, Tatī *kīna*, Galīnqaya *kina*, *čina*, versus Pers. *ḵāna*; marginal lexeme in Pers. *kanīz* and Kurdish *kinik*); Old Iranian **kata-* "home, house" (Dimlī *kaya*, *čē*, Ṭālešī *ka*, Gūrānī *ka*, Tatī *kā*, Galīnqaya *kar*, Harzanī *kar*, *čār*, Aftarī *kiye*; cf. in the Central dialects Ḵūnsārī *kī(y)a*, Nāʾīnī *kiya*; marginal lexeme in Pers. *kade* and Kurdish *kadī kirin* "to domesticate (animals)"); Old Iranian **ragu-* "quick, swift" (Parth. *raγ*, Dimlī *r̄au*, Harzanī *rav*, Ṭālešī *ra*, Tatī *rav*, Semnānī *rayk*, cf. Oss. *räw*, *rog* "light," versus Pers. *zūd*); Old Iranian **uz-ayara-* "yesterday" (Av. *uzaiiara-* "afternoon," Dimlī *vīžēr(ī)*, *vīžēr*, Gūrānī *uzera*, Harzanī, Tātī *zīr*, Tākistānī, Ṭālešī *azīra*, Aftarī *yezze*, versus Pers. *dī-rūz*); Old Iranian **waxš-* "burn" (Parth. *wxšyndg* "blazing," Dimlī *vaš* or *viš-*, Harzanī *vaš-*, Ṭālešī *vaš-*, Tatī *vaš-*, versus **sauc-* in Pers. *sūḵtan*, etc.); Old Iranian and common Northwest Middle Iranian **xšwipta-* "milk" (Av. *xšuuipta-*, Parth. *šift*, Dimlī *š/sit*, Gūrānī *šit*, *šifta*, Ṭālešī *šit*, Harzanī, Aftarī *šet*, Tātī *še(r)t*, versus Pers., Kurdish *šīr* < **xšīra-*); Old Iranian **upa-sar(a)daka-* "spring(time)" (Mid. Pers. *ābsālān*, Dimlī *ūsār̄(ō)*, *vazārī*, Ṭālešī *āvāsōr*, Harzanī *āvāsōr*, classical Pers. *ābsālān*); Avestan *vazdah-* "fat" (Dimlī *vazd* "fat, oil"; cf. Kurdish *baz*); and Parthian *wāš* "fodder" (Dimlī *văš/s*, Ṭālešī, Māzandarānī *vāš*, Aftarī *vāšt*, Semnānī *voš*, versus Parthian *gwyʾw*, Pers., Kurdish *giyāh*, *gīhā*). Also to be noted is Dimlī *r̄īz*, *r̄ēs* "rice" (<OIr. **wrĭzna-*; cf. Sogd. *ryz-*, versus Pers., Kurdish, etc., *berenǰ* < **wrĭnza-*). Relatives of the negative particle Dimlī *činyō/ā* "no, not" are found in Harzanī *čini(ya)* and Āzarī *čĭnĭ*.

Words found only in Dimlī include *angāz*, *hangāž* "plough handle" (< **han-gāza-* < **gāza-* "take, accept" found in Sogd. *ptγʾz-*, Khotanese *pajāys-*, etc.; it cannot be from Armenian; see Vahman and Asatrian, p. 272); *āz* "generation, offspring" (Man. Mid. Pers. *āzn(ān)*, Arm. lw. < Parth. *azn* "people, generation," *azniw* "noble"); *āz(i)* "branch" (Mid.Pers. *azg*, Arm. loanword from Parthian *azg* "race, kind, nation"); *ask(i)* "goat" (Avestan *aza-*, Mid. Pers. *az(ag)*; different from Kurdish *āsk* "deer" from **āsuka-*, cf. Mid. Pers. *āhūg*, Pers. *āhū*); *gauš* "weak, coward, greedy" and *gaušakay* "weakness, cowardice" (possibly related to Sogd. *γβs-* "to be fatigued"); *haw(i)* or *hiw(i)* "laughter," *hawāyīšʾ* present stem *hwĭn-* "to laugh" (cf. Oss. *xūdɨn*); *kay* "play, game" (Mid. Pers *kadag* "game, joke," Sogd. *kʾtʾk-*, Arm. lw. < Parth. *katak* "joke"; cf. Jowšaqānī *koy* "game"); *sīr-*, in present stem *sīn(a)n-* "I love" (< OIr. **srīra-*; cf. Av. *srīra-* "beautiful," Sogd. *šyr'kk* "good," Parth. *šīr-gāmag* "friend"; probably not from Arm. *sēr*, *sir-* "love"; see Asatrian, 1987, pp. 166-67); and *vistiš* and *fĭnāyīš* (or *finā-*) "to throw," *fīnyāyīš* "to be thrown" (Mid. Pers. *wistan* "to shoot," present stem from **wid-na-*) with *r̄ā-vistiš* "to spread, lay, put" (Galīnqaya *fest-*, *fesn-* "to throw, spread"), cf. Lorī *bistan* "to put down, to cast a foal" (before time).

Dimlī words without clear Iranian etymologies include *dĭǰn(i)* or *dĭžn(i)* "rain" (< OIr. **danǰa-*? cf. IE **dheng^uo-*); for "rain" *vāris*, *vārān* and Turkish *yāḡmūr* are also used in Dimlī.

Of the numerous borrowings from Armenian (exceeding perhaps those from Kurdish or even Turkish) the following may be mentioned: *aks/cʾīg* "woman, girl," *āvilīk* "broom," *bōč*, *pōč* "tail," *būǰūr* "small," *gāb* "*Rheum* L.," *hārs* "bride," *hēsān* "whetstone," *čirtʿān* "waterpipe," *gōǰăg(i)* "button," *gōm(a)* "cattle shed," *hāst* "hard, rigid," *hāgōs(i)* "furrow," *hīm* "root, base," *hēǰ* "cross" (Arm. *xačʿ*), *hōllik* "hut, shack," *hūrăkʿ* "hatchet, ax," *ǰāγ/x(i)* "wire mesh," *kʿa/irōn* "beam, girder," *kāl* "thrashing floor," *kālān(i)* "scabbard, sheath," *kʿalandī* "scythe," *kiray* "lime," *kirya*, *kirē* "Sunday," *kirīk* "neck," *kōra/ēk* "a kind of lentil," *kʿušna/i* "rye," *ōzōr* "branch," *pāč* "pod, grain," *pʿanǰār* "vegetable," *pʿūrt* "wool," *sāvār* "pearl barley, spelt," *sēmiga* "threshold," *sūnk/g* "mushroom," *xēγ(ō)*, *xīntʿ* "mad, insane," *xōr* "deep," *xōnj*, *xōz* "pig," *zīl(ik)* "sprout."

Literature in Dimlī

The earliest surviving literary works in the Dimlī language are two poems with identical titles, *Mawlūd* (Genesis), dating from the late 19th and early 20th centuries. The earlier, consisting of 756 eleven-syllable verses, is by Malā Ahmedē Ḵāsī, the other by ʿOṯmān Efendī, mufti of Siverek. There is also a minstrel tradition going back to the medieval period; a number of Dimlī bards have composed both in their mother tongue and in Turkish, for example, Daymī, Dāvūt Solārī, Pīr Solṭān, ʿAlī-Akbar Čīčak, Yāvūz Tōp, Arif Sāḡ, Sulaymān Yildiz, and Rahmī Sāltok (Zilfi, p. 6). Nevertheless, Dimlī has attained genuine literary status only in recent decades, owing to the activities of a number of writers, poets, and political leaders (e.g., Eulbekir Pamukçu, Ališan Karsan, Hesen Dewran, Zilfi, Malmisanic, K. Astare, Reme Bir, Hesen Uşen, Heyder, Usḵan), who now live abroad, mainly in western Europe. At present numerous newspapers, magazines, and bulletins are being published in Dimlī (e.g., *Piya* [formerly *Ayre*], *Raştiye*, *Ware*, *Raya Zazaistani*), and the number is increasing.

Bibliography: A. Abeghian, *Der armenische Volksglaube*, Leipzig, 1899. N. Adontz, *Towards the Solution of the Armenian Question*, London, 1920. Andranik, *Tersim* (Dersim), Tblisi, 1900. G. S. Asatrian, "O 'brate i sestre zagrobnoĭ zhizni' v religioznykh verovaniyakh ezidov" ("The brothers and sisters of the afterlife" in the religious beliefs of the Yazidis), *Strany i narody Blizhnego i Srednego Vostoka* [Yerevan] 13, 1985, pp. 262-71. Idem, "Yazyk zaza i armyanskiĭ" (The Zāzā language and Armenian), *Patma-banasirakan Handes* [Yerevan] 1, 1987, pp. 159-71. Idem, "Eshche raz o meste zaza v sisteme iranskikh yazykov (Zametki po novoiranskoĭ dialektologii)" (More on the place of Zāzā among the Iranian languages [Notes on New Iranian dialectology]), *Patma-banasirakan Handes* 4, 1990, pp. 154-63. Idem, "Unutulmuş bir halk. Zazalar," *Raştiye* 4 (Paris), 1991, pp. 5-12. Idem, "Nekotorye voprosy traditsionnogo mirovozzreniya zaza" (Some questions concerning the traditional Zāzā cosmology), *Traditsionnoe mirovozzreniya u narodov Peredneĭ Azii*, Moscow, 1, 1992a, pp. 102-10, 210-12. Idem, "Zazaların ulusal dünya görüsü," *Raştiye* 5, 1992b, pp. 6-9. Idem, "Zaza dilinin iran dilleri sistemindeki yeri," *Raştiye*, 7, 1992c, pp. 12-18. Idem, "Zaza zhoḡovurdə," *Azatamart* 3, 1993, p. 7. Idem and N. Kh. Gevorgian, "Zaza Miscellany. Notes on Some Religious Customs and Institutions," in *A Green Leaf. Papers in Honour of Prof. Jes P. Asmussen*, Acta Iranica 28, Leiden, 1988, pp. 499-508. J. Blau, "Gurânî et Zâzâ," in R. Schmitt, ed., *Compendium Linguarum Iranicarum*, Wiesbaden, 1989, pp. 336-40. M. van Bruinessen, *Agha, Shaikh and State. On the Social and Political Organization of Kurdistan*, Rijswijk, the Netherlands, 1978. Idem, "Religion in Kurdistan," *Kurdish Times* 4/1-2, 1991, pp. 5-24. R. L. Cabolov, "Zamechaniya o vokalizme zaza" (Remarks on Zāzā system of vowels), in M.N. Bogolyubov et al., eds., *Iranskoe yazykoznanie. Ezhegodnik 1981* (Iranian linguistics), Moscow, 1985, pp. 65-70. N. Dersimi, *Kurdistan tarihinde Dersim*, Aleppo, 1952. G. S. Erevanian, *Patmutʿiwn čʿarsanǰaki hayocʿ*, Beirut, 1956. V. Fontanier, *Voyages en Orient*, Paris, 1829. H. H. Gasparian, "Dersim (Patma-azgagrakan aknark)," *Patma-banasirakan handes* 2, 1979, pp. 195-210. K. Hadank, *Kurdisch-persische Forschungen von O. Mann Abt. 3 (Nordwestiranisch)* IV. *Mundarten der Zâzâ, hauptsächlich aus Siwerek und Kor*, Berlin, 1932. G. Halajian, *Dersimi hayeri azgagrutʿyun*, pt. 1, Yerevan, 1973. Idem, *Dersimi azgagrakan nyutʿer*, pt. 5 (a collection of valuable ethnographic materials on Dersim and its population, kept in the archive of the Institute of Archeology and Ethnography of the Academy of Sciences, Republic of Armenia). S. Haykuni, "Dersim," *Ararat* (Vałaršapat) 2-3, 1896, pp. 84-87, 132-34. W. B. Henning, "Two Manichaean Texts with an Excursus on the Parthian ending *-ēndēh*," *BSO(A)S* 12, 1947, pt. 1, pp. 39-66. Idem, "The Ancient Language of Azerbaijan," *TPS*, 1954, pp. 157-77. P. Lerch, *Forschungen über die Kurden und die iranischen Nordchaldäer* I, St. Petersburg, 1857. D. N. MacKenzie, "Kurmandzhi, kurdi, gurani," in *Narody Azii i Afriki* (Moscow) I, 1963, pp. 162-70. Malmisanic, *Zazaca-türkçe sözlük*, Uppsala, 1987. Idem, *Herakleītos*, Uppsala, 1988 (a selection of Dimlī poetry). Idem, "Dimli ve kurmancı lehcelerinin köylere göre dağılımı I, II, III," *Berham* (Stockholm) 2, 1988, pp. 8-17; 3, pp. 62-67; 4, pp. 53-56. V. Minorsky, *La domination des dailamites*, Paris, 1932. Idem, "The Gūrān," *BSO(A)S* 11/1, 1943, pp. 75-103. Idem, *Studies in Caucasian History*, London, 1953. Idem, "L'ouvrage de Markwart sur l'Arménie méridionale," *REA*, N.S., 2, 1965, pp. 143-64. A. Mkrtčʿian, "Dlmikner," in G. A. Ałaneancʿ, ed., *Lumay, grakan handēs*, girkʿ B, Tbilisi, 1898, pp. 49-58. L. Molyneux-Seel, "A Journey in Dersim," *The Geographical Journal* 44, 1914, pp. 49-68. K. E. Müller, *Kulturhistorische Studien zur Genese pseudoislamischer Sektengebilde in Vorderasien*, Studien zur Kulturkunde 22, Wiesbaden, 1967. S. Šaljian, "Delmiknerə ev nrancʿ aršavankʿnerə depi Hayastan," *Tełekagir SSRM GA Haykakan Filiali* (Yerevan) 5-6, 1941, pp. 107-15. F. Spiegel, *Erânische Altertumskunde*, 3 vols., Leipzig, 1871-73. N. Taławarian, *Kʿristoneakan bołokʿakanutʿean ew gəzəlpašneru ałandin cnundə*, Constantinople, 1914. R. Tēr Minasean, *Hay yełapʿoxakani mə hišatakner* III. *Taroni ašxarh (1906)*, Beirut, 1974. S. Trowbridge, "The Alevis, or Deifiers of Ali," *Harvard Theological Review* 2, 1909, pp. 340-53. F. Vahman and G. S. Asatrian, "Gleanings from Zāzā Vocabulary," in *Iranica Varia. Papers in Honour of Prof. E. Yarshater*, ed. D. Amin and M. Kasheff, Leiden, Acta Iranica 30, 1990, pp. 267-75. G. Windfuhr, "New West Iranian," in R. Schmitt, ed., *Compendium Linguarum Iranicarum*, Wiesbaden, 1989, pp. 251-62. K. N. Yuzbashian, "Deylamity v 'Provestvovanii' Aristakesa Lastiverttsi" (Deylamites in the history of Aristakes of Lastivert), *Palestinskiĭ sbornik* 7/70, 1962, pp. 146-51. Zilfi, *Lawikê Pir Sultanj*, Berlin, 1989.

(GARNIK S. ASATRIAN)

DĪN MOḤAMMAD KHAN b. Olūs Khan, the Uzbek prince who, with his brother ʿAlī Solṭān, joined Shah Ṭahmāsb's camp in 943/1536-37 during the latter's campaign in Khorasan against ʿObayd-

Allāh Khan, the Uzbek ruler of Bukhara. He was given the governorship of Nesā and Abīvard. In 945/ 1538-39 he regained Kᵛārazm from ʿAbd-al-ʿAzīz, son of ʿObayd-Allāh Khan.

Bibliography: Ī. Afšār, ed., *ʿAlamārā-ye Šāh Ṭahmāsb*, Tehran, 1370 Š./1991, pp. 80-81. Eskandar Beg, I, pp. 104-05. Ḥasan Rūmlū, ed. Navāʾī, I, pp. 306, 361, 376-79, 394-95, 405.

(EIr.)

AL-***DĪN*** WAʾL-***ḤAYĀT***, a bi-weekly religious magazine published in Tabrīz, 1346-50/1928-31, replacing another Tabrīz religious magazine, *Tadakkorāt-e dīnī*. Starting with its second year, it became a monthly magazine. Its owner and director, and probably also the writer of all of its articles, was Hājj Mīrzā ʿAlī Moqaddas, a Tabrīzī cleric about whom little is known. It contained only religious articles, all bearing Arabic titles and filled with Arabic words and phrases.

This journal was typographed in the Saʿādat and Ḥaqīqat printing houses and had 18 to 30 single-columned pages. In the first year its size was 18 x 22 and in the second year 14 x 21.5 cm. The annual subscription during the first year was 10 *qerān*s and during the second year 12 *qerān*s, to which postal charges for delivery outside Tabrīz were added. Complete sets are kept in the central library of Tehran University, in the Āstān-e Qods-e Rażawī Library in Mašhad, at the Asian Institute in Shiraz University, and at Princeton University Library.

Bibliography: R. Mach and R.D. McChesney, "A List of Persian Serials in the Princeton University Library," unpub. monograph, Princeton, 1971. Ṣadr Hāšemī, *Jarāʾed o majallāt* I, pp. 259-60. M. Solṭānī, *Fehrest-e majallahā-ye fārsī az ebtedā tā sāl-e 1320*, Tehran, 1356 Š./1977. Idem, *Fehrest-e majallāt-e mawjūd dar Ketāb-ḵāna-ye Āstān-e Qods-e Rażawī*, Mašhad, 1361 Š./1982, pp. 152-53.

(NASSEREDDIN PARVIN)

DINAR (NPers. *dīnār*, Mid. Pers *dēnār* < Lat. *denarius aureus*), a gold coin.

i. *In pre-Islamic Persia.*
ii. *In Islamic Persia.*

i. IN PRE-ISLAMIC PERSIA

From the period of the Roman Republic the word *denarius* was used for coinage in the east, whereas in Rome and the west *aureus* was used. The dinar was a gold coin, struck mainly for purposes of prestige, especially harking back to the Achaemenid tradition embodied in the gold daric (q.v.). Monetary bimetalism did not really exist among the various pre-Islamic dynasties. The Achaemenid empire remained until the end of the 5th century B.C.E. "a country without a proper currency" (Curiel and Schlumberger, pp. 16, 26), that is, a currency having a nominal value. The gold daric, introduced by Darius I (q.v.; 522-486 B.C.E.) and minted as a royal prerogative, was valued only as bullion, and the silver siglos circulated only in Greek cultural areas of Asia Minor. With the arrival of Alexander the Great (q.v.), however, the situation changed; Alexander withdrew the older issues, in order to expand the use of silver coins, which until then had not been attested in any part of the Persian empire except Asia Minor.

There are no surviving gold pieces from the Parthian period. Dinars began to be issued only under the Sasanians. From the reign of Ardašīr I (224-40 C.E.; q.v.) to that of Šāpūr III (383-88) their weight varied from 7 to 7.4 g. Like the silver derhams (q.v.), they bore on the obverse a bust of the crowned king facing right and on the reverse the fire altar flanked by two figures. Probably because it was primarily a ceremonial coin, the dinar is hardly attested in Iranian literary sources; nevertheless, in the trilingual inscription of Šāpūr I (240-70; ŠKZ, Parth. l. 4) it is mentioned that after the victory of the Sasanians at Misikhe (Pērōz-Šābuhr) the Romans had to pay the sum of 500,000 dinars (*dynr*, Gk. *dinaríon*) as ransom for the life of the emperor Philip the Arab and his family, a sum that Ernest Honigmann and André Maricq (p. 122) considered modest. Šāpūr struck dinars at Marv, including the mint name, which was unusual on gold coins. Under Šāpūr II (309-79), who often resided at Marv, the great proportion of dinars was minted in the Persian east, in order to pay for the costs of war (Gignoux, pp. 196-200).

Double dinars, introduced by Ardašīr, were struck only through the reign of Hormozd II (302-09). One-sixth dinars are attested from the reign of Bahrām II (274-93) through that of Kavād I (488-531). Already under Bahrām IV (388-99) the dinar of 7 g was no longer issued. Under Pērōz (459-84) it fell to 3.5 g, but it rose to 4.2 g under his successors. Bahrām IV introduced the minting of gold pieces of 4.54 g, corresponding to the Roman solidus and issued a 1.5-dinar piece. He and two of his successors, Yazdegerd I (399-420) and Yazdegerd II (438-57), also struck one-third dinars of 1.5 g. The dinar thus served as a trade commodity, sold by weight and fineness. The majority of kings minted dinars; a few did not, though the reasons are unknown. Legends on the dinars of Kavād I and Ḵosrow I (531-79) provide evidence that such issues marked accession to the throne.

Šāpūr I is supposed to have restruck Roman double dinars as drachmas, perhaps, as Robert Göbl has suggested (pp. 334), after the capture of Antioch, the principal mint city for the eastern Romans; such restriking would explain the generally poor quality of these coins. The dinars of the usurper Bahrām Čōbīn (r. 590-91; q.v.) are of fine workmanship, though reflecting close dependence on Byzantine models.

Under Pērōz most dinars were struck at the mint at

Balḵ, though some were also issued at Weh-Ardašīr. The abundance of dinars issued in eastern Persia can no doubt be explained by the preference of the great Kushans of Bactria for this gold coinage; in fact, they did not mint silver. Probably in the late 1st or early 2nd century C.E. Vima Kadphises, son of the first king, Kujula Kadphises, issued four series of gold coins to a weight standard based on the *aureus* of Augustus, and this monetary type persisted throughout the entire history of Kushan coinage. The inscriptions were in Greek and Indian (in kharoshthi script), then, beginning in the reign of the third king, in Bactrian (written in an alphabet derived from the Greek alphabet). Kushan numismatics is an independent field of study, largely dominated by the work of Göbl, D.W. MacDowall, and Helmut Humbach, as well as of a number of scholars in the former Soviet Union. The primary original feature of these coins is the image of a divinity on the reverse, as had already occurred among the Greco-Bactrian kings. Although only Shiva is represented on the coins of Vima Kadphises, those of third king, Kanishka, included a varied pantheon of about thirty gods of diverse origins. Under Vasudeva, however, Shiva alone was represented once again. After the conquest of Bactria by Šāpūr I in 265-69 (?) the Sasanian Kūšānšāhs carried on the regional tradition, issuing gold dinars imitating those of the last Kushan kings but with representations of fire altars and inscriptions that emphasized adherence to the Mazdean faith.

A large number of false dinars have been produced by modern forgers with images of the first Sasanian kings up to Bahrām IV.

See also COINS AND COINAGE.

Bibliography: R. Curiel and D. Schlumberger, *Trésors monétaires d'Afghanistan*, MDAFA 14, Paris, 1953. Ph. Gignoux, "Les nouvelles monnaies de Shāpūr II," *St. Iran.* 19/2, 1990, pp. 195-204. R. Göbl, *System und Chronologie der Münzprägung des Kušānreiches*, Vienna, 1984. E. Honigmann and A. Maricq, *Recherches sur les Res Gestae Divi Saporis*, Brussels, 1953. V. G. Lukonin, "Kušano-sasanidskie monety" (Kushano-Sasanian coins), *Epigrafika Vostoka* 18, 1967, pp. 16-33. A. Maricq, *Classica et Orientalia*, Paris, 1965. M. I. Mochiri, *Études de numismatique iranienne sous les Sassanides*, 2 vols., Tehran, 1972-77. B. Ya. Staviskiĭ, *La Bactriane sous les Kushans. Problèmes d'histoire et de culture*, ed. and tr. P. Bernard et al., Paris, 1986.

(PHILIPPE GIGNOUX)

ii. IN ISLAMIC PERSIA

In Arabic of the classical period, the word *dīnār* had the double sense of a gold coin and of a monetary unit which might not be precisely embodied by actual coins. The word occurs once in the Koran (3:75). In the time of the Prophet, gold coins were issued by the Byzantine empire; the Sasanian empire also minted gold coins, but these are extremely rare today and were probably little used in commerce. Gold coins were not issued by Muslims until 72/692. The earliest of them deliberately resembled Byzantine gold issues (*solidus*) and had the same weight (ca. 4.55g; Plate XXVII.a). Starting in 77/696, new Islamic dinars were minted in Damascus, the Omayyad capital, with Koranic inscriptions in Arabic and a new weight of 4.25 grams (Plate XXVII.b). Although they may have circulated to a limited extent in Persia, the main currency there was the silver dirham, as it was in Sasanian times.

In 132/750, when the Omayyad caliphate was overthrown by the ʿAbbasids, the caliphal mint for gold was removed to Iraq, the former territory of the Sasanian empire, where the ʿAbbasids established their capital. About 146/763-64 the capital and the mint were settled in Madīnat-al-Salām (i.e., Baghdad; q.v.). This is known only indirectly, because early ʿAbbasid dinars, like those of the Omayyads, had no mint name on the coin (Plate XXVII.c). Presumably there was no need to specify the mint, as was done on silver dirhams, since there was only one mint for gold coins. These coins were without the name of the caliph. Their inscriptions were purely Koranic, except for a date written in words.

A second ʿAbbasid dinar mint was established in Egypt in 170/786. Dinars were occasionally issued at other places in the western caliphate, but no dinars were issued in Persia until, apparently, the year 220/835 in Marv. Other eastern cities soon began issuing dinars as well. Among the most important mints in the 9th and early 10th centuries were Ahvāz and nearby mints (Sūq-al-Ahvāz, Tostar, etc.), Moḥammadīya (i.e., Ray), Samarqand, and Marv. George Miles (*Cambr. Hist. Iran*, pp. 370-71) enumerated thirteen ʿAbbasid gold mints in Persia, in addition to others in Iraq, Azerbaijan, and the Caucasus. All these mints also issued silver dirhams.

These ʿAbbasid dinars of Persia were all struck after the coinage standardization carried out in the caliphate of al-Maʾmūn (198-201/813-17). They carried uniform inscriptions which were continued by all dynasties that recognized the ʿAbbasid caliphate until the 13th century (Plate XXVII.d). Most of these inscriptions were the same as those originally introduced by the Omayyad ʿAbd-al-Malek in 78/697. The obverse had three or more horizontal lines in the center beginning with *lā elāh ellā Allāh waḥdaho, lā šarīk laho* (There is no god but God alone, none is associated with him). If there was a subordinate ruler named on the coin, such as the heir to the caliphate or a local dynast, his name most often appeared below these lines, while the caliph and the de-facto ruler were named on the reverse; but this rule was not always followed. Two circular inscriptions surrounded the central field. The inner inscriptions had the mint and date in the formula *besm Allāh żoreba hāḏaʾl-dīnār be-*(mint) *sana* (year in words),

PLATE XXVII

a. Dinar, probably issued in Damascus 692-94, ANS 1002.1.107. b. Dinar, probably issued in Damascus, dated 77/697, ANS 1002.1.406. c. Dinar, probably issued in Baghdad, dated 156/772-73, ANS 1917.215.134. d. Dinar, Madīnat al-Salām (Baghdad) mint, with the name of the ʿAbbasid caliph al-Moʿtaṣem, dated 222/836-37, ANS 1917.215.340. e. Dinar, Nīšāpūr mint, with names of the Samanid Amīr Naṣr b. Aḥmad and the ʿAbbasid caliph al-Rāżī, dated 328/939-40, ANS 1922.211.52. f. Dinar, Sūq al-Ahvāz mint, with names of the Buyid Moʿezz-al-Dawla and the ʿAbbasid caliph al-Qāder, dated 398/1007-08, ANS 1968.216.9. g. Dinar, Herat mint, with names of the Ghaznavid Sultan Maḥmūd and the ʿAbbasid caliph al-Qāder, dated 404/1013-14, ANS 1972.288.20. h. Dinar, Balḵ mint (?), with names of the Saljuq Sultan Sanjar and the ʿAbbasid caliph al-Mostaršed, dated 515/1121-22, ANS 1979.213.1. i. Dinar, Shiraz mint, with names of the Salghurid queen Ābeš Ḵātūn and the il-khan Abaqa, dated 675/1276-77, ANS 1970.81.2. Collection of American Numismatic Society. Scale 1:1.

"In the name of God this dinar was struck in...year..." The outer circular inscription was *le'llāh al-amr men qabl wa men baʿd wa-yawmaʾeḏen yafraḥo al-moʾmenūn be-naṣr Allāh*, "the command is God's, in the past and in the future, and on that day the believers shall rejoice in God's victorious help" (Koran 30. 4-5), which was first used in 198/814 when al-Maʾmūn's forces took Baghdad.

On the reverse, at the top of the inner field, nearly all dinars had the word *le'llāh*, meaning "to God," "for God," or "belonging to God," with a significance still not fully understood. The main central inscription, in three or more horizontal lines, began with *Moḥammad rasūl Allāh*, "Moḥammad [is] the messenger of God," which was often followed (when space allowed) by the formula *ṣallā Allāh ʿalayhe wa sallam*, "God bless him and grant him salvation." This was followed by the caliph's title, using only his honorific such as al-Motawakkel ʿalā Allāh and, when appropriate, by the secular ruler's name and titles. The field was surrounded by a circular inscription: *Moḥammad rasūl Allāh arsalaho be'l-hodā wa dīn al-ḥaqq le-yoẓheraho ʿalā al-dīn kollehe wa law kareha al-mošrekūn*, "Moḥammad is the messenger of God, who sent him with guidance and the religion of truth to make it supreme over all other religions even though the polytheists may detest it" (Koran 9. 33).

This was the standard type for the Samanids, Buyids, Ghaznavids, Saljuqs, and their contemporaries from the 10th to 13th centuries (Plate XXVII.e). The prolix titulature and multiple sovereignties of the 10th and 11th century made the central field inscriptions often very crowded (Plate XXVII.f). As a solution, die engravers put names or parts of names and titles in smaller letters above, below, or, vertically, to the right or left of the main inscriptions. Further variation within the standard format was achieved by the use of different scripts, small floral or abstract ornaments, and variant proportions of the different elements of the design (Plate XXVII.g). Especially in the east, in Khorasan under the late Samanids and their successors, die engraving became a highly developed art; sometimes engravers even signed their dies in tiny script that can scarcely be read without magnification. Very rarely the accepted canons of coin design were abandoned completely or in part; again, this was primarily an eastern development (Plate XXVII.h). In the 10th century, while most of the mints mentioned above continued to be important, Nīšāpūr became by far the most productive mint for dinars and continued to be important until the Mongol invasion. Isfahan, Moḥammadīya/Ray, and Ahvāz were also important centers, but some forty cities issued dinars under the Saljuqs at one time or another.

In the early 11th century minting of silver dirhams ceased in Persia. Copper *folūs* had stopped in the early 9th century. The gold dinar was left as the only currency under the Saljuqs and their contemporaries. Since the dinar was a valuable coin, it is not clear how smaller transactions were made. Perhaps older silver coins continued to circulate. After the early 12th century even gold coinage almost disappeared in Persia. Toward the end of the century minting of dinars as well as other coins revived somewhat in furthest eastern Persia under the Ghurids and Ḵᵛārazmšāhs. There are even a very few dinars and debased silver coins with the name of Jengiz Khan, but under his Mongol successors there was virtually no Persian coinage for most of the 13th century, except in Azerbaijan, where the Il-khans made their capital, and in Shiraz under the Salghurid vassal state (Plate XXVII.i).

Another development of the 11th century was the abandonment of fixed weight standard for coined dinars. Dinars of the 11th and 12th centuries vary randomly from less than one dinar's weight to as much as five or six times the standard weight (Nègre). This meant that the value of any individual gold coin had to be determined by weighing it, while conversely the payment of a specified number of dinars was accomplished by weighing coins in bulk with a balance against the correct number of standard dinar weights. This was probably the result of very low minting charges for dinars, which made the monetary value of a dinar coin very close to the commercial value of the gold in it, leaving little margin for the variation in weight which was unavoidable when coins were made by hand. It seems to have been easier for all concerned to weigh all payments than to weigh coins one by one. Transactions by bulk weighing rather than by counting were in any case a common feature of all monetary systems before the advent of machine minting; the abandonment of standard weights for individual gold coins was merely a practical response to economic realities. Gold coins from Egypt to Central Asia continued to be irregular in weight until the 15th century.

In 695/1296 the Il-khan Ḡāzān and his minister Rašīd-al-Dīn initiated a new system intended to standardize the coinage of all their realm (Smith and Plunkett). The dinar was the basic monetary unit, defined as the equivalent of six silver dirhams, each of 4.30 grams. It was a unit of account, not an actual coin. Gold coins were also part of the new system, but they were called *meṯqāl*s, not dinars, and their value in relation to dirhams and dinars was not fixed. As Il-khanid rule collapsed and was replaced by competing warlord states, the weight of the dirham was frequently reduced, and the value of the dinar, as an accounting multiple of the dirham, declined in proportion. By the end of the 14th century the dinar was a very small amount of money. The toman, 10,000 dinars, became an everyday unit of account. In 1310 Š./1931 the dinar was re-defined as a hundredth of the rial. Its value today is miniscule.

See also COIN AND COINAGE.

Bibliography: There are scarcely any studies or catalogues on dinars alone; see the general bibliography under COINS AND COINAGE. Nor are there any general catalogues or studies of the coinage of any of the Persian dynasties until the Il-khanids. For the Omayyad dinar, see M. L. Bates, "History, Geography, and Numismatics in the First Century of Islamic Coinage," *Revue suisse de numismatique* 65, 1986, pp. 231-62. The history of the coinage of one city through the centuries is presented in G. C. Miles, *The Numismatic History of Rayy*, American Numismatic Society, Numismatic Studies 2, New York, 1938. Idem, "Numismatics," *Cambr. Hist. Iran* IV, pp. 364-77. Some data on alloy is provided by A. S. Ehrenkreutz, "Studies Provided by the Monetary History of the Near East in the Middle Ages, II. The Standard of Fineness of Western and Eastern *Dīnārs* before the Crusades," *Journal of the Economic and Social History of the Orient* 6, 1963, pp. 243-77. The phenomenon of irregular weights from the 11th to the 13th centuries is analyzed by A. Nègre, "Le Monnayage d'or des sept derniers califes abbasides," *Stud. Isl.* 47, 1978, pp. 165-75. For the end of the dinar as a real coin, see J. M. Smith, Jr., and F. Plunkett, "Gold Money in Mongol Iran," *Journal of the Economic and Social History of the Orient* 11, 1968, pp. 275-97.

(MICHAEL BATES)

DĪNĀR, MALEK b. Moḥammad (d. 591/1195), a leader of the Oghuz Turkmen in Khorasan and, in the latter years of the 12th century, ruler of Kermān.

He is first mentioned as one of the Oghuz tribal chiefs who in 548/1153 brought about the downfall of the Saljuq sultan Sanjar (511-52/1118-57) in Khorasan (Ebn al-Aṯīr, XI, p. 176). Duri ng the subsequent Oghuz domination there Malek Dīnār was himself forced by pressure from the Khwarazmian Solṭānšāh b. Il-Arslan to move south from Nīšāpūr after the death of its Oghuz amir Ṭoḡanšāh b. Ay Aba (Ebn al-Aṯīr, XI, pp. 377-79). Oghuz tribesmen had already begun infiltrating peaceably into Kermān during the internecine strife of the last years of Saljuq rule there. In 581/1185 Dīnār appeared in Kermān and, at Jīroft, included his own name in the *ḵoṭba* (Friday sermon) and started minting his own coins. In Rajab 583/September 1187 he entered the capital, Bardasīr, from which the last Saljuq amir, Moḥammadšāh, had fled the previous year.

During his eight-year rule in Kermān Malek Dīnār showed a certain degree of statesmanship, in that he allowed his vizier, Jamāl-al-Dīn, to take measures for the restoration of agriculture and commerce, which had been devastated during the preceding disorders. Malek Dīnār conciliated the *ʿolamāʾ* and sought to legitimize his rule by marrying a daughter of the Saljuq amir Ṭoḡrelšāh b. Moḥammad (r. 551-65/1156-70), Ḵātūn-e Kermānī. He also extended his suzerainty over the rulers of the Persian Gulf coast; he received presents from the ruler of Hormoz and in 589/1193 negotiated with the ruler of the island of Qays/Kīš concerning the latter's designs on Hormoz.

After his death Malek Dīnār was briefly succeeded by his incompetent son Farroḵšāh, who himself died in 592/1196; two years later Oghuz domination in Kermān ended with the invasion of the troops of the Ḵᵛārazmšāh.

Bibliography: Afżal-al-Dīn Aḥmad Kermānī, *ʿEqd al-ʿolā le'l-mawqef al-aʿlā*, ed. ʿA.-M. ʿĀmerī Nāʾīnī, Tehran 1326 Š./1947. Aḥmad ʿAlī Khan Wazīrī, *Tārīḵ-e Kermān*, ed. M.-E. Bāstānī Pārīzī, Tehran, 1340 Š./1961, pp. 116-17, 124-32. C. E. Bosworth, "The Early Ghaznavids," in *Camb. Hist. Iran* V, pp. 162-97, esp. pp. 173-75. M. T. Houtsma, "Zur Geschichte der Selǵuqen von Kermân," *ZDMG*, 39, 1885, pp. 388-401. Moḥammad b. Ebrāhīm, *Tārīḵ-e Saljūqīān-e Kermān*, in Houtsma, *Recueil* I, pp. 138-201.

(C. EDMUND BOSWORTH)

DĪNĀRĀNĪ. See BAḴTĪĀRĪ.

DĪNAVAR (occasionally vocalized Daynavar), in the first centuries of Islam an important town in Jebāl, now ruined. Its site lies northeast of modern Kermānšāh, at 34° 35' N, 47° 26' E, on an upland plain (elev. 1,600 m) traversed by what the medieval traveler Abū Dolaf called the river of Dīnavar (p. 49, comm. pp. 93, 97).

Dīnavar was an important fortified point of the Sasanian empire, to which the Turkish Khazars were said to have penetrated in the early 6th century (Balāḏorī, *Fotūḥ*, p. 194). It was also the seat of the Syrian Christian bishopric of Mādkai. It was founded at least as early as the Seleucid period in the heartland of ancient Media, which probably accounts for the element *māh* in Māh al-Kūfa, the early Islamic name for the region of Dīnavar, distinct from Māh al-Baṣra, which was centered on Nehāvand. Dīnavar was conquered by Arabs from Baṣra immediately after the defeat of the Persians at Nehāvand in 21/642 (Balāḏorī, *Fotūḥ*, p. 307) but soon afterward became the center of the region allocated to the Arabs of the Kūfa garrison.

The Arab geographers expatiated on the prosperity of Dīnavar. According to Ebn Ḥawqal (p. 362; tr. Kramers, p. 354), it was two-thirds the size of Hamadān but surpassed the latter in production of such scholars and literary men as Ebn Qotayba and Abū Ḥanīfa Dīnavarī (qq.v.). Maqdesī (Moqaddasī, pp. 384, 395) called it the "elegant" (*ẓarīfa*) Dīnavar, the inhabitants of which were all adherents of the legal school of Sofyān Ṯawrī. Its fine Friday mosque had been built of stone by the local Kurdish ruler Ḥasanūya b. Ḥosayn (ca. 348-69/959-80; Ebn al-Aṯīr, VIII, p. 281). Dīnavar was, in fact, the center of the Ḥasanuyid principality and regained its prosperity after having been sacked by the Deylamites (q.v.) under Mardāvīj in 319/931.

From Yāqūt's repetitious reports and his vagueness about where Dīnavar actually lay (*Boldān* II, p. 545), it appears that by the beginning of the 13th century the town had fallen into decline; it had been plundered by the Oghuz Turkmen of the Īvā tribe in 568/1172-73 (Ebn al-Aṯīr, XI, p. 177). According to *Nozhat al-qolūb* (ed. Le Strange, p. 107; tr. p. 106), in the 14th century it was still a small town in a fertile region, but it was devastated by Tīmūr at the end of the century, and only a field of ruins is now visible.

Bibliography: Abū Dolaf Mesʿar b. Mohalhel, *Resāla al-ṯānīa*, ed. and tr. V. Minorsky as *Abu-Dulaf's Travels in Iran (circa A.D. 950)*, Cairo, 1955. *Ḥodūd al-ʿālam*, tr. Minorsky, p. 132. Le Strange, *Lands*, pp. 189-90, 227. L. Lockhart, "Dīnawar," in *EI*[2] II, pp. 299-300. Schwarz, *Iran*, pp. 473-77.

(C. EDMUND BOSWORTH)

DĪNAVARĪ, ABŪ ḤANĪFA AḤMAD b. Dāwūd b. Vanand (d. between 281/894 and 290/903), grammarian, lexicographer, astronomer, mathematician, and Islamic traditionist of Persian origin, who lived at Dīnavar (q.v.) and in several cities in Iraq in the 9th century. There is little information on his life, but he is known to have attended the lectures of Esḥāq Sekkīt and his son Yaʿqūb b. Esḥāq, both renowned philologists.

Dīnavarī has been compared to his older contemporary Jāḥeẓ (d. 255/869), but he differed in that he was interested in mathematics and the Islamic sciences. He was the author of about fifteen works, which are enumerated by Ebn al-Nadīm (ed. Flügel, I, p. 86; cf. Brockelmann, *GAL*, S I, p. 187; Sezgin, *GAS* IV, pp. 338-43; V, pp. 262-63, 428; VI, pp. 158-59; VIII, pp. 168-70) and in later biographies. They ranged from a commentary on the Koran to treatises on arithmetic (*Ketāb al-baḥṯ fī ḥesāb al-Hend*), algebra (*Ketāb al-jabr wa'l-moqābala*), and popular astronomy (*Ketāb al-anwāʾ*). Dīnavarī was an adherent of the purist reaction against "errors" in language (*Ketāb mā yalḥan fīh al-ʿāmma*), took an interest in the history of poetry (*Ketāb al-šeʿr wa'l-šoʿarāʾ*), and even published a manual of erotism (*Ketāb al-bāh*). All these works are lost or at least have not been found, but it is not impossible that traces of them can be recognized in later writings, notably those of Ebn Qotayba Dīnavarī, whom Masʿūdī accused of having borrowed extensively from, if not actually having plagiarized (*Morūj*, ed. Pellat, par. 1327), Dīnavarī's works, particularly *Ketāb al-anwāʾ*; several passages of various lengths from the latter work are also quoted in *Moḵaṣṣaṣ* by the Andalusian Ebn Sīdoh (d. 458/1066).

Otherwise, from the list of Dīnavarī's works only one text has been preserved in its entirety; another, which is partially preserved, has been complemented from numerous quotations in the later literature. The first, entitled *Ketāb al-aḵbār al-ṭewāl* (q.v.; ed. V. Guirgass, Leiden, 1888; preface, variants, and index by I. Yu. Krachkovsky, Leiden, 1912), is a history of Islam, although Dīnavarī has never been considered a historian; the work is written from a Persian point of view, with particular emphasis on events involving Persia. A clear idea of the second work, which has long aroused the interest of scholars, can be obtained from the preserved and restored sections. It is entitled *Ketāb al-nabāt*, a botanical treatise consisting of an alphabetical dictionary and a series of monographs on plants with specific uses. The portion of the dictionary from *alef* to *zayn* was edited by Bernhard Lewin (*The Book of Plants of Abū Ḥanīfa ad-Dīnawarī. Part of the Alphabetical Sections (Alif-Zayn)*, Uppsala, 1953) and that from *sīn* to *yā* by M. Hamidullah (*Le dictionnaire botanique d'Abū Ḥanīfa ad-Dīnawarī*, Cairo, 1973). The monographs were also published by Lewin (*The Book of Plants. Part of the Monograph Section*, Wiesbaden, 1974). This work is of the greatest importance for the study of the flora of ancient Arabia; it is based on written sources, information furnished by bedouin, and the personal observations of the author. Subsequent studies and commentaries have included those by B. Silberberg and Thomas Bauer.

Bibliography: (For cited works not given in detail. see "Short References.") T. Bauer, *Das Pflanzenbuch des Abū Ḥanīfa ad-Dīnawarī*, Wiesbaden, 1988. B. Lewin, "al-Dīnawarī," *EI*[2] II, p. 300. Kaḥḥāla, I, pp. 218-19. *Kašf al-ẓonūn*, ed. Flügel, V, p. 358. ʿAlī b. Yūsof Qefṭī, *Enbāh al-rowāt ʿalā anbāh al-noḥāt* I, Cairo, 1950, pp. 42-44. O. Rescher, *Abriss der arabischen Litteraturgeschichte* II, Istanbul, 1925, pp. 198-200. B. Silberberg, "Das Pflanzenbuch des Dinawari," *ZA* 24, 1910, pp. 225-65; 25, 1911, pp. 39-88. Jalāl-al-Dīn ʿAbd-al-Raḥmān Soyūṭī, *Ketāb boḡyat al-woʿāt*, Cairo, 1326/1908, p. 132. Yāqūt, *Odabāʾ* III, pp. 26-32.

(CHARLES PELLAT)

DĪNAVARĪ, ABŪ MOḤAMMAD ʿABD-ALLĀH b. Ḥamdān b. Wahb b. Bešr (d. 308/902; incorrectly identified with ʿAbd-Allāh b. Mobārak Dīnavarī, q.v., by Brockelmann, *GAL* I, p. 204, Suppl. I, p. 334, and Sezgin, *GAS* I, p. 42), traditionist and *ḥāfeẓ* (preserver of the Koranic text). He conversed in the circle of Abū Zorʿa Rāzī (d. 264/878) and seems to have preserved Hadith material going back to Sofyān Ṯawrī that was not known in Kūfa, where Sofyān had lived.

Bibliography: Šams-al-Dīn Moḥammad Ḏahabī, *Taḏkerat al-ḥoffāẓ*, 4 vols., Hyderabad, 1375/1955, pp. 754 ff. no. 756. Idem, *Mīzān al-eʿtedāl fī naqd al-rejāl*, ed. ʿA.-M. Bejāwī, Cairo, 1382/1963, nos. 4566, 4281 (ʿAbd-Allāh b. Ḥamdān b. Wahb), 4679 (ʿAbd-Allāh b. Wahb). Idem, *al-ʿEbar fī aḵbār al-bašar memman ʿabar* II, ed. Ṣ Monajjed and F. Sayyed, Kuwait, 1960-65, p. 137, ll. 2 ff.

Ebn Ḥajar ʿAsqalānī, *Lesān al-mīzan* III, Hyderabad, 1329/1911, pp. 344-45 no. 1406. Ḵalīl b. Aybak Ṣafadī, *Ketāb al-wāfī beʾl-wafayāt* XVII, Wiesbaden, 1984, p. 540 no. 460. ʿAbd-Allāh b. Asad Yāfeʿī, *Merʾāt al-janān wa ʿebrat al-yaqẓān fī maʿrefat ḥawādeṯ al-zamān* II, Hyderabad, 1337/ 1919, p. 249.

(JOSEF VAN ESS)

DĪNAVARĪ, ABŪ MOḤAMMAD ʿABD-ALLĀH b. Mobārak (d. first half of the 10th century), author of a *tafsīr* (koranic exegesis) entitled *al-Wāżeḥ fī tafsīr al-Qorʾān*, which is preserved in several manuscripts (Brockelmann, *GAL* I, p. 204, S. I, p. 334; Sezgin, *GAS I*, p. 42, in both of which the author is incorrectly identified and his name garbled). The material is presented in a sober fashion, with short explanations and almost without quotation of earlier works; it stands fully in the eastern Persian tradition of Ebn ʿAbbās and Kalbī and was transmitted in Nīšāpūr, as well as in Samarqand. Ṯaʿlabī used it, as did members of the Karrāmīya, an ascetic movement with heterodox (especially anthromorphic) tendenfies which had spread in eastern Persia.

Bibliography: Šams-al-Dīn Moḥammad b. ʿAlī Dāwūdī, *Ṭabaqāt al-mofasserīn*, ed. ʿA. M. ʿOmar, I, Cairo, 1972, p. 244, no. 233. J. van Ess, *Ungenützte Texte zur Karrāmīya. Eine Materialsammlung*, Heidelberg, 1980, pp. 44 no. 8, 50 ff. I. Goldfeld, ed., *Mofasserū šarq al-ʿālam al-eslāmī fī arbaʿat al-qorūn al-hejrīya al-ūlā. Našr maḵṭūṭāṭ moqaddemat al-Ṯaʿlabī le-ketāb al-Kašfwaʾl-bayān ʿan tafsīr al-Qorʾān*, Acre, 1984, pp. 52; ll.7 ff.

(JOSEF VAN ESS)

DĪNAVARĪ, AḤMAD b. Moḥammad. See EBN ḴĀZEN.

DĪNĀVARĪYA (Ar. and Pers.< Mid. Pers. *dēnāwar* "having religion, pious, upright"), in Manichean usage originally "the elect." The term was ultimately derived from the Iranian substantive (attested in Mid. Pers. *dēnawar*, Parth. *dēnāβar*, and Sogd. *δēnāβar* and its feminine derivation *δynʾβrʾnc*, pl. *δyʾβrʾšt*). Judging from the Arabic form, the early New Persian form was **dēnāvar*; the derivation *dēnāvarī* "follower of the *dīnāvarān*" is attested in the plural form *dēnāvarīān* in Gardīzī (ed. Ḥabībī, p. 268). The Arabic word derived from it is mentioned in the section on Mani and his teachings and writings by Ebn al-Nadīm (ed. Flügel, pp. 66-67, 97-98; ed. Tajaddod, pp. 399-400; tr., p. 792) and by Jāḥeẓ (p. 77). In the 7th century the Chinese traveler Hsüan-tsang transcribed the word as *ti-na-ba* (Chavannes and Pelliot, 1913, p. 150), but in the so-called "Manichean treatise" a later Chinese form, *dian-na-wu*, is attested (Chavannes and Pelliot, 1911, pp. 554-55). From the form *tinaba* H. H. Schaeder deduced that *dīnāvar* was already in use in the 7th

century (p. 80 n. 2), but the rendering *diannawu* contradicts his conclusion, as do the common Arabic parallel forms of the place name Daynavar and Daynovar (on all these forms, cf. Sundermann, 1984, pp. 305-06; idem, 1986, p. 271).

The New Persian form with *ā* in the second syllable, distinct from the Islamic Persian place name Dīnavar (cf. the Mid. Pers. attributive name *dēnawarī* but Parth. [?] *Dēnāβarān*; see Markwart, *Provincial Capitals*, par. 29), seems to have been the only one to appear in Manichean usage. It did not originally designate a place or a person (Chavannes and Pelliot, 1911, p. 554, n. 1). As *a* was already attested in Middle Persian, while *ā* occurred in Parthian and Sogdian, *dēnawar* must have been the original Persian form; New Persian *dīnāvar* must thus be explained as a derivation from Parthian or a neologisim. The variants *ā/a* occur in similar New Persian double forms such as *kīnavar/kīnāvar*. Wilhelm Eilers correctly emphasized (p. 273) that *ā* reflects a lengthening that also occurred in forms with *-āwand/-awand* and *-ākar*. The suffix can thus be traced back to Old Iranian *-bara-* "carrying," rather than to *ā-bar-* "to bring." (Already in Avestan *bara-*, as in the form of *-uuara-*, had caused lengthening of a preceding *a*, as in *gaošāuuara-* "earring.")

That Mani himself introduced the Middle Persian term *dēnawar* into the terminology of his church is clear from its frequent appearance in *Šābuhragān* (MacKenzie, p. 304, where the reading *[dy](n)wryḫ* is possible instead of *[dyn](ʾ)wryḫ*). It was certainly for that reason that the title retained a special status in Manichean tradition, above that of similar and formally related *dēndār*, lit., "having the religion." Although *dēnāwar* predominated in Middle Iranian Manichean texts, in Buddhist texts *dēndār* was preferred, and, at least in some cases, *dēnāwar* was used to designate non-Buddhist priests.

The frequent use of the title among the Manicheans also suggests that in their linguistic usage the abstract Parthian *dēnāβarīft* (cf. Man. Sogd. ms. 18140 II r 6: *δy-nʾβry-ʾ* "community of the elect") was also understood as a collective designation for the Manichean church as a whole, including the lay members who were not, strictly speaking, *dēnāβarān*. This usage is confirmed by the Parthian homily published by W. B. Henning (pp. 30-31), in which catechumens belonging to the *[dyn]ʾbryft* were admonished to zealous charity toward the elect (ms. M 6020 l. 3).

The self-designation of Manicheans of the Middle East and Central Asia as *dēnāβarīft* and the like is certainly attested from the period around 630 C.E., when Hsüan-tsang visited Central Asia and reported that the heresy of the *tinaba* was widespread in the Persian kingdom; Josef Markwart recognized the term *tinaba* as a rendering of *dēnāβar* (p. 502; cf. Chavannes and Pelliot, 1913, p. 150). Schaeder connected this report with the name of the Manichean priest Mār Šād Ohrmazd, who died in 600 and was apparently so influential that later the Manicheans took his death year as an epoch of their religious era (pp. 79-80). Schaeder considered that his name was reflected in the term *dīnāvarīya*, referring to those who had led the Manichean church of Central Asia into schism at the end of the 6th century. This schism is described by Ebn al-Nadīm (ed. Flügel, pp. 66-67, 97-98; ed. Tajaddod, p. 397; tr. pp. 791-93), who locates the schismatics "on the other side of the Balḵ river"; they disputed the supreme authority of the see in Babylon, which clearly suggests that the leader residing in Transoxania (in Samarqand?) was recognized as the highest authority within his own community. The split was healed in the time of the Omayyad Walīd b. ʿAbd-al-Malek (86-96/705-15). Nevertheless, in the Manichean-Sogdian letters cited above, dated to the 9th (?) century, the Central Asian *dīnāvarān* were still criticizing the religious laxity that had appeared among their western brethren.

Although the schism did become known as that of the *dīnāvarīya*, it would nevertheless be incorrect to consider the *dīnāvarīya* as Manichean heretics per se. The designation persisted as a regional name for the Manichean church in Central Asia even after the reconciliation with the mother church in Mesopotamia (as shown, e.g., by the Parthian homily mentioned above), and it is probable a priori that the name had actually been in use before the schism itself had occurred.

Jāḥeẓ distinguished three Manichean communities: the *moṣaddeqīya* (or *moṣaddaqīya*?; not to be interpreted as *mazdaqīya*, pace Klima, p. 358) in the Arabic-speaking lands (and Persia?); the *dīnāvarīya* of Iranian Central Asia; and the *toḡozḡozīya* in the Central Asian steppe kingdom of the Uighurs (p. 88). From this evidence it follows that both the Arabic-speaking and the Central Asian Manicheans identified themselves by the names of the elect of their communities. Those of the Uighur kingdom did the same; aside from the improbability that they actually called themselves *toḡozḡozīya*, it is clear from the Turfan texts that they often called themselves *dīnāvarān*. For example, in a Sogdian communal letter probably from the Turfan oasis in the 9th century the elect of the original Mesopotamian party of believers (or at least one group of them) known as Mehryānd and Meqlāsīqt were interpreted as designated *δenāβarānšt*, and the same term applied to the elect of the Central Asian community itself (Sundermann, 1984, pp. 305-09). In the 11th century Gardīzī reported on the worshipful gathering of "three to four hundred" members of the *dīnāvar* community with their "prefect" (*ʿāmel*) in the Toḡozḡoz kingdom (ed. Ḥabībī, p. 268; for interpretation of the passage, see Alfaric, p. 87, n. 1).

The period when Central Asian Manicheans were first designated as *dēnāwarān* is not clear. As already noted, Schaeder connected it with the schism within this community (pp. 78-80), citing as evidence M2, which he considered a document of the schism; this document contains the legend of Mar Ammō, in which the spread of Mani's message in Central Asia is recounted (Mir. Man., II, pp. 301-06). Actually, however, at least the etiological portion involving the introduction of the title *dēnāwar* is of a later date. It must have been written at a time when New Persian had already replaced Middle Persian (and Parthian) in Central Asia, which could hardly have taken place before the 8th century and more probably in the 10th century (Sundermann, 1986, pp. 270-73). Furthermore, the purpose of this section was to provide a popular etymology explaining the origin of the name of the *dēnāwarān* (i.e., *dēn-āwar* "bringer of religion"), not of the community itself. It is thus clearly impossible to determine precisely when the name *dīnāvarīya* was first applied to the Central Asian Manichean church, but it is most likely that it had already been introduced in the 3rd century, as claimed in the Ammō legend, and remained in use until Manicheism disappeared in Central Asia (13th century?).

Bibliography: P. Alfaric, *Les écritures manichéennes*, Paris, 1918. E. Chavannes and P. Pelliot, in *JA*, 10th ser., 18, 1911, pp. 499-617; 11th ser., 1, 1913, pp. 99-394. W. Eilers, "Der Name Demawend," *Archív Orientalní* 22, 1954, pp. 267-374. W. B. Henning, "A Grain of Mustard," *AION* 50, 1965, pp. 30-31. Jāḥeẓ, *Ketāb al-tarbīʿ wa'l-tadwīr*, ed. C. Pellat, Damascus, 1955. D. N. MacKenzie, "Mani's Šābuhragān," *BSOAS* 43, 1980, pp. 288-310. J. Markwart, *Osteuropäische und ostasiatische Streifzüge*, Leipzig, 1903. H. H. Schaeder, "Iranica," *Abhandlungen der Gesellschaft der Wissenschaften zu Göttingen* 3/10, 1934, pp. 1-88. W. Sundermann, "Probleme der Interpretation manichäisch-soghdischer Briefe," in J. Harmatta, ed., *From Hecataeus to Al-Ḫuwārizmī*, Budapest, 1984, pp. 289-316. Idem, "Studien zur kirchengeschichtlichen Literatur der iranischen Manichäer II," *Archiv für Altorientalische Forschungen* 13, 1986, pp. 239-317.

(WERNER SUNDERMANN)

DINKHA TEPE. See DENḴĀ TEPE.

DINON (fl. approximately 360-30 B.C.E., based upon a reference in his work to the reconquest of Egypt by Artaxerxes III (q.v.) in 343-42 B.C.E.; Jacoby, *Fragmente* IIIC, no. 690, fragm. 30), author of a historical work on the Ancient Orient. He was a citizen of Colophon in Asia Minor and father of the historian Cleitarchus (q.v.). His work was divided into at least three sections, which seem to have corresponded to the three sections of his predecessor Ctesias (q.v.), *Assyriaká, Mēdiká,* and *Persiká* (Jacoby, *Fragmente* 1, 2, 3; Müller, *Fragmenta* II, 21, 4, 8). The thirty surviving fragments seem to prove that Dinon adapted and continued Ctesias' work, which ended in 398-97 B.C.E.

Starting with legendary times (queen Semiramis) and coming to an end with the Persian reconquest of Egypt, the following themes of major interest were treated: the name of Zoroaster, the prophecy on Cyrus' future glory as foretold to the Median king Astyages (q.v.), the genealogy of Cambyses, description of a custom at Xerxes' table, the supposed guarantee of protection that Themistocles received from Xerxes—Artaxerxes I according to the authentic tradition—when Themistocles left Greece for Asia Minor, a very corrupted genealogy of a sister of Artaxerxes I, the life of Artaxerxes II as preserved in Plutarch's biography from 398-97 B.C.E. onward (where Ctesias ended), and Persian manners (Jacoby, *Fragmente* 5, 9, 11-27; Müller, *Fragmenta* 5, 7, 11, 12, 15, 19-29).

The surviving fragments show that Dinon composed his work for readers with a taste for fabulous, strange, and erotic elements. Nevertheless the Roman biographer Cornelius Nepos thought of him as the most credible source on Persian history (Conon 5.4), and Antheaeus as well as Plutarch have repeatedly made use of his work along with and againstCtesias; his name is also found a few times in the work of Pliny the Elder.

Bibliography: E. Schwartz, "Dinon," Pauly-Wissowa V/1, 1903, col. 654. H. Peter, *Wahrheit und Kunst. Geschichtsschreibung und Plagiat im klassischen Altertum*, Leipzig, 1911, p. 70 (2nd ed., Hildesheim, 1965).

(Wolfgang Felix)

DĪNŠĀH ĪRĀNĪ. See IRANI, DINSHAH.

DIO CASSIUS (more correctly, Cassius Dio; b. Nicea, Bithynia, ca. 160, d. Nicea, after 229), Roman official whose *Rhomaikē Historia* (ed. U. P. Boissevain, 3 vols., Berlin, 1896-1901) is important for the study of Parthian history. He was the son of a government official under Marcus Aurelius and during the reign of Commodus (180-93) went to Rome, where he began his public career. Under Septimius Severus (193-211) he was named pretorius (193) and consul (ca. 211). He accompanied Caracalla (211-17) on his campaign to Armenia in 216, remaining in the east for several years, and under Severus Alexander (222-35) he was proconsul of Africa, then of Dalmatia and Upper Pannonia (225-28), and in 229 consul again. He soon retired from public life, however, and returned to his native land, where he remained for the rest of his days (*Prosopographia*; Gabba, pp. 289 ff.).

At the age of forty years he settled in Capua, in order to prepare himself to write his history. By his own report (72.23), he spent ten years assembling his materials and the next twelve writing his text, up to the death of Septimius Severus; the rest of the work must have been completed under Severus Alexander (Christ et al., pp. 796-97). The work originally consisted of eighty books, beginning with the arrival of Aeneas in Rome and ending in the year 229 C.E. Only books 36-60 have been completely preserved; they contain the history of the years 68 B.C.E. to 47 C.E., a critical period in Roman relations with the Parthians. For the subsequent years only extracts from an 11th-century epitome prepared by the Byzantine Joannes Xiphilinus survive (Ziegler, 1964, pp. 73 ff.); books 1-35 were already missing from the manuscript consulted by Xiphilinus, but in the following century they were known to another Byzantine historian, Joannes Zonaras, who drew upon them for books 7-12 of his *Chronicle* (von Gutschmid, pp. 549-62; Schwartz; Boissevain's preface to vol. III, pp. iii-xiii; Christ et al., pp. 795-99). It should be noted that in the *Suda* (II, pp. 116-17) the *Persica* by Dinon (q.v.) of Colophon is mistakenly attributed to Dio.

Dio described contemporary personalities and events at first hand or from official documents; his history is thus the principal source on the Roman campaign against the Parthians in 197-99 (76 (75.9-11); Debevoise, pp. 256 ff.), during which Seleucia, Babylon, and Ctesiphon were captured and Septimius Severus then unsuccessfully laid siege to Hatra twice in a period of several months (76 (75.10-12); Rubin, pp. 421 ff., who expresses unfounded doubts about the truth of Dio's unique account). Dio is also the sole reliable, athough succinct, source on the campaign of Caracalla (78 (77.12.1[2]). Before his final retirement to Bithynia he recorded the defeat of the Parthians by the Sasanian Ardašīr I (q.v.) in 224, emphasizing the danger of Ardašīr's having established a foothold in Mesopotamia and Syria and his threat to reconquer all the territory that had formerly belonged to Persian empire (80. 3-4). In several places in the history Parthians are mentioned as if they were still in power, suggesting that Dio did not revise his text after the fall of the Arsacids (Hartmann, pp. 75 ff.; Millar, pp. 30, 177, 206).

It is not always easy to identify Dio's sources for periods before his lifetime. Books 36 and 37 (abridged by Xiphilinus) were based mainly on Sallust's *Histories* (Reinach, pp. 449-51), but recent research has revealed that the work of the Alexandrine historian Timagenes (2nd half of the 1st century B.C.E.), who was partial to the Parthians, may also have been used (Clementini). For the more detailed account of Crassus' Parthian campaigns in Book 40, containing information not in Plutarch's parallel account, Dio's principal source was the *Roman History* of Livy, and he also drew on Arrian's *Parthica* (Hartmann, pp. 74 ff.). The account of the nine-month journey to Rome of the Parthian Tiridates, brother of Balāš I (ca. 51-80, q.v.), and his coronation as king of Armenia by the emperor Nero deserve special attention (63.1-7; cf. Cumont, pp. 145-54; Lemosse, pp. 462 ff.) as an important contribution to the history of the relations among the Parthians, Rome, and Armenia after the agreement of Rhandeia in 63 C.E., providing detail that is lacking in the works of Tacitus and Suetonius. For Trajan's Parthian war (68.17-31; cf. Longden, pp. 1-35; Debevoise, pp. 213-39) Dio relied largely on Arrian's *Parthica*, which he consulted in the original (fragments ed. by Roos and Wirth, Leipzig, 1968, pp. 205-24; cf. see Roos, pp. 30 ff., esp. pp. 38-39; Hartmann, pp. 82 ff.).

Bibliography: R. Adinolfi, in *Puteoli* 3, 1979, pp. 35-40. G. Alföldy, in *Theinisches Museum* 114, 1971, pp. 360-68. W. von Christ, W. Schmid, and O. Stählin, *Geschichte der griechischen Literatur*, 6th ed., II/2, Munich, 1924. G. Clementini, in Invigi*liata Lucernis* 7-8, 1985-86, pp. 141-60. F. Cumont, in *Rivista di filologia*, N.S. 11, 1936, pp. 147-51. N. C. Debevoise, *A Political History of Parthia*, Chicago, 1969. E. Gabba, "Sulla storia romana di Cassio Dione," *Rivista storica italiana* 6, 1955. A. von Gutschmid, *Kleine Schriften* VI, Leipzig, 1891. K. Hartmann, in Phi*lologus* 74, 1917, pp. 73-91. M. Lemosse, "Le couronnement de Tiridate," in *Mélanges en l'honneur de Gilbert Gidel*, Paris, 1961, pp. 455-58. R. P. Longdon, in *Journal of Roman Studies* 21, 1931, p. 135. F. Millar, *A Study of Dio Cassius*, Oxford, 1964. *Prosopographia Imperii Romani* II^2, 1936, pp. 115-17. T. Reinach, *Mithridate Eupator, roi du Pont*, Paris, 1890. A. G. Roos, *Studia Arrianea*, Leipzig, 1912. Z. Rubin, in Ch*iron* 5, 1975, pp. 419-41. E. Schwartz, "Cassius 40," in Pauly-Wissowa, cols. 1684-722. A. Stepanian, in *Revude des études arméniennes* 11, 1975, pp. 216-18. *Suda*, ed. A. Adler, Leipzig, 1928-38. K. H. Ziegler, *Die Beziehungen zwischen Rom und dem Partherreich*, Wiesbaden, 1964. Idem, "Xiphilinos," in Pauly-Wissowa IXA/2, cols. 2132-34.

(Marie Louise Chaumont)

DIO CHRYSOSTOM. See DIO COCCEIANUS.

DIO COCCEIANUS , surnamed Chrysostom (golden-mouthed), a travling scholar who in his 36th *Oration* (known as the "Borysthenian" or "Olbian" from its dramatic setting), written about 100 C.E., purports to summarize a hymn composed by Zoroaster and sung by the magi "in secret rites" (text and commentary in Bidez and Cumont, II, pp. 142-53; tr. H. Lamar Crosby, *Dio Chrysostom*, vol. 3, Loeb Classical Library, pp. 455-75). The hymn is actually two cosmological myths. In the first (pars. 39-53), the universe is likened to a team of horses corresponding to the elements of fire, air, water, and earth. The team, under the governance of its divine charioteer, usually runs in harmony, but periodic disasters of conflagration and deluge are caused by the fiery ardor of the first and mightiest of the horses and by the sweat of the third. In a final catastrophe the entire universe is consumed and melted down like wax into the horse of fire. The second myth tells of the re-creation of the world from the fructifying union of the gods Zeus and Hera (54-end).

If genuine, the hymns would belong to the Iranian people known as the Magusaeans, the descendants of those left in Anatolia after Alexander's reconquest. Their communities flourished into Roman times (Boyce, Chaps. VIII-X), and it would have been perfectly possible for Dio, himself a native of Prusa in Bithynia and widely traveled in Asia Minor, to have learned the hymns from them. The fact that the hymns differ widely from any other Zoroastrian liturgical works could be due to the Magusaeans' divergence from the main stream of the faith and the considerable degree of hellenization that they underwent from the surrounding culture. Cumont (Bidez and Cumont, I, p. 97), who believed strongly in the hymns' genuineness, argued that the Stoicism with which they are thoroughly imbued, came from the Magusaeans themselves and not from their redactor Dio.

On the other hand, the hymns may equally well be pure inventions by Dio. Greek authors had no inhibitions about enhancing their own material by attributing it to oriental sages, and the setting of the hymns as a myth at the end of a philosophical discourse is precisely the sort of literary context where, by convention, the freest rein could be given to imagination. The problem is that there are no other extant remains of Magusaean liturgy or doctrine against which Dio's material might be tested, and in their default it is probably sounder to attribute to Dio himself that which is manifestly occidental and in the Greek philosophical tradition. That said, it remains possible that the myths themselves, apart form the cosmogonic and eschatological meanings which Dio imposes on them, may contain kernels of stories actually recited by the Magusaeans magi in a real liturgical context. Somthing about the ill fit of the interpretations with the underlying narratives (espe-cially the first), an allegorical dissonance on which Dio himself remarks several times, suggests as much.

Bibliography: R. Beck, "Thus Spake not Zarathuštra. Zoroastrian Pseudepigrapha of not the Greco-Roman World," in Boyce and Grenet, *Zoroastrianism* III, pp. 491-565, esp. pp. 539-48. J. Bidez and F. Cumont, *Les Mages helénisés*, 2 vols., Paris, 1938, repr. 1973. F. Cumont "La fin du monde selon les magesd coccidentaux," *RHR* 103, 1931, pp. 29-96.

(Roger Beck)

DIODORUS SICULUS, Greek historian from Agyrium in Sicily, hence called Siculus (the Sicilian). Diodorus came to Rome in the middle of the first century B.C.E. and there wrote *Bibliotheca Historia*, a universal history in forty books (only 1-5 largely legendary early history, and 11-20, covering 480-301 B.C.E., survive), from the origins to the age of Caesar.

The work is a compilation, normally epitomizing one earlier histoian at a time, with insertions from Diodorus' other readings and moral reflections of his own, and then changing over to another history where the previous one runs out. The quality of his sources varies, and his uses of them is often inaccurate. He misreports Herodotus' Median king list (Herodotus 1.95 ff.) and names Pharnabazus instead of Tissaphernes as the satrap active against Athens in the Peloponnnesian war (bk. 13) and as warning Artaxerxes II against Cyrus the Younger (qq.v.; 14.22.1, but correct in 14.80.6), an error not likely to have been in his fourth-century source). Characteristic of more serious errors is his confusion (16.40 ff) of Artaxexes III's unsuccessful expedition against Egypt in 351-50 with his successful one in 344-43. His presentation is annalistic, chiefly dating to Athenian archons and Roman consuls, whose entry upon office, by the second century, was six months apart. He also likes to follow a story over many years, while dating it under a particular year in which some significant part of it occurred. Thus the story of Themistocles, from his ostracism (471-70) throug his escape to "Xerxes" (Thucydides 1.137 gives Artaxexes: 465) to his death (probably about 460), is all under 471-70. This makes Diodorus' chronology difficult to use even when (as is most often the case) it is by his own standard correct. Subject to those limitations, he is important as the only surviving historian who gives an account of Persian relations with the Greeks between Xexes' defeat and the outbreak of the Peloponnesian war, with some information on the king's administratiors in his western provinces; for his account of the first part of the fourth century he is often judged superior to Xenophon, since his ultimate source appears to be the anonymous Greek history which has since been discovered in Oxyrhynchus (*Hellenica Oxy-rhynchia*). After minor contributions to the history of Alexander the Great (bk. 17: his longest, probably based on the novelistic work of Cleitarchus, q.v.), he follows Hieronymus of Cardia in books 18-20, providing our best account of the struggles of Alexander's successors, including Antigonus' conquest of Iran in book 18 and Seleucus' conquest of Babylonia and western Iran (he unfortunately ignores eastern Iran) in book 19.

Bibliography: The Loeb edition (Greek and English: *A Library of History*, 12 vols., 1933-67; various editors and translators), with an excellent index, uses the best available texts and includes the surviving fragments of the lost books, found in various Byzantine collections (chiefly Photius and the extracts compiled for Constantine Porphyrogenitus) and varying in length and importance. It gives a bibliography of earlier editions. A Budé edition (Greek and French), with good textual notes and commentaries of varying length, was begun in 1969 and is slowly proceeding. For the most recent treatment, with ample bibliography, see Kenneth Sacks, *Diodoros Siculus and the First Century*, Princeton, 1990. See also E. Schwartz, "Diodorus 38," in Pauly-Wissowa, V, cols. 663-704.

(Ernst Badian)

DIODOTUS, the satrap of Bactria-Sogdiana, who revolted against his Seleucid soverign Antiochus II (q.v.) and proclaimed himself king, thus laying the foundation of the Graeco-Bactrian kingdom. The date of his revolt has been a subject of much debate. It has been placed between 256 and 239 B.C., the majority of scholars arguing for about the year 250. He was succeeded by his son Diodotus II .

Apart from the classical sources, our knowledge of Diodotus depends, to a great extent, on numismatic evidence. His gold and silver coins can be divided into two distinct groups. In the first group, while keeping his sovereign's name, Diodotus introduced his own portrait instead of the portrait of Antiochus II, and replaced the most common Seleucid reverse type, Apollo seated on the Omphalus, by a fulllength figure of a thundering Zeus with an eagle at his feet. By minting these coins in the name of Antiochus II but with his own portrait, Diodotus showed a formal attachment to his Seleucid sovereignty while taking a revolutionary step towards independence, without taking the royal title. In the second group, not only the portrait and the reverse type, but also the name are those of Diodotus. It is evident that Diodotus, by minting them, took the final step to declare openly his independence. The date of the emergence of the Seleucid satrapy of 1,

PLATE XXVIII

a.

b.

a. Silver tetradrachm, Diodotos in the name of Antiochus (Cabinet des Médailles, Bibliothèque Nationale, Paris, no. R.3681.26). b. Silver tetradrachm, Diodotos in the name of Diodotos (BM, no. 1880.5.1.1.; copyright British Museum).

Bactria-Sogdiana as a totally independent kingdom may be placed at around 239-38 B.C.E.

Bibliography: P. Bernard, *Fouilles d'Aï Khanoum* IV. *Les monnaies hors trésors. Questions d'histoire gréco-bactrienne*, MDAFA 27, Paris, 1985. O. Bopearachchi, *Monnaies gréco-bactriennes et indo-grecques, Catalogue raisonné*, Bibliothèque nationale, Paris, 1991. R. Curiel and G. Fussman, *Le Trésor monétaire de Qunduz*, MDAFA 20, Paris, 1965. M. Mitchiner, *Indo-Greek and Indo-Scythian Coinage* I, London, 1975. A. K. Narain, *The Indo-Greeks*, Oxford, 1957. E. T. Newell, *The Coinage of the Eastern Seleucid Mints from Seleucos I to Antiochos III*, New York, 1941. W. W. Tarn, *The Greeks in Bactria and India* , 2nd ed., Cambridge, 1951, repr. Chicago, 1984. Willrich, "Diodotos 7," in Pauly-Wissowa, V/1, cols. 714-15.

(OSMUND BOPEARACHCHI)

DIOGENES LAERTIUS, author of a biographically arranged history of Greek philosophy in ten books that also deals with the Persian Magi, especially in the first book on the origins of philosophy. Of his life nothing is recorded, but according to the internal evidence in his work he must have lived in the 3rd century C.E. Diogenes Laertius gathered his material from (lost) second- or third-hand sources without citing the chain of tradition completely. He claimed to have based his statements upon the chief authorities that he quoted by name, though he rarely knew their works other than by means of citations. Moreover legendary tradition is not separated from facts. Hence each reported tradition must be examined critically.

According to the Hellenistic (pseudo-Aristotelian or rather peripatetic) view, philosophy must have originated from the barbarians. Rejecting this opinion in the proem of his book (1. 6-9), Diogenes mentions the position and cult of the Magians and, in a completely fantastical manner, refers to the time and name of Zoroaster. Elsewhere he lays great stress on the relations of prominent philosophers to the Magians: a Magian is said to have foretold to Socrates his death (2.45); Plato, interested in getting into touch with them, is said to have been prevented from doing so by war (3.7); a Persian Mithridates is mentioned as Plato's pupil (3.25). It is also stated that Pythagoras, Democritus, and Pyrrho had contacts with the Magians (8.3; 9.34.61).

Historical facts found in the book include: reference to the uprising of the Ionians against the Persians in a (spurious) letter of Pythagoras to Anaximenes (8.49) and the latter's fictious response (2.5); the relations of Xenophon to the younger Cyrus and the retreat of the 10,000 (2.49-51); the fictious correspondence of Heraclitus with Darius (9.12-14); and mention of the next-of-kin marriage among the Persians (9.83).

Bibliography: R. Hope, *The Book of Diogenes Laertius*, New York, 1930. E. Schwartz, "Diogenes Laertios 40," in Pauly-Wissowa, V/1, cols. 738-63, repr. in idem, *Griechisch Geschichtsschreiber*, Leipzig, 1957, pp. 453-91.

(WOLFGANG FELIX)

DIONYSIUS (Gk. Dionysios) of Miletus, Greek historiographer, who may have lived in the 5th century B.C.E. and is said to have written a book about Persian history after the death of Darius I (q.v.; cf. Suda, s.v., where five books of *Events after Darius* and *Persiká*, written in the Ionian dialect, are listed among his works). As in the only surviving historical notice, preserved in a scholium to Herodotus, there is reference to the removal of the false Smerdis, it seems probable that the fragment belongs to the introductory, "retrospective" part of Dionysius' books and that the detailed description of Persian history began only with the death of Darius.

Bibliography: Jacoby, *Fragmente* IIIC, pp. 410-11. [E.] Schwartz, "Dionysios. 112," in Pauly-Wissowa, V/cols. 933-34.

(RÜDIGER SCHMITT)

DIPLOMACY. See FOREIGN RELATIONS

DĪRAKVAND, Lor tribe belonging to the Bālā Garīva group and inhabiting a mountainous area between Ḵorramābād and Dezfūl (q.v.) in the Pīš-Kūh region of Lorestān. According to Albert Houtum-Schindler (p. 86), the Dīrakvand comprised about 2,000 families in 1294/1877; Arnold Wilson (p. 26), reported about 3,000 families in 1330/1912 and Henry Field (p. 183) about 8,000-10,000 individuals in 1307 Š./1928. The absence of more recent data on the tribe suggests that it has lost its separate identity.

According to H.-L. Rabino, the Dīrakvand claimed to be of Qorayšī origin, and their leaders believed themselves to be descendants of Imam ʿAlī's elder brother ʿAqīl; the *atābegs* of Lorestān were supposedly from the Dīrakvand (Rabino, p. 23), but Vladimir Minorsky maintained that they were from the Jangrūʾī tribe (p. 828).

According to Wilson (p. 27), the Dīrakvand were "notorious for their predatory habits," especially along the Dezfūl-Borūjerd road, an important trade route; they also robbed and pillaged one another, and blood feuds were "one of the chief pre-occupations of their chiefs." Rabino (p. 23) reported that as a result of an attack on the camp of Tīmūr (771-807/1370-1405) part of the tribe was massacred. They were also allegedly punished on several occasions by Shah ʿAbbās I (996-1038/1588-1629). At the beginning of the 20th century they suffered further reverses. According to Wilson (p. 26), around 1318/1900 they were crushed by a force led by Ḥešmat-al-Dawla, governor of Lorestān, and Ḥosaynqolī Khan Feylī, governor of Pošt-e Kūh. Many of the Dīrakvand were taken prisoner, and several chiefs were deported to Kermānšāh. In 1320/1902, after attacking the Baḵtīārī on the Kārūn river 30 km from Šūštar, the tribe was thoroughly defeated by Esfandīār Khan Baḵtīārī.

The Dīrakvand were divided into two branches: the Bahārvand (q.v., composed of thirteen clans or *tīras*) and the Qalāvand (composed of twelve clans; Field, p. 183).

Bibliography: (For cited works not given in detail see "Short References.") Curzon, *Persian Question* II, pp. 279, 384. C. J. Edwards, "Luristan. Pish-i Kuh and Bala Gariveh," *The Geographical Journal* 59, 1922, pp. 335-56. H. Field, *Contributions to the Anthropology of Iran*, Chicago, 1939. A. Houtum-Schindler, "Reisen im südwestlichen Persien," *Zeitschrift der Gesellschaft für Erdkunde zu Berlin* 14, 1879, pp. 81-124. H. Īzadpanāh, *Āṯār-e bāstānī wa tārīḵī-e Lorestān*, 2 vols., 1350-55 Š./1971-76, II, table facing p. 4. M. Mardūḵ Kordestānī, *Tārīḵ-e Kord wa Kordestān wa tawābeʿ yā Tārīḵ-e Mardūḵ*, 2nd. ed., 2 vols. in one, Tehran, 1353 Š./1974, I, p. 92. V. Minorsky, "Lur-i Kūčik," *EI*² V, pp. 828-29. H.-L. Rabino, *Les tribus du Louristan*, Paris, 1916. A. T. Wilson, *Military Report on South-West Persia* V. *Luristan*, Simla, 1912.

(PIERRE OBERLING)

DĪRGHANAKHA-SŪTRA, a Buddhist text in which the Buddha expounds the merits of observing the eight commandments to a *parivrājaka* named Dīrghanakha. It was translated into Chinese by I-tsing early in the 8th century (*Taishō Tripiṭaka* XIV, no. 584) and the complete Sogdian version translated from the Chinese is extant. Its title is rendered in Sogdian as *pwty prβʾyrtk βrznʾxʾn δynδʾry wpʾrs pwstk* "Sūtra spoken by Buddha at the question of a religious man (named) Long-nailed" (cf. Sk. title *Dīrghanakha-parivrājaka-paripṛcchā-sūtra* reconstructed from the Chinese by Nanjio, no. 734).

The Sogdian version, which was the first Buddhist Sogdian text to be published, was first studied by Robert Gauthiot. His edition was extensively commented upon by Friedrich Weller and later revised by Émile Benveniste (pp. 74-81, 200-01; on which see Henning, pp. 730-31, 735).

The scroll containing the *Dīrghanakha-sūtra* discovered at Tun-huang (ms. Pelliot sogdien 5 [P5]) has recently been shown by Yutaka Yoshida, the present author, to be from the same manuscript as Pelliot sogdien 17 ([P17]; Benveniste, pp. 145-47, 231). The original scroll, which was dismembered into two parts with a loss of several dozen lines in between was composed of two sections, namely *Dīrghanakha-sūtra* (P5, 1-88) and a formula for receiving the eight commandments (P5, 89-125 and P17), the title of the whole text being *βrz nʾxʾn δynδʾr ZY ʾštʾ škšʾpt pwstk* "Sūtra of the religious Dīrghanakha and the eight commandments" (P17, 42).

The text of the second section was revised by Yoshida, who, referring to its five subsections, compares it with the Tun-huang Chinese manuscripts of similar content. The five subsections are: 1. invitations of deities as witnesses to the confession of sins (P5, 90-105); 2. a confession of sins (P5, 105-25); 3. presumably a *triśaraṇa* (the three-hold refuge formula of the Buddhists) lost in a lacuna; 4. reception of the eight commandments (P17, 1-33); and 5. the expression of the wish to obtain Buddhahood (P17, 34-41). Yoshida suggests that the Sogdian text seems more likely to be adapted than translated from such Chinese texts (for the Chinese texts, see Yoshida, p. 170, n. 4).

Bibliography: É. Benveniste, *Textes sogdiens*, Paris, 1940. R. Gauthiot, "Le sūtra du religieux ongles-longs," *MSL* 17, 1911-12, pp. 357-67. W. B. Henning, "The Sogdian Texts of Paris," *BSOAS* 11, 1946, pp. 713-40. B. Nanjio, *A Catalogue of the Chinese Translation of the Buddhist Tripiṭaka*, Oxford, 1883. *Taishō Tripiṭaka*, ed. J. Takakusu and K. Watanabe, Tokyo, 1924-32. F. Weller, "Bemerkungen zum soghdischen Dīrghanakha-sūtra," *Asia Major* 10, 1935, pp. 221-28. Y. Yoshida, "On the Sogdian Formula for Receiving the Eight Commandments," *Orient* 20, 1984, pp. 157-72.

(YUTAKA YOSHIDA)

DIRHAM (< Gk. *drakhmḗ* "drachma"; Mid. Pers. *drahm*, Pers. *derham*), a unit of silver coinage and of weight.

i. *In Pre-Islamic Persia.*
ii. *In the Islamic period.*

I. IN PRE-ISLAMIC PERSIA

The dirham retained a stable value of about 4 g throughout the entire pre-Islamic period. The tetradrachm, or stater (> Pahl. *stēr*), was equivalent to 4 drachmas and was already in circulation in the Achaemenid period at the time of Alexander's departure for Persia. The minting of "lion staters" continued in use in Babylon and Susa until the period of Antiochus I (ca. 324-261 B.C.E.). From that time on the Attic talent served as the weight standard for the Seleucid tradrachms (e.g., gold staters of Andragoras and the Bactrian kings).

Under the Arsacids circulation of money in northern Persia was similar to that in the rest of the Seleucid empire, but the drachma was preferred at Bactria (q.v.) and Hecatompylos, whereas at Ecbatana the tetradrachm still predominated. The standard weight in the 3rd century B.C.E. remained at about 4 g. On the obverse of the Seleucid coins the royal portrait head was represented, on the reverse Apollo seated on the omphalos and holding a bow. The oldest surviving Parthian coins come from a hoard found in the Atrak valley (west of Bojnūrd), includ ing one tetradrachm and 1,500 drachmas, still based on Hellenistic models, recognizable in the *bāšlīg* diadem of the nomads, already known among satraps of the Achaemenid period, worn by an unbearded figure (Sellwood, p. 279). The archer remained the main reverse type throughout the Parthian period. The weight of the drachma varied between 3.5 and 4.2 g. The use of the dynastic name Arsaces, rather than the personal names of the kings, in the inscriptions before the advent of the Sasanians in the 3rd century C.E. makes it difficult to clarify the sequence in which these coins were issued. Drachmas and silver obols (=one-sixth of a drachma, which later became the Persian *dāng*), as well as bronze coins, are attested from the reign of Mithridates I in the 2nd century B.C.E. The head is represented bearded (Sellwood, p. 281). Tetradrachms of more than 16 g, from the years 140-38 B.C.E., were struck only at Seleucia. Several mint names appear in abbreviated form beginning with the reign of Phraates III (73-57 B. C. E.). The drachmas of Orodes II (57-37 B.C.E.) are known in the thousands and must have been struck by the millions. The titulature, including the epithet philhellene, remained in use until the end of the Parthian period. The last Parthian drachmas issued at Susa and in Khorasan were those of Vardanes I struck in 42 C.E. Under Vologeses I (ca. 51-80; see Balāš I) the Greek language was abandoned on drachmas in favor of Parthian. By the beginning of the 3rd century the drachmas had evolved quite far from their Greek prototypes. At the same period tetradrachms and drachmas were being issued in Persis (present-day Fārs) with Aramaic inscriptions in the name of the *prataraka*. They weigh about 4 g, but the novel feature is the representation on the reverse of the fire temple with the winged figure of Ahura Mazdā (q.v.). Coinage in the Elymais continued to follow Seleucid prototypes (silver tetradrachms of Kamnaskires I, with inscriptions in Greek). After 45 C.E. the tetradrachms weighed 14 g. and the drachmas 3.5 g. In Characene, at Spasinu Charax, tetradrachms were issued with Greek inscriptions. (Sellwood, p. 310 ff.)

The basic coinage of the Sasanians (224-632 C.E.) was the silver drachma and, along with Arab-Sasanian dirhams, it constituted the main coinage of the Arab conquerors in Persia for for a long time. From the beginning to the end the Sasanian drachma weighed the same as its Parthian predecessor, about 4 g, attesting a remarkable financial stability. One important change was the introduction of the large, thin drachma, the first thin money in history (Göbl, 1968, p. 27). The thirty kings of the Sasanian dynasty were represented on the obverse of their drachmas with different and characteristic crowns, which facilitate establishment of a precise sequence of issues. The portrait of the king is not frontal, as on Parthian coins, but facing to the right. On the reverse is the fire altar, which may be flanked by two personages (both priests or perhaps the king and a priest) and also sometimes appears with a bust in the flames. Šāpūr II (309-79) must have increased production of coinage to finance his wars, as did Pērōz (459-84) during his conflict with the Hephthalites. A large propotrion of minted coinage was used to pay troops. Enormous quantities were thus struck under Kavāḏ I (488-96, 498-531), Ḵosrow I (531-79), and Ḵosrow II (590-628), who were engaged in foreign wars. The tax reform of Kavād and Ḵosrow I simultaneouslly lightened the burden on the population and ensured higher returns for the treasury by making the poll tax (on men between twenty and fifty years old) more equitably assessed (Christensen, *Iran Sass.*, p. 366; Göbl, 1968, p. 26) The tetradrachm fell into disrepute in the time of Bahrām I (271-74), for it was made almost entirely of copper with only a tiny amount of silver. Half-drachmas appeared only at the beginning of the Sasanian period, obols and half-obols sporadically for gifts on the occasion of investitures or to be thrown to crowds. The inscriptions in Middle Persian included on the obverse the titles and name of the king and on the reverse, beginning with Bahrām IV, the mint and regnal year.

The Pahlavi *Vīdēvdād* and the late religious literature provide an idea of the purchasing power of the drachma: One sheep cost three *stērs* (*Vd.* 4.2); a cow 12, 14, or 30 *stērs*, depending on whether it was of inferior, medium, or superior quality (*Vd.* 7.41); and a man 125 *stērs*. According to *Mādayān ī hazār dādestān* (12.7-9), a slave was sold for 500 drachmas and a sheep for 10 (104.6), but a good piece of land was worth more than 500 drachmas (*Vd.* 4.2).

Sins had to be redeemed by fines that, depending on their gravity, were set between 1 drachma and 300 *stērs* (Kotwal, p . 115 table). A passage from the *Dēnkard* VI (Shaked, p. 179) includes the story of two poor priests who refused a gift of 2,000 *dirhams* that a *mowbedān mowbed*, moved by compassion, had sent to them; it must have represented a significant sum.

The drachma weight (Pahl. *dram-sang*) is mentioned on Sasanian vessels, where next to the name of the owner the weight of the object is sometimes given in drachmas or *stērs* (Smirnov, no. 61, pl. 33: 330 *dlmsng*).

See also COINS AND COINAGE.

Bibliography: D. H. Bivar, "Achaemenid Coins, Weights and Measures," in *Camb. Hist. Iran* II, pp. 610-39. R. Curiel and D. Schlumberger, *Trésors monétaires d'Afghanistan*, MDAFA 14, Paris, 1953. M. A. Dandamaev and V. G. Lukonin, *The Culture and Social Institutions of Ancient Iran*, tr. P. L. Kohl and D. J. Dadson, Ney York etc., 1989, pp. 195 ff. H. Gaube, *Arabosasanidische Numismatik*, Brunswick, 1973. R. Göbl, *Die Münzen der Sasaniden im koniglichen Münzkabinett*, The Hague, 1962. Idem, *Sasanidische Numismatik*, Brunswick, 1968; Engl. ed. Sasanian Numismatics, Brunswick, 1971. Idem, "Sasanian Coins," in

Camb. Hist. Iran III, pp. 322-39. F. M. P. Kotwal, *The Supplementary Texts to the Šāyest nē Šāyest*, Copenhagen, 1969. A. Perikhanian, *Sasanidskiĭ sudebnik* (The Sasanian law code), Yerevan, 1973. D. Sellwood, "Parthian Coins," in *Camb. Hist. Iran* III, pp. 279-98; Idem, "Minor States in Southern Iran," in *Camb. Hist. Iran* III, pp. 299-321. S. Shaked, *The Wisdom of the Sasanian Sages (Dēnkard VI)*, Boulder, Colo., 1979. J. Smirnov, *Argenterie orientale*, St. Petersburg, 1909. J. Walker, *A Catalogue of the Arab-Sassanian Coins*, London, 1941; repr. London, 1967.

(Philippe Gignoux)

ii. In the Islamic Period

For Muslims in the classical period, any silver coin was a dirham, and a dirham was also a monetary unit that might or might not be represented by a circulating coin. A dirham was also a small weight unit, usually not the same as the weight of a monetary dirham.

Under the Sasanian emperors, numerous mints throughout Persia issued large quantities of silver *drahms* (Plate XXIX.a), while scarcely any silver coins were issued elsewhere in the world. These coins have the image and name of the Sasanian emperor on the obverse and on the reverse a Zoroastrian fire altar with two attendants and inscriptions in Pahlavi giving the date and mint.

Since the Arabs knew and used Sasanian coins, it was natural that they allowed minting of silver coins like those of the Sasanians to continue when they conquered Persia in the mid-7th century. At first, the coins had no indication of Arab authority, but all coins issued after the death of the last Sasanian emperor have an additional brief Arabic inscription in the margin such as *bism Allah* "in the name of God" (Plate XXIX.b). About 50/670 it began to be customary to substitute the name of an Arab official, written in Pahlavi script, for the name of the Sasanian emperor (Plate XXIX.c).

In 80/699 new Arabic Islamic dirhams were invented at Damascus and introduced at about thirty mints throughout Persia (Plate XXIX.d). These coins are anonymous, bearing only Islamic religious inscriptions in Arabic, principally the *šahāda*. There is no god but God alone; none is associated with Him), and the date and mint of issue. These inscriptions remained standard throughout the Omayyad period (until 132/750) and were retained with some additions and changes until the 16th century.

The weight standard of the new dirhams was 7/10 of the old Sasanian standard. In the 7th century, as the 9th century Arab historian Balaḏorī explains (*Fotūḥ*, p. 465), weight standards in Persia were expressed as a relationship to the *meṯqāl*, in a formula such as "dirhams weight of ten" meaning that ten dirhams at such a standard weighed ten *meṯqāl*s, while ten "dirhams weight of seven" weighed seven *meṯqāl*s. Since in his account the original dirhams were "weight of ten," it follows that the *meṯqāl* in 7th century Persia was the weight of the heaviest circulating silver coins, or just over 4 grams (there were minor local variations in this standard). There were, however, other weight standards such as "weight of eight" (8/10 *meṯqāl*) and "weight of five" (1/2 *meṯqāl*). The standard of the new Islamic dirham was fixed in Persia, perhaps as a compromise, at "weight of seven" or 7/10 of the old standard, usually between 2.80 and 2.85 grams though there are heavier dirhams, up to 2.95 grams, resulting from local variation.

Commencing with the ʿAbbasid caliphate (132/750), a series of changes in the appearance and weight standard of the dirham were made, ending with the beginning of the reign of al-Moʿtaṣem (218/833), when the dirham, as well as the gold dinar, was fixed in the form it would retain until the 11th century. The earliest was the introduction of *Moḥammad Rasūl Allāh* (Moḥammad [is] the messenger of God) as the standard reverse central inscription, in place of a longer inscription that had characterized Omayyad dirhams. Starting in 145/762, dirhams began to bear the names of caliphs and other officials (Plate XXIX.e). A second obverse marginal inscription, the Koranic verse beginning *le'llāh al-amr men qabl wa men baʿd* (command is God's, in the past and in the future), was first used in 199/814 and became standard about 206/821. Al-Moʿtaṣem amd his successors established the rule that no one but the caliph and his heir could be named on coins (Plate XXIX.f), but later viziers and *amir-al-omarā*ʾs (q.v.) at the center and certain powerful governors in the provinces were allowed to be named as well. All the independent secular rulers of the 4th to 7th centuries, such as the Saffarids, Samanids, Buyids, Ghaznavids, and Saljuqs, used the classical ʿAbbasid design and inscriptions on their coins, but added the rulers' names and titles to those of the caliph (Plate XXIX.g). Otherwise their coinage in Persia followed the ʿAbbasid pattern (see dīnār for the full inscriptions of the standard type, which was the same for gold and silver).

Also during the 8th and 9th centuries, the definition of the *meṯqāl* was changed to make it equal to the weight of the Islamic gold dinar (as had already been true in Egypt and Syria). The weight standard of the dirham continued to be defined as 7/10 of this *meṯqāl* of 4.25 grams, and the 7:10 ratio between the weight of the silver dirham and the gold dinar became a tenet of Muslim Šarīʿa law. The value of the two coins was, however, never fixed. The dinar and dirham were two separate currencies, with their relative value set in the marketplace.

Around the beginning of the 11th century, dirhams in Persia became increasingly debased in alloy and scarce, finally disappearing completely. There are virtually no Saljuq dirhams, for example. The economic reasons for this are not clear, but it seems that

PLATE XXIX

a.

b.

c.

d.

e.

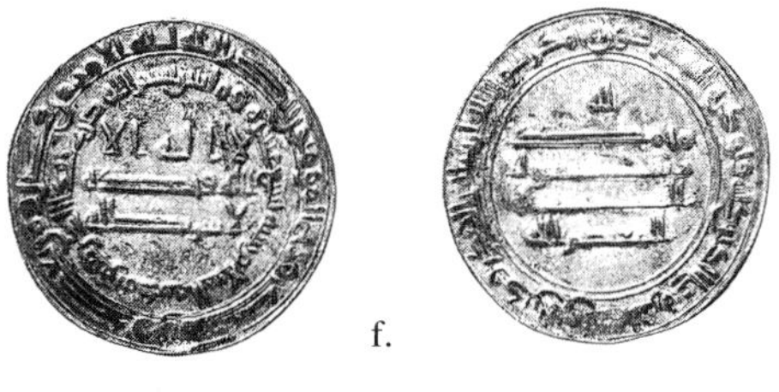
f.

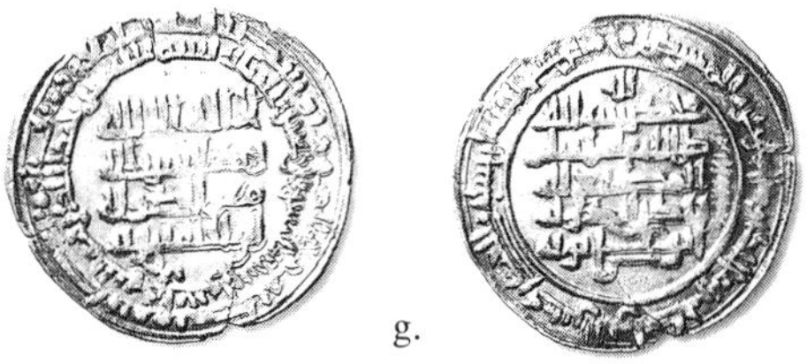
g.

h.

a. Dirham, Bīšāpūr mint, 25th year of K̲osrow II (C.E. 614), American Numismatic Society, 1959.123.1. b. Dirham, Dārābgerd mint, with name of K̲osrow, dated 30th year of Yazdegerd III (C.E. 661-62), American Numismatic Society 1975.238.40. c. Dirham, Garmkermān (Bardasīr) mint, with name of ʿAmr b. Laqīt̲, governor of Kermān, dated 83/702-03, American Numismatic Society 1975.238.1. d. Dirham, Ray mint, dated 94/712-13, American Numismatic Society 1952.80.12. e. Dirham, Ray mint, with name of al-Mahdī Moḥammad son of the commander of the believers, dated 145/762-63, American Numismatic Society 1958.222.10. f. Dirham, Madīnat-al-Salām (Baghdad) mint, with name of ʿAbbasid caliph al-Moʿtaṣem, dated 219/834-35, American Numismatic Society 1921.53.10. g. Dirham, Sūq al-Ahvāz mint, with names of Buyids Moʿezz-al-Dawla and Rokn-al-Dawla and ʿAbbasid caliph al-Moṭīʿ, dated 342/953-54, American Numismatic Society 1980.35.37. h. Dirham, Solṭānīya mint, with name of Il-khan Abū Saʿīd dated 33 Il-khani era (*sana t̲ālet̲ wa t̲alāt̲īn īlk̲ānīya*; 1333-34), 1974.26.108. Collection of American Numismatic Society. Scale 1:1.

silver had become relatively scarce throughout the world. For Persia and its neighbors in particular, the shortage of silver might be connected with the enormous export of dirhams from eastern Persia across Russia to Scandinavia to pay for northern imports. This export, however, had gone on for some two centuries without slackening; its sudden termination at the beginning of the 11th century must also be explained by the exhaustion of some major source of silver, such as the mines of Panjhīr/Panjšīr in Afghanistan.

In the late 12th century, silver coinage resumed in Syria and Anatolia, and in 629/1231-32 at Baghdad. By 642/1244-45, the Mongols initiated silver dirham coinage at their Persian capital, Tabrīz. In subsequent years, silver coinage spread gradually to other Persian cities, but a uniform silver dirham coinage at nearly every urban center began only with the general monetary reform of the Il-khan Ḡāzān and his vizier Rašīd-al-Dīn Fażl-Allāh in 696/1296-97 (Rašīd-al-Dīn, *Jāmeʿ-al-tawārīḵ*, Baku, pp. 490-94). In the new system, the weight of the dirham was set at that of the *meṯqāl*, about 4.30 grams, and the dinar, formerly a gold coin of 4.25 grams, was defined as six silver dirhams. The gold coins of the Il-khans were called *meṯqāl*s and were not fixed in relation to the dinar of six dirhams.

Throughout the 14th century, under the Il-khans and their successors, successive reductions in the weight standard of the dirham followed rapidly. To distinguish these various weight standards, the dirhams of the Il-khans and their successors show a variety of designs (Plate XXIX.h), in contrast to the uniformity of the classical dirham type. By the middle of the 14th century, a coin denominated as six dirhams, or one dinar, weighed and was worth less than the original one-dirham coin of 1296. Timur's conquest of Persia swept all this away and introduced a new silver coin called the *tanka*. The term dirham was not used thereafter in Persia for coinage, being replaced by such denominations as *šāhī* and *rīāl*. It survived only in literary and legal contexts.

As a weight unit, in later medieval and modern Persia the dirham varied between 3.2 and 3.3 grams.

See also COINS AND COINAGE.

Bibliography: (For cited works not given in detail see "Short References.") S. Album, "Studies in Ilkhanid History and Numismatics. I. A Late Ilkhanid Hoard (743/1342)," *Studia Iranica* 13, 1984, pp. 49-116. Idem, "Studies in Ilkhanid History and Numismatics. II. A Late Ilkhanid Hoard (741/1340) as Evidence for the History of Diyar Bakr," *Studia Iranica* 14, 1985, pp. 43-76. Idem, "The Coinage of Nūr-Āward, Atabeg of Lur Buzurg, 751-57 H./A.D. 1350-56," *American Numismatic Society Museum Notes* 22, 1977, pp. 213-39. Idem, *A Checklist of Popular Islamic Coins*, Santa Rosa, CA, 1993. M. L. Bates, "Islamic Numismatics," *Middle East Studies Association Bulletin* 12/2, May 1978, pp. 1-16; 12/3, December 1978, pp. 2-18; 13/1, July 1979, pp. 3-21; 13/2, December 1979, pp. 1-9. M. R. Cowell and N. M. Lowick, "Silver from the Panjhīr Mines," *Metallurgy and Numismatics* 2, London, 1988, pp. 65-74. S. H. Gaube, *Arabo-Sasanidische Numismatik*, Braunschweig, 1973. R. Göbl, *Sasanian Numismatics*, Braunschweig, 1971. Lane-Poole, *Catalogue of Oriental Coins in the British Museum*, London, 1875-90. G. C. Miles, "Dirham," in *EI²* II, pp. 319-20. Idem, "Numismatics," in *Camb. Hist. Iran* IV, pp. 364-77. J. Masson Smith, Jr., "The Silver Currency of Mongol Iran," *Journal of the Economic and Social History of the Orient* 12, 1969, pp. 16-41. J. Walker, *A Catalogue of the Muhammadan Coins in the British Museum*. I. *A Catalogue of the Arab-Sassanian Coins (Umaiyad Governors in the East, Arab-Ephthalites, ʿAbbasid Governors in Tabaristan and Bukhara*, London, 1941; II. *A Catalogue of the Arab-Byzantine and Post-Reform Umaiyad Coins*, London, 1956.

(MICHAEL BATES)

DĪV (demon, monster, fiend), often confused with *ḡūl* (orge, ghoul) and jinn in both folk and literary traditions (Massé, *Croyances*, pp. 352-53; Qazvīnī, pp. 383-95), expresses not only the idea of "demon," but also that of "ogre," "giant," and even "Satan." The translators of Ṭabarī's commentary render the Arabic *eblīs*, (Satan) as *dīv* (I, p. 32, II, pp. 307, 446, 461, 471, 543, III, p. 551), while at the same time translating Arabic *jinn* into Persian *dīv* or *parī*. This indicates a confusion between the notions of *jinn* and *ḡūl* on the one hand, and *dīv* and *parī* on the other (Ṭabarī, II, pp. 458, 543, III, p. 552). The same confusion is found in the *Šāh-nāma*, where not only every demon, but also *eblīs* is sometimes called *dīv* rather than *ahrīman* (II, ed. Khaleghi, pp. 50-51, 95).

The description of the demons in the Persian epic literature is echoed in later literature and other genres. Except for an instance where Ferdowsī uses the word *dīv* as a metaphor for "evil people" (Moscow, IV, p. 310, vv. 140-41), demons are generally portrayed as beings completely independent of, and different from humans. They are often black (*Šāh-nāma*, ed. Khaleghi, I, pp. 22 v. 33, 166. v. 64; Moscow, VII, p. 34 v. 498; Asadī, pp. 80, v. 16, 111, v. 1; *Farāmarz-nāma*, pp. 80, 241, 341, 349), with long teeth, black lips, blue eyes (*kabūd-čašm*), claws on their hands, and large bodies covered with thick hair. Often they eat people (*Šāh-nāma*, ed. Khaleghi, II, p. 36, v. 479; Moscow, IV, pp. 312-13; Asadī, pp. 273, 281, 283; *Farāmarz-nāma*, pp. 93, 241, 341). Some demons have several heads, while others have monstrous ears or teeth (Asadī, pp. 15-18, 92). The epics tell of demon lands, the most important of which in the *Šāh-nāma* is called Māzandarān (not to be confused with the modern namesake province in Persia). There, they have a king, with all the trappings of kingship including armies, demon generals, cities, fortresses, farms, herds, etc. (ed. Khaleghi, I, pp. 223, v. 881, 10, vv. 115-18, 15, v. 188, 35-40, etc.; *Farāmarz-nāma*, pp. 335-38). Mention is made of an island of demons, the inhabitants of which had their own language and were so fond of iron that they would swim up to vessels passing by their island in order to exchange jewels for this metal. They fought with great stones, sticks, or other primitive tools of war (Asadī, pp. 15-18, 164, 242, 341-42). However sometimes they appear as warriors with armor, weapons, and retainers or armies (*Šāh-nāma*, ed. Khadeghi, II, pp. 42, v. 570, 54, v. 735, 466, v. 651; *Farāmarz-nāma*, pp. 350-51). Thus, they may not have always been perceived as supernatural "spirits."

One of their most curious characteristics is that they tend to be contrary in their behavior, doing the opposite of what they are asked to do. For this reason, they are often called *vārūna*, (backwards, inside out), or *vārūna-ḵūy* (contrary; *Šāh-nāma*, ed. Khaleghi, I, pp. 22, v. 33, 47, v. 108, 48, v. 112, 55, v. 38, Moscow, IV, pp. 272, v. 969, 305-06). Not unrelated to their contrariness is their tendency to sleep during the day and roam about at nights (*Šāh-nāma*, ed. Khaleghi, II, p. 41, v. 555). Demons are capable of transformation. They can change themselves into other beings such as people, dragons, lions, and more commonly onagers or horses (*Šāh-nāma*, ed. Khaleghi, I, pp. 46-51, II, pp. 4, 428, Moscow, IV, pp. 302-04, VIII, p. 405; *Farāmarz-nāma*, pp. 27, 338). Demons, being essentially supernatural beings, sometimes overcome their opponents by means of magic (*Šāh-nāma*, ed. Khaleghi, I, pp. 55, 57, 75, v. 325, II, p. 10, v. 115-18). In the story of Kāvūs' attack on Māzandarān, he and his army are captured easily, because they were made blind by the sorcery of the white demon (motif, D 2062.2). Rostam cures the nobles by applying the blood of the white demon to their eyes (motif D 1505.14, "animal liver cures blindness"; cf. D 1505.19, "giant's gall restores sight"; Coyajee, 1928, p. 184).

Demons who were overcome by a king or a hero, would often serve him as his slave. The primordial kings, Ṭahmūraṯ and Jamšēd could control the demons. Ṭahmūraṯ received the title *dīvband* (binder of demons) because of his victory over them (*Šāh-nāma*, ed. Khaleghi, I, pp. 35-37). This title in the *Šāh-nāma* has been also used of Rostam (ed. Moscow, pp. 252, v. 675, 282, v. 1137, 292, v. 1283). Jamšēd, however, was more of a Solomonic figure, ruling all living beings including the demons. When the demons served a ruler, they either taught him something such as writing, or they served him as great builders (*Šāh-nāma*, ed. Khaleghi, I, pp. 6, v. 50, 37, vv. 39-45, 43, vv. 35-38, II, pp. 93-94). This characteristic of the demons (motif F531.6.6. "giants as builders") is not limited to Iranian tradition (cf. Höttges, pp. 49-65). The demons often organize themselves in great armies and fight a primordial king whose forces are made up of animals (e.g., *Šāh-nāma*, ed. Khaleghi, I, pp. 24-25, 50-66). This is reminiscent of the war of Rāma and his army of animals with the Rakṣasa king Rāvaṇa and his demon army (Buck, pp. 239f).

In the short epic tale *Rostam o babr-e bayān*, which is incorporated into the *Farāmarz-nāma*, Rostam fights and overcomes a demon called *Galīmīna-gūš*, who goes into Rostam's service (p. 18). When Farāmarz defeats a black demon, he pierces his ears placing therein two horse shoes as the mark of the latter's servitude. The demon goes on to serve Farāmarz so faithfully that he is even dispatched to ask for the hand of a princess on behalf of the hero (pp. 351, 364). This willingness of a vanquished demon to serve the victor is explicitly stated in the Persian folktales, where often demons offer to wrestle a hero saying: "If you win, I will be your slave" (e.g., Enjavī, 1979, I, p. 133). There may be a connection between this motif with the story of Garšāsp, who is offered rulership by Żaḥḥāk, as he overcomes the three-headed monster in the final days of the world (Unvala, pp. 95, 108).

A list of ten demons is provided in the *Šāh-nāma*. These are, in order of importance, *āz* (greed), *nīāz* (need), *ḵašm* (wrath), *rašk* (envy), *nang* (dishonor), *kīn* (vengeance), *nammām* (tell-tale), *do-rūy* (two-faced), *nāpāk-dīn* (heretic), and, although not explicitly named, ungratefulness (*Šāh-nāma*, Moscow, VIII, pp. 195-96).

Dīv in the oral epics. A greater variety of demons than those found in the *Šāh-nāma* reside in the oral tradition. They typically have more colorful names associated with their physical characteristics, or activities. For instance we find two and twelve headed demons (Enjavī, 1976a, pp. 213, 220). There is a seven-headed demon, who like the Hydra of the Greek myth grows a new head every time one of its heads is cut off (Enjavī, 1975, p. 88). We meet a demon called *Hūsang-e čehel dast-e dīv* (Hūsang the forty-armed demon; Enjavī, 1976a, p. 138) and another with only one eye (Enjavī, 1979, p. 97). The "white demon" is prominent, as is the *dīb-e sar safīd* (the white headed demon; ibid, pp. 73-77). There is even one demon named for his association with water (*dīv-e ğawwāṣ*, the diving demon; Enjavī, 1976a, p. 221). The oral epics further clarify the family relationships of a number of demons. We find out that Akvān-e Dīv had a brother called Owrang-e Dīv, and a son, who was put in charge of the well in which Bīžan was imprisoned. Both of these demons were killed by Rostam (Enjavī, 1976a, pp. 152, 258-59). Sometimes the narrative of the oral epics drastically deviates from that of the *Šāh-nāma*. Demons are introduced into scenes where the literary epics make no mention of them. For instance according to one tale, it is Zāl's mother aided by a demon, who tries to kill the hero shortly after his birth. The reason given in the tale is that the child was born "blonde," whereas in the *Šāh-nāma* it was the hero's father Sām who attempted to destroy him because he was born an albino (Enjavī, 1976a, pp. 186-88). Key Kāvūs is captured by the demon Akvān (q.v.) after his misguided Nimrodian adventure. One tale suggests that the bow was invented to fight the demons (Enjavī, 1979, pp. 38, 70). Mention is made of demons who serve heroes. Notable among them is the servant of the hero Sām, who is called Farhang-e Dīv. The form of this demon's name, meaning also culture and civility, may be influenced by his civilized behavior in Sām's service (Enjavī, 1976a, p. 67).

Dīv in the folktales. Many demons figure in Iranian folktales (Marzolph, s.v. *daemon*). They may act as villains, sorcerers, ogres, fools, or helpers of the protagonist (Ṣobḥī, I, pp. 103-05, II, pp. 28, 35-36; Dehqānī, I, pp. 140-43; Amīnī, pp. 4, 45). They may be summoned for help when a bit of their hair, which has been left with the hero for this purpose, is put into the fire (Enjavī, 1978, I, p. 141; cf. summoning the Sīmorḡ by putting her feathers in fire). Demons of the folktales may be many headed, or they may have only heads and no body. When thus handicapped, they roll rather than walk (ibid., I, pp. 180, 188-89). They come in different colors: white, yellow, and black (Dehqānī, I, pp. 46-49; Ṣobḥī, II, p. 16). They have a tendency to alternate long periods of wakefulness and sleep, each lasting several days, and to become sleepy in sunlight. Typically this unfortunate habit proves to be their undoing (e.g., Ṣobḥī, II, p. 10; cf. Enjavī, 1975, p. 89; idem, 1979, p. 77; idem, 1976a, p. 228). They are capable of magic and transformation (Enjavī, 1978, I, pp. 115, 142; cf. Ṣobḥī, II, p. 143; Amīnī, p. 17). Sometimes their approach may be deduced from changes in temperature, or by a foul smell in the air. They are quite fond of human women, whom they steal or forcibly marry (Enjavī, 1978, p. 113-14, III, pp. 113-14; Ṣobḥī, II, pp. 7, 16; Dehqānī, I, p. 46). Although usually the human mate of the demon is an unwilling bride, sometimes a woman wooed by a demon, grows so amorous of her demon husband as to agree to harm her own kin at his bidding (Faqīrī, pp. 103-07; Dehqānī, I, pp. 46-49). Some demons give away a sister in marriage to a human male (Enjavī, 1978, I, p. 134), however, they generally prefer to steal human maidens, whom they take to their home, which is usually at the bottom of a well, place their heads upon her lap, and sleep for several days at a time (e.g., Dehqānī, I, p. 99). Many demons have an external soul (motif E711), the destruction of which is the sole way to kill them. This they may keep hidden in a box (motif E712.4), in a live fish (motif E715.2), or in the body of some other animal (motif E715; Enjavī, 1978, I, pp. 138-39; Ṣobḥī, II, pp. 12-13, 18; Dehqānī, I, pp. 100-02; cf. Penzer, I, pp. 129-32, VIII, pp. 106-07).

A curious folktale which normally has animals for its protagonists, has found itself a home in the Rostam saga of the classical epics. Tale Type 1310, "Drowning the crayfish as punishment; eel, crab, turtle, etc. express fear of water and are thrown in," and the related Type 1634E* "throwing the thief over the fence. Thief caught red-handed says: do your worst only don't throw me over the fence. When thrown over, he escapes" (motifs K584, K581-K581.4). The story of Rostam and the trick which he plays on the demon Akvān is clearly based on this tale type.

Before a demon-slayer fights a demon, he typically comes upon his opponent while the latter is asleep. He always wakes the demon up by piercing him in the foot by his sword or dagger. Then he proceeds to fight his adversary, often cutting a limb off of the demon in the course of the combat (cf. Rostam and the White Demon). The demon is finally killed either by weapons, or by means of breaking the container in which he keeps his external soul. In the latter case, he turns into smoke and disappears into thin air (Enjavī, 1978, I, pp. 115, 139, 145, 155; Ṣobḥī, II, p. 13; Behrangī, I, p. 100; Faqīrī, p. 67; Massé, *Croyances*, p. 352). Sometimes the hero does not kill the demon after overcoming him in battle. In exchange for his life, the demon agrees to serve the hero as his slave, and to indicate his servitude, the hero places an iron ring or a nail from his shoe in the demon's ear lobe (Enjavī, 1979, I, p. 133).

Folk tradition makes demons responsible for a number of mental and physical maladies. The very Persian word *dīvānagī* (insanity) betrays the association of all mental illness with demonic possession. Other such minor conditions as fever blisters *tab-ḵāl*, also called *āfat-e dīv* (the demon's malady) are attributed to demons. There is a variety of demon who causes nightmares or deceptive dreams (Qomī, II, pp. 355-56; *Šāh-nāma*, ed. Khaleghi, II, p. 422; cf. Massé, *Croyances*, p. 354). According to folk tradition, *dīv*s and *jenn*s are said to fear the sound of the dog and the white rooster (Eʿtemad-al-Salṭana, p. 37; Dhabhar, p. 25; Balʿamī, ed. Bahār, I, p. 118; Soyūṭī, pp. 9-11).

See also *DAIVA; DĒW.

Bibliography: A. Aarne, and S. Thompson, *The Types of the Folktale*, Helsinki, 1973. A. Amīnī, *Sī afsāna az afsānahā-ye maḥallī-e Eṣfahān*, Isfahan?, 1960. Abū Naṣr ʿAlī b. Aḥmad Asadī Ṭūsī, *Garšāsp-nāma*, ed. Ḥ. Yaḡmāʾī, Tehran, 1975. *Bānū-gošasb-nāma*, see *Farāmarz-nāma*. Ṣ. Behrangī and B. Dehqānī, *Afsānahā-ye Āḏarbāyjān*, Tabrīz, 1965. W. Buck, *Ramayana: King Rama's way*, New York, 1978. J. C. Coyajee, "Some Shāhnāmah Legends and Their Chinese Parallels," *Journal and Proceedings of the Asiatic Society of Bengal* 24, 1928, pp. 177-203. E. B. Dhabhar, ed., *Saddar Nasr and Saddar Bundahesh*, Bombay, 1909. A. Enjavī, *Mardom o Ferdowsī*, Tehran, 1976a. Idem, *Mardom o Šāh-nāma*, Tehran, 1975. Idem, *Qeṣṣahā-ye īrānī* III. *ʿArūsak-e sang-e ṣabūr*, Tehran, 1976b. Idem, *Qeṣṣahā-ye īrānī* I. *Gol bā ṣenowbar če kard*, Tehran, 1978. Idem, *Ferdowsī-nāma. Mardom o qahramānān-e Šāh-*

nāma, Tehran, 1979. Moḥammad-Ḥasan Khan Eʿtemād al-Salṭana, *Ketāb al-tadwīn fī aḥwāl jebāl Šervīn*, Tehran, 1311/1893. A. Faqīrī, *Qeṣṣahā-ye mardom-e Fārs*, Tehran, 1970. *Farāmarz-nāma*, ed. R. Taftī, Bombay, 1324/1907 (a collection of two *Farāmarz-nāma*s, *Bānū-gošasp-nāma*, and a small epic called *Rostam o Babr-e bayān*). V. Höttges, *Typenverzeichnis der deutschen Riesen- und riesischen Teufelssagen*, Folklore Fellows Communications, no. 122, Helsinki, 1937. U. Marzolph, *Typologie des persischen Volksmärchens*, Beirut, 1984. N. M. Penzer, *The Ocean of Story*, 10 vols., London, 1927. Qazvīnī, *ʿAjāyeb al-maḵlūqāt*, ed. N. Ṣabūḥī, Tehran, 1983. Abu'l-Ḥasan ʿAlī Qomī, *Tafsīr al-Qomī*, 2 vols., ed. M. Jazāʾerī, Najaf, 1386/1966. *Rostam o Babr-e bayān*, see *Farāmarz-nāma*. F. Ṣobḥī, *Afsānahā*, 2 vols., Tehran, 1959-63. Soyūṭī, *Ketāb al-wadīk fī fażl al-dīk*, Cairo(?), 1322/1904. A. Ṭabāṭabāʾī, "Dīv wa jowhar-e asāṭīrī-e ān," *NDA Tabrīz* 16, 1343 Š./1964, pp. 39-45. S. Thompson, *Motif-Index of Folk-Literature*, 6 volumes, Bloomington, 1955-58. M. R. Unvala, ed., *Dārāb Hormazyār's Rivāyat*, 2 vols., Bombay, 1922.

(MAHMOUD OMIDSALAR)

DĪV SOLṬĀN, title of ʿALĪ BEG RŪMLŪ, a *qezelbāš* officer first mentioned at the battle of Šarūr (907/1501), in which the Safavid Esmāʿīl I (q.v.) defeated the Āq Qoyūnlū prince Alvand (*Jahāngošā-ye Ḵāqān*, p. 138). Dīv Solṭān was present at the decisive battle of Marv (916/1510), which enabled Esmāʿīl to recover Khorasan from the hands of Moḥammad Šībānī (Šeybak) Khan Uzbek. In 919/1513, after having carried out a punitive expedition in the region of Šoborqān, Andḵūy, and Balḵ (qq.v.), he was appointed governor of Balḵ (Ḥasan Rūmlū, ed. Navāʾī, p. 181, ed. Seddon, I, p. 139; *Ḥabīb al-sīar*, Tehran, IV, p. 540). In 921/1515 Dīv Solṭān visited Esmāʿīl's court at Tabrīz to inform the shah of the complete expulsion of the Uzbeks from Khorasan and the inefficiency of Zeynal Khan Šāmlū, the governor of Herat (Ḥasan Rūmlū, ed. Navāʾī, pp. 201-02, Seddon, p. 154). Dīv Solṭān did not return to Khorasan, but was sent on a number of expeditions to Georgia; the first two, in 922/1516 and 923/1517, were to the Samtzkhe district in support of Malek Qorqora against his rival Manūčehr; the third, in 927/1520, was directed against the rebellious Lavand Beg, ruler of the Kakheti district (Ḥasan Rūmlū, ed. Navāʾī, pp. 211-12, 218, 225; ed. Seddon, p. 173).

In 930/1523 the *wakīl* Dīv Solṭān was appointed to the important office of *amīr al-omarā* (q.v.), superseding Čāyān Solṭān (Eskandar Beg, I, p. 46, tr., I, p. 77; Ḥasan Rūmlū, ed. Navāʾī, p. 236, ed. Seddon, p. 181), or his son Bāyazīd Solṭān, the latter having died the previous year (Bodāq Monšī Qazvīnī, fol. 293b; Bedlīsī, II, p. 169). After the death of Shah Esmāʿīl (930/1524), Dīv Solṭān, by virtue of a testamentory disposition of the late shah, retained the office of *amīr al-omarā* and was made *atābeg* (guardian) of the young prince Ṭahmāsb, who succeeded his father at the age of ten and a half. Dīv Solṭān thus became the de facto ruler of the state. Less than a year later, he put to death the vizier Jalāl-al-Dīn Moḥammad Tabrīzī (Ḥasan Rūmlū, ed. Navāʾī, p. 240; Eskandar Beg, I, p. 159, tr., I, p. 251). He was initially supported by the Rūmlū, Takkalū and Ḏu'l-Qadar tribes, by most of the Šāmlū amirs, and by some Ostājlūs. However, the powerful Ostājlū amir Kopek Solṭān, the brother of the former *amīr al-omarā* Čāyān Solṭān, refused to swear allegiance to him at Lār. After a period of negotiation, a triumvirate was formed consisting of Dīv Solṭān Rūmlū, Čūha Solṭān Takkalū, and Kopek Ostājlū, but civil war broke out between rival *qezelbāš* factions in 932/1526. Kopek Solṭān was killed in 933/1526-27, and Čūha Solṭān succeeded in persuading Shah Ṭahmāsb that Dīv Solṭān was the cause of the discord. On 5 Šawwāl 933/5 July 1527, when Dīv Solṭān entered the *divān*, the Shah gave the signal for his execution by the royal guards (Ḥasan Rūmlū, ed. Navāʾī, pp. 245-54, 259-61, 268; Bedlīsī, II, pp. 172-73; for full details of the manoeuvrings of rival *qezelbāš* amirs for control of the state after the accession of Ṭahmāsb, and for a discussion of the complicated relationship between the offices of *wakīl* and *amīr al-omarā*, see Savory).

Bibliography: (For cited works not given in detail see "Short References.") Šaraf al-Dīn Bedlīsī, *Šaraf-nāma*, ed. V. Véliaminof-Zernof, St. Petersburg 1860-62. Bodāq Monšī Qazvīnī, *Jawāher al-aḵbār*, Leningrad Library MS, Dorn 288. *Jahāngošā-ye Ḵāqān*, ed. A. Możṭar, Islamabad, 1350 Š./1971. R. M. Savory, "The Principal Offices of the Ṣafawid State during the Reign of Ṭahmāsp I (930-84/1524-76)," *BSO(A)S* 24, part 1, 1961, pp. 65-85; repr. in Idem, *Studies on the History of Ṣafawid Iran*, London, 1987.

(ROGER M. SAVORY)

DĪVĀL-E ḴODĀYDĀD (31°15'-31°16' N, 62°06'-62°09' E), an extensive area of historic remains in the center of an ancient canal system fed by the rivers Helmand and Ḵāšrūd. It is located between the eastern border of the Hāmūn-e Aškīnʿām and the lower Ḵāšrūd, about 45 km to the northeast of Zaranj in southwest Afghanistan.

The remains consist of low mounds and about twenty mud-brick ruins that once formed the so-called "*ayvān*-courtyard-houses" (see AYVĀN). These rectangular structures are invariably situated with one smaller side towards the northwest thus protecting its inhabitants against the "wind of the 120 days" (*bād-e sad o bīst rūz*) blowing during the summer months from northwest to southeast and thus transporting the typical Sīstānī moving sand dunes. In the course of the years and centuries sand dunes cover and again set free partially dried-up riverbeds, abandoned fields, and deserted houses. Therefore archeological maps of Sīstān/Nīmrūz usually reflect only the present state of field surveys recently completed by air photography. The "*ayvān*-courtyard-house" is entered in the southeastern small side by a more or less decorated door. To both sides of the central court are situated square or rectangular rooms. To the northwest the edifice is closed and protected by an *ayvān*, an oblong hall covered by barrel vaulting; it was probably designed as the seat of the feudal owner and reception room and is modestly embellished with mud-brick patterns with squares, crosses, or triangles. In the *ayvāns*, rooms, *bāzār*-like buildings, and a cistern we observed various modes of Iranian constructions adopted to features of Islamic type settlements (tunnel vaults, pendentive structures, squinch-domes, even superimposed domes). In the houses and the open plains between them we found sherds of Iranian and Islamic pottery; besides atypical, unglazed wares types from Ghaznavid glazed ceramics and Ghurid glazed decorated ware in early Islamic graffito (to be dated from the 11th to 13th centuries according to the excavations in the residence of Laškarī Bāzār), as well as Il-khanid and Timurid multi-colored varieties known from Iranian lands throughout 13th-15th centuries. Neither this ruin field nor adjoining ones can be identified according to Islamic sources. Dīvāl-e Ḵodāydād seems to have been a rural estate (*rostāq*) situated in the vicinity of artificially irrigated fields. The settlement seems to have been established after the Arab conquest of Persia and Central Asia and may have flourished untill 785/1383 when Tīmūr raided Sīstān, destroying irrigation systems, villages, and fortresses and reducing the population (Šāmī, pp. 91-94). Later on parts of Sīstān were again converted to arable land but it never regained the former wealth.

Bibliography: W. Ball and J.-C. Gardin, *Archaeological Gazetteer of Afghanistan*, 2 vols., Paris, 1982, I, p. 93. K. Fischer, "Nimruz and the Archaeology of Afghanistan," *Afghanistan* 26/3, 1973, pp. 1-16. Idem, "Archaeological Field Survey of Afghan Sistan 1968-72," *AMI* 6, 1973, pp. 213-30. Idem, D. Morgenstern and V. Thewalt, eds., *Nimruz. Geländebegehungen in Sistan 1955-1973 und die Aufnahme von Dewal-i Khodaydad 1970*, 2 vols., Bonn, 1974-76. Idem, "Architecture au Séistan Islamique," *Afghanistan Historical and Cultural Quarterly* 27/1, 1974, pp. 12-34. Idem, "Fortified and Open Settlements in Medieval Sistan," *Storia della Città. International Review of Town Planning History* 7, 1978, pp. 59-63. Idem, "From the Rise of Islam to the Mongol Invasion," in *The Archaeology of Afghanistan from Earliest Times to the Timurid Period*, ed. F. R. Allchin and N. Hammond, London, 1978 p. 368. Neẓām-al-Dīn Šāmī, *Ẓafar-nāma* I, ed. F. Tauer, Beirut, 1937.

(KLAUS FISCHER)

DĪVĀN, archive, register, chancery, government office; also, collected works, especially of a poet.

i. *The term.*

ii. *Government office.*

iii. *Collected works of a poet.*

i. THE TERM

Dīvān is a Persian loan-word in Arabic and was borrowed also at an earlier date into Armenian. It is attested in Zoroastrian Middle Persian in the spellings *dpyw'n* and *dyw'n*. It has long been recognized that the word must go back to some derivative of Old Persian *dipi-*, (inscription, document), itself borrowed, via Elamite, from Akkadian *ṭuppu* and ultimately from Sumerian *dub* (clay tablet). Compare also Persian *debīr* (scribe), Middle-Persian *dibīr*, from **dipī-var-*. Armenian *divan*, which occurs already in the translation of the Bible, could in theory represent an Arsacid Parthian **dēvān*, but such a form would be most difficult to explain, as it is hardly imaginable that *dipi-* should have become **dē-*. But the Armenian form could equally well be a later borrowing from Sasanian Middle-Persian *dīvān* (with *-ī-*), which (following Bailey) could continue an earlier Middle-Persian **diβi-vān*, from the adjective **dipi-vān-* (relating to documents) with contraction of *-iβi-* to *-ī-*. In this case, must one assume that the word was borrowed into Armenian after the Middle-Persian shift of post-vocalic *-p-* to *-b/β-* (i.e., not before the 3rd century) and, moreover, that the correct Middle-(and early New-)Persian form is *dīvān*, not **dēvān*. To be sure, there is an often quoted fanciful etymology (e.g., in Aṣmaʿī, apud Jawāleqī, p. 70), according to which the Persians called the chancery *dīvān* because they considered the bureaucrats to be devils (*dēvān*), - a variant of this says that it was because they were crazed (*dēvāna*); either version seems to presuppose the pronunciation *dēvān*, but one need not attach much importance to this obviously facetious story. It does, however, seem that, probably as a result of this sort of popular etymology, there was a secondary pronunciation *dēvān*, which still survives in Tājīkī. (For the treatment of the Iranian vowels in Armenian loan-words see ARMENIA AND IRAN iv).

Bibliography: (For the cited works not given in detail see "Short References.") H.W. Bailey, in *BSOS* 7, 1933, pp. 76-77. Horn, *Etymologie*, p. 119. Hübschmann, *Persische Studien*, p. 60. Idem, *Armenische Grammatik*, pp. 143-44. Abū Manṣūr Jawāleqī, *Ketāb al-moʿarrab men kalām al-ʿajamī*, ed. E. Sachau, Leipzig, 1867. Nyberg, *Manual* II p. 64.

(FRANÇOIS DE BLOIS)

ii. GOVERNMENT OFFICE

The origins of the *dīvān* lie in the earliest years of the Arab caliphate in Medina, when the caliph ʿOmar

b. Ḵaṭṭāb is said to have instituted a register (*dīvān*) in which were recorded tax payments, as well as the names of Arab warriors entitled to stipends (*ʿaṭāʾ*) and the appropriate rates (Ṭabarī, I, p. 2412). In the Arabic sources, this innovation was in imitation of fiscal and administrative practice in Byzantine Syria and Sasanian Persia, the latter associated with the name of a Persian secretary in Sasanian Iraq, Fayrūzān (Pērōzān; Jahšīārī, p. 11; Balāḏorī, *Fotūḥ*, pp. 450-61; Ṭabarī, I, pp. 2749-50; Sprengling, pp. 177-81; Kennedy, pp. 68-69).

By the beginning of the Omayyad period (41-132/661-750) the central administration in Damascus had to be more specialized than the single *dīvān* of the first four caliphs in Medina and Kūfa. The central *dīvān*, called *dīvān al-ḵarāj*, was concerned with assessments and receipts, as well as taxation in the conquered lands. It was backed by a *dīwān al-rasāʾel* for official correspondence; a *dīwān al-ḵātam* for sealing these documents and checking on possible forgeries; and a *dīwān al-jond* responsible for military affairs and keeping up to date the payrolls for Arab warriors. In addition, there were *dīvāns* responsible for collection of the poor tax (*ṣadaqa*), administration of revenues from state domains, manufacture of the *ṭerāz* (official textiles), and running the postal and courier services (*barīd*, q.v.). The caliph Moʿāwīa (41-64/661-80) seems to have been the guiding hand in the formation of these new organs.

It is difficult to assess the degree of continuity, with the previous Sasanian administration, though it must have been extensive in Iraq and Persia itself, where most official personnel there under Arab provincial governors were undoubtedly either Persianized Arameans or ethnic Persians; certainly Persian remained the language of official business in the eastern provinces of the caliphate until the adoption of Arabic toward the end of the 7th century. The sources bearing on this process are confused and contradictory, but it was almost certainly gradual, rather than abrupt, as implied by those authors who attribute the decisive influence to Ḥajjāj b. Yūsof, governor of Iraq under ʿAbd-al-Malek (65-86/685-705). Moʿāwīa's earlier viceroy there, Zīād b. Abīhi, seems to have first employed the Persian Zādān-Farroḵ in his *dīwān al-ḵarāj*, and others of the same family followed him there. His son Mardānšāh is supposed to have opposed the process of arabization, but Ḥajjāj resolved to carry it through in 78/697, following the advice and with the technical assistance of another Persian, Ṣāleḥ b. ʿAbd-al-Raḥmān Sīstānī, who had been a subordinate official of Zādān-Farrok (Jahšīārī, p. 23; Balāḏorī, *Fotūḥ*, pp. 300-01; Sprengling, pp. 183-201; Zarrīnkūb, pp. 45-48). In the farther provinces like Khorasan, however, the change from Persian did not take place until almost the end of the Omayyad period (Hawting, pp. 63-64).

The ʿAbbasids (after 132/750) established their capital in Iraq, eventually at Baghdad. A shift in orientation toward the east is discernible, encouraged by increased receptiveness to Persian cultural influence and the roots of the ʿAbbasid revolution in Khorasan (Kennedy, pp. 134-37). The ʿAbbasid central administration became increasingly complex; the financial administration in particular was subdivided into departments responsible for financial control and accounting (*dīvān al-zemām/al-azemma*), the caliphs' personal domains (*dīvān al-żīāʿ al-ḵāṣṣa*), confiscation of the estates of fallen officials (*dīwān al-moṣādara*), and so on. The military department retained a special importance (see Hoernerbach, pp. 257-90), but there was further specialization there too, under its chief(*ʿāreż*); for example, the *dīwān al-mawālī wa'l-ḡelmān* was responsible for the new, professional slave army that increasingly replaced traditional Arab troops during the 9th century, and the *dīwān al-jond wa'l-šākerīya*, responsible, according to M. A. Shaban (pp. 64-65) for personal retainers brought into the ʿAbbasid army by Persian and Turkish magnates from Central Asia (on the ʿAbbasid *dīvāns* in general, see Levy, pp. 305-07, 322-27; Dūrī).

It was on from these caliphal institutions that the administrations of the successor states in Persia were formed after the relaxation of the caliphal grip on outlying provinces from the 9th century on. Such provincial capitals as Shiraz, Marāḡa, and Marv and later Nīšāpūr, Zarang, and Sīrjān must already have had local *dīvāns* for collection of the provincial revenues and employees responsible to the chief tax collectors (*ʿāmel* or *bondār*); virtually nothing is known, however, about the working of these officials or their subordinates.

All that is known of the administration of the Taherid governors in Nīšāpūr, for example, is that the treasuries of the last of them, Moḥammad b. Ṭāher (II) b. ʿAbd-Allāh, were plundered by the Saffarid Yaʿqūb b. Layṯ when he captured the city in 259/873 (Gardīzī, ed. Ḥabībī, p. 140); presumably they were part of a financial *dīvān*. At that time the *dīvān* of Khorasan was situated in the center of the city, but in the 10th and early 11th centuries it was located in the more salubrious suburb of Šādyāḵ (Bosworth, *Ghaznavids*, pp. 160-61). A little more is known about the administration of the Saffarids, founded by Yaʿqūb (r. 253-65/867-79), who had a *dīwān al-ʿarż*, in which his soldiers and their pay allotments were registered; it and other offices were located in the *dār al-emāra*, or government building, at Zarang (Bosworth, 1968, p. 549). His successor, ʿAmr b. Layṯ (q.v., r. 265-88/879-901) had three separate treasuries, which suggests a degree of specialization; the second, responsible for the *māl-e ḵāṣṣ*, corresponds to the ʿAbbasid *dīwān al-żīāʿ al-ḵāṣṣa*. The chief secretary must have presided over a *dīvān al-rasāʾel/al-enšāʾ*, though its precise name is unrecorded in the sources (for Saffarid administration, see Bosworth, 1992, ch. VII).

The Buyids (q.v.) took control of lands in northern, western, and southern Persia that had been administered directly by the caliphate, so that an appreciable amount of administrative continuity was to be expected, not only in Baghdad, which Moʿezz-al-Dawla Aḥmad took over in 334/945, but also in the capitals of other members of the Buyid confederacy: Isfahan, Ray, and Shiraz. Nevertheless, the very nature of this family's rule implied a certain degree of decentralization, compared with the ʿAbbasid bureaucracy. At the head of the Buyid system were the three great departments: the *dīwān al-wazīr* for finance, the *dīwān al-rasāʾel* for correspondence, and the *dīwān al-jayš* for military affairs. Several other *dīvān*s were directly continued from their ʿAbbasid predecessors, for example, those of the *barīd*, the *zemām*, and the *al-żīāʿ al-ḵāṣṣa*. A *dīvān al-ḵelāfa* controlled what remained of the puppet ʿAbbasid caliphs' executive powers in Baghdad and oversaw liaison between them and the Buyid amirs. In the time of ʿAżod-al-Dawla (q.v.; 367-72/978-83) the special section of the central financial department responsible for revenues from the rich Mesopotamian agricultural plains, the *dīwān ḵarāj al-savād*, was transferred to Shiraz, the capital of southern and western Persia (Busse, pp. 310-17). As the Buyid confederation was essentially the military domination of a Deylamite-Turkish elite, the department of military affairs was of premier importance, and the sources for the period include much information about the activities of its chief (*ʿāreż al-jayš*). At the zenith of the dynasty's fortunes, under ʿAżod-al-Dawla and his son Bahāʾ-al-Dawla (379-403/989-1012) there were actually two separate *ʿāreż*es, one for the Deylamite troops and one for the Turks, Arabs, and Kurds, hence the term *dīwān al-jayšayn* (department of the two armies; Bosworth, 1965-66, pp. 162 ff.; Busse, pp. 339 ff.).

Information about the structure of the Samanid central at Bukhara (q.v.) is available from Naršaḵī's listing of the various *dīvān*s there in the time of the amir Naṣr b. Aḥmad (303-31/913-43) and from material on their procedures and techniques given by Ḵᵛārazmī. Naršaḵī mentioned the *dīvān*s of the *wazīr*, the chief secretary (*ʿamīd al-molk*), the treasurer and accountant (*mostawfī*), the commander of the guard (*ṣāḥeb-e šoraṭ*), the postmaster and intelligence chief (*ṣāḥeb-e barīd*), the controller and inspector of finances (*mošref*), the intendant (*ṣāḥeb*) of the amir's personal domains (*mamlaka-ye ḵāṣṣ*), the market inspector and custodian of public morals (*moḥtaseb*), the comptroller of pious endowments (*awqāf*), and the judiciary (*qażā*; Naršaḵī, p. 31; tr. Frye, p. 26; Barthold, *Turkestan*³, pp. 229-32). The reliance on the ʿAbbasid model is apparent, reflecting a distinct sophistication, as is further apparent in the material provided by Ḵᵛārazmī, apparently himself a secretary in the administration at Bukhara. Naršaḵī did not mention the office for military affairs (unless he subsumed it under the *dīvān-e ṣāḥeb-e šoraṭ*), but Ḵᵛārazmī devoted special sections to the *dīwān al-jayš* and its procedures, including the use of the black register (*al-jarīda al-sawdāʾ*), the master register of troops, their fighting skills, equipment, pay entitlements, and so on (Ḵᵛārazmī, pp. 56, 64-66; Bosworth, 1969).

As the Ghaznavids arose from the slave guard of the Samanids, it was likely that the administration in their capital, Ḡazna, would follow in essentials that of Bukhara, especially as there was some continuity of personnel between the two centers. Five central *dīvān*s served the sultan: those of the vizier, the chief secretary (*dīvān-e rasāʾel*), the army (*dīvān-e ʿarż*), the internal spy and police system (*dīvān-e šoḡl-e ešrāf-e mamlakat*), and the official (*wakīl-e ḵāṣṣ*) responsible for operation and supply of the royal palaces and gardens. Similar organs existed on a reduced scale in the provincial centers of the extensive Ghaznavid empire, like Nīšāpūr and Lahore. Remarkable insight into the workings of the Ghaznavid bureaucracy, with a detail unparalleled in medieval Persian history, can be gained from the history of Abu'l-Fażl Bayhaqī (see Nāẓim, pp. 130-50; Bosworth, *Ghaznavids*, pp. 48-97, 122-26, 137-38; idem, *Later Ghaznavids*, pp. 33-35, 69-74).

In Transoxania the Turkish Qarakhanids succeeded the Samanids; the predominance of this nomadic steppe group meant a lightening of administrative and fiscal burdens in Transoxania, and it must be assumed that the requirements for a Qarakhanid bureaucracy were much reduced and that much of the complex Samanid government machinery fell into disuse. Unfortunately, no direct information is available on the administrative arrangements of the Qarakhanids, though, as Reşat Genç has pointed out (pp. 254-62), Yūsof Ḵāṣṣ Ḥājeb's didactic poem *Qutadgu bilig* (comp. 461/1069), permits inference of the existence at least of organs corresponding to a great *dīvān* and a *dīvān-e enšāʾ*. The same process of simplification in both central and local administration is observable, though on a less drastic scale, in the lands south of the Oxus, where the Saljuqs replaced the Ghaznavids and Buyids (Klausner, pp. 9-13).

The Saljuqs were also originally nomadic pastoralists, and the Great Saljuq sultans tended to maintain a somewhat peripatetic existence, with their capital shifting among various Persian cities, like Nīšāpūr, Ray, Isfahan, Hamadān, and also, in the 12th century, Baghdad. The sultan was, moreover, often absent on long military campaigns. The Saljuq administration was directed from a supreme *dīvān* (*dīvān-e aʿlā*) presided over by the vizier, who, at least at first, played a greater role in the state than previously, exercising civil, military, and religious responsibilties; the careers of statesmen like Abū Naṣr Kondorī and Ḵᵛāja Neẓām-al-Molk illustrate this change. The raising of funds for the sultan was naturally one of the vizier's prime duties, but he also directed a secretariat (*dīvān-al-enšāʾ wa'l-ṭoḡrā*), an accounting department (*dīvān al-zemām wa'l-estīfā*ʾ), and a department concerned with financial control and oversight of provincial officials (*dīvān-e ešrāf*). From the end of the 11th century the *mostawfī* might on occasion wield an influence in the state comparable with that of the vizier, whose authority would then be correspondingly restricted. There are also references in the sources to *dīvān*s concerned with redress of grievances (*maẓālem*), the sultans' private domains (*ḵāṣṣ*), the *awqāf*, land grants (*eqṭā*ʿ, q.v.), and confiscations (*moṣādarāt*), though they may not all have functioned continuously. The military department, led by the *ʿāreż*, retained its importance, and this office was often a stepping stone to the vizierate itself. Only the earlier *dīvān-e barīd* was allowed to fall into disuse (Neẓām al-Molk, ch. X). Mo st government departments must have remained in the capital of the time, but the vizier normally accompanied the sultan on his progresses and military expeditions, and it is probable that the privy treasury, kept in the *dīwān al-ḵāṣṣ*, also went with the ruler. The pattern of central administration was partly repeated in the provinces, as at Marv under Sultan Sanjar (511-52/1118-57; Horst, pp. 25-60; Lambton, *Camb. Hist. Iran*, pp. 247 ff.; idem, 1988, pp. 28-48; idem, in *EI*²; Klausner, pp. 15-21).

Not much is known about the administrative arrangements of the Ḵᵛārazmšāhs, but they appear to have followed the lines of those of the Great Saljuqs, normally headed by a vizier in his *dīvān-e aʿlā*. In 615/1218 ʿAlāʾ-al-Dīn Moḥammad replaced his vizier with a body of six high officials (*wakīldār*s), one of whom is described as head of the chancery (*dīvān-e enšā*ʾ); whether there was any shared responsibility among these officials is unclear (Horst, p. 25).

The Mongol invasion, however disastrous for Persia in regard to population, land use, and economic life, did not entail a traumatic break in the remarkably resilient Persian administrative tradition. In the decades immediately after the establishment of the Il-khanids in the mid-13th century members of minority groups were employed as officials, for example, the Jewish Saʿd-al-Dawla under Arḡūn Khan (q.v.; 683-90/1284-91). But, as usually happened, incoming rulers eventually turned to Muslim Persians to run the financial and administrative system, even though there was a certain simplification of the latter, compared even with Saljuq practice; once the Il-khans themselves became Muslims at the end of the 13th century, there was a distinct revival of the Persian Islamic bureaucratic ethos. The *dīvān-e aʿlā* remained necessary, and the chief minister was still the vizier, though occasionally known as the deputy (*raʾīs*) of the ruler, but there was a tendency for the supervision of financial affairs to pass to the *ṣāḥeb-e dīvān*, whose power might at times equal or surpass that of the vizier. For example, for several years toward the end of the 13th century the vizier ʿAṭā-Malek Jovaynī shared power with the *mošref al-mamālek* Majd-al-Molk Yazdī; and, when in 699/1299-1300 Rašīd-al-Dīn Fażl-Allāh became *ṣāḥeb-e dīvān* for Ḡāzān Khan (694-703/1295-1304), he was entrusted with the general supervision of the Il-khanid realm, including finance, administration of crown domains, appointment of subordinate officials, operation of the postal and courier service (*yām*; Morgan, pp. 105-07), and general promotion of the development and prosperity of the empire (*Tārīḵ-e Waṣṣāf*, p. 347, cited in Lambton, *EI*²).

The Il-khanid financial departments operated under the direction of a group of senior secretaries, the *uluḡ bitikčī*s; they included the *dīvān-e estīfā*ʾ or *dīvān-e ešrāf* and a bureau for overseeing the Il-khans' private domains, *īnjū* or, tautologically, *īnjū-ye ḵāṣṣa*. The Mongol chancery was inaugurated by the body of Chinese, Uighur, Nestorian Christian, and Muslim *bitikčī*s whom Čengīz Khan and the first Il-khanids had employed. The diplomacy of the Il-khanids was far-flung, and there was always a need to communicate, not only with the unconquered rulers of the Muslim world, particularly the Mamluks, but also with the Frankish Christians, the Byzantines, the Il-khanids' pagan kindred in Inner Asia, and the Chinese. The Il-khanid secretaries thus not only performed such routine duties as affixing to documents the khans' seals (*āl tamḡā* and *altūn tamḡā*, qq.v.) and preparing and issuing tablets of authority (*pāyza*, Mong. *gerege*) but also the inditing of correspondence in a formidable array of languages and scripts. Jovaynī mentioned that the chancery had secretaries specifically for issuing decrees in Persian, Uighur Turkish, North Chinese (*ḵetāʾī*), Tibetan, Tangut, and so on (ed. Qazvīnī, III, p. 89; tr. Boyle, II, pp. 606-07).

The absence, at least initially, of a specific military department is, however, noteworthy, reflecting the fact that the original Mongol army was coterminous with the free, adult, male nation, thus differing fundamentally from the armies of earlier rulers in Persia. Only during Ḡāzān Khan's reign were new recruitment and pay arrangements, including allocation of *eqṭā*ʿs, introduced, bringing the Mongol army more in line with earlier Persian armies; eventually, at an unspecified date, a *dīvān-e ʿarż* appeared. The Il-khanids themselves followed a seminomadic or transhumant way of life similar to that of the Saljuq sultans. Although Oljāytū, for example, built a capital at Solṭānīya in northwestern Persia between 705/1305 and 713/1313, he often moved his military camp (*ordū*) between winter and summer quarters and was accompanied by a mobile administration, as well as the army; this administration usually included the vizier and at least some chancery officials (*monšī*s or *bitikčī*s/*baḵšī*s, *mošref*s, and *mostawfī*s), but their spheres of duty are somewhat imprecise in the sources (Melville, pp. 55, 60-61; for the Il-khanid administration, see Spuler, *Mongolen*¹ pp. 282 ff.; Uzunçarşılı, pp. 198-241; Lambton, in *EI*²; idem, 1988, pp. 50-67).

Under the Il-khans there had been in practice an administrative division between military (Mongol and Turkish) and the civilian (Persian) populations, which remained under the Timurids. In the time of Tīmūr himself (771-807/1370-1405) the *dīvān-e aʿlā* assessed and collected tribute (*māl-e amān*) from the conquered provinces and towns and was also responsible for collection of taxes, though the ruler himself might well modify the assessments. The title borne by the head of the supreme *dīvān* is unscertain. The official historian of Tīmūr's reign, Neẓām-al-Dīn Šāmī, seldom mentioned the term *wazīr* and then only in the plural, as the term for a group of leading state dignitaries (*omarāʾ wa wozarāʾ wa arkān-e dawlat*); he also mentioned a *dīvān-e ḵāṣṣ*. This paucity of reference indicates that under Tīmūr the chief of the *dīvān-e ḵāṣṣ* had only limited authority and was closely supervised by the khan (Manz, pp. 200-02). A century later, under Solṭān-Ḥosayn Bayqarā, the administrative-ethnic division still persisted below the level of the *dīvān-e aʿlā*, which was responsible for both civil and military, Turkish and Persian spheres of affairs. Subordinate to it, first, was the organ charged with Turkish and military matters, the *dīvān-e bozorg-e amārat*, led by a *dīvānbegī*, with a staff of *bitikčīs*/*baḵšīs*; the *tavajī dīvānī* "department of the army inspector" (i.e., of an official corresponding to the *ʿāreż* as muster master) was probably a subdivision of this *dīvān*. Second, the *dīvān-e ʿālī* or *Sart* (Mong. and Turk. "Persian, Tajik") *dīvānī* was responsible for affairs of the Persian population and was staffed by secretaries (*nevīsandagān-e tājīk*); the *dīvān-e māl* must have been a subdivision of this *dīvān* (Hinz, cited in Morvārīd, comm., p. 169).

The Turkmen dynasties that succeeded the Il-khanid state in western Persia and Iraq, the Jalayerids, the Qara Qoyunlū, and the Āq Qoyunlū, probably inherited the administrative institutions of the Il-khanids, though little specific is known about the workings of the individual *dīvān*s. It seems that Moḥammad b. Hendūšāh Naḵjavānī, author of *Dastūr al-kāteb*, worked in the chanceries of both the Il-khanid Abū Saʿīd (717-36/1316-35) and the Jalāyerid Šayḵ Oways (757-76/1356-74; Storey, III, pp. 5-9, 246-47). The civil administration of the Qara Qoyunlū, as well as of the Āq Qoyunlū, was headed by a supreme *dīvān-e aʿlā/aʿẓam*, with a vizier who oversaw central and provincial administration in general. Under the Āq Qoyunlū there was also a secretarial department, the *dīvān-e parvānačī*, corresponding to the older *dīvān-e rasāʾel/enšāʾ*, where official documents (*parvāna*) were drawn up and sealed. The revenue department of the Āq Qoyunlū was presided over by the *ṣāḥeb(-e) dīvān*, whose Persian title *ḵᵛāja* could be traced back to the Samanids; the *dīvān-e ṣadārat*, directed by the *ṣadr*, or head of the religious institution, seems to have originated under the Timurids (Savory, 1961, p. 103). In the military sphere the term *dīvān* appeared in the title of the Āq Qoyunlū *amīr-e dīvān*, a soldier who functioned as viceroy or deputy for the sultan; virtually nothing is known, however, about his duties or his supporting staff. The equivalent of the earlier *dīvān-e ʿarż* was the *dīvān* of the *tavajī*s, a group of senior military officers (for the term, see Deny, pp. 160-61) who possibly constituted in a sort of "general staff" (Minorsky, 1939, p. 163); the duties of this *dīvān* included keeping a register (*daftar*, q.v.) of the names and qualifications of the troops (on administrative arrangements of the Turkmen dynasties, see Uzunçarşılı, pp. 286-308; Minorsky, 1939, pp. 162-63, 169-71; idem, 1957, pp. 28, 101).

Documentation for the Safavid administration is much more comprehensive than that for the preceding periods in Persia, though one of the most detailed and important sources, the *Taẕkerat al-molūk* of Mīrzā Samīʿā, was not compiled until around 1137/1725, at the very end of effective Safavid rule. The elucidation of this material nevertheless poses problems that are inherent in the nature and evolution of the Safavid state. First, there was from the beginning a mingling of a Turkmen-dominated secular monarchy not very dissimilar from the Āq Qoyunlū and the Timurids with a theocratic kingship, messianic and Shiʿite, in which the shah was spiritual director (*moršed-e kāmel*) of the Ṣafawīya Sufi order. Second, it is not easy to demarcate the various spheres of competence of the *dīvān-e aʿlā*, which functioned both as royal court (*dargāh*) and as central government; equally, the functions of civil, military, and religious officials are frequently difficult to distinguish. Third, the Safavid state evolved considerably over the two and a quarter centuries of its existence; Roger Savory (*Camb. Hist. Iran*, pp. 351-72) has distinguished three phases: the formative phase (907-96/1501-88), during which spheres of authority were not yet clearly defined and clashes and changes could occur; inauguration of a new system by Shah ʿAbbās I (996-1038/1588-1629); and "gradual sclerosis and consequent decline" (1038-1135/1629-1722).

At first, under Shah Esmāʿīl I (907-30/1591-24) and Shah Ṭahmāsb I (930-84/1524-76), the head of the *dīvān-e aʿlā* was also the shah's chief deputy (*wakīl*) for both civil and military affairs. The vizier was of little importance at that time; only toward the end of Ṭahmāsb's reign did his power increase as he became *wazīr-e aʿẓam* or *wazīr-e mostaqell* (Savory, 1960, pp. 93-99, 102); in the 17th century he acquired the official title *eʿtemād-al-dawla*. All financial transactions, both civil and military, were supervised by the *dīvān-e aʿlā*, and subordinate viziers were responsible for overseeing various groups connected with the court, eunuchs, falconers, and the like. The military responsibilities of the *dīvān* obviously included payment of the professional troops, commanded initially by the *amīr al-omarāʾ* but increasingly by the *qūrčī-bāšī*, commander-in-chief of the Turkmen tribal cavalry (Savory, 1960, pp. 99-101; idem, 1961, pp. 77-79). The *dīvān* itself had two important divisions: the *dīvān-e mamālek* under the *mostawfi'l-mamālek*, concerned with taxation and general administration of the Safavid empire and those provinces and districts administered directly by governors; and the *dīvān-e ḵāṣṣa* under the *nāẓer-e boyūtāt* (lit., "superintendent of the royal workshops"). As the operations of the latter, which included supervision of the crown domains, were so close to the shah, the *nāẓer* was a powerful figure, whose authority at times encroached on that of the grand vizier.

The Safavid chancery (*dār al-enšāʾ*) also evolved during the three periods distinguished by Savory. It was originally under the *monši'l-mamālek* but subsequently became more complex, as new types of registers and documents were issued in greater numbers, especially those concerning grants of taxation (*barāt*) and land (*soyūrḡāl, tīūl*). Under Shah ʿAbbās the *majlesnevīs* or *wāqeʿanevīs* expanded his duties to include issuing of diplomas for provincial governors and amirs, court officials, and the like, while the *monši'l-mamālek* receded into the background and was reduced to issuing diplomas for minor provincial officials; hence in the 17th and early 18th centuries there were both an "old chancery" and a "new chancery," the latter predominant; because of it chief's closeness to the shah he even rivaled the grand vizier.

It should be further noted that, according to *Taḏkerat al-molūk* (tr. Minorsky, p. 44, comm. pp. 113-14; cf. Savory, in *Camb. Hist. Iran*, pp. 353-54), there was a state advisory council, also called *dīvān* and later *jānqī* (a Mongol term suggesting an Il-khanid or Timurid origin for the institution), to which in later Safavid times certain members of the *dīvān-e aʿlā* also belonged; they included the grand vizier; the *dīvānbegī*, or chief justiciar; and the *majlesnevīs* or chief secretary. This council was outside the normal pattern of central administration.

Provinces like Khorasan and Azerbaijan were governed through regional administrations. In the 16th century a centrally nominated official with the title *wazīr-e koll* (general vizier) administered each province, and, in the absence of specific information, it seems reasonable to assume that he had his own *dīvān*, staffed by revenue officials and secretaries. The *wazīr-e koll* oversaw the finances of the province, including those of any *ḵāṣṣa* lands situated there, ensuring a regular flow of collected taxes to the central treasury; an important additional part of his duties was to act as a check on the activities of the *beglerbegī*, or provincial governor.

From this sketch of the functioning of *dīvān*s in the Safavid period, it is clear that, though there is considerable information on some aspects, it is patchy, making it extremely difficult to perceive an orderly pattern and to distinguish the functions of officials known by frequently changing or evolving titles (Savory, *Camb. Hist. Iran*, pp. 351-72; Lambton, *EI*[2]; Rohrborn, 1966; idem, 1979, pp. 17-57; Savory, 1987, arts. IV-VII; *Taḏkerat al-molūk*, ed. Minorsky, commentary).

For the administrative systems of the Zands and Qajars, see ADMINISTRATION i.

Bibliography: (For the cited works not given in detail see "Short References.") ʿAbd-Allāh Morvārīd, *Šaraf-nāma*, facs. ed. and tr. H. R. Roemer as *Staatsschreiben der Timuridenzeit. Das Šaraf-Nāma des ʿAbdallāh Marwārīd in kritisches Auswertung*, Wiesbaden, 1952. C. E. Bosworth, "Military Organisation under the Būyids of Persia and Iraq," *Oriens* 18-19, 1965-66, pp. 143-67. Idem, "The Armies of the Ṣaffārids," *BSO(A)S* 31, 1968, pp. 534-54. Idem, "Abū ʿAbdallāh al-Khwārazmī on the Technical Terms of the Secretary's Art. A Contribution to the Administrative History Mediaeval Islam," *JESHO* 12, 1969, pp. 113-64. Idem, *The History of the Saffārids of Sistan and the Maliks of Nimruz*, Costa Mesa, Calif., 1994. H. Busse, *Chalif und Grosskönig. Die Buyiden im Iraq (945-1055)*, Wiesbaden, 1969. J. Deny, "Osmanli ancien *tovija (dovija)*," *JA* 221, 1932, pp. 160-61. ʿA. ʿA. Dūrī, "Dīwān i. The Caliphate," in *EI*[2] II, pp. 323-27. Ebn Ḵaldūn, *al-Moqaddema*, tr. F. Rosenthal as *The Muqaddimah. An Introduction to History*, New York, 1958. R. Genç, *Karahanlı devlet teşkilâtı. XI Yüzyıl*, Istanbul, 1981. G. Hawting, *The First Dynasty of Islam. The Umayyad Caliphate AD 661-750*, London, 1986. W. Hoenerbach, "Zur Heeresverwaltung der ʿAbbāsiden. Studie über Abulfarağ Qudāma: *Dīwān al-ğaiš*," *Der Islam* 29, 1950, pp. 257-90. H. Horst, *Die Staatsverwaltung der Grosselğūqen und Ḫōrazmšāhs (1038-1231)*, Wiesbaden, 1964. Abū ʿAbd-Allāh Moḥammad Jahšīārī, *Ketāb al-wozarāʾ wa'l-kottāb*, Baghdad, 1357/1938. Abū ʿAbd-Allāh Moḥammad b. Aḥmad Ḵʷārazmī, *Mafātīḥ al-ʿolūm*, ed. G. van Vloten, Leiden, 1895. H. Kennedy, *The Prophet and the Age of the Caliphates*, London, 1986. C. L. Klausner, *The Seljuk Vezirate. A Study of Civil Administration 1055-1194*, Cambridge, Mass., 1973. A. K. S. Lambton, "The Internal Structure of the Saljuq Empire," in *Camb. Hist. Iran* V, pp. 203-82. Idem, *Continuity and Change in Medieval Persia. Aspects of Administrative, Economic and Social History, 11th-14th Century*, London, 1988. Idem, "Dīwān iv. Iran," in *EI*[2] II, pp. 332-36. R. Levy, *The Social Structure of Islam*, Cambridge, 1957. B. Lewis, *The Political Language of Islam*, Chicago, 1988. B. F. Manz, "Administration and the Delegation of Authority in Temur's Dominions," *Central Asiatic Journal* 20, 1976, pp. 191-207. C. Melville, "The Itineraries of Sultan Öljeytü, 1304-16," *Iran* 28, 1990, pp. 55-70. V. Minorsky, "A Civil and Military Review in Fārs in 881/1476," *BSOS* 10, 1939, pp. 141-78. Idem, *Persia in A.D. 1478-1490*, London, 1957. M. Morgan, *The Mongols*, Oxford, 1986. M. Nāẓim, *The Life and Times of Sulṭān Maḥmūd of Ghazna*, Cambridge, 1931. Ḵʷāja Neẓām-al-Molk Ṭūsī, *Sīar al-molūk (Sīāsat-nāma)*, ed. H. Darke, 2nd.

ed., Tehran, 1347 Š./1968. K. Rohrborn, *Provinzen und Zentralgewalt Persiens im 16. und 17. Jahrhundert*, Berlin, 1966. Idem, *Regierung und Verwaltung Irans unter den Safaviden*, HO, pt. 1, VI/5, Leiden and Cologne, 1979. Neẓām-al-Dīn Šāmī, *Ẓafar-nāma*, ed. F. Tauer, Beirut, 1937. R. M. Savory, "The Principal Offices of the Ṣafawid State during the Reign of Ismaʿīl I (907-30/1501-24)," *BSO(A)S* 23, 1960, pp. 91-105. Idem, "The Principal Offices of the Ṣafawid State during the Reign of Ṭahmāsp I (930-84/1524-76)," *BSO(A)S* 24, 1961, pp. 65-85. Idem, "The Safavid Administrative System," in *Camb. Hist. Iran* VI, pp. 351-72. Idem, *Studies on the History of Ṣafawid Iran*, Variorum Reprints, London, 1987. M. A. Shaban, *Islamic History, A New Interpretation. A.D. 750-1055 (A.H. 132-448)*, Cambridge, 1976. M. Sprengling, "From Persian to Arabic," *AJSLL* 56, 1939, pp. 175-224, 325-36. I. H. Uzunçarşılı, *Osmanlı devleti teşkilâtına medhal*, Istanbul, 1941. ʿA. Zarrīnkūb, "The Arab Conquest of Iran and Its Aftermath," in *Camb. Hist. Iran* IV, pp. 1-56.

(C. EDMUND BOSWORTH)

iii. COLLECTED WORKS OF A POET.

The word *dīvān* is widely used both in Arabic and Persian to designate the collected poems of a particular author, generally without his or her long poems (*maṯnawī*s). The Arabic philologists of the Abbasid period (many of them of Persian origin) assembled the works of the pre-Islamic Arab poets, which had until then survived only through oral transmission, into collections which they called *dīvān*s, evidently by analogy to the registers or archives in which financial documents were preserved. Then the literate Arabic poets of the Abbasid period often collected their own poems in a *dīvān*, but in some cases their *dīvān*s were put together by others after their death, evidently because they had no time to do so themselves; this is the case, for example, with Motanabbī.

Many of the surviving *dīvān*s of pre-Mongol Persian poets are known only from manuscripts copied in the last two or at most three centuries and evidently represent collections assembled by literati of the Safavid period such as Taqī Kāšī (e.g., the *dīvān*s of Farroḵī, Lāmeʿī, Manūčehrī, and ʿOnṣorī). In the absence of old manuscripts it is difficult to say whether the Safavid prototypes of these *dīvān*s were based on earlier, lost, copies, or whether they were assembled ad hoc from the stray poems quoted in anthologies. Other published *dīvān*s were put together by their 20th-century editors. On the other hand, some early *dīvān*s, such as those of Azraqī or Sanāʾī, survive in good 13th-century manuscripts. In any case, Persian *dīvān*s did certainly exist at a very early date. Thus Nāṣer-e Ḵosrow writes that in the year 438/1046 the poet Qaṭrān "came to me and brought the *dīvān* of Monjīk and the *dīvān* of Daqīqī" (now both lost) and the same author speaks in his poems of his own 'two *dīvān*s' in Arabic and Persian. Neẓāmī Ganjavī indicates that he collected his own *dīvān* before 584/1188 (very early in his career) and his contemporary Farīdal-Dīn ʿAṭṭār also assembled his own *dīvān*, as he tells us in the introductions to two of his other works (*Moḵtār-nāma* and *Ḵosrow-nāma*). On the other hand the *dīvān* of Ẓahīr Fāryābī was assembled after the author's death by the poet Shams-al-Dīn Sojāsī, who wrote a preface to it in prose.

In the post-Mongol period it is commonplace for poets to publish their own *dīvān*s. Amīr Ḵosrow collected his own poems at various stages in his life in five different *dīvān*s, for each of which he composed a prose introduction. His example was followed in the three *dīvān*s of Jāmī. By contrast, Saʿdī's shorter poems are not assembled in a *dīvān* but rather are contained, together with his longer poems and his prose writings in the 'complete works' (*kollīyāt*) put together after his death by ʿAlī b. Aḥmad b. Abī Bakr b. Bīsotūn.

In most manuscripts (and modern editions) the poems in a given *dīvān* are grouped by genre (usually with *qaṣīda*s first, then strophic poems, *ḡazal*s, *qeṭʿa*s, and *robāʿī*s last) and then within each section the poems are arranged alphabetically by the last letter. However, in early manuscripts the poems are generally not arranged alphabetically, and often not separated by genre either, but often grouped by subject, or by their dedicatee. Both alphabetical and non-alphabetical ordering can be observed in early copies of Arabic *dīvān*s as well; it is thus likely that both systems were used for Persian *dīvān*s from an early date.

Bibliography: Nāṣer-e Ḵosrow, *Dīvān*, ed. M. Mīnovī and M. Moḥaqqeq, Tehran 1353 Š./1974, *qaṣīda* 64 v. 46; *qaṣīda* 177 v. 51. Idem, *Safar-nāma*, ed. M. T. Dabīrsīāqī, Tehran 1354 Š./1976, p. 9. Neẓāmī Ganjavī, *Laylī o Majnūn*, ed. A. A. Aleskerzade and F. Babayev, Moscow 1965, p. 39. Storey/de Blois, V (for the manuscripts of Persian *dīvāns*). Ẓahīr Fāryābī, *Dīvān*, ed. T. Bīneš, Mašhad, 1337 Š./1959, pp. 2-9.

(FRANÇOIS DE BLOIS)

DĪVĀN-E KEŠVAR. See JUDICIARY.

DĪVĀNA NAQQĀŠ, 15th-century painter whose work is known primarily from single-page paintings preserved in the Topkapı Sarayı library, Istanbul. His name is inscribed on five pages now mounted in a *moraqqaʿ* (album; ms. no. H.2160), which contains paintings and calligraphy of various dates, including many linked to Sultan Yaʿqūb (883-96/1478-90) or other members of the Āq Qoyunlū dynasty (Tanındı, pp. 38-39). He may also be identified with a poet known as Dīvāna Naqqāš, mentioned by the early 16th-century writer Sām Mīrzā (p. 190), who described him as a native of Tabrīz and an intimate of Sultan Yaʿqūb.

The pages in the Istanbul album bearing Dīvāna's name in either signatures or attributions provide an indication of his artistic achievements. On the most revealing of these pages his name is given as Fażl-Allāh Dīvāna; it contains painted sketches of plants, animals, and human figures (Tanındı, figs. 22, 67) that link his style with a variety of chinoiserie often ascribed to other painters at Sultan Yaʿqūb's court, for example, Šayḵī Naqqāš; in all these works quotations from Chinese paintings or drawings are combined with elements from the Persian repertoire (Tanındı, pp. 38-39, figs. 105, 107-13). Āq Qoyunlū court painters also illustrated manuscripts in a more traditional Persian style. One such painting in a manuscript of the Maḵzan al-asrār by Ḥaydar Ḵᵛārazmī, dated to 883/1478 (Spencer Collection, New York Public Library, Persian ms. no. 41) and dedicated to Sultan Yaʿqūb, has been attributed to Dīvāna Naqqāš (Soucek, pp. 5-7).

Bibliography: Sām Mīrzā Ṣafawī, *Toḥfa-ye al-sāmī*, ed. Ḥ Waḥīd Dastgerdī, Tehran, 1354 Š./1975. P. Soucek, "The New York Public Library *Makhzan al-asrār* and Its Importance," *Ars Orientalis* 18, 1988, pp. 1-37. Z. Tanındı, "Some Problems of Two Istanbul Albums, H. 2153 and 2160," *Islamic Art* 1, 1981.

(PRISCILLA P. SOUCEK)

DĪVĀNBEGĪ

i. *The Timurid period.*
ii. *The Safavid period.*

i. THE TIMURID PERIOD

Dīvānbegī was the designation for the highest-ranking officer in the Timurid office of finance and justice (*dīvān-e aʿlā*). The *dīvānbegī* (cf. Pers. *amīr-e dīvān*) was responsible for placing the seal on decrees and was particularly concerned with increasing tax revenues and associated problems (Herrmann, p. 188). The Timurid administration was organized in two main branches, the top personnel of which consisted of *tovāčībegī*s (Pers. *tovāčī*), military inspectors, and of *dīvānbegī*s, respectively. These two amir-/beg-groups together constituted the grand amirs (*omarāʾ-e ʿeẓām*), with the title *ologh beg*. The chiefs of both branches were called *amīr al-omarāʾ* (q.v.), which explains why in Timurid sources two *amīr al-omarāʾ* are sometimes reported as having simultaneously served a single ruler. The office of the *dīvānbegī*s, i.e., *dīvān-e aʿlā*, is already attested under Tīmūr (771-807/1370-1405), but the earliest mention of the office of *tovāčībegī*s (i.e., *dīvān-e tovāčī*, *dīvān-e laškar*, or *tork dīvānī*) is after the reign of Šāhroḵ (807-50/1405-47). Other synonyms for *dīvān-e aʿlā* were *dīvān-e molk wa māl*, *dīvān-e māl*, and *sart dīvānī* (Mīr ʿAlī-Šīr, p. 29; Ando, pp. 224-27). Ḵᵛāndamīr reported (fols. 20b, 21a) that, according to the Mongol customary law (*yāsā*, *tūrā*), the *omarāʾ-e dīvān-e māl* ranked second after the *omarāʾ-e dīvān-e tovāčī*. It seems that at the same time several *dīvānbegī*s were attested. For example, in 771/1370 Tīmūr named eight members of his entourage as *tovāčī* and six as *amīr-e dīvān* (*dīvānbegī*; Yazdī, fol. 141b). Most *dīvānbegī*s were of Turkish origin, but especially under Solṭān-Ḥosayn Bayqarā (875-912/1470-1506) there were reports of the activities of Persian *dīvānbegī*s. The Timurids tended not to appoint members of tribes considered aristocratic, like the Barlās or the Arlāt, to influential posts as *dīvānbegī*s, but rather only personal intimates of the ruler (Ando, pp. 234-39).

Bibliography: ʿAbd-Allāh Morvārīd, *Šaraf-nāma*, facs. ed. and tr. H. R. Roemer as *Staatschreiben der Timuridenzeit. Das Šaraf-nāmä des ʿAbdallāh Marwārīd*, Wiesbaden, 1952, pp. 169 ff. Mīr ʿAlī-Šīr Navāʾī, *Waqfīya*, ed. A. Ḥekmat and B. Čūbānzāda, Baku, 1926. S. Ando, *Timuridische Emire nach dem Muʿizz al-ansāb*, Berlin, 1992. Yu. Bregel, "Dīwān-begī," in *EI*², S., pp. 227-28. G. Herrmann, *Der historische Gehalt des "Nāmä-ye nāmī" von Ḫāndamīr*, Ph.D. diss., Göttingen University, 1968. Ḡīāṯ-al-Dīn Moḥammad Ḵᵛāndamīr, *Nāma-ye nāmī*, Bibliothèque Nationale, Paris, ms. Suppl. pers. 1842. *Moʿezz al-ansāb*, Bibliothèque Nationale, Paris, ms. Pers. ancien fonds. 67. Šaraf-al-Dīn ʿAlī Yazdī, *Ẓafar-nāma*, ed. A. Urunbayev, Tashkent, 1972. A. Z. Velidi Togan, "Ali Şîr," *İA* I, pp. 349-57.

(SHIRO ANDO)

ii. IN THE SAFAVID PERIOD

In the Safavid administrative system, the *dīvānbegī* was one of the high-ranking amirs (addressed *ʿālī-jāh*) residing at court (*omarā-ye dawlat-ḵāna*). From the time of Shah ʿAbbās I (q.v.) onwards, there were normally seven *ʿālī-jāh amīr*s who together constituted the council of state (*dīvān*, *jānqī*)). As an official of the internal palace administration, the *dīvānbegī* had the status of *moqarrab al-ḵāqān* (*Taḏkerat al-molūk*, ed. Minorsky, pp. 44, 56ff; Savory, p. 355). Minorsky's designation of the *dīvānbegī* as "Lord High Justice" (*Taḏkerat al-molūk*, p. 119) is close to the mark. Although the *dīvānbegī* could not rule on cases involving one of the four capital crimes under *šarīʿa* law (murder, rape, the breaking of teeth, and blinding) unless the *ṣadr*s were present (*Taḏkerat al-molūk*, pp. 42. 50), the *dīvānbegī*'s court was the highest appellate court in the land, and received appeals from the courts of the *qāżī*s and from that of the *šayḵ al-eslām* (*Taḏkerat al-molūk*, p. 120, quoting Chardin, ed. Langlès, VI, pp. 54-55).

On four days a week, including Saturdays and Sundays when he was joined by the *ṣadr-e ḵāṣṣa*, the *dīvānbegī* presided over a court in the *kešīk-ḵāna* (guard house) at the ʿĀlī Qāpū palace (q.v.). On other days he heard cases involving customary law (*ʿorf*) in his own home. In both courts, if the case concerned *dīvān* revenue, or was a suit brought against an official of the central bureaucracy, the case was sent on to the vizier. If the case concerned *qūrčīs*, *ḡolāms* or members of other military units, or employees of the royal workshops (see BOYŪTĀT-E SALṬANATĪ), it was referred to the senior official (*rīš-safīd*) of the appropriate department. Cases not involving *dīvān* revenue were decided by the *dīvānbegī* himself. Plaintiffs from the provinces who had grievances against provincial governors and other officials and had not presented their cases heard in the vizier's court, could apply to have their cases heard before the *dīvānbegī* (Mīrzā Rafīʿā, p. 88; *Taḏkerat al-molūk*, pp. 42, 50-51). The salary of the *dīvānbegī* was set at 500 toman, but could be as much as 1,000 toman; in addition, he received a *toyūl* (assignment; *Taḏkerat al-molūk*, p. 152) officially evaluated at 15 toman but yielding in reality 92 toman, 3,845 *dīnārs*; Mīrzā Rafīʿā (p. 88) states that this *toyūl* had "recently" been cancelled.

Although the *dīvānbegī* was one of seven *ʿālī-jāh amīrs*, his was not "high-profile" position, and the holders of this office are mentioned relatively rarely in the sources. The first person recorded as holding this office is Mīrzā ʿAlī Solṭān Qājār, who was the *dīvānbegī* at the time of the death of Shah Ṭahmāsb (984/1576; Eskandar Beg, I, p. 140; tr. Savory, I, p. 226). This leads one to suppose that, during the earlier, formative period of the Safavid state, the legal functions of the *dīvānbegī* were performed by officials such as the *qāżī al-qożāt*, the *qāżī ʿaskar*, and the *šayḵ al-eslām*. Qezelbāš amirs continued to hold the post of *dīvānbegī* until toward the end of the reign of Shah ʿAbbās I, when the appointment is recorded in 1036/1626-27 of the aide-de-champ (*yasāvol-e ṣoḥbat*) Rostam Beg, who continued to hold the office under Shah Ṣafī (Eskandar Beg, II, p. 1060; tr. Savory, II, p. 1283) and was succeeded in office by his son, Ṣafīqolī Beg (Waḥīd Qazvīnī, p. 221). Occasionally, the holder of the office of *dīvānbegī* also held that of *ešīk-āqāsī-bāšī* (e.g., ʿAlīqolī Khan Šāmlū and Kalb-ʿAlī Khan; see Eskandar Beg, II, pp. 887, 1040, tr. Savory, II, pp. 1104, 1261; Mofīd Bāfqī, III, p. 214). The office of *dīvānbegī* also existed in the Uzbek administrative system in Transoxania in the late 16th and early 17th centuries (e.g., Eskandar Beg, I, pp. 456, 548, 553, II pp. 706, 927; tr. Savory, II, pp. 629, 728, 734, II, p. 898, 1145).

Bibliography: Mīrzā Rafīʿā, *Dastūr al-molūk*, ed. M.-T. Dānešpažūh, *MDAT*, nos 63-70, 1347-48 Š./1968-69. Moḥammad Mofīd Mostawfī Bāfqī, *Jāmeʿ-e mofīdī*, ed. Ī. Afšār, Tehran 1340 Š./1961. R. M. Savory, "The Safavid Administrative System," in *Cam. Hist. Iran* VI, 1986. Moḥammad-Ṭāher Waḥīd Qazvīnī, *ʿAbbās-nāma*, ed. E. Dehgān, Arāk, 1329 Š./1950.

(ROGER M. SAVORY)

DĪVĀNĪ, ḴAṬṬ-E. See CALIGRAPHY.

DĪVDĀD b. Dīvdast **OŠRŪSANĪ**. See BANŪ SĀJ.

DIVINATION (Per. *morvā*, *morḡvā*, *šogūn zadan*, *fāl*, *fāl gereftan/zadan*, *tafaʾʾol*), the art or technique of gaining knowledge of future events or distant states by means of observing and interpreting signs. Various objects or events may serve as media of divination. Here we discuss only those interpretive acts which have the general structure of "A is a sign of B" (e.g., seeing a black cat is a bad omen).

Classical and early Muslim sources refer to the practice of divination among Persians (Rapp, pp. 76-94). Herodotus (7.37) reports that the Magi interpreted the eclipse of the sun as the waning of the fortune of the Greeks, against whom the Persian king was marching. Agathias (2.25) refers to the Zoroastrian priests who told the future events by looking into flames. Ebn al-Nadīm (ed. Flügel, p. 314) refers to a number of Persian works on divination, which seem to have been translated into Arabic. Balʿamī (ed. Bahār, pp. 1130-31) reports that Persians had a book of divination (*ketāb-e fāl*) in which they had listed all that they had used for divining during their dominion. A story reported by Ebn Qotayba (I, p. 149) of a Persian warlord seems to suggest that Persians wrote names or words on the shafts of their arrows. The inscribed word was interpreted as an omen when an arrow was pulled out to shoot at the enemy. The same warlord interpreted the actions of his enemy, who changed his mounts from elephant to horse, mule, and donkey, as evidence of his waning fortune (Balʿamī, ed. Bahār, II, p. 1032; Ebšīhī, II, pp. 91-94). References about divination are scattered throughout the *Šāh-nāma* (e.g., ed. Khaleghi, I, pp. 71, 77, 269; II, p. 300; Moscow, VI, pp. 229-30, VII, pp. 164, 354, VIII, pp. 161-62, 347). In the story of Alexander the sages divine the demise of the king from the birth of a monstrous child (*Šāh-nāma*, Moscow, VII, pp. 102-03; cf. Ṭūsī, p. 421). Ḵosrow II Parvēz divined his own death and the demise of the Sasanian dynasty from the accidental fall of a quince from the top of his throne (*Šāh-nāma*, Moscow, IX, pp. 259-60; Ṯaʿālebī, *Ḡorar*, p. 720). A sage forecasts that Persia will fall into chaos during the rule of Šērōya, because he sees the prince hitting a dried wolf claw against an animal horn (*Šāh-nāma*, Moscow, IX, p. 218; Ṯaʿālebī, *Ḡorar*, pp. 712-13). The sage Bozorgmehr (q.v.) divines that the three objects concealed in a box are three pearls, one bored, one half-bored, and one intact. He reaches this insight from his chance meeting on the road with three women, one married and with child, one married and childless, and a virgin (*Šāh-nāma*, Moscow, VIII, pp. 262-63; Ṯaʿālebī, *Ḡorar*, p. 635). Meeting with unattractive or deformed individuals was considered a bad omen and such individuals were avoided or even attacked (Marzbān, p. 221; Ebšīhī, II, p. 96; cf.

pseudo-Ḵayyām, pp. 82-88). The aversion to unattractive individuals seems to have been motivated by the belief that outward unattractiveness indicates inward or moral defect, itself a form of divination. Quite often evil deeds, such as destruction of a Persian city or slaying of a monarch, were attributed to unattractive men who were usually red-headed, green or blue-eyed, hairy, and cross-eyed. These men often had large teeth and noses (*Šāh-nāma*, Moscow, IX, pp. 191, 281; Ṯaʿālebī, *Ḡorar*, pp. 726-27; cf. ʿĀmelī, II, p. 403). Conversely, a beautiful face was valued as a good omen. The Arscasid king Ardavān reportedly had his concubine Golnār awaken him every morning so that her beautiful face would be the first sight he laid eyes on (*Šāh-nāma*, Moscow, VII, p. 127; cf. pseudo-Ḵayyām, pp. 82, 85-88). According to pseudo-Ḵayyām (pp. 40-43), Persians considered certain plants such as barley as auspicious, and old women used barley in divination. Secondary sources report divination by interpreting the twitching of different parts of the body to be common among Persians. Ebn al-Nadīm (ed. Flügel, p. 314) lists a book on *Eḵtelāj aʿżāʾ* among the oeuvres of the Persians. In the story of *Ḵosrow o Šīrīn*, the princess interprets the twitching of her *del* (abdomen, chest?) as a sign of impending misfortune, while she expects the twitching of her eyelid to be the sign of some important unknown event (Neẓāmī, p. 134).

Divination by means of animals involves not only interpreting their behavior but also any fluctuation in their numbers (Dīnavarī, p. 74; Ebšīhī, II, p. 97). Ebn Qotayba reports a number of animal divinations from the Arabic translation of a lost Middle Persian text called *Ketāb al-āʾīn* (Ebn Qotayba, I, pp. 151-53; cf. Balʿamī, ed. Bahār, pp. 115, 118; pseudo-Ḵayyām, p. 67). Mostawfī relates that the hero Rostam divined that Kay-Ḵosrow would not be harmed by Afrāsīāb, when the hero untypically missed a shot taken at a game (apud Mīnovī, p. 21).

The Islamic period. Permissibility of taking good omens from people's names or chance events has support not only in literary sources (Dīnavarī, p. 282; Sūzanī, p. 446) but also in some compendia of prophetic traditions (ʿAbd al-Bāqī, III, p. 71; Qomī, II, p.102; Kolaynī, II, p. 246; Balāḡī, p. 307). There exist, however, other traditions according to which taking bad omens from random events is prohibited (e.g., ʿĀmelī, II, pp. 193-94). The author of *Ketāb al-wāfī* writes that whereas seeking guidance (*esteḵāra*) from God by means of the Koran is permissible, divination (*tafaʾʾol*) is not permissible because through it the diviner seeks to gain knowledge of future events, which is an ability reserved for God (apud Balāḡī, p. 307; cf. Ḥakamī, pp. 161-62; Ḵarāʾeṭī, pp. 270, 274-75). Shiʿite scholars generally look down upon divination, considering it an irrational if not impious act (ʿĀmelī, II, p. 193; Balāḡī, pp. 306-07; Kolaynī, I, p. 370 tradition 235; Fahd, pp. 195-204). Moḥammad b. Monnawar (pp. 26-27, 175) describes the manner of divination by the Koran. It seems that divination was carried over into Islam from a pre-Islamic tradition (Bayhaqī, II, pp. 10, 212).

One of the meanings of the word *fāl* is reported to have been divination by randomly heard names or words (e.g., Ebn Qotayba, I, p. 146; Ebšīhī, II, pp. 94-5; cf. *Baḵtīār-nāma* p. 126). The positive form of this kind of divination, which had prophetic and religious approval (Karāʾeṭī, p. 276), reportedly was practiced by many of the early companions of the prophets and especially by Muslim generals engaged in early conquests (e.g., Balāḏorī, *Fotūḥ*, p. 257; Ṯaʿālebī, *Ḡorar*, p. 739; Dīnavarī, pp. 167, 282; Mostawfī, p. 177). Diviners were popular among the general populace of Persia and could charge their customers for their services (e.g., *Čahār maqāla*, ed. Qazvīnī, text, pp. 93-94, 102-04; cf. Fozūnī, p. 338).

Many varieties of divination are attested in Persian literature and folk practice. They include interpretation of objects which appear haphazardly, interpretation of involuntary bodily actions (sneezing, twitching, itches, etc.), observing animal behavior, divining by playing cards (*fāl-e waraq*) or chickpeas (*fāl-e noḵod*), bibliomancy (e.g., *fāl-e Ḥāfeẓ*), divination by means of mirrors and lenses (*āʾīna-bīnī*), observation of the liver of a slain animal (*jegar-bīnī*), divination by means of the flame of a lamp, etc. (Baskin, pp. 178-79; Balāḡī, pp. 333-34). Some involve special props or should be practiced at special places. Fozūnī (p. 492; Ṭūsī, p. 442) reports of a village near Ḡūr, in which there was a tree similar to the willow. At the vernal equinox every spring a villager brought a crystal bowl under that tree, hit the rim of the bowl, and forecast the events of the coming year. It was believed that had he practiced his art under some other tree he would have caused bad luck for the village. Bibliomancy using the *dīvān* of Ḥāfeẓ is the most popular for this kind of divination, but by no means the only kind. The Koran, as well as the *Maṯnawī* of Rūmī may also be used. *Fāl-e Ḥāfeẓ* may be used for one or more persons. In group bibliomancy, the *dīvān* will be opened at random, and beginning with the ode of the page that one chances upon, each ode will be read in the name of one of the individuals in the group. The ode is the individual's *fāl*. Assigning of the odes to individuals depends on the order in which the individuals are seated and is never random. One or three verses from the ode following each person's *fāl* is called the *šāhed*, which is read after the recitation of the *fāl*. According to another tradition the *šāhed* is the first or the seventh verse from the ode following the *fāl* (Zarrīnkūb, p. 557). An ode which had already been used for one individual in the group is disqualified from serving as the *fāl* for a second time (Balāḡī, p. 309).

Kat-bīnī is another form of divination in which the shoulder bone of a sacrificial sheep is "read." The sheep should be slaughtered at a moon-lit night in the name of the person for whom divination is being performed. Both the slaughterer and the seeker's clothing and persons should be ritually clean. The animal should be slaughtered close to running water and its right shoulder bone taken. The bone should be carefully cleared of flesh without getting scratched or damaged by the knife. When reading the bone (presumably the next day), the diviner should sit with his back to the sun, paying attention to every detail (Balāgī, pp. 335-36; Zarrīnkūb, p. 551; Ṭūsī, p. 598). A number of other types of divination are reported in the classical sources, e.g., divination by reading of the palm and by looking at the manner in which mice have gnawed something (Ṭūsī, p. 598; for a list see Zarrīnkūb, pp. 550-59).

Divination in folk tradition. Certain things, colors (e.g., Behrūzī, p. 52), or events are considered auspicious or inauspicious in Persian folk tradition. Shooting stars may be good or bad omens, but they usually presage someone's death (Wadīʿī, p. 17; cf. Hedāyat, p. 80). The number thirteen and certain days of the week (Hedāyat, p. 101; Wilson, pp. 222-23), howling of dogs, braying of a sitting donkey, and untimely crowing of cocks are signs of misfortune or death (Šakūrzāda, pp. 309, 316, 321; Aʿẓamī-e Sangesarī, 1349a, p. 55; idem, 1349b, p. 53; Tawakkolī, p. 71; Ṭāhbāz, p.7 1; Dānešvar, II, p. 230). A widespread belief considers a single sneeze to be a sign that one must stop whatever one is doing. This is called *ṣabr āmad* (patience is in order). Apparently in order to ward off evil during the short period of waiting after sneezing, some believe that one should recite the formula of praising the prophet and his family three to seven times. A double sneeze, called (*jakt/d*, i.e., *jahd*, effort), is a sign that one should speed up whatever one is doing (Aʿẓamī-e Sangesarī, 1349a, p. 51; Hedāyat, p.75; cf. Onians, pp. 103-5, 138-40, 197).

One of the most common folk practices concerns divination by a twitching of ones eyelids which may be auspicious or inauspicious depending on whether it occurs in the left or the right eye and in the upper or the lower eyelid (Hedāyat, p. 75-7; Aʿẓamī Sangesarī, 1349a, p. 52; Šakūrzāda, pp. 315-16). The folk practice uses virtually everything in the environment, from animals, to the behavior of children, weather, insects, and even the chance movements of smoke rising from a fire, as a means of divination (Šakūrzāda, pp. 319-20, 322-43, 307; Aʿẓamī Sangesarī, 1349a, pp. 49-55; idem, 1349b, p. 54; Tawakkolī, p. 71; Sāʿedī, 1342, p. 169; idem, 1344, pp. 202-04; Ṭāhbāz, p. 72; Mūsawī, p. 31). There is an ethnic Persian group called Marāgīān, who are also called also *kalla-bozī* (lit. goat-head) by their detractors because of their skill in divination by studying the severed heads of goats (Pūr-e Dāwūd, p. 244).

Persians believe that certain days are especially good for divination. During the last Wednesday of the year, called Čahāršanba-sūrī (q.v.), divination, especially by listening to the conversations of the passers by and interpreting that which is heard (*fālgūš*) as a sign is quite common (Šakūrzāda, pp. 79, 87). Fortunetellers, (*fālgīr*), who are mostly gypsies, are still active in some parts of Persia. Šakūrzāda has published specimens of their discourse (pp. 281-91, 292-98).

Bibliography: (For cited works not given in detail see "Short References.") Bahāʾ-al-Dīn ʿĀmelī, *al-Kaškūl*, ed. Ṭ-A. Zāwī, 2 vols., Cairo, 1380/1961. M.-F. ʿAbd-al-Bāqī, *al-Loʾloʾ wa'l-marjān fī mā ettafaq ʿalayhi al-šayḵān*, 3 vols., Beirut, 1986. Moḥammad b. Jaʿfar Ḵarāʾeṭī, *Masāwī al-aḵlāq wa maḏmūmohā*, ed. M. S. Ebrāhīm, Cairo, n.d. Moḥammad ʿAwfī, *Pānzdah bāb-e jawāmeʿ al-ḥekāyāt*, facs. ed., Tehran, 1335 Š./1956. Č. Aʿẓamī Sangesarī, "Bāvarhā-ye ʿām(m)īāna-ye mardom-e Sangesar," *Honar o mardom*, N.S., no. 92, 1970a, pp. 47-56, no. 93, 1970b, pp. 53-56. *Baḵtīār-nāma*, ed. M. Rowšan, Tehran, 1367 Š./ 1988. ʿA. Balāgī, *Tārīḵ-e Nāʾīn*, Tehran, 1369 Š./1990. W. Baskin, *The Sorceres's Handbook*, New York, 1974. Ebrāhīm b. Moḥammad Bayhaqī, *al-Maḥāsen wa'l-masāwī*, ed. M. A. Ebrāhīm, 2 vols., Cairo, 1961. ʿA-N. Behrūzī, in *Honar o mardom*, 1349 Š./1970, N.S., no. 99. Chardin, IV, pp. 430-44. M. Dānešvar, *Dīdanīhā wa šanīdanīhā-ye Īrān*, 2 vols., Tehran, 1327-28 Š./1948-49. Dīnavarī, *Aḵbār al-ṭewāl*, ed. ʿAbd-al-Āmer, Cairo, 1960. Ebn-Qotayba, *ʿOyūn al-aḵbār*, 4 vols., Cairo, 1343/1925. Bahāʾ-al-Dīn Moḥammad Ebšīhī, *al-Mostaṭraf fī koll fann mostaẓraf*, 2 vols., Cairo, 1371/1952. T. Fahd, *La Divination Arabe*, Leiden, 1966. Maḥmūd Fozūnī Estarābādī, *Boḥayra*, Tehran, n.d. Ḥāfeẓ b. Aḥmad Ḥakamī, *Aʿlām al-sonna al-manšūra*, ed. Š.-A. Ḵalīl Salafī, Cairo, 1989. Ṣ. Hedāyat, *Ney-rangestān*, Tehran, 1343 Š./1964. pseudo-Ḵayyām, *Nowrūz-nāma*, ed. ʿA. Hoṣūrī, Tehran, 1357 Š./1978. Abū Jaʿfar Moḥammad Kolaynī, *al-Rawża men al-kāfī*, ed. M. B. Kamaraʾī, 2 vols., Tehran, 1382/1962. D. S. Margoliouth, in *Encyclopaedia of Religion and Ethics*, ed. J. Hastings et al., 1908-26, IV, pp. 816-18. Marzbān b. Rostam, *Marzbān-nāma*, ed. M. Qazvīnī, Leiden, 1908, repr. Tehran, n.d. M. Mīnovī, "Dāstānhā-ye ḥamāsī-e Īrān dar maʾāḵeḏ-ī gayr az *Šāh-nāma*," *Sīmorg*, 1975, pp. 9-29. Moḥammd b. Monawwar, *Asrār al-tawḥīd fī maqāmāt al-Šayḵ Abī Saʿīd*, ed. A. Bahmanyār, Tehran, 1333 Š./1934. Ḥamd-Allāh Mostawfī, *Tārīḵ-e gozīda*, ed. ʿA.-Ḥ. Navāʾī, 2nd ed., Tehran, 1362 Š./1983. Ḥ. Mūsawī, *Gūšahā-ī az farhang o ādāb o rosūm-e mardom-e Kūhmarra, Nowdān Jarūq, wa Sorḵī-e Fārs*, Shiraz, 1362 Š./ 1983. Neẓāmī Ganjavī, *Ḵosrow o Šīrīn*, ed. Ḥ. Pežmān Baḵtīārī, Tehran, 1363 Š./1964. R. B. Onians, The *Origins of European Thought*, Cambridge, 1988. E. Pūr-e Dāwūd, *Ānāhītā*, ed. M. Gorjī, Tehran, 1363 Š./1964. ʿA. Qomī, *Safīnat al-beḥār wa madīnat al-ḥekam wa'l-āṯār*, 2 vols.,

Tehran, 1365 Š./1986. A. Rapp, in *ZDMG* 20, pp. 49-141. H. J. Rose, in *Encyclopaedia of Religion and Ethics*, ed. J. Hastings et al., Edinburgh, 1908-26, IV, pp. 775-80. Ḡ.-Ḥ. Sāʿedī, *Īlḵčī,* Tehran, 1362 Š./1963. Idem, *Ḵīāv yā Meškīnšahr*, Tehran, 1364 Š./1965. E. Šakūrzāda, *ʿAqāyed o rosūm-e mardom-e Ḵorāsān,* 2nd ed., Tehran, 1362 Š./1983. Sūzanī Samarqandī, *Dīvān*, ed. N. Šāh-Ḥosaynī, Tehran, 1338 Š./1959. S. Ṭāhbāz, *Yūš*, Tehran, 1342 Š./1963. M.-R. Tawakkolī, *Joḡrāfīā wa tārīḵ-e Bāna-ye Kordestān*, 2nd ed., Tehran, 1363 Š./1984. L. Thornkike, *A History of Magic and Experimental Science*, 8 vols., New York, 1934-60. Moḥammad b. Maḥmūd Ṭūsī, *ʿAjāyeb al-maḵlūqāt*, ed. M. Sotūda, Tehran, 1345 Š./1966. J. Wadīʿī, in *Honar o mardom*, no. 176, 1977, pp. 14-18. S. G. Wilson, *Persian Life and Customs*, 3rd rev. ed., New York etc., 1899. ʿA.-Ḥ. Zarrīnkūb, in *Soḵan* 13/5, 1341Š./1962, pp. 545-60.

(MAHMOUD OMIDSALAR)

DIVORCE, legal termination of marriage. In the following series of articles only those communities are taken into consideration which are either Iranian or are focussed in Persia. For this reason Jewish and Christian practices have not been included.

i. *In the Achaemenid period.*
ii. *In the Parthian and Sasanian periods.*
iii. *In Shiʿite law.*
iv. *In modern Persia.*
v. *Among modern Zoroastrians.*
vi. *Among Babis and Bahais.*

i. IN THE ACHAEMENID PERIOD

There is hardly any available information on divorce in Persia itself during the Achaemenid period; there is evidence only for certain of the western satrapies of the Achaemenid empire. It can be presumed that in the polygamous families of ancient Persia divorce was practiced only on rare occasions and that, in all probability, only the husband had the right to divorce his wife; perhaps in such an instance a mere declaration was sufficient to dissolve a marriage.

A number of marriage contracts with divorce clauses have been preserved from Babylonia. From these documents it can be determined that, if a divorce was initiated by the husband, he had to pay a predetermined sum, usually 6 minas (ca. three kg) of silver, and the divorced wife would be free to go wherever she wished. In all divorce clauses it was anticipated that the reason for dissolving the marriage would be the husband's desire to marry another woman (Roth, pp. 188 ff.). In a few marriage contracts it was specified that the husband could marry another woman if his first wife proved unable to bear children (Cardascia, p. 84). It was also possible for a husband to divorce his wife because of her extramarital sexual activity, although in one series of marriage contracts it was stipulated that adultery would result in the death penalty for the wife (for references, see Roth, pp. 197 ff.). In the ancient Near East a man's extramarital sexual activity was not considered an offense against his wife (Roth, p. 186 n. 1). From Achaemenid Babylonia there is no documentary evidence that a wife was entitled to divorce her husband.

According to Hebrew law, a husband had the right to divorce his wife upon the delivery of a "note of divorce," which permitted her to remarry (Deuteronomy 24:1-2), but what constituted grounds for divorce was not specified. There is no statement in the Pentateuch that a wife could divorce her husband (Driver and Miles, pp. 290 ff.). In contrast to the situation in some other communities, however, Jewish families at Elephantine in Egypt were monogamous, and husbands did not have the right to take second wives while still married. Three Aramaic marriage contracts have been preserved from Elephantine; they contain provisions for divorce on the initiative of either the husband or the wife. It is thus clear that spouses had equal rights in this respect, in contrast to the provisions of most ancient law (Bresciani, p. 158; Seidl, pp.79-80). This equality probably reflected specific conditions in Egypt,where women seem to have enjoyed a more privileged position (Yaron, p. 53). The initiating party had to announce the divorce before an assembly of witnesses and to pay a specified sum to the partner. If the initiating party was the wife the sum was 7.5 shekels of silver plus the return of her *mohar* (bride price); upon payment she was free go wherever she wished. If the initiator was the husband he had to pay divorce money (in one instance 200 shekels of silver) and to return the dowry (Porten and Yardeni, pp. 30 ff., 62 ff., 78 ff.). If a wife had committed adultery, her husband could divorce her, but she was not subject to additional punishment; this arrangement was in sharp contrast to that under biblical and most other ancient codes of law, in which such faithlessness was considered a criminal offense and punished severely (Muffs, pp. 51-62; Volterra; Yaron, pp. 53-64).

Bibliography: E. Bresciani, "La satrapia d'Egitto," *Studi Classici e Orientali* 7, 1958, pp. 132-88. G. Cardascia, "Le statut de la femme dans les droits cunéiformes," *Recueils de la Société Jean Bodin* XI. *La femme*, pt. 1, Brussels, 1959, pp. 79-94. G. R. Driver and J. C. Miles, *The Babylonian Laws* I, Oxford, 1968. Y. Muffs, *Studies in the Aramaic Legal Papyri from Elephantine*, Studia et Documenta ad Iura Orientis Antiqui Pertinentia 8, New York, 1973. B. Porten and A. Yardeni, *Textbook of Aramaic Documents from Ancient Egypt* II. *Contracts*, Jerusalem, 1989. M. T. Roth, "'She Will Die by the Iron Dagger.' Adultery and Neo-Babylonian Marriage," *JESHO* 31, 1988, pp. 196-206. E. Seidl, *Ägyptische Rechtsgeschichte der Saiten- und Perserzeit*, Ägyptologische Forschungen 20, Glückstadt, Germany, 1968. E. Volterra, "Osservazioni sul divorzio nei documenti aramaici," in *Studi orientalistici in onore di Giorgio Levi della Vida* II, Rome, 1956, pp. 586-600. R. Yaron, *Introduction to the Law of the Aramaic Papyri*, Oxford, 1961.

(MUHAMMAD A. DANDAMAYEV)

ii. IN THE PARTHIAN AND SASANIAN PERIODS

In pre-Islamic Zoroastrian canon and civil law the dissolution of marriage (Parth. *abihirzan—cf. Arm. apaharzan "divorce" [Hübschmann, Armenische Grammatik, p. 104, no. 43], Younger Av. *(apa-) harəzana-* "leaving" [*AirWb.*, col. 1794], OPers. *ava-hard-* "to abandon" [Kent, *Old Persian*, p. 214]; Mid. Pers. *hilišn* "abandonment"; *abēzārīh* "repudiation," cf. Arm. *apizar* "separated, free" [*EIr.*, II, p. 460]; *hištārīh*) was by law; it could be affected either by mutual consent or if the wife was barren or guilty of a deadly (*marg-arzān* "deserving death") sin/offence. The Riwāyat ī Ēmēd ī Ašawahištān (chap. 7) gives a thorough account of the cases that entitle the husband to divorce his legitimate (*pādixšāyīhā*) wife without her consent. It states: "The repudiation (*abēzārīh*) of a legitimate wife by the legitimate husband is only allowed by their mutual consent, unless the woman is found guilty of a proven sin (*wināhkārīh ī ēwarīhā*)...such as whoring, sorcery, failure to fulfill the obligatory duties (*ān-iš frēzwānīg kardan*), refusing to submit herself unto the husband, failure to observe the monthly period of confinement (i.e., retiring and keeping aloof when in menses), sleeping with her husband when in menses, concealing the menstruation (*daštān*), submitting herself to another man, or committing any other deadly sin or any sin that may harm the body or the soul. If the man divorces his wife for some other offence or against her will, the divorce (*hištārīh*) is not valid and he becomes guilty of a sin to the degree of one *tanāpuhl* (a deadly sin), whereas the (innocent) woman remains his legal wife." However, on the death of the husband the property held by the wife passes to the family of the husband, unless on her entering into marriage there has been settled some other agreement or arrangement (*pašn ud ēstišn*) as regards her private property (*wāspuhragān*). At all event she is entitled to food, maintenance, and bed-clothes (*xuft-paymōxt*, a 9th-century term) in conformity with her social station (*čand pāyag passazagīhā abayišnīg*), beyond which she has no other title to the estate left by the deceased husband. If her alimony is in excess of her needs, it should not be taken away from her; but if the husband has left less than her needs, it should be made up from the husband's estate. And if he has given away his estate as alms, so much of it should be retrieved as is necessary for her maintenance. In the case of a *čakar* (q.v.) wife, she should be regarded as exempt from any obligation to the *čakar* husband; therefore, there is no need for any statement in respect to her repudiation, as she is divorced (*abēzār*) from him by her own status (*xwad aziš abēzār*; Shaki, 1983, pp. 46-47).

The antiquity of the law of divorce is attested to by Justin's report (41.3) that in the Parthian period the low-class women could not remarry in the lifetime of their husbands; that is, as in Sasanian practice they could not seek the dissolution of marriage. In contrast to the legal limitations imposed upon the commoners, the noblewomen could easily divorce their husbands. This class privilege, judging by the tenacity of legal and social institutions, must have continued in Sasanian times. Similarly, the Parthian husband could divorce his wife only if she were barren or guilty of sorcery, adultery, or concealing her menstruation.

The *Mādayān ī hazār dādestān* and the 9th-century Pahlavi legal texts have generally passed over the case of woman's barrenness. The Persian *Ṣad dar-e naṯr* (chap. 92), however, in agreement with the Parthian tradition, mentions it in conjunction with adultery, sorcery, and concealing of menstruation as justifications for divorce. But according to the late *Persian Rivāyat of Dārāb Hormazyār* (I, p. 189) a man may divorce his barren wife if he does not conclude a second marriage. And the *Dēnkard* (ed. Madan, pt. 2, p. 749) refers to the maintenance of a barren woman or wife (*zan ī starwan*) and that of a pregnant wife, which, by implication, asserts her title to a "separate maintenance." Because sleeping with a barren woman (*zan ī anāpus*) as a case of "wasting semen" (*šusr/toxm wanīnīdan*, pp. 490, 807) is considered a grave sin (*tanāpuhl*), the judicial separation is the obvious alternative to divorce. Of interest is the evidence of Ṯaʿālebī giving adultery, sorcery, and apostasy as reasons for divorce (*Ḡorar*, p. 260).

The guardianship (*sālārīh*) over the wife being an indispensable condition for the legality of marriage, its dissolution is equally essential to the validity of divorce. If the guardianship is not renounced together with (the marriage contract), divorce will not take effect (*ka-š sālārīh abāg be nē hilēd hilišn be nē bawēd*; *Mādayān*, pt. 1, p. 87). That is why in the certificate of divorce first the guardianship is terminated and then divorce considered (*ān-iz pad hilišn-nāmag naxust sālārīh hanjāmēnd ud pas hilišn nigerīdan*, p. 87). In case the wife is divorced and given in marriage and guardianship to another person who rejects to assume her guardianship, then according to some jurists the divorce is not effective, as the jurist Wahrām has maintained: "marriage cannot be contracted apart from guardianship" (pp. 4-5).

The significant element of guardianship in matrimonial relations offers the husband a wide scope to manipulate the wife. The transferring of guardianship to the wife and giving freedom over her own person results in a partial divorce or legal separation that makes it possible for the husband to set his wife to various undertakings. Thus the *Mādayān ī hazār dādestān* (pt. 1, pp. 3-4) states: "If a person divorces his wife in such a way that makes the woman her own guardian and gives freedom over her own person (*pad xwēš tan sālār ud pādixšāy kunēd*—the technical formula for legal separation), and does not place her under the guardianship of another person, and that woman in the lifetime of that husband marries and gives birth to children, those offspring belong to that man who divorced her in that manner." In this way a man without male issue can make his wife to undertake a *čakarīhā* marriage in his own favor (pt. 1, p. 3), or to appoint her to assume a *stūrīh* marriage (pt. 1, p. 49), in order to provide a deceased co-religionist with a male progeny.

In case the wife is divorced by her consent, she does not receive the property that the husband has given her (pt. 1, p. 4), nor can she retrieve the earnings (*windišn*) that she has transferred to the husband on her own accord (pt. 2, p. 2). The jurists were divided on a woman's title to a property which she claims, against the husband, to have been promised her in case of divorce (pt. 1, p. 95). According to some jurists, on divorce the wife is only entitled to that which she has brought with her in connection with marriage, such as her dower (*pēšīgān/ passāzagān*?) and private property (*wāspuhragān*), but her earnings during matrimony remain with the husband. It is stressed that this orthodox traditional practice (*kardag*) is retained unchanged in the modified civil code (*u-š kardag aōn abāg ku gaštag be bawēd*, ms. *šawēd*, by copyist's error; pt. 1, p. 4; Shaki, 1974, p. 329). If a man divorces his wife and marries her to his under-age child, who dies in infancy, the *stūrīh* of that man does not devolve upon that woman (pt. 1, p. 4). A bodily mature maiden of nine years given in marriage with the consent of her guardian, on reaching her prime, at fifteen years of age, is not entitled to renounce the wedlock; should she abandon her husband, she would become *marg-arzān* ("deserving death"; *The Pahlavi Rivāyat of Āturfarnbag*, chap. 14); but a youth under age married to a mature woman, on coming of age may dissolve the arranged match only if he had not acted according to the contract (chap. 15).

The only case in which the husband may divorce his innocent legitimate wife against her will is when he offers her in marriage to a co-religionist who is in want of wife and children because of poverty (*niruzdīh*; *Mādayān*, pt. 1, p. 101; Bartholomae, I, pp. 29-30, 36-37), an injunction that echoes the *Vidēvdād*, chap. 4.44. This is interpreted by the *Dēnkard* (ed. Madan, pt. 2, p. 715) as making a charitable gift to the amount of one human being (*dāsr ī wīr-masāy*).

On remarrying his divorced wife, the promises made by the husband during the former term of cohabitation may not be binding on him (*Mādayān*, pt. 1, pp. 104-05), but if the husband makes an agreement on an allocation of property with his wife, who is his partner, and then divorces her, that promise remains binding on him (p. 4).

A divorced wife given in marriage to someone reverts to her former husband if she is found to suffer from an injury (*rēš*, p. 105).

Bibliography: Ch. Bartholomae, *Zum sassanidischen Recht* I-V., Heidelberg, 1918-23. S. J. Bulsara, *"The Laws of the Ancient Persians as Found in the Mātīkān ē Hazār Dātastan" or "The Digest of a Thousand Points of Law,"* Bombay, 1937. M. Macuch, *Das sasanidische Rechtsbuch "Mātakdān ī Hazār Dātistān*," Pt. 2, Wiesbaden, 1981. *The Pahlavi Rivāyat of Āturfarnbag and Farnbag-Srōš*, ed. B.T. Anklesaria, 2 vols., Bombay, 1969. *The Pahlavi Rivâyat Accompanying the Dâdestân-î Dînîk*, ed. B. N. Dhabhar, Bombay, 1913. A. G. Perikhanian, *Sasanidskiĭ sudebnik (Mātakdān ī hazār dātastān)*, Yerevan, 1973. *The Persian Rivayats of Dârâb Hormazyâr Frâmarz*, ed. M. R. Unvala, 2 vols., Bombay, 1922. *Rivāyat ī Ēmēd ī Ašawahištān*, ed. B. T. Anklesaria, *Rivâyat-î Hêmît-î Ašavahištān*, Bombay, 1962. *Ṣad dar-e naṯr*. M. Shaki, "The Sasanian Matrimonial Relations," *Archív Orientální* 39, 1971, pp. 322-45. Idem, "Two Middle Persian Legal Terms for Private Property," in Ph. Gignoux and A. Tafazzoli, eds., *Mémorial Jean de Menasce*, Louvain, 1974, pp. 327-36. Idem, "Two Chapters of the Rivāyat ī Ēmēd ī Ašawahištān," in *Oriental Studies*, D. Kobidze Memorial Volume, Tbilisi, 1983, pp. 45-53.

(MANSOUR SHAKI)

iii. IN SHIʿITE LAW

The term *ṭalāq* was employed in pre-Islamic times and in the Koran to refer to the separation of a married couple. In the Islamic law, *ṭalāq* means to sever the bond of marriage and is the exclusive right of the husband; the terms *ḵolʿ* and *mobārāt* are used to refer to two forms of *ṭalāq* with compensation given to the husband. In the following the views of the Jaʿfarī (Twelver Shiʿite) school are explained, with brief mention of the most important points on which the Sunnite schools diverge from it.

The pillars of divorce. Four pillars (*rokn*) are recognized: the formula (*ṣīḡa*), the divorcer (*moṭalleq*), the divorcée (*moṭallaq*), and the witness (*šāhed*). The Malikite and Shafiʿite schools also mention four pillars but replace witnesses with intention (*qaṣd*). The Hanafite and Hanbalite schools recognize only the first as a pillar and discuss the rest under headings such as conditions (*šorūṭ*; Jazīrī, IV, pp. 280-90).

1. The formula. The word *ṭāleq* must be used in the formula, and the woman must be designated clearly by name or pronoun (e.g., *ante ṭāleq* "You are divorced"). If the husband is mute, gestures can replace the formula. According to the Sunnite schools, the use of the word *ṭāleq* is not mandatory;

divorce can take place through other words or metaphorical expressions. The Sunnites maintain that the formula can be expressed in writing, but Shiʿite authorities differ on this point; those who allow it stipulate that the husband must be absent and two witnesses present with him. No conditions may be attached to the formula (Jazīrī, IV, p. 281; Zayn-al-Dīn ʿĀmelī, VI, pp. 12-16).

2. The divorcing man has to fulfill four conditions: He must have reached puberty (*bolūḡ*), be compos mentis, act on his own free will (*ektīār*), and have the intention (*qaṣd*) to divorce. A divorce by a husband who has not reached puberty is invalid, even if permitted by his guardian. The Hanbalite school, however, maintains that such divorce is valid if the meaning and consequence of the divorce is understood by the husband. Insanity or temporary loss of rationality (*ʿaql*) invalidates the pronouncement of the formula. The Sunnite schools maintain that if the loss of rationality is caused by alcohol or drugs and the man knew that these things would cause its loss, the formula is valid; otherwise it is invalid. If a man is coerced (*ekrāh*) into divorcing his wife, the divorce is invalid (in all schools except the Hanafite). Since the right to divorce belongs to the husband, he can give his wife the power of attorney (*wakāla*) to divorce herself or some other wife. In pronouncing the formula, the husband must have the intention of divorcing his wife; a divorce formula pronounced in jest or by mistake is invalid (Zayn-al-Dīn ʿĀmelī, V, pp. 17-21; Jazīrī, IV, p. 281-82).

3. The divorcée. a. The woman must be a wife through a legitimate, permanent marriage. A wife by temporary marriage (*motʿa*) and one who has not been married in accordance with the *šarīʿa* are not dealt with as objects of divorce. b. If the marriage has been consummated and the wife is not pregnant while her husband lives with her, she must be in a state of purity from menstruation or the confinement of childbirth. Divorce at the time of menstruation or confinement is prohibited. If the marriage has not been consummated, or the woman is pregnant, or the husband is absent from her, divorce is permissible. Opinions differ as to how long the husband should have been absent (one month, three months), but all agree that he must have no knowledge of his wife's situation. c. The husband cannot have had coitus with his wife in the *ṭohr* ("period of purity" the time between two menstrual periods) during which he wants to divorce her, unless she does not menstruate for some reason, has reached menopause, or is pregnant. d. If the marriage has not been consummated, the wife is entitled to one-half of the dower (*mahr*); otherwise she is entitled to the whole dower (Zayn-al-Dīn ʿĀmelī, V, p. 351; VI, pp. 24-29).

4. The witnesses. Two male witnesses must be present at the time of pronouncing the formula. The witnesses are neither a pillar nor a condition of divorce in the Sunnite schools (Ḥellī, II, p. 57; Jazīrī, IV, pp. 280-96).

Categories of divorce. Divorce is divided into two categories of traditional (*sonnī*) and non-traditional (*bedʿī*). Though prohibited, non-traditional divorce is valid in the Sunni schools; it is invalid in the Jaʿfarī law. Nontraditional divorce includes the following: a. A formula that is pronounced after the marriage has been consummated while the wife is menstruating or in confinement and not pregnant and while her husband is present. b. A formula pronounced when the wife is in a state of purity but her husband has had coitus with her during her present *ṭohr*. c. Three formulae pronounced at once. The four Sunnite schools hold that it is permissible for a man to divorce his wife by pronouncing the formula three times at once or simply by mentioning the number three; thus if he says, "You are divorced with three divorces," the divorce is complete. The Jaʿfarī school maintains that only a single formula can be pronounced at a time; hence this particular formula is counted as one pronouncement; another view holds that this formula is totally invalid (Zayn-al-Dīn ʿĀmelī, VI, pp. 17, 30-32; Jazīrī, IV, p. 341).

Traditional divorce observes the conditions set down for the woman in the third pillar of divorce; in addition, one formula is pronounced in each of three *ṭohrs*. Many *ʿolamāʾ* hold that it is permissible to pronounce more than one formula if the wife is pregnant; opinions differ as to whether divorce is valid if the man pronounces the formula, returns (*rejʿa*) to his wife but does not have coitus, divorces her again and returns, and then does the same for a third time, such that all three pronouncements are issued within a single *ṭohr*. The more prevalent opinion holds that the divorce is valid; others hold that each pronouncement of the formula must occur in a different *ṭohr* (Zayn-al-Dīn ʿĀmelī, VI, pp. 40-44).

Traditional divorce can be divided into two kinds (or, according to some authorities, three): a. Irrevocable (*bāʾen*), in which case the husband cannot return to his wife after pronouncing the formula of divorce if the marriage has not been consummated, the wife has not reached puberty or has reached menopause, the divorce takes the form known as *kolʿ* or *mobārāt* (see below), or the formula has been pronounced for the third time. b. Revocable (*rejʿī*), which allows the husband to return to his wife during her waiting period (*ʿedda*, see below) without her consent (Koran 2:228); he actualizes the return by a verbal expression such as "I am returning to you" or by some action that is permitted only between married couples, such as kissing or embracing. In the latter case, he must have the intention to return, while in the former case, pronouncing the words establishes the return. Return nullifies the effect of having pronounced the formula and reestablishes a full marital bond. Coitus is not a condition for the return. c. *Ṭalāq ʿedda*, in which coitus takes place during the return, is considered a third kind of traditional divorce by some Shiʿites, while others make it a second form of revocable divorce (Zayn-al-Dīn ʿĀmelī, VI, pp. 35-37).

A man can pronounce the divorce formula and then return to his wife twice (Koran 2:229). If he wants to remarry a woman whom he has divorced irrevocably, he has to do so with a new marriage contract. If the irrevocable divorce has taken place through three declarations of the formula, she has to marry someone else (known as *moḥallel*) according to a legitimate permanent marriage contract; she has to consummate the marriage and then be divorced by the second husband and observe the waiting period (Koran 2:230). In cases of irrevocable divorce where three formulae have not been pronounced, the *moḥallel* is not necessary. If the woman who has been divorced with three formulae remarries her first husband and then he divorces her irrevocably twice more for a total of nine formulae, she becomes unlawful to him forever (Ḥellī, II, pp. 57-58).

K̲olʿ and *mobārāt*. *K̲olʿ* (to remove) is used in the sense of removing a garment in accordance with the Koran (2:187): "They [women] are a garment (*lebās*) for you, and you are a garment for them." *Mobārāt* means to declare one another free. The two terms refer to two forms of irrevocable divorce in which the woman asks her husband to divorce her in exchange for compensation. The difference between the two is that in *k̲olʿ* the woman dislikes (*ekrāh*) her husband, while in *mobārāt* the feeling is mutual. In the former case, it is permissible for the amount of the compensation to exceed the amount of the dower, while in the latter this is not permissible. In Jaʿfarī and Hanafite law, *mobārāt* is discussed separately from *k̲olʿ*, but in the other Sunnite schools no distinction is drawn. In the Hanafite school, the husband receives no compensation for *mobārāt*; rather, the two parties drop their claims on each other. The pillars of *k̲olʿ* and *mobārāt* are the same as for ordinary divorce. In general, anything of value that can be given as dower can also be given as compensation. However, these two forms of divorce are not one-sided like normal divorce, since the wife must fulfill the conditions for a transaction. If the husband is not capable of divorce (e.g., he has not yet reached puberty), he cannot divorce his wife, even if she requests *k̲olʿ* or *mobārāt*. The jurists enter into detailed discussions concerning the validity of *k̲olʿ* when a person other than the wife or guardian offers to pay compensation; according to most authorities, this is not permitted (Zayn-al-Dīn ʿĀmelī, VI, pp. 87-94; Hamilton, p. 116).

The formula for *k̲olʿ* is pronounced by the man, employing the word *k̲olʿ* (or its derivatives), while any formula can be used for *mobārāt* with the condition that it be followed by the formula for divorce. Although *k̲olʿ* and *mobārāt* are irrevocable, if the wife reclaims the compensation during her waiting period, then the husband must return it and the divorce turns into a revocable divorce; in this case he can return to her, though he is not under any obligation to do so (Ḥellī, II, pp. 69-73).

The waiting period (*ʿedda*). This is the period in which the woman waits after divorce in order to be sure that she is not pregnant (Koran 2:228), or it is the period during which the woman must refrain from remarrying after the death of her husband (2:234). There is no waiting period if the marriage was not consummated, the wife has not reached puberty, or she has reached menopause; otherwise she must wait three *qorʾ*s. The Jaʿfarite, Malekite, and Shafeʿite schools take *qorʾ* to mean *ṭohr*. The Hanafites and Hanbalites understand it to mean menstrual period. If the wife is of a menstruating age but does not menstruate for some reason, the waiting period is three months. The waiting period of a pregnant woman lasts until she gives birth or miscarries the child (Zayn-al-Dīn ʿĀmelī, VI, pp. 57-72; Jazīrī, IV, pp. 540-48).

During the waiting period of revocable divorce, the husband is obliged to support his wife in the same manner as he did before the divorce. During this period it is prohibited to expel the wife from the house in which the divorce takes place (Koran 65:1). In case the divorce takes place in a house less suitable for living than the house in which the woman normally resides, she has the right to demand a better house from the man. During this period, the woman cannot leave the house except for necessities. During the waiting period for irrevocable divorce, the woman is not supported by the man unless she is pregnant, in which case he is obliged to support her until she gives birth (Koran 65:6).

Besides the above-mentioned cases, there are also religious (*šarʿī*) divorces issued by a judge in various circumstances, and annulment (*fask̲*). Grounds for annulment include physical or mental causes that make the continuation of marriage relationships difficult or impossible, such as insanity, emasculation, and impotence for men and insanity, leprosy, a blocked vagina, and blindness for women. A spouse with grounds for annulment refers to a religious judge, who issues a formal statement. If the husband makes an oath not to have coitus with his wife (*īlāʾ*; Koran 2:226), or says to his wife "You are to me as my mother's back" (*ẓehār*; Koran 58:2), or accuses his wife of infidelity or denies her parenthood of a child (*leʿān*), either divorce or annulment takes place, unless he breaks his oath and pays expiation (*kaffāra*) for breaking it, or he repents of the accusation and receives the punishment of eighty lashes for false accusation (Ḥellī, II, pp. 74-91; Zayn-al-Dīn ʿĀmelī, VI, pp. 117-218; Murata, pp. 33-37).

Bibliography: Šahīd T̲ānī Zayn-al-Dīn b. ʿAlī ʿĀmelī, *al-Rawża al-bahīya fi šarḥ al-Lomʿa al-demašqīya*, ed. S. M. Kalāntar, 10 vols., Najaf, 1390/1970, VI, pp. 1-114. B. Abu'l-ʿAynayn Badrān, *al-Zawāj wa'l-ṭalāq fe'l-Eslām*, Alexandria, 1970, pp. 342-412. C. Hamilton, *The Hedaya. A Commentary on the Mussulman Laws*, Lahore, 1963. ʿAbd-al-Raḥmān Jazīrī, *Ketāb al-feqh ʿalā madāheb al-arbaʿa*, Cairo, 1969, IV, pp. 278-552. Moḥammad b. Ḥasan Ḥorr ʿĀmelī, *Wasāʾel al-Šīʿa*, ed. ʿA.-R. Rabbānī Šīrāzī, 20 vols., Tehran, 1383/1963, XV, pp. 266-505. Moḥaqqeq Ḥellī, *Šarāʾeʿ al-Eslām fī masāʾel al-ḥalāl wa'l-ḥarām*, 2 vols., Beirut, 1930, II, pp. 53-73. S. Murata, *Temporary Marriage (Mutʿa) in Islamic Law*, London, 1987, pp. 18-26. A. M. Šāfeʿī, *al-Ṭalāq wa ḥoqūq al-awlād wa'l-aqāreb*, Beirut, 1986. J. Schacht, "Ṭalāḵ," in *EI*[1] IV, pp. 636-40. Shaikh Abū Jaʿfar Moḥammad Ṭūsī, *Masāʾel al-ḵelāfā*, Tehran, 1377/1958, pp. 213-51. M. T. Zāyed, *Dīwān al-ṭalāq*, Cairo, 1980.

(Sachiko Murata)

iv. In Modern Persia

Twelver Shiʿite laws of marriage and divorce, legitimacy, and custody of children (see iii above) were incorporated in the Civil code (Qānūn-e madanī) that was enacted and revised in the 1930s. The registration of marriages and divorces in the state registries (Dafāter-e rasmī-e ṯabt-e ezdewāj wa ṭalāq) became compulsory by the Marriage Act of 1931 (Article 1041). The important statute of reform pertaining to women and the family affairs, including divorce, was the Family protection law (Qānūn-e ḥemāyat-e ḵānevāda) of 1346 Š./1967. This law contained 23 articles and, though it did not concentrate exclusively on divorce, its most significant reforms pertained to the curtailment of men's unilateral prerogatives regarding divorce and polygamy. According to Article 8, the husband could not divorce his wife without first applying to the court for a certificate of non-reconciliation. The court in turn was required to do all that was within its jurisdiction to bring about a reconciliation between the two parties. If the court failed in its efforts for reconciliation, then it would issue a certificate of non-reconciliation. Without such a certificate the divorce registration offices could not lawfully revoke the marriage. The law was enforced despite opposition from the conservative elements, particularly the religious leaders and the *bāzārī*s (Abrahamian, pp.450-73).

The law was abolished after the establishment of the Islamic Republic in 1979. However, a modified verion of its provisions on divorce was adopted on 1 Mehr 1358 Š./23 September 1979 by the law of Special civil court (Dādgāh-e madanī-e ḵāṣṣ); the courts were established in November. Only after the judge has been unsuccessful in bringing about a reconciliation would the court schedule to hear the case and make a decision concerning the divorce. It has been claimed that some 65 percent of cases brought to the court are reconciled. However, this law allows those couples who have mutually consented to divorce to go to an Office of marriage and divorce registration (Dartar-e rasmī-e ezdewāj o ṭalāq) and register their divorce before two witnesses. It is the number of these divorces, cases not brought to the court, that have been increasing (Faʿʿālīyat, p. 2).

Table 33
CRUDE DIVORCE RATE IN PERSIA: 1954-1986

	Year	Divorce per thousand
Before family protection law:	1954-59	182
	1960-65	na
During family protection law:	1967-76	100
	1977-78	88
During post-revoltionary period:	1979-80	71
	1981-82	84
	1983-84	90
	1985-86	100
	1987-88	96
	1989-90	83
	1991-92	88

Source: for 1954-65, Vatandust, p. 122; for 1966-86, *Sāl-nāma-āmārī-e kešvar*, various issues. Rates are spread as number as number of divorce per 1000 mariages in the period.

Offices of marriage and divorce registration are required by law to send a monthly report to the Bureau of the civil registration of the Ministry of interior (Sāzmān-e ṯabt-e aḥwāl-e kešvar) and to the Statistical bureua of the ministry of justice (Edāra-ye āmār-e qażāʾī). In the last two decades these data have been published in statistical yearbooks (*Sāl-nāma-ye āmārī-e kešvar*). Table 33 shows the trend in divorce rate since 1954.

Three different patterns are rcognized: 1. the period before the 1967 Family protection law with a relatively high divorce rate; 2. the period of declining divorce rate between 1967-77; and 3. a period of rising divorce rate in the 1980s. The declining trend in the second period could be due to the Family protection law, which was a significant obstacle toward unilateral, easy divorce. The tedious legal proceedings required excessive time and caused embarrassment. Furthermore, the requirement to produce evidence to justify a divorce tended to change the inclinations of husbands. Both the numerical level and divorce rate have been rising in Persia since 1981. The main reason for this trend has been the ease of obtaining a divorce without going to court. But there have been other contributing factors as well. Right after the 1978-79 Revolution there was strong encouragement for marriage and having children. Many young men and women, mostly ill-prepared to assume family responsibilities, rushed into marriage and soon began their own families. But economic hardships in the following years (increasing unemployment, rising costs of living, and black-market prices as the war with Iraq continued) made daily life more conducive to divorce. Furthermore, there has been an increasing number of remarriages of war widows, some into polygamous marriages. Such marriages may have been more vulnerable to divorce. In 1976 there were 11 men with more than one wife per 1,000 married men. This ratio rose to 24 per 1,000 in 1986 (Aghajanian, 1990a).

The eight years of war with Iraq disrupted the social and economic structure of Persian society and disturbed the daily life of families and individuals, especially refugee families from southern and southwestern areas. Many of these families lost their homes, jobs, and for years lived in temporary camps. Adjustment to this new life also contributed to family quarrels and breakups (Aghajanian, 1990b). Currently the divorce rate in Persia is about 88 per 1,000 marriages. In an effort to reduce the rate of divorce, a law was enacted in 1994 to improve the legal status of divorced women. Under this law, if the special civil court determines that a man is divorcing his wife without any acceptable reason, the wife receives half of the joint property (Yazdī).

No national study has been conducted on the differentials in family instability in modern Persia. Some tentative conclusion can, however, be drawn about the situation in the 1970s, based on local and provincial studies (Aghajanian, 1986). Age at first marriage seems to be a major difference between women who were divorced and those who were not; those who were older were more likely to be divorced subsequently. More than 50 percent of family breakups occurred before children were born. The absence of children evidently made decisions about divorce easier. As in other modern industrial societies, the wife's employment is associated with a higher probability of divorce in Persia.

Bibliography: M. Abd al-ʿAti, *The Family Structure in Islam*, New York, 1977. E. Abrahamian, *Iran between Two Revolutions*, Princeton, N.J., 1982. A. Aghajanian, "Some Notes on Divorce in Iran," *Journal of Marriage and the Family* 48, 1986, pp. 749-55. Idem, "The Changing Status of Women in Iran. 1966-86," paper presented at the American Sociological Society, Washington, D.C., August 11-15, 1990a. Idem, "War and Migrant Families in Iran. An Overview of Social Disaster," *International Journal of Sociology of the Family* 20, 1990b, pp. 97-107. F. R. C. Bagley, "The Iranian Family Protection Law of 1967. A Milestone in the Advance of Women's Rights," in C. E. Bosworth, ed, *Iran and Islam*, Edinburgh, 1971, pp. 47-64. "Faʿʿālīyat-e dādgāhhā-ye madanī-e ḵāṣṣ," *Keyhān* 11795, Bahman 1361 Š./February 1982, pp. 1-2. P. Higgins, "Women in the Islamic Republic of Iran. Legal, Social, and Ideological Changes," *Journal of Women in Culture and Society* 1/3, 1985, pp. 477-94. Sāzmān-e zanān-e Īrān, *Barrasī-e āmārī-e ezdewāj wa ṭalāq*, Tehran, 1978. G. R. Vatandoust, "The Status of Iranian Women during the Pahlavi Regime," in A. Fathi, ed., *Women and the Family in Iran*, Leiden, 1985, pp. 107-30. J. R. Weeks, *Population*, Belmont, Calif., 1994, pp. 270-73. M. Yazdī, "Qawānīn-e ṭalāq be nafʿ-e zanān taġyīr mīkonad," *Iran Times* 1202, December 1994, p. 99.

(AKBAR AGHAJANIAN)

v. DIVORCE AMONG MODERN ZOROASTRIANS

The approach to divorce in the Zoroastrian community seems to have changed considerably in the period following the Arab conquest. The early 9th-century *Rivāyat of Āturfarnbag and Farnbag-Srōš* mentioned divorce in the example of a man whose wife was "bad" and "insubordinate" (*aburd-framān*) and who slept with non-Iranians while her husband was away from home (chap. 29). In such an instance the legitimate (*pādixšāy*) marriage was dissoluble, provided the wife had consented. But the husband could choose to keep his wife with the intention of improving her, because by "doing so he reinforces the truth and goodness of the true faith in this world" (Hjerrild, p. 69). This attitude toward divorce was reinforced in the later *Riwāyat ī Ēmēd ī Ašawahištān*, where the husband was allowed to divorce his legitimate wife only with her consent, unless misdemeanors had been discovered (see DIVORCE ii). Zoroastrian divorce laws, however, were "subject to alteration and modification that reflect different exigencies at different times" (Hjerrild, p. 71).

In the later *Rivāyats of Hormazyār Frāmarz* (tr. Dhabhar) the matter of divorce was again raised, following a detailed discussion regarding the age of marriage, the negotiating of marriage contracts, the five kinds of marriage, the marriage ceremony, and the division of the patrimony. A lay person (*behdīn*) was allowed to take a second wife only if the first wife could not bear children, but he wis not allowed to divorce the latter; nor was male impotence grounds for divorce (*Persian Rivayats*, tr. Dhabhar, p. 204). According to these *Rivāyats*, if an adulteress was repentant, then she was still to be regarded as the wife if authority in the land was not in the hands of Zoroastrians. If Zoroastrians were in power and a man caught his wife in adultery or heard of it from another source, then she was to be put to death (p. 204). It seemed to be recognized in these *Rivāyats* that the only Zoroastrian grounds for divorce in a time of Muslim rule were apostasy and adultery. The divorced woman was allowed to remarry with her husband's consent.

In the modern period, in both Persia and India, the attitude toward divorce remains one of reluctance. Although marriage is regarded not as a sacrament but rather as a contract, the sanctity of married life is considered very important, and any violation of it is frowned upon by many. Some members of the community would attribute the low rate of divorce to the predominance of arranged marriages and the belief that such a marriage is an eternal bond. Until recently it was common for young widows never to remarry. M. M. Fischer (1978, p. 213) maintains that divorce is a 20th-century innovation among Zoroastrians in Persia and reports that today Zoroastrians are under a uniform legal code, the *Āyīn-nāma-ye Zartoštīān*, which was adopted by the community around 1334 Š./1935 and which approximates Muslim codes. This innovation followed the introduction in 1312 Š./1933 of a Persian law that permitted minority religious groups to have personal lawsuits adjudicated according to their own customs (Fischer, 1973, p. 196).

The Persian Zoroastrian community has an established council of *mobeds* (priests), one of whose functions is to preside over and decide upon divorce suits. Couples seeking divorce must first file a suit with the Family protection court (Dādgāh-e ḥemāyat-e ḵānavāda), which then refers it to the council. The verdict of the council is communicated to the court, which issues the final decree, including decisions regarding alimony and the custody, education, and maintenance of children (Irani, p. 26). The divorce then must be registered at the Bureau of statistics and registration of status (Edāra-ye āmār wa ṯabt-e aḥwāl).

When more educated Persians began to accept divorce more readily, a problem arose for divorced Zoroastrian women, who often received little or no financial support from their ex-husbands. They were expected to live on their *mahrīyas* (bridal money payable on demand, especially in the instance of divorce), despite the fact that the formal *mahr*, as specified in the *Rivāyats*, is no longer contracted. The emphasis in a modern divorce is on the groom's paying the bride at a rate fixed at half the male portion of patrimony (similar to the inheritance), rather than according to the actual ratio of the value contributed by her family. Fischer (1978, p. 201) maintains that the pattern of marriage exchanges in Persia is similar for Muslims, Zoroastrians, and Jews and apparently originated in quite ancient times in Mesopotamia).

With the influence of the British legislative system on Indian social structures, the Parsis had to contend with the introduction of legislation on marriage and divorce from the mid-19th century onward. There have been several Parsi Marriage and Divorce Acts since the mid-19th century, the most recent being that of 1936, which was amended by the Parsi Marriage and Divorce (amendment) Act of 1988. The first Parsi Marriage and Divorce Act was passed in 1865 and resulted from a legal suit ten years earlier filed by a Parsi woman for maintenance and restoration of conjugal rights, which had been ruled out of the jurisdiction of the Supreme Court on its ecclesiastical side (Fischer, 1973, p. 91). This and other such demands on the British legal system operating in India led to the formation of a commission of inquiry and the Act of 1865.

Following the 1936 Act and its amendment in 1988, no Parsi is able to contract any marriage under this act or any other law in the lifetime of his or her spouse, whether a Parsi or not, except after lawful divorce or the declaration of the marriage as null and void or dissolved. The copy of the decree for divorce, nullity, or dissolution is sent to the local registrar general of births, deaths, and marriages. Since 1865 special Parsi chief matrimonial courts, consisting of Parsi delegates, have been designated to hear suits under the act in Calcutta, Madras, Bombay, and some other towns (Karaka, II, app. B, pp. 303-04).

At present the grounds for divorce by any married Zoroastrian include willful refusal to consummate the marriage within a year after its solemnization; continuing mental disorder since the time of the marriage (provided that the plaintiff was unaware of it at the time of the marriage) or for at least two years immediately preceding the suit; the defendant's pregnancy by a third party at the time of the marriage, provided that no marital intercourse has taken place since the plaintiff learned about it; adultery, bigamy, or rape after marriage; cruelty toward the spouse; infecting the spouse with venereal disease; the husband's forcing his wife into prostitution; completion by the defendant of a year or more of at least a seven-year jail sentence; desertion for at least two years; award to the plaintiff of separate maintenance by the magistrate, followed by abstention from marital intercourse for at least two years; and apostasy.

Bibliography: (For cited works not found in this bibliography, see "Short References.") B. Hjerrild, "Zoroastrian Divorce," in *A Green Leaf. Papers in Honour of Prof. Jes P. Asmussen*, Acta Iranica 28, Leiden, 1988, pp. 63-71. G. Irani, "Our Faith Is One," *Parsiana* 12/7, January 1990. D. F. Karaka, *History of the Parsis. Including Their Manners, Customs, Religion and Present Position*, 2 vols., London, 1884. M. M. Fischer, *Zoroastrianism in Iran. Praxis and Myth*, Chicago, 1973. Idem, "On Changing the Concept and Position of Persian Women," in L. Beck and N. Keddie, eds., *Women in the Muslim World*, Cambridge, Mass., 1978, pp. 189-215. J. J. Modi, *The Religious Customs and Ceremonies of the Parsees*, Bombay, 1986. *The Pahlavi Rivāyat of Āturfarnbag and Farnbag-Srōš*, ed. and tr. B. T. Anklesaria, 2 vols., Bombay, 1969.

(JENNY ROSE)

vi. AMONG BABIS AND BAHAIS

The law of divorce given by the Bāb (q.v.) in the Persian *Bayān* (q.v.; *wāḥed* 6, chap. 12) discourages divorce and makes it permissible only under pressing circumstances (*eżṭerār*). Even then it is necessary to wait for one whole year, called the "year of patience, or waiting" (*sāl-e tarabbos*). If during that time affection returns between the couple then the divorce is annulled. At the end of that time, however, the divorce is final. If subsequently the couple wish to remarry, they may do so provided that nineteen days have passed.

Bahāʾ-Allāh (q. v.) also commended marriage and discouraged divorce (*Divorce*, p. 5). In the *Ketāb-e aqdas* (pars. 67-70) he confirmed the Bāb's provision concerning a year's period of waiting before divorce can be effected. He provided for remarriage to the same person and rejected the principle of simply reciting the divorce divorce formula three times, which is accepted in Islam. He defined desertion and provided for remarriage in such cases. If estrangement occurs between the husband and wife during a journey, the husband is responsible for ensuring the safe return of his wife to their home and for providing her with expenses for a year. In instances of the wife's proven infidelity, however, no maintenance is payable.

Most of the writings of ʿAbd-al-Bahāʾ and Shoghi Effendi on this subject are taken up with strong condemnations of divorce. In their role of authorized interpreters of the Bahai teachings, however, they amplified Bahāʾ-Allāh's rulings, declaring that the woman has an equal right to initiate divorce; clarifying that during the year of patience the couple are not to live together; and by establishing that the husband is normally responsible for the wife's maintenance during that year.

The procedure for divorce is carried out in the Bahai community under the supervision of the local spiritual assembly (*maḥfel-e rūḥānī*; in some areas of the world, the procedure is still supervised by a committee of the National spiritual assembly). It is the duty of this institution to establish that antipathy and aversion exist between the two parties; they are the only recognized grounds for separation. A date may then be set for the year of patience. The couple must live separately during the year of patience, and no sexual intercourse may occur. During this period attempts are made under the supervision of the spiritual assembly to effect a reconciliation, and neither party is permitted to seek a new partner. The assembly also tries to establish an agreement between the couple regarding the financial arrangements and access to the children. The norm is for the husband to support his wife and children during the year unless there is mutual agreement to a different arrangement (e.g., if the woman has been the main provider of income for the household). The husband also normally remains responsible for his children's upkeep after the divorce. If there is a reconciliation during the year of patience then the procedure for divorce is abandoned.

If no reconciliation has been effected by the end of the year, then the assembly may pronounce the divorce final and will attempt to obtain mutual agreement between the couple in matters of finance and access to the children. The couple must also obtain the civil divorce of the country in which they live and abide by any decisions on finances and access to children made by the civil court. Bahai divorce is not considered complete until a civil divorce has also been granted. Remarriage to the same or a different partner may occur anytime thereafter.

Bibliography: Bahāʾ-Allāh, *The Kitāb-i Aqdas. The Most holy Book*, Haifa, 1992. *Divorce* (no. 18 in a series of compilations issued by the Universal House of Justice, Oakham, U.K., 1986. A. Ešrāq Ḵāvarī, *Ganjīna-ye ḥodūd wa aḥkām*, Tehran, 128 Badīʿ/1971, pp. 276-91. *Ketāb-e aqdas*, in A. Tumanski, *Kitabe Akdes*, Mémoires de l'Académie Impériale des Sciences de St. Petersbourg, 8th ser., 3/6, St. Petersburg, 1899. *Ketāb-e mostaṭāb-e bayān*, n.p., n.d. Fāżel Māzandarānī, *Amr wa ḵalq* IV, Langenheim, Germany, 1986, pp. 183-96.

(MOOJAN MOMEN)

DIZK. See JIZAK.

DJEITUN WARE. See CERAMICS i.

DO-BARĀDARĀN. See HAFT-OWRANG; NOJŪM.

DO-BAYTĪ, a quatrain of sung poetry in many Persian dialects. In popular speech and publications the quatrains are commonly described as *tarānahā-ye maḥallī/rūstāʾī* (regional/rural songs). Many of the verses, however, are widely diffused in Persia, in part through inexpensive printed collections. Regional differences are perhaps most pronounced in the melodies to which the quatrains are sung.

Each hemistich of a *do-baytī* normally has eleven syllables, although singers sometimes add or subtract one or two syllables. The melodies used for singing the *do-baytī* accommodate twenty-two syllables, and the final note of the melody is usually lower in pitch than the note to which the eleventh syllable is sung. For the second half of one *do-baytī*, singers repeat the same melody with slight variations. The rhyme scheme is aaba.

In performance (at weddings, circumcisions, or intimate gatherings of family and friends) singers group together several quatrains in a freely chosen order, perhaps inserting a conventional refrain of fifteen to twenty-two syllables between each quatrain. The singer may be accompanied by an instrumentalist playing the *ney* (end-blown flute), the *kamānča* (spike fiddle), or one of several plucked lutes (*dotār*, *dambūra*, etc.), but most singers perform *do-baytī* without accompaniment. Many, but not all, of the metric patterns used by singers and instrumentalists are variants of the *hazaj* meter associated with the literary *do-baytī* (see ʿARUŻ)

Among the topics most commonly treated in the *do-baytī* are traveling, loneliness, rejection, discomfort, and other misfortunes. Quatrains on these topics are termed *ḡarībī* or *qarāʾī* (in eastern Persia) and *felak* (among the mountain Tajiks of Afghanistan), as well as *čahār-baytī*. The third line of a quatrain usually modifies, qualifies, or intensifies the preceding thought, as in the following examples: *Hawā garma vo sar-sāya neyāya / Ṣedā-ye kelkel-e pāya mīāya / Ṣedā-ye kelkel-e pāya ne čandān / Ṣedā-ye kafš-e jānāna mīāya* (The air is hot; no shadow falls. / The clatter of footsteps is heard. / It is less than the clatter of footsteps. / It is the sound of my loved one's slippers). *Ḥoseynā mīravī rā-ye to dūray / Ḥoseynā sūḵta-ye bād-e samūray / Del-e to meyl-e nān-e garma dāray / Bar ū sabze-y ke dar pāy-a tanūr-ay* (Ḥoseynā, you are going; your path is a long one. / Ḥoseynā has been scorched by the simoon. / Your heart is desirous of warm bread. / Upon it the greens lying beside the oven).

See also FAHLAVĪYĀT; ROBĀʿĪ.

Bibliography: A. ʿAbd-Allāhī, *Hezār tarāna az tarānahā-ye rūstāʾī wa maḥallī-e Īrān*, Tehran, 1346 Š./1967. J. ʿAnāṣerī, "Tarānahā-ī az . . . īlāt wa ʿašāyer-e Sangesarī," *Nāma-ye nūr* 7-8, 1358 Š./1980, pp. 104-22. "Baythā-ye Boir Aḥmadī," *Nāma-ye nūr* 10/11, 1359 Š./1981, pp. 146-72. S. Blum, "Persian Folksong in Meshhed (Iran), 1969," *Yearbook of the International Folk Music Council* 6, 1974, pp. 86-114. Ḥ. Deljū and ʿA. Ārām, *Hezār tarāna be-lahja-ye rūstāʾī*, Tehran, 1346 Š./1967. A. Faqīrī, "Tarānahā-ye ʿāmīāna-ye Šīrāz," *Honar o mardom* 119-20, 1351 Š./1972, pp. 64-68. Idem, "Tarānahā-ye maḥallī-e Šīrāz," *Payām-e novīn* 1352 Š./1973, 10/4, pp. 26-28; 10/5, pp. 62-63; 10/6, pp. 40-41. R. Gerīgorīān, *Tarānahā-ye rūstāʾī-e Īrān*, Tehran, 1327 Š./1948. Ṣ Homāyūnī, *Tarānahā-ī az janūb*, Tehran, 1346 Š./1967. Idem, *Yak-hezār o čahār-ṣad tarāna-ye maḥallī*, Shiraz, 1348 Š./1969. Idem, "Dīgar wīžagīhā-ye tarānahā-ye maḥallī," *Kāva* 13/3, 1354 Š./1976, pp. 60-64; 13/4, pp. 45-51. W. Ivanow, "Rustic Poetry in the Dialect of Khorasan," *J(R)ASB*, N.S. 21, 1925, pp. 233-313. Ḥ. Kūhī Kermānī, *Haft-ṣad tarāna az tarānahā-ye rūstāʾī-e Īrān*, Tehran, 1345 Š./1966. M.-T. Moqtaderī, "Čahār-baytīhā-ye afḡānī," *Aryānā* 12, 1333 Š./1954, pp. 30-33. J. Ṣadāqat-nežād, *930 Tarāna az tarānahā-ye rūstāʾī wa maḥallī-e Īrān*, Tehran, 1346 Š./1967. E. Šakūrzāda, *Tarānahā-ye rūstāʾī-e Ḵorāsān*, Tehran, 1338 Š./1959. M. Ṣeddīq, "Tarānahā-ye ʿāmīāna dar Kohgīlūya wa Boir Aḥmad," *Honar o mardom* 81, 1356 Š./1977, pp. 70-77. M. Slobin, "Persian Folksong Texts from Afghan Badakhshan," *Iranian Studies* 3/2, 1970, pp. 91-103. A. Šoʿūr, "Do-baytīhā," *Folklor*, 1352 Š./1973, 1, pp. 81-94; 2-3, pp. 94-100; 4-5, pp. 45-52. J. W. Weryho, "Sīstānī-Persian Folklore," *IIJ* 5, 1962, pp. 276-307. V. A. Zhukovskiĭ, *Materialy dlya izucheniya persidskikh narechiĭ* (Materials for the study of Persian dialects), St. Petersburg, 1888-1922.

(STEPHEN BLUM)

DO-PAYKAR. See NOJŪM.

DOʿĀ, the act of offering supplicatory or petitionary prayer, a principal manifestation of Muslim piety. *Doʿā*, with the literal meaning "calling" or "summoning," frequently signifies worship as such in the Koran (e.g., 6:56, 17:110, 52:19), but the technical definition of *doʿā* as a distinct practice is "seeking the occurrence or nonoccurrence of a thing with a wording that combines the praise and exaltation of God with the confession of one's own weakness and helplessness" (Tahānawī, I, pp. 503-04). Sufis, however, speak of *doʿāʾ al-ḥāl*, the nonverbal, implicit prayer that a given condition of neediness may silently express, and even praise it as the form of *doʿā* most likely to elicit a positive response (Qošayrī, *Resāla*, p. 526, tr., p. 276; Ebn ʿArabī, III, p. 208).

Several verses of the Koran encourage the believer to engage in *doʿā*, e.g., "When My servants ask you concerning Me, (say) I am indeed close, responding to the prayer of the suppliant when he calls on Me, so let them respond to Me and believe in Me in order to be guided" (2:186). Commenting on this verse, Qošayrī remarked that God's promise to answer prayers comes before the injunction to supplicate, so that here divine generosity (*takrīm*) precedes the imposition of a duty (*taklīf*; 1390/1971, I, pp. 156-57; echoed in Meybodī, I, p. 502). The Koran (40:60) also guarantees the divine answering of prayer: "Call on Me and I will respond to you; those who do not worship Me shall enter Hell in humiliation." Qošayrī suggested that by equating *doʿā* with worship and condemning as arrogant those who disdain it this verse effectively makes of *doʿā* a duty for the believer (Qošayrī, 1390/1971, II, p. 313).

In principle the petitioner may formulate his own *doʿā*, in any language of his choosing, but prayers in Arabic and hallowed by tradition are generally preferred as a matter of practice. The numerous formulas of *doʿā* that the Koran itself contains are those most favored for recitation because of the divine authority with which they are imbued. The entirety of the first sura (*Fāteḥa*) counts as a *doʿā*, and it is frequently recited as such in order to ensure a favorable outcome for a wide variety of undertakings. Individual verses containing or consisting of supplicatory prayers are 2:286, 3:8, 3:16, 3:147, 3:191-94, 17:24, 17:80, and 23:118. In addition, the Koran ascribes a whole series of supplicatory prayers to the prophets: Noah (23:26, 23:29, 26:117-18, 51:26-28), Abraham (2:126-29, 15:35-41, 26:83-89, 37:99), Moses (7:151, 20:25-35, 28:16, 28:21), Solomon (38:35), Joseph (12:101), Lot (26:169, 29:30), and Zacharia (3:38, 19:5-6, 21:89). The prophet Moḥammad is instructed in his turn to utter certain particular prayers (21:114, 21:112, 23:93-94). The Koran also depicts the angels who bear the divine throne as engaged in *doʿā* for the sake of the believers (42:5).

The importance of *doʿā* is confirmed by numerous traditions of the Prophet, as well as of the imams. After reciting Koran 40:60 the Prophet described *doʿā* as the kernel (*mok̲k̲*) of worship, a description indicating in the view of Qošayrī (1966, p. 526; tr., p. 275) that by making *doʿā* man acknowledges God as the sole source of help, this being the very essence of monotheism (*tawḥīd*). In another tradition the Prophet is reported to have said that any prayer not having a sin as its object or tending to the severance of kinship will yield one of three results: immediate fulfillment; a fulfillment postponed to the hereafter; or the averting from the petitioner of a significant evil of which he may be unaware (Meybodī, I, p. 499). Other traditions specify categories of petitioners whose prayers will be answered forthwith, namely the oppressed, the sick, just rulers, those who pray for the welfare of their brethren, those who invoke God's name abundantly, and fathers who pray for their sons. Another category of traditions relate to times and circumstances that are especially recommended for making *doʿā*, examples being the final hours of a night vigil, the breaking of the fast during Ramażān, and retreat or isolation, particularly at a distance from human habitation (Meybodī, I, pp. 501-02).

Although *doʿā* is distinct from the canonical prayer (*ṣalāt* or *namāz*), which is clearly obligatory in nature and has fixed times and forms, formulas of *doʿā* are in fact interwoven with every stage of the prayer, beginning with the *doʿā-ye eftetāḥ* (prayer of commencement) that is recited after the *takbīr* that inaugurates the prayer and ending with the *taʿqībāt* or *moʿaqqebāt-e namāz*, i.e., the lengthier and more varied formulas of supplication that follow its conclusion. In addition, a formula of *doʿā* known as *qonūt* is recited, while standing, by Sunnites in the last *rakʿa* of the supererogatory prayer called *wetr* that is performed after the evening prayer and by Shiʿites in the second *rakʿa* of every prayer (Sajjādī, III, pp. 1515-16). Likewise, there are traditional formulas of *doʿā*, most of them ascribed to the Prophet, for recitation in conjunction with other major devotional duties like fasting and pilgrimage, and still others (*aʿmāl al-yawm wa 'l-nahār*) that are prescribed for recitation at certain times of the day. A final category of traditional supplicatory prayers consists of those relating to everyday acts like sleeping, rising, eating, entering a house, departing on a journey, and going to a bathhouse. The most authoritative compendium of all these categories of *doʿā* is, for Sunnites, *al-Ad̲kār al-montak̲aba men kalām sayyed al-abrār* compiled by Abū D̲akarīyāʾ Nawawī (d. 676/1277-78); this work is almost completely unknown in Persia.

A special type of *doʿā* is that in which God is besought to visit misfortune on a given person or group, that is, an imprecation. Koran 4:148 ("God does not love that evil should be uttered in clear speech, except by one who has been wronged; certainly God hears and knows all things") is sometimes seen as justifying this kind of *doʿā*, but, as the Prophet engaged in it but rarely, preferring to pray for the guidance of his enemies, its practice is generally discouraged, particularly with regard to one's personal adversaries (Çağırcı, pp. 297-98).

Sufis have paid particular attention to the theory and practice of *doʿā*. Although Koran 2:186 ("responding to the prayer of the suppliant when he calls Me") might be taken to suggest unconditional divine willingness to answer supplicatory prayer (Qošayrī, 1390/1971, I, p. 155), several Sufi authors have laid down *ādāb* (norms or conditions) that ought to govern the making of *doʿā*. Anṣārī listed five conditions: contrition (*del-šekastagī*); uttering the prayer softly and in privacy (cf. Koran 7:55: "Call on your Lord with humility and hiddenness"); preceding the *doʿā* with an act of worship or charity; persistence (in accordance with the Hadith "God loves those who are insistant in supplication"); and making the content of one's request general, rather than specific, in nature (Meybodī, I, p. 500). Ḡazālī (I, pp. 268-72) stipulated ten: the choice of a blessed day and time; the attainment of a proper inward state; orientation to the *qebla*; uttering the *doʿā* softly; the avoidance of rhyming phrases (in order, presumably, to prevent the degeneration of *doʿā* into a kind of literary exercise); complete humility; uttering the prayer three times (cf. the Hadith "Whenever the servant says, 'O my Lord!' three times, God Almighty will respond, "Here I am, o servant of Mine!'" cited in Meybodī, I, p. 500); beginning the prayer with a mention of divine attributes instead of proceeding forthwith to the presentation of one's request; and cultivating a state of regret and repentance for one's sins. To these varied injunctions may be added the external detail that, while *doʿā* is being made, the hands are held apart, on a level with the breast, with the palms facing upward, except in the case of the prayer for rain (*doʿā-ye estesqā*), when they face downward.

As the devotional life of the Sufis was elaborated into a complex and codified system, formulas of *doʿā* were stipulated for recitation on such occasions as the initiation of novices, the donning of ritual garments (especially the turban), the performance of *d̲ekr* (q.v.), the consumption of communal meals, and entering or leaving retreat (e.g., Sohravardī, pp. 93, 97, 129; Bāk̲arzī, passim). Certain prominent Sufis, especially the eponyms of the Sufi orders, also composed a special type of *doʿā* known as *awrād*, prescribed for daily recitation, generally after the dawn prayers, by members of the orders. *Awrād* are pastiches of koranic verses, traditional prayers, and sentences composed by the Sufi masters themselves. The best-known example of *awrād* from the Persian-speaking and Persian-influenced world are the *Awrād-e bahāʾīya*, attributed to K̲ᵛāja Bahāʾ-al-Dīn Naqšband (d. 791/1389) and the *Awrād-e fatḥīya* attributed to the Kobrawī saint ʿAlī Hamādānī (d.

786/1384), which have been widely recited beyond the confines of the Kobrawī order (Komoškānavī, I, pp. 16-25). In addition, the Sufi practice of invoking the mediatory powers of the saints (*tawassol*) led to the composition of versified formulas of *doʿā* in which all the names comprising an initiating chain would be enumerated (e.g., Fārūqī, pp. 479-80).

Perhaps the most distinctive Sufi contribution to the literature of *doʿā* consists of intimate supplications (*monājāt*), which were composed for the most part in Persian. Defined by Abū Naṣr Sarrāj (p. 349) as the "addressing of secrets to God, the Almighty Sovereign, in a state of pure recollection," *monājāt* differ from other forms of *doʿā* in their complete eschewal of worldly concerns and its frequent recourse to what might be termed the ecstatic impudence sometimes displayed by even the soberest of Sufis. The earliest Persian *monājāt* are probably those ascribed to Abu'l-Ḥasan Ḵaraqānī (q.v., d. 425/1033; Mīnovī, pp. 53, 61-64, 93, 96, 118-19, 147-48). This genre of devotional literature is, however, more commonly associated with his younger contemporary, ʿAbd-Allāh Anṣārī (q.v.); indeed, so closely linked to the name of Anṣārī is the whole category of *monājāt* that compositions of diverse and frequently unknown authorship have been unquestioningly assigned to him (e.g., the collection published with Engish translation by Morris and Sarfeh). The authentic *monājat* of Anṣārī are scattered in his *Rasāʾel* and *Ṭabaqāt al-ṣūfīya*, as well as in Meybodī's *Kašf al-asrār*. They have been assembled from these works by Moḥammad Fekrat. Several hundred of Rūmī's quatrains have *monājāt* as their themes (quatrains 65-69, 93, 150, 153, 170, 216), as do many of the somewhat more stylized quatrains of ʿAbd-al-Raḥmān Jāmī.

Despite all the foregoing, *doʿā* appeared problematic to many Sufis because of its connotations of concern for the self and the tension or even contradiction that they perceived between it and the virtues of *reżā* (satisfaction with divine decree), *taslīm* (surrender), and *tafwīż* (assignation of one's affairs to God). Thus Qošayrī pointed out that, although *doʿā* is desirable because it is an act of worship, the silent endurance of need is also meritorious because of the acceptance of God's will that it implies. He attempted to resolve the problem by suggesting that *doʿā* with the tongue be combined with silence in the heart; that one pray for one's fellow Muslims and not for oneself; and that one engage in *doʿā* only if it results in *basṭ* (spiritual expansion). He also maintained that in any event *doʿā* takes on different forms with different classes of men: words with the commonalty, deeds with the ascetics, and inner states with the gnostics (1966, pp. 526-29; tr., pp. 276-78). When asked what might motivate the people of *taslīm* and *tafwīż* to engage in *doʿā* a sheikh replied: "They make *doʿā* either to increase the adornment of their limbs, *doʿā* being a form of service, or in order to obey God's command to engage in it" (Sarrāj, pp. 262-63); in other words, their *doʿā* is free of all egoistic desire. A related dilemma was posed by Yaḥyā b. Moʿāḏ: How could a man presume to beseech God, given his sinfulness, and how could he refrain from doing so, given God's generosity? The view of ʿAbd-Allāh b. Monāzel was, by contrast, categorical: "I have not made a prayer in fifty years, nor do I wish another to make a prayer for my sake" (Qošayrī, 1966, p. 532; tr., p. 280).

As most formulas of *doʿā* include the mention of at least one divine name, the selection being determined by the nature of the petitioner's request, *doʿā* clearly overlaps with *ḏekr*, the invocation of God's names; it is not accidental that Hadith relating to *ḏekr* and *doʿā* are often grouped together in a single chapter in some collections of traditions, like the *Ṣaḥīḥ* of Moslem. Nonetheless, the two practices are conceptually distinct, and Sufis sought accordingly to establish which of the two is more meritorious. *Ḏekr* was generally favored over *doʿā*, not least because of this *ḥādīṯ qodsī*: "I give more to the one who is so occupied with invocation/remembrance of Me that he does not ask things of Me than I give to the suppliants" (Qošayrī, 1966, p. 526; Ḡazālī, 1361 Š./1982, I, p. 253).

Sufis also addressed themselves to the problem of prayers remaining unanswered. Popular among them was a Hadith to the effect that God delays fulfilling the request of those He most loves because of His delight in hearing them address Him repeatedely; less favored petitioners have their prayers answered without delay (Meybodī, I, p. 501). Attention was drawn to the concluding words of the Koran, 2:186 ("in order to be guided"), which suggest that the true purpose of *doʿā* is the attainment of guidance, not of the object sought in prayer, and to a Hadith that promises the opening of the gates of God's mercy in exchange for the regular practice of *doʿā* (Qošayrī, 1390/1971, I, p. 157). The most subtle and imaginative answer was, however, that intimated by Ḥosayn b. Manṣūr Ḥallāj (244-309/857-922) and propounded repeatedly by Rūmī: that, as God makes it possible for man to engage in *doʿā*—indeed even invites him to do so—every *doʿā* contains its response within itself or is even identical with that response (bk. 1 l. 1578, bk. 2 l.691, bk. 3 l. 195, bk. 4 l. 3993, bk. 5, l. 4162).

Shiʿite piety is also extremely rich in supplicatory prayers, including many believed to have been composed by the imams themselves; it can even be said that these prayers constitute, for the mass of the believers, both the chief textual legacy of the imams and the principal means by which they commune with them. Of the prayers attributed to ʿAlī b. Abī Ṭāleb (q.v.) the most frequently recited is the *doʿā-ye Komayl*, so called because ʿAlī taught it, on the authority of Ḵeżr, to a companion named Komayl b. Zīād Nakaʿī; its recitation on Thursday nights (i.e., during the early hours of Friday, according to the traditional method of reckoning time) is strongly recommended. Varyingly attributed to the Prophet himself and to ʿAlī b. Abī Ṭāleb are two formulas of *doʿā* to be recited for protection in battle, the *jawšan-e kabīr* (the great cuirass) and the *jawšan-e ṣaḡīr* (the small cuirass); these prayers, the effectiveness of which is said to extend to other situations of danger, are often found in Sunnite and Shiʿite manuals of *doʿā*. Much favored, too, is the prayer recited by Imam Ḥosayn on the day of ʿArafa, the eve of the Festival of Sacrifice that concludes the pilgrimage season. The *doʿā-ye semāt*, recited during the final hours of Friday, is attributed to the imams Moḥammad al-Bāqer and Jaʿfar al-Ṣādeq. Imam Mūsā al-Kāẓem maintained that *doʿā* might, under certain circumstances, avert the decree of fate and himself composed prayers of some sublimity. To his successor, Imam ʿAlī al-Reżā (q.v.), is owed the prayer commonly recited at dawn by Shiʿites throughout the month of Ramażān, the *doʿā-ye saḥar*. There is also a *doʿā* attributed to the Twelfth Imam, conveyed from him during his occultation. The *doʿā* recited on the fifteenth day of Šaʿbān is attributed collectively to all the imams.

It is, however, the fourth imam, ʿAlī al-Sajjād, who stands alone as the reputed author of a complete collection of supplicatory prayers, known after him as *al-Ṣaḥīfa al-sajjādīya*, a book of great beauty that is rich in metaphysical as well as spiritual content (for an analysis of the work as well as Shiʿite supplications in general, see Chittick, in ʿAl al-Sajjādī, pp. xv-xvi).

In addition to prayers attributed to the imams, there are others of unknown origin, prescribed for recitation on every day of religious significance, as well as for pilgrimages to the resting places of the imams, whether accomplished in both spirit and flesh or in the spirit alone. The definitive compendium of Shiʿite suppications, found in virtually every religious household in Persia, is the *Mafātīḥ al-jenān*, compiled by Sheikh ʿAbbās Qomī (d. 1359/1940).

In modern Persia the Shiʿite practice of *doʿā* came under ferocious attack from Aḥmad Kasrawī, who equated it—together with all the other principal manifestations of Shiʿism—with superstition and fatalism. A rationalist defense of *doʿā* was undertaken by Mahdī Bāzargān. It was above all Ayatollah Khomeini (Ayāt-Allāh Ḵomeynī) who defended the practice of *doʿā* from the strictly traditional point of view, first in *Kašf al-asrār* (pp. 30, 68-80) and later, after the triumph of the Revolution of 1357 Š./1978-79, in his televised lectures on *Sūrat al-Fāteḥa*, in which he described the books of prayer as means for "making true human beings out of men" 1368 Š./1989, pp. 77-82; tr. in Algar, pp. 400-03). Khomeini's emphatic interest in *doʿā* had, in fact, been plain from the very beginning of his scholarly career, one of his earliest writings being a metaphysical commentary in Arabic on *doʿā-ye saḥar*. The practice of *doʿā* has accordingly enjoyed great visibility in the Islamic Republic. Various *doʿā*s are regularly broadcast on radio and television, and *doʿā-ye Komayl* was regularly recited in the trenches every Thursday night throughout the war with Iraq. The ceremonies at Khomeini's funeral on 19 Ḵordād 1368 Š./9 June 1989 included a recitation of *doʿā-ye Komayl* into which phrases in Persian tending to associate him with the imams were inserted.

In folk religion recourse to *doʿā* has often assumed the aspect of magic, its general purpose being to secure protection (especially for children) against maleficent jinn and the evil eye. The formulas of *doʿā* serve not as texts for recitation and meditation; instead, written on paper, cloth, or occasionally deerskin, they are transformed into objects imbued with magical power that are to be carried or worn as amulets at all times. In addition, the paper on which the *doʿā* is written is sometimes soaked in water, which is then drunk by the person seeking protection. The writing of prayers and the preparation of amulets was traditionally the function of persons known as *doʿānevīs* (see DOʿA-NEVĪSĪ), who also laid claim to power over the jinn. The texts used in this way, although called *doʿā*, appear more frequently to have been passages from the Koran, supplemented with incantatory words of no evident meaning and talismanic signs (Donaldson, pp. 20, 25, 37, 39, 132-33, 203). This approach to *doʿā*, simultaneously magical and mechanistic in its assumptions, is fast becoming extinct in Persia under the dual impact of modernity and the vigorous propagation of standard religious practice by the authorities of the Islamic Republic.

Bibliography: (For cited works not found in this bibliography and abbreviations found here, see "Short References.") H. Algar, *Islam and Revolution*, Berkeley, 1981. Imam ʿAlī al-Sajjād, *al-Ṣaḥīfa al-sajjādīya*, tr. W. C. Chittick as *The Psalms of Islam*, London, 1988. ʿA. Baḥr-al-ʿOlūm, *Ażwāʾ ʿalā doʿā Komayl*, Beirut, 1403/1983. Abu'l-Mafāḵer Yaḥyā Bāḵarzī, *Awrād al-aḥbāb wa foṣūṣ al-ādāb*, ed. Ī. Afšār, Tehran, 1358 Š./1979. M. Bāzargān, *Doʿā, termūdīnāmīk-e ensān*, Tehran, 1340 Š./1961. Moḥammad Boḵārī, *Ṣaḥīḥ* VIII, Cairo, n.d., pp. 82-96. M. Çağırcı, "Beddua," in *Türkiye Diyanet Vakfī İslam Ansiklopedisi* V, pp. 297-98. B. A. Donaldson, *The Wild Rue*, London, 1938. Ebn ʿArabī, *al-Fotūḥāt al-makkīya*, 4 vols., Būlāq, 1293/1876. C. Ernst, *Words of Ecstasy in Sufism*, Albany, N.Y., 1985. Abu'l-Ḵayr Fārūqī Naqšbandī, *Maqāmāt-e aḵyār*, Delhi, 1394/1974. M.-A. Fekrat, *Monājāt wa goftār-e pīr-e Herāt*, Kabul, 1355 Š./1976; tr. S. de Laugier de Beaurecueil as *Cris du coeur*, Paris, 1988. L. Gardet, "Duʿā'" in *EI*[2] II, pp. 617-18. Abū Ḥāmed Moḥammad Ḡazālī, *Eḥyāʾ ʿolūm al-dīn* I, Beirut, n.d., pp. 268-90; bk. 9 tr. K. Nakamura as *Invocations and Supplications*, Cambridge, 1990. Idem, *Kīmīā-ye saʿādat*, ed. Ḥ. Ḵadīv Jam, 2 vols., Tehran, 1361 Š./1982. M. Ḡazālī, *al-Doʿāʾ wa'l-ḏekr*, tr. Y. Talal de Lorenzo as *Remembrance and*

Prayer. The Way of Prophet Muhammad*, Leicester, 1986. Abū Jaʿfar Moḥammad Kolaynī, *Oṣūl al-kāfī*, ed. and tr. S. Ḥ. Rasūlī, IV, Tehran, n.d., pp. 210-393. Żīāʾ-al-Dīn Komošḵānavī, *Majmūʿat al-awrād*, Istanbul, 1298/1881. Ayatollah Ḵomeynī, *Kašf al-asrār*, Tehran, 1323 Š./1944. Idem, *Šarḥ doʿāʾ al-saḥar*, ed. S. A. Fehrī, Tehran 1362 Š./1983; tr. S. A. Fehrī, Tehran, 1359 Š./ 1980. Idem, *Tafsīr-e sūra-ye ḥamd*, ed. ʿA.-A. Rabbānī Ḵalḵālī, Tehran, 1368 Š./1989. K. Kufralı, "Dua," in *İA* III, pp. 650-52. Moḥammad-Bāqer Majlesī, *Beḥār al-anwār*, Tehran, 1398/1978, XCIV-XCV; XCVII, pp. 133-385. Abu'l-Fażl Meybodī, *Kašf al-asrār wa ʿoddat al abrār*, ed. ʿA.-A. Ḥekmat, 10 vols., Tehran, 1344 Š./1965. M. Mīnovī, *Aḥwāl wa āṯār-e Šayḵ Abu'l-Ḥasan Ḵaraqānī*, Tehran, 1354 Š./1975. Moḥammad b. Monawwar, *Asrār al-tawḥīd fī maqāmāt al-Šayḵ Abī Saʿīd*, ed. M. R. Šafīʿī Kadkanī, I, Tehran, 1366 Š./1987, pp. 319-23; tr. J. O'Kane as *The Secrets of God's Mystical Oneness*, Costa Mesa, Calif., 1992, pp. 497-503. L. Morris and R. Sarfeh, *Munajat. The Intimate Prayers of Khwajih ʿAbd Allah Ansari*, New York, 1975. Abu'l-Ḥosayn Moslem Nīšābūrī, *Ṣaḥīḥ*, tr. A. H. Siddiqi as *Sahih Muslim* IV, Lahore, 1973, pp. 1408-30. S. H. Nasr, H. Dabashi, and S. V. R. Nasr, eds., *Shiʿism. Doctrines, Thought, and Spirituality*, Albany, N.Y., 988, pp. 243-53. Abū Zakarīyāʾ Yaḥyā Nawawī, *Rīāż al-ṣāleḥīn*, Delhi, n.d., pp. 513-23. C. Padwick, *Muslim Devotions*, London, 1961. ʿAbbās Qomī, *Safīnat al-beḥār* I, Tehran, n.d., pp. 447-62. Abu'l-Qāsem Qošayrī, *al-Resālat al-qošayrīya*, ed. ʿA. Maḥmūd and M. Šarīf, Cairo, 1966, p. 526; tr., B. R. von Schlegell as *Principles of Sufism*, Berkeley, Calif., 1992. Idem, *Laṭāʾef al-ešārāt*, ed. E. Basyūnī, 5 vols., Cairo, 1390/1971. Jalāl-al-Dīn Moḥammad Balḵī Rūmī, *Maṯnawī*, ed. and tr. R. A. Nicholson, 6 vols., London, 1925-33. Idem, *Dīvān-e šams*, 3rd ed., ed. B. Forūzānfar, Tehran, 1352 Š./1973. S. J. Sajjādī, *Farhang-e maʿāref-e eslāmī*, Tehran, 1366 Š./1987. Abu Naṣr Sarrāj, *Ketāb al-lomaʿ fi'l-taṣawwof*, ed. R. A. Nicholson, London, 1914. Moḥammad b. ʿAlī Šawkānī, *Toḥfat al-ḏākerīn be-ʿeddat al-ḥeṣn al-ḥaṣīn men kalām sayyed al-morsalīn*, Cairo, n.d. A. Schimmel, *The Triumphal Sun*, London and the Hague, 1978, pp. 352-66. A. H. Siddiqi, *Prayers of the Prophet*, Lahore, n.d. Mīrzā Abu'l-Qāsem Šīrāzī, *Meṣbāḥ al-šarīʿa wa meftāḥ al-ḥaqīqa*, Tehran, 1363/1944, pp. 390-423. Abu'l-Najīb Żīāʾ-al-Dīn Sohravardī, *Ādāb al-morīdīn*, ed. N. Māyel Heravī, Tehran, 1363 Š./1984. Šehāb-al-Dīn Sohravardī, *ʿAwāref al-maʿāref*, in supplementary volume to Ḡazālī, *Eḥyāʾ ʿolūm al-dīn*, Beirut, n.d., pp. 196-201. M.-Ḥ. Ṭabaṭabāʾī, *al-Mīzān fī tafsīr al-Qorʾān*, Tehran, 1397/1977, II, pp. 209-42, XVII, pp. 362-63. Idem, *A Shiʿite Anthology*, tr. W. C. Chittick London, 1980, pp. 91-133. Moḥammad ʿAlī Tahānawī, *Kaššāf esṭelāḥāt al-fonūn*; repr. Istanbul, 1984. A. Zomorrodīān, *ʿAlī wa Komayl. Šarḥ-ī bar doʿā-ye Komayl*, Tehran, 1341 Š./1962.

(Hamid Algar)

DOʿĀ-NEVĪSĪ, the act of writing charms against various evils. *Doʿā* in this sense refers to spoken or written words assumed to have properties that can either avert harm, cure physical or mental sickness, or bring about a desired effect. A person who makes a living from writing *doʿā*s is called *doʿānevīs*. A variety of *doʿā* called *taʿwīḏ* (amulet) has been common for many centuries (see CHARM). *Taʿwīḏ* involves suras or verses from the Koran, often the two last suras, which begin with *qol aʿūḏo* (Say: I seek refuge), and for this reason these two suras are called *moʿawweḏatayn*. It is believed that carrying, reciting, and blowing (*fūt kardan*) of certain verses from the Koran may avoid calamity, sickness, or the effects of the evil eye. It is important to note that, although the word *doʿā* may mean the religiously sanctioned prayers recited during worship to attain pious goals, in its special meaning of an incantation it is in no way related to the canonical form, even when words or passages from the canonical prayers are borrowed and used in it. The practice of wearing the *doʿā* on one's person is well attested among the pre-Islamic Arabs, who called such things *tamīma* (pl. *tamāʾem*). Ordinarily these *tamīma*s were made of either beads of baked clay or of small pebbles with natural designs on them. These were made into a necklace and worn around the neck of the individual who sought to partake of their magical property. Infants were especially adorned with these charms, which, however, would be removed after the infant had grown into a child. Similar necklaces are also used in Persia. They are made of copper, silver, or gold, depending on the means of the family. Sometimes these charms are made of forty small silver plates, on each of which the koranic verse *besmellāh al-raḥmān al-raḥīm*, is carved. This variety of charm is called *čehel besmellāh* (forty *besmellāh*s; Dehḵodā, s.v.). In a photograph of Moḥammad-Reżā Shah as a child, in which he is sitting on his father's lap, one of these charms can be seen around his neck (Wilber, pl. 12). Either Sura 112 or the last four suras of the Koran, which begin with the word *qol* (*čahār qol*) could be carved on the forty plates of the necklace or written on a piece of gazelle skin and carried as a charm. Sometimes seven verses from Sura 36 that end in the word *mobīn* (*haft mobīn*) were used instead. Another variety of these charms is called *ḥerz*, which may be made of a thin piece of leather (preferably gazelle skin) on which verses from the Koran or religious prayers are written in saffron (cf. Ḵāqānī, p. 203). This piece of leather is placed in a small metal container, made of gold for women and silver for men, and tied around the arm or worn around the neck (cf. Neẓāmī, 1363 Š./1984b, p. 701; idem, 1984a, p. 5; cf. *Dehḵodā*, s.v. *taʿwīḏ*). Once the *doʿā* is written and placed in its container, it should not be taken out, nor should it be unrolled and read. The containers for *ḥerz* are usually cylindrical. Some of the most famous kinds of these charms are *ḥerz-e yamānī*, *ḥerz-e Fāṭema-ye zahrā*, *ḥerz-e roqʿat al-jayb* (attributed to Imam ʿAlī al-Reżā, q.v.), and the very popular *ḥerz-e Jawād* (attributed to Imam Moḥammad al-Taqī).

According to the 1301 Š./1922 census of Tehran, there were twenty-five *doʿānevīs*es in the city (Šahrī, I, p. 84). Traditionally they may be divided into two groups. One group consists of those who use established religious texts in the preparation of their charms. They usually have some sort of authorization (*ejāza*) from their master who sometimes is their father. Some of them may be associated with a Sufi sect, and some claim to have studied the supernatural sciences under Indian or Arab masters. They may sometimes teach a certain magical formula to their customers, which the latter are supposed to recite at specific times. These *doʿānevīs*es are objects of reverence and are believed to possess blessing (*baraka*) in their breath or pens. Sometimes one of them attempts to cure various maladies by writing a charm on a piece of paper, which is then washed in water; the sick person is made to drink that water. The second group of *doʿānevīs*es consists of those who do not use religious texts in their charms. Instead they employ certain magical forms, geometric or otherwise; numbers; and sentences formed of Hebrew, Arabic, and Persian words. Furthermore, they engage in a variety of other activities like fortune telling, palm reading, and using a child to reconstruct crime scenes for the discovery of the guilty party. These individuals are usually active in poorer quarters of large cities in Persia. Many of their customers are uneducated women who consult them for various problems (e.g., help in begetting male children, winning their husbands' love, getting rid of rival wives). Some do not even have specific places of business and walk around in certain quarters of the city hawking their skills to potential customers. The tools of the trade are usually a brass bowl with incised designs, an object similar to an astrolabe, several mirrors, colorful crystal balls, and pieces of string with knots tied in them.

Bibliography: (For cited works not found in this bibliography see "Short References.") Dāʾūd Anṭākī, *Taḏkarat ūli'l-albāb wa jāmeʿ le'l-ʿajab al-ʿojāb* II, Beirut, n.d., s.vv. "Ramal," pp. 147 ff., "Roqya," pp. 166 ff. A. Enjavī Šīrāzī, *Jašnhā wa ādāb wa moʿtaqedāt-e zemestān* II, Tehran, 1354 Š./1975, pp. 58, 191. Ṣ. Homāyūnī, "Doʿāhā dar Šīrāz," *Kāva* 12/2-3, 1353 Š./1974, pp. 74-77. Ḵāqānī Šervānī, *Dīvān*, ed. ʿA. ʿAbd-al-Rasūlī, Tehran, 1316 Š./1937. Neẓāmī Ganjavī, *Leylī o Majnūn*, ed. Ḥ Waḥīd Dastgerdī, Tehran, 1363 Š./ 1984a. Idem, *Šaraf-nāma*, ed. Ḥ Waḥīd Dastgerdī, Tehran, 1363 Š./1984b. J. Šahrī, *Tārīḵ-e ejtemāʿī-e Tehrān dar qarn-e sīzdahom* V, Tehran, 1368 Š./ 1989, pp. 252-68. E. Šakūrzāda, *ʿAqāyed wa rosūm-e mardom-e Ḵorāsān*, 2nd. ed., Tehran, 1363 Š./ 1984, pp. 272-73, 299-303. D. Wilber, *Reza Shah Pahlavi. The Resurrection and Reconstructioon, 1878-1944*, Hicksville, N.Y., 1975.

(AḤMAD MAHDAWĪ DĀMḠĀNĪ)

DOĀB-E MĪḴZARĪN (Doab-i Mekhe Zarin; 35°15′-35°16′ N, 67°58′-68°01′ E), a group of archeological sites with numerous pre-Islamic mud-brick ruins on either side of the Sorḵāb river, on the road from Bāmīān to Došī, opposite the entrance to the Kahmard valley.

There are remains of large fortresses on both banks of the Sorḵāb river, for example, on a natural hill commanding the passage to the Kahmard valley. Of art-historical interest are constructions from cut limestone carrying edifices built of large mud bricks, for example, in two-storied elliptical tunnel vaults in the style of an Iranian *ayvān* (q.v.), thus attesting a cultural presence in this region of the Hindu Kush from late Sasanian times (6th-7th centuries). Finds of plain ceramics indicate the same chronological range.

Bibliography: (For abbreviations found in this bibliography, see "Short References.") W. Ball and J.-C. Gardin, *Archaeological Gazetteer of Afghanistan*, 2 vols., Paris, 1982, pp. 302-03. M. Le Berre et al., *Monuments pré-islamiques de l'Hindukush central*, MDAFA XXIV, Paris, 1987, pls. 29-35. K. Fischer, "Indo-Iranian Contacts as Revealed by Mud-Brick Architecture from Afghanistan," *Oriental Art* N.S. 12/1, 1966, pp. 25-31, esp. p. 27 fig. 4. Idem, "Preliminary Remarks on Archaeological Survey in Afghanistan," *Zentralasiatische Studien des Seminars für Sprach- und Kulturwissenschaft Zentralasiens der Universität Bonn* 3, 1969, pp. 344-45.

(KLAUS FISCHER)

DOCUMENTS, production and registration of.

i. *In pre-Islamic periods.*
ii. *Babylonian and Egyptian documents in the Achaemenid period.*
iii. *In the modern period.* See DAFTAR-E ASNĀD-E RASMĪ.

i. IN PRE-ISLAMIC PERIODS

The function of a notarial institution is not explicitly set forth in the extant records for all pre-Islamic periods, but allusions to procedures for drawing up and executing documents suggest the existence of some sort of notarial practice.

The Achaemenid period. In the Achaemenid period documents related to private and social affairs were registered on clay tablets in Elamite and Akkadian, some with Aramaic endorsements on the sides, and on parchment and papyrus in Aramaic.

Tablets found in the treasury and fortifications at Persepolis attest the early registration of documents in the court chancery. The numerous texts from fortifications, written at many sites in the area encompassing Persepolis and Susa and recording transfers of supplies, date from 509 to 494 B.C.E. (13th-28th years of Darius I, q.v.), whereas the much smaller number of Treasury tablets from Persepolis and the vicinity include records of silver payments in the years 492-58 B.C.E. (the 30th year of Darius I to the 7th year of Artaxerxes I, q.v.; Cameron; Hallock, p. 588). The treasury tablets were written under the supervision of the chief economic official, the Persian Farnaka, who, as head of an extensive administrative apparatus, oversaw the correspondence, most of which bears subscripts naming the scribes (Hallock, p. 590). They were deposited in the chancery, a royal registry. In addition, about 200 broken stone plates, pestles, and mortars inscribed in Aramaic were discovered at Persepolis; the inscriptions are records of the manufacture of these objects by artisans in Arachosia (Bowman; Levine). In addition to clay tablets and stone objects, a number of other documents were written in Aramaic on more perishable materials, which have survived in much smaller quantities (Cameron, pp. 24-31; Greenfield, p. 704). The widespread use of parchment for transactions, agreements, contracts, and the like in the Achaemenid empire may be assumed from the existence of a "guild" of parchment makers in Babylonia (Eilers, p. 49 n. 1; cf. Oppenheim, p. 579). That some scribes were well versed in Aramaic is also clear from a gracefully written parchment translation of the inscription of Darius I at Bīsotūn (q.v.), found at Elephantine in Upper Egypt, and from the "Aršāma (q.v. 2) letters," written on leather in Susa and Babylon (Greenfield, p. 703). The Akkadian and Elamite languages, traditionally written on more cumbersome clay tablets, were in time superseded by the more expedient Aramaic written on parchment, thus promoting the development of the Persian scribal tradition. Tablets continued to be used occasionally until the mid-Parthian period, however (Oppenheim, p. 571). It has been plausibly suggested that bullae were originally attached to documents of this period written in Aramaic (Cross, pp. 46-51). There is also rich economic and legal documentation from ancient Babylonia and Egypt, a substantial part of which is dispersed in various museums and remains unpublished. As the social and economic environments of these highly advanced Achaemenid dependencies were in many respects distinct from those prevailing in Persia, these documents seem to fall into a different cultural category.

The Parthian period. During the Seleucid and Parthian periods Greek was in use concurrently with Aramaic, and eventually the Greek system of preparing documents was introduced into Persia and adopted by Persian scribes. This change is apparent from the Avroman documents and parchments from Dura-Europos (qq.v.), which together provide the earliest evidence for the registration of deeds and contracts under the Parthians (see CONTRACTS ii). These documents attest that a developed law of obligations existed in Parthian domains and that Iranian scribes had already contrived an elaborate system for drawing up contractual agreements. The registry or archive of a royal wine storehouse (*mdwst*) containing more than 2,000 ostraca of the 1st century B.C.E. has come to light at Nisa, the Parthian capital located in what is now southern Turkestan. The documents, written in Aramaic script, are primarily notations not intended to be kept long; their contents were entered into a permanent document, probably on parchment, which constituted a running total of wine deliveries to the storehouse. Among these ostraca are dozens of emphyteutic leases of royal vineyards situated in the precincts of Mihrdādkerd (D'yakonov and Livshits; Lukonin, p. 694). Three Sogdian contracts between private persons have also been preserved among the documents from Mount Mug, drafted in the second half of the 7th or at the beginning of the 8th century (*Dokumenty*). Chinese archeologists have recently discovered another Sogdian document recording the sale of a Samarkand slave woman in 638 (Yoshida and Moriaso).

The Sasanian period. A large number of Middle Persian papyri and a few parchments have been discovered in Egypt; they contain fragments of documents and official letters from the period of the Sasanian occupation (ca. 619-28). They are complemented by Greek papyri of the same period. From Persia itself there is a hoard of 199 discovered by Ernst Herzfeld near Ray and dated by him to the 6th century. The texts are related to supplies of wine and other commodities and have been interpreted either as treasury records (Weber) or as authorizations to warehouse workers to issue supplies (de Blois). In addition, repeated references to drawing up, signing, and sealing (*nibišt ud āwišt*) legal deeds confirm the existence of some sort of registry in the highly legalistic Sasanian state. Further confirmation is a complete model Zoroastrian marriage contract (*paymān ī zanīh*) from the Islamic period (*Pahlavi Texts*, ed. Jamasp-Asana, II, pp. 141-43), which, despite a number of modifications and adaptations of the marriage articles to conform to a predominantly Islamic environment, still retains the character of its Sasanian prototype. Consistent with Sasanian tradition, the Yazdegerdī year 627 (the era beginning with the 20th year of Yazdegerd III, i.e., 1278 C.E.) and the Zoroastrian month and day are used; the identities of all participants are to be registered by their names and the names of their fathers and grandfathers and the domiciles (districts and provinces) of the couple specified. At the end the contract is to be signed by three witnesses, whose identities are to be similarly recorded. Although officiation at marriages, divorces, and adoption ceremonies was within the competence of a priest (*mōbed*), there is no information in the text on whether it was drawn up by the *mōbed* himself or a scribe (see DABĪR i). There is, however, no reference in the Sasanian law book *Mādayān ī hazār dādestān* to scribal functions, with one exception, in which the emphasis is on the maximum number of scribes to be engaged to record the minutes in tribunals of inquiry (pt. 1, p. 78). The general tenor of numerous legal cases, as well as the social environment of the Sasanians, suggests that documents were, as a rule, drawn up according to prescribed forms by people who were well versed in the subtle phraseology of Middle Persian, especially juridical terminology. They were then signed and sealed by the parties concerned, their witnesses, and in some instances officials like *mōbed*s or *rad*s (high-ranking spiritual or religious leader or judge, eminent religious personality; *Mādayān*, pt. 2, p. 18).

Presumably the only literate people who could handle the technicalities of Middle Persian were the religious authorities and the scribes, who formed a stratum of the clergy. There are instances in which documents were only signed and sealed by *mōbed*s or *rad*s; the scribal part in the process of registration thus seems to have been indispensable. But, unlike the Achaemenid notaries, who managed registries, checked documents, and stored the copies (*ham-paččēn*) in archives, the function of the Sasanian scribes seems to have been essentially confined to writing. In Sogdian legal documents (contracts and receipts) the names of the scribes are usually given.

A number of formalities and conventions of Sasanian notarial practice are given in the *Madayān*. For example, the cost of preparing documents in duplicate (*uzēnag ī pad nāmag-passāz*) in traditional law (*kardag*) was 2 of every 9 drahms (dirhams) or 3 of every 10 drahms of the value of the property involved, whereas in civil law (*dādestān*, q.v.) expenses did not exceed 2 of every 18 drahms. The expenses for a condemned person (*marg-arzān*) could not be more than 95 drahms (*Mādayān*, pt. 2, p. 15). When a contract involved two partners with unequal assets or interests the original (*mādagwar*) went to the person with the greater share and the copy to the other (*Mādayān*, pt. 2, p. 33). In accordance with the pronouncements (*pad čāštag*) of eminent jurists, the ordeal document (*yazišn-nāmag*, drawn up by the judge or *rad* recommending or ordering a trial by ordeal) was attested on the day of Ardwahišt but, in accordance with traditional law, on the day of Hordād (*Mādayān*, pt. 2, p. 13). The text of a testament could be changed when formulated and revoked at any time until it was signed and sealed (*Mādayān*, pt. 2, p. 10). A "separate seal" (*muhr-wēxt*), "detached seal" (*muhr-brīd*), or "loose seal" (*muhr-wišād*) in a document was tantamount to its having been "ripped open" (*wišād-dib*; *Mādayān*, pt. 1, p. 102).

Middle Persian legal terminology is rich in distinctive technical terms, which were, however, not always strictly respected by scribes. The least specific term is *nibēg* "letter, writing, book" (*Mādayān*, pt. 1, p. 110). *Nāmag* generally meant "book, account, chronicle" and legally "decree, unsealed document," which when sealed became *wizīr* "executed document." *Wizīr* is defined as "the sealing wax plus document" (*gil ud nāmag*; *Mādayān*, pt. 2, p. 34). *Nāmag* was also used for "edict" (*nāmag ī kār-framān* "edict of executive office"; *Mādayān*, pt. 2, p. 38). It occurs as an element in various compounds: *hilišn-nāmag* "certificate of divorce," *āzād-nāmag* "deed of manumission," *uzdād-nāmag* "ordeal warrant" (*Mādayān*, pt. 1, p. 78), and *nāmag-niyān* "archives" (lit., "document store"; *nāmag-niyān ī ātaxš ī Ḥuram-Ardašīr* "archives of the fire of Ḥuram-Ardašīr," *Mādayān*, pt. I, p. 78). *Dib* was "a decree, a binding official document," as in *dib ī pādixšāy-kard* "decree of executive authority" (*Mādayān*, pt. 2, p. 38). *Frawardag*, synonymous with *nāmag*, most often meant "letter, epistle" and generally also "document, edict." *Nibištag*, literally, "a writing," legally denoted "report, record" (cf. *nibištag kardan* "to record (an offense)"; *az nibištag hištan* "to remove (an offense) from the official report"; *Mādayān*, pt. 1, p. 97). *MGLTʾ* (Aram. *megiltā*), interpreted as "*nāmag*," denoted "scroll." *Git*, *gitāk* meant "legal document, testament" (cf. Ak. *giṭṭu* "tablet," Aram. *giṭā* "document," Syr. *geṭṭā* "testament"). *Pādixšīr* meant "treaty, covenant giving title to transfer of property for religious purposes" (inscription of Kerdīr at Kaʿba-ye Zardošt, 2-3; Back, pp. 389-92).

In Middle Persian legal texts various seals with distinct legal force are mentioned: "personal seal" (*muhr ī xwēš*), "seal of office" (*muhr ī pad kār-framān*); and "trustworthy seal" (*muhr ī ēwar*), "authentic seal" (*muhr ī wizurd*), and "credible seal" (*muhr ī wābarigān*), providing different degrees of reliability as evidence.

See also CONTRACTS.

Bibliography: (For cited works not found in this bibliography and for abbreviations found here, see "Short References.") *Mādayān ī hazār dādestān*, tr. S. J. Bulsara as *The Laws of the Ancient Persians as Found in the Mâtîkân ê hazâr Dâttastân*, 2 vols., Bombay, 1937; tr. A. G. Perikhanian as *Sasanidskiĭ Sudebnik*, Yerevan, 1973. M. Back, *Die sassanidischen Staatsinschriften*, Acta Iranica 18, Liège, 1978. F. de Blois, review of D. Weber, *Ostraca, Papyri and Pergamente*, *BSOAS* 56, 1993, pp. 37-38. R. A. Bowman, *Aramaic Ritual Texts from Persepolis*, Chicago, 1970. G. C. Cameron, *Persepolis Treasury Tablets*, Chicago, 1948. M. A. R. Colledge, *The Parthians*, London, 1967, chap. 4. F. M. Cross, "Papyri of the Fourth Century B.C. from Dâliyeh," in D. N. Freedman and J. C. Greenfield, eds., *New Directions in Biblical Archaeology*, Garden City, N.Y., 1971, pp. 46-51. I. M. D'yakonov and V. A. Livshits, *Dokumenty iz Nisy. Novye nakhodki dokumentov v staroi Nise i peredneaziatskiĭ sbornik* (Documents from Nisa. New finds of documents in ancient Nisa and the

Near Eastern collection) II, Moscow, 1960, pp. 135-57. W. Eilers, *Iranische Beamtennamen in der keilschriftlichen Überlieferung* I, Leipzig, 1940. J. C. Greenfield, "Aramaic in the Achaemenian Empire," *Camb. Hist. Iran* II, pp. 698-713. R. T. Hallock, "The Evidence of the Persepolis Tablets," *Camb. Hist. Iran* II, pp. 588-609. B. A. Levine, "Aramaic Texts from Persepolis," *JAOS* 92, 1972, pp. 70-79. V. G. Lukonin, "Political, Social and Administrative Institutions, Taxes and Trade," *Camb. Hist. Iran* III/2, pp. 681-746. E. H. Minns, "Parchments of the Parthian Period from Avroman in Kurdistan," *Journal of Hellenistic Studies* 35, 1915, pp. 22-65. A. L. Oppenheim, "The Babylonian Evidence of Achemenian Rule in Mesopotamia," *Camb. Hist. Iran* II, pp. 529-87. D. Weber, *Ostraca, Papyri and Pergamente*, Corpus Inscr. Iran., pt. 3, IV-V, London, 1992. C. B. Welles et al., *The Excavations at Dura-Europos. Final Report* V/1. *The Parchments and Papyri*, New Haven, Conn., 1959. Y. Yoshida and P. Moriaso, "A Sogdian Document Recording Sale of a Samarkand Slave Woman in 638," *Annals of Foreign Studies* 19, Studies on the Inner Asian Languages 4, 1988, pp. 1-50.

(Mansour Shaki)

ii. Babylonian and Egyptian Documents in the Achaemenid Period

No documents composed in Old Persian and other Iranian languages are known. In Persia and Media private parties apparently did not conclude written transactions, though some Persians and other Iranians who lived in Babylonia actively participated in business and made various deeds with local individuals following traditional Babylonian legal norms. The documents of the royal household in Persia were written partly in Elamite and partly in Aramaic.

About 6,000 legal, economic, and administrative documents from Babylonian private and temple archives of the Achaemenid period have so far been published. They are written on clay tablets in the late-Babylonian dialect of Akkadian. These documents include promissory notes; mortgages; contracts for the sale and lease of land and houses; receipts for tax payments; records of court proceedings; and so on, including about 500 official and private letters. The majority of these texts belong to the reigns of Cyrus, Cambyses, and Darius I (qq.v.; 539-486 B.C.E.). About two dozen of them were drafted in Ecbatana, Persepolis, Humadeshu (in the vicinity of Persepolis), Susa, and other cities of western and southwestern Iran. They represent transactions by Babylonians who came to Persia as merchants and businessmen or, in a few instances, had settled there.

From the archives of the Eanna temple in Uruk and the Ebabbar temple in Sippar, both in Mesopotamia, there is especially abundant information about the economy and social institutions of Babylonia. Among private archives the most important are those of the Egibi, Murashû, and several other business houses. Most of the Egibi documents were drafted in the vicinity of Babylon, but some were composed in other cities, including Ecbatana, where the firm was engaged in business (Dandamaev, pp. 12-22). The Murashû documents come mainly from the region of Nippur, but a certain number were composed in Babylon, Susa, and other cities. They constitute the largest single source for the economic history of Babylonia in the second half of the 5th century B.C.E. and for changes introduced by the Achaemenid administration into policies on property and the system of land tenure. They also provide extensive information on Persian and other Iranian soldiers and officials settled around Nippur (Stolper, pp. 1, 23-24).

Various documents written in Egyptian demotic on papyrus have been preserved from Achaemenid Egypt. Among them the Ryland Papyri comprise a number of documents of various periods, one of which, the "petition of Petesi," concerns the illegal appropriation of property by priests in the early Achaemenid period. It provides valuable insight into the Egyptian legal system. Cambyses' decree limiting the property of Egyptian temples and Darius I's edict codifying Egyptian laws are also of great importance. The correspondence of local priests with Pherendates, satrap of Egypt under Darius I, provides information on the administrative system of the country. Other demotic documents include leases for fields and livestock, the sales of slaves, hiring of labor, records of self-sale, and the like (Seidl, pp. 51-83; Cruz-Uribe, pp. 103-11).

About 200 Aramaic documents are known from Egypt. They include marriage contracts, promissory notes, leases for land, and other business documents. Some also contain information on Persian administrative policies in Egypt. All these texts are written on papyrus. Thirteen letters of Arshama (q.v.), satrap of Egypt in the second half of the 5th century B.C.E., contain instructions for management of the estates of Persian nobles in Egypt. They are written on leather. Finally, Aramaic documents from the Achaemenid province of Samaria include private documents (marriage contracts, manumission of slaves, etc.) drafted between 375 and 335 B.C.E. (Porten and Yardeni).

See also CONTRACTS i.

Bibliography: E. Cruz-Uribe, *Saite and Persian Demotic Cattle Documents. A Study in Legal Forms and Principles in Ancient Egypt*, American Studies in Papyrology 26, Chico, Calif., 1985. M. A. Dandamaev, *Slavery in Babylonia from Nabopolassar to Alexander the Great*, DeKalb, Ill., 1984. B. Porten and A. Yardeni, *Textbook of Aramaic Documents from Ancient Egypt*, 3 vols., Jerusalem, 1986-93. E. Seidl, *Ägyptische Rechtsgeschichte der Saiten- und Perserzeit*,

Glückstadt, Germany, 1968. M. W. Stolper, *Entrepreneurs and Empire. The Murašû Archive, the Murašû Firm, and Persian Rule in Babylonia*, Leiden, 1985.

(MUHAMMAD A. DANDAMAYEV)

DŌDĀ-BĀLĀÇ. See BALUCHISTAN iii/II.

DODDER. See AFTĪMŪN.

DOG (*Canis familiaris*; Pers. *sag*; *sagtūla* "puppy"; Av. *span-*, Median **spaka-*; Lorī *say*, *lās* "bitch," *sayu* "puppy" [Digard, 1981, p. 34]; Pašto *spay*, *spie* "bitch" [Dupree, p. 49]; Semnānī *esbá*; Sang. *əsbá*; Kajalī of K̲alk̲āl *esbé*; Ṭālešī of Vīzna *səba*; Abyānaī *kuyā*).

Bibliography: J.-P. Digard, *Techniques des nomades Baxtyâri*, Cambridge and Paris, 1981. L. Dupree, *Afghanistan*, Princeton, N.J., 1978; repr. Princeton, N.J., 1980.

i. *In literature and folklore.*
ii. *In Zoroastrianism.*
iii. *Ethnography.*

i. IN LITERATURE AND FOLKLORE

The dog was the first animal to be domesticated (Olsen, p. xi), probably from the wolf (*Canis lupus*), according to the fossil record. At paleontological sites in northern China and elsewhere hominids (*Homo erectus pekinensis*) and small wolves (*Canis lupus variabilis*) were found together in Middle Pleistocene levels, dating approximately 500,000-200,000 years ago (Hall and Sharp; Olsen, pp. 15, 41-42). The prevailing hypothesis is that wolves would have been attracted to human encampments by the smell of food and refuse; their territorial growling at intruders then came to serve as an early-warning system for the camp. Canid bones are found in refuse heaps near but not in Paleolithic camps, whereas bones of domesticated dogs are first found within Neolithic camps, evidence that the process of domestication must have been slow and gradual (Olsen, p. 18; La Barre, p. 48). F. E. Zeuner (pp. 39, 83) has rejected this hypothesis, however, suggesting that it was the scavenging habits of wolves that brought the animals into human camps and that some pups may have been adopted by the inhabitants, leading eventually to domestication of the animal.

The earliest remains of the domestic dog in the Near East, predating those in Europe, were found in Palegawra cave in northeastern Iraq; they have been dated to 12,000 B.P. and seem to be structurally close to the so-called "Kurdish dog" (Olsen, pp. 71-72). In a study of the beginning of animal and plant domestication in southern Persia Frank Hole and his colleagues concluded from osteological evidence, first, that the dog had probably been domesticated in K̲ūzestān by 5500 B.C.E.; second, that it was probably descended from the local variety of wild wolf (*Canis lupus pallipes*); and, third, that the condition of some canid bones is evidence that dogs were used as food in some areas (cf. Olsen, pp. 74-75). Remains of domesticated dogs have also been found at the site of Ḥājī Fīrūz in Azerbaijan (radiocarbon-dated to 5500-5100 B.C.E.; Meadow, p. 6).

Four kinds of Persian hunting hounds were reported by the classical authors: Elymaeans from the northeastern shore of the Persian Gulf; Hyrcanians and Carmanians, known for their savagery; and Medians, which were great fighters (Aelian, 3.2, 7.38; Grattius; Pollux, *Onomasticon*; cf. Hull, pp. 26-29). Aside from Zoroastrian funerary rites (see ii, below), pre-Islamic Persians used the dog not only for hunting and herding but also in war (Fiennes, pp. 28-29; cf. Aelian, 7.38). Persians, Greeks, Assyrians, and Babylonians used large mastiffs as shock troops; one Athenian dog so distinguished itself against the Persians at the battle of Marathon (490 B.C.E) that its likeness was supposedly placed on Greek victory monuments (Aelian, 7.38). Indian dogs were highly prized among the Persian aristocracy; Xerxes I (486-65 B.C.E.) reportedly took a large number of them with his army when he marched against Greece (Herodotus, 7.187). One of the Persian satraps of Babylon assigned the revenues derived from four large villages in that province to the care of his Indian hounds (Herodotus, 1.192). A dog belonging to Darius III (q.v.; 336-30 B.C.E) supposedly refused to leave his corpse after he had been struck down by Bessus (q.v.; Aelian, 6.25, 7.10). Dogfights must also have been common in ancient Persia (Grattius, apud Fiennes, p. 11). Alexander the Great (q.v.) was said to have received a gift of four fighting dogs from Indians (Aelian, 8.1). The Persian phrase *sag-e kārzārī* (war dog) may refer either to canine warriors or merely to dogs trained for dogfights (*Šāh-nāma*, Moscow, III, p. 166).

Myths about the Creation and Domestication of the Dog.

Pre-Islamic myths. According to the *Bundahišn* (13.10), all animals were created from the purified semen of the primordial bull. Ten varieties of dog are mentioned (13.18; tr. Anklesaria, p. 121; tr. Bahār, p. 79), of which only the guard dog, the sheep dog, and the hunting dog can properly be considered dogs. The dog is said to have been created to protect man's possessions against wolves; in its opposition to evil it cooperates with the cock and is able to repel evil by its mere gaze (*Bundahišn* 24.38, 24.48; tr. Anklesaria, pp. 201, 203; tr. Bahār, p. 103). In ancient Persian folk etymology the word *sag* (dog) was derived from *seh-yak* (one third) because one third of its essence is human (*Bundahišn* 13.28; tr. Anklesaria, pp. 123-25; tr. Bahār, pp. 79-80).

Islamic myths. Three distinct myths of the creation of the dog can be reconstructed from Islamic texts. According to a tradition related on the authority of ʿAlī b. Abī Ṭāleb (q.v.), when Adam and Eve were cast out of paradise Satan came to the beasts of the earth and encouraged them with violent cries to attack and devour the couple; his spittle flew out of his mouth, and God fashioned a male and a female dog from it. The male was sent to guard Adam and the female to protect Eve. The enmity between the dog and wild animals was thus initiated (Damīrī, II, p. 298; Jazāʾerī, pp. 57-58; ʿAbbās Qomī, II, p. 488; Ḥāʾerī, XXV, p. 99; cf. *Persian Rivayats*, ed. Unvala, I, p. 256). In a second version God created the dog from the clay left over (*baqīyat al-ṭīn*) from His creation of Adam (Fozūnī, p. 490; cf. Anwarī, I, p. 88), which may lie behind the assertion in some sources that dog bones and tissue may be grafted to the human body (Balāgī, p. 204; Tonokāboni, p. 222). The third myth may be deduced from a tradition about the taboo on eating the dog's flesh because the animal is "metamorphosed" (*mamsūḵ*; Kolaynī, VI, p. 245); the implication is that human sinners are transformed into dogs and that eating the flesh would be a form of cannibalism. This notion of transformation of sinners is widely attested in Muslim lore and literature. For example, Ebn Abī Donyā (d. 281/894) cited a tradition according to which those who use foul language against others will be resurrected in the form of dogs (p. 404). Rašīd-al-Dīn Meybodī, author of a Sufi exegesis on the Koran (comp. ca. 520/1126), declared that usurers would be raised as dogs and pigs on the Day of Judgment (I, p. 747). Baʿlam (Meybodī, III, p. 271; Ḥakīm Termeḏī, p. 17) and Šemr b. Ḏi'l-Jawšan (d. 66/686), the slayer of Imam Ḥosayn, supposedly suffered punishment by being transformed into dogs (Massé, *Croyances*, pp. 185-86; Šakūrzāda, p. 308 n. 1; ʿAbbās Qomī, II, p. 539). In about 1935 in Mašhad a woman who had ridiculed the miraculous events associated with the death of Imam Ḥosayn was supposed to have been transformed into a dog (Donaldson, p. 159).

A tradition about the domestication of the dog was related on the authority of Ebn ʿAbbās: When Adam was cast out of heaven and attacked by Satan, God reassured him and sent Moses' staff as a means of defense; Adam struck a dog with it, but God commanded him to pat the animal on the head. The animal thus became domesticated, befriending Adam and his seed (Ḥakīm Termeḏī, p. 16).

The dog in Islamic law.

Dogs are mentioned four times in the Koran (5:4, 7:176, 18:18, 22). Ignaz Goldziher argued that in the time of the Prophet Moḥammad the dog was not considered unclean (pp. 9-10). In later Islamic legal texts they are said to be unclean (*najes be'l-ʿayn*), but the use of guard dogs, sheep dogs, and especially hunting dogs is allowed (Moḥammad b. Ḥosayn Ṭūsī, I, pp. 92, 94), as trained dogs are considered livestock (*bahīma)*. Their sale, purchase, and rental are permissible (Moḥammad b. Ḥosayn Ṭūsī, II, pp. 165-66, III, pp. 57, 250). The flesh of game killed by a hunting dog is not unclean, provided that it is not itself a forbidden animal (Moḥammad b. Ḥosayn Ṭūsī, VI, pp. 256-62; Meybodī, III, p. 32; ʿAlī Qomī, I, pp. 162-63; Kolaynī, VI, pp. 202-04, 207; Ebn Taymīya, p. 325). There are, however, some qualifications in Sunni law books regarding the use of hunting dogs trained by non-Muslims. In one tradition, disallowed by some authorities, it is alleged that the Prophet Moḥammad forbade the flesh of game brought down by a hunting dog trained by Zoroastrians (Albānī, p. 170). Shiʿite legal authorities hold, however, that, if the hunter himself is Muslim, it does not matter who trained the dog (Moḥammad b. Ḥosayn Ṭūsī, VI, p. 262). There is some doubt about the permissibility of the flesh of game brought down by a black dog (Kolaynī, VI, p. 206), which may reflect a general Near Eastern association of the black dog with the devil (cf. Thompson, motifs G303.6.1.6, G303.3.3.3.11; Woods, s.vv. dog, black dog; see below).

Mālek b. Anas (d. 179/796) permitted the use of money from the sale of a dog for making the pilgrimage to Mecca (Damīrī, II, p. 291). Trained dogs taken as spoils of war could be given by the imam to whoever might need them (Moḥammad b. Ḥosayn Ṭūsī, II, p. 31; Damīrī, II, p. 291). Killing or maiming a dog requires payment of fines to the owner (Jāḥeẓ, I, pp. 217, 293; ʿAbbās Qomī, II, p. 488). Conversely, the owner is legally responsible for personal injury or damage to property committed by his dog (Moḥammad b. Ḥosayn Ṭūsī, VIII, p. 79), as well as for preventing the dog from being a nuisance (Ḡazālī, I, p. 523; Damīrī, II, p. 291). The question whether or not animals may enter paradise seems to have engaged a number of legal authorities, who reached a compromise according to which only three (in some sources four) animals were said to be allowed to enter, the faithful dog of the "Seven Sleepers of Ephesus" (Aṣḥāb al-kahf) being one of them (ʿAbbās Qomī, II, p. 488; Mobārakšāh, p. 268; cf. Jāḥeẓ, III, p. 395; Damīrī, II, p. 262).

The dog in epic and legend.

Accounts of feral children raised by various animals are widely attested (Thompson, motif B535), though often legendary, but it can be verified that human children have been nursed by dogs (Jāḥeẓ, II, pp. 155-56; Gutman, p. 40; cf. Radbill). Several heroes, gods, and legendary figures of antiquity were supposed to have been nursed by dogs (Leach, pp. 273-75; Binder, pp. 17-57). Herodotus (1.122) reported a legend according to which Cyrus the Great (q.v.) had been suckled by a bitch. Similarly the author of *Mojmal* (ed. Bahār, p. 104) attributed the violent nature of "the father of Soqlāb" to his having been nursed by a dog. In the *Bahman-nāma* violent men are repeatedly likened to those who have been nursed by dogs (Īrānšāh, p. 268 v. 4379). In some oral versions of the *Šāh-nāma* Afrāsīāb (q.v.) is said to have owed his violent temper to his having been suckled by a bitch (Enjavī, 1354 Š./1975, pp. 96-97);

the wicked king Żaḥḥāk is said to have been nursed by a she-wolf (Enjavī, 1357 Š./1978, p. 23). Another ruthless epic character, Boḵtonnaṣr (Nebuchadnezzar), was supposedly so hideous that his parents had no choice but to expose him, but he survived, thanks to a bitch who came to nurse him three times a day (Enjavī, 1973b, p. 27).

The legendary Armenian king Ardāvāzd was said to have been put in chains on Mount Māsīs; his hunting dogs tried to free him by chewing through his chains. Armenian blacksmiths ceremonially pound their anvils before quitting work at the end of each week, in order magically to restore the tyrant's chains (Thompson, motif A1074.7; Enjavī, 1357 Š./1978, pp. 316-17). According to a contemporary Boir Aḥmadī (q.v.) story, the messianic ruler Kayḵosrow is hidden with his horse and hunting dog in a cave in the province of Fārs (Enjavī, 1354 Š./1975, pp. 294-95). Aside from the expected association of kings with hunting dogs in epic literature, dogs fulfill other roles in Persian heroic tales. According to a famous tale in the *Šāh-nāma* and other sources, Bahrām V (q.v.) was awakened to the oppression of his tyrannical vizier as a result of witnessing a shepherd's treatment of his treacherous sheep dog, which, having grown enamored of a she-wolf, was allowing the latter to ravage his master's flocks (Thompson, motif B267.1; Mostawfī, p. 113; Neẓām-al-Molk, pp. 25-26). In a curious version of the epic of Ardašīr I (q.v.) a great dog, rather than the ram usually mentioned in the text, is said to have followed him during his flight (Fozūnī, p. 418).

The dog in mystical literature.

Because of the dog's humble position in Persian life, it became a symbol of humility in mystical literature (see Nurbakhsh). According to some Muslim sources, Jesus scolded his apostles for criticizing the stench of a dog's carcass, rather than appreciating the whiteness of its teeth (Zamaḵšarī, II, p. 175; Jāḥeẓ, II, p. 163; ʿAṭṭār, 1364 Š./1985, p. 302). Noah (Nūḥ, in popular etymology derived from an Arabic root associated with mourning) is said to have received his name because God scolded him for expressing disgust at a dog, which inspired him to bitter lamentation for his deed (Meybodī, IV, pp. 381-82). The mystic Maʿšūq Ṭūsī once struck a dog with a stone, and immediately a divine horseman appeared and whipped him, exclaiming that in the eyes of God the ascetic is essentially no better than the creature that he mistreats (ʿAṭṭār, 1351 Š./1972, pp. 46-47). Many mystics proclaimed that dogs had first taught them humility (ʿAṭṭār, 1351 Š./1972, pp. 155-56; idem, 1364 Š./1985, pp. 196, 314-15; Meybodī, I, p. 447; Bahāʾ-al-Dīn ʿĀmelī, 1268/1852, pp. 14-17; Damīrī, II, p. 257; Fozūnī, p. 533). According to one tradition from the Prophet, dogs are better than some base humans (Meybodī, I, p. 615; Damīrī, II, p. 253). In a similar vein a mystic cursed a *moʾaḏḏen* for his call to prayer while praising a dog because its bark was praising God (Meybodī, III, p. 172; cf. Damīrī, II, pp. 251, 257).

The dog in folk medicine.

Reflecting the belief that bones and tissue from a dog could be successfully grafted to the human body (see above), the Persian physician Bahāʾ-al-Dawla, in his *Ḵolasat al-tajāreb* (comp. 906/1501 at Ray; apud Elgood, p. 229), reported that an Indian doctor residing there had successfully grafted a piece of dog's skin to the scalp of a patient suffering from impetigo (*saʿfa*). He first removed the patient's scalp under anesthesia, then grafted the dog skin to the scalp and treated the wound with various ointments. The transplant worked, and the patient was cured.

Rabies, the disease that most dramatically affects the dog, aroused much concern because it is highly communicable to humans. Many pre-Pasteurian cures are mentioned in the folk medicine of various peoples (Thompson, motif D1515.5; cf. Forbes, pp. 13-14). In one of the earliest Arabic medical texts a remedy for rabies made from the spleen or liver of a rabid dog is included (Ṭabarī, p. 426; cf. Jorjānī, pp. 640, 651; Mostawfī, p. 49; Ebn Boḵtīšūʿ, fol. 93a; Tonokābonī, p. 222; cf. Aelian, 14.20; for other reported treatments of rabies, see Damīrī, II, pp. 252, 297; Ḥāseb Ṭabarī, pp. 51, 110; Šakūrzāda, pp. 253, 275).

Dog's milk was considered a strong antidote against poison, and drinking it was supposed to facilitate the exit of the dead fetus and the placenta from the womb. Women were allowed to suckle newborn dogs, in order to relieve the blockage and pain of gorged breasts (Tonokābonī, p. 222; Katīrāʾī, p. 36). Dog's urine was used in treatment of abscesses and warts. Dogs were also used in treatment of infectious and poisonous bites (for other alleged uses of dogs in treating diseases, see Ebn Boḵtīšūʿ, fols. 7b, 15b, 94a; Hedāyat, p. 115; Jāḥeẓ, I, p. 245, II, p. 205, VII, p. 89; Jorjānī, pp. 395-96, 651; Massé, *Croyances*, pp. 339, 345; Šakūrzāda, pp. 249, 628; cf. Forbes pp. 13-14; Selous, pp. 229-30).

The dog in magic.

The association of the dog with the devil may have motivated several attempts at eradicating the animal. The Prophet Moḥammad (and later Yūsof b. Ḥajjāj) was said to have ordered all dogs to be put to death but to have modified his order to apply only to black dogs, especially those with two spots (*noqtatayn*) over their eyes (Meybodī, III, p. 31; Jāḥeẓ, I, pp. 262, 291-93, II, pp. 153, 293, IV, p. 295; Ebn Qotayba, II, p. 81; Ḥoṣrī, p. 184; Zamaḵšarī, III, p. 451; Balʿamī, ed. Bahār, pp. 987-88; Damīrī, II, pp. 288-89; cf. Rāḡeb, II, p. 665; Donaldson, p. 159; Rudkin).

The black dog figures prominently in magic. Its satanic connections mean that harming it may bring injury or misfortune to the perpetrator (Hedāyat, p. 138; Massé, *Croyances*, p. 197). In Khorasan it is believed that he who kills a dog will lose a child or experience seven years of bad luck (Šakūrzāda, p. 321). Such beliefs may at least partly reflect pre-Islamic taboos against harming dogs (see ii, below), reinterpreted to conform to the Islamic association of the animal with evil. For example, by the 9th century Zoroastrian concern for the welfare of dogs had already come to be viewed as an attempt to avert the evil eye. ʿAmr b. Baḥr Jāḥeẓ (II, p. 131; cf. Zamaḵšarī, III, p. 452) reported that the Persians, fearing the evil eye, did not eat in front of animals, especially dogs. In at least one Shiʿite source this prohibition was attributed to ʿAlī b. Abī Ṭāleb (Ḥāʾerī, XXV, p. 100); nevertheless, according to one tradition, Imam Ḥasan was seen eating in front of a dog, to which he gave a piece of bread for each piece that he ate himself (ʿAbbās Qomī, II, p. 488; cf. Bayhaqī, V, p. 189). According to folk belief, withholding food from a watching dog causes bulimia (*maraż-e jūʿ*; Hedāyat, pp. 138-39, cf. Massé, *Croyances*, p. 205). Bess Allan Donaldson (p. 159) reported that Persians do not allow dogs near them at mealtime for fear of their evil breath. The pre-Islamic ritual of *sagdīd* was also reinterpreted and rationalized by some Muslim authors. Jāḥeẓ (I, p. 375, II, p. 289; cf. Moḥammad b. Maḥmūd Ṭūsī, p. 583), for instance, explained that the reason Zoroastrians exposed their dead to dogs was that the animals' sharp sense of smell would permit them to ascertain whether indeed the persons had died or were merely unconscious (for mistaken attribution of *sagdīd* to the Romans, rather than the Zoroastrians, see ʿAbbās Qomī, II, p. 487; Damīrī, II, p. 252).

Dogs are believed able to see devils and fairies (Thompson, motif E421.1.3), and this belief figures in some prophetic traditions (Damīrī, II, pp. 257, 288-90; Zamaḵšarī, II, p. 579, III, p. 451; cf. Donaldson, pp. 36, 45, 159; Penzer, II, p. 117). It may have given rise to stories of the animals' forecasting the rise and fall of great men (see, e.g., Moḥammad b. Maḥmūd Ṭūsī, p. 497, on the demise of Neẓām-al-Molk). They were also believed to served as mounts for witches (Damīrī, II, p. 259).

A number of practices connected with sympathetic magic involved dogs or things associated with dogs in efforts to cause conflict in or ruin a household (Ebn Boḵtīšūʿ, fol. 94a; Tonokābonī, p. 222; for a story connecting dogs with drunkenness, see Moḥammad b. Maḥmūd Ṭūsī, pp. 323-24; Fozūnī, p. 476; cf. Ḥāseb Ṭabarī, pp. 39, 207). Belief in the evil nature of the dog is expressed in such superstitions as that seeing a dog first thing in the morning is a bad omen and that passing between two dogs brings bad luck (Šakūrzāda, p. 321; Massé, *Croyances*, p. 289). Dogs were also to be avoided if one were wearing certain charms, for their gaze or proximity would nullify the effects (Moḥammad b. Maḥmūd Ṭūsī, p. 148). In the village of Kohnak in Ḵūzestān a more widespread belief that throwing water on a cat will cause warts on the hands has been extended to the dog (Karīmī, p. 44).

Naturally such a potent animal would occasionally be of use against harm as well. Wearing the canine teeth of a rabid dog on the forearm or carrying the tongue of a black dog would ward off attacks by rabid animals; hanging the teeth of a dog around the neck of a teething child would facilitate the process. Wearing the dried penis of a dog on one's thigh would increase sexual appetite (Ṭabarī, p. 426; Damīrī, II, pp. 296-97; Ḥāseb Ṭabarī, pp. 19, 24, 207; Ebn Boḵtīšūʿ, fol. 94a; cf. Donaldson, pp. 30, 160-61; Katīrāʾī, p. 91; Kalāntarī, p. 28). The brain of a whelp might be used in magic rituals (Hedāyat, p. 116; Massé, *Croyances*, p. 314). Pouring diluted dog's milk on the head of the bewitched and fumigating a house suspected of bewitchment with smoke from the dung of a white dog have been considered strong apotropaics in this century (Donaldson, pp. 160-61). Dogs were also believed able to procure the potent mandrake (*mehr-gīāh*) root (cf. *sagkan* "uprooted by dogs," one of the Persian names for the mandrake; Hedāyat, p. 122; Katīrāʾī, p. 354; cf. Penzer, III, pp. 153, 158; Frazer, II, p. 381; Moḥammad b. Maḥmūd Ṭūsī, p. 326; Ginzberg, V, p. 298; Balāḡī, p. 217).

In dream lore a dog generally represents a weak enemy, a hunting dog a wise one (*došman-e ʿālem*); Kurdish and Turkish dogs are interpreted as foreign enemies. Dreaming of a dog that tears one's flesh or clothes is a warning of an impending fierce fight or a base rival who may overcome the dreamer. Similarly a bitch symbolizes a shrewish wife (*Ḵᵛāb-goḏārī*, pp. 337-38; cf. Damīrī, II, p. 297). It is related that the Prophet dreamed that a spotted dog was lapping his blood; upon awakening he interpreted the dream as a harbinger of the martyrdom of his grandson Ḥosayn at the hands of a man suffering from vitiligo (Damīrī, II, p. 255). There is almost unanimous agreement in Persian folklore regarding the ominousness of a howling dog (Šakūrzāda, p. 321; Hedāyat, p. 138; Massé, *Croyances*, p. 191; Ṭāhbāz, p. 71; Karīmī, p. 44; Aʿẓamī Sangesarī, 1349 S./1970b, p. 53; Dānešvar, II, p. 230; Enjavī, 1352-54 Š./1973-75, I, p. 10; Tawakkolī, p. 71). Not only death but also earthquakes and pestilence may be divined from the howling of dogs (Donaldson, p. 159). Weather is also predicted from dogs' behavior: A dog rolling in dust signals the approach of stormy weather, whereas lying down in the shade in the cold foretells approaching warm weather (Šakūrzāda, p. 338; Ṣadīq, p.75). In Gīlān, if jackals howl and dogs howl back, the weather will be good the next day (Rabino, tr., p. 34). In Shiraz the first snowfall is called "dog snow" (*barf-e sag*), and it is believed that no one should eat it (Faqīrī, p. 71). Belief in the association of dogs with weather conditions led to a number of magical practices aimed at improving the latter. In Ḵorram Darra in Azerbaijan, for instance, a ritual called *sag-davānī* (running the dog) is aimed at halting cold weather and blizzards. The inhabitants find and surround a dog, chasing and beating it until it is completely exhausted; having driven it away, they believe they have also cast out cold weather (Enjavī, 1352-54 Š./1973-75, II, p. 9).

Practical uses of the dog (see iii, below).

Hunting dogs were highly prized by both nobility and commoners (*Mojmal*, ed. Bahār, pp. 70, 364). It was believed that they should have long limbs, small heads, and protruding eyeballs (*Nozhat al-qolūb*, ed. Le Strange, p. 49). Royal hunting dogs were ordinarily adorned with gold and fine fabrics (ʿAṭṭār, 1341 Š./1962, p. 149-50; Asadī Ṭūsī, p. 416). Aristocrats also used dogs as official tasters. The mother of the caliph Hārūn al-Rašīd (170-93/786-809) was said to have averted death by giving a dish suspected of poison to a dog (*Mojmal*, ed. Bahār, p. 340). According to a number of stories, some kings kept ferocious dogs to which they threw their opponents to be devoured (Neẓāmī Ganjavī, pp. 146-49; Fozūnī, p. 531; Ebn Baṭṭūṭa, II, 57-60; cf. Penzer, II, p. 121; Thompson, motif Q415.1; Faqīhī, pp. 194-95; Margoliouth and Amedroz, *Eclipse*, p. 58).

Frequent reference to testing the sharpness of a blade on dogs is also found in Persian texts (*Mojmal*, ed. Bahār, p. 331; ʿAṭṭār, 1338 Š./1959, pp. 162, 413; Ṣafā, p. 7). In a related vein swords were treated with a concoction of dog's blood and human urine, in order to ensure that wounds would be fatal (Ḥāseb Ṭabarī, p. 209).

Although the Prophet forbade animal fights (see Tawḥīdī, 1408/1988, I, p. 210; cf. Albānī, s.v. *Jehād* 30; Abū Dāwūd, s.v. *Jehād* 51), the practice is well attested in the Persian cultural area in the Islamic period (Jāḥeẓ, II, pp. 163-64, V, p. 246; *Šāh-nāma*, Moscow, III, pp. 16, 177-78 n. 23). Sometimes dogs were made to fight other animals. Jāḥeẓ reported an instance of a fight between a cock and a dog (I, p. 376; cf. *Čahār maqāla*, ed. Qazvīnī, p. 60). Evidently those of a yellow or reddish color were preferred (Moḥammad b. Maḥmūd Ṭūsī, p. 584; Ebn Boḵtīšūʿ, fol. 91a).

There seems to have been a class of people called *sagbān* or *sag-banda* (dog keeper), whose profession was caring for dogs (Meybodī, I, p. 615). Dogs were trained and highly prized for particular abilities. Jāḥeẓ mentioned dogs trained to balance lamps on their heads and to carry lists and money to grocers, who would place the required merchandise in pouches to be carried to the dogs' masters (II, p. 179; cf. Zamaḵšarī, IV, pp. 435-36). There are also reports of bestiality involving dogs (Jāḥeẓ, I, pp. 369-71, 373, III, p. 203; Rāḡeb, III, p. 257).

Dogs in fable and folktale.

Many fables about dogs in the Aesopian corpus are also found in Persian folklore and literature. Perhaps the most famous is about the dog that drops meat (or a bone) for its reflection in the water (Thompson, motif J1791.4; Arne and Thompseon, type 34A; Bodker, p. 950; Thompson and Roberts, p. 270; Daly, no. 133; Amīnī, p. 283; cf. ʿAṭṭār, 1364 Š./1985, p. 154; Boḵārī, p. 66; Brockelmann). Others have been classified by Ulrich Marzolph (s.v. *Hund*), who has also provided a convenient list of tale types about dogs in Persian folk narrative.

Tales of the dog's fidelity are particularly well represented in oral and written sources. In one version (Arne and Thompson, type 178A; Thompson, motif B331.2) a dog (or sometimes a mongoose) saves a child from a serpent by biting the latter to death; the child's father sees the dog's bloody mouth and, thinking that it has eaten his child, kills the animal, then finds out the truth (Boḵārī, p. 214). A related story (Arne and Thompson, type 178B) is more common. A man leaves his faithful dog as security for a debt; the dog saves the creditor's life, and the latter sends the dog back to its master with an appreciative note tied around its neck, forgiving the debt. Seeing the dog approaching, the debtor thinks that it has escaped and thus dishonored him. Angrily he kills it and then finds the letter (Fozūnī, p. 531; for a study of this tale, see Emmeneau). In other tales a murdered man's hound either attacks and kills its master's slayers or points them out to the authorities by barking (Ebn al-Jawzī, p. 244; Damīrī, II, pp. 253-54; Fozūnī, pp. 531-32); this type of tale goes back to the ancient Greeks (Aelian, 7.113). The dog's fidelity unto death is exemplified in the tale of a man whose dog remains with his corpse and dies from the canine equivalent of a broken heart (e.g., Mostawfī, p. 282; cf. Aelian, 6.25, 7.10). There are also reports of dogs who supposedly rescued their masters from death or danger (Zamaḵšarī, IV, p. 421; Ebn al-Jawzī, pp. 223-24, 245-46; Fozūnī, p. 532-34; Enjavī, 1973a, pp. 353-55, 402-03, idem, 1973b, pp. 209-10, idem, 1976; pp. 168-71).

Turning people into dogs by magic or by wishing is commonly attested in the folk and written traditions (Rāzī, IX, p. 16; Meybodī, III, p. 790; Qorṭobī, VII, pp. 320-21; Enjavī, 1973a, pp. 375-76, 384-85, 396-97). Alternatively a persecuted individual may hide in a hound's skin and live a dog's life, rather than risk discovery (Enjavī, 1973a, pp. 80-83).

Bibliography: (For cited works not found in this bibliography and abbreviations found here, see "Short References.") A. Aarne and S. Thompson, *The Types of the Folktale*, 2nd ed., Helsinki, 1973. Abū Dāwūd Solaymān b. Ašʿaṯ Sejestānī, *Sonan Abī Dāwūd*, ed. M. M. ʿAbd-al-Ḥamīd, 4 vols., Beirut, 1970. M. N. Albānī, *Żaʿīf sonan al-Termeḏī*, ed. M. Z. Šāwīš, Beirut, 1991. Bahāʾ-al-Dīn ʿĀmelī, *Nān o ḥalwā*, n.p., 1268/1852. A. Amīnī, *Dāstānhā-ye amṯāl*, 2nd ed., Isfahan, 1333 Š./1954. Awḥad-al-Dīn Moḥammad Anwarī, *Dīvān-e Anwarī*, ed. M.-T. Modarres Rażawī, 2 vols., Tehran, 1337-40 Š./1958-61. Asadī Ṭūsī, *Garšāsp-nāma*, ed. Ḥ. Yaḡmāʾī, Tehran 1333 Š./1954. Farīd-al-Dīn ʿAṭṭār, *Asrar-nāma*, ed. Ṣ. Gowharīn, 1338 Š./1959; repr. Tehran, 1361 Š./1982. Idem, *Manṭeq al-ṭayr*, ed. M.-J. Maškūr, Tehran, 1341 Š./1962.

Idem, *Elāhī-nāma*, ed. F. Rūḥānī, Tehran, 1351 Š./1972. Idem, *Moṣībat-nāma*, ed. ʿA. Nūrānī Weṣāl, Tehran, 1364 Š./1985. Č. Aʿẓamī Sangesarī, "Bāvarhā-ye ʿāmīāna-ye mardom-e Sangesar," *Honar o mardom* 92, 1349 Š./1970a, pp. 47-56; 93, 1349 Š./1970b, pp. 53-56. ʿA. Balāḡī, *Ketāb-e tārīḵ-e Nāʾīn*, Tehran, 1369/1949. Aḥmad b. Ḥosayn Bayhaqī, *Šoʿab al-īmān*, ed. M. Zaḡlūl, 9 vols., Beirut, 1410/1990. G. Binder, *Die Aussetzung des Königskindes Kyros und Romulus*, Meisenheim am Glan, Germany, 1964. L. Bodker, *Indian Animal Tales*, Helsinki, 1957. Moḥammad b. ʿAbd-Allāh Boḵārī, *Dāstānhā-ye Bīdpāy*, ed. P. N. Ḵānlarī and M. Rowšan, Tehran, 1361 Š./1982. C. Brockelmann, "Fabel und Tiermärchen in der älteren arabischen Literatur," *Islamica* 2, 1926, pp. 96-128. *Bundahišn*, tr. M. Bahār as *Farnbaḡ-dādagī (Bondaheš)*, Tehran, 1369 Š./1990. L. W. Daly, *Aesop without Morals*, New York and London, 1961. Moḥammad b. Mūsā Damīrī, *Ḥayāt al-ḥayawān al-kobrā*, 2 vols., Cairo, 1970; repr. Qom, 1364 Š./1985. M. Dānešvar, *Dīdanīhā wa šanīdanīhā-ye Īrān*, 2 vols., Tehran, 1327-28 Š./1948-49. B. A. Donaldson, *The Wild Rue. A Study of Muhammadan Magic and Folklore in Iran*, London, 1938. ʿAbd-Allāh Ebn Abī Donyā, *Ketāb al-ṣamt wa ādāb al-lesān*, ed. N. ʿA. Ḵalaf, Beirut, 1406/1986. Ebn Boḵtīšūʿ, *Manāfeʿ al-ḥayawān*, The Pierpont Morgan Library, New York, ms. no. M 500. ʿAbd al-Raḥmān Ebn al-Jawzī, *Aḵbār al-aḏkīāʾ*, ed. M. M. Ḵūlī, Cairo, 1970. ʿAbd-Allāh Ebn Qotayba, *ʿOyūn al-aḵbār*, 4 vols., Cairo, n.d. (1964). Aḥmad Ebn Taymīya, *al-Eḵtīārāt al-feqhīya men fatāwā Šayḵ-al-Eslām Ebn Taymīya*, ed. M. Ḥ. Feqī, Beirut, 1980. C. Elgood, "Bahaʾ-ul-Douleh and the Quintessence of Experience," in E. A. Underwood, ed., *Science, Medicine, and History. Essays on the Evolution of Scientific Thought and Medical Practice Written in Honour of Charles Singer*, I, London, 1953, pp. 224-31. M. B. Emmeneau, "The Faithful Dog as Security for a Debt. A Companion to the Brahman and Mongoose Story-Type," *JAOS* 61, 1941, pp. 1-17; 62, 1942, pp. 339-41.

A. Enjavī Šīrāzī, *Gol beh ṣenowbar če kard?* Tehran, 1352 Š./1973a; repr. Tehran, 2537=1357 Š./1978. Idem, *Tamṯīl o maṯal*, Tehran, 1352 Š./1973b; repr. Tehran, 2537=1357 Š./1978. Idem, *Jašnhā o ādāb o moʿtaqedāt-e zemestān*, 2 vols., Tehran, 1352-54 Š./1973-75. Idem, *ʿArūsak-e sang-e ṣabūr*, Tehran, 1355 Š./1976. Idem, *Mardom o Šāh-nāma*, Tehran, 1354 Š./1975. Idem, *Mardom o qahramānān-e Šāh-nāma*, Tehran 2537=1357 Š./1978; repr. Tehran, 1366 Š./1987. E. P. Evans, *The Criminal Prosecution and Capital Punishment of Animals*, London, 1906. ʿA.-A. Faqīhī, *Šāhanšāhī-e ʿAżod-al-Dawla*, Tehran, n.d. (1968). A. Faqīrī, "Moʿtaqadāt-e mardom-e Šīrāz," *Honar o mardom*, 123, 1351 Š./1972, pp. 67-72. R. and A. Fiennes, *The Natural History of the Dog*, London, 1968. T. R. Forbes, "The Madstone," in W. H. Hand, ed., *American Folk Medicine. A Symposium*, Berkeley and Los Angeles, 1976, pp. 11-21. Fozūnī Estarābādī, *Boḥayra*, Tehran, 1328/1910. J. G. Frazer, *Folk-Lore in the Old Testament*, 3 vols., London, 1919. Moḥammad Ḡazālī, *Kīmīā-ye saʿādat*, ed. Ḥ. Ḵadīv Jam, 2 vols., Tehran, 1361 Š./1982. L. Ginzberg, *The Legends of the Jews*, 7 vols., Philadelphia, 1909-38; repr. Philadelphia, 1967-69. I. Goldziher, "Islamisme et parsisme," *RHR* 43, 1901, pp. 1-29. Grattius, "Cynegeticon," in J. W. Duff and A. M. Duff, eds., *Minor Latin Poets*, Cambridge, Mass, 1958, pp. 161-70. J. M. Gutman, *Through Indian Eyes*, New York, 1982.

M.-Ḥ. Ḥāʾerī, *Ketāb moqtabes al-aṯar*, 30 vols., Tehran, 1350 Š./1971. Moḥammad Ḥakīm Termeḏī, *al-Amṯāl men al-ketāb wa al-sonna*, ed. ʿA.-M. Bajāwī, Cairo, n.d. (1975). R. L. Hall and H. S. Sharp, eds., *Wolf and Man. Evolution in Parallel*, New York, 1978. Moḥammad b. Ayyūb Ḥāseb Ṭabarī, *Toḥfat al-ḡarāʾeb*, ed. J. Matīnī, Tehran, 1371 Š./1992. Ṣ. Hedāyat, *Neyrangestān*, Tehran, 1342 Š./1963. F. Hole, K. V. Flannery, and J. A. Neely, *Prehistory and Human Ecology of the Deh Luran Plain*, Memoirs of the Museum of Anthropology 1, Ann Arbor, Mich., 1969. Ebrāhīm b. ʿAlī Ḥoṣrī Qayrawānī, *Jamʿ al-jawāher fi'l-molaḥ wa'l-nawāder*, ed. ʿA. M. Bajāwī, Cairo, 1353/1934; repr. Beirut, 1407/1987. D. B. Hull, *Hounds and Hunting in Ancient Greece*, Chicago, 1964. Īrānšāh b. Abi'l-Ḵayr, *Bahman-nāma*, ed. R. ʿAfīfī, Tehran, 1370 Š./1991. ʿAmr b. Baḥr Jāḥeẓ, *al-Ḥayawān*, ed. ʿA. M. Hārūn, 2nd ed., 8 vols., Cairo, 1387/1968. Neʿmat-Allāh Jazāʾerī, *al-Nūr al-mobīn fī Qeṣaṣ al-anbīāʾ wa'l-morsalīn*, 2nd ed., Beirut, 1398/1978. Esmāʿīl b. Ḥosayn Jorjānī, *Ḏaḵīra-ye ḵʷārazmšāhī*, ed. ʿA.-A. Saʿīdī Sīrjānī, Tehran, 2535=1355 Š./1976. *Ḵʷāb-goḏārī*, ed. Ī. Afšār, Tehran, 1346 Š./1967. M. Kalāntarī "Īl-e Mīlān," *Honar o mardom* 43, 1345 Š./1966, pp. 20-31. A. Karīmī, "Kohnak," *Honar o mardom* 85, 1348 Š./1969, pp. 35-44. M. Katīrāʾī, *Az ḵešt tā ḵešt*, Tehran, 1348 Š./1969. Abū Jaʿfar Moḥammad Kolaynī, *Ketāb al-kāfī*, ed. ʿA.-A. Ḡaffārī, 8 vols., Tehran, 1367 Š./1988. W. La Barre, *The Human Animal*, Chicago, 1954. M. Leach, *God Had a Dog. Folklore of the Dog*, New Brunswick, N.J., 1961. C. Lévi-Strauss, *Le cru et le cuit*, Paris, 1964; tr. J. and D. Weightman as *The Raw and the Cooked*, New York, 1969; repr. Chicago, 1983. U. Marzolph, *Typologie des persischen Volksmärchens*, Berliner Texte und Studien 31, Beirut, 1984. R. H. Meadow, "The Vertebrate Faunal Remains from Hasanlu Period X at Hajji Firuz. The Neolithic Settlement," in M. M. Voigt, ed., *Hajji Firuz Tepe, Iran. The Neolithic Settlement*, Hasanlu Excavation Reports I, University of Pennsylvania, University Museum Monograph 50, Philadelphia, 1983, pp. 369-422. Abu'l-Fażl Rašīd-al-Dīn Meybodī, *Kašf al-asrār wa ʿoddat al-abrār*, ed. ʿA.-A. Ḥekmat, 10 vols., Tehran, 1357 Š./1978. Moḥam-mad b. Manṣūr Mobārakšāh (Fak̲r-e Modabber), *Ādāb al-ḥarb wa'l-šajāʿa*, ed. A. Zajaczkowski as *Le traité iranien de l'art militaire, Ādāb al-ḥarb wa-š-šaǧā'a, du XIIIe siècle*, Warsaw, 1969. Ḥamd-Allāh Mostawfī, *Tārīk̲-e gozīda*, ed. ʿA.-Ḥ Navāʾī, Tehran, 1363 Š./1984. Neẓām-al-Molk, *Sīāsat-nāma*, ed. M. Qazvīnī and M. Modarresī, Tehran, 2537=1357 Š./1978. Neẓāmī Ganjavī, *Leylī o Majnūn*, ed. Ḥ. Pežmān Bak̲tīārī, Tehran, 1347 Š./1968. J. Nurbakhsh, *Dogs. From the Sufi Point of View*, London, 1989. S. J. Olsen, *Origins of the Domestic Dog. The Fossil Record*, Tucson, Ariz., 1985. N. M. Penzer, *The Ocean of Story*, 10 vols., London, 1925; repr. Bombay, 1968. ʿAbbās b. Moḥammad-Reżā Qomī, *Safīnat al-beḥār wa madīnat al-ḥekam wa'l-āthār*, 2 vols., Beirut, 1355/1936; repr. Beirut, 1405/1985. ʿAlî b. Ebrāhīm Qomī, *Tafsīr Qomī*, 2 vols., ed. Ṭ. Jazāʾerī, Najaf, 1386/1967. Moḥammad b. Aḥmad Qorṭobī, *al-Jāmeʿ le-aḥkām al-Qorʾān*, 20 vols., Cairo, 1387/1967. H. L. Rabino, *Les provinces caspiennes de la Perse. Le Guîlân*, tr. J. K̲ammāmīzāda as *Welāyāt-e dār al-marz-e Īrān*, Tehran, 1350 Š./1971. S. Radbill, "The Role of the Animals in Infant Feeding," in W. D. Hand, ed., *American Folk Medicine. A Symposium*, Berkeley and Los Angeles, 1976, pp. 21-31. Abu'l-Qāsem Ḥosayn Rāḡeb Eṣfahānī, *Moḥāżarāt al-odabāʾ wa moḥāwarāt al-šoʿarāʾ wa'l-bolaḡāʾ*, 4 vols. in 2, Beirut, 1961. Abu'l-Fotūḥ Rāzī, *Rawż al-jenān wa rawḥ al-janān fī tafsīr al-Qorʾān* IX-XVII, ed. M.-M. Nāṣeḥ and M.-J. Yāḥaqqī, Mašhad, 1367 Š./1988. E. H. Rudkin, "The Black Dog," *Folklore* (London) 49, 1938, pp. 111-31.

M. Ṣadīq, "Gūšahā-ī az zendagī-e mardom-e dehkada-ye samīya," *Honar o mardom* 158, 1354 Š./1975, pp. 70-76. Ḏ. Ṣafā, "Do šāʿer-e gom-nām," *MDAT* 2/3, 1334 Š./1955, pp. 1-7. E. Šakūrzāda, *ʿAqāyed o rosūm-e mardom-e K̲orāsān*, 2nd ed., Tehran, 1362 Š./1983. E. Selous, "The Hair of the Dog That Bit Him," *Folklore* (London) 23, 1912, pp. 229-30. ʿAlī b. Sahl Rabban Ṭabarī, *Ferdaws al-ḥekma*, ed. M. Z. Siddiqi, Berlin, 1928. S. Ṭāhbāz, *Yūš*, Tehran, 1342 Š./1963. M.-R. Tawakkolī, *Joḡrāfīā wa tārīk̲-e bāna-ye Kordestān*, 2nd ed., Tehran, 1362 Š./1983. Abū Ḥayyān Tawḥīdī, *Ketāb al-emtāʿ wa'l-moʾānasa*, ed. A. Amīn and A. Zayn, 3 vols., Beirut, 1973. Idem, *al-Baṣāʾer wa al-ḏak̲āʾer*, ed. W. Qāżī, 10 vols., Beirut, 1408/1988. S. Thompson, *Motif-Index of Folk-Literature*, rev. ed., 6 vols., Bloomington, Ind., 1955. Idem and W. Roberts, *Types of Indic Tales*, Helsinki, 1960. Moḥammad-Moʾmen Tonokābonī (Ḥakīm Moʾmen), *Toḥfa-ye Ḥakīm Moʾmen* Tehran, 1277/1860; repr. Tehran, 1338 Š./1959. Moḥammad b. Ḥosayn Ṭūsī, *al-Mabsūṭ fi'l-feqh al-emāmīya*, 8 vols., ed. M.-B. Behbūdī, Tehran, 1351 Š./1972. Moḥammad b. Maḥmūd Ṭūsī, *ʿAjāyeb al-mak̲lūqāt*, ed. M. Sotūda, Tehran, 1345 Š./1966. B. A. Woods, *The Devil in Dog Form. A Partial Type-Index of Devil Legends*, Berkeley and Los Angeles, 1959. Maḥmūd b. ʿOmar Zamak̲šarī, *Rabīʿ al-abrār wa noṣūṣ al-ak̲bār*, ed. S. Noʿaymī, 4 vols., Baghdad, 1976-82. F. E. Zeuner, *A History of Domesticated Animals*, New York, 1963.

(MAHMOUD OMIDSALAR AND TERESA P. OMIDSALAR)

ii. IN ZOROASTRIANISM

There was evidently an Indo-European belief in supernatural dogs of death (Schlerath), and these appear in the *Rigveda* as the "four-eyed" hounds of Yama, who watch along the path which departed souls take to their future abode (Keith, II, pp. 406-07). In *Vidēvdād* 19.30 two dogs are said to stand at the Činvat bridge (see ČINWAD PUHL), by the female figure (the Daēna, q.v.) who there confronts the soul, and in *Vidēvdād* 13.9 these are called the "two bridge-protecting dogs" (*spāna pəšu.pāna*).

Mortal dogs receive a striking degree of attention in the "legal" (*dādīg*) books of the Avesta, notably in the *Vidēvdād* and the almost wholly lost *Duzd-sar-nizad*, the contents of which are known from *Dēnkard* (q.v.) 8. The two chief categories of dog (*Vd.* 13.8 and passim; *Ardā Wīrāz nāmag* 48.4) are the herd dog (*pasuš.haurva*, lit., "cattle protecting"; Pahl. *sag ī šubānān*) and house dog (*viš.haurva*, lit. "house protecting"; Pahl. *sag ī mānbānān*). Their duties only are defined (*Vd.* 13.17-18). To them are added the *vohunazga* (*Vd.* 13.8), which other Avestan and Pahlavi contexts suggest was a masterless dog, loosely attached to the local community; and finally the *tauruna* (*Vd.* 13.15), apparently a young dog (linked by a simile with a youth who has put on the sacred girdle; *Vd.* 13.23), presumably not yet trained.

Gratitude is required of men toward the herd and house dog, for Ahura Mazdā (q.v.) is represented as declaring: "No house would stand *firmly founded* for me on the Ahura-created earth were there not my herd dog or house dog" (*nōiṯ mē nmānəm vīδātō hištənti ząm paiti ahuraδātąm yezi mē nōiṯ åŋhāṯ spā pasuš.haurvō vā viš.haurvō vā*; *Vd.* 13.49). Responsibility toward dogs is repeatedly linked with responsibility toward humans. In the Huspārām Nask the proper quantities of food are listed for man, woman, child, and the three kinds of dogs (*Dēnkard* 8.37.1). A sick dog is to be looked after as carefully as a sick person (*Vd.* 13.35), a bitch in whelp as solicitously as a woman with child (*Vd.* 15.19). Puppies are to be cared for for six months, children for seven years (*Vd.* 15.45). There is a partly playful account of how the dog combines the characteristics of eight kinds of people (*Vd.* 13.44-48), and a description of him as created by Ahura Mazdā "self-clothed, self-shod, alertly watchful, sharp-toothed, sharing the food of men, to watch over (man's) possessions" (*hvāvastrəm xᵛā.aoθrəm zaēni.buδrəm tiži.dąsurəm vīrō.draonaŋhəm gaēθanąm harəθrāi*;

Vd. 13.39). "Having/sharing the food of men" (*vīrō.draonaŋhəm*) is to be taken literally. In *Vidēvdād* 13.28 it is enjoined that a dog is to be given milk and fat together with meat (*xšvisca āzūitišca gə̄uš maṯ*), staple articles of the diet of pastoralists.

According to a lost Avestan passage, preserved through Pahlavi translation in the *Bundahišn* (tr. Anklesaria, 13.28), the dog was created "from the star station . . . for the protection of beneficent animals, as if blended of beneficent animals and people" (*az star pāyag . . . pānagīh ī gōspandān rāy, čun gumēzag az gōspandān ud mardōhmān*). Because he was held to be of moral character, his corpse was thought to be surrounded, like a good person's, by triumphant evil powers, and so was highly contaminating. Hence one of the places where earth suffers most is where the bodies of men and dogs are buried (*Vd.* 3.8). If a dog dies in a house, fire is to be taken out of that house, as when a person dies (*Vd.* 5.39-40), and the dog's body is to be carried like a human's to a place of exposure (*Vd.* 8.14).

Like a human's, it contaminates the path over which it is carried, which is then to be purified by a living dog being led over it, for a dog was thought capable of driving away Nasu, the corpse demon which brings putrefaction. The dog used for this task was ideally "tawny with four eyes (or) white with tawny ears" (*zairitəm caθru.cašməm spaētəm zairi.gaošəm*; *Vd.* 8.16). There seems an echo here of the supernatural four-eyed dogs of Yama, though for a mortal creature the characteristic is understood, by later Zoroastrians at least, as having two flecks of different-colored hairs just above the eyes (Jackson; Boyce, *Stronghold*, p. 140 and n. 3).. Because of the belief that a dog could drive away contaminating demons it was also to be present at the ritual cleansing known later as the *barašnom-e nō šaba* (*Vd.* 8.37, 8.38; see BARAŠNOM).

It seems probable that this power came to be attributed to the dog because dogs are the animals always referred to in the Avesta as devouring corpses, and, as they (presumably, that is, the *vohunazga* dogs, which would have followed the corpse bearers to the exposure place) were able to do this with impunity, it was plain that the corpse demon could not harm them. (On similar corpse eating by the dogs of modern African pastoralists see Boyce, p. 100 n. 56; see also CORPSE; DEATH). Thus a Pahlavi gloss on the *vohunazga* dog of *Vidēvdād* 13.19 is "he smites Nasu" (*nasūš ē zanēd*; *Pahlavi Vendidād*, p. 283.)

Respect for dogs was maintained in later Zoroastrianism, with most of the usages enjoined in the Avesta being continued, and some even elaborated. With the general building of funerary towers, the disposal of corpses was left to carrion-eating birds; but the dog was still used to help drive off Nasu at the *barašnom-e nō šaba*, and the additional rite of *sagdīd* (lit., "seen by the dog") was evolved, evidently from the belief that he has the power to do so. For this rite a dog (male and at least four months old) was brought to look at a corpse before it was carried to the *daḵma*, in order to lessen the contamination. The rite is first attested in the late Sasanian *Šāyest nē šāyest* (chap. 2), with what appears to be a supportive interpolation in the *Vidēvdād sāde* (between 7.2 and 7.3; given in *Avesta*, tr. Darmesteter, II, p. 97). In time the rite came to be performed three times for each corpse (at death, when it was placed on the bier, and outside the *daḵma*) and also during each *gāh* if the funeral were delayed (Modi, pp. 58, 63).

The dog was induced to go up to the corpse by three bits of bread being placed on or by it. For Iranians bread had long replaced meat as the staple of diet, and three pieces of bread had become the recognized "portion for the dog" (in Zor. Pers. the *čom-e šwa*, in Parsi Gujarati the *kutrā-nō būk*). In *Saddar naṯr* 31.1 it is enjoined that "whenever people eat, they should keep back three morsels from themselves and give them to a dog," and this was general practice in the Irani and Parsi communities down into the present century (Boyce, *Stronghold*, pp. 143, 145 n. 11). In one of the *Persian Rivāyats* (ed. Unvala, I, pp. 256.19-257.4; tr. Dhabhar, p. 259) it is said that, if a person does this, he will be saved from even due torments in hell, while Ardā Wīrāz sees the soul of a man suffering in hell who had withheld food from dogs (*Ardā Wīrāz nāmag* 48.4). In *Saddar naṯr* 31.5 it is said that food was given because the donor hoped that the dogs of the Činvat bridge would aid his soul, and sometimes still in recent usage the daily *čom-e šwa* was given at sunset in the name of someone departed, in the hope of helping him or her in the hereafter (Boyce, *Stronghold*, p. 144).

At every Zoroastrian religious service there is invocation of the *fravašis*, the souls of the dead, and the link of the dog with death and the soul brought it about that on holy days and at memorial rites the *čom-e šwa* was augmented by portions of everything consecrated at the "outer" religious service, including always a whole egg, symbol of immortality. This was given to a dog by someone (preferably, at a memorial service, a close relative) in a state of ritual purity and with recital of Avestan. A portion of the food offerings for the dead was thus always given to a dog (Boyce, *Stronghold*, pp. 143-44, 158; Modi, pp. 404, 350). During the three days after death, if there were no house dog, a lane dog would be tied up in the courtyard (Persia) or on the verandah (Gujarat) and given food for the soul's sake at every mealtime, and then, in Persia, once a day outside the house for the next forty days (Boyce, *Stronghold*, pp. 153 and n. 30, 158).

As a distinct usage, the tongue of every sacrificed animal was consecrated with a *Hōm drōn* (service dedicated to Haoma) and given to a dog to eat (Boyce, *Stronghold*, p. 158). Until the mid-20th century when a house dog died its body was wrapped in an old sacred shirt tied with a sacred girdle, and was carried to a barren place (cf. *Šāyest nē šayest* 2.7), and brief rituals were solemnized for its spirit

(Boyce, *Stronghold*, pp. 162-63). All rites in which dogs are concerned have been under attack by reformists since the mid-19th century, and have by now been wholly abandoned by them, and are much curtailed even by the orthopractic.

Bibliography: (For cited works not found in this bibliography, see "Short References.") M. Boyce, *Zoroastrianism. Its Antiquity and Constant Vigour*, Columbia Iranian Series 7, Costa Mesa, Calif., 1992. A. V. W. Jackson, *Persia Past and Present*, New York, 1909; repr. New York, 1975. A. B. Keith, *The Religion and Philosophy of the Veda and Upanishads*, 2 vols., Harvard Oriental Series 31-32, Cambridge, Mass., 1925; repr. Delhi, 1970. J. J. Modi, *The Religious Ceremonies and Customs of the Parsees*, Bombay, 1937; repr. New York, 1986. *Pahlavi Vendidād*, tr. B. T. Anklesaria, Bombay, 1949. B. Schlerath, "Der Hund bei den Indo-germanen," *Paideuma* 6, 1954, pp. 25-40.

(Mary Boyce)

iii. Ethnography

In contrast to attitudes toward the dog in pre-Islamic Persia (see ii, above), those of Persian and Afghan Muslims, like those of the majority of Muslims everywhere, are generally hostile (Bousquet). They consider the animal unclean (*najes*) and as much as possible avoid direct contact with it. Consumption of the flesh of the dog, like that of all carnivores, is absolutely proscribed (*ḥarām*). According to Imam Jaʿfar al-Ṣādeq, it is even forbidden (*makrūh*) to keep a dog in the house (Donaldson, p. 159). Canine pets are thus unknown in Persia, except among the most westernized minority in the northern quarters of Tehran. In Afghanistan there is "an urban pet, called *papi*, [that] at least superficially resembles the spitz of southern Siberia and farther north" (Dupree, p. 50), but that is a marginal instance; the general tendency in the Iranian world is to avoid, even to maltreat dogs, to the point that in Afghanistan "Europeans have been known to spend time in local jails for taking issue with an Afghan flogging his dog" (Dupree, p. 49).

Such attitudes have resulted in the proliferation of stray dogs, especially in the cities, where they find nourishment in various kinds of garbage, thus playing a not insignificant role as scavengers; they also pose numerous problems of health (e.g., rabies) and security, however, justifying periodic extermination drives. As for Afghanistan, according to Louis Dupree (p. 50), "packs of dogs nocturnally roam the streets of the larger cities, particularly Kabul. Periodically, the police liberally distribute poisoned meat throughout Kabul. The survivors, however, live quite well off the land. I tend to grade the level of poverty in Asian cities by examining the state of the urban dog-population. Those in Kabul appear fatter and healthier than most I have seen elsewhere in Asia."

Despite this prevailing hostility, there is no shortage of examples in Persian culture of opinions and behavior less unfavorable to the dog. Already in the *Vidēvdād* important virtues were recognized, and in one passage it was prescribed that six-month-old puppies be fed by young girls, who would thus earn the same merit as if they had been guardians of the sacred fire (Voutsy, 1989, p. 369; cf. Hovelacque, passim). An analogous message is to be found in a poem by Saʿdī (p. 85). A man finds a thirsty dog in a desert. Using his hat and turban, he draws water from a well to serve the dog. For this meritorious act God forgives all his sins. Some Sufi masters held the dog in high esteem because of its virtues: courage, devotion, fidelity, and so on. Their few negative comments have recently been explained with considerable condescension (Nurbakhsh) as having resulted from the inevitable influence exercised on Sufi literature by surrounding Muslim tradition.

At any rate, it is clear that in practice Persians recognize and treat differently several categories of dog. In fact, since antiquity hunting dogs and sheep dogs have been distinguished from the mass of roaming city and country dogs. The hunting dogs were mainly coursers (Pers. *tāzī*, Afghan *bārakzā*), used for hunting gazelles, onagers, and rabbits. They were often very expensive and received special training and care, as well as exceptionally favorable treatment. Hunting with such dogs was strictly codified; they were not to be trained by non-Muslims and were not permitted to kill the game (Donaldson, p. 159). This kind of hunting, an aristocratic privilege par excellence, has almost disappeared in Persia, though it remained common in Afghanistan in the 1970s (Dupree, pp. 215-17).

On the other hand, sheep dogs (in Persia *sag-e galla*, in Afghanistan *sag-e rama*, *sag-e torkestānī*, Pašto *da ramay spay*) are working animals and are very widely used. In contrast to Western sheep dogs (Planhol), they are essentially only mastiffs, which do not intervene except to defend domestic flocks against thieves and predatory animals (e.g., wolves, bears, lynxes, panthers). They are thus often provided with spiked collars or straps (Papoli-Yazdi, p. 332), and sometimes their tails and ears are clipped, in order to provide less purchase for the teeth of carnivores and to increase the acuity of their hearing (Digard, 1981, p. 63). These dogs (two to five per flock) are fed (coarse bread or wheat-flour cakes) only by the shepherds, to whom they become attached; they are aggressive and dangerous toward strangers. Such dogs can also be very important in guarding cultivated fields (Digard, 1981, p. 246), caravans (Dupree, pp. 49-50), and nomad tents and thus play a substantial role in the internal organization of encampments (Digard, 1980). All guard dogs are treated fairly harshly. Nevertheless, only these dogs and horses are given proper names: Gallepā (guardian of the flocks), Ḵersī (like a bear), Palang (panther), Nahang (crocodile, not to be confused with its recent meaning "whale"), and so on.

A few animals are selected for their size and fierceness and trained as fighting dogs. Until recently such fights took place every Friday in Kabul, where they were the occasion for considerable betting (Dupree, pp. 50, 217). In Persia and Afghanistan (as formerly in many other parts of the Islamic world) the dog thus has a highly ambiguous status, depending ultimately more on the functions that the animal fulfills than on social norms, which are often contradicted or simply ignored in practice.

Bibliography: (For abbreviations found in this bibliography, see "Short References.") G.-H. Bousquet, "Des animaux et de leur traitement selon le Judaïsme, le Chris-tianisme et l'Islam," *Stud. Isl.* 9, 1958, pp. 31-48. J.-P. Digard, "Chiens de campement et chiens de troupeau chez les nomades Baxtyâri d'Iran," *Stud. Ir.* 9/1, 1980, pp. 131-39. Idem, *Techniques des nomades Baxtyâri d'Iran*, Cambridge and Paris, 1981. Idem, *L'homme et les animaux domestiques. Anthropologie d'une passion*, Paris, 1990. B. A. Donaldson, *The Wild Rue. A Study of Muhammadan Magic and Folklore in Iran*, New York, 1938; repr. New York, 1973. L. Dupree, *Afghanistan*, Princeton, N.J., 1978; repr. Princeton, N.J., 1980. A. Hovelacque, *Le chien dans l'Avesta. Les soins qui lui sont dus, son éloge*, Paris, 1876. Dj. Nurbakhsh, *Dogs from a Sufi Point of View*, London, 1989. M.-H Papoli-Yazdi, *Le nomadisme dans le nord du Khorassan*, Paris and Tehran, 1370 Š./1991. X. de Planhol, "Le chien de berger. Développement et signification géographique d'une technique pastorale," *Bulletin de l'Association des Géographes Français* 370, 1969, pp. 355-68. Saʿdī, *Būstān*, ed. Ḡ.-Ḥ. Yūsofī, Tehran, 1363 Š./1985. F. Viré, "À propos des chiens de chasse *saluqi* et *zagari*," *REI* 41/2, 1973, pp. 321-40; repr. in *Production pastorale et Société* 16, 1985, pp. 71-77. M. Voutsy, "Un chien en Sorbonne. Vers une anthro-pologie du chien," in *Une galaxie anthropologique. Hommage à Louis-Vincent Thomas*, Saint-Mandé, France, 1989, pp. 353-79.

(JEAN-PIERRE DIGARD)

DOḠLAT, MĪRZĀ MOḤAMMAD ḤAYDAR. See Supplement.

DOGONBADAN. See GAČSARĀN.

DOJAYL. See KĀRŪN.

DOḴĀNĪYĀT (tobacco projects), referring to the State tobacco-monopoly law (Qānūn-e enḥeṣār-e dawlatī-e doḵānīyāt) of 29 Esfand 1307/20 March 1909 and to the state monopoly of tobacco products itself.

After an abortive attempt to tax unprocessed tobacco through a national monopoly in 1307/1890 (see Tobacco Régie) the Persian government imposed the cured-tobacco excise tax (Qānūn no. 1076) on 18 Ḏu'l-qaʿda 1333/27 September 1915. World War I made it impossible to exercise the state monopoly effectively, however, and a new law had to be passed in 1336/1918. Moreover, many officials in charge of collecting the tax found the regulations difficult to understand. Initially merchants paid the tax by purchasing banderoles for the packets to be marketed, but this system did not work well, especially for water-pipe tobacco (*tanbākū*), and was dropped. After June 1919 a system proposed by the tobacco merchants themselves was gradually introduced throughout Persia: Tobacco to be consumed locally was taxed directly, that taken to Tehran or other provinces at its destination. The tax, 20 percent ad valorem on cigarette tobacco (*tūtūn-e sīgār*) and 30 percent ad valorem on pipe tobacco (*tūtūn-e čopoq*) and water-pipe tobacco, was levied not on the growers but on the merchants. The General bureau of tobacco (Edāra-ye koll-e doḵānīyāt), established in the Ministry of finance (Wezārat-e mālīya), was charged with collecting the tobacco excise. From November 1919 to September 1920 collection was farmed out in the six important tobacco-growing regions identified in the law (Kordestān, Hamadān, Kāšān, Golpayagān, Šāhrūd, and Semnān) because the government lacked the funds and staff to collect the tax effectively. Nevertheless, the tax farming was resented by local merchants, who tried to sabotage its operation; its success was also negatively affected by the general insecurity and political anarchy prevailing in Persia (Nezam-Mafi, pp. 6-10).

In 1299 Š./1920 the grand vizier Mīrzā Ḥasan Khan Mošīr-al-Dawla abolished farming of the tobacco excise and merged the General bureau with the opium-excise bureau in a new General bureau of restrictions on opium and tobacco (Edāra-ye taḥdīd-e teryāk wa doḵānīyāt). Żīāʾ-al-Dīn Ṭabāṭabāʾī, during his short government in 1299-1300 Š./1921, raised the tobacco excise by 50 percent for cigarette tobacco and 33 percent for pipe tobacco. After his fall the old rates were reinstated (Ḵosravānī, p. 5) .

Under the new system the merchants were to report their tobacco purchases to the bureau, which would then grant permission to store them. When the processed tobacco was ready for sale it was transferred to government warehouses, where it was sorted into four categories: for local consumption, sale in Tehran, sale in the rest of Persia, and export. Tobacco to be sold in Persia outside Tehran was taxed when it left the government warehouse; that to be sold in Tehran was taxed on arrival in the city. No excise was levied on tobacco to be exported; it had to be accompanied by a permit (*jawāz*) identifying the owner, quantity, origin, destination, and price of the tobacco. To prevent fraud, the owner had to put up an export bond, but he received the money back upon presenting the permit signed by the customs office (Ḵosravānī, p. 5; Jamālzāda, pp. 129-30; Great Britain, Foreign Office 416/72: Millspaugh to Imperial

Bank of Persia, 20 April 1923, fol. 99).

The tobacco-excise law was revised on 27 Esfand 1303 Š./18 March 1925 (Qānūn-e eṣlāḥ-e qānūn-e dokānīyāt). The main change introduced in this law was categorization of processed tobacco into three types (*tanbākū*, *tūtūn-e čopoq*, and *tūtūn-e sīgār*), which were taxed at different fixed rates. Tobacco to be exported remained free of this tax (*Majmūʿa*, n.d.a, pp. 18-19).

On 29 Esfand 1307 Š./20 March 1929 the tobacco-excise law underwent major structural revisions; a new state tobacco-monopoly law was enacted by the Majles. Thenceforth the purchase, sale, importing, exporting, processing, and storage of tobacco, as well as the transport of processed and finished tobacco products, were a government monopoly. The tax was levied on growers, at rates varying with quality and location (*Majmūʿa*, n.d.b, pp. 25-28). By the end of the 1920s tobacco was almost as important a source of revenue (3.5 percent of the total) as opium (see AFYŪN), but it was no longer an important export commodity (Lingeman, 1928, p. 12; idem, 1930, p. 16; Hadow, 1925, p. 13). To improve the quality of Persian cigarette tobacco, the state monopoly imported new varietiest from Turkey, Russia, and the United States; distributed seed free to growers; and took other measures to increase production (Gray, pp. 23, 24), but for tobacco imports in general the monopoly served as a barrier to trade.

In 1309 Š./1931 the state tobacco-monopoly law was revised yet again, and on 26 Esfand 1311/17 March 1933 a new law was passed. The next year Šerkat-e dokānīyāt-e Īrān, a syndicate for centralizing the purchase and sale of tobacco from the state monopoly, was established with initial capitalization of 10 million rials (Simmonds, p. 32). In 1316 Š./1937 the Dokānīyāt opened a state tobacco factory in Tehran, managed by Greeks, and drove all private factories out of business. At about the same time a tobacco-research institute was established in Tīrtāš in Māzandarān. All processing of tobacco was centralized in the Tehran factory, where the Greek managers trained Persian staff in various aspects of the business. Despite government efforts to increase output, however, monopoly and price controls led to an actual decline; by 1319 Š./1940 total acreage under tobacco cultivation totaled only about 30,000 acres, with an annual output of about 13,500 tons, sufficient to meet domestic demand. In the same year production of cigarettes reached 12 million a day (*Persia*, pp. 310, 445, 460; "Tabacs"; *Sāl-nāma . . . 1356*, p. 550).

The situation did not change significantly after World War II. Cigarette tobacco was produced in the Caspian provinces, around Reżāʾīya (Urmia) and Koy, and in Kordestān, whereas pipe tobacco was produced mainly in Fārs, Isfahan, and Kāšān provinces (for particulars of production and manufacture, see "Šerkat-e dokānīyāt," p. 498). A new factory for filter cigarettes was built in Tehran in 1339 Š./1960 and a *tūtūn*-packaging plant in Isfahan. Additional tobacco-processing plants were in operation in Reżāʾīya, Sārī, and Gorgān. By 1346 Š./1967 the total work force of the Dokānīyāt comprised about 750,000 people, 350,000 farmers and an equal number of people involved in sales; the remainder were factory workers and headquarters staff (*Sāl-nāma . . .1346*, p. 563). All were eligible for various government-sponsored educational and credit programs introduced in the next decade ("Šerkat-e dokānīyat," pp. 498-500; *Sāl-nāma . . . 1356*, pp. 551-53).

With regular adjustments in the tax rates the Persian tobacco monopoly remains in effect today (for a summary of the objectives of the Dokānīyāt and the types of tobacco produced, see *Sal-nāma . . . 1346*, pp. 559-61). The Dokānīyāt operates three tobacco factories, at Tehran, Isfahan, and Rašt, employing 7,500 people; a limited amount of water-pipe tobacco is exported to neighboring countries. In 1365 Š./1986 about 30 billion cigarettes were sold in Persia, an increase of 7 percent over the preceding years; almost 60 percent were produced in Persia (*Sāl-nāma . . . 1367*).

Bibliography: F. A. G. Gray, *Report on Economic and Commercial Conditions in Iran*, London, 1937. R. H. Hadow, *Report on the Trade and Industry of Persia*, London, 1923. Idem, *Report on the Trade and Industry of Persia*, London, 1925. M.-ʿA. Jamālzāda, *Ganj-e šāyegān*, Berlin, 1335/1917. M.-M. Kosravānī, "Mālīyāt-e ḡayr-e mostaqīm-e Īrān. Dokānīyāt," *Majalla-ye ʿolūm-e mālīya wa eqteṣād* 1/3, 1303 Š./1924, pp. 2-8. E. R. Lingeman, *Report on the Finance and Commerce of Persia 1925-27*, London, 1928. Idem, *Economic Conditions in Persia*, London, 1930. *Majmūʿa-ye qawānīn wa moṣawwabāt-e Majles-e moqaddas-e šūrā-ye mellī dar čahār dawra-ye taqnīnīya*, Tehran, 1302 Š./1923. *Majmūʿa-ye qawānīn-e mawżūʿa wa moṣawwabāt-e dawra-ye panjom-e taqnīnīya*, Tehran, n.d.a. *Majmūʿa-ye qawānīn-e mawżūʿa wa moṣawwabāt-e dawra-ye haftom-e qānūn-goḏārī*, 2nd. ed., Tehran, n.d.b. M. E. Nezam-Mafi, "Merchants and Government, Tobacco and Trade. The Case of Kordestan, 1333 AH/1919 AD," *Iranian Studies* 20, 1987, pp. 1-15. *Persia*, London, 1942. *Sāl-nāma-ye kešvar-e Īrān 1346*, Tehran, 1346 Š./1967. *Sāl-nāma-ye kešvar-e Īrān 1356*, Tehran, 1356 Š./1977. *Sāl-nāma-ye kešvar-e Īrān 1366*, Tehran, 1366 Š./1987. *Sāl-nāma-ye kešvar-e Īrān 1367*, Tehran, 1367 Š./1988. "Šerkat-e dokānīyāt-e Īrān-rā bešenāsīd," in *Šāhanšāhī-e Āryāmehr. Dawrān-e taḥawwol-e ṣanʿat wa honar-e Īrān*, Tehran, 1348 Š./1969, pp. 496-500. S. M. Simmonds, *Economic Conditions in Iran*, London, 1935. "Tabacs. Culture, commerce et manufacture," *Bulletin de la Banque Mellie Iran* 20, August 1938, pp. 286-326.

(WILLEM FLOOR)

DOKKĀN. See BĀZĀR i.

DOKKĀN-E DĀWŪD (lit., "shop of David"), rock-cut tomb of the Achaemenid period in the Zagros range a few kilometers southeast of Sar-e Pol-e Ḏohāb, in the province of Kermānšāhān. It was discovered by Henry C. Rawlinson in 1836 (pp. 38-39), but, owing to its position high on the rock face (12 m above a recess, which is in turn 10 m above the foot of the cliff; cf. Hüsing, p. 15), a plan of the interior of the monument drawn by Pascal Coste in 1840 (Flandin and Coste, IV, pl. 211) remained the sole source of information until 1972, when some details of the plan were corrected by the present author (von Gall, 1974, p. 147, fig. 3; Figure 19). The tomb consists of an antechamber 9.60 m wide at the double frame of the entrance (Plate XX) and 7.32 m wide at the back; it is 1.95 deep on the floor and 2.60 m high. Of the two columns in the antechamber (not rectangular pillars, as shown in Flandin and Coste, IV, pl. 211) only the bases and the capitals, of abacus form, are preserved. The bases are of simple shape, with plinths 0.83 m^2 topped by remains of round parts (cf. the columned hall on the Tall-e Taḵt at Pasargadae; Stronach, pp. 147-49, pls. 111-12). The surfaces of both bases have been smoothed, including an elevation like a pivot on the left one, suggesting that broken column shafts may have been repaired and replaced (in stucco?) in antiquity (von Gall, 1974, p. 147 fig. 4). In the middle of the back wall a door (1.50 m high, 1 m wide) leads into a rectangular, barrel-vaulted tomb chamber (2.31 m deep, 2.83 m wide, 2.18 m high), with five small niches probably intended for lamps (cf. Flandin, I, pp. 462-63). On the left side of this chamber a cavity like a trough extends the full depth of the room; its floor is 70 cm lower than that of the chamber. This

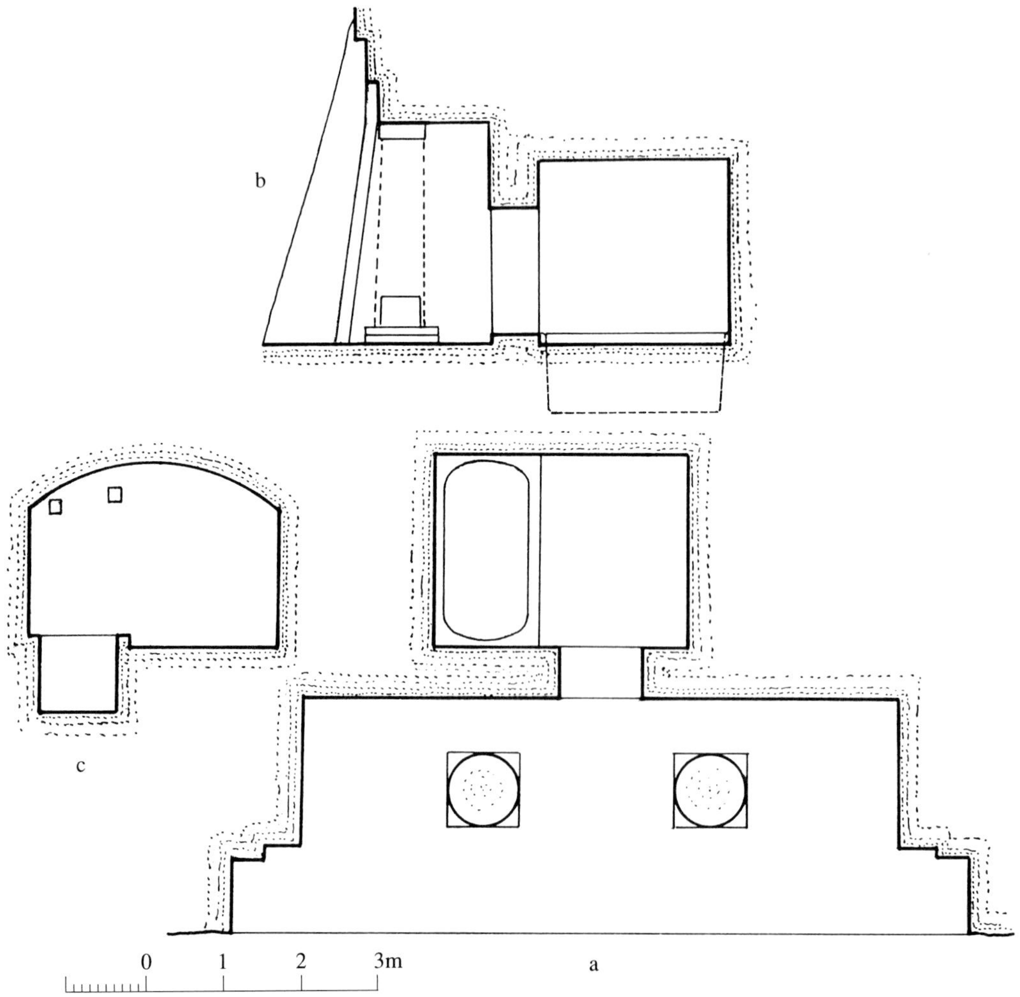

Figure 19. Dokkān-e Dāwūd, plan and sections. a. Plan. b. Longitudinal section. c. Cross section through vaulted tomb chamber.

PLATE XX

Dokkān-e Dāwūd, general view.

PLATE XXI

Relief known as Kel-e Dāwūd, below Dokkān-e Dāwūd.

cavity is the sole provision for a burial in the tomb (von Gall, 1988, pl. 29c; Figure 19b, c).

Dokkān-e Dāwūd is one of several rock-cut tombs in northwestern Persia and Iraqi Kurdistan that were identified as "Median" by Ernst Herzfeld (Sarre and Herzfeld, pp. 122-23; Herzfeld, 1920, p. 13; idem, 1940, p. 208). "Median" is to be understood in the geographical, rather than the historical sense (von Gall, 1966), however, as details at similar but more elaborate rock-cut tombs like that of Kizkapan (von Gall, 1988) and Fak̲rīka (Huff, 1971) clearly exclude a dating before the Achaemenid period. In the interiors of the latter two tombs the cavities are too short to have permitted burial in an extended position; they were probably *astōdān*s (q.v.), as was first argued by A. Shapur Shahbazi (pp. 131-34) and Hubertus von Gall (1974, p. 142; cf. idem, 1988, pp. 562-63; see DEH-E NOW). If the appearance of *astōdān*s was a later development from monumental Median tombs with columns in the antechamber, then Dokkān-e Dāwūd and the larger tomb at Saḥna (Herzfeld, 1920, pp. 8-10; von Gall, 1966, pp. 21-23), with their cavities measuring more than 2 m, appear to represent this older type.

About 8 m below Dokkān-e Dāwūd there is a small bas-relief (1.50 m x 0.90 m), known as Kel-e Dāwūd (Kurd. "tombstone of David"), carved out of an earlier and wider panel that was originally intended to be extended higher but was unfinished (Plate XXI). This relief represents a priest with a *barsom* bundle and a headdress that projects forward as does the headdress in the images of the Frataräka kings on coins of Persis (beginning with Wahbarz; Alram, pls. 17-18), suggesting that Kel-e Dāwūd probably belongs to the early Hellenistic period, considerably later than the tomb above it. The image of a priest, presumably representing a funeral guard of magi, as was recorded on the tomb of Cyrus the Great (q.v. v; Arrian, *Anabasis* 6.29.4; cf. von Gall, 1972, p. 280 n. 98), suggests the importance of Dokkan-e Dāwūd in antiquity.

The name Dāwūd may represent more than a fanciful connection with a biblical and koranic hero: A modern cemetery below the rock monument belongs to the Ahl-e Ḥaqq (q.v.), who consider Dāwūd one of the helper angels and the Dōkkān-e Dāwūd a holy place (Gabriel, p. 17, pp. 35-36).

Bibliography: (For abbreviations found in this bibliography, see "Short References.") M. Alram, *Nomina Propria Iranica in Nummis*, Iranisches Personennamenbuch 4, Vienna, 1986. E. Flandin, *Voyage in Perse. Relation du voyage*, 2 vols., Paris, 1851. Idem and P. Coste, *Voyage en Perse*, 6 vols, Paris, 1843-54. A. Gabriel, *Religionsgeographie von Persien*, Vienna, 1971. H. von Gall, "Zu den 'medischen' Felsgräbern in Nordwestiran und Iraqi Kurdistan," *Archäologischer Anz.* 1966, pp. 19-43. Idem, "Persische und medische Stämme," *AMI*, N.F. 5, 1972, pp. 261-83. Idem, "Neue Beobachtungen zu den sog. medischen Felsgräbern," in *Proceedings of the IInd Annual Symposium on Archaeological Research in Iran 1973*, Tehran, 1974, pp. 139-54. Idem, "Das Felsgrab von Qizqapan. Ein Denkmal aus dem Umfeld der achämenidischen Königsstrasse," *Bagdader Mitteilungen* 19, 1988, pp. 557-82. M. Golzārī, *Kermānšāhān-e bāstān*, Tehran, n.d. (ca. 1974). E. Herzfeld, *Am Tor von Asien*, Berlin, 1920. Idem, *Iran in the Ancient East*, London and New York, 1941. D. Huff, "Das Felsengrab von Fakhrikah," *Istanbuler Mitteilungen* 21, 1971, pp. 161-71. G. Hüsing, *Der Zagros und seine Völker. Eine archäologisch-ethnographische Skizze*, Der Alte Orient 9/3-4, Leipzig, 1908. H. C. Rawlinson, "Notes on a March from Zohab . . . to Kirmanshah, in the Year 1836," *JRGS* 9, 1839, pp. 26-116. F. Sarre and E. Herzfeld, *Iranische Felsreliefs*, Berlin, 1910. A. Sh. Shahbazi, *The Irano-Lycian Monuments. The Principal Antiquities of Xanthos as Evidence for Iranian Aspects of Achaemenid Lycia*, Tehran, 1975. D. Stronach, *Pasargadae. A Report on the Excavations*, Oxford, 1978.

(HUBERTUS VON GALL)

DOḴTAR-E NŌŠERVĀN (lit., "daughter of Nōšervān"), rock-cut architectural complex with important wall paintings in the Ḵolm valley in northern Afghanistan, discovered in 1924 (Godard et al., pp. 65-74, figs. 25-27, pls. XLI-XLIII). Of the two niches in the complex the upper one contains a large painting in a very fragmentary state but of particular iconographic importance. The painted framework consists of an architectural form similar to an arcade, originally resting on four columns. Within the central pair of columns are the remains of a painted personage seated on a throne. On the basis of new tracings by Deborah Klimburg-Salter (1989, pl. LXXXVII), this image can now be recognized as an enthroned deity, worshiped by two donors (Figures 20-21). The throne, supported by two horse protomes, recurs in the early medieval art of Sogdia as an emblem of a supreme deity, most probably Ahura Mazdā (Sogd. Xurmazd[ā]; Mode). In the Kushan period (2nd-3rd centuries C.E.) MOZDOOANO (*mazdā *vana-*, i.e., Ahura Mazdā, q.v.; Colpe 1986) was depicted as a king riding a double-headed horse (Göbl, p. 42, pl. 167), probably a forerunner of the "deity with two horses." The crown of the seated figure at Doḵtar-e Nōšervān is partly damaged; only the upper portion, with a pair of wings surmounted by a ram's head, has survived. It is reminiscent of crown types from the Hunnic-Hephthalite period (5th-6th centuries). Surrounding the deity's head is a tripartite nimbus with attached animal protomes. This complex system seems to emphasize the supernatural force of the "king of gods" as ultimate creator of all life. Two elephant protomes (only one of them partly preserved) seem to have been either emanations from the deity's shoulders (Figure 20) or parts of the throne back (Figure 21). They recall an "Indian" element in the iconography of Xurmazd, whom the Sogdians identified with Indra (whose *vāhana*, or vehicle, is the elephant; Belenitskii and Marshak, p. 33; Humbach, pp. 398-402). Most probably, the fragmentary wall painting at Doḵtar-e Nōšervān should be dated to the early 8th century, reflecting a synthesis of strong Sogdian elements with elements from farther south, at Bāmīān (q.v.), as well as a few vague survivals from Sasanian

Figure 20. Doḵtar-e Nōšervān, variant reconstruction of central image, based on Klimburg-Salter, 1989, pl. LXXXVII.

Figure 21. Doḵtar-e Nōšervān, second variant reconstruction of central image, based on Klimburg-Salter, 1989, pl. LXXXVII.

Persia.

Bibliography: G. Azarpay, *Sogdian Painting*, Berkeley and Los Angeles, 1981. A. M. Belenitskii and B. I. Marshak, "The Paintings of Sogdiana," in G. Azarpay, *Sogdian Painting*, Berkeley and Los Angeles, 1981, pp. 13-77. C. Colpe, "Ōhrmazd 1," in H. W. Haussig, ed., *Wörterbuch der Mythologie* I/4, Stuttgart, 1986, p. 413. R. Göbl, *System und Chronologie der Münzprägung des Kušānreiches*, Vienna, 1984. A. Godard, Y. Godard, and J. Hackin, eds., *Les antiquités bouddhiques de Bāmiyān*, MDAFA 2, Paris and Brussels, 1928. H. Humbach, "Vayu, Śiva und der Spiritus Vivens im ostiranischen Synkretismus," in *Acta Iranica* 4, 1975, pp. 397-408. D. Klimburg-Salter, "Dokhtar-i Noshirvan. An Ideology of Kingship," in M. S. Nagaraja Rao, ed., *Kusumāñjali. New Interpretation of Indian Art and Culture. Sh. C. Sivaramamurti Commemoration Volume* I, Delhi, 1987, pp. 61-76. Idem, *The Kingdom of Bāmiyān. Buddhist Art and Culture of the Hindu Kush*, Naples and Rome, 1989, pp. 74-75, 183-86, figs. 114-15. Idem, "Dokhtar-i-Noshirvan (Nigār) Reconsidered," in *Essays in Honor of Oleg Grabar,* Muqarnas 10, Leiden, 1993, pp. 355-68. M. Mode, "The Great God of Dokhtar-e Noshirwān," *East and West* 42, 1992, pp. 473-83.

(MARKUS MODE)

DOKTARĀN-E ĪRĀN (lit., "Daughters of Iran"), a monthly variety magazine for girls published in Shiraz from 1 Mordād 1310 Š./23 July 1931 to Āḏar 1311 Š./November 1932. The publisher and editor was "Zand-doḵt Šīrāzī" (Faḵr-al-Molūk Zandpūr, 1327-71=1331 Š./1909-52), one of the pioneers in seeking women's rights in Persia; she founded the Society for women's revolution (Majmaʿ-e enqelāb-e neswān) and was the first woman in Shiraz in modern times to appear in public unveiled (Roknzāda Ādamīyat, pp. 665-66). The content was varied but generally concerned the life of women. A number of scholars and journalists in Tehran contributed to the magazine, including Ṣadīqa Dawlatābādī (q.v.), Kāẓemzāda Īrānšahr, Saʿīd Nafīsī, and Rašīd Yāsamī; although the magazine was published for girls, the works of women and girls were rarely included in it.

The title page of *Doḵtarān-e Īrān* included an epigraph with illustrations of the Ayvān-e Kesrā (q.v.) at Ctesiphon (q.v.), girls and women in Persian local costumes, an angel with wings spread, and Reżā Shah (1304-20 Š./1925-41). The magazine was typeset in forty to forty-four single-column pages measuring 14 by 19 cm and printed at the Farhūmand-Ḵāvar and Etteḥādīya printing shops in Tehran; it included black-and-white illustrations. The last issue was double, nos. 6-7. An annual subscription cost 30 rials, 40 (later 50) rials abroad. Scattered issues are available in the central library of the University of Tehran; the library of Princeton University, Princeton, N.J., possesses a single copy.

Bibliography: (For cited works not found in this bibliography and abbreviations found here, see "Short References.") Ṭ. Baṣṣārī, *Zand-doḵt pīšāhang-e nahżat-e āzādī-e bānovān-e Īrān,* Tehran, 1346 Š./1967. R. Mach and R. D. McChesney, "A List of Persian Serials in the Princeton University Library," Princeton, N.J., 1971, unpublished. ʿA.-A. Mošīr Salīmī, *Zanān-e soḵanvar*, Tehran, 1335 Š./1956, p. 219. S. Nafīsī, "Maṭbūʿāt," in Komīsīūn-e mellī-e Yūnesko dar Īrān (UNESCO), *Īranšahr* II, Tehran, 1343 Š./1964, p. 1255. ʿA. Nāhīd, *Zanān-e Īrān dar jonbeš-e mašrūṭa*, n.p., n.d.; repr. Saarbrücken, 1989. M.-Ḥ. Roknzāda Ādamīyat, *Dānešmandān wa soḵansarāyān-e Fārs* II, Tehran, 1338 Š./1959. Ṣadr Hāšemī, *Jarā'ed o majallāt* II, pp. 280-81. N. Saʿīdī, "Tārīḵča-ye rūznāma-negārī-e zanān dar Īrān," in *Taḥqīqāt-e rūznāma-negārī* 5/18-19, 1348-49 Š./1969-70, p. 20. M. Solṭānī, *Fehrest-e majallahā-ye fārsī az ebtedā tā sāl-e 1320 šamsī*, Tehran, 1356 Š./1977, p. 92. L. Sūdbaḵš, *Fehrest-e našrīyāt-e adwārī dar ketāb-ḵāna-ye markazī-e Fārs*, Shiraz, n.d., p. 361.

(NASSEREDDIN PARVIN)

DOKUZ (DOQUZ) ḴĀTŪN (d. 29 Šaʿbān 663/16 June 1265), chief wife of the Il-khan Hülegü (Hūlāgū; 654-63/1256-65) and granddaughter of Wang (Ong) Khan, leader of the Nestorian Christian Kereyit (Karāyet) tribe domiciled near present-day Ulan Bator. After Wang Khan's defeat by the future Čengīz Khan in 1203 she was given to the latter's youngest son, Tolui (Tūlī). The marriage was apparently not consummated, and, when Tolui died in 630/1233 she passed into the care of his son Hülegü, who married her during his expedition to Persia in 654-56/1256-58. He had considerable respect for her judgment, and she was able to intercede for the Christians after the Mongol sack of Baghdad in 656/1258; she was also instrumental in securing the election of Mar Denha as Nestorian catholicus in 1265. A mobile church with bells was erected in her camp (*ordu*). She survived Hülegü by only four months; there is no evidence to support the thirteenth-century Armenian historian Stephanos Orbelian's claim (pp. 234-35) that she was poisoned by the *ṣāḥeb-dīvān* (i.e., Jovaynī).

Although Doquz Ḵātūn produced no children, Hülegü had offspring from several concubines in her entourage, and her influence continued to be felt; she helped to ensure the succession for his son Abaqa (q.v.; 663-80/1265-82).

Bibliography: (For abbreviations found here, see "Short References.") Bar Hebraeus, *Chronicon Syriacum*, ed. and tr. E. A. Wallis Budge, I, Oxford and London, 1932, pp. 419, 435, 444. Š. Bayānī, *Zan dar Īrān-e ʿaṣr-e moğūl*, Tehran, 1352 Š./1973. E. Dulaurier, "Les Mongols d'après les historiens arméniens," *JA*, 5th ser., 11, 1858, pp. 491, 507-08; 5th ser., 16, 1860, pp. 290-91, 308-09. Haithon, *Flos Historiarum Terre Orientis*, in Recueil des historiens des croisades. Documents arméniens 2, Paris, 1906, p. 301. *Histoire de Mar Jabalaha III patriarche des Nestoriens*, tr. C.-B. Chabot, Paris, 1895. H. H. Howorth, *History of the Mongols* III. *The Mongols of Persia*, London, 1888 (esp. pp. 209-12). E. Hunter, "The Conversion of the Kerait to Christianity in A.D. 1007," *Zentralasiatische Studien* 22, 1989-91, pp. 142-63. S. Orbelian, *Histoire de la Siounie*, tr. M. Brosset, I, St. Petersburg, 1864. Rašīd-al-Dīn, *Jāmeʿ al-tawārīḵ* (Baku), pp. 6-7, 24, 96. Idem, *Jāmeʿ al-tawārīḵ*, ed. E. Quatremère as *Raschid-eldin. Histoire des Mongols de la Perse*, Paris, 1836, pp. 92-97. B. Spuler, "Le christianisme chez les Mongols aux XIIIe et XIVe siècles," in W. Heissig et al., eds., *Tractata Altaica*, Wiesbaden, 1976, pp. 621-31.

(CHARLES MELVILLE)

DOLAFIDS, family of Arab origin that became politically prominent in western Persia during the 9th century. Some members were also significant Arabic literary figures. The Dolafids belonged to the Arab tribe of ʿEjl b. Lojaym, among the first Muslim conquerors of central Iraq (cf. Donner, appendices; Caskel, s.v. ʿIǧl b. Luǧaym; Ṭabarī, II, p. 994). The precise ancestry of the family within the tribe was the subject of dispute among various informants, however. The first member of the family mentioned in the surviving historical record was Edrīs b. Maʿqel, said to have dealt in perfumes and sheep at Kūfa (Balāḏorī, *Fotūḥ*, p. 314; Ebn Ḥazm, p. 313; Krenkow, p. *alef*). Edrīs and his brother ʿĪsā b. Maʿqel were reportedly imprisoned in Kūfa during the caliphate of Hešām b. ʿAbd-al-Malek (105-25/724-43), but the reasons are unclear. Perhaps, as Balāḏorī claimed (*Fotūḥ* p. 314), Edrīs had assaulted a merchant. Other reports suggest that the brothers may have been suspected of revolutionary activity against the Omayyads; the future organizer of the ʿAbbasid revolution in Khorasan, Abū Moslem, is said to have been their personal servant, purchased from them by the ʿAbbasids during a visit in prison (Ṭabarī, II, pp. 1726-27, 1769; Ebn al-Aṯīr, V, pp. 191-92; Ebn Ḵallekān, II, p. 502; *Mojmal*, ed. Bahār, pp. 308, 315-16; Yaʿqūbī, *Boldān*, p. 207). It is possible, however, that these claims were fabricated by the Dolafids at a later date, in order to enhance their standing with their ʿAbbasid patrons.

Edrīs apparently became wealthy and moved with his family to the Zagros region, where he became an owner of estates and settled in the village of Mass near Hamadān. He may already have owned estates in the Isfahan area before 132/750 (Ebn al-Aṯīr, V, p. 191). Samʿānī noted simply that his son ʿĪsā, father of Abū Dolaf (q.v.), was an Arab of ʿEjl who came to the Isfahan area with his sons and engaged in brigandage; then, in the time of al-Mahdī (158-69/775-85), he repented and settled his family at Karaj between Isfahan and Hamadān, which he irrigated and began to develop, building up its fortresses (ed. Margoliouth, fol. 477b; Balāḏorī, *Fotūḥ*, p. 314). The fertile region around Karaj became the center of the Dolafid patrimony, particularly Āstāna near the modern village of Qadamgāh (cf. Luther). It flourished during the 9th century, as the Dolafids, especially ʿĪsā b. Edrīs and his son Abū Dolaf, extended its cultivated area and constructed palaces, fortresses, and other buildings for themselves and their followers.

The most prominent member of the Dolafid family was Abū Dolaf Qāsem b. ʿĪsā (q.v., for further details of his career), who was appointed governor of Jebāl province by Hārūn al-Rašīd (170-93/786-809) and seems to have been successful in suppressing turbulent Kurdish and Arab tribesmen. In the civil war between Hārūn's sons al-Amīn (193-93/809-13) and al-Maʾmūn (198-218/813-33) he sided with the former but was pardoned by the latter and reappointed governor of Jebāl; he was chosen as one of the caliph's boon companions and was well known as a poet. Abū Dolaf also served al-Maʾmūn's successor, al-Moʿtaṣem (218-27/833-42), as boon companion, military commander, and possibly governor of Damascus. He died in Baghdad in 225/839-40. His brother Maʿqel b. ʿĪsā seems to have lived in his shadow but was also affiliated with the ʿAbbasid court, serving as a military commander; he was also known for his poetry (*Aḡānī*[1], Cairo, XVIII, pp. 194-95; Ebn Qotayba, III, p. 10; Aštar, p. 123 n. 3; Krenkow, p. *waw-zay*).

After Abū Dolaf's death the main base of the family's power and activity remained Karaj and Isfahan. Two of his sons earned some historical mention. Hešām was a subordinate military commander in ʿAbbasid service in Iraq in 251/865-66 (Ṭabarī, III, pp. 1605, 1617, 1619, 1623-24), but leadership of the Dolafid family passed to ʿAbd-al-ʿAzīz, who was apparently recognized as his father's successor in Jebāl. He seems to have attempted to act independently of Samarra, for two punitive expeditions are recorded in 253/867, during one of which Karaj was ransacked (Ṭabarī, III, pp. 1685-87; Ebn Ḥazm, p. 313; Krenkow, p. *alef*; *Mojmal*, ed. Bahār, p. 363). Although ʿAbd-al-ʿAzīz's ultimate fate is unclear, his son Dolaf was recognized by the ʿAbbāsids as his successor in Jebāl; when Dolaf was killed by a rebel in Isfahan in 265/878-79 he was succeeded as head of the family by his brother Aḥmad (Ṭabarī, III, pp. 1916, 1929; Ebn al-Aṯīr, VII, p. 227), who was responsible for destroying the army of the Saffarid ʿAmr b. Layṯ (q.v.) in 273/886-87 (Ṭabarī, III, pp. 1937, 1940, 2024, 2112, 2122, 2135; Ebn al-Aṯīr, VII, pp. 226, 231, 233, 253, 259, 291, 317-18). The uneasy and shifting relationship between the Dolafids and the central ʿAbbasid government was reflected in a campaign by al-Moʿtamed's brother al-Mowaffeq against Karaj in 276/889-90 (Ṭabarī, III, pp. 2115-16; Ebn al-Aṯīr, VII, pp. 304-05). Aḥmad died in 280/894-95, and his brothers Bakr and ʿOmar openly disputed the leadership of the family. The ʿAbbasids exploited this split to reassert their power in Jebāl (Ṭabarī, III, pp. 2137, 2152, 2154-59; Ebn al-Aṯīr, VII, pp. 327-28, 332, 334).

Some of Abū Dolaf's descendants were said to have become prominent in Qazvīn (*Tārīḵ-e gozīda*, ed. Browne, p. 847); a scholar from the family, a certain Moḥammad b. Ebrāhīm, in the eighth generation after Abū Dolaf, is also mentioned (Rāfeʿī, I, p. 148).

Bibliography: (For cited works not found in this bibliography, see "Short References.") ʿAbd-al-Karīm Aštar, *Šeʿr Deʿbel b. ʿAlī al-Ḵozāʿī*, Damascus, 1964. W. Caskel, *Ǧamharat an-nasab. Das genealogische Werk des Hišām b. Muḥammad al-Kalbī*, 2 vols., Leiden, 1966. F. M. Donner, *The Early Islamic Conquests*, Princeton, N.J., 1981. Ebn Ḥazm, *Jamharat ansāb al-ʿArab*, Cairo, 1971. ʿAbd-Allāh b. Moslem Ebn Qoṭayba, *Ketāb ʿoyūn al-aḵbār*, 4 vols., Cairo, 1924-30. F. Krenkow, *Šeʿr Bakr b. ʿAbd-al-ʿAzīz b. Dolaf b. Abī Dolaf al-Qāsem b. ʿĪsā al-ʿEjlī al-Karajī*, Delhi, 1337/1918-19 (in same edition with Krenkow, *Šeʿr al-Noʿmān b. Bašīr al-Anṣārī*). K. A. Luther, "The Site of Karaj-i Abī Dulaf," *Art and Archaeology Research Papers* 1, 1972, pp. 34-40. ʿAbd-al-Karīm Abu'l-Qāsem Rāfeʿī, *al-Tadwīn fī aḵbār Qazvīn*, ed. ʿA. ʿAṭāredī Ḳabūšānī, Beirut, 1987.

(FRED M. DONNER)

DOLDOL (or Doldūl, in Ar. lit., "large porcupine"), name of a female mule that Moqawqes, governor of Egypt, sent to the Prophet Moḥammad as a gift. Toward the end of his life the Prophet gave it and his armor to ʿAlī b. Abī Ṭāleb, an act that is viewed by Shiʿites as one of the important indicators of ʿAlī's special status.

In the Islamic folk tradition Doldol is sometimes confused with Borāq, the mount upon which the Prophet is believed to have ascended physically to heaven; in popular paintings of the Prophet's ascension Borʿāq is usually depicted with a horse's body and a human face, however. Although in biographical and mystical texts in Arabic and Persian, as well as in much Persian poetry, the name Doldol is reserved for the Prophet's mule, the phrase *šāh-e doldol sawār* "the king riding the *doldol*" refers to Imam ʿAlī (Saʿdī, p. 36; Dehḵodā, s.v.).

Bibliography: (For cited sources not found in this bibliography and abbreviations found here, see "Short References.") Moḥammad b. Mūsā Damīrī, *Ḥayāt al-ḥayawān al-kobrā*, 2 vols., Damascus 1989, s.v. Doldol. Ebn al-Aṯīr, II, p. 314. Majd-al-Dīn Ebn al-Aṯīr, *al-Nehāya fī ǧarīb al-ḥadīṯ* II, Cairo, 1385/1965, p. 139. ʿAbbās b. Moḥammad-Reżā Qomī, *Safīnat al-beḥār wa madīnat al-ḥekam wa'l-āṯār* I, Najaf, 1355/1936, p. 461. Moṣleḥ-al-Dīn Saʿdī, *Būstān-e Saʿdī*, ed. Ḡ.-Ḥ. Yūsofī, Tehran, 1359 Š./1970. *Tāj al-ʿarūs* VII, Cairo, 1307/1889, s.v. Doldol.

(AḤMAD MAHDAWĪ DĀMḠĀNĪ)

"DOLGORUKOV MEMOIRS," document published under the title *Eʿterāfāt-e sīāsī yā yāddāšthā-ye Kenyāz Dolqorūkī* (Political confessions or memoirs of Prince Dolgorukov) in the historical portion of the "Khorasan yearbook," issued in Mašhad in 1322 Š./1943. A new edition was published in Tehran the following year, and there have been many others since. According to these memoirs, the Russian Dimitri Dolgorukov came to Persia in the 1830s, converted to Islam, learned Persian and Arabic, and even studied at Karbalāʾ; he then repudiated Islam, instigated the Bāb (q.v.) to put forward his claims, and subsequently assisted Bahāʾ-Allāh (q.v.) in Baghdad and later in Edirne and ʿAkka.

A simple reading of the text of this work reveals it immediately to be a clumsy forgery, and it was denounced as such by reputable Persian academics like ʿAbbās Eqbāl (*Yādgār* 5/8-9, 1328 Š./1949, p. 148) and Mojtabā Mīnovī (*Rāhnemā-ye ketāb* 6/1-2, 1342 Š./1963, p. 22). Even Sayyed Aḥmad Kasrawī, in his anti-Bahai (q.v.) work *Bahāʾīgarī* (pp. 79-80), acknowledged that the memoirs are fraudulent. No original manuscript has ever been produced, and the work is riddled with errors and contradictions showing that its author was poorly informed about Babi and Bahai history and even about the names of Russian czars. Dimitri Ivanovich Dolgorukov was in fact a high-ranking diplomat, and at the very time that he was supposedly in Persia and conspiring with the Bāb, he was actually serving successively in the Hague, Naples, and Istanbul. Furthermore, in 1939 the Russian scholar Mikhail Ivanov published all the dispatches relating to the Babi movement that he had found in the archives of the Soviet foreign ministry (appendix), about six years before the "memoirs" appeared. From these documents it is clear that, far from having been interested in the Babi movement, Dolgorukov had largely ignored it until 1848, when, as Russian minister to Tehran, he had requested the Persian government to remove the Bāb from Mākū near the Russian border, for fear that he might stir up discontent among the Russian Muslims (Momen, pp. 72-73).

Despite all this evidence, these spurious memoirs have acquired a life of their own because of their usefulness in polemics against the Bahais. They are regularly cited in anti-Bahai literature disseminated by the Persian government and have even been translated into Arabic (as *Moḏākarāt Dālkorūkī*, Beirut, n.d.).

Bibliography: *Baḥṯ-ī dar radd-e Yāddāšthā-ye majʿūl-e montaseb be Kenyāz Dālgorūkī*, Tehran,

1352 Š./1973. "Dolgorkov," *Gūšahā-ye fāšnašoda-ī az tārīḵ. Čand časma az ʿamalīyāt-e ḥayrat - angīz-e Kenyāz Dālgorūkī, jāsūs-e asrār āmīz-e Rūsīya-ye tezārī, wa nokāt-e jāleb-e tawajjoh az paydāyeš-e maḏhab-e bābī wa bahāʾī dar Īrān*, 3rd ed., Tehran, n.d. M. Ivanov, *Babidskie vosstaniya v Irane (1848-52)* (The Babi uprising in Iran [1848-52]), Moscow, 1949. A. Kasrawī, *Bahāʾī-garī*, Tehran, n.d. D. MacEoin, *The Sources for Early Bābī Doctrine and History. A Survey*, Leiden, 1992, pp. 170-71. M. Momen, ed., *The Bábí and Baháʾí Religions, 1844-1944. Some Contemporary Western Accounts*, Oxford, 1980.

(MOOJAN MOMEN)

DOLICHE, city in the Roman province of Syria conquered together with the surrounding area by Šāpūr I (240-70) during his second campaign against Rome in 252 or 253 (Back, p. 303, ŠKZ, Parth. l. 7, Gk. l. 17; for the date see DICHŌR). The name is no longer legible in the Middle Persian version of Šāpūr's *Res Gestae* (cf. Sprengling, pl. 7 l. 10), and the Parthian form *dwrhw* is mysterious. The identification of Dolichē, on the ancient trade route from Antioch to Edessa, with Dülük in modern Turkey is certain (see Wagner, 1976, sketch 3; on the various forms of the name, see Honigmann, 1923, p. 182 n. 264). Also enigmatic is the sequence Dura (Parth. *dwl'y*), Dolichē in the Greek version, which complicates reconstruction of the route followed by the Sasanian army (see DURA-EUROPOS). It is often assumed that after the capture of Antioch Dolichē was taken, together with Germanikeia and Batna, which are also mentioned, on Šāpūr's return march (cf. Baldus, p. 265), but absolute certainty is not possible. The city is known as the birthplace of the local deity Baʿal, who became famous as Jupiter Dolichenus.

Bibliography: (For abbreviations found here, see "Short References.") M. Back, *Die sassanidischen Staatsinschriften*, Acta Iranica 18, Tehran and Liège, 1978. H. R. Baldus, *Uranius Antoninus. Münzprägung und Geschichte*, Antiquitas 3/11, Bonn, 1971, esp. pp. 263-65. I. Benzinger, "Doliche 4," in Pauly-Wissowa V/1, col. 1276. F. Cumont, *Études syriennes*, Paris, 1917, pp. 173-202. M. H. Dodgeon and S. N. C. Lieu, eds., *The Roman Eastern Frontier and the Persian Wars (AD 226-363)*, London, 1991, p. 362. F. K. Dörner, *Der Thron der Götter auf dem Nemrud Dağ*, 2nd ed., Bergisch Gladbach, Germany, 1987, pp. 147-48, 216 ff. R. Dussaud, *Topographie historique de la Syrie antique et médiévale*, Paris, 1927, pp. 229, 434, 445, 472, 478-79. W. Ensslin, *Zu den Kriegen des Sassaniden Schapur*, Sitzb. der Bayerischen Akademie der Wissenschaften. Phil.-hist. Kl., 1947/5, Munich, 1949, p. 103 and n. 4. P. Gignoux, *Glossaire des inscriptions pehlevies et parthes*, Corpus Inscr. Iran., Suppl. 1, London, 1972, p. 50. H. Hellenkamper, *Der Limes am nordsyrischen Euphrat in Studien zu den Mili-tärgrenzen Roms* II, Cologne and Bonn, 1977, p. 470. E. Honigmann, "Historische Topographie von Nordsyrien im Altertum," *Zeitschrift des Deutschen Palästina-Vereins* 46, 1923. Idem, *Recherches sur les* Res Gestae Divi Saporis, Académie Royale de Belgique, Classe des lettres, 47/4, Brussels, 1953, pp. 147, 154. E. Kettenhofen, *Die römisch- persischen Kriege des 3. Jahrhunderts n. Chr.*, TAVO Beihefte B 55, Wiesbaden, 1982, pp. 74-77. D. O. A. Klose, "Nikopolis und Doliche," *Jahrbuch für Numismatik und Geldgeschichte* 34, 1984, p. 66. D. J. MacDonald, "The Genesis of the 'Res Gestae Divi Sapori,'" *Berytus* 27, 1979, pp. 77-83. A. T. Olmstead, "The Mid-Third Century of the Christian Era," *Classical Philology* 37, 1942, pp. 409, 414. M. I. Rostovtzeff, "*Res Gestae Divi Saporis* and Dura," *Berytus* 8, 1943, p. 26. M. Sprengling, *Third Century Iran. Sapor and Kartir*, Chicago, 1953, pl. 2 l. 13, pp. 95-96. J. Wagner, *Seleukeia am Euphrat/Zeugma*, TAVO, Beihefte B 10, Wiesbaden, 1976. Idem, "Neue Denkmäler aus Doliche," *Bonner Jahrbücher* 182, 1982, pp. 133-66.

(ERICH KETTENHOFEN)

DOLMA (or *dūlma*), Turkish term (Doerfer, III, pp. 203-04) for stuffed vegetable or fruit dishes common in the Middle East and in Mediterranean countries. Versions have been known in Persia since at least as early as the 17th century (Afšār, pp. 217, 238-39). Mīrzā ʿAlī-Akbar Khan Āšpaz-bāšī, chef to the court of Nāṣer-al-Dīn Shah (1264-1313/1848-96), recorded *dolma* as a category of Persian cuisine and gave recipes for stuffing grape leaves, cabbage leaves, cucumbers, eggplants, apples, and quinces (pp. 42-43). Stuffings included ground meat, sautéed mint, rice, and saffron. Rice had not not been an ingredient of Safavid *dolma*s (Afšār, pp. 217, 238-39).

The most popular *dolma*s in Persia today are stuffed grape leaves, which are prepared by lightly parboiling the fresh leaves in salted water, then stuffing them with a mixture of ground meat, rice, chopped herbs like parsley, split peas, and seasoning. The *dolma*s are then simmered in a sweet-and-sour mixture of vinegar or lemon juice, sugar, and water. Stuffings vary, however, from region to region and even from family to family. Stuffed cabbage and grape leaves are the only *dolma*s that can be served hot or cold. When intended to be served cold they generally do not contain meat, however. Fruit *dolma*s are probably a specialty of Persian cuisine. The fruit is first cooked, then stuffed with meat, seasonings, and sometimes tomato sauce; the *dolma*s are then simmered in meat broth or a sweet-and-sour sauce. In recent decades new variations have been introduced, largely under Western influence: Potatoes, artichokes, green peppers, onions, tomatoes, and other vegetables are also stuffed.

Bibliography: Ī. Afšār, ed., *Āšpazī-e dawra-ye ṣafawī. Matn-e do resāla az ān dawra*, Tehran, 1360 Š./1981. Mīrzā ʿAlī-Akbar Khan Āšpaz-bāšī, *Sofra-ye aṭʿema*, Tehran, 1353 Š./1974. T. Mallos, *The Complete Middle East Cookbook*, New York, 1979. R. Monteẓamī, *Majmūʿa-ye ḡeḏāhā-ye īrānī wa farangī*, Tehran, 1347 Š./1968, pp. 499-510. M. R. Ghanoonparvar, *Persian Cuisine*, 2 vols., Lexington, Ky., 1982-84. N. Ramazani, *Persian Cooking*, Charlottesville, Va., 1982, pp. 41-51. M. Tehrānī, *Ṭabbāḵī-e kadbānū*, Tehran, 1346 Š./1967, pp. 72-79.

(M. R. Ghanoonparvar)

DOLOMITAE. See DEYLAMITES i.

DOMAN, city in the Roman province of Cappadocia, conquered along with the surrounding area by the Sasanian Šāpūr I (240-70) during his second campaign against Rome (ŠKZ, Parth, l. 8: *dwm'n*; Gk. l. 18; not extant in Middle Persian; Back, p. 305). It is probably to be identified with Domana, a city mentioned by the geographer Ptolemy (5.7.3); according to the itineraries, it was located on the road between Satala (modern Sadak in Turkey) and Trapezous (modern Trabzon). Ernst Honigmann has suggested a localization at Köse, north of Sadak. Less probable are identifications with Tomla (Olmstead) and Domankaya near Şebinkarahisar (Garstang, apud Olmstead).

It is generally assumed that both Doman and Satala were targets of raids undertaken in Cappadocia at an uncertain date by Šāpūr's son Hormizd, great king of Armenia. The precise dating of this campaign is still open, however, as it did not necessarily coincide with Šāpūr's advance into Syria.

Bibliography: (For abbreviations found here, see "Short References.") M. Back, *Die sassanidischen Staatsinschriften*, Acta Iranica 18, Tehran and Liège, 1978. H. R. Baldus, *Uranius Antoninus*, Antiquitas 3/11, Bonn, 1971, p. 232. M.-L. Chaumont, "Conquêtes sassanides et propagande mazdéenne (IIIème siècle)," *Historia* 22, 1973, pp. 672-73. F. and E. Cumont, *Studia Pontica* II. *Voyage d'exploration archéologique dans le Pont et la Petite Arménie*, Brussels, 1906, pp. 354-55. M. H. Dodgeon and S. N. C. Lieu, eds., *The Roman Eastern Frontier and the Persian Wars (AD 226-363)*, London, 1991, p. 363. W. Ensslin, *Zu der Kriegen des Sassaniden Schapur*, Munich, 1949, p. 104. P. Gignoux, *Glossaire des inscriptions pehlevies et parthes*, Corpus Inscr. Iran., Suppl. 1, London, 1972, p. 50. E. Honigmann, *Recherches sur les* Res Gestae Divi Saporis, Brussels, 1953, pp. 158-59. E. Kettenhofen, *Die römisch-persischen Kriege des 3. Jahrhunderts n. Chr.*, TAVO, Beihefte B 55, Wiesbaden, 1982, pp. 83-87. T. B. Mitford, "Cappadocia and Armenia Minor. Historical Setting of the Limes," *Aufstieg und Niedergang der römischen Welt* II 7/2, Berlin, 1980, pp. 1209-17. Idem, "Some Inscriptions from the Cappadocian *Limes*," *Journal of Roman Studies* 64, 1974, p. 169. A. T. Olmstead, "The Mid-Third Century of the Christian Era," *Classical Philology* 37, 1942, pp. 409-10. M. I. Rostovtzeff, "Res Gestae Divi Saporis and Dura," *Berytus* 8, 1943-44, p. 42. W. Ruge, "Domana 1," in Pauly-Wissowa V/1, col. 1294. M. Sprengling, *Third Century Iran. Sapor and Kartir*, Chicago, 1953, pl. 2 l. 16, p. 96.

(Erich Kettenhofen)

DOMES, circular vaulted roofs or ceilings. The variety of forms and decoration of Persian domes is unrivaled.

The Sasanian and early Islamic periods. The dome on squinches first appeared in Persia in the Sasanian period in the palace at Fīrūzābād (q.v.) in Fārs and at nearby Qalʿa-ye Doḵtar, both erected by Ardašir (224-40) in the early 3rd century. Although the dome chambers at these sites are impressive in size, their conical squinches (arches across the corners of a cube, forming a zone of transition) are crude in design and execution (Plate XXII). The rubble masonry was so haphazardly applied that it is difficult to distinguish the outer edges of the squinches from the corbeled walls between them. The extreme thickness of the walls in proportion to the height of the dome is another indication that these chambers stood at the beginning of the series. There is no evidence of precursors. Roman domes on circular bases or smaller domes on pendentives obviously sprang from a different tradition (Ward-Perkins, p. 338). Evidence for the simpler pitched-brick dome exists from as early as the 3rd millenium B.C.E. in Mesopotamia (Reuther, p. 501; see ČAHĀRṬĀQ i), but the absence of any known intermediaries between them and the Fīrūzābād domes, even from the Parthian period, attests to the originality of the Sasanian examples.

The most numerous surviving Sasanian domes are those over *čahārṭāq*s, frequently the central chambers of fire temples. It is in the large dome of the structure variously identified as a palace and a fire temple at Sarvestān in Fārs that two constant features of later dome design first become apparent: the use of lighter materials, in this instance brick, for the dome itself and decorative emphasis on the zone of transition, which at Sarvestān is carefully set off by dogtooth moldings above and below and lightened by four windows between the squinches. The squinches are also more clearly articulated, each consisting of intersecting segments of two tunnel vaults (Bier, figs. 24-28). These features are, however, consistent with an early Islamic rather than a late Sasanian date for Sarvestān, a possibility also

PLATE XXII

Detail of dome chamber, palace of Ardašīr I, Fīrūzābād, 3rd century.

mooted for several *čahārṭāq*s.

The survival of the dome on squinches in the Islamic period may have been encouraged by the transformation of several *čahārṭāq*s into mosques, documented in a few instances (see ČAHĀRṬĀQ ii; *EIr.* V, *Addenda and Corrigenda*). The building of isolated dome chambers to serve as mosques ("kiosk mosques") may have followed, though the evidence comes not from the usually cited congregational mosques of major cities but from a few, mostly Saljuq examples in small villages in Khorasan.

It was the appearance of the domed mausoleum that was to prove most important for the development of the dome in early Islamic Persia. Despite initial Islamic hostility to tomb structures, by the 10th century several had probably been built by the ʿAbbasid caliphs for themselves (Allen). Domed tombs had also been erected over the graves of many Shiʿite martyrs (Blair, 1983, pp. 83-84), and the respect paid to them by pilgrims may well have hastened the spread of the form. Two early mausoleums in Transoxania stand out: that of the Samanids in Bukhara (before 331/943) and the ʿArab Atā at Tīm (possibly 367/977-78), between Bukhara and Samarqand. In the zone of transition in the former the squinches are of the same width as the arches between them, resulting in a regular octagonal plan at this level; this scheme was followed in virtually all later examples. At Tīm the zone of transition is further unified by trilobed squinches composed of large *moqarnas* (oversailing courses of niche sections) separated by trilobed arches. This mausoleum is also the earliest extant to incorporate a *pīšṭāq* (an arched portal projecting vertically or horizontally from a facade), a feature that also became usual in domed-square mausoleums but that, even at this early stage, often made its impact at the expense of the dome.

Tomb towers represent another tradition in Persian mausoleums; many survive from the beginning of the 11th century onward. They are circular or polygonal in plan, thus reducing the importance of the zone of transition, and they frequently have conical roofs masking interior domes. Although the domes of the earliest tomb towers are plain, the shafts often display the inventive decorative brickwork of the period, as at the Pīr-e ʿĀlamdār (417/1026-27) and Čehel Doḵtarān (446/1054-55) at Dāmḡān (q.v.). Two other notable examples are at Ḵarraqān on the Qazvīn-Hamadān road 33 km west of Āb-e Garm (460/1067 and 486/1093); the earlier had the first masonry double dome known from Persia.

The Saljuq period. The introduction by the Saljuqs of a *maqṣūra* (enclosure) in front of the mihrab of the hypostyle mosque helped to transform the skylines, characteristically punctuated with domes, of Persian towns. Although in the early Islamic period dome chambers may have been used for small neighborhood mosques, it was only after the vizier Neẓām-al-Molk introduced the domed *maqṣūra* (ca 479-80/1086-87) in the congregational mosque at Isfahan that dome chambers on the *qebla* become the norm in Persian congregational mosques. It was the largest masonry dome in the Islamic world in its time and embodied a new form of squinch, in which a barrel vault above two smaller quarter domes was substituted for the weaker central unit of the squinch at ʿArab Atā. The classic status of this squinch form is clear from numerous copies, not only in the Isfahan oasis (Barsīān, Ardestān [qq.v.], Zavāra), but also in Khorasan (Rebāṭ-e Šaraf) and Transoxania (Yarty [Yortī] Gonbad; Karriev et al., pp. 88-89). At the Isfahan mosque Neẓām-al-Molk's rival Tāj-al-Molk built a second dome chamber (481/1088) on the axis opposite the southern chamber, for purposes that are still unclear (see Blair, 1992, pp. 166-67). It is justly famous as the cynosure of Saljuq domes (Pope). The emphasis on verticality and on lightening the walls of the lower square became typical of Il-khanid dome chambers. The interior of the dome of Tāj-al-Molk is patterned with interlacing ribs that form pentagons and five-pointed stars, among other geometric figures. This arrangement represents a considerable technical advance over the eight ribs in the southern dome and could well have inspired subsequent designers of patterns for this hitherto neglected surface. The much smaller domes over the bays of the hypostyle portion of the Isfahan mosque also display a wealth of geometric ornamentation (Galdieri, I, pls. 60-62).

The numerous Saljuq dome chambers of northwestern Persia usually have much simpler zones of transition than those at Isfahan but, perhaps in compensation, are abundantly decorated with carved stucco and are also sometimes articulated on the exterior (Hillenbrand, 1976). This concern is most apparent in the largest Saljuq domed chamber, the tomb of Sultan Sanjar at Marv. Although the dome is decorated on the interior with a system of intersecting ribs, the squinches and lower walls are plain. The exterior zone of transition received the greatest emphasis, with the squinches disguised by alternating large and small arches, echoed by smaller superposed arches at the base of the double-shelled dome. Stucco work on the soffits of the main arcade, probably by the same artisans who had earlier worked at Rebāṭ-e Šaraf (cf. Cohn-Wiener, pl. VIII; Hill and Grabar, fig. 546), underlines the new importance of this zone.

The Il-khanid period. The dome chamber of the congregational mosque in Varāmīn provides an example of changes in Persian domes in the Il-khanid period. Its taller proportions result primarily from the increased height of the zone of transition, with the addition of a sixteen-sided zone above the main zone of *moqarnas* squinches. Extra light enters through eight windows in this upper tier, although, as the Persian climate necessitated avoidance of sunlight during most of the year, architects of Persian dome chambers never aspired to the walls of light that characterized Ottoman examples.

The major Il-khanid domes were those of the mausoleums of Ḡāzān Khan at Tabrīz and Öljeitü (Ūljāytū) at Solṭānīya, each at the center of a larger complex of buildings. Ḡāzān's mausoleum was twelve-sided; although it is no longer extant, its magnificence may be judged by that of Ōljeitü, which was built to rival it. The dome of Öljeitü's mausoleum is 50 m high and nearly 25 m in diameter, dimensions unsurpassed in later Persian examples. The decoration of tile, stucco, and painting (the last forming part of a remodeling of the interior; Blair, 1987) is the finest surviving from the period. The thin double-shelled dome was reinforced by arches between the shells. Galleries on the upper part of the octagonal exterior differ from earlier arcades in that they were easily accessible. They were the first in a series that can be traced through Timurid and Shaybanid examples to a culmination at the Taj Mahal in Agra.

In the Il-khanid period tomb towers mirroring the splendors of Öljeitü's mausoleum proliferated. Several have *moqarnas* domes. This feature was found in brick at the Saljuq congregational mosque at Sīn, and an example covered with painted plaster in the congregational mosque at Nāʾīn may date from as early as the 10th century (Hillenbrand, 1987, fig. 11). In Il-khanid examples they usually consist of plaster shells masking the underlying structures. The finest example is probably that at the tomb of ʿAbd-al-Ṣamad in Naṭanz. The form may have been adopted from the tomb of Shaikh Sohravardī, founder of the order to which ʿAbd-al-Ṣamad belonged, near Baghdad (Blair, 1986). In the Mesopotamian examples (that of Imam Dūr at Samarra, 478/1085-86, is the earliest) the *moqarnas* are frequently expressed on the exterior as well. This form is occasionally found in Persia, for example, at the *emāmzāda* (q.v.) of Mīr Moḥammad on Ḵarg island, dated 738/1337 (Watson, p. 187). A plaster slab discovered at Taḵt-e Solaymān in Kordestān is incised with a plan of the *moqarnas* vaulting for a room restored by Abaqa Khan (671-74/1271-74; Harb).

The dome over the chamber adjoining the Do Manār Dardašt in Isfahan marks a major advance in dome design. If contemporary with the gravestone of Solṭān-Baḵt Āqā inside (753/1351-52; Honarfar, *Eṣfahān*, p. 317), it is the earliest known example of a double dome in which the inner and outer shells have substantially different profiles. It has been claimed that the dome of the Solṭānīya complex in Cairo (probably built by Sultan Ḥasan, ca. 1356-60) was the origin of this form, which then spread to Persia (Meinecke, p. 175), but the interior buttressing at the Solṭānīya complex betrays the influence of a brick tradition, suggesting a Persian origin. The trend toward taller drums continued in the Timurid period, finally reaching the inordinate proportions of the ʿEšrat-ḵāna in Samarqand (ca. 869/1464). One factor responsible was the increasing height of *pīštāq*s, which at the *boqʿa* (shrine) of Zayn-al-Dīn Ḵᵛāfī at Tāybād (848/1444-45) led the architect to abandon the outer shell of the dome altogether (Plate XXIII). Where the drum was retained, however, it usually rose straight from a lower square, resulting in the loss of an external zone of transition.

There were two divergent trends in the interior decoration of domed chambers from the Saljuq period onward. The most prominent was the substitution of plain or painted plaster for brick. The other was increased use of tilework. A spectacular early example of nearly complete tile revetment is the dome chamber of the congregational mosque at Yazd (765/1364; Plate XXIV). The same craftsman's signature appears in the dome of this monument and in the congregational mosque at Sāva (O'Kane, 1984, p. 84). The interiors of several of the mausoleums in the Šāh-e Zenda in Samarqand (e.g., that of Šād-e Molk, 773/1371) are totally reveted in tilework.

In the 15th-17th centuries. After the turn of the 15th century the Timurids built very few freestanding mausoleums, attaching them instead to *madrasa*s (religious schools), often in pairs. The dome chambers erected within these *madrasa*s revolutionized the design of interiors, as in the *madrasa* of Gowhar Šād at Herat (820-36/1417-33) and the *madrasa* at Ḵargerd (ca. 840-46/1436-43; O'Kane, 1987, nos. 14, 22). This change probably originated in 14th-century experiments with small lantern domes set at right angles to the main transverse vaults, from

PLATE XXIII

Exterior of the dome of the *boqʿa* of Zayn-al-Dīn K̲ᵛāfī, Tāybād, 848/1444-45, from the southwest.

PLATE XXIV

Interior of dome faced with tiles, congregational mosque, Yazd, 765/1364.

PLATE XXV

Domed carpet market (Tīm-e bozorg), Qom, 19th century.

which arose the concept of using intersecting arches to support a dome with a diameter smaller than the width of the square below. The chamber was also modified, with a deep recess added to each side to produce a cruciform plan. The result was a much more fluid space than had been possible with the rigid tripartite division of lower square, zone of transition, and dome. In particular, the intersecting arches provide a visual link between the dome and the dado level, an illusion, as the thrusts are taken up by concealed masonry (O'Kane, 1987, pp. 108-09). In the *madrasa* of Gowhar Šād the dome is actually a triple shell, the first of its kind; the intermediate dome presumably was added for reinforcement.

The tilework of the Qara Qoyunlū Moẓaffarīya mosque (also known as the Blue Mosque, 870/1465) at Tabrīz is outstanding. Above a marble dado the whole of the interior of the dome chamber on the *qebla* was faced with dark-blue hexagonal tiles with stenciled gilding, creating a richness that was unparalleled until construction of the mosque of Shaikh Loṭf-Allāh in Isfahan (1012-28/1603-18), the quintessential Persian dome chamber. In the latter the blending of the square, zone of transition, and dome was achieved by unifying the first two, rather than the upper two, as in the Timurid examples with intersecting arches. The form of the squinches is plain, recalling those of Sarvestān and the Saljuq domes of northwestern Persia, but the way in which the framing arches and the enclosed tilework patterns continue in an uninterrupted sweep down to dado level was an innovation. The four identical arches between the squinches are edged by a bold twisted turquoise cable, lending the interior a new unity and simplicity. The exterior of the dome displays another innovation, the use of multiple levels of arabesque, interwoven with the brick ground with such finesse that it has often been mistakenly presumed that the ground, too, was glazed. The domes of the 17th-century Masjed-e Šāh and Mādar-e Šāh madrasa in Isfahan show how effective a similar arabesque pattern can be against a light-blue tiled ground.

In Transoxania and neighboring regions the Uzbeks carried on the Timurid tradition of dome building with little change, though dome chambers were sometimes surrounded with axial *ayvān*s (q.v.) and corner rooms, as in the *ḵānaqāh* (Sufi monastery) of Qāsem Shaikh in Kermān (Golombek, fig. 16). Where these corner rooms are part of an octagonal plan and on two stories, as in the shrine of Ḵᵛāja Pārsā at Balḵ (ca. 1598), the form was a prototype for the major

PLATE XXVI

Domed cistern with wind funnel (*bādgīr*, q.v.), at Bašnīgān, near Yazd.

Indian mausoleums of Persian inspiration, that of Homāyūn in Delhi and the Taj Mahal. The domed *tīmčas* (markets) that survive at major intersections in Shaybanid Bukhara (McChesney) are among the earliest survivors of the type.

In the 19th and 20th centuries. In the Qajar period the major architectural focus was the *ayvān*, leading to comparative neglect of the dome, even when it was on the *qebla* axis (as at the Solṭānī mosque in Semnān, 1242/1826-27, and the Sepahsalār *madrasa* in Tehran, 1296/1878-79). The "onion dome," with an exaggerated swelling above a short drum, first appeared in Persia in this period (e.g., at Šāh Čerāḡ in Shiraz, 1269/1852-53), but it is difficult to view the resulting top-heavy appearance as other than an aesthetic step backward. More impressive are the Qajar *tīmčā*s at Qom (Plate XXV) and Kāšān, each of which features a sea of stalactites supporting a central dome flanked by two smaller ones (Ministry, pp. 218-19, 228-33).

In the 20th century the dome has declined further in importance, especially since reinforced steel has usurped its role as a substitute for wooden beams. It has remained central in mausoleums, however, perhaps echoing an original paradise symbolism (Daneshvari), as at the 20th-century tombs of Ḥāfeẓ and Saʿdī in Shiraz and those of Reżā Shah in Ray (now destroyed) and Ruhollah Khomeini (Rūḥ-Allāh Ḵomeynī) in Tehran.

In vernacular architecture. Throughout Persian history the dome also played an important role in vernacular architecture. On many parts of the Persian plateau where wood is scarce whole villages with domed roofs are to be observed (Beazley, fig. 1). From Sasanian to Qajar times caravansaries (q.v.) were frequently constructed with the domed bay as the module. Domed cisterns (*āb-anbār*, q.v.; Plate XXVI) and icehouses (*yakčāl*s), still common sights in the Persian countryside (Beazley), are other reminders of the variety, pervasiveness, and permanence of the dome in Persian history.

Bibliography: T. Allen, "The Tombs of the ʿAbbāsid Caliphs in Baghdād," *BSO(A)S* 46, 1983, pp. 421-31. E. Beazley, "Some Vernacular Buildings of the Plateau," in R. W. Ferrier, ed., *The Arts of Persia*, London, 1989, pp. 109-17. L. Bier, *Sarvistan. A Study in Early Iranian Architecture*, University Park, Pa., 1986. S. Blair, "The Octagonal Pavilion at Natanz. A Reexamination of Early Islamic Architecture in Iran," *Muqarnas* 1, 1983, pp. 69-94. Idem, *The Ilkhanid Shrine Complex at Natanz, Iran*, Cambridge, Mass., 1986. Idem, "The Epigraphic Program of the Tomb of Uljaytu at Sultaniyya. Meaning in Mongol Architecture," *Islamic Art* 2, 1987, pp. 43-96. Idem, *The Monumental Inscriptions from Early Islamic Iran and Transoxiana*, Leiden, 1992. E. Cohn-Wiener, *Turan*, Berlin, 1930. A. Daneshvari, *Medieval Tomb Towers of Iran. An Iconographical Study*, Lexington, Ky., 1986. E. Galdieri, *Esfahān. Masǧid-i Ǧumʿa*, 3 vols., Rome, 1972-84. A. Godard, "Les coupoles," *Āṯār-é Īrān* 4, 1949, pp. 259-325. L. Golombek, "From Tamberlane to the Taj Mahal," in A. Daneshvari, ed., *Essays in Islamic Art and Architecture in Honor of Katharina Otto-Dorn*, Malibu, Calif., 1981, pp. 43-50. U. Harb, *Ilkhanidische Stalaktitengewölbe*, AMI, Ergänzungsbd. 4, Berlin, 1978. D. Hill and O. Grabar, *Islamic Architecture and Its Decoration*, London, 1967. R. Hillenbrand, "Saljūq Dome Chambers in North-West Iran," *Iran* 14, 1976, pp. 93-102. Idem, "ʿAbbāsid Mosques in Iran," *Rivista degli Studi Orientali* 59, 1985, pp. 175-212. A. K. Karriev et al., *Pamyatniki arkhitektury Turkmenistana* (Architectural monuments of Turkmenistan), Leningrad, 1974. R. D. McChesney, "Economic and Social Aspects of the Public Architecture of Bukhara in the 1560's and 1570's," *Islamic Art* 2, 1987, pp. 217-42. M. Meinecke, "Mamluk Architecture. Regional Architectural Traditions. Evolution and Interrelations," *Damaszener Mitteilungen* 2, 1985, pp. 163-75. Ministry of housing and development, *Masterpieces of Iranian Architecture*, n.p. (Tehran), n.d. (1970). B. O'Kane, "Timurid Stucco Decoration," *Annales Islamologiques* 20, 1984, pp. 61-84. Idem, *Timurid Architecture in Khurasan*, Costa Mesa, Calif., 1987. A. U. Pope, "Notes on the Aesthetic Character of the North Dome of the Masjid-i Jāmiʿ of Iṣfahān," in *Studies in Islamic Art and Architecture in Honour of K.A.C. Creswell*, Cairo, 1965. O. Reuther, "Sāsānian Architecture. A. History," in *Survey of Persian Art* I, pp. 493-578. J. Sauvaget, "Observations sur quelques mosquées seldjoukides," *Annales de l'Institut d'Études Orientales, Université d'Alger* 4, 1938, pp. 81-120. E. B. Smith, *The Dome. A Study in the History of Ideas*, Princeton, N.J., 1950. D. Stronach and T. C. Young, "Three Octagonal Seljuq Tomb Towers from Iran," *Iran* 4, 1966, pp. 1-20. J. B. Ward-Perkins, *Roman Imperial Architecture*, Harmondsworth, U.K., 1981. O. Watson, *Persian Lustre Ware*, London, 1985. D. Wilber, *The Architecture of Islamic Iran. The Il Khanid Period*, Princeton, N.J., 1955.

(BERNARD O'KANE)

DOMESTIC ANIMALS (Pers. *ḥaywān-e ahlī*; cf. *ahlī kardan/šodan* "to domesticate, be domesticated"), a group of animals raised or maintained in captivity so that they can provide products, services, or entertainment. These animals, the methods of raising and exploiting them, their general treatment, and the ways in which they are represented by human beings constitute the "system of domestication" (Digard, 1990, pp. 176-79). This article is devoted to the principal characteristics of the predominant systems of domestication in Afghanistan and Persia, what they owe to neighboring or preceding systems, how they have departed from them, and whether or not it is possible to speak of a typically Iranian system of domestication. For domestication of individual species, the general history of domestication, and related topics, individual articles on those species and topics should be consulted (e.g., ASB; BOZ; CAMEL; CAT; CATTLE; ČŪPĀN; DĀMDĀRĪ; DOG; DONKEY).

Table 34 presents a panorama of the systems of domestication in Afghanistan and in Persia, encompassing the various species and their uses. The species constitute a broad and fairly heterogeneous zoological ensemble, ranging from large herbivorous mammals through primates, carnivorous mammals, and birds to insects. Not all these species are domesticated to the same degree. Some, like cattle, dogs, and chickens, are domestic species in the most common sense of the term. Others are represented by animals captured in their natural habitats, raised in captivity, and trained in varying degrees for specific purposes (cheetahs and hunting falcons; performing bears and monkeys; fighting crickets, quails, and partridges; and canaries, nightingales, mynas, parrakeets, and other singing or talking birds; Kühnert, 1980; Roux, 1981; Nogge, 1973). Still others, like bees, are kept and exploited in conditions close to those in nature (Schneider, 1976). There is one species raised in entirely artificial conditions and owing its survival only to man's interest in its produce, that is, the *Bombyx*, or silkworm moth (Reut, 1983; see ABRĪŠAM). Finally, of course, there are hybrids produced by human intervention, like the *bok̲ta*/*bok̲tī* resulting from the crossing of camel and dromedary and the mule from donkey and horse (see below).

The type and number of uses also vary widely from one species to another. In Table 34 the most polyvalent, or versatile, animals are listed at the left, the most specialized at the right; at the top are the products for which animals are exploited, at the bottom their work, behavioral, and semiotic or symbolic benefits. Aside from the extraction of certain products (notably meat from a limited number of species: sheep and goats, cattle, poultry) and sacrifices for religious purposes, which presuppose slaughter, Iranians exhibit a strong preference for exploiting living animals. Among the polyvalent animals two main subgroups can be distinguished: those like the small ruminants that must be slaughtered to be fully exploited and those, basically donkeys, horses, and mules, that are useful only while alive. Cattle occupy an intermediate position between these two subgroups. The least versatile of utilitarian animals, like the chicken and the pigeon, belong to a separate class.

With the exception of the bee (from which honey and wax are obtained), the *Bombyx* (from the cocoon of which silk is produced), and the cat (useful as a predator against pests), all the specialized animals are exploited for enjoyment, and some rank as luxuries. They give pleasure (nightingales and other singing birds), serve as ornaments (peacocks), furnish traveling entertainment (monkeys and bears) or spectacle (fighting crickets, quails, and partridges), or are used in hunting by the upper classes (cheetahs and trained birds of prey, which are thus highly valued in both money and prestige).

The most noteworthy species are doubtless the horse and the dog. The former can be subdivided into saddle horses (almost always stallions in Persia and Afghanistan) and less valuable workhorses (although the term *yābū* is frequently used interchangeably for both). Among dogs coursers (*tāzī*) are distinguished from the mastiffs that guard flocks and dwellings, particularly among the nomads (de Planhol, 1969a; Digard, 1980), and from the wandering dogs that scavenge in cities and villages. Such distinctions can be justified from both biological and cultural points of view, which are, of course, inseparable when dealing with domesticated animals. Ownership of both saddle horses and hunting dogs is limited, if only because of their cost, to social and economic elites that draw status from them and use them for activities that also confer status (war and hunting). For this reason these animals are carefully selected, raised and trained under special conditions, and treated with a consideration unknown to the mass of their fellows. This inequality of treatment is particularly flagrant among dogs. The esteem in which hunting dogs are held is all the more striking in comparison with the blows and stoning continually administered to the general canine population of Afghanistan and Persia.

Finally, what structuralists would call the "symmetrical and inverse" positions occupied by the common dog and the cat should be noted. Among Muslims the dog, though "familiar," is considered unclean (Viré, 1978), whereas the cat, a distant predator, clearly enjoys a more favorable status (Pitton de Tournefort, 1982, pp. 80-81); among Zoroastrians, on the contrary, it is the cat that is considered "unclean" and "a creature of darkness" (Boyce, *Stronghold*, p. 163) while the dog is "honoured as the creature nearest in dignity to man" (Boyce, *Reader*, pp. 302-03; cf. Hovelacque; Brackert and Kieffens, pp. 24, 57-59; Boyce, *Stronghold*, passim). There is also a clear similarity between Zoroastrian respect for the dog and the relatively conciliatory attitude toward this animal in certain branches of Persian Sufism (Nurbakhsh), a similarity that certainly reflects Zoroastrian influence on Persian Islam, at least in certain locations; in other locations differences in the treatment of dogs clearly distinguish the two communities (Boyce, *Stronghold*, pp. 141-43).

It is clear that there are shadings in Persian attitudes toward domestic animals, reflecting vestiges of successive cultural strata in the history of domestication in the Iranian world. The first great wave of domestication, of cattle, pigs, goats, sheep, and so on, took place in the Neolithic and lasted for several millennia. The rise of states and cities in antiquity

Table 34

DOMESTIC ANIMALS AND THEIR USES IN PERSIA AND AFGHANISTAN

Use[a]	Sheep	Goats	Cattle	Dromedaries, hybrids	Horses	Riding horses	Mules	Donkeys	Elephants	Poultry	Pigeons	Dogs	Greyhounds	Cats	Cheetahs	Birds of prey	Singing birds	Partridges	Crickets	Bears	Monkeys	Peacocks	Bees	*Bombyx sp.*
PHYSICAL PRODUCTS																								
Meat	■	■	■							■														
Offal	■	■	■							■														
Blood																								
Fat																								
Food	■	■	■																					
Light	■	■	■																					
Other	■	■	■																					
Secretions																								
Liquid	■	■	■																					
Solid (bezoard)	■	■	■																					
Silk																								■
Membranes	■	■	■																					
Tendons	■	■	■																					
Bones	■	■	■																					
Teeth and tusks	■	■	■																					
Horns and antlers	■	■	■																					
Skin																								
Fur	■	■																						
Leather	■	■	■																					
Hair	■	■																						
Wool																								
Felt	■	■		■																				
Yarn	■	■		■																				
Feathers																								
Feathers																								
Down										■														
Excrement																								
Urine																								
Feces																								
Surfacing, cement			■																					
Fuel			■	■	■	■	■	■																
Manure	■	■	■								■													

a. Underscored uses require that the animal be dead, italicized uses apply to animals either alive or dead, and other uses are for live animals.

Use	Sheep	Goats	Cattle	Dromedaries, hybrids	Horses	Riding horses	Mules	Donkeys	Elephants	Poultry	Pigeons	Dogs	Greyhounds	Cats	Cheetahs	Birds of prey	Singing birds	Partridges	Crickets	Bears	Monkeys	Peacocks	Bees	*Bombyx sp.*
Milk																								
With full cream																								
Cooked and uncooked	X	X	X	X																				
Fermented (yogurt)	X	X	X	X																				
Cream																								
Butter	X	X	X	X																				
Ghee	X	X	X	X																				
Casein																								
Curds	X	X	X	X																				
Cheese	X	X	X	X																				
Sugar																								
Alcoholic drinks																								
Eggs																								
Food										X														
Shells																								
Honey																							X	
ENERGY																								
Threshing			X		X	X	X	X																
Carrying																								
Pack saddle			X	X	X	X	X	X	X															
Litter				X	X	X	X	X	X															
Saddle			X			X	X																	
Draft																								
Travois																								
Harnessed																								
Threshing			X		X		X	X																
Plowing			X		X																			
Drawing carts			X		X																			
Roundabout																								
Lifting water			X	X																				
Mills			X	X																				
Treadmills																								
Other																								

Use	Sheep	Goats	Cattle	Dromedaries, hybrids	Horses	Riding horses	Mules	Donkeys	Elephants	Poultry	Pigeons	Dogs	Greyhounds	Cats	Cheetahs	Birds of prey	Singing birds	Partridges	Crickets	Bears	Monkeys	Peacocks	Bees	*Bombyx sp.*
BEHAVIOR																								
Food supply and predatory																								
Cleaning																								
Human excrement												■												
Other refuse			■																					
Rodent destruction														■										
Hunting auxiliary													■		■	■								
Gathering auxiliary																								
Territorial																								
Warning												■												
Guarding												■												
Conveying messages											■													
Social																								
Pets																								
Singing																	■							
Decoys																								
Leading herds		■																						
Fighting	■		■	■								■						■	■					
Racing				■		■																		
Entertainment and games						■					■									■	■			
SIGNS																								
Divination																								
Sacrifice	■	■	■	■						■														
Status and wealth																								
Herds	■	■	■	■	■	■			■															
Individual animals				■		■			■				■		■	■						■		
Monetary units																								

generated needs that led to development of specialized animal products (Briant, 1982; Zeder, 1991). At the same time in the religious sphere the value of the dog (see above) and especially of the ox rose; the latter represented "the prototype of animal sacrifice" (Boyce, *Reader*, p. 141; cf. Brentjes; Simoons and Simoons; Planhol, 1969b; Briant, 1982).

In the 7th century Muslim attitudes and beliefs about animals penetrated onto the Persian plateau (Bousquet; Pellat), including prohibition of the consumption of pork (Henninger; Viré) and blood, contempt for the dog, and greater appreciation of the horse, the camel, the sheep, and so on. Beginning in the 11th century, the influences of the Turks and Mongols began to make themselves felt, especially in the lexicon of zootechnology (Digard, de Planhol, and Bazin) and in methods of animal husbandry. Crossbreeding of the camel and the dromedary (Tapper) and similar developments were followed by the gradual spread in mountainous regions of large-scale nomadic pastoralism (de Planhol, 1968) and the cultural traits linked to it: management and exploitation of large flocks of herbivores (Digard, 1981) and idealization, even ritualization, of mountain pasturage and animals (Parkes, a study dedicated to the Kafirs of the Hindu Kush but including descriptions of phenomena frequent among Persian tribes). The pastoral specialization acquired by nomadic tribal societies no doubt explains the minimal interest in zootechnological matters apparent in sources written by sedentary authors, despite koranic exhortations (Zeghidour, pp. 363-64); exceptions are texts related to saddle horses, hunting dogs, and trained birds of prey. Otherwise, there is either total silence or caricature, for example: "The Persians (*Furs*) claim that viviparous quadrupeds . . . can be divided into only two classes: the caprids (*ma'z*) and ovines (*da'n*). For them, buffalo are the ovines of the bovines (*da'n al-baqar*) [cf. Pers. *gāv-mīš*]. Bactrian camels (*bokht*) are the ovines of the camels (*da'n al-hilil*) and beasts of burden (*barādhin*) the ovines of the equines (*khayl*)" (Jāḥeẓ, tr., p. 80; cf. Massé, *Croyances*, pp. 185-207; de Fouchécour, pp. 137-62).

In the 17th and 18th centuries there was intensive development of land and maritime commmerce with Mughal India. The army of Kabul received domestic elephants, a practice already attested in the Sasanian and the Ghaznavid periods and one that survived well into the 20th century, imposing winter pasturing of the animals at Jalālābād, where the climate is less harsh. On the other hand, from the Persian Gulf ports (especially Bušehr) there was substantial traffic in Arabian horses, Persian cats, and Pathan mastiffs going to northern India, a traffic paralleled from Kabul to the Ganges plain (Kolff, pp. 11-12; Digard, in press).

The westernization of Persia that began in the second half of the 19th century, though pervasive, affected animal domestication only sporadically. For example, it produced profound dislocations in the breeding of silkworms in Gīlān (Bromberger), but, on the other hand, the great majority of Persians remained untouched by the Western fondness for pets and corresponding zoophiliac tendencies.

Throughout history, then, Afghanistan and Persia seem to have been a sort of crucible for innovations in domestication and zootechnology from various origins. The system of domestication that predominates in those countries is in fact characterized by a mixture of elements clearly borrowed from neighboring systems or inherited from previous periods, in patterns that vary considerably in different regions: first, fairly ubiquitous Turkish elements like crossbreeding of the camel and the dromedary and the zootechnological vocabulary; second, Indian elements (cf. *Āʾīn-e akbarī*, ed. Blochmann, passim), which were particularly numerous in Afghanistan, including relatively free circulation of cows, ensuring the clearing of city pathways and gutters (*jūy*), and use of elephants for both fighting and riding (especially in royal hunts); and, third, Zoroastrian, the only genuinely indigenous, elements, though of quite modest, even uncertain importance (e.g., the equivocal status of the dog).

Like any cultural system, a system of domestication consists of a stable core, here essentially made up of large domestic herbivores and fighting animals, and a more unstable periphery, where species come and go, exemplified in the modern period, on one hand, by the introduction of the bee, which was domesticated in Kashmir but not introduced into Afghanistan until the 19th century (Irwin, p. 1006), and, on the other, by the disappearance of the elephant, the last one being attested at Kabul in 1306 Š./1927. The mule illustrates in an entirely different fashion the contrast between the core and the periphery. Mating the ass with the mare has been widely practiced in Persia (Digard, 1981, p. 33), probably since antiquity (Negahban), but farther east it has been strictly limited to the Solaymān mountains in Afghanistan, specifically to the high Kurram, in the territory of the Jājī (in Afghanistan) and the Tūrī (in Pakistan) tribes. This distribution was already attested at the beginning of the 19th century: "Mules are scarcely raised in Toorkistan, the best are bred in Khoorasan; a slender species, but yet hardy, is bred in Pothwar and the neighbouring districts [i.e., Punjab]. They are raised in the vallies of Jajee and Foree [Turi] in Teera [Tīrāh, the country of the Afridis north of Kurram] and some other places" (Irwin, p. 1009). Another 19th-century witness emphasized the difference between Afghanistan and Persia on this point: "The religious prejudices of the Afghans object to mules, hence they are uncommon in Afghanistan. In Persia it is by mules that all the rapid travelling and quick conveyance of goods takes place; they convey heavy loads rapidly by long marches and exist upon miserable fare. When mules are well cared for, it is marvellous what an amount of work they will do" (Aitchison, p. 136). The author thus suggested that this difference had a religious origin. There are in fact some Hadith that condemn breeding the ass and the mare (Pellat); though of doubtful authenticity, they could have led here and there to a divergence between Sunnite and Shiʿite practice. According to this hypothesis, the presence of mules in the territory of a Shiʿite Pashtun tribe (Tūrī) might very well have fostered their introduction into the territory of neighboring Sunnite tribes (Jājī).

It thus appears that the prevailing system of domestication in Afghanistan and Persia does not differ fundamentally from a more widespread "Middle Eastern" system, in which the influence of Islam is preponderant. Rather than an "Iranian system of domestication" properly speaking, there is an "Iranian" variant of this Middle Eastern system.

Bibliography: J. E. T. Aitchison, "Notes to Assist in a Further Knowledge of the Products of Western Afghanistan and of North-Eastern Persia," *Transactions of the Botanical Society of Edinburgh* 18, 1891, pp. 1-228. D. Balland, "Une spéculation originale. L'astrakan en Afghanistan," *Hannon* (Beirut) 7, 1972, pp. 89-113. G.-H. Bousquet, "Des animaux et de leur traitement selon le judaïsme, le christianisme et l'Islam," *Stud. Isl.* 9, 1958, pp. 31-48. H. Brackert and C. van Kieffens, *Histoire des chiens et des hommes*, Paris, 1991. B. Brentjes, "Zur ökonomischen Funktion des Rindes in den Kulturen des Alten Orients," *Klio* 55, 1973, pp. 43-78. P. Briant, *État et pasteurs au Moyen-Orient ancien*, Cambridge and Paris, 1982. Idem, "Chasses royales macédoniennes et chasses royales perses. Le thème de la chasse au lion sur *La chasse de Vergina*," *Dialogues d'histoire ancienne* 17/1, 1991, pp. 211-55. C. Bromberger, "Changements techniques et transformation des rapports sociaux. La sériculture au Gilân dans la seconde moitié du XIXe siècle," in Y. Richard, ed., *Entre l'Iran et l'Occident. Adaptation et assimilation des idées et techniques occidentales en Iran*, Paris, 1989, pp. 71-90. M. J. Casimir, "The Biological Phenomenon of Imprinting—Its Handling and Manipulation by Traditional Pastoralists," *Production pastorale et société* 11, 1982, pp. 23-237. J.-P. Digard, "Chiens de campement et chiens de troupeau chez les nomade Baxtyâri d'Iran," *Stud. Ir.* 9/1, 1980, pp. 131-39. Idem, *Techniques des nomades Baxtyâri d'Iran*, Cambridge and Paris, 1981. Idem, *L'homme et les animaux domestiques. Anthropologie d'une passion*, Paris, 1990. Idem, "Chah des chats, chat de chah? Sur les traces du chat persan," in *Mélanges en hommage à Xavier de Planhol*, in press. Idem, X. de Planhol, and L. Bazin, "Éléments turcs dans le vocabulaire pastoral baxtyâri," *Production pastorale et société* 11, 1982, pp. 5-11. R. Dollot, *L'Afghanistan*, Paris, 1937. L. Dupree, *Afghanistan*, Princeton, N.J., 1973. C.-H. de Fouchécour, *La description de la nature dans la poésie lyrique persane du XIe siècle*, Paris, 1969. H. Henninger, "Nouveaux débats sur l'interdiction du porc dans l'Islam," in J.-P. Digard, ed., *Le cuisinier et le philosophe. Hommage à Maxime Rodinson*, Paris, 1982, pp. 29-40. A. Hovelacque, *Le chien dans l'Avesta. Les soins qui lui sont dûs, son éloge*, Paris, 1876. Irwin, "Memoir on the Climate, Soil, Produce, and Husbandry of Afghanistan and the Neighbouring Countries III," *Journal of the Asiatic Society of Bengal* 8, 1839, pp. 1005-15. Abū ʿOṯmān ʿAmr Jāḥeẓ, *al-Ḥayawān*, abr. and tr. L. Souami as *Le cadi et la mouche. Anthologie du livre des animaux*, Paris, 1988. B. C. Karmyševa, "Arten der Viehhalgung in den Südbezirken von Uzbekistan and Tadshikistan," in L. Földes, ed., *Viehwirtschaft und Hirtenkultur*, Budapest, 1969, pp. 112-26. D. H. A. Kolff, *Naukar, Rajput and Sepoy. The Ethnohistory of the Military Labour Market of Hindustan, 1450-1850*, Cambridge, 1990. G. Kühnert, *Falknerei in Afghanistan*, Bonn, 1980. T. Lewicki, "Średniowieczne źródła arabskie i perskie o hodowli zwierząt domowych u słowian," *Kwartalnik Historii Kultury Materialy* (Warsaw) 2, 1954, pp. 444-68. B. A. Litvinskij, "Schaf und Ziege in der Glaubenswelt der Pamir-Tadschiken," in P. Snoy, ed., *Ethnologie und Geschichte. Festschrift für Karl Jettmar*, Beiträge zur Südasien-Forschung 86, Wiesbaden, 1983, pp. 389-98. E. O. Negahban, "Horse and Mule Figurines from Marlik," in L. de Meyer and E. Haerinck, eds., *Archaeologia Iranica et Orientalis. Miscellanea in Honorem Louis vanden Berghe* I, Ghent, 1989, pp. 287-309. G. Nogge, "Vogeljagd am Hindukusch," *Natur und Museum* 103/8, 1978, pp. 276-79. Dj. Nurbakhsh, *Dogs from a Sufi Point of View*, London, 1989.

P. Parkes, "Livestock Symbolism and Pastoral Ideology among the Kafīrs of the Hindu Kush," *Man* 22/4, 1987, pp. 637-60. C. Pellat, "Baghl," in *EI*[2] I, p. 909. J. Pitton de Tournefort, *Relation du voyage du Levant*, Lyons, 1717; new ed., II. *Voyage d'un botaniste*, Paris, 1982. X. de Planhol, *Les fondements géographiques de l'histoire de l'Islam*, Paris, 1968. Idem, "Le chien de berger. Développement et signification géographique d'une technique pastorale," *Bulletin de l'Association de Géographes Français* 370, 1969a, pp. 355-68. Idem, "Le bœuf porteur dans le Proche-Orient et l'Afrique du Nord," *JESHO* 12/3, 1969b, pp. 298-321. A. Pour-Fickoui and M. Bazin, *Élevage et vie pastorale dans le Guilân (Iran septentrional)*, Publications du Départment de Géographie de l'Université de Paris-Sorbonne 7, Paris, 1978. G. Redard, "Camelina. Notes de dialectologie iranienne II," in *Indo-Iranica. Mélanges présentés à Georg Morgenstierne*, Wiesbaden, 1964, pp. 155-62. M. Reut, *La soie en Afghanistan. L'élevage du ver à soie en Afghanistan et l'artisanat de la soie à Herât*, Beiträge zur Iranistik 11, Wiesbaden, 1983. J. de Rochechouart, *Souvenirs d'un voyage en Perse*,

Paris, 1867. J.-P. Roux, "Le combat d'animaux dans l'art et la mythologie irano-turcs," *Arts Asiatiques* 36, 1981, pp. 5-11. P. Schneider, "Honigbienen und ihre Zucht in Afghanistan," *Afghanistan Journal* 3/3, 1976, pp. 101-04; 4/1, 1977, pp. 36-38. F. Sigaut, "Un tableau des produits animaux et deux hypothèses qui en découle," *Production pastorale et société* 7, 1980, pp. 20-36. F. Simoons and J. Simoons, *A Ceremonial Ox of India—The Mithan in Nature, Culture, and History, with Notes on the Domestication of Common Cattle*, Madison, Wisc., 1968. R. Tapper, "One Hump or Two? Hybrid Camels and Pastoral Cultures," *Production pastorale et société* 16, 1985, pp. 55-69. E. and A. Thornton, *Leaves from an Afghan Scrapbook*, London, 1910. F. Viré, "Kalb," in *EI*² IV, pp. 489-92. M. A. Zeder, *Feeding Cities. Specialized Animal Economy in the Ancient Near East*, Washington, D.C., 1991. S. Zeghidour, *La vie quotidienne à la Mecque de Mahomet à nos jours*, Paris, 1989.

(DANIEL BALLAND AND JEAN-PIERRE DIGARD)

DONALDSON, BESS ALLEN (b. Galesburg, Ill., 7 December 1879, d. Lakeland, Fla., 20 December 1974) and DWIGHT MARTIN (b. Washington, O., 16 December 1884, d. Lakeland, Fla., 11 May 1976), American Presbyterian missionaries and writers about Persia. Bess Allen went to Tehran in 1910 as a teacher at the Iran Bethel Girl's School (renamed Nūrbakš School in 1940), a Presbyterian mission school; she subsequently became principal. Dwight Donaldson was a missionary of the American Presbyterian Church in Mašhad from 1915. They were married in Tehran on 28 June 1916 and undertook evangelical work in Mašhad until 1940, when foreign missionary teachers were expelled from Persia and their schools nationalized. Dwight Donaldson then became principal of the Henry Martyn Institute of Islamic Studies at Aligarh in India, where the couple remained until his retirement in 1951.

Dwight Donaldson's major scholarly contributions were *The Shiʿite Religion. A History of Islam in Persia and Irak* (London, 1933) and *Studies in Muslim Ethics* (London, 1953). For the latter he drew on many lectures delivered in Persia, India, and the United States, as well as on his Persian experiences. He was for several years a member of the editorial board of *The Muslim World*, in which he published "Modern Persian Law" (October 1934, pp. 341-49). In *International Review of Missions* he published "The First Missionaries to the Parthians" (18, 1929, pp. 481-94), "What to Conserve, and What to Abandon" (20, 1931, pp. 422-28), and "Intellectual Awakening in Modern Iran" (25, 1936, pp. 172-83). Donaldson's scholarly credentials and the legacy of his work are incontrovertible.

During thirty years of sharing her husband's missionary work, giving Bible instruction, and teaching English, particularly to women, Bess Donaldson gathered material for *The Wild Rue* (London, 1938), a unique study of Persian folklore and myths, ranking with but based on more direct personal experience than Henri Massé's *Croyances et coutumes persanes*. . . . In her book she treated such topics as the evil eye, childbirth practices, love and marriage, pilgrimage, burial practices, angels, cosmology and astronomy, names and numbers, the calendar, the Koran, the significance of flora and fauna, personal hygiene, and talismans and signs. It is indispensable to any serious student of Persia and popular Islam. She also published *Prairie Girl* and *Prairie Girl in Iran and India* (Galesburg, Ill., 1971 and 1972, respectively).

Biographical details on the couple and Bess Donaldson's correpondence are held at the Department of History, Presbyterian Church (USA), Philadelphia.

Bibliography: J. Addison, *The Christian Approach to the Muslims*, New York, 1942. W. M. Miller, *My Persian Pilgrimage*, Pasadena, Calif., 1989. Idem, sermon preached on D. M. Donaldson's death, Philadelphia, 27 August 1976, ms. at Department of History, Presbyterian Church (USA), Philadelphia. L. Vander Werff, *Christian Mission to Muslims. The Reward*, Pasadena, Calif., 1977.

(PETER AVERY)

DONBA, the fatty part of the sheep's tail, traditionally used as a cooking fat, sometimes in melted form, or as an inexpensive meat substitute. Nowadays it is less frequently used because of the harmful effects of animal fat.

Bibliography: Mīrzā ʿAlī-Akbar Ašpāz-bāšī, *Sofra-ye aṭʿema*, Tehran, 1353 Š./1974, pp. 27, 51, 56. Ḥājī Mohammad-ʿAli Bāvarčī Bag̱dādī, *Kārnāma dar bāb-e ṭabbāḵī wa ṣanʿat-e ān*, in Ī. Afšār, ed., *Āšpāzī-e dawra-ye ṣafawī. Matn-e do resāla az ān dawra*, Tehran, 1360 Š./1981, pp. 53, 54, 62. A. Mīrzāyef, *Abū Esḥāq wa faʿʿālīyat-e adabī-e ū*, Dushanbe, 1971.

(M. R. GHANOONPARVAR)

DONBAK. See TONBAK.

DONBĀVAND. See DAMĀVAND.

DONBOLĪ, name of a turkicized Kurdish tribe in the Ḵoy and Salmās regions of northwestern Azerbaijan and of the leading family of Ḵoy since the 16th century. Šaraf-al-Dīn Bedlīsī (tr., pt. 1, p. 169) reported that, according to the "most authentic" theory, the Donbolī came from Boḵtān, a region between Siirt and Cizre in what is now southeastern Turkey, and the tribe was thus called Donbolī-e Boḵt. Its first leader seems to have been a certain ʿĪsā Beg, whose descendants were known as the ʿĪsā

Begī. The Donbolī were supposedly Yazīdīs for a considerable time before becoming Shiʿite Muslims (for other theories about the origin and early history of the Donbolī, see Nikitine, pp. 110-18). The ʿĪsā Begī held the district of Sokmanābād (modern Zūravā) some years before the establishment of the Āq Qoyunlū dynasty in 780/1378. Shaikh Aḥmad Beg, a descendant of ʿĪsā Beg, became an important official in the Āq Qoyunlū administration and conquered both the fortress of Bāy (which, for a long time, remained under Donbolī control) and a part of Hakkārī territory southeast of Lake Van (Bedlīsī, tr., pt. 1, pp. 169-70).

In the Safavid period. The Safavid shah Ṭahmāsb I (930-84/1524-76) combined Ḵoy with Sokmanābād in a single district (*eyālat*) and named Shaikh Aḥmad Beg's grandson Ḥājī Beg governor, with the honorary title *ḥājī solṭān*. He also entrusted Ḥājī Beg with the defense of the frontiers of the empire, including the province of Van. In 955/1548 Eskandar Pasha, governor of Van, at the instigation of the Kurdish chief Ḥasan Beg, attacked and killed Ḥājī Beg in Ḵoy (Bedlīsī, pt. 1, pp. 170-72; Ḥasan Rūmlū, ed. Seddon, II, p. 153). Donbolī allegiance to the shah then became increasingly tenuous, and Shah Ṭahmāsb's troops, sent to subdue the tribe by force, massacred a large number of its leaders. Manṣūr Beg, a nephew of Ḥājī Beg, survived and fled to the Ottoman empire, where he was appointed governor of the *sanjāq* of Qotūr Deresī (Qotūr valley) and Bargīrī and was able to gather the remnants of the Donbolī tribe under his leadership (Bedlīsī, tr., pt. 1, pp. 172-73).

During the reign of Shah ʿAbbās I (996-1038/1588-1629) most of the Donbolī once more shifted their allegiance to Persia, and several tribal leaders achieved distinction. Among them were Jamšīd Solṭān, who participated in the shah's expedition to Balḵ in the summer of 1011/1602 and was appointed governor of Marand after the capture of Tabrīz in the autumn of 1012/1603; Salmān Solṭān, who was for many years governor of Čūrs and Salmās and was a hero of the Persian defense of Azerbaijan against the Ottomans in the summer of 1025/1616; Ṭahmāsbqolī Šīra, who in 1035/1625-26 set off on a diplomatic mission to Istanbul but was murdered en route, allegedly by Ottoman officials who "did not consider it in their interests to allow the ambassador to reach Istanbul"; Maqṣūd Solṭān, governor of Barkošāṭ in Qarābāḡ; and Qelīč Beg, who received a fief from Shah ʿAbbās (Eskandar Beg, II, pp. 643, 783, 882, 901-02, 1031, 1057, 1064, 1086; tr. Savory, II, p. 832-33, 847, 980, 1117-18, 1252, 1281, 1287-88, 1313).

In the 18th century. Najafqolī Khan (1125-99/1713-85), the son of Šahbāz Khan Donbolī, entered the service of Nāder Shah (1148-60/1736-47) after the latter took Ḵoy from the Ottomans in 1147/1734 (Bedlīsī, repr., p. 399; Nāder Mīrzā, p. 154) and was soon appointed chief musketeer (*tofangčī āqāsī*). He accompanied Nāder Shah on his military expeditions to India, Georgia, and Dāḡestān and while in India was raised to the rank of *amīr al-omarāʾ* (q.v.; Donbolī, 1349 Š./1970, I, pp. 58-68; Marvī, p. 999 n. 3). He maintained his position under Nāder Shah's successors.

In late 1163/1750, when Āzād Khan Afḡān took control of Tabrīz and Urmia, Najafqolī Khan's nephew Šahbāz Khan Donbolī joined with several influential Afšār khans and leaders of the mountain tribes of Azerbaijan in his support. Šahbāz Khan performed many services for Āzād Khan, but at the battle of Urmia in the spring of 1170/1757 he switched sides and pledged allegiance to Moḥammad-Ḥasan Khan Qājār. In early 1171/late 1757, at the head of 6,000 men, he helped Moḥammad-Ḥasan Khan take Isfahan but withdrew his support after the Qājār leader failed to wrest Shiraz from Karīm Khan Zand (1163-93/1750-79) a few months later. Šahbāz Khan then concentrated his energies on extending his own power base in Azerbaijan; he and Najafqolī Khan already controlled much of the province, but an alliance with Fatḥ-ʿAlī Khan Afšār Arašlū strengthened them further. When, in the spring of 1172/1759, Āzād Khan passed through Azerbaijan after a period of exile in Baghdad, Šahbāz Khan and Fatḥ-ʿAlī Khan defeated him at Marāḡa. A year later the two leaders prevented Karīm Khan Zand from seizing Tabrīz and forced him to withdraw from Azerbaijan, then a few months later defeated Āzād Khan once more near Tabrīz. In the spring of 1175/1762 Karīm Khan Zand again invaded Azerbaijan and took Šahbāz Khan and Najafqolī Khan's son ʿAbd-al-Razzāq Beg (q.v.) to Shiraz as hostages. There Šahbāz Khan once more switched sides and was appointed governor of Ḵoy and Salmās, and his daughter Ṣāḥeb Solṭān Ḵānom was married to Karīm Khan's son Abu'l-Fatḥ Khan (Perry, pp. 49, 57, 66, 68, 70, 73, 81, 83-84, 88, 92, 98).

In 1177/1763 Karīm Khan appointed Najafqolī Khan governor of large parts of Azerbaijan and in 1183/1769 governor of the province of Tabrīz (Nāder Mīrzā, pp. 154, 249, 271). At a time when the central government was weak and in decline Najafqolī Khan kept the province of Azerbaijan completely under control (Bāmdād, *Rejāl* VI, pp. 19, 49, 170, 283). When Moḥammad-Ḥasan Khan Qājār captured Azerbaijan in 1171/1757-58 he appointed his own minor son Aqā Moḥammad Khan (q.v.) but appointed Najafqolī Khan and ʿAlī Khan Qīlījlū joint guardians. After a severe earthquake in 1193/1779 Najafqolī Khan devoted himself to rebuilding Tabrīz. He constructed a strong fortified city wall, with eight gates; built the Daftar-ḵāna-ye šāhī, the government palace, which continued in use under the Qajars; and enlarged and restored the small Moʿīnī mosque, which became known as Maqām-e Ṣāḥeb-al-Amr. Najafqolī Khan died in 1199/1785 and was buried in Najaf near the tomb of Imam ʿAlī (Āqāsī, 1350 Š./1971, p. 191; Donbolī, 1349 Š./1970, I, pp. 86-89;

idem, 1350 Š/1971, II, pp. 263-64; Nāder Mīrzā, pp. 152 ff.; Rūžbayānī, pp. 370-71; Bāmdād, *Rejāl* IV, pp. 333-34). He was succeeded briefly at Tabrīz by his son Ḵodādād Khan.

Šahbāz Khan had died in 1187/1773 and was succeeded as governor of Ḵoy by his brother Aḥmad Khan. Aḥmad Khan was killed in 1200/1786, and his son Ḥosaynqolī Khan became governor (Āqāsī, 1350 Š./1971, pp. 209-10; Rūžbayānī, p. 373; Nāder Mīrzā, p. 151; Rīāḥī, p. 20). In the spring of 1205/1791 he concluded a friendship pact with Āqā Moḥammad Khan Qājār (1193-1212/1779-97) and, in addition to being reconfirmed as governor of Ḵoy, was appointed governor of Tabrīz, Ardabīl, and other parts of Azerbaijan (Fasāʾī, I, p. 232; Hedāyat, *Rawżat al-ṣafā* I, p. 230; Donbolī, 1351 Š./1972, p. 21; Nāder Mīrzā, p. 156; Rīāḥī, p. 21; Āqāsī, 1350 Š./1971, p. 209). The next year he accompanied Āqā Moḥammad Khan on a campaign against Ebrāhīm Ḵalīl Khan Javānšīr, governor of Qarābāḡ, and was rewarded with the title *amīr al-omarāʾ* of Azerbaijan and the governorship of Qarāča Dāḡ. But he apparently aroused suspicion by marrying Javānšīr's daughter, and Aqā Moḥammad Khan appointed his brother Jaʿfarqolī Khan to govern Ḵoy and other towns of Azerbaijan (Hedāyat, *Rawżat al-ṣafā* I, pp. 309, 329; Rūžbayānī, pp. 373-74). When Fatḥ-ʿAlī Shah succeeded to the Qajar throne in 1211/1797 Ḥosaynqolī Khan once more came into favor and was reappointed governor of Ḵoy, Tabrīz, and Qarāča Dāḡ.

During Ḥosaynqolī Khan's terms as governor of Ḵoy he built several mosques, including the great Masjed-e Ḵān. He completed the Askarīyīn tomb at Samarra in Iraq, begun by his father (Nāder Mīrzā, p. 151). In Tabrīz he restored the congregational mosque, which had been completely destroyed in an earthquake, and built three additional mosques and several baths (Āl-e Dāwūd, pp. 79-80, 107; Āqāsī, 1350 Š./1971, p. 220). Ḥosaynqolī Khan was also a patron of learning and poetry; among the literary men in his service were Abu'l-Ḥasan Ḥarīf Jandaqī (d. 1230/1814), who composed *qaṣīdas* in his praise (Āl-e Dāwūd, pp. 93-99, 113), and Mīrzā Moḥammad-Ḥasan Fānī Zonūzī, author of *Rīāż al-jenna* (partial ed. ʿA. Rafīʿī, Qom, 1371 Š./1992) and *Baḥr al-ʿolūm* (unpublished). Ḥosaynqolī Khan died in 1213/1798 and was buried in the tomb at Sāmarrā; Fath-ʿAlī Khan Ṣabā Kāšānī composed the *qaṣīda* engraved on his tombstone (Bāmdād, *Rejāl* I, p. 468).

When news of his brother's death reached Jaʿfarqolī Khan he assumed his brother's posts. After a period of rebellion he appealed to Fatḥ-ʿAlī Shah for forgiveness but rebelled again in 1214/1799. The crown prince, ʿAbbās Mīrzā (q.v.), then marched on Ḵoy, and in September Jaʿfarqolī Khan, with an army of 15,000 horse met him at Dīlmaqān, near Salmas but was defeated (Brydges, pp. 39, 50, 68, 71-72, 88-90). For the rest of his life he served the Russian government and on 10 December 1806 was appointed governor of the district of Šekkī in eastern Transcaucasia. He died in 1229/1814 and was succeeded by his son Esmāʿīl Khan, who died in 1819 (Minorsky, "Shekkī," p. 347; Jawāher-al-Kalām, p. 216).

Other leaders of the Donbolī tribe had remained loyal to the Qajars, and several became important figures in the 19th century. Foremost among them was a great-grandson of Najafqolī Khan by the same name, who rebuilt the citadel at Tabrīz in 1224/1809 (Minorsky, "Tabrīz," p. 590). The best-known member of the Donbolī tribe in the 20th century was Ḥājī Mīrzā Yaḥyā Imam Jomʿa Ḵoyī, who died in 1324 Š./1945 (Mojtahedī, pp. 24-26).

According to J. M. Jouannin, the tribe numbered some 12,000 families at the time of Jaʿfarqolī Khan (Dupré, II, p. 459), but only about forty years later Lady Sheil (p. 396) estimated their number at a mere 2,000 families. Today the Donbolī have been sedentary for a long time and have completely lost their tribal identity. Apparently, when the Donbolī of Ḵoy and Salmās moved to northwestern Persia, some families remained behind in southeastern Anatolia. This group was mentioned by Bedlīsī (pt. I, p. 174) in the 16th century, as well as by Carsten Niebuhr (p. 419), who reported in the second half of the 18th century that it was located south of Dīārbakr and comprised about 500 tents. Also in the 18th century there was a group of Donbolī Kurds (presumably not turkicized) in the province of Yerevan (*Taḏkerat al-Molūk*, ed. Minorsky, pp. 101, 166).

Bibliography: (For cited works not found in this bibliography and for abbreviations found here, see "Short References.") ʿA. ʿAbd-al-ʿArīz, *Āṯār al-Šīʿa al-emāmīya* IV, tr. ʿA. Jawāher-kalām, Tehran, 1307 Š./1928. ʿA. Āl-e Dāwūd, *Aḥwāl wa ašʿār-e Ḥarīf Jandaqī*, Tehran, 1366 Š./1987. M. Āqāsī, *Tārīḵ-e Ḵoy*, Tabrīz, 1350 Š./1971. Idem, *Gūša-ī az tārīḵ-e Ḵoy* I, Tabrīz, 1355 Š./1976. Šaraf-al-Dīn Khan Bedlīsī, *Šaraf-nāma* I, ed. Veliaminof-Zernof, St. Petersburg, 1861; repr. Cairo, 1931; tr. F. B. Charmoy as *Chéref-Nâmeh* II, St. Petersburg, 1873, pt. 1, pp. 169-77; pt. 2, pp. 123-31. H. J. Brydges, *Dynasty of the Kajars*, London, 1833. ʿAbd-al-Razzāq Beg Donbolī, *Tajrebat al-aḥrār wa taslīat al-abrār*, 2 vols., Tabrīz, ed. Ḥ. Qāżī Ṭabāṭabāʾī, 1349-50 Š./1970-71. Idem, *Maʾāṯer-e solṭānīya*, 2nd ed., ed. Ḡ.-Ḥ. Ṣadrī Afšār, Tehran, 1351 Š./1972, pp. 21-26, 29, 47. A. Dupré, *Voyage en Perse fait dans les années 1807, 1808 et 1809*, Paris, 1819. O. A. Efendiev, *Azerbaidzhanskoe Gosudarstvo Sefevidov* (The state of Azerbaijan under the Safavids), Baku, 1961. A. Jaubert, *Voyage en Arménie et en Perse*, Paris, 1821. ʿAbd-al-ʿAzīz Jawāher-al-Kalām "Omarā-ye Danābela dar Ḵoy wa Āḏarbāyjān," in *Āṯār al-Šīʿa al-emāmīya*, Tehrān, 1307 Š./1928, pp. 205-17. Moḥammad-Kāẓem Marvī, *ʿĀlamārā-ye nāderī*, ed. M.-A. Rīāḥī, III, Tehran, 1364 Š./1985. V. Minorsky, I"Shekkī," in *EI*[1] IV, pp. 346-48. Idem, "Tabrīz," in *EI*[1] IV, pp. 583-93. Idem, "Kurds, Kurdistān iii," in *EI*[2] V, pp. 447-64. M. Mojtahedī, *Rajāl-e Āḏarbāyjān dar ʿaṣr-e mašrūṭīyat*, Tehran, 1327 Š./1948. Nāder Mīrzā, *Tārīḵ wa joḡrāfīā-ye dār-al-salṭana-ye Tabrīz*, ed. M. Mošīrī, Tehran, 1360 Š./1981. C. Niebuhr, *Reisebeschreibung nach Arabien und andern umliegenden Ländern* II, Copenhagen, 1774, pp. 415-22. B. Nikitine, "Les Afšārs d'Urumiyeh," *JA*, January-March 1929, pp. 67-123. E. Pakravan, *Abbas Mirza. Un prince réformateur*, Tehran, 1337 Š./1958. J. R. Perry, *Karim Khan Zand*, Chicago, 1979. M.-J. Rūžbayānī, "Emārat wa farmān-rava'ī-e Donbolīān dar Tabrīz wa manāṭeq-e arbaʿa," in *Majmūʿa-ye soḵanrānīhā-ye šešomīn kongera-ye taḥqīqāt-e īrānī* II, Tabrīz, 1357 Š./1978, pp. 352-77. M. L. Sheil, *Glimpses of Life and Manners in Persia*, London, 1856.

(ʿALĪ ĀL-E DĀWŪD AND PIERRE OBERLING)

DONBOLĪ, ʿABD-AL-RAZZĀQ BEG. See ʿABD-AL-RAZZĀQ BEG.

DONBOLĪ, AMĪR BEHRŪZ. See Supplement.

DONKEY (*Equus hydrunitinus*, *Equus asinus asinus*, etc.; Pers. *ḵar*, *darāz-gāš*), domesticated species descended from the wild ass (*Equus africanus*; Uerpmann), probably first bred in captivity in Egypt and western Asia, where by 2500 B.C.E. the domesticated donkey was in use as a beast of burden (Clutton-Brock, p. 65). Because of its jolting gait, it was almost never used in hunting or battle (Clutton-Brock, p. 66; for a rare exception, see Aelian, 10.40, 12.34). In southern Persia remains of the domestic donkey have been identified from the 3rd millennium B.C.E. at Tall-e Malīān (Zeder).

In Persian tradition. According to the *Bundahišn*, donkeys were created from the purified seed of the primordial ox and belonged to the family of horses and mules (TD_2, pp. 95-96; tr. Bahār, p. 78). The "cat-footed" (*gorba-pāy*) donkey was the chief of all asses (TD_2, p. 120; tr. Bahār, p. 89). Nevertheless, the donkey's braying was considered unpleasant, resembling the voice of the evil spirit (TD_2, p. 187; tr. Bahār, p. 122; cf. Koran 31:19-20: "the harshest of sounds"; Hedāyat, pp. 178-79).

In the *Šāh-nāma* (ed. Khaleghi, I, p. 31) domestication of the donkey is credited to Hūšang, though in the 13th century Moḥammad b. Manṣūr Mobārakšāh (p. 405) attributed it to Tahmūraṯ. Either Jamšīd ([Pseudo] Ḵayyām, p. 17) or Tahmūraṯ was supposed to have been the first to mate horses and donkeys to breed mules (Balʿamī, ed. Bahār, I, p. 129). There is a Muslim tradition that such breeding is undesirable, though not unlawful (Abū Dāwūd, III, p. 27).

In biblical times donkeys, especially white ones, were among the preferred mounts for persons of rank (Judges 5:10, 10:3-4; II Samuel 16:2). In Muslim tradition, too, the they were the mounts favored by prophets (Balʿamī, ed. Bahār, I, p. 509; Ṭūsī, p. 562; cf. Zamaḵšarī, IV, p. 401). Nevertheless, Moses was ordered to remove shoes made of donkey skin before approaching holy ground (Ṭabarī, IV, p. 1017; cf. II, p. 477).

Sunnite theologians consider the flesh of donkeys forbidden, though Abū Dāwūd Sejestānī cited a tradition implying that it is permissible in dire need (cf. Termeḏī, IV, p. 82, V, p. 184; Ebn Ḥajar, XVI, pp. 44, 46-67, 62-63, 65; Abū Dāwūd, III, pp. 356-57). The prohibition was extended to the flesh of mules and similar animals resulting from the copulation of donkeys with other breeds (Zohaylī, III, p. 508). On the basis of one koranic verse (16:5) Shiʿite authorities do not consider donkey flesh forbidden but merely disapprove of it (Ḥorr ʿĀmelī, XVI, pp. 315, 322-29; Kolaynī, VI, pp. 244, 246, 313 n. 9; Ṭabarsī, XVI. pp. 174-76; Maḡnīya, IV, p. 370; Šahīd Ṯānī, VII, pp. 268-69).

There are references to the prices of donkeys in some early texts (Moḥammad Ḡaznavī, p. 284; Kolaynī, VI, p. 535), but the dependability of such reports cannot be ascertained. Some people have taken great pride in their donkeys and have gone to great lengths to adorn their beasts (for Tehran in the 19th century, see Šahrī, VI, pp. 377-81). Donkey dealers, on the other hand, were often unscrupulous and lowly people; some painted their larger animals brown and sold them as mules. Apparently the Persian expression *ḵar rang ḵon* (lit., "donkey dyer"), referring to a tricky person who takes advantage of the simplicity of his fellow man, is rooted in this questionable commercial practice (Šahrī, I, p. 345, V, p. 27 n. 1). Donkeys, like other domesticated animals in the Middle East, are often abused or overworked (see, e.g., Šahrī, II, p. 291). From as early as the time of Aristotle (d. 322 B.C.E.; p. 107) donkeys have been thought to be insensitive to pain, which may account for their especially harsh treatment.

In Persian folk belief. Perhaps the most famous donkey in Muslim tradition is the white one that will carry the Dajjāl (q.v.), the Antichrist (Hedāyat, pp. 178-79; Yāḥaqqī, s.v. *dajjāl*).

The speaking donkey is a common motif in folklore (Thompson, V237) and is well attested in Persian literature (e.g., Balʿamī, ed. Bahār, I, p. 509; Ṭabarī, III, p. 569; Meybodī, III, p. 788). The Prophet Moḥammad had such a donkey, ʿOfayr or Yaʿfūr (Mobārakšāh, p. 268), which supposedly threw itself down a well after his death (Ebn Ḥajar, XII, p. 9; Ebn al-Jawzī, I, pp. 293-94). The Prophet used to dispatch him to summon people (Mojāhed, p. 369). According to one tradition, donkeys bray because they see demons (Nesāʾī, p. 63) or other supernatural beings (Zamaḵšarī, II, p. 578-79; cf. Numbers 22:23-72; Leach, p. 276). Measures recommended to stop braying ranged from the ancient practice of tying a stone to the animal's tail (cf. Aelian, 9.55) or a string to its ears to oiling its anus, the latter measure probably on the assumption that the animal would avoid braying for fear of soiling itself (Ḥāseb Ṭabarī, pp. 24, 30; Ḥobayš, p. 381; Jamālī Yazdī, pp. 36-37).

Divinations were made from the behavior or presence of donkeys. One Sasanian warlord supposedly interpreted an enemy leader's change of mount from an elephant to a donkey as evidence of his waning fortunes (Balʿamī, ed. Bahār, II, p. 1032). In the Middle Ages tales of witches' turning their victims into donkeys were publicly narrated (Bayhaqī, pp. 904-05). In modern Khorasan the braying of a seated donkey is taken as an omen of death (Šakūrzāda, pp. 309); it may also simply foretell rainy weather (Aʿẓamī Sangesarī, p. 55; cf. Šakūrzāda, p. 341).

In the Middle Ages donkeys could not be included in a woman's dowry (*mahr*; Tawḥīdī, 1408/1988, III, p. 140). In 19th-century Tehran brides rode white horses in their nuptial processions if they were virgins but donkeys if they were widows (Šahrī, II, p. 60). Midwives were transported about their business by female donkeys that had already borne colts; these donkeys could not be black, and drivers were not allowed to beat them (Šahrī, V, pp. 655-66).

A number of magical properties have been attributed to various parts of the donkey's anatomy. The head, for example, has been supposed to have apotropaic properties against the evil eye (ʿAṭṭār, 1361 Š./1982, p. 134; Saʿdī, p. 139; Balāḡī, p. 234). To gain control of her mate or ensure his unfailing love, a woman could serve him donkey brains (Katīrāʾī, p. 419 n. 3; Balāḡī, p. 217). Generally however, consuming donkey's brains was thought to cause stupidity (Tonokābonī, p. 94; ʿAṭṭār, 1341 Š./1962, p. 142; idem, 1361 Š./1982, p. 134), reflecting the ancient belief that donkeys are stupid (Aristotle, p. 121; Koran 61:6; Jāḥeẓ, II, pp. 99, 255; Boḵārī, pp. 209-11; cf. Aarne and Thompson, no. 52). The *Šāh-nāma* includes the story of a donkey that went to the cows to obtain a pair of horns but instead lost its ears (Moscow, IX, p. 37); another story, in which the devil uses a donkey to gain admission to Noah's ark, is also well represented in the Persian literary tradition (Aarne and Thompson, type 825; *Mojmal*, ed. Bahār, p. 185; Ṭabarī, III, p. 732; Zamaḵšarī, IV, p. 401; cf. Utley, for greater detail on the type). The Persian expression *yāsīn be gūš-e ḵar ḵᵛāndan* "to recite (the koranic sura) Yāsīn in an ass's ear" means to waste advice on a fool (Dehkodā, s.v. *yāsīn*). On the other hand, Jāḥeẓ, departing from the accepted wisdom of his time, suggested that donkeys are capable not only of distinguishing among certain voice commands (VII, p. 87) but also of engaging in a variety of primitive reasoning (II, p. 75). It was believed that the donkey, like the mule, would never forget a path it had trodden once (Jamālī Yazdī, p. 36; Tawḥīdī, 1973, I, p. 186).

Cutting the penis off a live donkey in order to cook it in hot spices, to be eaten as an aphrodisiac, has also been reported (Tonokābonī, p. 94). Abū Bakr Moṭahhar Jamālī Yazdī noted that keeping a hair pulled from the tail of a male donkey that has mounted a female increases a man's sexual prowess to the point that he can produce erections at will. Applying a concoction of powdered donkey's penis and olive oil has the more modest effect of making one's hair grow long (Jamālī Yazdī, pp. 36, 39). Donkey urine was used to remove certain types of stubborn spots from laundry (Ḥobayš, p. 438). Treating blades with concoctions of donkey urine, blood, milk, or hoof by-products would ensure that their blows were fatal (Ḥāseb Ṭabarī, pp. 209-10; Ḥobayš, pp. 337, 339-40; Jamālī Yazdī, pp. 38-39). Donkeys or various parts of their anatomy were further used in rain-making magic (Hedāyat, p. 196; Šakūrzāda, pp. 311, 346-47; for other charms and magical practices involving parts of donkeys, see Jamālī Yazdī, pp. 37, 39; Ḥāseb Ṭabarī, p. 100).

Among the most important set of Persian beliefs about the magical properties of the donkey is that connected with folk medicine, which may reflect an association with Christ. This association is implied in the name *ambar(-e) naṣārā* "amber of the Christians" for donkey dung (q.v.), a commonly used remedy (Bolūkbāšī, p. 137; Partovī, 1356 Š./1977, p. 70; Hedāyat, p. 114; Ṭūsī, p. 561). Applying three drops of liquid extracted from the dung, either alone or mixed with other ingredients, is thought to stop most nosebleeds and heal most wounds. Fumigation with smoke from burning ass's dung is considered medicinally effective in general (e.g., Jorjānī, pp. 557, 560; Hedāyat, p. 114; Massé, *Croyances*, p. 338; cf. Thorndike, I, pp. 733-34, 739-40). Burning donkey's hooves to fumigate the genitals of women in labor was once thought to help in difficult childbirths (Ḥobayš, p. 436).

From medieval times women used a "stone" (*mohra-ye ḵar*, *ḵar-mohra*), possibly a petrified gland (*ḡodda*) from the donkey's neck, to prevent pregnancy (Ebn Boḵtīšūʿ, p. 61; Ṭūsī, p. 140; Donaldson, p. 160; cf. Thorndike, I, pp. 739-40). It has also been described as a small stone found under the tongue of the newborn donkey, which is swallowed if not taken immediately after birth (Katīrāʾī, pp. 416-17). The *ḵar-mohra* hardens into a yellow-white stone if placed in water and is thought efficacious against most poisons (Jamālī Yazdī, pp. 36-39; Ḥāseb Ṭabarī, p. 53).

The flesh and milk of the donkey have also been considered effective antidotes to poisons. The milk must be taken chilled, however, as drinking it warm is fatal unless the patient ingests dried human feces. Donkey's milk is also considered effective in treatment of many diseases (Kolaynī, VI, pp. 338-89; Jorjānī, p. 648; Ebn Boḵtīšūʿ, p. 59; Ṣadīq, p. 71; Massé, *Croyances*, p. 338), which may have some basis in fact (Iacono et al.). The pain of a scorpion's sting may be transferred to a donkey if the victim whispers in the animal's ear (Pliny, *Historia Naturalis* 28.42; Ḥāseb Ṭabarī, p. 36; Jamālī Yazdī, p. 37; Thorndike, I, p. 88) or rides the animal seven paces while facing the tail (Ebn Boḵtīšūʿ, p. 58).

Although the ass is a symbol of stupidity (see above), in some folktales it functions as a trickster (e.g., Marzolph, types 103C*, 122J) or entertainer. For example, ʿAmr b. Baḥr Jāḥeẓ mentioned "donkey fights" (II, p. 163). Sprinkling a fistful of dirt from a place where a donkey has rolled under the cloth upon which people are eating supposedly results in the entire party's collapsing in guffaws (Jamālī Yazdī, pp. 36-39; cf. Ḥāseb Ṭabarī, p. 90; Ḥobayš, pp. 405-06, 410).

Bibliography: (For cited works not found in this bibliography and abbreviations found here, see "Short References.") A. Aarne and S. Thompson, *The Types of the Folktale*, 2nd ed., Helsinki, 1973. Abū Dāwūd Solaymān b. Ašʿaṯ Sejestānī, *Sonan Abī Dāwūd*, ed. M.-M. ʿAbd al-Ḥamīd, 4 vols., Beirut, 1970. A. Amīnī, *Dāstānhā-ye amṯāl*, 2nd ed., Isfahan, 1333 Š./1954. Aristotle, *Minor Works*, tr. W. S. Hett, Cambridge, Mass., 1980. Farīd-al-Dīn ʿAṭṭār, *Asrār-nāma*, ed. Ṣ. Gowharīn, Tehran, 1338 Š./1959; repr. Tehran, 1361 Š./1982. Idem, *Manṭeq al-ṭayr*, ed. M.-J. Maškūr, Tehran, 1341 Š./1962. Idem, *Moṣībat-nāma*, ed. ʿA. Nūrānī Weṣāl, Tehran, 1364 Š./1985. Č. Aʿẓamī Sangesarī, "Bāvarhā-ye ʿāmīāna-ye mardom-e Sangesar," *Honar o mardom* 92, 1349 Š./1970, pp. 47-56. ʿA. Balāḡī, *Ketāb-e tārīḵ-e Nāʾīn*, Tehran, 1369 Š./1990. Ebrāhīm b. Moḥammad Bayhaqī, *Ketāb al-maḥāsen wa'l-masāwī*, 2 vols., ed. M. A. Ebrāhīm, Cairo, 1961. Moḥammad b. ʿAbd-Allāh Boḵārī, *Dāstānhā-ye Bīdpāy*, ed. P. N. Ḵānlarī and M. Rowšan, Tehran, 1361 Š./1982. ʿA. Bolūkbāšī, "Darmān-e bīmārīhā wa nāḵošīhā dar pezeškī-e ʿāmīāna," *Ketāb-e Hafta* 103, 1342 Š./1963, pp. 132-39. *Bundahišn*, tr. M. Bahār as *Farnbag-dādagī (Bondaheš)*, Tehran, 1369 Š./1990. J. Clutton-Brock, *Horse Power. A History of the Horse and the Donkey in Human Societies*, Cambridge, Mass., 1992. ʿA.-A. Dehḵodā, *Amṯāl o ḥekam*, 4 vols., Tehran, 2537=1357 Š./1978. B. A. Donaldson, *The Wild Rue. A Study of Muhammadan Magic and Folklore in Iran*, London, 1938. Ebn Boḵtīšūʿ, *Manāfeʿ al-ḥayawān*, The Pierpont Morgan Library, New York, ms. no. M 500. Aḥmad Ebn Ḥajar ʿAsqalānī, *Fatḥ al-bārī be šārḥ al-Boḵārī*, ed. T.-ʿA. Saʿd et al., 28 vols., Cairo, 1978. ʿAbd-al-Raḥmān Ebn al-Jawzī, *Ketāb al-mawżūʿāt*, ed. ʿA. M. ʿOṯmān, 3 vols., Medina, 1389/1966-68. Moḥammad b. Ayyūb Ḥāseb Ṭabarī, *Tohfat al-ḡarāʾeb*, ed. J. Matīnī, Tehran, 1371 Š./1992. Ṣ. Hedāyat, *Neyrangestān*, Tehran, 1342 Š./1963. Ḥobayš b. Ebrāhīm Teflīsī, *Bayān al-ṣanāʿāt*, ed. Ī. Afšār, *FIZ* 5, 1336 Š./1957, pp. 298-447. Moḥammad b. Ḥasan Ḥorr ʿĀmelī, *Wasāʾel al-Šīʿa elā taḥṣīl masāʾel al-šarīʿa*, ed. ʿA. Rabbānī Šīrāzī, 5th ed., 9 vols. in 20, Beirut, 1983. G. Iacono et al., "Use of Ass Milk in Multiple Food Allergy," *Journal of Pediatric Gastroenterology and Nutrition* 14/2, 1992, pp. 177-81. ʿAmr b. Baḥr Jāḥeẓ, *al-Ḥayawān*, ed. ʿA. M. Hārūn, 2nd ed., 8 vols, Cairo, 1387/1968. Abū Bakr Moṭahhar Jamālī Yazdī, *Farroḵ-nāma*, ed. Ī. Afšār, Tehran, 1346 Š./1967. Esmāʿīl b. Ḥosayn Jorjānī, *Ḏaḵīra-ye ḵᵛārazmšāhī*, ed. ʿA.-A. Saʿīdī Sīrjānī, Tehran, 2535=1355 Š./1976. M. Katīrāʾī, *Az ḵešt tā ḵešt*, Tehran, 1348 Š./1969. [Pseudo] ʿOmar Ḵayyām, *Nowrūz-nāma*, ed. ʿA. Ḥosūrī, Tehran, 1357 Š./1978. Abū Jaʿfar Moḥammad Kolaynī, *Ketāb al-kāfī*, ed. ʿA.-A. Ḡaffārī, 8 vols., Tehran, 1367 Š./1988. M. Leach, *God Had a Dog. Folklore of the Dog*, New Brunswick, N.J., 1961. M. J. Maḡnīya, *Feqh al-Emām Jaʿfar al-Ṣādeq*, 6 vols. in 3, Qom, 136? Š./198?. U. Marzolph, *Typologie des persischen Volksmärchens*, Berliner Texte und Studien 31, Beirut, 1984. Rašīd-al-Dīn Aḥmad Meybodī, *Kašf al-asrār wa ʿoddat al-abrār*, ed. ʿA.-A. Ḥekmat, 10 vols., Tehran, 1357 Š./1978. Moḥammad b. Manṣūr Mobārakšāh (Faḵr-e Modabber), *Ādāb al-ḥarb wa'l-šajāʿa*, ed. A. Zajaczkowski as *Le traité iranien de l'art militaire, Ādāb al-ḥarb wa-š-šağā'a, du XIIIe siècle*, Warsaw, 1969. Sadīd-al-Dīn Moḥammad Ḡaznavī, *Maqāmat-e Žanda Pīl*, ed. Ḥ. Moʿayyad, Tehran, 1345 Š./1966. Mojāhed ʿAlī b. Dāwūd Rasūlī Ḡassānī, *al-Aqwāl al-kāfīa wa'l-foṣūl al-šāfīa fi'l-ḵayl*, ed. Y. W. Jabbūrī, Beirut, 1987.

Aḥmad b. Šoʿayb Nesāʾī, *Tahḏīb Ketāb al-esteʿāḏa*, ed. H. ʿAbd-al-Ḥamīd, Cairo, 1989. M. Partovī, "Rīšahā-ye tārīḵī-e amṯāl o ḥekam," *Honar o mardom* 172, 2535=1356 Š./1977, pp. 69-71. ʿAbbās Qomī, *Safīna al-behār wa madīna al-ḥekam wa'l-āṯār*, 2 vols., Tehran, 1344 Š./1965. Saʿdi, *Būstān*, ed. Ḡ.-Ḥ. Yūsofī, Tehran, 1359 Š./1970. M. Ṣadīq, "Gūšahā-ī az zendagī-e mardom-e dehkada-ye Samīya," *Honar o mardom* 158, 1354 Š./1975, pp. 70-76. Zayn-al-Dīn b. ʿAlī Šahīd Ṯānī, *Rawża al-bahīya fī šarḥ al-lomʿa al-demašqīya*, 10 vols., Qom, 1395-96/1975-76. J. Šahrī, *Tārīḵ-e ejtemāʿī-e Tehrān dar qarn-e sīzdahom*, 6 vols., Tehran, 1367-68 Š./1988-89. E. Šakūrzāda, *ʿAqāyed o rosūm-e mardom-e Ḵorāsān*, 2nd ed., Tehran, 1362 Š./1983. Moḥammad b. Ḥosayn Šarīf Rażī, *Ḵaṣāʾeṣ Amīr al-Moʾmenīn ʿAlī b. Abī Ṭāleb*, Beirut, 1406/1986. Jalāl-al-Dīn ʿAbd-al-Raḥmān Soyūṭī, *Jāmeʿ al-aḥādīṯ le'l-Jāmeʿ al-ṣaḡīr wa zawāʾedeh wa al-Jāmeʿ al-kabīr*, ed. ʿA.-A. Ṣaqr and A. ʿAbd al-Jawwād, 9 vols., Damascus, n.d. (1979-81). Moḥammad b. Jarīr Ṭabarī, *Tafsīr*, ed. and tr. H. Yaḡmāʾī as *Tarjoma-ye Tafsīr-e Ṭabarī*, 7 vols., Tehran, 1339 Š./1960. H. Ṭabarsī, *Mostadrak al-wasāʾel wa mostanbaṭ al-masāʾel*, 18 vols., Beirut, 1987-88. Abū Ḥayyān Tawḥīdī, *Ketāb al-emtāʿ wa'l-moʾānasa*, ed. A. Amīn and A. Zayn, 3 vols., Beirut, 1973. Idem, *al-Baṣāʾer wa'l-ḏaḵāʾer*, ed. W. Qāżī, 10 vols., Beirut, 1408/1988. Moḥammad b. ʿĪsā Termeḏī, *Sonan al-Termeḏī*, ed. ʿE. ʿObayd-al-Daʿʿās, 10 vols., Homs, Syria, 1965. S. Thompson, *Motif-Index of Folk-Literature*, rev. ed., 6 vols., Bloomington, Ind., 1955. L. Thorndike, *A History of Magic and Experimental Science*, 8 vols., New York, 1934-60. Moḥammad-Moʾmen Tonokābonī (Ḥakīm Moʾmen), *Tohfa-ye Ḥakīm Moʾmen*, Tehran, 1277/1859; repr. Tehran, 1338 Š./1959. Moḥammad b. Maḥmūd Ṭūsī, *ʿAjāyeb al-maḵlūqāt*, ed. M. Sotūda, Tehran, 1345 Š./1966. H. P. Uerpmann, *The Ancient Distribution of Ungulate Mammals in the Middle East*, TAVO Beihefte 27, Wiesbaden, 1987. F. L. Utley, "The Devil in the Ark [AaTh 825]," in K. Ranke, ed., *Internationaler Kongress der Volkserzählungsforscher in Kiel und Kopenhagen*, Berlin, 1961, pp. 447-63. M.-J. Yāḥaqqī, *Farhang-e asāṭīr o ešārāt-e dāstān-e dar adabīyāt-e fārsī*, Tehran, 1369 Š./1990. Maḥmūd b. ʿUmar Zamaḵšarī, *Rabīʿ al-abrār wa nosūs al-aḵbār*, ed. S. Noʿaymī, 4 vols., Baghdad, 1976-82. M. A. Zeder, "The Equid Remains from Tal-e Malyan, Southern Iran," in R. H. Meadow and H.-P. Uerpmann, eds., *Equids in the Ancient World*, TAVO A 19/1, Wiesbaden, 1986, pp. 194-206. W. Zoḥaylī, *al-Feqh al-eslāmī wa adellatoh*, 8 vols., Damascus, 1984.

(Mahmoud Omidsalar and Teresa P. Omidsalar)

DONYĀ (lit., "The world"), name of several Persian journals and newspapers.

1. The earliest *Donyā* was a Marxist monthly journal published in Tehran from Bahman 1312 Š./February 1933 until Ḵordād 1314 Š./June 1935. Its founder and editor was Taqī Arānī (q.v.), a chemist who had become a Marxist while studying in Berlin. *Donyā* was the first theoretically oriented Marxist journal in Persia. Because of official and popular opposition, however, communism was never openly promoted in its pages. In the first issue the editorial aims were explained in detail, particularly adherence to dialectical materialism and rejection of "idealism." "It attempts to make the reader's thinking familiar with the level of civilization of mankind today; its style and orthography will not conform to any restrictions of conservatism."

The journal was divided into four main sections, devoted to science, industry, philosophy, and society respectively, with commentary on political and economic events overseas under the heading "Manẓara-ye donyā" (World view). In fact, much of the space in *Donyā* was devoted to scientific reports. Because Persian politics were not covered, the journal was never suppressed. Although contributors alluded to dialectical materialism in obscure academic language, they avoided controversy. The major writers were Arānī, who sometimes wrote under the pseudonym Aḥmad Qāżī; Īraj Eskandarī, who wrote under the name A. Jamšīd; and Bozorg ʿAlawī, who wrote under the name Ferīdūn Nāḵodā. *Donyā* was usually printed at the Eṭṭelāʿāt printing

house in Tehran, in issues of thirty-two double-column pages, measuring 14 by 21 cm; the normal print run was 200 copies (Amīr Ḵosravī and Āḏarnūr, p. 34). The journal was illustrated, and advertising was restricted to books. An annual subscription cost 25 rials, a single issue 2 rials.

Publication of *Donyā* was suspended after twelve issues, perhaps owing to lack of funds (Kāmaʾī, p. 83), or Arānī's appointment to a government position (Amīr Ḵosravī and Āḏarnūr, p. 48). When Arānī and his colleagues were put on trial in 1317 Š./1938 the publication of *Donyā* was cited against them in court.

Collections of *Donyā* are preserved in the Malek Library, Tehran, and in the Central Library of Fārs in Shiraz; the works of Arānī, including his writings for *Donyā*, were published under the title *Āṯār o maqālāt* in Florence in 1975.

Donyā was revived as the theoretical organ of the Tudeh party in exile (see COMMUNISM iii) in 1960 and was published in Europe until 1974; the contributors were anonymous. The journal began as a quarterly of 96-120 pages, measuring 15 by 22 cm, but later it was reduced to appearing twice a year, with 140-60 pages, measuring 11 by 15.5 cm and in smaller print. The price of a single copy was 40 rials in Persia and 50 cents or the equivalent elsewhere. A third series was launched in the summer of 1975, also in Europe; it was published in Stassfurt, near Magdeburg, in former East Germany, and carried an address in Stockholm. In this series Donyā became a political, rather than a theoretical, research-oriented publication. It appeared monthly, in the same format as the previous series but with 56-64 pages. Each issue cost 15 rials.

The fourth series was initiated in Tehran in March 1979; the journal appeared monthly, with 156-224 pages in approximately the same dimensions as those of the third series. *Donyā* was distributed as a supplement to the newspaper *Nāma-ye mardom*, the organ of the Tudeh party. Each issue cost 150 rials. During this period the owner of the franchise was Manūčehr Behzādī and as before the names of other contributors were not listed.

After the Tudeh party was banned in Persia a fifth series of *Donyā* began irregular publication in Germany in 1984 but also carried an address in Stockholm.

In addition to political articles all these series of *Donyā*, especially the fourth, included poetry and brief historical and literary notices. They carried no advertisements and few illustrations. Complete runs exist in some European and American libraries, but, because the Tudeh party and its publications were usually banned in Persia, only the fourth series, which was published in Tehran, can be found in Persian libraries.

2. A weekly newspaper including political commentary was published in Tehran by ʿAbd-al-Karīm Ṭabāṭabāʾī from Mehr 1324 Š./September 1945. In

the autumn of 1328 Š./1949, publication was suspended, and Kāẓem Etteḥād Sarkešīkzāda issued the newspaper *Etteḥād*, edited by Ṭabāṭabāʾī in its place. Two months later its editors returned to the name *Donyā*. In the summer of 1352 Š./1973 the government closed *Donyā*, along with 134 other publications. In the winter of 1357 Š./1978 the newspaper resumed publication, but, with the success of the revolution in Persia, it was once again suppressed. From 1327 Š./1948 the newspaper also issued a yearbook.

Donyā normally consisted of four six-column pages, with many advertisements but few illustrations. During most of its run the price of a single issue was 2 rials.

There are only incomplete collections of this *Donyā* in major Persian libraries.

3. The British published a monthly propaganda magazine in Persian and English in Delhi from December 1945 to May 1946. It consisted mainly of news photographs from India and occasionally neighboring countries, with bilingual captions. The names of contributors were not listed. The publisher of record was United Publications, and the magazine was printed in twenty-four double-column pages. Although the price for a single issue was 4 annas, the magazine was distributed free to the British embassies in Persia and Afghanistan. Issues can be found in the Persian National Library and the India Office in London.

Bibliography: (For abbreviations found here, see "Short References.") P. Abu'l-Żīāʾ and N. Morādī, *Rāhnemāhā-ye rūz-nāmahā-ye Īrān. 1352*, Tehran, 1352 Š./1973, p. 5. ʿA. Āgāhī, "Rastāḵīz-e *Donyā*," *Donyā*, 2nd ser., 1, Ordībehešt 1339 Š./April 1960, pp. 1-5. Idem, "Doktor Taqī Arānī. Čehra-ī tābān dar tārīḵ-e jonbeš-e kārgarī wa komūnīstī-e Īrān," *Donyā*, 4th ser., 1/5, 1979, pp. 150–56. B. Amīr Ḵosravī and F. Āḏarnūr, *Ḵāṭerāt-e sīāsī-e Īraj Eskandarī*, Saint Cloud, France, 1366 Š./1987, pp. 18-23, 26-31, 34-51. Idem, "Rowšan bād ḵāṭera-ye Doktor Taqī Arānī be monāsabat-e haftād o panjomīn sāl-e zādrūz," *Donyā* 4/5, 1979,pp. 28-30. W. Behn, *Islamic Revolution or Revolutionary Islam in Iran*, Berlin, 1980, p. 49. Idem and W. M. Floor, *Twenty Years of Iranian Power Struggle*, Berlin, 1982, p. 33. A. Ḵāmaʾī *Panjāh nafar . . . wa seh nafar*, 4th ed., I, Tehran, 1363 Š./1984, pp. 73-83. E. Pūrqūčānī, *Fehrest-e rūz-nāmahā-ye mawjūd dar ketāb-ḵānahā-ye markazī-e Āstān-e qods-e rażawī*, Mašhad, 1364 Š./1985, pp. 153-54. W.-M. Ṣādeqī-nasab, *Fehrest-e rūz-nāmahā-ye fārsī-e sāl-e 1320-1332 šamsī*, Tehran, 1360 Š./1981, p. 88. Ṣadr Hāšemī, *Jarāyed o majallāt*, pp. 293-96. B. Sartīpzāda and K. Ḵodāparast, *Fehrest-e rūz-nāmahā-ye mawjūd dar ketāb-ḵāna-ye mellī-e Īrān*, Tehran, 1356 Š./1977, pp. 100-01 no. 212; 130 no. 241. U. Sims-Williams, *Union Catalogue of Persian Serials and Newspapers in British Libraries*, London, 1985, p. 126, no. 124. L. Sūdbakš, *Fehrest-e našrīyāt-e adwārī dar ketāb-ḵāna-ye markazī-e Fārs*, Shiraz, 1368 Š./1989, p. 375.

(NASSEREDDIN PARVIN)

DONYĀ-YE EMRŪZ (Today's world), name of a weekly magazine published in Tehran and two weekly newspapers founded in Qazvīn and Isfahan respectively.

1. A cultural weekly was published in Tehran from 26 Ṯawr 1301/16 May 1922 until mid-Asad (7 August) of that year. The licensee (*ṣāḥeb-e emtīāz*) and editor of the magazine was H. Bāḏīl, and the staff included Ḡolām-Reżā Rašīd Yāsemī and ʿAlī-Aṣḡar Ḥekmat. The journal was ordinarily printed at the Majles printing press, in thirty-two double-column pages, measuring 19.5 by 27.5 cm. It included illustrations and a few advertisements. A three-month subscription cost 15 *qerān*s in Persia and 20 *qerān*s abroad; a single issue sold for 30 *šāhī*s. Incomplete collections of this magazine are preserved in the Majles library, Tehran, and the central library of the University of Tehran.

2. In Qazvīn a weekly newspaper entitled *Donyā-ye emrūz* was published from Mehr 1303 Š./September-October 1924 to Ordībehešt 1304 Š./April-May 1925. The licensee and editor-in-chief was Sayyed Ḥosayn Tonokābonī, and the editor was Ḡolām-Ḥosayn Šams. The newspaper was focused on local news and matters of religious interest. No extant issue has been found in any public library.

3. In Isfahan *Donyā-ye emrūz* was focused on news and politics; established as a weekly, it was published somewhat irregularly, beginning in 1323 Š./1944; from Mehr 1324 Š./September-October 1945 to Mordād 1332 Š./July-August 1953 it was published in Tehran and was considered favorable to the Tudeh party (see COMMUNISM ii). Its licensee and editor-in-chief was Ḥosayn Faršīd (Elwell-Sutton, p. 87). Copies are available in the Persian national library, the central library of Tehran University, and the library of Princeton University, Princeton, N.J.

Bibliography: (For abbreviations found here, see ("Short References.") L. P. Elwell-Sutton, "The Iranian Press, 1941-1947," *Iran* 6, 1968, pp. 65-104. K. Ḵodāparast and F. Ḵoršīdī, *Fehrest-e rūz-nāmahā-ye mawjūd dar ketāb-ḵāna-ye mellī-e Īrān* II, Tehran, 1363 Š./1984, p. 330. R. Mach and R. D. McChesney, "A List of Persian Serials in the Princeton University Library," Princeton, N.J., 1971, unpublished. "Registre analytique annoté de la presse persane (depuis la guerre)," *RMM* 60, 1925, p. 56. W. M. Ṣādeqī-nasab, *Fehrest-e rūz-nāmahā-ye fārsī (1320-1332 Š.)*, Tehran, 1360 Š./1981, p. 89. Ṣadr Ḥāšemī, *Jarāyed o majallāt* II, pp. 296-97. M. Solṭānī, *Fehrest-e majallahā-ye fārsī az ebtedā tā sāl-e 1320*, Tehran, 1356 Š./1977, pp. 57-58 .

(NASSEREDDIN PARVIN)

DOORS AND **DOOR FRAMES** (*dar o sardar*), in Persian architecture major foci of decoration, varying in size and elaboration with the function and importance of the building and the location of the entrance in relation to the total composition.

i. *From the medieval through the Safavid periods.*

ii. *In the Qajar and Pahlavi periods.*

i. From the Medieval through the Safavid Periods

Doors. In the Islamic period doors were usually made of wood, either large planks or joined pieces, and the finest examples were elaborately decorated. City gates were normally of huge sturdy planks with metal fittings, which were often the only parts to survive. The Ḥaẓīra gate at Yazd, for example, had iron plates decorated with figures, elephants, and a foundation inscription naming the amirs who funded the work in 432/1040-41; the city gate at Ganja (now Kirovabad) was inscribed with the names of the ruler and the *qāżī* (religious judge) who supervised the work in 455/1063 (Blair, 1992, nos. 41, 49). In both these inscriptions the smiths who made the fittings were named, and, as some of the earliest craftsmen to have signed their work, they must have been considered important artisans. City gates also had symbolic and apotropaic associations and were thus often removed by conquerors and reinstalled elsewhere as signs of sovereignty.

More elaborate doors were made of joined wood, sometimes inlaid with ivory and other precious materials and closed with bronze fittings inlaid with silver and gold. The standard arrangement comprised a pair of leaves, each with two vertical stiles connected by four or more rails enclosing three or more panels. The middle panel was often larger than the upper and lower ones. The pairs of doors still in situ at the shrine of Aḥmad Yasavī (799-801/1397-99) in the city of Turkestan, northwest of Tashkent, one at the main portal and another at the entrance to the mausoleum, exemplify the finest Timurid workmanship (cf. Lentz and Lowry, pp. 208-09; cf. pp. 46-49). Each wing reflects the traditional tripartite division into three rectangular panels: a larger vertical one sandwiched between smaller ones. The upper panels are inscribed, and the lower ones contain geometric medallions. The glory of the doors, however, is the superb carving of the central panels, with arched cartouches and arabesque tracery and palmettes on a delicate scrolled ground; the spandrels are filled with naturalistic vegetal tracery and peonies, other flowers, and leaves. These designs recall contemporary bookbindings and carpets and were based on the designs of court artists. A pair of doors made by the master carpenter Ḥasan (or Ḥosayn) b. Moḥammad in 846/1442 (Iran Bastan Museum, Tehran, no. 1135/3308; ht. 208 cm., w. 148 cm; *Arts of Islam*, no. 458) is evidence that the style was widespread.

The same arrangement of three rectangular panels continued on doors in the Safavid period, but the technique of decoration changed: The surfaces were painted with gold and polychrome pigments, then coated with resin varnish (see Plate XXVII), a technique often erroneously identified as "lacquer." Cartouches on the panels are decorated with figures adapted from book illustration (Plate XXVIII). The paintings are executed in red, blue, green, and other colors against dark grounds that contrast with the gold brushstrokes in the surrounding field. The spandrels around the field are filled with arabesques, also on dark grounds. More elaborate examples, in which the fields around the cartouches are also painted with figural scenes, are probably 19th-century interpretations of Safavid work (Eastman).

PLATE XXVII

Applewood doors, painted, lacquered, and gilded, in the manner of Reżā ʿAbbāsī, Persia, 16th-17th centuries, City of Detroit Purchase 26.7. Courtesy Detroit Institute of Arts.

PLATE XXVIII

Painted cartouche, detail of central medallion of right-hand wing of door shown in Plate XXVII. Courtesy Detroit Institute of Arts.

Door frames. Doors were often the focus of elaborate surrounds of carved stucco or stone and framed by a flat masonry or brick structure known as a *pīštāq*. The *pīštāq* was already known at 8th-century palaces in Iraq and the ruined structure at Sarvestān in Fārs, of contemporary date but uncertain purpose (Bier, pp. 21, 50-51); by the 10th century elaborate portals with *pīštāqs* had been introduced in Persian mosques and mausolea. In the 9th century the congregational mosque at Isfahan, rebuilt in the time of the ʿAbbasid caliph al-Moʿtaṣem (217-27/833-42), had had an articulated exterior facade, but the doorways were only slightly larger than the other blind arches and decorated with a gently arched motif (Galdieri). The Jorjīr mosque in Isfahan (late 10th century), on the other hand, has a projecting portal with intricate decoration, though the original height of the doorway is uncertain. The facade of the ʿArab-Atā mausoleum (367/978) at Tim near Samarqand (Figure 22) consists of an elaborately framed arch, but, as it occupies the entire facade of the building, it differs from the typical *pīštāq* of later times, which projects above a visible roof line.

By the 12th century most important buildings in Persia had portals projecting from and above the main facade. The elaboration of the doorway complemented the development of the four-*ayvān* plan, in which the tall axial *ayvān* (q.v.) preceded the dome chamber and the *pīštāq* matched it in height and general form. The entrance to Rebāṭ-e Malek, a caravansary/residence in the steppe between Bukhara and Samarqand rebuilt in 471/1078-79, is preceded by a pointed semidome, framed in a wide band of eight-pointed stars in relief (Plate XXIX). At Rebāṭ-e Šaraf, between Mašhad and Saraḵs (508/1114-15; Godard, fig. 3), the portal is heavily decorated in relief brickwork. The trio of 12th-century mausoleums built by the Qarakhanids at Ūzgand in the Fargāna valley (Hill and Grabar, figs. 112-19; Ettinghausen and Grabar, pl. 302) have squarish, shallow *pīštāqs* that mask the tomb chambers behind them. The portal added to one corner of the congregational mosque at Herat in Afghanistan in 596/1200 (Melikian-Chirvani, pls. VII-VIII) is embellished with an inscription in "knotted Kufic" script (see CALLIGRAPHY) highlighted in light-blue tile.

From the 13th through the 17th centuries the *pīštāq*, usually centered on the main facade, became proportionately taller and larger, as did the interior *ayvāns* to which it corresponded formally. The standard design, nascent in the 10th century, was canonized: The entry bay comprised a relatively small doorway below a tall, deep vault enclosing a pointed semidome, frequently filled with *moqarnas* (oversailing courses of niche sections set at angles to one another). The flanks of this entry bay were filled with decorative panels, epigraphic bands, and modest niches; the frame of the arch was composed of tiers of flat niches and decorative and epigraphic bands running along three sides of the *pīštāq*. The bands contained the foundation inscription with the patron's name and the date of construction or foundation, koranic quotations, and sometimes excerpts from endowment deeds. Tile decoration was mandatory; early examples include the *ḵānaqāh* of ʿAbd-al-Ṣamad at Naṭanz (707/1307; Plate XXX; cf. Wilber, pp. 133-34 no. 39, pls. 52-54) and the congregational mosque at Varāmīn (722/1322; Wilber, pp. 158-59 no. 64, pls. 129, 131; Blair, 1986, pp. 65-68, pls. 2, 145-56). By the 15th century the entire *pīštāq* was covered with tilework, as at the "Blue mosque" in Tabrīz (870/1465; Golombek and Wilber, I, pp. 407-09 no. 214, II, pls. 415-16). In a few instances, like the "mosque of Bībī Ḵānom" at Samarqand (801-08/1398-1405; Blair and Bloom, pl. 49), twin minarets flank or surmount the *pīštāq*. At the congregational mosque at Yazd (14th century) the *pīštāq* is twice as high as the facade to which it is attached (Golombek and Wilber, I, pp. 414-18 no. 221; *Survey of Persian Art*, pl. 439A-B; Blair and Bloom, pl. 17); the *pīštāq* could also occupy as much as half the main facade, as at the *madrasa* (religious school) built by Ulug Beg in Samarqand (820-23/1417-21; Golombek and Wilber, I, pp. 263-65 no. 30, II, pls. 88, 95). In the Shah mosque at Isfahan (1021-47/1612-38; *Survey of Persian Art*, pls. 463-64; Blair and Bloom, pls. 236, 238) the *pīštāq* had developed into an entry complex that reorients the visitor to-

Scale 1:20 m 1 0.5 0 1 2

Figure 22. Drawing, facade of the ʿArab-Atā mausoleum (367/978) at Tim, near Samarqand. After Pugachenkova.

PLATE XXIX

Portal of Rebāṭ-e Malek, a caravansary/residence between Bukhara and Samarqand, rebuilt in 471/1078-79. After *Survey of Persian Art*, pl. 272.

PLATE XXX

Portal of the *ḵānaqāh* of ʿAbd-al-Ṣamad at Naṭanz (707/1307). Photograph S. Blair.

ward the *qebla* (direction of Mecca) and provides a transition from the public *maydān* (open square) to the more private court of the mosque.

Bibliography: *Arts of Islam*, London, 1976. L. Bier, *Sarvistan. A Study in Early Iranian Architecture*, University Park, Pa., 1986. S. S. Blair, *The Ilkhanid Shrine Complex at Natanz, Iran*, Cambridge, Mass., 1986. Idem, *The Monumental Inscriptions from Early Islamic Iran and Transoxiana*, Leiden, 1992. Idem and J. M. Bloom, *The Art and Architecture of Islam, 1250-1800*, New Haven, Conn., 1994. A. C. Eastman, "Palace Doors from the Throne-Room of Shāh ʿAbbās," *Bulletin of the Detroit Institute of Arts* 7, 1926, pp. 49-52. R. Ettinghausen and O. Grabar, *The Art and Architecture of Islam. 600-1250*, Harmondsworth, U.K., 1987. E. Galdieri, "The Masǧid-i Ǧuma Isfahan. An Architectural Facade of the 3rd Century H.," *Art and Archeology Research Papers* 6, December 1974, pp. 24-34. A. Godard, "Khorāsān," *Āṯār-è-Īrān* 4, 1949, pp. 7-68. L. Golombek and D. Wilber, *The Timurid Architecture of Iran and Turan*, 2 vols, Princeton, N.J., 1988. D. Hill and O. Grabar, *Islamic Architecture and Its Decoration*, Chicago, 1964. T. W. Lentz and G. D. Lowry, *Timur and the Princely Vision. Persian Art and Culture in the Fifteenth Century*, Los Angeles, 1989. A. S. Melikian-Chirvani, "Eastern Iranian Architecture à propos of the Ghūrid Parts of the Great Mosque of Harāt," *BSOAS* 33, 1970, pp. 322-27. G. A. Pugachenkova, *Mavzoley Arab-ata*, Tashkent, 1963. D. N. Wilber, *The Architecture of Islamic Iran. The Il Khānid Period*, Princeton, N.J., 1955.

(SHEILA BLAIR)

ii. IN THE QAJAR AND PAHLAVI PERIODS

In the Qajar period the designs and methods of construction of doors and door frames continued those from preceding periods.

Doors. Doors were generally made of wood from plane and mulberry trees but also from semihard forest woods like beech, maple, alder, elm, and walnut (personal communications from members of the carpenter's guild, Tehran). Whether large or small, traditional doors were constructed to revolve on the outer stiles, which were extended to fit into sockets in the lintels and sills; more recently they have been attached to door frames by means of metal hinges (Wulff, *Crafts*, p. 86). Large double doors, more than twice the size of ordinary house doors, were used for the portals of citadels, city gates, and entrances to mosques, caravanseries, *bāzārs* (qq.v.; Gluck and Gluck, p. 368 and pls.), palaces, and other monumental buildings. Usually a smaller door, known as *ḡolāmrow* (page's passage), was set into one of the wings of the main door, to provide easy access, as the main portals remained closed for security reasons.

The simplest doors were decorated with rows of metal bosses (*gol-mīḵ*), strips, and knockers (Michell, p. 120 pls. 27-28; Plate XXXI). The bosses, placed in double rows on the upper and lower sections of the door, helped to prevent the wooden panels from cracking. Door knockers (*kūba*) were often signed by the smiths. All doors were bolted from the inside with *kolūn*s (tumbler locks; Wulff, *Crafts*, pp. 67-69 figs. 99-101). The traditional lock for the exterior was the *čeft-e varza*, in which the solid end of a narrow metal strip (*čeft*) was fastened to the door, either directly or by means of a chain; a slit in the other end of the *čeft* fitted over a metal half-loop (*bast*) set into the lintel. A padlock then secured the two parts.

Doors of palaces, principal mosques, and places of pilgrimage were more elaborately decorated. In addition to being fitted with bosses and knockers, they were sometimes carved, inlaid, or plated with engraved metal panels or even sheets of precious metal (for examples from the Pahlavi Marmar palace in Tehran, see Gluck and Gluck, pp. 365 pl. upper right, lower left and right, 367 pl.). The standard composition of the door resembled those for carpets and bookbindings, with features like a central me-

PLATE XXXI

Wooden house door of the period of Reżā Shah but in the Qajar tradition, with metal bosses and knockers, Tehran. Photograph M. Momayyez.

dallion, cartouches, and corner pieces. Openwork wooden screens set in carved wooden frames often served as doors at tombs and shrines (Gluck and Gluck, p. 157 pl.). The shapes of doors generally conformed to the shapes of the openings, for example, curved on top in an arched door frame; sometimes the arched tympanum of the door was filled with openwork in brick, wood, or metal (for openwork on courtyard doors [1367 Š./1968] at the Nāranjestān mansion, Shiraz, see Gluck and Gluck, pp. 389 pl., 390 pl. top).

House doors were made in similar shapes and materials, though on a scale closer to the average height of a man. The degree of sophistication and the lavishness of the decoration depended on the status and wealth of the owner. In some regions of Persia the decoration of residential doors reflected specific foreign influences; for example, motifs in Ḵūzestān and the coastal area along the Persian Gulf recall African and Indian originals (see Michell, p. 120 pl. 27). The designs of late Qajar and early Pahlavi wooden doors also reflect European prototypes, usually mediated through Russia and Turkey. Traditional designs based on *gol-mīḵ* gave way to framing devices and diaper patterns (Plate XXXII). During the same period it became fashionable to paint doors in flat colors, whereas previously they had been left in their natural wood colors and maintained by annual polishing with vegetal oils. Toward the end of the reign of Reżā Shah Pahlavī (1304-20 Š./1925-41) European art nouveau and art deco styles were adopted for doors in Persia; the results were largely devoid of artistic merit or character. As with door frames (see below), there was also a tendency under the Pahlavis to revive historic styles, particularly of the Achaemenid, Sasanian, and Safavid periods (Gluck and Gluck, pp. 365 pls. upper right, lower left, 383 pl.)

The doors of shops and other places of trade differed in being divided into several wooden panels, which slid back and forth independently in grooves on the upper and lower parts of the door frame. To lock these panels, a long metal rod with a slit at one end, like a *čeft*, was passed through metal rings and locked onto a *bast*. More recently these door panels have been vertically hinged, so that they fold back.

Doors of village houses, storage spaces, and stables have only single wings, simply decorated with wood and a few bosses. The *čeft-e varza* is the only locking device used on such doors.

Finally, doors in the interiors of buildings were also fashioned from wood, though more delicately than outer doors; they usually consisted of two wings, and their surfaces were articulated with framing elements. In some instances the upper frames were filled with colored glass; the tympanum above such a door might be filled with stained glass (Gluck and Gluck, p. 390 pl. top), including the image of a half-sun. In the homes of the wealthy interior doors were often lacquer-painted with floral, vegetal, and bird motifs. Even more luxurious were the interior doors of palaces and important shrines, where marquetry, encrustation with precious stones, and layering with sheets of precious metals were common (see, e.g., Gluck and Gluck, p. 367 pl.).

Door frames. The gateways of large monuments were composed of several parts: an outer gate, a transitional space known as *rewāq*, and the door itself, which opened to the interior of the building. The vaulted space of the *rewāq* was often decorated with *moqarnas* (oversailing courses of niche sections set at angles to one another) of the same materials as those on the outer facade of the gateway (for a Europeanizing stucco version at the Hotel Shah ʿAbbās in Isfahan, 1346-47 Š./1967-68, see Gluck and Ġluck, p. 387 pl. bottom left). In private houses the transitional space is usually a small octagon or portion of an octagon, hence its name *haštī* (or *keryās*). The ceiling of the *haštī* may be plain or decorated with *moqarnas*. The ceiling and walls are sometimes whitewashed, and there may be stone dados. Most *haštī*s are equipped with small benches providing the visitor with a place to rest while awaiting permission to enter the house. A vestibule with shallow recesses on the side walls is known as a *dargāh*. The materials and methods of construction and decoration of the *dargāh* are the same as for the *rewāq* and the *haštī*.

PLATE XXXII

Painted wooden house door in Tehran, of the period of Reżā Shah, reflecting European taste for shaped and recessed paneling and including a mail slot. After Solṭānzāda, p. 64 fig. 78.

Door frames consist of two major parts, the jambs flanking the opening and the lintel or arch connecting them at the top. The latter was usually the main focus of decoration; the jambs were articulated with engaged columns, either full length, with base, shaft, and capital, or half length, with shaft and capital supported on a volute. The architectural and decorative compositions of Qajar and Pahlavi door frames can be divided into two major types. One is associated with large buildings, where the apex of the arched opening intersects the horizontal line of the rectangular frame, leaving two spandrels filled with decorative patterns in glazed tile, stucco, or brick, in addition to rectangular bands of varying widths that border the frame. The second is characterized by a larger decorative surface above the opening, usually patterned in brick; this decoration is often quite elaborate, with an inscription on the lintel and a tympanum resting on two full columns, or it may be confined to an inscription band framing the doorway. The decoration of columns and lintels ranged from traditional types, as in the door frames of mosques, to those derived from Achaemenid and Sasanian prototypes or the European baroque (Plates XXXIIII, XXXIV).

Door frames were mainly built of bricks and surfaced with plain, molded, or carved bricks, often combined in patterns. Glazed tiles, stucco, stone, and occasionally unbaked bricks could also be used in the decoration of door frames, depending on the function and importance of the building. Glazed tiles in vegetal or geometric patterns appeared on religious buildings, whereas in secular buildings they might also include human and animal figures. By the middle of the Qajar period traditional designs were being combined with imported Victorian motifs, including human, animal, and landscape subjects. Expensive stone was rarely used in the decoration of door frames but was reserved for palaces or state buildings; one extant example is the stone door frame at the Marmar palace. Stucco decoration is often relegated to the interior faces of door and

PLATE XXXIII

Doorway in Tehran, period of Reżā Shah, combining jambs inspired by the Qajar tradition and a highly individual choice of various Western decorative elements. After Solṭānzāda, p. 55 fig. 59.

PLATE XXXIV

Doorway in Tehran, period of Reżā Shah, incorporating various elements of European inspiration. After Solṭānzāda, p. 59 fig. 67.

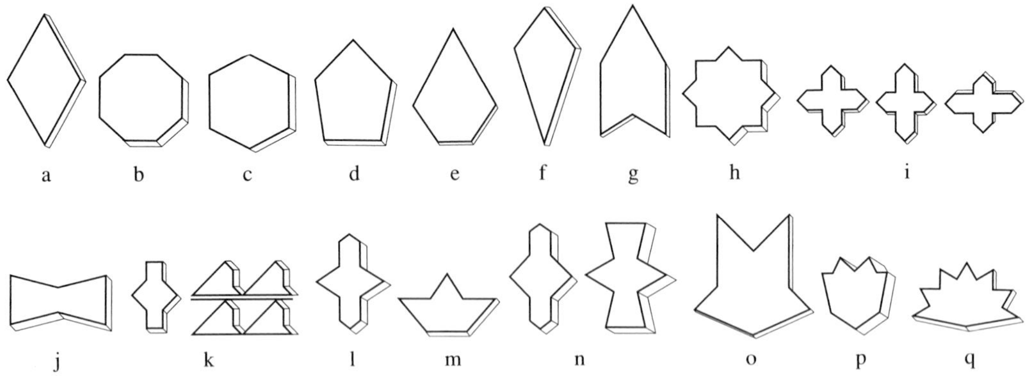

Figure 23. Independent tile or brick elements. a. *Almāstarāš*. b. *Hašt*. c. *Naqš-e čašm-e gāvī*. d. *Sellī*. e. *Kīsa-ye sormadān*. f. *Pā bārīk*. g. *Pābozī*. h. *Setāra-ye īrānī*. i. Three types of *bāzūband*. j. *Gīva*. k. Two versions of *ālat-e čīnī-band-e rūmī*. l. *Sormadān*. m. *Abābīl*. n. *Sormadān-e morabbaʿ*, *sormadān-e lowzī*. o. *Čūb-ḵaṭṭ*. p. *Barg-e čenārī*. q. *Šamsa-ye tah borīda*.

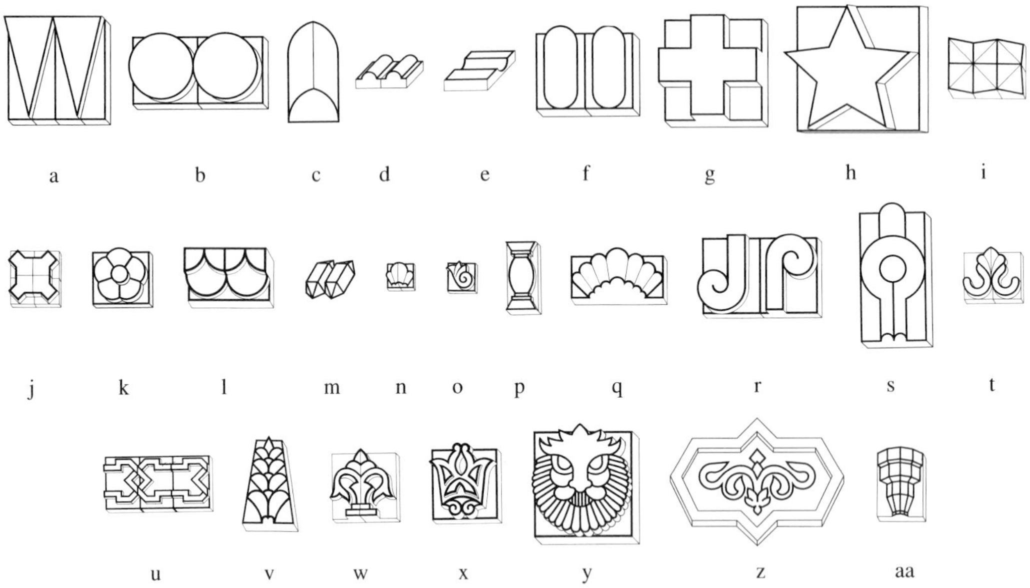

Figure 24. Molded or carved elements. a. *Gūš-gorgī*. b. *Ḥāšīa-ye gūy-nešān*. c. *Ḥāšīa*. d. *Fetīla*. e. *Šīār-qāšoqī*. f. *Nīm-gerd*. g. *Ṣalīb*. h. *Setāra*. i. *Ḥāšīa-ye tazʾīn*. j. *Morabbaʿ-e bāzūbandī*. k. *Gol-e panj par*. l. *Falsī*. m. *Ḥāšīa-moqarnas*. n. *Ḥāšīa-ye bozorg*. o. *Ḥalazūnī*. p. *Ḥāšīa-goldān*. q. *Ḵoršīdī-e kala dar*. r. *Pīčak*. s. *Kelīdī*. t. *Zanjīra-ye šāḵ o bargī*. u. *Zanjīra*. v. *Kākol*. w. *Nīm-toranj*. x. *Tāj*. y. *Naqš-e šīr*. z. *Mowj*. aa. *Sar-sotūn*.

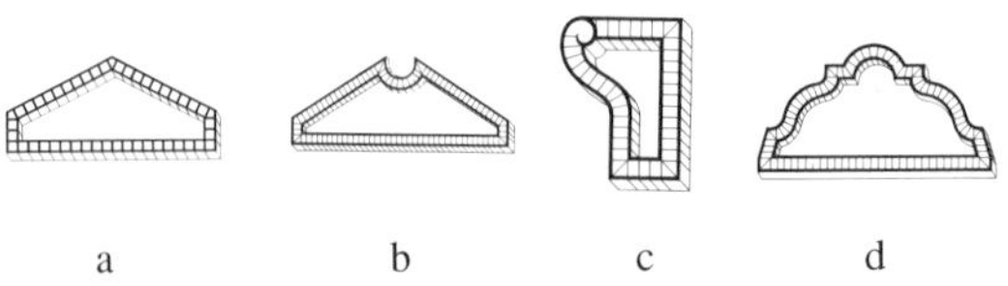

Figure 25. Composite relief elements. a. *Kalla-santūrī*. b. *Kalla-santūrī-e šekasta*. c. *Zānūʾī*. d. *Sar-tāj*.

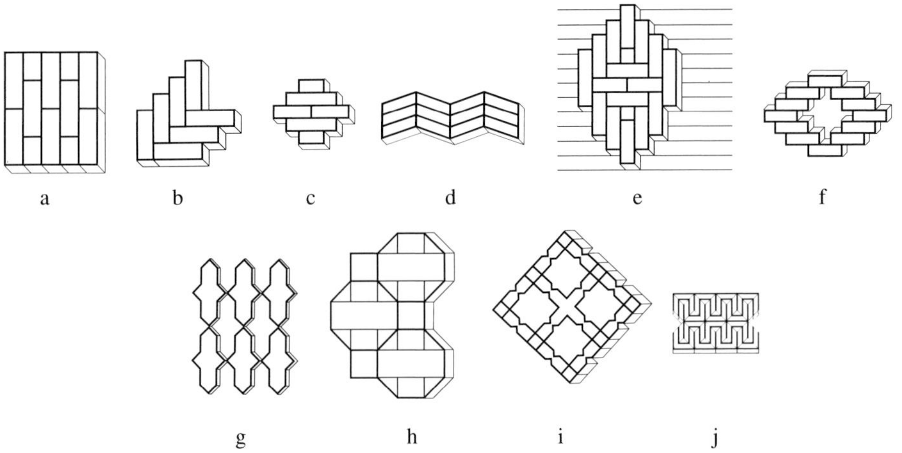

Figure 26. Patterns composed from individual elements. a. *Band-e ʿalamī*. b. *Naqš-e ḥaṣīrī*. c. *Čandragī*. d. *Ragčīn-e jenāġī*. e. *Čandragī-e ḥāšīadār*. f. *Čandragī*. g. *Ālat-e čīnī-band-e rūmī*. h. *Ṣalīb*. i. *Ālat-e jaʿfarī-e čūḵaṭṭī*. j. *Čahār langa-ye ḥāšīadār*.

window frames. Unbaked brick is still found on the door frames of village houses.

The decorative motifs found on door frames were mainly derived from the repertoire of Persian chinoiserie and arabesques. Single units of plain brick and glazed tiles were employed to form intricate and beautiful geometric patterns (for the Qajar Masjed-e Šāh at Qazvīn, see *EIr*. II, p. 628, pl. XVIII; cf. *Survey of Persian Art*, pl. 494A-B). The great variety of brickwork pattern elements used for door frames is apparent from the repertoire still common in Tehran (Figures 23-26; cf. Wulff, *Crafts*, p. 123 fig. 187). Among the simplest basic shapes (Figure 23) are *almāstarāš* or *lowzī* (lozenge shape); *hašt* (octagon); *naqš-e čašm-e gāvī* (lit., "cow's eye"; hexagon); *sellī* (a pentagon with two longer sides); *kīsa-ye sormadān* (lit., "case of the *sormadān*"; an elongated pentagon designed to fit between *sormadān* in patterns; see below); *pā bārīk* (kite-shaped element); *pā-bozī* (lit., "goat's foot"; a vertical rectangle with an elongated pointed top and a shallower point cut from the base); *setāra-ye īrānī* or *zohra-ye hašt par* (eight-pointed star); *bāzūband* (a cross with pointed ends, either symmetrical or with one longer arm); *gīva* (lit., "shoe"; shaped like a bow tie); *ālat-e čīnī-band-e rūmī* (a vertical bar bisected horizontally by a rectangle or an irregular pointed element); *sormadān* (one of several elongated shapes, with or without pointed ends, bisected horizontally by a rectangle or lozenge shape); *abābīl* (a three-pointed element with a flat base); *sormadān-e morabbaʿ* (lit., "*sormadān* with rectangle"); *sormadān-e lowzī* (lit., "*sormadān* with lozenge"); *čūb-ḵaṭṭ* (an angular tooth shape); *barg-e čenārī* (lit., "plane-tree leaf"; irregular leaf-shaped heptagon); and *šamsa-ye tah borīda* (seven radial points on a slightly angular base).

Molded and carved bricks (Figure 24) include *gūš-gorgī* (raised triangle on a vertical rectangular base); *ḥāšīa-ye gūy-nešān* (raised disk on a square base, intended for borders); *ḥāšīa* (semicylinder, also used for borders); *fetīla* (vertical rectangle with a semicylinder in relief); *šīār-qāšoqī* (lit., "spoon-shaped groove"; rectangular tile bisected by a semicylindrical groove); *nīm-gerd* (raised ellipse on a vertical rectangular base); *ṣalīb* (equilateral cross in relief on a square base); *setāra* (five-pointed star in relief on a square base); *ḥāšīa-ye tazyīn* (square base with a two-faceted top, designed to be set in groups of four); *morabbaʿ-e bāzūbandī* (square base with a raised section resembling a smaller square with projections at the corners); *gol-e panj par* (five-petaled flower with raised center, the whole raised on a square base); *falsī* (lit., "scaled"; a horizontal rectangular base with two levels of overlapping scallops in relief); *ḥāšīa-moqarnas* (independent faceted element resting on a flat surface, with three exposed long sides tapering at each end to a point formed of three triangles); *ḥāšīa-ye bozorg* (tripartite fan shape raised on a square base); *ḥalazūnī* (lit., "snail shell"; curled half-palmette with volute in relief on a square base); *ḥāšīa-goldān* (vertical rectangle with "newel post" in relief); *ḵoršīdī-e kalla dar* (fluted fan in relief on a horizontal rectangular base); *pīčak* (lit., "ivy"; rectangular base with a volute in relief, intended to be set in alternating directions); *kelīdī* (lit., "key-shaped"; a vertical rectangular base with a relief design consisting of a semicylinder at the top interrupted by a circle in the center supported on two narrower semicylinders at the base); *zanjīra-ye šāḵ o bargī* (vertical rectangular base with half-leaf supported on a volute in relief, meant to be laid in alternate directions to form a continuous frieze); *zanjīra* or *zanjīrī* (vertical rectangular base, with raised bands forming interlocking arrow shapes when laid in a frieze); *kākol* (lit., "crest"; vertical base tapering toward the top with relief plant consisting of successively smaller elements aligned vertically); *nīm-toranj* (plant in a vase standing on a two-stepped platform, all in relief on a square base); *tāj* (crown; elaborate floral form in relief on a square base); *naqš-e šīr* (lion's head in relief on a square base); *mowj* or *modāḵel* (element shaped like a *sormadān-e lowzī* placed horizontally, with raised border and molded composition of volutes in the center); and *sar-sotūn* (vertical rectangular base, with four courses of multifacted relief producing the effect of an engaged column capital).

More elaborate composite elements with relief (Figure 25) include *kalla-santūrī* (lit., "head of the musical instrument *santūr*"; gable-shaped tympanum with raised border); *kalla-santūrī-e šekasta* (like the preceding but with a semicircular gap replacing the upper point); *zānūʾī* (lit., "knee-shaped"; vertical rectangular base with raised border, broadened into a volute at the top of one side); and *sar-tāj* (tympanum with raised border of alternating curves and angles).

Among specific patterns in which these elements are combined (Figure 26) are *band-e ʿalamī* (bricks laid vertically); *naqš-e ḥaṣīrī* (basketweave); the basic form of *čandragī* (six horizontal bricks forming a cross); *rag čīn-e jenāḡī* (herringbone); *čandragī-e hāšīadār* (central *čandragī* element within larger frame of vertical bricks); a variant of *čandragī* in which a larger frame of horizontal bricks surrounds a negative of the basic form); *ālat-e čīnī-band-e rūmī* (*sormadān* placed vertically); *ṣalīb* (staggered courses of octagons with inscribed crosses, separated by squares in each course); *ālat-e jaʿfarī-e čūḵaṭī* (a diaper pattern composed of eight-pointed stars and crosses); and *čahār langa-ye ḥāšīadār* (an interlocking design of relief with gabled profiles, the dark lines representing mortared joints).

Other terms include *vārū* (lit., "upside down"; fan-shaped?); *barg-e kangarī* (cardoon or artichoke leaf); *barg o morvārīd* (leaf and pearl); *toka* (arrow without point; cf. Wulff, *Crafts*, p. 123 fig. 187: an elongated triangle set on its short base); *jeqqa* (aigrette); *dom-kalāḡī* (lit., "crow's tail"); *rīša* (root?); *ṣadaf* or *gūšmāhī* (shells); *ḵofta wa rāsta* (various horizontal and vertical forms?); *čahār ḵāna* (grid); *dandān mūšī* (lit., "mouse teeth"; crenellated); *abrī* (cloud pattern); *band-e jaʿfarī* and *band-e rūmī* (types of diaper work).

Bibliography: (For cited works not found in this bibliography, see "Short References.") Ī. Afšār, *Yādgārhā-ye Yazd*, 3 vols., Tehran, 1348-54 Š./1969-75. J. Gluck and S. H. Gluck, *A Survey of Persian Handicraft. A Pictorial Introduction to the Contemporary Folk Arts and Art Crafts of Modern Iran*, Tehran, 1977. A. Ḥājj ʿAlī Moḥammadī, *Noqūš-e sardarhā-ye ḵānahā-ye Tehrān-e qadīm*, Tehran, 1372 Š./1993. G. Michell, ed., *Architecture of the Islamic World. Its History and Social Meaning*, London, 1978. Ḥ Solṭānzāda, *Fażāhā-ye worūdī-e ḵānahā-ye Tehrān-e qadīm*, Tehran, 1371 Š./1992. P. Tanavoli and J. T. Wertime, *Locks from Iran. Pre-Islamic to Twentieth Century*, Washington, D.C., 1976.

(MORTAŻĀ MOMAYYEZ)

DŌRĪ (Pashto Ḍôrəy; Aslanov, p. 432), river in southern Afghanistan, the main tributary of the Arḡandāb (q.v.). It originates about 2,500 m above sea level in the Tōba highlands of northern Baluchistan, about 50 km east of the Afghan boundary (for details, see Wylie; summarized in Hughes-Buller, p. 14; *Gazetteer of Afghanistan* V, pp. 199 ff.) and receives the waters of the Arḡestān (344 km long) and Tarnak (353 km long) rivers on its right bank before its confluence with the Arḡandāb below Qandahār, at an altitude of 890 m. On the left bank it skirts the barren Rēgestān desert. On the upper part of its course it is known as the Kadanay. The total length of the river is 227 km within Afghan territory, where its basin covers 31,955 km^2, almost 5 percent of the total area of the country.

The hydrology of the Dōrī is poorly known, as only one water-gauging station has been established on its length, at Taḵt-e Pol (alt. 1,050 m), 99 km above the junction with the Arḡandāb. Furthermore, measurements are available only for the period October 1976 to September 1978. They show a mean discharge of 1.35 m^3/sec. At the confluence with the Arḡandāb, however, that would rise to 11 m^3/sec, almost twice as much water as is left in the Arḡandāb below the Qandahār oasis (Garbovskiĭ, p. 122).

At Taḵt-e Pol the Dōrī registers extreme seasonal irregularity; the ratio of maximum to minimum mean monthly discharge is above 1,000 (Garbovskiĭ, p. 184 fig. 5.25). It is determined entirely by rainfall, which at these latitudes is low and scarce. The seasonal peak flows are recorded in July and August after heavy but short-lived monsoon rains in the Solaymān and Tōba mountains (absolute maximum 154 m^3/sec on 21 August 1978, highest mean monthly discharge 7.78 m^3/sec in August; Garbovskiĭ, p. 211). Much lower peak flows result from winter cyclonic precipitation (absolute maximum recorded in winter 59.6 m^3/sec). In the long periods between successive rain events the flow falls well below 1 m^3/sec (lowest mean monthly discharge 0.04 m^3/sec in November), and the river may run dry for some time, with only shallow pools in the riverbed.

Although the water of the Dōrī is brackish, it is nevertheless heavily diverted into irrigation channels by means of traditional small earth dams, especially on its upper course (Hughes-Buller; Tate, pp. 240-41). Above Taḵt-e Pol, for example, it has been estimated that 82 percent of the total flow of the river, about 5.80 m^3/sec, is diverted for agricultural use (Garbovskiĭ, p. 122). The biannual peak flows permit growing of two crops a year (*Gazetteer of Afghanistan* V, p. 469; for a list of the major canals between Šāh Pasand and Taḵt-e Pol, see pp. 139-40, 470).

Bibliography: M. G. Aslanov, *Afgansko-russkiĭ slovar'* (Afghan-Russian dictionary), Moscow, 1966. E. A. Garbovskiĭ, *Inzhenernaya gidrologiya rek Afganistana* (Engineering hydrology of the rivers of Afghanistan), Leningrad, 1989. R. Hughes-Buller, *Quetta-Pishin District,* Baluchistan District Gazetteer Series 5, Ajmer, 1907; repr. in *Balochistan through the Ages*, 2 vols., Quetta, 1979. Ministry of Water and Power, *Hydrological Yearbook 1961-1975*, pt. II-4B. *Arghandab River Basin*, Kabul, 1976. Idem, *Hydrological Yearbook 1976-1978*, pt. II. *Rivers of Helmand Basin. Ghazni and Helmand,* Kabul, 1982. G. P. Tate, *The Frontiers of Baluchistan, Travels on the Borders of Persia and Afghanistan*, London, 1909; repr. Lahore, 1976. H. Wylie, *Summary of Report on Toba* (1879), India Office Records, London, L/P & S/7/23/1477-82. Idem, *Report on the Toba Plateaux and the Roads Leading Thereto from Pishin and Kadanai*, 1879, India Office Records, London, L/P & S/7/23/1482-90.

(DANIEL BALLAND)

DORN, JOHANNES ALBRECHT BERNHARD (Boris Andreevich; b. Scheierfeld, Saxe-Coburg, Germany, 29 April 1805, d. St. Petersburg, 19 May 1881), pioneer in many areas of Iranian studies in Russia. Dorn studied philology and theology at the universities of Halle and Leipzig, learning Hebrew, Arabic, Syriac, Persian, Turkish, Pashto, Sanskrit, and Ethiopian. In 1825 he received a doctorate in theology and philosophy from Leipzig and was appointed lecturer in oriental languages. The next year C. M. Fraehn, director of the Asiatic Museum of the Imperial Russian Academy of Sciences in St. Petersburg, recommended that Dorn be appointed to the newly established department of oriental languages at the University of Kharkov. The formalities took almost two years, during which time Dorn traveled in western Europe.

From 1829 through 1835 he taught in Kharkov; in the latter year he moved to St. Petersburg, where he taught the history and geography of the Muslim east in the Asiatic department of the Russian Ministry of foreign affairs (until 1843); from 1838 to 1842 he also taught Sanskrit at the University of St. Petersburg and in 1855-57 Pashto, the first such course taught in Europe (Kulikova, 1975; idem, 1982). In 1839 he began a long career at the Imperial Russian Academy of Sciences, reaching the level of academician in 1852. From 1842 he was also director of the Asiatic Museum and head of the oriental section of the Imperial public library.

Despite his administrative obligations, Dorn published indefatigably in Iranian studies. His broad conception of the field, particularly his insistence that grasping the meaning of historical events depends on knowledge of the geography, languages, and life of a people, was apparent in his active collecting of oriental manuscripts, documents, books, coins, and artifacts. For almost fifty years he guided Russian scientists and travelers in their gathering of eastern materials and acquired a number of private collections for the Asiatic Museum: During his tenure the total of Persian manuscripts tripled, and collections of Pashto and Kurdish manuscripts were begun. Dorn gradually turned the museum into an academic research institution, now the St. Petersburg branch of the Institute of Oriental Studies of the Russian Academy of Sciences. At the same time he introduced the newly acquired manuscripts, especially those in Iranian languages, to the scientific world through a series of publications extending from 1827 to 1881.

One main focus of his work was on concise annotated lists and catalogues (Akimushkin and Borshevskiĭ). He undertook catalogues of oriental manuscripts (*Catalogue des manuscrits et xylographes orientaux de la Bibliothèque Impériale publique de St. Pétersbourg*, St. Petersburg, 1852) and printed books ("Catalogue des ouvrages arabes, persanes et turcs, publiés à Constantinople, en Égypte et en Perse, qui se trouvent au Musée Asiatique de l'Académie," *Bulletin de l'Académie Impériale des Sciences de St. Pétersbourg* [*Bulletin . . .*] 10, 1866, cols. 168-213; "Chronologisches Verzeichniss der seit dem Jahre 1801 bis 1866 in Kazan gedruckten arabischen, türkischen, tatarischen und persischen Werke," *Bulletin . . .* 11, 1867, cols. 305-85). He also published more than thirty articles on Sasanian and Islamic numismatics (Livotova and Portugal, pp. 54-56).

Dorn was particularly interested in the Pashtun and published annotated editions and translations of texts on tribal history (e.g., *Die Geschichte Tabaristans und der Serbedare nach Chondemir*, ed. and tr., St. Petersburg, 1850, esp. p. 4; Neʿmat-Allāh Heravī, *Maḵzan-e afḡānī* [1021/1613], ed. and tr. as *The History of the Afghans*, 2 vols., London, 1829-36; cf. Storey, I, pp. 393-95; Miklukho-Maklaĭ, pp. 346-48). He also compiled what at the time was the most complete available list of 254 Pashtun tribes, as well as the history and traditions of the Dor(r)ānī (q.v.), Ḡelzī, Lōdī, and other confederations ("Verzeichniss afghanischer Stämme," *Bulletin . . .* 3/17, 1838, cols. 257-66; "Beitrag zur Geschichte des afghanischen Stammes der Jusufsey," *Bulletin . . .* 4/1, 1838, cols. 23-31; "Über eine sechste von mir benützte Handschrift von Ni'metullahs Geschichte der Afghanen," *Bulletin . . .* 9/13-14, 1842, cols. 217-19; "Über die ursprüngliche und richtige Schreibung einiger afghanischen Benennungen," *Bulletin . . .* 10/5, 1842, cols. 60-73; "Zur Geschichte des af-ghanischen Emires Chandschehan Lodi, nach Ni'met-Ullah," *Mémoires de l'Académie Impériale des Sciences de St. Pétersbourg* [*Mémoires . . .*], ser. 6 no. 7, 1847, pp. 373-400). Although some of his conclusions have since been disproved, his works remain valuable.

Dorn never visited Afghanistan, but he nevertheless established the scientific basis for Afghan studies, particularly the first systematic description of Pashto ("Nachträge zur Grammatik der afghanischen Sprache," *Bulletin* . . . 10/23, 1842, cols. 356-68; "Grammatische Bemerkungen über das Puschtu, oder die Sprache der Afghanen," *Mémoires* . . ., 6 ser. no. 5, 1845, pp. 1-163; "Zusätze zu den grammatischen Bemerkungen über das Puschtu," *Mémoires* . . ., 6 ser. no. 5, 1845, pp. 435-87; "Auszüge aus afghanischen Schriftstellern," *Mémoires* . . ., ser. 6 no. 5, 1845, pp. 581-643). In 1847 he published the first anthology of Pashto literature (*A Chrestomathy of the Pushtū or Afghan Language*, ed., St. Petersburg, 1847), with excerpts from historical texts and poetry, accompanied by commentary and a Pashto-English glossary; it was used for many years as a textbook at the University of St. Petersburg.

Dorn also extended his comprehensive approach to study of the Caspian region, compiling information on the history and historical geography of Gīlān, Māzandarān, Ṭabarestān, Šīrvān, and neighboring regions. A group of Persian manuscripts accompanied by commentaries and partial translations was published mainly in two series, Beiträge zur Geschichte der kaukasischen Länder und Völker aus morgenländischen Quellen (1840-48) and Muhammedanische Quellen zur Geschichte der südlichen Küstenländer des Kaspischen Meers (1850-58), as well as in several separate books and articles ("Auszüge aus zwei morgenländischen Schriftstellern, betreffend das Kaspische Meere und angrenzende Länder," *Bulletin* . . . 16, 1871, cols. 15-41; "Morgenländische Benennungen der Fahrzeuge auf dem Kaspischen Meere und angrenzende Länder,"*Bulletin* . . . 16, 1871, cols. 15-45; "Auszüge aus vierzehn morgenländischen Schriftstellern, betreffend das Kaspische Meer und angrenzende Länder" *Bulletin* . . . 17, 1872, cols. 466-94; 18, 1873, cols. 299-320; 19, 1874, cols. 198-215, 292-320; *Kaspii. O pokhodakh drevnikh russkikh v Tabaristan* . . . [The Caspian. On early Russian expeditions in Ṭabarestān . . .], St. Petersburg, 1875). Dorn collected linguistic material during an expedition to the Caucasus and the southern shore of the Caspian Sea in 1860-61 ("Bericht über eine wissenschaftliche Reise in dem Kaukasus und den südlichen Kustenländern des Kaspischen Meeres," *Bulletin* . . . 4, 1862, cols. 344-93). The results were published jointly with Mirza Muhammad Schafy in the series Beiträge zur Kenntniss der iranischen Sprachen (1860-66), which included *Masanderanische Sprache* (I-II/1, 3, St. Petersburg, 1860-66) and surveys of Gīlakī, Tatī, and Ṭālešī, as well as verse by Amir Pāzvārī Māzandarānī (Akimushkin et al., nos. 1375-77). Dorn himself published only a small part of this material; the remainder has served as a prime source for compilation of the appropriate section in the *Grundriss der iranischen Philologie* (*Grundriss* I/2, pp. 344-80; Aziatskiĭ Muzeĭ, pp. 306-07).

Bibliography: (For cited works not found in this bibliography, see "Short References.") O. F. Akimushkin and Yu. E. Borshevskiĭ, "Materialy dlya bibliografii rabot o persidskih rukopisyakh" (Materials for a bibliography of works on Persian manuscripts), *Narody Azii i Afriki*, 1963/3, pp. 165-72; 1963/6, pp. 228-41. O. F. Akimushkin et al., *Persidskie i tadzhikskie rukopisi Instituta Narodov Azii AN SSSR* I, Moscow, 1964. *Aziatskiĭ Muzeĭ—Leningradskoe otdelenie Instituta vostokovedeniya AN SSSR* (The Asiatic Museum—The Leningrad branch of the Institute of Oriental Studies), Moscow, 1972. "B. A. Dorn," *Zapiski Imperatorskoĭ Akademii nauk* 40/2, 1882, pp. 44-45. "B. A. Dorn," file 776, Trudy Arkhiva AN SSSR 16 (Moscow and Leningrad), 1959, pp. 252-54. *Istoriya otechestvennogo vostokovedeniya do serediny XIX veka* (History of national oriental studies up to the mid-19th century), Moscow, 1990. G. Dugat, *Histoire des orientalistes de l'Europe du XIIe au XIXe siècle* I, Paris, 1868 (for a bibliography of Dorn's publications up to that time, see pp. 72-99). V. V. Grigoriev, "B. A. Dorn," *Novoye vremya* 1878, 1881, p. 3; 1924, 1881, p. 3. I. Yu. Krachkovskii, *Ocherki po istorii russkoi arabistiki* (Survey of the history of Russian Arabic studies), Moscow and Leningrad, 1950, pp. 75-76, 123-25. A. M. Kulikova, "B. A. Dorn i universitetskoe vostokovedenie v Rossii" (B. A. Dorn and university oriental studies in Russia), *Narody Azii i Afriki* 2, 1975, pp. 220-28. Idem, *Stanovlenie universitetskogo vostokovedeniya v Peterburge* (Emergence of university oriental studies in St. Petersburg), Moscow, 1982. Idem, *Vostokovedenie v rossiiskikh zakonodatelnykh aktakh (konets XVII v.-1917 g.)* (Russian legislative acts concerning oriental studies [End of the 17th century to 1917]), St. Petersburg, 1994. O. E. Livotova and V. B. Portugal, *Vostokovedenie v izdaniyakh Akademii nauk. 1726-1917. Bibliografiya* (Oriental studies in publications of the Academiya Nauk. 1726-1917. Bibliography), Moscow, 1966, pp. 54-62. V. A. Livshits and I. M. Oranskii, "Izuchenie afganskogo yazyka (pashto) v otechestvennoĭ nauke" (The study of the Afghan language [Pashto] in national scholarship), in *Ocherki po istorii izucheniya iranskikh yazykov* (Survey of the history of the study of Iranian languages), Moscow, 1962, pp. 69-73. N. D. Miklukho-Maklaĭ, *Opisanie persidskih i tadzhikskih rukopiseĭ Instituta vostokovedeniya* III. *Istoricheskie sochineniya* (Description of the Persian and Tajik manuscripts in the Institute of Oriental Studies III. Historical texts), Moscow, 1975. V. A. Romodin, "Iz istorii izucheniya afgantsev i Afganistana v Rossii" (From the history of the study of Afghans and Afghanistan in Russia), in *Ocherki po istorii russkogo vostokovedeniya* (Survey of the history of Russian oriental studies) I, Moscow, 1953, pp. 155-58. V. S. Sokolova and A. L. Gryunberg, "Istoriya izucheniya bespis'mennykh iranskikh yazykov" (History of the study of Iranian languages that lack writing), in *Ocherki po istorii izucheniya iranskikh yazykov* (Survey of the history of the study of Iranian languages), Moscow, 1962, pp. 135-37.

(N. L. LUZHETSKAYA)

DORNĀ. See CRANE.

DORR. See PEARL.

DORRĀNĪ (sg. Dorrānay), probably the most numerous Pashtun tribal confederation (q.v.), from which all Afghan dynasties since 1160/1747 have come. It has always played a leading role in modern Afghan politics (Yusufzai; see AFGHANISTAN X).

Tribal composition. The Dorrānī confederation is a political grouping of ten Pashtun tribes of various sizes, which are further organized in two leagues of five tribes each. The Panjpāy (or Panjpāw) league includes three major tribes, the ʿAlīzī, Esḥāqzī (q.v.; or simply Sākzī), and Nūrzī, as well as two minor ones, the Mākōzī (known as Mākōhī until the mid-19th century, sometimes simply Mākō) and K̲ōgānī (or K̲awgānī/K̲agwānī, not to be confused with the K̲ōgīānī of eastern Afghanistan). The Zīrak (or Jīrak) league includes the Mastīzī (an unimportant group, called Mūsāzī by Ḥayāt Khan), Al(e)kōzī, Pōpalzī (or Fōfalzī), and Bārakzī (q.v.), with the latter's offshoot the Acakzī (cf. Glatzer, 1983, p. 220, quoting an Acakzay version of the story in which the Bārakzī are said to be descended from the Acakzī; see ACƎKZĪ). The political leadership of the confederation has always belonged to the Zīrak league, shifting between the Pōpalzī and Bārakzī. Affiliations with tribe and confederation are the only ones currently in use; the leagues, though consistently mentioned in local chronicles, are never referred to spontaneously, and it remains to be ascertained whether they have ever functioned as autonomous political bodies.

In the genealogical idiom of the Pashtuns the confederation reputedly encompasses tribes descended from a common patrilinear ancestor, Abdāl (Awdal), who himself, it is further claimed, was descended from Qays ʿAbd-al-Rašīd, the ultimate ancestor of all Pashtun tribes (481
34); hence the original name of the confederation, Abdālī (q.v.; or Awdalī; cf. Dorn, p. 257), later changed to Dorrānī (see below). The initial heterogeneity of the confederation is reflected, however, in both its tribal terminology and genealogical organization. Although Zīrak/Jīrak (Pashto "intelligent"), the sobriquet for Solaymān II (Leech, p. 450; Ḥayāt Khan, tr., table), is claimed as a common ancestor for all tribes of the Zīrak league (a denomination like *Zīrakī would be more likely), Panjpāy simply means "five legs" (i.e., "five septs") and refers to the grouping of five independent tribes, without reference to a common ancestor. Moreover, the Panjpāy tribes Mākōhī and K̲ōgānī lack the typical Pashto suffix -*zī* (sg. -*zay* "tribe"), which supports the tradition that they were allogeneous tribes (Ferrier, p. 11; Ḥayāt Khan, tr., table and p. 67, referring to a tradition that the K̲ōgānī are descended from Abdāl's second wife while the "Mākō" are truly an "adopted" tribe; cf. McMahon, who reported a tradition that the K̲ōgānī and Mākō are descended from the same father; Table 35); such genealogical imprecision generally typifies a process of adoption. It must also be stressed that the Adōzī tribe, though reputedly descended from Abdāl, does not seem to have ever been clearly included in the confederation (cf., however, Ḥayāt Khan, tr., p. 64, claiming that it is incorporated in the ʿAlīzī), reinforcing the idea that the confederation was originally of a political, rather than a genealogical, nature.

No serious estimate of the present strength of the various Dorrānī tribes is available, but collectively they may include at least 2 million people. Earlier tentative estimates are conflicting and unreliable, though suggesting that the Nūrzī and Bārakzī were, and probably still are, the two largest Dorrānī tribes (Table 36). The whole confederation reputedly comprised 60,000 families in the time of Nāder Shah (1148-60/1736-47), but this figure does not seem to have included the many nomadic components (Elphinstone, p. 400).

History. The origin of the Dorrānī confederation has not clearly been determined. A proposed connection between the name Abdālī and the ancient Hephthalite dynasty seems extremely tenuous (Masson, I, p. xiii). According to some traditions, the Abdālī tribes entered southern Afghanistan (from Ḡōr?) in the early 15th century (*Taḏkerāt al-molūk*, tr., p. 13). The earliest mention of a confederation by that name dates from the 16th century, when Shah ʿAbbās I (q.v.; 996-1038/1588-1629) bestowed supreme command of it upon the chief of the Pōpalzay tribe (Elphinstone, p. 397; Malcolm, II, pp. 410-11). This report suggests that some kind of political union had already been achieved among the Abdālī tribes, perhaps in order to fight against rival tribes like the Yūsofzī, Mohmand, and others that they successfully expelled from Arachosia at that time (cf. *Tārīḵ-e moraṣṣaʿ*), and that the Safavid state was simply institutionalizing it.

At about the same time the Abdālī were mentioned as a sheep-herding (i.e., nomadic) "tribe" living, at least partly, east of Qandahār (*Āʾīn-e akbarī*, tr. Blochmann, II, p. 403). In the mid-17th century Abdālī "tribes" were again reported living near Qandahār (ʿEnāyat Khan, p. 484). Driven from that area by Ḡilzay pressure in the early 18th century, the Abdālī (or at least part of them) then took refuge in "the mountains of Herat" (Ḥayāt Khan, tr., pp. 61,

Table 35
THE DORRĀNĪ TRIBES WITHIN PASHTUN GENEALOGY

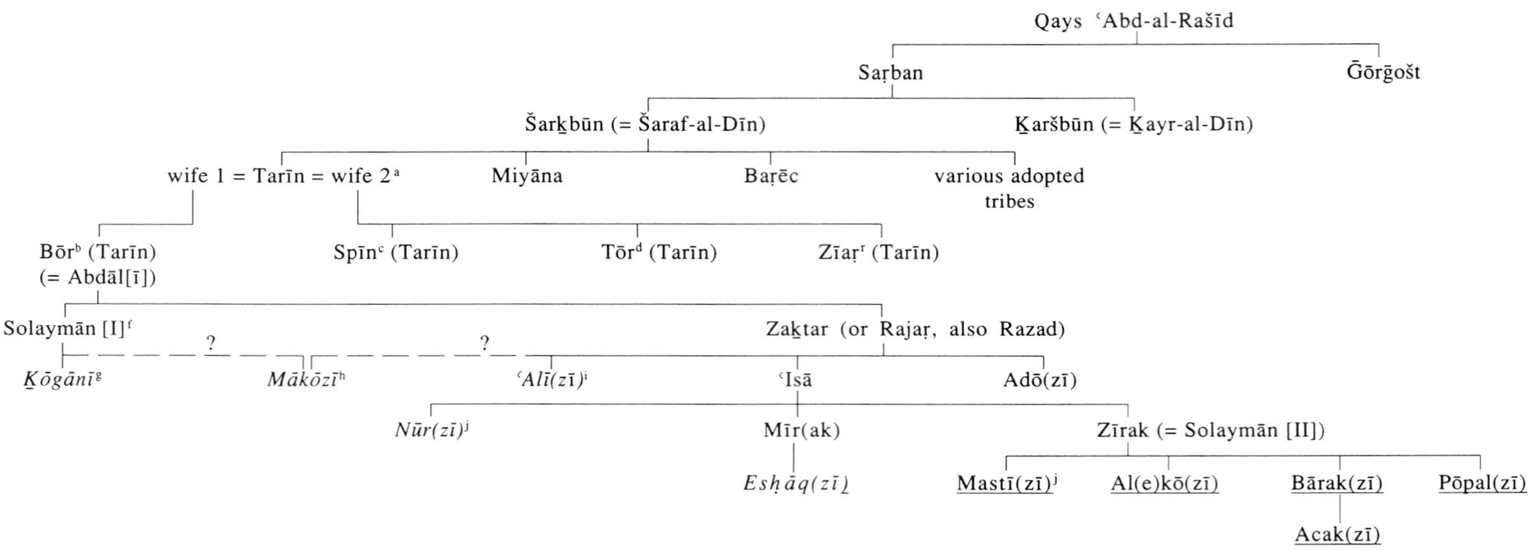

a. Leech, p. 449.

b. Pashto "brown."

c. Pashto "white."

d. Pashto "black."

e. Pashto "yellow."

f. Son of Abdāl's second wife, hence Zaḵtar's half-brother, sometimes confused (e.g., McMahon) with the homonymous son of ʿIsā.

g. Italics indicate tribes of the Panjpāy league.

h. The filiation of Mākō is uncertain; according to some traditions, he was Ḵōgānī's brother (e.g., McMahon), but he is generally reckoned to have been Zaḵtar's son.

i. Sometimes inverted with Nūr in the line of descent (e.g., *Taḏkerāt al-molūk*, tr., p. 12).

j. Solid underscores indicate tribes of the Panjpāy league, dotted underscores tribes of the Zīrak league.

Table 36
ESTIMATES OF THE STRENGTH OF THE DORRĀNĪ TRIBES AT VARIOUS DATES
(in numbers of families)

Tribes	About 1740[a]	About 1810[b]	About 1865[c]
Panjpāy			
Esḥāqzī	10,000	10,000	11-12,000
Nūrzī	30,000	30,000	35,000
ʿAlīzī	10,000	15,000	16,000
K̲ōgānī	6,000	? ("small clan")	? ("very few")
Mākōhī	10,000	? ("small clan")	? ("very few")
Zīrak			
Bārakzī	40,000	30,000	35,000
Acakzī	—	3,000	4,000
Pōpalzī	20,000	12,000	13,000
Al(e)kōzī	20,000	10,000	15,000
Mastīzī	?	?	? ("a few families")
Total	146,000 or 195,000?[d]	110,000	130,000

a. Ferrier, p. 9.
b. Elphinstone, pp. 398-99, 421.
c. Ḥayāt Khan, tr., pp. 65 ff.
d. Ferrier, p. 8.

67; Leech, p. 467), whence they fought against the Persians, gained control of Herat, raided in Khorasan, and "in the course of a very few years greatly increased in numbers" (Ferrier, p. 30), suggesting that outsiders were joining the confederation en masse. Nāder Shah managed to bring them under control, however, and raised from their ranks a contingent of 12,000 cavalry under the command of an ʿAlīzay chief (Ferrier, p. 67). At Nāder Shah's death they felt strong enough to proclaim their independence. At a *jerga* (assembly of elders) held at the holy shrine of Šēr-e Sork̲, 5 km southeast of Qandahār, they elected as their supreme chief Aḥmad Khan, a young member of the Sadōzī clan of the Pōpalzī tribe, son of an Al(e)kōzay mother; soon after he was formally crowned as Aḥmad Shah (1160/1747).

It was on that occasion that the name of the confederation was changed to incorporate the royal title *dorr-e dorrān* (pearl of pearls, i.e., primus inter pares), allegedly referring to "the distinctive custom of the Abdālī tribe of wearing a small pearl studded ring in the right ear"; Bellew, p. 31). The Dorrānī were thus explicitly supporters of the king, as were the so-called "Bar Dorrānī" (upper Dorrānī), a now obsolete designation for several eastern Pashtun tribes unconnected with the Dorrānī proper (Elphinstone, p. 325). From that time on the history of the Dorrānī effectively coincides with the history of the Afghan state. Unlike most other Pashtun tribes they have generally remained loyal to the dynasties sprung from their ranks and have only seldom rebelled. Notable exceptions were Ayyūb Khan's revolt in 1297-98/1880-81 (arising from the long-standing rivalry between the Sadōzī Pōpalzī and Moḥammadzī Bārakzī for political leadership of the confederation and of Afghanistan) and a riot in Qandahār in 1338 Š./1959. The long tradition of Dorrānī loyalty to the state may explain why tribesmen did not join anti-communist guerrillas until comparatively late, after 1358 Š./1979 (Roy, p. 136; for similar late involvement of the Dorrānī in the anti-British uprising of 1256-57/1841-42, see Yapp, 1963, p. 312; idem, 1964, p. 373). On the other hand, two centuries of political domination of Afghanistan, with associated privileges (see examples in Kakar, pp. 73-74, 83, 99), certainly explain their claim to social superiority over all other ethnic groups in Afghanistan, including other Pashtun tribes (Tapper, 1991, pp. 38 ff.). In the last decades of the royal regime, however, as actual political power became more and more restricted to a narrow circle comprising the Moḥammadzay royal clan and a handful of leading Dorrānī families who had settled in Kabul as clients of the court, educated non-Moḥammadzī Dorrānī of lower or provincial extraction gradually sought alternative sources of promotion, rallying to communist groups, mainly Parčam, where they were heavily represented in the politburo, rather than to Islamic parties, in which they were totally absent from the leadership (Rubin, pp. 87-88; see CONSTITUTIONAL HISTORY OF AFGHANISTAN; COMMUNISM iv).

Tribal affiliation among Dorrānī gained an entirely new geographical consistency when Nāder Shah returned to them the lands they had lost to the Ḡilzī in southern Afghanistan (Leech, p. 469; Lockhart, p. 120). He allotted them on a tribal basis that has been broadly retained since that time: Zīrak tribes were given the tracts east of the Helmand and around Qandahār and Panjpāy tribes those in the west between the Helmand and Sīstān. The former are well watered, and Zīrak tribesmen have therefore become mostly agriculturalists; in the early 19th century, however, many peasant families were still living in tents, a clear indication of their former nomadic life (Elphinstone, p. 407). In the western territories, on the contrary, scarcity of water and poorer agricultural potential account for better conservation of nomadic traditions among Panjpāy tribes. Actually the tribal geography is much more complex than a simple opposition between east and west (for details, see Ḥayāt Khan, tr., pp. 65 ff.). For example, while some Nūrzī were settled east of Qandahār (Rawlinson, p. 512; Wylie, fol. 1480), Bārakzī and Acakzī clans are also found around Šīndand, in the very heart of Nūrzī territory (*Gazetteer of Afghanistan* III, pp. 344-45; Table 37). On the other hand, in the late 18th century conquests of the Hazāra expanded Dorrānī territory toward the north, into lower Orozgān (Rawlinson, p. 517). The present tribal geography is therefore blurred, all the more so as migrations and deportations have resulted in the spread of the Dorrānī from their homeland in southern Afghanistan, always for political, rather than demographic, reasons.

Northern Afghanistan has been the main target of Dorrānī out-migration. Two different waves of colonization, both sponsored by successive Afghan governments, can be distinguished. The first and least documented followed Aḥmad Shah's imperial conquests (Ross, p. 31; de Planhol, 1973, p. 8; idem, 1976, p. 286, noting the toponym Sākzay, of unequivocal Dorrānay origin). The second, more important wave of colonization took place in the late 19th and early 20th centuries, when the Afghan amirs systematically organized the colonization of depopulated Bādḡīs (q.v.) and Afghan Turkestan, relying massively on their Dorrānī cotribalists. Several thousand Dorrānī families migrated north, most of them from the nomadic clans of the Panjpāy tribes (Esḥāqzī, then Nūrzī; Tapper, 1973; idem, 1983; Table 37). Known locally as "Qandahārī," wherever they actually came from, in their new locations they succeeded in acquiring political and economic leadership out of proportion to their numbers (e.g., only 10 percent of the total population of Sar-e Pol district in the 1970s; Tapper, 1991, p. 30).

Aside from the Acakzī, whose tribal territory straddles the present Afghan-Pakistani boundary between Qandahār and Quetta, several Dorrānī tribes also include minorities established east of Afghanistan, even as far as the Deccan (Ḥayāt Khan, tr., p. 66). They are concentrated mainly in the Punjab. Best known among them are the so-called Multani Pathans, actually Sadōzī (Pōpalzī) tribesmen. In the mid-17th century some members of the clan fled from Khorasan to Multān, in order to escape allegiance to Persia (Nabi Khan, p. 3); they were further reinforced by fellow tribesmen expelled by the Ḡilzay chief Mīr Ways Khan in the early 18th century (Ḥayāt Khan, tr., p. 71; Ibbetson, p. 93). Small colonies from the Pōpalzī, ʿAlīzī, and Al(e)kōzī tribes are also scattered in various other parts of the Punjab (Rose, III, p. 339; Ḥayāt Khan, tr., pp. 65-66, 72 ff.).

Substantial changes in the geographical distribution of the Dorrānī in and around Afghanistan occurred during the 1980s. Information is scanty, and it remains to be seen whether or not all these changes will last. First, it has been reported that the civil war has produced a flow of return migration of Pashtuns from northern to southern Afghanistan. Second, there has been massive emigration from southern Afghanistan to neighboring Pakistan and Persia (see DIASPORA ix, x). According to a sample survey in 1988, nearly 75 percent of all Afghan refugees in the southern part of Persian Khorasan were Dorrānī, that is, about 280,000 people (Papoli-Yazdi, p. 62).

Sociocultural characteristics. Although a majority of Dorrānī are now sedentary peasants or citydwellers (no figures are available), more than 20,000 families, about 110,000 people, were still nomads in 1357 Š./1978 (Table 37). Most of them belonged to the Panjpāy league for historical reasons (see above). Their summer pastures are mainly in the mountains of Ḡōr (Balland), where they compete with the local Aymāq (q.v.) populations for access to grazing lands. In sharp contrast to the situation in neighboring Hazārajāt, where the Hazāra villagers have been overpowered by Pashtun nomads (mainly Ḡilzī), the Aymāq have succeeded in keeping control of their territory; the Dorrānī nomads are considered only *hamsāya* (clients). Free legal right to pastureland is normally restricted to owners of springs or arable land in the vicinity, and Dorrānī nomads must therefore either pay grazing fees to local Aymāq owners or purchase springs or agricultural lands, which they then rent to Aymāq tenants (Glatzer, 1977, pp. 97 ff.). Some have settled on land they have bought and become seminomads, on the way to "aymaqization" (e.g., ten Al(e)kōzī families at Sōfak, 10 km northwest of Čaḡčarān).

Seminomadism is otherwise infrequent among Dorrānī, except in northern Afghanistan (Table 37). Joint families, however, frequently split into purely sedentary households that till the jointly owned lands and purely nomadic ones that take care of the jointly owned herds; shifting from one way of life to the

Table 37

PASTORAL NOMADISM AMONG DORRĀNĪ TRIBES IN AFGHANISTAN (1978)

Tribes	Southern Afghanistan[a]		Northern Afghanistan[b]		Western Afghanistan[c]		Other Regions		Total		
	A[d]	B[e]	A[d]	B[e]	A[d]	B[e]	A[d]	B[e]	A[d]	B[e]	Total
Panjpāy											
Nūrzī	2,890	50	1,466	661	3,099	405	—	—	7,455	1,116	8,571
Esḥāqzī	2,258	10	3,128	1,931	3,280	—	—	—	8,666	1,941	10,607
ʿAlīzī	699	122	532	38	345	15	—	—	1,576	175	1,751
Mākōzī	400	—	—	—	—	—	—	—	400	—	400
Zīrak											
Al(e)kōzī	243	—	200	60	52	—	60	38	555	98	653
Bārakzī	412	20	340	954	357	—	—	30	1,109	1,004	2,113
Acakzī	124	170	325	782	285	85	—	—	734	1,037	1,771
Pōpalzī	180	—	185	184	35	—	—	—	400	184	584
Total	7,206	372	6,176	4,610	7,453	505	60	68	20,895	5,555	26,450

a. Includes all provinces from Farāh to Qandahār.
b. Includes all provinces from Bādgīs to Qondūz.
c. Includes Herat province..
d. Number of nomadic families.
e. Number of seminomadic families.
Source: Afghan Nomad Survey (1978), unpublished.

other is easy (Glatzer, 1982; cf. Ḥayāt Khan, tr., p. 66, referring to the Nūrzī). Symbiotic relationships between settled and nomadic populations have thus been achieved on a much larger scale among Dorrānī than among Ḡilzī.

Dorrānī pastoral culture also differs in a number of ways from that of other Pashtun nomads, though this topic has never been thoroughly studied (Ferdinand, 1969, pp. 146 ff.). For example, Dorrānī use specific types of camel saddle and butter churn, as well as a black barrel-vaulted tent probably of the same origin as that used by the Baluch (Ferdinand, 1959, pp. 37 ff.); they wear somewhat different felt cloaks and shoes; the sexual division of labor among them is also unique, with the men fetching water and the women milking animals; they have a more pronounced handicraft tradition (female weaving, including weaving of the tent cloth); hunting (with hounds) plays a more important role in their daily life; and, finally, trade has never been introduced as an important component of their pastoral life, probably because their winter and summer quarters in Afghanistan are not complementary, with the exception of the Acakzī clans that migrate across the Afghan-Pakistan boundary to the Tōba highlands (Hughes-Buller, p. 71).

The Dorrānī confederation has traditionally been governed by a powerful hierarchy of hereditary tribal chiefs (*sardārs*). Kings depended on their support, and they held high positions in both central and provincial governments. Originally responsible for recruiting a feudal cavalry, they were consequently assigned rent-free tenancies (Turk. *toyūl*; Doerfer, II, p. 667-69) and were paid allowances in proportion to the number of horsemen they retained (for an extensive survey, see Rawlinson). They thus became a powerful and respected aristocracy, though also a potential threat to the monarch. Aristocratic government and pervasive state influence, combined with comparatively slight human pressure on agricultural and pastoral lands in southern Afghanistan, explain why feuds were traditionally uncommon among Dorrānī, aside from competition among chiefs for political power, and their country reputedly quiet (Elphinstone, pp. 389, 404; *Gazetteer of Afghanistan* V, pp. 145-46).

This peaceful situation has had durable consequences. First, Dorrānī customary law (*nark̲*) differs sharply from the standard *paṣ̌tūnwālī*; for example, the Panjpāy tribes ignore the *maraka* (customary law court for minor disputes) and even consider the *jerga* (assembly of elders for settlement of important problems) a rather unusual institution (oral information; see also Elphinstone, pp. 404-05; Atayee, p. 67). Second, fortified settlements (*qalʿa*), the architectural expression of mutual distrust between tribal neighbors, are much less common among Dorrānī than in the rest of the Pashtun area and are restricted to the landed aristocracy (Elphinstone, pp. 407-08). A final distinctive feature of the Dorrānī is their Pashto dialect, characterized by the so-called "soft" consonants (described in Penzl; see AFGHANISTAN v, vi).

Bibliography: (For cited works not found in this bibliography and abbreviations found here, see "Short References.") M. I. Atayee, *A Dictionary of the Terminology of Pashtun's Tribal Customary Law and Usages*, Kabul, 1358 Š./1979. D. Balland, *Afghanistan—Nomadismus und Halbnomadismus*, TAVO A 10/12.7, Wiesbaden, 1989. H. W. Bellew, *The Races of Afghanistan*, Calcutta, 1880; repr. Lahore, 1976. A. Bonner, *Among the Afghans*, Durham, N.C., 1987. B. Dorn, "Verzeichniss afghanischer Stämme," *Bulletin scientifique publié par l'Académie Impériale des Sciences de Saint-Petersbourg* 3/17, 1838, cols. 257-66. M. Elphinstone, *An Account of the Kingdom of Caubul, and its Dependencies in Persia, Tartary, and India*, London, 1815; repr. Graz, 1969. ʿEnāyat Khan, *Šāh Jahān-nāma*, tr. A. R. Fuller, ed. W. E. Begley and Z. A. Desai as *The Shah Jahan Nama of ʿInayat Khan*, Delhi, 1990. K. Ferdinand, "The Baluchistan Barrel-Vaulted Tent and Its Affinities," *Folk* (Copenhagen) 1, 1959, pp. 27-50. Idem, "Nomadism in Afghanistan, with an Appendix on Milk Products," in L. Földes, ed., *Viehwirtschaft und Hirtenkultur*, Budapest, 1969, pp. 127-60. J. P. Ferrier, *History of the Afghans*, London, 1858. B. Glatzer, *Nomaden von Gharjistān. Aspekte der wirtschaftlichen, sozialen und politischen Organisation nomadischer Durrānī-Paschtunen in Nordwestafghanistan*, Beiträge zur Südasien-Forschung 22, Wiesbaden, 1977. Idem, "Processes of Nomadization in West Afghanistan," in P. C. Salzman, ed., *Contemporary Nomadic and Pastoral Peoples. Asia and the North*, Studies in Third World Societies 18, Williamsburg, Va., 1982, pp. 61-86. Idem, "Political Organisation of Pashtun Nomads and the State," in R. Tapper, ed., *The Conflict of Tribe and State in Iran and Afghanistan*, London, 1983, pp. 212-32.

Moḥammad Ḥayāt Khan, *Hayāt-e afḡān*, tr. H. Priestley as *Afghanistan and Its Inhabitants*, Lahore, 1874; repr. Lahore, 1981. R. Hughes-Buller, ed., *Quetta-Pishin District*, Baluchistan District Gazetteer Series, Ajmer, 1907. D. Ibbetson, *Panjab Castes*, Lahore, 1916; repr. New Delhi, 1981; repr. Lahore, 1982. H. K. Kakar, *Government and Society in Afghanistan. The Reign of Amir ʿAbd al-Rahman Khan*, Austin, Tex., 1972. R. Leech, "An Account of the Early Abdalees," *Journal of the Asiatic Society of Bengal* 14/162, 1845, pp. 445-70. L. Lockhart, *Nadir Shah*, London, 1938; repr. Lahore, 1976. A. H. McMahon, "The Origin of Duranis" (genealogical tree), National Archives of India, New Delhi, Foreign Department, Secret F, August 1895, no. 346. J. Malcolm, *Histoire de la Perse*, 4 vols., Paris, 1821. C. Masson, *Narrative of Various Journeys in Balochistan, Afghanistan, and the Panjab*, 3 vols., London, 1842; repr.

Karachi, 1974; repr. Graz, 1975. A. Nabi Khan, *A History of the Saddozai Afghāns of Multān*, Publications of the Research Society of Pakistan 44, Lahore, 1977. M. H. Papoli-Yazdi, "Cultures et géopolitique en Iran. Les réfugiés afghans dans le Khorāssān," *Géographie et cultures* 3, 1992, pp. 57-70. H. Penzl, *A Grammar of Pashto. A Descriptive Study of the Dialect of Kandahar, Afghanistan*, Washington, D.C., 1955. X. de Planhol, "Sur la frontière turkmène de l'Afghanistan," *Revue Géographique de l'Est* 13/1-2, 1973, pp. 1-16. Idem, "Le repeuplement de la basse vallée afghane du Murghāb," *Stud. Ir.* 5/2, 1976, pp. 279-90. H. C. Rawlinson, "Report on the Dooranee Tribes, 19th April 1841," in C. M. MacGregor, ed., *Central Asia* II. *A Contribution towards the Better Knowledge of the Topography, Ethnology, Resources, and History of Afghānistān*, Calcutta, 1871, pp. 823-69; repr. with numerous typographical errors in *Gazetteer of Afghanistan* V, pp. 509-77. H. A. Rose, ed., *A Glossary of the Tribes and Castes of the Punjab and North-West Frontier Province*, 3 vols., Lahore, 1919; repr. Lahore, 1978. F. E. Ross, ed., *Central Asia. Personal Narrative of General Josiah Harlan 1823-1841*, London, 1939. O. Roy, *L'Afghanistan. Islam et modernité politique*, Paris, 1985. B. R. Rubin, "Political Elites in Afghanistan. Rentier State Building, Rentier State Wrecking," *IJMES* 24/1, 1992, pp. 77-99. N. Tapper, "The Advent of Pashtūn māldārs in North-Western Afghanistan," *BSOAS* 36/1, 1973, pp. 55-79. Idem, "Abd al-Rahman's North-West Frontier. The Pashtun Colonisation of Afghan Turkistan," in R. Tapper, ed., *The Conflict of Tribe and State in Iran and Afghanistan*, London, 1983, pp. 233-61. Idem, *Bartered Brides. Politics, Gender and Marriage in an Afghan Tribal Society*, London, 1991. *Taḏkerāt al-molūk*, partial tr. in H. G. Raverty, *A Grammar of the Puk'hto, Pus'hto, or Language of the Afghāns*, 2nd ed., London, 1860, pp. 5-14. *Tārīḵ-e moraṣṣaʿ*, partial tr. in T. C. Plowden, *Translation of the Kalid-i-Afghani*, Lahore, 1901, pp. 167-208. H. Wylie, *Summary of Report on Toba* (1879), India Office Records, London, L/P & S/7/23/1477-82. M. E. Yapp, "Disturbances in Western Afghanistan, 1839-41," *BSOAS* 26/2, 1963, pp. 288-313. Idem, "The Revolutions of 1841-2 in Afghanistan," *BSOAS* 27/2, 1964, pp. 333-81. R. Yusufzai, "Influence of Durrani-Ghalji Rivalry in Afghan Politics," *Regional Studies* (Islamabad) 1/4, 1983, pp. 42-66.

(DANIEL BALLAND)

DORRĀNĪ, AḤMAD SHAH. See AFGHANISTAN x.

DORRĀNĪ DYNASTY. See AFGHANISTAN x.

ḎORRAT, maize or (Indian) corn, *Zea mays* L. (fam. Gramineae), with many varieties and hybrids (see Ṭabāṭabāʾī, pp. 140-62).

Terminology. This important cereal, of American origin, was introduced into India in about 1500 by the Portuguese, and from there it reached southern Persia in the Safavid period (907-1145/1501-1732), probably through Portuguese and Spanish merchants (Pūr(-e) Dāwūd, p. 137). In India, Persia, and other Middle Eastern countries its names are not reminiscent of its native American name *mahiz/mays*; instead, the names of familiar cereals, especially millet, sorghum, and wheat were applied to it, sometimes with modifiers. In India vernacular designations for millet or sorghum included *jo/awār* (for other variants, see Platts, s.v. *jowār*), originally referring to *Sorghum sudanense* (Piper) Stapf (cf. Pashto [*ḡaṭ-*] *jwār*, lit., "(big) millet," *jo/awārī* "sorghum" in the 16th-century text of Abūnaṣrī Heravī, pp. 100-01) and Hindī *mak(k)ā/makāʾī* "Meccan" because of the supposed Arabian provenience of sorghum (for hypotheses about the diffusion routes of sorghum from East Africa, see Watson, chap. 2; Dymock et al., III, pp. 579-80; cf. obsolete Persian *ḏorrat-/gandom-e Makka* "millet/wheat of Mecca," given as synonyms for *g/jāvars* in Tonokābonī, s.vv.; Azeri Turk. *maka/matša* < *maka būḡdā*, lit., "Mecca wheat"; eastern Gīlakī *makā-ba/ī/ūj*, lit., "Mecca rice"). Other terms for millet or sorghum applied to corn include Persian *ḏorrat* (Kurd. *zoř̄āt*, Ar. *ḏor(r)a* < Akkadian *durra* "a certain kind of millet"; Hrozný, tr., pp. 147-48; cf. *ḏora ṣafrāʾ* "yellow sorghum" in Syria, *ḏora šāmīyya* "Syrian sorghum" in Egypt), *mısır* (*darı*) "Egyptian (millet)" in Turkey, and Yazdī *goʾars*, originally "millet." Terms for wheat (Pers. *gandom*) applied to corn include *bābā-gandam*, lit., "daddy wheat" (probably an allusion to the beard-like corn silk) in western Gīlān, *kū-gand/nem* "mountain wheat" in Māzandarān, and *gan/rma šāmī* "Syrian wheat" and *ganmok*, probably "little wheat," in Kurdish (see Hažār, s.vv.). Other appellations for maize, of uncertain origin, include Māzandarānī *kāve*, Lāsgerdī *zorok*, and Kurdish *sardārī* (probably related to a certain *sardār* "chief, general") and *ganma pēḡambarāna*, lit., "prophets' wheat."

Cultivation. According to the most recent available statistics (for 1367 Š./1988-89) the areas under cultivation of corn in Persia included 48,560 ha producing 156,450 metric tons of *ḏorrat-e dānaʾī* (lit., "seed corn," i.e., sweet corn) and 32,390 ha producing 581,090 metric tons of *ḏorrat-e ḵūšaʾī* (sorghum) and *ḏorrat-e ʿolūfaʾī* (lit., "fodder corn," i.e., varieties of field corn; Markaz-e āmār, pp. 17, 40). The larger areas under cultivation of "seed corn" were in the *ostān*s of Fārs, Ḵūzestān, Sīstān and Baluchistan, and Māzandarān, in that order; those under cultivation of both "field corn" and sorghum were in the *ostān*s of Tehran, East Azerbaijan, Sīstān and Baluchistan, and Fārs, in that order (Markaz-e āmār, pp. 96, 119).

Uses. In Persia, sorghum and "field corn" are used mainly for cattle feed and "seed corn" for poultry and occasionally cattle feed. In some poor rural districts cornmeal is occasionally added to wheat flour to make an inferior bread. The most conspicuous use of corn is in the form of *balāl* (probably from, or akin to, Hindī *bāl* "ear of corn"; Platts, s.v.), ears of sweet corn with soft, milky grains (*šīr balāl*, lit., "milk corncob") roasted over charcoal in sidewalk braziers or in the open, then dipped in salt water, and eaten on the spot in the summer. Popcorn (*čos-e fīl*) is also made.

In popular medicine an infusion of *kākol-e d̲orrat/balāl* (corn silk), alone or with *dom-e gīlās* (bigarreau-cherry stalks), is recommended as a diuretic and a lithotriptic, for treatment of gout, nephritis, and infections of the urinary tract (Jazāyerī, pp. 116-18).

Bibliography: Qāsem b. Yūsof Abūnaṣri Heravī, *Eršād al-zerāʿa*, ed. M. Moširī, Tehran, 1346 Š./1967. W. Dymock et al., *Pharmacographia Indica . . .*, 3 vols., London, 1890-93. ʿAbd-al-Raḥmān Šarafkandī Hažār, *Farhang-e kordī-fārsī*, 2 vols., Tehran, 1368-69 Š./1989-90. B. Hrozný, *Die älteste Geschichte des Vorderasiens und Indiens*, 2nd ed., Prague, 1943; tr. M. David as *Histoire de l'Asie antérieure, de l'Inde et de la Crète depuis les origines jusqu'au début du second millénaire*, Paris, 1947. Ḡ. Jazāyerī, *Zabān-e ḵorākīhā*, 3rd ed., I, Tehran, 1354 Š./1975. Markaz-e āmār-e Īrān, *Sar-šomārī-e ʿomūmī-e kešāvarzī-e 1367. Natāyej-e tafṣīlī-e koll-e kešvar* V, Tehran, 1371 Š./1992. J. T. Platts, *A Dictionary of Urdū, Classical Hindī, and English*, London, 1930; repr. Oxford, 1982. E. Pūr(-e) Dāwūd, *Hormazd-nāma*, Tehran, 1331 Š./1952. M. Ṭabāṭabāʾī, *Gīāhšenāsī-e kārbordī . . . I. Gīāhān-e zerāʿathā-ye bozorg*, Tehran, 1365 Š./1986. Moḥammad-Moʾmen Ḥosaynī Tonokābonī (Ḥakīm Moʾmen), *Toḥfat al-moʾmenīn (Toḥfa-ye Ḥakīm Moʾmen)*, Tehran 1360 Š./1981(?). A. M. Watson, *Agricultural Innovation in the Early Islamic World. The Diffusion of Crops and Farming Techniques, 700-1100*, Cambridge, 1983.

(HŪŠANG AʿLAM)

DORRAT-AL-MAʿĀLĪ, FAṬEMA (b. Tehran, 1295/1873, d. Tehran, Šahrīvar 1344=1303 Š./1924), pioneer in female education in Persia. Her father, Sayyed ʿAlī Ḥakīm Šams-al-Maʿālī, was a physician in the service of Nāṣer-al-Dīn Shah, but, as was typical of the period, no information on her mother was recorded. Dorrat al-Maʿālī was educated at home, at first by her father and then by a series of tutors.

Dorrat-al-Maʿālī and her sister, whose name is not given in the sources, founded several schools for girls in Tehran: Dabestān-e moḵaddarāt-e eslāmīya in 1323/1905, Dabestān-e pardagīān, Mastūrāt, Ḵawātīn, and finally Dorrat-al-madāres in 1342/1923 (*Īrān-e now*, 29 Šaʿbān 1327/15 September 1909; 3 Rabīʿ I 1328/16 March 1910; Qawīmī, pp. 128-31). She also established adult literacy classes and opened a reading room for women (Qerāʾat-ḵāna-ye neswān; Īraj Mīrzā, p. lii). In a letter written to *Īrān-e now* on 29 Šaʿbān 1327 Dorrat-al-Maʿālī and her sister explained their motivation for establishing the first two schools mentioned above: "We were seeking a way to take a step to serve the children of our homeland. . . . [Women] are the first teachers of children. The first words are taught by mothers to children. Children mirror their mothers' manners and morals. . . . Thus [we thought] we had best establish [schools] for the girls of our homeland, so that in future every household may be headed by a learned lady well versed in home management, child education, sewing, cooking, and cleaning and from whose breast may flow the milk of patriotism into the mouths of the newborn, who, when necessary, will prove worthy of serving and sacrificing [themselves for] the country."

Opening schools for girls gained impetus after the constitutionalist victory over Moḥammad-ʿAlī Shah (1324-27/1907-1909; see CONSTITUTIONAL REVOLUTION ii). A number of women's associations were formed to support the new government and to involve women more actively in the social and political life of the country. In the spring of 1910 Dorrat-al-Maʿālī, together with other principals of girls' schools and other women activists, held a number of meetings (*Īrān-e now*, 3 Rabīʿ I 1328/16 March 1910, 4 Rabīʿ I 1328/17 March 1910, 18 Rabīʿ I 1328/30 March 1910; Bāmdād, II, pp. 13-14) that led to formation of Anjoman-e etteḥādīya-ye moḵaddarāt-e waṭan (Association of women of the homeland), in which she played an important role. In its initial declaration the association declared "At this dreadful juncture it is incumbent upon every Iranian to strive and [even] to offer his/her life to preserve the country's independence and to perpetuate Iranianism and the nation's honor." It was proposed that women should deposit contributions in the Bānk-e šāhī (Imperial bank; see BANKING IN IRAN) and that the association keep a record of all such donations; the association was to "report the result of its campaign to the sacred National Consultative Assembly and will ask the assembly what to do with the funds" (*Īrān-e now*, 21 Rabīʿ I 1328/2 April 1910). Members of the association were active in promoting consumption of Persian goods like textiles and sugar and campaigned for a boycott of imported products (Qawīmī, p. 129).

Several of Dorrat-al-Maʿālī's letters were published in *Šokūfa*, a women's journal (1330-33/1912-15) edited by the educator Mozayyen-al-Salṭana. These letters reflect their shared concern that the new schools for girls should come under greater scrutiny and tighter supervision of the Ministry of education (Wezārat-e maʿāref), lest they become tainted by accusations of morally corrupting influences or, even worse, become in fact places of moral corruption (*Šokūfa*, 10 Ramażān 1332/2 August 1914, pp. 2-3).

In 1303 Š./1924 Dorrat-al-Maʿālī and one Nadīm-al-Molūk headed a delegation of principals of girls' schools that welcomed the poet Īraj Mīrzā upon his return to Tehran from Khorasan. The delegation presented him with a poem and a letter, along with a silver vase and cigarette box, in appreciation of his public support of women's causes. He thanked them in turn in a poem entitled "Do hadīya" (Two gifts; pp. 198-99; Āryanpūr, *Az Ṣabā tā Nīmā* II, pp. 388-89). After Dorrat-al-Maʿālī's death from a heart attack he composed two elegies for her, both entitled "Dar reṯāʾ-e Dorrat-al-Maʿālī" (Īraj Mīrzā, pp. 5, 219).

Dorrat-al-Maʿālī had two daughters, Šams-al-Nahār Mahdawī and Šams-al-Żoḥā Ḵāqānī, and two sons, ʿAlī-Reżā Hūšī Fīlsūf-al-Dawla and Moḥammad Hūšī (Qawīmī, p. 131).

Bibliography: (For cited works not found in this bibliography, see "Short References.") Badr-al-Molūk Bāmdād, *Zan-e īrānī az enqelāb-e mašrūṭa tā enqelāb-e safīd*, 2 vols., Tehran, 1347-48 Š./1968-69. Īraj Mīrzā, *Taḥqīq dar aḥwāl o āṯār o afkār o ašʿār-e Īraj Mīrzā wa ḵānadān o nīākān-e ū*, ed. M.-J. Maḥjūb, Tehran, 1342 Š./1963; repr. Los Angeles, 1989. F. Qawīmī, *Kār-nāma-ye zanān-e mašhūr-e Īrān* . . ., Tehran, 1352 Š./1973.

(AFSANEH NAJMABADI)

DORRAT AL-NAJAF (Pearl of Najaf), monthly religious journal published in Persian at Najaf in southern Iraq at the end of the first decade of the 20th century. It was preceded by the monthly *al-Ḡarī*, which began publication on 18 Ḏu'l-ḥejja 1327/31 December 1909; the second issue, dated 18 Ṣafar 1328/29 February 1910, was, however, seized by the Ottoman governor of Iraq. After obtaining new permission for publication the publisher changed the name of the journal to *Dorrat al-Najaf*; the first issue appeared on 20 Rabīʿ I 1328/1 April 1910. It ceased publication with the combined nos. 7 and 8, which appeared in Ḏu'l-qaʿda 1328/November 1910.

The proprietor and publisher of *Dorrat al-Najaf* was Ḥājj Ḥosayn Eṣfahānī, the editor-in-chief Āqā Moḥammad Maḥallātī; both were connected with Āḵūnd Mollā Moḥammad-Kāẓem Ḵorāsānī (q.v.), one of the great Shiʿite leaders and a supporter of the Constitutional movement (q.v.) in Persia. Among noteworthy contributors was the Shiʿite scholar Shaikh Āqā Bozorg Ṭehrānī (q.v.). The articles were written in very complex Persian, rich in Arabic terms and idioms used by Shiʿite clerics. It may have been for that reason that the journal did not achieve a wide audience and ceased publication after only a few issues.

Dorrat al-Najaf was printed from lead type at the ʿAlawī publishing house in Najaf. It consisted of between thirty-two and sixty-two pages, measuring 14 by 21 cm, and carried no illustrations or advertisements. A number of koranic quotations appeared on the cover, along with the title and the date of publication. An annual subscription cost 2 Ottoman *majīdī*s. Issues of the journal are available in the library of the Faculty of theology (Dāneškada-ye elāhīyāt) and the central library at Tehran University, the library of Āstān-e qods-e rażawī in Mašhad, and the library of Isfahan University.

Bibliography: (For abbreviations found here, see "Short References.") L. B., "Livres et Revues. En Perse," *RMM* 13, p. 191. S.-A. Ḥasanī, *Tārīḵ al-ṣaḥāfat al-ʿerāqīya*, Baghdad, 1957, pp. 27-28. M. Modarresī Čahārdehī, "Naḵostīn maṭbūʿāt-e fārsī-e ʿErāq," *Āyanda* 6/9-12, 1359 Š./1980, pp. 882-83. M. Moḥīṭ Ṭabāṭabāʾī, *Tārīḵ-e taḥlīlī-e maṭbūʿāt-e Īrān*, Tehran, 1366 Š./1987, pp. 248, 267. Ṣadr Hāšemī, *Jarāʾed o majallāt* I, p. 260, II, pp. 283-84. M. Solṭānī, *Fehrest-e majallahā-ye fārsī az ebtedā tā sāl-e 1320 šamsī*, Tehran, 1356 Š./1977, pp. 54-55. Idem, *Fehrest-e majallāt-e mawjūd dar ketāb-ḵāna-ye Āstān-e qods-e rażawī* I, Mašhad, 1361 Š./1982, pp. 146, 213-14. *Ṭūs* (Mašhad) 29, Rabīʿ I 1328/13 March, 1910, p. 4.

(NASSEREDDIN PARVIN)

DORRI EFENDI. See DÜRRI EFENDI.

DORŪD, a town in Lorestān province, situated at the foot of Oštorānkūh, at an altitude of 1,460 m (33° 28′ N, 49° 3′ E), on the route from Tehran to Ḵorramābād at the confluence of the rivers Tīra and Mārbara. The town enjoys temperate summers and fairly cold winters. It owes its rapid growth from a simple village into a sizable town to its location on the Persian railroad, which led to commercial and industrial development in the last few decades. According to the general census (q.v.) of 1365 Š./1986, the population of Dorūd was 62,517 (11,099 households), with a 67 percent literacy rate among the 47,943 individuals six years of age and older (Markaz-e āmār, p. 20). Modern facilities include electricity, piped water, and a telephone network. The people speak a Lorī dialect of Persian.

Dorūd contains one of the largest cement-producing complexes in Persia, comprising three factories that together produce about 4,500 tons of cement daily and employ more than 2,100 workers. The first factory began production in 1338 Š./1959, and the other two were opened in 1348 Š./1969 and 1359 Š./1980 respectively. The Farsit plant was completed in 1350 Š./1971; it produces pipe, corrugated sheet metal, rubber, and cast-iron joints and employs about 850 people (Farajī et al., p. 1105).

The town of Dorūd is surrounded by several mounds of historical interest, located in the villages of Sīākala, Sangar, Rezvar, Somba-deh, and Kolangona (Īzadpanāh, p. 515).

Bibliography: ʿA. Farajī et al., *Joḡrāfīā-ye kāmel-*

e Īrān II, Tehran, 1366 Š./1987. Ḥ. Īzadpanāh, *Āṯār-e bāstānī wa tārīḵī-e Lorestān* II, Tehran, 1355 Š./1976. Jehād-e Sāzandagī, *Farhang-e ejtemāʿī-e dehāt o mazāreʿ-e ostān-e Lorestān. Āmār-gīrī-e sāl-e 1360 Š.*, Tehran, 1363 Š./1984, I, p. 29, II, pp. 29, 32-36. Markaz-e āmār-e Īrān, *Farhang-e ābādīhā-ye kešvar bar asās-e sar-šomārī-e mehr-e 1365. Šahrestān-e Borūjerd*, Tehran, 1365 Š./1986, pp. 18-19. Idem, *Sar-šomārī-e ʿomūmī-e nofūs o maskan, sāl-e 1365. Šahrestān-e Borūjerd*, Tehran, 1367 Š./1988, pp. 20-21. M.-Ḥ. Pāpolī Yazdī, *Farhang-e ābādīhā wa makānhā-ye maḏhabī-e kešvar*, Mašhad, 1367 Š./1989, pp. 241, 253.

(ʿALĪ ĀL-E DĀWŪD)

DŌŠĪ, small town and district on the northern slope of the central Hindu Kush in Afghanistan. The town is situated at the junction of the Sorḵāb and Andarāb, the valleys of which are traversed by two old caravan tracks linking Kabul with Qaṭaḡan. The one, along the Sorḵāb via Bāmīān (q.v.) and the Šebar pass, was the usual post road at the end of the 19th century (Peacocke, p. 404); the other, along the Andarāb, passed through the Panjšēr valley and the Ḵāwāk pass. Dōšī was thus a transit point between southeastern and northeastern Afghanistan. In 1343 Š./1964 modernization of the once difficult but more direct road to Kabul through the Sālang pass, which branches off the Andarāb road at Ḵenjān 22 km east of Dōšī, has greatly enhanced the activity of the town, accounting for numerous teahouses and a busy *bāzār* of 120 shops, to meet travelers' requirements (Grötzbach, p. 87); modern hotel accommodations and petrol refueling are lacking, however, both having been located in the smaller *bāzār* at Ḵenjān. Dōšī has some religious significance, as it is the usual residence of the *sayyed*s (claiming descent from the Prophet Moḥammad) of Kayān, a leading Ismaʿili lineage from Dara-ye Kayān, a left bank tributary of the Sorḵāb.

Dōšī is also the administrative headquarters of a district (*woloswālī*) of 1,735 km^2 belonging to the province of Baḡlān (q.v.). The population of the district includes Larḵābī Tajik and Pashtun newcomers (mostly from the Sāfī tribe) in its lower northern part, and Ismaʿili Šēḵ-ʿAlī Hazāra in the higher southern part. In 1886 it was estimated at 935 families, of which 49 percent were identified as Hazāra, 34 percent as Pashtun, and 17 percent as seminomadic Tajiks (Maitland, p. 440; reproduced, with errors, in *Gazetteer of Afghanistan* I, pp. 63-64). In 1922 it was put at 2,399 households, approximately 9,000 inhabitants (Koshkaki, p. 52). In 1979 the first demographic census (q.v.) found 37,600 permanent inhabitants in the district, 22 inhabitants/km^2. Although little more than estimates, these figures suggest impressive demographic growth.

Bibliography: (For cited works not found in this bibliography and abbreviations found here, see "Short References.") E. Grötzbach, *Städte und Basare in Afghanistan*, TAVO Beihefte B 16, Wiesbaden, 1979. M. B. K. Koshkaki, *Qataghan et Badakhshān*, tr. M. Reut, Travaux de l'Institut d'Études Iraniennes 10, Paris, 1979. P. J. Maitland, *Diary, with Notes on the Population and Resources of Districts Visited 1884 to 1887*, Afghan Boundary Commission, Records of Intelligence Party 2, Simla, 1888. W. Peacocke, *Diary between September 1884 and October 1886*, Afghan Boundary Commission, Records of Intelligence Party 3, Simla, 1887.

(DANIEL BALLAND)

DOŠMANZĪĀRĪ, name of two Lor tribes in southern Persia, the Došmanzīārī-e Mamasanī and the Došmanzīārī-e Kūhgīlūya.

The Došmanzīārī-e Mamasanī were one of the four principal components of the Mamasanī tribal confederation. They were greatly weakened in the power struggle following the execution of their chief, Moḥammad-Reżā Khan, in 1256/1840 (de Bode, p. 269). By the early 1900s they had already settled in what is today the *dehestān* of Došmanzīārī, southeast of Fahlīān in the subprovince of Kāzerūn in western Fārs (Field, p. 224). According to Gustave Demorgny (p. 127), the tribe comprised about 1,500 families in 1331/1913, a figure repeated by Maḥmūd Kayhān (*Jogrāfīā* II, p. 90). Henry Field (p. 224) was informed that in 1335/1918 the tribe had consisted of some 2,000 families, but he noted that this figure was probably exaggerated. According to Persian army files, in 1337 Š./1958 the tribe comprised the following clans (*tīras*): Serenjelāk (300 families), Baḵšī (300 families), Maḥmūdī (300 families), Tīrtājī (300 families), Kolāhsīāh (200 families), Tawakkolī (200 families), Ḥasanī (200 families), Harāyjānī (300 families), Mašāyeḵ (300 families), Ardešīrī (100 families), Rūdbālī (200 families), and Bābā Šams-al-Dīnī (150 families).

The Došmanzīārī-e Kūhgīlūya were one of the four components of the Čahār Bonīča tribal confederation, which also included the Boir Aḥmadī (q.v.), Čorām, and Novī. Their leader at the time of Nāder Shah (1148-60/1736-47), Moḥammad Khan Goštāsbī, was head of the entire confederation. He built an impressive residence for himself in the village of Dehdašt, 4 km northeast of Qalʿa-ye Kalāt, the main tribal center and today capital of the *dehestān* of Došmanzīārī northeast of Behbahān in the governorate of Kūhgīlūya in western Fārs (Fasāʾī, II, pp. 273-74). Ḥājī Mīrzā Ḥasan Fasāʾī estimated (II, p. 273) the tribe at no more than 400 families in the early 1890s, Kayhān at about 700 in 1311 Š./1932 (*Jogrāfīā* II, p. 89), Maḥmūd Bāvar at about 500 in 1324 Š./1945 (p. 107), Manūčehr Żarrābī at about 1,200 in 1340 Š./1961 (p. 302), Hūšang Kešāvarz at about

1,840 in 1347 Š./1968 (p. 1), and Sāzmān-e omūr-e ʿašāyer at about 2,150 in 1360 Š./1981 (cf. Afšār Sīstānī, p. 595). Many of these Došmanzīārī have remained nomadic, 1,057 families according to a recent survey (Sāzmān-e barnāma). Their summer quarters (*yeylāq*) are in the mountainous regions of Jowkār, Reven, Dālven and Gol-Aspīd, their winter quarters (*qešlāq*) around Ābrīz, Bīdanjār, Rūd-e Šūr, Zīrnā, Qalʿa-ye Kalāt, and Qalʿa-ye Rāk (Afšār Sīstānī, pp. 595-96). The settled tribesmen are scattered in villages throughout the *dehestān*. The tribe is divided into four subtribes: the Elyāsī, Bāvar(-e) Dīnārī, Sādāt, and Novī. The Elyāsī comprise the clans of Šīr-Moḥammadī, Raʾīs, Goštāsbī, Ḵᵛāja, Kolī, and Šāh-Ḥosaynī; the Bāvar Dīnārī the clans of Qalandarī, Būyrī, Šayḵ-ʿĀlī, and Solṭān ʿAlī; the Sādāt the clans of Sādāt-e ʿEsmāʿīlī, Sādāt-e ʿAbbāsī, Sādāt-e Mašhadī, Sādāt-e Kordlī, and Sādāt-e ʿAlāʾī (Afšār Sīstānī, p. 594).

Bibliography: (For cited works not found in this bibliography and for abbreviations found here, see "Short References.") Ī. Afšar Sīstānī, *Īlhā, čādornešīnān wa ṭawāyef-e ʿašāyerī-e Īrān* I, Tehran, 1336 Š./1987. M. Bāvar, *Kūhgīlūya wa īlāt-e ān*, Gačsārān, 1324 Š./1945. C. A. de Bode, *Travels in Luristan and Arabistan* I, London, 1845. G. Demorgny, "Les réformes administratives en Perse. Les tribus du Fars," *RMM* 22, 1913, pp. 116. H. Field, *Contributions to the Anthropology of Iran*, Chicago, 1939. H. Kešāvarz, *Barrasī-e ejtemāʿī wa eqṭesādī-e Došmanzīārī*, Tehran, 1347 Š./1968. Persian army files at Tehran, consulted in 1337 Š./1958. Sāzmān-e barnāma wa Būdja-ye ostān-e Kūhgīlūya *sāl-e 1362 šamsī*, Tehran, 1362 Š./1983. Sāzmān-e omūr-e ʿašāyer, *Gozāreš*, Tehran, 1360 Š./1981. M. Żarrābī, "Ṭawāyef-e Kūhgīlūya," *FIZ* 9, 1340 Š./1961, pp. 278-302.

(PIERRE OBERLING)

DŌST MOḤAMMAD KHAN (b. Qandahār December 1792, d. Herat, 21 Ḏu'l-ḥejja 1279/9 June 1863), first ruler (1242-55/1826-39, 1259-79/1842-63) of the Bārakzay/Moḥammadzay dynasty of Afghanistan. He was the eleventh son of Sardār Pāyenda Khan (Sarfarāz Khan), chief of the Bārakzay clan, who was put to death by Shah Zamān Sadōzī (1208-15/1793-1800) in 1214/1799. Dōst Moḥammad Khan was raised by his Qezelbāš mother, from the Persian tribe of Sīāh Manṣūr and reportedly Pāyenda Khan's favorite wife, though not of noble stock. Later, when ʿAbd-al-Majīd Khan, a cousin of Dōst Moḥammad Khan, forcibly married her, Dōst Moḥammad Khan came under the tutelage of his eldest brother, Sardār Fatḥ Khan, vizier during the second reign of Shah Maḥmūd Sadōzī (1215-18/1800-03, 1224-34/1809-18; Fayż Moḥammad, pp. 75-88; Mohan Lal, I, pp. 11-36).

Dōst Moḥammad Khan first achieved distinction as an aide to his brother and then as governor of Kūhestān. While with Fatḥ Khan on campaign in Herat in 1232/1817 he was sent to seize the assets of a local notable named Ḥājī Fērūz-al-Dīn. Much innocent blood was spilled, and some members of the harem were assaulted by Dōst Moḥammad Khan's party. Fearing retaliation by his brother and Shah Maḥmūd, both of whom had great respect for Ḥājī Fērūz-al-Dīn, Dōst Moḥammad Khan fled to Kashmir. Sardār Fatḥ Khan captured Herat and was preparing to launch an attack on Persia, but his success alarmed Shah Maḥmūd and his son Kāmrān, and the latter immediately set out for Herat from Qandahār. After an uneasy coexistence lasting three months Kāmrān blinded Fatḥ Khan, whose brothers vowed to avenge him. Dōst Moḥammad Khan and two brothers, Sardār Yār Moḥammad Khan and Sardār Pīr Moḥammad Khan, left Kashmir for Kabul, entering it unopposed in 1234/1819. Shah Maḥmūd and Kāmrān decided to recapture the city, taking with them the blinded vizier, Fatḥ Khan; on the way, in Sayyedābād, Kāmrān murdered him, however. Dōst Moḥammad Khan then went out to intercept the forces of Shah Maḥmūd and his son, who fled without a battle. Kabul came under the control of Sardār Moḥammad ʿAẓīm Khan, the second most senior brother of Dōst Moḥammad Khan, who became governor of Ḡaznī. Dōst Moḥammad Khan dreamed of ruling all Afghanistan, however, a dream that he never relinquished. When Moḥammad ʿAẓīm Khan died in 1238/1822-23 his son Sardār Ḥabīb-Allāh Khan took control of Kabul but was later defeated by Dōst Moḥammad Khan, who also, with the help of the Qezelbāš of Kabul, repelled the challenge of another brother, Sardār Solṭān Moḥammad Khan. Dōst Moḥammad Khan took effective control of the city in 1242/1826 (Fayż Moḥammad, pp. 88-108; Mohan Lal, I, pp. 90-150).

After Dōst Moḥammad Khan established himself in Kabul he began to extend his rule throughout Afghanistan. He took Ḡaznī and defeated Shah Šojāʿ-al-Dawla Sadōzī in Qandahār but failed to restore Afghan sovereignty over Peshawar in 1250/1834 and again in 1253/1837. He adopted the title *amīr-al-moʾmenīn* (commander of the faithful) in 1254/1838 and waged what he claimed was *jehād* (holy war) against the Sikhs in Send. The following verse was inscribed on the first coinage that he issued, in 1254/1838: "Amīr Dōst Moḥammad resolved to wage *jehād* / And to mint coins, may God grant him victory." From that time on he was known as Amīr-e Kabīr, despite a three-year interruption in his rule. In 1255/1839, with the help of British forces, he was ousted from Kabul, and Shah Šojāʿ-al-Dawla was installed as ruler. After some attempts to regain his throne Dōst Moḥammad Khan surrendered to the British government and was exiled to India. The tumultuous period between his dethronement and his return to Kabul as amir in 1258/1842 is known as the First Anglo-Afghan War (see ANGLO-AFGHAN WARS i).

It was during his second reign that Dōst Moḥammad

Khan was able to bring all of Afghanistan under his direct control, with the exception of Peshawar and Kashmir, which have remained separate. He conquered Bāmīān and Hazārajāt in 1266/1849, naming his son Moḥammad Akram Khan as governor. During an expedition to Turkestan in 1271/1854 Balḵ, Maymana, and Šebergān were subjugated, and Prince Moḥammad Afżal Khan was appointed governor there. The amir extended his rule over Qandahār after the death, in 1272/1855, of his brother Sardār Kohandel Khan, ruler of that region. Dōst Moḥammad Khan's last campaign resulted in the conquest of Herat, but he died there of natural causes in 1279/1863 (Fayż Moḥammad, pp. 121-222; Mohan Lal, II, passim; Reštīā, pp. 52-160).

Amir Dōst Moḥammad Khan was the first to bring the region that today constitutes Afghanistan under the control, occasionally tenuous, of a single central government. It could thus be argued that he laid the foundations of the modern Afghan state, which was developed by his descendants. He managed to rule Afghanistan by playing one segment of society against another. Unruly tribes were forcibly crushed. The chiefs of the Ḡelzī, the main rivals of the Bārakzī, were especially harshly treated, though overall Dōst Moḥammad Khan can be considered merciful in the treatment of his adversaries. He allied himself with Shiʿites, particularly the Qezelbāš and Hazāra tribes, and made use of them in his military and civil administrations. Marriage was another political instrument that he used effectively; at the time of his death he had sixteen wives. The result of these alliances was a great number of offspring, twenty-seven sons and twenty-five daughters at his death, the cause of much discord among the Moḥammadzī. Three of his sons ruled in Afghanistan as amirs: Šēr ʿAlī Khan (1280-82/1863-65, 1285-97/1868-79), Moḥammad Afżal Khan (1283-84/1866-67), and Moḥammad Aʿẓam Khan (1284-85/1867-68). Other noteworthy sons were Moḥammad Akbar Khan, Ḡolām Ḥaydar Khan, and Moḥammad Amīn Khan (Fayż Moḥammad, pp. 230-51; Gregorian, pp. 73-81; Mohan Lal, II, passim).

See also AFGHANISTAN x, xi; DORRĀNĪ.

Bibliography: Fayż Moḥammad Kāteb, *Serāj-al-tawārīḵ* I, Kabul, 1331/1913. V. Gregorian, *The Emergence of Modern Afghanistan*, Stanford, Calif., 1969, pp. 73-81. J. Harlan, *Central Asia. Personal Narrative of General Josiah Harlan, 1832-1841*, London, 1939. K. A. Haye, "Amir Dost Muhammad Khan Barakzai," *Proceedings of the Pakistan Historical Conference* 2, 1952, pp. 235-44. Mīrzā Yaʿqūb ʿAlī Ḵāftī, *Pādšāhān-e mota'aḵḵer-e Afḡānestān* I, Kabul, 1334/1916, pp. 7-79. Mohan Lal, *Life of the Amir, Dost Mohammad Khan of Kabul*, 2 vols., London, 1846; repr. Karachi, 1978. S. Q. Reštīā, *Afḡānestān dar qarn-e nōzdāh*, Kabul, 1346/1928, pp. 44-168.

(AMIN H. TARZI)

DOTĀR, long-necked lute of the *tanbūr* family, usually with two strings (*do tār*). Several different types are current in the area between Turkey and Central Asia, sometimes with other names (generally derived from the word *tanbūr*). The principal feature is the pear-shaped sound box attached to a neck that is longer than the box and faced with a wooden soundboard. *Dotār*s can be classified in several different types.

The Central Asian *dotār* is the largest (total length ca. 125 cm) and is equipped with two silken strings; the box is made of wooden strips glued together (Plate XXXV). It is tuned in fifths, in fourths, and sometimes in unison. Its sonority is grave and noble, and it is as suitable for accompanying popular songs as for solos and interpretation of the classical repertoire (e.g., Šaš maqām, Oniki muqam).

The *dotār* of Khorasan (in the broad sense) is narrower and shorter (total length ca. 100-10 cm); it was formerly strung with silk or gut, materials that in the 20th century have been supplanted by steel. It is tuned in fifths or fourths. The box is carved from a single mulberry log, and the neck is often fitted with metallic frets, sometimes of silver. This *dotār* is played by the Turkman, Karakalpaks, Turks, Kurds, and Persians, as well as the Afghans, of Khorasan (Plate XXXVI). It is the favored instrument of the troubadours (*baḵšī*, q.v.) and is also played as a solo instrument. It has a very light, brilliant timbre, and the technique of playing it is based on ornamentation, basically a very rapid tremolo. Several subcategories can be distinguished, corresponding to the various ethnic traditions in the region (Baily and During). A close variation is the Kurdish and Lorī *tanbūr*, the sharp cord of which has recently been doubled (Plate XXXVI).

The sound box and neck of the *dotār* (or *dombra*) used in the popular music of Tajikistan are carved from a single piece of apricot wood. There are no frets, and the gut (or nylon) strings are no more than 60 cm long, the total length of the instrument being 75 cm (Sakata, p. 72). In contrast to the other types, its sounding board is of poplar wood, rather than mulberry.

The *dotār* of Herat has undergone certain recent modifications. The gut strings have often been replaced by metal ones, and a third string has been added. In the 1960s, under the influence of Indian instruments, strings for resonance and a drone bass were added, which led to a change in the technique of playing (with a metal pick) and to a change in proportions (Baily, pp. 31-33).

The musical function of the *dotār* determines its status. In the province of Herat it has been relegated to the array of rustic instruments, but in Persian Khorasan it retains its former nobility, especially in Torbat-e Jām, one of the great musical centers of the region. It is often richly decorated with inlays, marquetry of bone and horn, and silver niello.

Despite differences in proportions, sonority, and

PLATE XXXV

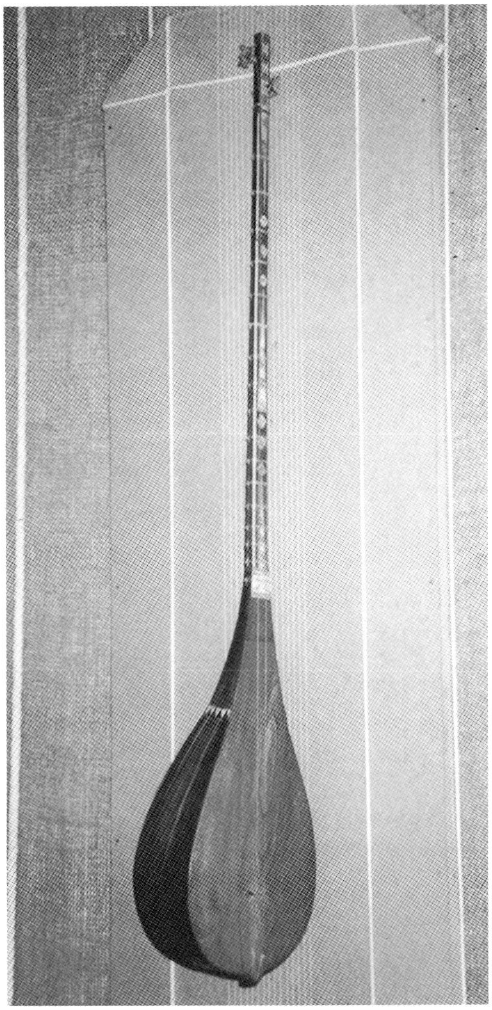

Dotār from Bukhara. Photograph J. During.

PLATE XXXVI

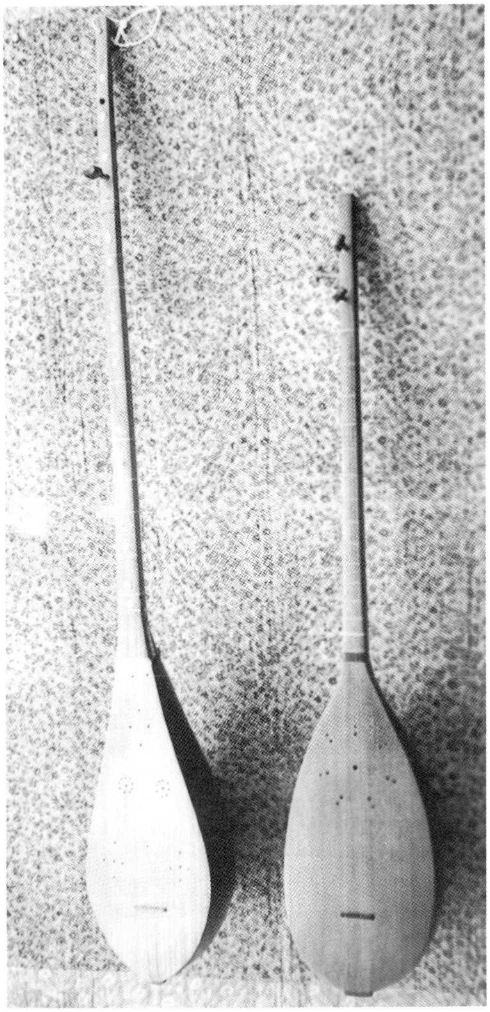

Left: *Dotār* from Afghanistan. Right: Kurdish *tanbūr* from Khorasan. Photograph J. During.

manufacture, all the *dotār*s (except the modern Afghan instrument) and many other *tanbūr*s and *dombra*s share one common feature: When played the two strings are plucked simultaneously in a single movement of the entire hand, including the index finger and one or several other fingers, without a plectrum or metal sheath, in such a way that the accented notes are sounded from high to low. This basic technique has been refined to varying degrees, incorporating different kinetic-rhythmic patterns and fingerings and reaching a consummation in the Tajik-Uzbek tradition.

The term *dotār* does not appear in early texts, but it is probable that this same instrument was described under the term *tanbūr*. In the 14th century Marāḡī (1367 Š./1988, pp. 200-01) described a two-string *tanbūr* that was tuned in fourths and equipped with ten frets (*dasātīn*, q.v.), producing the Pythagorean scale based on limma and comma; he doubtless drew his description from Ṣafī-al-Dīn Ormavī. Marāḡī also described two other two-string *tanbūr*s (the *torkī* and the *šervānī*).

It may be supposed that the original *tanbūr*, which, with the *ʿūd*, occupied the central position in early musicological writings (especially those of Farābī, q.v.), gave rise to variations with three or more strings, called *tanbūr*, *setār*, *čahārtār*, and so on and that the two-string type was then distinguished by the more popular term *dotār* (or *dombra*).

This type of instrument is rarely represented in pre-Islamic art, though there are innumerable representations of the *barbaṭ* (q.v.; Karomatov, Meskeris, and Vyzgo, pp. 92-93) and later of the *ʿūd*. To judge from medieval miniature paintings, the *dotār* or two-stringed *tanbūr* lost its place among the classical instruments of Persia for a considerable period, doubtless supplanted by the *setār*, which is represented frequently.

Bibliography: J. Baily, *Music of Afghanistan. Professional Musicians in the City of Herat*, Cambridge, 1988. Idem and J. During, "Dutār," in S. Sadie, ed., *The New Grove Dictionary of Musical Instruments*, London, 1984, s.v. Dotār. *Central Asia. The Masters of the Dotār* (compact disk with booklet), Geneva, 1993. F. M. Karomatov, V. A. Meskeris, and T. S. Vyzgo, *Mittelasien*, Musikgeschichte in Bildern 2/9, Leipzig, 1987. ʿAbd-al-Qāder b. Ḡaybī Marāḡī, *Maqāṣed al-alḥān*, ed. T. Bineš, Tehran, 2536=1356 Š./1977. Idem, *Jāmeʿ al-alḥān*, ed. T. Bineš, Tehran, 1367 Š./1988. L. Sakata, "Afghan Musical Instruments. The Dambura," *Afghanistant Journal* 5/4, 1978, pp. 170-52. Idem, "Afghan Musical Instruments. The Dotar and Tanbur," *Afghanistan Journal* 5/4, 1978b, pp. 150-52.

(JEAN DURING)

DOZĀLA, kind of flute consisting of two parallel pipes pierced with holes and fitted with a removable vibrating mouthpiece made by cutting a U-shaped incision into a thin reed. The principle of this instrument is used in different forms in the Mediterranean and western Islamic world (in instruments like the *mezmār*, *motbej*, *mejwez*, and *čefta*, Turk. *çifte*) and as far east as Central Asia (as in the *qošney*). It is attested from as early as the New Kingdom in Egypt (Hickmann, p. 121). The principle of the *dozāla* flute was described by Farābī (p. 272) in the 10th century but not in its doubled form. On the other hand, it is not mentioned in later works and is never represented in miniatures.

In Persia today the *dozāla* (sometimes called *zammāra*, *qošma*, or *joft ney*) is played in Khorasan, Azerbaijan, and Kurdistan. Most examples are made of reeds, but the Kurdish examples are made of eagle bone set in wax, each pierced with six holes; they are 16-17 cm long without the vibrating reed, which is 5 cm long. The *dozāla* is played according to the principle of circular breathing, which produces an uninterrupted sound. It is used only in popular music, except in the Tajik-Uzbek tradition, in which the technique of playing it has been refined to the needs of art music.

Bibliography: J. During, "Dozāle," in S. Sadie, ed., *The New Grove's Dictionary of Musical Instruments*, London, 1984, s.v. Idem, "Mezmār," in S. Sadie, ed., *The New Grove's Dictionary of Musical Instruments*, London, 1984, s.v. Farābī, *Ketāb al-mūsīqī al-kabīr*, tr. R. d'Erlanger as *La musiqe arabe* I, Paris, 1930. H. Hickmann, *Ägypten*, Musikgeschichte in Bildern 2/1, Leipzig, 1961.

(JEAN DURING)

DOZDĀB. See ZĀHEDĀN.

DOZY, REINHARD PETRUS ANNE (b. Leiden, 21 February 1820, d. Leiden, 29 April 1883), Dutch orientalist renowned especially as a lexicographer of Arabic and a historian of Muslim Andalusia. He began his studies at Leiden University in 1834 with H. E. Weijers (1804-40), who introduced him to Arabic philology through the rich Warner collection of manuscripts in the university library. Dozy received a prize from the Royal Institute (later the Royal Dutch Academy of Sciences) for his first publication (*Dictionnaire détaillé des noms des vêtements chez les Arabes*, Leiden, 1843). In 1845 he visited libraries in Germany and England, which inspired him to launch a series of editions of Arabic texts, for which he started international fund raising. Through this initiative he gave a new impetus to all oriental studies in the Netherlands. It led to the publication of many Arabic, Persian, and Turkish texts by Dutch scholars during the second half of the 19th century. Simultaneously Dozy, together with M. J. de Goeje (q.v.) and others, embarked on the cataloguing of the oriental manuscripts in Leiden (*Catalogus Codicum Orientalium Bibliothecae Academiae Lugduni Batavorum*, 6 vols., Leiden, 1851-77). Description of the Persian manuscripts in this catalogue was entrusted to Piet de Jong and M. T. Houtsma. In 1850 Dozy was appointed to the chair of medieval history at Leiden University, and from that time on he devoted most of his attention to his pioneering study of Muslim Spain (*Histoire des Musulmans d'Espagne*, Leiden, 1861). During his later years, however, he returned to lexicographical research, which resulted in his two-volume *Supplément aux dictionnaires arabes* (Leiden, 1881), in which he assembled words and meanings found in medieval texts but missing from indigenous Arabic dictionaries. It is of lasting importance for knowledge of postclassical Arabic and includes many Persian loanwords and other materials for Persian lexicography.

Bibliography: J. Brugman, "Dozy, a Scholarly Life According to Plan," in W. Otterspeer, ed., *Leiden Oriental Connections 1850-1940*, Leiden, 1989, pp. 62-81.

(J. T. P. DE BRUIJN)

DRAGON. See AŽDAHĀ.

DRAINAGE, the carrying away of excess surface water through runoff in permanent or intermittent streams. On Persian territory, because of seasonal variations in the climate, surface runoff also varies considerably at different times and in different places.

There are basically three sources of water for drainage: rainfall remaining after evapotranspiration and infiltration into the ground, water released from storage, and water held in aquifers. Persia is characterized by generally scanty but seasonal patterns of precipitation. Owing to the geomorphology of the country, precipitation is markedly higher on the periphery, especially in the northern and western regions, whereas the central, eastern, and southeastern areas are extremely arid (see DESERT), with extremely limited surface runoff through only a few stream systems. Permanent streams can be found especially along the northern slopes of the Alborz (q.v.) mountain range, which receive considerable rainfall during most of the year, though there is a distinct peak during the winter months; these mountains block the movement of moist air masses to the south. Farther to the west, in the Zagros mountain range, surplus water is collected in extended stream systems and discharged through exterior drainage, that is, ultimately into the world oceanic system. Most of Persian territory, on the other hand, is characterized by endorheic basins, that is, by interior drainage.

Persia can be divided into four main drainage regions (for terminology, see Krinsley, p. 32): the Caspian region, the Lake Urmia region, the Persian Gulf region, and the interior (Table 38). The Caspian drainage region encompasses a narrow zone along the southern coast of the Caspian Sea. Of several hundred mainly minor tributaries only a few catchment areas have longer extensions, for example, the Safīdrūd in the southwestern part of the Caspian basin and the Atrak river in the Dašt-e Gorgān. Although classified as an exterior drainage basin, the Caspian is itself endorheic, with no outlet to the oceans. Lake Urmia is also endorheic, forming a body of water 4,000 km^2 in the spring but varying with the seasonal discharge rates of its main tributaries, the Talḵarūd and the Zarrīnarūd. The Persian Gulf system is by far the most important single drainage system of Persia. Covering more than 350,000 km^2, it drains the western Zagros mountains, with its large watersheds, characterized by extremely complex geomorphology (Oberlander, 1965); snows are retained in the valleys through the winter, and in the spring permanent streams from the Zagros may carry a volume of runoff ten times greater than the minimum discharge in late summer (Oberlander, *Camb. Hist. Iran*, p. 267). The Kārūn river, one of the largest in Persia, and some of its tributaries are examples of such annual variation. The interior drainage region is the largest in Persia; because of its particularly complex geomorphic structure, it can be subdivided into eleven watersheds, some of which extend across national boundaries (Table 39). The watersheds themselves are further divided into basins, for example, the Dašt-e Kavīr and Dašt-e Lūt (Table 39, Figure 27). Almost all the Persian watersheds are drained primarily by intermittent streams; only the Zāyandarūd, the Helmand, and some smaller streams are permanent, discharging their waters into intermittent lakes or interior basins.

Altogether the Persian drainage system reflects the ecological differentiation of the country (see ECOLOGY). Surface runoff is used to a large degree for irrigation, and peripheral regions are thus more favored. Agriculture in Gīlān and Māzandarān, as well as in Ḵūzestān and in the garden belt around Isfahan, would be impossible without the availability of sufficient surface water. Surface drainage is also important for the development of hydroelectric power. Only permanent streams and their catchment areas in the Alborz and the western Zagros receive enough runoff to provide suitable sites for construction of dams for energy and irrigation. One important aspect of drainage systems, that is, navigability, is totally absent from Persian streams, with the esception of the lower sections of the Arvandrūd up to Ḵorramšahr.

See also ĀBYĀRĪ; AGRICULTURE.

Table 38
DRAINAGE REGIONS OF PERSIA

Region	Area (in km^2)	Percentage of Total Land Surface
Caspian	193,161	11.9
Lake Urmia	54,747	3.4
Persian Gulf	335,864	21.9
Interior	1,626,520	61.8
Total	2,210,292	100.0

Source: Krinsley, p. 448 table 1.

Table 39
WATERSHEDS OF THE INTERIOR DRAINAGE REGION

Watershed	Area (in km^2)	Percentage of Regional Land Surface
Qom	92,332	9.0
Dāmġān	19,863	1.9
Dašt-e Kavīr	200,747	19.6
Mašhad	43,496	4.3
Bejestān highlands	91,349[a]	8.9
Dašt-e Lūt	166,160	16.2
Sīstān	90,813	8.9
Jāz Mūrīān	75,193	7.4
Yazd	105,291	10.3
Isfahan	97,802	9.6
Zagros mountains	39,702	3.9
Total	1,022,748	100.0

a. Does not include 10,600 km^2 in Afghanistan.
Source: Krinsley, p. 448 table 1.

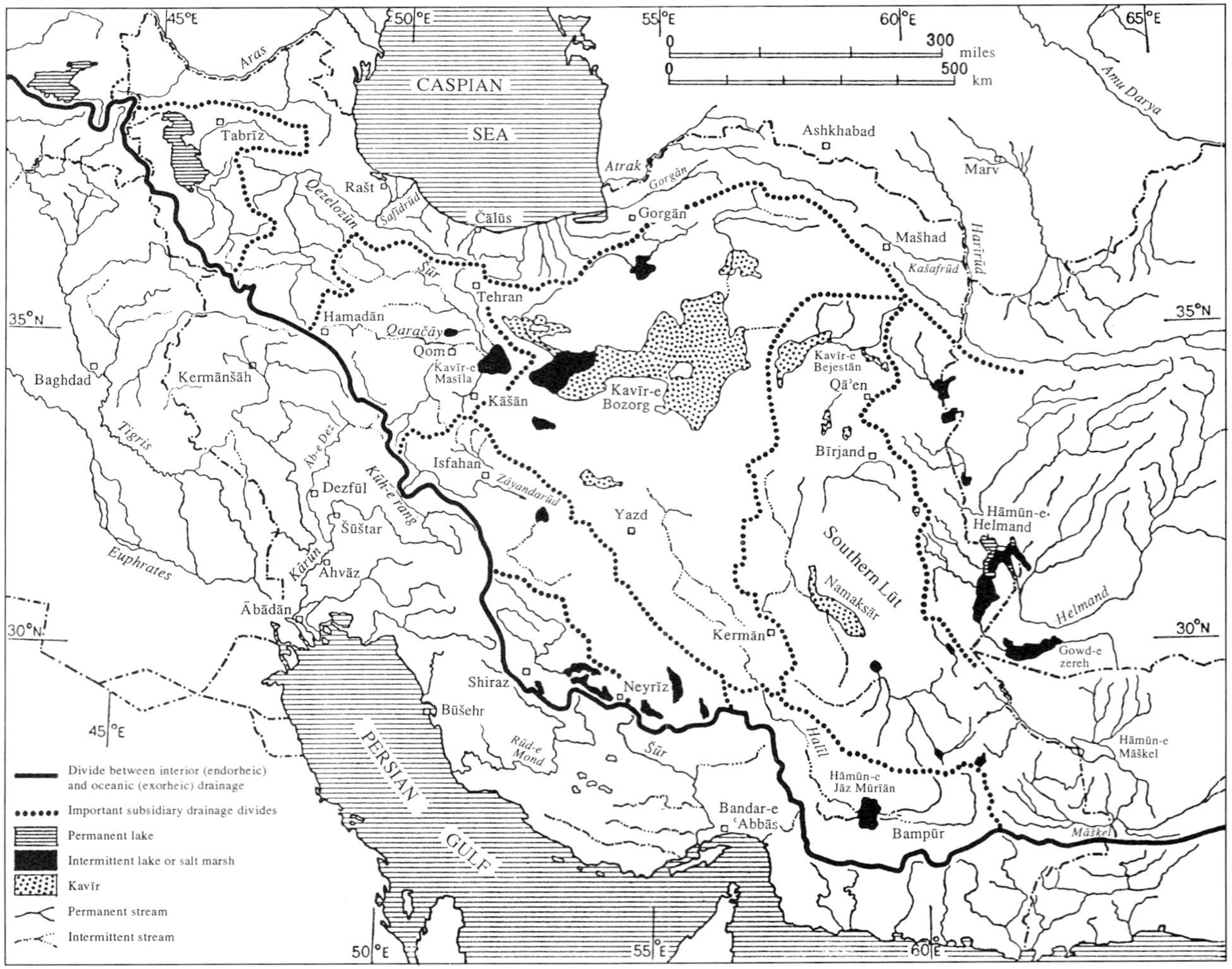

Figure 27. The hydrography of Persia. After Oberlander, *Camb. Hist. Iran*, p. 270 fig. 87.

Bibliography: (For cited works not found in this bibliography, see "Short References."). D. B. Carter, C. W. Thornthwaite, and J. R. Mather, "Three Water Balance Maps of Southwest Asia," Laboratory of Climatology, Publications in Climatology 11/1, Centerton, N.J., 1958. D. B. Krinsley, *A Geomorphological and Climatological Study of the Playas of Iran*, U.S. Dept. of the Interior, Geological Survey, Washington, D.C., 1970. T. M. Oberlander, *The Zagros Streams*, Syracuse, N.Y., 1965. Idem, "Hydrography," in *Camb. Hist. Iran* I, pp. 264-79.

(ECKART EHLERS)

DRAMA, in formal Western terms a relatively new art form in Persia, though various types of dramatic performance, including religious plays and humorous satirical skits, have long been a part of Persian religious and folk tradition. *Taʿzīya* (q.v.) is a form of Persian religious drama that developed in the 16th century and commemorates the suffering of Shiʿite martyrs; it is usually presented in verse and is the only traditional form of Persian drama in which written texts are used (Yarshater, 1979). Traditional comic entertainments are usually presented on special occasions like weddings; they include *baqqāl-bāzī* (q.v.), *rūḥawżī* or *taḵt-ḥawżī* (usually performed over a courtyard pool covered with boards to make a stage), *sīāh-bāzī* (in which the central comedian appears in blackface), *ḵīāl-bāzī* (shadow play), *ḵayma-šab-bāzī* (marionette show), and *ʿarūsak-bāzī* or *ʿarūsak-e pošt-e parda* (puppet show). Most of these plays have stock characters and involve domestic quarrels, lovers' conflicts, and relations between rich and poor. Traditionally they were not written down. Professional performers followed standard plots, improvising the dialogue from performance to performance. These performances were often used as vehicles for social criticism, particularly of high officials, the rich, and clerics (Beyżāʾī, 1344 Š./1965a, pp. 175-98; Malekpūr, I, pp. 269-78; see COFFEEHOUSE; DALQAK).

Despite government censorship, religious restrictions, and public infatuation with newer forms of entertainment (Kapuscinski, 1988; Ghanoonparvar and Green, p. x) both traditional religious drama and comedies have continued to evolve to the present day, and modern Persian dramatists have drawn on them for their own works.

Beginnings of Persian drama. Modern Persian drama had its beginnings in the 19th century, when educated Persians became acquainted with Western theater. Students sent to Europe to acquire knowledge of Western technology returned with a taste for other aspects of Western culture, including theater. Initially Western plays were translated into Persian and performed for the royal family and courtiers in the first Western-style theater in Persia, on the site of the later Dār al-fonūn (q.v.). Molière's *Le misanthrope* was the first of them, translated as *Gozāreš-e mardomgorīz* by Mīrzā Ḥabīb Eṣfahānī (Istanbul, 1286/1869) with much liberty taken in the rendering of the characters' names and personalities, so that the play was more Persian than French (Browne, *Lit. Hist. Persia* IV, pp. 327-28).

In addition to direct adaptations, Persian drama was also indirectly influenced by Western theater through the works of the reform-minded civil servant and writer Mīrzā Fatḥ-ʿAlī Āḵūndzāda (q.v.), whose plays, written in Azeri Turkish and published in a newspaper in the Caucasus in 1851-56 (tr. M. J. Qarāčadāḡī as *Tamṯīlāt* "The comedies," Tehran, 1349 Š./1970; Malekpūr, I, pp. 136-37), stimulated Mīrzā Āqā Tabrīzī (q.v.) to try his hand at writing plays in Persian. Three of Tabrīzī's four plays, written in the 1870s, were initially published erroneously under the name of Mīrzā Malkom Khan Nāẓem-al-Dawla in Berlin in 1301 Š./1922; later all four were published under the title *Čahār tīātr* (Four plays) in Tabrīz (ed. M.-B. Moʾmenī, 1355 Š./1976). They deal essentially with government corruption and other social ills. In *Sargoḏašt-e Ašraf Ḵān* (The story of Ašraf Khan) Tabrīzī focused on the practice of bribery in the Qajar government. The protagonist is obliged to pay bribes to every official, from the king down to the groom, in order to continue in his post as governor of Ḵūzestān, where he expects to be able to extort a great deal more from his subjects. In *Ṭarīqa-ye ḥokūmat-e Zamān Ḵān-e Borūjerdī* (The method of government of Zamān Khan Borūjerdī) Tabrīzī examined the manner in which local governors coerced the people into paying bribes, and in *Ḥekāyat-e Karbalāʾ raftan-e Šāhqolī Mīrzā* (The story of Šāhqolī Mīrzā's pilgrimage to Karbalāʾ) he addressed the family relationships of the Qajar rulers, also governed by greed and extortion. Finally, in *Ḥekāyat-e ʿāšeq šodan-e Āqā Hāšem* (The story of Āqā Hāšem's falling in love) he attacked the importance placed on wealth and the prevalence of superstitious beliefs and practices like fortune-telling.

These plays are not entirely successful, owing to Tabrīzī's unfamiliarity with the formal aspects of Western drama; although some have been staged in recent decades, they remain important primarily to historians of Persian drama. In particular their themes are significant, comparable to those embodied in contemporary fiction and poetry. Indeed, Persian drama has remained primarily a vehicle of social criticism since these early attempts, though later playwrights created more sophisticated and experimental works.

From these initial attempts interest in Western-style drama began to grow in Persia in the later decades of Qajar rule. A national theater was established in Tehran in 1329/1911, and a number of playwrights began experimenting with musical comedies and dramas in verse. Among the most prominent were Mortażāqolī Khan Fekrī Eršād Moʾayyad-al-Mamālek (1288-1337/1868-1917), who wrote five plays: *Sīrūs-e kabīr* (Cyrus the Great; Tehran, 1332/1914), *Sargoḏašt-e yek rūz-nāmanegār* (The story of a journalist; Tehran, 1332/1914), *Ešq-e pīrī* (Love in old age; Tehran, 1332/1914), *Ḥokkām-e qadīm, ḥokkām-e jadīd* (Old rulers, new rulers; Tehran, 1334/1916), and *Se rūz dar mālīya* (Three days in the department of finance; Tehran, 1334/1916). Although Fekrī Eršād's plays are technically superior to those of Tabrīzī, they are focused on similar themes. For example, in *Ḥokkām-e qadīm, ḥokkām-e jadīd* he dealt with government corruption after the Constitutional Revolution (q.v.) in ways reminiscent of *Sargoḏašt-e Ašraf Ḵān*. Other contemporary playwrights included Aḥmad Maḥmūdī Kamāl-al-Wezāra (1292-1349=1309 Š./1875-1930), author of *Ḥājī Rīāʾī Ḵān yā Tārtūf-e šarqī* (Ḥājī Rīāʾī Khan, or the oriental Tartuffe; Tehran, 1336/1918) and *Ostād Nowrūz-e pīnadūz* (Master Nowrūz the cobbler; Tehran, 1337/1919); Mīrzāda Ešqī (1272-1344=1303 Š./1893-1925), who wrote *Rastākīz-e salāṭīn-e Īrān* (The resurrection of Persian kings; Tehran, 1334/1916); and Abu'l-Ḥasan Forūḡī (1301-79=1338 Š./1883-1959), author of *Šīdūš o Nāhīd* (Šīdūš and Nāhīd; Tehran, 1339/1921).

Under the Pahlavis. When Reżā Shah came to power in the early 1920s his efforts to westernize Persia included new support for Western-style theater. Nonetheless, the government strictly censored plays deemed critical of the regime (see CENSORSHIP; CINEMA iv). Only those with historical and nationalistic themes, often glorifying pre-Islamic Persia, were supported and promoted by the government. Still, some dramatists of the period satirized the new preoccupation with the glorious Persian past and the shah's efforts to establish a modern military force. Examples include Saʿīd Nafīsī's *Āḵerīn yādgār-e Nāder Šāh* (The last memento of Nāder Shah; Tehran, 1305 Š./1926), set during the war with Russia and revolving around the character of an old soldier from Nāder Shah's army, who dwells on memories of past victories, oblivious to the passage of time and Persian defeat. Another example is Ḥasan Moqaddam's popular *Jaʿfar Ḵān az farang āmada* (Jaʿfar Khan has returned from Europe; Tehran, 1301 Š./1922; 2nd ed., Tehran, 1357 Š./1978), one of the earliest plays to focus on the comic confusion arising from encounters between Persian and European cultures. Moqaddam mocked the Persian penchant for superficial imitation of Westerners, on one hand, and rampant superstition and decadent ideas in Persian society, on the other. Ḏabīḥ Behrūz (1309-81=1350 Š./1891-1971) wrote the farce *Jījak-ʿAlīšāh* (Tehran, 1302 Š./1923), ʿAlī Naṣr (1311-81=1340 Š./1893-1962) wrote *Arūsī-e Ḥosayn Āqā* (Ḥosayn Āqā's wedding), and Ṣādeq Hedāyat (1321-70=1330 Š./1903-51) wrote *Parvīn doḵtar-e Sāsān* (Parvīn, daughter of Sāsān; Tehran, 1309 Š./1930; 2nd ed., Tehran, 1333 Š./1954), a sentimental and nationalistic play.

After Reżā Shah's abdication in 1320 Š./1941 there was a decade of relative freedom of expression. Various new political parties and groups used drama as a propaganda tool, and once again playwrights turned to sociopolitical themes. In 1326 Š./1947 ʿAbd-al-Ḥosayn Nūšīn (1280-1350 Š./1901-71), a graduate of the Conservatoire de Toulouse and an active member of the communist Tudeh party, gathered a number of professional actors to stage translations of Western dramas in Tehran. The initial success of two such plays persuaded a wealthy merchant to invest in the Ferdowsī theater, in which additional translations of Western dramas directed by Nūšīn were staged. The first production, a translation of J. B. Priestley's *An Inspector Calls* (*Mostanṭeq*), met with great success and was followed without interruption by other translated plays until 15 Bahman 1327 Š./4 February 1948, when the Tudeh party was banned and its leading members, including Nūšīn, jailed after an attempt on the shah's life. Colleagues of Nūšīn carried on his work, however, in 1330 Š./1951by opening the Saʿdī theater, in which translations of Western plays continued to be staged with success. The Saʿdī theater was burned in the coup d'etat of 1332 Š./1953 (q.v.) and some of its actors jailed (Oskūʾī, pp. 185-222). With the fall of the government of Moḥammad Moṣaddeq, martial law and strict censorship were imposed, and Persian dramatists focused their attention of necessity on artistic aspects of drama and production techniques. Even though a large number of theaters and theater groups were established in the two decades after the abdication, few critically significant plays were written in Persia, at first because of political confusion and then because of censorship. Nevertheless, this period afforded Persian playwrights and audiences the opportunity to become more acquainted with Western theater. Instrumental in this spread was the arrival of Patrick Quinby of Bowdoin College in Maine to teach drama at the University of Tehran. Classic European plays, including examples by Ben Jonson, William Shakespeare, and Molière, and modern plays by George Bernard Shaw and Jean-Paul Sartre were translated and staged.

By the early 1960s a younger generation of playwrights had appeared on the scene, ushering in a new era in Persian drama, which lasted two decades, until the Islamic Revolution of 1357 Š./1978. Ḡolām-Ḥosayn Sāʿedī, Bahrām Beyżāʾī, ʿAlī Naṣīrīān, Bahman Forsī, Bīžan Mofīd, Esmāʿīl Ḵalaj, Parvīz Ṣayyād, Arsalān Pūryā, ʿAbbās Naʿlbandīān, Parvīz Kārdān, Saʿīd Solṭānpūr, Maḥmūd Dawlatābādī, Moḥsen Yalfānī, Ebrāhīm Makkī, Nāder Ebrāhīmī, Moṣṭafā Raḥīmī, Nāṣer Šāhīnpar, and Nāṣer Īrānī contributed to the flourishing of this art form in Persia. As a literary form drama also appealed to writers of fiction like Ṣādeq Čūbak and poets like Aḥmad Šāmlū. On the other hand, dramatists like Sāʿedī and Beyżāʾī also wrote fiction and made films (Ghanoonparvar and Green, pp. ix-xxix; Kapuscinski,

1987, pp. 392, 397; see CINEMA ii).

Important factors in the development of Persian drama in this period were the continued translation and production of European, American, and occasionally Arab and Asian plays. They ranged from the works of classical Greek dramatists like Sophocles and Euripides to Shakespeare, Johann Wolfgang von Goethe, and Friedrich Schiller. More significant, however, were the many modern plays by Shaw, Oscar Wilde, Henrik Ibsen, Nikolai Gogol, Anton Chekhov, Bertolt Brecht, Max Frisch, Friedrich Dürrenmatt, Samuel Beckett, Eugène Ionesco, Harold Pinter, John Osborne, Tennessee Williams, and Heinrich Böll.

This floruit of the drama reflected not only the relative novelty of the genre, with its potential for experimentation, but also the general intellectual climate in Persia, which was partly encouraged by the government of Moḥammad-Reżā Shah (1320-57 Š/1941-78). The Ministry of culture and arts (Wezārat-e farhang o honar) established an acting school; a division of dramatic arts was added to the Faculty of fine arts at Tehran University; and Persian national television sponsored a theater workshop that produced plays for television and the stage. Beginning in 1346 Š./1967 the government also sponsored the Shiraz arts festival, which became an international forum for experimental theater, attracting Western playwrights and theater groups. Nevertheless, the official attitude toward some notable Persian dramatists and their works was ambivalent. Although the government sought to promote Persian drama to international status, it was unable to tolerate explicit or even subtle criticism of the regime; many works were strictly censored. Such measures, usually coupled with harassment and incarceration of writers, resulted in frequent bans on publication and production of such plays as *Amūzgarān* by Yalfānī and *Ḥasanak* by Solṭānpūr. It was perhaps partly for this reason that Persian dramatists, like Persian poets and fiction writers, took refuge in often enigmatic symbolism (see Ghanoonparvar) that had to be decoded by the audience.

Fascinated by this situation, playwrights became even more interested in innovative techniques. Forsī represented a generation of younger playwrights who seemed to focus their work on experimentation with metaphor, symbol, and language. The language and form of his first play, *Goldān* (The vase; Tehran, 1340 Š./1961), attracted the attention of the critics. More advanced examples of this school include the work of Naʿlbandīān, whose first play, *Pažūheš-ī žarf wa setorg wa now dar sangvārahā-ye dawra-ye bīst-o-panjom-e zamīn-šenāsī* (Profound, strong, and new research on the fossils of the twenty-fifth geological era; Tehran, 1347 Š./1968), which was performed at the Shiraz arts festival in 1347 Š./1968, alluded to various Persian and non-Persian traditions that even many educated Persians found difficult to decipher. Even the works of more popular playwrights like Sāʿedī, who wrote under the pseudonym Gowhar Morād, were often characterized by similar approaches. For example, in *Māh-e ʿasal* (Honeymoon; Tehran, 1355 Š./1976), an allegory in which Persia in the 1970s is presented as a police state, a newlywed couple is forced by a government agency to accept an oddly dressed old woman as a permanent guest in their apartment. Before long their personal relationship is under the absolute control of the woman and the agency she represents. Through a series of arbitrary actions and nonsensical speeches the couple has been totally brainwashed by the end of the play. Not all of Sāʿedī's plays belong to the theater of the absurd, however; in fact, despite his use of symbols to convey several levels of meaning, he is often described as a realist, probably because he set his works in everyday urban and rural situations and dealt with topical issues. He was a particular master of dialogue reflecting all walks of Persian life, which enhanced the realistic character of his work.

The works of Beyżāʾī, whose book *Nemāyeš dar Īrān*, is the definitive work on the history of Persian theater since the mid-1960s, are also characterized by language, style, and symbolism that require deciphering by a sophisticated audience. *Čahār ṣandūq* (Four boxes; Tehran, 1358 Š./1979), written in 1346 Š./1967, is a study of how a society manufactures its own dictators. Four characters appear on stage as four colors: yellow, green, red, and black, symbolizing intellectuals, clergy, merchants, and laborers respectively. At the beginning, in order to safeguard the interests of his own class, each contributes to the making of a scarecrow as guardian against some unknown external threat. Soon, however, the scarecrow comes to life and is able to break their alliance and force them to build four boxes, in which each is confined. This confinement is, however, self-imposed, for each character is more afraid of the others than of the despotic scarecrow. Beyżāʾī, who is also a successful filmmaker, is known for mythical and historical characters caught in ontological dilemmas. In his plays he succeeds in presenting universal philosophical ideas in fully dramatic terms. His language is poetic, in both formal and colloquial Persian; in the latter he achieves this effect by means of rapid rhythmic exchanges among characters.

Other playwrights of the period relied on more traditional forms. Beyżāʾī himself used such forms in many of his plays. Naṣīrīān, a well-known actor, writer, and director in both theater and films, relied on them extensively. His *Sīāh* (Black) and *Bongāh-e teʾātrāl. Nemāyeš-e tak̲t-ḥawżī dar do bak̲š*, (The theatrical agency. A *tak̲t-ḥawżī* show in two parts, 1357 Š./1978) are modern adaptations of *rūḥawżī* and *tak̲t-ḥawżī*. For subject matter he often turned to old Persian tales, as in *Bolbol-e sargašta* (The wandering nightingale; 2nd ed., Tehran, 1354 Š./1975), a reworking of a popular children's story. Nevertheless, his guiding themes were contemporary social issues, particularly the clash between traditional and newer ways of life.

Mofīd also drew on Persian tales. His *Šahr-e qeṣṣa* (City of tales; Tehran, 1348 Š./1969), perhaps the most popular of all Persian plays, was written in traditional rhythmic style that resulted in a kind of musical drama. Although it seems at first glance to have been written for children, its main audience, it is in fact a parable about contemporary sociopolitical issues. Akbar Rādī, one of the realist playwrights, set his works in Gīlān province and on the Caspian shores. The critically acclaimed *Ofūl* (The descent; Tehran, 1343 Š./1964) and *Ṣayyādān* (The fishermen; Tehran, 1348 Š./1969; 2nd ed., 1355 Š./1976) established his reputation. In the former he focused on the conflict between generations: A young engineer tries to introduce changes on the estate of his wealthy and old-fashioned father-in-law. In *Ṣayyādān* a group of fishermen rise up against a large fishing firm but are defeated. In *Marg dar pāʾīz* (Death in the autumn; Tehran, 1349 Š./1970) Rādī dealt with the disintegration and destruction of the way of life of an old farmer and his family, symbolized by the departure of the farmer's son, who fears being drafted into the army, and by the death of the farmer's only horse, which could have helped him work in his old age. Rādī's incorporation of colloquial Persian, especially the dialects of the northern provinces, may also help to preserve threatened aspects of local culture. Ḵalaj, whose generally realistic plays are focused on the urban poor, addicts, pimps, and prostitutes, achieved his effects with minimal dialogue. A typical play is *Pātūğ* (The hangout; Tehran, 1350 Š./1971), set in a teashop in the infamous red-light district of Tehran before the Islamic Revolution. Ḥosayn, a tough, is in love with the prostitute Zarī and wishes to marry her, but she is unfaithful; at the end of the play he learns that she is having a relationship with one of his old friends. Ḵalaj wrote other plays on similar themes. For example, in *Goldūna Ḵānom* (Mrs. Goldūna; Tehran, 1350 Š./1971) he experimented with techniques perhaps inspired by the cinema. In the published editions of his plays he used a peculiar transcription of Persian in which silent letters are omitted and a single letter stands for several letters that have the same sound in Persian. They are thus difficult to read. His focus on a segment of Persian society with which most of his audience was not familiar was a form of implied social criticism.

Under the Islamic Republic. Political allegories and plays implicitly criticizing the Persian government and social institutions, as well as dramas dealing with the influence of alien, particularly Western, cultures and social ills like poverty, prostitution, and drug addiction, remained popular in the Persian theater until the Revolution. As government censorship and control diminished in the late 1970s and before new censorship measures were imposed after the Revolution there was a brief period during which enigmatic symbolism gave way to more direct political expression in the Persian theater, sometimes by less well-known but politically active playwrights. Maḥmūd Rahbar, in *Qānūn* (The law; Tehran, 1356 Š./1977) wrote about a prominent senator near the end of the Pahlavi period who finds himself in jail after having served the regime faithfully for many years. His dialogue with a general gave Rahbar the opportunity to expose unethical practices of the government. Another example is Farāmarz Ṭālebī's *Pādegān dar šāmgāh* (The barracks in the evening; Tehran, 1356 Š./1977); it deals with military brainwashing of simple young villagers, which turns them into killers of demonstrators. During this period Solṭānpūr wrote his popular *ʿAbbās Āqā, kārgar-e Īrān nāsīonāl* (ʿAbbās Āqā, worker for the Īrān nāsīonāl company), which was reportedly performed in the streets. The period of comparative freedom of expression was very brief, however, and ended with the triumph of the Islamic Revolution; Solṭānpūr was executed for leftist activities in the spring of 1360 Š./1981, and censorship was reimposed on all the Persian arts.

Even before the Islamic Revolution Persian religious authorities and devout people had strongly disapproved of Western-style theater, which, like the cinema, was regarded as sinful. Particularly among older generations few such people ever visited a theater (Malekpūr, I, p. 309). Naturally, after the Revolution many assumed that at least a temporary suspension of dramatic performances would ensue, a view seemingly confirmed by the harsh treatment of individuals connected with the performing arts and the flight abroad of many Persian playwrights, actors, and directors (Sāʿedī, 1363 Š./1984). In fact, in the months before the Islamic government was able to consolidate its power a variety of literary journals and other works were published without censorship, but this freedom did not last long. With the start of the war with Iraq in 1359 Š./1980 and the growing power of the Islamic regime to impose internal controls, various official and semiofficial government agencies began to review materials written and produced for the theater. Contrary to expectations, however, the government found dramatic performances useful propaganda tools, and the expected taboo on drama never fully materialized. Nevertheless, the official attitude has been ambivalent, perhaps reflecting the continuing struggle between conservative religious groups and more liberal factions. The former have remained suspicious of modern art as a manifestation of anti-Islamic and Western cultural influence (Ashraf).

On the whole the 1980s should be considered a transitional period in Persian drama. Two factors contributed to heightening the changes in this genre beyond those in other literary forms. First, the sociopolitical content of plays was transformed, owing to alterations in the political system and, more important, a fundamental transformation in the general values and social attitudes of the Persian people. Second, in the staging of plays official attitudes on issues like dress restrictions for both men and women and the interaction between male and female performers dictated changes in playwriting itself. At the same time more conventional storytelling techniques replaced the experimentation of the 1960s and 1970s and helped to attract general audiences. Experimentation remains important in the Persian theater, however.

Postrevolutionary Persian drama can be classified in two general categories: plays written in Persia under Islamic rule and plays written by Persians living abroad. In Persia government restrictions have promoted direct propaganda in support of the regime and its objectives, as well as mandating adherence to the new social mores. Incentives are provided by various government agencies, especially the Ministry of culture and Islamic guidance (Wezārat-e farhang o eršād-e eslāmī), that finance theater groups throughout Persia and organize theater festivals. As a result dozens of amateur and professional groups have appeared, and there are many young playwrights. In 1367 Š./1988, for instance, it was reported that the number of theatrical groups had reached 100. In January 1989 some of them presented fifty-two plays at the Fajr theater festival in Tehran (*Keyhān-e farhangī* 9, Bahman 1366 Š./February 1988; 10, Esfand 1366 Š./March 1988; 11, Bahman 1367 Š./February 1989). A number of journals and other publications regularly include reports on the theater and interviews with younger playwrights and directors.

Most dramatists continue on the course established in the 1960s and 1970s (*Ketāb-e ṣobḥ*, spring 1368 Š./1989; summer and fall 1368 Š./1989; see also issues of *Faṣl-nāma-ye teʾātr* and *Nemāyeš*, two journals devoted to theater and drama). For example, a play by Salmān Fārsī Ṣāleḥzehī, *Āb, bād, ḵāk* (Water, wind, land; Tehran, 1368 Š./1989), written in 1366 Š./1987, deals with conflicts between peasants and landlords. It opens with a peasant uprising, but the landlords, represented as torchbearers, though driven from the villages, have not given up and return to set the wheat fields on fire. Sacrifice by the village headman and other villagers is required to protect the crops and prevent the return of the old order. This theme was not new in Persian drama, having been treated by Sāʿedī and other earlier dramatists. Formally Ṣāleḥzehī made use of symbolic actions in several scenes that are at times reminiscent of the work of Beyżāʾī. Another example is *Šegerd-e āḵer* (The last technique; Tehran, 1368 Š./1989) by Ḥamīd-Reżā Aʿẓam, written in 1365 Š./1986. It is a work of propaganda in the service of the regime and its role in the war with Iraq. The audience, however, may not recognize it as a religious play or one with Islamic overtones. Aʿẓam chose as his protagonist a traditional *naqqāl*, who has told tales from the *Šāh-nāma* in teahouses all his life and acquired a great reputation. In the course of his career he has trained a number of apprentices. As the story unfolds through a performance by him and one of the apprentices, the audience expects to hear stories from the Persian epic tradition, particularly the battle of Rostam and Sohrāb. But the old *naqqāl*, having become aware of the heroism of the young people fighting in the war with Iraq, tells their story instead, in the traditional language of performance. More important, he decides to experience heroism and the battlefield at first hand, the "last technique" of the title, which in effect he teaches to the younger *naqqāl* and the audience.

Among playwrights who had already gained a reputation before the Revolution and remained active under Islamic rule, Beyżāʾī and Rādī are the most prominent. Beyżāʾī, still a prolific playwright, director, and filmmaker, wrote and produced *Marg-e Yazdegerd* (The death of Yazdegerd) in 1358 Š./1979). The play is his deconstruction and reconstruction of the murder of Yazdegerd III by a miller in 651, revealing a thematic parallel between the shah's departure from Persia and the story of the last Sasanian king, who escaped from his capital in hopes of raising an army to return and fight the Arab invaders of Persia. More directly topical is Rādī's *Āhesta bā gol-e sorḵ* (Slowly with the rose), produced in 1367 Š./1988 (Tehran, 1368 Š./1989). It is a psychological and sociological study of a Persian family, focusing on the different value systems underlying the imminent external and internal changes in Persian society. Another noteworthy play is *Man be bāḡ-e ʿerfān* (I to the garden of mysticism) by Parī Ṣāberī, highlighting the mystical dimensions of the life and work of the poet Sohrāb Sepehrī (1307-59 Š./1928-80). It was staged in an abstract form with dance and music and received negative reviews from critics in Persia, but it was a significant box-office success, owing to public interest in Sepehrī.

Although restrictions on expression of antiestablishment sentiments and themes that do not conform to the religious and revolutionary guidelines laid down by the Islamic government have promoted a kind of Persian propaganda theater, the absence of such restrictions outside Persia has resulted in quite another sort of propaganda theater. Persian dramatists have continued to write in exile, particularly in Europe and the United States. The most renowned among them is Sāʿedī, who until his death in 1364 Š./1985 continued to write prolifically and published a number of plays, beside contributing articles and short stories to the journal *Alefbā*, which he published in France. His best-known plays written in exile are *Pardadārān-e āʾīna-afrūz* (The mirror-polishing storytellers) and *Otello dar sarzamīn-e ʿajāyeb* (Othello in wonderland), published posthumously in a single volume (Paris, 1364 Š./1986). The first is an antiwar play in which Sāʿedī also made use of the *naqqālī* tradition. It is performed by three *pardadār*s (storytellers) with large canvases on which scenes from the war with Iraq are depicted; various portions of the canvases are lit in turn to accompany the narrations. In the first act two *pardadārs* tell the general story of modern warfare and destruction; in the second, a black comedy, the third tells of two families whose sons are martyred in the fighting with Iraq. Although the tone is satirical, the antiwar message is clear throughout. *Otello dar sarzamīn-e ʿajāyeb* is even more satirical. Sāʿedī took advantage of the Islamic regime's stated support for the arts, particularly the theater, to create a farce about the production of Shakespeare's *Othello* in Persia, where it is transformed into a propaganda tool for the revolutionary government and its opposition to the superpowers. Under official supervision and watched by a revolutionary guard armed with a machine gun, the director and actors are forced to transform the character of Othello into a revolutionary fighter representing the downtrodden and Iago into a counterrevolutionary. Even Shakespeare, sometimes called Brother Shakespeare and confused by the official in charge with the character of Othello in the play, is thought to have been a Muslim who lived, anachronistically, in pre-Islamic times. The government agents also force the female actors to cover themselves from head to foot in full Islamic dress and even object to Othello's speaking affectionately to Desdemona.

A second well-known figure in the Persian theater in exile is Ṣayyād, who, in addition to his very active role in the production of several films, has also written and staged a number of plays in the United States, including *Moḥākama-ye sīnemā Reks* (The Rex cinema trial) and *K̲ar* (Jackass). The former deals with the deaths of about 400 people in a fire at the Rex cinema in Ābādān in 1356 Š./1977 and the question of who was responsible for the arson. In the staged trial of several officials of the shah's regime, accused by the new Islamic government of the crime, Ṣayyād presents a skeptical view of justice in Islamic Persia, intimating that the actual perpetrators of the crime are the judges and prosecutors in a farcical kangaroo court. *K̲ar* deals with the issue of imposed conformity in Persian society; the actors wear masks to represent this conformity. At the end of the play some of the characters reject uniformity of thought, but all turn into jackasses with no consciousness even of their own metamorphosis.

Yalfānī has published a number of plays in France in recent years. He is essentially interested in psychological states and underlying tensions in relationships between individuals and chooses for his characters mainly young Persian revolutionaries. He generally begins with a stereotypical revolutionary and then focuses on him as an individual, providing the audience with a subtler view and an opportunity for self-examination, both as revolutionaries and as human beings. In *Molāqāt* (Visit; Paris, 1369 Š./1990), written in 1358 Š./1979, a husband and wife who appear to be truly in love reveal when she visits him in jail that their commitment to their cause is more important to them than their relationship. *Qawītar az šab* (Stronger than the night; Paris, 1369 Š./1990), set in the Islamic Republic, is about a group of revolutionaries in a "safe house"; for some of them being revolutionaries has become a way of life, justifying even their escape into exile, while others are simply caught in a web from which they are trying to free themselves. In *Bonbast* (Dead end; Paris, 1369 Š./1990) a former revolutionary, who has broken with the cause in order to live a normal life, comes to the realization that he will suffer from hallucinations and guilt for the rest of his life.

From this brief survey of modern Persian drama some general conclusions can be drawn. As in the immediate prerevolutionary period, the themes of Persian drama continue to be predominantly sociopolitical. In prerevolutionary Persia antiestablishment art became an unofficial institution, often tolerated by the regime if the message was not openly stated, but in the 1980s sociopolitical concerns were more overt, perhaps because most plays published and staged in Persia must receive a seal of approval from the Islamic regime and in some way further its ideology. At the same time Persian drama in exile is often overtly political because playwrights are free from government censorship. Since the Islamic Revolution plays written both in Persia and abroad have been affected by the religious attitudes and terminology of the regime. Playwrights working in Persia must consciously practice self-censorship and restrict their work in terms of the dress, actions, and appearance of their characters, in order to receive permission for performance.

See also THEATER; articles on individual dramatists.

Bibliography: M.-ʿA. Afrāšta, *Nemāyeš-nāmahā, taʿzīahā, safar-nāma*, Tehran, 1360 Š./1981. Āryanpūr, *Az Ṣabā tā Nīmā* I, pp. 322-66; II, pp. 288-315. A. Ashraf, "Theocracy and Charisma. New Men of Power in Iran," *International Journal of Politics, Culture, and Society* 4, 1990, pp. 113-52. W. O. Beeman, "A Full Arena. The Development and Meaning of Popular Performance Traditions in Iran," in M. E. Bonine and N. R. Keddie, eds., *Continuity and Change in Modern Iran*, Albany, N.Y., 1981a, pp. 285-305. Idem, "Why Do They Laugh? An Interactional Approach to Humor in Traditional Iranian Improvisatory Theater," *Journal of American Folklore* 94, 1981b, pp. 506-26. Idem, *Culture, Performance and Communication in Iran*, Tokyo, 1982. B. Beyżāʾī, *Matarsakhā dar šab wa ʿarūsakhā*, Tehran, 1341 Š./1962. Idem, *Se nemāyeš-nāma-ye ʿarūsakī*, Tehran, 1342 Š./1963. Idem, *Nemāyeš dar Īrān*, Tehran, 1344 Š./1965a. Idem, *Pahlavān Akbar mīmīrad*, 3rd ed., Tehran, 1344 Š./1965b. Idem, *Donyā-ye maṭbūʿatī-e Āqā-ye Asrārī*, Tehran, 1345 Š./1966. Idem, *Majles-e dīvān-e Balk̲*, Tehran, 1347 Š./1968. Idem, *Haštomīn safar-e Sendbād*, Tehran, 1350 Š./1971. Idem, *Mīrāt̲*, Tehran, 1356 Š./1977. Idem, *Fatḥ-*

nāma-ye Kalāt, Tehran, 1362 Š./1983. *The Cambridge Guide to World Theatre*, ed. M. Banham, Cambridge, 1988, pp. 664-76. P. Chelkowski, ed., *Taʿziyeh. Ritual and Drama in Iran*, New York, 1979.

H. Dabashi, *Theater of the Diaspora*, Costa Mesa, Calif., 1993. M. Dawlatābādī, *Tangnā*, Tehran, 1349 Š./1970. Idem, *Qoqnūs*, Tehran, 1361 Š./1982. N. Ebrāhīmī, *Ejāza hast Āqā-ye Berešt?* Tehran, 1349 Š./1970. Idem, *Wosʿat-e maʿnā-ye enteẓār*, Tehran, 1355 Š./1976. B. Forsī, *Čūb-e zīr-e baḡal*, Tehran, 1341 Š./1962. Idem, *Mūš*, Tehran, 1342 Š./1963. Idem, *Ṣedā-ye šekastan*, Tehran, 1350 Š./1971. F. Gaffary, "Evolution of Rituals and Theater in Iran," *Iranian Studies* 17/4, 1984, pp. 361-89. Idem, "Persian Secular Theater," in *McGraw-Hill Encyclopedia of World Drama* III, New York, 1972, pp. 58-65. M. R. Ghanoonparvar, "Literary Ambiguity," in *Prophets of Doom. Literature as a Socio-Political Phenomenon in Modern Iran*, Lanham, Md., 1984, pp. 149-77. Idem and J. Green, eds., *Iranian Drama. An Anthology*, Costa Mesa, Calif., 1989. H. Gūrān, *Kūšešhā-ye nāfarjām. Sayrī dar ṣad sāl tīātr-e Īrān*, Tehran, 1360 Š./1981. Ṣ. Hedāyat, *Māzīār*. Tehran, 1312 Š./1933. N. Īrānī, *Se nemāyeš-nāmā-ye kesālatāvar*, Tehran, 1347 Š./1968. Idem, *Qatl*, Tehran, 1358 Š./1969. Idem, *Dar pāyān*, Tehran, 1350 Š./1971. Idem, *Ḥofra*, Tehran, 1356 Š./1977. A.-Q. Jannatī-ʿAṭāʾī, *Bonyād-e nemāyeš dar Īrān*, 2nd ed., Tehran, 1356 Š./1977. G. Kapuscinski, *Modern Persian Drama. An Anthology*, Lanham, Md., 1987. Idem, "Modern Persian Drama," in E. Yarshater, ed., *Persian Literature*, New York, 1988, pp. 381-402.

J. Malekpūr, *Adabīyāt-e nemāyešī dar Īrān*, 2 vols., Tehran, 1363 Š./1984. B. Mofīd, *Māh wa palang*, Tehran, 1348 Š./1969. Idem, *Jān-neṯār*, Tehran, 1352 Š./1973. ʿA. Naʿlbandīān, *Agar Fost yak kam maʿrefat ba ḵarj dāda būd*, Tehran, 1349 Š./1970a. Idem, *Ṣandalī kenār-e panjera begozārīm wa benešīnīm wa be šab-e derāz-e tārīk-e ḵāmūš-e sard-e bīābān negāh konīm*, Tehran, 1349 Š./1970b. Idem, *Qeṣṣa-ye ḡarīb-e safar-e Šād Šīn-e Šangūl bā dīār-e ādamkošān wa amardān wa jodāmīān wa dozdān wa dīvānagān wa rūspīān wa kāfkešān*, Tehran, 1351 Š./1972. ʿA. Naṣīrīān, *Lūna-ye šaḡāl*, Tehran, 1348 Š./1969. Idem, *Hālū wa čand nemāyeš-nāma-ye dīgar*, Tehran, 1355 Š./1976. M. Oskūʾī, *Pažūhešī dar tārīḵ-e teātr-e Īrān*, Moscow, 1370 Š./1991. A. Rādī, *Erṯīya-ye īrānī*, Tehran, 1347 Š./1968. Idem, *Dar meh beḵᵛān*, Tehran, 1354 Š./1975. Idem, *Az pošt-e šīšahā*, 2nd ed., Tehran, 1355 Š./1976. E. Rahbar, *Mehr-abānān wa se nemāyeš-nāmā-ye dīgar*, Tehran, 1348 Š./1969. M. Raḥīmī, *Tīyāla*, Tehran, 1353 Š./1974. Idem, *Ānāhītā*, 3rd ed., Tehran, 1354 Š./1975. Idem, *Dast bālā-ye dast*, Tehran, 1357 Š./1978. M. Rezvani, *Le théâtre et la danse en Iran*, Paris, 1962. Ḡ.-Ḥ Sāʿedī, *Bāmhā wa zīr-e bāmhā*, Tehran, 1340 Š./1961. Idem, *Dah lāl-bāzī*, Tehran, 1342 Š./1963. Idem, *Behtarīn bābā-ye donyā*, Tehran, 1344 Š./1965a. Idem, *Čūb be-dasthā-ye varazīl*, Tehran, 1344 Š./1965b. Idem, *Panj nemāyeš-nāma az enqelāb-e mašrūṭīyat*, Tehran, 1345 Š./1966. Idem, *Ḵāna-rowšanī*, Tehran, 1346 Š./1967. Idem, *Dīkta wa zāwīa*, Tehran, 1347 Š./1968. Idem, *Parvārbandān*, Tehran, 1348 Š./1969. Idem, *Vāy bar maḡlūb*, Tehran, 1351 Š./1972. Idem, *Kārbāfakha dar sangar*, Tehran, 1353 Š./1974. Idem, *Āy-e bī kolāh, āy-e bā kolāh*, Tehran, 1357 Š./1978a. Idem, "Nemāyeš dar ḥokūmat-e nemāyešī," *Alefbā* 5, 1363 Š./1984, pp. 197-211. M. Sepānlū, "Nemāyeš-nāma-nevīsī," in *Nevīsandegān-e pīšrow-e Īrān*, Tehran, 1362 Š./1983. M. Yalfānī, *Mard-e motowasseṭ wa ṭelā*, Tehran, 1352 Š./1974. E. Yarshater, "Modern Literary Idiom," in E. Yarshater, ed., *Iran Faces the Seventies*, New York, 1971, pp. 284-320. Idem, "Taʿzīya and Pre-Islamic Mourning Rites in Iran," in P. J. Chelkowski, ed., *Taʿziyeh. Ritual and Drama in Iran*, New York, 1979, pp. 88-94.

(M. R. GHANOONPARVAR)

DRANGIANA (or Zarangiana), territory around Lake Hāmūn (q.v.) and the Helmand river in modern Sīstān. The name of the country and its inhabitants is first attested as Old Persian *z-r-k* (i.e., Zranka) in the great Bīsotūn (q.v. iii) inscription of Darius I (q.v.; col. I l. 16), apparently the original name. This form is reflected in the Elamite (Sir-ra-an-qa and variants), Babylonian (Za-ra-an-ga), and Egyptian (*srng* or *srnḳ*) versions of the Achaemenid royal inscriptions, as well as in Greek Zarángai, Zarangaîoi, Zarangianḗ (Arrian; Isidore of Charax), and Sarángai (Herodotus) and in Latin Zarangae (Pliny). Instead of this original form, characterized by non-Persian *z* (perhaps from proto-IE. palatal * or * ʰ), in some Greek sources (chiefly those dependent upon the historians of Alexander the Great, q.v.) the perhaps hypercorrect Persianized variant (cf. Belardi, p. 183) with initial *d-*, *Dranka (or even *Dranga?), reflected in Greek Drángai, Drangḗ, Drangēnḗ, Drangi(a)nḗ (Ctesias; Polybius; Strabo; Diodorus; Ptolemy; Arrian; Stephanus Byzantius) and Latin Drangae, Drangiana, Drangiani (Curtius Rufus; Pliny; Ammianus Marcellinus; Justin) or Drancaeus (Valerius Flaccus, *Argonautica* 6.106, 6.507) occurs. Gherardo Gnoli (p. 43) has suggested that the form with initial *z-* attested in the royal inscriptions was the official one, which had first entered the administrative nomenclature of the Medes (p. 46), whereas the Persianized *d* form first appeared in the work of Ctesias, who lived at the royal court, and belonged exclusively to the spoken language. It is more likely, however, that Zranka is distinct from the many Median borrowings in Old Persian, as it does not conform to the customary use of the Median or Persian forms observed without exception in the different versions of the Bīsotūn inscription; it must thus be regarded as an East Iranian form that entered Old Persian directly.

The etymology of Zranka/*Dranka is far from clear. Whereas most scholars prefer a connection with Old Persian *drayah-* (Av. *zraiiah-*, Mid.Pers. *zrēh*, NPers. *daryā* "sea, lake") and, because of the location in the Hāmūn basin, have interpreted it as "sea land," that interpretation raises serious morphological problems; Georg Morgenstierne (p. 43) linked Zranka with New Persian *zarang* "mountain peak" (Bal. *d(ə)rəng* "precipice") and suggested that it may have been "originally the name of the mountain, which dominates the province: Kōh-i Khwāja." The ancient name Zranka lived on in the toponym Zarang (Ar. Zaranj), name of the medieval capital of Sīstān, now the ruins of Nād ʿAlī (Ball, pp. 189-90 no. 752).

According to Strabo, the northern part of Drangiana was bordered both on the north and the west by Aria, whereas most Drangian territory extended south of the Parapamisus and was bordered on the west by Carmania, on the south by Gedrosia, and on the east by Arachosia. Strabo also reported that the province formed a single tax district with Aria, information that applies only to Parthian times (11.10.1, 15.2.9). The land was characterized as rich in tin (Strabo, 15.2.10), and the inhabitants were said to imitate the Persian way of life but to have little wine. The most detailed description, though riddled with errors, is that of Ptolemy (6.19), according to whom Drangiana was bounded in the west and north by Aria, in the east by Arachosia, and in the south by Gedrosia; a river, supposedly a branch of the Arabis, flowed through it. Ptolemy also mentioned individual tribes living there: the Darandae near the Arian border, the Batrians near Arachosia, and the inhabitants of Tatakḗnē (or the like) between, perhaps reflecting the subdivision of Drangiana in Seleucid and Parthian times (cf. Tomaschek, col. 1666, correcting the first and third names to Drangae and Paraitakḗnē respectively). He listed a number of towns and villages, of which Prophthasía (cf. 8.25.8) and Ariáspē are known from other sources as well: Strabo (11.8.9, 15.2.8) and Pliny (*Historia Naturalis* 6.61) named Prophthasía, located on or near Lake Hāmūn on the network of major roads, and Stephanus Byzantius (s.v. Phráda) knew its pre-Alexandrian name Phráda; both this city and Ariáspē were mentioned as rich and illustrious by Ammianus Marcellinus (23.6.71). Isidore of Charax (*Mansiones Parthicae* 17) mentioned only Párin (to be emended to Zárin) and Korók among Drangian towns. From all these reports Paolo Daffinà (p. 30) concluded that in the Hellenistic period Drangiana was not restricted to the lower Helmand basin but extended northeast toward the Hindu Kush. Pliny listed the Zarangians among a large number of peoples living between the Caucasus and Bactria, side by side with the Drangians (*Historia Naturalis* 6.48, 6.94), obviously confusing information on a single people taken from different sources.

The Drangians were listed among the peoples ruled by the legendary King Ninus before the Achaemenids (Diodorus, 2.2.3, apud Ctesias in Jacoby, *Fragmente* IIIC, p. 422, fr. 1, par. 2.3). There is no evidence on the situation of the country during the Median period; it may well have belonged to the Median empire, but it may instead have belonged to an eastern Iranian state centered on Marv and Herat (Henning, pp. 42-43, based on Herodotus, 3.117.1). Herodotus, perhaps following Hecataeus, reported a large plain ringed by mountains and bordered by the Chorasmians, Hyrcanians, Parthians, Sarangians (Drangians), and Thamanaeans (surprisingly omitting the Arians); from it flowed the Akes (q.v.), perhaps the modern Harīrūd, which irrigated the fields of all these peoples before the Persian conquest. This plain may indeed be sought somewhere in Chorasmia (q.v.), Herat, or Drangiana/Sīstān, but "with the clues given it fits no more easily on a map than the Garden of Eden" (Cook, p. 195).

In Achaemenid royal inscriptions Drangiana is listed as a separate province, but its position varies; it was located either between Parthia and Aria (DB, DPe, and the restored portion of DSm), between Chorasmia and Arachosia (DNa, the restored portion of DSe, and the late tomb inscription A?P), or even, owing to an awkward rearrangement of the text, before Parthia and Aria and after Armenia (XPh). On the other hand, in Herodotus' tribute list (3.93.2) the Sarangians, Sagartians, Thamanaeans, Utians, Mycians (i.e., all the peoples living in the lands extending from the Iranian central desert through Baluchistan to the Persian Gulf), and neighboring islanders were included in the fourteenth tax district, required to pay the relatively high amount of 600 talents annually. In Xerxes' army the Sarangian contingent was led by Pherendátēs, son of Megabazus; the men were armed with Median bows and lances and wore brightly colored clothes and knee-high boots (Herodotus 7.67.1). Barsaḗntēs, satrap of Arachosia and Drangiana, was one of the accomplices of the usurper Bessos (q.v.) against the last Achaemenid king, Darius III (q.v.; Arrian 3.21.1; cf. Curtius Rufus, 6.6.36); the combination of these two provinces in a single satrapy cannot be dated exactly.

Alexander the Great came to the capital of Drangiana in pursuit of Bessos and his followers (Arrian, 3.25.8; cf. Diodorus, 17.78.4; Strabo, 15.2.10) in the winter of 330-29 B.C.E. and subdued the entire satrapy (Arrian, 3.28.1, 7.10.6, who used the forms Drángai and Zarángai or Zarangaîoi interchangeably; cf. Justin, 12.5.9). Early in the summer of 325 B.C.E. Alexander sent Craterus with part of the army from India via Arachosia, Drangiana, and Carmania (Arrian, 6.17.3; cf. Strabo, 15.2.5). At that time Stasanor of Soli was satrap of Aria and Drangiana, having succeeded one Arsames (Curtius Rufus, 8.3.17; Arrian, 6.27.3; cf. Justin, 13.4.22); his appointment was confirmed by Perdiccas after Alexander's death (Diodorus, 18.3.3). Unlike

Craterus Alexander himself made a dangerous march across the Gedrosian desert, ordering racing camels and pack animals sent to him in Carmania from "Parthia, Drangiana, Aria, and the other countries bordering on the desert" (Diodorus, 17.105.7). As part of the great mingling of Greco-Macedonian and Oriental customs and institutions initiated by Alexander, which culminated in the famous mass wedding ceremonies at Susa in 324 B.C.E., Zarangian, Bactrian, Sogdian, and Arachosian cavalry units were included in the royal horse guards (Arrian, 7.6.3).

In 321 B.C.E., when Antipater redistributed the satrapies, Stasander of Cyprus received Aria and Drangiana (Diodorus, 18.39.6, 19.14.7). According to Polybius (11.34.13), after the Greco-Bactrian king Euthydemus had subdued the Sogdians, Arachosians, Drangians, and Arians (Justin, 41.6.3), Antiochus III marched against him; he returned in the winter of 206-05 B.C.E., crossing Arachosia, the Erymanthus (i.e., the Etymand(r)us or Helmand) river, Drangiana, and Carmania in turn. Some time in the mid-2nd century B.C.E. Drangiana became part of the Arsacid empire under Mithridates I. Ammianus Marcellinus (23.6.14) incorrectly listed Drangiana, between the Paropamisus and Arachosia, as one of the provinces of the Sasanian empire.

Bibliography: (For abbreviations found here, see "Short References.") W. Ball, *Catalogue des sites archéologiques d'Afghanistan* I, Paris, 1982. W. Belardi, "Sul nome dell'Egitto nel persiano antico," *AI(U)ON*, Sezione linguistica 2, 1960, pp. 171-84. J. M. Cook, *The Persian Empire*, London, 1983. P. Daffinà, *L'immigrazione dei Sakā nella Drangiana*, Rome, 1967, esp. pp. 23 ff. G. Gnoli, *Ricerche storiche sul Sīstān antico*, Rome, 1967, esp. pp. 41 ff. W. B. Henning, *Zoroaster, Politician or Witch-Doctor?* Oxford, 1951. G. Morgenstierne, "Notes on Balochi Etymology," *NTS* 5, 1932, pp. 37-53. [W.] Tomaschek, "Drangai," in Pauly-Wissowa, V/2, cols. 1665-67.

(RÜDIGER SCHMITT)

DRÁPSAKA, Greek name of a Bactrian city in northern Afghanistan, the first town captured by Alexander the Great after crossing the Hindu Kush (Arrian, *Anabasis* 3.29.1). Shorter forms (< ancient Iranian *drafša-* "banner") include Dárapsa (Strabo, 11.11.2), Ádrapsa (Strabo, 15.2.10), Drépsa (Ptolemy, *Geography* 6.12.6, confusing its location with that of Marakanda-Samarkand, probably because the rivers flowing near them were both called Dargamánēs, designating the Qondūz river and the Dargom channel), and Drepsa (Ammianus Marcellinus, 23.6.59). The name also appears in the great foundation inscription from Surkh Kotal (Sork̲ Kotal; Ball, I, no. 1123; Harmatta, pp. 453-55) in the Bactrian form Lrafo, referring to the citadel where the "gods" (i.e., statues) were transported when the temple was temporarily abandoned during the 2nd century C.E.

Since Franz von Schwarz first made the suggestion in 1893 there has been a consensus that Drápsaka should be identified with the Bālā Ḥeṣār at Qondūz (Ball, I, pp. 222-23 no. 931; cf. Holt, p. 28 n. 67), which is the correct distance from Alexandria (q.v.) sub Caucaso (probably Begram) to correspond to the fifteen-day march mentioned by Strabo; an archeological survey (Gardin and Lyonnet, pp. 135-36) has revealed an Achaemenid occupation there. Nevertheless, two even larger fortified sites situated farther upstream should perhaps not be excluded, as they lie closer to Surkh Kotal: They are ʿAlīābād (with evidence of occupation from pre-Achaemenid times; Ball, I, p. 34 no. 29) and Qalʿa-ye Ḡūrī (near Surkh Kotal but still unsurveyed; Ball, I, p. 207 no. 846).

Bibliography: (For abbreviations found here, see "Short References.") W. Ball, *Archaeological Gazetteer of Afghanistan*, 2 vols., Paris, 1982. P. Bernard and H.-P. Francfort, *Études de géographie historique sur la plaine d'Aï Khanoum (Afghanistan)*, Paris, 1978, pp. 14-15, 75. J.-C. Gardin and B. Lyonnet, "La prospection archéologique de la Bactriane orientale (1974-1978). Premiers résultats," *Mesopotamia* 13-14, 1978-79, pp. 99-154. F. Grenet , in G. Lazard, F. Grenet, and C. de Lamberterie, "Notes bactriennes," *Stud. Ir.* 13, 1984, pp. 199-232, esp. pp. 205-207. J. Harmatta, "The Great Bactrian Inscription," *AAASH* 12, 1964, pp. 373-471. F. L. Holt, *Alexander the Great and Bactria. The Formation of a Greek Frontier in Central Asia*, Leiden, 1988. S. Mizuno and N. Odani, "Durman Tepe," in S. Mizuno, ed., *Durman Tepe and Lalma. Buddhist Sites in Afghanistan Surveyed in 1963-1965*, Kyoto, 1968, pp. 93-108, esp. p. 95. F. von Schwarz, *Alexander des Grossen Feldzüge in Turkestan*, Munich, 1893, p. 28. [W.] Tomaschek, "Darapsa," in Pauly-Wissowa, IV/2, col. 2152. Idem, "Drepsa," in Pauly-Wissowa V/2, cols. 1698-99.

(FRANTZ GRENET)

DRAWING, an art form primarily dependent on expressive line. The high quality of Persian drawings maintained from the late 13th to the early 20th century provides a clear indication that this art form was appreciated by the Persian cultural elite. All artists were trained in ateliers under an arduous apprenticeship system, absorbing through practice and emulation Persian artistic traditions and ideals.

There are two main categories of Persian drawings: preparatory or exploratory and finished works of art (Swietochowski and Babaie, p. 8). The first category includes underdrawings, the skeleton of all Persian painting, invisible in the final product (e.g., Swietochowski and Babaie, fig. 5); rare practice sketches filling every corner of paper scraps; drawings of figures or groups, animals, landscape and architectural elements that served as models for finished drawings or elements in compositions of varying complexity (e.g., Swietochowski and Babaie, fig. 15); preparatory drawings transferred to another surface by means of pouncing (Swietochowski and Babaie, fig. 3, no. 22; Atıl, fig. 60); and decorative drawings to be used as patterns on media other than paper: ceramics, textiles and costumes, leather, wood, and the like. A number of the last type survive in albums in the Topkapı Saray, Istanbul, and in the "Diez album" in the Staatsbibliothek, Berlin (e.g., Lentz and Lowry, no. 91). One of the Istanbul albums (ms. no. H 2153, fol. 98r) includes a report on the progress of work, believed to be in the hand of Jaʿfar Tabrīzī, director of the manuscript atelier (*ketāb-ḵāna*) of the Timurid prince Bāysonḡor (q.v.; d. 837/1433). Beside manuscripts the artists were preparing decorative drawings for a saddle, a book-binding, a chest, and tent poles, and one artist was busy exclusively with designs for binders, illuminators, tentmakers, and tilemakers (Thackston, p. 325). On the other hand, the finish and detail of some drawings are evidence that they were intended as works of art. They range from fully developed compositions that are the visual equivalent of paintings and are often embellished with restrained touches of color to seemingly spontaneous sketches executed for the artist's own pleasure, as a gift for a friend, or even in hopes of a sale. Often internal evidence alone is all that helps to distinguish these groups, but occasionally the artist inscribed his drawing with details of the circumstances in which he made it (Swietochowski and Babaie, pp. 18, 20).

The Il-khanid period. Any attempt at a summary of the history of Persian drawings is hindered by insufficient surviving examples, especially from the earlier periods, and insufficient information from surviving contemporary texts. Nevertheless, it seems that Persian drawing developed as an art form under the Il-khanids at the turn of the 14th century, when the first wave of Chinese influence manifested itself in Persian art (Ettinghausen, pp. 52-56, figs. 6-9). A painting style in which line is dominant and colors washed in emerged, as in two fragmentary manuscripts of Rašīd-al-Dīn's *Jāmeʿ al-tawārīḵ* of 706/1307 and 714/1314 (Rice; Gray, 1978), in marked contrast to an earlier style characterized by areas of flat, strong color. In Persia this early style and the new Chinese elements become integrated during the course of the 14th century, but the new emphasis on line gave impetus to an independent evolution of drawing.

A clue to the development of Persian drawing is provided by the 16th-century Persian artist Dūst-Moḥammad Heravī (q.v.) in his famous preface to the album (Topkapı Saray, ms. no. H 2154) he prepared in 951/1544 for the Safavid prince Bahrām Mīrzā (q.v.): "Amir Dawlatyar, a slave (*gulam*) of Sultan Abu- Saʿid (717-36/1317-35), was ennobled by being a pupil of Master Ahmad Musa and was outstanding in this regard, especially in *qalam-sīyahi* . . ."; it was Aḥmad Mūsā who "lifted the veil from the face of depiction, and the [style of] depiction that is now current was invented by him" (Thackston, p. 345). Dūst-Moḥammad thus provided an unequivocal statement that an artist of the first half of the 14th century was particularly esteemed for his black-and-white drawings. Several examples signed by Mīr Dawlatyār survive in the Istanbul and Diez albums (Tanindi, p. 38; Kühnel, p. 68 fig. 2). According to Dūst-Moḥammad, one of his pupils, Šams-al-Dīn, was trained in the time of the Jalayerid sultan Ovays (757-76/1356-74; Thackston, p. 345); a finished drawing in the Diez album, showing a stylistic affinity with the drawings of his teacher, is ascribed to Šams-al-Dīn (Kühnel, p. 69).

Under the Jalayerids (736-835/1336-1432). After the fall of the Il-khanids the Jalayerids succeeded to their western and northwestern domains. The Jalayerids were dedicated patrons of the book arts, and under their tutelage the classic canons of Persian painting and drawing evolved. Although varying considerably in subject matter and finish, drawings, by their immediacy, provide a closer view of artistic creativity in this period than would surviving paintings alone. The Istanbul and Diez albums contain preliminary sketches, usually undated and unsigned, that can be identified as Jalayerid from comparison with dated paintings and from internal evidence. Human figures tend to be elongated and long-waisted, with tall caps or turbans pulled down on one side. The horses are small in body and have proportionally smaller heads; other animals, like lions, appear in both naturalistic and improbable poses, while swimming ducks and birds in flight are abundant. Landscape elements are very diverse. Hunting and animal-combat scenes were particularly popular (e.g., Topkapı Saray, ms. no. H 2152, fols. 8r, 14r, 34v, 53r, 63v, 45v, 70, 74v, 79r, 90v, 51r, 53r, 64v, 68r, 91, 45v, 50v, 83v, 95r, 98v; Lentz and Lowry, nos. 75-79, 82, 83). These drawings help to clarify artistic relations between the Jalayerids and the contemporary Muzaffarid rulers (713-95/1314-93) of Fārs, on one hand, and the Timurid courts of the 15th century, on the other. The Muzaffarid style appears to have been a provincial offshoot of the Jalayerid.

Dūst-Moḥammad reported that ʿAbd-al-Ḥayy, a pupil of Šams-al-Dīn, "instructed Sultan Aḥmad [784-813/1382-1410] in depiction so that the sultan himself produced a scene . . . in *qalam-siyahi*" (Thackston, p. 345). Tīmūr, who invaded Persia in 795/1392, took ʿAbd al-Ḥayy back to Samarqand, where he remained the rest of his life and "all masters imitated his work" (Thackston, p. 345). Moḥammad Ḵayyām, though not mentioned by Dūst-Moḥammad, was a prolific and imaginative Jalayerid master, who frequently signed his drawings (PlateXXXVII). His output included single animals, especially lions, and animal and human combat scenes, all characterized by a simple, undifferentiated line, with the addition of spots of gold and red (Lentz and Lowry, nos. 82-83 n. 91; Kühnel, figs. 4-10). Two of his drawings (Kühnel, figs. 4, 5) are after drawings by ʿAbd-al-Ḥayy. A single artistic lineage can thus be traced from Aḥmad Mūsā in the time of the Il-khanid Abū Saʿīd to Moḥammad Ḵayyām in the early 15th century. Although Moḥammad Ḵayyām apparently lived long enough to be employed in Bāysonḡor's *ketāb-ḵāna* (Sakisian, pp. 60-61, mentioning a piece of calligraphy dated 812/1409), his style remained quintessentially Jalayerid (e.g., Kühnel, figs. 6-8; Lentz and Lowry, no. 83).

The culminating achievements of Jalayerid art are the marginal drawings (actually each seeming a full-page drawing with text panels superimposed) of the *Dīvān* of Sultan Aḥmad Jalāyer, from the opening years of the 15th century and now in the Freer Gallery of Art, Washington, D.C. These drawings, with touches of gold and washes of blue, are imbued with a combination of naturalism and lyricism in which Chinese influence is evident but in which there is also a suggestion of familiarity with European manuscript painting (Atıl, nos. 1, 4; Plate XXXVIII).

The Timurid period. Sultan Aḥmad Jalāyer's son-in-law Eskandar Solṭān, Timurid governor of Fārs from 812/1409 to 817/1414 during the reign of his uncle Šāhroḵ (807-50/1405-47), fell heir to the Jalayerid tradition of cultivated patronage. A series of manuscripts made for Eskandar Solṭān, who seemed to prefer small portable volumes like two miscellanies of 813/1410-11 (in the Gulbenkian Foundation, Lisbon, and the British Museum, London, respectively), are adorned with lively and delicate decorative drawings, in addition to their painted illustrations: "Another distinguishing element of several of Iskandar's manuscripts is the accompanying illumination and drawing . . . in the margins, in scalloped medallions, and on entire pages" (Lentz and Lowry, p. 119 no. 36; Akimushkin and Ivanov, pl. IX; Plate XXXIX). When Eskandar Solṭān was blinded for rebelling against Šāhroḵ in 817/1414 the center of court patronage shifted to the Timurid capital, Herat, under the aegis of Bāysonḡor. The tradition established under the Jalayerids and carried on by Eskandar Solṭān was further developed at Herat. Timurid court artists adopted similar subject matter, though their work was less experimental and varied than that produced under the Jalayerids. For example, a drawing that has been labeled "Bāysonḡor Slays a Wolf," representing the theme of princely valor and skill, is characterized by economy of line and a sense of effortless power (Lentz and Lowry, no. 33). The face of the prince is too idealized to justify identification with Bāysonḡōr, however; he seems to have been more accurately depicted in frontispieces to manuscripts made for him (Lentz and Lowry, pp. 66, 125).

Timurid decorative designs, often within shaped

PLATE XXXVII

Drawing of Ḵosrow spying Šīrīn bathing, Moḥammad Ḵayyām; ink on paper, 12.7 x 20.9 cm.; probably Baghdad, 1400-50. Musée d'Art et d'Histoire, Geneva, no. 1971-107/398.

PLATE XXXVIII

Page from the *Dīvān* of Sultan Aḥmad Jalāyer with marginal drawings, including a vignette based on images of the Virgin and Child with Joseph; ink on paper, 29.5 x 20.4 cm; Baghdad, ca. 1400. Courtesy of the Freer Gallery of Art, Smithsonian Institution, Washington, D.C., no. 32.30.

PLATE XXXIX

Ornamental drawing from a horoscope prepared for Eskandar Sultan; opaque watercolors, ink, and gold on paper, 26.5 x 16.7 cm; Shiraz, 813/1411. Wellcome Institute Library, London, no. Persian 474, fol. 1a.

cartouches, follow their predecessors so closely that distinguishing material from the two periods is very difficult (see, e.g., Lentz and Lowry, nos. 75, 90-96). Although much of the vocabulary in these drawings had originally been borrowed from China, by the 15th century it had been thoroughly assimilated. Nevertheless, a renewed interest in Chinese art may have been stimulated by missions to and from China during the reign of Šāhrok̲, as suggested by a drawing of two arhats copied from a Yüan dynasty original (Swietochowski and Babaie, no. 2). Extant underdrawing from the early Timurid period attests the mastery of draftsmanship achieved by court artists (see, e.g., Soucek, fig. 4; Lentz and Lowry, nos. 64, 65).

In his aforementioned preface Dūst-Moḥammad described Herat as an artistic center during the reign of Sultan Ḥosayn Bāyqarā (875-912/1470-1506). He had high praise for Behzād (q.v.), best known for his paintings but demonstrably also a great draftsman. A late 15th-century drawing of a youth teasingly removing a bottle from the reach of an older man has been assigned to him by Stuart Cary Welch; the economy of line and keen observation of the figures seem to confirm the attribution (Lentz and Lowry, no. 158). Among other late 15th-century Herat artists one was particularly recognized for his drawings. In *Tārīk̲-e rašīdī* Mīrzā Moḥammad-Ḥaydār Dog̲lāt (905-58/1500-51), a Central Asian cousin of Bābor, founder of the Mughal dynasty, praised Šāh Moẓaffar even above Behzād: "His pen and ink drawings (*qalam-sīāhī*) are to be found in the possession of some people [and] the masters of this art consider them very dear" (Thackston, p. 361). Little of Šāh Moẓaffar's work seems to have survived, perhaps because he died at the age of twenty-four years; it is not clear whether two of his unpublished works in the Bahrām Mīrzā album are drawings or paintings (Lentz and Lowry, p. 326 n. 376; Stchoukine, pp. 18-20, mentioning a citation to Šāh Moẓaffar in a chronicle but without identification of his work).

Although the chroniclers did not mention artists who worked for the contemporary Turkman sultans, two Istanbul albums (mss. nos. H 2153, H 2160) are treasure troves of Turkman paintings and drawings through the reign of the Āq Qoyunlū sultan Yaʿqūb (883-96/1478-90). Quite a number bear what appear to be valid ascriptions to the artists Šayk̲ī and Dārvīš Moḥammad (Çağman, pp. 31-33; Tanindi, p. 38). More problematic are works ascribed to Moḥammad Sīāh-qalam (lit., "black pen," suggesting his preference for drawing as a medium). This name is most closely associated with a series of pictures of demons and nomads in black and reddish tones that have aroused much speculation but are not relevant here; there are also a few drawings ascribed to him that seem to fit stylistically into the period of Sultan Yaʿqūb (e.g., ms. no. H 2160, fols. 34r, 75r, 78r; Çağman, fig. 461).

The Safavid period. The Timurid dynasty came to an end in Persia with the death of Sultan Ḥosayn. In 907/1501 the first Safavid shah, Esmāʿīl I (907-30/1501-24), was crowned in Tabrīz, and in 916/1510 he took Herat from the Uzbek conquerors. The Safavid court style thus developed from a combination of the Timurid Herat style with the Āq Qoyunlū style of Tabrīz.

Shāh Ṭahmāsb (930-84/1524-76) was, like his father, a great patron of the arts during the first half of his reign. Under his patronage there seems to have been increased appreciation of drawings, for a considerable number of finished examples survive. The themes continued to parallel those of painting (see, e.g., Atıl, no. 14; Swietochowski and Babaie, nos. 7, 9). The two artists of this period who received the most unstinted praise from Dūst-Moḥammad were Solṭān-Moḥammad and Āqā Mīrak (Thackston, p. 348); although both were superb draftsmen, it is for their paintings that they are admired today. Welch has convincingly attributed to Solṭān-Moḥammad several border drawings in a dispersed copy of Saʿdī's *Golestān*, executed in shades of gold and silver and filled with real and imagined beasts and birds, figures, and angels amid trees, foliage, and rocks. Āqā Mīrak was noted for his ornamental drawings and was cited by Ṣādeqī Beg Afšār in *Qānūn-e ṣowar* for his animal designs; Welch has attributed to him the original borders of a manuscript of Neẓāmī's *K̲amsa* in the British Museum, with birds, beasts, and foliage in silver and shades of gold (S. C. Welch, 1979, no. 52).

In the mid-16th century the Safavid capital was moved from Tabrīz to Qazvīn, but Ṭahmāsb himself turned away from artistic patronage, and court artists sought employment with such cultivated princes as the shah's brother Bahrām Mīrzā and the latter's son Ebrāhīm Mīrzā, as well as at the Mughal court of Homāyūn at Kabul and later at Delhi. Paintings and drawings for albums (*moraqqaʿ*s) began to overshadow manuscript illustrations in importance as sources of patronage spread outward from court circles; more affordable drawings were increasingly in demand among discerning but less affluent collectors. Patrons sought the drawings of individual artists, who became increasingly aware of their own worth and began to sign their works more frequently. A number of talented artists, most notably Shaikh̲ Moḥammad, Moḥammadī, and Ṣādeqī Beg, became fascinated by the innovative possibilities of line drawings. Unlike their manuscript illustrations, their drawings tend to be of single or paired figures and occasional scenes unrelated to any narrative (Plate XL). Stimulated by one another's work, they developed a fluid, calligraphic style at the court of Qazvīn before migrating to Khorasan in search of princely patronage there. Shaikh Moḥammad, for example, was also a calligrapher who exploited the calligraphic line in his drawings (for an extensive study of his work, see Dickson and Welch, pp. 166-68; S. C. Welch, 1979, nos. 73, 76, 77, 80, 84; idem, 1976, pls. 39, 41, 46, 47, 48; cf. A. Welch, 1974, pp. 459-66; Simpson, pp. 99-112). After leaving Shah Ṭahmāsb's atelier he accompanied Ebrāhīm Mīrzā to Mašhad, remaining in his employ from about 1556 to about 1576, then serving at the court at Qazvīn until the accession of Shah ʿAbbās I (996-1038/1588-1629). As Welch noted, "Shaykh-Muhammad's spirited drawings were eagerly sought after. . . . It could be argued that he was responsible for the surge of interest in drawing for its own sake. . . ." (S. C. Welch, 1979, pp. 190-91). Moḥammadī is admired today principally for his delicately rendered pastoral drawings heightened with colored washes and for graceful figures derived from those of his predecessors in Ṭahmāsb's atelier (Robinson, 1965, pl. 39; idem, 1976, pl. V). Ṣādeqī Beg worked at the court of Esmāʿīl II (984-85/1576-78), moved on to Khorasan, then served as head of the royal library of Shāh ʿAbbās for approximately ten years. He was an exponent of the calligraphic line, which swells, diminishes, disappears, re-emerges, yet defines form, face, and drapery (A. Welch, 1973, no. 2).

The "Qazvīn style" influenced the greatest artist of the late 16th and early 17th centuries, Reżā ʿAbbāsī (d. 1045/1635), also known as Āqā Reżā, son of the painter ʿAlī-Aṣg̲ar and universally recognized not only as the greatest artist of the reign of Shāh ʿAbbās I but also as one of the most talented in the history of Persian painting and drawing (A. Welch, 1974. pp. 478-82; Canby, pp. 71-84). Even as a young man his influence on his contemporaries was profound, and his style and subject matter dominated the 17th century. His drawings reveal not only his mastery of fluid line contrasted with sputtering strokes but also nuances of form, drapery folds, and textures, as well as psychological depth (see, e.g., A. Welch, 1973, no. 9). Among his preferred subjects were studies of single figures, especially graceful youths and contemplative older men, often darvishes (A. Welch, 1973, no. 7; Atıl, nos. 19, 32; Canby, nos. 9, 11, 13; Swietochowski and Babaie, no. 32; Plate XLI). He also drew closely observed genre scenes (e.g., Atıl, no. 33, a camp scene, dated 1048/1639). That Reżā drew from life is known from his sketch of a bald man holding his turban and scratching his head; according to the inscription, it was drawn in Mašhad on Friday, 10 Moḥarram 1007/13 August 1598 in the house of Mīrzā K̲ᵛājagī, from which it can be deduced that the figure was a pilgrim to the holy city, that the evening was uncomfortably warm, and that Reżā's host on this anniversary of Shiʿite martyrdom was a pious man (Swietochowski and Babaie, fig. 4). Reżā copied works of Behzād and was familiar with those of Moḥammadī and Shaikh̲ Moḥammad. Ṣadeqī Beg in turn imitated Reżā's calligraphic line.

What may be a self-portrait of Reżā's son Moḥammad-Šafīʿ ʿAbbāsī is mounted next to a portrait of his father in the so-called "Reżā ʿAbbāsī album" in the Freer Gallery (Atıl, no. 47); it shows a sharp-featured youth absorbed in a flower drawing (Stchoukine, 1964, p. 90). A remarkable early drawing (dated 1038/1627-28) of Yūsof at the court of Zolayk̲ā, filled with figures, architecture, and landscape elements, appears to have been a cartoon for a mural like those in the Čehel Sotūn in Isfahan; if so, it is the only one surviving from the Safavid period (Rogers, no. 58). Although Šafīʿ ʿAbbāsī could produce fine drawings in the accepted 17th-century mode (see, e.g., Falk, no. 88), he is particularly noted for bird and flower paintings and drawings, a departure from the usual subjects of the time. The vogue that he introduced lasted into the 20th century. The largest extant collection of his works, in the so-called "Cobb album" in the British Museum includes drawings dated from 1050/1640 until his death in 1082/1672. The European source for at least one of them was verified by Basil Gray, who concluded that the floral drawings were designs for textile patterns (1959). No doubt designs of this sort were transferred to other media, but many of the pieces from this album are finished drawings inscribed by the artist, in the manner of Reżā, a practice unlikely in pattern books (Farhad, p. 198).

PLATE XL

Drawing of a hero and dragon; ink, transparent colors, and gold on paper, 22 x 13.3 cm; Qazvīn, third quarter of the 16th century. The Metropolitan Museum of Art, New York, no. 223.83.7, gift of George D. Pratt, 1925.

PLATE XLI

Drawings of an old man and a youth, inscribed Reżā ʿAbbāsī; ink, transparent and opaque colors, and gold on paper, 12.7 x 5.4 cm; Isfahan, second quarter of the 17th century. The Metropolitan Museum of Art, New York, no. 25.68.5, Fletcher Fund, 1925.

The drawings of three of the most prominent artists working in the mid-17th century "style of Isfahan," where the Safavid capital had been moved, grew directly out of the work of Reżā. Moḥammad-Qāsem, Moḥammad-Yūsof, and Moḥammad-ʿAlī evolved a style that, despite individual differences, was fluently linear, though somewhat mannered, with repetitive patterns of lines creating both decorative and dynamic effects. The same single figure types, particularly of contemplative older men and idealized androgynous young men and women, are generally shown at ease in landscapes with touches of washed color and occasional brighter accents. Moḥammad-Qāsem was the most innovative of the three (Plate XLII), but all were highly accomplished. By far the most gifted of Reżā's students was Moʿīn Moṣawwer, whose career lasted from the 1630s to the end of the century. He was extraordinarily prolific, producing manuscript and detached illustrations and drawings of single figures or small

PLATE XLII

Drawing of the chastisement of a pupil, inscribed Moḥammad-Qāsem; ink, transparent and opaque colors, and gold on paper, 24.5 x. 15.9 cm, mid-17th century. The Metropolitan Museum of Art, New York, no. 11.84.14, Frederick C. Hewitt Fund, 1911.

PLATE XLIII

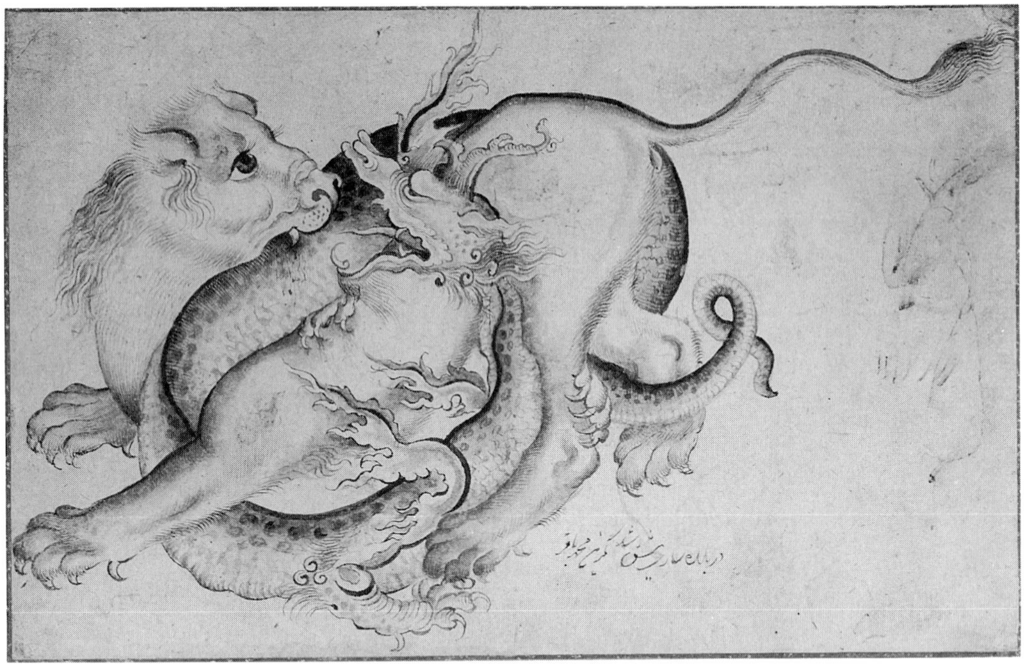

Drawing of a lion and dragon in combat, inscribed Moḥammad-Bāqer; ink and transparent colors on paper, 14 x 22.9 cm; second half of the 18th century. The Metropolitan Museum of Art, New York, no. 1974.20, Rogers Fund, 1974.

groups. His famous painted portrait of Reżā, begun, according to the inscription, in 1044/1635, shortly before the master's death, and completed forty years later, confirms his sure and sensitive draftsmanship (A. Welch, 1973, no. 76). Moʿīn adopted Reżā's habit of jotting notations on his drawings, some of which reveal that the sketches were spontaneous, if not drawn from life (Atıl, nos. 34, 41). A drawing of the unusual subject of a youth carrying a rooster attests his powers of observation; according to the inscription, it was drawn in haste for his son Āqā Zamān on 15 Ḏu'l-Hejja 1066/4 October 1656 (Farhad, 1990, fig. 4). The most detailed notation by the artist appears on a drawing made at the end of February 1672 in his own home, in order to distract himself from the extreme rigors of winter. At the palace gates a lion, a royal gift to Shah Solaymān (1077-1105/1666-94), had suddenly attacked and killed a youth, tearing away half his face. Moʿīn was probably not present at this event, but his drawing has the drama of an eyewitness rendition, except that the lion has been adorned with tiger stripes (A. Welch, 1973, no. 75). Moʿīn was active until about 1697 and appears to have had many pupils.

The 18th century was a turbulent period in Persian history, and the production, or at least survival, of works of art on paper diminished dramatically. Artists seem to have turned away from manuscripts and album pages to produce lacquer paintings on penboxes and other luxury objects. Nevertheless, surviving works by Moḥammad-Bāqer (Swietochowski and Babaie, no. 19; Plate XLIII) and others demonstrate that there was still a market for drawings and artists who were fine draftsmen. Moḥammad-Bāqer carried on the tradition of Šafīʿ ʿAbbāsī in painting and drawing flowers, birds, and insects.

During the 19th century Qajar patrons preferred oil painting and portraiture, but artists of the 19th and 20th centuries continued to draw subjects evolved in the 15-17th centuries.

Bibliography: O. F. Akimushkin and A. A. Ivanov, "The Art of Illumination," in B. Gray, ed., *The Arts of the Book in Central Asia. 14th-16th Centuries*, Boulder, Colo., 1979, pp. 35-58. E. Atıl, *The Brush of the Masters. Drawings from Iran and India*, Washington, D.C., 1978. F. Çağman, "On the Contents of Four Istanbul Albums H. 2152, 2153, 3154 and 2160," *Islamic Art* 1, New York, 1981, pp. 31-36. S. R. Canby, "Age and Time in the Life of Riza," in S. R. Canby, ed., *Persian Masters. Five Centuries of Painting*, Bombay, 1990, pp. 71-84. M. B. Dickson and S. C. Welch, *The Houghton Shahnameh*, 2 vols., Cambridge, Mass., 1981. R. Ettinghausen, "On Some Mongol Miniatures," in

E. Kühnel, ed., *Kunst des Orients* 3, 1959, pp. 44-65. T. Falk, ed., *Treasures of Islam*, Geneva, 1985. M. Farhad, *Safavid Single Page Painting 1629-1666*, Ann Arbor, Mich., 1988. Idem, "The Art of Muʿin Musavvir. A Mirror of His Times," in S. R. Canby, ed., *Persian Masters. Five Centuries of Painting*, Bombay, 1990, pp. 113-28. B. Gray, "An Album of Designs for Persian Textiles," in R. Ettinghausen, ed., *Aus der Welt der islamischen Kunst*, Berlin, 1959, pp. 219-25. Idem, *The World History of Rashid al-Din. A Study of the Royal Asiatic Society Manuscript*, London, 1978. E. Kühnel, "Malernamen in den Berliner 'Saray'-Alben," in *Kunst des Orients* 3, 1959, pp. 66-77. T. Lentz and G. Lowry, *Timur and the Princely Vision. Art and Culture in the Fifteenth Century*, Los Angeles, 1989. Qāżī Aḥmad, tr. Minorsky. D. T. Rice, *The Illustrations to the "World History" of Rashid al-Din*, ed. B. Gray, Edinburgh, 1976. B. W. Robinson, *A Descriptive Catalogue of the Persian Paintings in the Bodleian Library*, Oxford, 1958. Idem, *Drawings of the Masters. Persian Drawings from the 14th through the 19th Century*, New York, 1965. Idem, *Persian Paintings in the India Office Library. A Descriptive Catalogue*, London, 1976. J. M. Rogers, *Islamic Art and Design. 1500-1700*, London, 1983. A. Sakisian, *La miniature persane du XIIe au XVIIe siècle*, Paris and Brussels, 1929. M. S. Simpson, "Shaykh-Muhammad," in S. R. Canby, ed., *Persian Masters. Five Centuries of Painting*, Bombay, 1990, pp. 99-112. P. P. Soucek, "Nizami on Painters and Painting," in R. Ettinghausen, ed., *Islamic Art in the Metropolitan Museum of Art*, New York, 1972. I. Stchoukine, *Les peintures des manuscrits tīmourides*, Paris, 1954. Idem, *Les peintures des manuscrits de Shāh ʿAbbās Ier à la fin des Safavīs*, Paris, 1964. M. L. Swietochowski and S. Babaie, *Persian Drawings in The Metropolitan Museum*, New York, 1989. W. M. Thackston, *A Century of Princes. Sources on Timurid History and Art*, Cambridge, Mass., 1989. Z. Tanindi, "Some Problems of Two Istanbul Albums," in *Islamic Art* 1, 1981, pp. 37-41. A. Welch, *Shah ʿAbbas and the Arts of Isfahan*, New York, 1973. Idem, "Painting and Patronage under Shah ʿAbbas I," in R. Holod, ed., *Studies on Isfahan. Proceedings of the Isfahan Colloquium* I. Iranian Studies. 7/1-2, 1974, pp. 458-507. S. C. Welch, *Persian Painting. Five Royal Safavid Manuscripts of the Sixteenth Century*, New York, 1976. Idem, *Wonders of the Age. Masterpieces of Early Safavid Painting, 1501-1576*, Cambridge, Mass., 1979.

(M. L. SWIETOCHOWSKI)

DRAXT Ī ĀSŪRĪG (The Babylonian tree), a versified contest over precedence between a goat and a palm tree, composed in the Parthian language, written in Book Pahlavi script, and consisting of about 120 verses. Probably in ancient times the Iranians adopted this literary genre, which has the characteristics of oral literature from Mesopotamia; examples are found in Sumerian and Akkadian texts (Asmussen, 1973, pp. 51-59; Brunner, pp. 194-202). The text has been edited and published from Codex MK, with collations from other manuscripts (*Pahlavi Texts*, ed. Jamasp-Asana, II, pp. 109-14).

Draxt ī āsūrīg begins with a riddle, posed by the poet, in which a brief description of a tree is given without specific identification (par. 1), though the reader or listener understands that it is a palm tree. Then the tree itself enumerates (1-20) for the goat the benefits it provides: fruits and useful objects made from its wood, leaves, and fibers. In the next section (21-53) the goat rises to the challenge, first ridiculing the palm tree, then enumerating the benefits it offers; foods made from its milk, milk for Zoroastrian religious ceremonies, and objects fashioned from its skin, wool, and gut. Finally, the poet proclaims the goat victorious (54). At the end there are prayers for the person who has recited, written down, or otherwise brought this poem into his possession and curses for his enemies (55-60).

According to some scholars, the contest represents the opposition between two faiths, with the goat representing Zoroastrianism and the palm tree representing the pagan religions of Assyria and Babylonia, in which the cult of the tree formed an important part (Smith). Others have better understood it as a manifestation of the contrast between pastoral life, symbolized by the goat, and the agricultural life, symbolized by the palm tree (Rūḥ-al-Amīnī, pp. 323-36).

Christian Bartholomae (pp. 23-28) was the first scholar to identify the language of the text as Parthian. His identification is confirmed by the presence of words and grammatical constructions that are exclusively Parthian: *ās-* "to come" (par. 49; Man. Parth. *ʾʾs-*, *ʾs-*), *awišt-* "to stand, to be" (20; Man. Parth. *ʾwyšt-*; see Henning, 1950, p. 643 n. 6), *bid* "again" (45, 46, 48; Man. Parth. *byd*), *burz* "high, tall" (22; Man. Parth. *bwrz*), *darg/γ* "long" (54; Man. Parth. *drγ*), *hā̆mhirz* "attendant" (36; Man. Parth. *hʾmhyrz*), *hawiž/hōyiž* "he, that too" (32, 44; Man. Parth. *hwyc*); *hirz-* "let" (19, Man. Parth. *hyrz-*), *kar-* "do, make" (6-8, 11-13, 16, 31, 34, etc.; Man. Parth. *kr-*), *kēž* "somebody" (31; Man. Parth. *kyc*; see Henning, 1950, p. 643 n. 12), *naxšag* "fine, good" (40; Man. Parth. *nxšg*), *šāx* "horn" (22, in *dēw šāx*; Tafażżolī, 1990), *wasnāδ* "for, for the sake of" (2, 8, 17, 28, 35, 38, 42, 47; Man. Parth. *wsnʾd*), *wāxt*, *wāž-* "tell, say" (20, 27, 51; Man. Parth. *wʾxt*, *wʾc-*), *wirāz-* "arrange" (6, 37, 38; Man. Parth. *wyrʾz-*), *yaδ ō* "until" (20, 25, 28, 30; Man. Parth. *yd (ʾw)*; see Henning, 1950, p. 643 n. 7), *ahēm* "I am" (29; Man. Parth. *ʾhym/ʾhyym*), *aʾi/ay* "thou art" (29, 53; Man. Parth. *ʾyy*), *čē* used as a particle in *eżāfa* (28, 43; Man. Parth. *cy*).

In the course of oral transmission by speakers of Middle Persian, the Parthian text came to include many words or constructions influenced by this language, for example, *āšyān* "nest" (instead of *āhyān(ag)*, par. 18), *buland* "high, tall" (instead of *burzend*, 2, 22, 25, 30), *ēwēn(ag)* "manner, way" (instead of *aβδēn*, 28, 41, 54), *morwārīd* "pearl" (instead of *moryārīd*, 34, 51), *pērōz* "victory" (instead of *paryōž*, 54), *pēš* "before" (instead of *parwān*, 51), *šīr* "milk" (instead of *šift*, 44), *šīrēn* "sweet" (instead of *šiftēn*, 1), *xurmāg* "dare" (instead of *amrāw*, 54), the abstract suffix *-īh* (instead of *-īf(t)*, e.g., *bundahišnīh* "original creation"), and frequent use of the particle *ī* in *eżāfa*.

In the manuscripts of *Draxt (ī) āsūrīg* the text is written in prose form; Émile Benveniste was the first to recognize it as poetry. From examination of certain sections of the text he concluded that some verses contain six syllables (pp. 194, 195, 204). His conclusion about the syllabic meter of the poem was criticized by W. B. Henning (1950), who argued that the meter of this poem is accentual, like those of other Middle Persian and Parthian poems. He established the versification of certain lines and the correct readings of certain words. The poem probably conforms to the principles and rules of Parthian poetic meter (e.g., return of the ictus at regular intervals, quantity of syllables) as described by Gilbert Lazard. But, owing to alterations in the course of oral transmission, redaction in Pahlavi script, and copying, as well as to the presence of unknown words, it has not yet been possible to establish the versification of the entire text. The effort by Māhyār Nawwābī to do so must be considered tentative.

The poetic diction of the text is simple and without embellishment, and the imagery is elementary, as in the likening of the shape of the date-palm (q.v.) leaf to that of the reed (*naδ*), the sweetness of the date to that of the grape (par. 1), the softness and whiteness of a maiden's breast and neck to the body (**handām*, Unvala, p. 661) of the goat (43), the body odor of a certain species of goat to the scent of a fragrant flower (*gul gētīg*, 43), and the immobility of the date palm to the nail of a loom (53). The expressions "casting pearls before swine" and "playing the harp before a mad camel" (51) were drawn from ancient Iranian proverbs (Widengren, pp. 36-37; Asmussen, 1968), and the idiom *kōy murdagān* "alley of the dead" (49) was probably a metaphor for cemetery (Henning, 1950, p. 645 n. 2).

Draxt (ī) āsūrīg is also a catalogue poem, that is, a poem containing lists of related words, the purpose of which was instruction and reinforcement of memory; in this aspect it also can be considered wisdom literature (Boyce, "Middle Persian Literature," p. 55). Such lists include items of clothing (*mōy* "shoe," par. 9, cf. Ar. lw. *mūq*; **nālēn* (?) "sandals," 10; *kamar* "belt," 34; *mōžag* "boot," 35; *angustbān* "finger guard, finger stall," 35; *xaz tuxārīg* "Tokharian marten furs," 42; see Henning, 1950, p. 644 n. 11), food and drink (*sik* "vinegar," 15 [Henning, 1950, p. 642 n. 8: *šīr* "milk," but cf. Shaki, p. 67]; *angubēn* "honey," l. 16; *nān* "bread," 20, 42; *pist/pust* "browned flour," 42; *panīr* "cheese," 42, 46; *rōyn-xwardīg* "sweetmeats," 42, Henning, 1950, p. 644 n. 10; *pēšpārag* "appetizer, hors-d'œuvre," 45, Henning, 1955, p. 603; *šīr* "milk," 46; *dōx* "churned sour milk," 46; *māst* "curds, sour milk," 46; *kašk* "dried buttermilk," 46; *afrušag* "beastings," 46; *wašag* "beer," 45, Henning, 1955; *hur*, an alcoholic drink, 45, Henning, 1955; *maδ* "wine," 20), musical instruments (*čang* "harp," 48, 51; *win* "vina, lute," 48; *kannār*, a kind of lute, 48; *barbat* "lyre," l. 48; *tambūr* "cittern, lute," l. 48), perfumes (*kāpūr* "camphor," 42; *mušk* "musk," 42), arms and battle equipment (*drōn* "bow," 40, Bailey, p. 472; *zīh* "bowstring," 40; *skuz* "saddle strap," 41, Tafażżolī, 1970; *zēn* "saddle," 41; **pilakxān "sling," 41, MacKenzie*; *kaškanjīr* "ballista," 41, Tafażżolī, 1966, idem, 1971; *meh pīl* "big elephant," 41; *zand pīl* "large, furious elephant," 41), objects of everyday and economic use (*gyāg-rōb* "broom," 6; *yawāz* "oil press," 7, Tafażżolī, 1966; *damēnag* "fan," 8; *rasan* "rope," 11; *mēx* "peg," 13; *tabangōg* "box, basket," 17; *mašk* "skin bag," 36; *maškīžag* "skin tablecloth," 37; *bāryāmag* "saddle bag," 33, Henning, 1950, p. 644 n. 2; *ambān* "skin bag," 42; *makōg* "ship," 4; *wādbān* "sail," 5; *frasp* "mast," 5), writing terms (*nāmag* "letter, book," *frawardag* "epistle," *dēwān* "register," *daftar* "register, account book," *pādixšīr* "treaty," 39), and religious terms (*jīw* "(consecrated) milk," 31; *hōm* "Haoma (juice)," 32; *gōšuru(n)* "soul of the cow," 32; *yazišn* "sacrifice, *yasna* ceremony," 32; *kustīg* "sacred girdle," 43; **padām*, as read by Unvala, p. 660, rather than *pašm*, as read by others, "sacred mouth mask," 43; *taškanag* "sacred undershirt," 43; *pādyāb* "ablution," 47; *māzdēsnān* "Mazdā worshipers," 47).

"The story of the vine and the ewe" (*raz o mīš*), a poem similar to *Draxt (ī) āsūrīg*, exists in Persian literature in two versions, one consisting of sixty-one distichs in Judeo-Persian (Asmussen, 1973, pp. 32 ff.), the other in forty-nine distichs in Persian (Qayṣarī, pp. 363-78). Both versions are versified contests over precedence and have the characteristics of oral literature, but neither is as eloquent or as high in literary quality as *Draxt (ī) āsūrīg*.

Bibliography: (For cited works not found in this bibliography and for abbreviations found here, see "Short References.") J. P. Asmussen, "Ein iranisches Wort, ein iranischer Spruch und ein iranische Märchenformel als Grundlage historischer Folgerungen," *Temenos* 3, 1968, pp. 7-18. Idem, *Studies in Judeo-Persian Literature*, Leiden, 1973. H. W. Bailey, "Arya III," *BSOAS* 24, 1961, pp. 470-83. C. Bartholomae, *Zur Kenntnis der mitteliranischen Mundarten* IV, Sb. der Heidelberger Akademie der Wissenschaften, Phil.-hist. Kl., Abh. 6, Heidelberg, 1922. E. Benveniste, "Le texte du *Draxt Asūrīk* et la versification pehlevie," *JA* 218, 1930, pp. 193-225. G. Bolognesi, "Osservazioni sul Draxt i Āsūrīk," *Rivista degli Studi Orientali* 28, 1953, pp. 174-81. C. J. Brunner,

"The Fable of the Babylonian Tree," *JNES* 30, 1980, pp. 197-202, 291-302. *Draxt (ī) āsūrīg*, ed. and tr. M. Nawwābī as *Manẓūma-ye Derak̲t-e āsūrīg*, Tehran, 1346 Š./1967. W. B. Henning, "A Pahlavi Poem," *BSO(A)S* 13, 1950, pp. 641-48. Idem, "The Middle Persian Word for 'Beer'," *BSOAS* 17, 1955, pp. 603-04. G. Lazard, "La métrique de la poésie parthe," *Papers in Honour of Professor Mary Boyce*, Acta Iranica 25, Leiden, 1985, pp. 371-99. D. N. MacKenzie, "Some Pahlavi Plums," *Orientala J. Duchesne-Guillemin Emerito Oblata*, Acta Iranica 23, Leiden, 1984, pp. 385-87. E. Qayṣarī, "Manẓūma-ī be šeʿr-e darī naẓīr-e *Derak̲t-e āsūrīg*" in *Majmūʿa-ye sok̲anrānīhā-ye haftomīn kongra-ye taḥqīqāt-e īranī*, ed. M.-R. Daryāgašt, II, Tehran, 1357 Š./1978, pp. 362-78. M. Rūḥ-al-Amīnī, "Jostārī mardom-šenāsī az manẓūma-ye Derak̲t-e āsūrīg," in Y. Mahdawī and Ī. Afšār, eds., *Haftād maqāla. Armaḡān-e farhangī be Doktor Ḡolām-Ḥosayn Ṣadīqī* I, Tehran, 1369 Š./1990, pp. 323-36. M. Shaki, "Observations on the Draxt ī Āsūrīg," *Archív Orientální* 43, 1975, pp. 64-75. S. Smith, "Notes on 'The Assyrian Tree'," *BSO(A)S* 4, 1926-28, pp. 69-76. A. Tafażżolī, "Do vāža-ye pārtī az *Derak̲t-e āsūrī*," *MDAT* 14, 1345 Š./1966, pp. 138-47. Idem, "Notes pehlevies I," *JA* 258, 1970, pp. 91-92. Idem, "Pahlavica I," *Acta Orientalia* 33, 1971, p. 199. Idem, "Pahlavica III," *Acta Orientalia* 51, 1990, pp. 58-59. J. M. Unvala, "Draxt i Asurīk," *BSO(A)S* 2, 1923, pp. 637-78. G. Widengren, *Iranisch-semitische Kulturbegegnung in par-thischer Zeit*, Cologne, 1960.

(AḤMAD TAFAŻŻOLĪ)

DREAMS AND DREAM INTERPRETATION.

i. *In pre-Islamic Persia.* See Supplement.
ii. *In the Persian tradition.*

ii. IN THE PERSIAN TRADITION

Dreams and their interpretation (*k̲ᵛāb*, *roʾyā*; *k̲ᵛāb-gozārī*), an integral part of the Persian world view, as well as the Shīʿite notion of "inner prophethood" (*nobowwat-e bāṭen*; Fahd, 1966b, p. 351). Dreams are divided into two main categories: those that occur only during sleep (*k̲ᵛāb, nawm, roʾyā*) and those that occur while awake or in a state of semiwakefulness (*wāqeʿa* "vision," *roʾyā*). They are further subdivided into those that are "true" and "false" (*ḥolm,ażḡāṯ-e aḥlām*, etc.). "True" dreams include those experienced by believers (*moʾmenūn*), saints (*awlīāʾ*), and prophets (*anbīāʾ*), both those that require interpretation and those that do not (Ebn Sīrīn, 1302/1884, p. 5).

A three-part typology of dreams can be drawn from the work of R. G. A. van Lieshout (pp. 12-34) and G. E. von Grunebaum (pp. 11-20). Type 1 is the "passive" or "enstatic" dream, of which there are three subtypes: a "recognizable" visual perception or a symbolic form; a message conveyed by a figure, recognized by the dreamer; and, less frequently, an "objective record," for example a piece of paper (*bāb*) found in the morning or marks on the dreamer's body (MacEoin, p. 56). Type 2, the "active" or "ecstatic" vision, is more prevalent in the Islamic and Persian experience than in the Greek tradition; it occurs in a special state "between sleep and wakefulness." The dreamer experiences either unusual ecstasy, awe-inspiring yet with cognitive elements; a departure from the body, often guided by an angel; or transformation into a winged creature that flies to fantastic realms. Type 3 is the dream that must be interpreted; this type is more often reported in popular literature, where dreams show the way to treasure, warn of imminent danger, or bring cures and the like.

In epic, legends, and popular tradition. In Persian myth and epic literature many dreams of kings and heroes are recounted. In one of the darkest mythic episodes, in the version compiled by Abū Manṣūr T̲aʿālebī, the evil king Żaḥḥāk dreams of his own demise: Three men enter his palace and kill him. His dream interpreters warn that he is to be brought down by a prince named Ferēdūn, as yet unborn, whose mother is descended from King Tahmūraṯ. Zāl foresees his marriage to Rūdāba in a dream. According to the *Bundahišn* and the *Kār-nāmag*, Bābak dreams that the sun and moon appear from Sāsān's forehead and cover the land (T̲aʿālebī, *Ḡorar*, pp. 12-14, 36, 221-22; cf. *K̲ᵛāb-gozārī*, p. 5). The only named interpreter of dreams in this work, however, is Bozorgmehr (see BOZORGMEHR-E BOK̲TAGĀN), who, while still a youth, gains royal favor by explaining Anōšīravān's dream after the *mōbeds* (priests) have failed (T̲aʿālebī, *Ḡorar*, p. 299).

In the *Šāh-nāma* eighteen dreams are reported, most of them not mentioned or in different versions from those mentioned by T̲aʿālebī. For example, Żaḥḥāk dreams of three men who strike him with a bull-headed mace and imprison him on Mount Damāvand (ed. Mohl, I, p. 37). Many dreams are predominantly informative, as when a horseman informs Sām that Zāl, the son whom he has abandoned in the wilderness, is alive (I, p. 111). Perhaps the most graphic dream recounted in the *Šāh-nāma* is that of Afrāsīāb (q.v.), who sees a desert full of serpents and a sky full of eagles; the wind blows his banner to the ground, and a hundred thousand Iranian soldiers carry him off to Kāvōs. The astronomers (*ak̲tar-šenāsān*) and wise men (*bek̲radān*) then interpret the destiny in store for Afrāsīāb (II, pp. 130-31; cf. Sīāvoš's dream of his own destiny, I, pp. 193-94). Among the few places in the *Šāh-nāma* where the angel Sorūš appears is Gōdarz's dream, in which the angel, seated on a cloud, informs him of God's command (II, p. 239). The angel provides a nonsymbolic message, which results in action without the necessity for interpretation. In another such "clear" dream Ṭōs sees a radiant "candle" rising from the water; on it Sīāvoš is seated on an ivory throne, manifesting the full Kayanid glory (*farra-ye kayānī*; III, p. 36; cf. IV, pp. 114 ff.). When Ferdowsī himself dreamed that Daqīqī assured him that his endeavors in compiling the *Šāh-nāma* were not in vain, the dream needed no interpretation because the message was clear, not symbolic (IV, pp. 180 ff.). The most elaborate dream episode in the *Šāh-nāma*, consisting of nine interrelated but separate dreams, is that involving the Indian king of Qannūj (V, pp. 57 ff.). These dreams are, however, symbolic and must be interpreted. The only person capable of doing so is Mehrān, a wise ascetic who lives in the wilderness with the animals and eats mountain herbs. According to him, the dreams are a warning of an imminent attack by Alexander (q.v.), which the king is not to resist (V, pp. 136 ff.). The only place in the *Šāh-nāma* where the term "dream interpreter" (*gozāranda-ye k̲ᵛāb*) occurs is in the episode of K̲osrow Anōšīravān and Bozorgmehr, in which Ferdowsī also expressed his own views: "Enlightened souls see in dreams all existing things" (VI, pp. 122, 123-24). In the final dream episode reported in the *Šāh-nāma* Bahrām Čōbīn (q.v.) regains his courage in his battle against the Arab invaders as the result of a dream and rearranges his army effectively (VI, pp. 306 ff.).

In Persian legends and popular narratives political authority is bestowed through dreams, as exemplified, for example, in tales about Abū Moslem K̲orāsānī (q.v.). In one such dream the Prophet Moḥammad, accompanied by Gabriel, appears to Abū Moslem and grants him the ax and other regalia of the *fotowwa* (q.v.), emblems of his authority. He receives his sword from Salmān Fārsī (Lecerf, p. 374). In the *Abū Moslem-nāma*, a romance by Abū Ṭāher Ṭarsūsī (pp. 2 ff.), each of Abū Moslem's forty companions, many of them representatives of guilds, dreams of events to come (Mélikoff, pp. 63-64) and receives magical powers, so that the blacksmith can make Abū Moslem's sword, the wood carver his ax, and so on. Abū Moslem's dream of the Prophet is typical of a genre that includes almost every royal figure, including Shaikh Ṣafī-al-Dīn, eponymous ancestor of the Safavid dynasty, who derived his authority from dreams of investment with miraculous powers (*k̲awāreq-e ʿādāt wa karāmāt*; Eskandar Beg, pp. 10-11, 13 ff.). Shah Ṭahmāsb claimed to have seen and conversed in a dream (*wāqeʿa*) with Imam ʿAlī, who foretold his victories in battle with the Uzbeks and others (*Tad̲kera*, pp. 15, 23 ff.). The Ahl-e Ḥaqq (q.v.) still equate true inner dreams with divine revelation (Mokrī). Other Persian legends of this genre are to be found in such popular works as *Fīrūzšāh-nāma*, *Dārāb-nāma* (q.v.), *Qeṣṣa-ye Ḥamza*, and *Dāstān-e Samak-e ʿAyyār* (see Hanaway; Meyerovitch; cf. Chauvin).

Dreams in religion. Dreams have an especially important place in Shiʿism; the infallible imams are all considered to have had "true dreams," which served as sources for their continued inspiration by God, even though revelation had ended with the Prophet (Corbin, tr., p. 385). The imams are considered to have been especially adept at interpreting symbolic dreams, which gave them access to esoteric knowledge. A work on dream interpretation, *Taqsīm*, has been widely attributed to the sixth imam, Jaʿfar al-Ṣādeq (for the inclusion of this book in a work by Teflīsī, see below). According to later Shiʿite jurists (see Majlesī), it was a major source of esoteric knowledge. One of the earliest jurists, Moḥammad b. Yaʿqūb Kolaynī (d. 329/940), whose *al-Oṣūl men al-kāfī* served as a model for development of Shiʿite jurisprudence, also wrote a work on dream interpretation, *Taʿbīr al-roʾyā* (see Kolaynī, p. 8). Moḥammad-Bāqer Majlesī (d. 1110/1698) quoted from Kolaynī's work on dream interpretation in his own chapter on the subject (pp. 176 ff.), where he also referred to *Ketāb al-taʿbīr ʿan al-aʾemma*, a collection of reported teachings on dreams by the imams. One of the significant principles stated there is that the dreams of "believers" are true (*roʾyā al-moʾmen ṣaḥīḥa*). The imams or other "signs" may appear to any believer, who will thus also gain access to esoteric knowledge. The occultation of the twelfth imam, who possessed a higher visionary knowledge (in Henry Corbin's terms a hierognosis; tr., p. 382), is of special significance in the Shiʿite view of dreams, for he "resides" in Ḥūrqalyā, a realm of the imagined world and may thus be "seen" through dreams (Corbin, tr., p. 405). Dreams thus inform the believer of "inner" knowledge (*bāṭen*) not apparent when he is awake and not associated with phenomenal existence. The believer must, however, perform certain acts in order to prepare for the imams to appear, inform, and guide him in dreams. The conditions are elaborated at length in several Shiʿite works (e.g., Nūrī, pp. 417-20).

Dreams also play a central role in legitimizing the Shiʿite institution of *welāya*, that is, the guardianship of the elect over the multitude. This channel is, for example, fully described in Shaikhi literature, especially by Shaikh Aḥmad Aḥsāʾī (q.v.; d. 1241/1826), who considered the authority of his own investiture dreams to be undisputed (MacEoin, p. 57). These dreams were closely paralleled in the visionary experiences of Moḥammad-ʿAlī the Bāb (q.v.), who reported a dream in which he drank blood from the severed head of Imam Ḥosayn (MacEoin, p. 84 n. 44; cf. Amanat, pp. 168-69). Bahāʾ-Allāh (q.v.), too, placed special emphasis on the revelatory function of dreams (pp. 34-35).

Among Persian works on dream interpretation Ḥobayš Teflīsī's *Kāmel al-taʿbīr* (13th century; p. 3) occupies a special place; in it the author refers to the earlier *Ketāb-e oṣūl* of Dānīāl-e Ḥakīm, *Taqsīm* of Jaʿfar al-Ṣādeq, Ebn Sīrīn's *Ketāb-e jawāmeʿ*, Ebrāhīm Kermānī's *Dastūr*, Jāber Maḡrebī's *Ketāb-*

e eršād, Esmāʿīl b. Ašʿaṯ's *Taʿbīr*, Moʾmenī's *Kanz al-roʾyā*, *Taʿbīr* of ʿAbdūs, *Ḥall* (Jamal in the printed text) *al-dalāʾel fi'l-manāmāt*, and *Īżāḥ al-taʿbīr* of Ṭāmūsī (see *Ḵᵛāb-gozārī*, p. 6; Afšār, pp. 1-9; for other works on dream interpretation, see Fahd, 1966a, pp. 330-63; Storey, II/3, pp. 466-72). The anonymous *Ḵᵛāb-gozārī* of the twelfth or thirteenth century has only partially survived; it is similar to Teflīsī's work and includes an extensive introduction to the subject of dream interpretation, in which the main koranic passages and pertinent prophetic traditions are cited.

Bibliography: (For cited works not found in this bibliography, see "Short References.") Ī. Afšār, "Andar fawāyed-e loḡawī-e kāmel al-taʿbīr," in S. Ḥ. Naṣr, ed., *Majmūʿa-ye maqālāt-e taḥqīqī-e ḵāvar-šenāsī-e ehdāʾ be Hānrī Māsa/Mélanges d'orientalisme offerts à Henri Massé*, Tehran, 1341 Š./1962, pp. 1-9. *ʿĀlamārā-ye Šāh Esmāʿīl*, ed. A. Montaẓer-Ṣāḥeb, Tehran, 1349 Š./1970. A. Amanat, *Resurrection and Renewal. The Making of the Babi Movement in Iran, 1840-1850*, Ithaca, N.Y., 1989. Bahā-Allāh, *Haft Vādī, Chahār Vādī*, Hofheim-Langenhain, Germany, 1988. V. Chauvin, "Les rêves du trésor sur le pont," *Revue des Traditions Populaires* 13, 1898, pp. 193-96. H. Corbin, *L'imagination créatrice dans le soufisme d'Ibn ʿArabī*, Paris, 1958; tr. R. Manheim as *Creative Imagination in the Ṣūfism of Ibn ʿArabī*, Princeton, N.J., 1969. Moḥammad Ebn Sīrīn, *Montaḵab al-kalām fī tafsīr al-aḥlām*, Cairo, 1302/1884; repr. Cairo, 1963. T. Fahd, "Les songes et leur interprétation selon l'Islam," in A.-M. Esnoul et al., eds., *Les songes et leur interprétation. Sources orientales* II, Paris, 1959. Idem, *La divination arabe*, Leiden, 1966a. Idem, "The Dream in Medieval Islamic Society," in G. E. von Grunebaum and R. Caillois, eds., *The Dream and Human Societies*, Berkeley and Los Angeles, 1966b, pp. 351-63. Abū Ḥāmed Ḡazālī, *Eḥyāʾ ʿolūm al-dīn. Ketāb ḏekr al-mawt* IV, Cairo, n.d., pp. 504-11. G. E. von Grunebaum, "Introduction. The Cultural Function of the Dream as Illustrated by Classical Islam," in G. E. von Grunebaum and R. Caillois, eds., *The Dream and Human Societies*, Berkeley and Los Angeles, 1966, pp. 3-21. W. Hanaway, "Formal Elements in the Persian Popular Romances," *Review of National Literature* 21, 1971, pp. 139-61. *Ḵᵛāb-gozārī*, ed. Ī. Afšār, Tehran, 1346 Š./1967. Moḥammad b. Yaʿqūb Kolaynī, *al-Oṣūl men al-kāfī* I, tr. M.-B. Kamareʾī, ed. M.-B. Behbūdī and ʿA.-A. Ḡaffārī, Tehran, 1382/1962. J. Lecerf, "The Dream in Popular Culture. Arab and Islamic," in G. E. von Grunebaum and R. Caillois, eds., *The Dream and Human Societies*, Berkeley and Los Angeles, 1966, pp. 366-79. R. G. A. van Lieshout, *Greeks on Dreams*, Utrecht, 1980. D. MacEoin, *From Shaykhism to Babism. A Study in Charismatic Renewal in Shīʿī Islam*, Ph.D. diss., The University of Cambridge, 1979. Moḥammad-Bāqer Majlesī, *Beḥār al-anwār. Ketāb al-samāʾ wa'l-ʿālam*, bk. LXI, Qom, n.d., pp. 151-244. J. Matīnī, "Ḵᵛābhā-ye Ahūrāʾī-e Ābtīn," *Īrān-šenāsī* 3/2, 1991, pp. 369-81. I. Mélikoff, *Abū Muslim, le "porte-hache" du Khorrassan. Dans la tradition épique turco-irannenne*. Paris, 1962. E. Meyerovitch, "Les songes et leur interprétation chez les Persans," in A.-M. Esnoul et al., eds., *Les songes et leur interprétation. Sources orientales* II, Paris, 1959, pp. 175-87. M. Mokri, "Les songes et leur interprétation chez les Ahl-e-Haqq du Kurdistan," in A.-M. Esnoul et al., eds., *Les songes et leur interprétation. Sources orientales* II, Paris, 1959, pp. 191-204. Mīrzā Ḥosayn Nūrī, *Najm-e ṯāqeb dar aḥwāl-e Emām-e ḡāyeb*, Tehran, 1306/1888. *Taḏkera-ye Šāh Ṭahmāsb*, Berlin, 1343/1924. Moḥammad b. ʿAlī Tahānawī, *Kaššāf eṣṭelāḥāt al-fonūn* I, ed. A. Sprenger, Calcutta, 1862, pp. 597-606. Abū Ṭāher Ṭarsūsī, *Abū Moslem-nāma* (*Ḥamāsa-ye Ḵorāsānī*), ed. E. Yaḡmāʾī, Tehran, 1355 Š./1976. Abu'l-Fażl Ḥobayš b. Moḥammad Teflīsī, *Kollīyāt-e kāmel al-taʿbīr . . .*, Tehran, n.d.

(HOSSEIN ZIAI)

DRESDEN, MARK JAN (b. Amsterdam, 26 April 1911; d. Philadelphia, 16 August 1986), American iranist of Dutch origin. He was born to a family of eminent musicians and studied classics and Indology at the University of Amsterdam, receiving a master's degree in 1937. He then transferred to the University of Utrecht, in order to study Vedic ritual texts with Jan Gonda; his doctoral dissertation was a translation entitled *Mānavagṛhyasūtra. A Vedic Manual of Domestic Rites* (Groningen, 1941). In 1937-38 Dresden studied with Émile Benveniste (q.v.) at the École Pratique des Hautes Études in Paris as a French government exchange fellow; in 1938-39 and again, after wartime hardships, in 1945-49 he taught Greek and Latin at the secondary school that he had himself attended in Amsterdam. During the same period he gradually shifted his interest from Indology to Iranian studies, under the influence of J. H. Kramers. His main publications from this period are two bibliographical guides in Dutch on Sogdian and Khotanese ("Iranica I. Bibliographia Sogdiana Concisa," *Ex Oriente Lux* 8, 1942, pp. 729-34; "Introductio ad Linguam Hvatanicam," *Ex Oriente Lux* 9, 1943-44, pp. 200-06) and a survey of postwar studies on Sogdian (in English, *Bibliotheca Orientalis* 6, 1949, pp. 28-31).

From 1947 to 1949 Dresden spent almost every summer in Cambridge, supported by the Dutch government, in order to study with H. W. Bailey and W. B. Henning. In 1948, while in England, Dresden met W. Norman Brown of the University of Pennsylvania in Philadelphia, who was then considering introducing Iranian studies into the curriculum; he invited Dresden to the university, where he taught Persian, then various Old and Middle Iranian languages from 1949 until his retirement in 1977.

Dresden continued to work on Khotanese secular, especially literary texts until his death. "The Jātakastava or 'Praise of the Buddha's Former Births'" (ed. and tr., *Transactions of the American Philosophical Society*, N.S. 45, pt. 5, Philadelphia, 1955, pp. 397-508) is a study of a collection of Late Khotanese jatakas (stories of the Buddha's former lives) in verse in a manuscript recovered from Dunhuang at the eastern end of the Tarim basin by Mark Aurel Stein. In addition to comparison with the jatakas known in other languages, he provided a grammatical and lexicological analysis, the first for Late Khotanese. His other significant works on this language include "Khotanese (Saka) Manuscripts. A Provisional Handlist," *Acta Iranica* 12, 1976, pp. 27-85, a classified list of all extant Khotanese manuscripts, with bibliographical notes; "Note on Khotanese Poetry" (in E. Bender, ed., *Indological Studies in Honor of W. Norman Brown*, New Haven, Conn., 1962, pp. 42-50); and "A Lyrical Poem in Khotanese" (in *Beiträge zur Indienforschung. Ernst Waldschmidt zum 80. Geburtstag gewidmet*, Veröffentlichungen des Museums für Indische Kunst 4, Berlin, 1977, pp. 81-103), his last published work. He was working on a sequel when illness struck him in 1982.

Dresden also wrote "Sogdian Language and Literature" (in *Camb. Hist. Iran* III/2, pp. 1216-29) and "Introductory Note" (in G. Azarpay, *Sogdian Painting. The Pictorial Epic in Oriental Art*, Berkeley and Los Angeles, 1981, pp. 1-10). He published a facsimile edition of the most important manuscript of the *Dēnkard* (q.v.; ed. Dresden), as well as a long introduction to the text ("Note on the 'B' Manuscript of the Dēnkart," in *J. M. Unvala Memorial Volume*, Bombay, 1964, pp. 198-268) and a survey of Pahlavi manuscripts in various universities and public libraries throughout the world ("Pahlavi Manuscripts," in *Sir J. J. Zarthoshti Madressa Centenary Volume*, Bombay, 1967, pp. 74-83). His article "Indo-Iranian Notes" (in *Henning Memorial Volume*, London, 1970, pp. 134-39) deals with a wide range of materials, from the Avesta and Old Persian to modern Iranian dialects.

In 1958 he and several associates compiled *A Reader in Modern Persian* (New York, 1958). One of the most useful tools for students of Iranian linguistics and philology is his general survey "Middle Iranian" (in T. Sebeok, ed., *Current Trends in Linguistics* VI, the Hague, 1970, pp. 26-63), containing lists of both primary and important secondary sources on each of the six Middle Iranian languages and descriptions of the grammatical characteristics of each. Every year from the early 1970s until illness made the work impossible he published a classified bibliography of the entire field of Iranian linguistics in the relevant section of *M.L.A. (Modern Language Association) International Bibliography*. He also wrote "Survey of the History of Iranian Studies" (*HO*, Abt. I, IV, pt. 2/1, Leiden, 1968, pp. 168-90) and "On the Genesis of Anquetil Duperron's Oupnek'hat" (in P. Gignoux and A. Tafazzoli, *Mémorial Jean de Menasce*, Louvain, 1974, pp. 35-43), dealing with a period when Indology and Iranian studies were not quite separate.

Bibliography: (For cited works not found in this bibliography, see "Short References."). *Répertoires* I. *Bio-bibliographies de 134 savants*, Acta Iranica 20, Leiden, 1979, pp. 122-24.

(Hiroshi Kumamoto)

DREYFUS-BARNEY, joint surname adopted by two leading Bahai figures of the 20th century.

i. *Hippolyte Dreyfus-Barney.*

ii. *Laura Clifford Dreyfus-Barney.*

i. Hippolyte Dreyfus-Barney

Hippolyte Dreyfus (b. Paris, 12 April 1873, d. Paris, 20 December 1928), son of a prominent French Jewish family, became a leading Bahai scholar, translator, and religious teacher. He received a degree in law from the Institut des Sciences Politiques in Paris and practiced before the Paris court of appeals. He was converted to the Bahai faith in about 1900 by May Ellis Bolles (later Maxwell), a Canadian living in Paris. In 1903 he was able to visit the Bahai leader ʿAbd-al-Bahāʾ (q.v.) in ʿAkkāʾ in Palestine. At about the same time he gave up his legal career to devote himself to oriental studies, enrolling in the religious-studies section of the École Pratique des Hautes Études in Paris, where he studied Arabic and Persian with Hartwig Derenbourg and Clément Huart, intending to translate Bahai scripture into French. He was the only Western Bahai of his generation who received such formal training.

In 1904 Dreyfus went to India and Burma to visit Bahai communities there. In the following year he met Moẓaffar-al-Dīn Shah (1313-24/1896-1907) in Paris and urged him to intervene to protect the Persian Bahais. Also in 1904 he visited Bahais in many Persian cities, as well as in the Caucasus and Turkestan, where he visited the large community in Ashkhabad (q.v.).

Dreyfus' first major translation was Bahāʾ-Allāh's *Ketāb-e īqān* (Book of certitude; Paris, 1904). He also published *Le babisme et le béhaïsme* (Paris, 1904), a lecture that he had delivered on 1 March 1904 at the École des Hautes Études Sociales. More influential was his later publication *Essai sur le béhaïsme* (Paris, 1909; 3rd ed. published as *Bahaïsme*), the first "handbook" on the faith, in which he dealt with the the history of the Babi and Bahai religions and such questions as religion and the state, universal peace, Bahaism and society, the house of justice, Bahaism and the individual, and the Bahai faith and patriotism. In 1905-06 he and Ḥabīb-Allāh Šīrāzī published a collection of Bahāʾ-Allāh's writings entitled *Les préceptes du Béhaïsme* (2 vols.,

Paris, 1905-06), which included *Haft wādī* (The seven valleys), *Kalemat-e maknūna* (The hidden words), *Lawḥ-e ḥekmat* (Tablet of wisdom), *Lawḥ-e aqdas* (The most holy tablet), and several other works. In 1907-09 Dreyfus collaborated with the American Bahai Laura Clifford Barney (see ii, below) on the publication of Persian, French, and English editions of the answers of ʿAbd-al-Bahāʾ to philosophical and theological questions that she had put to him (published as *Mofāważāt-e mobāraka*, *Les leçons de Saint Jean d'Acre*, and *Some Answered Questions* respectively). In later years he translated several more of Bahāʾ-Allāh's books: *al-Ketāb al-aqdas* and *Soʾāl o jawāb* (both unpublished), *Lawḥ-e Šayḵ* (Paris, 1913), and a three-volume collection of Bahāʾ-Allāh's works containing his own earlier translations and some new ones (Paris, 1923-28). He also published a number of books and scholarly articles on Bahai topics.

In 1911 he married Barney, and both took the surname Dreyfus-Barney. In the same year he served as translator when ʿAbd-al-Bahāʾ visited Paris. The Dreyfus-Barneys continued their travels, visiting China and French Indochina in 1914. During World War I Hippolyte worked as a postal censor in Marseilles. In 1920 the couple once again visited Southeast Asia.

Dreyfus-Barney was greatly respected by ʿAbd-al-Bahāʾ, who encouraged him in his travels and relied on him in various delicate matters. When ʿAbd-al-Bahāʾ died in November 1921 the Dreyfus-Barneys were among those summoned to Haifa by the new leader, Shoghi Effendi Rabbānī. Hippolyte made use of his legal and linguistic skills to represent the Bahais in conflicts involving the status of the Bahai shrines in Palestine, the seizure of Bahāʾ-Allāh's house in Baghdad, and the persecution of the Bahais of Egypt (1925-27).

Bibliography: ʿA. ʿAzīzī, *Tāj-e wahhāj*, Tehran, 1976. A. Fāżel Māzandarānī, *Ẓohūr al-ḥaqq* VIII/2, Tehran, 132 B.E./1975, pp. 1184-85. L. Henuzet, "Dreyfus-Barney, Hippolyte and Laura Clifford," in *A Short Encyclopedia of the Bahá'í Faith*, Wilmette, Ill., forthcoming. K. Joneidi, "Une biographie de Hippolyte Dreyfus, le premier croyant français," *Bahá'í France* 17, January 1989. Reinach, "Hippolyte Dreyfus," *Revue archéologique*, 5th ser., 29, 1929, p. 173. Shoghi Effendi S. Rabbānī, "Hippolyte Dreyfus-Barney. An Appreciation," in *The Bahá'í World* 3, Wilmette, Ill., 1928-30, pp. 210-11, 214.

(Shapour Rassekh)

ii. Laura Clifford Dreyfus-Barney

Laura Clifford Barney (b. Cincinnati, O., 30 November 1879, d. Paris, 18 August 1974) became a leading American Bahai teacher and philanthropist. The daughter of Albert and Alice Pike Barney, a socially prominent artist from Washington, D.C., she was educated by private tutors. While continuing her studies in Paris Laura met May Ellis Bolles (later Maxwell), a Canadian Bahai, and was converted to the faith in about 1900. Her mother was converted soon afterward.

Laura Barney financed the visit of the Persian Bahai scholar Mīrzā Abu'l-Fażl Golpāyagānī (q.v.) to the United States in 1901-04, in order to propagate the faith there, and helped to publish the translation of his *Ḥojaj al-bahīya* (Cairo, 1342/1925; tr. Ali-Kuli Khan as *The Bahá'í Proofs*, New York, 1902; 2nd ed., ed. J. R. I. Cole, Wilmette, Ill., 1983). In 1904 she visited ʿAbd-al-Bahāʾ in ʿAkkāʾ, Palestine, where she remained about two years, acquiring a working knowledge of Persian and becoming an intimate of his household. During that time she arranged to have ʿAbd-al-Bahāʾ's answers to her questions, mainly on philosophy and Christian theology, recorded by his secretaries. She collaborated with her future husband, Hippolyte Dreyfus (see i, above), on the editing and translation of this work (*al-Nūr al-abhā fī mofāważāt ʿAbd-al-Bahāʾ*, Leiden, 1908; tr. L. C. Barney and H. Dreyfus as *Some Answered Questions*, London, 1908; tr. H. Dreyfus as *Les leçons de Saint Jean d'Acre*, Paris, 1909). In 1905-06 she visited Persia, the Caucasus, and Russia with Dreyfus. After their marriage in April 1911, when they both adopted the surname Dreyfus-Barney, she traveled extensively with him.

During World War I Laura Dreyfus-Barney served in the American Ambulance Corps (1914-15) and the American Red Cross (1916-18) in France and helped to establish the first children's hospital in Avignon (1918). The remainder of her life was devoted to international humanitarian and philanthropic activities, most connected with the League of Nations and the United Nations. For her services she was named *chevalier* (1925) and *officier* (1937) of the French Légion d'Honneur. There is a copy of her unpublished memoirs in the Bahai national archives in France.

Bibliography: Bahá'í International Community, United Nations Office, *Report to the United Nations and Public Information Policy Committee*, New York, 21 July 1988 (on celebration of the centennial of the International Council of Women in honor of the memory of Laura Dreyfus-Barney). A. Fāżel Māzandarānī, *Ẓohūr al-ḥaqq* VIII/2, Tehran, 132 B.E./1975. U. R. Giachery, "Laura Clifford Dreyfus-Barney, 1879-1974" in *The Bahá'í World* 16, 1978, pp. 535-38. R. Meḥrāb-Ḵānī, *Zendagī-e Mīrzā Abu'l-Fażl Golpāyagānī*, Langenhain, Germany, 1988, p. 277. *Who Was Who in America, 1897-1942* I, Chicago, 1968, p. 59.

(Shapour Rassekh)

DRIWAY- (or Driβi-), Younger Avestan noun from the *Vidēvdād*; it is not a substantive but an adjective in *-i-* referring to a defect of the body defined as "the mark of Aŋra Mainiiu" (see AHRIMAN; *Vd.* 2.29) or, in the compound *akaranəm.driβi-* "eternal *driβi*," to the fly that embodies the demon of corpses *(nasu; Vd.* 7.2). It is also the name of a *daēuua* (see *DAIVA-; *Vd.* 19.43). It is not certain whether the vowel *i* in the first syllable is original or whether a derivation from reconstructed *$*d(h)ṛb(h)i-$ must be assumed. Beside being attested only in late texts, the word *driβi-* belongs to a vocabulary so special that its etymology cannot be taken as certain, despite suggestions put forward by Jarl Charpentier and H. W. Bailey. A relation with *driβika-* (*Vd.* 1.8), rendered as "sobs" by the Pahlavi translator (*Avesta*, tr. Darmesteter, II, p. 10 n. 21), is also uncertain. The word probably referred either to a skin disease (*AirWb.*, pp. 46, 778; cf. Charpentier: *Flecken*) or to drooling (Bailey).

Bibliography: (For cited works not found in this bibliography and abbreviations found here, see "Short References.") J. Charpentier, "Zur arischen Wortkunde," *ZVS* 40, 1907, pp. 460-62. H. W. Bailey, "Avestan *driβi-*," *Professor Jackson Memorial Volume*, Bombay, 1954, pp. 1-7.

(JEAN KELLENS)

DṚNABĀJIŠ, name of the fifth month (July-August) of the Old Persian calendar, equivalent to Akkadian Ābu and Elamite Zillatam (several attestations in the Persepolis tablets only; see Hinz and Koch, pp. 1164, 1299-1300, 1305; cf. CALENDARS i). It is one of three month names that are not attested in the original Old Persian form; it can be reconstructed only from the Elamite rendering Tur-na-ba-(iz-)-zí(-iš), Tu-ur-na-, Tar-na- (and some minor variants). In some instances the variant Tur/Tar-na-ba-(iz-)zí-ya-iš, reflecting *Dṛnabājya-, occurs (cf. the Elamite doublet Bakeyatiyaš/Bakeyatiš, reflecting OPers. *Bāgayādya-/Bāgayādiš, q.v., with corrigenda; see Hinz, p. 66). The various renderings lead to reconstruction of an original form *Dṛna-bāji- or the like, the etymological interpretation of which is not fully established, though the second element is surely Old Persian *bāji-* "tribute, duty, tax"; Walther Hinz (p. 66: *bāži-*) understands the form as "(month of) the harvest tax."

Bibliography: W. Hinz, *Neue Wege im Altpersischen*, Wiesbaden, 1973. Idem and H. Koch, *Elamisches Wörterbuch*, 2 parts, Berlin, 1987, pp. 292, 369-70, 387.

(RÜDIGER SCHMITT)

DRŌN (Mid. Pers. *drōn*, Bk. Pahl. *dlwn* < Av. *draonah-* "portion of food"; Gujarati Parsi *darūn*), Zoroastrian ritual term originally meaning "sacred portion" and designating a ritual offering to divine beings (*Y.* 33.8), for example, the portion of a sacrificial animal presented to the *yazata* Haoma (Hōm; *Y.* 11.4). In later Zoroastrian tradition, as reflected in the Pahlavi books and contemporary Parsi practice, however, *drōn* denotes only the flat, round unleavened wheat bread that constitutes the regular offering. According to stipulations preserved in *Nērangestān* (1.8.A-C), *drōn* must be prepared from dry, ritually clean, unleavened wheat flour moistened with pure water and kneaded only by priests or their wives (*Aērpatastān*, pp. 86-104; *Ērbadistān*, fols. 28r-34r; *Nērangestān*, fols. 39v-47v, 48v-49v). During preparation each *drōn* is marked on one side with znine shallow incisions, arranged three by three, while the words *humata*, *hūxta*, and *hvaršta* are recited thrice each. *Frasast*, unmarked wheat bread of the same type, is also made and consecrated with the *drōn* by the *zōt* "officiating priest" (*Y.* 8.1; Modi, pp. 279-80, 335). Zoroastrians in Persia now make *drōn* from leavened dough (Boyce, *Stronghold*, p. 38).

As one of the *myazd*, or votive offerings, *drōn* is a ritual requisite for the *yasna*, *yašt ī drōn*, *vidēvdād*, *visperad*, and *āfrīnagān* ceremonies. Because *yašt ī drōn* "service [for consecration] of the *drōn*" (*Y.* 3-8), a ceremony of worship and thanksgiving with a *šnūman*, or dedication, in Avestan to any Zoroastrian divinity, may also be performed as a *bāj* (q.v.), or consecration, before eating, Parsis have come to call it by that term and know it as the *bāj* of *panj tāy* (Modi, p. 340). Zoroastrians in Persia, on the other hand, have abbreviated the name of the service simply to *drōn* (Boyce and Kotwal, p. 65). One *drōn* is required for consecration during the *yasna*, *vidēvdād*, *visperad*, and *āfrīnagān* ceremonies. *Yašt ī drōn* services usually require consecration of two *drōn*s and two *frasast*s. One exception is the service in honor of Sraoša (Srōš), which requires three *drōn*s and three *frasast*s.

Parsi priests place clarified butter, representing the *gōšodāg* (< Av. *gaoš.huδå*), in the center of the *drōn* and consecrate them together. The bread is believed to represent the vegetable kingdom and to have been made for protection of the body and is also compared to the material world (K. J. Jamasp-Asa, p. 203), whereas *gōšodāg* is thought to symbolize the animal kingdom (Boyce and Kotwal, p. 63). Consecration of the *drōn* and *gōšodāg* consists of the recitation of *Yasna* 3-8, which takes place as part of the *yasna* service; the *zōt*, while reciting *Yasna* 8.4, ritually tastes (makes *čāšnī* of) both (Boyce and Kotwal, p. 63; Modi, p. 281). In a separate *yašt ī drōn* service, for which the text is the same, the *frasast* is also tasted (Modi, pp. 340-41). Afterward members of the congregation may partake of these consecrated foods. Four *yašt ī drōn* are performed, in honor of Vayu (Wāy), Rašnu (Rašn) and Arštāt (Aštād), Sraoša, and the *fravaši*s just before the dawn following the third night after a Zoroastrian's death and during each of the ten days of *frawardīgān*. The service is a basic preliminary for all other high ceremonies as well (K. M. Jamasp-Asa).

Bibliography: (For cited works not found in this bibliography and for abbreviations found here, see

"Short References.") *Aērpatastān and Nīrangastān*, tr. S. J. Bulsara, Bombay, 1915. M. Boyce and F. M. Kotwal, "Zoroastrian *bāj* and *drōn*," *BSOAS* 34, 1971, pp. 56-73, 298-313. *Ērbadistān ud Nīrangistān*, ed. F. M. Kotwal and J. W. Boyd, Cambridge, Mass., 1980 (ms. no. TD). K. J. Jamasp-Asa, "On the Symbolism of the Darun," in *The Dastur Hoshang Memorial Volume*, Bombay, 1918, pp. 201-05. K. M. Jamasp-Asa, "On the Drôn in Zoroastrianism," *Acta Iranica* 24, 1985, pp. 335-56. J. J. Modi, *The Religious Ceremonies and Customs of the Parsees*, 2nd ed., Bombay, 1937; repr., Bombay, 1986. *Nērangestān*, ed. P. Sanjana as *Nirangistan*, Bombay, 1894 (ms. no. HJ).

(JAMSHEED K. CHOKSY)

DRUGS (Pers. *dārū*, Pers-Ar. *dawā*, pl. *adwīa*), in medieval Muslim literature any vegetable, mineral, or animal substance that acts on the human body, whether as a medicament, a poison, or an antidote.

Pre-Islamic Persia. Information on drugs in the pre-Islamic period is very scarce and, apart from clues in sources from after the Islamic conquest, limited to a few mentions in the Avesta (q.v.) and other ancient texts. They indicate that ancient Iranians were aware of the therapeutic properties of various substances and made deliberate use of them. In a travel narrative sometimes ascribed to Pythagoras (Pseudo Pythagoras, tr., p. 54) unspecified herbal drugs are mentioned, including a sleeping draft said to have been used by Zoroaster. Herbal treatment is also mentioned in the Avesta (*Yt.* 3.3), where frequent reference is made to the plant *haoma* (Mid. Pers. *hōm*, identified by Flattery and Schwartz as harmal), which "gives good cures," "keeps death away," and "implants strength" (*Y.* 9-11, 20; *Yt.* 10.23). Mazdeans believed that Ohrmazd had created at least one herb to cure each disease (Christensen, *Iran Sass.*, p. 419). The most cogent evidence for ancient Iranian interest in pharmacy is the Iranian origin of many drug names in medieval medical and pharmacological treatises (Browne, p. 22). The first writers in the Persian empire to discuss drugs and their properties were mainly physicians from the college at Gondēšāpūr in Ḵūzestān or their pupils; their works were the sources on which later writers relied (cf. *al-Ḵūz*, a source for Bīrūnī, 1992, pp. 530, 611; and Rāzī, 1955-71, XXI, pp. 45, 70, which seems a reference to the physicians at Gondēšāpūr; *Konnāš al-ḵūz*, mentioned by Bīrūnī, 1888, p. 205, seems to be the title of a book on pharmacology composed there).

The caliphate until the rise of the Buyids. The medical college at Gondēšāpūr remained active under the Omayyads, but very little is known about the work of Persian physicians and pharmacologists there. In keeping with the ancient theory of humors, drugs were classified as cold, hot, moist, or dry (e.g., Ṭabarī, p. 400). The essential function of a drug, according to this theory, is to help the body keep or recover a stable balance among the humors and temperaments. Contrary to the modern medical assumption that patients normally react to a drug in the same way, medieval physicians thought that reactions varied with the temperament of the patient, as well as the nature of the drug. Drugs were classified as "simple" (*mofrad*, *ʿaqqār*, pl. *ʿaqāqīr*) and "compound" (*morakkab*, *qarābāḏīn*, *aqrābāḏīn* < Gk. *graphidion*, lit., "small treatise"). Compounds were designed to achieve a balance among the component simple drugs (see, e.g., Ebn Sīnā, II, p. 222).

One of the first known Persian pharmacologists was Māsarjūya (Pers. Māsargōya), a prominent Jewish physician from Baṣra who lived in the early ʿAbbasid period and was said to have written books about drugs, including *Qowā al-ʿaqāqīr wa manāfeʿehā wa mażārrehā* (Ebn al-Qefṭī, pp. 324-25); his treatise on substitute drugs still survives. It was, however, the arrival of Jorjīs b. Boḵtīšūʿ (see BOḴTĪŠŪʿ) from Gondēšāpūr at the court of the caliph al-Manṣūr (136-58/754-75) that marked the beginning of the transmission of Persian pharmacological knowledge in the ʿAbbasid capital, whence it was diffused throughout the Muslim world. Jorjīs himself was said to have written *al-Konnāš*, a collection of essays on medical and pharmacological subjects. His pupil at Gondēšāpūr ʿIsā b. Ṣahārboḵt (Čahārboḵt) Jondīsābūrī wrote *Qowā al-adwīa al-mofrada* (Ebn al-Nadīm, p. 356; cf. Sezgin, *GAS* III, p. 243) on simple drugs. Another noted contemporary was Māsūya, who practiced pharmacology at Gondēšāpūr for forty years (Ebn al-Qefṭī, pp. 383-84; cf. Sezgin, *GAS* III, p. 229). His son Yūḥannā (d. 243/857) wrote essays on the subject, including *al-Adwīa al-moshela* and *Eṣlāḥ al-adwīa al-moshela* on aperient drugs, which were cited several times by Rāzī (1955-71, XV, p. 234, VI, p. 109, XX, pp. 105, 133, XXI, p. 653; cf. Sezgin, *GAS* III, pp. 231-36). From remarks by Ebn Abī Oṣaybeʿa (I, p. 157) about the experiences of pharmacists in the camp of Afšīn during the war against Bābak the Ḵorramī (qq.v.) in the early 9th century, it appears that early pharmacists constituted a professional or occupational class, including untrained quacks.

One of the most widely used pharmacological books written in the 9th century was a treatise on compound drugs, *Aqrābāḏīn*, by Sābūr (Šāpūr) b. Sahl Jondīsābūrī (d. 355/869; Ebn al-Nadīm, p. 355); it included formulas for pills, ointments, poultices, and other drugs (Bābā, 1976, p. 579). At about the same time Boḵtīšūʿ b. Jebrāʾīl (d. 256/870) wrote *Naṣāʾeḥ al-rohbān fi'l-adwīa al-morakkaba*, of which a manuscript survives in the Taymūrīya library in the Dār al-kotob, Cairo (Sezgin, *GAS* III, p. 243; Sāmarrāʾī, I, p. 391; cf. Ebn al-Qefṭī, p. 103).

The outstanding physician of the ʿAbbasid period was, however, Ḥonayn b. Esḥāq (192-260/816-73), who wrote and translated many works, including a book about drugs, *Eḵtīār al-adwīa al-mojarraba*, and another about antidotes, *al-Teryāq* (Ebn al-Nadīm, p. 353; Ebn al-Qefṭī, pp. 173-74). One of his translations, *al-Adwīa al-mofrada*, was a pharmacopoeia attributed to Galen, and the seventh discourse (pp. 147-58) of his ʿAšar maqālāt is about simple drugs in general. Ḥonayn followed the old classification of drugs according to humors and further subdivided them by the degree of change induced in the human organism (pp. 152-53). He also revised Esṭefān b. Basīl's Arabic translation of a portion of the Greek *De Materia Medica* by Dioscorides (Dīosqoredīs) under the title *Hayūlā'l-ṭebb fi'l-ḥašāʾeš wa'l-somūm*. This work had a strong influence on pharmacology in Ḥonayn's lifetime and subsequently (Sezgin, *GAS* III, p. 59), but its importance was more theoretical than practical because many of the cited drugs were unobtainable in the eastern part of the caliphate and could not be tested or prescribed; local pharmacists relied on Persian and Indian drugs instead (Bābā, 1977, pp. 188-89).

The medical treatise *Ferdaws al-ḥekma* by the Persian physician ʿAlī b. Rabban Ṭabarī (d. ca. 250/864) also deserves mention. It includes chapters on simple and compound drugs; uses of drugs made from the bodies of animals (pp. 420-23); oils, juices, seeds (pp. 374-99), and antidotes (p. 449-66); and various antitoxic and anticholeric pills and remedies (pp. 467-72). Ṭabarī wrote another treatise, on the medical uses of different foods, drinks, and simple drugs, *Manāfeʿ al-aṭʿema wa'l-ašreba wa'l-ʿaqāqīr* (Ebn al-Nadīm, p. 354; for a different title, see Sezgin, III, p. 240), an abridged version of which, by Mūsā Motaṭabbeb Yamānī (ca. 1250/1834), survives in a private library at Aleppo (Sezgin, *GAS*, pp. 236-40; Sāmarrāʾī, I, p. 471).

Pharmacology was often linked in the early sources with the study of botany, alchemy, mineralogy, and even zoology. In fact, these studies were often motivated by the desire for pharmacological knowledge (Ṣeddīqī, p. 448; Naṣr, p. 459), and any general medical treatise usually included a chapter on simple and compound drugs. Abū Bakr Moḥammad b. Zakarīyāʾ Rāzī (d. early 10th century) devoted three volumes of his great medical encyclopaedia *al-Ḥāwī fi'l-ṭebb* to pharmacology. His precise and highly technical studies of drugs and compounding were positively influenced by his knowledge of alchemy. The various drugs are discussed in alphabetical order; for each entry the theories of earlier pharmacologists are given first, then varieties and properties. Sometimes the Greek or Syriac name is also given. Rāzī's main achievement in this field, however, was to bring the practice of pharmacy under scientific scrutiny. In a preliminary essay he pointed out that pharmacology is not a branch of medicine but a tool in its service; the best physicians were also qualified pharmacists, and one who knew only about the characteristics of drugs was not a physician

(1955-71, XXII, pp. 2, 4; idem, 1977, pp. 2, 3, 13; cf. Elgood, 1951, p. 272). He also emphasized the importance of freshly gathered herbs and mentioned the sources of supply for many. He even noted the volumes and weights to be used in mixing drugs and measuring doses and provided tables highlighting different names (1955-71, XXII, pp. 2-66). Rāzī wrote several other books on pharmacology, including *al-Aqarābāḏīn al-kabīr*, *al-Qarābāḏīn al-ṣaḡīr*, *al-Adwīa al-mawjūda be-koll makān*, and *Abdāl al-adwīa* (Ebn al-Qefṭī, p. 274; Sezgin, *GAS* III, pp. 274-94).

The Samanids and Buyids. In Samanid Bukhara Abū Bakr Aḵawaynī (q.v.) wrote a medical textbook, *Hedāyat al-motaʿallemīn*. Although it is not primarily concerned with pharmacology, it includes descriptions of about 3,000 simple and compound drugs, many with Persian names, in connection with relevant diseases. The author apparently intended to write a separate book on drugs (p. viii). Aḵawaynī claimed to have personally tested most of the drugs mentioned in his book (pp. 407, 455, 589) and did not hesitate to criticize earlier physicians for misusing them (pp. 457, 560, 580). He also classified them as foods, drugs, medicinal foods, and poisons (p. 3). Whenever possible, he gave the Persian, Arabic, Syriac, and Greek names of each drug. From the same period is preserved the oldest surviving pharmacological work in Persian, *Ketāb al-abnīa*, by Abū Manṣūr Mowaffaq Heravī (q.v.), in which 584 drugs are described (Meyerhof, pp. xvi-xvii). Aḥmad b. Abi'l Ašʿat (d. 360/970), a Persian physician living in Mosul and author of many medical books, wrote a manual of simple drugs, *Ketāb al-adwīa al-mofrada*, and a book on compound drugs, *Tarkīb al-adwīa* (Ebn Abī Oṣaybeʿa, I, pp. 246-47; Sezgin, *GAS* III, pp. 301-02).

The great Avicenna (q.v.; Ebn Sīnā) completed his major work, *al-Qānūn fi'l-ṭebb*, in the early 11th century. Books 2 and 5 are devoted to simple and compound drugs respectively. Avicenna, who had personally prepared and tested many drugs, recommended balanced remedies blending the four basic humors (II, p. 224); the properties of such remedies could be ascertained by experimentation and inference (II, p. 223 ff.). Whenever a simple drug failed to cure a given sickness, proved harmful to another part of the body, or was found to be excessively hot, cold, dry, or moist, it was to be mixed with other simple drugs in order to strengthen its curative properties, counteract its harmful effects, and balance the nature of the drug (III, p. 309 ff.). Avicenna provided the earliest descriptions of a number of remedies, including opium (*al-teryāq al-kabīr*) for stomach and liver disorders (III, p. 321). According to Ebn al-Qefṭī (p. 418), he also wrote a monograph on cardiac drugs, *al-Adwīa al-qalbīya*.

The Ghaznavids and Saljuqs. The outstanding pharmacological work of the later 11th century is *Ketāb al-ṣaydana* (comp. 442/1050) by Abū Rayḥān

Bīrūnī (q.v.). It begins with definitions of the terms "pharmacy" (*ṣaydana*) and "simple drug," a substance intermediate between a food and a poison that can neutralize either; like his predecessors Bīrūnī emphasized that drugs can be evaluated only by expert physicians (pp. 9-10). He distiguished two kinds of substitute for scarce or unobtainable drugs: an inferior variety or a different drug (pp. 12-13) with similar curative properties. He also observed that a given drug may have different effects, depending on whether it is administered as a potion, a poultice, or an ointment (p. 13). He then described individual drugs in alphabetical order, with Arabic, Persian, Greek, Indian, and Syriac names as appropriate. One of his sources was probably the Syriac *Poššāq šmāhē* (Explanation of the names), which some Christians had permitted him to see; it was also known as *Čahār nām* (Four names) because it included the Persian, Syriac, Greek, and Arabic names of drugs (Bīrūnī, *Ṣaydana*, pp. 16-17; cf. Ebn Abī Oṣaybeʿa, I, p. 318; Ullmann, pp. 335-36). In the medieval Persian translation of the *Ṣaydana* 819 drugs are mentioned; the chapter on properties of drugs, including only 799 entries, is a later addition (1992, p. xxvii).

The leading author in the 12th century was Sayyed Esmāʿīl Jorjānī (d. ca. 531/1136), who devoted book 10 of his lengthy medical encyclopedia *D̲ak̲īra-ye k̲ᵛārazmšāhī* to pharmacology (pp. 651-745). In the first discourse he described drugs in thirty-eight categories according to their effects on various ailments. The second discourse begins with a discussion of experimentation and analogy as methods for determining the curative properties of drugs (p. 686). His view of circumstances calling for compound drugs was broadly similar to those of Avicenna and Bīrūnī. Book 9 comprises four discourses on poisons, antidotes, and harmful herbal, mineral, and animal drugs (pp. 626-51). At the end of the Saljuq period Najīb-al-Dīn Moḥammad b. ʿAlī Samarqandī (d. 619/1222) wrote the lengthy treatise *Qarābād̲īn* on compound drugs, classified by the diseases they helped relieve, and a work on simple drugs, both preserved in manuscript (*al-D̲arīʿa* XVII, p. 60).

The Mongols and Timurids. The *Tansūk̲-nāma-ye īl-k̲ānī*, a treatise on precious stones and rare minerals ascribed to Naṣīr-al-Dīn Ṭūsī, includes discussion of medical uses, for example, powdered pearls for certain eye diseases, headaches, and bleeding in the throat (p. 105) and lapis lazuli for bilious dysentery and melancholia (pp. 116-17). Similarly ʿAbd-Allāh Kāšānī, in his book on precious stones and perfumes, mentioned medical properties attributed to such substances as diamonds, rubies, mercury, and camphor (q.v.; pp. 36, 82, 212, 262), which are known to have actually been used as remedies for several diseases in later centuries (see, e.g., Chardin, V, p. 187). Zakarīyāʾ Qazvīnī (d. 682/1283) attributed medical properties to the hair, skull, blood, and other parts of the human body, as well as to parts of the bodies of asses, camels, giraffes, hares, and so on (pp. 253-55, 264-340).

Large hospitals (see BĪMĀRESTĀN) had specialized pharmacists and pharmaceutical laboratories (*šarāb-k̲āna, bayt al-adwīa, dārū-k̲āna*) headed by officials called *mehtar-e šarāb-k̲āna* or *k̲āzen* (Rašīd-al-Dīn, 1977, pp. 42, 146, 148; Qalqašandī, III, p. 472, X, p. 4, V, pp. 469-70). The Il-khanid vizier Rašīd-al-Dīn Fażl-Allāh founded a hospital and dispensary in the Rabʿ-e Rašīdī at Tabrīz, where drugs were dispensed to patients every Monday and Thursday. They had to be prescribed by a physician and were administered under his direct supervision or in the presence of the pharmacist (*šarābdār*) and the manager of the pharmacy (*k̲āzen*; 1977, pp. 146-47). Rašīd-al-Dīn ordered that drugs be obtained from every city and declared that one of his reasons for traveling to India was to arrange for medical supplies (1945, pp. 16, 53-54).

On the other hand, concoction and sale of drugs by unqualified pharmacists and itinerant vendors became so widespread that in every city special regulations were adopted; they were enforced by the *moḥtaseb* (market supervisor), who was empowered to enter the premises of any apothecary, even at night, without the owner's permission, in order to inspect substances and equipment and to ensure conformity with the official formulary, in principle that of Ebn Abi'l-Bayyān (d. 640/1242) or that of Ebn al-Telmīd̲ (d. 560/1165); the latter survives in manuscript but has not been published. Druggists were forbidden, for example, to dilute simple drugs like essence of violets with such substances as lemon juice. Violations were punishable under Islamic law (Ebn al-Ok̲ūwwa, pp. 115-25).

The great influence of *Jāmeʿ al-mofradāt* by Ebn al-Bayṭār (d. 646/1248), a work on pharmacology, throughout the Muslim world can be seen in Naṣīr-al-Dīn Jovaynī's *Mā lā yasaʿo'l-ṭabība jahloho* (comp. mid-14th century), in two parts on simple and compound drugs respectively. Jovaynī claimed (fol. 4a) that his book replicates *Jāmeʿ al-mofradāt* but is an independent work, insofar as Persian names of many drugs are given; he attempted to find Persian equivalents for many Syriac, Greek, Indian, and Arabic drug names. Some of these drugs cannot yet be identified, for example *arand sorand*, a bulb (fol. 12a); *oštorḡān*, called *ṭāk̲ak* in Ṭabarestān (fol. 13a); *k̲oškanjabīn* (fol. 83b); *bādāmak*; and *bārzad* (fol. 31b). In one respect his book is superior to that of Ebn al-Bayṭār: More attention is given to appraising the properties of drugs and specifying quantities to be used in compounds. Jovaynī also noted undesirable side effects of certain drugs and discussed appropriate countermeasures (fols. 3b-4a).

Among authors of the Timurid period the most distinguished were Najīb-al-Dīn Samarqandī, whose works survive in manuscript (e.g., *Oṣūl-e tarkīb-e adwīa* and *Tarkīb al-adwīa al-qalbīya*, Ketāb-k̲āna ye Majles-e Senā, Tehran, ms. nos. 536-37) and

Borhān-al-Dīn Nafīs.

The Safavids, Afsharids, and Zands. In the 16th-18th centuries few physicians and pharmacists presented new ideas or original research. ʿAlī Afżal Qāṭeʿ, apparently a hospital administrator at Qazvīn in the Safavid period (ca. 1051/1641), characterized his *Manāfeʿ-e afżalīya* as a selection of excerpts from the works of earlier authorities (fol. 1b); after classifying diseases and drugs according to the four humors (fols. 8a-20b), he discussed aperients, sedatives, and drugs for stomach and liver disorders (fols. 20b-finis). Many pharmacological books of the Safavid period include the word *qarābāḏīn* in the title, for example, *Qarābāḏīn-e Šefāʾī* by Moẓaffar b. Moḥammad Ḥosaynī Šefāʾī (d. 963/1556), a work preserved in numerous manuscripts (*al-Ḏarīʿa* XVII, p. 61; Monzawī, *Noskahā* I, p. 580), the main source for the *Pharmacopoeia Persica* of Father Angelus, published in France in 1681 (Elgood, 1970, p. 34). A large number of medical and pharmacological treatises were written in India in the Persian language, often with Sanskrit or Urdu, as well as Persian, drug names, for example, *Ektīārāt-e qoṭbšāhī* (on simple and compound drugs; ca. 972/1563) by Mīr Majd-al-Dīn Moḥammad Ḥosaynī Kāšānī, *Ganj-e bādāvard* (1035/1624) by Amān-Allāh Khan b. Mahābat Khan, *Alfāẓ al-adwīa* (1038/1627) by Nūr-al-Dīn ʿAbd-Allāh Šīrāzī, *Qarābāḏīn* by Moḥammad-Hāšem ʿAlawī Khan (d. 1162/1749), *Qarābāḏīn-e jalālī* by Jalāl al-Dīn Amrūdahī, and *Majmūʿa-ye Ḥakīm-al-Molk* by Ḥakīm-al-Molk Gīlānī (Wāseṭī, pp. 51, 91, 115-16; Šahmardān, p. 684).

In contrast to the practice in earlier periods, in the 17th century it was customary for apothecaries (*ʿaṭṭār*) to examine sick customers in their shops and to prescribe drugs (Elgood, 1970, p. 31). Sometimes (Chardin, V, p. 176) a physician and a druggist might consult on the diagnosis and prescription. The English traveler Thomas Herbert (in Persia 1627-28) praised Persian physicians and remarked on their preference for vegetable, rather than mineral, drugs (Elgood, 1951, pp. 406-07), but his countryman John Fryer (in Persia 1676-78) criticized their ignorance of the medicinal properties of juices and extracts from plants and roots; nevertheless, Fryer found the apothecary shops unequaled in the world for the variety of drugs and medicinal herbs on offer (Elgood, 1951, pp. 392-406). Jean Chardin noted that physicians kept collections of medicinal herbs for use in training apprentices (V, p. 175). Among the drugs then in common use in Persia were *šīrkešt* and *gazangabīn* (two kinds of manna), *morr-e makkī* (Meccan myrrh), *folūs* (cassia), *senā* (senna), *rīvand* (rhubarb), *šīrīn-bayān* (licorice), *nošāder* (sal ammoniac), *saqmūnīā* (scammony), and *čūb-e čīnī* (China root; Chardin, V, pp. 187-88).

The most eminent physician of Safavid Persia was Ḥosayn Nūrbakš, who drew on both experience and precedent in his medical treatise *Kolāṣat al-tajāreb* (957/1550), several chapters of which were devoted to pharmacology and the pharmacopoeia. In chapter 26 he defined poisons and antidotes, distinguishing toxic substances from drugs with harmful side effects, then named and described various poisons (fols. 308b-10a); vegetable antidotes included *jadvār* or *māhparvīn* (zedoary), *zarāvand* (birthwort), *zoronbād* (broad-leaved ginger), and *mūrd* (true myrtle), and among mineral and animal antidotes he mentioned Armenian bole, black and white naphtha, and rhinoceros horn (fols. 320a-25b). In chapter 27 he described compound drugs of his own invention, including *ḥabb al-šefā* (cure pills), *ḥāfeẓ al-ṣeḥḥa* (health preserver), *teryāq-e jadīd* (new theriaca), and *teryāq al-ṭīn-e jadīd* (new mud theriaca; fols. 335a-34b), several aperients, and such potions as *čahār-šarbat* (four syrups, fol. 337b) and *pālūda-ye ṭebbī* (medicinal *pālūda*, a sort of jelly, fol. 338a-b). Chapter 28 is about technical terms and weights and measures used in compound drugs (fols. 340b-41a).

The most widely used pharmacological manual in the Safavid period was *Toḥfat al-moʾmenīn* by Moḥammad-Zamān Tonakābon, personal physician to Shah Esmāʿīl I (907-30/1501-24), and his son Moḥammad-Moʾmen. It consists of two parts, the first with names and descriptions of drugs, the second explaining preparations. The authors noted the regions and seasons in which the plants grow (pp. 6-9) and their corresponding effectiveness. There is also a chapter on poisons and treatment of poisoning (pp. 883 ff.).

No information about pharmacology survives from the Afsharid period, apart from some references by personal physicians of Nāder Shah (1148-60/1736-47) to drugs that they themselves prepared (Bazin, tr., pp. 31-32). A report by Antony Forbes in 1726 shows that drugs in use at the hospital of the English East India Company (q.v.) at Gombroon (Bandar-e ʿAbbās, q.v.) included pills, pastes, salts, juices, seeds, and roots, all apparently imported from India (Elgood, 1951, p. 409).

An important pharmacopoeia, *Makzen al-adwīa*, was compiled in the reign of Karīm Khan Zand (1163-93/1750-79) by Moḥammad-Ḥosayn ʿAqīlī Korāsānī. The author drew his material from pre-Safavid works, listing simple and compound drugs in respective sections, each organized alphabetically. In ʿAqīlī's opinion the effects of drugs depended on their properties and generic types (p. 4). On the assumptions that every drug is a substance from one of the three "kingdoms" (mineral, vegetable, animal) or a compound of such substances and that, as the ancients believed, these kingdoms are subject to influences from the seven planets, he argued that the medical properties of drugs depend on the "temperaments" of the planets. He therefore included in his book several diagrams of these influences and linkages (pp. 59, 66-79). As a consequence of these relations, drugs of demonstrated medicinal value in one region would not necessarily be as effective in others (p. 23). ʿAqīlī also discussed in detail how long drugs remain usable and proper storage (pp. 36-37).

The Qajar period and the beginnings of modern pharmacy. A long time passed before the work of a few European physicians in the employ of the Persian court or foreign diplomatic and commercial establishments had any significant impact on traditional Persian theories and methods. The first European officially licensed to practice pharmacy in Persia was apparently William Cormick (q.v.), who ran an apothecary business in Tabrīz in about 1260/1844 (Wright, p. 124). There is also a record of a Mr. Gerald at the East India Company hospital at Būšehr (Elgood, 1951, p. 485). The work of foreign physicians and the efforts of such Persian leaders as ʿAbbās Mīrzā (q.v.) to spread knowledge of European science, particularly medicine, paved the way for the introduction of modern pharmaceutical studies at the Dār al-fonūn (q.v.), which opened at Tehran in 1268/1852.

The first professor of chemistry and pharmacy at the Dār-al-Fonūn was the Austrian Fochetti. Dr. Eduard Jakob Polak also taught pharmacy, as well as medicine and surgery. Among the numerous textbooks that Polak wrote during his stay in Persia was one on simple and compound drugs (*Mofradāt-e ṭebb*). Mīrzā Kāẓem Maḥallātī, known as Šīmī, succeeded Fochetti as professor of pharmacy in 1279/1862 (Maḥbūbī, pp. 14, 53; Najmābādī, 1975, pp. 205-06; Naranjīhā, p. 35-36). Later a Frenchman, one Dr. Georges, took charge of the pharmacy department (Najmābādī, 1975, p. 210). The best-known professor of medicine at Dār al-fonūn was, however, Dr. Johann Schlimmer, whose *Terminologie médico-pharmaceutique* was the first Persian medical dictionary in the European style; it included currently used medical terms and names of drugs in French, Latin, English, German, Persian, and Arabic as used in Persia. Several translations of other works by Schlimmer appeared in this period, among them *Meftāḥ a-ḵawāṣṣ* on drugs and *Asbāb al-adwīa* on methods of preparing simple and compound drugs (Maḥbūbī, p. 25; Najmābādī, 1975, p. 318).

During the later Qajar period Western missionary groups established hospitals and dispensaries in several Persian cities (see CHRISTIANITY viii). Owing to dedicated workers like Mary Bird, who opened a dispensary for women at Isfahan in 1308/1891, they gradually won public trust. Clinics and dispensaries maintained by foreign legations and consulates and the Indo-European Telegraph Department also served members of the public free of charge (Wright, pp. 118-20, 126). Among prominent Persians Mīrzā Ḥosayn Khan Sepahsālār (prime minister 1288-90/1871-73) built a hospital beside the Sepahsālār Madrasa and appointed a pharmacist and an apprentice to work there (S. Nafīsī, p. 19). There was some opposition to European pharmacology; for example, the physician Mīrzā Bābā Moḥammad-Taqī Šīrāzī wrote *Jawharīya*, in which he condemned European drugs as harmful (Fīlsūf-al-Dawla, I, pp. 242-43). Nevertheless, increasing public demand prompted composition or translation of several books on modern scientific pharmacology. One of them was *Meftāḥ al-adwīa-ye nāṣerī* by Ḥosayn Khan Hanjan Neẓām-al-Ḥokamāʾ. It covers the properties, manufacture, and uses of drugs in treating diseases. The author claimed to have discovered the antipyretic value of a plant of the thistle family, the effects and applications of which he discussed in detail (pp. 522-25). Much the same ground was covered in *Terāpūtīk wa dārūsāzī-ye ṭebbī* by Abu'l-Ḥasan Khan Doktor Tafrešī, who declared in his preface that he had based his work on European books about drugs and their therapeutic functions. Also worthy of note is *Asrār al-ḥekma*, translated by Mīrzā ʿAlī-Naqī Khan Efteḵār-al-Aṭebbāʾ, "chief physician of the army in Persia," from a work by Sydney Rinkser, "professor of clinical research and director of the university hospital in England." This work is devoted to European drugs, most of which were already in use in Persia. The medical treatise *Pezeškī-nāma* (comp. 1314/1879) by ʿAlī-Akbar Khan Nafīsī Nāẓem-al-Aṭebbāʾ became extremely popular; it included Arabic, French, Latin, Greek, and Persian names for the drugs described.

After the departure in 1316/1898 of Roquebrune, who had been director of the pharmacy department at Dār al-fonūn since 1313/1895, it was headed successively by the German Schwerin and the Frenchman Mauléon (Nāranjīhā, p. 36). In 1322-23/1904 the French pharmacist Gustave Lecomte was hired by the Persian government; he established a pharmaceutical laboratory at Takīya-ye dawlat, where he trained students (Maḥbūbī, p. 363).

Despite these advances, modern drugs were not yet available in all Persian cities and towns. In about 1910 the English medical officer at the quarantine station at Bandar-e ʿAbbās had to obtain necessary drugs from the British consulate, for the stocks in town were rotten or too old to be used (Sadīd-al-Salṭana, p. 169). Although some modern apothecaries had been established in Tehran, their customers were mainly embassy officials, resident Europeans, and highly educated Persians; few members of the general public patronized them. Schwerin opened a retail pharmacy on Nāṣerīya avenue but encountered violent public opposition. The traditional apothecaries (*ʿaṭṭār*), who usually also gave medical advice, remained prosperous and influential throughout the Qajar period (Šahrī, 1958, p. 29; idem, 1990, IV, pp. 327-28).

The modern period. Real progress in the teaching and practice of modern pharmacology in Persia began in 1301 Š./1922, when a pharmacy department was established in the College of medicine, which had been split off from Dār al-fonūn in 1297 Š./1918. Initially the three-year course was taught by professors at the College of medicine. In 1304 Š./1925 a Dr. Papariyan from Turkey was engaged by the

Persian government to teach pharmacology; he remained four years, and at his suggestion preparations were made to compile a manual of the laws and rules governing pharmacy in Persia. Among other teachers in the early years were Drs. ʿAlīm-al-Molk (pharmacodynamics), Ḥakīm-al-Salṭana (drug preparation), and Maḥmūd Šīmī (chemistry). From 1304 Š./1925 to 1313 Š./1934 the number of graduates from the pharmacy department totaled 114 (Maḥbūbī, p. 363; *Rāhnemā-ye Dāneškada*, pp. 49, 67). The first set of regulations governing the sale of drugs was issued in 1298 Š./1919 by the Ministry of education (Wezārat-e maʿāref). One requirement was that every seller of drugs be licensed (Komīsīūn, II, p. 144).

In the second biannual report of the Persian Department of public health (Ṣeḥḥīya-ye koll) in 1305/1926 attention was drawn to the need for drug-manufacturing facilities in Persia, which led to establishment of pharmaceutical laboratories in several hospitals and plans for others (*Dovvomīn*, pp. 5, 13-14, 16). New regulations were also announced. They provided that only those with certification from approved training colleges in Persia or abroad could compound drugs and that all apothecaries had to be licensed by the Department of public health (*Dovvomīn*, p. 222). In the statutes of the College of medicine enacted in 1307 Š./1928 a diploma from lower secondary school was made the minimum prerequisite for acceptance in the department of pharmacy (*Rāhnemā-ye Dāneškada*, p. 201). In the same year Dr. Heinrich Strunk, then director of the German technical school (Madrasa-ye ṣanʿatī-e ālmān) in Tehran, began teaching pharmaceutical chemistry in the department of pharmacy, and in 1309 Š./1930 Dr. Mahdī Nāmdār, Dr. Ṣādeq Moqaddam, and Dr. Fatḥ-Allāh Aʿlam, all graduates of French schools, joined the staff (Maḥbūbī, p. 364). In the same year the pharmacy course was fixed at five years (*Rāhnemā-ye Dāneskada*, p. 90). In 1316 Š./1937, three years after incorporation of the Medical college into Tehran University, it was decided to require completion of secondary school before admission to the pharmacy department (*Rāhnemā-ye Dānešgāh* I, p. 33). In 1318 Š./1939, when Charles Oberlin became dean of the faculty of medicine, plans were drawn up for the creation of eight chairs of pharmacology. Among the faculty at that time were Drs. Nāṣer Mālek, Nāmdār, and Ārmāʾīs Vartānī (*Rāhnemā-ye Dāneškada*, pp. 80-81). The curriculum included Galenic pharmacology, chemical pharmacology, simple (herbal) drugs, organic chemistry, toxicology, biochemistry, pharmacodynamics, and botany. Chairs in chemical analysis and pharmacological physics were added in 1322 Š./1943 (Maḥbūbī, p. 365). Nāmdār served as technical director of the department and was later succeeded by Moqaddam in 1316 Š./1937.

In 1318 Š./1939 the Central pharmaceutical company (Šerkat-e markazī) was established to centralize procurement of drugs in Persia (Komīsīūn, II, p. 1426), and the next year inspection of pharmacists' shops and stocks and coordinated distribution of drugs were instituted (*Rāhnemā-ye Dāneškada*, p. 97). In 1323 Š./1944 the University council (Šūrā-ye dānešgāh) changed the length of the degree course in pharmacology to four years and the period of study for the doctorate to at least one year (*Rāhnemā-ye Dāneškada*, p. 204).

In early 1942 responsibility for matters pertaining to drugs was transferred to the General pharmaceuticals commission (Bongāh-e koll-e dārūʾī) in the Ministry of finance (Wezārat-e dārāʾī). Ten years later the Ministry of health (Wezārat-e behdārī) was authorized to set up a directorate-general of pharmaceuticals (Bongāh-e dārūʾī-e koll-e kešvar), in order to procure drugs, medical and surgical equipment, and laboratory apparatus (Komīsīūn, II, p. 1426). A syndicate of pharmacists was established in 1333 Š./1954; it later became the Persian pharmacists' association (Jāmeʿa-ye dārūsāzān-e Īrān). The association lapsed in 1337 Š./1958, owing to internal disunity, but resumed its activities in 1341 Š./1962 (*Māh-nāma-ye dārū-pezeškī* 40, Ḵordād-Tīr 1347 Š./May-July 1968, pp. 24-25).

In 1335 Š./1956 the Department of pharmacy became the independent Faculty of pharmacology (Dāneškada-ye dārūsāzī) within Tehran University, with Nāmdār as its first dean (Maḥbūbī, p. 365). Two courses were offered, a four-year degree course, the graduates of which were entitled to practice pharmacy, and a three-year postgraduate course leading to the doctorate (Maḥbūbī, p. 366). Nāmdār was succeeded in 1341 Š./1962 by Dr. Nāderqolī Šarqī, who was succeeded in turn by Dr. Alī Zargarī in 1348 Š./1969.

Over the years pharmacology departments were also established in the universities of Isfahan, Tabrīz, Ahvāz, Mašhad, and Shiraz, as well as in the Mellī university (now Beheštī university) in Tehran.

By 1370 Š./1991 the sale of drugs in Persia was subject to the general laws governing medical matters, which required that a special license be obtained from the Ministry of hygiene, health care, and medical education (Wezārat-e behdārī). Such a licence could be granted only to a qualified pharmacist, who was legally responsible in all matters pertaining to the preparation and issue of drugs. Deviation from a physician's prescription by a pharmacist was categorically forbidden, and pharmacists were not allowed to give medical treatment other than first aid (ʿEbādī, pp. 62-64). Nevertheless, traditional remedies remain in use in many Persian villages and towns. Many believers in herbal medicine still prefer to consult traditional practitioners, who also often prescribe for them (Bolūkbāšī, p. 136). Today some traditional herbal remedies are sold in modern packages bearing descriptions of their benefits and instructions for their use. Preparations like camel thorn (q.v.; *taranjabīn*), licorice, absinthium, rice husks, wild tea (*čāy-e kūhī*), almond oil, and castor oil are taken mainly for relief of diarrhea, constipation, stomachache, skin diseases, pellagra, gout, and renal calculus (Jazāʾerī, pp. 85-88).

Bibliography: (For cited references not found in this bibliography and for abbreviations found here, see "Short References.") Abu'l-Ḥasan Khan Doktor, *Terāpūtīk wa dārū-sāzī-e ṭebbī*, Tehran, 1304/1887. Abū Manṣūr Mowaffaq Heravī, *Ketāb al-abnīa ʿan ḥaqaʾeq al-adwīa*, ed. A. Bahmanyār, Tehran, 1346 Š./1967. Abū Bakr Aḵawaynī Boḵarī, *Hedāyat al-motaʿallemīn*, ed. J. Matīnī, Mašhad 1344/1965. ʿAlī Afżal Qāṭeʿ, *Manāfeʿ-e afżalīya*, Tehran University, central library, ms. no. 2546. Moḥammad-Ḥosayn ʿAqīlī Ḵorāsānī, *Maḵzen al-adwīa*, Calcutta, 1844; repr. Tehran, n.d. M.-Z. Bābā, "al-Aqrābāḏīnāt aw dasātīr al-adwīa al-ʿarabīya," *Abḥāṯ al-nadwat al-ʿālamīya al-ūlā le-taʾrīḵ al-ʿolūm ʿend al-ʿArab* (Aleppo) 1, 1976, p. 579. Idem, "Maṣāder al-adwīa al-mofrada aw al-ʿaqāqīr fi'l-ṭebb," in *Abḥāṯ al-moʾtamar al-sanawī al-ṯānī le'l-jamʿīyat al-Sūrīya le-taʾrīḵ al-ʿolūm*, Aleppo, 1977. P. L. Bazin, *Lettres*, tr. ʿA.-A. Ḥarīrī as *Nāmahā-ye ṭabīb-e Nāder Šāh*, ed. Ḥ. Yaḡmāʾī, Tehran, 1340 Š./1961. Abū Rayḥān Bīrūnī, *Ketāb al-jamāher fī maʿrefat al-jawāher*, Hyderabad, 1305/1888. Idem, *Fehrest kotob-e Rāzī*, ed. M. Moḥaqqeq, Tehran, 1366 Š./1987. Idem, *Ketāb al-ṣaydana fi'l-ṭebb*, ed. ʿA. Zaryāb Ḵoʾī, Tehran, 1370 Š./1992; tr. Abū Bakr Kāšānī, ed. Ī. Afšār and M. Sotūda, Tehran, 1358 Š./1979. ʿA. Bolūkbāšī, "Darmān-e bīmārīhā wa nāḵōšīhā dar pezeškī-e ʿāmma," *Ketāb-e hafta* 101, 1342 Š./1963, pp. 134-41; 102, 1342 Š./1963, pp. 134-39; 103, 1342 Š./1963, pp. 73-84. Borhān-al-Dīn Nafīs, *Šarḥ al-asbāb wa'l-ʿalāmāt*, Calcutta, 1251/1835. E. G. Browne, *Arabian Medicine*, Cambridge, 1902. *Dovvomīn rāport-e šeš-māha-ye Ṣeḥḥīya-ye koll*, Tehran, 1305 Š./1926.

Š. ʿEbādī, *Ḥoqūq-e pezeškī*, Tehran, 1368 Š./1989. Ebn Abi'l-Bayyān, *Aqrā bāḏīn*, ed. P. Sbath as *al-Dostūr al-bīmārestānī fi'l-adwīa al-morrakkaba* Cairo, 1932-33. Ebn Abī Oṣaybeʿa, *ʿOyūn al-anbāʾ fī ṭabaqāt al-aṭebbāʾ*, 2 vols. in 1, Cairo, 1299/1882. Moḥammad b. Moḥammad Ebn al-Oḵowwa, *Maʿālem al-qorba fī aḥkām al-ḥesba*, ed. R. Levy, Cambridge, 1937. Ebn al-Qefṭī, *Tārīḵ al-ḥokamāʾ*, ed. J. Lippert, Leipzig, 1903. Ebn Sīnā (Avicenna), *al-Qānūn fi'l-ṭebb*, 3 vols., Būlāq (Cairo), 1294/1877. C. Elgood, *A Medical History of Persia and the Eastern Caliphate*, Cambridge, 1951. Idem, *Safavid Medical Practice*, London, 1970. Mīrzā ʿAbd-al-Ḥosayn Khan Fīlsūf-al-Dawla, *Maṭraḥ al-anẓār fī tarājem aṭebbāʾ al-aʿṣār wa falāsefat al-amṣār*, Tehran, 1334/1916. D. S. Flattery and M. Schwartz, *Haoma and Harmaline. The Botanical Identity of the Indo-Iranian Sacred Hallucinogen "Soma" and Its Legacy in Religion, Language, and Middle-Eastern Folklore*, Berkeley, Calif., 1989. Ḥonayn b. Esḥāq, *al-ʿAšar maqālāt fi'l-ʿayn*, ed. M. Meyerhof, Cairo, 1928. Ḡ. Jazāʾerī, "Manšaʾ-e peydāyeš-e ṭebb-e sonnatī," in *Ṭebb-e sonnatī-e Īrān*, Tehran, 1362 Š./1983. Sayyed Esmāʿīl Jorjānī, *Ḏaḵīra-ye ḵʷārazmšāhī*, facs. ed., ed. ʿA.-A. Saʿīdī Sīrjānī, Tehran 1355 Š./1976. Naṣīr-al-Dīn Yūsof b. Esmāʿīl Jovaynī, *Mā lā yasaʿo' al-ṭabība jahloho*, Tehran University, central library, ms. no 1999. Abu'l-Qāsem ʿAbd-Allāh Kāšānī, *ʿArāʾes al-jawāher wa nafāʾes al-aṭāyeb*, ed. Ī. Afšār, Tehran, 1345 Š./1966. Yaʿqūb b. Zakarīyā Kaškarī, *al-Konnāš fi'l-ṭebb*, facs. ed. F. Sezgin, Frankfurt, 1405/1989. Komīsīūn-e mellī-e Yūnesko (UNESCO), *Īrān-šahr*, 2 vols., Tehran, 1342-43/1963-64.

Ḥ. Maḥbūbī Ardakānī, *Tārīḵ-e taḥawwol-e Dānešgāh-e Tehrān wa moʾassasāt-e ʿālī-e āmūzešī dar Īrān*, Tehran, 1350 Š./1971. Māsarjūya, *Fī abdāl al-adwīa wa mā yaḵūm maqām ḡayrehe menhā*, tr. M. Levey in *Substitute Drugs in Early Arabic Medicine . . .*, Stuttgart, 1971. M. Meyerhof, *Introduction to Šarḥ asmāʾ al-ʿoqqār*, Cairo, 1940. J. Moḥammad Mūsā, "al-Adwīa al-mofrada wa maʿrefat qowāhā," *Abḥāṯ al-nadwat al-ʿālamīya al-ūlā le-taʾrīḵ al-ʿolūm ʿend al-ʿArab* (Aleppo) 1, 1976, pp. 805-08. ʿA. Nafīsī, "Barḵī az gīāhān," *Jašn-nāma-ye Ebn Sīnā* III, Tehran, 1344 Š./1965, pp. 55-58. ʿAlī-Akbar Khan Nafīsī Nāẓem-al-Aṭebbāʾ, *Pezeškī-nāma dar ʿelm-e terāpūtīk*, Tehran, 1317/1899. S. Nafīsī, "Tārīḵ-e bīmārestānhā-ye Īrān," *Majalla-ye šīr o koršīd-e sorḵ-e Īrān* 3/9-10, 1329-31 Š./1950-52. M. Najmābādī, "Tārīḵ-e ṭebb wa behdāšt dar Īrān-e bāstān," *Našrīya-ye Dāneškada-ye adabīyāt-e Dānešgāh-e Eṣfahān* 7, 1350 Š./1971, pp. 81-92. Idem, "Ṭebb-e Dār-al-Fonūn wa kotob-e darsī-e ān," in Q. Rawšanī Zaʿfarānlū, ed., *Amīr-e Kabīr wa Dār-al-Fonūn*, 1354 Š./1975, pp. 202-37. Ī. Nāranjīhā, "Tārīḵča-ye dārū-sāzī dar Īrān," *Māh-nāma-ye dārū-pezeškī* 3/28, 1343 Š./1964, pp. 33-36; 4/38, 1345 Š./1966. S. Ḥ. Naṣr, "Tārīḵ-e ṭebb," tr. Ḥ. Marandī, in *Tārīḵ-e falsafa dar Eslām* III, ed. M.-M. Šarīf, Tehran, 1367 Š./1988, p. 459. Sayyed Ḥosayn Khan Hanjan Nāẓem-al-Ḥokamāʾ, tr., *Meftāḥ al-adwīa*, ed. Amīn-al-Aṭebbāʾ Tabrīzī, Tehran, 1309/1892. Bahāʾ-al-Dawla Ḥosayn Nūrbaḵš, *Ḵolāṣat al-tajāreb*, University of Tehran, central library, ms. no. 1400. Pseudo Pythagoras (Fīṯāḡūres), *Sīyāḥat-nāma-ye Fīṯāḡūres dar Īrān*, tr. Y. Eʿteṣāmī, Tehran, 1363 Š./1984. Abu'l-ʿAbbās Aḥmad Qalqašandī, *Ṣobḥ al-aʿšā*, ed. E. Ebyārī, 16 vols., Cairo, 1963. J. Š. Qanawātī, *Taʾrīḵ al-ṣaydala wa'l-ʿaqāqīr*, Cairo, 1950. Zakarīyāʾ b. Moḥammad Qazvīnī, *ʿAjāʾeb al-maḵlūqāt wa ḡarāʾeb al-mawjūdāt*, Beirut, n.d. *Rāhnemā-ye Dānešgāh-e Tehrān*, Tehran, 1317-18 Š./1938-39. *Rāhnemā-ye Dāneškada-ye ṭebb wa dārū-sāzī wa dandān-pezeškī wa bīmārestānhā wa āmūzešgāhhā-ye vābasta*, Tehran, 1332 Š./1953. Rašīd al-Dīn Fażl-Allāh, *Mokātabāt*, ed. M. Šafīʿ, Lahore, 1364/1945. Idem, *Waqf-nāma-ye Rabʿ-e rašīdī*, ed. Ī. Afšār, Tehran, 1356 Š./1977. Moḥammad b. Zakarīyā Rāzī, *Ketāb al-ḥāwī fi'l-ṭebb*, 23 vols. in 15, Hyderabad (Deccan), 1374-90/1955-71. Idem, *Qeṣaṣ wa ḥekāyāt al-marżā*, ed. and tr. M. Najmābādī, Tehran, 1356 Š./1977. S. Rinkser (sic), tr. Mīrzā ʿAlī-Naqī Khan Efteḵār-al-Aṭebbā as *Asrār al-ḥekma*, Tabrīz, 1325/1908. Moḥammad-ʿAlī Sadīd-al-Salṭana Kabābī, *Bandar-e ʿAbbās wa Ḵalīj-e Fārs*, ed. A. Eqtedārī, Tehran, 1363 Š./1984. R. Šahmardān, "Kār-nāma-ye Ḥakīm-al-Molk Gīlānī dar Hend," *Mehr* 10, 1365 Š./1986, p. 689. J. Šahrī, *Gūša-ī az tārīḵ-e ejtemāʿī-e Tehrān-e qadīm*, Tehran, 1357 Š./1958. Idem, *Tārīḵ-e ejtemāʿī-e Tehrān-e dar qarn-e sīzdahom*, 6 vols., Tehran, 1369 Š./1990. K. Sāmarrāʾī, *Moḵtaṣar taʾrīḵ al-ṭebb al-ʿarabī*, 2 vols., Baghdad, 1984-85. J. Schleifer and S. M. Stern, "Aḳrābādhīn," in *EI²* I, pp. 344-45. Salīm-al-Zamān Ṣeddīqī, "Šīmī," tr. H. Aʿlam, in *Tārīḵ-e falsafa dar Eslām* III, ed. M.-M. Šarīf, Tehran, 1368 Š./1989, p. 448. Abu'l-Ḥasan ʿAlī b. Rabban Ṭabarī, *Ferdaws al-ḥekma fi'l-ṭebb*, ed. M. Z. Ṣeddīqī, Berlin, 1938. Moḥammad Moʾmen Ḥosaynī Tonokābonī, *Toḥfat al-moʾmenīn (Toḥfa-ye Ḥakīm Moʾmen)*, Tehran, 1402/1986. Naṣīr-al-Dīn Ṭūsī (attributed), *Tansūḵ-nāma-ye īl-ḵānī*, ed. M.-T. Modarres Rażawī, Tehran, 1363 Š./1984. M. Ullmann, *Die Medizin im Islam*, Leiden, 1970. N. Wāseṭī, *Tārīḵ-e rawābeṭ-e pezeškī-e Īrān wa Pākestān*, Rawalpindi, 1974. D. Wright, *The English amongst the Persians during the Qajar Period 1787-1921*, London, 1977.

(Ṣādeq Sajjādī)

DRUJ-, Avestan feminine noun defining the concept opposed to that of *aša-* (q.v.). Controversies about the meaning of the latter word have naturally had implications for the understanding of *druj-*. The corresponding verbal root in Indic (*druh*: *drúhyati*) seems to have the basic meaning "to blacken" (Mayrhofer, *Dictionary* II, pp. 79 ff.), perhaps preserved in Avestan in *Yašt* 5.90 and 8.5. In view of the opposition of the two words, if the meaning of *aša-* is "truth," then that of *druj-* must be "lie," but, if the meaning of the former is "order, justice," than *druj-* must mean "error, deceit." Christian Bartholomae prudently gave both meanings: "falsehood, deceit" (*AirWb.*, cols. 778-82). Considering that the meaning "falsehood" corresponds to a certain kind of derivation (see the discussion of *draoga-/drauga-*, below) and that the meaning "deceit" results from a specific contextual usage (cf. the verb *druj:druža-*, below), the opposition was probably between "real order" and "illusory, deceptive order," the first being linked to the lights of the day, the second to the shadows of the night (Kellens, 1991, pp. 46 ff.).

The opposition of the Iranian Mazdean conceptions of Aša and Druj reflected the revision and systematization of an old schema of Indo-Iranian ideology, but the opposition was not simply that between *ṛtá* (order, truth) and *ánṛta* (chaos, lie), as in the Vedic religion, a detail that also argues for an interpretation different from "truth versus lie." Rather, it underlay all aspects of the religion, including cosmogony (see COSMOGONY AND COSMOLOGY i), ritual, and eschatology (q.v. i), and thus appears to have been the foundation of Mazdean dualism (q.v.).

Druj- is attested eighteen times in the Old Avesta and is often found explicitly and systematically opposed to *aša-*, as in *aša varatā karapā . . . drujəm* "the Karapan preferred Druj to Aša" (32.12). The debasement of both the word and the principle that it defined is reflected metrically, for the word occurs as an excess of syllables at the end of the second hemistich of *ahunavaitī* meter, probably reflecting a bungled recitation (Kellens and Pirart, p. 89). In one way or another the principle of *druj* motivates the action of the *daēuuas* (32.3; see *DAIVA). The defeat of Druj is hoped for or sought (31.4, 48.1), and victory over her will either make her the prisoner of Aša (30.8, 44.14) or detach her from the side of the enemy (44.13). In the metaphor of the cosmic dwelling place that illustrates Old Avestan cosmogony the dwelling place erected by Aša, as the agent of Ahura Mazdā (q.v.), is opposed to that erected by Druj (46.6, 51.10; Kellens, 1989). Just as Aša is the point of reference for the *ratu* "archetypal planes" and the *mąra* "formulas" of Ahura Mazdā, Druj is the reference point for the fabricated words of the bad divinities (31.1, 53.6). In the eschatological sphere the refuge for the souls of the dead depends upon their merits: either the "residence" (*dam-*) of Ahura Mazdā or that of Druj (46.11, 49.11, 51.11: *drūjō dəmānē*). It should be noted that *druj-*, like all words expressing negative concepts, is not attested in the *Yasna Haptaŋhāiti*. The negative present participle *adrujiiaṇt-* "who does not deceive" is attested once in the Gathas (31.15).

Many mentions of *druj* in the Younger Avesta are direct calques of passages in the Old Avesta; for example, *vainit̰ aša drujəm* (*Y.* 60.5) and analogous passages are based on *yezī . . . ašā drujəm və̄ŋghaitī* "as he will conquer the Druj through the agency of Aša" (41.1). *Yašt* 13.12-13, in which the Younger Avestan cosmogony is explicitly described as the arena for the dual confrontation between Aša and Druj and between the two *mainiius*, deserves special mention: "If the mighty *fravašis* of the just had not given me aid . . . to the Drug would have been the power, to the Drug the rule, to the Drug corporeal life; of the two spirits the Drug would have sat down between earth and heaven" (Boyce, *Zoroastrianism* I, p. 269). In references to female demons in the *Vīdēvdad druj-* was sometimes substituted for *pairikā-* or for the feminine *daēuua-* (Boyce, *Zoroastrianism* I, p. 279 n. 11). It is possible that a similar usage appeared in Vedic (Spiegel, pp. 215 ff.). *Druj-*, apparently in the nominative form, is the first term in the compounds **druxš.vī.druj-* "who abjures deception of the deception" (*Vd.* 19.16) and *druxš.manah-* "who has deception for thought" (*Yt.* 1.18) and in the accusative in *drujim.vana-* "who conquers deception" (*Y.* 9.19-20), all of which are hapax legomena (Kellens, 1974, p. 39).

The personal forms of the verb *druj:druža-* (< *drúǰ(h)i̯a-*), frequently with the prefix *aiβi*; compounds in which *druj-* is the second term (e.g., *adruj-* "who does not deceive," *tanu.druj-* "who has deception in his body," *miθrō.druj-* "who betrays the contract," **druxš.vi.druj-* "who abjures the deception of the deception"); and derivations with a passive adjectival sense (*anādruxta-*, *anaiβidruxta-*) or the noun of action (*anaiβidruxti-*) are used almost exclusively in connection with deception practiced on the occasion of a contract (*miθra-*), when there is a question of its not being respected or of having a fraudulent clause introduced into it (Kellens, 1974, pp. 40 ff.).

The full-fledged Younger Avestan derivation in *-a-*, *draoga* (OPers. *drauga-*) has the obvious meaning "lie," which the noun of agent *draojina-* "liar" (OPers. *draujana-*) also expresses. In Old Persian *drauga-* and the personal forms of the verb *druj:durujiya-* connote more specifically the lie about dynastic legitimacy. It is in this sense that *drauga-* represents the first sin in the triad of calamities mentioned in inscription DPd 19-20, the other two being the enemy army (*hainā-*) and famine (*dušiyāra-*; see Dumézil, pp. 617 ff.; Boyce, *Zoroastrianism* II, pp. 120, 123). The passive adjective *duruxta-* is used as an antonym for *hašiya-* "truth" (DB 4.6-8).

In Avestan *druj-* also has a secondary derivation, the adjective *drəguuaṇt-* (Younger Av. *druuaṇt-*) "partisan of deception, deceiver," of which the superlative *draojišta-* and perhaps also the comparative *draoj(ii)ah-* are attested (Kellens, 1977, pp. 69 ff.).

Bibliography: (For cited works not found in this bibliography and for abbreviations found here, see "Short References.") G. Dumézil, *Mythe et épopée*, Paris, I, 1968. J. Kellens, *Les noms-racines de l'Avesta*, Wiesbaden, 1974. Idem, "Remarques sur le Farvardīn Yašt," *AAASH* 25, 1977, pp. 69-73. Idem, "Huttes cosmiques en Iran," *MSS* 50, 1989, pp. 65-78. Idem, *Zoroastre et l'Avesta ancien*, Paris, 1991. Idem and E. Pirart, *Les textes vieil-avestiques* I, Wiesbaden, 1988. F. Spiegel, *Die arische Periode und ihre Zustände*, Leipzig, 1887.

(JEAN KELLENS)

DRUMS, large group of percussion instruments.

Structure. Persian drums can be classified in three families, according to structure.

The first group consists of tambourines, or wooden frame drums, of various dimensions. In antiquity they were frequently represented in a variety of contexts, though more such representations survive from western than from eastern Persia; they were beaten with the hand, rather than with sticks. The two principal types are the *daff* and *dāyera* (q.v.), usually equipped with metallic rings on the interior face, and the more modern *dāyera zangī*, with small metallic disks.

The second group consists of drums with sound boxes covered with skin (or skins), which is struck with the fingers. There are two main types. First are the double-headed drums, cylindrical or barrel-shaped (e.g., the Azeri *naqqāra*, which is played on only one of the drumheads, and the Baluch *doholak*, which is played on both) or hourglass-shaped (the *kūba*, which has disappeared from the Persian cultural sphere, and perhaps the *tabīra*). They are always of wood and were frequently depicted (often being played by monkeys) until the 7th century in Bactria and Tokharistan and in Khotan as early as the 2nd century (Karomatov, Meskeris, and Vyzgo, pp. 89, 151). They seem to have disappeared from those regions after the 14th century and survive now only in Indian cultural areas. Single-headed drums constitute the second type; they have the shape of a goblet, like the Persian *tombak* (or *żarb*) and the Afghan *zīrbağalī*, and are made of wood or pottery. A small drum of this type, made of horn, has been found in kurgan II at Pazyryk (4th century B.C.E.; Karomatov, Meskeris, and Vyzgo, p. 53), but the type was rarely represented in wall paintings.

The third group encompasses those drums, also with sound boxes covered with skin, that are struck with drumsticks, either simple pieces of wood the striking ends of which are curved or covered with cloth. They include double-headed wooden drums (*dohol*, *ṭabl*, *dammām*), which are still played, and single-headed drums (like kettledrums) played singly or in pairs (e.g., the *naqqāra*, *kūs*, and *tās* of the Qāderī dervishes of Kurdistan and the Azeri *qoša naqqāra*) made of metal or pottery and sometimes of turned wood. In Persian miniatures they are depicted in different sizes (e.g., Gray, 1961, p. 43; idem, 1979, p 230 ill. 134) and are sometimes carried by camels; some appear to be as much as a meter high. Such illustrated drums doubtless correspond to some varieties known from texts (see below). This type was formerly used principally for military and ceremonial purposes, but it is going out of use at present.

Function. Drums used for art music (*bazmī*) are often distinguished from military instruments (*razmī*), though in practice this distinction can become blurred, as when military percussion instruments are played at religious festivals. The names of percussion instruments gathered from texts are very numerous and often difficult to identify with accuracy.

The best-known percussion instruments of the Persian cultural sphere are the double kettledrums (*naqqāra*) of metal or pottery, supposedly invented by the legendary king Hōšang (Farmer, 1937, p. 14); the *kūs* (< Aram. *kūsā*; Farmer, in *A Survey of Persian Art*, p. 2786 and n. 3; the *kūs* is mentioned in the *Šāh-nāma*, e.g., Borūḵīm ed., I, p., 76 vv. 256,

259, p. 91 v. 558), a type of enormous kettledrum often carried in pairs on the backs of camels or elephants (Farmer, 1966, p. 193) and also played in pairs; the *dohol*, a large double-headed drum played with sticks, which is the origin of the large European military drums (Koch, s.v.); the *doholak*, a two-faced, barrel-shaped drum played with the hand; the *senj* (large cymbals); the *k̠om* (or *k̠onb*), a war drum (Mašḥūn, p. 19), probably of pottery; and a smaller variant called *k̠onbak* (Caron and Savfate, p. 179).

Among rarer instruments were the *tabīra* mentioned in early sources (e.g., *Šāh-nāma*, Borūk̠īm ed., p. 92 v. 559), a drum in the shape of an hourglass; the *šandaf*, a kind of *dohol*; the *ṭabl-e bāz*, a drum used for calling falcons; the *jām*, a large metal kettledrum; and the *gūrga* or *gūrgā*, a drum larger than the *naqqāra* and made of pottery covered with sheepskin (Farmer, 1966, p. 193; Mašḥūn, pp. 18, 22). G. H. Farmer (*Survey of Persian Art*, p. 2799; idem, 1966, p. 193) defined this last instrument, which he called *korka* or *korga*, as a "monster kettle-drum" and the symbol of military power under the Il-khanids.

In addition, a number of instruments mentioned in texts cannot yet be defined with certainty or vary considerably. For example, *ṭabl* is currently used as a general term, but in Persia and neighboring lands it also refers to a small two-headed cylindrical drum played with sticks, a smaller version of the *dohol*. Two variants in Baluchistan are the *raḥmānī* and the smaller *keysal* (Rīāḥī, p. 7). Baluch women play the *kunzag*, a clay jar half filled with water. The *kūba* (or *kūma*, according to Mašḥūn, p. 21) is a drum shaped like an hourglass and is related to Central Asian drums (Koch, pp. 550-51), but, according to Emām Šūštarī (p. 154), the term *kūba*, derived from *kūftan*, also denoted the stick used to beat the drum. Such drums were also called *fenjān*. The *ṭās*, a small metal drum struck with two sticks, was used by the Qāderī order in Kurdistan (During, 1989, p. 255). The *dammāma* or *dabdaba* was a small double-headed drum from southern Persia, but the *dammāma* has been defined by Farmer (p. 2799) as a kettledrum. The *tombak* was, according to Farmer (1966, p. 193), a small kettledrum that varied in form and may have been the ancestor of the Arab *tablak*; the term seems later to have referred to a chalice-shaped drum of the *żarb* type made of pottery. The *mandal* and the *mohrī* (Mašḥūn, p. 21) have not been identified, nor have the *āʾīn-e pīl*, the *darāʾī*, and the *qāšoqak*; the last consists of two or three slightly concave pieces of wood connected by an elastic cord, making a sound somewhat like that of castanets (Joneydī, p. 232).

Bibliography: (For cited works not found in this bibliography and for abbreviations found here, see "Short References.") J. Baily, *Music of Afghanistan. Professional Musicians in the City of Herat*, Cambridge, 1988. N. Caron and D. Safvate, *Iran. Les traditions musicales*, Paris, 1966. J. During, *Musique et mystique dans les traditions de l'Iran*, Paris, 1989. M.-ʿA. Emām Šūštarī, *Īrān gāhvāra-ye dāneš o honar. Honar-e mūsīqī-e rūzgār-e eslāmī*, Tehran, 1348 Š./1969. H. G. Farmer, "Ṭabl," in *EI*[1], Suppl., pp. 215-17. Idem, *Turkish Instruments of Music*, London, 1937. Idem, "An Outline History of Persian Music and Musical Theory," in *Survey of Persian Art* III, pp. 2783-2804. Idem, *Islam. Musikgeschichte in Bildern* III, 2nd ed., Leipzig, 1966. B. Gray, *Persian Painting*, Geneva, 1961. Idem, ed., *The Arts of the Book in Central Asia, 14th-16th Centuries*, Boulder, Colo., 1979. F. Joneydī, *Sarzamīna-ye šenāk̠t-e mūsīqī-e īrānī*, Tehran, 1361 Š./1982. F. M. Karomatov, V. A. Meskeris, and T. S. Vyzgo, *Mittelasien. Musikgeschichte in Bildern* II, 9th ed., Leipzig, 1987. K. P. Koch, "Persia," in S. Sadie, ed., *The New Grove Dictionary of Music and Musicians*, London, 1980, pp. 549-52. Ḥ. Mašḥūn, *Naẓar-ī be mūsīqī-e żarbī-e Īrān*, Shiraz, 1348 Š./1969, ʿA. Rīāḥī, *Zār o bād o Balūč*, Tehran, 1352 Š./1973.

(Jean During)

DRUSTBED (Pahl. *drwdstpt*; Syr. lw. *drwstbyd*; Margoliouth, p. 94; Ar. lw. *drwst'bḏ*) "chief physician" in the Sasanian period. As the title does not occur in the early Sasanian sources and those who are known to have held it were all recorded as having lived toward the end of this period, it seems reasonable to assume that it was a late innovation, on the model of such official titles as *dibīrbed* "chief secretary." Sometimes *drustbed* was used in the Pahlavi texts simply as a synonym for *bizešk* "doctor, physician" (e.g. *Dēnkard*, ed. Madan, p. 14.19; tr., p. 37; *Škand-gumanīg Wizār*, ch. 4.102, p. 58), though it seems to have referred to a higher rank and social status, as may be inferred from some passages in the *Dēnkard*. For example, it is stated (ed. Madan, p. 159.1-2; tr., p. 159) that in the material world the function of medicine (*gētīg bizeškīh*) is treating the bodies of individuals according to the teachings of the chief physicians (*drustbedān *hammōg*). Another distinction was made between the two terms: The *drustbed* was said to have the function of protecting (*pādār*) the souls of men against sin and their bodies against illness, whereas the latter was simply healing (*bēšāzēnīdārīh*; *Dēnkard*, pp. 159.19-160.5; tr., p. 160). This distinction seems to have been based on etymological suppositions, however (i.e., *drustbed*/*pādār*, *bizešk*/*bēšāzēnīdār*).

Non-Zoroastrians could be promoted to the rank of *drustbed*, for example, the Christian Gabriel of Šiggār, the private physician of Khosrow II (591-628), who enjoyed the king's favor (Hoffmann, p. 66; Labourt, p. 219; Christensen, *Iran Sass.*, p. 488; Ebn al-Qifṭī, p. 133, where the title is recorded in Arabic as *drwstʾbʾḏ* for *drustabaḏ*; see Bailey, *Zoroastrian Problems*, p. 85 n. 3).

The chief *drustbed* was called *ērān-drustbed* "chief

physician of Iran, archiater" and was probably nominated by the king himself. The selection and appointment of a chief physician and his appointment to the position of "the chief physician of Iran" (*ērān-drustbedīh*) depended on his perfection in treating people of high rank (*Dēnkard*, p. 163.7-9; tr. pp. 162-63). The *ērān-drustbed* was expected to be "soul loving" (*ruwān-dōst*); "possessed of subtle insight" (*bārīg-wēnišn*); "reading much" (*was-xwānišn*); "knowing books by heart" (*warm-nibēg*); "knowing about the power of the substance, transformations, and nature of the body" (*nērōg ī gōhr, wihērišn ī ǰadagān ud čihr ī tanān āgāh*); "knowing about changes" (*wardišn-šnās*); "knowing about illnesses and their remedies" (*wēmārīh ud darmān-šnās*); "free of envy" (*nēst-arešk*); "soft in speech" (*čarb-ēwāz*); "friendly to the ill" (**wēmārān dōst*); "willing to give service" (*paristīdār*); dextrous (*sbuk-dast*); and the like (*Dēnkard*, p. 161.7-16; tr., p. 161). The examination, selection, and authorization of a physician to treat the body (*tan bizešk*) were the duty of the *ērān-drustbed* (*Dēnkard*, p. 165.3, tr., p. 164).

Bibliography: (For cited works not found in this bibliography, see "Short References.") *Dēnkard*, tr. J. de Menasce as *Le trosième livre du Dēnkart*, Paris, 1973. Ebn al-Qeftī, *Ta'rīḵ al-ḥokamā'*, ed. J. Lippert, Leipzig, 1903. J. Hampel, *Medizin der Zoroastrier im vorislamischen Iran*, Husum, Germany, 1982. G. Hoffmann, *Auszüge syrischen Akten persischer Märtyrer*, Leipzig, 1880. J. Labourt, *Le christianisme dans l'empire perse*, Paris, 1904. J. P. Margoliouth, *Supplement to the Thesaurus Syriacus*, Oxford, 1927. *Škand-gumanīg Wizār*, ed. J. de Menasce, Fribourg, 1945.

(AḤMAD TAFAŻŻOLĪ)

DRVĀSPĀ (or Drwāspā, Druuāspā, lit., "with solid horses"), Avestan goddess. Her name suggests that she must have been a divinity responsible for the health of horses. From the time of James Darmesteter (q.v.), it has been customary to compare her to the Celtic Epona (*Avesta*, tr. Darmesteter, II, pp. 431-40). Nevertheless, despite the clarity of her name and the anchoring of her function in Indo-European tradition, she remains enigmatic, for she is a strangely discreet goddess. Although in Avestan Mazdaism the *Druuāsp Yašt* (*Yt.* 9), consisting of thirty-three sentences in seven *karde*, was dedicated to her, the formulary material contains no original elements. Rather, the text reproduces, with the necessary substitution of the proper name, sentences 27-52 of *Yašt* 17, dedicated to Aši, in which the notable votaries who had officiated for the goddess in the past are enumerated. Only in the first two sentences are specific epithets connected to Druuāspā, as the object of *yazamaide* "we sacrifice."

Otherwise the goddess is mentioned only in the *Sīrōza* (1.14), in which *gōš*, the fourteenth day of the month, is said to be under the patronage of three divinities responsible for protecting the animal world, Gəuš Tašan, Gəuš Uruuan, and Druuāspā; this association is confirmed by the fact that the Pahlavi title of *Yašt* 9 was *Gōš Yašt*, which led Darmesteter to claim that Druuāspā "is Gəuš guarding the horse." On the other hand, Mary Boyce thinks that the word *druuāspa-* could originally have been an epithet for Āši, from which it eventually developed into the name of an independent divinity (*Zoroastrianism* I, p. 82).

Outside the Avestan tradition the name appears in the masculine form DROOASPO beneath the image of a male god on the reverse of a Kushan coin. This form is to be identified with the Middle Persian name Lwhl'sp/Lohrāsp of the father of Vīštāspa, though the identification is somewhat problematic as, in the Avestan tradition, the latter is called Auruuaṯ.aspa- "of the rapid horses" (Davary, p. 220).

Bibliography: (For cited works not found in this bibliography, see "Short References.") A. Christensen, *Études sur le zoroastrisme de la Perse antique*, Copenhagen, 1928, pp. 36-41. G. D. Davary, *Baktrisch*, Heidelberg, 1982. H. Lommel, *Die Yäšt's des Awesta*, Göttingen and Leipzig, 1927.

(JEAN KELLENS)

DRYPETIS (Gk. Drypĕtis [Arrian] or Drypêtis [Diodorus]), daughter of Darius III Codomannus (q.v.; Arrian, 7.4.5) and younger sister of Stateira (Diodorus, 17.107.6); in the collective wedding arranged by Alexander the Great (q.v.) at Susa in 324 B.C.E. she was given in marriage to Hephaestion (Arrian, 7.4.5; Diodorus, 17.107.6). After Alexander's death, which was lamented by "Hephaestion's widow," according to Curtius Rufus (10.5.20), his wife, Roxane, out of jealousy, ordered Stateira "and her sister" (i.e., Drypetis) murdered and thrown into a well (Plutarch, *Alexandros* 77.6). The Iranian original form of the name and its etymological interpretation have been the subject of unconvincing speculation (see most recently, Werba, pp. 164-65).

Bibliography: (For abbreviations in this bibliography, see "Short References.") [F.] Stähelin, "Drypetis," in Pauly-Wissowa, Suppl. III, col. 415. C. Werba, *Die arischen Personennamen und ihre Träger bei den Alexanderhistorikern*, Ph.D. diss., Vienna, 1982.

(RÜDIGER SCHMITT)

ḎU'L-AKTĀF. See ŠĀPŪR II.

ḎŪ-BAḤRAYN, a term in Persian and Arabic prosody designating a poem that can be scanned according to two or more different meters (*baḥr*). Traditionally it has been considered a rhetorical embellishment (*badīʿ*; q.v.) and known as *šeʿr-e molawwan* or *motatawwan* (lit., "variegated poem").

In Persian poetry the two meters *ramal* (– ⏑ – – / – ⏑ – – / – ⏑ –) and *sarīʿ* (– ⏑ ⏑ – / – ⏑ ⏑ – / – ⏑ –) are considered the most compatible and have often been used in this genre. *Majmaʿ al-baḥrayn* by Kātebī Nīšāpūrī (d. 838 or 839/1435) and *Seḥr-e ḥalāl* by Ahlī Šīrāzī (d. 942/1535-36) were composed entirely in these two meters (e.g., *Sāqī az ān šīša-ye Manṣūr-dam / Bar rag o bar rīša-ye man ṣūr dam*; Ahlī, p. 626).

A verse may be scanned as a *dū-baḥrayn* if the final short vowels can be scanned as long vowels, if final long vowels followed by initial vowels can be changed to short vowels, and if initial *hamza*s can be eliminated.

Some verses may be scanned in more than two meters, for example, *Lab-e to marham-e ʿāšeq, ḵaṭṭ-e to ḵāma-ye Mānī / Ḡam-e to mūnes-e ḵāṭer, qadd-e to sāya-ye ṭūbā*. It can be scanned in three, the third being *baḥr-e mojtaṯ*: ⏑ – – – / ⏑ – – – / ⏑ – – – / ⏑ – – – ; ⏑ ⏑ – – / ⏑ ⏑ – –/ ⏑ ⏑ – – / ⏑ ⏑ – – ; or ⏑ – ⏑ – / ⏑ ⏑ – – / ⏑ – ⏑ – / ⏑ ⏑ – – . Verses of this kind have been called *jāmeʿ al-boḥūr* (Wāʿeẓ Kāšefī, p. 122). Mīrzā Naʿīm Sedehī (b. 1272/1855-56) wrote a poem that can be scanned in seven different ways (*To serr-e ḥaqq-ī o to kaštī-e Nūḥ / To ḥaqq-e serr-ī o to yaḥyī* [sic; probably to be read *moḥyī*]*-e jān*), in *baḥr-e ramal-e maḵbūn*, *baḥr-e ramal*, *hazaj*, *sarīʿ*, *motaqāreb*, *ḵafīf*, and *qarīb-e aḵrab*. Rašīd-al-Dīn Vaṭvāṭ (p. 54) mentioned a book of poetry, *Kanz al-ḡarāʾeb* by the 11th-century poet Aḥmad Manšūrī, that reportedly contained a verse that could be scanned in more than thirty different ways.

See also ʿARŪŻ.

Bibliography: Ahlī Šīrāzī, *Dīvān*, ed. Ḥ Rabbānī, Tehran, 1344 Š./1965. A. Najafī, "Eḵtīārāt-e šāʿerī," *Jong-e Eṣfahān* 10, 1352 Š./1973, pp., 147-89. Rašīd Vaṭvāṭ, *Ḥadāʾeq al-seḥr fī daqāʾeq al-šeʿr*, ed. ʿA. Eqbāl Āštīānī, Tehran, 1362 Š./1983. S. Šamīsā, *Āšnāʾī bā ʿarūż wa qāfīa*, Tehran, 1366 Š./1987. Ḥosayn Wāʿeẓ Kāšefī, *Badāyeʿ al-afkār fī ṣanāyeʿ al-ašʿār*, ed. M. J. Kazzāzī, Tehran, 1369 Š./1990.

(SĪRŪS ŠAMĪSĀ)

ḎU'L-FAQĀR (lit., "provided with notches, grooves, vertebrae"), the "miraculous sword" of Imam ʿAlī b. Abī Ṭāleb (q.v.), with two blades or points, which became a symbol of his courage on the battlefield. According to some sources, it was taken as booty at the battle of Badr (2/624) by the Prophet Moḥammad, who gave it to ʿAlī at the battle of Oḥod (3/625). A voice is supposed to have recited *lā sayf ellā Ḏu'l-Faqār wa lā fatā ellā ʿAlī* (There is no sword but Ḏu'l-Faqār, and there is no one brave but ʿAlī; Ṭabarī, I/3, pp. 1359, 1402; in the Shiʿite tradition *lā fatā* . . . comes first; Balʿamī, ed. Rowšan, III, p. 169; Dehḵodā, s.v. Ḏu'l-Faqār; cf. Dozy, II, s.v. *faqara*; both versions of this formula became popular as inscriptions on swords throughout the Islamic world; Mittwoch).

Some early Shiʿites believed that Ḏu'l-Faqār was brought down from heaven by the archangel Gabriel and given, together with other relics of the Prophet, as a sign to the imams (Kolaynī, I, pp. 337 ff.; cf. Donaldson, pp. 82-83). It supposedly bore the inscription *wa lā yoqtal Moslem be-kāfer* (no Muslim shall be slain by an unbeliever; Ebn Saʿd, apud Mittwoch; 1960, p. 486; cf. Moosa, pp. 186-87, 365). On the day of resurrection ʿAlī is supposed to wield the apocalyptic Ḏu'l-Faqār (Ayoub, p. 229).

In *Omm al-ketāb* it is claimed that Ḏu'l-Faqār was imbued with spiritual power by God's command, according to sayings attributed to the fifth imam, Moḥammad al-Bāqer (d. ca. 117/735; cf. Moosa, p. 72). Later it was supposedly in the possession of Imam ʿAlī al-Reżā (q.v.; d. 203/818; Kolaynī, I, pp. 339-40) and was said eventually to have fallen into the hands of the ʿAbbasids (Mittwoch). The sword also figured in the beliefs of the Ahl-e Ḥaqq (q.v.) of western Persia (Moosa, p. 207), where it represented the angel Moṣṭafā, incarnation of divine fury (Mokri, p. 378; tr., p. 132; for beliefs about Ḏu'l-Faqār in other Shiʿite sects, see Moosa, pp. 71, 337-38).

Ḏu'l-Faqār became the most prominent ʿAlid symbol and is omnipresent in Shiʿite rituals. In Turkish and Persian *maqtal-nāma*s (martyrdom narratives), down to Ḥosayn Wāʿeẓ Kāšefī's 16th-century *Rawżat al-šohadāʾ*, Imam Ḥosayn carries it in his hand at the battle of Karbalāʾ (Calmard, pp. 226, 528). The "avenger" of Ḥosayn's blood, Moḥammad b. Ḥanafīya, also fights with it (Calmard, p. 264). ʿAlī (Ḥaydar-e Karrār "the impetuous lion") and Ḏu'l-Faqār were often celebrated in Persian classical poetry by Šahīd Balḵī, Farroḵī, Manučehrī, Nāṣer-e Ḵosrow, Masʿūd-e Saʿd, Sūzanī, Ḵāqānī, and others (Dehḵodā, s.vv.), as well as in Sunni, Shiʿite, and especially Sufi devotional poetry. In the 13th century Jalāl-al-Dīn Moḥammad Rūmī portrayed Ḏu'l-Faqār as the incarnation of al-Ḥaqq (lit., "divine truth," in a Sufi context referring to God; Moosa, p. 71). Shah Esmāʿīl I "Ḵaṭāʾī," (907-30/1501-24), in his Azeri Turkish *Dīvān*, also claimed to carry it as a sign (Calmard, p. 480).

Although it was used particularly for finials on banners and standards in Safavid and Qajar Persia, Ḏu'l-Faqār seems to have been more popular in Ottoman and Mughal domains. This impression may result partly from the fact that in the Persian lion-and-sun emblem the lion, symbolizing ʿAlī, generally does not wield a two-bladed sword (Malcolm, pp. 565-66; cf. Jamālzāda; Nayyer Nūrī; Ḏokāʾ). Double-bladed or double-pointed swords were represented on coins, however. There are also representations with notched, undulating two-edged blades and a small double point (Ḏokāʾ, 1344 Š./1965, pp. 21-22, figs. 17, 19; cf. *Survey of Persian Art*, pl. 1423E). In the hierarchy of the *fotowwa* (lit., "brotherhoods"), the Persian origin of which has now been demonstrated (Baldick), Ḏu'l-Faqār was the em-

Figure 28. The name ʿAlī written twice in mirror image, topped by a crown (*ṭāj*) and interlaced at the bottom with a pair of double-bladed swords; Turkish, influenced by letter symbolism propagated by the Persian and Turkish Ḥorūfīya Sufi sect. The inscription reads *lā fatā ellā ʿAlī, lā sayf ellā D̲u'l-Faqār*. Drawing by Jacqueline Calmard after Aksel, p. 108.

blem of the intermediate level, "those of the sword" (Ṣarrāf, p. 108; cf. Baldick, p. 351). Images of the double-pointed sword on banners carried among the *marāteb* ("dignities") in Moḥarram processions in India are called *barzak̲ī* or *qodratī*, perhaps reflecting Savafid usage (Šarīf, pp. 160-61, fig. 11: a pair of scissors). The main banner of the Qoṭbšāhīs of Golconda (901-1098/1496-1697) was provided with two large "arms" representing ʿAlī's sword (Greenfield, p. 269).

As ʿAlī and his family are venerated by most Muslims, representations of D̲u'l-Faqār are common in both official and popular iconography. In Sufi letter symbolism the *lām-alef*, considered a single letter, is often compared to a sword (or to scissors) and particularly to D̲u'l-Faqār (Schimmel,

Figure 29. The invocation *yā ʿAlī*, with reference to ʿAlī also in the human-faced lion and the double-bladed sword; Turkish, influenced by letter symbolism propagated by the Persian and Turkish Ḥorūfīya Sufi sect. Drawing by Jacqueline Calmard after Aksel, p. 88.

p. 419; for other types of imagery, cf. Lassy, p. 214; Figures 28, 29). In popular Turkish iconography the letter *yā'* in ʿAlī's name is often extended to form a two-bladed sword (Aksel, pp. 49, 61, 124-25). D̲u'l-Faqār was also abundantly represented in 17th-century Mughal miniature paintings (Titley, index, s.v. D̲ū'l-fak̲ār).

In Islamic folklore D̲u'l-Faqār is connected with magic, and from as early as Fatimid times there have been many legends about its miraculous origin and its two blades or points, effective against the evil eye or any enemy (Zawadowski, p. 37). The image of ʿAlī and D̲u'l-Faqār was popular on amulets accompanied by the koranic verses used against the evil eye (68:51-52; Donaldson, pp. 130-31, 240). Many mountain passes are said to have been cut by ʿAlī's magic sword, and some actually bear the name D̲u'l-Faqār, particularly those near Torbat-e Jām, Tang-e Šamšīrbor, Fīrūzkūh, and Ṭāq-e ʿAlī near Kermān (Massé, *Croyances* II, p. 411; Dehk̲odā, s.v.). Warm springs near Mašhad are also said to be the result of such a stroke. Whenever ʿAlī drew D̲u'l-Faqār the mountain of Qāf is supposed to have trembled (Donaldson, pp. 90, 150; cf. Moosa, p. 71).

D̲u'l-Faqār also became a widely used *laqab* (honorific), often attached to another title ("beg," "khan," "pasha," "sultan," etc.).

Bibliography: (For cited works not found in this bibliography and abbreviations found here, see "Short References.") M. Aksel, *Türklerde dinî resimler*, Istanbul, 1967. M. Ayoub, *Redemptive Suffering in Islam*, the Hague, 1978. J. Baldick, "The Iranian Origin of the Futuwwa," *AIUON* 50/4, 1990, pp. 345-61. J. Calmard, *Le culte de l'Imām Ḥusayn. Étude sur la commémoration du drame de Karbalā dans l'Iran pré-safavide*, Ph.D. diss., Université de Paris III (Sorbonne), 1975. Y. D̲okā', "Tārīk̲ča-ye tag̲yīrāt wa taḥawollāt-e derafš wa ʿalāmat-e dawlat-e Īrān . . .," *Honar o mardom* 31, 1344 Š./1965, pp. 13-24; 32-33, 1344 Š./1965, pp.

21-38. B. A. Donaldson, *The Wild Rue*, London, 1938. R. Dozy, *Supplément aux dictionnaires arabes*, 2nd ed., II, Leiden and Paris, 1927. Ebn Saʿd, *Ṭabaqāt* I, Beirut, 1960, p. 486. K. Greenfield, "Shia Standards of Hyderabad," *The Moslem World* 27, 1937, pp. 269-72. M.-ʿA. Jamālzāda, "Beyraqhā-ye Īrān dar ʿahd-e Ṣafawīya," *Honar o mardom* 39-40, 1344 Š./1965, pp. 10-13. T. W. Juynboll [P. Voorhoeve], "Atjèh," in *EI²* I, pp. 739-43. Abū Jaʿfar Moḥammad Kolaynī, *Oṣūl al-kāfī*, ed. and tr. Ḥ. S. J. Moṣṭafawī, 4 vols. in 2, Tehran, n.d. R. Kriss and H. Kriss-Heinrich, *Volksglaube im Bereich des Islam* II, Wiesbaden, 1962. I. Lassy, *Persiska mysterier*, Helsingfors, 1917. J. Malcolm, *History of Persia* II, London, 1815. E. Mittwoch, "Dhū'l-Faḳār," in *EI²* II, p. 233. M. Mokri, ed. and tr., *La grande assemblée des fidèles de vérité au tribunal sur le mont Zagros en Iran. Dawra-ī dīwānā-gawra*, Paris, 1977. M. Moosa, *Extremist Shiites. The Ghulat Sects*, Syracuse, N.Y., 1987. Ḥ. Nayyer Nūrī, "Ḏayl-ī bar selsela-ye maqālāt . . .," *Honar o mardom* 77-78, 1345-48 Š./1966-69, pp. 61-74. A. Schimmel, *Mystical Dimensions of Islam*, Chapel Hill, N.C., 1978. J. Šarīf, *Qānūn-e Eslām*, tr. G. A. Herklots as *Islam in India*, 2nd ed., London, 1921; repr. London, 1972. M. Ṣarrāf, *Rasāʾel-e javānmardān*, Tehran and Paris, 1352 Š./1973. N. Titley, *Miniatures from Persian Manuscripts*, London, 1977. Ḥosayn Wāʿeẓ Kāšefī, *Rawżat al-šohadāʾ* . . ., ed. M. Ramażānī, Tehran, 1344/1955. G. Zawadowski, "Note sur l'origine magique du Dhoû-l-faqâr," in *En terre d'Islam* (Lyons), 3ème sér. 21, 1943/1, pp. 36-40.

(JEAN CALMARD)

ḎU'L-FAQĀR KHAN AFŠĀR, governor (*ḥākem*) of Ḵamsa province (ca. 1177-94/1763-80) under the Zand dynasty. Of the Imīrlū clan of Afšārs, which had long been established at Zanjān, the chief city of the province, Ḏu'l-Faqār was evidently already a local leader of some consequence before Karīm Khan Zand (1163-93/1750-79), on his way south after subjugating Azerbaijan, formally appointed him *ḥākem* of strategic Ḵamsa province in 1177/1763; Ḵamsa lay between Azerbaijan, Gīlān, and the Zand chieftain's home range in the province of Qalamrow-e ʿAlī Šakar (Hamadān; Röhrborn, p. 8). In 1186/1772 Ḏu'l-Faqār fell behind in his tax remittances to Shiraz and was reported to be plotting a bid for independence. Karīm Khan, already threatened by a Qajar revolt in the Caspian provinces, summoned him to the capital. Instead Ḏu'l-Faqār sent his aging mother (Ḡaffārī, pp. 306-07; Hedāyat, *Rawżat al-ṣafā* IX, p. 83; Nāmī, p. 169: his son), who assured the Zand ruler that the delinquent was a loyal and diligent servant and persuaded him to grant a respite. This ploy was repeated soon after, whereupon Karīm sent two forces under ʿAlī-Morād Khan Zand (q.v.) and ʿAlī-Moḥammad Khan Zand to dismiss and arrest Ḏu'l-Faqār. ʿAlī-Moḥammad Khan met Ḏu'l-Faqār and a Šaqāqī Kurdish army at Abhar and defeated them in a fierce battle; Ḏu'l-Faqār fled but was captured and taken to Shiraz, together with his family and forfeited property (Ḡaffārī, pp. 307-08; Hedāyat, *Rawżat al-ṣafā* IX, p. 83; Tafrešī, fol. 217; Rostam-al-Ḥokamāʾ, pp. 378-79; tr., pt. 2, pp. 633-34).

On the intercession of his mother, however, he was soon granted a full pardon and reinstated at Zanjān, though his family and dependents were detained as hostages in Shiraz (Ḡaffārī, p. 309; Perry, p. 122). In the spring of 1191/1777 Ḏu'l-Faqār cooperated in Karīm Khan's campaign against the Ottomans in Kurdistan, leading one arm of a three-pronged advance on Sanandaj, in which the Turks were defeated at Šahrazūr (Ḡaffārī, p. 366; Perry, p. 191).

Two years later Ḏu'l-Faqār took advantage of the anarchy following Karīm Khan's death to gather a large army and occupy Qazvīn, threatening both the Zand and the Qajar contestants for control of the region between Gīlān and Tehran. While ʿAlī-Morād Khan, acting on behalf of the late ruler's brother and would-be successor, Ṣādeq Khan, was at Isfahan after a defeat by Jaʿfarqolī Khan Qājār, Ḏu'l-Faqār sent a force against Tehran. It was repelled by the Zands (Ḡaffārī, p. 489) or, according to pro-Qajar sources, by the Qajars (Hedāyat, *Rawżat al-ṣafā* IX, p. 136). Ḏu'l-Faqār then invaded Gīlān, captured the governor (*beglerbegī*), Hedāyat-Allāh Khan, and imprisoned him at Zanjān, appointing his own governor at Rašt. He next invaded Qalamrow. ʿAlī-Morād Khan, who was again at Isfahan, had declared himself against the latest Zand claimant, Zakī Khan; after the latter had been killed by his own men at Īzadḵᵛāst in 1193/1779 ʿAlī-Morād Khan marched against Ḏu'l-Faqār. In the ensuing clash at Šarrāʾ (northwest of Arāk) Ḏu'l-Faqār's force, notably his elite corps of 300 men, came close to defeating the Zand army, but ʿAlī-Morād Khan's Bābān Kurdish reinforcements carried the day. Ḏu'l-Faqār fled to Zanjān, where his prisoner Hedāyat-Allāh was released by a faction of citizens and Ḏu'l-Faqār found himself besieged in his house as a pursuing Zand force approached the city. Breaking through a wall, he escaped with two or three followers to Ḵalḵāl, where he was seized and handed over to ʿAlī-Morād Khan at Zanjān. He was beheaded in late 1194/1780 or early 1195/1781 (Ḡaffārī, pp. 490-96; Hedāyat, *Rawżat al-ṣafā* IX, pp. 159-60; Nāmī, pp. 129-31; Fasāʾī, I, p. 221; tr. Busse, p. 11).

ʿAlī-Morād Khan then appointed one ʿAlī Khan Afšār to govern Ḵamsa province, but Ḏu'l-Faqār's family remained influential well into Qajar times (Nāmī, p. 255; Hedāyat, *Rawżat al-ṣafā* X, pp. 672, 713-14), later adopting Ḏu'l-Faqārī as surname (Bāmdād, *Rejāl* I, p. 506).

Bibliography: (For cited works not found in this bibliography and abbreviations found here, see

"Short References.") Abu'l-Ḥasan Ḡaffārī Kāšānī, *Golšan-e morād*, ed. Ḡ Ṭabāṭabāʾī Majd, Tehran, 1369 Š./1990. Moḥammad-Ṣādeq Nāmī Eṣfahānī, *Tārīḵ-e gītīgošā*, ed. S. Nafīsī, Tehran, 1317 Š./1938. J. R. Perry, *Karim Khan Zand*, Chicago, 1979. K. M. Röhrborn, *Provinzen und Zentralgewalt Persiens im 16. und 17. Jahrhundert*, Berlin, 1966. Moḥammad-Hāšem Āṣaf Rostam-al-Ḥokamāʾ, *Rostam al-tawārīḵ*, ed. M. Mošīrī, Tehran, 1348 Š./1969; tr. B. Hoffmann as *Persische Geschichte 1694-1835 erlebt, erinnert und erfunden. Das* Rustam ut-tawārīḫ *in deutscher Bearbeitung*, 2 pts., Bamberg, 1986. Rażī-al-Dīn Tafrešī, untitled, British Library, London, ms. no. Add. 6587, fols. 185-216 (Rieu, *Persian Manuscripts* II, p. 798, sec. 15).

(JOHN R. PERRY)

ḎU'L-FAQĀR ŠĪRVĀNĪ, MALEK-AL-ŠOʿARĀʾ QEWĀM-AL-DĪN ḤOSAYN b. Ṣadr-al-Dīn ʿAlī (d. ca. 691/1291), Persian poet and panegyrist of the Il-khanid period. Through the intercession of the vizier Ḵʷāja Moḥammad Māstarī he obtained the patronage of Atābak Yūsofšāh I of the Fażlūya branch of the Atābakān-e Lorestān (q.v.); Yūsofšāh was governor of Ḵūzestān, Kūhgīlūya, the city of Fīrūzān (near Isfahan), Golpāyagān, and Lorestān (672-88/1273-89). Ḏu'l-Faqār dedicated a number of panegyrics to him. The poet also wrote poems in praise of the Il-khanid Gayḵātū Khan (690-94/1291-94); the Qara Khitay amir Jalāl-al-Dīn Soyūrḡatmeš b. Qoṭb-al-Dīn Moḥammad, who ruled Kermān in 681-91/1282-91; and Jalāl-al-Dīn's half-sister Pādšāh Ḵātūn, who succeeded him and governed in 691-94/1291-94.

According to some sources (e.g., Dawlatšāh, ed. Browne, p. 146), Ḏu'l-Faqār had been employed by Moḥammad Ḵʷārazmšāh (d. 617/1220) and had recorded in verse the circumstances of the sultan's flight to Iraq during the Mongol invasion of 614-15/1217-18, but that would mean that the poet lived to be a hundred years old; none of his memorialists or biographers has noted such longevity. He is reported to have died in 679/1280 (Hedāyat, p. 219) or 689/1290 (*Ātaškāda*, p. 5), but, as he dedicated poems to Gayḵātū, Jalāl al-Dīn Soyūrḡatmeš, and Pādšāh Ḵātūn, he could not have died before 691/1291 (cf. Ṣafā, *Adabīyāt*, 2nd ed., 1356 Š./1977, p. 518). His tomb is in Maqbarat al-Šoʿarāʾ in the Sorḵāb quarter of Tabrīz.

Ḏu'l-Faqār's *dīvān* includes 9,000 verses (ed. M. Edward, London, 1934). He was generally recognized as a master of versification (*ṣanāyeʿ-e šeʿrī*), and his poems have a charming, lyrical quality. Among his more important works is *Mafātīḥ al-kalām wa madayeḥ al-kerām*, dedicated to Moḥammad Māstarī. It is a lengthy panegyric ode (*qaṣīda-ye maṣnūʿī*) with two opening verses (*maṭlaʿ*) encompassing every possible combination of meter (*dāʾera*) and elision (*zeḥāfāt*), written in acrostic form (*tawšīḥ*); it is also remarkable in that from every few lines certain words can be strung together to form new distichs (*abyāt*) with different meters. The poet was rewarded for this work with seven bales (*ḵarvār*) of silk. Other odes of his have survived: one on *ṭard o ʿaks* (making a statement, then reversing it, as in *Būstān bar sarv dārad ān negār-e delsetān / Ān negār-e delsetān bar sarv dārad būstān*)) and one of thirty-eight verses with three different rhyme schemes (*qāfīa*), a *ḥājeb* (identical repeating arrangement of syllables or auxiliary rhyme), and a refrain (*radīf*). The poet's skillful use of semantics and thematic material (*ṣanāyeʿ-e lafẓī o maʿnawī*), particularly in *Mafātīḥ al-kalām*, influenced later poets, many of whom wrote imitative verses (*esteqbāl*) in response to his and one another's work; they include *Šarḥ-e momarrad* by Salmān Sāvajī (d. 778/1376), *Maḵzan al-boḥūr* by Šams-e Faḵrī (d. after 758/1357), *Maḵzan al-maʿānī* by Ahlī Šīrāzī (q.v.; d. 942/1535), and *Badāyeʿ al-asḥār fī ṣanāyeʿ al-ašʿār* by Qīāmī Moṭarrazī.

Bibliography: (For cited works not found in this bibliography and abbreviations found here, see "Short References.") Dawlatšāh Samarqandī, *Taḏkerat al-šoʿarā*, ed. M. ʿAbbāsī, I, Tehran, 1337 Š./1958, pp. 146-51. Reżāqolī Khan Hedāyat, *Majmaʿ al-foṣahāʾ*, Tehran, 1284/1867, p. 219. Moḥammad b. Badr Jājarmī, *Mūnes al-aḥrār fī daqāyeq al-ašʿār*, ed. M. S. Ṭabībī, 2 vols., Tehran, 1337-50 Š./1958-71. Loṭf-ʿAlī Beg (Āḏar Bīgdelī), *Ātaškada*, ed. H. Sādāt Nāṣerī, I, Tehran, 1336 Š./1957, pp. 195-97. Ṣafā, *Adabīyāt* III, pp. 518-23. Tarbīat, *Dānešmandān-e Āḏarbāyjān*, 2nd ed., 1356 Š./1977, pp. 153-55 and sources cited there.

(MOḤAMMAD DABĪRSĪĀQĪ)

ḎU'L-JANĀḤ, Imam Ḥosayn's winged horse, known from popular literature and rituals. Ḏu'l-Janāḥ was mentioned in medieval narratives of Ḥosayn's martyrdom at Karbalāʾ (*maqātel*), for example, Ebn Aʿṯam Kūfī's 9th-century *Ketāb al-fotuḥ* and *al-Lohūf* by Ebn Ṭāʾūs Ṭāʾūsī (d. 664/1266), which became sources for later Turkish and Persian *maqtal-nāmas*. In *al-Lohūf* the horse, unnamed but said to be descended from the Prophet Moḥammad's mount, is supposed to have dipped its head in its master's blood and attacked the enemy. It then returned, smeared with Ḥosayn's blood, to the tents of the Ahl-e Bayt (q.v.). As it approached, Ḥosayn's infant daughter Sokayna began to cry, joined by the other women in the family (pp. 98-99; cf. Calmard, p. 120). The Turkish *Dāstān-e maqātel-e Ḥosayn* (763/1362) by Šādī Maddāḥ contains a similar account but includes the name Ḏu'l-Janāḥ (Mélikoff, p. 142; Calmard, pp. 225-26). Ḥosayn Wāʿeẓ Kāšefī, in *Rawżat al-šohadāʾ* (comp. 908/1502), recounted a detailed story, partly based on Ebn Aʿṯam's text, in which Ḏu'l-Janāḥ, instead of behaving aggressively, weeps (p. 363; cf. Calmard, p. 396; Ebn Aʿṯam, tr., pp. 538-39). According to various traditions, Ḏu'l-Janāḥ eventually killed itself or disappeared into the desert (Wāʿeẓ Kāšefī, p. 349).

At least from Safavid times representations of Ḥosayn's horse were led in the processions and pageants that developed into *taʿzīa* performances of the martyrdom of Ḥosayn. This "nationalist" tradition also found its way into the literature of such plays (Pelly, II, p. 173; Calmard, p. 396). Ḏu'l-Janāḥ appears in various other *taʿzīa* episodes, for example, Qāsem b. Ḥasan's marriage at Karbalāʾ: Ḥosayn orders the horse brought to his daughter Fāṭema, who rides it to the bridal chamber (Humayuni, p. 14). Ḏu'l-Janāḥ was also represented in Moḥarram processions in India (Pelly, I, p. xxii) and is still included at Lucknow, Delhi, and probably elsewhere (Jaffri, pp. 224-25).

A connection between using horses in Shiʿite rituals and pre-Islamic Persian practices has been suggested (see ʿAZĀDĀRĪ).

Bibliography: (For abbreviations found here, see "Short References.") J. Calmard, *Le culte de l'Imām Ḥusayn. Étude sur la commémoration du drame de Karbalā dans l'Iran pré-safavide*, Ph.D. diss., Université de Paris III (Sorbonne), 1975. Ebn Aʿṯam Kūfī, *Ketāb al-fotūḥ*, partial tr. Moḥammad b. Aḥmad Mostawfī Heravī [596/1199], Bombay, 1300/1882. Ebn Ṭāʾūs Ṭāʾūsī, *al-Loḥūf*, tr. F. Wüstenfeld as *Der Tod des Ḥusein ben Ali und die Rache*, Göttingen, 1883. S. Humayuni, "An Analysis of the Taʿziyeh of Qāsem," in P. Chelkowski, ed., *Taʿziyeh. Ritual and Drama in Iran*, New York, 1979, pp. 12-23. S. H. A. Jaffri, "Muharram Ceremonies in India," in P. Chelkowski, ed., *Taʿziyeh. Ritual and Drama in Iran*, New York, 1979, pp. 222-27. I. Mélikoff, "Le drame de Kerbelâ dans la littérature épique turque," *REI* 34, 1966, pp. 133-48. L. Pelly, *The Miracle Play of Hasan and Husain*, 2 vols., London, 1879. Ḥosayn Wāʿeẓ Kāšefī, *Rawżat al-šohadāʾ* . . ., ed. M. Ramażānī, Tehran, 1344/1955.

(JEAN CALMARD)

ḎU'L-LESĀNAYN "possessor of two tongues," epithet often bestowed upon bilingual poets. It appears to have originated in Arabic as an honorific indicating unusual eloquence in a single language, Arabic, as was the case with Mowallah b. Kaṭīf, a Companion of the Prophet (Sami, p. 2228). Poets writing in both Arabic and Persian were fairly numeorous in Transoxania and Khorasan in the tenth century, a circumstance easily explained by the persistence of Arabic as a major literary idiom in Persian-speaking lands (Zand). So common was the phenomenon of bilingual literary composition in that period that by no means all poets writing in the two languages were designated Ḏu'l-Lesānayn; the example of Ḥosayn b. Ebrāhīm Adīb Naṭanzī (q.v.; d. 497/1103-04), who did bear the epithet, appears to have been unusual (Modarres, *Rayḥānat al-adab*, II, p. 271). Most prominent classical Persian poets tried their hands at composing Arabic verse (e.g., Saʿdī's Arabic *qaṣīdas*, pp. 73-90), in addition to which acrostic verses may occasionally be encountered in their *dīvāns*. None of these poets can, however, be said to have been truly bilingual in the sense of contributing in comparable measure to both Arabic and Persian literature or composing approximately similar quantities of verse in the two languages.

Significant instances of poets writing in Persian and one other language are to be found chiefly outside Persia. Many were products of the bilingual urban environment of Timurid and, more especially, post-Timurid Central Asia, where both Persian and Chaghatay (q.v.) were current; examples include the illustrious ʿAlī-Šīr Navāʾī (d. 907/1501) and Allāhyār Ṣūfī (d. 1136/1724), who wrote didactic *maṯnawī*s that are less familiar to scholars but more widely read than the works of Navāʾī. The poetic works of the Mughal general Bayrām Khān (d. 968/1561) may be regarded as a short-lived extension on Indian soil of this joint cultivation of Persian and Chaghatay.

Other bilingual poets flourished in areas where Persian was not spoken to any appreciable extent but enjoyed great cultural prestige, for example, pre-Ottoman Turkey and India. The earliest important Turkish poet in this category was Solṭān Walad (Sultan Veled; d. 711/1312), who, in addition to a Persian *dīvān* and *maṯnawī*s, composed a slender but valuable *dīvān* in Turkish. The rise of Ottoman Turkish brought such bilingualism to an end; although many Ottoman poets wrote verse in Persian, they did so more as a type of literary exercise, comparable to Persian poets' composing Arabic verse. The Indian tradition of bilingual Persian and Urdu poetic expression was far more fecund and lasted longer than its Ottoman counterpart, presumably because of the relatively late and slow maturation of Urdu as a literary medium. Among the principal exemplars of this tradition were Mīrzā Maẓhar Jānjānān (d. 1195/1781), Ḵʷāja Mīr Dard (d. 1199/1785), Mīrzā Asad-Allāh Ḡāleb (d. 1286/1869), and Muhammad Iqbal (d.1357/1938).

A third category of bilingual poets lived in regions where poetic expression in vernaculars belonging to the Iranian language family was overshadowed by the appeal of Persian, the prime example being Kurdistan, where all poets of significance have cultivated Persian at least as much as Kurdish (Ṣafīzāda). Finally, Azerbaijan, where the Turkish and Persian worlds overlap, has also produced many poets at home in two languages, including such diverse figures as the Safavid shah Esmāʿīl I "Ḵaṭāʾī" (d. 930/1524), Foẓūlī (d. 963/1556), Mīrzā Šafīʿ Wāẓeḥ (d. 1268/1852), and the contemporary poet Moḥammad-Ḥosayn Šahrīār (d. 1367 Š./1988).

Bibliography: (For cited works not found in this

bibliography, see "Short Referrences.") Saʿdī, *Kolliyāt*, ed. M.-ʿA. Forūḡī, Tehran, 1342 Š./1963. Ṣ. Ṣafīzāda, *Pārsī-gūyān-e kord*, Tehran, 1366 Š./1987. Ş. Sami, *Kâmûs el-a'lâm* III, Istanbul, 1306/1889. M. Zand, "Some Light on Bilingualism in Literature of Transoxiana, Khurasan and Western Iran in the 10th Century A.D.," in *Yádnáme-ye Jan Rypka*, Prague and the Hague, 1967, pp. 161-64.

(HAMID ALGAR)

DU MANS, FATHER RAPHAEL (b. Jacques Dutertre, Le Mans, France, where he was baptized 27 August 1613 at the cathedral of St.-Julien, d. Isfahan, 1 April 1696), author of important descriptions of Persia. His father was a lawyer attached to the presidial court of Le Mans, a member of the *noblesse de robe* (a hereditary class of magistrates), and a former magistrate of the town. Young Jacques, after apparently having received a good basic education, decided to enter the Capuchin order and made his profession at the monastery of Le Mans on 16 July 1636, adopting the name Raphaël du Mans. He seems to have taken his vows in 1637 and to have been ordained a priest in 1641 or 1642.

In 1645 or 1646 he was sent on his first foreign mission. He stayed first at the Capuchin monastery in Cairo, then, in May 1647, he joined the French Capuchins (q.v.) at Isfahan, where they had been established since 1038/1628. They were under the supervision of the custody at Aleppo, a dependency of the ecclesiastical province of Touraine. The superior at Isfahan, Ambroise de Preuilly, and the experienced missionary Valentin d'Angers assisted Father Raphaël with their knowledge of the country and its languages and introduced him to their protectors at the Safavid court. At the end of 1649 Father Raphaël himself became superior of the hospice at Isfahan. Until 1655-57 the Capuchins primarily carried out a ministry of preaching and spiritual guidance among the Armenians of the city of Isfahan proper. After Shah ʿAbbās II (1052-77/1642-66) transferred all Armenians to the suburb of New Jolfā Father Raphaël intensified his efforts to obtain permission to establish a Capuchin hospice in the heart of the new community, but he was unsuccessful.

Cultivated and gifted at languages, Father Raphaël soon made a number of friends in the literary circles of Isfahan; his library was renowned, and his knowledge of astronomy highly prized. In 1664-65, shortly before his death, Shah ʿAbbās himself received him. Father Raphaël enjoyed a long friendship with the court historian Moḥammad-Ṭāher Waḥīd. From about 1650 until his death he was principal interpreter at the Safavid court, translating the many letters brought by ambassadors and envoys from European states. As a result he was admired, feared, and criticized by those visitors. Reports about him by diplomats and travelers are abundant, for almost all of them had had something to do with him. The pages devoted to him in the works of Jean-Baptiste Tavernier, Jean de Thévenot, Jean Chardin, Petrus Bedik, John Fryer, and Engelbert Kaempfer are well known. Because he was linked with the French religious party, which since 1660 had supported the first failed attempt to establish a company of merchants that would support missions in the east, he had a thankless role to play when envoys, including Protestant merchants, arrived in Isfahan in 1664 to establish the Compagnie Française des Indes (see EAST INDIA COMPANY, THE FRENCH).

The many Capuchin hospices, or convents, in the Near East, Persia, and India played a major role in providing couriers and disseminating news, particularly to India and the Far East. Father Raphaël himself seems to have written many such despatches, and the several dozen of his letters that have been preserved reveal his own immense interest in the "news of the day." Possessing a lively intelligence, he was able to keep abreast on every topic, owing to his good relations with Armenian notables, certain members of the court, and the agents of the British East India Company (q.v.) and the Dutch Vereenigde Oostindische Compagnie (V.O.C.; see DUTCH-PERSIAN RELATIONS). People eagerly sought his advice, and he gave it generously to the numerous travelers who stayed at the Capuchin hospice in Isfahan. Some, however, received his advice with suspicion, notably during the Turkish siege of Vienna in 1683, when negotiations for an alliance among Poland, the Holy Roman Empire, and Safavid Persia were in progress; they accused him of secretly supporting Louis XIV's unacknowledged policy of pro-Ottoman neutrality.

Father Raphaël was very hostile to the Jesuits and looked with equal disfavor upon the permanent establishment of a Latin Catholic bishopric in Isfahan, an attitude that he made clear during the visit in 1682 of the appointed bishop, Monsignor François Picquet, a former consul in Aleppo. He strongly upheld the goals of the first Capuchin missionaries in Persia: to maintain the best possible relations with the Safavid court in hopes of achieving some conversions to Roman Catholicism, while at the same time striving for the emancipation of Armenian Christians and their union with the apostolic see at Rome. Father Raphaël seems to have been esteemed by the Armenians of Isfahan and their clergy because of the austere life that he led.

Although he published nothing, he was nevertheless the author of several memoirs of the greatest importance for the history of Safavid Persia. Best known is *L'estat de la Perse en 1660*, probably prepared at the request of his superiors, preserved first in the library of Jean Baptiste Colbert and now in the Bibliothèque Nationale, Paris. Charles Schefer published it with an introducton on the history of relations between Persia and Europe, including the text of a letter from Father Raphaël to the minister of finance, Colbert, in 1670 (Paris, 1890). Chardin had seen a copy of Father Raphaël's memoir on the establishment of the Jesuit mission at Isfahan, written in about 1662; an autograph copy is preserved in the archives of the Missions Étrangères at Paris, and there is an abridged Latin version in the archives of Propaganda Fide at Rome. In another *Estat de la Perse*, datable to about 1665, Father Raphaël described, perhaps for Nicolas de Lalain, the court of ʿAbbās II and its institutions; the preserved copy, made by François Pétis de la Croix at Isfahan, is in the Bibliothèque Nationale (ms. no. Fr. 6114). *Réponse de quelques savants de Perse . . . sur la magie, etc.*, mentioned by the same Pétis in about 1674, seems to have been lost. The autograph of *De Persia*, written in Latin in 1684 for two members of the Swedish embassy of Ludwich Fabritius, Kaempfer, and his companion Gotfredus Pristaf, is preserved in the Sloane collection at the British Library, London, along with other texts collected by Kaempfer. A Turkish grammar, written for Kaempfer in Father Raphaël's hand, is also preserved at the British Library, and a Turkish dictionary, copied by Balthazar de Lauzières, is in the library of the University of Uppsala. Some memoirs or reports written by Father Raphaël seem to have been incorporated into Tavernier's *Six Voyages*, though the originals are lost. No text in Persian or Turkish has been preserved in his hand, though he was renowned for his perfect knowledge of these languages.

The writings of Father Raphaël merit serious attention. He was both an attentive observer of Persian society in the Safavid capital and a critical and uncompromising moralist. He thus provided an extremely colorful description of the functioning of Safavid institutions, of great value to social historians and linguists; in particular he transcribed the contemporary Isfahan pronunciation of a very large number of words and expressions, as well as common proverbs. His various memoirs were among the major sources of pubished travel accounts, notably those of Tavernier, Fryer, Kaempfer, and Chardin; as for de Thévenot, he stayed a long time in the hospice at Isfahan and was an intimate of the Capuchins.

Father Raphaël emerges from these works as an original and attractive personality; his interest in Persian institutions and customs, which impressed both Persian Muslims and European travelers, made him something of the model for the French *pādrī* (< Portuguese *padre*) in the Safavid capital.

Bibliography: F. Richard, *Raphaël du Mans, missionnaire en Perse au XVIIème siècle*, 2 vols., Paris, 1994. C. Schefer, *P. Raphaël du Mans. Estat de la Perse en 1669 . . .*, Paris, 1890.

(FRANCIS RICHARD)

ḎU'L-NŪN MEṢRĪ, ABU'L-FAYŻ ṮAWBĀN b. Ebrāhīm (b. Aḵmīm in Upper Egypt, ca. 175/791, d. Jīza [Giza], between 245 and 248/859 and 862), early Sufi master. He lived mainly in Lower Egypt (Meṣr) and is known to have visited Mecca and possibly also Yemen, as well as traveling extensively in Palestine and Syria, becoming familiar with Syrian asceticism. During his active years he was opposed by two groups: the Mālekī jurists of Egypt, particularly ʿAbd-Allāh b. ʿAbd-al-Ḥakam (d. 214/829), who condemned him for public teaching about mystical experience, and the Moʿtazilites, whose persecution during the *meḥna* forced him to flee Egypt in 228/843 (van Ess, p. 100). He preached at the court of al-Motawakkel (232-47/847-61) in Samarra and visited Sufi circles in Baghdad on his way there; he may have been imprisoned in Baghdad for a short while, presumably for maintaining the "uncreatedness" of the Koran, but was released on al-Motawakkel's orders and returned to Egypt.

Extant primary sources include traces of two strands of tradition on Ḏu'l-Nūn. The Egyptian strand is reflected in *Taʾrīḵ ʿolamāʾ ahl Meṣr* by Ebn Ṭaḥḥān (d. 416/1025), who derived his sparse information from *Aʿyān al-mawālī al-meṣrīyīn* by Abū ʿOmar Kendī (d. 360/971; *GAS* I, p. 358). References by Abū Bakr b. Moḥammad Mālekī (d. 356/967; p. 223) to the Mālekī ascetic Abū ʿAlī Šaqerān b. ʿAlī of Qayrawān (d. 186/802?) as a teacher of Ḏu'l-Nūn, repeated by Abū Zayd Dabbāḡ (d. 696/1296; I, p. 209, with reference to Solamī's lost *Taʾrīḵ al-ṣūfīya*), raise chronological and geographical difficulties. Ḏu'l-Nūn's transmissions of prophetic Hadith, which he received through intermediaries on the authority of Mālik b. Anas (d. 179/795), Layṯ b. Saʿd (d. 175/791), and Sofyān b. ʿOyayna (d. 198/814) appear historically plausible, however. Accounts of his ability to read hieroglyphs (Masʿūdī, *Morūj*, ed. Pellat, I, p. 307; Abū Noʿaym, IX, pp. 339, 367), though untenable, may function as a topos expressing his links with an Egyptian Hellenistic wisdom tradition.

Large segments of the Syrian and Iraqi tradition were preserved by Abū Noʿaym Eṣfahānī (d. 430/1038; IX, pp. 331-95, X, pp. 3-4), Ebn Ḵamīs Mawṣelī (d. 522/1157; fols. 17a-34a), and Ebn ʿAsāker (d. 571/1176; facs. ed., VI, pp. 147-71; ed. Badrān, V, pp. 271-88; cf. Ebn Manẓūr, VIII, pp. 246-54). In addition, many of Ḏu'l-Nūn's sayings are scattered throughout the works of Abū Naṣr Sarrāj, Abū ʿAbd-al-Raḥmān Solamī, Abu'l-Qāsem Qošayrī, Ḵᵛāja ʿAbd-Allāh Anṣārī, and Ebn al-Jawzī; Farīd-al-Dīn ʿAṭṭār collected and embellished many anecdotes about him (I, pp. 114-34). In two later hagiographies of Ḏu'l-Nūn, by Ebn ʿArabī (d. 638/1240) and Jalāl-al-Dīn Soyūṭī (d. 911/1505), selected anecdotes and sayings are accompanied by extensive glosses. Conjectures that Fāṭema of Nīšāpūr (d. 223/838) was Ḏu'l-Nūn's spiritual master at Mecca, derived from incidental references in these sources (Deladrière, pp. 21-22), have a weak historical basis. More reliable is information on the transmitters of Ḏu'l-Nūn's sayings, among whom

Saʿīd b. ʿOṯmān (d. 294/906-07) and Yūsof b. Ḥosayn Razī (d. 304/916-17) were the most important. Claims of a master-disciple relationship between Ḏu'l-Nūn and Sahl Tostarī (d. 283/896) are tenuous (cf. Böwering, pp. 50-55) and his purported role as redactor of Jaʿfar al-Ṣādeq's commentary on the Koran (Massignon, p. 206) unsubstantiated.

It is impossible to be certain whether or not Ḏu'l-Nūn studied medicine, alchemy, and magic, though he is cited as the author of alchemical writings from the 9th century onward (*GAS*, I, pp. 643-44, IV, p. 273; Ullmann, pp. 196-97; cf. Ebn al-Nadīm, ed. Tajaddod, p. 423). Ḏu'l-Nūn combined knowledge of Islamic tradition with profound mystical experience; his most influential contributions to Sufism remain his teachings on ecstasy (*wajd*) and gnosis (*maʿrefa*) and his description of the soul's journey to God along a path of stages (*maqāmāt*) and states (*aḥwal*), frequently called the "seven steps" of the Sufi path. He defined gnostics (*ʿārefūn*) as those who exist in God and contemplate His face within their hearts, so that He reveals Himself to them in a way not accorded to others. It appears that Ḏu'l-Nūn's notion of *maʿrefa* reflected his own experience of the inner knowledge of God, rather than simply a Hellenistic theory of gnosis. Persian mystics, however, tended to view him as a Muslim exponent of Hellenistic tradition. Yaḥyā Sohravardī (d. 587/1191) dubbed the wisdom tradition of the ancient sages "the pre-eternal leaven" (*al-ḵamīra al-azalīya*) and considered his own philosophy of illumination (*ešrāq*) as having arisen from the confluence of the two principal strands of this wisdom tradition, the Greek (transmitted through Hermes) and the Persian (transmitted through Kayḵosrow). For Sohravardī Ḏu'l-Nūn and Tostarī were transmitters of the Greek strand, Muslim mystics who handed the Neoplatonic and Neopythagorean wisdom tradition on to Sufi philosophical circles (Böwering, p. 52).

Bibliography: (For cited works not found in this bibliography and abbreviations found here, see "Short References.") Abū Noʿaym Eṣfahānī, *Ḥelyat al-awlīāʾ wa-ṭabaqāt al-aṣfīāʾ*, 10 vols., Cairo, 1351-57/1932-38. Ḵᵛāja ʿAbd-Allāh Anṣārī, *Ṭabaqāt al-ṣūfīya*, ed. ʿA. Ḥabībī, Kabul, 1340 Š./1961. A. J. Arberry, "A Biography of Dhul-Nun al-Miṣri," in M. Ram and M. D. Ahmad, eds., *ʿArshi Presentation Volume*, New Delhi, 1965. Farīd-al-Dīn ʿAṭṭār, *Taḏkerat al-awlīāʾ*, ed. R. A. Nicholson, 2 vols., London, 1905-07. G. Böwering, *The Mystical Vision of Existence in Classical Islam*, Berlin, 1980. Abū Zayd ʿAbd-al-Raḥmān b. Moḥammad Dabbāḡ, *Maʿālem al-īmān*, 2 vols., Tunis, 1320/1902. Šams-al-Dīn Moḥammad Ḏahabī, *Sīar aʿlām al-nobalāʾ*, ed. Š. Arnaʾūṭ and Ṣ. Samar, XI, Beirut 1402/1982, pp. 532-36. R. Deladrière, *La vie merveilleuse de Dhû-l-Nûn l'Égyptien*, Paris, 1988. Ebn ʿArabī, *al-Kawkab al-dorrī*, Topkapı Saray library, Istanbul, ms. no. Ahmet III 1378. Ebn ʿAsāker, *Taʾrīḵ madīna Demašq*, facs. ed., 19 vols., ʿAmmān, n.d.; ed. ʿA. Badrān, 2nd ed., 7 vols., Damascus, 1399/1979. Ebn al-Jawzī, *Ṣefat aṣ-ṣafwa*, 4 vols., Beirut 1409/1989. Idem, *Talbīs Eblīs*, Cairo, n.d. Ebn Ḵallekān, ed. ʿAbbās. Ebn Ḵamīs Mawṣelī, *Manāqeb al-abrār*, Topkapı Saray library, Istanbul, ms. no. Ahmet III 2904. Ebn Manẓūr, *Moḵtaṣar Taʾrīḵ Demašq*, 29 vols., Damascus, 1405/1985. J. van Ess, "Biobibliographische Notizen zur islamischen Theologie (8)," *Die Welt des Orients* 12, 1981, pp. 99-106. R. Gramlich, *Die schiitischen Derwischorden Persiens*, 3 vols., Wiesbaden, 1965-81. U. Haarmann, "Evliyā Çelebīs Bericht über die Altertümer von Gize," *Turcica* 8, 1976, pp. 157-230. ʿAlī b. ʿOṯmān Hojvīrī, *Kašf al-maḥjūb*, ed. V. A. Zhukowskiĭ, Leningrad, 1926; repr. Tehran, 1358 Š./1979. Jāmī, *Nafaḥāt*. Abū Bakr Kalābāḏī, *Ketāb al-taʿarrof*, ed. A. J. Arberry, Cairo, 1933. Ḵaṭīb Baḡdādī, *Taʾrīḵ Baḡdād* VIII, Cairo, 1349/1931, pp. 393-97. Abū Bakr ʿAbd-Allāh Mālekī, *Rīāż al-nofūs*, ed. Ḥ. Moʾnes, Cairo, 1951. L. Massignon, *Essai sur les origines du lexique technique de la mystique musulmane*, Paris, 1968. Abu'l-Qāsem Qošayrī, *al-Resāla*, Cairo, 1368/1948. B. Reinert, *Die Lehre vom Tawakkul in der klassischen Sufik*, Berlin, 1968. H. Ritter, *Das Meer der Seele*, Leiden, 1955. Ṣalāḥ ad-Dīn Ḵalīl b. Aybak Ṣafadī, *al-Wāfī be'l-wafāyāt*, ed. Š. Fayṣal, XI, Beirut, 1401/1981, pp. 22-24 no. 37. Abū Naṣr Sarrāj, *Ketāb al-lumaʿ fi'l-taṣawwof*, ed. R. A. Nicholson, London, 1914. Abū ʿAbd-al-Raḥmān Solamī, *Ṭabaqāt al-ṣūfīya*, ed. J. Pedersen, Leiden, 1960, pp. 23-32; ed. N. Šorayba, Cairo, 1372/1952, pp. 15-26. Jalāl-al-Dīn Soyūṭī, *al-Serr al-maknūn*, Süleimaniye library, Istanbul, ms. no. Laleli 2051. M. Ullmann, *Die Natur- und Geheimwissenschaften im Islam*, Leiden, 1972.

(GERHARD BÖWERING)

ḎU'L-QADR (arabicized form of Turk. Dulgadır), a Ghuzz tribe (*Taḏkerat al-molūk*, ed. Minorsky, p. 194) that became established mainly in southeastern Anatolia under the Saljuqs. In 738/1337 one of their leaders, Zayn-al-Dīn Qarāja b. Ḏu'l-Qadr, founded a principality incorporating the towns of Albestān and Marʿaš. These princes were clients first of the Mamlūks of Egypt and later of the Ottomans. The dynasty came to an end in 928/1522, when ʿAlī Beg, the tenth ruler, and his entire family were executed by order of the Ottoman Sultan Solaymān I (926-74/1520-66; Mordtmann; Mordtmann and Ménage).

The Ḏu'l-Qadr often opposed the Āq Qoyunlū (q.v.), but in 860/1456 contingents of them joined Uzun Ḥasan (857-82/1453-78) before the battle on the Tigris and again in 878/1473 at the battle of Bāškent (Woods, pp. 97, 131-34, 212). As the Ḏu'l-Qadr principality crumbled, many tribesmen entered the service of Shah Esmāʿīl Ṣafawī (907-30/1501-24) and formed one of the most important of the

Qezelbāš tribes. Several of their leaders were prominent during the reigns of Shah Ṭahmāsb I (939-84/1524-76) and Shah ʿAbbās I (996-1038/1588-1629; Eskandar Beg, pp. 140, 1085; tr. Savory, pp. 225, 1310); according to Eskandar Beg (p. 1084), under Shah ʿAbbās only the Šāmlū tribe had more prominent amirs than the Ḏu'l-Qadr. Yet it was in the same period that the decline of the tribe began. In the stiff competition for power and wealth the Šāmlū, Qājār, and Afšār tribes grew stronger, whereas the Ostāljū, Takalū, Ḏu'l-Qadr, and others gradually lost strength and subsequently disintegrated (Reid, p. 10).

During the Safavid period Ḏu'l-Qadr were found in Azerbaijan, in Fārs, and around Ganja; they were still present in the last area until the 1920s (Ḥasan Rūmlū, pp. 143, 151; Eskandar Beg, p. 458; tr. Savory, p. 631; *Taḏkerat al-molūk*, ed. Minorsky, p. 194; Valili Baharlu, pp. 61-96). The Ḏu'l-Qadr of Azerbaijan settled in the southern part of the province and the adjacent region of Ḵamsa. According to Lady Sheil (p. 397), they comprised some 200 households in 1849. Today the only vestige of that group is a village by the name of Ḏu'l-Qadr, 31 km south of Sareskand (Razmārā, *Farhang* IV, p. 234). The Ḏu'l-Qadr tribe of Fārs has left no trace, even though men from that tribe governed the province throughout most of the 16th century (Reid, pp. 55, 64 n. 88).

Bibliography: (For cited works not found in this bibliography and abbreviations found here, see "Short References.") Eskandar Beg, pp. 31-33, 47-48; tr. Savory, pp. 50-53, 80-83. Ḥasan Rūmlū, ed. Seddon, II, passim. J. H. Mordtmann, "Dulkadırlılar," in *İA* III, pp. 654-62. Idem and V. L. Ménage, "Ḏhū'l-Ḳadr," in *EI²* II, pp. 239-40. J. Reid, *Tribalism and Society in Islamic Iran*, Malibu, Calif., 1983. Lady [M. L.] Sheil, *Glimpses of Life and Manners in Persia*, London, 1856. F. Sümer, *Oğuzlar*, Ankara, 1967, pp. 152, 282, 285-86, 338. Idem, *Sefevi devletinin kuruluşu ve gelişmesinde Anadolu Türklerin rolu*, Ankara, 1976. H. Valili Baharlu, *Azerbaycan. Coğrafi, tabii, etnoğrafi ve iktisadi mülāhazāt*, Baku, 1921. J. E. Woods, *The Aqqoyunlu. Clan, Confederation, Empire*, Minneapolis, Minn., 1976. M. H. Yınanç, "Akkoyunlular," *İA* I, pp. 251-70.

(PIERRE OBERLING)

ḎŪ QĀR, watering place near Kūfa in Iraq where a battle was fought between Arab tribesmen and Persian forces in the early 7th century. In the 6th century the Sasanians relied on the Arab Lakhmid dynasty, with its capital at Ḥīra in Iraq, for defense of their southwestern frontier against incursions by Arab tribes. Nevertheless, in the second half of the century Arab tribes sometimes defeated Lakhmid forces and also attacked Persian caravans (Jād al-Mawlā et al., pp. 2-5, 94-98, 107-08; Ḥellī, p. 367; Simon, p. 30). In 602 Ḵosrow II Parvēz (590-628, with interruption) imprisoned the Lakhmid Noʿmān b. Monḏer and abolished the dynasty, appointing Īās b. Qabīṣa, an Arab of the tribe of Ṭayyeʾ, as governor. Subsequently, at an indeterminate date, an open clash between the Persians and their Arab auxiliaries, on one hand, and Arab tribesmen, on the other, occurred at Ḏū Qār. According to certain Muslim traditions, the battle took place in the year 1/623 or 2/624 (Ḥellī, pp. 158, 192). Ebn Ḥabīb (p. 360) dated it earlier, between 606 and 622, but modern scholars have narrowed this range to 604-11 (Rothstein, p. 123; Caussin de Perceval, p. 184; Bosworth, p. 608).

In the Arab sources the Persian force is numbered at 2,000 soldiers, with 3,000 Arabs led by Īās b. Qabīṣa. The enemy was from the Bakr b. Wāʾel, a large tribal confederation whose territory extended from southwestern Iraq into the eastern Arabian peninsula (Donner, pp. 16-18, 28; Ṭabarī, I, pp. 1030-31; Ḥellī, pp. 410-11). The most prominent constituent tribe was Šaybān, the other groups being Banū Ejl, Banū Ḏohl, Banū Qays b. Thaʿlaba, Banū Taym-Allāh b. Thaʿlaba, and Banū Yaškor. These groups do not seem to have coordinated their efforts on the battlefield, nor did they have a single commander-in-chief. Rather, leadership seeems to have shifted among various warriors. Nevertheless, the Bakrīs defeated the combined Persian and Arab forces.

Arab authors pieced together elements from disparate traditions on the battle of Ḏū Qār. The outlines of two main versions are discernible, one ultimately traceable to Abū ʿObayda (d. 209/824), the other to Ebn Kalbī (d. 204/819). According to Abū ʿObayda's more anecdotal version, Ḵosrow Parvēz was angry with the Ḥīran king Noʿmān for refusing to give him his daughter in marriage and insulting Persian women; he therefore imprisoned Noʿmān, who died in prison. Subsequently Ḵosrow sent armed forces against the Šaybānī leader Hānīʾ b. Qabīṣa, who refused to hand over to him Noʿmān's family and armor, but these forces were defeated at Ḏū Qār. According to Ebn Kalbī's version, when Noʿmān was deposed Bakrī tribesmen raided Persian territory in Iraq. The Šaybānī Qays b. Masʿūd made an agreement with Ḵosrow by which he received tracts of land in return for preventing Arab incursions into Persian territory. Qays's rivals within his own tribe deliberately continued the raids in order to foil this contract, and, indeed, Ḵosrow imprisoned Qays and demanded Bakrī hostages as a condition for his release (or as a guarantee against further incursions). The Bakrīs refused to give such hostages, and Ḵosrow sent armies against them, meeting with defeat at Ḏū Qār. Modern scholars generally prefer Ebn Kalbī's version, on the grounds that it is less colorful and therefore more plausible. Persian sources on the Sasanian period are silent about this battle; the relatively small number of soldiers involved, as well as the Persian defeat, may explain this silence.

Religious, as well as Arab, sentiment must have played a part in shaping accounts of Ḏū Qār. The Prophet Moḥammad (allegedly) said "This is the first battle in which the Arabs took equitable vengeance on the Persians, and they achieved this victory through me" (Ṭabarī, I, 1031; Mottaqī Hendī, no. 30301; Eṣfahānī, XX, p. 138). Ignaz Goldziher (p. 100) noted the connection between Arab disdain for Persians and elaboration on the victory at Ḏū Qār.

Some scholars, apparently influenced by the Muslim tradition (e.g., Ḥellī, p. 422; Yaʿqūbī, II, p. 46), have interpreted the battle of Ḏū Qār as part of a prolonged Arab rebellion against the Persians, which culminated in the Muslim conquest of the Persian empire. As Šaybānī tribesmen, led by Moṯannā b. Ḥāreṯa, assisted in the conquest of Iraq, it has been argued that the Bakr, and especially the Šaybān, had followed a distinct anti-Sasanian policy since Ḏū Qār. Fred Donner has shown (pp. 28-30), however, that the Šaybān who supported the Muslims and those who were prominent at Ḏū Qār belonged to different, even rival clans; some Šaybānī leaders allied themselves with the Persians after Ḏū Qār, and others even opposed the Muslims during the conquest of Iraq. The battle of Ḏū Qār thus appears to have had ideological and symbolic meaning for the Arabs far beyond its military and political significance.

Bibliography: (For cited works not found in this bibliography and abbreviations found here, see "Short References.") Abū Helāl ʿAskarī, *Ketāb al-awāʾel*, Beirut, 1987, pp. 289-91. Balʿamī, ed. Bahār, II, pp. 1098-1137. E. Bräunlich, *Bisṭām Ibn Qays*, Leipzig, 1925. C. E. Bosworth, "Iran and the Arabs before Islam," in *Camb. Hist. Iran* III/1, pp. 593-612. A. P. Caussin de Perceval, *Essai sur l'histoire des Arabes* II, Paris, 1847, pp. 171-85. F. Donner, "The Bakr b. Wāʾil Tribes and Politics in Northeastern Arabia on the Eve of Islam," *Stud. Isl.* 51, 1980, pp. 5-38. Ebn al-Balḵī, pp. 105-06. Ebn Ḥabīb, *Ketāb al-moḥabbar*, Beirut, n.d. (esp. pp. 144, 153, 360). Ebn Kalbī, *Jamharat al-nasab*, Beirut, 1986 (esp. pp. 492, 506, 510, 536). Abu'l-Faraj Eṣfahānī, *Ketāb al-aḡānī*, ed. A. Šanqīṭī, II, Cairo, n.d. (esp. p. 29); XX, Cairo, n.d. (esp. pp. 132-40). M. Faraj, *al-Fatḥ al-ʿarabī be'l-ʿErāq wa-Fārs*, Cairo, 1966 (esp. pp. 45-66). I. Goldziher, *Muslim Studies* I, London, 1967. Abu'l-Baqāʾ Hebat-Allāh Ḥellī, *al-Manāqeb al-mazyadīya fī aḵbār al-molūk al-asadīya* I, ʿAmmān, n.d. (esp. pp. 158, 192, 393-422). M. A. Jād-al-Mawlā, A. M. Bejāwī, and M. A. Ebrāhīm, *Ayyām al-ʿArab fi'l-jāhelīya*, Cairo, n.d. (pp. 6-39). M. Morony, *Iraq after the Muslim Conquest*, Princeton, N.J., 1984 (esp. pp. 152-53, 220). Mottaqī Hendī, *Kanz al-ʿommāl*, Beirut, 1979. Nöldeke, *Geschichte der Perser* (esp. pp. 303-45). G. Rothstein, *Die Dynastie der Laḫmiden in al-Ḥīra*, Berlin, 1899 (esp. pp. 120-23). R. Simon, *Meccan Trade and Islam*, Budapest, 1989. Ṭabarī, I (esp. pp. 1028-37). Yaʿqūbī, *Taʾrīḵ* I, Beirut, 1960 (esp. pp. 215, 225), II, Beirut, 1960 (esp. p. 46).

(ELLA LANDAU-TASSERON)

ḎŪ'L-QARNAYN. See ESKANDAR.

ḎU'L-RĪĀSATAYN, ḤĀJJ MĪRZĀ ʿABD-AL-ḤOSAYN MŪNES-ʿALĪŠĀH (b. Shiraz, 1290/1873, d. Tehran, 25 Ḵordād 1332 Š./15 June 1953), for thirty years leader (*qoṭb*) of a principal branch of the Neʿmatallāhī Sufi order. The title Ḏū'l-Rīāsatayn ("possessor of two kinds of supremacy") refers to his reportedly exceptional command of both the exoteric and esoteric sciences (Nurbakhsh, p. 117). He is said to have received this title from Aḥmad Shah (1327-44/1909-25), but his father and predecessor, Ḥājj ʿAlī Āqā Wafā-ʿAlīšāh (d. 1336/1918) had also borne it, and it may well have come with the position of *qoṭb*. Owing to the length of Mūnes-ʿAlīšāh's tenure, the entire Neʿmatallāhī line descended from his grandfather, Ḥajj Moḥammad Āqā Monawwar-ʿAlīšāh (d. 1301/1884), is often called the "line of Ḏū'l-Rīāsatayn."

Mūnes-ʿAlīšāh initially studied at home with such tutors as Sayyed Moḥammad-Nabī Karbalāʾī and is said to have mastered Arabic and the fundamentals of jurisprudence by the age of sixteen years. He then began an intensive study of all the traditional sciences, culminating in a reading of Ebn ʿArabī's *Foṣūṣ al-ḥekam* under the guidance of Shaikh Ḥosayn Sabzavarī and Shaikh-al-Moḥaqqeqīn Eṣṭahbānātī. Part of his spiritual training was supervised by Ayatollah Jaʿfar Maḥallātī, but it was his father who initiated him into the Neʿmatallāhī order. The two went on a pilgrimage to Mecca in 1306/1889, a journey that resulted in the composition of one of Mūnes-ʿAlīšāh's earliest treatises, *Anīs al-mohājerīn*.

Both father and son were convinced adherents of the constitutional cause in Persia (see CONSTITUTIONAL REVOLUTION), and together they established at Shiraz the Anjoman-e anṣār to support it. Ḏū'l-Rīāsatayn's patriotic fervor manifested itself again during World War I, when he donned military garb with the aim of combating the British troops in Fārs and began drilling his father's disciples in the courtyard of the Masjed-e Now in Shiraz, where normally he delivered sermons. Also symptomatic of his political interests, which in his later years he totally abandoned, was his publication in Shiraz of the newspaper *Eḥyā*.

When Wafā-ʿAlīšāh died in 1336/1918 his designated successor was not a member of his family but Sayyed Esmāʿīl Ojāq Ṣādeq-ʿAlīšāh, presumably because Mūnes-ʿAlīšāh was still relatively young. Wafā-ʿAlīšāh is said to have made his choice of Ṣādeq-ʿAlīšāh conditional on his renouncing the right to name his own successor, however (Gramlich,

p. 59). In any event, when he died in 1340/1922 the succession passed smoothly to Mūnes-ʿAlīšāh. In the same year Ḏū'l-Rīāsatayn made another pilgrimage to Mecca. Seven years later he moved from Shiraz to Tehran, where he established his headquarters in the Čahār Sūq ḵānaqāh, remaining there until his death; in accordance with his instructions, his body was taken to Kermānšāh for burial in a ḵānaqāh built there by Ṣādeq-ʿAlīšāh.

It is not clear that Ḏū'l-Rīāsatayn ever appointed a successor, which may help to explain the profusion of claimants to his mantle. It was his nephew and son-in-law Jawād Nūrbaḵš who took control of the Čahār Sūq *ḵānaqāh* and was best placed to assert his claims. According to one account, Nūrbaḵš was unable to produce an *ejāza-nāma* (letter of appointment) and drew up instead a protocol, witnessed by the shaikhs of the order, in which he pledged to act as interim leader until Ḏū'l-Rīāsatayn's grandson Moḥammad Āqā should come of age; subsequently, however, he broke this pledge (Modarresī Čahārdehī, 1360 Š./1981, pp. 227, 231). Nūrbaḵš himself claims to have been posthumously invested as *qoṭb* by Ḏu'l-Rīāsatayn on the very night of his death (Nurbakhsh, p. 157).

Of Ḏū'l-Rīāsatayn's writings only his *Dīvān* (Tehran, 1345 Š./1966) and one treatise, *Yūnosīya* (said to be derived largely from *Kebrīt-e aḥmar* by Moẓaffar-ʿAlīšāh [d. 1315/1800] and printed by Nūrbaḵš under the title *Čerāḡ-e rāh*, Tehran, n.d.) have been published for general circulation; the pamphlet *Mūnes al-sālekīn* was distributed exclusively among neophytes (for unpublished works, see *Mūnes al-sālekīn*, pp. 8-9; Nurbakhsh, p. 125).

Bibliography: M.-Ḥ. Roknzāda Ādamiyyat, *Fārs wa jang-e bayn-al-melal*, Tehran, n.d., pp. 127, 153. R. Gramlich, *Die schiitischen Derwischorden Persiens* I. *Die Affiliationen*, Abh. für die Kunde des Morgenlandes 36/1, Wiesbaden, 1965, pp. 59-60. M. Homāyūnī, *Tārīḵ-e selselahā-ye ṭarīqat-e neʿmatallāhīya dar Īrān*, 4th ed., London, 1992, pp. 233-34. N. Modarresī Čahārdehī, *Selselahā-ye ṣūfīya-ye Īrān*, Tehran, 1360 Š./1981. Idem, *Sayr-ī dar taṣawwof. Dar šarḥ-e ḥāl-e mašāyeḵ wa aqṭāb*, Tehran, 1361 Š./1982, pp. 133-35. J. Nurbakhsh, *Masters of the Path. A History of the Masters of the Niʿmatullahi Sufi Order*, New York, 1980. Idem, "The Nimatullāhī," in S. H. Nasr, *Islamic Spirituality. Manifestations*, New York, 1991, pp. 144-61. N. Pourjavady and P. L. Wilson, *Kings of Love. The History and Poetry of the Niʿmatullāhī Sufi Order of Iran*, Tehran, 1978, pp. 164-66.

(HAMID ALGAR)

ḎU'L-RĪĀSATAYN. See FAŻL B. SAHL.

ḎU'L-ŠAHĀDATAYN. See AŠRAF ḠAZNAVĪ.

DUALISM, feature peculiar to Iranian religion in ancient and medieval times. There is general agreement on this point, though some scholars have minimized the importance of dualistic elements in Zoroastrian doctrine and even denied their existence, in order to emphasize monotheistic or crypto-monotheistic aspects (e.g., Shroff; Moulton, pp. 125-26; Gray, 1929, p. 3), perceived as incompatible with any form of dualism (cf. Duchesne-Guillemin, 1958, pp. 1 ff.; idem, 1962, pp. 385 ff.; Herrenschmidt, pp. 217 ff.). From a strictly religious-historical perspective, however, dualism should not be conceived as opposed to monotheism (as polytheism must be); on the contrary, it can be viewed as "monotheism itself in two opposite and contrary aspects" (Pettazzoni, pp. 96, 112 n. 109). Although this definition cannot be applied to every dualistic religious conception (cf. Bianchi, 1986, p. 109), it fits Zoroastrianism, in which a monotheistic tendency and a strong dualism coexisted. The problem is complicated by the fact that Iranian dualism was not unitary and static but a developing concept (Gnoli, 1984). Heterogeneity within the Iranian religious world must also be taken into account; in fact, the fundamentally ethical and philosophical dualism of Zoroaster (as found in the Gathas and in part of Zoroastrian tradition) must be distinguished from a metaphysical and ontological dualism in which two coexisting entities are opposed by their intrinsic natures, rather than by choice (see below). This distinction is rejected by those who maintain the ontological nature of dualism in the Gathas and argue that reference to the two *mainiius* "spirits" (*Y.* 30.5) is at most a "statement regarding their essence" (Bianchi, 1978, p. 376). Nevertheless, the pivotal role of choice in Zoroastrianism has been established by Herman Lommel (pp. 156-65) and others, and Ilya Gershevitch has argued effectively for the ethical character of the gathic opposition between the two spirits (1964, pp. 12-14; cf. Gnoli, 1984, p. 118).

The most lucid evaluation of dualism as a fundamental element of the Gathas is that of W. B. Henning: "Any claim that the world was created by a good and benevolent god must provoke the question why the world, in the outcome, is so very far from good. Zoroaster's answer, that the world had been created by a good *and* an evil spirit of equal power, who set up to spoil the good work, is a complete answer: it is a logical answer, more satisfying to the thinking mind than the one given by the author of the Book of Job, who withdrew to the claim that it did not behove man to inquire into the ways of Omnipotence" (1951, p. 46). According to Henning, Zoroaster came to formulate his dualistic conception "only by thinking" and "by very clear thinking." Whether he was correct that it was a protest against monotheism or whether it was an integral part of gathic monotheism is unclear. It can reasonably be concluded, however, that dualism lay at the heart of Zoroaster's message and that gathic dualism cannot be dismissed on grounds that Ahura Mazdā (q.v.) stood above the two opposed spirits or that an eschatological expectation of the triumph of good pervades the Gathas. These elements are, in fact, common to other dualistic conceptions in which the final triumph of good is implicit.

The following passage from the Gathas (*Y.* 30.3-4) is fundamental to understanding Iranian dualism: "The two primeval Spirits (*mainiiū pauruiiē*) who are twins (*yə̄mā*) were revealed [to me] in sleep. Their (*hī*) ways of thinking, speaking, and behaving are two: the good and the evil (*vahiiō akəmčā*). And between these two [ways] the wise men (*hudå̄ŋhō*) have rightly chosen, and not the foolish ones (*duždå̄ŋhō*). And when these two Spirits met, they established at the origin (*paouirīm*) life and non-life (*gaēmcā ajiiāitīmcā*) and that at the end (*apə̄məm*) the worst existence (*aŋhuš acištō*) will be for the followers of Falsehood (*drəguuatąm*) and for the follower of Truth (*ašāunē*) the Best Thinking (*vahištəm manō*)." Although the interpretation of this passage is uncertain (for a different translation, see Kellens and Pirart, p. 111), its dualistic content is beyond doubt. Equally clear is the paradigmatic character of the choice between two spirits, the prototype of the choice that man must make between the paths of truth and falsehood (Gershevitch, 1964, pp. 13, 32). Among the many other gathic texts in which dualism is emphasized are *Yasna* 45.2, in which the two spirits are juxtaposed in several modes of expression, and *Yasna* 47.3, in which the twinship of the two spirits is implicitly clarified by affirmation that Ahura Mazdā is the "father" of the beneficent spirit: Both are, in a certain sense, sons of the same father (Gershevitch, 1964, pp. 13, 33). Interpretation of "twins" as a metaphor for "the equality in state of the two unrelated beings, and their coevity" (Boyce, *Zoroastrianism* I, p. 194) is unconvincing. Instead, the fundamental role of choice in Zoroastrian dualism should be kept in mind; the relationship between God and the devil did not involve direct dependence, because the notion of "childbirth" implicit in the concept of twin spirits refers to derivation from God of an undifferentiated spirit, which splits into twin spirits of opposite allegiance once human free will has emerged (Gershevitch, 1964, p. 13).

Zoroaster's dualism was therefore a wholly transcendent or "spiritual" dualism, not based on the opposition *mēnōg* versus *gētīg*, which can be very approximately translated as "spiritual" and "material" respectively. The latter duality recurs particularly in 9th-century Pahlavi texts, reflecting a complex theoretical systematization (Shaked, 1971). It has clear Avestan antecedents in the Gathas, in the idea of two states of being (*uba- ahu-*), *ahu- manaŋhō* (or *manahiia-*) and *ahu- astuuaṇt* (lit., "bony," i.e., "corporeal"; cf. Pahl. *axw ī astōmand*) or *sti-* "existence," *mainiiauua-* and *gaēiθiia-*. In this context *gētīg* is negative not by nature but because it is the place where the two spirits intermingle, in which God's creation is contaminated by the assault (Pahl. *ēbgat*) by Ahriman (q.v.). In 9th-century Zoroastrian theology Ahriman was not considered the author of a *gētīg* creation, as Ohrmazd was (*Bundahišn*, chap. 1; tr. Anklesaria, pp. 17-21): "Of Ahriman it is said that he has no *gētīg*"; "The creation of Ohrmazd is both *mēnōg* and *gētīg*, while that of the demon has no *gētīg*" (*Dādistān ī dēnīg*, pt. 1, 18.2, 36.51). In the *Dēnkard* (q.v.) it is said that "Ahriman never existed and does not exist" and that "the gods exist while the demons do not" (*Dēnkard* 6.278, 6.98; tr. Shaked, 1979, pp. 39, 109). It may therefore be concluded that "Ahriman's presence in the world is not an ontological fact, but merely an anthropological and psychological phenomenon. This does not deny the reality of Ahriman as such: it merely marks his totally negative, hence also non-material, character" (Shaked, 1967, p. 232). This doctrine, too, has Avestan antecedents: Avestan *gaēiθiia-* (> Pahl. *gētīg*) may refer to the *yazata*s but not to the *daēuua*s (Gnoli, 1963, pp. 182-83 n. 61; see *DAIVA; DĒW). The existence of evil forces is only "spiritual" or "mental"; Iranian dualism is a dualism not between spirit and matter but between two spirits, who choose between truth (*aša*, q.v.; gathic *ašå̄uuan-*) and falsehood (*drug*; gathic *drəguuaṇt-* or Younger Av. *druuaṇt-*; see DRUJ-) in the same way that men do (Gnoli, 1963, pp. 180-90; idem, 1971, pp. 77-78, 97-98).

There is no doubt that Aŋra Mainiiu, like Ahura Mazdā, was a "creating divinity," an idea that occurs in the Avesta (e.g., *Yt.* 13.76 = *Y.* 57.17, with an explicit reference to creation by the two spirits; cf. Kreyenbroek, pp. 44, 45, 85-86; *Vd.* 1, with a list of "countries" created by Ahura Mazdā and the countercreations of Aŋra Mainiiu; cf. Christensen, 1943, pp. 50 ff.). The crucial element is the fundamental difference between the two kinds of creation (*Y.* 44.7; for references, see Gray, 1929, p. 176). Aŋra Mainiiu's creation has a negative character because it begins in opposition to that of Ahura Mazdā (or, in the gathic formulation, of Spəṇta Mainiiu). The *gētīg* state is the creation of Ohrmazd; Ahriman can only attack, contaminate, and corrupt it. The *mēnōg* nature of Ahriman's creation is amply documented in Pahlavi literature (*Dēnkard* III, sec, 10; *Dādistān ī dēnīg*, pt. 1, 18, 30; cf. de Menasce, 1968; idem, 1973, pp. 107, 393). From this perspective the preeminently "mental" or "spiritual" character of the demons can be explained: The *daēuua*s are false gods or chimeras without real existence (Gershevitch, 1975, pp. 79-80; Zaehner, 1961, p. 216), an idea traceable to the gathic notion (*Y.* 30.4) that Spəṇta Mainiiu and Aŋra Mainiiu are related to life and to nonlife (*gaēmčā ajiiāitīmcā*) respectively. Pahlavi *gētīg* "worldly" corresponds to Avestan *gaēiθiia-* "having corporeal life, material" (*AirWb.*, col. 479) and is therefore connected to *jī-* (*juua-*) "to live," *gaiia-* "life." Zoroastrian "pandemonium"

(Gray, 1929, pp. 175 ff.; cf. Christensen, 1941), with its classes of demonic beings symmetrically opposed to the angelic ones, results from an elaborate analysis of the superhuman world divided between good and evil, virtues and vices, opposed forces that, like man, may belong to the world of truth or of falsehood. All things are divided into two categories, even language itself, in order to distinguish between activities proper to beings that conform to truth and those who choose falsehood (Frachtenberg; Güntert; Gray, 1927; Burrow, pp. 128-33; Boyce, *Zoroastrianism* I, p. 298).

Zoroastrian dualism was based on the idea of choice, and the argument that one who chooses evil follows his own nature (Bianchi, 1978, pp. 361-62) does not affect that principle. In the *Bundahišn* (1.20-22; tr. Anklesaria, pp. 6-9) Ohrmazd offers peace to the evil spirit (*ganāg mēnōg*), who may thus become "deathless and unaging, unfeeling, incorruptible," but the evil spirit rejects the offer and threatens to take over the entire universe. From this passage it appears that Ahriman freely chooses his own destiny: Dualism is thus characterized by "choice," not by the essence or nature of the protagonists. Further confirmation comes from the Armenian Christian writer Eznik Kołbacʿi, in whose work Ahriman says: "'It is not that I cannot create anything good, but that I will not.' . . . Do you see? He is evil through his own wish, not from the fact of his birth" (Zaehner, 1955, p. 438). Abnormal aspects suggesting that Ahriman is capable of creativity comparable to that of Ohrmazd are debatable or absolutely secondary in Zoroastrian dualism, the ethical nature of which is a constant element from the Gathas to Pahlavi literature. Yet Zoroastrian and Iranian dualism generally did undergo historical transformations, impelled by inner tendencies and contacts with other religions (Shaked, 1994).

The transformation of Zoroaster's original dualism was determined by the progressive assimilation of Ahura Mazdā and Spəṇta Mainiiu, a process favored by the idea that God created everything through the beneficent spirit (*Y.* 44.7), defined in the Younger Avesta (*Yt.* 10.143) as a "creator" (*daδuuå spəṇtō mainiiuš*) not unlike Ahura Mazdā himself (Gershevitch, 1964, p. 14); there is no real evidence in the Avesta that the opposition between Spəṇta Mainiiu and Aŋra Mainiiu was transferred to Ahura Mazdā and Aŋra Mainiiu, however. As Gershevitch (1964, p. 15) has noted, such a transformation was documented in the Greek sources as early as the 4th century B.C.E. and in Zoroastrian texts of the 9th century C.E.: "In the place of Falsehood now stands the Fiendish Spirit, in the place of Truth, God himself. Zoroaster's religion has become an uncompromising dualism, in which two aboriginal deities, Ohrmazd and Ahriman, God and the Devil, face each other and contend for ultimate victory." Aristotle, in a fragment of the *Perì philosophías* (apud Diogenes Laertius, 1.8), explained the teaching of the Magi as presupposing the existence of two principles, Zeus or Oromasdes and Hades or Areimanios. In the *Metaphysics*, too, he cited the Magi in Asia, because of their dualism, as forerunners of Plato immediately after Pherecydes in Greece (cf. Benveniste, p. 17; Bidez and Cumont, I, p. 102). A similar notion was expressed by his disciple Eudemus of Rhodes (apud Damascius, p. 322; cf. Gnoli, 1988). In *De Iside et Osiride* Plutarch attributed such a dualistic formula to Zoroastres the Magus (Bidez and Cumont, II, p. 71).

In the 9th-century Pahlavi literature the dualism between Ohrmazd and Ahriman is omnipresent. In the first chapter of the *Bundahišn* there is a powerful representation of Ohrmazd as omniscient and good, residing on high in the infinite light (*asar rōšnīh*), which is also its own space (*gāh*) and place (*gyāg*). Ahriman, endowed with "knowledge after the fact" (*pas-dānišnīh*, knowledge of effects, rather than causes, as only Ohrmazd is able to foresee) and a desire for destruction (*zadār-kāmīh*), resides in the abyss (*zofr-pāyag*) in infinite darkness (*asar tārīgīh*), which is its own place. Between them is the void (*tuhīgīh*), or atmosphere (*way*), where the mingling (*gumēzišn*) of the two spirits (*mēnōg*) takes place (*Bundahišn* 1.1-5; tr. Anklesaria, pp. 4-5).

It should be noted, however, that this new formulation of Zoroastrian dualism, in which God is degraded to the level of devil's antagonist, was part of a unitary body of doctrine that remained essentially unchanged for centuries. Within certain limits a historical development can be partially reconstructed from the heterogeneous sources. It can be assumed that the gathic formulation (of Ahura Mazdā and opposed twin spirits) was succeeded by a formulation in which Ahura Mazdā was directly opposed to the evil spirit, with the addition in some instances of another entity, time (Zurwān), conceived as the father of the twins Ohrmazd and Ahriman. The supremacy of time in some sources, both Iranian and non-Iranian, related to the religion of the Magi or even in the 9th-century Zoroastrian religious literature, has been interpreted as attesting to Zurvanism, defined either as the continuation of an Iranian religion parallel to Mazdaism, a Mazdean heresy, or simply a theological trend peripheral to orthodoxy (Nyberg, 1929; idem, 1931; Zaehner, 1955; for further references, cf. Gnoli, 1980, pp. 211-12; Boyce, 1990; idem, *Zoroastrianism* III, pp. 412, 423-24, 463-64). It seems that Zurvanism, "with its speculation on Time, its apparatus of numbers, and the idea of the world-year, is the outcome of contact between Zoroastrianism and the Babylonian civilization" in the 5th-4th centuries B.C. (Henning, 1951, p. 49; see BABYLONIA ii). The various references to the opposition between Oromasdes and Areimanios in Greek and Latin sources, particularly the passage from Eudemus, can be interpreted as evidence that Zurvanism already existed in the latter half of the Achaemenid period. The historical development of

Iranian dualism can therefore be viewed as having taken place in three principal stages: gathic dualism (Ahura Mazdā + Spəṇta Mainiiu and Aŋra Mainiiu), Zurvanite dualism (Zruuan + Ahura Mazdā and Aŋra Mainiiu), and the simplified dualism of the Pahlavi texts (Ohrmazd and Ahriman), in which the two principles are represented in almost symmetrical opposition (pace Bianchi, 1958; Molé).

In the Zurvanite myth as transmitted by hostile and foreign sources, chiefly Syrian and Armenian Christian writers (cf. Schaeder, 1941), Zurwān, or time, fathered the twins Ohrmazd and Ahriman; having promised the scepter to the firstborn, he made Ahriman, who came to light first, king for 9,000 years, a "limited time," after which kingship was to be bestowed on Ohrmazd for "endless time." This myth attests a religious and philosophical mentality quite different from that of original Zoroastrianism. The historical development of Iranian dualism under the influence of Babylonian astronomy and astrology and the astral religion of Mesopotamia, far from preserving Zoroastrian moral values and belief in the dignity and freedom of man, caused a radical subversion of those values. In gathic dualism Ahura Mazdā and man, his earthly and corporeal symbol, stood above and in the center of everything, with the two opposing spirits offering free choice. Syncretistic Iranian-Mesopotamian dualism reduced Ahura Mazdā to the level of Aŋra Mainiiu and raised time above everything. Whereas in the Gathas the role and value of God and man's moral freedom were exalted above all, in the syncretistic version the role and value of the creator God were debased and man subjugated to the omnipotence of time (*zamān*), from which the soul cannot release itself: "Time is more powerful than the two creations, the creation of Ohrmazd and the creation of the Evil Spirit" (*Bundahišn* 1.43; tr. Anklesaria, pp. 12-15; cf. Nyberg, 1929, pp. 214-15; Henning, 1935, p. 11; Zaehner, 1955, pp. 281, 297 ff., 315-16). In these conceptions lie the foundations of a religious fatalism that deeply influenced medieval Persia (cf. Ringgren, 1952, pp. 72 ff.).

The transformation of gathic dualism into Zurvanite dualism was not simply a theological development without consequences for the Zoroastrian religious life and world view, as has been suggested (Boyce, 1990, p. 25). In fact, the Zurvanite conception of the world-year and exaltation of time above the protagonists in the cosmic drama represented adaptation of the Zoroastrian tradition to the religious, philosophical, and scientific tendencies prevailing in the Near East during the Achaemenid and Hellenistic periods, when the notions of a universal law regulating the eternal movement of the orbs and of the celestial vault were widely accepted (on these aspects of Babylonian religion, see, e.g., Meissner, chap. xviii; Bottéro, pp. 142-43). It is certainly paradoxical to consider dualism as a monistic attempt to subjugate dualism to Zurwān (Pétrement, 1947, pp. 323 ff.).

It was during this period, too, that Iranian dualism influenced Judaism (Bousset, 1926; Colpe; Duchesne-Guillemin, 1958, pp. 86 ff.; Hultgård; Shaked, 1984), as is especially clear from the Qumran texts (Wilderberger; Michaud; Duchesne-Guillemin, 1957; Winston; Widengren, 1966; Ringgren, 1967; see DEAD SEA SCROLLS); early Christianity (Clemen; Duchesne-Guillemin, 1962, pp. 264 ff.; Widengren, 1975); and Gnosticism (Bousset, 1907; Widengren, 1952; idem, 1967). Research in these different fields is particularly rich and complex, and opinions often differ widely. It is nevertheless difficult to deny an influence of Iranian dualism on the religions of the Near East from the Achaemenid period to the early centuries of the present era (for a recent discussion see Boyce, *Zoroastrianism* III, pp. 361-490; cf. Gnoli, 1984; see also BIBLE ii).

Even clearer is the influence of Iranian dualism on Manicheism, despite the present tendency to consider the origins of Manicheism within the general framework of Judaism and Christianity (see, e.g., Boyce, *Zoroastrianism* III, p. 460-65). In formulating his version of dualism Mani abided by one of the fundamental tenets of Mazdaism, that creation is the work of a good, wise, and omniscient God (Puech, p. 142), but in Manicheism there is particular emphasis on an omnipresent evil, which man must fight with all his force during his earthly life. This dualism is based on the opposition of light and darkness, God and matter, conceived as principles preceding and transcending the drama of human existence in the mediating moment of their "intermingling" (Pahl. *gumēzišn*), as in the 9th-century Zoroastrian texts. In Mani's dualism man was again at the center; Ohrmazd was redeemed from the degradation into which he had fallen in Zurvanite theology and identified as primordial man, who, in Manichean Gnosticism was the true divine savior (Gnoli, 1984, pp. 134-35). Manichean and Turkish documents from Central Asia demonstrate that Manicheans reacted against Zurvanite dualism by attacking those who affirmed that Ohrmazd and Ahriman were brothers or that God had created both good and evil, referred to in the Manichean Middle Persian text M 28 (Henning, 1951, p. 50) and the Uighur confession text *Xwāstwānīft* I.C.3-4 (Asmussen, p. 194; cf. the texts collected in Zaehner 1955, pp. 431 ff.; Puech, pp. 140-41). The occurrence of such a condemnation in a 9th-century Zoroastrian text undoubtedly reflects the influence of polemics between Manicheans and Christians (*Dēnkard* 9.30.4: "Ohrmazd and Ahriman were two brothers in one womb"; Junker, p. 144; Schaeder, 1930, pp. 288-91; Benveniste, 1932-33, pp. 209-11; Zaehner, 1955, pp. 429-31; Molé, pp. 464-65). Any trace of Zurvanite dualism was to be eradicated and replaced by the new Zoroastrian orthodoxy, in which the dualism between Ohrmazd and Ahriman was preeminent.

Islamic hostility to dualism also influenced the Zoroastrian communities in Persia. In fact, condemnation of dualists (*tanawīya, ahl al-iṯnayn*) was almost a topos in Muslim refutations of Manichean, Mazdakite, and even Mazdean doctrines; the last was, however, given special attention by such authors as Abū Bakr Moḥammad Bāqellānī (Monnot, 1977), ʿAbd-al-Jabbār b. Aḥmad (Monnot, 1974), and Abu'l-Fatḥ Moḥammad Šahrestānī (Gimaret and Monnot, pp. 635-54; cf. Monnot, 1986, pp. 119, 38, 41, 86, 124, 141 ff., 157 ff.). After the Muslim conquest of Persia and the exodus of many Zoroastrians to India and after having been exposed to both Muslim and Christian propaganda, the Zoroastrians, especially the Parsis in India, went so far as to deny dualism and to view themselves as outright monotheists (Dhalla, pp. 46-53, 156-73, 247-68, 337 ff.; Duchesne-Guillemin, 1953, pp. 161 ff.; idem, 1962, pp. 373-74; Boyce, 1979, pp. 197, 207, 213, 220). After several transformations and developments one of the defining features of the Zoroastrian religion thus gradually faded and has almost disappeared from modern Zoroastrianism.

Nevertheless, Iranian dualism spread widely east and west of the Iranian world, especially through Manicheism. Traces can still be found in Central Asian and particularly Tibetan cosmogonies (Klimkeit, 1986, pp. 46, 48; Tucci, 1949, pp. 730-31; idem, 1980, pp. 214, 271 n. 5; Gnoli, 1962, pp. 127-28; Hoffmann, pp. 102 ff.; Blondeau, p. 313; cf. Uray; Kværne). In the West, although the connections are uncertain and the historical development difficult to reconstruct, religious dualism can be identified in the beliefs of Priscillianus and his followers in the late Roman empire, the Paulicians in the Byzantine empire, and later the Bogomils (see, e.g., Söderberg; Runciman; Loos; for a sound survey of the history and problems, see Manselli; for further references, see Couliano, pp. 223-81; Rudolph, pp. 402 ff., 423 n. 191).

Bibliography: (For cited works not found in this bibliography and abbreviations found here, see "Short References.") J. P. Asmussen, *Xᵘāstvānīft. Studies in Manichæism*, Copenhagen, 1965. E. Benveniste, *The Persian Religion According to the Chief Greek Texts*, Paris, 1929. Idem, "Le témoignage de Théodore bar Kônay sur le zoroastrisme," *Le Monde Oriental* 26, 1932-33, pp. 170-215. U. Bianchi, *Zamān ī Ōhrmazd. Lo zoroastrismo nelle sue origini e nella sua essenza*, Turin, 1958. Bianchi, "Alcuni aspetti abnormi del dualismo persiano," *Atti del convegno internazionale sul tema: La Persia nel Medioevo*, Rome, 1971, pp. 149-64. Idem, "La doctrine zarathoustrienne des deux esprits," in U. Bianchi, *Selected Essays on Gnosticism, Dualism and Mysteriosophy*, Leiden, 1978, pp. 361-89. Idem, *Problemi di storia delle religioni*, 2nd ed., Rome, 1986. J. Bidez and F. Cumont, *Les Mages hellénisés. Zoroastre, Ostanès et Hystaspe d'après la tradition greque*, 2 vols., Paris, 1938. A.-M. Blondeau, "Les religions du Tibet," in H.-C. Puech, ed., *Histoire des religions* III, Paris, 1976, pp. 233-329. J. Bottéro, *La religion babylonienne*, Paris, 1952. W. Bousset, *Hauptprobleme der Gnosis*, Göttingen, 1907. Idem, *Die Religion des Judentums im späthellenistischen Zeitalter*, 3rd ed., ed. H. Gressmann, Tübingen, 1926. M. Boyce, *Zoroastrians. Their Religious Beliefs and Practices*, London, 1979. Idem, "Some Further Reflections on Zurvanism," in *Iranica Varia. Papers in Honor of Professor Ehsan Yarshater*, Acta Iranica 30, Leiden, 1990, pp. 20-29. T. Burrow, "The Proto-Indoaryans," *JRAS*, 1973, pp. 123-40. L.-C. Casartelli, *La philosophie religieuse du mazdéisme sous les Sassanides*, Louvain, 1884. A. Christensen, *Essai sur la démonologie iranienne*, Det Kgl. Danske Videnskabernes Selskab., Hist.-fil. Medd. 27/1, Copenhagen, 1941. Idem, *Le premier chapitre du Vendidad et l'histoire primitive des tribus iraniennes*, Det Kgl. Danske Videnskabernes Selskab., Hist.-fil. Medd. 29/4, Copenhagen, 1943. C. Clemen, *Religionsgeschichtliche Erklärung des Neuen Testamentes*, Giessen, 1924. C. Colpe, *Die religionsgeschichtliche Schule. Darstellung und Kritik ihres Bildes vom gnostischen Erlösermythus*, Göttingen, 1961. I. P. Couliano, *Les gnoses dualistes d'Occident. Histoire et mythes*, Paris, 1990.

Damascius, *Dubitationes et Solutiones in Platonis Parmenidem*, ed. C. A. Ruelle, Paris, 1889. J. Darmesteter, *Ohrmazd et Ahriman*, Paris, 1877. M. N. Dhalla, *Zoroastrian Theology. From the Earliest Times to the Present Day*, New York, 1914; repr. New York, 1972. J. Duchesne-Guillemin, *Ormazd et Ahriman. L'aventure dualiste dans l'antiquité*, Paris, 1953. Idem, "Le zervanisme et les manuscrits de la Mer Morte," *Indo-Iranian Journal* 1, 1957, pp. 96-99. Idem, *The Western Response to Zoroaster*, Oxford, 1958. Idem, *La religion de l'Iran ancien*, Paris, 1962. L. J. Frachtenberg, "Etymological Studies in Ohrmazdian and Ahrimanian Words in Avestan," in J. J. Modi, ed., *Spiegel Memorial Volume. Papers Written on Iranian Subjects . . .*, Bombay, 1908, pp. 269-89. I. Gershevitch, "Zoroaster's Own Contribution," *JNES* 23, 1964, pp. 12-38. Idem, "Die Sonne das Beste," in J. R. Hinnells, ed., *Mithraic Studies* I, Manchester, 1975, pp. 68-89. D. Gimaret and G. Monnot, eds., *Shahrastani. Livre des religions et des sectes* I, Louvain, 1986. G. Gnoli, "Un particolare aspetto del simbolismo della luce nel Mazdeismo e nel Manicheismo," *AIUON*, N.S. 12, 1962, pp. 95-128. Idem, "Osservazioni sulla dottrina mazdaica della creazione," *AIUON*, N.S. 13, 1963, pp. 163-93. Idem, "Problems and Prospects of the Studies on Persian Religion," in *Problems and Methods of the History of Religions*, Numen 19, suppl., Leiden, 1971, pp. 67-101. Idem, *Zoroaster's Time and Homeland*, Naples, 1980. Idem, "L'évolution du dualisme iranien et le problème zurvanite," *RHR*

201, 1984, pp. 115-38. Idem, "A Note on the Magi and Eudemus of Rhodes," in J. Duchesne-Guillemin and D. Marcotte, eds., *A Grean Leaf. Papers in Honour of Professor Jes P. Asmussen*, Acta Iranica 28, Leiden, 1988, pp. 283-88. L. H. Gray, "The 'Ahurian' and 'Daevian' Vocabularies in the Avesta," *JRAS*, 1927, pp. 427-41. Idem, *The Foundations of the Iranian Religions*, The Journal of the K. R. Cama Oriental Institute 15, 1929. H. Güntert, *Über die ahurischen und daēvischen Ausdrücke im Awesta. Eine semasiologische Studie*, Sb. der Heidelberger Akademie der Wissenschaften, Phil.-hist. Kl., Abh. 13, Heidelberg, 1914. W. B. Henning, review of H. S. Nyberg, *Hilfsbuch des Pehlevi*, *Göttingische Gelehrte Anzeigen* 197, 1935, pp. 1-19. Idem, *Zoroaster. Politician or Witch-Doctor?* London, 1951. C. Herrenschmidt, "Once upon a Time, Zoroaster," *History and Anthropology* 3, 1987, pp. 209-37. H. Hoffmann, *Tibet. A Handbook*, Bloomington, Ind., 1975. A. Hultgård, "Das Judentum in der hellenistisch-römischen Zeit und die iranische Religion," *ANRW* II, pp. 512-90.

H. Junker, *Über iranische Quellen der hellenistischen Aion-Vorstellung*, Leipzig and Berlin, 1923. S. N. Kanga, "The Doctrine of Dualism in the Gathas," in *Prof. A. V. W. Jackson Memorial Volume*, Bombay, 1954, pp. 171-86. J. Kellens, *Zoroastre et l'Avesta ancien. Quatre leçons au Collège de France*, Paris, 1991. Idem, *Le panthéon de l'Avesta ancien*, Wiesbaden, 1994. Idem and E. Pirart, *Les textes vieil-avestiques* I, Wiesbaden, 1988. H.-J. Klimkeit, *Die Begegnung von Christentum, Gnosis und Buddhismus an der Seidenstrasse*, Rheinisch-Westfälische Akademie der Wissenschaften. Vorträge G 283, Opladen, Germany, 1986. G. Kreyenbroek, *Sraoša in the Zoroastrian Tradition*, Leiden, 1985. P. Kværne, "Dualism in Tibetan Cosmogonic Myths and the Question of Iranian Influence," in C. I. Beckwith, ed., *Silver on Lapis. Tibetan Literary Culture and History*, Bloomington, Ind., 1987, pp. 163-74. H. Lommel, *Die Religion Zarathustras nach dem Awesta dargestellt*, Tübingen, 1930. M. Loos, *Dualist Heresy in the Middle Ages*, Prague, 1974. R. Manselli, *L'eresia del male*, Naples, 1963. B. Meissner, *Babylonien und Assyrien* II, Heidelberg, 1925. J. de Menasce, "L'origine mazdéenne d'un mythe manichéen," *RHR* 174, 1968, pp. 161-67. Idem, *Le troisième livre du Dēnkart*, Paris, 1973. H. Michaud, "Un mythe zervanite dans un des manuscrits de Qumrân," *Vetus Testamentum* 5, 1955, pp. 137-47. M. Molé, "Le problème zurvanite," *JA* 247, 1959, pp. 431-69. G. Monnot, *Penseurs musulmans et religions iraniennes. ʿAbd al-Jabbār et ses devanciers*, Paris, 1974. Idem, "La réponse de Bāqillānī aux dualistes," in *Recherches d'islamo-logie. Recueil d'articles offert à Georges C. Anawati et Louis Gardet par leurs collègues et amis*, Louvain, 1977, pp. 247-60. Idem, *Islam et religions*, Paris, 1986. J. H. Moulton, *Early Zoroastrianism*, London, 1913. H. S. Nyberg, "Questions de cosmogonie et de cosmologie mazdéennes," *JA* 214, 1929, pp. 193-310; 219, 1931, pp. 1-134, 193-244. S. Pétrement, *Le dualisme chez Platon, les gnostiques et les manichéens*, Paris, 1947; repr. Brionne, France, 1982. R. Pettazzoni, *La religione di Zarathustra nella storia religiosa dell'Iran*, Bologna, 1920. H.-C. Puech, *Sur le manichéisme et autres essais*, Paris, 1979. H. Ringgren, *Fatalism in Persian Epics*, Uppsala, 1952. Idem, "Qumran and Gnosticism," in U. Bianchi, ed., *Le origini dello gnosticismo/The Origins of Gnosticism*, Numen 12, suppl., Leiden, 1967, pp. 378-88. K. Rudolph, *Die Gnosis. Wesen und Geschichte einer spätantiken Religion*, 3rd ed., Göttingen, 1990. S. Runciman, *Le manichéisme médiéval. L'hérésie dualiste dans le christianisme*, Paris, 1949; repr. Paris, 1972. H. H. Schaeder, *Urform und Fortbildungen des manichäischen Systems*, Leipzig, 1927. Idem, "Zandik-Zindiq," in *Iranische Beiträge* I, Schriften der Königsberger Gelehrten Gesellschaft 6, Geisteswiss. Kl. 5, Halle, 1930, pp. 274-91. Idem, "Der iranische Zeitgott und sein Mythos," *ZDMG* 95, 1941, pp. 288-99. J. Scheftelowitz, *Die Zeit als Schicksalsgottheit in der indischen und iranischen Religion (Kāla und Zurvan)*, Stuttgart, 1929. S. Shaked, "Some Notes on Ahreman, the Evil Spirit, and His Creation," in E. E. Urbach, R. J. Z Werblowsky, and C. Wirszubski, eds., *Studies in Mysticism and Religion, Presented to Gershom G. Scholem . . .*, Jerusalem, 1967, pp. 227-34. Idem, *The Wisdom of the Sasanian Sages (Dēnkard VI)*, Boulder, Colo., 1979. Idem, "Iranian Influence on Judaism. First Century B.C.E. to Second Century C.E.," in W. D. Davis and L. Finkelstein, eds., *The Cambridge History of Judaism* I, Cambridge, 1984, pp. 308-25. Idem, *Dualism in Transformation. Varieties of Religion in Sasanian Iran*, London, 1994. P. J. Shroff, "The Sublime Teachings of the Gathas," in *K. R. Cama Oriental Institute Golden Jubilee Volume*, Bombay, 1969, pp. 153-67. M. Söderberg, *La religion des Cathares. Étude sur le gnosticisme de la Basse Antiquité et du Moyen Âge* Uppsala, 1949.

G. Tucci, *Tibetan Painted Scrolls*, 3 vols., Rome, 1949. Idem, *The Religions of Tibet*, London, 1980. G. Uray, "Tibet's Connections with Nestorianism and Manichæism in the 8th-10th Centuries," in E. Steinkellner and H. Tauscher, eds., *Contributions on Tibetan Language, History and Culture*, Vienna, 1983, pp. 399-429. G. Widengren, "Der iranische Hintergrund der Gnosis," *Zeitschrift für Religions- und Geistes-geschichte* 4, 1952, pp. 87-114. Idem, "Iran and Israel in Parthian Times with Special Reference to the Ethiopic Book of Enoch," *Temenos* 2, 1966, pp. 139-77. Idem, "Les origines du gnosticisme et l'histoire des religions," in U. Bianchi, ed., *Le origini dello gnosticismo/The Origins of Gnosticism*, Numen 12, suppl., Leiden,

1967, pp. 28-60. Idem, "'Synkretismus' in der syrischen Christen-heit," in A. Dietrich, ed., *Synkretismus im syrisch-persischen Kulturgebiet*, Göttingen, 1975, pp. 38-64. H. Wilderberger, "Der Dualismus in den Qumranschriften," *Asiatische Studien/Études asiatiques* 8, 1954, pp. 163-77. D. Winston, "The Iranian Component in the Bible, Apocrypha and Qumran. A Review of the Evidence," *History of Religions* 5, 1966, pp. 183-216. R. C. Zaehner, *Zurvan. A Zoroastrian Dilemma*, Oxford, 1955. Idem, *The Dawn and Twilight of Zoroastrianism*, London, 1961.

(GHERARDO GNOLI)

DUBAI (Dobayy), second largest of the seven emirates constituting the United Arab Emirates (U.A.E.) on the southern shores of the Persian Gulf. It rivals Abu Dhabi (Abū Ẓabī) for preeminence within a federal structure that provides for considerable autonomy among its constituents (Dubai, p. 29). The twin cities of Dubai and Daireh (Dayra) are located around a creek (*ḵawr*) and have thus functioned as a center of commerce on the Persian Gulf. The emirate encompasses about 3,200 km^2, and in 1993 it had an estimated 501,000 inhabitants, 27 percent of the total population of the U.A.E. ("United Arab Emirates," p. 2897). Most of the population of the U.A.E. and of Dubai in particular consists of immigrants; nationals account for only 20.7 percent of the total population of the federation (Middle East Research Institute, p. 131). Almost half the inhabitants of Dubai are from the Indian subcontinent; 100,000-150,000 are of Persian origin (Farāzanda, p. 34). This Persian community, the largest in the U.A.E., has been instrumental in promoting ties between Persia and Dubai.

Relations with Persia before 1357 Š./1979. Toward the end of the 19th century the Persian port of Lenga lost its free-trade status, and nearby Dubai became the leading entrepôt in the area. The liberal policies of the emir of Dubai persuaded many Persian merchants to move there from Lenga. Dubai thus became the major port for trade with Persia. In addition, the growing Persian community provided opportunities for special cultural ties between the two countries. Nevertheless, Dubai, as a member of the Trucial States, was still under British control, and its relations with Persia were governed by the overall relations between Great Britain and Persia.

In January 1968 Great Britain announced its decision to withdraw from the Persian Gulf, including the Trucial States, by 1971; in the resulting power vacuum the government of Persia was concerned about its own claims and geopolitical interests in the area (Ramazani, pp. 408-27). When the idea of forming the U.A.E. was put forward by Great Britain Persian support was conditional on recognition of the islands of Abū Mūsā (q.v.) and the two Tonbs (also claimed by the emirates of Sharjah [Šāreqa] and Ras al-Khaimah [Ra'ʾs-al-Ḵayma]) as Persian territory. Despite Arab opposition to this demand, relations between Shaikh Rāšed (1958-90), emir of Dubai, and Moḥammad-Reżā Shah (1320-57 Š./1941-79) remained friendly. The emir, on a state visit to Persia in October 1969, expressed support for Persian preeminence over Iraq in the Persian Gulf (Alam, pp. 93-94), reflecting the political and socioeconomic realities in Dubai. Persia was able to exploit the rivalry between Dubai and Abu Dhabi by developing close ties with the emir of Dubai. A consulate was opened in Dubai in July 1952; it was elevated to consulate general in 1954. On the other hand, the trade-oriented economy of Dubai ensured the emir's greater interest in Persia than in his immediate neighbors. In the early 1970s more than half of about 50,000 trading dhows in Dubai were engaged primarily in re-export trade with Persia (Wezārat-e bāzargānī, p. 130). Cultural relations flourished as well, as Persia sponsored educational, health, and other institutions in Dubai. Students from Dubai attended Persian universities, particularly in Shiraz.

The postrevolutionary period. The conservative Arab countries viewed the Persian revolution of 1357 Š./1979 as a threat to the stability of the Persian Gulf. The formation of the Gulf Cooperation Council (G.C.C.) and its support for Iraq in the war with Persia in the 1980s attest the council members' fears of the Persian revolutionary regime. The U.A.E. was, however, more temperate than Kuwait and Saudi Arabia in its support for Iraq, primarily owing to the influence of Dubai and Sharjah. The emirs of both distrusted Iraq, and neither wished to sacrifice trade relations with Persia. In addition, the Persian community in Dubai, conservative, predominantly Sunnite, rather than Shiʿite, merchants, meant that it posed less of a threat as a "fifth column" than might otherwise have been so. The trade route thus not only remained open, but transactions between Persia and the U.A.E., mainly Dubai, reached a peak of 1 billion dirhams during the war (Yazdānīnīā, pp. 50-51, 55; Eilts, p. 22). The end of the war and subsequent developments in the Persian Gulf area, including the Iraqi invasion of Kuwait, only strengthened ties between Persia and Dubai. Many hospitals, schools, banks, recreation clubs, workers' cooperatives, and other institutions in Dubai are run directly by the Persian government or semigovernmental organizations (Wezārat-e omūr-e ḵāreja, pp. 36-37). If no new major crises occur capitalist initiatives adopted recently by the Persian government should strengthen relations with Dubai in the near future.

Bibliography: A. A. Alam, *The Shah and I*, ed. A. N. Alikhani, London, 1991. Dubai, Ministry of Culture and Information, *United Arab Emirates 1971-1986. Fifteen Years of Progress*, Dubai, n.d. H. F. Eilts, "Foreign Policy Perspectives of the Gulf States," in H. R. Sindler, ed., *Crosscurrents in the Gulf*, Washington, D.C., 1988, pp. 16-37. H. Farāzanda, *Šakl-gīrī-e sīāsat-e ḵārejī-e emārāt*,

Tehran, 1362 Š./1983. Middle East Research Institute, *The MERI Report. United Arab Emirates*, 1985. R. Ramazani, *Iran's Foreign Policy. 1941-1973*, Charlottesville, Va., 1975. "The United Arab Emirates," in *The Europa World Year Book. 1993* II, London, 1993, pp. 3011-24. Wezārat-e bāzargānī, Moʾassassa-ye moṭālaʿāt o pažūheshā-ye bāzargānī (Institute for commercial studies and research), *Emārāt-e mottaḥeda-ye ʿarabī*, Negāh-ī kūtāh be kešvarhā 17, Tehran, 1365 Š./1986. Wezārat-e omūr-e ḵāreja, *Ketāb-e sabz*, Tehran, 1368 Š./1989. Abu'l-Qāsem Yazdānīnīā, *Sīāsat-e ḵārejī-e emārāt-e ʿarabī-e mottaḥeda bā takīa bar jang-e taḥmīlī*, Tehran, 1359 Š./1980.

(SUSSAN SIAVOSHI)

DUCK (*morḡābī* < *morḡ-e ābī* "aquatic fowl" or *ordak* < Turk. *ördäk*), technically any species of the family Anatidae but in Persian popular usage including similar waterfowl from other families, particularly some geese and grebes.

François Hüe and R. D. Etchécopar recorded (pp. 106-33) eight genera comprising twenty-three species of Anatidae, either nesting in or migrating through Persia (cf. Read, pp. 3-5: eleven genera and twenty-two species; Scott et al., pp. 54-71: nine genera and twenty-one species).

It should be noted that the vernacular, or "Persian," terminology "officially" adopted by Sāzmān-e ḥefāẓat-e moḥīṭ-e zīst (Department for the protection of the environment) and recorded by D. A. Scott and his colleagues includes only a few authentic names for some of the better-known nesting ducks and that most of those assigned to migratory or sporadic species are arbitrary adaptations of the respective Latin, English, or French names. Careful study of the vernacular terminology of the avifauna of different regions of Persia will help to exclude many such arbitrary names. For instance, though further verification is required, the Gīlakī names for ducks observed in Gīlān and recorded by Aḥmad Marʿašī (s.vv.) and Maḥmūd Pāyanda Langarūdī (pp. 188-89) may be adopted; they include *sīā-ḵūt/d* for *Aythya fuligula*, *jaq(q)ə-dār* for *Clangula hyemalis*, *kallə-sorḵū* for *Netta rufina*, *set-k/gar* and *rūḵənə-mūrḡay* for *Mergus albellus*, *čū/obrāk* for *Anas clypeata*, and *sīā-kar* for *Bucephala clangula*. Similarly, the vaguely defined Kurdish names for ducks (*mrāwī* or *māmərāwī*, lit., "aquatic fowl," *sōnə*, *wordek/wardak*) recorded by Moḥammad Mokrī and ʿAbd-al-Raḥmān Šarafkandī Hažār (s.vv.), if identified more precisely, may prove helpful, as in these examples (pronunciation varies in different Kurdish dialects): *bōrčīn*, female *sər-səwz* (mallard, lit., "green-headed"); *merīšk(-ī/-ē) āwī* (a kind of large duck, lit., "aquatic hen"); *pēbəqangə* (a kind of small duck); *sūr-ə qāng* (a kind of duck the size of a mallard); *sūr-əwīk* (a kind of red duck); and *ḡūtkə-ḵorə* (a kind of small, diving duck (lit., "diver").

Although the Šūrā-ye ʿālī-e ḥefāẓat-e moḥīṭ-e zīst (High council for the protection of the environment) has prohibited the hunting of some rare species of ducks (especially the ruddy shelduck, the white-headed duck, and the marbled duck) and has fixed heavy fines for violations (decree dated 10 Šahrīvar 1366 Š./1 September 1987), illegal duck hunting goes on in Persia wherever wild ducks and other waterfowl flock together. Various methods and devices are used. The following are brief descriptions of those used in Māzandarān (Badīʿ-Allāh Īmānī, personal communication). The *čelā-sū* (< *čelā* "duck hunting by night" + *sū* "(lamp/torch)light") method is used on large ponds, *ābendūn*s/*ūndūn*s/*ennūn*s, serving as open-air reservoirs. A group of three persons in a *nū* (a canoe carved from a tree trunk; cf. Pers. *nāv*) is arranged so that one person wields a long-handled fork behind a torch or *čerāḡ-tūrī* (an oil lamp with an incandescent mantle and a piston to atomize the oil) fixed on the bow; behind him the second man (*tašt-ko/eten*) strikes monotonous muted notes on a *tašt*, a special plate made from an alloy of seven metals (Pers. *haft-jūš*), while the third person rows. At an appointed moment the lamps in a group of *nū*s are lighted, and the canoes begin to move, silently converging on the place where ducks are resting; after a while the *tašt* beaters begin "playing" in unison. As if hypnotized by the dazzling light and the soporific sound, the sleepy ducks allow themselves to be caught by the fork handlers, who twist the wings of each duck and place it in a sack. This kind of hunt may be repeated several times in winter. A second kind of hunting, involving live decoys, takes place at dawn or dusk. From a *kīmé* (an improvised small hut; Pers. *kūma*) of reeds screened by a blind of reeds on the edge of an *ābendūn* the hunter launches a few decoys among the wild ducks flying about or resting on the pond. When the ducks have been lured to the blind, the hunter drops a large net over them. The decoys are trained to escape through a hole in the net. In the *dūm* (Pers. *dām* "trap") method the hunter stretches a large net (ca. 15-20 x 5 m) vertically between two poles at the edge of a paddy or shallow *ābendūn*. His companions rush toward the ducks, driving them away toward the net; the bewildered flock, flying low before soaring, hits the net, which the hunter, hidden in a *kīmé*, lets drop at the right moment, enveloping the whole lot. This method has been specifically forbidden by the Sāzmān-e moḥīṭ-e zīst (p. 32; for variants of these methods in Gīlān, see Pāyanda Langarūdī, pp. 475-78).

In rural parts of Gīlān, Māzandarān, and other provinces, wherever there is a nearby pond or watercourse, flightless domestic ducks are kept for eggs and meat. As duck meat has a strong taste, it is usually cooked in highly seasoned dishes, especially *fesenjān* (q.v.; for a recipe, see Ramazani, p. 155). *Ḵūtkā-kabāb* (broiled teals) is a gourmet dish in Gīlān.

Bibliography: F. Hüe and R. D. Etchécopar, *Les oiseaux du Proche et du Moyen Orient . . .*, Paris, 1970. A. Marʿašī, *Vāža-nāma-ye gūyeš-e gīlakī . . .*, Rašt, 1363 Š./1984. M. Mokrī, *Farhang-e nāmhā-ye parandagān dar lahjahā-ye ğarb-e Īrān (lahjahā-ye kordī) . . .*, 3rd ed., Tehran, 1361 Š./1982. M. Pāyanda Langarūdī, *Farhang-e Gīl o Deylam (fārsī be gīlakī)*, Tehran, 1366 Š./1987. N. Ramazani, *Persian Cooking. A Table of Exotic Delights*, New York, 1974. S. H. J. Read, *A Provisional Check-List of the Birds of Iran*, Tehran, 1337 Š./1958. ʿA. Šarafkandī Hažār, *Farhang-e kordī-fārsī*, 2 vols., Tehran, 1368-69 Š./1989-90. Sāzmān-e ḥefāẓat-e moḥīṭ-e zīst, *Kolāṣa-ī az moqarrarāt-e šekār o ṣayd*, Tehran, 1354 Š./1975. D. A. Scott, Ḥ. Morawwej Hamadānī, and ʿA.-A. Mīr-Ḥosaynī, *Birds of Iran/Parandagān-e Īrān*, Tehran, 1354 Š./1975.

(HŪŠANG AʿLAM)

DŪĞ, beverage made of yogurt and plain or carbonated water and often served chilled as a refreshing summer drink or with meals, especially with kebabs or *čelow-kabāb* (q.v.). The term occurred in Persian as early as the 11th century, when it apparently meant skim milk to which yogurt was sometimes added (Dehḵodā, s.v.). Traditionally *dūğ* was made by shaking a sheepskin (see CHURNS AND CHURNING) filled with milk and yogurt until the fat separated and could be removed. Today it is more often made simply by beating the yogurt with a spoon or in a blender, then adding still or carbonated water, salt, and dried mint, celery leaves, or other herbs. Carbonated *dūğ* is also made commercially and sold in bottles.

Sometimes grated or chopped cucumbers, onions, and bread or dried flat bread are added to *dūğ* and served as a light dish known as *ābdūğ-ḵīār*.

According to the Safavid cook Moḥammad-ʿAlī Bāvarčī (p. 77), *dūğ* was used as a substitute for yogurt in yogurt soup (*māstbā*), prepared with lamb, rice, and green herbs. The Qajar chef Mīrzā ʿAlī-Akbar Āšpaz-bāšī recommended using it to bleach cooked rice (p. 8) and also as an ingredient in various kinds of *āš* (q.v.; pp. 33, 50, 68, 75, 80).

See also CHEESE.

Bibliography: (For cited works not found in this bibliography, see "Short References.") Mīrzā ʿAlī-Akbar Khan Āšpaz-bāšī, *Sofra-ye aṭʿema*, Tehran, 1353 Š./1974. N. Batmanglij, *Food of Life*, Washington, D.C., 1984, p. 230. Ḥājī Moḥammad-ʿAlī Bāvarčī Bağdādī, *Kār-nāma dar bāb-e ṭabbāḵī wa ṣanʿat-e ān*, in Ī. Afšār, ed., *Āšpazī-e dawra-ye ṣafawī. Matn-e do resāla az ān dawra*, Tehran, 1360 Š./1981. M. R. Ghanoonparvar, *Persian Cuisine* I. *Traditional Foods*, Lexington, Ky., 1982, p. 210. N. Ramazani, *Persian Cooking. A Table of Exotic Delights*, Charlottesville, Va., 1982, p. 78.

(M. R. GHANOONPARVAR)

DŪĞ-E WAḤDAT "beverage of unity," concoction made from adding hashish extract (*jowhar-e ḥašīš*) to diluted yogurt (Šahrī, VI, pp. 412, 423). The resulting tonic is drunk by certain mystics as a hallucinogen during their rites. ʿAlī-Akbar Dehḵodā, in his compendium of Persian proverbs and dicta (1339 Š./1960, I, p. 255), quoted a verse from Kamāl-al-Dīn Ḵojandī (d. 803/1399) in which the use of the narcotic by a Sufi sheikh is mentioned. Apparently some less scrupulous Sufis used the drink to attract followers (Šahrī, VI, p. 419).

A similar draft called *bangāb* was made from boiling cannabis leaves in water or milk or simply by adding powdered *bang* (q.v.) to water, which was sweetened with sugar. Those who sold this tonic were called *bangābī* or *bangābsāz* (Dehḵodā, s.v.). Whether or not it contained *dūğ* it was known by the generic name *dūğ-e waḥdat* and also as "cannabis tea." In early 20th-century Isfahan *dūğ-e waḥdat* was reportedly called by the generic name *bang*. It had a noxious smell, and drinking it sometimes caused death (Mahdawī, p. 102). According to Jaʿfar Šahrī, a drink containing more than two grains would be fatal to the nonaddict (III, p. 748). The medieval pharmacologist ʿAlī Heravī (ca. 447/1055) also mentioned the danger of overdosing on *bang* drinks, though he set the acceptable amount of the drug as no more than half a grain in a single draft. Those who overdose first lose sensation in their limbs, then foam at the mouth and develop redness in the eyes. As countermeasures Heravī suggested forcing down milk to induce vomiting (p. 88).

The wide distribution and long history of use of cannabis led Weston La Barre to suggest that it has been part of a "religio-shamanic complex of at least Mesolithic age," paralleling that of the more famous *soma* (pp. 93, 95-96). Drinking *bang* is well attested in classical Persian poetry (e.g., Farroḵī, p. 212 l. 4245; cf. Faqīhī, p. 729; Qazvīnī, IV, pp. 56-57; Browne, pp. 521, 569 n. 1, quoting Ḥāfeẓ and Jalāl-al-Dīn Rūmī).

The active ingredient of *dūğ-e waḥdat* is *bang*, extracted from the leaves of the cannabis plant; the chemical agent is tetrahydrocannabinol (THC). Among the best-known effects of the drug are anxiety followed by euphoria, a sense of excited well-being, rapid emotional change, heightened sensory awareness, feelings of enhanced insight, fragmented thought, impaired short-term memory, altered perceptions of time and space, a shifting sense of identity, hunger, and restlessness and hyperactivity followed by drowsiness and sleep (La Barre, p. 104). Most such feelings lend themselves well to what is known of mystical experience.

The chemistry of cannabis is nevertheless not well known, though it is certain that the mode of preparation influences its interaction with the human body. The part of the plant that is used may also influence the nature of the "high" (Segelman et al., p. 273). Tetrahydrocannabinol is a chief chemical component of cannabis, but it is by no means certain that it is the chief pharmacodynamic element. La Barre mentioned, for example, that "the whole marihuana fluid extract is approximately three times as potent as equivalent amounts of tetrahydrocannabinol." Furthermore, the absorption of THC when smoked is three times as effective as when it is ingested. Because THC is soluble in body fats, its effects are cumulative, which may account for the widely varying experiences described by those who have taken it (La Barre, pp. 103-04; cf. Williams-Garcia, p. 142).

Bibliography: (For cited works not found in this bibliography and abbreviations found here, see "Short References.") E. G. Browne, *A Year amongst the Persians*, Cambridge, 1926. ʿA.-A. Dehkhodā, *Amṯāl o ḥekam*, Tehran, 1339 Š./1960. ʿAlī-Aṣḡar Faqīhī, *Āl-e Būya wa awżāʿ-e zamān-e īšān*, Tehran, 1365 Š./1986. Abu'l-Ḥasan ʿAlī Farroḵī, *Dīvān-e Ḥakīm Farroḵī Sīstānī*, ed. M. Dabīrsīāqī, Tehran, 1363 Š./1984. ʿAlī Heravī, *al-Abnīa ʿan ḥaqāʾeq al-adwīa*, Tehran, 1344 Š./1965. W. La Barre, "History and Ethnography of Cannabis," in W. La Barre, ed., *Culture in Context. Selected Essays of Weston La Barre*, Durham, N.C., 1980, pp. 93-108. M. Levey, "Ḥas͟hīs͟h," *EI*[2] III, pp. 266-67. M. Mahdawī, *Dāstānhāʾī az panjāh sāl*, Tehran, 1348 Š./1969. M. Qazvīnī, *Yāddāšthā-ye Qazvīnī*, ed. Ī. Afšār, 10 vols., Tehran, 1363 Š./1984. V. Rubin, ed., *Cannabis and Culture*, the Hague, 1975. J. Šahrī, *Tārīḵ-e ejtemāʿī-e Tehrān dar qarn-e sīzdahom*, 6 vols., Tehran, 1368 Š./1989. A. B. Segelman, R. D. Sofia, and F. H. Segelman, "*Cannabis Sativa* L. (Marihuana) VI. Variations in Marihuana Preparations and Usage—Chemical and Pharmacological Consequences," in V. Rubin, ed., *Cannabis and Culture*, the Hague, 1975, pp. 269-93. R. Williams-Garcia, "The Ritual Use of Cannabis in Mexico," in V. Rubin, ed., *Cannabis and Culture*, the Hague, 1975, pp. 133-47.

(MAHMOUD OMIDSALAR)

DUGDŌW, the name of Zoroaster's mother, which appears in several different spellings in the Pahlavi texts, mostly more or less corrupted from an original attempt at representing the Avestan form. The *Dēnkard* has consistently the best spelling, *dwktʾwbʾ*, to be pronounced Dugdōw or Duγdōw. In different manuscripts of selections from *Zādspram* (5.1) it appears corrupted to *dwktkʾ* (possibly for **dwktwk*) and *dwtkwb* (probably from **dwktwb*). In the manuscripts of the Greater *Bundahišn* it is always written *dwγtʾby* (TD_1 203.10-11; TD_2 236.10-11; DH 107.1), which appears transliterated into Pāzand letters as *duγdā* in the Indian version (ms. K20, fol. 128v, l. 14). Lastly, in *Šāyest nē šāyest* there occur (10.4) *dwkdʾwʾ* and the variants *dwktkʾwʾ* and *dwtkʾw* (12.11) for earlier **dwktʾw*. The Avestan form is preserved only in a single fragment (FrD 4), corrupted in both manuscripts. It can, however, be reliably reconstructed as Duγdōwā-, interpreted as "with milked cows." Whether as cause or effect, this name presumably refers to the tradition, preserved in its fullest form in the *Dēnkard* (VII, chap. 2), according to which some virgin heifers belonging to Dugdōw's husband, Pōrušasp, began to give milk (*awēšān gāwān 2 azādagān pēm be mad*), in which the vegetable essence (*gōhr*) of Zoroaster was mixed. Pōrušasp instructed his wife to milk those heifers. He had already acquired, through divine intervention, some *haoma* twigs containing the *frawahr*, the guardian spirit, of Zoroaster. When this *haoma* was pressed and the juice mixed with the milk both parents drank of it, thus imbibing both the *frawahr* and the *gōhr* of the future prophet. As Dugdōw had carried the *xwarrah* of Zoroaster within her since her birth, causing her to radiate light about her, the three elements, *xwarrah*, *frawahr*, and *tan-gōhr* "physical essence" were united in the embryo of Zoroaster.

Bibliography: (For cited works not found in this bibliography and for abbreviations found here, see "Short References.") Boyce, *Zoroastrianism* I, pp. 277 ff. *Iranisches Personennamenbuch* I/1, Vienna, 1977, pp. 36-37. R. Zwanziger, "Zum Namen der Mutter Zarathustras," *Anz. der phil.-hist. Klasse der Österreichischen Akademie der Wissenschaften* 114, 1977, pp. 251 ff. (with complete text references).

(D. N. MACKENZIE)

DULAFIDS. See DOLAFIDS.

DUMAQU (or Domoko), administrative center of the eastern region of the Khotan oasis in Chinese Turkestan (q.v.). About 20 km to the north are the ruins of Old Domoko, a settlement abandoned in 1840. Manuscript fragments to which the name Dumaqu or Domoko has become attached were actually excavated by native treasure hunters in the numerous ruined towns of the region dating from the 6th-8th centuries; they were purchased by traveling scholars from dealers on the spot or in Kašgar and Khotan (Gropp, pp. 23-25, 364, 368, fig. 2/65, with references to earlier excavation reports). Sir Mark Aurel Stein labeled a few manuscript fragments in Khotanese, Old Indian, and Chinese in the British Library, London, with the letters DK (for Domoko), though they actually came from the ruins of Uzun Tati and Balawaste. Many of the texts bought in 1914 by A. H. Francke for the Museum für Völkerkunde, Munich, and in 1928 by Ernst Trinkler for the Preussische Akademie in Berlin were labeled with the same letters. The beautiful manuscripts of the *Suvarṇabhāsa Sutra* in Khotanese and the *Saddharmapuṇḍarīka Sutra* in Sanskrit, which are divided among many collections, also belong to this group (Bechert, p. 21; Yuyama, pp. 29, 49).

Bibliography: H. W. Bailey, *Indo-Scythian Studies* V. *Khotanese Texts*, Cambridge, 1963, p. 106.

H. Bechert, *Über die "Marburger Fragmente" des Saddharmapuṇḍarīka*, Nachrichten der Akademie der Wissenschaften zu Göttingen, Phil.-hist. Kl., 1, 1972. G. Gropp, *Archäologische Funde aus Khotan, Chinesisch-Ostturkestan. Die Trinklersammlung im Überseemuseum, Bremen*, Monographien der Wittheit zu Bremen 11, Bremen, 1974. S. Konow, *Zwölf Blätter einer Handschrift des Suvarṇabhāsasutra in Khotan-Sakisch*, SPAW, Phil.-hist. Kl., 18, Berlin, 1935. A. Yuyama, *A Bibliography of the Sanskrit Texts of the Saddharmapuṇḍarīkasūtra*, Oriental Monograph Series 5, Canberra, 1970.

(GERD GROPP)

DUNG, human and animal excrement (*pehen, pehīn* "cow, horse dung," *sargīn* "cow dung" [for etymology, see Emmerick], *peškel* "sheep, goat dung," *čalḡūz* "bird dung," *madfūʿ, borāz* "human dung," *kūd* "natural fertilizer"), widely used in Persia and Afghanistan for fuel and fertilizer.

Fuel. In most parts of Persia wood is scarce (see CHARCOAL), and it is probable that throughout history the principal fuel has been dried dung (Adams, p. 135). In the Safavid period there was a dung market in Isfahan, where prices were competitive with those for wood and charcoal. In Tabrīz, too, dung from the stables, rather than expensive firewood, was used as fuel (Membrè, 1969, p. 59; idem, 1993, p. 52). According to the Dutch painter Cornelis de Bruin (q.v.), who visited Isfahan in 1113/1701, dung was used for cooking; its market price was the equivalent of 30 pence for a load of 220-30 pounds (tr., I, p. 228). A year later Fransz Casper Schilliger (p. 238) reported that the rich in Tabrīz used wood as fuel but the poor dung cakes sold by villagers and brought to the city on camelback. In the 19th century in both town and village whatever animal droppings were not consumed by dung beetles (*sūsk-e sargīnḵor*) or collected by *kannās*es (lit., "sweepers") for fertilizer (*kūd*) were used for fuel. They were first mixed with water and straw, camel thorn (q.v.; Wilson, p. 273), or ashes, then kneaded with the hands or feet, formed into round cakes, pressed flat against a wall to dry in the sun, and stored or sold (Wilson, pp. 268-69; Höltzer, p. 77). In the cities the *kannās*es themselves may have done this work; in Isfahan, for example, a group of men made and sold dung cakes in a caravansary (q.v.) in the Jewish quarter (Höltzer, p. 77). In the villages the work was done by women, who molded the dung into cakes and into bowls and covers for ovens and skylights, in the latter instance perhaps to keep out the snow (Wilson, pp. 268-69). There was a pile of dung cakes on the outskirts of every Persian village (for a photograph, see Powell, opposite p. 225). They were used for baking bread, burning limestone or brick, and heating baths (Wilson, p. 273). As recently as 1301 Š./1922 M. A. Hall (p. 191) reported a manure pile just outside the hotel room in which he was staying. Fuel for public baths could also be purchased from caravansaries (q.v.) or, if there was none in the neighborhood, in dried form, in sacks weighing 15 *mans* (ca. 80 kg) for 10 *šāhīs* each, from the stables of wealthy people in the cities (Mostawfī, *Šarḥ-e zendagānī* I, p. 169; Bird, p. 383). There were thus both commercial and domestic markets for dung fuel, which persisted into the 1960s and probably still function, at least in villages.

Fertilizer. Until the development of the petrochemical industry in Persia in the early 1960s animal manure was the most common and in many areas the only fertilizer used in Persia. According to a popular belief, animal manure fertilizes the soil for seven years, but it has always been in short supply, owing to the great demand for dung fuel. After the harvest fields are either thoroughly cleared of stubble, which is used for feed or fuel, or left to sheep and goats to graze, in which instance the land is fertilized by their droppings. Almost no other measures have been taken to increase soil productivity. "The growing of crops as green manure specifically for soil improvement is uncommon" (Overseas Consultants, III, p. 29). Furthermore, some parts of the country are too arid to permit natural decomposition of manure (Lambton, *Landlord and Peasant*, p. 362 and n. 1). In Semnān, for example, manure was still the fertilizer most commonly used in 1349 Š./1970, but its rapid oxidation in the hot climate limited its effectiveness (Connell, pp. 97-98; Overseas Consultants, III, p. 29).

Available historical data suggest that Persian farmers and landowners have long been aware of the value of dung as fertilizer. For example, in *Ketāb al-aḥyāʾ wa'l-āṯār* (Book of living creatures and monuments), a lost treatise on practical matters by the Il-khanid vizier Rašīd-al-Dīn (ca. 645-718/1247-1318), chapter 10 was entitled "On the use of dung, its different kinds, its usefulness, and its various properties" (Rašīd-al-Dīn, p. cxiii). The many pigeon towers around Isfahan, most between 9 and 13 m tall, have supplied bird dung for cultivation of melons and pear trees (Lambton, *Landlord and Peasant*, p. 362; Polak, p. 135; Wills, p. 130) since at least as early as the 17th century (see BORJ i); the use of pigeon towers in Persian agriculture seems to date from much earlier times, however (see, e.g., Naršaḵī, p. 41; tr. Frye, pp. 29, 125 n. 134). Traditionally the dung is removed once a year from the central well in each tower (Landor, I, p. 352; cf. de Bruin, tr., I, p. 228). In the 17th century a special dung tax was levied on the more than 3,000 pigeon towers in Isfahan (Chardin, III, p. 386; for various kinds of dung, its preparation, and use for agricultural purposes, see IV, pp. 103-04).

In the 19th century, whenever it was economically feasible, agricultural lands were fertilized with dirt collected from old buildings, manure, ashes, and human refuse (Wilson, p. 274: Fraser, II, p. 65; Forbes, p. 171). In particular ashes from dung that had been burned as fuel were used as fertilizer (Adams, p. 135). On the outskirts of towns higher-quality manure was available from night soil and other sewage. In towns the *kannās*es cleaned the cesspools of private houses, as well as of public bathhouses (q.v.) and mosques. The contents were mixed with ashes and stored in fields until they decomposed into an odorless manure that could be sold as fertilizer (see, e.g., Taḥwīldār, p. 121; Wills, p. 365). Around 1276/1859-60 there were 150 *kannās*es in Isfahan (Höltzer, p. 23). Some mosques had very large public toilet facilities. For example, in the late Qajar period the Masjed-e Šāh in Tehran had forty toilets in a space covering more than 1,000 m^2. The "key money" (*sar-qoflī*) to operate these toilets was 30,000-40,000 tomans, and the revenues were 10-12 tomans a day. The twelve public toilets at the congregational mosque in the same city earned 4 tomans a day in rent (*ejāra*), and those in other mosques earned from 5 *qerān*s to 3 tomans (Šahrī, p. 29). The dung beetle was also an important sanitary "worker": "Through the activity of these insects very little horse-dung, save that which is trodden, is seen on the roads" (Wills, p. 216). With the development of modern views on sanitation, the *kannās* has largely disappeared, though advanced sewage systems and sanitary public latrines are still lacking. On the Persian plateau deep latrines seem to meet sanitary standards (Overseas Consultants, II, p. 56).

In Kermān manure and other fertilizers are still widely used on summer cash crops but, because of the need for fuel during the cold months, much less often on winter cereals. In winter "only sheep and goat manure and night soil are available for the fields. Mountain villagers sell manure to agriculturalists on the plains in the spring, after the underground shelters in which the goats and sheep are housed during the winter have been cleaned. Privy cleaners sell night soil the year round. Chemical fertilizers are used mainly on the estates of landed proprietors" (English, pp. 122-23).

Afghanistan. The situation in Afghanistan is not much different from that in Persia. As recently as the 1970s dung cakes and brush were the most common fuels (U.S. Government, p. 112). Dung is used as a fertilizer in areas like eastern Afghanistan, where sufficient wood for fuel is still available in the mountains. Even there, however, dung is used for fuel in the lower valleys. Higher in the mountains, where there are also more animals, dung is kept in compost heaps (also including plant residues and soil) near the farms and in the fields (Wald, p. 39).

Central Asia. Dung cakes have also been widely used in Central Asia, beginning in early times and continuing to the present (Naršaḵī, p. 41; tr. Frye, pp. 29, 125). For example, in Kirghizia 88 percent of rural households used dung cakes as their main cooking and heating fuel in 1994 (World Bank).

Bibliography: (For cited works not found in this bibliography, see "Short References.") I. Adams, *Persia by a Persian*, Washington, D.C., 1900. F. L. Bird, "Modern Persia and Its Capital," *The National Geographic Magazine* 39, April 1921, pp. 353-416. C. de Bruin (Le Brun), *Voyage de Corneille Le Brun par la Moscovie, en Persia, et aux Indes Orientales*, 6 pts. in 2 vols., Amsterdam, 1718; tr. as *Travels into Muscovy, Persia . . .*, 2 vols., London, 1737. J. Connell, ed., *Semnan. Persian City and Region*, London, 1970. R. E. Emmerick, "r-/n- Stems in Khotanese," in M. Meyrhofer at al., eds., *Lautgeschichte und Etymologie. Akten der VI. Fachtagung der Indogermanischen Gesellschaft, Wien, 24.-29. September 1978*, Wiesbaden, 1980, pp. 166-72, esp. p. 172. P. W. English, *City and Village in Iran*, Madison, Wisc., 1966. F. Forbes, "Route from Turbat Haideri, in Khorasan, to the River Heri Rud, on the Borders of Sistan," *JRGS* 14, 1844, pp. 145-92. J. B. Fraser, *A Winter's Journey from Constantinople to Tehran*, 2 vols., London, 1838. M. A. Hall, *Journey to the End of an Era*, New York, 1947. E. Höltzer, *Persien vor hundert und dreizehn Jahren. Text und Bilder* I. *Isfahan*, ed. and tr. M. Āsemī, Tehran, 2535=1355 Š./1976. A. H. S. Landor, *Across Coveted Lands; or, a Journey from Flushing (Holland) to Calcutta, Overland*, 2 vols., New York, 1903. M. de Membrè, *Relazione di Persia*, ed. G. R. Cardona, Naples, 1969; tr. A. H. Morton as *Mission to the Lord Sophy of Persia (1539-1542)*, London, 1993. Overseas Consultants Inc., *Report on [the] Seven Year Development Plan for the Plan Organization*, 5 vols., New York, 1949. J. E. Polak, "Beitrag zu den agrarischen Verhältnissen in Persien," *Mittheilungen der kaiserlich-königlichen geographischen Gesellschaft* 6, 1862, pp. 107-43. E. A. Powell, *By Camel and Car to the Peacock Throne*, New York, 1923. Rašīd-al-Dīn Fażl-Allāh, *Jāmeʿ al-tawārīḵ*, partially ed. and tr. É. Quatremère as *Histoire des Mongols de la Perse*, Paris, 1836; repr. Amsterdam, 1968. J. Šahrī, *Tehrān-e qadīm* I, Tehran, 1357 Š./1978. Fransz Caspar Schilliger, *Persianische und ost/indianische Reis*, Nuremberg, 1707. Mīrzā Ḥosayn Khan Taḥwīldār, *Jog̣rāfīā-ye Eṣfahān*, ed. M. Sotūda, Tehran, 1342 Š./1963. U.S. Government, *Area Handbook for Afghanistan*, 4th ed., Washington, D.C., 1973. H.-J. Wald, *Landnutzung und Siedlung der Pashtunen im Becken von Khost*, Opladen, Germany, 1969. C. J. Wills, *In the Land of the Lion and the Sun*, London, 1883. S. G. Wilson, *Persian Life and Customs*, New York, 1895. The World Bank, "Household Energy Survey," appendix to *Energy Sector Review—Kyrgyz Republic*, Washington, D.C., 1995.

(WILLEM FLOOR)

DŪNQEŠLĀQ (Dong Qešlaq), group of pre-Islamic and Islamic archeological sites on the Emām Ṣāḥeb plain in the Qondūz province of Afghanistan, about 10 km south of the Oxus, 37° 10′ N, 68° 59′ E. The pre-Islamic sites date mainly from the Hephthalite-Turkish period (5th-9th centuries), and there are also traces of Islamic settlements of the 10th-13th centuries (Ball and Gardin, I, no. 307). Earlier traces include abandoned canal systems providing evidence that artificial irrigation was practiced in this area from prehistory. Mud-brick ruins and pottery finds are classified according to local type sites: Watagan Tepe, Emām Sayyed, Majar, Tepe Dūnqešlāq, Tepe Afḡānī, and Tūrānī. Field research was interrupted by political and military events in 1358 Š./1979.

Bibliography: W. Ball and J.-C. Gardin, *Archaeological Gazetteer of Afghanistan*, 2 vols., Paris, 1982. K. Fischer, "Preliminary Remarks of Archaeological Survey in Afghanistan," *Zentralasiatische Studien des Seminars für Sprach-und Kulturwissenschaft Zentralasiens der Universität Bonn* 3, 1969, p. 351. J.-C. Gardin and B. Lyonnet, "La prospection archéologique de la Bactriane orientale (1974-1978). Premiers résultats," *Mesopotamia* 13-14, 1978-79, pl. V.

(KLAUS FISCHER)

DUPREE, LOUIS (b. Greenville, N.C., 23 August 1925, d. Durham, N.C., 21 March 1989), American anthropologist who specialized in Afghan studies (Plate XLIV). During World War II Dupree, as a teenager, joined the U.S. Merchant Marine, but toward the end of the war he transferred to the 11th Airborne Division of the U.S. Army. He was stationed in the Philippines, where he fought with native guerrilla units behind Japanese lines, an experience that he later credited with having inspired his interest in ethnology. After the war Dupree studied Asian archeology and ethnology at Harvard University, receiving his B.A., M.A., and Ph.D. degrees in 1949, 1953, and 1955 respectively. Although he had intended to return to the Philippines, the rejection of his research application by the Philippine government and a fortuitous invitation to join an archeological survey in Afghanistan in the summer of 1949 led to his lifelong interest in southwestern Asia.

Following the completion of his Ph.D. degree Dupree taught at the Air University at Maxwell Air Force Base and Pennsylvania State University. Between 1959 and 1983 he he was affiliated with the American Universities Field Staff (A.U.F.S.) as its expert on Afghanistan and Pakistan. In this capacity Dupree spent two thirds of the next nineteen years conducting research, principally in Afghanistan; every third year he spent lecturing in turn at the twelve universities that sponsored the A.U.F.S. program. Beginning in 1983 Dupree held visiting appointments at Princeton University, the U.S. Military Academy, and the University of North Carolina at Chapel Hill. In 1985 he also became senior research associate in Islamic and Arabic development studies at Duke University, a position he held at the time of his death. During his career Dupree also served as adviser to several governments, including those of West Germany, France, Denmark, Sweden, and Great Britain, and he consulted with the U.S. State Department and other government agencies, as well as with the United Nations.

PLATE XLIV

Louis Dupree, Kabul, 1976. Photograph courtesy Nancy Hatch Dupree.

Dupree's research interests were diverse, reflecting both his own predilections and the inclusive nature of his mandate as an associate of A.U.F.S. These interests comprised but were not limited to archeology, ethnology, folklore, history, economic development, and contemporary politics. His most original and significant work was probably in archeology related to early human habitation in Afghanistan during the Middle and Upper Paleolithic. Among his notable achievements in this area was the discovery of more than 20,000 flint tools from the Upper Paleolithic at several sites near the village of Aq Kupruk south of Balḵ. From the same area and period came a small limestone pebble carved with the face of a man and reported to be the oldest piece of portable cave art found in Asia to date (L. Dupree, 1968; idem, 1980, p. 262; N. H. Dupree, p. 128).

After the Marxist coup d'etat in Afghanistan in

April 1978 Dupree was briefly imprisoned before being deported from the country (N. H. Dupree, p. 129). From then on he lived principally in North Carolina but returned frequently to Peshawar, in Pakistan, to monitor the progress of the Afghan war. On several occasions he joined Afghan guerrillas on sorties into Afghanistan. Dupree died only a month after the Soviet withdrawal from Afghanistan.

Among his extensive publications were *Afghanistan*, 3rd ed., Princeton, N.J., 1980; *Afghanistan in the 1970s*, New York, 1974; "The Changing Character of South-Central Afghanistan Villages," *Human Organization 14/4*, 1956, pp. 26-29; "Tribalism, Regionalism, and National Oligarchy. Afghanistan," in K. H. Silvert, ed., *Expectant Peoples. Nationalism and Development*, New York, 1963, pp. 41-76; "Functions of Folklore in Afghan Society," *Asian Affairs*, N.S. 66/1, 1979, pp. 51-61; and "Tribal Warfare in Afghanistan and Pakistan. A Reflection on the Segmentary Lineage System," in A. S. Ahmed and D. M. Hart, eds., *Islam in Tribal Society*, London, 1984, pp. 266-86.

Bibliography: "Louis Dupree," *The New York Times*, 23 March 1989, p. D22. L. Dupree, "The Oldest Sculptured Head?" *Natural History* 77/5, 1968, pp. 26-27. Idem, *Afghanistan*, 3rd ed., Princeton, N.J., 1980. *Curriculum Vitae 1925-1989*, Peshawar, 1992. N. H. Dupree, "Louis Dupree—American Lover of Afghanistan," *Central Asia* (Peshawar), 33, winter 1993, pp. 119-30.

(DAVID B. EDWARDS)

DURA EUROPOS, ruined city on the right bank of the Euphrates between Antioch and Seleucia on the Tigris, founded in 303 B.C.E. by Nicanor, a general of Seleucus I. It flourished under Parthian rule. The site is in modern Syria, on a plateau protected on the east by a citadel built on bluffs overlooking the river, on the north and south by wadis, and on the west by a strong rampart with powerful defensive towers. Its military function of the Greek period was abandoned under the Parthians, but at that time it was the administrative and economic center of the plain extending 100 km between the confluence of the Ḵābūr and Euphrates rivers and the Abū Kamāl gorge to the south.

i. *Archeology and history.*
ii. *The inscriptions.*

i. ARCHEOLOGY AND HISTORY

Initial archeological exploration of the city took place in 1920-22, under the direction of Franz Cumont and the sponsorship of the Académie des Inscriptions et Belles-Lettres in Paris. From 1929 to 1937 Yale University and the Académie sponsored excavations under the initiative of M. I. Rostovtzeff, who published *Dura-Europos and Its Art*, a synthesis of the history of the town and of its civilization, formed from Greek, Semitic, and Iranian components. This work has served as the basis for all subsequent studies of the site. In fact, however, understanding of Dura Europos depended mainly on written materials (parchments, papyri, inscriptions, and grafitti; see ii, below), paintings, tombs, and portable objects (e.g., coins, bronzes, and lamps) from the excavations, and very little attention has been paid to the architectural remains. Although nearly a third of the town has been excavated, a large number of buildings have been published only summarily or not at all. It therefore became necessary to resume the work of publication, and for this reason the Mission Franco-Syrienne de Doura-Europos was formed in 1986 under the joint direction of the author and Assad Al-Mahmoud; the major objectives are to reexamine the archeological data, to make available the entire mass of documentation from previous excavations, as well as to save the monuments from destruction.

Dura Europos was brought into the Iranian cultural sphere after the Parthian conquest in about 113 B.C.E. (Bellinger; Welles). This domination lasted three centuries, interrupted by a Roman occupation in 115-17 C.E., during Trajan's expedition to Ctesiphon (q.v.). In 165 Dura was conquered by Avidius Cassius and became a stronghold in the Roman defensive system along the eastern frontier of the empire. Nevertheless, despite an impressive effort to reinforce its defenses, the town was unable to withstand the great offensive launched by the Sasanian Šāpūr I (240-70) in 256; it was taken after a bitter siege, and the population was deported (see DEPORTATIONS ii), thus putting an end to the town's existence.

The Parthian period. According to recent discoveries, Dura Europos, originally a fortress, was constituted as a city only in the late Hellenistic period and had been only sparsely populated throughout the Greek period. It was under the Parthians, however, that the city assumed its essential aspect, as revealed by the excavations, a configuration only partly modified by the Roman occupation, except for transformation of the northern sector into a Roman camp (see Figure 30). Recent work by the Mission Franco-Syrienne has permitted some refinement of this picture; certain buildings that had formerly been attributed to the Parthians can now be dated to the Hellenistic period. For example, according to Armin von Gerkan, the cut-stone fortifications of Dura Europos had been built by the Parthians, fearful that the Greek wall of unbaked bricks would be insufficient against a Roman attack. Only the northern section of the original western wall survived, which he took as proof that the project had been rendered unnecessary by the peace concluded between the Parthians and Augustus in 20 B.C.E. (pp. 4-51). This conclusion was based more on probabilities extrapolated from the reports of ancient historians than on archeological discoveries and has been contradicted by the results of recent soundings and clearing of earlier

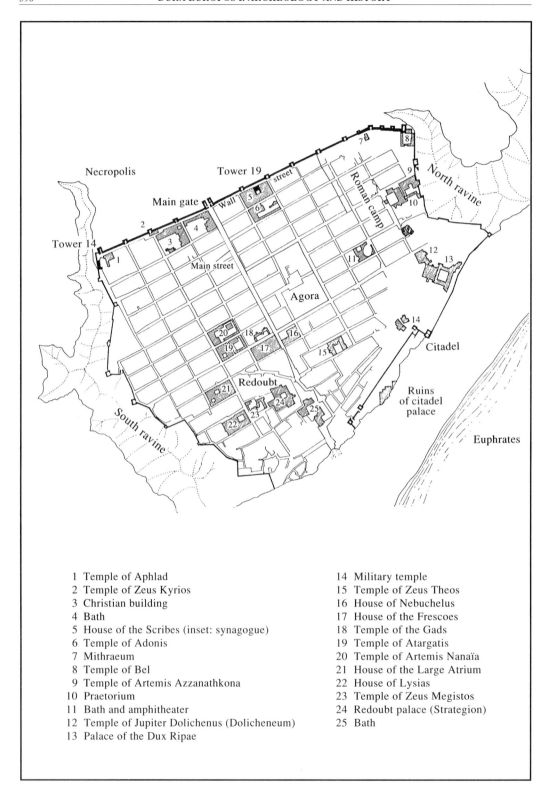

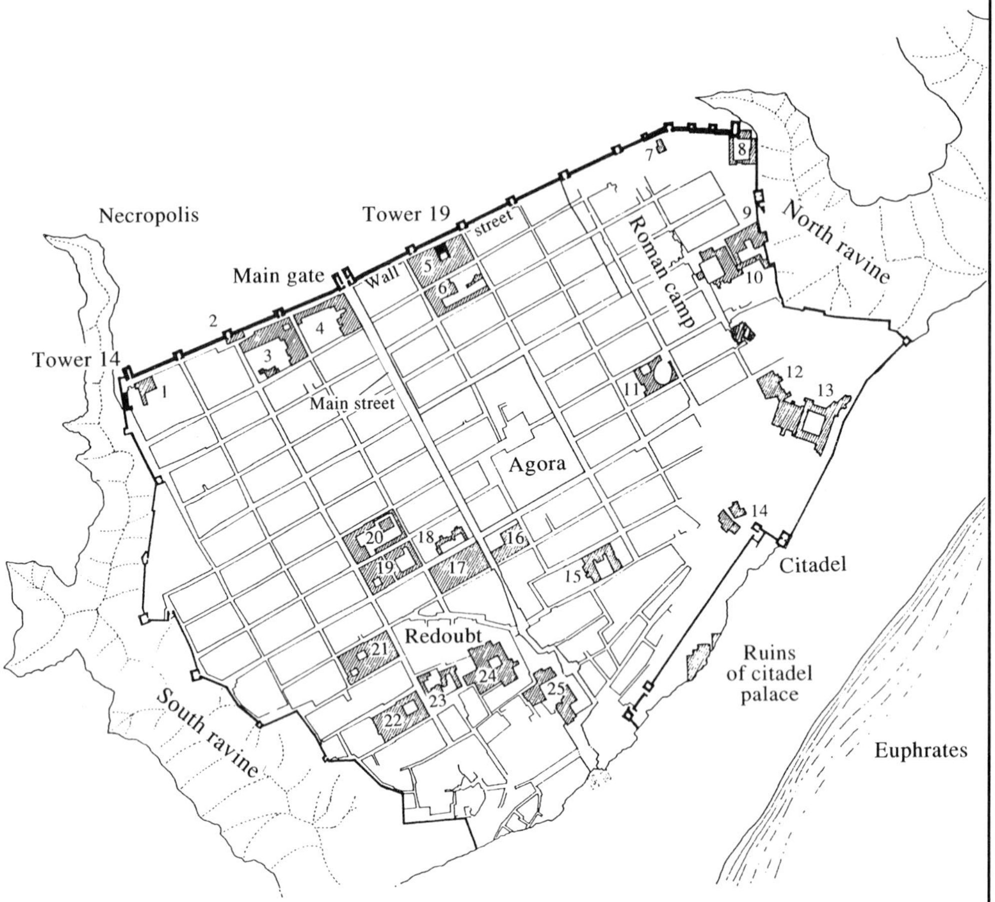

1 Temple of Aphlad
2 Temple of Zeus Kyrios
3 Christian building
4 Bath
5 House of the Scribes (inset: synagogue)
6 Temple of Adonis
7 Mithraeum
8 Temple of Bel
9 Temple of Artemis Azzanathkona
10 Praetorium
11 Bath and amphitheater
12 Temple of Jupiter Dolichenus (Dolicheneum)
13 Palace of the Dux Ripae
14 Military temple
15 Temple of Zeus Theos
16 House of Nebuchelus
17 House of the Frescoes
18 Temple of the Gads
19 Temple of Atargatis
20 Temple of Artemis Nanaïa
21 House of the Large Atrium
22 House of Lysias
23 Temple of Zeus Megistos
24 Redoubt palace (Strategion)
25 Bath

Figure 30. Plan of Dura Europos in the Roman period. After Matheson, p. 18.

trenches. It is now clear that it was the Greeks themselves who built the stone fortifications, in the second half of the 2nd century B.C.E., and that the use of mud bricks resulted from the imminent threat from the Parthians, which forced the builders to finish the wall with more easily obtained material (Leriche and Mahmoud, 1990). Similarly, the reconstruction of the palace of the strategus (the redoubt palace; Figure 30/24) and its extension to the north, as well as construction of the second palace in the citadel, which shows a number of similarities, had been attributed to the Parthian period, but recent excavations in the interior and at the base of the facade of the former building have revealed that it belongs to the 2nd century B.C.E., that is, the Greek period. In a recent study Susan Downey (1988) has also called into question the restoration of one palace with an *ayvān* (q.v.), which was suggested in the Yale publications and would imply a Parthian construction.

The Parthian period thus appears to have been primarily a phase of expansion at Dura Europos, an expansion favored by abandonment of the town's military function. All the space enclosed by the walls gradually became occupied, and the installation of new inhabitants with Semitic and Iranian names alongside descendants of the original Macedonian colonists contributed to an increase in the population (Welles et al.). In his celebrated *Caravan Cities* Rostovtzeff had argued that this prosperity could have resulted from the town's position as a trading center and caravan halt, but this hypothesis has been abandoned, for nothing uncovered by the excavations has confirmed it. Instead, Dura Europos owed its development to its role as a regional capital, amply illustrated by the contents of inscriptions, parchments, and papyri.

In the Parthian period Greek institutions remained in place (Arnaud), and the property-zoning scheme established in the Hellenistic period was respected in new construction; that is, buildings were kept within the limits of pre-existing blocks 35 x 70 m laid out uniformly over the entire surface of the plateau, even to a large extent in the interior wadis. The only exceptions were the quarter of the town southeast of the citadel, which had apparently already been occupied before the division into lots, and a sector of the agora that had been invaded by domestic buildings. The ramparts were neglected: Domestic trash accumulated along the periphery, finally forming a mass so thick that it prevented access to certain towers on the western wall.

The architecture of the Parthian period was characterized by a progressive evolution of Greek concepts toward new formulas in which regional traditions, particularly those derived from Babylonia, played an increasing role. These innovations affected both religious and domestic buildings. No secular public building is known to have been built during the Parthian period, with the possible exception of a bath constructed of cut stone in the northeast sector of the town (Figure 30/25). The evolved Parthian forms generally persisted into the Roman period, except for buildings in the Roman camp in the northern third of the town, for example, the palace of the Dux Ripae and the praetorium (Figure 30/10, 13).

The architecture of private dwellings varied in detail according to the wealth of the owner. The systematic layout of the Greek city, in which each house was supposed to cover one-eighth of a block (ca. 300 m^2), was abandoned or modified through subdivision and consolidation resulting from sales or inheritance (Saliou). The smallest houses covered one quarter or even less of a Greek lot, whereas other, more luxurious examples might cover up to half a block. But the organizing principle of the house remained fundamentally the same: The street door, often situated at a corner of the house, opened onto a corridor leading into a central courtyard, which provided access and light to the various rooms of the house. The principal room, the *andrón*, was usually situated on the south side, opening to the north, and was surrounded on all four walls by a masonry bench; it served as a reception room (Allara). Some houses incorporated columns, but gabled roofs disappeared in favor of terraces, rooms became irregular in shape, and several houses had second stories.

Religious architecture underwent a comparable evolution, traceable through numerous excavated buildings: the temples of Artemis Nanaïa II and Zeus Megistos II (Figure 30/20, 23), the necropolis temple, and the temples of Artemis Azzanathkona, Zeus Kyrios, Atargatis, Bel, Aphlad, Zeus Theos, Gad, and Adonis (Figure 30/9, 2, 21, 8, 1, 15, 18). This architecture diverged more and more from the hypothetical Greek model, if in fact such a model had ever been introduced at Dura Europos (Downey, 1988, p. 176). All the temples of the Parthian period have the same basic plan, with variations in detail. A generally square temenos is enclosed by a blank wall; the naos stands at the back of the interior courtyard facing the entrance. Against the interior face of the enclosure wall are a series of rooms for service or secondary cults, usually built by donors. When the naos is set against the back wall of the temenos, a narrow space is left between them to provide a separation of the cella from the exterior world. The building is small, usually square in plan, and raised on a podium of two or three steps, with one or more altars in front. The interior is divided in two: the pronaos, which occupies the full width of the building and is sometimes furnished with tiers of benches on either side of the entrance, and the cella, usually flanked by two chapels or lateral sacristies. The cult image on the wall opposite the entrance, either mounted on a pedestal or painted directly on the surface. All that remains from the Greek tradition is the occasional presence of a columned facade in front of the temple or porticoes along the sides of the courtyard, as at the temple of Bel (Figure 30/8).

It is thus clear that at Dura Europos entirely original architectural formulas were perfected during the Parthian period, in both religious and domestic constructions; the Babylonian element predominated, though with a certain Greek dressing, but no unequivocal Iranian influence appears. The formula for religious buildings was followed in all temples, whatever the form of worship to which they were consecrated, Greek or Semitic.

The only Iranian cult known at Dura Europos was that of Mithra, which paradoxically had been introduced into the city by Roman troops in 168. The mithraeum, located near the western wall in the Roman camp (Figure 307), belongs to the type dedicated to the cult throughout the Roman world and has no features in common with the other religious buildings at Dura Europos, except that it stands on a podium. It appears to have been a single room of modest dimensions with a bench on each of the longer sides; above the central aisle there was a raised ceiling with a clerestory. At the end of the room was a niche containing two cultic bas-reliefs with an altar before them. The entire surface of the room was covered with painted decoration: scenes from the life of Mithra, representations of magi and the zodiac around the bas-reliefs in the niche, and mounted hunting scenes on the side walls.

Although Iranian influence is difficult to find in the architecture of Dura Europos, in figurative art it is much more pronounced. In fact, owing to landfill that preserved religious buildings along the western wall (see below), Dura has provided the main evidence of a decorative art that seems to have developed in Parthian domains, reflecting a synthesis of the traditions of the ancient Near East (linear drawing, two-dimensional forms, stiff poses) and the Hellenic world (the use of architectural decoration and friezes, types of dress). Furthermore, in religious settings, those most fully represented, the principle of "Parthian frontality" prevailed. This convention, according to which all figures, human or divine, face directly forward, with eyes fixed on the spectator, made its appearance at Dura very early, in the oldest painting, of the sacrifice of Conon, in the temple of Bel (probably 1st century C.E.; Figure 30/8). It persisted until the destruction of the city, as attested in the frescoes of the synagogue, dating from 245 (Figure 30/5). It was equally apparent in sculpture and terra-cottas (except for a statue of Artemis with the tortoise, which comes from a Hellenistic center) and, for example, in two reliefs of the Gads of Dura and Palmyra. On the other hand, in frequent narrative scenes of combat and hunting on horseback, like those in the mithraeum (Figure 30/7), the horses and wild beasts are portrayed in a flying gallop, a characteristic that was to be developed in Sasanian art.

The siege of Dura Europos. The Sasanian siege of Dura Europos in 256 brought an end to the town's existence and immobilized Šāpūr's army for several months. The determined resistance put up by the inhabitants forced the assailants to adopt various siege tactics, which eventually resulted in conquest of the city; the defensive system, the mines, and the assault ramp were left in place after the deportation of the population, which permits modern investigators to gain an exact idea of the military techniques of the Sasanians and the Romans in the mid-3rd century.

It is not known where the Sasanians located their camp, but traces of their operations against the city wall still survive (du Mesnil du Buisson). To guard against the attack, which was clearly expected from the time that the Sasanian empire was established, the Romans had heightened and reinforced the external faces of the western and northern ramparts by masking them with thick layers of fill covered by a mud-brick glacis and thus burying the buildings along the inside of the wall. The Persians undermined towers 19 and 14 (Figure 30) on the western wall in order to bring them down, but, owing to the filling and the glacis, the towers were not really destroyed. At the southeast corner of the town they built an assault ramp 40 m long and 10 m high against the wall to permit troops to enter; it consisted of a mass of fill packed between two walls of brick and paved with baked bricks, which made it possible to move a siege machine close to the wall. Two tunnels, each wide enough to permit several men to advance abreast, were dug near the body of the ramp. There is no surviving textual description of the siege of Dura Europos, but Ammianus Marcellinus' account of the siege of Amida (q.v.) a century later, in which the same techniques were used, permits reconstruction of the operations at Dura; the main siege weapons were catapults, movable towers, and even elephants. Clearly the Sasanian armies had a sophisticated knowledge of siege techniques.

The discovery of the body of a Sasanian soldier in one of the trenches has also yielded precious information. He was equipped with a coat of mail, a sword ornamented with a jade disk of Central Asian type, and an iron helmet made in two halves with an iron crest running vertically down the center of the front, of clearly Mesopotamian and Iranian origin. This type of helmet served as a model for those adopted in the Roman empire in the 3rd century (James).

The chronology of the siege operations has given rise to a debate that is still far from having been resolved. The discovery of Pahlavi inscriptions on the frescoes of the synagogue does not prove that the town had first been occupied by the Sasanians during a campaign in 253, three years before the final siege. It is also improbable that a house near the triumphal arch on the main street, in which there was a fresco of Sasanian type showing a fight between cavalrymen, belongs to this putative first occupation. It seems now that this fresco, several ostraca in Pahlavi found in the palace of the Dux Ripae (Figure 30/13), and the tombs discovered in the town and along the river resulted from temporary installation of a small Persian detachment in the town after the victory of 256 (MacDonald; Leriche and Al Mahmoud, 1994).

Bibliography: The results of the French-Syrian campaigns have been published in P. Leriche, ed., *Doura-Europos. Études* I-III (*DEE*), published in *Syria*, 1986, 1988, 1992. The fourth volume is forthcoming in the series Bibliothèque Archéologique et Historique, Beirut.

A. Allara, "Les maisons de Doura-Europos. Questions de typologie," in *DEE* I, pp. 39-60. P. Arnaud, "Doura-Europos. Microcosme grec ou rouage de l'administration arsacide?" in *DEE* I, pp. 135-55. A. R. Bellinger, "The Evidence of the Coins," *Berytus* 9, 1948, pp. 51-67. A. Bounni, "Un nouveau bas-relief palmyrênien de Doura-Europos," *Comptes Rendus de l'Académie des Inscriptions et Belles-Lettres*, 1994, pp. 11-18. F. Cumont, *Fouilles de Doura-Europos (1922-1926)*, Paris, 1926. S. B. Downey, "The Citadel Palace at Dura-Europos," in *DEE* I, pp. 28-37. Idem, *Mesopotamian Religious Architecture. Alexander through the Parthians*, Princeton, N.J., 1988. A. von Gerkan, "The Fortifications," in M. I. Rostovtzeff, ed., *The Excavations at Dura-Europos. Preliminary Reports* VII-VIII, New Haven, Conn., 1939, pp. 4-61. R. Ghirshman, *Iran. Parthians and Sasanians*, tr. S. Gilbert and J. Emmons, London, 1962 (for illustrations). C. Hopkins, *The Discovery of Dura-Europos*, New Haven, Conn., 1979 (with an almost complete bibliography on the site up to that time). S. James, "Evidence from Dura Europos for the Origins of Late Roman Helmets," in *DEE* I, pp. 107-34. P. Leriche, "Chronologie du rempart de briques crues," in *DEE* I, pp. 61-82. Idem, "Techniques de guerre sassanides et romaines à Doura-Europos," in F. Vallet and M. Kazanski eds., *L'armée romaine et les Barbares du IIIe au VIIIe siècle*, Paris, 1993, pp. 83-100. Idem and A. Al Mahmoud, "Bilan des campagnes de 1986 et 1987 de la mission franco-syrienne à Doura-Europos," in *DEE* II, 1988, pp. 3-24. Idem, "Bilan des campagnes de 1989 et 1990 à Doura-Europos," in *DEE* III, pp. 3-28. Idem, "Doura-Europos. Bilan des recherches récentes," *Comptes-Rendus de l'Académie des Inscriptions et Belles-Lettres*, 1994, pp. 395-420. D. MacDonald, "Dating the Fall of Dura-Europos," *Historia* 35, 1986, pp. 45-68. S. Matheson, *Dura Europos*, New Haven, Conn., 1982. R. du Mesnil du Buisson, "Les ouvrages du siège de Doura-Europos," *Mémoires de la Société nationale des antiquaires de France* 81, 1944, pp. 5-60. A. Perkins, *The Art of Dura-Europos*. Oxford, 1973. M. I. Rostovtzeff, ed., *The Excavations at Dura-Europos. Preliminary Reports*, 9 vols., New Haven, Conn., 1929-52. Idem, *Caravan Cities*, Oxford, 1932. Idem, "Dura and the Problem of Parthian Art," *Yale Classical Studies* 5, 1935, pp. 157-304. Idem, *Dura-Europos and Its Art*, Oxford, 1938. Idem, and A. Perkins, eds., *The Excavations at Dura-Europos. Final Reports*,, 11 vols., New Haven, Conn., 1943-77. C. Saliou, "Les quatre fils de Polémocratès," in *DEE* III, Paris, 1990, pp. 65-100. D. Schlumberger, *L'Orient hellénisé*, Paris, 1970. C. B. Welles, "The Chronology of Dura-Europos," *Eos* 48, 1957, pp. 467-74. Idem, *The Parchments and Papyri*, The Excavations at Dura-Europos. Final Report 5/1. New Haven, Conn., 1959.

(Pierre Leriche)

ii. Inscriptions

Beside the many documents in Greek, Latin, and Aramaic, there are several written traces of an Iranian presence in Dura Europos. On the paintings on the walls of the synagogue (Figure 30/5) three graffiti have been scratched in Parthian script and another twelve written in ink in Middle Persian. One more in Parthian and five in Persian are written in ink on the walls of the House of the Frescoes (Figure 30/17), and a last in Parthian at the entrance to the redoubt. Two further graffiti in Parthian are to be found incised on the walls of the temple of Zeus Megistos (Figure 30/23), one being a precise date: *ŠNT 522 YRḤʾ ʾdʾr sḥt 11 pty hwnn* "year 522, month Adar (i.e., March 211 or 212 C.E.), on the 11th in the morning." Finally, a long graffito in Persian is scratched on the north jamb of the main door of the synagogue. All these graffiti have been published in facsimile, but, because most are partially illegible, no fully satisfactory readings or complete interpretations have been achieved so far. The type of the synagogue graffiti is, however, clear. They mostly begin with a date, the name of the Zoroastrian month, the number of the year (presumably the 14th and 15th regnal years of the unnamed king Šāpūr I, 240-70 C.E.), and the name of the day. Then comes the name of the writer, in almost every instance qualified by the description "scribe" (*dibīr*), and sometimes those of his fellow visitors, followed by the text of his message. A typical and practically certain Persian example (no. 42) is written on the himation of a figure on panel WC 2: /1/ *BYRḤ prwrtyn QDM* /2/ *ŠNT X III II WYWM lšny* /3/ *ʾMT yzdʾntḥ[m]pr[n]b(g)* /4/ *dpywr ZY tḥmy ʿL* /5/ *ZNH BYTʾ* [*YʾTWNt*] *ʾPš ZNH nkʾl* /6/ *ps(nd)yt* "(It was the 1st) month of Frawardīn in the year 15 and the (18th) day Rashn when the scribe Yazdān-tahm-farrbay, the strong, [came] to this house, and he liked this picture."

In addition to the graffiti, more than a dozen inscribed ostraca have been found at half a dozen different sites. Nearly all these inscriptions are written in Parthian. Those that are most legible are clearly lists of deliveries of different quantities measured in *grbn* (i.e. *grīβān* "modii"), and so probably of grain, from persons identified by name and either profession or patronymic. In three of them the same person is mentioned, *ršnw hštrp*, Rašn *šahrab* (satrap), presumably an official organizing the collections of grain, almost certainly under Roman administration. The purpose of the one Middle Persian ostracon is obscure. It contains a list of some twenty-seven professions, in no evident logical sequence. They range from the humble *nʾnpʾk* "baker," *kpškly* "shoemaker," and *kštkly* "plowman" to officeholders like *zyndʾnyk* "jailer," *dpylpty* "chief scribe," and *šʾpstn* "harem keeper."

Finally, three pieces of parchment with Parthian and Middle Persian text have been found at two different sites. Two are parts of letters, one in each language; the other is a tiny fragment apparently of a Persian document. The Parthian letter consists only of the beginning "From Sānēsarakān to Husraw-(?)" and three lines of polite introductory formulas. The Persian letter, written on both sides in a rather imperious tone, contains enough text to suggest that it was sent by "a highly-placed army-general to another of slightly inferior rank," probably "during the brief occupation of Dura by the Persians in A.D. 253" (Henning, 1959).

Bibliography: (For abbreviations found here, see "Short References.") R. N. Frye, ed., *The Parthian and Middle Persian Inscriptions of Dura-Europos*, Corpus Inscr. Iran. III/3, portf. I, London, 1968. B. Geiger, "The Middle Iranian Texts," in C. H. Kraeling, *The Synagogue*, The Excavations at Dura-Europos. Final Report 8/1, New Haven, Conn., 1956, pp. 283-317. P. Gignoux, *Glossaire des inscriptions pehlevies et parthes*, Corpus Inscr. Iran., Suppl. I, London, 1972 (with full secondary bibliography to date, pp. 11, 44). W. B. Henning, "Mitteliranisch," pp. 41-42, 46. Idem in C. B. Welles, *The Parchment and Papyri*, The Excavations at Dura-Europos. Final Report 5/1, New Haven, Conn., 1959, pp. 414-17, pl. 70.

(D. N. MACKENZIE)

DURAND, HENRY MORTIMER (b. Sehore, Bhopal State, India, 14 February 1850, d. Polden, Somerset, England, 8 June 1924), British diplomat and envoy to Tehran at the end of the 19th century. The second son of a British military family, he was educated in England and entered the Indian Civil Service in 1870. During the second Anglo-Afghan War (q.v. ii; 1878-80) he served as political secretary to General Sir Frederick Sleigh Roberts at Kabul. In 1893, as foreign secretary to the government of India, he returned to Kabul to negotiate the northern and eastern boundaries of Afghanistan (see BOUNDARIES iii). Impressed by Durand's distinguished service in India and Afghanistan, the Liberal British prime minister Lord Rosebery, despite Russian protests, appointed him minister to Tehran, where he arrived on 17 November 1894. He spoke Persian fluently, but he nonetheless found his tour in the country trying. Russian influence predominated in Tehran, and at the same time Great Britain was preoccupied with events elsewhere, particularly the Boer war, and unable to counter the Russians.

In private letters, as well as in official analyses dated 27 September 1895 (Foreign Office [F.0.] 60/566) and 12 February 1899 (F.0. 60/608), Durand identified discouraging trends and recommended remedies. Lord Curzon (q.v.), in a famous dispatch of 21 September 1899 (F.0. 60/615), followed his assessments closely. Durand had outlined three alternative British policies for Persia: agreement with Russia for joint development of the country, which ran counter to the established Russian pattern; clear warnings that advances in the north would provoke responses in the south, which seemed too aggressive; and continuation of the traditional policy of upholding the independence and integrity of Persia under increasingly adverse conditions, which Durand and Curzon favored.

Although Durand's conduct of affairs in Persia aroused criticism from the Conservative prime minister Lord Salisbury and Herbert Bowen, the American minister in Tehran, he did enjoy some success. Appreciating the strategic importance of Sīstān, he pushed for its development as one of the pillars of British policy; as a result in 1896 the trade route between Quetta and Nushki (Noškī) was reopened, and by 1902 the British were "appreciably gaining ground" in Sīstān (U.S., XI, Griscom to Hay, 25 November 1902). He also raised the standard of professional training, strengthened the consular service, and persuaded the British government to protect and expand the telegraph network.

Durand sustained his most serious defeat in negotiations to obtain a British loan for the Persian government after the assassination of Nāṣer-al-Dīn Shah (17 Ḏu'l-qaʿda 1313/1 May 1896). His efforts foundered on the opposition of the British treasury and the banks' lack of confidence in Persian credit after cancellation of Persian concessions (q.v.) to Baron Julius de Reuter (1290/1873) and the Tobacco Régie (1309/1892), as well as Malkom Khan's lottery concession. In September 1899 Durand set out on an extended trip through southwest Persia (F.O. Confidential Print 6765), accompanied by his wife and some of the legation staff. The Qajar prince and governor Masʿūd Mīrzā Ẓell-al-Solṭān (Ẓell-e Solṭān) was their host in Isfahan. Then they explored the region around the Kārūn river, inspected the new trade route where H. F. B. Lynch and A. Taylor were working, and met several Baḵtīārī chiefs. They returned to Tehran via Lorestān, in order to study the feasibility of a trade route for which the Imperial Bank had acquired rights. The entire tour of 1,200 miles lasted eighty-eight days and involved crossing and recrossing the Baḵtīārī and Lor ranges. The party arrived in Tehran on 14 December 1899.

Although Durand opposed dividing Persia into spheres of influence, he had sketched a line from Ḵāneqīn, then on the Ottoman-Persian border, through Hamadān, Isfahan, Yazd, and Kermān to Sīstān, defining the northernmost limits of clear British ascendance, in order to bring into focus the region where British energies should be concentrated. In London the Liberals used this so-called "Durand line" to defend the Anglo-Russian Convention of 1907 (q.v.) in Parliament, arguing, over Durand's own denial, that the policies of the previous British government had simply been carried forward.

Durand's departure from Persia in April 1900 coincided with the granting of a Russian loan, accompanied by severe political restrictions, including continuation of a ban on railway building. Although Lord Salisbury did not blame Durand for the failure of the British loan negotiations, he did hold him partly responsible for the rift with the grand vizier, Mīrzā ʿAlī-Aṣḡar Khan (see ATĀBAK-E AʿẒAM). Durand liked Persia and its people, but he left without regret, confessing that in Tehran he had felt "like a jellyfish in a whirlpool" (Lord Newton, p. 232).

After serving as ambassador to Madrid Durand was suddenly transferred to Washington, D.C. Sir Edward Grey recalled him in 1906. After his return to England he devoted much of his time to writing.

Bibliography: Unpublished sources. Private Papers. India Office Library. Durand Collection. Mss. Eur. D. 727. See specifically Letterbooks: (letters from) no. 5, April 1885-95; no. 6, Persia, 1886-99 and 1899-1903; no 18, official papers, 1887-1908. Lord Salisbury: India Office Library and Hatfield House. Lord Curzon and Lord z Hamilton: India Office Library. Lord Kimberley (privately held). Lord Mayo and Sir Charles Hardinge (First Baron Hardinge of Penshurst): University of Cambridge Library. Sir John Ardagh (PRO 30/40/2).

Public Record Office: FO 60/566, 596, 601, 608, 610, 615, 619, 630, 631, 676; 65/1528, 1529, 1547.

American Department of State, Persia, Diplomatic Despatches: VIII, IX, X.

Printed Documents: *British Documents on the Origins of the War, 1898-1914* IV (London, 1929). *Cd. 3882, Persian, no. 1 (1908).* James Rives Childs, *Perso-Russian Treaties and Notes of 1828-1931* (typescript, n.d.), New York Public Library. *Krasnyi Arkhiv*: LIII, LVI. J. C. Hurewitz, *Diplomacy in the Near and Middle East* I, nos. 101, 105 (New York, 1956). *Parliamentary Debates*, Fourth Series, Commons, XXVII, LXXIII, LXXIX, LXXXII; Lords, CLXXXIII.

Published Works: His own and Lady Durand's. Lady E. R. Durand, *An Autumn Tour in Western Persia*, 1902. Sir Mortimer Durand, *The Charm of Persia*, London, 1912. *Nadir Shah. An Historical Novel*, London, 1908. *Life of the Right Hon. Sir Alfred Comyn Lyall . . .*, Edinburgh, 1913. *The Life of Field Marshall Sir George White*, 2 vols., Edinburgh, 1915.

Books and Articles: M. Entner, *Russo-Persian Commercial Relations, 1828-1914*, Gainesville, Fla., 1965. R. L. Greaves, "British Policy in Persia, 1892-1903," *BSOAS* 28 1965, pp. 34-60. S. Gwynn, ed., *The Letters and Friendships of Sir Cecil Spring Rice*, 2 vols., London, 1928. F. Kazemzadeh, *Russia and Britain in Persia 1864-1914*, New Haven, Conn., 1968. H. F. B. Lynch, *The Future of British Relations with Persia*, London, 1908. D. McLean, *Britain and Her Buffer State. The Collapse of the Persian Empire, 1890-1914*, London, 1979. Lord Newton, *Lord Lansdowne*, London, 1929. P. Sykes, *The Right Honourable Sir Mortimer Durand . . .*, London, 1926.

Dictionary of National Biography, 1922-30, pp. 277-79. "Spy" cartoon, *Vanity Fair*, 12 May 1904.

The Times, 19 November 1894, 2 and 7 May 1896, 13 January 1897, 2 August 1898, 31 August 1901.

(ROSE L. GREAVES)

DŪRAOŠA-, Avestan word, attested once in the Older Avesta (*Y.* 32.14), in the Younger Avesta the preferred and exclusive epithet of *haoma*, the ritual liquid. Although the equivalent term in Sanskrit *duróṣa*(*s*)- is attested three times, in only one instance is it connected with the soma. It is therefore not certain that the single Old Avestan usage refers to *haoma*; another possibility is strongly suggested by the fact that it occurs in the form *dūraošəm*, the object of the causative *saočaiia-* "to set alight," whereas in the Rigveda (4.21.6) *duróṣa*(*s*)- is an epithet of Agni (32.14; Kellens and Pirart, p. 92). H. W. Bailey has identified the Khotanese *durauśa* as a survival of this term (1964, p. 4), but doubt has been cast on this identification by Ronald Emmerick (in Flattery and Schwartz, p. 64 n. 28).

Both the etymology and the meaning of the word are uncertain. The great majority of scholars have recognized it as a compound and have agreed that the second term is *aoša-* "death"; this interpretation is, however, not entirely convincing, for the meaning of *aoša-* is more specifically "destruction by fire." Furthermore, interpretation of the first term has caused considerable difficulty. Although the Pahlavi translator rendered *dūra-* as "distant," leading to an interpretation of the compound as "whose death is distant" or "who keeps death at a distance," the parallel with *duróṣa(s)-* seems to exclude that solution. Christian Bartholomae (*AirWb.*, cols. 751-52) was thus led to dissociate the Iranian and Indian words, but more recent scholars, from Jarl Charpentier to D. S. Flattery and Martin Schwartz (p. 130), have attempted to minimize the difference by invoking the individual instance and popular etymology respectively.

Alternative interpretations also present insurmountable difficulties. Bailey (1936, pp. 95-97) reconstructed **dura-*, derived from *dvar* "to run"; the compound would thus be translated "from whom destruction flees," though Bailey himself did not propose a compound (see below). He also suggested a reconstruction from Baluchi *dōr* "sadness." Ilya Gershevitch (p. 49) proposed "painkiller," apparently with the improbable subject *dur-*. One problem with all the interpretations is that gathic *dūraoša-* contains three syllables, whereas the compound (**dūraʾ(a)uša-*) would not be contracted (Kellens and Pirart, p. 260). The initial element might be more satisfactorily explained by the Indo-Iranian prefix **dus*, but that suggestion also raises doubts, for in Iranian there is no sandhi in which *s* becomes *r*; furthermore, the proposed consonant modification to **dužauša-* "charred" (Karl Hoffmann, cited in Humbach, pp. 300-01) has no known Iranian equivalent. It can be asked also whether *dūraoša-/ duraóṣa(s)-* is not simply a fossil word, attesting a root and suffix that had otherwise become extinct. Bailey (1957) followed this line of reasoning, reconstructing a root *dur* "injure" with a derived adjective meaning "pungent in taste," but his arguments are not persuasive.

Bibliography: (For cited works not found in this bibliography and abbreviations found here, see "Short References.") F. C. Andreas and J. Wackernagel, "Die erste, zweite und fünfte Ghāthā des Zuraˣthuštro," *Nachrichten der göttinger Gesellschaft der Wissenschaften*, 1913, pp. 363-85. H. W. Bailey, "Indo-Iranica," *TPS*, 1936, pp. 95-97. Idem, "Dvārā matīnām," *BSOAS* 20, 1957, pp. 53-58. Idem, "Lyrical Poems of the Sakas," in *Dr. J. M. Unvala Memorial Volume*, Bombay, 1964, pp. 1-5. Idem, "Durauzha the Drink Exhilarant," *South Asian Studies* 1, 1985, pp. 157-64. J. Charpentier, "Kleine Mitteilungen," *WZKM* 27, 1913, pp. 236-44. J. Duchesne-Guillemin, *Les composés de l'Avesta*, Liège and Paris, 1936, pp. 168, 272. D. S. Flattery and M. Schwartz, *Haoma and Harmaline. The Botanical Identity of the Indo-Iranian Sacred Hallucinogen "Soma" and Its Legacy in Religion, Language, and Middle Eastern Folklore*, Berkeley and Los Angeles, 1989. B. Geiger, *Die Aməša Spəntas*, Vienna, 1916, pp. 77-78 n. 2. I. Gershevitch, "An Iranianist's View of the Soma Controversy," in P. Gignoux and A. Tafazzoli, eds., *Mémorial Jean de Menasce*, Louvain, 1974, pp. 45-75. H. Humbach, *Deutsche Literaturzeitung* 78, 1957, pp. 300-01. J. Kellens and E. Pirart, *Les textes vieil-avestiques* III, Wiesbaden, 1991.

(JEAN KELLENS)

DŪRĀSRAW, according to the Pahlavi tradition the name of two legendary personages in the history of Zoroastrianism. The Pahlavi spelling *dwlʾ-* or *dwlyd-slwbʹ* is ambiguous (despite Pazand Durāsro) and points to an Avestan original, either *Dūrā- or, more likely, *Dūraēsrauuah-, literally "far-famed" (cf. Av. Dūraēsrūta-).

1. One of the three sons of Mānuščihr (Av. Manuščiθra-), king of Ērān. In the *Bundahišn* (TD_2, pp. 230-37; tr. Anklesaria, chaps. 35.15, 35.37, 35.52, 35A.3-4, pp. 294-303) his brothers are named as *Fraš and Nōdar (Av. *Naotara-). Through his son Rajan and his grandson Ayazim, he was the ancestor of Spitāma and thus in the thirteenth generation of Zoroaster; through his grandson *Frašn of *Frānag (Av. *Frəni-), who married Kay Kawād, he was the begetter of the Kayanian dynasty and of Waxš, ancestor of the family of *mobeds* including Ādurbād ī Māraspandān (see ĀDURBĀD Ī MAHRSPANDĀN). In Ṭabarī (I, p. 533) the name appears as Dwrsrw b. Manūšihr but is also corrupted as Xwrʾsrw (I, p. 681; tr., IV, p. 77), probably via *Jūrāsraw, based on a misreading of the Pahlavi form as **ywl-*. In Bīrūnī (*Āṯār*, p. 104) it is reduced to Dwrsr and in Masʿūdī (*Morūj* II, p. 124) augmented to Dwrwsrwr. In some redactions of the *Šāh-nama* (e.g., ed. Mohl, I, p. 178; ed. Vullers, I, pp. 141, 215) his place as son of Manūčihr is taken by Zarăsp.

2. According to the Zoroaster legend in Book 7 of the *Dēnkard* (ed. Madan, pp. 614-22; ed. Dresden, pp. 345-37; Molé, pp. 26-37), the name of an evil *karb* priest (Av. *karapan-*) famed as a sorcerer and *dēw* worshiper, consulted by Zoroaster's father, Pōrušasp, about the miracles occurring at his son's birth. Dūrāsraw conceived a bitter hatred for the future prophet and persuaded Pōrušasp to kill the baby, first by cremating him, then by having him trampled by oxen and afterward by horses, and finally by having him thrown into the lair of a she-wolf whose cubs had been killed. Each time Zoroaster was miraculously saved. When the boy was seven years old Dūrāsraw came to his home, with another *karb* named Brādrōrēš, intending to damage the mind of the lad but was again foiled. When about to render sacrifice to the *dēws*, Dūrāsraw was three times stupefied by the prophet. He then fled, but, after covering some leagues, died, apparently as a result of his semen's bursting through his skin and his side's breaking open and becoming detached from his thighs. In the late, apocryphal *Wizīrkard ī dēnīg* (31-40; Molé, pp. 124-31) this legend is corrupted.

Bibliography: (For cited works not found in this bibliography and abbreviations found here, see "Short References.") Ferdawsī, *Šāh-nāma*, ed. J. A. Vullers as *Firdusii Liber Regum . . .*, 3 vols., Leiden, 1877-84. Justi, *Namenbuch*, p. 87. M. Molé, *La légende de Zoroastre*, Paris, 1967.

(D. N. MACKENZIE)

DURIS of Samos (Gk. Doûris), Greek historiographer of the early Hellenistic period (b. ca. 340 B.C.E., d. ca. 270 B.C.E. or at least after 281 B.C.E.). Duris attended the lectures of Theophrastus of Eresus and was said to have been tyrant of his native town, perhaps as heir to his father, Scaeus (Athenaeus 4.128a, 8.337d).

Under the influence of the Peripatetics he wrote a variety of books on literature, art, and music; his main contribution, however, was historiographic, and he was noted for introducing the new "tragic" style in the writing of history, a style characterized by emphasis on pathos and emotion and especially a straining after effect. Only fragments of all these writings are known , from casual quotations, mainly by Athenaeus and Plutarch; they have been collected by Felix Jacoby (*Fragmente* IIA, pp. 1136-58 [text], IIC, pp. 115-31 [commentary]). The most important are from the historical work *Makedoniká* (sometimes also *Historíai*), which Duris may have written in his old age. It originally consisted of twenty-six or more books and dealt with the history of Macedonia from 370 B.C.E. to the war between Seleucus and Lysimachus and the latter's death (in 281) or perhaps later (Jacoby, *Fragmente* IIA, frag. 55). In connection with the campaigns of Alexander and others Persia was mentioned explicitly in a quotation from book VII (IIA, frag. 5, apud Athenaeus 10.434ef), in which Duris apparently dealt with Persian customs and a feast in honor of the god Mithra; in another fragment (IIA, frag. 54, apud Strabo 1.3.19, without mention of the title or book) a Greek etymology for the name of the town Rhágai (< OPers. Ragā) is given.

Bibliography: (For cited works not found in this bibliography and abbreviations found here, see "Short References.") [E.] Schwartz, "Duris. 3," in Pauly-Wissowa, V/2, cols. 1853-56.

(RÜDIGER SCHMITT)

DŪRMEŠ (or Dormeš) KHAN b. ʿAbdī Beg TAVĀČĪ ŠĀMLŪ, powerful Qezelbāš amir, brother-in-law and confidant of Shah Esmāʿīl I (907-30/1501-24; *ʿĀlamārā-ye ṣafawī*, pp. 148-49; *Ḥabīb al-sīar*, Tehran, IV, pp. 555, 558). In 909/1503 Dūrmeš Khan was appointed governor of Isfahan but remained at court in Tabrīz and sent Mīrzā Shah Ḥosayn Eṣfahānī to act for him (*Tārīḵ-e Šāh Esmāʿīl*, fol. 112b). At the battle of Čālderān (q.v.) in 920/1514 Dūrmeš commanded the right wing of the Safavid army (*Tārīḵ-e Šāh Esmāʿīl*, fol. 249b; *Ḥabīb al-sīar*, Tehran, IV, p. 545: left wing) and proposed the fatal delay in attacking the Ottoman positions that led to Safavid defeat (Ḥasan Rūmlū, pp. 189-90; *ʿĀlamārā-ye ṣafawī*, pp. 484-85). In *Tārīḵ-e Qezelbāš* (p. 19) Dūrmeš Beg is described as *qūrčī-bāšī* during the battle of Dīārbakr (which took place in about 920/1514; 924/1518, given in the source, cannot be correct), but there seems to be no corroboration in other sources (Savory, IV, p. 101). In later years Shah Ṭahmāsb was said to have cursed the name of Dūrmeš Khan whenever the battle of Čālderān was mentioned (Ḵᵛoršāh, fol. 473a), but in fact the shah seems to have borne no grudge, for in 923/1517 he appointed Dūrmeš Khan *lala* (guardian) of his new-born son Sām Mīrzā (*Ḥabīb al-sīar*, Tehran, IV, p. 555). In 924-25/1518-19 Dūrmeš Khan conducted successful campaigns in Māzandarān against rebellious local rulers (Ḥasan Rūmlū, pp. 218-19; *Ḥabīb al-sīar*, Tehran, IV, pp. 558-60, 562-64), and in 926/1520 he was sent to Baghdad to check the advance of the Ottoman Sultan Salīm, but the death of the sultan ended the threat (*Tārīḵ-e Šāh Esmāʿīl*, fol. 284b).

In a decree appointing Dūrmeš Khan governor-general of Khorasan in 927/1521 Esmāʿīl called him "the one who has the status of a son" (*rotba-ye farzandī*) to himself. The new governor reached Herat on 19 Ḏu'l-Ḥejja/20 November, followed by Sām Mīrzā on 17 Ramażān 928/10 August 1522. Dūrmeš Khan was unable to prevent Moḥammad Ẓahīr-al-Dīn Bābor from occupying Qandahār in May 1522 (*Ḥabīb al-sīar* IV, pp. 587-88, 590, 592), but in 930/1523-24 he successfully defended Herat against a prolonged siege by ʿObayd Khan Uzbeg; he was confirmed as governor-general by Shah Ṭahmāsb (930-84/1524-76) but died in 931/1525 (Ḥasan Rūmlū, pp. 241-45, 248).

Bibliography: (For cited works not found in this bibliography, see "Short References.") *ʿĀlamārā-ye ṣafawī*, ed. Y. Šokrī, Tehran, 1350 Š./1971. *ʿĀlamārā-ye Šāh Esmāʿīl*, ed. A. Montaẓer-e Ṣaḥeb, Tehran, 1349 Š./1970. Ḥasan Rūmlū, *Aḥsan al-tawārīḵ*, ed. ʿA.-Ḥ. Navāʾī, Tehran, 1357 Š./1929. Ḵᵛoršāh b. Qobād Ḥosaynī, *Tārīḵ-e īlčī-e Neẓāmšāh*, British Library, London, ms. no. Add. 25,513. R. Savory, "The Consolidation of Ṣafawid Power in Persia," *Der Islam* 41, 1965, pp. 87-88; repr. in *Studies in the History of Ṣafawid Iran*, London, 1987, III, pp. 87-88. Idem, "The Principal Offices of the Ṣafawid State during the Reign of Ismaʿīl I (907-30/1501-24)" *BSOAS* 23, 1960, p. 101; repr. in *Studies in the History of Ṣafawid Iran*, London, 1987, IV, p. 101. *Tārīḵ-e Qezelbāš*, ed. Mīr Hāšem Moḥaddeṯ, Tehran, 1361 Š./1982. *Tārīḵ-e Šāh Esmāʿīl-e Ṣafawī*, British Library, London, ms. no. Or. 3248.

(ROGER M. SAVORY)

DŪRNEMĀ-YE ĪRĀN, weekly of politics and culture edited and published by the Persian writer, scholar, and filmmaker ʿAbd-al-Ḥosayn Sepantā (b. Tehran, 1286/1907, d. Isfahan, 1348 Š./1969) in Bombay from 9 Āḏar 1307 Š./30 November 1928 to Farvardīn 1308 Š./March 1929.

Sepantā had moved to Bombay in 1306 Š./1927. *Dūrnemā-ye Īrān* was a Persian nationalist publication and supported the policies of Reżā Shah Pahlavī (1304-20 Š./1925-41), particularly the emancipation of women and discarding the veil.

The journal, which measured 21 x 33 cm, was printed from lead type in four two-column pages at Hoor Press; it included illustrations and advertising.

A subscription in India cost 4 rupees; foreign subscriptions also included the cost of postage. Single issues sold for 1 anna each.

Dūrnemā-ye Īrān does not seem to be held in Persian or foreign libraries.

Bibliography: (For abbreviations in this bibliography, see "Short References.") F. Ābādānī, *Zendagī-nāma-ye ʿAbd-al-Ḥosayn Sepantā*, Isfahan, 1348 Š./1969. Bāmdād, *Rejāl* IV, p. 138. E. Naqavī, *Fārsī ṣaḥāfat. Tārīḵ-e adabīāt-e Mosolmānān-e Pākestān wa Hend* V, Lahore, 1972, p. 627. Ṣadr Hāšemī, *Jarāʾed o majallāt* II, pp. 299-302.

(Nassereddin Parvin)

DÜRRI EFENDI (Dorrī Afandī), Aḥmad (b. Van, date unknown, d. Istanbul, 1135/1722), Ottoman poet, civil servant, and diplomat who served as ambassador to Tehran and wrote *Sefārat-nāma*, the first Turkish account of Safavid Persia. Nothing is known of his early life and education; he made his career in Istanbul, rising through the bureaucratic ranks.

The Ottoman empire had lost western territories as a result of its defeat by Austria and Venice and the treaty of Passarowitz (20 Šaʿbān 1130/21 July 1718). The government hoped to compensate itself by acquiring territories from Persia, which was weak and torn by internal conflict. Dürri Efendi's official mission was to help smooth the path for Persian merchants crossing Ottoman territory to Austria, but his real task was to assess the situation. According to his *Sefārat-nāma*, he left Baghdad and crossed the border near Kermānšāh on 1 Moḥarram 1133/2 November 1720, passing through Kermānšāh, Darjazīn, Hamadān, and Qazvīn to Tehran, where he delivered letters to Shah Solṭān-Ḥosayn, who was in residence there (1105-35/1694-1722), and the vizier. He was accompanied on his return (18 Safar 1134/5 December 1721) by the Persian ambassador Mortażāqolī Khan, who carried letters to their Ottoman counterparts. Some time later the Ottomans declared war on Persia, most of which was by then under Afghan control.

Dürri Efendi was known for his virtuosity in casting chronograms and composed a *majmūʿa*, the manuscript of which is kept in the Süleimaniye library (Esat Efendi, no. 3409). His fame is based mainly on his *Sefārāt-nāma*, however. Aside from valuable information on Persia, it is also useful for the study of "embassy literature." It was first published in lithograph (*Relation de Dourry Effendy, ambassadeur de la Porte Ottomane* . . ., Paris, 1820; repr. in *Rāšed tarīḵī* III, Istanbul, 1153/1740, pp. 93-100; 2nd ed., V, Istanbul, 1282/1865, pp. 372-98; a Persian translation of this edition has not survived). It was translated into French by Louis Langlès (*Relation de Dourry Efendi* . . ., Paris, 1810) and into Latin by Father Tadeusz Krusiński (*Prodomus ad Tragicam Bertentis Belli Persici Historiam seu Legationis* . . .); an abridged version of the latter was translated into Turkish by Ibrahim Müteferrika (*Tārīḵ-e sayyāḥ*, Istanbul, 1277/1860-61), which was in turn translated into Persian by ʿAbd-al-Razzāq Donbolī (*Baṣīrat-nāma*, Tehran, 1369 Š./1991). The most recent Persian translation is by Moḥammad-Amīn Rīyāḥī (in *Sefārāt-nāmahā-ye Īrān. Gozarešhā-ye mosafarat wa maʾmūrīyat-e safīrān-e ʿoṯmānī dar Īrān* (Tehran, 1368 Š./1989, pp. 49-98).

Bibliography: M. Aktepe, "Dürri Ahmet Efendi'nin İran sefâreti," *Belgelerle Türk Tarihi Dergisi* 1, 1985, pp. 56-61. F. Babinger, *Die Geschichtsschreiber der Osmanen und ihre Werke*, Leiden, 1927; tr. C. Üçok as *Osmanlı tarih yazarları ve eserleri*, Ankara, 1982, pp. 354-55. *Ḥayāt* (Istanbul) I/38, 1926, pp. 14-15; I/69, 1926, pp. 323-24. Šayḵī Meḥmed (Moḥammad) Afandī, *Waqāyeʿ al-fożalāʾ*, ed. A. Özcan, Istanbul, 1989, pp. 737-39. F. R. Onat, *Osmanlı sefirleri ve sefaretnameleri*, Ankara, 1968, p. 59-61. Qāżīasker Sālim Efendi, *Tāḏkera*, Istanbul, 1311/1893-94, pp. 239-44. Meḥmet (Moḥammad) Süreyya, *Sejell-e ʿoṯmānī* II, Istanbul, (1891?); repr. Westmead, Hants., U.K., 1971, pp. 337-38. B. M. Tahir, *Osmanlı müellifleri* III, Istanbul, 1924, p. 8. A. Talay, *Bizim eller Van*, Istanbul, 1988, p. 82.

(Tahsin Yazici)

DUSHANBE (Pers. Došanba "Monday"; in Russian known as Dyushambe until 1929, Stalinabad from 1929 to 1961, and Dushanbe after 1961), capital and most populous city of Tajikistan. It is located in the Hisor (Pers. Ḥeṣār, Russian Gissar) valley, at an average altitude of approximately 823 m, on the Dushanbe river (Russian Dushanbinka), the lower course of the Varzob (Pers. Varzāb) at the confluence with the Luchob (Lūčāb). According to tradition, the name reflects an earlier practice of holding a market in the area on Mondays.

There is archeological evidence of human habitation in the Dushanbe region since the late Neolithic era. Speculation that there may have been a large ancient settlement on the site remains controversial. The earliest historical references to a village named Dushanbe are from the 17th and 18th centuries; by the early 18th century a small fort was associated with it ("Dushanbe," p. 353). Dushanbe and its environs were long subject to the beg of Hisor. In the 19th century the village of Dushanbe was a center for regional trade and artisanal production, including weaving, tanning, and ironworking (Ghafurov, p. 199). After a prolonged, though intermittent, struggle for control of the Hisor area among various local and regional rulers, the tsarist government allocated it to the amir of Bukhara in 1868, as compensation for the loss of other parts of his realm to the Russian governorship-general of Turkestan (Bartol'd, pp. 291, 430-31; Spuler, p. 247).

The civil war that followed the Russian Revolution caused extensive damage in Dushanbe. The last amir of Bukhara, Sayyed ʿĀlem Khan, fled to Dushanbe at the end of August 1920 to escape advancing Red Army forces from Tashkent. For the next half-year he used Dushanbe as a base for directing his fight against the communists. The Red Army took Dushanbe on 21 February 1921; the amir fled farther east and eventually reached Afghanistan. Basmachi forces besieged the communist garrison in Dushanbe twice in the fall and winter of 1921-22. The derogatory term *basmachi* (lit., "bandit") was applied by the Soviet authorities to those who fought against them in Central Asia during the civil war; though it was not a self-designation, it has gained widespread currency. The second siege, commanded by Enver Pasha, was successful, and Dushanbe fell in February 1922. The village remained in Basmachi hands until July of that year, when the Red Army retook it (Akademiya nauk, pp. 92, 99-100, 102, 110, 112, 118). As a result of the turmoil the population of the town declined from 3,140 in 1920 to 283 in 1924. Most of its buildings had been destroyed during the civil war; only about forty houses were still standing in 1924 (Veselovskiĭ et al., p. 61).

Dushanbe was transformed in the Soviet era. With the return of the Red Army in 1922 the village became the center of Soviet power in eastern Bukhara. In 1924 the Tadzhikistan Autonomous Soviet Socialist Republic was created as part of the Uzbekistan Soviet Socialist Republic, and Dushanbe became its capital; the government began functioning there formally in March 1925. As part of this process, Dushanbe was officially redefined as a city, and two nearby villages, Sari Osiyo (Pers. Sar-e Āsīā) and Shohmansur (Šāh Manṣūr), were incorporated into it. The city developed slowly during the 1920s. Some of the most important cultural figures and official organizations of Tajikistan were located elsewhere in Uzbekistan and only gradually moved to Dushanbe; for example, the state publishing department of Tajikistan was located in Samarqand (Ikromi, p. 3). The city's first telegraph link, with Bukhara, began operation late in 1923, and the first railroad line (from Termez, Uzbekistan) reached it in 1929. Dushanbe's growth was planned and directed largely by Russian and Ukrainian architects and construction personnel, beginning in 1926 (subsequent plans were adopted in 1938, 1965, and 1983; Veselovskiĭ et al., pp. 63-65, 132, 135, 137). In the interwar years most of the new buildings were single-story structures of mud brick.

In 1929 Tajikistan became a Soviet Socialist Republic separate from Uzbekistan, with Dushanbe remaining its capital. Since the 1930s the city has acquired an increasing number of larger public and official buildings (including a sports stadium, a theater for opera and ballet, government headquarters, and a post office) in architectural styles typical of the Soviet Union at the time, though many have decorative details drawn from local traditions. In the 1950s the city government began to construct increasingly tall residential housing, at first four-story apartment buildings, and, since the 1970s, an ever-increasing number of medium- and high-rise apartment buildings, although some neighborhoods of small mud-brick houses remain.

Modern Dushanbe has expanded from its original core on the left bank of the river along both banks and along the Luchob as well. It is divided into four administrative units (*raions*): Rohi Ohan (Pers. *rāh-e āhan* "railroad," Russian *zheleznodorozhnyi*), Markazi (Pers. *markazī* "central," Russian Tsentral'nyi), Oktiabr' (October, Russian Oktyabr'skii), and Frunze (Russian Frunzenskii, after M. V. Frunze, 1885-1925, commander of the Red Army in Turkestan during the civil war).

The few industries in Dushanbe during the 1920s and 1930s were primarily oriented toward local demand and processing locally produced raw materials. They included meat packing; production of soap, bricks, lumber, silk thread, leather, and clothing; and generation of electric power. The city's industrial development was stimulated by the Moscow government's decision during World War II to relocate some of the Soviet Union's production facilities east of the Urals, farther from the war zone. In Dushanbe the effects were felt primarily in such light industries as textile manufacturing and food processing. Today the city is a major industrial center of Tajikistan, with approximately 100 factories and other production facilities, and is home to about one third of the industrial labor force and white-collar personnel of the republic, even though less than 10 percent of the total population of the country lives there (Fedorova, p. 18; Nasyrov, p. 26). It has several factories producing industrial machinery (including machines for the oil and textile industries), parts for farm machinery, consumer durables (like refrigerators and furniture), and textiles and thread (silk and cotton), as well as numerous facilities for processing meat, fruit, vegetables, and other locally produced raw materials. The city is also the center of publishing, television and radio broadcasting, and film production in Tajikistan.

There are a number of institutions of higher education and culture in the city, including the main campus of Tajikistan State University, the State Pedagogical University, the State Medical University, the State Polytechnic University, the State Agricultural University, the Technological University, and other institutions for the study of art, physical culture, and, in the Soviet era, Russian language and literature (now the Institute of Foreign Languages). The Tajik Academy of Sciences and the Firdavsi (Ferdowsī) National Library, with its collection of more than 2,000 oriental manuscripts, are also located in Dushanbe. The performing arts are represented by a symphony orchestra, opera and ballet companies, a youth theater, and a puppet theater.

Dushanbe has a resident circus and many movie theaters. Its main museums include the Behzod (Behzād) regional studies museum and the ethnographic museum of the Academy of Sciences. For many years during the Soviet era there were only one legally recognized mosque in the city and an unknown number of unofficial ones; beginning in the late 1980s changes in the Soviet Union made possible the opening of many new mosques in Tajikistan, as in other parts of the country where Muslim inhabitants are concentrated. In 1990 an Islamic institute was opened in Dushanbe. The city also has a Russian Orthodox cathedral.

Dushanbe was the scene of conflict in the 1990s, part of the dispute over who would wield power in late Soviet and independent Tajikistan. In this period there were large and prolonged demonstrations, serious shortages of basic necessities, hostage taking, seizure of public buildings, and armed clashes. Although much of this activity was politically motivated, violent crime also increased. The design of the contemporary city includes several squares, around which government offices are located. There are also parks and outdoor recreational facilities. In addition to shops along the streets, Dushanbe has two large *bāzārs*. Several large public teahouses decorated in traditional fashion are located around the city. There are also a central railway station and an airport. After Tajikistan declared its independence on 9 September 1991 the authorities replaced some Soviet designations and monuments with new ones symbolizing the Tajiks' pan-Iranian cultural heritage. For example, Lenin Street became Rūdakī Street, and a statue of V. I. Lenin in downtown Dushanbe was replaced by a statue of Ferdowsī.

The population of Dushanbe grew from 5,600 in 1926 (Fedorova, p. 8) to 604,000 (including 2,000 from the surrounding villages), according to the 1989 census ("Dar borai," p. 3; see DEMOGRAPHY iii). The increase resulted from immigration of Russians and other Soviet Europeans (an especially crucial factor in the early decades of the Soviet period, as they constituted most of the skilled and white-collar workers); rural-to-urban migration within the republic; and, especially in recent years, the natural increase of the existing urban population (Fedorova, p. 42; Alimov et al., p. 11). Another factor was the redrawing of Dushanbe's boundaries to include nearby villages. In the 1989 census, for example, 8,000 people were classified as inhabitants of rural areas subject to the city government. Data on the ethnic composition of Dushanbe's popularion are available from the 1989 census. Of a total of 602,000 who actually lived in the city the largest groups were Tajiks, 39.1 percent; Russians, 32.4 percent; Uzbeks 10.4 percent; Tatars, 4.1 percent; and Ukrainians, 3.5 percent. The remaining 10.4 percent included Jews, Kirghiz, Turkmen, and others (*First Book*, p. D-8). Since the 1970s the trend has been toward an increase in the Tajik proportion of the population. According to the 1970 and 1979 censuses, Dushanbe had a larger proportion of Russian inhabitants (42 and 39 percent respectively) and a smaller proportion of Tajiks (26 and 30.7 percent respectively) than in 1989 (Vinnikov, p. 20; "Faktku raqamho," p. 124). The population of Dushanbe dropped as a consequence of the breakdown of the Soviet Union and the ensuing civil war in Tajikistan, although estimates of the numbers vary. Concerns about the standard of living, the status of non-Central Asians, and turmoil associated with the post-Soviet power struggle prompted people of various nationalities to leave the city. Anecdotal information suggests that Russians and other non-Central Asians, many of them professional people, left in particularly large numbers. The civil war also drove other population groups into Dushanbe, as they fled the area of heaviest fighting, in southern Tajikistan.

Bibliography: Akademiya Nauk Tadzhikskoĭ SSR, *Istoriya tadzhikskogo naroda* III/1. *Perekhod k sotsializmu* (History of the Tajik people III/1. The transition to socialism), Moscow, 1964. R. K. Alimov, Sh. Shoismatulloev, and M. Saidov, "Migratsionnye protsessy i natsional'nyi vopros" (Migration processes and the national question), *Kommunist Tadzhikistana* 5, May 1990, pp. 10-17. V. V. Bartol'd, "Istoriya kul'turnoi zhizni Turkestana" (History of the cultural life of Turkestan), in V.V. Bartol'd, *Sochineniya* (Collected works) II/1, Moscow, 1963, pp. 169-433. "Dar borai natijahoi peshakii baruikhatgirii umumiittifoqii aholi dar soli 1989," *Tojikistoni soveti*, 7 May 1989, p. 3. "Dushanbe," *Entsiklopediyai Sovetii Tojik* II, Dushanbe, 1980, pp. 353-55. "Faktku raqamho," *Kommunisti Tojikiston* 5, May, 1987, pp. 123-27. T. I. Fedorova, *Goroda Tadzhikistana i problemy rosta i razvitiya* (The cities of Tajikistan and the problems of growth and development), Dushanbe, 1981. *First Book of Demographics for the Republics of the Former Soviet Union*, Shady Side, Md., 1992. B. Gh. Ghafurov, *Tojikon* II, Dushanbe, 1985. J. Ikromi, "Sabaqhoi ustod," *Tojikistoni soveti*, June 17, 1990, p. 3. Institut Etnografii, Akademiya Nauk SSSR, *Sotsiai'no-kul'turnyi oblik sovetskikh natsii* (Sociocultural features of the Soviet nations), Moscow, 1986. E. M. Nasyrov, "Professional'naya podgotovka rabochikh kadrov Tadzhikistana" (Professional training of workers' cadres of Tajikistan), *Sotsiologicheskie issledovaniia* 4, 1986, pp. 25-31. B. Spuler, "Central Asia. The Last Three Centuries of Independence," *The Muslim World* III. *The Last Great Muslim Empires*, ed. and tr. F. R. C. Bagley, Leiden, 1969, pp. 219-59. V. G. Veselovskiĭ et al., *Arkhitektura sovetskogo Tadzhikistana* (The architecture of Soviet Tajikistan), Moscow, 1987. Ya. R. Vinnikov, "Natsional'nye i etnograficheskie gruppy Sredneĭ Azii po dannym etnicheskoi statistiki" (National and ethnic groups in Central Asia, according to data from ethnic statistics), in

Etnicheskie protsessy u natsional'nykh grupp SredneĭAzii i Kazakhstana (Ethnic processes among national groups of Central Asia and Kazakhstan), Moscow, 1980, pp. 11-42.

(MURIEL ATKIN)

DŪST-ʿALĪ MOʿAYYER-AL-MAMĀLEK. See MOʿAYYER-AL-MAMĀLEK.

DŪST-MOḤAMMAD b. Solaymān HERAVĪ (d. probably Qazvīn, shortly after 972/1564), master calligrapher, the only artist whom Shah Ṭahmāsb I (930-84/1524-76) kept with him after having gradually dismissed all the others from his direct service (Bodāq, fol. 111a; Qāżī Aḥmad, p. 99; tr. Minorsky, p. 147). Although Dūst-Moḥammad may have been involved with ornamentation or other activities connected with the art of the book (Sām Mīrzā, pp. 138-39; Qāżī Aḥmad, p. 99; tr. Minorsky, p. 147), he is not to be confused with his contemporary Dūst-Moḥammad Moṣawwer (q.v.).

Dūst-Moḥammad studied with the master calligrapher Qāsem Šādīšāh (Bodāq, fol. 111a); his earliest signed work (National Public Library, Saint Petersburg, ms. no. Dorn 147, fols. 37a and 37b; cf. Adle, 1993, fig. 1), produced in Herat in 917/1511-12, includes his father's name and his *nesba* (attributive name), Heravī. Another page, dated in Herat 938/1531 (Topkapı Saray library, Istanbul, ms. no. H. 2156, fol. 31b; cf. Adle, 1993, fig. 2), and a Koran, also copied in Herat and dated 944/1538 (Adle, 1993, p. 229; Plate XLV), show that he had not yet left this city. The colophon of a *maṯnawī* attributed by Bernhard Dorn (q.v.) to Farīd-al-Dīn ʿAṭṭār (National Public Library, St. Petersburg, ms. no. Dorn 354, fol. 112a; cf. Dorn, pp. 331-32), signed "Dūst-Moḥammad al-kāteb al-šāhī . . . year 947/1540-41" (Adle, 1993, fig. 3), is evidence that he had left Herat and entered the service of Shah Ṭahmāsb, a position he retained for the rest of his life (Adle, 1993, pp. 226-30). His last known work appears to be a copy of *Majāles al-ʿoššāq* by Kamāl-al-Dīn Ḥosayn Gāzorgāhī dated 972/1564, now in the Madrasa-ye Sepahsālār in Tehran (ms. no. 2715; Bayānī, *Ḵošnevīsān* I, p. 191).

Dūst-Moḥammad's main achievement was an album (*moraqqaʿ*) of calligraphic pieces and paintings by great masters that he finished assembling in 951/1544 for Prince Bahrām Mīrzā (q.v.), brother of Shah Ṭahmāsb; it is now in the library of the Topkapı Saray (ms. no. H. 2154). It is both a masterpiece and a major contribution to knowledge of post-Mongol Irano-Turkic artistic culture (Adle, 1990, pp. 219-56). It includes an introduction by Dūst-Moḥammad on the lives of calligraphers and painters (Chaghtai; Bayānī, *Ḵošnevīsān* I, pp. 192-203; Thackston, pp. 335-49) and appears to be the earliest known example of an album of expressly selected pieces, rather than a random assemblage of pages (Adle, 1993, pp. 221 n. 4, 265-66 n. 174, 278-83).

PLATE XLV

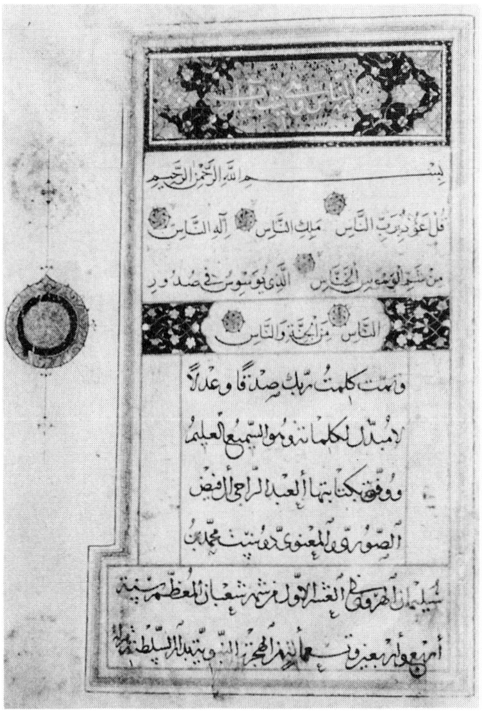

Colophon of a Koran manuscript signed by Dūst-Moḥammad b. Solaymān Heravī at Herat in the first ten days of Šaʿbān 944/3-13 January 1538; private collection. Photograph courtesy C. Adle.

Bibliography: (For cited works not found in this bibliography, see "Short References.") C. Adle, "Autopsia, in absentia. Sur la date de l'introduction et de la constitution de l'album de Bahrâm Mirzâ par Dust-Moḥammad en 951/1544," *Stud. Ir.* 19/2, 1990, pp. 219-56. Idem, "Les artistes nommés Dust-Moḥammad au XVIᵉ siècle," *Stud. Ir.* 22/2, 1993, pp. 219-96. Bodāq Monšī Qazvīnī, *Jawāher al-aḵbār*, National Public Library, Saint Petersburg, ms. no. Dorn 288. M. A. Chaghtai, *A Treatise on Calligraphers and Painters*, Lahore, 1936. B. Dorn, *Catalogue des manuscrits xylographes orientaux de la Bibliothèque Impériale de St. Petersbourg*, St. Petersburg, 1852. Sām Mīrzā Ṣafawī, *Taḏkera-ye toḥfa-ye sāmī*, ed. R. Homāyun Farroḵ, Tehran, n.d. (1347 Š./1968?). W. M. Thackston, "Preface to the Bahram Mirza Album," in *A Century of Princes. Sources on Timurid History of Art*, Cambridge, Mass., 1989, pp. 335-49.

(CHAHRYAR ADLE)

DŪST MOḤAMMAD KHAN BĀRAKZĪ. See DŌST MOḤAMMAD KHAN.

DŪST-MOḤAMMAD MOṢAWWER (also Dūst-e Dīvāna "fool, eccentric," Dūst-e Moṣawwer; d. India in 1560 or shortly afterward), master painter, not to be confused with the contemporary calligrapher Dūst-Moḥammad b. Solaymān (q.v.; D̲okāʾ). It is remotely possible that he was identical with Dūst-Moḥammad b. ʿAbd-Allāh Heravī Qāṭeʿ (Adle, 1993, pp. 235-38; see CUT PAPER).

Dūst-Moḥammad was renowned in the Indo-Persian world and even among the Ottomans as a painter (*moṣawwer*), paper cutter (*qāṭeʿ*), calligraphic tracer/outliner (*moḥarrer*), and perhaps binder (*saḥḥāf*) and gilder (*mod̲ahheb*). Bodāq Monšī (fols. 111v-112r), secretary to the Safavid prince Bahrām Mīrzā (q.v.), a great collector and connoisseur and very well informed about art, characterized the artist as the best pupil of Behzād (q.v.). When Behzād was appointed head of the court scriptorium by Shah Esmāʿīl I (907-30/1501-24; K̲ᵛāndamīr, fols. 152b-54b) in about 1520 (Akimushkin, p. 142), Dūst-Moḥammad may have accompanied him. Later he was among the artists with whom Shah Ṭahmāsb (930-84/1524-76) surrounded himself when he succeeded his father at the age of ten years in 930/1524 (Bodāq fols. 296a-b). Four paintings in Bahrām Mīrzā's album of 951/1544 (Topkapı Sarayı Library, Istanbul, ms. no. H. 2154, fols. 71a, 121b, 138b, 140b; Adle, 1990; idem, 1993, figs. 9-12; Plate XLVI) and "Haftvād's daughter finding the magic worm in her apple" (Sadruddin Aga Khan's collection, Geneva, ms. no. M. 199; Dickson and Welch, I, pl. 14) date from the period when he was in the shah's service. The last was part of the great *Šāh-nāma* made for Ṭahmāsb, known to contemporaries as *Šāh-nāma-ye šāhī* "the shah's *Šāh-nāma*" (Dūst-Moḥammad Heravī in the *Moraqqaʿ* of Bahrām Mīrzā, fol. 17a; tr. Thackston, p. 348), which was dismembered in the 1970s.

A heavy drinker (Bāyazīd, p. 66), Dūst-Moḥammad seems to have been not much affected by the shah's ban on drink after his own "first repentance" (*tawba*) in 940/1532, as he was close to Behzād, whose drinking the shah feigned to ignore (Bodāq, fol. 111b; Adle, 1993, pp. 238-42). Conditions changed when Behzād died in 942/1535-36 (Dūst-Moḥammad Heravī, fol. 16b; tr. Thackston, p. 347) and the shah's interest in the arts began to wane. Dūst-Moḥammad left Persia in the late 1530s and joined the Mughal prince Kāmrān b. Bābor, who had royal ambitions and had rebelled against his brother, the Mughal emperor Homāyūn (937-63/1530-56, with interruption), in Kabul no later than the 1530s (Bāyazīd, p. 66; Lowick, pp. 159-60; Adle, 1993, pp. 244-48). When Homāyūn took Kabul on his return from Persia in 952/1545 Dūst-Moḥammad joined his court; in the late 1540s he was still the leading artist in Kabul (Bāyazīd, pp. 66, 69; Adle, 1993, pp. 249-51). In 957/1550 he painted one of his best works, "Homāyūn and Hendāl in the orange grove of a Kabul mountain pass" ("Jahāngīr album," Staatsbibliothek Preussischer Kulturbesitz, Orientabt., Berlin, ms. no. Libr. Pict. A 117, fol. 15a; Welch, fig. 85; Adle, 1993, pp. 251-52). After the arrival of Mīr Sayyed ʿAlī Moṣawwer and ʿAbd al-Ṣamad Šīrīn-Qalam (q.v.; Adle, 1993, pp. 256-57) from Persia toward the end of 956/1549, Dūst-Moḥammad lost his preeminent position there, however (Dickson and Welch, I, pp. 119, 178, 248 n. 18), and in 962/1554-55 he accompanied Homāyūn on his expedition to reconquer India (Bāyazīd, pp. 176-77), where he died during the reign of Akbar. In India Dūst-Moḥammad painted his last known work, a portrait of Šāh Abu'l-Maʿālī (Sadruddin Aga Khan's collection M. 126; Adle, 1993, pp. 272-75, fig. 16).

PLATE XLVI

Dūst-Moḥammad Moṣawwer, "The young Shah Ṭahmāsb offering flowers to a maiden," ca. 937/1530; album of Bahrām Mīrzā, Topkapı Sarayı library, Istanbul, ms. no. H. 2154, fol. 121b.

He was the master of the renowned Persian painter, calligrapher, and gilder Šayk̲ Moḥammad (Bodāq, fol. 112b) and may also be considered one of the artists who contributed most to the emergence of the early Mughal school of painting. His miniatures were admired and copied in both Persia and India (Sotheby's, lot 148; "Jahāngīr album," fol. 14a;

Adle, 1993, pp. 276-84, figs. 14-15; Beach, 1987, pp. 23-26; idem, 1992, pp. 304-10).

Bibliography: C. Adle, "Autopsia, in absentia. Sur la date de l'introduction et de la constitution de l'album de Bahrâm Mirzâ par Dust-Moḥammad en 951/1544," *Stud. Ir.* 19/2, 1990, pp. 219-56. Idem, "Les artistes nommés Dust-Moḥammad au XVIe siècle," *Stud. Ir.* 22/2, 1993, pp. 219-96. O. F. Akimushkin, "Legenda o khudožnike Bekhzade i kalligrafe Makhmud Nišapuri," *Narody Azii i Afriki* 6, 1963, pp. 140-43. M. C. Beach, *Early Mughal Painting*, Cambridge, Mass., 1987. Idem, "Persian Culture and Mughal India," in A. Soudavar, ed., *Art of Persian Courts*, New York, 1992, pp. 304-10. Bāyazīd Beyāt, *Taḏkera-ye Homāyūn wa Akbar*, ed. H. Hosain, Calcutta, 1941. M. B. Dickson and S. C. Welch, *The Houghton Shahnameh*, 2 vols., Cambridge, Mass., 1981. Y. Ḏokā, "Dūst-Moḥammad-e Moṣawwer, Dūst-Moḥammad-e Kāteb, Dūst-e Moṣawwer," *Āyanda* 8/5, 1361 Š./1982, pp. 244-53. Ḡīāṯ-al-Dīn Ḵᵛāndamīr, *Nāma-ye nāmī*, Biblithèque Nationale, Paris, ms. no. Suppl. Pers. 1842. N. M. Lowick, "Some Countermarked Coins of the Shaybanids and Early Moghuls," *Journal of the Numismatic Society* 27, 1965, pp. 157-69. Sotheby's, *Oriental Manuscripts and Miniatures*, London, 12 October 1990. W. M. Thackston, "Preface to the Bahram Mirza Album," in *A Century of Princes. Sources on Timurid History of Art*, Cambridge, Mass., 1989, pp. 335-49. S. C. Welch, *India. Art and Culture, 1300-1900*, New York, 1985.

(CHAHRYAR ADLE)

DUTCH-PERSIAN RELATIONS, from the 16th century to the present, encompassing commercial, political, and cultural contacts, including Persian studies in the Netherlands. Until the 16th century the Dutch knew little of Persia and nothing of its language. Franciscus Raphelengius (1539-97), a professor at Leiden University, drew up a short list of Persian words based on the first Persian text ever printed, the translation of the Pentateuch published in Hebrew characters in Istanbul in 1546 (see BIBLE vii; ČĀP). Raphelengius called attention to the similarities between certain Persian and Dutch words, but until the older Iranian and Indian languages became known in the 19th century (see CODICES HAFNIENSES) this first attempt at comparative Indo-European linguistics could lead no farther. Joseph Scaliger (1540-1609), another Leiden professor, expanded Raphengelius' list into a concise Persian-Latin vocabulary (Leiden University library, cod. ar. 267; de Bruijn, p. 166; cf. Emmerick). Although unpublished, it can be considered the first example of Persian academic studies in Europe.

For 136 years, from 1033/1623 to 1174/1759, the Vereenigde Oostindische Compagnie (V.O.C., Dutch East Indies company) was the most important single foreign trading firm in Persia (e.g., Thévenot, II, p. 138), though it did not, of course, go unchallenged, particularly by the British East India Company (q.v.). Dutch documents on relations with Persia consist almost exclusively of V.O.C. records from the 17th and 18th centuries; except for the years 1623-38 (Dunlop, 1930), however, they have not been published, though a few studies have been based on them (Floor, 1978b; idem, 1979b; idem, 1980; idem, 1983c; idem, 1987). Most are kept in the national archives (Algemeen Rijks Archief) in the Hague, including the 19th- and 20th-century Dutch legation files (Gast). Some reports, journals, and letters by individual Dutch travelers to Persia have also been published (e.g., Hotz, 1908; Roobacker; van Dam; Valentijn; Floor, 1979a; idem, 1982b; idem, 1982c; idem, 1984; idem, 1365 Š./1986). Nevertheless, it is surprising, in view of the long and substantial presence of the V.O.C. in Persia, that so few Dutchmen wrote about their experiences; on the other hand, various staff members were instructed to buy Persian manuscripts and to collect indigenous herbs for shipment to the Netherlands (Valentijn, p. 242).

There is also very little information about the Dutch, occasionally called Valandīs or Holandīs, in Persian sources, perhaps because many state records were destroyed by the Afghans in the mid-18th century and also perhaps because merchants were of little interest to the Persian upper classes. That Persians visited the Netherlands is clear from François Valentijn's remark that he "need not describe the Persians, neither how they are dressed nor their nature, because there are many of them in Amsterdam, where one can see them every day" (V, p. 208).

The reign of Shah ʿAbbās I (q.v.; 996-1038/1588-1629). Foremost among Dutch travelers who contributed to diffusion of knowledge about Persia was Jan van Linschoten (1563-1611), whose account of his voyage in 1589 was influential throughout Europe. Visits to the Netherlands in 1016/1607 by Shah ʿAbbās' ambassador Zayn-al-Dīn Beg and in 1020/1611 by Robert Sherley, who was seeking to promote military and commercial relations between Persia and Europe, whetted an interest in Persian silk (Dunlop, 1930, pp. 1-3; *Chronicle*, I, p. 170; Glamann, p. 112; see ABRĪŠAM). Nevertheless, because the V.O.C., which had been founded in 1602, was at first preoccupied with fierce commercial competition with the Portuguese and British in southeast Asia, it was unable to act on its intentions in Persia until 1031/1622, when the East India Company drove the Portuguese from their base on Hormuz. The V.O.C. was quick to take advantage of the new opportunities: In 1033/1623 Huybert Visnich, an experienced merchant, arrived to establish a trading station in Isfahan (Lockhart, p. 381; Gaube and Wirth, p. 282; for a description, see Hotz, 1908, pp. 136-37 n. 138) and to conclude a commercial treaty with the shah (Meilink-Roelofsz, p. 11). The latter saw the Dutch as an outlet for Persian products, thus providing an additional and immediate source of precious metals, whereas the V.O.C. officials saw Persia mainly as a link in the larger Asian trade. On 30 Moḥarram 1033/17 November 1623 the shah signed a treaty granting the V.O.C. the right to import into Persia a specified quantity of selected products at fixed prices and toll free. In return he was to supply the Dutch with a fixed quantity of silk at higher-than-market price, which was 50 tomans per carga (ca. 300 lbs.; Dunlop, 1930, pp. 677-82; Meilink-Roelofsz, pp. 18-19; Heeres, I, pp. 186-91). The firm opened a rest house in Lār for Dutch caravans plying between Isfahan and the coast (Hotz, 1908, p. 47).

The East India Company repeatedly attempted to interfere with V.O.C. trade in Persia, for example, pressing a claim to 50 percent of the tolls from Hormuz/Gombroon (see BANDAR-E ʿABBĀS) under a treaty signed with Persia in 1032/1622; owing to Visnich's excellent relations with the shah and Emāmqolī Khan, governor of Fārs, these efforts were unsuccessful, however. Nevertheless, as the V.O.C. was generally short of cash, Visnich was forced to remit less for the silk than he was supposed to, despite the protests of Molayem Beg, the shah's factor and mint master (Ferrier, p. 62 fig. 7). Eventually the shah had to intervene personally (Meilink-Roelofsz, pp. 20, 22); over the objections of the V.O.C. he sought to establish closer political relations with the Dutch government by sending one Mūsā Beg as his ambassador to the Hague. Mūsā Beg embarked with several merchants carrying silk for sale in the Netherlands on 2 Jomādā I 1034/10 February 1625, on a company ship sailing via Batavia. The mission was not very successful diplomatically, commercially, or personally, and Mūsā Beg was forced to leave the Netherlands, embarking on 14 March 1627 for the return trip by way of Java and India. He was accompanied by Jan Smidt, ambassador of both the Estates-General and the V.O.C. (Floor, 1978a, pp. 40-58; Vermeulen, 1975-78b).

Meanwhile, in 1035/1626 Visnich had concluded a three-year contract with Molayem Beg for annual V.O.C. payments of 40,000 tomans (Dfl. 1.6 million), one-fourth in cash, the rest in specified goods at fixed amounts, in return for silk (Dunlop, 1930, pp. 184-86). The most important commodity to be provided by the V.O.C. was pepper: 750,000 pounds at 12,000 tomans. The most important exchange commodity was specie (gold and silver), which the Dutch exported from Persia illegally at first. Other Persian exports included small quantities of all kinds of dried fruit, pistachios, almonds (see BĀDĀM), hazelnuts, madder (see CARPETS ii), wine and rose water from Shiraz, and medicinal drugs. V.O.C. imports to Persia, aside from pepper, were considerable and varied: spices, textiles, tin, camphor, Japanese copper (q.v.), powdered and lump sugar, zinc, indigo, sappanwood, chinaroot (*Smilax china*, Pers. *čūb čīnī*), gum lac, benzoin, iron, steel, and sandalwood. Trade was conducted through brokers, and merchants usually received credit; a variety of drafts, money orders, and the like were used (Floor, 1978b, chap. 1). Molayem Beg did not find the contract to his advantage, however, and Visnich himself did not comply with its terms, continuing to turn over less cash than was due or even none at all. His relations at court were still strong enough to protect him from Molayem Beg (Steensgaard, p. 383; Meilink-Roelofsz, pp. 22-23), but Smidt, who arrived on 14 Rajab 1038/8 February 1629, listened favorably to Visnich's detractors and the allegations of British rivals and Molayem Beg.

Apart from commercial relations, the main point of contact between Persia and the Netherlands in the 17th century was art. Especially in the forty-five years after 1029/1620 a number of Dutch painters were active in Persia, though their possible influence on Persian painting has not yet been studied. From available sources it is clear that Dutch artists were employed by the shahs and members of the Persian political and commercial elite. For example, Jan van Hasselt, who lived in Isfahan from 1029/1620 to 1038/1628, was appointed court artist and executed paintings for Shah ʿAbbās' palace at Ašrāf in Māzandarān (see BEHŠAHR). When he returned home the shah appointed him his political agent in the Netherlands.

During this period travelers brought back increasing numbers of Persian manuscripts to the West. In particular, Thomas Erpenius (1584-1624) and Jacobus Golius (1596-1667), both of Leiden University, acquired better knowledge of Persian through their study of manuscripts in Arabic script. Golius, who was for some time assisted by the same Azerbaijani who had assisted Adam Olearius (Floor, 1983b), read Saʿdī's *Golestān* with his students and also prepared a Persian-Latin dictionary, which was published after his death (Castellus). His own extensive personal library was sold at auction twenty-five years later; most of it was purchased by Narcissus Marsh, Archbishop of Armagh, who bequeathed it to the Bodleian Library, Oxford (McCarthy, pp. 25, 47, 49). Golius' students contributed still further to Persian studies in the Netherlands. Lodewijk (Louis) de Dieu (q.v.) published the first Persian grammar in Latin (*Rudimentae Linguae Persicae*, Leiden, 1639). Levinus Warner published an annotated collection of Persian proverbs with translations (*Proverbiorum et Sententiarum Persicarum Centuria*, Leiden, 1644) and, while serving as Dutch consul in Istanbul, bought a large number of manuscripts in Arabic, Persian, and Turkish. His library, which he bequeathed to Leiden University, still constitutes the most important part of its collection of oriental manuscripts.

The reign of Shah Ṣafī I (1038-52/1629-42). Shah ʿAbbās and the governor-general of the V.O.C., Jan Pietersz Coen, died in the same year. On 1 Šaʿbān 1039/16 March 1630 Smidt sailed for Batavia, having obtained from ʿAbbās' successor, Shah Ṣafī I, limited confirmation of the earlier V.O.C. treaty (for

period of conflict Dutch artists and
nued to find success in Isfahan. The
ampen was working there in
nd van Sichem probably painted
r's cathedral in the suburb of
loor, 1979b, pp. 147-48). A
were also active, includ-
kens, a diamond cutter,
Cornelis Walraven and
any of them has been
ffkens was appointed
) at a salary of Dfl.

man authorities arrested him on suspicion of spying for Persia and executed him. Meanwhile, van Hasselt had been successful in obtaining trading privileges for Persians in the Netherlands, effective 7 February 1631 (Vermeulen, 1979; Valentijn, pp. 296-97; Alexandrowicz).

Between 1035/1626 and 1050/1640 silk was the main commodity exported from Persia by the V.O.C., but high prices, varying quality, and competition of silk from Bengal kept the profits from Persian silk low. Furthermore, despite the treaty terms, the shah supplied silk only irregularly and in smaller quantities than stipulated. The Dutch therefore also bought silk from private individuals, without paying customs duties on it. Pieter del Court, who had been appointed to succeed Visnich, was an ineffective administrator and was dismissed in 1044/1634; he was replaced by Nicolaas Jacobus Overschie, who in 1045/1635 was instructed to attempt to corner the silk market and to borrow the necessary cash (at 20 percent annual interest). His efforts were unsuccessful (Dunlop, 1930, pp. 410-12, 435; Steensgaard, pp. 391-93), and, to make matters worse, in 1047/1637 Mīrzā (Sārū) Taqī, the grand vizier, demanded payment of customs duties on the silk purchased from private merchants, pointing out that the V.O.C. had been granted exemption only on what it purchased from the shah. The Dutch refused to pay, insisting that the treaty guaranteed tax-free trade in Persia unconditionally, and Mīrzā Taqī then seized 4,309 tomans from Overschie by force. He went farther still; as he was having difficulty disposing of the shah's silk, he forced the Dutch to buy 300 bales at the stipulated high price of 50 tomans a carga. The V.O.C. then ordered its staff to reduce silk purchases in Persia.

1,000 a year; he died in Isfahan in 1066/1656.

The reign of Shah ʿAbbās II (q.v.; 1052-77/1642-66). The V.O.C. continued to protest Mīrzā Taqī's high-handedness without positive result; in 1054/1644 the firm therefore decided on military action (Floor, 1978b, pp. 46-48). In May 1645 seven men-of-war blockaded Bandar-e ʿAbbās on the Persian Gulf coast and seized all Persian vessels there. The fleet bombarded the Safavid fortress on Qešm island (Plate XLVII) but failed to seize it. The company then shifted most of its operations from Isfahan to Bandar-e ʿAbbās, which became its main trading station (Plate XLVIII). The shah promised the Dutch redress for their earlier losses at the hands of Mīrzā Taqī and invited them to send a plenipotentiary to court. In 1057/1647 Nicolaes Verburch and Willem Basting arrived; although they were unable to reach an agreement with the shah, the V.O.C. did continue trading with Persia tax-free. Even the appearance of a Dutch fleet on the roadstead of Bandar-e ʿAbbās in 1059/1649 did not cause further deterioration in political and commercial relations between the two countries (Floor, 1978b, pp. 48-51). Nevertheless, between 1055/1645 and 1062/1652 the V.O.C. exported no silk at all from Persia.

In 1061/1651 Joan Cunaeus arrived in Persia and negotiated a new agreement, which, with minor changes, remained the basis for V.O.C. trade with Persia until 1180/1766. The Dutch were to buy from the shah 300 bales of silk at 48 tomans a carga, in exchange for toll-free trade of 20,000 tomans a year; export of specie from the country was prohibited, and V.O.C. goods were exempted from inspection and road tolls. The company was not satisfied with the 20,000-toman limit or the prohibition on export of specie. Furthermore, in no year thereafter did the

PLATE XLVII

Drawing of Safavid fortress on Qešm island, ca. 1645. Photograph Algemeen Rijks Archief, the Hague, Collection Leupe, no. 866.

PLATE XLVIII

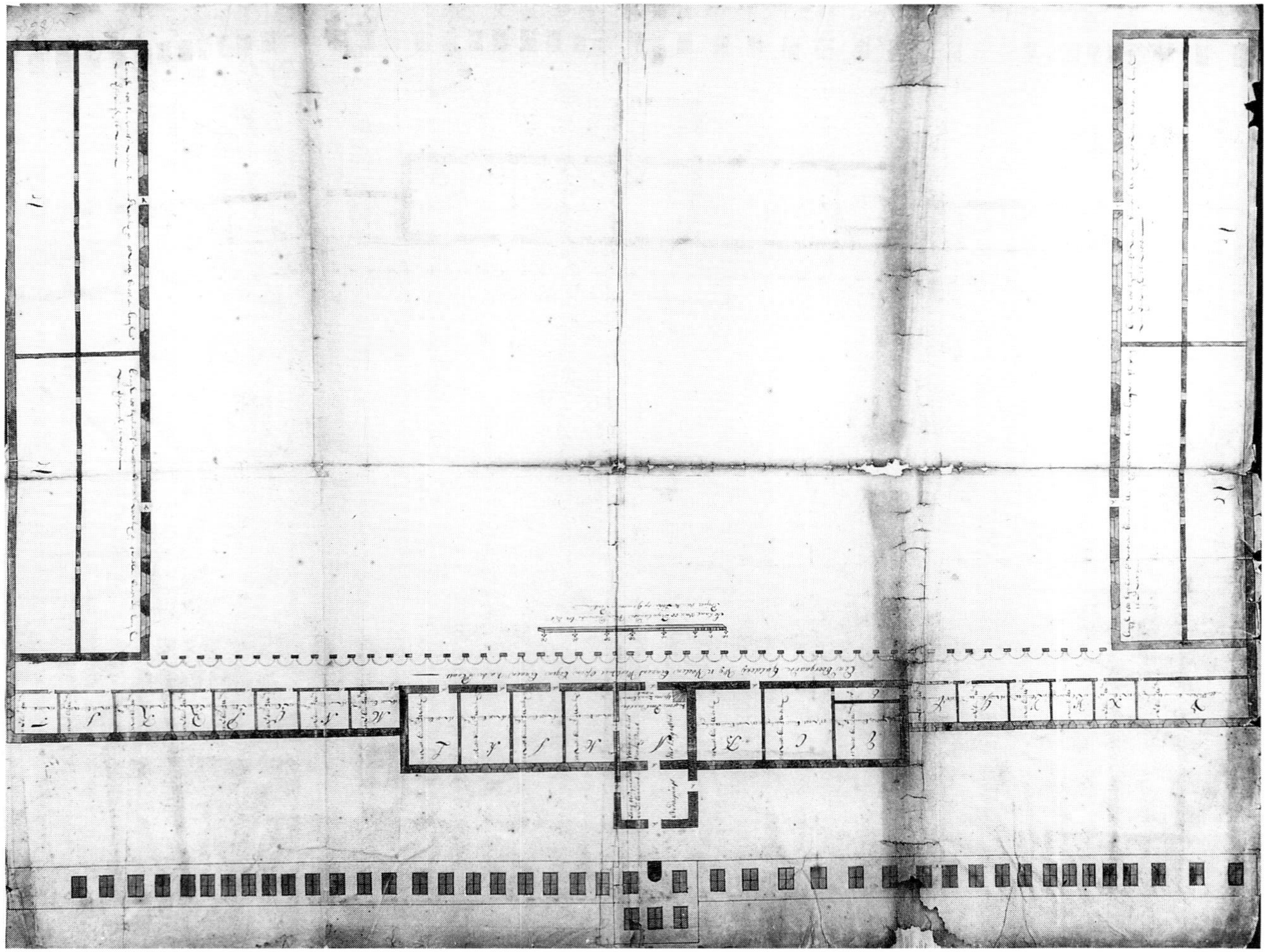

Front elevation and plan of Dutch factory, Bandar-e ʿAbbās, 1702. Photograph Algemeen Rijks Archief, the Hague, Collection Leupe, no. 865.

shah provide the promised 300 bales of silk, though the Dutch did enjoy tax-free trade (Hotz, 1908, pp. 355-62). Until 1108/1696 silk deliveries remained irregular because the shahs preferred to sell in the Levant when the price was better. Nevertheless, despite occasional problems over illegal export of specie, which was in fact the country's most important export commodity, the V.O.C. continued to prosper in Persia. Precise data for the 17th century are lacking, but gross profits in the years 1033-50/1624-50 had averaged about Dfl. 200,000; under the new treaty they began a gradual rise in 1062/1652, eventually reaching Dfl. 400,000 (van Dam, pp. 317-18; Table 40). A Dutch trading station was opened at Kermān in 1069/1659, when the V.O.C. began to buy wool there; it remained in operation, with interruptions, until 1157/1744. The firm had a standing order for 70,000 pounds of red wool annually, though it never actually received that much in any given year (Matthee; Floor, 1978b, p. 39; idem, forthcoming, chap. 5).

Between 1061/1651 and 1065/1655 Philip Angel not only made paintings for Shah ʿAbbās but also instructed him in the art. Other Dutch artists in Persia during this period included Hendrinck Boudewijn van Lockhorst, who worked there in 1053-57/1643-47; Juriaen Ambdis, who took service as a gunner in the shah's army in 1058/1648; a man named Romeyn, whose presence in 1065/1655 is attested; Jan de Hart, who was there the next year; Adriaan Gouda, there in 1071/1661; and an unnamed painter from Brabant in the later 17th century (Floor, 1979b).

Problems created by the governor of Fārs prompted the V.O.C. to send Huybert de Lairesse as envoy to the Persian court in 1076-77/1666, in order to ensure continuation of good relations and profitable trade. He was the last Dutch ambassador to have an audience with Shah ʿAbbās and the first to be received by his successor, Shah Ṣafī II.

The reign of Shah Ṣafī II (Solaymān I; 1077-1105/1666-94). One result of de Lairesse's mission was renewed confirmation of the commercial privileges granted to the V.O.C. (Coolhaas, III, pp. 571-72, 598). Other Dutch travelers also visited Persia in this period, but little information is available on

Table 40

AVERAGE ANNUAL V.O.C. PROFITS IN THE PERSIAN TRADE, 1700-54
(in Dfl.)

1700-09	402,859
1710-19	363,728
1720-29	185,856
1730-39	72,587
1740-49	73,912
1750-54	137,131

Source: Floor, 1992.

what they observed ... was shipwrecked ... (1082/1671), left ... which was trans... printed more ti... warranted (Fl... student of C... (1076-81/166... of the V.O.C., but ... been preserved. ... mented on his vast kno... which many of them drew ... works. Jean Chardin (q.v.), for e... his collaboration on the description ... pp. 287-89). Engelbert Kaempfer praise... ing and reported on their joint outings to collect plants and other information (Meier-Lemgo, pp. 112, 122; cf. Thévenot, II, p. 104).

Although the V.O.C. generally did very well in Persia in this period, it did have difficulties with the governor of Bandar-e ʿAbbās, who sought "arrears" in rent for the Dutch-owned station there, and with the grand vizier Šayḵ-ʿAlī Khan (Lockhart, pp. 366-67; Chardin, IX, pp. 71-72). In 1089/1678 the firm threatened armed action against the governor and abandonment of its trading activities in Persia. A protest at court resulted in orders to the governor to cease interference with Dutch trade or traders. Nevertheless, the grand vizier, in response to a deteriorating Persian economy, forced the Dutch to accept more silk than previously, and the next year the government demanded payment of road tolls. In 1091/1680 the V.O.C., engaged in military action elsewhere in Asia, instructed its staff to ask for deliveries of only 150 cargas of Persian silk; the grand vizier refused to comply and sent the usual quantity to the Dutch factory, where it was turned away. He then seized payment by force, and the Dutch agent was beaten. The V.O.C. finally decided on war; in 1096/1685 a fleet of five ships blockaded Bandar-e ʿAbbās, seized Persian vessels, and took Qešm island. A delegation that included de Jager was unable to reach an agreement with the shah (van Dam, p. 318; Valentijn, p. 249; Coolhaas, IV, pp. 299-300, 358-63, 582-83, 740-43, 826-27).

The generally tense atmosphere was temporarily relieved by the arrival in 1102/1691 of Johan van Leene as ambassador. He reached an agreement with Ṣafī II, who again granted tax-free trading privileges for maximum annual imports and exports of 20,000 tomans each and exemption from road duties. Persian officials were not to open Dutch trade goods, and in exchange the Dutch were to buy annually 300 cargas of silk from the shah at 44 tomans each. The next year the Heeren XVII gave instructions that all V.O.C. transactions were to take place at Bandar-e ʿAbbās and that goods were no longer to be transported to Isfahan (van Dam, pp. 319-21; Valentijn, pp. 250-70). The Isfahan office remained open, however, in order to maintain good relations with the court and to purchase silk and specie to be forwarded to Bandar ʿAbbās. The history of other trading stations on the Persian Gulf in this period was also somewhat checkered (Floor, 1985).

Toward the end of the 17th century V.O.C. profits began to diminish as a result of the general economic decline in Persia. Interest in Persian studies was also waning in the Netherlands, though scholars trained by Golius, George Gente and Daniel Havart, did publish Dutch translations of Saʿdī's *Būstān* (q.v.) in 1688 and his *Golestān* in 1694.

The reign of Shah Solṭān-Ḥosayn (1105-35/1694-1722). After his accession to the throne Shah Solṭān-Ḥosayn confirmed Dutch privileges in Persia, but in 1108/1696, when he was unable to sell silk to the V.O.C., his government proposed abolishing the obligatory delivery of silk and receiving from the V.O.C. an annual fixed volume of goods instead. The company declined, and in 1113/1701 Ambassador Jacobus Hoogkamer negotiated a new agreement, which did not differ in essentials from earlier ones. In exchange for taking 100 cargas of silk at 44 tomans each and supplying a certain quantity of "treaty goods," the V.O.C. was entitled to tax-free trade of 20,000 tomans a year (Valentijn, pp. 270-86; Floor, 1978b, ch. 1). Trade remained reasonably profitable for the Dutch, though between 1107/1696 and 1126/1714 silk was delivered to the V.O.C. only three times and after 1126/1714 it ceased to figure among Dutch exports (Steensgaard, pp. 391-96; van Dam; Floor, 1978b).

In 1124/1712 an internal conflict on the V.O.C. staff led to the departure of the Isfahan agent, Pieter Macare. He asked the shah for protection, in return for which he lent him 14,000 tomans of the company's funds (Dfl. 595,000), which were never repaid. He also gave the Persian government access to the V.O.C. factory and books, which led to a demand that the company pay taxes on goods that it had traded above the specified tax-free amount. The Dutch demanded that both Macare and the books be handed over to them and continued to maintain that they were not liable for taxation. The shah did send Macare to Batavia, in the company of Mīrzā Jaʿfar; they arrived in the spring of 1127/1715. Johan Josua Ketelaar arrived at Bandar-e ʿAbbās in June 1716 and quickly reached an agreement with the Persian court; the new treaty was essentially the same as that of 1113/1701, except that the V.O.C. had to permit inspection of its goods and pay duty on the export of specie. The directors were not pleased (Floor, 1978b, pp. 58-60), but Ketelaar was not to blame for these relatively unfavorable terms, which in fact reflected an increasingly unstable political situation in Persia. The decline in V.O.C. profits continued. After the fall of the vizier Fatḥ-ʿAlī Dāḡestānī (q.v.) in December 1720 the new government once again raised issues that were supposed to have been resolved by the Ketelaar mission. Nevertheless, in late September 1722 the V.O.C. lent 17,000 tomans to Shah Solṭān-Ḥosayn.

Cultural contacts also declined in this period. The only Dutch painter known to have been in Persia after 1076/1666 was Cornelis de Bruin (q.v.), who was in Isfahan in 1114/1702 and left an important travel account, enriched with many engravings of notables, ordinary people, plants, buildings, and the like. Furthermore, in the Netherlands there was only one important contemporary Dutch scholar of the Persian language, Adriaan Reland of the University of Utrecht, who used his knowledge of such literary works as the poems of Neẓāmī Ganjavī as the basis for a study of Islam (*De Religione Mohammedica*, Utrecht, 1717) that was less biased than had previously been customary and was frequently translated into other European languages. Reland also urged the study of Persian to improve understanding of ancient history.

The Afghan interval (1135-42/1722-30). Before the disagreements between Solṭān-Ḥosayn's administration and the V.O.C. could became more serious the Safavid state was effectively brought to an end by the invasion of Maḥmūd Afḡān, who took Isfahan in October 1722 (Lockhart, pp. 93 ff.). The Dutch, who were kept virtual prisoners in their factory, left a vivid diary of the siege, the most complete available account of those crucial days (for a Persian translation, see Floor, 1365 Š./1986, ch. 5). Having already suffered the loss of the money it had lent to Solṭān-Ḥosayn, the company then lost a further 6,000 tomans worth of "gifts" and property when the Afghans searched the Isfahan trading station and wreaked severe damage on the factory itself; in 1139/1727 it had to be abandoned altogether because the inner city was to be reserved for Afghans only. The Dutch staff moved to Jolfā. Bandar-e ʿAbbās was not occupied by the Afghans until that year; the Dutch residents there had a military garrison and an escape route by sea.

Total V.O.C. profits from the Persian trade dropped steeply during this period. In 1141/1729 the Dutch attempted to move their factory from Bandar-e ʿAbbās to the island of Hormuz, which led to the death of the agent and his deputy and open warfare between the Dutch and the Afghan garrison on the island. Nevertheless, after consolidating their power the Afghan rulers tried to induce the Dutch to resume commercial activities; Ašraf (see AŠRAF ḠILZAY), Maḥmūd's successor, even granted the V.O.C. trading privileges. But Afghan rule was insecure, the population of Persia impoverished, and prospects for trade non-existent. Furthermore, after the Safavid victory over Ašraf the Afghan troops fled the country (Floor, 1365 Š./1986; idem, 1367 Š./1988; Dunlop, 1912, pp. 258-60).

The reign of Shah Ṭahmāsb II (1135-45/1722-32). Under Shah Ṭahmāsb II the Dutch at first fared well, as he appreciated the support they had given to his father, Solṭān-Ḥosayn, and hoped to receive similar assistance. His general Nāder Shah Afšār (see

AFSHARIDS) made increasing demands for money and naval assistance, however. In 1143/1730 he demanded Dutch naval support in operations against Masqat and later against the Hūwala Arabs of the Persian Gulf coast; it was given but not without protest. In the same year the firm's total claim on Persia amounted to Dfl. 1,721,060, an enormous sum (Floor, 1365 Š./1986, pp. 223-25, 237; Dunlop, 1912, p. 258); furthermore, increased expenditures for security and a vastly reduced volume of trade meant that thenceforth the V.O.C. actually lost money in the Persian trade.

The Afsharids (1148-1210/1736-95). Once Nāder Shah had proclaimed himself shah, the Dutch refused to sell him ships to build his own navy. In 1150/1738 the company opened a new trading station in Būšehr (q.v.); six years later it closed the one in Kermān, though continuing to buy wool there. In 1160/1747 the V.O.C. discontinued trading activities in Isfahan. When Nāder Shah was assassinated later that year the Dutch—and most Persians—were greatly relieved (Floor, 1983c; idem, 1987). Although Nāder Shah's nephew Ebrāhīm Shah (1161/1748) offered them the same privileges that they had enjoyed under his uncle, the Dutch refused to side with any of the Afsharid contenders for the throne. This entire period had in fact been disastrous for V.O.C. trade in Persia. Not only had the purchasing power of the population been greatly reduced, but also Nāder Shah had increased the cost of maintaining a presence in the country through his continual demands for presents, loans, and ships. After his death there was a commercial upsurge, but it was only temporary.

The Zands (1163-1209/1750-94). In February 1752, when ʿAlī-Mardān Khan Baḵtīārī invaded Lārestān, the V.O.C. agent at Bandar-e ʿAbbās abandoned the station there to two caretakers. The Dutch opened a new factory on Ḵārg island, in order to escape the extortions of mainland rulers. The Baron Tido von Kniphausen, formerly V.O.C. agent in Baṣra, built the Mosselsteyn fortress on the island and proceeded to blockade the Šaṭṭ-al-ʿArab, in order to recover money extorted from him and the firm. He was successful and began to build relations with the local shaikhs of Rīg, Būšehr, Lenga, Kuwait, and the Banū Kaʿb, but open conflict resulted when Mīr Mohannā Zaʿābī of Bandar-e Rīg, in retreat from Karīm Khan Zand (1163-93/1750-79), sought to reclaim Ḵārg island, his natural refuge. A year later the V.O.C. closed the station at Būšehr. Finally, as the Persian trade had become a losing proposition, in 1171/1758 the company decided to abandon it entirely, closing down the station at Bandar-e ʿAbbās (Floor, 1989a); a year later it ceased to buy wool in Kermān (Floor, 1978b, ch. 5; idem, forthcoming, chap. 5).

Eventually, in 1179/1766, despite the presence of two ships in the roadstead, the Dutch were forced to surrender the fortress and the goods stored on Ḵārg island. Although William Eaton, the Dutch consul in Baṣra, tried to persuade the V.O.C. to resume trading activities in the Persian Gulf, the firm declined (Floor, 1979a; idem, 1992; Perry). Only in 1185/1771 did it began voyages to Masqat, primarily to sell sugar; these voyages continued on a fairly regular basis until the end of the 18th century, but there was no further direct connection with Persia (Floor, 1982a; idem, 1982b).

Throughout the 18th century Dutch power had been declining in Europe, which was reflected in the Dutch position in Persia and the Persian Gulf. There are no reports of Dutch artists or craftsmen active in Persia in the later 18th century, apart from those who were employed by the V.O.C.

In the Qajar period (1193-1342/1779-1924). It was not until the reign of Fatḥ-ʿAlī Shah (1212-50/1797-1834) that trade relations between the Netherlands and Persia were resumed on a fairly regular basis; in 1239/1824 the government of the Dutch East Indies sent the *Baron van der Capellen*, under the command of one M. Cantor, to Bandar-e ʿAbbās with a typical 18th-century cargo: sugar, tin, copper, spices, steel, nails, iron, and sappanwood, a total value of Dfl. 125,000. At Bandar-e ʿAbbās Cantor was able to sell his goods and load horses, rose water, gallnuts, opium, and especially specie, which accounted for two-thirds of the value of the cargo on the return trip. The profits were reasonable enough to encourage the Nederlandse Handels Maatschappij (N.H.M., or Dutch Trading Company), which had no connecetion with the V.O.C., to finance four other voyages of a single ship each between 1828 and 1831. There already existed an informal trade between Java and Persia, carried on by Armenian merchants living in Java; Cantor had letters of introduction from an Armenian merchant in Batavia to Messrs. Arakil and Arathun, an Armenian firm in Būšehr (den Tex, pp. 23-27). But, as security on the Persian Gulf coast was uncertain and the shaikh at Būšehr somewhat arbitrary in business matters, the N.H.M. eventually decided to discontinue trade in Persia.

That the Dutch had no agent representing their interests on the spot was a disadvantage. In 1273/1857 a commercial treaty was signed in Paris by ambassadors from Nāṣer-al-Dīn Shah (1264-1313/1848-96) and Willem III (text in Dunlop, 1912, pp. 575-79; cf. Floor, 1367 Š./1988), but the Dutch parliament never ratified it. Various private Dutch merchants continued to trade with Persia, sending mainly sugar from Java and bringing back wheat, dried fruit, and dates. The value of this trade increased from Dfl. 300,000 in 1855 to Dfl. 1,690,000 in 1865, when 100,000 picols (1 picol: 125 lb.; den Tex, pp. 28-31) of sugar were traded; imports from Persia in the same years totaled Dfl. 100,000 and 200,000 respectively. After repeated requests for appointment of a consul in Persia to protect the budding Dutch (East Indies) trade the government of the Netherlands invited J. L. Schlimmer, a Dutch physician in Persian service during the 1860s and 1870s, to become honorary consul-general in Tehran. He declined, however, on grounds that he lacked the necessary means to maintain such a prominent position.

In 1866 exports from Java to Persia began gradually to decline in volume, and the composition of the cargoes changed. Whereas initially spices, coffee, timber, tea, and textiles had been exported in addition to sugar, the trade had shifted almost exclusively to sugar. Richard Keun was appointed consul at Būšehr in 1285/1868. His family was part of the old Dutch community in Smyrna (Izmir, Turkey), and he was familiar with the Middle East, its culture, and its languages. He built a large house named Holandarābād outside Būšehr (Plate XLIX). An ambitious man, eager to increase his small capital, Keun attempted to promote Dutch trade and his own share in it in various ways, including establishment of Perzische Handels Vereeniging (P.H.V.). His efforts sometimes led to conflict with the British political resident in Būšehr and with local merchants, who accused him of misusing his diplomatic position for his own gain (B 149, various letters between 1871 and 1875). The Russian legation, which oversaw Dutch interests in Tehran, had to intervene on his behalf. In 1872 the Dutch government therefore again invited Schlimmer to accept the post of consul-general; he again refused but did agree to act as commercial agent. He was officially appointed in February 1873, and from that time on Keun was supposed to address all requests to the Persian government through him, but, despite official reprimands, he did not do so (B 149, memo to M, 19.10.75). Schlimmer died in March 1876 (B 149, Keun to Willebois, 20.7.76), two years after publishing *Terminologie médico-pharmaceutique* (Tehran, 1874; repr. Tehran, 1970), still a treasure trove for historians.

In 1296/1879 Keun himself was given the title consul-general and was able to obtain Persian agreement to a new commercial treaty granting the right of entrepôt to the Netherlands; it had been denied to Russia and Great Britain. The Dutch parliament was not really interested in the treaty, however, and the text also posed "legal" problems (Floor, 1367 Š./1988). In 1883 Mīrzā Jawād Khan, Persian minister in Belgium, was also accredited to the Netherlands.

Nevertheless, the overall drop in Dutch East Indian exports to Persia was dramatic: from Dfl. 1,440,000 in 1866 to Dfl. 160,000 in 1884. After that no ships sailed from Java for the Persian Gulf, and Persia no longer figured in the trade statistics of the Dutch East Indies. Exports from Persia to Java, which had reached about Dfl. 200,000 a year, also declined and were discontinued at about the same time as imports. These changes primarily reflected

PLATE XLIX

Holandarābād, near Būšehr, ca. 1875. Photograph Algemeen Rijks Archief, the Hague, Legatie Perzie.

the opening of the Suez canal, for Java sugar could no longer compete with sugar from the West Indies. Nevertheless, some people believed that sugar and tea from Java could be profitably marketed in Persia if a direct steamboat line were to link them via Bombay (Hotz, 1896, pp. 725-26, 739).

In 1306/1889 Nāṣer-al-Dīn Shah and in 1318/1900 Moẓaffar-al-Din Shah visited the Netherlands on their way to England, but these visits attracted little attention in either Dutch or Persian sources (Schweiger; Eʿtemād al-Salṭana, *Rūz-nāma-ye ḵāṭerāt*, pp. 648-49; Hotz, 1904, p. 676 n. 2). The generally low-key nature of Dutch-Persian relations was also reflected in the workload of the Dutch representative in Persia in the period 1309-31/1892-1913 (Gast; Hotz, 1904). In fact, in the Netherlands it was generally believed that no consul in Persia was necessary, but pressure from commercial interest groups in both the Netherlands (Hotz, 1904, pp. 675-76) and the Dutch East Indies led to the appointment in 1307/1890 of F. N. Knobel as "consul-general"; he served until 1314/1896. Knobel lived in Tehran and, in contrast to other European representatives, was accredited to the Persian court, rather than to the ministry of foreign affairs. He was succeeded by F. W. Bosschart, then served another term himself, and was succeeded again by J. E. de Sturler. It was owing to Knobel's efforts that the Dutch printing firm J. Enschede & Zoon won a contract to print Persian postage stamps. In 1310/1893 he was also instrumental in establishing the Tehran Toko, a Dutch department store created with the financial participation of many leading Persians, including Amīn-al-Solṭān (q.v.). Other Dutch commercial activities were generated by J. C. P. Hotz & Zoon, an import-export firm that had been established in 1874, at Keun's suggestion. It had agents in Isfahan, Shiraz, Solṭānābād, Yazd, Būšehr, and Iraq and was engaged particularly in the carpet trade. A. Hotz undertook many projects to develop the wealth of Persia. He was the first to drill for oil (near Dālakī) and had interests in the development of coal mines, the Imperial Bank of Persia, the carpet industry, and the potential of the Kārūn river, proposed in 1324/1906 by a Dutch engineer, D. L. Graadt van Roggen; unfortunately, the last project came to nothing, owing to British opposition (Dunlop, 1912, pp. 551-64). In 1321/1903 the Hotz firm went bankrupt, largely owing to the dishonesty of a Persian business partner (Floor, 1983a); in the same year the Tehran Toko also went bankrupt, as a result of poor management (Hotz, 1904, p. 677).

Indirect trade between Java and Persia continued through Calcutta and Bombay, involving mostly sugar and tea (Hotz, 1904, pp. 812-13), but the Dutch share in total Persian foreign imports was only 0.75 percent (2.1 million krans) in 1320/1902. The Dutch representative in Persia became discouraged, but others perceived a challenge to do better (Hotz, 1904). Although Dutch trade did not become much more important than before, some Dutchmen were able to market their goods in Persia or to do business there. P. P. ter Meulen, for example, established a thriving import-export business in Ahvāz in 1318 Š./1900 (Hotz, 1906, p. 376). In Tehran two Dutch general stores, Joost Vos and de Pater, were opened to serve the well-to-do (Kuss, IV, pp. 28, 32). Many Dutch insurance firms were also interested in the Persian market (see records in the municipal archives in Amsterdam).

Although there is only one 19th-century Dutch travel account of Persia, by T. M. Lycklama à Nyeholt, a rich though somewhat shady character who wanted to ingratiate himself in Dutch society, Persian studies became more popular in the Netherlands as a result of growing interest in comparative Indo-European liguistics. The many editions of manuscripts published by R. P. A. Dozy and M. J. de Goeje (qq.v.), especially those of geographical texts from the Islamic period, also stimulated Persian studies. In the 1880s M. T. Houtsma was appointed reader of Persian and Turkish at Leiden University; he was interested in medieval Persian history and published Bondarī's history of the Saljuqs (q.v. Suppl.; Houtsma, *Recueil*). Furthermore, Hotz and his collaborator Henryk Dunlop were active not only as businessmen but also in trying to stir greater Dutch interest in Persia. To that end Dunlop wrote a history of the country and edited the V.O.C. records for the years 1623-38. Hotz edited historical texts (e.g., the report of the 1651 embassy) and promoted trade with Persia in many publications. His characterization of the Persians was sympathetic, showing none of the usual superior European attitude (Hotz, 1906, p. 364). It is therefore not surprising to find both men mentioned positively by contemporary Persians (Forṣat, p. 539, Sadīd-al-Salṭana, pp. 620-29). Hotz bequeathed many artifacts that he had collected during his travels in Persia to the anthropological museums of Amsterdam, Leiden, and Rotterdam; they include a collection of photographs taken by him in the 1870s-90s.

Maurits Wagenvoort wrote an account of his journey to Persia in 1324-25/1906-07 (1926), as well as two other works on the Babis (q.v.). In 1327/1909 the post of consul-general was upgraded to envoy extraordinary and minister plenipotentiary, and W. J. Oudendijk arrived to take it up in January 1910; he remained until 1331/1913 (Gast, p. 2). In 1328/1910 the Dutch were asked to organize, train, and provide officers for the urban police and the gendarmerie in Persia, but they declined to do so, and the Swedes took on the task instead. In the same year a third consulate was established, at Ahvāz, supplementing those at Tehran and Būšehr. The first Persian ambassador to live in the Netherlands was Mīrzā Ṣamad Khan, who arrived in 1902. From 1331/1913 until 1338/1920, however, Italy represented Dutch interests in Persia; they were then taken over by the United States.

In the Pahlavi period (1304-57 Š./1925-79). The abolition of the Persian capitulations (q.v.) in 1305 Š./1927 included abrogation of the Dutch-Persian treaty of 1274/1857. In response to urging by the Persian government, the Netherlands appointed a special envoy to assess the need and desirability for permanent representation in Persia. The recommendation was favorable, and a new treaty was signed in 1309 Š./1930. The Dutch have been officially represented in Persia ever since. The two countries were unable to agree on a commercial treaty, however, owing to differences over consular regulations. In 1313 Š./1935 the Dutch chief of mission in Persia, designated successively consul-general, minister-resident, chargé d'affaires, and ambassador, was given jurisdiction over all Dutch consuls in Persia (Gast, p. 2). He dealt mainly with sugar imports from the Dutch East Indies and the export of Persian opium to the latter; the Persian government insisted on a fixed ratio between these two commodities. Trade continued between the Netherlands and Persia throughout the Pahlavi period. Persia exported mainly opium, dried fruit, and textiles, whereas the Netherlands exported agricultural and industrial products to Persia. The pioneering KLM airline route from Amsterdam to Batavia passed through Iraq and Persia, where the government was not always cooperative. There were also Persian requests for experts on tea cultivation (see ČAY) and other agricultural matters, mineral prospecting, and harbor construction. In the 1940s Dutch representation was merely formal because the Netherlands was occupied by the Germans and most of its colonies by the Japanese (Gast, pp. 2-3). The Dutch embassy regained some importance, however, when Royal Dutch Shell assumed the role of coordinator within the international oil consortium between 1332 Š./1953 and 1352 Š./1973. In fact, its officials focused on the growing commercial relations between the two countries and also concluded a cultural treaty in 1338 Š./1959. In the 1960s the trade balance shifted in favor of Persia, which began to export large quantities of oil to the Netherlands. Dried fruit and textiles also continued to be traded. The Netherlands exported mainly agricultural, industrial, and chemical goods to Persia.

In 1301 Š./1922 J. H. Kramers became reader of Persian and Turkish at Leiden University and later professor of Arabic. His main interest was in the Arab geographers, rather than in Persia, but his successor, Karl Jahn, specialized in Persian historiography. He published and translated many parts of the *Jāmeʿ al-tawārīḵ* of Rašīd al-Dīn (de Bruijn).

The Islamic Republic of Persia (1358 Š.-/1979-). At present (1995) the Netherlands has an embassy in Tehran, and Persia has one in the Hague. Trade between the two countries has increased, owing to Dutch refusal to participate in economic sanctions against Persia after the Revolution of 1358 Š./1979. The balance of trade continues in Persia's favor. In 1365 Š./1986 it exported $500 million worth of goods, mainly crude oil, to the Netherlands, which in turn exported $300 million of agricultural goods, chemicals, machinery, and raw materials, in almost equal proportions, to Persia. Persian studies are still included in the curricula of the universities of Leiden, Utrecht, and Nijmegen (de Bruijn; de Groot and Peters).

Bibliography: (For cited works not found in this bibliography and abbreviations found here, see "Short References.") A. C. H. Alexandrowicz, "A Persian-Dutch Treaty in the Seventeenth Century," in *The India Yearbook of International Affairs* VII, Madras, 1958, pp. 201-16. J. T. P. de Bruijn, "Iranian Studies in the Netherlands," *Iranian Studies* 20, 1988, pp. 161-78. E. Castellus, *Lexicon Heptagloton . . . et Persicum Separatim*, London, 1669. *A Chronicle of the Carmelites in Persia and the Papal Mission of the XVIIth and XVIIIth Centuries*, 2 vols., London, 1939. W. P. Coolhaas, ed., *Generale Missieven der Vereenigde Oostindische Compagnie*, 7 vols., the Hague, 1960-78. P. van Dam, *Beschrijvinge van de Oost Indische Compagnie*, ed. F. W. Stapel, Rijks Geschiedkundige Publicatiën 83, the Hague, 1939. H. Dunlop, *Perzie. Voorheen en Thans*, Harlem, 1912. Idem, ed., *Bronnen tot de Geschiedenis der Oost Indische Compagnie in Perzie*, Rijks Geschiedkundige Publicatiën 72, the Hague, 1930.

R. E. Emmerick, "The Beginnings of Iranian Comparative Philology," in R. N. Frye, ed., *Neue Methodologie in der Iranistik*, Wiesbaden, 1974, pp. 49-56. R. W. Ferrier, "The Terms and Conditions under Which English Trade Was Transacted with Ṣafavid Persia," *BSOAS* 49/1, 1986, pp. 48-66. W. M. Floor, *Awwalīn sofarā-ye Īrān wa Holand*, Tehran, 1357 Š./1978a. Idem, *Commercial Conflict between Iran and the Netherlands, 1712-1719*, Durham Occasional Papers 37, Durham, 1978b. Idem, "Description of the Persian Gulf and Its Inhabitants in 1756," *Persica* 8, 1979a, pp. 163-86. Idem, "Dutch Painters in Iran during the First Half of the 17th Century," *Persica* 8, 1979b, pp. 145-61. Idem, "Het Nederlands-Iraanse Conflict van 1645," in *Verslagen en Aanwinsten 1978-79 van de Stichting Cultuurgeschiedenis van de Nederlanders Overzee*, Amsterdam, 1980, pp. 46-51. Idem, "Dutch Trade with Masqaṭ in the Second Half of the Eighteenth Century," *Asian and African Studies* 16, 1982a, pp. 197-213. Idem, "First Contacts between the Netherlands and Masqaṭ, or A Report on the Discovery of the Coast of ʿOman in 1666. Translation and Introduction," *ZDMG* 132, 1982b, pp. 289-307. Idem, "Pearl Fishing in the Persian Gulf in 1757," *Persica* 10, 1982c, pp. 209-22. Idem, "Hotz versus Mohammad Shafiʿ. A Study in Commercial Litigation in Qajar Iran 1888-1894," *IJMES* 15, 1983a, pp. 185-209. Idem, "New Facts on the Holstein Embassy to Iran in 1637," *Der Islam* 60, 1983b, pp. 302-08. Idem,

"The Revolt of Sheikh Ahmad Madani in Larestan and the Garmsirat (1730-1733)," *Stud. Ir.* 12, 1983c, pp. 63-93. Idem, "The Bahrain Project of 1754," *Persica* 11, 1984, pp. 129-48. Idem, "A Description of Masqat and Oman in 1673 AD/1084 Q," *Moyen Orient & Océan Indien* 2, 1985, pp. 1-69. Idem, *Bar-oftādan-e Ṣafawīān wa bar-āmadan-e Maḥmūd Afḡān*, ed. and tr. A. Serrī, Tehran, 1365 Š./1986. Idem, "The Iranian Navy in the Gulf during the Eighteenth Century," *Iranian Studies* 20, 1987, pp. 31-53. Idem, *Ašrāf Afḡān bar taḵtegāh-e Eṣfahān*, ed. and tr. A. Serrī, Tehran, 1367 Š./1988. Idem, "The Decline of the Dutch East Indies Company in Bandar ʿAbbās (1747-1759)," *Moyen Orient & Océan Indien* 6, 1989a, pp. 45-80. Idem, *Ḥokūmat-e Nāder Šāh*, ed. and tr. A. Serrī, Tehran, 1368 Š./1989b. Idem, "The Dutch on Khark—A Commercial Mishap," *IJMES* 24/3, 1992, pp. 441-60. Idem, "The Dutch on Khark Island. The End of an Era. The Baron von Kniphausen's Adventures," in *Européens en Orient au XVIIIe S.*, Moyen Orient & Océan Indien 11, 1994, pp. 157-202. Idem, "Fact or Fiction. The Most Perilous Journeys of Jan Jansz. Struys," in J. Calmard, ed., *Études safavides*, Tehran and Paris, 1995, pp. 57-68. Idem, *The Persian Textile Industry, Its Products and Their Use (1500-1925)*, forthcoming. Moḥammad-Naṣīr Forṣat Šīrāzī, *Āṯār-e ʿajam*, Tehran, 1316/1898.

C. D. Gast, *Inventaris van het Archief van de Nederlandse Legatie te Teheran 1903-1945*, ms. report, Ministerie van Buitenlandse Zaken, the Hague, 1972. H. Gaube and E. Wirth, *Der Bazar von Isfahan*, Wiesbaden, 1978. K. Glamann, *Dutch Asiatic Trade, 1620-1740*, Copenhagen and the Hague, 1958. A. de Groot and R. Peters, *A Bibliography of Dutch Publications on the Middle East and Islam 1945-1981*, Nijmegen, 1981. J. E. Heeres, *Corpus Diplomaticum Neerlando-Indicum. Verzameling van politieke Contracten en verdere Gedragen door de Nederlanders in het Oosten gesloten*, 6 vols., the Hague, 1907. A. Hotz, "Java-Bombay-Perzische Golf. Een nieuwe Stoomvaartlijn," *De Economist* 2, 1896, pp. 723-57. Idem, "Perzië. Medelingen," *Tijdschrift Aardrijkskundig Genootschap* 31, 1897, pp. 713-58. Idem, "Perzie met Betrekking tot Nederland," *De Economist* 2, 1904, pp. 673-700, 801-20. Idem, "Onze Handel met Perzie en de Levant," *De Economist* 24, 1906, pp. 357-82. Idem, *Journaal der Reis van den Gezant der O.I. compagnie, Joan Cunaeus naar Perzie in 1651-52*, Amsterdam, 1908. P. A. Leupe, "Nederlandsche Schilders in Persie en Hindostan in de eerste Helft der 17e Eeuw," *De Nederlandsche Spectator* 33-34, 1873, pp. 260-66. W. Kuss, *Handelsratgeber für Persien*, Berlin, 1911. J. H. van Linschoten, *Navigatio ac Itinerarium Iohannis Hygonis Linscotani . . .*, 2 vols., the Hague, 1599. L. Lockhart, *The Fall of the Safavi Dynasty and the Afghan Occupation*, London, 1956. T. M. Lycklama à Nyeholt, *Voyage en Russie, au Caucase, en Perse, etc. en 1866-68*, 4 vols., Paris and Amsterdam, 1872-75.

M. McCarthy, *All Graduates and Gentlemen. Marsh's Library*, Dublin, 1980. R. Matthee, "The East India Company Trade in Kerman Wool, 1658-1730," in J. Calmard, ed., *Études safavides*, Tehran and Paris, 1995, pp. 343-83. K. Meier-Lemgo, *Die Reisetagebuecher Engelbert Kaempfers*, Wiesbaden, 1968. M.-A. Meilink-Roelofsz, "The Earliest Relations between Persia and the Netherlands," *Persica* 6, 1975, pp. 1-50. C. Niebuhr, *Reisebeschreibung nach Arabien und andern umliegenden Ländern*, Copenhagen, 1774. W. J. Oudendijk, *Ways and By-ways in Diplomacy*, London, 1979. J. Perry, "Mīr Muhannā and the Dutch. Patterns of Piracy in the Persian Gulf," *Stud. Ir.* 2, 1973, pp. 79-95. C. C. Roobacker, *Scheeps Journal Gamron-Basra (1645). De eerste Reis der Nederlanders door de Perzische Golf*, ed. A. Hotz, Leiden, 1907. Moḥammad-ʿAlī Sadīd al-Salṭana Kabābī, *Bandar-e ʿAbbās wa Ḵalīj-e Fārs*, ed. A. Eqtedārī, Tehran, 1342 Š./1963. T. Schweiger, "Een vorstelijke Bezoek uit Perzië in het jaar 1889," *Ons Amsterdam* 11, 1959, pp. 142-47. N. Steensgaard, *Carracks, Caravans and Companies. The Structural Crisis in the European-Asian Trade in the Early 17th Century*, Lund, 1973. J. Struys, *Drie aanmerkelijke en seer rampspoedige Reysen door Moscovien, Tartarijen, Medien, Persien, etc.*, Amsterdam, 1676. N. J. den Tex, "Onze Handel in de Perzische Golf en in de Roode Zee," *De Economist* 1, 1871, pp. 1-41. F. Valentijn, *Oud-en Nieuw Oost-Indiën . . .* V, Dordrecht, 1726. U. Vermeulen, "L'ambassade néerlandaise de Jan Smit en Perse (1628-1630)," *Persica* 7, 1975-78a, pp. 155-62. Idem, "L'ambassade persan de Musa Beg aux Provinces-Unies (1625-1628)," *Persica* 7, 1975-78b, pp. 145-54. Idem, "La mission de Jan L. van Hasselt comme agent du Shah de Perse aux Provinces Unies (1629-1631)," *Persica* 8, 1979, pp. 133-44. M. Vermeulen-Forrier, "De Organisatie van de Handelsbedrijvigheid van de VOC in Perzie, 1623-1638," *Tijdschrift van Geschiedenis* 80, 1967, pp. 472-85. M. Wagenvoort, *Een Karavaanreis door Zuid-Perzie, 1906-07*, Santpoort, the Netherlands, 1926.

(WILLEM FLOOR)

DŪZAḴ (Av. *dužaŋhu*: *Yt.* 19.44, *daožahu-*: *Vd.* 19.47; OIr. **daušaxva-*; Mid. Pers. *dwšḥwʾ*/*došaxw*/ *dušox*; Inscriptional Middle Persian *dwšḥwy*; Man. Mid. Pers. *dwšwx*/*dušox*; Man. Parth. *dwjx*/*dōžax*; Arm. lw. *džox*; lit., "evil existence") "hell" (q.v.).

In the Zoroastrian doctrine of the future life *dūzaḵ* consists of a series of grades, extending to the restoration (*frašegird*), in which the damned are punished for their earthly misdeeds, in order to bring about their spiritual and corporeal purgation and final salvation. Aryan eschatological belief in heaven and hell, already identified in the *Rigveda* (10.14.8) as a paradise on high and a shadowy netherworld respectively (Boyce, *Zoroastrianism*, I, p. 115), was expressed by Zoroaster himself in the Gathas and elaborated in Younger Avestan and Middle Persian texts (see ESCHATOLOGY). In the *Yasna* (46.10-11) the prophet pronounced that "everyone who hearkens to his commandments will cross the bridge of the separator" (*AirWb.*, col. 596; Insler, p. 83) or of the "accumulator" (Kellens) into heaven, a theme elaborated with varying details in Middle Persian texts (see ČINWAD PUHL; DĒN). His opponents the Karapans (pagan priests) and the Kavis will, however, fail to cross the bridge and will become "guests of the house of the deceit/lie"; that is, they will suffer in hell (Insler, p. 83). The prophet also referred to hell as a place where the wicked experience "a long life of darkness, foul food and crying/word of woe" (*Y.* 31.20; cf. Insler, p. 83; Boyce, 1979, p. 279) and as Ačista- Demāna- Manah- "the abode of worst thinking/purpose" (*Y.* 32.13; cf. Insler, p. 49; Boyce, 1984, p. 37; see below). Zoroaster thus preached that the wicked who have adhered to the lie are destined to suffer pain in hell, which, because of its demonic nature, is necessarily a creation of the evil spirit (*Y.* 30.4, 31.1; cf. Insler, p. 33; Boyce, 1984, p. 35).

Among Younger Avestan texts the canonical account of the fate of the soul after death is preserved in the fragmentary Haδōxt Nask. The third chapter is devoted to the fate of the wicked soul. When a sinner dies the soul hovers near the head for three days: "At the end of the third night . . . it is as if the soul of the wicked man were in a wilderness and breathing in stenches." Then from the northerly quarter (i.e., from hell) a foul-smelling wind blows on it. The first step that the soul takes is "evil thought," the second "evil speech," and the third "evil deed" (the first, second, and third forecourts of hell respectively). With the fourth step the wicked soul enters "endless darkness" (i.e., hell proper; Boyce, 1984, pp. 81-82; *Avesta*, tr. Darmesteter, II, pp. 311-12). These four grades later came to be considered by most authorities as the canonical definition of hell.

The future life is treated in other sections of the Avesta, some of which are preserved in Middle Persian epitome in the *Dēnkard* (q.v.; chaps. VIII, IX). In the Pahlavi Sūdgar Nask hell is described as dark, abysmal, obnoxious, foul, close, and frightful (*Dēnkard*, ed. Madan, pp. 808-09; West, 1892, pp. 209-10). The cursory accounts of a few types of punishment for sinners suggest that this *nask* may originally have dealt with the topic in greater detail (*Dēnkard*, ed. Madan, p. 806; West, 1892, p. 205). In the Pahlavi version of the Spand Nask hell is also described as the most abysmal and worst of places, where the wicked are to be punished in accordance with their misdeeds (*Dēnkard*, ed. Madan, pp. 691-92; West, 1892, pp. 32-34).

In the thirty-fourth chapter of the *Bundahišn* there is a vivid account of the resurrection (*ristāxēz*) and the final body, that is, ultimate existence (*tan ī pasēn*). In the 12th millennium of the Zoroastrian world people will gradually lose their appetites, and finally, when they can live without eating, Sōšyans (the savior, a posthumous son of Zoroaster) will be born and, with his helpers, will perform the Yasna and restore the dead. Then all the people of the world will assemble in their natural bodies, presided over by Isadwāstar (the proper name of Sošyans); in a second reckoning the righteous will be separated from the wicked, who will be cast back into hell, in order to experience severe punishment for three days, this time in their material bodies. In the process of restoration the god Ādur and Airyaman (q.v.) will melt the metal contained in rocks and mountains, and it will surge in rivers through the world. All men, regardless of their deserts, will pass through the molten metal and be purified. Then Sōšyans will immolate the bull Hadayans; from its rendered fat mixed with the white Hōm he will prepare ambrosia (*anōš* "[beverage of] immortality"), which all men will swallow, thus becoming immortal. The demons will be seized and destroyed by the Amahraspands (see AMƎŠA SPƎNTA) and Srōš; Ahreman (see AHRIMAN) and the archdemon Āz (q.v.) will be rendered powerless when Ohrmazd celebrates the gathic liturgy and will be driven from the world into the gloomy den from which they had emerged. Finally the molten metal will flow over hell, consuming its stench and impurity; hell will thus be swept clean and restored to the pure world (*Bundahišn*, TD_2, chap. 34, pp. 282-92; Boyce, 1984, pp. 52-53).

In sharp contrast to all other accounts is that of the eminent 9th-century authority Manūščihr, son of Juwān-(Gušn-)Jam (see *DĀDESTĀN Ī DĒNĪG*), who put forward an unorthodox schema of the grades of hell, perhaps derived from the teaching of his eminent forefathers. In his version the souls of the wicked, upon departing the bodies, remain in one of three internal stages (*wimand*), in accordance with the degree of their misdeeds. Those whose evil deeds outweigh their good deeds dwell in the *hammistagān* of the wicked, also called "mixture" (*gumēzag*; cf. Av. *misvan gātu* "the place of the mixed"; *Vd.* 19.36); it is a frightful place, dark, foul, and grievous with pain. The second stage, "the worst existence" (*waddom axwān*, synonymous with *dōšaxw*/*dušox*), is the abode of dreadful demons; there all is punishment without comfort. The last stage is *drujasgān* (Av. *drujaskanā-* "abode of the *druj*es"; *Vd.* 19.41), the infernal abyss, the abode of the archdemon (*dēwān kamālīg*); it is the home of all gloom and evil. Collectively these three stages of the underworld constitute *dušox* "hell," which is north, downward, underneath the earth, extending to the utmost declivity of the sky. Its gate is in the northern Arezūr ridge, on the peak of which the assembly of all demons is held (*Dādistān ī dēnīg*, chap. 32, pp. 65-68; West, 1880, pp. 74-75). Manūščihr, moreover, also described another *hammistagān* for the righteous, for souls whose meritorious deeds outweigh their sins but who are not good enough to enter directly into heaven (*Dādistān ī dēnīg*, chap. 24; West, 1880, p. 55). This singular conception of two *hammistagān*s contradicts all other authoritative teachings. In fact the word *hammistagān* is derived from Avestan *hammiias-* "to be mixed in equal proportions" (*AirWb.*, col. 1190). It is said to be "the final (judgment) for those whose falsity and honesty are balanced" (*Y.* 33.1). In *Mēnōg ī xrad* (chap. 6.18) *hammistagān* is a place between hell and heaven, extending from the earth up to the station of the fixed stars, the abode of those whose sins and good works are equal and who thus experience no suffering other than heat and cold. Unlike the purgatory of other revealed religions, the Mazdean *hammistagān* is not a preparatory stage for entering heaven.

The last house of hell is described in the *Mēnōg ī xrad* (chap. 7.27-31) as partly cold as the coldest ice and partly scorching hot, with wild rapacious animals and a foul stench; its darkness is so dense that it can be seized by hand. In the *Ardā Wirāz-nāmag*, a visionary revelation of the joys of heaven and retributions for misdeeds in the netherworld, the last stage of hell, situated beneath the *činwad* bridge, is depicted as a place far more frightful than the previous stations. It is a narrow pit, an abyss "to the bottom of which thousands of cries could not reach, as narrow as the distance between the ear and the eye, packed with the souls of sinners like hairs on the mane of a horse; no one sees the other, everyone feels lonely . . . extremely cold and fiery hot" (chap. 54.2-5).

The supposed immutability of the Mazdean principle of justice requires that even in hell punishment should fit the crime. The enforcement of this discipline is entrusted to the Amahraspand Ardwahišt (q.v.), who supervises and restrains the demons from punishing the damned more than is fitting (*Bundahišn*, TD_2, chap. 26.35). According to the Pahlavi version of the Spand Nask, the punishment of the wicked in hell should be commensurate with their misdeeds (Dēnk*ard*, ed. Madan, p. 691; West, 1892, pp. 32-34). Similarly, in the Pahlavi version of the Sūdgar Nask it is enjoined that punishment (in the netherworld) should be meted out in accordance with the canon of the faith (*Dēnkard*, ed. Madan, p. 505; West, 1892, p. 204).

For the Islamic period, see HELL.

Bibliography: (For cited works not found in this bibliography and abbreviations found here, see "Short References"). M. Boyce, *Zoroastrians. Their Religious Beliefs and Practices*, London, 1979. Idem, ed. and tr., *Textual Sources for the Study of Zoroastrianism*, Manchester, 1984; repr. Chicago, 1990. *Dokumenty s gory Mug* (Documents from Mt. Mūḡ), Moscow, 1963. P. Gignoux, ed. and tr., *Le livre d'Ardā Vīrāz*, Éditions Recherche sur les Civilisations 14, Paris, 1984. S. Insler, ed. and tr., *The Gathas of Zarathustra*, Acta Iranica 8, Leiden, 1975. J. Kellens, "Yima et la mort," in *Languages and Cultures. Studies in Honor of Edgar C. Polomé*, Berlin, 1988, pp. 329-34. D. P. Sanjana, ed. and tr., *The Dînâ î Maînû î Khrad. Dādestān ī Mēnōg ī Xrad*, Bombay, 1895. E. W. West, tr., *Dâdistân-î Dînîk*, SBE XVIII, Oxford, 1880. Idem, tr., *Dēnkard* IV. *Contents of the Nasks*, SBE XXXVII, Oxford, 1892; repr. Delhi, 1969, pp. 209-10R. R. C. Zaehner, *The Teachings of the Magi*, London, 1956, pp. 131-50.

(MANSOUR SHAKI)

DUŽYĀIRYA (Av.; OPers. *dušiyāra*; *AirWb.*, col. 759; Kent, *Old Persian*, p. 192), a compound (Duchesne-Guillemin, 1936, pp. 145, 192) meaning basically "bad year" or "bad harvest," attested only in *Tištar Yašt* (*Yt.* 8), a hymn dedicated to the star Sirius (Tištriia) that incorporates the myth of the liberation of the waters. The compound occurs both as a neuter noun (8.36) and as a feminine adjective (here bahuvrihi, lit., "whose year is bad") applied to a *pairikā* "witch" (8.51, 8.54-55) and is conceived as the antithesis to *huiiāiriia-* "good year" (Duchesne-Guillemin, 1936, p. 189). This opposition is explicit in *Yašt* 8.36 and 8.51: After a description of the battle between Tištriia and the demon Apaoša there is an account of the astral combat between the fixed stars, guided by Sirius, and the shooting stars (*pairikā* or *stārō kərəmå*) led by Pairikā Dužiiāiriiā, sent by Aŋra Mainyu (see AHRIMAN) to overthrow the cosmic order and bring drought (Panaino, 1986b). The opposition is further confirmed by the expression *yā dužiiāiriia yąm maṣ̌iiāka auui dužuuacaŋhō huiiāiriiąm nąma aojaite* "the bad-year witch, whom, contrarily, evil-speaking men call by the name good-year." This formula, which has also been interpreted differently (Benveniste, 1938; Panaino, 1986a; idem, 1990b, pp. 139, 141), must nevertheless imply an apotropaic usage in which the witch of the bad year is referred to as "that of the good year" (cf. Christensen, pp. 14-15). According to *Yašt* 8.54-55, the earthly havoc wreaked by the Pairikā Dužiiāiriiā would have been substantial if Tištriia had not defeated her (on "the linking god" and the symbolism of the nodes in this episode, see Éliade, p. 18).

In the inscription DPd (13-24) three calamities are mentioned: *hāinā-* (a hostile army), *dušiyāra-*, and *drauga-* (a lie), in order to avoid which Darius invokes Ahura Mazdā (qq.v.). In *Yašt*s 8.56-61 and 14.48-53 the god is invoked to prevent his Aryan countries from being stricken by any of the following calamities (Panaino, 1987; 1991): *hāena* "hostile forces," *vōiγna* "famine," *pąma* "leprosy," *kapastiš* "plague," *haēniiō raθō*, "enemy chariot," and *uzgərəptō drafšō* "the banner (of war) fluttering on high" (cf. *Yt.* 8.54-56). This type of formula, which has been explained by Georges Dumézil and Jacques Duchesne-Guillemin (1972, pp. 59-60) as reflecting the tripartite ideology, has been connected by Gherardo Gnoli (pp. 67-68) instead with several supplication formulas characteristic of the Mesopotamian tradition (e.g., in the Assyrian and Mari inscriptions).

As for Middle Persian Manichean *dwšy'ryy* (*Šābuhragān* M477 V14), compared by Duchesne-Guillemin (1936, p. 40) to Old Persian *dušiyāra-*, W. B. Henning (p. 171) preferred the interpretation *dwšw'ryy* "misfortune." Mary Boyce (*Reader*, p. 79 n. to par. 11) accepted, though with doubts, the original reading *dwšy'ryy* (*dušyārī*; cf. Boyce, 1977, p. 37) and translated the passage in question (*'wd dwšy'ryy 'wd nyxrwst cn'nd*) "and they (i.e., surviving humanity) will shake-off famine (?) and reproaches. . . ." D. N. MacKenzie (1979, p. 508 l. 134) also read *dwšy('ryy)* as "famine" (1980, p. 304).

Bibliography: (For cited works not found in this bibliography and abbreviations found here, see "Short References.") E. Benveniste, "Une différenciation de vocabulaire dans l'Avesta," in W. Wüst, ed., *Studia Indo-Iranica. Ehrengabe für Wilhelm Geiger zur Vollendung des 75. Lebensjahres 1856-21. Juli-1931*, Leipzig, 1931, pp. 219-26. Idem, "Traditions indo-iraniennes sur les classes sociales," *JA* 230, 1938, pp. 529-49. M. Boyce, *A Word-List of Manichaean Middle Persian and Parthian*, Acta Iranica 9a, Tehran and Liège, 1977. W. Brandenstein and M. Mayrhofer, *Handbuch des Altpersischen*, Wiesbaden, 1964. A. Christensen, *Essai sur la démonologie iranienne*, Copenhagen, 1941. J. Duschesne-Guillemin, *Études de morphologie iranienne. Les composés de l'Avesta*, Liège and Paris, 1936. Idem, "La religion des Achéménides," in G. Walser, *Beiträge zur Achämenidengeschichte*, Wiesbaden, 1972, pp. 59-82. G. Dumézil, "Les 'trois fonctions' dans le ṚgVeda et les dieux indiens de Mitani," *Bulletin de l'Académie Royale de Belgique*, 5th sér., 47, 1961, pp. 265-98. M. Éliade, "Le 'dieu lieur' et le symbolisme des noeuds," *RHR* 134, 1947-48, pp. 5-36. G. Gnoli, "Politica religiosa e concezione della regalità sotto gli Achemenidi," in *Gururājamañjarikā. Studi in onore di Giuseppe Tucci* I, Naples, 1975, pp. 23-88; tr. as "Politique religieuse et conception de la royauté sous les Achéménides," in *Commémoration Cyrus. Hommage universel* II, Acta Iranica 2, Tehran and Liège, 1974, pp. 117-90. L. H. Gray, "The 'Ahurian' and 'Daevian' Vocabularies in the Avesta," *JRAS*, 1927, pp. 427-41. Idem, *The Foundations of the Iranian Religions*, Bombay, 1929, p. 205. W. B. Henning, "Das Verbum des Mittelpersischen der Turfanfragmente," *ZII*, 1933, pp. 158-253; repr. in W. B. Henning, *Selected Papers* I, Acta Iranica 14, Tehran and Liège, 1977, pp. 65-160. W. Hinz, *Neue Wege im Altpersischen*, Wiesbaden, 1973. D. N. MacKenzie, "Mani's *Šābuhragān*," *BSOAS* 42/3, 1979, pp. 500-34; 43/2, 1980, pp. 288-310. A. Panaino, "Un'espressione avestica per indicare il doppio linguaggio degli adoratori dei daēva," *Atti del Sodalizio Glottologico Milanese* 26, 1986a, pp. 20-24. Idem, "Tištrya e la stagione delle piogge," *ACME, Annali della Facoltà di Lettere e Filosofia dell'Università degli Studi di Milano* 39/1, January-April 1986b, pp. 125-33. Idem, "hāinā-, dušiyāra-, drauga-. Un confronto antico-persiano avestico," *Atti del Sodalizio Glottologico Milanese* 27, 1987, pp. 95-102. Idem, "Sulla supposta dipendenza di *Yašt* VIII da *Yašt* XIV," in G. Gnoli and A. Panaino, eds., *Proceedings of the First European Conference of Iranian Studies* I. *Old and Middle-Iranian Studies*, Rome, 1990a, pp. 239-51. Idem, *Tištrya* I. *The Avestan Hymn to Sirius*, Rome, 1990b. Idem, "Ancora sulle tre calamitá," *Atti del Sodalizio Glottologico Milanese* 32, 1991, pp. 70-83. O. G. von Wesendonk, *Das Weltbild der Iranier*, Munich, 1933, p. 131.

(ANTONIO PANAINO)

DVIN, city in Armenia located at 40° N, 44° 41′ E, north of Artaxata (q.v.) on the left bank of the Azat (Garnīčāī), about 35 km south of the present Armenian capital at Yerevan. It remained a significant center from the Sasanian period to the 13th century, and its pleasant climate was mentioned by many authors (for maps, see Hewsen, 1987; idem, 1988a; idem, 1988b; idem, 1989).

In Old Armenian sources the name of the city is almost always given as Dowin (e.g., Faustus, pp. 29-30; tr. Garsoïan, p. 75; Pʿarpecʿi, p. 292; Sebêos, p. 67). Later authors (e.g., Samuel of Ani; see *Narratio*, p. 141) wrote Dvin, which is the most common form in the scholarly literature. The assertion by Moses of Khorene (3.8) that the name means "hill" in Persian resulted from his misunderstanding of Faustus (3.8). In fact no plausible Iranian etymology can be traced from a supposed **duwīn* (D. N. MacKenzie, personal communication, 1991; cf. Minorsky, 1930, who suggested that the name was borrowed by the Arsacids from the Turkmen steppe, their original homeland). The reading *'dḇyl* for Dvin in *Šahrestānīhā-ī Ērān* (cf. Nyberg, *Manual* II, p. 9) can no longer be accepted (cf. Gignoux, pp. 14-15). Procopius (2.25), Menander (p. 214 frag. 23.11), and Theophanes of Byzantium (apud Photius, p. 78 no. 64) wrote Doubios; other forms of the name that occur in Greek texts are *Tibin (invariable; cf. use in genitive and accusative in *Narratio*, pp. 39, 43), Tibion or Tibios (with genitive Tibiou in Cedrenus, II, pp. 558, 561), Tibi (Constantine Porphyrogenitus, *De Adm. Imp.* 44.4), and Tibēn (*Narratio*, p. 156). In Latin the name appears as Dubios (*Ravennatis Anonymi Cosmographia*, p. 23); in Syriac as *'dbyn* (cf. Thopdschian, p. 71), *dwyn* (Zacharias, 12.7), *d'wyn*, and *dwbyn* (cf. Ghazarian, p. 209); in Arabic as Dabīl (the most frequent form; cf. BGA IV, p. 61, s.v.) and occasionally Dawīn/Duwīn (Ebn Ḥawqal, tr. Kramers, pp. 339, 335). Yāqūt (*Boldān*, II, pp. 548, 632) included both forms under different lemmas, without recognizing that they referred to a single city (for other citations from Arabic sources, see Canard, p. 678).

Excavations by Soviet teams have shown that the beginnings of settlement on the site of Dvin can be traced back to the 3rd, possibly even the 4th millennium B.C.E. (Kafadaryan, 1966). It remains uncertain whether occupation was continuous. The excavations have yielded numerous finds from the Hellenistic period (Kocharyan). The hill at Dvin was, in the opinion of the excavators, enclosed within a defensive wall and inhabited in the time of the Armenian Arsacids (Kafadaryan, 1965, p. 284). Possibly in the first half of the 4th century C.E. (the dating is uncertain; cf. Hewsen, 1978-79) the Armenian king K̲osrow is supposed to have established a hunting park (OPers. *paridaidā*) there (Faustus, 3.8). The often expressed view that K̲osrow had previously shifted the capital from Artaxata to Dvin is based on an unreliable report of Moses of Khorene (9th century), who relied on the much shorter text of Pseudo Faustus.

After the division of Armenia between Rome and Persia in 384 (?) Vałarshapat was in the Persian portion, of which it was the capital; Dvin was also part of the Persian portion. When the Arsacid kingdom was abolished in Armenia in 428 Dvin became the capital (Arm. *ostan*; cf. Hübschmann, p. 460) of Persian Armenia, from which the *marzbān* (Arm. *marzpan*) ruled. The palace and archives (*dīvān*; see ARMENIA AND IRAN ii, p. 432) were located there. The earliest numismatic finds contain the portrait of the Sasanian king Bahrām V (420-38; Mushegyan, 1962, p. 57). According to the so-called *Armenian Geography* of Anania Širakacʿi, the *ostan* of Dvin extended as far as the canton of Ayrarat (q.v.; Hübschmann, pp. 365-66). Probably in the second half of the 5th century (the date is controversial) it was also the seat of the Armenian patriarch (catholicus) and the center of the Armenian church, where a number of synods were convened (e.g., the first in 505 or 506, the second in 552, 554, or 555; at the latter the council of Chalcedon was condemned and the specifically Armenian calendar adopted; other synods were held in 604? 607? 644? and 646?). As capital and economic and industrial center (particularly famed for "purple" carpets, q.v. ii) Dvin became important in trade with Central Asia (cf. Procopius, *De Bello Persico* 2.25.3-4; Arakelyan and Martirosyan, pp. 44-46), which Artaxata had previously dominated. The reputation of the local manufactures was still known to authors of the Islamic period.

Sasanian efforts to impose the Zoroastrian religion in Armenia never ceased. The construction of a fire temple in Dvin led to a revolt in 571-72. The city was thenceforth often involved in the conflict between Byzantines and Sasanians (cf. Sebêos, p. 68). After the the Sasanian K̲osrow II (590-628) ceded the larger portion of Persian Armenia to the Byzantines in 591 Dvin lay directly on the newly established border, though still within Persian territory (cf. *Narratio*, p. 237; cf., on the other hand, Hage, pp. 44-48; Hewsen, 1965, p. 336). In a campaign against the Sasanians the emperor Heraclius captured and destroyed the city in 623 (cf. Manandean, 1950, plan 1). The city was conquered by the Muslims on 17 Šawwāl 19/6 October 640 and subsequently lost much of its importance. It subsequently became the seat (Arm. *ostekan*) of the caliph's governor and remained so until 173/789. In the 9th and 10th centuries it was caught up in the conflicts between the Armenian Bagratids (q.v.) and Arab amirs (for detailed references on the early Islamic period, see Canard); no ruler was able to dominate there for long. Early in the 10th century the residence of the catholicus was moved to Coravankʾ in Vaspurakan. Also in the 10th century the Byzantines reentered the history of Dvin. The city flourished again during the period when the Bagratid king Gagik I (990-1020) was semi-independent in Armenia and able to eliminate the rival amirates. Most of the archeological finds at the site are from the Bagratid period. Dvin remained a bone of contention between Kurdish and Deylamite amirs of Iranian origin; after 1100 the city was briefly ruled by the Turks. A late flowering took place in the time of the Armenian Zakʿarids (after 1200) until the Mongol conquerors again destroyed the city, between 1233 and 1236, thus bringing about its definitive decline. Today there is only a small settlement on the site.

The site of Dvin has been continuously excavated since 1937, except for a period during World War II. The finds have been widely published, though certain conclusions must be treated with reserve, for example, the reconstruction of the temple that S. T. Eremyan believed was founded by Tiridates I (1st century C.E.) to honor his ancestors (p. 49). Also dubious is that of the "great throne hall," which has been identified as part of a palace building from the time of King K̲osrow (330s; Kafadaryan, 1966). Slightly more reliable is the schematic reconstruction of the palace of the Sasanian *marzbān*, possibly of the 5th century (debatable), as well as those of the palaces that were rebuilt after the earthquake of 893. The reconstructions of the palace of the catholicus of the second half of the 5th century, a church with a 6th-century nave (the "martyrium of Yazdbōzēd"; cf. Kafadaryan, 1952, pp. 101-10), and the three-aisled cathedral church with porticoes on three sides of a courtyard, which was dedicated in the mid-5th century to Saint Gregory the Illuminator, deserve special attention. According to the reports of Armenian authors (e.g., Tʿomas Arcʿruni, 2.1), the last was supposed to have been built on the site of a Sasanian fire temple. After it was destroyed in the early 7th century it was rebuilt with fortifications (cf.

Kafadaryan, 1952, pp. 111-22; for drawings, see Khatchatrian, pp. 11-13).

Bibliography: (For cited works not found in this bibliography and abbbreviations found here, see "Short References."). Primary Sources. Georgius Cedrenus, ed. I. Bekker, *Corpus Scriptorum Historiae Byzantinae* 33, II, Bonn, 1838. Eṣṭaḵrī, pp. 191-93. Menander Protector, *The History of Menander the Guardsman*, ed. and tr. R. C. Blockley, Liverpool, 1985. *La Narratio de Rebus Armeniae*, ed. G. Garitte, CSCO 132, Louvain, 1952 (with abundant material). Muqaddasī, p. 377. Łazar P'arpec'i, *Patmut'iwn Hayoc'*, ed. V. Mamikonian, rev. G. Ter-Mkrtchyani and S. Malkhasyanc'i, Yerevan, 1982; tr. R. W. Thomson as *The History of Lazar P'arpec'i*, Atlanta, 1991. Photius, *Bibliotheca*, ed. and tr. R. Henry as *Bibliothèque* I, Paris, 1959. *Ravennatis Anonymi Cosmographia . . .*, ed. J. Schnetz, Itineraria Romana 2, Stuttgart, 1940. Sebêos, *Patmut'iwn i Herakln*, ed. G. V. Abgaryan as *Patmut'iwn Sebêosi* (*History* of Sebêos), Yerevan, 1979; tr. F. Macler as *Histoire d'Héraclius par l'évêque Sebèos*, Paris, 1904. Zacharias Rhetor, *Historia Eccle-siastica* II, ed. F. W. Brooks, CSCO 84, Louvain, 1921; repr. Louvain, 1953.

Modern sources (most works in Armenian include Russian summaries). N. Adontz, *Armenia v epokhy Yustiniana*, tr. N. G. Garsoïan as *Armenia in the Period of Justinian. The Political Conditions Based on the* Naxarar *System*, Lisbon, 1970, esp. p. 435 n. 18. B. A. Arakelyan and A. A. Martirosyan, "Arkheologicheskoe izuchenie Armenii za gody sovetskoĭ vlasti" (Archeological studies of Armenia during the years of Soviet power), *Sovetskaya Arkheologiya*, 1967/4, pp. 26-47. V. M. Arutyunyan, *Arkhitekturnye pamyatniki Dvina V-VII vv. (Po materialam raskopok 1937-1939 gg.)* (Architectural monuments of Dvin in the 6th-7th centuries [According to materials from the excavations of 1937-39]), Arkheologicheskie raskopki v Armenii (Archeological excavations in Armenia) 2, Yerevan, 1950 (in Armenian).

W. Baumgartner, "Dubios," in Pauly-Wissowa, V/2, p. 1751. M. Canard, "Dwin," in *EI*² II, 1965, pp. 678-81. S. T. Eremyan, *Armeniya po "Ashkhartsuĭts" -u (Arm-yanskaya geografiya VII veka)* (Armenia according to Ašxarc'oyc' [Armenian geography of the 7th century]), Yerevan, 1963 (in Armenian). G. Garitte, "Documents pour l'étude du livre d'Agathange," *Studi e Testi* 127, 1946, pp. 210-11. N. G. Garsoïan, "Dwin," in *Dictionary of the Middle Ages* IV, New York, 1984, pp. 323-25. Idem, "The Early-Medieval Armenian City. An Alien Element?" *The Journal of the Ancient Near Eastern Society* 16-17, 1984-85, pp. 67-83; repr. in *Ancient Studies in Memory of Elias Bickerman*, New York, 1987, pp. 67-83. M. Ghazarian, "Armenien unter der arabischen Herrschaft bis zur Entstehung des Bagra-tidenreiches. Nach arabischen und armenischen Quellen bearbeitet, *Zeitschrift für armenische Philologie* 2, 1904, pp. 161-225. P. Gignoux, "L'organisation administrative sasanide. Le cas du *marzbān*," *Jerusalem Studies in Arabic and Islam* 4, 1984, pp. 1-29. R. Grousset, *Histoire de l'Arménie des origines à 1071*, Paris, 1947.

W. Hage, "Armenien," in *Theologische Realenzyklopädie* IV, Berlin, 1979, pp. 40-57. H. Hewsen, "Armenia According to the Ašxarhac'oyc'," *Revue des Études Arméniennes* 2, 1965, pp. 319-42. Idem, "The Sucessors of Tiridates the Great. A Contribution to the History of Armenia in the Fourth Century," *Revue des Études Arméniennes* 13, 1978-79, pp. 99-123. Idem, *Armenia and Georgia. Christianity and Territorial Development from the 4th to the 7th Century*, TAVO B VI/14, Wiesbaden, 1987. Idem, *Armenia and Georgia in the 10th and 11th Century*, TAVO B VII/16, Wiesbaden, 1988a. Idem, *Armenia and Georgia circa 1200*, TAVO B VII/17, Wiesbaden, 1988b. Idem, *Armenia and Georgia. Christianity in the Middle Ages (7th-17th Century)*, TAVO B VIII/4, Wiesbaden, 1989. E. Honigmann, *Die Ostgrenze des byzantinischen Reiches . . .*, Brussels, 1935. H. Hübschmann, "Die altarmenischen Ortsnamen mit Beiträgen zur historischen Topographie Armeniens," *Indogermanische Forschungen* 16, Strassburg, 1904; repr. Amster-dam, 1969, pp. 279, 365-66, 422. Ł. Inčičean, *Storagrut'iwn hin Hayastaneayc'*, Venice, 1822, pp. 462-69. V. Inglisian, "Chalkedon und die armenische Kirche," in A. Grillmeier and H. Bacht, eds., *Das Konzil von Chalkedon* II, Würzburg, 1953, esp. pp. 361-83. K.

G. Kafadaryan, *Gorod Dvin i ego raskopki* (The city of Dvin and its excavations), Yerevan, 1952 (in Armenian); French summary H. Berbérian in *Revue des Études Arméniennes* 2, 1965, pp. 459-60; Russian summary tr. H. Berbérian as "Les fouilles de la ville de Dvin (Duin)," *Revue des Études Arméniennes* 2, 1965, pp. 283-301. Idem, "O vremeni osnovaniya goroda Dvina i o yazycheskom khrame na vyshgorode" (On the period of the foundation of the city of Dvin and on the pagan temple in the upper city), *Patma-banasirakan Handes*, 1966/2, pp. 41-58 (in Armenian). Idem, *Gorod Dvin i ego raskopki* II. *Rezul'taty rabot arkheologicheskoĭ ėkspeditsii AN ArmSSSR 1951-1972 godov* (The city of Dvin and its excavations II. Results of the work of the archeological expedition of the Academy of Sciences, Armenian S.S.R.), Yerevan, 1982 (in Armenian). A. A. Kalantaryan, "Raskopki tsentral'nogo kvartala gor. Dvina (1964-65 gg.)" (Excavations in the central quarter of the city of Dvin [1964-65]), *Patma-banasirakan Handes*, 1967/1, pp. 214-21. Idem, *Material'naya kul'tura Dvina V-VIII vv.* (The material culture of Dvin, 5th-8th centuries), Arkheologicheskie pamyatniki Armenii (Archeological monuments of Armenia) 5/1, Yerevan, 1970 (in Armenian, with

English summary). Idem, *Rannesrednevekovye bully Dvina* (Early medieval bullae from Dvin), Arkheo-logicheskie pamyatniki Armenii (Archeological monuments of Armenia) 15, Yerevan, 1981 (in Armenian). A. Khatchatrian, *L'architecture arménienne du IVe au VIe siècle*, Paris, 1971a, pp. 53-58, 61-65; figs. 67-74. Idem, "Dvin," in *Reallexikon zur byzantinischen Kunst* II, Stuttgart, 1971b, pp. 9-22. G. Kocharyan, "Keramika Dvina ellinisticheskoĭ epokhi" (Ceramics from Dvin in the Hellenistic period), *Lraber*, 1974/5, pp. 82-97 (in Armenian). G. A. Koshelenko, ed., *Arkheologiya SSSR. Drevneĭ gosudarstva Kavkaza i Sredneĭ Azii* (The archeology of the U.S.S.R. The ancient states of the Caucasus and Central Asia), Moscow, 1985. K. Kh. Kushnareva, *Drevneĭshie pamyatniki Dvina* (Ancient monuments of Dvin), Yerevan, 1977. H. A. Manandean (Ya. A. Manandyan), "Les invasions arabes en Arménie (notes chronologiques)," *Byzantion* 18, 1948, pp. 163-95. Idem, "Marshruty persidskikh pokhodov imperatora Irakliya" (The lines of march of the Persian campaign of the emperor Heraclius), *Vizantiĭskiĭ Vremmenik* 3, 1950, pp. 133-53. Idem, *O torgovle i gorodakh Armenii v svyazi s mirovoĭ torgovleĭ drevnikh vremen*, 2nd ed., Yerevan, 1954; tr. N. G. Garsoian as *The Trade and Cities of Armenia in Relation to Ancient World Trade*, Lisbon, 1965. Markwart, *Ērānšahr*, p. 122. Idem, *Südarmenien und die Tigrisquellen nach griechischen und arabischen Geographen*, 1930, esp. pp. 562-70. J. Mécérian, "Histoire et institutions de l'église arménienne," *Recherches de l'Institut de Lettres Orientales de Beyrouth* 30, 1965, pp. 59-115. V. Minorsky, "Le nom de Dvin en Arménie," *Revue des Études Arméniennes* 10, 1930, pp. 117-23; repr. in V. Minorsky, *Iranica. Twenty Articles*, Tehran, 1964, pp. 1-11. Idem, *Studies in Caucasian History*, London, 1953, esp. pp. 104-07, 116-24. Idem, "Transcaucasica. Le nom de Dvin," *JA* 217, 1930, pp. 41-56. Kh. A. Mushegyan (Mušhełyan), *Denezhnoe obrashchenie Dvina po numizmaticheskim dannym* (Monetary circulation at Dvin, according to the numismatic data), Yerevan, 1962; French summary H. Berbérian, *Revue des Études Arméniennes* 2, 1965, pp. 464-68. Idem, "Bilan comparé des découvertes numismatiques à Ani et à Duin," *Revue des Études Arméniennes* 18, 1984, pp. 461-69. H. S. Nyberg, "Die sassanidische Westgrenze und ihre Verteidigung," in *Septentrionalia et Orientalia. Studia Bernhardo Karlgren . . .*, Kungl. Vitterhets Historie och Antikvitets Akademiens Handlingar 91, Stockholm, 1959, pp. 319-26. M. d'Onofrio, *The Churches of Dvin*, Rome, 1973. Idem, "Certains palais résidentiels de l'Arménie du Ve au VIIe siècle après J.-C.," *Reports of the Second International Symposium on Armenian Art* II, Yerevan, 1981, pp. 90-110. J. Sturm, "Persarmenia," in Pauly-Wissowa, XIX/1, pp. 932-38. A. Ter-Ghewondyan, in "*Izvestiya Akad. Nauk Arm. S.S.R. [Tełekagir]*, 1956/12, pp. 81-89; tr. as "Duin (Dvine) sous les Salarides," *Revue des Études Arméniennes*, N.S. 1, 1964, pp. 233-42. Idem, in *Izvestiya Akad. Nauk Armyansk S.S.R. [Tełekagir]*, 1957/10, pp. 85-98; tr. as "Chronologie de la ville de Dvin (Duin) aux 9e et 11e siècles," *Revue des Études Arméniennes*, N.S. 2, 1965, pp. 303-18. Idem, *Arabakan Amir-ayutʿyunneṙe bagratunyacʿ haystanum*, Yerevan, 1967; tr. N. Garsoïan as *The Arab Emirates in Bagratid Armenia*, Lisbon, 1976. Idem, *Armeniya i arabskiĭ khalifat* (Armenia and the Arab caliphate), Yerevan, 1977. E. Ter-Minassiantz, *Die armenische Kirche in ihren Beziehungen zu den syrischen Kirchen bis zum Ende des 13. Jahr-hunderts nach den armenischen und syrischen Quellen bearbeitet*, Leipzig, 1904. H. Thopdschian, "Armenien vor und während der Araberzeit," *Zeitschrift für armenische Philologie* 2, 1904, pp. 50-71. N. M. Tokarskiĭ, *Arkhitektura Armenii IV-XIV vv.* (The architecture of Armenia, 4th-14th centuries), Yerevan, 1961, pp. 52-61, 88-90, 101-04, 262-68; review A. Khatchatrian, *Revue des Études Arméniennes* 2, 1965, pp. 222-38; 3, 1966, pp. 119-41.

(ERICH KETTENHOFEN)

D'YAKONOV, MIKHAIL MIKHAĬLOVICH (b. St. Petersburg, 26 June 1907, d. Moscow, 8 June 1954), Russian scholar of Iranian studies. The son of an economist, he spent his youth in Norway and in 1924-26 studied with Georg Morgenstierne at the University of Oslo, specializing in Iranian studies. He continued his studies, particularly in ancient and modern European and eastern languages, at the University of Leningrad with V. V. Bartol'd, A. A. Freĭman, A. A. Romaskevich, and others until 1930. In 1930-31 D'yakonov was a researcher in both the regional museum and the Uzbek Scientific Research Institute in Samarqand, and in 1931 he spent several months in a similar position at the Ukrainian Institute of Oriental Studies in Kharkov. From then until 1941 he was at the State Hermitage Museum in Leningrad, becoming head of the Iranian and Near Eastern section in 1934 and director of the Oriental Department in 1938. His first dissertation, *Bronzovyĭ vodoleĭ 1206 g. n.e.* (A Bronze aquamanile dated A.D. 1206) was published in *III. Mezhdunarodnyi Kongress po Iranskomy Iskusstvu i arkheologii. Doklady (*Third International Congress on Iranian Art and Archaeology. Proceedings; Moscow and Leningrad, 1939, pp. 45-52), and in 1938 he was named docent at the University of Leningrad; throughout this period he lectured there and at the Academy of Fine Arts. After military service in World War II he served briefly as vice-dean of the faculty of history at the University of Moscow, but in 1945 he returned to the Hermitage. In 1949 he was promoted to university professor, and in 1951 he became secretary of the Leningrad branch of the Institute of the History of Material Culture, subsequently rising to director. In 1953 he returned to the University of Moscow as professor in the faculty of history.

D'yakonov's first scholarly publication was a study, in collaboration with L. T. Gyuzal'yan, of the manuscripts of Ferdowsī's *Šāh-nāma* in Leningrad collections (*Rukopisi Shakh-Name v Leningradskikh sobraniyakh* [Manuscripts of the *Šāh-nāma* in Leningrad collections], Leningrad, 1934); they then examined the miniatures in these manuscripts (*Iranskie miniatyury v rukopisyakh Shakh-Name Leningradskikh sobraniĭ* [Persian miniatures in manuscripts of the *Šāh-nāma* in Leningrad collections], Leningrad, 1935). Subsequently D'yakonov published many excellent translations of selections from the text, as well as from the works of Fak̲r-al-Dīn Gorgānī, Neẓāmī, Jāmī, and others (for bibliographies of his works, see Belenitskiĭ; Fajans).

D'yakonov's important article "Bronzovaya plastika pervykh vekov khidzhry" (Bronze sculpture of the early centuries *hejrī*; *Trudy Otdela Vostoka, Gosudarstvennogo Ermitazha* 4, 1947, pp. 155-79 (with French summary), dealt with Persian metalwork up to the early 13th century. In 1939 he began archeological work and in 1946 became the principal excavator of the Sogdian-Tajik expedition (from 1952 the Tajik archeological expedition, with D'yakonov as director), sponsored jointly by the Tadzhikistan branch of the Institute of the History of Material Culture of the Soviet Academy of Sciences and by the Hermitage. His major contribution as an archeologist was to clarify the positions of Sogdia and Bactria in the history of Central Asia. He was one of the first to investigate Sogdian painting (at Panjīkant) and to clarify its importance in the history of Asian art. His excavations on the Kobādīān ("Arkheologicheskie raboty v nizhnem techenii reki Kafirnigana/Kobadian 1950-1951 gg." [Archeological work on the lower course of the Kafīrnegān/Kobādīān river, 1950-51], in *Materialy i issledovaniya po arkheologii SSSR* [Materials and investigations on the archeology of the U.S.S.R.] XXXVII, Moscow and Leningrad, 1953, pp. 252-93) and Tūpk̲āna (Tūp-khāna) for the first time yielded stratigraphic evidence for the evolution of culture in ancient Bactria.

A skilled epigrapher, D'yakonov participated in decipherment and initial publication, with I. M. D'yakonov and V. V. Livshits, of Parthian inscriptions from Nisa ("Dokumenty iz drevneĭ Nisy. Rasshifrovka i analiz" [Documents from ancient Nisa. Decipherment and analysis], in I. M. D'yakonov and V. A. Livshitz, eds., *Materialy yuzhnoturkmenistanskoĭ arkheologicheskoĭ kompleksnoĭ ekspeditsii* [Materials from the general southern Turkmenistan archeological expedition] II, Moscow and Leningrad, 1951, pp. 21-65; "Parfyanskiĭ arkhiv iz drevneĭ Nisy" [The Parthian archive from ancient Nisa], *Vestnik drevneĭ istorii* 4, 1953, pp. 114-30).

In his last years he wrote a series of synthetic works on the culture and archeology of Central Asia and Persia. They included detailed studies of the ancient history of Bactria ("Slozhenie klassovogo obshchestva v severnoĭ Baktrii" [The constitution of class society in northern Bactria], *Sovetskaya arkheologiya* 19, 1954, pp. 120-40; *U istokov drevneĭ kul'tury Tadzhikistana* [Toward the source of the ancient culture of Tajikistan], Stalinabad, 1956), as well as several works on Sogdian art ("Rospisi Pendzhikenta i zhivopis' Sredneĭ Azii" [Mural paintings from Panjīkant and the pictorial art of Central Asia], in *Zhivopis' drevnego Pyandzhikenta* [The painting of ancient Panjīkant], Moscow, 1954, pp. 83-158). His *Ocherki istorii drevnego Irana* (An outline history of ancient Iran, Moscow, 1961), a revised and expanded version of his second dissertation, was the first such synthesis published in Russian; in it he brought together evidence from literary sources, archeological monuments, and exhaustive study of the secondary literature in European languages. Although he also intended to write a survey of the history of medieval Persia, he never did so.

Bibliography: A. Bank, "M. M. D'yakonov (1907-1954). (Nekrolog)," *Soobshcheniya Gosudarstvennogo Ermitazha* 7, 1955, p. 2. A. M. Belenitskiĭ, "Pamyati Mikhaila Mikhaĭlovicha D'yakonova" (Memories of Mikhail Mikhailovich D'yakonov), *Kratkie soobshcheniya o dokladakh i polevykh issledovaniyakh Instituta istorii material'noĭ kul'tury* 55, 1954, pp. 155-58. L. C. Bretanitskiĭ, "Mikhail Mikhaĭlovich D'yakonov. K shestidesyatiletiyu so dnya rozhdeniya" (Mikhail Mikhaĭlovich D'yakonov. On the sixtieth anniversary of his birth), *Narody Azii i Afriki*, 1967/3, pp. 188-91. S. Fajans, "The Publications of Mikhail Mikhailovich D'iakonov," *Ars Orientalis* 2, 1957, pp. 512-19. "Mikhail Mikhaĭlovich D'yakonov. 1907-1954," *Vestnik drevneĭ istorii*, 1964/3, pp. 122-23. S. P. Tolstov, "Mikhail Mikhaĭlovich D'yakonov," *Sovetskaya Etnografiya*, 1954/3, pp. 122-23.

(Boris Litvinsky)

DYES. See CARPETS ii; PIGMENTS.

E

EAGLES (Ar. and Pers. *ʿoqāb*; also obsolete Pers. *dāl*< Mid. Pers. *dālman*; also obsolete Pers. and Mid. Pers. *āloh*), large, diurnal, raptorial birds of the family *Accipitridae* in several genera (45-90 cm long, wing-span 110-250 cm).

i. *Species in Persia and Afghanistan.*
ii. *The eagle in Persian literature.*

i. Species in Persia and Afghanistan

Ten species of eagles occur at least seasonally in Persia, nine of which also occur in Afghanistan. Eagles have strong, hooked bills and powerful talons adapted to their flesh-eating mode of life. They catch their prey with their feet and the claws of the rear toe and the central of the front three toes close together powerfully, killing their victims. The length of the toes and claws is more closely correlated with the size of the prey than with the size of the eagle itself. The fish-eating, white-tailed eagle has barbs on its toes. The "true" eagles of the genus *Aquila* feed on mammals, including small predators, and have feathered legs, which presumably protect the leg from struggling, sharp-toothed and clawed prey. The short toes and claws of the short-toed eagle provide a more effective grip on its reptilian prey, especially snakes. Some eagles, such as the golden and Bonelli's, are used with greyhounds to hunt gazelles in the deserts of the South. But while these feeding adaptations and preferences distinguish several species, most supplement their diets with reptiles, amphibians, birds, small mammals, and carrion.

The flight of eagles is powerful and often soaring; a few, such as the short-toed and white-tailed eagles, may hover. Some that take their prey on the ground, swoop down on it from hunting perches on cliffs or branches. Like other raptors, eagles regurgitate pellets containing undigested feathers, hair, and bone fragments; ornitholgists use these to study the birds' feeding habits in a particular region.

Many, including the golden and Bonelli's eagles, nest on ledges or inaccessible cliff faces; others, including the short-toed eagle, nest in trees. The female, usually larger than the male, chooses the nesting site and does most of the building. Eagles tend to renew old nests, adding only twigs and lining; such nests may be used year after year and for many generations. Most eagles lay two to three eggs. Incubation begins with the laying of the first egg, so that the firstborn is older and larger than its siblings; often the older chick kills the younger ones, although abundance of prey and adequate provisioning by the male may enable nesting pairs to raise two or three offspring in good years.

Eagles, like other birds of prey, have been hunted for sport and trophies and because they endanger newborn livestock—particularly sheep and poultry—and because they are believed to compete with human hunters for game. In fact, many species take large numbers of rodents and hares and thus reduce populations of agricultural pests. In many areas of the world, eagle populations have declined along with other predatory and insect-eating birds because of secondary poisoning by pesticides, particularly the fat-soluble organochlorines, which become increasingly concentrated at higher levels of food chains and reach doses that interfere with the reproduction of top predators, like eagles and other raptors. As most eagles are migratory, even those which nest far from agricultural areas become vulnerable to these poisons in the course of their travels.

The following species are known to occur in Persia and Afghanistan: Pallas's fish eagle, *Haliæetus leucoryphus* (*oqāb-e daryāʾī-e pālās*), ranges throughout Asia, is vagrant in Persia, eastern Arabia, and Oman, and is probably a winter visitor in western Afghanistan. It breeds from the Caspian to central China and Mongolia. Its habitat is inland lakes and rivers, though it occasionally winters in coastal regions (Scott et al., p. 78; Paz, p. 54; Hollom et al., p. 49; Plate L).

The white-tailed eagle, *Haliæetus albicilla* (*oqāb-e daryāʾī-e dom-safīd*) ranges throughout the trans-Palearctic, from Greenland through Europe into Asia. Adults reside and breed on the southern coast of the Caspian Sea and winter in northern and western Persia, the Persian Gulf coast, and the Sīstān basin. The young often disperse in winter, occasionally reaching Egypt, Israel, Iraq, and southern Persia. The bird is presumably a passage migrant and winter visitor in Afghanistan. Its habitat is wetlands, rivers, lakes, and coasts. It nests in trees or on cliffs (Scott et al., p. 79; Paz, p. 54; Hollom et al., p. 49).

The short-toed eagle, *Circaetus gallicus* (*ʿoqāb-e mārḵor),* ranges throughout southern and eastern Europe, North Africa, the Middle East, India, and Central Asia; it resides in Persia along the Persian Gulf; it breeds as a summer visitor throughout Persia, and is a passage migrant in Afghanistan. As a summer visitor, it also breeds in Lebanon, Syria, Turkey, and Libya, and perhaps Egypt, Saudi Arabia, and Oman. Few winter in Arabia. Its habitat is arid

PLATE L

Pallas's fish eagle.

stony foothills, semidesert, and open or lightly wooded plains. It nests in trees (Scott et al., p. 95; Paz, p. 58; Hollom et al., p. 53; Plate LI).

The lesser spotted eagle, *Aquila pomarina* (*ʿoqāb-e jangalī),* is a breeding summer visitor in northwestern Persia and on the Caspian coast as well as in eastern Germany, Russia, the Balkans, and Turkey. It breeds in moist wooded plains and dry mountain woods. It winters in East Africa from southern Sudan to Zimbabwe, and occasionally in the eastern Mediterranean, and nests in trees (Scott et al., p. 91; Paz, p. 65; Hollom et al., p. 58).

The spotted eagle, *Aquila clanga* (*ʿoqāb-e tālābī),* is a resident of the south coast of the Caspian Sea, a winter visitor throughout Persia, and a passage migrant or winter visitor in Afghanistan. It breeds from eastern Europe to Manchuria. Its western Palearctic population winters in northern Italy, the Balkans, Turkey, Iraq, Persia, Israel, and the Nile delta. Its habitat is usually near water, especially in marshes with some trees (Scott et al., p. 90; Paz, pp. 65-66; Hollom et al., p. 64; Plate LII).

The steppe eagle or tawny eagle, *Aquila rapax orientalis* (*ʿoqāb-e daštī),* mainly resides in breeding areas; the subspecies *A. r. orientalis* breeds east of the Black Sea through the high steppes of Central Asia to Mongolia; most winter in tropical Africa. It is resident in southern Baluchistan, a winter visitor in southwestern Persia, and a passage migrant or winter visitor in Afghanistan. Its habitat is dry regions in mountains or plains and rubbish dumps in desert towns. It nests on mounds, ruins, or small trees (Scott et al., pp. 89-90; Paz, p. 66; Hollom et al., p. 64).

PLATE LI

The short-toed eagle.

PLATE LII

The spotted eagle.

The imperial eagle, *Aquila heliaca heliaca* (*ʿoqāb-e šāhī),* breeds from the Balkans to Central Asia; is a resident in the eastern Alborz Mountains and western Kopet Dag; is a partial migrant; winters in Afghanistan, Turkey, Persia, Iraq, Egypt, Israel, Oman, Yemen, and central and eastern Saudi Arabia; and is a vagrant in Syria, Libya, and Morocco. Its habitat is parklike plains, steppes, and marshes; it builds substantial nests in large trees (Scott et al., pp. 91-92; Paz, pp. 66-67; Hollom et al., p. 65).

The golden eagle, *Aquila chrysaetos* (*ʿoqāb-e ṭelāʾī),* ranges across the Holarctic. Found in Europe, Asia, and North America, its range in the Palearctic region extends from the Sahara and the shores of the Mediterranean to the tundra of northeastern Asia. *A. c. homeyeri* is distributed from Spain and North Africa east through Turkey and Persia; is a resident in mountainous and upland areas of western and northern Persia; and also breeds in highland Turkey, isolated areas of North Africa, Saudi Arabia, Oman, Israel, and possibly Afghanistan. Its habitat is barren mountainsides, and locally it can also be found in upland and lowland forests, and on plains and semideserts with trees. It nests on rocky ledges, sometimes in trees (Scott et al., p. 92; Paz, pp. 64-65; Hollom et al., p. 65).

The booted eagle, *Hieraaetus pennatus* (*ʿoqāb-e parpā*), breeds as a summer visitor in North Africa, Spain, southern Europe, Turkey, Iraq, northern Persia, southern Russia, and Mongolia, and probably in Nūrestān, Afghanistan. It winters in sub-Saharan Africa and India; a few winter in Yemen, and occasionally eastern Arabia, the eastern Mediterranean, and North Africa. Its habitat is deciduous and pine forests with clearings; it is seldom found far from trees. It usually nests in trees but also on cliffs; it breeds in broadleaf forests and in mixed woodland on the slopes of mountains (Scott et al., pp. 84, 89; Paz, p. 68; Hollom et al., p. 66; Plate LIII).

Bonelli's eagle, *Hieraaetus fasciatus fasciatus* (*ʿoqāb-e do-barādarān),* is a resident in North Africa, the Mediterranean basin, India, and southern China, but shows some dispersal. It is also a resident throughout Persia, except the northwest and the Caspian coast, and is a vagrant several places in eastern and northwestern Arabia. It breeds in scattered mountainous regions of Turkey, Persia, Iraq, Israel, Jordan, Arabia, and North Africa; it is recorded from Afghanistan (Paludan, 1959, p. 19). Its habitat is rocky, mountainous country, but seldom at great altitudes; it descends to the plains and

PLATE LIII

The booted eagle.

PLATE LIV

Bonelli's eagle.

semideserts in winter and nests on precipitous rock-faces, occasionally in trees (Scott et al., p. 89; Paz, pp. 67-68; Hollom et al., p. 66; Plate LIV).

See also BIRDS IN IRAN, BĀZDĀRĪ.

Bibliography: J. P. Asmussen, "Sīmurγ in Judeo-Persian Translations of the Hebrew Bible," in *Iranica Varia. Papers in Honor of Professor Ehsan Yarshater,* ed. D. Amin and M. Kasheff, Acta Iranica 30, Leiden, 1990, pp. 1-5. W. T. Blanford, *Eastern Persia. An Account of the Journeys of the Persian Boundary Commission, 1870-72*, London, 1876, II, pp. 110-12. H. Heinzel, R. Fitter, and J. Parslow, *The Birds of Britain and Europe with North Africa and the Middle East*, 3rd ed., London, 1974. P. A. D. Hollom, R. F. Porter, S. Christensen, and I. Willis, *Birds of the Middle East and North Africa*, Vermillion, S. D., 1988. R. Howard and A. Moore, *A Complete Checklist of the Birds of the World*, Oxford, 1980. S. H. Jervis Read, "Ornithology," in *Camb. Hist. Iran* I, pp. 372-92. K. Paludan, "The 3rd Danish Expedition to Central Asia. Zoological Results 25," *Videnskabelige Meddelelser fra Dansk Naturhistorisk Forening I København* 122, 1959, pp. 1-332. U. Paz, *The Birds of Israel*, Lexington, Mass., 1987. U. Schapka, *Die persische Vogelnamen,* Würzburg, 1972. R. Schmitt, "Der Adler in alten Iran," *Die Sprache,* 16/1, 1970. D. A. Scott, Ḥ. Morawwej Hamadānī and ʿA. Adhamī Mīrḥosaynī, *Parandagān-e Īrān*, Tehran, 1354 Š./1975. C. Vaurie, *The Birds of the Palearctic Fauna*, 2 vols., London, 1959-65.

(STEVEN C. ANDERSON)

ii. THE EAGLE IN PERSIAN LITERATURE

The eagle (*ʿoqāb*) is used frequently by poets as an image of soaring flight, speed, power, nobility, and independence. Šahīd of Balḵ compares a horse (?) with an eagle because of its abilities to traverse mountains and heights (Lazard, I:65, II:30). Masʿūd-e Saʿd-e Salmān (*Dīvān*, p. 30) describes the pace of a horse as making an eagle seem slow. Moʿezzī (*Dīvān*, p. 58) says his horse descends slopes as swiftly as an eagle. Another horse is as rebellious and independent (*sarkeš*) as an eagle (ibid., p. 55). The eagle is the king of birds (ibid., p. 69), and like a ruler it is at the apex of a hierarchy of power: *Nehīb-e ḵalq ze mīrān nehīb-e mīrān zū / balā-ye kabkān bāz o balā-ye bāz ʿoqāb* (Qaṭrān, *Dīvān*, p. 37). The eagle's (and the ruler's) power is emphasized by contrast with the weakness of its prey: *Šavad be amn-e to āhū bara nadīm-e hožabr / šavad be farr-e to tīhū-bača qarīn-e ʿoqāb* (Moʿezzī, p. 61). These qualities of the eagle are summed up in P. N. Ḵānlarī's poem "ʿOqāb" (*Māh dar mordāb*, pp. 107-16). An aging eagle laments his approaching death and asks a crow why crows live many years while his life must be short. The crow attributes its longevity to keeping close to the ground and to eating carrion. Tempted by the crow to try these remedies, the eagle becomes disgusted by the carrion and disappears into the sky, declaring that if he must die in the skies, he cannot abide living in squalor and eating carrion (for Ḵānlarī's "*ʿOqāb*," see also CROW).

With all its noble qualities, the eagle is also seen as arrogant and proud. Nāṣer-e Ḵosrow's version of an old fable (*Dīvān*, p. 499) beginning *rūzī ze sar-e sang...* portrays an eagle which is shot down by an arrow fletched with an eagle's feather. The message of the poem is in the words, now a proverbial expression, *az mā'st ke bar mā'st*. (For earlier versions of this fable, see Aeschylus, II, p. 425; Aesop, p. 110). In the poem "Jogd-e jang," M.-T. Bahār (q.v.; *Dīvān*, I, pp. 796-99) uses the *ʿoqāb-e āhanīn* ("iron eagle") as a powerful image of a Western bomber dropping bombs on Eastern peoples.

Bibliography: Aeschylus, ed. H. Lloyd-Jones, Loeb Classical Library, 2 vols., Cambridge, 1957. Aesop, *Fables*, ed. T. James, London, 1848. M.-T. Bahār, *Dīvān*, 2 vols., Tehran, 1344-45 Š./1965-67. P. N. Ḵānlarī, *Māh dar mordāb*, Tehran, 1343 Š./1964; for an analysis of this poem, see Ḡ.-Ḥ. Yūsofī, "Owj o forūd" in his *Čašma-ye rowšan*, Tehran, 1369 Š./1990, pp. 676-89; for English tr., see *Life and Letters* 63, no. 148, December 1949, pp. 240-44, and A. J. Arberry, *Persian Poems*, London, 1954, pp. 141-46. G. Lazard, *Les Premiers poètes persans*, 2 vols., Paris, 1964. Masʿūd-e Saʿd-e Salmān, *Dīvān*, ed. Ḡ. Rašīd Yāsamī, Tehran, 1339 Š./1960. Moʿezzī Nīšābūrī, *Dīvān*, ed. ʿA. Eqbāl, Tehran, 1318 Š./1939. Nāṣer-e Ḵosrow, *Dīvān*, ed. N. Taqawī, Tehran, 1339 Š./1960; Eng. tr. in A. Schimmel, *Make a Shield from Wisdom*, London, 1993, pp. 92-93. Qaṭrān Tabrīzī, *Dīvān*, ed. M. Naḵjavānī, Tabrīz, 1333 Š./1954.

(WILLIAM L. HANAWAY, JR.)

EARTH IN ZOROASTRIANISM. See ELEMENTS IN ZOROASTRIANISM.

EARTHQUAKES. Persia and Afghanistan lie on the great alpine belt that extends from the Azores in the Atlantic Ocean through the Indonesian archipelago and forms the world's longest collision boundary, between the Eurasian plate in the north and several former Gondwanan blocks in the south, including the so-called "Iranian plates" and "Afghan plates" (Schöler, pp. 29f.). Hence, it is not surprising that they are regions of high seismic activity.

i. *In Afghanistan.*
ii. *In Central Asia.*
iii. *In Persia.*
iv. *The historical record of earthquakes in Persia.*

i. IN AFGHANISTAN

Inside Afghan territory a major suture line is the Herat fault which runs from west to east throughout the country over 1,200 km and extends on a further 300 km inside Tajikistan, where it is called the Central Pamir fault. It is actually a dextral (right-lateral) transform fault with a W-E direction west of Čārīkār (q.v.) and a SW-NE direction east of that point. Russian geologists distinguish these two segments by calling them respectively Main Hari Rôd fault (*glavnyi gerirudskiiĭ razlom)* and Central Badaḵšān fault (Dronov, pp. 465f.). South of it, a network of transform faults delimits several intra-Gondwanan blocks of various sizes. The most important is the S-N Čaman sinistral fault (800 km, out of which 650 km inside Afghanistan), between the Afghan and Indian plates, which is the second major structure of Afghanistan (Wellman). It joins the Herat fault near Čārīkār; from it splay off two secondary sinistral faults, the Gardēz fault, which forms the eastern limit of the Kabul block, and the Moqor-Qandahār fault, which is the western limit of the Qalat-e Ḡilzay block (Carbonnel, pp. 145f.). On the other hand, two dextral faults, the NW-SE Sarobī (150 km) and SW-NE Konar faults delimit the Nūrestān and Jalālābād blocks (Prévot, pp. 6, 113).

Present-day Afghan territory is therefore criss-crossed by a network of transform faults of high tectonic activity; hence no surprise if it is a region of high seismic activity. The frequency of detectable earthquakes occurring within, or near, the borders of the country has been assumed to be in the order of 5,000 events per year. Of this large number at least 500 would be classified as significant earthquakes, i.e., earthquakes recorded by seismic stations located outside Afghanistan (Heuckroth and Karim, 1970, p. 4). High as they are, these figures are underestimates, however.

Contemporary data show sharp regional contrasts in the frequency of earthquakes (Table 1; also Schöler and Bauer). Out of 1,039 events with a reported magnitude of 4.5 or greater recorded for the period 1900-1983, 534, or 51.4 percent, occurred in the Hindu Kush region of NE Afghanistan, where a remarkably persistent source of earthquakes is located along the Central Badaḵšān fault in the Kūh-e Ḵᵛāja Moḥammad, between the Warsaj and upper Kōkča valleys, at about 36°30 N and 70°30 E—a very isolated and less accessible area; major events originating from that source may cause cracks in buildings in Kabul (250 km SW) and are felt up to distances of more than 1,000 km from the epicenter (e.g., in 1937, 1960, 1962, 1964-65). Another series of 473 major events, or 45.5 percent, were located along the nearby eastern part of the Afghan-Soviet border. But only thirty-two occurred in other parts of the country, including the area of the Čaman fault which thus appears to have been recently less active along its Afghan northern section (the sectio Ḡaznī-Čārīkār being actually inactive; Carbonnel, p. 147) than along its Pakistani southern extremity, where a major shock destroyed Quetta on 31 May 1935, causing a loss of about 30,000 lives (Jackson; Quittmeyer and Jacobs, pp. 793ff.; Yeats et al.; Prévot, pp. 61ff., similarly stresses the low level of microseismic activity south of Moqor. Only one earthquake out of these thirty-two events was recorded in west Afghanistan (the shocks of 19 Sonbola 1310 Š./10 September 1931 and 2 Mīzān 1329 Š./24 September 1950, famous for having reportedly caused the collapse of three minarets in Herat, are not recorded, probably on account of an intensity below 4.5; Ambraseys and Melville, p. 197, n. 16). The level of modern seismic activity is therefore minimal in western and southern Afghanistan and maximal in NE Afghanistan, in rough accordance with the uneven distribution of transform faults in the country. In the broader Asian context, western and southern Afghanistan are clearly areas of "seismic quiescured cence" between the much more unstable Persian and Himalayan regions, with NE Afghanistan being definitely included into the latter (Schöler and Bauer; Ambraseys and Melville, p. 140; Table 41).

Average surface-wave magnitudes (measured on the Richter scale) do not show any significant regional variation (Table 41). Between 1900 and 1983, however, extreme magnitudes have been recorded only in NE Afghanistan: out of nineteen earthquakes with a magnitude of 7.0 or greater, eighteen occurred in the Hindu Kush and one in the nearby Soviet-Afghan border region. The greatest magnitude recorded has been 8.1 for the 215 km-deep earthquake of 14 Rabīᶜ I 1340/15 November 1921 in Kūh-e Ḵᵛāja Moḥammad (Riad and Meyers, p. 115). Somewhat lighter events occurring at smaller depths may be more destructive, however: the Saygān-Kahmard earthquake of 19 Jawzā 1335 Š./9 June 1956, located north of the Herat fault, with a magnitude of 7.3 (some reports say 7.6; Quittmeyer and Jacob, p. 796) and a focal depth of only 60 km, caused an estimated 300 to 400 deaths and extensive damage in northern Hazārajāt (Riad and Meyers, map); it was preceded by one foreshock (8 June) and followed by five aftershocks within two days which delineated a rupture zone of some 50 km in length and 25 km in width (Quittmeyer and Jacobs, p. 796).

Sources for Afghan historical seismicity in both archives and published literature still remain to be thoroughly studied. The only available survey lists no more than sixty-two earthquakes from the origin to 1900, and only two between 445/1053 and 1247/1831—an altogether insignificant number (Heuckroth and Karim, 1970, pp. C5ff.). Though preliminary, the present knowledge of historical seismicity in Afghanistan suggests that areas which have been recently free from earthquakes have been badly hit in the past. Such is, for instance, the case for western Afghanistan, where Herat was shocked in 234/849 and again, more severely, in 495/1102 and 765/1364 (Heuckroth and Karim, 1970, pp. 50, C5; Ambraseys and Melville, pp. 37, 41, 44; see idem, p. 140, for excessive downgrading of historical seismicity in western Afghanistan).

The oldest earthquake recorded so far damaged the Greco-Bactrian city of Āy Ḵānom (q.v.) in the period 50 B.C.E.-50 C.E. (Heuckroth and Karim, 1970, pp. 48ff.). In 203/819 a catastrophic earthquake destroyed a quarter of Balḵ (q.v.) and affected the whole area between Fāryāb (q.v.) to Toḵarestān (Ambraseys and Melville, p. 37). The same city was again hit in 813/1410 (idem, p. 44). In 444/1052-53 a destructive earthquake occurred along the Gardēz fault in the Urgūn area (Heuckroth and Karim, 1970, p. 50). Of all the major seismic events in the past, however, the most significant definitely was the Pağmān earthquake of 3 Ṣafar 911/6 July 1505, located on the northern extremity of the Čaman fault, with an estimated magnitude of 8. Surface faulting was observed and extended for about 60 km along the base of the Pağmān range where vertical displacements of several meters were recorded. Its effects were felt as far as Agra, a distance of more than 1,000 km, and several aftershocks were perceptible every day during the following month (*Bābur-nāma*, tr. Beveridge, p. 247; Heuckroth and Amin, 1970, pp. 50f.; Quittmeyer and Jacob, pp. 789f.).

Information is slightly less scanty for the earthquakes of the 19th century. The Badaḵšān seism of 19 Ramażān 1247/21 February 1832 appears to be the first documented earthquake known to have originated from the Hindu Kush; it severely hit the upper Kōkča valley (Heuckroth and Amin, 1970, pp. 51f.). On 8 Moḥarram 1258/19 February 1842 another major earthquake occurred along the Gardēz fault, with maximum intensity in the Alīngār valley and Jalālābād basin; several hundred individuals were killed; the radius of perceptibility of the event was 900 km, and numerous aftershocks were felt for many months (Quittmeyer and Jacob, p. 791). The Jabal Serāj earthquake of 7 Ramażān 1291/18 October 1874 was the third major seismic disturbance of the 19th century. It seems to have been connected with a rupture along the Herat fault, but evidence is not strong (Quittmeyer and Jacob, p. 803). According to some reports, as a result of this earthquake

Table 41

REGIONAL DISTRIBUTION OF EARTHQUAKES WITH A MAGNITUDE OF 4.5 OR GREATER, AFGHANISTAN (1900-1983)

Flinn-Engdahl seismic regions	Number of Events	Average Magnitude (Richter scale)	Mean Depth (Km)
Turkmen-Afghan border	–	–	–
NW Afghanistan	1	4.0	33
SW Afghanistan	–	-	–
Afghanistan (Central andSE)	31	4.8	43
Uzbeko-Tajik-Afghan border	471	4.7	116
Hindu Kush	534	4.8	158

Source: Riad and Meyers.

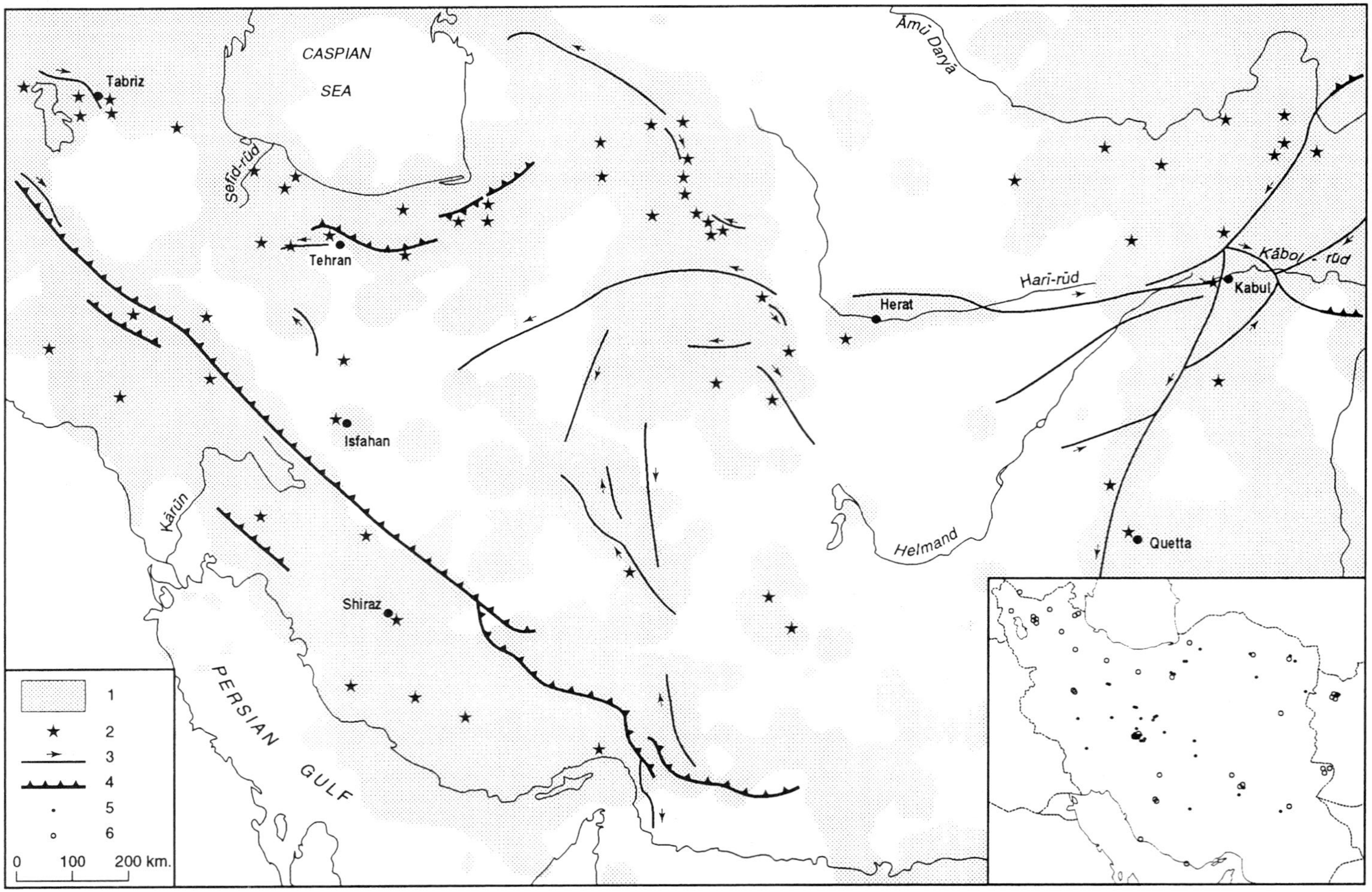

Figure 31. Seismic map of Persia and Afghanistan. Main map: seismicity in Persia and Afghanistan. 1: Areas affected by historical destructive earthquakes (tentative). 2: Major destructive earthquakes. 3: Main transform faults (the arrows indicate their directions). 4: Thrust surfaces. Inset. Distribution of free-standing structures built in Persia before the 16th century. 5: Existent Structures. 6: Ruined structures (after Ambrasyes and Melville, p. 149).

Jabal Serāj, Golbahār, and portions of Kūhestān were completely destroyed, and ground cracks were observed. On 30 Jumādā I 1310/20 December 1892 another severe earthquake was recorded in the Spīn Bōldak border area of southern Afghanistan, along the Čaman fault; left-lateral strike-slip movement of at least 75 cm was observed near the town of Sanzal; it damaged the railway line between Quetta and Čaman; the horizontal extent of the surface faulting was at least 30 km (Griesbach; McMahon, p. 402; Quittmeyer and Jacob, p. 791). According to information gathered by McMahon from local elders, other events had occurred previously—a total of three times during the elders' life, and similar accounts of repeated movements along the Čaman fault in this vicinity were handed down in oral history.

As one enters the 20th century, information becomes more and more numerous and instrumentally documented (see above). A seismological observatory, equipped with a seismograph, the only one operating in the country, was established in the Faculty of Engineering of Kabul University in 1347 Š./1968 (Heuckroth and Amin 1970, p. 3). Among the significant contemporary events, one may cite the destructive earthquake which leveled most of Paštūn Kōt (Fāryāb province) on 14 Ḥamal 1313 Š./ 3 April 1934, but caused only little damage in Maymana, less than 10 km away (magnitude 5.4); the Hindu Kush earthquake of 13 Ḥūt 1327 Š./4 March 1949, one of the most severe in the present century (magnitude 7.5, depth 230 km), damaging extensively the entire northeastern part of the country but causing comparatively little loss of life; the Golrān series of light shocks in Asad-Sonbola 1334 Š./August 1955, which destroyed only some houses, stand distinctively among the very few events detected for western Afghanistan; the Saygān-Kahmard earthquake of 1335 Š./1956, already referred to; the Tāšqorḡān (Ḵolm) earthquake of 28 Ḥūt 1355 Š./19 March 1976, located along an offshoot of the Herat fault (magnitude 5.5, depth 33 km), which took the lives of about fifty people and destroyed some 1,200 houses, including the whole village of Saygānčī, which was quickly rebuilt through Australian assistance and according to antiseismic standards (independently supported roof) used for the first time in Afghanistan (Carbonnel and Denizot; Sibtain).

Bibliography: N. N. Ambraseys and C. P. Melville, *A History of Persian Earthquakes*, Cambridge, 1982. *The Bābur-nāma*, tr. A. S. Beveridge, London, 1922, repr. London, 1969. J.-P. Carbonnel, "La limite de la plaque indienne en Afghanistan. Nouvelles données géologiques et sismologiques," in *Recherches géologiques dans les chaînes alpines de l'Asie du sud-ouest. Livre à la mémoire de Albert F. de Lapparent*, Paris, 1977, pp. 145-152. Idem and F. Denizot, "Le tremblement de terre de Tachkourgan (N. Afghanistan) du 19-20 mars 1976," *Revue de Géormorphologie Dynamique* 26/4, 1977, pp. 121-133. J.-L. Chatelain, *Étude fine de la sismicité en zone de collision continentale au moyen d'un réseau portable: Région Pamir-Hindu-Kush*, Thèse troisième cycle, Grenoble Univ., 1978. V. I. Dronov, "Krupneishie razlomy Afganistana," in Sh. Abdulla and V. M. Chmyrov, eds., *Geologiya i poleznye iskopaemye Afganistana*, Moscow, 1980, I, pp. 464-73. E. A. Flinn and E. R. Engdahl, "A Proposed Basis for Geographical and Seismic Regionalization," *Review of Geophysics* 3/1, 1965, pp. 123-49. C. L. Griesbach, "Notes on the Earthquake in Balûchistân on the 20th December 1892," *Records of the Geological Survey of India* 26/2, 1893, pp. 57-61.

L. E. Heuckroth and R. A. Karim, *Earthquake History. Seismicity and Tectonics of the Regions of Afghanistan*, Kabul, 1970. Idem, "Afghan Seismotectonics," *Philosophical Transactions of the Royal Society of London*, A 274, 1973, pp. 389-95. R. Jackson, *Thirty Seconds at Quetta. The Story of an Earthquake*, London, 1960. R. D. Lawrence and R. S. Yeats, "Geological Reconnaissance of the Chaman Fault in Pakistan," in A. Farah and K. A. De Jong, eds., *Geodynamics of Pakistan*, Quetta, 1979, pp. 351-57. A. H. McMahon, "The Southern Borderlands of Afghanistan," *Geographical Journal* 9/4, 1897, pp. 393-415.

R. D. Prévot, *Sismicité superficielle du nord-est de l'Afghanistan*, Thèse troisième cycle, Grenoble Univ., 1979. R. C. Quittmeyer, A. Farah, and K. H. Jacob, "The Seismicity of Pakistan and its Relation to Surface Faults," in A. Farah and K. A. De Jong, eds., *Geodynamics of Pakistan*, Quetta, 1979, pp. 271-84 (covers much of Afghanistan, too). R. C. Quittmeyer and K. H. Jacob, "Historical and Modern Seismicity of Pakistan, Afghanistan, N.W. India and S.E. Iran," *Bulletin of the Seismological Society of America* 69/3, 1979, pp. 773-823. S. Riad and H. Meyers, *Earthquake Catalog for the Middle East Countries 1900-1983*, World Data Center A for Solid Earth Geophysics, Report SE-40, Boulder (Col.), National Geophysical Data Center, 1985. S. Schöler, *Aktuelle und historische Seismizität im Vorderen und Mittleren Orient*, Wiesbaden, 1992. Idem and E. Bauer, *Vorderer Orient—Seismotektonik, geschichtliche Beben*, Wiesbaden, 1984, TAVO Sheet A II 3 (suggestive although coverage is poor for Afghanistan). S. N. Sibtain, *To Build a Village. Earthquake-Resistant Rural Architecture—A Technical Handbook*, Sydney, 1982. H. W. Wellman, "Active Wrench Faults of Iran, Afghanistan, and Pakistan," *Geologische Rundschau* 55, 1966, pp. 716-35. R. Wolfart and H. Wittekindt, *Geologie von Afghanistan*, Berlin and Stuttgart, 1980. R. S. Yeats et al., "Surface Effects of the 16 March 1978 Earthquake, Pakistan-Afghanistan Border," in A. Farah and K. A. De Jong, eds., *Geodynamics of Pakistan*, Quetta, 1979, pp. 359-61.

(DANIEL BALLAND)

ii. In Central Asia

Central Asia lies in the Mediterranean-Himalayan seismic belt (see Tables 42, 43) and comprises two distinct regions of high seismic activity. The first, in southwest Turkmenistan, includes two seismic zones: i) the Krasnovodsk area, along the eastern coast of the Caspian Sea, which is associated with the larger zone of the conjunction of the uplifted Kuba Dagh-Greater Balkan tectonic structure with the Transcaspian depression; ii) the Ashkhabad area, which borders on a highly active region in northern Persia. Most of the epicenters in the latter zone lie near the Kopet Dag fault, where the greatest tectonic activity is concentrated (Medvedev, pp. 300-13).

The second region includes the territories of Tajikistan, Kirgizstan, southeastern Uzbekistan, southeastern Kazakhstan, and eastern Sinkiang Province in China. A heterogeneous tectonic area, including territories of Caledonian, Variscan, and Alpine folding, this region is enlaced by a fairly complicated network of faults characterized by both horizontal and vertical displacements of recent development (Nalivkin, pp. 533f; Leith, pp. 1-22). Researchers have proposed that seismic activity in the region derives from continental collision between the Indian and Eurasian plates, beginning about 40 million years ago (Molnar and Tapponnier). The longest fault in the region, the Talas-Fargāna fault, is oriented NW-SE and extends for over 1,500 km, cross-cutting the Tien Shan mountain range for over 600 km. For approximately 700 km along the southern boundary of the Tien Shan, another zone of seismicity several tens of kilometers wide follows the EW-oriented Gissar(Ḥeṣār)-Kokshal fault zone. The two other major faults are the Darvāz-Karakul and Central Pamir faults, both of which extend from the Tarim Basin to the Hindu Kush, skirting the

Table 42
SELECTIVE LIST OF LARGE-SCALE EARTHQUAKES BEFORE 1900

Earthquake	Location	Est. Magnitude (M_s)*	Intensity**
2nd Millen. B.C.E.	Ak Tepe (near Ashkhabad)	7.1	X
3rd Cent. B.C.E.	Chiguchin (SE Kazakhstan)	6.1	IX
1st Cent. B.C.E-1st Cent. C.E.	Nisa (Nesā)	7.1	X
500	S.E. Kazakhstan	6.7	VIII
819 (June)	Balḵ-Ṭāleqān-Jūzjān-Fārīāb	7.5	VIII
838 (23 November)	Fargāna	n.a.	n.a.
914 (April)	Bukhara	n.a	n.a.
942 (June)	Bukhara	6.7	IX
943 (August)	Nisa (Nesā)	7.6	X
1175	Kerki (E. Turkmenia)	7.1	X
1208	Gorgānj	6.1	IX
1390 (April)	Bukhara	6.1	VIII
1410	Balḵ-Bukhara	n.a.	n.a.
1428	Tāleqān	6.5	n.a.
1475	Balāsagūn (Kazakhstan)	6.4	IX
1490 (20 February)	Samarkand	5.8	XIII
1620	Fargāna	5.8	IX
1716	Āqsū (E. Turkestan)	7.5	IX
1799	Urgut (near Samarkand)	6.0	IX
1817-22	Samarkand-Bukhara	6.4	XIII
1822 (September)	Ḵᵛoqand	6.2	IX
1832 (January)	Badaḵšān	7.4	IX
1868 (3 April)	Tashkent	6.5	VIII
1885 (2 August)	Belovodsk (Kirgizia)	6.9	X
1887 (8 June)	Alma-Ata	7.3	X
1889 (11 July)	Chilik (N.E. of Alma Ata)	8.3	X
1895 (8 July)	Krasnovodsk (W. Turkmenia)	8.2	X
1895 (4 August)	Tāšqorgān (E. Turkestan)	6.5	VIII
1896 (23 September)	Pamir-Hindu Kush	7.5	VI
1897 (17 November)	Ūrāteppa (Tajikistan)	6.7	VIII

* A measure of energy released by the shock; here "surface magnitude" is used. ** A "Modified Mercalli Scale," an index signifying the effect of an earthquake on buildings and/or the earth itself in a given location.

Sources: Ambraseys, pp. 34-68, 158-62; Dunbar, pp. 144-57; Kondorskaya, pp. 176-79, 204-13; Medvedev, pp. 28-29.

northern Pamirs (Burtmen; Kristy; Molnar and Qidong).

Between these two active regions, there is another of lesser activity, with only isolated known foci, along the lower course of the Oxus river, encompassing the regions of Marv, Čārjū (Āmol), Bukhara, and K̲ᵛārazm—the sites of the oldest extant cultural monuments in Central Asia. However, several earthquakes have been reported in this area in the last millennium. Even the northward shift of the course of the Oxus has reputedly been ascribed, in Khivan the tradition, to a strong earthquake (Ambraseys, p. 149).

The earthquakes listed in Table 42 have been identified principally from historical sources but also, in a few cases, from archaeological or geological evidence. The earliest traces of macroseismic activity in Central Asia may be in Ak-Tepe, in the vicinity of

Table 43

SELECTIVE LIST OF EARTHQUAKES IN THE 20TH CENTURY

Earthquake	Location	Magnitude(M_s)	Intensity	Casualties
22 August 1902	Singkiang-Kirgizia	7.7	IX	2,500
16 December 1902	Andejān (E. Uzbeks.)	6.4	IX	4,500
21 October 1907	Qarātāḡ (W. Tajiks.)	7.8	IX	12,000
3 January 1911	Kebin (SE. Kazakhs.)	8.7	X	450
18 February 1911	Sarēz (Tajikistan)	7.4	IX	90
28 December 1923	Gardan: Ūrāteppa-Mastčāh (Tajikistan)	6.4	XIII	n.a.
6 & 12 July 1924	S. Kirgizia	6.5	IX	n.a.
3 June 1929	Chiili (S. Kazakhstan)	6.4	VII	n.a.
22 September 1930	Fayẓābād (Tajikistan)	6.3	n.a.	175
31 August 1934	Arḡānkūl (Tajikistan)	6.5	IX	n.a.
20 June 1938	Kemin-Chu (N. Kirgizia)	6.9	IX	n.a.
20 April 1941	Ḡarm (Cen. Tajikis.)	6.4	IX	n.a.
11 January 1943	Fayẓābād (Tajikistan)	6.0	IX	n.a.
27 September 1944	Eastern Pamirs	6.7	0	n.a.
November 1946	Chatkal (Kirgizia)	7.6	X	n.a.
4 November 1946	Kazanjik (W. Turkmenia)	7.0	IX	400
5 October 1948	Ashkhabad	7.2	X	19,800
10 July 1949	Ḥāʾeṭ (Tajikistan)	7.4	X	n.a.
23 January 1954	Jowšangāz (Tajikistan)	5.8	VIII	n.a.
15 April 1955	Ulugchat (Sinkiang)	7.1	VII	n.a.
1 & 13 April 1961	N.E. Sinkiang	6.6	0	n.a.
16 October 1963	Karakul (E. Tajikistan)	6.5	X	n.a.
25 April 1966	Tashkent	5.1	VIII	n.a.
5 June 1970	Sarykamysh (SE. Kazakhstan)	6.6	IX	n.a.
8 April 1976	Gazli (Uzbekistan)	7.3	IX	n.a.
17 May 1976	Gazli (Uzbekistan)	7.3	X	n.a.
31 January 1977	Esfara (N. Tajikistan)	6.1	VIII	n.a.
21 March 1978	Alma-Ata	7.2	VII	n.a.
1 November 1978	E. Tajikistan	6.8	IX	n.a.
19 March 1984	Gazli (Uzbekistan)	7.1	IX	n.a.
26 October 1984	Jergatal-Ḡarm (Central Tajikistan)	6.2	VII	n.a.
13 October 1985	N. Tajikistan	6.0	IX	29+
22 January 1989	Šarāra-Ḥeṣār (Tajikis.)	5.5	VII	274
25 March 1990	Pamirs (Tajikistan)	6.3	VI	n.a.
15 May 1992	Osh-Andejān (Kirgizia-Uzbekistan)	6.2	VII	3
19 August 1992	N. Kirgizia	7.5	IX	75

Sources: Dunbar, pp. 144-57; Kondorskaya, pp. 180-202, 213-305; Medvedev, pp. 28-29; National Geographical Data Center and World Data Centers A for Solid Earth Geophysics, Boulder (Col.).

Ashkhabad, where archaeological evidence suggests that an earthquake during the second millennium B.C.E. damaged a building structure (Kondorskaya, pp. 519f.). Evidence for the strong earthquake that destroyed old Nisa (Nesā) west of Ashkhabad for the first time is also archaeological, so that the date remains only approximate (idem). Literary sources, however, describe a second earthquake that destroyed the city in Ḏu'l Hejja 331/August 943), taking more than 5,000 lives (Gardīzī, ed. Ḥabībī, p. 155; Ebn al-Aṯīr, VIII, p. 404). Abū Dolaf also describes the destruction of dozens of villages in the Salmaqān valley by the same earthquake (Ambraseys, p. 39). The Kerki earthquake of 1175 presents a case where historical sources corroborate the geomorphological evidence (Kondorskaya, p. 525).

Owing to lack of historical evidence, incidents in the more earthquake-prone regions of Central Asia are less represented in Table 42 than in Table 43. Tajikistan is among these regions: on the average, it suffers a destructive earthquake every ten to fifteen years, with an annual incidence of thousands of recordable seismic events (Kukhtikova; Roecker). Most of these smaller events lie below the threshold of human perception, but a traditional *Now-rūz* custom reveals that they may be strong enough to displace an egg on a flat mirror, a sign of the beginning of the new year.

The fact that Central Asia possesses the highest level of seismicity in the continental territory of the former Soviet Union has made it the subject of a strikingly large number of seismological and seismotectonic studies. As part of a countrywide network—first Russian and then Soviet—the following seismic stations were installed prior to the Second World War: Tashkent (1902), Alma Ata [formerly Vernyi] (1907), Frunze [formerly Pishpek] (1927), Andejān (1929), Samarkand (1929), and Čimkent (1934) (Ambraseys, pp. 134-37). It was not until one year after the highly destructive Fayżābād earthquake sequence of 1943 that a seismic station was set up in Dushanbe, followed by one in Ashkhabad in 1947 (idem). In the 1950s, further development of seismic studies of Central Asian territories resulted from two catastrophic earthquakes: that of 1948 in Ashkhabad, whose toll of 19,800 lives was kept secret by the Soviet Union until the late 1980s, and that of 1949 in Ḥāʾeṭ, during which an enormous landslide buried the center of that Tajik district, and 150 other settlements suffered heavy damage (Kukhtikova).

Active work on earthquake prediction began after the Tashkent earthquake of 1966, the focus of which appeared beneath the center of the city, causing significant destruction despite its relatively low magnitude. Seismic outposts called "polygons," containing extensive instrumentation for earthquake prediction, were installed in the regions of Ashkhabad, Tashkent, Frunze-Alma Ata, Osh, and Dushanbe-Ḡarm, all being regions calculated to be particularly vulnerable to earthquakes (Nersesov). An improved version of the seismic zoning map of the Soviet Union, originally published with a scale of 1:5,000,000 during the mid-1950s (Medvedev, p. 65), was republished with a scale of 1:1,500,000 in the 1970s. Subsequently, more detailed maps were prepared for individual regions of Central Asia (Sodovsky; Asimov et al.).

During the détente years of the early 1970s, scientific agreements for environmental protection between the United States and the Soviet Union led to several joint studies aimed at earthquake prediction. Under this agreement a number of Western researchers visited Central Asia and, in conjunction with the republics' Academies of Sciences, conducted field studies on the seismicity and seismotectonics in the region. In recent years, continued seismological studies in Central Asia have been conducted under the "Joint Seismic Program" (IRIS Consortium). A prominent institution for the study of earthquakes in Central Asia is currently the Institute of Seismic Resistant Construction and Seismology of the Academy of Sciences of Tajikistan, founded in 1951. This organization has conducted both experimental and theoretical research and has participated in major construction and engineering projects in Tajikistan (Asimov and Negmatov). In the 1980s, the institute issued the annual publication *Zemletryaseniy v sredney Azii i Kazakhstana* (Earthquakes in Central Asia and Kazakhstan) and *Prognoz zemletryasenii* (Earthquake Prediction).

Bibliography: N. N. Ambraseys and C. P. Melville, *A History of Persian Earthquakes*, Cambridge, 1982. M. S. Asimov and N. N. Negmatov, "Tajik Soviet Socialist Republic: Science and Scientific Institutions," *Great Soviet Encyclopaedia* (tr. from 1976 Russian ed.), XXV, A. M. Prokharov, ed., New York, 1980, pp. 300-03. M. S. Asimov et al., "On the State of Research Concerning Earthquake Prediction in the Soviet Republics of Central Asia," *Earthquake Prediction: Proceedings of International Symposium on Earthquake Prediction*, Tokyo, 1984, pp. 585-95. V. S. Burtman, "Faults of Middle Asia," *American Journal of Science* 280, 1980, pp. 725-44. P. K. Dunbar, P. A. Lockridge, and L. S. Whiteside, eds., *Catalogue of Significant Earthquakes 2150 B. C.-1991 A. D.*, World Data Center A, Boulder (Col.), 1992. IRIS Consortium, "Installation of Seismic Stations," *1993 Annual Report*, Arlington (Va.), 1994, pp. 22-26. N. V. Kondorskaya, and N. V. Shebalin, eds., *New Catalog of Strong Earthquakes in the USSR from Ancient Times through 1977*, World Data Center A for Solid Earth Geophysics, Boulder (Col.), 1982. M. J. Kristy and D. W. Simpson, "Seismicity Changes Preceding Two Recent Central Asian Earthquakes," *Journal of Geophysical Research* 85/B9, 1980, pp. 4829-37. T. I. Kukhtikova et al., "Zilzila," *Entsiklopediyai sovetii tojik*, 2 vols., M. S. Osimi (ʿĀṣemī), ed., Dushanbe, 1980, II, pp. 490-92. W.

Leith, *The Tajik Depression, USSR: Geology, Seismicity and Tectonics*, unpubl. Ph.D. dissert., Columbia University, 1984. S. V. Medvedev, ed., *Seismic Zoning of the USSR* (tr. from 1968 Russian edition), Jerusalem, 1976. P. Molnar and D. Qidong, "Faulting Associated with Large Earthquakes and the Average Rate of Deformation in Central and Eastern Asia," *Journal of Geophysical Research* 89, 1984, pp. 6203-27. P. Molnar and P. Tapponnier, "Cenozoic Tectonics of Asia: Effects of a Continental Collision," *Science* 189/4201, 1975, pp. 419-26. D.V. Nalivkin, *Geology of the USSR* (tr. from Russian, Moscow-Leningrad, 1962), Edinburgh, 1973. S. W. Roecker, "Velocity Structure of the Pamir-Hindu Kush Region: Possible Evidence of Subducted Crust," *Journal of Geographical Research* 87/B2, 1982, pp. 945-59. M. A. Sadovsky and I. L. Nersesov, "Earthquake Prediction Problems in the USSR," *Proceedings of the Seminar on Earthquake Prediction Case Histories*, Geneva, 1983, pp. 35-49.

(HABIB BORJIAN)

iii. IN PERSIA

Sources and state of current knowledge. Based on numerous but fragmentary observations of earthquakes over a long period of time, it is only since the middle of the 20th century that there has been an attempt at systematic study of seismic activity in Persia and that macroseismic data collected at international stations have been refined in relation to the Persian situation, through the establishment of a network of local seismological stations, in Tehran (1337 Š./1958); Shiraz (1338 Š./1959); Safīdrūd (1341 Š./1962); Tabrīz, Mašhad, and Kermānšāh (1343-44 Š./1964-65); Būšehr (1354 Š./1975); Isfahan (1355 Š./1976); and Sāva (1356 Š./1977), each the center of a constellation of substations. After early, incomplete, and imperfect attempts at cataloguing earthquakes in Persia (A. T. Wilson), the first comprehensive seismotectonic map of the country was published; it was limited to north central Persia and was drawn to a scale of 1:1 million (Tchalenko et al.). It was soon followed by a map of the entire country, drawn to a scale of 1:2.5 million, with supplementary maps of the epicenters of destructive earthquakes in the period 1318-96=1279-1355 Š./1900-76, of the principal faults in the country, and of earthquakes recorded since the 4th century B.C.E., all drawn to a scale of 1:5 million (Berberian). The historical study was taken up again in a fundamental work by N. N. Ambraseys and Charles Melville (1982), who drew upon a much broader range of documentary sources; their work is a model of its kind, encompassing not only a general study, but also reconstructed maps of the areas of destruction connected with a number of major historical earthquakes. More recently these data have been integrated into a much less detailed synthesis and then into a general seismic map of the entire Near and Middle East (Schöler and Bauer; Schöler). Nevertheless, it must be admitted that our knowledge of past earthquakes is still insufficient, owing particularly to the extreme unevenness of the documentation for different regions; indeed, for many sparsely populated desert areas it is almost entirely absent, both from textual sources and from the archeological record. The broad outlines of seismotectonics have thus been established, but they cannot yet be filled in without some hesitation and approximation.

General features of the seismological geology of Persia. The main relevant feature is the great Zagros fault line, where the Arabian and central Iranian plates overlap. In this zone, 1,600 km long and on average 250 km wide, seismic activity is extreme. Historical data suggest that there has been continuous seismic activity, with occasional local tremors, but chiefly a large number of mild earthquakes bearing little relation to tectonic fractures in the region or to visible traces of recurrence; nor can they be linked with major faults. In certain parts of the Zagros nomadic tribes report that the earth trembles more or less regularly every year, setting off notable rock slides. At Bandar-e ʿAbbās in 1031/1622, besides a major earthquake on 28 Ḏu'l-qaʿda/4 October, there were six or seven minor tremors, but the residents reported to a European traveler that there was usually an average of only one earthquake a year (Della Valle, III, p. 590). Altogether, however, this zone seems to have been relatively free from major earthquakes, and, despite continual deformation of the earth's crust, most episodes have had no serious seismic consequences. Throughout its history Shiraz has experienced numerous tremors in which varying numbers of buildings have collapsed, but only one truly cataclysmic earthquake, that of 26 Rajab 1269/5 May 1853, in which about 9,000 people died.

Northeast of the Zagros central Persia corresponds broadly to a mosaic of Gondwanian plates, the details of which have not yet been sufficiently defined; altogether, they constitute a stable zone. Major earthquakes are rare there, and it is the region in which the largest number of early minarets are preserved (at Isfahan, Yazd, and Kermān; for Isfahan, see Ambraseys, 1979). Earthquakes there seem to be essentially local reverberations from major events in other regions. Movements resulting from the subsidence of the Zagros are, however, transmitted through the central Iranian plates toward the northern and eastern zones, tracing a gigantic triangle.

These northern and eastern zones thus experience the most intense seismic responses to the general drift of Arabia toward Eurasia. It is there that most serious earthquakes occur, throughout the length of the so-called Iranian Crescent, which extends from Azerbaijan through the Alborz, Khorasan and the Kopet Dag, Kūhestān, and Sīstān east of the Dašt-e Lūt as far as Makrān, for which sources are rare. Important earthquakes can also occur in the regions of central Persia along the edges of the Iranian Crescent, thus in the Ṭabas (earthquake of 27 Šahrīvar

1357 Š./16 September 1978, which left 6,300 dead, 3,600 in the town itself) or in the fault area around Kāšān (15 Ḏu'l-qaʿda 1192/15 December 1778, in which more than 8,000 died). This seismic activity between tectonic plates does not appear to depend on the apparent surface tectonics or on the major Quaternary faults; rather it is correlated with minor faults, tilted and sometimes very recent, that have cut across earlier instances. Relatively long periods of quiescence separate major paroxysms, which thus seem totally unpredictable. For example, Nīšāpūr was affected by serious cataclysms in 605/1209, 669/1270, 808/1405 (leaving 30,000 dead), and 1084/1673 but has remained almost free of earthquakes since (Melville, 1980). Only Azerbaijan, particularly in the region of Tabrīz, is distinguished by apparently continuous seismic activity. More or less severe shocks were experienced in the city in 244/858, 434/1042, 672/1273, 704/1304, 746/1345, 864/1459, 957/1550, 1060/1650, 1068/1657, 1075/1664, 1130/1717, 1134/1721, 1195/1780, 1235/1819, 1253/1837, 1259/1843, 1273/1856, 1314/1896, and 1349=1309 Š./1930; those of 434/1042, 1134/1721, and 1195/1780 were particularly destructive, each doubtless causing 20,000-50,000 deaths. It has been suggested that seismic activity alternates somewhat between the northern and eastern parts of Persia, the former seeming to be enjoying a period of relative calm at present (with the exception of the Rūdbār earthquake in 1990), while the latter is undergoing a peak of activity (Ambraseys and Melville, p. 153).

Earthquakes in the beliefs and daily life of the Persians. In Persian popular belief the origins of earthquakes are attributed to the position of the globe on the horns of a bull, itself resting on a fish. When the bull is tired or, according to others, when there is too much injustice in the world, he becomes impatient and shifts the globe from one horn to the other, with resulting earthquakes. Some people claim that earthquakes occur where the earth falls directly onto the bull's horn (Massé, *Croyances et Coutumes* I, p. 181). This notion is actually quite widespread all across the Islamic civilization of the Middle East, but Persian versions can be adduced, interpolation showing the influence of Shiʿism. The earthquake that destroyed Qūčān in Khorasan in 1313/1895 was explained by the fact that a son of the Imam ʿAlī al-Reżа (q.v.), whose tomb is located there, had gone to visit his father, who is buried at Mašhad, thus leaving the city defenseless against the elements (Donaldson, p. 264).

Recourse to astrologers was common during cataclysmic occurrences, and there were also individuals who predicted earthquakes. The astrologer Abū Ṭāher Šīrāzī was reported to have predicted the exact date of the earthquake that destroyed Tabrīz during the night of 14 Ṣafar 434/3 October 1042 and killed more than 40,000 people. He was consequently chosen to direct the reconstruction of the city and announced that in the future Tabrīz would no longer be in danger. Ḥamd-Allāh Mostawfī, writing in 741/1340, noted that the prediction had proved correct (*Nozhat al-qolūb*, ed. Le Strange, pp. 75-76; tr., pp. 78-79; Ebn al-Aṯīr, IX, p. 513). After an earthquake at Urmia in 1300/1883 an astrologer from Tehran sent a telegram informing the population that the earth would continue to tremble for forty days. Armenian priests consulted their books and announced a new shock for the next morning at 11 o'clock. A mulla from Tabrīz predicted an aftershock for the following Sunday at 2:00 p.m., which set off a panic among the population. As his prediction did not come true, the mulla was arrested (S. G. Wilson, pp. 224-25). On 21 Jomādā I 1261/28 May 1845, at about four hours before nightfall, a tremor was felt 2 parasangs (ca. 14 km) from Mašhad just at the place where the European traveler J. P. Ferrier was preparing to camp for the night; his guide concluded that the tremor was a bad omen and moved the camp (Ferrier, I, p. 260).

In such a situation of permanent danger it is paradoxical that no systematic adaptation of traditional Persian construction techniques to the frequency of earth tremors has been attempted, at least until very recently (Ambraseys and Melville, p. 25). After the great earthquake of 1194/1780 at Tabrīz the inhabitants began to build their walls as low as possible, using wood instead of brick and stucco, and to roof the *bāzārs* with planks, rather than with domes (Morier, pp. 278-79). Nevertheless, in 1232/1817 they again rebuilt the city walls to a considerable height (Johnson, p. 212). In the same city it was apparently Westerners in the service of the crown prince ʿAbbās Mīrzā (q.v.) who first introduced construction methods that provided a certain security, particularly wood-frame structures with flexible joints (known as *taḵta-pūš*); while such methods seem to have been reserved for temporary shelters in gardens (Ker Porter, II, p. 502), the old houses were rebuilt in the traditional fashion. After the earthquake of 1288/1871 at Qūčān a new type of emergency shelter appeared: beams removed from the ruins were assembled in "A" frames or used as ridge poles, the walls being plastered with earth (MacGregor, II, pp. 85-86). When such a house had to be enlarged, an identical building was constructed parallel to the first and the space between enclosed with walls and covered with a flat roof. Houses of this type, consisting of one to three rooms, withstood the earthquakes of 1311/1893 and 1313/1895 and were still in place in 1322/1904 (Huntington, p. 236, pl. 27). But these ephemeral improvements do not seem to have had any long-term impact. In the 1960s there were private attempts in the comfortable neighborhoods of northern Tehran to bring spherical houses, already ill-adapted to the sloping terrain, up to antiseismic standards (Ambraseys and Melville, pp. 25-26, pl. 26), but no official regulations were ever adopted. In fact, Persia, which includes some of the most seismically active regions in the world, seems never to have been seriously concerned about the danger and the need for preventive measures. Daily life is marked by indifference and appears not to have been noticeably affected by major episodes. The historical repercussions have been none the less significant, particularly for the fates of certain cities. The decline of Qūmes in the 9th century, of Sīrāf in the 11th, and of Nīšāpūr after the 12th-14th centuries seems to have been largely owing to destructive earthquakes (Ambraseys and Melville, p. 109).

Bibliography: (For cited works not given in detail, see "Short References.") R. Afsarī, "Zelzelahā-ye Kermān...," *Waḥīd*, nos. 219-20, 1356 Š./1977, pp. 69-78. N. N. Ambraseys, "A Test Case of Historical Seismicity. Isfahan and Chahar Mahal, Iran," *Geographical Journal* 145, 1979, pp. 56-71. Idem and C. P. Melville, *A History of Persian Earthquakes*, Cambridge, 1982. M. Berberian, *Contribution to the Seismotectonics of Iran*, Geological Survey of Iran Report 39, Tehran, 1976. ʿA. Dawlatābādī, "Zelzelahā-ye Tabrīz," *NDA*, Tabrīz 16, 1343 Š./1964, pp. 137-62. P. Della Valle, *Voyages* . . ., 4 vols., Paris, 1663-65. M. D. Donaldson, *The Shiite Religion. A History of Islam in Persia and Irak*, London, 1937. J. P. Ferrier, *Voyages en Perse* . . ., 2 vols., Paris, 1860. W. B. Fisher, "The Land," in *Camb. Hist. Iran* I, pp. 3-110 E. Huntington, "The Basin of Eastern Persia and Sistan," in R. Pumpelly, *Explorations in Eastern Turkestan*, Washington, D.C., 1905. J. Johnson, *Voyage de l'Inde en Angleterre, par la Perse* . . ., 2 vols., Paris, 1818. R. Ker Porter, *Travels in Georgia, Persia* . . ., 2 vols., London, 1822. C. M. MacGregor, *Narrative of a Journey through the Province of Khorassan and the N.W. Frontier of Afghanistan in 1875*, 2 vols., London, 1879. C. Melville, "Earthquakes in the History of Nishapur," *Iran* 18, 1980, pp. 103-20. Idem, "Historical Monuments and Earthquakes in Tabriz," *Iran* 19, 1981, pp. 159-77. J. Morier, *A Journey through Persia* ..., London, 1812. A. Nīkū-hemmat, "Zelzelahā-ye tārīḵī-e kāšān," *Waḥīd*, nos. 260-61, 1358 Š./1979, pp. 62-65. S. Schöler, *Aktuelle und historische Seismizität im Vorderen und Mittleren Orient*, Beihefte TAVO, A 17, Wiesbaden, 1992. Idem and E. Bauer, *Vordere Orient—Seismotektonik, geschichtliche Beben*, TAVO, A. II. 3, Wiesbaden, 1984. J. S. Tchalenko et al., *Materials for the Study of Seismotectonics of Iran. North-Central Iran*, Geological Survey of Iran, Report 29, Tehran, 1974. A. T. Wilson, "Earthquakes in Persia," *BSO(A)S* 6, 1930, pp. 103-31. S. G. Wilson, *Persian Life and Customs*, 3rd ed., New York, 1900.

(XAVIER DE PLANHOL)

iv. THE HISTORICAL RECORD OF EARTHQUAKES IN PERSIA

Introduction. The Iranian plateau, characterized by active faulting, active folding, recent volcanic activities, and considerable elevation contrasts along the Alpine-Himalayan mountain belt, has been frequently struck by catastrophic earthquakes during recorded history. These earthquakes have resulted in great loss of life and, by rendering large numbers of people homeless and disrupting the agricultural and industrial bases of their lives, have wasted natural resources.

Archaeoseismicity. Large, destructive earthquakes are very infrequent. The dormant period between large-magnitude earthquakes on a particular fault or fault segment in Persia ranges from many centuries to millennia (Berberian, 1981, pp. 44-45; Ambraseys and Melville, 1982, pp. 158-62; Berberian et al., 1992, pp. 1728-31). The great length of the earthquake cycle for most active faults in Persia results in a paucity of historical (pre-1900) and instrumental (20th century) data from which to assess earthquake hazards or derive an understanding of the mechanism of faulting. Unlike instrumental and historical seismic records, the archaeological and geological records of earthquake activity extend many earthquake cycles into the past. Archaeological sites and historical monuments may yield direct or indirect evidence of earthquake activity. They may contain episodes of rebuilding or repairs following earthquakes.

Several archaeological sites and monuments have provided earthquake information on Persia: Sagzābād about the middle of the 3rd millennium B.C.E. (Negahbān, 1973, pp. 11-13; Berberian et al., 1993, pp. 100-102), Ak-Tapa of 4,000 B.C.E. (Golinsky, 1982, p. 519), Gowdīn-Tapa of 4,000-3,350 B.C.E. (Young, 1968, p. 160), Mārlīk of 3,000-2,000 B.C.E. (Negahbān, 1990, p. 146; Berberian et al., 1992, pp. 1728-31), Parthian Nesā of 10 B.C.E.-10 C.E. (Golinsky, 1982, p. 519), Kangāvar Anāhītā Temple of the 17th century B.C.E. and 224-642 C.E. (Kāmbaḵš-Fard, 1974, p. 47), Bīšāpūr city of 293-302 and 531-79 C.E., late 10th century (Sarfarāz, 1987, pp. 45, 56, 71, and personal communication, January 1994; Berberian, 1994, p. 221), Nīšāpūr of 1145 and 1270 (Wilkinson, 1975, pp. xxxv, xxxvi), and Masjed-e-Jāmeʿ of Qāen of 1066 (Nāderī, 1980, pp. 103-07). The decline of civilization in the following cities seems to have been partly, if not largely, due to large-magnitude earthquakes, some of which were associated with long surface faulting: Sagzābād, Mārlīk, Kūmeš (after the 856 earthquake), Zarang/Sīstān (around 734, 805, and 815 C.E.), Sīrāf (978 and 1008 C.E.; Ṭāherī), Nīšāpūr (1145, 1209, 1251, 1270, 1389, and 1405), and Jīzd (1336). (For more information, see Berberian, 1994, pp. 53-161.)

Historical (pre-1900) earthquakes. Historical records of catastrophic earthquakes have survived for centuries. At least nine destructive earthquakes in Nīšāpūr/Šādyāḵ have reduced the size and changed the location of the city several times (Melville, 1980, pp. 116-17). Ray has been devastated at least six times in its recorded history (Ambraseys, 1974, pp.

50-68; Berberian et al., 1985, pp. 221-30, 287). Almost all monuments in Tabrīz were destroyed or severely damaged by at least eight large-magnitude earthquakes, especially by the one on 29 D̲u'l-Hejja 1193/7 January 1780, which reduced all buildings to rubble. Unfortunately, except for the Blue Mosque (Masjed-e-Moẓaffarīya) built in 870/1465, the city now has very few historical monuments (Ṭabāṭabā'ī-Tabrīzī, 1294/1877, p. 121; Berberian and Aršadī, 1976, pp. 397-418; Melville, 1981, p. 167; Golombeck and Wilber, 1988, pp. 31, 407-409). Table 44 below lists the most important historical earthquakes in the Iranian plateau. (For more precise information, see Ambraseys and Melville, 1982, pp. 158-62; Berberian, 1994, pp. 11-413; Figure 32.)

20th-century earthquakes. Since the beginning of this century at least 126,000 people have lost their lives in destructive earthquakes in Persia. These losses cannot be justified in light of existing scientific knowledge and expertise in disaster management. Table 45 lists the most important earthquakes in Persia since 1900.

The Ṭabas-e-Golšan earthquake of 25 Šahrīvar 1357/16 September 1978 (Ms=7.4; Berberian, 1979, pp. 1861-87; 1982, pp.449-530) and the Rūdbār-Ṭārom earthquake of 31 Ḵordād 1369/20 June 1990 (Ms=7.4; Berberian et al., 1992, pp. 1726-55) were the most catastrophic earthquakes to have occurred in Persia to date in the 20th century. The Ṭabas-e-Golšan earthquake destroyed or severely damaged

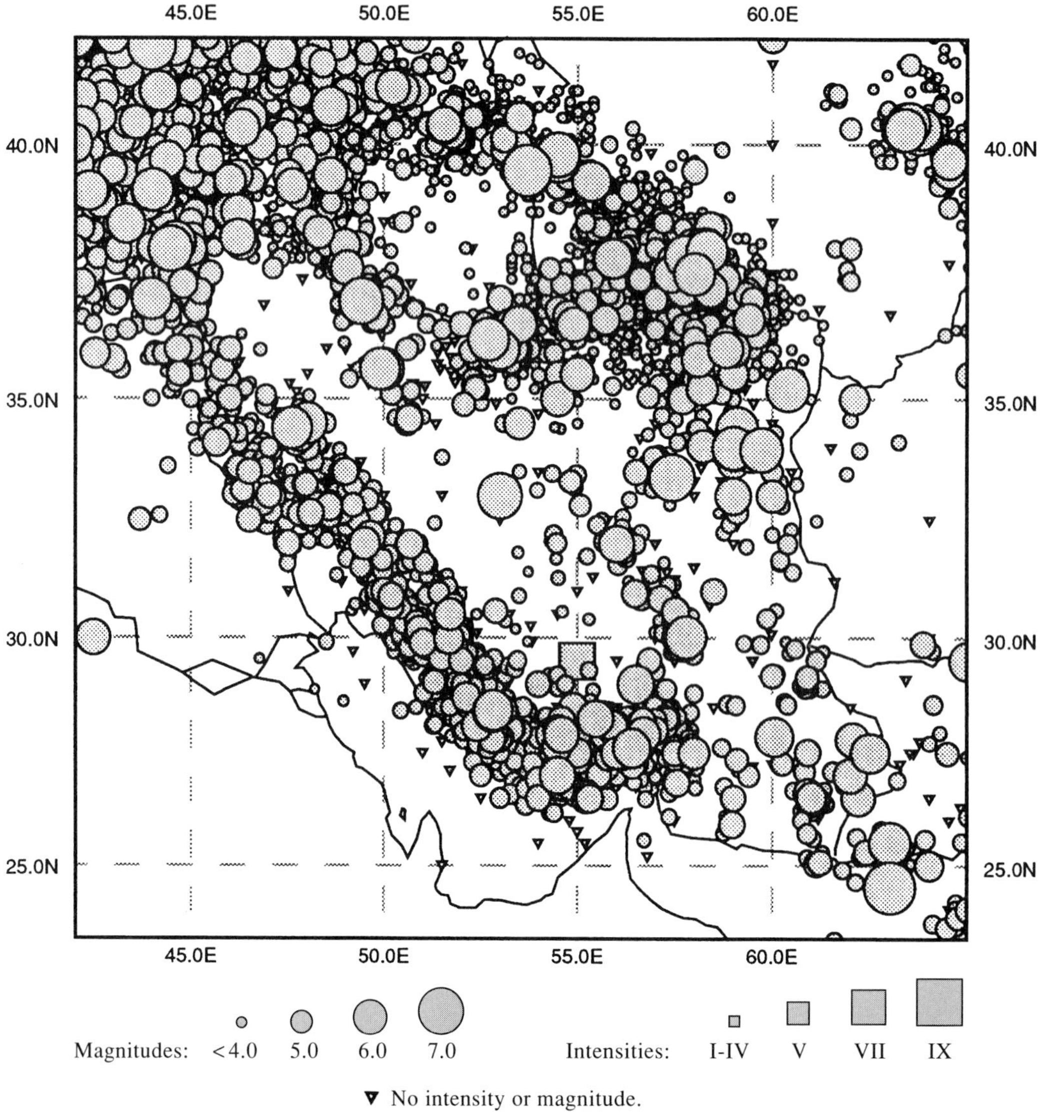

Figure 32. Seismicity of Persia, by the author

Table 44

HISTORICAL (PRE-1900) DESTRUCTIVE EARTHQUAKES IN PERSIA

Date	Location	Reported Casualties
10 B.C.E.-10 C.E.	Parthian Nesā	K+
ca. 734/111-120	Zarang/Sīstān	n.a.
743/125	Tang-e Sār Darra	K
840/225	Ahvāz	K
855/241	Ray	K+
856/242	Dāmḡān/Kūmeš	45,096
872/258	Saymara-Darra Šahr	20,000
943/331	Samalqān	5,000
958/346	Ray-Rūyān	K
1008/398	Dīnavar	16,000+
1008/398	Sīrāf (Tāharī)	K
1042/434	Tabrīz	40,000
1052/444	Bayhaq (Sabzavār)	K
1052/444	Arjān	K
1107/500	Kargsar/Dīnavar	K
1119/513	Qazvīn	K
1127/521	Farīm	K
1177/572	Ray-Karaj-Qazvīn	K
1209/605	Nīšāpūr	10,000
1270/669	Nīšāpūr	10,000
1273/671	Tabrīz	250
1301/700	Farīm	K
1304/704	Tabrīz	K
1336/737	Jīzd-Zūzan	20,000
1389/791	Nīšāpūr	K+
1405/808	Nīšāpūr	30,000
1440/844	Kārzīn-Qīr	10,000
1485/890	Šakūr-Tonekābon	K+
1493/898	Nowzād	K+
1497/902	Hormoz-Bandar-e ʿAbbās	K+
1498/903	Jorjān (old Gorgān)	1,000
1593/100	Lār	K
1608/1017	Rūdbarāt-Tāleqān	K+
1619/1028	Dūḡābād	800
1641/1050	Dehḵᵛārqān-Tabrīz	K+
1665/1075	Damāvand	K
1666/1076	NW Ardal	K
1673/1084	Mašhad	5,600
1678/1088	Lāhījān	K
1678/1089	Gonābād	K
1695/1106	Esfarāyen	K+
1721/1133	Šeblī-Tabrīz	40,000
1780/1194	Tabrīz	50,000
1808/1223	Rešm	K
1809/1224	Āmol	K
1825/1239	Harāz	K
1830/1245	Damāvand	K
1838/1254	Noṣratābād	K
1844/1260	Mīāna-Garmīrūd	K+
1851/1267	Sarvelāyat	2,000+
1871/1288	Qūčān	K
1879/1296	SE Bozqūš	2,000+
1890/1307	Tāš	K+
1893/1311	Qūčān	10,000+

- *Continued on next page* -

Table 44 (Continued)
HISTORICAL (PRE-1900) DESTRUCTIVE EARTHQUAKES IN PERSIA

Date	Location	Reported Casualties
1895/1312	Qūčān	1,000
1896/1313	Sangābād-Ḵalḵāl	1,100+

K: Unspecified number of fatalities; K+: Heavy casualties.

Source: Ambraseys and Melville, 1982, pp. 158-62; Berberian, 1994, pp. 11-413.

Table 45
DESTRUCTIVE EARTHQUAKES IN 20TH-CENTURY PERSIA

Date	Time (GMT)	MAG. (M$_s$)	Location	Casualties
1282Š./1903.09.25	01:20	5.9	Toršīz/Kāšmar	350
1287Š./1909.01.23	02:48	7.4	Sīlāḵor	6,000
1290Š./1911.04.18	18:14	6.2	Rāvar-Lakar Kūh	50
1302Š./1923.05.25	22:21	5.5	Kāj Deraḵt	2,200
1302Š./1923.09.22	20:47	6.7	Lālahzār	290
1308Š./1929.05.01	15:37	7.3	Baḡān-Garmāb	3,800
1309Š./1930.05.06	22:34	7.7	Salmās	2,500
1313Š./1934.06.13	22:10	6.9	Makrān	n.a.
1314Š./1935.04.11	23:14	6.8	Ḵosūt/Tajan Rūd	400
1324Š./1945.11.27	21:56	8.0	Makrān	4,100
1326Š./1947.08.05	14:24	7.6	Makrān	n.a.
1326Š./1947.09.23	12:28	6.8	Dūstābād	500
1327Š./1948.10.05	20:12	7.2	Ashkhabad	10,000
1331Š./1953.02.12	08:15	6.5	Torūd	930
1336Š./1957.07.02	00:42	6.8	Sangčāl	1,100
1336Š./1957.12.13	01:45	6.7	Farsīnaj	1,200
1337Š./1958.08.16	19:13	6.6	Fīrūzābād	130
1340Š./1961.06.11	05:10	6.5	Deh-Kūya	60
1341Š./1962.09.01	19:20	7.2	Būyīn Zahrā	12,200
1347Š./1968.08.31	10:47	7.4	Dašt-e-Bayāż	10,000
1347Š./1968.09.01	07:27	6.4	Ferdows	1,000
1351Š./1972.04.10	02:06	6.9	Qīr-Kārzīn	5,010
1356Š./1977.03.21	21:18	7.0	Ḵūrgū	152
1356Š./1977.04.06	13:36	6.1	Naḡān	366
1357Š./1978.09.16	15:35	7.4	Ṭabas-e-Golšan	20,000
1358Š./1979.11.14	02:21	6.6	Korīzān	171
1358Š./1979.11.27	17:10	7.1	Kolī	20
1360Š./1981.06.11	07:24	6.7	Golbāf	1,400
1360Š./1981.07.28	17:22	7.1	Sīrč	1,300
1369Š./1990.06.20	21:00	7.4	Rūdbār-Ṭārom	40,000
1369Š./1990.11.06	18.45	6.7	Fūrg	22
1372Š./1994.02.23	08:02	6.1	Safīdāba	6

MAG.: Magnitude. Ms:Surface-wave magnitude.

Source: Berberian, 1979, p. 1862; idem, 1981, pp. 42-50; idem et al., 1992, p. 1731; Ambraseys and Melville, pp. 164-66.

about ninety villages, slightly damaged another fifty villages in the region, and completely demolished the oasis town of Ṭabas-e-Golšan, where 85 percent of the inhabitants (11,000 out of 13,000) perished. Total fatalities were more than 20,000 with thousands injured. This earthquake, strongly felt over an area of 1,130,000 square km, destroyed over 15,000 housing units and thirty *qanāts* (q.v.) in the epicen-

tral region (Berberian, 1989, pp. 1861-87). The Rūdbār-Ṭārom earthquake, the largest in this century to affect an urban area in Persia, killed over 40,000 people, injured 60,000, and left more than 500,000 homeless. The earthquake destroyed three towns (Rūdbār, Manjīl, and Lowšān) and 700 villages and damaged another 300 villages in Gīlān and Zanjān provinces of northwest Persia, southwest of the Caspian Sea. Nearly 100,000 buildings were destroyed or badly damaged. Water supplies in 283 villages were destroyed or reduced by 70 percent, several thousand livestock were buried under debris, and farms and irrigation canals were seriously damaged. In addition, 1,200 km of rural roads now require repair or reconstruction (Berberian et al., 1992, pp. 1726-55). Economic losses caused by this earthquake have been estimated at $7.2 billion, constituting 7.2 percent of the GNP (UNESCO, *DHA News*, Department of Humanitarian Affairs, 1992, p. 30). The long-term effects of this catastrophic event, such as the disruption of major economic links between three large provinces, the resettlement of populations from at least three large towns and 700 villages, and the reconstruction of buildings according to modern standards will take decades to accomplish and will absorb a considerable part of the country's resources.

Bibliography: N. N. Ambraseys, "Historical Seismicity of North-Central Iran," *Materials for the Study of Seismotectonics of Iran. North Central Iran,* Geological Survey of Iran, Tehran, 1974, rep. no. 29, pp. 47-95. N. N. Ambraseys and C. P. Melville, *A History of Persian Earthquakes*, Cambridge, 1982. Ebn Marzbān Bahmanyār, *Jām-e jahān-nomā,* eds. ʿA. Nūrānī and M.-T. Dānešpažūh, Tehran, 1362 Š./1983. M. Berberian, *Contribution to the Seismotectonics of Iran*, pt. II, Geological Survey of Iran 39, Tehran, 1976; pt. III, Tehran, 1977. Idem, "Earthquake Faulting and Bedding Thrust Associated with the Tabas-e-Golshan (Iran) Earthquake of September 16, 1978," *Bulletin of the Seismological Society of America* 69/6, 1979, pp. 1861-87. Idem, "Active Faulting and Tectonics of Iran," in H. K. Gupta and F. M. Delany, eds., *Zagros-Hindu Kush-Himalaya Geodynamic Evolution*, Geodynamics Series III, American Geophysical Union, Washington, D.C., 1981, pp. 33-69. Idem, "The Southern Caspian: A Compressional Depression Floored by a Trapped, Modified Oceanic Crust," *Canadian Journal of Earth Science* 20/2, 1983, pp. 163-83. Idem, *Continental Deformation in the Iranian Plateau (Contribution to the Seismotectonics of Iran*, pt. IV), Geological Survey of Iran 52, 1983 (625 pp. in English; 74 pp. in Persian). Idem, .*Natural Hazards and The First Earthquake Catalogue of Iran;* I: *Historical Hazards in Iran Prior to 1900*. UNESCO/IIEES publication during UN/IDNDR, Paris and Tehran, 1994. M. Berberian and S. Arshadi, "On the Evidence of the Youngest Activity of the North Tabriz Fault and the Seismicity of Tabriz City," *Geological Survey of Iran* 39, Tehran, 1976, pp. 397-418. M. Berberian, J. A. Jackson, M. Qorashi, and M. H. Kadjar, "Field and Teleseismic Observations of the 1981 Golbaf-Sirch Earthquakes in SE Iran," *Geophysical Journal of Royal Astronomical Society* (London) 77, 1984, pp. 809-38. M. Berberian, M. Qorayšī, B. Aržangrāveš, and A. Mohājer-Ašja'ī, "Pažūheš o barrasī ..." (Recent Tectonics, Seismotectonics and Earthquake-fault Hazard Study of the Greater Tehran Region), *Contribution to the Seismotectonics of Iran,* pt. V. Geological Survey of Iran 56, Tehran, 1985; 2nd ed. 1371 Š./1992; and pt. VI, 61, Tehran, 1993. M. Berberian, M. Qorashi, J. A. Jackson, K. Priestley, and T. Wallace, "The Rudbar-Tarom Earthquake of June 20, 1990 in NW Iran: Preliminary Field and Seismotectonic Observations and its Tectonic Significance," *Bulletin of the Seismological Soceity of America* 82/4, 1992, pp. 1726-55. G. L. Golinsky, "Description of the Major Earthquakes in Western Turkmenia SSR," in N.V. Kondorskaya and N. V. Shebalin, eds., *New Catalog of Strong Earthquakes in the USSR from Ancient Times through 1977,* World Data Center A, U.S. National Oceanic and Atmospheric Administation , Denver (Col.), Report SE-31, 1982, pp. 519-24. L. Golombek and D. Wilber, *The Timurid Architecture of Iran and Turan*, 2 vols., Princeton, 1988. G. P. Gorshkov, *Zemletryaseniya Turkmenii* (Earthquakes of Turkmenia), *Trudy Seismol.*, no. 122, Akademi Nauk, Moscow, 1947. K. H. Jacob and R. C. Quittmeyer, "The Makran of Pakistan and Iran: Trench-arc System with Active Plate Subduction," in A. Farah and K. De Jong, eds., *Geodynamics of Pakistan,* Geological Survey of Pakistan, Quetta, 1979, pp. 305-17. S. Kāmbak̲š-Fard, "Kāvešhā-ye ʿelmī ..." (Excavations at Ānāhītā Temple, Kangāvar). *Bāstānšenāsī o honar-e Īrān*, ... Archaeological Institute, nos. 11-12, 1353 Š./1974, pp. 40-49. Šaraf-al-Dīn Moḥammad Masʿūdī Marvazī, *Do resāla dar āṯār-e ʿolwī*, ed. M.-T. Dānešpažūh, Tehran, 1337 Š./1958. C. P. Melville, "Earthquakes in the History of Nishapur," *Iran* XVIII, 1980, pp. 103-22. Idem, "Historical Monuments and Earthquakes in Tabriz," *Iran* XIX, 1981, pp. 159-71. Ḥamd-Allāh Mostawfī Qazvīnī, *Nozhat al-qolūb*, Pers. tr. M. Dabīrsīāqī, Tehran, 1336 Š./1957; Eng. tr. Le Strange. Moses Khorene, *History of the Armenians*, tr. Thompson. B. Nāderī, "Masjed-e-Jāmeʿ-e Qāen," *Našrīya-ye sāzmān-e mellī-e ḥefāzat-e āṯār-e bāstānī* (Bulletin of the National Organization for the Protection of Ancient Heritage) 10, 1359 Š./1980, pp. 103-07. Nāṣer-e K̲osrow, *Safar-nāma wa zād al-mosāferīn,* ed. M. Dabīrsīāqī, Tehran, 1355 Š./1976. E. O. Negahbān, "Gozāreš-e moqadamātī ..." (Preliminary Report of the Excavation of Sagzābād, 1970 Season), *Mārlīk* I, Esfand 1351 Š./March 1973, pp. 11-13. Idem, "Silver Vessels of Marlik with Gold Spouts and Impressed Gold Designs," Iranica Varia 16, 1990, pp. 144-51. A.-A. Sarfarāz, "Bīšāpūr," in *Šahrhā-ye Īrān* (Iranian Cities), ed., M.-Y. Kīānī, Tehran, 1366 Š./1987, pp. 23-74. Šāhmardān b. Abi'l-K̲ayr, *Nozhat-nāma-ye ʿAlāʾī*, ed. F. Jahānpūr, Tehran 1362 Š./1983. M.-R. Ṭabāṭabāʾī-Tabrīzī, *Tarīk̲-e-awlād al-aṯhār*, Tabrīz, 1304/1887, and Tehran, 1314/1896. Moḥammad b. Maḥmūd b.

Aḥmad Ṭūsī, *ʿAjāʾeb al-maḵlūqāt wa ğarāʾeb al-mawjūdāt*, ed. M. Sotūda, Tehran, 1345 Š./1966. T. Cuyler Young, Jr., "Godin Tepe," *Iran* VI, 1968, pp. 160-61. Idem, "Godin Tepe," *Iran* X, 1972, pp. 184-86. T. Cuyler Young, Jr., and H. Weiss, "Godin Tepe," *Iran* XII, 1974, pp. 207-11. Zakarīyā Qazvīnī, Zakarīyā b. Moḥammad ..., *Aṯār al-belād wa aḵbār al-ʿebād*, ed. F. Wüstenfeld, Göttingen, 1848; partial Pers. tr. ʿA.-R. Šarafkandī, Tehran, 1366 Š./1987.

(MANUEL BERBERIAN)

EAST AFRICA, Persian relations with the lands of the East African coast, particularly Somalia, Kenya, and Tanzania.

i. *Economic, political, and cultural relations through 1900.*
ii. *Persian loanwords in Swahili.*
iii. *Baluchi and Parsi communities.*
iv. *Bahai communities.*

i. ECONOMIC, POLITICAL, AND CULTURAL RELATIONS THROUGH 1900

From early times monsoon winds have permitted rapid maritime travel between East Africa and Western Asia. Persian relations with the African coastal regions were largely via this maritime trade network (Hourani, pp. 4-6, 38, 79-82). Although large-scale Persian settlement in East Africa is unlikely and the only known Persian inscription in East Africa comes from an imported glazed tile, now lost, decorating a tomb at Tongoni (Freeman-Grenville and Martin, p. 116), Persian cultural and religious influences nonetheless were felt. Ki-Swahili, the language of the East African coastal regions, contains Persian loan words (q.v.), mainly nautical terms. Archeological evidence from East Africa shows economic connections with the ports of southern Persia from the 3rd to the 15th centuries C.E., and African traditional history connects the founding of some of the East African ports with Shiraz.

Sasanian interest in East Africa seems to have been largely directed toward the Red Sea and the northern coast of Somalia. Competition between Ethiopian and Persian merchants for the lucrative Indian trade may have been one cause of the Persian campaigns in Yemen during the reign of Ḵosrow I (r. 531-79), which campaigns led to Sasanian control of the Red Sea route to the Indian Ocean (Cosmas Indicopleustes apud Wolska-Conus, pp. 141, 159, 197; Procopius, *de bello Persico* 1.20.9-12). Persia may also have been after slaves, who in the pre-Islamic period were obtained from the Horn of Africa. Duan Chengshi, in *Yuyang za zu* (ca. 850 C.E.), describing an earlier period, also refers to "Possu" (probably here meaning "Persian") merchants on the coast of Bobali (possibly northern Somalia) who formed caravans of several thousand men to obtain ivory and ambergris (Duyvendak, pp. 13-14). Before trading, these merchants were forced to draw blood and swear an oath. Persian ceramics of the 3rd/ 5th centuries C.E. have been found at the site of Ras Hafun (probably ancient Opone) in northern Somalia (Smith and Wright, pp. 125, 138-40), though 5th century ceramics, very similar to those from Ras Hafun, have been claimed from Chibuene in southern Mozambique and from the island of Ngazidja in the Comoro archipelago (Sinclair, p. 190). The 4th/10th-century *Ḥodūd al-ʿālam* (tr. Minorsky, pp. 163-64, with commentary), the only surviving early Persian geographical text with detained evidence on East Africa, describes the coast, termed Zangestān, as lying opposite Fārs, Kermān, and Sind; the people are described as extremely black, with curly hair and the nature of wild animals. Three towns are noted: M.ljān (possibly Unguja, the original name of Zanzibar Island), the port visited by foreign merchants; Sofāla, the royal capital, in modern Mozambique; and Hwfl (a corruption of Waqwāq?), the richest in goods. Gold is important, and ancient gold mines are well known from the basement rock complex of southern Africa (Summers, pp. 11-17, 31-104; settlement sites in the interior, such as Mapungubwe/K2, were in contact with the coast by at least the 10th century C.E. and probably much earlier (Hall, pp. 74-90).

Masʿūdī (*Morūj*, ed. Pellat, I, pp. 112-13, 124-25; II, p. 113), who last visited East Africa in 304/916 on a ship owned by two brothers from Sīrāf, suggests that regular voyages were made from Oman and Sīrāf to the Belād al-Zanj, and in particular to the port of Qanbalū (most likely Pemba Island). Masʿūdī (who was writing after the Zanj revolt) suggests ivory was the main export. Jāḥeẓ suggests (*Rasāʾel*, written ca. 235/850, para. 210-213) that many Zanj slaves came from Lanjuya (Unguja, Zanzibar Island) and Qanbalū. These claims are supported by recent archaeological work that has yielded 6th-century-C.E. radiocarbon dates from Unguja Ukuu on Zanzibar and 3rd-4th/9-10th century occupation at Ras Mkumbuu and Mtambwe Mkuu on Pemba. Other African exports were ambergris and timber, especially mangrove poles. Ebn Ḥawqal (q.v.; tr. Kramers, p. 277) records that Sīrāf was built with *sāj* (teakwood) and other kinds of wood from East Africa.

The ports in the Lamu archipelago, though not mentioned in the literary sources, are known from archeological evidence to have also played a central part in the maritime trade. Excavations at Manda (Chittick, pp. 65-106) and Shanga (Horton, forthcoming) have produced ceramic assemblages very similar to those from Sīrāf, including numerous unglazed storage jars that were actually made in Sīrāf as well as the more widely distributed Sasanian-Islamic glazed jars and white-glazed wares. Chinese stonewares have also been found at these levels.

By the 5th/11th century the Indian Ocean trade had shifted to the ports at the head of the Persian Gulf, in particular Kīš and Hormoz (Ricks, pp. 352-55), which traded East African products to India, the Far East, and the West. In East Africa, the shift was marked by the appearance of sgraffito pottery manufactured in the Makrān. During the late 7th/13th century, the main center of the East African trade moved to the South Arabian coast. Though some Persian Gulf pottery found its way to East Africa in the 9th/15th century, by the time of Portuguese contact, East Africa was trading directly with either Aden or the ports of western India, not with the Persian Gulf itself.

African traditional history recognizes early connections with the Persian Gulf. The most pervasive are stories of origin from Shiraz. The *Ketāb al-solwa fī ak̲bār Kelwa* (BM Or. 2666; excerpts and summary in Freeman-Grenville, 1962, pp. 45ff.) tells of the voyage of seven ships manned by a father who, after a dream, left Shiraz with his six sons for East Africa, founding towns at Mandakha, Shaugu, Yanbu, Mombasa, Pemba, Kilwa, and Hanzuan. Another tradition recorded by the Portuguese in the 16th century tells of a migration of seven brothers from Laçah [al-Ḥasā in eastern Arabia], but it is unclear whether this is another version of the same story or a distinct tradition (J. de Barros, *Decadas da Asia*, ed. A. Baiao, Coimbra, 1930, I/8/4; trans. in Freeman-Grenville, 1962, pp. 31-32).

Chronicles from Mombasa, Vumba, and the Comoros give local elaborations of the Shirazi origin myth; the coastal peoples who claimed these origins often termed themselves "Shirazi," and a political party—the "Afro-Shirazi" party—was formed in 1957. Explanations for this myth—no modern scholar accepts that any substantial migration took place from Shiraz—range from the extensive trade links with Sīrāf/Shiraz to religious and political factors. Allen (pp. 116-18, 179) suggests that the Shirazi myth is an Islamization of indigenous origin myths, particularly those associated with Shungwaya. Alternatively, the African courts may have looked to Buyid Shiraz as a model. Hints of this come from the descriptions of court practice and apparel. These were observed by Ebn Baṭṭūṭa (q.v.) in Mogadishu (pp. 179-96; tr. Defrèmery and Sanguinetti, II, pp 179-96; tr. Gibb, II, pp. 373-83), where state processions in which the ruler dressed in turban and cloak, shaded by ceremonial parasols, were preceded by a band, and followed by barefoot court officials including viziers and amirs. The Song annals (*Song Shu* 490, f 20 verso) describe a delegation of Africans from Zangistan who reached China in the late 11th century. The annals call the African ruler by the Buyid title Amīr-e amīrān (Chin. *Ameiluo Ameilan*; Hirth and Rockhill, p. 127; see AMĪR-AL-OMARĀʾ). This use of Shirazi practice may explain the observance of the Persian New Year, "Siku ya Mwaka," on Zanzibar (Gray, 1954; 1962, p. 20), although this could equally well be linked to seafarers' use of Now-Rūz (*Nairuzi*) in the navigational calendar (Tibbetts, pp. 361-66). The surviving titles such as Sheha (locally elected chief) and dīvānī (ruler) have also been cited as evidence for Persian links, but are more likely the result of the adoption of general Arabic terms for government offices by Swahili Muslims.

Islamization of the East African coast may have followed trade contacts with Sīrāf/Shiraz. A 10th-century mosque at Shanga is very similar to family mosques in Sīrāf (Horton, 1991, p. 43). The floriated and plaited Kufic inscriptions on *meḥrābs* at Kizimkazi (Plate LV) and Tumbatu in Zanzibar resemble inscriptions carved at Sīrāf in the 11th and 12th centuries (Whitehouse, p. 56), although the style of the polyloped arch seems to draw more upon North African or Spanish influences; local coral is used for the Zanzibar inscriptions . Two Persians were recorded on Arabic inscriptions from Mogadishu during the 13th century: Abū ʿAbd-Allāh b. Moḥammad b. Aḥmad al-Nīsabūrī al-K̲orāsānī on a tombstone, dated 614/1217, and K̲osrow b. Moḥammad al-Šīrāzī on a *meḥrāb* inscription at the ʿArbaʿa Rokūn mosque, dated 667/1268-69 (Freeman-Grenville and Martin, pp. 102-03).

PLATE LV

Meḥrāb of mosque at Kizimkazi, Dimbari, Zanzibar, dated 500/1107, with a Kufic inscription very similar to those found in Sīrāf and Shiraz. Courtesy of 1M. Horton

The last period of Persian influence came in the 19th century when Saʿīd bin Solṭān (1806-56), the Omani ruler of Zanzibar, took two Persian wives. The first—Šāhzāda, daughter of Ḥosayn-ʿAlī Mīrzā Farmānfarmā, the governor of Fārs—came from Shiraz. She went to Zanzibar in 1832 and left with the dissolution of the marriage in 1833. The second marriage was in 1849 to a daughter of Īraj Mīrzā, an alleged son of Moḥammad Shah; this, too, was dissolved a few years later.

Palaces built in Zanzibar to accommodate Persian tastes fashionable at the time, including baths, have survived. Those at Kidichi, probably built in 1832, were elaborately decorated in stucco by masons brought from Persia (*Zanzibar Guide*, p. 64). Saʿīd b. Solṭān relied on Baluchi mercenaries, recruited at Gwadur and Mukulla, to secure Zanzibar and the coastal regions. They were garrisoned at the fort in Zanzibar but acted more as police than as a standing army. They rarely numbered more than eighty.

Bibliography: (For cited works not given in detail, see "Short References.") J. de V. Allen, *Swahili Origins. Swahili Culture and the Shungwaya Phenomenon*, London, 1993. H. N. Chittick, *Manda. Excavations at an Island Port on the Kenyan Coast*, Nairobi, 1984. J. J. L. Duyvendak, *China's Discovery of Africa*, London, School of Oriental and African Studies Occasional Paper, 1949. G. S. P. Freeman-Grenville, *The Medieval History of the Coast of Tanganyika*, Oxford, 1962. Idem, "Shi'i Rulers at Kilwa," *Numismatic Chronicle*, 7th ser., 1978, pp. 187-90. Idem and B. G. Martin, "A Preliminary Handlist of the Arabic Inscriptions of the East African Coast," *JRAS*, 1972, pp. 98-122. H. A. R. Gibb, tr., *The Travels of Ibn Battuta. AD 1325-1354* II, London, 1962. J. Gray, "Nairuzi, or Siku ya Mwaka," *Tanganyikan Notes and Records* XXXVIII (Dar es Salaam), 1954, pp. 1-23; XXXXI, 1954, pp. 68-72. Idem, *A History of Zanzibar from the Middle Ages to 1856*, London, 1962. M. Hall, *The Changing Past. Farmers, Kings, and Traders in Southern Africa, 200-1860*, Cape Town and Johannesburg, 1987. F. Hirth and W. W. Rockhill, *Chau Ju-kua. His Work on the Chinese and Arab Trade in the 12th and 13th Centuries, entitled Chu-fan-chi*, St. Petersburg, 1911. M. C. Horton, "Primitive Architecture and Islam in East Africa," *Muqarnas* 8, 1991, pp. 103-06. Idem, *Shanga. A Muslim Trading Settlement on the East African Coast*, Nairobi, forthcoming. A. Hourani, *Arab Seafaring in the Indian Ocean in Ancient and Medieval Times*, Princeton, 1951. Al-Jāḥeẓ, *Rasāʾel*, ed. H. Sandabi, Cairo, 1933. T. M. Ricks, "Persian Gulf Seafaring and East Africa, Ninth-Twelfth Centuries," *African Historical Studies* 3/2, 1970, pp. 339-57. P. P. J. Sinclair, "Archaeology in Eastern Africa. An Overview of Current Chronological Issues," *Journal of African History* 32, 1991, pp. 179-219. M. C. Smith and H. T. Wright, "The Ceramics from Ras Hafun in Somalia. Notes on a Classical Maritime Site," *Azania* 23, 1982, pp. 115-43. R. Summers, *Ancient Mining in Rhodesia*, National Museum of Rhodesia, Memoir 3, Salisbury, 1969. G. R. Tibbetts, *Arab Navigation in the Indian Ocean before the Coming of the Portuguese*, London, 1971. D. Whitehouse, "Siraf. An Islamic City and Its Rôle in Art," *Storia della Città* 7, 1978, pp. 54-58. W. Wolska-Conus, *La topographie chrétienne de Cosmas Indicopleustes. Théologie et sciences au VIe siècle, Bibliothèque byzantine. Études* 3, Paris, 1962. *Zanzibar Guide*, 2nd ed., Zanzibar, 1949.

(MARK HORTON)

ii. PERSIAN LOANWORDS IN SWAHILI

The earliest Bantu-speaking communities entered eastern Africa during the last five centuries B.C.E. Swahili is a member of the Bantu subgroup known as Sabaki. Proto-Sabaki was likely spoken on or near the East African coast during the first half of the first millennium C.E., and Proto-Swahili on the coast a century or two later. Based on archeological and linguistic data, the earliest Swahili settlements along the coast from southern Somalia to Mozambique are usually assigned to 800 C.E. or slightly earlier. A set of 1,400 lexical reconstructions for Proto-Sabaki and thus Proto-Swahili (Nurse and Hinnebusch, chap. 3 and apps.) show that few were necessarily derived from Persian (or Arabic) during most of the first millennium C.E.; that is, either the items are also attested in Arabic and/or Indic languages in an identical or similar form, which means these languages could also be the source, or they are not cognate across the Swahili dialect spectrum, which means that, although we tentatively reconstructed them from the early protostage, they more likely entered Swahili later. The paucity of lexical material at this stage as well as the total absence of nonlexical material suggest very light Persian influence. The few items of general reference at this stage include **(m)pula* "steel," **bwana* "man, gentleman," **(m)pamba* "cotton," and **(n)kasa* "turtle," which correlate with Middle Persian *pōlāwad, bān, pambag,* and *kašawag*.

By about 1700, when the first recorded documents in Swahili appeared, Swahili vocabulary was much as it is today, containing several hundred items from Persian (Krumm; Knappert) and many more from Arabic. Thus, most of these entered Swahili between 800 and 1700. The recentness of their arrival is corroborated by their having undergone only recent and local sound shifts affecting Swahili. They cluster in certain categories—tools, ornaments, spices, plants, household items, and maritime and kinship terms—and contain few general items. This pattern derives from trading contact rather than sustained political intertwining. As with the small, earlier set, it is possible that many entered Swahili indirectly via Arabic or Indic languages. Many are also attested in Comorian and Mwani, a Swahili-like language on the Mozambique coast.

Bibliography: J. Knappert, "Persian and Turkish Loanwords in Swahili," *Sprache und Geschichte in Afrika* 5, 1983, pp. 111-44. B. Krumm, *Words of Oriental Origin in Swahili*, London, 1961. D. Nurse and T. J. Hinnebusch, *Swahili and Sabaki. A Linguistic History*, Berkeley, 1993. A. N. Tucker, "Foreign Sounds in Swahili," *BSO(A)S* 11, 1946, pp. 854-71; 12, 1947, pp. 214-32.

(DEREK NURSE)

iii. BALUCHI AND PARSI COMMUNITIES

Members of the Baluchi and Parsi communities, both of which have had historical links with Persia, began settling in East Africa in the 19th century. A small group of the Baluchis first went to Zanzibar around 1837 as bodyguards of the Arab sultan of the Būsaʿīdī dynasty. They spoke a variant of Persian, and, unlike the majority of the other Sunni Muslims (who were Shafi2ʿite), they followed the Hanafite school of Islamic law (Salvadori, p. 138). They became traders over the years (Gregory, p. 33), and intermarried extensively with Arabs and Swahilis with the result that some of the youths today speak Swahili as their mother-tongue.

On the other hand, the Parsis (q.v.), who had originally emigrated from Persia to India after the Islamic conquest in the 7th century, in order to preserve their Zoroastrian faith, vigorously retained their identity as Zoroastrians. In time, the Parsis became "Indianized" in language and culture, adopting Gujarati as the language of communication and prayers. However, cardinal features of Zoroastrian identity were retained: the consecration of the sacred fire from Persia, the establishment of burial places ("the towers of silence"), and the creation of the *anjoman*, the community. These features were recreated in Zanzibar (and later elsewhere in East Africa), where, beginning in about 1845, the Parsis settled.

In East Africa, as elsewhere in their diaspora, the Parsis have distinguished themselves as a dynamic community which places a high premium on education. Although a community of relatively small numbers, their contribution has been significant, particularly as traders—the firm of Cowasjee Dinshaw was one of the pioneer firms in Zanzibar—and as members of the professions (lawyers, doctors, accountants, etc.). Today, however, the Parsis are faced with an issue that is far-reaching in its implications for the continuity of their identity: whether a child born of a non-Zoroastrian parent should be accepted as a Zoroastrian Parsi. It is a modern challenge which they did not have to face in East Africa in the 19th century.

Bibliography: R. G. Gregory, *The Rise and Fall of Philanthropy in East Africa. The Asian Contribution*, New Brunswick, 1992. C. Salvadori, *Through Open Doors. A View of Asian Cultures in Kenya*, Nairobi, 1983.

(FAROUK TOPAN)

iv. BAHAI COMMUNITIES

The earliest contact of Persian Bahais with East Africa followed plans developed in 1950 by the then Guardian of the Bahai faith Shoghi Effendi (q.v.). The national Bahai community of Persia had direct responsibility for settling Italian Somaliland, one of twelve designated areas in East Africa, though Persian Bahais settled in other territories, including Ethiopia, Uganda, Tanzania, and Kenya, the first areas in the world to experience mass conversion to the Bahai faith. During the formative years of Bahai communities in East Africa, the area received eighty Bahai settlers, "pioneers," forty of whom were Persians. Forty percent of the Persian Bahais were women. In 1993 there were an estimated 223,000 Bahais in East Africa and 1,268 Bahai local governing councils ("Statistical Table, Six-Year Plan Final Figures," in *The Bahá'í Encyclopedia*).

The Ethiopian Bahai community was established as early as 1933 by an Egyptian Bahai, Ṣabrī Elyās. The Italian invasion of Ethiopia caused Elyās to leave the country, only to return in 1944 with his spouse, Fahīma Yakot; they remained until 1954 when they left for Djibouti. Between 1953 and 1963, a large influx of Bahais from Persia, Egypt, and the United States resulted in conversions sufficiently numerous to undertake active Bahai work in many parts of the country. The area, however, attracted only two Persian couples, namely the Monajjems and Dr. and Mrs. Farhūmand; the latter donated land and national and regional Bahai centers to the Bahais of Ethiopia. Formed in 1956, the National Spiritual Assembly of the Bahais of Ethiopia was legally incorporated in 1992. One finds Bahais in several hundred localities at present.

The Uganda Bahai community. A leading center for Bahai expansion, the Uganda Bahai community was formed considerably later. In 1951 six Bahais, four of whom Persians, arrived in the country. Among the most notable Persian Bahais were Mūsā Banānī (1886-1971), in 1952 appointed a "Hand of the Cause" (*Ayādī-e Amr-Allāh;* q.v.), his wife Samīḥa, his daughter Violette, and his son-in-law ʿAlī Naḵjavānī. Many Ugandans accepted the Bahai faith rapidly. A number of them traveled westward across Africa to open new territories to the Bahai faith. In 1956 the National Spiritual Assembly of the Bahais of Uganda was formed. In 1961 the first Bahai House of Worship in Africa was dedicated in Kampala. During the 1970s the Bahai community of Uganda lost its legal recognition, as did many other religious communities during Idi Amin's rule, but by 1979 recognition was restored. Uganda has several Bahai schools and in 1992 had more than 335 local Bahai governing councils (more properly known as "spiritual assemblies").

The Tanzania Bahai community. Tanzania attracted the greatest number of Persian Bahais, namely eighteen. The foundation of the Bahai community was laid in 1951 by Jalāl Naḵjavānī (1917-1982), the first contemporary pioneer to settle in Africa, his wife Daraḵšanda Naʿīmī, his brother-in-law Farhang Naʿīmī, and ʿEzzat Zahrāʾī. The Egyptian Bahai Ḥasan Ṣabrī and the American Isobel Ṣabri were also influential in promoting the work of the new faith in Tanzania. Farzāna Yazdānī, her husband, and their family arrived in 1952 in Dar es Salaam, the former capital and chief port of Tanzania. In 1954 Dr. Farhūmand left Tehran and settled in the country with his three children; his wife followed. Dr. Farhūmand was particularly noted for his founding a multiracial clinic in Dar es Salaam and eventually served as personal physician to the first president of Tanzania. In the course of these early years, many Tanzanians became Bahais. The death of a Persian Bahai, Mrs. Afrūḵta, widow of a professor of medicine at Tehran University, provided the opportunity for the still emerging Bahai community of Dar es Salaam to establish the first multiracial cemetery in that city. Bahais can be found in 508 localities, of which 191 have spiritual assemblies (Yazdani, "Tanzania").

The Kenyan Bahai community. Like those of Uganda and Tanzania, the Bahai community in Kenya started to take shape in the early 1950s. Kenya was the recipient of the second largest contingent of Persian Bahais, namely thirteen individuals. This group included ʿAzīz Yazdī, a businessman from Tehran, and his family; the ʿAlāʾī family; the ʿAlīzādas; Manūčehr Maʿānī; the Sohaylīs; and the Fanānāpaḏīrs. The Bahai presence is greatest in the Western Province. The national spiritual assembly of the Bahais of Kenya was formed in 1964. There are now over 700 spiritual assemblies (Sohaili, "Kenya").

The Somalian Bahai community. The Bahai situation in Somalia is strikingly different from that in the four other East African countries. The growth of the Bahai community was much slower in Somalia. The notable Persians who settled in Italian and British Somaliland were Sohayl and Cyrus Samandarī (1934-58), Šīdān Fatḥ-Aʿẓam, and Mahdī and Ursula Samandarī. The last couple stayed for twenty years. There were Bahais in only one locality (Smandari, "Somalia").

Aside from activities that have led to a dramatic growth of the Bahai faith in East Africa, Persian Bahais, through the establishment of local and national Bahai governing councils, the donation of land and buildings, and support of the African Bahai Temple erected in Uganda in 1964, have made a significant contribution to the consolidation of the Bahai faith in Africa as a whole. Persians have also assisted Western Bahai "pioneers" in settling in East Africa.

Bibliography: *Africa Teaching Committee Records*, National Bahai Archives, Wilmette, Ill. A. Banani, "Musa Banani," *Bahāʾī World* 15, 1979, pp. 421-23. M. Bossi, "Jalal Nakhjavanī," *Bahāʾī World* 18, 1978, pp. 797-800. M. and U. Samandari, "Cyrus Samandari," *Bahāʾī World* 12, 1956, pp. 925-6. *The Bahá'í Encyclopedia* (forthcoming) is the source for the following references: Will. C. van den Hoonaard, "Africa"; idem, "An Annotated Index of the United Africa Teaching Committee Minutes and Correspondence: Bahá'i History in 25 African Countries"; S. Samandari, "Somalia"; M. Sohaili, "Kenya"; and F. Yazdani, "Tanzania."

(WILL. C. VAN DEN HOONAARD)

EAST INDIA COMPANY (THE BRITISH), a

trading company incorporated on 31 December 1600 for fifteen years with the primary purpose of exporting the staple production of English woolen cloths and importing the products of the East Indies.

i. *The Safavid period.*
ii. *The Afsharid, Zand, and Qajar periods.*

i. THE SAFAVID PERIOD

The East India Company initially had 125 shareholders and was capitalized at £72,000 for separate trading voyages to the East Indies. While Portugal was politically united with Spain, from 1580 to 1640, the company encountered opposition from Portuguese trading interests, which were already established on the Indian mainland, islands in the Indian Ocean, and particularly in the Persian Gulf area. There the Portuguese controlled the small island Hormoz, off the southwest coast of Persia. Dutch merchants joined together in 1602 to form a powerful national United East India Company (see DUTCH-PERSIAN RELATIONS) on behalf of the States General and achieved early commercial success from their main base at Batavia on Java. Another international, commercial competitor on the Persian scene was the French Compagnie des Indes Orientales (French East India Company; q.v.), founded in 1664.

The East India Company established its first base at the port of Surat in Gujarat in 1612, but its factors soon realized that sale of cloth was disappointing and resolved to expand its market possibilities in Persia, where an indirect trade was already carried on by the (British) Levant Company, established on 11 September 1581 by its agents through Aleppo. Inevitably, this trade caused friction between the companies, and some questioned whether it was worthwhile offending the Ottomans for a hypothetical advantage with the Persians, arguing that the overland routes from northern Persia to the eastern Mediterranean ports would not be diverted for economic or political reasons (Roe, *The Embassy to the Moghul*, pp. 313-14).

Nevertheless, desire for a Persian outlet prevailed, and a small consignment was dispatched to Jāsk on the ship *James*, carrying goods to the value of £6,333 15s 11d, which arrived on 4 December 1616 under agent Edward Connock, who had previously served as a merchant in Turkey. It was not an auspicious beginning, for the port was a paltry place and the reception unwelcoming, but Connock was optimistic. In the course of a year he laid the foundations of a trade and negotiated a treaty for exports of silk and imports of cloth on satisfactory terms, without recourse to a great outlay of ready money, and with the possibility of supplanting Portuguese trade there. Shah ʿAbbās I (q.v.), in conflict with the Ottomans, welcomed the opportunity to divert silk exports away from Turkey, thereby depriving the Ottomans of silk supplies and transit dues, and to acquire a potential ally against the Portuguese. He resented the Portuguese occupation of Hormoz, against whom he had no shipping leverage to enable him to expel them. This cooperation appeared mutually advantageous, but neither side could fulfill its part of the bargain.

Shah ʿAbbās I was never strong enough to dispense with the interdependent economic and political ties between the Ottomans and the Persians. Although he aspired to control Persian trade, which he did much to encourage and in which he greatly assisted Armenian enterprise, he did not completely succeed. The company never had the financial resources nor the goods in exchange to become the prominent supplier in the Persian market, and could not rival the superior organization and greater range of products that the Dutch possessed after their settlement at Bandar(-e) ʿAbbās (then Gombroon) in 1623. By detaining the company's silk purchase in 1622, Shah ʿAbbās I forced it to assist him with its fleet in the taking of Hormoz and rewarded it with an agreement for a half share of the customs revenue, but this revenue was seldom properly paid (Lockhart, pp. 361-63).

With the death of Shah ʿAbbās I and the accession of Shah Ṣafī, royal influence over trade diminished. Armenian control increased, and Persian-Ottoman relations improved. This proved a mixed blessing for the company. Apart from its general Asian trade, it sponsored three separately financed voyages to Persia with large deliveries of cloth and other English commodities in exchange for silk, for which demand was growing. The results were disappointing. In the 1630s, as the state of India improved, the growth in local trade between India and Persia, some of it carried on company ships, the share of customs' revenue, and rivalry with the Dutch kept the factors in Persia.

However, the constitutional troubles in England, competition from illegal interlopers, and the outbreak of the first Anglo-Dutch war made the mid-century period one of declining value for the company, although the area trade continued and the Dutch prospered. Following the restoration of the monarchy in England, the termination of the Anglo-Dutch wars, and the revival of trade and the economy, the company's prospects improved. Although the company, unlike its Dutch rival, had not hitherto undertaken territorial acquisition, this changed in 1668 when Bombay, ceded in 1665 to Charles II as part of a marriage settlement from the Portuguese crown, became the seat of the company's western presidency in place of Surat. These events were followed by the dominance of Sir Josiah Child in the councils of the company and by a more energetic direction of its activities in the face of growing rivalry at home. Correspondingly, the Dutch company was faltering in its competitiveness, and local merchants were becoming more active. Thus, to some extent, while Asian commerce was increasing, the volume traded by the two major European companies was proportionally declining, although the local freightage carried by their shipping rose, as did the personal participation of their factors in it (Ferrier, 1970, pp. 189-98).

After a period of severe retrenchment in supplies, expenses, and staff in Persia, in the mid-1660s the company made efforts to improve the standing and trading of its Persian agency. Unsettled conditions in Mughal India, as much as the company's need to increase its sales of British goods, necessitated diversification. The agency of Thomas Rolt, 1670-77, reflected both the determination to implement a more forward approach to Persia and the acknowledgment that royal trade had lessened while "the young King [Solaymān] spends his time wholly in pleasure," leaving the chief minister "governing all these kingdoms as he pleases" (India Office [IO] G/36/106, 27 January 1671/72). Meanwhile, Rolt recommended more aggressive action to enforce the payment of the customs share; the company's president, Aungier, sensibly advocated caution. Moderation, not force, was the policy. Nevertheless, the incentive to expand trade to Persia was powerful; Armenian interests were entrenched in the overland trade to Aleppo (Chardin, IV, p. 165).

In spite of disappointments, the company resolved "to find a good vent for our English manufactures in Persia" (IO E/3/89 Company to Persia, 20 May 1681), so that "the trade of Persia shall not be fallow to the English nation, as it hath done too long" (IO E/3/90 Company to Persia, 6 September 1682). The factors were instructed to obtain Persian goods in exchange, even to purchase them and to provide a comprehensive freightage service to and from India to compete with Portuguese and Dutch vessels. Unfortunately, success was not commensurate with the effort, and the company believed the poor results were due to the failure of their servants, but also partly to "the miserable condition" of Persia, which was suffering from insecurity, intolerance, corruption, and a collapsing currency (IO G/40/4, Surat to Company, 21 January 1677/78). The Dutch company experienced the same adverse conditions, but took more forceful measures to assert itself.

In the last decade or so of the 17th century the objectives of the company in Persia remained the same, but the approach changed. Failing by itself to penetrate the market sufficiently or to obtain royal support, the company proposed in June 1688 to form a close association with members of the Armenian community in Isfahan (see ARMENIANS OF MODERN IRAN) for "carrying on a great part of the Armenian trade to India and Persia and from thence to Europe by way of England" (IO, Courts Minutes, 22 June 1688). This agreement had been negotiated by Sir Josiah Child; Jean Chardin (q.v.), the Huguenot jeweler and traveler to Persia; and K̲ᵛāja Pānūs Kalendar, an Armenian merchant of Isfahan. The company hoped by this commercial coup to secure the professional expertise and market knowledge of the Armenians, and thereby reverse the flow of Persian trade and enhance the company's exports. Such an agreement would fulfill the earlier expectations for complementary silk and cloth commerce envisaged during the reign of Shah ʿAbbās I.Five particular Armenian merchants to whom another proposal was addressed were unwilling to jeopardize their existing interests for the sake of anticipated attractions. The large cargoes dispatched by the *Nassau* and *Mary* were disregarded by them, as was another consignment carried on the *Charles II* in 1697 (IO, Company to Persia, 3 January, 1693/4). The Armenian community in Isfahan had become desperately factionalized as a result of persecution during the reign of Shah Solaymān, and the merchants felt menaced by the offer of cooperation. They were unimpressed by the agency's suggestion, had no confidence in its staff, and were unfavorably influenced by the company's detractors. Although Shah Solṭān Ḥosayn confirmed the company's privileges in 1704, Persia was thought "to be in a very tottering condition" (IO G/36/10/A, Isfahan to Surat, 14 February 1703). In this deteriorating situation the company was ill-served by its servants and suffered attacks from Muscat coastal raiders and incursions from eastern regions against its factory in Bandar(-e) ʿAbbās, though it was still hoping to revive its trade. The freight trade made a reasonable return, and goat wool from the Kermān area made acceptable merchandise, although this trade partly revived in the Zand period.

See also GREAT BRITAIN.

Bibliography: (For cited works not given in detail, see "Short References.") A. A. Amin, *British Interests in the Persian Gulf*, Leiden, 1967. K. N. Chaudhuri, *The English East India Company. The Study of an Early Joint-Stock Company, 1600-1640*, London, 1965. Idem, *The Trading World of Asia and the English East India Company, 1660-1760*, Cambridge, 1973. K. N. Chaudhuri and A. Dasgupta, "Foreign Trade," in T. Raychaudhuri and Irfan Habib, eds., *The Cambridge Economic History of India*, 2 vols., Cambridge, 1981-1983, I, pp. 382-433. N. Falsafī, *Zendagānī-e Šāh ʿAbbās* ..., 4 vols., Tehran, 1346 Š./1967, IV, pp. 251-69. R. W. Ferrier, "The Agreement of the East India Company with the Armenian Nation, 22 June 1688," *REA*, n.s., 7, 1970, pp. 427-43. Idem, "The Trade between India and the Persian Gulf and the East India Company in the 17th Century," *Bengal: Past and Present* LXXXIX, July-December 1970, pt. II. Idem, "The Armenians and the East India Company in Persia in the Seventeenth and Early Eighteenth Century," *Economic History Review*, 2nd ser., 26/1, 1973, pp. 38-61. Idem, "An English View of Persian Trade in 1618," *JESHO* XIX, 1976, pp. 182-214. Idem, "The Terms and Conditions under which English Trade Was Transacted with Safavid Persia," *BSAOS* XLIX, pt. 1, 1986, pp. 48-66. Idem, "Trade from the Mid-14th Century to the End of the Safavid Period," in *Camb. Hist. Iran* VI, pp. 412-90. W. Foster, *England's Quest of Eastern Trade*, London, 1933. L. Lockhart, *The Fall of the Safavid Dynasty and the Afghan Occupation of Persia*, Cambridge, 1958. Sir Thomas Roe, *The Embassy to the Moghul*, ed. Sir William Foster, London, 1926. W. R. Scott, *The Constitution and Finance of English, Scottish, and Irish Joint-Stock Companies to 1720*, Cambridge, 1912. N. Steensgaard, *Carracks, Caravans and Companies. The Structural Crisis in the European-Asian Trade in the Early 17th Century*, Copenhagen, 1973. A. T. Wilson, *The Persian Gulf*, London, 1928. A. C. Wood, *A History of the Levant Company*, Oxford, 1935. See also M. Zarnegār in *Rahāvard* 9/35, 1373 Š./1994, pp. 77-84.

(R. W. FERRIER)

ii. THE AFSHARID, ZAND, AND QAJAR PERIODS

The fall of the Safavid Dynasty in 1722, the Afghan occupation, and subsequent anarchy naturally depressed trade throughout Persia. With the accession of Nāder Shah in 1736, attempts were made by agents of the British "Russia Company" to expand their trade across the Caspian Sea to northern Persia with Nāder's support, but Russian opposition forced the end of this venture by 1746 (see ELTON). The East India Company maintained its factories in Kermān and Isfahan throughout Nāder's reign, but a renewal of civil war after his assassination in 1747—and lack of encouragement by Nāder's immediate successors—persuaded them to withdraw from Isfahan to Bandar(-e) ʿAbbās (q.v.) in 1750. A representative stayed at Kermān until 1758, and an Armenian interpreter into the 1760s. In 1763 their last outpost in Persia, at Bandar(-e) ʿAbbās, was evacuated (after a bloody skirmish with the khan of Lār) to Baṣra, in the Ottoman domains, where the company was already represented. Within a few months, however, Shaikh Nāṣer b. Mad̲kūr of Būšehr invited them to set up an agency at his port, strategically located in respect of Shiraz, which was now in effect the capital of the new ruler of western Persia, Karīm Khan Zand. In July a commercial treaty was concluded with Karīm's brother and viceroy Ṣādeq, and trade initially prospered: during 1763-67 more than half of the company's sale of woolens in the Persian Gulf (annually averaging 1,407 bales) went through Būšehr (Amin, pp. 50, 73-75, 79, 82, 151, 155; Perry, pp. 256-60).

The Zand ruler, however, expected in the bargain that the company's ships would aid him in operations against rival Arab polities on the Persian coast, which the Bombay presidency, concerned for the company's neutrality, refused to sanction. The new agent at Baṣra, Henry Moore, was resolutely opposed to negotiating with Karīm Khan, and within three years relations with Shiraz were at a breaking point. There are garbled allusions to these events in the Persian chronicles: in the *Golšan-e morād*, the company's envoy George Skipp is misidentified as a Russian ambassador (Ḡaffāri, pp. 286-87 and note 143; Perry, pp. 261-62, 305) and in the *Rostam al-tawārik̲*, Skipp's visits to Shiraz in 1767 and 1768 are conflated with the episode of the expulsion of the Dutch from K̲ārg island in 1766 (Rostam-al-Ḥokamāʾ, pp. 386-90, tr. Hoffmann, pt. 2, pp. 236ff.; Perry, p. 267 note 96). In 1769 Moore attempted to seize K̲ārg island, but was forestalled by a landing by Karīm Khan's troops; fearing reprisals, the factors at Būšehr hastily withdrew to Baṣra. Despite misgivings by the presidency and repeated feelers from Shaikh Nāṣer, they were not to return until 1775.

An epidemic that struck Baṣra in 1773, and the siege and occupation by Zand forces in 1775-76, crippled the city economically and twice forced the temporary evacuation of the agency to Bombay. A company ship was captured by boats from Bandar(-e) Rīg, and two company employees on board were sent to Shiraz to serve for two years as hostages for the resumption of trade at Būšehr. This Moore refused to countenance, but was finally overridden by the presidency; in April 1775 the company's ship and personnel were restored by Karīm Khan, and its flag was once more hoisted at Būšehr (Perry, pp. 261-67).

However, trade had slumped considerably since the occupation of Baṣra, and with the anarchy that ensued on the death of Karīm Khan in 1779 it was not to revive for decades. Both Baṣra and Būšehr were downgraded to the status of company residencies and, with the threat of renewed war with France, were maintained more as communications links with India than for their waning commercial value. As the company's fortunes elevated it to the very government of India, involving it in a closer relationship with the British government, so its interest in Persia and the Persian Gulf declined. In 1789 Bombay sent a Persian, Mahdī-Qolī Khan, as resident at Būšehr, as much for political as for commercial advantages, i. e., to incline Fatḥ-ʿAlī Shah to the British, rather than the French, cause. In 1800 and again in 1810, the governor general at Bombay dispatched Sir John Malcolm with a flotilla to the Persian Gulf as envoy to the Qajar monarch; but Whitehall's appointment of Sir Harford Jones as ambassador formalized direct diplomatic relations between London and Tehran, and the company's role in Persia was virtually ended (see BRYDGES).

Even in India, the company's trading monopoly was abolished in 1813, and by the 1850s it was little more than a managing agency for the British government's administration of India. After the Indian mutiny in 1857, for which the company was held partly to blame, it was liquidated and its assets transferred to the crown on 2 August 1858.

The meticulous records and letters of the company's employees provide a valuable source for the history of Persia during the 17th and 18th centuries. They are preserved in the India Office Library in London, under the headings *Persia and the Persian Gulf Records* and *Bombay Public Consultations* (or *Proceedings*); in the National Archives of India at New Delhi; and in the Maharashtra State Archives, Bombay (Basra and Gombroon factory diaries). Particulars are to be found in Abdullah Thabit, Amin, and Perry.

Bibliography: A. A. Amin, *British Interests in the Persian Gulf*, Leiden, 1967. Abu'l-Ḥasan Ḡaffārī Kāšānī, *Golšan-e morād*, ed. by Ḡ.-R. Ṭabāṭabāʾī Majd, Tehran, 1369 Š./1990. John R. Perry, *Karim Khan Zand. A History of Iran 1747-1779*, Chicago, 1979. Moḥammad-Hāšem Āṣaf Rostam-al-Ḥokamāʾ, *Rostam al-tawārik̲*, ed. by M. Mošīrī, Tehran, 1348 Š./1969, tr. and annotated by Birgitt Hoffmann as *Persische Geschichte 1694-1835 erlebt, erinnert und erfunden. Das Rustam at-tawārīḫ in deutscher Bearbeitung*, 2 pts., Bamberg, 1986. Abdullah Thabit, *The Political Economy of Merchants and Trade in Basra, 1722-1795*, unpubl. doctoral dissertation, Department of History, Georgetown University, 1992.

(JOHN R. PERRY)

EAST INDIA COMPANY (THE DUTCH).

See DUTCH-PERSIAN RELATIONS.

EAST INDIA COMPANY (THE FRENCH),

a company established in 1664 to conduct all French commercial operations with the Orient. Colbert, minister of Louis XIV, had been aware of the great profits earned by the Dutch and English merchants in importing and selling Asian goods to the French (Kaepplin, p. 3). He wanted to deprive foreigners of such a profitable market and, therefore, founded a chartered company modeled on the Dutch company, which could, with the support of a reviving merchant marine and the protection of the king's vessels, carry on trade with countries east of the Cape of Good Hope. Subscriptions were raised, though with few results; the king and his court had to be the main contributors, since French traders were rather suspicious of a state-launched venture. The geography of France also engendered rivalry between Atlantic-oriented merchants and those looking toward the Mediterranean Sea, who were already using the overland routes to the Persian Gulf.

The company's statutes provided for a settlement in Madagascar which would serve as the base for activities on the model of Batavia (Java), the center of Dutch trade in Asia. The company was to contribute to the propagation of Christianity by supporting Catholic missionaries (Furber, pp. 103-07).

Colbert had been informed by Father Raphaël du Mans (q.v.), a Capuchin friar active in the convent of Isfahan since 1054/1644, that Shah ʿAbbās II (q.v.), like his predecessors, had spoken in favor of establishing diplomatic and commercial relations between Persia and France. The French jeweler Isaac de l'Étoile, who belonged to a group of European craftsmen working for the shah and his court, corroborated the information. Colbert and the company's directors decided to send representatives to Persia and India to request from the sovereigns a trading license like the one obtained by the English and Dutch companies. Three merchants, Mariage, Beber, and Dupont, were chosen to carry out the mission, and as a matter of prestige, Louis XIV named two gentleman, Nicolas de Lalain and François de La Boullaye Le Gouz, to be the king's representatives and to conduct negotiations. La Boullaye, who belonged to the king's chamber, had traveled in the Orient, and Lalain, a member of the parliament in Provence, would give the mission dignity and significance. Unfortunately, the five men never agreed. In Isfahan, Father Raphaël du Mans, acting as interpreter, did his best to coordinate the negotiations and to instill coherence into the French envoys' demands (Schefer, in Raphaël du Mans, pp. l-li). In 1076/1665, the shah issued a firman granting the company the right to free trade, the use of a house in Bandar-e ʿAbbās (q.v.), and the right to make wine in Shiraz for its employees. After a trial period of three years, these privileges were to be reexamined with the obligation of once again offering presents to the shah and his attendants. New authorized envoys were to be sent and would receive, as accredited guests of the shah, a daily allowance, *taʿyīn*, as had the five Frenchman of this mission (Kroell, pp. 5-6).

Mariage went to Bandar-e ʿAbbās to take possession of the house and arrange storerooms where the company merchandise would be unloaded. In 1079/1669, three small vessels were sent from Surat by François Caron, a defector from the Dutch Company who had been recruited by Colbert to handle French trade in Asia. Only the *Marie*, with a light freight of pepper and indigo, anchored at Bandar-e ʿAbbās; the *Force* and the *Salomon* went on to Baṣra, where they traded their cargo with profit (Martin, I, pp. 199-209).

The company settlement in Madagascar turned out to be a disaster, and financial problems became so pressing that no advantage was taken of the privileges granted by Shah ʿAbbās II and renewed by Shah Solaymān in 1082/1671. Louis de l'Étoile, Isaac's son, had come to Surat to conduct his own business. He persuaded Guêton, recently arrived as a company director, to travel to Isfahan to present the promised gifts to the shah and to reaffirm France's determination to pursue its trade with Persia. Guêton and his suite sailed to Bandar-e ʿAbbās on the *Saint Paul*, carrying rich presents (Raphaël du Mans, pp. 334-35) and an important cargo of India goods. Following Guêton's sudden death at Shiraz, the Carmelite missionaries, fearing the whole enterprise would collapse, advised Jonchères, captain of the *Saint Paul*, to take over; he did so, but, according to Chardin's testimony, with flippancy (Chardin, III, pp. 222-25, 232-46). Nevertheless, the privileges were renewed for three years, again, with no concrete results on behalf of the company. The house in Bandar-e ʿAbbās was soon deserted, and the missionaries were left utterly disappointed, considering it worthless to invoke the protection of a king whose ships seldom sailed the Persian Gulf. Alexandre de l'Étoile, Isaac's grandson, still held the title of company's agent and the right to make wine in Shiraz (Kroell, p. 7).

In Persia, political unrest was aggravated by the threat of Arab hegemony in the Persian Gulf. The powerful Imam of Oman's navy, based at Muscat, multiplied its attacks against merchant-ships, avoiding the most heavily armed vessels. Safavid ministers, remembering the 1032/1622 capture of Hormoz, thought of mounting a similar expedition against Muscat, with European naval support. Dutch and English agents eluded the proposed alliance, as it would have required the mobilization of an important task force and troops that the Safavid state, harassed on its frontiers, appeared unable to muster. The French missionary Martin Gaudereau, having heard of the plan, asserted that the capture of Muscat would secure the French company a permanent base in the Indian Ocean and free trade with Persia. He repeatedly encouraged French authorities to enter Muscat (Lockhart, pp. 66-69, 434-36.). From this time on, the overthrow of the Omani power became the dream of a few Frenchmen who were convinced that it would revive a moribund company. Étienne Pilavoine, then chief at the Surat factory, flatly denied that the project had any sense. He knew of the Omani naval strength and of the failure of a Portuguese undertaking in 1110-11/1699, when vessels sent from Goa had waited at Bandar Kung for Persian troops that never came. Moreover, France did not maintain sufficient naval forces in the region. Jérôme de Pontchartrain, Trade and Navy secretary of state (1110-127/1699-1715), assumed the same prudent attitude when Pierre Victor Michel, French envoy to Shah Solṭān-Ḥosayn, resumed previous agreements in 1120/1708 and later, when Moḥammad-Reżā Beg, Persian ambassador at Versailles (1127/1715), proposed military action against Oman. A treaty was signed and ratified in 1134/1722, establishing diplomatic and commercial relations, but with no mention of an alliance (Lockhart, pp. 437-68; Kroell, pp. 36-41, 56-57.).

The expansion of war in Europe "had sealed the fate of Colbert's Company," which had been periodically insolvent since the beginning (Furber, p. 207). Pontchartrain granted the company privileges to a group of Saint-Malo merchants willing to invest in inter-Asian trade, or "country trade." Not until 1131/1719 did two Malouin ships anchor at Bandar-e ʿAbbās to unload goods freighted at Chandernagor, Bengal, and did the supercargoes manage to obtain from the Šāhbandar (customs office) all trading facilities (Kroell, p. 64.). After Louis XIV's death in 1715, an astute banker, John Law, appointed by the new government, invented an overseas trading consortium that merged all the existing companies. This second "Compagnies des Indes," 1131-83/1719-69, outlived Law's financial bankruptcy (Furber, p. 210). In Persia Ange de Gardane, chief consul at Isfahan (1129-42/1716-30), and Étienne Padery, consul at Shiraz (1131-36/1718-23), were its representatives. They differed totally on the Muscat affair. Padery had been secretly entrusted to negotiate a French military assistance, while Gardane earnestly denied the reality of the project. Fearing retaliation from the Omani navy on French merchant-ships, he wrote long pleading letters to the French ministers, successfully asking them to dismiss Padery (Kroell, pp. 58-76).

Already on the verge of collapse, the Safavids could no longer ensure an effective commercial policy. Despite its incidental efforts, the French East India Company could not, even in subsequent years, establish any permanent commercial links with Persia (Otter, I, pp. 224-25, II, pp. 32-34, 86-87; Masson, pp. 533-43).

Bibliography: (For cited works not given in full, see "Short References.") B. Carré, *The Travels of the Abbé Carré in India and the Near East, 1672 to 1674*, ed. C. Fawcett, 3 vols., London 1947. J. Chardin, *Voyages*. L. Dermigny, *Le fonctionnement des Campagnies des Indes. Sociétés et Compagnies de Commerce en Orient et dans l'Océan Indien*, Actes du huitième colloque international d'histoire maritime, Paris, 1970, pp. 443-66. R. Ferrier, "Trade from the Mid-14th Century to the End of the Safavid Period," in *Camb. Hist. Iran* VI, pp. 412-90. H. Furber, *Europe and the World in the Age of Expansion. Rival Empires of Trade in the Orient, 1600-1800*, Minneapolis, 1976. Ph. Haudrère, *La Compagnie française des Indes au XVIIIe siècle, 1719-1795*, 4 vol., Paris, 1989. P. Kaeppelin, *La Compagnie des Indes Orientales et François Martin*, Paris, 1908. A. Kroell, *Louis XIV, la Perse et Mascate*, Paris, 1977. Idem, *Alexandre de Lestoille, dernier agent de la Compagnie royale des Indes en Perse, Moyen-Orient et Océan Indien*, Paris, 1984, I, pp. 65-72. L. Lockhart, *The Fall of the Safavi Dynasty and the Afghan Occupation of Persia*, Cambridge, 1958. F. Martin, *Mémoires, 1665-1696*, ed. A. Martineau, 3 vols., Paris, 1931-1934. P. Masson, *Histoire du commerce français dans le Levant au XVIIe siècle*, Paris, 1896. Idem, *Histoire du commerce français dans le Levant au XVIIIe siècle*, Paris, 1911. Raphaël du Mans, *Estat de la Perse en 1660*, ed. C. Schefer, Paris, 1890. J. Otter, *Voyage en Turquie et en Perse avec une relation des expéditions de Tahmasp Quli Khan*, 2 vols., Paris, 1748. J. Savary des Bruslons, *Dictionnaire universel de commerce, d'histoire naturelle et des arts et métiers*, nouvelle éd., 5 vols., Copenhagen, 1759.

(ANNE KROELL)

EASTERN IRANIAN LANGUAGES, term used to refer to a group of Iranian languages most of which are or were spoken in lands to the east of the present state of Persia. In terms of both historical and typological linguistics, the distinction between Western and Eastern Iranian is generally regarded as the most fundamental division in Iranian dialectology. Each of these two major groups is sometimes subdivided along the opposite axis, giving a potential four-way distinction between South-Western, North-Western, South-Eastern, and North-Eastern Iranian. These conventional terms correspond only partially to the real geographical situation of the languages and their speakers. Thus Ossetic, an Eastern Iranian language, is spoken in the Caucasus, further west than many Western Iranian languages, while Baluchi (q.v.), a North-Western Iranian language, is spoken chiefly in Pakistan, in the south-eastern corner of the Iranophone area. However, the great majority of the Eastern Iranian languages have or had their main centers in areas to the east and north-east of Persia, in what are now Turkmenistan, Uzbekistan, Tajikistan, Afghanistan, Pakistan, and China.

The term "Eastern Iranian" is of limited utility with reference to the Old Iranian period. Of the two attested Old Iranian languages, Old Persian is a typical representative of South-Western Iranian. Avestan geographically belongs to the eastern Iranian area (see AVESTAN GEOGRAPHY), but shows few if any of the distinctive characteristics of the later Eastern Iranian languages. (A possible example is provided by the Av. third person plural verbal ending *-āire* < **-ārai*, which has its only precise cognates in the Eastern Iranian languages Khotanese, Chorasmian, and Yaghnobi.) One may suppose that at this stage the Iranian languages had only recently begun to diverge from one another, and that only the more peripheral languages had already developed markedly individual traits. Among such peripheral languages one would include Old Persian in the extreme south-west, which displays such unique developments as those of Indo-European **ḱ* and **ǵ(h)* to *θ* and *d* (as in *maθišta-* "greatest;" *adam* "I") and of **ḱw* and **ǵ(h)w* to *s* and *z* (as in *asa-* "horse;"

hạzan- "tongue"). At the opposite end of the Iranian world the languages of the nomadic Saka peoples of the Eurasian steppes show a different but equally distinctive development of *ḱw and *ǵ(h)w to *š* and *ž* (cf. Khot. *aśśa* [aša-], Wakhi *yaš* "horse;" Khot. *biśāa-* [βižā] "tongue," etc.). In Avestan, however, as in the great majority of Iranian languages, *ḱ and *ǵ(h) become *s* and *z* (Av. *masišta-*, Parth. *masišt* "greatest," Khot. *mästa-* "great;" Av.*azəm*, Parth. *az*, Sogd. *'zw*, Khot. *aysu* [azu], Pashto *ze* "I") while *ḱw and *ǵ(h)w become *sp* and *zb* (Av. *aspa-*, Sogd. *'sp-*, Orm. *yâsp* "horse;" Parth. *'zb'n*, Sogd.*'zβ'k*, Pashto *žeba*, Yazgh. *zveg* "tongue," etc.). At least in respect to these features, Avestan may be regarded as representative of a central group within Old Iranian, in which the developments that later distinguish Eastern from Western Iranian had not yet taken place (Sims-Williams 1993, pp. 162-63; on the relationship between Khotanese and Wakhi, see P.O. Skjærvø in Schmitt, p. 375). Of the less well attested Old Iranian languages, the meager remains of ancient Scythian (Schmitt, pp. 92-3) have been claimed as Eastern Iranian.

By the Middle Iranian stage, when a larger number of distinct languages are attested, a classification into Western and Eastern Iranian becomes more meaningful. While Western Middle Iranian is represented by Middle Persian and Parthian, the chief Eastern Middle Iranian languages are Khotanese (with the closely related Tumshuqese), Sogdian, Chorasmian, and Bactrian, to which one may add the remnants of such languages as Sarmatian and Alanic (R. Bielmeier in Schmitt, pp. 236-45; cf. also Sims-Williams, ibid., pp. 165-67), together with the "Parnian" stratum in Parthian (Sims-Williams, ibid., p. 171) and reconstructed proto-forms of Eastern Iranian languages attested only in the modern period, e.g., "proto-Pashto." It should be noted that, while the above division is universally accepted by specialists in Iranian dialectology, the dividing-line between Western and Eastern Iranian is in fact by no means clear-cut. The attested Middle Iranian languages seem rather to form a continuum from Middle Persian (South-Western) via Parthian (North-Western) to Bactrian, Chorasmian, and Sogdian (North-Eastern), with the Saka languages (Khotanese and Tumshuqese) at the opposite end of the spectrum. Bactrian, in particular, seems to occupy an intermediate position between Western and Eastern Iranian, sharing almost as many features with Parthian as with Chorasmian and Sogdian (Sims-Williams in Schmitt, pp. 165-72).

The Modern Eastern Iranian languages are even more numerous and varied. Most of them are classified as North-Eastern: Ossetic; Yaghnobi (which derives from a dialect closely related to Sogdian); the Shughni group (Shughni, Roshani, Khufi, Bartangi, Roshorvi, Sarikoli), with which Yazghulami (Sokolova 1967) and the now extinct Wanji (J. Payne in Schmitt, p. 420) are closely linked; Ishkashmi, Sanglichi, and Zebaki; Wakhi; Munji and Yidgha; and Pashto. According to Morgenstierne (1926, pp. 14-39; 1929; cf. also C. Kieffer in Schmitt, pp. 451ff.), Parachi and Ormuri occupy a special position as a "South-Eastern Iranian" group.

Typical features of Eastern Iranian. The Eastern Iranian languages are distinguished from the Western by both archaisms and innovations. A typical phonological archaism of Eastern Iranian is the widespread preservation of Old Iranian *θ*, as in Sogd. and Chor. *myθ*, Shughni *mēθ*, Yazgh. *miθ* (but Sanglichi *mēi*, Munji *mīx̌*) "day" < **maiθā̆-*; Sogd. *prθwty*, Shughni *θud-*, Wakhi *θət-* "burnt," cf. O. Pers. *θav* "to burn." Sometimes *θ* even develops to a stop as in Western Yagh. *mēt* (Eastern Yagh. *mēs*) "day;" Khot. *paṭhuta*, Sanglichi *təδ*, Zeb. *ted* (but Ishkashmi *sId*) "burnt;" Alanic *fourt*, Oss. D. *furt*, Wakhi *pɨtr* "son" < **puθra-*. Most Eastern Iranian languages (but not Sogdian, Yaghnobi, Yidgha-Munji or Parachi) have developed a dental affricate *c* (= *ts*), in some contexts *j* (= *dz*) or *s*, from the OIr. palatal *č*: cf. Khot. *tcahora*, Tumshuqese *tsahari*, Chor. *cf'r*, Bactr. *sofaro* (unpublished), Oss. D. *cuppar*, Shughni *cavōr*, Ishkashmi *cIfur*, Wakhi *cəbɨr*, Pashto *calōr*, Orm. *cār* < **čaθwar-* "four." Many of these languages preserve *č* in special contexts or have created a new *č*, e.g., by secondary palatalization of old *k*, resulting in contrast between *c* and *č* (sometimes also *ç̌*). While the weakening of postvocalic *b, d, g* to *v, δ, γ* (sometimes with further changes, such as *v* > *w* or *δ* > *l*) is common throughout Iranian, the same changes in initial position are specific to Eastern Iranian. However, Parachi and Ormuri do not take part in this development, nor is it carried through consistently in all of the North-Eastern languages. (Some apparent inconsistencies may be due to reversal of a sound change. Thus, Yagh. *v-, d-, γ-* may derive from Sogd. *v-, δ-, γ-*, with a late change of *δ* to *d* analogous to that of *θ* to *t* in Western Yaghnobi.) Another widespread but not quite universal North-Eastern Iranian development is the voicing of OIr. **ft*, **xt* to *vd, γd*: cf. Khot. *hauda*, Tumshuqese **hoda* (in the ordinal *hodama-*), Chor. *'βd*, Oss. *avd*, Shughni *ūvd*, Sanglichi *ōvδ*, Wakhi *ɨb*, Munji *ōvda*, Pashto *ōwə* < **hafta* "seven;" Khot. *dūta* (= *δūda*?), Tumshuqese *duḏa*, Chor. *δγd* (= *δuγda*), Bactr. *logda*, Oss. I. *-dɨγd* (in *xodɨγd* "sister-in-law"), Yazgh. *δoγd*, Sanglichi *wuδəγδ*, Wakhi *δəγd*, Yidgha *luγdo* < **duxtā* (nom.) "daughter." Sogdian has the partially voiced clusters *vt* and *γt* (e.g., *'βt'*, *δwγt'*), whence Yaghnobi reverts to *ft* and *xt*. The voicing did not take place in the South-Eastern languages (cf. Par. *hō̆t, dut*).

The Eastern Middle Iranian languages preserve OIr. final syllables to a large extent (cf. the forms of the word for "daughter" quoted above, and contrast Mid. Pers. and Parth. *duxt*). Many of the resulting final vowels survive in the modern Eastern Iranian languages. The accent has a distinctive function in several languages, e.g., Ossetic (Iron *xǽdzar* "the house," *xädzár* "a house"), Pashto (perfective *préγ̌dəm* to imperfective *preγ̌də́m* "I leave") and Ormuri (*á saṛai* "this man," *a-saṛái* "the man").

The preservation of final vowels has important implications for the morphology of Eastern Iranian, which tends to be much more complex and conservative than that of Western Iranian. In particular, Khotanese, Sogdian, and Pashto have well-preserved case-systems, fairly strict rules of concord, and a variety of declensions. Several languages (Sogdian, Chorasmian, Ossetic, Pashto, Parachi; but also Western Iranian Sivandi) have special forms of nouns used after numerals in certain cases; some such forms derive from OIr. duals. A notable isogloss is provided by the second person pl. pronouns with prefixed *t-*: Bactr. *tŏmaxo* (unpublished), Shughni *tama*, Yazgh. *təmox*, Sanglichi *təmux* (cf. also Pashto *tāse*, Orm. *tōs*?). A triple system of deictic pronouns based on the stems **ayam*/*iyam*/*ima-* "this," **aiša-*/*aita-* "this, that" (middle distant or near the person addressed) and **hău*/*awa-* "that (yonder)" can be reconstructed on the basis of data in Sogdian, Shughni, Sanglichi-Ishkashmi, Wakhi, and Yidgha-Munji (Sims-Williams, 1994). Typical Eastern Iranian verbal forms include causatives and denominatives in **-āwaya-* (Khot. *-ev-*, Chor. *-'wy-*, Wakhi *-ɨv-*, Munji *-ōv-*, Pashto and Orm. *-aw-*, Par. *-ēw-*; contrast Western Iranian **-ānaya-*).

For the numerous vocabulary items attested exclusively in Eastern (as distinct from Western) Iranian a few examples must suffice:

**abi-ar-* "to find, obtain": Sogd. *βyr*, Chor. *βyr-*, Man. Bactr. *'βyr-*, Oss. D. *yerun*, Yagh. *vīr-*, Shughni *viri-*, Yazgh. *vir-*, Ishkashmi *avir-*.

**anda-* "blind" (OInd. *andhá-*, Av. *aṇda-*): Khot. *hana-*, Sogd. *'nt*, Munji *yāndəy*, Pashto *ṛ-ūnd*, Orm. *hōnd*.

**drawa-* "hair": Khot. *drau-*, Sogd. *žw-*, Oss. D. *ärdo*, Yagh. *dirau*, Shughni *cīw*, Yazgh. *cŭ*, Orm. *drī*.

**gari-* "mountain" (OInd. *girí-*, Av. *gairi-*), often also "rock" or "pass" in the modern languages: Khot. *ggara-*, Sogd. *γr-*, Yagh. *γar*, Shughni *žīr*, Yazgh. *γar*, Wakhi *γar*, Munji *γār*, Pashto *γar*, Orm. *grī*, Par. *gir*.

**kapă-* "fish": Khot. *kavā-*, Sogd. *kp-*, Chor. *kb*, Scythian *Pantikápēs* "Fish-path" (place-name), Oss. *käf*, Wakhi *kūp*, Munji *kop*, Pashto *kab*.

**kuta-*, *kutī-* "dog" (cf. Prakrit *kutta-*, *kuttī-*): Sogd. *'kwt-*, Chor. *'kt*, Oss. D. *kui*, I. *kɨdz*, Yagh. *kut*, Shughni *kud*, Yazgh. *kʷod*, Sanglichi *kud*.

**maiθă-* "day": see forms listed above.

Eastern Iranian as a group. The best evidence for the unity of Eastern Iranian is provided by shared innovations such as the voicing of *xt* to *γd*, or the use of **kapă-* for "fish" in place of older **masyă-* (cf. OInd. *mátsya-*, Av. *masiia-*, Parth. *m'sy'g*, Pers. *māhī*), since they can hardly have come about everywhere independently. Archaisms such as the preservation of *θ* or of **gari-* "mountain," as opposed to the innovative use of **kaufa-* in this sense in Western Iranian, cf. Parth. *kwf*, Pers. *kūh*, etc. (also Av. *kaofa-*), are less significant in this respect. Within Eastern Iranian one can establish several sub-groups of languages which are particularly closely related to one another, e.g.: Alanic, Sarmatian and Ossetic; Khotanese and Tumshuqese; Sogdian and Yaghnobi; the Shughni group and Yazghulami. However, it does not seem possible to regard the Eastern Iranian group as a whole—even excluding Parachi and Ormuri—as a genetic grouping. Such a conception would imply the existence of an ancestral "proto-Eastern Iranian" intermediate between "common Iranian" and the attested Eastern Iranian languages; but if one reconstructs "proto-Eastern Iranian" in such a way as to account for all the features of the group, it proves to be identical to the "common Iranian" reconstructible as the ancestor of the whole Iranian family. It is therefore more plausible to conceive of Eastern Iranian as a "Sprachbund" or areal grouping of languages. In this case the members of the "Sprachbund" happen to be genetically related, but the special features which mark them out as a group result rather from centuries of contiguity, during which innovations will have spread from one language of the group to another and neighboring languages will have supported each other in the retention of shared features.

The most pervasive external influence on Eastern Iranian has been that exerted by the neighboring Indian languages, as is most evident in the development of aspirates (Khotanese, Parachi, Ormuri) and retroflex consonants (Khotanese, Pashto, etc.). However, similar developments are found in Baluchi (North-Western Iranian), which is also spoken in close proximity to Indian. Indian loanwords are found already in most Eastern Middle Iranian languages (but also in Parthian) and increase in number in the modern period.

See also ALANS; AVESTAN LANGUAGE; BACTRIAN LANGUAGE; BARTANGI; CHORASMIA III; THE CHORASMIAN LANGUAGE; DIALECTOLOGY.

Bibliography: Apart from works referred to above in the text, this list includes etymological dictionaries or vocabularies of individual languages of the group and important comparative studies of the Eastern Iranian languages. V. I. Abaev, *Istoriko-ètimologicheskiĭ slovar' osetinskogo yazyka*, 4 vols., Moscow and Leningrad, 1958-89. M. S. Andreev and E. M. Peshchereva, *Yagnobskie teksty. Sprilozheniem Yagnobsko Russkogo slovar', sostavlennogo M. S. Andreev, V. A. Livshitsem i A. K. Pisarchik*, Moscow and Leningrad, 1957. H. W. Bailey, *Dictionary of Khotan Saka*, Cambridge, 1979. D. I. Edelman, "History of the consonant systems of the North-Pamir languages," *IIJ* XXII, 1980, pp. 287-310. Idem (Edel'man), *Sravnitel'naya grammatika vostochnoiranskikh yazykov*, 2 vols., Moscow, 1986, 1990. V. A. Efimov and D. I. Edel'man, "Novoiranskie yazyki: vostochnaya gruppa" in *Jazyki Azii i Afriki* II, Moscow, 1978, pp. 198-253. W. B. Henning, "Mitteliranisch," in HO, I/IV/1, Leiden and Cologne, 1958, pp. 20-130. G. Morgenstierne, *Report on a Linguistic Mission to Afghanistan*, Oslo, 1926. Idem, *An etymological Vocabulary of Pashto*, Oslo, 1927. Idem, *Indo-Iranian Frontier Languages; I: Parachi and Ormuri*, Oslo, 1929; II: *Iranian Pamir Languages*, Oslo, 1938. Idem, "Neu-iranische Sprachen," in HO, I/IV/1, Leiden and Cologne, 1958, pp. 155-78. Idem, *Irano-Dardica*, Wiesbaden, 1973. Idem, *Etymological Vocabulary of the Shughni group*, Wiesbaden, 1974. T. N. Pakhalina, *Issledovanie po sravnitel'no-istoricheskoĭ fonetike pamirskikh yazykov*, Moscow, 1983. V. S. Rastorgueva, ed., *Opyt istoriko-tipologicheskogo issledovaniya iranskikh yazykov*, 2 vols., Moscow, 1975. R. Schmitt, ed., *Compendium Linguarum Iranicarum*, Wiesbaden, 1989. N. Sims-Williams, "Le lingue iraniche," in A. Giacalone Ramat and P. Ramat, eds., *Le lingue indoeuropee*, Bologna, 1993, pp. 151-79. Idem, "The Triple System of Deixis in Sogdian," *TPS*, 92, 1994, pp. 41-53. V. S. Sokolova, *Geneticheskie otnosheniya yazgulyamskogo yazyka i shugnanskoĭ yazykovoĭ gruppy*, Leningrad, 1967. Idem, *Geneticheskie otnosheniya mundzhanskogo yazyka i shugnano-yazgulyamskoĭ gruppy*, Leningrad, 1973.

(NICHOLAS SIMS-WILLIAMS)

PLATE LVI

Aḥmad ʿEbādī playing the *setār*, Tehran, Photograph Faḵr-al-Dīn Faḵr-al-Dīnī, courtesy M. Kasheff.

ʿEBĀDĪ, AḤMAD (b. Tehran, 1305/1906, d. 1371 Š./1993), one of the outstanding modern masters of Persian music. He was a grandson of ʿAlī-Akbar Farāhānī (d. ca. 1275/1858) and a son of Mīrzā ʿAbd-Allāh (1261-1336/1845-1918), the great masters of their own times. ʿEbādī began accompanying his father on the *żarb* (see DRUMS) at the age of seven years, then took lessons on the *setār* from his two sisters Mawlūd Ḵānom and Molūk Ḵānom before studying briefly with his father (Ḵāleqī, pp. 128, 453-54) . In 1303 Š./1924, at the age of eighteen years, he appeared in his first public concert, accompanying the singer Molūk Żarrābī. Subsequently, however, he became an official in the Tehran municipal government and later in the Ministry of Culture (Wezārat-e farhang), deferring his public career until 1321 Š./1942 (Behrūzī, p. 116). For the next ten years he participated actively in the development of the musical radio series *Golhā-ye jāvīdān*, directed by Dāwūd Pīrnīā. It was through the radio that he attracted a growing audience for the *setār*. In 1337 Š./1958 he played in concert in Paris and thereafter in several European countries. He continued to perform regularly in Persia until 1358 Š./1979. He generally appeared as a soloist or accompanied by the *żarb* and frequented private circles of music lovers, where the special charm of his playing was appreciated.

ʿEbādī played a leading role in popularizing the *setār*; the appeal of his performance resulted partly from the development of a new style involving slight technical and acoustical modifications to the instrument, which he undertook upon his disappointment caused by hearing recordings of his own first radio performances. In contrast to the traditional style of playing, his own was much less rapid, with sharper contrasts in timbre and intensity and less systematic reliance on the drone on all the strings (During, 1984, pp. 45-46); it was characterized by a rich sonority resulting from a firm and broad attack, made easier by a slight displacement of the strings from the sounding board and the use of strings 10-20 percent thicker than usual. Another of his contributions was a very large number of different tunings (*kūk*), which allowed him to play the traditional musical modes (*dastgāh*, q.v.) in unfamiliar tonalities that lent them original coloration (for a list of his tunings, see ʿEbādī, *Šīvahā*). On the other hand, ʿEbādī never shifted the frets of his instrument, which were at fixed intervals (analyzed by During, 1985, pp. 110-18; idem, 1991, pp. 49-52), regardless of the mode. Available recordings include performances of the *dastgāh*s Māhūr and Daštī (cf. Zonis) and *Šīvahā-ye novīn-e kūk-e setār* (cf. ʿEbādī).

ʿEbādī had no children and trained very few students, but his style inspired not only players of the *setār* but also most of the instrumentalists of the period 1329-59 Š./1950-80. Although he was extremely generous with advice, he played no role in transmission of the repertory (*radīf*), placing innnovative improvisation and development of a personal style above academic knowledge. For ʿEbādī the *setār* had to touch the heart, but, though its tone is naturally melancholy, it had also to be able to express joy; he believed that it should never be played in the open air or in an orchestra, where it could have only a secondary role (Behrūzī, p. 119). As for his audience, according to Mīrzā ʿAbd-Allah, "Two listeners are not enough; three are too many" (Behrūzī, p. 117).

Bibliography: Š. Behrūzī, *Čehrahā-ye mūsīqī-e Īrān* I, Tehran, 1372 Š./1993, pp. 113-19. J. During, *La musique iranienne. Tradition et évolution*, Paris, 1984. Idem, "Théorie et pratiques des gammes iraniennes," *Revue de Musicologie* 71/1-2, 1985, pp. 79-118. Idem, *Le répertoire-modèle de la musique persane. Radif de târ et de setâr de Mirzâ ʿAbdollâh,* Tehran (Sorūš), 1991. A. ʿEbādī, *Šīvahā-ye novīn-e kūk-e setār*, 2 cassettes, Tehran (Sorūš), ca. 1369 Š./1990. R. Ḵāleqī, *Sargozašt-e mūsīqī-e Īrān*, 2 vols. Tehran, 1333-35 Š./1955-56. Ḥ. Naṣīrīfar, *Mardān-e mūsīqī-e sonnatī o novīn-e Īrān*, Tehran, 1369 Š./1990, pp. 226-29. E. Zonis, comp., *Classical Modes of Iran. The Dastgāh System*, 2 vols., Folkways 8831-32.

(JEAN DURING)

EBĀḤĪYA (or **EBĀḤATĪYA**), a polemical term denoting either antinomianism or groups and individuals accused thereof. It occurs generally in the context of condemning pseudo-Sufis, although it is sometimes used in connection with a variety of other religious deviants. The word is derived from *ebāḥat,* which in the terminology of Islamic jurisprudence means the permissibility which is inherent in all things unless canceled or modified by specific provisions of the law; the error of the antinomians lies in their rejection of all such provisions. The principal hallmarks of the Ebāḥīya are generally identified as the rejection of all ritual worship and indulgence in sexual promiscuity.

Several early Sufi writers who were at pains to dissociate their discipline from the deviants that claimed allegiance to it did not have recourse to the term *ebāḥīya* (Kalābāḏī, p. 20; Qošayrī, pp. 20-21; Abū Naṣr Sarrāj, pp. 2-3). The earliest and also fullest treatment of the phenomenon of pseudo-Sufi antinomianism using the term *ebāḥīya* is an acephalic treatise by Abū Ḥāmed Ḡazālī (q.v.) written in Persian, probably while he was teaching at the Neẓāmīya *madrasa* in Nīšāpūr in 499/1105 (Pretzl, Per. tr., pp. 63-118). Ḡazālī describes the antinomians as the most difficult group of the misguided to redeem through proof and argumentation, for they are mere idiots, cast into the lap of Satan by lustfulness and lethargy. Many of them simply welcome the special opportunities to sin that are provided by the cover of a Sufi exterior; others, however, advance arguments which may point to doubt or confusion (*šobhat*) on their part. Of the eight instances of *šobhat* Ḡazālī addresses, only half—the third, fourth, fifth, and eighth—are related to a faulty understanding or practice of Sufism: those who, disappointed with their inability to rid themselves entirely of lowly characteristics completely, abandon the struggle; those who, beholding certain paranormal phenomena in the course of ascetic practice, imagine themselves to have reached the goal and therefore to be free of all need to pray; those who, having been vouchsafed certain genuine insights, believe they have transcended the law; and those who claim that the poverty essential to Sufism includes divesting oneself even of meritorious acts. The remaining four sources of antinomian error are simply four common forms of skepticism, not tied to Sufism in any way: the belief that worship is superfluous, since God does not stand in need of our prayers; the assumption that God's forgiveness is unconditional and not balanced by His wrath; the deterministic notion that worship cannot affect man's fate in the hereafter; and the straightforward denial of resurrection and judgment. Ḡazālī reserves his harshest condemnation for those whose antinomianism is rooted in this denial which, he remarks, "has become common in this age" (p. 23), and he proclaims their extermination to be the duty of the ruler.

Six of the eight sources of *ebāḥīya* listed by Ḡazālī are reproduced, in a somewhat different order, by the Hanbalite jurist Ebn al-Jawzī (d. 592/1200) in his *Talbīs Eblīs* (pp. 411-18). Since there is no reason to assume that Ebn al-Jawzī knew Persian, this may indicate that Ḡazālī's treatise had been translated into Arabic, or that its contents had been incorporated into an Arabic work accessible to Ebn al-Jawzī. While Ḡazālī does not name any pseudo-Sufi group or individual guilty of antinomianism, Ebn al-Jawzī mentions a certain Moḥammad b. Ṭāher al-Maqdesī as exemplifying the trend (pp. 185-86). In his brief evocation of the Ebāḥīya, Hojvīrī (d. 464/1071) mentions (pp. 164, 334) the Fāresīān, the followers of a certain Fāres who claimed falsely to be a disciple of Ḥallāj.

In general, however, it appears that the pseudo-Sufi antinomians represented a tendency rather than a coherent school; it is in this sense that ʿAbd-al-Karīm Samʿānī (d. 562/1166) denounces as exemplifying *ebāḥīya* all who deny resurrection and disregard sexual prohibitions (*Ketāb al-ansāb*, GMS XX, f. 15b).

A writer as late as ʿAbd-al-Raḥmān Jāmī (d. 898/1492) defined the Ebāḥīya as a people who sought unjustifiably to assimilate themselves with the Sufis (*motašabbeh-e mobṭel be īšān*) while completely lacking "the adornment of their beliefs and states" (*Nafaḥāt al-ons*, pp. 9-10). Gradually, however, the term *ebāḥīya* came to lose its particular resonance, becoming virtually interchangeable with *ḥolūlīya* (in-carnationism), *bāṭenīya* (extreme esotericism), and *zandaqa* (heresy) in a series of epithets that were affixed to heterodox movements of all stripes.

It may finally be noted that historians of Mughal India described as Ebāḥatīya a Tantric sect of Hinduism, found especially in Orissa (I. H. Qureshi, "Ibāḥatīya," *EI*[2] III, p. 663).

Bibliography: (For cited works not given in detail, see "Short References.") Hojvīrī, *Kašf al-maḥjūb*, ed. V. A. Žukovskii, Leningrad, 1926. ʿAbd-al-Rahmān Jāmī, *Nafaḥāt al-ons*, ed. M. ʿĀbedī, Tehran, 1370 Š./1991. Ebn al-Jawzī, *Talbīs Eblīs*, ed. Ḵayr-al-Dīn ʿAlī, Beirut, n.d. C. Ernst, *Words of Ecstasy in Sufism*, Albany (N.Y.), 1985, pp. 118-120. Kalābāḏī, *al-Taʿarrof le maḏhab ahl al-taṣawwof*, eds. ʿA.-H. Maḥmūd and Ṭ. ʿAbd-al-Bāqī Sorūr, Cairo, 1380/1960.

W. Madelung and M. G. S. Hodgson, "Ibāḥa II," *EI*[2] III, pp. 662-63. O. Pretzl, *Die Streitschrift des Ġazâlī gegen die Ibāḥīja*, in *Sitzungsberichte der Bayerischen Akademie der Wissenschaften, Philosophisch-historische Abteilung*, 1933:7; repr. with a Persian tr. of Pretzl's introduction by Čangīz Pahlavān, *Zamīna-ye Īrān-šenāsī*, Tehran, 1364 Š./1985. Qošayrī, *al-Resālat al-qošayrīya*, eds. ʿA.-H. Maḥmūd and M. Šarīf, Cairo, 1385/1966. Najm-al-Dīn Rāzī, *Merṣād al-ʿebād*, ed. M.- A. Rīāḥī, Tehran, 1365 Š./1986, pp. 261, 396. Sayyed Jaʿfar Sajjādī, *Farhang-e maʿāref-e eslāmī*, Tehran, 1366 Š./1987, I, p. 26. Abū Naṣr Sarrāj, *Ketāb al-lomaʿ fi'l-taṣawwof*, ed. R. A. Nicholson, GMS XXII. Moḥammad-ʿAlī Tahānawī, *Kaššāf eṣṭelāḥāt al-fonūn*, repr., Istanbul, 1984, I, p. 114.

(HAMID ALGAR)

EBER-NĀRI (Aram. Abar Naharā, "Beyond/ Across the river"), the Akkadian name used in Assyrian and Babylonian records of the 8th-5th centuries B.C.E. for the lands to the west of the Euphrates—i.e., Phoenicia, Syria, and Palestine (Parpola, p. 116; Zadok, p. 129; see ASSYRIA ii). These regions apparently passed from Neo-Babylonian to Persian control in 539 B.C.E. when Cyrus the Great conquered Mesopotamia.

In 535 B.C.E. Cyrus made Babylonia and Eber-Nāri into a single satrapy that included almost all the territory of the previous Neo-Babylonian kingdom. From Babylonian legal documents the following satraps, all evidently Persians residing in Babylon, are known: Gubāru (535-525 B.C.E.), Uštānu (521-516 B.C.E.), Ḫuta [...], son of Pagakanna (486 B.C.E.). Eber-Nāri also had its own governors subordinate to the satrap of the united province. This post was held by Tattannu, about 518-02 B.C.E. (Dandamayev, pp. 3-4, 73-79, 84, 139-41; Ephʿal, p. 154; Stolper, p. 290).

Some time between 486 and 450 B.C.E. the satrapy of Babylonia and Eber-Nāri was divided into two administrative units of equal status (Stern, p. 78). Probably the separation occurred soon after 482 when Xerxes crushed the rebellion of the Babylonians against Persia. Soon this satrapy, now also including Cyprus, occupied a leading position in the western part of the Achaemenid empire. Babylonian legal documents from 407-01 B.C.E. mention Bēlšunu, son of Bēl-uṣuršu (Belesys), as governor of Eber-Nāri (Stolper, p. 290; Xenophon, *Anabasis* 1.4.10, 7.8.25). Another Belesys, governor of Syria under Artaxerxes III (r. 358-38 B.C.E.) is mentioned by Diodorus (16.42.1); he may have lived in Damascus or Sidon. In 349 B.C.E. the Phoenician cities revolted against the Persians; thereafter, in about 344 B.C.E. Eber-Nāri was joined to Cilicia, whose satrap Mazaeus had led an army against the Phoenicians. His coins are inscribed with the Aramaic legend "Mazaeus who is over Abar Nahār and Cilicia" (Cooke, p. 346). In 332 B.C.E. the satrapy was occupied by Alexander.

Eber-Nāri included three areas with distinct types of administrative status: Phoenicia, Judah and Samaria, and the Arabian tribes. The Phoenician cities of Tyre, Sidon, Byblos, and Aradus were vassal states ruled by hereditary local kings who struck their own silver coins and whose power was limited by the Persian satrap and local popular assemblies. The economies of these cities were mainly based on maritime trade. During military operations, the Phoenicians were obliged to put their fleet at the disposal of the Persian kings (Elayi, pp. 13ff.; Ephʿal, pp. 156f.). Judah and Samaria enjoyed considerable internal autonomy. Bullae and seal impressions of the end of the 6th and beginning of the 5th centuries mention the province of Judah (Ephʿal, pp. 160f.). Its governors included Sheshbazzar and Zerubbabel under Cyrus and Darius I; Nehemiah (ca. 445-32); Bagohi, who succeeded Nehemiah and whose ethnicity is difficult to determine; and "Yehizkiyah the governor" and "Yohanan the priest," known from coins struck in Judah in the 4th century B.C.E. From the second half of the 5th century the province of Samaria was governed by Sanballat and his descendants (Ephʿal, pp. 151-52). Finally, the Arabian tribes in the area between Egypt and the Euphrates were ruled by their tribal chiefs (Ephʿal, p. 162).

Bibliography: (For cited works not given in detail, see "Short References.") G. A. Cooke, *A Text-Book of North Semitic Inscriptions*, Oxford, 1903. M. Dandamayev, *Iranians in Achaemenid Babylonia*, Columbia Lectures on Iranian Studies 6, Costa Mesa, Calif., 1992. J. Elayi, "The Phoenician Cities in the Persian Period," *The Journal of the Ancient Near Eastern Society of Columbia University* 12, 1980, pp. 13-28. I. Ephʿal, "Syria-Palestine under Achaemenid Rule," *CAH*[2] IV, 1988, pp. 139-64. S. Parpola, *Neo-Assyrian Toponyms*, Alter Orient und Altes Testament. Veröffentlichungen zur Kultur und Geschichte des Alten Orients und des Alten Testaments 6, Neukirchen-Vluyn, 1970. Th. Petit, *Satrapes et satrapies dans l'empire achéménide de Cyrus le Grand à Xerxès Ier*, Bibliothèque de la Faculté de Philosophie et Lettres de l'Université de Liège, fasc. 254, Paris, 1990, pp. 189-92, 197-99. E. Stern, "The Persian Empire and the Political and Social History of Palestine in the Persian Period," *The Cambridge History of Judaism* I, Cambridge etc., 1984, pp. 70-87. M. W. Stolper, "The Governor of Babylon and Across-the-River in 486 B.C.," *JNES* 48, 1989, pp. 283-305. R. Zadok, *Geographical Names According to New and Late-Babylonian Texts*, Beihefte zum Tübinger Atlas des Vorderen Orients, Répertoire Géographique des Textes Cunéiformes 8, Wiesbaden, 1985.

(MUHAMMAD A. DANDAMAYEV)

EBERMAN, VASILIĬ ALEKSANDROVICH (b. St. Petersburg, 1899, d. Orel, 1937), scholar of early Persian poets writing in Arabic. Born in the family of a surgeon of German origin, Eberman studied Arabic and Persian in 1917-21 at the Department of Oriental Languages at the University of Petrograd. As a researcher he was active only from 1919 to 1930, working at the Asiatic Museum of the Academy of Sciences (researcher, first rank, 1919-20) and the State Academy of the History of Material Culture (researcher, second rank, 1920-30). In 1924-29 he taught Arabic at Leningrad University (docent, 1925-29). In June 1930 he was charged with counterrevolutionary activities and sent to the Solovkilabor camp, whence he was moved to Belbaltlag labor camp. Having learned geology at the new labor camp, he worked as a geologist. He was discharged ahead of schedule in July 1933 for having performed, in his own words, "shock work." He resumed teaching as a docent at the Leningrad Institute for the History of Philosophy and Linguistics, but was dismissed on 15 January 1934, arrested again, and sent on 7 March 1934 to Sevvost (northeastern) labor camp in Magadan ("Response of the Federal Service of Counterintelligence," St. Petersburg, to the Institute of Oriental Studies, dated 29 April 1994; no. 10/16-11449). In 1936 he returned from the labor camp and settled in Orel, where it was impossible to continue his research. He drowned while swimming in 1937.

Eberman's earliest article was a study of oriental topics in Russian poetry (1923), but his chief interest was the contribution of non-Arabs, primarily Persians, to early Islamic culture and Arabic literature. His first major article dealt with the Jondīšāpūr school of medicine (1925). In his "Persians among the Arabic poets of the Umayyad era" (1929, pp. 113-54) he argued that Persians "created a poetical literature important even on a world scale" (p. 114). Finding no evidence that Sasanian poetry had survived into Islamic times, he held that the beginnings of New Persian poetry "are to be sought in Arabic, in the poetry of the first century of ʿAbbasid rule (p. 115, n. 3) This article investigates the preceding period and discusses all available information concerning the earliest Arabic poets of Persian extraction: Ważżāḥ, K̲orra, K̲osrow, Ebn Mofarreḡ, Mūsā Šahawāt, Abu'l-ʿAbbās, and Esmāʿīl b. Yasār. Eberman continued this line of research with a study of K̲oraymī (3rd/9th century; 1930b). He also catalogued a small collection of Persian manuscripts (1927b) and published in German an excellent survey of Arabic studies in Russia in 1914-27 (1927a, 1930a).

Bibliography: Eberman's works relating to Persia are as follows: V. Eberman, "Arabi i persi v russkoĭ poezii" (Arabs and Persians in Russian poetry), *Vostok, zhurnal literaturi, nauki i iskusstva* 3, 1923, pp. 108-25. Idem, "Meditsinskaya shkola v Jundishapure" (The medical school of Jondīšāpūr), *Zapiski Kollegii Vostokovedov pri Aziatskom muzee Akademii nauk SSSR* 1, 1925, pp. 47-72. Idem, "Opisanie sobraniya arabskikh rukopiseĭ, pozhertvo-vannykh v Aziatskiĭ Muzeĭ v 1926 g. Polnomochnym Predstavitel'stvom SSSR v Persii" (Description of the collection of Arabic manuscripts donated to the Asiatic Museum in 1926 by the plenipotentiary representative of the USSR in Persia), *Izvestiya Akademii Nauk*, 6th ser., 21, 1927b, pp. 315-24. Idem, "Persi sredi arabskikh poetov epokhi Omeĭyadov" (Persians among the Arabic poets of the Umayyad era), *Zapiski Kollegii Vostokovedov pri Aziatskom Muzee Akademii Nauk SSSR* 2, 1929, pp. 113-54. An autobiography of Eberman and a memoir of him by I. Y. Kratchkovskiĭ, kept in the Central State Archives of St. Petersburg (fund no. 328, list 2, no. 1920), were made available by Ya. V. Vasil'kov.

(A. B. KHALEDOV)

EBIR NĀRĪ. See EBER-NĀRI.

EBLĀĞ (lit., "communication"), title of five Persian language newspapers.

1. A Constitutionalist weekly published in Tabrīz by the printer Maḥmūd Eskandānī, who also published *Nażmīya* (1326/1908). The first issue was published on Thursday, ʿĪd-e Ḡadīr, 18 D̲u'l-Ḥejja, probably in 1325, corresponding to 22 January 1908 (Rabino, no. 1, gives 1326/1909, and Browne, *Press and Poetry*, no. 22, gives 1324/1907; neither corresponds to a Thursday). No more than five issues appeared. Its prose was old-fashioned and its content religious. Format was four two-column pages, 22 x 34 cm, lithographed in *nask̲*. Copies are accessible at Reżā ʿAbbāsī Museum (Tehran), Cambridge University library (England), and Bibliothèque Nationale (Paris).

2. A biweekly newspaper published in Tehran by Mīrzā ʿAlī Āqā Eblāḡ Jahromī between Rabīʿ II 1343/September-October 1924 and 1345/1926. Ṣadr Hāšemī thought incorrectly that it was published in Shiraz. Format was four three-column pages, 41 x

56 cm, typeset. Copies are accessible at Majles Library II (Tehran).

3. A continuation ("3rd year") of the biweekly above, published in Bombay by the same Eblāḡ between April 1927 and the end of the year. Format was four four-column pages, 28 x 41.5 cm, lithographed. A copy of one issue is at the University of Isfahan library.

4. A government broadside published in Kabul one to three times a week during the years 1300-05 Š./1921-26. It was posted on walls in major Afghan towns. It contained summaries from other official newspapers and was used to promulgate laws and make official announcements. The public called it *Aḵbār-e rāygān*, "the free news," or *Moft-e dīvārī*, "the free poster." It was edited by Mīrzā Moḥammad-Akbar Khan and later Sayyed Moḥammad Īšān Ḥosaynī, a noted calligrapher in whose handwriting the newspaper was published. Format was one page, 24 x 34 cm, later 33 x 50 cm, with one or two columns, lithographed in *nastaʿlīq*. Some copies are accessible at major Afghan libraries.

5. A magazine said to have been published in Urmia in 1312 Š./1933. No extant copies are known.

Bibliography: (For cited works not given in detail, see "Short References.") M.-K. Āhang, *Sayr-e žūrnālīsm dar Afḡānestān*, Kabul, 1349 Š./1970, pp. 164-66. N. Māyel Heravī, *Moʿarrefī-e rūz-nāmahā, jarāyed, majallāt-e Wezārat-e Maṭbūʿāt*, Kabul, 1341 Š./1962, p. 40. Ḥ. Naḵjavānī, "Tārīḵča ye entešār-e rūz-nāmahā wa majallāt dar Āḏar-bāyjān," *NDA Tabrīz* 15, Spring 1342 Š./1963, p. 4. Ḥ. Omīd, *Tārīḵ-e farhang-e Āḏarbāyjān* II, Tabrīz, 1334 Š./1955, p. 20. Š. Peymānī, *Fehrest-e rūz-nāmahā-ye mawjūd dar Ketāb-ḵāna-ye Markazī-e Dānešgāh-e Eṣfahān*, Isfahan, 1362 Š./1983, p. 6. Rabino, *Ṣūrat-e jarāʾed*. Ṣadr Hāšemī, *Jarāʾed o majallāt*, nos. 12-15. Ṣ. Sardārīnīā, *Tārīḵ-e rūz-nāmahā wa majallāt-e Āḏarbāyjān*, Tehran, 1360 Š./1981, pp. 108-09. U. Sims-Williams, *Union Catalogue of Persian Serials*, no. 204. M.-ʿA. Tarbīat, *Dānešmandān-e Āḏarbāyjān*, Tehran, 1314 Š./1935, p. 406.

(NASSEREDDIN PARVIN)

EBLĪS IN PERSIAN SUFI TRADITION. The word Eblīs, a Koranic designation for the devil, appears to derive ultimately from the Greek *diabolos*. Some authorities have nonetheless imaginatively connected it with Arabic *ublisa* ("he was rendered hopeless"), with reference to the accursedness that befell Eblīs as a result of his rebellion (Maybodī, I, p. 145). Of the eleven Koranic verses in which the name Eblīs occurs (2:34, 7:11, 15:31-32, 17:61, 18:50, 20:116, 26:95, 34:20, 38:74-75), ten refer to this rebellion and the events immediately preceding and following it; the exception, 26:95, speaks of "the hosts of Eblīs" (*jonūd Eblīs*) being cast into Hellfire on the Day of Judgement. Eblīs is, therefore, a name peculiarly connected with the refusal to bow down before Adam and the reasons and motives that led to it; it occurs far less frequently in the Koran than *al-šayṭān* (Satan), which is used to designate the devil in the context of his maleficent plots against man. The distinction between the two names can be seen clearly in 20:116-120. The first verse in this sequence reads: "When We said to the angels, 'Prostrate yourselves before Adam, they prostrated, but not Eblīs; he refused." And the last: "But Satan whispered evil to him. ..." There are relatively few Hadith in which the name Eblīs occurs, the most frequently cited being that in which the Prophet speaks of Eblīs having a throne "on the Waters," which serves as the base from which he sends forth his hosts (*Ṣaḥīḥ Muslim* IV, p. 1472). The majority of the traditions included by Boḵārī in his *Bāb ṣefat Eblīs wa jonūdehe* (chapter on the description of Eblīs and his hosts) refer to *al–šayṭān* rather than Eblīs (*Ṣaḥīḥ al-Boḵārī* IV, pp. 147-53). A minor distinction between the two names is that Eblīs as a proper name does not have a plural (at least in the Koran; in Persian texts the broken plurals *abālīs* and *abālesa* are sometimes encountered; Mojtabāʾī, p. 598), whereas *šayṭān* forms the plural *šayāṭīn* (6:112, for example, speaks of "satans among mankind and jinn"). The most significant difference with respect to Sufi tradition is that Eblīs gradually evolves into "a complex mythic personality" (Awn, p. 46), while *šayṭān* remains fixed as the designation for a being of pure malevolence.

The complexities surrounding Eblīs begin with the exegetical questions pertaining to his original nature. The wording of 2:34, 7:11, 17:61, and 18:50 (*fa-sajadū ellā Eblīs*) might be taken to suggest that Eblīs was an angel until the refusal of divine command. However, as Bayżāwī (II, p. 300) points out, such an interpretation would contradict the general principle that angels are constitutionally incapable of disobedience ("they rebel not against God in aught that He commands them, and they do whatever they are commanded"; 66:6). Furthermore, 18:50 says clearly of Eblīs, "he was from the jinn" (although it has been argued that the word *al-jenn* in this verse means *ḵazanat al-janna*, the angelic custodians of Paradise; Nīsābūrī, p. 6). The nature of Eblīs as jinn also seems to be confirmed by his boast, "You created me from fire" (55:15), this being the element from which the jinn were fashioned. Maybodī therefore concludes that the particle *ellā* in the verses that speak of Eblīs' refusal to prostrate himself does not imply an exception of Eblīs from the otherwise obedient category of angels and has instead the sense of "by contrast with" or "unlike" (Maybodī, I, p. 144). Some exegetes, most notably Ṭabarī (I, pp. 173-74) attempt to solve the problem by suggesting that the jinn were in some fashion derived from the angels or formed a subdivision of them so that the term *al-malāʾeka* (angels) in the problematic verses could be taken as implicitly including the jinn who are fully capable of refusing God's command.

This theory was buttressed by various narratives, for the most part unsupported by Koran or Hadith, that detailed Eblīs' transition from the status of jinn to that of angel, or vice versa, within a single category of supernatural being. He is thus said to have originated as the commander of a troop of 7,000 angels worshipping God in the seventh heaven for 8,000 years; then, because of an innate wretchedness (*šaqāwat*) manifest long before his rebellion, he aspired, not to ascend beyond the seventh heaven to the divine throne, but to descend from it through each of the remaining heavens. After spending 8,000 years worshipping God in each heaven, Eblīs finally reached the earth where he quelled a rebellion of the jinn and ruled on behalf of God for eight more millennia until Adam was created and appointed viceregent in his place, inspiring him to rebel (Nīsābūrī, pp. 6-7). Alternatively, Eblīs is presented as being originally a jinn inhabiting the earth, who by virtue of the asceticism that set him apart from his fellows was elevated by God into the company of the angels, ultimately becoming their supreme instructor at the foot of the divine throne (Awn, p. 30). Most of the mythic narrations concerning Eblīs agree that until the time of his rebellion against God he was known as ʿAzāzīl, a word which rhyming with Jebrāʾīl, Mīkāʾil, Esrāfīl, and the like was understood to reflect his inclusion among the archangels. Of Hebrew origin, the name has the meaning "the one empowered by God" (Tuğ, p. 312; among the Biblical verses where it occurs, possibly also as a designation for the devil, may be cited Leviticus 16:8-10, 13:21, and 17:7). Nonetheless, a number of authors sought to connect ʿAzāzīl with Arabic *ʿazl* (dismissal, removal), as if the very name of Eblīs in his archangelic state had presaged his fall and disgrace (Maybodī, I, p. 145). Eblīs is generally understood, even by authors who regard him as fallen angel, as the father of the jinn, just as his adversary Adam was the father of mankind; extra-Koranic narratives attribute to him in addition the procreation of a named offspring, specifically and recognizably his own, each child being entrusted with the fostering of a different vice among men. This theme was taken up by Ḡazālī (*Eḥyāʾ* III, p. 38), who lists seven names, and by ʿAṭṭār (*Taḏkerat al-Awlīyāʾ*, pp. 529-31), who depicts Eblīs as tricking Adam into eating one of his sons, Ḵannās, thereby fatally ingesting the very substance of Eblīs. In general, however, it is less the narrative details of these mythic accounts that interest the Sufis than the general theme of Eblīs' downfall, a theme rich in didactic possibilities.

Many of them regarded as the main source of his undoing the egoism that expressed itself in the boast, "I am better than him (= Adam)" in the Koran, 7:12. Thus Ḡazālī observes, "The story of Eblīs has been related to you not as a mere fable, but so that you might understand the outcome of pride, for it was pride that impelled him to say, 'I am better than him'" (*Kīmīā-ye saʿādat* II, p. 257); ʿAṭṭār has Eblīs counseling Moses, "Never say 'I' lest you become like me" (*Manṭeq al-ṭayr*, p. 163); Bahāʾ-al-Dīn Walad goes so far as to say "Eblīs and all demons are identical with egoism" (*Maʿāref*, p. 364); and Rūmī warns, "The disease of Eblīs was 'I am better,' and this sickness is in every creature's soul" (*Maṯnawī*, bk. I, line 3216). According to Rūzbehān Baqlī, it is true, the gnostic may legitimately exclaim, in a state of spiritual expansion (*basṭ*), "I am better than so-and-so," but although Baqlī is relatively well-disposed to Eblīs, following in the footsteps of Ḥallāj, he takes pains to clarify that the state of Eblīs was one of contraction (*qabż*), not expansion (*Mašrab al-arwāḥ*, pp. 185-86). This was also the view of ʿAbd-al-Karīm Jīlī (*al-Ensān al-kāmel*, p. 40).

One consequence of Eblīs' egoistic pride was that he counted on the eons of worship he had performed both to rebel against God and to avoid the resulting divine wrath. According to Bahāʾ-al-Dīn Walad, his devotions weighed heavily only in his own scales, not in God's reckoning, and when he defied the command to incline before Adam, all his millennia of worship were revealed as counterfeit (*Maʿāref*, p. 80). In the opinion of ʿAbd-Allāh Anṣārī, the devotions of Eblīs were invalidated by his disdain for Adam, God's chosen friend, since all worship is futile unless accompanied by love for God's friends (*Rasāʾel* I, pp. 54-55). For other Sufis, the case of Eblīs was proof that worship alone, irrespective of quality or quantity, can never suffice (Ḥātem b. Aṣamm, quoted in *Kīmīā-ye saʿādat* II, p. 414; Hojvīrī, p. 255; ʿAṭṭār, *Manṭeq al-ṭayr*, p. 92; Rūmī, *Maṯnawī*, bk. II, line 2617).

Eblīs' boast of superiority to Adam by virtue of his creation from a superior element (fire as opposed to clay) gave rise to a condemnation of him for engaging in *qīās* (comparison or, in the terminology of Islamic jurisprudence, analogical reasoning) in an attempt to refute God's categorical command. Recording a tradition to this effect from Ebn ʿAbbās ("the first to engage in *qīās* was Eblīs"), Maybodī (III, p. 566) observes that the comparison was wrong because clay and fire are equal, insofar as they are both elements, and that, if there is any superiority involved, it belongs to clay because of its stability and durability. For Bahāʾ-al-Dīn Walad, Eblīs' comparison was flawed because God had given Adam inner knowledge and the inner is by definition superior to the outer, the sole realm to which Eblīs has cognitive access (*Maʿāref*, p. 271), while Rūmī dismisses it on the grounds that Adam's excellence, like that of his descendants, is based on asceticism and piety, not lineage and origin (*Maṯnawī*, bk. I, lines 3396-99).

Envy (*ḥasad*) is also discerned as one of the fatal vices of Eblīs (Ḡazālī, *Kīmīā-ye saʿādat* II, p. 130; Rūmī, *Maṯnawī*, bk. I, lines 428-29), as is subjugation to delusion (*wahm*). The association between delusion and Eblīs was made in passing by ʿAṭṭār

("Your delusions are all Eblīs, a malevolent demon;" *Asrār-nāma*, p. 70), and more fully by ʿAzīz-al-Dīn Nasafī (*Ketāb al-Ensān al-kāmel*, p. 143). Nasafī's remarks on the subject were no doubt influenced by the teachings of Ebn ʿArabī (q.v.; "Eblīs is the faculty of delusion (*al-qowwat al-wahmīya*)"; *Tafsīr al-Qorʾān al-Karīm* I, p. 39), but it may be relevant to note that an Ismāʿīlī doctrine equates Eblīs (under the name of Hāreṯ b. Morra) with the evil imagination of the Third Intelligence (Corbin, pp. 45-46).

Finally, Sufis attribute the downfall of Eblīs to an unbridled inquisitiveness. He is said to have conducted a furtive examination of the physical form of Adam in its pre-animate state. According to Rūmī, he compounded this offense by expressing disgust at the blood and putrid matter the body of Adam contained and denying his dignity (*Fīhe ma fīh*, p. 27). Najm-al-Dīn Dāya presents the same theme in an extended narrative which has Eblīs concluding from his examination of Adam: "There is no cause for alarm. This person is hollow; he needs food and is subject to lust like other animals; we may soon gain mastery over him," but expressing concern over what might be hidden in his heart, the only part of his person he had been unable to penetrate (*Merṣād al-ʿebād*, p. 78). Describing Eblīs as "a spy on the path" (*jāsūs-e rāh*), ʿAṭṭār suggests in his treatment of the theme that Eblīs did perceive the mystery contained within Adam, and that it was in fact for this reason that he was punished. God had commanded the angels to prostrate themselves before the form of Adam so they could not see Him placing the mystery in Adam's heart, and it was only Eblīs, with his head insolently raised, who witnessed the act, thereby violating the primordial intimacy of God with His viceregent (*Manṭeq al-ṭayr*, pp. 181-82).

It is in large part by promoting his own vices among men that Eblīs deludes and misguides them; in addition, sins such as lust, gluttony, acquisitiveness, and, above all, anger provide dangerous inroads for Eblīs into the human soul (Ḡazālī, *Kīmīā-ye saʿādat* II, p. 165; *Eḥyāʾ ʿOlūm al-Dīn* III, pp. 31-40). Often, however, in keeping with his consummate cunning, Eblīs persuades people to perform good acts for ultimately malicious purposes, an example being the ascetic whom he persuaded to nurse a sick girl in the knowledge that the ascetic would sooner or later fall prey to her charms (*Eḥyāʾ ʿolūm al-dīn* III, p. 30). Alternatively, he might impel his victims to perform a minor good deed in order to forestall the accomplishment of a greater good, a case in point being the reminder he gave to Moʿāwīya to perform his prayers promptly in order to deprive him of the benefit of heartfelt repentance (Rūmī, *Maṯnawī*, bk. II, lines 2604-2743). When behaving in such deceptively solicitous fashion, Eblīs may appear even in the role of a spiritual guide (*moršed; Maṯnawī*, bk. II, lines 256-58). Occasionally, however, Eblīs' wiliness rebounds against him as when a sinner whom he has deluded attains Paradise by means of a repentance that would not have occurred without his intervention (Ḡazālī, *Kīmīā-ye saʿādat* II, p. 326).

It is plain that for the Sufis Eblīs, as the agent of temptation, has a real existence external to man. Many of his characteristics are, however, identical with those of the *nafs*, the unredeemed self, and certain utterances of the Sufis suggest that Eblīs is indistinguishable from the sinful inclinations of man and is therefore internal to him. Thus Najm-al-Dīn Kobrā says, "Know that the *nafs*, Satan and angels are not things external to you; rather you are they. ..." (*Die Fawaʾeḥ al-jamāl*, p. 32), and human shortcomings such as egoism were seen by Bahāʾ-al-Dīn Walad as equivalent to Eblīs (*Maʿāref*, p. 364). The perspectives of externality and internality are, however, ultimately reconcilable in view of the hadith, frequently quoted by Sufis, that "Satan flows in man's bloodstream" (Boḵārī, IV, p. 150).

It is, however, only the prophets and the saints, the invincible adversaries of Eblīs, that he is said to have confronted in visible or audible form. Thus he once appeared to the Prophet Moḥammad while he was praying; the Prophet restrained himself with some difficulty from strangling him, mindful, no doubt, of the purpose for which he had been created (Muslim, I, pp. 273-74). ʿAṭṭār describes another encounter of Eblīs with the Prophet, in the course of which he asked him whether during the *meʿrāj* he had seen the abandoned tokens of his archangelic glories (*Moṣībat-nāma*, pp. 244-45). Noah is recounted to have invited Eblīs to repent by prostrating before the tomb of Adam, thereby redeeming his primordial disobedience; he refused, arguing that, if he had rejected obeisance to a living Adam, he was even less inclined to bow before his remains (Maybodī, I, p. 146). The same exchange is said to have taken place between Eblīs and Moses, the outcome differing only in that Eblīs favored Moses with the advice to avoid vices such as anger, avarice, and keeping the company of women (Ḡazālī, *Kīmīā-ye saʿādat* I, p. 541, II, p. 54). In a contrasting anecdote, Eblīs is said to have informed Sahl b. ʿAbd-Allāh Tostarī that he did prostrate himself penitently before the tomb of Adam a thousand times, but desisted when he heard a voice telling him, "Do not tire yourself; We do not want you" (Maybodī, I, pp. 160-61). According to Ḡazālī (*Kīmīā-e saʿādat* I, p. 240), Eblīs tempted Abraham (see EBRĀHĪM) to disobey the divine indication that he should sacrifice his son, an element not found in the relevant Koranic passage (37:99-107). As for Job, Eblīs could not persuade him to do more than moan in the face of his tribulations (*Kīmīā-ye saʿādat* I, p. 568). Jesus, together with his mother, was singularly privileged in being the only human being at whose birth Eblīs was not present (*Eḥyāʾ ʿolūm al-dīn* III, p. 33), but in later life he, too, was not exempt from visitations by the evil one: Eblīs once upbraided him for claiming detachment from the world despite his use of a stone as a headrest (Makkī, *Qūt al-qolūb*, I, p. 538; Ḡazālī, *Kīmīā-ye saʿādat* II, p. 323; Kobrā, p. 15), and, according to Ebrāhīm b. Adham, on another occasion tempted him to break the rigorous fast in which he was engaged (Makkī, *ʿElm al-qolūb*, p. 216). Surmounting the challenges of Eblīs is thus an integral part of the prophetic experience.

Numerous anecdotes relate his encounters with Sufis, at least the foremost of whom were regarded as falling within the category of God's "purified servants" (Koran, 15:40) who lie beyond the reach of his powers; they represented, therefore, particularly challenging targets (Kalābādī, p. 75; Makkī, *Qūt al–qolūb* II, pp. 92-93). On occasion, the saints are said, indeed, to have taken the offensive against Eblīs; Abū Saʿīd b. Abi'l-Ḵayr is said by a single sneeze to have transported Eblīs from Mayhana to Anatolia (Monawwar, I, p. 275), and Bāyazīd Bestāmī went so far as to attempt to crucify him at the gates of Besṭām (*Taḏkerat al–awlīā*ʾ, p. 175). More commonly, however, it is Eblīs who initiates the encounter: thus he persistently plagued Ebrāhīm b. Adham soon after his renunciation of worldly power (ibid.), and also accosted Rābeʿa ʿAdawīya, who was able to repel him swiftly and with ease (ibid., p. 77). On other occasions, playing the role of a *moršed*, Eblīs reproaches Sufis for slight but significant shortcomings, thus fulfilling a positive purpose, even if his intent be simply to shame. He thus informed Abū Saʿīd Ḵarrāz that the saint had abandoned all things which would place him in his grasp except the company of beardless young men (Qošayrī, I, p. 129; it was no doubt the presence of young men at sessions of *samāʿ* [music] that prompted certain Sufis to infer that Eblīs also frequented such gatherings). Eblīs would frequently insinuate himself into the dreams of the Sufis, attempting, among other things, to dazzle them with the flashes of light emanating from his throne (Sarrāj, p. 428). Ḵarrāz and Jonayd are both reported to have dreamed of Eblīs walking naked before men; when they upbraided him for his shamelessness, Eblīs retorted, "These are not men; true men are those gathered at the mosque in Šonayzīya who keep me ailing and gaunt"—Šonayzīya being a suburb of Baghdad renowned as a gathering place for the devout (Qošayrī, II, p. 721; *Kīmīā-ye saʿādat* I, p. 635). When Ḵarrāz dreamed of Eblīs on another occasion, the saint was about to attack him with a stick when a voice told him, "he has no fear of that, only of a light that is in the heart," so he desisted (Qošayrī, I, pp. 729-30). By contrast, Abū Żaḥḥāk did come to grips with Eblīs and succeeded in throwing him down from a roof, only to be tricked by him into entering a perilously deep river (Jāmī, p. 250).

It is remarkable that none of these otherwise vivid accounts of confrontation contain any description of the physical appearance of Eblīs. He is sometimes described as one-eyed, an attribute shared with the Dajjāl (q.v.), who as the prime manifestation of evil at the end of time fulfills a function somewhat akin to that of Eblīs at its beginning, but this seems to have the allegorical sense of Eblīs' inability to perceive the treasure concealed within Adam (Rūmī, *Maṯnawī*, bk. III, line 2759; bk. IV, lines 824, 1616-17; bk. V, line 3452). Ḡazālī observes, however, that Eblīs sometimes assumes the form of animals such as dogs, pigs, and frogs, each corresponding to a vice being instilled in his victim (*Eḥyāʾ ʿolūm al-dīn* III, p. 40).

The most distinctive feature of the portrayal of Eblīs in Persian Sufism is, perhaps, the attempt to depict him as both more and less than purely satanic, an enterprise that ranged from simple exculpation to outright glorification and the chief protagonists of which were Ḥallāj, Aḥmad Ḡazālī, ʿAyn-al-Qożāt Hamadānī, Sanāʾī, and Rūzbehān Baqlī. At its simplest, this involved the predestinarian argument that Eblīs was compelled to rebel against God. Thus Abū Saʿīd b. Abi'l-Ḵayr placed these words in the mouth of Eblīs: "If it had been up to me, I would have prostrated the very first day. He (=God) tells me, 'prostrate yourself,' but He does not want me to. If He had wanted me to, I would have prostrated myself on that very day" (Monawwar, I, p. 254). Similarly, in a poem of Sanāʾī, Eblīs laments: "He (=God) wished to make me the target of his curse; He did what He wanted, that Adam of clay was but an excuse!" and, "I read on the Preserved Tablet that someone was to be cursed; I thought it might be anyone, but never myself" (*Dīvān*, p. 871). Picking up the same theme, Dāya observes in his narrative concerning the downfall of Eblīs: "It was found desirable to lay the foundation of punishment, to hoist someone onto the scaffold, so that throughout the realms of Kingship and Dominion none should dare to claim viceregency or to oppose that of Adam. Eblīs ... was, therefore, seized on the charge of robbery and bound with the rope of wretchedness" (*Merṣād al–ʿebād*, p. 86); in other words, Eblīs was punished less for his own sins than for, so to speak, reasons of state. In a similar vein, Eblīs is sometimes presented as a victim of divine guile (*makr*). According to one tradition, Jebrāʾīl and Mīkāʾīl wept uncontrollably after the disgracing of Eblīs out of fear that they, too, would fall prey to God's guile, and He told them approvingly, "Be thus; do not feel safe from My guile" (Qošayrī, I, p. 314; *Kīmīā-ye saʿādat* II, p. 411). Eblīs himself complains, in the poem of Sanāʾī, "Secretly He placed the trap of His guile in my path, and then He put Adam in the ring of that trap" (*Dīvān*, p. 871).

Once it is assumed that God both willed Eblīs to disobey Him and intended all the consequences of his disobedience, a contradiction necessarily arises between the divine will (*erāda*) and the divine command (*amr*) to make prostration before Adam. In an encounter with Bāyazīd Bestāmī, Eblīs is thus recounted to have said, "It was a command of testing (*ebtelāʾ*), not of willing; otherwise I would never have disobeyed," (Maybodī, I, p. 161), attempting thereby both to resolve the contradiction between will and command and to exculpate himself. In the view of ʿAlaʾ-al-Dawla Semnānī, God willed two things by His command, that the angels should obey it and that Eblīs should disobey it, so that will has a priority over command which does away with all contradiction between the two (*Moṣannafāt*, p. 197).

A more significant consequence of God having willed the rebellion of Eblīs is that his malevolent activity must be seen as having a divinely mandated purpose and cannot, therefore, be integrally evil. Eblīs is, for example, the polar opposite of Adam: whereas Adam sought forgiveness for his act of primordial disobedience and accepted responsibility for it (Koran, 7:23), Eblīs complained at having been led astray (Koran, 15:39); Adam is thus the manifestation of neediness before God (*efteqār*) and Eblīs of obstinate pride (*eftek̲ār*) (Monawwar, I, p. 303). Moreover, if Adam sinned primordially it was out of passionate desire (*šahwat*), and Eblīs was inspired by arrogance, a more serious vice in that encroaches on God's majesty (Maybodī, p. 145); and Adam is characterized by love (*ʿešq*), and Eblīs by mere mental dexterity (*zīrakī*) (Rūmī, *Maṯnawī*, bk. IV, line 1402). But insofar as Eblīs is the antipole of Adam, he is also his complement, derived from the same substance and fulfilling ultimately the same purpose. The matter is expressed metaphorically by Maybodī when he compares Adam to the sugar-coated almonds that are scattered at a wedding, and Eblīs to the blackened almonds that are strewn over a corpse before burial; the gardener who planted the almond tree from which both were plucked is one and the same (I, p. 160). The polarity of Adam and Eblīs sets, moreover, a pattern that is necessarily repeated throughout sacred history, in the oppositions of Moses and the Pharoah (who through his own assertion of ego in Koran, 79:24, hears a special affinity to Eblīs), Abraham and Nimrod, and the Prophet Moḥammad and Abū Jahl (Bahāʾ-al-Dīn Walad, *Maʿāref*, p. 376; Rūmī, *Fīhe ma fih*, p. 80).

With considerable boldness, Ḥallāj proposed a more positive pairing of Eblīs, with none other than the Prophet Moḥammad himself, by asserting that "the claims of none were justified except those of Eblīs and Aḥmad (=the Prophet)," in that Eblīs rejected the command to prostrate himself before Adam, and the Prophet, in the course of his ascension, resisted the temptation to gaze around him ("his gaze swerved not nor wandered," Koran, 53:17); common to both was an orientation to God that excluded awareness of His creation (*Ketāb al-ṭawāsīn*, p. 41; Fr. tr. in Massignon, III, p. 326; Turkish tr. in Öztürk, p. 109). The difference between them was, however, that Eblīs fell from favor (*saqaṭa ʿan al-ʿayn*), whereas "the essence of the essence was revealed to Aḥmad (*košefa lahū ʿan ʿayn al-ʿayn*) (Öztürk's understanding of these phrases is to be preferred to that of Massignon, who seems to have missed the polyvalence of *ʿayn*). Even after his fall, Eblīs persisted in justifying his refusal: "My denial is an assertion of Your sanctity, and my mind is distraught before You" (*Ketāb al-ṭawāsīn*, p. 43; *Dīvān al-Ḥallāj*, p. 48), and he willingly accepted the attribute of "disgraced" (*mahīn*) because such is the state of the lover (ibid., p. 52). Even the name ʿAzāzīl, in which so many other Sufis saw a hint of Eblīs' ultimate fate, was interpreted positively by Ḥallāj, each of its letters being the initial of a virtuous quality (ibid.). As for the attribution to Eblīs of spiritual chivalry (*fotowwat*), this stems, in the view of Massignon (III, p. 374), from an interpolation in the text of the *Ṭawāsīn*.

Post-Hallajian Sufi tradition retained, from this depiction of Eblīs, principally the themes of Eblīs as the monotheist despite God and as the lover of God who remained patient in the face of eternal rejection. Thus Aḥmad Ḡazālī is said to have proclaimed, "Whoever does not learn monotheism from Eblīs is a heretic" (*zendīq*; cited in Awn, p. 132), and he ascribed to him the sublime degree of love that recognizes only an unattainable beloved to be worthy of devotion (*Savāneḥ*, p. 49), as well as delight in the curse that had befallen him, because it came from God and was exclusively his (cited in Massignon, II, p. 174). The correlation between true love and the acceptance of separation from the beloved as inevitable caused Aḥmad Ḡazālī's master, Abu'l-Qāsem Gorgānī, to award Eblīs the title of "the supreme one among the abandoned" (*sarvar-e mahjūrān*; Jāmī, p. 420).

The positive re-evaluation of Eblīs reaches its apotheosis with ʿAyn-al-Qożāt Hamadānī. He propounded a thoroughgoing complementarity between Eblīs and the Prophet: while it is the function of the Prophet to call men to God, it is that of Eblīs to guard His threshold by denying access to the unworthy (*Tamhīdāt*, pp. 74-75, 228-29). Just as the Prophet is a manifestation of the divine names Compassionate (*raḥmān*) and Merciful (*raḥīm*), Eblīs manifests the names Coercer (*jabbār*) and Wrathful (*qahhār*), and insofar as the divine attributes are knowable in terms of their opposites, the existence of Eblīs is as necessary as that of the Prophet (ibid., p. 227). Eblīs and the Prophet also have in common the fact that their powers respectively to mislead and guide are not grounded in their own beings but derive from appointment by God (ibid., p. 186). It thus becomes permissible to say that, if the Prophet is the luminous cheek of the divine beloved, Eblīs is His black tress (ibid., p. 178). Eblīs has, indeed, his own luminosity, a black light that is the shadow of the Prophet's pure and colorless light (ibid., p. 248). ʿAyn-al-Qożāt illustrates this theme by citing a cryptic quatrain by Abu'l-Ḥasan Bostī: "We saw the world's origin and its inner aspect, and passed with ease beyond all sickness and disgrace./Know that black light to be higher than the dotless letters (the *lā* of *lā elāha ella' llāh*); beyond that too we passed, neither this nor that remained" (Pūrjawādī, p. 55). ʿAyn-al-Qożāt's understanding of this quatrain (shared by Aḥmad Ḡazālī, who cites it in *Savāneḥ*, p. 20) is that the black light of Eblīs lies beyond the final negation of all other than God, so that to transcend it is to cross the last barrier to the divine presence.

Since the role delineated for Eblīs by Ḥallāj, Aḥmad Ḡazālī, and ʿAyn-al-Qożāt requires precisely that he remain eternally damned, they hold out no more hope for his ultimate redemption than do Sufis with less nuanced views of the evil one. However, ʿAṭṭār suggests that he may ultimately be rehabilitated (*Moṣībat-nāma*, p. 244), and Nasafī forecasts that he will at least be reconciled with Adam (*Ketāb al-ensān al-kāmel*, p. 178). It is Jīlī alone who asserts with full confidence that Eblīs will be fully redeemed and forgiven, after Hellfire itself has passed away (*al-Ensān al-kāmel*, p. 40). Insofar as the Yazīdī sect may have originated as a form of Sufism, it is also relevant to note that for the Yazīdīs Eblīs has already been forgiven and restored to his archangelic glory, so that those who recognize him may hope for his special protection (Guest, p. 29).

It remains only to remark that Eblīs makes a last appearance in the role of devout rebel in the *Jāvīd-nāma* of the Indo-Persian poet Moḥammad Eqbāl (*Kollīyāt-e ašʿār-e fārsī*, pp. 344-47).

Bibliography: (For cited works not given in detail, see "Short References.") K̲ᵛāja ʿAbd-Allāh Anṣārī, *Rasāʾel*, ed. M. Sarvar Mawlāʾī, 2 vols., Tehran, 1372 Š./1993. ʿAṭṭār, Farīd-al-Dīn, *Asrār-nāma*, ed. Ṣ. Gawharīn, 2nd ed., Tehran, 1361 Š./ 1982. Idem, *Manṭeq al-ṭayr*, ed. Ṣ. Gawharīn, 4th ed., Tehran, 1365 Š./1986. Idem, *Moṣībat-nāma*, ed. Nūrānī Weṣāl, Tehran, 1338 Š./1950. Idem, *Taḏkerat al-awlīāʾ*, ed. M. Esteʿlāmī, 3rd ed., Tehran, 1360 Š./1981. P. Awn, *Satan's Tragedy and Redemption. Iblis in Sufi Psychology*, Leiden, 1983. Rūzbehān Baqlī, *Mašrab al–arwāḥ*, ed. Nazif Hoca, Istanbul, 1973. Idem, *Šarḥ-e šaṭḥīyāt*, ed. H. Corbin, repr. Tehran, 1360 Š./1981. ʿAbd-Allāh b. ʿOmar Bayżāwī, *Anwār al–tanzīl*, 2 vols., Cairo, 1344/1925. Bok̲ārī, *Ṣaḥīḥ al-Bok̲ārī*, 9 vols., Cairo, n.d. W. C. Chittick, *The Sufi Path of Knowledge*, Albany (N.Y.), 1989, pp. 24, 194, 197, 277, 330. Idem, *The Vision of Islam*, New York, 1994, pp. 145-47. H. Corbin, *Cyclical Time and Ismaili Gnosis*, London, 1983. Najm-al-Dīn Dāya, *Merṣād al-ʿebād*, ed. M.-A. Rīāḥī, 2nd ed., Tehran, 1365 Š./1984. Ebn ʿArabī, *Tafsīr al-Qorʾān al-Karīm*, 2 vols., Beirut, 1387/1968. Idem, *Hekāyat Eblīs be mā ak̲bara behe al–nabī al–moʿaẓẓam*, pr. on pp. 27-32 of *Šajarat al-kawn*, Cairo, n.d. C. W. Ernst, *Words of Ecstasy in Sufism*, Albany (N.Y.), 1985, pp. 74-80. Abū Ḥāmed Ḡazālī, *Eḥyāʾ ʿolūm al–dīn*, 5 vols., Beirut, n.d. Idem, *Kīmīā-ye saʿādat*, ed. Ḥ. K̲adīv-Jam, 2 vols., Tehran, 1361 Š./1982. Aḥmad Ḡazālī, *Savāneḥ*, ed. N. Pūrjawādī, Tehran, 1359 Š./1980. J. S. Guest, *The Yezidis*, London, 1987. Manṣūr Ḥallāj, *Dīwān al–Ḥallāj*, ed. M. Kāmel Šībī, 2nd ed., Baghdad, 1404/1984. Idem, *Ketāb al-tawāsīn*, ed. L. Massignon, Paris, 1913. ʿAyn-al-Qożāt Hamadānī, *Tamhīdāt*, ed. ʿA. ʿOsayrān, Tehran, 1341 Š./1962. Hojvīrī, *Kašf al-maḥjūb*, ed. V. Zhukovskii, repr., Tehran, 1358 Š./1979. M. Eqbāl, *Kollīyāt-e ašʿār-e fārsī*, ed. A. Sorūš, Tehran, 1343 Š./1964. ʿAbd-al-Raḥmān Jāmī, *Nafaḥāt al-ons*, ed. M. ʿĀbedī, Tehran, 1370 Š./1991. ʿAbd-al-Karīm Jīlī, *al-Ensān al-kāmel*, Cairo, 1304/1886. Najm-al-Dīn Kobrā, *Fawāʾeḥ al-jamāl wa fawāteḥ al-jalāl*, ed. Fritz Meier, Wiesbaden, 1957. Abū Ṭāleb Makkī, *ʿElm al-qolūb*, Cairo, 1384. Idem, *Qūt al-qolūb*, 2 vols., Cairo, 1381/1961. Al-Kalābāḏī, *Ketāb al–taʿarrof li maḏhab ahl al–taṣawwof*, eds. ʿAbd-al-Bāqī Sorūr and ʿAbd-al-Ḥalīm Maḥmūd, Cairo, 1380/1960. L. Massignon, *La passion de Hallaj*, new ed., 4 vols., Paris, 1975. Rašīd-al-Dīn Maybodī, *Kašf al–Asrār wa 'Oddat al–abrār*, ed. ʿA.- A. Ḥekmat, 10 vols., 4th ed., 1361 Š./1982. F. Mojtabāʾī, "Eblīs: 4, dar adab-e fārsī wa ʿerfān," *DMBE* V, pp. 597-605. Moḥammad b. Abī Monawwar, *Asrār al-tawḥīd*, ed. M. R. Šafīʿī-Kadkanī, 2 vols., Tehran, 1366 Š./1987. Muslim, *Ṣaḥīḥ Muslim*, Eng. tr., A. H. Siddiqi, 4 vols., Karachi, 1975. ʿAzīz-al-Dīn Nasafī, *Ketāb al–ensān al–kāmel*, ed. M. Molé, Tehran and Paris, 1362 Š./1983. Abū Esḥāq Nīsābūrī, *Qeṣaṣ al–anbīyāʾ*, ed. Ḥ. Yagmāʾī, 2nd ed., Tehran, 1359 Š./ 1980. Yasşar Nuri Öztürk, *Hallac-ı Mansur ve Eseri*, Istanbul, 1976. N. Pūrjawādī, *Zendagī wa āṯār-e Abu'l-Ḥasan Bostī*, Tehran, 1362 Š./1983. Abu'l-Qāsem Qošayrī, *al-Resālat al-Qošayrīya*, eds., ʿA.-Ḥ. Maḥmūd and M. b. al-Šarīf, 2 vols., Cairo, 1385/1966. Jalāl-al-Dīn Rūmī, *Fīhe mā fīh*, ed. B.-Z. Forūzānfar, 5th ed., Tehran, 1362 Š./ 1983. Idem, *Maṯnawī*, ed. Nicholson. Sanāʾī, *Dīvān*, ed. Modarres Rażawī, Tehran, 1341 Š./1962. Abū Naṣr Sarrāj, *Ketāb al-lomʿa*, ed. R. A. Nicholson, repr. London, 1963. A. Schimmel, *The Triumphant Sun*, London and The Hague, 1978, pp. 141, 254-55, 272. ʿAlāʾ-al-Dawla Semnānī, *Moṣannafāt*, ed. N. Māyel Heravī, Tehran, 1369 Š./1990. S. Tuğ, "Azāzīl," *Türkiye Diyanet Vakfi Islam Ansiklopedisi* IV, pp. 311-12. Ṭabarī, *Tafsīr*, 30 vols., Cairo, 1321/1903. Bahāʾ-al-Dīn Walad, *Maʿāref*, ed. B.-Z. Forūzānfar, Tehran, 1333 Š./1954. A. J. Wensinck and L. Gardet, "Iblīs," *EI²* III, pp. 668-69.

(HAMID ALGAR)

EBN ʿABBĀD. See ṢĀḤEB B. ʿABBĀD.

EBN ABHAR, MOḤAMMAD-TAQĪ (1270-1337/ 1854-1919), Bahai teacher and one of the "hands of the cause" (see AYĀDĪ-E AMR-ALLĀH). He was one of two Bahai sons of Mirza ʿAbd-al-Raḥīm Eṣfahānī (d. 1290/1872), the Shiʿite *mojtahed*, a crypto-Babi and Bahai, and Belqīs K̲ānom. His zealous Bahai teaching in Zanjān, Qazvīn, Tehran, Yazd, Kermān, and elsewhere led to his frequent imprisonment, for the first time in 1295/1878. At various times resident or imprisoned in Abhar, between Qazvīn and Zanjān, he was entitled Ebn(-e) Abhar ("son of Abhar") by Bahāʾ-Allāh (q.v.) in about 1300/1883. Around 1305/1887 Bahāʾ-Allāh appointed him one of the "hands of the cause." Ebn(e) Abhar was imprisoned in Tehran in 1308-12/1890-94, and because he was chained with the same heavy chain that Bahāʾ-Allāh had worn in 1268-69/1852, the latter referred to him as his "chainmate" (*ham-zanjīr*). He became a permanent member of the first Central Spiritual Assembly established in Tehran at ʿAbd-al-Bahāʾ's direction in 1314/1897. In 1316/1899, on the advice of ʿAbd-al-Bahāʾ, he married Monīra (d. 1326/1918), a daughter of a "hand of the cause," ʿAlī-Akbar Šahmīrzādī (q.v.). As a Bahai teacher, he visited Turkey and the Caucasus and lived for a while in Ashkhabad. He went to India in 1325/1907 accompanied by Mīrzā Maḥmūd Zarqānī and two American Bahais, Harlan Ober and Hooper Harris. In 1331/1913 he settled in Tehran. He visited Bahāʾ-Allāh or ʿAbd-al-Bahāʾ on more than ten occasions. He and his wife were active supporters of female education and emancipation.

Bibliography: ʿA. ʿA. ʿAlāʾī, ed., *Moʾassasa-ye Ayādī-e Amr-Allāh,* Tehran, 130 B.E./1973, pp. 402-49. H. Balyuzi, *Eminent Baháʾís in the Time of Baháʾuʾlláh*, Oxford, 1985, p. 268. Ebn-(e) Abhar [as told to his nephew Faḵr-al-Dīn], "The Story of Ebn Abhar," *Star of the West* 13/12, March 1923, pp. 333-39. A. Fāżel Māzandarānī, *Tārīḵ-e ẓohūr al-ḥaqq* VI, Bahá'í World Center MS, fols. 329ff.; VIII/1, Tehran, 131 B.E./1974, pp. 321-27. M.-Ṭ. Mālmīrī, *Tārīḵ-e šohadā-ye Yazd*, Cairo, 1343/1924, p. 80. Idem, *Ḵāṭerāt-e Mālmīrī*, Hofheim-Langenhain, Germany, 149 B.E./1992. K. Samandar, *Tārīḵ-e Samandar o molḥaqāt*, Tehran, 1975 pp. 236-43. A. Taherzadeh, *The Revelation of Baháʾuʾlláh* IV, Oxford, 1987, pp. 304-12.

(STEPHEN LAMBDEN)

EBN ABIʾL ḤADĪD. See ʿABD-AL-ḤAMĪD B. ABUʾL ḤADĪD.

EBN ABĪ JOMHŪR AḤSĀʾĪ, Moḥammad b. Zayn-al-Dīn Abiʾl-Ḥasan ʿAlī b. Ḥosām-al-Dīn Ebrāhīm (b. ca. 837/1433-34; d. after 25 Ḏu ʾl-Qaʿda 904/4 July 1499). Shiʿite thinker. He lived and taught in his home town of Aḥsā in Baḥrayn, Najaf, and Mašhad during the last half of the 15th century. His best known work, the *al-Mojlī*, which is actually his commentary and super-commentary on a *kalām* treatise by himself, is important as an example of the immediate scholastic precursor to the kind of Shiʿite intellectual synthesis which would flower during the Safavid period and come to be called *ḥekmat-e elāhī* and whose most famous exponent was Mollā Ṣadrā (d. 1050/1640). This synthesis relies on the Islamic *kalām* tradition, the Islamic peripatetic tradition most prominently represented in the work of Avicenna (d. 1037; q.v.), the *Ešrāqī* tradition issuing from the work of Sohrawardī (k. 587/1193), and finally the high Sufism of the ontologists who relied on the oeuvre of Ebn al-ʿArabī (d. 638/1240; q.v.). Madelung (p. 150) has called the *Mojlī* "a mirror of the religious ideas and aspirations of the previous three centuries." But it must be remembered that these ideas are presented by Aḥsāʾī in their distinctive (and apparently Twelver) Shiʿite form. Thus he and the more famous Ḥaydar Āmolī (d. after 787/1385-86) and the more obscure Rajab Borsī (d. 714/1411) may be seen as a trio of post-Mongol, near-contemporary Shiʿite authors who were attracted to the world of images (*ʿālam al-meṯāl*) as the most likely place for their utopia to be established. None of them seems to have ever anticipated the kind of worldly theocracy (functioning under the direct supervision of the Hidden Imam) that the Safavids eventually would be able to establish. It remains nonetheless beyond dispute that the success of the project depended heavily on the type of piety found in the *Mojlī*.

An example of this synthesis in his work is the all-important Shiʿite topic of *walāya*. Aḥsāʿī relies heavily upon Ebn al-ʿArabī's formulation: *Walāya* represents a universal and supreme relationship to the divine, according to which every prophet is also a bearer of *walāya* and may therefore be designated, in some sense, as a *walīy* (see AWLĪAʾ). However, not every *walīy* is the bearer of *nobūwa* (prophecy). Thus, while Moḥammad is a prophet (*nabīy*), he is also a *walīy*. It is this fact that renders *walāya* superior to prophecy. Aḥsāʾī sees in such a formulation grounds for the theological elevation of the Imams, preeminently represented by ʿAlī (q.v.; *Mojlī*, p. 488). The metaphysical theory supporting this doctrine is the distinctive emanation scheme called *tajallī* (the self-manifestation of God). Again, Aḥsāʾī appropriates Ebn al-Arabī's vision, which came to be known as *waḥdat al-wojūd* (unity of being), to Shiʿite theology (*Mojlī*, pp. 204-05). Another example is his interpretation of the *basmala*. Ebn Abī Jomhūr takes as his starting point the statement of Ebn al-ʿArabī in the *Fotūḥāt*, that the *bāʾ* should be interpreted according to its three modes: form, sound, and voweling. The form of the *bāʾ* corresponds to the *malakūt*, the pronunciation to the *jabarūt*, and the voweling represents the testimony of *molk*. Ebn Abī Jomhūr adds the characteristically Shiʿite comment that the hidden (*maḥḏūfa*) *alef* (the one that disappears when the Arabic words *be* and *esm* are connected) represents the Hidden Imam, the eventual *Qāʾem* (viz., upright alef; *Mojlī*, p. 5).

Ebn Abī Jomhūr was a prolific writer dealing with the usual range of Islamic learned topics and is dubbed a mystic (*ʿāref)*, a traditionist (*moḥaddeṯ*), and a legist (*faqīh; al-Ḏarīʿa* XX, p. 13). In addition to the very old and rare printed edition of the *Mojlī*, one of his collections of Hadith has been published recently. The most complete list of his works is in Madelung (pp. 151-53). It seems certain that Ebn

Abī Jomhūr's thought had a special influence on the formation of the early 19th century religious movement founded by Shaikh Aḥmad Aḥsāʾī (q.v.), who apparently fell heir to his library; this movement was to issue eventually in the Bābī and Bahāʾī religions (Corbin, IV, p. 222). The most recent discussion of his life and work is given in *DMBE*.

Bibliography: (For cited works not given in detail, see "Short References.") Aḥsāʾī, Ebn Abī Jomhūr Aḥsāʾī, *al-Awālī al-laʾāla al-ʿazīzīya fiʾl-aḥādīṯ al-dīnīya*, 4 vols., Qom, 1403/1983. Idem, *(Ketāb) al-Mojlī (al-Maslak al-afhām waʾl-nūr al-monjī men al-ẓalām)*, ed. Shaikh Aḥmad Šīrāzī, Tehran, 1329/1911. H. Corbin, *En Islam iranien*, 4 vols., Paris, 1971-72. *DMBE* II, pp. 634-37. W. Madelung, "Ibn Abī Ǧumhūr al-Aḥsāʾī's Synthesis of *Kalām*, Philosophy, and Sufism," in *La signifiance du bas moyen âge dans l'histoire et la culture du monde musulman*, Actes du 8° Congrès de l'Union Européenne des Arabisants et Islamisants: Aix-en-Provence, 1978, pp. 147-56. Idem, "Ibn Abī Djomhūr al-Aḥsāʾī," *EI*², suppl., p. 380.

(TODD LAWSON)

EBN ABĪ ṢĀDEQ, ABU'L-QĀSEM ʿABD-al-RAḤMĀN b. ʿAlī b. Aḥmad NAYŠĀBŪRĪ (Nīšāpūr, 5th/11th century), medical author known in the century after his death, at least in Khorasan, as "the second Hippocrates" (Bayhaqī, p. 107), and reportedly a student of Avicenna (q.v.; Ebn Abī Oṣaybeʿa, II, p. 22). His commentaries on Hippocrates' *Aphorisms* (*Foṣūl*) and *Prognostics* (*Taqdemat al-maʿrefa*) Galen's *De usu partium* (*Manāfeʿ al aʿżāʾ*) *Masāʾel fiʾl-ṭebb* of Ḥonayn b. Esḥāq (d. 264/877)—completed in 460/1068 (Ebn Abī Oṣaybeʿa, II, p. 22)—and the *Šokūk ʿalā Jālīnūs* of Rāzī (d. 313/925) approximate a core course in medicine. The dates of his commentary on *Prognostics* and his rebuttal of Rāzī's reservations about Galen, both lost, are unknown.

His reputation rests chiefly on quotations by Esmāʿīl Jorjānī (d. 531/1136; Richter-Bernburg, *Persian Medical Manuscripts*, index), on the gnomological literature (see references below), and on Ebn Abī Oṣaybeʿa. Although known in Khorasan in his lifetime, Ebn Abī Oṣaybeʿa reports that it took nearly two centuries for his work to reach Damascus. A manuscript of Ebn Abī Ṣādeq's works copied directly from the author's autograph was acquired by Ebn Abī Oṣaybeʿa's father (Ebn Abī Oṣaybeʿa, II, pp. 22, 266) and may be the source of the Syrian tradition of his work preserved, for example, in two Cairene codices (cf. Ebrāhīm Šabbūḥ, *Fehrest al makṭūṭ al-moṣawwara* (Maʿhad al-makṭūṭ al-ʿarabīya), qesm III, jozʿ 2, Cairo, 1959, pp. 116f., nos. 148, 149).

Bibliography: (For cited works not given in detail, see "Short References.") **A**) Gnomological and biographical sources: ʿAlī b. Zayd "Ebn Fondoq" Bayhaqī, *Tatemmat Ṣewān al-ḥekma*, ed. M. Šafīʿ, Lahore, 1351/1932, pp. 107-09, no. 63. Šams-al-Dīn Moḥammad b. Maḥmūd Šahrazūrī, *Rawżat al-afrāḥ wa nozhat al-arwāḥ*, ed. Khurshid Ahmad, Hayderabad, 1398/1979. Ebn Abī-Oṣaybeʿa, *ʿOyūn al-anbāʾ fī ṭabaqāt al-aṭebbāʾ*, ed. Emraʾ al-Qays b. Ṭaḥḥān [i.e., August Müller], Cairc, 1299/1882 and Königsberg, 1884. *Nāma-ye dānešvarān-e nāṣerī* I, Tehran, 1296/1878, p. 297. **B**) Modern studies, including lists of mss: *GAL* I., pp. 206, 484; S I, pp. 367f.; *GAS* III, pp. 30, 107, 250, 411. A. Dietrich, *Medicinalia Arabica*, Abhandlungen der Akademie der Wissenschaften in Göttingen, Philos.-histor. Klass, Dritte Folge, no. XXX, pp. 20f., 43f., nos. 3, 15. L. Richter-Bernburg, *Persian Medical Manuscripts at the University of California, Los Angeles. A Descriptive Catalogue*, Malibu (Calif.), 1978. M. Ullmann, *Die Medizin im Islam*, Leiden and Cologne, 1970, pp. 68f., 160.

(LUTZ RICHTER-BERNBURG)

EBN ABĪ ṬĀHER ṬAYFŪR, ABU'L-FAŻL AḤMAD (204-80/819-93), littérateur (*adīb*) and historian of Baghdad, of a Khorasani family. His extensive *adab* (q.v.) works include treatises on poets and singing, praised by Abu'l-Faraj Eṣfahānī in his *Ketāb al-aḡānī*, and the partially extant literary anthology *Ketāb al-manṯūr wa'l-manẓūm* (Cairo, 1326/1908), used by, among others, Abū Ḥayyān Tawḥīdī (q.v.) in his *al-Baṣāʾer wa'l-ḏaḵāʾer* (see the list of Ebn Abī Ṭāher's works in Ebn al-Nadīm, ed. Tajaddod, pp. 163-64; tr. Dodge, I, pp. 320-22).

His *Ketāb Baḡdād* treated the history of the city up to the caliphate of al-Mohtadī (255-56/869-70), but only the greater part of volume 6 is extant, that dealing with al-Maʾmūn's caliphate. Ṭabarī used this volume almost verbatim (though he mentioned Ebn Abī Ṭāher only once, III, p. 1516) for some three-fifths of the account of al-Maʾmūn's reign in his own *History*. Ebn Abī Ṭāher was a lively writer of history, careful to cite documents and contemporary sources, and with a special interest in cultural history and anecdote. His book is thus a pioneer work of local and urban history. On Persian history it gives information about the appointments of Ṭāher Ḏu'l-Yamīnayn and his son Ṭalḥa to the governorship of the East, military operations in Azerbaijan against the Ḵorramī rebel Bābak (q.v.), and various local revolts in Khorasan and at Qom during al-Maʾmūn's caliphate. Ebn Abī Ṭāher's son Abu'l-Ḥosayn ʿObayd-Allāh (d. 313/925-26), also a well-respected *adīb*, continued his father's history up to al-Moqtader's reign (Ebn al-Nadīm, p. 164; tr. Dodge, I, p. 322).

Bibliography: (For cited works not given in deteail, see "Short References.") C. E. Bosworth, in Ṭabarī, tr., XXXII, pp. 3, 7. F. Rosenthal, *A*

*History of Muslim Historiography*², Leiden, 1968, pp. 152-3 and index. Idem, s.v. "Ibn Abī Ṭāhir," *EI*². Sezgin, *GAS* I, pp. 348-49. *Sechster Band des Kitāb Bagdād*, ed. and German tr. H. Keller, Leipzig, 1908 (with intro.), ed. Moḥammad Zāhed Kawṯar, Cairo, 1949. See also *DMBE* II, pp. 672-76.

(C. EDMUND BOSWORTH)

EBN AMĀJŪR. See BANŪ AMĀJŪR.

EBN ʿĀMER. See ʿABD-ALLĀH B. ʿĀMER.

EBN AL-ʿAMĪD, cognomen of two famous viziers of the 4th/10th century: Abu'l-Fażl and his son Abu'l-Fatḥ. The father of the first was called Ḥoseyn. Tawḥīdī claims that this Ḥoseyn was of humble origin, a *naḵḵāl* (wheat-sifter) in the grain market of Qom (*Aḵlāq al-wazīrayn*, p. 82). This, however, is probably not true. After occupying major administrative posts, Ḥosayn was appointed chief of the chancery (*dīwān al-rasāʾel*) at the court of the Sāmānid amir Nūḥ b. Naṣr in Khorasan and was given two honorific titles: "ʿAmīd" (chief; doyen) and "Shaikh."

Not much is known about Ḥosayn's son, Abu'l-Fażl before he became the vizier of Rokn-al-Dawla, the Buyid sultan who ruled a district which included Ray, Hamadān, and Isfahan; but the fact that he occupied such a post indicates that he took the same line as his father. His early education combined Arabic poetry and Greek sciences and philosophy. His fame as a vizier spread far and wide, and many poets and men of letters were attracted to his court. The poet Motanabbī in one of his panegyrics speaks of him as one who had met Aristotle, Alexander, and Ptolemy. Meskawayh and Tawḥīdī both confirm his interest in philosophy, but the latter adds that Abu'l-Fażl did not hesitate to kill his adversaries—a trait not quite befitting a philosopher. During his vizirate, Abu'l-Fażl won several honorific titles: "Raʾīs," "Ostād," "the second Jāḥeẓ," etc.

Apart from a collection of epistles and some poetry, Abu'l-Fażl left no books. Tawḥīdī copied some wise sayings and proverbs from a book by him entitled *al-Ḵalq wa' l-ḵolq*, but this book remained in draft form (*Aḵlāq al-wazīrayn*, p. 328; *al-Baṣāʾer* VI, p. 165). In his style, he was not as fond of *sajʿ* (rhymed prose) as his contemporary Ṣāḥeb b. ʿAbbād was. He admired Jāḥeẓ's style a great deal, but could not emulate it well. This was due, according to Tawḥīdī, to the fact that Abu'l-Fażl lacked several of the natural and circumstantial qualities which Jāḥeẓ possessed (*Emtāʿ*, I, p. 66).

When Abu'l-Fażl died in 360/971, he was succeeded in the vizirate by his son of twenty-two years, Abu'l-Fatḥ, who served two Buyid sultans: Rokn-al-Dawla and his son Moʾayyad-al-Dawla. Abu'l-Fatḥ was a good prose writer, in the manner of the secretaries of the *dīvān* (q.v.), and was highly respected by the military. For this reason, he was given the title "Ḏu'l-kefāyatayn," that is, master of both the pen and the sword. Six years into his vizirate, in 366/977, he was killed after having fallen out of favor with the powerful Buyid sultan ʿAżod-al-Dawla; he had also indulged excessively in pleasures, to the point of being oblivious to the intrigues being concocted around him. According to Ṣābī, however, his violent end was due to two factors: a) Rokn-al-Dawla's lenient treatment of him, and b) the fact that he had inherited rather than earned the vizirate (Ṯaʿālebī, *Yatīma* II, p. 217).

Bibliography: (For cited works not given in detail, see "Short References.") Abū Hayyān Tawḥīdī, *Aḵlāq al-wazīrayn*, ed. M. b. Tāwīt al-Ṭanjī, Damascus, 1965. Idem, *al-Emtāʾ wa'l-moʾānasa*, 3 vols., ed. A. Amīn and A. Zayn, Cairo, 1939-44. Idem, *al-Baṣāʾer wa'l-ḏaḵāʾer* 10 vols., ed. W. Qāḍī, Beirut, 1988. Meskawayh, *Tajāreb al-omam*, 3 vols., Cairo, 1914. Ṯaʿālebī, *Yātima*, 4 vols., ed. M. M. ʿAbd al-Ḥamīd. Ebn Ḵallekān, *Wafayāt al-aʿyān*, 8 vols., ed. E. ʿAbbās, Beirut, 1968-72. Yāqūt-al-Ḥamawī, *Moʿjam al-odabāʾ*, 7 vols., ed. E. ʿAbbās, Beirut, 1993.

(IHSAN ABBAS)

EBN AL-ʿARABĪ, MOḤYĪ-al-DĪN Abū ʿAbd-Allāh Moḥammad Ṭāʾī Ḥātemī (b. 17 Ramażān 560/28 July 1165; d. 22 Rabīʿ II 638/10 November 1240), the most influential Sufi author of later Islamic history, known to his supporters as *al-Šayḵ al-akbar*, "the Greatest Master." Although the form "Ebn al-ʿArabī," with the definite article, is found in his autographs and in the writings of his immediate followers, many later authors referred to him as 'Ebn ʿArabī', without the article, to differentiate him from Qāżī Abū Bakr Ebn al-ʿArabī (d. 543/1148).

Life, views, terminology.

He was born in Murcia in Spain, and his family moved to Seville when he was eight. He experienced an extraordinary mystical "unveiling" (*kašf*) or "opening" (*fotūḥ*) at about the age of fifteen; this is mentioned in his famous account of his meeting with Averroes (Addas, pp. 53-58; Chittick, 1989, pp. xiii-xiv). Only after this original divine "attraction" (*jaḏba*) did he begin disciplined Sufi practice (*solūk*), perhaps at the age of twenty (Addas, p. 53; Chittick, 1989, pp. 383-84). He studied the traditional sciences, Hadith in particular, with many masters; he mentions about ninety of these in an autobiographical note (Badawi). In 597/1200 he left Spain for good, with the intention of making the *ḥajj*. The following year in Mecca he began writing his monumental *al-Fotūḥāt al-makkīya*; the title, "The Meccan Openings," alludes to the inspired nature of the book. In 601/1204 he set off from Mecca on his way to Anatolia with Majd-al-Dīn Esḥāq, whose son Ṣadr-al-Dīn Qūnawī (606-73/ 1210-74) would be his most influential disciple. After moving about for several years in the central Islamic lands, never going as far as Persia, he settled in Damascus in 620/1223. There he taught and wrote until his death.

Ebn al-ʿArabī was an extraordinarily prolific author. Osman Yahia counts 850 works attributed to him, of which 700 are extant and over 450 probably genuine. The second edition of the *Fotūḥāt* (Cairo, 1329/1911) covers 2,580 pages, while Yahia's new critical edition is projected to include thirty-seven volumes of about five hundred pages each (vol. 14, Cairo, 1992). By comparison, his most famous work, *Foṣūṣ al-ḥekam* (Bezels of widsom), is less than 180 pages long. Scores of his books and treatises have been published, mostly in uncritical editions; several have been translated into European languages.

Although Ebn al-ʿArabī claims that the *Fotūḥāt* is derived from divine "openings"—mystical unveilings—and that the *Foṣūṣ* was handed to him in a vision by the Prophet, he would certainly admit that he expressed his visions in the language of his intellectual milieu. He cites the Koran and Hadith constantly; it would be no exaggeration to say that most of his works are commentaries on these two sources of the tradition. He sometimes quotes aphorisms from earlier Sufis, but never long passages. There is no evidence that he quotes without ascription, in the accepted style, from other authors. He was thoroughly familiar with the Islamic sciences, especially *tafsīr*, *feqh*, and *kalām*. He does not seem to have studied the works of the philosophers, though many of his ideas are prefigured in the works of such authors as the Ekwān-al-Ṣafāʾ (q.v.; Rosenthal; Takeshita). He mentions on several occasions having read the *Eḥyāʾ* of Ḡazālī, and he sometimes refers to such well known Sufi authors as Qošayrī.

In short, Ebn al-ʿArabī was firmly grounded in the mainstream of the Islamic tradition; the starting points of his discussions would have been familiar to the *ʿolamāʾ* in his environment. At the same time he was enormously original, and he was fully aware of the newness of what he was doing. Most earlier Sufis had spoken about theoretical issues (as opposed to practical teachings) in a brief or allusive fashion. Ebn al-ʿArabī breaks the dam with a torrent of exposition on every sort of theoretical issue related to the "divine things" (*elāhīyāt*). He maintains a uniformly high level of discourse and, in spite of going over the same basic themes constantly, he offers a different perspective in each fresh look at a question. For example, in the *Foṣūṣ al-ḥekam*, each of twenty-seven chapters deals with the divine wisdom revealed to a specific divine word—a particular prophet. In each case, the wisdom is associated with a different divine attribute. Hence, each prophet represents a different mode of knowing and experiencing the reality of God. Most of the 560 chapters of the *Fotūḥāt* are rooted in similar principles. Each chapter represents a "standpoint" or "station" (*maqām*) from which reality, or a specific dimension of reality, can be surveyed and brought into the overarching perspective of the "oneness of all things" (*tawḥīd*).

Ebn al-ʿArabī assumed and then verified through his own personal experience the validity of the revelation that was given primarily in the Koran and secondarily in the Hadith. He objected to the limiting approaches of *kalām* and philosophy, which tied all understanding to reason (*ʿaql*), as well as to the approach of those Sufis who appealed only to unveiling (*kašf*). It may be fair to say that his major methodological contribution was to reject the stance of the *kalām* authorities, for whom *tašbīh* (declaring God similar to creation) was a heresy, and to make *tašbīh* the necessary complement of *tanzīh* (declaring God incomparable with creation). This perspective leads to an epistemology that harmonizes reason and unveiling.

For Ebn al-ʿArabī, reason functions through differentiation and discernment; it knows innately that God is absent from all things—*tanzīh*. In contrast, unveiling functions through imagination, which perceives identity and sameness rather than difference; hence unveiling sees God's presence rather than his absence—*tašbīh*. To maintain that God is either absent or present is, in his terms, to see with only one eye. Perfect knowledge of God involves seeing with both eyes, the eye of reason and the eye of unveiling (or imagination). This is the wisdom of the prophets; it is falsified by those theologians, philosophers, and Sufis who stress either *tanzīh* or *tašbīh* at the expense of the other.

If Ebn al-ʿArabī's methodology focuses on harmonizing two modes of knowing, his actual teachings focus more on bringing out the nature of human perfection and the means to achieve it. Although the term *al-ensān al-kāmel* "the perfect human being" can be found in earlier authors, it is Ebn al-ʿArabī who makes it a central theme of Sufism. Briefly, perfect human beings are those who live up to the potential that was placed in Adam when God "taught him all the names" (Koran 2:30). These names designate every perfection found in God and the cosmos (*al-ʿālam*, defined as "everything other than God"). Ultimately, the names taught to Adam are identical with the divine attributes, such as life, awareness, desire, power, speech, generosity, and justice. By actualizing the names within themselves, human beings become perfect images of God and achieve God's purpose in creating the universe (Chittick, 1989, especially chap. 20).

Even though all perfect human beings—i.e., the prophets and the "friends" (*awlīāʾ*) of God—are identical in one respect, each of them manifests God's uniqueness in another respect. In effect, each is dominated by one specific divine attribute—this is the theme of the *Foṣūṣ*. Moreover, the path to human fulfillment is a never-ending progression whereby people come to embody God's infinite attributes successively and with ever-increasing intensity. Most of Ebn al-ʿArabī's writings are devoted to explaining the nature of the knowledge that is unveiled to those who travel through the ascending stations or standpoints of human perfection. God's friends are those who inherit their knowledge, stations, and states from the prophets, the last of whom was Moḥammad. When Ebn al-ʿArabī claimed to be the "seal of the Moḥammadan friends" (*ḵātam al-awlīāʾ al-moḥammadīya*), he was saying that no one after him would inherit fully from the prophet Moḥammad. Muslim friends of God would continue to exist until the end of time, but now they would inherit from other prophets inasmuch as those prophets represent certain aspects of Moḥammad's all-embracing message (Chodkiewicz, 1986).

The most famous idea attributed to Ebn al-ʿArabī is *waḥdat al-wojūd* "the oneness of being." Although he never employs the term, the idea is implicit throughout his writings. In the manner of both theologians and philosophers, Ebn al-ʿArabī employs the term *wojūd* to refer to God as the Necessary Being. Like them, he also attributes the term to everything other than God, but he insists that *wojūd* does not belong to the things found in the cosmos in any real sense. Rather, the things borrow *wojūd* from God, much as the earth borrows light from the sun. The issue is how *wojūd* can rightfully be attributed to the things, also called "entities" (*aʿyān*). From the perspective of *tanzīh*, Ebn al-ʿArabī declares that *wojūd* belongs to God alone, and, in his famous phrase, the things "have never smelt a whiff of *wojūd*." From the point of view of *tašbīh*, he affirms that all things are *wojūd*'s self-disclosure (*tajallī*) or self-manifestation (*ẓohūr*). In sum, all things are "He/not He" (*howa lā howa*), which is to say that they are both God and other than God, both *wojūd* and other than *wojūd*.

The intermediateness of everything that can be perceived by the senses or the mind brings us back to imagination, a term that Ebn al-ʿArabī applies not only to a mode of understanding that grasps identity rather than difference, but also to the World of Imagination, which is situated between the two fundamental worlds that make up the cosmos—the world of spirits and the world of bodies—and which brings together the qualities of the two sides. In addition, Ebn al-ʿArabī refers to the whole cosmos as imagination, because it combines the attributes of *wojūd* and utter nonexistence (Chittick, 1989).

Influence on Persian Sufis and Philosophers.

Tracing Ebn al-ʿArabī's influence in any detail must await an enormous amount of research into both his own writings and the works of later authors. Most modern scholars agree that his influence is obvious in much of the theoretical writing of later Sufism and discernible in works by theologians and philosophers.

Waḥdat al-wojūd, invariably associated with Ebn al-ʿArabī's name, is the most famous single theoretical issue in Sufi works of the later period, especially in the area under Persian cultural influence. Not everyone thought it was an appropriate concept, and scholars such as Ebn Taymīya (d. 728/1328) attacked it vehemently. In fact, Ebn Taymīya deserves much of the credit for associating this idea with Ebn al-ʿArabī's name and for making it the criterion, as it were, of judging whether an author was for or against Ebn al-ʿArabī (on this complex issue, see Chittick, forthcoming).

Although Ebn al-ʿArabī's name is typically associated with theoretical issues, this should not suggest that his influence reached only learned Sufis. He was the author of many practical works on Sufism, including collections of prayers, and he transmitted a *ḵerqa* that was worn by a number of later shaikhs of various orders. As M. Chodkiewicz (1991) has illustrated, his radiance permeated all levels of Sufi life and practice, from the most elite to the most popular, and this has continued down to modern times. Today, indeed, his influence seems to be on the increase, both in the Islamic world and in the West. The Muhyiddin Ibn ʿArabi Society, which publishes a journal in Oxford, is only one of many signs of a renewed attention to his teachings.

Ebn al-ʿArabī's first important contact with Persian Islam may have come through one of his teachers, Makīn-al-Dīn Abū Šojāʿ Zāher b. Rostam Eṣfahānī, whom he met in Mecca in 598/1202 and with whom he studied the *Ṣaḥīḥ* of Termeḏī. He speaks especially highly of Makīn-al-Dīn's elderly sister, whom he calls Šayḵat-al-Ḥejāz ("Mistress of Ḥejāz"), Faḵr-al-Nesāʾ ("Pride of womankind") bent Rostam, adding that she was also Faḵr-al-Rejāl ("Pride of men") and that he had studied Hadith with her. It was Makīn-al-Dīn's daughter, Neẓām, who inspired Ebn al-ʿArabī to write his famous collection of poetry, *Tarjomān al-ašwāq* (Nicholson, pp. 3-4; Jahāngīrī, pp. 59-62).

In 602/1205 Ebn al-ʿArabī met the well-known Sufi Awḥad-al-Dīn Kermānī (d. 635/1238) in Konya and became his close friend; he mentions him on a number of occasions in the *Fotūḥāt* (Chodkiewicz et al., pp. 288, 563; Addas, pp. 269-73). Awḥad-al-Dīn's biographer tells us that Ebn al-ʿArabī entrusted his stepson Qūnawī to Awḥad-al-Dīn for training (Forūzānfar, pp. 86-87), and Qūnawī confirms in a letter that he was Kermānī's companion for two years, traveling with him as far as Shiraz (Chittick, 1992b, p. 261).

Qūnawī is the most important intermediary through which Ebn al-ʿArabī's teachings passed into the Persian-speaking world. He taught Hadith for many years in Konya and was on good terms with Jalāl-al-Dīn Rūmī, but there is no evidence in Rūmī's works to support the oft-repeated assertion that he was influenced by the ideas of Ebn al-ʿArabī or Qūnawī (Chittick, forthcoming). Nevertheless, Rūmī's commentators typically interpreted him in terms of Ebn al-ʿArabī's teachings, which had come to define the Sufi intellectual universe.

Qūnawī is the author of about fifteen Arabic works,

including seven books and a number of relatively short treatises. These works are much more systematic and structured than those of his master. His focus on certain specific issues in Ebn al-ʿArabī's writings, such as *wojūd* and the perfect human being (*al-ensān al-kāmel*), helped ensure that these would remain the central concern of the school. Certain terms typically ascribed to Ebn al-ʿArabī, such as *al-ḥażarāt al-elāhīya al-ḵams*, "the five divine presences," seem to be Qūnawī's coinages. In *al-Fokūk* (ed. M. Ḵᵛājavī, Tehran, 1371Š./1992), Qūnawī explains the significance of the chapter headings of the *Foṣūṣ*; this work was used directly or indirectly by practically all the *Foṣūṣ* commentators (Chittick, 1984).

Qūnawī wrote a few minor Persian works, but probably not *Tabṣerat al-mobtadī* or *Maṭāleʿ-e īmān*, both of which have been printed in his name (Chittick, 1992b, pp. 255-59). However, from at least 643/1245 he taught the *Tāʾīya* of Ebn al-Fāreż in Persian, and his lectures were put together as a systematic commentary on the poem by his student Saʿīd-al-Dīn Farḡānī (d. 695/1296) as *Mašāreq al-darārī* (ed. S. J. Āštīānī, Mašhad, 1398/1978). This work was extremely popular, but even more so was his much expanded Arabic version of the same work, *Montaha'l-madārek* (Cairo, 1293/1876).

The most widely read Persian work by Qūnawī's students was no doubt the *Lamaʿāt* of Faḵr-al-Dīn ʿErāqī (d. 688/1289), which is based on Qūnawī's lectures on Ebn al-ʿArabī's *Foṣūṣ* (Chittick and Wilson). Moʾayyed-al-Dīn Jandī (d. ca. 700/1300), who was initiated into Sufism by Qūnawī, wrote in Arabic the first detailed commentary on the *Foṣūṣ* (ed. Āštīānī, Mašhad, 1361 Š./1982) as well as a number of Persian works, including *Nafḥat al-rūḥ* (ed. N. Māyel Heravī, Tehran, 1362 Š./1983; despite the editor's claim of a unique Tehran manuscript, there are at least two other copies in Istanbul [Şehit Ali Paşa 1439, Haci Mahmud Efendi 2447], the first an expanded version).

Jandī taught the *Foṣūṣ* to ʿAbd-al-Razzāq Kāšānī (d. 730/1330), who wrote one of the most widely disseminated commentaries (Cairo, 1386/1966); it often summarizes or paraphrases Jandī's text. Kāšānī wrote several other important works, both in Arabic and Persian, all of which are rooted in Ebn al-ʿArabī's universe of discourse. His *Taʾwīl al-Qorʾān* has been published in Ebn al-ʿArabī's name (Beirut, 1968; for passages in English, see Murata); although permeated with Ebn al-ʿArabī's basic world view, there are important differences of perspective that mark Kāšānī as an independent thinker (Lory; Morris, 1987, pp. 101-06). A Persian work on *fotowwat* (*fotūwa*) has also been published (*Toḥfat al-eḵwān fī ḵaṣāʾeṣ al-fetyān*, ed. M. Ṣarrāf in *Rasāʾel-e javānmardān*, Tehran, 1973).

Persian commentaries on the *Foṣūṣ* are frequently based on the Arabic commentary of Kāšānī's student, Dāwūd Qayṣarī (d. 751/1350), author of a dozen other Arabic works. His systematic philosophical introduction to *Šarḥ al-Foṣūṣ* (Tehran, 1299/1882; Bombay, 1300/1883) itself became the object of commentaries (for the latest, see Āštīānī, 1385/1966). Certainly, Qayṣarī's influence is obvious and acknowledged in the first Persian commentary on the *Foṣūṣ*, *Noṣūṣ al-ḵoṣūṣ* (partly edited by R. Mażlūmī, Tehran, 1359 Š./ 1980), written by his student Bābā Rokn-al-Dīn Šīrāzī (d. 769/1367). The Persian commentary by Tāj-al-Dīn Ḥosayn b. Ḥasan Ḵᵛārazmī (d. ca. 835/1432; ed. N. Māyel Heravī, Tehran, 1364 Š./1985) is almost a verbatim translation of Qayṣarī. Other Persian commentaries include *Ḥall-e Foṣūṣ* by Sayyed ʿAlī Hamadānī (d. 786/1385); this work has been wrongly attributed to Ḵᵛāja Pārsā in its printed edition (ed. J. Mesgarnežād, Tehran, 1366 Š./1987; see Māyel Heravī, 1988, pp. xxi-xxvii). In his comprehensive list of the more than one hundred commentaries on the *Foṣūṣ*, Osman Yahia mentions ten in Persian, some of which, however, may be repeats (introduction to Āmolī, pp. 16-36). Persian commentaries that he does not mention include the following: 1. *Ḵātam al-Foṣūṣ*, attributed to Shah Neʿmat-Allāh Walī (d. 834/1437); this is much longer than any of Shah Neʿmat-Allāh's printed *rasāʾel* (manuscripts include Nadwat al-ʿOlamāʾ 35; Andhra Pradesh State Oriental Manuscript Library, *Taṣawwof* 254, *Jadīd* 715; Ḵodābaḵš, Fārsī 1371). 2. Another long commentary is also attributed to Shah Neʿmat-Allāh (Andhra Pradesh, *Taṣawwof* 185). 3. Shaikh Moḥebb-Allāh Mobārez Elāhābādī (d. 1048/1648), Ebn al-ʿArabī's most faithful Indian follower, wrote a lengthy Persian commentary and a shorter Arabic commentary. 4. Ḥāfeẓ Ḡolām-Moṣṭafā b. Moḥammad-Akbar from Thaneswar wrote *Šoḵūṣ al-hemam fī šarḥ Foṣūṣ al-ḥekam*, a commentary of 1024 pages in the Andhra Pradesh copy (*Taṣawwof* 296), apparently in the 11th/18th century. The last Persian commentary on the *Foṣūṣ* in India seems to be *al-Taʾwīl al-moḥkam fī motašabah Foṣūṣ al-ḥekam* by Mawlawī Moḥammad-Ḥasan Ṣāḥeb Amrūhawī; he was living in Hyderabad (Deccan) when this 500-page work was published in Lucknow in 1893.

A number of Qūnawī's contemporaries not directly connected to his circle were important in making at least some of Ebn al-ʿArabī's teachings available to Persian speakers. Saʿd-al-Dīn Ḥamūya (d. 649/1252), a Persian disciple of Najm-al-Dīn Kobrā, corresponded with Ebn al-ʿArabī and spent several years in Damascus, where he met both Ebn al-ʿArabī and Qūnawī. He wrote works in both Arabic and Persian; these are often extremely difficult, especially because the author delighted in letter symbolism (for a Persian work, see *al-Meṣbāḥ fi'l-taṣawwof*, ed. N. Māyel Heravī, Tehran, 1362 Š./1983). His disciple ʿAzīz-al-Dīn Nasafī (d. before 700/1300) was responsible for making some of Ebn al-ʿArabī's terminology well-known in Persian; his popularizing works can hardly be compared in sophistication to those of

ʿErāqī or Farḡānī (see, e.g., his *Ensān-e kāmel*, ed. M. Molé, Tehran, 1962; an English paraphrase of his *Maqṣad-e aqṣā* was published by E. H. Palmer as *Oriental Mysticism*, London, 1867; see also Morris, pp. 745-51). Šams-al-Dīn Ebrāhīm Abarqūhī began to write *Majmaʿ al-baḥrayn* (ed. N. Māyel Heravī, Tehran, 1364 Š./1985) in 714/1314. The work represents an early effort to integrate Ebn al-ʿArabī's teachings into Persian Sufism; more sophisticated than Nasafī, the author does not have the strong philosophical orientation typical of Qūnawī and his circle.

Among early Persian poets influenced by Ebn al-ʿArabī's teachings and terminology were ʿErāqī, Maḡrebī, and Maḥmūd Šabestarī (d. ca. 720/1320). Moḥammad Lāhījī (d. 912/1506) commented on Šabestarī's thousand-verse *Golšan-e rāz* in *Šarḥ-e Golšan-e rāz*, a long Persian work rooted in the writings of Kāšānī and Qayṣarī. One of Ebn al-ʿArabī's most learned and successful popularizers was the poet ʿAbd-al-Raḥmān Jāmī (d. 898/1492), especially through his *ḡazal*s and *maṯnawī*s; about 1,000 verses of his *Selselat al-ḏahab* carefully follow the text of Ebn al-ʿArabī's *Ḥelyat al-abdāl* (Māyel Heravī, 1988, pp. xxxvii-xl). Jāmī's Persian prose works dealing with Ebn al-ʿArabī's teachings—the *Lawāʾeḥ*, *Lawāmeʿ*, *Ašeʿʿat al-lamaʿāt*, and *Naqd al-noṣūṣ fī šarḥ Naqš al-Foṣūṣ*—as well as his Arabic commentary on the *Foṣūṣ*, were also widely read (see introduction to Jāmī, 1977). Jāmī was especially popular in India, and most of the numerous followers of Ebn al-ʿArabī in the subcontinent—who were much more likely to write in Persian than in Arabic—are indebted to his explications of the Shaikh's works (Chittick, 1992d). Moḥammad b. Moḥammad, who was known as Shaikh-e Makkī (d. 926/1020) and considered himself a disciple of Jāmī, defended Ebn al-ʿArabī against attacks by narrow-minded critics in his Persian *al-Jāneb al-ḡarbī fī ḥall moškelāt al-šayḵ Mohyī-al-Dīn Ebn ʿArabī* (ed. Māyel Heravī, Tehran, 1364 Š./1985).

The poet and Sufi master Shah Neʿmat-Allāh Walī was one of Ebn al-ʿArabī's most fervent admirers and followed closely in the tracks of Kāšānī and Qayṣarī. He wrote over one hundred *rasāla*s (treatises) on theoretical and practical Sufism that fit squarely into Ebn al-ʿArabī's universe; four of these comment on the *Foṣūṣ* or *Naqš al-Foṣūṣ*, Ebn al-ʿArabī's own treatise on the essential ideas of the *Foṣūṣ*. The Perso-Indian poet Mīrzā ʿAbd-al-Qāder Bīdel (=Bēdil, q.v.; d. 1133/1721) demonstrates an intimate knowledge of Ebn al-ʿArabī's school in such *maṯnawī*s as *ʿErfān*.

Even Sufi authors critical of Ebn al-ʿArabī's teachings adopted much of his terminology and world view. Thus in Persia ʿAlāʾ-al-Dawla Semnānī (d. 736/1337) and in India Shaikh Moḥammad Ḥosaynī, known as Gīsū-Derāz (d. 825/1422), and Shaikh Aḥmad Serhendī (d. 1034/1634) do not diverge markedly from most of the teachings established by him and his immediate followers. Most Sufis did not take the criticisms of these authors too seriously. Typical are the remarks of Sayyed Ašraf Jahāngīr Semnānī (d. probably in 829/1425), who studied with ʿAlāʾ-al-Dawla Semnānī but sided with Kāšānī in his defense of Ebn al-ʿArabī against Semnānī's criticisms (see Landolt, 1973). After providing the views of the participants in this debate and those of a number of observers, Sayyed Ašraf tells us that Semnānī had not understood what Ebn al-ʿArabī was saying and that he had retracted his criticisms before the end of his life (Yamanī, *Laṭāʾef-e ašrafī, laṭīfa* 28, pp. 139-45; Māyel Heravī, 1367, pp. xxxi-xxxv). In a similar manner, Shah Walī-Allāh Dehlawī (d. 1176/1762) wrote a work showing that there was no fundamental difference between Ebn al-ʿArabī's *waḥdat al-wojūd* and Serhendī's *waḥdat al-šohūd*.

From the 8th/14th century onward Ebn al-ʿArabī's influence is clearly present in many works written by authors known primarily as theologians or philosophers. Among Shiʿites, Sayyed Ḥaydar Āmolī (d. 787/1385) was especially important in bringing Ebn al-ʿArabī into the mainstream of Shiʿite thought. He wrote an enormous commentary on the *Foṣūṣ*, *Naṣṣ al-noṣūṣ*, the 500-page introduction of which has been published (representing about 10 percent of the text). Āmolī investigates the meaning of the *Foṣūṣ* on three levels: *naql* (the Koran and Hadith, making special use here of Shiʿite sources), *ʿaql* (meaning *kalām* and *falsafa*), and *kašf* (referring both to his own experience and the writings of major members of Ebn al-ʿArabī's school). Āmolī also wrote several Arabic works on metaphysics; especially significant is *Jāmeʿ al-asrār* (ed. Corbin and Yahia, Tehran, 1347 Š./1969; see Morris, 106-08), which was written in his youth during his initial movement into Ebn al-ʿArabī's universe.

Ṣāʾen-al-Dīn ʿAlī Torka Eṣfahānī (d. 835/1432) completed a commentary on the *Foṣūṣ* in 831/1427; his treatise on *wojūd* "being," *Tamhīd al-qawāʿed* (ed. S. J. Āštīānī, Tehran, 1396/1976), frequently paraphrases Jandī's *Foṣūṣ* commentary. A number of Torka's Persian treatises (*Čahārdah rasāʾel*, eds. S. ʿA. Mūsawī Behbahānī and S. E. Dībājī, Tehran, 1351 Š./1972) make explicit or implicit reference to Ebn al-ʿArabī's teachings. Mollā Ṣadrā (d. 1050/1641) frequently quotes at length from the *Fotūḥāt* in his *Asfār*. His student Mollā Moḥsen Fayż Kāšānī (d. 1090/1679) wrote an epitome of the *Fotūḥāt* and frequently quotes from Ebn al-ʿArabī in his works (*EI*[2] V, p. 476). Even Mollā Moḥammad-Bāqer Majlesī (d. 1110/1669), well-known as a critic of Sufis in general and Ebn al-ʿArabī in particular, quotes on occasion from Ebn al-ʿArabī in his monumental *Beḥār al-anwār* (Beirut, 1983; e.g., *baʿż ahl al-maʿrefa* in vol. 67, p. 339, refers to Ebn al-ʿArabī in the *Fotūḥāt*, Cairo, 1911, vol. 2, p. 328.15). In the modern period, Āyat-Allāh Khomeini differentiated himself from many other influential *ʿolamāʾ* by his intense interest in Ebn al-ʿArabī (Knysh, 1992b).

The first of Ebn al-ʿArabī's works to be translated into Persian was the *Foṣūṣ*, not as an independent work, but rather in the midst of the commentaries by Bābā Rokn-al-Dīn and others. A translation without commentary was made by ʿAbd-al-Ḡaffār b. Moḥammad-ʿAlī; an autograph version, written in 1008/1685, is found in the Salar Jung Library in Hyderabad (Deccan) (*Taṣawwof* 33; other copies are found in the Andhra Pradesh State Library, *Taṣawwof* 464 and *Jadīd* 4248). Several short works by Ebn al-ʿArabī on Sufi practice, including *al-Anwār*, *Asrār al-ḵalwa*, *Ḥaqīqat al-ḥaqāʾeq*, and *Ḥelyat al-awlīāʾ* were translated in the 8-9th/14-15th centuries (for the Persian text of these and other minor works, see Māyel Heravī, 1988). A manuscript (Andhra Pradesh, *Jadīd* 1461) called *Šarḥ-e Fotūḥāt*, probably by Shaikh Moḥebb-Allāh Elāhābādī, is the second volume (fols. 357-747) of a work that includes translations of and commentary on long passages from the *Fotūḥāt*. Several of Elāhābādī's long Persian works provide extensive translations from the *Fotūḥāt*.

Among Persian Sufis who were especially influential in the Arabic-speaking countries of Islam, one can mention ʿAbd-al-Karīm Jīlī (d. 832/1428), author of numerous independently-minded works, who settled in the Yemen and contributed to the widespread interest in Ebn al-ʿArabī's writings there (see Knysh, 1992a). Finally, it is worth noting that most followers of Ebn al-ʿArabī in Persia wrote their theoretical works in Arabic. In contrast, the Indian subcontinent witnessed an enormous outpouring of Persian writing pertaining to this school of thought, a legacy largely ignored by modern scholars, even in the subcontinent itself (Chittick, 1992d).

Bibliography: (For cited works not given in detail, see "Short References.") The most comprehensive and best documented account of Ebn al-ʿArabī's life is C. Addas, *Ibn ʿArabī ou La quête du Soufre Rouge*, Paris, 1989; tr. as *Quest for the Red Sulphur*, Cambridge, 1993. N. Z. Abū Zayd, *Falsafat al-taʾwīl*, Cairo, 1983. H. Algar, "Reflections of Ibn ʿArabī in Early Naqshbandī Tradition," *Journal of the Muhyiddin ibn ʿArabi Society* 10, 1991, pp. 45-66. Sayyed Ḥaydar Āmolī, *al-Moqaddemāt men naṣṣ al-noṣūṣ*, eds. H. Corbin and O. Yahia, Tehran, 1975. M. Asin Palacios, *El Islam cristianizado*, Madrid, 1931. S. J. Āštīānī, *Šarḥ-e moqaddema-ye Qayṣarī bar Foṣūṣ al-ḥekam*, Mašhad, 1385/1966. Idem, *Rasāʾel-e Qayṣarī*, Mašhad, 1357 Š./1978. A. Badawi, "Autobibliografía de Ibn ʿArabī," *al-Andalus* 20, 1955, pp. 107-28. Awḥad-al-Dīn Balyanī, *Épître sur l'unicité absolue*, tr. M. Chodkiewicz, Paris, 1982. M. Bayrakdar, *La philosophie mystique chez Dawud de Kayseri*, Ankara, 1990. W. C. Chittick, "The Last Will and Testament of Ibn ʿArabī's Foremost Disciple and Some Notes on its Author," *Sophia Perennis* 4/1, 1978, pp. 43-58. Idem, "The Perfect Man as the Prototype of the Self in the Sufism of Jāmī," *Stud. Isl.* 49, 1979, pp. 135-57. Idem, "The Five Divine Presences. From al-Qūnawī to al-Qayṣarī," *Muslim World* 72, 1982a, pp. 107-28. Idem, "Ibn ʿArabī's own Summary of the *Fuṣūṣ*. 'The Imprint of the Bezels of Wisdom'," *Journal of the Muhyiddin Ibn ʿArabi Society* 1, 1982b, pp. 30-93. Idem, "The Chapter Headings of the *Fuṣūṣ*," *Journal of the Muhyiddin Ibn ʿArabi Society* 2, 1984, pp. 41-94. Idem, *The Sufi Path of Knowledge. Ibn al-ʿArabī's Metaphysics of Imagination*, Albany, 1989. Idem, "Ibn al-ʿArabī and his School," in *Islamic Spirituality. Manifestations*, ed. S. H. Nasr, New York, 1991, pp. 49-79. Idem, "The Circle of Spiritual Ascent According to al-Qūnawī," *Neoplatonism and Islamic Thought*, ed. P. Morewedge, Albany, 1992a, pp. 179-209. Idem, *Faith and Practice of Islam. Three Thirteenth Century Sufi Texts*, Albany, 1992b. Idem, "Spectrums of Islamic Thought. Saʿīd al-Dīn Farghānī on the Implications of Oneness and Manyness," in *The Legacy of Medieval Persian Sufism*, ed. L. Lewisohn, London, 1992c, pp. 203-17. Idem, "Notes on Ibn al-ʿArabī's Influence in India," *Muslim World* 82, 1992d, pp. 218-41. Idem, "Rumi and Waḥdat al-Wujūd," in *The Heritage of Rumi*, ed. A. Banani and G. Sabagh, Cambridge, forthcoming. Idem and P. L. Wilson, *Fakhruddin ʿIraqi. Divine Flashes*, New York, 1982. M. Chodkiewicz, *Le sceau des saints. Prophétie et sainteté dans la doctrine d'Ibn Arabī*, Paris, 1986; tr. as *The Seal of the Saints*, Cambridge, 1993. Idem, "The Diffusion of Ibn ʿArabī's Doctrine," *Journal of the Muhyiddin Ibn ʿArabi Society* 9, 1991a, pp. 36-57. Idem, "The *Futūḥāt Makkīya* and its Commentators. Some Unresolved Enigmas," in *The Legacy of Medieval Persian Sufism*, ed. L. Lewisohn, London, 1991b, pp. 219-32. Idem, *Un océan sans rivage. Ibn ʿArabī, le Livre et la Loi*, Paris, 1992; tr. as *An Ocean without Shore*, Albany, 1993. M. Chodkiewicz et al., *Les Illuminations de la Mecque/The Meccan Illuminations. Textes choisis/Selected Texts*, Paris, 1988. H. Corbin, *Creative Imagination in the Ṣūfism of Ibn ʿArabī*, Princeton, 1969. Idem, *En Islam iranien*, III, Paris, 1973. Idem, *Spiritual Body and Celestial Earth*, Princeton, 1977. B. Forūzānfar, ed., *Manāqeb-e Awḥad-al-Dīn ... Kermānī*, Tehran, 1347 Š./1968. Y. Friedmann, *Shaykh Aḥmad Sirhindī. An Outline of His Thought and a Study of His Image in the Eyes of Posterity*, Montreal, 1971. S. Ḥakīm, *al-Moʿjam al-ṣūfī*, Beirut, 1981. N. L. Heer, *The Precious Pearl. al-Jami's al-Durrat al-Fakhirah*, Albany, 1979. S. Hirtenstein and M. Notcutt, eds., *Muhyiddin Ibn ʿArabi. A Commemorative Volume*, Shaftesbury, Dorset, 1993. T. Izutsu, *Sufism and Taoism*, Los Angeles, 1983. M. Jahāngīrī, *Moḥyī-al-Dīn Ebn al-ʿArabī*, Tehran, 1361 Š./1982. ʿAbd-al-Raḥmān Jāmī, *Naqd al-noṣūṣ fī šarḥ Naqš al-Foṣūṣ*, ed. W. C. Chittick, Tehran, 1977. Idem, *Lawāʾeḥ*, text and French tr. Y. Richard, *Les jaillissements de lumière*, Paris, 1982; text and English tr. E. H. Whinfield and M. M. Kazwīnī, London, 1906. A. Knysh, "Ibn ʿArabi in the Yemen. His Admirers and Detractors," *Journal of the Muhyiddin Ibn ʿArabi Society* 11, 1992a, pp. 38-63. Idem, "Irfan Revisited. Khomeini and the Legacy of Islamic Mystical Philosophy," *Middle East Journal* 46, 1992b, pp. 631-53. H. Landolt, "Der Briefwechsel zwischen Kāšānī und Simnānī über Waḥdat al-Wuǧūd," *Der Islam* 50, 1973, pp. 29-81. Idem, "Simnānī on *Waḥdat al-Wojūd*," in *Majmūʿa-ye sok̲anrānīhā wa maqālahā*, ed. M. Moḥaqqeq and H. Landolt, Tehran, 1971, pp. 91-111. L. Lewisohn, *A Critical Edition of the Divan of Muhammad Shirin Maghribi*, Tehran and London, 1993. P. Lory, *Les Commentaires ésotériques du Coran d'après ʿAbd al-Razzāq al-Qāshānī*, Paris, 1981. N. Māyel Heravī, *Rasāʾel-e Ebn-e ʿArabī. Dah resāla-ye fārsī-šoda*, Tehran, 1367 Š./1988. A. Mīr-ʿĀbedīnī, *Dīvān-e kāmel-e Šams-e Maḡrebī ... be enżemām-e Resāla-ye jām-e jahānnomā*, Tehran, 1358 Š./1979. J. Morris, "Ibn ʿArabī and his Interpreters. Part I: Recent French Translations," *JAOS* 106, 1986, pp. 539-51; "Part II. Influences and Interpretations," *JAOS* 106, 1986, pp. 733-56; 107, 1987, pp. 101-19. S. Murata, *The Tao of Islam. A Sourcebook on Gender Relationships in Islamic Thought*, Albany, 1992. S. ʿA. Mūsawī Behbahānī, "Aḥwāl wa āṯār-e Ṣāʾen-al-Dīn Torka Eṣfahānī," in *Majmūʿa-ye sok̲anrānīhā wa maqālahā*, ed. M. Moḥaqqeq and H. Landolt, Tehran, 1971, pp. 97-145. S. Nafīsī, *Kollīyāt-e ʿErāqī*, Tehran, 1338 Š./1959. I. R. Netton, *Allah Transcendent. Studies in the Structure and Semiotics of Islamic Philosophy, Theology, and Cosmology*, London, 1989. R. A. Nicholson, *The tarjumān al-ashwāq. A Collection of Mystical Odes by Muḥyi'ddīn ibn al-ʿArabī*, London, 1911. H. S. Nyberg, *Kleinere Schriften des Ibn al-ʿArabī*, Leiden, 1919. F. Rosenthal, "Ibn ʿArabī between 'Philosophy' and 'Mysticism'," *Oriens* 31, 1988, pp. 1-35. A. Schimmel, *Mystical Dimensions of Islam*, Chapel Hill, 1975, pp. 263-86 and passim. M. Takeshita, *Ibn ʿArabī's Theory of the Perfect Man and its Place in the History of Islamic Thought*, Tokyo, 1987. O. Yahia, *Histoire et classification de l' oeuvre d'Ibn ʿArabī*, Damascus, 1964. Neẓām-al-Dīn Yamanī, *Laṭāʾef-e ašrafī*, Delhi, 1219/1804. ʿA. Zarrīnkūb, *Donbāla-ye jostojū dar taṣawwof-e īrānī*, Tehran, 1362 Š./1983.

(WILLIAM C. CHITTICK)

EBN ʿARABŠĀH, ŠEHĀB-AL-DĪN ABU'L-ʿABBĀS AḤMAD b. Moḥammad ... Ḥanafī ʿAjamī (b. Damascus, 791/1389, d. Cairo, 854/1450), literary scholar and biographer of Tamerlane (Tīmūr). According to the autobiography quoted by Ebn Taḡrīberdī, when Tīmūr conquered Damascus in 803/1401, Ebn ʿArabšāh and his family were transported to Tīmūr's capital, Samarkand. He spent the next eight years in Transoxiana and Chinese Turkestan, where he learned Persian and Mongolian and studied with Sayyed Šarīf Moḥammad Jorjānī, Saʿd-al-Dīn Masʿūd Taftāzānī, and Šams-al-Dīn Moḥammad Jazarī. Later, in K̲ᵛārazm, Sarāy, Astrakhan, and the Crimea, he associated with the ruling elite, scholars, and litterateurs. Around 815/1412, he entered the service of the Ottoman sultan Moḥammad I, holding the office of confidential secretary (*kāteb al-serr*). At this time, he translated several religious works from Arabic into Turkish and ʿAwfī's *Jāmeʿ al-ḥekāyāt wa lāmeʿ al-rewāyāt* from Persian into Turkish. Ebn ʿArabšāh returned to Syria and reentered Damascus in 825/1422 after the death of Moḥammad I. There he occupied several minor religious posts and completed his celebrated biography of Tīmūr, *ʿAjāʾeb al-maqdūr fī nawāʾeb Tīmūr* (q.v.). Sometime after 841/1438, he settled in Cairo, where he became acquainted with the historians Ebn Taḡrīberdī and Sak̲āwī (Sak̲āwī, II, pp. 128-29, 130-31). He initially secured the favor of the Mamlūk sultan Jaqmaq and composed several works in his name, including an adaptation of the *Marzbān-nāma* entitled *Fākehat al-k̲olafāʾ wa mofākahat al-ẓorafāʾ*, written in 852/1448. In 854/1450, Jaqmaq imprisoned him for a few days as the result of a rival's complaint. Ebn ʿArabšāh died twelve years after his release.

Bibliography: (For cited works not given in detail, see "Short References.") For his life, see the notices in Ebn Taḡrīberdī, *al-Manhal al-ṣāfī wa' l-mostawfī baʿd al-wāfī* II, ed. M. M. Amīn, Cairo, 1984-90, pp. 131-45, and ʿAbd-al-Raḥmān Sak̲āwī, *al-Żawʾ al-lāmeʿ le ahl al-qarn al-tāseʿ* II, Cairo, 1353-55/1934-36, pp. 126-31, from which other accounts are derived. Secondary accounts include: Browne, *Lit. Hist. Persia* III, pp. 181, 183, 185, 197 n., 198, 203, 321 n., 355-56; İ. Kafesoğlu, *İA* II, pp. 698-701; J. Pedersen, *EI*² III, pp. 711-12; and *DMBE* IV, pp. 221-23. For his works, see *Kašf al-ẓonūn*, ed. Flügel, II, pp. 128, 352, 510; IV, pp. 190-91, 345; VI, p. 544; and Brockelmann, *GAL* II, pp. 28-30; SII, p. 25. Published texts include: *ʿAjāʾeb al-maqdūr fī nawāʾeb* (or *akhbār*) *Tīmūr* (ed. most recently by ʿA. M. ʿOmar, Cairo, 1979, and A. F. al-Ḥemsī, Beirut, 1986; *Fākehat al-k̲olafāʾ wa mafākahat al-ẓorafāʾ*, ed. G. W. Freytag, *Fructus imperatorum et jocatio ingeniosorum ...*, 2 vols., Bonn, 1832-52; and *al-Taʾlīf al-ṭāher fī šīam Šayk̲ al-Malek al-Ẓāher al-qāʾem be noṣrat al-ḥaqq Abī Saʿīd Jaqmaq*, partially ed. S.A. Strong, *JRAS*, 1907, pp. 395-96; Arabic text, pp. 1-27.

(JOHN E. WOODS)

EBN AṢDAQ, MĪRZĀ ʿALĪ-MOḤAMMAD (b. Mašhad 1267/1850; d. Tehran, 1347/1928), prominent Bahai missionary. He was given the honorific designation Ebn(-e) Aṣdaq in certain Bahai scriptural writings. Toward the end of his life Bahāʾ-Allāh counted him a living martyr and referred to him as *Šahīd ebn-e*

Šahīd ("martyr, son of a martyr"). He was a son of the Šayḵī, Bābī and Baha'i Mollā Ṣādeq Moqaddas-e Ḵorāsānī (d.1306/1889), who was entitled Esm-Allāh al-Aṣdaq by the Bāb. The father was posthumously referred to as one of the *Ayādī-e Amr-Allāh* (q.v.; "Hands of the Cause of God") by ʿAbd-al-Bahāʾ in 1919, and Ebn-e Aṣdaq was so designated by Bahāʾ-Allāh around 1305/1887. Around 1278/1861-2, he was imprisoned with his father for over two years in the Sīāh Čāl (dungeon) in Tehran. During this time he was attended by the Jewish physician Ḥakīm Masīḥ, who was subsequently converted and is often considered to be the first Jewish [Bābī] Bahai. As a Bahai missionary, Ebn-e Aṣdaq visited many parts of Persia, Iraq, India, Burma, and Caucasia, as well as Ashkhabad and Marv. He was a permanent member of the first Central Spiritual Assembly established at ʿAbd-al-Bahāʾ's direction in Tehran in 1316/1897. During his lifetime he frequently visited Bahāʾ-Allāh and ʿAbd-al-Bahāʾ in Palestine. The latter entrusted him with various tasks such as the presentation of his Resāla-ye Sīāsīya ("Treatise on Politics" written in 1311/1893) to Nāṣer-al-Dīn Shah, to contemporary religious authorities, and to Persian notables. His wife, ʿAḏrāʾ Ḵānom Żīāʾ-al-Ḥājīa, a great-granddaughter of Moḥammad Shah, was the sister-in-law of Enteẓām-al-Salṭana, a socially prominent Bahai. In 1919 ʿAbd-al-Bahāʾ gave him and Aḥmad Yazdānī the responsiblity of delivering his Tablet addressed to the *Central Organization for a Durable Peace, The Hague (Lawḥ-e lāha)*. Shoghi Effendi reckoned Ebn-e Aṣdaq the nineteenth of the nineteen Apostles of Bahāʾ-Allāh.

Bibliography: ʿAbd al-Bahāʾ, *Memorials of the Faithful*, tr. M. Gail ,Wilmette, Ill., 1971, pp. 5-8 (Esm-Allāh al-Aṣdaq). ʿAbd-al-ʿAlī ʿAlāʾī, ed., *Moʾassesa-ye Ayādī-e Amr-Allāh*, Tehran, 130 Badīʿ/1973-4, pp. 465-93. Hasan Balyuzi, *Eminent Bahá'ís in the Time of Bahá'u'lláh*, Oxford, 1985, pp. 171-176. Mīrzā Asad-Allāh Fāżel Māzandarānī, *Tārīḵ-e ẓohūr al-ḥaqq* VI, MS in Afnān Library (England), fols. 34 -37, VIII/1, Tehran, 131 Badīʿ/ 1974, pp. 375-77. M. Momen, ed., "Esslemont's Survey of the Bahāʾī Community, 1919-1920, pt. 1: Iran by Ibn-i Aṣdaq and ʿAzīzuʾllāh Varqā," *Bahāʾī Studies Bulletin* 1/1, June 1982, pp. 2-10. ʿAzīz-Allāh Solaymānī, *Maṣābīh-e Hedāyat* VII, pp. 374-418 (Esm-Allāh al-Aṣdaq), Tehran, 129 Badīʿ/1973. Shaikh Kāẓem Samandar, *Tārīḵ-e Samandar o molḥaqāt*, Tehran, 1975, pp. 163-71. Adib Taherzadeh, *The Revelation of Bahá'u'lláh* IV, Oxford, 1987, pp. 301-04.

(STEPHEN LAMBDEN)

EBN AL-AṮĪR, ʿEZZ-AL-DĪN ABU'L-ḤASAN ʿALĪ b. Moḥammad Jazarī (b. Jazīrat Ebn ʿOmar [modern Cizre, in eastern Turkey] 4 Jomādā I 555/13 May 1160; d. Mosul, Šaʿbān 630/June 1233), major Islamic historian and important source for the history of Persia and adjacent areas from the Samanids to the first Mongol invasion.

Life and works. Ebn al-Aṯīr's family were landowners and officials of the Zengid dynasty in Mosul. His elder brother, Majd-al-Dīn (d. 606/1209), was an administrator and author. His younger brother, Żīāʾ-al-Dīn (d. 637/1239), was a vizier and literary critic. There is no evidence that he himself held any official position. Writing about Ṭabarī, he mentions approvingly "his contentment with his income from a village in Ṭabarestān left him by his father" (Ebn al-Aṯīr, VIII, p. 136). Some similar arrangement may have allowed Ebn al-Aṯīr to follow his scholarly career. He studied in his home town and Mosul, and, after a pilgrimage to Mecca in 576/1181, in Baghdad. After the recovery of Jerusalem, he was for a while with Saladin in Syria. From 584/1188 until his death he alternated between Mosul, where he enjoyed the patronage of Badr-al-Dīn Loʾloʾ, and Syria, where the atabeg of Aleppo, Šehāb-al-Dīn Ṭoḡrol, supported him (Ebn Ḵallekān, ed. ʿAbbās, III, p. 349).

Ebn al-Aṯīr wrote two histories: *al-Kāmel fi'l-taʾrīḵ* (The complete history), a universal history ending in 628/1231, and a monograph on the Zengid dynasty, *al-Taʾrīḵ al-bāher fi'l-dawlat al-Atābakīya* (The brilliant history of the Atabeg dynasty, ed. A. A. Tolaymat, Cairo, 1962). The latter was written sometime between 609/1212 and 615/1218, when its patron, the Zengid Sultan Qāher, died. It has much in common with the corresponding parts of the *Kāmel*, but, being didactic and dedicated to the dynasty, it is more partial and selective. It deals mainly with events in Mesopotamia and Syria. Two other works of Ebn al-Aṯīr survive: *al-Lobāb fī tahḏīb al-ansāb*, a revised version of Samʿānī's famous manual of *nesbas*, and *Osd al-ḡāba fī maʿrefat al-ṣaḥāba (*Lions of the thicket concerning knowledge of the Prophet's companions; *GAL* I, pp. 402, 422-23, S I, p. 587).

Ebn al-Aṯīr on Persian history. The *Kāmel* is an important source for Persian history, both for Ebn al-Aṯīr's times and for preceding centuries. In it he made intelligent use of a wide range of sources, many of them no longer extant. Its first draft, entitled *al-Mostaqṣā fi'l-taʾrīḵ* (A study of history), was completed in about 600/1203. At the command of Badr-al-Dīn, Ebn al-Aṯīr revised, enlarged, and retitled his chronicle in about 620/1223. Five years later he probably made further additions and then did so regularly until the end of 628/1231 (Richards, pp. 76-84).

In his detailed introduction Ebn al-Aṯīr says that he intended to create a single convenient compilation from the writings of Ṭabarī and his continuators, aiming at a balanced coverage of the whole Islamic world. His style, while sensitive to literary effect, avoids over-elaborateness. He tried to give his narrative a flowing character, conflating his sources into a single consistent version whenever possible and often devoting an extended section to connected events stretching over a number of years. This breaking of the strict annalistic form was not his own innovation, although he has at times been given exaggerated credit for it. On the other hand, he has been criticized for his general failure to identify his sources. Even when it is possible to make lexical and structural comparisons with extant works or with what is thought to have been the content of lost works, one can never be sure whether Ebn al-Aṯīr used texts directly or through intermediary compilations, possibly some unknown to us.

For Ebn al-Aṯīr the whole of human history is an unfolding of God's purposes for mankind. All actions are subject to the will of God, which is the ultimate explanation of all events. Without taking account of the contradictions involved in his constant invoking of God's sovereign will, Ebn al-Aṯīr also applied moral judgements to history. He looked upon history as a source of "good example" (*ʿebra)* and a moral proving ground, in which those who adhere to Islamic norms win just rewards and lasting repute (Richards, pp. 93ff.). In practice, the *Kāmel* takes account of political aims and interests.

Ṭabarī was his fundamental source for early periods, supplemented by other sources. For pre-Islamic Persian history the *Kāmel* follows Ṭabarī, but Ebn al-Aṯīr expresses disdain for the "inane fabrications of the Persians." He only includes them to show "the folly of the Persians," who affect to despise the ignorance of the Arabs, and because there would otherwise be a blank in the record (I, p. 66; cf. pp. 76, 166, 247). Ebn al-Aṯīr's history of the Islamic east down to the 3rd/early 10th century is also based on Ṭabarī's history, which ends in 302/915 (Ebn al-Aṯīr, I, p. 3). For the later years, sketchily treated in Ṭabarī, he begins to rely on the fuller accounts of such continuators as Meskawayh (q.v.). Ebn al-Aṯīr gives us concise and usable accounts of Samanid and Buyid history (vols. VII-IX). He probably used the history of the Samanids by Sallāmī, for Gardīzī's Persian quotations from it resemble Ebn al-Aṯīr's account (Barthold, *Turkestan*[3], pp. 10-11). Basic to the historiography of the 4/10th century and the first half of the 5/11th century are the writings of members of the Ṣābeʾ family, whose interests centered on Iraq and the ʿAbbasid caliphate. Ṯābet b. Senān, the first of them, was probably known to Ebn al-Aṯīr through the *Tajāreb al-omam* of Meskawayh, which he names four times, mostly to dispute a point (VII, p. 118; VIII, pp. 86, 186, 321). Cahen speculated that Ebn al-Aṯīr's detailed account of the first half of the 5/11th century was based directly on the work of Ṯābet's successor, Helāl Ṣābeʾ (Cahen, 1962, p. 60).

For the Great Saljuqs (5/11th-6/12th centuries), who did not have their own dynastic historians, Ebn al-Aṯīr gives the most complete and continuous account available (IX, p. 473-XII, p. 108). He used the continuators of the central ʿAbbasid tradition, whom he often characterizes simply as "the Iraqis," although he names Ebn al-Jawzī (d. 597/1200; *Kāmel* XI, p. 333). For the semi-legendary early history of the Seljuqs, Ebn al-Aṯīr used an Arabic version of the *Malek-nāma*, originally written in Persian for Alp Arslān (Cahen, 1949). The lost *Mašāreb al-tajāreb* of Ebn al-Fondoq Beyhaqī (q.v.) was probably an important source for his account of the Seljuq decline in the east and the rise of the K̲ᵛārazmšāhs. Unfortunately, the only explicit citation of this work concerns the events of 568-595/1172-1198, although Beyhaqī is thought to have died in 565/1166. Cahen has argued that this work would have been particularly valuable for Ebn al-Aṯīr because it was written in Arabic, and there is no real evidence that he knew Persian. However, his younger contemporary, the historian Nasawī, citing the scope of Ebn al-Aṯīr's coverage of eastern lands, speculates that he must have had Persian-language sources (Nasawī, p. 34). There is no obvious Arabic source, for example, for his detailed information on Ghurid history for the period 559-604/1163-1207.

His celebrated account of the initial Mongol attack on the Islamic east is based on first-hand accounts of merchants, envoys, and refugees. In one of his set-pieces he vividly expresses the horror of these events (XII, pp. 358-68). He did not, however, attach eschatological significance to the coming of the Mongols, seeing them as a passing scourge and viewing the Franks as a greater danger to Islam.

Bibliography: (For cited works not given in detail, see "Short References.") Ebn K̲allekān, ed. E. ʿAbbās, III, pp. 348-50. Nasawī, *History of Djalāl ed-Dīn Mankobirti*, ed. H. H. Hamdi, Cairo, 1953. Ṣafadī, *al-Wāfī be'l-wafayāt*, ed. R. Baalbaki, Wiesbaden, 1983, XXII, pp. 136-37. The standard edition is *al-Kāmel fi'l-taʾrīḵ*, ed. C. J. Tornberg as *Ibn-el-Athiri Chronicon quod Perfectissimum Inscribitur*, Leiden, 1851-76; repr. Beirut, 1385-87/1965-67, the ed. used here. Another ed. was published in Cairo, 1303/1886. An incomplete Persian tr. exists: *Kāmel, tārīḵ-e bozorg-e Eslām o Īrān*, tr. ʿA. K̲alīlī, Tehran, n.d. An English tr. of the section on the Saljuqs is being prepared by D. S. Richards.

Studies: Claude Cahen, "Le Malik-nameh et l'histoire des origines seljukides," *Oriens* II, 1949, pp. 31-65. Idem, "The Historiography of the Seljuqid Period," in B. Lewis and P. M. Holt, eds., *Historians of the Middle East*, London, 1962, pp. 59-78. D. S. Richards, "Ibn al-Athīr and the Later Parts of the *Kāmil*. A Study of Aims and Methods," in D. O. Morgan, ed., *Medieval Historical Writing in the Christian and Islamic Worlds*, London, 1982, pp. 76-108.

(D. S. Richards)

EBN ʿAṬṬĀŠ. See ʿAṬṬĀŠ.